LONGMAN

Active Study

Dictionary

PEARSON
Longman

NEW EDITION

Pearson Education Limited
Edinburgh Gate, Harlow, Essex CM20 2JE
England and Associated Companies throughout the world

www.longman.com/dictionaries

First edition published 1983
Second edition 1991
Third edition 1998
This edition 2004
Seventeenth impression 2009

ISBN

Paperback   978-0-582-79453-5
Paperback + CD   978-1-4058-6228-8

Library of Congress Cataloging-in-Publication Data
A catalog record for this book is available from the Library of Congress.

British Library Cataloguing-in-Publication Data
A catalogue record for this book is available from the British Library.

Set in Nimrod by Letterpart, UK
Printed in China
GCC/17

Acknowledgements

Director
Della Summers

Senior Publisher
Laurence Delacroix

Managing Editor
Stephen Bullon

Associate Lexicographer
Michael Murphy

Senior Editor
Elizabeth Manning

Editors
Evadne Adrian-Vallance
Rosalind Combley
Sheila Dignen
Martin Stark

Lexicographers
Daniel Barron, Elizabeth Beizai,
Gill Francis, Lucy Hollingworth,
Julie Moore, Carole Murphy,
Elizabeth Potter, Penny Stock,
Jenny Watson, Deborah Yuill

Project Manager
Alan Savill

Production Manager
Clive McKeough

Editorial Manager
Sheila Dallas

Senior Production Editor
Michael Brooks

Project and Database Administrator
Denise McKeough

Technical Support Manager
Trevor Satchell

Network Administrator
Kim Larkin

U.S. Reader
Julie B. Plier

Pronunciation Editor
Dinah Jackson

Language notes
Diane Nicholls
Liz Potter

Exercises
Richard Northcott

Proofreaders
Irene Lakhani
Philippa Logan

Design
Paul Price-Smith
Mick Harris

Keyboarder
Pauline Savill

Artwork
Chris Pavely, Graham Humphries,
Oxford Designers and Illustrators,
Dave Bowyer, Maltings Partnership

Photography credits
IMS Communications Ltd for pages 88, 100 (top), 127, 642, 698, 731, 794; **Corbis** for pages 121, 201, 268,
680, 739; **DK Picture Library** for page A4; **PhotoDisc** for pages 3, 59, 98, 100 (bottom), 105, 122, 135, 184,
186, 198, 212, 216, 226, 229, 236, 253, 281, 292, 296, 367, 407, 429, 433, 480, 511, 527, 566, 599, 604, 619,
640, 644, 657, 684, 705, 710, 719, 750, 783, 831, 839, 870, A6, A9; **Oxford Designers and Illustrators** for
page 67; **Gareth Bowden** for pages 179, 266 (bottom); **Maltings Partnership** for page A12; **Brand X Pictures**
for page A5; **Hemera Technologies Inc** "Copyright ©2004 (Pearson Education) and its licensors. All rights
reserved" for pages 50, 62, 69, 76, 83, 85, 92, 103, 109, 124, 133, 147, 215, 239, 251, 266 (top), 302, 321,
338, 343, 346, 349, 363, 401, 416, 424, 456, 465, 473, 483, 506, 548, 667, 685, 683, 726, 766, 807, 825, 838,
869

CONTENTS

GUIDE TO THE DICTIONARY

Definitions explain the meaning of the word in clear simple language, using the 2000-word Longman Defining Vocabulary.

Useful natural examples show you how you can use the word.

Part of speech is shown first, then information about whether a word is countable, uncountable, transitive, intransitive etc.

Information about irregular forms of verbs and nouns is shown at the beginning of the entry.

Phrasal verbs are listed in alphabetical order after the main verb.

Thesaurus boxes help you to increase your vocabulary by showing you words related to the word you are using.

Common grammar patterns are shown before the examples, so that you can see clearly how the word operates in a sentence.

Common prepositions are also shown before the examples.

This dictionary has full coverage of both American and British English.

If a word is used mainly in spoken English, it is labelled spoken.

---

abacus /'æbəkəs/ *n* [C] a wooden frame with small balls which are moved along wires, used for counting and calculating

abandon /ə'bændən/ *v* [T] **1** to leave a person or thing, especially one that you are responsible for, and not go back for them: *The baby had been abandoned outside a hospital.* | *The thieves abandoned the car nearby.* **2** to stop doing or using something because of problems: *The new policy had to be abandoned.* —**abandonment** *n* [U]

abbot /'æbət/ *n* [C] a man who is in charge of a MONASTERY

abbreviate /ə'bri:vieit/ *v* [T] *formal* to make a word, story etc shorter

abhor /əb'hɔ: $ əb'hɔːr, æb-/ *v* [T] abhorred, abhorring *formal* to hate something because you think it is morally wrong: *He abhorred violence in any form.* → see box at **HATE** —**abhorrence** /əb'hɒrəns $ -'hɔː-/ *n* [U]

abound /ə'baʊnd/ *v* [I] *literary* to exist in large numbers: *a river where fish abound*
abound in/with sth *phr v* to contain a lot of something: *The park abounds with wildlife.*

accident /'æksɪdənt/ *n* [C]
1 a situation in which someone is hurt or something is damaged without anyone intending it to happen: **car/traffic/road etc accident** *Her parents were killed in a car accident.* | *Sam **had an accident** at work and had to go to hospital.* | *I didn't do it on purpose, **it was an accident**.*

THESAURUS

crash/collision – an accident in which a vehicle hits something else
wreck *AmE* – an accident in which a car or train is badly damaged
pile-up – an accident that involves several cars or trucks
disaster – something that happens which causes a lot of harm or suffering
catastrophe – a very serious disaster

2 by accident in a way that is not intended or planned [≠ on purpose]: *The cure was discovered almost by accident.* | *I met her **quite by accident**.*

accuse /ə'kju:z/ *v* [T] to say that someone has done something wrong or illegal **accuse sb of (doing) sth** *Are you accusing me of lying?* | *He was accused of theft.*
—**accuser** *n* [C]

acquisition /,ækwɪ'zɪʃən/ *n* **1** [U] the process of getting or learning something: +*of the acquisition of wealth* **2** [C] something that you have obtained, especially by buying it: *This sofa's a new acquisition.*

action 'replay *n* [C] *BrE* an exciting moment in a sports game that is shown again on television immediately after it happens [= instant replay *AmE*]

actually /'æktʃuəli, -tʃəli/ *adv especially spoken* **1** used to emphasize that something is true, especially when it is a little surprising or unexpected: *Prices have actually fallen.* | *Disappointed? No, actually I feel rather glad.* | *Actually he's 45.*
2 used to politely give more information, give your opinion etc: *I've known him all my life, actually.* | *Actually, I think I prefer this one.*

AD /ˌeɪ ˈdiː/ **Anno Domini** used to show that a date is a particular number of years after the birth of Christ [➡ **BC**]: 453 AD

added /ˈædɪd/ adj more than what is usual or natural [= **extra**]: This method has an **added** advantage. | fruit juice with no added sugar

Synonyms (=words with the same meaning), opposites, and related words are shown after the definition.

adept /ˈædept, əˈdept $ əˈdept/ adj good at doing something that needs care or skill [≠ **inept**]: He became adept at cooking her favourite dishes. —**adeptly** adv

affirm /əˈfɜːm $ -ɜːrm/ v [T] formal to say definitely that something is true: The President affirmed his intention to reduce taxes. —**affirmation** /ˌæfəˈmeɪʃən $ ˌæfər-/ n [C,U]

Labels before the definition show you if a word is used in informal, formal, literary, legal, or technical English.

afternoon /ˌɑːftəˈnuːn◂ $ ˌæftər-/ n [C,U] the period of time after the morning and before the evening [➡ **morning, evening**]: **in the afternoon** It was very hot in the afternoon. | **on Monday/ Friday etc afternoon** I'll see you on Tuesday afternoon. | Do you want to go swimming **this afternoon** (=today in the afternoon)? | **yesterday/tomorrow afternoon** We met yesterday afternoon. | an afternoon sleep
→ **GOOD AFTERNOON**

Active words are printed in red letters. This shows you which are the most important words to know.

Collocations are shown before the examples, or highlighted in bold in the examples.

ago /əˈɡəʊ $ əˈɡoʊ/ adv used to say how far back in the past something happened: **10 years/a moment/a long time etc ago** Jeff left an hour ago. | We went there a long time ago.

Pronunciation is shown using the International Phonetic Alphabet.

GRAMMAR

ago, for, since
Ago, for, and **since** are all used to talk about time.
Ago is used with the simple past tense to say how far back in the past something happened. It follows a length of time: My grandfather died two years ago.
For is used with the present perfect or simple past tense to say how long a situation or event has lasted. It is followed by a length of time: She's been here for three days. | The party lasted for five hours.
Since is used with the present perfect tense to say when something started. It is followed by an exact day, date, or time: He's been here since Sunday. | I've been working here since 1998.

Grammar boxes give you extra grammatical information about a word, and help you avoid making mistakes.

aground /əˈɡraʊnd/ adv **run/go aground** if a ship runs aground, it becomes stuck because the water is not deep enough

aim² v
1 [I] to try or intend to achieve something: **aim to do sth** We aim to finish by Friday. | **+for** We're aiming for a reduction in pollution levels. | **(be) aimed at doing sth** a program aimed at creating more jobs

Idioms and fixed phrases are shown in dark type and have a definition which explains the whole phrase.

2 aim sth at sb to do or say something that is intended for a particular person or group: advertising aimed at children | criticism aimed at the government
3 [I,T] to point a weapon at someone or something that you want to hit: **+at** The gun was aimed at his head.

The meanings of each word are listed in order of frequency. The most common meaning is shown first.

aimless /ˈeɪmləs/ adj without a clear purpose or reason —**aimlessly** adv

Derived words are shown at the end of the entry.

Labels used in this Dictionary

Words which are only or mainly used in either Britain or the U.S. are labelled:

BrE British English   *AmE* American English

Words that are only or mainly used in a particular situation, context, or type of language are labelled:

formal – used in formal speech or writing, but not usually used in ordinary conversation
informal – used in normal situations when you are speaking or writing to people you know well, but not suitable in essays, business letters etc
spoken – used only, or almost only, in spoken conversation
written – used only, or almost only, in written English
approving – used when you approve of someone or something
disapproving – used when you do not approve of someone or something
humorous – used in a joking way
literary – used mainly in books, not in normal speech or writing
old-fashioned – used in the past or by old people
technical – used by doctors, scientists and other people who have special knowledge about a subject
law – used by lawyers
trademark – used as the official name of a product

Parts of Speech are labelled:

adj = adjective
adv = adverb
auxiliary verb (the verbs 'be', 'do' and 'have')
determiner
linking word (a word that joins words, phrases and clauses together, for example 'and')
modal verb (verbs such as 'could', 'might' and 'shall')

n = noun
number
phr v = phrasal verb
prefix
prep = preposition
pron = pronoun
suffix
v = verb

Grammar Codes used in this Dictionary

[C] **countable** – a noun that has a singular and a plural form
[C usually singular] – a countable noun that is usually used in the singular form
[C usually plural] – a countable noun that is usually used in the plural form
[U] **uncountable** – a noun that does not have a plural form and can be used without a determiner such as 'a' or 'the' before it
[singular] – a noun that does not have a plural form, always has a determiner before it, and is always followed by a singular verb
[plural] – a noun that is used in the plural form and is followed by a plural verb
[T] **transitive** – a verb that is followed by an object (a noun phrase, a pronoun, or a relative clause)
[I] **intransitive** – a verb that is not followed by an object
[I + adv/prep] – a verb that is always followed by an adverb or preposition
[not before noun] – an adjective that never comes before a noun
[only before noun] – an adjective that always comes before a noun
[only after noun] – an adjective that always comes after a noun
[linking verb] – a verb used in descriptions, such as 'be' or 'seem'

Abbreviations used in this Dictionary

sb = somebody   sth = something

A, a

A, a /eɪ/ n [C,U] plural **A's, a's** **1** the first letter of the English alphabet **2** the sixth note in the musical SCALE of C MAJOR, or the musical KEY based on this note **3** the highest mark that a student can get in an examination or for a piece of work: *I got an A in French.*

a /ə; *strong* eɪ/ also **an** (before a vowel sound) *determiner*
1 used to show that you are talking about something or someone that has not been mentioned before, or that the listener does not know about [➡ **the**]: *There was a problem with the car.* | *I saw a really good film last week.*
2 used to show that you are talking about a general type of thing, not a specific thing [➡ **the**]: *Do you have a car?* | *Her boyfriend is an artist.* | *Have a look at this* (=Look at this).
3 one: *a thousand pounds* | *a dozen eggs*
4 used in some phrases that say how much of something there is: *a few weeks from now* | *a lot of people*
5 every or each: *A square has 4 sides.* | **once a week/$100 a day etc** (=one time each week, $100 each day etc) *He gets paid $100,000 a year.*
6 used before two nouns that are often mentioned together: *a knife and fork*

> **GRAMMAR**
>
> **a, an**
> If the word that follows starts with a consonant sound, use a: *a car* | *a brown egg* | *I bought a CD today.*
> If the word that follows starts with a vowel sound (the sounds shown by the letters a, e, i, o, or u), use an: *an apple* | *an orange sweater* | *I waited an hour.*
> ➔ ANY

aback /ə'bæk/ *adv* **be taken aback** to be very surprised or shocked: *I was taken aback by Linda's rudeness.*

abacus /'æbəkəs/ n [C] a wooden frame with small balls which are moved along wires, used for counting and calculating

abandon /ə'bændən/ v [T] **1** to leave a person or thing, especially one that you are responsible for, and not go back for them: *The baby had been abandoned outside a hospital.* | *The thieves abandoned the car nearby.* **2** to stop doing or using something because of problems: *The new policy had to be abandoned.* —abandonment n [U]

abandoned /ə'bændənd/ *adj* not being used or looked after any more: *an abandoned building*

abashed /ə'bæʃt/ *adj* embarrassed or ashamed: *They both looked slightly abashed.*

abate /ə'beɪt/ v [I] *formal* to become less strong: *The storm showed no signs of abating.*

abattoir /'æbətwɑː $ -ɑːr/ n [C] *BrE* a place where animals are killed for their meat [= **slaughterhouse**]

abbey /'æbi/ n [C] a large church, especially one used by a group of MONKS or NUNS

abbot /'æbət/ n [C] a man who is in charge of a MONASTERY

abbreviate /ə'briːvieɪt/ v [T] *formal* to make a word, story etc shorter

abbreviation /ə,briːvi'eɪʃən/ n [C] a shorter form of a word: **+for/of** *'Dr' is the written abbreviation for 'Doctor'.*

abdicate /'æbdɪkeɪt/ v **1** [I] to officially give up the position of being king or queen **2 abdicate (your) responsibility** *formal* to refuse to continue being responsible for something —abdication /,æbdɪ'keɪʃən/ n [C,U]

abdomen /'æbdəmən, æb'dəʊ- $ -'doʊ-/ n [C] *technical* the part of your body between your chest and the top of your legs, including your stomach —abdominal /æb'dɒmɪnəl $ -'dɑː-/ *adj*

abduct /əb'dʌkt, æb-/ v [T] to take someone away by force: *Police believe that the woman has been abducted.* —abduction /əb'dʌkʃən, æb-/ n [C,U]

aberration /,æbə'reɪʃən/ n [C,U] *formal* something that is completely different from what usually happens or from what someone usually does: *a temporary psychological aberration*

abet /ə'bet/ v abetted, abetting ➔ aid and abet at AID[2]

abhor /əb'hɔː $ əb'hɔːr, æb-/ v [T] abhorred, abhorring *formal* to hate something because you think it is morally wrong: *He abhorred violence in any form.* ➔ see box at HATE —abhorrence /əb'hɒrəns $ -'hɔː-/ n [U]

abhorrent /əb'hɒrənt $ -'hɔːr-/ *adj formal* behaviour or beliefs that are abhorrent seem very bad and morally wrong

abide /ə'baɪd/ v **can't abide sb/sth** to hate someone or something very much: *I can't abide his stupid jokes.*
abide by sth *phr v* to obey a law, agreement etc: *You have to abide by the rules of the game.*

abiding /ə'baɪdɪŋ/ *adj* [only before noun] *literary* an abiding feeling or belief continues for a long time: *her abiding love of the English countryside* ➔ LAW-ABIDING

ability /ə'bɪləti/ n [C,U] plural **abilities** the state of being able to do something, or your level of skill at doing something: **ability to do sth** *A manager must have the ability to communicate well.* | **athletic/academic/linguistic etc ability** *a young girl with great musical ability* | *We just have to play* **to the best of our ability** (=as well as we can).

abject /'æbdʒekt/ *adj* **1 abject poverty/misery/failure** when someone is extremely poor, unhappy, or unsuccessful **2 abject apology** an abject apology shows that you are ashamed of what you have done

ablaze /ə'bleɪz/ *adj* [not before noun] **1** burning with a lot of flames: *The ship was set ablaze by the explosion.* **2** very bright with colour or light: *a garden ablaze with summer flowers*

able /'eɪbəl/ *adj*
1 be able to do sth a) to have the power, skill, knowledge etc you need to do something

[≠ **unable**]: *I'd love to be able to play the piano.* → see box at **CAN b)** to be in a situation where it is possible for you to do something [≠ **unable**]: *Will you be able to come tonight?*
2 clever or good at doing something: *a very able student*

-able /əbəl/ *suffix* used to say that something can have something done to it: *a washable fabric* | *a noticeable change*

,able-'bodied *adj* physically strong and healthy, especially when compared with someone who is DISABLED: *a team of both disabled and able-bodied athletes*

ably /'eɪbli/ *adv* skilfully or well: *The director was ably assisted by his team of experts.*

abnormal /æb'nɔːməl $ -'nɔːr-/ *adj* different from what is normal, especially in a way that is strange, worrying, or dangerous [≠ **normal**]: *abnormal behaviour* | *abnormal levels of chlorine in the water* —**abnormally** *adv* —**abnormality** /,æbnɔː'mælɨti $ -nər-/ *n* [C,U] *a serious genetic abnormality*

aboard /ə'bɔːd $ ə'bɔːrd/ *adv, prep* on or onto a ship, plane, or train: *The boat swayed as he climbed aboard.* | *Everyone aboard the plane was killed.*

abode /ə'bəʊd $ ə'boʊd/ *n* [C] *formal* the place where you live: **right of abode** (=the right to live in a country)

abolish /ə'bɒlɪʃ $ ə'bɑː-/ *v* [T] to officially end a law, system etc: *plans to abolish the death penalty* —**abolition** /,æbə'lɪʃən/ *n* [U] *the abolition of slavery*

abominable /ə'bɒmɪnəbəl, -mənə- $ ə'bɑː-/ *adj* extremely unpleasant or bad —**abominably** *adv*

aborigine /,æbə'rɪdʒɨni/, **aboriginal** /,æbə'rɪdʒɨnəl◂/ *n* [C] a member of the race of people who have lived in Australia from the earliest times —**aboriginal** *adj*

abort /ə'bɔːt $ -ɔːrt/ *v* [T] **1** to stop an activity because it would be too difficult or dangerous to continue: *The flight had to be aborted because of computer problems.* **2** to deliberately end a PREGNANCY when the baby is still too small to live

abortion /ə'bɔːʃən $ ə'bɔːr-/ *n* [C,U] when a PREGNANCY is deliberately ended while the baby is still too small to live: *She considered having an abortion.*

abortive /ə'bɔːtɪv $ ə'bɔːr-/ *adj* an abortive action or attempt to do something is not successful

abound /ə'baʊnd/ *v* [I] *literary* to exist in large numbers: *a river where fish abound*
abound in/with sth *phr v* to contain a lot of something: *The park abounds with wildlife.*

about¹ /ə'baʊt/ *prep*
1 concerning a particular subject, thing, or person: *a book about astrology* | *What was he talking about?* | *We're all very upset about it.* | *Tell me all about it* (=everything about) *it.*
2 *BrE* in many different directions or in different parts of a place [= **around**]: *Clothes were scattered about the room.*
3 what/how about sb/sth *spoken* **a)** used to make a suggestion: **what/how about doing sth** *How about coming round for a barbecue?* | *'What shall I get Simon?' 'What about a CD?'* **b)** used to ask someone to consider and talk about something

one or something else involved in a situation: *What about Jack? We can't just leave him here.*
4 do something about sth to do something to solve a problem: *We must do something about the shower – it's still dripping.*
5 in the character or nature of a person or thing: *There's something odd about him.*

about² *adv*
1 a little more or less than a number or amount [= **approximately, roughly**]: *I live about 10 miles from here.* | *We left the restaurant at round about 10.30.*
2 be about to do sth to be ready to start doing something: *We were about to leave when Jerry arrived.*
3 just about almost: *Dinner's just about ready.*
4 *BrE* in many different directions or in different parts of a place [= **around**]: *People were lying about on the floor.*
5 *BrE* near to where you are now [= **around**]: *Is Patrick about? There's a phone call for him.*

a,bout-'face also **a,bout-'turn** *BrE* *n* [singular] a complete change in the way someone thinks or behaves

above /ə'bʌv/ *adv, prep*
1 in or to a higher position than something else [≠ **below**]: *Raise your arm above your head.* | *There's a light above the entrance.* | *The noise came from the room above.* → see picture on page A8
2 more than a number, amount, or level [≠ **below**]: *Temperatures rose above zero today.* | **and/or above** suitable for children aged 7 and above
3 louder than other sounds: *He couldn't hear her voice above the noise.*
4 *formal* before, in the same piece of writing [≠ **below**]: *Write to the address above for further information.*
5 above all *formal* most importantly: *Above all, I would like to thank my parents.*
6 higher in rank, more powerful, or more important: *officers above the rank of lieutenant*
7 be above suspicion/criticism etc to be so good that no one can doubt or criticize you

a,bove 'board / $.'. ./ *adj* [not before noun] something such as a business deal that is above board is honest and legal

abrasive /ə'breɪsɪv/ *adj* **1** rude and not gentle: *his abrasive manner* **2** having a rough surface that can be used to rub off the surface of other things

abreast /ə'brest/ *adv* **1 keep abreast of sth** to make sure that you know the most recent facts about a subject: *I listen to the radio to keep abreast of the news.* **2 two/three/four abreast** with two, three, or four people moving along next to each other: *The cyclists were riding three abreast, so no one could pass them.*

abridged /ə'brɪdʒd/ *adj* an abridged form of a book, play etc has been made shorter [≠ **unabridged**]: *the abridged version of the novel* —**abridge** *v* [T]

abroad /ə'brɔːd $ ə'brɒːd/ *adv* in or to a foreign country: *He often has to go abroad on business.* | *Did you enjoy living abroad?* | *the President's image both at home and abroad* (=in this country and in other countries) | **from abroad** *workers hired from abroad*

abrupt /ə'brʌpt/ *adj* **1** sudden and unexpected: *an abrupt change in the attitudes of voters* **2** not polite or friendly, especially because you do not want to waste time: *She was rather abrupt on the phone.* —**abruptly** *adv* —**abruptness** *n* [U]

abs /æbz/ *n* [plural] *informal* the muscles on your ABDOMEN (=stomach): *exercises that improve your abs*

abscess /'æbses/ *n* [C] a swollen place on your body that is infected and contains a yellow liquid

abscond /əb'skɒnd, æb- $ æb'skɑːnd/ *v* [I] *formal* to leave a place without permission, or to leave somewhere after stealing something: *She had absconded from a children's home.*

abseil /'æbseɪl/ *v* [I] *BrE* to go down a cliff etc by sliding down a rope and pushing against the cliff with your feet

abseiling

absence /'æbsəns/ *n* **1** [C,U] when you are not in a place that you are expected to be normally: **+from** *frequent absences from work* | **in/during sb's absence** *The vice president will handle things in my absence.* **2** [U] the lack of something: **In the absence of** *any firm evidence (=because there wasn't any), the police had to let him go.*

absent /'æbsənt/ *adj* **1** not in the place you are normally expected to be [≠ **present**]: **+from** *Why was she absent from school yesterday?* | *I had to do the work of an absent colleague.* **2** *formal* not in a place, thing, or situation: *Controversy was rarely absent.*

absentee /ˌæbsən'tiː◂/ *n* [C] **1** *formal* someone who is supposed to be in a place but is not there **2** **absentee landlord/owner** the owner of a building or piece of land who lives far away

absenteeism /ˌæbsən'tiːɪzəm/ *n* [U] regular absence from work or school without a good reason

absently /'æbsəntli/ *adv* in a way that shows you are not interested or not thinking about what is happening: *Rachel smiled absently and went on with her work.*

ˌabsent-'minded *adj* someone who is absent-minded often forgets or does not notice things because they are thinking of something else —**absent-mindedness** *n* [U] —**absent-mindedly** *adv*

absolute /'æbsəluːt/ *adj* **1** complete and total: *There was absolute silence.* | *a ruler with absolute power* **2** used to emphasize your opinion: *You're an absolute genius!* **3** definite and not likely to change: *I can't give you any absolute promises.*

absolutely[1] /'æbsəluːtli, ˌæbsə'luːtli/ *adv* completely or totally: *Are you absolutely sure?* | *This is absolutely delicious!* | **absolutely no/nothing** (=none or nothing at all) *He knows absolutely nothing about politics.* → see box at **COMPLETELY**

absolutely[2] *spoken* used to say 'yes' or show that you agree in a strong way: *'Do you think I should go?' 'Absolutely.'* | *'Don't you believe me?' ' Absolutely not* (=no).*'*

absolve /əb'zɒlv $ -ɑːlv/ *v* [T] *formal* to say publicly that someone should not be blamed for something, or to forgive them

absorb /əb'sɔːb, əb'zɔːb $ -ɔːrb/ *v* [T] **1** if something absorbs liquid, heat etc, it takes it in through its surface: *The towel absorbed most of the water.* **2** **be absorbed in sth** to be very interested in something that you are doing, watching etc: *I was completely absorbed in the book.* **3** to learn, understand, and remember new information: *She's a good student who absorbs information quickly.* **4** if something is absorbed, it becomes part of something larger: **be absorbed into sth** *countries that had become absorbed into the Soviet Union* —**absorption** /-ɔːpʃən $ -ɔːr-/ *n* [U]

absorbent /əb'sɔːbənt, -'zɔː- $ -ɔːr-/ *adj* something that is absorbent can take in liquids through its surface: *absorbent paper*

absorbing /əb'sɔːbɪŋ, -'zɔː- $ -ɔːr-/ *adj* very interesting and keeping your attention: *an absorbing article about space travel* → see box at **INTERESTING**

abstain /əb'steɪn/ *v* [I] **1** *formal* to not do something that you would normally enjoy doing: **+from** *Patients were advised to abstain from alcohol.* **2** to deliberately not vote —**abstention** /əb'stenʃən/ *n* [C,U]

abstinence /'æbstɪnəns/ *n* [U] when someone stops doing something that they would normally enjoy, especially for religious reasons

abstract /'æbstrækt/ *adj* **1** based on ideas rather than specific examples or real events: *Beauty is an abstract idea.* | *abstract arguments about justice* **2** abstract art consists of shapes and patterns that do not look like real things or people → see picture at **PAINTING**

absurd /əb'sɜːd, -'zɜːd $ -ɜːrd/ *adj* completely unreasonable or silly: *an absurd situation* | *It seems absurd to go all that way just for the day.* —**absurdly** *adv* —**absurdity** *n* [C,U]

abundance /ə'bʌndəns/ *n* [singular, U] *formal* a very large quantity of something: *There is an abundance of creative talent.* | **in abundance** *Wild flowers grow here in abundance.*

abundant /ə'bʌndənt/ *adj* existing in large quantities: *an abundant supply of fresh fruit*

abundantly /ə'bʌndəntli/ *adv* **1** **abundantly clear/plain** very easy to understand: *He made it abundantly clear that he was dissatisfied.* **2** in large quantities

abuse[1] /ə'bjuːs/ *n* **1** [C,U] when someone uses something in a way that it should not be used: **+of** *government officials' abuse of power* | **drug/alcohol abuse** (=when people take illegal drugs or drink too much) **2** [U] cruel or violent treatment of someone: *a police investigation into child abuse* | *victims of sexual abuse* **3** [U] rude and insulting things that someone says when they are angry: *The family suffered constant verbal abuse.*

abuse[2] /ə'bjuːz/ *v* [T] **1** to do cruel or violent things to someone: **sexually/physically abused** *He was sexually abused as a child.* **2** to use something too much or in the wrong way: *He*

A

had **abused** his **position** as mayor by offering jobs to his friends. **3** to say rude and insulting things to someone

abusive /ə'bjuːsɪv/ adj using words that are rude and insulting: an abusive letter

abysmal /ə'bɪzməl/ adj very bad: the country's abysmal record on human rights → see box at **BAD** —**abysmally** adv

abyss /ə'bɪs/ n [C] **1** a very dangerous or frightening situation: the abyss of nuclear war **2** literary a very deep hole or space that seems to have no bottom

academic¹ /ˌækə'demɪk◂/ adj **1** relating to education, especially in a college or university: students' **academic achievements** | **academic work/study/research** | **the academic year** (=the period of the year when there are school or university classes) → see box at **QUALIFICATION 2** if a subject in a discussion is academic, it is not important to discuss it because you cannot change the situation: We don't have any money, so the question of where to go on holiday is purely academic. **3** good at studying: She was never a very academic child.

academic² n [C] a teacher in a college or university

academy /ə'kædəmi/ n [C] plural **academies 1** a school or college that trains students in a special subject or skill: a military academy **2** an organization whose purpose is to encourage the development of art, science, or literature

accede /ək'siːd, æk-/ v
accede to sth phr v formal to agree to a request or demand

accelerate /ək'seləreɪt/ v **1** [I] if a car driver accelerates, they start to go faster: Melissa accelerated as she drove onto the highway. **2** [I,T] if a process accelerates or if you accelerate it, it starts to happen more quickly: a plan to accelerate economic growth —**acceleration** /əkˌselə'reɪʃən/ n [U]

accelerator /ək'seləreɪtə $ -ər/ n [C] the part of a car that you press with your foot to make it go faster → see picture on page A12 → see box at **DRIVE**

accent /'æksənt $ 'æksent/ n [C]
1 a way of pronouncing words that someone has because of where they were born or live: **English/Indian/American etc accent** a man with an Irish accent | She speaks French with a Swiss accent. | **broad/strong/slight etc accent** He's got a strong northern accent. **2 the accent on sth** the importance given to something: a training programme with the accent on safety **3** a mark written above some letters, for example é or â

accentuate /ək'sentʃueɪt/ v [T] to make something easier to notice

accept /ək'sept/ v
1 [I,T] to take or agree to something that someone offers you or suggests: They offered me the job and I accepted. | **accept an offer/invitation** We would be happy to accept your invitation. | **accept advice/suggestions** Jackie won't accept any advice. | **accept sth from sb** officials accused of accepting bribes from criminals

accepting

yes, please: 'Would you like some wine?' 'Yes, please.'
I'd love to: 'Why don't you come round here for a meal?' 'Thanks, I'd love to.'
that sounds nice/good/great/(like) fun: 'We could go to the cinema.' 'That sounds great.'
why not? informal spoken: 'Have a chocolate.' 'Oh, why not.'
→ **AGREE, OFFER, REFUSE**

When someone asks you to do something, you **agree** to do it. Never say 'accept to do something': Britain has agreed to provide military aid.
You **accept** an invitation, a job, an offer etc: Teachers have accepted the government's pay offer.

2 [T] to admit that an unpleasant fact or difficult situation is true: +**that** I accept that we've made mistakes. | Arthur soon **accepted the fact that** he wasn't going to get the job. | Everyone **accepts the need** for change.
3 [T] to let someone join an organization, university course etc [≠ reject]: She applied to Columbia College and was accepted.
4 [T] to let someone new become part of a group and to treat them in the same way as other members: It was a long time before the other kids at school accepted him.
5 [T] to let customers pay for something in a particular way [→ take]: We don't accept credit cards.
6 accept responsibility/blame for sth to admit that you are responsible for something bad that has happened: The company have accepted responsibility for the accident.

acceptable /ək'septəbəl/ adj
1 good enough, especially for a particular purpose: +**to** an agreement which is acceptable to everyone | **acceptable level/standard/quality** Do staff provide an acceptable level of service?
2 if behaviour is acceptable, people approve of it and think that it is appropriate [≠ unacceptable]: It is socially acceptable for men to marry younger women. | It's simply not an acceptable way to do business. | Her suggestion seems perfectly acceptable.
—**acceptability** /əkˌseptə'bɪləti/ n [U]

acceptance /ək'septəns/ n [U] **1** when you agree to accept something that is offered to you: +**of** The board has recommended acceptance of the offer. | She gave a brief **acceptance speech** (=a speech to accept an award, a position etc). **2** when people agree that something is right or true: +**of** There is widespread acceptance of the need for economic reform. | +**that** the general acceptance that global temperatures have risen | **gain/find acceptance** (=become popular) His ideas soon gained acceptance from scientists. **3** when you decide that there is nothing you can do to change an unpleasant situation **4** when someone is allowed to become part of a group or society: +**into** the immigrants' gradual acceptance into the community

accepted /ək'septɪd/ *adj* an accepted idea or way of doing something is one that most people think is right or reasonable: **generally/widely/universally etc accepted** *a generally accepted principle of international law*

access[1] /'ækses/ *n* [U] **1** the right to enter a place, use something, see someone etc: **+to** *In some areas there is no access to clean water.* | *Students need to **have access to** the computer system.* **2** the way you enter a building or get to a place, or how easy this is: **+to** *The only access to the farm is along a narrow track.* | **+for** *improved access for disabled customers* | **get/gain access (to sth)** *formal* (=enter) *The thieves gained access through the upstairs window.*

access[2] *v* [T] to find and use information, especially on a computer: *software for accessing the Internet*

accessible /ək'sesɪbəl/ *adj* **1** easy to reach, find, or use [≠ **inaccessible**]: *The park is not accessible by road.* | *a wide range of information that is **easily accessible*** **2** easy to understand and enjoy [≠ **inaccessible**]: **+to** *He makes a difficult subject accessible to the ordinary reader.* —**accessibility** /ək,sesə'bɪlɪti/ *n* [U]

accessory /ək'sesəri/ *n* [C] plural **accessories** **1** something such as a bag, belt, or jewellery that you wear or carry because it is attractive: *fashion accessories* **2** something that you can add to a machine, tool, car etc which is not necessary but is useful or attractive **3** *law* someone who helps a criminal

accident /'æksɪdənt/ *n* [C]

1 a situation in which someone is hurt or something is damaged without anyone intending it to happen: **car/traffic/road etc accident** *Her parents were killed in a car accident.* | *Sam **had an accident** at work and had to go to hospital.* | *I didn't do it on purpose, **it was an accident**.*

THESAURUS

crash/collision – an accident in which a vehicle hits something else
wreck *AmE* – an accident in which a car or train is badly damaged
pile-up – an accident that involves several cars or trucks
disaster – something that happens which causes a lot of harm or suffering
| **catastrophe** – a very serious disaster

2 by accident in a way that is not intended or planned [≠ **on purpose**]: *The cure was discovered almost by accident.* | *I met her **quite by accident**.*

accidental /,æksɪ'dentl◂/ *adj* if something that happens is accidental, it was not planned or intended [≠ **deliberate**]: *insurance against accidental damage* | *Was the explosion accidental or deliberate?*
—**accidentally** *adv*: *I accidentally set off the alarm.*

accident-prone *adj* someone who is accident-prone often has accidents

acclaim /ə'kleɪm/ *n* [U] a lot of public praise for someone or something: **international/great/widespread etc acclaim** *His first novel received widespread acclaim.* | *The show won critical acclaim.*

acclaimed /ə'kleɪmd/ *adj* praised by a lot of people: **highly/widely acclaimed** *the band's highly acclaimed debut album* —**acclaim** *v* [T]

acclimatize also **-ise** *BrE* /ə'klaɪmətaɪz/ also **acclimate** *AmE* /ə'klaɪmət $ 'ækləmeɪt, ə'klaɪmət/ *v* [I,T] to become used to the weather, way of living etc in a new place, or to make someone do this: **+to** *It takes the astronauts a few days to **get acclimatized** to conditions in space.* —**acclimatization** /ə,klaɪmətaɪ'zeɪʃən $ -tə-/ *n* [U]

accolade /'ækəleɪd/ *n* [C] praise given to someone because people think they are very good, or a prize given to them for their work

accommodate /ə'kɒmədeɪt $ ə'kɑː-/ *v* [T] **1** to have enough space for a particular number of people or things: *The hall can accommodate 300 people.* **2** to give someone a place to live, stay, or work: *A new hostel was built to accommodate the students.* **3** *formal* to provide someone with what they need, or do what they want: *The centre is designed to **accommodate the needs** of all visitors.*

accommodating /ə'kɒmədeɪtɪŋ $ ə'kɑː-/ *adj* helpful and willing to do what someone else wants

accommodation /ə,kɒmə'deɪʃən $ ə,kɑː-/ *BrE*, **accommodations** *plural AmE n* [U] a place to live, stay, or work: *The college **provides accommodation** for all new students.* | *Rented accommodation is very expensive.*

THESAURUS

hotel – a building where you pay to sleep and eat when you are travelling or on holiday: *a one-star hotel* (=least comfortable type) | *a five-star hotel* (=most comfortable type)
motel *especially AmE* – a hotel for people travelling by car, where you can park outside the room you stay in
guesthouse *BrE* – a small hotel that is also the hotel owner's home
guesthouse *AmE* – a separate building next to someone's home, where visiting family or friends can stay
bed and breakfast (B&B) – a room in a private house that is also the owner's home, where they give you breakfast in the morning but no other meals.
self-catering accommodation *BrE* – a house, flat etc where you do the cooking yourself
villa – a house you rent, especially in France, Italy, or Spain
chalet – a house you rent, usually in a mountain area
campsite *BrE*/**campground** *AmE* – a place where you camp in a tent
→ HOTEL

GRAMMAR

In British English, there is no plural form of **accommodation**.
In American English, the plural **accommodations** is very common and the singular form is rare: *The accommodations are plain but comfortable.*

accompaniment /ə'kʌmpənimənt/ *n* [C] **1** *formal* something that is good to eat or drink with another food: **+to** *White wine is an excel-*

A

lent accompaniment to fish. **2** music played while someone sings or plays another instrument: *a piano accompaniment*

accompany /əˈkʌmpəni/ v [T] **accompanied, accompanying, accompanies 1** *formal* to go somewhere with someone: **+to** *I accompanied her to the station.* | **be accompanied by sb** (=have sb with you) *Children under 12 must be accompanied by an adult.* **2** to play a musical instrument while someone is playing or singing the main tune **3** to happen, exist etc with something else: *Depression may be accompanied by fear in some cases.*

accomplice /əˈkʌmplɪ̯s $ əˈkɑːm-, əˈkʌm-/ n [C] someone who helps a criminal to do something wrong

accomplish /əˈkʌmplɪʃ $ əˈkɑːm-, əˈkʌm-/ v [T] to succeed in doing something: *The new government has accomplished a great deal.*

accomplished /əˈkʌmplɪʃt $ əˈkɑːm-, əˈkʌm-/ adj very skilful, especially in art, writing, music etc: *a highly accomplished poet*

accomplishment /əˈkʌmplɪʃmənt $ əˈkɑːm-, əˈkʌm-/ n **1** [C] *formal* a skill, especially in art, writing, music etc **2** [U] when you succeed in doing something: **+of** *the accomplishment of his ambition*

accord[1] /əˈkɔːd $ -ɔːrd/ n **1 of your own accord** willingly, and not because someone has asked you or forced you to do something: *He left of his own accord.* **2 in accord (with sb/sth)** *formal* in agreement with someone or something, or the same as something: *These results are in accord with earlier research.* **3** [C] an official agreement

accord[2] v [T] *formal* to treat someone or something in a special way, or give them special attention: *On his return he was accorded a hero's welcome.*

accordance /əˈkɔːdəns $ əˈkɔːr-/ n **in accordance with sth** *formal* according to a system or rule: *Safety checks were made in accordance with the rules.*

accordingly /əˈkɔːdɪŋli $ əˈkɔːr-/ adv **1** in a way that is suitable for a particular situation: *If you work extra hours, you will be paid accordingly.* **2** *formal* as a result of something [= **therefore**]

acˈcording to prep
1 as shown by something or said by someone: *According to our records she hasn't paid her bill.* | *According to Angela, he's married.*
2 in the way that has been planned or that is based on a system: *Everything went according to plan and we arrived on time.* | *The game must be played according to the rules.*

accordion /əˈkɔːdiən $ əˈkɔːr-/ n [C] a musical instrument like a box that you hold in both hands. You play it by pulling the sides in and out and pushing buttons to produce different notes.

accost /əˈkɒst $ əˈkɔːst, əˈkɑːst/ v [T] if someone you do not know accosts you, they come and speak to you in an unpleasant or threatening way

account[1] /əˈkaʊnt/ n [C]
1 a written or spoken description of something that has happened: **+of** *She was able to give an account of the accident.* | *Holroyd has written a detailed account of the war.* | **eye-witness/**

first-hand account (=description of events by someone who saw them) *his eye-witness account of the shootings*
2 also **bank account** an arrangement with a bank that allows you to keep your money there and take money out when you need it: *Would you like to open an account* (=make this arrangement)? | *Your salary will be paid into your bank account.* | *I've withdrawn £250 from my account.* | *What's your account number?*

You **open** an **account** at a bank. You **pay, put,** or **deposit money into** your **account.** You **take money out of/withdraw money from** your **account.** You can do this at a bank or you can use an **ATM** (=a machine that you use with a card). An ATM is also called a **cash machine** or a **Cashpoint™** *BrE.*
When there is money in your account, you are **in credit** *BrE/*have a **credit balance** *AmE.* When the amount of money in your account is less than zero, you are **overdrawn** *BrE.*

current account *BrE/***checking account** *AmE* – one that you use regularly for making payments etc
deposit account *BrE/***savings account** *AmE* – one where you leave money for longer periods of time, and which pays you a higher rate of interest than a current account

3 take account of sth/take sth into account to consider particular facts when judging or deciding something: *These statistics do not take account of age.*
4 on account of sth because of something: *Some trains were cancelled on account of the storm.*
5 accounts [plural] a record of the money that a business has received and spent: *Their annual accounts showed a loss of £4 million.* → see box at **RECORD**
6 an arrangement with a shop or company that allows you to buy things or use a service now and pay later: **on account** *Can I buy this on account?* | *I'd like to charge this to my account* (=pay using this arrangement). | *an Internet account* | **pay/settle your account** (=pay what you owe) *You must settle your account within thirty days.*
7 by/from all accounts according to what people say: *He was, by all accounts, a shy man.*
8 not on my account *spoken* not for me or because of me: *Don't stay up late on my account.*
9 on no account/not on any account *formal* used to emphasize that someone must not do something: *On no account open the door to a stranger.*

account[2] v
account for sth *phr v* **1** to be a particular part of an amount: *Oil and gas account for 60% of our exports.* **2** to be the reason for something, or to explain the reason for something: *If he's taking drugs, that would account for his behaviour.* | *Can you account for what you did?*

accountable /əˈkaʊntəbəl/ adj [not before noun] responsible for what you do and willing to explain it or accept criticism: **+to** *The govern-*

ment is accountable to the people. | **+for** *Managers must be accountable for their decisions.* | *If students fail exams, can their teachers be **held accountable** (=considered responsible)?* —accountability /əˈkaʊntəˈbɪlɪti/ *n* [U]

accountancy /əˈkaʊntənsi/ *BrE*; **accounting** /əˈkaʊntɪŋ/ *AmE n* [U] the job of being an accountant

accountant /əˈkaʊntənt/ *n* [C] someone whose job is to write or check financial records

accredited /əˈkredɪtɪd/ *adj* having official approval

accumulate /əˈkjuːmjʊleɪt/ *v* [I,T] to gradually increase in amount, or to make the amount of something gradually increase: *Dirt and dust had accumulated in the corners of the room.* | **accumulate money/knowledge/wealth etc** *He had accumulated over £300,000.* —accumulation /əˌkjuːmjʊˈleɪʃən/ *n* [C,U]

accuracy /ˈækjʊrəsi/ *n* [U] the quality of being exact or correct [≠ **inaccuracy**]: *He passes the ball with amazing accuracy.*

accurate /ˈækjʊrət/ *adj* exact and correct [≠ **inaccurate**]: *Patients should be given **accurate information** about their treatment.* | *These figures are not completely accurate.* | *an accurate shot* → see box at **RIGHT** —accurately *adv*

accusation /ˌækjʊˈzeɪʃən/ *n* [C] a statement saying that someone has done something wrong or illegal: **+against** *Both boys **made serious accusations** against each other.*

accuse /əˈkjuːz/ *v* [T] to say that someone has done something wrong or illegal: **accuse sb of (doing) sth** *Are you accusing me of lying?* | *He was accused of theft.* —accuser *n* [C]

accused /əˈkjuːzd/ *n* **the accused** [singular or plural] the person or people who are accused of a crime in a court of law

accusing /əˈkjuːzɪŋ/ *adj* showing that you think someone has done something wrong: *She gave him **an accusing look**.* —accusingly *adv*

accustom /əˈkʌstəm/ *v* **accustom yourself to (doing) sth** to make yourself get used to something and accept it: *He had accustomed himself to living alone.*

accustomed /əˈkʌstəmd/ *adj formal* **be accustomed to (doing) sth** to be used to something and accept it as normal: *She was accustomed to a life of luxury.* | **become/get/grow accustomed to sth** *Ed's eyes quickly grew accustomed to the dark.*

ace[1] /eɪs/ *n* [C] **1** a PLAYING CARD with one symbol on it, that has the highest or lowest value in a game: **+of** *the ace of hearts* → see picture at **PLAYING CARD** **2** a first hit in tennis or VOLLEYBALL that is so good that your opponent cannot reach it **3** someone who is very skilful at doing something: *a soccer ace*

ace[2] *adj informal* very good or skilful → see box at **GOOD**

ache[1] /eɪk/ *v* [I] **1** if part of your body aches, you feel a continuous pain there: **ache from (doing) sth** *My legs were aching from walking so far.* **2** to want to do or have something very much: **+to** *Jenny was aching to go home.* | **+for** *I was aching for sleep.*

ache[2] *n* [C] a continuous pain: **have a headache/backache/toothache etc** (=have a continuous pain in your head etc) *Tommy has an earache.* | *a bad stomach ache* —achy *adj*

achieve /əˈtʃiːv/ *v* [T] to succeed in getting a good result or in doing something you want: *Most of our students **achieve** excellent exam results.* | **achieve an aim/ambition/goal** *She had finally **achieved** her **ambition** to sail around the world.* —achiever *n* [C] *a high achiever* (=someone who is very successful) —achievable *adj*

achievement /əˈtʃiːvmənt/ *n* **1** [C] something good and impressive that you succeed in doing: **great/major/remarkable etc achievement** *Putting a man on the moon was one of our greatest achievements.* | *an impressive achievement of 144 points* **2** [U] when you succeed in doing or getting something you want: **+of** *the achievement of a lifetime's ambition* | *educational achievement* | *the **sense of achievement** you get from doing a job well*

acid[1] /ˈæsɪd/ *n* [C,U] a liquid chemical substance. Some types of acid can burn holes in things or damage your skin: *hydrochloric acid* —acidic /əˈsɪdɪk/ *adj* —acidity /əˈsɪdɪti/ *n* [U]

acid[2] *adj* **1** having a very sour taste **2** **acid remark/comment** something you say that uses humour in an unkind way to criticize someone **3** containing acid: *an acid solution*

acid 'rain *n* [U] rain that contains acid chemicals, for example from factory smoke and cars, and that is harmful to the environment → see box at **ENVIRONMENT**

acknowledge /əkˈnɒlɪdʒ $ -ˈnɑː-/ *v* [T] **1** to accept or admit that something is true or official: **+(that)** *Angie acknowledged that she'd made a mistake.* | *They are refusing to acknowledge the court's decision.* **2** [usually passive] to recognize how good or important someone or something is: **acknowledge sth as sth** *These beaches are acknowledged as the cleanest in Europe.* | **acknowledge sth to be sth** *He's widely acknowledged to be the best in his field.* **3** to write to someone telling them that you have received something they sent you: *They still haven't acknowledged my letter.* **4** to show someone that you have seen them or heard what they said: *Tom **acknowledged** her **presence** with a quick smile.*

acknowledgement, **acknowledgment** /əkˈnɒlɪdʒmənt $ -ˈnɑː-/ *n* **1** [C,U] when you show that you accept something is true: **+of** *He bowed his head **in acknowledgement** of defeat.* **2** [C] a letter that tells you someone has received something you sent them: *Have you **received an acknowledgement** yet?* **3** [singular, U] when you make a movement to show you have noticed someone or heard what they said: **a nod/smile/wave etc of acknowledgement** **4** **acknowledgements** [plural] a short piece of writing in a book in which the writer thanks the people who have helped with it

acne /ˈækni/ *n* [U] a skin problem that causes spots to appear on the face and is common among young people

acorn /ˈeɪkɔːn $ -ɔːrn, -ərn/ *n* [C] the nut of an OAK tree → see picture at **PLANT**

A

acoustic

acoustic guitar

electric
guitar

amplifier

lead BrE/
cord AmE

acoustic /ə'ku:stɪk/ adj **1** relating to sound and the way people hear things **2** an acoustic musical instrument is not electric: an acoustic guitar

acoustics /ə'ku:stɪks/ n [plural] the way in which the shape and size of a room affect how well or badly you can hear music, speech etc

acquaintance /ə'kweɪntəns/ n **1** [C] someone you know, but do not know well **2 make sb's acquaintance** formal to meet someone for the first time

acquainted /ə'kweɪntɪd/ adj formal **1** if you are acquainted with someone, you have met them a few times but do not know them very well: Doug and I are already acquainted. **2 be acquainted with sth** to know about something, because you have seen it, read it, used it etc: My lawyer's already acquainted with the facts.

acquiesce /ˌækwi'es/ v [I] formal to agree to do what someone wants, or to allow something to happen, although you do not like it —**acquiescence** n [U]

acquire /ə'kwaɪə $ ə'kwaɪr/ v [T] formal **1** to get something, especially by buying it: The museum acquired the painting for £6.8 million. **2** to learn something: **acquire knowledge/skills** He's acquired some knowledge of Arabic.

acquisition /ˌækwɪ'zɪʃən/ n **1** [U] the process of getting or learning something: +of the acquisition of wealth **2** [C] something that you have obtained, especially by buying it: This sofa's a new acquisition.

acquit /ə'kwɪt/ v [T usually passive] **acquitted**, **acquitting** to decide in a court of law that someone is not guilty of a crime: **acquit sb of sth** Simons was acquitted of murder.

acquittal /ə'kwɪtl/ n [C,U] an official statement in a court of law that someone is not guilty

acre /'eɪkə $ -ər/ n [C] a unit for measuring an area of land, equal to 4840 square yards or about 4047 square metres

acrid /'ækrɪd/ adj having a very strong and unpleasant smell that hurts your nose or throat: a cloud of acrid smoke

acrimonious /ˌækrɪ'məʊniəs◄ $ -'moʊ-/ adj an acrimonious meeting, argument etc involves a lot of anger and disagreement: an acrimonious divorce —**acrimoniously** adv

acrobat /'ækrəbæt/ n [C] someone who does skilful physical actions to entertain people, for example balancing on a high rope —**acrobatic** /ˌækrə'bætɪk◄/ adj

acrobatics /ˌækrə'bætɪks/ n [plural] skilful actions like those of an acrobat

acronym /'ækrənɪm/ n [C] a word made from the first letters of the name of something. For example, NATO is an acronym for the North Atlantic Treaty Organization.

across /ə'krɒs $ ə'krɔːs/ adv, prep
1 from one side of something to the other side: the first flight across the Atlantic | There wasn't a bridge so we swam across. | **go/run/come etc straight across** (=go across in a direct line or without stopping) The road runs straight across the desert. | **10 feet/5 metres etc across** (=used to show how wide something is) In places, the river is two km across. → see picture on page A8
2 on the opposite side of something: Andy lives **across the road**. | **across (sth) from sb/sth** France is just across the Channel from here.
3 across the board affecting everyone or everything: a pay increase of 8% across the board

acrylic /ə'krɪlɪk/ adj acrylic paints or cloth are made from chemical substances, not natural ones

act[1] /ækt/ v
1 [I] to do something: Unless the UN acts soon, more people will die. | **act on advice/orders/instructions** (=do what someone says) We're acting on the advice of our lawyer.
2 [I] to behave in a particular way: Nick's been **acting strangely** recently. | Do you think the company **acted reasonably**? | +**like** Stop acting like a baby! | **act cool/crazy/tough etc** a gang of boys trying to act tough | He's not really upset – he's **just acting** (=pretending to be upset)!
3 [I,T] to perform in a play or film: She started acting when she was 12. | Which character are you acting?
4 [I] to have a particular use or effect: +**as** Salt acts as a preservative. | +**on** the way that drugs act on the brain | **act as agent/chairman/consultant etc** (=do a particular job, especially for a short time) Mr Compton has kindly agreed to act as Secretary for this event.

act sth ⇔ out phr v to show how something happened by performing it like a play: The children read the story and then acted it out.

act up phr v if a child acts up, he or she behaves badly

act[2] n
1 [C] something that you do: +**of** an act of kindness | **in the act of doing sth** (=at the moment that you are doing something) The man was **caught in the act of** leaving the building. | a criminal act
2 also **Act** [C] a law that has been officially accepted by the government: The Criminal Justice Act | **Act of Congress/Parliament**
3 also **Act** [C] one of the main parts of a play, OPERA etc: Hamlet kills the king in Act 5.
4 [C] a short piece of entertainment on television or stage: a **comedy act**
5 [singular] behaviour that is not sincere: He never loved me – it was **just an act**.
6 get your act together informal to start to do things in a more organized way: You'll have to get your act together before the exams.
7 get in on the act informal to become involved in a successful activity that someone else has started

acting[1] /ˈæktɪŋ/ *adj* **acting manager/director etc** someone who does an important job until the usual person comes back, or until a new person is chosen

acting[2] *n* [U] the job or skill of performing in plays or films

action /ˈækʃən/ *n*

1 [U] when you do something, especially to achieve a particular thing: *The government must* ***take action*** *to stop the rise in crime.* | **course/ plan of action** (=way of dealing with a situation) *The* ***best course of action*** *is to tell her the whole story.* | **firm/tough/direct etc action** *He realized the need for immediate action.* | *Most people are against* ***military action****.*
2 [C] something that you do: *You cannot be responsible for other people's actions.* | **quick/ swift/prompt action** *Tanya's prompt action saved his life.*
3 in action doing a particular job, activity, or sport: *photos of ski jumpers* ***in action*** | *a chance to see the new technology* ***in action***
4 out of action broken and not working, or injured and not able to do things such as sport: *The photocopier's* ***out of action*** *again.* | *His injury* ***put*** *him* ***out of action*** *for a month.*
5 [U] *informal* exciting things that are happening: *New York's* ***where the action is****.* | **an action movie** (=one with a lot of fast, exciting scenes) | **action-packed** *holidays for teenagers*
6 the action the events in a story, film, play etc: *The action takes place in southern Italy.*
7 [U] fighting in a war: *Ann's husband was* ***killed in action****.* | *buildings destroyed by* ***enemy action***
8 [C,U] the process of deciding something in a court of law: *They threatened to* ***take legal action*** *against him.*
9 [singular] the way something moves or works, or the effect it has on something: **+of** *the action of the heart* | *the action of bacteria on the skin*

ˌaction ˈreplay *n* [C] *BrE* an exciting moment in a sports game that is shown again on television immediately after it happens [= **instant replay** *AmE*]

activate /ˈæktɪ̥veɪt/ *v* [T] *formal* to make something start working: *This switch activates the alarm.*

active[1] /ˈæktɪv/ *adj*

1 always doing things, or moving around a lot [≠ **inactive**]: *games for active youngsters* | *She's 80, but still very active.*
2 involved in an organization or activity by doing things for it: **active member/supporter** *an active member of the local football club* | *Students should* ***take an active part*** *in discussions.*
3 *technical* something that is active is ready or able to work as expected: *The virus is active even at low temperatures.* | *an* ***active volcano*** (=able to explode at any time)
4 *technical* an active verb or sentence has the person or thing doing the action as its SUBJECT. In 'The boy kicked the ball', the verb 'kick' is active. [≠ **passive**]
→ **PROACTIVE**

active[2] *n* **the active (voice)** the active form of a verb [➡ **passive**]

actively /ˈæktɪvli/ *adv* in a way that involves doing things or taking part in something: *Parents must be* ***actively involved*** *in their children's education.*

activist /ˈæktɪ̥vɪ̥st/ *n* [C] someone who works to achieve social or political change

activity /ækˈtɪvɪ̥ti/ *n plural* **activities**

1 [C *usually plural*] something that you do for enjoyment in a regular organized way: **leisure/ recreational/social etc activities** *outdoor activities such as hiking and climbing*
2 [C,U] things that people do to achieve a particular aim: **political/business/economic etc activity** *the department's research activities* | *terrorist activity*
3 [U] when a lot of things are happening, or when people are moving around [≠ **inactivity**]: *The house is full of activity once the kids get home.*

actor /ˈæktə $ -ər/ *n* [C] someone who performs in a play or film → see box at **FILM**

actress /ˈæktrɪ̥s/ *n* [C] a woman who performs in a play or film → see box at **FILM**

actual /ˈæktʃuəl/ *adj* real or exact: *Were those his actual words?* | *Germany won, but I don't know the actual score.* | **In actual fact** (=actually), *she's older than me.*

actually /ˈæktʃuəli, -tʃəli/ *adv especially spoken*

1 used to emphasize that something is true, especially when it is a little surprising or unexpected: *Prices have actually fallen.* | *Disappointed? No, actually I feel rather glad.* | *Actually he's 45.*
2 used to politely give more information, give your opinion etc: *I've known him all my life, actually.* | *Actually, I think I prefer this one.*

acumen /ˈækjə̥mən, əˈkjuːmən/ *n* [U] the ability to think quickly and make good decisions: *business acumen*

acupuncture /ˈækjə̥ˌpʌŋktʃə $ -ər/ *n* [U] a way of treating pain or illness by putting thin needles into parts of the body

acute /əˈkjuːt/ *adj* **1** very serious or severe: *an* ***acute shortage*** *of teachers* | *acute pain* | *an* ***acute infection*** *of the throat* **2** good at understanding things quickly and clearly: *an* ***acute mind*** **3** an acute sense or feeling is very strong: *an* ***acute sense*** *of smell* | *acute feelings of anxiety* **4** *technical* an acute angle is less than 90 degrees

acutely /əˈkjuːtli/ *adv* feeling or noticing something very strongly: *We are* ***acutely aware*** *of the problem.* | *acutely embarrassed*

ad /æd/ *n* [C] *informal* an advertisement

AD /ˌeɪ ˈdiː/ *Anno Domini* used to show that a date is a particular number of years after the birth of Christ [➥ **BC**]: *453 AD*

adage /ˈædɪdʒ/ *n* [C] a well-known phrase that says something wise about life

adamant /ˈædəmənt/ *adj formal* determined not to change your opinion, decision etc —**adamantly** *adv*

ˌAdam's ˈapple / $ ˈ.. ˌ../ *n* [C] the lump at the front of your neck that moves when you talk or swallow

adapt /əˈdæpt/ *v* **1** [I,T] to change your behaviour or ideas because it is necessary in a new

A

situation: **+to** *Children may find it hard to adapt to a new school.* | **adapt yourself/itself etc (to sth)** *Insects adapt themselves to many environments.* → see box at **CHANGE** **2** [T] to change something so that it is suitable for a different purpose: **+to** *Our car has been adapted to take unleaded fuel.* | **adapt sth for sb/sth** *Her first novel was adapted for television* (=changed and made into a film or television programme). **3 be well adapted to sth** to be especially suitable for something: *flowers that are well adapted to the cold winters*

adaptable /ə'dæptəbəl/ *adj* able to change and be successful in new and different situations —**adaptability** /ə,dæptə'bɪlɨti/ *n* [U]

adaptation /,ædæp'teɪʃən/ *n* **1** [C] a play, film, or television programme that is based on a book **2** [U] when someone or something changes in order to be suitable for a new situation: **+to** *successful adaptation to retirement*

adapter, **adaptor** /ə'dæptə $ -ər/ *n* [C] an object you use to connect two pieces of electrical equipment, or to connect more than one piece of equipment to the same power supply

add /æd/ *v*
1 [T] to put something with something else, or with a group of other things: *Just add a little water.* | **add sth to sth** *Do you want to add your name to the mailing list?* → see box at **RECIPE**
2 [T] to put numbers or amounts together to calculate the total [≠ **subtract**]: **add sth and sth** *Add 5 and 3 to make 8.* | **add sth to sth** *The interest will be added to your savings every six months.* → see box at **CALCULATE**
3 [I,T] to increase the amount or cost of something: **add (sth) to sth** *Sales tax adds 15% to the bill.* | *Let's try not to add to the problem.*
4 [T] to say something extra about what you have just said: *'It's too late anyway,' he added.* | **+that** *The judge added that this case was the worst she had ever seen.* → see box at **SAY**
5 add insult to injury to make a bad situation even worse for someone who has already been treated badly

add sth ⇔ on *phr v* to put another part or amount on something, so that it is bigger: *They're going to add on another bedroom.* | **+to** *A service charge will be added on to your bill.*

add up *phr v* **1** to calculate the total of several numbers or amounts: **add sth ⇔ up** *Add your scores up and see who's won.* **2 not add up** to not seem true or reasonable: *His story* (=explanation) *doesn't add up.*

added /'ædɨd/ *adj* more than what is usual or natural [= **extra**]: *This method has an added advantage.* | *fruit juice with no added sugar*

adder /'ædə $ -ər/ *n* [C] a small poisonous snake

addict /'ædɪkt/ *n* [C] **1** someone who is unable to stop taking drugs: *a heroin addict* **2** someone who likes something very much and does it a lot: *television addicts*

addicted /ə'dɪktɨd/ *adj* **1** unable to stop taking a drug: **+to** *Marvin soon became addicted to sleeping pills.* **2** liking something so much that you do not want to stop doing it or having it: **+to** *My kids are addicted to surfing the Net.* —**addiction** /ə'dɪkʃən/ *n* [C,U] *addiction to nicotine* —**addictive** *adj*: *a highly addictive drug*

addition /ə'dɪʃən/ *n*
1 in addition used to add another piece of information to what you have just said: *The group meets four times a week; in addition we have individual counselling sessions.* | **+to** *In addition to her teaching job, she plays in a band.*
2 [U] the act of adding something to something else: **the addition of sth** *The addition of herbs and spices improves the flavour.*
3 [U] the process of adding together several numbers or amounts to get a total [➔ **subtraction**]
4 [C] something that is added: *The tower is a later addition to the cathedral.*

additional /ə'dɪʃənəl/ *adj* more than you already have, or more than was agreed or expected [➔ **extra**]: *Additional information can be obtained from the centre.* —**additionally** *adv*

additive /'ædɨtɪv/ *n* [C usually plural] a substance that is added to food to make it taste or look better or to keep it fresh

address¹ /ə'dres $ ə'dres, 'ædres/ *n* [C]
1 the details of where someone lives or works, including the number of the building, name of the street and town etc: *What's your new address?* | *Please notify us of any change of address.*
2 a series of letters or numbers used to send an email to someone, or to reach a page of information on the Internet: *Give me your email address.*
3 a formal speech: *the Gettysburg Address*

address² /ə'dres/ *v* [T]
1 to write a name and address on an envelope, package etc: **address sth to sb** *There's a letter here addressed to you.*
2 *formal* to speak directly to a person or a group: *A guest speaker then addressed the audience.* | **address sth to sb** *You should address your question to the chairman.*
3 *formal* if you address a problem, you start trying to solve it: **address a problem/issue/question** *We are now starting to address the problem of oil on the beaches.*
4 to use a particular name or title when speaking or writing to someone: **address sb as sth** *The President should be addressed as 'Mr. President'.*

adept /'ædept, ə'dept $ ə'dept/ *adj* good at doing something that needs care or skill [≠ **inept**]: *He became adept at cooking her favourite dishes.* —**adeptly** *adv*

adequate /'ædɪkwɨt/ *adj* **1** enough in quantity or of a good enough quality for a particular purpose [≠ **inadequate**]: *Her income is hardly adequate to pay the bills.* **2** fairly good, but not excellent: *Her performance was adequate but lacked originality.* —**adequately** *adv* —**adequacy** *n* [U]

adhere /əd'hɪə $ -'hɪr/ *v* [I] to stick firmly to something: **+to** *The eggs of these fish adhere to plant leaves.*

adhere to sth *phr v* to continue to behave according to a particular rule, agreement, or belief: *I have adhered strictly to the rules.*

adherent /əd'hɪərənt $ -'hɪr-/ *n* [C] someone who supports a particular belief, plan, political party etc —**adherence** *n* [U] *adherence to democratic principles*

adhesion /əd'hiːʒən/ n [U] when one thing sticks to another thing

adhesive /əd'hiːsɪv/ n [C,U] a substance such as glue that can stick things together —**adhesive** adj: adhesive tape

ad hoc /æd 'hɒk◂ $ -'haːk◂, -'hoʊk◂/ adj done when necessary, rather than planned or regular: I work for them **on an ad hoc basis**. —**ad hoc** adv

adj. also **adj** BrE the written abbreviation of **adjective**

adjacent /ə'dʒeɪsənt/ adj formal next to something: a door leading to the adjacent room | **+to** buildings adjacent to the palace

adjective /'ædʒɪ̞ktɪv/ n [C] a word that tells you more about a noun. 'Big', 'funny', and 'hot' are all adjectives.
—**adjectival** /ˌædʒɪ̞k'taɪvəl◂/ adj: an adjectival phrase

adjoining /ə'dʒɔɪnɪŋ/ adj next to something, and connected to it: adjoining rooms —**adjoin** v [T]

adjourn /ə'dʒɜːn $ -ɜːrn/ v [I,T] to stop a meeting or a legal process for a short time or until a later date: The committee adjourned for an hour. —**adjournment** n [C,U]

adjudicate /ə'dʒuːdɪkeɪt/ v [I,T] formal to be the judge in a competition or make an official decision about a problem or argument: The European Court was asked to adjudicate in the dispute. —**adjudicator** n [C] —**adjudication** /əˌdʒuːdɪ'keɪʃən/ n [U]

adjust /ə'dʒʌst/ v **1** [I,T] to make small changes to the way you do things in order to get used to a new situation or condition: **+to** We're gradually adjusting to the new way of working. **2** [T] to change or move something slightly to improve it or make it more suitable for a particular purpose: Check and adjust the brakes regularly. → see box at **CHANGE** —**adjustable** adj: an adjustable lamp

adjustment /ə'dʒʌstmənt/ n [C,U] **1** a small change made to a machine, system, or calculation: I've **made** a few **adjustments to** our original calculations. **2** a change in the way you behave or think: a **period of adjustment**

ad-lib /ˌæd 'lɪb/ v [I,T] **ad-libbed, ad-libbing** to say things that you have not prepared or planned to say when you are performing or giving a speech: She forgot her lines and had to ad-lib. —**ad-lib** n [C]

administer /əd'mɪnɪ̞stə $ -ər/ v [T] **1** to manage the work or money of a company or organization: officials who administer the transport system **2** to provide or organize something officially as part of your job: **administer sth to sb** The test was administered to all 11-year olds. **3** formal to give someone a drug or medical treatment: The medicine was administered in regular doses.

administration /ədˌmɪnɪ̞'streɪʃən/ n [U] **1** also **admin** the activities that are involved in managing the work of a company or organization: Have you any experience in administration? **2** the government of a country at a particular time: the Kennedy Administration

administrative /əd'mɪnɪ̞strətɪv $ -streɪtɪv/ adj relating to the work of managing a company or organization: The job is mainly administrative. —**administratively** adv

administrator /əd'mɪnɪ̞streɪtə $ -ər/ n [C] someone whose job involves managing the work of a company or organization

admirable /'ædmərəbəl/ adj having many good qualities that you respect and admire: an admirable achievement —**admirably** adv

admiral /'ædmərəl/ n [C] an officer who has a very high rank in the Navy

admiration /ˌædmə'reɪʃən/ n [U] a feeling of great respect and liking for something or someone: **in admiration** He gazed at her in admiration. | **+for** I'm **full of admiration** for the people who built this.

admire /əd'maɪə $ -'maɪr/ v [T]
1 to respect and like someone because they have done something that you think is good: **admire sb for (doing) sth** I always admired my mother for her courage and patience. | I really **admire the way** she brings up those kids.
2 to look at something and think how beautiful or impressive it is: We stopped halfway to admire the view.
—**admirer** n [C] I'm a great admirer of yours. —**admiring** adj: He took an admiring look at himself in the mirror. —**admiringly** adv

admissible /əd'mɪsɪ̞bəl/ adj formal admissible reasons, facts etc are acceptable or allowed, especially in a court of law [≠ **inadmissible**]: admissible evidence

admission /əd'mɪʃən/ n **1** [C] when you admit that something is true or that you have done something wrong: **+of** If he resigns, it will be an admission of guilt. **2** [C,U] permission given to someone to enter a building or place, or to become a member of a school, club etc: **+to** Tom has applied for admission to Oxford next year. **3** [C,U] the process of taking someone into a hospital for treatment, tests, or care: There are 13,000 hospital admissions annually due to playground accidents. **4** [U] the price charged when you go to a film, sports event, concert etc: Admission $6.50

admit /əd'mɪt/ v **admitted, admitting**
1 [I,T] to agree unwillingly that something is true or that you have done something wrong [≠ **deny**]: 'OK, I was scared,' she admitted. | **+(that)** You may not like her, but you have to admit that she is good at her job. | **+to** He'll never admit to the murder.
2 [T] to allow someone to enter a public place to watch a game, performance etc: Only ticket holders will be admitted into the stadium.
3 be admitted to be taken into hospital because you are ill

admittance /əd'mɪtəns/ n [U] permission to enter a place: Journalists were refused admittance to the meeting.

admittedly /əd'mɪtɪ̞dli/ adv used when you are admitting that something is true: This has led to financial losses, though admittedly on a fairly small scale.

admonish /əd'mɒnɪʃ $ -'maː-/ v [T] literary to tell someone that they have done something wrong —**admonishment** n [C,U]

ado /ə'duː/ n **without more/further ado** without any more delay

A

adolescence /ˌædəˈlesəns/ n [U] the period when a young person is developing into an adult, usually between the ages of 12 and 18

adolescent /ˌædəˈlesənt/ n [C] a young person who is developing into an adult —**adolescent** adj → see box at **YOUNG**

adopt /əˈdɒpt $ əˈdɑːpt/ v **1** [I,T] to take someone else's child into your home and legally become its parent: *Sally was adopted when she was four.* **2** [T] to begin to use a particular plan or way of doing something: *The police are adopting more forceful methods.* **3** [T] to formally approve a suggestion: *The committee voted to adopt our proposals.* —**adoption** /əˈdɒpʃən $ əˈdɑːp-/ n [C,U] *children put up for adoption | the adoption of new technology* —**adopted** adj: *their adopted daughter*

adoptive /əˈdɒptɪv $ əˈdɑːp-/ adj [only before noun] an adoptive parent is one who has adopted a child

adorable /əˈdɔːrəbəl/ adj very attractive: *an adorable little puppy*

adore /əˈdɔː $ əˈdɔːr/ v [T] **1** to love and admire someone very much: *Tim absolutely adores his older brother.* **2** to like something very much: *I simply adore chocolate.* —**adoration** /ˌædəˈreɪʃən/ n [U] —**adoring** adj: *Kylie's adoring fans*

adorn /əˈdɔːn $ -ɔːrn/ v [T] formal **be adorned with sth** to be decorated with something: *church walls adorned with religious paintings* —**adornment** /əˈdɔːnmənt $ -ɔːr-/ n [C,U]

adrenalin /əˈdrenələn/ n [U] a chemical produced by your body that gives you more energy when you are frightened, excited, or angry

adrift /əˈdrɪft/ adv **1** a boat that is adrift is not tied to anything, and is moved around by the ocean or wind **2 come adrift** if something comes adrift, it becomes separated from the thing it should be fastened to

adroit /əˈdrɔɪt/ adj clever and skilful, especially at thinking and speaking —**adroitly** adv

adulation /ˌædʒʊˈleɪʃən/ n [U] formal praise and admiration for someone that is more than they really deserve

adult[1] /ˈædʌlt, əˈdʌlt/ n [C] a fully grown person or animal

adult[2] adj **1** [only before noun] fully grown or developed: *an adult lion | the adult population | He lived most of his adult life in Scotland.* **2** typical of an adult: *an adult view of the world* **3** [only before noun] adult films, magazines etc are about sex or related to sex

adultery /əˈdʌltəri/ n [U] sex between someone who is married and someone who is not their wife or husband: *She had committed adultery on several occasions.* —**adulterous** adj

adulthood /ˈædʌlthʊd, əˈdʌlt-/ n [U] the time when you are an adult [→ **childhood**]

adv. also **adv** BrE the written abbreviation of **adverb**

advance[1] /əˈdvɑːns $ əˈdvæns/ n **1 in advance (of sth)** before something happens or is expected to happen: *The airline suggests booking tickets 21 days in advance.* **2** [C,U] a change, discovery, or invention that brings progress: *medical advances* **3** [C] a movement forward to a new position, especially by an army [≠ **retreat**]:

Napoleon's advance towards Moscow. **4** [C, usually singular] money paid to someone before the usual time: +**on** *Could I have a small advance on my salary?* **5 advances** [plural] an attempt to start a sexual relationship with someone: *She accused her boss of **making advances** to her.*

advance[2] v **1** [I,T] to develop or progress, or to make something develop or progress: *Their analysis does not really advance our understanding of the problem. | He agreed to take the job because he hoped it would **advance** his **career**.* **2** [I] to move forward to a new position [≠ **retreat**]: +**on** *Troops advanced on the rebel stronghold.* —**advancement** n [C,U] *the advancement of science*

advance[3] adj [only before noun] done or given before an event: **advance planning/warning/ booking etc** *advance warning of a hurricane | You can make an advance booking with your credit card.*

advanced /ədˈvɑːnst $ ədˈvænst/ adj **1** very modern: *advanced technology | advanced weapon systems* → see box at **MODERN** **2** studying or dealing with a school subject at a difficult level: *advanced learners of English | advanced physics* **3** having reached a late point in time or development: *By this time, the disease was too far advanced to be treated.*

advantage /ədˈvɑːntɪdʒ $ ədˈvæn-/ n [C,U] **1** something that helps you to be better or more successful than other people [≠ **disadvantage**]: +**of** *the advantages of a good education | +**over** Her computer training gave her an advantage over the other students.* **2** a good or useful quality or condition that something has: +**of** *Good public transport is just one of the advantages of living in a big city. | +**over** The printer has several advantages over conventional printers.* **3 take advantage of sth/sb a)** to use a situation to help you do or get something you want: *I took advantage of the good weather to paint the shed.* **b)** to treat someone unfairly in order to get something for yourself: *I don't mind helping, but I resent being taken advantage of.* **4 use/turn sth to your advantage** to use something that you have or that happens in order to achieve something: *How could he turn the situation to his advantage?*

advantageous /ˌædvənˈteɪdʒəs, ˌædvæn-/ adj helpful and likely to make you more successful [≠ **disadvantageous**]

advent /ˈædvent/ n **the advent of sth** the time when something first begins to be used a lot or by a lot of people: *the advent of the computer*

adventure /ədˈventʃə $ -ər/ n [C,U] an exciting experience in which dangerous or unusual things happen: *a great adventure | an adventure story* —**adventurer** n [C]

adventurous /ədˈventʃərəs/ adj **1** also **adventuresome** /ədˈventʃəsəm $ -tʃər-/ AmE wanting to do new, exciting, or dangerous things: *Andy is a very adventurous rock-climber.* **2** exciting and involving danger —**adventurously** adv

adverb /ˈædvɜːb $ -vɜːrb/ n [C] a word that adds to the meaning of a verb, an adjective, another adverb, or a whole sentence, such as 'slowly' in 'He ran slowly', 'very' in 'It's very hot', or 'naturally' in 'Naturally, we want you to come'
—**adverbial** adj

adversary /ˈædvəsəri $ ˈædvərseri/ n [C] plural **adversaries** formal a country or person you are fighting or competing against

adverse /ˈædvɜːs $ -ɜːrs/ adj formal not good or favourable: the recession's **adverse effect on** the building industry | **adverse weather** conditions
—**adversely** adv

adversity /ədˈvɜːsɪ̩ti $ -ɜːr-/ n [C,U] difficulties or problems in your life: his courage **in the face of adversity**

advert /ˈædvɜːt $ -ɜːrt/ n [C] BrE an advertisement

advertise /ˈædvətaɪz $ -ər-/ v [I,T]
1 to tell the public about a product or service in order to persuade them to buy it or use it: a poster advertising sportswear | I saw your car advertised in the evening paper. | We can't afford to advertise all year round.
2 to make an announcement, for example in a newspaper, that a job is available, an event is going to happen etc: +**for** RCA is advertising for an accountant.
—**advertiser** n [C]

advertisement /ədˈvɜːtɪ̩smənt $ ˌædvərˈtaɪz-/also **ad** informal, **advert** BrE n [C] a picture, set of words, or a short film, which is intended to persuade people to buy a product or use a service, or that gives information about a job that is available, an event that is going to happen etc: +**for** The Sunday papers are full of advertisements for cars.

THESAURUS

commercial – an advertisement on TV or radio
poster – an advertisement on a wall, often with a picture on it
flyer – a piece of paper with an advertisement on it, often given to you in the street
junk mail – unwanted letters in the post advertising things
spam – unwanted e-mails advertising things
want ads AmE/**small ads** BrE/**classified ads** – short advertisements in a newspaper, in which people offer things for sale

advertising /ˈædvətaɪzɪŋ $ -ər-/ n [U] the business of advertising things on television, in newspapers etc: a career in advertising | advertising executives

advice /ədˈvaɪs/ n [U] the things you say to someone when you tell them what you think they should do: +**on/about** a book that's full of advice on babycare | Can you **give** me some **advice** about buying a house? | Beth decided to **ask** her doctor's **advice**. | **legal/medical/financial etc advice** If I were you, I'd get some legal advice. | **take/follow sb's advice** (=do what they advise you to do) Did you take your father's advice? | Let me give you a **piece of advice**.

COMMUNICATION

giving advice

you ought to ...: You ought to see the doctor.
you should ...: I think you should write to her.
if I were you, I'd ...: If I were you, I'd ask for my money back.
why don't you ...: Why don't you catch the later train?
you'd better ...: You'd better ask your teacher.
it would be a good idea to ...: It would be a good idea to book early.

advisable /ədˈvaɪzəbəl/ adj something that is advisable should be done in order to avoid problems or risks [≠ **inadvisable**]: It is advisable to wear a safety belt at all times. —**advisability** /əd,vaɪzəˈbɪlɪ̩ti/ n [U]

advise /ədˈvaɪz/ v
1 [I,T] to tell someone what you think they should do: **advise sb to do sth** The doctor advised me to take more exercise. | **advise (sb) against (doing) sth** I'd advise you against saying anything to the press. | **advise (sb) on sth** Franklin advises us on financial matters. | **advise (sb) that** The doctor advised him that a period of complete rest was the only remedy.
2 you would be well advised to do sth used to strongly advise someone to do something: You would be well advised to see a lawyer.
3 [T] formal to officially tell someone something: You will be advised when the work is completed.

adviser, advisor /ədˈvaɪzə $ -ər/ n [C] someone whose job is to give advice about a subject: a financial adviser

advisory /ədˈvaɪzəri/ adj having the purpose of giving advice: an advisory committee

advocate¹ /ˈædvəkeɪt/ v [T] formal to publicly say that something should be done: Extremists were openly advocating violence. —**advocacy** /-kəsi/ n [U]

advocate² /ˈædvəkɪ̩t, -keɪt/ n [C] **1** someone who publicly supports someone or something: +**of** an advocate of prison reform **2** law a lawyer who defends someone in a court of law

aerial¹ /ˈeəriəl $ ˈer-/ adj [only before noun] from a plane or happening in the air: aerial photos | aerial attacks

aerial² n [C] BrE a piece of metal or wire used for receiving or sending radio or television signals [= **antenna** AmE] → see picture on page A12

aerobic /eəˈrəʊbɪk $ eˈroʊ-/ adj aerobic exercise makes your heart and lungs stronger

aerobics /eəˈrəʊbɪks $ eˈroʊ-/ n [U] active physical exercise done to music, usually in a class: Are you going to aerobics tonight? → see box at EXERCISE

aerodynamics /ˌeərəʊdaɪˈnæmɪks $ ˌeroʊ-/ n [U] the scientific study of how objects move through the air —**aerodynamic** adj

aeroplane /ˈeərəpleɪn $ ˈer-/ BrE; **airplane** AmE n [C] a flying vehicle with wings and at least one engine [= **plane**]

aerosol /ˈeərəsɒl $ ˈerəsɑːl/ n [C] a small metal container in which a liquid substance is kept under pressure. You press a button on the container to make the liquid come out in very small drops.

A

A

aeroplane *BrE*/**airplane** *AmE*

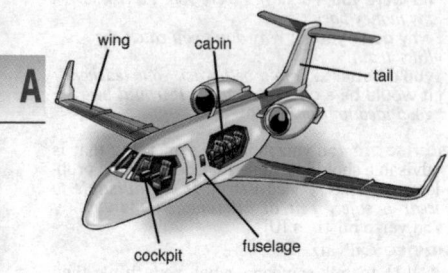

wing   cabin

tail

cockpit   fuselage

aerospace /ˈeərəʊspeɪs $ ˈeroʊ-/ *n* [U] the industry that designs and builds aircraft and space vehicles: *the aerospace industry*

aesthetic also **esthetic** *AmE* /iːsˈθetɪk, es- $ es-/ *adj* relating to beauty and the study of beauty: *the aesthetic qualities of literature* —**aesthetically** /-kli/ *adv*: *aesthetically pleasing*

aesthetics also **esthetics** *AmE* /iːsˈθetɪks, es- $ es-/ *n* [U] the study of beauty, especially beauty in art

afar /əˈfɑː $ əˈfɑːr/ *adv* **from afar** *literary* from a long distance away

affable /ˈæfəbəl/ *adj* friendly and easy to talk to [= **pleasant**]: *an affable guy* —**affably** *adv*

affair /əˈfeə $ əˈfer/ *n* [C]
1 affairs [plural] **a)** public or political events and activities: *a foreign affairs correspondent for CNN* **b)** things connected with your personal life, your financial situation etc: *I don't want to discuss my financial affairs.*
2 an event or a set of related events, especially unpleasant ones: *the Watergate affair* | *The whole affair was a disaster.*
3 a secret sexual relationship between two people, when at least one of them is married to someone else: +**with** *Ed's having an affair with his boss's wife.*
4 be sb's affair if something is your affair, you do not want other people to know about it or become involved in it
→ **LOVE AFFAIR, CURRENT AFFAIRS, STATE OF AFFAIRS**

affect /əˈfekt/ *v* [T]
1 to cause a change in someone or something, or to change the situation they are in: *Help is being sent to areas affected by the floods.* | *decisions which affect our lives*
2 [usually passive] to make someone feel strong emotions: *We were all deeply affected by her death.*

affectation /ˌæfekˈteɪʃən/ *n* [C,U] *disapproving* when someone behaves or speaks in a way that is not natural or sincere

affected /əˈfektɪd/ *adj* not sincere or natural [≠ **unaffected**]: *an affected laugh*

affection /əˈfekʃən/ *n* [C,U] a feeling of liking or loving someone: +**for** *Barry felt a great affection for her.*

affectionate /əˈfekʃənɪt/ *adj* showing that you like or love someone: *an affectionate child* —**affectionately** *adv*

affidavit /ˌæfɪˈdeɪvɪt/ *n* [C] *law* a written statement that you swear is true, used in a court of law

affiliate /əˈfɪlieɪt/ *v* [I,T usually passive] if a group or organization affiliates to or with another larger one, it forms a close connection with it —**affiliated** *adj*: *The Society is not affiliated with any political party.* —**affiliation** /əˌfɪliˈeɪʃən/ *n* [C,U] *What are the group's political affiliations?*

affinity /əˈfɪnɪti/ *n* plural **affinities 1** [singular] the feeling you have when you like and understand someone or something: +**for/with/between** *She felt a natural affinity for these people.* **2** [C,U] a close relationship between two things because of qualities or features that they share

affirm /əˈfɜːm $ -ɜːrm/ *v* [T] *formal* to say definitely that something is true: *The President affirmed his intention to reduce taxes.* —**affirmation** /ˌæfəˈmeɪʃən $ ˈæfər-/ *n* [C,U]

affirmative /əˈfɜːmətɪv $ -ɜːr-/ *adj formal* an affirmative answer or action means 'yes' or shows agreement [≠ **negative**]: *an affirmative nod* —**affirmative** *n* [C] *She answered in the affirmative.* —**affirmatively** *adv*

affix /ˈæfɪks/ *n* [C] *technical* a group of letters added to the beginning or end of a word to change its meaning or use, for example 'un' or 'ness' [➡ **prefix, suffix**]

afflict /əˈflɪkt/ *v* [T] *formal* to affect someone or something in an unpleasant way, and make them suffer: **afflict sb/sth with/by sth** *Towards the end of his life he was afflicted with blindness.* | *a country afflicted by famine* —**affliction** /əˈflɪkʃən/ *n* [C,U]

affluent /ˈæfluənt/ *adj* having a lot of money, nice houses, expensive things etc [➡ **wealthy**]: *an affluent suburb of Paris* | *affluent families* —**affluence** *n* [U]

afford /əˈfɔːd $ -ɔːrd/ *v* [T]
1 can/could afford a) to have enough money to pay for something: *I wish we could afford a new computer.* | **afford to do sth** *I can't afford to buy a new car.* **b)** to have enough time to do something: *Dad can't afford any more time off work.* **c)** if you cannot afford to do something, you must not do it because it could cause serious problems for you: **afford to do sth** *We can't afford to offend our regular customers.*
2 *formal* to provide something: *The walls afforded some protection from the wind.* —**affordable** *adj*: *affordable housing*

affront /əˈfrʌnt/ *n* [singular] a remark or action that offends or insults someone: *The accusation was an affront to his pride.*

afield /əˈfiːld/ *adv* **far/further afield** far or further away: *As he grew more confident, he started to wander further afield.*

afloat /əˈfləʊt $ əˈfloʊt/ *adj* **1** floating on water **2 keep (sb/sth) afloat/stay afloat** to have enough money to pay your debts and continue in business: *She had to borrow more money just to keep the company afloat.*

afoot /ə'fʊt/ *adj* [not before noun] being planned or happening: *There were plans afoot for a second attack.*

afraid /ə'freɪd/ *adj* [not before noun]
1 frightened because you think that you may get hurt or that something bad may happen [= **frightened, scared**]: *There's no need to be afraid.* | **+of** *kids who are afraid of the dark* | **afraid to do sth** *She was afraid to go back into the house.* → see box at **FRIGHTENED**
2 worried about something: **afraid of doing sth** *A lot of people are afraid of losing their jobs.* | **afraid to do sth** *Don't be afraid to ask for help.* | **+(that)** *He was afraid that the other kids would laugh at him.* | **afraid for sb/sth** (=worried that something bad may happen to a particular person or thing) *I thought you were in danger and I was afraid for you.*
3 I'm afraid *spoken* used to politely tell someone something that may annoy, upset, or disappoint them: *I won't be able to come with you, I'm afraid.* | **+(that)** *I'm afraid this is a no smoking area.* | *'Are we late?' 'I'm afraid so* (=yes).*' | *'Are there any tickets left?' 'I'm afraid not* (=no).*'*

afresh /ə'freʃ/ *adv* **start afresh** to start again from the beginning: *We decided to move to Sydney and start afresh.*

African American /ˌæfrɪkən ə'merɪ̩kən/ *n* [C] an American with dark skin, whose family originally came from the part of Africa south of the Sahara Desert

Afro-Caribbean /ˌæfrəʊ kærɪ̩'biːən $ ˌæfrou-/ *adj* relating to a person whose family originally came from Africa, and who was born or whose parents were born in the Caribbean

after /'ɑːftə $ 'æftər/ *prep, linking word, adv*
1 when a particular time or event has happened, or when someone has done something [≠ **before**]: *What are you doing after class?* | *After you called the police, what did you do?* | **after doing sth** *After leaving school, he worked in a restaurant.* | **the day/week/year etc after (sth)** *I'll see you again tomorrow or the day after.* | **an hour/2 weeks etc after (sth)** *We left an hour after daybreak.* | *He discovered the jewel was a fake a month after he bought it.* | **soon/not long/shortly after (sth)** *We arrived soon after they did.*
2 when a particular amount of time has passed [≠ **before**]: *After 10 minutes remove the cake from the oven.* | *After a while, the woman returned.*
3 following someone or something else in a list or a piece or writing, or in order of importance: *Whose name is after mine on the list?* | *After football, tennis is my favourite sport.*
4 following someone in order to stop or speak to them: *Go after him and apologize.*
5 *AmE* used to say how many minutes past the hour it is when saying the time [= **past** *BrE*]: *It's 10 after five.*
6 day after day/year after year etc continuously for a very long time: *Day after day we waited, hoping she'd call.*
7 one after the other/one after another if a series of events or actions happen one after another, each one happens soon after the previous one: *Ever since we moved here it's been one problem after another.*
8 because of something that has happened: *I'm surprised he came, after the way you treated him.*
9 when someone has left a place or has finished doing something: *I spend all day cleaning up after the kids.*
10 in spite of something: *After all the trouble I had, Reese didn't even say thank you.*
11 be after sb/sth a) to be looking for someone or something: *He's always in trouble – the police are after him again.* **b)** to want to have something that belongs to someone else: *You're just after my money!*
12 after all a) used to say that what you expected did not happen: *Rita didn't have my pictures after all. Jake did.* | *It didn't rain after all.* **b)** used when saying something that shows why you are right: *Don't shout at him – he's only a baby, after all.*
13 be called/named after sb to be given the same name as someone else: *She was named Sarah, after my grandmother.*

'after-ef,fect *n* [C usually plural] a bad effect that remains after something has ended: **+of** *the after-effects of an illness*

afterlife /'ɑːftəlaɪf $ 'æftər-/ *n* [singular] the life that some people believe you have after you die

aftermath /'ɑːftəmæθ $ 'æftər-/ *n* [singular] the time after an important or bad event: **in the aftermath of** *the refugee crisis in the aftermath of the civil war*

afternoon /ˌɑːftə'nuːn◂ $ 'æftər-/ *n* [C,U] the period of time after the morning and before the evening [➡ **morning, evening**]: **in the afternoon** *It was very hot in the afternoon.* | **on Monday/Friday etc afternoon** *I'll see you on Tuesday afternoon.* | *Do you want to go swimming **this afternoon*** (=today in the afternoon)*?* | **yesterday/tomorrow afternoon** *We met yesterday afternoon.* | *an afternoon sleep*
→ **GOOD AFTERNOON**

aftershave /'ɑːftəʃeɪv $ 'æftər-/ *n* [C,U] a liquid with a nice smell that a man puts on his face

aftertaste /'ɑːftəteɪst $ 'æftər-/ *n* [C usually singular] a taste that stays in your mouth after you eat or drink something: *a drink with a strong aftertaste*

afterthought /'ɑːftəθɔːt $ 'æftərθɒːt/ *n* [C usually singular] something that you mention or add later because you did not think of it before: *'Bring Clare too,' he added as an afterthought.*

afterwards /'ɑːftəwədz $ 'æftərwərdz/ also **afterward** *AmE adv* after an event or time that has been mentioned: *Charles arrived **shortly afterwards**.* | *For years afterwards, I felt guilty about what happened.* | *Two days afterwards, I received a call.* | *Afterwards, he told me they were getting married.*

again /ə'gen, ə'geɪn $ ə'gen/ *adv*
1 one more time: *Could you say that again? I didn't hear.* | *I'll never go there again.* | **yet/once again** (=used to emphasize that something has happened before) *He had to apologize yet again.* | *The cake burned so we had to start **all over again*** (=from the beginning).

2 back to the same condition, situation, or place as before: *I'll come and see you when I'm well again.* | *It's great to have you home again.*
3 again and again many times: *He read the letter again and again.*
4 then/there again *spoken* used to add a fact that is different from what you have just said or makes it seem less true: *I prefer showers but then again I do like having a bath occasionally.*

against /ə'genst, ə'geɪnst $ ə'genst/ *prep*
1 not agreeing with something: *John was against the idea of selling the house.* | *We are against testing cosmetics on animals.*
2 used to say who is affected by something in a bad way: *violence against elderly people* | *discrimination against women*
3 used to say who someone is competing or fighting with: *The team will play against Hungary on Saturday.*
4 trying to stop something from happening: *the battle against crime* | *We must take action against homelessness.*
5 against the law/the rules not allowed by the law or the rules: *It is against the law to sell alcohol to children.*
6 against sb's wishes/advice/orders etc if you do something against someone's wishes etc, you do it even though they tell you not to do it: *She got married against her parents' wishes.*
7 touching a surface: *The cat's fur felt soft against her face.* | *Chris leaned back against the wall.* → see picture on page A8
8 in the opposite direction to the movement or flow of something: *sailing against the wind*
9 protecting you from something: *insurance against injury*
10 have sth against sb/sth to dislike or disapprove of someone or something: *I have nothing against dogs but I don't want one myself.*

age[1] /eɪdʒ/ *n*
1 [C,U] the number of years someone has lived or something has existed: *games for children of all ages* | *Patrick is the same age as me.* | **at the age of 12/50 etc** *formal* *She married at the age of 19.* | **4/15 etc years of age** *formal* (=4, 15 etc years old) | **over/under the age of 16/30 etc** *people over the age of 65* | **(of) his/her etc own age** (=of the same age as him/her etc) *He doesn't have many friends of his own age.* | **for his/her age** (=compared with other people the same age) *Judy's very tall for her age.*
2 [U] the age when you are legally old enough to do something: *You can't buy alcohol, you're **under age**.* | **retirement/school/voting age** (=when you are old enough to stop working, start going to school, vote) *I went back to work when the children reached school age.*
3 [C,U] a period in someone's life: *women of childbearing age* | *The teens are often a difficult age.*
4 [U] when something is old: **with age** *Wine often improves with age.*
5 ages [plural] *informal* a long time: *It's ages since I saw him.* | **for ages** *I haven't been there for ages.*
6 [C] a period of history: *the modern age* | **+of** *the age of new technology*
7 come of age a) to reach the age when you are legally an adult **b)** if something comes of

age, people start to accept and respect it: *The festival has finally come of age.*
→ MIDDLE-AGED, OLD AGE, UNDER-AGE

age[2] *v* [I,T] present participle **aging** or **ageing** to become or look older, or to make someone look older: *He has aged a lot since his wife died.*
—**ageing** *BrE*, **aging** *AmE adj: an aging rock star*

aged[1] /eɪdʒd/ *adj* **aged 5/15 etc** 5, 15 etc years old: **+between** *Police are searching for a man aged between 25 and 30.*

aged[2] /'eɪdʒɪd/ *adj* **1** very old: *his aged parents* **2 the aged** old people: *the cost of caring for the sick and aged*

'age group *n* [C] the people between two ages, considered as a group: *people **in the** 18–44 **age group***

ageist /'eɪdʒɪst/ *adj* treating older people unfairly because of a belief that they are less important than younger people —**ageism** *n* [U]

ageless /'eɪdʒləs/ *adj* never seeming old or old-fashioned: *furniture with an ageless quality*

agency /'eɪdʒənsi/ *n* [C] plural **agencies** **1** a business that provides a particular service for people or organizations: *an advertising agency* **2** an organization or government department that does a particular job: *the UN agency responsible for helping refugees* → TRAVEL AGENCY

agenda /ə'dʒendə/ *n* [C] **1** a list of things that an organization is planning to do: **on the agenda** *This has put environmental issues on the political agenda.* | **be high on/top of the agenda** (=be one of the most important things that should be done first) *Health care reforms are high on the President's agenda.* | *The government set an agenda for constitutional reform.* **2** a list of the subjects that will be discussed at a meeting: **on the agenda** *The next item on the agenda is finance.* **3 hidden agenda** *disapproving* the secret purpose behind something that you do: *Was there a hidden agenda behind their decision?*

agent /'eɪdʒənt/ *n* [C] **1** a person or company that arranges services or does work for other people: *Our agent in Rome handles all our Italian contracts.* **2** someone who tries to get secret information about another government or organization → ESTATE AGENT, TRAVEL AGENT

'age-old *adj* having existed for a very long time: *age-old traditions*

aggravate /'æɡrəveɪt/ *v* [T] **1** to make a bad situation, illness, or injury worse: *Exercise may aggravate the injury.* **2** to annoy someone —**aggravating** *adj* —**aggravation** /ˌæɡrə'veɪʃən/ *n* [C,U]

aggregate /'æɡrɪɡət/ *n* [C,U] *formal* a total —**aggregate** *adj*

aggression /ə'ɡreʃən/ *n* [U] angry or violent behaviour or feelings: *an **act of aggression*** | **+towards** *Our dogs have never shown any aggression towards other dogs.*

aggressive /ə'ɡresɪv/ *adj*
1 behaving in an angry or violent way towards someone: *an aggressive attitude*
2 very determined to succeed: *aggressive marketing* —**aggressively** *adv* —**aggressiveness** *n* [U]

aggressor /ə'ɡresə $ -ər/ *n* [C] a person or country that starts a fight or war

aggrieved /ə'ɡriːvd/ *adj* angry or unhappy because you think you have been treated unfairly

aghast /ə'ɡɑːst $ ə'ɡæst/ adj [not before noun] *written* shocked: **+at** *They were aghast at the verdict.* | *She stared at him aghast.*

agile /'ædʒaɪl $ 'ædʒəl/ adj **1** able to move quickly and easily: *She was strong and agile.* **2** someone who has an agile mind is able to think quickly and intelligently —**agility** /ə'dʒɪlᵻti/ n [U]

agitate /'ædʒᵻteɪt/ v [I] *formal* to protest in order to achieve social or political changes: **+for/against** *workers agitating for higher pay* —**agitator** n [C]

agitated /'ædʒᵻteɪtᵻd/ adj very worried or upset: *He was in an agitated state.* —**agitation** /ˌædʒᵻ'teɪʃən/ n [U]

AGM /ˌeɪ dʒiː 'em/ n [C] *BrE* **annual general meeting** a meeting that a business or organization has every year

agnostic /æɡ'nɒstɪk, əɡ- $ -'nɑː-/ n [C] someone who believes that it is not possible to know whether God exists [➡ **atheist**] —**agnostic** adj —**agnosticism** /-tᵻsɪzəm/ n [U]

ago /ə'ɡəʊ $ ə'ɡoʊ/ adv used to say how far back in the past something happened: **10 years/a moment/a long time etc ago** *Jeff left an hour ago.* | *We went there a long time ago.*

GRAMMAR

ago, for, since

Ago, for, and since are all used to talk about time.

Ago is used with the simple past tense to say how far back in the past something happened. It follows a length of time: *My grandfather died two years ago.*

For is used with the present perfect or simple past tense to say how long a situation or event has lasted. It is followed by a length of time: *She's been here for three days.* | *The party lasted for five hours.*

Since is used with the present perfect tense to say when something started. It is followed by an exact day, date, or time: *He's been here since Sunday.* | *I've been working here since 1998.*

agonize also **-ise** *BrE* /'æɡənaɪz/ v [I] to think and worry for a long time about a decision: **+about/over** *For a long time she had agonized about what she should do.*

agonizing also **-ising** *BrE* /'æɡənaɪzɪŋ/ adj extremely painful or difficult: *an agonizing decision* —**agonizingly** adv

agony /'æɡəni/ n [C,U] plural **agonies** very severe pain, sadness, or worry: **in agony** *He was lying on the floor in agony.* | **+of** *the agony of loneliness*

'agony ˌaunt n [C] *BrE* someone who answers people's letters in a magazine or newspaper, giving them advice about their personal problems

agree /ə'ɡriː/ v
1 [I,T] to have the same opinion as someone else [≠ **disagree**]: **+with** *I agree with Karen. It's much too expensive.* | **+that** *Most doctors agree that the condition is caused by stress.* | **+about/on** *My first husband and I never agreed about anything.*

COMMUNICATION

agreeing
yes/yeah

you're right
that's right
that's true
exactly/absolutely/definitely
sure (thing) *AmE* 'See you Friday.' 'Yeah, sure.'
→ ACCEPT, SUGGEST

2 [I,T] to say yes to a suggestion, plan etc [≠ refuse]: **agree to do sth** *She agreed to stay at home with Charles.* | **+to** *He would never agree to such a plan.*
3 [I,T] to make a decision with someone after discussing something: **agree to do sth** *We agreed to meet next week.* | **+on** *We're still trying to agree on a date for the wedding.* | **+that** *It was agreed that the elections would be held in May.*
4 [I] if two pieces of information agree, they say the same thing: **+with** *The names you've given me don't agree with those on my list.*

agree with sb/sth phr v **1** to think that something is the right thing to do: *I don't agree with the decision at all.* **2 not agree with sb** if something that you ate or drank does not agree with you, it makes you feel ill

agreeable /ə'ɡriːəbəl/ adj **1** *old-fashioned* pleasant: *an agreeable man* **2** acceptable: **+to** *a solution that's agreeable to both parties* **3 be agreeable to sth** *formal* to be willing to do or allow something —**agreeably** adv: *I was agreeably surprised.*

agreed /ə'ɡriːd/ adj **1** an agreed price, method, arrangement etc is one that people have discussed and accepted **2 be agreed** if people are agreed, they all agree about something: **+on** *Are we all agreed on the date for the meeting?*

agreement /ə'ɡriːmənt/ n
1 [C] an arrangement or promise to do something, made by two or more people, organizations etc: *a trade agreement* | **+between** *an agreement between Britain and Germany* | **+on** *an international agreement on environmental standards* | **come to/reach an agreement** *Lawyers on both sides finally reached an agreement today.*
2 [U] when people have the same opinion [≠ disagreement]: **+on** *There is general agreement on the need for prison reform.* | **+that** *There was unanimous agreement that the meeting should be cancelled.* | **in agreement** *All parties were in agreement.*

agriculture /'æɡrɪˌkʌltʃə $ -ər/ n [U] the work or study of growing crops and keeping animals on farms
—**agricultural** /ˌæɡrɪ'kʌltʃərəl◂/ adj

aground /ə'ɡraʊnd/ adv **run/go aground** if a ship runs aground, it becomes stuck because the water is not deep enough

ah /ɑː/ *spoken* used to show surprise, happiness etc or that you have just understood something: *Ah, yes, I see what you mean.*

aha /ɑː'hɑː/ *spoken* used when you suddenly understand or realize something: *Aha! So that's where you've been hiding!*

ahead /ə'hed/ adv
1 in front of someone or something: *She was staring straight ahead.* | **+of** *Jane was walking ahead of him.* | **up ahead** *We could see the lights of the city up ahead.*
2 in or into the future: **+of** *We have a busy day ahead of us.* | **the months/years/weeks**

ahead *The months ahead are going to be difficult for him.* | *You need to **plan ahead** (=plan for the future).*
3 before someone or something else: **+of** *He's giving a series of concerts ahead of his international tour.* | *There were two people ahead of me at the doctor's.*
4 making more progress or more developed than other people or things: **+of** *She is well ahead of the rest of her class.* | *a design that's way ahead of others* | **get/stay ahead** *You need to work hard if you want to get ahead.* | **ahead of your/ its time** (=very advanced or new and not understood or accepted)
5 winning in a game, competition etc: *Two shots from Gardner **put** the Giants 80–75 **ahead**.* → see box at **WIN**
6 ahead of schedule/time earlier than planned: *The building was completed ahead of schedule.*

aid¹ /eɪd/ *n* **1** [U] money, food, or services that an organization or government gives to help people: *The UN is sending aid to the earthquake victims.* | *a £15 billion aid package* | **military/ financial/medical etc aid** **2 with/without the aid of sth** using or not using something to help you do something: *We finally got there with the aid of a map.* **3 in aid of sth** in order to collect money for a CHARITY **4 come/go to sb's aid** to help someone: *The school is hoping that businesses will come to its aid and finance the project.* **5** [C] a thing that helps you do something: *study aids*

aid² *v* [T] **1** *formal* to help someone, or help something to happen: *Exercise can aid relaxation.* **2 aid and abet** *law* to help someone do something illegal

aide also **aid** *AmE* /eɪd/ *n* [C] someone whose job is to help a person who has an important job: *a presidential aide*

AIDS /eɪdz/ *n* [U] **Acquired Immune Deficiency Syndrome** a very serious disease that stops your body from defending itself against infection: *the AIDS virus* | *AIDS sufferers*

ailing /'eɪlɪŋ/ *adj* weak or ill: *an ailing economy* | *his ailing mother*

ailment /'eɪlmənt/ *n* [C] an illness that is not very serious: *minor ailments*

aim¹ /eɪm/ *n*

1 [C] something that you want to achieve: **+of** *The aim of the research is to discover what causes the illness.* | *Our **main aim** is to provide a good service.* | **with the aim of doing sth** *I flew to the US with the aim of finding a job.* → see box at **PURPOSE**
2 take aim to point a weapon at someone or something: **+at** *He took aim at the target.*
3 [singular,U] someone's ability to hit the thing they are trying to hit: *Mark's aim wasn't very good.*

aim

aim² *v*
1 [I] to try or intend to achieve something: **aim to do sth** *We aim to finish by Friday.* | **+for** *We're aiming for a reduction in pollution levels.* | **(be) aimed at doing sth** *a program aimed at creating more jobs*
2 aim sth at sb to do or say something that is intended for a particular person or group: *advertising aimed at children* | *criticism aimed at the government*
3 [I,T] to point a weapon at someone or something that you want to hit: **+at** *The gun was aimed at his head.*

aimless /'eɪmləs/ *adj* without a clear purpose or reason —**aimlessly** *adv*

ain't /eɪnt/ a way of saying or writing 'am not', 'is not', 'are not', 'has not', or 'have not', which many people think is incorrect

air¹ /eə $ er/ *n*
1 [U] the gases around the Earth, which we breathe: **in the air** *There was a smell of burning in the air.* | *Let's go outside and get some **fresh air**.* | *air pollution*
2 the air the space above the ground or around things: **into the air** *David threw the ball up into the air.*
3 by air travelling by or using a plane: *Most people travel to the islands by air.*
4 air travel/safety etc travel, safety etc involving or relating to planes: *the world's worst air disaster*
5 be in the air a) to be likely to happen very soon: *Romance is in the air.* **b)** if a feeling is in the air, a lot of people have it: *There was a tension in the air.*
6 [singular] a quality that someone or something seems to have: **+of** *There was an air of mystery about her.*
7 be on/off (the) air to be broadcasting or not broadcasting on television or radio
8 be up in the air if something is up in the air, no one has made a decision about it yet
9 airs [plural] a way of behaving that shows someone thinks they are more important than they really are: *You shouldn't have to **put on airs** with your own friends.*
→ **MIDAIR** → **thin air** at **THIN¹** → **in the open air** at **OPEN¹ (12)**

air² *v* **1** [T] to express your opinions publicly: **air your views/grievances/complaints** *Everyone will get a chance to air their views.* **2** [I,T] to broadcast a programme on television or radio: *Star Trek first aired in 1966.* **3 air out** *AmE* [I,T] to put clothes outdoors or in a warm place so that they smell clean **4 air out** *AmE* [I,T] to let fresh air into a room —**airing** *n* [singular]

airbag /'eəbæg $ 'er-/ *n* [C] a bag in a car that fills with air to protect the driver or passenger in an accident

airborne /'eəbɔːn $ 'erbɔːrn/ *adj* flying or carried through the air

'air con,ditioning *n* [U] a system that makes the air in a room, building, or vehicle stay cool —**air conditioned** *adj*

aircraft /'eəkrɑːft $ 'erkræft/ *n* [C] plural **aircraft** a plane or other vehicle that can fly

'aircraft ,carrier *n* [C] a ship that planes can fly from and land on → see box at **SHIP**

airfare /'eəfeə $ 'erfer/ n [C] the price of a ticket to fly somewhere

airfield /'eəfi:ld $ 'er-/ n [C] a place where military or small planes fly from [➡ **airport**]

'**air force** n [C] the part of a country's military organization that uses planes to fight

airhead /'eəhed $ 'er-/ n [C] informal someone who behaves in a stupid way

'**air ,hostess** n [C] BrE old-fashioned a woman who serves food and drink to passengers on a plane [➡ **flight attendant**]

airily /'eər $ li $ 'er-/ adv in a way that shows you do not think something is important: 'I know all that,' she said airily.

'**airing ,cupboard** n [C] BrE a warm cupboard where you keep sheets and clothes that have just been washed and dried

airless /'eələs $ 'er-/ adj without fresh air

airlift /'eə,lıft $ 'er-/ n [C] an occasion when people or things are taken to a place by plane, because it is too difficult or dangerous to get there by road —**airlift** v [T]

airline /'eəlaın $ 'er-/ n [C] a company that carries passengers by plane

airliner /'eə,laınə $ 'er,laınər/ n [C] a large plane for passengers

airmail /'eəmeıl $ 'er-/ n [U] the system of sending letters and packages by plane: Do you want to send this by airmail?

airman /'eəmən $ 'er-/ n [C] plural **airmen** /-mən/ someone who is a member of a country's air force ➔ see picture at ARMED FORCES

airplane /'eəpleın $ 'er-/ n [C] AmE a vehicle with wings and an engine that flies in the air [= aeroplane BrE; = plane]

airplay /'eəpleı $ 'er-/ n [U] the number of times that a particular song is played on the radio: The new single is getting lots of airplay.

airport /'eəpɔːt $ 'erpɔːrt/ n [C] a place where planes take off and land, with buildings for passengers to wait in

At the airport you go into the **terminal**. You **check in** (=show your ticket, leave your bags etc) at the **check-in desk**, usually two hours before your **flight** leaves. You go through **airport security** where passengers and their bags are checked for weapons etc. You wait in the **departure lounge** until your **flight number** is called. You go through the **departure gate** before **boarding** (=getting on) the plane. The plane **takes off** from the **runway**. When the plane **lands/touches down**, you get off. If you have travelled from another country, you show your **passport** as you go through **immigration** and then you **go through customs** where your bags may be checked before leaving the airport.
➔ PASSPORT, TRAVEL

'**air raid** also '**air strike** n [C] an attack by military planes

airship /'eə,ʃıp $ 'er-/ n [C] a large aircraft with an engine but no wings, which is filled with gas

airspace /'eəspeıs $ 'er-/ n [U] the sky above a particular country, which is controlled by that country

'**air strike** n [C] an air raid

airstrip /'eə,strıp $ 'er-/ n [C] a long narrow piece of land that planes can fly from and land on

airtight /'eətaıt $ 'er-/ adj not allowing air to get in or out: airtight containers

airtime /'eətaım $ 'er-/ n [U] the amount of time that a radio or television station gives to a particular subject, advertisement etc

airwaves /'eəweıvz $ 'er-/ n **the airwaves** informal radio and television broadcasts: a subject that's been debated on the airwaves

airy /'eəri $ 'eri/ adj an airy room or building has a lot of space and fresh air

aisle /aıl/ n [C] a passage between rows of seats in a church, theatre, or plane, or between rows of shelves in a shop

ajar /ə'dʒɑː $ ə'dʒɑːr/ adj [not before noun] a door that is ajar is slightly open

a.k.a. /,eı keı 'eı, 'ækə/ adv also **known as** used when giving someone's real name together with the name they are known by: John Phillips, a.k.a. The Mississippi Mauler

akin /ə'kın/ adj formal **akin to sth** similar to something: He looked at her with something akin to pity.

alarm¹ /ə'lɑːm $ ə'lɑːrm/ n

1 [C] a piece of equipment that makes a noise to warn people of danger: **burglar/fire/smoke alarm** | He set off the alarm (=made it start ringing) by accident. | Someone's car **alarm** was **going off** (=making a noise).

2 [U] a feeling of fear because something bad might happen: +**at** Many people expressed alarm at the plans. | **in alarm** They both jumped back in alarm.

3 [C] an alarm clock: I've **set the alarm** for six o'clock.

4 raise/sound the alarm to warn people that something bad is happening: A neighbour heard shouting and raised the alarm.

5 alarm bells ring if alarm bells ring, you worry that something bad is about to happen: When she didn't arrive by 9, alarm bells started to ring.
➔ false alarm at FALSE

alarm² v [T] to make someone feel worried or frightened —**alarmed** adj: He was rather alarmed to find her there.

a'larm clock n [C] a clock that makes a noise to wake you up ➔ see picture at CLOCK¹

alarming /ə'lɑːmıŋ $ -ɑːr-/ adj making you feel worried or frightened: an alarming increase in crime

alarmist /ə'lɑːm $ st $ -ɑːr-/ adj making people feel worried about dangers that do not exist: alarmist reports of health risks

alas /ə'læs/ formal used when mentioning a fact that you wish was not true

albatross /'ælbətrɒs $ -trɒːs, -trɑːs/ n [C] a very large sea bird

albeit /ɔːl'biː $ t $ ɒːl-/ linking word formal although

albino /æl'biːnəʊ $ æl'baınoʊ/ n [C] plural **albinos** a person or animal who has pink eyes and white skin and hair

album /'ælbəm/ n [C] **1** a CD, record, or TAPE with several songs on it: Their latest album will *be released next week.* **2** a book that you put photographs, stamps etc in: *a photograph album*

alcohol /'ælkəhɒl $ -hɔːl/ *n* [U]

1 drinks such as beer or wine that can make you drunk: *Avoid drinking alcohol if you're driving.* | **alcohol abuse/problems** (=when someone regularly drinks too much) *the effects of alcohol abuse*

2 the substance in beer, wine etc that makes you drunk

alcoholic¹ /ˌælkə'hɒlɪk◂ $ -'hɔː-/ *adj* containing alcohol [≠ **non-alcoholic**]: *an alcoholic drink*

alcoholic² *n* [C] someone who regularly drinks too much alcohol and cannot stop: *His father was an alcoholic.*

alcoholism /'ælkəhɒlɪzəm $ -hɔː-/ *n* [U] the medical condition of being an alcoholic

alcove /'ælkəʊv $ -koʊv/ *n* [C] a place in the wall of a room that is built further back than the rest of the wall

ale /eɪl/ *n* [U] a type of beer

alert¹ /ə'lɜːt $ -ɜːrt/ *adj* always watching and ready to notice anything strange, unusual, or dangerous: *I knew that I had to remain wide awake and alert.* | **+to** *Cyclists must always be alert to the dangers on a busy road.*

alert² *v* [T] to warn someone of a problem or of possible danger: *As soon as we suspected it was a bomb, we alerted the police.*

alert³ *n* **1 on the alert** ready to notice and deal with a problem: **+for** *Police are on the alert for trouble.* | *All our troops are on **full alert** (=ready to deal with a serious problem).* **2** [C] a warning to be ready for possible danger: *a flood alert*

A level /'eɪ ˌlevəl/ *n* [C] an examination in a particular subject taken in England and Wales, usually at the age of 18

algae /'ældʒiː, -giː/ *n* [U] a very simple plant without stems or leaves that grows in or near water

algebra /'ældʒɪbrə/ *n* [U] a type of mathematics that uses letters and signs to show numbers and amounts —**algebraic** /ˌældʒɪ'breɪ-ɪk◂/ *adj*: *algebraic formulae*

alias¹ /'eɪliəs/ *prep* used when you are giving a name that someone uses instead of their real name: *the spy Margaret Zelle, alias Mata Hari*

alias² *n* [C] a false name used by a criminal → see box at **NAME**

alibi /'æləbaɪ/ *n* [C] something that proves that someone was not where a crime happened and therefore could not have done it: **+for** *He had an alibi for the night of the murder.*

alien¹ /'eɪliən/ *adj* **1** very different and strange: **+to** *Her way of life is totally alien to me.* **2** relating to creatures from other worlds: *alien life-forms*

alien² *n* [C] **1** *formal* someone who lives and works in a country but is not a citizen: *The clinic provides health care for illegal aliens.* **2** a creature that comes from another world

alienate /'eɪliəneɪt/ *v* [T] **1** to do something that makes someone stop supporting you: *The latest tax increases will alienate many voters.* **2** to make someone feel they no longer belong to your group: *We don't want to alienate kids who*

already have problems at school. —**alienated** *adj* —**alienation** /ˌeɪliə'neɪʃən/ *n* [U] *a feeling of alienation from society*

alight¹ /ə'laɪt/ *adj* [not before noun] **1** burning: *Several cars were **set alight** by rioters.* **2** if your face or eyes are alight, they look happy and excited

alight² *v* [I] *formal* **1** if a bird or insect alights on something, it stops flying and comes down onto it **2** to step out of a vehicle at the end of a journey: **+from** *She alighted from the train.*

align /ə'laɪn/ *v* [I,T] **1 be aligned with sb/align yourself with sb** to say that you support a political group, country, or person: *Some Democrats have aligned themselves with the Republicans on this issue.* | *a country closely aligned with the West* **2** to arrange something so that it is in the same line as something else: *It looks like your wheels need aligning.* —**alignment** *n* [C,U]

alike¹ /ə'laɪk/ *adj* [not before noun] very similar: *All small cars look alike to me.*

alike² *adv* **1** in a similar way: *When we were younger we dressed alike.* **2** equally: *The new rule was criticized by teachers and students alike.*

alimony /'æləməni $ -moʊni/ *n* [U] money that someone has to pay regularly to their former wife or husband after a DIVORCE

alive /ə'laɪv/ *adj* [not before noun]

1 living and not dead: *They didn't expect to find anyone alive after the explosion.* | *My grandparents are **still alive**.* | *I'm amazed my plants have **stayed alive** in this weather.* | *He was **kept alive** on a life-support machine.*

2 continuing to exist: *Ancient traditions are very much alive in rural areas.*

3 full of energy or activity: **+with** *The stadium was alive with excitement.* | *The streets **come alive** after ten o'clock.*

all¹ /ɔːl $ ɒːl/ *determiner, pron*

1 the whole of an amount or period of time: *Have we spent all the money?* | *I've been waiting all day for him to call.* | **+of** *All of this land belongs to me.* | *Bill talks about work **all the time** (=very often).*

2 every one of a group of people or things: *Did you answer all the questions?* | *We all wanted to go home.* | **+of** *Listen, all of you, I have an important announcement.* → see box at **EACH, ANY**

3 the only thing: *Is that all you're going to eat?* | *He had dark hair. That's all I can remember.*

4 all sorts/kinds/types of sth very many different types of things, people, or places: *You can buy all kinds of things in the bazaar.*

5 (not) at all used to say that something is not even slightly true, or to ask if something is even slightly true: *The place hasn't changed at all.* | *Was anyone at all interested in my idea?*

6 for all ... in spite of something: *For all his faults, he was a good father.*

→ **after all** at **AFTER** → **all the same** at **SAME²**

GRAMMAR

Use **all** with a singular verb when you are using a U noun: *All the wine is finished.*

Use **all** with a plural verb when you are using a plural noun form: *All my friends are coming to the party.*

→ **EVERY**

all² adv

1 completely: *Ruth was sitting all alone.* | *She got all upset when he had to leave.* | *The judges were dressed all in black.*

2 all over **a)** in every part of a place: *We've been looking all over for you.* | *There were papers all over the floor.* **b)** finished: *I'm just glad it's all over.*

3 5 all/20 all etc used to say that the two players or teams in a game both have the same number of points: *The score was 2 all at half-time.*

4 be all for sth *informal* to support something strongly: *I'm all for the idea of women priests.*

5 all but almost completely: *It was all but impossible to find anywhere to park.*

6 all along during all of a period of time: *I knew all along that I couldn't trust him.*

7 all through sth through the whole time that something continues: *He sat there quietly all through the film.*

8 all in all considering everything: *All in all, the evening went well.*

9 all the better/easier etc used to emphasize that something was better or easier etc because of the situation: *The job was made all the easier by having the right tools.*
→ ALL RIGHT¹

Allah /'ælə/ n the Muslim name for God

,all-a'round adj [only before noun] *AmE* good at doing a lot of different things, especially in sports [= all-round *BrE*]: *a good all-around player*

allay /ə'leɪ/ v [T] *formal* **allay sb's worries/ fears/suspicions etc** to make someone feel less worried, frightened etc: *I did my best to allay her fears.*

,all 'clear n **the all clear** a message saying that it is safe to do something: *We have to wait for the all clear from the safety committee before we can start.*

allegation /,ælɪ'geɪʃən/ n [C] a statement saying that someone has done something wrong or illegal, which is not supported by proof: **+that** *There are allegations that the police tortured prisoners.* | **+against** *The teacher made serious allegations against a colleague.* | **+of** *He faces allegations of fraud.*

allege /ə'ledʒ/ v [T] *formal* to say that someone has done something wrong or illegal, without showing proof: *Baldwin is alleged to have killed two people.*

alleged /ə'ledʒd/ adj [only before noun] *formal* supposed to be true, but not proved: *the group's alleged connections with organized crime*
—**allegedly** /ə'ledʒɪdli/ adv

allegiance /ə'liːdʒəns/ n [C] loyalty or support that you give to a leader, country, or idea: **+to** *I pledge allegiance to the flag of the United States of America.*

allegory /'ælɡəri $ -ɡɔːri/ n [C,U] plural **allegories** a story, poem, or painting in which the events and characters represent good and bad qualities

allergic /ə'lɜːdʒɪk $ -ɜːr-/ adj **1** if you are allergic to something, you become ill if you eat, touch, or breathe it: **+to** *He's allergic to cats.*
2 caused by an allergy: *an allergic reaction to the bee sting*

allergy /'ælədʒi $ -ər-/ n [C] plural **allergies** a condition that makes you ill when you eat, touch, or breathe something: **+to** *He has an allergy to peanuts.*

alleviate /ə'liːvieɪt/ v [T] *formal* to make something less bad or severe: *These tablets will allevi-ate the pain.*

alley /'æli/ also **alleyway** /'æliweɪ/ n [C] a narrow street between buildings

alliance /ə'laɪəns/ n [C] an agreement between countries or groups of people to work together or support each other: **+between** *an alliance between an American and a Japanese company* | **+with** *The Liberals formed an alliance with the new Social Democratic Party.*

allied /'ælaɪd, ə'laɪd/ adj joined by a political or military agreement: *allied soldiers* | *The two leaders were closely allied during the Gulf War.*

alligator /'ælɪɡeɪtə $ -ər/ n [C] a large animal like a CROCODILE that lives in the US and China

alliteration /ə,lɪtə'reɪʃən/ n [U] the use of a series of words that begin with the same sound in order to make a special effect, for example in 'Round the rocks runs the river'

allocate /'æləkeɪt/ v [T] to decide to use an amount of money, time etc for a particular purpose: **allocate sth for sth** *The hospital has allocated $500,000 for AIDS research.*

allocation /,ælə'keɪʃən/ n **1** [C] an amount of something that you have decided to use for a particular purpose **2** [U] the decision to allocate something: **+of** *the allocation of state funds to the university*

allot /ə'lɒt $ ə'lɑːt/ v [T] **allotted, allotting** to use an amount of something for a particular purpose, or give an amount of something to a particular person: **allot sth to sth/sb** *He allotted 20 minutes a day to exercise.* | **allot sb sth** *Each person was allotted two tickets.*

allotment /ə'lɒtmənt $ ə'lɑːt-/ n **1** [C,U] when an amount of something is given to someone as their share: **+of** *the allotment of funds* **2** [C] *BrE* a small area of land that people can rent for growing vegetables

,all 'out adv **go all out to do sth** to try to do something with a lot of effort and determination: *We'll be going all out to win.* —**all-out** adj: *an all-out effort*

allow /ə'laʊ/ v [T]

1 to give someone permission to do something or have something: *Smoking is not allowed in the library.* | **allow sb to do sth** *My parents would never allow me to stay out late.* | **allow sb sth** *We're allowed four weeks holiday a year.* | **allow sb in/out/up etc** *You're not allowed in here.*

THESAURUS

Allow is used in both formal and informal English: *You're not allowed to wear earrings to school.*

Let is informal and is used a lot in spoken English: *Will your Mum let you come to the party?*

Permit is formal and is mainly used in written English: *Smoking is not permitted in this building.*

2 to make it possible for something to happen or for someone to do something: **allow sb/sth to**

do sth *The new headlights allow drivers to see even in very foggy weather.* | *We mustn't allow the situation to get any worse.*

3 to plan that a particular amount of time, money etc will be needed for a particular purpose: *Allow 14 days for delivery.* | **allow yourself sth** *Allow yourself two hours to get to the airport.*
—**allowable** *adj*

allow for sth *phr v* to include the possible effects of something in your plans so that you can deal with them: *Even allowing for delays, we should finish early.*

allowance /ə'lauəns/ *n* [C usually singular]
1 an amount of money that you are given: *His father gives him a small monthly allowance.* | *a travel allowance* **2** an amount of something that you are allowed to have: *Passengers' baggage allowance is 75 pounds per person.* **3 make allowances for sb** to be kind to someone and not criticize because you know that they have a problem or disadvantage

alloy /'ælɔɪ $ 'ælɔɪ, ə'lɔɪ/ *n* [C] a metal made by mixing two or more different metals

,all-'purpose *adj* [only before noun] able to be used in any situation: *an all-purpose cleaner*

all 'right¹ *adj* [not before noun] *adv spoken*
1 satisfactory, but not very good: *'How's the food?' 'It's all right, but I've had better.'* | *Did everything **go all right** (=happen in a satisfactory way)?*
2 well and happy: *Kate was looking very pale – I hope she's all right.* | *Are you **feeling all right**?*
3 that's all right a) used to reply when someone thanks you: *'Thanks for your help!' 'That's all right.'* **b)** used to tell someone you are not angry when they say they are sorry: *'Sorry I'm late!' 'That's all right!'*
4 suitable or convenient [= okay]: *We need to fix a time for our meeting. Would Thursday afternoon be all right?*
5 is it all right if...? used to ask for someone's permission to do something: *Is it all right if I close the window?*

all 'right² *spoken* used to say that you agree with a plan or suggestion: *'Let's go now.' 'All right.'*

,all-'round *adj* [only before noun] *BrE* good at doing a lot of different things, especially in sports [= all-around *AmE*]: *an all-round athlete*
—**all-rounder** *n* [C]

'all-time *adj* used when you compare things to say that one of them is the best, worst etc that there has ever been: **an all-time high/low** *The price has reached an all-time low.* | *my **all-time favorite** film*

allude /ə'luːd/ *v*
allude to sb/sth *phr v formal* to mention something or someone in an indirect way

allure /ə'ljuə $ ə'lur/ *n* [U] an exciting quality that attracts people: **+of** *the allure of travel*

alluring /ə'ljuərɪŋ $ ə'lur-/ *adj* very attractive: *an alluring smile*

allusion /ə'luːʒən/ *n* [C,U] *formal* when you mention something or someone in an indirect way: *His poetry is full of historical allusions.*

ally¹ /'ælaɪ $ 'ælaɪ, ə'laɪ/ *n* [C] plural **allies**
1 a country that helps another country during a war: *the US and its European allies* **2** a person who supports you in a difficult situation

ally² /ə'laɪ $ ə'laɪ, 'ælaɪ/ *v* [I,T] allied, allying, allies
ally yourself to/with sb to join with another person, organization, or country and support them

almighty /ɔːl'maɪti $ ɒl-/ *adj* **1** having the power to do anything: *Almighty God* | **the Almighty** (=God) **2** [only before noun] very big or loud: *We heard an almighty crash.*

almond /'ɑːmənd $ 'ɑː-, 'æ-, 'æl-/ *n* [C] a flat white nut with a slightly sweet taste

almost /'ɔːlməust $ 'ɒːlmoust, ɒːl'moust/ *adv* nearly but not completely: *Are we almost there?* | *It was almost midnight.* | *Almost all children like to read.* | *I'm sorry, I almost forgot to call you.*

alms /ɑːmz $ ɑːmz, ɑːlmz/ *n* [plural] *old-fashioned* money and food given to poor people

aloft /ə'lɒft $ ə'lɔːft/ *adv literary* high up in the air: *They held the banner aloft for everyone to see.*

alone /ə'ləun $ ə'loun/ *adj, adv*
1 [not before noun] without any other people: *She lives alone.* | *I was **all alone** (=completely alone) in a strange city.* | *You shouldn't **leave** a child alone in the house.* | *My wife and I like to spend time **alone together** (=away from everyone else).*
2 sb/sth alone only one person or thing: *You alone must make this decision.* | *This disease cannot be cured by drugs alone.*
3 leave/let sb alone to stop annoying someone: *'Leave me alone!' she screamed.*
4 leave/let sth alone to stop touching something: *Leave that clock alone or you'll break it.*

along¹ /ə'lɒŋ $ ə'lɔːŋ/ *prep*
1 from one place on a line, road, river etc to another place on it: *We took a walk along the river.* | *She looked anxiously along the line of faces.* | *They've put up a fence along the road.*
2 at a particular place on a line, road, river etc: *The house is somewhere along this road.*

along² *adv*
1 going forward: *I was driving along, listening to the radio.*
2 go/come along to go or come to a place where something is happening: *We're going out – you're welcome to come along!*
3 take/bring sb/sth along to take someone or something with you to a place: *Do you mind if I bring a friend along?*
4 be/come along to arrive: *The next bus should be along in a minute.*
5 get/come along to develop or make progress: *How are you getting along in your new job?* | *Your English is coming along very well.*
6 along with in addition to someone or something else: *Dunne was murdered along with three other men.*
→ **all along** at **ALL²**

alongside /ə,lɒŋ'saɪd $ ə,lɔːŋ-/ *adv, prep*
1 next to the side of something: *We parked alongside a white van.* **2** working or doing something with someone else: *Charles spent a week working alongside the miners.*

aloof /ə'luːf/ *adj* **1** deliberately staying away from other people or not talking to them, especially because you think you are better than they are: *She seemed cold and aloof.* **2** if you stay aloof from something, you do not become involved in it

aloud /ə'laʊd/ adv in a voice that people can hear: *Will you please read the poem aloud?* | *He cried aloud with pain.*

alphabet /'ælfəbet/ n [C] a set of letters that are used when writing a language: *the Greek alphabet*

alphabetical /ˌælfə'betɪkəl◂/ adj arranged according to the letters of the alphabet: *The names are listed in alphabetical order.* —**alphabetically** /-kli/ adv

,alpha 'male n [C] **1** the male with the highest rank in a group of animals such as CHIMPANZEES **2** *humorous* the man who has the most power and influence and the highest social position in a particular group

alpine /'ælpaɪn/ adj relating to the Alps or other high mountains: *alpine flowers*

already /ɔːl'redi $ ɒːl-/ adv

1 before now, or before a particular time: *I've seen that film already.* | *By the time he arrived, the room was already crowded.*

2 sooner than expected: *Are you leaving already?* | *I've forgotten the number already.*

alright /ˌɔːl'raɪt $ 'ɒːl-/ adv another spelling of ALL RIGHT that some people consider to be incorrect

also /'ɔːlsəʊ $ 'ɒːlsoʊ/ adv in addition to something you have mentioned: *We specialize in shoes, but we also sell handbags.* | *She sings beautifully and also plays the piano.*

Also is more formal than **too**, and is used more often in writing than in speech: *Tom was also hungry.*
Too and **as well** are less formal and more often used in spoken English: *The dog's hungry, Tom's hungry too, and I am as well.* Do not say 'Tom was also not hungry.' Say 'Tom was not hungry either.'

Use **also** before a verb, unless the verb is 'be': *Ron also speaks Italian.* | *His wife is also a doctor.*
If there are two or more verbs together, **also** comes after the first one: *Patty can also speak Italian.*

altar /'ɔːltə $ 'ɒːltər/ n [C] a kind of holy table, especially used in a church for religious ceremonies

alter /'ɔːltə $ 'ɒːltər/ v [I,T] to change, or to make something or someone change: *Her face hadn't altered much over the years.* | *They had to alter their plans.* → see box at CHANGE

alteration /ˌɔːltə'reɪʃən $ ˌɒːl-/ n [C,U] a change in something, or the process of changing it: +**to** *I have just made a couple of minor alterations to the drawings.*

altercation /ˌɔːltə'keɪʃən $ ˌɒːltər-/ n [C] *formal* a noisy argument

alternate[1] /ɔːl'tɜːnət $ 'ɒːltər-, 'æl-/ adj [only before noun] **1** happening in a regular way, first one thing and then the other thing: *Arrange the meat and rice in alternate layers.* **2** **alternate days/weeks etc** one of every two days, weeks etc: *We visit my parents on alternate*

Sundays. **3** used to replace another thing of the same type [= **alternative**] —**alternately** adv

alternate[2] /'ɔːltəneɪt $ 'ɒːltər-, 'æl-/ v [I,T] if two things alternate, or if you alternate them, first you do one thing or one thing happens, then the other, then the first one again: +**between** *Her moods alternated between joy and sadness.* —**alternating** adj: *alternating layers of sand and stone*

alternative[1] /ɔːl'tɜːnətɪv $ ɒːl'tɜːr-, æl-/ adj [only before noun]

1 used instead of something else: *The main road is blocked, so drivers should choose an alternative route.*

2 different from what is usual or accepted: *an alternative lifestyle* | *alternative medicine*

alternative[2] n [C] something you can choose instead of something else: *There are a number of alternatives.* | +**to** *Milk is a healthier alternative to cream.* | *I had no alternative but to report him to the police.*

alternatively /ɔːl'tɜːnətɪvli $ ɒːl'tɜːr-, æl-/ adv used to suggest an alternative to your first suggestion: *I could come to your house, or alternatively we could meet in town.*

although /ɔːl'ðəʊ $ ɒːl'ðoʊ/ linking word

1 in spite of the fact that something is true: *Although the car's old, it still runs well.* | *He lent his friend £20, although he didn't have much money himself.*

2 but: *You can copy my answers, although I'm not sure they're right.*

altitude /'æltɪtjuːd $ -tuːd/ n [C,U] the height of something above sea level: **high/low altitude** *Breathing becomes more difficult at high altitudes.*

alto /'æltəʊ $ -toʊ/ n [C,U] plural **altos** a female singer with a low voice, or a male singer with a high voice

altogether /ˌɔːltə'geðə◂ $ ˌɒːltə'geðər◂/ adv

1 completely: *Bradley seems to have disappeared altogether.* | *I'm not altogether sure what this word means.*

2 including everything or everyone: *There were five of us altogether.*

Altogether does not mean the same as **all together**.
Use **altogether** to talk about the total amount of people or things: *You owe me £5 altogether.*
Use **all together** to say that people or things are together in a group: *When we're all together, we have a great time.*

3 in general, considering everything: *It did rain a lot, but altogether I'd say it was a good trip.*

altruistic /ˌæltru'ɪstɪk◂/ adj caring more about other people's needs and happiness than about your own —**altruism** /'æltruɪzəm/ n [U]

aluminium /ˌæljə'mɪniəm/ *BrE*; **aluminum** /ə'luːmɪnəm/ *AmE* n [U] a silver-white metal that is light and easy to bend

alumni /ə'lʌmnaɪ/ n [plural] the former students of a school, college etc

always /'ɔːlwɪz, -weɪz $ 'ɒːl-/ adv

1 every time, or at all times: *Always lock your car.* | *We're always ready to help you.* → see box at STILL

A

THESAURUS

permanently – every time or at all times: *The door is permanently locked.*
all the time/the whole time – constantly: *It rains here all the time.*

2 for ever: *I will always love you.*

THESAURUS

permanently – for ever or for a very long time: *His eyesight may be permanently damaged.*
forever – for all time in the future: *I could stay here forever.*
for life – for the rest of your life: *Marriage is supposed to be for life.*
for good – used to say that a change is permanent: *I've given up smoking for good.*

3 for a very long time: *I've always loved his music.* | *I've always wanted to go to China.*
4 very often: *The stupid car is always breaking down!*
5 you could always... *spoken* used to make a polite suggestion: *You could always try calling her.*

GRAMMAR

Use **always** before a verb, unless the verb is 'be': *We always go on holiday in August.* | *Jeff's always late for school.*
If there are two or more verbs together, **always** comes after the first one: *I have always lived in this town.*

Alzheimer's disease /ˈæltshaɪməz dɪˌziːz $ -mərz-/ *n* [U] a disease that affects someone's brain, and makes it difficult for them to remember things

am /m, əm; *strong* æm/ the first person singular present tense of the verb BE

a.m. also **am** *BrE* /ˌeɪ ˈem/ used in times from 12 o'clock at night until 12 o'clock in the day [➔ **pm**]: *I start work at 9:00 a.m.*

amalgamate /əˈmælɡəmeɪt/ *v* [I,T] to join two organizations together to become a bigger organization, or to join together in this way: *The two companies are amalgamating to form a huge multi-national corporation.* —**amalgamation** /əˌmælɡəˈmeɪʃən/ *n* [C,U]

amass /əˈmæs/ *v* [T] *formal* if you amass money, knowledge, information etc, you gradually collect a large amount of it: *He amassed a fortune in the years before the war.*

amateur[1] /ˈæmətə, -tjʊə, -tʃə, ˌæməˈtɜː $ ˈæmətʃʊr, -tər/ *adj* doing something because you enjoy it, not because it is your job: *an amateur boxer* | *amateur football*

amateur[2] *n* [C] **1** someone who does something because they enjoy it, not because it is their job [≠ **professional**] **2** someone who is not very good at doing something: *It looked as if the building had been decorated by a bunch of amateurs.*

amateurish /ˈæmətərɪʃ, -tjʊə-, -tʃə-, ˌæməˈtɜːrɪʃ $ ˈæmətʃʊr-, -ˈtɜːr-/ *adj* done in a way that is not very skilful: *his amateurish attempts at painting*

amaze /əˈmeɪz/ *v* [T] to make someone feel very surprised: *Kay amazed her friends by saying she was getting married.* | *It amazes me how much she has improved.*

amazed /əˈmeɪzd/ *adj* [not before noun] very surprised: **+at/by** *We were amazed at how quickly the kids learned the song.* | **+(that)** *I'm amazed that you remember him.* ➔ see box at **SURPRISED**

amazement /əˈmeɪzmənt/ *n* [U] when you feel very surprised: **in amazement** *I stared at him in amazement.* | **to sb's amazement** *To my amazement, Neal got up and left without a word.*

amazing /əˈmeɪzɪŋ/ *adj* very surprising: *What an amazing story!* ➔ see box at **SURPRISING**
—**amazingly** *adv*: *an amazingly generous offer*

ambassador /æmˈbæsədə $ -ər/ *n* [C] an important official who represents his or her government in a foreign country: **+to** *the Mexican ambassador to Canada* —**ambassadorial** /æmˌbæsəˈdɔːriəl/ *adj*

amber /ˈæmbə $ -ər/ *n* [U] **1** a hard yellowish-brown clear substance that is used for making jewellery: *an amber necklace* **2** a yellowish-brown colour: *The traffic lights turned to amber.* —**amber** *adj*

ambidextrous /ˌæmbɪˈdekstrəs◂/ *adj* able to use both your hands equally well

ambience also **ambiance** *AmE* /ˈæmbiəns/ *n* [U] the character of a place and the way this makes you feel: *a restaurant with a lovely friendly ambience*

ambiguity /ˌæmbɪˈɡjuːəti/ *n* [C,U] plural **ambiguities** when something can have more than one possible meaning: **+in** *There were several ambiguities in the letter.*

ambiguous /æmˈbɪɡjuəs/ *adj* something that is ambiguous has more than one possible meaning: *His answer was ambiguous.*

ambition /æmˈbɪʃən/ *n* **1** [C] a strong desire to do or achieve something: *Her ambition is to climb Mount Everest.* | *Miles had finally achieved his ambition of being an author.* **2** [U] a strong determination to become successful or powerful: *a young politician with a lot of ambition*

ambitious /æmˈbɪʃəs/ *adj*
1 determined to be successful or powerful: *He is young and very ambitious.*
2 an ambitious plan aims to achieve something very great but very difficult: *the most ambitious engineering project of modern times*

ambivalent /æmˈbɪvələnt/ *adj* not sure whether you like something or whether you want it: *I think Carla's ambivalent about getting married.* —**ambivalence** *n* [U]

amble /ˈæmbəl/ *v* [I] to walk slowly in a relaxed way

ambulance /ˈæmbjʊləns/ *n* [C] a special vehicle for taking ill or injured people to hospital: *the ambulance service* | **by ambulance** *Mike had to be taken by ambulance to hospital.*

ambush /ˈæmbʊʃ/ *n* [C] a sudden attack by people who have been waiting and hiding: *Two soldiers were killed in an ambush near the border.* ➔ see box at **ATTACK** —**ambush** *v* [T]

ameliorate /əˈmiːliəreɪt/ *v* [T] *formal* to make something better

amen /ɑːˈmen, eɪ-/ *spoken* said at the end of a Christian or Jewish prayer

amenable /əˈmiːnəbəl $ əˈmiːn- əˈmen-/ *adj* willing to listen or do something: **+to** *I'm sure they'll be amenable to your suggestions.*

amend /əˈmend/ *v* [T] to make small changes or improvements, especially to something that has been written: *The law has been amended several times.*

amendment /əˈmendmənt/ *n* [C,U] a change made in the words of a law or document: *constitutional amendments* | **+to** *an amendment to the new Finance Bill*

amends /əˈmendz/ *n* **make amends** to do something to show that you are sorry for something bad or wrong that you did: *I tried to make amends by inviting him to lunch.*

amenity /əˈmiːnɪ̯ti $ əˈme-/ *n* [C usually plural] plural **amenities** something that makes a place comfortable and easy to live in: *The hotel's amenities include a pool and two bars.*

American[1] /əˈmerɪ̯kən/ *adj* from or connected with the United States: *Her mother is American.* | *American cars*

American[2] *n* [C] someone from the United States → NATIVE AMERICAN

A,merican 'football *n* [U] *BrE* a game played in the US in which two teams wearing HELMETS and special protective clothes carry, kick, or throw an OVAL ball [= **football** *AmE*]

A,merican 'Indian *n* [C] NATIVE AMERICAN

Americanism /əˈmerɪ̯kənɪzəm/ *n* [C] a word or phrase that is typically used in American English

Americanize also **-ise** *BrE* /əˈmerɪ̯kənaɪz/ *v* [T] to change a society, language, system etc so that it becomes more like America —**Americanization** /əˈmerɪ̯kənaɪˈzeɪʃən $ -nə-/ *n* [U]

amethyst /ˈæmɪ̯θɪ̯st/ *n* [C,U] a purple stone used in jewellery

amiable /ˈeɪmiəbəl/ *adj* friendly and pleasant: *an amiable young man* —**amiably** *adv* —**amiability** /ˌeɪmiəˈbɪlɪ̯ti/ *n* [U]

amicable /ˈæmɪkəbəl/ *adj* friendly and without arguments: *an amicable divorce* —**amicably** *adv*

amid /əˈmɪd/ also **amidst** /əˈmɪdst/ *prep formal* among something, or while something is happening: *surviving amid the horrors of war*

amiss[1] /əˈmɪs/ *adj* if something is amiss, there is a problem: *She sensed something was amiss.*

amiss[2] *adv* **1 take sth amiss** to feel offended or upset about something someone has said or done **2 sth would not go/come amiss** to be useful or suitable in a particular situation: *Two hundred pounds wouldn't go amiss right now.*

ammonia /əˈməʊniə $ -ˈmoʊ-/ *n* [U] a clear liquid with a strong bad smell that is used for cleaning things or in cleaning products

ammunition /ˌæmjᵿˈnɪʃən/ *n* [U] things such as bullets, bombs etc that are fired from guns

amnesia /æmˈniːziə $ -ʒə/ *n* [U] the medical condition of not being able to remember anything

amnesty /ˈæmnɪsti/ *n* [C,U] plural **amnesties** **1** an official order by a government that allows prisoners to be free: **+for** *an amnesty for political*

prisoners **2** a period of time when you can admit to doing something illegal without being punished

amoeba /əˈmiːbə/ *n* [C] a very small creature that has only one cell

amok /əˈmɒk $ əˈmɑːk/ *adv* **run amok** to behave in an uncontrolled way

among /əˈmʌŋ/ also **amongst** /əˈmʌŋst/ *prep* **1** in a particular group of people or things: *The decision has caused a lot of anger among women.* | *Relax, you're among friends here.* | *When they were children they were always fighting among themselves.*
2 in the middle of, through, or between: *We found him hiding among the bushes.* | *Rescue teams searched among the wreckage for survivors.* → see box at BETWEEN
3 if something is divided or shared among a group of people, each person is given a part of it: *His money will be divided among his three children.*
4 used when you are mentioning one or two people or things from a larger group: *Swimming and diving are among the most popular Olympic events.* | *We discussed, among other things, ways to raise money.*

amoral /eɪˈmɒrəl, æ- $ eɪˈmɔːr-, -ˈmɑː-/ *adj* behaving in a way that shows you do not care if what you are doing is wrong

amorous /ˈæmərəs/ *adj* full of sexual desire or feelings of love

amorphous /əˈmɔːfəs $ -ɔːr-/ *adj* without a definite shape

amount[1] /əˈmaʊnt/ *n* [C] how much of something there is: **+of** *I was surprised at the amount of work I had to do.* | *They spent a considerable amount* (=a lot) *of time on the project.* | *Please pay the full amount* (=all the money you owe) *by the end of the month.* | *There's a certain amount of risk* (=some risk) *with any investment.*

amount[2] *v*
amount to sth *phr v* **1** to have the same meaning or effect as something, without being exactly that thing: *What he said amounted to an apology.* **2** to add up to a particular total: *Jenny's debts amount to $1000.*

amp /æmp/ also **ampere** /ˈæmpeə $ -pɪr/ *n* [C] **1** a unit for measuring electric current **2** *informal* an AMPLIFIER

amphetamine /æmˈfetəmiːn, -mɪ̯n/ *n* [C,U] a drug that gives people more energy and makes them feel excited

amphibian /æmˈfɪbiən/ *n* [C] an animal such as a FROG that can live on land and in water

amphibious /æmˈfɪbiəs/ *adj* able to live on both land and water: *amphibious creatures*

amphitheatre *BrE*; **amphitheater** *AmE* /ˈæmfɪ̯θɪətə $ -ər/ *n* [C] a large circular building without a roof and with many rows of seats, where people can sit and watch public performances

ample /ˈæmpəl/ *adj* more than enough: *You'll have ample time for questions later.* | *There's ample room in here for everyone.* —**amply** *adv*

amplifier /ˈæmplɪ̯faɪə $ -faɪər/ *n* [C] a piece of electronic equipment used to make music and other sounds louder → see picture at ACOUSTIC

amplify /'æmplɪfaɪ/ v [T] **amplified, amplifying, amplifies 1** to make sounds louder using electronic equipment **2** *formal* to make something such as a feeling stronger: *These stories only amplified her fears.* —**amplification** /ˌæmplɪfɪ'keɪʃən/ n [U]

amputate /'æmpjʊteɪt/ v [I,T] to cut off someone's arm, leg, finger etc during a medical operation: *After the accident, the doctors had to amputate her leg.* —**amputation** /ˌæmpjʊ'teɪʃən/ n [C,U]

amuse /ə'mjuːz/ v [T] **1** to make someone laugh or smile: *Harry's jokes always amused me.* **2** to make time pass in an enjoyable way, so that you don't get bored: *She brought along some games to amuse the children on the flight.* | *The kids amused themselves playing hide-and-seek.*

amused /ə'mjuːzd/ adj **1** smiling or laughing because something is funny: *The man looked a little amused.* | **+at/by** *Ellen seemed amused by the whole situation.* | *I could see she was highly amused* (=very amused). **2 keep sb amused** to entertain or interest someone for a long time so that they do not get bored: *It's hard work trying to keep the kids amused on rainy days.*

amusement /ə'mjuːzmənt/ n **1** [U] the feeling you have when something makes you laugh or smile: **in/with amusement** *She looked at him in amusement.* **2** [C,U] something that entertains you and makes time pass in an enjoyable way: *childhood amusements* | *What do you do for amusement* (=in order to enjoy yourself) *in this town?*

a'musement arˌcade n [C] *BrE* a place where people can play games on machines by putting coins in them

a'musement ˌpark n [C] a large park where people can ride on big machines, for example ROLLER COASTERS

amusing /ə'mjuːzɪŋ/ adj funny and entertaining: *a highly amusing* (=very amusing) *story* | *I didn't find your comment amusing.* → see box at FUNNY

an /ən; *strong* æn/ determiner used instead of 'a' when the following word begins with a vowel sound [➡ a]: *an orange* | *an X-ray* | *an hour*

anachronism /ə'nækrənɪzəm/ n [C] someone or something that seems to be in the wrong historical time: *The royal family seems something of an anachronism nowadays.* —**anachronistic** /əˌnækrə'nɪstɪk/ adj

anaemia *BrE*; **anemia** *AmE* /ə'niːmiə/ n [U] a medical condition in which you do not have enough red cells in your blood —**anaemic** adj

anaesthetic *BrE*; **anesthetic** *AmE* /ˌænəs'θetɪk/ n [C,U] a drug that stops you feeling pain, used during a medical operation: **under anaesthetic** *The operation will be done under anaesthetic* (=using anaesthetic). | *The doctor gave him a local anaesthetic* (=one that only affects a particular part of your body). | *You will need to have a general anaesthetic* (=one that makes you completely unconscious).

anaesthetist *BrE*; **anesthetist** *AmE* /ə'niːsθətɪst $ ə'nes-/ n [C] someone whose job is to give anaesthetics to people in hospitals

anaesthetize also -ise *BrE*; **anesthetize** *AmE* /ə'niːsθətaɪz $ ə'nes-/ v [T] to make someone unable to feel pain by giving them an anaesthetic

anagram /'ænəgræm/ n [C] a word or phrase made by changing the order of the letters in another word or phrase: *'Silent' is an anagram of 'listen'.*

anal /'eɪnl/ adj relating to the ANUS

analogous /ə'næləgəs/ adj *formal* similar to another situation or thing: **+to/with** *Operating the system is analogous to driving a car.*

analogy /ə'nælədʒi/ n [C,U] plural **analogies** a way of explaining something by saying it is similar to something else: **+between** *We can draw an analogy* (=make a comparison) *between the brain and a computer.*

analyse *BrE*; **analyze** *AmE* /'ænəl-aɪz/ v [T] to examine or think about something carefully in order to understand it: *We're trying to analyse what went wrong.* | *The patient's blood is tested and analyzed.*

analysis /ə'næləsɪs/ n plural **analyses** /-siːz/ [C,U] careful examination of something in order to understand it better or find out what it consists of: **+of** *The team are carrying out a detailed analysis of the test results.* | *statistical analysis* | **for analysis** *Blood samples were sent to the laboratory for analysis.*

analyst /'ænəlɪst/ n [C] **1** someone whose job is to analyse a subject and advise other people about it: *a computer analyst* **2** a PSYCHOANALYST

analytical /ˌænəl'ɪtɪkəl/, **analytic** /-'ɪtɪk/ adj using methods that help you examine things carefully: *an analytical mind*

analyze /'ænəlaɪz/ the American spelling of ANALYSE

anarchist /'ænəkɪst $ -ər-/ n [C] someone who believes that governments, laws etc are not necessary —**anarchism** n [U]

anarchy /'ænəki $ -ər-/ n [U] a situation in which no one obeys rules or laws and there is no control or government: *The nation is in danger of falling into anarchy.* —**anarchic** /æ'nɑːkɪk $ -ɑːr-/ adj

anathema /ə'næθɪmə/ n [singular, U] *formal* something you hate because it is the opposite of what you believe in: **+to** *His political views were anathema to me.*

anatomy /ə'nætəmi/ n **1** [U] the scientific study of the structure of the body: *human anatomy* **2** [singular] the structure of a living thing, organization, or social group, and how it works: **+of** *the anatomy of modern society* —**anatomical** /ˌænə'tɒmɪkəl $ -'tɑː-/ adj —**anatomically** /-kli/ adv

ancestor /'ænsəstə $ -sestər/ n [C] a member of your family who lived a long time ago, before your grandparents [➡ descendant]: *His ancestors came from Italy.* —**ancestral** /æn'sestrəl/ adj

ancestry /'ænsəstri, -ses- $ -ses-/ n [C,U] plural **ancestries** the members of your family who lived in past times: *people of Scottish ancestry*

anchor[1] /'æŋkə $ -ər/ n [C] **1** a heavy metal object that is lowered into the water to prevent a ship or boat from moving **2** *AmE* someone who reads the news on television or radio and is in charge of the programme [= newsreader *BrE*]

anchor² v [I,T] **1** to lower the anchor of a ship or boat to prevent it from moving: *Three tankers were anchored in the bay.* **2** to fasten something firmly so that it cannot move: *We anchored the tent with strong ropes.*

anchovy /'æntʃəvi $ 'æntʃouvi/ n [C,U] plural **anchovies** a small fish that tastes of salt

ancient /'eɪnʃənt/ adj

1 belonging to a time in history that was thousands of years ago: *ancient Rome* → see box at **OLD**

2 *humorous* very old: *I look absolutely ancient in that photograph!*

and /ənd, ən; *strong* ænd/ *linking word*

1 used to join two words or parts of sentences: *a knife and fork* | *They started shouting and screaming.* | *Martha was going to the store, and Tom said he'd go with her.*

2 used to say that one thing happens after another: *Grant knocked and went in.*

3 *spoken* used instead of 'to' after certain verbs such as 'come', 'go', 'try': *Try and finish your homework before dinner.*

4 used in numbers and when adding numbers: *Six and four make ten.* | *three and a half*

5 used to say that one thing is caused by something else: *I missed lunch and I'm starving!*

android /'ændrɔɪd/ n [C] a ROBOT that looks completely human

anecdotal /ˌænɪk'dəʊtl◂ $ -'doʊ-/ adj consisting of stories based on someone's personal experience: *The report is based on anecdotal evidence rather than serious research.*

anecdote /'ænɪkdəʊt $ -doʊt/ n [C] a short interesting story about a particular person or event

anemia /ə'niːmiə/ n the American spelling of ANAEMIA —**anemic** adj

anesthetic /ˌænəs'θetɪk◂/ n the American spelling of ANAESTHETIC

anesthetist /ə'niːsθətɪst $ ə'nes-/ n the American spelling of ANAESTHETIST

anesthetize /ə'niːsθətaɪz $ ə'nes-/ v the American spelling of ANAESTHETIZE

anew /ə'njuː $ ə'nuː/ adv *literary* in a new or different way: *She started life anew in New York.*

angel /'eɪndʒəl/ n [C] **1** a SPIRIT who is God's servant in heaven, and who is often shown as a person dressed in white with wings **2** *spoken* a very kind person: *Oh, thanks! You're an angel!* —**angelic** /æn'dʒelɪk/ adj

anger¹ /'æŋgə $ -ər/ n [U] a strong feeling of wanting to hurt or criticize someone because they have done something bad to you or been unkind to you: *insults that aroused his anger* | +**at** *Emily was filled with anger at the way she had been treated.* | **in anger** (=when you are angry) *You should never hit a child in anger.*

anger² v [T] to make someone feel angry: *The court's decision angered environmentalists.*

angle¹ /'æŋgəl/ n [C]

1 the space between two lines or surfaces that meet or cross each other, measured in degrees: *an angle of 45°*

2 at an angle sloping, not upright or level: *The tree was growing at an angle.*

3 a way of considering a problem or situation: *Let's try to look at the problem from a different angle.*

4 the direction from which you look at something: *From that angle, he could just see the corner of the roof.*
→ **RIGHT ANGLE**

angle² v [T] **1** to turn or move something so that it is not straight or upright: *You could angle the table away from the wall.* **2** to present information from a particular point of view for a specific group of people: *The book is angled towards a business audience.*

angle for sth *phr v* to try to get something you want without asking directly for it: *I think she's angling for an invitation to the party.*

Anglican /'æŋglɪkən/ adj relating to the Church of England —**Anglican** n [C] —**Anglicanism** n [U]

angling /'æŋglɪŋ/ n [U] the activity of fishing with a hook and a line —**angler** n [C]

Anglo- /æŋgləʊ $ -gloʊ/ prefix relating to England or Britain and another country: *Anglo-American relations*

angry /'æŋgri/ adj feeling or showing anger: *He was beginning to get angry.* | +**with/at** *She was angry with him because he had lied to her.* | *Jess laughed, which made me even angrier.* | +**about** *Don't you feel angry about the way you've been treated?* | +**that** *The workers are angry that they haven't been paid for the week.*

—**angrily** adv

angst /æŋst/ n [U] strong feelings of anxiety that you have over a long period of time when you are worried about your life

anguish /'æŋgwɪʃ/ n [U] *written* very great pain or worry: *the anguish of not knowing the truth* —**anguished** adj: *anguished cries for help*

angular /'æŋgjʊlə $ -ər/ adj having sharp corners

animal¹ /'ænɪməl/ n [C]

1 any living creature, like a cow or dog, that is not a bird, insect, fish, or person: *farm animals* | *wild animals* | *the enormous diversity of the animal kingdom*

2 any living creature that can move around: *Humans are highly intelligent animals.*

animal² adj connected with or made from animals: *animal fats*

animate /'ænɪmət/ adj *formal* living [≠ inanimate]

animated /'ænɪmeɪtɪd/ adj **1** showing a lot of interest and energy: *an animated debate* **2 animated cartoon/film etc** a film in which pictures and MODELS seem to move and talk → see box at **FILM** —**animatedly** adv

A

animation /ˌænɪˈmeɪʃən/ n **1** [U] the process of making animated films **2** [U] energy and excitement: **with animation** *They were talking with animation.*

animosity /ˌænɪˈmɒsɪti $ -ˈmɑː-/ n [C,U] plural **animosities** *formal* strong dislike or hatred: *There was a lot of animosity between the two leaders.*

ankle /ˈæŋkəl/ n [C] the part of your body where your foot joins your leg → see picture on page A3

annals /ˈænlz/ n **in the annals of sth** in the whole history of a particular subject: *one of the most unusual cases in the annals of crime*

annex /əˈneks $ əˈneks, ˈæneks/ v [T] to take control of a country or area next to your own, especially by using force —**annexation** /ˌænekˈseɪʃən/ n [C,U]

annexe *BrE*; **annex** *AmE* /ˈæneks/ n [C] a separate building that has been added to a larger one: *a hospital annexe*

annihilate /əˈnaɪəleɪt/ v [T] to destroy something or defeat someone completely: *Their army was annihilated in just three days.* —**annihilation** /əˌnaɪəˈleɪʃən/ n [U]

anniversary /ˌænɪˈvɜːsəri $ -ɜːr-/ n [C] plural **anniversaries** a date on which something special or important happened in a previous year: *Our **wedding anniversary** is May 3.* | +**of** *the 50th anniversary of India's independence*

Anno Domini /ˌænəʊ ˈdɒmɪnaɪ $ ˌænoʊ ˈdɑː-/ *formal* → AD

announce /əˈnaʊns/ v [T]
1 to officially tell people about something so that everyone knows: *The winner of the competition will be announced shortly.* | +**(that)** *A police spokesman announced that a man had been arrested.*
2 to say something in a loud and confident way: +**(that)** *Liam suddenly announced that he was leaving the band.*

announcement /əˈnaʊnsmənt/ n
1 [C] an important official statement about something that has happened or will happen: *We all waited for the captain to **make an announcement**.* | +**(that)** *We were shocked by the announcement that the mayor was resigning.*
2 [singular] when someone tells a lot of people about something: +**of** *the announcement of the election results*

announcer /əˈnaʊnsə $ -ər/ n [C] someone who gives information or introduces people on television or radio

annoy /əˈnɔɪ/ v [T] to make someone feel a little angry: *Jane wouldn't stop complaining and it was beginning to annoy me.*

annoyance /əˈnɔɪəns/ n **1** [U] the feeling of being annoyed: *Mia's annoyance never showed.* **2** [C] something that annoys you: *The dog next door is a constant annoyance.*

annoyed /əˈnɔɪd/ adj a little angry: +**with** *Are you annoyed with me just because I'm a bit late?* | +**at/about** *She was really annoyed at the way he just ignored her.* | +**(that)** *My sister's annoyed that we didn't call.* → see box at ANGRY, NERVOUS

annoying /əˈnɔɪ-ɪŋ/ adj making you feel annoyed: *an annoying habit of interrupting* |

It's annoying that we didn't know about this before.
—**annoyingly** adv

annual¹ /ˈænjuəl/ adj **1** happening once every year: *the annual conference* → see box at REGULAR **2** calculated over a period of one year: *He has an annual income of around $500,000.* —**annually** adv

annual² n [C] **1** a plant that lives for one year or season **2** a book, especially for children, that is produced once a year with the same title but different stories, pictures etc

annuity /əˈnjuːɪti $ əˈnuː-/ n [C] plural **annuities** a fixed amount of money that is paid each year to someone, usually until they die

annul /əˈnʌl/ v [T] **annulled, annulling** *formal* to officially state that a marriage or legal agreement no longer exists —**annulment** n [C,U]

anomalous /əˈnɒmələs $ əˈnɑː-/ adj *formal* different from what you expected to find: *a highly anomalous situation*

anomaly /əˈnɒməli $ əˈnɑː-/ n [C,U] plural **anomalies** *formal* something that is noticeable because it is different from what is usual: *In those days, a woman professor was still an anomaly.*

anon /əˈnɒn $ əˈnɑːn/ the written abbreviation of **anonymous**, used especially to show that the writer of a poem or song is not known

anonymity /ˌænəˈnɪmɪti/ n [U] when other people do not know who you are or what your name is: *The author prefers anonymity.*

anonymous /əˈnɒnɪməs $ əˈnɑː-/ adj **1** not known by name: *the anonymous author of a collection of poems* | *The person concerned wishes to **remain anonymous**.* **2** done, sent, or given by someone who does not want their name to be known: *an anonymous letter* —**anonymously** adv

anorak /ˈænəræk/ n [C] *BrE* a short coat with a HOOD that keeps out the wind and rain

anorexia /ˌænəˈreksiə/ also **anorexia nervosa** /ˌænəˌreksiə nɜːˈvəʊsə $ -nərˈvoʊ-/ n [U] a mental illness that makes people, especially young women, stop eating so that they become dangerously thin

anorexic /ˌænəˈreksɪk◂/ adj suffering from or relating to anorexia

another /əˈnʌðə $ -ər/ determiner, pron
1 one more person or thing of the same kind: *Do you want another beer?* | *Buy one CD and we'll give you another, completely free.*
2 a different person or thing: *You'll just have to find another job.* | *She lives in another part of the country.* | *He left his wife for another woman.*
→ ONE ANOTHER

answer¹ /ˈɑːnsə $ ˈænsər/ v
1 [I,T] to say something to someone when they have asked you a question or spoken to you: *'I don't know,' she answered.* | *I had to **answer** a lot of questions about my previous job.* | *Why don't you answer me?* | +**(that)** *Clare answered that she was not interested in their offer.*
2 [T] to reply to a question in a test, competition etc: *Please answer as many questions as you can.*
3 answer the telephone/door to pick up the telephone when it rings or go to the door when

someone knocks or rings the bell → see box at
TELEPHONE
4 [I,T] to send a letter as a reply to an advertisement or to a letter that someone has sent to you
answer back *phr v* to reply in a rude way to
someone you are supposed to obey: **answer sb
back** *Don't answer me back, young man!*
answer for sth *phr v* to explain to people in
authority why you did something wrong or why
something happened, and be punished if necessary: *One day you'll have to answer for this.*

answer² *n*

1 [C,U] something you say when you reply to a
question that someone has asked you: *Give me
an answer as soon as possible.* | +**to** *Mark never
got an answer to his letter.* | *In answer to your
question, I think Paul's right.* | *I told you before,
the answer is no!*
2 [C] something that you write or say in reply to
a question in a test or competition: *What was the
answer to question 7?* | **the right/wrong/
correct/incorrect answer** *Score two points for
each correct answer.*
3 [C] something that solves a problem: *There is
no simple answer.* | +**to** *A bit more money would
be the answer to all our problems.*

'answering ma,chine also **answerphone**
BrE /'ɑːnsəfəʊn $ 'ænsərfoʊn/ *n* [C] a machine
that records messages from people who telephone you when you are not there

ant /ænt/ *n* [C] a small black or red insect that
lives in large groups

antagonism /æn'tægənɪzəm/ *n* [U] when people strongly dislike or oppose someone or something: +**between** *the longstanding antagonism
between the two countries* | +**towards** *their
antagonism towards tourists*

antagonistic /æn'tægə'nɪstɪk◂/ *adj* opposing
an idea or plan, or showing that you dislike
someone: +**to/towards** *groups which are antagonistic to one another*

antagonize also **-ise** *BrE* /æn'tægənaɪz/ *v* [T] to
make someone feel angry or unfriendly towards
you: *He was deliberately trying to antagonise her.*

Antarctic /æn'tɑːktɪk $ -ɑːr-/ *n* **the Antarctic**
the very cold area around the South Pole [➡ **the
Arctic**] —**Antarctic** *adj*

antelope /'æntɪ̩ləʊp $ 'æntəl-oʊp/ *n* [C] an
animal with long horns that can run very fast

antenatal /ˌæntɪ'neɪtl◂/ *adj BrE* relating to the
medical care given to women who are going to
have a baby [= **prenatal**; ➡ **postnatal**]: *an antenatal clinic*

antenna /æn'tenə/ *n* [C] **1** plural **antennae**
/-niː/ one of two long thin parts on an insect's
head that it uses to feel things → see picture on
page A2 **2** plural **antennas** especially *AmE* a
wire or piece of metal that receives or sends
television or radio signals [= **aerial** *BrE*] → see
picture on page A12

anthem /'ænθəm/ *n* [C] a special song that is
sung at religious, sports, or political ceremonies
→ NATIONAL ANTHEM

anthology /æn'θɒlədʒi $ æn'θɑː-/ *n* [C] plural
anthologies a set of stories, poems etc by different people collected together in one book

anthrax /'ænθræks/ *n* [U] a serious disease
affecting cattle and sheep, which can affect
humans

anthropology /ˌænθrə'pɒlədʒi $ -'pɑː-/ *n* [U]
the scientific study of people, societies, customs,
and beliefs —**anthropologist** *n* [C]
—**anthropological** /ˌænθrəpə'lɒdʒɪkəl◂ $ -'lɑː-/
adj

anti- /ænti $ ænti, æntaɪ/ *prefix* **1** strongly
opposed to something or someone, or strongly
disliking something or someone [≠ **pro-**]: *anti-
American feeling* **2** having the effect of preventing something: *antifreeze* (=liquid added to a
car's engine to prevent freezing)

antibiotic /ˌæntɪbaɪ'ɒtɪk◂ $ -'ɑː-/ *n* [C usually
plural] a drug that is used to kill BACTERIA and
cure infections —**antibiotic** *adj*

antibody /'æntɪˌbɒdi $ -'bɑː-/ *n* [C] plural **anti-
bodies** a substance produced by your body to
fight disease

anticipate /æn'tɪsɪpeɪt/ *v* [T] to expect something to happen and to prepare for it: *We don't
anticipate any problems.* | +**(that)** *It is antici-
pated that prices will rise.*

anticipation /ænˌtɪsɪ'peɪʃən/ *n* [U] **1** happy
feelings when you think something good is going
to happen: *Her eyes sparkled with anticipation.*
2 in anticipation of sth because you expect
something to happen: *He raised his fists in anticipation of a fight.*

anticlimax /ˌæntɪ'klaɪmæks/ *n* [C,U] an event
that seems disappointing because it happens
after something that was much better: *The rest
of the journey was an anticlimax.*

anticlockwise /ˌæntɪ'klɒkwaɪz◂ $ -'klɑːk-/
adj, adv BrE in the opposite direction to the way
the hands of a clock move [= **counterclockwise**
AmE; ≠ **clockwise**]: *Turn the handle anticlockwise.*

antics /'æntɪks/ *n* [plural] funny, silly, or strange
behaviour

antidepressant /ˌæntɪdɪ'presənt/ *n* [C] a drug
used to treat DEPRESSION (=a medical condition in
which you are very unhappy)

antidote /'æntɪdəʊt $ -doʊt/ *n* [C] **1** some-
thing that makes an unpleasant situation better:
+**to** *Laughter is a good antidote to stress.* **2** a
substance that stops the effects of a poison

antifreeze /'æntɪfriːz/ *n* [U] a liquid that is put
in the water of a car's engine to stop it from
freezing

antipathy /æn'tɪpəθi/ *n* [U] formal a feeling of
strong dislike towards someone or something:
+**to/towards** *his antipathy to women*

antiquated /'æntɪ̩kweɪtɪ̩d/ *adj* old-fashioned
and not suitable for modern needs or conditions:
antiquated laws

antique /ˌæn'tiːk◂/ *n* [C] a piece of furniture,
jewellery etc that is old and valuable: *priceless
antiques* | *an antique shop* (=one that sells
antiques) → see box at OLD —**antique** *adj*: *beautiful antique furniture*

antiquity /æn'tɪkwɪ̩ti/ *n* plural **antiquities**
1 [U] ancient times: **in antiquity** *In antiquity a
variety of methods were used.* **2** [U] the state of
being very old: *a building of great antiquity*
3 [C usually plural] a building or object made in
ancient times: *Roman antiquities*

anti-semitism /ˌænti'semɪ̩tɪzəm/ *n* [U] hatred
of Jewish people —**anti-semitic**
/ˌæntɪsɪ̩'mɪtɪk◂/ *adj*

A

antiseptic /ˌæntɪˈsɛptɪk◂/ n [C,U] a medicine that you put onto a wound to stop it becoming infected —**antiseptic** adj: antiseptic cream

anti-'social adj **1** antisocial behaviour upsets, harms, or annoys other people **2** unwilling to meet other people and talk to them: I'm feeling a bit antisocial at the moment.

antithesis /ænˈtɪθəsɪs/ n [C] plural **antitheses** /-siːz/ formal the exact opposite of something: +**of** Love is the antithesis of selfishness.

antler /ˈæntlə $ -ər/ n [C] one of the two horns on the head of male DEER ➔ see picture on page A2

antonym /ˈæntənɪm/ n [C] technical a word that means the opposite of another word [➡ synonym]

anus /ˈeɪnəs/ n [C] the hole in your bottom through which solid waste leaves your body

anvil /ˈænvɪl/ n [C] an iron block on which pieces of hot metal are shaped using a hammer

anxiety /æŋˈzaɪəti/ n plural **anxieties 1** [C,U] the feeling of being very worried about something: +**about/over** his anxiety about the future | My mother's ill health was a constant source of anxiety. **2** [U] a feeling of wanting to do something very much: **anxiety to do sth** I nearly fell in my anxiety to get downstairs.

anxious /ˈæŋkʃəs/ adj **1** worried about something: +**about** I'm quite anxious about my exams. | an anxious look | **anxious moment/time etc** (=one in which you feel worried) ➔ see box at WORRIED **2** feeling strongly that you want to do something or want something to happen: **anxious to do sth** I was anxious to get home. | +**(that)** We're very anxious that no one else hears about this. —**anxiously** adv: Mom waited anxiously by the phone.

any¹ /ˈeni/ determiner, pron **1** some or even the smallest amount or number – usually used in questions and negative statements: Have you got any money? | It won't make any difference. | +**of** They didn't invite any of us. | Are there any other questions? | 'Don't you want butter?' 'I couldn't find any.' ➔ see box at SOME **2** used to refer to a person or thing of a particular type when what you are saying is true of all people or things of that type: a question that any child could answer | Any help would be welcome.

USAGE

Do not say 'Any parents love their children'. Say 'All parents love their children'.
Do not say 'Any teacher must deal with these problems'. Say 'Every teacher must deal with these problems'.

3 any moment/minute/day etc (now) very soon: He'll be here any minute. ➔ see box at SOON ➔ **in any case** at CASE ➔ **at any rate** at RATE¹

GRAMMAR

any, a
Use **any** with U nouns or plural noun forms: Do you have any money?
Use **a** with singular noun forms: Do you have a car?
➔ A

any² adv even a small amount – used before a COMPARATIVE form, usually in questions and negative statements: Are you feeling any better? | Is she any happier now? | I can't run any faster.

anybody /ˈeniˌbɒdi, ˈenibədi $ -ˌbɑːdi/ pron ANYONE

anyhow /ˈenihaʊ/ adv informal ANYWAY

any more, **anymore** /ˌeniˈmɔː $ -ˈmɔːr/ adv **not any more** if something does not happen any more, it used to happen in the past but it does not happen now: Nick doesn't live here any more.

anyone /ˈeniwʌn/ also **anybody** pron **1** a person – used in questions and negative statements: Is anyone at home? | I haven't seen anyone all day. | Do you know **anyone else** who wants a ticket? **2** any person or any people, when it does not matter who: Anyone can learn to cook. | We offer advice to anyone who is unemployed.

anyplace /ˈenipleɪs/ adv AmE ANYWHERE

anything /ˈeniθɪŋ/ pron **1** any thing, event, situation etc, when it is not important which one: Take anything you want. | Anything would be better than feeling like this. | Can I do anything to help? **2** something – used in questions and negative statements: Do you need anything? | Her father didn't know anything about it. | Would you like **anything else** to eat? | **or anything** spoken (=or anything similar) It's not dangerous or anything. **3 anything but** not at all: Maria is anything but stupid. **4 anything like sb/sth** similar in any way to something or someone: Belinda doesn't look anything like her sister. | If you're anything like me, you hate ironing. **5 as important/clear/big etc as anything** informal extremely important, clear etc: He's as excited as anything.

anyway /ˈeniweɪ/ also **anyhow** informal adv **1** in spite of the fact that you have just mentioned: Tom was ill, but I went to the party anyway. | This idea probably won't work, but let's try it anyway. **2** used when you are adding something to support or explain what you have just said: I haven't got time to do it now. **And anyway**, I don't have the right tools. | He decided to sell his bike – he never used it anyway. **3** used when you are changing the subject of a conversation or returning to a previous subject: Anyway, how are things with you? | I think she's around my age, **but anyway**, she's pregnant. **4** used when adding something that corrects or slightly changes what you have just said: I'm not thinking of changing my job. Not this year, anyway.

anywhere /ˈeniweə $ -wer/ also **anyplace** AmE adv **1** in or to any place, when it is not important where: Sit anywhere you like. | I could study anywhere. | I wouldn't want to live **anywhere else**. **2** used in questions and negative statements to mean 'somewhere' or 'nowhere': Did you go anywhere last night? | Have you looked **anywhere else**? | I don't have anywhere to live. **3 not anywhere near** not at all: She doesn't practise **anywhere near as** much as Sam.

4 anywhere between one and ten/20 and 30 etc used to mean any age, number, amount etc between the ones that you say: *She could have been anywhere between 45 and 60 years of age.*

apart /ə'pɑːt $ -ɑːrt/ *adv*

1 if people or things are apart, they are not close to each other or touching each other: *Plant the seeds 8 inches apart.* | *They have offices as far apart as India and Peru.* | *He and his wife are now living apart.* | **+from** *Tim and Kate sat together, slightly apart from the others.*

2 if something comes apart, or if you take it apart, it separates into different pieces: *He took the camera apart to clean it.*

3 if two events are a particular time apart, that is the length of time between them: *Our birthdays are only two days apart.*

4 fall apart if something falls apart, it fails completely: *His marriage fell apart.*

a'part from *prep* **1** except for: *Apart from the ending, it's a really good film.* | *I don't see any of my family, apart from my sister.* **2** in addition to: *Apart from Rory, Claire has two other children.*

apartheid /ə'pɑːtaɪt, -teɪt, -taɪd $ -ɑːr-/ *n* [U] the system that used to exist in South Africa, in which only white people had full political and legal rights

apartment /ə'pɑːtmənt $ -ɑːr-/ *n* [C] *especially AmE* a set of rooms on one floor of a large building, where someone lives [= **flat** *BrE*] → see box at **HOUSE**

a'partment ,building, a'partment ,house *n* [C] *AmE* a building that is divided into separate apartments

apathetic /ˌæpə'θetɪk◂/ *adj* not interested in something, and not willing to make any effort to change things: **+about** *He's totally apathetic about politics.*

apathy /'æpəθi/ *n* [U] the feeling of not being interested in something, and not willing to make any effort to change things: *public apathy about the coming election*

ape /eɪp/ *n* [C] an animal that is similar to a monkey but has no tail or only a very short tail

aperitif /əˌperə'tiːf/ *n* [C] an alcoholic drink that you have before a meal

aperture /'æpətʃə $ 'æpərtʃʊr/ *n* [C] *formal* a small hole, especially one that lets light into a camera

apex /'eɪpeks/ *n* [C] *formal* **1** the top or highest part of something pointed or curved: *the apex of the roof* **2** the most important position in an organization or society

aphrodisiac /ˌæfrə'dɪziæk◂/ *n* [C] a food, drink, or drug that makes someone want to have sex

apiece /ə'piːs/ *adv* each: *Roses cost £2 apiece.*

Apocalypse /ə'pɒkəlɪps $ ə'pɑː-/ *n* **the Apocalypse** the destruction and end of the world

apocalyptic /əˌpɒkə'lɪptɪk◂ $ ə'pɑː-/ *adj* warning people about terrible events that will happen in the future

apolitical /ˌeɪpə'lɪtɪkəl◂/ *adj* not interested in politics, or not connected with any political party

apologetic /əˌpɒlə'dʒetɪk◂ $ ə'pɑː-/ *adj* showing or saying that you are sorry that you did something bad or were responsible for it: *The manager was very apologetic.* | *an apologetic smile* —**apologetically** /-kli/ *adv*

apologize also **-ise** *BrE* /ə'pɒlədʒaɪz $ ə'pɑː-/ *v* [I] to tell someone that you are sorry that you have upset them or caused them problems: **apologize for (doing) sth** *He apologized for being late.* | **+to** *Apologize to your sister now!* | *I apologise. I was selfish.*

A

COMMUNICATION

Ways of apologizing

I'm sorry
I'm so sorry
I owe you an apology
please accept my apologies *formal*

apology /ə'pɒlədʒi $ ə'pɑː-/ *n* [C] plural **apologies** something that you say or write to someone to show them that you are sorry for upsetting or causing them problems: *I received a written apology from the council.*

apostle /ə'pɒsəl $ ə'pɑː-/ *n* [C] one of the 12 men chosen by Christ to teach people about the Christian religion

apostrophe /ə'pɒstrəfi $ ə'pɑː-/ *n* [C] **a)** the sign (') that is used in writing to show that numbers or letters have been left out, for example, 'don't' (=do not) and '86 (=1986) **b)** the sign (') used before or after the letter 's' to show that something belongs or relates to someone or something, for example 'Laura's coat' or 'the boys' father' **c)** the sign (') used before 's' to show the plural of letters and numbers: *Your r's look like v's.*

appal *BrE*; **appall** *AmE* /ə'pɔːl $ ə'pɒːl/ *v* [T] **appalled, appalling** if something appals you, it shocks and upsets you: *I was appalled by their racism.* —**appalled** *adj*

appalling /ə'pɔːlɪŋ $ ə'pɒː-/ *adj* **1** terrible and shocking: *children living in appalling conditions* → see box at **BAD** **2** *informal* very bad: *The weather was appalling.* —**appallingly** *adv*

apparatus /ˌæpə'reɪtəs $ -'ræ-/ *n* [C,U] plural **apparatus** or **apparatuses** a set of equipment that is used for a particular purpose: *firemen wearing breathing apparatus*

apparel /ə'pærəl/ *n* [U] *formal* clothes

apparent /ə'pærənt/ *adj* **1** easy to notice: *It soon became apparent that he hadn't read the report.* | *Suddenly, for no apparent reason, she started to cry.* **2** seeming to be real or true, although it may not be: *He was frustrated by his apparent lack of progress.*

apparently /ə'pærəntli/ *adv*

1 used to say that you have heard that something is true, although you are not completely sure about it: *Apparently, it's not the first time she's left him.* | *The conference was apparently a great success.*

2 according to the way someone looks or a situation appears, although you cannot be sure: *the unexplained death of an apparently healthy baby*

apparition /ˌæpə'rɪʃən/ *n* [C] **1** a GHOST **2** someone who looks strange or frightening

A

appeal¹ /ə'piːl/ *n*

1 [C] an urgent public request for help, money, information etc: **+for** *Police have issued an appeal for information.* | *The girl's parents have made a public appeal for her safe return.* | *The hospital has launched an appeal to raise £150,000.*

2 [C,U] a formal request to a court or to someone in authority asking for a decision to be changed: **+to** *an appeal to the European Court of Human Rights* | **+against** *He lost his appeal against a 6-month jail sentence.*

3 [U] if something has appeal, people think it is attractive or interesting: **+of** *the popular appeal of football*

→ **SEX APPEAL**

appeal² *v*

1 [I] to make a serious public request for help, money, information etc: **+for** *The President has appealed for calm.* | *Police are appealing for witnesses.* | **appeal to sb (to do sth)** *Hungary has appealed to foreign zoos to find the animals a home.*

2 [I,T] to make a formal request to a court or someone in authority asking for a decision to be changed: **+against** *He plans to appeal against his conviction.*

3 [I] if something appeals to you, you think it is attractive or interesting: **+to** *That idea doesn't appeal to me at all.*

appealing /ə'piːlɪŋ/ *adj* attractive or interesting

appear /ə'pɪə $ ə'pɪr/ *v*

1 [linking verb] to seem: **appear to be/do sth** *The noise appeared to come from the bedroom.* | *Richard appeared worried.* | *It appears that she's changed her mind.*

2 [I] if someone or something appears, they can suddenly be seen or they suddenly arrive [≠ **disappear**]: *A man suddenly appeared from behind a tree.* | *Ruth appeared in the doorway.*

3 [I] to take part in a film, play, concert, television programme etc: **+in/on** *He is currently appearing in 'Blood Brothers' at the Lyric Theatre.*

4 [I] to be written or shown in a newspaper, book, magazine etc: **+in** *The article appeared in the Independent on 31st August.*

5 [I] to become available or known about for the first time: *The calendars will appear in the shops in September.*

appearance /ə'pɪərəns $ ə'pɪr-/ *n*

1 [C,U] the way that someone or something looks or seems: *Annette was always very concerned about her appearance.* | *The government wanted to give the appearance of doing something.*

2 [C] when someone takes part in a public event, play, concert, television programme etc: *I made my first TV appearance in 1957.* | *a series of public appearances*

3 [singular] when something new begins to exist or starts being used: **+of** *the appearance of the mini-skirt in 1965*

4 [C usually singular] the unexpected or sudden arrival of someone or something: **+of** *The sudden appearance of her daughter startled her.*

appease /ə'piːz/ *v* [T] *formal* to make someone less angry by giving them something that they want: *an attempt to appease critics of his regime* —**appeasement** *n* [C,U]

append /ə'pend/ *v* [T] *formal* to add something to a piece of writing

appendage /ə'pendɪdʒ/ *n* [C] *formal* something that is attached to something bigger or more important

appendicitis /ə,pendɪ'saɪtɪs/ *n* [U] an illness in which your appendix swells and causes pain

appendix /ə'pendɪks/ *n* [C] **1** plural **appendixes** a small organ near your BOWEL, which has little or no use **2** plural **appendixes** or **appendices** /-dɪsiːz/ a part at the end of a book that has additional information

appetite /'æpɪtaɪt/ *n* [C,U] **1** a desire for food: *I seem to have lost my appetite lately.* **2** a desire or liking for a particular activity: **+for** *her amazing appetite for work*

appetizer also **-iser** *BrE* /'æpɪtaɪzə $ -ər/ *n* [C] a small amount of food that you eat at the beginning of a meal [= **starter** *BrE*]

appetizing also **-ising** *BrE* /'æpɪtaɪzɪŋ/ *adj* food that is appetizing looks or smells very good

applaud /ə'plɔːd $ ə'plɒːd/ *v* **1** [I,T] to hit your hands together to show that you have enjoyed a play, concert, speaker etc [= **clap**]: *The audience applauded.* **2** [T] *formal* to praise something that someone does: *She should be applauded for her honesty.*

applause /ə'plɔːz $ ə'plɒːz/ *n* [U] the sound of people hitting their hands together to show that they have enjoyed a play, concert, speaker etc: *He was given a big round of applause* (=period of applause).

apple /'æpəl/ *n* [C,U] a hard round fruit that has a green, red, or yellow skin and is white inside: *apple pie* → see picture at **FRUIT**

appliance /ə'plaɪəns/ *n* [C] a piece of electrical equipment, such as a REFRIGERATOR or a WASHING MACHINE, that is used in people's homes

applicable /ə'plɪkəbəl, 'æplɪkəbəl/ *adj* affecting or concerning a particular person, group, or situation: **+to** *The legislation will be applicable to the whole country.*

applicant /'æplɪkənt/ *n* [C] someone who has formally asked, usually in writing, for a job, university place etc

application /,æplɪ'keɪʃən/ *n*

1 [C] a formal request, usually in writing, for something such as a job, a university place, or permission to do something: **+for** *an application for a grant* | *job applications* | *You'll need to fill in an application form.* → see box at **JOB**

2 [C,U] a practical purpose for which a machine, idea etc can be used: *The research has many practical applications.*

3 [C] a piece of computer software which does a particular job

4 [C,U] when you put something such as paint or a cream onto a surface

applied /ə'plaɪd/ *adj* **applied science/ physics/linguistics etc** a subject that is studied for a practical purpose [→ **pure**]

apply /ə'plaɪ/ **applied, applying, applies** *v*

1 [I] to make a formal request, usually in writing, for something such as a job, a university place, or permission to do something: **+for** *Rob's applied for a job in Canada.* | *The company is* *applying for permission to demolish the building.* | **apply to do sth** *I've applied to join the army.* → see box at **JOB**

2 [I] to affect or concern a particular person, group, or situation: **+to** *Do the same rules apply to part-time workers?*

3 [T] to use something such as a method, idea, or law: **apply sth to sth** *the value of applying these techniques to archaeology*

4 apply yourself (to sth) to work very hard and carefully on something, especially for a long time: *If only he had applied himself to his studies!*

5 [T] to put something such as paint or a cream onto a surface: *Apply the paint using a sponge.* | **apply make-up/lipstick etc**

appoint /ə'pɔɪnt/ *v* [T] to formally give someone a job or position: *The school's just appointed a new head teacher.* | **appoint sb to sth** *She's been appointed to the Board of Directors.* | **appoint sb (as) sth** *He was appointed Chief Engineer.*

appointed /ə'pɔɪntɪd/ *adj* **the appointed day/time/place etc** the time, date etc that has or had been decided: *I reported to H.Q. at the appointed time.*

appointment /ə'pɔɪntmənt/ *n*
1 [C] an arrangement for a meeting at an agreed time and place, for a particular purpose: **+with** *She has an appointment with a client at 10.30.* | *Ring your doctor and make an appointment.*
2 [C,U] when someone is formally given a job or position: **+of** *the appointment of a new Archbishop*

apportion /ə'pɔːʃən $ -ɔːr-/ *v* [T] *formal* to decide how something should be shared between various people: *We are not here to apportion blame* (=say who deserves to be blamed).

appraisal /ə'preɪzəl/ *n* [C,U] an official description of how valuable, effective, or successful someone or something is: *an annual appraisal of employees' work*

appraise /ə'preɪz/ *v* [T] *formal* to carefully decide how valuable, important etc something is: *She appraised her handiwork.*

appreciable /ə'priːʃəbəl/ *adj formal* noticeable or important: *Three years in China had had an appreciable effect on him.* —**appreciably** *adv*

appreciate /ə'priːʃieɪt/ *v* [T] **1** to understand how serious or important a situation or problem is or what someone's feelings are: *He did not fully appreciate the significance of signing the contract.* | **+that/how etc** *I don't think you appreciate how busy I am.* **2** to be grateful for something: *Aunt Kate really appreciated the card you sent.* | *I'd appreciate it if you came along tonight* (=please come). **3** to understand how good or useful someone or something is: *The Americans, however, appreciated his talents.*

appreciation /ə,priːʃi'eɪʃən/ *n* **1** [U] pleasure you feel when you realize something is good, useful, or well done: **+of** *She has a fine appreciation of music.* **2** [U] a feeling of being grateful to someone: *Let's show our appreciation by buying her a small gift.* **3** [C,U] an understanding of the importance or meaning of something: **+of** *The course helped me gain a better appreciation of children's needs.*

appreciative /ə'priːʃətɪv/ *adj* showing that you have enjoyed something or feel grateful for it —**appreciatively** *adv*

apprehend /,æprɪ'hend/ *v* [T] *formal* if the police apprehend a criminal, they catch them and take them to a police station [= **arrest**]

apprehension /,æprɪ'henʃən/ *n* [U] anxiety or fear about something in the future: *She felt sick with apprehension.*

apprehensive /,æprɪ'hensɪv/ *adj* anxious or afraid about something in the future —**apprehensively** *adv*

apprentice /ə'prentɪs/ *n* [C] someone who works for an employer for a fixed amount of time in order to learn a skill

apprenticeship /ə'prentɪsʃɪp/ *n* [C,U] the job of being an apprentice, or the period of time in which you are an apprentice

approach¹ /ə'prəʊtʃ $ ə'proʊtʃ/ *v*
1 [I,T] to move nearer to someone or something: *Slowly, he approached the bed.* | *A car approached and stopped.*
2 [T] to ask someone to do something, especially when you are not sure if they will want to do it: *She's been approached by two schools about a teaching job.*
3 [I,T] if an event or a particular time is approaching, or if you are approaching it, it will happen soon: *It was approaching 4.15 p.m.*
4 [T] to begin to deal with a situation or problem in a particular way

approach² *n* **1** [C] a way of doing something or dealing with a problem: **+to** *a new approach to teaching languages* **2** [C] a request: **+to** *An approach to the landlord may be necessary.* **3 the approach of sth** the fact that a future time or event is getting closer: *the approach of winter* **4** [U] movement nearer to something: *Our approach frightened the birds.* **5** [C] a road or path leading to a place: *an approach road*

approachable /ə'prəʊtʃəbəl $ ə'proʊtʃ-/ *adj* friendly and easy to talk to [≠ **unapproachable**]

approbation /,æprə'beɪʃən/ *n* [U] *formal* praise or approval

appropriate¹ /ə'prəʊpri-ɪt $ ə'proʊ-/ *adj* suitable for a particular time, situation, or purpose [≠ **inappropriate**]: **+for** *clothes that are appropriate for a job interview* | **+to** *an education system which is more appropriate to the needs of the students* | *It would not be appropriate for me to discuss that now.*
—**appropriately** *adv* —**appropriateness** *n* [U]

appropriate² /ə'prəʊprieɪt $ ə'proʊ-/ *v* [T] *formal* to steal or take something

approval /ə'pruːvəl/ *n* [U]
1 when a plan, decision, or person is officially accepted: **+for** *We have obtained approval for the funding.* | *The president has already given his approval to the plan.*
2 the opinion that someone or something is good [≠ **disapproval**]: *I was always trying to win my father's approval.* | *Does the design meet with your approval* (=do you like it)?

approve /ə'pruːv/ *v*
1 [T] to officially accept a plan or idea: *We are waiting for our proposals to be approved.*

A

2 [I] to think that someone or something is good, right, or suitable [≠ **disapprove**]: +**of** *My parents didn't approve of my friends.* | *I don't approve of taking drugs.*

approving /ə'pruːvɪŋ/ *adj* showing support or agreement for something [≠ **disapproving**]: *an approving nod* —**approvingly** *adv*

approx /ə'prɒks $ ə'prɑːks/ the written abbreviation of **approximately**

approximate[1] /ə'prɒksɪmɪt $ ə'prɑːk-/ *adj* not exact, but nearly right: *These figures are only approximate.*

approximate[2] /ə'prɒksɪmeɪt $ ə'prɑːk-/ *v* [I, linking verb] *formal* to be similar to but not exactly the same as something else —**approximation** /ə,prɒksɪ'meɪʃən $ ə,prɑːk-/ *n* [C,U]

approximately /ə'prɒksɪmətli $ ə'prɑːks-/ *adv* a little more or less than an exact number, amount etc: *The plane will be landing in approximately 20 minutes.*

apricot /'eɪprɪkɒt $ 'æprɪkɑːt/ *n* [C] a small soft yellow fruit with one large seed

April /'eɪprəl/ *n* [C,U] written abbreviation **Apr.** the fourth month of the year, between March and May: **next/last April** *I'm going to Cuba next April.* | **in April** *Our new office opened in April.* | **on April 6th** *The meeting was on April 6th.* → see box at **MONTH**

April 'Fool's Day *n* [singular] April 1, a day when people play tricks on each other

apron /'eɪprən/ *n* [C] a piece of clothing that you wear to protect your clothes, especially when you are cooking

apt /æpt/ *adj* **1 be apt to do sth** to be likely to do something: *They're good kids but apt to get into trouble.* **2** exactly suitable: *an apt remark* —**aptly** *adv*

aptitude /'æptɪtjuːd $ -tuːd/ *n* [C,U] a natural ability to do something well

aquarium /ə'kweəriəm $ ə'kwer-/ *n* [C] **1** a clear glass or plastic container for fish and other water animals **2** a building where people go to look at fish and other water animals

aquarium

Aquarius /ə'kweəriəs $ ə'kwer-/ *n* **1** [U] the sign of the Zodiac of people born between January 21 and February 19 **2** [C] someone who has this sign

aquatic /ə'kwætɪk, ə'kwɒ- $ ə'kwæ-, ə'kwɑː-/ *adj* living or happening in water: *aquatic plants* | *aquatic sports*

aqueduct /'ækwɪdʌkt/ *n* [C] a structure like a bridge that takes water across a valley

Arab /'ærəb/ *n* [C] someone whose language is Arabic and whose family come from the Middle East or North Africa —**Arab** *adj*: *Arab countries*

Arabic /'ærəbɪk/ *n* [U] the language of Arab people and the religious language of Islam

arable /'ærəbəl/ *adj* relating to growing crops: *arable land*

arbiter /'ɑːbɪtə $ 'ɑːrbɪtər/ *n* [C] **1** someone who settles an argument between two opposing sides **2 arbiter of fashion/taste etc** someone who judges what is fashionable, attractive etc

arbitrary /'ɑːbɪtrəri, -tri $ 'ɑːrbɪtreri/ *adj* decided or arranged without any reason or plan, often unfairly: *an **arbitrary** decision* —**arbitrarily** /'ɑːbɪtrərəli $,ɑːrbɪ'trerɪli/ *adv*

arbitrate /'ɑːbɪtreɪt $ 'ɑːr-/ *v* [I,T] to officially judge how an argument between two opposing sides should be solved —**arbitrator** *n* [C] —**arbitration** /,ɑːbɪ'treɪʃən $,ɑːr-/ *n* [U]

arc /ɑːk $ ɑːrk/ *n* [C] part of a circle or any curved line

arcade /ɑː'keɪd $ ɑːr-/ *n* [C] **1** a place where people go to play games on machines: *an **amusement arcade*** **2** also **shopping arcade** *BrE* a large building where there are a lot of shops

arch[1] /ɑːtʃ $ ɑːrtʃ/ *n* [C] plural **arches** **1** a structure with a curved top that supports the weight of a bridge or building: *We walked under an arch into a small courtyard.* **2** the curved middle part of the bottom of your foot —**arched** *adj*: *an arched doorway*

arch[2] *v* [I,T] to form a curved shape, or to make something form a curved shape: *The cat arched her back and hissed.*

archaeology also **archeology** *AmE* /,ɑːki'ɒlədʒi $,ɑːrki'ɑː-/ *n* [U] the study of ancient societies by examining what remains of their buildings, tools, places they were buried etc —**archaeologist** *n* [C] *The site is being studied by archaeologists.* —**archaeological** /,ɑːkiə'lɒdʒɪkəl $,ɑːrkiə'lɑː-/ *adj*: *an archaeological site*

archaic /ɑː'keɪ-ɪk $ ɑːr-/ *adj* very old-fashioned or no longer used: *archaic words*

archbishop /,ɑːtʃ'bɪʃəp $,ɑːrtʃ-/ *n* [C] a Christian priest of the highest rank, who is in charge of all the churches in a particular area

archeology /,ɑːki'ɒlədʒi $,ɑːrki'ɑː-/ an American spelling of ARCHAEOLOGY

archery /'ɑːtʃəri $ 'ɑːr-/ *n* [U] the sport of shooting ARROWS from a BOW —**archer** *n* [C]

archetype /'ɑːkɪtaɪp $ 'ɑːr-/ *n* [C usually singular] a perfect example of something, because it has all the most important features, qualities etc of that thing —**archetypal** /,ɑːkɪ'taɪpəl $,ɑːr-/ *adj*: *Byron was the archetypal Romantic hero.*

architect /'ɑːkɪtekt $ 'ɑːr-/ *n* [C] someone who designs buildings

architecture /'ɑːkɪtektʃə $ 'ɑːrkɪtektʃər/ *n* [U]

1 the style and design of buildings: *medieval architecture*

2 the job or skill of designing buildings —**architectural** /,ɑːkɪ'tektʃərəl $,ɑːr-/ *adj*

archive /'ɑːkaɪv $ 'ɑːr-/ *n* [C usually plural] a place where a lot of historical records are stored, or the records that are stored

archway /'ɑːtʃweɪ $ 'ɑːrtʃ-/ *n* [C] a passage or entrance under an ARCH

Arctic[1] also **arctic** /'ɑːktɪk $ 'ɑːrk-/ *adj* **1** relating to the most northern part of the world near the North Pole **2** extremely cold: *arctic conditions*

Arctic[2] *n* the very cold area around the North Pole [➡ **the Antarctic**]

ardent /'ɑːdənt $ 'ɑːr-/ *adj* supporting or wanting something very strongly: *an ardent football supporter* | *an ardent desire to win*

ardour *BrE*; **ardor** *AmE* /'ɑːdə $ 'ɑːrdər/ *n* [U] *formal* very strong admiration or love

arduous /'ɑːdjuəs $ 'ɑːrdʒuəs/ *adj* involving a lot of strength and hard work: *an **arduous** task* | *an **arduous** journey*

are /ə; *strong* ɑː $ ər; *strong* ɑːr/ the present tense plural and second person singular of 'be'

area /'eəriə $ 'eriə/ *n* [C]
1 a part of a country, town etc: *Dad grew up in the Portland area.* | **+of** *a **working-class area** of Birmingham* | *a **residential area***

> **region** – a large area of a country or the world: *the north-west region of Russia*
> **zone** – an area that is different in a particular way from the areas around it: *a no-parking zone*
> **district** – a particular area of a city or the country: *the financial district of London*
> **neighbourhood** *BrE*/**neighborhood** *AmE* – an area of a town where people live: *a friendly neighbourhood*
> **suburb** – an area outside the centre of a city, where people live: *a suburb of Boston*
> **slum** – an area of a city that is in very bad condition, where many poor people live: *the slums of London*
> **ghetto** – an area of a city where poor people of a particular race or class live

2 a part of a house, office, garden etc that is used for a particular purpose: *Their apartment has a large kitchen area.*
3 a particular subject or type of activity: *The course covers three main **subject areas**.*
4 the size of a flat surface: *an area of 200 square miles*
→ **CATCHMENT AREA, NO-GO AREA**

ˈarea ˌcode *n* [C] the part of a telephone number that you have to add for a different town or country

arena /əˈriːnə/ *n* **1** [C] a building with a large flat central area surrounded by raised seats, used for sports or entertainment: *a sports arena*
2 the political/public/international etc arena all the people and activities connected with politics, the government etc: *Women are entering the political arena in larger numbers.*

aren't /ɑːnt $ 'ɑːrənt/ **a)** the short form of 'are not': *They aren't here.* **b)** the short form of 'am not', used in questions: *I'm in big trouble, aren't I?*

arguable /'ɑːɡjuəbəl $ 'ɑːr-/ *adj* **1 it is arguable that** used to say that something might be true: *It's arguable that the new law will make things better.* **2** not certain, or not definitely true, and therefore easy to doubt: *Whether he's the right person for the job is arguable.*

arguably /'ɑːɡjuəbli $ 'ɑːr-/ *adv* used to say that there are good reasons for saying that something is true: *Senna was arguably the greatest racing driver of all time.*

argue /'ɑːɡjuː $ 'ɑːr-/ *v*
1 [I] to shout and say angry things to someone because you disagree with them: *We could hear the neighbours arguing.* | **+about/over** *They always seem to be arguing about money.* | **+with** *Stop arguing with me!*

> **fight/have a fight**: *My mom and dad were always fighting.*
> **have an argument**: *We've had serious arguments before but never split up.*
> **have a row**: *We have had another family row.*
> **quarrel/have a quarrel** – to have an angry argument: *Let's not quarrel about money.* | *They've had a quarrel about some girl.*
> **squabble/bicker** – to argue about unimportant things: *The kids were bickering over what program to watch.*

2 [I,T] to clearly explain why you think something is true or should be done: **+that** *She argued that most teachers are underpaid.* | **+for/against** *Baker argued against cutting the military budget.* | *She **argued the case** for changing the law.*

argument /'ɑːɡjᵿmənt $ 'ɑːr-/ *n* [C]
1 a situation in which people shout and say angry things to each other because they disagree with each other: **+about/over** *an argument about who was responsible for the accident* | **+with** *a serious argument with my husband* | *My parents **had** a big **argument** last night.* → see box at **ARGUE**
2 a set of reasons that show that something is true or untrue, right or wrong etc: **+for/against** *a powerful argument against smoking* | **+that** *the familiar argument that the costs outweigh the benefits*

argumentative /ˌɑːɡjᵿˈmentətɪv $ ˌɑːr-/ *adj* someone who is argumentative often argues or likes arguing

aria /'ɑːriə/ *n* [C] a song that is sung by only one person in an OPERA

arid /'ærᵻd/ *adj formal* very dry and with very little rain: *arid land* | *an arid climate*

Aries /'eəriːz, 'eəriiz $ 'eriːz/ *n* **1** [U] the sign of the Zodiac of people born between March 21 and April 20 **2** [C] someone who has this sign

arise /əˈraɪz/ *v* [I] past tense **arose** /əˈrəʊz $ əˈroʊz/ past participle **arisen** /əˈrɪzən/ **1** if a problem or difficult situation arises, it begins to happen: *A crisis has arisen in the Foreign Office.*
2 *literary* to get out of bed, or to stand up

aristocracy /ˌærᵻˈstɒkrəsi $ -ˈstɑː-/ *n* [C] plural **aristocracies** the people in the highest social class, who traditionally have a lot of land, money, and power: *a member of the aristocracy* —**aristocrat** /'ærᵻstəkræt, əˈrɪs- $ əˈrɪs-/ *n* [C] *a wealthy aristocrat* —**aristocratic** /ˌærᵻstəˈkrætᵻk/ *adj*

arithmetic /əˈrɪθmətᵻk/ *n* [U] the science of numbers involving adding, multiplying etc [➜ **mathematics**] —**arithmetic** /ˌærᵻθˈmetᵻk◂/ *adj* —**arithmetically** /-kli/ *adv*

arm[1] /ɑːm $ ɑːrm/ *n* [C]
1 one of the two long parts of your body between your shoulders and your hands: **left/right arm** *He had a tattoo on his left arm.* | *I put my **arms** around him.* | *They walked along **arm in arm** (=with their arms bent around each other's).* | **cross/fold your arms** (=bend your arms so that they are resting on top of each

other against your body) | **under your arm** *I was carrying a pile of books under my arm.* → see picture on page A3
2 the part of a piece of clothing that covers your arm [= **sleeve**]
3 the part of a chair that you rest your arm on
4 arms [plural] weapons: *the sale of arms to other countries* | *the **arms trade*** | *an **arms dealer*** (=a company that sells weapons) | *a new international agreement on **arms control*** (=limiting the number of weapons that countries are allowed to have)
5 be up in arms about sth to be very angry about something: *The whole town is up in arms about the closure of the hospital.*
6 welcome sb/sth with open arms to show that you are very happy and eager to see someone or to accept an idea or plan: *We welcomed the offer with open arms.*
7 a long part of an object or piece of equipment: *The cutting wheel is on the end of a steel arm.*
→ **twist sb's arm** at TWIST¹

arm² *v* [I,T] to provide weapons for someone [≠ **disarm**]

armaments /'ɑːməmənts $ 'ɑːr-/ *n* [plural] weapons and military equipment: *nuclear armaments*

armband /'ɑːmbænd $ 'ɑːrm-/ *n* [C] a band of material that you wear around the top part of your arm

armchair /'ɑːmtʃeə, ,ɑːm'tʃeə $ 'ɑːrmtʃer, ,ɑːrm'tʃer/ *n* [C] a comfortable chair with sides that you can rest your arms on → see picture at SEAT¹

armed /ɑːmd $ ɑːrmd/ *adj* **1** carrying weapons: *an armed guard* | **+with** *The suspect is armed with a shotgun.* | *He got ten years in prison for **armed robbery*** (=stealing using a gun). **2 armed with sth** having something useful that you need: *I went into the meeting armed with a copy of the report.*

soldier   airman   **armed forces**
sailor

,armed 'forces *n* **the armed forces** a country's military organizations such as the army → see box at ARMY

armistice /'ɑːmɪstɪs $ 'ɑːrm-/ *n* [C] an agreement to stop fighting

armour *BrE*; **armor** *AmE* /'ɑːmə $ 'ɑːrmər/ *n* [U] **1** metal or leather clothing worn in past times by men in battle: *a suit of armour* **2** a layer of strong material that protects something

armoured *BrE*; **armored** *AmE* /'ɑːməd $ 'ɑːrmərd/ *adj* protected against bullets or other weapons by a strong layer of metal: *an armoured car*

armoury *BrE*; **armory** *AmE* /'ɑːməri $ 'ɑːr-/ *n* [C] plural **armouries** a place where weapons are stored

armpit /'ɑːm,pɪt $ 'ɑːrm-/ *n* [C] the hollow place under your arm where it joins your body

'arms race *n* [C usually singular] the competition between different countries to have a larger number of powerful weapons

army /'ɑːmi $ 'ɑːr-/ *n* [C] plural **armies**
1 a military force that fights wars on land: *He joined the army when he was 17.* | **in the army** *Her son is in the army.* | *the US army*

THESAURUS

An army consists of **soldiers** or **troops**.
If you **join up** *BrE*/**enlist** *AmE*, you join the army.
If you are **called up** *BrE*/**drafted** *AmE*, you are ordered to serve in the army by the government.
You can use **armed forces**, **the military services** *BrE*/**the service** *AmE* to talk in a general way about the army, navy, and air force.

2 a large group of people or animals involved in the same activity: **+of** *an army of ants*

A-road /'eɪ rəʊd $ -roʊd/ *n* [C] a main road in Britain that is smaller than a MOTORWAY

aroma /ə'rəʊmə $ ə'roʊ-/ *n* [C] a strong pleasant smell: **+of** *the aroma of fresh coffee* → see box at SMELL —**aromatic** /,ærə'mætɪk◂/ *adj*: *aromatic oils*

aromatherapy /ə,rəʊmə'θerəpi $ ə,roʊ-/ *n* [U] the use of pleasant smelling plant oils to make you feel healthy and relaxed —**aromatherapist** *n* [C]

arose /ə'rəʊz $ ə'roʊz/ *v* the past tense of ARISE

around /ə'raʊnd $ also **round** *BrE* *adv, prep*
1 surrounding something or someone: *We put a fence around the yard.* | *Mario put his arms around her.*
2 in a circular movement: *Water pushes the wheel around.* | *They danced around the bonfire.*
3 to or in many parts of a place: *Stan showed me around the office.* | *an international company with offices **all around** the world*
4 in or near a particular place: *Is there a bank around here?* | *Is your dad around?* → see box at LOCALLY
5 on or to the other side of something: *There's a door around the back.*
6 existing: *That joke's been around for years.*
7 used to say that someone or something turns so that they face in the opposite direction: *I'll turn the car around and pick you up at the door.*
8 also **about** *especially BrE* used when guessing a number, amount, time etc, without being exact [= **approximately**]: *The stadium seats around 50,000 people.*

arouse /ə'raʊz $ ə'raʊz/ *v* [T] **1** to make someone have a particular feeling: *Her behaviour aroused the suspicions of the police.* **2** to make someone feel sexually excited —**arousal** *n* [U]

arrange /əˈreɪndʒ/ v

1 [I,T] to make plans and preparations for something to happen: *I've arranged a meeting with Jim.* | **arrange to do sth** *Have you arranged to play football on Sunday?* | **arrange for sb to do sth** *Dave arranged for someone to drive us home.* | **+that** *We arranged that I would go and stay with them for the weekend.*
2 [T] to put a group of things or people in a particular order or position: *The list is arranged alphabetically.* | *She arranged the flowers in a vase.*

ar‚ranged 'marriage n [C,U] a marriage in which your parents choose a husband or wife for you

arrangement /əˈreɪndʒmənt/ n

1 [C usually plural] plans and preparations that you must make so that something can happen in the future: **+for** *Lee's still making arrangements for the wedding.* | *We haven't finalized our travel arrangements yet.*
2 [C,U] something that has been organized or agreed on [= **agreement**]: **+with** *We have a special arrangement with the bank.* | **arrangement to do sth** *Max cancelled our arrangement to meet.*
3 [C] a group of things in a particular position or order: *a flower arrangement*

array /əˈreɪ/ n [C usually singular] a group of people or things, especially one that is large or impressive: **+of** *a dazzling array of young dancers*

arrears /əˈrɪəz $ əˈrɪrz/ n [plural] **1 be in arrears** to owe someone money because your regular payment to them is late: *We're six weeks in arrears with the rent.* **2** money that is owed and should already have been paid: *You'll have to pay off the arrears later.*

arrest[1] /əˈrest/ v [T]

1 if the police arrest someone, the person is taken away because the police think they have done something illegal: **arrest sb for sth** *The police arrested Eric for shoplifting.*
2 *formal* to stop something happening: *drugs that are used to arrest the spread of the disease*

arrest[2] n [C,U] when the police take someone away and guard them because they may have done something illegal: *The police expect to make an arrest soon.* | **under arrest** *A man is under arrest following the murder of two teenage girls.* → see box at **POLICE**

arrival /əˈraɪvəl/ n

1 [U] when you arrive somewhere [≠ **departure**]: *Shortly after our arrival in Florida, Lottie got robbed.*
2 the arrival of sth the time when a new idea, method, product etc is first used or discovered: *The arrival of the personal computer changed the way we work.*
3 [C] a person or thing that has arrived recently: *a new arrival at the school*

arrive /əˈraɪv/ v [I]

1 to get to a place: *Your letter arrived yesterday.* | **+in/at** *The train finally arrived in New York at 8.30 pm.* | *He arrived late as usual.* | *We arrived home at ten o'clock.*
2 to happen: *At last the big day arrived!*
3 arrive at a decision/solution/conclusion etc to reach a decision, solution etc

4 to begin to exist or to start being used: *Our sales have doubled since computer games arrived.*
5 to be born: *It was just past midnight when the baby arrived.*

arrive in, arrive at
Use **arrive in** with the name of a country, city, town etc: *He arrived in Australia on 24th July.* | *We arrived in Paris at four in the afternoon.*
Use **arrive at** with a building or place: *Ian arrived at the hotel just before ten.* | *By the time she arrived at Victoria Station, the train had already left.*

A

arrogant /ˈærəgənt/ adj behaving in an unpleasant or rude way because you think you are more important than other people: *an arrogant, selfish man* → see box at **PROUD** —**arrogantly** adv —**arrogance** n [U]

arrow /ˈærəʊ $ ˈæroʊ/ n [C] **1** a thin straight weapon with a point at one end that you shoot from a **bow** **2** a sign in the shape of an arrow, used to show direction

arsenal /ˈɑːsənəl $ ˈɑːr-/ n [C] a large number of weapons, or the building where they are stored

arsenic /ˈɑːsənɪk $ ˈɑːr-/ n [U] a very strong poison

arson /ˈɑːsən $ ˈɑːr-/ n [U] the crime of deliberately making a building burn —**arsonist** n [C]

art /ɑːt $ ɑːrt/ n

1 [U] the activity or skill of producing paintings, photographs etc, or paintings etc that are produced using this skill: *He's very good at art.* | **modern/contemporary art** | *lovers of fine art* (=paintings etc that are considered to be very high quality) | *important works of art*

painting, drawing, photography, sculpture (=the art of making objects out of stone, wood, clay), **ceramics** (=the art of making pots, plates etc from clay)
artist, painter, photographer, sculptor, potter

2 the arts [plural] art, music, theatre, film, literature etc all considered together: *Government funding for the arts has been reduced.*
3 arts also **the arts** [plural] subjects you can study that are not scientific, for example history, languages etc → see box at **UNIVERSITY**
4 [C,U] the skill involved in making or doing something: **+of** *the art of writing*
→ **CLIP ART, MARTIAL ART, PERFORMING ARTS**

artefact especially BrE; **artifact** especially AmE /ˈɑːtɪfækt $ ˈɑːr-/ n [C] an object such as a tool or weapon that was made in the past and is historically important: *Egyptian artefacts*

artery /ˈɑːtəri $ ˈɑːr-/ n [C] plural **arteries 1** one of the tubes that takes blood from your heart to the rest of your body [→ **vein**] **2** *formal* a main road, railway line, or river

artful /ˈɑːtfəl $ ˈɑːrt-/ adj good at deceiving people —**artfully** adv

'art ‚gallery n [C] a building where paintings are shown to the public

arthritis /ɑːˈθraɪtɪs $ ɑːr-/ n [U] a disease that causes the joints of your body to become swollen and very painful —**arthritic** /-ˈθrɪtɪk/ adj: *arthritic fingers*

artichoke /ˈɑːtɪtʃəʊk $ ˈɑːrtɪtʃoʊk/ n [C] a round green vegetable with thick pointed leaves and a firm base

article /ˈɑːtɪkəl $ ˈɑːr-/ n [C]

1 a piece of writing in a newspaper or magazine: **+on/about** *an article on fishing* | *I read a very interesting article about the problem of teenage pregnancy.* → see box at NEWSPAPER
2 a thing: *The museum has some very valuable articles.* | *an article of clothing*
3 technical in grammar, the word 'the' (=the definite article), or the words 'a' or 'an' (=the indefinite article)

articulate¹ /ɑːˈtɪkjʊlət $ ɑːr-/ adj able to express your thoughts and feelings clearly [≠ inarticulate]: *a bright and articulate child* —**articulately** adv

articulate² /ɑːˈtɪkjʊleɪt $ ɑːr-/ v [T] to put your thoughts or feelings into words: *She found it difficult to articulate her fears.*

articulated /ɑːˈtɪkjʊleɪtɪd $ ɑːr-/ adj especially BrE an articulated vehicle has two parts joined together to make it easier to turn: *an articulated lorry*

artifact especially AmE /ˈɑːtɪfækt $ ˈɑːr-/ n [C] another spelling of ARTEFACT

artificial /ˌɑːtɪˈfɪʃəl $ ˌɑːr-/ adj

1 not real or not made of natural things but made to be like something that is real or natural [≠ natural]: *a vase of artificial flowers* | *an artificial leg* | *foods that contain artificial flavourings and sweeteners* → see box at NATURAL
2 disapproving not natural or sincere [≠ genuine]: *an artificial smile* —**artificially** adv

artificial inˈtelligence n [U] written abbreviation *AI* the science of how to make computers do things that people can do, such as make decisions and understand language

artificial respiˈration n [U] a way of making someone breathe again when they have stopped, by blowing air into their mouth

artillery /ɑːˈtɪləri $ ɑːr-/ n [U] big heavy guns, usually on wheels

artisan /ˌɑːtɪˈzæn $ ˈɑːrtɪzən/ n [C] formal someone who does skilled work, making things by hand

artist /ˈɑːtɪst $ ˈɑːr-/ n [C]

1 someone who produces art, especially paintings → see box at ART
2 a professional performer such as a singer or dancer

artiste /ɑːˈtiːst $ ɑːr-/ n [C] formal a professional performer such as a singer or dancer

artistic /ɑːˈtɪstɪk $ ɑːr-/ adj **1** [only before noun] relating to art or culture: *the artistic director of the Metropolitan Opera* **2** good at painting, drawing etc: *She was so artistic and creative.* —**artistically** /-kli/ adv

artistry /ˈɑːtɪstri $ ˈɑːr-/ n [U] great skill in a particular activity

artwork /ˈɑːtwɜːk $ ˈɑːrtwɜːrk/ n **1** [U] pictures, photographs etc that are prepared for a book, magazine etc **2** [C,U] paintings and other pieces of art: *an exhibition of contemporary artworks*

arty /ˈɑːti $ ˈɑːrti/ BrE; **artsy** /ˈɑːtsi $ ˈɑːrt-/ AmE adj disapproving showing an interest in art in a way that seems pretended: *an arty film*

as /əz; strong æz/ adv, prep, linking word

1 used to compare people or things: **as...as** *Her hands were as cold as ice.* | *We must decide* **as soon as possible** (=very soon). | *You're* **the same** *age* **as** *me.* | *Tom works* **just as** *hard as the others.*
2 used to say what job someone has or what purpose something has: *Mum worked* **as** *a teacher before she married.* | *What can we use* **as** *a bandage?*
3 in a particular way or state: *Please leave my desk* **as** *it is.*
4 used when what you are saying is already known about: **As you know**, *I'm leaving at the end of this month.* | **As I said before**, *money is our biggest problem.*
5 while something is happening: **As** *I was walking home, I realized I had left my bag behind.* | *The phone rang* **just as** *I was leaving.*
6 because: **As** *you've apologised, I won't tell anyone.*
7 as for sb used when you are starting to talk about a different person: *John's ill and as for me, I'm too busy to help.*
8 as if/as though used when you are saying how someone or something seems: *She looked* **as if** *she had been crying.* | *It looks* **as though** *it might rain.*
9 as of/as from today/next week etc formal starting from a particular time: *The change comes into effect as of January 1.*
→ **as long as** at LONG² → **as a matter of fact** at MATTER¹ → **such as** at SUCH → **as well (as sb/sth)** at WELL¹ → **as yet** at YET¹ → **so as to do sth** at SO²

asap /ˌeɪ es eɪ ˈpiː, ˈeɪsæp/ adv the abbreviation of as soon as possible

asbestos /æsˈbestəs/ n [U] a grey material that does not burn and was used in buildings in the past

ascend /əˈsend/ v [I,T] formal **1** to move to a higher position [≠ descend]: *The plane ascended rapidly.* **2 ascend the throne** to become king or queen **3 in ascending order** arranged so that each thing in a group is bigger, more important etc than the one before: *Their ages, in ascending order, are four, seven, 10, and 14.*

ascendancy also **ascendency** /əˈsendənsi/ n [U] formal a position of increasing power, influence, or control: *Conservative ideals are* **in the ascendancy.**

ascent /əˈsent/ n formal **1** [C usually singular] when someone or something moves to a higher position [≠ descent]: *the ascent of Mount Everest* **2** [U] when someone becomes more important or successful **3** [C] a path or hill that goes upwards: *a steep ascent*

ascertain /ˌæsəˈteɪn $ ˈæsər-/ v [T] formal to discover the truth about something: **ascertain who/whether/what etc** *The investigation failed to ascertain how she died.*

ascetic /əˈsetɪk/ adj living a simple life with no physical comforts

ASCII /'æski/ *n* [U] **American Standard Code for Information Exchange** a system that makes computers recognize letters and numbers in the same way

ascribe /ə'skraɪb/ *v*

ascribe sth to sb/sth *phr v formal* to say that something is caused by a particular person or thing: *Can we ascribe the rise in asthma to an increase in pollution?*

asexual /eɪ'sekʃuəl/ *adj technical* not having or using sexual organs: *asexual reproduction*

ash /æʃ/ *n* **1** [U] the grey powder that is left after something has burned: *cigarette ash* **2 ashes** [plural] the powder that remains after a dead body has been CREMATEd (=burned) **3** [C,U] a type of tree that grows in forests in Britain and North America

ashamed /ə'ʃeɪmd/ *adj* [not before noun] feeling embarrassed or guilty about something: **+of** *Mike felt ashamed of his own behaviour.* | *Some children are ashamed of their parents.* | *Crying is* **nothing to be ashamed of** (=you shouldn't feel ashamed). | **be ashamed to do sth** *I'm ashamed to admit I only scored 20.* | **+that** *They were ashamed that they had not offered to help.*

ashen /'æʃən/ *adj* very pale because of shock or fear: *Her face was ashen.*

ashore /ə'ʃɔː $ ə'ʃɔːr/ *adv* towards the side of a lake or sea: *His body was washed ashore.*

ashtray /'æʃtreɪ/ *n* [C] a small dish used to collect cigarette ASH (=the powder that is produced when it burns)

Asian /'eɪʃən, 'eɪʒən $ 'eɪʒən, 'eɪʃən/ *n* [C] someone who comes from Asia, or whose family came from Asia —**Asian** *adj*

aside[1] /ə'saɪd/ *adv* **1** if you keep something aside, you keep it so that you can use it or think about it later: **set/put sth aside** *Set aside an hour a week for practice.* **2** if you move something aside, you move it away from you, to the side: **move/step/push etc aside** *Bob pushed her aside in disgust.* **3 aside from sb/sth** except for someone or something

aside[2] *n* [C] something funny you say quietly so that only a few people hear

ask /ɑːsk $ æsk/ *v* [I,T]

1 to say to someone that you want them to tell you something: *'What time is it?' she asked* | *Can I ask a question?* | *Let's ask the way.* | **ask sb sth** *I don't like it when people ask me my age.* | **ask (sb) who/what/if etc** *The officer asked who we were.* | *Ask Tom if he's got a spare pen.* | **ask (sb) about sth** *Did they ask about your experience?* | *She asked me about my job.*

THESAURUS

order – to ask for food or drink in a restaurant: *Have you ordered some wine?*

demand – to ask for something in a firm or angry way: *They're demanding immediate payment.*

request – to ask for something officially: *The men request permission to go ashore, sir.*

beg – to ask for something in an urgent way that you want very much: *'Please can I have one?' she begged.* | *I begged her to stay.*

question/interrogate – if the police question or interrogate someone, they ask them a lot of questions in order to get information: *The*

two men are being questioned by police about the robbery.

inquire/enquire *especially BrE* – to ask someone for information or facts about something: *I'm writing to inquire about the job you advertised.*

2 to make a request for help, advice, or permission: *If you need anything, just ask.* | **ask (sb) for sb/sth** *I had to ask my parents for money.* | *She rang the hospital and asked for Dr Harvey* (=asked whether she could speak to him). | **ask sb to do sth** *I asked Paula to email me the file.* | **ask (sb) if/whether** *Ask your mom if you can stay over.* | *I asked if I could use the phone.* | **ask to do sth** *Karen has asked to leave early on Friday.*

3 to invite someone to go somewhere: **ask sb out** (=invite someone to a film, restaurant etc because you like them) *Mark's too shy to ask girls out.* | **ask sb in/into sth** (=invite someone into your house, room etc) *Don't ask strangers into your house.* | **ask sb over/round** *informal* (=invite someone to your house) *They asked us over for a meal.*

4 to want a particular amount of money for something you are selling: *How much are you asking for the house?* | **ask £20/$2000 etc for sth** *They're asking £5,000 for their old car.*

5 be asking for trouble/it *informal* used to say that doing something will cause problems

6 ask yourself sth to think very carefully and honestly about something: *Have you asked yourself whether you're doing the right thing?*

7 if you ask me *spoken* used to emphasize your opinion: *If you ask me, you're all wrong.*

8 ask after sb to ask someone about another person's health: *Jill was asking after you.*

9 don't ask me! *spoken informal* used to say that you do not know the answer to a question: *'When will you be finished?' 'Don't ask me!'*

askew /ə'skjuː/ *adv, adj* [not before noun] not straight or level: *His tie was askew and he smelt of brandy.*

asleep /ə'sliːp/ *adj* [not before noun] sleeping [≠ awake]: *Quiet! The baby's asleep.* | **fast/sound asleep** (=sleeping very deeply) | *I fell asleep* (=started sleeping) *in front of the fire.* | *I was* **half asleep** (=very tired) *by the time we got home.*

asparagus /ə'spærəgəs/ *n* [U] a long thin green vegetable

aspect /'æspekt/ *n* [C] one part of a situation, plan, or subject: **+of** *What's the most interesting aspect of your work?*

aspersion /ə'spɜːʃən, -ʒən $ ə'spɜːrʒən/ *n* [C] *formal* an unkind remark or an unfair judgment: *No one is* **casting aspersions on** *you or your work.*

asphalt /'æsfælt $ 'æsfɔːlt/ *n* [U] a hard black substance used on the surface of roads

asphyxiate /æs'fɪksieɪt, əs-/ *v* [T] *formal* to stop someone breathing [= suffocate]: *Three children were asphyxiated by smoke.* —**asphyxiation** /æs,fɪksi'eɪʃən, əs-/ *n* [U]

aspiration /,æspə'reɪʃən/ *n* [C usually plural, U] a strong desire to have or achieve something: **+of** *the political aspirations of their leaders*

aspire /ə'spaɪə $ ə'spaɪr/ *v* [I] to have a strong desire to achieve something: **+to** *students who* *aspire to a career in law* —**aspiring** *adj* [only before noun] *an aspiring politician*

aspirin /'æsprɨn/ *n* [C,U] plural **aspirin** or **aspirins** a drug sold as small TABLETS that reduces pain and fever: *I took an aspirin and went to bed.*

ass /æs/ *n* [C] *old-fashioned* a DONKEY

assailant /ə'seɪlənt/ *n* [C] *formal* someone who attacks another person [= **attacker**]

assassin /ə'sæsɨn/ *n* [C] someone who murders an important person: *Who was Kennedy's assassin?*

assassinate /ə'sæsɨneɪt $ -səneɪt/ *v* [T] to murder an important person: *a plot to assassinate the President* → see box at **KILL** —**assassination** /ə,sæsɨ'neɪʃən $ -sən'eɪ-/ *n* [C,U] *an assassination attempt*

assault¹ /ə'sɔːlt $ ə'sɒːlt/ *n* **1** [C,U] *formal* the crime of attacking a person: **+on/against** *sexual assaults on women* | *He was **charged** with assault.* → see box at **ATTACK, CRIME 2** [C] an attack by an army to take control of a place: **+on** *an assault on enemy lines*

assault² *v* [T] to attack someone violently: *He claims the teacher assaulted him.*

assemble /ə'sembəl/ *v* **1** [I,T] if you assemble people or things, or if people assemble, they are brought together in the same place: *A crowd had assembled in front of the White House.* **2** [T] to put the different parts of something together: *The bookcase was quite easy to assemble.* → see picture at **BUILD¹**

assembly /ə'sembli/ *n* plural **assemblies 1** [C] a group of people who are elected to make decisions for a country or organization: *the United Nations General Assembly* **2** [C,U] a regular meeting of all the students and teachers in a school: *I'll see you after assembly.* **3** [U] the process of making something by joining its different parts together

as'sembly ˌline *n* [C] a system for making large quantities of things in a factory. The products move past a line of workers who each check or make one part.

assent /ə'sent/ *n* [U] *formal* official agreement: *They will be asked to give their assent to the proposal.* —**assent** *v* [I]

assert /ə'sɜːt $ -ɜːrt/ *v* [T] **1** to say firmly that something is true: **+that** *The company has vigorously asserted that it is not breaking the law.* **2** to behave in a determined and confident way to make people respect you: **assert your rights/ independence etc** *A teacher must assert his authority.* | **assert yourself** —**assertion** /ə'sɜːʃən $ -ɜːr-/ *n* [C,U] *a confident assertion*

assertive /ə'sɜːtɪv $ -ɜːr-/ *adj* behaving confidently to make people listen to you —**assertiveness** *n* [U] —**assertively** *adv*

assess /ə'ses/ *v* [T] **1** to make a judgment about a person, situation etc after considering it: *a study to assess the impact of crime on people's lives.* **2** to calculate the value, cost, or level something has: **assess sth at £100/31 per cent etc** *The cost of the earthquake was assessed at $2.2 billion.* —**assessment** *n* [C,U] *reading assessment tests*

asset /'æset/ *n* **1** [C usually singular] something or someone that helps you to succeed: **+to** *You're an asset to the company, George.*

2 assets [plural] a company's assets are the things it owns: *a firm with $1.3 billion in assets*

assiduous /ə'sɪdjuəs $ -dʒuəs/ *adj* *formal* working with great care —**assiduously** *adv*

assign /ə'saɪn/ *v* [T] *formal* to give something to someone: **assign sth to sb** *We assigned a different task to each student.* | *Victoria has been assigned a personal bodyguard.*

assignment /ə'saɪnmənt/ *n* [C,U] a job or piece of work that is given to someone: *Students have to do three written assignments.* | **on assignment** (=doing a job) *He's on assignment in Russia at the moment.* → see box at **UNIVERSITY**

assimilate /ə'sɪmɨleɪt/ *v* **1** [T] to learn and understand information: *The children were quick to assimilate new ideas.* **2** [I,T] if people assimilate, or if they are assimilated, they gradually become part of a new group or country they have joined: **+into** *The immigrants soon assimilated into Canadian society.* —**assimilation** /ə,sɪmɨ'leɪʃən/ *n* [U]

assist /ə'sɪst/ *v* [I,T] *formal* to help someone do something: **assist (sb) in/with sth** *She returned to the kitchen to assist in the preparations.* | *Shall I assist you with carrying your bags?*

assistance /ə'sɪstəns/ *n* [U] *formal* help: *Shall I give you some assistance?* | *Can I **be of any assistance** (=help you)?* | *A passer-by **came to her assistance** (=helped her).* | **financial/legal/ military etc assistance** | *with the assistance of sb/sth We put the shed up with the assistance of a few friends.*

assistant /ə'sɪstənt/ *n* [C]

1 someone whose job is to help someone more important: *Meet Jane, my new assistant.*
2 *BrE* someone whose job is to help customers in a shop [= **clerk** *AmE*]: *a sales assistant*
3 assistant manager/director/editor etc someone whose job is just below the position of manager, director etc → see box at **POSITION**

as,sisted 'suicide *n* [C,U] when a doctor or other person helps a person who is seriously ill to kill themselves in order to end their suffering

associate¹ /ə'səʊʃieɪt, ə'səʊsi- $ ə'soʊ-/ *v* **1** [T] if you associate two people or things, or if they are associated, you see that they are connected in some way: **associate sb/sth with sth** *You don't normally associate sunshine with England.* | *Cancer is definitely associated with smoking.* **2 be associated with sth/associate yourself with sth** to show support for someone or something
associate with sb *phr v* *formal* to spend time with someone: *I don't like the people she associates with.*

associate² /ə'səʊʃiɨt, ə'səʊsi- $ ə'soʊ-/ *n* [C] someone that you work or do business with: *business associates*

associate³ *adj* [only before noun] an associate position or job is at a lower level and has fewer rights than similar positions or jobs

association /ə,səʊsi'eɪʃən, ə,səʊʃi- $ ə,soʊ-/ *n*
1 [C] an organization for people who do the same kind of work or have the same interests: *the Association of University Teachers* → see box at **ORGANIZATION**
2 [C,U] a connection or relationship with another person or group: **in association with sb** *The award was presented by Hydro UK in*

association with the Fellowship of Engineering. |
his **close associations** *with the Green Party*
3 [C, usually plural] a memory or feeling that is
related to a particular place, event etc: *a building with romantic associations*

assorted /ə'sɔːtɪd $ -ɔːr-/ *adj* of various differ-
ent types: *a box of assorted cookies*

assortment /ə'sɔːtmənt $ -ɔːr-/ *n* [C] a mix-
ture of different types of the same thing: **+of** *an
assortment of cakes and biscuits*

assume /ə'sjuːm $ ə'suːm/ *v* [T]　**1** to think
that something is true, although you have no
proof: **+(that)** *Your light wasn't on, so I assumed
you were out.* | **let's assume that/assuming
that** *Let's assume for a moment that you were the
father of that child.*　**2** *formal* to take control,
power, or a particular position: **assume power/
responsibility/authority etc** *Mark will assume
the role of Managing Director.*　**3** to pretend to
feel something or be something you are not: *Gail
assumed an air of indifference.*

assumed /ə'sjuːmd $ ə'suːmd/ *adj* if you have
an assumed name or IDENTITY you use a false
name or pretend to be someone else → see box at
NAME

assumption /ə'sʌmpʃən/ *n*　**1** [C] something
that you think is true although you have no
proof: **+that** *We're working on the assumption
that prices will rise.* | **+about** *Don't make
assumptions about people you don't know.*
2 [singular] when someone starts to have power,
control, or a new position

assurance /ə'ʃʊərəns $ ə'ʃʊr-/ *n*　**1** [C] a prom-
ise that something is true or will happen: **+that**
*He gave me an assurance that the work would be
complete by now.*　**2** [U] confidence in your abilities or the truth of what you are saying: *Cindy
spoke with quiet assurance.*

assure /ə'ʃʊə $ ə'ʃʊr/ *v* [T]　**1** to tell someone
that something is definitely true or will happen,
to try to stop them worrying: **assure sb (that)**
She kept assuring me that she felt quite well. | *I
can assure you, the painting is quite genuine.*
2 to make something certain to happen or be
successful: *enough money to assure the success of
the project*

assured /ə'ʃʊəd $ ə'ʃʊrd/ *adj*　**1** showing confi-
dence in your abilities [= self-assured]: *a mature
assured manner*　**2** certain to be achieved: *A
Republican victory seemed assured.*　**3** **be/feel
assured of sth** if you are assured of something,
you are sure that it will happen: *The Queen can
be assured of a warm welcome in Australia.*

asterisk /'æstərɪsk/ *n* [C] a mark like a star (*),
used in writing to point out that something is
interesting, important, or missing

asteroid /'æstərɔɪd/ *n* [C] a large object made
of rock, that moves around in space → see box at
SPACE

asthma /'æsmə $ 'æzmə/ *n* [U] an illness that
makes it difficult to breathe: *people who suffer
from asthma* | *an asthma attack* —**asthmatic**/
æs'mætɪk $ æz-/ *adj*

astonished /ə'stɒnɪʃt $ ə'stɑː-/ *adj* very sur-
prised: **+at/by** *We were astonished at her
ignorance.* | **+that** *He was quite astonished that
she actually agreed.* | **astonished to see/learn/
discover etc** *I was astonished to discover she*

was younger than me. → see box at SURPRISED
—**astonish** *v* [T] *The result astonished everyone.*

astonishing /ə'stɒnɪʃɪŋ $ ə'stɑː-/ *adj* very sur-
prising: *an astonishing decision* | *It's astonish-
ing that you didn't know about this.* → see box at
SURPRISING —**astonishingly** *adv*

astonishment /ə'stɒnɪʃmənt $ ə'stɑː-/ *n* [U]
complete surprise: **in astonishment** *We all
stared in astonishment.* | **to sb's astonishment**
To her astonishment, she won.

astound /ə'staʊnd/ *v* [T] to make someone feel
very surprised: *The result astounded us.*
—**astounding** *adj*: *an astounding success*
—**astounded** *adj*: *I was absolutely astounded
when he told me.* —**astoundingly** *adv*

astray /ə'streɪ/ *adv*　**1 go astray** to be lost: *The
letter went astray in the post.*　**2 lead sb astray**
to encourage someone to do bad or immoral
things

astride /ə'straɪd/ *adv, prep* with one leg on
each side of something: *a girl* **sitting astride** *a
motorbike*

astrology /ə'strɒlədʒi $ ə'strɑː-/ *n* [U] the
study of the position and movements of PLANETS
and stars and how they might affect people's
lives [➡ astronomy] —**astrologer** *n* [C]
—**astrological** /ˌæstrə'lɒdʒɪkəl◂ $ -'lɑː-/ *adj*:
astrological predictions

astronaut /'æstrənɔːt $ -nɒːt, -nɑːt/ *n* [C]
someone who travels in a spacecraft → see box
at SPACE

astronomical /ˌæstrə'nɒmɪkəl◂ $ -'nɑː-/ *adj*
1 *informal* astronomical prices are very high →
see box at EXPENSIVE　**2** [only before noun] connected with the scientific study of the stars and
PLANETS —**astronomically** /-kli/ *adv*

astronomy /ə'strɒnəmi $ ə'strɑː-/ *n* [U] the
scientific study of the stars and PLANETS
—**astronomer** *n* [C]

astute /ə'stjuːt $ ə'stuːt/ *adj* quick to under-
stand a situation and how to get an advantage
from it: *an astute businessman*

asylum /ə'saɪləm/ *n*　**1** [U] protection that a
government gives to people who have left their
country because they are in danger for political
reasons: *He arrived in Britain and* **applied for
asylum**. | *He was granted* **political asylum**.
2 [C] *old-fashioned* a hospital for people with
mental illness

a'sylum-ˌseeker *n* [C] someone who escapes to
another country because they are in danger for
political reasons [= refugee]

asymmetrical /ˌeɪsɪ'metrɪkəl/ *adj* having two
sides of different shapes or lengths

at /ət; *strong* æt/ *prep*

1 used to say where someone or something is or
where something happens: *I met my husband at
university.* | *Does this train stop at Preston?* | **at
the top/bottom/end etc (of sth)** *We live at the
end of the street.* | *We're meeting at Mike's
(=Mike's house).* | *John's at work* (=in the place
where he works).

2 used to say when something happens: *The
movie starts at 8:00.* | *at night* | *What are you
doing at the weekend?*

3 used to show the price, speed, level etc of
something: *gas selling at $2.75 a gallon* | *a car
traveling at 50 mph*

A

4 used to show who or what a particular action or feeling is directed towards: *That guy's staring at me.* | *None of the kids laughed at his joke.* | *I'm really surprised at you.*

5 used to say which activity you are talking about when you say how well someone can do it: **good/bad etc at (doing) sth** *I'm pretty good at maths.*

6 in a particular state: *children at risk* | *The two countries were at war.*

7 the symbol @, used in EMAIL addresses
→ **(not) at all** at ALL[1] → **at first** at FIRST[1] → **at least** at LEAST[1]

ate /et, eɪt $ eɪt/ *v* the past tense of EAT

atheist /'eɪθi‿ɪst/ *n* [C] someone who does not believe in God [➨ **agnostic**] —**atheism** *n* [U]

athlete /'æθliːt/ *n* [C] someone who competes in sports such as running or jumping

athletic /æθ'letɪk, əθ-/ *adj* **1** physically strong and good at sport: *a tall man with an athletic build* **2** [only before noun] connected with athletes or athletics

athletics /æθ'letɪks, əθ-/ *n* [U] **1** *BrE* sports such as running and jumping **2** *AmE* sports in general: *high school athletics*

atlas /'ætləs/ *n* [C] a book of maps: *a road atlas*

ATM /ˌeɪ tiː 'em/ *n* [C] *AmE* **Automated Teller Machine** a machine that you use with a card to get money from your bank account [**cash machine** *BrE*] → see box at ACCOUNT

atmosphere /'ætməsfɪə $ -fɪr/ *n*
1 [C usually singular, U] the feeling that a place, situation, or event gives you: *The atmosphere at home was tense.* | *a hotel with a relaxed atmosphere* | **+of** *an atmosphere of excited expectation*
2 [singular] the mixture of gases that surrounds the Earth or another PLANET
3 [singular] the air in a room: *a small pub with a smoky atmosphere*

atmospheric /ˌætməs'ferɪk◂/ *adj* **1** relating to the Earth's atmosphere: *atmospheric pressure* **2** if a place or sound is atmospheric, it seems beautiful and mysterious: *atmospheric music*

atom /'ætəm/ *n* [C] the smallest part of an ELEMENT that can exist alone: *carbon atoms*

atomic /ə'tɒmɪk $ ə'tɑː-/ *adj* relating to atoms and the energy produced by splitting them: *the atomic bomb*

atone /ə'təʊn $ ə'toʊn/ *v* [I] *formal* to do something to show that you are sorry for having done something wrong: **+for** *Richard was anxious to atone for his crimes.*

atop /ə'tɒp $ ə'tɑːp/ *prep written* on top of something

atrium /'eɪtriəm/ *n* [C] a large open space with a glass roof in the centre of a building

atrocious /ə'trəʊʃəs $ ə'troʊ-/ *adj* very bad or severe: *Your spelling's atrocious.* | *atrocious weather* → see box at BAD —**atrociously** *adv*

atrocity /ə'trɒsɪ̩ti $ ə'trɑː-/ *n* [C,U] plural atrocities a very cruel or violent action: *the atrocities of war*

attach /ə'tætʃ/ *v* [T]
1 to fasten or join one thing to another: **attach sth to sth** *Please attach a photograph to your application.* | **the attached cheque/form etc**

Please sign and return the attached slip. → see box at FASTEN

2 be attached to sb/sth to like someone or something very much because you have known them for a long time: *Tom was very attached to his old teddy-bear.*

3 to connect a document or FILE to an email so that you can send them together

4 attach importance/value etc to sth to believe that something is important, valuable etc: *Don't attach much importance to what Nick says.*

5 be attached to sth to belong to or be part of a bigger organization: *The Medical School is attached to the University of Sussex.*

attachment /ə'tætʃmənt/ *n* **1** [C,U] *formal* a strong feeling of loyalty, love, or friendship: **+to/for** *his strong attachment to his sister* **2** [C] a part that you fasten to a machine to make it do a particular job: *Use the brush attachment to clean wooden floors.* **3** [C] a FILE that you send with an email message: *I can't open the attachment.*

attack[1] /ə'tæk/ *v* **1** [I,T] to try to hurt or kill someone: *She was attacked as she walked home from school.* | *The rebel army attacked on Sunday.* | **attack sb/sth with sth** *The man attacked him with a knife.* **2** [T] to criticize someone strongly: **attack sb for (doing) sth** *The government has been attacked for failing to tackle street crime.* **3** [T] if a disease, insect, or substance attacks something, it damages it: *The virus attacks the body's immune system.* **4** [I,T] in sport, to move forward in order to score points —**attacker** *n* [C]

attack[2] *n*
1 [C,U] a violent action that is intended to hurt or kill someone: **+on** *the terrorist attack on the World Trade Center* | **bomb/knife/arson etc attack** *fears of a nuclear attack* | *The army launched an attack.* | **be/come under attack** *We were under attack from enemy forces.*

THESAURUS
Military attack
invasion – when an army enters a country and takes control of it
raid – a short surprise military attack on a place
assault – an attack by an army to take control of a place
ambush – a sudden attack by people who have been waiting and hiding
counterattack – an attack that you make against someone who has attacked you
Physical attack on a person
assault – the crime of attacking someone
mugging – the crime of attacking and robbing someone in a public place
rape – the crime of forcing someone to have sex
→ CRIME

2 [C,U] strong criticism: **+on** *He launched a personal attack on the President.* | **be/come under attack** *He came under fierce attack for his ideas.*

3 [C] a short period of time when you are ill, worried, afraid etc: **+of** *an attack of flu* | *She suffers from panic attacks.*

4 [C,U] in sport, an attempt by the players in a team to get points: **in attack** (=when a team is attacking) *Brazil look very impressive in attack.*
→ HEART ATTACK

attacker /ə'tækə $ -ər/ n [C] someone who attacks someone else: *Her attacker dragged her into the bushes.* → see box at CRIME

attain /ə'teɪn/ v [T] to achieve something after trying for a long time: *More women are now attaining high positions in business.* —attainment n [C,U] —attainable adj

attempt¹ /ə'tempt/ n [C] when you try to do something: **attempt to do sth** *All attempts to resolve the problem have failed.* | **+at** *his first attempt at this exam* | *He* **made no attempt** *to hide his anger.* | **in an attempt** *In an attempt to save money, I offered to do the work myself.*

attempt² v [T] to try to do something, especially something difficult: *The second question was so difficult I didn't even attempt it.* | **attempt to do sth** *Now I will attempt to explain why the revolution started.*

attempted /ə'temptɪd/ adj [only before noun] tried, but not successfully achieved: *He was charged with attempted murder.*

attend /ə'tend/ v [I,T] formal to go to an event such as a meeting or a class: *More than 2000 people are expected to attend the conference. Please let us know if you are unable to attend.*
  attend to sb/sth phr v formal to give attention to someone or something: *I may be late – I've got some things to attend to.*

attendance /ə'tendəns/ n [C,U] **1** the number of people who attend an event, such as a meeting, concert etc: *Church attendances have fallen in recent years.* **2** when someone goes to a meeting, class etc: **+at** *The course involves 8 hours attendance at college each week.*

attendant /ə'tendənt/ n [C] someone whose job is to look after customers in a public place: *a car parking attendant*

attention /ə'tenʃən/ n [U]
1 when you watch, listen, or think carefully because you are interested in something: *You should* **pay** *more* **attention** *in class.* | *We need to* **give** *more* **attention** *to the needs of older people.* | *My* **attention** *wasn't really* **on** *the game.* | *The game is fun and will* **keep the attention of** *any child.* | **Attention to detail** *is essential in this job.* | *Most children have a short* **attention span** (=period of time that they are interested in watching, listening etc to something). → **undivided attention** at UNDIVIDED
2 when people notice something or are interested in it: *She waved to* **attract the attention of** *the waiter.* | *We wanted to* **draw attention to** *this problem* (=make people notice it). | **public/ media/press attention** *Her story attracted a lot of media attention.* | *Johnny enjoyed being* **the centre of attention** (=the person that everyone is interested in).
3 special care or treatment: *Some of the children required urgent* **medical attention.**
4 stand at/to attention if soldiers stand to attention, they stand very straight, with their feet together

attentive /ə'tentɪv/ adj **1** listening or watching carefully: *an attentive audience* **2** making

sure that someone has everything they need: *an attentive host* —attentively adv

attic /'ætɪk/ n [C] a room at the top of a house, just below the roof

attire /ə'taɪə $ ə'taɪr/ n [U] formal clothes

attitude /'ætɪtjuːd $ -tuːd/ n [C,U] what you think and feel about something: **+to/towards** *Many people have* **negative attitudes** *towards old age.* | *He has a very* **positive attitude** *towards his work.* | *These people have a different* **attitude of mind** (=way of thinking). → see box at OPINION

attorney /ə'tɜːni $ -ɜːr-/ n [C] AmE a lawyer

attract /ə'trækt/ v [T]
1 to make someone like something or feel interested in it: **attract sb to sth** *What attracted me to the job was the chance to travel.* | **attract attention/interest etc** *The story has attracted a lot of attention from the media.*
2 to make someone come to a place: *The exhibition has attracted a lot of visitors.*
3 be attracted to sb to like someone in a sexual way: *I've always been attracted to blondes.*
4 if something attracts things it makes them move towards it: *Left-over food attracts flies.*

attraction /ə'trækʃən/ n **1** [C,U] a feeling of liking someone, especially in a sexual way: *The attraction between them was immediate.* **2** [C] something that is interesting or enjoyable to see or do: *The beautiful beaches are the island's* **main attraction.** | *The castle is a major* **tourist attraction** (=place that many tourists visit).

attractive /ə'træktɪv/ adj
1 pretty or pleasant to look at: *an attractive young woman* | *Women seem to* **find** *him* **attractive.**

2 interesting or exciting: **+to** *a political movement that is attractive to young people* —attractively adv

attribute¹ /ə'trɪbjuːt $ -bjət/ v
  attribute sth **to** sb/sth phr v **1** to believe or say that a situation or event was caused by something: *The increase in crime can be attributed to social changes.* **2** to believe that something was written, said, or made by a particular person: *a painting attributed to Rembrandt*

attribute² /'ætrɪbjuːt/ n [C] a good or useful quality: *What attributes should a good manager have?*

attributive /ə'trɪbjʊtɪv/ adj an attributive adjective comes before a noun and describes the noun. For example, in the phrase 'big city', 'big'

A

is an attributive adjective, and in the phrase 'school bus', 'school' is a noun in an attributive position. [➡ **predicative**]

aubergine /ˈəʊbəʒiːn $ ˈoʊbər-/ n [C] BrE a large dark purple vegetable [= **eggplant** AmE] → see picture at **VEGETABLE**

auburn /ˈɔːbən $ ˈɒːbərn/ adj auburn hair is a reddish brown colour

auction /ˈɔːkʃən $ ˈɒːk-/ n [C] an event at which things are sold to the person who offers the most money —**auction** v [T]

auctioneer /ˌɔːkʃəˈnɪə $ ˌɒːkʃəˈnɪr/ n [C] someone who is in charge of an auction

audacity /ɔːˈdæsᵻti $ ɒː-/ n [U] when someone is brave enough to do something that seems shocking or rude: I can't believe he **had the audacity to** ask for more money. —**audacious** /ɔːˈdeɪʃəs $ ɒː-/ adj

audible /ˈɔːdᵻbəl $ ˈɒː-/ adj loud enough to be heard [≠ **inaudible**]: Her voice was barely audible. —**audibly** adv

audience /ˈɔːdiəns $ ˈɒː-, ˈɑː-/ n [C also + plural verb BrE]
1 the people who watch or listen to a performance: One **member of the audience** described the opera as boring. | The audience were (=each member was) clapping and cheering. → see box at **THEATRE**
2 BrE the people who watch a particular television programme, read a particular book or magazine etc: The show attracts a regular audience of 20 million viewers. | a new magazine aimed at a teenage audience
3 a formal meeting with someone who is very important: +**with** an audience with the Pope

audio /ˈɔːdiəʊ $ ˈɒːdioʊ/ adj [only before noun] for recording and broadcasting sound: audio tapes | audio equipment

audiovisual /ˌɔːdiəʊˈvɪʒuəl $ ˌɒːdioʊ-/ adj [only before noun] using recorded pictures and sound: audiovisual equipment

audit /ˈɔːdᵻt $ ˈɒː-/ n [C] when someone officially examines a company's financial records to check that they are correct —**audit** v [T] —**auditor** n [C]

audition /ɔːˈdɪʃən $ ɒː-/ n [C] a short performance by an actor, singer etc to test whether he or she is good enough to perform in a play, concert etc —**audition** v [I,T]

auditorium /ˌɔːdᵻˈtɔːriəm $ ˌɒː-/ n [C] the part of a theatre where people sit to watch a performance

augment /ɔːgˈment $ ɒːg-/ v [T] formal to increase the size or value of something

augur /ˈɔːgə $ ˈɒːgər/ v **augur well/ill** formal to be a sign that something good or bad will happen in the future

August /ˈɔːgəst $ ˈɒː-/ n [C,U] written abbreviation **Aug.** the eighth month of the year, between July and September: **next/last August** I was there last August. | **in August** His birthday's in August. | **on August 6th** The new store opened on August 6th. → see box at **MONTH**

aunt /ɑːnt $ ænt/ also **auntie** /ˈɑːnti $ ˈæn-/ informal n [C] the sister of your father or mother, or the wife of your UNCLE → see box at **RELATIVE** → **AGONY AUNT**

au pair /əʊ ˈpeə $ oʊ ˈper/ n [C] a young person who stays with a family in a foreign country and looks after their children

aura /ˈɔːrə/ n [C] a quality or feeling that seems to come from a person or place: Inside the church there was an aura of complete tranquillity.

aural /ˈɔːrəl/ adj relating to the sense of hearing [➡ **oral**]: aural skills

auspices /ˈɔːspᵻsᵻz $ ˈɒː-/ **under the auspices of sth** formal with the help and support of an organization: The research was done under the auspices of Harvard Medical School.

auspicious /ɔːˈspɪʃəs $ ɒː-/ adj formal an auspicious time or event makes you expect success in the future [≠ **inauspicious**]

austere /ɔːˈstɪə, ɒ- $ ɒːˈstɪr/ adj **1** very plain and simple: Life in the monastery was very austere. | an austere style of painting **2** very strict and serious: a cold, austere woman

austerity /ɔːˈsterᵻti, ɒ- $ ɒː-/ n [U] bad economic conditions in which people do not have enough money to live: the austerity of the post-war years

authentic /ɔːˈθentɪk $ ɒː-/ adj something that is authentic really is what it seems to be: authentic Indian food | an authentic Picasso painting —**authentically** /-kli/ adv —**authenticity** /ˌɔːθenˈtɪsᵻti $ ˌɒː-/ n [U]

author /ˈɔːθə $ ˈɒːθər/ n [C] someone who has written a book [= **writer**]: a well-known American author | +**of** Robert Louis Stevenson was the author of 'Treasure Island'.

authoritarian /ɔːˌθɒrᵻˈteəriən $ ɒːˌθɑːrᵻˈter-, ə,θɑː-/ adj forcing people to obey strict rules or laws and not allowing any freedom: an authoritarian regime

authoritative /ɔːˈθɒrᵻtətɪv, ə- $ ɒːˈθɑːrᵻteɪtɪv, əˈθɑː-/ adj **1** an authoritative book, statement etc can be trusted because it was written by someone who knows a lot about a subject: an authoritative textbook on European history **2** behaving or speaking in a confident, determined way that makes people respect and obey you: The captain spoke in a calm and authoritative voice. —**authoritatively** adv

authority /ɔːˈθɒrᵻti, ə- $ ɒːˈθɑː-, əˈθɒː-/ n plural **authorities**
1 [U] the power someone has because of their official position: +**over** Which country has authority over these islands? | **in authority** Could I speak to someone in authority (=who has a position of power) please? | He is now **in a position of authority**. | **authority to do sth** She doesn't have the authority to dismiss staff.
2 [C] an organization or government department that makes official decisions and controls public services: Write a letter of complaint to the **local authority**. | the San Diego Water Authority | an agreement between the US and Columbian authorities
3 [C] someone who is respected because of their knowledge about a subject: +**on** Dr Ballard is a **leading authority** on tropical diseases. → see box at **EXPERT**

authorize also -**ise** BrE /ˈɔːθəraɪz $ ˈɒː-/ v [T] to give official permission for something: an authorized biography | **authorize sb to do sth**

No one authorized you to spend this money.
—**authorization** /ˌɔːθəraɪˈzeɪʃən $ ˌɔːθərə-/ n
[C,U]

autistic /ɔːˈtɪstɪk $ ɒː-/ adj having a mental
condition that makes people unable to communicate properly or to form relationships

auto /ˈɔːtəʊ $ ˈɒːtou/ adj especially AmE relat-
ing to cars [= **motor** BrE]: *the auto industry* | *auto
insurance*

autobiography /ˌɔːtəbaɪˈɒɡrəfi
$ ˌɒːtəbaɪˈɑː-/ n [C] plural **autobiographies** a book
that someone writes about their own life
—**autobiographical** /ˌɔːtəbaɪəˈɡræfɪkəl $ ˌɒː-/
adj

autograph /ˈɔːtəɡrɑːf $ ˈɒːtəɡræf/ n [C] if a
famous person gives you their autograph, they
sign their name on something for you
—**autograph** v [T] *an autographed picture*

automated /ˈɔːtəmeɪtɪd $ ˈɒː-/ adj using com-
puters and machines to do a job rather than
people: *The production process is now fully automated.* —**automation** /ˌɔːtəˈmeɪʃən $ ˌɒː-/ n [U]

automatic[1] /ˌɔːtəˈmætɪk $ ˌɒː-/ adj

1 an automatic machine is designed to work by
itself without much human control: *an automatic gearbox*
2 certain to happen because of a rule or system:
We get an automatic pay increase every year.
3 done without thinking: *an automatic reaction*
—**automatically** /-kli/ adv: *You shouldn't automatically assume that your teacher is right.*

automatic[2] n [C] **1** a weapon that can shoot
bullets continuously **2** a car with a system of
GEARS that operate themselves

automobile /ˈɔːtəməbiːl $ ˈɒːtəmoʊ-/ n [C]
AmE a car

automotive /ˌɔːtəˈməʊtɪv $ ˌɒːtəˈmoʊ-/ adj
[only before noun] relating to cars: *automotive
technology*

autonomous /ɔːˈtɒnəməs $ ɒːˈtɑː-/ adj having
the power to make independent decisions or
rules: *an autonomous state* —**autonomy** n [U]
The region wants political autonomy.

autopsy /ˈɔːtɒpsi $ ˈɒːtɑːp-/ n [C] plural **autop-
sies** AmE an official examination of a dead body
to discover why the person has died [= **post
mortem** BrE]

autumn /ˈɔːtəm $ ˈɒː-/ n [C,U] the season
between summer and winter, when the leaves
fall off the trees [= **fall** AmE]
—**autumnal** /ɔːˈtʌmnəl $ ɒː-/ adj

auxiliary /ɔːɡˈzɪljəri, ɔːk- $ ɒːɡˈzɪljəri, -ˈzɪləri/
adj giving extra help or support: *auxiliary
nurses* —**auxiliary** n [C]

auxiliary 'verb n [C] a verb that is used with
another verb to form questions, negative sentences, and tenses. In English the auxiliary
verbs are 'be', 'do', and 'have'.

avail[1] /əˈveɪl/ n **to no avail** without success:
They had searched everywhere, but to no avail.

avail[2] v **avail yourself of sth** formal to accept
an offer or use an opportunity: *Students should
avail themselves of every opportunity to improve
their English.*

available /əˈveɪləbəl/ adj

1 if something is available, you can have it, buy
it, or use it: **+at/in/from** *Tickets are available
from the box office.* | **+to** *not enough data is*
available to scientists | **+for** *land that is available
for development* | **readily/widely available** *Ille-
gal drugs are readily available in our cities.*
2 [not before noun] someone who is available is
not busy and has enough time to talk to you: *Dr
Wright is not available at the moment.*
—**availability** /əˌveɪləˈbɪləti/ n [U]

avalanche /ˈævəlɑːntʃ $ -læntʃ/ n [C] **1** a
large amount of snow that falls down the side of
a mountain **2 an avalanche of sth** a very
large number of things that happen or arrive at
the same time: *The school received an avalanche
of letters.*

avant-garde /ˌævɒŋ ˈɡɑːd $ ˌævɑːŋ ˈɡɑːrd/
adj avant-garde literature, music, or art is very
modern and different from existing styles: *an
avant-garde film*

avarice /ˈævərɪs/ n [U] formal an extreme
desire for wealth [= **greed**]

Ave. also **Ave** BrE the written abbreviation of
Avenue: *36, Rokesly Ave*

avenge /əˈvendʒ/ v [T] literary to punish someone because they have harmed you or your family: *He wanted to avenge his brother's death.*

avenue /ˈævˌnjuː $ -nuː/ n [C] **1** a road in a
town: *Fifth Avenue* → see box at ROAD **2** a
possible way of achieving something: *We must
explore every avenue in order to achieve peace.*

average[1] /ˈævərɪdʒ/ adj

1 [only before noun] the average amount is the
amount you get when you add together several
figures and divide this by the total number of
figures: *The average cost of making a movie has
risen by 15%.* | *Last winter was colder than
average.*
2 [only before noun] an average person or thing
is the usual or most typical size or type: *They
have an average size garden.* | *In an average
week I drive about 250 miles.* → see box at NORMAL
3 not very good but not very bad: *I didn't think it
was a great movie – just average really.*

average[2] n

1 [C] the amount that you get by adding several
figures together and then dividing the result by
the number of figures: **+of** *The average of 3, 8
and 10 is 7.* | *Each person raised an average of
£60.*
2 on average based on a calculation of what
usually happens: *On average, men still earn more
than women.*
3 [C,U] the usual level or amount for most people
or things: **above/below average** *students of
above average ability*

average[3] v [T] to be a particular amount as an
average: *The train travelled at speeds averaging
125 mph.*
average out phr v to result in a particular
average amount: **+at** *Our weekly profits average
out at about $750.*

averse /əˈvɜːs $ -ɜːrs/ adj formal **not be averse
to sth** to quite enjoy something: *Charles was not
averse to the occasional cigar.*

aversion /əˈvɜːʃən $ əˈvɜːrʒən/ n [singular] for-
mal a strong dislike of something: **+to** *She has a
strong aversion to cats.*

avert /əˈvɜːt $ -ɜːrt/ v [T] formal **1** to prevent
something unpleasant from happening: *negotiations aimed at averting a crisis* **2 avert your
eyes/gaze** to look away from something

aviary /'eɪviəri $ 'eɪvieri/ *n* [C] plural **aviaries** a large CAGE in which birds are kept

aviation /ˌeɪvi'eɪʃən $ ˌeɪ-, ˌæ-/ *n* [U] the activity of flying or making aircraft

avid /'ævɪd/ *adj* [only before noun] eager: *an avid reader of romantic novels* —**avidly** *adv*

avocado /ˌævə'kɑːdəʊ $ -doʊ/ *n* [C,U] plural **avocados** a fruit with a thick dark green skin that is green inside and has a large seed in the middle → see picture at **FRUIT**

avoid /ə'vɔɪd/ *v* [T]
1 to prevent something bad from happening: **avoid doing sth** *The refugees left to avoid getting bombed.* | *Alan **narrowly avoided** an accident.*
2 to deliberately stay away from someone or something: *I have the impression John's trying to avoid us.*
3 to deliberately not do something: **avoid doing sth** *Try to avoid spending too much.*
—**avoidance** *n* [U] —**avoidable** *adj*

await /ə'weɪt/ *v* [T] *formal* **1** to wait for something: *Briggs is awaiting trial for murder.* **2** if a situation or event awaits someone, it is going to happen to them: *A warm welcome awaits you.*

awake¹ /ə'weɪk/ *adj* [not before noun] not sleeping: *How do you **stay awake** during boring lectures?* | *Emma **lay awake** half the night, worrying.* | *The noise brought him **wide awake** (=completely awake).* | *The storm **kept us awake** all night.*

awake² *v* [I,T] past tense **awoke** /ə'wəʊk $ ə'woʊk/ past participle **awoken** /ə'wəʊkən $ ə'woʊkən/ *formal* to wake up, or to wake someone up: *I awoke early the next morning.*

awaken /ə'weɪkən/ *v formal* **1** [I,T] to wake up, or to make someone wake up: *The noise awakened me.* **2** [T] to make someone have a sudden feeling: *Several strange events had already occurred to awaken our suspicions.*

  awaken sb to sth *phr v formal* to make someone begin to realize something: *We must awaken people to the dangers of pollution.*

awakening /ə'weɪkənɪŋ/ *n* [singular, U] when you suddenly start to realize a fact or experience a feeling: *His political awakening took place in 1943.*

award¹ /ə'wɔːd $ -ɔːrd/ *n* [C]
1 a prize that someone gets for something that they have achieved: +**for** *She **won** an **award** for her book.*
2 an amount of money that is given to someone because of a judge's decision: +**for** *an award for unfair dismissal*

award² *v* [T] to officially give someone a prize or money: **award sth to sb** *A prize will be awarded to the winner.* | **award sb sth** *The judge awarded me first prize.* → see box at **GIVE**

aware /ə'weə $ ə'wer/ *adj*
1 [not before noun] if you are aware of something, you know about it or realize that it is there [≠ **unaware**]: +**of** *The children are aware of the danger.* | *He was aware of the wind in his face.* | +**that** *Were you aware that Joe had a problem with his knee?*
2 interested in something and knowing a lot about it: **politically/socially/environmentally etc aware** *Young people are becoming more politically aware.*

awash /ə'wɒʃ $ ə'wɔːʃ, ə'wɑːʃ/ *adj* [not before noun] **1** covered with water: *The streets were awash with flood water.* **2** having too much of something: +**with** *Hollywood is awash with rumours.*

away¹ /ə'weɪ/ *adv*
1 moving further from a place, or staying far from a place: *Go away!* | *Diane drove away quickly.* | +**from** *Keep away from the fire!*
2 in a different direction: *Tim turned away and looked out of the window.* | *She blushed and looked away.*
3 not at home, at work, or in school: *Kate is away on holiday.* | +**from** *Simon's away from school.*
4 used to say how far it is to a place, thing, or time in the future: **five miles/10 feet etc away** *Geneva is only 20 miles away.* | *Christmas is only a month away.*
5 used to say how close someone is to achieving something or experiencing something: +**from** *At one point they were only two points away from victory.*
6 into a safe place: *Put your money away, I'm paying.*
7 used to say that something disappears or is removed: *The music died away.* | *Cut away all the dead wood.* | *He gave his money away to charity.*
8 without stopping: *They've been hammering away all day.*
9 if a team plays away, they play at their opponent's field or sports hall
→ **right away** at **RIGHT²**

away² *adj* **away game/match** a sports game that is played at your opponent's field or sports hall [≠ **home**]

awe /ɔː $ ɒː/ *n* [U] a feeling of great respect for someone or something: **in awe of sb** *We were all in awe of the headmaster* (=we respected him a lot).

'awe-in,spiring *adj* very impressive: *an awe-inspiring achievement*

awesome /'ɔːsəm $ 'ɒː-/ *adj* very impressive, often in a way that is slightly frightening: *an awesome responsibility*

awful /'ɔːfəl $ 'ɒː-/ *adj*
1 very bad or unpleasant: *The weather was awful.* | *He's a pretty awful driver.* → see box at **BAD**
2 [only before noun] *spoken* used to emphasize how much, how good, how bad etc something is: *It's going to cost **an awful lot of** (=a large amount of) money.* | *She made me feel an awful fool.*
3 look/feel awful to look or feel ill

awfully /'ɔːfəli $ 'ɒː-/ *adv spoken* very: *I'm awfully sorry – I didn't mean to disturb you.*

awkward /'ɔːkwəd $ 'ɒːkwərd/ *adj*
1 embarrassing: *I hope he won't ask any **awkward questions**.* | *an **awkward silence***
2 not relaxed: *Geoff looked uneasy and awkward.* | *I had been sitting in an awkward position.*
3 difficult to deal with or use: *The cupboard was an awkward shape and wouldn't fit into the room.*
4 not suitable: *They came at an awkward time.*
—**awkwardly** *adv* —**awkwardness** *n* [U]

awning /'ɔːnɪŋ $ 'ɒː-/ *n* [C] a sheet of material outside a shop, tent etc to keep off the sun or the rain

awoke /ə'wəʊk $ ə'woʊk/ *v* the past tense of AWAKE

awoken /ə'wəʊkən $ ə'woʊ-/ *v* the past participle of AWAKE

awry /ə'raɪ/ *adj* **go awry** to not happen in the way that was planned: *All their plans had gone awry.*

axe¹; ax *AmE* /æks/ *n* [C] a tool used for cutting wood, with a wooden handle and a metal blade

axe²; ax *AmE* *v* [T] *informal* to get rid of a plan, service, or someone's job: *a decision to axe 2000 staff*

axis /'æksɪ̱s/ *n* [C] plural **axes** /-siːz/ **1** the imaginary line around which a large round object, such as the Earth, turns → see picture at **GLOBE** **2** a line at the side or bottom of a GRAPH, used for marking measurements

axle /'æksəl/ *n* [C] the bar that connects two wheels on a vehicle

aye /aɪ/ *adv spoken informal* a word meaning 'yes', used especially in Scotland and the North of England

A

B, b

B, b /biː/ *n* [C,U] plural **B's, b's** **1** the second letter of the English alphabet **2** the seventh note in the musical SCALE of C MAJOR, or the musical KEY based on this note **3** a mark given to a student's work to show that it is good but not excellent: *I got a B in history.*

BA, B.A. /ˌbiː ˈeɪ/ *n* [C] **Bachelor of Arts** a university degree in a subject such as history or literature [➔ **BSc**]

babble /ˈbæbəl/ *v* [I] to talk quickly in a way that is silly or difficult to understand: *What are you babbling on about?* —**babble** *n* [U]

babe /beɪb/ *n* [C] **1** *literary* a baby **2** *spoken informal* an attractive young woman

baboon /bəˈbuːn $ bæ-/ *n* [C] a large monkey

baby /ˈbeɪbi/ *n* [C] plural **babies**

1 a very young child: *She had a baby in her arms.* | *a newborn baby* | *Muriel is expecting a baby.* | *She had a baby* (=gave birth to a baby) *last year.* | **baby boy/girl**

> **TOPIC**
>
> When babies **crawl**, they move around on their hands and knees. Babies usually crawl before they learn how to walk.
> A very young baby who cannot walk or talk yet is called an **infant**. A baby who has learned how to walk is called a **toddler**.
> When you take a baby somewhere, you can push them there in a **pram** *BrE*/**baby carriage** *AmE*, which is like a bed on wheels. You can push an older baby along in a **buggy** *BrE*/**stroller** *AmE*, which is like a chair on wheels.
> ➔ **CHILD**

2 baby bird/rabbit/elephant etc a very young animal

ˈbaby ˌboomer *n* [C] someone born during a period when a lot of babies were born, especially between 1946 and 1964

ˈbaby ˌcarriage also **ˈbaby ˌbuggy** *n* [C] *AmE* a thing like a bed on wheels that you put a baby in and push along [= pram *BrE*] ➔ see box at **BABY**

babysitter /ˈbeɪbiˌsɪtə $ -ər/ *n* [C] someone who looks after children while their parents go out for a short time —**babysitting** *n* [U] *I earn some extra money from babysitting.* —**babysit** *v* [I]

bachelor /ˈbætʃələ $ -ər/ *n* **1** [C] a man who has never been married **2 Bachelor of Arts/ Science/Education etc** a university degree

back¹ /bæk/ *n* [C]

1 the part of your body from your neck and shoulders down to your bottom: *Always sit with your back straight.* | *He fell and injured his back.* | *He lay on his back listening to music.* | *people who suffer from back pain*

2 [usually singular] the part of something that is furthest from the front [≠ front]: **on the back (of sth)** *a T-shirt with a picture of a snake on the back* | *Write your name on the back of the cheque.* | **in the back (of sth)** (=in the part of a vehicle behind the driver) *Do you want to sit in the back of the car?* | **at the back (of sth)** (=in the part of a room or building that is behind the front) *We sat at the back of the hall.* | *My bedroom's at the back of the house.* | **out back** *AmE* (=behind a building)

3 the part of a seat that you lean against when you are sitting: **+of** *He rested his arm on the back of the sofa.*

4 back to back a) with the backs of two people or things towards each other: *Stand back to back and see who's tallest.* **b)** happening one after the other: *The team had a couple of wins back to back.*

5 back to front *BrE* with the back of something where the front should be: *You've got your sweater on back to front.*

6 behind sb's back without someone knowing, especially in an unkind way: *They're always talking about her behind her back.*

7 at/in the back of your mind if a thought is at the back of your mind, it is there even when you are thinking about other things: *There was a slight worry at the back of his mind.*

8 be on sb's back *informal* to tell someone to do something again and again, or to criticize them a lot

9 get off sb's back *informal* to stop annoying someone or asking them to do something

10 be glad/pleased etc to see the back of sb/sth *informal* to be happy that someone is leaving or that something is ending

➔ **turn your back on sb/sth** at **TURN¹**

back² *adv*

1 where someone or something was before: **+in/ to/into etc** *Put the milk back in the refrigerator.* | *When do you go back to school?* | *The jumper didn't fit so I took it back to the shop.* | *I'll be back* (=return) *in an hour.* | *He ran all the way back home.*

2 into the state that someone or something was in before: **+to** *Would you go back to being married?* | *I couldn't get back to sleep.*

3 in the direction that is behind you: *Dan walked away and didn't look back.*

4 doing the same thing to someone that they have done to you: *I'll call you back later.* | *Gina smiled, and the boy smiled back.*

5 at or to a time in the past: **+to** *I often think back to my childhood.* | **three years/two months etc back** *This all happened about two years back.*

6 away from someone or something: *'Keep back* (=stay away)*!' shouted one of the firefighters.* | **+from** *The house was set back from the road.*

7 back and forth in one direction and then in the opposite direction several times

back³ *v*

1 [T] to support someone or something, especially by using your money or power: *The Bank gave £45,000 to back the programme.* | *Several witnesses came forward to back him.*

2 [I,T] to move in the direction that is behind you, or to make a vehicle move in this way: **back (sth) into/out of/away etc** *He slowly backed away from the dog.* | *Teresa backed the car into the garage.*

3 [T] to risk money by guessing that a particular horse, team etc will win something: *I backed Goliath at 10–1.*

back down *phr v* to agree not to do something, or to admit that you are wrong: **+on** *The government has backed down on its proposal.* | *Neither side was prepared to back down.*

back off *phr v* **1** to move away from something: *She backed off, turned, and ran.* **2** *especially AmE spoken* to stop telling someone what to do, or to stop criticizing them: *Back off! I don't need your advice.*

back onto sth *phr v* if a building backs onto a place, the back of the building faces it: *The house backs onto the river.*

back out *phr v* to decide not to do something that you had promised to do: **+of** *They backed out of the deal at the last minute.*

back up *phr v* **1 back sb/sth ⇔ up** to support what someone is saying, or show that it is true: *Will you back me up?* **2 back sth ⇔ up** to make a copy of information stored on a computer: *Don't forget to back up your files.* **3** to move backwards, or to make a vehicle go backwards: **back sth ⇔ up** *He backed the car up a few feet.*

back⁴ *adj* [only before noun]

1 at the back of something: *the back door* | *in the back garden* | *Mum sat in the back seat of the car.* **2 back street/road** a street that is away from the main streets **3 back rent/taxes/pay** money that someone owes from an earlier date **4 take a back seat** to be less involved in something than you used to be

backache /'bækeɪk/ *n* [C,U] a pain in your back

backbench /ˌbæk'bentʃ◂/ *adj* [only before noun] *BrE* a backbench Member of Parliament is one who does not have an important official position —**backbencher** *n* [C]

backbenches /ˌbæk'bentʃɪz/ *n* **the backbenches** [plural] *BrE* the seats in Parliament where backbench politicians sit

backbone /'bækbəʊn $ -boʊn/ *n* **1** [C] the bone down the middle of your back [= spine] → see picture on page A3 **2 the backbone of sth** the most important part of something: *A good manager is the backbone of the team.*

backbreaking /'bækbreɪkɪŋ/ *adj* backbreaking work is very hard physical work

backdate /ˌbæk'deɪt $ 'bækdeɪt/ *v* [T] to make something have its effect from an earlier date: **backdate sth to/from sth** *The pay increase will be backdated to January.*

backdrop /'bækdrɒp $ -drɑːp/ *n* **1** the situation in which something happens: *a love story set against the backdrop of war* **2** also **backcloth** /-klɒθ $ -klɔːθ/ the painted cloth at the back of a stage

backer /'bækə $ -ər/ *n* [C] someone who supports a plan, especially by providing money

backfire /ˌbæk'faɪə $ 'bækfaɪr/ *v* [I] if something you do backfires, it has the opposite effect to the one you wanted

backgammon /'bækgæmən/ *n* [U] a game for two players, using flat round pieces and DICE on a board

background /'bækgraʊnd/ *n*

1 [C] someone's education, family, and experience: *All the kids here come from very different*

backgrounds. | *He **has a background in** Computer Science.* | **social/cultural/family** etc **background** *What's her educational background?* **2** [singular, U] the general situation in which something happens: **+to** *Let me explain the background to this case.* | **against a background** *The deal came against a background of rising political tension.* | *He gave us some background information.* **3** [C usually singular] the area that is behind the main things that you look at in a picture: **in the background** *You can see some houses in the background.* | **on/against a background** *a pattern of roses on a blue background* **4 in the background** if someone stays in the background, they work or do things quietly, so that other people do not notice them: *A waiter stood quietly in the background.* **5** [singular] sounds that are in the background are not the main ones that you can hear: *There was a lot of **background noise**.* | **in the background** *I could hear music playing in the background.*

backhand /'bækhænd/ *n* [C usually singular] a way of hitting the ball in tennis etc, with the back of your hand turned towards the ball

backing /'bækɪŋ/ *n* [U] support or help, especially with money: *We managed to get **financial backing** for the project.*

backlash /'bæklæʃ/ *n* [C] a strong reaction from people against an idea or person: **+against** *a public backlash against the President*

backlog /'bæklɒg $ -lɔːg, -lɑːg/ *n* [C usually singular] a lot of work that needs doing and that you should have done earlier

backpack¹ /'bækpæk/ *n* [C] a bag used to carry things on your back, especially when you go walking → see picture at **BAG¹**

backpack² *v* [I] to go walking or travelling carrying a backpack —**backpacker** *n* [C] —**backpacking** *n* [U]

backpedal /ˌbæk'pedl $ 'bæk,pedl/ *v* [I] **backpedalled, backpedalling** *BrE*, **backpedaled, backpedaling** *AmE* to change your opinion or not do something that you had said you would do [= backtrack]: *They are backpedalling on the commitment to cut taxes.*

backside /'bæksaɪd/ *n* [C] *informal* the part of your body that you sit on [= bottom]

backslash /'bækslæʃ/ *n* [C] a line (\) used in writing to separate words, numbers, or letters

backstage /ˌbæk'steɪdʒ◂/ *adv, adj* behind the stage in a theatre

backstroke /'bækstrəʊk $ -stroʊk/ *n* [singular] a style of swimming on your back → see picture at **SWIM¹**

back-to-back *adj* [only before noun] happening one after another: *The team has had five back-to-back wins.*

backtrack /'bæktræk/ *v* [I] to change your opinion or not do something that you had said you would do [= backpedal]: *The minister denied that he was backtracking.*

backup /'bækʌp/ *n* **1** [C,U] extra help or support that can be used if it is needed: *Four more police cars **provided backup**.* **2** [C] a copy of a computer document or program that you can use if the original one is lost or damaged: **+of** *Have you made a backup of the file?*

backward /ˈbækwəd $ -wərd/ *adj* **1** [only before noun] in the direction that is behind you: *She gave a backward glance.* **2** developing or learning more slowly than normal: *a backward child*

backwards /ˈbækwədz $ -wərdz/ also **backward** *especially AmE adv*
1 in the direction that is behind you [≠ **forwards**]: *She stepped backwards in surprise.*
2 towards the past or the beginning of something [≠ **forwards**]: *Count backwards from 100.*
3 with the back part in front: *You've got your T-shirt on backwards.*
4 backwards and forwards first in one direction, then in the opposite direction several times

backwater /ˈbækwɔːtə $ -wɒtər, -wɑː-/ *n* [C] a quiet uninteresting town

backyard /ˌbækˈjɑːd $ -ˈjɑːrd/ *n* [C] **1** *BrE* a small enclosed area behind a house covered with a hard surface **2** *AmE* an area of land behind a house [= **garden** *BrE*]

bacon /ˈbeɪkən/ *n* [U] meat from a pig that has been put in salt and cut into thin pieces: *bacon and eggs* → see box at **MEAT**

bacteria /bækˈtɪəriə $ -ˈtɪr-/ *n* [plural] very small living things that sometimes cause disease —**bacterial** *adj*

bad /bæd/ *adj* comparative **worse** /wɜːs $ wɜːrs/, superlative, **worst** /wɜːst $ wɜːrst/ **1** not good or pleasant: *I'm afraid there's some bad news.* | *a bad smell* | *That's bad luck.* | *Dad's in a bad mood today.*

2 of a low quality or standard: *That was the worst meal I've ever had.* **3** if you are bad at something, you cannot do it very well: **+at** *I'm really bad at spelling.* **4** serious or severe: *a bad cold* | *The situation's getting worse.* **5 not bad** spoken quite good: *The movie wasn't bad.* **6 be bad for sb/sth** to be harmful: *Smoking is bad for you.* | *It's bad for your teeth to eat sweets.* **7 a bad time/moment** a time that is difficult or unsuitable: *Is this a bad time to call?* **8** not morally good or not behaving well: *He was a bad man.* | *a bad dog* **9 too bad** spoken **a)** *BrE* used to say that you do not care about something: *'We need the report by tomorrow.' 'Too bad, I can't finish it until next week.'* **b)** *especially AmE* used to say that you are sorry about some-

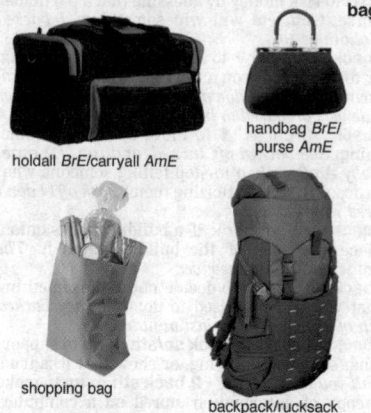

bags

holdall *BrE*/carryall *AmE*

handbag *BrE*/ purse *AmE*

shopping bag

backpack/rucksack

thing that has happened: *It's too bad she missed all the fun.* **10 feel bad** to feel ashamed or sorry about something: **+about** *I felt really bad about missing your birthday.* **11 bad heart/leg/back etc** a heart, leg etc that is injured or does not work properly **12** food that is bad is not safe to eat because it is not fresh: *The milk has gone bad.* **13 bad language** words that are rude or used for swearing → **be in sb's bad books** at **BOOK**[1]

baddie, baddy /ˈbædi/ *n* [C] *BrE informal* a bad person in a film or book [≠ **goody**]

bade /bæd, beɪd/ *v* the past tense and past participle of **BID**

badge /bædʒ/ *n* [C] *BrE* a piece of metal, plastic, or cloth with writing or a picture on it, that you wear to show which school you go to, which job you do etc [= **button** *AmE*, **pin** *AmE*]: *the school badge* | *Her badge said '4 today!'* | *a sheriff's badge*

badger[1] /ˈbædʒə $ -ər/ *n* [C] an animal with black and white fur that lives under the ground

badger[2] *v* [T] to keep trying to persuade someone to do or allow something: *My friends keep badgering me to get a cell phone.* | *Tom badgered me into going.*

badly /ˈbædli/ *adv* comparative **worse** /wɜːs $ wɜːrs/ superlative **worst** /wɜːst $ wɜːrst/
1 in a way that is not good [≠ **well**]: *The book was badly written.* | *Rob did badly in the test.*
2 very much or very seriously: *The refugees badly need clean water.* | *Our roof was leaking badly.* | *I could see that he was badly injured.*

badly 'off *adj* [not before noun] *especially BrE* poor or in a bad situation [≠ **well-off**]

badminton /ˈbædmɪntən/ *n* [U] a game in which you hit a small object with feathers on it over a net

badmouth /ˈbædmaʊθ/ *v* [T] *especially AmE informal* to criticize someone

bad-'tempered *adj* someone who is bad-tempered is easily annoyed → see box at **ANGRY**

baffle /ˈbæfəl/ *v* [T] if something baffles you, you cannot understand it: *Her behaviour baffled me.* —**baffling** *adj*

bag[1] /bæg/ n [C]

1 a) a container that you can carry things in: *a shopping bag* | *a brown paper bag* | *a carrier bag* **b)** *BrE* a container that women use for carrying money and personal things [= hand-bag]: *a black leather bag* **c)** a large container used to carry clothes when you are travelling: *John packed his bags and left.*
2 the amount a bag can contain: +of *He ate a whole bag of sweets.*
3 bags of sth *especially BrE informal* a lot of something: *They've got bags of money!*
4 bags under your eyes dark circles or loose skin under your eyes
→ **let the cat out of the bag** at CAT → SHOULDER BAG, SLEEPING BAG, TOILET BAG

bag[2] v [T] bagged, bagging **1** also **bag up** to put things in a bag **2** *informal* to get something before other people get it: *I'll get there early and bag some seats.*

bagel /'beɪɡəl/ n [C] a type of bread, shaped like a ring → see picture at BREAD

baggage /'bæɡɪdʒ/ n [U] **1** the bags that you carry when you are travelling [= luggage]: *Check your baggage in at the desk.* **2** problems and emotional difficulties that you continue to have from a situation in the past: *She's carrying a lot of emotional baggage.*

GRAMMAR

Baggage does not have a plural form. You can say **some baggage**, **any baggage**, or **pieces of baggage**: *Do you have any baggage?*

baggy /'bæɡi/ adj baggy clothes are big and loose [≠ tight] → see box at CLOTHES

'bag ,lady n [C] *informal* an offensive word for a homeless woman who carries all her possessions with her

bagpipes /'bæɡpaɪps/ n [plural] a musical instrument played especially in Scotland, by blowing air into a bag and forcing it out through pipes

baguette /bæ'ɡet/ n [C] a long thin LOAF of bread

bail[1] /beɪl/ n [U] when someone pays money to a court so that they can stay out of prison until they appear before the court, or the amount of money that they pay: **grant/refuse sb bail** *The defendant was granted bail until April 27.* | **release/free sb on bail** (=let someone go free when bail is paid)

bail[2] v [T usually passive] *BrE* if someone is bailed, they pay an amount of money and are allowed to stay out of prison until they appear in a court of law
  bail sb ⇔ **out** phr v **1** to help someone get out of trouble, especially by giving them money: *Young people often expect their parents to bail them out.* **2** to leave money with a court of law so that someone can stay out of prison until they appear in court

bailiff /'beɪlɪf/ n [C] **1** *BrE* someone whose job is to take people's property when they owe money **2** *AmE* someone whose job is to guard prisoners in a court of law

bait[1] /beɪt/ n [singular, U] **1** food that you use to attract fish or animals so that you can catch them **2** something that is offered to someone to persuade them to do something

bait[2] v [T] **1** to put food on a hook or in a trap to catch fish or animals **2** to deliberately try to annoy someone by laughing at them or making jokes about them

bake /beɪk/ v [I,T] to cook something such as bread or cakes in an OVEN: *I'm baking a cake.* | *baked potatoes* | **bake (sth) at 180/200 etc degrees** *Bake at 250 degrees for 20 minutes.* → see box at COOK

,baked 'beans n [plural] beans that are cooked in a tomato sauce and sold in cans

baker /'beɪkə $ -ər/ n [C] **1** someone whose job is making bread, cakes etc **2 baker's** *BrE* a shop that sells bread, cakes etc → see box at SHOP

bakery /'beɪkəri/ n [C] plural **bakeries** a place where bread, cakes etc are made or sold → see box at SHOP

baking /'beɪkɪŋ/ adj very hot: *a baking hot day* → see box at HOT

balance[1] /'bæləns/ n

1 [U] when you are able to stand and walk steadily, without falling: *I put my arms out to help me keep my balance.* | *Jim lost his balance on the ice.* | *The blow knocked his opponent off balance.*
2 [singular,U] when you give the right amount of importance to different things in a sensible way: *Try to keep a balance between work and play.* | *It's not always easy to strike the right balance.*
3 [singular,U] when the correct relationship exists between different things [≠ imbalance]: +between *the need to maintain the balance between cost and profit* | +of *pesticides that upset the balance of nature*
4 [C] **a)** the amount of money that you have left to use: *Can I check my bank balance please?* **b)** the amount of money that you owe for something: *You can pay a deposit now and the balance later.*
5 on balance used to tell someone your opinion after considering all the facts: *On balance, I prefer the new system.*
6 be/hang in the balance if something hangs in the balance, you do not know yet whether the result will be bad or good: *The president's future hung in the balance.*

balance[2] v

1 [I,T] to be in a steady position, without falling, or to put something in this position: +on *Can you balance on one leg?* | **balance sth on sth** *The woman was balancing a large vase on her head.*
2 [T] to consider one thing in relation to something else, especially so that you give the right amount of importance to both: **balance sth against sth** *Our rights have to be balanced against our responsibilities.* | **balance sth and sth** *It can be hard to balance family life and a career.*
3 also **balance out** [I,T] if two or more things balance, or if one balances the other, the effect of one equals the effect of the other: *Job losses in some departments were balanced by increases in others.*
4 balance the books/budget to make sure that you do not spend more money than you have

balanced /'bælənst/ *adj* **1** fair and sensible: *a balanced approach to the problem* **2** including a good mixture of things: *a balanced diet* → **WELL-BALANCED**

,balance of 'payments also **,balance of 'trade** *n* [singular] *especially BrE* the difference between the amount of money that a country earns from selling goods and services abroad and the amount it spends

,balance of 'power *n* **the balance of power** the way in which power is divided between people, countries, or organizations

'balance sheet *n* [C] a written statement of how much a business has earned and how much it has spent

'balancing ,act *n* [singular] when you are trying to please two different people or groups, or achieve two different things: *The Prime Minister is attempting a difficult balancing act.*

balcony /'bælkəni/ *n* [C] plural **balconies 1** a structure built onto an outside wall of a building, that you reach through an upstairs door **2** the seats upstairs in a theatre → see box at **THEATRE**

bald /bɔːld $ bɒːld/ *adj* **1** someone who is bald has no hair or very little hair on their head **2** [only before noun] bald facts or statements are very direct —**baldness** *n* [U]

balding /'bɔːldɪŋ $ 'bɒːl-/ *adj* losing hair on your head

baldly /'bɔːldli $ 'bɒːld-/ *adv* in a clear direct way, without trying to be polite: *'I want you to leave,' she said baldly.*

bale¹ /beɪl/ *n* [C] a large amount of something such as paper or HAY, tied tightly together

bale² *v*
bale out *BrE*; **bail out** *AmE phr v* to escape from a plane, using a PARACHUTE

baleful /'beɪlfəl/ *adj formal* angry or evil

balk /bɔːk, bɔːlk $ bɒːk, bɒːlk/ *v* the American spelling of BAULK

ball /bɔːl $ bɒːl/ *n* [C]
1 a round object that you throw, hit, or kick in a game or sport: *tennis balls* | *Do you want to come and play ball* (=play a game with a ball)?
2 something rolled into a round shape: +**of** *a ball of wool* | *Form the pastry into a ball.*
3 a large formal occasion where people dance
4 **have a ball** *informal* to enjoy something very much: *We had a ball last night!*
5 **the ball of the foot/hand** the rounded part at the base of the toes or at the base of the thumb
6 **be on the ball** *informal* to be able to think or react very quickly
7 **set/start the ball rolling** *informal* to start something happening: *Just a small donation will start the ball rolling.*
→ **play ball** at **PLAY¹**

ballad /'bæləd/ *n* [C] a long song or poem that tells a story

ballerina /,bælə'riːnə/ *n* [C] a woman who dances in ballets

ballet /'bæleɪ $ bæ'leɪ, 'bæleɪ/ *n* **1** [C,U] a type of dancing that tells a story with music but no words, or a performance of this type of dancing: *We went to see a ballet in London.* | *I'm going to the ballet* (=going to watch a ballet) *this evening.* | *a ballet dancer* → see box at **THEATRE**

2 [C] a group of ballet dancers who work together: *the Royal Ballet*

'ball game *n* [C] **1** *AmE* a game of baseball, football or BASKETBALL **2** *informal* **a whole new ball game/a different ball game** a situation that is very different from the one you are used to

ballistic /bə'lɪstɪk/ *adj* **go ballistic** *informal* to suddenly become very angry

bal,listic 'missile *n* [C] a powerful weapon that can travel very long distances through the air

balloon¹ /bə'luːn/ *n* [C] a small coloured rubber bag that you blow air into and use as a toy or decoration: *Can you blow up these balloons?* | *Suddenly the balloon burst.* → **HOT AIR BALLOON**

balloon² *v* [I] to suddenly become much larger: *The company's debt ballooned to $350 billion.*

ballot¹ /'bælət/ *n* [C,U] a system of voting in secret, or an occasion when people vote in this way: *Workers held a ballot and rejected strike action.* | *a ballot paper* (=piece of paper that you use to vote) | *He won 54% of the ballot* (=the number of votes in an election).

ballot² *v* [T] *especially BrE* to ask people to vote for something: *We will ballot our members to find out how much support there is for a strike.*

'ballot box *n* [C] **1** **the ballot box** the system of voting in an election: *Voters will make their views known through the ballot box.* **2** the box where people put the papers they have used for voting

ballpark /'bɔːlpɑːk $ 'bɒːlpɑːrk/ *n* [C] **1** *AmE* a field for playing baseball, with seats for people to watch the game **2** **in the right/same etc ballpark** *informal* used to say that numbers or amounts are almost correct, almost the same etc: *All the bids are expected to be in the same ballpark.* **3** **a ballpark figure/estimate** a number or amount that is almost but not exactly correct

ballpoint pen /,bɔːlpɔɪnt 'pen $,bɒːl-/ also **ballpoint** *n* [C] a pen with a small ball at the end, which rolls ink onto the paper

ballroom /'bɔːlrʊm, -ruːm $ 'bɒːl-/ *n* [C] a large room for formal dances

,ballroom 'dancing *n* [U] a formal type of dancing that is done with a partner and has different steps for different types of music

balmy /'bɑːmi $ 'bɑːmi, 'bɑːlmi/ *adj* balmy air or weather is warm and pleasant: *a balmy evening*

baloney /bə'ləʊni $ -'loʊ-/ *n* [U] *informal* something that is silly or not true: *Don't give me that baloney!*

balustrade /,bælə'streɪd $ 'bæləstreɪd/ *n* [C] a row of posts along the edge of a BALCONY or bridge

bamboo /,bæm'buːˑ/ *n* [U] a tall tropical plant with hollow stems, often used for making furniture

bamboozle /bæm'buːzəl/ *v* [T] *informal* to trick or confuse someone

ban¹ /bæn/ *n* [C] an official order saying that people must not do something: +**on** *The government imposed* (=started) *a ban on tobacco advertising.* | *The committee agreed to lift* (=end) *the ban on meat imports.*

ban² v [T] **banned, banning** to officially say that people must not do something: *Smoking is banned inside the building.* | **ban sb from doing sth** *He was banned from driving for a year.*

banal /bəˈnɑːl, bəˈnæl/ *adj* ordinary and not interesting: *a banal conversation* —**banality** /bəˈnælɪti/ n [C,U]

banana /bəˈnɑːnə $ -ˈnæ-/ n [C] a long curved yellow fruit → see picture at **FRUIT**

band¹ /bænd/ n [C]

1 [also + plural verb *BrE*] a group of musicians who play popular music together: *He used to play in a band called 'Adventure'.* | *The band was playing old Beatles' songs.* | *the band members* | **rock/jazz/pop band**

2 a group of people who have the same beliefs or aims: **+of** *a loyal band of supporters*

3 a narrow piece of something, with one end joined to the other to form a circle: *papers held together with a* **rubber band**

4 a range of numbers or amounts in a system: **tax/age/income band** *taxpayers in higher tax bands*

5 a narrow area of colour or light that is different from the areas around it: *a fish with a black band along its back*

→ **BOY BAND, ELASTIC BAND**

band² v

band together *phr v* if people band together, they work with each other to achieve something: *Local people have banded together to fight the company's plans.*

bandage¹ /ˈbændɪdʒ/ n [C] a long piece of cloth that you tie around a wound or injury

bandage² also **bandage up** v [T] to tie a bandage around a wound or injury

'Band-Aid n [C] *trademark AmE* a small piece of material that you stick over a small wound on your skin [= **plaster** *BrE*]

bandanna, bandana /bænˈdænə/ n [C] a piece of coloured cloth that you wear around your head or neck

B and B, B & B /ˌbiː ənd ˈbiː/ n [C] the abbreviation of **bed and breakfast**

bandit /ˈbændɪt/ n [C] someone who robs people who are travelling through hills or mountains

bandstand /ˈbændstænd/ n [C] a structure in a park, used by a band playing music

bandwagon /ˈbændˌwægən/ n [C] an activity or idea that suddenly becomes popular or fashionable: *the keep-fit bandwagon of the 1980s* | *All the political parties are trying to* **jump on the** environmental **bandwagon** (=start supporting it because it is fashionable).

bandwidth /ˈbændwɪdθ/ n [U] *technical* the amount of information that can be carried through a telephone wire or computer connection at one time

bandy /ˈbændi/ v **bandied, bandying, bandies be bandied about/around** to be mentioned by a lot of people: *Rumours of an affair had been bandied about in the media.*

bane /beɪn/ n **be the bane of sb/sth** to be the person or thing that annoys someone or causes problems for them: *Commuting is the bane of my life.*

bang¹ /bæŋ/ n [C] **1** a sudden loud noise such as an explosion or something hitting a hard

surface: *There was a loud bang, followed by the sound of breaking glass.* | *The door closed with a bang.* → see picture on page A7 **2** when part of your body hits something: **+on** *He got a nasty bang on the head.* **3 bangs** [plural] *AmE* hair that is cut straight across the front of your head, above your eyes [= **fringe** *BrE*] → see picture at **HAIR 4 go with a bang** *informal* if an event goes with a bang, it is very successful: *ideas to make sure your party goes with a bang*

bang² v [I,T] **1** to make a loud noise, especially by hitting something against something hard: **+on** *Someone was banging on the door.* | **bang sth on sth** *She banged her fists on the table.* | *A door banged downstairs.* → see box at **HIT 2** to hit part of your body against something by accident: **bang sth on sth** *I banged my knee on the corner of the bed.* | **+into** *He banged into the doorpost.*

bang³ *adv informal* **1** directly or exactly: *The train arrived bang on time.* | *The technology is bang up to date.* **2 bang goes sth** *BrE spoken* used to show that you are unhappy because something you had planned will not happen: *Oh well, bang goes our night out.*

banger /ˈbæŋə $ -ər/ n [C] *BrE informal* **1** a SAUSAGE **2** an old car in bad condition **3** a FIREWORK that makes a loud noise

bangle /ˈbæŋgəl/ n [C] a band of metal, wood etc that you wear around your wrist

banish /ˈbænɪʃ/ v [T] **1** to get rid of something: *facial massage that can help banish wrinkles* | **banish sth from sth** *a show that's been banished from our TV screens* | **banish the thought/feeling etc** *She tried to banish the memory from her mind.* **2** to make someone leave a place as a punishment: **banish sb from/to sth** *He was banished from the country.* —**banishment** n [U]

banister /ˈbænɪstə $ -ər/ n [C] the piece of wood that you hold onto at the side of stairs

banjo /ˈbændʒəʊ $ -dʒoʊ/ n [C] plural **banjos** a musical instrument with a round body and strings that you pull with your fingers → see picture on page A6

bank¹ /bæŋk/ n [C]

1 the company or place where you can keep your money or borrow money: **in the bank** *I think I'll put the money in the bank.* | *I need to* **go to the bank.** | *a bank loan* → see box at **ACCOUNT**

2 land along the side of a river or lake: **+of** *the banks of the River Thames* | *the river bank*

3 a store of something that is kept until people need it: *a blood bank* | *a data bank* | **+of** *a bank of information*

4 a large sloping mass of snow, earth, sand etc: *a grassy bank* | **+of** *a huge bank of earth*

5 a mass of cloud or FOG

→ **BOTTLE BANK, FOOD BANK, PIGGY BANK**

bank² v **1** [T] to put money in a bank: *Have you banked the cheque yet?* **2** [I] to use a particular bank: **+with/at** *I bank with the National Bank now.* **3** [I] if a plane banks, it slopes to one side when it is turning

bank on *sb/sth phr v* to depend on something happening: *I was banking on him being here.*

'bank ac,count n [C] an arrangement that allows you to keep your money in a bank and take it out when you want to → see box at ACCOUNT

'bank ,balance n [C] the amount of money someone has in their bank account

banker /'bæŋkə $ -ər/ n [C] someone who has an important job in a bank

,bank 'holiday n [C] BrE an official holiday when banks and most companies are closed

banking /'bæŋkɪŋ/ n [U] the business of a bank

'bank note n [C] a piece of paper money [= note BrE; = bill AmE]

bankroll /'bæŋkrəʊl $ -roʊl/ v [T] to provide the money that someone needs for a business, a plan etc [= finance]: Who is bankrolling the campaign?

bankrupt¹ /'bæŋkrʌpt/ adj without enough money to pay your debts: Many small businesses went bankrupt last year.

bankrupt² v [T] to make someone become bankrupt: The deal nearly bankrupted us.

bankruptcy /'bæŋkrʌptsi/ n [C,U] plural bankruptcies when a person or company cannot pay their debts: a company on the verge of bankruptcy

banner /'bænə $ -ər/ n [C]   **1** a long piece of cloth with writing on it: The crowds were cheering and waving banners.   **2 under the banner of sth   a)** doing something because of a principle or belief: an election fought under the banner of social justice   **b)** doing something as part of a particular organization: a force operating under the NATO banner

banquet /'bæŋkwɪt/ n [C] a very formal meal for a lot of people

banter /'bæntə $ -ər/ n [U] friendly conversation with a lot of jokes in it: He always enjoyed a bit of banter with his customers.

bap /bæp/ n [C] BrE a round soft bread ROLL

baptism /'bæptɪzəm/ n [C,U] a religious ceremony in which a priest puts water on someone to make them a member of the Christian church [➠ christening] —**baptismal** /bæp'tɪzməl/ adj

Baptist /'bæptɪst/ n [C] a member of a Christian group that believes baptism should only be for those old enough to understand its meaning

baptize also -ise BrE /bæp'taɪz $ 'bæptaɪz/ v [T] to make someone a member of the Christian church by a baptism

bar¹ /baː $ baːr/ n [C]

1   a) a place where alcoholic drinks are sold and can be drunk: We met in the hotel bar.   **b)** BrE one of the rooms inside a PUB
2 a COUNTER where alcoholic drinks are served: **at the bar** They stood at the bar. | **behind the bar** The woman behind the bar was very friendly.
3 coffee/snack/burger etc bar a place where a particular type of food or drink is served
4 a small block of something: **+of** a bar of soap | a bar of chocolate | a candy bar → see picture at PIECE
5 a long narrow piece of metal or wood: iron bars
6 bar to (doing) sth something that prevents something else from happening: His lack of a formal education was not a bar to his success.
7 a group of notes in printed music, separated from others by a vertical line

8 a row of pictures on a computer screen that you can choose and CLICK on: the menu bar
9 behind bars informal in prison: He was back behind bars last night.
10 the bar the profession of being a lawyer, or lawyers considered as a group

bar² v [T] barred, barring   **1** to officially prevent someone from doing something: **bar sb from (doing) sth** He was barred from playing in the tournament.   **2** to prevent someone from going somewhere by putting something in front of them: A tall gate barred their way.   **3** to close and lock a door or window

bar³ prep   **1** except: It was a great performance, bar one mistake.   **2 bar none** used to emphasize that someone or something is the best: It's the best restaurant in town, bar none.

barbarian /baː'beəriən $ baːr'ber-/ n [C] someone who is rough, violent, and uneducated and does not respect art, education etc

barbaric /baː'bærɪk $ baːr-/ also **barbarous** /'baːbərəs $ 'baːr-/ adj violent and cruel: a barbaric act of terrorism —**barbarism** n [U]

barbarous /'baːbərəs $ 'baːr-/ adj literary cruel and shocking: barbarous crimes —**barbarously** adv

barbecue /'baːbɪkjuː $ 'baːr-/ n [C] BBQ   **1** an occasion when you cook and eat food outdoors: We had a barbecue on the beach.   **2** a piece of equipment for cooking food outdoors → see picture on page A5 —**barbecue** v [T] barbecued sausages

barbed /baːbd $ baːrbd/ adj a barbed remark is unkind

,barbed 'wire n [U] wire with sharp points on it, used to stop people getting into a place

barber /'baːbə $ 'baːrbər/ n [C] a man whose job is to cut men's hair

'bar chart also **'bar graph** n [C] a picture of boxes of different heights, in which each box represents a different amount or quantity

'bar code n [C] a row of black lines on a product that a computer can read to get information such as the price

bard /baːd $ baːrd/ n [C] literary a poet

bare¹ /beə $ ber/ adj   **1** not covered by clothes: children running around in bare feet | **bare-chested/bare-legged etc   2** empty, or not covered by anything: The room was very bare. | a bare hillside → see box at EMPTY   **3** basic and with nothing extra: a report giving just the bare facts | a room with the bare minimum of furniture | **the bare necessities/essentials** (=the basic things you need)   **4 with your bare hands** without using a weapon or tool: Firefighters dug with their bare hands to rescue survivors. —**bareness** n [U]

bare² v [T] to let people see part of your body by removing something that is covering it: I don't usually bare my skin to the sun. | The dog bared its teeth and growled.

barefoot /'beəfʊt $ 'ber-/ adj, adv not wearing any shoes or socks: walking barefoot in the sand

barely /'beəli $ 'berli/ adv   **1** only just: They had barely enough money to live on. | I could barely stay awake. | The cabin was barely visible in the rain.   **2** used to emphasize that something happens immediately after something else: He'd barely sat down when the phone rang.

barf /baːf $ baːrf/ v [I] *AmE informal* to VOMIT
—**barf** n [U]

bargain[1] /ˈbaːgɪn $ ˈbaːr-/ n [C]　**1** something
you buy cheaply or for less than its usual price:
The table was a real bargain. | *books at bargain prices* | *bargain hunters* (=people looking
for things that are cheap) ➔ see box at **CHEAP**
2 an agreement between two or more people, in
which each person agrees to do something in
return for something else: **make/strike a bargain** *I'll make a bargain with you. You cook and
I'll wash up.* | *I've kept my side of the bargain
and I expect you to keep yours.*　**3 into the
bargain** *especially BrE* in addition to everything
else: *She found a new job and a new husband into
the bargain.*

bargain[2] v [I]　to discuss the conditions of a
sale, agreement etc in order to get a fair deal:
+**with** *people bargaining with traders* | +**for**
They're trying to bargain for better pay. | +**over**
union leaders bargaining over wages
　bargain for/on sth *phr v* to expect that something will happen: *I hadn't bargained on getting
stuck in traffic.* | *The thief got more than he
bargained for when his victim fought back.*

barge[1] /baːdʒ $ baːrdʒ/ n [C] a boat for carrying goods on a CANAL or river ➔ see box at **SHIP**

barge[2] v [I,T] to walk somewhere so quickly or
carelessly that you push people or hit things:
+**through/past** *He barged past the guards at the
door.* | *She barged her way through the crowds.*
　barge in also **barge into** sth *phr v* to enter
somewhere rudely, or to rudely interrupt someone: *Sorry to barge in while you're having a
meal.*

baritone /ˈbærɪtəʊn $ -toʊn/ n [C] a male singing voice that is fairly low, but not the lowest

bark[1] /baːk $ baːrk/ v　**1** [I] when a dog barks, it
makes a short loud sound: +**at** *The dog always
barks at strangers.*　**2** also **bark out** [I,T] to say
something in a loud angry voice: *The teacher
barked instructions at us.* | +**at** *'What are you
doing?' he barked at her.*　**3 be barking up the
wrong tree** *spoken* to be doing something that
will not get the result you want

bark[2] n　**1** [C] the rough, loud sound that a dog
makes　**2** [U] the outer covering of a tree ➔ see
picture at **PLANT**

barley /ˈbaːli $ ˈbaːrli/ n [U] a grain used for
making food and alcohol

barmaid /ˈbaːmeɪd $ ˈbaːr-/ n [C] *BrE* a woman
who serves drinks in a bar [= **bartender** *AmE*]

barman /ˈbaːmən $ ˈbaːr-/ n [C] plural **barmen**
/-mən/ *BrE* a man who serves drinks in a bar
[= **bartender** *AmE*]

bar mitzvah /ˌbaː ˈmɪtsvə $ ˌbaːr-/ n [C] the
religious ceremony held when a Jewish boy
reaches the age of 13

barmy /ˈbaːmi $ ˈbaːrmi/ adj *BrE informal*
slightly crazy

barn /baːn $ baːrn/ n [C] a large farm building
for keeping crops or animals in

barometer /bəˈrɒmɪtə $ -ˈraːmɪtər/ n [C]
1 something that shows any changes in a situation: +**of** *an industry that's a good barometer of
the state of the economy*　**2** an instrument for
measuring changes in air pressure and weather

baron /ˈbærən/ n [C]　**1** a man in Britain or
Europe of a high social rank　**2** someone who
has a lot of power in a particular business:
press/drug barons

baroness /ˈbærənɪs/ n [C] a woman in Britain
or Europe of a high social rank

baroque /bəˈrɒk, bəˈrəʊk $ bəˈroʊk, -ˈraːk/ adj
relating to the style of art, music, building etc
popular in Europe in the 17th century

barrack /ˈbærək/ v [I,T] *BrE* to shout criticism at
a speaker, performer, or sports player: *He was
barracked by a section of the crowd.*

barracks /ˈbærəks/ n [plural] a group of buildings where soldiers live

barrage /ˈbæraːʒ $ bəˈraːʒ/ n　**1** [singular] a lot
of complaints, questions etc: +**of** *We've received
a barrage of complaints from viewers.*　**2** [C
usually singular] the continuous shooting of
guns

barred /baːd $ baːrd/ adj a barred window has
bars across it

barrel /ˈbærəl/ n [C]　**1** a large container for
liquids such as beer: *a beer barrel* | +**of** *a barrel
of oil*　**2** the part of a gun that bullets are fired
through

barren /ˈbærən/ adj barren land or soil is not
good enough for plants to grow

barricade[1] /ˈbærɪkeɪd, ˌbærɪˈkeɪd/ n [C] something that is put across a road or door to stop
people going through: *Demonstrators erected barricades across the streets.*

barricade[2] v [T] to use a barricade to prevent
someone or something from going somewhere:
barricade sb in/into sth *Students barricaded
themselves in and refused to leave.*

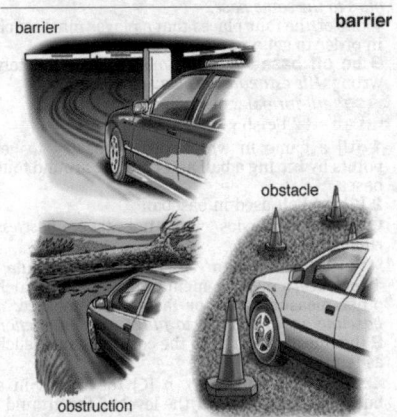

barrier　　　　　　　　　　　　　　　　**barrier**

obstacle

obstruction

barrier /ˈbæriə $ -ər/ n [C]　**1** something that
prevents people from doing something: *a new
deal to abolish trade barriers* | *The **language
barrier** prevents many people from working
abroad.* | +**to** *Disability need not be a barrier to
success.*　**2** an object that keeps people or things
separate or prevents people from entering a
place: *barriers to hold back the crowds*

barring /ˈbaːrɪŋ/ prep unless something happens: *Barring accidents, she should win.*

barrister /ˈbærɪ̯stə $ -ər/ n [C] a lawyer in Britain who can work in the higher law courts

barrow /ˈbærəʊ $ -roʊ/ n [C] a small vehicle that is pushed or pulled along

bartender /ˈbɑːˌtendə $ ˈbɑːrˌtendər/ n [C] *especially AmE* someone whose job is to serve drinks in a bar

barter /ˈbɑːtə $ ˈbɑːrtər/ v [I,T] to exchange goods or services without using money: **barter sth for sth** *Farmers bartered grain for machinery.* —**barter** n [U]

base[1] /beɪs/ v [T] to use somewhere as your main place of business: *The company is based in Denver.* | **London-based/Tokyo-based etc** a *London-based publisher*

base sth on/upon sth *phr v* to use something as the thing you develop something else from: *The movie is based on the author's childhood experiences.*

base[2] n [C]

1 the lowest part of something: +**of** *the base of the skull*

2 a situation or idea that something else can develop from: +**for** *The research has been used as a base for many other studies.*

3 a place where people in the army, navy etc live and work: *an army base*

4 the main place where someone works or stays, or from which work is done: *The firm has its main base in London.* | +**for** *The hotel is an ideal base for sightseeing.*

5 the people who support a person or organization: *Mandela had a broad base of political support.* | *a company with a large client base*

6 the main part of a substance, to which other things can be added: *You can add different colours to the same base.*

7 one of the four places that a player must touch in order to get a point in baseball

8 be off base *AmE informal* to be completely wrong: *His estimate was way off base.*

base[3] *adj formal* morally bad: *base instincts*

baseball /ˈbeɪsbɔːl $ -bɒːl/ n

1 [U] a game in which two teams try to get points by hitting a ball and running around four bases

2 [C] the ball used in baseball

baseless /ˈbeɪsləs/ *adj* not true: *baseless rumours*

baseline /ˈbeɪslaɪn/ n [C usually singular]

1 *technical* a measurement or fact against which other measurements or facts are compared: *a baseline against which to judge waste reduction*

2 the line at the back of the court in games such as tennis

basement /ˈbeɪsmənt/ n [C] the rooms in a building that are below the level of the ground

bases /ˈbeɪsiːz/ n the plural of BASIS

bash[1] /bæʃ/ v **1** [I,T] to hit something or someone hard: **bash sth on/against sth** *He bashed his head on the back of the seat.* **2** [T] *informal* to criticize someone publicly

bash[2] n [C] **1** *informal* a party: *a birthday bash* → see box at PARTY **2** a hard hit **3 have a bash at (doing) sth** *BrE spoken* to try to do something

bashful /ˈbæʃfəl/ *adj* shy —**bashfully** *adv*

basic /ˈbeɪsɪk/ *adj*

1 basic things are the most simple or most important things [➡ **basics**]: *the basic principles of chemistry* | *The basic idea is simple.*

2 something that is basic is simple, with nothing extra: *The rooms are fairly basic.* | *food and basic necessities*

basically /ˈbeɪsɪkli/ *adv*

1 *spoken* used to give a simple explanation of something: *Basically, I'm just lazy.*

2 in the most important ways, without considering small details: *All cheeses are made in basically the same way.*

basics /ˈbeɪsɪks/ n [plural] the most important facts or things that you need: +**of** *I know the basics of first aid.* | *people without basics like food and education*

basil /ˈbæzəl $ ˈbeɪ-/ n [U] a HERB with a strong smell and taste

basin /ˈbeɪsən/ n [C] **1** *BrE* a round container attached to a wall, in which you wash your hands and face [= **sink** *AmE*] → see picture at BATHROOM **2** *BrE* a bowl for liquids or food: *Pour the hot water into a basin.* **3** *technical* a large area of land that is lower at the centre: *the Amazon basin*

basis /ˈbeɪsɪ̯s/ n [C] plural **bases** /-siːz/

1 the information, facts, or thing on which something is based: **form/provide a basis for sth** *The video will provide a basis for class discussion.* | **the basis for/of sth** *Bread forms the basis of their daily diet.* | **on the basis of sth** (=using particular facts or reasons) *On the basis of the present evidence, he is not guilty.*

2 on a... basis used to say how something is organized or done: *They work on a **voluntary basis**.* | *We offer this service on a **commercial basis**.* | **on the basis that** *He was employed on the basis that he would work 37 hours per week.* | **on a regular/daily/weekly etc basis** *Meetings are held on a regular basis.*

bask /bɑːsk $ bæsk/ v [I] **1** to enjoy sitting or lying in the warmth of the sun: +**in** *A lizard was basking in the sun.* **2** to enjoy the approval that you are getting from other people: +**in** *Nigel was still **basking in the glory** of his first book.*

basket /ˈbɑːskɪ̯t $ ˈbæ-/ n [C]

1 a container made from thin pieces of wood, plastic, wire etc, used to carry things or put things in: *a **shopping basket*** | *a wicker **laundry basket*** (=for dirty clothes) | +**of** *a basket of fruit*

2 the net in basketball

→ WASTEPAPER BASKET

basketball /ˈbɑːskɪ̯tbɔːl $ ˈbæskɪ̯tbɒːl/ n

1 [U] a game between two teams, in which each team tries to throw a ball through a net

2 [C] the ball used in this game

bass /beɪs/ n **1** [C] a very low male singing voice, or a man with a voice like this **2** [U] the lower half of the whole range of musical notes **3** also **,bass guiˈtar** [C,U] an electric GUITAR that plays low notes **4** [C] a DOUBLE BASS

bassoon /bəˈsuːn/ n [C] a very long wooden musical instrument with a low sound that you play by blowing into it → see picture on page A6

baste /beɪst/ v [I,T] to pour liquid or melted fat over food that is cooking

bastion /'bæstiən $ -tʃən/ *n* [C] a place, organization etc that protects old beliefs or ways of doing things

bat¹ /bæt/ *n* [C] **1** a piece of wood used to hit the ball in games such as baseball and CRICKET: *a cricket bat* **2** a small animal that flies at night, like a mouse with wings

bat² *v* **batted**, **batting 1** [I] to be the person or team that is trying to hit the ball in CRICKET or baseball **2 not bat an eyelid/eye** to not be upset or surprised by something

batch /bætʃ/ *n* [C] a group of things or people that arrive or are dealt with at the same time: **+of** *She had just baked another batch of cookies.*

bated /'beɪtɪd/ *adj* **with bated breath** feeling very anxious or excited

bath¹ /bɑːθ $ bæθ/ *n* [C]
1 *BrE* a long container in which you wash yourself [= **bathtub** *AmE*] → see picture at **BATHROOM**
2 [usually singular] when you wash your body in the water that you put in a bath: **have/take a bath** *Suzy had a bath and went to bed.* | *All I wanted was a nice hot bath* (=wash with hot water). | *Shall I run a bath* (=put water in a bath) *for you?*
3 a bathroom, used especially in advertising: *All our bedrooms have a private bath.*

bath² *v* [I,T] *BrE* to wash yourself or someone else in a bath [= **bathe** *AmE*]: *Mum's upstairs bathing the baby.*

bathe /beɪð/ *v* **1** [I,T] *especially AmE* to wash yourself or someone else in a bath **2** [T] to put water or another liquid on part of your body as

a medical treatment **3** [I] *BrE old-fashioned* to swim **4 be bathed in light** if something is bathed in light, a lot of light is shining on it

bathing suit /'beɪðɪŋ suːt, -sjuːt $ -suːt/ *n* [C] *especially AmE old-fashioned* a SWIMSUIT

bathrobe /'bɑːθrəʊb $ 'bæθroʊb/ *n* [C] a loose piece of clothing like a coat that you wear before or after a bath (=dressing gown)

bathroom /'bɑːθrʊm, -ruːm $ 'bæθ-/ *n* [C]
1 a room where there is a bath and often a toilet: *a house with two bathrooms*
2 *AmE* a room where there is a toilet: *I need to go to the bathroom* (=use a toilet).

bathtub /'bɑːθtʌb $ 'bæθ-/ *n* [C] *especially AmE* a long container in which you wash yourself [= **bath** *BrE*]

baton /'bætɒn, -tn $ bæ'tɑːn, bə-/ *n* [C] **1** a stick that a police officer uses as a weapon **2** a stick used to control the way music is played by a group of musicians **3** a stick passed from one runner to another in a race

batsman /'bætsmən/ *n* [C] plural **batsmen** /-mən/ the person who is trying to hit the ball in cricket

battalion /bə'tæljən/ *n* [C] a large group of soldiers

batter¹ /'bætə $ -ər/ *v* [I,T] to hit someone or something very hard many times: *He was battered to death.* | **+at/on/against etc** *People were battering at the door.*

batter² *n* **1** [C,U] a mixture of flour, eggs, and milk, used in cooking **2** [C] the person who is trying to hit the ball in baseball

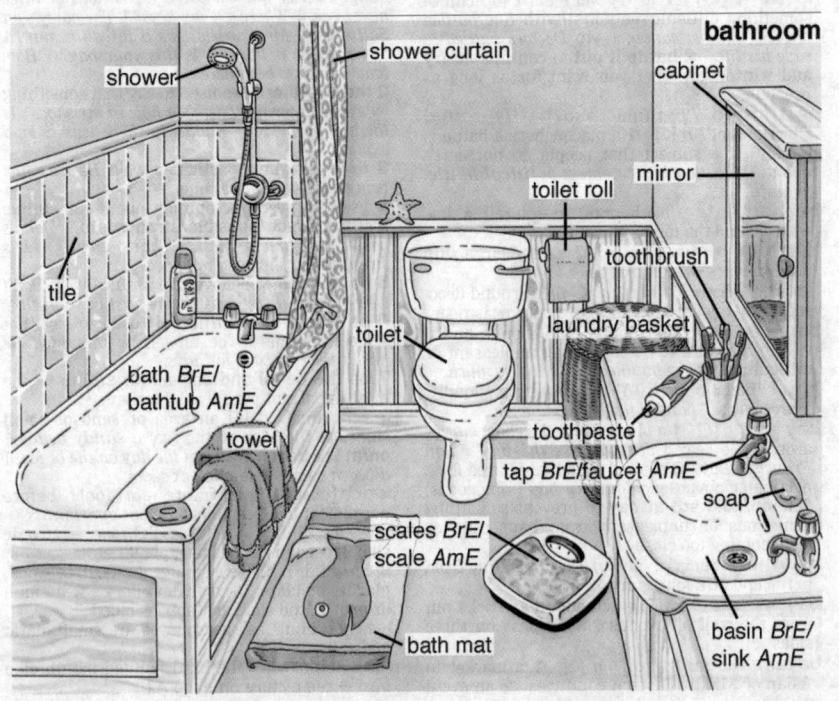

bathroom

shower · shower curtain · cabinet · mirror · toilet roll · toothbrush · laundry basket · toothpaste · tap *BrE*/faucet *AmE* · soap · basin *BrE*/sink *AmE* · bath mat · scales *BrE*/scale *AmE* · towel · bath *BrE*/bathtub *AmE* · toilet · tile

battered /'bætəd $ -ərd/ *adj* **1** old and in bad condition: *a battered suitcase* **2 battered woman/wife/baby etc** someone who has been attacked by their husband, a parent etc

battery /'bætəri/ *n plural* **batteries**
1 [C] an object that provides electricity for something such as a radio, car, or toy: *It needs a new battery.* | **flat battery** *BrE*/**dead battery** *AmE* (=one with no power) | **rechargeable batteries**
2 battery chickens/hens chickens that are kept in very small cages, so the farm can produce a lot of eggs
3 [U] *law* the crime of hitting someone: *He was charged with assault and battery.*
→ **recharge your batteries** at **RECHARGE**

battle¹ /'bætl/ *n*
1 [C,U] a fight between two armies or groups, especially in a war: *the battle of Trafalgar* | **in battle** *Her son was killed in battle.*
2 [C] a situation in which people or groups compete or argue with each other: **+with/between** *a long battle with my parents about clothes* | **+for** *the battle for power* | *a legal battle*
3 [C] an attempt to stop something happening or to achieve something difficult: **+against** *the battle against disease* | **the battle to do sth** *the battle to protect the English countryside* | *We're fighting a losing battle* (=trying to do something but not succeeding). | **win/lose a battle** (=succeed or not succeed in doing something)
4 be half the battle to be an important part of achieving something: *Having enough confidence is half the battle.*

battle² *v* [I,T] **1** to try very hard to achieve something difficult: **+against/with** *She battled bravely against cancer.* | **+to** *Doctors battled to save his life.* **2 battle it out** to continue to try and win or get what you want for as long as possible

battlefield /'bætlfi:ld/ also **battleground** /'bætlɡraʊnd/ *n* [C] **1** a place where a battle is fought **2** a subject that people do not agree about: *Education has become a political battleground.*

battlements /'bætlmənts/ *n* [plural] a low wall around the top of a castle

battleship /'bætl‚ʃɪp/ *n* [C] a very large ship used in wars → see box at **SHIP**

bauble /'bɔːbəl $ 'bɒː-/ *n* [C] *BrE* a round decoration that is used to decorate a CHRISTMAS TREE

baulk *BrE*; **balk** *AmE* /bɔːk, bɔːlk $ bɒːk, bɒːlk/ *v* [I] to not want to do something unpleasant or difficult: **+at** *They baulked at paying so much.*

bawl /bɔːl $ bɒːl/ *v* [I,T] to shout or cry loudly: *'Fares please!' bawled the bus conductor.*

bay /beɪ/ *n* [C] **1** a place where the coast curves around the sea: *a view across the bay* | *San Francisco Bay* **2** a small area that is used for a particular purpose: *a loading bay* (=for goods) **3 keep/hold sth at bay** to prevent something dangerous or unpleasant from happening or from coming too close

bayonet /'beɪənət, -net/ *n* [C] a long knife fixed to the end of a long gun

bay 'window *n* [C] a window that sticks out from the wall of a house, with glass on three sides

bazaar /bə'zɑː $ -'zɑːr/ *n* [C] **1** a market in Asian or Middle Eastern countries **2** an event when people sell a lot of different things to collect money for an organization: *a church bazaar*

BBC /‚biː biː 'siː◂/ *n* **the BBC** the British Broadcasting Corporation the British radio and television company that is paid for by the state

BBQ *n* [C] the written abbreviation of **barbecue**

BC /‚biː 'siː/ *adv* **before Christ** used after a date [➡ **AD**]: *2600 BC*

be¹ /bɪ; *strong* biː/ *auxiliary verb* past tense **was/were**, past participle **been**, present participle **being**
1 used with a present participle to form the CONTINUOUS tenses of verbs: *Jane was reading by the fire.* | *He isn't leaving, is he?*
2 used with a past participle to form the PASSIVE: *Smoking is not permitted on this flight.* | *The house is being painted.*
3 used to talk about imagined situations, in CONDITIONAL sentences: **if sb was/were (to do) sth** *If I were rich, I'd buy a Rolls Royce.* | *If he was to offer me the job, I'd accept.*
4 sb is to do sth *formal* **a)** used to say what must happen: *You are not to go out.* **b)** used to say what will happen: *They are to be married in June.*
5 sb/sth is to be seen/found/heard etc *formal* used to say that someone or something can be seen etc: *The only sound to be heard was the birds' singing.*

be² *v* [linking verb]
1 used to give or ask for information about someone or something, or to describe them: *I'm hungry.* | *Her name's Sally.* | *Tom will be three next week.* | *Where are my keys?* | *The party's on Saturday.* | *Mr Cardew was a tall thin man.* | *Their house is huge.* | *Is this your bag?* | *How long have you been here?*
2 there is/there are used to say that something exists or happens: *There's a hole in my shoe.* | *Is there a problem?* | *Suddenly there was a loud explosion.*
3 to behave in a particular way: *He was just being silly.* | *Don't be rude.*
4 used to give your opinion about something: **it's/that's nice/possible/strange etc** | *'John's passed his driving test.' 'That's great!'* | *It's strange that she hasn't phoned.*
5 be yourself to behave in a natural way: *Don't worry about impressing them – just be yourself.*
6 sb is not himself/herself used to say that someone seems to be unwell or unhappy: *He hasn't been himself for days.*
7 be the be-all and end-all (of sth) to be the most important part of a situation

beach /biːtʃ/ *n* [C] an area of sand or small stones at the edge of the sea: *a sandy beach* | **on/at the beach** *We spent the day on the beach.* | *a beach resort* → see box at **SHORE**

beachfront /'biːtʃfrʌnt/ *adj* [only before noun] next to a beach: *beachfront apartments*

beacon /'biːkən/ *n* [C] a light or electronic signal, used to guide boats, planes etc

bead /biːd/ *n* [C] **1** a small round ball of wood, plastic, or glass, used in jewellery **2** a small drop of liquid such as water or blood

beady /'biːdi/ *adj* beady eyes are small, dark, and shiny

beak /biːk/ *n* [C] the hard pointed mouth of a bird → see picture on page A2

beaker /'biːkə $ -ər/ *n* [C] *BrE* a cup with straight sides and no handle

beam¹ /biːm/ *n* [C] **1** a line of light or energy: **+of** *the beam of the flashlight* | *a laser beam* **2** a long piece of wood or metal used in building houses, bridges etc **3** a big happy smile → see box at SMILE

beam² *v* **1** [I] to smile very happily: **+at** *Grandad beamed at us proudly.* **2** [T] to send a radio or television signal: **beam sth across/up/to etc sth** *News from any part of the world can be beamed to us by satellite.*

bean /biːn/ *n* [C]

1 a seed or a case that seeds grow in, cooked as food: *kidney beans* | *green beans* **2** **coffee/cocoa beans** the seeds used in making coffee or chocolate

bear¹ /beə $ ber/ *v* [T] past tense **bore** /bɔː $ bɔːr/ past participle **borne** /bɔːn $ bɔːrn/

1 can't bear sb/sth to dislike someone or something very much, or to feel unable to do something because it is so unpleasant [= **can't stand**]: *She really can't bear him.* | **can't bear (sb) doing sth** *I can't bear people shouting at me.* | *He can't bear the thought of starting again.* | **can't bear to do sth** *It was so horrible I couldn't bear to watch.* **2** to bravely accept or deal with something that is unpleasant [= **stand, tolerate**]: *For Etty, the loss was very hard to bear.* | *The pain was almost more than she could bear.* | *They just had to grin and bear it* (=not complain). **3 bear in mind sth** to not forget a fact or idea: **+that** *Bear in mind that this method may not work.* **4** to be responsible for something: **bear the responsibility/blame** *He must bear some of the blame.* | **bear the burden/costs 5 bear a resemblance/relation to sb/sth** to be similar to or related to someone or something: *The child bore a striking resemblance to his father.* **6** *formal* to have a particular name or appearance [= **have**]: *the company that bore her father's name* | *The town still bore the scars of war.* **7 bear fruit** if a plan or decision bears fruit, it is successful **8 bear witness to sth** *formal* to show that something is true or exists: *The film bears witness to her skill as a director.* **9** to support the weight of something [= **hold**]: *Her ankle was sore, but it was bearing her weight.* **10** *formal* to bring or carry something: *They came bearing gifts.* **11** *formal* to have bad feelings towards someone: *I don't bear a grudge* (=still feel angry about something). **12 bear with me** *spoken* used to politely ask someone to wait while you do something: *Bear with me for a moment and I'll check.* **13 bear right/left** to turn towards the right or left: *Bear left at the lights.* **14** *formal* to give birth to a baby **15 sth doesn't bear thinking about** used to say that something is very upsetting or shocking: *The long-term effects don't bear thinking about.*

→ **bear the brunt of sth** at BRUNT

bear down on sb/sth *phr v* to move quickly towards someone or something in a threatening way: *The truck bore down on them.*

bear sth ⇔ **out** *phr v* to show that something is true: *Our fears were borne out by the research.*

bear up *phr v* to succeed in being brave and determined during a difficult or upsetting time: *How's she bearing up?*

bear

bear² *n* [C] a large strong animal with thick fur → POLAR BEAR, TEDDY BEAR

bearable /'beərəbəl $ 'ber-/ *adj* something that is bearable is possible to accept or deal with, although it is very unpleasant

beard /bɪəd $ bɪrd/ *n* [C] the hair that grows on a man's chin

—**bearded** *adj* → see picture at HAIR

bearer /'beərə $ 'berər/ *n* [C] someone who brings or carries something: **+of** *the bearer of bad news*

bearing /'beərɪŋ $ 'ber-/ *n* **1 have a bearing on sth** to have an influence or effect on something: *His age had no bearing on our decision.* **2 lose your bearings** to become confused about where you are **3 get your bearings** to find out where you are or what you should do

beast /biːst/ *n* [C] *literary* a wild animal

beat¹ /biːt/ *v* past tense **beat** past participle **beaten** /'biːtn/

1 [T] to get more points, votes etc than other people in a game or competition: *Spain beat Italy 3–1.* | *It was clear that the Democrats could not beat the Republicans.* | **beat the record/ score etc** (=do something better, faster etc than it has been done before) *He beat the world record by eleven seconds.* **2** [T] to hit someone or something violently many times: *He had been badly beaten.* | *The girl was beaten to death.* | **beat the door down/in** (=hit it until it opens or breaks) **3** [I,T] to hit against the surface of something continuously, or to make something do this: **+on/against** *The rain beat loudly on the roof.* | **beat sth on/against sth** *A bird was beating its wings against the wire netting.* **4** [T] to mix food together quickly using a fork or a kitchen tool: *Beat the eggs.* → see box at RECIPE → see picture on page A4 **5** [I] to make a regular movement or sound: *My heart was beating.* | *We could hear drums beating.* **6** [T] to deal successfully with a problem, illness etc: *The government has promised to beat inflation.* | *advice on how to beat depression* **7** [T] *spoken* to be better or more enjoyable than something: **beat doing sth** *It beats going to* *work.* | **You can't beat** *a good book* (=nothing is better).

8 (it) beats me *spoken* used to say that you do not understand or know something: *'What's his problem?' 'Beats me!'*

9 beat about/around the bush to avoid talking about something unpleasant or embarrassing: *Don't beat about the bush – what is it?*

10 beat a (hasty) retreat to leave very quickly, in order to avoid trouble

→ **off the beaten track/path** at **BEATEN**

beat down *phr v* **1** if the sun beats down, it shines brightly and is hot **2** if the rain beats down, it rains very hard

beat sb/sth ⇔ **off** *phr v* to succeed in defeating someone who is attacking you

beat sb **to** sth *phr v* to get or do something before someone else: *I applied for the job but someone beat me to it.*

beat sb ⇔ **up** *phr v* to hit someone until they are badly hurt

beat² *n* **1** [C] one of a series of regular movements or sounds: **+of** *the steady beat of his heart* **2** [singular] the pattern of sounds in a piece of music **3** [singular] the area that a police officer walks around regularly: *We need more police on the beat* (=walking around the streets).

beat³ *adj especially AmE informal* very tired → see box at **TIRED**

beaten /ˈbiːtn/ *adj* **off the beaten track/path** far away from places that people usually visit

beating /ˈbiːtɪŋ/ *n* [C] **1** when someone is hit many times, for example in a fight: *a brutal beating* **2 take a beating** to lose very badly in a game or competition

'beat-up *adj informal* a beat-up car, bicycle etc is old and in bad condition

beautician /bjuːˈtɪʃən/ *n* [C] someone whose job is to give beauty treatment to your skin, hair etc

beautiful /ˈbjuːtɪfəl/ *adj*

1 extremely attractive to look at: *She was the most beautiful woman in the world.* | *a stunningly beautiful area* → see box at **ATTRACTIVE**

2 very good or giving you great pleasure [= lovely]: *The weather was beautiful.* | *a beautiful piece of music*

—**beautifully** *adv*

beauty /ˈbjuːti/ *n plural* **beauties**

1 [U] the quality of being beautiful: *a woman of great beauty* | **+of** *the beauty of the Swiss Alps* | **beauty treatments/products** (=to make you more attractive)

2 [C] *informal* something that is very good or impressive: *That motorcycle's a real beauty.*

3 the beauty of sth is … used to explain why something is especially good: *The beauty of email is that it's fast.*

4 [C] *old-fashioned* a woman who is very beautiful

'beauty ˌsalon / $ '.. .,./ also **'beauty ˌparlor** *AmE n* [C] a place where you can have beauty treatments for your skin, hair etc

'beauty spot *n* [C] a beautiful place in the countryside

beaver¹ /ˈbiːvə $ -ər/ *n* [C] a North American animal with thick fur and a wide flat tail

beaver² *v*

beaver away *phr v* to work hard in a very busy way

became /bɪˈkeɪm/ *v* the past tense of **BECOME**

because /bɪˈkɒz, bɪkəz $ bɪˈkɒːz, bɪkəz/ *linking word*

1 used when you are giving the reason for something: *You can't go because you're too young.* | **partly/largely/mainly because** *I'd never leave, partly because I'd get homesick.* | *Students lose marks* **simply because** *they haven't read the question properly.* | **because of sth/sb** *We didn't have a picnic because of the rain.*

2 just because … *spoken* used to say that although one thing is true, it does not mean that something else is true: *Just because you're older, it doesn't mean you can tell me what to do.*

beck /bek/ *n* **be at sb's beck and call** to always be ready to do what someone wants

beckon /ˈbekən/ *v* [I,T] to move your hand to show that you want someone to move towards you: **beckon (to) sb to do sth** *He beckoned to them to follow him.*

become /bɪˈkʌm/ *v past tense* **became** /-ˈkeɪm/ *past participle* **become**

1 [linking verb] to begin to be something, or to feel something: *Kennedy became the first Catholic president.* | *It is becoming harder to find good staff.* | *Helen was becoming increasingly anxious.*

THESAURUS

You can use **get** and **go** to mean the same as **become** in front of adjectives: *It's getting dark outside.* | *I was getting very tired.* | *My hair's going grey.* But you must use **become** in front of a noun: *He wants to become a teacher.* In spoken English, you usually say **get** or **go**. **Become** is more formal.

---

2 become of sb/sth to happen to someone or something: **Whatever became of** *those old photos?* | *I don't know* **what will become of** *him when she dies.*

beds

sheet

single bed

pillow

double bed

bunk beds

duvet *BrE*/comforter *AmE*

camp bed *BrE*/
cot *AmE*

cot *BrE*/crib *AmE*

bed /bed/ *n*

1 [C,U] a piece of furniture for sleeping on: **in bed** *Sam lay in bed thinking.* | **get into/out of bed** *She had just got out of bed.* | *Jamie usually* **goes to bed** (=for the night) *at around 7 o'clock.* |

Have you made your bed (=tidied the covers)? | **a single/double bed** (=for one person or two people)
2 [C] the ground at the bottom of the ocean, a river, or a lake: *the sea bed*
3 [C] an area of ground that has been prepared for plants to grow in: *flower beds*
4 [singular] a layer of something that is a base for something else: **on a bed** *prawns on a bed of lettuce*
→ **bunk beds** at BUNK → CAMP BED

,bed and 'breakfast also **B&B** *n* [C] a house or a small hotel where you pay to sleep and have breakfast → see box at ACCOMMODATION

bedclothes /'bedkləʊðz, -kləʊz $ -kloʊðz, -kloʊz/ *n* [plural] BEDDING

bedding /'bedɪŋ/ *n* [U] **1** the sheets, BLANKETS etc that you put on a bed **2** something soft that an animal sleeps on, such as dried grass

bedlam /'bedləm/ *n* [U] a situation where there is a lot of noise and confusion: *When the bomb exploded, there was bedlam.*

bedraggled /bɪ'dræɡəld/ *adj* wet and untidy

bedridden /'bed,rɪdn/ *adj* not able to get out of bed because you are old or ill

bedrock /'bedrɒk $ -rɑːk/ *n* [singular] the ideas, people, or facts which provide a strong base for something: *Honesty is the bedrock of a good relationship.*

bedroom /'bedrum, -ruːm/ *n* [C] a room for sleeping in: *John's in his bedroom.* | *a two-bedroom flat*

bedside /'bedsaɪd/ *n* [C] the area around a bed: *a bedside table*

bedsit /,bed'sɪt/, **bedsitter** /,bed'sɪtə $ -ər/, **,bed-'sitting room** *n* [C] *BrE* a rented room which you live and sleep in

bedspread /'bedspred/ *n* [C] a large cover that goes on top of a bed

bedtime /'bedtaɪm/ *n* [C,U] the time when you usually go to bed: *It's past your bedtime!*

bee /biː/ *n* [C] a black and yellow flying insect that makes HONEY

beech /biːtʃ/ *n* [C,U] a large tree that has a smooth grey surface

beef¹ /biːf/ *n* [U] meat from a cow: *roast beef* | *a joint of beef* → see box at MEAT → GROUND BEEF

beef² *v*
  beef sth ⇔ **up** *phr v informal* to improve something, especially by making it bigger or stronger: *Security around the palace has been beefed up since the attack.*

beefburger /'biːfbɜːɡə $ -bɜːrɡər/ *n* [C] *BrE* very small pieces of beef made into a flat round shape and cooked [= hamburger, burger]

beefy /'biːfi/ *adj informal* a beefy man is big and strong

beehive /'biːhaɪv/ *n* [C] a place where BEES are kept to produce HONEY [= hive]

beeline /'biːlaɪn/ *n* **make a beeline for sb/sth** *informal* to go quickly and directly towards someone or something: *The children made a beeline for the food.*

been /biːn, bɪn $ bɪn/ *v* **1** the past participle of BE **2** **have been to (do) sth** used to say that someone has gone to a place and come back: *Kate has just been to Japan.* | *Have you been to see the new James Bond film yet?*

beep /biːp/ *v* **1** [I] if a machine beeps, it makes a short high sound: *The heart monitor started beeping.* **2** [I,T] if a horn beeps, or you beep it, it makes a loud noise —**beep** *n* [C]

beeper /'biːpə $ -ər/ *n* [C] a small machine that you carry with you, which makes a sound to tell you to telephone someone [= pager]

beer /bɪə $ bɪr/ *n* [C,U] an alcoholic drink made from grain, or a glass of this drink: *a pint of beer* | *Would you like a beer?*

beet /biːt/ *n* [C,U] **1** also **sugar beet** a vegetable that sugar is made from **2** *AmE* a dark red vegetable that is the root of a plant [= beetroot *BrE*]

beetle /'biːtl/ *n* [C] an insect with a hard round back

beetroot /'biːtruːt/ *n* [C] *BrE* a dark red vegetable that is the root of a plant [= beet *AmE*]

befall /bɪ'fɔːl $ -'fɔːl/ *v* [I,T] past tense **befell** /-'fel/ past participle **befallen** /-'fɔːlən $ -'fɔːlən/ *formal* if something unpleasant or dangerous befalls you, it happens to you: *the terrible things that had befallen him*

befit /bɪ'fɪt/ *v* [T] **befitted, befitting** *formal* to seem suitable or good enough for someone: *a funeral befitting a national hero*

before¹ /bɪ'fɔː $ -'fɔːr/ *prep*
1 earlier than something or someone [≠ after]: *I usually shower before breakfast.* | *We got home before the others.* | *You need to check in an hour before your flight.* | *We got back **the day before yesterday** (=two days ago).*
2 in front of someone or something else in a list or order [≠ after]: *S comes before T in the alphabet.*
3 used to say that one thing or person is considered more important than another: *She always puts her family before her career.*
4 if one place is before another as you go towards it, you will reach it first [≠ after]: *Turn right just before the station.*
5 *formal* in front of: *The priest knelt before the altar.*

before² *adv* at an earlier time: *They'd met before, at one of Sally's parties.* | **the day/week/month etc before** *We were in Paris last week and Rome the week before.*

before³ *linking word*
1 earlier than the time when something happens: *John wants to talk to you before you go.*
2 so that something does not happen: *You'd better lock your bike before it gets stolen.* | *I sat down before she could change her mind.*

beforehand /bɪ'fɔːhænd $ -'fɔːr-/ *adv* before something happens: *When you give a speech, it's natural to feel nervous beforehand.*

befriend /bɪ'frend/ *v* [T] to become someone's friend, especially someone who needs your help

befuddled /bɪ'fʌdəld/ *adj* completely confused

beg /beɡ/ *v* **begged, begging** **1** [I,T] to ask for something in a way which shows you want it very much: **beg (sb) to do sth** *I begged her to stay, but she wouldn't.* | *a prisoner begging to be released* | **beg (sb) for sth** *They begged for mercy.* | *He rang a friend to beg for his help.* → see box at ASK **2** [I] to ask someone for food, money etc because you are very poor: *children begging in the streets* **3** **I beg your pardon** *spoken*

B

a) used to ask someone politely to repeat something: *'It's 7 o'clock.' 'I beg your pardon?' 'I said it's 7 o'clock.'* **b)** *formal* used to say sorry for something you have said or done: *Oh, I beg your pardon, did I step on your toe?* **c)** *formal* used to show that you strongly disagree: *'New York's a terrible place.' 'I beg your pardon, that's my home town!'*

beggar /'begə $ -ər/ n [C] someone who lives by asking people for food and money

begin /bɪ'gɪn/ v past tense **began** /-'gæn/ past participle **begun** /-'gʌn/ present participle **beginning**

1 [I,T] to start doing something, or to start to happen or exist: *The meeting will begin at 10:00.* | *Tomorrow the President will begin talks with several European heads of state.* | **begin to do sth** *It's beginning to rain.* | *He began to cry.* | **begin doing sth** *I began teaching in 1992.*
2 [I] **a)** if you begin with something or begin by doing something, you do it first: **+with** *Let's begin with exercise 5.* | **begin by doing sth** *May I begin by thanking you all for coming.* **b)** if a book, film, word etc begins with something, that is how it starts: *It begins with a description of the author's home.*
3 to begin with a) used to introduce the first or most important point: *To begin with, you mustn't take the car without asking.* **b)** used to say what something was already like before something else happened: *I didn't break it! It was like that to begin with.* **c)** in the first part of an activity or process: *The children helped me to begin with, but they soon got bored.*

beginner /bɪ'gɪnə $ -ər/ n [C] someone who has just started to do or learn something: *a class for beginners*

beginning /bɪ'gɪnɪŋ/ n [C, usually singular] the start or first part of something: **+of** *the beginning of the war* | *We've been here since the beginning of the year.* | **at the beginning** *At the beginning of the film, she's in London.* | **from the beginning** *Read it again, from the beginning.* | **in the beginning** *You should have told me in the beginning if there was a problem.*

begrudge /bɪ'grʌdʒ/ v [T] to feel upset and angry about something: *Honestly, I don't begrudge him his success.* | *I begrudge spending so much money on train fares.*

beguiling /bɪ'gaɪlɪŋ/ adj literary attractive and interesting

begun /bɪ'gʌn/ v the past participle of BEGIN

behalf /bɪ'hɑːf $ bɪ'hæf/ n **on behalf of sb/on sb's behalf** instead of someone: *He agreed to speak on my behalf.*

behave /bɪ'heɪv/ v [I]

1 to do things of a particular kind: *He's been behaving very oddly recently.* | *He began behaving differently towards me.* | *She behaved in a very responsible way.* | **+like** *Stop behaving like a child!*
2 to be polite and not cause trouble [≠ misbehave]: *Will you boys please behave!* | **behave yourself** *If you behave yourself you can have an ice-cream.* | **well-behaved/badly-behaved** *a badly-behaved class*

behaviour *BrE*; **behavior** *AmE* /bɪ'heɪvjə $ -ər/ n [U]

1 the things that a person or animal does: *I'm*

not very pleased with your behaviour.* | **good/bad behaviour** *Reward your children for good behaviour.* | **+towards** *violent behaviour towards police officers* | **human/social/sexual etc behaviour** *normal patterns of human behaviour*
2 *technical* the things that something in science normally does: *the behaviour of cancer cells*
—**behavioural** adj

behead /bɪ'hed/ v [T] to cut someone's head off as a punishment

beheld /bɪ'held/ v the past tense and past participle of BEHOLD

behind¹ /bɪ'haɪnd/ prep

1 at the back of something: *the person standing behind me* | *He stepped out from behind the counter.* | *The car park is **right behind** (=just behind) the supermarket.* → see picture on page A8
2 not as successful or making as much progress as someone or something else: *We're three points behind the other team.* | *The building work is three months **behind schedule** (=later than it should be).*
3 responsible for something or causing it to happen: *The same gang is believed to be behind all the robberies.*
4 supporting a person, idea etc: *We're all behind the plan.*
5 behind the times old-fashioned

behind² adv

1 at the back of something: *George was following close behind.* | **from behind** *He grabbed me from behind.*
2 in the place where someone or something was before: *I decided to **stay behind** and work.* | *When I got there I realized I'd **left** the tickets behind.*
3 be/get behind to be late or slow in doing something: *We are three months behind with the rent.*

behind³ n [C] informal the part of your body that you sit on [= bottom]

behold /bɪ'həʊld $ -'hoʊld/ v [T] past tense and past participle **beheld** /-'held/ literary to see something —**beholder** n [C]

beige /beɪʒ/ n [U] a pale brown colour —**beige** adj

being¹ /'biːɪŋ/ v the present participle of BE

being² n **1** [C] a living person or imaginary creature: *strange beings from outer space*
2 come into being to begin to exist: *a law that came into being in 1912*

belated /bɪ'leɪtɪd/ adj happening or arriving late: *a belated birthday card* —**belatedly** adv

belch /beltʃ/ v **1** [I] to let air come out noisily through your mouth from your stomach [= burp]
2 [T] to produce a lot of smoke or fire: *factories belching black smoke* —**belch** n [C]

beleaguered /bɪ'liːgəd $ -ərd/ adj formal having a lot of problems: *the country's beleaguered motor industry*

belie /bɪ'laɪ/ v [T] belied, belying, belies formal to give you a wrong idea about something: *He has an energy that belies his 85 years.*

belief /bɪ'liːf/ n plural beliefs

1 [singular, U] the feeling that something is definitely true or definitely exists: **+that** *the belief that children learn best through playing* |

+in *a strong belief in magic* | *Contrary to popular belief* (=despite what most people believe), *exercise is not always good for you.*
2 [singular] the feeling that someone or something is good, important, or right: **+in** *He has a strong belief in the importance of education.*
3 [C usually plural] an idea or set of ideas that you think are true: *different communities with different religious beliefs*
4 beyond belief used to emphasize that something is very bad, good, strange etc: *It seemed cruel beyond belief.*

believe /bɪˈliːv/ *v*
1 [T] to think that something is true or that someone is telling the truth: *Do you believe his story?* | *I don't believe you!* | **+(that)** *I can't believe he's only 25!* | *I found his explanation hard to believe.* → see box at **THINK**
2 [T] to have a particular opinion about something, without being completely sure: **+(that)** *I believe she'll be back on Monday.* | *It is believed that three people were killed in the accident.*
3 [T] used in some phrases to show that you are surprised or shocked: **can't/don't believe sth** *I can't believe you lied to me!* | **Would you believe it**, *he even remembered my birthday!* | *He could hardly believe his eyes* (=was very surprised) *when he looked out of his window.*
4 believe it or not *spoken* used when something is true but surprising: *Believe it or not, I don't actually dislike him.*
5 [I] to have religious faith
—believable *adj*
  believe in sth *phr v* **1** to be sure that something or someone definitely exists: *Do you believe in ghosts?* **2** to think that someone or something is good, important, or right: *We believe in democracy.* | *I believe in being honest and telling the truth.*

believer /bɪˈliːvə $ -ər/ *n* [C] **1** someone who believes that a particular idea or thing is very good: **firm/great believer in sth** *I'm a great believer in healthy eating.* **2** someone who believes in a particular religion

belittle /bɪˈlɪtl/ *v* [T] *formal* to say that something is less important than it really is: *Why do they always try to belittle our efforts!*

bell /bel/ *n* [C]
1 a piece of electrical equipment that makes a ringing sound: *I rang the front door bell but no one answered.*
2 a metal object that makes a ringing sound when you hit it or shake it
→ **ring a bell** at **RING²**

belligerent /bɪˈlɪdʒərənt/ *adj formal* wanting to fight or argue

bellow /ˈbeləʊ $ -loʊ/ *v* [I,T] to shout something in a very loud voice

belly /ˈbeli/ *n* [C] plural **bellies** *informal* your stomach, or the part of your body between your chest and the top of your legs

'belly ,button *n* [C] *informal* the small hole just below your waist on the front of your body [= navel]

belong /bɪˈlɒŋ $ bɪˈlɔːŋ/ *v* [I]
1 if something belongs in a place, that is the place where it should go: **+in/on/by etc** *Books like that don't belong in the classroom.* | *Please put the chair back where it belongs.*

2 if you belong somewhere, you feel happy there: *She felt she didn't belong in the city.*
  belong to sb/sth *phr v* **1** if something belongs to you, you own it: *Does this umbrella belong to you?* **2** if you belong to an organization, you are a member of it: *I don't belong to the tennis club.*

belongings /bɪˈlɒŋɪŋz $ bɪˈlɔːŋ-/ *n* [plural] the things that you own, especially things that you carry with you: *Please take all your personal belongings with you.* → see box at **OWN**

beloved /bɪˈlʌvɪd/ *adj literary* loved very much: *my beloved wife, Fiona*

below /bɪˈləʊ $ -ˈloʊ/ *adv, prep*
1 in a lower place or position than someone or something else [≠ above]: *Jake lives in the apartment below.* | *fish that feed just below the surface of the water* → see picture on page A8
2 less than a particular number or amount [≠ over]: *Anything below £500 would be a good price.* | *The temperature was well below zero.*
3 on a later page or lower on the same page [≠ above]: *For more information, see below.*
4 lower in rank: *Is a captain below a general?*

belt¹ /belt/ *n* [C]
1 a band of leather or cloth that you wear around your waist → see picture at **CLOTHES**
2 a circular band of material such as rubber that moves parts of a machine: *the car's fan belt*
3 a large area of land: *America's farming belt*
4 have sth under your belt to have already done something useful or important: *I want to get this qualification under my belt.*
→ **CONVEYOR BELT, GREEN BELT, SAFETY BELT, SEAT BELT**

belt² *v* [T] *informal* to hit someone or something hard
  belt sth ⇔ **out** *phr v* to sing a song very loudly

belying /bɪˈlaɪ-ɪŋ/ *v* the present participle of BELIE

bemoan /bɪˈməʊn $ -ˈmoʊn/ *v* [T] *formal* to say that you are unhappy about something: *He was bemoaning the fact that lawyers charge so much.*

bemused /bɪˈmjuːzd/ *adj* slightly confused: *a bemused expression*

bench /bentʃ/ *n*
1 [C] a long wooden seat for two or more people: *We sat on a park bench to eat our sandwiches.* **2 the bench** *law* the judges who work in a court

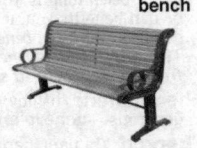
bench

benchmark /ˈbentʃmɑːk $ -mɑːrk/ *n* [C] something that is used for comparing and measuring other things: **+for** *The test results provide a benchmark for measuring student achievement.*

bend¹ /bend/ *v* past tense and past participle **bent** /bent/
1 [I,T] to move a part of your body so that it is not straight or so that you are not standing upright: *Bend your knees slightly.* | **+down/over** *He bent down to tie his shoelace.* → see picture on page A11
2 [T] to push or press something so that it is no longer flat or straight: *You've bent the handle.*

3 bend over backwards to try very hard to help someone: *Our new neighbours bent over backwards to help us when we moved house.*
→ **bend the rules** at RULE¹

bend² *n* [C] a curve in something, especially a road or river: *a sharp bend in the road* → HAIRPIN BEND

beneath /bɪˈniːθ/ *adv, prep*
1 under or below something: *the warm sand beneath her feet* | *He stood on the bridge, looking at the water beneath.*
2 if someone or something is beneath you, you think that they are not good enough for you: *She seemed to think that talking to us was beneath her.*

benefactor /ˈbenɪˌfæktə $ -ər/ *n* [C] *formal* someone who gives money or help to someone else

beneficial /ˌbenɪˈfɪʃəl◂/ *adj* helpful or useful: **+to** *The agreement will be beneficial to both groups.*

beneficiary /ˌbenɪˈfɪʃəri $ -ˈfɪʃieri/ *n* [C] plural **beneficiaries** *formal* someone who gets an advantage from something which happens: *Businesses were the main beneficiaries of the tax cuts.*

benefit¹ /ˈbenɪfɪt/ *n*
1 [C,U] an advantage or improvement that you get from something: **+of** *What are the benefits of contact lenses?* | *The new credit cards will be of great benefit to our customers.* | **for sb's benefit** (=in order to help them) *Liu Han translated what the minister said for my benefit.*
2 [C,U] *BrE* money that you get from the government when you are ill or when you do not have a job [= **welfare** *AmE*]: *You may be entitled to unemployment benefit.* | **on benefit(s)** (=receiving benefits) *All his family are on benefits.* → see box at MONEY
3 [C] a performance, concert etc that makes money for a CHARITY
4 give sb the benefit of the doubt to believe or trust someone even though it is possible that they are lying or are wrong
→ **CHILD BENEFIT, FRINGE BENEFIT**

benefit² *v* [I,T] past tense and past participle **benefited** or **benefitted**, present participle **benefiting** or **benefitting** if you benefit from something or if it benefits you, it helps you: *The new policy changes mainly benefit small companies.* | **+from/by** *Most of these children would benefit from an extra year at school.*

benevolent /bɪˈnevələnt/ *adj formal* kind and generous —**benevolence** *n* [U]

benign /bɪˈnaɪn/ *adj* **1** *technical* a benign TUMOUR is not caused by CANCER [≠ **malignant**] **2** *formal* kind and gentle

bent¹ /bent/ *v* the past tense and past participle of BEND

bent² *adj* **1** no longer straight or flat: *a bent nail* | *She was bent double* (=with the top part of her body leaning forward) *in pain.* **2 be bent on (doing) sth** to be determined to do something or have something: *Mendoza was bent on getting a better job.* **3** *BrE informal* someone who is bent is not honest

bent³ *n* [singular] *formal* a skill or interest that someone has: *readers of a more literary bent*

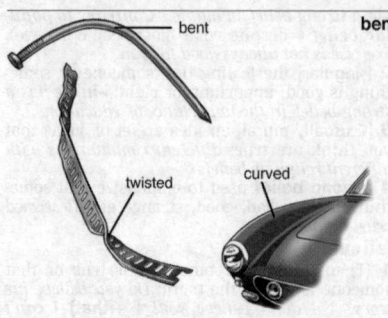

bent   bent
twisted   curved

bequeath /bɪˈkwiːð, bɪˈkwiːθ/ *v* [T] *formal* to arrange that someone will get something you own after you die

bequest /bɪˈkwest/ *n* [C] *formal* something that you arrange to give to someone after you have died

berate /bɪˈreɪt/ *v* [T] *formal* to speak angrily to someone because they have done something wrong

bereaved /bɪˈriːvd/ *adj formal* if someone is bereaved, someone they love has died —**bereavement** *n* [C,U]

bereft /bɪˈreft/ *adj formal* **1 bereft of sth** completely without something: *bereft of all hope* **2** feeling sad and alone

beret /ˈbereɪ $ bəˈreɪ/ *n* [C] a soft round flat hat → see picture at HAT

berry /ˈberi/ *n* [C] plural **berries** a small soft fruit with small seeds

berserk /bɜːˈsɜːk, bə- $ bɜːrˈsɜːrk, ˈbɜːrsɜːrk/ *adj* **go berserk** *informal* to become very angry and violent in a crazy way: *The guy went berserk and started hitting Paul.*

berth /bɜːθ $ bɜːrθ/ *n* [C] **1** a place to sleep on a train or boat **2** the place where a ship comes to land

beseech /bɪˈsiːtʃ/ *v* [T] past tense and past participle **besought** /-ˈsɔːt $ -ˈsɒːt/ or **beseeched** *literary* to eagerly and anxiously ask someone for something [= **beg**]

beset /bɪˈset/ *v* [T] past tense and past participle **beset**, present participle **besetting** *formal* to cause trouble for someone: *The family was beset by financial difficulties.*

beside /bɪˈsaɪd/ *prep*
1 next to or very close to someone or something: *Gary sat down beside me.* | *a cabin right beside the lake* → see picture on page A8
2 used to compare two people or things: *This year's sales figures don't look very good beside last year's.*
3 be beside the point to not be important: *'I'm not hungry.' 'That's beside the point, you need to eat!'*
4 be beside yourself (with anger/fear/grief/ joy etc) to feel a particular emotion very strongly: *The boy was beside himself with fury.*

besides /bɪˈsaɪdz/ *adv, prep* **1** *spoken* used when adding another reason: *I wanted to help her out. Besides, I needed the money.* **2** in addition to something or someone else: *Was there* *anyone else you knew besides Steve?* | **besides doing sth** *Besides going to college, she works fifteen hours a week.*

besiege /bɪˈsiːdʒ/ v **1 be besieged by people/worries/thoughts etc** to be surrounded by a lot of people or to be very worried etc: *a rock star besieged by fans* **2 be besieged with letters/questions/demands etc** to receive a lot of letters, be asked a lot of questions etc: *The radio station was besieged with letters of complaint.* **3** [T] if an army besieges a place, soldiers surround it

besotted /bɪˈsɒtɪd $ bɪˈsɑː-/ adj loving someone or something so much that you seem silly: **+with** *He's completely besotted with her.*

besought /bɪˈsɔːt $ -ˈsɒːt/ v the past tense and past participle of BESEECH

bespectacled /bɪˈspektəkəld/ adj formal wearing glasses

best[1] /best/ adj [the superlative of 'good'] better than anyone or anything else: *the best player on the team* | *What's the **best way** to get to El Paso?* | *The **best thing** to do is to ask Mum first.* | *Who is your **best friend**?*
→ SECOND BEST

best[2] adv [the superlative of 'well']
1 more than anyone else or anything else: *Helen knows him best.* | *Which song do you like best?* | *She's **best known** for her role in 'Friends'.*
2 in a way that is better than any other: *It works best if you warm it up first.*
3 as best you can as well as you can: *She would have to manage as best she could.*

best[3] n **1 the best a)** someone or something that is better than any others: *Which stereo is the best?* **b)** the most successful situation or results you can achieve: *All parents want the best for their children.* **2 do/try your best** to try as hard as you can to achieve something: *I did my best, but I still didn't pass.* **3 at best** used to emphasize that something is not very good, even when you consider it in the best possible way: *You should get 10 or, at best, 11 thousand dollars pension.* **4 at your best** doing something as well as you are able to: *The movie shows Hollywood at its best.* **5 make the best of sth** to accept a bad situation and do what you can to make it better: *It's not going to be easy, but we'll just have to make the best of it.* **6 be (all) for the best** used to say that something seems bad now, but might have a good result later: *I'll be sad to see her leave, but maybe it's for the best.*

,best 'man n [singular] a friend of a BRIDEGROOM (=man who is getting married), who helps him to get ready and stands next to him during the wedding → see box at WEDDING

bestow /bɪˈstəʊ $ -ˈstoʊ/ v [T] formal to give someone something of great value or importance

bestseller /ˌbestˈselə $ -ər/ n [C] a popular product, especially a book, which a lot of people buy —**best-selling** adj [only before noun] *a best-selling novel*

bet[1] /bet/ v past tense and past participle **bet**, present participle **betting**
1 [I,T] to try to win money by saying what the result of a race, game, or competition will be: **bet (sb) that** *I bet him £5 that he wouldn't win.* |

bet (sth) on sth *She bet all her money on a horse that came last.*
2 I bet, I'll bet spoken **a)** used to say that you are sure that something is true or happened: *I bet they'll be late.* | *I bet she was surprised when she saw you at the party.* **b)** used to show that you agree with someone or understand how they feel: *'I was furious.' 'I bet you were!'* **c)** used to show that you do not believe someone: *'I'm definitely going to give up smoking.' 'Yeah, I bet.'*
3 you bet! spoken used to say 'yes' in a very definite way: *'Would you like to come?' 'You bet!'*
—**betting** n [U]

bet[2] n [C]
1 a) if you have a bet on something, you try to win money by saying what the result of a game, race, or competition will be: **+on** *I had a bet on the match.* | **win/lose a bet** *If he scores now, I'll win my bet.* **b)** the money that you risk in order to try to win more money: *a $10 bet*
2 your best bet spoken used when advising someone what to do: *Your best bet would be to avoid the motorway.*
3 a good/safe bet something that is likely to be useful or successful: *This shop is always a good bet for presents.*
→ hedge your bets at HEDGE[2]

betray /bɪˈtreɪ/ v [T] **1** to behave dishonestly towards someone who loves you or trusts you: *Her husband had betrayed her by lying to her.* **2** to be disloyal to your country, company etc, for example by giving secret information to its enemies **3** to show feelings that you are trying to hide: *His voice betrayed his nervousness.*

betrayal /bɪˈtreɪəl/ n [C,U] when someone betrays another person

better[1] /ˈbetə $ -ər/ adj
1 of higher quality, or more useful, interesting, skilful etc [≠ worse]: *We need a better computer.* | **+than** *Your stereo is better than mine.* | **+at** *My sister's better at maths than I am.* | **much/a lot/far better** *We now have a much better understanding of the disease.* | **better still/even better** *It was even better than last year.* | *Your English is **getting better** (=improving).*
2 less ill than you were, or no longer ill [≠ worse]: *She's a little better today.* | *Are you feeling better?* | *I hope your sore throat gets better soon.*
3 it is better/it would be better used to give advice about what someone should do: **it is better to do sth** *It's much better to get a proper written agreement.* | **+if** *It would be better if you stayed here.*
4 the sooner the better/the bigger the better etc used to say that something should happen as soon as possible, be as big as possible etc: *Fetch a large vase, the bigger the better.*
5 have seen better days informal to be in a bad condition: *The sofa had seen better days.*

better[2] adv
1 to a higher standard or quality: **+than** *He speaks English better than I do.*
2 more: *This jacket suits me better.* | **+than** *I knew her better than anyone else.*
3 had better spoken **a)** used to say what someone should do: *You'd better go and get ready.* | *I think I'd better leave now.* **b)** used to

threaten someone: *You'd better keep your mouth shut about this.*
4 do better to perform better or reach a higher standard: **+than** *We did better than all the other schools.*

better³ *n* **1 the better** the one that is the higher in quality, more suitable etc when you are comparing two similar people or things: *It's hard to decide which one's the better.* **2 get the better of sb a)** if a feeling gets the better of you, you do not control it when you should: *His curiosity got the better of him and he opened the letter.* **b)** to defeat someone **3 for the better** in a way that improves the situation: *a definite change for the better*

better⁴ *v* [T] *formal* to achieve something that is better than something else: *Jim's total of five gold medals is unlikely to be bettered.*

better 'off *adj* **1** if you are better off, you have more money than you had before: *We plan to reduce taxes and make all families better off.* **2** happier, improved, more successful etc: **+with/ without** *She's better off without him.* **3 you/he/she etc would be better off doing sth** *spoken* used to say what someone should do: *You'd be better off doing the exam next year, when you're ready for it.*

'betting ,shop *n* [C] *BrE* a place where people go to BET on the results of races, games etc [= bookmaker]

between /bɪˈtwiːn/ *adv, prep*

1 also **in between** with one thing or person on each side: *He sat between the two women on the sofa.* | *two houses with a narrow path in between* → see picture on page A8

THESAURUS

Between and **among** are both used to talk about the position of someone or something. Use **between** when there is one other person or thing on each side of someone or something: *I sat between Alex and Sarah.* Use **among** when there are two or more people or things on each side of someone or something: *The hut was hidden among the trees.*

2 used to say that a place is in the middle with other places at a distance from it: *Oxford is between London and Birmingham.*
3 used to say which two places are connected by something: *They're building a new road between Manchester and Sheffield.*
4 also **in between** after one event or time and before another: *I didn't see my parents at all between Christmas and Easter.* | *He had a year off between leaving school and going to university.* | *I have a lesson at nine o'clock and another at three o'clock, but nothing in between.*
5 used to show a range of amounts, by giving the largest and smallest: *My journey to school takes between 30 and 40 minutes.* | *children aged between 7 and 11*
6 used to show who is involved in a relationship, agreement, fight etc: *The relationship between them has always been friendly.* | *an agreement between the company and the trade unions* | *the war between England and France*
7 used to say that something is shared by each

person in a group: *Tom divided his money between his children.*
8 used to say which two things or people you are comparing: *the contrast between town and country life*
9 if people have an amount of money between them, that is the total amount they have: *We had ten dollars between us.*
→ GO-BETWEEN

beverage /ˈbevərɪdʒ/ *n* [C] *formal* a drink: *We don't sell alcoholic beverages.*

beware /bɪˈweə $ -ˈwer/ *v* [I,T] used to warn someone to be careful: **+of** *Beware of the dog!* | **beware of doing sth** *They should beware of making hasty decisions.*

bewildered /bɪˈwɪldəd $ -ərd/ *adj* confused and not sure what to do or think: *The children looked bewildered and scared.* —**bewilderment** *n* [U]

bewildering /bɪˈwɪldərɪŋ/ *adj* confusing: *a bewildering variety of choices*

bewitch /bɪˈwɪtʃ/ *v* [T] if something bewitches you, you are so interested in it that you cannot think about anything else: *He was bewitched by her smile.*

beyond /bɪˈjɒnd $ -ˈjɑːnd/ *prep, adv*

1 if something is beyond a place, it is on the side of it that is farthest away from you: *There was a forest beyond the river.* | *We got a lovely view of the river, and the mountains beyond.*
2 past a particular time or date: *The project will continue beyond 2007.* | *our plans for the year 2008 and beyond*
3 more than a particular amount, level, or limit: *Inflation has risen beyond the 5% level.*
4 outside the limits of what someone or something can do: *Such tasks are far beyond the abilities of the average student.*
5 used to say that something cannot be done: *The TV is beyond repair.* | *The concert was cancelled due to circumstances beyond our control.*
6 it's beyond me *spoken* used to say that you do not understand something: *It's beyond me why she's so popular.*
7 used to mean 'except' in negative sentences: *The island doesn't have much industry beyond tourism.*

bi- /baɪ/ *prefix* two: *He's bilingual* (=able to speak two languages well).

bias /ˈbaɪəs/ *n* [singular,U] an opinion about a person, group, or idea which makes you treat them unfairly or differently: **political/gender/ racial etc bias** *He has accused his employers of racial bias.* | **+against/towards/in favour of** *Some employers have a bias against women.*

biased /ˈbaɪəst/ *adj* supporting one person or group in an unfair way, when you should treat everyone fairly: *The referee was definitely biased!* | **+against/towards/in favour of** *Some newspapers are biased in favour of the government.*

bib /bɪb/ *n* [C] a piece of cloth or plastic that you tie under a baby's chin to protect its clothes when it is eating

bible /ˈbaɪbəl/ *n* **1 the Bible** the holy book of the Christian religion **2** [C] a copy of the Bible —**biblical** /ˈbɪblɪkəl/ *adj*

bibliography /ˌbɪbliˈɒɡrəfi $ -ˈɑːg-/ n [C] plural **bibliographies** a list of books on a particular subject

bicentenary /ˌbaɪsenˈtiːnəri $ -ˈtenəri, -ˈsentəneri/ especially BrE, **bicentennial** /-ˈteniəl/ AmE n [C] plural **bicentenaries** the day or year exactly 200 years after an important event: **+of** the bicentenary of Mozart's death

bicep /ˈbaɪsep/ n [C usually plural] the large muscle on the front of your upper arm

bicker /ˈbɪkə $ -ər/ v [I] to argue about something unimportant: **+about/over** The kids were bickering about who was the fastest runner. → see box at **ARGUE**

bicycle /ˈbaɪsɪkəl/ n [C] a vehicle with two wheels that you ride by pushing the PEDALS with your feet: Can he **ride a bicycle**? | **by bicycle** She came by bicycle.

bid¹ /bɪd/ n [C]   **1** an offer to pay a particular price for something: **+for** We made a bid of £400 million for the company. | a takeover bid for the company   **2** an offer to do work for someone at a particular price: **+for** The company accepted the lowest bid for the cleaning contract.   **3** an attempt to achieve or get something: **+for** a bid for power | **bid to do sth** a desperate bid to save the child's life

bid² v past tense and past participle **bid**, present participle **bidding** [I,T] to offer to pay a particular price for something that several people want to buy: **bid (sb) sth for sth** She bid $50,000 for the painting. —**bidder** n [C]

bid³ v [T] past tense **bade** /bæd, beɪd/ or **bid**, past participle **bid** or **bidden** /ˈbɪdn/ present participle **bidding** literary **bid sb good morning/goodbye etc** to greet someone

bidding /ˈbɪdɪŋ/ n [U]   **1** when people bid for goods in an AUCTION   **2** **do sb's bidding** formal to do what someone tells you to do

bide /baɪd/ v **bide your time** to wait until the right time to do something

bidet /ˈbiːdeɪ $ bɪˈdeɪ/ n [C] a large bowl that you sit on to wash your bottom

biennial /baɪˈeniəl/ adj a biennial event happens once every two years

big /bɪg/ adj

1 something that is big is large or larger than average size [≠ **small**]: a big red balloon | the biggest city in the world | How big is their new house? → see box at **FAT**

THESAURUS

huge: huge sums of money
enormous: an enormous cake
vast: The birds nest here in vast numbers.
gigantic: gigantic waves
Big and **large** mean the same thing, but **large** is slightly more formal: That's a big piece of cake! | It's the largest hotel in Birmingham.
Use **large** not **big** to describe amounts: a large amount of money
Use **big** not **large** to describe something that is important: a big opportunity | That's the big question.

bicycle

seat/saddle
gears   handlebars   crossbar
brake
lamp
mudguard
pump
tyre BrE/
tire AmE
spoke
frame
valve   pedal   chain
wheel

2 important or serious [≠ **small**]: *a big decision* | *This is a very big match for our team.* | *We have some* **big problems.** | *It was the* **biggest mistake** *of my life.*
3 *informal* successful or popular: *His last film was a big hit.* | *He'll never* **make it big** (=become successful) *as a professional golfer.*
4 big sister/big brother *informal* your older sister or brother
5 big deal *spoken* used when you do not think something is as important as someone else thinks it is: *It's just a game. If you lose, big deal.* | **It's no big deal** (=it's not important).
6 big money also **big bucks** *AmE* a lot of money: *He was offered big money for his life story.*

bigamy /'bɪgəmi/ *n* [U] the crime of being married to two people at the same time —**bigamist** *n* [C]

,**big 'business** *n* [U] very large companies, considered as a powerful group with a lot of influence

big-headed /,bɪg'hedɪd◂/ *adj disapproving* too proud of yourself, especially of what you can do → see box at **PROUD**

,**big 'name** *n* [C] a famous person or group, especially an actor, singer etc

bigot /'bɪgət/ *n* [C] someone who has strong and unreasonable opinions and will not listen to other people's opinions

bigoted /'bɪgətɪd/ *adj* someone who is bigoted has strong and unreasonable opinions and will not listen to other people's opinions

bigotry /'bɪgətri/ *n* [U] bigoted behaviour or beliefs

'**big shot** *n* [C] *informal* someone who has an important or powerful job

,**big-'ticket** *adj* [only before noun] *AmE informal* expensive: *big-ticket items such as cars or jewelry*

'**big time**[1] *adv especially AmE spoken* a lot, or very much: *He messed up big time.*

big time[2] *n* **the big time** *informal* when someone is very famous or important, for example in politics or sports: *The 46-year-old author has finally* **hit the big time.** —**big-time** *adj* [only before noun] *big-time drug dealers*

bigwig /'bɪgwɪg/ *n* [C] *informal* an important person

bike[1] /baɪk/ *n* [C] *informal*
1 a bicycle: *He likes riding his bike.* | **by bike** *I came here by bike.*
2 a MOTORCYCLE
→ **MOUNTAIN BIKE**

bike[2] *v* [I + adv/prep] *informal* to ride a bicycle

biker /'baɪkə $ -ər/ *n* [C] someone who rides a MOTORCYCLE

bikini /bɪ'kiːni/ *n* [C] a piece of clothing in two parts that women wear on the beach when it is hot

bilateral /baɪ'lætərəl/ *adj* involving two groups or countries: *a bilateral trade agreement* | *bilateral negotiations between Israel and Syria* —**bilaterally** *adv*

bile /baɪl/ *n* [U] a bitter green-brown liquid produced by your LIVER, which helps you to DIGEST fat

bilingual /baɪ'lɪŋgwəl/ *adj* **1** able to speak two languages very well **2** written or spoken in two languages: *a bilingual dictionary*

bill[1] /bɪl/ *n* [C]
1 a list of things that you have bought or that someone has done for you, showing how much you have to pay for them: **+for** *The bill for the repairs came to $650.* | **phone/electricity/gas/water etc bill** *Have you* **paid** *the gas bill?*
2 a list showing how much you have to pay for a meal that you have eaten in a restaurant [= **check** *AmE*]: *Can we have the bill, please?* → see box at **RESTAURANT**

COLLOCATIONS

If you have eaten in a restaurant and are ready to pay, you **ask for the bill.**
If someone who eats with other people pays for the entire meal, they **pick up the bill.**
If people share the cost of the meal between them, they **split the bill.**

3 *AmE* a piece of paper money [= **note** *BrE*]: *a ten-dollar bill* → see box at **MONEY**
4 a plan for a new law: *The new education bill was* **passed** (=became law) *last week.*
5 fit/fill the bill to be exactly what you need: *This car fits the bill perfectly.*
6 a programme of entertainment at a theatre, concert etc
7 a bird's beak
→ **foot the bill** at **FOOT**[2]

bill[2] *v* [T] to send a bill to someone: **bill sb for sth** *They've billed me for things I didn't order.*
bill sth as sth *phr v* to advertise or describe something in a particular way: *The boxing match was billed as 'the fight of the century'.*

billboard /'bɪlbɔːd $ -bɔːrd/ *n* [C] a big sign next to a road, that is used to advertise something [= **hoarding** *BrE*]

billet /'bɪlɪt/ *v* [T] to put soldiers in people's houses to live for a short time —**billet** *n* [C]

billfold /'bɪlfəʊld $ -foʊld/ *n* [C] *AmE* a small flat case that you use for carrying paper money [= **wallet** *BrE*]

billiards /'bɪljədz $ -ərdz/ *n* [U] a game played on a table that is covered in cloth, in which you hit balls with a CUE (=long stick) and try to knock them into pockets at the edge of the table

billing /'bɪlɪŋ/ *n* [U] the importance of the position of a performer's name, for example at the beginning of a film: *He promised me I'd get* **top billing.**

billion /'bɪljən/ *number* plural **billion** or **billions**
1 the number 1,000,000,000: **two/three/four etc billion** *3.5 billion years ago* | **billions of pounds/dollars etc**
2 an extremely large number of things or people: **a billion** *A billion stars shone in the sky.* | **billions of sth** *There are billions of things I want to say.*
—**billionth** *adj* —**billionth** *n* [C]

billow /'bɪləʊ $ -loʊ/ *v* [I] **1** also **billow out** if something made of cloth billows, it moves in the wind and fills with air: *The boat's sails billowed in the wind.* **2** if smoke billows, a lot of it rises into the air: **+out of/up etc** *Smoke billowed out of the chimney.* —**billow** *n* [C]

bimbo /'bɪmbəʊ $ -boʊ/ *n* [C] plural **bimbos** *informal* an offensive word meaning an attractive but stupid woman

bimonthly /baɪ'mʌnθli/ *adj* appearing or happening once every two months or twice each month: *a bimonthly trade magazine* —**bimonthly** *adv*

bin /bɪn/ *n* [C]
1 a large container where you put small things that you no longer want: *She threw the letter in the bin.* | *a wastepaper bin*

> **THESAURUS**
>
> **litter bin/rubbish bin/waste bin** *BrE*, **garbage can/trashcan** *AmE* – a container in a public place for paper, cans etc that people throw away
> **dustbin** *BrE*, **garbage can/trashcan** *AmE* – a large container outside your home, where you put waste so that it can be taken away
> **wastepaper basket/bin** *especially BrE*, **wastebasket** *AmE* – a small container inside a building where you put paper and things you do not want
> → **RUBBISH**

2 a container that you use to store things: *a flour bin*

binary /'baɪnəri/ *adj* **the binary system** *technical* a system of counting that only includes the numbers 0 and 1, used especially in computers: *The binary system was discovered by a Hungarian.*

bind[1] /baɪnd/ *v* past tense and past participle **bound** /baʊnd/ **1** [T] to tie something together firmly, with string or rope: *They bound his legs with a rope.* **2** also **bind together** [T] *formal* to form a strong connection between two people, groups, or countries: *Their shared experiences helped to bind the two men together.* **3** [T usually passive] if you are bound by an agreement or promise, you must do what you agreed or promised to do: *Each country is bound by the treaty.* **4** [I,T] *technical* to stick together in a mass, or to make small pieces of something stick together **5** [T] to fasten the pages of a book together and put them in a cover: *The book was printed and bound in India.*

bind[2] *n* **a bind** *informal* an annoying or difficult situation: *It's a real bind having to look after the children.*

binding[1] /'baɪndɪŋ/ *adj* a contract or agreement that is binding must be obeyed: *The contract isn't binding until you sign it.*

binding[2] *n* [C] the cover of a book

binge /bɪndʒ/ *n* [C] *informal* an occasion when you eat or drink a lot in a very short time: *He goes on alcohol binges that last all weekend.* —**binge** *v* [I] *I sometimes binge on chocolate.*

bingo /'bɪŋgəʊ $ -goʊ/ *n* [U] a game played for money or prizes in which numbers are chosen and called out. If you have the right numbers on your card, you win.

binoculars /bɪ'nɒkjɡləz, baɪ- $ -'nɑːkjɡlərz/ *n* [plural] an object like a large pair of glasses that you hold up and look through to see things that are far away

binoculars

biochemistry /ˌbaɪəʊ'kemɪstri $ ˌbaɪoʊ-/ *n* [U] the scientific study of the chemistry of living things —**biochemist** *n* [C] —**biochemical** *adj*

biodegradable /ˌbaɪəʊdɪ'ɡreɪdəbəl $ ˌbaɪoʊ-/ *adj* a material that is biodegradable can be destroyed by natural processes, in a way that does not harm the environment: *biodegradable plastic* → see box at **ENVIRONMENT**

biodiversity /ˌbaɪəʊdaɪ'vɜːsɪti, -dɪ- $ ˌbaɪoʊdaɪ'vɜːr-, -dɪ-/ *n* [U] *technical* the number of different plants and animals in a place

biographer /baɪ'ɒɡrəfə $ -'ɑːɡrəfər/ *n* [C] someone who writes a biography of someone else

biography /baɪ'ɒɡrəfi $ -'ɑːɡ-/ *n* [C] plural **biographies** a book about a person's life —**biographical** /ˌbaɪə'ɡræfɪkəl/ *adj*

biological /ˌbaɪə'lɒdʒɪkəl $ -'lɑː-/ *adj*
1 relating to the natural processes performed by living things: *a biological process*
2 relating to biology
3 **biological weapons/warfare/attack etc** weapons, attacks etc that involve the use of living things, including **BACTERIA**, to harm people —**biologically** /-kli/ *adv*

biology /baɪ'ɒlədʒi $ -'ɑːl-/ *n* [U] the scientific study of living things —**biologist** *n* [C]

biopsy /'baɪɒpsi $ -ɑːp-/ *n* [C] plural **biopsies** the removal of cells from someone's body to find out more about a disease they may have

biotechnology /ˌbaɪəʊtek'nɒlədʒi $ ˌbaɪoʊtek'nɑː-/ *n* [U] the use of living things such as cells and **BACTERIA** to make drugs, destroy waste matter etc

bipartisan /ˌbaɪpɑːtɪˈzæn $ baɪ'pɑːrtɪzən/ *adj* involving two political parties: *a bipartisan committee*

birch /bɜːtʃ $ bɜːrtʃ/ *n* [C,U] a tree with smooth **BARK** and thin branches, or the wood from this tree

bird /bɜːd $ bɜːrd/ *n* [C] an animal with wings and feathers that can usually fly
→ **kill two birds with one stone** at **KILL**[1]

birdie /'bɜːdi $ 'bɜːrdi/ *n* [C] *AmE* a small object with feathers that you hit across a net in the game of **BADMINTON** [= **shuttlecock** *BrE*]

bird of 'prey *n* [C] plural **birds of prey** a bird that kills and eats other birds and small animals

Biro /'baɪərəʊ $ 'baɪroʊ/ *n* [C] plural **biros** *trademark BrE* a type of pen

birth /bɜːθ $ bɜːrθ/ *n*
1 give birth if a woman gives birth, she produces a baby from her body: **+to** *She's just given birth to twins.*

2 [C,U] the time when a baby comes out of its mother's body: **at birth** (=when someone is born) *She weighed 3kg at birth.* | **from/since birth** *He has been blind from birth.* | **date of birth** *especially BrE*/**birth date** *especially AmE*: *What's your date of birth?*

3 [U] someone's family origin: **by birth** *Her father was French by birth.*

4 birth parent/mother/father someone's birth parent is their real mother or father, rather than someone who looked after them or ADOPTED them

5 [singular] the time when something new starts to exist: **+of** *the birth of a nation*

birth cer,tificate *n* [C] an official document that shows when and where you were born

birth con,trol *n* [U] methods of stopping a woman becoming PREGNANT

birthday /'bɜːθdeɪ $ 'bɜːr-/ *n* [C] the date in each year on which you were born [➔ **anniversary**]: *When's your birthday?* | **birthday card/gift/party etc** | **happy birthday!** (=what you say to someone on their birthday)

birthmark /'bɜːθmɑːk $ 'bɜːrθmɑːrk/ *n* [C] an unusual mark on someone's skin that is there when they are born

birthplace /'bɜːθpleɪs $ 'bɜːrθ-/ *n* [C usually singular] the place where someone was born

birthrate /'bɜːθreɪt $ 'bɜːrθ-/ *n* [C] the average number of babies born during a particular period of time in a country or area

biscuit /'bɪskɟt/ *n* [C]
1 *BrE* a thin sweet cake [= **cookie** *AmE*]: *a chocolate biscuit* → see picture on page A5
2 *AmE* a kind of bread that you bake in small round shapes

bisexual /baɪ'sekʃuəl/ *adj* sexually attracted to both men and women —**bisexual** *n* [C] —**bisexuality** /,baɪsekʃu'æl̩ti/ *n* [U]

bishop /'bɪʃəp/ *n* [C] a Christian priest with a high rank who is in charge of the churches and priests in a large area

bison /'baɪsən/ *n* [C] plural **bison** or **bisons** an animal that looks like a large cow with long hair on its head and shoulders, and lives in the United States [= **buffalo**]

bistro /'biːstrəʊ $ -troʊ/ *n* [C] plural **bistros** a small restaurant

bit¹ /bɪt/ *n* [C]
1 a bit *especially BrE* slightly: *Could you turn the TV up a bit?* | *Aren't you being **a little bit** unfair?* | *Carol looks **a bit like** my sister.* | **a bit better/older/easier etc** *I feel a bit better now.* | **not a bit/not one bit** (=not at all) *You're not a bit like your brother.*
2 a small piece of something: **+of** *a few bits of broken glass* | *The car was **blown to bits** (=broken into small pieces) in the explosion.*
3 a bit *especially BrE informal* a small amount of something: **+of** *He may need a bit of help.*
4 *BrE informal* a part of something: **+of** *the best bit of the film*
5 quite a bit a fairly large amount: *She's quite a bit older than him.* | **+of** *He does quite a bit of travelling.*
6 a bit *especially BrE* a short period of time or a short distance: *I'll see you in a bit.* | **in a bit** *I'll see you in a bit.* | **for a bit** *We sat around for a bit chatting.* | **after a bit** *After a bit, he got used*

to the idea. | *I walked on a bit and then turned back.*

7 a bit of a sth *especially BrE* used to show that the way you describe something is only true to a limited degree: *The news came as a bit of a shock.*

8 every bit as important/bad/good etc *especially BrE* equally important, bad etc as something else: *Peter was every bit as good-looking as his brother.*

9 bit by bit *especially BrE* gradually: *Bit by bit, I was starting to change my mind.*

10 to bits *BrE informal* very much: *I **love** him **to bits**.*

11 bits and pieces *informal* any small things of various kinds

12 do your bit *informal* to do a fair share of the work or effort that is needed to achieve something

13 the smallest unit of information that a computer uses

14 the sharp part of a tool for cutting or making holes: *a drill bit*

15 a metal bar that is put in the mouth of a horse and used to control its movements

bit² *v* the past tense of BITE

bitch¹ /bɪtʃ/ *n* **1** [C] a female dog **2** [C] an offensive word for a woman that you dislike: *She's such a bitch!* **3 be a bitch** *informal* to cause problems or be difficult: *I love this sweater but it's a bitch to wash.*

bitch² *v* [I] **1** *informal* to make unpleasant remarks about someone: **+about** *He never bitches about other members of the team.* **2** *AmE* to complain continuously

bitchy /'bɪtʃi/ *adj informal* unkind and unpleasant about other people —**bitchily** *adv* —**bitchiness** *n* [U]

bite¹ /baɪt/ *v* past tense **bit** /bɪt/ past participle **bitten** /'bɪtn/ present participle **biting**
1 [I,T] to use your teeth to cut or chew something: *Be careful of the dog. Jerry said he bites.* | **+into/through/at/down** *She bit into an apple.* | *An adult conger eel can bite through a man's leg.* | **bite sth off** *a man whose arm was bitten off by an alligator* | *I wish I could stop **biting** my **nails** (=biting the nails on my fingers).*
2 [I,T] if an insect or snake bites, it injures someone by making a hole in their skin [➔ **sting**]: *I think I've been bitten.* | *The dog's been bitten by fleas.*
3 [I] to start to have an unpleasant effect: *The new tobacco taxes have begun to bite.*
4 bite the dust *informal* to die, fail, or be defeated: *Their hopes of winning the championship have finally bitten the dust.*
5 bite the bullet to start dealing with an unpleasant situation because you can no longer avoid it: *I finally bit the bullet and paid.*

bite² *n*
1 [C] when you cut or chew something with your teeth: **take/have a bite (of sth/out of sth)** *He took a bite of the cheese.* | *Can I have a bite of your apple?* | **give sb a bite** *The dog gave her a nasty bite.* | *Antonio ate half his burger in one bite.*
2 [C] a wound made when an animal or insect bites you [➔ **sting**]: **snake/mosquito/ant etc bites** *I'm covered in mosquito bites!*

3 a bite (to eat) *informal* a small meal: *Let's have a bite to eat before we go.*

biting /'baɪtɪŋ/ *adj* **1** a biting wind is extremely cold **2** a biting criticism or remark is cruel or unkind

bitten /'bɪtn/ *v* the past participle of BITE

bitter[1] /'bɪtə $ -ər/ *adj*

1 angry and upset because you feel you have been treated unfairly: **+about** *I feel very bitter about what happened.* | *a bitter old man* | *She gave a bitter laugh.*

2 [only before noun] making you feel very unhappy and upset: **a bitter disappointment/ blow** *His exam results were a bitter disappointment to his parents.* | *She knew from bitter experience that they wouldn't agree.*

3 a bitter argument is one in which people feel very strong anger or hatred towards each other: *The couple are locked in a bitter legal dispute over the children.* | *They are bitter enemies.*

4 something that is bitter has a strong taste that is not sweet [≠ sweet; → sour]: *a fruit with a horrible bitter taste*

5 bitter weather is extremely cold: *a bitter wind*

6 to/until the bitter end continuing until the end, even though this is difficult: *They say they will fight the closure to the bitter end.*
—**bitterness** *n* [U]

bitter[2] *n* [C,U] *BrE* beer with a bitter taste, or a glass of this: *A pint of bitter, please.* | *Two bitters, please.*

bitterly /'bɪtəli $ -ər-/ *adv* **1** with a lot of anger or sadness: *I was bitterly disappointed.* | *He complained bitterly.* **2 bitterly cold** very cold

bitter-'sweet *adj* making you feel both happy and sad: *bitter-sweet memories*

bizarre /bɪˈzɑː $ -ˈzɑːr/ *adj* very unusual and strange: *a bizarre coincidence* —**bizarrely** *adv*

black[1] /blæk/ *adj*

1 having the darkest colour, like coal or night: *a black dress* | *her jet black* (=very black) *hair* | *Outside, it was pitch black* (=completely black). → see picture at PATTERN

2 belonging to a race of people who have dark brown skin [→ white]: *Over half the students here are black.*

3 black coffee or tea does not have milk in it [≠ white]

4 sad and without hope for the future: *a mood of black despair*

5 black humour/comedy humour that makes jokes about serious subjects

6 angry or disapproving: *He gave me a black look.*

7 black mark if there is a black mark against you, someone has a bad opinion of you because of something you have done

8 black and blue *informal* having a lot of BRUISES on your body

9 black and white showing pictures or images only in black, white, and grey: *an old black and white film*
—**blackness** *n* [U]

black[2] *n*

1 [C,U] the dark colour of coal or night: *She was wearing black.*

2 also **Black** [C] someone belonging to a race of

people with dark skin: *discrimination against blacks*

3 be in the black to have money in your bank account [≠ in the red]

4 in black and white written or printed: *The rules are there in black and white.*

black[3] *v*

black out *phr v* to suddenly become unconscious [→ blackout]: *Sharon blacked out and fell to the floor.*

'black belt *n* [C] a high rank in JUDO and KARATE, or someone who has this rank

blackberry /'blækbəri $ -beri/ *n* [C] plural **blackberries** a small sweet black fruit

blackbird /'blækbɜːd $ -bɜːrd/ *n* [C] a common bird, the male of which is completely black

blackboard /'blækbɔːd $ -bɔːrd/ *n* [C] a dark smooth board that you write on with CHALK in schools → see picture at CLASSROOM

blackcurrant /ˌblækˈkʌrənt $ -ˈkɜːr-/ *n* [C] a small blue-black fruit

blacken /'blækən/ *v* [I,T] **1** to become black, or make something black: *Smoke had blackened the kitchen walls.* **2 blacken sb's name** to say unpleasant things about someone so that other people have a bad opinion of them

ˌblack 'eye *n* [C] an area of dark skin around someone's eye that is the result of them being hit

ˌblack 'hole *n* [C] an area in outer space into which everything, including light, is pulled → see box at SPACE

blacklist /'blæklɪst/ *v* [T] to put someone or something on a list of people or things that are considered bad or dangerous: *Members of the Communist Party have been blacklisted and are unable to find work.* —**blacklist** *n* [C]

ˌblack 'magic *n* [U] evil magic connected with the Devil

blackmail /'blækmeɪl/ *n* [U] when someone makes you pay them money or do what they want by threatening to tell your secrets —**blackmail** *v* [T] *He had tried to blackmail me.* —**blackmailer** *n* [C]

ˌblack 'market *n* [C] when things are bought or sold illegally: **on the black market** *drugs that were only available on the black market*

blackout /'blækaʊt/ *n* [C] **1** a period of darkness caused by failure of the electricity supply **2** a situation in which people are not allowed to report news **3** a period during a war when lights must be turned off or covered at night **4** when you suddenly become unconscious: *He's suffered from blackouts since the accident.*

ˌblack 'sheep *n* [C] someone who is considered to be bad or embarrassing by the rest of their family

blacksmith /'blæk smɪθ/ *n* [C] someone who makes and repairs things made of iron

blackspot /'blækspɒt $ -spɑːt/ *n* [C] *BrE* a place where the situation is very bad: *an accident blackspot* (=where there are a lot of road accidents)

ˌblack 'tie *adj* a black tie event is one at which people wear special formal clothes

blacktop /'blæktɒp $ -tɑːp/ *n* [U] *AmE* the thick black substance used to cover roads [= Tarmac *BrE*]

bladder /'blædə $ -ər/ n [C] the part of your body where URINE is stored before it leaves your body → see picture on page A3

blade /bleɪd/ n [C] **1** the flat sharp cutting part of a knife, tool, or weapon: *the blade of a knife* | *a* **razor blade** **2** the flat wide part of an OAR or PROPELLER **3 blade of grass** a single thin flat leaf of grass

blah /blɑː/ n **blah, blah, blah** *spoken* used instead of completing what you are saying, because it is boring or easy to guess: *She was saying, 'He's great, he's so cool, blah, blah, blah.'*

blame¹ /bleɪm/ v [T]

1 to say that someone or something is responsible for something bad: *Don't blame me – it's not my fault.* | **blame sb/sth for sth** *Marie still blames herself for Patrick's death.* | *Poor weather conditions were blamed for the accident.* | **blame sth on sb** *She blamed the broken computer on me.* | *I'm sure he was* **to blame** *for the fire.* | *The increase in interest rates was* **widely blamed** *for the crisis.*

2 I don't blame you/you can hardly blame them etc *spoken* used to say that you can understand why someone did something: *'She's left her husband.' 'I don't blame her, after the way he treated her.'*

blame² n [U] responsibility for a mistake or something bad: **+for** *I always* **get the blame** *for his mistakes.* | *You can't expect Terry to* **take all the blame.** | *Sue stole it but she's trying to* **put the blame** *on me.*

blameless /'bleɪmləs/ adj not guilty of anything bad: *a blameless life*

blanch /blɑːntʃ $ blæntʃ/ v [I] *literary* to become pale because you are afraid or shocked: *Nick blanched at the news.*

bland /blænd/ adj **1** without any excitement, strong opinions, or special qualities: *a bland TV quiz show* **2** bland food has very little taste: *a very bland white sauce* → see box at **TASTE**

blank¹ /blæŋk/ adj

1 something that is blank has nothing written or recorded on it: *a blank cassette* | **Leave** *the last page* **blank**.
2 a blank expression or look shows no emotion, understanding, or interest [➡ **blankly**]
3 go blank if your mind goes blank, you are suddenly unable to remember something: *When she saw the exam questions, her mind went blank.*
→ **POINT-BLANK**

blank² n [C] an empty space on a piece of paper, for you to write a word or letter in: **Fill in the blanks** *on the form.* → **draw a blank** at **DRAW**¹

,blank 'cheque *BrE*; **,blank 'check** *AmE* n [C] a cheque that has been signed, but has not had the amount written on it

blanket¹ /'blæŋk₁t/ n

1 [C] a cover for a bed, usually made of wool
2 [singular] a thick layer of something that covers something: **+of** *The hills were covered with a* **blanket of snow.**

blanket² v [T] to cover something completely: **be blanketed in/with sth** *The coast was blanketed in fog.*

blanket³ adj **blanket statement/rule/ban** a statement, rule etc that affects everyone or includes all possible kinds of something: *a blanket ban on all types of hunting*

blankly /'blæŋkli/ adv without showing any emotion or understanding: *Anna stared blankly at the wall.*

blare /bleə $ bler/ also **blare out** v [I,T] to make a very loud unpleasant noise: *Horns blared in the street outside.* | *music blaring out from her car* —**blare** n [singular]

blasphemy /'blæsfɪ̯mi/ n [C,U] plural **blasphemies** something you say or do that insults God or insults people's religious beliefs —**blasphemous** adj: *blasphemous talk* —**blaspheme** /blæs'fiːm/ v [I]

blast¹ /blɑːst $ blæst/ n **1** [C] a sudden strong movement of wind or air: **+of** *a blast of icy air* **2** [C] an explosion: *a bomb blast* | *Thirty-six people died in the blast.* **3** [C] a sudden very loud noise: *a long trumpet blast* **4 (at) full blast** as strongly or loudly as possible: *The TV was on full blast.* **5 a blast** *AmE* an enjoyable and exciting experience: *We* **had a blast** *at Mitch's party.*

blast² v **1** [I,T] to break something into pieces using explosives: *They blasted a tunnel through the side of the mountain.* **2** also **blast out** [I,T] to produce a lot of loud noise, especially music: **+from** *Dance music blasted from the stereo.* | *a loudspeaker blasting rock music* **3** [T] to attack a place or person with bombs or guns: *Two gunmen blasted their way into the building.*

blast³ *spoken* used when you are annoyed about something: *Blast! I've lost my keys!*

blatant /'bleɪtənt/ adj done openly, with no effort to hide bad or dishonest behaviour: *a blatant lie* —**blatantly** adv

blaze¹ /bleɪz/ n **1** [C] a large fire: *Helicopters were used to* **fight the blaze.** → see box at **FIRE** **2 a blaze of light/colour** a lot of very bright light or colour: *The garden was a blaze of colour.* **3 (in a) blaze of glory/publicity** receiving a lot of praise or public attention: *He launched the new paper in a blaze of publicity.*

blaze² v [I] to burn or shine very brightly and strongly: *a huge log fire blazing in the hearth* → see box at **FIRE**

blazer /'bleɪzə $ -ər/ n [C] a jacket, sometimes with the special sign of a school or club on it: *a school blazer*

blazing /'bleɪzɪŋ/ adj **1** extremely hot: *a blazing summer day* **2** very angry: *a blazing row*

bleach¹ /bliːtʃ/ n [U] a chemical used to clean things or make them whiter

bleach² v [T] to make something white or lighter in colour by using chemicals or the light from the sun: *Her hair had been bleached by the sun.*

bleachers /'bliːtʃəz $ -ərz/ n [plural] *AmE* rows of seats where people sit to watch sports games

bleak /bliːk/ adj **1** without anything to make you feel happy or hopeful: *Without a job, the future seemed bleak.* **2** cold and unattractive: *a bleak November day* | *the bleak landscape of the northern hills* —**bleakness** n [U]

bleary /'blɪəri $ 'blɪri/ adj unable to see clearly because you are tired or have been crying: *Sam came down to breakfast looking* **bleary-eyed.** —**blearily** adv

bleat /bliːt/ v [I] **1** to make the sound that a sheep or goat makes **2** *informal* to complain in a silly or annoying way: *He's always bleating about wanting more money.* —**bleat** n [C]

bleed /bliːd/ v past tense and past participle **bled** /bled/ [I] to lose blood because of an injury: *His head was bleeding badly. | Tragically, she **bled to death**.* —**bleeding** n [U] *Tom kept pressure on the vein to try and stop the bleeding.*

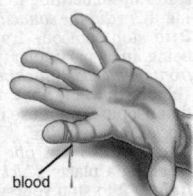
bleed

blood

bleep /bliːp/ n [C] a high electronic sound: *the shrill bleep of the alarm clock* —**bleep** v [I]

bleeper /'bliːpə $ -ər/ n [C] *BrE* a small electronic machine you carry with you that makes a high sound when it receives a message for you [= **pager**]

blemish /'blemɪʃ/ n [C] a mark that spoils something: *a blemish on her cheek* → see box at **MARK** —**blemished** adj

blend¹ /blend/ v **1** [I,T] to combine two different features: *a story that blends fact and fiction* **2** [T] to mix two or more things together thoroughly: *Blend the butter and sugar together.*
  blend in phr v if something blends in, it looks suitably similar to everything around it: +**with** *curtains that blend in with the wallpaper*

blend² n [C] a mixture of two or more things: +**of** *a unique blend of Brazilian and Colombian coffee | the right blend of sunshine and soil for growing grapes*

blender /'blendə $ -ər/ n [C] a small electric machine that you use to mix food

bless /bles/ v [T] past tense and past participle **blessed** or **blest** /blest/ **1 bless you** *spoken* words you say when someone SNEEZES **2 bless him/her etc** *spoken* used to show you really like someone or are pleased by them: *He's always willing to help. Bless him!* **3 be blessed with sth** to be lucky and have a special ability or good quality: *George was blessed with good health.* **4** to ask God to protect someone or something, or to make something holy: *Their mission had been blessed by the Pope.*

blessed /'blesɪd/ adj **1** [only before noun] *spoken* used to show that you are annoyed: *Now where have I put that blessed book?* **2** [only before noun] enjoyable or desirable: *a moment of blessed silence* **3** *formal* holy and loved by God: *the Blessed Virgin Mary*

blessing /'blesɪŋ/ n **1** [C] something good that improves your life or makes you happy: *The rain was a real blessing after all that heat.* **2** [U] someone's approval or encouragement: **with/without sb's blessing** *They were determined to marry, with or without their parents' blessing.* **3 a mixed blessing** something that is both good and bad: *Living close to the office was a mixed blessing.* **4 a blessing in disguise** something that seems to be bad but that you later realize is good: *The lack of tourism on the island could be a blessing in disguise.* **5 count your blessings** to be glad because of the good things that you have

6 [singular, U] protection and help from God, or the prayer in which you ask for this

blew /bluː/ v the past tense of BLOW

blight¹ /blaɪt/ n [singular, U] something which damages or spoils things: +**on** *the poverty that is a blight on our nation*

blight² v [T] to damage or spoil something: *an area blighted by unemployment*

blimey /'blaɪmi/ *BrE spoken informal* used to express surprise: *Blimey, look at that!*

blind¹ /blaɪnd/ adj
1 a) unable to see: **totally/completely/almost/partially blind** *She's almost blind in her right eye. | He was slowly **going blind** (=becoming unable to see). | Beverley was **born blind**.* **b) the blind** people who cannot see: *special facilities for the blind*
2 be blind to sth to completely fail to notice or realize something [→ **blindly**]: *He was blind to the faults of his own children.*
3 turn a blind eye (to sth) to ignore something that you know should not be happening: *Teachers were turning a blind eye to smoking in the school.*
4 blind faith/loyalty/panic etc strong feelings that make you do things without thinking – used to show disapproval: *a story about blind loyalty*
5 blind corner/bend a corner in a road that you cannot see round when you are driving —**blindness** n [U] → **COLOUR-BLIND**

blind² v [T] **1** to make someone unable to see, either permanently or for a short time: *The deer was blinded by our headlights.* **2** to make someone unable to notice or realize the truth about something: **blind sb to sth** *Being in love blinded me to his faults.*

blind³ n [C] a piece of cloth or other material that you pull down to cover a window

blind 'date n [C] a romantic meeting arranged between a man and a woman who have not met each other before: *They met on a blind date.*

blindfold¹ /'blaɪndfəʊld $ -foʊld/ n [C] a piece of cloth that is put over someone's eyes so that they cannot see

blindfold² v [T] to cover someone's eyes with a piece of cloth so that they cannot see: *The hostages were blindfolded and led to the cellar.*

blinding /'blaɪndɪŋ/ adj **1** a blinding light is very bright: *Suddenly there was a blinding flash of light.* **2 blinding headache** a very painful headache

blindly /'blaɪndli/ adv **1** without thinking or understanding: *Don't blindly accept what they tell you.* **2** not seeing or not noticing what is around you: *She sat **staring blindly** out of the window.*

'blind spot n [C] **1** something that you are unable or unwilling to understand: *He has a blind spot for computers.* **2** a part of the road that you cannot see when you are driving

bling bling /blɪŋ 'blɪŋ/ n [U] *informal* expensive objects, for example JEWELLERY, that are worn in a way that is very easy to notice

blink¹ /blɪŋk/ v **1** [I,T] to close and open your eyes quickly: *He blinked as he stepped out into the sunlight.* **2** [I] if a light blinks, it goes on and off

blink[2] n **1 on the blink** informal not working properly: *The phone's on the blink.* **2** [C] the action of blinking

blinkered /'blɪŋkəd $ -ərd/ adj refusing to accept new or different ideas: *a **blinkered attitude** to life*

blip /blɪp/ n [C] **1** a flashing light on the screen of a piece of electronic equipment **2** informal a small temporary change from what usually happens: *This month's rise in prices could be just a blip.*

bliss /blɪs/ n [U] complete happiness: *I didn't have to get up 'til 11 – sheer bliss!*

blissful /'blɪsfəl/ adj very happy: *the first blissful weeks after we married* —**blissfully** adv: *She seemed blissfully unaware of the problems ahead.*

blister /'blɪstə $ -ər/ n [C] a small area of skin that is swollen and full of liquid because it has been rubbed or burned → see box at **MARK** —**blister** v [I,T]

blistering /'blɪstərɪŋ/ adj **1** extremely hot: *blistering heat* **2 blistering attack/criticism etc** remarks expressing angry criticism: *a blistering attack on the government*

blithely /'blaɪðli/ adv without thinking about dangers or problems: *They blithely ignored the danger.* —**blithe** adj

blitz /blɪts/ n **1 the Blitz** the attack on British cities from the air during the Second World War **2** [C] when you use a lot of effort to achieve something in a short time: *The campaign starts next month with a TV advertising blitz.* —**blitz** v [T]

blizzard /'blɪzəd $ -ərd/ n [C] a storm with a lot of wind and snow → see box at **SNOW**

bloated /'bləʊtɪd $ 'bloʊ-/ adj full of liquid, gas, food etc, so that you look or feel much larger than normal: *I feel bloated after that meal.*

blob /blɒb $ blɑːb/ n [C] a small drop of a thick liquid: *+of a few blobs of paint*

bloc /blɒk $ blɑːk/ n [C] a group of countries with the same political aims, working together: *the former Soviet bloc*

block[1] /blɒk $ blɑːk/ n [C]

1 a solid piece of wood, stone etc: *+of a block of concrete* | *a model made of wooden blocks* → see picture at **PIECE**
2 AmE the distance along a street from one road that crosses it to the next that crosses it: *It's just three blocks to the store from here.*
3 BrE a large building divided into a lot of homes, offices, or CLASSROOMS: *+of a block of flats* | *an office block* | *an apartment block* | *the school science block*
4 a group of buildings with four streets that go around it: *Let's walk around the block.* | *the other kids on the block* (=living in the buildings)
5 something that makes it difficult to move or progress: *+to This incident could be a block to the peace process.*
6 an amount of something: *+of a block of text*
7 have a block (about sth) to be unable to think clearly or remember something for a short time: *I had a mental block about his name.*
→ **BUILDING BLOCK** → **be a chip off the old block** at **CHIP**[1] → **SUN BLOCK, TOWER BLOCK**

block[2] v [T]

1 also **block up** to prevent people or things from moving through something: *A fallen tree was blocking the road.* | **block sb's way/path/exit etc** *A ten foot wall blocked my escape.* | **be blocked (up)** (=contain something that is preventing movement) *The drain's blocked up.*
2 to stop something from happening or developing: *Why did the council block the plan?*
3 to stop someone from seeing something by being in a particular position: *A tall man in front of me was blocking my view.*

block sth ⇔ off phr v to close a road or path so that people cannot use it: *The freeway exit's been blocked off by police.*

block sth ⇔ out phr v **1** to stop light from reaching a place: *Thick smoke blocked out the light.* **2** to stop yourself thinking about something unpleasant: *She waited, trying to block out her anxiety.*

blockade /blɒ'keɪd $ blɑː-/ n [C] when an army or navy surrounds a place to stop people or supplies from leaving or entering: *a blockade of the city* | *a naval blockade* —**blockade** v [T]

blockage /'blɒkɪdʒ $ 'blɑː-/ n [C] something that is blocking a tube or pipe: *There seems to be a blockage in the pipe.*

blockbuster /'blɒk,bʌstə $ 'blɑːk,bʌstər/ n [C] informal a film or book that is very exciting and successful: *the latest Hollywood blockbuster* → see box at **POPULAR**

block 'capitals also **,block 'letters** n [plural] letters in their large form, for example A, B, C, instead of a, b, c

bloke /bləʊk $ bloʊk/ n [C] BrE informal a man → see box at **MAN**

blonde[1], **blond** /blɒnd $ blɑːnd/ adj **1** blonde hair is pale or yellow **2** someone who is blonde has pale or yellow hair

blonde[2] n [C] informal a woman who has pale or yellow hair: *a good-looking blonde*

blood /blʌd/ n

1 [U] the red liquid that flows around your body: *Blood was flowing from the wound.* | *She lost a lot of blood in the accident.* → see picture at **BLEED**
2 [U] the family that you belong to: *a woman of royal blood*
3 be/run in sb's blood to be a strong and natural part of someone's character: *A love of politics was in his blood.*
4 new blood new people in an organization who bring new ideas and energy
5 bad blood feelings of anger and hate between people
→ **in cold blood** at **COLD**[1] → **your own flesh and blood** at **FLESH**[1]

bloodbath /'blʌdbɑːθ $ -bæθ/ n [singular] when a lot of people are violently killed

bloodcurdling /'blʌd,kɜːdlɪŋ $ -ɜːr-/ adj a bloodcurdling sound is very frightening: *We heard a bloodcurdling scream.*

'blood ,donor n [C] someone who gives their blood to be used in medical treatment

'blood group n [C] BrE one of the types of blood that human blood is divided into [= **blood type** AmE]

bloodhound /'blʌdhaʊnd/ n [C] a large dog which can find things using its sense of smell

bloodless /'blʌdləs/ adj without killing or violence: *a bloodless revolution*

'blood ,pressure n [U] the force with which your blood moves around your body: *Older people often have high blood pressure.*

bloodshed /'blʌdʃed/ n [U] when people are killed in fighting or war: *talks aimed at avoiding further bloodshed*

bloodshot /'blʌdʃɒt $ -ʃɑːt/ adj bloodshot eyes are slightly red

'blood sport n [C] a sport that involves killing animals

bloodstain /'blʌdsteɪn/ n [C] a mark or spot of blood: *bloodstains on the carpet* —**bloodstained** adj: *his bloodstained clothes*

bloodstream /'blʌdstriːm/ n [singular] the blood flowing in your body: *The drug is injected straight into the bloodstream.*

bloodthirsty /'blʌd,θɜːsti $ -ɜːr-/ adj enjoying killing and violence

'blood trans,fusion n [C, U] a medical treatment that involves putting more blood into someone's body

'blood type n [C] AmE one of the types of blood that human blood is divided into [= **blood group** BrE]

'blood ,vessel n [C] one of the tubes in your body that blood flows through [➡ **artery, vein**]

bloody[1] /'blʌdi/ adj **1** covered in blood: *a bloody nose* **2** with a lot of killing and injuries: *a bloody battle*

bloody[2] adj, adv BrE spoken used to emphasize what you are saying in a slightly rude or angry way: *It's bloody cold out there.* | *Where's my bloody hat?* | *That was a bloody stupid thing to do.*

bloom[1] /bluːm/ n [C] **1** a flower: *beautiful yellow blooms* **2** in (full) bloom with the flowers fully open: *The roses were in bloom.*

bloom[2] v [I] **1** if a plant blooms, its flowers open **2** to be happy, healthy, and successful: *Jo seemed to be blooming.*

blossom[1] /'blɒsəm $ 'blɑː-/ n [C,U] a flower or the flowers on a tree or bush: *huge white blossoms* | in blossom (=with the flowers open) → see picture at PLANT

blossom[2] v [I] **1** if trees blossom, they produce flowers **2** also **blossom out** to become happier, more beautiful, or more successful: +**into** *She blossomed into a beautiful young woman.*

blot[1] /blɒt $ blɑːt/ v [T] **blotted, blotting** to dry wet spots on something using soft paper or a cloth

blot sth ⇔ **out** phr v **1** to cover or hide something completely: *Black clouds blotted out the sun.* **2** to stop yourself thinking about something unpleasant: *He tried to blot out the memory of that night.*

blot[2] n [C] a drop of liquid such as ink that has fallen onto a piece of paper

blotch /blɒtʃ $ blɑːtʃ/ n [C] a pink or red mark on your skin or a coloured mark on something —**blotchy** adj: *blotchy leaves*

'blotting ,paper n [U] soft paper used for drying ink on a page

blouse /blaʊz $ blaʊs/ n [C] a shirt for a woman or girl: *She was wearing a silk blouse.*

blow[1] /bləʊ $ bloʊ/ v past tense **blew** /bluː/ past participle **blown** /bləʊn $ bloʊn/

1 [I] if wind or air blows, it moves: *A cold wind was blowing hard.* | *A sudden draught of air blew in.*

2 [I,T] to move to or in the wind, or to make something move somewhere in the wind: +**in** *Her hair was blowing in the breeze.* | **blow sth across/ into etc sth** *The wind blew leaves across the path.* | **blow (sth) in/out/down etc** *My ticket blew away.* | *Trees had been blown down.* | **blow (sth) open/shut** *The door blew shut behind me.*

3 [I,T] to push air out through your mouth: **blow (sth) into/onto/through etc sth** *Renee blew on her soup to cool it down.* | *He blew the smoke right into my face.*

4 [I,T] to make a sound by pushing air into a whistle, horn, or musical instrument: *The referee's whistle blew.* | *A truck went by and blew its horn at her.*

5 **blow sth off/away/out etc** to damage or destroy something violently with an explosion or shooting: *Part of his leg had been blown off.*

6 **blow your chances/blow it** informal to lose a good opportunity by making a mistake: *By failing this exam I've blown my chances of getting into university.*

7 [T] informal to spend a lot of money in a careless way: *He blew all his savings on a trip to Hawaii.*

8 **blow your nose** to clear your nose by forcing air through it into a cloth or piece of paper

9 [I,T] if electrical equipment blows, it suddenly stops working because too much electricity has passed through: *My hairdryer's blown a fuse.*

blow sb away phr v spoken to make someone feel very surprised and pleased: *Their kindness just blew me away.*

blow sth ⇔ **out** phr v to blow air on a flame and make it stop burning: *Blow out all the candles.*

blow over phr v if an argument or storm blows over, it ends

blow up phr v **1** to destroy something, or to be destroyed, with an explosion: *Their plane blew up in mid-air.* | **blow sth** ⇔ **up** *The bridge was blown up by terrorists.* **2** **blow sth** ⇔ **up** to fill something with air or gas: *Come and help me blow up the balloons.*

blow[2] n [C]

1 something very sad and disappointing that happens to you: *Her mother's death was a terrible blow.*

2 a hard hit with a hand, tool, or weapon: +**to/on** *The victim suffered several blows to the head.*

3 when you blow air out of your mouth or nose: *One blow and the candles were out.*

4 **come to blows** if two people come to blows, they start fighting
→ BODY BLOW

,blow-by-'blow adj **a blow-by-blow account/ description etc** a description of an event that gives all the details exactly as they happened

'blow dry v [T] to dry your hair using an electric HAIRDRYER —**blow-dry** n [singular] *a cut and blow-dry*

blown /bləʊn $ bloʊn/ v the past participle of BLOW

blowout /'bləʊaʊt $ 'bloʊ-/ n [C] informal **1** a tyre that bursts suddenly **2** a big expensive meal or a large party

B

blubber[1] /'blʌbə $ -ər/ also **blub** /blʌb/ v [I] *BrE informal* to cry noisily

blubber[2] n [U] the fat of sea animals, especially WHALES

bludgeon /'blʌdʒən/ v [T] to hit someone several times with something heavy: *He was bludgeoned to death.*

blue[1] /bluː/ adj

1 having the colour of the sky on a fine day: *the blue lake* | **dark/light/pale/bright blue** *a dark blue dress* → see picture at PATTERN

2 [not before noun] *informal* sad: *I've been feeling kind of blue lately.*

3 blue joke/movie a joke or film about sex
→ **black and blue** at BLACK[1] → NAVY BLUE → **once in a blue moon** at ONCE[1] → ROYAL BLUE

blue[2] n [C,U]

1 the colour of the sky on a fine day: *I like greens and blues best.* | *She was dressed in blue.*

2 blues also **the blues** [plural] a slow sad style of music that came from the southern US: *He sings the blues.*

3 have/get the blues *informal* to feel sad and alone

4 out of the blue *informal* if something happens out of the blue, it is unexpected: *The letter came completely out of the blue.*

bluebell /'bluːbel/ n [C] a small plant with blue flowers that often grows in forests

blueberry /'bluːbəri $ -beri/ n [C] plural **blueberries** a small round dark blue fruit

blue-'blooded adj a blue-blooded person belongs to a royal or NOBLE family

'blue-chip adj **blue-chip companies/shares etc** companies or SHARES that are very unlikely to lose money

blue-'collar adj blue-collar workers do physical work, rather than working in offices [➡ white-collar]

blueprint /'bluːprɪnt/ n [C] a plan for achieving something, or showing how to build something: **+for** *a blueprint for health care reform* | *the blueprint for a new shopping mall*

blue 'ribbon n [C] the first prize in a competition, sometimes a small piece of blue material

bluff[1] /blʌf/ v [I,T] to pretend that you are going to do something or that you know about something, in order to get what you want: *I don't believe you – I think you're bluffing!*

bluff[2] n **1** [C,U] an attempt to make someone believe that you are going to do something when you do not really intend to: *He threatened to resign, but I'm sure it's a bluff.* **2 call sb's bluff** to tell someone to do what they are threatening to do because you do not believe they will really do it

blunder[1] /'blʌndə $ -ər/ n [C] a careless or stupid mistake: *a political blunder*

blunder[2] v [I] **1** to move in an unsteady way as if you cannot see properly: **+into/past/through etc** | *Jo came blundering down the stairs.* **2** to make a careless or stupid mistake

blunt[1] /blʌnt/ adj **1** not sharp or pointed: *a blunt knife* → see picture at SHARP[1] **2** saying exactly what you think, even if it upsets people: *Julian's blunt words hurt her.* —**bluntness** n [U]

blunt[2] v [T] to make someone's feelings less strong: *Too much alcohol blunted my reactions.*

bluntly /'blʌntli/ adv speaking in a direct, honest way that sometimes upsets people: *To put it bluntly, you're not going to pass the exam.*

blur[1] /blɜː $ blɜːr/ n [singular] something that you cannot see clearly or cannot remember clearly: *Below me, the island was already a blur.* | *The crash is just a blur in my mind.*

blur[2] v [I,T] blurred, blurring to become less clear, or to make something less clear: *His writing blurred beneath her tired eyes.* | *Electronic resources have blurred the distinction between learning and play.*

blurb /blɜːb $ blɜːrb/ n [singular] a short description giving information about a book or new product

blurred /blɜːd $ blɜːrd/ also **blurry** /'blɜːri/ adj not clear: *blurry photos* | *a blurred memory*

blurt /blɜːt $ blɜːrt/ also **blurt out** v [T] to say something suddenly and without thinking, especially something that you should keep secret: *Pete blurted out the news at a party.*

blush /blʌʃ/ v [I] to become red in the face, especially because you are embarrassed: *The way he looked at her made her blush.* | **+with** *Toby blushed with pride.* —**blush** n [C]

blusher /'blʌʃə $ -ər/ also **blush** *AmE* n [C,U] cream or powder that you put on your face to make it look pink and attractive

bluster /'blʌstə $ -ər/ v [I] to speak in a loud angry way —**bluster** n [U]

blustery /'blʌstəri/ adj blustery weather is very windy: *a blustery winter day*

boar /bɔː $ bɔːr/ n [C] **1** a male pig **2** a wild pig

boards

chessboard

skateboard

ironing board

cheese board

board[1] /bɔːd $ bɔːrd/ n

1 [C] a piece of wood or plastic on a wall where you can write or put information: **on the board** *The teacher wrote a few words on the board.* | *Can I put this notice on the board?* | *Remember to check the board for dates and times.*

2 [C] a flat piece of wood or plastic that you use for a particular purpose: *a chopping board* (=for chopping food) | **a chess/darts etc board** (=for playing these games)

3 also **Board** [C also + plural verb] *BrE* the group of people in a company or organization who

make important decisions: **+of** *The Board of Directors met yesterday.* | *a board meeting* | *one of the **board members***
4 Board used in the names of some organizations: *the Electricity Board* | *the Board of Trade*
5 [C] a long thin flat piece of wood used for making floors, fences etc
6 on board on a ship, plane, or spacecraft: *There were over 1000 passengers on board.*
7 [U] the meals that are provided for you when you pay to stay somewhere: **full board/half board** (=all meals or only breakfast and dinner) *How much is a single room with full board?* | **board and lodging** *BrE*/**room and board** *AmE* (=meals and a room) *The cost covers the student's board and lodging.*
8 across the board affecting everyone or everything: *Prices have been reduced **right across the board**.*
→ BULLETIN BOARD, DIVING BOARD, DRAINING BOARD, DRAWING BOARD, IRONING BOARD

board² *v* **1** [I,T] to get on a plane, ship, or train: *Passengers in rows 15 to 25 may now board.* | **boarding card/pass** (=a card you must show in order to get on a plane) → see box at AIRPORT
2 be boarding if a plane or ship is boarding, passengers are getting on it: *Flight 503 for Lisbon is now boarding.* **3** [I] to pay to stay in a room in someone's house: *Most students board with local families.* **4** [I] *especially BrE* to live at school rather than going home at night
　board sth ⇔ **up** *phr v* to cover windows or doors with wooden boards: *The house next door has been boarded up for months.*

boarder /ˈbɔːdə $ ˈbɔːrdər/ *n* [C] **1** *especially BrE* a child who lives at school **2** *AmE* someone who pays to live in someone else's house and have meals there [= **lodger** *BrE*]

'board game *n* [C] an indoor game that you play by moving small pieces around on a special board

'boarding house *n* [C] a private house where you pay to sleep and eat

'boarding school *n* [C] a school where students live rather than going home at night

boardroom /ˈbɔːdruːm, -rʊm $ ˈbɔːrd-/ *n* [C] a room where the important people in a company have meetings

boardwalk /ˈbɔːdwɔːk $ ˈbɔːrdwɒːk/ *n* [C] *AmE* a raised path made of wood, usually built next to the sea

boast¹ /bəʊst $ boʊst/ *v* **1** [I] to talk too much about your own abilities and achievements in a way that annoys other people: **+about** *He's always boasting about how much money he has.* **2** [T] if a place boasts something good, the place has it: *The health club boasts an Olympic-sized swimming pool.*

boast² *n* [C] something that you like telling people because you are proud of it: *Her proud boast was that she had never had a day's illness.*

boastful /ˈbəʊstfəl $ ˈboʊst-/ *adj* talking too much about your own abilities and achievements —**boastfully** *adv*

boat /bəʊt $ boʊt/ *n* [C]
1 a vehicle that travels across water [➙ **ship**]: **by boat** *You can only get to the island by boat.* | **a fishing/sailing/rowing etc boat**
2 be in the same boat (as sb) to be in the same

unpleasant situation as someone else: *We're all in the same boat, so stop complaining.*
→ HOUSEBOAT, MOTORBOAT, SAILBOAT → **miss the boat/ bus** at MISS¹ → **rock the boat** at ROCK²

boating /ˈbəʊtɪŋ $ ˈboʊt-/ *n* [U] the activity of travelling in a small boat for pleasure: *a boating holiday in Norfolk*

bob¹ /bɒb $ bɑːb/ *v* [I] **bobbed, bobbing** to move up and down on water: *a small boat **bobbing up and down***

bob² *n* [C] a way of cutting your hair so that it hangs straight down to the level of your chin → see picture at HAIR

bobbin /ˈbɒbɪn $ ˈbɑː-/ *n* [C] a small round object that you wind thread onto, especially on a SEWING MACHINE

bobby /ˈbɒbi $ ˈbɑːbi/ *n* [C] plural **bobbies** *BrE informal old-fashioned* a policeman

'bobby pin *n* [C] *AmE* a thin piece of metal that women use to hold their hair in place [= **hairgrip** *BrE*]

bode /bəʊd $ boʊd/ *v* **bode well/ill** *literary* to be a good or bad sign for the future: *The recent survey bodes ill for the Democrats.*

bodice /ˈbɒdɪs $ ˈbɑː-/ *n* [C] the part of a woman's dress above her waist

bodily¹ /ˈbɒdɪli $ ˈbɑː-/ *adj* relating to the human body: *He did not suffer any bodily harm.*

bodily² *adv* if you move someone bodily, you lift them or carry them: *I had to **lift** him **bodily** onto the bed.*

body /ˈbɒdi $ ˈbɑːdi/ *n* plural **bodies**
1 [C] **a)** the physical structure of a person or animal: *He had mud and dirt all over his body.* | *the **human body*** | *exercise that's good for the body and mind* **b)** the central part of a person or animal's body, not including the arms, legs, or head: *Keep your arms close to your body.* **c)** the dead body of a person: **+of** *The body of a girl has been found in the river.*
2 [C] an official group of people who work together: *the official body responsible for safety at work*
3 body of sth **a)** a large amount of information, knowledge etc: *There's a **body of evidence** in favour of this idea.* **b)** the main part of something: *The first paragraph should prepare the way for the body of your essay.*
4 [C] the main structure of a vehicle, not the engine, wheels etc: *The body of the plane was not damaged.*
5 [U] hair that has body is thick and healthy

'body blow *n* [C] a serious disappointment or shock

'body ,building *n* [U] doing physical exercises to make your muscles bigger and stronger —**body builder** *n* [C]

B

bodyguard

bodyguard /ˈbɒdigɑːd $ ˈbɑːdigɑːrd/ n [C] someone whose job is to protect an important person

ˈbody ˌlanguage n [U] movements you make without thinking, that show what you are feeling or thinking: *I could tell from his body language that he was nervous.*

bodywork /ˈbɒdiwɜːk $ ˈbɑːdiwɜːrk/ n [U] the metal structure of a vehicle, not the engine, wheels etc

bog¹ /bɒg $ bɑːg, bɔːg/ n [C,U] an area of soft muddy ground

bog² v **get/be bogged down (in sth)** to be unable to make any progress because you have become so involved with a problem: *Let's not get bogged down in minor details.*

bogeyman /ˈbəʊgimæn $ ˈboʊ-/ n [C] plural **bogeymen** /-men/ an evil SPIRIT, especially in children's imagination or stories

boggle /ˈbɒɡəl $ ˈbɑː-, ˈbɔːɡi/ v **the/your mind boggles** *spoken* used to say that something is difficult to imagine or believe: *The amount of money involved makes your mind boggle.*

boggy /ˈbɒɡi $ ˈbɑː- ˈbɔːɡi/ adj boggy ground is wet and muddy

ˌbog-ˈstandard adj BrE informal disapproving not special in any way

bogus /ˈbəʊɡəs $ ˈboʊ-/ adj not true or real, although someone is pretending that it is: *bogus insurance claims*

bohemian /bəʊˈhiːmiən, bə- $ boʊ-, bə-/ adj living in a very relaxed way and not accepting society's rules of normal behaviour —**bohemian** n [C]

boil¹ /bɔɪl/ v [I,T]

1 if a liquid boils, or if you boil it, it becomes hot enough to change into steam: *Drop the noodles into boiling salted water.* | **+at** *Water boils at 100°C.*

2 a) to cook something in boiling water: *Boil the rice for 10 minutes.* | *a boiled egg* → see box at **COOK** → see picture at **POTATO** **b)** to heat a container so the liquid in it boils: *Will you boil the kettle and make some tea?* | *The kettle's boiling.*

boil down to sth *phr v* if a situation or statement boils down to something, that is the most important fact or the basic meaning: *It all boils down to how much money you have.*

boil over *phr v* **1** to boil and flow over the sides of a pan **2** if a situation or an emotion boils over, people begin to get angry

boil² n **1 the boil** BrE; **a boil** AmE a state of boiling: *Bring the soup to the boil.* | *Wait until the water comes to the boil.* **2** [C] a painful infected swelling under your skin

boiler /ˈbɔɪlə $ -ər/ n [C] a container for heating water, that provides hot water in a house or steam for an engine

ˈboiler suit n [C] BrE a piece of loose clothing like trousers and a shirt joined together, that you can wear over your clothes to protect them when you are working

boiling /ˈbɔɪlɪŋ/ adj extremely hot: *It's boiling hot in here.* → see box at **HOT**

ˈboiling point n [singular] the temperature at which a liquid boils

boisterous /ˈbɔɪstərəs/ adj noisy and full of energy: *boisterous children*

bold¹ /bəʊld $ boʊld/ adj **1** confident and willing to take risks: *a bold and imaginative plan* | *She was bold enough to ask for more money.* **2** very clear and strong or bright: *a bold, bright red* | *The graphics are bold and colourful.* —**boldly** adv —**boldness** n [U]

bold² n [U] a style of printed letters that are darker and thicker than ordinary letters: *The chapter headings are in bold.*

bollard /ˈbɒləd, -lɑːd $ ˈbɑːlərd/ n [C] BrE a short thick post in the street, used to control traffic

bolster /ˈbəʊlstə $ ˈboʊlstər/ also **bolster up** v [T] to improve something by giving support and encouragement: *She tried to bolster his confidence.*

bolt¹ /bəʊlt $ boʊlt/ n [C] **1** a metal bar that slides across to fasten a door or window **2** a screw with no point, used with a NUT to fasten things together **3 a bolt from the blue** something that is completely unexpected: *Her promotion was a bolt from the blue.*

bolt² v **1** [I] to run away suddenly: *A gun fired, and the horse bolted.* **2** [T] to fasten two things together, using a bolt: *The chairs are bolted to the floor.* **3** [T] to lock a door or window with a bolt **4** also **bolt down** [T] to eat something very quickly: *He bolted down his lunch.*

bolt³ adv **sit/stand bolt upright** to sit or stand with your back very straight: *He suddenly sat bolt upright in bed.*

bomb¹ /bɒm $ bɑːm/ n [C]

1 a weapon made of material that will explode: **a bomb goes off/explodes** *The bomb went off in a crowded street.* | **plant/drop a bomb** *Bombs were dropped on the city.* | *protests against* **the bomb** (=nuclear bombs)

2 a bomb *informal* a lot of money: *It costs a bomb to have leather dry-cleaned.*
→ **TIME BOMB**

bomb² v **1** [T] to attack a place with bombs: *Terrorists bombed the railway station.* **2** [I] *informal* to be unsuccessful: *Her latest movie bombed.* **3** [I always + adv/prep] BrE informal to move very quickly

bombard /bɒmˈbɑːd $ bɑːmˈbɑːrd/ v [T] **1** to attack a place for a long time with guns and bombs: *They bombarded the enemy camp.* **2** to ask a lot of questions or give a lot of information or criticism, so that it is difficult for someone to deal with: *Viewers bombarded the TV station with complaints.* —**bombardment** n [C,U]

'bomb dis,posal *n* [U] the job of making bombs safe when they have not yet exploded

bomber /'bɒmə $ 'bɑːmər/ *n* [C] **1** a plane that drops bombs **2** someone who puts a bomb somewhere

bombshell /'bɒmʃel $ 'bɑːm-/ *n* [C] a shocking piece of news: *Then she **dropped** the **bombshell**: she was pregnant.*

bona fide /ˌbəʊnə 'faɪdi $ 'bəʊnə faɪd/ *adj* real and not intending to deceive anyone: *The pool is for bona fide members only.*

bonanza /bə'nænzə, bəʊ- $ bə-, bəʊ-/ *n* [C] a situation in which people make a lot of money: *The discovery could represent an amazing cash bonanza.*

bond[1] /bɒnd $ bɑːnd/ *n* [C] **1** a shared feeling or interest that unites people: **+between** *the bond between a mother and child* | **+with** *Britain has a special bond with the US.* **2** an official document promising that a government or company will pay back money that it has borrowed, often with INTEREST: *government bonds*

bond[2] *v* [I] **1** if two things bond, they become firmly fixed or glued together **2** to develop a special relationship with someone: *You all have to bond as a team.* —**bonding** *n* [U]

bondage /'bɒndɪdʒ $ 'bɑːn-/ *n* [U] a situation in which people have no freedom [➡ **slavery**]

bone /bəʊn $ boʊn/ *n* [C,U]
1 one of the hard parts that form the frame of the body: *Sam **broke** a **bone** in his foot.* | **hip/ thigh/cheek etc bone** *She was so thin her hip bones stuck out.* | *fragments of bone*
2 the bare bones (of sth) the most basic and important details of something
3 make no bones about (doing) sth to say or do something in an open way, because you are not ashamed about it: *She makes no bones about her ambitions.*
4 a bone of contention something that causes arguments

,bone 'dry *adj* completely dry

'bone ,marrow *n* [U] the substance in the middle of bones [= **marrow**]

bonfire /'bɒnfaɪə $ 'bɑːnfaɪr/ *n* [C] a large outdoor fire → see box at FIRE

'Bonfire ,Night *n* [U] November 5th, when people in Britain light FIREWORKS and have large outdoor fires

bonkers /'bɒŋkəz $ 'bɑːŋkərz/ *adj informal* crazy

bonnet /'bɒnɪt $ 'bɑː-/ *n* [C] **1** *BrE* the front part of a car, that covers the engine [= **hood** *AmE*] → see picture on page A12 **2** a hat that ties under the chin, worn by babies or by women in the past

bonny /'bɒni $ 'bɑːni/ *adj BrE* pretty and healthy – used mainly in northern Britain: *a bonny baby*

bonus /'bəʊnəs $ 'boʊ-/ *n* [C] **1** money added to someone's usual pay, especially as a reward for good work: *a Christmas bonus* **2** something good that you do not expect in a situation: *We work well together – the fact that we're friends is a bonus.*

bony /'bəʊni $ 'boʊ-/ *adj* **1** very thin: *bony fingers* **2** containing a lot of bones: *bony fish*

boo[1] /buː/ *v* [I,T] to shout 'boo' to show that you do not like a person, performance etc —**boo** *n* [C]

boo[2] *spoken* said loudly and suddenly to someone in order to frighten them, as a joke

boob /buːb/ *n* [C] *informal* **1** [usually plural] a woman's breast **2** *BrE* a silly mistake

booby prize /'buːbi praɪz/ *n* [C] a prize given as a joke to the person who is last in a competition

'booby trap *n* [C] a hidden bomb that will explode when anyone or anything touches something connected to it —**booby-trapped** *adj*

book[1] /bʊk/ *n* [C]

1 a set of printed pages held together in a cover so that you can read them: **+by** *a book by Zadie Smith* | **+about/on** *a book on Ethiopia* | *I'm reading a good book.* | **cookery/history/ grammar etc book** *The poetry books are on this shelf.*

THESAURUS

Books which describe real things or events are called **non-fiction**. Books which describe imaginary events are called **fiction**. Fiction that people think is important is also called **literature**.
Books which you look at to find specific information are called **reference books**, for example **dictionaries** and **encyclopedias**.
Books that are used in schools are called **textbooks** or **coursebooks**.
hardback *BrE*/**hardcover** *AmE* – a book which has a hard stiff cover
paperback – a book which has a soft cover
novel – a book about imaginary events
science fiction – books about imaginary events in the future

---

2 sheets of paper that you can write on held together in a cover: *a red **address book*** | *a **sketch book***
3 a set of things such as stamps or tickets held together inside a paper cover: **+of** *a book of raffle tickets* | *a **cheque book***
4 books [plural] written records of a company's financial accounts: *a company that is having problems **balancing the books***
5 by the book exactly according to the rules: *They **do** everything **strictly by the book**.*
6 a closed book a subject that you do not understand anything about
7 be in sb's good/bad books *informal* used to say that someone is pleased or annoyed with you
→ PHONE BOOK, PHRASE BOOK

book[2] *v*

1 [I,T] to arrange to have or do something at a particular time in the future: **book a ticket/ flight/seat/room etc** *Have you booked a holiday this year?* | **book ahead/in advance** *The restaurant is very popular so it's best to book ahead.* | *The flight is **fully booked** (=there are no seats left).* → see box at HOTEL
2 [T] to arrange for someone to perform at a particular place and time: *We've booked a jazz band for the wedding.*
3 [T] to arrange for someone to stay in a hotel, fly on a plane etc: **book sb sth** *I've booked you a*

room at the Plaza. | **book sb into/onto sth** *I was booked onto the early flight.*
4 [T] to ARREST someone
5 [T] *BrE* if a REFEREE in a sports game books a player, they write their name in an official book because they have broken the rules

book in also **book into sth** *phr v BrE* to arrive at a hotel and say who you are [= **check in**]

bookcase /'buk-keɪs/ *n* [C] a piece of furniture with shelves to hold books

bookie /'buki/ *n* [C] *informal* a BOOKMAKER

booking /'bukɪŋ/ *n* [C] an arrangement to use a hotel room, travel by train etc, at a particular time in the future: *Can I make a booking for next Saturday?*

'booking ,office *n* [C] *BrE* a place where you buy train or bus tickets

bookkeeping /'buk,ki:pɪŋ/ *n* [U] the job or activity of recording the financial accounts of an organization —**bookkeeper** *n* [C]

booklet /'buklət/ *n* [C] a small book that gives information [= **leaflet**]: *a booklet on immunization*

bookmaker /'buk,meɪkə $ -ər/ *n* [C] *formal* someone whose job is to collect money that people BET (=risk) on the result of games, races etc and to pay them if they win

bookmark /'bukmɑ:k $ -mɑ:rk/ *n* [C] **1** a piece of paper that you put in a book so that you can find the page you want **2** a way of saving the address of a page on the Internet so that you can find it easily —**bookmark** *v* [T]

bookshelf /'bukʃelf/ *n* [C] plural **bookshelves** /-ʃelvz/ a shelf that you keep books on

bookshop /'bukʃɒp $ -ʃɑːp/ *especially BrE*; **bookstore** /'bukstɔː $ -stɔːr/ *AmE n* [C] a shop that sells books

bookstall /'bukstɔːl $ -stɔːl/ *n* [C] *BrE* a small shop with an open front that sells books and magazines, especially at a railway station

bookworm /'bukwɜːm $ -wɜːrm/ *n* [C] *disapproving* someone who likes reading very much

boom¹ /buːm/ *n* **1** [singular] a sudden increase in business activity or in the popularity of something [≠ **slump**]: +**in** *a boom in sales* | *the postwar property boom* | *The economic boom is over.* **2** [C] a deep loud sound, like the sound of an explosion

boom² *v* **1** [I] if business or the ECONOMY is booming, it is very successful and growing quickly **2** [I,T] to make a loud deep sound —**booming** *adj*: *a booming economy*

boomerang /'buːməræŋ/ *n* [C] a curved stick that comes back to you when you throw it

boon /buːn/ *n* [C] something that is useful and makes your life easier or better: *My new car is a boon.*

boorish /'buərɪʃ $ 'bur-/ *adj literary* rude

boost /buːst/ *v* [T] to increase or improve something: *The publicity boosted sales by 30%.* | *Winning really boosts your confidence.* —**boost** *n* [singular] *The news gave a boost to the economy.*

booster /'buːstə $ -ər/ *n* [C] **1** something that increases or improves something, especially a person's confidence: *His speech was a real morale booster.* **2** a small quantity of a drug that increases the effect of one that was given before **3** a ROCKET that provides extra power for a SPACECRAFT

boot¹ /buːt/ *n* [C]
1 a type of shoe that covers your whole foot and the lower part of your leg: *She wore high-heeled boots.* | **walking/hiking/football boots** ➔ see picture at **SHOE¹**
2 *BrE* an enclosed space at the back of a car, used for carrying bags etc [= **trunk** *AmE*] ➔ see picture on page A12
3 get/be given the boot *informal* to be forced to leave your job [= **get the sack**]
➔ **CAR BOOT SALE**

boot² *v* **1** also **boot up** [I,T] to start the program that makes a computer ready to be used: *My PC won't boot.* ➔ see box at **COMPUTER** **2** [T] *informal* to kick someone or something hard

booth /buːð $ buːθ/ *n* [C] a small enclosed area, often used for doing something privately: *a voting booth* | *a telephone booth*

bootleg¹ /'buːtleg/ *adj* [only before noun] bootleg products are made and sold illegally

bootleg² *n* [C] a musical recording that has been made illegally

booty /'buːti/ *n* [U] valuable things taken by a group of people, especially an army that has won a battle

booze¹ /buːz/ *n* [U] *informal* alcoholic drink

booze² *v* [I] *informal* to drink a lot of alcohol

border¹ /'bɔːdə $ 'bɔːrdər/ *n* [C]
1 the official line that separates two countries or states: +**between** *the border between England and Wales* | +**with** *an area of Brazil on the border with Bolivia* | **across/over the border** *He escaped over the border.* | *This is where we cross the border into Canada.*
2 a band around the edge of something: *paper with a black border*

border² *v* [T] **1** to share a border with another country: *Arab states that border Israel* **2** to form a line along the edge of something: *trees bordering the river*

border on sth *phr v* to be very close to being something extreme or bad: *a relaxed attitude bordering on negligence*

borderline¹ /'bɔːdəlaɪn $ 'bɔːrdər-/ *adj* nearly not good enough or close to not reaching a particular standard: *In borderline cases a second examiner will review your work.*

borderline² *n* [singular] the point at which one quality, condition etc ends and another begins: *the borderline between sleep and being awake*

bore¹ /bɔː $ bɔːr/ *v* **1** [T] to make someone feel bored: *Am I boring you?* | **bore sb with sth** *I won't bore you with the details.* **2** [I,T] to make a deep round hole in a hard surface: *They bored a tunnel into the rock.*

bore² *n* **1** [singular] something that is not interesting or annoys you: *School is such a bore.* **2** [C] someone who talks too much about uninteresting things

bore³ *v* the past tense of BEAR

bored /bɔːd $ bɔːrd/ *adj* tired and impatient because something is uninteresting or you have nothing to do: *I'm bored – let's go!* | *After an hour people started to get bored.* | +**with** *She's bored with doing the same thing every day.* | *I'm so bored with my job.* | **bored stiff/bored to tears** (=extremely bored)

boredom /ˈbɔːdəm $ ˈbɔːr-/ n [U] the feeling you have when you are bored: *They sang songs to* **relieve the boredom**.

boring /ˈbɔːrɪŋ/ adj not interesting in any way: *His job sounds so boring.* | *I got stuck talking to a really boring man.*

THESAURUS

dull: *'How was the party?' 'A bit dull, actually.'*
tedious: *The job is quite tedious.*
not (very/that/at all) interesting
→ INTERESTING

born¹ /bɔːn $ bɔːrn/ v
1 be born when a person or animal is born, they come out of their mother's body or out of an egg: *Where were you born?* | *lambs that have only just been born* | +**in** *His wife was born in India.* | *Shakespeare was born in 1564.* | +**on** *Her baby was born on May 5th.* | **be born into sth** (=be in a particular situation when you are born) *children born into poor families*
2 be born when something such as an idea is born, it starts to exist
3 be born to do sth to be very suitable for a particular job or activity: *She was born to perform.*

born² adj **born leader/teacher etc** someone who has a natural ability to lead, teach etc

born-again ˈChristian n [C] someone who has started to have very strong religious beliefs

borne /bɔːn $ bɔːrn/ v the past participle of BEAR → AIRBORNE

borough /ˈbʌrə $ -roʊ/ n [C] a town or part of a large city that is responsible for managing its own schools, libraries, roads etc

borrow /ˈbɒrəʊ $ ˈbaːroʊ, ˈbɔː-/ v
1 [I,T] to use something that belongs to someone else and give it back to them later [→ lend, loan]: *Can I borrow the car tonight, dad?* | **borrow sth from sb** *She borrowed money from her friends.* | +**from** *The company had to borrow from the bank.* → see box at LEND
2 [I,T] to take or copy ideas or words: **borrow sth from sth/sb** *English has borrowed many words from French.* | +**from** *His act borrows heavily* (=a lot) *from other comedians.*
—**borrowing** n [C,U] —**borrower** n [C]

bosom /ˈbʊzəm/ n **1** [singular] the front part of a woman's chest **2** [C, usually plural] one of a woman's breasts **3 bosom friend/buddy** a very close friend

boss¹ /bɒs $ bɔːs/ n [C]
1 someone who employs people or is in charge of people in an organization: *She asked her boss for the day off.* | *We've got a new boss at work.* | *I like being* **my own boss** (=working for myself, not an employer).
2 the person who controls a relationship or situation: *You have to show a dog that you're the boss.*

boss² also **boss around** v [T] to tell people to do things, especially when you have no authority to do it: *Stop bossing me around!*

bossy /ˈbɒsi $ ˈbɔːsi/ adj always telling other people what to do, in a way that is annoying: *a bossy little girl* —**bossily** adv —**bossiness** n [U]

botany /ˈbɒtəni $ ˈbaː-/ n [U] the scientific study of plants —**botanist** n [C] —**botanical** /bəˈtænɪkəl/ adj

botch /bɒtʃ $ baːtʃ/ also **botch up** v [T] *informal* to do something badly and carelessly: *The surgeon really botched the operation.*

both /bəʊθ $ boʊθ/ determiner, pron
1 used to talk about two people or things together [→ either, neither]: *Anne and John are both scientists.* | *They can both speak Spanish.* | *Hold it in both hands.* | *She loved them both parents.* | +**of** *Both of his sisters are blonde.* | *We could go bowling, or dancing, or both.*
2 both ... and ... used to emphasize that something is true not only of one thing or person but also of another: *a game enjoyed by both adults and children*

GRAMMAR

both, both of
Do not say 'The both men were killed'. Say *Both of the men were killed, Both men were killed*, or *Both the men were killed.*
Do not say 'his both sisters'. Say *both of his sisters* or *both his sisters.*

bother¹ /ˈbɒðə $ ˈbaːðər/ v
1 [I,T] to make the effort to do something: **bother to do sth** *He didn't bother to lock the door.* | **bother doing sth** *Did anyone bother filling in the form?* | +**with/about** *I'm not going to bother with changing my clothes.* | *'Shall I get you a ticket?' – 'No,* **don't bother.***'*
2 [I,T] to make someone feel slightly annoyed, worried, or upset: *It was noisy, but that didn't bother me.* | *Does* **it bother** *you* **that** *he forgets your name?*
3 [T] to annoy someone, especially by interrupting what they are doing: *Stop bothering me – I'm trying to work.*
4 can't be bothered (to do sth) *BrE* used to say that you do not have enough interest or energy to do something: *I can't be bothered to cook tonight.*

bother² n especially *BrE* [U] trouble or difficulty caused by small problems: +**with** *He's had some bother with his back.* | *'Thanks.' 'That's okay –* **it's no bother** (=I am happy to help).*'*

bother³ *BrE spoken* used when you are annoyed about something

bothered /ˈbɒðəd $ ˈbaːðərd/ adj [not before noun] *spoken* **1** worried or upset: *He doesn't seem at all* **bothered about** *what she said.* **2 not bothered** especially *BrE* used to say that something is not important to you: *'What shall we have to eat?' – 'I'm not bothered.'*

botox /ˈbəʊtɒks $ ˈboʊtaːks/ n [U] a substance that is put into areas of your face so that they do not move and get lines

bottle¹ /ˈbɒtl $ ˈbaːtl/ n [C]
1 a) a glass or plastic container with a narrow top, used for keeping liquids in: +**of** *a bottle of beer* | **a wine/beer/water etc bottle b)** the amount that a bottle contains: +**of** *She drank a whole bottle of milk.*
2 a container for a baby to drink from with a rubber part on the top: *Will you give Joe his bottle?*
→ HOT-WATER BOTTLE

bottle² v [T] to put a liquid into a bottle: *This wine is bottled in Burgundy.* —**bottled** adj: *bottled water*

bottle sth ⇔ **up** phr v to not allow yourself to show strong feelings: *It's not good to bottle up anger.*

'bottle bank n [C] a container in the street that you put empty bottles in, so that the glass can be used again

bottleneck /'bɒtlnek $ 'bɑː-/ n [C] **1** a place where traffic cannot pass easily, so that there are delays **2** a part of a process that causes delays

bottom¹ /'bɒtəm $ 'bɑː-/ n

1 the bottom the lowest part or side of something [≠ top]: +**of** *Hold the bottom of the ladder.* | **at the bottom (of sth)** *a picture with his name at the bottom* | *She stood at the bottom of the stairs.* | **on the bottom (of sth)** *What's that on the bottom of your shoe?* | **in the bottom (of sth)** *I found my keys in the bottom of my bag.*
2 the bottom the lowest position in an organization or company [≠ top]: **at the bottom (of sth)** *United are at the bottom of the league.*
3 the bottom the ground under an ocean, river, pool etc: *I can't touch the bottom at the deep end.* | **at the bottom (of sth)** *creatures that live at the bottom of the sea*
4 [C] the part of your body that you sit on
5 [C usually plural] the part of a set of clothes that you wear on the lower part of your body: **pyjama/bikini bottoms**
6 get to the bottom of sth to find out the cause of a problem or situation
7 be at the bottom of sth to be the basic cause of a problem or situation
→ **ROCK BOTTOM** → **from top to bottom** at **TOP¹**

bottom² adj

1 [only before noun] in the lowest place or position: **the bottom drawer/shelf/corner etc** *Dictionaries are on the bottom shelf.*
2 the least successful or important: **be/come bottom** *I was bottom in the spelling test.*

bottomless /'bɒtəmləs $ 'bɑː-/ adj extremely deep, or seeming to have no limit: *a bottomless hole* | *The government does not have a bottomless pit* (=a supply with no limits) *of money to spend on public services.*

,bottom 'line n **the bottom line** the most basic and important fact about a situation: *The bottom line is that we have to finish the project on time.*

bough /baʊ/ n [C] literary a large tree branch

bought /bɔːt $ bɒːt/ v the past tense and past participle of **BUY**

boulder /'bəʊldə $ 'boʊldər/ n [C] a very large rock

boulevard /'buːlvɑːd $ 'bʊləvɑːrd, 'bʊ-/ n [C] a wide road in a town or city

bounce¹ /baʊns/ v **1** [I,T] if something such as a ball bounces, or if you bounce it, it hits a surface and then immediately moves away from it: +**off** *The ball bounced off the post and into the goal.* | **bounce sth on/against etc sth** *Two boys were bouncing a basketball against the wall.*
2 [I] to jump up and down on a soft surface: +**on** *Don't bounce on the bed.* → see picture at **JUMP¹**
3 [I,T] if you write a cheque and it bounces, or your bank bounces it, the bank will not pay the amount written on the cheque because there is not enough money in your bank account **4** [I] to

walk quickly and with a lot of energy: +**into/along etc** *The children came bouncing into the room.* **5** also **bounce back** [I,T] if an email that you send bounces or is bounced, it is returned to you and the other person does not receive it because of a technical problem or error: *I sent you three emails, but they all bounced back.*

bounce back phr v to feel better after being ill, or to become successful again after failing or being defeated: *The team bounced back after a series of defeats.*

bounce² n [C] when something bounces

bouncer /'baʊnsə $ -ər/ n [C] someone whose job is to keep people who behave badly out of a club or bar

bouncy /'baʊnsi/ adj **1** something that is bouncy bounces easily: *a bouncy ball* **2** someone who is bouncy is happy and full of energy

bound¹ /baʊnd/ v the past tense and past participle of **BIND**

bound² adj [not before noun]

1 be bound to do sth to be very likely to do something or to happen: *Madeleine's bound to make friends.* | *Interest rates are bound to go up.*
2 be bound (by sth) to be forced to do what a law or agreement says you must do: *The company is bound by law to provide us with safety equipment.*
3 be bound up with sth to be closely related to something: *Jake's self-image is very much bound up with his job.*
4 written a ship, plane etc that is bound for a particular place is going there: +**for** *a ship bound for Peru* | *a Tokyo-bound flight*

bound³ v [I] to move quickly with long steps and a lot of energy: +**up/towards/across etc** *Grace came bounding down the stairs.*

bound⁴ n **1 bounds** [plural] the limits of what is possible or acceptable: *That behaviour is beyond the bounds of decency.* **2 out of bounds** if a place is out of bounds, you are not allowed to go there: *This room is out of bounds for children.* **3** [C] written a long or high jump

boundary /'baʊndəri/ n [C] plural **boundaries**
1 the line that marks the edge of an area of land [➡ border]: +**between** *The Ohio River forms a natural boundary between Ohio and Kentucky.*
2 the limit of what is acceptable or thought to be possible: +**of** *the boundaries of human knowledge*

boundless /'baʊndləs/ adj having no limit or end: *boundless energy*

bountiful /'baʊntɪfəl/ adj literary if something is bountiful, there is more than enough of it: *a bountiful supply of fresh food*

bounty /'baʊnti/ n [C] plural **bounties** money that is given to someone as a reward for helping to catch a criminal

bouquet /bəʊˈkeɪ, buː- $ boʊ-, buː-/ *n* [C] a number of flowers fastened together, that you give to someone

a bouquet of flowers

bourbon /ˈbʊəbən $ ˈbɜːr-/ *n* [U] a type of American WHISKY

bourgeois /ˈbʊəʒwɑː $ bʊrˈʒwɑː/ *adj disapproving* too concerned with having a lot of money, possessions, and a high position in society

bourgeoisie /ˌbʊəʒwɑːˈziː $ ˌbʊr-/ *n* **the bourgeoisie** the people in a society who are rich, educated, own land etc [➡ **middle class**]

bout /baʊt/ *n* [C] **1** a short period of illness: **+of** *a bout of flu* **2** a BOXING or WRESTLING match

boutique /buːˈtiːk/ *n* [C] a small shop that sells fashionable clothes

bovine /ˈbəʊvaɪn $ ˈboʊ-/ *adj technical* relating to cows

bow¹ /baʊ/ *v* [I,T] to bend the top part of your body forward in order to show respect for someone: *The actors bowed and left the stage.* | **+before/to** *He bowed respectfully to the king.*
bow out *phr v* to decide to stop doing something that you have been doing for a long time: **+of** *It's time for him to bow out of politics.*
bow to sb/sth *phr v* to finally agree to do something that people want you to do, even though you do not want to do it: *The government will have to bow to the wishes of the people.*

bow² /baʊ/ *n* [C] **1** when someone bows **2** the front part of a ship [➡ **stern**]

bow³ /bəʊ/ *n* [C] **1** a band of cloth or string with a knot in the middle and a circle on each side, used as decoration in your hair or to tie shoes: *hair tied back in a bow* **2** a weapon that you use for shooting ARROWS **3** a long piece of wood with material fastened to it, used for playing instruments with strings, such as a VIOLIN

bowel /ˈbaʊəl/ *n* [C usually plural] the part inside your body that carries solid waste food away from your stomach and out of your body

bowl¹ /bəʊl $ boʊl/ *n* [C]
1 a round container that is open at the top, in which you put food or liquid [➡ **dish**]: *a soup bowl*
2 also **bowlful** /ˈbəʊlfʊl $ ˈboʊl-/ the amount that a bowl will hold: **+of** *a bowl of rice*
3 bowls an outdoor game in which you roll large wooden balls towards a smaller ball

bowl² *v* [I,T] **1** to roll a ball along a surface when you are playing the games of BOWLS or BOWLING **2** to throw a ball towards the BATSMAN in cricket ➡ see box at **THROW**
bowl sb ⇔ over *phr v* to make someone very pleased, excited, or surprised: *When Ian met Sue, he was completely bowled over.*

bow-legged /ˌbəʊˈlegd◂, -ˈlegɪd◂ $ ˌboʊ-/ *adj* a bow-legged person has legs that curve out at their knees

bowler /ˈbəʊlə $ ˈboʊlər/ *n* [C] **1** a player who throws the ball towards the BATSMAN in CRICKET

2 *BrE* also **,bowler 'hat** a hard round black hat that businessmen sometimes wear

bowling /ˈbəʊlɪŋ $ ˈboʊ-/ *n* [U] an indoor game in which you roll a heavy ball along a wooden track in order to knock over pieces of wood called PINS

bow tie /ˌbəʊ ˈtaɪ $ ˌboʊ taɪ/ *n* [C] a man's tie fastened in the shape of a BOW

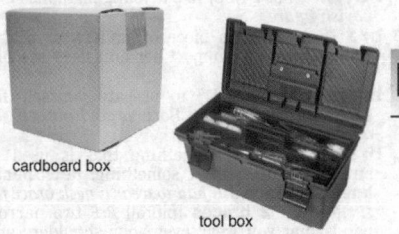

boxes

cardboard box

tool box

box¹ /bɒks $ bɑːks/ *n* [C]
1 a container for putting things in, especially one with four straight sides, or the amount that this container can hold: *a cardboard box* | **+of** *a box of chocolates* → see picture at **CONTAINER**
2 a small area of a theatre or court that is separate from where other people are sitting: *the jury box*
3 a small square on a page where you write a figure or other information: *Tick the box if you would like to join our mailing list.*
4 box (number) 25/232 etc a number used instead of an address, especially in newspaper advertisements [➡ **PO Box**]
5 the box *especially BrE informal* the television → **BALLOT BOX, CALL BOX, TELEPHONE BOX**

box² *v* **1** also **box up** [T] to put things in boxes: *It took us a day to box up everything in the study.*
2 [I] to take part in the sport of BOXING
box sb/sth ⇔ in *phr v* to surround someone or something so that they cannot get out or get away

boxer /ˈbɒksə $ ˈbɑːksər/ *n* [C] someone who does boxing as a sport

'boxer ,shorts *n* [plural] loose cotton underwear for men → see picture at **CLOTHES**

boxing /ˈbɒksɪŋ $ ˈbɑːk-/ *n* [U] a sport in which two people wearing big leather GLOVES hit each other

'Boxing Day *n* [C,U] *BrE* December 26th, the day after Christmas Day, which is a national holiday in the UK

'box ,office *n* [C] a place in a theatre, concert HALL etc where you buy tickets → see box at **THEATRE**

boy¹ /bɔɪ/ *n* [C]
1 a male child or a young man [➡ **girl**]: *a school for boys* | *a group of teenage boys* → see box at **MAN**
2 a son: *How old is your little boy now?*
→ **PAPER BOY**

boy² *AmE spoken informal* used to emphasize what you are saying: *Boy, that chicken smells good!*

'boy band *n* [C] a group of attractive young men who make POP records

B

boycott /'bɔɪkɒt $ -kɑːt/ v [T] to refuse to buy or use something as a protest: *Catholic groups plan to boycott the movie.* → see box at **PROTEST** —**boycott** n [C]

boyfriend /'bɔɪfrend/ n [C] a man that you are having a romantic relationship with [➡ **girlfriend**]

boyhood /'bɔɪhʊd/ n [U] the time during a man's life when he is a boy

boyish /'bɔɪ-ɪʃ/ adj like a young man: *his slim, boyish figure*

bra /brɑː/ n [C] a piece of underwear that a woman wears to support her breasts → see picture at **CLOTHES**

brace[1] /breɪs/ v [T] to prepare yourself for something unpleasant: *Boris braced himself for a fight.*

brace[2] n **1** [C] something that is used to strengthen or support something: **neck/back/knee etc brace** *Jill had to wear a neck brace for six weeks.* **2 braces** [plural] *BrE* two narrow bands that you wear over your shoulders and fasten to your trousers to stop them from falling down [= **suspenders** *AmE*] **3** [C] also **braces** *AmE* [plural] a wire frame that some people wear to make their teeth straight

bracelet /'breɪslᵻt/ n [C] a piece of jewellery that you wear around your wrist → see picture at **JEWELLERY**

bracing /'breɪsɪŋ/ adj bracing air or weather is cold and makes you feel healthy: *a bracing sea breeze*

bracken /'brækən/ n [U] a plant that often grows in forests and becomes reddish brown in the autumn

bracket[1] /'brækᵻt/ n [C] **1** one of the pairs of signs ( ) put around words to show additional information [= **parenthesis** *AmE*]: **in brackets** *Last year's sales figures are given in brackets.* **2 income/tax/age etc bracket** a particular level of income, tax etc: *Price's new job puts him in the highest tax bracket.* **3** a piece of metal or wood fixed to a wall to support a shelf

bracket[2] v [T] **1** to consider a group of people or things as similar: *Don't bracket us with those idiots.* **2** to put brackets around a word

brag /bræg/ v [I] **bragged, bragging** to talk too proudly about yourself [= **boast**]: **brag about sth** *Ray likes to brag about his success with women.*

braid[1] /breɪd/ n **1** [U] a narrow band made of threads that are twisted together, used to decorate the edges of clothes: *gold braid* **2** [C] *AmE* a length of something, especially hair, made by twisting three pieces together [= **plait** *BrE*] → see picture at **HAIR** —**braided** adj

braid[2] v [T] *AmE* to twist three long pieces of hair, rope etc together to make one long piece [= **plait** *BrE*]

braille /breɪl/ n [U] a type of printing that blind people can read by touching the page

brain /breɪn/ n

1 [C] the part of your body inside your head which you use to think, feel, and move: *Jorge suffered brain damage in the accident.* | *a brain tumour* → see picture on page A3
2 [C usually plural,U] the ability to think well: *If you had any brains, you'd know what I mean.* | *Come on, use your brain, John.*
3 [C usually plural] *informal* someone who is

very intelligent: *Some of the best brains in the country are here tonight.*
4 be the brains behind sth to be the person who thought of and developed a plan, system, organization etc, especially a successful one: *He's the brains behind the company's success.*
→ **pick sb's brain(s)** at **PICK**[1] → **rack your brain(s)** at **RACK**[2]

brainchild /'breɪntʃaɪld/ n [singular] *informal* an idea, plan, organization etc that one person has thought of: **+of** *The personal computer was the brainchild of Steve Jobs.*

brainless /'breɪnləs/ adj completely stupid

brainstorm /'breɪnstɔːm $ -stɔːrm/ n [singular] *informal* **1** an American word for **BRAINWAVE** **2** *BrE* when you are suddenly unable to think clearly

brainstorming /'breɪnstɔːmɪŋ $ -ɔːr-/ n [U] when a group of people meet in order to try to develop ideas or solve problems

brainwash /'breɪnwɒʃ $ -wɒːʃ, -wɑːʃ/ v [T] to force someone to believe something that is not true by telling them many times that it is true: *People are brainwashed into believing that being fat is some kind of crime.* —**brainwashing** n [U]

brainwave /'breɪnweɪv/ n [C] *BrE* a very good idea that you have suddenly [= **brainstorm** *AmE*]

brainy /'breɪni/ adj *informal* intelligent

brake[1] /breɪk/ n [C] **1** the part of a vehicle that makes it go more slowly or stop: *You need good brakes on a motorbike.* | *cars fitted with anti-lock brakes* → see box at **DRIVE** → see picture on page A12 **2 put a brake on sth/act as a brake on sth** to make something develop more slowly or happen less

brake[2] v [I] to make a vehicle go more slowly or stop, using its brake: *Brake gently as you approach the bend.*

bramble /'bræmbəl/ n [C] a wild **BLACKBERRY** bush

bran /bræn/ n [U] the crushed skin of wheat and other grain, often used in bread

branch[1] /brɑːntʃ $ bræntʃ/ n [C]

1 a part of a tree that grows out from the **TRUNK** (=the main part) → see picture at **PLANT**
2 a local business, shop etc that is part of a larger business etc: *The shop has opened branches all over the country.*
3 one part of a large subject of study or knowledge: **a branch of medicine/physics/philosophy etc**

branch[2] also **branch off** v [I] to divide into two or more smaller, narrower, or less important parts: *When you reach Bread Street, the road branches into two.*

branch out *phr v* to start doing something different from the work or activities that you normally do: **+into** *The bank has begun to branch out into selling insurance.*

brand[1] /brænd/ n [C] **1** a product that a particular company makes: **+of** *a new brand of soap* **2** a particular quality or way of doing something: *Nat's special brand of humour*

brand[2] v [T] **1** to describe someone as a very bad type of person: **brand sb (as) sth** *Ryan was branded a liar by the media.* **2** to make or burn a mark on an animal in order to show who it belongs to

B

branded /ˈbrændɪd/ *adj* a branded product is made by a well-known company and has the company's name on it

brandish /ˈbrændɪʃ/ *v* [T] to wave a weapon around in a threatening way: *Chisholm burst into the office brandishing a knife.*

ˈbrand ˌname *n* [C] the name a company gives to a product it makes

ˌbrand-ˈnew *adj* completely new: *a brand-new car*

brandy /ˈbrændi/ *n* [C,U] plural **brandies** a strong alcoholic drink made from wine, or a glass of this drink

brash /bræʃ/ *adj disapproving* behaving too confidently and speaking too loudly: *a brash young senator*

brass /brɑːs $ bræs/ *n* [U] **1** a shiny yellow metal that is a mixture of COPPER and ZINC **2 a)** musical instruments that are made of metal, such as the TRUMPET: *a brass band* **b) the brass (section)** the people in an ORCHESTRA or band who play musical instruments that are made of metal
→ see box at **ORCHESTRA**

brat /bræt/ *n* [C] *informal* a badly behaved child: *a spoiled brat*

bravado /brəˈvɑːdəʊ $ -doʊ/ *n* [U] behaviour that is intended to show that you are brave and confident, even when you are not

brave¹ /breɪv/ *adj* behaving with courage in a frightening situation: *brave firefighters* | *Marti's brave fight against cancer* | *It was brave of you to tell her the truth.*
—**bravely** *adv*: *The troops fought bravely until the end.* —**bravery** *n* [U] *medals awarded for bravery*

brave² *v* [T] to be brave enough to do something difficult, dangerous, or unpleasant: *The crowd braved icy wind and rain to see the procession.*

bravo /ˈbrɑːvəʊ, brɑːˈvəʊ $ -voʊ/ *spoken* something that you shout to show that you like something

brawl /brɔːl $ brɒːl/ *n* [C] a noisy fight among a group of people: *a drunken brawl* → see box at **FIGHT** —**brawl** *v* [I]

brawn /brɔːn $ brɒːn/ *n* [U] physical strength —**brawny** *adj*: *brawny arms*

brazen¹ /ˈbreɪzən/ *adj* used to describe a person or the actions of a person who is not embarrassed about behaving in a wrong or immoral way: *a brazen lie* —**brazenly** *adv*

brazen² *v*
brazen sth **out** *phr v* to deal with a situation in which you have done something bad by continuing to say that you acted correctly

brazier /ˈbreɪziə $ -ʒər/ *n* [C] a metal container that holds a fire and is used to keep people warm outside

breach /briːtʃ/ *n* [C,U] when you break a law, rule, or agreement: **+of** *You are in breach of your contract.* —**breach** *v* [T]

bread
bagel
sliced bread
croissant
toast
loaf of bread

bread /bred/ *n* [U] a common food made by baking a mixture of FLOUR and water: *a loaf of bread* | *a slice of bread* | **white/brown/rye etc bread**

breadcrumbs /ˈbredkrʌmz/ *n* [plural] very small pieces of bread, often used in cooking

breadline /ˈbredlaɪn/ *n* **the breadline** a very low level of income which allows people to eat but not have any extra things: *a family living on the breadline*

breadth /bredθ, bretθ/ *n* **1** [C,U] the distance from one side of something to the other [= **width**] **2** [U] the quality of including a lot of different people, things, or ideas: **+of** *No one could equal Dr Brenninger's breadth of knowledge.* **3 a hair's breadth** a very small distance or amount: *The bullet missed his heart by a hair's breadth.*

breadwinner /ˈbred,wɪnə $ -ər/ *n* [C] the person in a family who earns most of the money that the family needs

break¹ /breɪk/ *v* past tense **broke** /brəʊk $ broʊk/ past participle **broken** /ˈbrəʊkən $ ˈbroʊ-/

1 [I,T] if something breaks, or if you break it, it separates into pieces, usually because it has been dropped, hit etc: *I had to break a window to get into the house.* | *Watch it — those glasses break easily.* | **break sth in half/two** *He broke the biscuit in half.*

THESAURUS

smash – used when a plate, glass etc breaks or is broken with a lot of force: *Angry crowds smashed windows in the city centre.*
shatter – used when a plate, glass etc breaks into a lot of small pieces: *The glass hit the floor, shattering everywhere.*
crack – used when a plate, glass etc is damaged so that there is a line between two parts of it: *Oh no! The vase is cracked.*
tear – used about paper or cloth: *I tore the letter to pieces.*
snap – to break into two pieces, making a loud noise: *The stick snapped in two.*

burst – used when a tyre or balloon with air inside it or a pipe with liquid inside it breaks: *Our pipes had burst in the freezing weather.* | *a burst tire*

2 [T] to damage a bone in your body by making it crack or split: **break your leg/arm etc** *She fell down and broke her hip.*

3 [I,T] if you break a tool or a machine, or if it breaks, it no longer works properly: *He was playing with the camera and broke it!*

4 [T] to disobey a law or rule: *Williams denied* **breaking** the **law.** | *Students who* **break** the **rules** *will be punished.*

5 [T] to not do what you promised to do: *The mayor* **broke** *a* **promise** *to improve schools.* | *You* **broke** *your* **word**.

6 [I,T] to stop for a short time in order to have a rest or eat something: **+for** *We broke for lunch at 12:30.* | *We can* **break** *our* **journey** *in Oxford.*

7 [T] to stop something from continuing: *The sound of gunfire* **broke the silence.**

8 break a habit to stop doing something that you do regularly, especially something that you should not do: *The program is designed to help drug addicts break their habit.*

9 break sb's heart to make someone very unhappy, especially by ending a relationship with them

10 break a record to do something faster, better etc than anyone has ever done it before: *an attempt to break the 10,000 metres* **world record**

11 break the news (to sb) to tell someone about something bad that has happened: *Ellie called him into her office to break the news.*

12 break sb's concentration to stop someone from being able to think about what they are doing: *A shout from the crowd broke the golfer's concentration.*

13 break loose/free to escape: *The cattle broke loose during the night.*

14 [I] if news about an important event breaks, it becomes known: *News of his resignation broke yesterday afternoon.*

15 break even to neither make a profit nor lose money: *We broke even in our first year of business.*

16 break the ice *informal* to make people who have just met feel less nervous and more willing to talk to each other: *I suggested a game to break the ice.*

17 [I] when a boy's voice breaks, it becomes lower and starts to sound like a man's voice

18 [I] if day or DAWN breaks, light begins to show in the sky as the sun rises

19 [I] if the weather breaks, it suddenly changes: *We went to the coast for a few days until the weather broke.*

20 [I] if a storm breaks, it begins

break away *phr v* **1** to move away from someone who is holding you: *She started crying and tried to break away.* **2** to leave a group or organization and form another group, usually because of a disagreement: **+from** *They broke away from the national union and set up their own local organization.*

break down *phr v* **1** if a car or a machine breaks down, it stops working: *My car broke down on the way to work.* **2** to fail: *Negotiations broke down after only two days.* | *She moved back*

to America when her **marriage broke down**.
3 if someone breaks down, they start crying: *Imelda* **broke down in tears** *at the funeral.*
4 break sth ⇔ down if you break down a door, you hit it so hard that it breaks and falls to the ground **5** if a substance breaks down, or if something breaks it down, it changes or separates into smaller parts as a result of a chemical process: **break sth ⇔ down** *Food is broken down in the stomach.*

break in *phr v* to use force to enter a building, especially in order to steal something: *Burglars broke in during the night and took the stereo.*

break into sth *phr v* **1** to use force to enter a building or car, especially in order to steal something: *They broke into the room through the back window.* **2** to suddenly start doing something: *He* **broke into a run** *as he came round the corner.* | *Her face suddenly* **broke into a smile**. **3** to become involved in a new job or business activity: *American companies are trying to break into Eastern European markets.*

break off *phr v* **1** if something breaks off, or if you break it off, it is separated from the main part of something: **break sth ⇔ off** *She broke off a piece of cheese.* | *One of the car's wing mirrors had broken off.* → see box at REMOVE **2 break sth ⇔ off** to end a relationship: *The US has broken off diplomatic relations with Iran.* | *She* **broke off** *their* **engagement** *a week before they were due to be married.* **3** to suddenly stop doing something or talking to someone: **break sth ⇔ off** *Without explanation, management broke off contract negotiations.*

break out *phr v* **1** if a disease, fire, or war breaks out, it starts: *Nine months later, war broke out in Korea.* → see box at FIRE **2** to escape from prison: **+of** *Two inmates broke out of prison and murdered a police officer.* **3 break out in spots/a rash/sweat etc** if you break out in spots etc, they appear on your skin

break through (sth) *phr v* to use force to get through something that is stopping you from moving forward: *Demonstrators tried to break through police lines.*

break up *phr v* **1 break sth ⇔ up** to separate something into smaller parts: *They plan to break the company up into several smaller companies.* **2** if something breaks up, or if you break it up, it breaks into small pieces: *The ship broke up on the rocks.* | **break sth ⇔ up** *We used shovels to break up the soil.* **3** to end a relationship with a husband, wife, BOYFRIEND etc: *Troy and I broke up last month.* | **+with** *She's broken up with Glen.* **4 break sth ⇔ up** to stop a fight or argument: *Three policemen were needed to break up the fight.* **5** if a meeting or party breaks up, people start to leave **6** *BrE* when a school breaks up, it closes for a holiday: **+for** *When do you break up for Easter?*

break with sb/sth *phr v* to leave a group of people or an organization, after a disagreement with them: *Yugoslavia under Tito soon broke with Stalin's Russia.*

break² *n* [C]

1 a period of time when you stop what you are doing in order to rest, eat etc: **have/take a break** *Let's take a ten-minute break.* | **lunch/ coffee/tea break** → see box at STOP

2 a short holiday: *We flew off for a week's break in Spain.* | **(the) Christmas/Easter/summer etc break** *Are you going anywhere over the Easter break?* | *luxury **weekend breaks***

3 the place where something, such as a bone in your body, has been broken: *The break has not healed correctly.*

4 a period of time when something stops happening before it starts again: **+in** *a break in the conversation*

5 a space or hole in something: **+in** *a break in the clouds*

6 a chance to become successful: *The band's **big break** came when they sang on a local TV show.*

7 break with tradition/the past a time when people stop following old customs and do something in a completely different way: *Clark made a complete break with the past and moved to Chile.*

8 the break of day *literary* the morning, when it starts getting light

breakable /ˈbreɪkəbəl/ *adj* made of a material that breaks easily: *Make sure you pack breakable ornaments carefully.*

breakage /ˈbreɪkɪdʒ/ *n* [C usually plural] something that someone breaks: *All breakages must be paid for.*

breakaway /ˈbreɪkəweɪ/ *adj* a breakaway group of people has separated from a larger group because of a disagreement: *a **breakaway group** of journalists*

breakdown /ˈbreɪkdaʊn/ *n* **1** [C,U] the failure of a relationship or system: **+of** *He moved away after the breakdown of his marriage.* | **+in** *a breakdown in the peace talks* **2** [C] a mental condition in which someone becomes unable to continue with their normal life: *Two years ago he had a **nervous breakdown**.* **3** [C] an occasion when a car or a piece of machinery stops working: *We **had a breakdown** on the motorway.* **4** [C] a statement explaining the details of something: **+of** *I'd like a breakdown of these figures, please.*

breaker /ˈbreɪkə $ -ər/ *n* [C] a large wave with a white top that rolls onto the shore

breakfast /ˈbrekfəst/ *n* [C,U] the meal you have in the morning: *I usually **have breakfast** at 7.30.* | **for breakfast** *Would you like tea or coffee for breakfast?* | **English breakfast** (=a cooked breakfast of BACON, eggs, TOAST etc) | **continental breakfast** (=a breakfast of coffee and bread with butter and JAM)
→ BED AND BREAKFAST

ˈbreak-in *n* [C] a situation in which someone enters a building by force, especially to steal things: *There was a break-in at the college last night.*

ˈbreaking ˌpoint *n* [U] when a person or system can no longer work well because there are so many problems: *The relationship has **reached breaking point**.*

breakneck /ˈbreɪknek/ *adj* **at breakneck speed/pace** extremely fast: *She was driving at breakneck speed.*

breakout /ˈbreɪkaʊt/ *n* [C] an escape from a prison, especially one involving a lot of prisoners

breakthrough /ˈbreɪkθruː/ *n* [C] an important new discovery or development: **+in** *Police have made a breakthrough in their hunt for the killers.*

breakup /ˈbreɪkʌp/ *n* [C] **1** the ending of a marriage or relationship **2** the separation of an organization or country into smaller parts: **+of** *the breakup of the Soviet Union*

breast /brest/ *n*
1 [C] one of the two round parts on a woman's chest that produce milk when she has a baby
2 [C,U] the front of a bird's body, or the meat from this: *turkey breast* → see picture on page A2
3 [C] *literary* the top of your body at the front
→ DOUBLE-BREASTED

ˈbreast-feed *v* [I,T] past tense and past participle **breast-fed** if a woman breast-feeds, she feeds a baby with milk from her breasts

breaststroke /ˈbrest-strəʊk $ -stroʊk/ *n* [U] a way of swimming in which you push your arms forward and then pull them back in a circle towards you → see picture at SWIM¹

breath /breθ/ *n*
1 [U] air that you send out of your lungs when you breathe: *He has **bad breath** (=his breath smells unpleasant).* | *I could **smell** alcohol **on his breath**.*
2 [C,U] air that you take into your lungs: **take a (big/deep/long) breath** *He took a **deep breath** and dived into the water.* | **out of/short of breath** (=having difficulty breathing, especially after exercise) *Eric ran in completely out of breath.* | **hold your breath** (=deliberately stop breathing for a short time) *Can you hold your breath under water?* → see box at BREATHE
3 get your breath back/catch your breath to rest after running, climbing etc until you can breathe normally again
4 a breath of fresh air a) something that is new, different, and enjoyable: *This exciting young designer has **brought a breath of fresh air** to the fashion world.* **b)** clean air outside: *I'm just going out for a breath of fresh air.*
5 don't hold your breath *spoken* used to say that something is not going to happen soon
6 take your breath away if something takes your breath away, it is very beautiful or exciting [➙ breathtaking]: *a view that will take your breath away*
7 under your breath in a quiet voice, so that other people cannot hear: *'I hate you,' he muttered under his breath.* → see box at HEAR

Breathalyzer also **-lyser** *BrE* /ˈbreθəl-aɪzə $ -ər/ *n* [C] *trademark* a piece of equipment used by the police to test whether a driver has drunk too much alcohol —**breathalyze** *v* [T]

breathe /briːð/ *v*
1 [I,T] to take air into your lungs and send it out again: *Grandad got up, **breathing heavily** (=with long slow breaths).* | *Relax and **breathe deeply** (=take in a lot of air).* | *Try not to breathe the fumes.*

THESAURUS

pant – to breathe quickly with short breaths, especially after exercising
wheeze – to breathe with difficulty, making a noise in your throat and chest, often because

B

you are ill
**be short of breath/be out of breath/gasp for
air** – to have difficulty breathing, often after
physical activity such as running or climbing

2 be breathing down sb's neck *informal* to
watch someone carefully and make them feel
nervous or annoyed: *I can't work with you
breathing down my neck.*
3 not breathe a word to not say anything about
something that is secret: *Promise not to breathe a
word to anyone.*
—**breathing** *n* [U]

breathe in *phr v* to take air into your lungs:
The doctor told her to breathe in. | **breathe sth
⇔ in** *They breathed in the fresh sea air.*

breathe out *phr v* to let air out of your lungs:
Jim breathed out deeply.

breather /'briːðə $ -ər/ *n* [singular] *informal* a
short rest from what you are doing: *Let's take a
breather.*

'breathing ,space *n* [singular, U] a short
period when you have a rest from doing something before starting again

breathless /'breθləs/ *adj* having difficulty
breathing because you are tired, excited, frightened etc: **+with** *They waited, breathless with
anticipation.* —**breathlessly** *adv*
—**breathlessness** *n* [U]

breathtaking /'breθ,teɪkɪŋ/ *adj* very impressive, beautiful, or surprising: *a breathtaking
view* —**breathtakingly** *adv*

breed[1] /briːd/ *v* past tense and past participle
bred /bred/ **1** [I] if animals breed, they have
babies: *Rats can breed every six weeks.* **2** [T] to
keep animals or plants in order to produce
young animals or develop new plants: *He breeds
cattle.* **3** [T] to cause a particular feeling, situation etc to develop: *Arguments can breed insecu-
rity in a child.*

breed[2] *n* [C] **1** a particular type of an animal:
+of *a rare breed of sheep* **2** a particular type of
person or thing: **+of** *The island is catering for a
new breed of tourists.*

breeder /'briːdə $ -ər/ *n* [C] someone who
breeds animals or plants: *a dog breeder*

breeding /'briːdɪŋ/ *n* [U] **1** when animals
produce babies: *the breeding season* **2** the
activity of keeping animals or plants in order to
produce others with particular qualities: *animal
breeding programmes*

'breeding ,ground *n* [C] **1** a place or situation where something bad develops: **+for** *Stale
milk is a breeding ground for germs.* **2** a place
where animals or birds go to breed

breeze[1] /briːz/ *n* [C] a gentle wind: *a light
breeze* → see box at **WIND**

breeze[2] *v* [I] to walk somewhere in a relaxed
confident way: **+in/out/along etc** *She breezed
into my office and asked for a job.*

breezy /'briːzi/ *adj* **1** a breezy person is confident and relaxed **2** if the weather is breezy,
there is quite a lot of wind —**breezily** *adv*

brethren /'breðrən/ *n* [plural] *old-fashioned*
the members of an organization, especially a
religious group

brevity /'brevɨti/ *n* [U] *formal* the quality of
being short and quick [➜ **brief**]: **+of** *the brevity of
human life* | *Michelle answered with brevity.*

brew[1] /bruː/ *v* **1** [T] to make beer **2** [T] to
make a drink of tea or coffee: *freshly brewed
coffee* **3** [I] if tea or coffee brews, it is left in hot
water for a few minutes so that the taste gets
stronger **4 be brewing** if trouble or a storm is
brewing, it will happen soon

brew[2] *n* [C] *informal* **1** a type of beer **2** a pot
of hot tea

brewer /'bruːə $ -ər/ *n* [C] a person or company
that makes beer

brewery /'bruːəri/ *n* [C] plural **breweries** a place
where beer is made, or a company that makes
beer

bribe[1] /braɪb/ *v* [T] to give someone money or a
gift to persuade them to do something, especially
something dishonest: **bribe sb to do sth** *He
bribed one of the guards to smuggle out a note.*

bribe[2] *n* [C] money or a gift that is given to
someone to persuade them to do something,
especially something dishonest: **accept/take a
bribe** *The judge admitted that he had accepted
bribes.*

bribery /'braɪbəri/ *n* [U] when someone offers
or accepts bribes

bric-a-brac /'brɪk ə ,bræk/ *n* [U] small objects
from people's houses that are not worth very
much money

brick /brɪk/ *n* [C,U] a hard block of baked clay
used for building walls, houses etc: *a brick
wall* | *The houses are made of brick.*

bricklayer /'brɪk,leɪə $ -ər/ *n* [C] someone
whose job is to build walls with bricks
—**bricklaying** *n* [U]

bridal /'braɪdl/ *adj* relating to a bride or a
wedding: *a bridal gown*

bride /braɪd/ *n* [C] a woman who is getting
married or has just got married [➜ **groom**] → see
box at **WEDDING**

bridegroom /'braɪdgruːm, -grʊm/ *n* [C] a man
who is getting married or has just got married →
see box at **WEDDING**

bridesmaid /'braɪdzmeɪd/ *n* [C] a girl or
woman who helps the bride on the day of her
wedding → see box at **WEDDING**

bridge

bridge[1] /brɪdʒ/ *n*

1 [C] a structure built over a river, road etc so
that people or vehicles can cross it: **+over/
across** *a bridge over the Mississippi* | *They
crossed the bridge over the railway line.*
2 [C] something that makes a connection
between two things: **+between** *The training programme is seen as a bridge between school and
work.* | *The police must build bridges*

(=develop a better relationship) *with the community.*

3 [C usually singular] the high part of a ship from which it is controlled

4 [U] a card game for four players

5 the bridge of your nose the upper part of your nose between your eyes

→ SUSPENSION BRIDGE

bridge² *v* [T]   **1** to reduce the difference between two things or people: **+between** *Are we doing enough to **bridge the gap** between rich and poor?*   **2** to build or form a bridge over something: *A fallen tree bridged the stream.*

bridle¹ /'braɪdl/ *n* [C] a set of leather bands that is put over a horse's head to control its movements

bridle² *v* [I,T] *written* to become angry or offended about something: **+at** *She bridled at the question.*

brief¹ /briːf/ *adj*

1 continuing for only a short time: *a brief visit*

2 using only a few words: *The letter was very brief.* | *a brief statement*

3 be brief to say or write something using only a few words: *Ladies and gentlemen, I'll try to be brief.*

—**briefly** *adv*

brief² *n* [C]   **1** instructions that explain someone's duties or jobs: *My brief is to increase our sales.*   **2 in brief** using only a few words: *Here is the sports news in brief.*   **3 briefs** [plural] men's or women's underwear worn on the lower part of the body

brief³ *v* [T] to give the information or instructions they need: **brief sb on sth** *The president has been **fully briefed** on the current situation.*

briefcase /'briːfkeɪs/ *n* [C] a flat case used to carry papers or books for work → see picture at CASE

briefing /'briːfɪŋ/ *n* [C,U] an occasion when people are given information or instructions: *a **press briefing** (=when people who report the news are given information)*

brigade /brɪ'ɡeɪd/ *n* [C] a large group of soldiers forming part of an army → FIRE BRIGADE

brigadier /ˌbrɪɡə'dɪə◂ $ -'dɪr◂/ *n* [C] an important officer in the British army

bright /braɪt/ *adj*

1 shining strongly or full of light: *bright lights* | *a large bright room* | *a **bright summer's day** (=with the sun shining)* → see box at SUN

2 intelligent: *Vicky is a very bright child.* | *He is always full of **bright ideas**.* → see box at INTELLIGENT

3 bright colours are strong and easy to see: *Her dress was bright red.*

4 happy or cheerful: *a **bright smile*** | *She sounded bright on the phone.*

5 a bright future is one that is likely to be successful: *Looking ahead, **the future looks bright**.*

—**brightly** *adv*: *brightly coloured balloons*

—**brightness** *n* [U]

brighten /'braɪtn/ *also* **brighten up** *v*   **1** [I,T] to become brighter or more pleasant, or to make something brighter or more pleasant: *The weather should brighten up in the*

afternoon. | *She bought flowers to brighten the room.*   **2** [I,T] to become happier, or to make someone happier: *She brightened up when she saw us coming.*

brilliant /'brɪljənt/ *adj*   **1** brilliant light or colour is very bright and strong: *brilliant sunshine* | *brilliant blue eyes*   **2** very clever, skilful, or successful: *a brilliant scientist* | *That's a **brilliant idea**!* | *He's had a **brilliant career**.* → see box at INTELLIGENT   **3** *BrE spoken* extremely nice or enjoyable: *'How was your holiday?' 'It was brilliant!'* → see box at GOOD, NICE

—**brilliance** *n* [U] —**brilliantly** *adv*

brim¹ /brɪm/ *n* [C]   **1** the bottom part of a hat that sticks out   **2** the top edge of a container: *The glass was **full to the brim** (=completely full).*

brim² *v* [I] brimmed, brimming   **1** if your eyes brim with tears, you start to cry   **2 be brimming (over) with sth** to have a lot of something: *Rob was brimming with confidence.*

brine /braɪn/ *n* [U] salty water, often used for preserving food

bring /brɪŋ/ *v* [T] past tense and past participle **brought** /brɔːt $ brɒːt/

1 a) to take something or someone with you to a place: *I brought these pictures to show you.* | **bring sb/sth with you** *Bring the children with you.* | **bring sb/sth to sth** *Our teacher brought a real owl to class.* **b)** to get something for someone and take it to them: **bring sb sth** *Rob brought her a glass of water.*

take – to move something from one place to another, or help someone go from one place to another: *Don't forget to take your umbrella.* | *I can take you home after the concert.*

get/fetch *especially BrE* – to go to another place and come back with something or someone: *Just a minute while I get my jacket.* | *Can you fetch the kids from school?*

2 to move something somewhere: **bring sth out/ up/down etc** *Bring your arms up level with your shoulders.* | *She reached into her bag and brought out a pen.*

3 to make something happen: *The strikes brought chaos.* | *His words brought a smile to her face (=made her smile).* | **bring sth to an end/close etc** (=make something stop) *The trial was brought to a sudden halt.* | *Bring the sauce to the boil (=make it boil by heating it).*

4 if something brings people to a place, it makes them go there: *The fair brings a lot of people to the town.*

5 to make something available for people to have or enjoy: **bring sth to sb/sth** *Investment has brought jobs to the region.* | **bring sb sth** *Football brought him wealth and fame.*

6 can't bring yourself to do sth to not be able to do something, especially because it is unpleasant: *I couldn't bring myself to look.*

bring sth ⇔ **about** *phr v* to make something happen: *The war brought about huge social and political changes.*

bring sb/sth **around/round** *phr v*   **1 bring the conversation around/round to sth** to deliberately and gradually change the subject of a conversation: *Helen tried to bring the conversation around to the subject of marriage.* **2** to make someone become conscious again

bring sth/sb ⇔ **back** *phr v* **1** to return from somewhere with something or someone: **+for** *I'll bring back some sweets for the kids.* **2** to start using something again that was used in the past: *Some people want to bring back the death penalty.* **3** to make you remember something: *Seeing him brought back a lot of memories.*

bring sb/sth **down** *phr v* **1** to reduce something to a lower level: *Better farming methods have brought down the price of food.* **2 bring down a government/president etc** to force a government etc to stop ruling a country **3** to make something or someone fall: *An enemy plane was brought down by rocket launchers.*

bring sth ⇔ **forward** *phr v* **1** to change the date or time of something so that it happens sooner: **+to** *The meeting was brought forward to Wednesday.* **2** *formal* to introduce new plans or ideas for people to discuss

bring sb/sth ⇔ **in** *phr v* **1** to introduce a new law: *The council will bring in new regulations to restrict parking.* **2** to ask someone with special knowledge, skills etc to do a particular job: **bring sb in to do sth** *The FBI were brought in to help with the search.* **3** to earn or produce an amount of money: *The sale should bring in more than £2 million.*

bring sth ⇔ **off** *phr v* to succeed in doing something difficult [= **pull off**]: *They brought off the most daring robbery in history.*

bring sth ⇔ **on** *phr v* to cause a pain or an unpleasant situation: *Stress can bring on a headache.*

bring sth ⇔ **out** *phr v* **1** to make something easier to notice: *The spices bring out the flavour of the meat.* **2** to produce something that will be sold to the public: *They're bringing out a new album next month.* **3 bring out the best/worst in sb** to make someone show the best or worst part of their character: *Becoming a dad has brought out the best in Dan.*

bring sb/sth **round** *phr v* → **BRING SB/STH AROUND**

bring sb ⇔ **together** *phr v* to make people do things together or feel more friendly to each other: *War brings a community together.*

bring sb/sth ⇔ **up** *phr v* **1** to start to talk about something [= **raise**]: *She wished she'd never brought up the subject of money.* **2** *especially BrE* to look after children until they are adults [= **raise** *AmE*]: *Rachel had been brought up by her grandmother.* | **bring sb up to do sth** (=teach a child at home to behave in a particular way) *We were brought up to be polite.* | **well/badly brought up** (=behaving well or badly because of the way you were taught at home) **3** *BrE* if you bring food up, it comes back up from your stomach and out of your mouth [= **vomit**]

brink /brɪŋk/ *n* **be on the brink (of sth)** to be almost in a new situation, especially a bad one: *The world seemed on the brink of war.*

brisk /brɪsk/ *adj* **1** quick or full of energy: *a brisk walk* | *Her voice sounded brisk.* **2** trade or business that is brisk is very busy and a lot of things are sold —**briskly** *adv* —**briskness** *n* [U]

bristle¹ /'brɪsəl/ *n* **1** [C,U] short stiff hair that feels rough: *His chin was covered with bristles.* **2** [C] a short stiff hair, wire etc on a brush —**bristly** *adj*

bristle² *v* [I] **1** to show that you are very annoyed: **+with** *She bristled with indignation.* **2** if an animal's fur bristles, it stands up stiffly because of fear or anger

bristle with sth *phr v* to be full of something: *streets bristling with tourists*

Brit /brɪt/ *n* [C] *informal* someone from Britain

British¹ /'brɪtɪʃ/ *adj* from or relating to Britain

British² *n* **the British** [plural] the people of Britain

Briton /'brɪtn/ *n* [C] *formal* someone from Britain

brittle /'brɪtl/ *adj* hard but easily broken: *The branches were dry and brittle.*

broach /brəʊtʃ $ broʊtʃ/ *v* **broach the subject/matter/question etc** to mention a subject that may be embarrassing or unpleasant: *At last he broached the subject of her divorce.*

B-road /'biː rəʊd $ -roʊd/ *n* [C] a type of road in Britain that is smaller than an A-ROAD

broad /brɔːd $ brɑːd/ *adj*
1 wide [≠ **narrow**; ➡ **breadth**]: *broad shoulders* | *He gave her a broad smile.*
2 including many different kinds of things or people [≠ **narrow**]: *a broad range of interests*
3 general, and without a lot of details: *a broad outline of the plan*
4 in broad daylight during the day, when it is light: *He was attacked in broad daylight.*
5 a broad ACCENT (=way of speaking) clearly shows where you come from [= **strong**]: *a broad Scottish accent*

broadband /'brɔːdbænd $ 'brɑːd-/ *n* [U] a system of connecting computers to the Internet and moving information at a very high speed —**broadband** *adj*

broadcast¹ /'brɔːdkɑːst $ 'brɔːdkæst/ *n* [C] a programme on radio or television: *a news broadcast*

broadcast² *v* [I,T] past tense and past participle **broadcast** to send out a radio or television programme: *The match will be broadcast live* (=while it is happening) *on Channel 5.* —**broadcasting** *n* [U]

broadcaster /'brɔːdkɑːstə $ 'brɔːdkæstər/ *n* [C] someone who speaks on radio and television programmes

broaden /'brɔːdn $ 'brɑːdn/ *v* [I,T] **1** to include more people, ideas, activities etc, or to make something do this [= **widen**]: *The social world of the child slowly broadens.* | *The party must broaden its appeal to younger voters.* | *Travel broadens the mind* (=helps you to understand more about people and the world). **2** also **broaden out** to become wider, or to make something wider: *The river broadens out here.*

broadly /'brɔːdli $ 'brɑːd-/ *adv* **1** in a general way: *We reached broadly similar conclusions.* | *Broadly speaking, there are two interpretations.* **2 smile/grin broadly** to have a big smile on your face

broad-minded /ˌbrɔːd'maɪndɪd◂ $ ˌbrɑːd-/ *adj* willing to accept behaviour or ideas that are very different from your own [≠ **narrow-minded**]

broadsheet /'brɔːdʃiːt $ 'brɒd-/ n [C] a serious newspaper printed on large sheets of paper [➡ **tabloid**] ➔ see box at NEWSPAPER

broadside /'brɔːdsaɪd $ 'brɒd-/ n [C] a strong criticism of someone or something

brocade /brə'keɪd $ brou-/ n [U] thick cloth that has a pattern of gold and silver threads

broccoli /'brɒkəli $ 'brɑː-/ n [U] a vegetable with green stems and green or purple flowers ➔ see picture at VEGETABLE

brochure /'brəʊʃə, -ʃʊə $ brou'ʃʊr/ n [C] a thin book that gives information or advertises something: *a holiday brochure*

broil /brɔɪl/ v [T] AmE to cook something under or over direct heat [= **grill** BrE]: *broiled chicken* ➔ see box at COOK

broiler /'brɔɪlə $ -ər/ n [C] AmE a special area of a STOVE used for cooking food under direct heat [= **grill** BrE]

broke[1] /brəʊk $ brouk/ adj [not before noun] *informal* **1** having no money at all: *I can't pay you now – I'm broke.* ➔ see box at POOR **2 go broke** if a business goes broke, it has to close because it has no money

broke[2] v the past tense of BREAK

broken[1] /'brəʊkən $ 'brou-/ adj
1 damaged or in small pieces because of being hit, dropped etc: *Be careful of the broken glass.* | **a broken arm/leg etc** (=one in which the bone is badly damaged) | *Wrap the plates up so they won't get broken.*
2 a machine or piece of equipment that is broken does not work: *The CD player's broken.*
3 not continuous: *a broken white line* | *Expect broken sleep in your baby's early months.*
4 broken home/family/marriage a family in which the husband and wife have ended their relationship and do not live together any more: *a broken marriage* | *kids from broken homes*
5 broken English/French etc if you speak in broken English, French etc, you speak the language slowly and not very well
6 a broken heart a feeling of great sadness, especially because someone you love has died or left you

broken[2] v the past participle of BREAK

broken-'down adj not working or in bad condition: *a broken-down truck*

broken-'hearted adj very sad, especially because someone you love has died or left you

broker[1] /'brəʊkə $ 'broukər/ n [C] someone whose job is to buy and sell property, insurance etc for someone else: *a real estate broker* ➔ STOCKBROKER

broker[2] v **broker a deal/settlement/treaty etc** to arrange the details of a deal, plan etc so that everyone can agree to it: *an agreement brokered by the UN*

brolly /'brɒli $ 'brɑːli/ n [C] plural **brollies** BrE *informal* an UMBRELLA

bronchitis /brɒŋ'kaɪtɪs $ brɑː-ŋ-/ n [U] an illness that affects your breathing and makes you cough

bronze /brɒnz $ brɑːnz/ n [U] **1** a dark red-brown metal **2** a dark reddish brown colour —**bronze** adj: *a bronze statue*

bronzed /brɒnzd $ brɑːnzd/ adj having skin that is attractively brown because you have been in the sun

bronze 'medal n [C] a prize, especially a round piece of bronze, that is given to someone who comes third in a race or competition

brooch /brəʊtʃ $ broutʃ/ n [C] a piece of jewellery that you fasten to your clothes with a pin

brood[1] /bruːd/ v [I] to keep thinking about something that you are worried, angry, or upset about: **+over/about/on** *You can't just sit there brooding over your problems.*

brood[2] n [C] a family of young birds

brook[1] /brʊk/ n [C] a small stream

brook[2] v formal **not brook sth/brook no sth** to not allow or accept something

broom /bruːm, brʊm/ n [C] a brush with a long handle, used for sweeping floors

broomstick /'bruːm,stɪk, 'brʊm-/ n [C] the type of broom that a WITCH is supposed to fly on, in stories

broth /brɒθ $ brɒːθ/ n [U] soup made with meat or vegetables: *chicken broth*

brothel /'brɒθəl $ 'brɑː-, 'brɒː-/ n [C] a house where men pay to have sex with PROSTITUTES

brother /'brʌðə $ -ər/ n [C]
1 a man or boy who has the same parents as you [➡ **sister**]: **older/younger brother** *Carla has two younger brothers.* | *I have to take my little brother* (=younger brother) *to school.* | *My big brother* (=older brother) *has always looked after me.* ➔ see box at RELATIVE
2 a man who belongs to the same race, religion, organization etc as you
3 a man who is a member of a religious group, especially a MONK

brotherhood /'brʌðəhʊd $ -ər-/ n **1** [U] a feeling of friendship between people: *the spirit of brotherhood* **2** [C] an organization of people who share the same political or religious ideas

'brother-in-law n [C] plural **brothers-in-law 1** the brother of your husband or wife **2** the husband of your sister

brotherly /'brʌðəli $ -ər-/ adj **brotherly love/ feeling** the kind of love or feeling you expect a brother to show

brought /brɔːt $ brɒːt/ v the past tense and past participle of BRING

brow /braʊ/ n [C] **1** *literary* the part of your face above your eyes and below your hair [= **forehead**] **2** an EYEBROW **3 the brow of a hill** BrE the top part of a hill

browbeat /'braʊbiːt/ v [T] past tense **browbeat**, past participle **browbeaten** /-biːtn/ to try to force someone to do something, especially in a threatening way

brown[1] /braʊn/ adj
1 having the colour of earth, wood, or coffee: *brown shoes* | *Jenny has light brown hair.* ➔ see picture at PATTERN
2 having skin that has become darker in the sun: *You look brown. Have you been on holiday?* —**brown** n [C,U] *Is the jacket available in brown?*

brown[2] v [I,T] if food browns, or if you brown it, you cook the food until it is brown

B

B

brownfield site /'braʊnfiːld ˌsaɪt/ *n* [C] *BrE* land in a city that used to have factories etc on it, but is now used for building new houses [→ **greenfield site**]

browse /braʊz/ *v* **1** [I] to look at the goods in a shop without looking for a particular thing to buy: *'Can I help you?' 'No thanks. I'm just browsing.'* **2** [I] to look through a book or magazine without a particular purpose: **+through** *I was browsing through the catalogue.* → see box at **READ** **3** [I,T] to search for information on a computer or on the Internet

browser /'braʊzə $ -ər/ *n* [C] a computer program that finds information on the Internet and shows it on your computer screen: *a Web browser*

bruise /bruːz/ *n* [C] a dark mark on your skin where you have fallen, been hit etc → see box at **MARK** —**bruise** *v* [T] *He fell and bruised his knee.* —**bruising** *n* [U]

brunch /brʌntʃ/ *n* [C,U] a meal eaten in the late morning, instead of breakfast and LUNCH

brunette /bruːˈnet/ *n* [C] a woman with dark brown hair

brunt /brʌnt/ *n* **bear/take the brunt of sth** to suffer the worst part of something unpleasant: *I had to bear the brunt of his anger.*

paintbrush

brushes

hairbrush

toothbrush

brush¹ /brʌʃ/ *n*

1 [C] a thing that you use for cleaning, painting, tidying your hair etc [→ **broom**]: *a scrubbing brush* | *a brush and comb*

2 [singular] a movement of brushing something: *I'll just give my hair a quick brush.*

3 [U] small bushes and trees that cover an area

4 brush with sth a time when something unpleasant almost happens to you: *a brush with death* | *His first brush with the law occurred when he was a teenager.*

→ **HAIRBRUSH, NAILBRUSH, PAINTBRUSH, TOOTHBRUSH**

brush² *v*

1 [T] to clean something or make something smooth and tidy, using a brush [→ **sweep**]: *Go brush your teeth.* | *Ella brushed her hair slowly.*

2 [T] to remove something with a brush or your hand: **brush sth off/from sth** *She brushed the crumbs off her lap.* | **brush sth away** *He brushed his tears away.*

3 [I,T] to touch someone or something lightly as you go past them: *Something brushed his shoulders.* | **+against/past** *Her hair brushed against my arm.*

brush sb/sth ⇔ **aside/off** *phr v* to refuse to listen to someone or what they say, especially by ignoring them: *He brushed aside her accusations.*

brush up (on) sth *phr v* to practise your skill or knowledge of something so that you are as good at it as you were in the past: *I have to brush up on my French before I go to Paris.*

'brush-off *n* [singular] *informal* rude or unfriendly behaviour that shows you are not interested in someone: *She gave me the brush-off.*

brusque /bruːsk, brʊsk $ brʌsk/ *adj* using very few words when you speak, in a way that seems rude: *a brusque manner* —**brusquely** *adv*

Brussels sprout /ˌbrʌsəlz 'spraʊt/ *n* [C] a small round green vegetable → see picture at **VEGETABLE**

brutal /'bruːtl/ *adj* **1** very cruel and violent: *a brutal attack* **2** not pleasant and not sensitive to people's feelings: *He replied with brutal honesty.* —**brutally** *adv*: *He was brutally murdered.* —**brutality** /bruːˈtæləti/ *n* [C,U]

brutalize also -**ise** *BrE* /'bruːtəl-aɪz/ *v* [T] to make someone violent, cruel, and unable to feel sympathy: *the brutalizing effects of war*

brute¹ /bruːt/ *n* [C] a cruel violent man

brute² *adj* **brute force/strength** physical strength rather than intelligence and careful thinking

BSc /ˌbiː es 'siː/ *BrE*; **B.S.** /ˌbiː 'es/ *AmE n* [C] Bachelor of Science; a university degree in a science subject

BSE /ˌbiː es 'iː/ *n* [U] bovine spongiform encephalopathy a disease of the brain that affects cows and usually kills them

bubble¹ /'bʌbəl/ *n* [C] a ball of air or gas in a liquid: **+of** *A few bubbles of air rose to the surface of the water.* | *champagne bubbles*

bubble² *v* [I] **1** to produce bubbles: *Heat the sauce until it starts to bubble.* **2** also **bubble over** to be excited: **+with** *Mary was bubbling over with excitement.*

'bubble gum *n* [U] a type of CHEWING GUM that you can blow into a bubble

bubbly /'bʌbli/ *adj* **1** cheerful and full of energy: *a bubbly personality* **2** full of bubbles

buck¹ /bʌk/ *n* [C] **1** *informal* a US, Canadian, or Australian dollar: *Could you lend me 20 bucks?* | *He was just trying to make a buck* (=earn some money). **2** the male of some animals, for example DEER and rabbits

buck² *v* [I] if a horse bucks, it kicks its back feet into the air, or jumps with all four feet off the ground

bucket /'bʌkɪt/ *n* [C]

1 a round open container with a handle over the top, used for carrying things, especially liquids

2 also **bucketful** /-fʊl/ the amount that a bucket holds: **+of** *a bucket of water*

buckle¹ /'bʌkəl/ *v* **1** [I,T] to bend because of heat or pressure, or to make something bend in this way: *The front wheel on my bike had buckled.* **2** [I] if your knees or legs buckle, they become weak and bend **3** also **buckle up** [I,T] to fasten a buckle or be fastened with a buckle: **buckle sth on** *He buckled on his sword.*

buckle down *phr v informal* to start working seriously: *You'd better buckle down or you'll never pass your exams.*

buckle[2] *n* [C] a thing made of metal, used for fastening a belt, shoe, bag etc → see picture at WATCH[2]

bud /bʌd/ *n* [C] a young flower or leaf before it opens → see picture at PLANT

Buddhism /'bʊdɪzəm $ 'buː-, 'bʊ-/ *n* [U] a religion of east and central Asia, based on the teaching of Buddha —**Buddhist** *n* [C] —**Buddhist** *adj*

budding /'bʌdɪŋ/ *adj* beginning to develop or be successful: *a budding relationship* | *a budding artist*

buddy /'bʌdi/ *n* [C] plural **buddies** *informal* a friend: *We're good buddies.*

budge /bʌdʒ/ *v* [I,T] *informal* **1** if someone or something does not budge, they do not move, or you cannot make them move: *The car won't budge.* | **+from** *Mark hasn't budged from his room all day.* **2** if someone will not budge or be budged, they refuse to change their opinion: *Once Dad's made up his mind, he won't budge.*

budgerigar /'bʌdʒərɪgɑː $ -gɑːr/ *n* [C] *BrE* a small brightly coloured bird that people keep as a pet

budget[1] /'bʌdʒɪt/ *n* [C] **1** the money that is available to an organization or person, or a plan of how it will be spent: **+of** *We have a budget of £100 a week for food.* | **defence/education/ training etc budget** *an increase in the public health budget* | **over/under budget** (=spending more or less than what was planned) *The project's gone over budget again.* | *The mayor is raising taxes in order to balance the budget* (=not spend more than is available). | *families on a tight budget* (=with only a small amount of money to spend) **2** *BrE* also **Budget** an official statement that a government makes about how much it intends to spend and what taxes it intends to raise necessary

budget[2] *v* [I] to carefully plan and control how you will spend your money: **+for** *We've budgeted for a new car next year.*

budget[3] *adj* very low in price – used in advertisements: *a budget flight*

budgetary /'bʌdʒɪtəri $ -teri/ *adj* relating to a budget: *budgetary control*

budgie /'bʌdʒi/ *n* [C] a BUDGERIGAR

buff[1] /bʌf/ *n* [C] **wine/computer/opera etc buff** someone who is interested in wine, computers etc and knows a lot about them

buff[2] also **buff up** *v* [T] to polish something with a cloth

buffalo /'bʌfələʊ $ -loʊ/ *n* [C] plural **buffaloes** or **buffalo** an animal that looks like a cow with very long horns

buffer /'bʌfə $ -ər/ *n* [C] someone or something that helps to protect a person or thing from being harmed or damaged: **+against** *Support from friends provides a buffer against stress.* —**buffer** *v* [T]

buffet[1] /'bʊfeɪ $ bə'feɪ/ *n* [C] a meal in which people get their own food from a table and then move away to eat

buffet[2] /'bʌfɪt/ *v* [T usually passive] if wind, rain, or the sea buffets something, it hits it with a lot of force: *Chicago was buffeted by storms last night.*

buffet car /'bʊfeɪ kɑː $ bə'feɪ kɑːr/ *n* [C] *BrE* the part of a train where you can buy food and drink

buffoon /bə'fuːn/ *n* [C] *old-fashioned* someone who does silly things that make you laugh

bug[1] /bʌg/ *n* [C] **1** *informal* an illness that people get very easily from each other but is not very serious: *There's a nasty bug going round* (=which a lot of people have caught). | *a stomach bug* (=illness affecting your stomach) **2** a small insect **3** a small mistake in a computer program that stops it from working correctly → see box at FAULT: *There's a bug in the system.* **4** a small piece of electronic equipment for listening secretly to other people's conversations **5** *informal* a sudden strong interest in doing something: **the travel/acting etc bug** *She's got the sailing bug.*

bug[2] *v* [T] **bugged, bugging** **1** *spoken* to annoy someone: *Stop bugging me!* **2** to use electronic equipment to listen secretly to other people's conversations

buggy /'bʌgi/ *n* [C] plural **buggies** *BrE* a light folding chair on wheels that you push small children in [= **stroller** *AmE*] → see box at BABY

bugle /'bjuːgəl/ *n* [C] a musical instrument like a TRUMPET —**bugler** *n* [C]

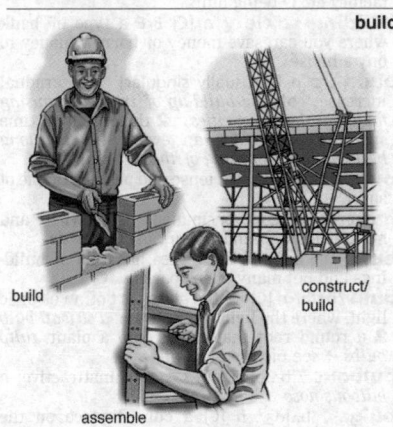

build

build

construct/ build

assemble

build[1] /bɪld/ *v* past tense and past participle **built** /bɪlt/

1 [I,T] to make a building, road, bridge etc: *They're building new houses for local people.* | *The Brooklyn Bridge was built in the 1870s.* | **be built of sth** *Most churches were built of stone.* | **+on** *Are there any plans to build on that land?*

2 also **build up** [T] to develop something slowly: *She had built a reputation as a criminal lawyer.* | *My father built up the business himself.*

build sth into sth *phr v* **1** to make something a permanent part of a wall, room etc: *There are three cash machines built into the wall.* **2** to make something a permanent part of a system, agreement etc

build on sth *phr v* **1** to use something you have done as a base for achieving more: *We hope to build on what we learned last year.* **2 build sth on sth** to base something on an idea or feeling: *Our relationship is built on trust.*

build up *phr v* **1** if something builds up, it gradually increases: *Excitement was building up* *inside her.* **2 build sb's hopes up** to make someone think they will get what they want, when in fact it is unlikely: *Don't build her hopes up.*

build² *n* [singular,U] the shape and size of someone's body: *Maggie's tall with a **slim build**.*

builder /'bɪldə $ -ər/ *n* [C] *especially BrE* a person or a company that builds or repairs buildings

building /'bɪldɪŋ/ *n*
1 [C] a structure such as a house, church, or factory that has a roof and walls: *We could see a tall building in the distance.* | *farm buildings*
2 [U] the process or business of building things: *land used for building*
→ **APARTMENT BUILDING, BODY BUILDING**

'building ,block *n* **1 building blocks** [plural] the pieces or parts which together make it possible for something big or important to exist: *Reading and writing are the building blocks of our education.* **2** [C] a block of wood or plastic for young children to build things with

'building ,site *n* [C] a place where a house, factory etc is being built

'building so,ciety *n* [C] *BrE* a type of bank where you can save money or borrow money to buy a house

'build-up *n* [C, usually singular] **1** a gradual increase: **+of** *The build-up of traffic is causing major problems in cities.* **2** the length of time spent preparing for an event: **+to** *the long build-up to the opening of the new mall*

built /bɪlt/ *v* the past tense and past participle of **BUILD**

,built-'in *adj* fixed permanently somewhere and not possible to remove: *built-in cupboards*

,built-'up *adj* a built-up area has a lot of buildings and not many open spaces

bulb /bʌlb/ *n* [C] **1** the glass part of an electric light, where the light shines from: *a 60 watt bulb* **2** a round root that grows into a plant: *tulip bulbs* → see picture at **PLANT**

bulbous /'bʌlbəs/ *adj* fat and unattractive: *a bulbous nose*

bulge¹ /bʌldʒ/ *n* [C] a curved place on the surface of something, caused by something under or inside it: *The gun made a bulge under his jacket.*

bulge² also **bulge out** *v* [I] to stick out in a rounded shape: *Jeffrey's stomach bulged over his trousers.* | **+with** *Her eyes were bulging with fear.*

bulimia /bjuː'lɪmiə, bʊ-, -'liː-/ *n* [U] an illness in which someone eats too much and then deliberately **VOMITS** as a way of controlling their weight —**bulimic** *adj*

bulk /bʌlk/ *n* **1 the bulk (of sth)** the main or largest part of something: *The bulk of the work has already been done.* **2** [U] the size of something or someone, especially a large size: *His bulk made it difficult for him to move quickly enough.* **3 in bulk** in large quantities: *It's cheaper to buy things in bulk.*

bulky /'bʌlki/ *adj* big and difficult to move: *a bulky package*

bull /bʊl/ *n* [C] a male cow, or the male of some other large animal such as an **ELEPHANT**

bulldog /'bʊldɒg $ -dɔːg/ *n* [C] a powerful dog with a short neck and short thick legs

bulldoze /'bʊldəʊz $ -doʊz/ *v* [T] to destroy buildings or move earth and rocks with a bulldozer

bulldozer /'bʊldəʊzə $ -doʊzər/ *n* [C] a large powerful vehicle used for destroying buildings or moving earth and rocks

bullet /'bʊlɪt/ *n* [C] a small piece of metal that is fired from a gun: *He was killed by a single bullet.* | *a **bullet wound** in the shoulder*

bulletin /'bʊlɪtɪn/ *n* [C] **1** a short news report on television or radio: *Our next **news bulletin** is at 6 o'clock.* **2** a regular letter or report that an organization produces to tell people its news

'bulletin ,board *n* [C]
1 *AmE* a board on a wall where you can put information for people to see [= **noticeboard** *BrE*] → see picture at **CLASSROOM**
2 a place in a computer system where you can leave or read messages

'bullet point *n* [C] a thing in a list, with a symbol in front of it

'bullet-,proof *adj* made of a material that stops bullets from going through it: *bullet-proof glass*

bullfight /'bʊlfaɪt/ *n* [C] a type of entertainment popular in Spain, in which a man fights and often kills a **BULL** —**bullfighter** *n* [C] —**bullfighting** *n* [U]

bullhorn /'bʊlhɔːn $ -hɔːrn/ *n* [C] *AmE old-fashioned* a piece of equipment that you hold up to your mouth to make your voice louder [= **megaphone**]

bullion /'bʊljən/ *n* [U] bars of gold or silver

bullish /'bʊlɪʃ/ *adj* feeling confident about the future: *He's bullish about the company's prospects.*

bullock /'bʊlək/ *n* [C] a young male cow

'bull's-eye *n* [C] the point in the exact centre of an object that you try to hit when shooting or in a game like **DARTS**

bully¹ /'bʊli/ *v* [T] **bullied, bullying, bullies** to deliberately frighten or upset someone who is smaller or weaker than you, especially to make them do something you want: **bully sb into (doing) sth** *He had bullied his wife into giving up her career.* —**bullying** *n* [U]

bully² *n* [C] plural **bullies** someone who deliberately frightens or upsets a person who is smaller or weaker than they are

bum¹ /bʌm/ *n* [C] *informal* **1** *BrE* the part of your body that you sit on [= **bottom**] **2** *AmE* someone who has no home or job

bum² *v* [T] **bummed, bumming** *informal* to ask someone if you can borrow or have something: *Can I bum a cigarette?*

bum around (sth) *phr v informal* to travel around, living very cheaply, without having any plans: *I spent the summer bumming around Europe.*

bumblebee /'bʌmbəl,biː/ *n* [C] a large **BEE**

bumbling /'bʌmblɪŋ/ *adj* [only before noun] not clever or skilful, and making a lot of mistakes

bumf /bʌmf/ *n* [U] *BrE informal* boring written information that you have to read

bummer /'bʌmə $ -ər/ *n informal* **a bummer** a situation that is disappointing or annoying

bump¹ /bʌmp/ *v* **1** [I,T] to hit or knock against something, especially by accident: *Mind you don't bump your head!* | **+into/against** *It was so dark I bumped into a tree.* **2** [I] to move in an

uneven way because the ground is not smooth:
+along *The truck bumped along the rough track.*
   bump into sb *phr v informal* to meet someone
when you were not expecting to: *Guess who I
bumped into this morning?*
   bump sb ⇔ **off** *phr v informal* to kill someone
   bump sth ⇔ **up** *phr v informal* to increase
something: *In the summer they bump up the
prices by 10 per cent.*
bump² n [C]   **1** a hard lump on your skin where
you have hit it on something: **+on** *Derek's got a
nasty bump on his head.*   **2** a small raised area
on a surface: **+in** *a bump in the road*   **3** a movement in which one thing hits against another
thing, or the sound that this makes: *Danny sat
down with a bump.*
bumper¹ /ˈbʌmpə $ -ər/ n [C] the bar across the
front and back of a car that protects it if it hits
anything
bumper² *adj* [only before noun] larger than
usual: *a bumper crop*
'**bumper ,sticker** n [C] a small sign with a
message on it on the bumper of a car

bumpy

bumpy   smooth

bumpy /ˈbʌmpi/ *adj* not smooth: *a bumpy road*
bun /bʌn/ n [C]   **1** *BrE* a small sweet cake: *We
had iced buns for tea.*   **2** bread that is made in a
small round shape: *a hamburger bun*   **3** a way of
arranging long hair by fastening it in a round
shape on the top of your head
bunch¹ /bʌntʃ/ n
   1 [C] a group of things that are held or joined
together: **+of** *a bunch of grapes* I *a beautiful
bunch of violets* → see box at **GROUP** → see picture
at **PIECE**
   2 [singular] *informal* a group of people: *My class
are a really nice bunch.* I **+of** *a bunch of idiots* →
see box at **GROUP**
   3 [singular] *AmE informal* a large amount: **+of**
The doctor asked me a bunch of questions.
   4 bunches [plural] *BrE* if a girl wears her hair
in bunches, she ties it together at each side of
her head
bunch² also **bunch up**, **bunch together** v
[I,T]   **1** to stay close together in a group, or to
make a group: *The children were bunched
together by the door.*   **2** to pull material together
tightly in folds: *My skirt got all bunched up in the
car.*
bundle¹ /ˈbʌndl/ n [C]   **1** a group of things that
are fastened or tied together: **+of** *a bundle of
newspapers* → see box at **GROUP**   **2 be a bundle
of nerves/fun etc** *informal* to be very nervous,
a lot of fun etc

bundle² v [T]   to make someone move by pushing them roughly: **bundle sb into/through/out
of etc** *The police bundled Jason into the back of
the van.*
   bundle sth ⇔ **up** *phr v* to make a bundle by
tying things together: *Bundle up the newspapers
and we'll take them to be recycled.*
bung¹ /bʌŋ/ n [C] *BrE* a round piece of rubber,
wood etc used to close the top of a container
bung² v [T] *BrE informal*   to put something
somewhere quickly and carelessly: **bung sth
in/on etc** *Bung the butter in the fridge, will you?*
   bung sth ⇔ **up** *phr v informal*   **1** to block a
hole by putting something in it   **2 be bunged
up** to be unable to breathe through your nose
because you have a cold
bungalow /ˈbʌŋɡələʊ $ -loʊ/ n [C] a house that
is built on one level → see box at **HOUSE**
bungee jumping /ˈbʌndʒi ˌdʒʌmpɪŋ/ n [U] a
sport in which you jump off something very
high with a long length of **ELASTIC** (=rope that
stretches) tied to your legs, so that you do not hit
the ground —**bungee jump** n [C] —**bungee
jumper** n [C]
bungle /ˈbʌŋɡəl/ v [T] to do something badly:
The builders bungled the job completely.
—**bungling** n [U]
bunk /bʌŋk/ n [C]   **1** a narrow bed on a train or
ship, which is joined to the wall   **2 bunk beds**
two beds that are one on top of the other → see
picture at **BED**   **3 do a bunk** *BrE informal* to
suddenly leave a place without telling anyone
bunker /ˈbʌŋkə $ -ər/ n [C]   **1** a strongly built
room under the ground, built to protect people
from bombs   **2** *BrE* a wide hole on a **GOLF COURSE**
filled with sand [= **sandtrap** *AmE*]
bunny /ˈbʌni/ also '**bunny ,rabbit** n [C] plural
bunnies a rabbit – used especially by children or
when you are talking to children
buoy¹ /bɔɪ $ ˈbuːi, bɔɪ/ n [C] an object that floats
on the sea to show which parts are safe or
dangerous
buoy² also **buoy up** v [T] to make someone feel
happier or more confident: *Jill was buoyed up by
success.*
buoyant /ˈbɔɪənt $ ˈbɔɪənt, ˈbuːjənt/ *adj*
   1 happy and confident: *Bob was in a buoyant
mood.*   **2** buoyant prices or profits are at a high
level   **3** able to float —**buoyancy** n [U]
burble /ˈbɜːbəl $ ˈbɜːr-/ v [I,T] to make a sound
like a stream flowing over stones
burden¹ /ˈbɜːdn $ ˈbɜːrdn/ n [C]   **1** something
difficult or worrying that you have to deal with:
+on *I don't want to be a burden on my children
when I'm old.*   **2** *formal* something heavy that
you have to carry
burden² v [T]   **1** to cause a lot of problems for
someone: **burden sb with sth** *We won't burden
her with any more responsibility.*   **2 be burdened (down) with sth** to be carrying something very heavy: *She struggled up the hill,
burdened down with shopping.*
bureau /ˈbjʊərəʊ $ ˈbjʊroʊ/ n [C] plural **bureaus**
or **bureaux** /-rəʊz $ -roʊz/   **1** an office or organi-
zation that collects or provides information: *an
employment bureau*   **2** *especially AmE* a government department: *the Federal Bureau of
Investigation*   **3** *BrE* a piece of furniture with
drawers and a sloping lid that you can open and
use as a desk

B

B

bureaucracy /bjuə'rɒkrəsi $ bju'rɑː-/ n plural **bureaucracies** **1** [U] an official system that is annoying or confusing because it has too many rules and takes too long to make decisions **2** [C,U] the officials in a government or business who are employed and not elected

bureaucrat /'bjuərəkræt $ 'bjur-/ n [C] someone who works in a government organization and uses official rules very strictly

bureaucratic /ˌbjuərə'krætɪk◂ $ ˌbjur-/ adj involving a lot of official rules and processes

burgeoning /'bɜːdʒənɪŋ $ 'bɜːr-/ adj formal growing quickly: *the burgeoning market for digital cameras*

burger /'bɜːgə $ 'bɜːrgər/ n [C] a mixture of meat or vegetables that is made into a round flat shape and cooked

burglar /'bɜːglə $ 'bɜːrglər/ n [C] someone who goes into buildings in order to steal things → see box at STEAL

'burglar aˌlarm n [C] a piece of equipment that makes a loud noise when a burglar gets into a building

burglarize /'bɜːgləraɪz $ 'bɜːr-/ v [T] AmE to go into a building and steal things

burglary /'bɜːgləri $ 'bɜːr-/ n [C,U] plural **burglaries** the crime of going into a building in order to steal things → see box at CRIME

burgle /'bɜːgəl $ 'bɜːr-/ v [T] BrE to go into a building and steal things: *Their house was burgled while they were away.* → see box at STEAL

burial /'beriəl/ n [C,U] when a dead body is put into the ground

burly /'bɜːli $ 'bɜːrli/ adj a burly man is big and strong

burn¹ /bɜːn $ bɜːrn/ v past tense and past participle **burnt** /bɜːnt $ bɜːrnt/ or **burned**

1 [T] to destroy or damage something with fire or heat: *We can burn all this rubbish.* | *The iron had burnt a hole in my shirt.* | *My toast is burning!*

2 [T] to hurt yourself or someone else with fire or something hot: **burn sb/sth on sth** *I burnt my hand on the iron.* | *She was badly burned in a road accident.*

3 [I] to produce heat and flames: *Is the fire still burning?* → see box at FIRE

4 [I,T] if the sun burns your skin, or if your skin burns, it becomes red and painful from the heat of the sun: *Don't forget, you can still get burned when it's cloudy.*

5 [T] if something burns a FUEL, it uses it to produce power, heat or light: *Cars burn gasoline.*

6 [I,T] if a part of your body burns, or if something burns it, it feels unpleasantly hot: *My eyes were burning from the smoke.*

7 **be/get burned** informal **a)** to have your feelings hurt **b)** to lose a lot of money, especially in a business deal

8 [I] literary if a light or lamp burns, it shines —**burned** adj

burn down phr v if a building burns down or is burned down, it is destroyed by fire: **burn sth ⇔ down** *The old church was burned down.*

burn sth ⇔ off phr v **1** to use energy that is stored in your body by doing physical exercise: *I decided to go for a run to try and burn off a few calories.* **2** to remove something by burning it

burn (itself) out phr v if a fire burns out, it stops burning because there is no coal, wood etc left

burn up phr v if something burns up or is burned up, it is completely destroyed by fire: **burn sth ⇔ up** *Most of the woodland has now been burnt up.*

burn² n [C] an injury or mark caused by fire or heat [➥ sunburn]: *Many of the victims suffered severe burns.*

ˌburned 'out also **ˌburnt 'out** adj **1** tired or ill because you have been working too hard: *I was completely burned out after my exams.* **2** a burned out building or car has had the inside of it destroyed by fire

burner /'bɜːnə $ 'bɜːrnər/ n **1** [C] the top part of a COOKER that produces heat or a flame **2** **put sth on the back burner** informal to delay dealing with something until a later time

burning /'bɜːnɪŋ $ 'bɜːr-/ adj **1** on fire: *a burning house* **2** feeling very hot: *burning cheeks* **3** **burning ambition/need etc** a very strong wish, need etc **4** **burning question/issue** a very important question that must be dealt with

burnished /'bɜːnɪʃt $ 'bɜːr-/ adj burnished metal has been rubbed until it shines —**burnish** v [T]

burnt¹ /bɜːnt $ bɜːrnt/ v a past tense and past participle of BURN

burnt² adj damaged or hurt by burning: *Sorry the toast is a little burnt.*

ˌburnt 'out adj BURNED OUT

burp /bɜːp $ bɜːrp/ v [I] informal if you burp, gas comes up from your stomach and makes a noise —**burp** n [C]

burrow¹ /'bʌrəu $ 'bɜːrou/ v [I,T] to make a hole or small TUNNEL in the ground: **+under** *Rabbits had burrowed under the wall.*

burrow² n [C] a hole in the ground made by an animal such as a rabbit

bursar /'bɜːsə $ 'bɜːrsər/ n [C] someone at a college or school who is responsible for money that is paid or received

bursary /'bɜːsəri $ 'bɜːr-/ n [C] plural **bursaries** BrE money that is given to a student to help them pay for their university studies [= scholarship]

burst¹ /bɜːst $ bɜːrst/ v past tense and past participle **burst**

1 [I,T] to break open suddenly and violently, or to make something do this: *The kids burst all the balloons with pins.* | *One of the tyres had burst.* → see box at BREAK

2 **be bursting with sth** to be very full of something: *Rome is always bursting with tourists.* | *Your mum's bursting with pride for you.* | *Classrooms are bursting at the seams* (=too full).

3 [I] to move quickly and suddenly: **+into/through etc** *Jenna burst into the room.* | *The door burst open and 20 or 30 policemen rushed in.*

4 **be bursting to do sth** informal to want to do something very much: *Becky's just bursting to tell you her news.*

burst in on sb/sth phr v to interrupt something by entering a room when people do not expect it: *I'm sorry to burst in on you like this.*

burst into sth phr v to suddenly begin doing something: *The car hit a tree and burst into flames* (=began burning). | *Ellen burst into tears* (=began crying).

burst out *phr v* **1 burst out laughing/crying** to suddenly start to laugh or cry **2** to suddenly say something quite loudly: *'I don't believe it!' Duncan burst out.*

burst² *n* [C] **1** a short sudden period of activity or noise: **+of** *a burst of applause* | *In a sudden burst of energy Denise cleaned the whole house.* **2** when something breaks suddenly, or the place where it has broken: *a burst in the water pipe*

burst³ *adj* broken, so that liquid or air can get out: *a burst pipe* | *burst blood vessels*

bury /'beri/ *v* [T] **buried, burying, buries**

1 to put a dead body into the ground: *She was buried in Woodlawn Cemetery.*

2 to cover something with something else so that it cannot be seen: *The dog was burying a bone.* | **bury sth under sth** *Dad's glasses were buried under a pile of newspapers.*

3 bury your face/head in sth to hide your face by pressing it into something, usually because you are upset: *She buried her face in her hands and began to cry.*

bus¹ /bʌs/ *n* [C] plural **buses** a large vehicle that people pay to travel on: **get on/off the bus** *She got on the bus at Clark Street.* | *Sally had to run to* **catch the bus.** | *Hurry up or we'll* **miss the bus!** | **by bus** *I usually go to school by bus.* → see picture at TRANSPORT

bus² *v* [T] **bussed, bussing** *BrE,* **bused, busing** *AmE* to take a group of people somewhere in a bus: **bus sb to/into etc** *Many children are being bussed to schools in other areas.*

bush /bʊʃ/ *n*

1 [C] a plant like a small tree with a lot of branches [➡ **shrub, tree**]: *a rose bush* | *The child was hiding in the bushes.*

2 the bush an area of Australia or Africa that is still wild

bushy /'bʊʃi/ *adj* bushy hair or fur grows thickly: *a bushy tail*

busily /'bɪzɪli/ *adv* in a busy way: *The class were all busily writing.*

business /'bɪznəs/ *n*

1 [U] the producing and selling of goods or services: *You need a lot of money to succeed in business.* | *He's thinking of* **going into business.** | *We* **do** *a lot of* **business** *with people in Rome.* | **the film business/the music business etc** *She has been in the advertising business for years.*

2 [U] the work that you do as your job to earn money: *Al's gone to Japan* **on business** (=as part of his job). | *a business trip*

3 [U] the amount of work a company is doing, or the amount of money a company is making: **business is good/bad/slow etc** *Business is always slow during the winter.*

4 go out of business if a company goes out of business, it closes because it is not making enough money: *Many small companies have recently gone out of business.*

5 [C] an organization that produces or sells things: *Graham* **runs** *a printing* **business.** | *a small family business* → see box at COMPANY

6 [U] if something is your business, it concerns you and other people do not have a right to know about it: *'Are you going out with Ben tonight?' 'That's my business.'* | *It's* **none of your business** *how much I earn.* | *'Who's that girl you were with?'* **'Mind your own business** (=don't ask

questions about something that does not concern you).'

7 [U] things that need to be done or discussed: *Okay, let's* **get down to business** (=start doing or discussing something).

8 [singular] a situation or event: *Her divorce was a very upsetting business.* | *Tanya found the* **whole business** *ridiculous.*

9 have no business doing sth/have no business to do sth to do something you should not be doing: *He was drunk and had no business driving.*

→ BIG BUSINESS, SHOW BUSINESS

'business ˌclass *n* [U] travelling conditions on an aircraft that are more expensive than the ordinary conditions, but not as expensive as FIRST-CLASS

businesslike /'bɪznəslaɪk/ *adj* sensible and practical in the way you do things: *a businesslike manner* → see box at ORGANIZED

businessman /'bɪznəsmən/ *n* [C] plural **businessmen** /-mən/ a man who works in business

businesswoman /'bɪznəsˌwʊmən/ *n* [C] plural **businesswomen** /-ˌwɪmɪn/ a woman who works in business

busk /bʌsk/ *v* [I] *BrE* to play music in a public place to earn money —**busker** *n* [C]

busk

busker

'bus pass *n* [C] a special ticket that gives you cheap or free bus travel

'bus stop *n* [C] a place at the side of a road, marked with a sign, where buses stop for passengers

bust¹ /bʌst/ *v* [T] past tense and past participle **bust** or **busted** *informal* **1** to break something: *Someone's bust my skateboard!* **2** if the police bust someone, they find them doing something illegal: *He got busted for possession of drugs.*

bust² *n* [C] **1** a woman's breasts, or the measurement around a woman's breasts and back: *a 34 inch bust* **2** *informal* a situation in which the police go into a place in order to catch people doing something illegal: *a major drug bust* **3** a MODEL of someone's head and shoulders, usually made of stone or metal: **+of** *a bust of Shakespeare*

bust³ *adj informal* **1 go bust** if a business goes bust, it has to close because it does not have enough money: *More and more small businesses are going bust each year.* **2** *informal* broken: *The TV's bust again.*

bustle¹ /'bʌsəl/ *n* [singular] busy and noisy activity: **+of** *the bustle of the big city* —**bustling** *adj*

bustle² *v* [I] to move around and do things in a quick, busy way: **+about/around** *Linda was bustling around in the kitchen.*

'bust-up *n* [C] *informal* a fight or argument

B

busy[1] /'bɪzi/ *adj*

1 someone who is busy has a lot of things that they must do: *Alex is busy studying for his exams.* | **+with** *I'm busy with a customer at the moment. Can I call you back?* | *There were lots of activities to* **keep** *the kids* **busy**.

2 a busy time is a time when you have a lot of things that you must do: *I've had a really* **busy day**. | *December is the busiest time of year for shops.*

3 a busy place is full of people or vehicles: *a busy airport* | *The roads were very busy this morning.*

4 *especially AmE* a telephone line that is busy is being used [= **engaged** *BrE*]
—**busily** *adv*

busy[2] *v* **busied, busying, busies busy yourself with sth** to make yourself busy by doing a particular job or activity: *Josh busied himself with cleaning the house.*

busybody /'bɪzi,bɒdi $ -,bɑːdi/ *n* [C] plural **busybodies** someone who is too interested in other people's private lives

but[1] /bət; *strong* bʌt/ *linking word*

1 used before you say something that is different or surprising: *Grandma didn't like the song, but we loved it.* | *Learning Chinese was difficult, but it meant that I got this job.*

2 used before you give the reason why something did not happen or was not possible: *Carla was supposed to come tonight, but her husband took the car.*

3 *spoken* used to show surprise at what someone has just said: *'I have to go tomorrow.' 'But you only just arrived!'*

4 *spoken* **but then (again) ...** used to add some information that makes what you have just said less surprising: *I didn't understand the film at all. But then I was really tired.*

5 *spoken* used after phrases such as 'excuse me' and 'I'm sorry': *Excuse me, but haven't we met before?*

but[2] *prep* except: *Joe can come any day but Monday.* | *Nobody but Liz knows the truth.*

butch /bʊtʃ/ *adj* an offensive word used to describe a woman who looks, dresses, or behaves like a man

butcher[1] /'bʊtʃə $ -ər/ *n* [C]   **1** someone who owns or works in a shop that sells meat   **2 butcher's** a shop that sells meat → see box at **SHOP**

butcher[2] *v* [T]   **1** to kill animals and prepare their meat as food   **2** to kill people in a cruel way: *Thousands of innocent people were butchered.*

butler /'bʌtlə $ -ər/ *n* [C] the most important male servant in a big house

butt[1] /bʌt/ *n* [C]   **1** *AmE informal* the part of your body that you sit on   **2** the end of a cigarette after it has been smoked   **3 be the butt of sth** to be the person that other people often make jokes about: *John is always the butt of the class's jokes.*   **4** the end of the handle of a gun

butt[2] *v* [I,T] to hit or push against someone or something with your head

butt in *phr v informal* to join a conversation or activity without being asked: *Sorry, I didn't mean to butt in.*

butter[1] /'bʌtə $ -ər/ *n* [U] a solid yellow food made from cream that you spread on bread or use in cooking: *a slice of bread and butter* | *Melt the butter in a pan.*

butter[2] *v* [T] to spread butter on something: *hot buttered toast*

butter sb ⇔ up *phr v informal* to say nice things to someone so that they will do what you want

buttercup /'bʌtəkʌp $ -ər-/ *n* [C] a small yellow wild flower

butterfly /'bʌtəflaɪ $ -ər-/ *n* [C] plural **butterflies**   **1** an insect with large coloured wings   **2 have butterflies (in your stomach)** *informal* to feel very nervous

buttock /'bʌtək/ *n* [C usually plural] one of the two parts of your body that you sit on

butterfly

button[1] /'bʌtn/ *n* [C]

1 a small round thing on a shirt, coat etc that you put through a hole to fasten the shirt etc: *a jacket with gold buttons* | *Sam undid* (=unfastened) *his buttons.* | **do up a button** *BrE* (=fasten a button)

2 a small part on a machine that you press to make it start, stop etc: **push/press a button** *Just press the 'on' button.* | *You can close the roof* **at the touch of a button**.

3 *AmE* a small piece of metal or plastic with a message or picture on it that you fasten to your clothes [= **badge** *BrE*]

button[2] also **button up** *v* [I,T] to fasten something with buttons, or to be fastened with buttons → see box at **FASTEN**

buttonhole /'bʌtnhəʊl $ -hoʊl/ *n* [C] a hole which you put a button through

buttress /'bʌtrəs/ *v* [T] *formal* to do something to support a system, argument etc

buxom /'bʌksəm/ *adj* a buxom woman has large breasts

buy[1] /baɪ/ *v past tense and past participle* **bought** /bɔːt $ bɒːt/

1 [I,T] to get something by paying money for it [≠ **sell**]: *Sam's just bought a new computer.* | **buy sb sth** *Let me buy you a drink.* | **buy sth for sb/sth** *He bought a diamond ring for his wife.* | **buy sth from sb** *I'm buying a car from a friend.* | **buy sth for $10/£20 etc** *She bought those shoes for £15.*

2 [T] *informal* to believe something that someone tells you: *I just don't buy that story.*

3 buy (sb) time *informal* to make more time for yourself to do something, especially by delaying something: *Keep him talking to buy us more time.*

buy into sth *phr v*   **1** to buy part of a business   **2** *informal* to believe an idea: *I don't buy into this idea that women must have perfect bodies.*

buy sb ⇔ off *phr v* to pay someone to stop causing you trouble

buy sb/sth ⇔ out *phr v* to get control of a business by buying all the SHARES in it

buy sth ⇔ **up** *phr v* to quickly buy as much as you can of something: *Property developers are buying up all the land in the area.*

buy² *n* **be a good/excellent etc buy** to be something that is good to buy because it is cheap, good quality etc: *The Brazilian wine is a good buy.*

buyer /'baɪə $ -ər/ *n* [C] someone who wants to buy something: +**for** *We've found a buyer for our house.*

buyout /'baɪaʊt/ *n* [C] a situation in which someone gets control of a company by buying all or most of its SHARES

buzz¹ /bʌz/ *v* [I] **1** to make a continuous noise like the sound of a BEE: *a loud buzzing noise* **2** to be full of activity, excitement, ideas etc: *The office was buzzing with activity.* | *My mind was buzzing with new ideas.*

buzz² *n* **1** [C] a continuous noise like the sound of a BEE: +**of** *the buzz of mosquitoes* → see picture on page A7 **2** [singular] *informal* a feeling of excitement or success: *I get a real buzz from living in New York.*

buzzer /'bʌzə $ -ər/ *n* [C] a small electronic thing that makes a buzzing sound when you press it: *Press your buzzer if you know the answer.*

buzzword /'bʌzwɜːd $ -wɜːrd/ *n* [C] a word or phrase from a particular area of activity which is fashionable because people think it refers to something important: *the latest management buzzwords*

by /baɪ/ *adv, prep*
1 used to show who did something or what caused something, especially after a PASSIVE verb: *a film made by Steven Spielberg* | *Sylvie was hit by a car.* | **a book/song/painting etc by sb** *a play by Shakespeare*
2 used to say what means or method you use to do something: *Send it by airmail.* | *Hold it by the handle.* | **by car/plane/train/bus etc** *We travelled across India by train.* | **by doing sth** *Carol earns extra money by babysitting.*
3 beside or near something: *I'll meet you by the bank.*
4 not later than a particular time: *Your report has to be done by 5:00.*
5 **by mistake/accident/chance** without intending to do something: *Hugh locked the door by mistake.*
6 according to something: *By law, you must be over 16 to marry.* | *It's 9.30 by my watch.*
7 past: *Sophie ran by me on her way to the bus.* | *Two cars went by, but nobody stopped.*
8 used to give the measurements of something,

or to multiply and divide numbers: *The room is 14 feet by 12 feet.* | *What's 7 **multiplied by** 8?* | **by the day/metre/hundred etc** (=used to show how the amount of something is measured) *Anne gets paid by the hour.*
9 (all) by yourself completely alone: *They left the boy by himself for two days!*
10 day by day/bit by bit/one by one etc used to mean gradually: *Day by day, he grew weaker.*
11 by day/by night during the day or night: *animals that hunt by night*
12 by and large used when you are talking generally about something: *By and large, I agree with what he said.*
→ **by the way** at **WAY¹**

bye /baɪ/ also **bye-'bye** *spoken* goodbye: *Bye Sandy! See you later.*

'by-e,lection *n* [C] *BrE* an election to replace a politician who has left Parliament or died

bygone /'baɪɡɒn $ -ɡɒːn/ *adj* **bygone days/ age/era etc** a period of time in the past

bygones /'baɪɡɒnz $ -ɡɒːnz/ *n* **let bygones be bygones** to decide to forget something bad that someone did to you in the past and to forgive them

bypass¹ /'baɪpɑːs $ -pæs/ *n* [C] **1** a road that takes traffic around the outside of a town: *the Winchester bypass* → see box at **ROAD** **2 (heart) bypass surgery** an operation on someone's heart to make the blood avoid the part that is not working properly

bypass² *v* [T] to go around or avoid something: *The road bypasses the town.* | *Why don't you bypass the agent and contact the seller directly?*

'by-,product *n* [C] **1** something that is made during the process of making something else: +**of** *Plutonium is a by-product of nuclear processing.* **2** an unplanned or unexpected result of something: +**of** *an unfortunate by-product of the war*

bystander /'baɪ,stændə $ -ər/ *n* [C] someone who is standing, walking etc near something that happens, for example an accident: *Several innocent bystanders were killed by the explosion.*

byte /baɪt/ *n* [C] a unit for measuring the amount of information a computer can use, equal to eight BITS (=the smallest unit of information)

byword /'baɪwɜːd $ -wɜːrd/ *n* **be/become a byword for sth** to be the name of someone or something that is well-known for having a particular quality: *Hollywood is a byword for glamour.*

B

C, c

cable car

C, c /siː/ *n* [C,U] plural **C's, c's** **1** the third letter of the English alphabet **2** the first note in the musical SCALE of C MAJOR, or the musical KEY based on this note **3** a mark given to a student's work to show that it is of average quality: *I got a C in geography.*

C **1** the written abbreviation of **Celsius** or **Centigrade** **2** the written abbreviation of **cent** **3** the written abbreviation of **century**

cab /kæb/ *n* [C] **1** a TAXI: *I took a cab to the airport.*

> **COLLOCATIONS**
>
> **call a cab** – to telephone and ask a cab to come to where you are
> **call sb a cab** – to telephone and ask a cab to come for someone else
> **hail a cab** – to stand outside and raise your arm so that a cab will stop for you

2 the part of a truck or train where the driver sits

cabaret /'kæbəreɪ $ ˌkæbə'reɪ/ *n* [C,U] entertainment such as music and dancing performed in a restaurant or club

cabbage /'kæbɪdʒ/ *n* [C,U] a large round vegetable with thick green or purple leaves → see picture at VEGETABLE

cabbie /'kæbi/ *n* [C] *informal* a taxi driver

cabin /'kæbɪn/ *n* [C] **1** a small house made of wood: *a log cabin* **2** a small room on a ship where you sleep **3** the area inside a plane where the passengers sit → see picture at AEROPLANE

cabinet /'kæbɪnət/ *n* [C] **1** a piece of furniture with doors and shelves, used for storing things: *a drinks cabinet* | *a bedside cabinet* → see picture at BATHROOM **2** also **the Cabinet** an important group of politicians who make decisions or advise the leader of a government: *a member of the Cabinet* | *cabinet meetings*

cable /'keɪbəl/ *n* **1** [C,U] a plastic or rubber tube containing wires that carry electronic signals, telephone messages etc: *an underground telephone cable* **2** [U] a system of broadcasting television by using cables under the ground: **on cable** *I'll wait for the movie to come out on cable.* | **cable network/ channel/programme** **3** [C,U] a thick strong metal rope

'cable car *n* [C] a vehicle that hangs from a metal rope and carries people up mountains

ˌcable 'television also **cable ˌTV** *n* [U] a system of broadcasting television by using cables under the ground

cache /kæʃ/ *n* [C] a number of things that are hidden, or the place where they are hidden: **+of** *a cache of weapons*

cackle /'kækəl/ *v* [I] to laugh in an unpleasant loud way → see box at LAUGH —**cackle** *n* [C]

cacophony /kə'kɒfəni $ kə'kɑː-/ *n* [singular] a loud unpleasant mixture of sounds

cactus /'kæktəs/ *n* [C] plural **cacti** /-taɪ/ or **cactuses** a desert plant covered with small sharp points

cactus

caddie also **caddy** /'kædi/ *n* [C] someone who carries the equipment for someone who is playing golf

cadence /'keɪdəns/ *n* [C] a regular pattern of sound, especially the sound of someone's voice rising or falling

cadet /kə'det/ *n* [C] someone who is training to be an officer in the army, navy, AIR FORCE, or police

cadge /kædʒ/ *v* [T] *BrE informal* to ask someone you know for money, food, cigarettes etc because you do not have any: **cadge sth from/off sb** *I managed to cadge ten quid off Dad.*

caesarean, **cesarean** /sɪ'zeəriən $ -'zer-/ also **cae,sarean 'section** *n* [C] an operation in which a woman's body is cut open to take a baby out

cafe, café /'kæfeɪ $ kæ'feɪ, kə-/ *n* [C]

1 a small restaurant which sells drinks and simple food: *a little Italian cafe* | **in/at a cafe** *We had coffee in a pavement cafe.* | **a transport/ motorway/station etc cafe** → see box at RESTAURANT

2 Internet/cyber cafe a public place where you can pay to use the Internet, buy drinks etc

cafeteria /ˌkæfɪ'tɪəriə $ -'tɪr-/ *n* [C] a restaurant where people get their own food and take it to a table to eat it: *the college cafeteria* → see box at OFFICE → and RESTAURANT

cafetiere /ˌkæfə'tjeə $ -'tjer/ *n* [C] a special pot for making fresh coffee

caffeine /'kæfiːn $ kæ'fiːn/ *n* [U] a substance in coffee, tea, and some other drinks that makes you feel more active

cage /keɪdʒ/ *n* [C] a structure made of wires or bars, used for keeping birds or animals: *a hamster cage*

—**caged** *adj: a caged animal*

cagey /'keɪdʒi/ *adj informal* not willing to talk about your plans, intentions etc: *He was very cagey about the deal.*

cagoule /kəˈguːl/ n [C] BrE a thin coat with a HOOD, that stops you from getting wet

cahoots /kəˈhuːts/ n **be in cahoots (with sb)** informal to be working secretly with others, especially to do something dishonest

cajole /kəˈdʒəʊl $ -ˈdʒəʊl/ v [T] to persuade someone to do something by being nice to them or making promises

cake /keɪk/ n

1 [C,U] a sweet food made by baking a mixture of flour, butter, sugar, and eggs: *Would you like some chocolate cake?* | **piece/slice of cake** *Have a piece of fruit cake.* | **birthday/wedding/ Christmas cake** *She blew out the candles on her birthday cake.* | **bake/make a cake** *Grandma bakes wonderful cakes.*
2 **fish/rice/potato etc cake** fish etc that is made into a flat round shape and then cooked
3 **have your cake and eat it** to have all the advantages of something without its disadvantages
→ **SPONGE CAKE**

caked /keɪkt/ adj **be caked in/with sth** to be covered with a thick layer of something: *boots caked with mud*

calamity /kəˈlæməti/ n [C,U] plural **calamities** an unexpected event that causes a lot of damage or suffering [= disaster]

calcium /ˈkælsiəm/ n [U] a silver-white metal that helps to form teeth, bones, and CHALK

calculate /ˈkælkjʊleɪt/ v [T]

1 to find out how much something will cost, how long something will take etc, by using numbers: **calculate how much/how many etc** *I'm trying to calculate how much paint we need.* | **+(that)** *Sally calculated that the trip would cost about £2000.*

THESAURUS

work out – a less formal word for calculate: *Let's try to work out how much this will cost.*
add sth and sth – to put two or more numbers together to find the total: *Add 7 and 5 to make 12.*
subtract sth from sth also **take sth away from sth** – to reduce one number by another number: *If you subtract 12 from 15, you get 3.* | *Take 2 away from 4 and you're left with 2.*
multiply – to add a number to itself a particular number of times: *4 multiplied by 10 is 40.*
divide – to calculate how many times one number contains another number: *10 divided by 2 equals 5.*
plus spoken – used between numbers to show that you are adding them together: *Two plus two equals four.*
minus spoken – used between numbers to show that you are taking one away from the other: *Six minus five is one.*

2 to guess something using the information you have: **+what/whether/how etc** *It's difficult to calculate what effect these changes will have.* | **+(that)** *He'd calculated that she would be home by now.*
3 **be calculated to do sth** to be intended to have a particular effect: *It seemed his letter was calculated to upset her.*

calculated /ˈkælkjʊleɪtɪd/ adj **1** **calculated risk/gamble** something you do after thinking carefully, although you know it may have bad results **2** done after thinking carefully, in a clever or dishonest way: *It was a calculated attempt to deceive the public.*

calculating /ˈkælkjʊleɪtɪŋ/ adj someone who is calculating makes careful plans to get what they want, without caring about how this affects other people: *a cold and calculating man*

calculation /ˌkælkjʊˈleɪʃən/ n [C,U]

1 when you use numbers to find out an amount, price etc: *a simple **mathematical calculation*** | **+of** *an approximate calculation of the cost* | **by/according to some/sb's calculations** *According to some calculations, nearly 80% of teenagers have tried drugs.* | **do/make a calculation** *Dyson did some **rough calculations** (=involving numbers that are not very exact).*
2 careful planning to get what you want, especially without caring about how it affects other people

calculator /ˈkælkjʊleɪtə $ -ər/ n [C] a small electronic machine that can add, multiply etc

calendar /ˈkæləndə $ -ər/ n [C]

1 a set of pages showing the days and months of a year, that you usually hang on a wall
2 **the Roman/Muslim/Jewish etc calendar** a system that divides and measures time in a particular way
3 **the golfing/sporting/racing etc calendar** all the events in a year that are important for a particular activity: *Wimbledon, the high point of the tennis calendar*
4 AmE a book with separate spaces for each day of the year, in which you write down the things you have to do [= diary BrE]
5 **calendar year/month** a period of time from the first day of the month or year to the last day of the month or year

calf /kɑːf $ kæf/ n [C] plural **calves** /kɑːvz $ kævz/ **1** the back of your leg between your knee and foot **2** a baby cow

calibre BrE; **caliber** AmE /ˈkæləbə $ -ər/ n **1** [U] someone's level of ability or quality: *players of the highest calibre* **2** [C] the width of a bullet or the inside of a gun

call¹ /kɔːl $ kɒːl/ v

1 [T] to use a particular name or word for someone or something, or to give someone a name: **call sb sth** *His friends call him Andy.* | *They finally decided to call the baby Joel.* | *What do you call this thing?* | **be called sth** (=have a particular name) *They have a dog called Toby.* | *We're meeting at a restaurant called Al Paso.*
2 [I,T] to telephone someone: *I called about six o'clock but no one was home.* | *I'll call you tomorrow.* | **call a doctor/the police/a taxi etc** (=telephone someone and ask them to come) *Has anyone called an ambulance?* | **call in sick** (=telephone your work place to say that you are too ill to come to work) → see box at **PHONE**
3 [T] to describe someone or something in a particular way: **call sb/sth sth** *Critics are already calling the film a hit.* | *Are you calling me a liar?* | **call sb names** (=use insulting names for someone) *The other kids used to call me names.*

C

4 [T] to ask or order someone to come to you: *I can hear Mom calling me.* | **call sb in/over/across etc** *The headmaster called me into his office.*

5 also **call out** [I,T] to say something loudly or to shout: *'I'm coming!' Paula called down the stairs.* | *Someone called out my name.* → see box at **SHOUT**

6 [I] if a train, ship, bus etc calls at a place, it stops there for a short time: **+at** *This train calls at all stations to Broxbourne.*

7 [T] to arrange for something to happen: **call a meeting/strike/election etc** *A meeting was called for 3 pm Wednesday.*

8 also **call by/round/in** [I] *BrE* to visit someone or their home for a short time: *Your friend Alex called earlier.* → see box at **VISIT**

9 call it a day *informal* to stop working, especially because you are tired: *Come on, guys, let's call it a day.*

10 call the shots/tune if someone calls the shots, they make the important decisions about what should be done

11 call collect *AmE* to make a telephone call that is paid for by the person who receives it [= **reverse the charges** *BrE*]

call back *phr v* **1** to telephone someone again: *Okay, I'll call back around three.* | **call sb back** *Sorry, she's busy. Can she call you back later?* **2** *BrE* to return to a place that you went to earlier: *I'll call back tonight to pick it up.*

call for sth/sb *phr v* **1** to demand something publicly: *Congressmen are calling for an investigation into the scandal.* **2** to need something: *It's a project that calls for careful planning.* **3** *BrE* to go to someone's home to collect them: *I'll call for you at about eight.*

call sth ⇔ **off** *phr v* to decide that a planned event will not happen [= **cancel**]: *The game was called off due to bad weather.*

call on/upon sb *phr v* to formally ask someone to do something: **call on sb to do sth** *The UN has called on both sides to start peace talks.*

call sb ⇔ **out** *phr v* to ask someone to come and deal with something difficult or dangerous: *The doctor's been called out to an emergency.*

call sb/sth ⇔ **up** *phr v* **1** especially *AmE* to telephone someone: *Why don't you call Suzie up?* **2 be called up** *BrE* to be ordered to join the army, navy, or AIR FORCE [= **draft** *AmE*] → see box at **ARMY**

call² *n* [C]

1 when you speak to someone on the telephone: **+for** *There's a phone call for you.* | **+from** *I got a call from Teresa yesterday.* | *Just give me a call from the airport.* | *Can I make a quick call?* | *Why didn't you return my calls* (=telephone me after I tried to telephone you)*?*

2 be on call to be ready to go to work if you are needed: *Heart surgeons are on call 24 hours a day.*

3 a shout or cry, or the sound that an animal makes: *a call for help* | **+of** *the call of an owl*

4 a short visit: *Should we pay a call on Nadia while we're in Paris?*

5 when people say publicly that they want something to happen: **+for** *a call for tougher controls* | **call for sb to do sth** *There have been calls for the minister to resign.*

6 there is no call for sth used to say that something is not needed or wanted: *There's no*

call for typewriters nowadays - everybody has got a computer on their desk.
→ **be at sb's beck and call** at **BECK** → **CONFERENCE CALL, ROLL CALL**

'call box *n* [C] **1** *BrE* a small structure containing a public telephone **2** *AmE* a public telephone beside a road or **FREEWAY** used to telephone for help

'call ,centre *BrE*; **call center** *AmE n* [C] an office where people answer customers' questions, make sales etc by using the telephone

caller /ˈkɔːlə $ ˈkɒːlər/ *n* [C] someone who makes a telephone call

'call-in *n* [C] *AmE* a radio or television programme in which people telephone to give their opinions [= **phone-in** *BrE*]

calling /ˈkɔːlɪŋ $ ˈkɒː-/ *n* [C] a strong feeling that you should do a particular kind of work, especially work that helps other people: *a calling to the priesthood*

callous /ˈkæləs/ *adj* not caring that other people are suffering —**callously** *adv* —**callousness** *n* [U]

'call-up *n* [C] *BrE* **1** an order to join the army, navy etc [= **draft** *AmE*] **2** an opportunity or invitation to play for a professional sports team, especially a national one

calm¹ /kɑːm $ kɑːm, kɑːlm/ *adj*

1 relaxed and not angry or upset: **keep/stay/remain calm** *Please, everyone, try to keep calm!* | *a calm voice* → see box at **CHARACTER**

2 if a place or situation is calm, there is not much activity or trouble: *The streets are calm again after last night's riots.*

3 a sea or lake that is calm does not have many waves: *The water was much calmer in the bay.* → see picture at **CHOPPY**

4 calm weather is not windy or stormy: *Calmer weather is expected later in the week.*
—**calmly** *adv* —**calmness** *n* [U]

calm² also **calm down** *v* [T] to make someone quiet after they have been angry, excited, or upset: *Matt was trying to calm the baby.*

calm down *phr v* to become quiet after you have been angry, excited, or upset: *Calm down and tell me what happened.*

calm³ *n* [singular, U] a time when it is peaceful and quiet: **+of** *the calm of the evening* | *The police appealed for calm* (=asked people to stay calm) *following the shooting.*

calorie /ˈkæləri/ *n* [C] a unit for measuring the amount of energy food produces: *An average potato has about 90 calories.* | **low calorie/high calorie** *a low-calorie diet*

calorific /ˌkæləˈrɪfɪk◂ / *adj* food that is calorific tends to make you fat

calves /kɑːvz $ kævz/ *n* the plural of **CALF**

camaraderie /ˌkæməˈrɑːdəri $ -ˈræ-, -ˈrɑː-/ *n* [U] the feeling that a group of people have when they enjoy being together, especially when they work together: **+of** *the camaraderie of office life*

camcorder /'kæm-,kɔːdə $ -,kɔːrdər/ *n* [C] a small video camera that you can carry around with you

camcorder

came /keɪm/ *v* the past tense of COME

camel /'kæməl/ *n* [C] a large desert animal with a long neck and one or two HUMPS

cameo /'kæmiəʊ $ -oʊ/ *n* [C] plural **cameos** a small part in a film or play acted by a famous actor: *Whoopi Goldberg makes a* **cameo** *appearance in the movie.*

camera /'kæmərə/ *n* [C] a piece of equipment used to take photographs, or make films or programmes: **television/video etc camera** *They posed for the TV cameras.* | **on/off camera** (=while a camera is recording or not recording) *The thieves were caught on camera.*

TOPIC

Before you can **take** any **pictures**, you need to **load film** into the **camera**.
Digital cameras do not need film because the pictures that you take are stored in the camera until you **download** them onto a computer.
When you take pictures, you need to **focus**, so the people or things in your picture will be clear. If you are taking a picture indoors, you might need to use a **flash**.
After you have taken pictures, you take the **film** to be **developed** and **printed**. The printed **photographs** are also called **prints**. When you get the prints, you also get the **negatives** which you can use in the future to get more photographs.

---

cameraman /'kæmərəmən/ *n* [C] plural **cameramen** /-mən/ someone who operates a camera for a television or film company

camouflage /'kæməflɑːʒ/ *n* [C,U] clothes or colours that hide you by making you look the same as the things around you: **in camouflage** *a soldier in camouflage* —**camouflage** *v* [T] *Hunters camouflage the traps with leaves.*

camp¹ /kæmp/ *n* [C,U]
1 a place where people stay in tents for a short time: *After hiking all morning, we returned to camp.* | *We* **set up camp** (=made the camping place ready) *at the lake.*
2 a place where children go to stay for a short time and do special activities: *summer camp*
3 **prison/army/refugee etc camp** a place where prisoners, soldiers etc have to stay in tents or temporary buildings
→ CONCENTRATION CAMP

camp² *v* [I] **1** also **camp out** to put up a tent and stay there for a short time: *Where should we camp tonight?* **2** **go camping** to have a holiday in which you sleep in tents —**camping** *n* [U] *camping equipment*

camp³ *adj* **1** a man who is camp moves or speaks in a way that people used to think was typical of HOMOSEXUALS **2** also **campy** /'kæmpi/ *AmE* clothes, decorations etc that are camp are very strange, bright, or unusual

campaign¹ /kæm'peɪn/ *n* [C] **1** a series of actions intended to get a particular social or political result: *an election campaign* | *an advertising campaign* | **+for/against** *a campaign for equal rights* **2** a series of military attacks

campaign² *v* [I] to do a series of things intended to get a particular social or political result: **+for/against** *The group were campaigning against the destruction of the rainforests.* —**campaigner** *n* [C]

,camp 'bed / $ '. ,./ *n* [C] *BrE* a narrow bed that folds flat and is easy to carry [= **cot** *AmE*] → see picture at BED

camper /'kæmpə $ -ər/ *n* [C] **1** someone who is staying in a tent for a short time **2** also **'camper van** *BrE* a vehicle that has cooking equipment and beds in it

campsite /'kæmpsaɪt/ *BrE*; **campground** /'kæmpgraʊnd/ *AmE n* [C] an area where people can stay in tents, often with a water supply and toilets → see box at ACCOMMODATION

campus /'kæmpəs/ *n* [C,U] the land and buildings of a college or university: **on campus** *Most first-year students live on campus.*

can¹ /kən; *strong* kæn/ *modal verb* negative short form **can't**

1 to be able to do something or to know how to do something: *You can swim, can't you?* | *Jess can speak French fluently.* | *I can't meet you now – I'm busy.* | **sb can see/hear/feel/taste/smell/ understand sth** (=used with these verbs to mean that someone is able to see etc something now) *I can see the sea!* | *He can't understand why you're so upset.*

USAGE

Use **can** and **be able to** to say that someone has the ability to do something. **Be able to** is more formal: *Can you swim?* | *He isn't able to run very fast.*
Use **could** to say that someone has the ability to do something, but does not do it: *He could do a lot better.*
Could is also the past form of **can**. Use **could** or a past form of **be able to** to say that someone had the ability to do something in the past: *She could ride a bike when she was three.* | *He was able to walk with a stick.*
Use **will be able to** to talk about future ability: *After only a few lessons, you will be able to understand basic Spanish.*

---

2 *spoken* used to ask someone to give you something or to do something: *Can I have a chocolate biscuit?* | *Can you help me lift this box?*
3 used to ask for permission to do something, or to give permission: *Can we go home now?* | *You can go out when you've finished your homework.* | *You can't park there!*
4 *spoken* used to offer to do something: *Can I help you?*
5 used to say that something is possible: *I'm sure it can be done.* | *Can he be alive after all this time?* | *We can't go on like this.*
6 *spoken* used in negatives and questions to say that you do not believe that something is true, or to express surprise or anger: *This can't be the right road.* | *You can't be serious!* | *How can you be so stupid?*

7 used to say what sometimes happens or how someone sometimes behaves: *It can be cold here at night.* | *He can be very charming.*

can² /kæn/ *n* [C]

1 a metal container in which food or liquid is kept without air [= tin *BrE*]: *a Coke can* | **+of** *a can of tuna fish* | *a can of paint* → see picture at **CONTAINER**

2 can of worms a complicated situation that causes a lot of problems when you start to deal with it

→ **GARBAGE CAN, WATERING CAN**

can³ *v* [T] **canned, canning** to preserve food by putting it in a closed metal container with no air [= tin *BrE*] —**canned** *adj*: *canned tomatoes* → see box at **FOOD**

canal /kə'næl/ *n* [C] a long narrow area of water made for ships or boats to travel along → see picture at **RIVER**

canary /kə'neəri $ -'neri/ *n* [C] plural **canaries** a small yellow bird that people often keep as a pet

cancel /'kænsəl/ *v* [I,T] **cancelled, cancelling** *BrE*, **canceled, canceling** *AmE*

1 to decide that something that was planned will not happen, or to tell someone this: *I had to cancel my trip to Rome.* | *You'll have to ring them and cancel.*

2 to end an agreement or arrangement that you do not want any more: *I phoned the hotel to cancel my reservation.*

—**cancellation** /ˌkænsə'leɪʃən/ *n* [C,U] *Passengers are fed up with cancellations and delays.*

cancel sth ⇔ **out** *phr v* if two things cancel each other out, each stops the other from having any effect: *The gains and losses will cancel each other out.*

cancer /'kænsə $ -ər/ *n* [C,U] a serious disease in which cells in someone's body start to grow in a way that is not normal: *lung cancer* | *He died of cancer.* —**cancerous** *adj*

Cancer *n* **1** [U] the sign of the Zodiac of people born between June 22 and July 23 **2** [C] someone who has this sign

candid /'kændɪd/ *adj* honest, even about things that are unpleasant or embarrassing [= frank]: *a candid article about his drug addiction* —**candidly** *adv*

candidacy /'kændɪdəsi/ *n* [C,U] plural **candidacies** the position of being a candidate: *She announced her candidacy at the convention.*

candidate /'kændɪdət $ -deɪt, -dət/ *n* [C] **1** someone who is being considered for a job or is competing in an election: **+for** *She's a likely candidate* (=likely to be chosen) *for the job.* | *a presidential candidate* **2** *BrE* someone who is taking an examination

candle /'kændl/ *n* [C] a stick of WAX that you burn to produce light: **light/blow out a candle** → see picture at **LIGHT¹**

candlelight /'kændl-laɪt/ *n* [U] the light that a candle produces —**candle-,lit** *adj*

candlestick /'kændl,stɪk/ *n* [C] an object used to hold a candle

candour *BrE*; **candor** *AmE* /'kændə $ -ər/ *n* [U] the quality of being honest, even about things that are unpleasant or embarrassing

candy /'kændi/ *n* [C,U] plural **candies** *especially AmE* a sweet food made of sugar or chocolate [= sweet *BrE*]: *a piece of candy*

cane¹ /keɪn/ *n* **1** [C,U] the hard stem of some plants, used to make furniture or to support plants in the garden: *cane furniture* **2** [C] a long thin stick used to help you walk **3** [C] a stick used by teachers in the past to hit children as a punishment

cane² *v* [T] to punish someone by hitting them with a cane

canine /'keɪnaɪn, 'kæ- $ 'keɪ-/ *adj* relating to dogs

canister /'kænɪstə $ -ər/ *n* [C] a metal container: *a gas canister*

cannabis /'kænəbɪs/ *n* [U] *especially BrE* an illegal drug that some people smoke [= marijuana]

canned /kænd/ *adj AmE* canned food is preserved in a round metal container [= tinned *BrE*]: *canned tomatoes* | *canned fruit*

cannibal /'kænɪbəl/ *n* [C] someone who eats human flesh —**cannibalism** *n* [U]

cannon /'kænən/ *n* [C] a large powerful gun used in the past to fire heavy iron balls

'cannon ball *n* [C] a heavy iron ball fired from a cannon

cannot /'kænət, -nɒt $ -nɑːt/ *modal verb* a negative form of 'can' [= can't]: *I cannot accept your offer.*

canny /'kæni/ *adj* clever and not easy to deceive

canoe /kə'nuː/ *n* [C] a long narrow boat that is pointed at both ends, which you move using a PADDLE —**canoe** *v* [I] —**canoeing** *n* [U]

canon /'kænən/ *n* [C] a Christian priest who works in a CATHEDRAL

'can ,opener *n* [C] a tool for opening cans of food [= tin opener *BrE*]

canopy /'kænəpi/ *n* [C] plural **canopies** a cover above a bed or seat, used as a decoration or for shelter

can't /kɑːnt $ kænt/ the short form of 'cannot': *I can't come today.*

cantankerous /kæn'tæŋkərəs/ *adj* getting annoyed easily and complaining a lot

canteen /kæn'tiːn/ *n* [C] *BrE* a place in a factory, school etc where people can get meals, usually cheaply → see box at **OFFICE** and **RESTAURANT**

canter /'kæntə $ -ər/ *v* [I,T] if a horse canters, it runs fairly fast but not as fast as it can [➡ gallop] —**canter** *n* [singular]

canvas /'kænvəs/ *n* **1** [U] a type of strong cloth used to make bags, tents, shoes etc: *a canvas bag* **2** [C] a painting done on canvas, or the cloth it is painted on

canvass /'kænvəs/ *v* **1** [I,T] to try to persuade people to vote for your political party in an election: **+for** *Someone was here canvassing for the Green Party.* **2** [T] to ask people what their opinion is about something: *The company canvassed 600 people who used their product.*

canyon /'kænjən/ *n* [C] a deep valley with steep sides: *the Grand Canyon*

cap¹ /kæp/ *n* [C]

1 a) a soft hat with a curved part sticking out at the front: *a baseball cap* → see picture at **HAT b)** a covering that fits closely to your head: *a swimming cap*

2 something that covers and protects the end or top of something [= **top**]: *Put the cap back on the bottle.*

→ ICE CAP

cap² *v* [T] **capped, capping** **1 be capped with sth** to have a particular substance on top: *mountains capped with snow* **2** to do or say something that is even better or worse than has already been done: *Lewis capped a brilliant season by beating the world record.* **3** to limit the amount of money that can be used or demanded: *Our council has had its spending capped.*

capability /ˌkeɪpəˈbɪləti/ *n* [C,U] plural **capabilities** the ability to do something, especially something difficult: **+to** *The country has the capability to produce nuclear weapons.*

capable /ˈkeɪpəbəl/ *adj* **1 capable of (doing) sth** having the qualities or ability needed to do something [≠ **incapable**]: **+of** *Do you think he's capable of murder?* **2** able to do things well: *Sue's an extremely capable lawyer.*

capacity /kəˈpæsəti/ *n* plural **capacities** **1** [singular] the amount that can fit inside a container, space, building etc: **+of** *The fuel tank has a capacity of 50 litres.* | *The theatre was filled to capacity* (=completely full). **2** [C,U] someone's ability to do something: **+for** *a child's capacity for learning* **3** [singular] someone's job, position, or duty: **(do sth) in your capacity as sth** *She travelled a lot in her capacity as a journalist.* **4** [singular, U] the amount that a factory or machine can produce: *The factory is working at full capacity* (=producing as much as it can).

cape /keɪp/ *n* [C] **1** a long loose coat without sleeves that fastens around your neck and hangs from your shoulders **2** a large piece of land surrounded on three sides by water: *Cape Cod*

caper /ˈkeɪpə $ -ər/ *n* [C] *informal* something you do for fun, especially something that is not sensible: *I'm too old for this sort of caper.*

capillary /kəˈpɪləri $ ˈkæpəleri/ *n* [C] plural **capillaries** a very small narrow tube that carries blood around your body [➤ **artery, vein**]

capital¹ /ˈkæpətl/ *n*
1 [C] an important city where the main government of a country, state etc is: **+of** *What's the capital of Poland?* | *a capital city*
2 [singular, U] money or property, especially when it is used to start a business or to make more money: *The government is eager to attract foreign capital.* | **capital gains** (=money made from businesses, property etc)
3 also **,capital 'letter** [C] a letter of the alphabet that is written in its large form, for example at the beginning of a name or sentence: *Write your name in capitals.* | *a capital 'T'*

capital² *adj* **capital offence/crime** a crime that can be punished by death

capitalism /ˈkæpətl-ɪzəm/ *n* [U] an economic and political system in which businesses belong mostly to private owners, not to the government [➤ **communism, socialism**] —**capitalist** *n* [C]

capitalize also **-ise** *BrE* /ˈkæpətl-aɪz/ *v*
capitalize on sth *phr v* to use something good that you have to get an advantage for yourself: *Ecuador has capitalized on its natural beauty to attract tourism.*

,capital 'punishment *n* [U] the punishment of killing someone who has committed a serious crime [➤ **death penalty**] → see box at **PUNISHMENT**

capitulate /kəˈpɪtʃəleɪt/ *v* [I] *formal* to accept or agree to something you have been opposing —**capitulation** /kəˌpɪtʃəˈleɪʃən/ *n* [C,U]

cappuccino /ˌkæpʊˈtʃiːnəʊ $ -noʊ/ *n* [C,U] plural **cappuccinos** Italian coffee made with hot milk

capricious /kəˈprɪʃəs/ *adj* likely to change very suddenly: *capricious spring weather*

Capricorn /ˈkæprɪkɔːn $ -kɔːrn/ *n* **1** [U] the sign of the Zodiac of people born between December 22 and January 20 **2** [C] someone who has this sign

capsize

capsize /kæpˈsaɪz $ ˈkæpsaɪz/ *v* [I,T] if a boat capsizes or you capsize it, it turns over in the water

capsule /ˈkæpsjuːl $ -səl/ *n* [C] **1** a very small tube of medicine that you swallow → see box at **MEDICINE** **2** the part of a spacecraft in which people live and work

captain¹ /ˈkæptən/ *n* [C]
1 the leader of a team or group of people: **+of** *Rod's captain of the football team.* | *the US team captain*
2 also **Captain** someone who is in charge of a ship or plane
3 also **Captain** a military officer with a fairly high rank

captain² *v* [T] to be the captain of a team, ship, or plane —**captaincy** *n* [U]

captaincy /ˈkæptənsi/ *n* [C,U] plural **captaincies** the position of being captain of a team

caption /ˈkæpʃən/ *n* [C] words written above or below a picture in a book, newspaper etc to explain what it is about

captivate /ˈkæptəveɪt/ *v* [T] to attract and interest you very much: *Alex was captivated by her beauty.* —**captivating** *adj*

captive¹ /ˈkæptɪv/ *adj* **1** kept somewhere and not allowed to leave: *captive animals* | *His son had been taken captive* (=made a prisoner) *during the raid.* **2** **captive audience** people who listen to or watch something because they have to, not because they want to

captive² *n* [C] someone who is kept as a prisoner, especially in a war

captivity /kæpˈtɪvəti/ *n* [U] when a person or animal is kept in a prison, cage etc and not allowed to leave: **in captivity** *Many animals won't breed in captivity.*

captor /ˈkæptə $ -ər/ *n* [C] *formal* someone who is keeping another person as a prisoner

capture¹ /'kæptʃə $ -ər/ v [T] **1** to catch a person or animal and keep them as a prisoner: *He was captured at the airport.* **2** to get control of something: *The town was captured by enemy troops after 10 days' fighting.* | *Sega and Nintendo soon captured half the market* (=the business available). **3** to succeed in showing or describing something, using pictures or words: *His new book captures what the 1920s were like.* **4 capture sb's imagination/attention etc** to make someone feel very interested in something

capture² n [U] **1** when someone captures a person or animal **2** when someone gets control of something: *the capture of the village*

car /kɑː $ kɑːr/ n [C]
1 a vehicle with four wheels and an engine, that can carry a small number of passengers: **by car** *Did you come by car?* | **get into/out of the car** *Joe got into the car.* | *You can't **park your car** there!* | *She was killed in a **car accident**.* | *He wasn't old enough to **drive a car**.*
2 dining/buffet/sleeping car *BrE* a part of a train used for eating or sleeping → see box at TRAIN
3 *AmE* one of the connected parts of a train [= carriage *BrE*] → see box at TRAIN → CABLE CAR, ESTATE CAR, SPORTS CAR, SQUAD CAR

carafe /kə'ræf, kə'rɑːf/ n [C] a glass container used for serving wine and water at meals

caramel /'kærəməl, -mel/ n [C,U] boiled sugar, butter, and milk used in food or made into a brown sweet

carat also **karat** *AmE* /'kærət/ n [C] a unit for measuring how pure gold is, or how heavy jewels are

caravan /'kærəvæn/ n [C] **1** *BrE* a vehicle that can be pulled by a car, and that people can live and sleep in [= trailer *AmE*] **2** *BrE* a vehicle that is pulled by a horse, and that people can live in [= wagon *AmE*]: *a gipsy caravan* **3** a group of people with animals or vehicles who travel together

carbohydrate /ˌkɑːbəʊ'haɪdreɪt, -drət $ ˌkɑːrboʊ-/ n [C,U] a substance in foods such as sugar, bread, and potatoes that provides your body with heat and energy

carbon /'kɑːbən $ 'kɑːr-/ n [U] a chemical substance that is found in all living things, and in coal, DIAMONDS, petrol etc

carbonated /'kɑːbəneɪt̬d $ 'kɑːr-/ adj carbonated drinks contain small bubbles [➡ fizzy]

ˌcarbon 'copy n [C] something or someone that is very similar to another thing or person: *The robbery is a carbon copy of the one last year.*

ˌcarbon di'oxide n [U] the gas produced when people or animals breathe out

ˌcarbon mo'noxide n [U] a poisonous gas produced when engines burn petrol

ˌcar 'boot ˌsale n [C] *BrE* an event when people sell things they do not want from the back of their cars

carburettor *BrE*; **carburetor** *AmE* /ˌkɑːbjʊ'retə, -bə- $ 'kɑːrbəreɪtər/ n [C] the part of a car engine where air and petrol mix

carcass /'kɑːkəs $ 'kɑːr-/ n [C] the body of a dead animal

carcinogen /kɑː'sɪnədʒən $ kɑːr- / n [C] technical a substance that can cause CANCER —**carcinogenic** /ˌkɑːsɪ̬nə'dʒenɪk $ ˌkɑːr-/ adj

card /kɑːd $ kɑːrd/ n
1 [C] a small piece of plastic or stiff paper that gives information about someone or something: *an **identity card*** | *Here's my business card.* | *a set of recipe cards* | *Please bring your **medical card**.*
2 [C] a small piece of plastic which you use to pay for goods or to get money: *my **credit card*** | *a **phone card***
3 [C] a folded piece of stiff paper with a picture on the front, that you send to people on special occasions: **birthday/greetings/Christmas etc card**
4 [C] one of a set of 52 small pieces of stiff paper with pictures or numbers on them that are used to play games [= playing card]: *Let's **play cards*** (=a game using cards). | **pack** (=complete set) **of cards** *BrE* /**deck of cards** *AmE*
5 [C] a POSTCARD
6 [U] *BrE* thick stiff paper [➡ cardboard]
7 red/yellow card a card that the REFEREE holds up in football to show that a player has done something wrong
8 [C] the thing inside a computer that the CHIPS are attached to, that allows the computer to do specific things: *a graphics card*
9 be on the cards *BrE* **be in the cards** *AmE* to seem likely to happen: *I've left Brenda. It's been on the cards for a long time.*
10 put/lay your cards on the table to be completely honest about your plans and intentions
→ CASH CARD, CHARGE CARD, CREDIT CARD, DEBIT CARD, SWIPE CARD

cardboard /'kɑːdbɔːd $ 'kɑːrdbɔːrd/ n [U] very stiff thick paper, used especially for making boxes → see picture at BOX¹

cardiac /'kɑːdi.æk $ 'kɑːr-/ adj [only before noun] technical relating to the heart: *cardiac arrest* (=when the heart stops working)

cardigan /'kɑːdɪɡən $ 'kɑːr-/ n [C] a piece of clothing like a SWEATER but with buttons that you fasten down the front

cardinal¹ /'kɑːdənəl $ 'kɑːr-/ n [C] a priest of high rank in the Roman Catholic church

cardinal² adj [only before noun] very important or basic: *a cardinal rule*

ˌcardinal 'number n [C] a number such as 1, 2 or 3, that shows how many of something there are [➡ ordinal number]

cardiovascular /ˌkɑːdiəʊ'væskjᵿlə $ ˌkɑːrdioʊ'væskjələr/ adj technical relating to the heart and the tubes through which blood flows in your body

care¹ /keə $ ker/ v
1 [I,T] to be concerned about or interested in someone or something: **+about** *He doesn't seem to care about other people.* | *A lot of people just don't care about politics.* | **+what/who/how etc** *I don't care what you do.*
2 [I] to like or love someone [➡ caring]: *Buy her flowers to show that you care.* | **+about/for** *She obviously cares about you a lot.*
3 who cares? spoken used to say that you do not think something is important or interesting: *It's rather an old car but who cares?*
4 I/he/they etc couldn't care less spoken used to say that someone is not at all concerned about

or interested in something: *I really couldn't care less what you think!*

5 would you care for sth?/would you care to do sth? *formal* used to ask someone if they want something or want to do something: *Would you care for a drink?*

care for sb/sth *phr v* **1** to look after someone or something [= **take care of**]: *Angie gave up her job to care for her mother.* **2 not care for sb/sth** *formal* to not like someone or something: *I don't care for his brother.*

care² *n*

1 [U] the process of looking after someone or something: *Your father will need constant medical care.* | **+of** *They shared the care of their children.* | **skin/hair/health etc care** advice on dental care | **in sb's care** (=being looked after by someone) *The children had been left in the care of a babysitter.*

2 take care of sb/sth a) to look after someone or something: *Who's taking care of the baby?* | *Karl took care of the house while we were on holiday.* **b)** to deal with something that needs doing: **take care of (doing) sth** *I'll take care of making the reservations.*

3 take care a) *informal* used to say goodbye to family or friends **b)** to be careful: **+to** *Take care to follow the instructions.*

4 [U] when you do something carefully in order not to make a mistake or damage something: *You need to put more care into your work.* | **with care** *Fragile! Handle with care.*

5 [C,U] a worry or problem: *Forget all your cares.* | *Alex looked as though he didn't have a care in the world* (=did not have any problems or worries).

6 in care *BrE* a child who is in care is being looked after by government organizations, not by their parents: *When their father was sent to prison, the kids were taken into care.*

→ DAY CARE, HEALTH CARE, INTENSIVE CARE

career¹ /kəˈrɪə $ -ˈrɪr/ *n* [C]

1 a job or profession that you have been trained for, and which you usually do for a long time: *a teaching career* | **+in** *a career in law* | **Career prospects** (=job opportunities) *within the company are excellent.* → see box at JOB

2 the time in your life that you spend working or doing a particular type of work: *Ted spent most of his career as a teacher.* | **+as** *My career as a writer didn't last long.*

career² *v* [I] *BrE* to move quickly forwards without control: **+down/through/off etc** *A couple of boys on bikes careered down the hill.*

carefree /ˈkeəfriː $ ˈker-/ *adj* without any problems or worries: *a carefree childhood*

careful /ˈkeəfəl $ ˈker-/ *adj*

1 trying very hard not to make mistakes, damage things etc [≠ **careless**]: *a careful driver* | **+to** *Anna was careful not to upset Steven.* | **+(that)** *We were very careful that he didn't find out.* | **(be) careful!** *spoken* (=used to tell someone to do this) *Be careful with that ladder!*

2 giving a lot of thought and attention to something: *Any school trip requires careful planning.* | **+about** *I'm always careful about what I buy.* —**carefully** *adv*: *Please listen carefully.*

careless /ˈkeələs $ ˈker-/ *adj* not giving enough thought and attention to something, so that you

make mistakes, damage things etc [≠ **careful**]: *a careless mistake* | **be careless of sb** *It was careless of you to leave your keys in the car.* —**carelessly** *adv* —**carelessness** *n* [U]

carer /ˈkeərə $ ˈkerər/ *n* [C] someone who looks after a child, or a person who is old or ill

caress /kəˈres/ *v* [T] *literary* to touch someone gently in a way that shows you love them —**caress** *n* [C]

caretaker /ˈkeəˌteɪkə $ ˈkerˌteɪkər/ *n* [C] *BrE* someone whose job is to look after a building, especially a school [= **janitor** *AmE*]

cargo /ˈkɑːɡəʊ $ ˈkɑːrɡoʊ/ *n* [C,U] plural **cargos** or **cargoes** goods that are carried in a ship or plane: **+of** *a cargo of oil* | *a cargo ship* → see box at SHIP

Caribbean /ˌkærɪˈbiːən ◂/ *adj* from or relating to the islands in the Caribbean sea, such as Jamaica and Barbados —**Caribbean** *n* [C]

caricature /ˈkærɪkətʃʊə $ -tʃʊr/ *n* [C,U] a funny drawing or description of someone that makes them seem silly → see box at PICTURE —**caricature** *v* [T]

caring /ˈkeərɪŋ $ ˈker-/ *adj* someone who is caring is kind to other people and tries to help them: *a warm and caring person*

carjacking /ˈkɑːˌdʒækɪŋ $ ˈkɑːr-/ *n* [U] the crime of forcing the driver of a car to give you the car or drive you somewhere, using a weapon —**carjacker** *n* [C]

carnage /ˈkɑːnɪdʒ $ ˈkɑːr-/ *n* [U] *formal* when a lot of people are killed or injured

carnal /ˈkɑːnl $ ˈkɑːrnl/ *adj* *formal* relating to sex: *carnal desire*

carnation /kɑːˈneɪʃən $ kɑːr-/ *n* [C] a white, pink, or red flower that smells nice

carnival /ˈkɑːnɪvəl $ ˈkɑːr-/ *n* [C,U] a public event when people play music, wear special clothes, and dance in the streets: *carnival time in Rio*

carnivore /ˈkɑːnɪvɔː $ ˈkɑːrnɪvɔːr/ *n* [C] an animal that eats meat —**carnivorous** /kɑːˈnɪvərəs $ kɑːr-/ *adj*

carol /ˈkærəl/ *n* [C] a song that people sing at Christmas: *Christmas carols*

carousel /ˌkærəˈsel/ *n* [C] **1** the moving thing at an airport from which passengers collect their bags **2** *AmE* a large machine at a FAIR which has toy animals, cars etc for people to ride on as it turns around [= **merry-go-round**]

carp¹ /kɑːp $ kɑːrp/ *n* [C,U] plural **carp** a large fish that lives in lakes or rivers and can be eaten

carp² *v* [I] *disapproving* to complain a lot about something: **+about** *people who constantly carp about the price of petrol*

'car park *n* [C] *BrE* an area or building where people can park their cars [= **parking lot** *AmE*]

carpenter /ˈkɑːpəntə $ ˈkɑːrpəntər/ *n* [C] someone whose job is making and repairing wooden objects

carpentry /ˈkɑːpəntri $ ˈkɑːr-/ *n* [U] the skill or work of a carpenter

carpet /ˈkɑːpɪt $ ˈkɑːr-/ *n*

1 [C,U] material for covering floors, often made of wool, or a piece of this material [➙ **rug**]: *All the rooms had fitted carpets* (=carpets cut to exactly fit a room). | *I'd like red carpet in the hall.* → see picture at RUG

2 a carpet of leaves/flowers etc *literary* a thick layer of leaves etc on the ground
—carpet *v* [T] → RED CARPET

carriage /'kærɪdʒ/ *n* [C] **1** *BrE* one of the separate parts of a train where passengers sit [= car *AmE*] → see box at TRAIN **2** a vehicle pulled by a horse and used for passengers

carriageway /'kærɪdʒweɪ/ *n* [C] *BrE* one of the sides of a MOTORWAY or main road, used by vehicles travelling in the same direction: *the north-bound carriageway* → DUAL CARRIAGEWAY

carrier /'kæriə $ -ər/ *n* [C] **1** a company that moves goods or passengers from one place to another: *an international carrier* **2** someone who passes a disease to other people without having it themselves → AIRCRAFT CARRIER

'carrier ,bag *n* [C] *BrE* a bag that you are given in a shop to carry the things you have bought

carrot /'kærət/ *n*

1 [C,U] a long orange vegetable that grows under the ground → see picture at VEGETABLE
2 [C] something that is offered to someone to persuade them to do something: **+of** *The government held out the carrot of lower interest rates.* | *a carrot and stick approach* (=both offering something good and threatening something bad)

carry /'kæri/ *v* carried, carrying, carries

1 [T] to hold something in your hands or arms, or on your back, as you go somewhere: *Let me carry that bag for you.* | **carry sth in/on sth** *Angie was carrying the baby in her arms.* | **carry sth to sth/sb** *The waiter carried our drinks to the table.* → see picture on page A11
2 [T] to take people or things from one place to another: *The bus was carrying 25 passengers.* | **carry sth into/across/through etc sth** *A network of pipes carries oil across the desert.*
3 [T] to have something with you in your pocket, bag etc as you go somewhere: *I never carry much money.* | *It's illegal to carry a gun.*
4 [T] to have a disease which can be given to others [→ carrier]: *Many diseases are carried by insects.*
5 [T] to contain a particular piece of information or news: *Tobacco products must carry a health warning.* | *The magazine carries articles on scientific developments.*
6 [T] to have a particular quality or result: *sports that carry a risk of injury* | **carry weight/authority** (=have influence over people) *He's someone whose opinion carries weight.* | *Murder carries a life sentence.*
7 [T] to support the weight of something: *Two columns carry the whole roof.*
8 [I] if a sound carries, it can be heard for a long way
9 be carried if a suggestion, proposal etc is carried, most of the people at a meeting vote for it: *The motion was carried by 20 votes to 12.*
10 carry sth too far/to extremes to do or say something too much or for too long: *It was funny at first, but you've carried the joke too far.*

be/get carried away *phr v* to be so excited, interested etc that you are not completely in control of what you do or say

carry sth ⇔ off *phr v* to do something difficult successfully: *No one believed he could carry the plan off.*

carry on *phr v* **1** to continue doing something: **carry on doing sth** *You'll get ill if you carry on working like that.* | **+with** *I decided to carry on with the course.* **2** to continue moving in the same direction: *Carry straight on to the traffic lights.*

carry sth ⇔ out *phr v* to do something that has been planned or discussed, or that someone has told you to do: *The students carried out a survey on attitudes to drugs.* | *Have you carried out her instructions?*

carry sth ⇔ through *phr v* to complete or finish something successfully

carryall /'kæri-ɔːl $ -ɒːl/ *n* [C] *AmE* a large soft bag [= holdall *BrE*]

carrycot /'kærikɒt $ -kɑːt/ *n* [C] *BrE* a small bed used to carry a baby

'carry-out *n* [C] *AmE* food that you can take away from a restaurant to eat, or a restaurant that sells food like this [= takeaway *BrE*]

carsick /'kɑːˌsɪk $ 'kɑːr-/ *adj* feeling sick when you are travelling in a car —carsickness *n* [U]

cart¹ /kɑːt $ kɑːrt/ *n* [C] **1** a vehicle pulled by a horse and used to carry things **2** *AmE* a large wire basket on wheels that you use in a SUPERMARKET [= trolley *BrE*]

cart² *v* [T] *informal* to carry or take something or someone somewhere, especially with difficulty: **cart sth around** *I'm sick of carting this suitcase around.*

carte blanche /ˌkɑːt 'blɑːnʃ $ ˌkɑːrt-/ *n* [U] the freedom to do something in exactly the way you want: *Her parents gave her carte blanche to organize a party.*

cartel /kɑːˈtel $ kɑːr-/ *n* [C,U] a group of companies that work together to control prices and increase their profits

cartilage /'kɑːtlɪdʒ $ 'kɑːrtəlɪdʒ/ *n* [C,U] a strong substance that can bend, which is around the joints in your body

cartography /kɑːˈtɒɡrəfi $ kɑːrˈtɑː-/ *n* [U] the skill or work of making maps —cartographer *n* [C]

carton /'kɑːtn $ 'kɑːrtn/ *n* [C] a box that contains food or drink, made from stiff paper or plastic: **+of** *a carton of juice* | *a milk carton* → see picture at CONTAINER

cartoon /kɑːˈtuːn $ kɑːr-/ *n* [C] **1** a film that uses characters that are drawn and not real → see box at TELEVISION **2** a funny drawing or set of drawings in a newspaper or magazine

cartoonist /kɑːˈtuːnɪst $ kɑːr-/ *n* [C] someone whose job is to draw cartoons

cartridge /'kɑːtrɪdʒ $ 'kɑːr-/ *n* [C] **1** a small container that you put inside something to make it work: *The printer needs a new ink cartridge.* **2** a tube containing explosive powder and a bullet, used in a gun

cartwheel /'kɑːt-wiːl $ 'kɑːrt-/ *n* [C] a movement in which you throw your body sideways onto your hands and bring your legs over your head —cartwheel *v* [I]

carve /kɑːv $ kɑːrv/ *v* **1** [T] to cut a piece of wood or stone in order to make an object or make a pattern on the surface: **carve sth from/out of sth** *All the figures are carved from a single tree.* | **carve sth on/onto sth** *Kids had carved their names on the desks.* **2** [I,T] to cut a large piece of cooked meat into thin pieces with a knife → see box at **CUT** → see picture at **CUT**[1]

   carve out sth *phr v* **carve out a career/ niche/role etc** to succeed in getting a job, position etc that suits you

   carve sth ⇔ **up** *phr v disapproving* to divide land, a company etc into smaller parts: *The country was carved up after the war.*

carving /ˈkɑːvɪŋ $ ˈkɑːr-/ *n* **1** [C,U] an object or pattern made by cutting wood, stone etc **2** [U] the activity of cutting wood, stone etc into objects or patterns

cascade /kæˈskeɪd/ *n* [C] *literary* something that flows or hangs down in large amounts: **+of** *Her hair was a cascade of soft curls.* —**cascade** *v* [I] *Waterfalls cascaded down the mountainside.*

cases

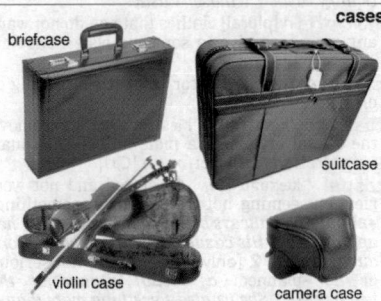

briefcase

suitcase

violin case

camera case

case /keɪs/ *n* [C]

1 a particular situation, or an example of that situation: *In this case there are several possible solutions.* | **in some/many/most etc cases** *In most cases, excessive speed was the cause of the accident.* | **in sb's case** *They say men don't age and in his case it was true.* | **In the case of** *special education, the issues are different.* | **+of** *a case of wrongful imprisonment*

2 (just) in case a) as a way of being prepared for something that might happen: *Take your umbrella in case it rains.* **b)** *AmE* if: *In case I'm late, start without me.*

3 in any case *spoken* used to give a reason for doing something, or to express determination to do it [= **anyway**]: *We'll take you home – we're going that way in any case.* | *I think I could win. In any case, I'm going to try.*

4 in that case if that is the situation: *'It will only take five minutes.' 'In that case, I'll wait.'*

5 be the case to be true: *It may be the case that science is badly taught in schools.*

6 something that is being dealt with by lawyers or the police: *a court case* | **+of** *a case of armed robbery* | *a murder case*

7 when someone has an illness, or someone who has an illness: **+of** *The first cases of AIDS were reported in 1978.*

8 [usually singular] a number of reasons why something should be done or believed: **+for/ against** *There's a strong case for changing the law.* | *Student representatives met to put forward their case.*

9 a) a container for storing or protecting something: *a packing case* | *a pencil case* | *Always keep your guitar in its case.* **b)** *BrE* a **SUITCASE**

10 in case of sth *formal* if or when something happens: *In case of fire, break the glass.*

11 it's a case of (doing) sth *spoken* used to say what is needed to do something: *Anyone can get fit. It's just a case of taking enough exercise.*

12 be on sb's case *informal* to criticize someone a lot in a way that seems unfair: *Dad's always on my case about something.*

13 be on the case *BrE* to be dealing with something

→ **LOWER CASE, TEST CASE, UPPER CASE**

ˈcase ˌstudy *n* [C] a detailed report about a person, group, or situation studied over a period of time

cash[1] /kæʃ/ *n* [U]

1 money in the form of coins and notes: *There's a small discount if you pay cash.* | **in cash** *I usually have about £50 in cash with me.* → see box at **MONEY**

2 *informal* money in any form: *I'm short of cash just now.* | *The company had problems raising cash for the deal.*

→ **hard cash** at **HARD**[1]

cash[2] *v* [T] to exchange a cheque for money

   cash in on sth *phr v disapproving* to get money or an advantage from a situation in a way that other people think is wrong

cashback /ˈkæʃbæk/ *n* [U] **1** a way of getting money from a shop when you pay for the things you are buying with a DEBIT CARD. The total amount is taken from your bank account. **2** an amount of money that is offered to customers who are buying a car, piece of furniture etc as a way of reducing what they have to pay for it

ˈcash card *n* [C] a plastic card used for getting money from a CASH MACHINE

ˈcash crop *n* [C] a crop that is grown to be sold, not used by the people growing it

ˈcash desk *n* [C] *BrE* the desk in a shop where you pay

cashew /ˈkæʃuː, kəˈʃuː/ *n* [C] a small curved nut

ˈcash flow *n* [U] the movement of money into and out of a business or someone's bank account: *I've had a few cash flow problems.*

cashier /kæˈʃɪə $ -ˈʃɪr/ *n* [C] someone whose job is to receive and pay out money in a bank, shop etc

ˈcash maˌchine also **ˈcash diˌspenser** *BrE* *n* [C] a machine that you get money from using a plastic card, especially in a wall outside a bank or SUPERMARKET [= **ATM**] → see box at **ACCOUNT**

cash machine *BrE/* **ATM** *AmE*

cashmere /ˈkæʃmɪə $ ˈkæʒmɪr, ˈkæʃ-/ *n* [U] a type of fine soft wool

Cashpoint /ˈkæʃpɔɪnt/ *n* [C] *trademark BrE* a CASH MACHINE → see box at **ACCOUNT**

ˈcash ˌregister *n* [C] a machine used in shops to keep money in and record the amount of money received [= **till**]

casing /ˈkeɪsɪŋ/ *n* [C] a layer of rubber, metal etc that covers and protects something, for example a wire

casino /kə'si:nəʊ $ -noʊ/ n [C] plural casinos a place where people try to win money by playing card games or ROULETTE

cask /kɑ:sk $ kæsk/ n [C] a round wooden container used to store alcohol

casket /'kɑ:skɪ̆t $ 'kæs-/ n [C] AmE the box a dead person is buried in [= coffin BrE]

casserole /'kæsərəʊl $ -roʊl/ n **1** [C,U] meat and vegetables in liquid cooked together slowly in an OVEN: chicken casserole **2** [C] a large covered dish used for cooking casseroles

cassette /kə'set/ n [C] a small flat plastic case with tape inside on which music, speech, a film etc has been recorded or can be recorded: **an audio/video cassette** | a blank cassette | **on cassette** (=with nothing recorded on it yet) | **on cassette** Is the album still available on cassette?
→ VIDEO CASSETTE RECORDER

cas'sette ,player n [C] a machine used for listening to cassettes

cast¹ /kɑ:st $ kæst/ v [T] past tense and past participle cast **1** to choose a particular actor for a part in a film, play etc: **cast sb as sb** Who was cast as Harry Potter? **2** literary to throw something somewhere, or send something in a particular direction: **cast sth across/on/into etc sth** The fishermen cast their nets into the sea. | The fire cast a soft light on her face. | **cast a look/glance at sb/sth** She cast an anxious glance at Guy. **3** cast doubt/suspicion on sth to make people feel less certain about something: Recent information has cast doubt on the evidence. **4** cast light on/onto sth to explain something or provide new information about it: Can you cast any light on these figures? **5** cast a shadow/cloud over sth to make people enjoy something less or feel less happy: The bad news cast a shadow over his visit. **6** cast an eye over sth to read or look at something quickly **7** cast a spell on/over sb/sth **a)** to use magic to make something happen **b)** to interest or attract people very much, as if by magic: Hong Kong casts a spell over its visitors as soon as they land. **8** [usually passive] to make an object by pouring hot metal into a hollow container: **cast sth in/from sth** a statue cast in bronze **9** cast a/your vote to vote in an election **10** cast your mind back to try to remember something that happened in the past: **+to** Try to cast your mind back to that first day at school.

cast around/about for sth phr v to try to find or get something: On leaving school he cast around for a job.

cast sb/sth ⇔ **aside** phr v to get rid of something or someone: Never cast aside your old friends.

cast off phr v to untie the rope that fastens a boat to something

cast² n [C] **1** all the actors in a film, play etc: an **all-star cast** (=all the actors are famous) **2** a PLASTER CAST

castaway /'kɑ:stəweɪ $ 'kæst-/ n [C] someone who is alone on an island after their ship has sunk

caste /kɑ:st $ kæst/ n [C,U] one of the social classes that people belong to in India: the **caste system**

caster, castor /'kɑ:stə $ 'kæstər/ n [C] one of a set of small wheels fixed to the bottom of a piece of furniture so that it can be moved about easily

castigate /'kæstɪ̆geɪt/ v [T] formal to criticize someone severely

'casting ,vote n [singular] the vote of the person in charge of a meeting, used to decide something when there are an equal number of votes supporting and opposing it

,cast 'iron n [U] **1** a type of iron that is very hard: a cast-iron frying pan **2 cast-iron excuse/alibi/guarantee etc** an excuse etc that is very definite and that people will believe

castle /'kɑ:səl $ 'kæ-/ n [C] a very large strong building with high walls, built in the past to protect the people inside from attack: a 12th century castle | Windsor Castle

'cast-offs n [plural] clothes that you do not want any more and give to someone else —**cast-off** adj

castor /'kɑ:stə $ 'kæstər/ n another spelling of CASTER

castrate /kæ'streɪt $ 'kæstreɪt/ v [T] to remove the sexual organs of a male animal or a man —**castration** /kæ'streɪʃən/ n [C,U]

casual /'kæʒuəl/ adj **1** relaxed and not worried, or seeming not to care about something: **+about** She's always been pretty casual about her appearance. | His **casual attitude** towards work annoyed me. **2** [only before noun] not serious or not planned: a casual glance at the newspapers | She wanted something more than a **casual relationship**. | the dangers of casual sex **3** casual clothes are comfortable and informal → see box at CLOTHES **4** casual work is temporary, or not regular: casual employment | people who work **on a casual basis** —**casually** adv: He was dressed casually in faded jeans.

casualty /'kæʒuəlti/ n plural casualties **1** [C usually plural] someone who is hurt or killed in an accident or war: road casualties | a battle with **heavy casualties** (=a lot of people hurt or killed) on both sides **2** be a casualty of sth to suffer because of a difficult economic situation or other event: The city library is the latest casualty of the financial cuts. **3** [U] BrE the part of a hospital that people are taken to when they need urgent treatment [= emergency room AmE]

cat /kæt/ n [C]

1 a small animal that people keep as a pet, and that often kills birds, mice etc [➡ feline] → see picture at PET¹

2 a large wild animal that is related to cats, such as a lion

3 let the cat out of the bag informal to tell someone a secret without intending to

cataclysm /'kætəklɪzəm/ n [C] literary a serious event that causes great changes or damage: the cataclysm of the First World War —**cataclysmic** /,kætə'klɪzmɪk◂/ adj

catalogue¹ also **catalog** AmE /'kætəlɒg $ -lɔ:g, -lɑ:g/ n [C] **1** a complete list of things that you can buy or look at: our new Spring catalogue | an on-line catalog **2** a catalogue of injuries/complaints/disasters etc a series of injuries etc that happen one after another

catalogue² also **catalog** AmE v [T] to make a complete list of something

catalyst /'kætl-ɪ̩st/ *n* [C] someone or something that causes important changes: **+for** *His election may act as a catalyst for reform.*

catamaran /ˌkætəmə'ræn/ *n* [C] a sailing boat with two separate HULLS (=the part that goes in the water)

catapult[1] /'kætəpʌlt/ *v* [T]   **1** to make someone or something move through the air very quickly: **catapult sb/sth across/through/into etc sth** *The explosion catapulted him into the air.*   **2 catapult sb to fame/stardom** to make someone suddenly become famous

catapult[2] *n* [C] *BrE* a small stick in the shape of a Y with a band of rubber between the ends, used by children to throw stones

cataract /'kætərækt/ *n* [C] a medical condition that affects the eye and makes you slowly lose your sight

catarrh /kə'tɑː $ -'tɑːr/ *n* [U] *BrE* thick liquid that blocks your nose and throat when you have a cold

catastrophe /kə'tæstrəfi/ *n* [C] a terrible event that causes a lot of destruction or suffering → see box at ACCIDENT —**catastrophic** /ˌkætə'strɒfɪk ◂ $ -'strɑː-/ *adj*: *the catastrophic effects of the floods*

catch[1] /kætʃ/ *v* past tense and past participle **caught** /kɔːt $ kɒːt/

1 [T] to stop and hold something that is moving through the air: *Tom leapt up and **caught the ball.*** | **catch sb/sth in sth** *She jumped and he caught her in his arms.* → see picture on page A11

2 [T]   **a)** to stop a person or an animal that is running away: *'You can't catch me,' she yelled over her shoulder.*   **b)** to get a fish or animal by using a trap, net, or hook   **c)** to find a criminal and put them somewhere so that they cannot escape [➦ **capture**]: *The police have caught the man suspected of the murder.*

3 [T] to see someone doing something wrong or secret: **catch sb doing sth** *I caught him looking through my letters.* | *The thieves were **caught in the act.*** | *She was **caught red-handed** taking the money.*

4 [T] to get an illness: *Put your coat on or you'll catch a cold.*

5 catch a bus/train/plane etc to get on a bus, train etc: *I caught the 7.30 train to London.* → see box at TRAIN[1]

6 [T] to not be too late to see something, talk to someone etc [≠ **miss**]: *We only caught the end of the movie.* | *If you hurry, you'll catch her before she leaves.*

7 [I] also **be/get caught** to become stuck on or in something by mistake: *His shirt caught on the fence and tore.*

8 catch sight/a glimpse of sb/sth to suddenly see someone or something for a moment: *Tony caught sight of Louisa in the crowd.* → see box at SEE

9 [T] if something catches your attention, you notice it and feel interested in it: **catch sb's attention/interest etc** *One article on the front page caught my attention.* | *There was one red dress that **caught my eye.***

10 catch fire to start burning, especially accidentally

11 [T] to hit a particular part of someone: **catch sb in/on sth** *The punch caught him in the face.*

12 be caught in/without etc sth to be unable to avoid an unpleasant situation: *We were caught in the rain.*

13 not catch sth *spoken* to not hear clearly what someone says: *I'm sorry, I didn't catch your name.*

14 catch sb by surprise/unawares/off guard if something catches you by surprise, it happens when you are not expecting it

15 catch the light if something catches the light, it is bright because of light shining on it

16 catch you later *spoken* used to say goodbye: *'I'm off now.' 'OK. Catch you later.'*

catch on *phr v*   **1** to become popular or fashionable: *The idea never caught on in this country.*   **2** to begin to understand something: *With careful training, a puppy will soon catch on.*

catch sb ⇔ out *phr v BrE* to make someone make a mistake, especially by asking a difficult question: *Some interviewers may try to catch you out.*

catch up *phr v*   **1** to reach someone in front of you by going faster than them: **+with** *I had to run to catch up with her.* | **catch sb up** *You go ahead, and we'll catch you up.*   **2** to reach the same standard as other people: *If you miss classes, it's difficult to catch up.*   **3 be/get caught up in sth** to become involved in something, especially without wanting to: *young people who get caught up in crime*

catch up on sth *phr v* to do something that you have not had time to do yet: **+on** *I need to catch up on some work this weekend.*

catch[2] *n* [C]   **1** an act of catching a ball: *Hey! Nice catch!*   **2** [usually singular] *informal* a hidden problem involved in something that seems good or cheap: *It's a very good deal – is there a catch?*   **3** a quantity of fish caught at one time   **4** a hook for fastening something and keeping it shut

Catch-22 /ˌkætʃ twenti'tuː/ *n* [singular] a situation in which, whatever you do, you are prevented from achieving what you want: *It's a **Catch-22 situation** because you can't get a job without experience and you can't get experience without a job.*

'catch-all *adj* intended to include all possibilities: *a vague catch-all clause in the contract*

catching /'kætʃɪŋ/ *adj* [not before noun] an illness or feeling that is catching spreads easily from one person to another

catchment area /'kætʃmənt ˌeəriə $ -ˌeriə/ *n* [C] *BrE* the area that a school, hospital, or business gets its students, PATIENTS, or customers from

catchphrase /'kætʃfreiz/ *n* [C] a short phrase that is well-known because a famous person often uses it

catchy /'kætʃi/ *adj* a catchy tune or phrase is easy to remember

catechism /'kætɪˌkɪzəm/ *n* [singular] a set of questions and answers about the Christian religion that people learn to become members of a church

categorical /ˌkætɪ'gɒrɪkəl $ -'gɔː-, -'gɑː-/ *adj* stating that something is completely certain: *a* *categorical assurance* —**categorically** /-kli/ *adv*: *He categorically denied the rumours.*

categorize also **-ise** *BrE* /'kætɪɡəraɪz/ *v* [T] to put people or things into groups according to what type, level etc they are: *The students were categorized according to ability.* | **categorize sb/sth as sth** *books categorized as 'modern classics'*

category /'kætɪɡəri $ -ɡɔːri/ *n* [C] plural **categories** a group of people or things that are all of the same type: **+of** *There are several categories of patients.* | *Voters* **fell into** (=belonged in) *three main* **categories**.

cater /'keɪtə $ -ər/ *v* [I,T] to provide and serve food and drinks at a party, meeting etc, especially as a business: **+for** *a company that caters for weddings* —**caterer** *n* [C]

cater for/to sb *phr v* to provide a particular group of people with what they need or want: *a hotel that caters for young children*

catering /'keɪtərɪŋ/ *n* [U] the job of providing and serving food and drinks at parties, meetings etc: *the catering industry*

caterpillar /'kætə,pɪlə $ -tər,pɪlər/ *n* [C] a small creature with a lot of legs, that eats leaves. It becomes a BUTTERFLY or MOTH

cathartic /kə'θɑːtɪk $ -ɑːr-/ *adj* helping you to get rid of unpleasant emotions: *a cathartic experience* —**catharsis** *n* [C,U]

cathedral /kə'θiːdrəl/ *n* [C] the most important church in an area

catholic /'kæθəlɪk/ *adj formal* including a great variety of things: *He had very catholic tastes in music.*

Catholic *adj* relating to the Roman Catholic church —**Catholic** *n* [C] —**Catholicism** /kə'θɒlɪsɪzəm $ kə'θɑː-/ *n* [U]

Catseye /'kætsaɪ/ *n* [C] *trademark BrE* one of the small objects in the middle of a road that shine when lit by a car's lights, and help the driver to see the road at night

catsup /'kætsəp/ *n* an American spelling of KETCHUP

cattle /'kætl/ *n* [plural] cows and BULLS kept on a farm: *a* **herd of** (=large group of) *cattle*

catwalk /'kætwɔːk $ -wɒk/ *n* [C] the path that MODELS walk on in a fashion show

Caucasian /kɔː'keɪziən $ kɔː'keɪʒən/ *adj* belonging to the race of people with white skin —**Caucasian** *n* [C]

caught /kɔːt $ kɒːt/ *v* the past tense and past participle of CATCH

cauldron, caldron /'kɔːldrən $ 'kɒːl-/ *n* [C] a large round metal pot for boiling liquids over a fire

cauliflower /'kɒlɪ,flaʊə $ 'kɔːli,flaʊər, 'kɑː-/ *n* [C,U] a vegetable with green leaves around a large firm white centre → see picture at VEGETABLE

cause¹ /kɔːz $ kɒːz/ *n*

1 [C] a person, event, or thing that makes something happen [➜ effect]: **+of** *Heart disease is a common* **cause of death**. | **main/major cause** *Sewage is a major cause of water pollution.* | *researchers* **investigating the causes** *of depression*

2 [C,U] a reason for doing something or having a particular feeling: **+for** *The birth of a baby is a*

cause for celebration. | **cause for concern/ alarm** *There is no cause for alarm.* | **have (good) cause to do sth** *I think you've good cause to complain.*

3 [C] an organization or aim that a group of people support or fight for: **+of** *the cause of freedom* | **good/worthy cause** (=an organization that helps people who need it) *I don't mind giving money if it's for a good cause.*

cause² *v* [T] to make something happen, especially something bad: *Heavy traffic is causing long delays.* | **cause sb sth** *The injury was causing him a lot of pain.* | **cause sb/sth to do sth** *Their divorce had caused her to feel very bitter.* | **cause problems/trouble/damage etc**

causeway /'kɔːzweɪ $ 'kɒːz-/ *n* [C] a raised road or path across wet ground or through water

caustic /'kɔːstɪk $ 'kɒːs-/ *adj* **1** a caustic remark criticizes someone in a way that is clever but unkind **2** a caustic substance contains chemicals that can burn through things

caution¹ /'kɔːʃən $ 'kɒː-/ *n* **1** [U] when you are very careful to avoid danger or taking risks: **with caution** *The animals should be handled with caution.* | **treat/view sth with caution** (=think about something carefully because it might not be true) *These statistics must be treated with caution.* **2** [C,U] a warning telling you to be careful: **word/note of caution** *A word of caution – be sure to make copies of all files.* **3** [C] *BrE* an official warning that a police officer or judge gives to someone who has done something wrong

caution² *v* **1** [I,T] to warn someone that something might be dangerous, difficult etc: **caution (sb) against sth** *Advisers have cautioned against tax increases.* **2** [T] *BrE* to warn someone officially that the next time they do something wrong they will be punished

cautionary /'kɔːʃənəri $ 'kɒːʃəneri/ *adj* giving a warning: *a* **cautionary tale** (=story used to warn people)

cautious /'kɔːʃəs $ 'kɒː-/ *adj* careful to avoid problems or danger: *a cautious driver* | **cautious about (doing) sth** *He was cautious about making any predictions.* —**cautiously** *adv*

cavalcade /,kævəl'keɪd, 'kævəlkeɪd/ *n* [C] a line of people on horses or in vehicles, moving along as part of a ceremony

cavalier /,kævə'lɪə◂ $ -'lɪr◂/ *adj* not caring enough about things that are important: *a cavalier attitude to human life*

cavalry /'kævəlri/ *n* [U] soldiers who fought on horses in the past

cave¹ /keɪv/ *n* [C] a large natural hole in the side of a cliff or hill, or under the ground

cave² *v*

cave in *phr v* **1** if the top or sides of something cave in, they fall down or inwards: *The roof caved in.* **2** to stop opposing something

caveat /'kæviæt, 'keɪv-/ *n* [C] *formal* warning that something may not be completely true, effective etc

caveman /'keɪvmæn/ *n* [C] plural **cavemen** /-men/ someone who lived in a cave a long time ago

cavern /'kævən $ -ərn/ *n* [C] a large deep cave

caviar, caviare /'kævɪɑː $ -ɑːr/ *n* [U] fish eggs, eaten as a very special expensive food

cavity /'kævₐti/ n [C] plural **cavities** **1** a hole or space inside something **2** a hole in a tooth, that a DENTIST fills

cavort /kə'vɔːrt $ -ɔːrt/ v [I + adv/prep] to jump or dance around in an excited or sexual way

cc /ˌsiː 'siː/ **1** the abbreviation of **cubic centimetre**: *a 2000 cc engine* **2** used in a business letter or email to show that you are sending a copy to someone else

CCTV /ˌsiː siː tiː 'viː/ n [U] BrE **closed circuit television** a system of cameras and television, used in public places to protect people from crime

CD /ˌsiː 'diːᵗ/ n [C,U] **compact disc** a small circular piece of plastic on which music or computer information is recorded

C'D ˌplayer n [C] a piece of equipment used to listen to music recorded on a CD

CD-R /ˌsiː diː 'ɑː $ -'ɑːr/ n [C,U] **compact disc recordable** a CD that you can use only once to record music or computer information

CD-ROM /ˌsiː diː 'rɒm $ -'rɑːm/ n [C,U] **compact disc read-only memory** a CD on which a lot of computer information is stored

CD-RW /ˌsiː diː ɑː 'dʌbəljuː $ -ɑːr-/ n [C,U] **compact disc rewritable** a CD that you can use several times to record music or computer information

cease /siːs/ v [I,T] formal to stop doing something, or stop happening: **cease to do sth** *The old hotel had ceased to exist.* | **cease doing sth** *After his son's death, Hugo ceased writing.*

ceasefire /'siːsfaɪə $ -faɪr/ n [C] an agreement between two countries or groups to stop fighting: *a ceasefire agreement*

ceaseless /'siːsləs/ adj formal continuing for a long time: *ceaseless rain* —**ceaselessly** adv

cedar /'siːdə $ -ər/ n [C,U] a tall EVERGREEN tree with leaves shaped like needles, or the wood of this tree

cede /siːd/ v [T] formal to give land, power etc to another country or person

ceiling /'siːlɪŋ/ n [C]
1 the inside surface at the top of a room [➡ roof]: *the bathroom ceiling* | *rooms with **high ceilings*** **2** the largest amount of something which is officially allowed: **+of** *a ceiling of 5.5% on wage increases*

celebrate /'selₐbreɪt/ v [I,T] to do something enjoyable because it is a special occasion or because something good has happened: *John passed his exams so we're having a party to celebrate.* | *How do you want to celebrate your birthday?*

celebrated /'selₐbreɪtₐd/ adj famous: *a celebrated actor*

celebration /ˌselₐ'breɪʃən/ n [C, U] when you celebrate something special, or an occasion or party when you celebrate something: *a time of joy and celebration* | *a celebration meal* | **anniversary/birthday/wedding etc celebrations** | **in celebration of sth** *a party in celebration of her 80th birthday* ➔ see box at PARTY

celebrity /sₐ'lebrₐti/ n [C] plural **celebrities** a famous living person: *TV celebrities*

celery /'selₐri/ n [U] a vegetable with long hard pale green stems, eaten raw or cooked: *a stick of celery* ➔ see picture at VEGETABLE

celestial /sₐ'lestiəl $ -tʃəl/ adj relating to the sky or heaven

celibate /'selₐbət/ adj someone who is celibate does not have sex —**celibacy** /-bəsi/ n [U]

cell /sel/ n [C] **1** the smallest part of a living thing: *red blood cells* **2** a small room where prisoners are kept: *a prison cell*

cellar /'selə $ -ər/ n [C] a room under a house, used for storing things

cellist /'tʃelₐst/ n [C] someone who plays the cello

cello /'tʃeləʊ $ -loʊ/ n [C] plural **cellos** a large wooden musical instrument that you hold between your knees and play by pulling a BOW (=special stick) across the strings [➡ **cellist**] ➔ see picture on page A6

Cellophane /'seləfeɪn/ n [U] trademark a thin transparent material used for wrapping things

'cell phone also **ˌcellular 'phone** n [C] especially AmE a telephone that you carry with you [= **mobile phone** BrE]

cellular /'seljₐlə $ -ər/ adj **1** relating to the cells in a plant or animal **2** relating to cellular phones: *cellular networks*

cellulite /'seljₐlaɪt/ n [U] fat just below someone's skin that makes it look uneven and unattractive

celluloid /'seljₐlɔɪd/ n [U] a substance like plastic, used in the past to make film

cellulose /'seljₐləʊs $ -loʊs/ n [U] a substance that forms the walls of plant cells

Celsius /'selsiəs/ n [U] a scale of temperature in which water freezes at 0° and boils at 100° [= **Centigrade**]

Celtic /'keltɪk, 'seltɪk/ adj relating to the Celts (=the people of Ireland, Scotland, or Wales) or their languages

cement[1] /sɪ'ment/ n [U] a grey powder used in building, that is mixed with sand and water and allowed to dry and become hard

cement[2] v [T] **1** to make a relationship, position etc stronger: *a deal that will cement their relationship* **2** to cover or fix something with cement

cemetery /'semₐtri $ -teri/ n [C] plural **cemeteries** a place where dead people are buried

censor[1] /'sensə $ -ər/ v [T] to examine books, films etc and remove anything that is offensive, politically dangerous etc —**censorship** n [U]

censor[2] n [C] someone whose job is to censor books, films etc

censure /'senʃə $ -ər/ v [T] formal to officially criticize someone —**censure** n [U]

census /'sensəs/ n [C] plural **censuses** an occasion when a government collects information about the number of people in a country, their ages, jobs etc

cent /sent/ n [C] 1/100th of the standard unit of money in some countries, for example the US

centenary /sen'tiːnəri $ -'ten-, 'sentəneri/ especially BrE, **centennial** /sen'teniəl/ especially AmE n [C] plural **centenaries** the day or year exactly one hundred years after an important event: **+of** *the centenary of the composer's birth*

center /'sentə $ -ər/ *n, v* the American spelling of CENTRE

Centigrade /'sentɨɡreɪd/ *n* [U] a scale of temperature in which water freezes at 0° and boils at 100° [= **Celsius**]

centimetre *BrE*; **centimeter** *AmE* /'sentɨ‚miːtə $ -ər/ *n* [C] written abbreviation *cm* a unit for measuring length. There are 100 centimetres in one metre.

central /'sentrəl/ *adj*
1 [only before noun] in the middle of an object or area: *central London* | *a central courtyard* | *Central Asia*
2 [only before noun] having control over the rest of a system, organization etc: *central and local* **government** | *the system's central control unit*
3 more important than anything else: *She had a* **central role** *in the negotiations.* | **+to** *the loving relationships that are central to family life*
4 a place that is central is near the centre of a town: *The hotel is very central.*
—**centrally** *adv*

‚central 'heating *n* [U] a system of heating buildings in which heat is produced in one place and taken to the rest of the building by pipes

centralize also **-ise** *BrE* /'sentrəlaɪz/ *v* [T] to control a country, organization, or system from one place: *plans to centralize the company's European operations* —**centralized** *adj* —**centralization** /‚sentrəlaɪ'zeɪʃən $ -lə-/ *n* [U]

‚central reser'vation *n* [C] *BrE* a narrow piece of ground that divides the two parts of a MOTORWAY or other main road

centre[1] *BrE*; **center** *AmE* /'sentə $ -ər/ *n* [C]
1 the middle part or point of something: **+of** *the center of a circle* | **in the centre (of sth)** *There was a table in the centre of the room.*
2 a building used for a particular purpose: *a* **sports centre** | **+for** *the Centre for Modern Art*
3 a place where there is a lot of a particular type of business or activity: **business/commercial/banking etc centre** *London is a major financial center.*
4 *BrE* the part in the middle of a city or town where most of the shops, restaurants etc are [= **downtown** *AmE*]: **town/city centre** *shops in the city centre* | **+of** *the centre of York*
5 **be (at) the centre of sth** to be very involved in something, or to have a very important part in something: *He's* **at the centre of a row** *over school fees.* | *Lizzy loves to be* **the centre of attention** (=the person everyone is talking to, looking at etc).
6 **be/take centre stage** if something or someone is centre stage, they have an important position and get a lot of attention
7 **the centre** a political position which does not support extreme views: **left/right of centre** *left of centre policies*
→ COMMUNITY CENTRE, GARDEN CENTRE, HEALTH CENTRE, LEISURE CENTRE, SHOPPING CENTRE

centre[2] *BrE*; **center** *AmE* *v* [T] to move something to a position at the centre of something else
centre on/around sth *phr v* if something centres on a particular thing, that is the most important thing in it or what it mainly concerns: *The film centres on his early life.*

‚centre of 'gravity *n* [singular] the point in an object around which its weight balances

centrepiece *BrE*; **centerpiece** *AmE* /'sentəpiːs $ -ər-/ *n* [singular] the most important, attractive, or noticeable part of something: **+of** *The painting will be the centrepiece of the exhibition.*

century /'sentʃəri/ *n* [C] plural **centuries** a period of 100 years, used especially in dates: **the 13th/19th/21st etc century** *The church was built in the 13th century* (=it was built between 1200 and 1299). | *life* **at the turn of the century** (=the beginning of the century)

CEO /‚siː iː 'əʊ $ -'oʊ/ *n* [C] **Chief Executive Officer** the person with the most authority in a large company

ceramics /sɨ'ræmɪks/ *n* [plural, U] pots, plates etc made from clay, or the art of making them → see box at ART —**ceramic** *adj*: *ceramic tiles*

cereal /'sɪəriəl $ 'sɪr-/ *n*
1 [C,U] breakfast food made from grain and usually eaten with milk: *a bowl of cereal*
2 [C] a plant grown to produce grain for food, for example wheat or rice: *cereal crops*

cerebral /'serɨbrəl $ sə'riː-, 'serɨ-/ *adj* [only before noun] *technical* relating to your brain

‚cerebral 'palsy *n* [U] a medical condition that affects someone's ability to move or speak, caused by damage to the brain at birth

ceremonial /‚serɨ'məʊniəl $ -'moʊ-/ *adj* used in a ceremony, or done as part of a ceremony: *a ceremonial procession*

ceremony /'serɨməni $ -moʊni/ *n* plural **ceremonies**
1 [C] a formal event that happens in public on special occasions: *a wedding ceremony* | *the opening ceremony of the Olympic Games*
2 [U] the formal actions and words always used on particular occasions: **with ceremony** *The statue was erected with great ceremony in 1905.*

certain /'sɜːtn $ 'sɜːr-/ *adj*
1 [not before noun] completely sure: **+(that)** *I'm* **absolutely certain** *I left the keys here.* | **+about/of** *Are you certain about that?* | **+what/how etc** *I'm not certain when it will happen.*
2 sure to happen or be true: **+that** *It seems certain that she will win.* | **certain to do sth** *Many people* **look certain** *to lose their jobs.* | *Prisoners faced* **certain death**.
3 [only before noun] used to talk about a particular person, thing etc without naming or describing them exactly: *The work must be done by a certain date.* | *You are not allowed to park in certain areas.* | *This only applies to certain people.*
4 **make certain a)** to check that something is correct or true: **+(that)** *He made certain no one could see him.* **b)** to do something in order to be sure something will happen: **+(that)** *I'll make certain he knows about it.*
5 **a certain a)** some but not a lot: *a certain amount of confusion* | **to a certain extent/degree** (=partly but not completely) *I agree with you to a certain extent.* **b)** difficult to describe exactly: *She had a certain elegance.*
6 **for certain** without any doubt [= **for sure**]: **know/say (sth) for certain** *Exactly what happened is not known for certain.*

certainly[1] /'sɜːtnli $ 'sɜːr-/ *adv* without any doubt [= **definitely**]: *His lawyers will **almost certainly** appeal.* | *She's certainly not shy.*

certainly[2] *spoken* used to agree or to give your permission: *'Can I use your phone?' 'Certainly!'*

certainty /'sɜːtnti $ 'sɜːr-/ *n* plural **certainties** **1** [U] when you are completely sure about something: **with certainty** *She knew with certainty that he was lying.* **2** [C] something that is definitely true or will definitely happen: *The job losses aren't a certainty.*

certificate /sə'tɪfɪkət $ sər-/ *n* [C] an official document that shows something is true or correct: *Keep all your exam certificates* (=showing the exams you have passed and their marks). | **birth/marriage/death certificate** (=giving details of someone's birth etc) → see box at QUALIFICATION

certify /'sɜːtɪfaɪ $ 'sɜːr-/ *v* [T] **certified, certifying, certifies** **1** to officially state that something is correct or true: **+(that)** *Engineers certified that the aircraft was safe.* **2** [usually passive] to give someone an official document to show that they have trained to work in a particular profession: *certified accountants*

cervix /'sɜːvɪks $ 'sɜːr-/ *n* [C] the entrance to a woman's UTERUS —**cervical** /'sɜːvɪkəl, sə'vaɪkəl $ 'sɜːrvɪkəl/ *adj*

cesarean /sɪ'zeəriən $ -'zer-/ *n* another spelling of CAESAREAN

cessation /se'seɪʃən/ *n* [C,U] *formal* when something stops: **+of** *a cessation of violence*

cesspit /'ses.pɪt/ also **cesspool** /'ses.puːl/ *n* [C] a large hole or container under the ground for collecting waste water from a building

cf used in writing to introduce something else that should be compared

CFC /ˌsiː ef 'siː/ *n* [C] **chlorofluorocarbon** a gas used in AEROSOLS and FRIDGES, which causes damage to the OZONE LAYER

chafe /tʃeɪf/ *v* [I,T] if part of your body chafes, or if something chafes it, your skin becomes sore because something is rubbing against it: *The shoes were chafing her heels.*

chagrin /'ʃægrɪn $ ʃə'grɪn/ *n* [U] *formal* when you feel disappointed and annoyed: **to sb's chagrin** *To her chagrin he got the job.*

chain[1] /tʃeɪn/ *n* **1** [C,U] a line of metal rings connected together: *He wore a gold chain around his neck.* | *My **bicycle chain*** (=that makes the wheels turn) *has come off.* | **in chains** (=having chains around your legs to stop you escaping) *The prisoners were in chains.* → see picture at BICYCLE **2** [C] a group of shops, hotels etc that are owned by the same person or company: **+of** *a chain of restaurants* | *a supermarket chain* **3** [C] a series of similar things in a line: *a mountain chain* | **+of** *a chain of islands* **4** [C] a series of related events or actions: *the **chain of events** leading up to the war* → FOOD CHAIN

chain[2] *v* [T] to fasten one thing or person to another, using a chain: **chain sb/sth to sth** *John chained his bicycle to the fence.*

chain re'action *n* [C] a series of related events or chemical changes, with each one causing the next

'chain-smoke *v* [I,T] to smoke cigarettes one after another —**chain-smoker** *n* [C]

'chain store *n* [C] one of a group of shops owned by the same company

chair[1] /tʃeə $ tʃer/ *n* **1** [C] a piece of furniture for one person to sit on: *a kitchen chair* | **in/on a chair** *He was sitting in a leather chair.* → see picture at SEAT[1] **2** [singular] someone who is in charge of a meeting or committee: **in the chair** *The president, Al Shaw, was in the chair.* **3** [singular] the position of being a university PROFESSOR: **+of** *She was **appointed to the chair** of Medicine.* → EASY CHAIR

chair[2] *v* [T] to be in charge of a meeting or committee

chairman /'tʃeəmən $ 'tʃer-/, **chairwoman** /'tʃeə,wʊmən $ 'tʃer-/, **chairperson** /'tʃeə,pɜːsən $ 'tʃer,pɜːrsən/ *n* [C] **1** someone who is in charge of a meeting or committee **2** someone who is in charge of a large company or organization: **+of** *the chairman of British Airways* —**chairmanship** *n* [C,U]

chalet /'ʃæleɪ $ ʃæ'leɪ/ *n* [C] a wooden house, especially one in a mountain area → see box at ACCOMMODATION

chalk[1] /tʃɔːk $ tʃɒːk/ *n* **1** [U] soft white rock **2** [C,U] a small stick of soft white or coloured rock, used for writing or drawing → see picture at CLASSROOM **3 be like chalk and cheese** *BrE* to be completely different from each other

chalk[2] *v* [T] to write or draw something with chalk

chalk sth ⇔ up *phr v* *informal* to succeed in doing something, especially winning a game, competition etc: *They've chalked up their third win of the season.*

chalkboard /'tʃɔːkbɔːd $ 'tʃɒːkbɔːrd/ *n* [C] *AmE* a BLACKBOARD

chalky /'tʃɔːki $ 'tʃɒː-/ *adj* similar to chalk, or containing chalk

challenge[1] /'tʃælɪndʒ/ *n* **1** [C,U] something that tests your skill or ability, especially in a way that is interesting: **+of** *I enjoy the challenge of a new job.* | *Together we can **meet** (=deal with) this **challenge**.* | *He still **faces** tremendous **challenges**.* | *The strike **posed a** (=was a) serious **challenge** to the government.* **2** [C] a situation in which other people want to take the power or the top position away from someone else: **+to** *The crisis resulted in a challenge to his leadership.* | **+for** *the challenge for the Championship* **3** [C] an invitation from someone to try to beat them in a fight, game, argument etc: **+to** *The club **accepted the challenge** to compete.* | *He looked at her as if **throwing down a challenge**.*

challenge[2] *v* [T] **1** to refuse to accept that something is right, fair, or legal: *She is **challenging** the court's **decision**.* **2** to invite someone to compete or fight against you: **challenge sb to sth** *I've challenged Mike to a game of tennis.*

challenger /'tʃælɪndʒə $ -ər/ *n* [C] someone who is trying to win a competition, position of power etc: *the main challenger for the world title*

challenging /'tʃælɪndʒɪŋ/ *adj* difficult in an interesting or enjoyable way: *a challenging year*

chamber /'tʃeɪmbə $ -ər/ n [C] **1** a room, especially one that is below the ground or used for something unpleasant: *a **burial chamber*** **2** a large room in a public building used for important meetings: *the Council chamber* **3** one of the two parts of a parliament: **upper/lower chamber** (=the House of Lords and the House of Commons, in Britain) **4** an enclosed space in your body or inside a machine

chambermaid /'tʃeɪmbəmeɪd $ -ər-/ n [C] a woman whose job is to clean and tidy hotel BEDROOMS

'chamber ,music n [U] CLASSICAL music for a small group of instruments

chameleon /kə'miːliən/ n [C] a LIZARD that can make its skin the colour of the things around it

champ /tʃæmp/ n [C] *informal* a champion

champagne /ʃæm'peɪn/ n [U] a French white wine with a lot of BUBBLES, drunk on special occasions

champion¹ /'tʃæmpiən/ n [C]
1 someone who has won a competition, especially in sport: *the **world** snooker **champion** | a champion cyclist* → see box at **WIN**
2 champion of sb/sth someone who fights for and defends an aim or idea: *a champion of women's rights*

champion² v [T] to publicly fight for and defend an aim or idea: *He **championed the cause** of the poor for many years.*

championship /'tʃæmpiənʃɪp/ n **1** [C] also **championships** [plural] a competition to find the best player or team in a particular sport: *the US basketball championships* **2** [singular] the position of being a champion

chance¹ /tʃɑːns $ tʃæns/ n
1 [C,U] a possibility that something will happen: **a good/fair/slight/slim chance (of sth)** (=used to say how likely something is) *There's **a** slight chance of rain.* | **some/little/no chance** *I think there's little chance of an agreement.* | **+(that)** *Is there any chance that he'll recover?* | **chance of doing sth** *Sue had no chance of winning.* | **sb's chances** (=how likely someone is to succeed) *What are his chances of getting the job?* | **(the) chances are (that) ...** *informal* (=it is likely that)
2 [C] an opportunity to do something that you want to do: **+to** *She had the chance to meet the leading actors.* | *I never get a chance to relax.* | *Will you give me a chance to explain? | Friday is our last chance to see the show.*
3 take a chance to do something that involves a risk: *I'm **not taking any chances**.* | **+on/with** *The Director took a chance on her and gave her the part.*
4 [U] when things happen without being planned or caused by people: **by chance** *By chance, I met her in town on Saturday.* | *It was **pure chance** (=not planned at all) that we ended up in the same office.*
5 by any chance *spoken* used to ask politely if something is true or possible: *Are you Loren, by any chance?*
6 any chance of...? *spoken* used to ask if you can have something or if something is possible: *Any chance of a coffee?*
7 no chance/not a chance! *spoken* used to

emphasize that you do not think something will happen
→ OFF-CHANCE

chance² v **1** [T] *informal* to do something that involves a risk: *The bus might get me there on time but I don't want to **chance it**.* **2** [I] *literary* to do something in a way that was not planned: **+to** *I chanced to hear their conversation.*

chance³ adj [only before noun] not planned or expected: *a chance meeting*

chancellor /'tʃɑːnsələ $ 'tʃænsələr/ n [C]
1 also **,Chancellor of the Ex'chequer** the British government minister in charge of taxes and government spending **2** the leader of the government in some countries **3 a)** *BrE* the person who officially represents a university or plays a special occasions **b)** *AmE* the person in charge of some universities

chandelier /,ʃændə'lɪə $ -'lɪr/ n [C] a frame that holds CANDLES or lights, hangs from the ceiling, and is decorated with many small pieces of glass

change¹ /tʃeɪndʒ/ v
1 [I,T] to become different, or to make someone or something become different: *She's changed a lot.* | *The club is changing its rules.* | **change from sth to sth** *The traffic lights changed from green to red.* | **change (sb/sth) into/to sth** *These caterpillars change into moths.* | *You can change the sofa to a bed.*

THESAURUS

alter – to change something: *Can we alter the date of the meeting?*
adapt/adjust/modify – to change something slightly, especially your behaviour, ideas etc: *He's modified his opinions since then.*
reform/reorganize/restructure – to change a system or organization: *plans to reform the tax system | The company has been restructured from top to bottom.*
transform/revolutionize – to change something completely: *They've completely transformed the city centre.* | *Computers have revolutionized the way we work.*
twist/distort/misrepresent – to deliberately change facts, information, someone's words etc: *He accused reporters of twisting his words.*

2 [I,T] to stop doing or using one thing, and start doing or using something else: *I changed jobs in May.* | *Are you changing your name?* | **change (from sth) to sth** *We've changed to a new computer system.* | *Let's **change the subject** (=start talking about something else).*
3 change your mind to change your decision or opinion about something: **+about** *I've changed my mind about leaving school.*
4 [I,T] to take off your clothes and put on different ones: *Tony shaved and changed his shirt.* | **+into/out of** *She changed into her swimsuit.* | *He's upstairs **getting changed**.*
5 [T] to put something new or different in place of something else: *Dad had to stop and change the tyre.* | **change the baby/a nappy** (=put a clean NAPPY on a baby) | **change the bed/the sheets** (=put clean sheets on a bed)
6 [I,T] to get out of one train, bus, or aircraft and into another in order to continue your journey:

+at *Change at Baker Street.* | *We had to change planes.*

7 [T] if you change money, you give it to someone and they give it back to you in smaller amounts, or in money from a different country: *Can you change a £20 note?* | **change sth into/for sth** *I'd like to change these pounds into euros.*

8 [T] *BrE* to take something you bought back to the shop and get something else instead, or to allow a customer to do this [= **exchange** *AmE*]

9 change hands to become someone else's property: *The hotel's changed hands.*

10 change your tune *informal* to start expressing a different opinion about something

change over *phr v* to stop doing or using one thing and start doing or using something different: **change over (from sth) to sth** *We're changing over to the new software next month.*

change² *n*

1 [C,U] something that has become different, or when something becomes different: **+in** *recent changes in the law* | *the need for political change* | *We'd like a bigger house but I hate change.* | **+of** *Tom's had a change of heart* (=his attitude has become different).

2 [C] an action or event that involves replacing one thing with another: *The car needs an oil change.* | **+of** *a change of government* | **change from sth to sth** *the change from sterling to euros*

3 [singular] something that is interesting or enjoyable because it is different from what is usual: *I need a change.* | *Let's eat out for a change.* | *'Ron was on time.' 'That makes a change.'*

4 [U] **a)** the money you get back when you pay more than something costs: *Here's your change, sir.* **b)** coins not paper money: **in change** *I have about a dollar in change.* → see box at **MONEY** **c)** coins or paper money that add up to the same value as a larger unit of money: **+for** *Do you have change for $1?*

5 change of clothes/underwear etc another set of clothes that you can use if necessary → **SMALL CHANGE**

changeable /'tʃeɪndʒəbəl/ *adj* likely to change or changing often: *changeable weather*

changeover /'tʃeɪndʒˌəʊvə $ -ˌoʊvər/ *n* [C] a change from one activity or system to another: *the changeover from military to civilian rule*

'changing room *n* [C] a room where you change your clothes when you play sport, try on clothes in a shop etc

channel¹ /'tʃænl/ *n* [C]

1 a television station: *What's on Channel 4?* | *Do you mind if I change channels?* | **channel hopping/surfing** (=when you change quickly from one channel to another many times) → see box at **TELEVISION**

2 [usually plural] a way that you use to communicate information, ideas etc: *Apply through the usual channels.* | **+of** *channels of communication*

3 a passage that water or other liquids flow along: *an irrigation channel*

4 a) the (English) Channel the narrow area of water between France and England **b)** the deepest part of a river, sea etc, especially where it is deep enough for ships to sail

channel² *v* [T] **channelled, channelling** *BrE*; **channeled, channeling** *AmE* to direct something towards a particular purpose, place, or situation: **channel sth into sth** *He began to channel his energies into sport.*

chant¹ /tʃɑːnt $ tʃænt/ *v* [I,T] **1** to repeat a word or phrase many times: *Protestors chanted anti-government slogans.* **2** to sing a religious song or prayer using only one or two notes

chant² *n* [C] **1** words or phrases repeated many times: **+of** *chants of 'Long Live the King!'* **2** a religious song or prayer that is sung using only one or two notes

chaos /'keɪ-ɒs $ -ɑːs/ *n* [U] a situation in which everything is confused and nothing is happening in an organized way: *The floods caused chaos.* | **in chaos** *The game ended in absolute chaos.* → see box at **ORGANIZED**

chaotic /keɪ'ɒtɪk $ -'ɑːtɪk/ *adj* confused and without any order: *The city was crowded and chaotic.*

chap /tʃæp/ *n* [C] *especially BrE informal* a man → see box at **MAN**

chapel /'tʃæpəl/ *n* [C] a small church or room in which Christians pray and have religious services

chaplain /'tʃæplɪn/ *n* [C] a priest who works for the army, a hospital, a university etc

chapped /tʃæpt/ *adj* chapped lips or hands are sore, dry, and cracked

chapter /'tʃæptə $ -ər/ *n* [C]

1 one of the parts into which a book is divided: *See Chapter 3.* → see box at **PART**

2 a particular period in someone's life or in history: **+of/in** *a terrible chapter of history*

character /'kærɪktə $ -ər/ *n*

1 [C,U] the qualities that make a person, place, or thing different from any other: *She has an interesting character.* | *The two brothers were totally different in character.* | *The character of the school has changed.* | **in character/out of character** (=typical or untypical of someone's character) *He swore, which was completely out of character.*

THESAURUS

Some good words about people
calm, cheerful, determined, energetic, kind, loyal, optimistic, organized, patient, sensible, sociable, sympathetic

Some bad words about people
critical, cruel, disorganized, fussy, impatient, insensitive, moody, pessimistic, stubborn, tense, vain

2 [C] **a)** a person in a book, play, film etc: *Julia Roberts played the main character.* **b)** a particular kind of person: *Dan's a strange character.* | **a (real) character** (=someone who is interesting and amusing)

3 [U] good qualities such as courage, loyalty, and honesty that people admire: *She had great strength of character.*

4 [U] qualities that make someone or something special and interesting: *a house with a lot of character*

5 [C] a letter, mark, or sign used in writing, printing, or on a computer

characteristic[1] /ˌkærɪktəˈrɪstɪk‹/ n [C usually plural] a quality or feature that is typical of someone or something and makes them different from others: **+of** *the characteristics of different schools* | *We inherit* **physical characteristics** *from our parents.*

characteristic[2] *adj* typical of a particular person or thing: **+of** *These problems are characteristic of modern life.* | *an organism's* **characteristic features** —characteristically /-kli/ *adv*

characterization also **-isation** *BrE* /ˌkærɪktəraɪˈzeɪʃən $ -tərə-/ n [U] the way that the people in a book, play etc are described

characterize also **-ise** *BrE* /ˈkærɪktəraɪz/ v [T] **1** to be typical of someone or something: *Bright colours characterize his paintings.* **2** to describe the qualities of someone or something in a particular way: **characterize sb/sth as (being) sth** *He is often characterised as a Catholic writer.*

charade /ʃəˈrɑːd $ ʃəˈreɪd/ n [C] a situation in which people pretend to think, feel etc something, although they clearly do not: *All their talk of unity was only a charade.*

charcoal /ˈtʃɑːkəʊl $ ˈtʃɑːrkoʊl/ n [U] a black substance made of burned wood, used as FUEL or for drawing

charge[1] /tʃɑːdʒ $ tʃɑːrdʒ/ n
1 [C,U] the amount of money you have to pay for something: **+of** *an admission charge of £2.50* | **+for** *charges for eye tests* | *We deliver* **free of charge** (=you do not have to pay for it). → see box at COST
2 [U] the position of having control over or responsibility for something or someone: **in charge (of sth)** *Who's in charge?* | *the officer in charge* | *Cathy's* **taken charge of** *the department.*
3 [C] a statement that says that someone has done something illegal or bad: **charge of assault/murder/robbery etc** (=an official statement that the police make) *He appeared in court on a charge of criminal damage.* | **bring/press charges** (=officially say that you think someone is guilty of a crime) | **charge that** *She rejected the charge that she had acted irresponsibly.*
4 [C] an attack in which people or animals move forward quickly
5 [U] electricity that is put into an item of electrical equipment such as a BATTERY
→ SERVICE CHARGE

charge[2] v
1 [I,T] to ask someone to pay a particular amount of money for goods, a service etc: **charge (sb) £10/$30 etc (for sth)** *We were charged £80.* | **+for** *Do you charge for delivery?* | *Many gyms* **charge** *a joining fee.*
2 [T] to state officially that someone might be guilty of a crime: **charge sb with sth** *Soames was charged with rape.* → see box at POLICE
3 [I,T] to move quickly forwards, especially in a threatening way: **+into/past/towards etc** *Police charged into the house, guns ready.*
4 also **charge up** [I,T] if a BATTERY charges, or if you charge it, it takes in and stores electricity

'charge card n [C] a plastic card from a particular shop that you can use to buy goods there and pay for them later [➥ credit card]

charged /tʃɑːdʒd $ tʃɑːrdʒd/ adj a charged situation is full of strong emotions: *the highly charged atmosphere of the trial*

chariot /ˈtʃæriət/ n [C] a vehicle with two wheels pulled by a horse, used in ancient times in battles and races

charisma /kəˈrɪzmə/ n [U] the natural ability to attract and influence other people —charismatic /ˌkærɪzˈmætɪk‹/ adj

charitable /ˈtʃærɪtəbəl/ adj **1** relating to charities and their work: **charitable donations** **2** kind and sympathetic —charitably adv

charity /ˈtʃærɪti/ n plural charities
1 [C,U] an organization that gives money, goods, or help to people who are poor, sick etc: **+for** *a charity for the homeless* | *The money raised will* **go to charity** (=be given to a charity). | **charity concert/dinner etc** (=an event etc organized to collect money for a charity)
2 [U] money or gifts given to help people who are poor, sick etc: *people who live on charity*
3 [U] *formal* kindness or sympathy towards other people

'charity shop n [C] *BrE* a shop that sells used clothes, books etc to collect money for a charity [= thrift shop *AmE*]

charlatan /ˈʃɑːlətən $ ˈʃɑːr-/ n [C] *literary disapproving* someone who pretends to have special skills or knowledge

charm[1] /tʃɑːm $ tʃɑːrm/ n **1** [C,U] a quality someone or something has that makes people like them: *Lee's boyish charm* | **+of** *the charm of Italy* **2** [C] something you wear, have etc because you believe it brings you good luck: *a lucky charm*

charm[2] v [T] to attract or please someone: *a story that has always charmed children* —charmer n [C]

charmed /tʃɑːmd $ tʃɑːrmd/ adj **have/lead a charmed life** to be very lucky, especially by succeeding in avoiding danger, injury etc

charming /ˈtʃɑːmɪŋ $ ˈtʃɑːr-/ adj very pleasing or attractive: *her charming brother* —charmingly adv

charred /tʃɑːd $ tʃɑːrd/ adj black from having been burned: *charred wood* —char n [I,T]

chart[1] /tʃɑːt $ tʃɑːrt/ n **1** a drawing, set of numbers, GRAPH etc that shows information: *The chart shows last year's sales.* **2 the charts** [plural] the official list of the most popular songs, produced each week **3** a map, especially of the sea or stars

chart[2] v [T] **1** to record information about something over a period of time: *Teachers chart each student's* **progress** *through the year.* **2** to make a map of an area of land, sea, or sky

charter[1] /ˈtʃɑːtə $ ˈtʃɑːrtər/ n **1** [C] a written statement of the principles, duties, and purposes of an organization: *the UN charter* **2** [U] when someone rents a boat, aircraft etc from a company, usually for a short time: **for charter** *yachts available for charter* | *a charter boat* | **charter flight/service** (=using aircraft that travel companies rent but do not own, so that the flight is usually cheaper than usual)

charter[2] v [T] to rent a boat, aircraft etc from a company

chartered /ˈtʃɑːtəd $ ˈtʃɑːrtərd/ adj [only before noun] *BrE* **chartered accountant/**

surveyor etc a trained ACCOUNTANT etc who has passed all the necessary examinations

charter 'member n [C] AmE someone who helps to establish a new organization or club [= **founder member** BrE]

chase¹ /tʃeɪs/ v

1 [I,T] to quickly follow someone or something, especially to catch them: *The car was chased by police.* | **+after** *'My glove,' he shouted, chasing after the dog.* | **chase sb away/off** (=make someone leave a place, by chasing them)

2 [I,T] to try very hard to get something: *Too many people are chasing too few jobs.* | **+after** *reporters chasing after a story*

chase² n [C] an act of following someone or something quickly to catch them: *a car chase* | *A policeman saw him and gave chase* (=chased him).

chasm /'kæzəm/ n **1** [C] a very deep space between two areas of rock or ice **2** [singular] a big difference between two people, groups, or things

chassis /'ʃæsiː/ n [C] plural **chassis** /-siːz/ the frame on which the body of a vehicle is built

chaste /tʃeɪst/ adj old-fashioned not having sex, or not showing sexual feelings

chasten /'tʃeɪsən/ v [T] formal to make someone realize that their behaviour was wrong

chastise /tʃæˈstaɪz/ v [T] formal to criticize or punish someone

chastity /'tʃæstɪti/ n [U] when someone lives without having sex: *a vow of chastity*

chat¹ /tʃæt/ v [I] **chatted, chatting** to talk in a friendly informal way, especially about unimportant things: **+to/with** *Jo was chatting to Sam.* | **+about** *We chatted about sailing.* → see box at **TALK**

chat sb ⇔ up phr v BrE informal to talk to someone in a way that shows you are sexually attracted to them

chat² n [C,U] a friendly informal conversation: **+with** *I've had a chat with Sue about it.*

château /'ʃætəʊ $ ʃæ'toʊ/ n [C] plural **châteaux** /-təʊz $ -'toʊz/ a castle or large country house in France

chatroom /'tʃætruːm, -rʊm/ n [C] a place on the Internet where you can have a conversation with people by writing messages to them and immediately receiving their reply → see box at **INTERNET**

'chat show n [C] BrE a television or radio show on which people are asked questions about themselves [= **talk show** AmE] → see box at **TELEVISION**

chatter /'tʃætə $ -ər/ v [I] **1** to talk quickly in a friendly way about unimportant things, especially for a long time **2** if your teeth are chattering, they are knocking together because you are cold or afraid —**chatter** n [U]

chatty /'tʃæti/ adj informal **1** liking to talk a lot in a friendly way **2** having a friendly informal style: *a chatty letter*

chauffeur /'ʃəʊfə, ʃəʊ'fɜː $ 'ʃoʊfər, ʃoʊ'fɜːr/ n [C] someone whose job is to drive a car for someone else —**chauffeur** v [T]

chauvinist /'ʃəʊvɪnɪst $ 'ʃoʊ-/ n [C] disapproving **1** a man who thinks that men are better than women **2** someone who believes

that their country or race is better than any other —**chauvinism** n [U]

cheap¹ /tʃiːp/ adj

1 costing little money, or less money than you expect [≠ **expensive**]: *The jacket was quite cheap.* | *Property's cheaper in Spain.* | *cheap flights* | **dirt cheap** informal (=extremely cheap)

THESAURUS

If something is **inexpensive**, it is not expensive and is usually of good quality.

If something is **reasonable**, it is not too expensive and seems fair: *The restaurant serves good food at reasonable prices.*

If something is **good/great/excellent value**, it is worth the price you pay for it: *The hotel offers great value for money.* | *At $3, it's great value for your money.*

If you think that something is worth more money than you paid for it, you can say that it is a **bargain**: *You can get some real bargains at the market.* | *bargain prices*

→ EXPENSIVE

2 disapproving low in price and quality: *cheap jewellery*

3 AmE disapproving not liking to spend money [= **mean** BrE]

—**cheaply** adv: *How did he buy the land so cheaply?* —**cheapness** n [U]

cheap² adv informal for a low price: *I got it cheap.* | *The house was going cheap* (=being sold for a lower price than normal).

cheapen /'tʃiːpən/ v **1** [I,T] to become lower in value or price, or to make something do this **2** [T] to make something or someone seem to deserve less respect: *Don't cheapen yourself by answering his insults.*

cheapo /'tʃiːpəʊ $ -oʊ/ adj [only before noun] informal low in price and low in quality [➞ **cheap**]: *a cheapo camera*

cheapskate /'tʃiːpskeɪt/ n [C] informal disapproving someone who does not like spending money

cheat¹ /tʃiːt/ v

1 [I] to behave in a dishonest way in order to win or get an advantage: **+at** *He always cheats at cards.* | **cheat in an exam** BrE / **cheat on an exam** AmE: *She was caught cheating in a maths test.*

2 [T] to deceive or trick someone: **cheat sb out of sth** *He cheated the old woman out of all her money.* | *I felt cheated* (=felt I had been treated unfairly).

cheat on sb phr v if someone cheats on their husband, girlfriend etc, they have a secret sexual relationship with another person

cheat² n [C] someone who cheats

check¹ /tʃek/ v

1 [I,T] to look at or test something carefully in order to be sure that it is correct, in good condition, safe etc: *You'd better check our tickets.* | *Check the eggs before you buy them.* | **+(that)** *Did you check that the door's locked?* | **+whether/ how/who etc** *He checked whether he was being followed.* | **double check** (=check something twice)

2 [I] to ask someone about something: **+(that)** *I called to check that they'd received my letter.* |

+with *Check with your doctor before going on a diet.*
3 [T] to stop something bad from getting worse: *measures to check the growth in crime*
4 [T] to suddenly stop yourself from saying or doing something: **check yourself** *Ruby wanted to laugh, but checked herself.*
5 [T] *AmE* to take your bags to a desk at an airport, so that they can be put on the plane [= **check in** *BrE*]
6 [T] *AmE* to put a mark by an answer to show that it is correct, or on a list to show that you have dealt with something [= **tick** *BrE*]
→ **DOUBLE-CHECK**

check in also **check into sth** *phr v* to go to the desk at an airport or hotel to say that you have arrived: *Check in two hours before your flight.* → see box at **AIRPORT** → and **HOTEL**

check sth ⇔ **off** *phr v* to put a mark next to something on a list to show that you have dealt with it

check (up) on sb/sth *phr v* to find out if something or someone is all right, doing what they should be doing etc: *I'll just go check on dinner.* | *Mom's always checking up on me.*

check out *phr v* **1 check sth** ⇔ **out** to get more information about something, especially to find out if it is true or correct: *Did you check out his story?* **2 check sb/sth** ⇔ **out** *informal* to visit a place or look at something or someone to see if you like them: *Check out our new website.* **3** to pay the bill and leave a hotel → see box at **HOTEL**

check² *n*
1 [C] a careful look at or test of something, to see if it is safe, correct, in good condition etc: **+on** *a safety check on gas appliances* | **carry out/run/make a check** *A medical check was carried out.*
2 [C usually singular] something that controls something else and stops it from increasing: **+on** *Higher interest rates are a check on public spending.* | **keep/hold sth in check** (=keep something under control) *He managed to keep his temper in check.*
3 [C,U] a pattern of squares, especially on cloth: *blue and white check trousers*
4 the American spelling of **CHEQUE**
5 [C] *AmE* a list that you are given in a restaurant showing what you have eaten and how much you must pay [= **bill** *BrE*]
6 [C] *AmE* a mark (✓) that you put next to an answer to show that it is correct or next to something on a list to show that you have dealt with it [= **tick** *BrE*]
→ **RAIN CHECK**

checkbook /'tʃekbʊk/ *n* the American spelling of **CHEQUEBOOK**

checked /tʃekt/ *adj* having a regular pattern of different coloured squares: *a checked shirt* → see picture at **PATTERN**

checkered also **chequered** *BrE* /'tʃekəd $ -ərd/ *adj* **1** marked with squares of two different colours: *a checkered flag* **2 checkered history/ past etc** periods of failure as well as success in someone's or something's past: *The car has had a chequered history.*

checkers /'tʃekəz $ -ərz/ *n* [U] *AmE* a game for two players, using 12 flat round pieces each and a special board with 64 squares [= **draughts** *BrE*]

'check-in *n* [singular] a place where you report your arrival at an airport, hotel etc: *The check-in desks seem to be crowded.* → see box at **AIRPORT**

'checking ac,count *n* [C] *AmE* a bank account that you can take money out of at any time [= **current account** *BrE*] → see box at **ACCOUNT**

checklist /'tʃek,lɪst/ *n* [C] a list that helps to remind you of all the things you have to do for a particular job or activity → see box at **LIST**

checkmate /'tʃekmeɪt/ *n* [U] the position in a game of **CHESS** when the **KING** cannot escape and the game has ended

checkout /'tʃek-aʊt/ *n* [C] the place in a **SUPER-MARKET** where you pay for goods

checkpoint /'tʃekpɔɪnt/ *n* [C] a place where an official person stops people and vehicles to examine them

checkup, check-up /'tʃek-ʌp/ *n* [C] an occasion when a doctor or **DENTIST** examines you to see if you are healthy: *It's important to **have** regular checkups.*

cheddar /'tʃedə $ -ər/ *n* [U] a firm smooth yellow cheese

cheek /tʃiːk/ *n*
1 [C] the soft round part of your face below each of your eyes: *Billy had rosy cheeks and blue eyes.* | *her tear-stained cheeks* → see picture on page A3
2 [singular,U] *BrE* behaviour that is rude or not respectful: **have the cheek to do sth** *He had the cheek to ask me for more money.*

cheekbone /'tʃiːkbəʊn $ -boʊn/ *n* [C] the bone just below your eye → see picture on page A3

cheeky /'tʃiːki/ *adj BrE* rude or showing no respect, sometimes in an amusing way: *a little boy with a cheeky grin* | *Don't be so cheeky!* → see box at **RUDE**

cheer¹ /tʃɪə $ tʃɪr/ *n* [C] a shout of approval, happiness, or encouragement

cheer² *v* [I,T] to shout approval, encouragement etc: *The spectators cheered him wildly.* → see box at **SHOUT**

cheer sb ⇔ **on** *phr v* to encourage a person or a team by cheering for them: *Her family and friends were cheering her on.*

cheer up *phr v* to become happier, or to make someone feel happier: *Cheer up! The worst is over.* | **cheer sb** ⇔ **up** *Here's a bit of news that will cheer you up.*

cheerful /'tʃɪəfəl $ 'tʃɪr-/ *adj*
1 happy, or behaving in a way that shows you are happy: *He is feeling more cheerful than before.* | **cheerful voice/smile/manner etc** *'I'm Robyn,' she said with a cheerful smile.* → see box at **CHARACTER**
2 bright, pleasant, and making you feel happy: *a cheerful kitchen*
—**cheerfully** *adv* —**cheerfulness** *n* [U]

cheerleader /'tʃɪə,liːdə $ 'tʃɪr,liːdər/ *n* [C] a member of a team of young women that encourages a crowd to cheer at a US sports event

cheerless /'tʃɪələs $ 'tʃɪr-/ *adj* cheerless weather, places, or times make you feel sad and bored: *a cheerless winter day*

cheers /tʃɪəz $ tʃɪrz/ *spoken* **1** what you say just before you drink a glass of alcohol with someone, to show friendly feelings towards them **2** *BrE informal* thank you **3** *BrE informal* goodbye

cheery /'tʃɪəri $ 'tʃɪri/ *adj* happy or making you feel happy: *a cheery smile* —**cheerily** *adv*

cheese /tʃiːz/ *n* [C,U] a solid food made from milk, that is usually white or yellow: *a cheese sandwich* | **a piece/bit/slice/lump etc of cheese** | *Sprinkle the pasta with **grated** cheese*.

cheeseburger /'tʃiːzbɜːgə $ -bɜːrgər/ *n* [C] a HAMBURGER cooked with a piece of cheese on top of the meat

cheesecake /'tʃiːzkeɪk/ *n* [C,U] a sweet cake made with soft white cheese: *a slice of strawberry cheesecake*

cheesy /'tʃiːzi/ *adj informal* cheap and not of good quality: *a cheesy soap opera*

cheetah /'tʃiːtə/ *n* [C] an African wild cat that has black spots and is able to run very fast

chef /ʃef/ *n* [C] a skilled cook, especially the most important cook in a restaurant

chemical[1] /'kemɪkəl/ *n* [C] a substance used in or produced by a chemical process: **toxic/hazardous/dangerous chemicals** *the disposal of toxic chemicals*

chemical[2] *adj* relating to substances, the study of substances, or processes involving changes in substances: *a chemical reaction* | *chemical weapons* —**chemically** /-kli/ *adv*

chemist /'kemɪst/ *n* [C] **1** a scientist who does work related to chemistry: *a research chemist* **2** *BrE* someone who is trained to prepare drugs and medicines for sale in a shop [= **pharmacist**] **3** also **chemist's** *BrE* a shop where you can buy medicines, beauty products etc [= **drugstore** *AmE*] → see box at **SHOP**

chemistry /'keməstri/ *n* [U] **1** the science that studies the structure of substances and the way that they change or combine with each other [➡ **biochemistry**] **2** the way substances combine in a process, thing, person etc: *a person's body chemistry* **3** if there is chemistry between two people, they like each other or work well together

chemotherapy /ˌkiːməʊ'θerəpi, ˌkem-$ -moʊ-/ *n* [U] the use of drugs to control and try to cure CANCER

cheque *BrE*/check *AmE*

signing a cheque

cheque *BrE*; **check** *AmE* /tʃek/ *n* [C] a printed piece of paper that you sign and use to pay for things: **+for** *a cheque for £100* | *Can I **pay by cheque**?* | **cash a cheque** (=get cash in exchange for a cheque) → **BLANK CHEQUE**

chequebook /'tʃekbʊk/ *n* [C] *BrE* a small book of cheques [= **checkbook** *AmE*]

'cheque card also **ˌcheque guaran'tee card** *n* [C] *BrE* a card given to you by your bank that you must show when you write a cheque, which promises that the bank will pay out the amount written on the cheque

chequered /'tʃekəd $ -ərd/ *adj* a British spelling of CHECKERED

cherish /'tʃerɪʃ/ *v* [T] **1** if you cherish something, it is very important to you: **cherish a hope/idea/dream etc** *Mary cherished the dream of being a pop star.* **2** to take care of someone or something you love very much

cherry /'tʃeri/ *n* plural **cherries** **1** [C] a small round red or black fruit with a stone in the middle: *a bunch of cherries* → see picture at **FRUIT** **2** [C,U] a tree that produces cherries, or the wood from this tree

cherub /'tʃerəb/ *n* [C] an ANGEL shown in paintings as a small child with wings

chess /tʃes/ *n* [U] a board game for two players in which you must trap your opponent's KING in order to win → see picture at **BOARD**

chest /tʃest/ *n* **1** [C] the front part of your body between your neck and stomach: *a hairy chest* | *chest pains* → see picture on page A3 **2** [C] a large strong box with a lid, that you use to keep things in: *a large wooden chest* **3** **get sth off your chest** *informal* to tell someone about something that has worried or annoyed you for a long time

chestnut /'tʃesnʌt/ *n* **1** [C] a smooth red-brown nut you can eat **2** [C] the tree on which these nuts grow **3** [U] a reddish brown colour —**chestnut** *adj*

ˌchest of 'drawers *n* [C] plural **chests of drawers** a piece of furniture with drawers, used for keeping clothes in [= **dresser** *AmE*]

chew /tʃuː/ *v* [I,T] **1** to bite food several times before swallowing it: *The meat's so tough I can hardly chew it.* **2** to bite something several times without eating it: **chew your lip/nails** *She chewed her lip and said nothing.*
　chew *sb* ⇔ **out** *phr v AmE informal* to speak angrily to someone who has done something wrong: *My boss chewed me out for being late.*
　chew *sth* ⇔ **over** *phr v* to think carefully about a problem, idea etc

'chewing gum also **gum** *n* [U] a type of sweet that you chew for a long time, but do not swallow

chewy /'tʃuːi/ *adj* needing to be chewed a lot before it can be swallowed: *chewy toffee*

chic /ʃiːk/ *adj* fashionable and showing good style

chick /tʃɪk/ *n* [C] a baby bird, especially a baby chicken

chicken[1] /'tʃɪkən/ *n* **1** [C] a farm bird that is kept for its meat and eggs [➡ **chick, cock, hen, rooster**] → see picture at **FARM**[1] **2** [U] the meat from a chicken: *roast chicken* | *chicken soup*

chicken[2] *v*
　chicken out *phr v informal* to decide at the last moment not to do something because you are not brave enough: *You're not chickening out, are you?*

chicken[3] *adj informal* not brave enough to do something [= **cowardly**]: *Dave's too chicken to ask her out.*

chicken pox /'tʃɪkɪn pɒks $ -paːks/ *n* [U] a common illness that children get, that causes a fever and red spots on the skin

chief[1] /tʃiːf/ *adj* [only before noun]

1 highest in rank: *the government's chief medical officer* → see box at POSITION

2 most important [= **main**; ⇒ **chiefly**]: *One of the chief causes of crime is drugs.* | *Safety is our chief concern.*

chief[2] *n* [C] **1** the leader of a group or organization: **+of** *the chief of police* **2** the ruler of a tribe

Chief Ex'ecutive *n* **the Chief Executive** the President of the US

chiefly /'tʃiːfli/ *adv* mainly: *a book that is intended chiefly for students of art*

chieftain /'tʃiːftɪn/ *n* [C] the leader of a tribe

chiffon /'ʃɪfɒn $ ʃɪ'faːn/ *n* [U] very thin soft cloth used for making women's clothing

child /tʃaɪld/ *n* [C] plural **children** /'tʃɪldrən/

1 a young person who is not yet an adult: *families with young children* | *The film is not suitable for children under 12.* | *I was very happy as a child* (=when I was a child).

THESAURUS

Child is a word that you can use to talk about **babies, young children**, and **teenagers**.
You are a **baby** when you are first born.
You are a **toddler** when you have just learnt to walk.
You are a **teenager** between 13 and 19.
Kid is an informal word for a child.
→ BABY

---

2 a son or daughter of any age: *Both our children are married now.* | *She has three grown-up children.* | *Alex is an only child* (=he has no brothers or sisters).

3 be child's play to be very easy to do: *Cooking for a family is child's play after running a restaurant.*

childbearing /'tʃaɪldbeərɪŋ $ -,ber-/ *n* [U]

1 the process of giving birth to children

2 childbearing age the period of a woman's life during which she can have babies

child 'benefit *n* [U] money that the British government gives every week to families with children

childbirth /'tʃaɪldbɜːθ $ -bɜːrθ/ *n* [U] the act of having a baby

childcare /'tʃaɪldkeə $ -ker/ *n* [U] an arrangement in which someone looks after children whose parents are at work

childhood /'tʃaɪldhʊd/ *n* [C,U] the time when you are a child: *Sara had a very happy childhood.*

childish /'tʃaɪldɪʃ/ *adj* **1** relating to or typical of a child: *a childish voice* **2** *disapproving* behaving in a silly way that makes you seem much younger than you are. *Stop being so childish.* —**childishly** *adv* —**childishness** *n* [U]

childless /'tʃaɪldləs/ *adj* having no children: *childless couples*

childlike /'tʃaɪldlaɪk/ *adj* having the good qualities of a child, such as natural or trusting behaviour: *childlike innocence*

childminder /'tʃaɪld,maɪndə $ -ər/ *n* [C] *BrE* someone who is paid to look after young children while their parents are at work —**childminding** *n* [U]

childproof /'tʃaɪldpruːf/ *adj* designed to prevent a child from being hurt: *a childproof lock*

children /'tʃɪldrən/ *n* the plural of CHILD

'child sup,port *n* [U] money that someone pays regularly to their former wife or husband in order to help look after their children [= **maintenance**]

chill[1] /tʃɪl/ *n* **1** [singular] a feeling of coldness: *There was a slight chill in the air.* **2** [C] a sudden feeling of fear: *The sound of his laugh sent a chill through her.* **3** [C] a slight illness like a cold: *Take off those wet clothes before you catch a chill.*

chill[2] *v* **1** [T] to make something or someone cold: *Champagne should be chilled before serving.* **2** [I] *informal* also **chill out** to relax instead of feeling angry or nervous: *Chill out, Dave, it doesn't matter.*

chilli *BrE*; **chili** *AmE* /'tʃɪli/ *n* plural **chillies** *BrE*, **chilies** *AmE* **1** [C,U] a small thin red or green vegetable with a very hot taste: *chilli sauce* **2** also **chilli con carne** *BrE*, **chili con carne** *AmE* /-kɒn 'kaːni $ -kaːn 'kaːrni/ [U] a dish made with beans, meat, and chillies → see picture on page A5

chilling /'tʃɪlɪŋ/ *adj* making you feel frightened: *the chilling sound of wolves howling*

chilly /'tʃɪli/ *adj* **1** cold enough to make you feel uncomfortable: *a chilly morning* | *It's a bit chilly in here.* → see box at COLD → and WEATHER **2** behaving in an unfriendly way: *The results received a chilly reception on the stock markets.*

chime /tʃaɪm/ *v* [I,T] if a clock or bell chimes, it makes a ringing sound: *The clock chimed six.* —**chime** *n* [C]

chime in *phr v* to say something in order to add your opinion to a conversation: *'The kids could go too,' Maria chimed in.*

chimney /'tʃɪmni/ *n* [C] a vertical pipe that takes smoke up from a fire and out through the roof, or the part of this pipe that is above the roof

'chimney sweep *n* [C] someone whose job is to SWEEP (=clean) the inside of chimneys

chimpanzee

chimpanzee /,tʃɪmpæn'ziː, -pən-/ also **chimp** /tʃɪmp/ *informal n* [C] an African animal like a monkey without a tail

chin /tʃɪn/ *n* [C] the front part of your face below your mouth: *He rubbed his chin thoughtfully.* → see picture on page A3

china /'tʃaɪnə/ *n* [U] **1** a hard white substance used for making plates, cups etc **2** plates, cups, and dishes made from china: *I'll get my best china out.*

chink /tʃɪŋk/ *n* [C] **1** a narrow crack or hole in something: *I could see light through a chink in the wall.* **2** *BrE* a high ringing sound made by metal or glass objects touching each other: *the chink of coins*

chinos /'tʃiːnəʊz $ -noʊz/ *n* [plural] loose trousers made from cotton

chintz /tʃɪnts/ *n* [U] smooth cotton cloth with flower patterns on it: *chintz covers on the chairs*

chip[1] /tʃɪp/ *n* [C]

1 [usually plural] *BrE* a long thin piece of potato cooked in oil [= **fries, French fry** *AmE*]: *fish and chips* | *a portion of chips*
2 *AmE* a thin flat round piece of food such as potato cooked in very hot oil and eaten cold [= **crisp** *BrE*]: *a bag of potato chips*
3 a small piece of SILICON with electronic parts on it, that is used in computers: *a silicon chip*
4 a small piece of wood, stone etc that has broken off something: *wood chips*
5 a small hole or mark on a plate, cup etc where a piece has broken off: *a bowl with a chip in it*
6 have a chip on your shoulder to have an angry attitude to life because you think you have been treated unfairly in the past: *He's always had a chip on his shoulder about not going to college.*
7 when the chips are down *spoken* in a serious or difficult situation
8 be a chip off the old block *informal* to be very similar to your mother or father in appearance or character
9 a small flat coloured piece of plastic used in GAMBLING games instead of money
→ **BLUE-CHIP**

chip[2] *v* **chipped, chipping 1** [I,T] if you chip something, or if it chips, a small piece accidentally breaks off: *She fell and chipped a tooth.*
2 [T] to break small pieces off something: **chip sth away/off** *Sandy chipped away the plaster covering the tiles.* —**chipped** *adj: a chipped cup*
chip away at sth *phr v* to gradually make something less effective or destroy it: *New laws are chipping away at the right to smoke in public places.*
chip in *phr v* **1** to interrupt a conversation by saying something: *'It won't be easy,' Jeff chipped in.* **2** if each person in a group chips in, they each give a small amount of money so that they can buy something together: *We all chipped in to buy Amy a present.* | **chip in (with) sth** *Fifty people chipped in $250 apiece.*

chiropodist /kɪ'rɒpədɪst, ʃɪ- $ -'rɑː-/ *n* [C] *BrE* someone whose job is to treat and care for people's feet [= **podiatrist** *AmE*] —**chiropody** *n* [U]

chirp /tʃɜːp $ tʃɜːrp/ *v* [I] if a bird or insect chirps, it makes short high sounds: *sparrows chirping in the trees* —**chirp** *n* [C]

chirpy /'tʃɜːpi $ tʃɜːrpi/ *adj BrE informal* happy and active: *You seem very chirpy this morning.*

chisel /'tʃɪzəl/ *n* [C] a metal tool with a sharp end, used to cut wood or stone

chit /tʃɪt/ *n* [C] an official note that shows that you are allowed to have something

chit-chat *n* [C,U] *informal* informal conversation about unimportant things

chivalrous /'ʃɪvəlrəs/ *adj formal* a man who is chivalrous behaves in a polite and honourable way to women —**chivalry** *n* [U]

chives /tʃaɪvz/ *n* [plural] the long thin leaves of a plant with purple flowers. Chives taste of onion and are used in cooking

chlorine /'klɔːriːn/ *n* [U] a yellow-green gas that is used to keep swimming pools clean

chock-a-block /,tʃɒk ə 'blɒk◂ $ 'tʃɑːk ə ,blɑːk/ *adj* **be chock-a-block (with sth)** *BrE* to be completely full of people or things

chock-'full *adj* [not before noun] *informal* completely full or containing a very large amount of something: **+of** *The pond was chock-full of weeds.*

chocolate /'tʃɒklət $ 'tʃɑːkələt, 'tʃɔːk-/ *n*

1 [U] a sweet brown food eaten as a sweet or used in cooking: **milk chocolate** | **plain/dark chocolate** (=chocolate with no milk and very little sugar) | *a chocolate bar*
2 [C] a small sweet covered with chocolate: *Would you like a chocolate?* | *a box of chocolates*
3 [U] a drink made from hot milk and chocolate: *a mug of hot chocolate*

choice[1] /tʃɔɪs/ *n*

1 [C,U] if you have a choice, you can choose between several things [➔ **choose**]: **+between** *Voters have a choice between three political parties.* | **+of** *You have a choice of hotel or self-catering accommodation.* | *He has to make some important choices.* | *They gave us no choice in the matter.* | *We had no choice but to destroy the animal.*
2 [singular] the range of people or things that you can choose from: **+of** *There is a choice of four colours.* | *We offer a wide choice of wines and beers.* | *Consumers these days are spoilt for choice* (=have a lot of things to choose from).
3 [C usually singular] the person or thing that someone has chosen: **+of** *I don't like her choice of shoes.* | *London was a good choice to go to.* | *The law was my first choice as a career* (=the career I wanted to do most).
4 sth of your choice the one that you would most like to choose: *Many children are not able to go to the school of their choice.*
5 by choice if you do something by choice, you do it because you want to: *She lives alone by choice.*
→ **MULTIPLE CHOICE**

choice[2] *adj* of high quality: *choice plums*

choir /kwaɪə $ kwaɪr/ *n* [C] a group of people who sing together, especially in a church or school: *Susan sings in the school choir.*

choke[1] /tʃəʊk $ tʃoʊk/ *v* **1** [I,T] to prevent someone from breathing or be prevented from breathing, because the throat is blocked or because there is not enough air: *The smoke was choking me.* | **+on** *He choked on a piece of bread.*
2 [I,T] to be unable to talk properly because of strong emotion: *He was choking with rage.*
3 also **choke up** [T] to fill a place so that things cannot move through it: **be choked (up) with sth** *The gutters were choked up with leaves.* | *roads choked with traffic*

C

choke sth ⇔ **back** *phr v* to control yourself so that you do not show how angry, sad etc you are: *Anna* **choked back tears** *as she tried to speak.*

choke² *n* [C] **1** a part of a car that controls the amount of air going into the engine **2** the sound someone makes when they are choking

choker /'tʃəʊkə $ 'tʃoʊkər/ *n* [C] a piece of jewellery or narrow cloth that fits closely around your neck

cholera /'kɒlərə $ 'kɑː-/ *n* [U] a serious disease that affects the stomach and BOWELS

cholesterol /kə'lestərɒl $ -roʊl/ *n* [U] a substance in your body which doctors think may cause heart disease

choose /tʃuːz/ *v* [I,T] past tense **chose** /tʃəʊz $ tʃoʊz/ past participle **chosen** /'tʃəʊzən $ 'tʃoʊ-/

1 to decide which one of several things or possibilities you want: +**between/from** *You can choose between ice cream and apple tart.* | **choose to do sth** *I chose to learn Italian rather than Spanish.* | **choose sb/sth to do sth** *They chose Donald to be their leader.* | **choose sb/sth for sth** *Why did you choose me for the job?*

> **THESAURUS**
>
> **pick**: *Pick any number from one to ten.*
> **select** *formal*: *All our wines have been carefully selected.*
> **opt for sth**: *Many drivers opt for Japanese cars.*
> **decide on sth**: *Have you decided on a name for the baby?*

2 to decide to do something: **choose to do sth** *I chose to ignore his advice.*
3 **there is little/nothing to choose between sth** used to say that two or more things are equally good

choosy /'tʃuːzi/ *adj* difficult to please: *Jean's very choosy about what she eats.*

chop¹ /tʃɒp $ tʃɑːp/ *v* [T] **chopped, chopping**
1 also **chop up** to cut something into smaller pieces: *He is outside chopping wood for the fire.* | *Can you chop up some carrots for me?* | **chop sth into pieces/chunks etc** *Chop the meat into small cubes.* → see box at CUT → and RECIPE → see picture at CUT¹ **2 chop and change** *BrE informal* to keep changing your opinion

chop sth ⇔ **down** *phr v* to make a tree fall down by cutting it with a sharp tool → see box at CUT

choppy

choppy

calm

chop sth ⇔ **off** *phr v* to remove something by cutting it with a sharp tool: *Be careful you don't chop your fingers off.*

chop² *n* [C] **1** a small flat piece of meat on a bone: *a pork chop* → see picture on page A5 **2 the chop** *BrE* if you get or are given the chop, you lose your job **3** a quick hard hit with the side of your hand or with a heavy sharp tool: *a karate chop*

chopper /'tʃɒpə $ 'tʃɑːpər/ *n* [C] *informal* a HELICOPTER

choppy /'tʃɒpi $ 'tʃɑːpi/ *adj* choppy water has a lot of waves and is not smooth to sail on

chopsticks /'tʃɒpstɪks $ 'tʃɑːp-/ *n* [plural] a pair of thin sticks used for eating food in China, Japan etc

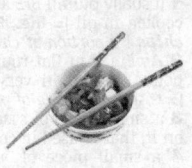

chopsticks

choral /'kɔːrəl/ *adj* related to music that is sung by a large group of people [➡ **chorus**]: *an evening of choral music*

chord /kɔːd $ kɔːrd/ *n* [C] two or more musical notes played at the same time

chore /tʃɔː $ tʃɔːr/ *n* [C] a job that you have to do, especially a boring one: *household chores*

choreography /ˌkɒri'ɒgrəfi, ˌkɔː- $ ˌkɔːri'ɑːg-/ *n* [U] the art of arranging how dancers should move during a performance —**choreographer** *n* [C] —**choreograph** /'kɒriəgrɑːf, 'kɔː- $ 'kɔːriəgræf/ *v* [T]

chortle /'tʃɔːtl $ 'tʃɔːrtl/ *v* [I] *written* to laugh, especially because you are pleased about something —**chortle** *n* [C]

chorus /'kɔːrəs/ *n* [C] **1** the part of a song that is repeated after each VERSE **2** a large group of people who sing together **3 the chorus** a group of singers, dancers, or actors who perform together in a show but do not have the main parts **4 a chorus of thanks/disapproval/criticism etc** something that a lot of people say at the same time: *The minister was greeted with a chorus of boos.*

chose /tʃəʊz $ tʃoʊz/ *v* the past tense of CHOOSE

chosen /'tʃəʊzən $ 'tʃoʊ-/ *v* the past participle of CHOOSE

Christ /kraɪst/ also **Jesus Christ** *n* the man who Christians believe is the son of God. Christianity is based on Christ's life, death, and teaching.

christen /'krɪsən/ *v* [T] **1** to officially give a child its name at a Christian religious ceremony [➡ **baptize**]: *She was christened Mary Ann.* **2** to give something or someone a name

christening /'krɪsənɪŋ/ *n* [C] a Christian ceremony in which a baby is officially given a name and becomes a member of a Christian church [➡ **baptism**]

Christian¹ /'krɪstʃən, -tiən/ *adj* related to Christianity: *Christian beliefs* | *the Christian Church*

Christian² *n* [C] someone whose religion is Christianity

Christianity /ˌkrɪstiˈænⱼti/ *n* [U] the religion that is based on the life and teachings of Jesus Christ

'Christian name *n* [C] someone's first name: *I can't remember his Christian name.* → see box at **NAME**

Christmas /ˈkrɪsməs/ *n* [C,U] the period around December 25th when Christians celebrate the birth of Christ and give each other presents: *Are you going home for Christmas?* | *Merry Christmas!* | *a **Christmas card** from her sister* | *an unwanted **Christmas present***
→ **FATHER CHRISTMAS**

Christmas 'carol *n* [C] a Christian song that people sing at Christmas

Christmas 'Day *n* [C,U] December 25th, the day when most Christians celebrate the birth of Christ

Christmas 'Eve *n* [C,U] December 24th, the day before Christmas Day

'Christmas tree *n* [C] a tree that people put inside their house and decorate for Christmas

chrome /krəʊm $ kroʊm/ also **chromium** /ˈkrəʊmiəm $ ˈkroʊ-/ *n* [U] a hard shiny silver metal that is used for covering objects: *doors with chrome handles*

chromosome /ˈkrəʊməsəʊm $ ˈkroʊməsoʊm/ *n* [C] *technical* a part of every living cell, which contains the GENES that control the size, shape etc that a plant or animal has

chronic /ˈkrɒnɪk $ ˈkrɑː-/ *adj* if a problem or illness is chronic, it is serious and likely to continue for a long time: *a chronic back problem* | *a chronic shortage of teachers* —**chronically** /-kli/ *adv*: *patients who are chronically ill*

chronicle /ˈkrɒnɪkəl $ ˈkrɑː-/ *n* [C] a written record of events which mentions them in the order in which they happened —**chronicle** *v* [T] *The book chronicles Flanagan's brave battle with cancer.*

chronological /ˌkrɒnəˈlɒdʒɪkəl◂ $ ˌkrɑːnəˈlɑː-/ *adj* arranged in the same order as events happened: *a list of World Cup winners **in chronological order*** —**chronologically** /-kli/ *adv*

chrysalis /ˈkrɪsəlⱼs/ *n* [C] a MOTH or BUTTERFLY at the stage of development when it has a hard outer shell and is changing into its adult form [→ COCOON] → see picture on page A2

chrysanthemum /krɪˈsænθⱼməm/ *n* [C] a garden plant that has large brightly coloured flowers

chubby /ˈtʃʌbi/ *adj* slightly fat: *chubby cheeks* → see box at **FAT**

chuck /tʃʌk/ *v* [T] *informal* to throw something: *Chuck that magazine over here.* → see box at **THROW**

chuck sth ⇔ **away** *phr v informal* to throw something away

chuck sth ⇔ **in** *phr v BrE informal* to leave your job: *If you hate the job so much, why don't you chuck it in?*

chuck sb/sth ⇔ **out** *phr v informal* **1** to throw something away: *We chucked out a lot of stuff when we moved.* **2** to make someone leave a place: **+of** *We were chucked out of the restaurant for smoking.*

chuckle /ˈtʃʌkəl/ *v* [I] to laugh quietly: *What are you chuckling about?* → see box at **LAUGH** —**chuckle** *n* [C]

chuffed /tʃʌft/ *adj* [not before noun] *BrE informal* very pleased or happy

chug /tʃʌg/ *v* [I] **chugged, chugging** if a car, train etc chugs somewhere, it moves there slowly, with the engine making a repeated low sound: **+along/up/around etc** *The little boat chugged slowly along the canal.*

chum /tʃʌm/ *n* [C] *old-fashioned* a good friend —**chummy** *adj*

chunk /tʃʌŋk/ *n* [C] **1** a large piece of something: **+of** *a chunk of cheese* → see picture at **PIECE** **2** a large part or amount of something: *Hospital bills took a big chunk out of her savings.*

chunky /ˈtʃʌŋki/ *adj* **1** thick, solid, and heavy: *chunky jewellery* **2** someone who is chunky has a broad, heavy body: *a short, chunky man*

church /tʃɜːtʃ $ tʃɜːrtʃ/ *n*
1 [C] a building where Christians go to pray [→ **cathedral**]
2 [U] the religious ceremonies in a church: *How often do you **go to church**?*
3 also **Church** [C] one of the separate groups within the Christian religion: *the Catholic Church*

GRAMMAR

Do not use 'a' or 'the' before **church** when you are talking about religious ceremonies: *I didn't see him **in church** this morning.* | *She used to **go to church** every Sunday.*

churchgoer /ˈtʃɜːtʃˌgəʊə $ ˈtʃɜːrtʃˌgoʊər/ *n* [C] someone who goes to church regularly

Church of 'England *n* **the Church of England** the state Christian organization in England [→ **Anglican**]

churchyard /ˈtʃɜːtʃjɑːd $ ˈtʃɜːrtʃjɑːrd/ *n* [C] a piece of land around a church where dead people are buried

churlish /ˈtʃɜːlɪʃ $ ˈtʃɜːr-/ *adj formal* not polite or friendly: *It seemed churlish to refuse her invitation.*

churn[1] /tʃɜːn $ tʃɜːrn/ *v* **1** [I] if your stomach churns, you feel sick because you are nervous or frightened: *Thinking about the exam made my stomach churn.* **2** also **churn up** [I,T] if water, mud etc churns, or if something churns it, it moves about violently: *The storm churned up the sea bed.* | *a brown, churning river* **3** [T] to make butter by using a churn

churn sth ⇔ **out** *phr v informal* to produce large quantities of something quickly, especially without caring about quality: *The nation's film industry churns out more than 50 movies a year.*

churn[2] *n* [C] **1** a container that is filled with milk and shaken to make butter **2** also **milk churn** *BrE* a large metal container used to carry milk

chute /ʃuːt/ *n* [C] **1** a long narrow structure that slopes down, so that things or people can slide down it: *a laundry chute* **2** *informal* a PARACHUTE

chutney /ˈtʃʌtni/ *n* [U] a cold mixture of fruit, sugar, and spices that is eaten especially with cheese or meat

CIA /ˌsiː aɪ ˈeɪ/ *n* **Central Intelligence Agency the CIA** the department of the US government that collects information about other countries, especially secretly

CID /ˌsiː aɪ ˈdiː/ *n* [U] **Criminal Investigation Department** the department of the British police that deals with serious crimes

cider /ˈsaɪdə $ -ər/ *n* [C,U] **1** *BrE* a drink made from apples that contains alcohol **2** *AmE* a drink made from apples that does not contain alcohol

cigar /sɪˈɡɑː $ -ˈɡɑːr/ *n* [C] a tube-shaped object made of tobacco leaves that people smoke

cigarette /ˌsɪɡəˈret $ ˈsɪɡəˌret, ˌsɪɡəˈret/ *n* [C] a paper tube filled with tobacco that people smoke [➜ **cigar**]: *a packet of cigarettes*

cilantro /sɪˈlæntrəʊ $ -ˈlɑːntroʊ/ *n* [U] *AmE* a herb, used especially in Asian cooking; [= **coriander** *BrE*]

cinch /sɪntʃ/ *n* **be a cinch** *informal* to be very easy: *The test was a cinch.*

cinder /ˈsɪndə $ -ər/ *n* [C] a very small piece of burnt wood, coal etc

cinema /ˈsɪnɪmə/ *n*

1 [C] *BrE* a building where you go to see films [= **movie theater** *AmE*]: *Shall we go to the cinema* (=go to see a film) *tonight?*
2 [U] the art or industry of making films: *the influence of Hollywood on Indian cinema*

cinnamon /ˈsɪnəmən/ *n* [U] a sweet-smelling spice

circa /ˈsɜːkə $ ˈsɜːr-/ *prep formal* used before a date to show that something happened close to that time, but you do not know exactly when: *He was born circa 1100.*

circle¹ /ˈsɜːkəl $ ˈsɜːr-/ *n* [C]

1 a round shape like the letter O, or a group of people or things arranged in this shape: **+of** *a circle of stones* | *The children were dancing in a circle.* ➔ see box at **SHAPE** ➔ see picture at **SHAPE¹**
2 a group of people who know each other and meet regularly, or who have the same interests or type of job: **+of** *She has a wide circle of friends.* | **in political/legal/academic etc circles** *Myers' new book has been praised in literary circles.*
3 the circle *BrE* the upper floor of a theatre, where the seats are in curved rows [= **balcony** *AmE*] ➔ see box at **THEATRE**
4 go around/round in circles to think or argue about something without achieving anything ➔ **TRAFFIC CIRCLE**, **VICIOUS CIRCLE**

circle² *v* **1** [I,T] to move in a circle around something: *Our plane circled the airport several times.* **2** [T] to draw a circle around something: *Circle the correct answer.*

circuit /ˈsɜːkɪt $ ˈsɜːr-/ *n* [C] **1** a set of wires etc that an electric current flows around: *an electrical circuit* **2 the tennis/lecture/club etc circuit** all the places that are usually visited by someone who plays tennis etc: *a well-known speaker on the international lecture circuit* **3** a path that forms a circle around an area, or a journey along this path: *We did a circuit of the old city walls.* **4** *BrE* a track where people race cars, bicycles etc

circuitry /ˈsɜːkɪtri $ ˈsɜːr-/ *n* [U] a system of electric circuits

circular¹ /ˈsɜːkjᵿlə $ ˈsɜːrkjᵿlər/ *adj* **1** shaped like a circle: *a circular table* ➔ see box at **SHAPE** **2** around in a large rough circle: *a circular walk*

circular² *n* [C] a printed advertisement or notice that is sent to lots of people at the same time

circulate /ˈsɜːkjᵿleɪt $ ˈsɜːr-/ *v* **1** [I,T] to move around within a system, or to make something do this: *Blood circulates around the body.* **2** [I] if information or ideas circulate, they become known by many people: *Rumours are circulating that the mayor's health is getting worse.* **3** [T] to give written information to a number of people: *I'll circulate the report at the meeting.*

circulation /ˌsɜːkjᵿˈleɪʃən $ ˌsɜːr-/ *n* **1** [singular, U] the movement of blood around your body: *Exercise can improve the circulation.* **2** [singular] the number of copies of a newspaper or magazine that are usually sold each day, week, month etc: **+of** *a magazine with a circulation of 400,000* **3 in/out of circulation** if something is in circulation, it is being used by people in a society and passing from one person to another: *Police believe there are thousands of illegal guns in circulation.*

circumcise /ˈsɜːkəmsaɪz $ ˈsɜːr-/ *v* [T] **1** to cut off the skin at the end of the PENIS (=male sex organ) **2** to cut off the CLITORIS (=part of the female sex organs) —**circumcision** /ˌsɜːkəmˈsɪʒən $ ˌsɜːr-/ *n* [C,U]

circumference /səˈkʌmfərəns $ sər-/ *n* [C,U] the distance around the outside of something round: *The earth's circumference is nearly 25,000 miles.*

circumspect /ˈsɜːkəmspekt $ ˈsɜːr-/ *adj formal* thinking carefully about things before doing them [= **cautious**]: *I advise you to be more circumspect about what you say in public.*

circumstance /ˈsɜːkəmstæns, -stəns $ ˈsɜːr-/ *n*

1 [C usually plural] the conditions that affect a situation, action, event etc: **under/in ... circumstances** *Under normal circumstances she would never have left her child with a stranger.* | *Non-members will be admitted only in special circumstances.*
2 under/in/given the circumstances used to say that a particular situation makes something necessary or acceptable when it would not normally be: *I think we did the best we could in the circumstances.*
3 under/in no circumstances used to emphasize that something must not happen: *Under no circumstances should you leave this house.*
4 sb's circumstances *formal* the conditions in which you live, especially how much money you have: *Everyone will be taxed according to their circumstances.*

circumstantial /ˌsɜːkəmˈstænʃəl◂ $ ˌsɜːr-/ *adj law* **circumstantial evidence** facts or signs that make something seem like it is true but do not definitely prove it: *The case against McCarthy is based largely on circumstantial evidence.*

circumvent /ˌsɜːkəmˈvent $ ˌsɜːr-/ *v* [T] *formal disapproving* to avoid having to obey a rule or law, especially in a dishonest way: *The senator is accused of circumventing the tax laws.*

circus /ˈsɜːkəs $ ˈsɜːr-/ *n* [C] a group of performers and animals that travel to different places doing tricks and other kinds of entertainment: *circus performers*

cistern /ˈsɪstən $ -ərn/ n [C] a large container that water is stored in → see picture at **BATHROOM**

citadel /ˈsɪtədəl, -del/ n [C] a strong castle where people in the past could go to be safe if their city was attacked

citation /saɪˈteɪʃən/ n [C] **1** an official statement publicly praising someone's actions or achievements: **+for** *a citation for bravery* **2** a phrase or sentence taken from a book, speech etc: *a citation from the Bible*

cite /saɪt/ v [T] **1** to mention something as an example or proof of something else: *The mayor cited the latest crime figures as proof of the need for more police.* **2** *AmE law* to order someone to appear before a court of law: *He was cited for speeding.*

citizen /ˈsɪtɪ̯zən/ n [C]

1 someone who lives in a particular town, state, or country [**➡ national**]: *The mayor urged citizens to begin preparing for a major storm.*
2 someone who has the legal right to live and work in a particular country: *a Brazilian citizen* → **SENIOR CITIZEN**

citizenship /ˈsɪtɪ̯zənʃɪp/ n [U] the legal right to belong to a particular country: *She's applied for French citizenship.*

citrus /ˈsɪtrəs/ also **'citrus fruit** n [C] plural **citrus** a fruit such as an orange or LEMON

city

city /ˈsɪti/ n [C] plural **cities**

1 a large important town: *Leeds is the third largest city in England.* | *Austria's* **capital city** (=where the government is) | *New York City*
2 the people who live in a city: *The city has been living in fear since last week's earthquake.*
→ **INNER CITY**

civic /ˈsɪvɪk/ adj relating to a town or city, or the people who live in it: *John Golden was an important civic and business leader.* | *It is your* **civic duty** *to vote in the local elections.*

civics /ˈsɪvɪks/ n [U] *AmE* a school subject dealing with the rights and duties of citizens and the way government works

civil /ˈsɪvəl/ adj **1** not related to military or religious organizations: *the civil aircraft industry* | *We were married in a civil ceremony, not in church.* **2** **civil unrest/disorder etc** violence involving different groups within a country **3** related to laws that deal with people's rights, not laws that are related to crimes: *a civil trial* | *civil law* **4** polite but not very friendly: *Please try to be civil.*

civil engi'neering n [U] the planning, building, and repair of roads, bridges, large buildings etc

civilian /sɪ̯ˈvɪljən/ n [C] anyone who is not a member of a military organization or the police: *Many innocent civilians were killed.* —**civilian** adj: *civilian clothes*

civilization also **-isation** *BrE* /ˌsɪvəlaɪˈzeɪʃən $ -vələ-/ n

1 [C,U] a society that is well organized and developed: *ancient civilizations*
2 [U] when people live in a well organized society and have a comfortable way of life: *all the benefits of* **modern civilization**

civilize also **-ise** *BrE* /ˈsɪvəl-aɪz/ v [T] to improve a society so that it is more organized and developed: *The Romans hoped to civilize all the tribes of Europe.*

civilized also **-ised** *BrE* /ˈsɪvəl-aɪzd/ adj **1** a civilized society is well organized and has laws and customs: *Care for the elderly is essential in a civilized society.* **2** behaving politely and sensibly: *Let's discuss this in a civilized way.*

civil 'liberties n [plural] also **civil liberty** [U] the right of all citizens to be free to do whatever they want while respecting the rights of other people

civil 'rights n [plural] the legal rights that every person has

civil 'servant n [C] someone who works in the civil service

civil 'service n **the civil service** all the government departments and the people who work in them

civil 'war n [C,U] a war between groups of people from the same country

CJD /ˌsiː dʒeɪ ˈdiː/ n [U] a brain disease that kills people, which may be caused by eating meat infected with BSE

cl the written abbreviation of **centilitre**

clad /klæd/ adj *literary* **1** wearing a particular kind of clothing: **+in** *a young man clad in shorts and a bike helmet* **2** **snow-clad/ivy-clad etc** covered in a particular thing

claim¹ /kleɪm/ v

1 [T] to say that something is true, even though it might not be: **+(that)** *Evans claimed that someone tried to murder him.* | **claim to do/be sth** *There's a man at the door claiming to be your son.* | *George claims to remember exactly what the gunman looked like.*
2 [I,T] to ask for something because you have a right to have it or because it belongs to you: *Elderly people can claim £10 a week heating allowance.* | *No one's claimed this wallet that was left behind.*
3 [T] *written* if a war, accident etc claims lives, people die because of it: *Officials say the violence has claimed 21 lives.*

claim² n [C]

1 a statement that something is true, even though it might not be: **+that** *Garcia denied claims that he was involved in drug smuggling.*
2 an official request for money that you think you have a right to: *insurance claims* | **+for** *She put in a* **claim** *for travel expenses.*
3 a right to have or do something: **+to/on** *Surely they* **have a claim** *to their father's land?*
4 **claim to fame** a place's or person's claim to fame is the most important or interesting fact

about them: *His claim to fame is once having played basketball with Michael Jordan.*

claimant /'kleɪmənt/ *n* [C] someone who claims something, especially money, from the government, a court etc because they think they have a right to it: *benefit claimants*

clairvoyant /kleə'vɔɪənt $ kler-/ *n* [C] someone who says they can see what will happen in the future

clam¹ /klæm/ *n* [C,U] a small sea animal with a shell, that people eat

clam² *v* **clammed, clamming**
  clam up *phr v informal* to suddenly stop talking: *Tom always clams up if you ask him about his girlfriend.*

clamber /'klæmbə $ -ər/ *v* [I] to climb over something with difficulty, using your hands and feet: **+over/out/up etc** *He clambered over the rocks.*

clammy /'klæmi/ *adj* slightly wet in an unpleasant way: *clammy hands*

clamour¹ *BrE*; **clamor** *AmE* /'klæmə $ -ər/ *n* [singular, U] **1** a loud noise made by a large group of people or animals: **+of** *a clamour of voices in the next room* **2** a complaint or a demand for something made by a lot of people: **+for** *the clamour for lower taxes*

clamour² *BrE*; **clamor** *AmE* *v* [I] to demand something loudly: **+for** *All the kids were clamouring for attention.*

clamp¹ /klæmp/ *v* [T] **1** to hold something tightly in a particular position so that it does not move: **clamp sth over/between etc sth** *He clamped his hand over her mouth.* **2** *BrE* to fasten a piece of equipment onto the wheel of a car that has been parked illegally, so that it cannot be moved [= **boot** *AmE*]
  clamp down *phr v* to become very strict in order to stop people from doing something: **+on** *The police are clamping down on drunk drivers.*

clamp² *n* [C] **1** a piece of equipment for holding things together **2** *BrE* a piece of equipment that can be fastened onto the wheel of a car that is illegally parked, so that it cannot be moved [= **boot** *AmE*]

clampdown /'klæmpdaʊn/ *n* [singular] sudden firm action to stop or reduce crime: **+on** *a clampdown on illegal immigration*

clan /klæn/ *n* [C] **1** *informal* a large family: *The whole clan will be here for Christmas.* **2** a large group of families that often share the same name: *the Campbell clan*

clandestine /klæn'destɪn/ *adj* secret: *a clandestine affair*

clang /klæŋ/ *v* [I,T] to make a loud sound like metal being hit: *The gate clanged shut behind him.* —**clang** *n* [C]

clank /klæŋk/ *v* [I] if a metal object clanks, it makes a loud heavy sound: *clanking chains* —**clank** *n* [C] *the clank of machinery*

clap¹ /klæp/ *v* **clapped, clapping**
  1 [I,T] to hit your hands together several times to show that you approve of something, or want to attract someone's attention [➡ **applause**]: *The audience was clapping and cheering.* | *The coach clapped his hands and yelled, 'OK, listen!'* → see picture on page A10
  2 clap sb on the back/shoulder to hit someone lightly on the back or shoulder with your hand in a friendly way
  3 clap your hand on/over/to sth to put your hand somewhere quickly and suddenly: *She clapped her hand over her mouth, realizing she had said too much.*
  —**clapping** *n* [U]

clap² *n* [C usually singular] **1** a sudden loud noise: *a clap of thunder* **2** the loud sound that you make when you clap

clarify /'klærɪfaɪ/ *v* [T] **clarified, clarifying, clarifies** to make something easier to understand: *I need you to clarify a few points.* —**clarification** /ˌklærɪfɪˈkeɪʃən/ *n* [C,U]

clarinet /ˌklærɪˈnet/ *n* [C] a wooden musical instrument like a long black tube that you play by blowing into it → see picture on page A6

clarity /'klærɪti/ *n* [U] the quality of being clear: *the clarity of Irving's writing style*

clash¹ /klæʃ/ *v* **1** [I] to fight, argue, or disagree: **+with** *Demonstrators clashed with police.* **2** [I] if colours or clothes clash, they do not look nice together: **+with** *That tie clashes with your jacket.* **3** [I] if two events clash, they happen at the same time, so you cannot go to one of them: **+with** *Unfortunately, the concert clashes with my class.* **4** [I,T] if two pieces of metal clash, they hit each other and make a loud sound

clash² *n* [C] **1** an argument or fight between two people, groups, or armies: **+between/with** *Ten soldiers were wounded in a clash with the rebels.* | *a clash between the President and Republicans in the Senate* **2** a loud sound made by two metal objects hitting together: *the clash of cymbals*

clasp¹ /klɑːsp $ klæsp/ *n* **1** [C] a small metal object used to fasten a bag, jewellery etc [= **grip**] **2** [singular] when you hold something tightly: *the firm clasp of her father's hand*

clasp² *v* [T] to hold someone or something tightly: **clasp sb/sth in your hands/arms** *She clasped the baby in her arms.*

class¹ /klɑːs $ klæs/ *n*
  1 [C also + plural verb *BrE*] a group of students who are taught together [➡ **classmate**]: **in a class** *Is Jodie in your class?* | *Gary was top of the class.* | **class of 1999/2002 etc** *AmE* (=all the students who finished school in 1999, 2002 etc) | *My class are going to the Lake District.*
  2 [C,U] a period of time when someone teaches a group of students [= **lesson** *BrE*]: **in class** (=during the class) *No talking in class.* | **maths/physics/music etc class** *What time is your Bible class?* → see box at **SCHOOL**
  3 [C] a set of classes in a particular subject [= **course** *BrE*]: **+in** *Sean's taking classes in art.* | **aerobics/pottery/French etc class** *Dance classes start at 7.30.* | **take/do/attend a class** *I'm doing an evening class next year.*
  4 [C,U] the social group that you belong to, based on your job, income, and education, or the system of dividing people in this way: **upper/middle/working class** *a working-class background* | *a member of the ruling classes* | *success based on class, not ability*
  5 [C] the group that people or things belong in when they are arranged according to their quality, abilities, or type: *What class of vehicle are you qualified to drive?* | **first/business/tourist**

etc class (=on a train, aircraft etc) *We traveled economy class.* | **first/second class post/mail** | **nice/better etc class (of sth)** *You get a nicer class of people in this area.* | *The car is in a class of its own* (=very good quality). | *a second class university degree*

6 [U] *informal* a high level of style or skill [➡ **classy**]: **have/show class** *The team showed real class today.* | *furniture that is guaranteed to add a touch of class to your home*
→ HIGH-CLASS, WORLD-CLASS

class² *v* [T] to put someone or something in a particular group: **class sth as sth** *Cocaine is classed as a hard drug.*

classic¹ /ˈklæsɪk/ *adj* [only before noun] **1** recognized as having good qualities that last and that people admire: *classic designs of the last century* | *a classic dark suit* **2** typical of a particular thing or situation: **classic example/ mistake/case** *Many students make the classic mistake of revising too much.*

classic² *n* **1** [C] a book, film, or play that is recognized as being important, serious, and with qualities that last for a long time: *'Moby Dick' is a classic of American literature.* **2 classics** [plural] the language, literature, and history of Ancient Rome and Greece

classical /ˈklæsɪkəl/ *adj* [only before noun] **1** using traditional styles and ideas and considered to be serious and important: **classical music/composer/dance etc** *classical ballet* **2** connected with the language, literature, and

history of Ancient Rome and Greece: *classical architecture* —**classically** /-kli/ *adv: a classically trained violinist*

classification /ˌklæsɪfɪ²ˈkeɪʃən/ *n* [C, U] the process of putting things in groups according to their age, type etc: **+of** *the classification of wines*

classified /ˈklæsɪ²faɪd/ *adj* classified information, documents etc are officially secret

classified 'ad *n* [C] a small advertisement that you put in a newspaper to buy or sell something [= small ad *BrE*; = want ad *AmE*] → see box at ADVERTISEMENT

classify /ˈklæsɪfaɪ/ *v* [T] **classified, classifying, classifies** to put things into groups according to their age, type etc: **classify sth as/under sth** *Whales are classified as mammals.*

classmate /ˈklɑːsmeɪt $ ˈklæs-/ *n* [C] someone who is in the same class as you at school or college

classroom /ˈklɑːs-rʊm, -ruːm $ ˈklæs-/ *n* [C] a room where students are taught

classwork /ˈklɑːswɜːk $ ˈklæswɜːrk/ *n* [U] work that students do in class, not at home [➡ homework]

classy /ˈklɑːsi $ ˈklæsi/ *adj informal* expensive and fashionable: *a classy restaurant*

clatter /ˈklætə $ -ər/ *v* [I,T] if something clatters, it makes a loud noise when it hits something: *The dishes clattered to the floor.* —**clatter** *n* [singular, U]

clause /klɔːz $ klɒːz/ *n* [C] **1** part of a legal document covering a particular subject: *clause*

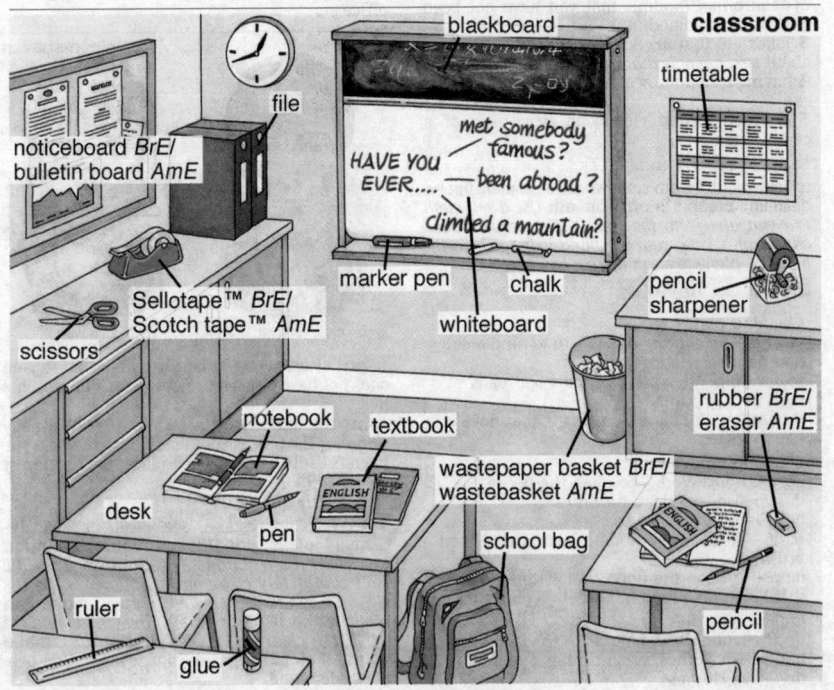

classroom

blackboard
timetable
file
noticeboard *BrE*/ bulletin board *AmE*
met somebody famous?
HAVE YOU EVER.... been abroad?
climbed a mountain?
marker pen
chalk
pencil sharpener
Sellotape™ *BrE*/ Scotch tape™ *AmE*
whiteboard
scissors
notebook
textbook
ENGLISH
rubber *BrE*/ eraser *AmE*
desk
pen
wastepaper basket *BrE*/ wastebasket *AmE*
school bag
ruler
pencil
glue

14(a) of the Disability Act **2** in grammar, a group of words that is part of a sentence → **MAIN CLAUSE, RELATIVE CLAUSE, SUBORDINATE CLAUSE**

claustrophobic /ˌklɔːstrəˈfəʊbɪk $ ˌklɒːstrəˈfoʊ-/ adj afraid of being in a small space or a crowd: *Elevators make me claustrophobic.* —**claustrophobia** n [U]

claw¹ /klɔː $ klɒː/ n [C] a sharp curved nail on an animal or bird → see picture on page A2

claw² v [I,T] **1** to tear or pull at something, using your fingers or nails: **+at** *The kitten clawed at my trousers.* **2** if you claw your way somewhere, you use a lot of effort and determination to reach a place or position: **claw your way up/back etc** *Hanson has clawed his way to the top.*

clay /kleɪ/ n [U] a type of heavy sticky earth that is used to make pots and bricks

clean¹ /kliːn/ adj

1 without any dirt, marks etc [➡ **cleanliness**]: *Have you any clean towels? | Her room is always nice and clean.* | **keep sth clean** *Work surfaces must be kept spotlessly clean.* | **wipe/sweep/scrub etc sth clean** *Wipe the sink clean when you're done.* | **clean air/energy/fuels etc** (=not containing dirty things that harm the environment) *the Clean Air Act*

2 honest or legal and showing that you have not broken any rules or made any mistakes: *a clean fight | a clean driving licence* | **clean sheet/slate** (=a record showing that someone has not made any mistakes or done anything wrong) | **come clean (about sth)/make a clean breast of it** informal (=admit that you have not been honest about something)

3 jokes etc that are clean are not offensive or about sex: *a movie that is just good clean fun*

4 having a smooth neat edge or surface: *a clean cut*

5 a clean sweep victory in every part of a competition

clean² v also **clean up** [I,T]

to remove dirt from somewhere or something [➡ **clean-up**]: **clean sth off/from sth** *Use a soft cloth to clean dirt from the lens.* | *The carpets need cleaning.* | *Does your husband help to clean the house?* | *plans to clean up our beaches*

THESAURUS

Cleaning plates etc
wash up BrE/**do the dishes** – to wash plates and pans after a meal
scour/scrub – to wash dirty pots and pans with a rough cloth
dry up – to dry plates, dishes etc that have been washed

Cleaning a house
do the housework – to clean the house
dust/polish – to clean furniture
hoover BrE/**vacuum** – to clean carpets
scrub – to clean the floor, usually with a hard brush
mop – to clean the floor with water and a soft brush on a long handle

Cleaning clothes
do the laundry/washing BrE – to wash clothes
handwash clothes, wash clothes by hand, dry-clean clothes

—**cleaning** n [U] *Who does your office cleaning?* —**clean** n [singular] BrE: *It's time you gave the car a good clean.* → **SPRING-CLEAN**

clean sb/sth out phr v **1 clean sth ⇔ out** to make the inside of a room, house etc clean or tidy: *We spent Sunday cleaning out the attic.* **2** informal if buying something cleans you out, it is so expensive you have no money left

clean sth ⇔ up phr v to remove crime, bad behaviour etc from a place or organization: *More police are needed to clean up our city centres.*

clean³ adv informal completely: *The thieves got clean away.* | *I clean forgot you were coming.*

clean-'cut adj approving someone who is clean-cut is clean and neat in their appearance

cleaner /ˈkliːnə $ -ər/ n **1** [C] BrE someone whose job is to clean offices, houses etc: *office cleaners* **2** [C,U] a machine or substance used to clean things: **toilet/bathroom/sink etc cleaner 3 take sb to the cleaner's** informal **a)** to defeat someone completely **b)** to cheat someone, taking all their money etc

cleanliness /ˈklenlinəs/ n [U] when you keep yourself or your things clean: *a high standard of cleanliness*

cleanly /ˈkliːnli/ adv **1** done quickly, smoothly, and neatly: *It snapped* (=broke) *cleanly in two.* **2** without producing dirt, harmful substances etc: *fuel that burns cleanly*

cleanse /klenz/ v [T] to carefully clean your skin

cleanser /ˈklenzə $ -ər/ n [C,U] **1** a creamy substance you use to clean your face **2** a substance used for cleaning surfaces in a house, office etc

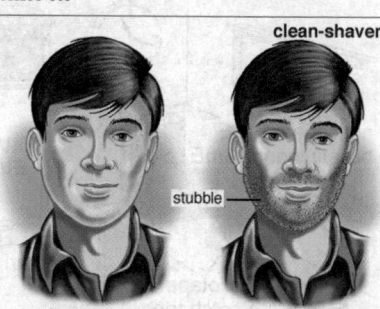

clean-shaven

stubble

clean-shaven · unshaven

clean-'shaven adj a man who is clean-shaven does not have a BEARD or MOUSTACHE (=hair on his face)

'clean-up also **cleanup** /ˈkliːnʌp/ n [C usually singular] the process of removing dirt, waste, or harmful substances from a place: *the cleanup of the oil spill*

clear¹ /klɪə $ klɪr/ adj

1 easy to understand, see, read, or hear [➡ clarity]: **clear idea/description/explanation etc** *clear instructions* | **+about/on** *The law isn't completely clear on this matter.* | **+to** *It's clear to me that you don't care.* | **make sth clear/make it clear (that)** *Hugh had made it perfectly clear he wasn't interested.* | **make yourself clear** (=express your ideas so that people understand) → see box at **NOTICEABLE**

2 impossible to doubt [➡ **clearly**]: *clear evidence* | *a clear victory* | **it is clear whether/how/what** etc *It's not clear how it happened.* | **it is clear (that)** *It became clear that she had lied.* | *a clear case of racism*

3 [not before noun] feeling sure that you understand something: **+about/on** *I'm not clear about what you want me to do.* | **+to** *He nodded as if things were now clear to him.*

4 weather that is clear is bright with no rain or clouds: *a clear sky*

5 a substance or liquid that is clear is easy to see through: *clear glass bottles* | *a crystal clear lake*

6 not blocked, hidden, or covered by anything: *The roads were clear last night.* | *clear skin* | **keep sth clear (of sth)** *Keep paths clear of weeds.* | **clear view/look** *a clear view over the bay*

7 a clear conscience when you know that you did the right thing and do not feel guilty

→ **the coast is clear** at COAST¹ → CRYSTAL CLEAR

clear² *v*

1 also **clear up** [T] to tidy or empty a place by removing things [➡ **clear-out**]: **clear sth off/from sth** *Please clear all books from the library desks.* | **clear sth of sth** *The roads had been cleared of snow.* | **clear sth away** (=put things where they belong) *John, clear your toys away, please.* | **clear sth out** (=remove things you do not want) *I spent the afternoon clearing out my desk.* | *After meals, I clear the table* (=remove the plates, glasses etc) *and start work.* | *Can you clear a space for my books?*

2 [T] to prove that someone is not guilty of something: **clear sb of (doing) sth** *Johnson was cleared of murdering his wife.*

3 [T] to give or get official permission to do something: *The plane has now been cleared for take-off.* | **clear sth with sb** *Has the order been cleared with Mr Herrick?*

4 also **clear up** [I] if the weather or sky clears, it gets brighter

5 clear your throat to cough a little so that you can speak clearly

6 [T] to go over a fence, wall etc without touching it

7 [I] if a cheque that is made out to you clears, the bank puts the money into your account

8 clear the air to talk about a problem in order to solve a disagreement with someone

clear off *phr v BrE informal* to leave a place quickly: *Clear off and leave me alone!*

clear up *phr v* **1 clear sth ⇔ up** to explain or solve something, or make it clearer: *I need to clear up some details with you.* **2** if an infection clears up, it gets better

clear³ *adv* away from someone or something: **+of** *Firefighters pulled the driver clear of the wreckage.* | **stand/stay/steer/keep clear (of sth/sb)** (=not see someone or do something that may cause you problems) *Steer clear of Neil – he's trouble.*

clear⁴ *n* **in the clear** not guilty of something

clearance /ˈklɪərəns $ ˈklɪr-/ *n* [C,U] **1** official permission to do something: *We're waiting for security clearance to enter the port.* | **+for** *clearance for landing* **2** the removal of unwanted things from a place: **snow/land/forest clearance** | **clearance sale** (=when things that

are not wanted are sold very cheaply) **3** the distance between two objects that is needed to stop them touching: *Allow 2 inches of clearance between the lights.*

ˈclear-cut *adj* certain or definite: *no clear-cut solutions*

ˌclear-ˈheaded *adj* able to think clearly and sensibly

clearing /ˈklɪərɪŋ $ ˈklɪr-/ *n* [C] a small area in a forest where there are no trees

clearly /ˈklɪəli $ ˈklɪrli/ *adv*

1 without any doubt: *Clearly, the situation was very serious.* | *She was clearly drunk.*

2 in a way that is easy to see, hear etc: *Speak slowly and clearly.*

3 if you cannot think clearly, you are confused

ˈclear-out *n* [C] *BrE* a process of removing things you do not want

cleavage /ˈkliːvɪdʒ/ *n* [C,U] the space between a woman's breasts

cleaver /ˈkliːvə $ -ər/ *n* [C] a knife with a large square blade: *a meat cleaver*

clef /klef/ *n* [C] a sign used in written music to show the PITCH of the notes

clemency /ˈklemənsi/ *n* [U] *formal* when someone is forgiven or punished less severely for a serious crime

clench /klentʃ/ *v* [T] to close your hands, mouth etc tightly: *Hal clenched his fists in anger.*

clergy /ˈklɜːdʒi $ ˈklɜːr-/ *n* **the clergy** [plural] the official leaders of organized religions

clergyman /ˈklɜːdʒimən $ ˈklɜːr-/, **clergywoman** /ˈklɜːdʒi,wʊmən $ -ɜːr-/ *n* [C] a man or woman who is a member of the clergy

cleric /ˈklerɪk/ *n* [C] a member of the clergy

clerical /ˈklerɪkəl/ *adj* **1** relating to office work: *clerical workers* **2** relating to the clergy

clerk /klɑːk $ klɜːrk/ *n* [C] **1** someone whose job is to do the written work or accounts in an office **2** *AmE* someone whose job is to help people in a shop [= **assistant** *BrE*] **3** *AmE* someone whose job is to help hotel guests when they arrive or leave: *Leave the keys with the desk clerk.*

clever /ˈklevə $ -ər/ *adj*

1 *especially BrE* someone who is clever is intelligent and understands things quickly [= **smart** *AmE*]: *a clever student* | *My brothers are all very clever.* | *It was very clever of you to work it out.* → see box at INTELLIGENT

2 things, ideas etc that are clever are skilfully designed: *clever advertising* | *a clever little gadget*

3 [not before noun] skilled in a particular activity [= **good**]: **clever at doing sth** *Heidi's quite clever at spotting a bargain.* | *He's always been clever with his hands* (=good at making things). —**cleverly** *adv* —**cleverness** *n* [U]

cliché /ˈkliːʃeɪ $ kliːˈʃeɪ/ *n* [C] a phrase that has been repeated so often that it is no longer effective or interesting: *tired old clichés* → see Thesaurus note at PHRASE —**clichéd** *adj*

click¹ /klɪk/ *v* **1** [I,T] to make a short hard sound, or to make something produce this sound: *The door clicked shut.* | *Ed clicked his fingers* (=made a sound by moving his thumb and fingers together quickly). **2** [I,T] to press a

button on a computer MOUSE to make the computer do something: +**on** *Double-click* (=click twice) *on the icon.* → see picture on page A7
3 [I] *informal* to suddenly understand the truth about something: *It all clicked into place – she was Jim's wife.* **4** [I] *informal* if two people click, they like each other straight away

click² *n* [C,U] a short hard sound: *the click of her heels*

client /'klaɪənt/ *n* [C] someone who pays a person or organization for a service: *an important client* → see box at CUSTOMER

clientele /ˌkliːənˈtel $ ˌklaɪənˈtel, ˌkliː-/ *n* [singular] the people who regularly use a shop, hotel etc: *Our clientele consists mainly of young people.*

cliff /klɪf/ *n* [C] a large area of rock with steep sides, often beside the sea: *the white cliffs of Dover* → see picture at ERODE

cliffhanger /'klɪfˌhæŋə $ -ər/ *n* [C] a situation in a story that excites you because you do not know what will happen next

climactic /klaɪˈmæktɪk/ *adj* forming the exciting or important part at the end of a story or event

climate /'klaɪmɪt/ *n*
1 [C] the typical weather conditions in an area: *a dry climate* | *research into climate change* (=permanent changes in weather conditions)
2 [C usually singular] the general feelings in a situation at a particular time: +**of** *a climate of racial tolerance* | **political/economic/ intellectual etc climate** *Small businesses are struggling in the present economic climate.*
—**climatic** /klaɪˈmætɪk/ *adj* [only before noun]

climax /'klaɪmæks/ *n* [C] the most important or exciting things that come at the end of a story or experience: +**of** *the climax of his career* | *The festival reaches a climax with a firework display.* —**climax** *v* [I]

climb /klaɪm/ *v*
1 also **climb up** [I,T] to move towards the top of something: *a cat climbing a tree* | *The aircraft was still climbing steadily.* | *the first man to climb Mount Everest* → see picture on page A11
2 [I] to move somewhere with difficulty, using your hands and feet: +**down/along/over etc** *We all climbed into the back of the truck.*
3 [I] if a number or amount climbs, it increases: *The temperature was climbing steadily.*
—**climb** *n* [C] *a steep climb*

climb down *phr v BrE* to admit that you were wrong about something: +**over** *The management had to climb down over the pay claim.*

climbdown /'klaɪmdaʊn/ *n* [C, usually singular] when someone is forced to admit that they are wrong: *a humiliating climbdown for the government*

climber /'klaɪmə $ -ər/ *n* [C] someone who climbs rocks or mountains as a sport

climbing /'klaɪmɪŋ/ *n* [U] the sport of climbing mountains or rocks: *The boys love to go climbing.* → see picture on page A9

clinch /klɪntʃ/ *v* [T] *informal* to succeed in getting something after trying hard: **clinch a match/race etc** *They clinched the cup with a last-minute goal.*

cling /klɪŋ/ *v* [I] past tense and past participle **clung** /klʌŋ/ **1** to hold someone or something

tightly because you do not feel safe: +**to/on/ together** *a little girl clinging to her mother* **2** to stick to something: +**to** *Sand clung to her arms and legs.*

cling on *phr v* to try to keep something, even though this is difficult: +**to** *He is clinging on to power.*

cling to sth *phr v* to continue to believe something, even though it may no longer be true: *She clung to the hope of rescue.*

Clingfilm /'klɪŋfɪlm/ *n* [U] *trademark BrE* thin transparent plastic used to wrap food [= **Saran Wrap** *AmE*]

clingy /'klɪŋi/ *adj* **1** *disapproving* someone who is clingy is too dependent on another person and will often hold onto them: *a clingy child* **2** clingy clothing or material sticks tightly to your body and shows its shape: *a clingy dress*

clinic /'klɪnɪk/ *n* [C] **1** a place where people get medical treatment: **dental/outpatient etc clinic** **2** *AmE* a group of doctors who share the same offices [= **practice** *BrE*]

clinical /'klɪnɪkəl/ *adj* **1** [only before noun] relating to medical tests or the treatment of people who are sick: **clinical trials/research** **2** *disapproving* not influenced by personal feelings: *His attitude was cold and clinical.* —**clinically** /-kli/ *adv*

clinician /klɪˈnɪʃən/ *n* [C] *technical* a doctor who examines and treats people who are sick rather than studying disease

clink /klɪŋk/ *v* [I,T] if glass or metal objects clink, or if you clink them, they make a short high sound when they touch: *Dad clinked his glass with a spoon.* —**clink** *n* [C,U]

clip¹ /klɪp/ *n* [C] **1** a small metal or plastic object used to hold things together **2** a short part of a film or television programme that is shown separately: +**from** *clips from the new Bond movie*

clip² *v* **clipped, clipping** **1** [I,T] to fasten things together, using a clip: **clip (sth) to/onto sth** *He clipped the dog's lead to its collar.* → see box at FASTEN **2** [T] to cut small amounts from something to make it neater: *clipped hedges* **3** [T] to hit something at an angle: *The truck clipped a parked car.*

'clip art *n* [U] pictures that you can copy from CD-ROMS or WEBSITES to use on your computer

clipboard /'klɪpbɔːd $ -bɔːrd/ *n* [C] **1** a small flat board with a clip that holds paper onto it **2** part of a computer MEMORY that stores information when you cut, copy, or move it

clipped /klɪpt/ *adj* a clipped voice is quick and clear but not very friendly: *a clipped military accent*

clippers /'klɪpəz $ -ərz/ *n* [plural] a tool used for cutting small pieces off something: *nail clippers*

clipping /'klɪpɪŋ/ *n* **1** [C] an article, picture etc that has been cut out of a newspaper or magazine **2** **clippings** [plural] small pieces that have been cut from something: *grass clippings*

clique /kliːk/ *n* [C] *disapproving* a small group of people who know each other well but who are not friendly towards other people —**cliquey** *adj*

clitoris /'klɪtərɪs/ *n* [C] a part of a woman's outer sex organs where she can feel sexual pleasure

cloak¹ /kləʊk $ kloʊk/ *n* **1** [C] a warm piece of clothing like a coat without sleeves **2** [singular] *disapproving* an organization or activity that deliberately keeps something secret: *a cloak for terrorist activities*

cloak² *v* [T usually passive] **1** to deliberately hide facts, feelings etc so that people do not see or understand them – used especially in news reports: *The talks have been **cloaked in secrecy**.* **2** *literary* to cover something, for example with darkness or snow

cloakroom /'kləʊkrʊm, -ruːm $ 'kloʊk-/ *n* [C] a small room where you can leave your coat, bag etc

clobber /'klɒbə $ 'klɑːbər/ *v* [T] *informal* **1** to hit someone hard **2** to defeat someone easily **3** to affect someone badly: *The steel industry was clobbered in the recession.*

clock¹ /klɒk $ klɑːk/ *n*

1 [C] an instrument that shows the time. Clocks are fixed on a wall or kept in a room: *What time does that clock say?* | **set a clock** (=adjust a clock so that it shows the correct time) *Mary set her **alarm clock** for 7.00 a.m.* | *The clock had stopped.* | **the clock is slow/fast** (=is showing an earlier or a later time than it should) | *the **ticking** of the clock* (=the sound it makes) | **by the church/bedside/kitchen etc clock** (=according to a particular clock) *It was 5.30 am by the kitchen clock.* | *The church clock **struck** three* (=rang three times, to show that it was three o'clock.) | **put the clocks forward/back** *BrE* (=change the time shown on a clock by one hour. In Britain, people have to do this twice a year.)

clock

alarm clock

2 around the clock round the clock *BrE* all day and all night without stopping: *Rescue teams worked around the clock.*
3 against the clock if you do something against the clock, you do it as fast as possible, because you do not have much time
4 turn/put the clock back to make a situation the same as it was in the past: *It's feared the new law will turn the clock back 50 years.*
5 [C] an instrument in a vehicle that tells you how far it has travelled or how fast it is going → O'CLOCK

clock² *v* [T] **1** to measure the speed at which someone or something is moving: *The police clocked him at 160 kilometres an hour.* **2** to cover a distance or reach a speed in a particular time: *Karen won the race, clocking 49.2 seconds.*

clock up sth *phr v* to reach a number or amount: *We clocked up 125,000 miles on our old car.*

clock-'radio *n* [C] a radio with a clock that you can set so that the clock wakes you up

clockwise /'klɒk-waɪz $ 'klɑːk-/ *adj, adv* in the same direction in which the hands of a clock move [≠ **anticlockwise, counter-clockwise**]: *Turn the dial clockwise.*

clockwork /'klɒk-wɜːk $ 'klɑːk-wɜːrk/ *n* **1 go/run like clockwork** to happen in exactly the way you planned: *The fire drill went like clockwork.* **2 (as) regular as clockwork** always happening in the same way at the same time **3** *BrE* [U] clockwork toys have parts inside that move when you turn a key

clog¹ /klɒg $ klɑːg/ also **clog up** *v* [I,T] **clogged, clogging** to block something completely: **clog sth up** *Leaves had clogged up the drain.*

clog² *n* [C] a shoe made of wood → see picture at **SHOE**¹

cloister /'klɔɪstə $ -ər/ *n* [C] a covered path between a church building and a garden

clone /kləʊn $ kloʊn/ *n* [C] *technical* an exact copy of an animal or plant, that scientists produce from one of its cells —**clone** *v* [T] *Scientists have managed to clone a sheep.*

close¹ /kləʊz $ kloʊz/ *v* [I,T]

1 to shut something, or to become shut [= **shut**; ≠ **open**]: *Do you mind if I close the window?* | *He closed the lid of the box.* | *The door closed quietly behind her.* | *Close your eyes and go to sleep.* → see box at OPEN
2 if a shop or building closes, or if someone closes it, it shuts for some time: *What time does the library close tonight?*
3 to stop existing or operating, or to stop something from existing or operating: *The factory closed last month.* | *I've closed my bank account.*
4 to finish something, or to finish: **close (sth) with sth** *He closed his speech with a quotation.*
5 close the gap to make the distance or difference between two things smaller: *an attempt to close the gap between rich and poor*
6 close a deal/sale/contract to successfully agree a business deal

close down *phr v* if a shop or business closes down, it stops existing: *The cinema will close down next year.* | **close sth ⇔ down** *They closed down their London offices last year.*

close in *phr v* **1** to move closer to someone or something, especially in order to attack them: **+on** *Rebel soldiers are closing in on the town.* **2** if night closes in, it starts to get dark

close sth ⇔ **off** *phr v* if a road or area is closed off, people cannot go into it

close² /kləʊs $ kloʊs/ *adj, adv*

1 not far from someone or something [➙ **closely**]: **+to** *The house was close to the beach.* | *The closest shops are a mile away.* | **+together** *They sat close together.* | **+behind** *I followed close behind.* | *Her parents lived **close by** (=near).* | *Close up* (=from a short distance), *he was less attractive.* | **at close range/quarters** (=from a short distance) → see box at NEAR → and LOCALLY
2 near to something in time: **+to** *It was close to midnight.* | **+together** *Our birthdays are quite close together.*
3 near to a number: **+to** *Inflation is now close to 6%.* | *They've been married for **close on** twenty years* (=nearly twenty years).
4 if you are close to something, you are likely to experience it soon: **close to (doing) sth** *They are close to agreeing a deal.* | *She was **close to tears**.* | *He **came close to death*** (=he almost died).

C

5 [only before noun] giving careful attention to something: *Pay close attention to this.* | *Take a closer look.* | *Keep a close eye on him.*
6 if people are close, they like or love each other very much: *We were very close friends.* | **+to** *Are you close to your sister?*
7 relating to a situation in which people work or talk well together: **close ties/links/ cooperation/relationship** *The government would seek closer ties with Europe.* | *She has kept in close contact with him over the years.*
8 a close competition or game is won or lost by only a few points
9 **(you're) close** *spoken* used to tell someone that they almost have the correct answer: *'He looks about 40.' 'You're close – he's 39.'*
10 **a close shave/thing/call** a lucky escape from a bad situation
11 **close relations/relatives/family** family members such as your parents, brother, or sister
12 *BrE* if the weather is close, it is warm and uncomfortable
—**closeness** *n* [U]

close³ /kləʊz $ kloʊz/ *n* [singular] the end of an activity or period of time: *The summer was drawing to a close.* | *It's time to bring the meeting to a close.* | **at the close of sth** *I was sent to Spain at the close of the war.*

closed /kləʊzd $ kloʊzd/ *adj*
1 not open [= shut]: *She kept her eyes tightly closed.* | *The door was firmly closed.*
2 if a shop or public building is closed, it is not open and people cannot go into it or use it [= shut]
3 restricted to a particular group of people or things [≠ open]: *a closed meeting*
4 **behind closed doors** privately, without involving other people: *The deal was made behind closed doors.*
5 not willing to accept new ideas or influences [≠ open]: *Don't go with a closed mind.*

,closed circuit 'television *n* [C,U] abbreviation *CCTV* cameras which are used in public places to help prevent crime

close-knit /,kləʊs 'nɪt◂ $,kloʊs-/ also **,closely-'knit** *adj* a close-knit family or group of people know each other well and help each other a lot

closely /'kləʊsli/ *adv* **1** very carefully: *I was watching him closely.* | *a closely guarded secret* **2** if you work closely with someone, you work with them and help them **3** **closely related/connected etc** having a strong connection: *The two problems are closely related.* **4** **follow closely** to happen soon after something else: *a flash of lightning followed closely by thunder*

close-set /,kləʊs 'set◂ $,kloʊs-/ *adj* close-set eyes are very near to each other

closet¹ /'klɒzᵻt $ 'klɑː-, 'klɔː-/ *n* [C] *especially AmE* a cupboard for keeping clothes in [= wardrobe *BrE*] → see box at **CLOTHES**

closet² *adj* [only before noun] used to describe someone who keeps their true opinions or way of life a secret: *a closet fascist*

close-up /'kləʊs ʌp $ 'kloʊs-/ *n* [C,U] a photograph that is taken from very near to someone or something

closing /'kləʊzɪŋ $ 'kloʊ-/ *adj* happening or done at the end of something: *the closing stages*

of the race | *his closing speech to the conference* | *The closing date* (=last possible date) *for applications is today.*

closure /'kləʊʒə $ 'kloʊʒər/ *n* **1** [C,U] when an institution, building, or road is closed: **+of** *the closure of the hospital* **2** [U] when a bad situation has ended and you can stop thinking about it

clot /klɒt $ klɑːt/ *n* [C] a mass of blood which has become almost solid —**clot** *v* [I,T]

cloth /klɒθ $ klɔːθ/ *n*
1 [U] material used for making clothes and other things: **cotton/woollen/silk cloth** *a coat made of thick woollen cloth*

Do not use **cloth** or **cloths** to mean 'things that you wear'. Use **clothes**: *My favourite clothes are jeans and a T-shirt.* | *a clothes shop*

2 [C] a piece of cloth that you use for cleaning things: *Wipe the surface with a damp cloth.*

clothe /kləʊð $ kloʊð/ *v* [T] to provide clothes for someone: *He needed money to feed and clothe his children.*

clothed /kləʊðd $ kloʊðd/ *adj formal* dressed: *He was fully clothed.*

clothes /kləʊðz, kləʊz $ kloʊðz, kloʊz/ *n* [plural] things such as shirts, skirts, or trousers that people wear: *He got up and put on his clothes.* | *She took off her clothes.* | *She was wearing her new clothes.* | **work/school clothes** | *Bring a change of clothes.* → **PLAIN-CLOTHES**

THESAURUS

tight: *tight jeans*
loose/baggy: *a baggy T-shirt*
fashionable: *fashionable clothes*
smart: *a smart suit*
casual: *casual dress* (=clothes that are comfortable and informal)
scruffy (=dirty and untidy): *scruffy shoes*
skimpy (=not covering much of the body): *a skimpy little dress*

TOPIC

You **look at clothes** in a shop and then **try** them **on**. You want to be sure that they **fit** you (=are the right size), and also that they **suit** you (=look nice on you). At home you **fold** them and put them in a drawer, or you **hang** them **up**, usually in a **wardrobe** *BrE* /**closet** *AmE*. If clothes are **creased** (=have lines in the material), you have to **iron** them. → **CLOTH**

GRAMMAR

There is no singular form of **clothes**. You have to say **a piece of clothing**, **an article of clothing**, or **an item of clothing**: *She picked up each piece of clothing and folded it carefully.*

clothesline /'kləʊðzlaɪn, 'kləʊz- $ 'kloʊðz-, 'kloʊz-/ *n* [C] a rope that you hang clothes on so that they will dry

'clothes peg *BrE*; **clothes pin** /'kləʊðzpɪn, 'kləʊz- $ 'kloʊðz-, 'kloʊz-/ *AmE n* [C] a small object that you use to fasten clothes to a clothesline

clothes

shirt

T-shirt

jacket

jumper

sweatshirt

skirt

waterproof jacket

dress

coat

gloves

tie

scarf

belt

socks

bra

boxer shorts

jeans

trousers BrE/ pants AmE

dungarees BrE/ overalls AmE

shorts

knickers BrE/ panties AmE

tracksuit

underpants

---

clothing /'kləʊðɪŋ $ 'kloʊ-/ n [U] *formal* clothes: *It's cold, so wear warm clothing.* | *I had brought a few **items of clothing**.*

clouds

cloud¹ /klaʊd/ n

1 [C,U] a white or grey mass in the sky, from which rain falls: *There were no clouds in the sky.* | ***Black clouds** were gathering overhead.* | ***Storm clouds** hung low over the island.*

2 [C] a mass of smoke, dust, or gas: **+of** *a huge cloud of dust*

3 [C] something that makes you feel worried or upset: **+of** *the cloud of economic recession* | *The*

only ***cloud on the horizon** was her mother's illness.* | ***every cloud has a silver lining*** (=every bad thing has a good side)

4 under a cloud affected by a bad or unpleasant situation: *He returned under a cloud of gloom and despair.*

5 on cloud nine *informal* very happy

6 be/live in cloud-cuckoo land to believe that a situation is much better than it really is

cloud² v **1** [T] to make it more difficult to form an opinion or to deal with a problem: *Don't allow personal feelings to **cloud** your **judgment**.* | *He should not be **clouding** the **issue** with irrelevant remarks.* **2** also **cloud up** [I,T] to become difficult to see through, or to make this happen: *The windows had clouded up.* | *Tears clouded his eyes.*

cloud over *phr v* if the sky clouds over, clouds appear or cover the sun

cloudless /'klaʊdləs/ *adj* a cloudless sky has no clouds

cloudy /'klaʊdi/ *adj*

1 if it is cloudy, there are a lot of clouds in the sky → see box at **SUN¹** → and **WEATHER¹**

2 a cloudy liquid is not clear: *The water looked cloudy.*

clout /klaʊt/ n informal **1** [U] the ability to influence important people: *He's still got some political clout.* **2** [singular] BrE when someone hits you

clove /kləʊv $ kloʊv/ n [C] **1** a piece of GARLIC **2** a strong sweet spice with a pointed stem

clover /'kləʊvə $ 'kloʊvər/ n [C] a small plant with three round leaves on each stem

clown[1] /klaʊn/ n [C] a person with a red nose, painted face, and funny clothes, whose job is to make people laugh

clown[2] also **clown around/about** v [I] to behave in a silly or funny way: *Stop clowning around!*

club[1] /klʌb/ n [C]

1 [also + plural verb BrE] an organization for people who share an interest or who enjoy similar activities: **football/rugby/golf etc club** | *I'm a member of the local drama club.* | *He's joined a health club.* | *She belongs to the tennis club.* | +**for** *a club for unemployed youngsters* | *The group has a huge fan club.* → see box at ORGANIZATION

2 the building used by a club: *We had lunch at the golf club.*

3 a place where people go to dance, listen to music, and meet socially: *Shall we go to a club?* | *a jazz club*

4 a stick used in golf to hit the ball [= golf club]

5 a heavy stick used as a weapon

6 clubs [plural] in card games, the cards with black symbols with three round parts: *the king of clubs* → see picture at PLAYING CARD, YOUTH CLUB

club[2] v [T] **clubbed, clubbing** to hit someone with a large heavy object: *The seals were clubbed to death.*

club together phr v if people club together, they all give money in order to pay for something together

clubbing /'klʌbɪŋ/ n [U] when people go to clubs to dance and be with friends: *She goes clubbing most weekends.*

clubhouse /'klʌbhaʊs/ n [C] the main building of a sports club where people can meet and talk

cluck /klʌk/ v [I] if a chicken clucks, it makes a short, low sound —**cluck** n [C]

clue /kluː/ n

1 [C] a piece of information or an object that helps to solve a crime or mystery: *The police are still searching for clues.* | +**(as) to** *He uncovered a clue as to her whereabouts.* | *The shoes could provide a clue to his identity.* | *I don't know – give me a clue!*

2 not have a clue informal to definitely not know or understand something: *'Where's Karen?' 'I haven't got a clue.'* | +**what/where/how etc** *I didn't have a clue what to do.*

clued-'up BrE; **clued-'in** AmE adj knowing a lot about something

clueless /'kluːləs/ adj disapproving having no understanding or knowledge of something

clump[1] /klʌmp/ n [C] a group of trees or plants growing together

clump[2] v [I + adv/prep] to walk with slow noisy steps

clumsy /'klʌmzi/ adj **1** moving in an awkward way often knocking things and making them fall over: *She was clumsy and shy.* **2** large, heavy,

and difficult to use: *big clumsy shoes* **3** if you say or do something in a clumsy way, you do it in a careless way, without considering other people's feelings: *Dave made a clumsy attempt to comfort us.* —**clumsily** adv —**clumsiness** n [U]

clung /klʌŋ/ v the past tense and past participle of CLING

cluster[1] /'klʌstə $ -ər/ n [C] a group of things that are close together: +**of** *a small cluster of buildings*

cluster[2] v [I,T] to form a group of people or things: +**around/round/together** *Everyone clustered around her.*

clutch[1] /klʌtʃ/ v [T] to hold something tightly: *She clutched her case.* | +**at** *She clutched at his arm* (=tried to hold it). → see box at HOLD

clutch[2] n [C] **1** the part of a car that you press with your foot to change GEAR → see picture on page A12 **2 sb's clutches** if you are in someone's clutches, they control you: *He was trying to escape his mother's clutches.* **3 a clutch of sth** a group of people or things

clutter[1] /'klʌtə $ -ər/ also **clutter up** v [T] to fill a space in an untidy way: *Piles of books cluttered up his desk.*

clutter[2] n [U] things that fill a space in an untidy way

cm the written abbreviation of **centimetre**

co- /kəʊ $ koʊ/ prefix with someone else, or together: *We co-wrote the book.*

c/o the written abbreviation of **care of**, used in addresses, for example when you are sending a letter to someone who is living in another person's house: *John Simms c/o Mrs R. Pearce*

Co. /kəʊ $ koʊ/ **1** the abbreviation of **Company**: *Hilton, Brooks & Co.* **2** the written abbreviation of **County**: *Co. Durham*

coach[1] /kəʊtʃ $ koʊtʃ/ n [C]

1 someone who trains a person or team in a sport: **basketball/football/tennis etc coach** → see box at TEACHER

2 BrE a bus with comfortable seats used for long journeys [= bus AmE]: **by coach** *We went to Paris by coach.* | **on a coach** *They came on a coach.* | **coach trip/tour**

3 BrE one of the parts of a train in which passengers sit [= car AmE]

4 a vehicle pulled by horses

coach[2] v [I,T] **1** to train a person or team in a sport: *He coaches the local football team.* **2** to give someone extra private lessons —**coaching** n [U]

coal /kəʊl $ koʊl/ n

1 [U] a hard black substance that you can burn to provide heat: *Put some coal on the fire.* | *a lump of coal* | *a coal fire*

2 coals [plural] burning pieces of coal

3 haul/rake sb over the coals to speak angrily to someone who has done something wrong

coalition /ˌkəʊəˈlɪʃən $ ˌkoʊə-/ n [C,U] when two or more groups work together, usually in politics: *The two parties have decided to form a coalition.* | *a coalition government*

coarse /kɔːs $ kɔːrs/ adj **1** rough and thick, not smooth or fine: *a coarse woollen blanket* **2** rude and offensive —**coarsely** adv —**coarseness** n [U]

coast[1] /kəʊst $ koʊst/ n [C]

1 the land next to the sea: +**of** *the west coast of Africa* | **on the coast** *They've rented a cottage on the coast.* | **off the coast** (=in the water near the land) *a small island off the coast* → see box at **SHORE**

2 the coast is clear if the coast is clear, there is no one around in a place, so no one will see you or catch you

coast[2] v [I] **1** to achieve something without effort: +**to** *He coasted to an easy victory.* **2** to move forward without using the engine of a car

coastal /ˈkəʊstl $ ˈkoʊstl/ adj [only before noun] near the coast: **coastal waters** | *a coastal town*

'coast guard n [C] a person or organization that helps people in danger on the sea

coastline /ˈkəʊstlaɪn $ ˈkoʊst-/ n [C,U] the land along the edge of the sea

coat[1] /kəʊt $ koʊt/ n [C]

1 a piece of clothing that you wear over other clothes to keep you warm when you go outside: *Put your coat on if you're going out.* → see picture at **CLOTHES**

2 a piece of clothing that a doctor wears over other clothes

3 an animal's fur

4 a layer of a substance such as paint: +**of** *a coat of varnish*

coat[2] v [T] to cover a surface with a layer of something: **coat sth with/in sth** *The books were coated with dust.*

coating /ˈkəʊtɪŋ $ ˈkoʊ-/ n [C] a layer of something that covers a surface: +**of** *a light coating of snow*

,coat of 'arms n [C] plural **coats of arms** a design that is the symbol of a family, town, or institution

coax /kəʊks $ koʊks/ v [T] to gently persuade someone to do something: **coax sb into doing sth** *We managed to coax him into eating something.* | **coax sb down/out/back etc** *Firefighters coaxed the man down.*

cobble /ˈkɒbəl $ ˈkɑː-/ also **cobblestone** /ˈkɒbəlstəʊn $ ˈkɑːbəlstoʊn/ n [C usually plural] a round stone that was used in the past for making road surfaces —**cobbled** adj: *cobbled streets*

cobbler /ˈkɒblə $ ˈkɑːblər/ n [C,U] old-fashioned someone whose job is to make or repair shoes

cobra /ˈkəʊbrə $ ˈkoʊ-/ n [C] a poisonous snake that can make its neck look wider when it is going to attack something

cobweb /ˈkɒbweb $ ˈkɑːb-/ n [C] a structure of fine threads made by a SPIDER

cocaine /kəʊˈkeɪn, kə- $ koʊ-/ n [U] an illegal drug

cock[1] /kɒk $ kɑːk/ n [C] **1** BrE a male chicken [= **rooster** AmE] **2** a rude word for a PENIS

cock[2] v [T] **1** to raise or move part of your head or face: *John cocked his head to one side.* **2 cock a snook at sb/sth** BrE to show clearly that you do not respect someone or something

cockerel /ˈkɒkərəl $ ˈkɑː-/ n [C] a male chicken

,cock-'eyed adj informal **1** not sensible or practical: *a cock-eyed idea* **2** not straight or level: *His hat was all cockeyed.*

cockney /ˈkɒkni $ ˈkɑːk-/ n **1** [C] a person from East London **2** [U] the form of English used by people from East London

cockpit /ˈkɒkˌpɪt $ ˈkɑːk-/ n [C] the part of a plane where the pilot sits → see picture at **AEROPLANE**

cockroach /ˈkɒkrəʊtʃ $ ˈkɑːkroʊtʃ/ n [C] a large insect that sometimes lives in places where there is food

cocktail /ˈkɒkteɪl $ ˈkɑːk-/ n **1** [C] an alcoholic drink which is a mixture of different drinks: *a cocktail party* **2 fruit/seafood/prawn cocktail** a mixture of fruit, SEAFOOD, etc **3** [C] a powerful or dangerous combination: +**of** *a poisonous cocktail of gases*

'cock-up n [C] BrE spoken informal a rude word for a mistake

cocky /ˈkɒki $ ˈkɑːki/ adj informal too confident, in a way which people do not like —**cockiness** n [U]

cocoa /ˈkəʊkəʊ $ ˈkoʊkoʊ/ n [U] **1** brown powder that tastes of chocolate **2** a hot chocolate drink

coconut /ˈkəʊkənʌt $ ˈkoʊ-/ n [C,U] a very large brown nut which is white inside and has liquid in the middle → see picture at **FRUIT**

cocoon[1] /kəˈkuːn/ n [C] **1** a silk cover around an insect **2** a situation in which you feel safe: *the cocoon of a loving family*

cocoon[2] v [T] to protect or surround someone: *She lay cocooned in her warm bed.*

cod /kɒd $ kɑːd/ n [C,U] plural **cod** a large sea fish that you can eat

code[1] /kəʊd $ koʊd/ n

1 [C] a set of rules or principles: *She followed a strict **moral code**.* | **code of conduct/behaviour** | **code of practice/ethics** (=rules that people in a particular business agree to obey)

2 [C] a set of numbers, letters, or symbols that gives information about something: *Please write the product code number on your order form.*

3 [C,U] a system of words, letters, or symbols, used instead of ordinary writing to keep something secret: **in code** *The messages were written in code.* | *a secret code* | *It took several months to crack the enemy's code* (=to understand it).

4 also **dialling code** [C] BrE the part of a telephone number that you use for a particular area or country [= **area code** AmE]: +**for** *The code for Manchester is 0161.*

→ AREA CODE, BAR CODE, ZIP CODE

code[2] v [T] to use a code to show something: *All the information was coded and entered into the computer.*

coded /ˈkəʊdɪd $ ˈkoʊ-/ adj using a system for giving information, for example with letters, symbols, or colours: *a coded message*

co-ed /ˌkəʊ ˈed◂ $ ˌkoʊ ed/ adj a co-ed school is one in which boys and girls study together

coerce /kəʊˈɜːs $ ˈkoʊɜːrs/ v [T] formal to force someone to do something by threatening them: *He was coerced into signing.* —**coercion** /kəʊˈɜːʃən $ koʊˈɜːrʒən/ n [U]

coexist /ˌkəʊɪɡˈzɪst $ ˌkoʊ-/ v [I] to exist together: +**with** *People can coexist with animals.* —**coexistence** n [U]

coffee /ˈkɒfi $ ˈkɒːfi, ˈkɑːfi/ n

1 [U] a hot dark brown drink that has a slightly bitter taste: *I don't like coffee.* | *Would you like a cup of coffee?* | **black/white coffee** (=without/with milk)

2 [C] *BrE* a cup of coffee: *Who wants a coffee?* | **black/white coffee** (=without/with milk) *Two black coffees, please.*

3 [U] whole coffee beans, crushed coffee beans, or a powder from which you make coffee: *a jar of coffee* | **instant coffee** (=coffee powder) | **real coffee** (=(crushed) coffee beans)

4 [U] a light brown colour: *a coffee-coloured blouse*

ˈcoffee ˌtable n [C] a low table in a LIVING ROOM

coffers /ˈkɒfəz $ ˈkɒːfərz, ˈkɑː-/ n [plural] the money that an organization has: *The firm's coffers are empty.*

coffin /ˈkɒfɪ̆n $ ˈkɒː-, ˈkɑː-/ n [C] a box in which a dead person is put [= casket *AmE*]

cog /kɒg $ kɑːg/ n [C] **1** a wheel that turns in a machine and makes another wheel turn **2 a cog in the wheel/machine** one of many people in an organization or situation

cogent /ˈkəʊdʒənt $ ˈkoʊ-/ adj formal a cogent explanation or opinion is clear and reasonable, and people will believe it

cognac /ˈkɒnjæk $ ˈkoʊ-, ˈkɑː-/ n [C,U] a strong alcoholic drink from France [= brandy]

cognitive /ˈkɒgnɪ̆tɪv $ ˈkɑːg-/ adj formal relating to the process of knowing, understanding, and learning something —**cognitively** adv

cohabit /kəʊˈhæbɪ̆t $ koʊ-/ v [I] formal to live as husband and wife, without being married —**cohabitation** /kəʊˌhæbɪ̆ˈteɪʃən $ koʊ-/ n [U]

coherent /kəʊˈhɪərənt $ koʊˈhɪr-/ adj **1** clear and easy to understand: *He put forward a coherent argument in favour of stricter laws.* **2** if someone is coherent, they are talking in a way that is easy to understand: *He was slightly drunk, and not very coherent.* **3** something that is coherent has parts that go together well: *They are not a coherent group.* —**coherently** adv

cohesion /kəʊˈhiːʒən $ koʊ-/ n [U] when all the people in a group are united and work together well

coil¹ /kɔɪl/ also **coil up** v [I,T] to wind or twist into a round shape, or to make something do this: *The snake coiled around the branch.* | *I coiled the rope around a post.*

coil² n [C] a piece of wire or rope that has been wound into a circular shape

coin¹ /kɔɪn/ n [C]

1 a round piece of money made of metal [➙ note, bill]: *a pound coin* → see box at MONEY

2 the other side of the coin a different fact or way of thinking about something

3 two sides of the same coin two ideas which are closely related

4 toss/flip a coin to decide something by throwing a coin into the air and guessing which side will show when it falls: *Let's flip a coin to see who goes first.*

coin² v [T] to invent a new word or phrase that many people start to use: *Who first coined the term 'acid rain'?*

coincide /ˌkəʊɪ̆nˈsaɪd $ ˌkoʊ-/ v [I] to happen at the same time as something else: **+with** *The show was timed to coincide with the launch of the book.*

coincidence /kəʊˈɪnsɪ̆dəns $ koʊ-/ n [C,U] when two things happen together, in a surprising way: *It was pure coincidence that we were on the same train.* | **by coincidence** *By coincidence, he was in London at the same time as I was.* | *It's no coincidence that most of the protesters are women.* —**coincidental** /kəʊˌɪnsɪ̆ˈdentl $ koʊ-/ adj —**coincidentally** adv

colander /ˈkʌləndə, ˈkɒ- $ ˈkʌləndər, ˈkɑː-/ n [C] a bowl with a lot of small holes in it, used for washing food or separating liquid from food

cold¹ /kəʊld $ koʊld/ adj

1 something that is cold has a low temperature [≠ hot, warm]: *The house was cold and empty.* | *We slept on the cold ground.* | *a blast of cold air* | **ice/stone/freezing cold** (=very cold) *freezing cold water* | *My coffee's gone cold.* | **be/feel/look/get cold** *I feel so cold!* | *It's cold outside.* | *The day was bitterly cold.*

2 cold food is cooked, but is not eaten hot: *a cold buffet* | *Serve the potatoes cold.*

3 without friendly feelings [≠ warm]: *a polite but cold greeting*

4 get/have cold feet informal to start to feel that you are not brave enough to do something: *She was getting cold feet about getting married.*

5 leave sb cold if something leaves you cold, you are not at all interested in it: *Most poetry leaves me cold.*

6 in cold blood in a cruel and deliberate way: *innocent civilians murdered in cold blood*

7 give sb the cold shoulder informal to deliberately ignore someone or be unfriendly to them, especially because they have upset or offended you
—**coldness** n [U]

cold² n

1 [C] a common illness that makes you cough, and makes it difficult to breathe through your nose: *I've got a bad cold.* | *Keep your feet dry so you don't catch a cold.*

2 [U] when you feel cold: *I was shivering with cold.*

3 the cold cold weather: *Come in out of the cold.*

4 be left out in the cold informal to not be included in an activity: *Anyone who didn't join the gang was left out in the cold.*

cold³ adv **1 out cold** informal unconscious **2** *AmE* suddenly and completely: *In the middle of his speech, he stopped cold.*

cold-blooded /ˌkəʊld 'blʌdɪd◂ $ ˌkoʊld-/ *adj*
1 cruel and showing no feelings: *a cold-blooded killer* **2** a cold-blooded animal, such as a snake, has a body temperature that changes with the temperature around it [➡ **warm-blooded**] —**cold-bloodedly** *adv*

cold-hearted /ˌkəʊld 'hɑːtɪd◂ $ ˌkoʊld 'hɑːr-/ *adj* showing no kindness or sympathy: *a cold-hearted man*

coldly /'kəʊldli $ 'koʊld-/ *adv* in a very unfriendly way: *Jan looked at her coldly.*

cold 'turkey *n* **go cold turkey** to feel ill because you have stopped taking a drug that you are ADDICTED to

coleslaw /'kəʊlslɔː $ 'koʊlslɒ:/ *n* [U] a SALAD made with thinly cut raw vegetables

colic /'kɒlɪk $ 'kɑː-/ *n* [U] pain in the stomach that babies often get

collaborate /kə'læbəreɪt/ *v* [I] **1** to work together to produce or achieve something: **+with** *She often collaborates with other writers.* | **+on** *Two companies collaborated on this project.* **2** to help an enemy army or government that controls your country: **+with** *It seems that he collaborated with the secret police.* —**collaborator** *n* [C] —**collaboration** /kəˌlæbə'reɪʃən/ *n* [U] —**collaborative** /kə'læbərətɪv $ -reɪ-/ *adj*

collage /'kɒlɑːʒ $ kə'lɑːʒ/ *n* [C,U] a picture made by sticking pieces of paper, cloth etc onto a surface, or the art of making pictures in this way

collapse¹ /kə'læps/ *v* [I] **1** to fall down suddenly: *Many buildings collapsed during the earthquake.* **2** to suddenly fall down or become unconscious because you are ill or very weak: *He collapsed with a dangerously high fever.* **3** to fail suddenly and completely: *The luxury car market has collapsed.*

collapse² *n* [C,U] **1** the sudden failure of a business, system, or plan: **+of** *the collapse of the Soviet Union* | *economic collapse* **2** when something suddenly falls down: *Floods caused the collapse of the bridge.* **3** when someone suddenly falls down or becomes unconscious because of an illness or injury: *The prisoner was in a state of collapse.*

collapsible /kə'læpsɪbəl/ *adj* something collapsible can be folded so that it can be stored or carried: *a collapsible table*

collar¹ /'kɒlə $ 'kɑːlər/ *n* [C]
1 the part of a shirt, coat, dress etc that fits around your neck: *a dress with a white collar*
2 a narrow band of leather or plastic that is fastened around an animal's neck
➔ **BLUE-COLLAR, WHITE-COLLAR**

collar² *v* [T] *informal* to catch and hold someone: *Two policemen collared him before he could get away.*

collarbone /'kɒləbəʊn $ 'kɑːlərboʊn/ *n* [C] one of the bones that go from the base of your neck to your shoulders ➔ see picture on page A3

collateral /kə'lætərəl/ *n* [U] *technical* property or money that you promise to give to someone if you cannot pay back a debt: *He offered his house as collateral for the loan.*

colleague /'kɒliːg $ 'kɑː-/ *n* [C] someone you work with: *my colleagues at the bank* ➔ see box at **WORK**

collect¹ /kə'lekt/ *v*
1 [T] to get things and bring them together: *I'll collect everyone's papers at the end of the test.*
2 [T] to keep objects of the same type because they interest you: *Ann collects teddy bears.*
3 [I,T] to ask people to give money for a particular purpose: **+for** *I'm collecting for Children in Need.*
4 [I] to come together in a place: *A crowd had collected at the scene of the accident.*
5 [T] *especially BrE* to go to a particular place and bring someone or something away [= **pick up**]: **collect sb from sth** *Can you collect the kids from school?*
6 collect yourself/your thoughts to make yourself calmer and able to think more clearly: *I want to collect my thoughts before the meeting begins.*

collect² *adj, adv AmE* **1 call/phone sb collect** if you call someone collect, the person who gets the telephone call pays for it [= **reverse the charges** *BrE*] **2 collect call** a telephone call that is paid for by the person who gets it

collected /kə'lektɪd/ *adj* **1** [only before noun] **collected poems/stories etc** all the poems, stories etc of a particular writer included together in one book: *the collected works of Shakespeare* **2** calm and in control of yourself and your thoughts and feelings

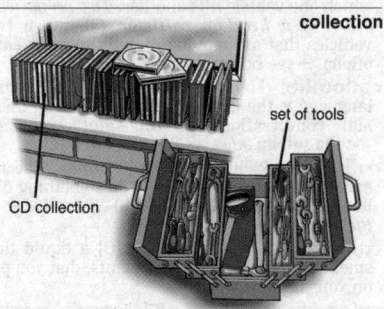

collection

set of tools

CD collection

collection /kə'lekʃən/ *n*
1 [C] a set of objects of the same type that you keep because they interest you: *my CD collection* | **+of** *a fine collection of paintings*
2 [U] when you bring together things of the same type from different places: **+of** *the collection of reliable information*
3 [C,U] when you ask people for money for a particular purpose: **+for** *a collection for cancer research*
4 [C,U] when something is taken away from a place: *Garbage collections are made every Tuesday.*
5 [singular] *informal* a group of people that are together in the same place: **+of** *There was an odd collection of people at the party.*

collective¹ /kə'lektɪv/ *adj* [only before noun] shared by every member of a group or society: *a collective decision* | *our collective responsibility for the environment* —**collectively** *adv*

collective² *n* [C] a business or organization owned and controlled by the people who work in it

collector /kə'lektə $ -ər/ n [C] **1 ticket/tax/debt etc collector** someone whose job is to collect tickets or money from people **2** someone who collects things that are interesting to them: *a stamp collector*

college /'kɒlɪdʒ $ 'kɑː-/ n

1 [C,U] a school for advanced education, especially in a particular profession or skill: *an art college* | **at college** *We were great friends at college.* | *I went to college in 1998.*
2 [C,U] AmE a university: *college students*
3 [C] a part of a university, especially in Britain: *King's College, Cambridge*
→ COMMUNITY COLLEGE, JUNIOR COLLEGE

GRAMMAR

Do not use 'a' or 'the' before **college** when you are talking about the time when someone is studying there: *They met while they were at college together.*

collide /kə'laɪd/ v [I] to crash violently into something or someone [→ **collision**]: *The two trains collided in a tunnel.* | **+with** *Her car collided with a lorry.*

colliery /'kɒljəri $ 'kɑːl-/ n [C] plural **collieries** BrE a coal mine and the buildings and machinery connected with it

collision /kə'lɪʒən/ n [C,U] a violent crash in which one vehicle hits another: *Two people were killed in a **head-on collision** (=between two vehicles that are moving directly towards each other).* → see box at ACCIDENT

colloquial /kə'ləʊkwiəl $ -'loʊ-/ adj colloquial language is the kind of language used in informal conversations: *a colloquial expression* —**colloquially** adv —**colloquialism** n [C]

collusion /kə'luːʒən/ n [U] formal a secret agreement between people to do something dishonest —**collude** /kə'luːd/ v [I] *She colluded in the plot.*

cologne /kə'ləʊn $ 'loʊn/ n [U] a liquid that smells slightly of flowers or plants, that you put on your neck or wrists

colon /'kəʊlən $ 'koʊ-/ n [C] the mark (:) used in writing to introduce a list or an example

colonel /'kɜːnl $ 'kɜːr-/ n [C] an officer with a high rank in the Army, Marines, or the US Air Force

colonial /kə'ləʊniəl $ -'loʊ-/ adj relating to colonialism or a colony: *the struggle against colonial rule*

colonialism /kə'ləʊniəlɪzəm $ -'loʊ-/ n [U] the system by which a powerful country rules another less powerful country [→ **imperialism**] —**colonialist** adj, n [C]

colonize also -**ise** BrE /'kɒlənaɪz $ 'kɑː-/ v [T] to get control of another country or area and make it a colony: *Australia was colonized in the 18th century.* —**colonist** n [C] —**colonization** /ˌkɒlənaɪˈzeɪʃən $ ˌkɑːlənə-/ n [U]

colony /'kɒləni $ 'kɑː-/ n [C] plural **colonies** **1** a country or area that is controlled by a more powerful country: *Algeria was formerly a French colony.* **2** a group of people with the same interests who live together: *an artists' colony* **3** a group of the same kind of animals living together: *an ant colony*

color /'kʌlə $ -ər/ n, v the American spelling of COLOUR

colossal /kə'lɒsəl $ kə'lɑː-/ adj extremely large: *They've run up colossal debts.*

colour¹ BrE; **color** AmE /'kʌlə $ -ər/ n

1 [C,U] red, blue, yellow etc: *What colour is your new car?* | *the colours of the rainbow* | **light/dark/bright etc colour** *houses painted in bright colours* | **in colour** *The meat should be pale pink in colour.* | *The sky slowly changed colour.*
2 [U] the quality of having colour: *flowers that will add colour to your garden*
3 colour photograph/film/television etc a photograph, film etc that shows all the different colours, not just black and white [≠ **black and white**]
4 [C,U] how dark or light someone's skin is: *people of all colours*
5 [U] the appearance of someone's skin, that shows how healthy they are: *The fresh air has brought some colour to her cheeks.*
6 [U] interesting or exciting qualities: *a story full of life, colour, and adventure*
7 colours [plural] the colours that are used to represent a team, school, club, country etc: *Australia's national colours are gold and green.*
→ OFF-COLOUR, PRIMARY COLOUR

colour² BrE; **color** AmE v [T] **1** to make something a particular colour: *Do you colour your hair or is it natural?* **2** also **colour in** to use paint, pencils etc to put colours inside the lines of a picture: *Draw a picture and colour it in.* **3 colour sb's judgment/opinion etc** to influence someone's opinion about something: *Personal feelings coloured his judgment.*

'colour-blind BrE; **color-blind** AmE adj not able to see the difference between some colours —**colour-blindness** n [U]

coloured BrE; **colored** AmE /'kʌləd $ -ərd/ adj having a colour or colours other than black or white: *coloured glass* | *a brightly-coloured shirt*

colourful BrE; **colorful** AmE /'kʌləfəl $ -lər-/ adj **1** having a lot of bright colours: *a garden full of colourful flowers* | *colourful costumes* **2** interesting, exciting, and full of variety: *He's led a very colourful life.*

colouring BrE; **coloring** AmE /'kʌlərɪŋ/ n **1** [U] the colour of someone's hair, skin, and eyes: *Mandy had her mother's dark colouring.* **2** [C,U] a substance used to give a particular colour to food: *green **food colouring***

colourless BrE; **colorless** AmE /'kʌlələs $ 'kʌlər-/ adj **1** having no colour: *a colourless liquid* **2** not interesting or exciting: *a colourless little man*

colt /kəʊlt $ koʊlt/ n [C] a young male horse

column /'kɒləm $ 'kɑː-/ n [C]

1 a tall, solid, upright, stone post used to support a building: *the marble columns of a Greek temple*
2 numbers or words written under each other down a page [→ **row**]: *Add up the numbers in each column.* | **+of** *a column of figures*
3 lines of print that go down the page of a newspaper or book
4 an article on a particular subject that appears regularly in a newspaper or magazine: *He writes a weekly column for 'The Times'.* | *a gardening column* → see box at NEWSPAPER

5 something with a long narrow shape: **+of** *a column of smoke*
6 a long moving line of people or vehicles: **+of** *a column of soldiers on the march*
→ GOSSIP COLUMN

columnist /'kɒləmɪˌst, -ləmnɪˌst $ 'kɑː-/ *n* [C] someone who regularly writes articles for a newspaper or magazine → see box at NEWSPAPER

coma /'kəʊmə $ 'koʊ-/ *n* [C,U] someone who is in a coma has been unconscious for a long time, usually because of a serious illness or injury: **in a coma** *Ben was in a coma for six days.*

comb¹ /kəʊm $ koʊm/ *n*

1 [C] a piece of plastic or metal with a row of thin teeth, that you use to make your hair tidy [➡ brush]
2 [singular] when you use a comb: *Your hair needs a good comb.*

comb² *v* [T] **1** to make your hair tidy with a comb: *Have you combed your hair?* **2** to search a place thoroughly: **comb sth for sth** *Police are combing the area for more bombs.*

combat¹ /'kɒmbæt $ 'kɑːm-/ *n* [C,U] fighting during a war: **in combat** *Her husband was killed in combat.* | **unarmed combat** (=without weapons)

combat² /'kɒmbæt, kəm'bæt $ kəm'bæt, 'kɑːmbæt/ *v* [T] combated or combatted, combating or combatting to try to stop something bad from happening or getting worse: *new technology to combat crime* | *measures to combat inflation*

combatant /'kɒmbətənt $ kəm'bætɪnt/ *n* [C] someone who fights in a war

combative /'kɒmbətɪv $ kəm'bætɪv/ *adj* ready to fight or argue: *Paul was in a combative mood.*

combination /ˌkɒmbɪˈneɪʃən $ ˌkɑːm-/ *n*

1 [C,U] two or more different things that are used, put, or mixed together: **+of** *Doctors now treat this disease with a combination of drugs.* | *a combination of bad management and inexperience*
2 [C] a set of numbers or letters you need to open a combination lock

combi'nation lock *n* [C] a lock that is opened by using a special set of numbers or letters

combine /kəmˈbaɪn/ *v*

1 [I,T] to join or mix two or more things together: **combine sth with sth** *Combine the flour with the milk and eggs.* | **combined with sb/sth** *Diets are most effective when combined with exercise.* | *The combined effects of the war and the drought resulted in famine.*
2 [T] to do two different activities at the same time: **combine sth with/and sth** *She manages to combine family life with a career.*

combustible /kəmˈbʌstɪˌbəl/ *adj* technical able to burn easily: *Gasoline is highly combustible* .

combustion /kəmˈbʌstʃən/ *n* [U] the process of burning

come /kʌm/ *v* [I] past tense **came** /keɪm/ past participle **come**

1 to move towards you or arrive at the place where you are [≠ go]: **+in/into/out of etc** *A young woman came into the room.* | **+to/towards** *Someone was coming towards me.* | *Can you come here for a minute?* | *What time are you coming home?* | **come and do sth** *Come and*

have dinner with us. | **come to do sth** *I've come to see Phil.* | **here comes sb/sth** spoken (=used to say that someone or something is coming towards you) *Here comes Karen now.*
2 to travel to a place: *Which way did you come?* | **+to/from/through etc** *They came over the mountains in the north.* | **come by car/train/bus etc** *Did you come by car?*
3 if someone comes with you, they go to a place with you: **+with** *I asked her if she'd like to come with us.*
4 if a letter or package comes, it is delivered to you by post: *The phone bill came yesterday.*
5 if a time or event comes, it arrives or starts to happen: *Spring came early that year.* | *The time has come to make some changes.*
6 to be in particular position in an order, a series, or a list: **come first/second/last etc** *I came last in the cycle race.* | **+before/after** *What letter comes after 'u'?*
7 to reach a particular level or place: **+up/down** *The water only came up to my knees.*
8 to be produced or sold with particular features: **+in** *The sweaters come in four sizes.*
9 come open/undone/loose etc to become open etc: *Your shoelace has come undone.*
10 come to do sth to begin to have a feeling or opinion: *I came to believe that he was innocent after all.*
11 come as a surprise/shock etc to make someone feel surprised etc: *Her death came as a shock to everyone.*
12 come naturally/easily (to sb) to be easy for someone to do, say etc: *Acting came naturally to Rae.*
13 in (the) years/days etc to come in the future: *I think we shall regret this decision in the years to come.*
14 come to think of it spoken used to add something that you have just realized or remembered: *Come to think of it, Cooper did mention the accident to me.*
15 come and go a) to be allowed to go into and leave a place whenever you want: *Students come and go as they please.* b) to keep starting and stopping: *The pain comes and goes.*
16 come of age to reach the age when you are legally considered to be an adult
→ **how come?** at HOW¹

come about phr v to happen or develop: *How did this extraordinary situation come about?*

come across phr v **1 come across sb/sth** to meet or find someone or something by chance: *I came across an old diary in her desk.* **2** if someone comes across in a particular way, they seem to have particular qualities: **+as** *He comes across as a nice guy.*

come along phr v **1** to develop or improve: *Terry's work has really come along this year.* **2** to appear or arrive: *I'm ready to take any job that comes along.* **3** to follow someone or go with them: *Can I come along too?*

come apart phr v especially BrE to break into pieces: *The book just came apart in my hands.*

come around phr v AmE → COME ROUND

come at sb phr v to move towards someone in a threatening way: *She came at him with a knife.*

come away phr v BrE **1** to become separated from the main part of something: *I pulled, and the handle came away.* **2** to leave a place with a particular feeling or idea: *We came away thinking we had done quite well.*

come back *phr v* **1** to return: *When is your sister coming back from Europe?* **2** if something comes back to you, you suddenly remember it: **+to** *Then, everything William had said came back to me.* **3** to become fashionable or popular again [➔ **comeback**]: *Long skirts are coming back.*

come between sb *phr v* to cause trouble between people: *I didn't want the question of money to come between us.*

come by *phr v* **1 come by sth** to get something that is rare or difficult to find: *How did you come by these pictures?* | *Jobs are very **hard to come by** in the winter months.* **2** to visit someone for a short time: *Veronica came by to see me today.* → see box at **VISIT**

come down *phr v* **1** if a price or level comes down, it gets lower: *Wait until prices come down before you buy.* **2** to fall to the ground: *A lot of trees came down in the storm.*

come down on sb/sth *phr v* **1** to punish someone or criticize them severely: *We need to come down hard on young offenders.* **2 come down on the side of sb/sth** to decide to support something or someone: *The court came down on the side of the boy's father.*

come down to sth *phr v* if a complicated situation or problem comes down to something, that is the single most important thing: *It all comes down to money in the end.*

come down with sth *phr v* to get an illness: *I think I'm coming down with flu.*

come forward *phr v* to offer help to someone, or offer to do something: *Witnesses are asked to come forward with information about the robbery.*

come from sth *phr v* **1** to be born, obtained from, or made somewhere: *His mother came from Texas.* | *A lot of drugs come from quite common plants.* | *The idea came from America.* **2** to be the result of something: **come from doing sth** *Most of her problems come from expecting too much of people.*

come in *phr v* **1** to enter a place: *Come in and sit down.* **2** to arrive: *What time does your train come in?* **3** to be received: *Reports are coming in of an earthquake in Japan.* **4** to become fashionable or popular: *I remember when miniskirts first came in.* **5** to finish a race: **come in first/second etc** *His horse came in second to last.* **6 come in useful/handy** to be useful: *Bring some rope – it might come in handy.* **7** when the TIDE comes in, the sea moves towards the land and covers the edge of it

come in for sth *phr v* to receive something, especially something unpleasant: *After the riots the police came in for a lot of criticism.*

come into sth *phr v* **1** to be involved in something: *Where do I come into all this?* **2** to receive money or property from someone who has died: *I came into some money when my grandfather died.*

come of sth *phr v* to result from something: *We wanted to start a pop group, but nothing ever came of it.*

come off *phr v* **1 come off sth** to become removed from something: *A button had come off his coat.* **2** to happen as planned: *In the end the trip never came off.* **3** to succeed: *It was a good*

idea, but it didn't quite come off. **4 come off well/badly etc** to get into a good or bad situation as a result of something: *If we have an argument, I always come off worst.* **5 come off it!** *spoken* used to tell someone that you do not believe what they are saying: *Oh, come off it! Don't pretend you didn't know.*

come on *phr v* **1** to start working: *The lights suddenly came on in the cinema.* **2 come on!** *spoken* **a)** used to tell someone to hurry, or to encourage them to do something: *Come on! We'll be late.* | *Come on, it's not that hard.* **b)** used to tell someone that you do not believe them: *Oh come on, don't lie to me!* **3** if an illness comes on, you start to be ill with it: *I can feel a headache coming on.*

come out *phr v* **1** to become known: *The truth will come out one day.* **2** if a book, record etc comes out, it becomes available for people to buy: *When does his new book come out?* **3** to state your opinions clearly and directly: *Why don't you just come out and say what you really think?* **4** if something you say comes out in a particular way, that is how it sounds or how it is understood: *I tried to explain, but it came out all wrong.* **5** if dirt or a mark comes out, it is removed by washing or cleaning it **6** if a photograph comes out, it shows a clear picture: *The wedding photos came out really well.* **7** if the sun, moon, or stars come out, they appear in the sky

come out in sth *phr v* **come out in spots/a rash** *BrE* to become covered in spots because you are ill

come out with sth *phr v* to say something, especially something that is not expected: *Tanya comes out with some stupid remarks.*

come over *phr v* **1** to visit you at your house: *Can I come over to your place tonight?* → see box at **VISIT** **2 come over sb** if a feeling comes over you, it affects you strongly: *A wave of sleepiness came over her.* | *I'm sorry I was so rude – I don't know what came over me!* **3** if someone or something comes over in a particular way, that is how they seem to people: **+as** *She comes over as a very cold woman.*

come round *BrE* also **come around** *AmE phr v* **1** to visit someone: *Paul is coming round to my house for tea.* → see box at **VISIT** **2** to change your opinion so that you now agree with someone: **+to** *I'm sure he'll come round to our way of thinking.* **3** to become conscious again: *When she came round her mother was sitting by the bed.* **4** to happen as a regular event: *Christmas will soon be coming round again.*

come through *phr v* **1 come through sth** to continue to exist or succeed after a difficult or dangerous time: *We've come through all kinds of trouble together.* **2** if a piece of news or a result comes through, it becomes known or arrives: *His divorce should come through next month.*

come to *phr v* **1 come to a conclusion/decision/agreement etc** to reach a particular result: *After a long discussion, we finally came to a decision.* **2 come to sth a)** to develop so that something bad happens: *We need to be prepared to fight, but hopefully it won't come to that.* **b)** to add up to a total amount: *That comes to $24.50.* **3 come to sb** if a thought or idea comes to you, you realize or remember it: *I can't*

remember her name just now, but it'll come to me.
4 to become conscious again: *When I came to, I was lying on the grass.*

come under sth *phr v* **1 come under attack/ fire/pressure etc** to be attacked, shot at etc: *The students have come under pressure to report their friends.* **2** to be controlled by something: *These schools come under the control of the Department of Education.* **3** to be in a particular part of a book or information system: *Skiing? That'll come under 'Sport'.*

come up *phr v* **1** if someone comes up to you, they come close to you, especially in order to speak to you: *One of the teachers came up and spoke to me.* **2** to be mentioned or suggested: *The subject didn't come up at the meeting.* **3 be coming up** to be happening soon: *Is your birthday coming up soon?* **4** if a problem comes up, it suddenly happens: *Something's come up, so I won't be able to go with you.* **5** when the sun or moon comes up, it appears in the sky

come up against sb/sth *phr v* to have to deal with problems or difficulties: *Black politicians often come up against racist attitudes.*

come up to sb/sth *phr v* to be as good as something: *This work doesn't come up to your usual standard.*

come up with sth *phr v* to think of an idea, plan, or reply: *They still haven't come up with a name for the baby.*

comeback /'kʌmbæk/ *n* [C usually singular] when someone or something becomes popular or successful again: *Miniskirts are **making a comeback**.*

comedian /kə'miːdiən/ *n* [C] someone whose job is to tell jokes and make people laugh

comedown /'kʌmdaʊn/ *n* [singular] *informal* a situation that is not as good as something you had before: *It was a comedown compared with his old job.*

comedy /'kɒmɪdi $ 'kɑː-/ *n* plural **comedies**
1 [U] entertainment intended to make people laugh: **comedy series/show/writer/actor etc** | **stand-up comedy** (=telling jokes in front of people)
2 [C] a funny film or play: *All my favourite films are comedies.* | *a TV comedy* → see box at **FILM**

comet /'kɒmɪt $ 'kɑː-/ *n* [C] a very bright object in the sky like a star with a tail → see box at **SPACE**

comfort¹ /'kʌmfət $ -ərt/ *n*
1 [U] when you feel physically relaxed, happy, and without pain [≠ discomfort]: *I dress for comfort, not fashion.* | **built/made/designed for comfort** *Our shoes are designed for comfort.* | **in comfort** *I prefer to travel in comfort.* | *Use the Internet to do your shopping from **the comfort of your own home**.*
2 [U] if someone or something gives you comfort, they make you feel happier when you are upset or worried: *Whenever Bob was upset, he turned to Meg for comfort.* | **give/provide/offer comfort** *a book which offers comfort to people with cancer* | **great/much/little comfort** *My faith is a **source of** great comfort.*
3 [singular] someone or something that helps you feel happier or less worried: **be a comfort (to sb)** *Ann's been a **great comfort** to me since Ian died.*

4 [U] when you have enough money to buy all the things you need: *They had enough money to **live in comfort**.*
5 comforts [plural] all the things that make your life easier and more comfortable: **home comforts**

comfort² *v* [T] to make someone feel happier when they are upset or worried: *The boy's mother tried to comfort him.* —**comforting** *adj*: *a comforting thought* —**comfortingly** *adv*

comfortable /'kʌmftəbəl, 'kʌmfət-$ 'kʌmfərt-, 'kʌmft-/ *adj*
1 something that is comfortable makes you feel physically relaxed: **comfortable chair/bed/ sofa etc** *The bed wasn't very comfortable.* | **comfortable room/lounge/hotel etc** *a comfortable flat* | **comfortable clothes/shoes/boots etc** *loose, comfortable clothing*
2 if you are comfortable, you feel physically relaxed: *Are you comfortable sitting on the floor?* | *Sit down and **make yourself comfortable**.*
3 emotionally relaxed and not worried: **+with** *I feel comfortable with him whenever we're together.*
4 having enough money to buy all the things you need or want: *a comfortable retirement* —**comfortably** *adv*: *The hotel is **comfortably furnished**.*

comforter /'kʌmfətə $ -fərtər/ *n* [C] *AmE* a cover for a bed that is filled with soft warm material [= **duvet** *BrE*] → see picture at **BED**

comfy /'kʌmfi/ *adj informal* comfortable

comic¹ /'kɒmɪk $ 'kɑː-/ *adj* funny or amusing: *a comic novel*

comic² *n* [C] **1** also **'comic book** a magazine that tells stories using sets of pictures **2** someone whose job is to tell jokes and make people laugh

comical /'kɒmɪkəl $ 'kɑː-/ *adj* funny: *She looked so comical I burst out laughing.* —**comically** /-kli/ *adv*

'comic strip *n* [C] a set of pictures in a newspaper or magazine that tell a short funny story

coming¹ /'kʌmɪŋ/ *n* **1 the coming of sth** when something new comes or begins: *The coming of the railways changed the town considerably.* **2 comings and goings** the movements of people as they arrive at and leave places: **+of** *the comings and goings of the visitors*

coming² *adj* [only before noun] *formal* happening soon: *the coming months*

comma /'kɒmə $ 'kɑːmə/ *n* [C] the mark (,) used in writing to show a short pause

command¹ /kə'mɑːnd $ kə'mænd/ *n*
1 [C] an order that must be obeyed: *Shoot when I give the **command**.*
2 [U] if someone is in command, they are responsible for deciding what people, especially soldiers, should do: **in command (of sth)** *Lieutenant Peters is in command.* | **under sb's command** *troops under the command of General Fox* | **take command (of sth)** (=begin controlling a group or situation and making decisions) *When the fire was discovered, Carl took command.* | **at sb's command** *He has a large staff at his command.*
3 [C] an instruction to a computer to do something

4 command of sth knowledge of something, especially a language: **good/excellent/poor etc command of sth** *He has a good command of English.*

command² *v* [T] **1** to order someone to do something: **command sb to do sth** *The king commanded him to stay.* **2** to control an army or group of soldiers: *Major Grey commanded the troops.* **3** to get something such as respect or attention because you do something well or are important or popular: *a teacher who commands respect*

commandant /ˌkɒmənˈdænt $ ˈkɑːməndænt/ *n* [C] the army officer in charge of a place or group of people

commandeer /ˌkɒmənˈdɪə $ ˌkɑːmənˈdɪr/ *v* [T] to take someone's property for military use: *The hotel was commandeered for use as a hospital.*

commander /kəˈmɑːndə $ kəˈmændər/ *n* [C] **1** an officer in charge of a military organization or group **2** an officer with a middle rank in the navy

commanding /kəˈmɑːndɪŋ $ kəˈmæn-/ *adj* [only before noun] **1** *approving* having great confidence which makes people respect and obey you: *his commanding presence* **2** a commanding position is one from which you are likely to win: *He now has a commanding lead in the championship.*

com,manding 'officer *n* [C] the officer in charge of a group of soldiers

commandment /kəˈmɑːndmənt $ kəˈmænd-/ *n* [C] one of ten rules given by God in the Bible that tell people how they must behave

commando /kəˈmɑːndəʊ $ kəˈmændoʊ/ *n* [C] plural **commandos** or **commandoes** a soldier who is trained to make quick attacks into enemy areas

commemorate /kəˈmeməreɪt/ *v* [T] if something commemorates an event or group of people, it exists so that people will remember that event or group with respect: *The monument commemorates the war of independence.* —**commemorative** /kəˈmemərətɪv/ *adj* —**commemoration** /kəˌmeməˈreɪʃən/ *n* [U]

commence /kəˈmens/ *v* [I,T] *formal* to begin: *Work on the building will commence soon.* —**commencement** *n* [C,U]

commend /kəˈmend/ *v* [T] *formal* to praise someone or something publicly or formally: *She was commended for her years of service to the community.* —**commendation** /ˌkɒmənˈdeɪʃən $ ˌkɑː-/ *n* [C,U]

commendable /kəˈmendəbəl/ *adj formal* deserving praise: *Your enthusiasm is* **highly commendable**. —**commendably** *adv*

commensurate /kəˈmenʃərɪt/ *adj formal* matching something in size, quality, or length of time: **+with** *The salary is commensurate with experience.*

comment¹ /ˈkɒment $ ˈkɑː-/ *n*
1 [C,U] an opinion that you give about someone or something: *Does anyone have any questions or comments?* | **+on/about** *He made rude comments about her.*

2 no comment *spoken* used when you do not want to answer a question

comment² *v* [I,T] to give your opinion about someone or something: **+on** *He refused to comment on the rumour.* | **+that** *She commented that the food was poor.*

commentary /ˈkɒməntəri $ ˈkɑːmənteri/ *n* [C,U] plural **commentaries 1** a spoken description on the television or radio of an event while it is happening: **+on** *the commentary on the race* **2** a book or article that explains or discusses a book, poem, idea etc: *political commentary*

commentator /ˈkɒmənteɪtə $ ˈkɑːmənteɪtər/ *n* [C] **1** someone on television or radio who describes an event as it is happening: *a sports commentator* **2** someone who knows a lot about a subject, and who writes about it or discusses it on the television or radio: *political commentators* —**commentate** *v* [I]

commerce /ˈkɒmɜːs $ ˈkɑːmɜːrs/ *n* [U] the activity of buying and selling things in business

commercial¹ /kəˈmɜːʃəl $ -ɜːr-/ *adj* relating to the buying and selling of things and with making money: *The film was a commercial success.* —**commercially** *adv*

commercial² *n* [C] an advertisement on television or radio: *TV commercials* → see box at **ADVERTISEMENT**

commercialized also **-ised** *BrE* /kəˈmɜːʃəlaɪzd $ -ɜːr-/ *adj disapproving* too concerned with making money: *The resort is too commercialized.* —**commercialism** *n* [U]

commiserate /kəˈmɪzəreɪt/ *v* [I] *formal* to express your sympathy for someone who is unhappy —**commiseration** /kəˌmɪzəˈreɪʃən/ *n* [U] also **commiserations** [plural]

commission¹ /kəˈmɪʃən/ *n* **1** [C] an official group whose job is to find out about or control an activity: *the International Whaling Commission* **2** [C,U] extra money that you are paid every time you sell something: *20% commission* **3** [C,U] a request for an artist, designer, or musician to do a piece of work

commission² *v* [T] to ask someone to do a particular piece of work for you: *The government commissioned the report last year.* | **commission sb to do sth** *He was commissioned to design a bridge.*

commissioner /kəˈmɪʃənə $ -ər/ *n* [C] someone with an important position in an official organization: *a police commissioner*

commit /kəˈmɪt/ *v* **committed, committing**

1 [T] to do something wrong or illegal: *the gang that* **committed the crime** | **commit murder/rape/arson etc** *Most murders are committed by men.* | **commit suicide** (=kill yourself deliberately)

2 [I,T] to say that you will definitely do something: **commit sb to (doing) sth** *He committed his government to solving the crisis.* | *Meeting them doesn't commit us to anything.* | **commit yourself** *I'd committed myself and there was no turning back.*

3 [T] to decide to use money, time, people etc for a particular purpose: **commit sth to sth** *A lot of money has been committed to the project.*

4 [T] to order someone to be put in a hospital or prison: *The judge committed him to prison.*

commitment /kəˈmɪtmənt/ n

1 [C] a promise or arrangement to do something: *a long-term commitment* | **commitment to do sth** *They made a commitment to work together.* | **+to** *a commitment to electoral reform* | *family commitments*

2 [U] determination to work hard and continue with something: *The team showed commitment.* | **+to** *her commitment to her job*

committed /kəˈmɪtɪd/ adj wanting to work hard at something: *a committed teacher*

committee /kəˈmɪti/ n [C also + plural verb BrE] an official group of people who meet to decide what needs to be done about something: **+of** *the International Committee of the Red Cross* | **+on** *a committee on safety* | **be on a committee** (=be a member of it) *He's on the finance committee.* | *a committee meeting* | *The committee have elected John as chairman.*

commodity /kəˈmɒdɪti $ kəˈmɑː-/ n [C] plural **commodities** a product that is bought and sold: *agricultural commodities*

common[1] /ˈkɒmən $ ˈkɑː-/ adj

1 something that is common is often seen or often happens [≠ **rare**]: *Rabbits are a common wild animal in this area.* | *a common mistake* | **+among** *The illness is common among children.* | *It's common for new fathers to feel jealous of their babies.* | **common practice** (=a usual way of doing something) *Working from home is common practice.*

2 shared by two or more people or things: *We have a common interest in films.* | *a common goal* | **+to** *These problems are common to all schools.* | **common ground** (=things that people or groups agree about or are interested in) *There was little common ground between the two sides.* | **the common good** (=what is best for everyone) *We need to work together for the common good.* | **common knowledge** (=something everyone knows) *It's common knowledge that he's an alcoholic.*

3 [only before noun] ordinary and not special in any way: *common salt* | **the common man** (=ordinary people)

4 *BrE* an offensive word used to describe someone from a low social class: *She's so common!*

common[2] n **1 have sth in common (with sb/sth)** to be similar in some way: *The two towns have many things in common.* | *I have a lot in common with him.* **2 in common with sb/sth** in the same way as someone or something else: *In common with other schools, we suffer from overcrowded classrooms.* **3** [C] a large area of grass in a town or village that people walk or play sport on

ˈcommon-law adj **common-law husband/ wife** someone you have lived with for a long time as if they were your husband or wife

commonly /ˈkɒmənli $ ˈkɑː-/ adv often or usually: *People with this illness commonly complain of headaches.*

commonplace /ˈkɒmənpleɪs $ ˈkɑː-/ adj very common and not unusual: *Divorce is commonplace.*

ˈcommon room n [C] *BrE* a room in a school or college that a group of teachers or students use when they are not teaching or studying

Commons /ˈkɒmənz $ ˈkɑː-/ n **the Commons** the larger and more powerful of the two parts of the British parliament, whose members are elected by citizens [➡ **the Lords**]

ˌcommon ˈsense n [U] the ability to do sensible things: *Use your common sense.*

Commonwealth /ˈkɒmənwelθ $ ˈkɑː-/ n **the Commonwealth** an organization of about 50 countries that were once part of the British EMPIRE

commotion /kəˈməʊʃən $ -ˈmoʊ-/ n [singular,U] sudden noise or activity: *They heard a commotion.*

communal /ˈkɒmjʊnəl, kəˈmjuːnl $ ˈkɑː-/ adj shared by a group of people: *a communal bathroom*

commune[1] /ˈkɒmjuːn $ ˈkɑː-, kəˈmjuːn/ n [C] a group of people who live together and share work and possessions

commune[2] /kəˈmjuːn/ v

commune with sb/sth phr v formal **1** to communicate with a person, god, or animal, especially in a mysterious, SPIRITUAL way **2 commune with nature** to spend time in the countryside, enjoying it in a quiet peaceful way

communicate /kəˈmjuːnɪkeɪt/ v [I,T] if people communicate with each other, they give each other information by speaking, writing letters etc: *We communicate by email.* | **+with** *It's difficult to communicate with people if you don't speak their language.* | **communicate sth to sb** *the way a conductor communicates his or her ideas to the orchestra* | *A baby communicates its needs by crying.*

communication /kəˌmjuːnɪˈkeɪʃən/ n

1 [U] when people talk to each other or give each other information: **+between** *communication between teachers and parents* | **be in communication with sb/sth** *The pilot stayed in communication with the control tower.* | *The Internet is an important means of communication.*

2 communications [plural] **a)** ways of sending and receiving information using computers, telephones, radios etc: *Modern communications enable people to work from home.* **b)** roads, railways etc that are used for travelling and sending goods: **+with** *Paris has good communications with many European cities.*

3 [C] formal a letter, message, or telephone call

communicative /kəˈmjuːnɪkətɪv $ -keɪtɪv/ adj someone who is communicative tells people things: *My son isn't very communicative.*

Communion /kəˈmjuːnjən/ n [U] also **Holy Communion** a Christian ceremony in which people eat bread and drink wine

communiqué /kəˈmjuːnɪkeɪ $ kəˌmjuːnɪˈkeɪ/ n [C] an official report or announcement

communism, Communism /ˈkɒmjʊnɪzəm $ ˈkɑː-/ n [U] a political system based on the idea that people are equal and that the state should own companies

communist, Communist /ˈkɒmjʊnɪst $ ˈkɑː-/ n [C] someone who believes in communism —**communist** adj: *the Communist Party*

community /kəˈmjuːnɪti/ n [C also + plural verb BrE] plural **communities**

C

1 a group of people who live in the same town or area: *The library serves the whole community.* | *a **rural community** (=people who live in the country)* | *the **local community**.*
2 a group of people who are similar in some way, for example because they have the same religion or do the same job: *ethnic communities* | *the gay/black/Asian etc community* protests from the gay community | *the business/academic/scientific etc community*

com'munity ,centre *BrE*; **community center** *AmE n* [C] a place where people from the same area can go for social events, classes etc

com'munity ,college *n* [C] **1** a SECONDARY SCHOOL in the UK that students from the local area can go to, and which also has classes for adults **2** a college in the US that students can go to for two years in order to learn a skill or prepare for university

com,munity 'service *n* [U] work that someone does to help other people without being paid, especially as a punishment for a crime → see box at PUNISHMENT

commute /kə'mju:t/ *v* [I] to regularly travel a long distance to work: +**to/from/between** *He commutes to York.* —**commute** *n* [C] *My morning commute takes 45 minutes.* —**commuter** *n* [C] *The train was packed with commuters.*

compact¹ /kəm'pækt, 'kɒmpækt $ kəm'pækt/ *adj* small and neat: *a compact design*

compact² /kəm'pækt/ *v* [T] to press something soft together so that it becomes smaller or more solid

,compact 'disc *n* [C] a CD

companion /kəm'pænjən/ *n* [C] someone you spend a lot of time with, or who travels somewhere with you: *his constant companion* | *a travelling companion*

companionship /kəm'pænjənʃɪp/ *n* [U] when you are not alone but have a friend with you: *She joined the club for companionship.*

company /'kʌmpəni/ *n* plural **companies**
1 [C also + plural verb *BrE*] a business that makes or sells things or provides a service: *Which company do you work for?* | *He runs a clothing **company**.* | *The **company** was set up in 1978.* | *The **company** have debts of £50 million.* | *software/insurance/tobacco etc company*

2 [U] when someone is with you and you are not alone: *I enjoy his company (=like being with him).* | *I'll stay here to keep you company (=be with you so you are not alone).* | *She had the dog as company.* | *Tim is good company (=someone you enjoy being with).* | *in sb's com-*

pany (=with someone) *He felt relaxed in the company of women.*
3 [C] a group of actors, dancers, or singers who work together: *a ballet company*
→ LIMITED COMPANY, PARENT COMPANY

comparable /'kɒmpərəbəl $ 'kɑːm-/ *adj formal* similar to something else in size, number, quality etc, so that you can make a comparison: *a car of comparable size*

comparative¹ /kəm'pærətɪv/ *adj* **1 comparative comfort/freedom/safety etc** comfort etc that is quite good when compared to how comfortable etc something or someone else is: *the comparative safety of the hut* **2 comparative study/analysis etc** a study etc that involves comparing something with something else: *She's working on a comparative study of the two writers.*

comparative² *n* **the comparative** the form of an adjective or adverb that you use when saying that something is bigger, better, more expensive etc than another thing or than before

comparatively /kəm'pærəṭɪvli/ *adv* compared with something else: *Videos are still comparatively expensive.*

compare /kəm'peə $ -'per/ *v*
1 [T] if you compare things, you examine them in order to find out how they are similar or different: *We went to different shops to compare prices.* | **compare sth with/to sth** *Compare this list with yours.* | **Compared to me**, *Al is very tall.* | *a 5% increase compared with last year*
2 [I,T] if you compare two things, you say that they are similar in some way: **compare sth to/with sth** *Critics have compared him to De Niro.*
3 sth doesn't/can't compare (with sth) if something does not compare with something else, it is not as good, large etc: *This CD doesn't compare with his last one.*
4 compare notes (with sb) *informal* to talk to someone to find out if their experience of something is the same as yours

comparison /kəm'pærɪ̣sən/ *n*
1 [C,U] when you compare things: +**of** *a comparison of prices* | **in comparison (with/to sth)** *In comparison to other video games, this one isn't very exciting.* | **by comparison (with sth)** *His brother's crime was minor by comparison.* | **for comparison (with sth)** *These figures are provided for comparison with previous studies.*
2 [C] a statement that something is like something else: +**between** *The article makes a comparison between the two poems.* | *The writer draws comparisons between the two men.*
3 there's no comparison *spoken* used when you think that one thing is much better than another: *There's no comparison between canned and fresh vegetables.*

compartment /kəm'pɑːtmənt $ -ɑːr-/ *n* [C]
1 a separate space or area inside something: *a purse with many compartments* **2** a separate area inside a railway carriage: *a first-class compartment*

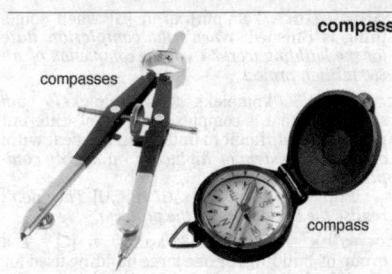

compass

compasses

compass

compass /'kʌmpəs/ *n* [C] **1** an instrument that shows the direction you are travelling in, with a needle that always points north **2** also **compasses** an instrument for drawing circles

compassion /kəm'pæʃən/ *n* [U] sympathy for someone who is suffering: **+for** *compassion for the sick*

compassionate /kəm'pæʃənɪt/ *adj* feeling sympathy for people who are suffering: *a compassionate man*

compatible /kəm'pætɪbəl/ *adj* **1** two people who are compatible have similar ideas or interests, and are able to have a good relationship **2** two things that are compatible are able to exist or be used together without problems: **+with** *Is the software compatible with your PC?* —**compatibility** /kəm,pætɪ'bɪlɪti/ *n* [U]

compatriot /kəm'pætriət $ -'peɪt-/ *n* [C] someone who is from the same country as you

compel /kəm'pel/ *v* [T] **compelled, compelling** to force someone to do something: **compel sb to do sth** *The bad weather compelled me to turn back.*

compelling /kəm'pelɪŋ/ *adj* **1** very interesting or exciting: *a compelling film* **2** a compelling argument, reason etc seems very strong or good: *a compelling reason for resigning*

compensate /'kɒmpənseɪt $ 'kɑːm-/ *v* **1** [I] to do something so that something bad has a smaller effect: **+for** *He bought her flowers to compensate for being late.* **2** [I,T] to pay someone money because they have suffered injury, loss, or damage: **compensate sb for sth** *The firm compensated workers for loss of earnings.*

compensation /,kɒmpən'seɪʃən $,kɑːm-/ *n* **1** [U] money that someone is given because they have been injured or badly treated: **in compensation** *The holiday company paid the Taylors £150 in compensation.* | **+for** *Farmers are demanding compensation for their losses.* **2** [C,U] something that makes a bad situation better: *Being unemployed has its compensations, like not having to get up early.*

compère /'kɒmpeə $ 'kɑːmper/ *n* [C] *BrE* someone who introduces the performers on a television programme, in a theatre show etc

compete /kəm'piːt/ *v* [I] to try to win something or to be more successful than someone else: **+in** *Ten runners are competing in the race.* | **+with/against** *We compete with teams from other villages.* | *Small firms cannot compete against large companies.* | **+for** *The stores are competing for customers.*

competent /'kɒmpɪtənt $ 'kɑːm-/ *adj* good at your work or able to do something well: *a highly competent doctor* —**competence** *n* [U] —**competently** *adv*

competing /kəm'piːtɪŋ/ *adj* [only before noun] **1** competing stories, ideas etc cannot all be right or accepted: *Several people gave competing accounts of the accident.* **2** competing products/brands/companies etc products etc that are trying to be more successful than each other

competition /,kɒmpɪ'tɪʃən $,kɑːm-/ *n*

1 [C] an organized event in which people or teams compete against each other: *an art competition* | *Who won the competition?* | *He decided to enter the competition.*
2 [U] a situation in which people or organizations compete with each other: **+for** *Competition for the job was intense.* | **+between/among** *fierce competition among supermarkets* | **be in competition with sb** *She is in competition with four other people.*
3 [singular,U] the people or groups that compete against you, especially in business or sport: *Our aim is to be better than the competition.* | *You'll have no competition.*

competitive /kəm'petɪtɪv/ *adj*

1 determined to be more successful than other people: *Boys are more competitive than girls.*
2 a competitive situation is one in which people or organizations try to be more successful than others: *a highly competitive industry* | *competitive sports*
3 competitive prices or products are fairly cheap: *Our rates are very competitive.*
—**competitiveness** *n* [U]

competitor /kəm'petɪtə $ -ər/ *n* [C] a person, team, or company that competes with another: *We sell more than our main competitors.*

compilation /,kɒmpɪ'leɪʃən $,kɑːm-/ *n* [C] a CD, record, or book which contains songs or stories from different CDs, records, or books: **+of** *a compilation of love songs*

compile /kəm'paɪl/ *v* [T] to make a book, list etc using different pieces of information

complacent /kəm'pleɪsənt/ *adj disapproving* too pleased with what you have achieved so that you no longer try to improve: *We mustn't get too complacent.* —**complacency** *n* [U] —**complacently** *adv*

complain /kəm'pleɪn/ *v* [I,T] to say that you are not satisfied with something or not happy about something: *They're complaining because the price has increased.* | *'No one ever tells me anything!' Ian complained.* | **+(that)** *Teachers complain that they do not get enough support from parents.* | **+about** *The kids complained about the food.* | **+to** *She complained to the manager.*

complain of sth *phr v* to say that you feel ill or have a pain: *He complained of stomach pains.*

complaint /kəm'pleɪnt/ *n*

1 [C,U] something that you say or write when you are not happy about something: **+about** *We've received complaints about the noise.* | **+against** *complaints against the police* | **+from** *complaints from residents* | **+to** *I made a complaint to the boss.* | *letters of complaint*
2 [C] something that you complain about: *My*

only complaint is that the restaurant is far too expensive.
3 [C] an illness that affects part of your body: *a chest complaint*

complement[1] /'kɒmpləmənt $ 'kɑːm-/ *n* [C]
formal **1** something that makes a good combination with another thing: **+to** *The wine was the perfect complement to the meal.* **2** the number of people or things that is needed or usual: **+of** *The school has its full complement of teachers.* **3** in grammar, a word or phrase that follows a verb and describes its subject

complement[2] /'kɒmpləment $ 'kɑːm-/ *v* [T] to make a good combination with something else: *The curtains complement the carpet.*

complementary /ˌkɒmpləˈmentəri◂ $ ˌkɑːm-/ *adj* complementary things go well together, although they are usually different: *Their skills are complementary – she is artistic and he is very good with money.*

ˌcomplementary 'medicine *n* [U] *especially BrE* complementary medicine uses treatments that are not part of traditional Western medicine

complete[1] /kəmˈpliːt/ *adj*
1 [only before noun] *informal* used when you are emphasizing something: *The police are in complete control of the situation.* | *The news came as a complete surprise.* | *a complete waste of time* | **complete fool/idiot etc** *I've been a complete fool.*
2 something that is complete has all the parts it should have [≠ **incomplete**]: *a complete set of china* | *the complete works of Shakespeare* | *The collection is complete.*
3 finished: *Work on the bridge is complete.*
4 **complete with sth** having particular equipment or features [≠ **incomplete**]: *The house comes complete with a sauna.*
—**completeness** *n* [U]

complete[2] *v* [T]
1 to finish doing or making something: *We hope to complete the work soon.* | *The building took a year to complete.*
2 to make something whole or perfect by adding what is missing: *I need one more stamp to complete the set.*
3 to write information on a form: *65 people completed the questionnaire.*

completely /kəmˈpliːtli/ *adv* in every way: *I completely forgot about your birthday.* | *Geoff's a completely different person since he retired.*

completion /kəmˈpliːʃən/ *n* [U] when something is finished: *When's the completion date for the building work?* | **+of** *the completion of an $80 million project*

complex[1] /'kɒmpleks $ ˌkɑːmˈpleks◂/ *adj* something that is complex has a lot of different parts and is difficult to understand or deal with: *a complex system of highways* | *a highly complex issue*
—**complexity** /kəmˈpleksəti/ *n* [C,U] *They don't realise the complexity of the problem.*

complex[2] /'kɒmpleks $ 'kɑːm-/ *n* [C] **1** a group of buildings or one large building used for a particular purpose: *a new shopping complex* **2** an emotional problem in which someone feels very anxious about something: *I think she's got an inferiority complex.*

complexion /kəmˈplekʃən/ *n* **1** [C,U] the natural colour and appearance of the skin on your face: *a young woman with a pale complexion* **2** [singular] the way something appears to be: *This puts an entirely new complexion on things* (=makes them seem completely different).

compliance /kəmˈplaɪəns/ *n* [U] *formal* when people obey a rule or law: **+with** *compliance with company regulations*

compliant /kəmˈplaɪənt/ *adj* willing to obey other people's wishes and demands

complicate /'kɒmpləkeɪt $ 'kɑːm-/ *v* [T] to make a problem or situation more difficult: *Don't tell Michael about this. It'll only complicate matters.*

complicated /'kɒmpləkeɪtəd $ 'kɑːm-/ *adj* something that is complicated has a lot of different parts and is difficult to understand or deal with [≠ **simple**]: *The instructions are much too complicated.* | *an extremely complicated process*

complication /ˌkɒmpləˈkeɪʃən $ ˌkɑːm-/ *n* **1** [C,U] a problem that makes a situation more difficult to understand or deal with: *The journey is difficult enough without further complications.* **2** [C usually plural] another medical problem or illness that happens when someone is already ill: *There were complications following surgery.*

complicity /kəmˈplɪsəti/ *n* [U] when someone allows another person to do something bad or illegal

compliment[1] /'kɒmpləmənt $ 'kɑːm-/ *n* [C] **1** something you say that shows you admire someone or something: *I was trying to pay her a compliment.* | *I wasn't sure exactly what they meant, but I took it as a compliment.* → see box at **PRAISE** **2** **with the compliments of sb/with sb's compliments** *formal* used by an organization when they send or give something to you: *Please accept these tickets with our compliments.*

compliment[2] /'kɒmpləment $ 'kɑːm-/ *v* [T] to say something nice to someone in order to praise them: **compliment sb on sth** *They complimented Jamie on his excellent English.*

complimentary /ˌkɒmpləˈmentəri◂ $ ˌkɑːm-/ *adj* **1** given free to someone: *complimentary tickets* **2** saying that you like something and think it is good: **+about** *He was very complimentary about the food.*

comply /kəm'plaɪ/ v [I] **complied, complying, complies** formal to obey an order or request: **+with** Anyone who fails to comply with the regulations will be fined.

component /kəm'pəʊnənt $ -'poʊ-/ n [C] one of the different parts of a machine or system: car components | **+of** Exercise is one of the key components of a healthy lifestyle.

compose /kəm'pəʊz $ -'poʊz/ v **1 be composed of sth** to be formed from a number of different things, parts, or people: The workforce is composed largely of women. **2** [T] to write a piece of music: Nyman composed the music for the film 'The Piano'. **3 compose yourself** to become calm after feeling angry, upset, or excited [➡ composed] **4** [T] to write a letter or speech, thinking very carefully about it as you write it

composed /kəm'pəʊzd $ -'poʊzd/ adj calm and not upset or angry [➡ composure]: She remained composed throughout the interview.

composer /kəm'pəʊzə $ -'poʊzər/ n [C] someone who writes music

composite /'kɒmpəzɪt $ kɑːm'pɑː-/ adj made up of different parts: a composite image —composite n [C]

composition /ˌkɒmpə'zɪʃən $ ˌkɑːm-/ n **1** [U] the way that something is made up of different parts, things, or people: **+of** the chemical composition of soil | the composition of the jury **2 a)** [C] a piece of music that someone has written: one of Beethoven's early compositions **b)** [U] the art or process of writing music or poetry **3** [U] the way in which the different parts of a painting or photograph are arranged **4** [C,U] a short piece of writing about a subject by a student [= essay]

compost /'kɒmpɒst $ 'kɑːmpoʊst/ n [U] a mixture of decayed leaves and plants that you add to the soil to help plants grow

composure /kəm'pəʊʒə $ -'poʊʒər/ n [singular, U] when someone appears or feels calm and confident: **regain/recover/keep your composure** She stopped crying and regained her composure.

compound¹ /'kɒmpaʊnd $ 'kɑːm-/ n [C] **1** a chemical compound is a substance that consists of two or more different substances **2** an area that contains a group of buildings and is surrounded by a wall or fence: a prison compound **3** also **compound noun/adjective/verb** two or more words that are used together as a noun, adjective, or verb

compound² /kəm'paʊnd/ v [T] to make a difficult situation worse: Our problems were compounded by appalling weather conditions.

comprehend /ˌkɒmprɪ'hend $ ˌkɑːm-/ v [I,T] formal to understand something: **comprehend what/how/why etc** They don't seem to comprehend how serious this is.

comprehensible /ˌkɒmprɪ'hensɪbəl $ ˌkɑːm-/ adj easy to understand [≠ incomprehensible]: **+to** language that is comprehensible to the average reader

comprehension /ˌkɒmprɪ'henʃən $ ˌkɑːm-/ n **1** [U] the ability to understand something: The whole situation is completely beyond my comprehension (=impossible for me to understand).

2 [C,U] an exercise to test how well students understand written or spoken language: a listening comprehension

comprehensive /ˌkɒmprɪ'hensɪv◂ $ ˌkɑːm-/ adj including everything: a comprehensive account of the war —comprehensively adv

comprehensive school also **comprehensive** n [C] a school in Britain for students aged between 11 and 18, who are of all levels of ability

compress /kəm'pres/ v [I,T] formal to press something or make something smaller so that it takes up less space or takes less time —compression /-'preʃən/ n [U]

comprise /kəm'praɪz/ v formal **1** [T] also **be comprised of** to consist of particular parts, groups, or people: The committee is comprised of 8 members. **2** [T] to form part of a larger group: Women comprise over 75% of our staff.

compromise¹ /'kɒmprəmaɪz $ 'kɑːm-/ n [C,U] when people or groups accept less than they really want, especially in order to make an agreement: **make/reach a compromise** Talks will continue until a compromise is reached. | **+between** a compromise between the government and trade unions

compromise² v **1** [I] to accept something that is not exactly what you want: President Chirac has said that he would be ready to compromise. **2** [T] to do something that is against your principles, beliefs etc and so seems dishonest or embarrassing: **compromise your beliefs/principles/integrity etc** artists who refuse to compromise their principles | **compromise yourself** The UN is afraid of compromising itself.

compromising /'kɒmprəmaɪzɪŋ $ 'kɑːm-/ adj making it seem that someone has done something dishonest or wrong: some compromising photographs of the President

compulsion /kəm'pʌlʃən/ n **1** [C usually singular] a strong desire to do something that is wrong: I had a sudden compulsion to hit her. **2** [U] when someone is forced to do something that they do not want to do [➡ compel]

compulsive /kəm'pʌlsɪv/ adj **1** compulsive behaviour is very difficult to stop or control: compulsive eating **2 compulsive liar/gambler etc** someone who has a strong desire to lie, GAMBLE etc, which they cannot control —compulsively adv

compulsory /kəm'pʌlsəri/ adj if something is compulsory, you must do it [≠ voluntary]: compulsory military service → see box at NECESSARY

compunction /kəm'pʌŋkʃən/ n **have no compunction about (doing) sth** to not feel guilty about doing something, even though other people may think it is wrong

computer /kəm'pjuːtə $ -ər/ n [C] an electronic machine that can store and arrange large amounts of information, which can be used to do many different things: The school has three new computers. | **on computer** All our data is kept on computer. | **computer technology/system/network etc** The new computer system at work is always going down. | **computer program/software/application etc** the latest computer graphics software | a new **computer game** → see box at OFFICE

TOPIC

You **start up/boot** a computer and **log in/on** in order to start using it.

People use computers to do a lot of different things, such as send and receive **emails**, look for information on **the Internet**, and work on **files** or other **documents**.

You need to **open** a **file** before you can work on it. When you have finished, you **save** your **work/file**, **close** the **document** or **file** that you were working on, and **shut down** the computer.

If your computer **crashes**, it suddenly stops working. You **reboot** the computer to make it start working again.

→ **EMAIL, INTERNET**

C

computerize also **– ise** BrE /kəm'pjuːtəraɪz/ v [T] to use a computer to store information or to control the way something is done: *plans to computerize all our financial records* —**computerization** /kəmˌpjuːtəraɪ'zeɪʃən $ -rə-/ n [U]

com,puter-'literate adj able to use a computer —**computer literacy** n [U]

computing /kəm'pjuːtɪŋ/ n [U] the use or study of computers

comrade /'kɒmrɪd, -reɪd $ 'kɑːmræd/ n [C] literary a friend, especially someone who fights together with you in a war —**comradeship** n [U]

con[1] /kɒn $ kɑːn/ v [T] **conned**, **conning** informal to trick someone in order to get something that you want: **con sb into (doing) sth** *You conned me into thinking I could trust you.* | **con sb out of sth** *She was conned out of £300.*

con[2] n informal [C usually singular] a trick to get someone's money or to make someone do something: *The website says they're offering free holidays, but it's all a big con.* → **the pros and cons (of sth)** at PRO

concave /ˌkɒn'keɪv◂, kən- $ ˌkɑːn'keɪv◂, kən-/ adj having a surface that curves inwards [≠ **convex**]: *a concave mirror*

conceal /kən'siːl/ v [T] to hide something carefully: *Cannabis was found concealed in the suitcase.* | **conceal sth from sb** *Sue tried hard to conceal her disappointment from the others.* —**concealment** n [U]

concede /kən'siːd/ v **1** [T] to admit that something is true, although you do not want to: **+(that)** *She reluctantly conceded that I was right.* **2** [T] to let someone have something although you do not want to: **concede sth to sb** *Japan was forced to concede the islands to Russia.* | *In the end the government conceded to the terrorists' demands* (=agreed to do what they asked). **3** [I,T] to admit that you are not going to win a game, argument etc: *Perot conceded defeat* (=accepted he had lost) *in the election.*

conceit /kən'siːt/ n [U] an attitude that shows that you are too proud of what you can do, how you look etc

conceited /kən'siːtɪd/ adj disapproving too proud of yourself, especially of what you can do: *I don't want to seem conceited, but I know I'll win.* → see box at PROUD —**conceitedly** adv

conceivable /kən'siːvəbəl/ adj something that is conceivable could possibly happen or be true

[≠ **inconceivable**]: **+that** *It is conceivable that the experts are wrong.* —**conceivably** adv

conceive /kən'siːv/ v **1** [I,T] to be able to imagine something: **+of** *It is impossible to conceive of the size of the universe.* **2** [T] to think of a new idea or plan: *How was the idea first conceived?* | **conceive sth as sth** *The exhibition was originally conceived as a temporary tourist attraction.* **3** [I,T] to become PREGNANT [➔ **conception**]

concentrate /'kɒnsəntreɪt $ 'kɑːn-/ v **1** [I] to think very carefully about something you are doing: *With all this noise, it's hard to concentrate.* | *Will you please concentrate!* | **+on** *I'm trying to concentrate on reading this article.* **2 be concentrated on/in/around etc sth** to exist in large numbers or amounts in a particular place: *Most of New Zealand's population is concentrated in the north island.*

concentrate (sth) on sth phr v to give most of your attention to one thing: *I want to concentrate on my career for a while before I have kids.* | **concentrate your efforts/attention/energy etc on sth** *They are concentrating their efforts on raising public awareness.*

concentrated /'kɒnsəntreɪtɪd $ 'kɑːn-/ adj **1** a concentrated liquid has been made stronger by removing most of the water from it: *concentrated orange juice* **2** [only before noun] showing a lot of effort or determination: *He made a concentrated effort to improve his French.*

concentration /ˌkɒnsən'treɪʃən $ ˌkɑːn-/ n **1** [U] when you think very carefully about something you are doing: *They soon get tired and lose their concentration.* | *She needed all her powers of concentration to stop herself slipping.* **2** [U] when you put a lot of attention, time or energy into one thing: **+on** *There was too much concentration on one type of industry.* **3** [C,U] a large amount of something in the same place: **+of** *high concentrations of minerals in the water*

concen'tration ,camp n [C] a prison where large numbers of people are kept in very bad conditions, usually during a war

concentric /kən'sentrɪk/ adj concentric circles are of different sizes and have the same centre

concept /'kɒnsept $ 'kɑːn-/ n [C] a general idea or principle: **+of** *the concept of freedom for all* —**conceptual** /kən'septʃuəl/ adj

conception /kən'sepʃən/ n **1** [C] a general idea about what something is like, or a way of understanding what something is like: **+of** *changing conceptions of the world* **2** [U] when a woman or female animal becomes PREGNANT [➔ **conceive**]

concern[1] /kən'sɜːn $ -ɜːrn/ n **1** [C,U] a feeling of worry about something important, or the thing that worries you: **+about/over** *There is growing concern about pollution in our cities.* | **+for** *concern for her children's welfare* | **+that** *renewed concern that the virus could spread* | *The research findings gave serious cause for concern* (=reason to worry). | *the concerns expressed by parents*

2 [C,U] something that is important to you or that involves you: *Our main concern is for passengers' safety.* | **of concern (to sb)** *The destruction of the rainforests is of concern to us all.*
3 [C] a company or business: *The restaurant is a family concern.*

concern² *v* [T] **1** to affect or involve someone: *What we're planning doesn't concern you.* **2** to make someone feel worried or upset: *The teenage drug problem concerns most parents.* **3** if a book, report etc concerns something, it is about it: *The film concerns a group of school friends.*
4 concern yourself (with sth) to become involved in something that interests or worries you: *You don't need to concern yourself with this, Jan.*

concerned /kən'sɜːnd $ -ɜːrnd/ *adj*
1 involved in something or affected by it: *Divorce is always painful, especially when children are concerned.* | **+with** *organizations concerned with animal welfare* | *It was a difficult time for **all concerned** (=everyone involved or affected).*
2 worried about something important: **+about** *I'm concerned about his eyesight.* | **+for** *We are all concerned for their safety.* | **+that** *Many people are concerned that the system is not safe.* → see box at **WORRIED**
3 as far as sb's concerned used to show someone's opinion: *As far as I'm concerned, the whole idea is crazy.*
4 as far as sth is concerned used to show which subject or thing you are talking about: *As far as money is concerned, the club is doing fairly well.*

concerning /kən'sɜːnɪŋ $ -ɜːr-/ *prep* about or relating to something: *Police are asking for information concerning the incident.*

concert /'kɒnsət $ 'kɑːnsərt/ *n* [C] a performance given by musicians or singers: *a rock concert* | *I like **going to concerts**.* | *The Youth Orchestra are **giving a concert** in the Town Hall tonight.*

concerted /kən'sɜːtɪd $ -ɜːr-/ *adj* **concerted effort/attempt/action etc** a very determined effort, attempt etc: *We should all **make a concerted effort** to raise this money.*

concerto /kən'tʃɜːtəʊ $ -'tʃertoʊ/ *n* [C] plural **concertos** a piece of CLASSICAL music, usually for one instrument and an ORCHESTRA

concession /kən'seʃən/ *n* [C] **1** something that you agree to in order to end an argument: *The government will never **make concessions** to terrorists.* **2** a special right given to someone by the government, an employer etc: *tax concessions for married people* **3** *BrE* a reduction in the price of tickets for certain groups of people, for example students

concessionary /kən'seʃənəri $ -neri/ *adj* **1** given as a concession **2** *BrE* specially reduced in price, for example for old people or children

conciliation /kən,sɪli'eɪʃən/ *n* [U] *formal* the process of trying to end an argument between people

conciliatory /kən'sɪliətəri $ -tɔːri/ *adj formal* intended to stop people arguing with you: *Both sides in the dispute have now adopted a more conciliatory approach.*

concise /kən'saɪs/ *adj* short and clear, without using too many words: *a concise answer* —**concisely** *adv*

conclude /kən'kluːd/ *v* **1** [T] to decide something after considering all the information you have: **+that** *The report concluded that the accident was preventable.* **2** [T] *formal* to complete something that you have been doing: *The study was concluded last month.* | **conclude an agreement/treaty/deal etc** (=to complete a political or business agreement successfully) **3** [I,T] to end a meeting, speech, book, or event by doing or saying one final thing, or to end in this way: **+with** *The seminar concluded with a question and answer session.* —**concluding** *adj*: *concluding remarks*

conclusion /kən'kluːʒən/ *n*
1 [C] something you decide after considering all the information you have: **+that** *I've **come to the conclusion** that she's lying.* | *The appeal court **reached** the same **conclusion**.* | *It's important not to **jump to conclusions** (=to decide something too quickly without all the facts).* | *We can **draw** two main **conclusions** from the data.*
2 [C] the end or final part of something: *the conclusion of his essay*
3 [U] when a political or business agreement is completed: **+of** *the conclusion of a peace agreement*
→ **FOREGONE CONCLUSION**

conclusive /kən'kluːsɪv/ *adj* proving that something is true: *There is no **conclusive evidence** connecting him with the crime.* —**conclusively** *adv*

concoct /kən'kɒkt $ -'kɑːkt/ *v* [T] **1** to invent a story, plan, or excuse, especially to deceive someone: *She concocted a story about her mother being sick.* **2** to make something unusual by mixing different things together —**concoction** /kən'kɒkʃən $ -'kɑːk-/ *n* [C, U]

concourse /'kɒŋkɔːs $ 'kɑːŋkɔːrs/ *n* [C] a large HALL or open place in a public building such as an airport

concrete¹ /'kɒŋkriːt $ 'kɑːŋ-/ *n* [U] a substance used for building that is made by mixing sand, water, small stones, and CEMENT —**concrete** *v* [T]

concrete² /'kɒŋkriːt $ kɑːn'kriːt/ *adj* **1** made of concrete: *a concrete floor* → see picture at **MATERIAL¹** **2** clearly based on facts, not on beliefs or guesses: **concrete information/evidence/facts etc** *We need concrete information about the man's identity.*

concur /kən'kɜː $ -'kɜːr/ *v* [I] **concurred, concurring** *formal* to agree with someone: **+with** *Dr. Hastings concurs with our decision.*

concurrent /kən'kʌrənt $ -'kɜːr-/ *adj* existing or happening at the same time: *He is serving two concurrent prison sentences.* —**concurrently** *adv*

concussion /kən'kʌʃən/ *n* [C,U] slight damage to your brain that makes you become unconscious or feel sick: *He was taken to hospital with concussion.* —**concussed** /kən'kʌst/ *adj*: *He was slightly concussed.*

condemn /kən'dem/ *v* [T] **1** to say very strongly that you do not approve of someone or something: *Politicians were quick to condemn the bombing.* **2** to give a severe punishment to someone who is guilty of a crime: *The murderer* *was condemned to death.* **3** to force someone to live in an unpleasant way or to suffer: **condemn sb to sth** *families who are condemned to a life of poverty* **4** to say officially that a building is not safe enough to be used

condemnation /ˌkɒndəm'neɪʃən, -dem-$ ˌkɑːn-/ *n* [C,U] an expression of very strong disapproval: **+of** *international condemnation of the plans*

condensation /ˌkɒnden'seɪʃən, -dən-$ ˌkɑːn-/ *n* [U] small drops of water that appear when steam or hot air touches a cold surface

condense /kən'dens/ *v* **1** [I,T] if gas or hot air condenses, it becomes a liquid as it becomes colder **2** [T] to make a speech or piece of writing shorter by using fewer words to say the same thing **3** [T] to make a liquid thicker by removing some of the water from it: *condensed milk*

condescend /ˌkɒndɪ'send $ ˌkɑːn-/ *v* [I] **1** to agree to do something even though you think you are too important to do it: **condescend to do sth** *He might condescend to see us later.* **2 condescend to sb** to behave as if you are better or more important than someone else —**condescension** /-'senʃən/ *n* [U]

condescending /ˌkɒndɪ'sendɪŋ $ ˌkɑːn-/ *adj* showing that you think you are better or more important than other people: *He gave us a condescending smile.*

condition¹ /kən'dɪʃən/ *n*

1 conditions [plural] the situation in which something happens: **under these/certain/ normal etc conditions** *Under such conditions, the plants will grow rapidly.* | *The trip was cancelled because of adverse **weather conditions**.* | *They managed to make a profit, despite difficult **economic conditions**.*

2 conditions [plural] the environment in which people live or work, that affects their life: **living/ working conditions** *protests against poor working conditions* | *Nurses are demanding better **pay and conditions**.*

3 [C,U] the state that something or someone is in: **+of** *the condition of the local roads* | **in (a) good/bad/terrible etc condition** *The bike is still in pretty good condition.* | **in (a) stable/ critical/comfortable etc condition** *The driver is in a critical condition in hospital.* | **in no condition to do sth** (=too ill, drunk, upset etc to do something) *Molly is in no condition to return to work.*

4 [C] something that you must agree to or must happen before something else can happen: **+for** *the conditions for getting into college* | *your **terms and conditions** of employment* | *The application was approved, **subject to** certain conditions.* | *We'll agree to your proposal **on condition that** we receive some of the money immediately.* | *You can go out **on one condition**: you must be home by eleven o'clock.*

5 [C] an illness: *a heart condition* | *a child with a serious **medical condition***

condition² *v* [T] **1** to make a person or animal behave in a particular way by training or influencing them over a period of time: **condition sb/sth to do sth** *The horses are conditioned to expect food from people.* **2** to add a special liquid to your skin or hair to keep it healthy —**conditioning** *n* [U]

conditional /kən'dɪʃənəl/ *adj* **1** if an offer, agreement etc is conditional, it will only happen if something else happens: **+on** *His college place is conditional on his exam results.* **2** a conditional sentence is one that begins with 'if' or 'unless', and expresses something that must happen before something else can happen

conditioner /kən'dɪʃənə $ -ər/ *n* [C,U] a liquid that you put on your hair after washing it to keep it in good condition

condo /'kɒndəʊ $ 'kɑːndoʊ/ *n* [C] plural **condos** *AmE informal* a condominium

condolence /kən'dəʊləns $ -'doʊ-/ *n* [C usually plural, U] sympathy for someone when someone they love has died: *Please offer my condolences to your mother.*

condom /'kɒndəm $ 'kɑːn-, 'kʌn-/ *n* [C] a thin piece of rubber that a man wears over his PENIS during sex to stop a woman becoming PREGNANT, or to protect against disease

condominium /ˌkɒndə'mɪniəm $ ˌkɑːn-/ *n* [C] *AmE* a building with several apartments, each of which is owned by the people living in it, or one of these apartments

condone /kən'dəʊn $ -'doʊn/ *v* [T] to accept or allow behaviour that most people think is wrong: *I cannot condone the use of violence.*

conducive /kən'djuːsɪv $ -'duː-/ *adj formal* **be conducive to sth** if a situation is conducive to something, it makes that thing possible or likely to happen: *The sunny climate is conducive to outdoor activities.*

conduct¹ /kən'dʌkt/ *v* **1** [T] to do or organize something: **conduct an experiment/test** *The pupils are conducting an experiment with two magnets.* | **conduct an interview/survey/ investigation etc** *We're conducting a survey into children's eating habits.* | *The group **conducted** a terrorist **campaign** in the 1970s.* **2** [I,T] to stand in front of musicians or singers and direct their playing or singing **3** [T] if something conducts electricity or heat, it allows the electricity or heat to travel along or through it **4 conduct yourself** the way that you conduct yourself is the way that you behave: *Public figures have a duty to conduct themselves correctly.*

conduct² /'kɒndʌkt $ 'kɑːn-/ *n* [U] **1** the way someone behaves, especially in public or in their job [= **behaviour**]: *standards of professional conduct* **2** the way an activity is organized and done: **+of** *complaints about the conduct of the election*

conductor /kən'dʌktə $ -ər/ *n* [C] **1** someone who conducts a group of musicians or singers → see box at ORCHESTRA **2** *BrE* someone whose job is to collect payments from passengers on a bus **3** *AmE* someone who is in charge of a train or the workers on it **4** something that allows heat or electricity to travel along or through it

cone /kəʊn $ koʊn/ *n* [C] **1** a hollow or solid object with a round base, sloping sides and a point at the top: *a traffic cone* **2 ice cream cone** a container for ICE CREAM that is shaped like a cone and that you can eat [= **cornet** *BrE*] **3** a thing that grows on PINE and FIR trees, which contains the seeds of the tree [= **pine cone**] → see picture at PLANT

confectionery /kən'fekʃənəri $ -neri/ *n* [U] sweets and cakes

confederation /kən,fedə'reɪʃən/ also
confederacy /kən'fedərəsi/ n [C] a group of
people, political parties, or organizations that
have joined together to achieve an aim
—**confederate** /kən'fedərₐt/ adj

confer /kən'fɜː $ -'fɜːr/ v conferred, conferring
1 [I] to discuss something with other people so
that everyone can express their opinion: **+with**
You may confer with the other team members.
2 confer a degree/honour etc on sb to officially give someone a degree etc

conference /'kɒnfərəns $ 'kaːn-/ n [C] a large
meeting, often lasting for several days, at which
members of an organization, profession etc discuss things related to their work: **+on** *an inter-
national conference on the Environment* |
conference centre/hall/facilities etc
→ PRESS CONFERENCE

'conference ,call n [C] a telephone call in
which several people can all talk to each other

confess /kən'fes/ v [I,T]
1 to admit that you have done something bad,
illegal, or embarrassing: **confess to (doing) sth**
He has confessed to the crime. | **+(that)** *Max
confessed that he'd forgotten my birthday.* | **I
have to/must confess** *spoken* (=used to admit
something embarrassing) *I have to confess, I
don't know much about it.*
2 to tell a priest or God about bad things you
have done
—**confessed** adj

confession /kən'feʃən/ n **1** [C] a statement
admitting that you have done something bad,
illegal, or embarrassing: *He made a full confes-
sion to the police.* | *I have a confession to make
– I've lost your keys.* **2** [C,U] when you tell a
priest or God about bad things you have done:
She decided to go to confession.

confetti /kən'feti/ n [U] small pieces of paper
that you throw over a man and woman who have
just got married

confidant /'kɒnf‚dænt, ‚kɒnf‚'dænt, -'dɑːnt
$ 'kɑːnf‚dænt/ n [C] someone you tell your
secrets to or who you talk to about personal things

confidante /'kɒnf‚dænt, ‚kɒnf‚'dænt, -'dɑːnt
$ 'kɑːnf‚dænt/ n [C] a female confidant

confide /kən'faɪd/ v [I,T] to tell someone about
personal things that you do not want other peo-
ple to know: *'I quite like him,' she confided.* |
confide to sb that *He had confided to friends
that he was unhappy.*
confide in sb phr v to tell someone about
something personal and secret, because you feel
you can trust them: *I've never been able to confide in my sister.*

confidence /'kɒnf‚dəns $ 'kaːn-/ n
1 [U] the feeling that you can trust someone or
something to be good or successful: **+in** *The
survey reveals a lack of confidence in the
police.* | *Most parents have total confidence in
the school.* | *a bid to restore confidence in the
government* | **public/business/consumer con-
fidence**
2 [U] belief in your ability to do things well or
be liked by people: **+in** *I didn't have any confi-
dence in myself.* | *My lack of confidence
showed.* | *The team is full of confidence.* |
confidence to do sth *I wouldn't have the confi-
dence to wear that.* | *Doing the course has given*

me a lot of confidence. | **with confidence** *It's
important that children learn to read with confidence.* → see box at CONFIDENT
3 gain/win/earn sb's confidence if you gain
someone's confidence, they start to trust you
4 in confidence if you say something in confidence, you tell someone something and trust
them not to tell anyone else
5 [C] a secret or some personal and secret information: *We spent the evening talking and sharing confidences.*

confident /'kɒnf‚dənt $ 'kaːn-/ adj
1 sure that something is true or that something
will happen in the way you want or expect:
+(that) *She was confident that the problem would
be sorted out.* | **confident of (doing) sth** *Owens
is confident of success.* | **+about** *I feel very confi-
dent about the future.*
2 sure about your ability to do things well or be
liked by people: **+about** *I'm much more confident
about my ability.* | **confident smile/manner/
voice etc**

THESAURUS

(antonyms)

insecure: *I always feel very insecure about my
appearance.*
unsure of yourself – not very confident about
yourself: *She's nervous and unsure of herself.*
lack confidence/be lacking in confidence – to
not believe that you have the ability to do
something well: *He is completely lacking in
confidence.*
timid – not having courage or confidence: *She
was too timid to ask for directions.*
shy – nervous and embarrassed about
meeting or talking to other people: *a shy
little girl*
introverted – not comfortable being with
other people

—**confidently** adv → SELF-CONFIDENT

confidential /‚kɒnf‚'denʃəl $ ‚kaːn-/ adj
secret and not intended to be shown or told to
other people: *confidential information* | **highly/
strictly confidential** *The report is highly confidential.* —**confidentially** adv —**confidentiality**
/‚kɒnf‚denʃi'ælₐti $ ‚kaːn-/ n [U]

configuration /kən,fɪgə'reɪʃən, -gjʊ- $ -gjʊ-/
n [C,U] formal or technical the shape or arrangement of the parts of something

confine /kən'faɪn/ v [T] **1** if you confine yourself or your activities to one thing, you do only
that thing, or you do something, using only that
thing: **confine sth to sth** *We confined our
research to young people.* | **confine yourself to
(doing) sth** *He confined himself to writing plays.*
2 to stop something bad from spreading: **confine sth to sth** *Firefighters managed to confine
the fire to the ground floor.* **3** to make someone
stay in a place: **confine sb to sth** *An accident
had confined him to a wheelchair.*

confined /kən'faɪnd/ adj **1 be confined to
sb/sth** to exist in or affect only a particular
place or group: *Demand for the book seems to be
confined to women.* **2** a confined space or area
is very small

confinement /kən'faɪnmənt/ n [U] when
someone is forced to stay in a place: *They were
held in confinement.* → SOLITARY CONFINEMENT

C

confines /ˈkɒnfaɪnz $ ˈkɑːn-/ n [plural] the limits or edge of something: *You must stay within the confines of the hotel.*

confirm /kənˈfɜːm $ -ɜːrm/ v [T]

1 to show or prove that something is true or right: *Blood tests confirmed the diagnosis.* | **+that** *Can you confirm that the money has been paid?* | **+what** *Today's events confirm what we already know.* | **confirm sb's suspicions/belief/fears** *A telephone call confirmed my suspicions.*

2 to tell someone that an arrangement is now definite: *Please confirm your booking.*

3 be confirmed to be made a full member of the Christian church in a special ceremony

confirmation /ˌkɒnfəˈmeɪʃən $ ˌkɑːnfər-/ n [C,U] **1** a statement, document etc saying that something is true or definite: **+of** *There is still no official confirmation of the report.* **2** a ceremony in which someone is made a full member of the Christian church

confirmed /kənˈfɜːmd $ -ɜːr-/ adj **confirmed bachelor/atheist etc** someone who has been something for a long time and is unlikely to change

confiscate /ˈkɒnfɪˌskeɪt $ ˈkɑːn-/ v [T] to officially take something away from someone: *Customs officers confiscated his passport.* —**confiscation** /ˌkɒnfɪˈskeɪʃən $ ˌkɑːn-/ n [C,U]

conflict¹ /ˈkɒnflɪkt $ ˈkɑːn-/ n [C,U]

1 a disagreement or fighting: **+between** *a conflict between rival gangs* | **+over** *conflicts over land* | **in conflict (with sb)** *She was always in conflict with her parents.*

2 a difference between two ideas, influences, needs etc: **+between** *the conflict between religion and science* | **in conflict (with sth)** *Individual aims may be in conflict with company aims.*

3 conflict of interest(s) a situation in which you cannot do your job fairly because you are personally affected by the decisions that you make

conflict² /kənˈflɪkt/ v [I] if two ideas, statements, needs etc conflict, they cannot both be true or exist together: **+with** *evidence that conflicts with previous findings* | *conflicting advice*

conform /kənˈfɔːm $ -ɔːrm/ v [I] **1** to behave in the way that people expect or in the same way as other people: *There's always pressure on children to conform.* | **+to** *He was determined not to conform to the stereotype of a police officer.* **2** to obey a law, rule etc: **+to** *Products must conform to safety standards.* —**conformity** n [U]

conformist /kənˈfɔːmˌɪst $ -ɔːr-/ adj thinking and behaving in the same way as everyone else [≠ **non-conformist**] —**conformist** n [C]

confound /kənˈfaʊnd/ v [T] to surprise people by showing that what they expected was wrong: *Her amazing recovery has confounded doctors.* | *He confounded his critics by winning the election.*

confront /kənˈfrʌnt/ v [T] **1** if a problem, difficulty etc confronts you, you have to do something about it: *the problems confronting the government* | **be confronted with sth** *Children are often shy when confronted with new situations.* **2** to do something to solve a difficult or unpleasant problem, situation etc: *We need to confront the issue.* **3** to stand in front of someone in a threatening way: *She was confronted by*

two men. **4** to try to make someone admit something, especially by showing them proof: *Eventually she confronted him about the affair.*

confrontation /ˌkɒnfrənˈteɪʃən $ ˌkɑːn-/ n [C,U] an argument or fight: **+with/between** *confrontations between countries*

confrontational /ˌkɒnfrənˈteɪʃənəl◂ $ ˌkɑːn-/ adj likely to cause arguments or make people angry: *a confrontational style of management*

confuse /kənˈfjuːz/ v [T]

1 to make someone feel that they cannot think clearly or understand something: *His directions really confused me.*

2 to think wrongly that a person or thing is someone or something else: **confuse sb/sth with sb/sth** *It's easy to confuse Sue with her sister.*

3 to make something more complicated or difficult to understand: *The media were accused of confusing the issue.*

confused /kənˈfjuːzd/ adj

1 unable to think clearly or understand something clearly: *He was totally confused.* | **+about** *I'm still confused about what happened.*

2 complicated and difficult to understand: *a confused situation*

confusing /kənˈfjuːzɪŋ/ adj difficult to understand: *It's all very confusing.* | *The results of the survey are confusing and contradictory.*

confusion /kənˈfjuːʒən/ n [C,U]

1 a feeling that you do not understand something or do not know what to do: **+over/as to/about** *There's a lot of confusion about the new rules.* | **in confusion** *Marcus frowned in confusion.*

2 when you wrongly think that a person or thing is someone or something else: *To avoid confusion, the teams were different colours.* | **+between** *confusion between flu and the common cold*

3 a confusing situation is one in which a lot of things are happening: **+of** *a confusion of noise and lights*

congeal /kənˈdʒiːl/ v [I] if a liquid such as blood congeals, it becomes thick or solid

congenial /kənˈdʒiːniəl/ adj formal pleasant in a way that makes you feel comfortable and relaxed: *a congenial atmosphere*

congenital /kənˈdʒenɪtl/ adj affecting someone from the time they are born: *a congenital heart problem*

congested /kənˈdʒestɪd/ adj full or blocked, especially with traffic: *The roads were heavily congested.* —**congestion** /-ˈdʒestʃən/ n [U]

conˈgestion ˌcharging n [U] BrE a way of reducing traffic in city centres by charging drivers money to enter

conglomerate /kənˈglɒmərɪt $ -ˈglɑː-/ n [C] a large company consisting of several companies that have joined together

conglomeration /kənˌglɒməˈreɪʃən $ -ˈglɑː-/ n [C] formal a group of many different things or people gathered together

congratulate /kənˈgrætʃʊˌleɪt/ v [T] to tell someone that you are happy because they have achieved something, or because something good has happened to them: **congratulate sb on (doing) sth** *I congratulated him on his success.* → see box at PRAISE

congratulations /kən‚græt∫ʊˈleɪʃənz/ *n* [plural] used to congratulate someone: *You won? Congratulations!* | **+on** *Congratulations on your engagement!* | **+to** *Congratulations to all the winners!*

congregate /ˈkɒŋgrɪɡeɪt $ ˈkɑːŋ-/ *v* [I] to come together in a group: *A group of protesters had congregated outside.*

congregation /‚kɒŋgrɪˈɡeɪʃən $ ‚kɑːŋ-/ *n* [C] the people who are in a church for a religious service

Congress /ˈkɒŋgres $ ˈkɑːŋgrəs/ *n* [C,U] the group of people elected to make laws for the US, consisting of the Senate and the House of Representatives

congress *n* [C] a large formal meeting of members of different organizations, countries etc

congressman /ˈkɒŋgrɪsmən $ ˈkɑːŋ-/ *n* [C] plural **congressmen** /-mən/ a man who is elected to be in Congress → see box at GOVERNMENT

congresswoman /ˈkɒŋgrɪs‚wʊmən $ ˈkɑːŋ-/ *n* [C] plural **congresswomen** /-‚wɪmɪn/ a woman who is elected to be in Congress → see box at GOVERNMENT

conical /ˈkɒnɪkəl $ ˈkɑː-/ *adj* shaped like a CONE

conifer /ˈkəʊnɪfə, ˈkɒ- $ ˈkɑːnɪfər/ *n* [C] a tree that keeps its leaves in winter and has CONES containing its seeds —**coniferous** /kəˈnɪfərəs $ koʊ-, kə-/ *adj*

conjecture /kənˈdʒekt∫ə $ -ər/ *n* [C,U] *formal* when you form ideas or opinions without having much information to base them on: *The statement is pure conjecture.* —**conjecture** *v* [I,T]

conjugal /ˈkɒndʒʊgəl $ ˈkɑːn-/ *adj* [only before noun] *formal* relating to marriage

conjugate /ˈkɒndʒʊgeɪt $ ˈkɑːn-/ *v* [T] to state the different forms that a verb can have —**conjugation** /‚kɒndʒʊˈgeɪʃən $ ‚kɑːn-/ *n* [C,U]

conjunction /kənˈdʒʌŋkʃən/ *n* [C] **1 in conjunction with sb/sth** working, happening, or being used with someone or something else: *The worksheets should be used in conjunction with the video.* **2** a word such as 'but', 'and', or 'because', which joins parts of a sentence

conjure /ˈkʌndʒə $ ˈkɑːndʒər, ˈkʌn-/ *v*
  conjure sth ⇔ **up** *phr v* **1** to bring a thought, memory, or picture to someone's mind: *Smells can often conjure up memories.* **2** to make, get, or achieve something, as if by magic: *Dean conjured up a last-minute goal.*

conjurer, conjuror /ˈkʌndʒərə $ ˈkɑːndʒərər, ˈkʌn-/ *n* [C] someone who does magic tricks

conjuring /ˈkʌndʒərɪŋ $ ˈkɑːn-, ˈkʌn-/ *n* [U] when someone does magic tricks and makes things appear and disappear

conman /ˈkɒnmæn $ ˈkɑːn-/ *n* [C] plural **conmen** /-men/ someone who tries to get money by tricking people

connect /kəˈnekt/ *v*

1 [T] to join two or more things together: *The M11 connects London and Cambridge.* | *Connect the speakers to the stereo.*

2 [T] to realize or show that a fact, event, person etc is related to or involved in something: **connect sb/sth with sth** *There is little evidence to connect him with the crime.*

3 [T] to join something to a supply of electricity, gas, or water, or to a computer or telephone network [≠ **disconnect**]: *Has the phone been connected yet?* | **+to** *Click here to connect to the Internet.*

4 [I] if a plane, train etc connects with another one, it arrives just before the other one leaves so you can change from one to the other: *a connecting flight to Rio*

connected /kəˈnektɪd/ *adj*

1 if two things are connected with each other, they are related in some way: **+with** *problems connected with homelessness* | *Bad diet is closely connected with many illnesses.*

2 joined to something else: **+to** *The computer is connected to a printer.*
→ WELL-CONNECTED

connection /kəˈnekʃən/ *n*

1 [C,U] a relationship between things: **+between** *the connection between smoking and cancer* | **+with/to** *Does this have any connection with the project?* | *the close connection between opera and poetry*

2 [C] a piece of wire or metal joining two parts of a machine together or to an electrical system

3 [C,U] when two or more machines or telephones are joined together or joined to a larger system, using an electrical connection: *free Internet connection* | **+to** *The socket allows connection to a PC.*

4 [C] a plane, train etc that is arranged so that people from an earlier plane, train etc can use it: *I missed my connection.*

5 in connection with sth concerning something: *Police are questioning a man in connection with the crime.*

6 connections [plural] people you know who can help you, especially because they are in positions of power: *He has connections in high places.*

connector /kəˈnektə $ -ər/ *n* [C] an object which is used to join two pieces of equipment together

connive /kəˈnaɪv/ *v* [I] to work secretly to do something bad or allow something bad to happen: **connive (with sb) to do sth** *Together, they connived to deceive her.* —**connivance** *n* [C,U]

connoisseur /‚kɒnəˈsɜː $ ‚kɑːnəˈsɜːr/ *n* [C] someone who knows a lot about something such as art, food, or music: **+of** *a connoisseur of fine wines* → see box at EXPERT

connotation /‚kɒnəˈteɪʃən $ ‚kɑː-/ *n* [C] an idea or quality that a word makes you think of, in addition to its basic meaning: **+of** *the word 'discipline' and its connotations of punishment*

conquer /ˈkɒŋkə $ ˈkɑːŋkər/ *v* **1** [I,T] to get control of a country or group of people by fighting: *The Normans conquered England in 1066.* **2** [T] to succeed in controlling something, especially a problem or strong feeling: *efforts to conquer inflation* | *I didn't think I'd ever conquer my fear of flying.* —**conqueror** *n* [C]

conquest /ˈkɒŋkwest $ ˈkɑːŋ-/ *n* [C,U] when someone gets control of a group of people, an area, or a situation: **+of** *the Spanish conquest of Central America* | *the conquest of space*

conscience /'kɒnʃəns $ 'kɑːn-/ n [C,U]
1 the part of your mind that tells you whether what you are doing is morally right or wrong: *He had a **guilty conscience** (=feeling of guilt).* | *I knew I could face them with a **clear conscience*** (=when you know you have done nothing wrong). | **pang/twinge of conscience** (=a slight feeling of guilt)
2 on sb's conscience making you feel guilty: *I lied and it's been on my conscience ever since.*

conscientious /ˌkɒnʃi'enʃəs◂ $ ˌkɑːn-/ adj
approving careful to do everything that it is your job or duty to do: *a conscientious teacher* —**conscientiously** adv

conscientious ob'jector n [C] someone who refuses to fight in a war because of their moral beliefs

conscious /'kɒnʃəs $ 'kɑːn-/ adj
1 [not before noun] noticing something or realizing that it exists: **conscious of (doing) sth** *People are increasingly conscious of the need to exercise.* | **+that** *John was conscious that she was watching him.*
2 awake and able to understand what is happening [≠ **unconscious**]: *Owen was still conscious when they got to the hospital.*
3 conscious effort/decision/attempt etc a deliberate effort, decision etc: *Lyn had made a conscious decision to have a baby.*
4 thinking that something is very important: **health-conscious/fashion-conscious etc** *fashion-conscious teenagers* | **+of** *She's very conscious of safety.*
—**consciously** adv → SELF-CONSCIOUS

consciousness /'kɒnʃəsn̩s $ 'kɑːn-/ n **1** [U] the condition of being awake and understanding what is happening: *She **lost consciousness** in the accident.* | *It was two weeks before he **regained consciousness**.* **2** [U] someone's mind, thoughts, and ideas: *research into human consciousness* **3** [singular,U] when you know that something exists or is important: **+of** *We need to increase public consciousness of the problem.*

conscript¹ /'kɒnskrɪpt $ 'kɑːn-/ n [C] someone who has been made to join the army, navy etc

conscript² /kən'skrɪpt/ v [T] to make someone join the army, navy etc —**conscription** /-'skrɪpʃən/ n [U]

consecrate /'kɒnsɪkreɪt $ 'kɑːn-/ v [T] to make something holy by performing a religious ceremony —**consecration** /ˌkɒnsɪ'kreɪʃən $ ˌkɑːn-/ n [U]

consecutive /kən'sekjᵿtɪv/ adj happening one after the other: *It rained for three consecutive days.* —**consecutively** adv

consensual /kən'senʃuəl/ adj formal
1 involving the agreement of all or most people in a group: *a consensual style of management* **2** consensual sexual activity is wanted and agreed to by the people involved

consensus /kən'sensəs/ n [singular,U] agreement between everyone in a group: **+on/about** *Ministers failed to **reach a consensus** on the issue.* | **+that** *a general consensus among teachers that the policy should be changed* | *The **consensus of opinion** is that Smith should resign.*

consent¹ /kən'sent/ n [U] permission: **without sb's consent** *He took the car without the owner's consent.* | *Her parents **gave** their **consent** to the marriage.*

consent² v [I] to give your permission for something, or agree to something: **+to** *He had not consented to medical treatment.*

consequence /'kɒnsᵻkwəns $ 'kɑːnsᵻkwens/ n [C]
1 something that happens as a result of something else: **+of** *the environmental consequences of road building* | **+for** *The policy will have serious **consequences** for Britain.* | *The accident happened **as a consequence of** poor safety procedures.* → see box at RESULT
2 of little/no consequence formal not important: *matters of little consequence*

consequent /'kɒnsᵻkwənt $ 'kɑːn-/ adj [only before noun] formal happening as a result of something else: *terrorism and the consequent decline in tourism*

consequently /'kɒnsᵻkwəntli $ 'kɑːnsᵻkwentli/ adv as a result: *He did no work and consequently failed the exam.*

conservation /ˌkɒnsə'veɪʃən $ ˌkɑːnsər-/ n [U] **1** the protection of natural things such as animals, plants, forests etc: **+of** *conservation of the countryside* | *conservation groups* **2** when you prevent something from being wasted: **+of** *the conservation of resources* —**conservationist** n [C]

conservatism /kən'sɜːvətɪzəm $ -ɜːr-/ n [U] dislike of change and new ideas

Conservative /kən'sɜːvətɪv $ -ɜːr-/ n [C] a member or supporter of the Conservative Party in Britain

conservative¹ adj **1** not willing to accept changes or new ideas: *a conservative attitude to education* **2 Conservative** belonging or relating to the Conservative Party in Britain: *a Conservative MP* **3 a conservative estimate/guess** a guess that is deliberately lower than the real amount probably is

conservative² n [C] someone who does not like changes

Con'servative ˌParty n **the Conservative Party** a political party in Britain that supports RIGHT-WING ideas

conservatory /kən'sɜːvətəri $ -'sɜːrvətɔːri/ n [C] plural **conservatories** a room with glass walls and a glass roof, that is joined to the side of a house

conserve /kən'sɜːv $ -ɜːrv/ v [T] to prevent something from being wasted, damaged, or destroyed: *the need to conserve the countryside*

consider /kən'sɪdə $ -ər/ v
1 [I,T] to think about something carefully, especially before making a decision: **consider doing sth** *I considered resigning.* | **+whether/what etc** *He was considering whether to apply for the job.* | *You should **consider the possibility of** hiring a lawyer.* → see box at THINK
2 [T] to think of someone or something in a particular way: **+that** *They considered that the film was not suitable for children.* | **consider sb/sth (to be) sth** *Mrs. Gillan was considered to be an excellent teacher.*

3 [T] to think about someone and their feelings so you do not upset them: *He doesn't consider my feelings at all.*

considerable /kənˈsɪdərəbəl/ *adj* large enough to be important or have an effect: *a considerable amount of money* —**considerably** *adv*

considerate /kənˈsɪdərɪt/ *adj* thinking about other people's feelings and needs [≠ **inconsiderate**]: *He was always kind and considerate.* → see box at **KIND** —**considerately** *adv*

consideration /kənˌsɪdəˈreɪʃən/ *n* **1** [U] *formal* careful thought and attention: **under consideration** *Several plans are under consideration.* **2** [C] a fact that you think about when deciding something: *financial considerations* **3 take sth into consideration** to think about something when making a decision: *We'll take into consideration the fact that you were ill.* **4** [U] when you think about other people's feelings and needs: **+for** *He shows no consideration for others.*

considered /kənˈsɪdəd $ -ərd/ *adj* **1 all things considered** when you think about all parts of a situation: *All things considered, I think the day went well.* **2** a considered opinion, judgment etc is one that you have thought about carefully

considering /kənˈsɪdərɪŋ/ *prep, linking word* used to say that you are thinking about a particular fact when giving your opinion: **+(that)** *She did very well considering it was her first attempt.*

consign /kənˈsaɪn/ *v*
consign sb/sth to sth *phr v* **1** to cause someone or something to be in a bad situation: *a decision that consigned him to political obscurity* **2** to put something somewhere, especially in order to get rid of it

consignment /kənˈsaɪnmənt/ *n* [C] a quantity of goods that is sent somewhere: **+of** *a consignment of toys*

consist /kənˈsɪst/ *v*
consist of sth *phr v* to be formed from two or more things or people: **consist mainly/entirely/ largely of sth** *The audience consists largely of teenagers.*

consistency /kənˈsɪstənsi/ *n* [C,U] plural **consistencies** **1** *approving* the quality of always happening or being done in the same way [≠ **inconsistency**]: **+in** *Consistency in approach is important.* **2** how thick, smooth etc a substance is: *a dessert with a creamy consistency*

consistent /kənˈsɪstənt/ *adj* **1** *approving* always happening or doing something in the same way [≠ **inconsistent**]: *the team's most consistent player* | **+in** *He is consistent in his opposition to the plan.* **2** containing facts, ideas etc that agree with other facts etc: **+with** *His story is not consistent with the facts.* —**consistently** *adv*: *consistently good marks*

consolation /ˌkɒnsəˈleɪʃən $ ˌkɑːn-/ *n* [C,U] something that makes you feel better when you are sad or disappointed: **+for/to** *The news will be little consolation for those who have lost their jobs.*

console¹ /kənˈsəʊl $ -ˈsoʊl/ *v* [T] to make someone feel better when they are sad or disappointed: *No one could console her when her dog*

died. | **console yourself with sth** *I consoled myself with the thought that I had done my best.*

console² /ˈkɒnsəʊl $ ˈkɑːnsoʊl/ *n* [C] a flat board that contains the controls for a machine, piece of electrical equipment, computer etc

consolidate /kənˈsɒlɪdeɪt $ -ˈsɑː-/ *v* [I,T] **1** to make your power or success stronger so that you continue to be successful: *The company has consolidated its position in the Japanese market.* **2** to combine things so that they are more effective or easier to manage: *a loan to consolidate debts* —**consolidation** /kənˌsɒlɪˈdeɪʃən $ -ˌsɑː-/ *n* [C,U]

consonant /ˈkɒnsənənt $ ˈkɑːn-/ *n* [C] any letter of the English alphabet except a, e, i, o, and u [➡ **vowel**]

consort /kənˈsɔːt $ -ɔːrt/ *v*
consort with sb *phr v formal* to spend time with someone who other people do not approve of

consortium /kənˈsɔːtiəm $ -ɔːr-/ *n* [C] plural **consortia** /-tiə/ or **consortiums** a group of companies or organizations who are working together: **+of** *a consortium of banks*

conspicuous /kənˈspɪkjuəs/ *adj* easy to notice [≠ **inconspicuous**]: *The notice must be displayed in a conspicuous place.* → see box at **NOTICEABLE** —**conspicuously** *adv*

conspiracy /kənˈspɪrəsi/ *n* [C,U] plural **conspiracies** a secret plan made by two or more people to do something bad or illegal: **conspiracy to do sth** *a conspiracy to evade taxes* | **+against** *a conspiracy against the police* → see box at **PLAN**

conspirator /kənˈspɪrətə $ -ər/ *n* [C] someone who is part of a group planning a conspiracy —**conspiratorial** /kənˌspɪrəˈtɔːriəl/ *adj*

conspire /kənˈspaɪə $ -ˈspaɪr/ *v* [I] **1** to secretly plan with other people to do something bad or illegal: **conspire to do sth** *The men admitted conspiring to steal cars.* **2** *formal* if events conspire to do something, they happen at the same time and have a bad result: **conspire to do sth** *Pollution and neglect have conspired to ruin the city.*

constable /ˈkʌnstəbəl $ ˈkɑːn-/ *n* [C] a British police officer of the lowest rank

constabulary /kənˈstæbjʊləri $ -leri/ *n* [C] plural **constabularies** the police force of a particular area or country

constant /ˈkɒnstənt $ ˈkɑːn-/ *adj*
1 happening regularly or all the time: *a constant stream of vehicles* | *the constant threat of violence* **2** staying the same: *a constant speed* —**constancy** *n* [U]

constantly /ˈkɒnstəntli $ ˈkɑːn-/ *adv* all the time or regularly: *The English language is constantly changing.* → see box at **OFTEN**

constellation /ˌkɒnstəˈleɪʃən $ ˌkɑːn-/ *n* [C] a group of stars that has a name → see box at **SPACE**

consternation /ˌkɒnstəˈneɪʃən $ ˌkɑːnstər-/ *n* [U] a feeling of shock or worry: **in consternation** *She stared at him in consternation.*

constipation /ˌkɒnstɪˈpeɪʃən $ ˌkɑːn-/ *n* [U] when someone is unable to get rid of solid waste easily out of their body —**constipated** /ˈkɒnstɪpeɪtɪd $ ˈkɑːn-/ *adj*

C

constituency /kənˈstɪtʃuənsi/ n [C] plural **constituencies** BrE an area of a country that elects someone to a parliament, or the people who live and vote there

constituent /kənˈstɪtʃuənt/ n [C] **1** someone who votes in a particular area **2** one of the parts that form something: **+of** the constituents of blood —**constituent** adj

constitute /ˈkɒnstɪtjuːt ˈkaːnstɪtuːt/ v linking verb **1** to be considered to be something: The rise in crime constitutes a threat to society. **2** if several parts constitute something, they form it: the 50 states that constitute the USA

constitution /ˌkɒnstɪˈtjuːʃən $ ˌkaːnstɪˈtuː-/ n [C] **1** also **Constitution** a set of laws and principles that a country or organization is governed by: the Constitution of the United States **2** someone's health and ability to fight illness: **(have) a strong/weak constitution**

constitutional /ˌkɒnstɪˈtjuːʃənəl $ ˌkaːnstɪˈtuː-/ adj relating to the constitution of a country: constitutional reform —**constitutionally** adv

constrain /kənˈstreɪn/ v [T] formal to limit something, or to stop someone from doing what they want to do: The project was constrained by lack of money.

constrained /kənˈstreɪnd/ adj **feel constrained to do sth** formal to feel that you must do something

constraint /kənˈstreɪnt/ n [C,U] something that limits your freedom to do what you want: **+on** The government has **placed constraints** on further research.

constrict /kənˈstrɪkt/ v **1** [I,T] to become narrower or tighter, or to make something do this: Her throat constricted. **2** [T] to limit someone's freedom to do what they want —**constriction** /-ˈstrɪkʃən/ n [C,U]

construct /kənˈstrʌkt/ v [T] to build something such as a house, bridge, road etc: The Empire State Building was constructed in 1931. → see picture at **BUILD**[1]

construction /kənˈstrʌkʃən/ n
1 [U] the process of building something such as a house, bridge, or road: **+of** the construction of a new airport | **under construction** (=being built) The hotel is under construction. | a road construction project
2 [C] formal something that has been built: a wooden construction
3 [C] the way in which words are put together in a sentence: difficult **grammatical constructions**

constructive /kənˈstrʌktɪv/ adj useful and helpful: constructive criticism —**constructively** adv

construe /kənˈstruː/ v [T] formal to understand a remark or action in a particular way: **construe sth as sth** Comments like that may be construed as sexist.

consul /ˈkɒnsəl $ ˈkaːn-/ n [C] a government official in a foreign city whose job is to help citizens of his or her own country who are there —**consular** /ˈkɒnsjʊlə $ ˈkaːnsələr/ adj

consulate /ˈkɒnsjʊlət $ ˈkaːnsələt/ n [C] the building in which a consul lives and works [→ embassy]

consult /kənˈsʌlt/ v **1** [T] to ask someone for advice or information, or to look for it in a book, map etc: Consult your doctor if the headaches continue. | **consult sb about sth** I consulted an accountant about tax. **2** [I,T] to discuss something with someone so that you can make a decision together: He sold the car without consulting me! | **+with** The President consulted with European leaders.

consultancy /kənˈsʌltənsi/ n [C,U] plural **consultancies** a company that gives advice on a particular subject, or the advice that they give: a management consultancy | consultancy fees

consultant /kənˈsʌltənt/ n [C] **1** someone whose job is to give advice about a particular subject: a marketing consultant **2** BrE a hospital doctor of the highest rank who knows a lot about a particular area of medicine → see box at **DOCTOR**

consultation /ˌkɒnsəlˈteɪʃən $ ˌkaːn-/ n **1** [C] a discussion or meeting that you have in order to get information or advice: **+between** consultations between teachers and parents | a medical consultation **2** [U] when you discuss something with someone in order to get information or advice: **for consultation** A counsellor is always available for consultation. | **in consultation with sb** The plans were drawn up in consultation with engineers. **3** [U] when you look for information in a book: **for consultation** Old exam papers are available for consultation.

consumables /kənˈsjuːməbəlz $ -ˈsuːm-/ n [plural] goods that people use and then buy again

consume /kənˈsjuːm $ -ˈsuːm/ v [T] **1** to use energy, goods, time etc: Only 27% of the paper we consume is recycled. **2** formal to eat or drink something **3** **be consumed with guilt/rage/passion etc** literary to feel extremely guilty, angry etc **4** if fire consumes something, it destroys it completely

consumer /kənˈsjuːmə $ -ˈsuːmər/ n [C] someone who buys or uses goods and services [→ consumption]: Consumers are enjoying lower airfares. | a wider choice of goods for **the consumer** (=consumers in general) → see box at **CUSTOMER**

consumerism /kənˈsjuːmərɪzəm $ -ˈsuː-/ n [U] the buying and selling of goods and services: the power of consumerism today

consuming /kənˈsjuːmɪŋ $ -ˈsuː-/ adj [only before noun] a consuming feeling or interest is very strong and important in your life: a consuming ambition

consummate[1] /kənˈsʌmət, ˈkɒnsəmət $ kənˈsʌmət/ adj formal showing great skill: He performed **with consummate skill**.

consummate[2] /ˈkɒnsəmeɪt $ ˈkaːn-/ v [T] to make a marriage or relationship complete by having sex —**consummation** /ˌkɒnsəˈmeɪʃən $ ˌkaːn-/ n [U]

consumption /kənˈsʌmpʃən/ n [U] **1** the amount of electricity, gas, oil etc that is used: **energy/fuel etc consumption** the need to reduce petrol consumption **2** formal when people eat or drink something: **+of** the consumption of alcohol

contact[1] /ˈkɒntækt $ ˈkaːn-/ n
1 [U] communication with a person, organiza-

tion, or country: **+with/between** *There is little contact between the two tribes.* | **be/get/keep/stay in contact (with sb)** *We stay in contact by email.* | *She moved away and they* ***lost contact****.* | *It'd be good to* ***make contact with*** *other local schools.*
2 [U] when two people or things touch against each other: **+with/between** *Babies need* ***physical contact*** *with a loving adult.* | *Don't let raw meat* ***come into contact with*** *other food.*
3 [C] someone you know who may be able to help you or give you advice: *Do you have any contacts in the area?*

contact² *v* [T] to telephone or write to someone: *Who can we contact in an emergency?* | *She contacted the police.*

'contact ˌlens *n* [C] a small round piece of plastic you put on your eye to help you see clearly

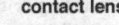

contact lens

contagious /kən'teɪdʒəs/ *adj*
1 a contagious disease can be passed from one person to another by touch **2** a feeling, attitude etc that is contagious spreads quickly among people: *Her laughter was contagious.*

contain /kən'teɪn/ *v* [T]
1 to have something inside: *His wallet contained $45.* | *This product may contain nuts.*
2 to include something: *Her letter contained information about his business activities.* | *Does the film contain violence?*
3 to control the emotions you feel: *Jane couldn't contain her amusement.* | **contain yourself** *He was so excited he could hardly contain himself.*
4 to stop something from spreading or escaping: *Doctors are struggling to contain the epidemic.*
—**containment** *n* [U] *formal*: *containment of public expenditure*

container /kən'teɪnə $ -ər/ *n* [C] something such as a box or bowl that you keep things in: *Ice cream is sold in plastic containers.*

contaminate /kən'tæmɪneɪt/ *v* [T] if a dirty or poisonous substance contaminates something, it gets into it and makes it dangerous: *Chemical waste had contaminated the water supply.* —**contamination** /kənˌtæmɪ'neɪʃən/ *n* [U]

contemplate /'kɒntəmpleɪt $ 'kɑːn-/ *v* [T] to think about something in a serious way: **contemplate doing sth** *Have you contemplated resigning?* —**contemplation** /ˌkɒntəm'pleɪʃən $ ˌkɑːn-/ *n* [U]

contemporary¹ /kən'tempərəri, -pəri $ -pəreri/ *adj*
1 belonging to the present time [**= modern**]: **contemporary music/art/dance etc** *an exhibition of contemporary art*

C

containers

Cola
can (of cola)
tube (of toothpaste)
PICKLES
jar (of pickles)
tub (of margarine)
Crisps
bag (of crisps BrE/ chips AmE)
Golden Valley
tin/can (of sweetcorn BrE/ corn AmE)
packet (of biscuits BrE/ cookies AmE)
English BLOSSOM
pot (of honey)
Orange FRESH
carton (of orange juice)
Magic SELECTION
box (of chocolates)

2 done or existing at the same time: ***contemporary accounts*** of the war | **+with** *letters contemporary with his earliest compositions*

contemporary² *n* [C] plural **contemporaries** someone who lives or works at the same time as someone else: *Mozart was admired by his contemporaries.*

contempt /kənˈtempt/ *n* [U] **1** the feeling that someone or something does not deserve respect: *Stuart treated his wife with* **utter contempt.** **2 contempt of court** *law* when someone does not obey a court of law

contemptible /kənˈtemptɪbəl/ *adj* not deserving any respect: *contemptible behaviour* —**contemptibly** *adv*

contemptuous /kənˈtemptʃuəs/ *adj* showing that you think someone or something deserves no respect: *a contemptuous glance* —**contemptuously** *adv*

contend /kənˈtend/ *v* **1** [I] to compete against someone to get something: **+for** *Twelve teams contended for the title.* **2** [T] to say or argue that something is true: **+that** *Democrats contend that the tax is unfair.*

contend with sth *phr v* to have to deal with something difficult or unpleasant: *The builders* **had to contend with** *bad weather.*

contender /kənˈtendə $ -ər/ *n* [C] someone who is competing to get or win something

content¹ /ˈkɒntent $ ˈkɑːn-/ *n*

1 contents [plural] **a)** the things that are inside a box, bag, room etc: **+of** *Suzy looked through the contents of her handbag.* | *The gallery's contents were damaged in the fire.* **b)** the things that are written in a letter, book etc: **+of** *He kept the contents of the letter a secret.* **2** [singular] the amount of a substance that something contains: **fat/protein/alcohol etc content** *the high fat content of cheese* **3** [singular] the ideas or information contained in a speech, book, programme etc: **+of** *Is the content of the magazine suitable for children?*

content² /kənˈtent/ *adj* [not before noun] satisfied and happy: **+with** *She seems content with her life.* | **content to do sth** *I was quite content to let Steve do the talking.* —**contentment** *n* [U] → **do sth to your heart's content** at **HEART**

content³ *v* **content yourself with (doing) sth** to accept something even though it is not what you really want: *We'll have to content ourselves with a cheaper holiday this year.*

contented /kənˈtentɪd/ *adj* satisfied and happy [≠ **discontented**]: *a contented smile* —**contentedly** *adv*

contention /kənˈtenʃən/ *n formal* **1** [C] a strong opinion that someone expresses **2** [U] arguments and disagreements between people **3 be in contention (for sth)** to be competing for something

contentious /kənˈtenʃəs/ *adj formal* likely to cause an argument

contest¹ /ˈkɒntest $ ˈkɑːn-/ *n* [C] a competition: **+for** *the contest for the world title* | *I only* **entered the contest** *for fun.* | *The election will be a* **close contest** (=one which either party, team etc could win, because they are equally popular, good etc).

contest² /kənˈtest/ *v* [T] **1** to say formally that you do not think something is correct or fair:

His brothers contested the will. **2** to try to win something, especially an election

contestant /kənˈtestənt/ *n* [C] someone who competes in a competition

context /ˈkɒntekst $ ˈkɑːn-/ *n* [C,U] **1** the situation, events etc that are related to something and help you understand it: **in context/out of context** (=in relation to this situation etc, or not) *You need to consider these events in their historical context.* **2** the words that come before and after a word or phrase and help you understand its meaning

continent /ˈkɒntɪnənt $ ˈkɑːn-/ *n* [C]

1 one of the seven main areas of land on the Earth: *the continent of Africa*
2 the Continent *BrE* Western Europe, not including Britain

continental /ˌkɒntɪˈnentl◂ $ ˌkɑːn-/ *adj* **1** relating to a continent but not its islands: *flights across the continental US* **2** *BrE* old-fashioned relating to the continent of Europe, not including Britain

contingency /kənˈtɪndʒənsi/ *n* [C] plural **contingencies** an event or situation that might happen in the future and could cause problems: *a* ***contingency plan***

contingent¹ /kənˈtɪndʒənt/ *adj formal* depending on something else in order to happen: **+on/upon** *Further investment is contingent on the company's performance.*

contingent² *n* [C] **1** a group of people at an event who all come from the same area, organization etc: *Has the Scottish contingent arrived?* **2** a group of soldiers sent to help a larger group

continual /kənˈtɪnjuəl/ *adj* [only before noun] happening all the time without stopping, or happening many times: *five weeks of continual rain* | *the continual threat of terrorism*

THESAURUS

Continual and **continuous** can be used in a very similar way: *a continual/continuous process*
Continual is also used when something happens many times, especially something annoying: *There were continual interruptions all day.*
Continuous is used to emphasize that there is no pause or break between things: *six continuous hours of meetings* | *a continuous line of trees*

—**continually** *adv*: *The phone rang continually.*

continuation /kənˌtɪnjuˈeɪʃən/ *n* **1** [C] something that follows something else and seems a part of it: **+of** *The book is a continuation of his autobiography.* **2** [singular, U] when something continues to exist or happen: *measures to ensure the continuation of food supply*

continue /kənˈtɪnjuː/ *v*

1 [I,T] to not stop happening, existing, or doing something [→ **discontinue**]: **+for** *The strike continued for four weeks.* | **+with** *Will the team continue with their research?* | **continue to do sth** *The city's population has continued to grow.* | **continue doing sth** *Most elderly people want to continue living at home.*
2 [I,T] to start again after a pause: *After a brief ceasefire, fighting continued.* | *Rescue teams will*

continue the search tomorrow. | **continue doing sth** *He picked up his book and continued reading.* **3** [I] to go further in the same direction: **+down/ along/into etc** *We continued along the road.*
—**continued** *adj: Thank you for your continued support.*

continuity /ˌkɒntɪ'njuːⁱti $ ˌkaːntⁱ'nuː-/ *n* [U] when something continues over a long period of time without stopping or changing: *There should be continuity of care between hospital and home.*

continuous /kən'tɪnjuəs/ *adj*

1 happening or existing without stopping: *a* **continuous flow** *of information* | *The problems have been continuous.* → see box at CONTINUAL
2 *technical* the continuous form of a verb shows that an action is continuing. In English, this is formed by the verb 'be' followed by a PRESENT PARTICIPLE as in 'I was watching TV'.
—**continuously** *adv* → see box at OFTEN

contort /kən'tɔːt $ -ɔːrt/ *v* [I,T] if your face or body contorts, or is contorted, it is twisted into an unnatural shape: **+with/in** *His body contorted in agony.* —**contortion** /-'tɔːʃən $ -ɔːr-/ *n* [C,U]

contour /'kɒntʊə $ 'kaːntʊr/ *n* [C] **1** the shape of the outer edges of something: *the contours of the hills* **2** also **'contour line** a line on a map joining points of equal height

contraband /'kɒntrəbænd $ 'kaːn-/ *n* [U] goods that are brought into a country illegally

contraception /ˌkɒntrə'sepʃən $ ˌkaːn-/ *n* [U] the methods that stop a woman becoming PREGNANT [= birth control]

contraceptive /ˌkɒntrə'septɪv‹ $ ˌkaːn-/ *n* [C] something that is used to stop a woman becoming PREGNANT —**contraceptive** *adj: the contraceptive pill*

contract¹ /'kɒntrækt $ 'kaːn-/ *n* [C] an official agreement between two or more people: *Read the* **contract** *carefully before you* **sign** *it.* | *She has* **agreed** *a three-year* **contract** *with a Hollywood studio.* | *What happens if you* **break** *your* **contract***?*
—**contractual** /kən'træktʃuəl/ *adj: a contractual arrangement*

contract² /kən'trækt/ *v* **1** [I] to become smaller [≠ **expand**]: *Metal contracts as it cools.* **2** [T] *formal* to get a serious illness: *Sharon contracted AIDS from a dirty needle.* **3** [I,T] to sign a contract with someone agreeing what you or they will do

contraction /kən'trækʃən/ *n* **1** [C] *technical* a very strong painful movement of a woman's muscles during the birth of her baby **2** [U] the process of becoming smaller [≠ **expansion**]: *the contraction of the coal industry* **3** [C] *technical* a shorter form of a word or words: *'Don't' is a contraction of 'do not'.*

contractor /kən'træktə $ 'kaːntræktər/ *n* [C] a person or company that does work or supplies goods for another company: *a building contractor*

contradict /ˌkɒntrə'dɪkt $ ˌkaːn-/ *v* **1** [I,T] to disagree with something, especially by saying that the opposite is true: *The article flatly* **contradicts** *their claims.* **2** [T] if one statement, story etc contradicts another, they are different, and both cannot be true: *The witnesses' accounts* **contradict each other.**

contradiction /ˌkɒntrə'dɪkʃən $ ˌkaːn-/ *n* **1** [C] a difference between two statements, facts etc which means they cannot both be true: **+between** *the contradiction between our figures and the official ones* **2** [U] when you say that someone else's opinion, statement etc is wrong

contradictory /ˌkɒntrə'dɪktəri‹ $ ˌkaːn-/ *adj* if two statements are contradictory, they are different and cannot both be true

contraption /kən'træpʃən/ *n* [C] a machine or piece of equipment that looks strange or unlikely to work

contrary¹ /'kɒntrəri $ 'kaːntreri/ *n formal* **1 on/quite the contrary** used to emphasize that the opposite of what someone has just said is actually true: *It wasn't a good thing; on the contrary it was a mistake.* **2 to the contrary** saying or showing the opposite of something: *Despite rumours to the contrary, their relationship is very good.*

contrary² *adj* **1** completely different from each other, or opposed to something: *They expressed contrary opinions.* | **+to** *The government's actions are contrary to the public interest.* **2 contrary to popular belief/opinion** opposite to what people think: *Contrary to popular belief, a desert can be very cold.*

contrast¹ /'kɒntraːst $ 'kaːntræst/ *n*

1 [C,U] a very noticeable difference between people, things etc: **+between** *the contrast between the rich and the poor* | **+with** *the marble makes a strong contrast with the wooden floor* **2 in/by contrast (to/with sth)** used when comparing two people, things etc that are very different from each other: *There was brilliant sunshine outside, in contrast to the interior.* **3** [C] something that is very different to something else: **+to** *The theatre was quite a contrast to the ones we'd performed in before.*

contrast² /kən'traːst $ -'træst/ *v*

1 [I] if two things contrast, the difference between them is very noticeable: **+with** *These results* **contrast sharply** *with other medical tests.* **2** [T] to compare two people, ideas, objects etc and show how they are different from each other: **contrast sth with sth** *The speaker contrasted this approach with earlier methods.*
—**contrasting** *adj: contrasting colours*

contravene /ˌkɒntrə'viːn $ ˌkaːn-/ *v* [T] *formal* to do something that is not allowed by a law or a rule —**contravention** /-'venʃən/ *n* [C,U]

contribute /kən'trɪbjuːt/ *v* [I,T]

1 to give money, help, ideas etc to something that other people are also involved in: *Everyone was expected to contribute £2.* | **contribute (sth) to/towards sth** *I hope you'll all contribute towards the discussion.* | *The volunteers contribute their own time to the project.*
2 to help to make something happen: **+to** *Alcohol contributes to 100,000 deaths a year in the US.*
3 to write for a newspaper or magazine
—**contributor** *n* [C]

contribution /ˌkɒntrⁱ'bjuːʃən $ ˌkaːn-/ *n* [C]

1 something that you give or do to help make something successful: **+to** *Einstein's enormous contribution to science* | *I'd like to think I'd* **made a contribution** *to society.*

C

2 an amount of money that you give to help pay for something: **+of** *A contribution of £25 will buy 15 books.*

contributory /kənˈtrɪbjʊ̩təri $ -tɔːri/ *adj* [only before noun] helping to cause something: *Smoking is a contributory factor in lung cancer.*

contrite /ˈkɒntraɪt $ ˈkɑːn-/ *adj formal* feeling guilty and sorry for something bad that you have done —**contritely** *adv* —**contrition** /kənˈtrɪʃən/ *n* [U]

contrive /kənˈtraɪv/ *v* [T] **1** *formal* to succeed in doing something difficult: **contrive to do sth** *Somehow she contrived to escape.* **2** to deliberately make something happen in a clever or dishonest way: *The companies are accused of contriving the oil shortage.*

contrived /kənˈtraɪvd/ *adj* seeming false and not natural: *The novel's characters seem contrived.*

control¹ /kənˈtrəʊl $ -ˈtroʊl/ *n*

1 [U] the power or ability to make someone or something do what you want: **+of/over** *Babies have very little control over their movements.* | *She's a good teacher who has control of her class.* | *Never lose control of the horse.* | *The car spun out of control and hit a tree.* | **under control** (=happening or behaving in the way you want) *'Do you need any help?' 'No, it's all under control, thanks.'*

2 [U] the power to decide how a country, place, company etc is organized, and what it does: **+of** *The family has control of the company.* | **in control (of sth)** *Rebel forces are still in control of the area.* | *China took control of the island in 1683.*

3 [C,U] when you limit something, or a rule, law etc that limits it: **+of** *the control of inflation* | **+on** *There are strict controls on international trade.* | **under control** (=being prevented from increasing) *Firefighters had the fire under control by midnight.*

4 [U] the ability to remain calm, even when you are angry, upset, or excited: *David lost control of himself and started yelling.*

5 [C] a thing that you press or turn to make a machine, television etc work: *the TV remote control*

6 [C,U] the place where something is officially checked: *passport control*
→ **BIRTH CONTROL**

control² *v* [T] **controlled, controlling**

1 to have the power to decide what will happen in an organization or place: *The Republicans now control the Senate.* | **Labour-/Republican-/Democrat- etc controlled** *a Conservative-controlled council*

2 to make someone or something do what you want, or to make something work in a particular way: *a teacher who can't control the kids* | *The temperature inside is carefully controlled.*

3 to limit the amount or growth of something: *a chemical used to control weeds*

4 to make yourself behave calmly, even if you feel angry, excited, or upset: *Sarah tried to control her anger.*
—**controller** *n* [C]

controversial /ˌkɒntrəˈvɜːʃəl◂ $ ˌkɑːntrəˈvɜːr-/ *adj* causing a lot of disagreement among people: *The site of the new road has been a controversial issue.* —**controversially** *adv*

controversy /ˈkɒntrəvɜːsi, kənˈtrɒvəsi $ ˈkɑːntrəvɜːrsi/ *n* [C,U] plural **controversies** a lot of disagreement about an idea or plan, involving many people: **+over/about** *There's been some controversy over increasing students' fees.*

conurbation /ˌkɒnɜːˈbeɪʃən $ ˌkɑːnɜːr-/ *n* [C] a group of towns that have spread and become joined together

convalesce /ˌkɒnvəˈles $ ˌkɑːn-/ *v* [I] to spend time getting well after an illness —**convalescence** *n* [U] *a long period of convalescence*

convection /kənˈvekʃən/ *n* [U] *technical* the movement caused by warm gas or liquid rising, and cold gas or liquid sinking

convene /kənˈviːn/ *v* [I,T] *formal* to come together or bring people together for a meeting

convenience /kənˈviːniəns/ *n* [U] the quality of being suitable or useful for a particular purpose [≠ **inconvenience**]: **the convenience of doing sth** *Most people like the convenience of using credit cards.* | **for convenience** *I bought a house near the station for convenience.*

con'venience ˌfood *n* [C,U] food that is prepared already and that is sold frozen or in cans, packages etc, so that it can be prepared quickly and easily

con'venience ˌstore *n* [C] a shop where you can buy food, alcohol, magazines etc, that is often open 24 hours each day → see box at **SHOP**

convenient /kənˈviːniənt/ *adj*

1 a convenient time is good for you because you are not doing anything else then [≠ **inconvenient**]: *Would 10:30 be a convenient time to meet?* | **+for** *11:00 is convenient for me.*

2 a convenient way of doing something is useful and easy [≠ **inconvenient**]: **convenient to do sth** *Mail order catalogues are a convenient way to shop.*

3 a convenient place is near and easy to get to [≠ **inconvenient**]: *The shops are very convenient.*
—**conveniently** *adv*

convent /ˈkɒnvənt $ ˈkɑːnvent/ *n* [C] a place where NUNS live

convention /kənˈvenʃən/ *n* **1** [C] a formal meeting of people who belong to the same profession, organization etc: *a teachers' convention* **2** [C] a formal agreement between countries: **+on** *the European convention on human rights* **3** [C,U] the normal and traditional way of behaving and thinking in a society: *social conventions*

conventional /kənˈvenʃənəl/ *adj*

1 [only before noun] of the usual type that has been used for a long time: *a conventional oven* → see box at **NORMAL**

2 thinking and behaving in the normal and traditional way [≠ **unconventional**]: **+in** *Tom is conventional in his approach to life.*

3 [only before noun] conventional weapons and wars do not use NUCLEAR power: *conventional forces*
—**conventionally** *adv*

converge /kənˈvɜːdʒ $ -ˈvɜːrdʒ/ *v* [I] to come from different directions and meet at the same place: **+on** *Reporters converged on the scene.*

conversant /kən'vɜːsənt $ -ɜːr-/ adj [not before noun] *formal* having knowledge or experience of something: **+with** *Staff members are conversant with the issues.*

conversation /ˌkɒnvə'seɪʃən $ ˌkɑːnvər-/ n [C,U] an informal talk between two or more people: **+with** *I had a short conversation with the teacher.* | **+about** *an interesting conversation about Italian opera* | *It's impossible to carry on a conversation with all this noise.* | *'Did you have a good journey?' he said, trying to make conversation* (=talk in order to be polite).
—**conversational** adj

converse¹ /kən'vɜːs $ -'vɜːrs/ v [I] *formal* to have a conversation with someone → see box at TALK

converse² /'kɒnvɜːs $ 'kɑːnvɜːrs/ n **the converse** *formal* the converse of a fact, word, statement etc is the opposite of it

conversely /kən'vɜːsli, 'kɒnvɜːsli $ kən'vɜːrsli, 'kɑːnvɜːrsli/ adv used when one situation is the opposite of another: *American consumers prefer white eggs; conversely, British buyers like brown eggs.*

conversion /kən'vɜːʃən $ -'vɜːrʒən/ n [C,U]
1 when you change something from one system or purpose to another: **+into/of/to** *the conversion of waste into energy* **2** when someone changes to a different religion or belief: **+to/ from** *her conversion to Catholicism*

convert¹ /kən'vɜːt $ -'vɜːrt/ v [I,T] **1** to change from one system or purpose to another, or to change something in this way: **+to/into** *a sofa that converts into a bed* | *The old houses have been converted into flats.* **2** to accept a different religion, opinion etc, or to make someone do this: **convert (sb) to sth** *Steve has converted to Islam.*

convert² /'kɒnvɜːt $ 'kɑːnvɜːrt/ n [C] someone who has been persuaded to change their religion or beliefs

convertible /kən'vɜːtɪbəl $ -ɜːr-/ n [C] a car with a roof that you can fold back or remove

convex /ˌkɒn'veks◂, kən-, 'kɒnveks $ ˌkɑːn'veks◂, kən-, 'kɑːnveks/ adj having a surface that curves OUTWARDS, like part of the outside of a ball or tube [≠ concave]

convey /kən'veɪ/ v [T] **1** to express ideas, feelings etc: *What does this poem convey?* **2** *formal* to take something from one place to another, especially in a vehicle

con'veyor belt n [C] a long moving band of rubber or metal, used to move things from one place to another

convict¹ /kən'vɪkt/ v [T] to officially decide in a court of law that someone is guilty of a crime [≠ acquit]: **convict sb of sth** *She was convicted of shoplifting.*

convict² /'kɒnvɪkt $ 'kɑːn-/ n [C] someone who has been proved guilty of a crime and sent to prison

conviction /kən'vɪkʃən/ n **1** [C,U] a very strong belief or opinion: **with/without conviction** *She spoke with great conviction* (=showing strong belief in what she said). **2** [C] a decision in a court of law that someone is guilty of a crime: **+for** *He had a conviction for theft.*

convince /kən'vɪns/ v [T]

1 to make someone feel certain that something

is true: *Her arguments didn't convince me.* | **convince sb (that)** *She convinced us she could do it.* | **convince sb of sth** *He tried to convince them of his innocence.*
2 to persuade someone to do something [= persuade]: **convince sb to do sth** *I couldn't convince Liz to come.*

convinced /kən'vɪnst/ adj [not before noun] completely certain that something is true: *You don't sound convinced.* | **+(that)** *I am convinced the treatment is safe.* | **+of** *Is she convinced of his guilt?*

convincing /kən'vɪnsɪŋ/ adj **1** making you believe that something is true or right: **convincing evidence/proof/arguments etc** *It was a convincing excuse.* | *He was utterly convincing in the role* (=he acted the part very well). **2 convincing victory/win** a victory that someone wins very easily —**convincingly** adv

convivial /kən'vɪviəl/ adj *formal* friendly and cheerful

convoluted /'kɒnvəluːtɪd $ 'kɑːn-/ adj *formal* complicated and difficult to understand

convoy /'kɒnvɔɪ $ 'kɑːn-/ n [C] a group of vehicles or ships travelling together: **+of** *a convoy of trucks*

convulsion /kən'vʌlʃən/ n [C] a sudden shaking movement of your body, caused by illness

coo /kuː/ v [I] **1** when DOVES or PIGEONS coo, they make a low soft sound **2** to speak in a soft, loving way

cook¹ /kʊk/ v

1 [I,T] to prepare food for eating, using heat: *Where did you learn to cook?* | **cook lunch/ dinner/supper etc** *It's your turn to cook dinner.* | **cook sb sth** *I've cooked you a delicious curry.* | **cook (sth) for sb** *Jamie's cooking for us tonight.* | *slices of cooked ham* → see box at PREPARE

THESAURUS

bake – to cook food such as bread in the oven
fry – to cook food in oil on the top part of the oven
roast – to cook meat or vegetables in an oven
grill – to cook food by placing it near to strong heat from above
sauté – to fry vegetables for a short time in a small amount of oil
broil – to cook meat or fish for a short time in the hottest part of the oven
boil – to cook vegetables in water on the top part of the oven
steam – to cook vegetables over water

2 [I] if food cooks, it is being prepared to eat, using heat: *While the pasta's cooking, grate some cheese.*

cook sth ⇔ up *phr v informal* to invent an excuse, plan etc, especially in order to deceive someone

cook² n [C] **1** someone whose job is to prepare and cook food [= chef] **2 good/bad/terrible etc cook** someone who is good, bad etc at cooking

cookbook /'kʊkbʊk/ *especially AmE* also **'cookery ˌbook** *BrE* n [C] a book that tells you how to prepare and cook food

cooker /'kʊkə $ -ər/ n [C] *BrE* a large piece of kitchen equipment used for cooking food [= **stove** *AmE*]: *a gas cooker* → see picture at KITCHEN

cookery /'kʊkəri/ n [U] *BrE* the art or skill of preparing and cooking food [= **cooking**]

cookie /'kʊki/ n [C]
1 *especially AmE* a small, flat, sweet cake [= biscuit *BrE*] → see picture on page A5
2 tough/smart cookie *informal* someone who is clever and knows how to get what they want

cooking /'kʊkɪŋ/ n [U]
1 the activity of preparing food and cooking it: *Who **does the cooking** in your house?* | *cooking implements*
2 food made in a particular way or by a particular person: *Indian cooking*

cool¹ /kuːl/ adj
1 fairly cold: *a lovely **cool drink*** | *a **cool breeze*** | *It gets quite **cool** in the evenings.* → see box at COLD → and WEATHER
2 calm and not nervous or excited: **keep/stay cool** *He's good at staying cool in a crisis.*
3 *informal* attractive, fashionable, or interesting in a way that people admire: *You **look cool** in that hat.* | *'He's in a band.' – 'Cool!'*
4 *spoken* used to say that you agree with something or are not annoyed about it: *If you want to go now, **it's cool with me.***
5 not as friendly as you expect: *I thought she was rather cool.*
—**coolness** n [U]

cool² v **1** [I,T] to become a little colder, or to make something a little colder: *Leave the cakes to cool.* | *We stopped to cool our faces in the stream.*
2 [I] if a feeling or relationship cools, it becomes less strong

cool (sb) down/off *phr v* **1** to return to a normal temperature after being hot: *Let's go for a swim to cool off.* **2** to become calm after being angry, or to make someone become calm: *She'll cool down in a day or two.*

cool³ n **1 keep your cool** to stay calm in a difficult situation: *Rick was yelling, but she kept her cool.* **2 lose your cool** to stop being calm in a difficult situation **3 the cool (of sth)** a temperature that is pleasantly cool: *the cool of the evening*

cooler /'kuːlə $ -ər/ n [C] a container for keeping food and drinks cold

coolly /'kuːl-li/ adv **1** in a way that seems unfriendly: *'Fine,' she said coolly.* **2** calmly: *He coolly walked over and kissed her.*

coop¹ /kuːp/ n [C] a building for chickens

coop² v **be cooped up** to be kept in a very small place, or to stay indoors: *I hate being cooped up in an office all day.*

cooperate also **co-operate** *BrE* /kəʊˈɒpəreɪt $ koʊˈɑːp-/ v [I]
1 to work with someone else to achieve something that you both want: **+with** *Many species cooperate with each other when hunting.* | **+on/in** *Several countries cooperated on the project.* | **+to** *Parents and teachers can cooperate to solve the problem.*
2 to be helpful by doing what someone wants you to do: **+with** *When questioned, he refused to co-operate with the police.*

cooperation also **co-operation** *BrE* /kəʊˌɒpəˈreɪʃən $ koʊˌɑːp-/ n [U] **1** when you work with someone else to achieve something that you both want: **+between** *the need for close co-operation between East and West* | **in cooperation with sb** *The study was done in cooperation with local businesses.* **2** when you are helpful and do what someone wants: *No smoking. Thank you for your cooperation.*

cooperative¹ also **co-operative** *BrE* /kəʊˈɒpərətɪv $ koʊˈɑːp-/ adj **1** willing to work [= **helpful**]: *She was very cooperative.* **2** done by people working together: *a cooperative effort*
—**cooperatively** adv

cooperative² also **co-operative** *BrE* n [C] a business or organization owned equally by all the people working there

coordinate¹ also **co-ordinate** *BrE* /kəʊˈɔːdɪneɪt $ koʊˈɔːr-/ v **1** [T] to organize an activity so that people work together effectively: *We need to coordinate our efforts.* **2** [T] to make the parts of your body move well together: *Some children find it hard to coordinate their movements.* **3** [I,T] if clothes or colours coordinate, or if you coordinate them, they look nice together

coordinate² also **co-ordinate** *BrE* /kəʊˈɔːdɪnət $ koʊˈɔːr-/ n [C] *technical* one of a set of numbers that give the exact position of a point on a map

coordination also **co-ordination** *BrE* /kəʊˌɔːdɪˈneɪʃən $ koʊˌɔːr-/ n [U] **1** the ability to make the different parts of your body do what you want: *Most sports will help to improve your coordination.* **2** the organization of people and things so that they work together well: **+of** *the coordination of military exercises*

coordinator also **co-ordinator** *BrE* /kəʊˈɔːdɪneɪtə $ koʊˈɔːrdɪneɪtər/ n [C] someone who organizes the way people work together

cop /kɒp $ kɑːp/ n [C] *informal* a police officer → see box at POLICE

cope /kəʊp $ koʊp/ v [I] to succeed in dealing with everything you have to do, especially when it is very difficult: *Sometimes I just can't cope.* | **+with** *How does she cope with six kids?*

copier /'kɒpiə $ 'kɑːpiər/ n [C] a PHOTOCOPIER

copious /'kəʊpiəs $ 'koʊ-/ adj [only before noun] large in quantity: *She took **copious** notes.*
—**copiously** adv

'cop-out n [C] *informal* something you do or say in order to avoid doing or accepting something: *He said he couldn't come because he was ill, but I think that was just a cop-out.*

copper /'kɒpə $ 'kɑːpər/ n **1** [U] soft orange-brown metal **2 coppers** [plural] *BrE informal* coins of low value, made of brown metal **3** [C] *BrE informal* a police officer

copse /kɒps $ kɑːps/ n [C] a small group of trees or bushes → see box at TREE

copy¹ /'kɒpi $ 'kɑːpi/ n [C] plural **copies**
1 a document, object etc that is exactly the same as an earlier or original one: **+of** *We'll need to make a copy of your birth certificate.* | *Always **make copies** of your files.* | *The chair is a copy of an original design.*
2 one of many books, magazines, CDs etc which have been produced: **+of** *Have you got a copy of*

today's paper? | *Their album sold millions of copies.*

→ CARBON COPY

copy² *v* copied, copying, copies

1 [I,T] to make a document, object etc that is exactly the same as an earlier or original one: *Copy the letter and send it out.* | **copy (sth) from sth** *The design was copied from an 18th century wallpaper.* | **copy sth into/onto sth** *You can copy the file onto a floppy disk.*

THESAURUS

photocopy – to copy a piece of paper with writing or pictures on it, using a special machine
forge – to illegally copy something written or printed: *He forged my signature.* | *forged ten pound notes*
pirate – to illegally copy and sell a film, book, CD, or DVD that was made and is owned by another person: *pirated videos*

---

2 [T] to do something that someone else has done, or behave like someone else: *Kids often copy what they see on TV.*
3 [I,T] to cheat by looking at someone's work and writing what they have written: *Stop copying me!*
4 also **copy down/out** [T] to write something exactly as it is written somewhere else: *I'd like you to copy down this poem.* | **copy sth into sth** *Here are some questions to copy into your books.*
  copy sb ⇔ in *phr v* to send someone a copy of an email message that you have written to someone else

copyright /ˈkɒpiraɪt $ ˈkɑː-/ *n* [C,U] the legal right to be the only person or company that produces or sells a book, play, film etc —**copyright** *adj*

coral /ˈkɒrəl $ ˈkɔː-, ˈkɑː-/ *n* [U] a hard pink, white, or red substance formed from the bones of very small sea animals

cord /kɔːd $ kɔːrd/ *n* **1** [C,U] a piece of thick string or thin rope **2** [C,U] wire covered with plastic for connecting equipment to a supply of electricity [= cable] → see picture at ACOUSTIC **3** cords [plural] trousers made from CORDUROY

cordial /ˈkɔːdiəl $ ˈkɔːrdʒəl/ *adj formal* friendly and polite —**cordially** *adv*

cordless /ˈkɔːdləs $ ˈkɔːrd-/ *adj* a cordless piece of equipment is not connected to its power supply by wires: *a cordless phone*

cordon¹ /ˈkɔːdn $ ˈkɔːrdn/ *n* [C] a line of police or soldiers around an area to stop people going there: *a police cordon*

cordon² *v*
  cordon sth ⇔ off *phr v* to surround and protect an area with police or soldiers: *Police cordoned off the street where the body was found.*

corduroy /ˈkɔːdʒ̩rɔɪ, -djʊ̩- $ ˈkɔːrdə-/ *n* [U] thick strong cotton cloth with raised lines on it

core /kɔː $ kɔːr/ *n* [C] **1** the hard central part of an apple or PEAR → see picture at FRUIT **2** the most important or central part of something: +**of** *Money is at the core of the problem.* | **core beliefs/subjects/skills etc** *Students have to study five core subjects.* **3** to the core completely or extremely: *The news shook me to the core.* **4** the central part of the earth or another PLANET → HARDCORE

coriander /ˌkɒriˈændə $ ˌkɔːriˈændər/ *n* [U] *BrE* a herb, used especially in Asian cooking [= cilantro *AmE*]

cork /kɔːk $ kɔːrk/ *n* **1** [U] material that comes from the BARK (=outer part) of a Mediterranean tree: *cork floor tiles* **2** [C] a small round piece of cork that is put into the top of a bottle to close it

corkscrew /ˈkɔːkskruː $ ˈkɔːrk-/ *n* [C] the tool you use to pull a cork out of a bottle

corn /kɔːn $ kɔːrn/ *n*
1 [U] *BrE* plants such as wheat, from which we get grain and seeds: *fields of corn* | *an ear of corn* (=the top part of the plant where seeds grow)
2 [U] *AmE* **a)** a tall plant with large yellow seeds [= maize *BrE*] **b)** the seeds of this plant eaten as food [= sweetcorn *BrE*] → see picture at VEGETABLE

corner¹ /ˈkɔːnə $ ˈkɔːrnər/ *n* [C]
1 the point at which two lines, edges, or walls meet: +**of** *Fold the corner of the page.* | **in the corner** *a room with a piano in the corner* | *Click the icon in the top left-hand corner of the screen.* | **on the corner** *She sat on the corner of the bed.*
2 the place where two roads or streets meet: +**of** *We walked to the corner of the street.* | **on/at the corner** *a hotel on the corner of 5th and Maine* | *Wait for me at the corner.* | **around the corner** *There's a bar just around the corner.*
3 the side of your mouth or eye: *I saw him out of the corner of my eye* (=without turning my head).
4 a difficult situation that you cannot easily escape from: **in/into a corner** *She found herself in a tight corner.* | *He forced me into a corner and I had to accept.*
5 a place that is far away and not well known: +**of** *She's gone to work in a remote corner of Africa.*
6 also **corner kick** a kick that one team is allowed to take from a corner at their opponent's end of the field
→ **cut corners** at CUT¹

corner² *v* **1** [T] to force someone into a position from which they cannot easily escape: *He cornered me and demanded an answer.* **2 corner the market** to get total control of the supply of a particular type of goods **3** [I] if a car corners, it goes around a corner

'corner shop *n* [C] *BrE* a small shop near houses, that sells food, cigarettes, and other things needed every day

cornerstone /ˈkɔːnəstəʊn $ ˈkɔːrnərstoʊn/ *n* [C] something that is very important because everything else depends on it: +**of** *Trust is the cornerstone of any relationship.*

cornet /ˈkɔːnɪ̩t $ kɔːrˈnet/ *n* [C] **1** a musical instrument like a small TRUMPET **2** a sweet food that you put ICE CREAM in, and hold in your hand to eat [= cone]

cornflakes /ˈkɔːnfleɪks $ ˈkɔːrn-/ *n* [plural] small flat pieces of corn, usually eaten at breakfast with milk

C

C

cornflour /'kɔːnflaʊə $ 'kɔːrnflaʊr/ *BrE*; **cornstarch** /'kɔːnstɑːtʃ $ 'kɔːrnstɑːrtʃ/ *AmE n* [U] a fine white flour made from corn, used in cooking

corny /'kɔːni $ 'kɔːrni/ *adj informal* very silly or repeated too often to be funny or interesting: *corny jokes* → see box at **FUNNY**

coronary¹ /'kɒrənəri $ 'kɔːrəneri, 'kɑː-/ *adj* relating to the heart: *coronary disease*

coronary² *n* [C] plural **coronaries** a HEART ATTACK

coronation /ˌkɒrəˈneɪʃən $ ˌkɔː-, ˌkɑː-/ *n* [C] an official ceremony in which someone is made a king or queen

coroner /'kɒrənə $ 'kɔːrənər, 'kɑː-/ *n* [C] an official whose job is to discover the cause of someone's death, especially when it is sudden or unusual

corporal /'kɔːpərəl $ 'kɔːr-/ *n* [C] a low rank in the army or AIR FORCE

corporal 'punishment *n* [U] punishment that involves hitting someone

corporate /'kɔːpərət $ 'kɔːr-/ *adj* [only before noun] relating to a corporation or the people in it: *Our corporate headquarters are in Houston.* | *corporate responsibilities*

corporation /ˌkɔːpəˈreɪʃən $ ˌkɔːr-/ *n* [C] a large company or organization → see box at **COMPANY**

corps /kɔː $ kɔːr/ *n* [C] plural **corps** /kɔːz $ kɔːrz/ **1** a group in an army, especially one with special duties: *the medical corps* **2** a group of people who do a particular job: *the press corps*

corpse /kɔːps $ kɔːrps/ *n* [C] a dead body

corpus /'kɔːpəs $ 'kɔːr-/ *n* [C] plural **corpuses** or **corpora** /-pərə/ *technical* a large collection of written or spoken language, used for studying the language

corral /kəˈrɑːl $ kəˈræl/ *n* [C] an enclosed area for cattle or horses, especially in the US

correct¹ /kəˈrekt/ *adj*

1 right or without any mistakes [= **right**; ≠ **incorrect**]: *He gave the correct answer.* | *'Is your name Ives?' 'Yes, that's correct.'* → see box at **RIGHT**
2 suitable for a particular situation: *Hold the wheel in the correct position.*
—**correctly** *adv*: *Have you spelled it correctly?*
—**correctness** *n* [U] → **POLITICALLY CORRECT**

correct² *v* [T]

1 to make something right or make it work the way it should: *Please correct the mistakes in your homework.* | *Most eyesight problems are easy to correct.*
2 to tell or show someone what mistakes they have made: *He always corrects my pronunciation.*

correction /kəˈrekʃən/ *n* [C,U] a change that makes something right or better, or when you change something in this way: *She made a few corrections to the text.*

corrective /kəˈrektɪv/ *adj formal* intended to make something right or better: *corrective lenses*

correlate /'kɒrɪleɪt $ 'kɔː-, 'kɑː-/ *v* [I,T] if two or more facts, ideas etc correlate or if you correlate them, they are closely connected to each other or one causes the other: **+with** *Poverty and poor housing correlate with a shorter life expectancy.*

correlation /ˌkɒrɪˈleɪʃən $ ˌkɔː-, ˌkɑː-/ *n* [C,U] a connection between two things, especially

when one causes the other: **+between** *There is a correlation between poverty and ill health.*

correspond /ˌkɒrɪˈspɒnd $ ˌkɔːrɪˈspɑːnd, ˌkɑː-/ *v* [I] **1** if two things correspond, they are the same or very similar: *The text and the pictures don't seem to correspond.* | **+with/to** *The French 'baccalauréat' exam corresponds to British 'A-levels'.* **2** if two people correspond, they write letters to each other

correspondence /ˌkɒrɪˈspɒndəns $ ˌkɔːrɪˈspɑːn-, ˌkɑː-/ *n* **1** [U] letters that people write, or the activity of writing and getting letters: *She keeps all her correspondence.* | *Their correspondence continued for years.* **2** [C] a relationship or connection between two things: *There's a close correspondence between their accounts.*

corre'spondence ˌcourse *n* [C] a course of lessons in which the student works at home and sends completed work to their teacher by post

correspondent /ˌkɒrɪˈspɒndənt $ ˌkɔːrɪˈspɑːn-, ˌkɑː-/ *n* [C] someone whose job is to report news from a particular area or on a particular subject: *Here's our sports correspondent.*

corresponding /ˌkɒrɪˈspɒndɪŋ $ ˌkɔːrɪˈspɑːn-, ˌkɑː-/ *adj* [only before noun] relating or similar to something else: *Sales are up 10% on the corresponding period last year.*
—**correspondingly** *adv*

corridor /'kɒrɪdɔː $ 'kɔːrɪdər, 'kɑː-/ *n* [C] a long narrow area between two rows of rooms: **in the corridor** *Please wait in the corridor.* | **along/ down the corridor** *Her office is just down the corridor.*

corroborate /kəˈrɒbəreɪt $ kəˈrɑː-/ *v* [T] *formal* to provide information that supports or proves someone's statement: *We have new evidence to corroborate her story.* —**corroboration** /kəˌrɒbəˈreɪʃən $ -ˌrɑː-/ *n* [U]

corrode /kəˈrəʊd $ -ˈroʊd/ *v* [I,T] if metal corrodes, or if water, chemicals etc corrode it, it is slowly destroyed: *Many of the pipes have corroded.*

corrosion /kəˈrəʊʒən $ -ˈroʊ-/ *n* [U] the gradual destruction of metal by water, chemicals etc —**corrosive** /-sɪv/ *adj*: *highly corrosive chemicals*

corrugated /'kɒrəɡeɪtɪd $ 'kɔː-, 'kɑː-/ *adj* **corrugated iron/cardboard** iron etc that is made in the shape of waves or folds

corrupt¹ /kəˈrʌpt/ *adj*

1 dishonest or immoral: *corrupt judges* | *a corrupt political system*
2 computer information that is corrupt has been damaged and spoiled

corrupt² *v* **1** [I,T] to make someone dishonest or immoral: *Power can corrupt.* | *films that corrupt people's minds* **2** [T] to damage the information on a computer so that it does not work properly: *Somehow the file got corrupted.*

corruption /kəˈrʌpʃən/ *n* [U] dishonest or immoral behaviour, especially by people with power: *Two officials were charged with corruption.*

corset /'kɔːsɪt $ 'kɔːr-/ *n* [C] a piece of tight underwear worn by women to make them look thinner, especially in the past

cos /kəz/ linking word BrE spoken informal because

cosmetic /kɒz'metɪk $ kɑːz-/ adj **1** intended to make your skin or body more beautiful: *cosmetic products* | *cosmetic surgery* (=medical operations to improve the way you look) **2** involving only small unimportant changes, instead of more important ones: *cosmetic changes to the law*

cosmetics /kɒz'metɪks $ kɑːz-/ n [plural] creams, powders etc that you use to make your face and body more attractive

cosmic /'kɒzmɪk $ 'kɑːz-/ adj relating to space or the universe

cosmonaut /'kɒzmənɔːt $ 'kɑːzmənɒːt/ n [C] an ASTRONAUT from the former Soviet Union → see box at SPACE

cosmopolitan /ˌkɒzmə'pɒlɪtən $ ˌkɑːzmə'pɑː-/ adj **1** a cosmopolitan place has people from many different parts of the world: *a vibrant, cosmopolitan city* **2** a cosmopolitan person, attitude etc shows a lot of experience of different people and places

cosmos /'kɒzmɒs $ 'kɑːzməs/ n **the cosmos** the whole universe

cost¹ /kɒst $ kɒːst/ n

1 [C,U] the amount of money that you have to pay in order to buy or do something: **+of** the *high cost of accommodation in London* | **at a cost (of sth)** *We repaired the roof at a cost of £15,000.* | *Baby seats are available at no extra cost.* | **running/living/travel etc costs** *The car has very low running costs.* | **the cost of living** (=the amount of money you need to spend on things like food and clothes)

<table>
<tr><td>**THESAURUS**</td></tr>
</table>

cost – the amount of money you pay for an activity, service, product etc: *The total cost of the trip was under $500.* | *the cost of accommodation*

price – the amount of money you must pay for something: *House prices in London keep going up.* | *the price of oil*

charge – the amount that you have to pay for a particular service or to use something: *There is an extra charge for advance booking.* | *telephone charges*

fee – the amount you have to pay to enter or join something, or that you pay to a lawyer, doctor etc: *There is no entrance fee to the museum.* | *Membership fee is £125 a year.* | *legal fees*

fare – the amount you have to pay to travel somewhere by bus, plane, train etc: *the bus fare*

rent – the amount you have to pay to live in or use a place that you do not own: *My rent is £500 a month.*

2 [singular] what you have to lose, give away etc in order to achieve something else: **+to** *The cost to the environment was high.* | *He saved his career, but at what cost to his marriage?* | **at all costs/at any cost** (=whatever you have to do to achieve something) *We must avoid a scandal at all costs.*

3 [singular, U] especially AmE also **'cost price** the price that someone paid for something they

are going to sell: *Her uncle let her have the car at cost.*

4 find/know/learn etc sth to your cost to know or find out about something because of an unpleasant experience

cost² v past tense and past participle **cost**

1 [linking verb] to have a particular price: *This dress cost $75.* | *How much did your computer cost?* | **cost sb sth** *A first class ticket will cost you a lot.* | **it costs sth to do sth** *It costs £6 to get into the museum.* | **cost (sb) a fortune/a bomb** *The meal cost a fortune.* | **not cost (sb) a penny/a thing** *A kind word doesn't cost you a thing.*

2 [T] to make someone lose something important: **cost sb sth** *That one mistake cost him his life.*

3 [T] past tense and past participle **costed** to calculate how much money is needed to pay for something: *Have you costed your proposals?*

co-star¹ /'kəʊ stɑː $ 'koʊ stɑːr/ n [C] one of two or more famous actors who appear together in a film or play

co-star² v [I] **co-starred, co-starring** to be working in a film or play with other famous actors: **+with/in** *Penelope Cruz co-starred with Tom Cruise.*

'cost-,cutting n [U] the things which a company or organization does in order to reduce its costs: *As part of a cost-cutting exercise, the company is reducing its workforce by 60 jobs.*

,cost ef'fective adj producing the best profits or advantages at the lowest cost: *a cost-effective solution*

costly /'kɒstli $ 'kɒːstli/ adj **1** costing a lot of money [= **expensive**]: *a costly procedure* **2** causing a lot of problems: *The mistake proved costly.*

costume /'kɒstjum $ 'kɑːstuːm/ n [C,U] **1** a set of clothes worn by an actor, or to make someone look like a particular type of person, animal etc [➡ **outfit**]: *the costumes for 'Hamlet'* | *She wore a rabbit costume.* **2** clothes that are typical of a particular country or time in the past: **in costume** | *dancers in national costume* → SWIMMING COSTUME

cosy BrE; **cozy** AmE /'kəʊzi $ 'koʊzi/ adj warm and comfortable: *a cosy bed*

cot /kɒt $ kɑːt/ n [C] **1** BrE a small bed with high sides for a young child [= **crib** AmE] → see picture at BED **2** AmE a CAMP BED → see picture at BED

'cot ,death n [C] BrE the sudden, unexpected and unexplained death of a baby while it is sleeping [= **crib death** AmE]

cottage /'kɒtɪdʒ $ 'kɑː-/ n [C] a small house in the country, especially an old one: *a country cottage* | *holiday cottages* → see box at HOUSE

,cottage 'cheese /ˌ $ ˌ.. ./ n [U] soft white cheese

,cottage 'industry n [C] an industry that consists of people working at home

cotton¹ /'kɒtn $ 'kɑːtn/ n [U]

1 cloth or thread made from the cotton plant: *a cotton shirt* | *a reel of black cotton* (=thread used for sewing)

2 a plant with white hairs used for making cotton cloth and thread

3 *AmE* a soft mass of cotton, used especially for cleaning your skin [= **cotton wool** *BrE*]

cotton² *v*

cotton on *phr v informal* to begin to understand something [= **realize**]: **+to** *I soon cottoned on to what he was doing.*

,cotton 'wool *n* [U] *BrE* a soft mass of cotton, used for cleaning the skin, wounds etc [= **cotton** *AmE*]

couch¹ /kaʊtʃ/ *n* [C] a long, comfortable piece of furniture on which you can sit or lie

couch² *v* **be couched in sth** to be expressed in a particular way: *His refusal was couched in polite terms.*

'couch po,tato *n* [C] *humorous* someone who spends a lot of time sitting and watching television

cough¹ /kɒf $ kɔːf/ *v* [I] if you cough, air suddenly comes out of your throat with a short loud sound, for example because you are ill: *He was awake coughing all night.*

cough up *phr v* **1** *informal* to give someone money, information etc when you do not really want to: *Come on, cough up!* | **cough sth ⇔ up** *I had to cough up £200 for a new printer.* **2 cough sth ⇔ up** if you cough up a substance such as blood, it comes from your lungs or throat into your mouth when you cough

cough² *n* [C]

1 when someone coughs, or the sound of someone coughing: *I heard a loud cough behind me.*
2 an illness that makes you cough: *Amy has a bad **cough**.*

could /kəd; *strong* kʊd/ *modal verb* negative short form **couldn't**

1 used as the past tense of 'can' to say what someone was able to do or was allowed to do in the past: *She said she couldn't find it.* | *The teacher said we could all go home.* | **sb could see/hear etc sth** (=saw, heard etc sth on a particular occasion) *I could hear laughter.* → see box at **CAN**
2 a) used to say that something is possible or might happen: *Most accidents in the home could be prevented.* | *You could be right, I suppose.* | *It could be weeks before we get a reply.* **b)** used to say that something was possible in the past, but did not actually happen: *She could have been killed.*
3 *spoken* used to make a polite request: *Could I ask you a couple of questions?* | *Could you open the window?*
4 used to suggest doing something: *You could try calling his office.* | *We could always stop and ask directions.*
5 *spoken* used to emphasize how happy, angry etc you are by saying how you want to express your feelings: *I was so angry I could have killed her.*

couldn't /'kʊdnt/ the short form of 'could not'

could've /'kʊdəv/ the short form of 'could have'

council /'kaʊnsəl/ *n* [C]

1 the organization that is responsible for local government in a particular area: *Northampton Borough Council* | *local council elections*
2 a group of people who make rules, laws, or decisions, or give advice: *the UN Security Council*
3 council house/flat a house or flat in Britain that is provided by the local council for a very low rent

'council es,tate *n* [C] *BrE* an area in a town or city with streets of council houses

councillor *BrE*; **councilor** *AmE* /'kaʊnsələ $ -ər/ *n* [C] a member of a council

counsel¹ /'kaʊnsəl/ *v* [T] **counselled, counselling** *BrE*; **counseled, counseling** *AmE* to advise or support someone who has problems: *a new unit to counsel alcoholics* —**counselling** *n* [U] *a counselling service for drug users* —**counsellor** *n* [C] *a marriage counsellor*

counsel² *n* [U] **1** a lawyer who speaks for someone in court: *counsel for the prosecution* **2** *literary* advice

count¹ /kaʊnt/ *v*

1 also **count up** [T] to try to find out how many people or things there are in a group: *It took hours to count all the votes.*
2 [I] to say numbers in the correct order: *Can you count in Japanese?*
3 [T] to think of someone or something in a particular way: **count sb/sth as sth** *I've always counted Rob as one of my best friends.* | *You should **count** yourself **lucky** that you weren't hurt.*
4 [I] to be important or valuable: **+for** *First impressions count for a lot.*
5 [I] to be allowed or accepted: *You cheated, so your score doesn't count.*
6 [T] to include someone or something in a total: *There are five in our family, counting me.*
7 don't count your chickens (before they're hatched) *spoken* used to say that you should not make plans that depend on something good happening, because it might not
8 count me in/out *spoken* used to say that you want to be involved in something or do not want to be involved

count on sb/sth *phr v* **1** to depend on someone or something: *You can always count on Doug in a crisis.* **2** to expect something: *We hadn't counted on so many people coming.*
count sth ⇔ out *phr v* to put things down one by one as you count them: *He counted out ten $50 bills.*

count² *n* [C] **1** the process of counting, or the total that you get when you count things: *Hold your breath for a count of ten.* **2 lose count (of sth)** to forget how many there are of something: *There have been so many accidents here, the police have lost count.* **3 on all/several/both etc counts** in every way, in several ways etc: *We were proved wrong on both counts.* **4** one of the crimes that the police say someone is guilty of: *Davis was found not guilty on all counts.* **5** a European man with a high social rank → **HEAD COUNT, POLLEN COUNT**

countable /'kaʊntəbəl/ *adj* a countable noun has both a singular and a plural form [≠ **uncountable**]

countdown /'kaʊntdaʊn/ *n* [C usually singular] **1** when numbers are counted backwards to zero before something happens: **+to** *the countdown to lift-off* **2** the period before an important event happens, when it gets closer and closer: **+to** *the countdown to the World Cup*

countenance[1] /'kaʊntɪnəns/ *n* [C] *literary* your face

countenance[2] *v* [T] *formal* to accept, support, or approve of something [= **tolerate**]

counter[1] /'kaʊntə $ -ər/ *n* [C]

1 the place where you pay or are served in a shop, bank etc: *He wondered if the girl **behind the counter** recognised him.*
2 *AmE* a flat surface in the kitchen where you prepare food [= **worktop** *BrE*]
3 a small round object used in some games that are played on a board
→ **OVER-THE-COUNTER**

counter[2] *v* [T] **1** to do something in order to prevent something bad from happening or to reduce its bad effects: *efforts to counter inflation* **2** to say something to show that what someone has just said is not true: *'That's not what the statistics show,' she countered.*

counter[3] *adv* **run/be counter to sth** *formal* to be the opposite of something: *ideas that run counter to the Church's traditional view of marriage*

counter- /kaʊntə $ -tər/ *prefix* the opposite of something: *counter-productive*

counteract /ˌkaʊntər'ækt/ *v* [T] to reduce or prevent the bad effect of something, by doing something that has the opposite effect: *Try relaxation exercises to counteract the effects of stress.*

counterattack /'kaʊntərəˌtæk/ *n* [C] an attack that you make against someone who has attacked you, in a sport, war, or argument → see box at **ATTACK** —**counterattack** *v* [I]

counterbalance /ˌkaʊntə'bæləns $ -tər-/ *v* [T] to have an equal and opposite effect to something else: *Riskier investments tend to be counterbalanced by high rewards.* —**counterbalance** /'kaʊntəˌbæləns $ -tər-/ *n* [C]

counterclockwise /ˌkaʊntə'klɒkwaɪz◂ $ -tər-'klɑːk-/ *adj, adv AmE* ANTICLOCKWISE [≠ **clockwise**]

counterfeit /'kaʊntəfɪt $ -tər-/ *adj* made to look exactly like the real thing in order to deceive people: *counterfeit money* → see box at **FAKE** —**counterfeit** *v* [T]

counterpart /'kaʊntəpɑːt $ -tərpɑːrt/ *n* [C] a person or thing that has the same job or purpose as someone or something else in a different place: *Belgian officials are discussing the matter with their French counterparts.*

counterproductive /ˌkaʊntəprə'dʌktɪv◂ $ -tər-/ *adj* causing the opposite result to the one you want: *Punishing children can be counterproductive.*

countersign /'kaʊntəsaɪn $ -ər-/ *v* [T] to sign a paper that has already been signed by someone else: *Your doctor should countersign the form.*

countess /'kaʊntɪs/ *n* [C] a European woman with a high social rank

countless /'kaʊntləs/ *adj* [only before noun] very many: *a drug that has saved countless lives*

country[1] /'kʌntri/ *n* plural **countries**

1 [C] an area of land that is controlled by its own government, president, king etc [➡ **nation**]: *the Scandinavian countries* | *developing countries* | *a foreign country*

2 the country a) land that is away from towns and cities [= **the countryside**]: *I've always lived in the country.* **b)** all the people who live in a country: *a government that has the support of the country*
3 [U] a type of land: *mountainous country*

country[2] *adj* [only before noun] in or relating to the countryside [= **rural**; ≠ **urban**]: *country people* | *country roads*

'country ˌclub *n* [C] a sports and social club, especially one for rich people

ˌcountry 'house *n* [C] *BrE* a large house in the countryside, especially one that is old and interesting → see box at **HOUSE**

countryman /'kʌntrimən/ *n* [C] plural **countrymen** /-mən/ someone from your own country

'country ˌmusic, also **ˌcountry and 'western** *n* [U] a type of music from the southern and western US

countryside /'kʌntrisaɪd/ *n* [U] land that is outside cities and towns [= **the country**]: *the beauty of the English countryside* | *open countryside*

county /'kaʊnti/ *n* [C] plural **counties** an area of a state or country that has its own local government

coup /kuː/ *n* [C] **1** also **coup d'état** /ˌkuː deɪ'tɑː $ -de'tɑː/ when a group of people suddenly take control of a country, especially by using force: *a military coup* → see box at **REVOLUTION** **2** [usually singular] an impressive achievement: *Winning that contract was a real coup.*

couple[1] /'kʌpəl/ *n*

1 a couple two or a few: **+of** *There were a couple of kids in the back of the car.* | *I'll be ready in a couple of minutes.* → see box at **TWO**
2 [C] two people who are married or have a romantic relationship: *the couple next door* | *married couples* → see box at **TWO**

couple[2] *v* **coupled with sth** together with something: *Low rainfall coupled with high temperatures destroyed the crops.*

coupon /'kuːpɒn $ -pɑːn/ *n* [C] **1** a small piece of printed paper that gives you the right to pay less for something or get something free: *a coupon for 30 pence off a jar of coffee* **2** a printed form, used when you order something, enter a competition etc

courage /'kʌrɪdʒ $ 'kɜːr-/ *n* [U] the quality you have when you do not let fear affect you in a frightening situation [= **bravery**; ≠ **cowardice**]: *She showed great courage throughout her illness.* | *Driving again after his accident must have taken a lot of courage.* | **the courage to do sth** *He did not **have the courage** to tell Nicola that he was leaving her.*
—**courageous** /kə'reɪdʒəs/ *adj*: *a courageous decision* —**courageously** *adv* → **pluck up (the) courage (to do sth)** at **PLUCK**[1]

courgette /kʊə'ʒet $ kʊr-/ *n* [C] *BrE* a long vegetable with a dark green skin [= **zucchini** *AmE*] → see picture at **VEGETABLE**

courier /'kʊriə $ -ər/ *n* [C] someone whose job is to deliver documents and packages

course¹ /kɔːs $ kɔːrs/ *n*

1 of course *spoken* **a)** used to show that what you are saying is expected or already known and so not surprising: *Of course there are exceptions to every rule.* | *The insurance has to be renewed every year, of course.* **b)** used to say yes very strongly or to give permission politely: *'Can I borrow your notes?' 'Of course you can.'*
2 of course not *spoken* used to say no very strongly: *'Do you mind if I'm a bit late?' 'Of course not.'*
3 [C] a series of lessons or a period of study in a particular subject [= **class** *AmE*]: *a three-day training course* | **take/do a course** *Andy's doing a computer course.* | **+in/on** *a degree course in engineering* → see box at **UNIVERSITY**
4 [C] one of the parts of a meal: *a three-course meal* | *the main course*
5 [singular] the way that something develops or happens: **+of** *events that changed the course of history* | **run/take its course** (=develop in the usual way) *You'll just have to let things take their course.*
6 in/during/over the course of sth during a period of time or a process: *During the course of our conversation, I found out that he had worked in France.*
7 in the course of time after some time passes: *The situation will improve in the course of time.*
8 [C] something that you can do to deal with a situation: *The best course of action would be to speak to her privately.*
9 course of treatment/antibiotics etc *especially BrE* medicine or medical treatment that someone has regularly for a period of time
10 [C,U] the planned direction taken by a boat or plane to reach a place: *The plane changed course to avoid the storm.* | **on/off course** (=going in the right or wrong direction) *The ship was blown off course.*
11 [C] an area of land or water where races are held, or an area of land designed for playing golf: *a race course* | *an 18-hole course*
12 be on course (for sth/to do sth) to be likely to achieve something because you have already had some success: *Hodson is on course to break the world record.*
→ **CORRESPONDENCE COURSE, CRASH COURSE** → in **due course** at **DUE¹** → as a **matter of course** at **MATTER¹**

course² *v* [I] *literary* to flow quickly: **+down/through** *Tears coursed down her cheeks.*

coursebook /'kɔːsbʊk $ 'kɔːrs-/ *n* [C] *BrE* a book that students use regularly during a set of lessons on a particular subject → see box at **BOOK**

coursework /'kɔːswɜːk $ 'kɔːrswɜːrk/ *n* [U] work that students do during a course of study, rather than in examinations, and that forms part of their final mark

court¹ /kɔːt $ kɔːrt/ *n*

1 [C,U] the people who make a legal judgment, for example about whether someone is guilty of a crime, or the place where these judgments are made: *the European Court of Justice* | *The court decided that West was guilty.* | *a court of law* | *The court case lasted six weeks.* | *If they don't pay, we'll take them to court* (=bring a legal case against them). | *He will appear in court today, charged with murder.*

TOPIC

In court, the person who is accused of committing a crime is called the **defendant**. The defendant's lawyers, who are called **the defence** *BrE*/**the defense** *AmE*, try to prove that the defendant is **not guilty**. The **prosecution** try to prove that the defendant is **guilty**. The **judge** and a **jury** listen to **testimony** and examine **evidence** in order to decide if the defendant is guilty or not guilty. Their decision is called the **verdict**.

2 [C] an area made for playing games such as tennis on: *a squash court* | **on court** *The players are due on court in an hour.* → see box at **SPORT**
3 [C] **a)** the place where a king or queen lives and works: *the royal courts of Europe* **b)** the king or queen, their family, and their friends, advisers etc: *Court officials denied the rumours.*

court² *v* **1** [T] to try to please someone so that they will support you: *Both parties are courting young voters.* **2** *old-fashioned* **be courting** if a man and a woman are courting, they are having a romantic relationship and may get married
3 court disaster to do something that is likely to have very unpleasant results

courteous /'kɜːtiəs $ 'kɜːr-/ *adj formal* very polite [≠ **discourteous**] —**courteously** *adv*

courtesy /'kɜːtɪ̣si $ 'kɜːr-/ *n plural* **courtesies**
1 [U] polite behaviour [≠ **discourtesy**]: *She didn't even have the courtesy to apologize.* **2 courtesies** [plural] things that you say or do to be polite in formal situations: *The President was exchanging courtesies with his guests.*
3 courtesy of sb used to say in a grateful way who provided or did something for you: *The winner will receive three CDs, courtesy of Hyperion Records.*

courthouse /'kɔːthaʊs $ 'kɔːrt-/ *n* [C] a building containing courts of law and government offices

courtier /'kɔːtiə $ 'kɔːrtɪr/ *n* [C] someone in the past with an important position at a royal court

court 'martial /ˌ $ ˈ. ˌ.ˌ./ *n* [C] a military court or an occasion when a soldier is judged by a military court —**court-martial** *v* [T]

courtroom /'kɔːtruːm, -rʊm $ 'kɔːrt-/ *n* [C] a room in a law court where cases are judged

courtship /'kɔːt-ʃɪp $ 'kɔːrt-/ *n* [C,U] *old-fashioned* when a man and a woman are having a romantic relationship before marrying

courtyard /'kɔːtjɑːd $ 'kɔːrtjɑːrd/ *n* [C] an open space surrounded by walls or buildings

cousin /'kʌzən/ *n* [C] a child of your **AUNT** or **UNCLE**: *Jane and I are cousins.* | **first cousin** (=a cousin) → see box at **RELATIVE**

cove /kəʊv $ koʊv/ *n* [C] part of the coast where a small area of sea is partly surrounded by land [➡ **bay**]

cover¹ /'kʌvə $ -ər/ *v* [T]
1 also **cover up** to put something over the top of something else to protect, close, or hide it [≠ **uncover**]: *Cover the pan and let the sauce simmer.* | *Cover the furniture up before you start painting.* | **cover sth with sth** *Dan covered his face with his hands.* | *tables covered with clean white cloths*

2 if something covers a surface, it forms a layer over it: *Snow covered the ground.* | **be covered in/with sth** *Your boots are covered in mud!*
3 to include or deal with something: *The course covers all aspects of business.*
4 to be enough money to pay for something: *The award should be enough to cover her college fees.* | *Will $200 cover the cost of textbooks?*
5 to travel a particular distance: *We had covered 20 kilometres by lunchtime.* | *A leopard can cover a lot of ground very quickly.*
6 used to say how big a town, forest etc is: *The city covers an area of 20 square kilometres.*
7 if your insurance covers you or your possessions, it promises to pay you money if you have an accident, something is stolen etc: **cover sb against/for sth** *This policy covers you against accident or injury.*
8 to report the details of an event for a newspaper, television, or radio: *I'd just returned from covering the Cambodian war.*
9 to aim a gun somewhere to protect someone from being attacked or to prevent someone from escaping: *Police officers covered the back entrance.*

cover for sb *phr v* **1** to do someone else's work because they are ill or are somewhere else: *I'll be covering for Sandra next week.* **2** to prevent someone from getting into trouble by lying for them, especially about where they are or what they are doing

cover sth ⇔ **up** *phr v* to prevent people from discovering a mistake or an unpleasant fact: *The whole thing was covered up and never reached the papers.*

cover² *n*
1 [C] something that is put on top of or around something else to protect it: *a cushion cover*

THESAURUS

lid – a cover for a container
top – the lid or cover for a container or a pen
wrapper – paper or plastic that is around something you buy
wrapping – cloth, paper etc that is put around something to protect it

---

2 [C] the outer front or back part of a book, magazine etc: **front/back cover** *His picture was on the front cover of Newsweek.* | *I read the book from cover to cover.*
3 [U] *BrE* the protection your insurance gives you, so that it pays you money if you are injured, something is stolen etc [= **coverage** *AmE*]: *temporary medical cover* | **+for/against** *cover against fire and theft*
4 [U] protection from bad weather or attack: *We took cover under a tree.* | *Everyone ran for cover when the shooting started.*
5 [singular] something that is used to hide someone's illegal activities: **+for** *The company is just a cover for the Mafia.*
6 the covers [plural] the sheets etc that are over you when you are in bed
→ **UNDERCOVER**

coverage /ˈkʌvərɪdʒ/ *n* [U] **1** when a subject or event is reported on television or radio, or in newspapers: **media/press coverage** *Her death attracted widespread media coverage.* **2** the range of subjects and facts included in a book,

website, class etc: **+of** *Dunn's website provides good coverage of the subject.* **3** *AmE* the protection your insurance gives you [= **cover** *BrE*]

coveralls /ˈkʌvərɔːlz $ -ɔːllz/ *n* [plural] *AmE*
OVERALLS

covering /ˈkʌvərɪŋ/ *n* [singular] something that covers or hides something: **+of** *a light covering of snow*

covering 'letter *BrE*; **'cover ˌletter** *AmE n* [C] a letter that you send with a document or package, which gives more information about it
→ see box at **JOB**

covert /ˈkʌvət, ˈkəʊvɜːt $ ˈkoʊvərt/ *adj* secret or hidden: *covert operations* —**covertly** *adv*

'cover-up *n* [C] an attempt to prevent the public from discovering the truth about something: *CIA officials denied there had been a cover-up.*

'cover ˌversion *n* [C] a new recording of a song that was originally recorded by a different person or group

covet /ˈkʌvɪt/ *v* [T] *literary* to want something very much, especially something that someone else has —**coveted** *adj*: *The FA Cup is the most coveted prize in English football.*

cow¹ /kaʊ/ *n* [C]
1 a large animal that is kept on farms and used to produce milk or meat [➔ **bull**]: *dairy cows* | *a herd of cows* → see picture at **FARM¹**
2 till the cows come home for ever

cow² *v* [T] to frighten someone in order to make them do something: *The children were cowed into obedience.*

coward /ˈkaʊəd $ -ərd/ *n* [C] someone who is not at all brave: *They called me a coward because I wouldn't fight.*
—**cowardly** *adj*: *a cowardly thing to do*

cowardice /ˈkaʊədɪs $ -ər-/ *n* [U] a lack of courage [≠ **bravery**]

cowboy /ˈkaʊbɔɪ/ *n* [C] **1** in the US, a man who rides a horse and whose job is to look after cattle **2** *BrE informal* someone whose work is bad or who is dishonest in business: *cowboy builders*

cower /ˈkaʊə $ -ər/ *v* [I] to bend low and move back because you are frightened: *The hostages were cowering in a corner.*

co-worker /ˌkəʊ ˈwɜːkə $ ˈkoʊ ˌwɜːrkər/ *n* [C] someone who you work with [➔ **colleague**] → see box at **WORK**

coy /kɔɪ/ *adj* **1** shy or pretending to be shy in order to attract people's interest: *a coy smile* **2** not wanting to tell people about something: *Tania was always coy about her age.* —**coyly** *adv*

coyote /ˈkɔɪ-əʊt, kɔɪˈəʊti $ ˈkaɪ-oʊt, kaɪˈoʊti/ *n* [C] a small wild dog that lives in North West America and Mexico

cozy /ˈkəʊzi $ ˈkoʊ-/ *adj* the American spelling of COSY

crab /kræb/ *n* [C,U] a sea animal with a round flat shell and ten legs, the front two of which have PINCERS on them, or the meat from this animal

crack¹ /kræk/ *v*
1 [I,T] if something cracks or is cracked, it breaks so that it gets a line on its surface, and may then break into pieces: *The ice was starting to crack.* | *cracked plates* | *He cracked a couple of eggs into a pan.* → see box at **BREAK**

2 [T] to hit someone or something hard: **crack sth on/against sth** *She fell and cracked her head on the step.*

3 [T] *informal* to find the answer to a difficult problem [= **solve**]: *Yes! I've finally cracked it! | This new evidence could help detectives to **crack** the case.*

4 [I] to become unable to deal with a situation because there is too much pressure on you: *She was beginning to **crack under the strain** of trying to do two jobs.*

5 [I,T] to make a sudden sharp sound, or to make something do this: *He **cracked his knuckles**. | Thunder cracked overhead.*

6 crack a joke *informal* to tell a joke

7 get cracking *BrE spoken* to start doing something or going somewhere quickly: *It's late, so we'd better get cracking.*

8 not all it's cracked up to be not as good as people think: *Life as a model isn't all it's cracked up to be.*

crack down *phr v* to become more strict in dealing with a problem and punishing the people involved: **+on** *The police are **cracking down** hard on violent crime.*

crack up *phr v informal* **1** to become mentally ill because you have a lot of problems **2** to start laughing

crack² *n*

1 [C] a thin line on the surface of something when it is broken but has not actually come apart: *A huge crack had appeared in the ceiling.*

2 [C] a weakness or fault in an idea, system, or organization: **+in** *The cracks in their relationship were starting to show.*

3 [C] a very narrow space between two things or two parts of something: **+in** *a crack in the curtains*

4 [C] a sudden loud sharp sound: *The firework exploded with a loud crack.*

5 [C] a clever joke or rude remark: **+about** *Stop making cracks about my sister!*

6 [C] *informal* an attempt to do something: **+at** *Okay, let's **have a crack** at fixing this bike.*

7 [U] a very dangerous illegal drug

8 at the crack of dawn very early in the morning

crack³ *adj* [only before noun] having a lot of experience and skill: *crack troops | He's a **crack shot** (=very good at shooting).*

crackdown /'krækdaʊn/ *n* [C usually singular] action that is taken to deal more strictly with bad or illegal behaviour: **+on** *a crackdown on drunk driving*

cracked /krækt/ *adj* something that is cracked has lines on the surface because it is damaged but not completely broken: *a cracked mirror | He escaped with a cracked rib.*

cracker /'krækə $ -ər/ *n* **1** [C] a thin BISCUIT often eaten with cheese **2** [C] a brightly coloured paper tube containing a small present, which people pull open at Christmas **3** [singular] *BrE informal* something that is very good: *Thompson's goal was a real cracker!*

crackers /'krækəz $ -ərz/ *adj* [not before noun] *BrE informal* crazy: *You're crackers!*

crackle /'krækəl/ *v* [I] to make a lot of short sharp noises: *the sound of logs crackling on the fire* → see picture on page A7

crackpot /'krækpɒt $ -pɑːt/ *adj* [only before noun] slightly crazy: *Whose crackpot idea was this?*

cradle¹ /'kreɪdl/ *n* **1** [C] a baby's bed with bars around the sides **2 the cradle of sth** the place where something important began: *Athens was the cradle of western democracy.*

cradle² *v* [T] to hold someone or something gently in your arms: *Tony cradled the baby in his arms.*

craft¹ /krɑːft $ kræft/ *n* [C] **1** plural **crafts** a skilled activity in which you make something using your hands: *traditional country crafts such as pottery and weaving* **2** plural **craft** a boat

craft² *v* [T] to make something with your hands, using a special skill: *Each doll is crafted individually by specialists.*

craftsman /'krɑːftsmən $ 'kræfts-/ *n* [C] plural **craftsmen** /-mən/ someone who is very skilled at making things with their hands: *furniture made by the finest craftsmen*

craftsmanship /'krɑːftsmənʃɪp $ 'kræfts-/ *n* [U] the skill of making something beautiful with your hands

crafty /'krɑːfti $ 'kræf-/ *adj* good at getting what you want by cleverly deceiving people: *He's a crafty old devil.* → see box at **INTELLIGENT** —**craftily** *adv*

crag /kræg/ *n* [C] a steep rough rock on a hill or mountain

craggy /'krægi/ *adj* **1** craggy ground is very steep and covered with large rocks **2** a craggy face has a lot of lines

cram /kræm/ *v* **crammed, cramming** **1** [T] to force a lot of people or things into a small space: **cram sth into sth** *She managed to cram all her clothes into one suitcase.* **2 be crammed with sth** to be full of people or things: *The streets were crammed with tourists.* **3** [I] to prepare yourself for an examination by learning a lot of information very quickly: *Julia stayed up all night cramming for her final.* —**crammed** *adj*: *a crammed train*

cramp /kræmp/ *n* [C,U] a bad pain in your muscles that makes it difficult to move: *I've got cramp in my foot.*

cramped /kræmpt/ *adj* a cramped room or building does not have enough space for the people or things in it → see box at **SMALL**

cranberry /'krænbəri $ -beri/ *n* [C] plural **cranberries** a small red sour fruit: *cranberry sauce*

crane¹ /kreɪn/ *n* [C] **1** a tall machine with a long metal arm for lifting heavy things **2** a water bird with very long legs

crane² *v* [I,T] to stretch your neck forward in order to see or hear something: *He craned his neck to get a better view of the stage.*

crank¹ /kræŋk/ *n* [C] **1** *informal* someone who has unusual ideas and behaves strangely: *a religious crank* **2** a handle that you turn to make a machine work

crank² *v*

crank sth ⇔ up *phr v informal* to make the sound of something, especially music, louder: *Crank up the volume!*

cranny /'kræni/ *n* [C] plural **crannies** a small narrow hole in a wall or rock → **every nook and cranny** at **NOOK**

crash[1] /kræʃ/ v

1 [I,T] to have an accident in a car, plane etc, especially by hitting something else [➡ **collide**]: *The jet crashed shortly after takeoff.* | **+into/through etc** *We crashed straight into the car in front.* | **crash a car/bus/plane etc** *He was drunk when he crashed the car.*

2 [I] to hit something hard, causing a lot of damage or making a loud noise: **+into/through/against etc** *A brick crashed through the window.* | *the sound of waves crashing against the rocks*

3 [I] to make a loud noise: *Thunder crashed and boomed outside.*

4 [I] if a computer crashes, it suddenly stops working → see box at **COMPUTER**

5 [I] if a STOCK MARKET crashes, prices suddenly fall by a large amount

crash[2] n [C]

1 an accident in which a vehicle hits something else [➡ **collision**]: *Six vehicles were involved in the crash.* | **car/plane/train etc crash** *All 265 passengers were killed in the plane crash.* | *a head-on crash between two trains* → see box at **ACCIDENT**

2 a loud noise made by something falling or breaking: *We were woken by the sound of a loud crash downstairs.* | **with a crash** *The tray fell to the floor with a crash.* → see picture on page A7

3 when a computer suddenly stops working

4 when prices on a STOCK MARKET suddenly fall by a large amount: *a stock market crash*

'crash ,barrier n [C] *BrE* a fence that divides the two sides of a road or that prevents a crowd from moving forward

'crash course n [C] a short course in which you study a subject very quickly

'crash ,helmet n [C] a hard hat worn by MOTOR-CYCLISTS, racing drivers etc to protect their heads

,crash-'land / $ '. ./ v [I,T] to bring a plane down to the ground in a more dangerous way than usual because the plane has a problem —**crash landing** n [C]

crass /kræs/ adj stupid and rude: *a crass remark*

crate /kreɪt/ n [C] a large box used for carrying fruit, bottles etc: *a crate of beer*

crater /'kreɪtə $ -ər/ n [C] **1** the round open top of a VOLCANO **2** a round hole in the ground made by something that has fallen on it or by an explosion

cravat /krə'væt/ n [C] a piece of loosely folded material that a man ties around his neck [➡ **tie**]

crave /kreɪv/ v [T] to want something very much: *He craved affection.*

craving /'kreɪvɪŋ/ n [C] a very strong desire for something: *a craving for chocolate*

crawl[1] /krɔːl $ krɒːl/ v [I]

1 to move on your hands and knees: **+into/out of/through etc** *We crawled through a hole in the fence.* → see box at **BABY** → see picture on page A11

2 if an insect crawls, it moves along the ground: **+over/up etc** *Flies were crawling all over the food.*

3 if a vehicle crawls, it moves very slowly: *We crawled all the way into town.*

4 *disapproving* to be very pleasant to someone because they are important or can help you: **+to** *He's always crawling to the boss.*

5 be crawling with sth to be completely covered with insects or people: *The tent was crawling with ants!*

crawl[2] n **1** [singular] a very slow speed: *cars moving along at a crawl* **2 the crawl** a way of swimming in which you lie on your stomach and move one arm, and then the other, over your head [➡ **backstroke, breaststroke, butterfly**] → see picture at **SWIM**[1]

crayon /'kreɪən, -ɒn $ -ɑːn, -ən/ n [C] a stick of coloured WAX that children use to draw pictures

craze /kreɪz/ n [C] a fashion, game, type of music etc that is very popular for a short time: *the latest craze to hit New York* → see box at **POPULAR**

crazed /kreɪzd/ adj behaving in a wild and uncontrolled way like someone who is mentally ill

crazy /'kreɪzi/ adj comparative **crazier**, superlative **craziest**

1 very strange or not sensible [= **mad**]: *Our friends all think we're crazy.* | *It's an absolutely crazy idea.*

2 angry or annoyed: *Stop it, you're **driving** me **crazy** (=making me very annoyed)!* | *Dad will **go crazy** when he hears about this.*

3 be crazy about sb/sth to like someone or something very much: *Lee's crazy about cats.* → see box at **LOVE**

4 mentally ill [= **mad**]: *a crazy old woman*

5 go crazy if a group of people go crazy, they become very excited: *England scored and the fans went crazy.*

6 like crazy very much or very quickly: *We're going to have to work like crazy to get this finished on time.*

—**crazily** adv —**craziness** n [U]

creak /kriːk/ v [I] if something such as a door or wooden floor creaks, it makes a long high noise when it moves: *The door creaked shut behind him.* —**creak** n [C] —**creaky** adj → see picture on page A7

cream[1] /kriːm/ n

1 [U] a thick white liquid that comes from milk: *strawberries and cream* | *fresh cream*

2 [C,U] a thick smooth substance that you put on your skin to make it softer or less painful: *face cream* | *sun cream*

3 the cream of sth the best people or things in a group: *the cream of Europe's footballers*

→ **ICE CREAM, SUN CREAM**

cream[2] adj pale yellow-white in colour: *a cream-coloured carpet*

,cream 'cheese / $ '. ./ n [U] a type of soft white cheese

creamy /'kriːmi/ adj containing cream or thick and smooth like cream: *The sauce was smooth and creamy.*

crease[1] /kriːs/ n [C] a line on cloth or paper where it has been folded or crushed: *She smoothed the creases from her skirt.*

crease[2] v [I,T] if a piece of cloth or paper creases, or you crease it, it becomes marked with a line after it has been folded or crushed [➡ **crumple**]: *Try not to crease your jacket.* —**creased** adj → see box at **CLOTHES**

create /kri'eɪt/ v [T]

1 to make something new exist or happen: *The new factory should create 450 jobs.* | *The increase in traffic has created a lot of problems.*

2 to invent or design something: *This dish was created by our chef Jean Richard.*
—**creator** n [C] *Walt Disney, the creator of Mickey Mouse*

creation /kri'eɪʃən/ n **1** [U] when something new is created: **+of** *the creation of a United Europe* | *a job creation scheme* **2** [C] something that has been created: *the artist's latest creation* **3 Creation** according to many religions, the time when the universe and everything in it was made by God

creative /kri'eɪtɪv/ adj **1** a creative person is good at thinking of new ideas: *one of Japan's most talented and creative film directors* **2** involving the use of imagination to produce new ideas or things: *a creative solution to the problem* —**creatively** adv —**creativity** /ˌkriːeɪˈtɪvəti/ n [U] *artistic creativity*

creature /'kriːtʃə $ -ər/ n [C]

1 an animal, fish, or insect: *We should respect all living creatures.*

2 an imaginary animal or person, or one that is very strange and frightening: *creatures from outer space*

3 beautiful/gorgeous/stupid etc creature someone who is beautiful, stupid etc

creature 'comforts n [plural] all the things that make life comfortable and enjoyable: *The hotel had all the creature comforts of his home in London.*

crèche /kreʃ $ kreʃ, kreɪʃ/ n [C] *BrE* a place where babies are looked after while their parents are at work [= **day care center** *AmE*]

credence /'kriːdəns/ n [U] when something is accepted as true: *This new evidence **lends credence to** the theory.*

credentials /krɪ'denʃəlz/ n [plural] **1** someone's education, achievements, and experience that prove they have the ability to do something: *She has excellent academic credentials.* **2** a document which proves who you are

credibility /ˌkredəˈbɪləti/ n [U] when someone or something can be trusted and believed by people: *The scandal has damaged the government's credibility.*

credible /'kredəbəl/ adj if someone or something is credible, people can trust them or believe them: *a credible witness*

credit[1] /'kredət/ n **1** [U] a way of buying goods in which you arrange to pay for them later: **on credit** *The TV and the washing machine were bought on credit.* **2** [U] praise given to someone for doing something: *It's not fair – I do all the work and he **gets** all the **credit**.* | **+for** *You've got to **give** him **credit** for trying.* **3 be a credit to sb/sth** to behave so well or be so successful that the people around you are proud of you: *You're a credit to the school.* **4 have sth to your credit** to have achieved something: *She already has two novels to her credit.* **5** [C] a successfully completed part of a course at a university or college **6** [C] a payment made into a bank account **7 be in credit** to have money in your bank account →

see box at **ACCOUNT**[1] **8 the credits** [plural] a list of the people who helped to make a television programme or film

credit[2] v [T] **1** to add money to a bank account [≠ **debit**]: **credit sth to sth** *The cheque will be credited to your account.* **2 credit sb with (doing) sth** to believe that someone has a good quality or has done something good: *Credit me with some intelligence, please!* **3 be credited to sb/sth** if something is credited to someone or something, they are said to have achieved it or be the reason for it: *Much of Manchester United's success can be credited to their manager.* **4** to believe that something surprising is true: *Would you credit it! He's won!*

creditable /'kredətəbəl/ adj deserving praise or approval: *The French team finished a creditable second.*

'credit card n [C] a small plastic card that you use to buy goods or services and pay for them later: **by credit card** *Can I pay by credit card?*

creditor /'kredətə $ -ər/ n [C] a person or organization that you owe money to

'credit ˌrating n [C] a judgment made by a bank or other company about how likely a person or business is to pay their debts

credo /'kriːdəʊ, 'kreɪ- $ -doʊ/ n [C] plural **credos** a short statement that expresses a belief or rule

creed /kriːd/ n [C] a set of beliefs or principles: *People of all creeds were there.* | *a **religious creed***

creek /kriːk/ n [C] **1** *BrE* a narrow area of water where the sea flows into the land **2** *AmE* a small narrow stream or river **3 be up the creek (without a paddle)** *spoken* to be in a difficult situation: *I'll really be up the creek if I don't get my passport by Friday.*

creep[1] /kriːp/ v [I] past tense and past participle **crept** /krept/

1 to move very quietly so that no one will notice you: **+down/in/out etc** *She crept down the stairs in the dark.* → see box at **WALK**

2 to move somewhere very slowly [➡ **crawl**]: *The car was creeping along in heavy traffic.*

3 to gradually start to happen: **+into/in/over etc** *A note of panic had crept into his voice.*

4 to gradually increase: **+up** *The total number of people out of work crept up to five million.*

creep up on sb *phr v* **1** to surprise someone by walking up behind them quickly: *I wish you wouldn't creep up on me like that!* **2** if a feeling, problem, or bad situation creeps up on you, it gradually affects you without you realizing it: *Tiredness can creep up on you when you're stressed at work.* **3** if an event creeps up on you, it seems to happen sooner than you expect: *Somehow, the end of term had crept up on us.*

creep[2] n **1** [C usually singular] someone who you dislike a lot: *Go away, you little creep!* **2 give you the creeps** to make you feel nervous or frightened: *That guy gives me the creeps!*

creeper /'kriːpə $ -ər/ n [C] a plant that grows up walls or along the ground

creepy /'kriːpi/ adj *informal* making you feel nervous and slightly frightened: *a creepy movie*

cremate /krɪ'meɪt $ 'kriːmeɪt/ v [T] to burn the body of a dead person at a funeral ceremony —**cremation** /krɪ'meɪʃən/ n [C,U]

crematorium /ˌkremə'tɔːriəm $ ˌkriː-/ *n* plural **crematoriums or crematoria** /-riə/ [C] a building in which the bodies of dead people are burned at a funeral ceremony

crept /krept/ *v* the past tense and past participle of CREEP

crescendo /krɪ'ʃendəu $ -dou/ *n* [C] plural **crescendos** when a piece of music becomes gradually louder

crescent /'kresənt, 'krez-/ *n* [C] **1** a curved shape that is wider in the middle and pointed at the ends: *a crescent moon* → see picture at SHAPE¹ **2 Crescent** used in the names of streets that have a curved shape: *Turn left into Woodford Crescent.*

crest /krest/ *n* [C] **1** the top of a hill or wave **2** a group of upright feathers on a bird's head **3** a special picture used as the sign of a school, town, important family etc

crestfallen /'krest,fɔːlən $ -,fɒːl-/ *adj formal* sad or disappointed

crevasse /krɪ'væs/ *n* [C] a deep open crack in the thick ice on a mountain

crevice /'krevɪ̥s/ *n* [C] a narrow crack, especially in rock

crew /kruː/ *n* [C]
1 all the people that work together on a ship, plane etc
2 a group of people who work together on something: *an ambulance crew* → see box at GROUP

crewman /'kruːmən/ *n* [C] plural **crewmen** /-mən/ a member of the crew on a boat or ship

crib /krɪb/ *n* [C] *AmE* a baby's bed with bars around the sides [= cot *BrE*] → see picture at BED

'crib death *n* [C] *AmE* the sudden, unexpected and unexplained death of a baby while it is sleeping [= cot death *BrE*]

cricket /'krɪkɪ̥t/ *n*
1 [U] a game in which two teams try to get points by hitting a ball and running between two sets of sticks
2 [C] a small brown insect that can jump and makes a rough sound by rubbing its wings together

cricketer /'krɪkɪ̥tə $ -ər/ *n* [C] *BrE* someone who plays cricket

crime /kraɪm/ *n*
1 [U] illegal activities in general: *There was very little crime when we moved here.* | *Women commit far less crime than men.* | *the reasons why people turn to crime* | *We need to focus more on crime prevention.* | *The town has a low crime rate.* | *As a teenager, he became involved in petty crime* (=crime that is not very serious).

THESAURUS

Crimes that involve stealing things
theft – the crime of stealing things: *car theft*
robbery – the crime of stealing money or valuable things from a bank, shop etc: *armed robbery*
burglary – the crime of going into someone's home in order to steal
shoplifting – the crime of taking things from shops without paying for them
Crimes that involve attacking people
assault – when someone is physically attacked
mugging – when someone is attacked and

robbed in a public place
murder – when someone is deliberately killed
rape – when someone is forced to have sex
Someone who commits crimes
criminal, offender, thief, robber, burglar, shoplifter, attacker, mugger, murderer, rapist
→ ATTACK, STEAL

2 [C] an illegal action that can be punished by law: *He committed a number of crimes in the area.* | *Rape is a very serious crime.*
3 it's a crime *spoken* used to say that something is morally wrong: *It's a crime to waste food.*
→ ORGANIZED CRIME, WAR CRIME

criminal¹ /'krɪmɪ̥nəl/ *adj*
1 [only before noun] relating to crime: *criminal behaviour* | *He has a long criminal record* (=an official record of the crimes he has committed). | *The case will be tried in a criminal court.*
2 wrong, dishonest, and unacceptable: *It's criminal that teachers are paid so little money.*
—**criminally** *adv*

criminal² *n* [C] someone who has done something wrong or illegal: *Police have described the man as a violent and dangerous criminal.* → see box at CRIME

crimson /'krɪmzən/ *adj* having a deep red colour —**crimson** *n* [U]

cringe /krɪndʒ/ *v* [I] **1** to feel embarrassed by something: *It makes me cringe when I think how stupid I was.* **2** to move away from someone or something because you are afraid: *She cringed away from him in horror.*

crinkle /'krɪŋkəl/ also **crinkle up** *v* [I,T] to become covered with small folds, or make something do this: *Mandy crinkled her nose in disgust.* —**crinkled** *adj* —**crinkly** *adj*

cripple¹ /'krɪpəl/ *n* [C] a word for someone who cannot walk properly that is now considered to be offensive

cripple² *v* [T] **1** to hurt someone so they can no longer walk: *He was crippled in a car accident.* **2** to seriously damage something or make it much weaker: *The country's economy has been crippled by drought.* —**crippled** *adj* —**crippling** *adj*: *a crippling illness* | *crippling debts*

crisis /'kraɪsɪ̥s/ *n* [C,U] plural **crises** /-siːz/ a time when a situation is very bad or dangerous [➙ emergency]: *The country now faces an economic crisis.* | *a major political crisis* | *an emotional crisis* | **in crisis** *The car industry is now in crisis.*
→ MIDLIFE CRISIS

crisp¹ /krɪsp/ *adj* **1** something that is crisp is hard, and makes a pleasant sound when you break it: *She kicked at the crisp leaves at her feet.* **2** fresh, firm, and pleasant to eat: *a nice crisp salad* **3** weather that is crisp is cold and dry: *a crisp winter morning* **4** cloth that is crisp looks clean and new: *crisp clean sheets* **5** a picture that is crisp is clear —**crisply** *adv*

crisp² *n* [C] *BrE* a thin, flat round piece of potato cooked in very hot oil and eaten cold as a SNACK [= chip *AmE*]: *a packet of crisps*

crispy /'krɪspi/ *adj* crispy food is pleasantly hard: *crispy bacon*

crisscross /'krɪskrɒs $ -krɒːs/ *v* [I,T] to make a pattern of straight lines that cross each other: *Motorways crisscross the countryside.*

criterion /kraɪˈtɪəriən $ -ˈtɪr-/ *n* [C usually plural] plural **criteria** /-riə/ a standard that you use to judge something or make a decision about something: **+for** *What are the criteria for selecting the winner?*

critic /ˈkrɪtɪk/ *n* [C] **1** someone whose job is to give their opinion of a film, book etc: *a literary critic for the Times* **2** someone who says that a person or idea is bad or wrong: **+of** *an outspoken critic of the government*

critical /ˈkrɪtɪkəl/ *adj* **1** if you are critical of someone or something, you say that you think they are bad or wrong: **+of** *Economists are critical of the plans.* | *She made some* **highly critical** *remarks.* **2** very important: **+to** *The talks are critical to the future of the peace process.* | *The effects of climate change are of* **critical importance.** **3** serious or dangerous: *The driver is still in a critical condition* (=seriously ill or injured) *in hospital.* **4** [only before noun] judging how good a play, film, book etc is: *a* **critical analysis** *of Shakespeare* —**critically** /-kli/ *adv*: *She's critically ill.*

criticism /ˈkrɪtɪˌsɪzəm/ *n*
1 [C,U] when you say that a person or thing is bad or wrong [≠ **praise**]: **+of** *I don't think his criticisms of the project are justified.* | **strong/harsh/severe criticism** *She faced harsh criticism when she resigned.* | **provoke/attract/draw criticism** *His speech attracted widespread criticism.* | **take/accept criticism** (=be willing to accept that it may be true) *Kate doesn't take criticism well.* | **constructive criticism** (=meant to help someone improve)
2 [U] when someone gives their judgment of a film, play, book etc: *literary criticism*

criticize also **-ise** *BrE* /ˈkrɪtɪˌsaɪz/ *v* [I,T] to say what faults you think someone or something has [≠ **praise**]: *You do nothing but criticize.* | **criticize sb for (doing) sth** *The regime has been criticized for its record on human rights.* | **criticize sth strongly/sharply/heavily etc** *The government's policies have been strongly criticized.* | *The new law has been* **widely criticized** (=criticized by a lot of people).

critique /krɪˈtiːk/ *n* [C] a piece of writing describing the good and bad qualities of a play, film, book etc

croak /krəʊk $ kroʊk/ *v* **1** [I] to speak in a low rough voice: *'Hello,' he croaked.* **2** [I] if a FROG croaks, it makes a low deep sound —**croak** *n* [C]

crochet /ˈkrəʊʃeɪ $ kroʊˈʃeɪ/ *v* [I,T] to make clothes by twisting wool together using a needle with a hook at one end —**crochet** *n* [U]

crock /krɒk $ kraːk/ *n* [C] *old-fashioned* a clay pot

crockery /ˈkrɒkəri $ ˈkraː-/ *n* [U] *BrE* cups, plates, and dishes

crocodile /ˈkrɒkədaɪl $ ˈkraː-/ *n* [C] a large REPTILE with a long mouth and sharp teeth, that lives in lakes and rivers in hot countries

crocus /ˈkrəʊkəs $ ˈkroʊ-/ *n* [C] a small purple, yellow, or white flower that appears in spring

croissant /ˈkwaːsɒŋ $ krɒːˈsaːnt/ *n* [C] a curved piece of soft bread, eaten for breakfast, especially in France → see picture at **BREAD**

crony /ˈkrəʊni $ ˈkroʊni/ *n* [C] plural **cronies** *informal disapproving* one of a group of friends who use their power or influence to help each other: *one of his* **political cronies**

crook¹ /krʊk/ *n* **1** [C] *informal* a criminal or dishonest person: *a bunch of crooks* **2** **the crook of sb's arm** the inside of someone's arm, where it bends

crook² *v* [T] if you crook your finger or arm, you bend it

crooked /ˈkrʊkɪd/ *adj* **1** not straight: *crooked streets* **2** *informal* dishonest

croon /kruːn/ *v* [I,T] to sing or speak softly about love

crop¹ /krɒp $ kraːp/ *n*
1 [C] a plant such as wheat, fruit, vegetables etc that farmers grow and sell: *Our main crops are rice and oats.*
2 [C] the amount of wheat, fruit etc that a farmer produces in a season: **+of** *a bumper crop* (=a very large amount) *of broad beans*
3 [singular] a group of people or things that arrive at the same time: **+of** *this year's crop of novels*
4 [C] a short whip used in horse riding
→ **CASH CROP**

crop² *v* [T] **cropped, cropping** to make something shorter by cutting it: *His hair was cropped short.* | *We use sheep to keep the grass cropped.*
crop up *phr v* to suddenly appear or happen: *A problem's cropped up.*

cropper /ˈkrɒpə $ ˈkraːpər/ **come a cropper** *BrE informal* **a)** to fail unexpectedly **b)** to fall over

croquet /ˈkrəʊkeɪ, -ki $ kroʊˈkeɪ/ *n* [U] a game played on grass in which you hit balls under bent wires using a wooden hammer

cross¹ /krɒs $ krɒːs/ *v*
1 also **cross over** [I,T] to go from one side of a road, river, room etc to the other: *Take care when you cross the road.* | *We crossed the border into Italy.* | **+to** *The boat had crossed over safely to the other side.* | *the first ship to cross the Pacific* | *A cheering crowd greeted the first runner to cross the finish line.*
2 [I,T] if two straight things cross, or if you cross them, they are arranged so that one goes over the other: *The road crosses the railway here.* | **cross your arms/legs/ankles** *She sat down and crossed her legs.*
3 **cross your fingers/fingers crossed** used to say that you hope something will happen
4 **cross your mind** if a thought crosses your mind, it suddenly comes into your mind: *It crossed my mind that he might think we were lovers.*
5 **cross yourself** to touch your head, chest, and shoulders in turn to show respect for God
6 [T] to mix two different types of animal or plant to produce young animals or plants: **cross sth with sth** *Wolves can be crossed with domestic dogs.*
7 [I,T] to pass the ball across the playing area in a game such as football: *Norbury crossed the ball into the penalty area.*
8 [T] to make someone angry by refusing to do what they want: *Those who crossed him soon had cause for regret.*
→ **DOUBLE-CROSS**

cross sth ⇔ **off** phr v to draw a line through something on a list to show that you have dealt with it: *Cross off their names as they arrive.*

cross sth ⇔ **out** phr v to draw a line through something you have written because it is not correct

cross² n [C]

1 a mixture of two things: +**between** *It looks like a cross between a dog and a rat.*

2 a) an upright wooden post with another post fixed across it. In the past, people were punished by being fastened to the post and left to die: **the cross** (=the cross that Christ died on) **b)** an object, sign etc in the shape of a cross, used to represent the Christian faith: *a tiny gold cross* | *He made **the sign of the cross** (=moved his hand in the shape of a cross).*

3 BrE a mark (x) put on paper to show where something is or that something is not correct: **put/mark a cross** *I've put a cross to show where the pub is.*

4 when a player kicks the ball across the playing area in a game such as football

cross³ adj BrE annoyed: +**with** *Are you cross with me?* | +**about** *She's still cross about losing all that money.* → see box at ANGRY

cross- /krɒs $ krɒːs/ prefix **1** going from one side of something to the other: *a cross-Channel ferry* | *cross-border fighting* **2** mixing two different things: *cross-cultural influences*

crossbar /ˈkrɒsbɑː $ ˈkrɒːsbɑːr/ n [C] **1** the bar that joins two GOALPOSTS **2** the bar on a bicycle that joins the seat and the HANDLEBARS → see picture at BICYCLE

crossbow /ˈkrɒsbəʊ $ ˈkrɒːsboʊ/ n [C] a weapon used to shoot ARROWS

cross-'country adj [only before noun] a cross-country race is one that goes across fields and not along roads —**cross-country** n [C,U]

cross-ex'amine v [I,T] to officially ask someone questions to discover whether they have been telling the truth: *In court, the two women were cross-examined.* —**cross-exami'nation** n [C,U]

cross-'eyed / $ ˈ. ./ adj having eyes that look inwards

crossfire /ˈkrɒsfaɪə $ ˈkrɒːsfaɪr/ n [U] **1** bullets travelling towards each other from different directions: *Red Cross workers were **caught in the crossfire**.* **2** a situation in which you are badly affected by a disagreement, even though it does not involve you: *I don't want to get **caught in** the political **crossfire**.*

crossing /ˈkrɒsɪŋ $ ˈkrɒː-/ n [C] **1** a place where you can safely cross a road, river etc **2** a place where two roads, lines etc cross **3** a journey across water → see box at JOURNEY

cross-legged /ˌkrɒs ˈleɡɪd◂ , -ˈleɡd◂ $ ˈkrɒːs ˈleɡɪd, -ˌleɡd/ adv, adj in a sitting position with your knees apart and one foot over the opposite leg: *Children **sat cross-legged** on the floor.*

crossover /ˈkrɒsəʊvə $ ˈkrɒːsoʊvər/ n [C,U] when something or someone is popular or successful in different areas or is liked by different types of people, for example when a popular song is liked by people who usually only like serious music: *The song has enjoyed crossover success on the country and pop charts.*

cross-'purposes n [plural] **at cross-purposes** if two people are at cross-purposes, they become confused because they think they are talking about the same thing, although they are not

cross-'reference / $ ˈ. ˌ.../ n [C] a note in a book telling you to look on a different page for more information

crossroads /ˈkrɒsrəʊdz $ ˈkrɒːsroʊdz/ n [C] plural **crossroads 1** a place where two roads cross each other [➔ T-junction, junction]: **at the crossroads** *Turn left at the crossroads.* **2** a time when you have to make an important decision about your future: **at a crossroads** *Neil is at a crossroads in his career.*

'cross ˌsection, cross-section n [C] **1** a picture of something that shows what it would look like if you cut it in half, or an object cut in this way **2** a group of people or things that is typical of a larger group: +**of** *a cross-section of the American public*

crosswalk /ˈkrɒswɔːk $ ˈkrɒːswɒːk/ n [C] AmE a marked place where people can cross a road safely [= pedestrian crossing BrE]

crossword /ˈkrɒswɜːd $ ˈkrɒːswɜːrd/ also **'crossword ˌpuzzle** n [C] a game in which you write the answers to CLUES (=questions) in boxes arranged in a black and white pattern: *I usually do the **crossword** in the newspaper.*

crotch /krɒtʃ $ krɑːtʃ/ also **crutch** BrE n [C] the place where your legs join at the top, or the part of a pair of trousers etc that covers this

crouch /kraʊtʃ/ also **crouch down** v [I] to bend your knees and back so you are close to the ground → see picture on page A11

crow¹ /krəʊ $ kroʊ/ n **1** [C] a large black bird that makes a loud sound **2 as the crow flies** used to describe the distance between two places when measured in a straight line

crow² v [I] **1** if a COCK (=male chicken) crows, it makes a loud sound **2** to talk very proudly about yourself or your achievements: +**about/ over** *She keeps crowing about her exam results.*

crowbar /ˈkrəʊbɑː $ ˈkroʊbɑːr/ n [C] a strong iron bar used to open things

crowd¹ /kraʊd/ n

1 [C] a large group of people in one place: +**of** *a large crowd of football supporters* | *A crowd gathered outside the building.* | *Police used tear gas to **disperse the crowd**.* | *Shop online and **avoid the crowds**.* → see box at GROUP

2 [singular] ordinary people: *He likes to **stand out from the crowd** (=be different from ordinary people).*

3 [singular] informal a group of people who know each other well

crowd² v [I,T] if people crowd somewhere, they are there in large numbers: +**around/into/in etc** *The students crowded round my desk for a better look.* | **be crowded together** *The prisoners were all crowded together in a small cell.* | *Holidaymakers crowd the beaches in high season.*

crowd sb/sth ⇔ **out** phr v to force someone or something to leave a place: *Supermarkets have crowded out the small grocery stores.*

crowded /ˈkraʊdɪd/ adj very full of people or things: *a crowded room* | *The train was **overcrowded** (=carrying too many people).*

crown[1] /kraʊn/ n [C]
1 a circle made of gold and jewels, which a king or queen wears on their head
2 the Crown the power and position of a king or queen, or their government
3 a cover that is fixed over a damaged tooth
4 the top of a hill, your head, or a hat: **+of** *the crown of the hill*

crown[2] v [I,T] **1** to put a crown on someone's head, as part of a ceremony that officially makes them the ruler of a country: **crown sb king/queen/tsar etc** *She was crowned queen 50 years ago.* **2** to make something complete or perfect by adding to it: *His career was crowned by a Nobel Prize.*

crowning /ˈkraʊnɪŋ/ adj [only before noun] better, more important etc than anything else: *Winning this award was the **crowning achievement** of his career.*

crucial /ˈkruːʃəl/ adj very important: **+to** *Money is crucial to the aid program.* → see box at IMPORTANT —**crucially** adv: *a crucially important meeting*

crucifix /ˈkruːsɪ̯fɪks/ n [C] a cross with a figure of Christ on it

crucify /ˈkruːsɪ̯faɪ/ v [T] **crucified**, **crucifying**, **crucifies 1** to kill someone by fastening them to a cross **2** *informal* to criticize someone very strongly —**crucifixion** /ˌkruːsɪ̯ˈfɪkʃən/ n [C,U]

crude /kruːd/ adj **1** [only before noun] crude oil, rubber etc is in a natural condition **2** offensive or rude: *His jokes are crude.* **3** not made to a high standard: *a crude shelter* **4** not exact or detailed: *a crude estimate* —**crudely** adv

crude 'oil also **crude** n [U] oil that is in its natural condition, as it comes out of an OIL WELL, before it is made more pure or separated into different products

cruel /ˈkruːəl/ adj hurting people or animals or making them suffer [≠ kind]: **+to** *People who are cruel to animals make me mad.* | *His death was a cruel blow.* → see box at CHARACTER → and UNKIND —**cruelly** adv: *She was treated very cruelly.*

cruelty /ˈkruːəlti/ n [C,U] plural **cruelties** behaviour or actions that are unkind or cause suffering [≠ kindness]: **+to** *cruelty to animals* | *cruelties committed in the name of religion*

cruise[1] /kruːz/ v [I] **1** if a plane, boat, car etc cruises, it moves at a steady speed **2** to win something easily: **cruise to victory/success etc**

cruise[2] n [C] a holiday on a large ship

cruise 'missile n [C] a powerful weapon that can be aimed from a very long distance away

cruiser /ˈkruːzə $ -ər/ n [C] a type of ship → see box at SHIP

crumb /krʌm/ n [C] **1** a very small piece of bread, cake etc **2** a very small amount: **+of** *She offered us a few crumbs of comfort.*

crumble /ˈkrʌmbəl/ v **1** [I,T] to break into small pieces, or to make something do this: *She crumbled the bread onto the ground.* | *The walls had crumbled away.* **2** [I] if a system or relationship crumbles, it fails: *His marriage had crumbled.*

crummy /ˈkrʌmi/ adj informal of poor quality: *a crummy hotel room*

crumple /ˈkrʌmpəl/ v [I,T] also **crumple up** to crush paper or cloth —**crumpled** adj: *crumpled sheets*

crunch[1] /krʌntʃ/ v [I,T] to make a noise like something being crushed: **+on/over** *I heard boots crunching on the gravel.* | *Rob crunched an apple.*

crunch[2] n **1** [singular] a noise like the sound of something being crushed: **+of** *the crunch of footsteps in the snow* → see picture on page A7 **2** [singular] *informal* the moment in a situation when you must make an important decision: *When it came to the crunch, I couldn't bring myself to do it.* **3** [C] an exercise in which you lie on the floor and move your head and shoulders up and down

crunchy /ˈkrʌntʃi/ adj food that is crunchy is pleasantly firm and makes a sound when you bite it

crusade /kruːˈseɪd/ n [C] a determined attempt to change something you feel is morally wrong: **+against/for** *a crusade against violence* —**crusade** v [I] —**crusader** n [C]

crush[1] /krʌʃ/ v [T]
1 to press something so hard that it breaks or is damaged: *The car was crushed by a falling tree.* | **crush sb/sth under/beneath/against etc sth** *She was crushed under the wheels of a car.* | *People were crushed to death by the crowd.* → see box at PRESS → see picture on page A4
2 to use severe methods to defeat someone: **crush a rebellion/uprising/revolt etc** *The revolt was crushed by the government.*
3 to make someone lose all hope, confidence etc: **crush sb's hopes/enthusiasm etc** *Her hopes were cruelly crushed.*

crush

crush[2] n **1** [C] a strong feeling of love for someone that continues only for a short time: *I had a huge **crush on** my tutor.* → see box at LOVE **2** [singular] a crowd of people in a very small space: *At last we managed to get through the crush.*

crushing /ˈkrʌʃɪŋ/ adj **1** very hard to deal with, and making you lose hope and confidence: *The army suffered a **crushing defeat**.* **2** a crushing remark, reply etc contains a very strong criticism

crust /krʌst/ n [C,U] **1** the baked outside part of bread, a PIE, etc **2** a hard layer on the surface of something: *the Earth's crust*

crusty /ˈkrʌsti/ adj food that is crusty has a hard crust: *nice crusty bread*

crutch /krʌtʃ/ n [C] **1** [usually plural] one of a pair of sticks that you lean on to help you walk: **on crutches** *I was on crutches for weeks.* **2** something that someone uses to help them, especially when this is not good for them: *Tom uses drugs as a crutch.* **3** BrE the place where your legs join at the top, or the part of a pair of trousers etc that covers this [= crotch]

crux /krʌks/ *n* [singular] the most important part of a problem or question: +**of** *The crux of the matter is whether he intended murder.*

cry¹ /kraɪ/ *v* **cried, crying, cries**

1 [I] when you cry, tears come from your eyes because you feel a very strong emotion, for example you are sad or in pain: +**over/about** *What are you crying about?* | +**for** *the sound of a baby crying for its mother* | +**with** *She could have cried with joy.* | *Sad movies always make me cry.*

THESAURUS

If someone **sobs** or **weeps**, they cry very hard and for a long time.
If someone **bursts into tears**, they suddenly start crying.

2 also **cry out** [I,T] *written* to say something loudly: *'Stop!' she cried.* | *He cried her name out in anguish.* | +**for** *voices crying for help* → see box at **SHOUT**

3 [I] if animals or birds cry, they make a loud, high sound

4 cry over spilt milk *informal* to worry about a mistake that cannot be changed

5 cry wolf to keep asking for help when you do not need it, so that when you really need help, no one believes you

6 be crying out for sth to need something urgently: *We're crying out for math teachers.*
—**crying** *n* [U] *the sound of crying* → **a shoulder to cry on** at **SHOULDER¹**

cry² *n* plural **cries**

1 [C] the sound someone makes when they feel a strong emotion, for example when they are very sad or are in pain: +**of** *He gave a cry of pain.* | *She let out a cry of delight.* | **cry of pain/joy/fear etc** *Letting out a cry of delight, he grasped her hands.* | +**for** *cries for help*

2 [singular] *BrE* when someone cries: **have a cry** | *You'll feel better after a good cry* (=crying for a long time).

3 a cry for help something someone does that shows they are unhappy and need help: *A suicide attempt is a cry for help.*

4 [C] a sound made by an animal or bird: *the cries of gulls*

5 be a far cry from sth to be very different from something else: *The Olympics were a far cry from the spectacle we see now.*

crying /ˈkraɪ-ɪŋ/ *adj* **1 it's a crying shame** *spoken* used to say that something is very sad **2 a crying need for sth** an urgent need for something: *There's a crying need for better public transport.*

crypt /krɪpt/ *n* [C] a room under a church

cryptic /ˈkrɪptɪk/ *adj* having a meaning that is hard to understand: *a cryptic comment*

crystal /ˈkrɪstl/ *n* **1** [U] high quality glass: *crystal wine glasses* **2** [C] a small evenly shaped object that forms naturally when a liquid becomes solid: *ice crystals* **3** [C,U] a type of clear pale rock

,crystal 'ball *n* [C] a glass ball that some people think can show future events

,crystal 'clear *adj* **1** clearly stated and easy to understand: *I made my orders crystal clear.* **2** completely clear and clean

crystallize also **-ise** *BrE* /ˈkrɪstəlaɪz/ *v* [I,T] **1** if liquid crystallizes, it forms crystals **2** if an idea or plan crystallizes, it becomes clear or certain

cub /kʌb/ *n* [C] a young bear, lion etc

cube /kjuːb/ *n* [C] **1** a solid square object with six equal sides: *an ice cube* → see picture at **SHAPE¹** **2** the cube of a number is the number produced when you multiply it by itself twice —**cube** *v* [T]

cubic /ˈkjuːbɪk/ *adj* relating to a measurement of space which is calculated by multiplying the length of something by its width and height: **cubic centimetre/inch etc**

cubicle /ˈkjuːbɪkəl/ *n* [C] a small separate area in a room: *a shower cubicle*

cuckoo /ˈkʊkuː $ ˈkuːkuː, ˈkʊ-/ *n* [C] a bird that lays its eggs in the NESTS of other birds and makes a sound like the sound of its name

cucumber /ˈkjuːkʌmbə $ -ər/ *n* [C] a long thin green vegetable that you eat raw → see picture at **VEGETABLE**

cuddle /ˈkʌdl/ *v* [I,T] to put your arms around someone or something as a sign of love: *Dan cuddled the puppy.* —**cuddle** *n* [C]
cuddle up *phr v* to lie or sit very close to someone: +**to** *Come and cuddle up to me.*

cuddle

cuddly /ˈkʌdli/ *adj* soft, warm, and nice to hold: *cuddly toys*

cue /kjuː/ *n* [C] **1** an action or event that is a signal for something else to happen: +**for** *That was a cue for us to leave.* **2** a word or action in a play that tells an actor to do something: *Tony waited nervously for his cue.* **3 (right/as if) on cue** happening at exactly the right moment: *As if on cue, Sam came in.* **4 take your cue from sb** to copy what someone else does because they do it correctly **5** a long straight wooden stick used to hit the ball in games such as **SNOOKER**

cuff¹ /kʌf/ *n* [C] **1** the end part of a sleeve, where it fastens **2 off the cuff** not prepared or thought about earlier: *an off-the-cuff-remark*

cuff² *v* [T] to hit someone lightly

'cuff link *n* [C] a small piece of jewellery that a man can use to fasten his shirt sleeves

cuisine /kwɪˈziːn/ *n* [U] a particular style of cooking: *French cuisine*

cul-de-sac /ˈkʌl də ˌsæk, ˈkʊl- $ ˌkʌl də ˈsæk, ˌkʊl-/ *n* [C] a street with no way out at the end

culinary /ˈkʌlɪnəri $ ˈkʌlɪneri, ˈkjuː-l-/ *adj* [only before noun] *formal* relating to cooking: *culinary skills*

cull /kʌl/ *v* [T] **1** to kill some of the animals in a group **2** *formal* to collect information from different places: **cull sth from sth** *The data was culled from many sources.* —**cull** *n* [C]

culminate /ˈkʌlmɪneɪt/ *v*
culminate in/with sth *phr v* to end with a particular event, especially a big or important one: *The meeting culminated in a vote.*

culmination /ˌkʌlmᵻˈneɪʃən/ n **the culmination of sth** something important that happens after a period of development: *The book is the culmination of 10 years' work.*

culpable /ˈkʌlpəbəl/ adj formal deserving blame —**culpability** /ˌkʌlpəˈbɪlᵻti/ n [U]

culprit /ˈkʌlprᵻt/ n [C] **1** someone who has done something wrong: *The police caught the culprit.* **2** informal the reason for a problem or difficulty: *Tax is the main culprit.*

cult /kʌlt/ n [C] **1** a small religious group whose members often have unusual beliefs: *a religious cult* **2** a film, POP group etc that has become very popular among a group of people: *a cult film* → see box at **POPULAR**

cultivate /ˈkʌltᵻveɪt/ v [T] **1** to prepare land for growing crops, or to grow a particular crop **2** to try to develop a friendship with someone who can help you: *You need to cultivate useful contacts.* **3** to work hard to develop a particular skill, attitude, or quality —**cultivation** /ˌkʌltᵻˈveɪʃən/ n [U]

cultivated /ˈkʌltᵻveɪtᵻd/ adj **1** someone who is cultivated is intelligent and knows a lot about music, art, literature etc: *a highly cultivated man* **2** cultivated land is used for growing crops or plants

cultural /ˈkʌltʃərəl/ adj

1 relating to a particular society and its way of life: *cultural differences* | *cultural traditions*
2 relating to art, literature, music etc: *the city's cultural life*
—**culturally** adv

culture /ˈkʌltʃə $ -ər/ n

1 [C,U] the ideas, way of life, traditions etc of a particular society: *You have to spend time in a country to understand its culture.* | *the differences between the two cultures* | **Western/American/ Japanese etc culture**
2 [U] art, music, literature etc: *If it's culture you're looking for, the city has several museums.* | *popular culture* (=the music, films etc that are liked by a lot of people)
3 [C,U] technical BACTERIA or cells grown for scientific use, or the process of growing them

cultured /ˈkʌltʃəd $ -ərd/ adj intelligent, polite, and interested in art, literature, music etc

'culture ˌshock n [singular,U] the feeling of being confused or anxious when you visit a country that is very different from your own

cumbersome /ˈkʌmbəsəm $ -bər-/ adj **1** heavy and difficult to move or use: *a cumbersome machine* **2** a process or system that is cumbersome is slow and difficult: *Getting a passport is a cumbersome process.*

cumin /ˈkʌmᵻn, ˈkjuː- $ ˈkʌmᵻn, ˈkuː-, ˈkjuː-/ n [U] the seeds of a plant, used in cooking

cumulative /ˈkjuːmjᵿlətɪv $ -leɪtɪv/ adj increasing gradually: *the cumulative effects of stress and overwork* —**cumulatively** adv

cunning /ˈkʌnɪŋ/ adj clever, especially in a dishonest or unfair way: *a cunning plan* | *a cunning opponent* → see box at **INTELLIGENT** —**cunning** n [U] —**cunningly** adv

cup¹ /kʌp/ n [C]
1 a small container with a handle that you drink from, or the drink that it contains [➡ saucer]: *a cup and saucer* | **of** *a cup of coffee*

2 a metal container that is given as a prize in a competition, or the competition itself: *They won the European Cup.*
3 a unit used in the US for measuring food when cooking: *Stir in a cup of flour.*

cup² v [T] **cupped, cupping** to form your hands into the shape of a cup: **+around** *She cupped her hands around the mug.*

cupboard /ˈkʌbəd $ -ərd/ n [C] a piece of furniture with doors and sometimes shelves, used for storing clothes, plates, food etc [➡ closet, wardrobe]: **kitchen/food/medicine etc cupboard** *Your coat's in the bedroom cupboard.* | *fitted cupboards* (=ones that are fixed in position and not possible to remove)
→ **AIRING CUPBOARD**

curable /ˈkjʊərəbəl $ ˈkjʊr-/ adj an illness that is curable can be cured

curate /ˈkjʊərᵻt $ ˈkjʊr-/ n [C] a priest of low rank whose job is to help the priest who is in charge of an area

curator /kjʊˈreɪtə $ -ər/ n [C] someone who is in charge of a MUSEUM

curb¹ /kɜːb $ kɜːrb/ n [C] **1** something that controls or limits something: **+on** *The new tax should act as a curb on spending.* **2** AmE the edge of the PAVEMENT, where it joins the road [= kerb BrE]

curb² v [T] to control or limit something: *new measures to curb crime*

curdle /ˈkɜːdl $ ˈkɜːrdl/ v [I,T] if a liquid curdles, it becomes unpleasantly thick: *Milk curdles in warm weather.*

cure¹ /kjʊə $ kjʊr/ v [T]

1 to make an illness or injury better [➡ heal]: *This type of cancer can be cured.* | **cure sb of sth** *90% of patients can be cured of the disease.*
2 to solve a problem, or improve a bad situation: *an attempt to cure unemployment*
3 to preserve food by drying it, hanging it in smoke, or covering it with salt: *cured ham*

cure² n [C] **1** a medicine or treatment that makes an illness go away: **+for** *a cure for AIDS* **2** something that solves a problem: **+for** *There's no easy cure for poverty.*

curfew /ˈkɜːfjuː $ ˈkɜːr-/ n [C] a law that forces people to stay indoors after a particular time at night: *The army imposed a curfew.*

curiosity /ˌkjʊəriˈɒsᵻti $ ˌkjʊriˈɑːs-/ n [singular,U] the desire to know about something: *I opened the box to satisfy my curiosity.* | **out of curiosity** (=because of curiosity) *She followed him out of curiosity.* | **+about** *Children have a natural curiosity about the world around them.*

curious /ˈkjʊəriəs $ ˈkjʊr-/ adj

1 wanting to know or learn about something: *Puppies are naturally curious.* | **+about** *I'm curious about how the system works.* | **curious to know/see/hear etc** *Sue was curious to know what happened.*
2 strange or unusual: *a curious noise* | **+that** *It's curious that she left without saying goodbye.*
—**curiously** adv

curl¹ /kɜːl $ kɜːrl/ v [I,T] to form a curve or curves, or to make something do this: *Her long hair curled down her back.* | **curl (sth) around/ round sth** *He curled his arm around her waist.*

curl up *phr v* **1** to lie or sit comfortably with your legs bent close to your body: *She curled up on the sofa.* **2** if paper, leaves etc curl up, the edges bend upwards

curl² *n* [C] something in the shape of a curve, especially a piece of hair: *a girl with blonde curls* | **+of** *a curl of smoke*

curler /ˈkɜːlə $ ˈkɜːrlər/ *n* [C] a small metal or plastic tube for making hair curl

curly /ˈkɜːli $ ˈkɜːrli/ *adj* curly hair has a lot of curls → see picture at HAIR

currant /ˈkʌrənt $ ˈkɜːr-/ *n* [C] a small dried GRAPE used in cakes

currency /ˈkʌrənsi $ ˈkɜːr-/ *n plural* **currencies**
1 [C,U] the type of money that a country uses: *foreign currency* | *the local currency* → see box at MONEY
2 [U] when something is accepted or used by a lot of people: *The idea soon gained currency.*

current¹ /ˈkʌrənt $ ˈkɜːr-/ *adj* happening, existing, or being used now: *her current boyfriend* | *The word is still current in some circles.* —**currently** *adv* → see box at NOW

current² *n* [C] **1** a flow of water or air in a particular direction: *Strong currents are dangerous for swimmers.* **2** a flow of electricity through a wire

ˈcurrent acˌcount *n* [C] *BrE* a bank account that you can take money out of at any time [= checking account *AmE*] → see box at ACCOUNT

ˌcurrent afˈfairs *n* [U] important political or social events that are happening now

curriculum /kəˈrɪkjɨləm/ *n* [C] *plural* **curricula** /-lə/ or **curriculums** the subjects that students learn at a school, college etc → see box at SCHOOL

curriculum vitae /kəˌrɪkjɨləm ˈviːtaɪ/ *n* [C] *BrE formal* abbreviation *CV* [= résumé *AmE*]

curry /ˈkʌri $ ˈkɜːri/ *n* [C,U] *plural* **curries** meat or vegetables cooked in a spicy sauce

curse¹ /kɜːs $ kɜːrs/ *v* **1** [I] to use rude language because you are angry [= swear]: *He cursed loudly.* **2** [T] to say or think bad things about someone or something because they have made you angry: **curse sb/sth for (doing) sth** *He cursed himself for believing her lies.*

curse² *n* [C] **1** a rude word or words that you use when you are angry **2** magic words that bring someone bad luck: *a witch's curse* **3** something that causes trouble or harm: **+of** *Noise is a curse of modern life.*

cursor /ˈkɜːsə $ ˈkɜːrsər/ *n* [C] a shape on a computer screen that moves to show where you are writing

cursory /ˈkɜːsəri $ ˈkɜːr-/ *adj* done very quickly and without much attention: *a cursory glance*

curt /kɜːt $ kɜːrt/ *adj* using very few words in a way that seems rude: *a curt reply* —**curtly** *adv* —**curtness** *n* [U]

curtail /kɜːˈteɪl $ kɜːr-/ *v* [T] *formal* to reduce or limit something: *The new law curtailed police powers.* —**curtailment** *n* [C,U]

curtain /ˈkɜːtn $ ˈkɜːrtn/ *n* [C] a piece of cloth that you pull across a window at night, use to divide a room etc: *a new pair of curtains* | *Lisa drew the curtains* (=opened or closed them).

curtsy, curtsey /ˈkɜːtsi $ ˈkɜːr-/ *v* [I] **curtsied, curtsying, curtsies** if a woman curtsies, she bends her knees with one foot in front of the other, as a sign of respect for an important person —**curtsy** *n* [C]

curve¹ /kɜːv $ kɜːrv/ *n* [C] a line or shape which bends round like part of a circle: *a sharp curve in the road* | *Look at the curve on this graph.*
→ LEARNING CURVE

curve² *v* [I,T] to bend or move in the shape of a curve, or to make something do this: *The ball curved through the air.* —**curved** *adj* → see picture at BENT²

cushion¹ /ˈkʊʃən/ *n* [C]
1 a bag filled with soft material that you put on a chair or the floor to make it more comfortable [➝ pillow]
2 something that stops one thing from hitting another: *Good sports shoes provide a cushion when running.*

cushion² *v* [T] **1** if something soft cushions a fall or a hit, it makes it less painful: *His landing was cushioned by the snow.* **2** to reduce the effects of something unpleasant

cushy /ˈkʊʃi/ *adj informal* a cushy job or situation is very easy or pleasant

cuss /kʌs/ *v* [I] *AmE spoken* to say rude words because you are angry [= swear]

custard /ˈkʌstəd $ -ərd/ *n* [U] *BrE* a thick sauce that you pour over sweet food

custodial /kʌˈstəʊdiəl $ -ˈstoʊ-/ *adj* **custodial sentence** *BrE* the punishment of being sent to prison

custodian /kʌˈstəʊdiən $ -ˈstoʊ-/ *n* [C] *formal* someone who takes care of a public building or something valuable

custody /ˈkʌstədi/ *n* [U] **1** the legal right to look after a child: **+of** *His ex-wife has custody of the kids.* **2** when someone is kept in prison until they go to court: **hold/keep sb in custody** → see box at POLICE¹

custom /ˈkʌstəm/ *n*
1 [C,U] something that people in a particular society do because it is traditional: **local/ancient/French etc custom** *She follows Islamic custom by covering her hair.* | **it is the custom (for sb) to do sth** *It's the custom for the bride's father to pay for the wedding.* → see box at HABIT
2 customs [plural] the place where your bags are checked for illegal goods when you enter a country [➝ immigration]: *All baggage must go through customs.* → see box at AIRPORT
3 [U] *formal* when people regularly use a particular shop or business: *The shop lost custom when a supermarket opened nearby.*

custom- /ˈkʌstəm/ *prefix* **custom-made/ custom-built/custom-designed etc** made, built etc for a particular person: *He always wore custom-made suits.*

customary /ˈkʌstəməri $ -meri/ *adj* usual or normal: **it is customary (for sb) to do sth** *It is customary for the bride to wear white.* —**customarily** /ˈkʌstəmərɨli $ ˌkʌstəˈmerɨli/ *adv*

customer /ˈkʌstəmə $ -ər/ *n* [C] someone who buys things from a shop or company: *a regular customer* | *the importance of good customer service*

cut

dice

slice

shred

chop

grate

carve

client – someone who pays for a service: *a business meeting with clients*
shopper – someone who goes to a shop looking for things to buy: *streets full of Christmas shoppers*
consumer – anyone who buys goods or uses services: *the rights of consumers*
guest – someone who pays to stay in a hotel: *The hotel has room for 120 guests.*
→ **SHOP**

customize also **-ise** *BrE* /ˈkʌstəmaɪz/ *v* [T] to change something to make it more suitable for a particular person or purpose

cut¹ /kʌt/ *v* past tense and past participle **cut**, present participle **cutting**

1 [I,T] to divide something into two or more pieces using a knife or scissors: *Shall I cut the cake?* | *She cut the string in half* (=into two pieces). | *cut the apple into slices.* | **cut sb a slice/piece (of sth)** (=separate a piece of something from the main part) *Can you cut me a piece of bread, please?* | **+along/across/round etc** *Cut along the dotted line.*

chop (up) – to cut meat, vegetables, or wood into pieces
slice – to cut bread, meat, or vegetables into thin pieces
dice – to cut vegetables or meat into small square pieces
peel – to cut the outside part off an apple, potato etc
carve – to cut pieces from a large piece of meat

2 [I,T] to make something shorter with a knife, scissors etc: **cut the lawn/grass/hedge etc** *The grass needs cutting.* | **have/get your hair cut** *It's time you got your hair cut.*

saw – to cut wood, using a saw (=a tool with a row of sharp points)
chop down – to make a tree fall down by cutting it
mow – to cut the grass in a garden, park etc
trim – to cut off a small amount of something to make it look tidy, for example hair or a hedge
snip – to cut something quickly, using scissors

3 [T] to reduce the amount of something: *Try to cut the amount of sugar in your diet.* | *70 jobs were lost in order to* **cut costs**.
4 [T] to hurt yourself with a knife or something else that is sharp: *I cut my finger chopping carrots.* | **cut yourself (on sth)** *Be careful you don't cut yourself.*
5 [T] to remove parts from a film, book, speech etc: *A sex scene was cut from the film.*
6 [T] to make a mark in the surface of something, open something etc using a sharp tool: **cut sth into sth** *Strange letters were cut into the stone.* | *Cut open the chillies and remove the seeds.*
7 [I] to go somewhere by a quicker and more direct way than usual: **+through/across etc** *I cut across the field.*
8 [T] to remove writing, a picture etc from a computer document: *Cut and paste the picture into a new file* (=remove it and move it to another place).
9 cut sth short to stop doing something earlier than you had planned: *The band had to cut short its concert tour.*
10 cut corners to do something less well than you should in order to save time, effort, or money
11 cut class/school *AmE informal* to deliberately not go to school
12 cut your losses to stop doing something that is failing so that you do not waste any more money, time, or effort

cut across sth *phr v* if a problem or feeling cuts across different groups of people, they are all affected by it: *The drug problem cuts across all social classes.*

cut back *phr v* to make an amount, number, cost etc smaller: **+on** *Hospitals are cutting back on staff.* | **cut sth ⇔ back** *Funding will be cut back.*

cut down *phr v* **1** to eat, drink, or use less of something, especially in order to improve your health: **+on** *I'm trying to cut down on cigarettes.*

2 cut sth ⇔ down to cut a tree so that the whole of it falls to the ground: *Large areas of forest have been cut down.*

cut in *phr v* to interrupt someone who is speaking by saying something

cut sb/sth ⇔ off *phr v* **1** also **cut sth off sth** to separate something from the main part with a knife etc: *His finger was cut off in the accident.* | *Cut the fat off the meat.* **2** to stop the supply of something to someone: *They'll cut off the electricity if you don't pay the bill.* | *The US has cut off aid to the country.* **3 be/get cut off** if you are cut off while you are talking on the telephone, the telephone suddenly stops working **4 be cut off** if a place is cut off it is difficult or impossible to get to: *The city was cut off by floods.*

cut out *phr v* **1 cut sth ⇔ out** to remove something by cutting it with a knife or scissors: **+from** *He was cutting out pictures from the magazine.* **2 cut it/that out!** *spoken* used when you want someone to stop doing something that is annoying you: *Hey, Kate, cut it out! That hurts!* **3 be cut out for sth/to be sth** to have the qualities that you need for a particular job or activity: *I wasn't cut out to be a teacher.* **4** if an engine cuts out, it suddenly stops working

cut sth ⇔ up *phr v* to cut something into small pieces: *Cut up the fruit into pieces.*

cut² *n* [C]

1 a reduction in the size, number, or amount of something: **+in** *a further cut in interest rates* | *the need to **make cuts** in spending* | **tax/pay/job etc cuts**

2 a wound that you get when something sharp cuts your skin: **+on** *He had bruises and cuts on his hands.*

3 a hole or mark in a surface made by something sharp: **+in** *Make a cut in the paper.*

4 [usually singular] a HAIRCUT

5 [usually singular] a share of something, especially money: **+of** *Do we all **get a cut** of the winnings?*

6 a piece of meat that comes from a particular part of an animal: *Use cuts of meat with less fat.*

7 be a cut above sb/sth to be better than someone or something else: *This movie is **a cut above the rest.***

→ **SHORT CUT**

,cut and 'dried *adj* a situation, decision, or result that is cut and dried cannot be changed

cutback /'kʌtbæk/ *n* [C usually plural] a reduction in something, especially to save money: **+in** *The government has **made cutbacks** in the armed forces*

cute /kjuːt/ *adj* attractive: *a cute little puppy* → see box at **ATTRACTIVE**

cutlery /'kʌtləri/ *n* [U] knives, forks, and spoons [= **silverware** *AmE*]

cutlet /'kʌtlɪt/ *n* [C] a small flat piece of meat on a bone: *a lamb cutlet*

'cut-off also **cutoff** /'kʌtɒf $ -ɔːf/ *n* [C] a time or level at which something stops: *April's the cut-off date.*

,cut-'price also **,cut-,rate** *especially AmE adj* cheaper than normal: *cut-price petrol*

cutter /'kʌtə $ -ər/ *n* [C] a tool used for cutting something: *wire cutters*

'cut-throat *adj* a cut-throat activity or business involves people competing with each other in an unpleasant way: *cut-throat competition*

cutting¹ /'kʌtɪŋ/ *n* [C] **1** a piece that you cut from a plant and use to grow a new plant **2** *BrE* a piece of writing that you cut from a newspaper or magazine [= **clipping** *AmE*]

cutting² *adj* a cutting remark is unkind and intended to upset someone

,cutting 'edge *n* the cutting edge (of sth) the newest design or way of doing something —**cutting-edge** *adj*: *cutting-edge technology*

CV /ˌsiː 'viː/ *n* [C] *BrE* curriculum vitae a list of your education and previous jobs, which you send to employers when you are looking for a job [= **résumé** *AmE*] → see box at **JOB**

cwt the written abbreviation of **hundredweight**

cyanide /'saɪənaɪd/ *n* [U] a very strong poison

cybercafé /'saɪbəkæfeɪ $ -bərkæˈfeɪ/ *n* [C] a CAFE where you can use computers connected to the Internet

cyberspace /'saɪbəspeɪs $ -bər-/ *n* [U] the imaginary place where electronic messages go when they travel from one computer to another

cycle¹ /'saɪkəl/ *n* [C] **1** a number of events that happen many times in the same order: **+of** *the cycle of the seasons* **2** *especially BrE* a bicycle or MOTORCYCLE

cycle² *v* [I] *especially BrE* to ride a bicycle [= **bike** *AmE*]: **+to/down/home etc** *She cycled to my house.* → see box at **TRAVEL** —**cyclist** *n* [C] —**cycling** *n* [U]

cyclic /'saɪklɪk/ also **cyclical** /'sɪklɪkəl, 'saɪ-/ *adj* happening again and again in a regular pattern

cyclone /'saɪkləun $ -kloun/ *n* [C] a very strong wind that moves in a circle

cygnet /'sɪgnɪt/ *n* [C] a young SWAN

cylinder /'sɪlɪndə $ -ər/ *n* [C] **1** an object in the shape of a tube → see box at **SHAPE** → see picture at **SHAPE¹** **2** the part of an engine that is shaped like a tube, where another part moves backwards and forwards —**cylindrical** /sɪ'lɪndrɪkəl/ *adj*

cymbal /'sɪmbəl/ *n* [C] one of a pair of round metal plates that you hit to make a musical sound

cynic /'sɪnɪk/ *n* [C] a cynical person —**cynicism** /-sɪzəm/ *n* [U]

cynical /'sɪnɪkəl/ *adj* unwilling to believe that people have good, honest, or sincere reasons for doing something: **+about** *The public is cynical about election promises.* —**cynically** /-kli/ *adv*

cyst /sɪst/ *n* [C] a LUMP containing liquid that grows in your body or under your skin

czar /zɑː $ zɑːr/ *n* [C] another spelling of TSAR

D, d

dam

D, d /diː/ n [C,U] plural **D's, d's** **1** the fourth letter of the English alphabet **2** the second note in the musical SCALE of C MAJOR, or the musical KEY based on this note **3** a mark given to a student's work to show that it is not very good: *I got a D in chemistry.*

-'d /d/ the short form of 'would' or 'had': *She'd like to come.* | *Nobody knew where he'd gone.*

D.A. /ˌdiː 'eɪ/ n [C] the abbreviation of **district attorney**

dab¹ /dæb/ v [I,T] **dabbed, dabbing** to touch something lightly several times, usually with a cloth: *She dabbed her eyes with a handkerchief.* | **dab sth on/onto sth** *Joe was dabbing sun lotion on his face.*

dab² n [C] **1** a small amount of something: **+of** *a dab of butter* **2** a light touch

dabble /'dæbəl/ v [I] to be involved in something in a way that is not very serious: **+in** *He dabbled in drugs.*

dad /dæd/ also **daddy** /'dædi/ n [C] *informal* father: *Dad took me to the zoo.* | *Dad, can I borrow the car?* → see box at RELATIVE

daffodil /'dæfədɪl/ n [C] a tall yellow flower that grows in spring

daft /dɑːft $ dæft/ adj BrE spoken informal silly: *Me, jealous? Don't be daft!*

dagger /'dægə $ -ər/ n [C] a short pointed knife used as a weapon

daily¹ /'deɪli/ adj

1 happening, done, or produced every day: *a daily newspaper* → see box at REGULAR

2 daily life the ordinary things that you do

3 relating to a single day: *a daily rate of pay* —**daily** adv: *The park is open daily.*

daily² n [C] plural **dailies** a newspaper that is printed and sold every day, or every day except Sunday

dainty /'deɪnti/ adj small, pretty, and delicate: *dainty white flowers* —**daintily** adv

dairy¹ /'deəri $ 'deri/ n [C] plural **dairies** **1** a place on a farm where milk is kept, and butter and cheese are made **2** a company that sells milk and makes cheese, butter etc

dairy² adj [only before noun] **1** made from milk: **dairy products/produce** **2** connected with the production of milk: **dairy farmer/farm/cattle**

daisy /'deɪzi/ n [C] plural **daisies** a small white flower with a bright yellow centre

dam /dæm/ n [C] a wall built across a river to stop the water and make a lake —**dam** v [T]

damage¹ /'dæmɪdʒ/ n

1 [U] physical harm that is done to something, so that it is broken or spoiled: **do/cause damage** *They claim the trade causes serious environmental damage.* | *The bomb caused extensive damage.* | **+to** *Was there any damage to your car?*

2 [U] a bad effect on someone or something: **+to** *The damage to his reputation was considerable.*

3 damages [plural] *law* money that a court orders someone to pay to someone else for harming that person or their property [➡ **compensation**]: *The court awarded her £5000 in damages.*

damage² v [T]

1 to cause physical harm to something: *The house has been badly damaged by fire.*

2 to have a bad effect on someone or something: *He claimed that the article had damaged his reputation.*

—**damaging** adj: *the damaging effects of sunlight*

dame /deɪm/ n [C] **1** a British title that is given to a woman because of her achievements: *Dame Judi Dench* **2** AmE old-fashioned a woman

damn¹ /dæm/ spoken used when you are annoyed or disappointed: *Damn! I forgot to bring my wallet!*

damn² also **damned** adv, adj spoken used to emphasize something: *Everything was so damn expensive.* | *Turn off that damn TV.* | *I'll do what I damn well want.*

damn³ n spoken **not give a damn** to not care at all about something: *I don't give a damn what he thinks.*

damn⁴ v [T] spoken **1 damn it/you etc** used when you are very angry: *Damn those kids!* **2 I'll be damned** used when you are surprised

damned /dæmd/ adj, adv another form of 'damn', used especially in writing

damning /'dæmɪŋ/ adj showing that someone has done something very bad or wrong: **damning indictment/evidence/report/criticism** *a damning report on the state of school discipline*

damp /dæmp/ adj slightly wet, usually in a cold and unpleasant way: *The house was cold and damp.* | *a damp cloth*

THESAURUS

Use **damp** when you want to say that something is slightly wet in an unpleasant way.

Use **humid** when you want to talk about weather that is slightly wet and makes you uncomfortable.

Use **moist** to say that something, especially food, is slightly wet in a pleasant way.

—**damp, dampness** n [U]

dampen /'dæmpən/ v [T] **1** also **dampen down** *BrE* to make something such as a feeling or activity less strong: *Nothing could dampen their enthusiasm.* **2** to make something slightly wet: *The fine rain dampened her hair.*

damper /'dæmpə $ -ər/ n **put a damper on sth** to stop something from being enjoyable: *Heavy rain put a damper on the event.*

damsel /'dæmzəl/ n [C] **damsel in distress** *humorous* a young woman who needs help

dance¹ /dɑːns $ dæns/ n
1 [C] a special set of movements performed to a particular type of music: *Let's have one more dance.* | *The only dance I know is the waltz.*
2 [U] the art or activity of dancing: *modern dance* | *dance lessons*
3 [C] a social event or party where you dance: *a school dance*

dance² v [I]
1 to move your body in a way that matches the style and speed of music: +**with** *Who's that dancing with Tom?* | *Do you want to dance?*
2 to move around quickly, because you are excited or full of energy: *She danced round him, trying to grab the letter.*
—**dancer** n [C] —**dancing** n [U]

dandelion /'dændɪlaɪən/ n [C] a small bright yellow wild flower

dandruff /'dændrəf, -drʌf/ n [U] small white pieces of dead skin from your head

danger /'deɪndʒə $ -ər/ n
1 [singular, U] the possibility that someone or something will be harmed, or that something bad will happen: +**of** *Is there any danger of infection?* | **in danger** (=in a dangerous situation) *They believe their lives are in danger.* | **be in danger of (doing) sth** *The bridge was in danger of collapsing.* | +**that** *There is a danger that these opportunities may be missed.*
2 [C] something or someone that may harm you: +**to** *He's a danger to others.* | +**of** *the dangers of smoking*

dangerous /'deɪndʒərəs/ adj able or likely to harm you: **be dangerous (for sb) to do sth** *It's dangerous to walk alone at night around here.* | +**to/for** *The virus is not dangerous to humans.* | *This man is highly dangerous.*
—**dangerously** adv: *They were standing dangerously close to the edge.*

dangle /'dæŋgəl/ v [I,T] to hang or swing loosely, or to make something do this: +**from** *The keys were dangling from his belt.* | **dangle sth in/over etc sth** *I dangled my feet in the water.*

dank /dæŋk/ adj unpleasantly wet and cold: *a dank cellar*

dapper /'dæpə $ -ər/ adj a dapper man is small and neatly dressed

dappled /'dæpəld/ adj marked with spots of colour, light, or shade: **dappled shade/sunlight**

dare¹ /deə $ der/ v **1** [I] to be brave enough to do something – used especially in negative sentences: *He wanted to ask her, but he didn't dare.* | **dare (to) do sth** *I daren't tell mum.* **2 how dare you/he etc** *spoken* used when you are very angry about what someone has said or done: *How dare you call me a liar!* **3 don't you dare** *spoken* used to tell someone that they must not do something: *Don't you dare talk to me like that!*

4 dare sb to do sth to try to persuade someone to do something dangerous: *I dare you to jump!* **5 I dare say** also **I daresay** *mainly BrE spoken* used when saying that something may be true: *I dare say things will improve.*

dare² n [C] something dangerous that you have dared someone to do

daredevil /'deədevəl $ 'der-/ n [C] someone who likes doing dangerous things —**daredevil** adj

daren't /deənt $ dernt/ the short form of 'dare not': *I daren't tell him. He'd be furious!*

daresay /,deə'seɪ $ 'derseɪ/ → DARE¹

daring /'deərɪŋ $ 'der-/ adj **1** willing to do dangerous things: *a daring rescue attempt* **2** new or unusual in a way that may shock people: *a daring new play* —**daring** n [U] —**daringly** adv

dark¹ /dɑːk $ dɑːrk/ adj
1 a dark place is one where there is little or no light [≠ **light**]: *Turn on the light; it's dark in here.* | **It gets dark** (=night begins) *early in winter.* | *Suddenly the room went dark* (=became dark).
2 closer to black than to white in colour [≠ **light, pale**]: *dark hair* | **dark blue/green/red etc** | *a dark suit*
3 a dark person has black hair, brown skin etc [≠ **fair**]: *a small, dark man*
4 mysterious or frightening: *a dark secret*
5 a dark time is unhappy or without hope: *the dark days of the war*
6 dark horse someone who is not well known, and who surprises people by winning a competition or doing something that you do not expect

dark² n
1 the dark when there is no light: *My son is afraid of the dark.*
2 after/before dark at night or before night begins: *I don't like walking home after dark.*
3 in the dark *informal* not knowing about something important because no one has told you about it: *We had been kept in the dark about the sale.*

darken /'dɑːkən $ 'dɑːr-/ v [I,T] to become darker, or to make something darker: *The sky darkened and rain began to fall.* | *a darkened room*

dark 'glasses n [plural] glasses that you wear to protect your eyes from the sun [= **sunglasses**]

darkly /'dɑːkli $ 'dɑːrk-/ adv in a sad, angry, or threatening way

darkness /'dɑːknɪs $ 'dɑːrk-/ n [U] when there is no light: *Darkness fell* (=it got dark) *around 5 pm.* | **in darkness** (=without any light) *The room was in darkness.*

darkroom /'dɑːkruːm, -rʊm $ 'dɑːrk-/ n [C] a room with a red light or no light, where film from a camera is made into photographs

darling¹ /'dɑːlɪŋ $ 'dɑːr-/ n [C] used when speaking to someone you love: *Come here, darling.*

darling² adj [only before noun] much loved: *my darling daughter*

darn¹ /dɑːn $ dɑːrn/ v [T] to repair a hole in clothes by stitching wool across it

darn² also **darned** /dɑ:nd $ dɑ:rnd/ adv, adj AmE spoken used to emphasize what you are saying: *a darn good idea*

darts

dart¹ /dɑ:t $ dɑ:rt/ n **1** [C] a small pointed object that is thrown in a game of darts or used as a weapon **2 darts** [U] a game in which you throw darts at a circular board: *a game of darts* **3** [C] a small fold stitched into a piece of clothing to make it fit

dart² v [I] to move suddenly and quickly in a particular direction: **+back/out/forward etc** *A child had darted out into the road.*

dash¹ /dæʃ/ v **1** [I] to go somewhere very quickly: **+into/across/out etc** *She dashed into the room.* | *Tim had to dash off after class.* → see box at **RUN** **2 I must dash/I have to dash** spoken used to say you have to leave quickly: *Must dash, I've got a meeting.* **3 dash sb's hopes** to destroy someone's hopes: *Hopes of peace have been dashed.* **4** [T] to make something hit violently against something else: **dash sth against/on sth** *The ship was dashed against the rocks.*

dash² n **1** [singular] a small amount of a liquid: *a dash of lemon* **2 make a dash for sth** to run very quickly towards something: *He made a dash for the door.* **3** [C] a mark (–) used in writing or printing to separate parts of a sentence

dashboard /'dæʃbɔ:d $ -bɔ:rd/ n [C] the part in front of the driver in a car that has the controls on it → see picture on page A12

dashing /'dæʃɪŋ/ adj a dashing man is attractive and confident: *a dashing young doctor*

data /'deɪtə, 'dɑ:tə/ n [U, plural] information or facts: *He's collecting data for his report.* | **data storage/retrieval**

database /'deɪtəˌbeɪs/ n [C] a large amount of information stored in a computer system

data 'processing n [U] the use of computers to store and organize information

date¹ /deɪt/ n [C]

1 a particular day of the month or of the year, shown by a number: *'What's today's date?' 'It's August the eleventh.'* | *Please write down your date of birth* (=the day you were born). | **set/fix a date** (=choose a day when something will happen) *Have you set a date for the wedding?*

2 an arrangement to meet someone, especially someone you like in a romantic way: *Mike's got a date tonight.* | *Let's make a date* (=arrange a time) *to meet up.*

3 AmE someone you go on a date with: *My date's taking me out to dinner.*

4 to date until now: *This is the best research on the subject to date.*

5 a sweet sticky brown fruit with a long seed → **OUT-OF-DATE, SELL-BY DATE, UP-TO-DATE**

date² v **1** [T] to write the date on something: *a letter dated May 1st, 1923* **2** [T] to find out the age of something that is very old: *Geologists can date the rocks by examining fossils in the same layer.* **3** [I,T] to seem old-fashioned, or to make something seem old-fashioned: *His designs have hardly dated at all.* **4** [I,T] AmE to have a romantic relationship with someone [= **go out with**]: *How long have you been dating Monica?*

date from sth also **date back to sth** phr v to have existed since a particular time: *The cathedral dates from the 13th century.*

dated /'deɪtᵻd/ adj not fashionable any more: *That dress looks a bit dated now.* → see box at **OLD-FASHIONED**

daub /dɔ:b $ dɒ:b/ v [T] to put paint or a soft substance on a surface in a careless way: *The walls are daubed with graffiti.*

daughter /'dɔ:tə $ 'dɒ:tər/ n [C] someone's female child: *They have two daughters.*

'daughter-in-law n [C] plural **daughters-in-law** the wife of someone's son

daunted /'dɔ:ntᵻd $ 'dɒ:n-/ adj feeling afraid or worried: **+by** *Don't be daunted by the technology.*

daunting /'dɔ:ntɪŋ $ 'dɒ:n-/ adj frightening or worrying: **daunting task/prospect/challenge**

dawdle /'dɔ:dl $ 'dɒ:-/ v [I] to take a long time to go somewhere: *Stop dawdling – we'll be late.*

dawn¹ /dɔ:n $ dɒ:n/ n [U] **1** the time of day when light first appears: **at dawn** *We were up at dawn.* | *As dawn broke* (=it started to get light) *the rain stopped.* **2 the dawn of civilization/time etc** the time when something began or first appeared

dawn² v [I] if day or morning dawns, it begins: *The morning dawned fresh and clear.*

dawn on sb phr v if a fact dawns on you, you realize it for the first time: *It dawned on me that Jo had been right all along.*

day /deɪ/ n

1 [C] a period of time equal to 24 hours [➔ **daily**]: *We went to Paris for ten days.* | *They arrived two days ago.* | *I'll call you in a couple of days.* | *'What day is it today?' 'It's Friday.'* | *I saw Jane the day before yesterday.* | *We're leaving the day after tomorrow.* | **the next/following day** *The following day, a letter arrived.*

2 [C,U] the period of time between when it becomes light in the morning and when it becomes dark in the evening [≠ **night**]: *The days begin to get longer in the spring.* | *It's rained all day.*

3 [C usually singular] the time during the day when you are usually awake: *My day usually begins at six o'clock.* | *It's been a long day* (=used when you had to get up early and were busy all day).

4 [C] the hours you work in a day: *Jean works an eight-hour day.*

5 [C] also **days** [plural] a particular time in the past: *In my day* (=when I was young) *very few people had cars.* | *Life was hard in those days* (=then).

6 one day on a day in the past: *She just walked in here one day.*

7 one day/some day at some time in the future: *I'd like to visit the States some day.*

8 these days used to talk about the situation that exists now: *Children have lots more opportunities these days.*

9 sb's days the time when someone is alive: *She ended her days in Kent.*

10 to this day until and including now: *To this day we don't know what really happened.*

11 the other day *spoken* a few days ago: *I saw Roy the other day.*

12 make someone's day *informal* to make someone very happy: *That card really made my day.*

13 have had its day to not be popular or successful any more: *I think the royal family has had its day.*

14 day after day/day in day out used to emphasize that something bad or boring continues to happen: *I'm sick of sitting at the same desk day after day.*

15 day by day slowly and gradually: *She was getting stronger day by day.*

→ DAY-TO-DAY, MODERN-DAY, OPEN DAY, PRESENT-DAY

GRAMMAR

Talking about days
Use **on** to talk about a particular day in the week: *I'm going to a party on Saturday.*
Use **next** to talk about a day after the present one: *I'll meet you next Tuesday.*
Use **last** to talk about a day before the present one: *He died last Friday.*
→ TODAY, TOMORROW, YESTERDAY

---

daybreak /'deɪbreɪk/ *n* [U] the time of day when light first appears [= dawn]: **at daybreak** *We set off at daybreak.*

'day care /'deɪkeə $ -ker/ *n* [U] care of young children, or of sick or old people, during the day

'day care ,center *AmE*; **day care centre** *BrE n* [C] a place where babies are cared for while their parents are at work [= nursery *BrE*]

'day ,centre also **'day care ,centre** *n* [C] *BrE* a place where people who are old or ill can be cared for during the day

daydream /'deɪdriːm/ *v* [I] to think about pleasant things so that you forget what you should be doing: **+about** *Jessica sat at her desk, daydreaming about Tom.* —**daydream** *n* [C] —**daydreamer** *n* [C]

daylight /'deɪlaɪt/ *n* [U] **1** the light produced by the sun during the day: *The park is open during daylight hours.* | *A young girl has been attacked in broad daylight* (=during the day when it is light). **2 scare/frighten the (living) daylights out of sb** *informal* to frighten someone a lot **3 beat the (living) daylights out of sb** to hit someone many times and hurt them badly **4 sth is daylight robbery** *BrE informal* used to say that something costs a lot more than is reasonable

,day re'turn *n* [C] *BrE* a train or bus ticket that lets you go somewhere at a cheaper price than usual, if you go there and back on the same day: *a day return to Oxford* → see box at TICKET

daytime /'deɪtaɪm/ *n* [U] the period between the time when it gets light and the time when it gets dark [≠ night-time]: **in/during the daytime** *Owls sleep in the daytime.* | *daytime television*

,day-to-'day *adj* [only before noun] happening every day as a normal part of your life: **day-to-day work/business/life etc** *the day-to-day running of the company*

daze /deɪz/ *n* **in a daze** confused and unable to think clearly: *He wandered around in a daze.*

dazed /deɪzd/ *adj* unable to think clearly, usually because you are shocked or have been in an accident: **dazed look/expression**

dazzle /'dæzəl/ *v* [T] **1** if a strong light dazzles you, it is so strong that you cannot see for a short time **2** if someone or something dazzles you, you think they are very impressive: *They were clearly dazzled by her talent and charm.*

dazzling /'dæzəlɪŋ/ *adj* **1** a dazzling light is so bright that you cannot see for a short time after you look at it **2** very impressive, exciting, or interesting: *a dazzling performance*

de- /diː, dɪ/ *prefix* used to talk about removing something or making it less: *decaffeinated coffee* (=coffee which has had the caffeine removed) | *The government have devalued the currency* (=reduced its value).

deacon /'diːkən/ *n* [C] a religious official in some Christian churches

deactivate /diːˈæktɪveɪt/ *v* [T] *formal* to make something stop working [≠ activate]: *Type in the code number to deactivate the alarm.*

dead¹ /ded/ *adj*

1 no longer alive: *Her mother's been dead for two years.* | *I think that plant's dead.* | *the dead body of a young boy* | *Two men were shot dead by the terrorists.*

USAGE

Dead is an adjective used to describe people or things that are no longer alive: *a dead fish*
Died is the past tense and past participle of the verb 'to die', used to talk about how and when someone died: *He died of a heart attack in 1992.*

---

2 an engine, telephone etc that is dead is not working because there is no power: *Is the battery dead?* | *Suddenly the phone went dead.*

3 no longer active or being used: *He says the peace plan is dead.*

4 a place that is dead is boring because nothing interesting happens there: *This place is dead during the week.*

5 a part of your body that is dead has no feeling in it for a short time: *My feet have gone dead.*

6 over my dead body *spoken* used when you are determined not to allow something to happen: *You'll marry him over my dead body!*

7 [only before noun] complete or exact: *We all stood waiting in dead silence.* | *The arrow hit the dead centre of the target.* | *The train came to a dead stop.*

8 a dead language is no longer used by people [≠ living]

dead² *adv informal* **1** completely or exactly: **dead right/wrong** *'It's a crazy idea.' 'You're dead right!'* | *She stopped dead when she saw us.* | *You can't miss it – it's dead ahead at the*

D

lights. | *The plane landed* **dead on time**. **2** *BrE spoken* very: **dead easy/simple/boring etc** *The film was dead good.*

dead³ *n* **1 the dead** people who are dead [≠ **the living**] **2 in the dead of night/winter** in the middle of the night or in the middle of winter

deaden /'dedn/ *v* [T] to make a feeling or sound less strong: *drugs to deaden the pain*

dead 'end *n* [C] **1** a street with no way out at one end **2** a situation from which no progress is possible

dead 'heat *n* [C] the result of a race in which two people finish at exactly the same time

deadline /'dedlaɪn/ *n* [C] a date or time by which you must finish something: *He failed to* **meet** *the* **deadline**.

deadlock /'dedlɒk $ -lɑːk/ *n* [singular, U] when people, organizations etc cannot agree: *an attempt to* **break the deadlock**

deadly¹ /'dedli/ *adj* very dangerous and likely to cause death: *a deadly poison*

deadly² *adv* **deadly serious/boring etc** very serious, boring etc

deadpan /'dedpæn/ *adj* sounding and looking completely serious when you are not

deaf /def/ *adj*

1 a) physically unable to hear, or unable to hear well [➡ **hearing impaired**]: *deaf children* | *Pa's going* (=becoming) *deaf.* → see box at **HEAR b) the deaf** [plural] people who are deaf: *a school for the deaf*

2 be deaf to sth unwilling to listen to something: *She was deaf to all his appeals.*

—**deafness** *n* [U]

deafen /'defən/ *v* [T] to make it difficult for you to hear anything —**deafening** *adj*: *The noise was deafening.* → see box at **LOUD**

deal¹ /diːl/ *n*

1 [C] an agreement or arrangement, especially in business or politics: *a business deal* | **do/make/strike a deal** *The union did a deal with the government.* | *'I'll go if you go.' 'OK, it's* **a deal**.

2 a great/good deal a large quantity of something [= a lot]: +**of** *I spend a great deal of time abroad.* | **a great deal more/longer/cheaper etc** *Ian is a great deal older than Sue.*

3 [C usually singular] the way someone is treated in a situation: **a good/fair etc deal** *Children deserve a better deal.* | **a rough/raw deal** (=unfair treatment) *He has had a raw deal.* → **big deal** at **BIG**

deal² *v* [I,T] past tense and past participle **dealt** /delt/ **1** also **deal out** to give playing cards to all of the players in a card game: *It's your* **turn to deal**. **2** to buy and sell illegal drugs: *He deals to finance his own habit.* **3 deal a blow (to sb/sth)** to harm someone or something: *The ban dealt a severe blow to local tourism.* —**dealing** *n* [U]

deal in sth *phr v* to buy and sell a particular product: *She deals in antiques.*

deal with sb/sth *phr v* **1** to do what is necessary, especially in order to solve a problem: *Who deals with complaints?* **2** to be about a particular subject: *Chapter 6 deals with taxation.* **3** to do business with someone: *We deal with companies all over Europe.*

dealer /'diːlə $ -ər/ *n* [C] **1** someone who buys and sells a particular product: *a car dealer* **2** the person who gives out the cards in a card game

dealership /'diːləʃɪp $ -ər-/ *n* [C] a business that sells a particular company's product, especially cars

dealings /'diːlɪŋz/ *n* [plural] business or personal relations with someone: +**with** *I've had dealings with Baylis before.*

dean /diːn/ *n* [C] **1** a priest with a high rank in the Christian church **2** a university official with a high rank: *the Dean of Arts*

dear¹ /dɪə $ dɪr/ **Oh dear** *spoken* used when you are surprised, upset, or annoyed: *Oh dear, I've broken it.*

dear² *n* [C] *spoken* used when speaking to someone you like or love: *You look nice, dear.*

dear³ *adj*

1 used before a name at the beginning of a letter: *Dear Mr. Todd, ...* | *Dear Meg, ...*

2 *BrE* [not before noun] expensive: *Petrol is a lot dearer in the UK.*

3 used to show that you like someone or something very much: *Mark's a very* **dear friend**. | **dear old Aunt Rose**

dearly /'dɪəli $ 'dɪrli/ *adv* very much: *Sam loved her dearly.* | *I would* **dearly like** *to see him.*

dearth /dɜːθ $ dɜːrθ/ *n* [singular] *formal* a lack of something: +**of** *the dearth of information*

death /deθ/ *n*

1 [C,U] the end of someone's life [≠ **birth**]: *her father's death* | *the* **cause of death** | +**from** *deaths from cancer* | **bleed/starve etc to death** (=die in this way) *He froze to death.* | **put/ sentence/condemn sb to death** (=to kill someone, or decide that they should be killed, as a legal punishment) *He was found guilty and sentenced to death.* → see box at **KILL**

2 the death of sth the permanent end of something: *the death of Communism*

3 be scared/bored etc to death *informal* be very frightened, bored etc

deathbed /'deθbed/ *n* **on his/her etc deathbed** when someone is dying

deathly /'deθli/ *adj, adv* reminding you of death or of a dead body: **deathly cold/white/ pale** *She turned deathly pale.* | *A* **deathly hush** (=complete silence) *fell over the room.*

death ,penalty *n* [singular] when someone is killed as a legal punishment [➡ **capital punishment**] → see box at **PUNISHMENT**

death row /,deθ 'rəʊ $ -'roʊ/ *n* [U] the part of a prison where prisoners are kept before they are killed as a punishment: *Troy is on death row.*

death squad *n* [C] a group of people who have been ordered to kill someone's political opponents

death toll *n* [singular] the number of people who have died in an accident, war etc: *As the unrest continues, the* **death toll** *has* **risen** *to 15.*

death trap *n* [C] *informal* a vehicle, building etc that is in such bad condition that it might injure or kill someone

debacle, débâcle /deɪ'bɑːkəl, dɪ-/ *n* [C] an event that is a complete failure: *We all remember the 1992 election debacle.*

debar /dɪˈbɑː $ -ˈbɑːr/ v [T] **debarred, debarring** *formal* to officially prevent someone from doing something: *groups which are debarred from voting*

debase /dɪˈbeɪs/ v [T] *formal* to make someone or something lose their value or people's respect —**debasement** n [C,U]

debatable /dɪˈbeɪtəbəl/ *adj* an idea, fact, or decision that is debatable may be right but it could easily be wrong: *It's debatable whether this book is as good as her last.*

debate¹ /dɪˈbeɪt/ n **1** [C,U] discussion of a subject that often continues for a long time and in which people express different opinions: *The school's future became the **subject of** much debate.* **2** [C] a formal discussion of a subject, for example in parliament, in which people express different opinions, and sometimes vote: **+on** *Friday's debate on immigration*

debate² v **1** [I,T] to discuss a subject formally so that you can make a decision or solve a problem: *The issue was debated on Monday.* **2** [T] to think about something carefully before making a decision: **debate who/what etc** *I debated whether to phone Kim.*

debauchery /dɪˈbɔːtʃəri $ dɪˈbɒː-, dɪˈbɑː-/ n [U] immoral behaviour involving drugs, alcohol, sex etc

debilitating /dɪˈbɪlɪteɪtɪŋ/ *adj formal* a debilitating illness or problem makes you very ill or weak

debit¹ /ˈdebɪt/ n [C] an amount of money that has been taken out of your bank account [≠ credit]

debit² v [T] when a bank debits your account, it takes money away from it because you have spent it [≠ credit]: *£25 has been debited from your account.*

ˈdebit card n [C] a plastic card that you can use to pay for things. The money is taken directly from your bank account.

debonair /ˌdebəˈneə◂ $ -ˈner◂/ *adj old-fashioned* fashionable and confident

debrief /ˌdiːˈbriːf/ v [T] to get information from someone such as a soldier by officially asking them questions about a job they have just done or an experience they have had [➡ brief] —**debriefing** n [C,U]

debris /ˈdebriː, ˈdeɪ- $ dəˈbriː, deɪ-/ n [U] the pieces remaining from something that has been destroyed: *debris from the explosion*

debt /det/ n

1 [C,U] if you have debts, or if you are in debt, you owe money to someone: *He sold the house to pay off his debts.* | **+of** *debts of £50 million* | **in debt (to sb)** *I was heavily in debt.* | **get/run/ fall into debt** | *a pile of **bad debts** (=debts that are unlikely to be paid)* → see box at OWE **2** [C usually singular] the degree to which you have been influenced by, or helped by, someone or something: *Years later, she acknowledged the debt she owed him for his help in London.* | **be in sb's debt** *formal* (=be thankful for something someone has done for you)

debtor /ˈdetə $ -ər/ n [C] someone who owes money

debunk /ˌdiːˈbʌŋk/ v [T] to show that an idea or belief is false

debut /ˈdeɪbjuː, ˈdeb- $ deɪˈbjuː, dɪ-/ n [C] the first time that a performer or sports player performs in public: *He made his debut for Wales in 98.* | **debut match/appearance etc** *He scored a brilliant goal in his debut match.* —**debut** v [I]

Dec. the written abbreviation of **December**

decade /ˈdekeɪd, deˈkeɪd/ n [C] a period of ten years

decadent /ˈdekədənt/ *adj* having low moral standards and interested only in pleasure —**decadence** n [U]

decaf /ˈdiːkæf/ n [C,U] *informal* decaffeinated coffee

decaffeinated /diːˈkæfɪneɪtɪd/ *adj* decaffeinated drinks have had the CAFFEINE removed

decapitate /dɪˈkæpɪteɪt/ v [T] to cut off someone's head

decay¹ /dɪˈkeɪ/ v [I] **1** to be slowly destroyed by a natural chemical process: *dead or decaying plants* **2** if buildings decay, they are slowly destroyed because no one takes care of them: *Many prisons are old and decaying.* —**decayed** *adj*

decay² n [U] when something decays: *tooth decay* | *The house fell into decay.*

deceased /dɪˈsiːst/ n **the deceased** someone who has recently died —**deceased** *adj*

deceit /dɪˈsiːt/ n [C,U] behaviour that tries to make people believe something that is not true: *lies and deceit* —**deceitful** *adj*

deceive /dɪˈsiːv/ v [T] to make someone believe something that is not true [= trick; ➡ deception]: *I was completely deceived.* | **deceive sb into doing sth** *He deceived his victim into giving him £500.* | **deceive yourself** *I thought she loved me, but I was deceiving myself.*

December /dɪˈsembə $ -ər/ n [C,U] written abbreviation **Dec.** the 12th month of the year, between November and January: **next/last December** *Last December they visited Prague.* | **in December** *We got married in December.* | **on December 6th** *The meeting was on December 6th.* → see box at MONTH

decency /ˈdiːsənsi/ n [U] morally correct behaviour: *At least he had the decency to apologize.*

decent /ˈdiːsənt/ *adj* **1** good enough or fairly good: *a decent salary* | *decent food* **2** honest and good: *ordinary decent people* **3** wearing enough clothes, so that you are not showing too much of your body: *Don't come in, I'm not decent!* —**decently** *adv*

decentralize also **-ise** *BrE* /ˌdiːˈsentrəlaɪz/ v [T] to change a government or organization so that decisions are made in a lot of different places, instead of only one place —**decentralization** /diːˌsentrəlaɪˈzeɪʃən $ -lə-/ n [U]

deception /dɪˈsepʃən/ n [C,U] the act of deliberately making someone believe something that is not true: *The money was obtained by deception.*

deceptive /dɪˈseptɪv/ *adj* something that is deceptive seems very different from how it really is: *She seems OK, but appearances can be deceptive.* —**deceptively** *adv*

decibel /ˈdesɪbel, -bəl/ n [C,U] a unit for measuring the loudness of sound

D

decide /dɪˈsaɪd/ v

1 [I,T] to make a choice or judgment about something: *'Where will you live?' 'We haven't decided yet.'* | **decide to do sth** *She decided to accept.* | **+(that)** *Ali decided that the house was too small.* | *I decided I would call her.* | **+whether/what/ when etc** *Have you decided what to wear?* | **decide against (doing) sth** (=decide not to do something) *They decided against taking the dog.*
2 [T] to be the reason why something has a particular result: *the goal that decided the match*
3 [T] to be the reason for someone making a particular choice: **decide sb to do sth** *What decided you to come all the way out here?*
  decide on sth *phr v* to choose one thing from among many: *Have you decided on a name for the baby?* → see box at **CHOOSE**

decided /dɪˈsaɪdɪd/ adj [only before noun] definite and easily noticed: *The new house was a decided improvement on the old one.*

decidedly /dɪˈsaɪdɪdli/ adv very much, in a way that is easy to notice: *Chris looked decidedly uncomfortable.*

deciduous /dɪˈsɪdʒuəs/ adj deciduous trees lose their leaves in winter [➡ **evergreen**]

decimal[1] /ˈdesɪməl/ n [C] a number, for example 0.8 or 0.263, which is less than one and is shown as a FULL STOP followed by the number of TENTHS, HUNDREDTHS etc

decimal[2] adj a decimal system is based on the number ten

decimal 'point n [C] the mark (.) in a decimal

decimate /ˈdesɪmeɪt/ v [T] to destroy a large part of something: *The village had been decimated by war.*

decipher /dɪˈsaɪfə $ -ər/ v [T] to find the meaning of something that is difficult to read or understand

decision /dɪˈsɪʒən/ n [C] a choice or judgment that you make: *I hope I've made the right decision.* | **decision to do sth** *Scott's decision to join the navy* | **take/reach/come to a decision** *The jury took three days to reach a decision.* | *The final decision is expected next week.*

decisive /dɪˈsaɪsɪv/ adj **1** having an important effect on the result of something: *a decisive moment in his career* **2** good at making decisions quickly and firmly: *a decisive leader* **3** a decisive victory, result etc is very definite and clear —**decisively** adv: *A manager must be able to act decisively.* —**decisiveness** n [U]

deck[1] /dek/ n [C] **1 a)** the flat top part of a ship, that you can walk on: **on deck** *Let's go up on deck.* **b)** one of the levels on a ship, plane, or bus: *the lower deck* **2** AmE a wooden floor built out from the back of a house, where you can sit outdoors **3** AmE a set of playing cards [= pack BrE]

deck[2] v [T] also **deck out** to decorate something with flowers, flags, etc: *The church was decked with flowers.*

deckchair /ˈdektʃeə $ -tʃer/ n [C] BrE a folding chair with a long seat made of cloth → see picture at **SEAT**[1]

decking /ˈdekɪŋ/ n [U] a wooden floor next to a house or in a garden

declaration /ˌdekləˈreɪʃən/ n [C,U] an official statement about something: *a declaration of war*

declare /dɪˈkleə $ -ˈkler/ v [T]

1 to state officially and publicly that a particular situation exists or that something is true: *She declared her intention to stand for president.* | *In 1853, Turkey declared war on Russia.* | **declare sb/sth (to be) sth** *The strike was declared illegal.* | **+(that)** *The company declared there was no risk.*
2 to say something in a clear firm way: *'It's not fair,' Jane declared.*
3 to state the value of things that you have bought or own, because you may have to pay tax on them

decline[1] /dɪˈklaɪn/ n [C,U] a decrease in the quality, quantity, or importance of something: **+in** *a decline in profits* | **in decline** *The city was in decline.*

decline[2] v **1** [I] to decrease in quantity, quality, or importance: *Coffee production declined.* | *His health continued to decline.* **2** [I,T] formal to say no to an invitation, offer, or request, usually politely: *Mary declined Jay's invitation to dinner.* | **decline to do sth** *Murray declined to comment.*

decode /ˌdiːˈkəʊd $ -ˈkoʊd/ v [T] to discover the meaning of a secret or complicated message

decommission /ˌdiːkəˈmɪʃən/ v [T] to stop using a ship, weapon, or NUCLEAR REACTOR and to take it to pieces

decompose /ˌdiːkəmˈpəʊz $ -ˈpoʊz/ v [I,T] to be slowly destroyed by a natural process: *a partially decomposed body*

decor /ˈdeɪkɔː $ -kɔːr/ n [C,U] the way that the inside of a building is decorated: *The decor was very modern.*

decorate /ˈdekəreɪt/ v

1 [T] to make something look more attractive by putting something pretty on it: *Paintings decorated the walls.* | **decorate sth with sth** *Decorate the cake with cherries.*
2 [I,T] BrE to paint or put paper onto the walls of a room or building: *We need to decorate the bathroom.* | *I spent Saturday decorating.*

decoration /ˌdekəˈreɪʃən/ n

1 [C,U] something pretty that you put onto something else in order to make it more attractive: *Christmas decorations* | *Save some of the nuts for decoration.*
2 [U] the style in which something is decorated, or the activity of decorating something: *changes in the decoration of churches*

decorative /ˈdekərətɪv $ ˈdekərə-, ˈdekəreɪ-/ adj pretty and used as a decoration: *decorative features* —**decoratively** adv

decorator /ˈdekəreɪtə $ -ər/ n [C] especially BrE someone who paints houses and puts paper on the walls as their job

decorum /dɪˈkɔːrəm/ n [U] formal behaviour that is polite and suitable for a particular occasion

decoy /ˈdiːkɔɪ/ n [C] a person or object that is used to trick a person or animal into going somewhere or doing something

decrease /dɪˈkriːs/ v [I,T] to become less, or to make something do this [≠ **increase**]: *Crime decreased by 30%.* | **+to** *By 1881, the population*

D

had decreased to 5.2 million. | *the need to decrease costs*

—**decrease** /ˈdiːkriːs/ *n* [C,U] *a decrease in sales*

decree /dɪˈkriː/ *n* [C] an official order or decision —**decree** *v* [T]

decrepit /dɪˈkrepᵻt/ *adj* old and in bad condition: *his decrepit car*

decriminalize also **-ise** *BrE* /diːˈkrɪmᵻnəlaɪz/ *v* [T] to state officially that something is not illegal any more —**decriminalization** /diːˌkrɪmᵻnəlaɪˈzeɪʃən $ -lə-/ *n* [U]

dedicate /ˈdedᵻkeɪt/ *v* [T] **1** to give all your attention and effort to one thing: **dedicate yourself/your life to (doing) sth** *She dedicated her life to helping the poor.* **2** to say that a book, film, song etc has been written, made, or performed for someone, to show that you respect or love them: *The book is dedicated to his wife.*

dedicated /ˈdedᵻkeɪtᵻd/ *adj* working very hard at something because you think it is important: *a dedicated musician*

dedication /ˌdedᵻˈkeɪʃən/ *n* **1** [U] when you work very hard because you believe that what you are doing is important | +**to** *his dedication to the sport* **2** [C] an act of dedicating something to someone, or a ceremony where this is done **3** [C] the words used when dedicating a book, film, song etc to someone

deduce /dɪˈdjuːs $ dɪˈduːs/ *v* [T] *formal* to decide that something is true using the information that you have

deduct /dɪˈdʌkt/ *v* [T] to take away an amount from a total: *Taxes are deducted from your pay.* —**deductible** *adj*

deduction /dɪˈdʌkʃən/ *n* **1** [C] an amount that is taken away from a total: *I earn about $2000 a month, after deductions.* **2** [C,U] when you decide that something is likely to be true, using the information that you have: *his formidable powers of deduction*

deed /diːd/ *n* [C] **1** *formal* something that someone does: *good deeds* **2** *law* an official paper that is a record of an agreement, especially an agreement concerning who owns property

deem /diːm/ *v* [T] *formal* to decide that something is true: *The material was deemed faulty.*

deep¹ /diːp/ *adj*

1 a) if something is deep, there is a long distance from the surface to the bottom or from the front to the back [≠ **shallow**; ➡ **depth**]: *The water's not very deep.* | *a deep shelf* | *a deep cut* ➔ see picture at **SHALLOW b) 3 centimetres/7 feet etc deep** measuring 3 centimetres, 7 feet etc from the surface to the bottom or from the front to the back: *The pool was 5 metres deep.*
2 serious or severe: *the deep divisions within the party* | *She's in deep trouble.*
3 if you take a deep breath or give a deep SIGH, you take a lot of air into your lungs before letting it out again
4 a deep feeling or belief is felt very strongly: *Colin felt a deep sense of despair.*
5 a deep sound or voice is very low
6 a deep colour is dark and strong [≠ **light, pale**]: *a deep blue carpet*
7 deep sleep if someone is in a deep sleep, it is difficult to wake them

8 serious and often difficult to understand: *some very deep aspects of philosophy*
9 deep in thought/conversation thinking or talking so much that you do not notice anything else
➔ **KNEE-DEEP**

deep² *adv*
1 a long way into or below the surface of something: *He thrust his hands deep in his pockets.* | *deep beneath the ground*
2 deep down a) if you feel or know something deep down, you are sure about it: *Deep down, I knew she was right.* **b)** if someone is kind, cruel etc deep down, that is what they are really like, even though they seem not to be
3 two/three etc deep if things or people are two deep, three deep etc, there are two, three etc rows or layers of them
4 run/go deep if a feeling runs deep or goes deep, people feel it very strongly: *Resentment against the police ran deep.*

deepen /ˈdiːpən/ *v* [I,T] to become worse, or make something become worse: *The crisis deepened.*

deep ˈfreeze *n* [C] a large metal box in which food can be stored at very low temperatures for a long time [= **freezer**]

deep ˈfried *adj* cooked in a lot of hot oil

deeply /ˈdiːpli/ *adv* extremely or very much: *She was deeply upset.*

deep-ˈseated also **deep-ˈrooted** *adj* a deep-seated feeling or idea is strong and very difficult to change

deep-ˈset *adj* deep-set eyes are deep in the surface of the face

deer /dɪə $ dɪr/ *n* [C] plural **deer** a large wild animal that can run very fast, eats grass, and has horns on its head

deface /dɪˈfeɪs/ *v* [T] to spoil the appearance of something by writing or making marks on it: *the vandals who defaced the statue*

defamation /ˌdefəˈmeɪʃən/ *n* [U] *law* when someone says or writes bad and untrue things about someone else —**defamatory** /dɪˈfæmətəri $ -tɔːri/ *adj*

default¹ /dɪˈfɔːlt $ -ˈfɔːlt/ *n* **1 by default** if something happens by default, it happens only because something else does not happen: *The other team never arrived, so we won by default.* **2** [C] the way in which things are arranged on a computer screen unless you decide to change them: *The default page length is 58 lines.*

default² *v* [I] to not do something that you have legally agreed to do: +**on** *He defaulted on his loan payments.*

defeat¹ /dɪˈfiːt/ *n* [C,U]
1 failure to win or succeed: *Italy suffered their 2nd defeat of the tournament.* | *On 2 March, they suffered their worst defeat of the war.*
2 victory over someone or something: +**of** *her defeat of Democrat Abe Robbins*

defeat² *v* [T]
1 to win a victory over someone in a war, competition, game etc [= **beat**]: *In the last match, Venus Williams defeated her sister 6–3, 6–4.*
2 if a problem or a piece of work defeats you, it is so difficult that you cannot solve it or do it: *It*

D

was the last question on the paper that defeated me.
3 to make something fail: *The plan was defeated by a lack of money.*

defeatist /dɪˈfiːtɪst/ *adj* behaving in a way that shows you expect to fail: *a defeatist attitude* —**defeatism** *n* [U] —**defeatist** *n* [C]

defecate /ˈdefɪkeɪt/ *v* [I] *formal* to get rid of solid waste from your body

defect¹ /dɪˈfekt, ˈdiːfekt/ *n* [C] a fault in the way something is made or the way it works: **+in** *defects in the product* → see box at **FAULT** —**defective** /dɪˈfektɪv/ *adj*: *defective machinery*

defect² /dɪˈfekt/ *v* [I] to leave your own country or group in order to go to or join an opposing one —**defector** *n* [C] —**defection** /dɪˈfekʃən/ *n* [C,U]

defence *BrE*; **defense** *AmE* /dɪˈfens/ *n*

1 a) [U] the act of protecting something or someone from attack: **+of** *the defense of human rights* **b)** [C] something that can be used to protect something or someone from attack: **+against** *The immune system is the body's defence against infection.*
2 [U] the weapons, soldiers etc that a country uses to protect itself from attack: *spending on defence* | *the Defense Department*
3 [C,U] something that you say or do in order to support someone or something who is being criticized: **in sb's/sth's defence** *Jill wrote a letter to their boss in Mike's defense.*
4 a) [C] the things that are said in a court of law to prove that someone is not guilty of a crime: *His defence was that he intended only to wound the thief.* **b) the defence** the lawyers in a court who try to prove that someone is not guilty of a crime: *The defense called only one witness.* → see box at **COURT**
5 [C,U] *BrE* the players in a game such as football whose main job is to stop the other team from getting points
→ **SELF-DEFENCE**

defenceless *BrE*; **defenseless** *AmE* /dɪˈfensləs/ *adj* weak and unable to protect yourself: *a defenceless child*

defend /dɪˈfend/ *v*

1 [T] to protect someone or something from attack: **defend sb/sth against/from sth** *a castle built to defend the island against invaders* | **defend yourself** *The course teaches women to defend themselves.*
2 [T] to say something to support someone or something that has been criticized: *The school has defended its decision.* | **defend yourself (against sth)** *He defended himself against the allegations.* | *She vigorously defended her husband.*
3 [T] to do something in order to allow something to continue: *It is important to defend democracy.*
4 [I,T] to try to prevent your opponents from getting points in a game such as football: *Liverpool defended well.*
5 [T] to try to win a competition that you won last time: *The team are preparing to defend their title.* | *the defending champion*
6 [I,T] to be the lawyer who tries to prove in court that someone is not guilty of a crime [≠ **prosecute**]

defendant /dɪˈfendənt/ *n* [C] the person in a court who has been ACCUSED of a crime → see box at **COURT**

defender /dɪˈfendə $ -ər/ *n* [C] **1** a player in a game such as football who defends their team's GOAL from the opposing team [➡ **forward**] **2** someone who defends a particular idea, belief, person etc: *a defender of democracy*

defense¹ /dɪˈfens/ *n* the American spelling of **DEFENCE**

defense² /dɪˈfens $ ˈdiːfens/ *n* [C,U] *AmE* the players in a game such as football who try to stop the other team from getting points [≠ **offense**]

defenseless /dɪˈfensləs/ *adj* the American spelling of **DEFENCELESS**

defensive¹ /dɪˈfensɪv/ *adj* **1** intended to protect people from attack: *defensive weapons* **2** behaving in a way that shows you think someone is criticizing you: *He was very defensive about his work.* —**defensively** *adv*

defensive² *n* **on the defensive** ready to defend yourself: *Jane was angry and on the defensive.*

defer /dɪˈfɜː $ -ˈfɜːr/ *v* [T] **deferred, deferring** *formal* to delay something until a later date: *Further discussions will be deferred until April.*

deference /ˈdefərəns/ *n* [U] *formal* behaviour that shows that you respect someone or something: **in deference to sb/sth** *They wore black in deference to tradition.* —**deferential** /ˌdefəˈrenʃəl◂/ *adj*

defiance /dɪˈfaɪəns/ *n* [U] when you refuse to obey a person or rule [➡ **defy**]: **act/gesture of defiance** *an act of defiance against his parents* | **in defiance (of sb/sth)** *Some stores opened in defiance of the law.*

defiant /dɪˈfaɪənt/ *adj* refusing to obey a person or rule: *a defiant gesture* —**defiantly** *adv*

deficiency /dɪˈfɪʃənsi/ *n* [C,U] plural **deficiencies 1** a lack of something that you need: *a vitamin deficiency* **2** a fault that makes something or someone not good enough: **+in/of** *the deficiencies of the system*

deficient /dɪˈfɪʃənt/ *adj* **1** not containing enough of something: **+in** *a diet that is deficient in iron* **2** not good enough: *a deficient immune system*

deficit /ˈdefɪsɪt/ *n* [C] the difference between the amount of something you have and the higher amount you need: **+of** *a trade deficit of $3 billion*

defile /dɪˈfaɪl/ *v* [T] *formal* to spoil something that is beautiful, good, or pure

define /dɪˈfaɪn/ *v* [T]

1 to describe something correctly and thoroughly: *We need to define our clients' needs.* | **clearly/well defined** *The aims need to be clearly defined.*
2 to explain the meaning of a word [➡ **definition**]: *It's difficult to define the word exactly.* | **define sth as sth** *A budget is defined as 'a plan of action expressed in money terms'.*

definite /ˈdefɪnɪt, ˈdefənɪt/ *adj*

1 without any doubt: *I can't give you a definite answer.* | *The study shows a definite link between sun exposure and skin cancer.*

2 a definite arrangement or promise is certain to happen: *We haven't made any definite arrangements.*
3 [not before noun] saying something firmly so that people are certain what you mean: **+about** *She's very definite about what she wants.*

definite 'article *n* [singular] the word 'the' in English [➡ **indefinite article**]

definitely /'defɪn‡tli, 'defən‡tli/ *adv* without any doubt [= **certainly**]: *That's definitely true.* | *The museum is definitely worth visiting.*

definition /ˌdefə'nɪʃən/ *n* [C]

1 a phrase or sentence that says what a word means: **+of** *There are many definitions of the word 'feminism'.*
2 by definition having a particular quality because all things or people of the same type have it: *Children are, by definition, immature.*

definitive /dɪ'fɪn‡tɪv/ *adj* **1** a definitive book is better than any other book on the same subject: *the definitive guide to wine* **2** a definitive agreement, statement etc is certain and unlikely to change: *I can't give a definitive answer yet.* —**definitively** *adv*

deflate /ˌdiː'fleɪt, dɪ-/ *v* **1** [T] to make someone feel less important or confident: *I felt deflated by his criticism.* **2** [I,T] if a tyre, BALLOON etc deflates, or if you deflate it, it gets smaller because the air comes out

deflect /dɪ'flekt/ *v* **1** [T] to do something to stop people paying attention to you and criticizing you: **deflect sth (away) from sth** *attempts to deflect attention away from his private life* **2** [T] to take someone's attention away from what they are trying to do: **deflect sb from sth** *She refused to be deflected from her aims.* **3** [I,T] to make something move in a different direction, especially after hitting something: *He deflected the ball away from the goal.* —**deflection** /-'flekʃən/ *n* [C]

deforestation /diːˌfɒrɪ'steɪʃən $ -ˌfɔː-, -ˌfɑː-/ *n* [singular, U] when all the trees in an area are cut down or destroyed ➡ see box at **ENVIRONMENT**

deformed /dɪ'fɔːmd $ -ɔːrmd/ *adj* something that is deformed has the wrong shape, especially because it has grown or developed wrongly: *deformed hands*

deformity /dɪ'fɔːm‡ti $ -ɔːr-/ *n* [C,U] plural **deformities** a part of someone's body that is not the normal shape: *children with physical deformities*

defraud /dɪ'frɔːd $ -'frɑːd/ *v* [T] to get money from an organization by deceiving them: **defraud sb of sth** *attempts to defraud the bank of almost $30 000*

defrost /ˌdiː'frɒst $ -'frɒːst/ *v* [I,T] **1** if frozen food defrosts, or if you defrost it, it becomes warmer and stops being frozen **2** to turn off a FREEZER or REFRIGERATOR so that the ice inside it melts

deft /deft/ *adj* quick and skilful: *deft movements* —**deftly** *adv*

defunct /dɪ'fʌŋkt/ *adj* not existing or useful any more

defuse /ˌdiː'fjuːz/ *v* [T] **1** to improve a difficult or violent situation by making people less angry: **defuse a situation/crisis/row** *an attempt to defuse the crisis* **2** to stop a bomb from exploding by removing the FUSE

defy /dɪ'faɪ/ *v* [T] **defied, defying, defies 1** to refuse to obey someone or something [➡ **defiance**]: *people who openly defy the law* **2 defy description/analysis/belief etc** to be impossible to describe or understand: *Its size defies description.* **3 defy sb to do sth** to ask someone to try to do something that you think is not possible

degenerate[1] /dɪ'dʒenəreɪt/ *v* [I] to become worse: **+into** *The discussion soon degenerated into an argument.*

degenerate[2] /dɪ'dʒenər‡t/ *adj* morally unacceptable: *his degenerate lifestyle* —**degenerate** *n* [C]

degrade /dɪ'ɡreɪd/ *v* [T] to treat someone in a way that makes people have less respect for them: *an advert which degrades women* —**degrading** *adj*

degree /dɪ'ɡriː/ *n*

1 [C] a unit for measuring temperature: **30 degrees Celsius/80 degrees Fahrenheit etc** (=30°C/80°F etc)
2 [C] a unit for measuring angles: *a 90 degree angle* (=90°)
3 [C,U] the level or amount of something: **+of** *an operation with a high degree of risk* | *The treatment has been used with varying degrees of success.* | **to a degree/to some degree/to a certain degree** (=partly) *Your weight depends to some degree on your genes.*
4 [C] a QUALIFICATION that you get when you finish a course at university: **+in** *She has a degree in physics.* | **do/take a degree** *He did a degree in French.*
→ see box at **UNIVERSITY** → **MASTER'S DEGREE**

dehydrated /ˌdiːhaɪ'dreɪt‡d $ diː'haɪdreɪ-/ *adj* not having enough water in your body —**dehydration** /ˌdiːhaɪ'dreɪʃən/ *n* [U]

deity /'deɪ‡ti, 'diː-/ *n* [C] plural **deities** a god or GODDESS

déjà vu /ˌdeɪʒɑː 'vjuː $ -'vuː/ *n* [U] the feeling that you are having exactly the same experience as you have had before: *I had a sudden feeling of déjà vu.*

dejected /dɪ'dʒekt‡d/ *adj* sad and disappointed: *He looked slightly dejected.*

delay[1] /dɪ'leɪ/ *n* [C,U] when you have to wait for something to happen, or the time you have to wait: *There are long delays on the motorway.* | *There may be a slight delay.* | **without delay** (=immediately) *He replied to the letter without delay.*

delay[2] *v*

1 [I,T] to wait until a later time to do something: *He agreed to delay the decision.* | **delay sth until sth** *The elections will be delayed until June.* | **delay doing sth** *Don't delay seeking help if your child is unwell.*
2 [T] to make someone or something late, or make something happen more slowly: *Our flight was delayed by bad weather.* | *A good diet can delay the onset of the disease.* → see box at **TRAIN**

delectable /dɪ'lektəbəl/ *adj formal* very pleasant, especially to taste or smell

delegate[1] /'delɪɡ‡t/ *n* [C] someone who has been chosen to represent a group at a meeting

delegate[2] /'delɪɡeɪt/ *v* [I,T] to give part of your work or responsibilities to someone else: *Some of the tasks can be delegated to assistants.*

D

delegation /ˌdelɪˈgeɪʃən/ n **1** [C] a group of people who represent a country or organization: **+of** a delegation of French officials **2** [U] when you give someone else part of your work or responsibilities: **+of** the delegation of responsibility

delete /dɪˈliːt/ v [T] to remove something from a piece of writing or from the information on a computer: **delete sth from sth** The data has been deleted from the file. —**deletion** /-ˈliːʃən/ n [C,U]

deli /ˈdeli/ n [C] a DELICATESSEN

deliberate¹ /dɪˈlɪbərət/ adj
1 intended or planned: a **deliberate attempt** to embarrass her | a deliberate mistake
2 slow and careful: His steps were slow and deliberate.

deliberate² /dɪˈlɪbəreɪt/ v [I,T] to think about something carefully

deliberately /dɪˈlɪbərətli/ adv
1 done in a way that is intended or planned [**≠ accidentally**]: The fire was started deliberately.
2 in a slow and careful way: He spoke deliberately.

deliberation /dɪˌlɪbəˈreɪʃən/ n [C,U] careful thought or discussion: **After much deliberation** the prize was awarded to Murray.

delicacy /ˈdelɪkəsi/ n plural **delicacies 1** [U] when something is soft, light, or easily damaged: the delicacy of the petals **2** [U] when you behave in a careful way so that you do not upset people: a situation that needs to be handled with delicacy **3** [C] a rare or expensive food that is good to eat: local delicacies

delicate /ˈdelɪkət/ adj
1 easily damaged or broken: delicate china
2 small and attractive: delicate flowers | her delicate hands
3 needing to be dealt with very carefully so that you do not upset people: This is a very delicate matter.
4 a delicate colour, taste, or smell is not very bright or strong: a delicate shade of pink
5 old-fashioned often ill: a delicate child
—**delicately** adv

delicatessen /ˌdelɪkəˈtesən/ n [C] a shop that sells good quality cheeses, cooked meats, SALADS etc → see box at SHOP

delicious /dɪˈlɪʃəs/ adj very pleasant to taste or smell: a delicious meal → see box at TASTE

delight¹ /dɪˈlaɪt/ n
1 [U] a feeling of great pleasure: **with/in delight** The children screamed with delight. | **to sb's delight** The plans were rejected to the delight of local people. | He **took** great **delight in** (=enjoyed) telling me I was wrong.
2 [C] something that gives you pleasure: The game was a delight to watch. | **the delights of sth** a chance to enjoy the delights of Tuscany

delight² v [T] to give someone great pleasure and enjoyment: **delight sb with sth** She delighted fans with her performance.
delight in sth phr v to enjoy something very much, especially something unpleasant: She delights in shocking people.

delighted /dɪˈlaɪtɪd/ adj very pleased: **delighted to do sth** Yoko will be delighted to see

you. | **+(that)** I'm delighted you can come. | **+with/by/at** Helen was absolutely delighted with the results.

delightful /dɪˈlaɪtfəl/ adj formal very pleasant: a delightful garden —**delightfully** adv

delinquency /dɪˈlɪŋkwənsi/ n [U] formal bad or illegal behaviour by young people —**delinquent** n [C] a young delinquent —**delinquent** adj: delinquent behaviour → JUVENILE DELINQUENT

delirious /dɪˈlɪriəs/ adj **1** talking in a confused way because you are ill **2** literary extremely happy —**deliriously** adv

delirium /dɪˈlɪriəm/ n [U] when someone is very confused because they are ill

deliver /dɪˈlɪvə $ -ər/ v
1 [I,T] to take something to a place: **deliver sth to sth** The letter was delivered to his home. | I'm having some flowers **delivered** for her birthday.
2 [T] to say something formally: **deliver a speech/lecture** etc He delivered a televised speech. | **deliver a judgment/verdict** The jury delivered a verdict of unlawful killing.
3 [I,T] to do the things that you have promised: **+on** It's time the government started delivering on its promises. | the failure of some services to **deliver the goods** (=do what they have promised)
4 [T] to help a woman give birth to her baby

delivery /dɪˈlɪvəri/ n plural **deliveries 1** [C,U] when something is taken to a place, or the things that are taken: There's free delivery on orders over £25. | a delivery service **2** [U] when people provide a service or do something that they have promised to do: **+of** the delivery of care for the elderly **3** [C,U] the process of giving birth to a baby

delta /ˈdeltə/ n [C] an area of low land near the sea where a river separates into many smaller rivers

delude /dɪˈluːd/ v [T] to make someone believe something that is not true: She deluded herself that she was in love.

deluge /ˈdeljuːdʒ/ n [singular] **1** a lot of things that happen or arrive at the same time: **+of** a deluge of complaints **2** formal a large flood —**deluge** v [T] We were deluged with mail.

delusion /dɪˈluːʒən/ n [C,U] something you believe that is not true: the delusion that things were better in the past

deluxe /dɪˈlʌks $ -ˈlʊks/ adj very good and expensive: a deluxe hotel

delve /delv/ v [I] **1** to try to find out more about something: **+into** attempts to delve further into the subject **2** to put your hand deep inside a bag or box in order to find something: **+into** He delved into his pocket and brought out a pen.

demand¹ /dɪˈmɑːnd $ dɪˈmænd/ n
1 [singular, U] the need or desire that people have for goods and services: **+for** There's a great demand for new housing. | the **growing demand** for organic produce | skills that are **much in demand**
2 [C] a very determined request for something: **+for** demands for political reform
3 demands [plural] the difficult or tiring things you have to do, or the skills you need: **+of** the demands of modern life | **+on** The play **makes** considerable **demands** on the actors' talents.

4 on demand whenever someone wants something: *Do you feed your baby on demand?*

demand² *v* [T]

1 to ask for something in a determined way: *The President demanded the release of all the hostages.* | **+that** *They demanded that he should resign.* | **demand to know/see etc sth** *They demanded to see my passport.* | *'Where are you going?' she demanded angrily.* → see box at **ASK**
2 if one thing demands another thing, it needs that thing in order to be successful: *Learning a language demands a great deal of time and effort.*

demanding /dɪˈmɑːndɪŋ $ dɪˈmæn-/ *adj*
1 needing a lot of time, ability, and effort: *a demanding job* **2** always wanting attention in a way that is annoying: *a demanding child*

demeaning /dɪˈmiːnɪŋ/ *adj* making you feel that you are not important or respected: *a demeaning job*

demeanour *BrE*; **demeanor** *AmE* /dɪˈmiːnə $ -ər/ *n* [singular, U] *formal* the way someone behaves, dresses, speaks etc: *her cheerful demeanour*

demented /dɪˈmentɪd/ *adj* behaving in a crazy way

dementia /dɪˈmenʃə, -ʃiə $ -tʃə/ *n* [U] an illness that gradually affects someone's brain and memory

demise /dɪˈmaɪz/ *n* [singular] *formal* **1** the end of something that used to exist: **+of** *the demise of the steel industry* **2** someone's death

demo /ˈdeməʊ $ -moʊ/ *n* [C] plural **demos**
1 *BrE* a DEMONSTRATION: *an anti-war demo* **2** an example of something that is produced to show what it is like or how it works: *demo software*

democracy /dɪˈmɒkrəsi $ dɪˈmɑː-/ *n* [C,U] plural **democracies** the political system in which everyone can vote to choose the government, or a country that has this system: *the struggle for democracy* | *Western democracies* → see box at **GOVERNMENT**

democrat /ˈdeməkræt/ *n* [C] someone who supports the idea of democracy

Democrat *n* [C] someone who supports the Democratic Party in the US

democratic /ˌdeməˈkrætɪk◂/ *adj*
1 a democratic government or leader has been elected by the people of a country
2 organized according to the idea that everyone should be involved in making decisions: *a democratic style of management*
—**democratically** /-kli/ *adv*: *He was democratically elected.*

Demoʹcratic ˌParty *n* **the Democratic Party** one of the two main political parties in the US [➡ **the Republican Party**]

demolish /dɪˈmɒlɪʃ $ dɪˈmɑː-/ *v* [T] **1** to destroy a building: *The house was demolished in 1968.* **2** to prove that an idea or opinion is completely wrong: *The theory has been demolished by recent research.* —**demolition** /ˌdeməˈlɪʃən/ *n* [C,U]

demon /ˈdiːmən/ *n* [C] an evil SPIRIT —**demonic** /dɪˈmɒnɪk $ -ˈmɑː-/ *adj*

demonstrate /ˈdemənstreɪt/ *v*
1 [T] to show that something is true: *The accident demonstrated the importance of wearing seatbelts.* | **+that** *The study demonstrates that fewer graduates are finding jobs.*
2 [T] to show someone how to do something or how something works: **+how** *Instructors should demonstrate how to use equipment.*
3 [I] to protest with other people in a public place: **+against** *Huge crowds demonstrated against war.* → see box at **PROTEST**
4 [T] to show that you have a particular skill, quality, or feeling: *Students must demonstrate an ability to work under pressure.*

demonstration /ˌdemənˈstreɪʃən/ *n*
1 [C] an occasion when a large group of people meet to protest or support something: **+against** *a demonstration against the government* | *Thousands of students took part in the demonstration.* → see box at **PROTEST**
2 [C,U] when you show someone how to do something or how something works: **+of** *She gave us a demonstration of how to use the software.* | *a cookery demonstration*
3 [C] something that shows someone or something has a particular quality or feeling: **+of** *This is a clear demonstration of the country's commitment to peace.*

demonstrative /dɪˈmɒnstrətɪv $ dɪˈmɑːn-/ *adj* willing to show that you care about someone

demonstrator /ˈdemənstreɪtə $ -ər/ *n* [C] someone who takes part in a demonstration

demoralized also **-ised** *BrE* /dɪˈmɒrəlaɪzd $ -ˈmɔː-, -ˈmɑː-/ *adj* no longer feeling confident or hopeful: *I came out of the interview feeling totally demoralized.*

demoralizing also **-ising** *BrE* /dɪˈmɒrəlaɪzɪŋ $ -ˈmɔː-, -ˈmɑː-/ *adj* making you feel less confident and hopeful: *They suffered a demoralizing defeat.* —**demoralize** *v* [T]

demote /dɪˈməʊt $ -ˈmoʊt/ *v* [T] to give someone a less important job [≠ **promote**] —**demotion** /-ˈməʊʃən $ -ˈmoʊ-/ *n* [C,U]

demure /dɪˈmjʊə $ -ˈmjʊr/ *adj* shy, quiet, and polite

den /den/ *n* [C] **1** the home of some wild animals **2** *informal* a room in a house where people can relax **3** a place where secret or illegal activities happen

denial /dɪˈnaɪəl/ *n* **1** [C,U] a statement saying that something is not true [➡ **deny**]: **+of** *The government issued an official denial of the reports.* **2** [U] when someone is not allowed to have or do something: **+of** *the denial of basic human rights*

denigrate /ˈdenɪɡreɪt/ *v* [T] to criticize someone or something unfairly

denim /ˈdenɪm/ *n* [U] strong cotton cloth used for making JEANS

denomination /dɪˌnɒmɪˈneɪʃən $ dɪˌnɑː-/ *n* [C] a religious group with slightly different beliefs from other groups in the same religion

denote /dɪˈnəʊt $ -ˈnoʊt/ *v* [T] to mean or represent something: *Each H on the map denotes a hospital.*

denounce /dɪˈnaʊns/ *v* [T] to criticize someone or something publicly: **denounce sb/sth as sth** *The election was denounced as a farce.*

dense /dens/ *adj* **1** containing a lot of things or people close together: *dense pine forests* **2** dense smoke or cloud is difficult to see through —**densely** *adv*

D

density /'densɪti/ n [C,U] plural **densities** **1** the number of people or things there are in an area, in relation to the size of the area: *Taiwan has a high population density.* | **+of** *the density of housing* **2** *technical* the relationship between an object's weight and the amount of space it fills

dent[1] /dent/ n [C] a hollow area in the surface of something, where it has been hit: *a dent in the car door*

dent[2] v [T] **1** to have a bad effect on something: *The affair severely dented his reputation.* **2** to make a hollow area on the surface of something by hitting it

dental /'dentl/ adj relating to teeth: *dental care*

dental 'floss n [U] special string that you use for cleaning between your teeth

dentist /'dentɪst/ n [C] someone whose job is to treat people's teeth: *I'm going to the dentist's this afternoon.*
—**dentistry** n [U]

dentures /'dentʃəz $ -ərz/ n [plural] a set of artificial teeth

denunciation /dɪ,nʌnsi'eɪʃən/ n [C,U] a public statement in which you criticize someone or something

deny /dɪ'naɪ/ v [T] **denied, denying, denies**

1 to say that something is not true [≠ **admit; ➡ denial**]: *In court they denied all the charges.* | **+(that)** *He strongly denied that he had taken the money.* | **deny doing sth** *Wilks denies murdering his wife.*

2 to not let someone have something: **deny sb sth** *Many people are being denied basic human rights.*

deodorant /di:'əʊdərənt $ -'oʊ-/ n [C,U] a substance that you put under your arms to stop your body smelling unpleasant

depart /dɪ'pɑːt $ -ɑːrt/ v [I] *formal* to leave: **+from** *The train will depart from Platform 4.* | **+for** *He departed for Rome immediately.*

department /dɪ'pɑːtmənt $ -ɑːr-/ n [C] one of the parts of a large organization such as a college, government, or company: *the marketing department* → see box at **PART**

de'partment ,store n [C] a large shop that sells many different types of things → see box at **SHOP**

departure /dɪ'pɑːtʃə $ -'pɑːrtʃər/ n **1** [C,U] when a person, plane, train etc leaves a place: *Check in at the airport an hour before departure.* | **+for** *her departure for Japan* → see box at **AIRPORT** **2** [C] a change from what is usual or expected: **+from** *a significant departure from previous methods*

depend /dɪ'pend/ v

it/that depends *spoken* used to say that you are not sure about something, because other things might affect what happens: *'Are you coming to my house later?' 'It depends. I might have to work.'*

depend on/upon sb/sth *phr v* **1** if something depends on something else, it is directly affected by that thing: *Your grade will depend on your performance in the final exam.* **2** to need help from someone or something: *We depend entirely on donations from the public.* **3** to trust someone or something: *I know I can always depend on Jon.*

dependable /dɪ'pendəbəl/ adj someone or something that is dependable will always do what you need them to do: *a dependable employee* | *a dependable car*

dependant *BrE*; **dependent** *AmE* /dɪ'pendənt/ n [C] a person, especially a child, who needs someone else to pay for their food, clothes etc

dependent /dɪ'pendənt/ adj **1** needing someone or something in order to exist, be successful, healthy etc [≠ **independent**]: **on/upon** *The local economy is dependent on tourism.* → see box at **NEED** **2 be dependent on/upon sth** *formal* to be directly affected by something else: *Starting salary is dependent on experience.*
—**dependence** also **dependency** n [U]

depict /dɪ'pɪkt/ v [T] to show someone in a picture or to describe them in a story: *The god is depicted as a bird with a human head.*
—**depiction** /dɪ'pɪkʃən/ n [C,U]

deplete /dɪ'pliːt/ v [T] to reduce the amount of something: *Many forests have been depleted by acid rain.* —**depletion** /dɪ'pliːʃən/ n [U] *the depletion of the ozone layer*

deplorable /dɪ'plɔːrəbəl/ adj *formal* very bad: *The prisoners were held in deplorable conditions.*

deplore /dɪ'plɔː $ -'plɔːr/ v [T] *formal* to say that you think something is very bad and that you strongly disapprove of it: *a statement deploring the use of chemical weapons*

deploy /dɪ'plɔɪ/ v [T] to move soldiers and military equipment to a place so that they can be used if necessary —**deployment** n [C,U] *the deployment of UN troops*

deport /dɪ'pɔːt $ -ɔːrt/ v [T] to force someone to leave a country and return to the country they came from —**deportation** /,diːpɔː'teɪʃən $ -pɔːr-/ n [C,U]

depose /dɪ'pəʊz $ -'poʊz/ v [T] to remove a leader from their position: *The king was recently deposed by the military.*

deposit[1] /dɪ'pɒzɪt $ dɪ'pɑː-/ n [C] **1** a part of the cost of something that you pay before paying the total amount later: *We put down a deposit on the house.* | **+of** *We require a deposit of 10%.* **2** an amount of money that you pay into a bank account [≠ **withdrawal**]: *I'd like to make a deposit please.* **3** money that you pay when you rent something such as an apartment or car, which will be given back if you do not damage it: *We paid one month's rent in advance, plus a deposit of $500.* **4** a layer of a mineral, metal etc that is left in soil or rocks through a natural process: *oil and mineral deposits*

deposit[2] v [T] **1** to put money into a bank account or valuable things into a safe place: *We deposited the money in a Swiss bank account.* → see box at **ACCOUNT** **2** *formal* to put something down in a particular place: *She deposited her bag by the front door.* **3** to gradually leave a layer of a substance on a surface: *The river deposits silt along its bed.*

de'posit ac,count n [C] *BrE* a bank account that pays **INTEREST** on the money that you leave in it → see box at **ACCOUNT**

depot /'depəʊ $ 'di:poʊ/ *n* [C] a place where buses, trains, planes etc are kept until they are needed

depraved /dɪ'preɪvd/ *adj* morally bad or evil: *Michael thought we were all depraved gamblers.*

depreciate /dɪ'pri:ʃieɪt/ *v* [I] to decrease in value or price: *A new car depreciates as soon as it is driven.* —**depreciation** /dɪ,pri:ʃi'eɪʃən/ *n* [U]

depress /dɪ'pres/ *v* [T] **1** to make someone feel very unhappy: *His films depress me.* **2** to reduce the value of something, or make something less successful: *The bad weather has depressed sales.* | *A war will depress the global economy.*

depressed /dɪ'prest/ *adj* **1** very unhappy: *She felt lonely and depressed.* → see box at **SAD** **2** not having enough jobs or business activity: *depressed inner-city neighbourhoods*

depressing /dɪ'presɪŋ/ *adj* making you feel sad: *a depressing book*

depression /dɪ'preʃən/ *n* [C,U] **1** a feeling of great sadness, or a medical condition that makes you have this feeling: *The patient is **suffering** from depression.* **2** a long period during which there is very little business activity and many people do not have jobs: *a severe **economic** depression*

deprive /dɪ'praɪv/ *v*
deprive sb of sth *phr v* to prevent someone from having something that they need or should have: *Prisoners were deprived of sleep for three days.*

deprived /dɪ'praɪvd/ *adj* not having the things that are necessary for a comfortable or happy life: *a deprived childhood* —**deprivation** /,deprɪ'veɪʃən/ *n* [U]

depth /depθ/ *n*
1 [C,U] **a)** the distance from the top of something to the bottom of it [→ **deep**]: **+of** *The lake has an average depth of 6 to 8 metres.* **b)** the distance from the front of an object to the back of it: **+of** *The depth of the shelves is about 35cm.* **2** [U] also **depths** how strong an emotion is or how serious a situation is: **+of** *People need to realize the depth of the problem.* | *I was in **the depths of depression** (=very unhappy).* **3 in depth** including all the details: *The book examines the issue in great depth.* **4 be out of your depth** to be in a situation that is too difficult for you to understand or deal with: *For the first week at her new job she felt hopelessly out of her depth.* **5 the depths of the ocean/forest etc** the part of an ocean etc that is furthest away from people, and most difficult to reach **6 the depths of winter** the middle of winter, when it is coldest
→ **IN-DEPTH**

deputy /'depjʊti/ *n* [C] plural **deputies** someone in an organization who is directly below another person in rank, and who is officially in charge when that person is not there

derail /,di:'reɪl, dɪ-/ *v* [I,T] if a train derails or is derailed, it goes off the tracks —**derailment** *n* [C,U]

deranged /dɪ'reɪndʒd/ *adj* behaving in a crazy or dangerous way: *a deranged criminal*

deregulation /di:,regjʊ'leɪʃən/ *n* [U] when rules and controls are removed in an area of business

derelict

a derelict warehouse

derelict /'derəlɪkt/ *adj* a derelict building or piece of land is in very bad condition because it has not been used for a long time

deride /dɪ'raɪd/ *v* [T] *formal* to say or show that you think that someone or something is silly or unimportant —**derision** /dɪ'rɪʒən/ *n* [U] —**derisive** /dɪ'raɪsɪv/ *adj*: *derisive laughter*

derisory /dɪ'raɪsəri/ *adj* an amount of money that is derisory is so small that it is not worth considering seriously: *a derisory pay increase*

derivation /,derɪ'veɪʃən/ *n* [C,U] what something developed from, especially a word

derive /dɪ'raɪv/ *v* **1** [T] to get something, especially an advantage or a pleasant feeling, from something: *It's important that I **derive** some pleasure from my work.* **2** [I,T] to develop or come from something: **+from** *The word is derived from Latin.*

dermatologist /,dɜ:mə'tɒlədʒɪst $,dɜ:rmə'taː-/ *n* [C] a doctor who treats skin diseases

derogatory /dɪ'rɒgətəri $ dɪ'rɑː gətɔːri/ *adj* insulting and disapproving: *derogatory remarks about his family*

descend /dɪ'send/ *v* **1** [I,T] *formal* to go down [≠ **ascend**]: *He slowly descended the steps.* **2 be descended from sb** to be related to someone who lived a long time ago: *She is descended from a family of French aristocrats.*

descendant /dɪ'sendənt/ *n* [C] someone who is related to a person who lived a long time ago [→ **ancestor**]: *a descendant of slaves*

descent /dɪ'sent/ *n* **1** [C,U] when a plane, person etc goes down to a lower place [≠ **ascent**]: *The plane began its descent.* **2** [U] your family origins, especially the country they lived in in the past: **of Italian/Russian etc descent** *a young man of Asian descent*

describe /dɪ'skraɪb/ *v* [T] to say what someone or something is like or to explain something that has happened: *Police asked the woman to describe her attacker.* | **describe sb/sth as sth** *The victim's neighbors described him as a gentle man who loved children.* | **describe sb/sth to sb** *Ava was just describing to me her trip to Egypt.* | **+how/what/why etc** *It's hard to describe how I felt.*

description /dɪ'skrɪpʃən/ *n* [C,U]
1 something you say or write that tells people what someone or something is like: **+of** *The police issued a **detailed description** of the missing woman.* | **brief/short/full/complete description** *The catalog gives a description of*

D

desert

each product. | **fit/match/answer a description** (=be like the person described)
2 a type of something: *I think it's a weapon of some description.* | *People of all descriptions came to see the show.*
→ JOB DESCRIPTION

descriptive /dɪˈskrɪptɪv/ *adj* a descriptive word or piece of writing describes something

desecrate /ˈdesɪkreɪt/ *v* [T] to damage something holy or respected —**desecration** /ˌdesɪˈkreɪʃən/ *n* [singular,U]

desert[1] /ˈdezət $ -ərt/ *n* [C,U] a large area of very hot dry land where few plants grow: *the Sahara desert*

desert[2] /dɪˈzɜːt $ -ˈzɜːrt/ *v* **1** [T] if you desert a person or a place, you leave them and never go back: *Her boyfriend deserted her when she got pregnant.* | *People have deserted the villages and moved to the cities.* **2** [I] to leave the army without permission —**desertion** /-ˈzɜːʃən $ -ɜːr-/ *n* [C,U]

deserted /dɪˈzɜːtɪd $ -ɜːr-/ *adj* a deserted place is empty and quiet: *At night the streets are deserted.* → see box at EMPTY

deserter /dɪˈzɜːtə $ -ˈzɜːrtər/ *n* [C] a soldier who leaves the army without permission

desert ˈisland *n* [C] a tropical island where nobody lives

deserve /dɪˈzɜːv $ -ɜːrv/ *v* [T] if you deserve something, you should get it because of something you have done: *After all that work you deserve a break.* | **deserve to do sth** *We didn't really deserve to win.* | *What had he done to deserve this punishment?* | *People who are sent to prison for drunk-driving* **get what they deserve**.
—**deserved** *adj*: *a well-deserved rest*
—**deservedly** /dɪˈzɜːvɪdli $ -ɜːr-/ *adv*

deserving /dɪˈzɜːvɪŋ $ -ɜːr-/ *adj* [only before noun] needing help and support: *The money is intended to help deserving students.*

design[1] /dɪˈzaɪn/ *n*
1 [C,U] the way that something is planned or made: *We've made some changes to the computer's original design.*
2 [C] a pattern used to decorate something: *curtains with a floral design*
3 [C,U] a drawing that shows how something will be made or what it will look like, or the process of making one of these drawings: *The new plane is in its final design stage.* | **+for** *the design for the new office building*
→ GRAPHIC DESIGN, INTERIOR DESIGN

design[2] *v* [T]
1 to draw or plan something that you will make or build: *The palace was designed by an Italian architect.*
2 to make something for a particular purpose or person: **design sth to do sth** *These exercises are designed to strengthen muscles.* | **be designed for sb/sth** *a computer specifically designed for children*

designate /ˈdezɪgneɪt/ *v* [T] to choose someone or something for a particular job or purpose: *The building was designated as a temporary hospital.* —**designation** /ˌdezɪgˈneɪʃən/ *n* [C,U]

designer[1] /dɪˈzaɪnə $ -ər/ *n* [C] someone whose job is to design new styles of clothes, cars etc: *a fashion designer* | *an interior designer* (=someone who designs the inside of a building)

designer[2] *adj* [only before noun] designer clothes are made by a famous fashion designer: *designer suits*

desirable /dɪˈzaɪərəbəl $ -ˈzaɪr-/ *adj* something that is desirable is something you want because it is good or useful: *a desirable neighborhood* —**desirability** /dɪˌzaɪərəˈbɪləti $ -ˌzaɪr-/ *n* [U]

desire[1] /dɪˈzaɪə $ -ˈzaɪr/ *n*
1 [C,U] a strong feeling that you want something very much: **+for** *a desire for peace* | **desire to do sth** *a desire to win at all costs* | *She had no desire to marry him.*
2 [U] when you feel strongly that you want to have sex with someone

desire[2] *v* [T] **1** *formal* to want something very much: *The hotel has everything you could possibly desire.* **2 have the desired effect/result** to have the effect or result you wanted: *Her remarks had the desired effect.* **3** to find someone sexually attractive

desk /desk/ *n* [C] a table where you sit and write or work → see box at OFFICE → see picture at CLASSROOM → CASH DESK

desktop /ˈdesktɒp $ -tɑːp/ *n* [C] **1** the main area on a computer where you can find the ICONS that represent PROGRAMS, and where you can do things to manage the information on the computer **2** the top surface of a desk

desktop ˈpublishing *n* [U] abbreviation *DTP* when you arrange the writing and pictures for a magazine, book etc using a computer

desolate /ˈdesələt/ *adj* **1** a place that is desolate has no people or activity and is not attractive: *a desolate highway* **2** someone who is desolate is very sad and lonely —**desolation** /ˌdesəˈleɪʃən/ *n* [U]

despair[1] /dɪˈspeə $ -ˈsper/ *n* [U] a feeling that you have no hope at all: *She killed herself in despair.*

despair[2] *v* [I] *formal* to feel that there is no hope at all: *Despite his illness, Ron never despaired.* —**despairing** *adj*

despatch /dɪˈspætʃ/ *n, v* a British spelling of DISPATCH

desperate /ˈdespərət/ *adj*
1 willing to do anything to change a bad situation, even if it is dangerous or unpleasant: *Joe had been unemployed for over a year and was getting desperate.* | *a desperate attempt to escape*

2 needing or wanting something very much: **+for** *The team is desperate for a win.* | **desperate to do sth** *After a week in the hospital he was desperate to go home.* → see box at **NEED**
3 a desperate situation is very bad or serious: *a desperate shortage of food*
—**desperately** adv: *The doctors tried desperately to save her life.* —**desperation** /,despə'reɪʃən/ n [U]

despicable /dɪ'spɪkəbəl, 'despɪ-/ adj extremely bad or cruel: *a despicable crime* —**despicably** adv

despise /dɪ'spaɪz/ v [T] to hate someone very much: *He was a nasty man who despised children.* → see box at **HATE**

despite /dɪ'spaɪt/ prep used to say that something happened or is true, even though this is not what you expected [= **in spite of**]: *She loved him despite the way he treated her.*

despondent /dɪ'spɒndənt $ dɪ'spɑːn-/ adj very unhappy and without hope: *Taylor was broke and increasingly despondent about finding work.* —**despondently** adv

despot /'despɒt, -ət $ 'despət, -ɑːt/ n [C] someone, especially a ruler, who uses power in a cruel and unfair way —**despotic** /de'spɒtɪk $ -'spɑː-/ adj —**despotism** /'despətɪzəm/ n

dessert /dɪ'zɜːt $ -ɜːrt/ n [C,U] sweet food that you eat after the main part of a meal: *What's for dessert?* → see box at **RESTAURANT**

destabilize also **-ise** BrE /diː'steɪbɪlaɪz/ v [T] to make something such as a government or ECONOMY become less successful or more likely to get worse

destination /,destɪ'neɪʃən/ n [C] the place that you are travelling to: *We have just enough fuel to reach our destination.*

destined /'destɪnd/ adj certain to do or become something: **destined to do sth** *She was destined to become her country's first woman Prime Minister.* | **+for** *He's destined for greatness.*

destiny /'destɪni/ n [C,U] plural **destinies** the things that will happen to someone in the future [= **fate**]: *a nation fighting to control its own destiny*

destitute /'destɪtjuːt $ -tuːt/ adj having no money, no home, no food etc: *The floods left thousands of people destitute.* → see box at **POOR** —**destitution** /,destɪ'tjuːʃən $ -'tuː-/ n [U]

destroy /dɪ'strɔɪ/ v [T] to damage something very badly, so that it can no longer be used or repaired: *The building was completely destroyed by fire.* | *Condon destroyed any evidence that linked him to the crime.*

destroyer /dɪ'strɔɪə $ -ər/ n [C] a small fast military ship with guns → see box at **SHIP**

destruction /dɪ'strʌkʃən/ n [U] when something is destroyed: **+of** *the destruction of the rainforest* —**destructive** /-tɪv/ adj: *the destructive power of a hurricane*

detach /dɪ'tætʃ/ v [T] to remove part of something that has been made so that you can remove it —**detachable** adj

detached /dɪ'tætʃt/ adj **1** not reacting to or involved in something in an emotional way: *Smith remained cold and detached throughout his trial.* **2** BrE a detached house is not joined to another house → see box at **HOUSE**

detachment /dɪ'tætʃmənt/ n **1** [U] when someone does not react in an emotional way or feel involved in something **2** [C] a group of soldiers who are sent to do something

detail¹ /'diːteɪl $ dɪ'teɪl/ n
1 [C,U] a fact or a piece of information about something: *The documentary included a lot of historical detail.* | **in detail** (=using a lot of details) *He describes the events in great detail.*
2 details [plural] information that helps to complete what you know about something: *She refused to give any details about what had happened.*

detail² v [T] to give all the facts or information about something: *The list detailed everything we would need for our trip.*

detailed /'diːteɪld $ dɪ'teɪld/ adj including a lot of information: *a detailed account of their conversation.*

detain /dɪ'teɪn/ v [T] if the police detain someone, they keep them in a POLICE STATION and do not allow them to leave —**detainee** /,diːteɪ'niː/ n [C]

detect /dɪ'tekt/ v [T] to notice something that is not easy to see, hear etc: *Paul detected a note of disappointment in his mother's voice.* —**detectable** adj —**detection** /-'tekʃən/ n [U]

detective /dɪ'tektɪv/ n [C] a police officer whose job is to discover who is responsible for crimes → see box at **POLICE**

detector /dɪ'tektə $ -ər/ n [C] a piece of equipment that tells you if there is a particular substance somewhere: *a metal detector*

detention /dɪ'tenʃən/ n **1** [U] when someone is kept in prison **2** [C,U] a school punishment in which you have to stay at school after the other students have left

deter /dɪ'tɜː $ -'tɜːr/ v [T] **deterred**, **deterring** if something deters you from doing something, it makes you not want to do it: *The security camera was installed to deter people from stealing.*

detergent /dɪ'tɜːdʒənt $ -ɜːr-/ n [C,U] a liquid or powder that you use for washing clothes, dishes etc

deteriorate /dɪ'tɪəriəreɪt $ -'tɪr-/ v [I] to become worse: *David's health deteriorated rapidly.* —**deterioration** /dɪ,tɪəri'reɪʃən $ -,tɪr-/ n [U]

determination /dɪ,tɜːmɪ'neɪʃən $ -ɜːr-/ n [U] the desire to continue trying to do something even when it is difficult: **determination to do sth** *I admire his determination to work his way through law school.*

determine /dɪ'tɜːmɪn $ -ɜːr-/ v [T] **1** to find out the facts about something: *Experts have been unable to determine the cause of the explosion.* **2** to directly influence or affect something: *Training will determine how well you perform in a race.* **3** to officially decide something: *The date of the court case has not yet been determined.*

determined /dɪ'tɜːmɪnd $ -ɜːr-/ adj wanting to do something very much, and not letting anyone or anything stop you: **determined to do sth** *She was determined to start her own business.* | **+(that)** *I'm determined that my children have the best education possible.* | *a determined effort to stop smoking* → see box at **CHARACTER**

determiner /dɪ'tɜːmɪnə $ -'tɜːrmɪnər/ n [C] in grammar, a word you use before a noun to show which thing you mean. In the phrases 'the car' and 'some new cars', 'the' and 'some' are determiners.

deterrent /dɪ'terənt $ -'tɜːr-/ n [C] something that makes people less likely to do something: *an effective deterrent to car thieves*

detest /dɪ'test/ v [T] *formal* to hate someone or something very much: *I was going out with a boy my mother detested.* → see box at **HATE**

detonate /'detəneɪt/ v [I,T] if you detonate a bomb, or if it detonates, it explodes —**detonation** /ˌdetə'neɪʃən/ n [C,U]

detonator /'detəneɪtə $ -ər/ n [C] a piece of equipment used to make a bomb explode

detour /'diːtʊə $ -tʊr/ n [C] a way of going somewhere that takes longer than the usual way —**detour** v [I,T]

detract /dɪ'trækt/ v
detract from sth *phr v* to make something seem less good: *One small mistake isn't going to detract from your achievements.*

detractor /dɪ'træktə $ -ər/ n [C] someone who says bad things about someone or something, in order to make them seem less good than they really are: *Even the President's detractors admit that his decision was right.*

detriment /'detrɪmənt/ n **to the detriment of sth** having a harmful effect on something: *He started working longer hours, to the detriment of his health.* —**detrimental** /ˌdetrɪ'mentl◂/ adj

devalue /diː'væljuː/ v **1** [I,T] to reduce the value of a country's money **2** [T] to make someone or something seem less important or valuable: *History has tended to devalue the contributions of women.* —**devaluation** /diːˌvæljʊ'eɪʃən/ n [C,U]

devastate /'devəsteɪt/ v [T] **1** to damage something very badly: *Bombing raids devastated the city of Dresden.* **2** to make someone feel extremely shocked and sad —**devastation** /ˌdevə'steɪʃən/ n [U]

devastating /'devəsteɪtɪŋ/ adj **1** causing a lot of damage: *Chemical pollution has had a **devastating effect** on the environment.* **2** making someone feel very sad and shocked: *Losing my job was a devastating experience.*

develop /dɪ'veləp/ v
1 [I,T] if something develops, or if you develop it, it gets bigger or becomes more important: *plans to develop the local economy* | +**into** *Wright is fast developing into one of this country's most talented players.* | +**from** *The book developed from a magazine article he had written earlier.*
2 [T] to make a new product or idea over a period of time: *Scientists are developing new drugs to fight AIDS.*
3 [T] to begin to have an illness or feeling: *Her baby developed a fever during the night.* | *Women are more likely to develop depression than men.*
4 [I,T] if a problem or difficult situation develops, it begins to happen or exist, or it gets worse: *A crisis seems to be developing within the Conservative Party.* | *The plane developed engine problems and crashed.*
5 [T] to make pictures from photographic film, using special chemicals → see box at **CAMERA**
6 [T] to build houses, offices etc on a piece of land
—**developed** adj

developer /dɪ'veləpə $ -ər/ n [C] a person or company that makes money by buying land and building houses, factories etc on it

development /dɪ'veləpmənt/ n
1 [U] the process of growing, changing, or becoming better: *Vitamins are necessary for a child's growth and development.* | +**of** *the development of computer technology*
2 [C] **a)** a new event that changes a situation: *Our reporter has news of the latest developments in Moscow.* **b)** a change that makes something better: *We've seen significant developments in the treatment of breast cancer.*
3 [C,U] a group of new buildings, or the process of building them: *a new **housing development*** | *The land was sold for development.*

deviant /'diːviənt/ also **deviate** /-viɪt/ *AmE* adj *formal* different, in a bad way, from what is considered normal: *deviant behaviour* —**deviant** n [C]

deviate /'diːvieɪt/ v [I] to change and become different from what is normal or expected: +**from** *The results of the survey deviate from what we expected.* —**deviation** /ˌdiːvi'eɪʃən/ n [C,U]

device /dɪ'vaɪs/ n [C]
1 a machine or tool used for a particular purpose: *a small electronic device*
2 a special way of doing something that makes it easier to do: *a memory device*

devil /'devəl/ n
1 the Devil the most powerful evil SPIRIT in some religions, especially in Christianity
2 [C] an evil SPIRIT
3 speak of the devil also **talk of the devil** *BrE spoken* used when you suddenly see someone that you have just been talking about

devilish /'devəlɪʃ/ adj **1** very evil: *devilish schemes* **2** morally bad, but in a way that is attractive: *He looked at her with a devilish grin.* —**devilishly** adv

devil's advocate n **play/be devil's advocate** to pretend to disagree with someone in order to have a good discussion with them

devious /'diːviəs/ adj using tricks or lies to get what you want: *a devious scheme for making money* —**deviously** adv —**deviousness** n [U]

devise /dɪ'vaɪz/ v [T] to think of a new way of doing something: *He's devised a game to help kids learn English.*

devoid /dɪ'vɔɪd/ adj **devoid of sth** to have no particular quality at all: *The area is completely devoid of charm.*

devote /dɪ'vəʊt $ -'voʊt/ v [T] to use most of your time, effort etc doing something: **devote your time/effort/energy etc (to sth)** *She devoted most of her spare time to tennis.*

devoted /dɪ'vəʊtɪd $ -'voʊ-/ adj giving someone or something a lot of love and attention: *a devoted father* | +**to** *She's devoted to her cats.* → see box at **LOVE** —**devotedly** adv

devotion /dɪ'vəʊʃən $ -'voʊ-/ n [U] **1** when you love someone a lot and show this by giving them a lot of attention: +**to** *Their devotion to each other grew stronger over the years.* **2** when you give a lot of effort or loyalty to something: +**to** *a musician's devotion to his art* | *a soldier's devotion to duty* **3** strong religious feeling

devour /dɪˈvaʊə $ -ˈvaʊr/ v [T] **1** to eat something quickly: *She devoured three burgers and a pile of fries.* → see box at **EAT** **2** to read something quickly and eagerly, or watch something with great interest → see box at **READ**

devout /dɪˈvaʊt/ adj very religious: *a devout Catholic* —**devoutly** adv

dew /dju: $ du:/ n [U] small drops of water that form on the surfaces of things that are outside during the night

dexterity /dekˈsterɪti/ n [U] skill in using your hands to make or do things

diabetes /ˌdaɪəˈbiːtiːz, -tɪs/ n [U] a disease in which your body cannot control the amount of sugar in your blood —**diabetic** /-ˈbetɪk/ adj —**diabetic** n [C]

diabolical /ˌdaɪəˈbɒlɪkəl $ -ˈbɑː-/ adj **1** evil or cruel: *a diabolical killer* **2** *BrE informal* very bad: *That hotel was diabolical.*

diagnose /ˈdaɪəgnəʊz $ -noʊs/ v [T] to find out what illness a person has: **diagnose sb with sth** *She was diagnosed with breast cancer.*

diagnosis /ˌdaɪəgˈnəʊsɪs $ -ˈnoʊ-/ n [C,U] plural **diagnoses** /-siːz/ when a doctor says what illness someone has

diagnostic /ˌdaɪəgˈnɒstɪk $ -ˈnɑː-/ adj **diagnostic methods/tests etc** methods, tests etc that are used to help make a diagnosis

diagonal /daɪˈægənəl/ adj **1** a diagonal line joins two opposite corners of a square shape **2** straight and sloping: *a dress with diagonal stripes* —**diagonal** n [C] —**diagonally** adv: *Tony was sitting diagonally opposite me.*

diagram /ˈdaɪəgræm/ n [C] a drawing that uses simple lines to show what something looks like, where something is, or how something works: **+of** *a diagram of a car engine*

dial¹ /daɪəl/ n [C] **1** the round part of a clock, watch, or machine that has numbers that show you the time or a measurement **2** the part of a radio, THERMOSTAT etc that you turn to change something, such as the radio station or temperature **3** part of an older telephone that you turn to dial a number

dial² v [I,T] **dialled, dialling** *BrE*; **dialed, dialing** *AmE* to press the buttons or turn the dial on a telephone: *I must have dialled the wrong number.* → see box at **TELEPHONE**

dial

dialect /ˈdaɪəlekt/ n [C,U] a form of a language that is spoken in one part of a country: *We couldn't understand the local dialect.*

dialogue also **dialog** *AmE* /ˈdaɪəlɒg $ -lɔːg, -lɑːg/ n [C,U] **1** a conversation in a book, play, or film: *a boring film with bad dialogue* **2** a discussion between two groups or countries: **+between/with** *an opportunity for dialogue between the opposing sides*

diameter /daɪˈæmɪtə $ -ər/ n [C,U] a line from one side of a circle to the other passing through the circle's centre: **3 inches/1 meter etc in diameter** *The wheel was about two feet in diameter.*

diametrically /ˌdaɪəˈmetrɪkli/ adv **diametrically opposed** completely different and opposite

diamond /ˈdaɪəmənd/ n
1 [C,U] a very hard, clear, valuable stone, used in jewellery: *a diamond ring*
2 [C] a shape with four straight but sloping sides of equal length that stands on one of its points
3 diamonds [plural] in card games, the cards with red diamond shapes on them: *the ace of diamonds* → see picture at **PLAYING CARD**
4 [C] the field where people play **BASEBALL**

diaper /ˈdaɪəpə $ ˈdaɪpər/ n [C] *AmE* a piece of soft cloth or paper you put on a baby's bottom to hold liquid and solid waste [= **nappy** *BrE*]

diaphragm /ˈdaɪəfræm/ n [C] **1** the muscle between your lungs and your stomach that controls your breathing **2** a round rubber object that a woman uses as a CONTRACEPTIVE

diarrhoea *BrE*; **diarrhea** *AmE* /ˌdaɪəˈrɪə/ n [U] an illness in which waste from your BOWELS is very watery

diary /ˈdaɪəri $ ˈdaɪri/ n [C] plural **diaries**
1 a book in which you write down things that have happened to you: *Tony kept a daily diary* (=wrote in a diary every day). → see box at **RECORD**
2 *especially BrE* a book with spaces for each day where you can write down meetings, events etc that are planned for the day [= **calendar** *AmE*]: *I'll put that meeting in my diary.* | *I think I'm free that day, but I'll just check my diary.*

diatribe /ˈdaɪətraɪb/ n [C] *formal* a piece of writing or speech full of criticism

dice¹ /daɪs/ n [C] plural **dice** a small block with six sides and a different number of spots on each side, used in games: ***Throw the dice* to start the game.**

dice² v [T] to cut food into small square pieces: *Dice the carrots.* → see box at **CUT** → see picture at **CUT¹** —**diced** adj

dicey /ˈdaɪsi/ adj *informal* slightly dangerous: *The future looks dicey for small businesses.*

dichotomy /daɪˈkɒtəmi $ -ˈkɑː-/ n [C] plural **dichotomies** *formal* the difference between two opposite things or ideas

dictate /dɪkˈteɪt $ ˈdɪkteɪt/ v **1** [I,T] to say words for someone else to write down: **dictate sth to sb** *She dictated the letter to her secretary.* **2** [I,T] to tell someone what they must do or how they must behave: **dictate who/what/how etc** *We can't dictate how the money will be spent.* **3** [T] to influence or control something: **dictate what/how etc** *Funds dictate what we can do.*

dictation /dɪkˈteɪʃən/ n **1** [U] when you say words for someone else to write down **2** [C,U] sentences that a teacher reads out to test a student's ability to hear and write the words correctly: *French dictation*

dictator /dɪkˈteɪtə $ ˈdɪkteɪtər/ n [C] a leader who has complete power —**dictatorial** /ˌdɪktəˈtɔːriəl/ adj

dictatorship /dɪkˈteɪtəʃɪp $ -ˈteɪtər-/ n [C,U] a system in which a dictator controls a country → see box at **GOVERNMENT**

D

diction /ˈdɪkʃən/ n [U] *formal* how clearly someone pronounces words

dictionary /ˈdɪkʃənəri $ -neri/ n [C] plural **dictionaries** a book that gives a list of words in alphabetical order, with their meanings in the same or another language: *a German-English dictionary* → see box at **BOOK**

did /dɪd/ v the past tense of **DO**

didn't /ˈdɪdnt/ the short form of 'did not'

die /daɪ/ v [I] **died, dying, dies**

1 to stop living: *He died at the age of 78.* | **+of** *patients who are dying of cancer* | **+from** *She eventually died from her injuries.* | *Mary died peacefully in her sleep.* | *The bullet entered his brain and he died instantly.* → see box at **DEAD**
2 to disappear or stop existing: *Poetry will never die.*
3 be dying for sth/to do sth *spoken* to want something very much: *I'm dying to see what it is.*
4 be dying of hunger/thirst/boredom etc to be very hungry, thirsty, bored etc

die away *phr v* if something, especially a sound, dies away, it becomes weaker and stops: *The footsteps died away.* | *Her voice died away into a mumble.*

die down *phr v* to become less strong, active, or violent: *The excitement finally died down.* → see box at **FIRE**

die out *phr v* to disappear or stop existing completely: *All but three of the lake's fish species have died out.*

diehard /ˈdaɪhɑːd $ -hɑːrd/ n [C] *informal* someone who is against change and refuses to accept new ideas

diesel /ˈdiːzəl/ n [U] a type of oil used in the engines of some vehicles

diet¹ /ˈdaɪət/ n

1 [C,U] the kind of food that you eat each day: **balanced/healthy/poor etc diet** *It is important to eat a healthy diet.* | **+of** *The animals live on a diet of fruit and insects.*
2 [C] a limited amount and range of food that you eat to become thinner or for your health: *a salt-free diet* | **be/go on a diet** *Lynn is always on a diet* (=trying to get thinner). → see box at **EAT**

diet² v [I] to eat less in order to become thinner: *Try to exercise when dieting.* → see box at **EAT**

diet³ adj [only before noun] diet drinks or foods contain less sugar or fat than ordinary ones

dietary /ˈdaɪətəri $ -teri/ adj related to the food someone eats

differ /ˈdɪfə $ -ər/ v [I] **1** to be different: **+from** *The new system differs from the old in important ways.* **2** to have different opinions: *We differ on this matter.*

difference /ˈdɪfərəns/ n

1 [C] the way in which one person or thing is different from another [≠ similarity]: **+between** *The main difference between them is their age.* | **+in** *Researchers found important differences in the way boys and girls learn.*
2 [singular] an amount by which one thing is different from another: **difference in age/size etc** *There's not much difference in price.* | *There's a 5-hour time difference between London and New York.*
3 make a/the difference to have an important effect or influence on someone or something:

+to *The programme made a big difference to my life.* | *Having a good teacher made all the difference to Alex.*
4 it makes no difference to sb used to say that it does not matter to someone which thing happens, is chosen etc: *Morning or afternoon. It makes no difference to me.*
5 our/your/their differences disagreements: *We're friends now but we've had our differences in the past.*
6 difference of opinion a slight disagreement

different /ˈdɪfərənt/ adj

1 not like something or someone else [≠ similar]: **+from** *Our sons are very different from each other.* | **+to** *Her jacket is completely different to mine.* | **+than** *AmE: He seemed different than he did in New York.* | *a slightly different way of doing things*
2 [only before noun] used to talk about two or more separate things: *I went to three different shops.* | *We can approach this problem in several different ways.* | **different types/kinds etc** *There are many different types of fabric.*
—**differently** adv

GRAMMAR

different from, different than, different to

You can use **different from** in both British and American English, but you can only use **different than** in American English.
In British English, some people also use **different to**, but many teachers think that this use is wrong.

differential /ˌdɪfəˈrenʃəl/ n [C] *formal* a difference between things: **wage/pay differentials**

differentiate /ˌdɪfəˈrenʃieɪt/ v [I,T] to recognize or express the difference between things or people: **+between** *It's important to differentiate between fact and opinion.*

difficult /ˈdɪfɪkəlt/ adj

1 hard to do, understand, or deal with [≠ easy]: *a difficult question* | **it is difficult to do sth** *It is difficult to see how we can save money.* | **it is difficult for sb to do sth** *It is difficult for me to travel now.* | *He's finding it difficult to get a job.*
2 involving problems or causing trouble or worry: *a difficult situation*
3 someone who is difficult never seems pleased or satisfied: *a difficult customer*

difficulty /ˈdɪfɪkəlti/ n plural **difficulties**

1 [U] when something is not easy to do: **have difficulty (in) doing sth** *Did you have difficulty finding the house?* | **with/without difficulty** *She stood up with difficulty.*
2 [U] a situation in which you have problems: *the country's severe economic difficulties* | **in difficulty** *Many families are in financial difficulty.*
3 [C] a problem: *We've had a few difficulties recently.* | **get/run into difficulties** *The boat ran into difficulties in rough seas.*

diffident /ˈdɪfədənt/ adj not behaving in a confident way

diffuse /dɪˈfjuːz/ v [I,T] to spread over a large area, or to make something spread over a large area: *These ideas diffused quickly across Europe.*

dig¹ /dɪg/ v past tense and past participle **dug** /dʌg/ present participle **digging**

1 [I,T] to move earth, snow etc so that you make a hole in the ground, especially using a tool such as a SPADE: *We'll have to **dig** a large **hole**.* | **dig sb/sth out of sth** *Two survivors were dug out of the rubble.* | **+down** *Dig down about 6 inches.* | **+for** *digging for treasure*

2 dig your heels in to refuse to do something that other people are trying to make you do

dig in also **dig (sth) into sth** *phr v* to push a hard or pointed object into something, or to press into something, often causing pain: **dig sth ⇔ in** *The cat dug its claws in.*

dig sth ⇔ up *phr v* **1** to take something out of the ground, using a tool: *Make sure that you dig up all the roots.* **2** to make holes in an area of ground or road: *It costs millions to dig up the streets and install cables.* **3** to find hidden or forgotten information by searching carefully: *Newspapers began to **dig up the dirt** (=find embarrassing information) on the President.*

dig² *n* [C] **1** *informal* an unkind thing that you say about someone in order to criticize them: *He's always **having a dig at** me about my weight.* **2** a quick hard push, using your finger or a sharp object: *a dig in the ribs* **3** the process or a place where people dig into the ground to find ancient objects to study: *an archaeological dig*

digest /daɪˈdʒest, dɔ̆-/ *v* [T] **1** when you digest food, your stomach changes it into a form that your body can use: *Babies can't digest the food that adults eat.* **2** to understand new or difficult information after thinking about it: *It took us a while to digest the news.* —**digestible** *adj*

digestion /daɪˈdʒestʃən, dɔ̆-/ *n* [C,U] the process of digesting food —**digestive** /-tɪv/ *adj*: *your digestive system*

digicam /ˈdɪdʒɪkæm/ *n* [C] a type of camera that takes pictures that can be stored on a computer rather than on film

digit /ˈdɪdʒɪ̆t/ *n* [C] a single number from 0 to 9: **three-digit/four-digit etc number** *Choose a four-digit number such as 3709.*

digital /ˈdɪdʒɪ̆tl/ *adj*

1 digital equipment, such as cameras or televisions, uses a system in which pictures and sound are recorded, stored, or sent out in the form of numbers: **digital TV/television/radio** → see box at CAMERA

2 showing information in a series of numbers: *a digital clock*

dignified /ˈdɪɡnɪ̆faɪd/ *adj* behaving in a calm and serious way that makes other people respect you: *a dignified leader*

dignitary /ˈdɪɡnɪ̆təri $ -teri/ *n* [C] plural **dignitaries** someone with an important official position

dignity /ˈdɪɡnɪ̆ti/ *n* [U] **1** the ability to behave in a calm serious way, even in difficult situations: **with dignity** *She spoke with courage and dignity.* | *He struggled to **maintain** his **dignity**.* **2** the quality of being serious and formal: *the dignity of the presidency*

digress /daɪˈɡres/ *v* [I] *formal* to begin to talk or write about something that is not related to what you were saying before —**digression** /daɪˈɡreʃən/ *n* [C,U]

dike /daɪk/ *n* [C] another spelling of DYKE

dilapidated /dɪˈlæpɪ̆deɪtɪ̆d/ *adj* a dilapidated building, vehicle, or piece of furniture is old and in bad condition

dilate /daɪˈleɪt/ *v* [I,T] if the PUPILS of your eyes dilate, they open and become wider: *dilated pupils*

dilemma /dɪˈlemə, daɪ-/ *n* [C] a situation in which you must make a difficult choice between two things: **in a dilemma** *He now finds himself in a terrible dilemma.* | *The president **faces a dilemma** about accepting these gifts.* | *a **moral dilemma***

diligent /ˈdɪlɪ̆dʒənt/ *adj formal* someone who is diligent works very hard and carefully: *a diligent student* —**diligently** *adv* —**diligence** *n* [U]

dilute /daɪˈluːt $ dɪˈluːt, daɪ-/ *v* [T] to make a liquid weaker by adding another liquid to it: *diluted fruit juice* —**dilute** /ˌdaɪˈluːt◂/ *adj*

dim¹ /dɪm/ *adj* **1** not bright, clear, or easy to see: *the dim light of a winter evening* **2** a dim memory is not very clear in your mind: *I had only a **dim memory** of my grandparents.* **3 take a dim view of sth** to strongly disapprove of something **4** *informal* stupid: *She can be a bit dim.* —**dimly** *adv*

dim² *v* [I,T] **dimmed, dimming** if a light dims, or if you dim it, it becomes less bright

dime /daɪm/ *n* [C] a coin worth 10 CENTS

dimension /daɪˈmenʃən, dɔ̆-/ *n* **1** [C] a particular part of a situation that affects the way you think about it: **+of** *the spiritual dimension of life* | **new/different/another dimension** *The baby has **added** a new **dimension to** their life.* **2 dimensions** [plural] the size of something measured by its length, width, and height: **+of** *What are the dimensions of the room?*

diminish /dɔ̆ˈmɪnɪʃ/ *v* [I,T] to become smaller or less important: *The country's political influence has diminished recently.*

diminutive /dɔ̆ˈmɪnjɵ̆tɪv/ *adj formal* very small: *a diminutive old lady*

dimple /ˈdɪmpəl/ *n* [C] a small hollow place on your cheek or chin that appears when you smile —**dimpled** *adj*

din /dɪn/ *n* [singular] a loud unpleasant noise that continues for a long time: *Her kids were **making** such a **din** upstairs!*

dine

dine

have a snack

dine /daɪn/ *v* [I] *formal* to eat a meal, especially in the evening: *He's dining with friends at the Ritz.*

dine out *phr v formal* to eat in a restaurant

diner /'daɪnə $ -ər/ n [C] **1** *especially AmE* a restaurant that serves cheap food → see box at **RESTAURANT** **2** someone who is eating in a restaurant

dinghy /'dɪŋgi, 'dɪŋi/ n [C] plural **dinghies** a small open boat: *a rubber dinghy* | *sailing dinghies*

dingy /'dɪndʒi/ adj a dingy place is dirty, dark, and unpleasant: *a dark, dingy office*

'dining room n [C] a room where you eat your meals in a house or hotel

dinner /'dɪnə $ -ər/ n
1 [C,U] the main meal of the day, which most people eat in the evening: *What's for dinner?* | *What time do you usually have dinner?* | *Let's go out for dinner* (=eat at a restaurant). | **Christmas/Thanksgiving dinner** | *a dinner party*
2 [C] a formal occasion in the evening when a large group of people eat a meal to celebrate something
→ **TV DINNER**

'dinner ˌjacket n [C] *BrE* a black or white jacket that men wear for formal occasions; [= **tuxedo** *AmE*]

dinosaur /'daɪnəsɔː $ -sɔːr/ n [C] a large animal that lived about 200 million years ago and is now **EXTINCT** (=no longer exists)

diocese /'daɪəsɪs/ n [C] the area that a **BISHOP** is in charge of

dip¹ /dɪp/ v **dipped**, **dipping** **1** [T] to put something into a liquid for a short time and lift it out again: **dip sth in/into sth** *Janet dipped her feet into the water.* | *strawberries dipped in chocolate* **2** [I] to go down to a lower level: *The sun dipped below the horizon.* | *Share prices have dipped sharply* (=quickly).
dip into sth *phr v* to use part of an amount of money: *Medical bills forced her to dip into her savings.*

dip² n **1** [C] a drop in the level or amount of something: **+in** *a dip in temperature* **2** [C] *informal* a quick swim: *She went for a dip in the pool.* **3** [C] a place where the surface of something goes down suddenly: **+in** *a dip in the road* **4** [C,U] a thick **SAUCE** that you dip food into before you eat it: *a sour cream dip*

diploma /dɪ'pləʊmə $ -'ploʊ-/ n [C] an official document that you are given when you have successfully finished a course of study: *a teaching diploma* | **+in** *a diploma in nursing* → see box at **QUALIFICATION**

diplomacy /dɪ'pləʊməsi $ -'ploʊ-/ n [U] **1** the job or skill of keeping the relationships between countries friendly: *international diplomacy* **2** the skill of dealing with people without upsetting them: *The situation demands tact and diplomacy.*

diplomat /'dɪpləmæt/ n [C] someone who officially represents their government in a foreign country

diplomatic /ˌdɪplə'mætɪk◂/ adj **1** relating to the relationships between countries: *The U.S. wants to establish diplomatic relations with China.* **2** good at dealing with people without upsetting them: *She's usually very diplomatic.*
—**diplomatically** /-kli/ adv

dire /daɪə $ daɪr/ adj very serious or bad: *It will have dire consequences for the stock market.* | *The farming industry is in dire straits* (=in a very difficult situation).

direct¹ /dɪ'rekt, daɪ'rekt◂/ adj
1 without other places, people, or processes coming between [≠ **indirect**]: *a direct flight to Egypt* | *staff who work in direct contact with the public* | *Keep medicines out of direct sunlight.* | *The building took a direct hit* (=was hit by a bomb). | **direct result/consequence** *10 people die every day as a direct result of smoking.* | *There's a direct link between poverty and crime.*
2 exact, without any changes: *a direct quote from the President*
3 saying exactly what you mean [≠ **indirect**]: *Can I ask you a direct question?*
—**directness** n [U]

direct² v
1 [T] to aim something at a particular person: **direct sth at/towards sb/sth** *His anger is mainly directed at his father.*
2 [I,T] to control the way a play, film, or television programme is made by telling the actors what they should do
3 [T] to tell someone how to get to a place: **direct sb to sth** *Can you direct me to the airport?*
4 [T] to control and organize something: *a police officer directing traffic*

direct³ adv
1 without stopping or changing direction: *You can fly direct from London to Nashville.*
2 without dealing with anyone else first: *Contact the bank direct.*

di,rect 'debit n [C] an instruction that you give to your bank to pay money regularly from your bank account to a particular person or organization: **by direct debit** *You can pay your bill by direct debit.*

direction /dɪ'rekʃən, daɪ-/ n
1 [C] the place or point that you are moving, facing, or pointing towards: *We met Jim coming in the opposite direction.* | **in a direction** *Jill pointed in my direction.* | *We walked in the direction of the hotel.* | **from a direction** *We heard a scream from the direction of the pool.* | *People were running in all directions.* | **right/wrong direction** *Are we going in the right direction?* | *Maurice changed direction and went back towards town.*
2 directions [plural] instructions about how to reach a place or do something: *Could you give me directions to the bus station?* | *Always read the directions before using weedkiller.*
3 [C] the general way that something develops: *Our lives have gone in very different directions.* | *This is a new direction for the company.* | *The law is a step in the right direction* (=a good development).
4 [U] the act of managing an organization and telling people what to do: **under sb's direction** *The company has expanded under his direction.*
5 [U] a purpose or aim: *I feel that there is a lack of direction in my life.*
6 sense of direction the ability to know which way to go: *Bill's always getting lost – he has no sense of direction.*

directive /dɪ'rektɪv, daɪ-/ n [C] an official order to do something: **+on** *the EU directive on maternity leave*

directly /dɪ'rektli, daɪ-/ adv
1 with no other person, process etc between: *You can order the book directly from the publisher.* | *Are you **directly involved** in planning the event?*
2 **directly opposite/in front/behind etc** exactly in a particular position: *Lucas sat directly behind us.*
3 done in a clear way that shows what you honestly feel: *He didn't **answer** my question directly.*

,direct 'object n [C] in grammar, the person or thing that is affected by the action of a TRANSITIVE verb, for example 'Mary' in the sentence 'I saw Mary' [➙ **indirect object**]

director /dɪ'rektə, daɪ- $ -ər/ n [C]
1 someone who controls or manages an organization or company: *the new marketing director* | **+of** *a director of the company* | *The company is run by a **board of directors** (=a group of directors).*
2 someone who is in charge of making a film, play, or television programme and who tells the actors etc what to do: *a famous **movie director*** | **+of** *the director of the 'Star Wars' films* → see box at **FILM, MANAGING DIRECTOR**

directory /daɪ'rektəri, dɪ-/ n [C] plural **directories** **1** a book or list of names, facts etc, arranged in alphabetical order: *the telephone directory* **2** a place on a computer where FILES or programs are kept

di,rect 'speech n [U] a way of reporting what someone says in which you say or write their actual words, as in ' 'I don't want to go,' said Julie' [➙ **indirect speech**]

dirt /dɜːt $ dɜːrt/ n [U]
1 a substance such as dust or mud that makes things dirty: *His hands were **covered in dirt**.*
2 earth or soil: *He left them lying in the dirt.* | **dirt track/road** (=one with a surface of soil and small stones)
3 *informal* secret information about someone's life, that would harm them if other people knew about it: **+on** *The papers were trying to **dig up the dirt** (=find harmful information) on the President.*

dirty¹ /'dɜːti $ 'dɜːr-/ adj
1 not clean: *dirty dishes* | *How did you get so dirty?*

2 relating to sex in a way that might offend people: *dirty jokes* | *He's got a **dirty mind** (=thinks about sex a lot).*
3 unfair or dishonest: *That was a **dirty trick**.*
4 **do sb's dirty work** to do an unpleasant or dishonest job for someone: *I told them to do their own dirty work.*

dirty² v [T] **dirtied, dirtying, dirties** to make something dirty

dis- /dɪs/ prefix **1** not: *a disrespectful remark* | *He acted dishonestly.* **2** used to talk about removing or stopping something: *Disconnect the plug.* | *Disinfect the wound.*

disability /ˌdɪsə'bɪləti/ n [C,U] plural **disabilities** a permanent illness or injury that makes it difficult for someone to do ordinary things such as seeing, walking etc: *wheelchair access for people with physical disabilities* | *Her child has a learning disability.*

disabled /dɪs'eɪbəld/ adj
1 someone who is disabled cannot use a part of their body properly: *a **severely disabled** patient* | ***mentally disabled** people*
2 **the disabled** people who are disabled

disadvantage /ˌdɪsəd'vɑːntɪdʒ $ -'væn-/ n [C,U] something that makes things more difficult to do or less pleasant for you: **+of** *the disadvantages of living in a city* | **be at a disadvantage** *Disabled people are at a disadvantage in the job market.*

disadvantaged /ˌdɪsəd'vɑːntɪdʒd $ -'væn-/ adj someone who is disadvantaged is poor and does not have a good education, good health etc: *disadvantaged kids from the inner cities*

disaffected /ˌdɪsə'fektɪd/ adj people who are disaffected are no longer happy with their lives or their government: *disaffected voters*

disagree /ˌdɪsə'griː/ v [I]
1 to have a different opinion from someone else [≠ **agree**]: **+with** *My boss doesn't like people disagreeing with her.* | **+about/on/over** *We disagree about most things.*
2 to be different: *The statements of the two witnesses disagree.*

disagreeable /ˌdɪsə'griːəbəl/ adj formal
1 unpleasant: *a disagreeable smell* **2** unfriendly and bad-tempered: *a rude, disagreeable woman*
—**disagreeably** adv

disagreement /ˌdɪsə'griːmənt/ n [C,U] when people express different opinions about something and sometimes argue: **+over/about/on** *There is some disagreement over the price.* | *He and his brother **had a disagreement** over money.* | **+between/among** *a disagreement between the two countries*

disallow /ˌdɪsə'laʊ/ v [T] to officially refuse to allow something, because a rule has been broken: *Their first goal was disallowed.*

disappear /ˌdɪsə'pɪə $ -'pɪr/ v [I]
1 if something disappears, you can no longer see it: *My keys have disappeared.* | *The sun briefly disappeared behind a cloud.* | **+from** *Some books have disappeared from the library.*
2 to stop existing: *The rain forests may disappear forever.*
—**disappearance** n [C,U] *Police are investigating the woman's disappearance.*

disappoint /ˌdɪsə'pɔɪnt/ v [T] to make someone unhappy because something they hoped for did not happen: *I'm sorry to disappoint you, but we can't go.*
—**disappointing** adj: *His exam results were very disappointing.*

disappointed /ˌdɪsə'pɔɪntɪd/ adj unhappy because something you hoped for did not happen, or was not as good as you expected: *disappointed customers* | **+at/with/about** *Jake seems bitterly disappointed* (=very disappointed) *with the result.* | **+in** *I'm very disappointed in you, Mark.* | **+that** *He was disappointed that Kerry couldn't come.* | **disappointed to hear/find/see etc sth** *I was very disappointed to hear you'd failed your test.*

disappointment /ˌdɪsə'pɔɪntmənt/ *n*
1 [U] a feeling of unhappiness because something is not as good as you expected, or has not happened in the way you hoped: **+at/about/over** *The family expressed their disappointment at the court's decision.* | *She tried to hide her disappointment.*
2 [C] someone or something that is not as good as you hoped or expected: *The party was a bit of a disappointment.*

disapprove /ˌdɪsə'pruːv/ *v* [I] to think that someone or something is bad or wrong: **+of** *Her parents strongly disapprove of her lifestyle.*
—**disapproving** *adj*: *She gave me a disapproving look.* —**disapproval** *n* [U]

disarm /dɪs'ɑːm $ -'ɑːrm/ *v* **1** [I] if a country disarms, it reduces the number of weapons and soldiers it has: *Both sides must disarm before the peace talks can begin.* **2** [T] to take away someone's weapons: *Police managed to disarm the gunman.* **3** [T] to make someone feel less angry and more friendly: *His tact and political skills disarmed his critics.* —**disarming** *adj*: *a disarming smile*

disarmament /dɪs'ɑːməmənt $ -'ɑːr-/ *n* [U] when a country reduces the number of soldiers and weapons it has: *nuclear disarmament*

disarray /ˌdɪsə'reɪ/ *n* [U] **be in disarray** to be very untidy, disorganized, or confused: *Her hair was in disarray.*

disassociate /ˌdɪsə'səʊʃieɪt, -sieɪt $ -'soʊ-/ *v* another form of DISSOCIATE

disaster /dɪ'zɑːstə $ dɪ'zæstər/ *n* [C,U]
1 an event such as an accident, flood, or storm that causes a lot of harm or suffering: *an air disaster in which 329 people died* | **ecological/environmental/natural etc disaster** *The drought was the worst natural disaster this century.* | *the Chernobyl nuclear disaster* | *The country is on the edge of economic disaster.* | **+for** *The flood could spell disaster for wildlife* (=cause a lot of harm in the future). → see box at ACCIDENT
2 something that is a complete failure: *Our Christmas party was a complete disaster.*

disastrous /dɪ'zɑːstrəs $ dɪ'zæ-/ *adj* very bad, or ending in failure: **disastrous consequences/results/effects** *Climate change could have disastrous effects on Earth.*

disband /dɪs'bænd/ *v* [I,T] *formal* to stop existing as an organization, or to make something do this

disbelief /ˌdɪsbɪ'liːf/ *n* [U] a feeling that you do not believe something: **in disbelief** *I looked at him in disbelief.* —**disbelieve** *v* [T] *I see no reason to disbelieve him.*

disc, disk /dɪsk/ *n* [C] **1** a round flat shape or object: *a revolving metal disc* **2** a record or CD **3** a computer DISK **4** a flat piece of soft bone between the bones in your back

discard /dɪs'kɑːd $ -ɑːrd/ *v* [T] *formal* to throw something away: *Discard any old cleaning materials.* | *discarded paper*

discern /dɪ'sɜːn $ -ɜːrn/ *v* [T] *formal* to see, notice, or understand something: *I could just discern the outline of the bridge in the fog.* —**discernible** *adj*

discerning /dɪ'sɜːnɪŋ $ -ɜːr-/ *adj* able to make good judgments, especially about art, style etc: *a superb hotel for the discerning traveller* —**discernment** *n* [U]

discharge /dɪs'tʃɑːdʒ $ -ɑːr-/ *v* [T] **1** to officially allow someone to leave a place: **discharge sb from sth** *Blanton was discharged from hospital last night.* **2** to send out gas, liquid, smoke etc: *Sewage is discharged directly into the sea.* **3** *formal* to perform a duty or promise: *The trustees failed to discharge their duties properly.* —**discharge** /'dɪstʃɑːdʒ $ -tʃɑːrdʒ/ *n* [U] *his discharge from the army*

disciple /dɪ'saɪpəl/ *n* [C] someone who believes in the ideas of a great teacher or leader, especially a religious one

disciplinarian /ˌdɪsɪplɪ'neəriən $ -'ner-/ *n* [C] someone who makes people obey strict rules: *Dad was always the disciplinarian in the family.*

discipline¹ /'dɪsɪplɪn/ *n*
1 [U] a way of training someone so that they learn to control their behaviour and obey rules: *The school has very high standards of discipline.* | *serious discipline problems in the police force*
2 [U] a way of training your mind or body, or of learning to control your behaviour: *It took him a lot of hard work and discipline to make the Olympic team.*
3 [C] a particular subject of study
→ SELF-DISCIPLINE

discipline² *v* [T] **1** to teach someone to obey rules and control their own behaviour: *Some parents are not very good at disciplining their children.* **2** to punish someone who has disobeyed an organization's rules —**disciplinary** /'dɪsɪplɪnəri, ˌdɪsɪ'plɪ- $ 'dɪsɪplɪneri/ *adj* [only before noun]

disciplined /'dɪsɪplɪnd/ *adj* a disciplined person obeys rules and controls their behaviour: *a disciplined, well-trained army*

'disc jockey *n* [C] a DJ

disclaim /dɪs'kleɪm/ *v* [T] *formal* to say that you are not responsible for something or do not know anything about it

disclaimer /dɪs'kleɪmə $ -ər/ *n* [C] a statement saying that you are not responsible for something, or that you do not know about it

disclose /dɪs'kləʊz $ -'kloʊz/ *v* [T] to make something publicly known, especially after it has been kept secret: *The newspaper refused to disclose where their information came from.* —**disclosure** *n* [C,U] *the disclosure of private medical information*

disco /'dɪskəʊ $ -koʊ/ *n* [C] plural **discos** a place or event where people dance to popular music

discolour *BrE*; **discolor** *AmE* /dɪs'kʌlə $ -ər/ *v* [I,T] to change colour, or to make something change colour, so that it looks unattractive

discomfort /dɪs'kʌmfət $ -ərt/ *n* **1** [U] slight pain, or a feeling of being physically uncomfortable: *Your injury isn't serious, but it may cause* some *discomfort.* **2** [C] something that makes you uncomfortable: *the discomforts of long-distance travel*

disconcerting /ˌdɪskən'sɜːtɪŋ◂ $ -ɜːr-/ *adj* making you feel slightly confused, embarrassed, or worried: *a disconcerting question* —**disconcerted** *adj*

disconnect /ˌdɪskə'nekt/ *v* [T] **1** to remove the supply of power, gas, water etc from a machine or piece of equipment: *Always disconnect the machine from the mains first.* **2** to separate two things that are connected

discontented /ˌdɪskən'tentɪd◂/ *adj* unhappy or not satisfied: +**with** *After two years, I became discontented with my job.* —**discontent** *n* [U]

discontinue /ˌdɪskən'tɪnjuː/ *v* [T] to stop doing something

discord /'dɪskɔːd $ -ɔːrd/ *n* [U] *formal* disagreement between people: *marital discord*

discount[1] /'dɪskaʊnt/ *n* [C] a reduction in the usual price of something: *Members **get a** 10% **discount.*** | **at a discount** *Employees can buy books at a discount.* —**discount** /dɪs'kaʊnt $ 'dɪskaʊnt/ *v* [T]

discount[2] /dɪs'kaʊnt $ 'dɪskaʊnt/ *v* [T] to consider something unlikely to be true or important: *Larry tends to discount any suggestion I ever make.*

discourage /dɪs'kʌrɪdʒ $ -'kɜːr-/ *v* [T]

1 to persuade someone not to do something [≠ **encourage**]: *attempts to discourage illegal immigration* | **discourage sb from doing sth** *They're trying to discourage staff from smoking at work.*

2 to make someone less confident or less willing to do something [≠ **encourage**]: *Don't let one failure discourage you.* —**discouragement** *n* [C,U]

discouraged /dɪs'kʌrɪdʒd $ -'kɜːr-/ *adj* no longer having the confidence you need to continue doing something: *Some players **get discouraged** and quit.* —**discouraging** *adj*

discourse /'dɪskɔːs $ -ɔːrs/ *n* [C,U] *formal* a serious talk, piece of writing, or discussion

discourteous /dɪs'kɜːtiəs $ -ɜːr-/ *adj formal* not polite

discover /dɪs'kʌvə $ -ər/ *v* [T]

1 to find someone or something, either by accident or because you were looking for them: *The body was discovered in a field.*

2 to learn something that you did not know about before: +**who/what/how etc** *Did you ever discover who sent you the flowers?* | +**(that)** *She discovered that she was pregnant.*

3 if someone discovers a new place, fact, substance etc, they are the first person to find it or know that it exists: *The Curies are best known for discovering radium.* —**discoverer** *n* [C]

discovery /dɪs'kʌvəri/ *n plural* **discoveries**

1 [C] a fact or piece of knowledge that someone learns about, when it was not known before: *Astronomers have **made** significant **discoveries** about our galaxy.* | +**that** *the discovery that bees can communicate with each other*

2 [U] when someone discovers something: +**of** *the discovery of oil in Alaska*

discredit /dɪs'kredɪt/ *v* [T] to make people stop trusting or respecting someone or something: *The defense lawyer will try to discredit our witnesses.*

discreet /dɪ'skriːt/ *adj* careful about what you say or do so that you do not upset or embarrass people: *Can you please be discreet about this?* —**discreetly** *adv*

discrepancy /dɪ'skrepənsi/ *n* [C,U] *plural* **discrepancies** a difference between two things that should be the same: +**between** *Police found discrepancies between the two men's statements.*

discretion /dɪ'skreʃən/ *n* [U] **1** if someone uses their discretion, they make a decision about exactly what should be done in a particular situation: *Promotions are left to the discretion of the manager.* | **at sb's discretion** *Tipping is entirely at the customer's discretion.* **2** when you are careful about what you say or do, so that you do not upset or embarrass people: *This situation must be handled with discretion.*

discretionary /dɪ'skreʃənəri $ -neri/ *adj* relating to or based on a decision by someone in a position of authority: **discretionary award/ grant etc**

discriminate /dɪ'skrɪmɪneɪt/ *v* [I] **1** to treat one person or group differently from another in an unfair way: +**against** *Under federal law, it is illegal to discriminate against women.* **2** to recognize a difference between two things

discriminating /dɪ'skrɪmɪneɪtɪŋ/ *adj* able to judge what is of good quality and what is not: *a book that will appeal to discriminating readers*

discrimination /dɪˌskrɪmɪ'neɪʃən/ *n* [U]

1 when one group of people is treated unfairly: +**against** *widespread discrimination against older people in the job market* | **racial/sex/ religious etc discrimination** *a victim of racial discrimination*

2 the ability to recognize the difference between two or more things: *children's shape discrimination*

discriminatory /dɪ'skrɪmɪnətəri $ -tɔːri/ *adj* *formal* treating one person or group differently from another in an unfair way

discus /'dɪskəs/ *n* [C] a heavy flat circular object which people throw as far as possible as a sport: *He came first in **the discus** (=the sport of throwing a discus).*

discuss /dɪ'skʌs/ *v* [T] to talk about something with someone in order to exchange ideas or decide something: *We're meeting today to discuss our science project.* | *If you would like to discuss the matter further, please call me.* | **discuss sth with sb** *I'd like to discuss this with my father first.* | +**what/who/where etc** *We are discussing how to deal with the situation.* → see box at **TALK**

discussion /dɪ'skʌʃən/ *n* [C,U] when people discuss something: +**about/on** *In class we **had a discussion** about global warming.* | +**of** *the discussion of important issues* | **under discussion** (=being discussed) *The project is under discussion.*

disdain /dɪs'deɪn/ *n* [U] *formal* a lack of respect for someone or something, because you think they are not important or good enough: +**for** *his disdain for manual labour* —**disdainful** *adj*: *He gave me a disdainful look.*

D

disease /dɪ'ziːz/ n [C,U] an illness which affects a person, animal, or plant: *heart disease* | *She suffers from a rare disease of the blood.* | *vaccinations against infectious diseases such as measles*

THESAURUS

Illness is usually used to describe the general condition of being ill: *She missed two weeks' work because of illness.*
A **disease** is a particular type of illness which often has a name: *childhood diseases such as measles and chickenpox*

—**diseased** adj

disembark /ˌdɪsɪm'bɑːk $ -ɑːrk/ v [I] to get off a ship or plane —**disembarkation** /ˌdɪsembɑː'keɪʃən $ -bɑːr-/ n [U]

disembodied /ˌdɪsɪm'bɒdid◂ $ -'bɑː-/ adj a disembodied sound or voice comes from someone who cannot be seen

disenchanted /ˌdɪsɪn'tʃɑːntɪd $ -'tʃænt-/ adj disappointed with someone or something, and no longer believing that they are good: +**with** *Anne was becoming disenchanted with her marriage.* —**disenchantment** n [U]

disengage /ˌdɪsɪn'geɪdʒ/ v [I,T] to separate two things that were connected: *Disengage the gears when you park the car.*

disentangle /ˌdɪsɪn'tæŋɡəl/ v [T] **1 disentangle yourself (from sb/sth)** to escape from a difficult situation that you are involved in **2** to untie ropes, strings etc that have become twisted or tied together

disfigure /dɪs'fɪɡə $ -'fɪɡjər/ v [T] to spoil someone's appearance: *His face was badly disfigured in the accident.* —**disfigurement** n [C,U]

disgrace /dɪs'ɡreɪs/ n **1 be a disgrace** to be very bad and unacceptable: *The UK rail system is a national disgrace.* | +**to** *Doctors like you are a disgrace to the medical profession.* **2** [U] when someone loses other people's respect because they have done something that other people strongly disapprove of: **in disgrace** *Harry left the school in disgrace.* —**disgrace** v [T] *How could you disgrace us all like that?*

disgraceful /dɪs'ɡreɪsfəl/ adj very bad: *Your behaviour has been disgraceful!* —**disgracefully** adv

disgruntled /dɪs'ɡrʌntld/ adj annoyed, disappointed, and not satisfied: *disgruntled employees*

disguise¹ /dɪs'ɡaɪz/ v [T] **1** to change your appearance or voice so that people will not recognize you: **disguise yourself as sb/sth** *She disguised herself as a man.* **2** to hide a fact or feeling so that people will not notice it: *Dan couldn't disguise his feelings for Katie.*

disguise² n [C,U] things that you wear to change your appearance and hide who you really are: *The glasses were part of his disguise.* | **in disguise** *The woman turned out to be a police officer in disguise.*

disgust¹ /dɪs'ɡʌst, dɪz-/ n [U] a strong feeling of dislike, annoyance, or disapproval: **with disgust** *Everybody looked at me with disgust.* | **in disgust** *We left in disgust.*

disgust² v [T] to make someone feel very annoyed or upset about something that is not

acceptable: *Pornography shocks and disgusts decent people.*
—**disgusted** adj: *We felt disgusted by the way we'd been treated.*

disgusting /dɪs'ɡʌstɪŋ, dɪz-/ adj **1** shocking and unacceptable: *The way he treats her is disgusting.* **2** extremely unpleasant and making you feel sick: *a disgusting smell* | *Smoking is a disgusting habit.* → see box at **HORRIBLE** → and **TASTE**
—**disgustingly** adv: *They're disgustingly rich.*

dish¹ /dɪʃ/ n [C] **1** a round container with low sides, used for holding food [↪ **bowl**]: *a serving dish* | +**of** *a large dish of spaghetti* **2** food cooked or prepared in a particular way: *a wonderful pasta dish* | *You can serve this soup as a **main dish** (=the biggest part of a meal).* **3 dishes** [plural] all the plates, cups, bowls etc that are used during a meal: **do/wash the dishes** *Who's going to do the dishes?*
→ **SATELLITE DISH**

dish² v
dish sth ⇔ out phr v informal to give something to people: *He's always dishing out unwanted advice.*

disheartened /dɪs'hɑːtnd $ -ɑːr-/ adj disappointed because you do not think you will be able to achieve something

disheartening /dɪs'hɑːtnɪŋ $ -ɑːr-/ adj making you lose hope and confidence: *It was disheartening to see how little had been done.*

dishevelled BrE; **disheveled** AmE /dɪ'ʃevəld/ adj having very untidy clothes and hair: *She looked tired and dishevelled.*

dishonest /dɪs'ɒnɪst $ -'ɑː-/ adj likely to lie, steal, or cheat [≠ **honest**]: *a dishonest politician* | *He's lazy and dishonest.*
—**dishonesty** n [U] —**dishonestly** adv

dishonour BrE; **dishonor** AmE /dɪs'ɒnə $ -'ɑːnər/ n [U] formal when people no longer respect you or approve of you because you have done something dishonest or immoral: *His behaviour brought dishonour on the family.*
—**dishonour** v [T] —**dishonourable** adj —**dishonourably** adv

dishtowel /'dɪʃˌtaʊəl/ n [C] AmE a cloth used for drying dishes [= **tea towel** BrE]

dishwasher /'dɪʃˌwɒʃə $ -ˌwɒːʃər, -ˌwɑː-/ n [C] a machine that washes dishes → see picture at **KITCHEN**

disillusion /ˌdɪsɪ'luːʒən/ v [T] to make someone realize that something they thought was true or good is not: *I hate to disillusion you, but she's never coming back.* —**disillusionment** n [U]

disillusioned /ˌdɪsɪ'luːʒənd◂/ adj unhappy because you have lost your belief that someone or something is true or good

disincentive /ˌdɪsɪn'sentɪv/ n [C] something that makes people less willing to do something: *High interest rates can be a disincentive to expanding a business.*

disinfect /ˌdɪsɪn'fekt/ v [T] to clean something with a chemical that destroys BACTERIA —**disinfection** /-'fekʃən/ n [U]

disinfectant /ˌdɪsɪn'fektənt/ n [C,U] a chemical that destroys BACTERIA

disinherit /ˌdɪsɪnˈherɪt/ v [T] to prevent someone from receiving any of your money or property after your death

disintegrate /dɪsˈɪntɪɡreɪt/ v [I] **1** to break up into small pieces: *The whole plane just disintegrated in mid-air.* **2** to become weaker and be gradually destroyed: *Pam kept the kids when the marriage disintegrated.* —**disintegration** /dɪsˌɪntɪˈɡreɪʃən/ n [U]

disinterested /dɪsˈɪntrəstɪd/ adj able to judge a situation fairly because you will not get any advantages for yourself from it: *disinterested advice* —**disinterest** n [U]

disjointed /dɪsˈdʒɔɪntɪd/ adj a disjointed speech or piece of writing is not easy to understand because the words or ideas are not arranged in a clear order

disk /dɪsk/ n [C]

1 a small flat piece of plastic or metal used for storing information in a computer
2 the American spelling of DISC
➔ **FLOPPY DISK, HARD DISK**

'disk drive n [C] the part of a computer where you put a disk when you want to copy information onto it or from it

'disk ˌjockey n [C] a DJ

dislike¹ /dɪsˈlaɪk/ v [T] to not like someone or something [≠ **like**]: *Why do you dislike her so much?* | **dislike doing sth** *I dislike being the centre of attention.*

dislike² /dɪsˈlaɪk, ˈdɪslaɪk/ n [C,U]

1 a feeling of not liking someone or something [≠ **liking**]: **+of/for** *She shared her mother's dislike of housework.* | *They* **took an instant dislike** *to each other.*
2 **dislikes** [plural] the things that you do not like: *I know all her* **likes and dislikes**.

dislocate /ˈdɪsləkeɪt $ -loʊ-/ v [T] to make a bone come out of its normal place: *I dislocated my shoulder playing football.* —**dislocation** /ˌdɪsləˈkeɪʃən $ -loʊ-/ n [C,U]

dislodge /dɪsˈlɒdʒ $ -ˈlɑːdʒ/ v [T] to force something to move when it is stuck somewhere: *Lee dislodged a few stones as he climbed over the wall.*

disloyal /dɪsˈlɔɪəl/ adj doing or saying things that do not support your friends, your country, or the group you belong to: *He felt he had been disloyal to his friends.* —**disloyalty** n [U]

dismal /ˈdɪzməl/ adj making you feel unhappy and without hope: *dismal weather* | *We faced a dismal future.*

dismantle /dɪsˈmæntl/ v [I,T] **1** to take something apart so that it is in separate pieces: *Chris dismantled the bike in five minutes.* **2** to gradually get rid of a system or organization: *an election promise to dismantle the existing tax laws*

dismay¹ /dɪsˈmeɪ/ n [U] a strong feeling of disappointment and worry: **to sb's dismay** *I found to my dismay that I had left my money behind.*

dismay² v [T] to make someone feel very disappointed and worried: *The poor election turn-out dismayed politicians.*

dismember /dɪsˈmembə $ -ər/ v [T] formal to cut a body into pieces

dismiss /dɪsˈmɪs/ v [T] **1** to refuse to consider someone's idea or opinion because you think it is not serious, true, or important: **dismiss sb/sth as sth** *He dismissed the idea as impossible.* **2** formal to make someone leave their job: *If you're late again you'll be dismissed!* **3** to send someone away or allow them to go: *Classes will be dismissed early tomorrow.* —**dismissal** n [C,U]

dismissive /dɪsˈmɪsɪv/ adj if you are dismissive of someone or something, you refuse to consider them seriously: **+of** *She tends to be dismissive of anyone who complains.* —**dismissively** adv

dismount /dɪsˈmaʊnt/ v [I] to get off a horse, bicycle, or MOTORCYCLE

disobedient /ˌdɪsəˈbiːdiənt◂, ˌdɪsəʊ- $ ˌdɪsə-, ˌdɪsoʊ-/ adj refusing to do what someone in authority tells you to do: *a disobedient child* —**disobedience** n [U] —**disobediently** adv

disobey /ˌdɪsəˈbeɪ, ˌdɪsəʊ- $ ˌdɪsə-, ˌdɪsoʊ-/ v [I,T] to refuse to do what someone with authority tells you to do: *She would never disobey her parents.*

disorder /dɪsˈɔːdə $ -ˈɔːrdər/ n **1** [U] when things or people are very untidy or disorganized: *The house was in a state of complete disorder.* **2** [U] a situation in which a lot of people behave in an uncontrolled, noisy, or violent way in public: **public/civil disorder 3** [C] an illness that prevents part of your body from working properly: *a rare liver disorder*

disordered /dɪsˈɔːdəd $ -ˈɔːrdərd/ adj formal **1** not tidy **2** mentally confused

disorderly /dɪsˈɔːdəli $ -ˈɔːrdər-/ adj **1** untidy: *clothes left in a disorderly heap* **2** disorderly behaviour is noisy or violent: *Jerry was charged with being* **drunk and disorderly**.

disorganized also -**ised** BrE /dɪsˈɔːɡənaɪzd $ -ˈɔːr-/ adj not arranged or planned very well: *The meeting was completely disorganized.*
➔ see box at **ORGANIZED** —**disorganization** /dɪsˌɔːɡənaɪˈzeɪʃən $ -ˌɔːrɡənə-/ n [U]

disoriented /dɪsˈɔːrientɪd/ also **disorientated** BrE /dɪsˈɔːriənteɪtɪd/ adj confused and not able to understand what is happening or where you are: *After the long flight, I was tired and disoriented for a week.* —**disorienting, disorientating** adj —**disorientation** /dɪsˌɔːriənˈteɪʃən/ n [U]

disown /dɪsˈəʊn $ -ˈoʊn/ v [T] to say that you no longer have any connection with someone or something: *Frankly, I'm not surprised her family disowned her.*

disparaging /dɪˈspærədʒɪŋ/ adj a disparaging remark or look shows that you do not think someone or something is very good or important: *She made some* **disparaging remarks** *about the royal family.*

disparate /ˈdɪspərət/ adj formal disparate things are very different and not related to each other: *a meeting covering many disparate subjects* —**disparity** /dɪˈspærəti/ n [C,U] *the disparities between rich and poor*

dispassionate /dɪsˈpæʃənət/ adj not influenced by personal feelings: *a dispassionate opinion* —**dispassionately** adv: *We must look at the situation dispassionately.*

dispatch¹ also **despatch** BrE /dɪˈspætʃ/ v [T] to send someone or something somewhere: *The packages were dispatched yesterday.*

dispatch² also **despatch** BrE n [C] **1** a message sent between military or government officials: *a dispatch from headquarters* **2** a report sent to a newspaper from one of its writers who is in another town or country

dispel /dɪˈspel/ v [T] **dispelled, dispelling** formal to make something go away, especially a belief, idea, or feeling: *Mark's calm words dispelled our fears.*

dispensary /dɪˈspensəri/ n [C] plural **dispensaries** a place where medicines are prepared and given out

dispensation /ˌdɪspənˈseɪʃən, -pen-/ n [C,U] special permission to do something that is not usually allowed

dispense /dɪˈspens/ v [T] **1** to give something to people: *The machines in the hall dispense drinks.* **2** to prepare and give medicines to people

dispense with sth phr v formal to not use something that people usually use, because it is not necessary: *Ann suggested that they dispense with speeches altogether at the wedding.*

dispenser /dɪˈspensə $ -ər/ n [C] a machine from which you can get things such as drinks or money: *a cash dispenser*

disperse /dɪˈspɜːs $ -ɜːrs/ v [I,T] to scatter in different directions, or to make something do this: *Police used tear gas to disperse the crowd.* —**dispersal** n [U]

dispirited /dɪˈspɪrɪ̥tɪ̥d/ adj sad and no longer hopeful: *She looked tired and dispirited.*

displace /dɪsˈpleɪs/ v [T] **1** to take the place of someone or something [= **replace**]: *The yen displaced the dollar as the world's most important currency.* **2** to make a group of people leave the place where they normally live: *Millions of people were displaced by war.* —**displacement** n [U] —**displaced** adj

display¹ /dɪˈspleɪ/ n [C]

1 an arrangement of objects for people to look at: +**of** *a display of African masks* | **on display** (=being displayed) *The pictures are on display in the cafeteria.*

2 a public performance or entertainment: *a firework display* | +**of** *a display of dancing*

3 the part of a piece of equipment that shows information, for example a computer screen: *A light flashed on the display.*

4 display of affection/temper etc an occasion when someone clearly shows a particular attitude or quality: *a shocking display of aggression*

display² v [T] **1** to put things in a place where people can see them easily: *a row of tables displaying pottery* | *Results will be displayed on the noticeboard.* **2** to clearly show a feeling or a quality: *He displayed no emotion at the funeral.* **3** if a computer displays information, it shows it: *An error message was displayed.*

displeased /dɪsˈpliːzd/ adj formal annoyed: *She looked displeased.* —**displeasure** /-ˈpleʒə $ -ər/ n [U]

disposable /dɪˈspəʊzəbəl $ -ˈspoʊ-/ adj intended to be used once or for a short time and then thrown away: *disposable nappies*

dis,posable 'income n [U] the amount of money that you have available to spend each month after you have paid for rent, food etc

disposal /dɪˈspəʊzəl $ -ˈspoʊ-/ n **1** [U] when you get rid of something: +**of** *the disposal of radioactive waste* **2 at sb's disposal** available for someone to use: *He had a lot of cash at his disposal.*

dispose /dɪˈspəʊz $ -ˈspoʊz/ v

dispose of sth phr v to get rid of something: *safer ways of disposing of waste*

disposed /dɪˈspəʊzd $ -ˈspoʊzd/ adj formal **1 well/favourably/kindly disposed to sb/sth** liking someone or something: *countries that are well disposed to the West* **2 be/feel disposed to do sth** to be willing to do something: *He did not feel disposed to argue.*

disposition /ˌdɪspəˈzɪʃən/ n [C] formal someone's usual character: *a cheerful disposition*

disproportionate /ˌdɪsprəˈpɔːʃənɪ̥t◂ $ -ɔːr-/ adj too much or too little in relation to something: *She gets a disproportionate amount of publicity.* —**disproportionately** adv

disprove /dɪsˈpruːv/ v [T] to show that something is definitely wrong or not true: *The facts disprove his argument.*

dispute¹ /dɪˈspjuːt, ˈdɪspjuːt/ n [C,U]

1 a serious argument or disagreement: +**with** *He was involved in a legal dispute with his neighbour.* | +**over** *The two men got into a dispute over money.* | **be in dispute (with sb)** *They are in dispute with a local building firm.* | **pay/industrial dispute** (=between employers and workers) *Flights have been disrupted by a pilots' pay dispute.*

2 beyond dispute if something is beyond dispute, everyone agrees that it is true: *His loyalty is beyond dispute.*

dispute² /dɪˈspjuːt/ v [T] to say that you think something is not correct or true: *He claims he won, but I dispute that.*

disqualify /dɪsˈkwɒlɪ̥faɪ $ -ˈkwɑː-/ v [T usually passive] **disqualified, disqualifying, disqualifies** to stop someone from taking part in an activity because they have broken a rule: **disqualify sb from sth** *He was disqualified from the race.* —**disqualification** /dɪsˌkwɒlɪ̥fɪ̥ˈkeɪʃən $ -ˌkwɑː-/ n [C,U]

disquiet /dɪsˈkwaɪət/ n [U] formal anxiety or unhappiness about something: +**about** *public disquiet about animal testing*

disregard /ˌdɪsrɪˈɡɑːd $ -ɑːrd/ v [T] to ignore something: *The judge told the jury to disregard that statement.* —**disregard** n [U] *He showed total disregard for my feelings.*

disrepair /ˌdɪsrɪˈpeə $ -ˈper/ n [U] buildings that are in disrepair are in bad condition because they have not been cared for: *The old house had fallen into disrepair.*

disreputable /dɪsˈrepjɪ̥tabəl/ adj dishonest, illegal, or bad [≠ **reputable**]: *a disreputable businessman*

disrepute /ˌdɪsrɪˈpjuːt/ n **bring sth into disrepute** formal to make people no longer admire or respect something: *behaviour which has brought the medical profession into disrepute*

disrespect /ˌdɪsrɪˈspekt/ n [U] lack of respect for something or someone: +**for** *his disrespect for the law* —**disrespectful** adj

disrupt /dɪsˈrʌpt/ v [T] to prevent something from continuing normally by causing problems: *Road works are seriously disrupting traffic.*

—**disruptive** adj: disruptive students
—**disruption** /-'rʌpʃən/ n [C,U]

dissatisfied /dɪ'sæt̬ɪ̬sfaɪd, dɪs'sæ-/ adj not happy because something is not as good as you had expected [≠ **satisfied**]: dissatisfied customers | +**with** If you are dissatisfied with our service, please let us know.
—**dissatisfaction** /dɪˌsæt̬ɪ̬s'fækʃən, dɪs'sæ-/ n [U]

dissect /dɪ'sekt, daɪ-/ v [T] to cut up the body of a plant or animal in order to study it

disseminate /dɪ'sem̬ɪ̬neɪt/ v [T] formal to spread information or ideas to as many people as possible: a network to disseminate medical information

dissent /dɪ'sent/ n [U] refusal to agree with an accepted opinion or decision: political dissent
—**dissent** v [I] Few historians dissent from this view. —**dissenter** n [C]

dissertation /ˌdɪsə'teɪʃən $ ˌdɪsər-/ n [C] a long piece of writing that you do for a university degree

disservice /dɪ'sɜːvɪ̬s, dɪs'sɜː- $ -ɜːr-/ n **do sb/sth a disservice** to make people have a bad opinion of someone or something, especially when this is unfair: The critics have done this play a great disservice.

dissident /'dɪsɪ̬dənt/ n [C] someone who publicly criticizes the government in a country where this is a crime —**dissident** adj: dissident writers

dissimilar /dɪ'sɪm̬ɪ̬lə, dɪs'sɪ- $ -ər/ adj not the same: The Breton language is not dissimilar to (=is quite like) Welsh. —**dissimilarity** /dɪˌsɪm̬ɪ̬'lær̬ɪ̬ti, dɪs,sɪ-/ n [C,U]

dissipate /'dɪsɪ̬peɪt/ v [I,T] formal to gradually disappear, or to make something do this

dissociate /dɪ'səʊʃieɪt, -sieɪt $ -'soʊ-/ v [T] to say that you do not agree with someone or something: **dissociate yourself from sth** He tried to dissociate himself from the chairman's remarks.

dissolution /ˌdɪsə'luːʃən/ n [U] when a parliament, marriage, or business arrangement is formally ended [➡ **dissolve**]

dissolve /dɪ'zɒlv $ dɪ'zɑːlv/ v **1** [I,T] if a solid dissolves, or if you dissolve it, it mixes with a liquid and becomes liquid itself: Stir the mixture until the sugar dissolves. | **dissolve sth in sth** Dissolve the tablets in water. **2** [T] to formally end a parliament, marriage, or business arrangement **3 dissolve into tears/laughter etc** to start crying or laughing a lot **4** [I] to gradually disappear: My shyness soon dissolved.

dissuade /dɪ'sweɪd/ v [T] formal to persuade someone not to do something: **dissuade sb from (doing) sth** a campaign to dissuade young people from smoking

distance[1] /'dɪstəns/ n

1 [C,U] the amount of space between two places or things: +**from/between** What's the distance from London to Harlow? | the distance between two cars | My house is just a **short distance** from here. | a **long distance** walk | **at a distance of** I followed at a distance of about 10 metres. | **within walking/driving/commuting distance** (=near enough to walk to, drive to etc) The school is within easy walking distance.

2 [singular] a place that is far away: **in the distance** I heard bells ringing in the distance. |

at/from a distance We watched from a safe distance.

3 keep your distance a) to stay far enough away to be safe: The dogs looked fierce, so I kept my distance. **b)** to avoid becoming too friendly with someone: He tends to keep his distance from employees.
→ **LONG-DISTANCE**

distance[2] v **distance yourself** to say that you are not involved with someone or something: The party is distancing itself from its violent past.

distant /'dɪstənt/ adj

1 far away in space or time: the sound of distant laughter | The building is a relic of **the distant past**.

2 not friendly or not interested: She seemed cold and distant.

3 [only before noun] not closely related to you [≠ **close**]: a distant relative
—**distantly** adv

distaste /dɪs'teɪst/ n [singular, U] a feeling that something or someone is unpleasant or offensive: +**for** her distaste for gossip

distasteful /dɪs'teɪstfəl/ adj unpleasant or offensive

distil, distill /dɪ'stɪl/ v [T] distilled, distilling **1** to make a liquid more pure by heating it until it becomes gas and then letting it cool: distilled water **2** to get the main ideas or facts from a large amount of information: The wisdom in this book has been distilled from years of experience.
—**distillation** /ˌdɪstɪ̬'leɪʃən/ n [C,U]

distillery /dɪ'stɪləri/ n [C] plural distilleries a factory where strong alcoholic drink such as WHISKY is produced

distinct /dɪ'stɪŋkt/ adj **1** clearly different or separate: Spanish and Catalan are two entirely distinct languages. **2** if something is distinct, you can see, hear, or notice it easily: There was a distinct smell of burning. **3 as distinct from** used to emphasize that you are talking about one thing and not another: I am talking about childhood as distinct from adolescence.
—**distinctly** adv: I distinctly remember his words.

distinction /dɪ'stɪŋkʃən/ n **1** [C] a clear difference between things: +**between** The law makes a **distinction** between children and adults. **2** [U] when someone or something is special and very good: an artist of great distinction **3** [C,U] a special mark given to a student whose work is excellent: She passed the exam with distinction.

distinctive /dɪ'stɪŋktɪv/ adj different from other things and very easy to recognize: The band have a distinctive sound. —**distinctively** adv

distinguish /dɪ'stɪŋgwɪʃ/ v **1** [I,T] to recognize or understand the difference between things or people: +**between** He is old enough to distinguish between fiction and reality. **2** [T] to be the thing that makes someone or something different from other people or things: What distinguishes us is the quality of our research. **3** [T] to be able to see or hear something, even if it is difficult: It was too dark for me to distinguish anything clearly. —**distinguishable** adj

distinguished /dɪ'stɪŋgwɪʃt/ adj successful and respected: a distinguished scientist

D

distort /dɪˈstɔːt $ -ɔːrt/ v [T] **1** to change the shape or sound of something so it is strange or unclear: *Tall buildings can distort radio signals.* **2** to report something in a way that changes its meaning: *The press distorted what I said.* → see box at CHANGE —**distorted** adj —**distortion** /dɪˈstɔːʃən $ -ɔːr-/ n [C,U] *a distortion of the facts*

distract /dɪˈstrækt/ v [T] to take someone's attention away from what they are doing: *Don't distract me while I'm driving!* | *The government is trying to distract attention from its failures.*

distracted /dɪˈstræktɪ̣d/ adj unable to think clearly because you are worried about something

distraction /dɪˈstrækʃən/ n **1** [C,U] something that takes your attention away from what you are doing: *I can't study at home – there are too many distractions.* **2 drive sb to distraction** to annoy someone very much

distraught /dɪˈstrɔːt $ -ˈstrɒːt/ adj extremely upset: *Friends comforted his distraught parents.*

distress¹ /dɪˈstres/ n [U] **1** a feeling of extreme unhappiness: *Their divorce caused him great distress.* **2** a very difficult situation where someone needs help: *charities who help families in distress*

distress² v [T] to make someone feel very upset: *The news distressed her.*

distressing /dɪˈstresɪŋ/ adj making you feel very upset: *a distressing dream* —**distressingly** adv

distribute /dɪˈstrɪbjuːt/ v [T] **1** to share things among a group of people: *I'll distribute copies of the report.* | **distribute sth to/among sb** *Food and blankets were distributed among the refugees.* → see box at GIVE **2** to supply goods to shops and companies in a particular area: *The tape is distributed by American Video.* —**distribution** /ˌdɪstrɪ̣ˈbjuːʃən/ n [U]

distributor /dɪˈstrɪbjɪ̣tə $ -ər/ n [C] a company or person that supplies goods to shops or companies

district /ˈdɪstrɪkt/ n [C] an area of a city or country: **shopping/residential/business etc district** *Edinburgh's main shopping district* | *the Ludhiana district of East Punjab* → see box at AREA

district at'torney n [C] AmE a lawyer who works for the government in one particular area

distrust¹ /dɪsˈtrʌst/ n [U] a feeling that you cannot trust someone [= mistrust]: **+of** *He had a deep distrust of the police.* —**distrustful** adj

distrust² v [T] to not trust someone or something [= mistrust; ≠ trust]: *Meg had always distrusted banks.*

disturb /dɪˈstɜːb $ -ɜːrb/ v [T]
1 to interrupt someone so that they cannot continue what they are doing: *Sorry to disturb you, but it's urgent.* | *Noise from the street disturbed her sleep.*
2 to make someone feel worried or upset: *Something about the situation disturbed him.*
3 to move something: *If you go into my office, please don't disturb anything.*

disturbance /dɪˈstɜːbəns $ -ɜːr-/ n **1** [C] a situation in which people behave violently in public: *a disturbance outside a bar* **2** [C,U] something that interrupts what you are doing: *The builders will cause as little disturbance as possible.*

disturbed /dɪˈstɜːbd $ -ɜːrbd/ adj not behaving in a normal way because of mental or emotional problems: *a disturbed child*

disturbing /dɪˈstɜːbɪŋ $ -ɜːr-/ adj worrying or upsetting: *a disturbing increase in crime*

disuse /dɪsˈjuːs/ n [U] when something is no longer used: *The building eventually fell into disuse.*

disused /ˌdɪsˈjuːzd◂/ adj [only before noun] no longer used: *a disused railway*

ditch¹ /dɪtʃ/ n [C] a long narrow hole dug at the side of a field or road to hold or carry away water

ditch² v [T] informal to get rid of something or someone: *The government quickly ditched the plan.*

dither /ˈdɪðə $ -ər/ v [I] to be unable to make a decision: **+over/about** *I was still dithering over what to wear.*

ditto¹ /ˈdɪtəʊ $ -toʊ/ adv used instead of repeating something, to say that what has been said is also true in another case: *Friday nobody showed up. Ditto Monday and Tuesday.*

ditto² n [C] plural **dittoes** a mark (") that you write under a word in a list so that you do not have to write the same word again

diva /ˈdiːvə/ n [C] a very successful female singer

divan /dɪˈvæn $ ˈdaɪvæn/ n [C] **1** a bed with a thick base **2** a long low soft seat with no arms or back

dive

dive¹ /daɪv/ v [I] past tense **dived** also **dove** /dəʊv $ doʊv/ AmE past participle **dived**
1 to jump into the water with your head and arms first: **+into/off etc** *Harry dived into the pool.* | *It is dangerous to dive off the cliffs.* → see box at JUMP
2 to swim under water using breathing equipment: *You can swim and dive in the crystal clear waters.*
3 to travel down through air or water: *The plane began to dive.* | **+down/onto etc** *Seabirds were diving down to catch fish.*
4 to move or jump quickly: **+into/after etc** *He dived into a doorway to get out of the rain.* | *Shots were heard and everyone dived for cover.*

dive² n [C] **1** a sudden movement in one direction: *She made a dive for the ball.* **2** a sudden fall in the amount, value, or success of something: *Share prices took a dive.* **3** a movement down through air or water: *The plane suddenly* *went into a dive.* **4** a jump into water with your head and arms first

diver /'daɪvə $ -ər/ *n* [C] someone who swims under water with breathing equipment

diverge /daɪ'vɜ:dʒ, dɪ̣- $ -ɜ:rdʒ/ *v* [I] to be different or to develop in a different way: **+from** *At this point his version of events diverges from hers.* —**divergence** *n* [C,U] —**divergent** *adj*: *divergent views*

diverse /daɪ'vɜ:s $ dɪ̣'vɜ:rs, daɪ-/ *adj formal* different from each other: *London is home to people of many diverse cultures.* —**diversity** *n* [U]

diversify /daɪ'vɜ:sɪ̣faɪ $ dɪ̣'vɜ:r-, daɪ-/ *v* [I,T] **diversified, diversifying, diversifies** to begin to make different products or get involved in new areas of business: **+into** *a cosmetics company that is diversifying into clothing* —**diversification** /daɪ,vɜ:sɪ̣fɪ̣'keɪʃən $ dɪ̣,vɜ:r-, daɪ-/ *n* [U]

diversion /daɪ'vɜ:ʃən, dɪ̣- $ -ɜ:rʒən/ *n* **1** [C,U] a change in the direction something is going in, or its purpose: **+of** *the diversion of a section of the river* **2** [C,U] an enjoyable activity that stops you from being bored: *Computer games can be a great diversion for kids.* **3** [C] something that takes your attention away from something else: *One man **creates a diversion** while the other steals your purse.* **4** [C] *BrE* a different way that traffic is sent when the usual way is blocked

divert /daɪ'vɜ:t, dɪ̣- $ -ɜ:rt/ *v* [T] **1** to change the direction or purpose of something: *We should **divert** more resources **into** research.* | *Traffic is being diverted to avoid the accident.* **2 divert (sb's) attention from** to take someone's attention away from something: *The war will divert attention from the government's problems.*

divest /daɪ'vest, dɪ̣-/ *v*
  divest sb/sth **of** sth *phr v formal* to remove something or get rid of something: *He divested himself of his coat.*

divide[1] /dɪ̣'vaɪd/ *v*
  1 [I,T] if something divides, or if you divide it, it separates into two or more parts: **divide sth into sth** *The teacher divided the class into groups.* | **+into** *The story divides into three sections.*
  2 also **divide off** [T] to keep two areas separate from each other: *The river divides the North and South sides of the city.* | **divide sth from sth** *A curtain divided his sleeping area from ours.*
  3 also **divide up** [T] to separate something into parts and give parts to different people, activities etc: **divide sth between/among sth/sb** *He divided the money equally among his children.* | *She divides her time between New York and London.*
  4 [T] to calculate how many times one number contains another number [➡ **multiply**]: **divide sth by sth** *15 divided by five is three.* → see box at **CALCULATE**
  5 [T] to make people disagree with each other: *The issue has divided voters.*

divide[2] *n* [C usually singular] a strong difference between the beliefs of two groups: *They're on opposite sides of the **political divide**.*

dividend /'dɪvɪ̣dənd, -dend/ *n* [C] **1** a part of a company's profit that is paid to people who have SHARES in the company **2 pay dividends** to bring a lot of advantages: *Exercise now will pay dividends when you're older.*

dividing line *n* [singular] the difference between two similar things: **+between** *the dividing line between popular fiction and serious literature*

divine /dɪ̣'vaɪn/ *adj* relating to God or a god: *divine power*

diving /'daɪvɪŋ/ *n* [U] **1** the sport of swimming under water using breathing equipment **2** the activity of jumping into water with your head and arms first

diving board *n* [C] a board above a SWIMMING POOL that people can jump from

divinity /dɪ̣'vɪnɪ̣ti/ *n* [U] **1** *AmE* the study of God and religious beliefs [= **theology** *BrE*] **2** being God or like a god

divisible /dɪ̣'vɪzɪ̣bəl/ *adj* able to be divided by a number: **+by** *27 is divisible by nine and three.*

division /dɪ̣'vɪʒən/ *n*
  1 [C,U] when you separate something into parts, or the way these parts are separated: **the division of sth into/between/among sth** *the division of words into syllables*
  2 [C,U] disagreement among the members of a group: **+within/among/between** *There are **deep divisions** within the party.*
  3 [U] when you calculate how many times one number contains another [➡ **multiplication**]
  4 [C] a group within a large company, army, or organization: *He heads our IT division.* | *They sent a division of tanks.*
  5 [C] one of the groups of teams that a sports competition is divided into: **First/Second etc Division** *Manchester City were in the First Division.*

divisional /dɪ̣'vɪʒənəl/ *adj* [only before noun] relating to a group within a large company, army, or organization: *a divisional manager*

divisive /dɪ̣'vaɪsɪv/ *adj* causing a lot of disagreement among people: *a very divisive issue*

divorce[1] /dɪ̣'vɔ:s $ -ɔ:rs/ *n* [C,U] the legal ending of a marriage [➡ **separation**]: *She wants to **get a divorce**.* | *Many marriages **end in divorce**.*

divorce[2] *v*
  1 [I,T] to legally end a marriage [➡ **separate**]: *His parents divorced when he was six.* | *Why did she divorce him?* | *They decided to **get divorced**.* → see box at **MARRIED**
  2 [T] *formal* to separate two things completely: **divorce sth from sth** *It is difficult to divorce religion from politics.*
  —**divorced** *adj*: *a divorced woman*

divorcee /dɪ̣,vɔ:'si:/ *n* [C] *BrE* someone who is divorced

divulge /daɪ'vʌldʒ, dɪ̣-/ *v* [T] to give someone secret information: *Doctors cannot divulge information about their patients.*

Diwali, Divali /dɪ'wɑ:li/ *n* a Hindu FESTIVAL, celebrated in the autumn

DIY /,di: aɪ 'waɪ/ *n* [U] *BrE* **do-it-yourself** when you make or repair things in your house yourself rather than paying other people to do the work → see box at **SHOP**

dizzy /'dɪzi/ *adj* feeling that you are losing your balance, for example because you have been spinning around or you are ill: *She felt dizzy when she stood up.* | *He suffers from **dizzy spells**.* —**dizziness** *n* [U]

D

DJ /ˌdiː ˈdʒeɪ◂/ n [C] **disk jockey** someone who plays records on the radio or in a club where you can dance

DNA /ˌdiː en ˈeɪ◂/ n [U] a substance that carries GENETIC information in a cell

do¹ /duː/ auxiliary verb past tense **did** /dɪd/ past participle **done** /dʌn/ third person singular **does** /dəz; strong dʌz/

1 used with another verb to form questions or negatives: *Do you like pasta?* | *What did he say?* | *I don't know her name.* | *Don't push me!*

2 used to form QUESTION TAGS: *You know Tom, don't you?* | *She didn't understand, did she?*

3 used to avoid repeating another verb: *She eats a lot more than I do.* | **so/neither do I** *'I have to go.' 'So do I.'* | *Paul didn't like it and neither did I.*

4 used to emphasize the main verb in a sentence: *He did tell me, but I forgot.* | *Do be careful.*

do² v past tense **did** past participle **done** third person singular **does**

1 [T] to perform an action or activity: *What are you doing?* | *I have to do my homework.* | *All he does is watch TV.* | **do something/anything** *Why isn't anybody doing anything to help?*

2 [I] used to talk or ask about how successful someone is: *How is he doing at university?* | **do well/badly** *She did well at school.*

3 [T] to have a particular effect on someone or something: *It will do you good to have a break.* | **do nothing/a lot/something etc for sb/sth** *The scandal has done nothing for his reputation.* | *The new job did a lot for her confidence.*

4 [T] to have a particular job: *What do you do?* | *She doesn't know what she wants to do.* → see box at JOB

5 [I] used to say that something is acceptable or enough: *Butter is best, but oil would do.* | *My old black shoes will have to do.* | *All these excuses just won't do.*

6 **what is sb/sth doing?** used when you are surprised or annoyed that someone or something is in a particular place or doing a particular thing: *What is my jacket doing on the floor?* | *What are you doing with my purse?*

7 **do your hair/nails/make-up etc** to make your hair etc look nice

8 [T] BrE to study a subject at school or college: *We didn't do Latin at school.* → see box at UNIVERSITY

9 [T] to cook a type of food: *I'm doing steak tonight.*

10 [T] to achieve a particular speed or distance: *He was doing over 90 miles an hour.*

11 [T] to provide a service or sell a product: *They do home deliveries.*

do away with sb/sth phr v informal **1** to get rid of something: *We should do away with those old customs.* **2** to kill someone

do sth **over** phr v AmE to do something again, especially because you did it wrong the first time

do up phr v **1** to fasten something, or to be fastened: *The dress does up at the back.* | **do** sth ⇔ **up** *Do up your shoelaces.* → see box at FASTEN **2** **do** sth ⇔ **up** to repair a building or car, and improve its appearance: *They bought an old house and did it up.*

do with sb/sth phr v **1** **could do with sth** to need or want something: *I could do with some help.* **2** **be/have to do with sb/sth** to be related to or involved with something or someone: *The conversation mostly had to do with work.* | *I'm sorry, but it's nothing to do with me* (=I am not responsible or involved). **3** **do sth with sth** to deal with something, usually by putting it somewhere: *I don't know what to do with these boxes.* | *What have you done with my bag* (=where have you put it)?

do without phr v **1** **do without (sth)** to live or manage without having something: *I couldn't do without a car.* **2** **could do without sth** used to say that something is annoying you or causing problems: *I could do without this noise.*

do³ n [C] plural **dos** informal **1** a party or other social event: *We're going to a do on Saturday.* → see box at PARTY **2** **dos and don'ts** things that you should and should not do: *the dos and don'ts of having a pet*

doable /ˈduːəbəl/ adj [not before noun] spoken informal able to be done or completed: *Is the task really doable?*

docile /ˈdəʊsaɪl $ ˈdɑːsəl/ adj quiet and easy to control: *a docile animal*

dock¹ /dɒk $ dɑːk/ n **1** [C] the place in a port where goods are taken on and off ships **2** **the docks** [plural] the area around and including a port **3** **the dock** the part of a law court where the person who is charged with a crime stands

dock² v **1** [I,T] if a ship docks, it sails into a dock **2** **dock sb's pay** to reduce the amount of money that you pay someone as a punishment: *The company has threatened to dock the officers' pay.*

ˈdock ˌworker also **dock worker** **docker** BrE /ˈdɒkə $ ˈdɑːkər/ n [C] a person whose job is to move goods on and off ships [= longshoreman AmE]

doctor¹ /ˈdɒktə $ ˈdɑːktər/ n [C]

1 written abbreviation **Dr.** someone who is trained to treat people who are ill: *You should go to the doctor with that cough.* | *Doctor Brown is busy at the moment.* | *For further advice, consult your family doctor.*

THESAURUS

GP BrE – a doctor you go to see in your local area, not in a hospital

surgeon – a doctor who does operations in a hospital: *a famous heart surgeon*

consultant – a doctor at a hospital who knows a lot about a particular area of medicine

physician especially AmE formal – a doctor

psychiatrist/psychoanalyst/psychotherapist – a doctor who treats mental illness

---

2 someone who has the highest level of degree given by a university: *a Doctor of Philosophy* → SPIN DOCTOR, WITCH DOCTOR

doctor² v [T] to change something in a dishonest way in order to gain an advantage: *Do you think the police doctored the evidence?*

doctorate /ˈdɒktərɪt $ ˈdɑːk-/ n [C] a university degree at the highest level

doctrine /ˈdɒktrɪn $ ˈdɑːk-/ n [C,U] a set of religious or political beliefs

document[1] /'dɒkjᵿmənt $ 'dɑːk-/ n [C]

1 a piece of paper that has official information written on it: *a legal document* | *historical documents*

2 a piece of work that you write and keep on a computer: *Click on the document you want to open.* → see box at COMPUTER

—**documentary** /,dɒkjᵿ'mentəri $,dɑːk-/ adj: *documentary evidence*

document[2] /'dɒkjᵿment $ 'dɑːk-/ v [T] to record information about something by writing about it, photographing it etc: *The programme documents the life of a teenager.*

documentary /,dɒkjᵿ'mentəri◂ $,dɑːk-/ n [C] plural **documentaries** a film or television programme that gives information about a subject: +**on/about** *They are making a documentary about volcanoes.* → see box at TELEVISION

documentation /,dɒkjᵿmən'teɪʃən, -men- $,dɑːk-/ n [U] documents that show that something is true or correct

doddle /'dɒdl $ 'dɑːdl/ n BrE informal **be a doddle** to be very easy: *The exam was a doddle.*

dodge[1] /dɒdʒ $ dɑːdʒ/ v **1** [I,T] to move quickly to avoid someone or something: +**between/through/into** etc *They dodged through the traffic.* | *We had to dodge the bullets.* **2** [T] to deliberately avoid discussing something or doing something: *The Senator dodged the crucial question.*

dodge[2] n [C] informal a way of avoiding something that you should do: *a tax dodge* (=a way of avoiding paying tax)

dodgy /'dɒdʒi $ 'dɑː-/ adj BrE informal **1** not working properly or not in good condition: *a dodgy hard disk* **2** dishonest, or not to be trusted: *dodgy business dealings*

doe /dəʊ $ doʊ/ n [C] a female rabbit or DEER

does /dəz; strong dʌz/ v the third person singular of the present tense of DO

doesn't /'dʌzənt/ v the short form of 'does not'

dogs

greyhound

labrador

terrier

poodle

dog[1] /dɒg $ dɒːg/ n [C]

1 a very common animal with four legs, fur, and a tail. Dogs are often kept as pets or as working animals [→ **puppy, bitch**]: *I could hear a dog barking.* | *What breed of dog is she?*

2 a male dog, FOX, or WOLF

→ GUIDE DOG, HOT DOG

dog[2] v [T] **dogged, dogging** if a problem dogs you, it causes trouble for a long time

'dog ,collar n [C] informal a white collar worn by priests

dog-eared /'dɒg ɪəd $ 'dɒːg ɪrd/ adj dog-eared books have been used so much that the corners of their pages are folded or torn

dogged /'dɒgᵻd $ 'dɒː-/ adj [only before noun] determined to do something even though it is difficult: *a dogged determination to succeed* —**doggedly** adv

doghouse /'dɒghaʊs $ 'dɒːg-/ n **1 be in the doghouse** informal to have annoyed someone or made them angry with you **2** [C] AmE a small building outdoors for a dog to sleep in [= **kennel** BrE]

dogma /'dɒgmə $ 'dɒːgmə, 'dɑːgmə/ n [C,U] beliefs that people are expected to accept as true without asking for any explanation: *religious dogma*

dogmatic /dɒg'mætɪk $ dɒːg-, dɑːg-/ adj someone who is dogmatic is completely certain of their beliefs and expects other people to accept them without arguing —**dogmatically** /-kli/ adv

do-gooder /du: 'gʊdə $ -ər/ n [C] informal someone who thinks they are helping others, but who often gets involved when they are not wanted

dogsbody /'dɒgz,bɒdi $ 'dɒːgz,bɑːdi/ n [C] plural **dogsbodies** BrE someone who has to do all the small boring jobs in a place: *I'm just the office dogsbody.*

doing[1] /'duːɪŋ/ n **1 be sb's (own) doing** to be someone's own fault: *His bad luck was all his own doing.* **2 take some doing** informal to be hard work: *Getting the place clean is going to take some doing.*

doing[2] v the present participle of DO

,do-it-your'self n [U] DIY

doldrums /'dɒldrəmz $ 'doʊl-, 'dɑːl-, 'dɔːl-/ n **in the doldrums a)** if something is in the doldrums, it is not doing well or developing: *Sales have been in the doldrums for months.* **b)** if you are in the doldrums you are feeling sad

dole[1] /dəʊl $ doʊl/ n [U] BrE money that the British government gives to people who are unemployed: **be/go on the dole** (=be receiving government money) *He's been on the dole for two years.*

dole[2] v

dole sth ⇔ **out** phr v informal to give money, food, advice etc to more than one person: +**to** *Vera was doling out candy to the kids.*

doleful /'dəʊlfəl $ 'doʊl-/ adj formal very sad: *a doleful song*

doll /dɒl $ dɑːl, dɔːl/ n [C] a toy that looks like a small person or baby: *a small wooden doll*

dollar /'dɒlə $ 'dɑːlər/ n [C]

1 written sign $; the standard unit of money in the US, Australia, Canada, and some other countries: *That will be three dollars, please.* | *a ten-dollar bill*

2 the dollar the value of US money in relation to the money of other countries: *The pound has* *risen against the dollar* (=increased in value in relation to the dollar).

dollop /'dɒləp $ 'dɑː-/ *n* [C] a small amount of soft food, usually dropped from a spoon: *a dollop of thick cream* → see picture at PIECE

dolphin

dolphin /'dɒlfɪn $ 'dɑːl-, 'dɔːl-/ *n* [C] a very intelligent sea animal with a long grey pointed nose

domain /də'meɪn, dəʊ- $ də-, doʊ-/ *n* [C] *formal* **1** an area of activity, interest, or knowledge, especially one that a particular person or organization deals with: **outside/within the domain of sth/sb** *This problem is outside the domain of medical science.* **2** an area that was controlled by someone in past times

dome /dəʊm $ doʊm/ *n* [C] a round roof on a building —**domed** *adj*

domestic /də'mestɪk/ *adj*
1 happening within one country and not involving any others: *US foreign and domestic policy*
2 [only before noun] relating to family relationships and life at home: *We share the domestic chores.* | *women who suffer from domestic violence* | **domestic appliances** (=machines used in the home) *such as washing machines*
3 someone who is domestic enjoys doing jobs in the home, such as cooking
4 [only before noun] a domestic animal lives on a farm or in someone's home

domesticated /də'mestɪkeɪtɪd/ *adj* domesticated animals work for people or live with them as pets

domesticity /ˌdəʊme'stɪsɪti $ ˌdoʊ-/ *n* [U] life at home with your family

dominant /'dɒmɪnənt $ 'dɑː-/ *adj* **1** strongest, most important, or most noticeable: *a company that is quite dominant in this market* **2** wanting to control people or events: *a dominant personality* —**dominance** *n* [U]

dominate /'dɒmɪneɪt $ 'dɑː-/ *v* **1** [I,T] to control someone or something: *Five large companies dominate the car industry.* **2** [I,T] to be the strongest, most important, or most noticeable feature of something: *Education issues dominated the election campaign.* —**domination** /ˌdɒmɪ'neɪʃən $ ˌdɑː-/ *n* [U]

domineering /ˌdɒmɪ'nɪərɪŋ◂ $ ˌdɑːmɪ'nɪr-/ *adj* trying to control other people too much: *a domineering father*

dominion /də'mɪnjən/ *n* **1** [U] *literary* the power or right to rule people **2** [C] *formal* the land owned or controlled by a ruler or government: *the king's dominions*

domino /'dɒmɪnəʊ $ 'dɑːmɪnoʊ/ *n* plural **dominoes** **1** [C] one of a set of small pieces of wood or plastic with spots on, used for playing a game **2 dominoes** [U] the game that you play using dominoes

don¹ /dɒn $ dɑːn/ *n* [C] *BrE* a university teacher

don² *v* [T] **donned, donning** *formal* to put on a piece of clothing

donate /dəʊ'neɪt $ 'doʊneɪt/ *v* [T] to give something, especially money, to a person or organization that needs help: **donate sth to sb/sth** *Our school donated £500 to the Red Cross.* → see box at GIVE

donation /dəʊ'neɪʃən $ doʊ-/ *n* [C,U] something, especially money, that you give to help a person or organization: **+to/from** *Please make a donation to the hospital fund.*

done¹ /dʌn/ *v* the past participle of DO

done² *adj* **1** finished or completed: *The job's nearly done.* | *I'll be glad when the exams are over and done with* (=completely finished). **2** cooked enough to eat: *Is the pasta done yet?* **3 be done for** *informal* to be in serious trouble or likely to fail: *If we get caught, we're done for.*

done³ *spoken* used to agree to and accept a deal: *'I'll give you $50 for it.' 'Done!'*

donkey /'dɒŋki $ 'dɑːŋki/ *n* **1** [C] a grey or brown animal like a small horse with long ears **2 for donkey's years** *BrE spoken* for a very long time: *I've known Kevin for donkey's years.*

'donkey ˌwork *n BrE* **do the donkey work** to do the hard or boring part of a job

donor /'dəʊnə $ 'doʊnər/ *n* [C] **1** someone who gives something, especially money, to an organization in order to help people: *The Museum received $10,000 from an anonymous donor.* **2** someone who gives some of their blood or part of their body to help a person who is ill: *a blood donor*

don't /dəʊnt $ doʊnt/ the short form of 'do not': *I don't know.*

donut /'dəʊnʌt $ 'doʊ-/ *n* [C] *especially AmE* another spelling of DOUGHNUT

doodle /'duːdl/ *v* [I,T] to draw shapes or patterns while you are thinking about something else: *I spent most of the class doodling in my notebook.* —**doodle** *n* [C]

doom¹ /duːm/ *v* [T] **be doomed to sth** if you are doomed to something unpleasant, it is certain to happen to you: *We are all doomed to die.* —**doomed** *adj*: *passengers on the doomed flight*

doom² *n* [U] when something very bad is certain to happen soon: *a sense of impending doom* (=coming very soon) | **doom and gloom/gloom and doom** (=when there seems to be no hope for the future) *Despite the bad figures, it's not all doom and gloom.*

door /dɔː $ dɔːr/ *n*
1 [C] the thing that you open and close to get into or out of a house, room, or car [➔ **gate**]: **open/close/shut the door** *Could you open the door for me?* | **front/back/side etc door** (=at the front, back etc of a house) *Is the back door shut?* | **kitchen/bathroom/bedroom etc door** *Don't forget to lock the garage door.* | *Can you* **answer the door** (=open it after someone has knocked)?
2 [C] the space made by an open door: **in/out of the door** *Rick ran out of the door.* | **in/out**

through the door *She walked in through the door.*

3 at the door if someone is at the door, they are waiting for you to open it so that they can come inside

4 out of doors outside: *I prefer working out of doors.*

5 (from) door to door a) *especially BrE* from one building to another: *How long is the journey, door to door?* **b)** going to each house on a street to sell something or talk to people: *The police went from door to door, asking if anyone had seen anything.* | *a door-to-door salesman*

→ NEXT DOOR

doorbell /'dɔːbel $ 'dɔːr-/ *n* [C] a button outside a house that makes a sound when you push it so that people inside know you are there

doorknob /'dɔːnɒb $ 'dɔːrnɑːb/ *n* [C] a round handle used to open a door

doorman /'dɔːmæn, -mən $ 'dɔːr-/ *n* [C] plural **doormen** /-men, -mən/ a man who works at the door of a hotel or theatre, helping people who are coming in and out

doormat /'dɔːmæt $ 'dɔːr-/ *n* [C] **1** a piece of material by a door for you to clean your shoes on **2** *informal* someone who lets other people treat them badly

doorstep /'dɔːstep $ 'dɔːr-/ *n* **1** [C] a step just outside a door to a building **2 on sb's/the doorstep** very near to where you live: *Wow! The beach is right on your doorstep!*

doorway /'dɔːweɪ $ 'dɔːr-/ *n* [C] the space where the door opens into a room or building

dope /dəʊp $ doʊp/ *n* [U] *informal* an illegal drug, especially MARIJUANA

dork /dɔːk $ dɔːrk/ *n* [C] *informal* a stupid person

dormant /'dɔːmənt $ 'dɔːr-/ *adj* not active now, but able to be active at a later time: *a dormant volcano*

dormitory /'dɔːmɪt̬əri $ 'dɔːrmɪtɔːri/ also **dorm** /dɔːm $ dɔːrm/ *n* [C] plural **dormitories 1** *especially BrE* a large room where a lot of people sleep **2** *AmE* a large building at a school or college where students live [= hall of residence *BrE*]

dosage /'dəʊsɪdʒ $ 'doʊ-/ *n* [C] the amount of a medicine that you should take: **+of** *a high dosage of morphine* → see box at MEDICINE

dose /dəʊs $ doʊs/ *n* [C] **1** a measured amount of medicine: **high/low dose** *Start with a low dose.* | **+of** *an extra dose of painkillers* **2** the amount of something that you experience at one time: *I quite like Jamie in small doses* (=in limited amounts but not often).

dosh /dɒʃ $ dɑːʃ/ *n* [U] *BrE informal* money

doss /dɒs $ dɑːs/ also **doss down** *v* [I] *BrE informal* to sleep somewhere that is not your usual place or not your usual bed: *I dossed down on the couch.*

dossier /'dɒsieɪ $ 'dɔːsjeɪ, 'dɑː-/ *n* [C] a set of papers that include detailed information about someone or something: **+on** *a dossier on the organization's political activities.*

dot¹ /dɒt $ dɑːt/ *n*

1 [C] a small round mark or spot: *a pattern of dots on the screen* | *The plane shrank to a black dot in the sky.*

2 on the dot *informal* exactly at a particular time: **at three o'clock/seven thirty etc on the dot** *He arrived at six on the dot.*

dot² *v* [T] **dotted, dotting 1** to mark something by putting a dot on it **2** to spread things out within an area: **be dotted with sth** *The lake was dotted with sailboats.*

dot-com, dot.com /ˌdɒt 'kɒm $ ˌdɑːt 'kɑːm/ *adj* [only before noun] *informal* a dot-com company is one whose business is done using the Internet

dote /dəʊt $ doʊt/ *v*

dote on/upon sb *phr v* to love someone very much, so that you cannot see their faults: *Steve dotes on his son.*

doting /'dəʊtɪŋ $ 'doʊ-/ *adj* [only before noun] doting parents love their children very much and cannot see their faults

dotted 'line *n* **1** [C] a line of small printed spots or lines: *Cut along the dotted lines.* **2 sign on the dotted line** *informal* to officially agree to something by signing a contract

dotty /'dɒti $ 'dɑːti/ *adj old-fashioned informal* slightly crazy

double¹ /'dʌbəl/ *adj*

1 having two parts that are similar or exactly the same: *the double doors of the cathedral* | *Don't park on double yellow lines.*

2 combining or involving two things of the same type: *a double murder case*

3 twice the usual amount, size, or number: *a double whiskey* | *walls of double thickness*

4 made to be used by two people [➔ single]: *a double bed* | *a double garage* → see box at TWO → see picture at BED

5 double figures *BrE*; **double digits** *AmE* the numbers from 10 to 99 [➔ single figures]

double² *n* **1** [C,U] something that is twice as big or twice as much as usual as something else: *Scotch and water please – make it a double.* | *'They offered me £10,000.' 'I'll give you double.'*

2 [C] a room for two people in a hotel [➔ single]

3 doubles [plural] a game played between two pairs of people, especially in tennis [➔ singles]

4 sb's double someone who looks very similar to someone else

double³ *v* [I,T] to become twice as large or twice as much, or to make something do this: *The church has doubled its membership.* | **double in size/number/value etc** *The company has doubled in size.* | **double the size/number/amount etc (of sth)** *We will double the number of police.*

double as sb/sth *phr v* to have a second use, job, or purpose: *The sofa doubles as a bed.*

double back *phr v* to turn around and go back the way you have just come: *He doubled back and headed for Howard Bay.*

double up/over *phr v* to bend at the waist because you are in pain or laughing a lot: **double up with pain/laughter** *They all doubled up with laughter.* —**doubled up** *adj*

double⁴ *determiner* twice as big, twice as much, or twice as many: **double the amount/ number/size etc** *We'll need double this amount for eight people.*

double-barrelled *BrE*; **double-barreled** *AmE* /ˌdʌbəl 'bærəld/ **1** a double-barrelled gun has two parts that bullets are fired through **2** *BrE* a double-barrelled family name has two parts

double bass /ˌdʌbəl 'beɪs/ n [C] a very large wooden musical instrument like a VIOLIN that you play standing up → see picture on page A6

double-breasted /ˌdʌbəl 'brestᵻd/ adj a double-breasted jacket or coat has two sets of buttons

double-'check v [I,T] to check something again so that you are completely sure: I think I turned off the oven, but I'll double-check.

double-'click v [I] to press a button on a computer MOUSE twice

double-'cross v [T] to cheat someone when you are involved in something dishonest together —double cross n [C]

double-decker /ˌdʌbəl 'dekə◂ $ -ər◂/ n [C] a bus with two levels

double 'glazing n [U] BrE two layers of glass in windows or doors, that help keep a room warmer and quieter —double glaze v [T]

double 'life n [C] if someone leads a double life, they have another secret family, job, or activity

double 'standard n [C] a rule or principle that is unfair because it treats one person or group differently from another: They accuse the government of double standards.

double 'take n do a double take to look at someone or something again because you are surprised by what you saw or heard

doubly /ˈdʌbli/ adv **1 doubly difficult/ important/interesting etc** much more difficult, important etc than usual: The journey will be doubly difficult in winter. **2** in two ways or for two reasons: You are doubly mistaken.

doubt¹ /daʊt/ n

1 [C,U] a feeling that you have when you are not certain whether something is true or possible: +about I have doubts about his ability to do the job. | +(that) There's no doubt that their marriage was a mistake. | NASA's report casts doubt on the findings.
2 beyond doubt/without doubt used to say that something is definitely true: The state must prove beyond reasonable doubt that he is guilty. | I knew without a shadow of doubt that I would lose.
3 be in doubt a) if something is in doubt, it may not succeed or be able to continue: The future of the peace talks are in doubt. **b)** if something is in doubt, you think that it may not be true: Her honesty was never in doubt.
4 no doubt used to say that you think something is true: No doubt they'll win. | She was a top student, no doubt about it (=used to emphasize that something is definitely true).

doubt² v [T]

1 to think that something may not be true or that it is unlikely: Do you doubt her story? | +(that) I doubt we will ever see her again. | He might come, but I doubt it.
2 to not trust or believe someone or something: Nobody doubts his ability to stay calm in a crisis. | Do you doubt my word (=think I am lying)?

doubtful /ˈdaʊtfəl/ adj **1** probably not true, or unlikely to happen: it is doubtful if/whether It is doubtful whether she will survive. **2** not

certain about something: +if/whether I'm still doubtful if I should take the job. —doubtfully adv

doubtless /ˈdaʊtləs/ adv used when saying that something is very likely to happen or be true: There will doubtless be someone at the party that you know.

dough /dəʊ $ doʊ/ n [U] a mixture containing flour that you use to make bread or PASTRY

doughnut, donut /ˈdəʊnʌt $ 'doʊ-/ n [C] a small cake that is usually shaped like a ring

dour /dʊə, 'daʊə $ daʊr, dʊr/ adj looking unfriendly and serious: a dour expression

douse, dowse /daʊs/ v [T] to pour water or another liquid over something: Firefighters quickly doused the blaze. | They doused the wood with petrol and set it alight.

dove¹ /dʌv/ n [C] a type of small white bird often used as a sign of peace

dove² /dəʊv $ doʊv/ v AmE a past tense of DIVE

dowdy /ˈdaʊdi/ adj unattractive or unfashionable

down¹ /daʊn/ adv, prep

1 towards or in a lower place [≠ up]: Dave bent down to tie his shoelace. | Get down off the table. | They came running down the stairs. | She looked down into the courtyard. | The bathroom is down those stairs. → see picture on page A8
2 into a sitting or lying position: Please sit down. | I think I'll go and lie down.
3 at or to a place which is further along a path, road etc: She's just gone down to the shops. | There's a cafe a hundred yards down the road. | A boy was running down the street.
4 in or towards the south [≠ up]: They drove all the way down from Boston to Miami. | He's bought a villa down south.
5 to or at a lower rate or amount [≠ up]: Keep your speed down. | Can you turn the radio down? | +to He cut his report down to three pages.
6 write/note/take etc sth down to write something on paper: I'll write down the address for you. | Start by jotting down a few ideas.
7 if you are down for something, you are on a list of people who will do something: +for Purvis is down for the 200 metres race.
8 from an earlier time to a later time: The story was handed down in the family from father to son. | +to traditions that have come down to us from medieval times

down² adj [not before noun] **1** unhappy: I've never seen Brett looking so down. → see box at SAD **2** behind in a game by a particular number of points: We were down by 6 points at half-time. **3** a computer that is down is not working

down³ v [T] to drink something quickly: Matt downed his coffee and left. → see box at DRINK

down⁴ n [U] thin soft feathers or hair

down-and-'out n [C] someone who has no home, job, or money —down-and-out adj

downcast /ˈdaʊnkɑːst $ -kæst/ adj **1** sad or upset **2** downcast eyes are looking down

downer /ˈdaʊnə $ -ər/ n informal **1** [singular] an experience that makes you feel unhappy: a movie that ends on a real downer **2** [C] a drug that makes you feel relaxed

downfall /ˈdaʊnfɔːl $ -fɒːl/ n [singular] when someone stops being successful: the scandal that led to his downfall

downgrade /'daʊngreɪd/ v [T] to make someone or something seem less important

downhearted /ˌdaʊn'hɑːtɪd ◄ $ -ɑːr-/ adj sad, especially because of not achieving what you want

downhill /ˌdaʊn'hɪl ◄/ adj, adv **1** towards the bottom of a hill, or on a slope that goes down [≠ **uphill**]: The truck rolled downhill. | downhill skiing **2 go downhill** to become worse: After Bob lost his job, things went downhill rapidly. **3 be all downhill/be downhill all the way** to become easier: The worst is over. It's all downhill from here.

Downing Street /'daʊnɪŋ striːt/ n [U] the government of Great Britain

download /ˌdaʊn'ləʊd $ 'daʊnloʊd/ v [T] to receive information or programs on a computer, especially using the INTERNET → see box at CAMERA

downmarket /ˌdaʊn'mɑːkɪt ◄ $ -ɑːr-/ adj BrE cheap and not of good quality [= **downscale** AmE]: They wanted to change their downmarket image.

down 'payment n [C] the first payment that you make when you are going to pay for something in regular payments: We've made a down payment on a new car.

downplay /ˌdaʊn'pleɪ $ 'daʊnpleɪ/ v [T] **downplayed, downplaying, downplays** to make something seem less important than it really is [= **play down**]: The police downplayed the seriousness of the situation.

downpour /'daʊnpɔː $ -pɔːr/ n [C usually singular] a lot of rain that falls in a short time → see box at RAIN

downright /'daʊnraɪt/ adv, adj used to emphasize what you are saying, especially when you are saying that something is bad: It's downright dangerous! | It's a downright disgrace.

downscale[1] /'daʊnskeɪl/ adj AmE downscale goods or services are cheap and not of very good quality [= **downmarket** BrE]

downshifting /'daʊnˌʃɪftɪŋ/ n [U] when you change your job so that you earn less but have a nicer life —**downshift** v [I]

downside /'daʊnsaɪd/ n [singular] the bad part of something: +**of** The downside of the plan is the cost.

downsize /'daʊnsaɪz/ v [I,T] to reduce the number of workers in a company —**downsizing** n [U]

'Down's ,Syndrome also **Downs** n [U] a condition that someone is born with, that stops them from developing normally both mentally and physically

downstairs /ˌdaʊn'steəz ◄ $ -'sterz ◄/ adj, adv on or towards a lower level of a building, especially a house [≠ **upstairs**]: Go downstairs and answer the door. | There was a sound from downstairs. | He was downstairs. | A light was on in one of the downstairs rooms.

downstream /ˌdaʊn'striːm ◄/ adv in the same direction that a river or stream is flowing [≠ **upstream**]

down-to-'earth adj practical and direct in a sensible honest way: She's very friendly and down-to-earth.

downtown /ˌdaʊn'taʊn ◄/ adj, adv especially AmE to or in the centre or main business area of

a city [≠ **uptown**]: Do you want to go downtown? | an office in downtown New York | **downtown offices/hotels**

downtrodden /'daʊnˌtrɒdn $ -ˌtrɑː-/ adj treated badly by people who have power

downturn /'daʊntɜːn $ -tɜːrn/ n [C usually singular] a time when there is less business activity and conditions become worse: +**in** a downturn in the economy

downwards /'daʊnwədz $ -wərdz/ especially BrE, **downward** especially AmE adv **1** moving or pointing towards a lower position [≠ **upwards**]: The balloon drifted slowly downwards. **2** decreasing to a lower level [≠ **upwards**]: The dollar moved downwards against the pound. —**downward** adj

downwind /ˌdaʊn'wɪnd/ adj, adv in the same direction that the wind is moving

dowry /'daʊəri $ 'daʊri/ n [C] plural **dowries** money or property which, in some societies, is given to a man by his wife's family when they marry

dowse /daʊs/ v another spelling of DOUSE

doze /dəʊz $ doʊz/ v [I] to sleep lightly, usually for a short time: Graham dozed for an hour.
    doze off phr v to fall asleep: I was just dozing off when they arrived.

dozen /'dʌzən/ number plural **dozen** or **dozens**
1 twelve: a dozen eggs | **two/three/four etc dozen** (=24, 36, 48 etc) The number of deaths has risen to more than two dozen. | Chris, Helen, and **half a dozen** others went on holiday together. | A **dozen or so** (=about 12) cars were parked near the entrance.
2 a lot of: **a dozen** I've heard this story a dozen times before. | **dozens of sth** We asked dozens of people.

Dr the written abbreviation of **Doctor**

drab /dræb/ adj not interesting or bright: Everything looked so drab and colourless. —**drabness** n [U]

draconian /drə'kəʊniən $ -'koʊ-/ adj extremely strict, in an unpleasant way: **draconian measures**

draft[1] /drɑːft $ dræft/ n [C] **1** a piece of writing or a drawing that is not yet in its finished form: +**of** the first draft of his novel | a **rough draft** | The final draft (=final form) had been completed. | a **draft report 2** a written order for money to be paid by a bank **3** the American spelling of DRAUGHT[1] **4 the draft** AmE a system in which people must join the armed forces

draft[2] v [T] **1** to write a plan, letter, report etc that will change before it is finished: The House plans to **draft a bill** on education. **2** AmE to order someone to join the armed forces [= **conscript**]: **draft sb into sth** Brad's been drafted into the army. → see box at ARMY

draft[3] adj the American spelling of DRAUGHT[2]

draftsman /'drɑːftsmən $ 'dræfts-/ n the American spelling of DRAUGHTSMAN

drafty /'drɑːfti $ 'dræfti/ adj the American spelling of DRAUGHTY

drag[1] /dræg/ v **dragged, dragging 1** [T] to pull someone or something somewhere: **drag sth away/along/through etc** He dragged his sledge through the snow. → see box at PULL → see picture at PULL[1] **2** [T] to move words, pictures etc on a computer screen by pulling them with the mouse: *You can drag and drop text like this.* **3** [T] to make someone go somewhere, although they do not want: **drag sb to/into/out of etc sth** *My mother used to drag me to church every week.* | **drag yourself away from the TV** (=stop watching TV) **4** [I] if time or an event drags, it seems to pass slowly and you feel bored: *History lessons always seemed to drag.* **5** [I] if something is dragging along the ground, part of it is touching the ground as you move: *Your coat's dragging in the mud.* **6 drag your feet/heels** to delay doing something: *The government were dragging their feet over reforms.*

drag sb/sth into sth *phr v* to involve someone or something in an unpleasant situation: *I'm sorry to drag you into this mess.*

drag on *phr v* to continue for too long: *The meeting dragged on all afternoon.*

drag sth ⇔ **out** *phr v* to make a situation or event last longer than necessary: *How much longer are you going to drag this argument out?*

drag sth **out of** sb *phr v* to force someone to tell you something

drag² *n* **1 a drag** *informal* something or someone that is annoying or boring: *'I have to stay in tonight.' 'What a drag.'* **2** [C] when someone breathes in smoke from their cigarette: *He took a drag on his cigarette.* **3 in drag** a man in drag is wearing women's clothes **4 the main drag** *informal especially AmE* the main road through a town → see box at **ROAD**

dragon /'drægən/ *n* [C] an imaginary animal that breathes fire and has wings and a tail

dragonfly /'drægənflaɪ/ *n* [C] plural **dragonflies** a flying insect with a long brightly-coloured body

drain¹ /dreɪn/ *v* **1 a)** [T] to make the water or liquid in something flow away: **drain sth from sth** *Drain the water from the peas.* | *Can you drain the pasta, please?* **b)** [I] if something drains, the liquid from it flows away: *Leave the dishes to drain.* **c)** [I] if a liquid drains away, it flows out: **+away/off/from** *The bath water slowly drained away.* **2 drain your glass/cup** to drink all the liquid in your glass or cup **3** [T] to make you very tired: *The experience drained her completely.* **4** [T] to use too much of something, especially money

drain² *n* [C] **1** a pipe or hole through which waste liquids are carried away: *a blocked drain* **2 a drain on sb/sth** something that uses too much time, money, or strength: *The war was an enormous drain on economic resources.* **3 down the drain** *informal* being wasted: *He doesn't want to see all his work going down the drain.*

drainage /'dreɪnɪdʒ/ *n* [U] the system or process by which water or waste liquid flows away from a place

drained /dreɪnd/ *adj* very tired: *Afterwards I felt completely drained.*

'draining board also **'drain board** *AmE n* [C] an area next to a kitchen SINK where you put wet dishes to dry

drainpipe /'dreɪnpaɪp/ *n* [C] *BrE* a pipe that carries rain water down from the roof of a building

drama /'drɑːmə $ 'drɑːmə, 'dræmə/ *n* **1** [C,U] a play for the theatre, television, or radio, or plays in general: *a new TV drama* | *perform-ances of dance, music, and drama* → see box at **TELEVISION 2** [U] the study of performing in plays: **drama classes** | *the new drama teacher* **3** [C,U] exciting or unusual things that happen: *a night of high drama*

dramatic /drə'mætɪk/ *adj* **1** sudden and sur-prising: *a dramatic change in temperature* **2** exciting and impressive: *a dramatic speech* **3** related to the theatre or plays: *Miller's dra-matic works* **4** showing your feelings in a way that makes other people notice you: *Tony threw up his hands in a dramatic gesture.* —**dramatically** /-kli/ *adv*

dramatist /'dræmətɪst/ *n* [C] someone who writes plays

dramatize also **-ise** *BrE* /'dræmətaɪz/ [T] **1** to make a book or event into a play: *a novel drama-tized for TV* **2** to make something seem more serious than it really is: *Do you always have to dramatize everything?* —**dramatization** /ˌdræmətaɪ'zeɪʃən $ -tə-/ *n* [C,U]

drank /dræŋk/ *v* the past tense of DRINK

drape /dreɪp/ *v* [T] to put cloth or clothing over or around something: **drape sth over/across/ around sth** *He draped his coat over a chair.* | **be draped in sth** *The coffin was draped in black.*

drapes /dreɪps/ *n* [plural] *AmE* long heavy cur-tains

drastic /'dræstɪk/ *adj* drastic action is extreme, and has an effect immediately: *The President promised drastic changes in health care.* —**drastically** /-kli/ *adv*: *Prices have been drasti-cally reduced.*

draught¹ *BrE*; **draft** *AmE* /drɑːft $ dræft/ *n* **1** [C] a current of air blowing through a room **2 on draught** beer that is on draught is served from a large container rather than from a bottle **3 draughts** *BrE* [U] a game played by two people, each with 12 round pieces, on a board of 64 squares [= checkers *AmE*]

draught² *BrE*; **draft** *AmE adj* [only before noun] draught beer is served from a large con-tainer rather than a bottle

draughtsman *BrE*; **draftsman** *AmE* /'drɑːftsmən $ 'dræfts-/ *n* someone who draws the parts of a new building or machine

draughty *BrE*; **drafty** *AmE* /'drɑːfti $ 'dræfti/ *adj* a draughty room has cold air blowing through it

draw¹ /drɔː $ drɔː/ *v* past tense **drew** /druː/ past participle **drawn** /drɔːn $ drɔːn/

1 [I,T] to make a picture of something with a pencil or a pen: *She was drawing a picture of a tree.* | **draw sb sth** *Can you draw me a map?* | *I can't draw very well.*

2 draw (sb's) attention to sb/sth to make someone notice something: *I'd like to draw your attention to the last paragraph.* | *She didn't want to draw attention to herself.*

3 draw conclusions to decide something, based on information that you have: *They have not drawn any conclusions from the data.*

4 draw a distinction/comparison to say that two things are different/similar: *The report drew a distinction between 'helping' and 'caring'.*

5 [T] to get a reaction, help, or support from someone or something: *His comments **drew** an angry response.* | **draw sth from sth** *I drew comfort from her kind words.*
6 [T] to take money from your bank account: *I'd just drawn £50 out of the bank.*
7 [T] to receive official payments, for example because you are ill or old: *I'll be **drawing** my pension soon.*
8 [T] to attract or interest someone: **draw sb to sth** *What first drew you to acting?* | *Her eye was drawn to a painting on the wall.*
9 [T] to pull something or someone in a particular direction: **draw sb/sth aside/up/into etc** *He drew her into his arms.* | **draw sth out/from sth** *He reached into his pocket and draw out a piece of paper.*
10 draw a gun/knife/sword to take a weapon from its container or from your pocket
11 draw blood to make blood come out of someone's skin
12 [I] to move in a particular direction: **+away/ out of/past** *The car drew away.*
13 [I,T] *especially BrE* if two teams or players draw, they have the same number of points: **+with** *Ireland drew with France.* | *They drew 3–3.*
14 draw the curtains to open or close curtains
15 [T] to pick tickets or cards in order to decide who will win a prize
16 draw near *literary* to move closer in time or space: *The summer holidays are drawing near.*
17 draw to an end/a close/a halt to end or stop: *Another year was drawing to an end.*
18 draw the line (at sth) to refuse to do something because you do not approve of it, although you will do other things: *I don't mind helping you, but I draw the line at telling lies.*
19 draw a blank to be unable to find something or think of something
20 draw breath a) to take air into your lungs **b)** to rest when you are busy: *I needed a moment to draw breath.*
21 be drawn (on sth) if you refuse to be drawn on a subject, you refuse to talk about it

draw in *phr v* if the days or nights are drawing in, it is getting dark earlier in the evening

draw sb into sth *phr v* to involve someone in something that they do not want to do: *Keith refused to be drawn into our argument.*

draw on sth *phr v* to use something, for example information or experience, for a particular purpose: *His books **draw heavily on** his experience as a therapist.*

draw up *phr v* **1 draw sth ⇔ up** to prepare a document: *We **drew up** a list of the options.* **2** if a vehicle draws up, it stops: *Another car drew up beside ours.*

draw² *n* [C] **1** *especially BrE* a game that ends with both teams or players having the same number of points: *The match **ended in a draw**.* | *a goalless draw* **2** when someone or something is chosen by chance, for example the winning ticket in a competition, or the teams who will play against each other in a competition: *a prize draw* | **+for** *the draw for the World Cup* **3** something that attracts visitors: *The museum will be a **big draw**.*

drawback /ˈdrɔːbæk $ ˈdrɒː-/ *n* [C] a disadvantage: **+of/to** *The only drawback to a holiday in Scotland is the weather.*

drawer /drɔː $ drɒːr/ *n* [C] part of a piece of furniture, which can be pulled out and is used for keeping things in: *Put it in the **desk drawer**.* | **the bottom/top/left-hand drawer**

drawing /ˈdrɔːɪŋ $ ˈdrɒː-/ *n*
1 [C] a picture you make with a pen or pencil: **+of** *She showed us a drawing of the house.*
2 [U] the art or skill of making pictures with a pen or pencil: *I've never been good at drawing.* → see box at **ART**

ˈ**drawing board** *n* **go back to the drawing board** to start working on a new plan or idea, because the one you tried before failed

ˈ**drawing pin** *n* [C] *BrE* a short pin with a wide flat top, used for fastening paper to a board [= **thumbtack** *AmE*]

ˈ**drawing room** *n* [C] *old-fashioned* a large room in a house where people can sit and talk and meet visitors

drawl /drɔːl $ drɒːl/ *v* [I,T] to speak slowly with long vowel sounds —**drawl** *n* [singular] *a slow Texas drawl*

drawn¹ /drɔːn $ drɒːn/ *v* the past participle of DRAW

drawn² *adj* looking tired, worried, or ill

ˌ**drawn-ˈout** *adj* continuing for a very long time: *a **long drawn-out** process*

dread¹ /dred/ *v* [T] to feel very worried about something that is going to happen: *Phil's really dreading his interview tomorrow.* | **dread doing sth** *I always dread going to the dentist's.* | *I **dread to think** what effect it will have* (=it will be very bad).

dread² *n* [U] a feeling of worry or fear: *She **lives in dread** of the disease returning.*

dreadful /ˈdredfəl/ *adj* very bad or unpleasant: *What dreadful weather!* → see box at **HORRIBLE** —**dreadfully** *adv*

dreadlocks /ˈdredlɒks $ -lɑːks/ *n* [plural] a style of arranging your hair so that it hangs in thick pieces like rope

dream¹ /driːm/ *n* [C]
1 a series of thoughts, images, and experiences that come into your mind when you are asleep [➡ **daydream**]: **+about** *I had a dream about you last night.* | *Did you have a **bad dream**?*
2 something that you hope will happen: *It was his dream to play football for his country.* | **+of** *He **fulfilled** his dream of becoming a police officer.* | **beyond your wildest dreams** (=better than anything you imagined or hoped) | *The whole experience has been a **dream come true** (=as good as I hoped).* | **the man/home/holiday etc of your dreams** (=the perfect man, home etc)
3 like a dream a) if something is like a dream, it does not seem real: *The last few days have seemed like a dream.* **b)** extremely well: *The plan **worked like a dream**.*
4 in a dream not noticing or paying attention to what is happening: *Ruth went about her tasks in a dream.*
5 a dream world a good situation which exists only in your imagination: *If you believe that, you're **living in a dream world**.*

dream² v past tense and past participle **dreamed** or **dreamt** /dremt/

1 [I,T] to have a dream while you are asleep [→ **daydream**]: **+(that)** *I often dream that I'm falling.* | **+about** *I dreamt about you last night.*

2 [I,T] to think about something that you would like to happen: **+of/about** *We dream of having our own home.* | **+(that)** *Cath never dreamt she'd be offered the job* (=she did not expect it to happen).

3 wouldn't dream of (doing) sth *spoken* used to say that you would never do something because you think it is wrong: *I wouldn't dream of letting her go on her own.*

dream sth ⇔ up *phr v* to think of a plan or idea, especially an unusual one: *Who dreams up these TV commercials?*

dream³ adj [only before noun] perfect, or exactly what you wanted: *They had built their **dream home**.*

dreamer /'dri:mə $ -ər/ n [C] someone who has plans or ideas that are not practical

dreamy /'dri:mi/ adj **1** imagining pleasant things and not paying attention: *a dreamy look* **2** pleasant, peaceful, and relaxing: *dreamy music* —**dreamily** adv

dreary /'drɪəri $ 'drɪri/ adj dull and uninteresting: *the same old dreary jobs* —**drearily** adv

dredge /dredʒ/ v [T] to move mud or sand from the bottom of a river or lake, or to search for something by doing this

dredge sth ⇔ up *phr v* to start talking about something bad or unpleasant that happened a long time ago: *Why do the papers have to dredge up that old story?*

dregs /dregz/ n [plural] a small amount of a drink, sometimes with bits in, left at the bottom of a cup, glass, or bottle

drench /drentʃ/ v [T] to make something completely wet —**drenched** adj: *I was **drenched** in **sweat**.*

dress¹ /dres/ n

1 [C] a piece of clothing worn by a woman or girl, which covers the top of her body and part or all of her legs [→ **skirt**]: *She was **wearing** a white **dress**.* | *a beautiful **wedding dress** →* see picture at CLOTHES

2 [U] clothing of a particular type: *The audience wore **evening dress*** (=formal clothes worn to important social events). | *He has no **dress sense*** (=ability to choose nice clothes). | *The club has a strict **dress code*** (=rules about what you can wear).

→ FANCY DRESS

dress² v

1 [I,T] to put clothes on someone or on yourself: *Can you dress the kids?* | *Hurry up and **get dressed**!*

2 be dressed to be wearing clothes: *Are you dressed yet?* | **be dressed in sth** *He was dressed in a suit.* | **smartly/elegantly/casually etc dressed** *a smartly dressed young officer* | **well/badly dressed** (=wearing tidy clothes or untidy clothes) | *She lay down on the bed **fully dressed*** (=wearing all her clothes).

3 [I] to wear particular clothes: *Dress warmly – it's cold outside.* | **+for** *a splendid hotel where*

*everyone **dresses for** dinner* (=wears formal clothes for an evening meal)

4 dress a wound/cut to clean and cover a wound to protect it

dress down *phr v* to wear clothes that are less formal than the ones you usually wear: *She dressed down in old jeans and a T-shirt.*

dress up *phr v* **1** to wear special clothes for fun: **+as** *I went to the party dressed up as a gorilla.* | **+in** *At Halloween, the kids dress up in costumes and collect candy.* **2** to wear clothes that are more formal than the ones you usually wear: *It's only a small party. You don't need to dress up.*

dresser /'dresə $ -ər/ n [C] **1** *BrE* a large piece of furniture with shelves for holding dishes and plates **2** *AmE* a piece of furniture with drawers for holding clothes [= **chest of drawers** *BrE*]

dressing /'dresɪŋ/ n **1** also **salad dressing** [C,U] a mixture of oil and VINEGAR that you pour over SALAD **2** [C] a piece of material used for covering a wound: *The nurse **changed** his **dressing**.*

'dressing gown n [C] *BrE* a long piece of clothing worn before going to bed or after getting out of bed [= **robe** *AmE*]

'dressing room n [C] a room where performers get ready for a show

'dressing ˌtable n [C] *BrE* a piece of furniture with a mirror in a bedroom, where you do your hair or MAKE-UP

'dress reˌhearsal n [C] the final practice for a show, with all the clothes and objects which will be used

drew /dru:/ v the past tense of DRAW

dribble /'drɪbəl/ v [I,T] **1** *BrE* if you dribble, liquid comes out of your mouth onto your face [= **drool** *AmE*]: *The baby's dribbling on your jacket.* **2** to flow slowly in irregular drops: **+from/down/out** *Blood dribbled down the side of his face.* **3** to move a ball using repeated movements of your arm or leg: *Dribble the ball up to the net.* —**dribble** n [C,U]

dribs and drabs /ˌdrɪbz ən 'dræbz/ n **in dribs and drabs** in small amounts, not all at once: *The guests arrived in dribs and drabs.*

dried /draɪd/ v the past tense and past participle of DRY

drier /'draɪə $ -ər/ n [C] another spelling of DRYER

drift¹ /drɪft/ v [I] **1** to move slowly on water or in air: **+out/towards/along etc** *The boat slowly drifted out to sea.* | *Smoke was drifting across the road.* **2** to move or do something gradually, without any plan or purpose: **+towards/across/away etc** *People were drifting out of the stadium.* | **your mind/thoughts drift** *His thoughts drifted back to their earlier conversation.* **3** if snow or sand drifts, the wind moves it into large piles

drift apart *phr v* if people drift apart, they gradually stop being friends

drift off *phr v* to gradually go to sleep: *I drifted off to sleep in front of the telly.*

drift² n [C] **1** a large pile of snow or sand that has been blown by the wind: *massive snow drifts* **2 catch/get the drift (of sth)** understand the general meaning of what someone is saying: *I* *think I caught the drift of his argument.* **3** a gradual movement from one place to another: *the drift away from the countryside to the big cities in the north.*

drill¹ /drɪl/ n

1 [C] a machine used for making holes in something hard: *an electric drill* | *a dentist's drill*
2 [C,U] a method of teaching something by making people repeat the same thing many times: *a pronunciation drill*
3 fire/emergency drill when you practise what you should do in a dangerous situation
4 [U] when soldiers practise marching

drill² v **1** [I,T] to make a hole with a drill: *Drill a hole in each corner.* | **drill for oil/gas etc** (=look for oil, gas etc under the ground) **2** [T] to teach someone by making them repeat the same thing many times

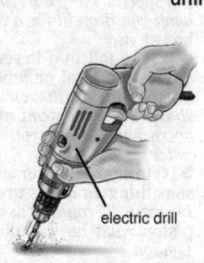

drill

electric drill

drily /'draɪli/ adv another spelling of DRYLY

drink¹ /drɪŋk/ v past tense **drank** /dræŋk/ past participle **drunk** /drʌŋk/

1 [I,T] to take liquid into your mouth and swallow it: *Would you like something to drink?* | *I drink too much coffee.* | *Is this water safe to drink?*

THESAURUS

sip also **take a sip** – to drink something very slowly
slurp informal – to drink something in a noisy way
gulp sth down also **down sth** – to drink all of something very quickly: *I downed my beer and left.*
knock sth back informal – to drink all of an alcoholic drink very quickly
swig informal also **take/have a swig** informal – to drink something quickly with large mouthfuls, especially from a bottle: *Can I have a swig of your beer?*
→ EAT

2 [I] to drink alcohol, especially regularly: *Ahmet doesn't drink, does he?* | *Don't drink and drive.*
—**drinking** n [U]
drink to sb/sth phr v to wish someone success, good health etc when you have an alcoholic drink: *Let's drink to Patrick's success in his new job.*

drink² n [C,U]

1 liquid that you drink: **+of** *Can I have a drink of water please?* | *Bring your own food and drink.* | *They sell snacks and soft drinks* (=non-alcoholic drinks).
2 an alcoholic drink: *We had a couple of drinks at lunch time.* | *Do you want to go for a drink after work?* | *She has a serious drink problem* (=drinks too much alcohol). → see box at PARTY

drink 'driving BrE; **drunk 'driving** AmE n [U] the crime of driving a car after drinking too much alcohol —**drink driver** n [C]

drinker /'drɪŋkə $ -ər/ n [C] someone who often drinks alcohol: *He's quite a heavy drinker* (=he drinks a lot).

'drinking ,water n [U] water which is clean enough to drink

drip¹ /drɪp/ v **dripped**, **dripping** [I,T] to let liquid fall in small drops: *That tap's still dripping.* | *Don't drip blood on the carpet!* | **+from/off/ through etc** *Water was dripping through the ceiling.* | **be dripping with water/sweat etc** *They were both dripping with sweat.* → see picture at FLOW²

drip² n **1** [C] a small drop of liquid that falls from something: *She put a bucket on the floor to catch the drips.* **2** [singular] the sound of a liquid falling in small drops: *the steady drip of rain from the roof* **3** [C] BrE a piece of hospital equipment used for putting liquids directly into a person's blood [= IV AmE]: **on a drip** *She was put on a drip after the operation.* **4** [C] informal someone who is boring and weak

drive¹ /draɪv/ v past tense **drove** /drəʊv $ droʊv/ past participle **driven** /'drɪvən/

1 a) [I,T] to make a car, bus, or truck move forward: *Can you drive?* | *Fiona drives a BMW.* **b)** to take someone somewhere in a car: **drive sb to sth** *Can I drive you to the station?* | *After the party, he drove her home.* **c)** [I] to travel somewhere in a car: **+to/down/off etc** *I drive to work every day.* | *Do you want to take a bus or drive?* → see box at TRAVEL → see picture at RIDE¹

TOPIC

When you get into your car, you **fasten** your **seatbelt**, then you turn the key in the **ignition**. You put the car **into first gear**. You **release** the **handbrake**. You look in your mirror before **pulling out**. You **press** the **accelerator (pedal)** BrE /**gas pedal** AmE with your foot to make the car go faster and you **press** the **clutch (pedal)** to **change gear**. When you turn left or right, you must **signal**. When you want to **slow down**, you **press** the **brake (pedal)** with your foot. When you **park** your car, you **put the handbrake on**.

2 [T] to force people or animals to move to a different place: *Crime drives business away from an area.*
3 [T] to strongly influence someone to do something: **drive sb to sth** *Marriage problems eventually drove her to drink.*
4 [T] to make someone very angry or excited: **drive sb crazy/mad/nuts/insane** (=make sb very angry) *This cough is driving me mad.*
5 [T] to hit something such as a stick or nail very hard into a surface: **drive sth into sth** *a tool for driving nails into floorboards*
6 [T] to make a person or animal work very hard: *Dad's driving himself too hard.*
7 [T] to provide the power for a machine: *a petrol-driven lawnmower*
8 what sb is driving at what someone is really trying to say: *Look, just what are you driving at?*
drive sb ⇔ away phr v to behave in a bad way that makes someone leave: *Her husband's violence finally drove her away.*

D

drive sb ⇔ **off** phr v to force someone to go away

drive² n

1 [C] a trip in a car: *Let's go for a drive along the coast.* | *Chris took the kids for a drive.* | **long/short drive** *It's a long drive home.*

2 [C] the road or area for cars between a house and the street [= **driveway**]

3 [C] a strong natural need: *the male sex drive*

4 [C] a planned effort to achieve a particular result: *500 jobs have gone as part of an economy drive* (=effort to save money). | **drive to do sth** *a nationwide drive to crack down on crime*

5 [U] determination and energy to succeed: *Mel's got tremendous drive.*

6 [C] a piece of equipment in a computer that can read and store information: *a CD-ROM drive*

7 [U] the power from an engine that makes the wheels of a vehicle go round: *a truck with four-wheel drive*

→ DISK DRIVE, ZIP DRIVE

'drive-by adj **drive-by shooting/killing etc** when someone is shot from a moving car

'drive-in adj **drive-in restaurant/cinema/movie** a restaurant, cinema etc where you can buy food or watch a film without leaving your car —**drive-in** n [C]

drivel /'drɪvəl/ n [U] nonsense: *He talks such drivel sometimes!*

driven /'drɪvən/ v the past participle of DRIVE

driver /'draɪvə $ -ər/ n [C]

1 someone who drives a car, truck, bus etc: *a taxi driver*

2 back seat driver a passenger in the back of a car who gives unwanted advice to the driver about how to drive

'driver's ,license n [C] AmE a DRIVING LICENCE

'drive-through adj **drive-through restaurant, bank etc** a restaurant, bank etc that you can use without getting out of your car

driveway /'draɪvweɪ/ also **drive** n [C] a small road that leads up to a person's house

driving¹ /'draɪvɪŋ/ adj **1 driving rain/snow** rain or snow that is falling very heavily and fast

2 driving force (behind sth) the person or organization who is mainly responsible for making something happen: *Her father is the driving force behind her tennis career.*

driving² n [U] when someone drives a car, or the way someone drives: *I'm having driving lessons.* | *He was convicted of dangerous driving.*

→ DRINK DRIVING

'driving ,licence BrE; **'driver's ,license** AmE n [C] an official card that says that you are legally allowed to drive a car

drizzle /'drɪzəl/ v [I] to rain very lightly: *It had just begun to drizzle.* → see box at WEATHER → and RAIN —**drizzle** n [U]

drone /drəun $ droun/ v [I] to make a low continuous noise: *A plane droned overhead.* —**drone** n [singular]

drone on phr v to talk in a boring way for a long time: +**about** *Joe kept droning on about work.*

drool /druːl/ v [I] **1** if you drool, the liquid in your mouth runs out onto your chin: *The dog was drooling at the sight of the food.* **2** to show in a silly way that you like someone or something a lot: +**over** *teenagers drooling over the lead singer*

droop /druːp/ v [I] if something droops, it hangs down, for example because it is weak or heavy: *The plants need watering. They're starting to droop.*

drop¹ /drɒp $ drɑːp/ v **dropped, dropping**

1 [T] to let something you are holding fall to the ground: *Tom dropped his bag by the door.* | *Enemy aircraft dropped bombs on the city.* → see picture on page A11

2 [I] to fall to or towards the ground: +**from/off/to etc** *She undid the zip and let her dress drop to the floor.*

3 [I] to visit someone you know, usually without telling them that you are coming: +**by/round/in** *I dropped by to see if you're feeling better.* | *Why don't you drop in for a drink one evening?* → see box at VISIT

4 [I,T] to fall to a lower level or amount, or to reduce the level or amount of something: *The number of deaths on this road has dropped sharply.* | *The temperature can drop to -15° overnight.* | *Have you asked them to drop the price?*

5 [T] to stop doing something or continuing with something: *Students are allowed to drop history in year 9.* | *I couldn't ask him to drop everything* (=stop what he was doing) *just to drive me to London.*

6 [T] to take someone to a place in a car, before continuing to somewhere else: *Just drop me here – I can walk the rest of the way.* | **drop sb off** *She drops the kids off at school on her way to work.*

7 [T] to decide not to include someone in a team: **drop sb from sth** *He's been dropped from the England squad for the second test.*

8 [T] to stop talking about something: *If you think I'm going to let it drop, you're wrong.* | *Just drop it, will you? I don't want to argue.*

9 drop dead informal to die suddenly and unexpectedly

10 drop sb a line informal to write a letter to someone

drop off phr v informal to go to sleep

drop out phr v to stop going to university or school before you have completed your studies, or to stop doing an activity before you finish it: +**of** *He had dropped out of college.*

drop² n

1 [C] a very small amount of liquid: +**of** *drops of rain* | *coffee with a little drop of brandy*

2 [singular] the distance from a high place to the ground: *There is a sheer drop to the valley below.*

3 [singular] a fall in the amount, level, or number of something: +**in** *a sudden drop in temperature*

4 a drop in the ocean BrE **a drop in the bucket** AmE an amount of something that is too small to have any effect

5 eye/ear drops liquid medicine that you put into your eye or ear one drop at a time

'drop-down ,menu n [C] a list of choices which appears on a computer screen when you CLICK on a place on the screen

droplet /'drɒplət $ 'drɑːp-/ n [C] a very small drop of liquid: +**of** *tiny droplets of water*

dropout /'drɒpaʊt $ 'drɑːp-/ n [C] **1** someone who leaves school or college without completing their course: *a highschool dropout* **2** someone who does not want to be part of normal society

droppings /'drɒpɪŋz $ 'drɑː-/ n [plural] solid waste from animals or birds

drought /draʊt/ n [C,U] a long period of dry weather when there is not enough water: *a region hit by severe drought*

drove /drəʊv $ droʊv/ v the past tense of DRIVE

droves /drəʊvz $ droʊvz/ n [plural] crowds of people: **in droves** *Tourists come in droves to see the White House.*

drown /draʊn/ v

1 [I,T] to die by being under water for too long, or to kill someone in this way: *The boys almost drowned in the river.* | *Hundreds of people were drowned when the ferry sank.* | *He saved his brother from drowning.*

2 also **drown out** [T] to prevent a sound from being heard by making a louder noise: *We put on some music to drown out their yelling.* → see box at HEAR

drowsy /'draʊzi/ adj tired and almost asleep [= sleepy]: *The tablets might make you feel drowsy.* —**drowsiness** n [U]

drudgery /'drʌdʒəri/ n [U] boring work: *the drudgery of housework*

drug[1] /drʌg/ n [C]

1 [usually plural] an illegal substance that people take to make them feel happy, relaxed, excited etc: **take/use drugs** *Many teenagers admitted taking drugs at some time.* | *No thanks, I don't do drugs.* | **on drugs** (=taking drugs) *She looks as though she's on drugs.* | **soft drugs** (=less strong drugs such as MARIJUANA) | **hard drugs** (=strong drugs such as COCAINE and HEROIN) | *Reports say he died of a drug overdose* (=he took too much of a drug).

2 a medicine or a substance for making medicines: *a new drug to treat depression* | *the cost of prescription drugs* (=medicines from your doctor) → see box at MEDICINE

drug[2] v [T] drugged, drugging **1** to give someone drugs, usually to stop them feeling pain or to make them sleep **2** to put a drug into someone's food or drink: *His wine had been drugged.*

'drug ,addict n [C] someone who cannot stop taking illegal drugs

drugstore /'drʌgstɔː $ -stɔːr/ n [C] AmE a shop where you can buy medicines, beauty products etc [= chemist's BrE] → see box at SHOP

drum[1] /drʌm/ n [C]

1 a round musical instrument played by hitting it with your hand or a stick [➡ drummer]: *Jason plays the drums.* | **bang/beat a drum** *1000 people marched, beating drums.* → see picture on page A6

2 a large round container for storing liquids such as oil or chemicals

drum[2] v [I,T] drummed, drumming to hit something many times in a way that sounds like drums: *I could hear the rain drumming on the roof.*

drum sth into sb phr v to say something to someone so often that they cannot forget it: *The risks of smoking were drummed into us at school.*

drum sth ⇔ up phr v to try to get help, money etc by asking a lot of people: *We need to drum up more support.*

drummer /'drʌmə $ -ər/ n [C] someone who plays the drums

drumstick /'drʌm,stɪk/ n [C] **1** the leg of a chicken, TURKEY etc, which has been cooked as food **2** a stick that you use to play a drum

drunk[1] /drʌŋk/ v the past participle of DRINK

drunk[2] adj unable to control your behaviour because you have drunk too much alcohol [≠ sober]: *Bill got really drunk at Sue's party.* | *He was too drunk to walk home.*

drunk[3] also **drunkard** /'drʌŋkəd $ -ərd/ n [C] someone who is drunk or who often gets drunk

drunken /'drʌŋkən/ adj [only before noun] behaving in a way that shows that you are drunk: *a drunken crowd* —**drunkenness** n [U]

dry[1] /draɪ/ adj

1 if something is dry, it has no water or other liquid inside it or on its surface [≠ wet]: *Is the washing dry yet?* | *Store in a cool, dry place.*

2 with very little rain [≠ wet]: *hot and dry weather* | *plants which grow in dry conditions*

3 if your mouth, skin, or hair is dry, it does not have enough natural liquid or oil in it: *She licked her dry lips.* | *shampoo for dry hair*

4 someone who has a dry sense of humour seems serious when they are making a joke

5 not interesting or exciting to read or listen to: *dry political debates*

6 dry wine does not have a sweet taste [≠ sweet] —**dryness** n [U] → BONE DRY

dry[2] v [I,T] dried, drying, dries to become dry, or to make something dry: *Hang on, I've just got to dry my hair.* | *I hung my towel up to dry.* | *Here, dry your eyes* (=wipe away your tears). —**dried** adj: *dried fruit* → BLOW DRY

dry off phr v to become dry, or to make something dry: *We dried off in the sun.* | **dry sth ⇔ off** *Clean the cut and dry it off carefully.*

dry out phr v to dry completely, or to dry something completely: *Put your coat on the radiator to dry out.*

dry up phr v **1** if a supply of something dries up, there is no more of it: *Our research project was cancelled when the money dried up.* **2** if a river or lake dries up, the water in it disappears **3** BrE to dry plates, dishes etc that have been washed: **dry sth ⇔ up** *Could you just dry those glasses up?*

,dry-'clean / $ ' . ./ v [T] to clean clothes with chemicals instead of water

,dry 'cleaner's n [C] plural **dry cleaner's** a shop where you take clothes to be dry-cleaned

dryer, drier /'draɪə $ -ər/ n [C] a machine that dries things, especially clothes or hair: *a hair dryer*

dryly, drily /'draɪli/ adv said in a way that sounds serious although you are really joking

dual /'djuːəl $ 'duːəl/ adj [only before noun] having two of something, or two parts: *a dual purpose vehicle* | *My wife has dual nationality. She has Swiss and British passports.*

,dual 'carriageway n [C] BrE a main road that has two lines of traffic travelling in each direction → see box at ROAD

dub /dʌb/ v [T] dubbed, dubbing **1** to change the original spoken language in a film or television programme into another language: **dub sth into sth** *an Italian film dubbed into English* **2** to give someone or something a name that describes them in some way: **dub sb sth** *They immediately dubbed him 'Fatty'.*

dubious /'dju:biəs $ 'du:-/ adj **1** [not before noun] not sure whether something is good or true: **+about** I'm very dubious about this idea. **2** not seeming honest, safe, or valuable: Some of his business activities seem a bit dubious.

duchess /'dʌtʃəs/ n [C] a woman with the highest social rank below a PRINCESS, or the wife of a DUKE: the Duchess of York

duck¹ /dʌk/ v **1** [I,T] to lower your body or head very quickly to avoid being hit or seen: She ducked her head to go through the doorway. | **+behind/under etc** He ducked behind a hedge. **2** [T] informal to avoid something that is difficult or unpleasant: The minister has been accused of ducking the real issue. **3** [T] BrE to push someone under water for a short time as a joke [= dunk AmE]

duck

duck² n [C,U] a common water bird with short legs and a wide beak, or the meat from this bird: roast duck
→ LAME DUCK

duckling /'dʌklɪŋ/ n [C] a young duck

duct /dʌkt/ n [C] **1** a tube in a building for carrying air or electric wires **2** a thin narrow tube inside your body that liquid or air goes through: a tear duct

dud /dʌd/ adj informal useless or not working: a dud light bulb —dud n [C]

dude /dju:d $ du:d/ n [C] especially AmE informal a man: Are you okay, dude?

due¹ /dju: $ du:/ adj

1 [not before noun] expected to happen or arrive at a particular time: **due to do sth** The film is due to start at 10.30. | **+in/on/at** The flight from Munich was due at 7:48 pm. | **+back** My library books are due back tomorrow. | **+for** The car's due for a service soon.
2 **due to sth** because of something: Our bus was late due to heavy traffic.
3 if an amount of money is due, it must be paid: The first payment of £25 is now due.
4 if you are due something, you deserve it, or someone owes it to you: He never got the recognition he was due.
5 **in due course/time** at a more suitable time in the future: Your complaints will be answered in due course.

due² adv **due north/south/east/west** exactly north, south etc

due³ n **1** **give sb his/her etc due** to admit that someone deserves something: But to give him his due, he is good at his job. **2** **dues** [plural] money that you pay regularly to be a member of an organization: union dues

duel /'dju:əl $ 'du:əl/ n [C] a fight between two people with guns or swords —duel v [I]

duet /dju'et $ du'et/ n [C] a piece of music for two performers

dug /dʌg/ v the past tense and past participle of DIG

duke /dju:k $ du:k/ n [C] a man with the highest social rank below a PRINCE

dull¹ /dʌl/ adj

1 not interesting or exciting: a pretty dull party | The meetings are usually **deadly dull** (=very dull). → see box at BORING
2 not bright or shiny: a dull green colour | a dull, cloudy day → see box at SUN¹
3 a dull sound is not clear or loud: I heard a **dull thud**.
4 a dull pain is not strong: a **dull ache** in my shoulder
—dully adv —dullness n [U]

dull² v [T] to make something become less severe or less clear: a drug to dull the pain

duly /'dju:li $ 'du:li/ adv formal at the correct time or in the correct way: His objection was duly noted.

dumb¹ /dʌm/ adj **1** informal stupid: What a dumb question! **2 a)** not able to speak because you are so surprised, angry etc: We were all **struck dumb** for a moment. **b)** old-fashioned someone who is dumb is not able to speak. Some people consider this to be offensive. —dumbly adv

dumb²

dumb sth ⇔ **down** phr v disapproving to present something in a way which is easy to understand, but which is too simple and not interesting: the dumbing down of TV news

dumbfounded /dʌm'faʊndɨd/ adj extremely surprised: He stared at me, absolutely dumbfounded. → see box at SURPRISED

dummy /'dʌmi/ n [C] plural dummies **1** a figure of a person: a dressmaker's dummy **2** a copy of a weapon, tool, vehicle etc that you cannot use: It wasn't a real gun, just a dummy. **3** BrE a rubber object that you put into a baby's mouth for it to suck [= pacifier AmE]

dump¹ /dʌmp/ v [T] **1** to put something somewhere in a careless way: **dump sth in/on/down etc** They dumped their bags on the floor and left. **2** to get rid of something that you do not want: Waste chemicals are simply dumped in the river. → see box at RUBBISH

dump² n [C] **1** a place where unwanted waste is taken and left: a rubbish dump **2** informal a place that is very dirty and ugly: This town's a real dump. **3 be down in the dumps** informal to feel very unhappy

dumpling /'dʌmplɪŋ/ n [C] a round mixture of flour and fat cooked in boiling liquid: chicken and dumplings

Dumpster /'dʌmpstə $ -ər/ n [C] trademark AmE a large metal container for holding waste [= skip BrE]

dumpy /'dʌmpi/ adj informal short and fat: a dumpy woman

dune /dju:n $ du:n/ n [C] a hill of sand

dung /dʌŋ/ n [U] solid waste from animals

dungarees /ˌdʌŋgə'ri:z/ n [plural] BrE trousers with thin pieces that go over your shoulders and

D

a square piece of cloth that covers your chest [= **overalls** *AmE*] → see picture at **CLOTHES**

dungeon /'dʌndʒən/ *n* [C] a dark underground prison used in the past

dunk /dʌŋk/ *v* **1** [T] to put something into a liquid for a short time and take it out again, especially something you are eating: *I like to dunk biscuits in my tea.* **2** [T] to push someone under water for a short time as a joke [= **duck** *BrE*]

dunno /'dʌnəʊ $ -nəʊ/ *spoken informal* a way of writing or saying 'I do not know', which many people think is incorrect

duo /'djuːəʊ $ 'duːəʊ/ *n* [C] plural **duos** two people who sing, dance etc together

dupe¹ /djuːp $ duːp/ *v* [T] to tell lies in order to make someone believe or do something: **dupe sb into doing sth** *She was duped into giving him the money.*

dupe² *n* [C] someone who is deceived by someone else

duplex /'djuːpleks $ 'duː-/ *n* [C] *AmE* a house that is divided into two parts, so that it has two separate homes in it → see box at **HOUSE**

duplicate¹ /'djuːplɪkeɪt $ 'duː-/ *v* [T] **1** to copy something: *Could you duplicate this letter for me?* **2** to repeat something in exactly the same way: *Staff were duplicating each other's work.* —**duplication** /ˌdjuːplɪ'keɪʃən $ ˌduː-/ *n* [U]

duplicate² /'djuːplɪkət $ 'duː-/ *adj* [only before noun] a duplicate copy of something is made so that it is exactly the same: *a **duplicate copy** of the letter*

duplicate³ *n* [C] an exact copy of something: **+of** *He made a **duplicate** of the key.*

durable /'djʊərəbəl $ 'dʊr-/ *adj* staying in good condition for a long time: *Plastic is a durable material.* —**durability** /ˌdjʊərə'bɪlɪti $ ˌdʊr-/ *n* [U]

duration /djʊ'reɪʃən $ dʊ-/ *n* [U] *formal* the length of time that something continues: *He slept **for the duration** of the journey.*

duress /djʊ'res $ dʊ-/ *n* [U] if you do something under duress, you do it because you are threatened by someone not because you want to: *The confession was obtained under duress.*

during /'djʊərɪŋ $ 'dʊr-/ *prep*
1 all through a period of time: *During the summer she worked as a waitress.* | *Foxes sleep during the day.*

THESAURUS

During is followed by a particular period of time and is used to say when something happens: *He was sick during the night.*
For is followed by words describing a length of time and is used to say how long something lasts: *She was in hospital for two weeks.*

2 at one point in a period of time: *The car was stolen during the night.*

dusk /dʌsk/ *n* [U] when it starts to get dark at the end of the day [➡ **dawn**]: **at dusk** *They arrived at dusk.*

dusky /'dʌski/ *adj literary* rather dark

dust¹ /dʌst/ *n* [U] very small bits of dirt or soil that look like a powder: *The furniture was cov-*

ered in dust. | *a thick **layer of dust** on the table* | *a **speck of dust*** | *The car drove off in a cloud of dust.*

dust² *v* [I,T] to clean the dust from something with a cloth: *He dusted the shelves.*
dust sth ⇔ off *phr v* to remove dust, dirt etc from something by brushing it with your hands: *He dusted off the crumbs.* | **dust yourself off** *He got to his feet and dusted himself off.*

dustbin /'dʌstbɪn/ *n* [C] *BrE* a large container outside your home where you put waste so that it can be taken away [= **garbage can** *AmE*] → see box at **RUBBISH**

duster /'dʌstə $ -ər/ *n* [C] a cloth for removing dust from furniture

dustman /'dʌstmən/ *n* [C] plural **dustmen** /-mən/ *BrE* someone whose job is to take away waste that people leave in dustbins [= **garbage collector** *AmE*]

dustpan /'dʌstpæn/ *n* [C] a flat container with a handle that you use with a brush to remove dust and waste from the floor

dusty /'dʌsti/ *adj* covered with dust: *dusty old bottles* → see box at **DIRTY**

dutiful /'djuːtɪfəl $ 'duː-/ *adj* a dutiful person does what they are expected to: *a dutiful son* —**dutifully** *adv*

duty /'djuːti $ 'duː-/ *n* plural **duties**
1 [C,U] something that you should do because it is right: *I promise I will **do my duty.*** | **duty to do sth** *It is our duty to help her.* | *Parents have a **duty** to protect their children.*
2 [C usually plural, U] something you have to do as part of your job: *Her duties included typing.* | *He was **carrying out** his **duties** as ambassador.*
3 on/off duty if a doctor, nurse, police officer etc is on or off duty, they are working or not working at a particular time: *Ann **goes on duty** (=starts working) at half past ten.* | *What time do you **go off duty** (=finish work)?*
4 [C,U] a tax you pay on something you buy: **+on** *the duty on cigarettes*
→ **HEAVY-DUTY, NIGHT DUTY**

duty-'free *adj* duty-free goods can be brought into a country without paying tax on them: *duty-free cigarettes* —**duty-free** *adv*

duvet /'duːveɪ, 'djuː- $ duː'veɪ/ *n* [C] *especially BrE* a thick warm cover that you put on top of you when you are in bed [= **comforter** *AmE*] → see picture at **BED**

DVD /ˌdiː viː 'diː/ *n* [C] a flat round object like a CD that you use on a computer or a piece of equipment called a DVD player to play films, pictures, and sound

dwarf¹ /dwɔːf $ dwɔːrf/ *n* [C] plural **dwarfs** or **dwarves** /dwɔːvz $ dwɔːrvz/ **1** an imaginary creature that looks like a small man: *Snow White and the Seven Dwarfs* **2** a person who is much shorter than usual. Many people think this use is offensive.

dwarf² *v* [T] something that dwarfs other things is so big that it makes them seem very small: *The church is dwarfed by skyscrapers.*

dwarf³ *adj* [only before noun] a dwarf plant or animal is much smaller than the usual size

dwell /dwel/ *v* [I] past tense and past participle **dwelt** /dwelt/ or **dwelled** *literary* to live in a particular place

dwell on/upon sth phr v to think or talk for too long about something unpleasant: *That is not a subject I want to dwell on.*

dweller /'dwelə $ -ər/ n [C] **city/town/cave etc dweller** someone who lives in a particular place

dwelling /'dwelɪŋ/ n [C] formal a house, apartment etc where people live

dwindle /'dwɪndl/ also **dwindle away** v [I] to gradually become less or smaller: *The town's population is dwindling.* —**dwindling** adj

dye¹ /daɪ/ n [C,U] a substance that you use to change the colour of hair, cloth etc

dye² v [T] past tense and past participle **dyed** present participle **dyeing** to change the colour of something, using a dye: *Her hair was dyed blonde.*

dying /'daɪ-ɪŋ/ v the present participle of DIE

dyke, dike /daɪk/ n [C] **1** a wall or bank built to keep back water and prevent flooding **2** especially BrE a long narrow hole cut in the ground to take water away

dynamic /daɪ'næmɪk/ adj **1** full of energy and ideas: *a dynamic businessman* **2** continuously changing: *a dynamic economy* **3** technical a dynamic force causes movement: *dynamic energy* —**dynamically** /-kli/ adv —**dynamism** /'daɪnəmɪzəm/ n [U]

dynamics /daɪ'næmɪks/ n [plural] the way in which things or people behave and affect each other: *group dynamics*

dynamite /'daɪnəmaɪt/ n [U] **1** a powerful explosive **2** something or someone that is exciting or likely to cause trouble

dynasty /'dɪnəsti $ 'daɪ-/ n [C] plural **dynasties** a family of rulers who have controlled a country for a long time: *the Ming dynasty* —**dynastic** /dɪ'næstɪk $ daɪ-/ adj

dysentery /'dɪsəntəri $ -teri/ n [U] a serious disease that causes severe DIARRHOEA

dysfunctional /dɪs'fʌŋkʃənəl/ adj not behaving or working normally

dyslexia /dɪs'leksiə/ n [U] a condition that makes it difficult for someone to read and spell —**dyslexic** adj

D

E, e

E, e /iː/ *n* [C,U] plural **E's, e's** **1** the fifth letter of the English alphabet **2** the third note in the musical SCALE of C MAJOR, or the musical KEY based on this note **3** a mark given to a student's work to show that it is of very low quality: *I got an E in physics.* **4** **Ecstasy** (=an illegal drug)

E the written abbreviation of **east** or **eastern**

e-, E- /iː/ *prefix* using or involving the Internet: *e-commerce* | *e-shopping*

each /iːtʃ/ *determiner, pron, adv* every person or thing: *She had a bottle in each hand.* | *Tickets cost £5 each* (=each ticket costs £5). | **+of** *Each of the children sang a song.* | *We were given ten minutes each* (=each of us was given ten minutes). | **each day/week/month etc** (=on each day, in each week etc) *I get one day off each week.*

THESAURUS

Each, every, and **all** are all used to talk about every person or thing in a group.
When you are considering them separately, use **each** with a singular noun: *Each child at the party was given a present.*
When you are considering them together, use **every** with a singular noun or **all** with a plural noun: *Every child in the class passed the test.* | *All the children enjoyed the trip.*

each 'other *pron* used to show that each of two or more people does something to the other or others [➡ **one another**]: *We all hugged and kissed each other.* | *Claire and Kay looked at each other.*

eager /ˈiːɡə $ -ər/ *adj* wanting to do something very much, or waiting with excitement for something to happen: **eager to do sth** *Rosie was eager to leave.* | **+for** *We were always eager for news from home.*
—**eagerly** *adv* —**eagerness** *n* [U]

eagle

eagle /ˈiːɡəl/ *n* [C] a very large strong bird, with a beak like a hook, that kills and eats small animals

ear /ɪə $ ɪr/ *n*

1 [C] one of the two parts of your body that you hear with: *'Darling,' he whispered in her ear.* | **be smiling/grinning etc from ear to ear** (=be smiling a lot) → see picture on page A3

2 [C] the top part of a plant such as wheat that produces grain: **+of** *an ear of corn*

3 [singular] the ability to learn music or copy sounds that you hear: **+for** *I've always had an ear for accents.*

4 **be all ears** *informal* be very interested to hear what someone is going to say: *Go ahead, I'm all ears.*

earache /ˈɪəreɪk $ ˈɪr-/ *n* [singular, U] a pain inside your ear: *I've got terrible earache.*

eardrum /ˈɪədrʌm $ ˈɪr-/ *n* [C] a thin piece of skin inside your ear that allows you to hear sound

earl /ɜːl $ ɜːrl/ *n* [C] a man with a high social rank

earlobe /ˈɪələʊb $ ˈɪr-/ *n* [C] the soft piece of flesh at the bottom of your ear

early /ˈɜːli $ ˈɜːrli/ comparative **earlier**, superlative **earliest** *adj, adv*

1 in the first part of a period of time or an event [≠ **late**]: *in the early 1960s* | *the early part of her career* | *the early morning sun* | **+in** *Harry was killed early in the war.* | *The store will open early next year.* | **early on** (=at an early stage) *I realized early on that I couldn't trust him.*

2 before the usual or expected time [≠ **late**]: *You're early! It's only five o'clock!* | **+for** *I was a few minutes early for my appointment.* | *They came home early.*

3 **at the (very) earliest** not before the time or date mentioned: *The tunnel won't open until July at the earliest.*

4 **the early hours** the time between MIDNIGHT and morning: *The attack happened in the early hours of Sunday morning.*

5 **it's early days** *BrE* used to say that it is too soon to know what the result of something will be

6 **early night** if you have an early night, you go to bed earlier than usual

earmark /ˈɪəmɑːk $ ˈɪrmɑːrk/ *v* [T] to decide that someone will do a particular job or something will be used for a particular purpose: **earmark sb/sth for sth** *The land was earmarked for a golf course.*

earn /ɜːn $ ɜːrn/ *v*

1 [I,T] to receive money for work that you do: *She earns £27,000 a year.* | *You don't earn much money being a nurse.* | *Dad did all sorts of jobs to earn a living* (=earn enough money for the things you need to live). → see box at **GAIN**

2 [T] to make a profit from business or from putting money in a bank: *You could earn a higher rate of interest elsewhere.*

3 [T] **a)** to deserve something, for example because you have worked hard: *I think we've earned a rest after all that work!* **b)** if your actions or qualities earn you something, you get it because of them: **earn sb sth** *That performance earned her an Oscar.* → see box at **GAIN**
—**earner** *n* [C] *He is the only wage earner in the family.*

earnest /ˈɜːnɪst $ ˈɜːr-/ *adj* **1** very serious and sincere: *an earnest young man* **2** **in earnest** if something starts happening in earnest, it starts happening properly or seriously: *On Monday your training begins in earnest!* **3 be in earnest** to really mean what you are saying —**earnestly** *adv*

earnings /ˈɜːnɪŋz $ ˈɜːr-/ *n* [plural] your earnings are the money that you earn by working: *Average earnings have risen by 3%.*

earphones /ˈɪəfəʊnz $ ˈɪrfoʊnz/ *n* [plural] a small piece of equipment that you put in or over your ears to listen to music so that only you can hear it

earplug /ˈɪəplʌg $ ˈɪr-/ *n* [C usually plural] a small piece of rubber that you put into your ear to keep out noise

earring /ˈɪərɪŋ $ ˈɪr-/ *n* [C] a piece of jewellery that you wear on your ear → see picture at JEWELLERY

earshot /ˈɪəʃɒt $ ˈɪrʃɑːt/ *n* **within earshot/out of earshot** near enough or not near enough to hear what someone is saying: *She waited until he was out of earshot before continuing.* → see box at HEAR

ˈear-ˌsplitting *adj* very loud: *an ear-splitting explosion* → see box at LOUD

earth /ɜːθ $ ɜːrθ/ *n*

1 also **the earth, the Earth** the PLANET that we live on [➦ world]: *The earth revolves around the sun.* | *when the space shuttle returns to earth* | **on earth** *one of the hottest places on earth* | *the future of planet Earth*
2 [U] the substance that plants grow in [= soil]: *the smell of wet earth* → see box at GROUND
3 [U] the hard surface of the world, as opposed to the sea or air: *We watched in horror as the plane fell to earth.* | *The earth began to shake beneath our feet.*
4 what/why/how etc on earth...? *spoken* used to ask a question when you are very surprised or angry: *What on earth did you do that for?*
5 cost/pay/charge the earth *informal* to cost, pay etc a very large amount of money: *That dress must have cost the earth!*
6 come down to earth/bring sb down to earth (with a bump) if you come down to earth, or if something brings you down to earth, something happens that makes you start having to deal with ordinary life and its problems again, after a period of great excitement
7 [C usually singular] *BrE* a wire that makes a piece of electrical equipment safe by connecting it with the ground [= ground *AmE*]
→ DOWN-TO-EARTH

earthenware /ˈɜːθənweə, -ðən- $ ˈɜːrθənwer, -ðən-/ *adj* an earthenware pot, bowl etc is made of very hard baked clay —**earthenware** *n* [U]

earthly /ˈɜːθli $ ˈɜːrθli/ *adj* **no earthly reason/ use etc** no reason, use etc at all: *There was no earthly reason to stay.*

earthquake /ˈɜːθkweɪk $ ˈɜːrθ-/ *n* [C] a sudden shaking of the earth's surface that often causes a lot of damage

ˈearth ˌscience *n* [C usually plural] a science such as GEOLOGY which involves the study of the physical world

earthworm /ˈɜːθwɜːm $ ˈɜːrθwɜːrm/ *n* [C] a thin brown WORM that lives in soil

earthy /ˈɜːθi $ ˈɜːrθi/ *adj* **1** tasting, smelling, or looking like earth or soil: *earthy colours*

2 talking about sex and the human body in a relaxed direct way: *earthy language*

ease[1] /iːz/ *n* [U] **1 with ease** if you do something with ease, it is very easy for you to do it: *They won with ease.* **2 at ease** feeling relaxed: **+with** *She felt completely at ease with Barry.* | *The nurse soon put me at my ease* (=made me feel relaxed). | *He looked shy and ill at ease* (=not relaxed).

ease[2] *v* [I,T] **1** if something unpleasant eases, or if you ease it, it gradually improves: *The doctor gave me something to ease the pain.* **2** to move someone or something slowly and carefully into a place: *Phil eased himself into an armchair.*

ease off *phr v* if something eases off, it becomes less: *The rain had eased off a bit.*

ease up *phr v* to work less hard or do something with less energy than before: *Just relax and ease up a little.*

easel /ˈiːzəl/ *n* [C] a frame that you put a painting on while you paint it

easily /ˈiːzḷli/ *adv* **1** without difficulty: *She found the house easily.* **2 could/can/might easily** used to say that something is possible or is very likely to happen: *Teenage parties can easily get out of control.* **3 easily the best/ biggest/most stupid etc** definitely the best, biggest etc: *She is easily the most intelligent girl in the class.*

east[1], **East** /iːst/ *n* [singular,U] written abbreviation *E*

1 the direction from which the sun rises: *Which way is east?* | **from/towards the east** *The army is approaching from the east.* | **to the east (of sth)** *the region to the east of Munich* → see picture at NORTH[1]
2 the east the eastern part of a country or area: *Rain will spread to the east later.* | **+of** *the east of Scotland*
3 the East a) the countries in Asia, especially China and Japan: *The Oriental is one of the most famous hotels in the East.* **b)** the countries in the eastern part of Europe and central Asia **c)** *AmE* the part of the US east of the Mississippi River, especially the states north of Washington DC

east[2], **East** *adj* [only before noun] written abbreviation *E*

1 in the east or facing the east: *the east coast of Africa* | *We live in East London.*
2 an east wind comes from the east

east[3] *adv* written abbreviation *E* towards the east: *We drove east along Brooklyn Avenue.* | **+of** *a small village 18 miles east of Paris*

eastbound /ˈiːstbaʊnd/ *adj* travelling or leading towards the east: *an eastbound train*

Easter /ˈiːstə $ -ər/ *n* [C,U] a holiday in March or April when Christians remember the death of Christ and his return to life: **at Easter** *We always go away at Easter.* | *the Easter holidays*

ˈEaster ˌegg *n* [C] **1** *BrE* a chocolate egg that people eat at Easter **2** *AmE* an egg that has been coloured and decorated to celebrate Easter

easterly /ˈiːstəli $ -ərli/ *adj* **1** towards or in the east: *We drove off in an easterly direction.* **2** an easterly wind comes from the east

eastern, Eastern /ˈiːstən $ -ərn/ *adj* written abbreviation *E*

1 in or from the east of a country or area: *the eastern shore of the island* | *Eastern Europe*
2 in or from the countries in Asia, especially China and Japan: *Eastern religions*

easternmost /'iːstənməʊst $ -ərnmoʊst/ *adj* furthest east: *the easternmost part of the country*

eastwards /'iːstwədz $ -wərdz/ also **eastward** *adv* towards the east: *We sailed eastwards.* —**eastward** *adj*: *We followed an eastward course up the river.*

easy[1] /'iːzi/ *adj*

1 not difficult [≠ **difficult, hard**]: *The test was really easy.* | *an easy job* | **easy to do sth** *It's a lovely car and very easy to drive.* | *Having a computer will* **make things** *a lot easier.*
2 comfortable, relaxed, and not worried: *I felt easy and at home.* | *He'll do anything for an easy life.*
3 I'm easy *informal* used to say that you are happy to do what other people want to do: *You choose – I'm easy.*

easy[2] *adv* **1 take it easy a)** also **take things easy** to relax and not do very much: *You should take it easy for a few days.* **b)** *spoken* used to tell someone to become less upset or angry: *Just take it easy and tell us what happened.* **2 go easy on sth** *informal* used to tell someone not to use, eat, or drink too much of something: *Go easy on salty foods.* **3 go easy on sb** *informal* to be more gentle and less strict or angry with someone: *Go easy on Peter – he's having a hard time at school.* **4 easier said than done** *spoken* used to say that something would be very difficult to do: *'Find him and bring him back.' 'That's easier said than done.'*

'easy chair *n* [C] a large comfortable chair

easygoing /ˌiːziˈɡəʊɪŋ◂ $ -ˈɡoʊ-/ *adj* not easily upset, annoyed, or worried

ˌeasy 'listening *n* [U] music with pleasant tunes that is relaxing to listen to

eat /iːt/ *v* [I,T] past tense **ate** /et, eɪt $ eɪt/ past participle **eaten** /'iːtn/

1 to put food in your mouth and swallow it: *We sat eating our sandwiches.* | *He began to eat.* | *Would you like* **something to eat**?

> **THESAURUS**
>
> If you eat something very quickly, you **devour** it, **gobble** it **up**, or **wolf** it **down**: *He devoured the rest of the cake.*
> If you **nibble (on)** something, you take small bites and eat only a little bit of it: *Sarah nibbled on a biscuit and sipped her coffee.*
> If you **pick at** your food, you eat only a little bit of it because you are not hungry.
> If you are **dieting**, or if you go **on a diet**, you eat less than normal in order to become thinner.
> If you are **fasting**, you do not eat for a period of time, often for religious reasons: *Muslims fast during the holy month of Ramadan.*
> → **DRINK**

2 to have a meal: *We usually eat at six.* | *Have you eaten lunch yet?*

eat away *phr v* to gradually remove or reduce something: **eat sth** ⇔ **away** *Rust had eaten the metal away.* | **+at** *Pollution was eating away at the stone.*

eat into sth *phr v* **1** to gradually use time, money etc so that less is available: *My job often eats into the weekend.* **2** to damage something: *Acid eats into the metal, damaging the surface.*

eat out *phr v* to eat in a restaurant: *Let's eat out for a change.*

eat up *phr v spoken* to eat all of something: *Eat up, there's a good girl.* | **eat sth** ⇔ **up** *He ate it all up.*

eater /'iːtə $ -ər/ *n* [C] **big/light/fussy etc eater** someone who eats a lot, not much, only particular things etc: *I've never been a big eater.*

'eating disˌorder *n* [C] a medical condition in which someone does not eat normal amounts of food, especially because they are frightened of getting fat [➡ **anorexia, bulimia**]

eaves /iːvz/ *n* [plural] the edges of a roof that stick out beyond the walls: *Birds had nested under the eaves.*

eavesdrop /'iːvzdrɒp $ -drɑːp/ *v* [I] **eaves-dropped, eavesdropping** to secretly listen to other people's conversations [➡ **overhear**] —**eavesdropper** *n* [C]

ebb[1] /eb/ *n* **1** also **ebb tide** [singular] the flow of the sea away from the land, when the TIDE goes out **2 be at a low ebb** to be weak and not strong: *His confidence is at a low ebb.* **3 ebb and flow** when something keeps increasing and decreasing: *the ebb and flow of the conversation*

ebb[2] *v* [I] **1** if the TIDE ebbs, it flows away from the land **2** also **ebb away** to gradually decrease: *Lucy's strength ebbed away.*

ebony /'ebəni/ *n* [U] a hard black wood —**ebony** *adj*

ebullient /ɪ'bʌliənt, ɪ'bʊ-/ *adj formal* very happy and excited: *his ebullient personality*

EC /ˌiː 'siː◂/ *n* **the EC** the European Community a former name for the EU

eccentric[1] /ɪk'sentrɪk/ *adj* strange or unusual: *Aunt Nessy was always a bit eccentric.* → see box at **STRANGE** —**eccentricity** /ˌeksen'trɪsˌti, -sən-/ *n* [C,U] *Kate's mother had a reputation for eccentricity.*

eccentric[2] *n* [C] someone who behaves in a way that is strange or unusual

ecclesiastical /ɪˌkliːzi'æstɪkəl/ also **ecclesiastic** /-'æstɪk◂/ *adj* relating to the Christian church or its priests: *ecclesiastical history*

echelon /'eʃəlɒn $ -lɑːn/ *n* [C usually plural] a level or rank in an organization, business etc, or the people at that level: **upper/higher/lower etc echelons (of sth)** *the upper echelons of government*

echo[1] /'ekəʊ $ 'ekoʊ/ *n* [C] plural **echoes 1** a sound that you hear again when it comes back off a wall or rock **2** something that is very similar to what has happened or been said before: **+of** *The article contains echoes of an earlier report.*

echo[2] *v* past tense and past participle **echoed** present participle **echoing** third person singular **echoes 1** [I] if a sound or place echoes, you hear sounds repeated when they come back off walls or rock: *Children's voices echoed through the big old house.* **2** [T] to repeat and agree with what someone else has said: *Kaletsky, writing in The Times, echoed this view.*

E

eclectic /ɪˈklektɪk/ *adj* including a mixture of many different things or people: *a wonderfully eclectic mix of furniture* | *His taste in music was eclectic.*

eclipse¹ /ɪˈklɪps/ *n* [C] when the sun or the moon seems to disappear, because one of them is passing between the other one and the Earth

eclipse² *v* [T] **1** to become more important, powerful, or famous than someone or something else, so that they are no longer noticed: *British cinema had been largely eclipsed by that of Hollywood.* **2** to make the sun or moon disappear in an eclipse

eco- /iːkəʊ $ iːkoʊ/ *prefix* relating to the environment: *ecofriendly products* | *an ecosystem*

ecofriendly /ˈiːkəʊˌfrendli $ ˈiːkoʊ-/ *adj* not harmful to the environment: *ecofriendly products* → see box at **ENVIRONMENT**

ecological /ˌiːkəˈlɒdʒɪkəl◂ $ -ˈlɑː-/ *adj* relating to the relationship of living things to each other and to their environment: *The ecological balance in the area could be destroyed.* | *an ecological disaster* —**ecologically** /-kli/ *adv*

ecology /ɪˈkɒlədʒi $ ɪˈkɑː-/ *n* [singular, U] the relationship of living things to each other and to their environment, or the scientific study of this —**ecologist** *n* [C]

e-commerce /ˈiː kɒmɜːs, $ -kɑːmɜːrs/ *n* [U] **electronic commerce** when people buy and sell goods and services using a computer and the Internet: *the growth of e-commerce*

economic /ˌiːkəˈnɒmɪk◂, ˌɪ- $ -ˈnɑː-/ *adj* **1** [only before noun] relating to trade, industry, and the management of money [➡ **economy**]: *the government's economic policy* | *Economic growth in Britain has been slow.* | *an economic crisis* **2** a business activity that is economic produces enough profit to continue: *It is no longer economic for us to run the service.* **3 economic migrant** someone who moves to a different country or area in order to find work —**economically** /-kli/ *adv*: *economically developed countries*

economical /ˌiːkəˈnɒmɪkəl, ˌɪ- $ -ˈnɑː-/ *adj* using money, time, products etc carefully and without wasting any: *a smaller and more economical car* —**economically** /-kli/ *adv*: *Food is produced as efficiently and economically as possible.*

economics /ˌiːkəˈnɒmɪks, ˌɪ- $ -ˈnɑː-/ *n* **1** [U] the study of the way in which money, goods, and services are produced and used: *a professor of economics* **2** [plural] the amount of money that something will cost and earn: *I think we need to look at the economics of the project again.*

economist /ɪˈkɒnəmɪ̈st $ ɪˈkɑː-/ *n* [C] someone who studies economics

economize also **-ise** *BrE* /ɪˈkɒnəmaɪz $ ɪˈkɑː-/ *v* [I] to reduce the amount of money or goods that you use: **+on** *We're trying to economize on heating.*

economy¹ /ɪˈkɒnəmi $ ɪˈkɑː-/ *n* plural **economies**
1 [C] the system by which a country's money and goods are produced and used, or a country considered in this way: *a capitalist economy* | *the slowdown in the Japanese economy* | *the economies of Eastern Europe*
2 [C,U] the careful use of things so that nothing

is wasted and less money is spent: *the need to make economies* | *For reasons of economy, we are not having a Christmas party this year.*
→ **MARKET ECONOMY**

economy² *adj* [only before noun] cheap or intended to save money: *an economy class air ticket* | *a large economy pack*

ecosystem /ˈiːkəʊˌsɪstɪ̈m $ ˈiːkoʊ-/ *n* [C] all the animals and plants in an area, and their relationship to each other and their environment

ecotourism /ˈiːkəʊˌtʊərɪzəm $ ˈiːkoʊˌtʊr-/ *n* [U] the business of organizing holidays to natural areas where people can visit and learn about the area in a way that will not hurt the environment —**ecotourist** *n* [C]

ecstasy /ˈekstəsi/ *n* plural **ecstasies 1** [C,U] a feeling of extreme happiness: *an expression of pure ecstasy* **2** also **Ecstasy** [U] an illegal drug that gives people a feeling of happiness and energy

ecstatic /ɪkˈstætɪk, ek-/ *adj* feeling extremely happy: *Peter was ecstatic when he heard the news.*

eczema /ˈeksɪ̈mə $ ˈeksɪ̈mə, ˈegz-, ɪgˈziːmə/ *n* [U] a medical condition in which someone's skin is dry, red, and sore

eddy /ˈedi/ *n* [C] plural **eddies** a circular movement of water or air

edge¹ /edʒ/ *n*
1 [C] the part of something that is furthest from the centre: **the edge of sth** *Billy sat on the edge of the bed.* | *He stood at the water's edge, staring across the lake.*
2 [C] the thin sharp part of a tool used for cutting: *the edge of the knife*
3 [singular] something that gives you an advantage over others: **+over/on** *That's where the Europeans have an edge over the Americans.*
4 [C] an area beside a very steep slope: *Don't stand so close to the edge.*
5 on edge nervous: *I'm a little on edge after what happened last night.*
→ **CUTTING EDGE**

edge² *v* **1** [I,T] to move slowly and gradually, or to make something do this: *The car edged forwards.* | **edge your way along/towards etc** *She edged her way along the path.* **2** [T] to put something along the edge of something to decorate it: *The city square was edged by trees.*

edgeways /ˈedʒweɪz/ also **edgewise** *AmE* /-waɪz/ *adv* with the part that is usually the edge facing forwards [= **sideways**]: *We carried it up the stairs edgeways.* → **get a word in (edgeways)** at **WORD¹**

edgy /ˈedʒi/ *adj* nervous and worried: *Are you OK? You seem a little edgy.*

edible /ˈedɪ̈bəl/ *adj* if something is edible, you can eat it [≠ **inedible**]

edict /ˈiːdɪkt/ *n* [C] *formal* an official order that is given by someone in a position of power

edifice /ˈedɪ̈fɪ̈s/ *n* [C] *formal* a large building

edit /ˈedɪ̈t/ *v* [T] to correct mistakes in a piece of writing or a film, and decide which parts to keep —**edit** *n* [C]

edition /ɪˈdɪʃən/ *n* [C] **1** one copy or form of a book, newspaper, magazine etc: **first/second/ third etc edition** *The first edition of the book was published in 1836, and the second edition a year later.* | *The paperback edition costs £7.95.* | *in* *today's edition of The Times* **2** one of a series of television or radio programmes that is broadcast regularly: *last week's edition of 'Friends'*

editor /'edɪtə $ -ər/ *n* [C] the person who decides what should be included in a book, newspaper, magazine etc, and checks for mistakes → see box at NEWSPAPER —**editorial** /ˌedɪ'tɔːriəl/ *adj: They made a few editorial changes.*

editorial /ˌedɪ'tɔːriəl◂/ *n* [C] a piece of writing in a newspaper that gives the editor's opinion about something

educate /'edjʊkeɪt $ 'edʒə-/ *v* [T] **1** to teach someone in a school or college: *He was educated at Westminster School.* **2** to give someone information about something so that they understand it: **educate sb about sth** *a campaign to educate teenagers about HIV* —**educator** *n* [C] *especially AmE*

educated /'edjʊkeɪtɪd $ 'edʒə-/ *adj* **1** an educated person has a high standard of knowledge and education: *a well-educated young woman* **2 educated guess** a guess that is likely to be correct because you have enough information

education /ˌedjʊ'keɪʃən $ ˌedʒə-/ *n* [singular, U] the process of teaching and learning, usually at school, college, or university: *The government has promised to spend more on education.* | *the education system* | *the importance of getting a good education*
→ FURTHER EDUCATION, HIGHER EDUCATION, PHYSICAL EDUCATION

educational /ˌedjʊ'keɪʃənəl◂ $ ˌedʒə-/ *adj* **1** relating to education: *universities and other educational institutions* → see box at QUALIFICATION **2** teaching you something: *Working in Tanzania was a very educational experience.* | *educational toys* —**educationally** *adv*

Edwardian /ed'wɔːdiən $ -'wɔːr-/ *adj* relating to the time of King Edward VII of Britain (1901-1910): *an Edwardian house*

eel /iːl/ *n* [C] a long thin fish that looks like a snake

eerie /'ɪəri $ 'ɪri/ *adj* strange and frightening: *an eerie sound* —**eerily** *adv*

effect¹ /ɪ'fekt/ *n*

1 [C,U] a change or result that happens because of an event or action: **+of** *We do not know the long-term effects of pollution.* | **+on** *My parents' divorce had a big effect on me.* → see box at RESULT

2 put/bring sth into effect to make a plan or idea happen: *It won't be easy to put the changes into effect.*

3 take effect a) also **come into effect** if a law, rule, or system takes effect or comes into effect, it officially starts: *The new rules come into effect in June.* **b)** to start to produce results: *The tablets soon began to take effect.*

4 in effect used when you are describing what you think are the real facts of a situation: *In effect, I'll be earning less than I was last year.*

5 [C] a feeling that an artist, speaker, book etc tries to give you: **+of** *The play's clever lighting created the effect of oil lamps.*

6 for effect if someone does something for effect, they do it in order to make people notice: *She paused for effect, then carried on speaking.*

7 to this/that effect used to say that you are giving the general meaning of what someone said, not their exact words: *The report says he's no good at his job, or words to that effect.*

8 effects [plural] *formal* someone's effects are the things that they own [= belongings]
→ AFTER-EFFECT, GREENHOUSE EFFECT, SIDE EFFECT

effect² *v* [T] *formal* to make something happen: *an attempt to effect major social change*

effective /ɪ'fektɪv/ *adj*

1 having the result that you want [≠ ineffective]: *an effective way to teach reading* | *a highly effective method*

2 [not before noun] if a law, agreement, or system becomes effective, it officially starts: **+from** *The new regulations are effective from April 5th.*
—**effectiveness** *n* [U] → COST EFFECTIVE

effectively /ɪ'fektɪvli/ *adv* **1** in a way that gets the result you want: *She controlled the class very effectively.* **2** used to describe what you think is really true or really happens: *The poor are effectively excluded from politics.*

effeminate /ɪ'femɪnət/ *adj* a man who is effeminate looks or behaves like a woman

effervescent /ˌefə'vesənt◂ $ ˌefər-/ *adj* **1** a liquid that is effervescent produces small bubbles of gas [= fizzy] **2** someone who is effervescent seems to be full of energy and happiness —**effervescence** *n* [U]

efficient /ɪ'fɪʃənt/ *adj* working well, without wasting time or energy: *an efficient way of organizing your work* | *an efficient secretary* → see box at ORGANIZED —**efficiently** *adv* —**efficiency** *n* [U]

effigy /'efɪdʒi/ *n* [C] plural **effigies** a model of a real person, which people sometimes burn as a protest

effluent /'efluənt/ *n* [C,U] *formal* liquid waste, especially chemicals or SEWAGE

effort /'efət $ 'efərt/ *n*

1 [U] hard work: *She puts a lot of effort into her work.* | **it takes effort (to do sth)** *It took a lot of effort to find him.* | *He lifted the box easily, without using much effort.*

2 [C,U] an attempt to do something: *Kim is making an effort to lose weight.* | **sb's efforts to do sth** *I was impressed with his efforts to stop smoking.* | **in an effort to do sth** *In an effort to reduce crime, more police are being hired.*

3 be an effort to be difficult or painful to do: *I was so weak that even standing up was an effort.*

effortless /'efətləs $ 'efərt-/ *adj* if something is effortless, you can do it very easily: *His running looks effortless.* —**effortlessly** *adv*

effusive /ɪ'fjuːsɪv/ *adj* showing your happiness, friendship etc in a very excited way: *an effusive greeting* —**effusively** *adv*

EFL /ˌiː ef 'el/ **English as a Foreign Language** the teaching of English to people who speak a different language

e.g. also **eg** *BrE* /ˌiː 'dʒiː/ the written abbreviation of **for example**: *science subjects eg chemistry and physics*

egalitarian /ɪˌɡælɪ'teəriən $ -'ter-/ *adj* based on the belief that everyone should have equal rights: *egalitarian principles* —**egalitarian** *n* [C]

E

egg¹ /eg/ n

1 [C] a round object that contains a baby bird, insect, snake etc: *Blackbirds **lay** their **eggs** in March.*

2 [C,U] an egg from a chicken that you can cook and eat: **fried/boiled/poached etc eggs** | *He had bacon and eggs for breakfast.*

3 [C] a cell produced inside a woman or female animal that can develop into a baby

4 put all your eggs in one basket to depend completely on one thing in order to get success so that you have no other plans if this fails

→ **EASTER EGG, NEST EGG**

egg² v

egg sb ⇔ **on** phr v to encourage someone to do something that they should not do: *He didn't want to jump, but his friends kept egging him on.*

eggcup /'eg-kʌp/ n [C] a container that holds a boiled egg while you eat it

eggplant /'egplɑːnt $ -plænt/ n [C,U] AmE a large vegetable with a smooth shiny purple skin [= **aubergine** BrE] → see picture at **VEGETABLE**

eggshell /'egʃel/ n [C,U] the hard outside part of an egg

'egg white n [C,U] the part of an egg that becomes white when cooked [➡ **yolk**]

ego /'iːgəʊ, 'egəʊ $ -goʊ/ n [C] plural **egos**
1 the good opinion that you have about yourself: **big/enormous ego** *He has an enormous ego* (=thinks he is very clever and important). | *The promotion **boosted** her **ego*** (=made her feel better about herself). **2 ego trip** disapproving if someone is on an ego trip, they think that they are better or more important than other people

egocentric /ˌiːgəʊ'sentrɪk◂, ˌeg- $ -goʊ-/ adj thinking only about yourself and not about other people

egotism /'iːgətɪzəm, 'eg-/ also **egoism** /'iːgəʊɪzəm, 'eg- $ -goʊ-/ n [U] the belief that you are much better or more important than other people —**egotist, egoist** n [C] —**egotistic** /ˌiːgə'tɪstɪk◂, ˌeg-/, **egoistic** /ˌiːgəʊ'ɪstɪk◂, ˌeg- $ -goʊ-/, **egotistical** adj

eh /eɪ/ spoken **1** BrE used to ask someone to say something again: *'You need a modem.' 'Eh?'* **2** used when you want someone to reply to you or agree with you: *Maybe he isn't as stupid as we thought, eh?*

eiderdown /'aɪdədaʊn $ -dər-/ n [C] a thick warm cover for a bed, filled with duck feathers

eight /eɪt/ number the number 8: *eight dollars* | *Dinner is at eight* (=eight o'clock). | *She is eight* (=eight years old).

eighteen /ˌeɪ'tiːn◂/ number the number 18: *Eighteen people were hurt.* | *Jim is eighteen* (=18 years old).

—**eighteenth** adj, pron: *his eighteenth birthday* | *I'm leaving on **the eighteenth*** (=the 18th day of the month).

eighth¹ /eɪtθ/ adj: *in the eighth century* | *her eighth birthday* —**eighth** pron: *He's arriving on **the eighth*** (=the eighth day of the month).

eighth² n [C] one of eight equal parts of something

eighty /'eɪti/ number
1 the number 80
2 the eighties also **the '80s, the 1980s** [plural] the years from 1980 to 1989: **the early/mid/late**

eighties *The band was very successful in the mid-eighties.*
3 be in your eighties to be aged between 80 and 89: **early/mid/late eighties** *Hilda Simpson was a woman in her early eighties.*
4 in the eighties if the temperature is in the eighties, it is between 80 degrees and 89 degrees Fahrenheit

—**eightieth** adj: *his eightieth birthday*

either¹ /'aɪðə $ 'iːðər/ linking word **either ... or** used when showing a choice: *We can either have lunch here or go out.* | *She's the kind of person you either love or hate.* | *Either she leaves or I will!*

either² determiner, pron

1 one of two things or people [➡ **any**]: *There's tea or coffee – you can have either.* | *She has a British and a Canadian passport so that she can live in either country.* | **+of** *Can either of you lend me £5?*
2 either side/end/hand etc both sides, ends, hands etc [= **each**]: *He sat in the back of the car with a policeman on either side.*

GRAMMAR

either, either of

Either is used with a singular noun form and a singular verb: *I can meet you on Wednesday or Thursday – either day is good for me.*
Either of is used with a plural noun form or pronoun, and the verb can be singular or plural: *Has/have either of them telephoned yet?*

---

either³ adv used in negative sentences to mean 'also' [➡ **neither**]: *I haven't seen the movie and my brother hasn't either.* | *'I don't like him.' 'I don't either.'* → see box at **ALSO**

ejaculate /ɪ'dʒækjʊˈleɪt/ v [I,T] when a male ejaculates, SEMEN comes out of his PENIS —**ejaculation** /ɪˌdʒækjʊ'leɪʃən/ n [C,U]

eject /ɪ'dʒekt/ v **1** [T] formal to make someone leave a place by using force: **eject sb from sth** *He was ejected from the club for fighting.* **2** [I,T] to make something come out of a machine by pressing a button: *How do I eject the CD?* **3** [I] if a pilot ejects from a plane, he or she escapes from it by using a special seat that throws the pilot out

eke /iːk/ v
eke sth ⇔ **out** phr v **1 eke out a living/existence** to live with very little money or food **2** to make a small supply of something last longer by only using small amounts of it

elaborate¹ /ɪ'læbərᵻt/ adj having a lot of small details or complicated parts: *an elaborate pattern* | *an elaborate plan* —**elaborately** adv

elaborate² /ɪ'læbəreɪt/ v [I,T] formal to give more details about something: **+on** *He refused to elaborate on his reasons for resigning.*

elapse /ɪ'læps/ v [I] formal if a period of time elapses, it passes

elastic /ɪ'læstɪk/ n [U] a rubber material that can stretch and then go back to its usual shape and size: *socks with elastic around the top* —**elastic** adj

e,lastic 'band n [C] BrE a thin circle of rubber for holding things together [= **rubber band**]

elated /ɪ'leɪtᵻd/ adj extremely happy: *He felt elated.* —**elation** /ɪ'leɪʃən/ n [U]

elbow[1] /'elbəʊ $ -boʊ/ *n* [C]
1 the joint in the middle of your arm, where your arm bends: *I've hurt my elbow.* → see picture on page A3
2 the part of a shirt etc that covers your elbow
3 elbow room enough space in which to move easily

elbow[2] *v* [T] to push someone with your elbow: **elbow your way through/past/into etc sth** *He elbowed his way through the crowd.*

elder[1] /'eldə $ -ər/ *adj especially BrE* the elder child in a family is the older one of two: *Their elder son is now at university.*

elder[2] *n* [C usually plural] **1 be sb's elder** *formal* to be older than someone else: **be two/ten etc years sb's elder** *Janet's sister is eight years her elder.* **2 sb's elders (and betters)** people who are older than you and who you should respect **3** a member of a social group who is important and respected because they are old: *the village elders*

elderly /'eldəli $ 'eldərli/ *adj* **1** an elderly person is old: *an elderly woman* → see box at OLD **2 the elderly** people who are old: *a home for the elderly*

eldest /'eldɪst/ *adj especially BrE* the eldest child in a family is the oldest one: *He is the eldest of six children.*

elect[1] /ɪ'lekt/ *v* [T]
1 to choose someone for a job by voting: **elect sb (as) president/leader/mayor etc** *She was elected President.*
2 elect to do sth *formal* to choose to do something: *He elected to stay at home.*

elect[2] *adj* **president-elect/governor-elect/prime minister-elect etc** the person who has been elected as president etc, but who has not yet officially started their job

election /ɪ'lekʃən/ *n* [C] an occasion when people vote to choose someone for a job: *He won the election for president.* | *The government will call an election next year.* | *Elections were held in May.*
—**electoral** /ɪ'lektərəl/ *adj* → BY-ELECTION, GENERAL ELECTION

elective /ɪ'lektɪv/ *adj formal* **1** an elective position is one that you must be elected for: *the House of Assembly's elective seats* **2** elective medical treatment is treatment that you choose to have, although you do not have to: *elective surgery such as hip replacements*

elector /ɪ'lektə $ -tər, -tɔːr/ *n* [C] someone who has the right to vote in an election [= voter]

electorate /ɪ'lektərɪt/ *n* [singular] all the people in a country who have the right to vote: *the British electorate*

electric /ɪ'lektrɪk/ *adj*
1 something that is electric works using electricity: **electric light/kettle/cooker etc** | *an electric guitar* | **electric current/power/charge** (=a flow of electricity)

Use **electric** before the names of things that work using electricity: *an electric kettle*
Use **electrical** to talk about things in general that use electricity, or people whose job is to make or repair these things: *faulty electrical equipment* | *an electrical engineer*

2 very exciting: *The atmosphere in the room was electric.* → see box at EXCITING

electrical /ɪ'lektrɪkəl/ *adj* using or relating to electricity: **electrical equipment/goods/appliances etc** | *an electrical fault* | *an electrical engineer* → see box at ELECTRIC

e,lectric 'chair *n* **the electric chair** a chair in which criminals are killed using electricity

electrician /ɪ,lek'trɪʃən, ,elɪk-/ *n* [C] someone whose job is to fit electrical wires and repair electrical equipment

electricity /ɪ,lek'trɪsɪti, ,elɪk-/ *n* [U] the power that is carried by wires and used to make lights and machines work: *The cooker works by electricity.* | *the electricity supply* | *the electricity bill*

electrics /ɪ'lektrɪks/ *n* [plural] *BrE* the parts of a machine that use electrical power

e,lectric 'shock *n* [C] a sudden painful feeling you get if you accidentally touch electricity

electrify /ɪ'lektrɪfaɪ/ *v* [T] **electrified, electrifying, electrifies 1** if a performance or a speech electrifies people, they think it is very interesting and exciting **2** to change a railway so that it uses electrical power, or to supply a place with electricity —**electrified** *adj* —**electrifying** *adj*: *Her words had an electrifying effect.*

electrocute /ɪ'lektrəkjuːt/ *v* [T] to kill someone by passing electricity through their body —**electrocution** /ɪ,lektrə'kjuːʃən/ *n* [U]

electrode /ɪ'lektrəʊd $ -troʊd/ *n* [C] a small piece of metal or a wire that sends electricity through something

electron /ɪ'lektrɒn $ -trɑːn/ *n* [C] a part of an atom that has a NEGATIVE electric CHARGE

electronic /,elɪk'trɒnɪk , ,lek- $ -'trɑː-/ *adj* electronic equipment uses electricity and MICROCHIPS —**electronically** /-kli/ *adv*

electronics /ɪ,lek'trɒnɪks, ,elɪk- $ -'trɑː-/ *n* [U] the science of making electronic equipment, such as computers or televisions: **electronics company/industry/firm etc** | *He's got a degree in electronics.*

elegant /'elɪgənt/ *adj* graceful and attractive: *an elegant woman* —**elegance** *n* [U] —**elegantly** *adv*

elegy /'elɪdʒi/ *n* [C] plural **elegies** a sad poem or song, especially about someone who has died

element /'elɪmənt/ *n* [C] **1** a simple chemical substance that consists of only one kind of atom [→ compound] **2 element of surprise/truth/risk/doubt etc** a small amount of surprise etc: *There's an element of risk in every sport.* **3** one part or feature of something: *Speed is an important element of the game.* **4** a group of people who are part of a larger group: *communist elements in the party* **5 the elements** [plural] the weather, especially bad weather: *A cave provided shelter from the elements.* **6** the part of a piece of electrical equipment that produces heat

elementary /,elɪ'mentəri/ *adj* **1** simple or basic: *an elementary mistake* **2** [only before noun] relating to the first and easiest part of a subject: *elementary science* **3** [only before noun] *AmE* elementary education is the first six years of children's education [= primary *BrE*]: *Fairbrook Elementary School*

E

elephant /'elɪfənt/ *n* [C] a large grey animal with big ears and a long TRUNK

elephant

elevate /'elɪveɪt/ *v* [T] *formal* to move someone or something to a higher position: **elevate sb/sth to sth** *He was elevated to Secretary of State.*

elevated /'elɪveɪtɪd/ *adj formal* in a high position or at a high level

elevation /ˌelɪ'veɪʃən/ *n* **1** [singular] a height above the level of the sea: **+of** *The village is situated at an elevation of 300 metres.* **2** [U] *formal* when someone moves to a more important position or rank: **+to** *her elevation to international stardom*

elevator /'elɪveɪtə $ -ər/ *n* [C] *AmE* a machine that takes you up and down in a building [= lift BrE]

eleven /ɪ'levən/ *number* the number 11: *She was sent to jail for eleven months.* | *I went to bed at eleven* (=11 o'clock). | *He is eleven* (=11 years old).

eleventh¹ /ɪ'levənθ/ *adj* coming after ten other things in a series: *her eleventh birthday* —**eleventh** *pron*: *I'm planning to leave on **the eleventh*** (=the 11th day of the month).

eleventh² *n* [C] one of eleven equal parts of something

elf /elf/ *n* [C] plural **elves** /elvz/ a small imaginary person with pointed ears and magical powers

elicit /ɪ'lɪsɪt/ *v* [T] *formal* to get information or a reaction from someone: *Her letter didn't **elicit** a response.*

eligible /'elɪdʒəbəl/ *adj* **1** if you are eligible for something, you have the right to have it or do it: **+for** *Are you eligible for a loan?* | **eligible to do sth** *If you are 18, you are eligible to vote.* **2** [only before noun] an eligible man or woman is good to marry because they are rich, attractive, and not married: *an **eligible bachelor*** —**eligibility** /ˌelɪdʒə'bɪlɪti/ *n* [U]

eliminate /ɪ'lɪmɪneɪt/ *v* [T] **1** to completely get rid of something that is unnecessary or unwanted: *Credit cards **eliminate** the need to carry cash.* | **eliminate sth from sth** *You should eliminate animal fats from your diet.* **2 be eliminated** if you are eliminated in a sports competition, you can no longer be in it, for example because you lost a game: *Pete was eliminated in the first game.*

elimination /ɪˌlɪmɪ'neɪʃən/ *n* [U] **1** the removal or destruction of something: **+of** *the elimination of nuclear weapons* **2** the defeat of a team or player in a competition, so that they no longer take part in it **3 process of elimination** a way of finding the right answer by proving that all the other answers are wrong

elite /eɪ'liːt, ɪ-/ *n* [C] a group of people who have a lot of power because they have money, knowledge, or special skills

elitist /eɪ'liːtɪst, ɪ-/ *adj* an elitist system is one in which a small group of people have much more power than others —**elitism** *n* [U]

Elizabethan /ɪˌlɪzə'biːθən◂/ *adj* relating to the time of Queen Elizabeth I of England (1558-1603): *Elizabethan drama*

elliptical /ɪ'lɪptɪkəl/ also **elliptic** /-tɪk/ *adj* shaped like a long circle but with slightly flat sides [= oval]

elm /elm/ *n* [C,U] a tall tree with broad leaves

elocution /ˌelə'kjuːʃən/ *n* [U] the skill of speaking clearly and correctly

elongated /'iːlɒŋgeɪtɪd $ ɪ'lɔːŋ-/ *adj* longer than normal

elope /ɪ'ləup $ ɪ'loup/ *v* [I] if two people elope, they leave home secretly to get married

eloquent /'eləkwənt/ *adj* able to express your ideas and opinions well: *an eloquent speaker* —**eloquently** *adv* —**eloquence** *n* [U]

else /els/ *adv* **1** used when talking about someone or something that is different from the one already mentioned: *Can I get you anything else?* | *He was sitting in someone else's seat.* | *Where else could she be?*
2 or else a) used to say that there will be a bad result if someone does not do something: *Hurry up or else we'll miss the train.* **b)** used to say what another possibility might be: *The salesman will reduce the price or else include free insurance.* **c)** used to threaten someone: *You'd better give it back or else!*

elsewhere /els'weə, 'elsweə $ 'elswer/ *adv* in or to another place: *goods imported from the US and elsewhere*

ELT /ˌiː el 'tiː/ *n* [U] *especially BrE* English Language Teaching the teaching of English to people whose first language is not English

elucidate /ɪ'luːsɪdeɪt/ *v* [I,T] *formal* to explain something by providing more information

elude /ɪ'luːd/ *v* [T] *formal* **1** to avoid being caught by someone, especially by tricking them: *He eluded the police for six weeks.* **2** if something you want eludes you, you do not find or achieve it: *Success eluded her.* **3** if a fact eludes you, you cannot remember it: *Her name eludes me at the moment.*

elusive /ɪ'luːsɪv/ *adj* difficult to find: *a shy and elusive animal*

elves /elvz/ *n* the plural of ELF

'em /əm/ *pron informal* sometimes used as a short form of 'them': *Go on, Bill, you tell 'em!*

emaciated /ɪ'meɪsieɪtɪd, -si-/ *adj* very thin because you are ill or do not have enough food → see box at THIN

email, e-mail /'iː meɪl/ *n*
1 [U] **electronic mail** a system for sending messages by computer: *Do you know how to use email?*

COLLOCATIONS

You can
read,
write,
send, and
receive an
email.
If you **check** your email, you look on your

computer to see if you have received any.
If you **reply** to an **email**, you write an email
to someone who has sent one to you.
If you get a **reply**, you receive an email from
someone you have written an email to.
If you **forward** an **email**, you send an email
that you have received to another person.
If you **send an attachment**, you send someone
a document which they can open and read
when they receive your **email message**.
If an **email bounces** or **bounces back**, it is sent
back to the sender, usually because the
address is wrong.
→ **INTERNET, COMPUTER, LETTER**

2 [C] a message sent by computer: *I got an email
from Joe.* | *I've sent her an email.* → see box at
MESSAGE
—**e-mail** *v* [T]

emanate /'emǝneɪt/ *v*
emanate from sth *phr v formal* if a smell, light
etc emanates from somewhere, it comes from
that place: *Wonderful smells emanated from the
kitchen.*

emancipate /ɪ'mænsɪpeɪt/ *v* [T] *formal* to give
people the political or legal rights that they did
not have before —**emancipated** *adj*
—**emancipation** /ɪˌmænsɪ'peɪʃǝn/ *n* [U]

embalm /ɪm'bɑːm $ -'bɑːm, -'bɑːlm/ *v* [T] to
preserve a dead body by using chemicals and
oils

embankment /ɪm'bæŋkmǝnt/ *n* [C] a wall of
earth or stones to stop water from flooding an
area, or to support a road or railway

embargo /ɪm'bɑːgǝʊ $ -'bɑːrgoʊ/ *n* [C] plural
embargoes an official order to stop trade with
another country: **impose/lift an embargo**
(=start or end one) *The UN lifted the oil embargo.*

embark /ɪm'bɑːk $ -ɑːrk/ *v* [I] to get on a ship
or plane —**embarkation** /ˌembɑː'keɪʃǝn
$ -bɑːr-/ *n* [C,U]
embark on/upon sth *phr v* to start something
new: *She left school to embark on a career as a
model.*

embarrass /ɪm'bærǝs/ *v* [T] to make someone
feel ashamed, stupid, or uncomfortable: *My parents always embarrass me.*

embarrassed /ɪm'bærǝst/ *adj* if you feel
embarrassed, you feel nervous or uncomfortable
about what other people think of you: **+about/at**
*I felt embarrassed about how untidy the house
was.* | **embarrassed to do sth** *He was too
embarrassed to admit his mistake.*

embarrassing /ɪm'bærǝsɪŋ/ *adj* if something
is embarrassing, it makes you feel embarrassed:
*It was very embarrassing being called up onto the
stage.* | *an embarrassing question*

embarrassment /ɪm'bærǝsmǝnt/ *n* **1** [U] the
feeling of being embarrassed: *Eric went red in
the face with embarrassment.* | **to sb's embar-
rassment** *To her embarrassment, she couldn't
remember his name.* **2** [C] something or someone that makes you feel embarrassed: **+to/for**
*The scandal is an embarrassment to the govern-
ment.*

embassy /'embǝsi/ *n* [C] plural **embassies** a
group of OFFICIALS who live and work in a foreign
country, and whose job is to help people from

their own country who are also living or working there. The building these people work in is
also called an embassy.

embattled /ɪm'bætld/ *adj formal* **1** [only
before noun] an embattled person, organization
etc has a lot of problems or difficulties: *The
embattled president had to resign.* **2** surrounded by enemies, especially in war or fighting: *the embattled capital, Sarajevo*

embed /ɪm'bed/ *v* [I,T] **embedded, embedding** to
put something firmly and deeply into something
else: **be embedded in sth** *A piece of glass was
embedded in her hand.*

embellish /ɪm'belɪʃ/ *v* [T] **1** to make something more beautiful by adding decorations
2 to make a story more interesting by adding
details that are not true —**embellishment** *n*
[C,U]

ember /'embǝ $ -ǝr/ *n* [C usually plural] a piece
of wood or coal that stays red and very hot after
a fire has stopped burning

embezzle /ɪm'bezǝl/ *v* [I,T] to steal money from
the place where you work —**embezzlement** *n*
[U]

embittered /ɪm'bɪtǝd $ -ǝrd/ *adj* angry or full
of hate because bad or unfair things have happened to you

emblazoned /ɪm'bleɪzǝnd/ *adj* [not before
noun] if something is emblazoned with a name
or design, it has that design on it where it can be
seen clearly

emblem /'emblǝm/ *n* [C] a picture, shape, or
object that is used to represent a country, organization etc

embodiment /ɪm'bɒdimǝnt $ ɪm'bɑː-/ *n* **the
embodiment of sth** someone or something that
represents an idea or quality, or is a typical
example of that idea or quality: *He is the embodiment of evil.*

embody /ɪm'bɒdi $ ɪm'bɑːdi/ *v* [T] **embodied,
embodying, embodies** to be a very good example of
an idea or quality: *She embodies everything I
admire in a teacher.*

embrace /ɪm'breɪs/ *v* [T] *formal* **1** to put your
arms around someone and hold them in a loving
way: *She warmly embraced her son.* **2** *formal* to
eagerly accept a new idea, opinion, religion etc:
*We hope these regions will embrace democratic
reforms.* **3** *formal* to include something: *This
course embraces different aspects of psychology.*
—**embrace** *n* [C] *He held her in a loving embrace.*

embroider /ɪm'brɔɪdǝ $ -ǝr/ *v* **1** [I,T] to deco-
rate cloth by sewing a picture or pattern on it
2 [T] to make a story more interesting by adding
details that are not true

embroidery /ɪm'brɔɪdǝri/ *n* plural **embroideries**
1 [C,U] a pattern sewn onto cloth, or cloth with
patterns sewn onto it **2** [U] the act of sewing
patterns onto cloth

embroil /ɪm'brɔɪl/ *v* [T] **be embroiled in sth** to
be involved in a difficult situation: *I didn't want
to become embroiled in their argument.*

embryo /'embriǝʊ $ -brioʊ/ *n* [C] plural **embryos**
an animal or human that has just begun to
develop inside its mother's body

embryonic /ˌembri'ɒnɪk◂ $ -'ɑːn-/ *adj* **1** at a
very early stage of development: *The plans are
only in embryonic form.* **2** relating to an
embryo: *embryonic cells*

E

emerald /'emərəld/ n [C] a bright green jewel

emerge /ɪ'mɜːdʒ $ -ɜːrdʒ/ v [I]   **1** to appear or come out from somewhere: **+from** *He emerged from his hiding place.*   **2** to become known: *Eventually the* **truth emerged.** | *Later it* **emerged that** *she had been having an affair.*   **3** to come out of a difficult experience: **+from** *She emerged from the divorce a stronger person.* —**emergence** n [U]

emergency /ɪ'mɜːdʒənsi $ -ɜːr-/ n [C] plural **emergencies** a dangerous situation that happens suddenly, and in which people might be hurt or killed: *Come quickly – it's an emergency!* | **in an emergency** *Make sure your children know what to do in an emergency.* | *In case of emergency,* *press the alarm button.* | **emergency exit/ supplies etc** (=used in an emergency)   → STATE OF EMERGENCY

e'mergency ,brake n [C] *AmE* a handle in a car that you pull up with your hand to stop the car from moving [= handbrake *BrE*] → see picture on page A12

e'mergency ,room n [C] *AmE* the part of a hospital where people are taken when they need urgent treatment [= casualty *BrE*]

e'mergency ,services n [plural] official organizations such as the police that deal with crimes, fires, or helping people who are badly hurt

emerging /ɪ'mɜːdʒɪŋ $ -ɜːr-/ also **emergent** /-dʒənt/ adj [only before noun] in an early state of development: *the country's emerging oil industry*

emigrant /'emɪgrənt/ n [C] someone who leaves their country to live in a different one [➤ immigrant]

emigrate /'emɪ̯greɪt/ v [I] to leave your country to go and live in a different one: **+to/from** *They emigrated to France.* —**emigration** /,emɪ̯'greɪʃən/ n [U]

eminent /'emɪnənt/ adj famous and respected: *an eminent scientist*

eminently /'emɪnəntli/ adv formal approving completely and certainly: *He's* **eminently suit- able** *for the role.*

emission /ɪ'mɪʃən/ n [C usually plural, U] a substance that is sent out into the air, or the act of sending it out: *gas emissions*

emit /ɪ'mɪt/ v [T] **emitted, emitting** to send out gas, heat, a sound etc

emotion /ɪ'məʊʃən $ ɪ'moʊ-/ n [C,U] a strong feeling such as love, hate, anger etc: **with emo- tion** *She trembled with emotion.* | **hide/show/ control emotion** *His face showed no* **sign of emotion.**

emotional /ɪ'məʊʃənəl $ ɪ'moʊ-/ adj con- nected with feelings such as anger, pity, sadness etc: *children with* **emotional problems** | *She* needs **emotional support.** | **become/get emo- tional** (=get upset, cry etc) *He becomes emotional easily.*
—**emotionally** adv: *an emotionally cold man*

emotive /ɪ'məʊtɪv $ ɪ'moʊ-/ adj causing strong feelings of anger, sadness etc: *Abortion is an* **emotive issue.**

empathize, also **-ise** *BrE* /'empəθaɪz/ v [I] to be able to understand someone else's problems,

especially because you have had similar prob- lems [➤ sympathize]: **+with** *I found it hard to empathize with her.*

empathy /'empəθi/ n [U] the ability to under- stand someone's feelings and problems [➤ sym- pathy]

emperor /'empərə $ -ər/ n [C] a man who rules an EMPIRE

emphasis /'emfəsɪ̯s/ n plural **emphases** /-siːz/

1 [C,U] special importance or attention that you give something: **(place/put) emphasis on (doing) sth** *The Japanese put a lot of emphasis on manners.*
2 [C usually singular] *technical* special impor- tance given to a word or phrase, for example by saying it louder [➤ stress]

emphasize also **-ise** *BrE* /'emfəsaɪz/ v [T] if you emphasize something you say or write, you give it special importance so that people will notice it: **emphasize that/how** *I emphasized that I was not criticizing her.* | *The report empha- sizes the importance of education.*

emphatic /ɪm'fætɪk/ adj expressing your meaning strongly: *an emphatic 'no'*
—**emphatically** /-kli/ adv

empire /'empaɪə $ -paɪr/ n [C] a group of coun- tries or organizations that are all controlled by one person, government etc: *the Roman Empire*

empirical /ɪm'pɪrɪkəl/ adj [only before noun] based on practical tests and experience, not ideas [≠ theoretical]: *empirical evidence*

employ /ɪm'plɔɪ/ v [T]
1 to pay someone to do a job: *The factory employs 2000 people.* | **employ sb as sth** *He was employed as a teacher.*
2 formal to use something: *The network employs the latest technology.*

employee /ɪm'plɔɪ-iː, ,emplɔɪ'iː/ n [C] some- one who receives a SALARY (=payment) to work for an organization, person, or company [= worker]: *government employees* | *employee rights* → see box at WORK

employer /ɪm'plɔɪə $ -ər/ n [C] an organiza- tion, person, or company that pays people to do a job: *Please give the name of your previous employer.* → see box at WORK

employment /ɪm'plɔɪmənt/ n [U]
1 when an organization, person, or company pays someone to do a job [≠ unemployment]: **in employment** *Are you in full-time employment?* | **+of** *We are opposed to the employ- ment of children.* | *employment rights for part- time workers* | **find/seek/offer employment** *What are her chances of finding employment?*
2 the number of people who have jobs: *Farm jobs represent 12% of the region's total employment.* | *You're never going to get* **full employment** (=when everyone has a job).
3 formal the use of a particular object or method to achieve something [= use]: **+of** *the employment of military force*

empower /ɪm'paʊə $ -'paʊr/ v [T] **1** to give someone confidence or skills so that they have more control over their life: *Education can empower you.* **2** formal to give someone the official power to do something

empress /'emprɪ̯s/ n [C] a woman who rules an EMPIRE, or the wife of an EMPEROR

empty

empty fridge   full fridge

empty¹ /'empti/ *adj* comparative **emptier**, superlative **emptiest**
1 an empty container or place has nothing or no one in it: *Noticing her empty wine glass, he refilled it. | By midnight, the streets were empty. | I've left an empty space for your signature. | The train was half-empty (=there were not many people on it).*

THESAURUS

bare – used about a room or area that has very little in it: *Apart from a bed, the room was bare.*
deserted – used about a place or building that has no people in it: *a deserted beach | By now, the streets were deserted.*
uninhabited – used about a place that has no people living in it: *an uninhabited island*
free – used about a seat, space, or room that no one is using: *Is this seat free?*
hollow – used about something that has an empty space inside: *The water flows through a hollow tube and into the drain.*

2 without meaning, value, or importance: **empty words/promises/threats etc** *a government's empty promises | Without him, my life would be empty.*
—**emptiness** *n* [U] *a feeling of emptiness*

empty² *v* **emptied, emptying, empties** **1** also **empty out** [T] if you empty a container, you remove everything from it: *The thieves had emptied out the desks. | **empty sth into/onto sth** Rachel emptied the soup into a pan.* **2** [I] if a place empties, people leave it: *The stores were already emptying.*

empty-'handed *adj* without getting what you wanted: *The thieves fled empty-handed.*

emulate /'emjʊˌleɪt/ *v* [T] *formal* if you emulate someone, you try to be like them because you admire them: *Children emulate their heroes.*

emulsion /ɪ'mʌlʃən/ also **e'mulsion paint** *n* [C,U] *BrE* a type of paint used on inside walls or ceilings that is not shiny when it dries

enable /ɪ'neɪbəl/ *v* [T] to make it possible for someone to do something or for something to happen: **enable sb/sth to do sth** *The money enabled me to buy a house.*

enact /ɪ'nækt/ *v* [T] **1** *law* to make a proposal become law: *Congress will not enact the Bill.* **2** *formal* to perform a story, event etc by acting it

enamel /ɪ'næməl/ *n* [U] **1** a hard substance used to decorate or protect things made of metal, clay etc **2** the hard surface on your teeth

enamoured *BrE*; **enamored** *AmE* /ɪ'næməd $ -ərd/ *adj* [not before noun] *formal* liking or loving someone or something very much: **+with** *You don't seem too enamoured with your job.*

encampment /ɪn'kæmpmənt/ *n* [C] a large temporary camp, especially of soldiers: *a military encampment*

encapsulate /ɪn'kæpsjʊˌleɪt $ -sə-/ *v* [T] *formal* to express or show something complicated in a short way [= **sum up**]: **encapsulate sth in sth** *Encapsulate your ideas in a few words.*

encase /ɪn'keɪs/ *v* [T] to cover something completely: **be encased in sth** *The reactor is encased in concrete.*

enchant /ɪn'tʃɑːnt $ ɪn'tʃænt/ *v* [T] **1** if something enchants you, it makes you feel happy, interested, and excited: *Her beauty enchanted us all.* **2** *literary* to use magic on someone or something —**enchanted** *adj: an enchanted castle*

enchanting /ɪn'tʃɑːntɪŋ $ ɪn'tʃæn-/ *adj* very pleasant or attractive: *She has an enchanting smile.*

encircle /ɪn'sɜːkəl $ -ɜːr-/ *v* [T] to surround someone or something: *a baby encircled by wolves*

enclave /'enkleɪv, 'eŋ-/ *n* [C] a small place that is different from the area around it because the people living there belong to a different nationality: *a Spanish enclave in Africa*

enclose /ɪn'kləʊz $ -'kloʊz/ *v* [T] **1** to put something in an envelope with a letter: *Please enclose your payment. | **Please find enclosed** the agenda for our meeting.* **2** to surround something with a fence or wall —**enclosed** *adj*

enclosure /ɪn'kləʊʒə $ -'kloʊʒər/ *n* [C] **1** an area that is separated by a wall or fence **2** something that you put in an envelope with a letter

encompass /ɪn'kʌmpəs/ *v* [T] *formal* **1** to include many ideas, subjects etc **2** to cover or surround an area

encore /'ɒŋkɔː $ 'ɑːŋkɔːr/ *n* [C] an extra piece of music a performer plays because the AUDIENCE wants it

encounter¹ /ɪn'kaʊntə $ -ər/ *v* [T] **1** to experience something that causes difficulty: **encounter problems/opposition etc** *The government encountered resistance to its plans.* **2** *formal* to meet someone when you did not plan to [= **come across**]: *I first encountered him at Oxford.*

encounter² *n* [C] an occasion when you meet someone or experience something when you did not plan to: **+with/between** *a chance encounter with a famous actor*

encourage /ɪn'kʌrɪdʒ $ ɪn'kɜːr-/ *v* [T]
1 to try to help someone succeed, for example by giving them confidence or determination [≠ **discourage**]: **encourage sb to do sth** *You are actively encouraged to contribute to school life. | **encourage sb in sth** My dad encouraged me in my ambitions.* **2** to make something more likely to happen: *Violent movies encourage anti-social behaviour.* —**encouraged** *adj* [not before noun] *I felt encouraged to continue.* —**encouragement** *n* [C,U] *words of encouragement | Henry needed no encouragement to work hard.* —**encouraging** *adj: encouraging news on jobs*

encroach /ɪn'krəʊtʃ $ -'kroʊtʃ/ *v*

E

encroach on/upon sth *phr v* to gradually take more of someone's time, power, space etc: *Don't let work encroach on your private life.*

encrusted /ɪnˈkrʌstɪd/ *adj* covered with a hard layer of something: **+with** *boots encrusted with mud*

encyclopedia also **encyclopaedia** *BrE* /ɪnˌsaɪkləˈpiːdiə/ *n* [C] a book or CD containing facts about many subjects, or detailed facts about one subject → see box at **BOOK**

end¹ /end/ *n*
1 [singular] the last part of a period of time, activity, book, etc [≠ **beginning, start**]: **+of** *I get paid at the end of the week.* | *By the end of the test she was sure she'd failed.* | *In the end* (=after a period of time) *we decided to go.* | *I watched the film from beginning to end.*
2 [singular] when something is finished or no longer exists: **put/bring an end to sth** *We must put an end to the war.* | **come to an end** *His life came to an abrupt end.* | **be at an end** *'This conversation is at an end,' she snapped.* | **the end of the road/line** *Our marriage had reached the end of the line.*
3 [C] the part of a place or thing that is furthest from its beginning or centre: **+of** *Walk to the end of the road with me.* | *We sat at opposite ends of the table.* | *desks arranged end to end* (=with their ends touching)
4 [C usually plural] a purpose, aim, or result: **political/military/personal etc ends** *She'd do anything to achieve her own ends.*
5 **days/hours etc on end** many days, hours etc without stopping: *It rained for days on end.*
6 **reach the end of your rope/tether** to get to the stage when you cannot deal with a bad situation
7 **no end of trouble/problems etc** *spoken informal* lots of trouble etc
8 **make ends meet** to get just enough money to buy what you need: *We could barely make ends meet after Ray lost his job.*
9 **it's not the end of the world** *spoken informal* used to say that a problem is not as bad as it seems
→ DEAD END, ODDS AND ENDS → **get (hold of) the wrong end of the stick** at **WRONG**

end² *v*
1 [I,T] to finish or stop, or to make something finish [≠ **begin, start**]: *What time does the film end?* | *talks aimed at ending the conflict* | **+with/in** *Their marriage ended in divorce.*
2 **the year/week etc ending sth** used to refer to a year that ends on a particular date: *accounts for the year ending 31 July 2004*
→ NEVER-ENDING

end up *phr v* to finally be in a particular place, situation, or state without intending to: **end up doing sth** *When I diet, I always end up putting weight back on.* | **+like/as** *I don't want to end up like my parents.*

endanger /ɪnˈdeɪndʒə $ -ər/ *v* [T] to put someone or something in a dangerous or harmful situation: *Smoking endangers your life.* | *The whale is an endangered species* (=one that may soon no longer exist).

endear /ɪnˈdɪə $ ɪnˈdɪr/ *v*

endear sb **to** sb *phr v* to make someone popular: *His remarks did not endear him to the audience.* —**endearing** *adj*: *an endearing smile*

endearment /ɪnˈdɪəmənt $ ɪnˈdɪr-/ *n* [C,U] words that express your love for someone

endeavour *BrE*; **endeavor** *AmE* /ɪnˈdevə $ -ər/ *v* [I] *formal* to try to do something new or difficult: **endeavour to do sth** *I endeavoured to reassure him.* —**endeavour** *n* [C,U] *Darwin's scientific endeavours*

endemic /enˈdemɪk, ɪn-/ *adj* an endemic disease or problem is always there [→ **epidemic**]: *Crime is endemic in cities.*

ending /ˈendɪŋ/ *n* [C] **1** the way that a story, film, activity etc ends: **+to** *cheese – the perfect ending to a meal* | **happy/surprise etc ending** *I like stories with a happy ending.* **2** the last part of a word: *Past participles have an 'ed' ending.*

endless /ˈendləs/ *adj* in large quantities or for long periods of time: *endless amounts of paperwork* —**endlessly** *adv*

endorse /ɪnˈdɔːs $ -ɔːrs/ *v* [T] to express support or approval of someone or something: *The president did not endorse the views of his deputy.* —**endorsement** *n* [C,U]

endow /ɪnˈdaʊ/ *v* [T] to give a college, hospital etc a large sum of money —**endowment** *n* [C,U]

endow sb/sth **with** sth *phr v formal* to make someone or something have a particular quality: *He was endowed with supernatural strength.*

ˈend-ˌproduct *n* [C] something that is produced at the end of a process or activity

ˌend reˈsult *n* [C usually singular] the final result of a process or activity: *The end result is likely to be fewer farms and farmers.*

endurance /ɪnˈdjʊərəns $ ɪnˈdʊr-/ *n* [U] the ability to continue doing something difficult or painful: *a test of physical and mental endurance*

endure /ɪnˈdjʊə $ ɪnˈdʊr/ *v* [T] to be in a difficult or painful situation for a long time without complaining

enduring /ɪnˈdjʊərɪŋ $ ɪnˈdʊr-/ *adj* continuing for a long time: *music's enduring appeal*

ˈend ˌuser *n* [C] the person who uses a product, rather than the people who made it

enemy /ˈenəmi/ *n* plural **enemies**
1 [C] someone who hates you and wants you to fail: *He made many enemies.* | *He's a dangerous enemy to have.* | **bitter/sworn enemy** *Jo and Jay are sworn enemies.*
2 [singular] the country that your country is fighting in a war: *territory controlled by the enemy* | **enemy aircraft/territory/fire etc**

energetic /ˌenəˈdʒetɪk◂ $ -ər-/ *adj* strong, active, and working hard: *a young energetic leader* | **energetic in doing sth** *The government could be more energetic in helping the poor.* → see box at **CHARACTER** —**energetically** /-kli/ *adv*

energy /ˈenədʒi $ -ər-/ *n* [C,U] plural **energies**
1 the physical and mental strength that makes you able to do things without getting tired: *Kids are always full of energy.* | **(have) the energy to do sth** *I didn't have the energy to walk.* | *Managers put time and energy into their artists' careers.*
2 power from oil, coal etc that produces heat, movement etc: **nuclear/solar etc energy** *renewable energies*

enforce /ɪn'fɔːs $ -ɔːrs/ v [T] to make people obey a rule or law: **enforce a law/ban etc** *We will enforce the speed limit.* —**enforcement** n [U] —**enforceable** adj

engage /ɪn'geɪdʒ/ v [T] formal **1** if something engages your interest or attention, it makes you stay interested: *The toy didn't engage her attention for long.* | **engage sb in sth** *I tried to engage him in conversation.* **2** formal to employ someone: **engage sb as sth/to do sth** *She was engaged as a nanny for their two children.*

engage in sth also **be engaged in sth** phr v formal to do an activity: *Ken was engaged in prayer.*

engaged /ɪn'geɪdʒd/ adj **1** if two people are engaged, they have agreed to marry: *Isn't she engaged to Phil?* | *Viv and Tony got engaged last year.* → see box at MARRIED **2** BrE if a telephone line is engaged, it is already being used [= **busy** AmE]: **engaged tone/signal** (=the sound you hear when this happens) → see box at TELEPHONE

engagement /ɪn'geɪdʒmənt/ n [C] **1** an agreement between two people to marry, or the period of time before they marry: *Their engagement was announced last week.* **2** an official arrangement for someone important to do something: *The Minister has a speaking engagement.*

engaging /ɪn'geɪdʒɪŋ/ adj pleasant and attractive: *an engaging smile*

engender /ɪn'dʒendə $ -ər/ v [T] formal to cause a particular situation or feeling: *a poster engendering racial hatred*

engine /'endʒ̣n/ n [C]
1 the part of a vehicle that produces the power that makes it move [→ **motor**]: **start/turn/switch an engine on/off** *He pulled in and turned off the engine.* | **car/jet etc engine** | *an engine that runs on gas*
2 a vehicle that pulls a railway train
→ FIRE ENGINE, JET ENGINE, SEARCH ENGINE

engineer¹ /ˌendʒ̣'nɪə $ -'nɪr/ n [C]
1 someone whose job is to design, build, or repair roads, bridges, machines etc: **mechanical/electrical/software etc engineer**
2 AmE someone whose job is driving a train

engineer² v [T] **1** to arrange something secretly: *the enemies who engineered his downfall* **2** to change the GENETIC structure of a plant or animal: *genetically engineered wheat*

engineering /ˌendʒ̣'nɪərɪŋ $ -'nɪr-/ n [U] the work of designing, building, or repairing roads, bridges, machines etc → GENETIC ENGINEERING

English /'ɪŋglɪʃ/ n
1 [U] the language used in Britain, the US, Australia, and some other countries: *Do you speak English?* | *He's Chinese, but his English is excellent.*
2 the English [plural] people from England
—**English** adj: *English literature*

engrave /ɪn'greɪv/ v [T] to cut words or pictures into metal, wood, glass etc: *a watch engraved with his initials*

engraving /ɪn'greɪvɪŋ/ n [C] a picture printed from a piece of engraved metal

engrossed /ɪn'grəʊst $ -'groʊst/ adj so interested in something that you do not think of anything else: **+in** *Dad was engrossed in the paper.*

engulf /ɪn'gʌlf/ v [T] **1** to have a very strong effect on a person, place, or thing: *Despair engulfed him.* **2** to completely surround something: *The house was engulfed in flames.*

enhance /ɪn'hɑːns $ ɪn'hæns/ v [T] to improve something: *Salt enhances flavour.* —**enhanced** adj —**enhancement** n [C,U]

enigma /ɪ'nɪgmə/ n [C] someone or something that is mysterious or difficult to understand: *Russia will always be an enigma.* —**enigmatic** /ˌenɪg'mætɪk◂/ adj: *an enigmatic smile*

enjoy /ɪn'dʒɔɪ/ v [T] to get pleasure from something: **enjoy doing sth** *My wife enjoys riding.* | **enjoy yourself** *Did you enjoy yourself at the party?*

enjoyable /ɪn'dʒɔɪəbəl/ adj giving you pleasure: *an enjoyable movie* → see box at NICE

enjoyment /ɪn'dʒɔɪmənt/ n [U] pleasure that something gives you: **give/bring sb enjoyment** *Music gives me great enjoyment.* | **+from** *He gets great enjoyment from driving.*

enlarge /ɪn'lɑːdʒ $ -ɑːrdʒ/ v [T] if you enlarge something, or if it enlarges, it gets bigger: *Can I have these photos enlarged?* —**enlargement** n [C,U]

enlarge on/upon sth phr v formal to provide more information about something you have already mentioned

enlighten /ɪn'laɪtn/ v [T] formal to explain something to someone: **enlighten sb as to/about sth** *Would you enlighten me as to your whereabouts?* —**enlightening** adj

enlightened /ɪn'laɪtnd/ adj approving having a sensible and modern attitude: *an enlightened approach to women's rights*

enlightenment /ɪn'laɪtnmənt/ n [U] formal when you understand something clearly, or when you help someone do this: *Isabel looked to Ron for enlightenment.*

enlist /ɪn'lɪst/ v **1** [I] to persuade someone to help you: *She enlisted help from friends.* **2** [I,T] to join the army, navy etc → see box at ARMY —**enlistment** n [C,U]

enliven /ɪn'laɪvən/ v [T] to make something more interesting: *Use games to enliven seminars.*

en masse /ˌɒn 'mæs $ ˌɑːn-/ adv together, as a group: *They resigned en masse.*

enmity /'enmɪti/ n [C,U] plural **enmities** formal a strong feeling of hatred towards someone: **+between/towards** *enmity between nations*

enormity /ɪ'nɔːmɪti $ -ɔːr-/ n [singular] how big, serious, or difficult something is: **+of** *the enormity of his crimes*

enormous /ɪ'nɔːməs $ -ɔːr-/ adj very big in size, amount, or degree: *It cost an enormous amount of money.* | *The team made an enormous effort.* → see box at BIG —**enormously** adv: *an enormously popular writer*

enough¹ /ɪ'nʌf/ adv
1 to the amount or degree that you need or want: **+for** *The water wasn't hot enough for a bath.* | **enough to do sth** *The room is just big enough to*

take a bed. | *Do you think this meat is cooked enough?*

2 if something is nice, good etc enough, it is fairly nice, good etc, but not very: **happy/nice/pleasant etc enough** *He seems a nice enough young man.*

3 sth is bad/difficult/hard etc enough (without sth) *spoken* used to say a situation is already bad, and you do not want it to get worse: *Life's hard enough if you were born here.*

4 strangely/oddly/funnily enough used to say that something is strange

→ **sure enough** at SURE

GRAMMAR

Use **enough** after adjectives or adverbs, or before nouns: *These jeans aren't big enough.* | *There isn't enough space in this office.*

enough² *determiner, pron*

1 as much or as many as you need or want: **(have) enough (sth) to do sth** *The police don't have enough evidence to convict him.* | *Have you had enough to eat?* | *Is there enough wine for everyone?* | *You've had* **more than enough** *time to prepare.*

2 have had enough (of sth) *spoken* used to say you are tired of a situation and you want it to end: *By 10.00 pm, I'd about had enough.*

enquire *especially BrE*; **inquire** *AmE* /ɪnˈkwaɪə $ -ˈkwaɪr/ *v* [I,T] to ask someone for information or facts about something: **+about/into** *I'm enquiring about trains to Newcastle.* → see box at ASK —**enquirer** *n* [C]

enquiry plural **enquiries** *BrE*; **inquiry** *AmE* /ɪnˈkwaɪəri $ ɪnˈkwaɪri, ˈɪŋkwəri/ *n* [C] a question you ask in order to get information: *Ask at the Enquiries desk.*

enrage /ɪnˈreɪdʒ/ *v* [T] to make someone very angry: *a programme that has enraged parents*

enrich /ɪnˈrɪtʃ/ *v* [T] to improve the quality of something by adding to it —**enrichment** *n* [U]

enrol *BrE*; **enroll** *AmE* /ɪnˈrəʊl $ -ˈroʊl/ *v* [I,T] **enrolled**, **enrolling** if you enrol at a college, university etc, or the college etc enrols you, you officially arrange to join a course there: **+on/for** *BrE* **+in** *AmE*: *I enrolled on the wine course.* —**enrolment** *n* [C,U]

en route /ˌɒn ˈruːt $ ˌɑːn-/ *adv* on the way: **+to/from** *a flight en route to Moscow*

ensconce /ɪnˈskɒns $ ɪnˈskɑːns/ *v* [T] to settle yourself in a place where you feel safe or comfortable: **+at/in/on etc** *Martha was firmly ensconced at the bar.*

ensemble /ɒnˈsɒmbəl $ ɑːnˈsɑːm-/ *n* [C] **1** *BrE* a small group of musicians, actors etc who perform together **2** a set of things that belong together

enshrine /ɪnˈʃraɪn/ *v* [T] *formal* if a right, power etc is enshrined, it is protected by law: **+in** *These rights are enshrined in the Constitution.*

enslave /ɪnˈsleɪv/ *v* [T] *formal* **1** to trap someone in a situation from which they cannot escape **2** to make someone a slave

ensue /ɪnˈsjuː $ ɪnˈsuː/ *v* [I] *formal* to happen after or as a result of something: *A long silence ensued.* —**ensuing** *adj* [only before noun]

en suite /ɒn ˈswiːt◂ $ ɑːn-/ *adj, adv BrE* a room that is en suite connects directly to another room: *en suite bathrooms*

ensure *especially BrE*; **insure** *AmE* /ɪnˈʃʊə $ -ˈʃʊr/ *v* [T] to make certain that something happens or is done: **+(that)** *Ensure that the fire doors are kept clear.*

entail /ɪnˈteɪl/ *v* [T] *formal* to involve something or make it necessary: *Does your job entail much travelling?*

entangle /ɪnˈtæŋɡəl/ *v* [T] **1** to make something become caught or twisted in a net, rope etc: **+in/with** *a fish got entangled with the line* **2** to involve someone in a situation that is difficult to get away from: **+in/with** *Jay became romantically entangled with her boss.* —**entanglement** *n* [C,U]

enter /ˈentə $ -ər/ *v*

1 [I,T] to go or come into a place [→ **entry**, **entrance**]: *Everyone stopped talking when he entered.* | *No one must enter this building.* | *We entered the city late at night.*

2 [T] to start working in a particular job: *He entered politics in 1990.*

3 [T] to start to become involved in something: *America entered the war in 1917.*

4 [I,T] to arrange to take part in a competition or examination, or to arrange for someone to do this: *She entered the competition and won.* | **enter (sb) for sth** *He was entered for a talent contest.*

5 [T] to put information onto a document or into a computer: **enter sth in/on etc sth** *Enter your name on the form.* | *Enter your password.* → see box at WRITE

6 [T] to begin a period of time: *The talks are now entering their third week.*

enter into sth *phr v* **1 enter into an agreement/contract etc** *formal* to make an official agreement to do something **2** to become involved in something: *Both sides must enter into negotiations.* **3** to affect a situation: *It was pure skill – luck didn't enter into it at all.*

enterprise /ˈentəpraɪz $ -tər-/ *n* **1** [C] a company or business: *a small family-run enterprise* **2** [C] a large and complicated project: *The film festival is a huge enterprise.* **3** [U] the ability to think of new ideas and make them work, especially in business: *a spirit of enterprise and adventure* → **FREE ENTERPRISE**

enterprising /ˈentəpraɪzɪŋ $ -tər-/ *adj* able to think of new ideas and make them work: *an enterprising young student*

entertain /ˌentəˈteɪn $ -tər-/ *v* **1** [T] to amuse people by doing something they enjoy watching or listening to: **entertain sb with sth** *A magician entertained the children with tricks.* **2** [I,T] to invite people to have food and drink with you: *I often have to entertain clients.* **3** [T] *formal* to consider an idea: *He would never entertain the thought of divorce.*

entertainer /ˌentəˈteɪnə $ -tərˈteɪnər/ *n* [C] someone whose job is to tell jokes, sing etc in order to entertain people

entertaining /ˌentəˈteɪnɪŋ◂ $ -tər-/ *adj* interesting and enjoyable: *an entertaining evening* | *an entertaining game*

entertainment /ˌentəˈteɪnmənt $ -tər-/ *n* [C,U] things such as television, films, and shows

that are intended to amuse or interest people:
The hotel offers live entertainment. | *Many
resorts have entertainments for children.* | **the
entertainment industry/business/world**

enthral *BrE*; **enthrall** *AmE* /ɪnˈθrɔːl $ -ˈθrɒːl/ *v*
[T] **enthralled**, **enthralling** if something enthrals
you, it makes you feel very interested or excited:
The audience was enthralled by his performance.
—**enthralling** *adj*

enthuse /ɪnˈθjuːz $ ɪnˈθuːz/ *v* [I] to talk about
something in a very excited way: **+about/over**
She enthused about the beauty of Lake Garda.

enthusiasm /ɪnˈθjuːziæzəm $ ɪnˈθuː-/ *n* [U] a
strong feeling of interest and enjoyment: **+for**
She shares your enthusiasm for jazz. | *He wel-
comed us with great enthusiasm.*
—**enthusiast** *n* [C]

enthusiastic /ɪnˌθjuːziˈæstɪk◂ $ ɪnˌθuː-/ *adj*
interested and excited: **enthusiastic about
(doing) sth** *Everyone was very enthusiastic about
the project.* | *She wasn't very enthusiastic about
going to London.* | *an enthusiastic crowd*
—**enthusiastically** /-kli/ *adv*

entice /ɪnˈtaɪs/ *v* [T] to persuade someone to do
something by offering them something nice:
entice sb into/away from etc *Good window
displays entice customers into the store.*
—**enticing** *adj*: *an enticing menu*

entire /ɪnˈtaɪə $ -ˈtaɪr/ *adj* [only before noun]
used to emphasize that you mean all of some-
thing: *It was the best day of my entire life.* | *The
hurricane destroyed entire villages.*

entirely /ɪnˈtaɪəli $ -ˈtaɪr-/ *adv* completely: *an
entirely different way of life* | *I'm not entirely
convinced about it.* | *The charity depends entirely
on donations.* → see box at **COMPLETELY**

entirety /ɪnˈtaɪərət̬i $ -ˈtaɪr-/ *n* **in its/their
entirety** *formal* including every part: *The film
will be shown in its entirety.*

entitle /ɪnˈtaɪtl/ *v* [T] **1** to give someone the
right to have or do something: **be entitled to
(do) sth** *Employees are entitled to free health
insurance.* | *You are not entitled to be here.* |
entitle sb to sth *a voucher which entitles you to
free membership of the club* **2 be entitled sth** if
a book, play etc is entitled something, that is its
name: *a poem entitled 'Pride of Youth'*
—**entitlement** *n* [C,U]

entity /ˈentət̬i/ *n* [C] plural **entities** *formal* something that exists as a single and complete unit:
The two stores are run as separate entities.

entourage /ˈɒntʊrɑːʒ $ ˈɑːn-/ *n* [C] a group of
people who travel with an important person: *the
president and his entourage*

entrance /ˈentrəns/ *n*
1 [C] a door or gate that you go through to enter
a place [≠ **exit**; ➡ **entry**]: **+to/of** *the entrance to the
tower* | *the school's main entrance* | *the hotel
entrance* | **front/back/side entrance** *We got in
through the back entrance.*
2 [U] the right to go into a place or join an
organization, college etc: **+to** *Entrance to the
museum is free.* | *There's a $30 entrance fee*
(=money you pay to get in somewhere). | *the
qualifications required for university entrance*
3 [C usually singular] when someone enters a
place: *Jane made a dramatic entrance.*

entrance

entrance

exit

entranced /ɪnˈtrɑːnst $ -ˈtrænst/ *adj* giving all
your attention to something or someone because
they are so beautiful or interesting: *She listened,
entranced.*

entrant /ˈentrənt/ *n* [C] *formal* someone who
enters a competition, organization, profession,
or examination: **+to** *new entrants to teaching*

entreat /ɪnˈtriːt/ *v* [T] *formal* to ask someone
for something in an emotional way [= **beg**]

entree /ˈɒntreɪ $ ˈɑːn-/ *n* [C] *AmE* the main part
of a formal meal [= **main course** *BrE*] → see box at
RESTAURANT

entrenched /ɪnˈtrentʃt/ *adj* entrenched ideas
have existed for a long time and are not likely to
change

entrepreneur /ˌɒntrəprəˈnɜː $ ˌɑːntrə-
prəˈnɜːr/ *n* [C] someone who starts a new business —**entrepreneurial** *adj*

entrust /ɪnˈtrʌst/ *v* [T] to make someone
responsible for something: **entrust sb with sth**
*I was entrusted with the task of looking after the
money.* | **entrust sth to sb** *The design of the new
building was entrusted to a young architect.*

entry /ˈentri/ *n* plural **entries**
1 [C,U] when someone goes into a place [≠ **exit**]:
+to/into *Entry to the gardens is free.* | *How did
the thieves gain entry* (=get in)*?* | *Refugees were
refused entry* (=they were not allowed in) *to the
country.* | *They were charged with illegal entry.*
2 [U] when someone joins an organization, college etc: **+into/to** *Britain's entry into the Euro-
pean Union* | *the entry requirements for a
university course*
3 [C] something you make or write in order to
try and win a competition: *The closing date for
entries is January 6.* | *the winning entry*
4 [C] a short piece of writing in a book contain-
ing information: *an entry in his diary* | *a diction-
ary entry*
5 [U] the process of putting information into a
computer: *data entry*
6 [C] a door or gate that you go through to enter
a place
→ **RE-ENTRY**

entwine /ɪnˈtwaɪn/ *v* [I,T] **1** to twist one thing
around another thing **2 be entwined** to be

closely related in a complicated way: *Physical and mental health are closely entwined.*

enumerate /ɪˈnjuːməreɪt $ ɪˈnuː-/ v [T] formal to name all the things on a list

envelop /ɪnˈveləp/ v [T] to cover or surround something completely: **be enveloped in sth** *The room was soon enveloped in flames.*

envelope /ˈenvələʊp $ -loʊp/ n [C] a paper cover that you put a letter in before you send it

enviable /ˈenviəbəl/ adj an enviable situation or quality is one that other people would like to have: *The hotel has an enviable position.*

envious /ˈenviəs/ adj wanting something that someone else has [➡ jealous]: **+of** *Tom became increasingly envious of his brother.* —**enviously** adv

environment /ɪnˈvaɪrənmənt/ n [C,U]
1 the environment the land, water, and air that people, animals, and plants live in: *new laws to protect the environment* | *chemicals that are damaging to the environment*

TOPIC

Things that are harmful to the environment
pollution – damage caused to air, water, soil etc by harmful chemicals and waste
the greenhouse effect – the warming of the air around the Earth as a result of the sun's heat being trapped by pollution
global warming – an increase in world temperatures, caused by an increase in carbon dioxide
acid rain – rain that contains acid chemicals from factory smoke, cars etc
deforestation – when all the trees in an area are cut down or destroyed
Describing things that are good for the environment
environmentally friendly/ecofriendly – products that are environmentally friendly or ecofriendly are not harmful to the environment when they are made or used
recycled – recycled glass, paper, or other material has been put through a special process so that it can be used again
biodegradable – a material that is biodegradable can be destroyed by natural processes, in a way that does not harm the environment
organic – organic food or organic farming does not use chemicals that are harmful to the environment

---

2 the people and things around you that affect your life: *Schools should provide a safe environment for children.* | **working/learning environment** *a pleasant working environment*

environmental /ɪnˌvaɪrənˈmentl◂/ adj relating to the land, water, and air on Earth: *serious environmental damage* | *environmental issues* | *environmental groups* (=groups who want to protect the environment) —**environmentally** adv: *chemicals that are environmentally safe*

environmentalist /ɪnˌvaɪrənˈmentəlɪst/ n [C] someone who tries to protect the environment

en·viron·men·tally ˈfriendly adj not harmful to the environment: *environmentally friendly products* ➜ see box at **ENVIRONMENT**

envisage /ɪnˈvɪzɪdʒ/ also **envision** /-ˈvɪʒən/ v [T] to think that something will be possible in the future: *I can't envisage moving from here.*

envoy /ˈenvɔɪ/ n [C] someone who is sent to another country as an official representative

envy¹ /ˈenvi/ v [T] envied, envying, envies to wish you had something that someone else has: *She has a lifestyle most people would envy.* | **envy sb (for) sth** *I envied her her good looks.* | *I don't envy you your job.*

envy² n [U]
1 the feeling of wanting something that someone else has [➡ jealousy]: **with envy** *He gazed with envy at the car.*
2 be the envy of sb to be something that other people admire and want: *Our facilities are the envy of most other schools.*

enzyme /ˈenzaɪm/ n [C] a chemical that is produced in plants and animals and causes a chemical process to start

ephemeral /ɪˈfemərəl/ adj formal existing only for a short time

epic¹ /ˈepɪk/ n [C] a long book, poem, or film with many exciting adventures

epic² adj long and exciting: *an epic journey*

epidemic /ˌepɪˈdemɪk◂/ n **1** [C] a situation in which a lot of people have a disease: *a flu epidemic* | **+of** *an epidemic of cholera* **2** [singular] a sudden increase in something bad: *an epidemic of car crime* —**epidemic** adj [only before noun]

epilepsy /ˈepɪlepsi/ n [U] a medical condition affecting someone's brain that can make them suddenly unconscious and unable to control their movements —**epileptic** /ˌepɪˈleptɪk◂/ adj: *an epileptic fit* —**epileptic** n [C]

epilogue /ˈepɪlɒg $ -lɔːg, -lɑːg/ n [C] a speech or piece of writing added to the end of a book, film, or play [➡ prologue]

episode /ˈepɪsəʊd $ -soʊd/ n [C] **1** one of the parts of a television or radio story that is broadcast separately: **+of** *He watches every episode of 'Friends'.* **2** an important event or period of time: *an exciting episode in her career*

epitaph /ˈepɪtɑːf $ -tæf/ n [C] a piece of writing on the stone over someone's GRAVE (=place where they are buried)

epitome /ɪˈpɪtəmi/ n **the epitome of sth** a very typical example of something: *She was the epitome of elegance.*

epitomize also **-ise** BrE /ɪˈpɪtəmaɪz/ v [T] to be a typical example of something: *a situation which epitomizes the problems in this industry*

epoch /ˈiːpɒk $ ˈepək/ n [C] a period of history

equal¹ /ˈiːkwəl/ adj
1 the same in size, value, or amount: **equal number/amount (of sth)** *There was an equal number of men and women.* | **of equal importance/value/size etc** *jobs of equal importance* | **+in** *two squares equal in size* | **+to** *One inch is equal to 2.54 centimetres.*
2 having the same rights and opportunities as everyone else: *Democracy is based on the idea that all people are equal.* | **equal rights/**

opportunities *Women do not yet have equal rights at work.*
3 be equal to sth **a)** to have the ability to do something successfully: *I'm not sure he's equal to the task.* **b)** to be as good as something else: *The architecture here is equal to any in the world.*

equal² *v* [T] **equalled, equalling** *BrE*; **equaled, equaling** *AmE* **1** to be the same size, number, or amount as something else: *Four plus four equals eight.* **2** to be as good as something or someone else: *Johnson has equalled the Olympic record.*

equal³ *n* [C] someone or something that is as good as another person or thing and has the same importance or value: *Men and women should be treated as equals.* | **be the equal of sb/sth** (=as good as someone or something) *a company that's the equal of its US competitors* | **without equal** (=better than anyone or anything else) *Good champagne is without equal.*

equality /ɪˈkwɒlɪti ＄ ɪˈkwɑː-/ *n* [U] when people have the same rights and opportunities [≠ **inequality**]: *the struggle for racial equality* | *They are demanding equality for men and women.* | **+of** *equality of opportunity* | **+between** *equality between the sexes*

equalize also **-ise** *BrE* /ˈiːkwəlaɪz/ *v* **1** [T] to make two things the same in size, value etc: *a vote to equalize wages* **2** [I] *BrE* to get a point in a game so that you have the same number of points as your opponent: *Spain equalized in the 75th minute.*

equally /ˈiːkwəli/ *adv*
1 to the same level or amount: *Diet and exercise are equally important in maintaining good health.*
2 in equal parts or amounts: *We divided the money equally.*
3 *spoken* used when you are saying something that is just as important as what you have just said: *There was no enthusiasm for the idea, but equally there was no opposition.*
4 in a way that is fair because it is the same for everyone: *We tried to treat everyone equally.*

'equals sign *BrE*; **'equal sign** *AmE* *n* [C] the sign (=) that you use in mathematics to show that two numbers, amounts etc are the same

equanimity /ˌiːkwəˈnɪmɪti, ˌekwə-/ *n* [U] *formal* calmness in the way you react to things

equate /ɪˈkweɪt/ *v* [T] *formal* to consider that two things are similar or related: **equate sth with sth** *Most people equate wealth with success.*

equation /ɪˈkweɪʒən/ *n* [C] a statement in mathematics showing that two amounts are equal: *In the equation 2y + 4 = 10, what is y?*

equator /ɪˈkweɪtə ＄ -ər/ *n* **the equator** the imaginary line around the Earth that is exactly the same distance from the North Pole and the South Pole → see picture at **GLOBE**

equestrian /ɪˈkwestriən/ *adj* relating to horse riding

equilibrium /ˌiːkwɪˈlɪbriəm/ *n* [singular, U] a balance between different things: *The government is anxious not to upset the economic equilibrium.*

equip /ɪˈkwɪp/ *v* [T] **equipped, equipping** **1** to provide someone with the tools or equipment they need: **equip sb/sth with sth** *The researchers equipped themselves with cameras.* | **be equipped with sth** *The hotel's rooms are*

equipped with a TV and telephone. | **well/fully/ poorly etc equipped** *a well equipped hospital* **2** to give someone the information and skills they need: **equip sb with sth** *We equip students with the skills they will need to succeed in life.* | **equip sb for sth** *training that will equip you for the job*

equipment /ɪˈkwɪpmənt/ *n* [U] the things that you need to do a job or sport: *new computer equipment* | *an expensive piece of equipment*

> **GRAMMAR**
>
> **Equipment** does not have a plural form. You can say **some equipment**, **any equipment**, or **pieces of equipment**: *We need to buy some extra equipment.*

equitable /ˈekwɪtəbəl/ *adj* *formal* fair and equal: *equitable treatment of all staff*

equity /ˈekwɪti/ *n* [U] *formal* when everyone is treated fairly and equally

equivalent¹ /ɪˈkwɪvələnt/ *adj* having the same value or meaning as something else: **+to** *a qualification that is equivalent to a degree*

equivalent² *n* [C] something that has the same value or meaning as something else: **+of** *He was fined £600 – the equivalent of two weeks' wages.* | *a French word with no English equivalent*

er /ɜː, ə ＄ ɜːr, ər/ *spoken* a sound you make when you are not sure what to say next: *Well, er, I don't really know.*

-er /ə ＄ ər/ *suffix* someone who does something: *a footballer* | *bad drivers*

ER /ˌiː ˈɑː ＄ -ˈɑːr/ *n* [C] *AmE* the abbreviation of **emergency room**

era /ˈɪərə ＄ ˈɪrə/ *n* [C] a period of time in history: *the post-war era* | **+of** *a new era of peace*

eradicate /ɪˈrædɪkeɪt/ *v* [T] to get rid of something such as a disease or social problem: *attempts to eradicate poverty* —**eradication** /ɪˌrædɪˈkeɪʃən/ *n* [U]

erase /ɪˈreɪz ＄ ɪˈreɪs/ *v* [T] **1** to remove written or recorded information: *Some of the names had been erased.* **2** to get rid of a memory or feeling: *He wanted to erase the memory of their last meeting.*

eraser /ɪˈreɪzə ＄ -ər/ *n* [C] a piece of rubber used for removing pencil marks from paper [= **rubber** *BrE*] → see picture at **CLASSROOM**

erect¹ /ɪˈrekt/ *v* [T] *formal* to build something, or put it in an upright position: *The church was erected in 1121.* | *The police erected barriers.*

erect² *adj* in a straight upright position: *He stood erect.*

erection /ɪˈrekʃən/ *n* **1** [C] if a man has an erection, his PENIS becomes stiff and upright because he is sexually excited **2** [U] when something is built or put in an upright position: **+of** *the erection of a fence*

ergonomics /ˌɜːɡəˈnɒmɪks ＄ ˌɜːrɡəˈnɑː-/ *n* [U] the way in which the careful design of equipment helps people to work better and more quickly —**ergonomic** *adj*: *a new ergonomic design* —**ergonomically** /-kli/ *adv*

E

The cliffs have been eroded by the sea.

erode /ɪˈrəʊd $ ɪˈroʊd/ v [I,T] **1** if the weather or sea erodes land or rocks, it gradually destroys them: *The coastline is being eroded.* **2** to gradually reduce someone's power or confidence: *Their political rights have been eroded.* —**erosion** /ɪˈrəʊʒən $ ɪˈroʊ-/ n [U]

erotic /ɪˈrɒtɪk $ ɪˈrɑː-/ adj involving sexual excitement: *erotic dreams*

err /ɜː $ ɜːr/ v [I] **err on the side of caution/generosity etc** to be more careful, generous etc than is necessary, in order to make sure nothing bad happens

errand /ˈerənd/ n [C] a short trip to do something for someone: *She's **running** an **errand** for me.*

errant /ˈerənt/ adj [only before noun] *formal* behaving badly: *his errant father*

erratic /ɪˈrætɪk/ adj changing often, or not following a regular pattern: *erratic behavior* —**erratically** /-kli/ adv

erroneous /ɪˈrəʊniəs $ ɪˈroʊ-/ adj *formal* not correct: *erroneous beliefs*

error /ˈerə $ ˈerər/ n [C,U] a mistake: **+in** *an error in our calculations* | *Police admitted they had **made** several errors.* | *a serious **error of judgment*** | **in error** (=because of a mistake) *The letter was opened in error.* | *an accident caused by **human error** (=a mistake by a person)* | *a computer **error message** (=message telling you the program cannot do what you want)*

erstwhile /ˈɜːstwaɪl $ ˈɜːrst-/ adj [only before noun] *formal* former: *his erstwhile friend*

erupt /ɪˈrʌpt/ v [I] **1** if a fight or argument erupts, it starts suddenly: *A political row has erupted.* **2** if a VOLCANO erupts, smoke, fire, and rock come out of it **3** if a place erupts, the people there suddenly become very angry or excited: *The stadium erupted when England scored.* —**eruption** /ɪˈrʌpʃən/ n [C,U] *a volcanic eruption*

escalate /ˈeskəleɪt/ v [I,T] **1** if an argument or fight escalates, or if someone escalates it, it quickly becomes worse: *Fighting has escalated in the area.* | **+into** *a dispute which has escalated into violence* **2** to increase, or make something increase: *Costs have escalated.* —**escalation** /ˌeskəˈleɪʃən/ n [C,U]

escalator /ˈeskəleɪtə $ -ər/ n [C] moving stairs that take people from one level of a building to another

escapade /ˈeskəpeɪd/ n [C] an exciting adventure

escape¹ /ɪˈskeɪp/ v

escape

1 [I,T] to get away from a dangerous place or unpleasant situation: **+from/through etc** *He escaped from prison.* | **+with** *She escaped with minor injuries.* | **escape unhurt/unharmed**

2 [I,T] to avoid something bad: **escape death/injury** *The driver narrowly escaped death.* | *Schools have not escaped criticism.*

3 [T] if something escapes you, you cannot remember it or do not notice it: *Her name escapes me.* | **escape sb's notice/attention** *His behaviour did not escape the notice of police.*

4 [I] if gas or liquid escapes from somewhere, it comes out

—**escaped** adj: *escaped prisoners*

escape² n

1 [C,U] when someone gets away from a place or situation: **+from** *Passengers talked about their escape from the wreckage.* | *She tried to **make** her **escape**.* | *The couple **had** a **lucky escape** (=were lucky not to be hurt or killed) when their car hit a tree.* | *the firm's **narrow escape** from bankruptcy*

2 [singular, U] a way to forget about your life and problems for a short time: **+from** *a welcome escape from the pressures of work*

→ FIRE ESCAPE

escapee /ˌeskeɪˈpiː, ɪˌskeɪˈpiː/ n [C] someone who has escaped

escapism /ɪˈskeɪpɪzəm/ n [U] activities or entertainment that help you forget about your life and problems for a short time: *Books were a form of escapism for him.* —**escapist** adj

escort¹ /ɪˈskɔːt $ -ɔːrt/ v [T] to take someone somewhere, especially in order to protect or guard them: **escort sb back/into etc sth** *Armed guards escorted the prisoners into the courthouse.*

escort² /ˈeskɔːt $ -ɔːrt/ n **1** [C,U] a person or group of people who go with someone in order to protect or guard them: *He was given a **police escort**.* | **under escort** *He was taken to prison under armed escort.* **2** [C] someone who goes with another person to a formal social event

Eskimo /ˈeskɪməʊ $ -moʊ/ n [C] plural **Eskimo** or **Eskimos** *old-fashioned* an INUIT. Many people now consider this word offensive.

ESL /ˌiː es ˈel/ n [U] English as a Second Language teaching English to students who are living in an English-speaking country, but whose first language is not English

esoteric /ˌesəˈterɪk◂, ˌiːsə-/ adj known or understood by only a few people who have special knowledge

esp. the written abbreviation of **especially**

especially /ɪˈspeʃəli/ adv

1 much more than usual, or much more than other people or things: *The town is very busy,* *especially in summer.* | *Good teaching is especially important.*

2 for one particular person or reason: **+for** *He played that song especially for me.* | *She bought new clothes especially for the trip.*

3 not especially not very much: *The hotel isn't especially nice.*

espionage /'espiɑːʒ/ *n* [U] the activity of finding out secret information and giving it to a country's enemies or a company's competitors [= **spying**]

espouse /ɪ'spaʊz/ *v* [T] *formal* to support an idea or belief

espresso /e'spresəʊ, ɪ'spre- $ -soʊ/ *n* [C,U] plural **espressos** strong black Italian coffee

essay /'eseɪ/ *n* [C] a piece of writing that discusses a subject: **+on/about** *He wrote an essay on French politics.* → see box at **UNIVERSITY**

essence /'esəns/ *n* **1** [singular, U] the most basic and important part of something: **+of** *The essence of his argument is simple.* | **in essence** (=basically) *In essence, we have three choices.* **2** [C,U] a liquid obtained from a flower or plant, that is used in cooking to give a particular flavour to food: *vanilla essence*

essential /ɪ'senʃəl/ *adj*

1 important and necessary: **+for/to** *A balanced diet is essential for good health.* | **It is essential that** *we make a decision soon.* | **it is essential to do sth** *It is essential to book tickets early.*

2 most important or basic: *The essential difference between them is their size.* → see box at **IMPORTANT** → and **NECESSARY**

essentially /ɪ'senʃəli/ *adv* used when giving the most basic fact about something: *It is essentially an old-fashioned romance story.*

es,sential 'oil *n* [C] an oil from a plant

essentials /ɪ'senʃəlz/ *n* [plural] things that are important and necessary: *They almost ran out of food and other essentials.*

establish /ɪ'stæblɪʃ/ *v* [T]

1 to start a company, organization, or system: *Our goal is to establish a new research center.* | *The company was established in 1974.*

2 establish relations/contacts/links etc to start a relationship with someone: *Many businesses have established links with local schools.*

3 to discover facts which prove something: *We have been unable to establish the cause of the fire.* | **+whether/what etc** *Detectives are trying to establish whether the crimes are related.* | **+that** *We have established that the disease is caused by a virus.*

4 to make people accept that you are good at doing something: *She has established a reputation in the fashion industry.* | **establish sb/sth as sth** *He has already established himself as a top chef.*

—**established** *adj*

establishment /ɪ'stæblɪʃmənt/ *n*

1 [C] *formal* an institution, organization, or business: *a research establishment*

2 the Establishment the people in a society or profession who have a lot of power and do not like new ideas: *a scandal that shocked the Establishment* | **the medical/military/religious etc establishment**

3 [U] when someone starts an organization, relationship, or system: **+of** *the establishment of NATO*

estate /ɪ'steɪt/ *n* [C] **1** a large area of land in the countryside that is owned by one person **2** *BrE* an area where a lot of houses or other buildings have been built: *a housing estate* | *an industrial estate* **3** all the property and money that someone leaves when they die **4** an estate car

es'tate ,agent *n* [C] *BrE* someone whose job is to buy and sell houses and land for people [= **real estate agent, Realtor** *AmE*]

es'tate car *n* [C] *BrE* a large car with a door at the back and a lot of space behind the back seats for bags etc [= **station wagon** *AmE*]

esteem[1] /ɪ'stiːm/ *n* [U] *formal* respect and admiration for someone: *She was held in high esteem.*

esteem[2] *v* [T] *formal* to respect and admire someone: *He was highly esteemed as a philosopher.*

esthetic /iːs'θetɪk $ es-/ *adj* an American spelling of **AESTHETIC**

estimate[1] /'estɪmeɪt/ *v* [T] to decide what you think the value, size etc of something is, partly by guessing and partly by calculating: **+that** *We estimate that 75% of our customers are teenagers.* | **estimate sth at sth** *The cost has been estimated at $1500.*

—**estimated** *adj*: *An estimated 10,000 people took part in the demonstration.*

estimate[2] /'estɪmət/ *n* [C]

1 what you think the value, size etc of something is, after calculating it quickly: *According to some estimates, two-thirds of the city was destroyed.* | **At a rough estimate**, *I'd say it's 300 years old.*

2 a statement of how much it will probably cost to build or repair something: *I got three estimates.*

estimation /,estɪ'meɪʃən/ *n* [U] someone's judgment or opinion: *Philip has really gone down in my estimation* (=I respect him less).

estranged /ɪ'streɪndʒd/ *adj* *formal* **1** no longer living with your husband or wife **2** no longer communicating with your family or friends because of an argument: **+from** *He was estranged from his family.* —**estrangement** *n* [C,U]

estrogen /'iːstrədʒən $ 'es-/ *n* the American spelling of **OESTROGEN**

estuary /'estʃuəri, -tʃəri $ -tʃueri/ *n* [C] plural **estuaries** where a river joins the sea

etc /et 'setərə/ *adv* et cetera used after a list to show that there are other similar things or people that could be added: *information in the form of books, leaflets, videos etc*

etch /etʃ/ *v* [I,T] **1** to make lines or patterns on metal, glass, or stone, using tools or chemicals **2 be etched in/on sb's memory/mind** to be impossible to forget: *Every detail is etched in my memory.*

eternal /ɪ'tɜːnəl $ -ɜːr-/ *adj* continuing for always: *the hope of eternal life* —**eternally** *adv*

eternity /ɪ'tɜːnɪti $ -ɜːr-/ *n* **1** [U] time that continues for always **2 an eternity** *informal* a very long time: *We waited for what seemed like an eternity.*

ethereal /ɪˈθɪəriəl $ ɪˈθɪr-/ *adj* delicate, and not seeming real: *ethereal beauty* —**ethereally** *adv*

ethic /ˈeθɪk/ *n* [C] **1** a belief that influences people's behaviour: *He had a strong work ethic* (=belief that work is important). **2 ethics** [plural] ideas or rules about what is morally right and wrong: *the medical ethics committee* **3 the ethics of (doing) sth** whether or not something is morally right: *a discussion on the ethics of capital punishment*

ethical /ˈeθɪkəl/ *adj* **1** connected with principles of what is right and wrong: **ethical issues/questions/problems 2** morally good and correct: *It would not be ethical to lie to them.* —**ethically** /-kli/ *adv*

ethnic /ˈeθnɪk/ *adj* relating to a particular race of people: *an ethnic minority*

ethnic ˈcleansing *n* [U] when people from a particular ethnic group are forced to leave an area

ethnicity /eθˈnɪsɪti/ *n* [U] the fact that someone belongs to a particular race of people

ethos /ˈiːθɒs $ ˈiːθɑːs/ *n* [singular] the moral attitudes within a group or institution: *The whole ethos of our society has changed.*

etiquette /ˈetɪket $ -kət/ *n* [U] the rules of polite behaviour

etymology /ˌetɪˈmɒlədʒi $ -ˈmɑː-/ *n* [U] the study of the origins and changing meanings of words —**etymological** /ˌetɪməˈlɒdʒɪkəl $ -ˈlɑː-/ *adj* —**etymologically** /-kli/ *adv*

EU /ˌiː ˈjuː/ *n* **the EU** the European Union the political and economic organization that most European countries belong to

eulogy /ˈjuːlədʒi/ *n* [C,U] plural **eulogies** a speech or piece of writing in which you praise someone or something very much

euphemism /ˈjuːfɪmɪzəm/ *n* [C,U] a word or phrase that is used to avoid saying something shocking or embarrassing —**euphemistic** /ˌjuːfɪˈmɪstɪk/ *adj* —**euphemistically** /-kli/ *adv*

euphoria /juːˈfɔːriə $ juː-/ *n* [U] extreme happiness and excitement —**euphoric** /-ˈfɒrɪk $ -ˈfɔː-, -ˈfɑː-/ *adj*

euro /ˈjʊərəʊ $ ˈjʊroʊ/ *n* [C] plural **euros** the unit of money used by most countries in the European Union

Euro- /jʊərəʊ $ jʊroʊ/ *prefix* relating to Europe or the EU: *the Euro-elections* (=elections for the European Parliament)

European¹ /ˌjʊərəˈpiːən $ ˌjʊrə-/ *adj* relating to Europe or the EU: *the European Parliament*

European² *n* [C] someone from Europe

European ˈUnion *n* the EU

euthanasia /ˌjuːθəˈneɪziə $ -ˈneɪʒə/ *n* [U] when someone is helped to die because they are suffering

evacuate /ɪˈvækjueɪt/ *v* [T] to move people to a safer place —**evacuation** /ɪˌvækjuˈeɪʃən/ *n* [C,U]

evacuee /ɪˌvækjuˈiː/ *n* [C] someone who was evacuated during a war

evade /ɪˈveɪd/ *v* [T] **1** to avoid doing something you should do, or avoid talking about something: *She evaded my question.* **2** to escape from someone who is trying to catch you: *He evaded capture.*

evaluate /ɪˈvæljueɪt/ *v* [T] *formal* to judge how good, useful, or successful something is [= **assess**]: *Teachers meet regularly to evaluate students' progress.* —**evaluation** /ɪˌvæljuˈeɪʃən/ *n* [C, U]

evangelical /ˌiːvænˈdʒelɪkəl/ *adj* **1** evangelical Christians believe that they must tell people about Christ **2** very keen to share your beliefs or ideas —**evangelical** *n* [C]

evaporate /ɪˈvæpəreɪt/ *v* **1** [I,T] if a liquid evaporates it changes into a gas: *The water had evaporated.* **2** [I] if a feeling evaporates, it disappears: *His fears evaporated.* —**evaporation** /ɪˌvæpəˈreɪʃən/ *n* [U]

evasion /ɪˈveɪʒən/ *n* [C,U] when you avoid doing something: *tax evasion*

evasive /ɪˈveɪsɪv/ *adj* trying to avoid doing something or saying something: *an evasive answer* —**evasively** *adv* —**evasiveness** *n* [U]

eve /iːv/ *n* **on the eve of sth** just before the day when something important happens: *Speaking on the eve of the match, he sounded confident.*

even¹ /ˈiːvən/ *adv*

1 used to emphasize something that is surprising or unexpected: *Even the youngest children enjoyed the concert.* | **not/never even** *I don't even know what he looks like.* | *He never even sent me a card.* | **may/might even** *He might even agree.*

2 even bigger/better/more etc used to emphasize that something is bigger, better etc: *If you could finish it today, that would be even better.* | *She knows even less about it than I do.*

3 used to add a word which is stronger or more exact: *He was surprised, even a little disappointed.*

4 even if/when/after used to emphasize that something will not or did not change a situation: *I'll never speak to her again, even if she apologizes.* | *Even when he found her, he couldn't stop crying.*

5 even so in spite of this: *They made more money that year, but even so the business failed.*

6 even now/then in spite of what happened: *Even now I find it hard to believe he lied.*

7 even though although: *She wouldn't go, even though Tom offered to take her.*

even² *adj*

1 flat, level, or smooth [≠ **uneven**]: *You need an even surface to work on.* | *He has lovely even teeth.*

2 an even rate or temperature does not change much: *an even body temperature*

3 involving equal amounts or numbers: *an even distribution of wealth* | *They have an even chance of winning.*

4 even numbers can be divided exactly by two [≠ **odd**]

5 get even (with sb) *informal* to harm someone as much as they have harmed you: *I'll get even with you one day!*

→ **break even** at **BREAK¹** → **on an even keel** at **KEEL¹**

even³ *v*

even out *phr v* if differences even out, or if you even them out, they become less: **even sth ⇔ out** *Things seem to have evened themselves out a bit.*

evening /ˈiːvnɪŋ/ n
1 [C,U] the end of the day and the early part of the night: *We visited them* **one evening**. | *I'll see you* **this evening**. | **on Monday etc evening(s)** *especially BrE*: *I have a class on Thursday evenings.* | **Monday etc evening(s)** *especially AmE*: *He was interviewed Friday evening.* | **in the evening(s)** *In the evenings it was very cold.* | *We spent a very pleasant evening with them.* | **evening class/paper/meal** *We had just finished our evening meal.*
2 (good) evening *spoken* used to greet someone when you meet them in the evening: *Evening, Rick.*

'evening dress n **1** [U] formal clothes that people wear for formal social events in the evening **2** also **evening gown** [C] a formal dress that a woman wears to a formal social event in the evening

evenly /ˈiːvənli/ adv **1** in an equal way: *a more* **evenly distributed** *workload* | *The Senate is* **split evenly** *between the two parties.* **2** in a regular or steady way: *He was breathing more evenly.* **3 evenly matched** having an equal chance of winning

event /ɪˈvent/ n [C]
1 something that happens, especially something important, interesting, or unusual: *The opening of the factory was a* **major event** *locally.* | *Police are trying to work out the* **sequence of events**. | *They were not happy about the* **course of events** (=the way things happened). | *Her* **version of events** (=what she said happened) *was completely different.*
2 a performance, competition, party etc that has been arranged for a particular date or time: **social/sporting events** | *The next event will be the 100 metres.*
3 in any event, at all events *especially AmE* whatever happens: *In any event, it seems likely that prices will rise.*
4 in the event of sth *formal* if a particular thing happens: *Britain agreed to support the US in the event of war.*
5 in the event used when saying what actually happened, especially when you expected something else: *In the event we didn't have to wait long for the results.*
6 in the normal course of events used to say what would usually happen: *In the normal course of events, she would not agree.*
→ NON-EVENT

eventful /ɪˈventfəl/ adj full of interesting or important events: *an eventful life*

eventual /ɪˈventʃuəl/ adj [only before noun] happening after a long time: *the eventual outcome* | *the eventual winner*

eventuality /ɪˌventʃuˈæləti/ n [C] plural **eventualities** *formal* something that might happen, especially something bad: *We must* **prepare for any eventuality**.

eventually /ɪˈventʃuəli, -tʃəli/ adv after a long time: *Eventually he got a job.* → see box at LASTLY

ever /ˈevə $ ˈevər/ adv
1 at any time – used mainly in questions and negative sentences: *Have you* **ever** *eaten snails?* | *Nothing* **ever** *makes Paula angry.* | *If you're ever in London, give us a call.* | **the best/biggest etc ever** *That was the best meal I've ever had.* | *They*

hardly ever (=almost never) *watch TV.* | *She* **never ever** *forgot him.*
2 hotter/thinner/better etc than ever even hotter etc than before: *I woke up the following morning feeling worse than ever.*
3 always or continuously: *Ever optimistic, I kept trying.* | *He joined the firm in 1980, and has been here* **ever since** (=continuously since then). | **ever-growing/ever-increasing etc** (=continuing to grow, increase etc) *the ever-growing population* | *Joe was late,* **as ever** (=like always).* | **as popular/bad/happy etc as ever** *She was looking as cheerful as ever.* | *His name will live* **for ever** (=always in the future).
4 ever so/ever such a *BrE spoken* used to emphasize what you are saying: *It's ever so cold in here.* | *He's ever such a nice man.*

GRAMMAR

You use **ever** when you ask a question, but not when you answer a question: *'Have you ever been to America?' 'Yes, I have been there.'*

evergreen /ˈevəgriːn $ -ər-/ adj an evergreen tree has leaves that do not fall off in winter [➡ **deciduous**] —**evergreen** n [C]

everlasting /ˌevəˈlɑːstɪŋ $ ˌevərˈlæ-/ adj continuing for ever: *everlasting peace*

evermore /ˌevəˈmɔː $ ˌevərˈmɔːr/ adv literary always in the future

every /ˈevri/ determiner
1 each one of a group of people or things: *Every student will take the test.* | **every single/last** (=with nothing or no one missing) *He told Jan every single thing.* → see box at ANY → and EACH
2 used to say how often something happens: **every day/month/year etc** (=on each day, in each month etc) *He goes running every day.* | *Every time the phone rang, she jumped.* | **every few feet/ten yards etc** *Every few yards she stopped.*
3 every now and then/every so often sometimes, but not often: *I still see her every now and then.* → see box at SOMETIMES
4 one in every hundred/two in every thousand etc used to show how common something is: *a disease that will kill one in every thousand babies*
5 the greatest possible: *I'll make* **every effort** *to be there.* | *There is* **every chance** *that he will succeed.*
6 every bit as good/important etc used to emphasize that something is as good, important etc as something else: *I dislike him* **every bit as much** *as you do.*
7 every other the first, third, fifth etc or the second, fourth, sixth etc: *Water the plants* **every other day**.
8 every which way *informal* in every direction: *People were running every which way.*

GRAMMAR

every, every one, everyone
These are all followed by a singular verb: *Almost every house has a computer nowadays.* | *Every one was different.* | *Everyone likes him.*
Every one is used to emphasize that you mean each person or thing in a group: *I've*

E

seen every one of his films.
Everyone means all the people in a group:
*Hello, everyone, I'd like to introduce Denise,
your new teacher.*
→ ALL¹

everybody /'evribɒdi, -bədi $ -baːdi/ *pron*
EVERYONE

everyday /'evrideɪ/ *adj* [only before noun]
ordinary, usual, or happening every day: *It's just
part of everyday life.*

everyone /'evriwʌn/ also **everybody** *pron*
every person: *Is everyone ready to go?* | *Everyone
else had gone.* → see box at EVERY

everyplace /'evripleɪs/ *adv AmE spoken* EVERY-
WHERE

everything /'evriθɪŋ/ *pron*
1 each thing or all things: *She criticizes every-
thing I do.* | *Is everything all right?* | *Jim does the
dishes, but I do **everything else**.*
2 and everything *spoken* used instead of mentioning other things: *He's a nice guy and everything, but not very bright.*
3 be/mean everything (to sb) to be more
important than anything else: *Money isn't everything.*

everywhere /'evriweə $ -wer/ *adv*
1 in or to every place: *I've looked **everywhere**
else.*
2 be everywhere to be very common

evict /ɪ'vɪkt/ *v* [T] to force someone to leave
their home, for example because they have not
paid rent → see box at RENT —**eviction** /ɪ'vɪkʃən/
n [C,U]

evidence¹ /'evɪdəns/ *n* [U]
1 facts or signs that prove the existence or truth
of something: *You must be able to **provide
evidence** of your ability.* | **+that** *Do you have
evidence that this treatment works?* | **+for** *There
is no evidence for these claims.* | *There is **not a
shred of evidence** to support such a theory.*
2 facts given or objects shown in a court of law
in order to prove that someone is guilty or not
guilty: *A vital **piece of evidence** was missing.* |
+against *There was very little evidence against
him.* → see box at COURT → and POLICE
3 give evidence to officially tell a court what
you know
4 be in evidence *formal* to be easily seen or
noticed

GRAMMAR

Evidence does not have a plural form. You can
say **some evidence**, **any evidence**, or **pieces of
evidence**: *There is some evidence that foods
rich in vitamin C can give protection against
cancer.*

evidence² *v formal* **be evidenced by/in sth** to
be shown or proven by something

evident /'evɪdənt/ *adj formal* easily noticed
[= obvious, clear]: *It was evident that they were
not satisfied.* | *Her deafness **became evident**
when she was 12.*

evidently /'evɪdəntli $ -dənt-, -dent-/ *adv*
1 used to say that something is true and can
easily be noticed [= obviously, clearly]: *The President was evidently unwell.* **2** used to talk about

something that you have heard about [= appar-
ently]: *He evidently studied hard and was popular.*

evil¹ /'iːvəl/ *adj*
1 very bad or harmful, or morally wrong: *his
evil deeds* | *an evil dictator*
2 connected with the devil: *evil spirits*
3 very unpleasant: *an evil smell*

evil² *n* [C,U] something that is very bad or harmful, or that is morally wrong: **+of** *the evils of
racism* | *They chose **the lesser of two evils** (=the
thing which seemed less bad).* | *They see the
process as **a necessary evil**.* | *the choice between
good and evil*

evocative /ɪ'vɒkətɪv $ ɪ'vaː-/ *adj* making you
remember or imagine something: **+of** *Her novel
is wonderfully evocative of village life.*

evoke /ɪ'vəʊk $ ɪ'voʊk/ *v* [T] to make someone
feel or remember something: *The film evoked
memories of my childhood.* —**evocation**
/ˌevə'keɪʃən, ˌiːvəʊ- $ ˌevə-, ˌiːvoʊ-/ *n* [C,U]

evolution /ˌiːvə'luːʃən, ˌevə- $ ˌevə-/ *n* [U]
1 the gradual development of plants and animals over millions of years: *Darwin's **theory of
evolution*** **2** the gradual development of an
idea, situation, or object: **+of** *the evolution of
computer technology* —**evolutionary** *adj*

evolve /ɪ'vɒlv $ ɪ'vaːlv/ *v* **1** [I,T] to develop, or
to make something develop: **+into** *Our relationship evolved into a warm friendship.* **2** [I] if
animals or plants evolve, they gradually develop
over a very long period

ewe /juː/ *n* [C] a female sheep

ex /eks/ *n* [C] *informal* someone who used to be
your husband, wife, boyfriend, or girlfriend

ex- /eks/ *prefix* former: **ex-wife/husband/
girlfriend etc**

exacerbate /ɪg'zæsəbeɪt $ -sər-/ *v* [T] to make
something worse: *This will only **exacerbate** the
problem.*

exact¹ /ɪg'zækt/ *adj*
1 correct in every detail: *I can remember his
exact words.* | *the **exact nature** of the problem* |
*I met her years ago – seven years ago, to be
exact.* | **exact date/time/number/amount** *I
can't remember the exact date.* | **exact location/
position/spot**
2 used to emphasize that something is the same
or precise [= very]: *He said **the exact same
thing**.* | *He's the **exact opposite** of his brother.* |
*He arrived **at the exact moment** I mentioned his
name.*
3 sth is not an exact science used to say that
something involves opinions and guessing,
rather than definite facts

exact² *v* [T] *formal* to take something from someone: *The war exacted a heavy price.*

exacting /ɪg'zæktɪŋ/ *adj* needing or demanding a lot of effort or care: *She set herself **exacting standards**.*

exactly /ɪg'zæktli/ *adv*
1 used to say that an amount, piece of information etc is or should be completely correct: *We
got home at **exactly** six o'clock.* | **exactly what/
how/where etc** *I know exactly where she
lives.* | **what/how/where etc exactly?** *What
exactly is going on?* | *That's **exactly right**.*
2 used to emphasize that something is the same
or different: *They were wearing **exactly the**

same dress. | *He was exactly the opposite of his brother.*
3 *spoken* used to show that you agree completely with someone: *'We should sell the car.' 'Exactly!'*
4 not exactly *spoken* **a)** used to reply that something is not completely true: *'Sheila's ill, is she?' 'Not exactly, she's just tired.'* **b)** used to say that something is definitely not true [= **hardly**]: *Why's Tim on a diet? He's not exactly fat.*

exaggerate /ɪɡ'zædʒəreɪt/ *v* [I,T] to make something seem better, larger, worse etc than it really is: *He says everyone hates him, but he's exaggerating.* | **grossly/wildly exaggerated** *The problems have been grossly exaggerated.*
—**exaggerated** *adj*: *He gave an exaggerated sigh.*
—**exaggeration** /ɪɡ,zædʒə'reɪʃən/ *n* [C,U] *It is no exaggeration to say that he saved my life.*

exalted /ɪɡ'zɔːltɪd $ -ɔːl-/ *adj formal* of a very high rank or highly respected: *an exalted position*

exam /ɪɡ'zæm/ *n* [C]
1 an official test of knowledge or ability in a particular subject: *He's taking his exams at the moment.* | *When do you get your exam results?* | **pass/fail an exam** | **chemistry/French etc exam**
2 *AmE* a set of medical tests: *an eye exam*

examination /ɪɡ,zæmɪ'neɪʃən/ *n*
1 [C] *formal* an official test of knowledge or ability in a particular subject: *The examination results will be announced in September.* | **pass/fail an examination** *He passed all his examinations.*
2 [C,U] when someone looks at or considers something carefully: **+of** *a detailed examination of the data* | *On closer examination, the painting was found to be a forgery.*
3 [C] a set of medical tests: *He was given a thorough medical examination.*

examine /ɪɡ'zæmɪn/ *v* [T]

examine

examining a patient

1 to look at something carefully in order to find out more about it: *The doctor examined her ankle.*
2 to consider an idea or plan carefully: *The proposals will be examined in detail.* | **+how/whether/what** *This chapter examines how the law actually operates.*
3 *formal* to test someone's knowledge of a subject

examiner /ɪɡ'zæmɪnə $ -ər/ *n* [C] the person who officially judges how well students perform in an examination

example /ɪɡ'zɑːmpəl $ ɪɡ'zæm-/ *n* [C]
1 something that you mention because it is typical of the kind of thing you are talking about: **+of** *Can you give me an example of an adverb?* | *She cited a number of examples.* | **good/typical/classic/prime example** *This is a prime example of the problems we face.*
2 for example used when you are giving an

example to show what you mean: *Food prices have increased greatly. For example, the price of meat has doubled.* | *Many countries, for example Mexico and Japan, have a lot of earthquakes.*
3 someone whose behaviour is good and should be copied, or their behaviour: **+to** *She's an example to us all.* | *Parents should set an example for their children* (=show them how to behave). | *I suggest you follow her example* (=do what she did).
4 make an example of sb to punish someone so that other people will not do what they did

exasperated /ɪɡ'zɑːspəreɪtɪd $ -'zæs-/ *adj* very annoyed: *I was so exasperated with him.*
—**exasperate** *v* [T]   —**exasperation** /ɪɡ,zɑːspə'reɪʃən $ -,zæs-/ *n* [U]

exasperating /ɪɡ'zɑːspəreɪtɪŋ $ -'zæs-/ *adj* very annoying

excavate /'ekskəveɪt/ *v* [I,T] to dig in the ground, especially in order to find ancient objects —**excavation** /,ekskə'veɪʃən/ *n* [C,U]

exceed /ɪk'siːd/ *v* [T] *formal* to go beyond a particular amount or level: *The cost must not exceed $150.* | *His performance exceeded our expectations.* | *She was fined for exceeding the speed limit.*

exceedingly /ɪk'siːdɪŋli/ *adv formal* extremely: *an exceedingly difficult task*

excel /ɪk'sel/ *v* [I] **excelled, excelling** *formal* **1** to do something very well: **+at/in** *I never excelled at sport.* **2 excel yourself** *BrE* to do something better than you have done it before

excellent /'eksələnt/ *adj*
1 extremely good or of very high quality: *What an excellent idea!* → see box at **GOOD**
2 *spoken* used to show that you approve of something: *'I'll bring them over tonight.' 'Excellent.'*
—**excellently** *adv* —**excellence** *n* [U] *a reputation for excellence in research*

except /ɪk'sept/ *linking word, prep*
1 not including a particular thing, person, or fact: *We're open every day except Monday.* | **+for** *Everyone went to the show, except for Scott.* | **+when/where/what etc** *I don't know anything about it, except what I've read.* | **+(that)** *I have earrings just like those, except they're silver.*
2 used to give the reason why something did not happen: *I would have gone, except we had visitors.*

excepted /ɪk'septɪd/ *adj formal* not included: *He doesn't have any interests, politics excepted.*

excepting /ɪk'septɪŋ/ *prep* not including [= **except**]: *All the students, excepting three or four, spoke fluent English.*

exception /ɪk'sepʃən/ *n* [C,U]
1 someone or something that is not included in a general statement: **+to** *There's an exception to every rule.* | **notable/important exception** *There was one notable exception.* | *He was generally rude, and today was no exception.* | **with the exception of sb/sth** *Everyone came to the party, with the exception of Mary.* | **without exception** *All of his films, without exception, have been a huge success.* | *We'll make an exception in your case* (=not include you in a rule).

2 the exception that proves the rule the only person or thing that makes a general statement not completely true

3 take exception to sth to be offended by something

exceptional /ɪkˈsepʃənəl/ *adj* **1** unusually good [= **outstanding**]: *an exceptional student* → see box at **GOOD 2** unusual and not likely to happen often: *We would do this only in exceptional circumstances.* —**exceptionally** *adv*

excerpt /ˈeksɜːpt $ -ɜːrpt/ *n* [C] a short piece taken from a book, poem, piece of music etc: **+from** *an excerpt from his poem*

excess¹ /ɪkˈses, ˈekses/ *n* **1** [singular, U] a larger amount of something than is suitable: **+of** *The problem was caused by an excess of enthusiasm.* **2 in excess of sth** more than an amount or level: *Our profits were in excess of $5 million.* **3 do sth to excess** to do something too much: *He smoked and drank to excess.* **4 excesses** [plural] harmful or bad things which people do too much: **+of** *the worst excesses of the rock star's lifestyle*

excess² /ˈekses/ *adj* [only before noun] more than is wanted or allowed: *He wanted to lose some excess weight.*

excessive /ɪkˈsesɪv/ *adj* too much or too great: *Avoid excessive amounts of coffee.* —**excessively** *adv*

exchange¹ /ɪksˈtʃeɪndʒ/ *n*

1 [C,U] when you give, send, or say something to someone, and they give, send, or say something to you: **+of** *Our main aim is to encourage the exchange of information.* | **exchange of ideas/views** *A very frank exchange of views took place.* | *There was an exchange of fire* (=both sides were shooting). | **in exchange for sth** *The Europeans traded weapons in exchange for gold.* **2** [C] a conversation, especially between people who are angry: *They had a heated exchange.* **3** [C] **a)** when you visit another student, usually in another country, and afterwards they visit you **b)** a temporary arrangement in which you have someone else's job or house, while you have your job or house **4** [U] *technical* money that is changed into money from another country: *foreign exchange* **5** [C] a STOCK EXCHANGE

exchange² *v* [T] to give, send, or say something to someone who gives, sends, or says something to you: *The two armies exchanged prisoners.* | **exchange sth for sth** *I'd like to exchange this shirt for a smaller one.* | **exchange information/ideas/views** *a place where people can chat and exchange ideas* | **exchange glances/greetings/words etc** *The two women exchanged glances and laughed.*

ex'change rate *n* [C] the value of money from one country compared with money from another country: *What's the exchange rate?*

excise /ˈeksaɪz/ *n* [C,U] tax on goods produced and used inside a country

excitable /ɪkˈsaɪtəbəl/ *adj* becoming excited very easily

excite /ɪkˈsaɪt/ *v* [T] **1** to make someone feel excited **2** *formal* to cause a particular feeling or reaction [= **arouse**]: *The photographs excited great interest.*

excited /ɪkˈsaɪtɪd/ *adj* happy, interested, or hopeful because something good has happened or is expected: **+about** *The kids are getting*

really excited about the trip. | **excited to do sth** *She was so excited to be home.* —**excitedly** *adv*

excitement /ɪkˈsaɪtmənt/ *n* [C,U] the feeling of being excited, or a situation in which you are excited: **+of** *the excitement of her new job* | *She was flushed with excitement.* | **in sb's/the excitement** *In his excitement, he had forgotten to switch his camcorder on.*

exciting /ɪkˈsaɪtɪŋ/ *adj* making you feel excited: *an exciting discovery* | *Their trip sounded really exciting.*

THESAURUS

thrilling – exciting and interesting: *a thrilling 3–2 victory*

gripping – a gripping film, story etc is very exciting and interesting

exhilarating – making you feel happy, excited, and full of energy: *an exhilarating ride*

nail-biting – very exciting, especially because you do not know what is going to happen next: *a nail-biting finish to the race*

electric – very exciting: *The effect/atmosphere was electric and the crowd cheered wildly.*

---

exclaim /ɪkˈskleɪm/ *v* [T] *written* to suddenly say something loudly, because you are surprised, excited, or angry: *'No!' she exclaimed angrily.*

exclamation /ˌekskləˈmeɪʃən/ *n* [C] something you say suddenly and loudly because you are surprised or angry

excla'mation mark *especially BrE* also **excla'mation point** *AmE n* [C] the mark (!) that is written after an exclamation

exclude /ɪkˈskluːd/ *v* [T] **1** to not allow someone to go into a place or take part in something: **exclude sb from (doing) sth** *Until 1994 the black population was excluded from voting.* **2** to not include something [≠ **include**]: **exclude sth from sth** *We have excluded this data from the report.* **3** to decide that something is not possible: *Police have excluded the possibility that she killed herself.*

excluding /ɪkˈskluːdɪŋ/ *prep* not including: *The cost of hiring a car is £180 a week, excluding insurance.*

exclusion /ɪkˈskluːʒən/ *n* **1** [U] when someone is not allowed to go into a place or take part in something [≠ **inclusion**]: *the exclusion of professional athletes from the Olympics* **2 do sth to the exclusion of sth** to do one thing so much that you do not do or think about something else: *She's been studying hard to the exclusion of everything else.*

exclusive¹ /ɪkˈskluːsɪv/ *adj* **1** available to only one person or group, and not shared: *an exclusive interview with Nelson Mandela* | *The club has exclusive use of the pool during the day.* **2** very expensive: *an exclusive hotel* **3 exclusive of sth** not including something [≠ **inclusive**]: *The price of the trip is $450, exclusive of meals.*

exclusive² *n* [C] a news story that is only in one newspaper or magazine

exclusively /ɪkˈskluːsɪvli/ *adv* only: *This offer is available exclusively to club members.*

excrement /ˈekskrɪmənt/ *n* [U] *formal* solid waste from a person's or animal's body

excrete /ɪk'skriːt/ v [I,T] *technical* to get rid of waste from the body —**excretion** /ɪk'skriːʃən/ n [C,U]

excruciating /ɪk'skruːʃieɪtɪŋ/ adj extremely painful: *The pain in my knee was excruciating.* —**excruciatingly** adv

excursion /ɪk'skɜːʃən $ ɪk'skɜːrʒən/ n [C] a short trip for pleasure: *an excursion to the island of Burano*

excusable /ɪk'skjuːzəbəl/ adj behaviour that is excusable can be forgiven [≠ **inexcusable**]

excuse¹ /ɪk'skjuːz/ v [T]

1 excuse me *spoken* **a)** used to politely get someone's attention: *Excuse me, is this the right bus for the airport?* **b)** used to politely say you are sorry for doing something: *Oh, excuse me, I didn't see you there.* **c)** used to politely tell someone that you are leaving a place: *Excuse me a moment, there's someone at the door.*

2 to forgive someone, usually for something that is not very serious: *Please excuse my bad handwriting.* | **excuse sb for (doing) sth** *Please excuse me for being so late.*

3 to allow someone not to do something: **excuse sb from (doing) sth** *You are excused classes for the rest of the week.*

4 if something excuses bad behaviour, it is the reason why it happened, which makes it possible to understand or forgive: *Nothing can excuse lying to your parents.*

excuse² /ɪk'skjuːs/ n [C]

1 a reason that you give to explain why you did something wrong: **+for** *What's your excuse for being late?* | *Jennifer started **making excuses** for her son's behaviour.* | *I'm sure he **has** a good **excuse** for not calling.* | *There is **no excuse** for such behaviour* (=it is not acceptable). → see box at REASON

2 a reason that you invent to explain why you do something: **excuse to do sth** *Karl was glad of an excuse to leave.* | *He **made** some **excuse** about a dentist's appointment and left.* | *At least it **gave** me an **excuse** to get out of the house.*

execute /'eksɪkjuːt/ v [T] **1** to kill someone as a punishment for a crime → see box at KILL **2** *formal* to do something that has been planned or ordered: *a carefully executed plan* —**execution** /ˌeksɪ'kjuːʃən/ n [U]

executioner /ˌeksɪ'kjuːʃənə $ -ər/ n [C] someone whose job is to kill criminals as a punishment

executive¹ /ɪg'zekjətɪv/ n [C] **1** an important manager in a company: *a sales executive* **2 the executive** the people in an organization who have the power to make decisions

executive² adj **1** relating to making decisions in a company or organization: *an executive committee* **2** expensive and suitable for people who have important jobs: *executive homes*

exemplary /ɪg'zempləri/ adj *formal* exemplary behaviour is excellent and can be used as an example for other people to copy

exemplify /ɪg'zemplɪfaɪ/ v [T] **exemplified, exemplifying, exemplifies** *formal* to be a typical example of something: *Stuart exemplifies the kind of student we like at our school.*

exempt¹ /ɪg'zempt/ adj not having to do something or pay for something: **+from** *He was exempt from military service.* | *Medical products are exempt from tax.*

exempt² v [T] to give someone permission not to do something: **exempt sb from sth** *Anyone who is mentally ill is exempted from military service.* —**exemption** /ɪg'zempʃən/ n [C,U]

exercise¹ /'eksəsaɪz $ -ər-/ n

1 [C,U] physical activity that you do to stay strong and healthy: *You can **do** special **exercises** to strengthen your back.* | *I really need to **take** more **exercise**.* | *Do you **get** much **exercise**?*

2 [C] something you do to help you practise a skill: *relaxation exercises*

3 [C] a set of written questions to test a student's knowledge: *For homework, do exercises 1 and 2.*

4 [C] a set of activities for training soldiers: *a military exercise*

exercise² v

1 [I,T] to do physical activities so that you stay strong and healthy: *It is important to exercise regularly.* | *You need to exercise the muscles in your back.*

> **TOPIC**
>
> People exercise so they can **keep fit** and **stay/keep in shape**. There are many different kinds of exercise, for example **jogging**, **lifting weights**, and **aerobics**. People often go to a **gym** or a **health club** to exercise. The series of exercises they do is called a **workout**. Before exercising, they **warm up** (=get their body ready) by **stretching** or jogging slowly.

2 [T] *formal* to use a power or right that you have: *She exercised her influence to get him the job.*

exert /ɪg'zɜːt $ -ɜːrt/ v [T] **1 exert authority/influence/pressure etc** to use your authority or influence to make something happen: **+on** *The UN is exerting pressure on the two countries to stop the war.* **2 exert yourself** to make a great effort

exertion /ɪg'zɜːʃən $ -ɜːr-/ n [C,U] when you make a great effort: *He was worn out by his exertions.*

exhale /eks'heɪl/ v [I,T] to breathe out [≠ **inhale**]: *Take a deep breath, then exhale slowly.*

exhaust¹ /ɪg'zɔːst $ -'zɒːst/ v [T] **1** to make someone very tired: *The trip totally exhausted us.* **2** to use all of something: *Eventually, the world's oil **supply** will be **exhausted**.*

exhaust

exhaust² n **1** also **ex'haust pipe** [C] a pipe on a car that waste gas comes out of → see picture on page A12 **2** [U] the waste gas that is produced when an engine is working: *exhaust fumes*

exhausted /ɪɡˈzɔːstɪd $ -ˈzɒːs-/ *adj* extremely tired: **+by/from** *I was still exhausted from the race.* → see box at TIRED
—**exhaustion** /ɪɡˈzɔːstʃən $ -ˈzɒːs-/ *n* [U] *He collapsed with exhaustion.*

exhausting /ɪɡˈzɔːstɪŋ $ -ˈzɒːs-/ *adj* making you feel extremely tired: *a long and exhausting journey*

exhaustive /ɪɡˈzɔːstɪv $ -ˈzɒːs-/ *adj* thorough and complete: *an exhaustive search of the area*

exhibit¹ /ɪɡˈzɪbɪt/ *v* **1** [I,T] to show something in a public place so that people can see it: *His paintings will be exhibited in the National Gallery.* **2** [T] *formal* to show a quality or feeling: *The prisoner exhibited no signs of remorse.*
—**exhibitor** *n* [C]

exhibit² *n* [C] an object that is shown in a public place for people to look at

exhibition /ˌeksəˈbɪʃən/ *n*
1 a) [C] a public show where people can go and see paintings, photographs etc: **+of** *an exhibition of historical photographs* **b)** [U] when something, such as a painting, is shown in public: **on exhibition** *The paintings are currently on exhibition in Paris.*
2 exhibition of sth when someone shows a skill, feeling, or kind of behaviour: *an impressive exhibition of athletic skill*

exhibitionist /ˌeksəˈbɪʃənɪst/ *n* [C] *disapproving* someone who likes to behave or dress in a way that makes other people notice them
—**exhibitionist** *adj*

exhilarated /ɪɡˈzɪləreɪtɪd/ *adj* extremely happy and excited: *He was exhilarated by the speed and the risk.* —**exhilaration** /ɪɡˌzɪləˈreɪʃən/ *n* [U]

exhilarating /ɪɡˈzɪləreɪtɪŋ/ *adj* making you feel extremely happy and excited: *an exhilarating experience* → see box at EXCITING

exhort /ɪɡˈzɔːt $ -ɔːrt/ *v* [T] *formal* to try to persuade someone to do something —**exhortation** /ˌeksɔːˈteɪʃən $ -ɔːr-/ *n* [C,U]

exile /ˈeksaɪl, ˈeɡzaɪl/ *n* **1** [U] when someone is forced to leave their country and live somewhere else, usually for political reasons: **in/into exile** *a writer who lives in exile* | *She went into exile.* **2** [C] someone who has had to leave their country and live somewhere else: *Cuban exiles living in the US* —**exile** *v* [T] *He was exiled from Russia in the 1930s.* —**exiled** *adj*

exist /ɪɡˈzɪst/ *v* [I] to happen or to be real or alive: *Do ghosts really exist?* | *a custom that still exists in some areas* | *Border controls will* **cease to exist** *after June.*

existence /ɪɡˈzɪstəns/ *n* **1** [U] when something exists: **+of** *Do you believe in the existence of God?* | **in existence** *Mammals have been in existence for many millions of years.* **2** [C, usually singular] the type of life that someone has: *He* **led a miserable existence***.*

existing /ɪɡˈzɪstɪŋ/ *adj* [only before noun] happening or being used now: *We need new computers to replace the existing ones.*

exit¹ /ˈeɡzɪt, ˈeksɪt/ *n* [C]
1 a door that you go through to leave a place: *There are two exits at the back of the plane.* | **emergency/fire exit** → see picture at ENTRANCE

2 when you leave a place: *The President* **made a quick exit** *after his speech.*
3 a place where you can leave a MOTORWAY: *Take exit 23 for the city.*

exit² *v* **1** [I] *formal* to leave a place: *The band exited through a side door.* **2** [I,T] to finish using a computer PROGRAM: *Press F3 to exit.*

exodus /ˈeksədəs/ *n* [singular] when a lot of people leave a place at the same time: *the exodus of Russian scientists to America*

exonerate /ɪɡˈzɒnəreɪt $ ɪɡˈzɑː-/ *v* [T] *formal* to officially say that someone who has been blamed for something is not guilty: *Ross was exonerated from all blame.*

exorbitant /ɪɡˈzɔːbɪtənt $ -ɔːr-/ *adj* an exorbitant price is much higher than it should be → see box at EXPENSIVE —**exorbitantly** *adv*

exorcize also **-ise** *BrE* /ˈeksɔːsaɪz $ -ɔːr-/ *v* [T] to force an evil SPIRIT to leave a place by using special prayers and ceremonies —**exorcism** /-sɪzəm/ *n* [C,U] —**exorcist** *n* [C]

exotic /ɪɡˈzɒtɪk $ ɪɡˈzɑː-/ *adj* something that is exotic seems unusual and exciting because it is from a foreign country: *an exotic flower* | *exotic food*

expand /ɪkˈspænd/ *v* [I,T] to become larger, or to make something larger: *The population* **expanded rapidly** *in the '60s.* | *Water expands as it freezes.* —**expandable** *adj*

expand on/upon sth *phr v* *formal* to add more details or information to something that you have already said: *Could you expand on your last comment, please?*

expanse /ɪkˈspæns/ *n* [C] a very large area of land, sea, or sky: *the vast expanse of the Pacific Ocean*

expansion /ɪkˈspænʃən/ *n* [U] when something increases in size, number, or amount: *a period of economic expansion*

expansionism /ɪkˈspænʃənɪzəm/ *n* [U] *disapproving* when a country or group tries to increase the amount of land or power it has —**expansionist** *adj*: *the country's expansionist policy*

expansive /ɪkˈspænsɪv/ *adj* very friendly and willing to talk a lot: *Alan was in an expansive mood.*

expatriate /eksˈpætriət, -trieɪt $ -ˈpeɪ-/ also **ex-pat** /ˌeksˈpæt/ *n* [C] someone who lives in a foreign country

expect /ɪkˈspekt/ *v* [T]
1 to think that something will probably happen: **expect (sb) to do sth** *Do you expect to travel a lot this year?* | *He expected me to drive him home!* | **+(that)** *We expect the meeting will finish about 5 o'clock.* | **As expected***, Rebecca passed easily.*
2 to believe that someone must do something because it is their duty: *The officer expects absolute obedience from his men.* | **expect sb to do sth** *We're expected to work late sometimes.*
3 to believe that someone or something is going to arrive: *I'm expecting a letter from Japan.* | *What time do you expect him home?* → see box at WAIT
4 be expecting (a baby) *informal* if a woman is expecting, she is going to have a baby
5 I expect *especially BrE* *spoken* used to say that you think something is probably true: **+(that)**

It's late and I expect you're tired. | *'Do you think he'll get the job?' 'Yes, I expect so.'*
—expected *adj*: *the expected rise in interest rates*

expectancy /ɪkˈspektənsi/ *n* [U] the feeling that something exciting or interesting is going to happen: *There was a look of expectancy on the children's faces.* → LIFE EXPECTANCY

expectant /ɪkˈspektənt/ *adj* **1** hopeful that something good or exciting will happen: *an expectant crowd* **2 expectant mother/father** a mother or father whose baby will be born soon —expectantly *adv*: *They looked at Jos expectantly.*

expectation /ˌekspekˈteɪʃən/ *n* **1** [C,U] what you hope or believe will happen: +**that** *the expectation that prices will rise* | +**of** *We have a reasonable expectation of success.* **2** [C usually plural] something good that you think will happen: *The trip didn't live up to our expectations* (=it wasn't as good as we hoped). | *Many refugees arrive in the country with high expectations.*

expedient[1] /ɪkˈspiːdiənt/ *adj* if something you do is expedient, it helps you but it is not morally right: *She thought it would be expedient to use a false name.* —expediency *also* **expedience** *n* [U]

expedient[2] *n* [C] a clever way of dealing with a situation

expedite /ˈekspɪdaɪt/ *v* [T] to make a process or action happen more quickly [= speed up]

expedition /ˌekspɪˈdɪʃən/ *n* [C] **1** a long and carefully organized journey: *an expedition to the North Pole* **2** a short trip that you make for a particular purpose: *a shopping expedition*

expel /ɪkˈspel/ *v* [T] **expelled, expelling** **1** to officially order someone to leave a school, organization, or country: **expel sb from sth** *Jake was expelled from school for smoking.* **2** *formal* to force air, water, or gas out of something

expend /ɪkˈspend/ *v* [T] *formal* to use money, time, or energy: *A lot of effort has been expended on creating the right image for the company.*

expendable /ɪkˈspendəbəl/ *adj* if something or someone is expendable, they are not needed and you can get rid of them: *workers who are regarded as expendable*

expenditure /ɪkˈspendɪtʃə $ -ər/ *n* [U] *formal* **1** the total amount of money that a government, organization, or person spends: +**on** *Expenditure on medical care has doubled.* **2** when someone spends money or uses time or effort: *the wasteful expenditure of time*

expense /ɪkˈspens/ *n*
1 [C,U] the amount of money you spend on something: **household/medical/living expenses** (=money that you spend for a particular purpose) *All his money went on medical expenses.* | *All rooms were fully equipped at great expense* (=costing a lot of money).
2 expenses [plural] money that you spend on travel, hotels etc when you are working, and then get back from your employer: *They pay £300 a week plus expenses.* | **on expenses** *Don't worry, I'll put the taxi on expenses.*
3 at the expense of sb/sth if something is done at the expense of something or someone else, it is achieved by harming the other person

or thing: *A medical career requires commitment at the expense of family life.*
4 at sb's expense a) if you do something at someone's expense, they pay for you to do it: *a trip to Japan at the tax-payer's expense* **b)** in a way that makes someone seem stupid: *Louis kept making jokes at his wife's expense.*

expensive /ɪkˈspensɪv/ *adj* something that is expensive costs a lot of money [≠ cheap]: *an expensive restaurant*

high – used about prices or amounts that are greater than normal or usual: *Petrol prices are very high in Europe.* | *If we want better public services, we will have to pay higher taxes.*
pricey *informal* – expensive: *The hotel was a bit pricey.*
overpriced – something that is overpriced is more expensive than it should be: *overpriced restaurants*
ripoff *informal* – if something is a ripoff, it is more expensive than it should be: *$125 for a shirt. What a ripoff!*
extortionate/astronomical/exorbitant – used about things that are much too expensive: *House prices in London are exorbitant.*
fancy *informal* – used about fashionable restaurants, cars, clothes etc that look expensive: *a fancy hotel in Manhattan*
posh *informal* – used about expensive hotels, restaurants, schools etc that rich people go to: *a posh boarding school*
→ CHEAP

experience[1] /ɪkˈspɪəriəns $ -ˈspɪr-/ *n*
1 [U] knowledge or skill that you learn when you do something yourself, or when something happens to you: *He's a very good teacher with a lot of experience.* | +**of/in/with** *Do you have any experience in marketing?* | *He has no previous experience of working with animals.* | **In my experience**, *a credit card is always useful.* | **know/learn/speak from experience** *I speak from personal experience.*
2 [C] something that happens to you: *I had a very strange experience last week.* | *Going to China was a wonderful experience.*

experience[2] *v* [T] if you experience something, it happens to you: **experience problems/difficulties etc** *We're experiencing a few problems with our website.* | *You may experience some pain.*

experienced /ɪkˈspɪəriənst $ -ˈspɪr-/ *adj* someone who is experienced has a lot of skill or knowledge because they have done something before [≠ inexperienced]: *a very experienced pilot* | +**in** *doctors who are experienced in these techniques*

experiment[1] /ɪkˈsperəmənt/ *n* [C]
1 a scientific test to find out or prove something: +**on/with** *experiments on rats* | **do/carry out/perform an experiment** *They carried out an experiment to test their theory.*
2 when you try something new to see if it will be successful: +**in/with** *an experiment in bilingual education*
—experimental /ɪkˌsperəˈmentl◂/ *adj*: *experimental farming techniques*

E

experiment[2] /ɪkˈsperəment/ v [I] **1** to try using different things or doing something in different ways: **+with** *Many teenagers experiment with drugs.* **2** to do a scientific test in order to find out or prove something: **+on/with** *Do you think it's right to experiment on animals?* —**experimentation** /ɪkˌsperəmenˈteɪʃən/ n [U]

expert /ˈekspɜːt $ -ɜːrt/ n [C] someone with special skills or knowledge of a subject: **+on/in** *an expert on ancient Egyptian art* | **medical/ technical/financial etc expert**

> **THESAURUS**
>
> **specialist** – someone who knows a lot about something because they have studied it for a long time: *Lowe is a specialist in immigration law.*
> **authority** – someone who is very respected because they know more about a subject than other people: *She is a leading authority on modern art.*
> **connoisseur** – someone who knows a lot about something such as art, food, or music: *a connoisseur of fine wines*

—**expert** *adj*: *expert advice* —**expertly** *adv*

expertise /ˌekspɜːˈtiːz $ -ɜːr-/ n [U] special skills or knowledge that you learn by experience or training: *medical expertise*

expiration /ˌekspəˈreɪʃən/ n [U] the end of a period of time in which an official document or agreement can be used: *the expiration date on your passport*

expire /ɪkˈspaɪə $ -ˈspaɪr/ v [I] if a document or legal agreement expires, the period of time in which you can use it ends

expiry /ɪkˈspaɪəri $ -ˈspaɪri/ n [U] BrE the end of a period of time in which something can be used, or the end of a period of authority: *What's the expiry date on your passport?* | *the expiry of the President's term of office*

explain /ɪkˈspleɪn/ v [I,T]
1 to tell someone about something in a way which makes it easy to understand: **explain (sth) to sb** *I explained the rules to Sara.* | **+how/ what/why etc** *Can someone explain how this thing works?* | **+that** *He explained that it had been a difficult film to make.*
2 to give the reason for something: **+why/how etc** *Brad never explained why he was late.* | **+that** *I explained that I'd missed the bus.*
  explain sth ⇔ **away** *phr v* to make something seem less important or less serious, by giving reasons for it: *Claire tried to explain away the bruises on her arm.*

explanation /ˌekspləˈneɪʃən/ n
1 [C] something you say or write to describe how something works or to make something easier to understand: **+of** *a detailed explanation of how to use the program* | *She gave a good, clear explanation.*
2 [C,U] the reasons why something happened or why you did something: **+for** *Is there any explanation for his behaviour?* | *I think you owe me an explanation* (=you should explain to me). | *Tom gave us no explanation for where he'd been.* →
see box at **REASON**

explanatory /ɪkˈsplænətəri $ -tɔːri/ adj giving information about something or explaining how something works: *an explanatory booklet* → **SELF-EXPLANATORY**

expletive /ɪkˈspliːtɪv $ ˈeksplətɪv/ n [C] formal a swear word

explicable /ekˈsplɪkəbəl/ adj something that is explicable can be easily understood or explained [≠ **inexplicable**]

explicit /ɪkˈsplɪsət/ adj **1** explaining something in a way that is very clear and easy to understand: *Could you be more explicit?* **2** showing or describing sex or violence in a detailed way: *explicit love scenes* —**explicitly** adv

explode /ɪkˈspləʊd $ -ˈsploʊd/ v
1 [I,T] to burst, or to make something burst, suddenly, with a lot of noise [➜ **explosion**]: *The car bomb exploded at 6:16.*
2 [I] to suddenly increase a lot in size or amount: *The population of the area exploded after the war.*
3 [I] to suddenly become very angry: *Susie exploded when I told her about the car.*

exploit[1] /ɪkˈsplɔɪt/ v [T] **1** to treat someone in an unfair way, by not paying as much as they deserve: *Many foreign workers are abused and exploited.* **2** to use something effectively so that you get as much advantage as possible from it: *We must exploit the country's mineral resources.* —**exploitation** /ˌeksplɔɪˈteɪʃən/ n [U]

exploit[2] /ˈeksplɔɪt/ n [C usually plural] something brave or interesting that someone has done: *a book about his exploits in Latin America*

exploratory /ɪkˈsplɒrətəri $ ɪkˈsplɔːrətɔːri/ adj done in order to find out more about something: *exploratory surgery*

explore /ɪkˈsplɔː $ -ˈsplɔːr/ v
1 [I,T] to travel around an area to find out what it is like: *We spent a week exploring the Oregon coastline.*
2 [T] to discuss or think about something carefully: **Explore** all **the possibilities** *before you make a decision.*
—**exploration** /ˌekspləˈreɪʃən/ n [C,U] *a voyage of exploration*

explorer /ɪkˈsplɔːrə $ -ər/ n [C] someone who travels to places that people have not visited before

explosion /ɪkˈspləʊʒən $ -ˈsploʊ-/ n [C]
1 when something such as a bomb explodes, or the noise it makes [➜ **explode**]: *We heard a huge explosion.* | *The force of the explosion shook the building.* | **bomb/nuclear etc explosion**
2 [usually singular] a sudden large increase: *the population explosion* | **+of** *the recent explosion of interest in African music*

explosive[1] /ɪkˈspləʊsɪv $ -ˈsploʊ-/ adj
1 something that is explosive can cause an explosion: *an explosive mixture of gases*
2 likely to make people become violent or angry: *an explosive situation* | *Abortion is an explosive issue.*

explosive[2] n [C] a substance that can cause an explosion

exponent /ɪkˈspəʊnənt $ -ˈspoʊ-/ n [C] an exponent of an idea or belief tries to persuade other people that it is good: *an exponent of socialism*

export[1] /'ekspɔːt $ -ɔːrt/ n
1 [U] the business of selling goods to another country [≠ **import**]: **+of** *the export of live animals*
2 [C] a product that is sold to another country [≠ **import**]: *Oil is now one of Malaysia's main exports.*

export[2] /ɪk'spɔːt $ -ɔːrt/ v [I,T] to sell goods to another country [≠ **import**]: **export (sth) to sb** *Japan exports electronic equipment to dozens of countries.*
—**exporter** n [C]

expose /ɪk'spəʊz $ -'spoʊz/ v [T]   **1** to show something that is usually covered or hidden: **expose sth to sth** *When a wound is exposed to the air, it heals more quickly.* **2** to put someone in a situation or place that may be harmful or dangerous: **be exposed to sth** *workers who were exposed to high levels of radiation* **3** to tell people the truth about something bad or dishonest: *The report exposed corruption among officials.* **4** to let someone experience new ideas, ways of life etc: **be exposed to sth** *Children who have been exposed to different cultures are less likely to be prejudiced.* **5** to allow light onto a piece of film in a camera in order to produce a photograph

exposé /ek'spəʊzeɪ $,ekspə'zeɪ/ n [C] a story in a newspaper or on television that shows the truth about something, especially something dishonest or shocking

exposed /ɪk'spəʊzd $ -'spoʊzd/ *adj* not protected from the weather: *an exposed hillside*

exposure /ɪk'spəʊʒə $ -'spoʊʒər/ n   **1** [C,U] when someone is put in a situation where they are not protected from something harmful: **+to** *Too much exposure to the sun can cause skin cancer.* **2** [C,U] when newspapers or television show the true facts about something bad or dishonest: *the exposure of his business dealings* **3** [U] the harmful effects of being outside for a long time when the weather is extremely cold: *Three climbers died of exposure.* **4** [C] the amount of film that is used each time you take a photograph: *a film with 36 exposures*

expound /ɪk'spaʊnd/ v [I,T] *formal* to explain or talk about something in detail: **+on** *Evans continued to expound on his theory.*

express[1] /ɪk'spres/ v [T]

1 to tell people what you are thinking or feeling: **express your views/opinions/concerns** *A number of people expressed their concern.* | *She expressed an interest in becoming a member.* | **express sth in/through/by sth** *The idea is difficult to express in words.* | **express yourself** (=clearly say what you think or feel) → see box at **SAY**
2 to show your thoughts or feelings by the way you look or your actions: *The look on Paul's face expressed utter despair.*

express[2] *adj* [only before noun]   **1** an express wish or purpose is clear and definite: *It was her express wish that you should inherit her house.* **2** an express train or bus is very fast

express[3] n [C] a fast train or bus which stops at only a few stations

expression /ɪk'spreʃən/ n
1 [C,U] when you say, write, or do something to show what you are thinking or feeling: **+of** *I'm sending these flowers as an expression of my*

gratitude. | **expression of thanks/regret/sympathy etc**
2 [C] a look on someone's face: **+of** *an expression of shock* | *He came back with a cheerful expression on his face.*
3 [C] a word or phrase that has a particular meaning: *What does the expression 'head over heels' mean?* → see box at **PHRASE**

expressionless /ɪk'spreʃənləs/ *adj* an expressionless face or voice does not show what someone is feeling or thinking

expressive /ɪk'spresɪv/ *adj* showing what someone is thinking or feeling: *expressive eyes*

expressly /ɪk'spresli/ *adv formal*   **1** clearly and firmly: *Students are expressly forbidden to enter.* **2** for a particular purpose: *a building expressly designed for the disabled*

expressway /ɪk'spreswei/ n [C] a wide road in a city on which cars can travel fast [→ **motorway**, **freeway**] → see box at **ROAD**

expulsion /ɪk'spʌlʃən/ n [C,U] when someone is officially ordered to leave a place [→ **expel**]: **+of/from** *his expulsion from the Soviet Union*

exquisite /ɪk'skwɪzɪt, 'ekskwɪ-/ *adj* beautiful and delicate: *an exquisite diamond ring*
—**exquisitely** *adv*

extend /ɪk'stend/ v   **1** [T] to make something continue for longer than previously arranged or planned: *Could you extend your visa for six months?* **2** [T] to make something include or affect more things or people: **extend sth to sth** *The UK wants to extend the ban to EU countries.* **3** [I] to cover a particular distance or area: **+across/over/through etc** *The river extends 2000 km to the south.* **4** [T] to make a building, road etc bigger: *plans to extend the road network* **5** [T] *formal* to officially offer help, thanks, sympathy etc: **extend sth to sb** *I'd like to extend a warm welcome to our visitors.* **6** [T] to stretch out your hand, arm, or leg: *Perry extended a hand in greeting.*

extended /ɪk'stendɪd/ *adj* [only before noun] long: *an extended period of neglect*

ex,tended 'family n [C] a family group that consists of parents, children, and also of grandparents, AUNTS, UNCLES etc [→ **nuclear family**]

extension /ɪk'stenʃən/ n   **1** [C,U] the process of making a building, road etc bigger, or a new part that is added to it: **+of** *the extension of the southern vineyards* | **+to** *BrE:* *We built an extension to the kitchen.* **2** [C usually singular] an extra period of time allowed for something: *I need an extension to finish my essay.* **3** [singular, U] the development of something so that it affects more things or people: **+of** *the extension of voting rights to women* **4** [C] one of several telephones that are connected to the same line: *What's your extension number?*

extensive /ɪk'stensɪv/ *adj* large in amount or area: *The exhibition received extensive media coverage.*

extent /ɪk'stent/ n [U] how big, important, or serious something is: **+of** *What is the full extent of his injuries?* | **to some/a certain extent** (=partly) *To a certain extent, it was my fault.* | **to a large/greater/lesser extent** | *Crime increased to the extent that people were afraid to go out.*

E

exterior /ɪkˈstɪəriə $ -ˈtɪriər/ n [C usually singular] **1** the outside of something [≠ interior]: +of *the exterior of the building* **2 calm/confident etc exterior** someone's behaviour, which does not show their real feelings or nature: *Beneath that calm exterior, she's angry.* —**exterior** *adj*

exterminate /ɪkˈstɜːmɪ̥neɪt $ -ɜːr-/ v [T] to kill all of a particular group or type of animals or people —**extermination** /ɪk‚stɜːmɪ̥ˈneɪʃən $ -ɜːr-/ n [C,U]

external /ɪkˈstɜːnl $ -ɜːr-/ adj

1 relating to the outside of a thing or person's body [≠ **internal**]: *repairs to the external walls* | *For external use only* (=used on medicines that you must put on your skin, not eat).

2 from outside your organization, country, university etc [≠ **internal**]: *external examiners*

extinct /ɪkˈstɪŋkt/ adj **1** a type of animal or plant that is extinct no longer exists: *Activists fear that the tiger may become extinct.* **2** an extinct VOLCANO does not ERUPT (=send out hot rock, smoke etc)

extinction /ɪkˈstɪŋkʃən/ n [U] when a type of animal or plant stops existing: *The whales are in danger of extinction.* | *They were hunted to extinction* (=all killed).

extinguish /ɪkˈstɪŋgwɪʃ/ v [T] formal to make a fire or light stop burning or shining [= put out]: *Please extinguish all cigarettes.*

extinguisher /ɪkˈstɪŋgwɪʃə $ -ər/ n [C] a FIRE EXTINGUISHER

extol /ɪkˈstəʊl $ -ˈstoʊl/ v [T] **extolled, extolling** formal to praise something very highly: **extol the virtues/benefits etc of sth**

extort /ɪkˈstɔːt $ -ɔːrt/ v [T] if someone extorts money from you, they threaten you to make you give them money —**extortion** /ɪkˈstɔːʃən $ -ɔːr-/ n [U]

extortionate /ɪkˈstɔːʃənət $ -ɔːr-/ adj disapproving extortionate prices, demands etc are too big → see box at EXPENSIVE

extra¹ /ˈekstrə/ adj, adv in addition to the usual things or amount: *pizza with extra cheese* | *Drivers should take extra care in icy conditions.* | *Dinner prices are fixed at $15, but wine is extra.* | *Do you get paid extra at weekends?* | *Henry's been working extra hard.* | *an extra hour in bed* | **one/a few/some extra** *I bought a few extra just in case.*

extra² n [C] **1** something that can be added to a product or service and that makes it cost more: *The DVD and scanner are optional extras.* **2** an actor in a film who has a small unimportant part

extract¹ /ɪkˈstrækt/ v [T] **1** formal to remove something from a place or thing: **extract sth from sth** *Precious gems are extracted from the mine.* | *I had a tooth extracted.* **2** if someone extracts information or money from you, they get it from you, even though you did not want to give it to them: **extract sth from sth** *The police failed to extract a confession from him.* —**extraction** /ɪkˈstrækʃən/ n [U]

extract² /ˈekstrækt/ n **1** [C] a small part taken from a story, poem etc: +from *an extract from the film* **2** [C,U] a substance that is removed from a plant: **vanilla/plant etc extract**

extracurricular /‚ekstrəkəˈrɪkjᵿlə◂ $ -ər-/ adj [only before noun] extracurricular activities are those that are not part of the course that a student is studying

extradite /ˈekstrədaɪt/ v [T] to send someone who may have committed a crime back to the country where it happened so that they can be dealt with there —**extradition** /‚ekstrəˈdɪʃən/ n [C,U]

extramarital /‚ekstrəˈmærᵻtl◂/ adj [only before noun] an extramarital sexual relationship is one that a married person has with a person who is not their husband or wife

extraneous /ɪkˈstreɪniəs/ adj formal not directly related to a particular subject: *extraneous details*

extraordinary /ɪkˈstrɔːdənəri $ ɪkˈstrɔːrdn-eri, ‚ekstrəˈɔːr-/ adj very unusual, surprising, or special: *It's extraordinary that he didn't tell you.* | *What extraordinary luck!* | *an extraordinary talent* → see box at SURPRISING —**extraordinarily** /ɪkˈstrɔːdənərᵻli $ ɪk‚strɔːrdnˈerᵻli, ‚ekstrəˈɔːrdn-erᵻli/ adv

extrapolate /ɪkˈstræpəleɪt/ v [I,T] formal to use facts about a current situation in order to say what might happen in another: **extrapolate (sth) from sth** *Extrapolating from these results, we predict future trends.*

extraterrestrial /‚ekstrətəˈrestriəl◂/ adj in or from a place that is not the Earth: *the search for extraterrestrial life*

extravagant /ɪkˈstrævəgənt/ adj **1** spending or costing too much money: *an extravagant lifestyle* **2** extravagant claims, promises etc are not likely to be true —**extravagantly** adv —**extravagance** n [C,U]

extravaganza /ɪk‚strævəˈgænzə/ n [C] a large expensive event or entertainment

extravert /ˈekstrəvɜːt $ -ɜːrt/ n another spelling of EXTROVERT

extreme¹ /ɪkˈstriːm/ adj

1 [only before noun] very great in amount or severity: *extreme poverty* | *extreme weather conditions* | **extreme cases/circumstances** *In extreme cases, the child may die.*

2 [only before noun] the furthest part of a place in a particular direction: *the extreme north*

3 extreme opinions are very strong and most people think they are unreasonable: *His views were extreme, and led to political isolation.*

4 [only before noun] extreme sports are done in a way that is more dangerous than the usual form of that sport: **extreme surfing/boxing etc**

extreme² n **1** [C] something that is much greater, more severe etc than usual: +of *Bacteria can withstand extremes of heat and cold.* | **at the other/opposite extreme** (=used when two things are as different as possible) *At the other extreme, Austria has almost zero unemployment.* | **take/carry sth to extremes/go to extremes** disapproving (=do something to the greatest possible extent) *Caution is sensible, but not if parents go to extremes.* **2 in the extreme** extremely: *These experiments are cruel in the extreme.*

extremely /ɪkˈstriːmli/ adv more than very: *I'm extremely sorry.* | *He finds it extremely difficult to talk about what happened.*

extremist /ɪkˈstriːmɪst/ *n* [C] *disapproving* someone with very strong political or religious opinions [➡ **fundamentalist**]: *left-wing extremists* —**extremist** *adj*: *an extremist group* —**extremism** *n* [U]

extremity /ɪkˈstrɛmɪti/ *n* [C] plural **extremities** *formal* the part that is furthest from the centre of something

extricate /ˈekstrɪkeɪt/ *v* [T] to get yourself or someone else out of a bad situation: **extricate yourself/sb from sth** *How could he extricate himself from the debt?*

extrovert, extravert /ˈekstrəvɜːt $ -ɜːrt/ *n* [C] someone who is confident and likes being with people [≠ **introvert**] —**extrovert**, **extroverted** /-vɜːtɪd $ -vɜːrt-/ *adj*

exuberant /ɪɡˈzjuːbərənt $ ɪɡˈzuː-/ *adj* very happy, excited, and full of energy: *an exuberant personality* —**exuberance** *n* [U]

exude /ɪɡˈzjuːd $ ɪɡˈzuːd/ *v formal* **1** [T] someone who exudes love, confidence, power etc shows a lot of love etc **2** [I,T] to flow out slowly, or to make something do this

eye¹ /aɪ/ *n* [C]
1 one of the two things in your face that you see with: *There were tears in her eyes.* | **close/shut/ open your eyes** *Close your eyes and go to sleep.* | **blue-eyed/one-eyed/bright-eyed etc** *a brown-eyed girl* | *He is blind in one eye.* | *I could tell he was lying because he didn't* **make eye contact** (=look back at my eyes). | **Look me in the eye** (=look at my eyes) *and tell me the truth.* | **run/ cast your eye over sth** (=read something quickly) ➔ see picture on page A3

COLLOCATIONS

open your eyes
close/shut your eyes (tight)
drop/lower your eyes – to look down
blink – to close your eyes – and open them again very quickly
squint – to close your eyes – partly, not fully, in order to see better, often because there is too much light
wink – to look at someone and quickly close and then open one eye – , in order to show them that you are joking or being friendly, or as a signal
Your **eyes narrow** if you are watching something carefully or thinking hard about something.
Your **eyes widen** if you are surprised, afraid etc.
Your **eyes sparkle** if you are excited or very happy.

2 a particular way of judging or understanding something: *He surveyed her with* **a critical eye.** | **in the eyes of sb** *Joe can do no wrong in the eyes of his partner.* | **through the eyes of sb** (=from a particular person's point of view) *a story seen through the eyes of a child* | **a (good) eye for sth** (=the ability to recognize or judge something) *To be a proofreader you need* **a good eye** *for detail.*
3 keep an eye on sb/sth to watch someone or

something to make sure nothing bad happens: *Police have* **kept a close eye on** *Taylor since she came out of prison.* | *Louise was* **keeping half an eye on** *the baby* (=watching without her full attention).
4 keep an eye open/out (for sb/sth) to be ready to notice something when it appears: *Keep an eye out for traffic.*
5 have your eye on sth to want something that you think might become available: *He's got his eye on the store next door.*
6 sb cannot take their eyes off sb/sth used to say that someone cannot stop looking at someone or something because they are attractive or interesting
7 set/lay/clap eyes on sb/sth *informal* to see someone or something, especially for the first time
8 do sth with your eyes open to do something when you know what problems you might have: *I went into the job with my eyes open, so I've only myself to blame.*
9 keep your eyes peeled/skinned (for sth) *spoken* to watch carefully for something
10 close/shut your eyes to sth to ignore something bad that is happening
11 be up to your eyes in sth *BrE informal* to be very busy doing something: *I'm up to my eyes in paperwork.*
12 the hole in a needle that you put the thread through
➔ **not bat an eye** at **BAT²** ➔ **could not believe your eyes** at **BELIEVE** ➔ **BLACK EYE** ➔ **turn a blind eye (to sth)** at **BLIND¹** ➔ **with/to the naked eye** at **NAKED**

eye² *v* [T] present participle **eyeing** or **eying** to look at someone or something with great interest

eyeball /ˈaɪbɔːl $ -bɒːl/ *n* [C] the whole of your eye, including the part inside your head

eyebrow /ˈaɪbraʊ/ *n* [C] the line of short hairs above your eye: *He raised his eyebrows in surprise.* ➔ see picture on page A3

'eye-ˌcatching *adj* unusual, attractive, or noticeable ➔ see box at **NOTICEABLE**

eyelash /ˈaɪlæʃ/ *n* [C] one of the small hairs growing on the edge of your eyelids ➔ see picture on page A3

eyelid /ˈaɪlɪd/ *n* [C] one of the pieces of skin that cover your eyes when you close them

eyeliner /ˈaɪˌlaɪnə $ -ər/ *n* [C,U] a type of MAKE-UP that you put in a thin line along the edges of your eyelids

'eye-ˌopener *n* [singular] an experience from which you learn something new or surprising

'eye-ˌshadow *n* [U] coloured MAKE-UP that you put on your eyelids

eyesight /ˈaɪsaɪt/ *n* [U] the ability to see: **poor/ good/perfect etc eyesight**

eyesore /ˈaɪsɔː $ -sɔːr/ *n* [C] a building or area that is very ugly

eyewitness /ˈaɪˌwɪtnɪs/ *n* [C] someone who sees a crime or accident: *According to eyewitnesses, four men were in the bank.* | *an* **eyewitness account** *of the incident*

E

F, f

F, f /ef/ n [C,U] plural **F's, f's** **1** the sixth letter of the English alphabet **2** the fourth note in the musical SCALE of C MAJOR, or the musical KEY based on this note

F the written abbreviation of **Fahrenheit**

fable /'feɪbəl/ n [C] a traditional story that teaches a moral lesson

fabled /'feɪbəld/ adj famous and often mentioned in traditional stories [= **legendary**]: *the fabled Fountain of Youth*

fabric /'fæbrɪk/ n **1** [C,U] cloth: **woollen/silk/ synthetic etc fabric** **2** [singular] the structure and customs of a society: *a change in the fabric of society* **3** [singular] the walls, floor, and roof of a building

fabricate /'fæbrɪkeɪt/ v [T] to invent a story or information in order to deceive someone: *The police were accused of fabricating evidence.* —**fabrication** /ˌfæbrɪ'keɪʃən/ n [C,U]

fabulous /'fæbjʊləs/ adj very good: *You look fabulous!*

facade, façade /fə'sɑːd, fæ-/ n [C] **1** [usually singular] a way of behaving that hides your real feelings or character: *Behind the cheerful facade, she's lonely.* **2** the front of a building

face¹ /feɪs/ n [C]

1 the front of your head, where your eyes, nose, and mouth are: *her beautiful face* | **the expression/look etc on sb's face** *There was a big smile on his face.* | *He was lying face down* (=with his face towards the ground). | **pale-faced/thin-faced etc** *a pale-faced boy*
2 the expression on someone's face that shows how they feel: *I saw the disappointment in her face.* | *His face lit up* (=suddenly looked happy). | *Sam's face fell* (=suddenly looked sad). | **make/pull a face** (=change your expression to show that you do not like something) *Roy took one bite and pulled a face.* | *When I heard this, I could hardly keep a straight face* (=stop myself from laughing).
3 a person: **new/famous/familiar etc face** *She's a familiar face to British audiences.*
4 face to face while physically close to someone: **meet/talk etc face to face** *I'd rather explain face to face, not on the phone.*
5 to sb's face if you say something to someone's face, you say it directly to them when you are with them
6 in the face of sth in a difficult situation: *courage in the face of danger*
7 the front or surface of something: *a clock face* | *a cliff face* → see picture at WATCH²
8 lose face/save face to lose the respect of other people, or to avoid losing their respect: *Is there any way that the government can save face?*
9 on the face of it when you first consider something, before you know the details: *On the face of it, it seemed reasonable.*
→ IN-YOUR-FACE

face² v [T]

1 also **be faced with** to have to deal with a difficult situation: **face problems/difficulty/a challenge etc** *The team faces the impossible task of beating Brazil.* | *Alan is faced with an uncertain future.*
2 also **face up to sth** to accept that an unpleasant situation exists: **face facts/the truth/the fact that** *Many couples can't face the fact that their marriage is over.* | *Let's face it – you'll never be a star player.*
3 sb can't face (doing) sth used to say that someone does not feel able to do something, especially because it upsets them
4 to be opposite or pointing towards someone or something: *Dean turned to face me.* | *Her apartment faces the sea.* | **north-facing/south-facing etc** *a south-facing garden*
5 face the music to experience the results of something bad you have done

faceless /'feɪsləs/ adj disapproving a faceless person, organization etc is not clearly known and seems unfriendly or not worth caring about: *faceless bureaucrats*

facelift /'feɪslɪft/ n [C] **1** a medical operation to make your face look younger **2** work to improve the appearance of a building, city etc: *The offices were given a facelift.*

facet /'fæsɪt/ n [C] one of several parts of someone's character, a situation etc [= **aspect**]

facetious /fə'siːʃəs/ adj disapproving saying things in order to be funny or clever, in a way that is silly and annoying: *facetious comments* —**facetiously** adv —**facetiousness** n [U]

face-to-'face adj [only before noun] a face-to-face meeting, conversation etc is one where you are with another person: *Do you prefer telephone or face-to-face interviews?*

face 'value n **1 take sth at face value** to accept what you are told without thinking carefully first: *Don't take what adverts tell you at face value.* **2** [singular, U] the value or cost shown on a coin, ticket etc

facial¹ /'feɪʃəl/ adj on or relating to your face: *facial hair*

facial² n [C] a beauty treatment to clean the skin on your face and make it softer

facile /'fæsaɪl $ 'fæsəl/ adj a facile remark, argument etc is too simple and shows a lack of careful thought or understanding: *a facile answer to a complex problem*

facilitate /fə'sɪlɪteɪt/ v [T] formal to make it easier for something to happen: *The Web could facilitate learning.* —**facilitator** n [C]

facility /fə'sɪlɪti/ n plural **facilities** **1 facilities** [plural] rooms, equipment, or services that are provided for a particular purpose: **library/ conference/leisure etc facilities** | *All rooms have private facilities* (=a private bathroom and toilet). **2** [C usually singular] a helpful service or feature that a machine or system has: *Does your bank offer an overdraft facility?* **3** [C] formal a building used for a particular activity: *a top-secret research facility*

facsimile /fæk'sɪməli/ n [C] an exact copy of a picture, piece of writing etc

fact /fækt/ *n*

1 [C] something that is true: **+about** *facts and figures about the Philippines* | **interesting/well-known fact** *It's a well-known fact that new cars lose their value quickly.* | **the fact that** *They lost, despite the fact that their opponents were reduced to 10 men.* | **in fact/as a matter of fact** (=used to add something surprising or unusual that is true) *It looks difficult, but in actual fact it's quite easy.* | **the fact (of the matter) is (that)** (=used to emphasize a fact) *The fact of the matter is, we need more time.* | *I know for a fact that she's married.* | *Just stick to the facts* (=only say what you know is true).

2 [U] things that really happen or exist [≠ **fiction**]: *A journalist must separate fact from fiction.*

3 a fact of life something bad that people must accept: *Violent crime is a fact of life in our cities.*

4 the facts of life if you tell a child the facts of life, you explain how people have sex to produce a baby

→ **MATTER-OF-FACT**

faction /'fækʃən/ *n* [C] a small group of people who are part of a larger group and who have different ideas that they want the other members to accept: *The President hopes to unite his party's warring factions.*

factor /'fæktə $ -ər/ *n* [C]   **1** one of several things that influence or cause a situation: **+in** *Vaccination is an important factor in improving the nation's health.* | **social/economic factor** *Crime is due to economic factors.*   **2** a particular position on a scale that measures the strength or effect something has: *factor 15 suncream*   **3 by a factor of five/ten etc** if something increases or decreases by a factor of five, ten etc, it increases or decreases by five times, ten times etc

factory /'fæktəri/ *n* [C] plural **factories** a building where goods are produced in large quantities: *a car factory*

factual /'fæktʃuəl/ *adj* based on or relating to facts: **factual information/knowledge etc** | *factual errors* —**factually** *adv*

faculty /'fækəlti/ *n* plural **faculties**   **1** [C] a group of departments in a university: **+of** *the Faculty of Law*   **2** [C,U] *AmE* all the teachers in a school or college   **3** [C usually plural] a natural ability, such as the ability to see, hear, or think: *the patient's mental faculties*

fad /fæd/ *n* [C] something that is very popular for a short period of time: *the latest health fad* → see box at **POPULAR**

fade /feɪd/ *v*

1 also **fade away** [I,T] to gradually disappear: *Hopes of peace are beginning to fade.*

2 [I,T] if material fades, or if something fades it, it becomes less bright: *The sunlight had faded the curtains.*

faeces *BrE*; **feces** *AmE* /'fiːsiːz/ *n* [plural] *formal* solid waste material from your BOWELS

fag /fæg/ *n* [C] *BrE informal* a cigarette

Fahrenheit /'færənhaɪt/ *n* [U] written abbreviation *F* a temperature scale in which water freezes at 32° and boils at 212°

fail¹ /feɪl/ *v*

1 [I] to not succeed in doing something that you try to do [≠ **succeed**]: **fail to do sth** *Doctors failed to save the girl's life.* | **+in** *The government has*

failed in its attempt to improve health services. | *The attempt failed.*

2 [I] to not do what is wanted, needed, or expected: **fail to do sth** *Your email failed to arrive.* | **+in** *teachers who fail in their duty to protect children*

3 [I,T] if you fail a test, or if someone fails you, you do not pass it [≠ **pass**]: *The Examination Board has no option but to fail you.*

4 [I] if a machine, a part of your body etc fails, it stops working: *The engine failed after take-off.* | *his failing eyesight*

5 [I] if a business fails, it cannot continue because it has no money

6 [T] if you fail someone, you do not do what they trusted you to do [= **let sb down**]: *I had failed my parents by not finishing my studies.*

7 sb's courage/nerve fails them used to say that someone suddenly loses the confidence they need to do something

8 I fail to see/understand why/how etc *spoken formal* used to say that someone has done something annoying and you do not know why —**failed** *adj*: *a failed marriage* | *failed efforts to reform the tax laws*

fail² *n* **without fail** if you do something without fail, you always do it: *Barry rings every Friday without fail.*

failing¹ /'feɪlɪŋ/ *n* [C] a fault or weakness

failing² *prep* **failing that** used to say that if one thing is not possible, there is something else you could try: *Try the specialist shops, or failing that, the Internet.*

failure /'feɪljə $ -ər/ *n*

1 [U] when someone or something does not succeed [≠ **success**]: *His career ended in failure.*

2 [C] someone or something that is not successful [≠ **success**]: *His last album was a total failure.* | *Business failures are expected to rise.*

3 failure to do sth the fact that someone has not done something that they should have done: *Failure to present a valid ticket will result in prosecution.*

4 [C,U] when a machine or part of your body stops working properly: **heart/kidney/liver etc failure** *He died of heart failure.* | *a power failure*

faint¹ /feɪnt/ *adj*

1 difficult to see, hear, or smell: *a faint noise*

2 faint possibility/chance/hope etc a very small possibility etc: *There's a faint hope they are still alive.*

3 if you feel faint, you feel weak and unsteady: **+with** *He was faint with hunger.*

4 not have the faintest idea (what/how etc) *informal* to not know anything at all about something —**faintly** *adv*

faint² *v* [I] if you faint, you become unconscious for a short time —**faint** *n* [C]

fair¹ /feə $ fer/ *adj*

1 reasonable, right, and accepted by most people [≠ **unfair**]: *It's fair to say that most scientists agree on the evolution theory.* | **not be fair on sb** *I can't work late every night – it's not fair on you.* | **to be fair** (=used to defend or excuse someone) *To be fair, she's only been in the job a week.* | **a fair deal/price/wage etc** *All we want is a fair wage.*

2 treating everyone equally or in the right way:
+to *The law is not fair to working mothers.* | *It's not fair – you always agree with Alice.*
3 neither very good nor very bad [= **average**]
4 fair hair or skin is light in colour [≠ **dark**]
5 have more than your fair share of sth to have more problems than other people, in a way that seems unfair
6 a fair size/number/amount etc quite a large size, number etc: *There's a fair chance of rain this afternoon.*
7 fair enough *BrE* used to say that what someone has said seems reasonable
8 fair weather is pleasant and without wind or rain
9 fair game if someone or something is fair game, it is reasonable and right to criticize them: *The singer's behavior made her fair game for the tabloid press.*
—**fairness** *n* [U]

fair² *adv* **1 fair and square** in a fair and honest way: *They won fair and square.* **2 play fair** to play or behave in a fair and honest way

fair³ *n* [C] **1** a large outdoor event where you can buy things, get information etc: **antiques/book/computer etc fair** *an art fair* | **job/careers fair** **2 funfair** *BrE* a form of outdoor entertainment where you can ride on exciting machines and play games to win prizes [= **carnival** *AmE*]

fairground /'feəɡraʊnd $ 'fer-/ *n* [C] an open space on which a fair takes place

fairly /'feəli $ 'ferli/ *adv*
1 more than a little, but much less than very [= **quite** *BrE*]: *She speaks English fairly well.* | *a fairly large room* → see box at **RATHER**
2 in a way that is fair and reasonable: *I felt that I wasn't treated fairly.*

,fair 'play *n* [U] when you play a game or treat people in a fair way, without cheating or being dishonest

fairway /'feəweɪ $ 'fer-/ *n* [C] the part of a GOLF COURSE that you hit the ball along towards the hole

fairy /'feəri $ 'feri/ *n* [C] plural **fairies** an imaginary magical creature like a very small person

'fairy tale *n* [C] a children's story in which magical things happen

faith /feɪθ/ *n*
1 [U] a strong feeling of trust in someone or something: **+in** *My faith in his ability was justified.* | *Everyone* **had faith** *in the doctor.* | *People will* **lose faith** *in the government.*
2 [U] belief and trust in God: *Her faith sustained her.* | **+in** *his faith in God*
3 [C] a religion: **the Christian/Muslim/Jewish etc faith**
4 keep/break faith with sb/sth to continue or stop supporting someone or something: *voters who have kept faith with the Labour Party*
5 good faith honest and sincere intentions: *I made the offer* **in good faith** *(=meaning to do what I said).*

faithful /'feɪθfəl/ *adj*
1 remaining loyal to someone or something and continuing to support them: *a faithful friend* | **+to** *She remained faithful to her principles.*
2 if you are faithful to your wife, husband etc, you do not have a sexual relationship with anyone else
3 representing an event or image exactly: *a faithful account of the battle* | *a* **faithful reproduction** *of the original picture*
—**faithfulness** *n* [U]

faithfully /'feɪθfəl-i/ *adv* **1** in a faithful way: *He served us faithfully for 30 years.* **2 Yours faithfully** *BrE* the usual polite way of ending a formal letter which begins Dear Sir or Dear Madam

fake¹ /feɪk/ *n* [C] a copy of a valuable object that is intended to deceive people: *The painting was a fake.*

fake² *adj* made to look or seem like something else in order to deceive people: *fake $20 bills* | *a fake German accent*

THESAURUS

false/imitation – not real, but intended to look real: *false teeth* | *imitation leather*
counterfeit – counterfeit money is made to look like real money in order to deceive people
phoney – not real and intended to deceive people: *a phoney British accent*
forged – used about writing or documents that have been illegally copied in order to deceive people: *forged £10 notes*

fake³ *v* **1** [T] to make something seem real in order to deceive people: *He faked his father's signature on the note.* **2** [I,T] to pretend to be ill, interested etc when you are not: *The doctors all thought I was* **faking it**.

falcon /'fɔːlkən $ 'fæl-/ *n* [C] a bird that eats small animals and can be trained to hunt

fall¹ /fɔːl $ fɔːl/ *v* past tense **fell** /fel/ past participle **fallen** /'fɔːlən $ 'fɔːl-/
1 [I] to drop down towards the ground: *Snow began to fall.* | **+out of/from** *The glass fell from his hands.* | **+down** *Something fell down the back of the fridge.*
2 [I] to suddenly go down onto the ground when you are standing, walking etc: *I fell and hurt my leg.* | **+down** *How did she fall down the stairs?* | **+in/into** *Pete slipped by the pool and fell in.* | **fall on/to your knees** (=suddenly kneel) *She fell on her knees and prayed.* → see picture on page A11

THESAURUS

trip – to hit your foot against something, so that you fall or nearly fall: *Be careful not to trip on that step.* | *He tripped over a fallen tree, breaking his leg.*
slip – to slide on something that is wet or icy, so that you fall or nearly fall: *She slipped on the ice and broke her leg.*
stumble – to put your foot down in an awkward way, so that you nearly fall: *She stumbled backwards and struck her head on the bed.*
lose your balance – to fall when you are, for example, climbing a ladder or riding a bicycle
plummet – if something plummets, it falls quickly from a very high place: *We watched, horrified, as the plane plummeted to the ground.*

3 [I] to go down to a lower level or amount [≠ **rise**]: *The temperature fell below zero.* | **+from/to** *Profits fell from $1.3 million to $750,000.* | *Crime fell sharply* (=by a large amount) *last year.*

4 [I, linking verb] to move into a different state: *I was so tired I fell asleep at the table.* | *She fell in love with a younger man.* | *Everyone fell silent.* | **+into** *They quickly fell into debt.*

5 [I] to be part of a particular group: **+into** *Both books fall into the category of historical fiction.* | **+within/under** *matters that fall within his jurisdiction*

6 fall short to be less than is needed or less than you want: **+of** *We fell short of our sales target this month.*

7 night/darkness falls if night falls, it starts to become dark

8 fall into place if things fall into place, they become clear or start to happen as you want: *Then it all fell into place and I realized what had happened.*

9 fall to pieces/bits to break into many parts, especially because of being old: *Her old car was falling to pieces.*

10 fall flat to fail to amuse or interest people: *All my jokes fell flat.*

11 fall into sb's hands/clutches if something falls into someone's hands, they get control over it and can use it to harm another person: *These papers must not fall into the wrong hands.*

12 fall into a trap to make a mistake: *Don't fall into the trap of feeling guilty.*

13 [I] to hang loosely: *Maria's hair fell in loose curls.*

14 [I] if light or shadow falls somewhere, it appears there: **+on/across etc** *His shadow fell across my page.*

15 sb's eyes fall/gaze falls on sth if your eyes fall on something, you notice it

16 [I] to lose power: *The government fell after only six months.*

17 [I] to happen on a particular day or date: **+on** *My birthday falls on a Friday this year.*

18 [I] *literary* to be killed in a war

fall apart *phr v* **1** to break into many pieces, especially because of being old: *This house is falling apart.* **2** to stop being effective or successful: *The economy was falling apart.*

fall back on sth *phr v* to use something or someone after other things or plans have failed: *If talks fail, they must fall back on the law.*

fall behind (sb/sth) *phr v* to make progress more slowly than other people or than you should: *He's fallen behind at school.* | *The project has fallen behind schedule.*

fall for sb/sth *phr v* **1** to be tricked into believing something that is not true: *I told him I was French and he fell for it!* **2** to start to love someone

fall off *phr v* **1** if part of something falls off, it becomes separated from the main part: *The handle fell off.* **2** to decrease: *Demand has fallen off recently.*

fall out *phr v* **1** to have a quarrel: **+with** *I don't want to fall out with you.* **2** if a tooth or your hair falls out, it is no longer attached to your body

fall over *phr v* **1 fall over (sth)** to fall to the ground: *I fell over on the ice.* | *She fell over the*

step (=fell after hitting the step with her foot) *and hurt herself.* **2 fall over yourself to do sth** to be very eager to do something: *They were falling over themselves to help her.*

fall through *phr v* to fail to happen or be completed: *The sale fell through at the last minute.*

fall to sb/sth *phr v* if an unpleasant job falls to someone, they have to do it: *It fell to me to tell them the bad news.*

fall² n

1 [C] a movement down towards the ground: *He had a bad fall from a horse.* | *the first fall of snow that winter*

2 [C] a decrease in the amount, level, or price of something [≠ **rise**]: **+in** *There has been a sharp fall in the temperature.* | **+of** *a fall of 25% in unemployment*

3 [singular,U] *AmE* the season between summer and winter, when the weather becomes colder [= **autumn**]: **this/that fall** *The trees were beautiful that fall.* | **in the fall** *Brad's going to college in the fall.*

4 [singular] a situation when someone or something loses their power or is defeated: **+from** *the Prime Minister's fall from power* | **+of** *the rise and fall of the Roman Empire*

5 falls [plural] a place where a river suddenly goes straight down over a cliff [= **waterfall**]

fallacy /ˈfæləsi/ *n* [C] plural **fallacies** a false idea or belief: *the fallacy that smoking helps you concentrate*

fallen /ˈfɔːlən $ ˈfɒːl-/ *v* the past participle of ⟶ FALL

ˈfall guy *n* [C] *informal* someone who is punished for someone else's crime or mistake

fallible /ˈfæləbəl/ *adj* able to make a mistake [≠ **infallible**]: *Humans are all fallible.*

fallout /ˈfɔːlaut $ ˈfɒːl-/ *adj* **1** the dangerous RADIOACTIVE dust that is in the air after a NUCLEAR explosion **2** the effects of an event: **+from** *We are still dealing with the fallout from his resignation.*

fallow /ˈfæləu $ -lou/ *adj* fallow land is dug but left without crops growing on it

false /fɔːls $ fɒːls/ *adj*

1 untrue or wrong: *He made false accusations.* | *Are these statements true or false?* | *The programme gave a false impression of the situation there.* → see box at **WRONG**

2 not real, but intended to seem real: *He adopted a false identity.* | **false teeth/eyelashes** → see box at **FAKE**

3 not sincere or honest: *a false laugh*

4 false alarm a situation in which people wrongly think that something bad is going to happen

5 false start an unsuccessful attempt to begin a process or event: *After two false starts, the race began.*

6 false economy something that is intended to save money but in fact costs more: *It's a false economy not to buy insurance.*

7 under false pretences if you get something under false pretences, you get it by deceiving people

—**falsely** *adv*: *I was falsely accused.*

falsehood /ˈfɔːlshud $ ˈfɒːls-/ *n* [C] *formal* a statement that is untrue [= **lie**] → see box at **LIE**

falsify /ˈfɔːlsɪ̯faɪ $ ˈfɒːl-/ v [T] **falsified, falsifying, falsifies** to change figures, records etc so that they contain false information: *They falsified the evidence.*

falter /ˈfɔːltə $ ˈfɒːltər/ v [I] **1** to become weaker: *His determination never faltered.* **2** to stop speaking or moving because you feel weak or afraid: *She faltered for a moment.*

fame /feɪm/ n [U] the state of being known about by a lot of people because of your achievements: **win/achieve/gain/find fame** *He first won fame as a singer.* | **rise/shoot to fame** *Kate rose to fame when she was only 17.* → **claim to fame** at CLAIM[2]

famed /feɪmd/ adj *written* well-known [= famous]: **+for** *a region famed for its beauty*

familiar /fəˈmɪliə $ -ər/ adj

1 well-known to you and easy to recognize: *a familiar face* | **look/sound familiar** *The voice on the phone sounded familiar.* | **+to** *This problem is familiar to most teachers.*
2 **be familiar with sth** to know about something: *Are you familiar with this software?*
3 friendly or informal: *The waiter was a bit too familiar.*
—**familiarly** adv: *Joseph, familiarly known as Joe*

familiarity /fəˌmɪliˈærᵻti/ n [U] **1** a good knowledge of something: **+with** *her familiarity with computers* **2** a relaxed feeling or way of behaving, because you know a person or place well: *He spoke to her with easy familiarity.*

familiarize also **-ise** *BrE* /fəˈmɪliəraɪz/ v **familiarize yourself with sth** to learn about something so that you know it well: *Familiarize yourself with the office routine.*

family /ˈfæməli/ n plural **families**

1 [C,U] a group of people who are related to each other, especially parents and their children: *Do you know the family that lives next door?* | *The whole family is invited.* | **+of** *a car big enough for a family of seven* | *Do you have any family in the States?* | **in sb's family** *Musical talent runs in her family.*

2 [C,U] children: *couples with young families* | *They want to start a family* (=have a child). | **bring up/raise a family** *Raising a family is hard work.*
3 [C] a group of related things, especially animals, plants, or languages: **the cat/dog etc family** | *The tiger is a member of the cat family.* | *the Celtic family of languages*
→ **EXTENDED FAMILY, NUCLEAR FAMILY**

'family ˌname n [C] the name someone shares with other members of their family [= surname]
→ see box at NAME

ˌfamily 'planning n [U] the practice of controlling how many children you have, by using CONTRACEPTION

ˌfamily 'tree n [C] a drawing that shows the names of the members of a family over a period of time and how they are related to each other

famine /ˈfæmᵻn/ n [C,U] a situation in which a large number of people have little or no food for a long time and some people die

famous /ˈfeɪməs/ adj

1 known about by a lot of people: *a famous actor* | **+for** *France is famous for its wine.*

2 **the famous** people who are famous
→ **WORLD-FAMOUS**

famously /ˈfeɪməsli/ adv **1** **get on/along famously** to get on with sb very well **2** in a way that is very well known: *Her cooking was famously awful.*

fan[1] /fæn/ n [C]

1 someone who likes something such as a sport, type of music, or singer very much: **football/film/rock etc fan** *Thousands of football fans filled the stadium.* | **+of** *He was a big fan of Elvis Presley.*
2 a machine, or a thing that you wave with your hand, that cools you by making the air move

fan[2] v [T] **fanned, fanning** to make air move by waving a fan, piece of paper etc: *She fanned herself with a magazine.*

fan out phr v if a group of people fan out, they walk forwards while spreading over a wide area: *The soldiers fanned out across the moor.*

fanatic /fəˈnætɪk/ n [C] **1** someone who has extreme religious or political ideas and may be dangerous [= extremist]: *religious fanatics* **2** someone who likes a particular thing or activity very much: *a golf fanatic* —**fanatical** adj —**fanatically** /-kli/ adv —**fanaticism** /-tˌsɪzəm/ n [U]

fanciful /ˈfænsɪfəl/ adj imagined rather than based on facts

fancy[1] /ˈfænsi/ v [T] **fancied, fancying, fancies** *BrE* **1** *informal* to like or want something [= feel like]: *Do you fancy a drink?* | **fancy doing sth** *I don't fancy going out tonight.* **2** *informal* to feel sexually attracted to someone: *I think he fancies you.* **3** **fancy/fancy that!** *spoken* used when you are surprised

fancy[2] adj **1** expensive and fashionable: *a fancy hotel* → see box at EXPENSIVE **2** unusual and complicated or having a lot of decoration: *I like simple food – nothing fancy.*

fancy[3] n **1** [singular] a feeling of liking something or someone: *He seems to have taken a fancy to you.* **2** **take sb's fancy** if something takes your fancy, you want to have it

ˌfancy 'dress n [U] *BrE* clothes that you wear, especially to parties, that make you look like a famous person, a character from a story etc: *a fancy-dress party* → see box at **PARTY**

fanfare /ˈfænfeə $ -fer/ *n* [C] a short loud piece of music played on a TRUMPET to introduce an important person or event

fang /fæŋ/ *n* [C] a long sharp tooth of an animal such as a snake or dog → see picture on page A2

fantasize also **-ise** *BrE* /ˈfæntəsaɪz/ *v* [I,T] to think about something that is pleasant or exciting, but unlikely to happen: **+about** *We all fantasize about winning the lottery.*

fantastic /fænˈtæstɪk/ *adj* **1** *informal* extremely good: *You look fantastic.* | *What a fantastic house!* | *'I got the job.' 'Fantastic!'* → see box at **NICE 2** a fantastic amount is very large **3** strange or unreal: *fantastic tales of knights and dragons* —**fantastically** /-kli/ *adv*

fantasy /ˈfæntəsi/ *n* [C,U] plural **fantasies** an experience or situation that you imagine but is not real: *I had fantasies about being an artist.*

FAQ /fæk, ˌef eɪ ˈkjuː/ *n* [C] **frequently asked questions** a list of answers to the questions that are most often asked about a subject, especially on the Internet

far¹ /fɑː $ fɑːr/ *adv* comparative **farther** /ˈfɑːðə $ ˈfɑːrðər/ or **further** /ˈfɜːðə $ ˈfɜːrðər/ superlative **farthest** /ˈfɑːðɪst $ ˈfɑːr-/ or **furthest** /ˈfɜːðɪst $ ˈfɜːr-/

1 a) a long distance: *Have you driven far?* | *See who can throw the farthest.* | **+from** *I work not far from here.* | **+away** *Her children have all moved far away.* | **+down/along etc** *They live further along the street.* **b)** used to ask or talk about distance: *How far is it to the station?* | *He didn't say how far he had walked.* | *I'll come with you as far as (=up to) the corner of the street.* → see box at **UNTIL**

2 very much, or to a great degree: **far better/easier etc** *The new system is far better than the old one.* | **far more/less** *It cost far less than I expected.* | **far too much/fat/early etc** *That's far too much for one person.* | *She is by far the best athlete in the school (=much better than anyone else).* | *As far as possible (=as much as possible), we use fresh local ingredients.*

3 used to talk about how much progress someone makes: *How far have you got with your book?* | *They only got as far as the first course before the phone rang.* | *She's very talented and should go far (=be very successful).*

4 a long time: **+ahead/back** *We need to plan further ahead.* | *This system was being used as far back as 1850.* | **+into** *They worked far into the night.*

5 go too far also **take too far** to do something that is too extreme: *I don't mind jokes but you've gone too far this time.*

6 go so far as to do sth to do something that seems surprising or extreme: *I wouldn't go so far as to call her a liar.*

7 so far until now: *We haven't had any problems so far.*

8 so far so good *spoken* used to say that something has been successful until now

9 far from sth used to say that something is not at all true: *The situation is far from ideal.* | *'Are you angry?' 'Far from it!' I'm delighted.'*

10 far and wide over a large area: *His fame spread far and wide.*

11 as far as I know/I can tell/I can remember etc *spoken* used to say that you think something is true, but you may be wrong: *As far as I know, Fran intends to come.*
→ **as far as sth is concerned** at **CONCERNED**

GRAMMAR

When you are talking about distances, you can use **far** in questions and negative sentences: *How far is it to the sea?* | *It's not very far.*
You can also use **far** after 'too', 'as', and 'so': *It's too far to walk.* | *I ran as far as I could.* | *I wish he didn't live so far away.*
But do not use **far** in other kinds of sentence. For example do not say 'It's far to London from here'. Say *'It's a long way to London from here.'*

far² *adj* comparative **farther** or **further**, superlative **farthest** or **furthest**

1 a long distance away [≠ **near**]: *We can walk to the restaurant – it's not far.* → see picture at **NEAR²**
2 the far side/end/corner etc the side, end etc most distant from where you are: *the far side of the street*
3 the far north/south etc the part of an area that is furthest to the north, the south etc: *They live in the far north of Scotland.*
4 the far left/right people who have extreme political opinions
5 be a far cry from sth to be very different from something: *His life as a pop star was a far cry from his childhood in Leeds.*

faraway /ˈfɑːrəweɪ/ *adj* **1** [only before noun] *literary* distant: *faraway places* **2 a faraway look** an expression on your face that shows that you are not thinking about what is around you

farce /fɑːs $ fɑːrs/ *n* **1** [singular] an event or situation that is very badly organized or not done properly: *The interview was a complete farce.* **2** [C,U] a humorous play or film with a lot of silly complicated situations —**farcical** *adj*

fare¹ /feə $ fer/ *n*
1 [C] the amount you pay to travel by train, plane, bus etc: **bus/train fare** *What's the bus fare into town?* | **air/rail fare** → see box at **COST**
2 [U] food, especially food served in a restaurant: *They serve traditional fare.*

fare² *v* **fare well/better/badly etc** *formal* to be successful or unsuccessful in a particular situation: *Girls fared better than boys in the tests.*

farewell /ˌfeəˈwel◂ $ ˌfer-/ *n* [C,U] the action of saying goodbye: *a party to bid farewell to their old house* | *a farewell speech*

far-fetched *adj* very unlikely to be true: *Her story was pretty far-fetched.*

far-flung *adj* very far away: *far-flung corners of the globe*

farm¹ /fɑːm $ fɑːrm/ *n* [C] an area of land used for growing crops or keeping animals: *a 4000-acre farm* | **on a farm** *I grew up on a farm.* | **pig/dairy/fruit etc farm**

farm² *v* [I,T] to use land for growing crops and keeping animals: *Our family has farmed here for generations.* | *They farm their land organically.* | **farmed salmon/rabbits etc** (=not wild)

F

farm animals

goat

sheep

horse

chicken

cow

farmer /'fɑːmə $ 'fɑːrmər/ *n* [C] someone who owns or manages a farm: **pig/dairy/fruit etc farmer**

farmhouse /'fɑːmhaʊs $ 'fɑːrm-/ *n* [C] the main house on a farm, where the farmer lives

farming /'fɑːmɪŋ $ 'fɑːr-/ *n* [U] the activity of keeping animals or growing crops on a farm: **organic farming** (=without using chemicals) | **factory farming** (=when animals are kept inside in small spaces)

farmland /'fɑːmlænd, -lənd $ 'fɑːrmlænd/ *n* [U] land used for farming

farmyard /'fɑːmjɑːd $ 'fɑːrmjɑːrd/ *n* [C] an area surrounded by farm buildings

far-'off *adj literary* a long distance away or a long time ago: *a far-off land*

far-'reaching *adj* having a big influence or effect: *far-reaching reforms*

farsighted /ˌfɑːˈsaɪtɪd◂ $ ˌfɑːr-/ *adj AmE* able to see or read things clearly only when they are far away from you [= **longsighted** *BrE*]

fart /fɑːt $ fɑːrt/ *v* [I] *informal* a rude word meaning to let air come out of your BOWELS —**fart** *n* [C]

farther /'fɑːðə $ 'fɑːrðər/ *adj, adv* a COMPARATIVE form of FAR

farthest /'fɑːðɪst $ 'fɑːr-/ *adj, adv* a SUPERLATIVE form of FAR

fascinate /'fæsɪneɪt/ *v* [T] to interest you very much: *The story fascinated her.*

fascinated /'fæsɪneɪtɪd/ *adj* extremely interested: *I am fascinated by space travel.*

fascinating /'fæsɪneɪtɪŋ/ *adj* extremely interesting: *a fascinating subject* | *She found him fascinating.* → see box at **INTERESTING**

fascination /ˌfæsɪˈneɪʃən/ *n* [singular, U] the state of being very interested in something: **+with/for** *He had a fascination with science.*

fascism /'fæʃɪzəm/ *n* [U] an extreme RIGHT-WING political system in which people's lives are completely controlled by the state

fascist /'fæʃɪst/ *n* [C] someone who supports fascism —**fascist** *adj*

fashion¹ /'fæʃən/ *n*

1 [C,U] something that is popular or thought to be good at a particular time: **+for** *There was a*

fashion for long hair. | **+in** *Fashions in education have changed.* | **in fashion** (=popular) *Hats are in fashion again.* | **come into/go out of fashion** *Those ideas went out of fashion years ago.* | *Being very thin **is the fashion** nowadays.*

2 [U] the business of making or selling clothes: **fashion magazine/photographer/show etc** *a world-famous fashion model*

3 in a ... fashion *formal* in a particular way: *Can we discuss this in a civilized fashion?*

fashion² *v* [T] *formal* to shape or make something with your hands or a few tools: *He fashioned a seat from a tree stump.*

fashionable /'fæʃənəbəl/ *adj* popular or thought to be good at a particular time [≠ **unfashionable**]: *Black is very fashionable now.* | *It was fashionable to be plump.* | **fashionable restaurant/shop/club etc** → see box at **CLOTHES** —**fashionably** *adv*

fast¹ /fɑːst $ fæst/ *adv*

1 at a great speed, or in not much time: *You're driving too fast!* | *How fast can you get the job done?* | *a **fast-moving**, exciting film*

THESAURUS

quickly/swiftly – used especially about movement: *I ran quickly down the stairs.* | *Anna looked swiftly up at him.*
rapidly/speedily – used especially about the speed at which something happens: *Unemployment rose rapidly.* | *special powers that would enable the government to deal with cases more speedily*

2 fast asleep sleeping very deeply

3 be stuck/held fast to be held very firmly: *The car was stuck fast in the mud.*

fast² *adj*

1 moving, happening, or doing something quickly: *a fast car* | *a fast learner* | *The metro is the fastest way to get around.*

2 [not before noun] showing a later time than the real time: *My watch is five minutes fast.*

fast³ *v* [I] to eat little or no food for a period of time, especially for religious reasons → see box at **EAT** —**fast** *n* [C]

fasten /'fɑːsən $ 'fæ-/ *v*

1 [I,T] to join together the two sides of something so that it is closed, or to become joined together: *Fasten your seat belts.* | *The skirt fastens at the back.*

fasten

fastening a seatbelt

THESAURUS

attach – to fasten something firmly to another object or surface
join – to connect or fasten things together
glue – to join things together using glue
tape – to fasten something using tape
staple – to fasten something using staples
clip – to fasten things together using a clip

tie – to fasten a tie or shoes etc by making a knot: *Don't forget to tie your shoelaces.*

do up – to fasten clothes or the buttons etc on clothes: *Can you do up my zip?*

button (up) – to fasten the buttons on a shirt, coat etc: *Craig buttoned up his jacket.*

zip up – to fasten clothes, bags etc with a zip: *I can't zip up these jeans.*

unfasten, untie, undo, unbutton, unzip

2 [T] to attach something firmly to another object or surface: **fasten sth to/onto sth** *I fastened the rope to a tree.*

3 [T] to close and lock a window, gate etc

fastener /ˈfɑːsənə $ ˈfæsənər/ *n* [C] *BrE* something such as a button or pin that you use to join something together

fastening /ˈfɑːsənɪŋ $ ˈfæs-/ *n* [C] something that keeps a door, window etc shut

'fast food *n* [U] food such as HAMBURGERS that is prepared and eaten quickly in a restaurant → see box at RESTAURANT

,fast-'forward *v* [I,T] to wind a tape or video forwards quickly without playing it —**fast forward** *n* [U]

fastidious /fæˈstɪdiəs/ *adj* very careful about small details: *He is fastidious about hygiene.* —**fastidiously** *adv*

'fast lane *n* **the fast lane a)** *informal* an exciting way of life that involves expensive or dangerous activities: *She loves **life in the fast lane**.* **b)** the part of a big road where people drive fastest

'fast track *n* [singular] a quick way to achieve something: *You're on the fast track to success.* —**fast-track** *adj*

fat¹ /fæt/ *adj*

1 having too much flesh on your body [≠ thin]: *You'll **get fat** if you eat all that.* | *a short, fat man*

2 thick or wide [≠ thin]: *a fat book*

3 worth a lot of money: **fat salary/paycheck/profits etc** *They wrote me a nice fat cheque.*

4 fat chance *spoken* used to say that something is very unlikely to happen

fat² *n*

1 [U] the substance under the skin of people and animals which helps to keep them warm

2 [C,U] a substance contained in foods such as milk, cheese, butter etc: **high/low in fat** *Choose foods that are lower in fat.* | **low-fat/high-fat/full-fat** *a low-fat diet* | *full-fat milk*

3 [C,U] an oily substance taken from animals or plants and used in cooking: *Fry the onions in bacon fat.*

fatal /ˈfeɪtl/ *adj* **1** resulting in someone's death: **fatal accident/injury/illness etc** *a fatal heart attack* **2** having a very bad effect: **fatal mistake/error** *Treating employees badly is a fatal mistake.* —**fatally** *adv*

fatalism /ˈfeɪtl-ɪzəm/ *n* [U] the belief that there is nothing you can do to prevent events from happening —**fatalist** *n* [C] —**fatalistic** /ˌfeɪtlˈɪstɪk◂/ *adj*

fatality /fəˈtæləti/ *n* [C] plural **fatalities** a death in an accident or a violent attack

fate /feɪt/ *n*

1 [C] the things that happen to someone, especially unpleasant events: **+of** *No one knows what the fate of the hostages will be.* | *The rest of Europe was to **suffer the same fate**.*

2 [U] a power that is believed to control what happens in people's lives: *Fate plays cruel tricks sometimes.* | **twist/quirk of fate** (=something unexpected that happens) *By a **strange twist of fate**, we were on the same plane.*

fated /ˈfeɪtɪd/ *adj* [not before noun] certain to happen or to do something because a mysterious force is controlling events: **be fated to do sth** *We were fated to meet.*

fateful /ˈfeɪtfəl/ *adj* having an important, usually bad, effect on future events: *a fateful decision* —**fatefully** *adv*

father¹ /ˈfɑːðə $ -ər/ *n* [C]

1 a male parent: *Ask your father to help you.* | *Andrew was very excited about becoming a father.* → see box at RELATIVE

2 also **Father** a priest, especially in the Roman Catholic Church: *Do you know Father Vernon?*

father² *v* [T] to become a male parent: *He fathered five children.*

,Father 'Christmas *n* *BrE* an imaginary man who wears red clothes, has a long white beard, and is said to bring presents to children at Christmas [= Santa Claus]

'father ,figure *n* [C] an older man who you trust and respect

fatherhood /ˈfɑːðəhʊd $ -ər-/ *n* [U] the state of being a father

'father-in-law *n* [C] plural **fathers-in-law** the father of your husband or wife

fatherly /ˈfɑːðəli $ -ðər-/ *adj* typical of a kind and caring father: *fatherly advice*

'Father's Day *n* [C] a day on which people give cards and presents to their father [→ Mother's Day]

fathom¹ /ˈfæðəm/ also **fathom out** *v* [T] to understand what something means after thinking about it carefully: *I still can't fathom out what she meant.*

fathom² *n* [C] a unit for measuring how deep water is, equal to 1.83 metres

fatigue /fəˈtiːɡ/ *n* [U] **1** extreme tiredness: *Sam's face was grey with fatigue.* **2** *technical* weakness in a substance such as metal that may cause it to break

F

fatten /ˈfætn/ v [T] to make an animal become fatter so that it is ready to eat

fatten sb/sth ⇔ **up** phr v to make a thin person or animal fatter: *My mum's always trying to fatten me up.*

fattening /ˈfætn-ɪŋ/ adj likely to make you fat: *Avoid fattening foods like chocolate.*

fatty /ˈfæti/ adj containing a lot of fat: *fatty foods*

fatuous /ˈfætʃuəs/ adj very silly or stupid: *a fatuous remark*

faucet /ˈfɔːsɪt $ ˈfɒː-/ n [C] AmE the thing that you turn on or off in order to control the flow of water from a pipe [= **tap** BrE]: *a leaky faucet* → see picture at **BATHROOM**

fault[1] /fɔːlt $ fɒːlt/ n

1 be sb's fault if something bad that happens is your fault, you are responsible for it happening: *I injured my back, but it was my own fault.* | *It's your fault that we're late.* | **be sb's fault for doing sth** *It's my fault for not checking* (=I should have checked).
2 be at fault to be responsible for something bad that has happened: *It was the other driver who was at fault.*
3 [C] something that is wrong with something: *a design fault* | **+in** *There's a fault in one of the loudspeakers.*

4 [C] a bad part of someone's character: *His worst fault is his arrogance.*
5 [C] a large crack in the rocks that form the Earth's surface: *the San Andreas fault*
→ **find fault with sb/sth** at **FIND**[1]

fault[2] v [T] to find a mistake in something: *Her performance could not be faulted.*

faultless /ˈfɔːltləs $ ˈfɒːlt-/ adj having no mistakes [= **perfect**]: *Yasmin spoke faultless French.*

faulty /ˈfɔːlti $ ˈfɒːlti/ adj **1** not working properly: *faulty wiring* **2** not correct: *faulty reasoning*

fauna /ˈfɔːnə $ ˈfɒː-/ n [C,U] technical all the animals living in a particular area [➔ **flora**]

favour[1] BrE; **favor** AmE /ˈfeɪvə $ -ər/ n

1 [C] something you do for someone in order to help them: *Could you do me a favour and tell Kelly I'm here.* | *He hired John as a favour to his father.* | *Paul, can I ask you a favour?*
2 [U] support, approval, or agreement for something: **in favour of sth** *He spoke in favour of the proposal.* | **find/gain/win favour (with sb)** *The idea may win favour with older people.*
3 in favour/out of favour if someone or something is in favour, people like them and approve of them: *Thompson was soon back in favour.* | **fall/go out of favour** (=become unpopular) *The custom fell out of favour at the beginning of the century.*
4 in sb's favour to someone's advantage, or so that someone wins: *The new rules should actually work in your favour.* | *The final score was 2–1 in Algeria's favour.*

5 abandon/drop etc sth in favour of sth to decide not to have one thing and have something else instead: *Plans for a tunnel were rejected in favour of the bridge.*

favour[2] BrE; **favor** AmE v [T] **1** to prefer something or someone to other things or people: *Both countries seemed to favour the agreement.*
2 to treat someone better than someone else in an unfair way: *tax cuts that favour the rich*

favourable BrE; **favorable** AmE /ˈfeɪvərəbəl/ adj **1** showing that you like or approve of someone or something: *The film received favourable reviews.* **2** suitable and likely to make something happen or succeed: *The disease spreads quickly under favourable conditions.*
3 make a favourable impression to make people like or approve of you: *Try to make a favourable impression on the interviewer.* —**favourably** adv

favourite[1] BrE; **favorite** AmE /ˈfeɪvərɪt/ adj [only before noun] your favourite person or thing is the one you like most: *a child's favourite toy* | *What's your favourite colour?*

favourite[2] BrE; **favorite** AmE n [C] **1** something that you like more than others of the same kind: *a sweater that's an old favourite* **2** someone who is liked and treated better than others by a teacher or parent: *She was always Dad's favourite.* **3** the team, player etc that is expected to win a race or competition: *Brazil were the favorites to win the World Cup.*

favouritism BrE; **favoritism** AmE /ˈfeɪvərɪˌtɪzəm/ n [U] when one person or group is treated better than another in an unfair way

fawn[1] /fɔːn $ fɒːn/ n **1** [C] a young DEER **2** [U] a pale yellow-brown colour

fawn[2] v [I] to praise someone and be friendly to them because you want something: **+on/over** *journalists who fawn over celebrities*

fax /fæks/ n

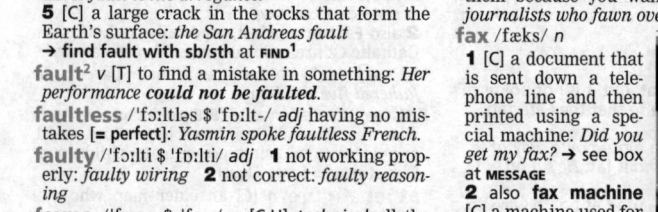

fax

fax machine

1 [C] a document that is sent down a telephone line and then printed using a special machine: *Did you get my fax?* → see box at **MESSAGE**
2 also **fax machine** [C] a machine used for sending and receiving faxes: *What's your fax number?*
3 [U] the system of sending documents using a fax machine: **by fax** *You can book tickets by fax.*
—**fax** v [T] *Can you fax me the details?*

faze /feɪz/ v [T] informal to make you feel confused or embarrassed, so that you do not know what to do: *Nothing seemed to faze him.*

FBI /ˌef biː ˈaɪ/ n **the FBI** the Federal Bureau of Investigation the US police department that is controlled by the government and is concerned with crimes that happen in more than one state

fear[1] /fɪə $ fɪr/ n

1 [C,U] the feeling you get when you are afraid or worried that something bad will happen: **+of** *a fear of flying* | **+that** *fears that prices might*

continue to rise | **+for** *She expressed fears for her daughter's safety.* | *Their **worst** fears became a reality.* | *People **lived in fear** of being arrested.*
2 for fear (that)/for fear of sth because you are worried that something bad will happen: *They travelled at night, for fear of being seen.*
3 No fear! *BrE spoken informal* used humorously to say that you are definitely not going to do something

fear² v

1 [I,T] to feel afraid or worried that something bad will happen or has happened: **+(that)** *Police fear there may be further attacks.* | *Hundreds of people are **feared dead**.* | *When he didn't come home, we **feared the worst** (=were afraid something very bad had happened).* | **+for** *We left because we **feared for** our lives.*
2 [T] to be afraid of someone: *As a leader, he was feared by his people.*

fearful /ˈfɪəfəl $ ˈfɪr-/ *adj* **1** *formal* afraid: **+of** *People are fearful of rising crime.* **2** *BrE* extremely bad: *The room was in a fearful mess.* —**fearfully** *adv*

fearless /ˈfɪələs $ ˈfɪr-/ *adj* not afraid of anything: *a fearless explorer* —**fearlessly** *adv* —**fearlessness** *n* [U]

fearsome /ˈfɪəsəm $ ˈfɪr-/ *adj* very frightening: *a fearsome sight*

feasible /ˈfiːzɨbəl/ *adj* possible, and likely to work: *a feasible solution*

feast¹ /fiːst/ *n* [C] **1** a large meal for a lot of people to celebrate a special occasion: *a wedding feast* **2** *informal* a good large meal: *That was a real feast!* **3** a religious holiday

feast² v **1** [I] to eat a large meal to celebrate something **2 feast your eyes on sb/sth** to look at someone or something with great pleasure

feat /fiːt/ *n* [C] an impressive achievement needing a lot of strength or skill: **+of** *an amazing feat of engineering* | **be no mean feat** (=be difficult to do) *Getting a doctorate is no mean feat!*

feather¹ /ˈfeðə $ -ər/ *n* [C] one of the light soft things that covers a bird's body: *an ostrich feather* → see picture on page A2

feather² v **feather your nest** to get money by dishonest methods

feathery /ˈfeðəri/ *adj* soft and light like feathers: *a fern with feathery leaves*

feature¹ /ˈfiːtʃə $ -ər/ *n* [C]

1 an important, interesting, or typical part of something: **+of** *An important feature of his paintings is their colours.* | *Striped tails are a **common feature** of many animals.*
2 a piece of writing about a subject in a newspaper or a magazine, or a special report on television or on the radio: **+on** *a special feature on holidaying with your dog*
3 [usually plural] a part of someone's face, such as their eyes, nose etc: *Her eyes are her best feature.*

feature² v [I,T] to include something as a special or important part, or to be included: *a new movie featuring Meryl Streep* | *Blake's name did not feature in the report.*

'feature film *n* [C] a film of normal length made for the cinema → see box at **FILM**

February /ˈfebruəri, ˈfebjuri $ ˈfebjueri/ *n* [C,U] written abbreviation **Feb.** the second month of the year, between January and March: **next/last February** *Mum died last February.* | **in February** *We can do it in February.* | **on February 6th** *He arrives on February 6th.* → see box at **MONTH**

feces /ˈfiːsiːz/ *n* the American spelling of FAECES

feckless /ˈfekləs/ *adj* a feckless person is not determined, effective, or successful

fed /fed/ v the past tense and past participle of FEED

federal /ˈfedərəl/ *adj* **1** consisting of a group of states that make some of their own decisions but are controlled by a central government: *Switzerland is a federal republic.* **2** relating to the national government of a country which consists of several states: *federal laws*

federation /ˌfedəˈreɪʃən/ *n* [C] a group of states or organizations that have joined together to form a larger group: *the International Boxing Federation*

fed 'up *adj* [not before noun] *informal* annoyed or bored and wanting change: **+with** *I'm fed up with this constant rain.*

fee /fiː/ *n* [C] an amount of money that you pay for professional services or that you pay to do something: *medical fees* | *college fees* | *The museum charges an **entrance fee**.* → see box at **COST**

feeble /ˈfiːbəl/ *adj* **1** extremely weak: *His voice sounded feeble.* **2** not good or effective: *a feeble excuse*

feed¹ /fiːd/ v past tense and past participle **fed** /fed/

1 [T] to give food to a person or animal: *Have you fed the cats?* | **feed sth to sb** *Children were feeding bread to the ducks.* | **feed sb on/with sth** *Her Mum fed her on stews and meat pies.*
2 [I] if animals or babies feed, they eat: **+on** *In winter, the birds feed on berries.*
3 [T] to give a substance to a plant to help it grow
4 [T] to provide enough food for a group of people: *money with which to feed and clothe their families*
5 [T] to supply something, or to put something into something else: **feed sth to sth** *The sound is fed directly to the headphones.*
→ **BREAST-FEED, SPOON-FEED**

feed² *n* **1** [C] *BrE* when milk is given to a small baby: *Has he had his feed yet?* **2** [U] food for animals: *cattle feed*

feedback /ˈfiːdbæk/ *n* [U] advice, criticism etc about how successful or useful something is: **+on** *Try to give the students some feedback on the task.*

feel¹ /fiːl/ v past tense and past participle **felt** /felt/

1 [linking verb, T] to experience a particular physical feeling or emotion: *Do you still feel hungry?* | *Marie immediately felt guilty.* | *Stop exercising if you feel any pain.* | *'How do you feel?' 'Better.'* | **+as if/as though/like** *I felt as though I'd won a million dollars.*
2 [T] to notice something that is touching you or happening to you: *He felt her breath on his cheek.* | **feel sb/sth do sth** *She felt his arms go*

round her. | **feel yourself doing sth** *I felt myself blushing.*

3 [linking verb] to seem to have a particular quality when touched or experienced by someone: **feel smooth/cold/damp etc** *Her hands felt rough.* | *The house felt hot and stuffy.* | *Seeing him again felt strange.* | *How does it feel to be 40?* | **+like** *It was a year ago, but it still feels like yesterday.*

4 [I,T] to have an opinion based on your feelings rather than on facts: **+(that)** *I feel that I should do more to help.* | **+about** *How would you feel about working with Nicole?* | **feel sure/certain** *She felt sure she'd made the right decision.*

5 feel like (doing) sth to want to have something or do something: *Do you feel like another drink?*

6 [T] to touch something with your fingers to find out about it: *Mum, feel this stone. Isn't it smooth?*

7 feel around/in sth etc (for sth) to try to find something by using your fingers: *She felt in her bag for a pencil.*

8 feel the force/effect/benefits etc of sth to experience the good or bad results of something: *They're beginning to feel the effects of the recession.*

9 feel your way a) to move carefully with your hands out in front of you because you cannot see well: *He felt his way across the room.* **b)** to do things slowly and carefully, because you are unsure about a new situation: **+towards** *The government is feeling its way towards a new policy.*

feel for sb *phr v* to feel sympathy for someone: *It was awful. I really felt for her.*

feel² *n* [singular]

1 the way that something seems to people: **+about** *The restaurant has a nice, relaxed feel about it.*

2 the way something feels when you touch it: **+of** *I like the feel of this cloth.* | *a soft feathery feel*

3 have/get a feel for sth *informal* to have or develop an understanding of something or ability with something: *Pete has a real feel for languages.*

feeling /'fiːlɪŋ/ *n*

1 a) [C,U] something that you experience in your mind: **+of** *terrible feelings of guilt* | *Don't try to hide your feelings.* | **negative/positive feelings** | *It was a wonderful feeling to be home again.* **b)** [C] something that you experience in your body: **+of** *feelings of dizziness*

2 sb's feelings [plural] whether someone is upset or not: *He doesn't care about my feelings.* | *It won't hurt my feelings* (=upset me) *if you change your mind.*

3 [C] a belief or opinion about something: **+on/about** *She has strong feelings on the issue of abortion.* | *My own feeling is that we should wait.* | **+(that)** *I had a feeling that he'd refuse.* | *Leslie got the feeling that she was being watched.*

4 [U] people's attitude about a subject: *anti-American feeling* | **+against/in favour of** *the depth of feeling against nuclear weapons*

5 [U] the ability to feel pain, heat, cold etc in your body: *He lost all feeling in his legs.*

6 I know the feeling *spoken* said when you understand how someone feels because you have

had the same experience: *'It's embarrassing when you can't remember someone's name.' 'I know the feeling.'*

7 bad/ill feeling anger or lack of trust between people: *The changes have caused ill feeling in the workforce.*

→ **gut feeling** at **GUT¹**

feet /fiːt/ *n* the plural of FOOT

feign /feɪn/ *v* [T] *formal* to pretend to have a feeling, be ill, be asleep etc: *Feigning a headache, I went to my room.*

feisty /'faɪsti/ *adj* having a strong determined character and a lot of energy

feline /'fiːlaɪn/ *adj* like a cat or relating to a cat

fell¹ /fel/ *v* the past tense of FALL

fell² *v* [T] **1** to cut down a tree **2** *written* to knock someone down

fellow¹ /'feləʊ $ -loʊ/ *n* [C] **1** *old-fashioned* a man: *What a strange fellow he is!* **2** *BrE* a member of an important society or college: *a Fellow of the Royal College of Surgeons*

fellow² *adj* **fellow workers/students/ passengers etc** people who work, study, travel etc with you

fellowship /'feləʊʃɪp $ -loʊ-/ *n* **1** [U] a feeling of friendship that people have because they have the same interests or experiences **2** [C] a group of people with the same beliefs or interests, who have meetings together: *a Christian youth fellowship* **3** [C] a job in a university that includes detailed study of a subject

felon /'felən/ *n* [C] *law* someone who is guilty of a serious crime: *a convicted felon*

felony /'feləni/ *n* [C,U] *law* plural **felonies** a serious crime such as murder

felt¹ /felt/ *v* the past tense and past participle of FEEL

felt² *n* [U] a soft thick cloth made from wool or other material that has been pressed flat

felt tip 'pen also **'felt tip** *BrE n* [C] a pen that has a hard piece of felt at the end that the ink comes through

female¹ /'fiːmeɪl/ *adj*

1 belonging to the sex that can have babies or produce eggs [≠ **male**; ➡ **feminine**]: *a female monkey* | *female workers* | *the female sex* → see box at **WOMAN**

2 a female plant or flower produces fruit [➡ **male**]

female² *n* [C] a person or animal that belongs to the sex that can have babies or produce eggs [≠ **male**; ➡ **feminine**]: *The female is smaller than the male.*

feminine /'femɪnɪn/ *adj*

1 having qualities that are thought to be typical of women, especially the qualities of being gentle, delicate, or pretty [➡ **masculine**]: *It was a very feminine room.*

2 in grammar, a feminine noun, adjective etc belongs to a class of words that have different INFLECTIONS from MASCULINE and NEUTER words [➡ **masculine**]

femininity /ˌfemɪˈnɪnɪti/ *n* [U] qualities that are thought to be typical of women [➡ **masculinity**]

feminism /'femᵻnɪzəm/ n [U] the belief that women should have the same rights and opportunities as men —**feminist** n, adj: *a feminist writer* | *militant feminists*

fence¹ /fens/ n [C]
1 a line of upright wooden posts with wire or wood between that surrounds an area of land: *the garden fence* | *a wooden fence*
2 a structure that horses jump over in a race or competition
3 *informal* someone who buys and sells stolen goods

fence² v [I] to fight with a sword as a sport —**fencing** n [U]
fence sth ⇔ in *phr v* to surround a place with a fence
fence sth ⇔ off *phr v* to separate one area from another with a fence: *We fenced off part of the field.*

fencing /'fensɪŋ/ n [U] **1** the sport of fighting with a long thin sword **2** fences, or the material used to make them

fend /fend/ v **fend for yourself** to look after yourself without help from other people: *The kids had to fend for themselves while their parents were away.*
fend sb/sth ⇔ off *phr v* to defend yourself when you are being attacked, asked unwelcome questions etc: *She managed to fend off her attacker.*

fender /'fendə $ -ər/ n [C] **1** *AmE* the side part of a car that covers the wheels [= wing *BrE*] → see picture on page A12 **2** *BrE* a low wall or bar around a FIREPLACE to prevent wood or coal from falling out

ferment¹ /fə'ment $ fər-/ v [I,T] if fruit, wine etc ferments or is fermented, the sugar in it changes to alcohol —**fermentation** /ˌfɜːmen'teɪʃən $ ˌfɜːrmən-/ n [U]

ferment² /'fɜːment $ 'fɜːrn-/ n [U] excitement or trouble in a country, caused especially by political change: **in ferment** *In the 1960s, American society was in ferment.*

fern /fɜːn $ fɜːrn/ n [C] a plant with green leaves shaped like large feathers but no flowers

ferocious /fə'rəʊʃəs $ -'roʊ-/ adj violent, dangerous, and frightening: *a ferocious-looking dog* | *a ferocious battle* —**ferociously** adv

ferocity /fə'rɒsᵻti $ fə'rɑː-/ n [U] extreme violence: *Police were shocked by the ferocity of the attack.*

ferret¹ /'ferᵻt/ n [C] a small animal, used for hunting rats and rabbits

ferret² v
ferret sth ⇔ out *phr v informal* to succeed in finding something, especially information: *She finally managed to ferret out the truth.*

ferry¹ /'feri/ n [C] plural **ferries** a boat that regularly carries people, often with their cars, across a narrow area of water: *a car ferry* → see box at **SHIP** → see picture at **TRANSPORT**

ferry² v [T] **ferried, ferrying, ferries** to regularly carry people or goods a short distance from one place to another: *a bus that ferries tourists from the hotel to the beach*

fertile /'fɜːtaɪl $ 'fɜːrtl/ adj **1** fertile soil is able to produce good crops: *fertile land* **2** able to become PREGNANT or make someone pregnant [≠ infertile] **3** **fertile imagination/mind** an

imagination or mind that produces lots of interesting and unusual ideas —**fertility** /fɜː'tɪlᵻti $ fər-/ n [U]

fertilize also **-ise** *BrE* /'fɜːtᵻlaɪz $ 'fɜːrtl-aɪz/ v [T] **1** if an egg is fertilized, the egg and a SPERM join together so that a baby can start to develop **2** to put fertilizer on the soil to help plants grow —**fertilization** /ˌfɜːtᵻlaɪ'zeɪʃən $ ˌfɜːrtl-ə'zeɪ-/ n [U]

fertilizer also **-iser** *BrE* /'fɜːtᵻlaɪzə $ 'fɜːrtl-aɪzər/ n [C,U] a substance that is put on the soil to make plants grow

fervent /'fɜːvənt $ 'fɜːr-/ adj believing or feeling something very strongly: *a fervent supporter of human rights* —**fervently** adv

fervour *BrE*; **fervor** *AmE* /'fɜːvə $ 'fɜːrvər/ n [U] very strong belief or feeling: *religious fervour*

fest /fest/ n **beer/song/food etc fest** an informal occasion when a lot of people drink, sing, eat etc together

fester /'festə $ -ər/ v [I] **1** if an unpleasant feeling or problem festers, it gets worse because it has not been dealt with: *Don't allow resentment to fester.* **2** if a wound festers, it becomes infected

festival /'festᵻvəl/ n [C]
1 an occasion when there are performances of many films, plays, pieces of music etc: *the Cannes film festival* | **+of** *a festival of Irish music*
2 a special occasion when people celebrate something such as a religious event: *the Muslim religious festival of Ramadan*

festive /'festɪv/ adj happy and special, because people are celebrating something: *festive occasions* | **the festive season** (=Christmas)

festivities /fe'stɪvᵻtiz/ [plural] also **festivity** [U] n things that people do to celebrate, such as dancing, eating, and drinking

festoon /fe'stuːn/ v [T usually passive] to cover something with flowers, long pieces of cloth etc, as a decoration: *streets festooned with flags*

fetal /'fiːtl/ adj the usual American spelling of FOETAL

fetch /fetʃ/ v [T]
1 *especially BrE* to go and get something or someone and bring them back: *Go and fetch your Dad.* | **fetch sb/sth from sth** *He fetched a blanket from upstairs.* | **fetch sb sth/fetch sth for sb** *Could you fetch me a drink?* → see box at **BRING**
2 to be sold for a particular amount of money: *The painting fetched $1.2 million.*

fetching /'fetʃɪŋ/ adj attractive: *She looks very fetching in that dress.*

fête¹ /feɪt/ n [C] **1** *BrE* an outdoor event with games, competitions, and things for sale **2** *AmE* a special occasion to celebrate something

fête² v [T usually passive] to honour someone by holding public celebrations for them: *The team was feted from coast to coast.*

fetish /'fetɪʃ/ n [C] **1** something unusual that someone gets sexual pleasure from: *a leather fetish* **2** something that someone does too much or thinks about too much

fetus /'fiːtəs/ n the usual American spelling of FOETUS

feud /fjuːd/ n [C] hatred or violence between two people or groups that continues for a long time: *a feud between rival gangs* —**feud** v [I]

feudal /'fjuːdl/ adj the feudal system was the social system in the Middle Ages in which people received land and protection from a lord whom they worked and fought for —**feudalism** n [U]

fever /'fiːvə $ -ər/ n

1 [C,U] an illness in which you have a very high temperature: **have/run a fever** *She's had a fever since last night.* | *Nick was ill with a **high fever.*** **2** [singular, U] a situation in which people feel very excited or anxious: *election fever* | +**of** *In a fever of excitement, Kay flew to Rome.* | **fever pitch** (=when people's excitement or anxiety is very great) BrE: *By 1918, these fears had **reached fever pitch.***
—**fevered** adj → HAY FEVER

feverish /'fiːvərɪʃ/ adj **1** suffering from a fever: *I'm still slightly feverish.* **2** done extremely quickly because the situation is urgent: *feverish activity* **3** very excited or worried: *feverish anxiety* —**feverishly** adv

few /fjuː/ determiner, pron, adj

1 a small number of things or people: **a few** *Let's go away for a few days.* | *A few people were staring.* | *'Are there any biscuits left?' 'A few.'* | +**of** *I've read a few of her books.* | **the last/past/ next few** *the last few weeks*
2 quite a few/a good few a fairly large number of things or people: *He's a good few years older than me.* | *'How many girlfriends have you had?' 'Quite a few.'* | +**of** *Quite a few of our residents have pets.*
3 not many things or people [≠ **many**]: *low-paid jobs that few people want* | +**of** *Very few of my friends still live here.* | *Women are having fewer children.* | *the candidate with the fewest votes* | *It is one of the few programmes I enjoy.*
4 no fewer than used to emphasize that a number is large: *He was arrested no fewer than seven times.*
5 be few and far between to not happen often or not be found often: *Good jobs were few and far between.*

fiancé /fi'ɒnseɪ $ ˌfiːɑːn'seɪ/ n [C] the man whom a woman is going to marry

fiancée /fi'ɒnseɪ $ ˌfiːɑːn'seɪ/ n [C] the woman whom a man is going to marry

fiasco /fi'æskəʊ $ -koʊ/ n [C] plural **fiascoes** or **fiascos** an event that is completely unsuccessful, in a way that is very embarrassing or disappointing: *He tried to blame the whole fiasco on me.*

fib /fɪb/ n [C] *spoken* a small unimportant lie: *You shouldn't **tell** fibs.* → see box at LIE —**fib** v [I] —**fibber** n

fibre BrE; **fiber** AmE /'faɪbə $ -ər/ n **1** [U] the parts of plants that you eat but cannot DIGEST, which help food to move through your body: *food that is high in dietary fibre* **2** [C,U] a mass of threads used to make rope, cloth etc: *Nylon is a man-made fibre.* **3** [C] a thin thread, or one of the thin parts like threads that form natural materials such as wood —**fibrous** adj

fibreglass BrE; **fiberglass** AmE /'faɪbəglɑːs $ -bərglæs/ n [U] a light material made from small glass threads pressed together

fickle /'fɪkəl/ adj **1** *disapproving* someone who is fickle is always changing their opinion about people or things: *Voters are fickle.* **2** something that is fickle, such as the weather, often changes suddenly

fiction /'fɪkʃən/ n
1 [U] books and stories about imaginary people and events [≠ non-fiction]: *She writes children's fiction.* → see box at BOOK
2 [C,U] something that people want you to believe is true but which is not true: *'The idea that organic food is better for you is a fiction,' he said.*
→ SCIENCE FICTION

fictional /'fɪkʃənəl/ adj fictional people or events are from a book or story, and are not real

fictitious /fɪk'tɪʃəs/ adj not true, or not real: *a fictitious address*

fiddle¹ /'fɪdl/ n [C] **1** a VIOLIN **2** BrE informal a dishonest way of getting money: *an insurance fiddle*

fiddle² v [T] BrE informal to give false information about something, in order to avoid paying money or to get extra money: *Bert had been fiddling his income tax for years.*
fiddle with sth *phr v* **1** to keep moving and touching something, especially because you are bored or nervous: *She began fiddling with her necklace.* **2** also **fiddle around/about with** sth BrE to keep moving parts of a machine in order to make it work, without knowing exactly what you should do: *He fiddled with the controls until he had produced a clear sound.*

fiddler /'fɪdlə $ -ər/ n [C] someone who plays the VIOLIN

fiddly /'fɪdli/ adj difficult to use or do because you have to move very small objects: *a fiddly little switch*

fidelity /fɪ'delɪti/ n [U] formal loyalty, especially to your wife or husband by not having sex with other people [≠ infidelity]

fidget /'fɪdʒɪt/ v [I] to keep moving your hands or feet, especially because you are bored or nervous: *Stop fidgeting!* —**fidgety** adj

field¹ /fiːld/ n [C]
1 an area of land in the country, where crops are grown or animals feed on grass: *the fields around the village* | +**of** *a field of wheat* | **corn/ rice/wheat etc field**
2 an area of ground where sports are played: **baseball/football etc field** → see box at SPORT
3 a subject that people study or a type of work that they are involved in: +**of** *experts in the field of psychology* | *economists **working in** this field*

4 the field all the people, companies, or horses that are competing against each other: *Troke was **leading the field** (=was the most successful) after the first round of the competition.*

5 magnetic/gravitational/force field the area in which a natural force has an effect

6 coal/oil/gas field an area where there is a lot of coal, oil, or gas under the ground

7 field of view/vision the whole area that you can see without turning your head

8 have a field day to have a chance to do a lot of something that you enjoy, especially a chance to criticize someone: *The press had a field day when Tom left his wife.*

→ PLAYING FIELD, TRACK AND FIELD

field[2] *v* **1** [T] if you field a team, an army etc, they represent you or fight for you in a competition, election, or war: *The Ecology Party fielded 109 candidates.* **2** [T] to answer questions, telephone calls etc, especially when there are a lot of them or they are difficult **3 be fielding** the team that is fielding in a game of CRICKET, baseball etc is the one that is throwing and catching the ball, rather than the one hitting it

fielder /'fiːldə $ -ər/ *n* [C] one of the players who tries to catch the ball in CRICKET, baseball etc

'field ˌhockey *n* [U] *AmE* HOCKEY played on grass

'field ˌmarshal *n* [C] an officer of the highest rank in the British army

'field trip *n* [C] when students go somewhere to learn about a subject: *a geography field trip to Italy*

fieldwork /'fiːldwɜːk $ -wɜːrk/ *n* [U] study which involves going somewhere, rather than working in a class or LABORATORY

fiend /fiːnd/ *n* [C] **1** *literary* an evil person: *a sex fiend* **2** someone who is very interested in something and does it a lot: *a crossword fiend*

fiendish /'fiːndɪʃ/ *adj* **1** very clever in an unpleasant way: *a fiendish plot* **2** very difficult: *a fiendish puzzle* —**fiendishly** *adv*

fierce /fɪəs $ fɪrs/ *adj*
1 done with a lot of energy and strong feelings: *fierce fighting in the city* | *the fierce competition between the two companies* | *The proposal came under fierce attack.*
2 a fierce person or animal looks very violent or angry and ready to attack: *a fierce dog* | *a fierce look*
3 fierce heat, cold, wind etc is very extreme or severe: *the fierce afternoon sun*
—**fiercely** *adv* —**fierceness** *n* [U]

fiery /'faɪəri $ 'faɪri/ *adj* **1** full of strong or angry emotion: *a fiery speech* | *her fiery temper* **2** looking like fire or involving fire: *a fiery sunset*

fiesta /fi'estə/ *n* [C] a religious holiday with dancing, music etc, especially in Spain and South America

fifteen /ˌfɪf'tiːn◂/ *number* the number 15: *a village fifteen miles south of Tourane* | *They met when she was fifteen (=15 years old).*
—**fifteenth** *adj, pron*: *her fifteenth birthday* | *I'm planning to leave on the fifteenth (=the 15th day of the month).*

fifth[1] /fɪfθ/ *adj* coming after four things in a series: *her fifth birthday* —**fifth** *pron*: *I'm planning to leave on the fifth (=the fifth day of the month).* —**fifthly** *adv*

fifth[2] *n* [C] one of five equal parts of something

fifty /'fɪfti/ *number*
1 the number 50
2 the fifties also **the '50s, the 1950s** [plural] the years between 1950 and 1959: **the early/mid/late fifties** *The play was written in the late fifties.*
3 be in your fifties to be aged between 50 and 59: **early/mid/late fifties** *He's in his early fifties.*
4 in the fifties if the temperature is in the fifties, it is between 50 degrees and 59 degrees F
—**fiftieth** *adj*: *her fiftieth birthday*

fifty-'fifty *adj, adv spoken* **1** divided equally between two people: *Let's divide the profits fifty-fifty.* **2 a fifty-fifty chance** an equal chance that something will happen or will not happen: *The operation has a fifty-fifty chance of success.*

fig /fɪɡ/ *n* [C] a small soft sweet fruit that is often eaten dried, or the tree on which this grows

fig. the written abbreviation of **figure**

fight[1] /faɪt/ *v past tense and past participle* **fought** /fɔːt $ fɒːt/
1 [I,T] to take part in a war or battle: **+in** *Her father fought in World War I.* | **+against** *rebels fighting against the Russians* | *Neither country is capable of fighting a long war.*
2 [I,T] if people fight, they hit each other: *Will you two boys stop fighting!* | **+with** *Fans fought with police.*
3 [I] to try hard to do or get something: **+for** *We will continue to fight for equal rights.* | *The boy is in hospital fighting for his life (=he may die).* | **fight to do sth** *Parents are fighting to save the school.*
4 [I,T] to try hard to prevent something or to get rid of something: **+against** *He fought against racism all his life.* | *Protestors are fighting the plans.*
5 [T] to try to win an election or a court CASE: *Together they fought the general election of 1974.*
6 [I] to argue: *Rachel and her boyfriend are always fighting.* | **+with** *She didn't want to fight with her mother.* | **+about/over** *We used to fight over money.* → see box at ARGUE
7 fight it out to fight physically, argue, or compete until one person wins: *We left them to fight it out.*

fight back *phr v* **1** to work hard to achieve or oppose something, especially in a situation where you are losing: *Lewis fought back to win the match.* **2** to use violence or arguments against someone who has attacked you or criticized you: *She fought back, grabbing at his throat.* **3 fight sth ⇔ back** to try hard not to have or show a feeling: *'Go away,' said Julia, fighting back the tears.*

fight sb/sth ⇔ off *phr v* **1** to keep someone away, or to stop them doing something to you, by fighting or opposing them: *He managed to fight off his attacker.* **2** to succeed in stopping other people getting something, and to get it for yourself: *He fought off tough competition to get a place in the final.*

F

fight² n

1 [C] a situation in which two people or groups hit each other: *Sam's always getting into fights at school.* | **+with** *He got drunk and had a fight with Jim.* | **+between** *A fight broke out* (=started) *between the two gangs.*

> **THESAURUS**
>
> **brawl** – a noisy fight among a lot of people
> **free-for-all** *informal* – a fight or argument involving a lot of people
> **scuffle** – a short fight
> **scrap** *informal* – a short fight
> **boxing match**
> **wrestling match**

2 [singular] the process of trying very hard to achieve something or prevent something: **+for** *the fight for democracy* | **+against** *the fight against AIDS* | **fight to do sth** *their fight to remain in the UK*
3 [C] an argument: **+with** *They've had a fight with their neighbours.* | **+over/about** *fights over money* → see box at ARGUE
4 [C] a battle between two armies: **+for** *the fight for Bunker Hill*

fighter /'faɪtə $ -ər/ n [C] **1** also **'fighter plane** a small fast military plane that can destroy other planes **2** someone who fights, especially as a sport **3** someone who keeps trying to achieve something in difficult situations → FIREFIGHTER

fighting /'faɪtɪŋ/ n [U] when people or groups fight each other in a war, in the street etc: *seven days of heavy fighting*

figment /'fɪgmənt/ n **a figment of sb's imagination** something that someone imagines is real, but which does not exist

figurative /'fɪgjʊrətɪv, -gə-/ adj a figurative use of a word is one where it does not have its normal or basic meaning. For example, in 'a mountain of debt', 'mountain' is used in a figurative way and means 'a large amount' not 'a high hill'. —**figuratively** adv

figure¹ /'fɪgə $ 'fɪgjər/ n [C]

1 a) [usually plural] a number representing an amount, especially an official number: **unemployment/sales/crime etc figures** *the latest unemployment figures* | *Figures show that violent crime is increasing.* **b)** a number from 0 to 9, written as a sign, not as a word: *Write the amount in words and figures.* | **four/five/six etc figure** (=in the 1000s, 10,000s, 100,000s etc) *six figure salaries*: **double figures** (=the numbers from 10 to 99) *Inflation was in double figures.* | **single figures** (=the numbers 0 to 9)
2 a particular amount of money: **+of** *A figure of $35m was apparently paid.*
3 a) someone who is important or famous in some way: *leading figures in the art world* **b)** someone with a particular type of appearance or character, especially when they are difficult to see: *I could see a dark figure in the distance.* **c)** a person in a picture
4 the shape of someone's body, especially a woman: *She had a good figure.*
5 figures [plural] *BrE* the activity of adding, multiplying etc numbers: *Ray's good at figures.*
6 a shape in mathematics: *a six-sided figure*

7 a numbered drawing in a book written abbreviation *fig.*
→ FATHER FIGURE, PUBLIC FIGURE

figure² v **1** [I] to be included as an important part of something: **+in** *Marriage didn't really figure in their plans.* **2** [T] *informal* to have a particular opinion after thinking about a situation: **+(that)** *I figured it was time to leave.* → see box at THINK **3 that figures/it figures** *especially AmE spoken* used to say that something that happens is expected or typical, especially something bad: *'It rained the whole weekend.' 'That figures.'*

figure sb/sth ⇔ out *phr v* to understand something or someone after thinking about them: **+how/why etc** *Can you figure out how to do it?* | *Women. I just can't figure them out.*

figurehead /'fɪgəhed $ 'fɪgjər-/ n [C] a leader who has no real power

figure of 'speech n [C] a word or phrase that does not have its normal or basic meaning

filament /'fɪləmənt/ n [C] a very thin thread or wire

file¹ /faɪl/ n [C]

1 a set of papers, records etc that contain information about a particular person or subject: **+on** *The school keeps files on all students.* | **on file** (=kept in an official file) *All the details are on file.* | *patients' medical files* → see box at RECORD
2 a box or folded piece of thick stiff paper in which you keep loose papers → see picture at CLASSROOM
3 information on a computer that you store under a particular name: **open/close a file** *Click on the icon to open the file.* | **create/copy/save/delete a file** → see box at COMPUTER
4 a metal tool with a rough surface that you rub on something to make it smooth
5 in single file moving in a line, with one person behind another: *The path was so narrow we had to walk in single file.*
→ NAIL FILE

file² v **1** [T] to store papers or information in a particular order or a particular place: *The letters are filed alphabetically.* **2** [I,T] *law* to give a document to a court or other organization so that it can be officially recorded and dealt with: *I intend to file a formal complaint.* **3** [I] if people file somewhere, they walk in a line, one behind the other: **+into/out of etc** *The jury filed into the courtroom.* **4** [T] to rub something with a metal tool to make it smooth or cut it: *She sat filing her nails.*

filet /'fɪlɪt $ 'fɪlɪt, -leɪ, fɪ'leɪ/ n, v the usual American spelling of FILLET

'filing ,cabinet *BrE*; **'file ,cabinet** *AmE* n [C] a piece of office furniture with drawers for storing important papers → see box at OFFICE

fill¹ /fɪl/ v

1 a) also **fill up** [I,T] to make something become full, or to become full: *She filled the kettle.* | *He kept filling our glasses up.* | **fill (sth) with sth** *Her eyes filled with tears.* **b)** [T] to be in all or most of the space somewhere: *the expensive ornaments that filled the apartment* | **be filled with sth** *The theatre was filled with smoke.*
2 [T] if a sound, smell, or light fills a place, you notice it because it is very loud or strong: *The smell of cooking filled the kitchen.* | **be filled**

with sth *The air was filled with the sound of birds.*
3 [T] if you are filled with an emotion, you feel it very strongly: **be filled with sth** *Elaine was suddenly filled with fear.* | **fill sb with sth** *The idea filled me with excitement.*
4 [T] to provide something that is needed or wanted: **fill a need/demand** *His book undoubtedly fills a need.* | *The company is filling a gap in the market.*
5 [T] if you fill a period of time with a particular activity, you spend that time doing it: **fill your time/the days etc (with sth)** *How do you fill your days?*
6 [T] to perform a particular job, activity, or purpose in an organization, or to find someone or something to do this: **fill a post/position/vacancy etc** *We need someone to fill the position of Editor.* | *The post has already been filled.*
7 also **fill in** [T] to put a substance into a hole, crack etc to make a surface level: *Fill any cracks in the wall before you paint.*

fill sb/sth **in** *phr v* **1 fill sth ⇔ in** to write all the necessary information on an official document, form etc: *You'll have to fill in an application form.* → see box at **WRITE** → and **JOB** **2** to tell someone about recent events: **+on** *I'll fill you in on all the news later.*

fill out *phr v* **1 fill sth ⇔ out** to write all the necessary information on an official document, form etc → see box at **WRITE** → and **JOB** **2** to get fatter: *Her face is beginning to fill out.*

fill² *n* **your fill** as much of something as you want, or can deal with: *I've had my fill of screaming kids today!*

fillet¹ *BrE*; **filet** *AmE* /ˈfɪlɨt $ ˈfɪlɨt, -leɪ, fɪˈleɪ/ *n* [C,U] a piece of meat or fish without bones

fillet² *BeE*; **filet** *AmE v* [T] to remove the bones from a piece of meat or fish

filling¹ /ˈfɪlɪŋ/ *adj* food that is filling makes your stomach feel full

filling² *n* **1** [C] a small amount of metal that is put into a hole in your tooth **2** [C,U] the food that is put inside a PIE, SANDWICH etc: *apple pie filling*

ˈfilling ˌstation *n* [C] a place where you can buy petrol for your car

film¹ /fɪlm/ *n*

1 [C] a story that is told using moving pictures, shown at a cinema or on television [= **movie**]: **watch/see a film** *I saw a great film last night.* | **+about** *a film about a young dancer* | *a horror film* (=very frightening film) | **film director/producer/crew etc** | **show/screen a film** *The film will be shown on Channel 4.* → see box at **TELEVISION**

THESAURUS

feature film – a full-length film made for the cinema
comedy – a film intended to make people laugh
romantic comedy – a film about love that is intended to make the people who watch it feel happy
thriller – an exciting film about murder or serious crimes
western – a film with cowboys in it
action film – a film that has lots of fighting,

explosions etc
horror film – a frightening film about ghosts etc
science fiction film – a film about imaginary events in the future
animated film/cartoon – a film with characters that are drawn or made using a computer
actor – a man or woman who acts in a film
actress – a woman who acts in a film
star – a famous actor or actress
director – the person who tells the actors and actresses in a film what to do
producer – the person who makes the arrangements for a film to be made and controls the film's budget (=the money available to make the film)
film crew – the people operating the camera, lights etc who help the director make a film

2 [U] the work of making films, considered as an art or a business: *I'd like to work in film.* | *the film industry*
3 [U] moving pictures of real events that are shown on television or at a cinema: *film footage* (=pictures) *of the riot*
4 [C,U] the thin plastic used in a camera for taking photographs or recording moving pictures: *a roll of film* → see box at **CAMERA**
5 [singular] a very thin layer of liquid, powder etc on the surface of something: **+of** *a film of sweat*

film² *v* [I,T] to make a film of something for the cinema or television: *The movie was filmed in China.*

ˈfilm-ˌmaker *n* [C] someone who makes films for the cinema or television

filter¹ /ˈfɪltə $ -ər/ *n* [C] a piece of equipment that you put gas or liquid through in order to remove solid substances that are not wanted: *a water filter*

filter² *v* **1** [T] to clean a liquid or gas using a filter: *filtered drinking water* **2** [I] if people filter somewhere, they gradually move there: *The audience began to filter into the hall.* **3** [I] if information filters somewhere, people gradually hear about it: *The news slowly filtered through to everyone in the office.*

filth /fɪlθ/ *n* [U] **1** dirt: *Wash that filth off your shoes.* **2** very offensive language, or pictures about sex

filthy /ˈfɪlθi/ *adj* **1** extremely dirty: *Doesn't he ever wash that jacket? It's filthy.* → see box at **DIRTY** **2** very rude or offensive, especially about sex: *filthy language*

fin /fɪn/ *n* [C] **1** one of the thin parts on the side of its body that a fish uses to swim → see picture on page A2 **2** part of a plane that sticks up at the back and helps it to fly smoothly

final¹ /ˈfaɪnəl/ *adj*

1 [only before noun] last in a series: *the final chapter of the book* | *students preparing for their final examinations* | *the final stages in their relationship*
2 if a decision, offer, or agreement is final, it cannot be changed: *Is that your final decision?* | *£300 is my final offer.*
3 [only before noun] happening at the end of a long process: *I can't wait to see the final product.*

F

final² *n* [C]

1 the last and most important game, race etc in a competition: *the World Cup Final* | *He didn't get through to the finals.*
2 finals [plural] *BrE* the examinations that students take at the end of their last year at university → see box at **UNIVERSITY**
3 *AmE* an important test that you take at the end of a class in high school or college
→ **SEMI-FINAL**

finale /fɪˈnɑːli $ fɪˈnæli/ *n* [C] the last part of a piece of music or a show, which is often the most exciting part: *Everyone was on stage for the grand finale.*

finalist /ˈfaɪnəl‑ɪst/ *n* [C] one of the people or teams that reaches the last part of a competition

finality /faɪˈnæləti/ *n* [U] when something is finished and cannot be changed: *the finality of death*

finalize also **-ise** *BrE* /ˈfaɪnəl‑aɪz/ *v* [T] to decide firmly on the details of a plan or arrangement: *Can we finalize the details of the deal?*

finally /ˈfaɪnəl‑i/ *adv*

1 after a long time [= **eventually**]: *After several delays, the plane finally took off at six o'clock.*
2 used when you are introducing the last of a series of things [= **lastly**]: *And finally, I'd like to thank my teachers.* → see box at **LASTLY**
3 in a way that does not allow changes: *It's not finally settled yet.*

finance /ˈfaɪnæns, fɪ̆ˈnæns $ fɪ̆ˈnæns, ˈfaɪnæns/ *n*

1 [U] the control of how money should be spent, especially in a company or government: *the finance department*
2 [U] money provided by a bank to help you to pay for something: *How will you get the finance to start your business?*
3 finances [plural] the money that a person or organization has: *The school's finances are limited.*
—**finance** *v* [T] *How will the new service be financed?*

financial /fɪ̆ˈnænʃəl, faɪ‑/ *adj* relating to money or the management of money: *a financial adviser* | *financial aid* | *The film was not a financial success* (=it did not make much money).
—**financially** *adv*: *He was successful and financially secure.*

financier /fɪ̆ˈnænsɪə, faɪˈnæn‑ $ ˌfɪnənˈsɪr/ *n* [C] someone who controls or lends large sums of money

finch /fɪntʃ/ *n* [C] a small wild bird with a short beak

find¹ /faɪnd/ *v* [T] past tense and past participle **found** /faʊnd/

1 to discover or get something that you have been looking for: *Will you help me find my bag?* | *I can't find my keys.* | *I have to find somewhere to live.* | **find sb sth** (=find something for someone) *I think we can find you a job.*
2 to discover something by chance: *She found a purse in the street.* | *We found a really good bar near the hotel.*
3 to see something: **find sb doing sth** *When the police arrived, they found him lying on the floor.* |

+**(that)** *Michael woke up to find that the bedroom was flooded.*
4 to discover or learn new information: *Scientists are still trying to find a cure for AIDS.* | +**that** *They found that men are better at reading maps than women.*
5 to have an opinion or feeling about someone or something: *I don't find his jokes at all funny.* | *She found the work very dull.* | **find it hard/easy etc to do sth** *I found it hard to understand her.*
6 to learn or know something by experience: +**that** *I soon found that it was quicker to go by bus.*
7 to have enough time, money, energy etc to be able to do what you want to do: *When do you find the time to read?*
8 be found to live or exist somewhere: *This species is only found in West Africa.*
9 find yourself somewhere to be in a place although you did not plan to be there: *At the end of the evening I found myself in the city centre.*
10 find your way (somewhere) to arrive at a place by discovering the way to get there: *Can you find your way, or do you need a map?*
11 find sb guilty/not guilty (of sth) *law* to officially decide that someone is guilty or not guilty of a crime: *He was found guilty of murder.*
12 find fault with sb/sth to criticize someone or something: *The teacher would always find fault with my work.*
13 find your feet to become confident in a new situation: *Matt's only been at the school two weeks and he hasn't found his feet yet.*

find out *phr v* **1** to get information about something or someone: **find sth** ⇔ **out** *We never found out her name.* | +**what/how/where etc** *He hurried off to find out what the problem was.* | +**about** *If Dad finds out about this, he'll go crazy.* | +**(that)** *I found out that my parents had never been married.* **2 find sb out** to discover that someone has been doing something dishonest or illegal: *What happens if we're found out?*

find² *n* [C] something good or useful that you discover by chance: *That little Greek restaurant was a real find.*

findings /ˈfaɪndɪŋz/ *n* [plural] the information that people have learned as a result of their study, work etc: *The Commission's findings are presented in a report.*

fine¹ /faɪn/ *adj*

1 satisfactory or acceptable: *'We're meeting at 8.30.' 'Okay, fine.'* | *In theory, the plan sounds fine.* | +**by** *If you want to meet up with us later, that's fine by me.*
2 healthy or reasonably happy: *'How are you?' 'I'm fine, thanks.'*
3 very good: *a fine performance by William Hurt* | *a selection of fine wines*
4 very thin or narrow, or made of very small pieces: *a fine layer of dust* | *a fine thread* | *fine sand*
5 fine details or differences are small or exact and difficult to see: *I didn't understand some of the finer points in the argument.*
6 fine weather is bright and sunny

fine² *adv* *informal* well: *'How's everything going?' 'Fine.'* | *The car's working fine now.*

fine³ n [C] money that you have to pay as a punishment for breaking a law or rule: *a parking fine* → see box at **PUNISHMENT**
—**fine** v [T] *He was fined £100 for speeding.*

finely /'faɪnli/ adv **1** into very small pieces: *finely chopped onion* **2** very exactly: *finely tuned instruments*

fine 'print n [U] SMALL PRINT

finesse /fɪ'nes/ n [U] if you do something with finesse, you do it with a lot of skill and style

fine-'tune v [T] to make very small changes to something such as a machine or a plan, so that it works as well as possible: *We fine-tuned the scheme and made some useful improvements.*
—**fine tuning** n [U]

finger¹ /'fɪŋgə $ -ər/ n
1 [C] one of the four long thin parts on your hand, not including your thumb: *We ate with our fingers.* → see picture on page A3
2 keep your fingers crossed *spoken* to hope that something will happen in the way you want it to: *We're keeping our fingers crossed that she's going to be OK.*
3 not lift a finger *spoken* to not make any effort to help someone: *I do all the work – Frank never lifts a finger.*
4 put your finger on sth to realize exactly what is wrong, different, or unusual about something: *There's something strange about him, but I can't put my finger on it.*
→ **INDEX FINGER, LITTLE FINGER**

finger² v [T] to touch or feel something with your fingers

fingernail /'fɪŋgəneɪl $ -gər-/ n [C] the hard flat part that covers the top end of your finger → see picture at **HAND¹**

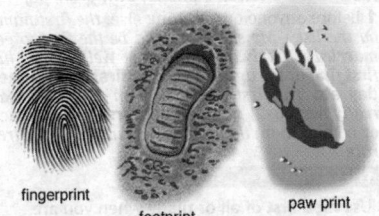

fingerprint

fingerprint

footprint

paw print

fingerprint /'fɪŋgə,prɪnt $ -gər-/ n [C] the mark made by the pattern of lines at the end of someone's finger

fingertip /'fɪŋgə,tɪp $ -gər-/ n **1** [C] the end of your finger **2 have sth at your fingertips** to have information easily available and ready to use

finicky /'fɪnɪki/ adj *disapproving* too concerned with small details and only approving of things that are correct in every way [= fussy]: *She's finicky about what she eats.*

finish¹ /'fɪnɪʃ/ v
1 also **finish off** [I,T] to come to the end of doing or making something [≠ start]: *Have you finished your homework?* | **finish doing sth** *Let me just finish typing this report.* | *I've done most of the work – I'll finish it off tomorrow.* | **finish (sth)**

with sth (=do something as the last thing) *He used to finish his act with a song.*
2 [I] *especially BrE* to end: *What time does the concert finish?*
3 also **finish up/off** [T] to eat, drink, or use all the rest of something: *Finish your breakfast before it gets cold, Tom.* | *Who finished off the cake?*
4 finish second/third etc to be in second, third etc position at the end of a race, competition etc: *He finished second in the 100 metres.*

finish up phr v *BrE informal* to arrive at a particular place, after going to other places first: *We finished up in Rome after a three week tour.*

finish with sb/sth phr v **1 have/be finished with sth** to no longer need to use something: *Have you finished with the scissors?* **2** *BrE* to end a romantic or sexual relationship with someone: *He's finished with Elise after all these years.*

finish² n **1** [singular] the end of something, especially a race: *It was a **close finish** (=the race ended with the competitors close together), but Jarrett won.* **2** [C] the way a surface looks after it has been painted or polished: *a table with a glossy finish* → **PHOTO FINISH**

finished /'fɪnɪʃt/ adj **1** [only before noun] completed: *the finished product* **2** [not before noun] if you are finished, you have finished doing something: *I'm almost finished.* **3** [not before noun] *informal* no longer able to continue successfully: *If the bank doesn't lend us the money, we're finished.*

finite /'faɪnaɪt/ adj having an end or a limit: *Earth's finite resources*

fir /fɜː $ fɜːr/ also **'fir tree** n [C] a tree with leaves shaped like needles that do not fall off in autumn

fire¹ /faɪə $ faɪr/ n
1 [C,U] uncontrolled flames and heat that destroy and damage things: *Fire destroyed part of the building.* | *a forest fire* | *One of the plane's engines had **caught fire**.* | **on fire** (=burning) *The house is on fire!* | *Police think that the fire was **started** deliberately.* | *An angry crowd **set fire to** several vehicles.* | *Sparks from the fireplace could easily **set** the curtains **on fire**.* | *It took firefighters two days to **put out** the fire* (=stop it burning).

THESAURUS

flames – the bright parts of a fire that you see burning in the air
blaze – a word for a large and dangerous fire, used in news reports: *Firemen fought to keep the blaze under control.*
inferno *literary* – a very large and very dangerous fire: *Soon, the house became a raging inferno.*
bonfire – a large outdoor fire that people make for a celebration
break out – to start suddenly
burn – to produce heat and flames
rage/blaze – to burn strongly for a long time over a large area
die down – to stop burning strongly
smoulder – to burn slowly with no flames and only a little smoke
go out/die – to stop burning completely

F

2 [C] a pile of burning wood or coal used to heat a room or cook food: *a camp fire* | *a coal fire* | *Come and sit in front of the fire.*

3 [C] *BrE* a piece of equipment that uses gas or electricity to heat a room: *an **electric fire*** | *Could you **turn the fire on***, please?

4 [U] when guns are fired: *Troops **opened fire** on the demonstrators.*

5 be/come under fire to be criticized

fire² *v*

1 [I,T] to shoot bullets from a gun: **+at/on/into** *Soldiers fired on the crowd.* | *He fired three shots.*

2 [T] to make someone leave their job [= **sack** *BrE*]: *She didn't want to get fired.* | **fire sb from sth** *I've just been fired from my job.*

3 also **fire up** [T] to make someone very excited or interested in something: *exciting stories that fired our imagination*

4 fire questions at sb to ask someone a lot of questions very quickly: *The reporters fired non-stop questions at him.*

5 oil/gas-fired *BrE* using oil or gas to produce heat or energy: *a coal-fired power station*

fire away *phr v spoken* used to tell someone that you are ready to answer questions: *'Do you mind if I ask you something?' 'Fire away.'*

'fire a,larm *n* [C] a piece of equipment that makes a loud noise to warn people of a fire in a building

firearm /'faɪərɑːm $ 'faɪrɑːrm/ *n* [C] *formal* a gun

'fire bri,gade *BrE*; **'fire de,partment** *AmE n* [C] the FIRE SERVICE

firecracker /'faɪə,krækə $ 'faɪr,krækər/ *n* [C] a small FIREWORK that makes a loud noise when it explodes

,fired-'up *adj* very excited, interested, or angry about something: *The crowd began to get all fired-up.*

'fire ,engine *n* [C] a large vehicle that carries FIREFIGHTERS and their equipment

'fire es,cape *n* [C] metal stairs on the outside of a building, that people can use to escape if there is a fire

'fire ex,tinguisher *n* [C] a piece of equipment used for stopping small fires

firefighter /'faɪə,faɪtə $ 'faɪr,faɪtər/ *n* [C] someone whose job is to stop fires burning

'fire ,hydrant *n* [C] a water pipe in the street used to get water for stopping fires burning

firelight /'faɪəlaɪt $ 'faɪr-/ *n* [U] the light produced by a small fire: *The room glowed in the firelight.*

fireman /'faɪəmən $ 'faɪr-/ *n* [C] plural **firemen** /-mən/ a man whose job is to stop fires burning

fireplace /'faɪəpleɪs $ 'faɪr-/ *n* [C] an open place in the wall of a room, where you can make a fire to heat the room

fireproof /'faɪəpruːf $ 'faɪr-/ *adj* something that is fireproof cannot be damaged by fire: *a fireproof door*

'fire ,service *n* [C] an organization that works to stop fires

fireside /'faɪəsaɪd $ 'faɪr-/ *n* [singular] the area around a small fire in a home: *a cat dozing by the fireside*

'fire ,station *n* [C] a building for FIREFIGHTERS and their equipment and vehicles

'fire truck *n* [C] *AmE* a FIRE ENGINE

firewall /'faɪəwɔːl $ 'faɪrwɒːl/ *n* [C] a system that protects a computer network from being used by people who do not have permission to do so

firewood /'faɪəwʊd $ 'faɪr-/ *n* [U] wood for burning on a fire

firework /'faɪəwɜːk $ 'faɪrwɜːrk/ *n* [C usually plural] an object that burns or explodes to produce coloured lights and noise in the sky: *a fourth of July **fireworks display***

'firing squad *n* [C] a group of soldiers whose duty is to shoot and kill a prisoner

firm¹ /fɜːm $ fɜːrm/ *adj*

1 not soft, and not easy to bend into a different shape: *a bed with a firm mattress* | *Choose the firmest tomatoes.*

2 [only before noun] definite and not likely to change: *No firm decision has been reached.* | *They remained **firm friends**.*

3 strong and in control: *This country needs firm leadership.* | **+with** *You need to be firm with children.*

4 strongly fixed in position, and not likely to move: *Make sure the ladder feels firm before you climb up.*

5 a firm grip/grasp/hold etc a way of holding something tightly and strongly: *Joe took her hand in his firm grip.*

—**firmly** *adv* —**firmness** *n* [U]

firm² *n* [C] a business or company: *an engineering firm* | *a law firm* → see box at COMPANY

firm³ *v* [T]

firm sth ⇔ up *phr v* **1** to make arrangements more definite: *We hope to firm up the deal next week.* **2** to make the muscles of your body harder and firmer

first¹ /fɜːst $ fɜːrst/ *number, adv, pron, adj*

1 before anyone or anything else: *the first name on the list* | *My sister said I'd be the first to get married.* | *Cindy arrived first.* | *Welles made his first film at the age of 25.* | **the first thing/time/day etc** *The first time I flew on a plane I was really nervous.* | **come/finish first** (=win a race or competition) *Jane came first in the 100 metres race.*

THESAURUS

Use **first, first of all** or **firstly** when you are giving a list of points, reasons etc: *There are three reasons for this. Firstly ...*
Use **first** or **first of all** to say what happens first in a series of actions: *First I checked my e-mail. Then I made a couple of calls.*
Use **at first** to say what happened at the beginning of a situation or time, when this changed later: *At first, we were very happy together.*

2 before anything else happens, or before doing anything else: *I always read the sports page first.* | *Do your homework first, then you can go out.*

3 when you first do something, it is new to you and you have not done it before: *I first met him in Paris.*

4 most important: *Our first priority must be to restore peace.* | *Ron's kids always **come first** (=are most important).*

5 first prize the prize for the person who wins a competition
6 at first in the beginning: *At first, Gregory was shy and hardly spoke.*
7 in the first place a) used to give the first in a list of reasons: *Quinn couldn't have committed the crime. In the first place he's not a violent man.* **b)** used to talk about the beginning of a situation: *Why did you agree to meet her in the first place?*
8 for the first time used to say that something has never happened or been done before: *For the first time in his life he felt truly happy.*
9 first/first of all a) before doing anything else: *First, I'd like to thank everyone for coming.* **b)** used before saying the first of several things you want to say: *I don't think Helen should go – first of all she's too young.*
10 first thing as soon as you wake up or start work in the morning: *I'll call you first thing tomorrow, okay?*
11 at first glance/sight the first time that you look at someone or something, before you notice any details: *At first sight, there didn't appear to be much damage.*
12 your first choice the thing or person you like best
→ HEAD-FIRST

first² n [C] **1** something that has never happened before: **+for** *The 3–0 defeat was a first for the team.* **2** the highest level of university degree you can get in Britain: *Helen got a first in law.*

,**first 'aid** n [U] simple medical treatment that is given as soon as possible to someone who is injured or who suddenly becomes ill

,**first-'class** adj **1** excellent: *Eric has proved himself a first-class performer.* → see box at **GOOD 2** a first-class ticket is a ticket for the most expensive type of seats on a plane or train —**first class** adv: *passengers travelling first class*

,**first 'floor** n [singular] **1** *BrE* the floor of a building just above the one at the bottom level **2** *AmE* the floor of a building at the bottom level, where you go into the building [= **ground floor** *BrE*] → see box at **FLOOR**

firsthand /ˈfɜːstˈhænd $ ˈfɜːrst-/ adj [only before noun] firsthand knowledge is knowledge that you get or learn yourself, not from other people: *officers with firsthand experience of war* —**firsthand** /ˌfɜːstˈhænd $ ˌfɜːrst-/ adv: *experience you have gained firsthand*

,**first 'language** n [C] the language that you first learn as a child

firstly /ˈfɜːstli $ -ɜːr-/ adv used before saying the first of several things: *Firstly, I would like to thank everyone who has contributed to this success.* → see box at **FIRST**

'**first name** n [C] a name that comes before your family name [➥ **last name, middle name**]: *My teacher's first name is Caroline.* → see box at **NAME**

,**first 'person** n [singular] **the first person** the form of the verb that you use with 'I' and 'we' [➥ **second person, third person**]

,**first-'rate** adj excellent: *a first-rate show*

fiscal /ˈfɪskəl/ adj relating to money and taxes that are managed by the government: *the city's fiscal policies*

fish¹ /fɪʃ/ n plural **fish** or **fishes**
1 [C] an animal that lives, breathes, and swims in water: *How many fish did you catch?*
2 [U] the flesh of a fish used as food: *We had fish for dinner.*

fish² v **1** [I] to try to catch fish: **+for** *Dad's fishing for salmon.* **2** [I,T] to search for something in a bag, pocket etc, or to bring it out when you have found it: **+about/around** *She fished around in her purse and pulled out a photo.* | **fish sth out** *Sally opened her briefcase and fished out a small card.*

fisherman /ˈfɪʃəmən $ -ʃər-/ n [C] plural **fishermen** /-mən/ a man who catches fish as a job or a sport

fishing /ˈfɪʃɪŋ/ n [U] the sport or job of catching fish: *Do you want to go fishing?*

'**fishing rod** also '**fishing pole** *AmE* n [C] a long stick with a string and a hook tied to it, used for catching fish

fishmonger /ˈfɪʃmʌŋɡə $ -mɑːŋɡər, -mʌŋ-/ n [C] *especially BrE* **1** someone who sells fish **2** also **fishmonger's** a shop that sells fish

fishy /ˈfɪʃi/ adj **1** *informal* seeming bad or dishonest: *There's something fishy about this business.* **2** tasting or smelling like fish

fist /fɪst/ n [C] a hand closed with all the fingers curled inwards: *She shook her fist angrily.*

fistful /ˈfɪstfʊl/ n [C] the amount that you can hold in your hand: **+of** *a man waving a fistful of cash*

fit¹ /fɪt/ v **fitted, fitting** *BrE*; **fit** or **fitted, fitting** *AmE*
1 [I,T] to be the right size and shape for someone or something: *I wonder if my wedding dress still fits me?* | *This lid doesn't fit very well.* → see box at **CLOTHES**
2 [I,T] to put or fix something in the place where it will be used: **fit sth on/in etc sth** *We're having new locks fitted on all the main doors.*
3 [I,T] if something fits into a place, there is enough space for it: **+in/into** *Will the cases fit in the back of your car?* | **fit sth in/into sth** *I can't fit anything else into this suitcase.*
4 [T] to be suitable for something: *The music fits the words perfectly.* | *The punishment should fit the crime.*
fit in phr v **1** if someone fits in, they are accepted by the other people in a group: *The new students all had a hard time fitting in.* **2 fit sb/sth ⇔ in** to manage to do something or see someone, even though you have a lot of other things to do: *Dr. Tyler can fit you in on Monday at 3:30.* **3** if something fits in with other things, it is similar to them or goes well with them: **+with** *A new building must fit in with its surroundings.*
fit sb/sth ⇔ out phr v to provide a person or place with the equipment, furniture, or clothes that they need: *The office had been fitted out in style.*

fit² adj
1 suitable or good enough: **+for** *This book is not fit for publication! | After the party he was not in a fit state to drive.*
2 *especially BrE* healthy and strong, especially because you exercise regularly [≠ **unfit**]: *Jogging helps me keep fit. | He was young and physically fit.*

F

3 see/think fit to do sth to decide that it is right to do something, even though other people may disagree: *Do whatever you think fit.*
→ **KEEP FIT**

fit³ *n* **1 have/throw a fit** *informal* to become very angry: *If your mother finds out about this she'll have a fit.* **2** [C] a short time during which you laugh or cough a lot, or become very angry, in a way that you cannot control: *a coughing fit | a fit of rage* **3** [C] a short period of time when someone loses consciousness and cannot control their body because their brain is not working properly: *an epileptic fit* **4 be a good/tight/perfect etc fit** to fit a person or a particular space well, tightly, perfectly etc: *The skirt's a perfect fit.*

fitful /'fɪtfəl/ *adj* something that is fitful is not continuous or regular: *a fitful sleep*

fitness /'fɪtnəs/ *n* [U] **1** when you are healthy and strong enough to play sports or do physical work: *physical fitness* **2** when someone or something is suitable: +**for** *He had doubts about her fitness for the job.*

fitted /'fɪtɪd/ *adj* **1 be fitted with sth** to have something as a permanent part: *Is your car fitted with an alarm?* **2** [only before noun] *BrE* made to fit a space exactly: *a fitted kitchen | a fitted carpet | fitted cupboards*

fitting¹ /'fɪtɪŋ/ *n* [C usually plural] *BrE* a piece of equipment in a house that seems to be attached to the house but can be removed so that you can take it with you if you sell the house [→ **fixture**]: *I like these light fittings.*

fitting² *adj formal* suitable: *The statue is a fitting tribute to the President.*

five /faɪv/ *number* the number 5: *The town is five miles away. | I'll be back by five* (=five o'clock). *| He is five* (=five years old).
→ **NINE-TO-FIVE**

fiver /'faɪvə $ -ər/ *n* [C] *BrE informal* a piece of paper money worth five pounds

fix¹ /fɪks/ *v* [T]

1 to repair something: *I've fixed your bike. | She fixed the problem.* → see box at **REPAIR**
2 to decide on an exact time, place, price etc: *Have you fixed a date for the wedding yet? | The interest rate was fixed at 6.5%.*
3 *BrE* to fasten something to something else so that it will not come off: **fix sth to/onto sth** *She fixed the shelf to the wall.*
4 *AmE* to prepare a meal or drink: *Mom was fixing dinner.*
5 *AmE* to make your hair or **MAKE-UP** look neat and attractive: *I need to fix my hair.*
6 to arrange an election or game dishonestly so that you get the result you want: *The deal was fixed in advance.*

fix sb/sth ⇔ up *phr v* **1** *BrE* to arrange an event or trip: *We need to fix up a meeting.* **2** to decorate or repair a room or building: *We fixed up the guest bedroom.* **3** to provide someone with something they want: +**with** *Can you fix me up with a bed for the night?*

fix² *n* **1 quick fix** something that solves a problem quickly but is only a temporary solution **2 (be) in a fix** to have a problem that is difficult to solve: *We'll be in a fix if we miss the bus.* **3** [singular] an amount of an illegal drug that someone takes and needs regularly

4 [singular] a result of a game or election that has been arranged in a dishonest way: *The election was a fix.*

fixation /fɪk'seɪʃən/ *n* [C] a very strong interest in someone or something, that is not natural or healthy: +**with/on/about** *He had a fixation with guns.* —**fixated** /-'seɪtɪd/ *adj*

fixed /fɪkst/ *adj* **1** firmly fastened in a particular position: **to/in/on** *a mirror fixed to the wall* **2** a time or amount cannot be changed: *The classes begin and end at fixed times. | fixed prices* **3 have fixed ideas/opinions** *disapproving* to have ideas or opinions that you will not change

fixedly /'fɪksədli/ *adv* without looking at or thinking about anything else: **stare/gaze/look fixedly at sth** *Ann stared fixedly at the screen.*

fixture /'fɪkstʃə $ -ər/ *n* [C] **1** *BrE* a sports event that has been arranged **2** [usually plural] a piece of equipment that is fixed inside a house and is sold as part of the house [→ **fitting**]

fizz /fɪz/ *n* [singular,U] the **BUBBLES** of gas in some drinks, or the sound they make: *The mineral water has lost its fizz.* —**fizz** *v* [I] → see picture on page A7

fizzle /'fɪzəl/ *v*
fizzle out *phr v* to gradually end in a weak or disappointing way: *Their relationship fizzled out.*

fizzy /'fɪzi/ *adj* a fizzy drink contains gas

flab /flæb/ *n* [U] *informal* soft, loose fat on a person's body

flabbergasted /'flæbəgɑːstɪd $ -bərgæs-/ *adj informal* very surprised → see box at **SURPRISED**

flabby /'flæbi/ *adj* a part of your body that is flabby has too much soft loose fat: *flabby arms*

flag¹ /flæg/ *n* [C]

1 a piece of cloth with a picture or pattern that is used as the sign of a country or organization: *the French flag | Children **waving flags** greeted the Russian leader.*
2 a piece of coloured cloth used in some sports as a sign or signal: *The flag went down and the race began.*

flag² *v* [I] **flagged, flagging** to become tired or weak: *By the end of the meeting we had begun to flag.* —**flagging** *adj*
flag sb/sth ⇔ down *phr v* to make the driver of a vehicle stop by waving at them: *I flagged down a taxi.*

flagpole /'flægpəʊl $ -poʊl/ *n* [C] a tall pole for a flag

flagrant /'fleɪɡrənt/ *adj* a flagrant action is shocking because it is done in a very noticeable way and shows no respect for the law, the truth etc: **flagrant abuse/violation/breach etc** *a flagrant abuse of power* —**flagrantly** *adv*

flagship /'flæɡʃɪp/ *n* [C usually singular] a company's best and most important product, building etc: *the flagship of the Ford range*

flagstone /'flæɡstəʊn $ -stoʊn/ *n* [C] a smooth flat piece of stone used for floors, paths etc

flail /fleɪl/ *v* [I,T] to move your arms and legs about in an uncontrolled way: *He flailed wildly as she held him down.*

flair /fleə $ fler/ *n* [singular,U] a natural ability to do something well: *He **has a flair** for languages. | **artistic/creative flair** a job that requires artistic flair*

flak /flæk/ n [U] *informal* criticism: *She got a lot of flak for that decision.*

flake¹ /fleɪk/ n [C] a small flat thin piece of something: *The paint was coming off the door in flakes.* —**flaky** *adj*

flake² v [I] to break off in small thin pieces: *The paint is flaking off.*

  flake out *phr v BrE informal* to fall asleep because you are very tired: *He flaked out on the sofa.*

flamboyant /flæm'bɔɪənt/ *adj* **1** behaving in a confident or exciting way that makes people notice you: *a flamboyant gesture* **2** brightly coloured: *flamboyant clothes*

flame¹ /fleɪm/ n

1 [C,U] a bright moving yellow or orange light that you see when something is burning: *Flames poured out of the building.* | *They doused the flames* (=poured water on them to stop them burning). → see box at **FIRE**

2 in flames burning in a way that is difficult to control: *The house was in flames.* | **go up in flames/burst into flames** *The plane burst into flames.*

→ **OLD FLAME**

flame² v [I,T] to send someone an angry or rude message on the Internet

flaming /'fleɪmɪŋ/ *adj* [only before noun] **1 a flaming row/temper** a very angry argument or temper **2** *BrE informal* used to emphasize what you are saying when you are annoyed: *You flaming idiot!* **3** burning brightly: *flaming torches*

flamingo

flamingo /flə'mɪŋɡəʊ $ -ɡoʊ/ n [C] plural flamingos or flamingoes a large pink tropical bird with long thin legs and a long neck

flammable /'flæməbəl/ *adj* materials or substances that are flammable burn very easily [= inflammable; ≠ non-flammable]

flan /flæn/ n [C] a PIE or cake without a top that is filled with fruit, cheese etc

flank¹ /flæŋk/ n [C] **1** the side of an animal's or person's body between the chest and the HIP **2** the side of an army in a battle

flank² v [T] to be on both sides of someone or something: *The gate is flanked by statues.*

flannel /'flænl/ n **1** [C] *BrE* a piece of cloth that you use to wash yourself **2** [U] a type of soft warm cloth

flap¹ /flæp/ n **1** [C] a flat piece of cloth or paper that is fastened by one edge to something: *the flap of the envelope* **2 a flap** *informal* a situation in which people feel very worried about something: **be/get in a flap** *She's in a flap over moving house.*

flap² v **flapped, flapping** **1** [I,T] if a bird flaps its wings, it moves them up and down **2** [I] if a piece of cloth flaps, it moves backwards and forwards: *The curtains flapped in the wind.* **3** [I] *BrE informal* to behave in an excited or nervous way: *There's no need to flap.*

flare¹ /fleə $ fler/ also **flare up** v [I] **1** to suddenly begin to burn very brightly: *The fire flared up.* **2** if trouble or anger flares, it suddenly starts or becomes more violent: *Tempers flared during the debate.*

flare² n [C] **1** a thing that produces a bright light and that someone shoots into the air as a sign that they need help **2** a sudden bright flame

flared /fleəd $ flerd/ *adj* flared trousers or skirts become wider towards the bottom

'flare-up n [C] a situation in which people suddenly become very angry or violent: *an angry flare-up during the match*

flash¹ /flæʃ/ v

1 [I,T] to shine brightly for a short time, or to make a light shine in this way: *Lightning flashed overhead.* | **flash sth into/at/towards sb/sth** *Why is that man flashing his headlights at me?* → see box at **SHINE**

2 [I] to move very quickly: **+by/past/through etc** *A police car flashed by.* | *Images of the war flashed across the TV screen.*

3 flash through sb's mind/head/brain if thoughts flash through your mind, you suddenly think of them: *The possibility that he was lying flashed through my mind.*

4 flash a smile/glance/look etc to smile or look at someone quickly: *'I love this city,' he said, flashing a big smile.*

5 [T] to show something to someone quickly: *He flashed his I.D. card.*

6 [T] to send information somewhere quickly by radio, computer, or SATELLITE: **flash sth across/to sth** *The news was flashed across the globe.*

flash² n

1 [C] a sudden quick bright light: **+of** *a flash of lightning*

2 [C,U] a bright light on a camera that you use to take photographs indoors → see box at **CAMERA**

3 in/like a flash also **(as) quick as a flash** very quickly: *I'll be back in a flash.*

4 flash of inspiration/brilliance/anger etc a sudden clever idea or strong feeling

5 a flash in the pan someone or something that is successful only for a very short time

flash³ *adj* **1 flash flood/fire** a flood or fire that happens very quickly or suddenly, and continues for only a short time **2** *BrE informal* looking very new, bright, and expensive – used to show disapproval: *a big flash car* **3** *BrE informal* liking to have expensive clothes and possessions so that other people notice you – used to show disapproval: *Chris didn't want to seem flash in front of his mates.*

flashback /'flæʃbæk/ n **1** [C,U] part of a film, play, book etc that shows something that happened earlier **2** [C] a sudden very clear memory of a past event

flashlight /'flæʃlaɪt/ n [C] *AmE* a small electric light that you carry in your hand [= torch *BrE*] → see picture at **LIGHT¹**

F

flashpoint /ˈflæʃpɔɪnt/ *n* [C] a place where trouble or violence might easily develop suddenly

flashy /ˈflæʃi/ *adj* very big, bright, or expensive: *a flashy car*

flask /flɑːsk $ flæsk/ *n* [C] **1** *BrE* a type of bottle for keeping liquids hot or cold: *a flask of coffee* **2** a type of bottle with a wide base, used in chemistry **3** a small flat bottle for carrying alcoholic drinks

flat¹ /flæt/ *adj* comparative **flatter**, superlative **flattest**

1 smooth and level, without any raised parts: *a flat surface* | *Holland is very flat.*
2 a flat rate or price is fixed and does not change: *They charge a flat rate for delivery.*
3 a tyre that is flat does not have enough air inside it
4 not very thick, deep, or high: *a flat box*
5 a drink that is flat has lost its gas: *This soda water has gone flat.*
6 a performance, book etc that is flat is not very interesting or exciting
7 *BrE* a flat BATTERY has lost its electrical power [= **dead** *AmE*]: *The batteries have gone flat.*
8 E flat/B flat etc a musical note that is slightly lower than E, B etc [➡ **sharp**]
9 if a musical note is flat, it is played or sung slightly lower than it should be
10 flat refusal/denial etc a refusal etc which someone will not change

flat² *n* [C]

1 *BrE* a set of rooms for someone to live in that is part of a larger building [= **apartment** *AmE*]: *a two-bedroom flat* | *a block of flats* (=a large building with many flats in it) ➔ see box at **HOUSE**
2 a tyre that does not have enough air inside: *The car has a flat.*
3 a musical note that is slightly lower than the usual note, or the sign (♭) used in written music to show this note
4 flats [plural] an area of land that is at a low level, especially near water: *mud flats*
5 the flat of sth the flat part or side of something: *He hit the desk with the flat of his hand.*

flat³ *adv*

1 in a position in which someone or something is smooth and level, with no parts that are raised or standing up: *The bed can be folded flat for storage.* | *He lay flat on his back.*
2 in 10 seconds/two minutes etc flat *informal* very quickly, in 10 seconds, two minutes etc: *He did his homework in ten minutes flat.*
3 flat out *informal* **a)** as fast as possible: *We've been working flat out.* **b)** *AmE* in a direct and complete way: **ask/tell sb flat out** *She asked him flat out if he was seeing another woman.*
➔ **fall flat** at **FALL¹**

flatly /ˈflætli/ *adv* **1 flatly refuse/deny etc** to say something in a very firm strong way: *She flatly refused to let me borrow her car.* **2** without showing any emotion: *'It's hopeless,' he said flatly.*

flatmate /ˈflætmeɪt/ *n* [C] *BrE* someone who shares a flat with other people [= **roommate** *AmE*]

ˈflat-pack also **ˈflat pack** *n* [C] *BrE* furniture that is sold in a box and has to be put together

flatten /ˈflætn/ *v* [I,T] to make something flat, or to become flat: *Use a rolling pin to flatten the dough.*

flatter /ˈflætə $ -ər/ *v* [T] **1** to say nice things about someone or show that you admire them, sometimes when you do not really mean it: *He flattered her, saying how nice she looked.* ➔ see box at **PRAISE 2 be/feel flattered** to feel pleased because someone has shown that they like or admire you: *When they asked me to come, I felt flattered.* **3** to make someone look as attractive as they can: *That dress flatters your figure.* **4 flatter yourself** to believe that your abilities or achievements are better than they really are: **+that** *She flatters herself that she could have been a model.* —**flatterer** *n* [C] —**flattering** *adj*: *a flattering photograph*

flattery /ˈflætəri/ *n* [U] nice things that you say about someone or something, but which you do not really mean: *She uses flattery to get what she wants.*

flaunt /flɔːnt $ flɔːnt, flɑːnt/ *v* [T] if you flaunt your money, success, beauty etc, you try to make other people notice it and admire you for it: *The rich flaunted their wealth.*

flautist /ˈflɔːtɪ̯st $ ˈflɔː-/ *n* [C] someone who plays the FLUTE [= **flutist** *AmE*]

flavour¹ *BrE*; **flavor** *AmE* /ˈfleɪvə $ -ər/ *n*

1 [C] the taste that a food or drink has: *Which flavour do you want – chocolate or vanilla?* | **+of** *a dry wine with a slight flavor of honey* | **nutty/smoky/bitter etc flavour** | **delicate/strong/rich etc flavour**
2 [U] when something tastes good: **add/give flavour to sth** *Herbs give food more flavour.*
3 [singular] a quality or feature that makes something have a particular style or character: *The stories have a regional flavour.*

flavour² *BrE*; **flavor** *AmE v* [T] to give food or drink a particular taste: *The sauce is flavoured with herbs.* | **orange-flavoured/chocolate-flavoured etc** *almond-flavored cookies*

flavouring *BrE*; **flavoring** *AmE* /ˈfleɪvərɪŋ/ *n* [C,U] something used to give food or drink a particular taste

flaw /flɔː $ flɔː/ *n* [C] **1** a mistake, mark, or weakness that stops something from being perfect: **+in** *a flaw in the glass* | *a flaw in his argument* ➔ see box at **FAULT 2** a bad part of someone's character

flawed /flɔːd $ flɒːd/ *adj* something that is flawed has mistakes or weaknesses and so is not perfect: *His theory is badly flawed.*

flawless /ˈflɔːləs $ ˈflɒː-/ *adj* something that is flawless has no mistakes, marks, or weaknesses [= **perfect**]: *Sue's flawless French* —**flawlessly** *adv*

flea /fliː/ *n* [C] a very small jumping insect that bites animals and drinks their blood

ˈflea ˌmarket *n* [C] a market where old or used goods are sold

fleck /flek/ *n* [C] a small mark or spot: **+of** *a black beard with flecks of gray*

flecked /flekt/ *adj* having small marks or spots: *red flowers flecked with white*

fledgling /ˈfledʒlɪŋ/ *adj* a fledgling country, organization etc is new and still developing: *a fledgling republic*

flee /fliː/ v [I,T] past tense and past participle **fled** /fled/ *formal* to leave a place very quickly in order to escape from danger: *She **fled** the country*.

fleece /fliːs/ n **1** [C,U] the wool that covers a sheep **2** [U] an artificial soft material used to make warm jackets —**fleecy** *adj*

fleet /fliːt/ n [C] a group of ships or vehicles: *the US seventh fleet* | **+of** *a fleet of taxis*

fleeting /ˈfliːtɪŋ/ *adj* happening for only a moment: *a fleeting smile*

flesh¹ /fleʃ/ n [U]

1 the soft part of your body, between your skin and your bones: *a fish with white flesh*
2 the skin of the human body: *naked flesh*
3 the soft part inside a fruit or vegetable: *Cut the melon in half and scoop out the flesh.* → see picture at **FRUIT**
4 in the flesh if you see someone in the flesh, you see them in real life, not in a picture: *I was thrilled to meet him in the flesh.*
5 your own flesh and blood someone who is part of your family
6 make sb's flesh creep/crawl to make someone feel frightened or nervous: *The way he stared at her made her flesh creep.*

flesh² v
flesh sth ⇔ **out** *phr v* to add more details to something: *You need to flesh out your essay with more examples.*

fleshy /ˈfleʃi/ *adj* having a lot of flesh: *the fleshy part of your hand*

flew /fluː/ v the past tense of **FLY**

flex¹ /fleks/ v [T] to bend part of your body so that your muscles stretch and become tight

flex² n [C] *BrE* a wire covered with plastic, used to connect electrical equipment [= **cord** *AmE*]

flexible /ˈfleksɪbəl/ *adj* **1** able to change easily [≠ **inflexible**]: *flexible working hours* | *Teachers have to be flexible.* **2** easy to bend: *a flexible tube* —**flexibility** /ˌfleksɪˈbɪləti/ n [U] *We need greater flexibility in how we use resources.*

flick /flɪk/ v **1** [T] to send something small through the air with a quick movement of your finger or hand: *He flicked the fly off his sleeve.* → see picture on page A10 **2** [I,T] to move with a quick sudden movement, or to make something move in this way: **+from/up/down** *The cow's tail flicked from side to side.* | *She flicked her hair back from her face.* **3** [T] to press a switch in order to start or stop electrical equipment: *He flicked the light switch on.* —**flick** n [C]
flick through sth *phr v* to look at a book, magazine etc quickly: *She was flicking through a magazine.* → see box at **READ**

flicker¹ /ˈflɪkə $ -ər/ v [I] **1** to burn or shine with an unsteady light: *The candle flickered.* → see box at **SHINE 2** *written* if an expression flickers across your face, it appears for a moment: **+across/through/on etc** *A smile flickered across her face.*

flicker² n [C] **1** an unsteady light that goes on and off quickly: **+of** *the flicker of the firelight* **2 a flicker of emotion/uncertainty/excitement etc** a feeling or an expression that continues for a very short time: *She saw a flicker of doubt in his eyes.*

flier /ˈflaɪə $ -ər/ n another spelling of **FLYER**

flies /flaɪz/ n the plural of **FLY²**

flight /flaɪt/ n
1 [C] a journey in a plane, or the plane making a particular journey: *She **booked** a **flight**.* | *They **caught** the next **flight** home.* | *We **missed** our **flight**.* | *Flight 453* → see box at **AIRPORT**
2 [U] when something flies through the air: **in flight** *a bird in flight*
3 flight of stairs/steps a set of stairs
4 [U] *formal* when you leave a place in order to escape from a dangerous situation: **+from** *his flight from South Africa*
→ **IN-FLIGHT**

'flight at,tendant n [C] someone whose job is to look after passengers on a plane

'flight deck n [C] the area of a plane where the pilot sits

flimsy /ˈflɪmzi/ *adj* **1** thin and light, and not thick or strong: *a flimsy cotton dress* | *a flimsy table* **2** a flimsy argument or excuse is not good enough for you to believe: *The evidence against him is very flimsy.*

flinch /flɪntʃ/ v [I] **1** to move backwards suddenly because you are afraid or hurt: *The child flinched as she touched him.* **2 not flinch from (doing) sth** to do something even though it is difficult or unpleasant: *She never flinches from the truth.*

fling¹ /flɪŋ/ v [T] past tense and past participle **flung** /flʌŋ/ to throw or put something somewhere with a lot of force or in a careless way: **fling** sth **at/into/on etc** sth/sb *Mike flung his coat down on the chair.* | *Val flung her arms around my neck.* | **fling yourself down/through etc** *He flung himself down on the bed.* → see box at **THROW**

fling² n [C] **1** a short and not very serious sexual relationship: *They **had** a brief **fling** last year.* **2** a short period of time when you enjoy yourself a lot

flint /flɪnt/ n [C,U] a type of very hard stone that makes a small flame when you strike it with steel

flip /flɪp/ v **flipped, flipping 1** [T] to move something or turn it over with a quick movement: **flip** sth **over** *She flipped the book over and looked on the back.* | *He flipped the lid open with his thumb.* **2** [T] to throw something flat up into the air so that it turns over: *Let's **flip** a **coin** to see who goes first.* **3** [I] *informal* to suddenly become very angry: *I just flipped and started screaming at them.* **4** [T] to move a control to start or stop electrical equipment: *You just flip a switch and the machine does everything for you.*
flip through sth *phr v* to look at a book or magazine quickly

'flip chart n [C] large sheets of paper which are joined at the top so that you can turn the pages over to present information to people

'flip-flops n [plural] *BrE* open summer shoes that have a V-shaped band to hold your foot

flippant /ˈflɪpənt/ *adj* not serious enough about something, in a way that shows a lack of respect: *You shouldn't be flippant about such things.* —**flippantly** *adv* —**flippancy** n [U]

flipper /ˈflɪpə $ -ər/ n [C] **1** a flat part of the body that some sea animals, for example **SEALS**, use for swimming **2** a large flat rubber shoe that you use for swimming under water

flipping /ˈflɪpɪŋ/ adj BrE informal used to emphasize that you are annoyed: Where's my flipping pen?

'flip side n [singular] informal the bad effects of something that also has good effects: The flip side is that the medicine may cause hair loss.

flirt¹ /flɜːt $ flɜːrt/ v [I] to behave as if you are sexually attracted to someone, but not in a very serious way: **+with** He's always flirting with the women in the office.

flirt with sth phr v **1** to think about doing something, but not be very serious about it: I've been flirting with the idea of moving to Greece. **2 flirt with danger/disaster** to do something that might be dangerous or have a very bad effect

flirt² n [C] someone who flirts with people: Dave is such a flirt!

flirtation /flɜːˈteɪʃən $ flɜːr-/ n **1** [C] when someone is interested in something for a short time: **+with** his brief flirtation with photography **2** [U] when you behave as if you are sexually attracted to someone, but not in a serious way

flirtatious /flɜːˈteɪʃəs $ flɜːr-/ adj behaving as if you are sexually attracted to someone, but not in a serious way

flit /flɪt/ v [I] **flitted, flitting** to move quickly from one place to another: Small birds flitted from branch to branch.

float

float

sink

float¹ /fləʊt $ floʊt/ v

1 [I, T] to stay on the surface of a liquid without sinking, or to make something do this: **+on** Oil floats on water. | **+in** She laying floating on her back in the pool. | **+down/along/past** leaves floating down the river | **float sth down/along etc** The huge logs are floated down the river.

2 [I] to stay in the air or move slowly through the air: The balloon floated up into the sky.

3 [T] to sell SHARES in a company to the public for the first time: The company was floated on the stock market last month.

float² n [C] a large vehicle that is decorated to be part of a PARADE

flock¹ /flɒk $ flɑːk/ n [C] **1** a group of sheep, goats, or birds: **+of** a flock of geese → see box at GROUP **2** a large group of people [= crowd]: **+of** a flock of tourists

flock² v [I] if people flock to a place, a lot of them go there: People have been flocking to see the play.

flog /flɒg $ flɑːg/ v [T] **flogged, flogging** to beat someone with a whip or stick as a punishment

flood¹ /flʌd/ v

1 [I,T] to cover a place with water, or to become

covered with water: The river floods the valley every spring. | The basement flooded and everything got soaked.

2 [I] to arrive or go somewhere in large numbers: **+in/into/across** Refugees flooded across the border.

3 be flooded with sth to receive so many letters, complaints etc, that you cannot deal with them all: After the show, they were flooded with calls from angry viewers.

4 [I] if a feeling or memory floods over you or floods back, you feel it or remember it very strongly: **+over** A feeling of relief flooded over me. | **+back** I saw her picture the other day, and it all came flooding back.

5 flood the market to sell something in very large quantities, so that the price goes down

6 [I] if light floods into a place, it becomes full of light: **+in/into** Sunlight flooded in through the kitchen window.

flood² n [C]

1 a very large amount of water that covers an area that is usually dry: Their homes were washed away by floods. | the worst floods in 50 years

2 flood of sth a very large number of things or people that arrive at the same time: We've had a flood of inquiries.

floodgate /ˈflʌdgeɪt/ n **open the floodgates** to suddenly make it possible for a lot of people to do something: The case could open the floodgates for thousands of other similar claims.

flooding /ˈflʌdɪŋ/ n [U] when an area that is usually dry becomes covered with water: The heavy rain has caused more flooding.

floodlight /ˈflʌdlaɪt/ n [C] a large bright light, used for lighting sports fields or public buildings

floodlit /ˈflʌdlɪt/ adj surrounded by floodlights

floor¹ /flɔː $ flɔːr/ n [C]

1 the surface that you stand on when you are inside a building: a cold stone floor | **on the floor** water spilt on the kitchen floor → see box at GROUND¹

2 one of the levels in a building: **on the first/ third/top etc floor** My office is on the third floor. | a ground floor flat → see box at OFFICE

In British English, the **ground floor** is the area of a building that is on the same level as the ground. In American English, this can also be called the **first floor**.
In British English, the **first floor** is one level up from the **ground floor**. In American English, this is called the **second floor**.
In American English, you can refer to the **first floor** of a hotel or other public building as the **lobby**. The elevator (=machine that takes you up and down in a building) will usually have the letter 'L' on the button that you press to go to this level.

3 an area where people work or do an activity: workers on the factory floor | the dance floor

4 ocean/forest etc floor the ground at the bottom of the ocean or in a forest

→ SHOP FLOOR

floor² v [T] **1** to surprise or shock someone so much that they do not know what to say: At first

she was completely floored by his question.
2 *AmE* to make a car go very fast

floorboard
/'flɔːbɔːd $ 'flɔːr-
bɔːrd/ *n* [C] a board in
a wooden floor

flooring /'flɔːrɪŋ/ *n*
[U] a material used to
cover floors

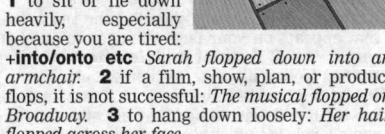
floorboards

'floor plan *n* [C] a
drawing of a room or
the inside of a build-
ing, as seen from
above

flop[1] /flɒp $ flɑːp/ *v*
[I] **flopped, flopping**
1 to sit or lie down
heavily, especially
because you are tired:
+into/onto etc *Sarah flopped down into an
armchair.* **2** if a film, show, plan, or product
flops, it is not successful: *The musical flopped on
Broadway.* **3** to hang down loosely: *Her hair
flopped across her face.*

flop[2] *n* [C] **1** a film, show, plan, or product that
is not successful: *The show's first series was a
complete flop.* **2** the noise or movement that
something makes when it falls down heavily: *He
fell with a flop into the water.*

floppy /'flɒpi $ 'flɑːpi/ *adj* soft and hanging
down loosely: *a floppy hat*

floppy 'disk also **floppy** *n* [C] a small flat
piece of plastic, used for storing information
from a computer

flora /'flɔːrə/ *n* [U] *technical* all the plants that
grow in a particular place: *the flora and fauna*
(=plants and animals) *of the island*

floral /'flɔːrəl/ *adj* made of flowers or decorated
with flowers: *a floral pattern*

florid /'flɒrɪd $ 'flɔː-, 'flɑː-/ *adj literary*
1 florid skin is red: *his florid complexion*
2 florid language, art, or music contains too
many unnecessary details

florist /'flɒrɪst $ 'flɔː-/ *n* [C] **1** also **florist's** a
shop that sells flowers **2** someone who works in
a shop that sells flowers

floss /flɒs $ flɑːs, flɔːs/ *v* [I,T] to clean between
your teeth with special string

flotation /fləʊ'teɪʃən $ floʊ-/ *n* [C,U] when
SHARES in a company are made available for
people to buy for the first time

flotilla /flə'tɪlə $ floʊ-/ *n* [C] a group of small
ships

flounce /flaʊns/ *v* [I] to walk in a way that
shows you are angry: **+out/off** *She flounced out
of the room.*

flounder /'flaʊndə $ -ər/ *v* [I] **1** to not know
what to do or say, because you are confused or
upset: *She floundered helplessly, unable to answer
his question.* **2** to move with difficulty because
you are in deep water or mud

flour /flaʊə $ flaʊr/ *n* [U] powder made from
grain, used for making bread and cakes → see
picture at **INGREDIENT**

flourish[1] /'flʌrɪʃ $ 'flɜːrɪʃ/ *v* **1** [I] to develop or
grow and be successful: *conditions in which busi-
nesses can flourish* | *Herbs flourished in her tiny*

garden. **2** [T] to wave something in your hand
to make people notice it: *Henry came out flour-
ishing a $100 bill.*

flourish[2] *n* **with a flourish** with a large confident movement that makes people notice you: *He
opened the door with a flourish.*

flout /flaʊt/ *v* [T] *formal* to deliberately disobey
a rule or law: *companies who flout the rules on
child labour*

flow[1] /fləʊ $ floʊ/ *n*

1 [C usually singular] a smooth steady movement
of something, such as a liquid, people, traffic, or
information: **+of** *They tried to stop the flow of
blood.* | *a steady flow of people leaving the
area* | *the free flow of information* | *measures to
help traffic flow*
2 [U] when ideas or a conversation can continue
easily without stopping: *Sorry, I didn't mean to
interrupt your flow.*
3 go with the flow *spoken* to decide to do the
same as other people, and not try to do something different
→ **CASH FLOW**

flow

pour

flow

drip

leak

flow[2] *v* [I]

1 if something flows, it moves in a smooth
steady way: **+over/down/through** *The River
Elbe flows through the Czech Republic.* | *A steady
stream of cars flowed past her window.*
2 if words, ideas, or conversations flow, they
continue easily without stopping: *After dinner,
the conversation flowed freely.*
3 if clothing or hair flows, it hangs down loosely
in an attractive way: *Her hair flowed down her
back.*
—**flowing** *adj*: *a fast-flowing river* | *long flowing
hair*

'flow chart *n* [C] a drawing that uses lines and
ARROWS to show how a series of actions or parts
of a system are connected with each other

flower[1] /'flaʊə $ -ər/ *n* [C]

1 the coloured part of a plant that produces the
seeds or fruit: *a tree with beautiful pink flowers* |
wild flowers by the roadside | *I bought Mum a*

F

bunch of flowers. | Can you pick some flowers from the garden? → see picture at PLANT

2 in flower if a plant is in flower, it has flowers on it

flower[2] v [I] if a plant or tree flowers, it produces flowers

flowerbed /ˈflaʊəbed $ -ər-/ n [C] an area of ground in which you grow flowers

flowered /ˈflaʊəd $ -ərd/ adj decorated with pictures of flowers: a flowered dress → see picture at PATTERN

flowerpot /ˈflaʊəpɒt $ -ərpɑːt/ n [C] a pot in which you grow plants

flowery /ˈflaʊəri/ adj **1** decorated with pictures of flowers: a flowery pattern **2** flowery speech or writing uses complicated and unusual words

flown /fləʊn $ floʊn/ the past participle of FLY

fl oz BrE; **fl.oz.** AmE the written abbreviation of **fluid ounce**

flu /fluː/ n [U] a common disease which is like a bad cold but is more serious [= influenza]: The whole team **has got flu**.

fluctuate /ˈflʌktʃueɪt/ v [I] if an amount fluctuates, it keeps changing from a higher to a lower level and back again: The price of copper fluctuated wildly. —**fluctuation** /ˌflʌktʃuˈeɪʃən/ n [C] fluctuations in temperature

flue /fluː/ n [C] a pipe through which smoke or heat from a fire can go out of a building

fluent /ˈfluːənt/ adj able to speak or write a language very well, without stopping or making mistakes: Jem can speak fluent Japanese. | **+in** Candidates must be fluent in two European languages. —**fluently** adv: She speaks Arabic fluently. —**fluency** n [U]

fluff[1] /flʌf/ n [U] small light pieces of wool, fur, or feathers: She picked the fluff off her sweater.

fluff[2] v [T] **1** also **fluff up/out** to make something soft appear larger by shaking it: **fluff sth up/out** The bird fluffed out its feathers. **2** informal to make a mistake or do something badly: Ricky fluffed the catch and we lost the game.

fluffy /ˈflʌfi/ adj very soft and light to touch: a fluffy kitten

fluid[1] /ˈfluːɪd/ n [C,U] technical a liquid: My doctor told me to rest and drink plenty of fluids.

fluid[2] adj **1** a situation that is fluid is likely to change **2** fluid movements are smooth and graceful

fluid ˈounce n [C] a unit for measuring liquid. There are 20 fluid ounces in a British PINT, and 16 in an American pint.

fluke /fluːk/ n [C] something that only happens because of luck: The goal was a fluke.

flung /flʌŋ/ the past tense and past participle of FLING

flunk /flʌŋk/ v [I,T] AmE informal to fail a test or course: I flunked my history exam.

flunk out phr v AmE informal to have to leave a school or college because your work is not good enough: **+of** Tim flunked out of Yale.

fluorescent /fluəˈresənt $ flʊ-, flɔː-/ adj **1** fluorescent colours are very bright and can be seen easily, even in the dark **2** a fluorescent light is made of a long glass tube filled with a special gas, which produces a very bright light

fluoride /ˈfluəraɪd $ ˈflʊr-/ n [U] a chemical that helps to protect teeth against decay

flurry /ˈflʌri $ ˈflɜːri/ n [C] plural **flurries** **1** when there is suddenly a lot of activity for a short time: **+of** There was a sudden flurry of excitement when the band appeared. **2** when it snows for a short time: a snow flurry

flush[1] /flʌʃ/ v **1** [I] to become red in the face, especially because you are embarrassed or angry [= blush]: Billy flushed deeply and looked down. | Her cheeks **flushed red**. **2** [I,T] if you flush a toilet, or if it flushes, you make water go through it to clean it **3** [T] to clean something by pouring water through it

flush sb ⇔ out phr v to make someone leave the place where they are hiding: The police managed to flush out the terrorists using tear gas.

flush[2] n **1** [C, usually singular] the red colour that appears on your face when you are embarrassed etc **2 flush of pride/excitement etc** a sudden feeling of pride, excitement etc

flush[3] adj [not before noun] **1** if two surfaces are flush with each other, they are at exactly the same level: Is that cupboard flush with the wall? **2** informal someone who is flush has plenty of money

flushed /flʌʃt/ adj **1** red in the face: Her face was a little flushed. **2 flushed with excitement/success** excited or pleased in a way that is easy to notice: Jill ran in, flushed with excitement.

flustered /ˈflʌstəd $ -ərd/ adj confused and nervous, often because you are doing something too quickly: He always **gets flustered** in job interviews. —**fluster** v [T] Don't fluster me, or I'll never be ready.

flute /fluːt/ n [C] a musical instrument like a thin pipe that you play by holding it across your lips and blowing over a hole [➡ flautist] → see picture on page A6

flutist /ˈfluːtɪst/ n [C] AmE someone who plays the flute [= flautist BrE]

flutter[1] /ˈflʌtə $ -ər/ v **1** [I] to wave or move gently in the air: Flags fluttered in the wind. **2** [I,T] if a bird or insect flutters its wings, it moves them quickly up and down **3** [I] if your heart or your stomach flutters, you feel very excited or nervous

flutter[2] n [C usually singular] **1** BrE informal if you have a flutter, you try to win money by GAMBLING **2** a fluttering movement

flux /flʌks/ n **be in (a state of) flux** to be changing a lot, so that you cannot be sure what will happen: The fashion world is in a state of constant flux.

fly[1] /flaɪ/ v past tense **flew** /fluː/ past participle **flown** /fləʊn $ floʊn/ third person singular **flies** **1** [I] to travel somewhere by plane: **+to** They flew to Paris for their honeymoon. | **+from/out of** The team is flying out of Heathrow airport this afternoon. → see box at TRAVEL **2** [I] if a plane, bird, or insect flies, it moves through the air: A helicopter flew overhead. | Something frightened the bird and it flew off. **3** [I,T] to be the pilot of a plane: Bill's learning to fly. | I've never flown an aeroplane before. **4** [T] to take something somewhere by plane: **fly sth into/out of sth** Medical supplies are being flown into the area.

5 [I] **a)** to suddenly move very quickly: **+down/ up/into/past** etc *Timmy flew down the stairs and out of the door.* | *The door suddenly flew open.* **b)** to suddenly move through the air: *Helena tripped and went flying* (=fell over). | *He knocked into the tray and sent the cups flying.*

6 [I] if time flies, it seems to pass very quickly: *Is it 5:30 already? Boy, time sure does fly!* | **+by/ past** *Last week just flew by.*

7 [I,T] to move in the air, or to make something move in the air: *The French flag was flying over the Embassy.* | *children flying kites in the park*

8 fly into a rage/temper also **fly off the handle** *spoken* to suddenly become very angry

fly around/about *phr v* if suggestions, ideas etc are flying around, a lot of people are talking about something: *There are a lot of rumours flying around.*

fly² *n* [C] plural **flies**

1 a small insect with two wings: *There were flies all over the food.*

2 also **flies** *BrE* the ZIP or row of buttons at the front of a pair of trousers: *Your fly is unzipped.*

flyer, flier /'flaɪə $ -ər/ *n* [C] **1** a piece of paper that advertises something: *people giving out flyers for a concert* → see box at **ADVERTISEMENT 2** *informal* someone who flies: *I'm a nervous flyer.*

flying¹ /'flaɪ-ɪŋ/ *n* [U] when you travel by plane: *I'm nervous about flying.*

flying² *adj* **1** able to fly: *a type of flying insect* **2 with flying colours** if you pass a test with flying colours, you are very successful in it **3 flying visit** a quick visit, because you do not have much time **4 get off to a flying start** to begin something such as a job or a race very well

flying 'saucer *n* [C] an object that some people say they have seen in the sky, which comes from space [= UFO]

flyover /'flaɪ-əʊvə $ -oʊvər/ *n* [C] *BrE* a bridge that carries one road over another road [= **overpass** *AmE*]

FM /ˌef 'em◂ / *n* [U] a system used for broadcasting radio programmes [➙ **AM**]

foal /fəʊl $ foʊl/ *n* [C] a very young horse

foam¹ /fəʊm $ foʊm/ *n* [U] **1** also **,foam 'rubber** soft rubber with lots of air in it, used in furniture: *a foam mattress* **2** a lot of very small BUBBLES on the surface of liquid: *white foam on the tops of the waves* **3** a thick substance with a lot of BUBBLES in it: *shaving foam* —**foamy** *adj*

foam² *v* [I] **1** to produce foam **2 be foaming at the mouth** *informal* to be very angry

fob /fɒb $ fɑːb/ *v* fobbed, fobbing *informal*

fob sb ⇔ off *phr v* **1** to tell someone something that is not true in order to stop them from complaining: **+with** *She fobbed him off with a promise to pay him the money next week.* **2** to give someone something that is not very good instead of the thing they really want: **+with** *They tried to fob me off with a cheap camera.*

focal point /'fəʊkəl pɔɪnt $ 'foʊ-/ *n* [C] the thing that people pay the most attention to: *the focal point of the picture*

focus¹ /'fəʊkəs $ 'foʊ-/ *v* focused or focussed, focusing or focussing **1** [I,T] to give all your attention to a particular thing: **+on** *In his speech he focused on the economy.* | **focus (your/sb's**

attention/mind) on sth *She tried to focus her mind on her work.* **2** [T] to move the controls on a camera or TELESCOPE so that you can see something clearly → see box at **CAMERA 3** [I,T] if you focus your eyes, or if your eyes focus, you are able to see clearly: *All eyes were focused on Maria.*

focus² *n* **1** [singular] the person or subject that people pay special attention to: **+of** *the main focus of his speech* | **focus of attention/ interest** *His private life became the focus of media attention.* | **+for** *The town became the focus for new development in the area.* **2** [U] if your focus is on something, it is what you give most attention to: **+on** *The school's focus is on basic reading and writing skills.* **3 out of focus** if a photograph is out of focus, you cannot see the picture clearly **4 in focus** if a photograph is in focus, you can see the picture clearly —**focused** *adj*

'focus group *n* [C] a small group of people who are asked questions by a company, political party etc in order to find out what they think of its products, actions etc

fodder /'fɒdə $ 'fɑːdər/ *n* [U] food for farm animals

foe /fəʊ $ foʊ/ *n* [C] *literary* an enemy

foetus, fetus /'fiːtəs/ *n* [C] a baby before it is born —**foetal** *adj*: *foetal abnormalities*

fog /fɒg $ fɑːg, fɔːg/ *n* [C,U] cloudy air near the ground, which is difficult to see through: **thick/ dense/heavy/freezing fog** *The accident happened in thick fog.*

fogey /'fəʊgi $ 'foʊ-/ *n* [C] plural **fogeys** or **fogies** someone who is old-fashioned and does not like change: *a couple of old fogies*

foggy /'fɒgi $ 'fɑːgi, 'fɔːgi/ *adj* **1** if the weather is foggy, there is fog: *a foggy day* → see box at **WEATHER 2 not have the foggiest (idea)** *informal* to not know something at all: *I haven't the foggiest idea where they are.*

foible /'fɔɪbəl/ *n* [C] a slightly strange habit that someone has: *It's just one of his little foibles.*

foil¹ /fɔɪl/ *n* [U] very thin metal, used for wrapping food: *aluminium foil*

foil² *v* [T] to prevent something bad that someone is planning to do: *A bank robbery has been foiled by police.*

foist /fɔɪst/ *v*

foist sth on/upon sb *phr v* to make someone accept something that they do not want: *These poor quality products are being foisted on the public.*

fold¹ /fəʊld $ foʊld/ *v*

1 [T] to bend a piece of paper or cloth by pressing one part over another: *He folded his clothes carefully.* | *Fold the paper in half.* | **fold sth up/over/back** etc *She folded back the sheets.* → see box at **CLOTHES**

2 [I,T] if something folds, or if you fold it, you bend part of it so that it is smaller: *Vic folded his sunglasses and put them in his pocket.* | *The table folds flat for easy storage.* | *a folding chair* | **fold (sth) away/up/down** etc *a bed that you can fold away*

3 fold your arms to bend your arms, so that they rest together against your body

F

4 [T] to cover something by wrapping something around it: **fold sth in sth** *a plant pot folded in newspaper*

5 [I] if an organization folds, it closes because it does not have enough money to continue

fold[2] *n* [C] **1** a line in paper or cloth where you have folded it **2** [usually plural] folds in cloth or skin are parts which hang down over other parts: *the folds of her skirt* **3 the fold** the group of people that you come from and belong to: *a former Republican who has returned to the fold* **4** a small enclosed area in a field, where sheep are kept

-fold /fəʊld $ foʊld/ *suffix* **1** of a particular number of kinds: *The purpose of a window is twofold: to let light in, and to let people see out.* **2** a particular number of times: *The value of the house has increased fourfold* (=it is now worth four times as much as before).

folder /ˈfəʊldə $ ˈfoʊldər/ *n* [C] **1** a container for keeping papers in, made of folded card or plastic **2** a group of related documents that you store together on a computer

foliage /ˈfəʊli-ɪdʒ $ ˈfoʊ-/ *n* [U] *formal* the leaves of a plant

folk[1] /fəʊk $ foʊk/ *n* **1** also **folks** *especially AmE* [plural] people: *Some folk will do anything for money.* | *ordinary folk* | *the old folk in the village* **2 folks** [plural] **a)** *especially AmE* your parents and family: *Is it OK if I call my folks?* **b)** used when talking to a group of people in a friendly way: *OK folks, it's time to go home.* **3** [U] FOLK MUSIC

folk[2] *adj* folk music, art, dancing etc is traditional and typical of a particular place: *an Irish folk song*

folklore /ˈfəʊklɔː $ ˈfoʊklɔːr/ *n* [U] the traditional stories, customs etc of a particular place

ˈfolk ˌmusic also **folk** *n* [U] traditional music from a particular place

folksy /ˈfəʊksi $ ˈfoʊ-/ *adj informal* friendly and informal, especially in a way that is typical of the countryside: *a small town with a folksy charm*

follicle /ˈfɒlɪkəl $ ˈfɑː-/ *n* [C] one of the small holes in your skin that hair grows from

follow /ˈfɒləʊ $ ˈfɑːloʊ/ *v*

1 [I,T] to walk or drive behind someone: *If you follow me, I'll show you to your room.* | *She thought someone was following her.* | **follow sb into/to etc sth** *She followed me into the kitchen.* | **followed by sb/sth** *A woman came in, closely followed by three children.*

2 [I,T] to happen immediately after something else: *The agreement followed months of negotiations.* | *In the years that followed, their friendship turned to love.* | **followed by sth** *a meeting followed by lunch* | **there follows sth** *After years of fighting, there followed a period of peace.*

3 [T] to do something in the way that someone has told or advised you: *I followed his advice.* | *Did you follow the instructions?* → see box at OBEY

4 [I,T] to do the same thing as someone else: *Budget airlines have been so successful that other airlines have been forced to follow suit* (=do the same thing) *and lower their fares.* | **follow sb's example/lead** *Other countries should follow*

their lead. | *Jane followed in her father's footsteps* (=did the same job as her father) *by becoming a doctor.*

5 as follows used to introduce a list of things: *The winners are as follows: in first place, Tony Gwynn; in second place...*

6 [T] to be interested in the progress of something: *Have you been following that crime series on television?*

7 [T] to continue on a road or path, or beside a river: *Follow the road for about 600m.* | *The road follows the river for six miles.*

8 [I,T] *informal* to understand something: *Sorry, I don't follow you* | **easy/difficult to follow** *The recipes are easy to follow.*

9 [I] if something follows, it is true because of something else that is true: **+from** *Two conclusions follow from this.* | *It doesn't necessarily follow that you will earn a lot of money if you're a graduate.*

follow sb around *phr v* to follow someone everywhere they go: *He followed them around with a camera.*

follow through *phr v* to do what needs to be done to complete something or make it successful: **follow sth ⇔ through** *Harry started training as an actor, but he never followed it through.*

follow sth ⇔ up *phr v* **1** to find out more about something: *I saw an advert in the paper and I decided to follow it up.* **2** to do something in addition to what you have already done: *If you don't get any response to your letter, follow it up with a phone call.*

follower /ˈfɒləʊə $ ˈfɑːloʊər/ *n* [C] someone who supports a person or believes in a set of ideas: **+of** *a follower of Karl Marx*

following[1] /ˈfɒləʊɪŋ $ ˈfɑːloʊ-/ *adj* **1 the following day/year/chapter etc** the day, year etc after the one you have just mentioned: *The letter arrived the following day.* **2 the following details/questions etc** the details, questions etc that will be mentioned next: *Payment can be made in the following ways: cash, cheque, or credit card.*

following[2] *n* **1** [singular] a group of people who support or admire someone: *The band has a huge following in the US.* **2 the following** the people or things that you are going to mention: *The following have been selected to play: Ann Smith, Yuri Tsumoto...*

following[3] *prep* immediately after something, or as a result of something: *Following the success of his latest movie, he has had several offers of work.*

ˈfollow-up 1 [C,U] something that is done to make sure that earlier actions have been successful or effective: *The hospital offers follow-up and support for all patients.* | *follow-up treatment* **2** [C] a film, book, event etc that is based on an earlier one: *The follow-up wasn't as good as the original film.* | **+to** *a follow-up to last year's hugely successful concert*

folly /ˈfɒli $ ˈfɑːli/ *n* [C,U] plural **follies** *formal* a very stupid thing to do: *It would be sheer folly to ignore the warnings.*

fond /fɒnd $ fɑːnd/ *adj*

1 be fond of sb/sth to like someone or something very much: *The children are very fond of* *each other.* | *She had **grown fond** of Bernard.* | *He's very fond of reading.*

2 [only before noun] showing that you like someone very much: *a fond gesture* | *As they parted, they said a **fond farewell**.*

3 fond memory someone or something that you remember with great pleasure: **+of** *I have fond memories of my time at Oxford.*

4 fond hope/belief/wish a hope, belief etc that something will happen, which seems silly because it will probably not happen
—**fondness** *n* [U]

fondle /ˈfɒndl $ ˈfɑːndl/ *v* [T] to touch someone's body in a way that shows love or sexual desire

fondly /ˈfɒndli $ ˈfɑːndli/ *adv* **1** in a way that shows you like someone or something very much: *Greta smiled fondly.* | *He is still fondly remembered by people who knew him.* **2 fondly imagine/believe/hope** to wrongly think that something is true or that something will happen: *He fondly imagined that things would improve.*

font /fɒnt $ fɑːnt/ *n* [C] **1** *technical* a set of letters of a particular size and style, used in printing or on a computer screen **2** a stone container in a church, that holds the water used for the ceremony of BAPTISM

food /fuːd/ *n*

1 [C,U] things that you eat: *a hotel that is famous for its good food* | *We sell a wide range of frozen foods.* | **Italian/Chinese/Indian etc food** *I love Chinese food.* | **dog/cat/pet food** (=food for dogs, cats etc)

THESAURUS

fresh – recently picked or prepared, and not dried, canned, or frozen
stale – used about bread or cake that is not good any more because it has become hard and dry
sour – used about milk or cream that tastes and smells bad and is not good any more
frozen – packed and stored at very low temperatures
tinned *BrE*/**canned** – stored and sold in cans
processed – processed food has chemicals in it to make it last longer
organic – produced without using harmful chemicals
nutritious/nourishing/wholesome – good for your health
vegetarian – food that has no meat or animal products in it
fast food – food such as hamburgers that you can buy quickly
junk food *formal* – food that is not healthy because it contains a lot of fat or sugar
→ TASTE

2 food for thought something that makes you think carefully

→ CONVENIENCE FOOD, FAST FOOD, HEALTH FOOD, JUNK FOOD

ˈfood bank *n* [C] *AmE* a place that gives food to poor people

ˈfood chain *n* **the food chain** animals and plants considered as a group, in which a plant is eaten by an insect or animal which is then eaten by another animal etc

ˈfood ˌpoisoning *n* [U] a stomach illness caused by eating food that contains harmful BACTERIA

ˈfood ˌprocessor *n* [C] a piece of electrical equipment used to prepare food by cutting and mixing it → see picture at KITCHEN

ˈfood stamp *n* [C] an official piece of paper that the US government gives to poor people so they can buy food

foodstuff /ˈfuːdstʌf/ *n* [C usually plural, U] something that you can eat: *There is now a shortage of basic foodstuffs.*

fool¹ /fuːl/ *n* [C]

1 a stupid person: *I felt such a fool, locking my keys in the car.* | *Like a fool, I accepted his offer.*

2 make a fool of yourself to do something silly or embarrassing: *He worried that he might make a fool of himself.*

3 make a fool of sb to deliberately try to make someone seem stupid: *She didn't like being made a fool of.*

4 any fool can do sth *informal* used to say that it is very easy to do something: *Any fool could see the plan wouldn't work.*

5 be no/nobody's fool to be difficult to trick because you have a lot of knowledge and experience

fool² *v* **1** [T] to make someone believe something that is not true: **fool sb into doing sth** *Don't be fooled into thinking it's easy to lose weight.* | **be fooled by sth** *Don't be fooled by appearances.* **2 you could have fooled me** *spoken* used to say that you do not believe what someone has told you: *'I'm not scared.' 'You could have fooled me!'*

fool around also **fool about** *BrE phr v* to behave in a silly way: *He's been fooling around in class.*

fool (around) with sth *phr v* to use something in a careless or dangerous way: *You shouldn't fool around with fireworks.*

foolhardy /ˈfuːlhɑːdi $ -ɑːr-/ *adj* taking stupid and unnecessary risks

foolish /ˈfuːlɪʃ/ *adj* not sensible: *It would be foolish to ignore his advice.* | *a foolish idea*
—**foolishly** *adv* —**foolishness** *n* [U]

foolproof /ˈfuːlpruːf/ *adj* a foolproof plan is certain to be successful

foot¹ /fʊt/ *n* [C]

1 plural **feet** /fiːt/ the part of your body that you stand on: *He always walks around in **bare feet** (=without shoes and socks).* | **on foot** (=walking) *It's easier to explore the city on foot.* | **on your feet** (=standing) *It's tiring being on your feet all day.* | **get/jump/rise to your feet** (=stand up after you have been sitting) → see picture on page A3

2 plural **foot** or **feet** written abbreviation **ft** a unit for measuring length, equal to 0.3048 metres: *He's six feet tall.*

3 the foot of sth the bottom of something: *the foot of the stairs* | *the foot of the bed* | *the foot of the page* | *the foot of a hill* → see box at MOUNTAIN

4 be back on your feet/be on your feet again to be healthy or successful again after being ill or having problems: *It's good to see you on your feet again.*

5 put your foot down a) to say very firmly that someone must or must not do something:

F

You've got to put your foot down! Don't let him treat you like that! **b)** to make a car go faster

6 put your feet up to relax, especially by sitting with your feet supported on something: *Go and put your feet up!*

7 put a foot wrong *BrE* to make a mistake, especially in your job: *She hardly put a foot wrong in 40 years of doing the job.*

8 put your foot in it to accidentally say something that embarrasses or upsets someone: *I think I may have put my foot in it.*

9 have/keep your feet on the ground to have a sensible attitude to life

10 fall/land on your feet to get into a good situation because you are lucky: *Jim always lands on his feet.*

11 be rushed/run off your feet to be very busy

12 get/keep/have a foot in the door to get your first opportunity to work in an organization

13 be/get under your feet to annoy you by being in the same place as you, and preventing you doing what you want: *The children were getting under my feet.*

14 a) left-footed/right-footed using your left or right foot when you kick a ball **b) flat-footed/four-footed** having a particular type or number of feet

→ **drag your feet** at DRAG¹ → **have/get cold feet** at COLD¹ → **set foot in sth** at SET¹ → **stand on your own two feet** at STAND¹

foot² *v* **foot the bill** *informal* to pay for something expensive or something that someone else should pay for: *It's the public who are being forced to foot the bill.*

footage /'fʊtɪdʒ/ *n* [U] film showing a particular event: *They showed some old footage of the war.*

football /'fʊtbɔːl $ -bɒːl/ *n*

1 [U] **a)** *BrE* a game played by two teams of 11 players who try to kick a ball into the other team's GOAL [= **soccer**]: *The children were **playing football**.* | *Which **football team** do you support?* | *a **football match*** | *a **football pitch*** **b)** *AmE* a game played by two teams of 11 players who try to carry or kick a ball into the other team's GOAL [= **American football** *BrE*]: *college **football games*** | *a football field*

2 [C] a ball used to play the game of football

—**footballer** *n* [C] *a professional footballer*

footbridge /'fʊtˌbrɪdʒ/ *n* [C] a narrow bridge used by people who are walking

foothills /'fʊtˌhɪlz/ *n* [plural] the smaller hills below a group of mountains: *the foothills of the Alps*

foothold /'fʊthəʊld $ -hoʊld/ *n* [C] **1** a position from which you can start trying to get what you want: *The company has struggled to **gain a foothold** in Europe.* **2** a small hole or crack where you can safely put your foot when climbing a rock

footing /'fʊtɪŋ/ *n* [singular] **1** the conditions or arrangements on which something is based: **put/place sth on a ... footing** *plans to put the business back on a firm financial footing* | *The companies are now able to compete **on a more equal footing** (=with the same advantages and disadvantages).* **2** a firm hold with your feet

when you are standing on a dangerous surface: **lose/miss your footing** *She lost her footing and fell into the water.*

footnote /'fʊtnəʊt $ -noʊt/ *n* [C] a note at the bottom of a page, which gives more information about something

footpath /'fʊtpɑːθ $ -pæθ/ *n* [C] *especially BrE* a path for people to walk along, especially in the countryside [= **trail** *AmE*]: *public footpaths*

footprint /'fʊtˌprɪnt/ *n* [C] a mark made by a foot or shoe: *footprints in the snow* → see picture at FINGERPRINT

footstep /'fʊtstep/ *n* [C] the sound of each step when someone is walking: *He **heard footsteps** in the hall.*

footstool /'fʊtstuːl/ *n* [C] a piece of furniture used to support your feet when you are sitting down

footwear /'fʊtweə $ -wer/ *n* [U] things you wear on your feet, such as shoes or boots

for¹ /fə; *strong* fɔː $ fər; *strong* fɔːr/ *prep*

1 used to say who will get something, or where something will be used: *That piece of cake is for Jane.* | *There's a letter for you.* | *We need a new battery for the radio.*

2 in order to help someone: *Let me carry the bag for you.* | *We looked after the house for them.*

3 used to say what the purpose of something is: *What's this button for?* | **for doing sth** *a knife for cutting bread* | *What did you do that for* (=why did you do it)?

4 in order to get or do something: *I paid $3 for a ticket.* | *We were waiting for the bus.*

5 used to say how long an action or situation continues: *Bake the cake for 40 minutes.* | *I've known Kim for a long time.* → see box at AGO → see box at DURING

6 used to show the time when something is planned to happen: *an appointment for 3:00*

7 because of something: **for doing sth** *an award for saving someone's life* | *For some reason he felt very tired.*

8 used to say where a person or vehicle is going: *Is this train for London?* | *I set off for work.*

9 used to talk about distance: *We walked for miles.*

10 used to show a price or amount: *a check for $100* | *an order for 200 copies of the book*

11 for Christmas/sb's birthday etc in order to celebrate Christmas, someone's birthday etc: *I gave him a watch for his birthday.* | *We went to my aunt's for Thanksgiving.*

12 for breakfast/lunch/dinner used to say at which meal you eat something: *We had steak for dinner last night.* | *'What's for lunch?' 'Hamburgers.'*

13 used to say which person you are talking about: *It's the ideal job for me.* | *It's difficult for me to take time off work.* | *I'm really happy for you.*

14 used to say which company, team etc you belong to: *Lou works for a small publishing company.* | *He plays for the Boston Red Sox.*

15 supporting, or agreeing with someone or something: *How many people voted for Mulhoney?* | *He explained the arguments for and against nuclear power.* | *Jane was **all for** the idea* (=she supported it completely).

16 for all sth in spite of something: *For all his faults, he's very organized.*
17 used to say what a word or sign means: *What's the Spanish word for oil?*
18 when you consider a particular fact: *Libby's very tall for her age.* | *It's cold for July.*

for² *linking word, literary* because

forage /ˈfɒrɪdʒ $ ˈfɑː-, ˈfɔː-/ *v* [I] to search for food or other things you need, especially outdoors: **+for** *animals foraging for food*

foray /ˈfɒreɪ $ ˈfɔː-, ˈfɑː-/ *n* [C] a short attempt at doing a job or activity: **+into** *a brief foray into politics*

forbid /fəˈbɪd $ fər-/ *v* [T] past tense **forbade** /-ˈbæd, -ˈbeɪd/ past participle **forbidden** /-ˈbɪdn/ present participle **forbidding**
1 *formal* to order someone not to do something [≠ **permit**]: **forbid sb to do sth** *He forbade her to see Philip again.* | *The law strictly forbids racial discrimination.* | **be forbidden from doing sth** *He was forbidden from leaving the country.*
2 God/Heaven forbid *spoken* used to emphasize that you hope something will not happen: *'Supposing I had an accident.' 'God forbid!'*

forbidden /fəˈbɪdn $ fər-/ *adj* not allowed because of a rule or law: *Alcohol is strictly forbidden in Saudi Arabia.* | *It is forbidden to smoke in the hospital.*

forbidding /fəˈbɪdɪŋ $ fər-/ *adj* looking frightening or unfriendly: *large forbidding buildings*

force¹ /fɔːs $ fɔːrs/ *n*
1 [C] a group of people who have been trained to do something, especially military or police work: *the **police force*** | *the company's **sales force*** | **the forces** *BrE* (=the army, navy, and air force) *Both sons are in the forces.*
2 [U] physical strength or violence: *The police **used force** to end the demonstration.* | **by force** *He had to be removed from the building by force.*
3 [U] the physical power of something: **+of** *The force of the explosion threw her backwards.* | *The building took the **full force** of the blast.* | *The waves were hitting the rocks **with great force**.*
4 [C] something or someone that has a very powerful effect: *Jones was **the driving force behind** the project* (=the person who made it happen). | **force for change/peace/democracy etc** (=someone or something that makes change etc more likely to happen)
5 [U] the powerful effect that someone or something has: *The village is now beginning to feel the **full force** of the tragedy.*
6 [C,U] a natural power or event: *the **forces of nature*** | *the force of gravity*
7 join/combine forces to work together to achieve something: **+with** *The company has joined forces with a Japanese firm.*
8 in force a) in large numbers: *Local people turned out **in force** to protest.* **b)** if a law or rule is in force, it already exists
9 bring sth/come into force if a new law comes into force, it starts being used: *The law comes into force next year.*
10 force of habit something you do because you have always done it: *Force of habit made him get up at 6:30.*

11 [C usually singular] a measure of wind strength: *gale force winds*
→ **TASK FORCE**

force² *v* [T]
1 to make someone do something they do not want to do: **force sb to do sth** *I had to force myself to get up this morning.* | *Many companies have been forced to close.* | **force sb into (doing) sth** *Bad health forced him into retiring.* | **force sb out of sth** *He was worried he might be forced out of his home.*
2 to use physical strength to move something or go somewhere: **force your way through/into etc sth** *Burglars had forced their way into the house.* | **force a door/lock/window** (=open a door etc using physical strength) | *He forced open the box.*
3 to make something happen: *The scandal forced his resignation.* | *an event which forced the pace of change* | **force prices/rates etc down/up** *The effect will be to force down wages.*
4 force a smile/laugh to smile or laugh even though you are angry or upset
force sth on/upon sb *phr v* to make someone accept something that they do not want: *people who try to force their views on you*

forced /fɔːst $ fɔːrst/ *adj* **1** a forced smile or laugh is not natural or sincere: *a mood of forced cheerfulness* **2** done suddenly because a situation makes it necessary or because someone makes you do it: *The plane had to make a **forced landing**.*

forceful /ˈfɔːsfəl $ ˈfɔːrs-/ *adj* expressing opinions strongly and clearly: *a forceful personality* | *forceful arguments* —**forcefully** *adv*

forceps /ˈfɔːseps, -sɪps $ ˈfɔːr-/ *n* [plural] a medical instrument for picking up and holding things

forcible /ˈfɔːsɪbəl $ ˈfɔːr-/ *adj* using physical force: *There were signs of forcible entry into the building.* —**forcibly** *adv*: *He was forcibly removed.*

ford /fɔːd $ fɔːrd/ *n* [C] a place where a river is not deep, so you can drive or walk across it

fore /fɔː $ fɔːr/ *n* **to the fore** into a position of importance: *Environmental issues came to the fore in the 1980s.*

forearm /ˈfɔːrɑːm $ -ɑːrm/ *n* [C] the part of your arm between your hand and your elbow

forebears /ˈfɔːbeəz $ ˈfɔːrberz/ *n* [plural] *formal* the members of your family who lived in the past [= **ancestors**]

foreboding /fɔːˈbəʊdɪŋ $ fɔːrˈboʊ-/ *n* [C,U] a feeling that something bad will happen soon: *We waited with a **sense of foreboding**.*

forecast¹ /ˈfɔːkɑːst $ ˈfɔːrkæst/ *n* [C] a description of what is likely to happen: *the **weather forecast***

forecast² *v* [T] past tense and past participle **forecast** or **forecasted** to say what is likely to happen: *Rain is forecast for the weekend.* | **+(that)** *They forecast that profits will increase next year.* —**forecaster** *n* [C]

forecourt /ˈfɔːkɔːt $ ˈfɔːrkɔːrt/ *n* [C] *BrE* an open area in front of a large building: *the hotel forecourt*

forefather /ˈfɔːˌfɑːðə $ ˈfɔːrˌfɑːðər/ *n* [C, usually plural] your forefathers are the people who were part of your family a long time ago

F

forefinger /ˈfɔːˌfɪŋgə $ ˈfɔːrˌfɪŋgər/ *n* [C] the finger next to your thumb

forefront /ˈfɔːfrʌnt $ ˈfɔːr-/ *n* **1 in/at/to the forefront of sth** in a leading position in an activity: *The Institute has been at the forefront of research into AIDS.* **2 in/at/to the forefront of sb's mind** if something is at the forefront of your mind, you are thinking about it a lot: *The world championships are in the forefront of my mind.*

forego /fɔːˈgəʊ $ fɔːrˈgoʊ/ *v* another spelling of FORGO

foregone conˈclusion *n* **be a foregone conclusion** if a result is a foregone conclusion, it is certain to happen: *The election result was a foregone conclusion.*

foreground /ˈfɔːgraʊnd $ ˈfɔːr-/ *n* **the foreground** the part of a picture that is nearest to you [≠ **background**]

forehand /ˈfɔːhænd $ ˈfɔːr-/ *n* [singular] a way of hitting the ball in tennis, with the flat part of your hand facing the direction of the ball [➡ **backhand**]

forehead /ˈfɒrɪd, ˈfɔːhed $ ˈfɔːrɪd, ˈfɑː-, ˈfɔːrhed/ *n* [C] the part of your face above your eyes → see picture on page A3

foreign /ˈfɒrɪn $ ˈfɔː-, ˈfɑː-/ *adj*
1 from or relating to a country that is not your own: *She spoke with a foreign accent.* | *foreign students* | *Do you speak any foreign languages?*
2 [only before noun] involving other countries, not just your own country [≠ **domestic**]: *the government's foreign policy* | *the Minister for Foreign Affairs*
3 be foreign to sb to be strange or difficult for someone to understand: *Their way of life was completely foreign to her.*
4 foreign body/matter/object something such as a piece of dirt that has got into a place where it does not belong, especially someone's body

foreigner /ˈfɒrɪnə $ ˈfɔːrɪnər, ˈfɑː-/ *n* [C] someone who comes from a different country

foreign exˈchange *n* [U] the system of buying and selling foreign money, or foreign money itself

foreleg /ˈfɔːleg $ ˈfɔːr-/ *n* [C] a front leg of an animal

foreman /ˈfɔːmən $ ˈfɔːr-/ *n* [C] plural **foremen** /-mən/ the worker in charge of a group of workers

foremost /ˈfɔːməʊst $ ˈfɔːrmoʊst/ *adj* [only before noun] the most famous or important: *the foremost novelist of her time*

forensic /fəˈrensɪk, -zɪk/ *adj* [only before noun] using scientific methods to solve crimes: *forensic evidence*

forerunner /ˈfɔːˌrʌnə $ -ər/ *n* [C] a type of something that existed at an earlier time: **+of** *Babbage's machine was the forerunner of the modern computer.*

foresee /fɔːˈsiː $ fɔːr-/ *v* [T] past tense **foresaw** /-ˈsɔː $ -ˈsɒː/ past participle **foreseen** /-ˈsiːn/ to expect that something will happen in the future [= **predict**]: *No one could have foreseen such a disaster.*

foreseeable /fɔːˈsiːəbəl $ fɔːr-/ *adj* **for/in the foreseeable future** continuing for as long as you can imagine: *I'll be in London for the foreseeable future.*

foreshadow /fɔːˈʃædəʊ $ fɔːrˈʃædoʊ/ *v* [T] if one event foreshadows another, it shows people that the second one will happen

foresight /ˈfɔːsaɪt $ ˈfɔːr-/ *n* [U] the ability to imagine what might happen in the future, and consider this in your plans: *Luckily I had the foresight to take an umbrella.*

foreskin /ˈfɔːˌskɪn $ ˈfɔːr-/ *n* [C] the loose skin covering the end of a man's PENIS

forest

forest /ˈfɒrɪst $ ˈfɔː-, ˈfɑː-/ *n* [C,U] a large area of land covered with trees [➡ **wood**]: *a tropical forest* → see box at **TREE**
—**forested** *adj*: *a thickly forested landscape* → **RAIN FOREST**

forestall /fɔːˈstɔːl $ fɔːrˈstɒːl/ *v* [T] to prevent something from happening

forestry /ˈfɒrɪstri $ ˈfɔː-, ˈfɑː-/ *n* [U] the science of planting and taking care of trees in forests

foretaste /ˈfɔːteɪst $ ˈfɔːr-/ *n* **be a foretaste of sth** to be a sign of what will happen in the future: *The riots were a foretaste of what was to come.*

foretell /fɔːˈtel $ fɔːr-/ *v* [T] past tense and past participle **foretold** /-ˈtəʊld $ -ˈtoʊld/ *formal* to say what will happen in the future

forethought /ˈfɔːθɔːt $ ˈfɔːrθɒːt/ *n* [U] careful thought or planning before you do something

forever /fərˈevə $ -ər/ *adv*
1 for all future time: *I'll remember you forever.* → see box at **ALWAYS**
2 *spoken* for a very long time: *It took forever to get to the airport.*
3 be forever doing sth *spoken* to do something often, especially in a way that annoys people: *He's forever making comments about my weight.*

forewarn /fɔːˈwɔːn $ fɔːrˈwɔːrn/ *v* [T] to warn someone about something bad that might happen: **forewarn sb of sth** *We'd been forewarned of the dangers.*

forewent /fɔːˈwent $ fɔːr-/ *v* the past tense of FOREGO

foreword /ˈfɔːwɜːd $ ˈfɔːrwɜːrd/ *n* [C] a short piece of writing at the beginning of a book about the book or its writer

forfeit /ˈfɔːfɪt $ ˈfɔːr-/ *v* [T] to give something up or have it taken away from you, usually because you have broken a rule: *Violent criminals have forfeited the right to freedom.*
—**forfeit** *n* [C]

forgave /fəˈgeɪv $ fər-/ *v* the past tense of FORGIVE

forge¹ /fɔːdʒ $ fɔːrdʒ/ *v* [T] **1** to develop a strong relationship with other groups: **forge a**

relationship/alliance/link (with sb) *In 1776 the United States forged an alliance with France.* **2** to illegally copy something to make people think it is real: *a forged passport* → see box at COPY

forge ahead *phr v* to do something successfully and confidently: *The team has forged ahead this season.*

forge² *n* [C] a place where metal is heated and shaped into objects

forger /ˈfɔːdʒə $ ˈfɔːrdʒər/ *n* [C] someone who illegally copies documents, paintings etc, to make people think they are real

forgery /ˈfɔːdʒəri $ ˈfɔːr-/ *n plural* **forgeries** **1** [C] something such as a document or painting that has been illegally copied [= **fake**] **2** [U] the crime of illegally copying something

forget /fəˈget $ fər-/ *v* [I,T] past tense **forgot** /-ˈgɒt $ -ˈgɑːt/ past participle **forgotten** /-ˈgɒtn $ -ˈgɑːtn/ present participle **forgetting**

1 to be unable to remember something: *I'm sorry, I've forgotten your name.* | **+(that)** *Don't forget that Linda's birthday is on Friday.* | **+about** *He completely forgot about the meeting.* | **+what/how/where etc** *I've forgotten what I was going to say!*

2 to not remember to do something that you should do: **forget to do sth** *I'm sorry – I forgot to post your letter.* | **(that)** *Dan forgot he was supposed to pick us up from school.* | *Give me your phone number before I forget* (=forget to get it).

3 to not remember to bring something that you need with you: *Oh no, I've forgotten my wallet.*

USAGE

You can say 'I forgot my passport'. You cannot say 'I forgot my passport at home'. When you want to talk about the place where you left something by mistake, you must use 'leave': *I left my passport at home.*

4 to stop thinking about someone or something: *I'll never forget him.* | **+about** *Just forget about work and relax.*

5 **forget it** used to tell someone that something is not important: *'I'm sorry I broke your mug.' 'Forget it.'*

6 **don't forget** used to remind someone about something: *Don't forget I'll be late home.* | **don't forget to do sth** *Don't forget to lock the door.*

forgetful /fəˈgetfəl $ fər-/ *adj* someone who is forgetful often forgets things: *Grandpa's getting a bit forgetful.*

forgive /fəˈgɪv $ fər-/ *v* [I,T] past tense **forgave** /-ˈgeɪv/ past participle **forgiven** /-ˈgɪvən/

1 to decide not to be angry or punish someone who has done something wrong: *I knew that my mother would forgive me.* | **forgive myself/yourself etc** *If anything happened to the kids, she'd never forgive herself.* | **forgive sb for (doing) sth** *She never forgave him for losing her ring.*

2 **forgive me for asking/saying sth etc** *spoken* used before you say or ask something that might seem rude: *Forgive me for saying so, but I don't think that's right.*

3 **sb could be forgiven for thinking/believing etc** used to say that you understand why someone would think or do something: *You could be forgiven for thinking that nobody lives here.*

forgiveness /fəˈgɪvnɪs $ fər-/ *n* [U] when someone forgives another person: *She begged for forgiveness.*

forgiving /fəˈgɪvɪŋ $ fər-/ *adj* willing to forgive: *a kind and forgiving man*

forgo, forego /fɔːˈgəʊ $ fɔːrˈgoʊ/ *v* [T] past tense **forwent** /-ˈwent/ past participle **forgone** /-ˈgɒn $ -ˈgɒːn/ *formal* not to do or have something that you want: *They had to forgo a pay rise.*

forgot /fəˈgɒt $ fərˈgɑːt/ *v* the past tense of FORGET

forgotten¹ /fəˈgɒtn $ fərˈgɑːtn/ *v* the past participle of FORGET

forgotten² *adj* a forgotten place or person is one that people have forgotten about: *He became the forgotten man of English football.*

fork¹ /fɔːk $ fɔːrk/ *n* [C]

1 a small tool that you use for picking up and eating food, with a handle and three or four points: *Put the **knives and forks** on the table.*

2 a tool used for digging and breaking up soil, with a handle and three or four points

3 a place where a road or river divides into two parts: *Turn left at the fork in the road.*

fork² *v* [I] **1** if a road or river forks, it divides into two parts: *The path forked in two directions.*

2 **fork left/right** to go left or right when a road divides into two parts: *Fork left at the bottom of the hill.*

fork out (sth) also **fork sth ⇔ over** *AmE phr v informal* to spend a lot of money: *We had to fork out nearly £300.*

forked /fɔːkt $ fɔːrkt/ *adj* with one end that divides into two parts: *Snakes have forked tongues.*

forlorn /fəˈlɔːn $ fərˈlɔːrn/ *adj* **1** sad and lonely: *a forlorn figure sitting by herself* **2** a forlorn hope, attempt, or struggle is not going to be successful

form¹ /fɔːm $ fɔːrm/ *n*

1 [C] one type of something: **+of** *The bicycle is a very economical form of transport.*

2 [C] the way something exists: *The medicine can be taken **in** liquid or tablet **form**.* | *The novel is written **in the form of** a series of letters.*

3 [C] an official document with spaces where you give information: **fill in/fill out a form** *Fill in the form using black ink.* | *I sent off for an **application form**.*

4 [C] a shape: *The building is **in the form of** an L.*

5 [C] a way of writing or saying a word that shows its number, tense etc: *'Men' is the plural form of 'man'.*

6 [U] *BrE* how well or badly someone is performing: *He's **in good form** (=playing well) at the moment.* | *He's been **off form** (=playing badly) lately.*

7 [C] *BrE old-fashioned* a class in a school

form² *v*

1 [T] to start an organization or business: *The United Nations was formed in 1945.*

2 [linking verb] to be something: *The river forms the boundary between Texas and Mexico.* | *Rice **forms** a large **part of** their diet.*

3 [I] to start to exist: *Ice had begun to form on the roads.* | *A queue quickly began to form.*

4 [T] to make something: *These rocks were formed over 4000 million years ago.* | *Fold the*

F

F

paper in two to form a triangle. | *In English the past tense is usually formed by adding '-ed'.*
5 form an opinion to develop an opinion based on information that you have

formal /'fɔːməl $ 'fɔːr-/ *adj*
1 suitable for official or serious occasions [≠ **informal**]: *I only wear a suit on formal occasions.* | *'How do you do?' is a formal expression.*
2 made or done officially: *We made a formal complaint.* | *We haven't reached a formal agreement yet.*
3 formal education/training/qualifications education, training etc that you get in a school or college
—**formally** *adv*

formality /fɔː'mælₐti $ fɔːr-/ *n* plural **formalities 1** [C] a formal or official part of a process that has to be done: *the legal formalities* | **just/only a formality** (=having to be done but not important) **2** [U] very polite, formal behaviour

formalize also **-ise** *BrE* /'fɔːməlaɪz $ 'fɔːr-/ *v* [T] to make a plan or decision official: *The contract has not yet been formalized.*

format¹ /'fɔːmæt $ 'fɔːr-/ *n* [C] the way something is organized or designed: *Next week's show will be in the new format.* | *a large format paperback*

format² *v* [T] **formatted, formatting 1** to organize the space on a computer DISK so that information can be stored on it **2** to arrange the pages of a book or the information on a computer into a particular design —**formatting** *n* [U] —**formatted** *adj*

formation /fɔː'meɪʃən $ fɔːr-/ *n* **1** [U] the process by which something starts or develops: **+of** *the formation of a new government* **2** [C,U] the shape in which something is made or exists: *rock formations* | *aircraft flying **in formation*** (=in a pattern)

formative /'fɔːmətɪv $ 'fɔːr-/ *adj* [only before noun] having an important influence on the way someone or something develops: *a child's formative years*

former¹ /'fɔːmə $ 'fɔːrmər/ *adj* [only before noun] happening, existing, or true in the past, but not now [➡ **present, previous**]: *former US president, Bill Clinton* | *the former Soviet Union* | *my former husband*

former² *n* **the former** *formal* the first of two things that you have just mentioned [≠ **latter**]: *Of the two theories, the former seems more likely.*

formerly /'fɔːməli $ 'fɔːrmərli/ *adv* in the past: *Kiribati, **formerly known as** the Gilbert Islands*

formidable /'fɔːmₐdəbəl, fə'mɪd- $ 'fɔːr-/ *adj* **1** powerful, impressive, and frightening: *a formidable opponent* **2** difficult and needing a lot of hard work or skill: *a formidable task*

formula /'fɔːmjₐlə $ 'fɔːr-/ *n* [C] plural **formulas** or **formulae** /-liː/ **1** a method used to make something successful: **+for** *There's no magic formula for success.* | *We're still searching for a **peace formula**.* **2** a group of numbers or letters that show a mathematical or scientific rule **3** a list of the different substances in a mixture

formulate /'fɔːmjₐleɪt $ 'fɔːr-/ *v* [T] **1** to develop a plan or idea and decide all the details: *The government is formulating a new policy.*

2 to think about what you want to say and say it clearly: *McLeish took a minute to **formulate** his reply.* —**formulation** /ˌfɔːmjₐ'leɪʃən $ ˌfɔːr-/ *n* [C,U]

forsake /fə'seɪk $ fər-/ *v* [T] past tense **forsook** /-'sʊk/ past participle **forsaken** /-'seɪkən/ *formal* **1** to leave a person or place [= **abandon**] **2** to stop doing or having something: *I won't forsake my principles.*

fort /fɔːt $ fɔːrt/ *n* [C] a strong building used by soldiers for defending a place

forte /'fɔːteɪ $ fɔːrt/ *n* **be sb's forte** if an activity is your forte, you are very good at it: *Cooking isn't really my forte.*

forth /fɔːθ $ fɔːrθ/ → **back and forth** at BACK² → **and so on/forth** at SO¹

forthcoming /ˌfɔːθ'kʌmɪŋ◂ $ ˌfɔːrθ-/ *adj* **1** [only before noun] happening soon: *the forthcoming election* **2** [not before noun] willing to give information: **+about** *Mike wasn't very forthcoming about his plans.* **3** [not before noun] if something is forthcoming, it is given or offered to someone: *When no reply was forthcoming, she wrote again.*

forthright /'fɔːθraɪt $ 'fɔːrθ-/ *adj approving* saying what you think honestly and directly: *Bill answered in his usual forthright manner.*

forthwith /fɔːθ'wɪθ, -'wɪθ $ fɔːrθ-/ *adv formal* immediately: *This sum is payable forthwith.*

fortification /ˌfɔːtₐfₐ'keɪʃən $ ˌfɔːr-/ *n* **1 fortifications** [plural] towers and walls built to protect a place **2** [U] the process of making something stronger

fortify /'fɔːtₐfaɪ $ 'fɔːr-/ *v* [T] **fortified, fortifying, fortifies 1** to build towers and walls around a place to defend it: *a fortified city* **2** to make someone feel physically or mentally stronger: *We fortified ourselves with a hearty breakfast.*

fortitude /'fɔːtₐtjuːd $ 'fɔːrtₐtuːd/ *n* [U] *formal* courage

fortnight /'fɔːtnaɪt $ 'fɔːrt-/ *n* [C usually singular] *BrE* two weeks: *The meetings take place once a fortnight.* | *a fortnight's holiday* | *a fortnight ago*

fortnightly /'fɔːtnaɪtli $ 'fɔːrt-/ *adj BrE* happening once a fortnight: *fortnightly meetings* —**fortnightly** *adv*

fortress /'fɔːtrₐs $ 'fɔːr-/ *n* [C] a big strong building used for defending a place

fortuitous /fɔː'tjuː-ₐtəs $ fɔːr'tuː-/ *adj formal* something that is fortuitous is lucky and happens by chance

fortunate /'fɔːtʃənət $ 'fɔːr-/ *adj* lucky [≠ **unfortunate**]: **fortunate (enough) to do sth** *We were fortunate enough to get tickets for the last show.* | **fortunate in (doing) sth** *I was fortunate in finding a job immediately.* | **+(that)** *It was fortunate that no one was hurt.*

fortunately /'fɔːtʃənətli $ 'fɔːr-/ *adv* happening because of good luck [= **luckily**; ≠ **unfortunately**]: *Fortunately the weather was excellent.*

fortune /'fɔːtʃən $ 'fɔːr-/ *n* **1** [C] a very large amount of money: *He **made a fortune** buying and selling property.* | *That dress must have **cost a fortune**!* | *We **spent a fortune** on holiday.* **2** [U] chance or luck: *I've **had the good fortune** to work with some brilliant people.* **3** [C usually plural] the good and bad things that happen to you: *The win marked a change in the team's* *fortunes.* **4 tell sb's fortune** to tell someone what will happen to them in the future

'fortune ,teller *n* [C] someone who tells you what will happen to you in the future

forty /'fɔːti $ 'fɔːrti/ *number*
1 the number 40
2 the forties also **the '40s, the 1940s** [plural] the years from 1940 to 1949: **the early/mid/late forties** *He spent several years in Paris in the late forties.*
3 be in your forties to be aged between 40 and 49: **early/mid/late forties** *She was in her mid forties.*
4 in the forties if the temperature is in the forties, it is between 40 degrees and 49 degrees
—**fortieth** *adj*

forum /'fɔːrəm/ *n* [C] an occasion or place where people can discuss an important subject: **+for** *The meeting provides a forum for debate.*

forward¹ /'fɔːwəd $ 'fɔːrwərd/ *adv* also **forwards**
1 towards a place in front of you [≠ **backwards**]: *He **leaned forward** to hear what they were saying.* | *The crowd moved forwards.*
2 towards greater progress or development: *The project cannot **go forward** without more money.*
3 towards the future [≠ **backwards**]: *Successful companies are always **looking forwards**.*
4 go forward to/into to successfully complete one stage of a competition so that you can compete in the next stage: *Germany go forward into the next round.*
→ **FAST-FORWARD** → **look forward to sth** at **LOOK¹**

forward² *adj* **1** [only before noun] closer to a place that is in front of you [≠ **backward**]: *Further **forward movement** was impossible.* **2 forward planning/thinking etc** plans or ideas that are helpful for the future: *Forward planning is essential.* **3** *disapproving* too confident and friendly with people you do not know very well

forward³ *v* [T] **1** to send letters or goods to someone at another address: *I forwarded the letter to my manager.* **2** to help something become successful: *I see this as a good chance to forward my career.*

forward⁴ *n* [C] an attacking player in a sport such as football [➡ **defender**]

'forwarding ad,dress /$ '... ,.../ *n* [C] a new address to which your mail is sent

'forward-,looking *adj* planning for the future by trying new ideas: *a forward-looking company*

forwards /'fɔːwədz $ 'fɔːrwərdz/ *adv* FORWARD

forwent /fɔːˈwent $ fɔːr-/ *v* the past tense of FORGO

fossil /'fɒsəl $ 'fɑː-/ *n* [C] the shape of an animal or plant that lived a very long time ago, preserved in rock

fossil

'fossil ,fuel *n* [C, U] a FUEL such as coal or oil that is produced by animals or plants decaying over millions of years

fossilized also ~**ised** *BrE* /'fɒsᵻlaɪzd $ 'fɑː-/ *adj* preserved in rock: *fossilized dinosaur bones*

foster¹ /'fɒstə $ 'fɑːstər/ *v* [T] **1** to encourage a feeling or skill to develop: *Training helps to foster team spirit.* **2** to take care of someone else's child for a period of time, without becoming their legal parent: *In the last ten years, she fostered six children.* [➡ **adopt**]

foster² *adj* **1 foster parents/family/mother etc** the people who foster a child **2 foster child** a child who is fostered

fought /fɔːt $ fɒːt/ *v* the past tense and past participle of FIGHT

foul¹ /faʊl/ *adj* **1** a foul taste or smell is very unpleasant [= **disgusting**]: *The soup tasted foul.* → see box at **HORRIBLE** **2** *especially BrE* very bad: *The weather's been foul all week.* | *She came home from work in a foul mood.* **3 foul language** rude and offensive words: *You should never use foul language in front of a customer.*

foul² *v* [T] **1** if a sports player fouls another player, they do something that is against the rules: *Berger was fouled in the penalty area.* **2** also **foul up** to make something very dirty
foul up *phr v informal* to do something very badly: **foul sth** ⇔ **up** *He really fouled that shot up.*

foul³ *n* [C] an action in sport that is against the rules

,foul 'play *n* [U] violence or a crime that leads to someone's death: *The police do not **suspect** foul play.*

found¹ /faʊnd/ *v* the past tense and past participle of FIND

found² *v* [T] **1** to start an organization: *The Academy was founded in 1666.* **2 be founded on/upon sth** to be based on a set of ideas or beliefs: *The US was founded on the idea of religious freedom.*

foundation /faʊnˈdeɪʃən/ *n* **1** [C] the solid base under the ground that supports a building: *It took the builders three weeks to **lay the foundations**.* **2** [C] a basic idea or belief that something is based on: **+of** *Justice and equality are the foundation of democracy.* | *This agreement will **lay the foundations** for peace.* | *The course gives students a **solid foundation** in computing.* **3** [C] an organization that gives money for special purposes: *the National Foundation for the Arts* **4** [singular] when an organization is first started **5 be without foundation/have no foundation** *formal* to not be true: *These rumours are without foundation.*

founder /'faʊndə $ -ər/ *n* [C] someone who starts an organization

,founder 'member *n* [C] *BrE* someone who helps to establish a new organization or club [= **charter member** *AmE*]

foundry /'faʊndri/ *n* [C] plural **foundries** a place where metals are melted and made into things

F

fountain /'faʊntᵻn $ 'faʊntn/ n [C] a structure that sends water up into the air

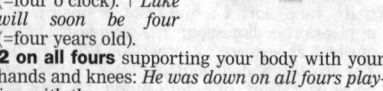
fountain

fountain pen n [C] a pen that you fill with ink

four /fɔː $ fɔːr/ number

1 the number 4: *She is married with four children.* | *They arrived just after four* (=four o'clock). | *Luke will soon be four* (=four years old).

2 on all fours supporting your body with your hands and knees: *He was down on all fours playing with the puppy.*

fourfold /'fɔːfəʊld $ 'fɔːrfoʊld/ adj four times as much or as many: *a fourfold increase in price* —**fourfold** adv

four-letter 'word n [C] a very rude word [= swear word]

four-poster 'bed also **four-'poster** n [C] a bed with four tall posts at the corners, a cover fixed at the top of the posts, and curtains around the sides

foursome /'fɔːsəm $ 'fɔːr-/ n [C] a group of four people doing something together: *I'll invite Jo to make up a foursome.*

fourteen /ˌfɔːˈtiːn◂ $ 'fɔːr-/ number the number 14: *He used to work fourteen hours a day.* | *I started playing the guitar when I was fourteen* (=14 years old).
—**fourteenth** adj, pron: *my fourteenth birthday* | *I'm planning to leave on the fourteenth* (=the 14th day of the month).

fourth /fɔːθ $ fɔːrθ/ adj coming after three other things in a series: *her fourth birthday* —**fourth** pron: *the fourth of July* —**fourthly** adv

fowl /faʊl/ n [C] plural **fowl** or **fowls** a bird such as a chicken that is kept for its meat and eggs

fox

fox¹ /fɒks $ fɑːks/ n [C] a wild animal like a dog with red-brown fur and a thick tail

fox² v [T] *BrE* if something foxes you, it is too difficult for you to understand

foyer /'fɔɪeɪ $ 'fɔɪər/ n [C] a room at the entrance to a public building [= lobby]

fracas /'fræka: $ 'freɪkəs/ n [singular] a short noisy fight

fraction /'frækʃən/ n **1** [C] a part of a whole number, for example ½ or ¾ **2** [singular] a very small amount of something: **+of** *She paused for a fraction of a second.*

fractional /'frækʃənəl/ adj very small: *a fractional increase*

fracture¹ /'fræktʃə $ -ər/ v [I,T] if something hard such as a bone fractures, or if you fracture it, it cracks or breaks: *He fell and fractured his arm.* | *a fractured skull*

fracture² n [C] a crack in a bone or other hard substance

fragile /'frædʒaɪl $ -dʒəl/ adj easily broken or destroyed: *fragile glassware* | *The ceasefire is fragile.*

fragment¹ /'frægmənt/ n [C] a small piece of something that has broken off: **+of** *fragments of glass*

fragment² /fræg'ment $ 'frægment, fræg'ment/ v [I,T] to break something into many small parts, or to be broken in this way: *Social changes have fragmented our communities.* —**fragmented** adj: *an increasingly fragmented society*

fragrance /'freɪgrəns/ n [C,U] a pleasant smell → see box at SMELL

fragrant /'freɪgrənt/ adj smelling pleasant: *a fragrant flower*

frail /freɪl/ adj thin and weak: *a frail old man*

frailty /'freɪlti/ n [C,U] plural **frailties** a physical or moral weakness: *human frailty*

frame¹ /freɪm/ n [C]

1 the wood or metal part around something such as a picture or window: *a picture in a wooden frame* | **door/window/picture frame**

2 the main structure of a building, vehicle, or piece of furniture: *a bicycle frame* → see picture at BICYCLE

3 the shape of someone's body: *her slender frame*

4 frames [plural] the part of a pair of GLASSES that holds the LENSES

5 frame of mind the way you feel: *I'll wait until she's in a more positive frame of mind.*
→ **TIME FRAME**

frame² v [T] **1** to surround something or someone and make them look attractive: *Her hair was cut so that it framed her face.* **2** to put a picture or photograph into a frame: *a framed portrait* **3** to deliberately make someone seem guilty of a crime when they are not: *Murphy claims he was framed by his partner.*

framework /'freɪmwɜːk $ -wɜːrk/ n [C] **1** a set of rules, facts, or beliefs that people use to make plans or decisions: **+of/for** *We must work within the framework of our budget.* | **theoretical/legal/ethical etc framework** *the theoretical framework for our research* **2** the main structure that supports something such as a building or vehicle

franchise /'fræntʃaɪz/ n **1** [C,U] permission given by a company to sell its products or services: *beer brewed in Britain under franchise* **2** [C] a business that operates as a franchise: *a fast food franchise* **3** [U] *formal* the legal right to vote in an election

frank /fræŋk/ adj **1** honest and direct: *I'll be frank with you – it's not good enough.* | *a frank discussion* **2 to be frank** *spoken* used when you are saying what you really think: *To be frank, I don't care.* —**frankly** *adv*

frankfurter /'fræŋkfɜːtə $ -fɜːrtər/ *n* [C] a long SAUSAGE [= **hot dog**]

frantic /'fræntɪk/ *adj* **1** extremely worried or upset: +**with** *Her parents were frantic with worry.* **2** hurrying in an anxious and disorganized way: *a frantic rush for tickets* —**frantically** /-kli/ *adv*

fraternal /frə'tɜːnl $ -ɜːr-/ *adj formal* **1** showing the friendly relationship between people who have the same interest or aim: *fraternal support and cooperation* **2** relating to brothers [= **brotherly**]: *fraternal love*

fraternity /frə'tɜːnˌti $ -ɜːr-/ *n* plural **fraternities** **1** **the teaching/hunting/criminal etc fraternity** people who are involved in an activity **2** [C] a club of male students at a US university [➡ **sorority**] **3** [U] *formal* a feeling of friendship among a group of people

fraternize also **-ise** *BrE* /'frætənaɪz $ -ər-/ *v* [I] to be friendly with someone, used especially to say that you disapprove of this: +**with** *Soldiers who fraternize with the enemy will be shot.*

fraud /frɔːd $ frɒːd/ *n* **1** [C,U] the crime of deceiving people in order to get money: *She was found guilty of fraud.* | **tax/insurance/benefit fraud** **2** [C] someone or something that is not what they claim to be: *He wasn't a real doctor – he was a fraud.*

fraudulent /'frɔːdjʊlənt $ 'frɒːdʒə-/ *adj* dishonest and illegal: *fraudulent insurance claims* —**fraudulently** *adv*

fraught /frɔːt $ frɒːt/ *adj* **1** **fraught with problems/difficulty/danger** full of problems, difficulty etc **2** very anxious or worried

fray[1] /freɪ/ *v* **1** [I,T] if cloth frays, or if something frays it, its threads become loose at the edge **2** [I] if someone's temper frays, they become annoyed: *As we waited, tempers began to fray.* —**frayed** *adj*

fray[2] *n* **the fray** a fight or argument: *More protesters soon entered the fray.*

freak[1] /friːk/ *n* [C] **1** *informal* someone who is extremely interested in something: **a health/ fitness/computer freak** **2** a person or animal that is very strange: *He looks like a freak with that hair.*

freak[2] *adj* very unusual and unexpected: *a freak result* | **a freak accident/storm/wave**

freak[3] also **freak out** *v* [I,T] *spoken* to suddenly become very anxious, upset, or afraid, or to make someone do this: *When she heard the news, she just freaked.* | *Horror films always freak me out.*

freckle /'frekəl/ *n* [C usually plural] freckles are small light brown spots on someone's skin → see box at **MARK** —**freckled** *adj*

free[1] /friː/ *adj, adv* **1** if something is free, it does not cost any money: *There's a free gift with this month's magazine.* | *Entrance to the club is free.* | *Pregnant women can get dental treatment free of charge.* | *Children under 5 travel free.* | **for free** *He fixed the car for free.*

2 not tied up or kept somewhere as a prisoner: *The UN demanded that the hostages be set free.* | *The bear broke free from its cage.* | *He walked from court a free man.*

3 not controlled or restricted by rules, laws, or government control [➡ **freely**]: *The government cannot restrict free speech* (=the freedom to say what you believe). | *The country held free elections last year.* | *a free press* | **free to do sth** *You're free to say no.* | +**from** *The Bank of England should be free from political control.*

4 not busy working or doing other things: *Yes, I'm free next weekend.* | *I never have any free time.*

5 not being used by anyone else: *Excuse me, is this seat free?* → see box at **EMPTY**

6 **a free hand** permission to do something the way you want to: *We gave the design team a free hand.*

7 not fixed or held in a particular position: *She undid her hair, letting it fall free.*

8 **feel free** *spoken* used to tell someone that they are allowed to do something: *Feel free to ask questions.*

9 without something, especially something harmful or unpleasant: +**of/from** *drinks that are free from artificial sweeteners* | *fat-free yoghurt* | **tax-free/duty-free**

free[2] *v* [T]

1 to allow someone to leave a prison or somewhere they have been forced to stay: *The terrorists have refused to free the hostages.* | **free sb from sth** *Atkins was freed from jail yesterday.*

2 to remove something unpleasant that is affecting someone: **free sb from sth** *drugs that can free people from pain*

3 to move someone or something so that they are no longer held, fixed, or trapped: *Firefighters freed two men trapped in the burning building.*

free sb/sth ⇔ up to make something or someone available, so that they can be used: *Hiring an assistant will free up your time to do other things.*

free 'agent *n* [C] someone who is free to do what they want, and is not legally responsible to anyone else

freebie /'friːbi/ *n* [C] *informal* something you are given that you do not have to pay for

freedom /'friːdəm/ *n*

1 [C,U] when you are allowed to do what you want without being stopped or controlled by anyone [➡ **liberty**]: *Kids have too much freedom nowadays.* | **freedom of speech/expression/ religion etc** (=the legal right to say what you want or choose your religion) | **freedom to do sth** *We want the freedom to live our lives as we please.* | *The new TV satellite channels offer viewers greater freedom of choice.*

2 [U] when someone is not in prison

3 **freedom from sth** when you are not affected by something bad: *freedom from fear and hunger*

'freedom ˌfighter *n* [C] *approving* someone who fights against the government or army that controls their country [➡ **terrorist**]

free 'enterprise *n* [U] when people can own and operate a business without much government control

ˌfree-for-'all *n* [C usually singular] *informal* a fight or argument involving a lot of people → see box at **FIGHT**

freehand /'friːhænd/ *adj, adv* a freehand drawing is drawn by hand without using any special tools

F

free 'kick n [C] an occasion during a football game when a REFEREE allows a player to kick the ball freely, because the other team has broken the rules

freelance /'friːlɑːns $ -læns/ adj, adv working independently for several different organizations: *a freelance journalist | I work freelance from home.* —**freelance** v [I] —**freelancer**, **freelance** n [C]

freely /'friːli/ adv **1** without anyone trying to control you or prevent you doing something: *We encourage our students to **speak freely**. | People can now **travel freely** across the border. | a **freely-elected** government* **2 freely available** very easy to obtain: *The information is freely available to the public.* **3 freely admit/ acknowledge** to say that something bad about yourself or your company is true: *He freely admits using drugs.* **4** in large amounts: *Her tears flowed freely.*

free 'market n [C] a system in which the buying and selling of goods is not controlled by the government

Freemason /'friː,meɪsən, ,friː'meɪsən/ n [C] a man who belongs to a secret society in which members help other members to be successful

free-'range adj free range eggs or meat are from animals that are allowed to move around outside and are not kept in small rooms or cages

free-'standing, freestanding /,friː'stændɪŋ/ adj a free-standing object is not fixed to a frame, wall, or other support: *a free-standing cooker*

free-to-'air adj BrE free-to-air television programmes do not cost extra money to watch

free 'trade n [U] when goods coming into or going out of a country are not controlled or taxed

freeway /'friːweɪ/ n [C] AmE a wide road on which cars can travel at a fast speed [= **motorway** BrE; ➡ **expressway, highway**] ➡ see box at ROAD

free 'will n [U] **1 of sth of your own free will** to do something because you want to, not because you have to: *She went of her own free will.* **2** the ability to make your own decisions about what to do, rather than being controlled by God or FATE

freeze¹ /friːz/ v past tense **froze** /frəʊz $ frouz/ past participle **frozen** /'frəʊzən $ 'frou-/

1 [I,T] if a liquid freezes, it becomes solid and hard because the temperature is very cold [➡ **melt, thaw**]: *The lake had frozen overnight.*
2 [T] to make food very cold, usually by putting it in a freezer, so that it stays in good condition for a long time: *I'm going to freeze some of this bread.*
3 [I] to feel very cold: *You'll freeze if you don't wear a coat.*
4 it freezes if it freezes, the temperature drops below FREEZING POINT: *It's going to freeze tonight.* ➡ see picture at MELT
5 [I] to suddenly stop moving and stay very still: *Hugh froze when he saw the snake.*
6 [T] to officially prevent money from being spent, or stop prices, wages etc from increasing: *Our budget for next year has been frozen.*

freeze² n **1** [C] when prices or wages are not allowed to increase: **price/pay/wage freeze** | +**on** *a freeze on pay rises* **2** [C usually singular] when an activity or process is stopped for a period of time: +**on** *There's a freeze on recruitment at the moment.* **3** [singular] a period of time when the weather is extremely cold

freezer /'friːzə $ -ər/ n [C] a piece of electrical equipment in which food is kept frozen [➡ **fridge**]

freezing¹ /'friːzɪŋ/ n **above/below freezing** above or below the temperature at which water freezes

freezing² adj informal extremely cold: *It's freezing in here! | We were freezing last night.* ➡ see box at COLD

'freezing ,point n [C,U] the temperature at which a liquid freezes

freight /freɪt/ n [U] goods carried by ship, train, or aircraft

'freight car n [C] AmE part of a train which carries goods [= **wagon** BrE]

freighter /'freɪtə $ -ər/ n [C] a ship or aircraft that carries goods ➡ see box at SHIP

French fries /,frentʃ 'fraɪz/ n [plural] especially AmE long thin pieces of potato cooked in hot oil [= **chips** BrE]

French 'windows n [plural] large glass doors

frenetic /frɪ'netɪk/ adj frenetic activity is fast and not very organized: *She rushes around at a frenetic pace.*

frenzied /'frenzid/ adj wild and uncontrolled: *He was killed in a frenzied attack.*

frenzy /'frenzi/ n [singular, U] a state of great anxiety or excitement, when you cannot control your behaviour: **in/into a frenzy** *He worked the fans up into a frenzy.* | +**of** *a frenzy of excitement*

frequency /'friːkwənsi/ n plural **frequencies**
1 [U] the number of times that something happens: +**of** *The frequency of his asthma attacks was increasing. | He misses school **with alarming frequency** (=very often).* **2** [C,U] the number of radio waves or sound waves that go past a point each second: *sounds of very high frequency*

frequent¹ /'friːkwənt/ adj happening often [≠ **infrequent**]: *Her headaches became more frequent. | Buses leave for the airport **at frequent intervals**. | He was a **frequent visitor** to our house.*

frequent² /frɪ'kwent $ frɪ'kwent, 'friːkwənt/ v [T] to go to a place often: *a café frequented by artists*

frequently /'friːkwəntli/ adv often: *Trains are frequently late.* ➡ see box at OFTEN

fresh /freʃ/ adj

1 new and different from what was done or used before: *Start again on a **fresh** sheet of paper. | We need some **fresh ideas**. | They decided to move to Australia and **make a fresh start**.*
2 recently picked or prepared, and not dried, tinned, frozen etc: **fresh fruit/vegetables/fish/ bread etc** *Make sure the fish is fresh. | fresh flowers from the garden* ➡ see box at NEW ➡ word FOOD
3 done or experienced recently: *fresh animal tracks* | **be fresh in sb's mind/memory** *The incident was still fresh in my mind.*
4 pleasantly clean or cool: *a fresh minty taste | Let's go and get some **fresh air** (=from outside a building). | You'll feel nice and fresh after a shower.*

5 fresh water water that contains no salt and comes from rivers and lakes
6 fresh from/out of sth having just left a place, especially a college or school: *a new teacher fresh from university*
—**freshness** n [U]

freshen /ˈfreʃən/
  freshen up *phr v spoken* to wash your hands and face, so that you feel clean and comfortable: *I'd like to freshen up before dinner.*

fresher /ˈfreʃə $ -ər/ n [C] *BrE* a student who has just started at a college or university

freshly /ˈfreʃli/ *adv* **freshly made/picked/dug etc** made, picked etc very recently: *freshly ground pepper* → see box at RECENTLY

freshman /ˈfreʃmən/ n [C] plural **freshmen** /-mən/ *AmE* a student in the first year of HIGH SCHOOL or university

freshwater /ˈfreʃwɔːtə $ -wɔːtər, -wɑː-/ *adj* [only before noun] containing or living in water that contains no salt: *a freshwater lake* | *freshwater fish*

fret /fret/ v [I] **fretted, fretting** to worry: **+over/about** *She frets about her son's health.*

fretful /ˈfretfəl/ *adj* anxious and complaining: *a fretful child*

Fri. also **Fri** *BrE* the written abbreviation of **Friday**

friar /ˈfraɪə $ -ər/ n [C] a MONK who travelled around teaching about Christianity in the past

friction /ˈfrɪkʃən/ n [U] **1** disagreement or angry feelings between people: **+between** *Money can cause friction between friends.* **2** when one surface rubs against another: *the heat produced by friction*

Friday /ˈfraɪdi, -deɪ/ n [C,U] written abbreviation **Fri.** the day between Thursday and Saturday → see examples at MONDAY → see box at DAY

fridge /frɪdʒ/ n [C] a piece of electrical equipment for storing food and keeping it cool [→ **freezer**]: *There's more milk in the fridge.* → see picture at KITCHEN

fried /fraɪd/ *adj* cooked in hot oil: *fried chicken* → see picture at POTATO

friend /frend/ n [C]
1 someone that you know well and enjoy spending time with: *This is my friend Kate.* | *He went out with some friends.* | **a friend of mine/yours/John's etc** *Lee is an old friend of mine* (=one that I have known for a long time). | **a good/close friend** *We're only inviting a few close friends.* | *Joe was my best friend.*

2 be friends to be someone's friend: **+with** *I'm friends with his sister.* | *Helen and I are old*

friends. | *He's not my boyfriend – we're just friends.*
3 make friends to start a friendly relationship: *He finds it hard to make friends.* | **+with** *I made friends with her in college.*
→ PEN FRIEND

friendly /ˈfrendli/ *adj*
1 behaving towards other people as if you like them and want to talk to them or help them [≠ **unfriendly, hostile**]: *a friendly smile* | *a school with a friendly atmosphere* | **+to/towards** *The locals are very friendly towards tourists.* → see box at NICE
2 be friendly with sb to be someone's friend: *My parents are friendly with his parents.*
—**friendliness** n [U] → ENVIRONMENTALLY FRIENDLY, USER-FRIENDLY

friendship /ˈfrendʃɪp/ n
1 [C] a relationship between friends: *Josh and I have a close friendship.* | **+between/with** *The friendship between the three girls began at school.*
2 [U] the feelings and behaviour of a friend: *I needed some friendship and support.*

fries /fraɪz/ n [plural] *AmE* long thin pieces of potato cooked in hot oil [= **chips** *BrE*]

frieze /friːz/ n [C] a decorated border along the top of a wall

frigate /ˈfrɪɡət/ n [C] a small fast ship used in a war to protect other ships → see box at SHIP

fright /fraɪt/ n [singular, U] a sudden feeling of fear: *The noise gave me a fright.* | *They both ran off in fright.*

frighten /ˈfraɪtn/ v [T] to make someone feel afraid: *Don't shout – you'll frighten the baby.* | *She was frightened by his threats.*
  frighten sb ⇔ away/off *phr v* to make a person or animal afraid or nervous so that they go away: *A scarecrow frightens birds away.* | *The violence has frightened off tourists.*
  frighten sb into sth *phr v* to make someone do something by frightening them: **frighten sb into doing sth** *They frightened him into confessing.*

frightened /ˈfraɪtnd/ *adj* feeling afraid: *Don't be frightened. I won't hurt you.* | **+of** *Are you frightened of the dark?* | **+that** *She is frightened that her father will find out.* | **frightened to do sth** *Some people are frightened to fly.*

frightening /ˈfraɪtn-ɪŋ/ *adj* making you feel afraid: *a frightening experience* | **It is frightening to realize that I could have been killed.**
—**frighteningly** *adv*

frightful /ˈfraɪtfəl/ *adj BrE old-fashioned* very bad [= **awful**]: *Her hair was a frightful mess.*

frightfully /ˈfraɪtfəli/ *adv BrE old-fashioned* very: *I'm frightfully sorry.*

frigid /ˈfrɪdʒɪd/ *adj* **1** a woman who is frigid gets no pleasure from sex **2** *literary* not friendly

frill /frɪl/ n [C] **1** a narrow piece of cloth with many folds, attached to something as a decoration **2 frills** [plural] attractive but unnecessary features: *a basic, comfortable apartment with no frills*

frilly /'frɪli/ adj frilly clothes are decorated with lots of frills

fringe¹ /frɪndʒ/ n [C] **1** *BrE* the part of your hair that hangs down above your eyes [= **bangs** *AmE*]: *She has long hair with a fringe.* → see picture at **HAIR** **2** a decorative edge of hanging threads on a curtain or piece of clothing **3 the fringe/fringes of sth a)** a small part of a group of people that is different from and not completely accepted by the rest of the group: **on the fringe/fringes** *an extremist who is on the fringes of politics* **b)** the edge of something: **on the fringe/fringes** *people living on the fringes of big cities*

fringe² adj [only before noun] not accepted by most people in a group: *a fringe organization*

fringe³ v [T] to be along the edge of something: *Palm trees fringe the shore.*

'fringe ,benefit n [C usually plural] something extra that you get with your job in addition to wages: *The company provides childcare, an important fringe benefit.*

frisk /frɪsk/ v [T] to search someone for hidden weapons, drugs etc by feeling their body

frisky /'frɪski/ adj full of energy and fun: *frisky lambs*

fritter /'frɪtə $ -ər/
fritter sth ⇔ away *phr v* to waste money or time on unimportant things: **+on** *Don't fritter your money away on clothes.*

frivolity /frɪ'vɒləti $ -'vɑː-/ n [C,U] plural **frivolities** something that is not serious or sensible

frivolous /'frɪvələs/ adj not serious or sensible, especially in a way that is not suitable: *a frivolous remark* | *Don't be so frivolous.*

frizzy /'frɪzi/ adj frizzy hair is very tightly curled

fro /frəʊ $ froʊ/ adv → **to and fro** at **TO³**

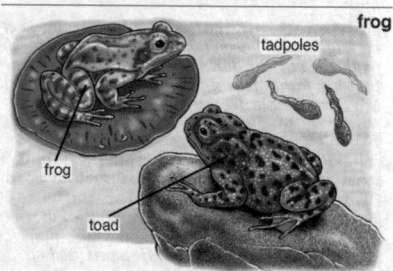

frog

tadpoles

frog

toad

frog /frɒg $ frɑːg, frɔːg/ n [C] a small green animal that lives near water and has long legs for jumping [➡ **toad**]

frogman /'frɒgmən $ 'frɑːg-, 'frɔːg-/ n [C] plural **frogmen** /-mən/ *BrE* someone whose job is to swim under water using special equipment to help them breathe

frolic /'frɒlɪk $ 'frɑː-/ v [I] **frolicked, frolicking** *literary* to play happily

from /frəm; *strong* frɒm $ frəm; *strong* frʌm, frɑːm/ prep

1 starting at a particular place, time, or level: *He drove all the way from Colorado.* | **from ... to ...** *the road from here to the airport* | *I have classes from 9.30 to 1.30.* | *Tickets cost from $8 to $25.* | *I will be teaching you from now on* (=starting now and continuing). | *We'll be in Spain 2 hours from now* (=in 2 hours, starting now).

2 used when you are saying how far away something is: *We live about ten miles from the airport.* | *It landed a few inches from my head.*

3 used to say who gave or sent something: *Who is the letter from?* | *I got the idea from Colin.* | *We buy our cheese from the market.* | *Get permission from your parents first.*

4 used to say where something is before it is removed: *She took a key from inside the drawer.*

5 used to say where someone was born, or where they usually live or work: *'Where are you from?' 'I'm from South Africa.'* | *We had a speaker from York University.*

6 used to say what someone or something was like before they changed: **from ... to/into ...** *She changed from a shy child to a confident young woman.* | *It was translated from Latin into English.*

7 used to say where you are when you see something: *We could see the house from the road.*

8 used to state the cause of something: *She's exhausted from the worry.* | *deaths from cancer*

9 used to state the reason for your opinion: *From what I've seen, he seems a nice man.*

10 used to say what is used to make something: *Beer is made from hops.*

11 used when you are comparing things: *He's quite different from his brother.*

frond /frɒnd $ frɑːnd/ n [C] a leaf of a **FERN** or **PALM**

front¹ /frʌnt/ n

1 the front a) the part of something that is furthest forward [≠ **back**]: **at/in the front (of sth)** *We got on the bus and sat at the front.* | *Can I ride in the front* (=of a car)? | **+of** *At last I got to the front of the queue.* **b)** the side or surface of something that faces forward: **+of** *the controls on the front of the machine* | *a shirt with stains down the front* | *He lay on his front* (=the front of his body). **c)** the most important side or surface of something, which you look at first [≠ **back**]: *a magazine with a picture of Elvis on the front* | **+of** *The front of the house was painted white.*

2 in front of sth/sb a) facing something [≠ **behind**]: *She stood in front of the mirror.* | *I spend hours in front of my computer* (=using it). **b)** near the entrance to a building, facing the street [≠ **behind**]: *You can park in front of the store.* **c)** where someone can see or hear you: *Don't swear in front of the children.*

3 in front a) further forward than someone or something else [= **ahead**; ≠ **behind**]: *The car in front braked suddenly.* | **+of** *Louise was in front*

of me in the queue. **b)** winning in a game or competition [= ahead; ≠ behind]: *His goal put Leeds back in front.*
4 on the business/political/sporting etc front in a particular area of activity: *We've had some good news on the business front.*
5 out front in the area near the entrance to a building: *The taxi is waiting out front.*
6 [C] a line where an area of warm air meets an area of cold air: **warm/cold front**
7 [C] a legal business that is used to hide illegal activity: **+for** *The casino was a front for their drugs operation.*
8 [singular] a way of behaving that hides how you really feel: *She was worried, but put on a brave front.*
9 the front also **the front line** a line along which fighting takes place during a war: *More troops were sent to the front.* | *front-line troops* → **upfront**

front² *adj* [only before noun] at or in the front of something [≠ back]: *His front teeth fell out.* | *She's on the front cover of every magazine.* | *The front door is red.* | *front row tickets*

front³ *v* [T] **1** *especially BrE* to be the person in something such as a band or television programme who leads it and is most well-known to the public: *He fronted his own band.* **2** to face something: *hotels fronting the lake*

frontal /ˈfrʌntl/ *adj* at or relating to the front part of something: *a frontal attack on their troops* | *the frontal lobe of the brain*

frontier /ˈfrʌntɪə $ frʌnˈtɪr/ *n* [C] **1** *especially BrE* the border of a country: **+between/with** *a town on the frontier between France and Spain* **2 the frontiers of knowledge/science etc** the limits of what is known about something

front ˈline *n* [C usually singular] the place where fighting happens in a war [= **the front**] —**front-line** *adj*: *front-line troops*

ˈfront-page *adj* **front-page news/article/story etc** news that is important enough to be on the front page of a newspaper

ˌfront-ˈrunner *n* [C] the person, company etc that is most likely to win or succeed: *the front-runner in the presidential election*

frost¹ /frɒst $ frɒːst/ *n* **1** [C,U] very cold weather, when water freezes: *There was a hard frost last night* (=it was extremely cold). | *plants killed by frost* **2** [U] a white powder of ice that covers things when the weather is very cold: *trees covered with frost* → see box at **SNOW**

frost² *v* [T] *AmE* to cover a cake with FROSTING [= ice *BrE*]

frostbite /ˈfrɒstbaɪt $ ˈfrɒːst-/ *n* [U] a condition in which your fingers, toes etc become frozen and are badly damaged —**frostbitten** /-bɪtn/ *adj*

frosted /ˈfrɒstɪd $ ˈfrɒːstɪd/ *adj* **frosted glass/window etc** glass that has a rough surface, so that you cannot see through it clearly

frosting /ˈfrɒstɪŋ $ ˈfrɒːstɪŋ/ *n* [U] *AmE* a sweet substance put on cakes, made from sugar and liquid [= **icing** *BrE*]

frosty /ˈfrɒsti $ ˈfrɒːsti/ *adj* **1** very cold or covered with FROST: *a frosty morning* | *frosty ground* → see box at **COLD** **2** unfriendly: *a frosty stare*

froth¹ /frɒθ $ frɒːθ/ *n* [singular, U] a mass of small BUBBLES on top of a liquid —**frothy** *adj*: *frothy coffee*

froth² *v* [I] to produce a lot of froth

frown¹ /fraʊn/ *v* [I] to make an angry or unhappy expression by moving your EYEBROWS together: **+at** *Mel frowned at me.*
frown on/upon sth *phr v* to disapprove of something: *Smoking is allowed, but frowned upon.*

frown² *n* [C] the expression on your face when you frown: *He looked at her with a puzzled frown.*

froze /frəʊz $ froʊz/ *v* the past tense of FREEZE

frozen¹ /ˈfrəʊzən $ ˈfroʊ-/ *v* the past participle of FREEZE

frozen² *adj*
1 frozen food has been stored at very low temperatures to preserve it [➡ **freeze**]: *frozen peas* → see box at **FOOD**
2 *spoken* feeling very cold: *You look frozen!*
3 changed into ice or made very hard because of very cold weather: *The ground was frozen.* | *a frozen lake*
4 unable to move, usually because of fear: *She stood there frozen with terror.*

frugal /ˈfruːɡəl/ *adj* careful to buy or use only what is necessary [≠ **extravagant**]: *He led a frugal existence.* —**frugally** *adv*

fruit /fruːt/ *n* plural **fruit** or **fruits**
1 [C,U] something such as an apple or orange, which grows on a plant, tree, or bush, and contains seeds: *a bowl of fruit* | *Eat plenty of fresh fruit.* | **fruit juice/yoghurt/salad etc**
2 the fruits of sth the good results from something, after you have worked hard
→ **bear fruit** at **BEAR¹**

fruitful /ˈfruːtfəl/ *adj* producing good results: *a very fruitful meeting*

fruition /fruˈɪʃən/ *n* **come to fruition** *formal* to start to be successful or have the effect you wanted: *It took many years for his plans to come to fruition.*

fruitless /ˈfruːtləs/ *adj* failing to produce any good result, especially after a lot of effort: *a fruitless attempt to resolve the dispute* —**fruitlessly** *adv*

fruity /ˈfruːti/ *adj* tasting or smelling strongly of fruit: *a fruity wine*

frustrate /frʌˈstreɪt $ ˈfrʌstreɪt/ *v* [T] **1** if something frustrates you, it makes you feel impatient or angry because you are unable to do what you want: *The slow pace of his learning frustrates him.* **2** to prevent someone's plans or efforts from succeeding: *Her plans were frustrated by her parents.*

frustrated /frʌˈstreɪtɪd $ ˈfrʌstreɪtɪd/ *adj* **1** feeling impatient or angry because you are unable to do what you want: **+with/at** *I get really frustrated with my computer sometimes.* **2 a frustrated poet/artist/actor etc** someone who would like to develop a particular skill but has not been able to

frustrating /frʌˈstreɪtɪŋ $ ˈfrʌstreɪtɪŋ/ *adj* making you feel impatient or angry because you cannot do what you want: *a frustrating experience* | *It's frustrating when nobody listens.*

F

fruit

plums, apples, peaches, flesh, stone BrE/pit AmE, pips, core, watermelon, mango, grapes, strawberries, lime, kiwi fruit, bananas, skin, coconut, pear, avocado, pineapple, oranges, peel, stalk, raspberries, cherries, lemons

frustration /frʌˈstreɪʃən/ n [C,U] the feeling of being impatient or angry because you are unable to do what you want

fry /fraɪ/ v [I,T] **fried, frying, fries** to cook something in hot oil, or be cooked in hot oil: *Do you want me to fry some eggs?* | *I could smell bacon frying.* | *fried mushrooms* → see box at **COOK** → and **RECIPE**

'frying ˌpan n [C] a round flat pan with a long handle, used for frying food → see picture at **KITCHEN**

ft. the written abbreviation of **foot**

fudge¹ /fʌdʒ/ n [U] a soft creamy sweet food

fudge² v [I,T] to avoid giving exact details or a clear answer about something: *The President tried to fudge the tax issue.*

fuel¹ /ˈfjuːəl/ n [C,U] a substance such as coal, gas, or oil, which can be burned to produce heat or power: *The plane was running low on fuel.* | *We compared the fuel consumption of several cars.*
→ **FOSSIL FUEL**

fuel² v [T] **fuelled, fuelling** BrE; **fueled, fueling** AmE to make a situation worse, or make someone's feelings stronger: *The photo fuelled the rumour that they had split up.* | *inflation fuelled by government spending*

fugitive /ˈfjuːdʒɪtɪv/ n [C] someone who is trying to avoid being caught by the police

fulfil BrE; **fulfill** AmE /fʊlˈfɪl/ v [T] **fulfilled, fulfilling 1 fulfil a promise/commitment/ obligation etc** to do something that you have promised to do, or do something that you should

do: *He fulfilled his promise to cut taxes.* | *Britain is not fulfilling the requirements of the treaty.* **2 fulfil a hope/wish/aim etc** to achieve the thing that you hoped for, wished for etc: *She never fulfilled her dream of becoming a dancer.* | *This merger will help the company fulfil its strategic aims.* **3 fulfil a role/function/need etc** to do or provide something that is needed: *Does the church still fulfil a need in society?* **4 fulfil your potential** to be as successful as you can be: *We want all our students to fulfil their potential.* **5** to make you feel satisfied because you are using all your skills and qualities: *Motherhood alone did not fulfil her.*

fulfilled /fʊlˈfɪld/ adj satisfied that you are doing interesting and important things in your life or job

fulfilling /fʊlˈfɪlɪŋ/ adj making you feel satisfied because you are doing interesting and important things: *Teaching is a very fulfilling career.*

fulfilment BrE; **fulfillment** AmE /fʊlˈfɪlmənt/ n [U] **1** the feeling of being satisfied, especially because you are doing interesting, useful, or important things: *Ann's work gives her a real sense of fulfilment.* **2** when someone does what they have promised to do, what they should do, or what they have always wanted to do: **+of** *The trip was the fulfilment of a childhood dream.*

full¹ /fʊl/ adj

1 if a container, room, space etc is full, it contains as many things or people as possible [≠ empty]: *The train was completely full.* | *We* *started with a full tank of petrol.* | **+of** *The garage is* ***crammed full*** *of junk.* | *The bottle was only* ***half full.*** | *The hotel is* ***full up.*** → see picture at **EMPTY¹**

2 [only before noun] complete and including all parts or details: *Please give your* ***full name*** *and address.* | *He has my* ***full support.*** | *Read the* ***full story*** *in today's paper!* | *We will pay* ***the full cost*** *of repairs.*

3 [only before noun] as high in level or great in amount as possible: *The government's goal is* ***full employment.*** | **at full speed/power/volume etc** *He plays his stereo at full volume.*

4 be full of sth/sb a) to contain many things or people of the same kind: *a garden full of flowers* | *Eric's essay is full of mistakes.* **b)** feeling or showing a lot of a particular quality: *We were full of excitement.*

5 also **full up** *BrE informal* having eaten so much food that you do not want to eat any more: *No more, thanks. I'm full.*

6 a full ten days/six inches etc or **ten full days/six full inches etc** used to emphasize a quantity or amount: *I told him about it a full three weeks in advance.*

7 [only before noun] with all the rights or duties that belong to a particular position: *Only full members can vote.* | *a full driving licence*

8 a full life/day etc a life or day in which you are very busy or active: *Tom was tired after his full day.*

9 be full of yourself *spoken, disapproving* to have a high opinion of yourself

10 made with a lot of material and fitting loosely: *a full skirt*

11 large and rounded in an attractive way: *a full figure*

12 having a pleasantly strong taste: *The coffee beans are roasted for a* ***fuller flavour.***

13 in full view of sb in a place where someone can easily see you: *She hit him in full view of the neighbours.*

14 be in full swing if an event such as a party is in full swing, it has reached its highest level of activity

full² *n* **1 in full** including the whole of something: *The debt must be* ***paid in full.*** **2 to the full** as completely as possible: *My mother* ***lived life to the full.***

full³ *adv literary* directly: **+on/in** *She kissed him full on the mouth.*

fullback /'fʊlbæk/ *n* [C] a player in a football team who plays in defence [= **defender**]

'full-blown *adj* at the most complete or advanced stage: *full-blown AIDS*

full-'fledged *adj AmE* completely developed, trained, or established [= **fully-fledged** *BrE*]

full-'grown *adj* a full-grown animal, plant, or person has developed to their full size and will not grow any bigger

full 'house *n* [C] an occasion at a theatre, concert hall etc when there are no empty seats

'full-length *adj* **1 full-length skirt/coat etc** a skirt etc that is long or reaches the ground **2 full-length play/film/novel etc** a play etc that is not shorter than the normal length

full 'marks *n* [plural] if you give someone full marks, you praise them for doing something very well: *He failed, but he deserves full marks for bravery.*

full 'moon *n* [singular] the moon when it looks completely round

full-'on *adj* as powerful, **INTENSE**, or extreme as possible: *a full-on performance*

full-'page *adj* [only before noun] covering all of one page in a newspaper or magazine: *a full-page advert*

full-'scale *adj* [only before noun] **1** as complete or thorough as possible: *the threat of full-scale nuclear war* | *We will conduct a full-scale inquiry.* **2** a full-scale drawing, model etc is the same size as the thing it represents

full 'stop *n* [C] *BrE* a mark (.) that shows the end of a sentence or the short form of a word [= **period** *AmE*]

full-'time *adj, adv* for all the hours of the week during which it is usual for people to work, study etc [➝ **part-time**]: *Both her parents* ***work full-time.*** | *a full-time job*

fully /'fʊli/ *adv* completely: *The restaurant is* ***fully booked.*** | *I'd like to discuss this more fully with you.*

fully-'fledged *adj BrE* completely developed, trained, or established [= **full-fledged** *AmE*]: *She's now a fully-fledged star.*

fumble /'fʌmbəl/ *v* [I] to try to hold or find something, using your hands in an awkward way: **+for/in/with** *I fumbled for the light switch.*

fume /fjuːm/ *v* [I] to be very angry: *She was fuming.*

fumes /fjuːmz/ *n* [plural] strong-smelling gas or smoke that is unpleasant to breathe in: *paint fumes* → see picture at **EXHAUST²**

fumigate /'fjuːmɪ̹geɪt/ *v* [T] to use special chemicals in order to get rid of infection or insects from a place —**fumigation** /ˌfjuːmɪ̹'geɪʃən/ *n* [U]

fun¹ /fʌn/ *n* [U]

1 enjoyment, or something that is enjoyable: *Did you have fun with your friends?* | **great fun/a lot of fun** *The picnic was great fun.* | **it is fun doing sth** *It was fun dressing up as somebody else.* | *It's* **no fun** (=not at all enjoyable) *being old.* | **(just) for fun** *The quiz is just for fun, so don't take it seriously.*

2 make fun of sb/sth to make unkind jokes about someone or something: *They made fun of him because he was fat.*

fun² *adj* **1** [only before noun] enjoyable: *It'll be a fun day out.* **2** a fun person is amusing and enjoyable to be with

function¹ /'fʌŋkʃən/ *n* [C] **1** the purpose that something has, or the job that someone does: *Lighting* ***performs*** *several* ***functions*** *in the home.* | *What is the function of a treasurer?* **2** a large party or official event: *The mayor was*

F

attending an official function. **3** one of the basic operations performed by a computer

function² *v* [I] **1** to work in the correct or intended way: *Rail services are now **functioning normally** again.* **2** to work in a particular way: *an understanding of how the economy functions*
  function as sth *phr v* to be used as another thing or to do what another thing usually does: *a phrase that functions as an adverb*

functional /'fʌŋkʃənəl/ *adj* **1** designed to be useful rather than attractive: *office furniture that is **purely functional*** **2** working correctly: *The new system is now **fully functional**.*

'function key *n* [C] one of the keys on a computer KEYBOARD, for example F1 or F2, that tell the computer to do something

fund¹ /fʌnd/ *n* [C]

1 funds [plural] the money that an organization needs or has: *We're trying to **raise funds** for a new sports hall.* | *The project was abandoned due to **lack of funds**.*
2 an amount of money that is kept for a particular purpose: *donations to the church restoration fund* | *the staff pension fund*

fund² *v* [T] to provide money for an activity, organization, event etc: *a project funded by the EU*

fundamental /ˌfʌndə'mentl◂/ *adj* relating to the most basic and important parts of something: *the fundamental cause of the problem* | *fundamental changes to the law* —**fundamentally** *adv*: *Their conclusions are fundamentally wrong.*

fundamentalist /ˌfʌndə'mentḷ̩st/ *n* [C] someone who follows religious laws very strictly —**fundamentalist** *adj* —**fundamentalism** *n* [U]

fundamentals /ˌfʌndə'mentlz/ *n* **the fundamentals of sth** the most important ideas, rules etc that something is based on: *the fundamentals of computer programming*

funding /'fʌndɪŋ/ *n* [U] money provided by an organization for a particular purpose: *government funding for universities*

'fund-ˌraising *n* [U] the activity of collecting money for a particular purpose, especially in order to help people —**fund-raiser** *n* [C]

funeral /'fjuːnərəl/ *n* [C] a ceremony for someone who has just died: *The funeral will be **held** on Friday.* | *His ex-wife did not **attend** the funeral.* | **funeral procession/service/mass etc**

'funeral diˌrector *n* [C] someone who is paid to organize a funeral [= undertaker *BrE*]

'funeral home also **'funeral ˌparlour** *n* [C] the place where a body is kept before a funeral

funfair /'fʌnfeə $ -fer/ *n* [C] *BrE* an outdoor event where you can ride on machines or play games to win prizes [= fair]

fungus /'fʌŋgəs/ *n* [C,U] plural **fungi** /-dʒaɪ, -gaɪ/ or **funguses** a simple type of plant that has no leaves or flowers and grows on wood or other surfaces. MUSHROOMS and MOULD are types of fungus.

funk /fʌŋk/ *n* [U] a style of popular music with a strong beat, based on JAZZ and African music

funky /'fʌŋki/ *adj informal* **1** funky music has a strong beat and is good to dance to **2** modern, fashionable, and interesting: *a funky Mexican restaurant*

funnel /'fʌnl/ *n* [C] **1** a tube with a wide top that you use for pouring a liquid into a narrow opening **2** *BrE* a metal CHIMNEY on top of a steam ship or train

funnily /'fʌnḷi/ *adv* **funnily enough** *spoken* used to say that something is unexpected or strange: *Funnily enough, I was just going to call you.*

funny /'fʌni/ *adj*

1 making you laugh: *You look funny in that hat.* | **funny story/joke/film etc** *She tells **hysterically funny** stories about her work.* | *I don't **find** him **funny** at all.* | *It's not funny* (=don't laugh) – *I could have been hurt!*

> ### THESAURUS
>
> **hilarious/hysterical** – extremely funny
> **witty** – using words in a funny and clever way: *witty remarks*
> **corny** – corny jokes etc have been told many times or are so silly that they are not funny
> **amusing/humorous** – slightly more formal ways to say that something is funny: *an amusing anecdote* (=a short, interesting, and funny story about an event or person)
> → FUN¹

2 strange or unusual: *I had a **funny feeling** I'd see you there.* | **it's funny how/that** *It's funny how I can never remember his name.* | *That's **funny**! I was just thinking about you when you called.* | **look/feel funny** *Are you OK? You look funny.* → see box at STRANGE
3 dishonest, illegal, or wrong: *There's **something funny** about this.* | *Remember, **no funny business** while I'm away.*

fur /fɜː $ fɜːr/ *n*

1 [U] the thick soft hair that covers the bodies of some animals such as cats and rabbits → see picture on page A2
2 [C,U] the fur-covered skin of an animal, used especially for making clothes, or a piece of clothing made from furs: *She never wears fur.* | **fur coat/hat etc** | **real/fake fur** *Is that real fur on the collar?*

furious /'fjʊəriəs $ 'fjʊr-/ *adj* **1** very angry: **+at/about** *He is furious at the court's decision.* | **+with** *She was furious with me.* | **+that** *I'm absolutely furious that nothing has been done.* → see box at ANGRY **2** done with a lot of speed, violence, or effort: *He worked **at a furious pace**.* —**furiously** *adv*

furl /fɜːl $ fɜːrl/ *v* [T] to roll or fold something such as an UMBRELLA or sail [≠ unfurl]

furlong /'fɜːlɒŋ $ 'fɜːrlɔːŋ/ *n* [C] a unit of distance, used in horse racing, equal to 1/8 of a mile or 201 metres

furnace /'fɜːnɪs $ 'fɜːr-/ *n* [C] an enclosed space with a very hot fire in it, used for melting metals or producing power or heat

furnish /'fɜːnɪʃ $ 'fɜːr-/ *v* [T] **1** to put furniture into a house or room: *They furnished the house with antiques.* **2** to provide someone with something that they need: *We can furnish you with a list of local solicitors.* —**furnished** *adj*: *a fully furnished apartment*

furnishings /'fɜːnɪʃɪŋz $ 'fɜːr-/ *n* [plural] the furniture and other things such as curtains in a room

F

furniture /'fɜːnɪtʃə $ 'fɜːrnɪtʃər/ *n* [U] large objects in a room such as chairs, tables, and beds: *office furniture* | *That bureau is a lovely piece of furniture*.

GRAMMAR

Furniture does not have a plural form. You can say **some furniture, any furniture,** or **pieces of furniture:** *When we first got married, we didn't have any furniture at all.*

furore *BrE*; **furor** *AmE* /fjʊ'rɔːri, 'fjʊərɔː $ 'fjʊrɔːr/ *n* [singular] *formal* a sudden expression of anger among a large group of people: *Darwin's theories caused a furore.*

furrow¹ /'fʌrəʊ $ 'fɜːroʊ/ *n* [C] **1** a deep line in the skin of someone's face **2** a wide deep line made in the ground, especially one in which to plant seeds

furrow² *v* [I,T] *literary* to make lines appear on someone's FOREHEAD: *Her brow furrowed in concentration.* —**furrowed** *adj*

furry /'fɜːri/ *adj* covered with fur or short threads: *small furry animals*

further¹ /'fɜːðə $ 'fɜːrðər/ *adv*

1 more, or to a greater degree or level: *I have nothing further to say.* | *His career had not progressed any further.* | **go further/take sth further** *Should we go further and ban smoking in the whole building?*

2 also **farther** at or to a longer distance away: *I can't walk any further.* | **+down/along etc** *They live further down the street.*

3 into the past or future: *Ten years further on, we still haven't found a cure.*

further² *adj* [only before noun] additional: *Are there any further questions?* | *Visit our website for further details.*

further³ *v* [T] *formal* to help something to succeed: *efforts to further the cause of peace*

further edu'cation *n* [U] *BrE* education for adults after leaving school that is not at a university

furthermore /ˌfɜːðə'mɔː $ 'fɜːrðərmɔːr/ *adv formal* in addition to what has already been said

furthest /'fɜːðɪst $ 'fɜːr-/ *adj, adv* at the greatest distance from a place or point in time: *He sat on the chair furthest from me.*

furtive /'fɜːtɪv $ 'fɜːr-/ *adj* behaving as if you want to keep something secret: *a furtive glance* —**furtively** *adv*

fury /'fjʊəri $ 'fjʊri/ *n* [singular, U] extreme anger: *She shook with fury.*

fuse¹ /fjuːz/ *n* [C] **1** a short wire inside a piece of electrical equipment or an electrical system, that melts if too much electricity passes through it, preventing damage **2** a part that is connected to a bomb, FIREWORK etc, that delays or starts the explosion → **blow a fuse** at **BLOW¹**

fuse² *v* [I,T] **1** to join together and become one thing, or to join two things together: *The bones of the spine had fused together.* | *His style fuses Indian music and hip-hop.* **2** *BrE* if an electrical system fuses, or if you fuse it, it stops working because the fuse has melted: *The lights had fused.*

fuselage /'fjuːzəlɑːʒ $ -sə-/ *n* [C] the main part of a plane → see picture at **AEROPLANE**

fusion /'fjuːʒən/ *n* [C,U] when two things are joined together or combined: *the fusion of hydrogen atoms*

fuss¹ /fʌs/ *n* **1** [singular, U] anxious or excited behaviour or activity, usually about unimportant things: *I don't see what all the fuss is about.* | *They wanted a quiet wedding without any fuss.* **2** **make a fuss/kick up a fuss** to complain angrily or noisily about something: *One customer made a big fuss because his food was cold.* **3** **make a fuss of sb** *BrE*, **make a fuss over sb** *AmE* to pay a lot of attention to someone and try to make them comfortable: *Grandma always makes a fuss of me.*

fuss² *v* [I] to behave in an anxious way, worrying over unimportant things: *Stop fussing! We'll be home soon!*

fuss over sb *phr v* to pay a lot of attention to making someone comfortable: *Don't fuss over me, mom, I'm fine.*

fussy /'fʌsi/ *adj* someone who is fussy is very careful about what they choose and is difficult to please: **+about** *He's very fussy about what he wears.* | *I'm not fussy about where we go tonight* (=I don't mind). | *She's a fussy eater.* → see box at **CHARACTER**

futile /'fjuːtaɪl $ -tl/ *adj* certain to be unsuccessful: *a futile attempt to put out the fire* —**futility** /fjuː'tɪlɪti/ *n* [U] *the futility of war*

futon /'fuːtɒn $ -tɑːn/ *n* [C] a MATTRESS that can be used as a bed or folded into a seat

future¹ /'fjuːtʃə $ -ər/ *adj* [only before noun]

1 likely to happen or exist in the future: *future patterns of climate change* | *We will preserve this forest for future generations.* | **future wife/ husband/son-in-law etc** (=someone who will be your wife, husband etc) *He met his future wife at college.*

2 the future tense in grammar, the form of a verb that is used for things that will happen in the future

future² *n*

1 the future the time after now: *What are your plans for the future?* | *In the future, people will be able to travel to other planets.* | *It may be useful at some time in the future.* | **in the near/ immediate future** (=soon) *I'm hoping to go to Atlanta in the near future.* → see box at **SOON**

2 [C] what someone will do, or what will happen to someone or something in the future: *My parents have already planned out my whole future.* | **+of** *He is optimistic about the future of the business.* | *I've decided to stay, no matter what the future holds.*

3 in future *BrE* from now: *In future, staff must wear identity badges.*

future 'perfect *n* **the future perfect** in grammar, the form of a verb that is used to show that an action will be completed before a particular time in the future: *I will have finished by tomorrow afternoon.*

futuristic /ˌfjuːtʃə'rɪstɪk◂/ *adj* something which is futuristic looks unusual and modern, as if it belongs in the future instead of the present: *a futuristic sports stadium*

fuzz /fʌz/ *n* [U] short soft hair or fur

fuzzy /'fʌzi/ *adj* **1** unclear: *Some of the photos are a little fuzzy.* **2** fuzzy hair is soft and curly

F

G, g

G, g /dʒiː/ n [C,U] plural **G's, g's** **1** the seventh letter of the English alphabet **2** the fifth note in the musical SCALE of C MAJOR, or the musical KEY based on this note

g a written abbreviation of **gram**

gabble /'gæbəl/ v [I,T] to talk so quickly that people cannot understand what you are saying

gable /'geɪbəl/ n [C] the top part of a wall of a house where it joins a roof, making a shape like a TRIANGLE

gadget /'gædʒɪt/ n [C] a small tool or machine that helps you to do something: *a neat gadget for sharpening knives*

gaffe /gæf/ n [C] an embarrassing mistake

gag¹ /gæg/ v **gagged, gagging** **1** [I] to be unable to swallow and feel as if you are about to bring up food from your stomach **2** [T] to cover someone's mouth with a piece of cloth so that they cannot talk: *They gagged her and tied her to a chair.* **3** [T] to stop people expressing their opinions: *an attempt to gag political activists*

gag² n [C] **1** informal a joke or funny story **2** a piece of cloth used to gag someone

gaggle /'gægəl/ n **1 a gaggle of tourists/ children etc** a noisy group of people: *a gaggle of schoolchildren* **2 a gaggle of geese** a group of GEESE

gaiety /'geɪɪti/ n [U] old-fashioned a feeling of fun and happiness

gaily /'geɪli/ adv in a happy, cheerful way

gain¹ /geɪn/ v

1 [T] to get or achieve something: *The country gained independence in 1957.* | **gain control/ power** *The army gained control of enemy territory.*

THESAURUS

Gain means to get something useful or necessary: *I've gained a lot of useful experience.*
Do not use **gain** to talk about getting money for the work you do. Use **earn**: *He earns more than I do.*
Get is a less formal way of saying **earn**: *I get £20 an hour.*
Win means to get a prize in a game or competition: *The first person to get all the answers right will win $100.*

2 [I,T] to get an advantage from something: **gain (sth) from (doing) sth** *There is much to be gained from getting expert advice.* | *Who really stands to gain* (=will get an advantage) *from these tax cuts?*

3 [T] to increase in size or weight: *I've gained a lot of weight recently.*

4 [I] if a clock gains, it works too quickly and shows a later time than the real time

5 gain ground to become more popular or stronger: *The anti-smoking lobby is gaining ground.*

gain on sb phr v to start getting closer to someone you are chasing

gain² n

1 [C] an advantage or an improvement: **+in** *substantial gains in efficiency* | **+to/from** *There are obvious gains for the student.* | *The party made considerable gains at local elections.*

2 [C,U] an increase in the amount or level of something: **+in** *a gain in weekly output* | *Try to avoid too much weight gain.*

gait /geɪt/ n [singular] the way that someone walks: *He had a slow ambling gait.*

gala /'gɑːlə $ 'geɪlə, 'gælə/ n [C] a special public performance or competition: *a charity gala evening* | *a swimming gala*

galaxy /'gæləksi/ n [C] plural **galaxies** one of the large groups of stars that make up the universe → see box at SPACE

gale /geɪl/ n [C] a very strong wind: *Our fence blew down in the gale.* → see box at WIND

gall /gɔːl $ gɒl/ n **have the gall to do sth** to do something rude and unreasonable: *He had the gall to blame Lucy.*

gallant /'gælənt/ adj old-fashioned **1** a gallant man is kind and polite towards women **2** brave: *a gallant attempt to save lives* —**gallantly** adv

'gall ,bladder n [C] the organ in your body in which BILE is stored

gallery /'gæləri/ n [C] plural **galleries** **1** a room or building where you can look at famous paintings and other types of art: *the Uffizzi gallery in Florence* **2** an upper floor inside a large room, where you can sit and watch what is happening in the room below

galley /'gæli/ n [C] **1** a kitchen on a ship or a plane **2** an ancient warship that was rowed by SLAVES

galling /'gɔːlɪŋ $ 'gɒː-/ adj something that is galling makes you feel upset and angry because it is unfair

gallon /'gælən/ n [C] a unit for measuring liquid, equal to 4.55 litres in Britain or 3.79 litres in the US

gallop /'gæləp/ v [I] if a horse gallops, it runs very quickly —**gallop** n [singular]

gallows /'gæləʊz $ -loʊz/ n [C] plural **gallows** a structure used for killing criminals by hanging them from a rope

galore /gə'lɔː $ -'lɔːr/ adj [only after noun] in large amounts: *There are bargains galore in the sales.*

galvanize also **-ise** BrE /'gælvənaɪz/ v [T] to shock or surprise someone so much that they do something: *The letter galvanized us into action.*

galvanized also **-ised** BrE /'gælvənaɪzd/ adj galvanized metal has been treated in a special way so that it does not RUST

gambit /'gæmbɪt/ n [C] something you do or say to get an advantage for yourself

gamble¹ /'gæmbəl/ v [I,T]

1 to try to win money by guessing the result of a horse race, by playing cards etc [➡ **gamble**]: **+on** *Jack loves gambling on the horses.*

2 to do something that involves a risk and might not succeed: **+on** *They're gambling on all the team being fit by Saturday.*
—**gambling** *n* [U] *Gambling is illegal in some states.* —**gambler** *n* [C]

gamble² *n* [singular] an action or plan that involves a risk but that you hope will succeed: **+on** *We cannot afford to take a gamble on a new product.*

game¹ /geɪm/ *n*

1 [C] an activity or sport in which people compete with each other according to agreed rules [➡ match]: **computer/card/ball etc game** *He doesn't like card games.* | *We used to play games like chess.* | **win/lose a game** *They've won their last three games.* | **a game of sth** *How about a game of cards?*

2 games [plural] *BrE* a lesson at school in which children do sport [= PE]: *Games is my favourite lesson.*

3 games [plural] an organized sports event: *the Olympic Games*

4 [C] an activity in which children play: **+of** *a game of hide-and-seek* | *The children are playing a game in the backyard.*

5 sb's game how well someone plays a game or sport: **improve/raise your game** *He's taking lessons to improve his game.*

6 give the game away to accidentally say something that lets someone guess a secret

7 play games to behave in a way that is dishonest or not serious: *We want a deal. We're not interested in playing games.*

8 [U] wild animals and birds that are hunted for food or as a sport → see box at MEAT
→ BALL GAME, BOARD GAME, VIDEO GAME

game² *adj* [not before noun] willing to try something: *I'm game if you are.*

gamekeeper /'geɪmkiːpə $ -ər/ *n* [C] someone whose job is to look after wild animals and birds that will be hunted

'game plan *n* [C] a plan for achieving success, especially in business or sport

'game show *n* [C] a television programme in which people play games in order to win prizes
→ see box at TELEVISION

gammon /'gæmən/ *n* [U] *BrE* meat from a pig that has been preserved using salt

gamut /'gæmət/ *n* [singular] the complete range of possibilities: **+of** *College opened up a whole gamut of new experiences.*

gang¹ /gæŋ/ *n* [C] **1** a group of young people, especially a group that often causes trouble and fights: *two rival street gangs* | **+of** *a gang of kids* | **in a gang** *Do you want to be in our gang?*
→ see box at GROUP **2** a group of criminals who work together: **+of** *a gang of smugglers* **3** *informal* a group of friends: *All the gang will be there.*

gang² *v*
gang up on/against sb *phr v* to join together in order to criticize or attack someone: *Helen thinks everyone's ganging up on her.*

gangland /'gæŋlænd, -lənd/ *adj* **gangland killing/murder/shooting etc** a killing etc relating to the world of organized and violent crime

gangling /'gæŋglɪŋ/ also **gangly** /'gæŋgli/ *adj* unusually tall and thin and not very graceful: *a gangly teenager*

gangrene /'gæŋgriːn/ *n* [U] a medical condition in which a person's flesh in part of their body starts to decay

gangster /'gæŋstə $ -ər/ *n* [C] a member of a group of violent criminals: *Al Capone was a Chicago gangster.*

gangway /'gæŋweɪ/ *n* [C] **1** *BrE* the space between two rows of seats in a theatre, bus, or train **2** a board or steps between a boat and the shore for people to walk down

gaol /dʒeɪl/ a British spelling of JAIL

gaoler /'dʒeɪlə $ -ər/ *n* [C] a British spelling of JAILER

gap

gap /gæp/ *n* [C]

1 a space between two things: **+in** *a gap in the traffic* | **+between** *the gap between two rows of seats*

2 a big difference between two things: **+between** *the widening gap between the rich and the poor* | *His films try to bridge the gap between tradition and modern life.*

3 something that is missing that stops something else from being good or complete: **+in** *His death has left a huge gap in my life.* | *Murphy will fill the gap left by Hurst's departure from the team.*

4 a period of time in which nothing happens or nothing is said: *I went back to university after a gap of two years.* | **+in** *an awkward gap in the conversation*
→ GENERATION GAP

gape /geɪp/ *v* [I] to look at something or someone in surprise, with your mouth open: **+at** *What are all these people gaping at?*

gaping /'geɪpɪŋ/ *adj* [only before noun] a gaping hole, wound, or mouth is wide and open

'gap year *n* [C] *BrE* a year between leaving school and starting university, in which someone travels or works

garage /'gærɪdʒ, -ɑːʒ $ gə'rɑːʒ/ *n* [C]
1 a building for keeping a car in: *I'll put the car in the garage.*
2 a place where cars are repaired: *My car's at the garage.* | *I'll take the car to the garage tomorrow.*
3 *BrE* a place where you buy petrol [= gas station *AmE*]

garb /gɑːb $ gɑːrb/ *n* [U] *formal* a particular style of clothing

garbage /'gɑːbɪdʒ $ 'gɑːr-/ *n* [singular,U] especially *AmE*

G

1 waste material, such as paper, empty containers, and food thrown away [= **rubbish** *BrE*]: *Can you take out the garbage?* → see box at **RUBBISH**
2 stupid words or ideas: *He's talking garbage!*

'garbage ˌcan *n* [C] *AmE* a container that you put waste in [= **dustbin** *BrE*] → see box at **BIN** → and **RUBBISH**

'garbage colˌlector *n* [C] *AmE* someone whose job is to collect waste from garbage cans [= **dustman** *BrE*]

garbled /ˈgɑːbəld $ ˈgɑːr-/ *adj* garbled speech or writing is very unclear and confusing: *a garbled phone message*

garden /ˈgɑːdn $ ˈgɑːr-/ *n* [C]
1 *BrE* an area of land next to a house, where there are flowers, grass, and other plants [= **yard** *AmE*]: *Our house has a small garden.* | *He's in the garden cutting the grass.* | **back/front garden**
2 *AmE* a part of the area next to your house, where you grow plants of a particular kind: *a herb garden*
3 gardens [plural] a large area of land where plants are grown for the public to see

'garden ˌcentre *n* [C] *BrE* a place that sells plants and equipment for gardens [= **nursery** *AmE*] → see box at **SHOP**

gardener /ˈgɑːdnə $ ˈgɑːrdnər/ *n* [C] someone who works in a garden, as a job or for pleasure

gardening /ˈgɑːdnɪŋ $ ˈgɑːr-/ *n* [U] work that you do in a garden: *I'll do some gardening this afternoon.* —**garden** *v* [I]

gargantuan /gɑːˈgæntʃuən $ gɑːr-/ *adj literary* extremely large

gargle /ˈgɑːgəl $ ˈgɑːr-/ *v* [I] to hold a liquid in your throat and blow air through it without swallowing it

garish /ˈgeərɪʃ $ ˈger-/ *adj* very brightly coloured and unpleasant to look at: *a garish carpet*

garland /ˈgɑːlənd $ ˈgɑːr-/ *n* [C] a ring of flowers or leaves

garlic /ˈgɑːlɪk $ ˈgɑːr-/ *n* [U] a small plant like an onion with a very strong taste, used in cooking: *Add a clove of garlic* (=a piece of garlic).

garment /ˈgɑːmənt $ ˈgɑːr-/ *n* [C] *formal* a piece of clothing: *Wash delicate garments by hand.*

garnish /ˈgɑːnɪʃ $ ˈgɑːr-/ *v* [T] to decorate food with small pieces of a fruit or vegetables —**garnish** *n* [C]

garret /ˈgærɪt/ *n* [C] a small room at the top of a house just under the roof

garrison /ˈgærɪsən/ *n* [C] a group of soldiers who live in a building or town and defend it

garters /ˈgɑːtəz $ ˈgɑːrtərz/ *n* [plural] pieces of ELASTIC fixed to a woman's underwear and to her STOCKINGS to hold them up [= **suspenders** *BrE*]

gas¹ /gæs/ *n plural* **gases** or **gasses**
1 [C,U] a substance such as air, which is not solid or liquid: *hydrogen gas* | *a cloud of toxic gas*
2 [U] a clear substance like air that is burned to give heat for cooking and heating: *a gas stove*
3 [U] *AmE* also **gasoline** a liquid that is used for producing power in car engines [= **petrol** *BrE*]: *I spend over $200 a month on gas.*
→ **NATURAL GAS**

gas² *v* [T] **gassed**, **gassing** to attack or kill someone with poisonous gas

'gas ˌchamber *n* [C] a large room in which people or animals are killed with poisonous gas

gash /gæʃ/ *n* [C] a deep cut —**gash** *v* [T]

'gas mask *n* [C] a piece of equipment that you wear over your face to protect you from breathing poisonous gases

gasoline /ˈgæsəliːn/ *n* [U] *AmE* a liquid that is used for producing power in car engines [= **gas**; = **petrol** *BrE*]

gasp /gɑːsp $ gæsp/ *v* [I] **1** to breathe in suddenly because you are surprised or in pain: **+in/with** *Ollie gasped with pain and fell to the ground.* **2** to quickly breathe in a lot of air because you are having difficulty breathing normally: *Brendan was gasping for breath.* —**gasp** *n* [C] *a gasp of surprise*

'gas ˌstation *n* [C] *AmE* a place that sells petrol [= **petrol station** *BrE*]

gastric /ˈgæstrɪk/ *adj technical* relating to your stomach: *a gastric ulcer*

gastronomic /ˌgæstrəˈnɒmɪk◂ $ -ˈnɑː-/ *adj* [only before noun] *formal* relating to cooking and eating good food

gate /geɪt/ *n* [C]
1 a door in a fence or outside wall [➡ **door**]: **open/close/shut a gate** *I ran back to close the gate.* | **front/back/main gate** *Make sure the back gate is locked.*
2 the place where you leave an airport building to get on the plane: *Please go to gate 4.*

gateau /ˈgætəʊ $ gɑːˈtoʊ/ *n* [C,U] *BrE plural* **gateaux** /-təʊz $ -ˈtoʊz/ a large cake decorated with cream, fruit, chocolate etc

gatecrash /ˈgeɪtkræʃ/ *v* [I,T] to go to a party when you have not been invited —**gatecrasher** *n* [C]

gateway /ˈgeɪtweɪ/ *n* **1** [C] an opening in a fence or wall where there is a gate **2 the gateway to sth** a place, especially a city, that you go through in order to reach another place: *St. Louis is the gateway to the West.*

gather /ˈgæðə $ -ər/ *v*
1 [I,T] if people gather somewhere, or if someone gathers them, they come together in the same place: *A crowd gathered to watch the fight.* | **+round/around** *Can you gather round so I can show you how it works?* | *If you gather the kids, I'll start the car.* | **be gathered** *Dozens of photographers were gathered outside Jackson's hotel.*
2 [T] to believe that something is true based on the information you have: **+(that)** *I gather you've had some problems with the computer.* | *You two know each other, I gather.*
3 [T] to bring things from different places together: *My job is to gather information on the subject.* | **gather sth up/together** *Anna gathered up her books.*
4 gather speed/force/momentum etc to move faster, become stronger, get more support etc: *The cart gathered speed as it rolled down the hill.*

gathering /ˈgæðərɪŋ/ *n* [C] a party or meeting when a large number of people spend time together: *a family gathering*

gauche /gəʊʃ $ goʊʃ/ *adj* someone who is gauche says or does things that are considered impolite because they do not know the right way to behave

gaudy /'gɔːdi $ 'gɒːdi/ adj unpleasantly bright and cheap: *gaudy jewellery*

gauge¹ /geɪdʒ/ n [C] **1** an instrument that measures the amount or size of something: *a fuel gauge* **2** a measurement of the width or thickness of something: *heavy gauge black polythene* **3 a gauge of sth** something that helps you make a judgment about a person or situation: *Sales are a gauge of consumer spending.*

gauge² v [T] **1** to judge what someone is likely to do or how they feel: *I looked at Chris trying to gauge his reaction.* | **+whether/what/how etc** *It is difficult to gauge what her next move will be.* **2** to calculate the size or amount of something

gaunt /gɔːnt $ gɒːnt/ adj very thin, pale, and unhealthy

gauntlet /'gɔːntlɪt $ 'gɒːnt-/ n **1 throw down the gauntlet** to invite someone to fight, argue, or compete with you **2 run the gauntlet** to be criticized or attacked by a lot of people: *The minister ran the gauntlet of demonstrators.* **3** [C] a long thick GLOVE that you wear to protect your hand

gauze /gɔːz $ gɒːz/ n [U] thin light cloth with small holes in it, often used for covering wounds

gave /geɪv/ v the past tense of GIVE

gawk /gɔːk $ gɒːk/ v [I] informal to look at someone or something for a long time, in a way that looks stupid: **+at** *Don't just stand there gawking at those girls.*

gawky /'gɔːki $ 'gɒːki/ adj someone who is gawky is tall and not graceful: *a gawky teenager*

gawp /gɔːp $ gɒːp/ v [I] BrE informal to look at something for a long time, especially with your mouth open because you are surprised: **+at** *What are you gawping at?*

gay¹ /geɪ/ adj **1** a gay person is sexually attracted to people of the same sex [= homosexual; ➡ lesbian]: *My son's just told me he's gay.* **2** old-fashioned bright or attractive: *gay colours* **3** old-fashioned happy and excited: *gay laughter*

gay² n [C] someone, especially a man, who is sexually attracted to people of the same sex [= homosexual]

gaze /geɪz/ v [I] to look at someone or something for a long time: **+at/into etc** *She sat gazing out of the window.* —**gaze** n [singular] *Judith tried to avoid his gaze.*

GB, Gb the written abbreviation of **gigabyte**

GCSE /ˌdʒiː siː es 'iː/ n [C] **General Certificate of Secondary Education** an examination that is taken by students aged 15 or 16 in Britain

GDP /ˌdʒiː diː 'piː/ n [U] **gross domestic product** the total value of all the goods and services produced in a country in one year, except for income received from abroad [➡ GNP]

gear¹ /gɪə $ gɪr/ n
1 [C,U] the machinery in a vehicle such as a car, truck, or bicycle that you use to go at different speeds: *The car has five gears.* | **in first/second etc gear** *We drove along in first gear.* | *I had to change gear halfway up the hill.* → see box at DRIVE → see picture at BICYCLE
2 [U] special equipment, clothing etc that you need for a particular activity: *camping gear*

gear² v **be geared to/towards sb/sth** to be organized in order to achieve a particular pur-

pose: *All his training was geared to winning an Olympic medal.* | *advertisements that are geared towards children*

gear up phr v to prepare for something: **+for** *They are gearing up for a conference in May.*

gearbox /'gɪəbɒks $ 'gɪrbɑːks/ n [C] the system of gears in a vehicle

'gear stick BrE also **'gear ˌlever** BrE; **'gear shift** AmE n [C] a stick that you move to change gears in a vehicle → see picture on page A12

GED /ˌdʒiː iː 'diː/ n **the GED General Equivalency Diploma** a document that is given to someone in the US who did not finish their HIGH SCHOOL education but has studied and passed an examination later

gee /dʒiː/ spoken informal especially AmE used to show that you are surprised or annoyed

geek /giːk/ n [C] informal someone who is not popular because they wear unfashionable clothes and do not know how to behave in social situations: *a computer geek*

geese /giːs/ n the plural of GOOSE

geezer /'giːzə $ -ər/ n [C] informal **1** BrE a man **2** AmE an old man

gel¹ /dʒel/ n [C,U] a thick liquid, especially one for cleaning or for arranging your hair: *hair gel* | *shower gel*

gel² v [I] **gelled, gelling** also **jell** especially AmE **1** if an idea gels, it becomes clearer or more definite: *Don't start writing until the idea has gelled in your mind.* **2** if people gel, they begin to work together well as a group **3** if a liquid gels, it becomes firmer and thicker

gelatine /'dʒelətiːn $ -tn/ BrE, **gelatin** /-tɪn $ -tn/ AmE n [U] a clear substance used when cooking liquid food, to make it thicker

gelignite /'dʒelɪgnaɪt/ n [U] a very powerful explosive

gem /dʒem/ n [C] **1** a valuable stone that has been cut into a particular shape to make a piece of jewellery [➡ jewel] **2** informal someone or something that is very special

Gemini /'dʒemɪnaɪ $ -niː/ n **1** [U] the sign of the Zodiac of people born between May 22 and June 21 **2** [C] someone who has this sign

gender /'dʒendə $ -ər/ n **1** [C,U] the fact of being male or female: *discrimination on the grounds of gender* (=because someone is male or female) | *society's traditional gender roles* **2** [U] the system in some languages of dividing nouns, adjectives, and PRONOUNS into MASCULINE, FEMININE, or NEUTER

gene /dʒiːn/ n [C] a part of a CELL in a living thing that controls how it develops. Parents pass genes on to their children.

general¹ /'dʒenərəl/ adj

1 relating to the whole of something or its main features, not the details [≠ specific]: **in general** *What are your hopes for the future, in general?* | *I've a general idea of what to say.* | *His general health is good.*

2 including most people or situations: **in general** *In general, women are paid less.* | *The drug is not available to the general public* (=most ordinary people). | *As a general rule, I pay in cash.* | *The drug is not yet available for general use.*

G

3 [only before noun] not limited to one subject or type: *a **general** knowledge quiz* | *Walford **General** Hospital*
4 used in the job title of someone who has complete responsibility for a particular area of work: *the **general** manager*

general², **General** *n* [C] an officer with a high rank in an army or air force

,**general anaes'thetic** *BrE*; **general anesthetic** *AmE n* [C,U] a substance used to make a patient who is having an operation unconscious so that they do not feel anything

,**general e'lection** *n* [C] an election in which all the voters in a country elect a new government

generalization also **-isation** *BrE* /ˌdʒenərəlaɪˈzeɪʃən $ -lə-/ *n* [C] *disapproving* a statement that may be true for most people or situations, but that is not true for all of them: **sweeping/broad generalization** *Don't make sweeping generalizations.* —**generalize** /ˈdʒenərəlaɪz/ *v* [I]

generally /ˈdʒenərəli/ *adv*
1 considering something as a whole, rather than its details: *The arrangements have **generally** worked well.* | ***Generally speaking**, cars are cheaper in Europe.*
2 by or to most people: *It's **generally accepted** that the story is true.*
3 usually: *I **generally** get to work early.*

,**general prac'titioner** *n* [C] a GP

,**general 'strike** *n* [C] a situation when most of the workers in a country refuse to work

generate /ˈdʒenəreɪt/ *v* [T] **1** to make something happen or start to exist: *Our discussion generated a lot of ideas.* | *Tourism generates a lot of **income** for the town.* **2** to produce energy, power, heat etc

generation /ˌdʒenəˈreɪʃən/ *n*
1 [C also + plural verb *BrE*] all the people in a society or family who are about the same age: **+of** *Three generations of the Lambe family have lived here.* | **younger/older generation** *The younger generation don't know what hard work is.* | **first-generation/second-generation etc** (=being of a member of the first people to live or be born in a particular country) *first-generation immigrant families* | *Our generation has never known a war.*
2 [C] the average period of time between your birth and the birth of your children: *A **generation** ago, no one had home computers.* | *Some families have lived here **for generations**.*
3 [C] machines that are at the same stage of development: **+of** *a **new generation** of cell phones* | *first-generation nuclear reactors* (=the first ones built or made)
4 [U] the process of producing power or energy: **+of** *the generation of solar power*

,**gene'ration ,gap** *n* [singular] a lack of understanding between older and younger people

generator /ˈdʒenəreɪtə $ -ər/ *n* [C] a machine that produces electricity

generic /dʒɪˈnerɪk/ *adj* **1** relating to a whole group of similar things, rather than just one of them **2** a generic product does not have a BRAND NAME (=a name showing it is made by a particular company) —**generically** /-kli/ *adv*

generosity /ˌdʒenəˈrɒsɪti $ -ˈrɑː-/ *n* [U] a generous attitude, or generous behaviour: **+to/towards** *I never forgot the generosity he **showed** to my parents.*

generous /ˈdʒenərəs/ *adj*
1 someone who is generous is kind and enjoys giving people things or helping them [≠ **mean**]: **+to/towards** *Billy was extraordinarily generous to his friends.* | **+with** *Jim is always generous with his time* (=is willing to spend time helping people). | *It was generous of you to offer to help.* | **generous offer/gesture/donation etc** *a very generous gift*
2 more than the usual amount: **generous amount/helping/portion etc** *a generous slice of cake*
—**generously** *adv*: *Please **give** generously to Cancer Research.*

genesis /ˈdʒenɪsɪs/ *n* [singular] *formal* the beginning of something

genetic /dʒɪˈnetɪk/ *adj* relating to GENES or GENETICS: *genetic research* | *genetic defects* —**genetically** /-kli/ *adv*

ge,netically 'modified also abbreviation **GM** *adj* genetically modified food, crops etc have been changed so that their GENE structure is different from the one they have naturally

ge,netic engin'eering *n* [U] the science of changing the GENES of a living thing

ge,netic 'fingerprinting *n* [U] the process of examining the pattern of someone's GENES to find out whether they are guilty of a crime

genetics /dʒɪˈnetɪks/ *n* [plural] the study of how GENES affect the development of living things —**geneticist** /-tɪsɪst/ *n* [C]

genial /ˈdʒiːniəl/ *adj* friendly, happy, and kind —**geniality** /ˌdʒiːniˈælɪti/ *n* [U] —**genially** *adv*

genie /ˈdʒiːni/ *n* [C] a magical creature in old stories who can make wishes come true

genitals /ˈdʒenɪtlz/ also **genitalia** /ˌdʒenɪˈteɪliə/ *n* [plural] *formal* the sex organs that are outside your body —**genital** *adj* [only before noun]

genius /ˈdʒiːniəs/ *n* **1** [U] very great and unusual intelligence, ability, or skill: **work/writer/woman etc of genius** *a work of pure genius* | *His solution to the problem was **a stroke of genius*** (=a very clever idea). **2** [C] someone who has an unusually high level of intelligence, ability, or skill in a particular subject: **musical/artistic etc genius** *Newton was a mathematical genius.*

genocide /ˈdʒenəsaɪd/ *n* [U] the murder of a whole race of people

genome /ˈdʒiːnəʊm $ -noʊm/ *n* [C] *technical* all the GENES in one cell of a living thing: *the human genome*

genre /ˈʒɒnrə $ ˈʒɑːnrə/ *n* [C] *formal* a type of art, music, literature etc that has a particular style or feature: *a fashionable literary genre*

gent /dʒent/ *n* [C] *BrE informal* **1** a gentleman **2 the gents** a public toilet for men [= **men's room** *AmE*]

genteel /dʒenˈtiːl/ *adj* polite in a way that was typical of people in the past who had a high social position

gentle /'dʒentl/ adj
1 kind and careful not to hurt anyone or anything [≠ **rough**]: *Arnold is a gentle, caring person.* | **gentle voice/smile**
2 not strong, extreme, or violent: **gentle exercise/walk etc** *We broke into a gentle run.* | *Melt the butter over a gentle heat.* | *a gentle breeze*
—**gentleness** n [U] —**gently** adv: *a gently sloping hill*

gentleman /'dʒentlmən/ n [C] plural **gentlemen** /-mən/
1 a polite word used for a man you do not know [➡ **lady**]: *Good evening ladies and gentlemen* (=used to begin a speech). → see box at **MAN**
2 a man who is polite and behaves well [➡ **lady**]: *Roy is a perfect gentleman.*
—**gentlemanly** adj

gentrification /ˌdʒentrɪfɪ'keɪʃən/ n [U] when a poor area improves after people who have money move there

gentry /'dʒentri/ n [plural] old-fashioned people of a high social class

genuflect /'dʒenjʊflekt/ v [I] formal to bend your knees in a church or other holy place as a sign of respect

genuine /'dʒenjuːn/ adj
1 a genuine feeling or desire is one that you really feel, not one that you pretend to feel [= **sincere**]: *There was genuine affection in his voice.* | *The killer showed genuine remorse.* | *Her enthusiasm seemed quite genuine.*
2 something that is genuine is real or true [= **real**]: *genuine diamonds*
3 approving someone who is genuine is honest and sincere [≠ **false**]: *She's a charming girl, and far more genuine than her sister.*
—**genuinely** adv

genus /'dʒiːnəs, 'dʒen-/ n [C] plural **genera** /'dʒenərə/ technical a group of animals or plants of the same general type [➡ **species**]

geography /dʒi'ɒgrəfi, 'dʒɒg- $ dʒi'ɑːg-/ n [U] the study of the countries, oceans, cities, populations etc of the world or of a particular area: +**of** *the geography of Asia* —**geographer** n [C] —**geographical** /ˌdʒiːə'græfɪkəl◀/ **geographic** adj

geology /dʒi'ɒlədʒi $ -'ɑːl-/ n [U] the study of rocks, soil, minerals etc and how they have changed over time —**geologist** n [C] —**geological** /ˌdʒiːə'lɒdʒɪkəl◀ $ -'lɑː-/ adj

geometric /ˌdʒiːə'metrɪk◀/ also **geometrical** /-trɪkəl/ adj **1** having a regular pattern of shapes and lines **2** relating to geometry

geometry /dʒi'ɒmɪtri $ -'ɑːm-/ n [U] the mathematical study of angles, shapes, lines etc

Georgian /'dʒɔːdʒən, -dʒiən $ 'dʒɔːrdʒən/ adj Georgian buildings, furniture etc were built or made in Britain in the 18th century

geranium /dʒə'reɪniəm/ n [C] a plant with red, pink, or white flowers and round leaves

geriatric /ˌdʒeri'ætrɪk◀/ adj [only before noun] relating to the medical care of old people: *geriatric medicine*

germ /dʒɜːm $ dʒɜːrm/ n
1 [C usually plural] a very small living thing that can make you ill [= **bacteria**]: *Sneezing spreads germs.* | *Kitchen cloths can harbour* (=contain) germs. | *fears of germ warfare* (=the use of germs to harm or kill people in a war)
2 [C usually singular] the early stages of something or a very small amount of an idea, feeling etc: **germ of an idea/theory etc** *The germ of the idea goes back to Ancient Rome.* | *There's a germ of truth in what he says.*

German measles /ˌdʒɜːmən 'miːzəlz $ ˌdʒɜːr-/ n [U] RUBELLA

germinate /'dʒɜːmɪneɪt $ 'dʒɜːr-/ v **1** [I,T] if a seed germinates, or if it is germinated, it begins to grow **2** [I] if an idea or feeling germinates, it starts to develop —**germination** /ˌdʒɜːmɪ'neɪʃən $ ˌdʒɜːr-/ n [U]

gerund /'dʒerənd/ n [C] technical a noun formed from the PRESENT PARTICIPLE of a verb, for example 'shopping' in the sentence 'I hate shopping'

gestation /dʒe'steɪʃən/ n [U] technical the process during which a baby grows inside its mother's body

gesticulate /dʒe'stɪkjʊleɪt/ v [I] to make movements with your arms and hands while speaking, usually because you are excited or angry

gesture¹ /'dʒestʃə $ -ər/ n [C] **1** a movement of your head, arm, or hand to express your feelings: +**of** *Jim raised his hand in a gesture of despair.* | *He's making rude gestures at us.*
2 something you do or say to show that you care about someone: +**of** *As a gesture of goodwill, the wine is free.* | *Sending flowers was a nice gesture.*

gesture² v [I] to move your head, arm, or hand in order to tell someone something: *Tom gestured for me to move.*

get /get/ v past tense **got** /gɒt $ gɑːt/ past participle **got** BrE, **gotten** /'gɒtn $ 'gɑːtn/ AmE present participle **getting**
1 [T] to receive, obtain, or buy something: **get sth from sb** *I got an email from Chris.* | **get sb sth** *Dad got him a job at the factory.* | **get sth for sb** *Could you get some information for me?* | **get sth from sb** *Pam ran to get help from a nearby house.* | **get sth for £5/$9 etc** *You can get a laptop for under £500.* | **get yourself sth** *He's gotten himself a new girlfriend already.* | **get £5/£45,000 etc** (=receive £5 etc as payment for something) *Hospital porters get £4.50 an hour.* | **get 90%/a good mark etc** (=receive 90% etc for a test, competition etc) *Who got the highest score?* → see box at **GAIN**
2 [T] to bring someone or something back from somewhere [= **fetch**]: **get sb sth** *Carrie, go and get me a towel.* | **get sth for sb** *He went to get cigarettes for his mom.* | **get sb/sth from sth** *I'll get the kids from school later.* → see box at **BRING**
3 [T] to have, do, or experience something: **have got sth** *I've got three sisters.* | *Has he got blue eyes?* | **get pleasure/a shock/a surprise etc** *I got the impression she didn't like me.*
4 [T] to begin to have an illness: **get a cold/the flu/cancer etc** *I think I'm getting a cold.*
5 [I, linking verb] to change to a new state, feeling, or situation [= **become**]: **get bored/angry/upset etc** *Children get bored very quickly.* | *Helen got drunk, as usual.* | **get cold/dark/late etc** *We should go – it's getting late.* | **get hurt/broken/stolen etc** *I got lost in the wood.* | **get married/divorced/engaged** *When*

G

are you getting married? | **get washed/dressed**
Isn't it time you got dressed? → see box at **BECOME**
6 [I] to arrive, go, or move somewhere: *When did
you get home?* | **+to** *How do I get to the station?* |
They somehow had to get past the guards. | *The
thieves* **got away** (=escaped). | *Liam* **got** *slowly
to his feet* (=stood up).
7 [T] to move something to a different position:
get sth into/through/across etc *Father got his
gun down from the shelf.*
8 [I] to reach a particular stage in a process
successfully: *She didn't* **get far** *with her
studies.* | *I'm* **not getting anywhere** (=not pro-
gressing successfully) *with this job.*
9 [T] if you get a bus, train etc, you travel on a
bus etc: *Pete always gets the bus to work.* → see
box at **TRAIN**
10 [T] to make or arrange for someone or something to do a particular job or action: **get sb/sth
to do sth** *I couldn't get the car to start.* | **get sth
done/fixed etc** *We'll have to get the roof
mended.*
11 [T] *informal* to hear or understand some-
thing: *Tracy didn't* **get the joke.** | *I just* **don't get
it** (=do not understand). | *Sorry, I didn't quite get
what you said.*
12 [T] to receive a punishment: *He got ten years
for robbery.*
13 [T] *informal* to prepare a meal: *Can I get you
anything for lunch?*
14 [T] *informal* to attack, hurt, or catch someone: *The gang had threatened to get him.*
15 [T] to answer the door or telephone:
Can you **get the door,** *please?*
16 get to do sth *informal* to have the opportunity to do something: *She's nice once you* **get to
know** *her.* | *I never* **get** *a chance* **to see** *you
anymore.*
17 get doing sth *spoken* to begin doing some-
thing: *We got talking about the old days.* | **get
going/moving** (=start doing something that you
must do) *It's late, we'd better get going.*

get about *BrE phr v* **1** to move or travel to
different places **2** if news or information gets
about, many people hear about it

get across *phr v* to be understood, or to make
someone understand something: **+to** *The mes-
sage isn't* **getting across** *to youngsters.* | **get sth
⇔ across** *What's the best way to* **get** *your* **ideas
across?**

get ahead *phr v* to be successful in your job,
work etc

get along *phr v* if people get along, they have a
friendly relationship: **+with** *Do you get along
well with your colleagues?*

get around *phr v* **1 get around (sth)** to go to
different places **2** if news or information gets
around, many people hear about it **3 get
around sth** to avoid something that will cause
problems: *There are ways of getting around the
law.*

get around to *sth phr v* to do something you
have been intending to do for a long time: *I must
get around to writing some cards.*

get at *sb/sth phr v* **1** to be able to reach
something: *We took up the carpet to get at the
wiring.* **2 be getting at sth** to be trying to
explain an idea: *Just what are you getting at?*
3 to discover information about something:

They were determined to **get at the truth.**
4 *informal* to keep criticizing someone

get away *phr v informal* to leave a place:
+from *I didn't get away from work until late.* | *I'd
love to* **get away from it all** (=leave your work,
duties etc for a holiday).

get away with *sth phr v* to not be caught or
punished for something: *He'll cheat if he thinks
he can get away with it.*

get back *phr v* **1** to return to a place: *It's time
we were getting back.* | **+to** *When did you get back
to London?* **2 get sth ⇔ back** to have something again after you had lost it or given it to
someone: *Did you get your purse back?* **3 get sb
back** also **get back at sb** to hurt someone
because they have hurt you: **+for** *I'll get you
back for this!*

get back to *sb/sth phr v* **1** to return to a
previous state, condition, or activity: *Life is
beginning to get back to normal.* **2** *informal* to
return a telephone call by speaking to the person who made the call

get behind *phr v* if you get behind with work
or a regular payment, you fail to do the work or
pay the money in time: **+with** *Whatever you do,
don't get behind with your rent.*

get by *phr v* to have only just enough of
something to be able to do the things you need to
do: **+on** *She gets by on just £80 a week.* | *I know
enough Italian to get by.*

get *sb/sth* **down** *phr v* **1** *informal* to make
someone feel unhappy: *Her illness gets her down.*
2 get sth ⇔ down to quickly write down what
someone says or what you think: *Let me get down
your address.* → see box at **WRITE**

get down to *sth phr v* to start doing something
that needs time or energy: *Isn't it time you got
down to some work?*

get in *phr v* **1** to be allowed or able to go into a
place: *I applied to college but didn't get in.*
2 when a train, bus etc gets in, it arrives: *My
train gets in at 10.* **3** to arrive home: *What time
did you get in?* **4** to be elected: *Do you think
Labour will get in again?*

get in on *sth phr v informal* to become
involved in something that other people are
doing: *We began a delivery service and now others want to get in on the act.*

get into *sth phr v* **1** to be accepted by an
organization, team etc: *Do you think he'll get into
the squad?* **2** to enter or arrive at a place **3** to
start being involved in a situation: **get into
trouble/debt/difficulties etc** | *He got into the
habit of arriving late.* **4** *informal* to start being
interested in something: *I got heavily into rap
music.* **5 what's got into sb?** *spoken* used to
say that someone is behaving very differently
from usual

get off *phr v* **1 get (sb) off (sth)** *informal* to
leave a place, or to help someone leave: *It's time
we got off.* | *What time do you get off work?* | **+to**
I must get the kids off to school. **2 get sth off** to
send a letter, package etc **3 get sth off** to
remove a piece of clothing you are wearing:
You'd better get those wet shoes off. **4 get (sb) off**
to receive little or no punishment for a crime, or
to help someone do this: *He got off lightly*
(=received a very small punishment). | *His
attorney got him off on a technicality* (=using a
legal detail). **5** *informal* to go to sleep: *I couldn't*

get off to sleep last night. **6 get off to a good/bad start** to begin something well or badly **7 get (sth) off (sb/sth)** *informal* to stop touching something or someone: *Get your hands off me!*

get off with sb *phr v BrE informal* to start a romantic relationship with someone

get on *phr v* **1** *BrE* if people get on, they have a friendly relationship: +**with** *She doesn't get on with my mum very well.* **2** to continue or to make progress with a job, work etc: +**with** *Stop talking and get on with it!* **3** to be successful in your work, job etc **4 be getting on** *informal* **a)** if time is getting on, it is quite late **b)** if someone is getting on, they are quite old

get onto sb/sth *phr v* **1** *informal* to write or speak to someone because you want them to help you: *We got onto the landlord about the damp.* **2** to be elected to a committee, position etc **3** to start talking about a particular subject: *How did we get onto the war?*

get out *phr v* **1 get (sb) out** to leave or escape from a place, or to help someone do this: +**of** *The Embassy advised tourists to get out of the country.* | *Firefighters tried to get them out.* **2 get sth** ⇔ **out** to take something from the place where it is kept or hidden: *He got out a knife and pointed it at me.* **3** if secret information gets out, people find out about it **4 get sth** ⇔ **out** to succeed in saying something

get out of sth *phr v* **1** to avoid doing something that you should do: **get out of doing sth** *I'm afraid I can't get out of going to the meeting.* **2 get sth out of sb** to persuade someone to tell or give you something **3 get sth out of sth** to enjoy an activity and feel you have gained something from it: **get sth out of doing sth** *Do you get a lot out of playing the violin?*

get over *phr v* **1 get over sth** to feel better after an illness or bad experience: *It takes weeks to get over the flu.* | *You feel bad now, but you'll get over it.* **2 get sth over (with)** to finish something difficult or unpleasant: *I'll feel better when I've got the test over with.* **3 get sth** ⇔ **over** to succeed in making people understand your ideas: +**to** *You'll get your message over if you stick to the point.*

get round *phr v BrE* → **GET AROUND**

get round to sth *phr v BrE* → **GET AROUND TO STH**

get through *phr v* **1** *informal* **get through sth** to use or deal with a particular amount of something: *I get through about 20 cigarettes a day.* | *I've got through a lot of work this month.* **2 get (sb) through sth** to reach the end of an unpleasant experience, test etc, or to help someone do this: *Her love got me through the death of my son.* **3** to succeed in telephoning someone: *I tried phoning, but I couldn't get through.* → see box at **TELEPHONE**

get (sth) through to sb *phr v* to succeed in making someone understand you: *How can I get through to you that I love you?*

get to sb *phr v informal* to upset someone

get together *phr v* **1** if people get together, they meet in order to do something nice: *We must get together for a drink.* **2 get sth/sb** ⇔ **together** to bring or collect several things or people so they are in one place: *He got some residents together to form an action group.* **3 get**

it/your life/yourself together to change the way you live so that you are better organized, happier etc

get up *phr v* **1 get (sb) up** to get out of your bed after sleeping, or to make someone do this: *Get me up at 8.* **2** to stand up

get up to sth *phr v informal* to do something that might be slightly bad: *What are the kids getting up to, I wonder?*

getaway /'getəweɪ/ *n* [C] an escape from a place after doing something wrong: *The gunmen made their getaway in a stolen car.*

'get-to,gether *n* [C] an informal meeting or party: *a family get-together* → see box at **PARTY**

ghastly /'gɑːstli $ 'gæstli/ *adj* very bad or unpleasant: *a ghastly mistake* | *a ghastly woman*

ghetto /'getəʊ $ -toʊ/ *n* [C] plural **ghettos** or **ghettoes** a part of a city where poor people of a particular race or class live → see box at **AREA**

ghost /gəʊst $ goʊst/ *n* [C] the SPIRIT of a dead person that people think they can see: +**of** *The ghost of Marie Antoinette haunts* (=often appears in) *the palace.* | *Do you believe in ghosts?* | *a scary ghost story*
—**ghostly** *adj*

'ghost town *n* [C] a town that is empty because the people who lived there have left

ghostwriter /'gəʊst,raɪtə $ 'goʊst,raɪtər/ *n* [C] someone whose job is to write books, speeches etc for another person, who then presents it as their own work

ghoul /guːl/ *n* [C] an evil SPIRIT in films, stories etc that steals and eats dead bodies

ghoulish /'guːlɪʃ/ *adj* getting pleasure from death, accidents etc

GI /,dʒiː 'aɪ/ *n* [C] a soldier in the US army

giant¹ /'dʒaɪənt/ *adj* [only before noun] much bigger than usual: *a giant TV screen*

giant² *n* [C] **1** a very tall strong man in stories **2** a very large successful company: *the music industry giant*

gibberish /'dʒɪbərɪʃ/ *n* [U] something that you write or say that has no meaning or is difficult to understand

gibe /dʒaɪb/ *n* another spelling of JIBE

giddy /'gɪdi/ *adj* feeling slightly sick and unable to stand up properly because everything seems to be spinning around [= **dizzy**]

gift /gɪft/ *n* [C]

1 something that you give to someone as a present: +**of** *a generous gift of £50* | +**from** *a wedding gift from my aunt*
2 a natural ability to do something: +**for** *a gift for languages*

gifted /'gɪftɪd/ *adj* having a natural ability to do one or more things extremely well: **gifted musician/artist/teacher etc** *She is a gifted poet.* | **gifted child** (=one who is extremely intelligent) → see box at **INTELLIGENT**

'gift ,token *BrE*, **'gift ,voucher** *BrE*; **'gift cer,tificate** *AmE* *n* [C] a special piece of paper that is worth a particular amount of money when it is exchanged for goods in a shop

'gift wrap *v* [T] to wrap a present with attractive coloured paper

gig /gɪg/ *n* [C] a concert at which musicians play popular music or JAZZ

G

gigabyte /'gɪgəbaɪt/ n [C] a unit for measuring computer information, equal to 1024 MEGABYTES

gigantic /dʒaɪ'gæntɪk/ adj extremely big: *a gigantic skyscraper* → see box at BIG

giggle /'gɪgəl/ v [I] to laugh quickly in a high voice, especially because you are nervous or embarrassed → see box at LAUGH —**giggle** n [C]

gild /gɪld/ v [T] to cover the surface of something with a thin layer of gold or gold paint

gill /gɪl/ n [C] one of the organs on the sides of a fish, through which it breathes → see picture on page A2

gilt /gɪlt/ adj covered with a thin layer of gold or gold-coloured paint: *a gilt chair* —**gilt** n [U]

gimme /'gɪmi/ informal a way of saying 'give me': *Gimme the ball!*

gimmick /'gɪmɪk/ n [C] disapproving something unusual that is used to make people notice something: *advertising gimmicks* —**gimmicky** adj

gin /dʒɪn/ n [C,U] a strong clear alcoholic drink made from grain

ginger[1] /'dʒɪndʒə $ -ər/ n [U] a light brown root with a strong hot taste that is used in cooking

ginger[2] adj BrE hair or fur that is ginger is bright orange-brown in colour: *a ginger cat*

gingerly /'dʒɪndʒəli $ -ər-/ adv if you do something gingerly, you do it in a slow careful way, because you are afraid it will be dangerous or painful: *Jack lowered himself gingerly onto the bed.*

gipsy /'dʒɪpsi/ n a British spelling of GYPSY

giraffe /dʒɪ'rɑːf $ -'ræf/ n [C] a tall African animal with a very long neck and legs and dark spots on its yellow-brown fur

girder /'gɜːdə $ 'gɜːrdər/ n [C] an iron or steel beam that supports a floor, roof, or bridge

girdle /'gɜːdl $ 'gɜːr-/ n [C] a piece of women's underwear that fits tightly around her waist and HIPS

girl /gɜːl $ gɜːrl/ n [C]
1 a female child [➔ **boy**]: *Both boys and girls can join the choir.* | *a teenage girl* | **five-year-old girl/girl of ten etc** *The patient was a girl of twelve.*
2 a daughter [➔ **boy**]: *Karen has two boys and a little girl* (=young daughter).
3 a young woman: *Steve's married to a Dutch girl.* → see box at WOMAN
4 the girls informal a woman's female friends [➔ **the lads**]: *I'm going out with the girls tonight.*
—**girlish** adj: *a peal of girlish laughter* → PAPER GIRL

girlfriend /'gɜːlfrend $ 'gɜːrl-/ n [C]
1 a girl or woman with whom you have a romantic relationship: *Do you have a girlfriend?*
2 especially AmE a woman or girl's female friend

girlhood /'gɜːlhʊd $ 'gɜːrl-/ n [U] the period of her life when a woman is a girl

girth /gɜːθ $ gɜːrθ/ n [C,U] the distance around something that is big and round: *the girth of the tree's trunk*

gist /dʒɪst/ n **the gist** the main idea and meaning of what someone has said or written: +**of** *The gist of his argument is that full employment is impossible.*

give[1] /gɪv/ v past tense **gave** /geɪv/ past participle **given** /'gɪvən/

1 [T] to let someone have something as a present, or to provide something for someone: **give sb sth** *What did Bob give you for your birthday?* | *Researchers were given a grant to continue their work.* | *I've got some jewellery that my grandmother gave me.* | **give sth to sb** *a ring which was given to him by his mother* | *Most people are willing to **give to charity**.*

THESAURUS

donate – to give money to an organization that uses it to help people: *Would you like to donate something to charity?*
leave – to give something to people after you die: *This house was left to me by my aunt.*
award – to officially give money or a prize to someone: *Mr Gilmartin was awarded the medal of honour.*

2 [T] to put something in someone's hand: **give sb sth** *Give me the letter, please.* | **give sth to sb** *He poured a cup of coffee and gave it to her.* | *She gave a spare key to her neighbour.*

THESAURUS

give out – to give something to each person in a group: *Students were giving out leaflets to everyone.*
hand/pass – to put something in someone's hand or where they can reach it: *Could you pass me the salt?*
hand out/pass around – to give something to each of the people in a group: *Our teacher handed out the question papers.* | *Pass those cookies around, please.*
share/share out BrE – to divide something into equal parts and give a part to each person: *Marty, could you share out the cake?*
distribute – to give things to a large number of people, especially in the streets: *Anti-war protesters were distributing leaflets.*

3 [T] to allow or make it possible for someone to do something: **give sb sth** *He gave us permission to leave.* | *Everyone will be given a chance to speak.* | *I asked him to give me more time to finish my essay.* | *Women were given the vote in the early 1900s.* | **give sth to sb** *This bill will give more power to local authorities.*
4 [T] to tell someone information or details about something, or tell someone to do something: *Let me give you some advice.* | **give orders/instructions** *They were given orders not to tell anyone.* | *Can you give me directions to the station* (=tell me how to get there)? | *He gives us jobs to do around the house.* | **give an account/description** *Today's newspaper gives an account of the murder.*
5 [T] to perform an action: *Don't move until I give the signal.* | **give a speech/performance etc** *He's giving a talk on early Roman pottery.* | **give sb sth** *Joel gave me a smile as I walked in.* | **give sb a call** also **give sb a ring** BrE (=telephone someone) *Give me a call around 8:00.*
6 [T] to make someone have or feel something: **give sb sth** *He gave us quite a shock.* | *That noise is giving me a headache.* | *The course has*

given me more confidence. | **give sb problems/ troubles/difficulties** *The new software has been giving us problems.* | **give sth to sb** *Their music has given a lot of pleasure to people.*

7 [T] to pay a particular amount of money for something: **give sb sth for sth** *They gave us £700 for our old car.*

8 give way   a) if a structure gives way, it falls down because it cannot support the weight on it   **b)** to stop or slow down when driving, in order to allow other vehicles to go first [= yield *AmE*]   **c)** to be replaced by something: +**to** *My sadness soon gave way to anger.*

9 give (sb) an impression/sense etc to make someone think about something in a particular way: *I didn't want to give him the wrong idea about the job.*

10 give a party to organize a party

11 give (sth) thought/attention/consideration etc to spend some time thinking about something carefully

12 give sb a hand *spoken* to help someone: +**with** *Can I give you a hand with that bag?* → see box at **HELP**

13 not give sth another/a second thought to not think or worry about something

14 [I] if something gives, it bends or stretches when pressure or weight is put on it: *The leather will give slightly as you wear the boots.*

give sb/sth away *phr v*   **1 give sth ⇔ away** to give something you own to someone without asking for money: +**to** *Give your old clothes away to charity.* | *We're giving away a free diary with tomorrow's paper.*   **2** to show or say something about someone that should be kept secret [➡ **giveaway**]: *Don't worry, I won't give you away.* | *The look on his face **gave the game away** (=showed something he wanted to keep secret).*

give (sb) sth ⇔ back *phr v* to return something to its owner: *You'll have to give the money back.* | *I have to give Rick his car back by 3.00.*

give in *phr v*   **1** to finally agree to do something that you did not want to do: *Eventually I gave in and said yes.* | +**to** *The government refused to give in to the union's demands.*   **2** to accept that you have lost a fight, game etc: *The rebels were eventually forced to give in.*   **3 give sth ⇔ in** *BrE* to give something such as an official paper or a piece of work to someone: *You were supposed to give in this work yesterday.*

give off sth *phr v* to produce a smell, light, heat, etc: *The burning wood gave off a sweet smell.*

give out *phr v*   **1 give sth ⇔ out** to give something to each person in a group: *Can you give the drinks out please?* | +**to** *Students were giving out leaflets to everyone in the street.*   **2** to stop working correctly: *My voice gave out half way through the song.*

give up *phr v*   **1 give sth ⇔ up** to stop doing something, especially something that you do regularly: *Why don't you give up smoking?* | **give up doing sth** *I gave up going to the theatre after that.*   **2** to stop trying to do something: *You shouldn't give up so easily.* | **give sth ⇔ up** *She has still not given up the search.*   **3 give yourself/sb up** to allow yourself or someone else to be caught by the police or enemy soldiers: +**to** *In the end his family gave him up to the police.*

give up on sb/sth *phr v* to stop hoping that someone or something will change or improve: *At that point I hadn't completely given up on the marriage.*

give² *n* [U] the ability of a material to bend or stretch when it is under pressure

give and 'take *n* [U] if there is give and take between two people, each person agrees to do some of the things that the other person wants: *In any relationship there has to be some give and take.*

giveaway¹ /'gɪvəweɪ/ *n* [singular] **be a giveaway** to make it easy to guess something: *His glazed eyes are a dead giveaway* (=make it very easy to guess) *that he's been taking drugs.*

giveaway² *adj* [only before noun] giveaway prices are extremely cheap

given¹ /'gɪvən/ *v* the past participle of GIVE

given² *adj* [only before noun] **any given day/ time/situation etc** any particular time, situation etc, used when giving an example of something: *They could arrive at any given moment.* | *In any given situation, there will be winners and losers.*

given³ *prep* taking something into account: *Given the circumstances, you've coped well.*

'given name *n* [C] *AmE* someone's FIRST NAME → see box at **NAME**

glacier /'glæsɪə $ 'gleɪʃər/ *n* [C] a large mass of ice that moves slowly down a mountain valley

glad /glæd/ *adj*

1 [not before noun] pleased and happy about something: *'I've decided to accept his offer.' 'I'm glad.'* | **glad to do sth** *I'm glad to be back home.* | +**(that)** *We're so glad you came.* | +**when** *I'll be glad when the conference is over.*

G

THESAURUS

Glad and **pleased** describe how you feel about a particular event or situation: *I'm glad you telephoned.* | *Are you pleased with your exam results?*
Happy can be used to describe a general feeling that you have: *They seem to be very happy together.* | *a happy child*

---

2 be glad of sth to be grateful for something: *Thanks, I'll be glad of the help.* | **be glad of the opportunity/chance/excuse to do sth** *They were glad of the chance to get some sleep.*

3 be glad to do sth to be willing and eager to do something: *We'd be glad to send you any information you need.*

glade /gleɪd/ *n* [C] *literary* a small open space in a wood or forest

gladiator /'glædieɪtə $ -ər/ *n* [C] a man who had to fight other men or animals as entertainment in ancient Rome

gladly /'glædli/ *adv* used to say politely that you are willing to do something: *She said she'd gladly pay for any damages.*

glamorize also **-ise** *BrE* /'glæməraɪz/ *v* [T] to make something appear more attractive than it really is: *TV has been accused of glamorizing crime.*

glamorous /'glæmərəs/ *adj* attractive, exciting, and related to wealth or success

glamour *BrE*; **glamor** *AmE* /'glæmə $ -ər/ *n* [U]
the attractive and exciting quality of being connected with wealth and success: +**of** *the glamour of television*

glance[1] /glɑːns $ glæns/ *v* [I] **1** to look at someone or something for a short time: +**at/up/down etc** *I glanced at my watch.* | *Emily glanced over her shoulder.* **2** to read something very quickly: +**at/through etc** *Can you glance through these figures for me?*

glance[2] *n* **1** [C] a quick look: *Jim gave him a quick glance and smiled.* **2 at a glance** if you know something at a glance, you know it as soon as you see it: *Beth saw at a glance what happened.*

glancing /'glɑːnsɪŋ $ 'glæn-/ *adj* **glancing blow** a hit that partly misses so that it does not have its full force

gland /glænd/ *n* [C] an organ in the body that produces a substance such as a HORMONE, SWEAT, or SALIVA —**glandular** /'glændjᵿlə $ -dʒələr/ *adj*

glandular 'fever *n* [U] *BrE* an infectious illness that makes you feel weak and tired for a long time afterwards [= **mono** *AmE*]

glare[1] /gleə $ gler/ *v* [I] **1** to look angrily at someone or something for a long time: +**at** *She glared at him accusingly.* **2** to shine with a strong bright light that hurts your eyes: *The sun glared down on us.*

glare[2] *n* **1** [singular, U] a strong bright light which hurts your eyes: **the glare of sth** *the glare of the sun* **2** [C] a long angry look: *She gave him an icy glare.*

glaring /'gleərɪŋ $ 'gler-/ *adj* **1** bad and very noticeable: *a glaring example of corruption* **2** too bright to look at: *a glaring light*

glass /glɑːs $ glæs/ *n*
1 [U] a hard transparent material that is used for making windows, bottles etc: *a glass bowl* | *a piece of broken glass* | **pane/sheet of glass** (=flat piece of glass with straight edges) *Double-glazed windows have two panes of glass.* → see picture at **MATERIAL**[1]
2 [C] a container made of glass used for drinking, or the drink in it [➔ **cup**]: *I'll just fetch some wine glasses.* | +**of** *She poured me a glass of water.*
3 glasses [plural] two pieces of specially cut glass or plastic in a frame, which you wear in order to see more clearly [= **spectacles**]: *Tom wears glasses.* | *I need a new pair of glasses.*
4 [U] objects made of glass: *a collection of Venetian glass*
→ **MAGNIFYING GLASS, STAINED GLASS**

glass 'ceiling *n* [singular] the fact that women are not given jobs at the highest level in a company

glass 'fibre *n* [U] FIBREGLASS

glasshouse /'glɑːshaʊs $ 'glæs-/ *n* [C] *BrE* a glass building used for growing plants [= **greenhouse**]

glassware /'glɑːsweə $ 'glæswer/ *n* [U] glass objects, especially ones used for drinking and eating

glassy /'glɑːsi $ 'glæsi/ *adj* **1** smooth and shining, like glass: *the glassy surface of the lake* **2** glassy eyes show no feeling or understanding

glaze[1] /gleɪz/ *v* **1** also **glaze over** [I] if your eyes glaze over, they show no expression because

you are bored or tired **2** [T] to cover clay pots, bowls etc with a thin liquid that gives them a shiny surface **3** [T] to put glass into a window frame —**glazed** *adj*

glaze[2] *n* [C] a liquid that is put on clay pots, bowls etc to give them a shiny surface

gleam[1] /gliːm/ *v* [I] **1** to shine softly and pleasantly: *The table was gleaming with wax polish.* **2** if your eyes or face gleam with a feeling, they show it: *His green eyes gleamed with pleasure.*

gleam[2] *n* [C] **1** a soft light: *a sudden gleam of light* **2** an emotion or expression that appears on someone's face for a short time: *She saw a gleam of amusement in his eyes.*

glean /gliːn/ *v* [T] to find out information slowly and with difficulty: **glean sth from sb** *We gleaned more information from other sources.*

glee /gliː/ *n* [U] a feeling of satisfaction and excitement: *The children laughed with glee.* —**gleeful** *adj* —**gleefully** *adv*

glen /glen/ *n* [C] a deep narrow valley in Scotland or Ireland

glib /glɪb/ *adj disapproving* said in a way that makes something sound simple, easy, or true when it is not: *Her answer sounded too glib.* —**glibly** *adv*

glide /glaɪd/ *v* [I] to move smoothly and quietly, as if without effort: +**across/over/down etc** *Couples glided over the dance floor.* —**glide** *n* [C]

glider /'glaɪdə $ -ər/ *n* [C] a light plane that flies without an engine → see picture on page A9

gliding /'glaɪdɪŋ/ *n* [U] the sport of flying a glider

glimmer[1] /'glɪmə $ -ər/ *n* [C] **1** a small sign of something such as hope or understanding: +**of** *a glimmer of hope for the future* **2** a light that is not very bright

glimmer[2] *v* [I] to shine with a light that is not very bright

glimpse[1] /glɪmps/ *n* [C] **1** a quick look at someone or something that does not allow you to see them clearly: +**of** *They caught a glimpse of a green car.* **2** a short experience of something that helps you to understand it: *a glimpse into the future*

glimpse[2] *v* [T] to see someone or something for a moment without getting a complete view of them: *I glimpsed a figure at the window.*

glint /glɪnt/ *v* [I] **1** if a shiny surface glints, it gives out small flashes of light: *His white teeth glinted in his brown face.* **2** if your eyes glint with pleasure, anger etc, they show pleasure, anger etc —**glint** *n* [C]

glisten /'glɪsən/ *v* [I] to shine because of being wet or oily: +**with** *His back was glistening with sweat.*

glitch /glɪtʃ/ *n* [C] a small fault in a machine or piece of equipment that stops it working: *a computer glitch*

glitter[1] /'glɪtə $ -ər/ *v* [I] to shine brightly with flashing points of light: *The river glittered in the sunlight.*

glitter[2] *n* [U] **1** brightness consisting of many flashing points of light: *the glitter of her diamond ring* **2** the attractiveness and excitement connected with rich and famous people or places: *the glitter of Las Vegas*

glittering /'glɪtərɪŋ/ *adj* **1** glittering objects shine with small flashes of light: *glittering jewels* **2** successful and impressive: *a glittering career in motor racing* | *a glittering Hollywood premiere*

glitzy /'glɪtsi/ *adj* exciting and attractive because of being connected with rich, famous, and fashionable people —**glitz** *n* [U]

gloat /gləʊt $ gloʊt/ *v* [I] to show in an annoying way that you are proud of your success or someone else's failure: *Dick was still gloating over his team's win.*

global /'gləʊbəl $ 'gloʊ-/ *adj* affecting or including the whole world: *the global economy* —**globally** *adv*

globalization also **-isation** *BrE* /ˌgləʊbəlaɪ'zeɪʃən $ 'gloʊbələ-/ *n* [U] when something such as a business operates or starts to operate in countries all over the world

ˌglobal 'warming *n* [U] an increase in world temperatures, caused by an increase in CARBON DIOXIDE around the Earth → see box at ENVIRONMENT

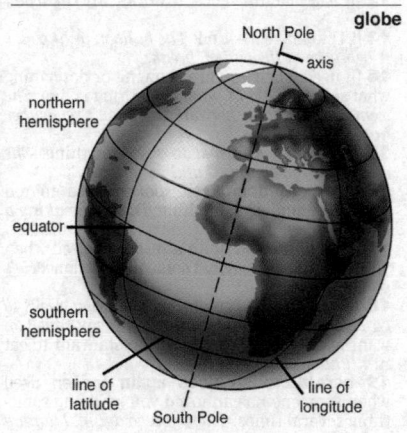

globe

North Pole

axis

northern hemisphere

equator

southern hemisphere

line of latitude

line of longitude

South Pole

globe /gləʊb $ gloʊb/ *n* **1** [C] a round object with a map of the earth drawn on it **2 the globe** the world: *Our company has offices all over the globe.* **3** [C] an object shaped like a ball

ˈglobe-ˌtrotting *n* [U] when someone spends a lot of time travelling to many different countries —**globe-trotting** *adj*

globule /'glɒbjuːl $ 'glɑː-/ *n* [C] a small drop of a liquid or of a melted substance: *globules of fat*

gloom /gluːm/ *n* [singular,U] **1** *literary* almost complete darkness **2** a feeling of great sadness and lack of hope

gloomy /'gluːmi/ *adj* **1** making you feel that a situation will not improve: *The report paints a gloomy picture of the economy.* → see box at SAD **2** sad because you think the situation will not improve: *the gloomy faces of the rescue workers* **3** dark, especially in a way that seems sad: *a gloomy room with one small window* —**gloomily** *adv*

glorified /'glɔːrɪ̯faɪd/ *adj* [only before noun] made to seem like something more important: *Many people still think of computers as glorified typewriters.*

glorify /'glɔːrɪ̯faɪ/ *v* [T] **glorified**, **glorifying**, **glorifies** **1** to make something seem more important or better than it really is: *films which glorify violence* **2** to praise someone, especially God —**glorification** /ˌglɔːrɪ̯fɪ̯'keɪʃən/ *n* [U]

glorious /'glɔːriəs/ *adj* **1** having or deserving praise and honour: *a glorious achievement* **2** very beautiful or impressive: *glorious views of the coast* —**gloriously** *adv*

glory[1] /'glɔːri/ *n* plural **glories** **1** [U] the importance, honour, and praise that people give someone they admire a lot: *The team finished the season covered in glory.* **2** [C] the things about a place or way of life which are beautiful or make people feel proud: *the glories of ancient Greece*

glory[2] *v* **gloried, glorying, glories** **glory in** sth *phr v* to enjoy or be proud of something: *They gloried in their new freedom.*

gloss[1] /glɒs $ glɔːs, glɑːs/ *n* [singular,U] a bright shine on a surface: *a shampoo that adds gloss to your hair* | *gloss paint*

gloss[2] *v* [T] to give a short explanation for a difficult word or idea **gloss over** sth *phr v* to avoid talking about something unpleasant, or to say as little as possible about it

glossary /'glɒsəri $ 'glɔː-, 'glɑː-/ *n* [C] plural **glossaries** a list of explanations of technical or unusual words, printed at the end of a book

glossy /'glɒsi $ 'glɔːsi, 'glɑːsi/ *adj* **1** shiny and smooth: *her glossy black hair* **2 glossy magazine/brochure etc** a magazine etc that is printed on good quality shiny paper, usually with lots of colour pictures

glove /glʌv/ *n* [C] a piece of clothing worn on your hand, with separate parts for the thumb and each finger: *a pair of gloves* → see picture at CLOTHES

ˈglove comˌpartment *n* [C] a small cupboard in a car in front of the passenger seat

glow[1] /gləʊ $ gloʊ/ *n* [singular] **1** a soft steady light: **+from** *The glow from the dying fire.* **2** the bright colour your face has when you exercise or are healthy **3 a glow of pleasure/pride/satisfaction etc** a strong feeling of pleasure, pride etc

glow[2] *v* [I] **1** to shine with a soft steady light: *The red tip of his cigarette was glowing in the dark.* → see box at SHINE **2** if your face glows, it is bright or hot because you have been doing exercise, or are feeling a strong emotion: *She was glowing with health.* **3 glow with happiness/pride/pleasure etc** to show in your expression that you are very happy, proud etc: *She glowed with happiness.* | *Their young faces glowed with interest.*

glower /'glaʊə $ -ər/ *v* [I] to look at someone in an angry way: **+at** *Jill glowered at her husband but said nothing.*

glowing /'gləʊɪŋ $ 'gloʊ-/ *adj* **glowing report/description etc** a report etc that praises someone or something

glucose /'gluːkəʊs $ -koʊs/ *n* [U] a natural form of sugar that exists in fruits

G

glue¹ /gluː/ *n* [C,U] a sticky substance used for joining things together: *Stick the ribbon on with glue.* → see picture at CLASSROOM

glue² *v* [T] present participle **gluing** or **glueing**

1 to join things together, using glue: **glue sth (back) together** *Cut out the pieces and glue the edges together.* → see box at FASTEN

2 be glued to sth *informal* to be looking at something with all your attention: *He was glued to the TV when the Olympics was on.*

glum /glʌm/ *adj* unhappy: *She looked glum.* | *a glum silence* → see box at SAD —**glumly** *adv*

glut /glʌt/ *n* [C usually singular] a bigger supply of something, especially a product or crop, than is needed [≠ **shortage**]: +**of** *a glut of oil on the world market*

glutinous /'gluːt̬n̩əs $ -tn-əs/ *adj* very sticky

glutton /'glʌtn/ *n* **1** [C] someone who eats too much **2 glutton for punishment** someone who seems to enjoy working very hard or doing something unpleasant

gluttony /'glʌt̬əni/ *n* [U] *formal* the bad habit of eating too much

gm a written abbreviation of **gram**

GM /ˌdʒiː 'em/ *adj BrE* **g**enetically **m**odified GM crops have had their GENETIC structure changed

GMT /ˌdʒiː em 'tiː/ *n* [U] **Greenwich Mean Time** the time as measured at Greenwich in London, used as an international standard for measuring time

gnarled /nɑːld $ nɑːrld/ *adj* rough and twisted: *a gnarled branch*

gnat /næt/ *n* [C] a small flying insect that bites

gnaw /nɔː $ nɒː/ *v* [I,T] to keep biting something hard: *A rat had gnawed a hole in the box.* | +**at/on** *a dog gnawing on a bone*

gnaw (away) at sb *phr v* to make you feel worried or anxious over a period of time: *Guilt had been gnawing at me all day.*

gnawing /'nɔːɪŋ $ 'nɒː-/ *adj* [only before noun] worrying, over a long period of time: *gnawing doubts*

gnome /nəʊm $ noʊm/ *n* [C] a creature in children's stories like a little old man with a pointed hat

GNP /ˌdʒiː en 'piː/ *n* [U] **Gross National Product** the total value of all the goods and services produced in a country, usually in a single year [➡ **GDP**]

go¹ /gəʊ $ goʊ/ *v* past tense **went** /went/ past participle **gone** /gɒn $ gɒːn/ third person singular **goes**

1 [I] to leave a place and move or travel somewhere else [➡ **come**]: *Should I stay or go?* | *Where are you going?* | +**to/into/inside etc** *Mom went into the kitchen.* | *Let's go home.*

2 [I,T] to travel: *It took an hour to go ten miles.* | *You're going too fast.* | **go by bus/plane/bike etc** *It's easier to go by train.* → see box at TRAVEL

3 [I] to move or travel somewhere in order to do something or be at an event: **go for a walk/drink/meal etc** *Shall we go for a swim?* | **go shopping/swimming/skiing etc** *Lucy and Paul have gone shopping.* | **go to do sth** *Mick's gone to buy a paper.* | **go (and) do sth** *Go see who's at the door.* | *He had a party but not many people went.* | +**to** *She goes to a lot of meetings.*

4 go flying/rushing/crashing etc to move somewhere in a particular way: *The ball went flying over my head.*

5 be going to do sth used to talk about what

will happen or what someone intends to do in the future: *It's going to rain.* | *I'm going to tell him what you did.*

6 [I] to reach or lead to a particular place: +**to/down etc** *Does this road go to the airport?*

7 [linking verb] to become: *The company went bankrupt.* | **go bad/sour etc** *The milk has gone sour.* | **go grey/red/brown etc** *My hair's going grey.* | **go deaf/blind/mad etc** *I think she's going deaf.* → see box at BECOME

8 [I] to happen or develop in a particular way: *How did your interview go?* | **go well/fine/wrong etc** *Everything started to go wrong.* | **how are things going/how's it going?** (=used to ask about someone's life, work, or progress)

9 [I] to belong or fit in a particular place or position: +**in/on** *Dictionaries go on the bottom shelf.* | *It won't all go in one suitcase.*

10 [I] to be sent or passed on: +**to/by/through etc** *The e-mail went to everyone in the company.*

11 [linking verb] to be or remain in a particular state: **go unheard/unanswered/unnoticed etc** *Her cries for help went unheard.* | *Many people went hungry* (=did not have enough to eat) *during the war.*

12 [I] if a machine goes, it works: *My car won't go.*

13 [I,T] to make a sound: *The balloon went pop.* | *A bell goes at the end of break.*

14 [I] used when you are showing or describing what someone did or what something is like: *She went like this with her hand.* | *I can't remember how the story goes.*

15 [T] *spoken informal* to say something: *She went, 'Are you coming?' and I went, 'No.'*

16 don't go doing sth *spoken* used to tell someone not to do something: *Don't go making a mess.*

17 have gone and done sth *spoken* used when you are annoyed by what someone has done: *He's gone and broken it!*

18 to go a) still remaining: *Only two weeks to go before the holidays!* b) used to say that you want to take food away from a restaurant to eat it: *I'll have large fries to go.*

19 here/there sb goes again *spoken* used when someone has annoyed you by doing something several times: *There you go again, blaming me!*

20 [I] to disappear: *Has your headache gone yet?*

21 [I] to become weak or damaged, or stop working: *Dad's hearing is starting to go.* | *One of the lights has gone.*

22 [I] if money goes, it is spent: +**on** *Most of her money goes on rent.*

23 [I] if time goes, it passes: *The hours go so slowly at work.*

24 [I] to look or taste good together: *Pink and yellow just don't go.* | +**with/together** *This wine would go well with fish.*

→ **NO-GO AREA**

go about sth *phr v* to do something or begin doing something: *You're going about this the wrong way.* | **go about doing sth** *How do you go about finding work?*

go after sb/sth *phr v* to try to get something or catch someone: *They both went after the same job.*

go against sb/sth *phr v* **1** to be or do the opposite of what someone believes, wants, advises etc: *Lying to him goes against all my principles.* **2** if a decision, vote etc goes against you, you do not get the result that you wanted: *His lawyer is afraid the case will go against him.*

go ahead *phr v* to happen or continue to do something as planned: *The railway strike looks likely to go ahead.* | **+with** *Are you going ahead with the conference?*

go along *phr v* **as you go along** while doing something, without previous planning or preparation: *I made the story up as I went along.*

go along with sb/sth *phr v* to agree with or support someone or something: *I'm happy to go along with your suggestion.*

go around also **go round** *BrE phr v* **1** to behave or dress in a particular way: **go around doing sth** *You can't go around accusing people like that.* | **+with/in etc** *She goes around in a T-shirt all the time.* **2** if an illness or a piece of news is going around, it is being passed from one person to another: *There's a rumour going around that they're engaged.* **3 go around with sb/go around together** to be friends and spend a lot of time with someone **4 enough/plenty to go around** enough for everyone

go at sb/sth *phr v* to start to do something with a lot of energy: *She went at the task with enthusiasm.*

go away *phr v* **1** to leave a place or a person: *Go away! Leave me alone!* **2** to spend some time away from home, especially on holiday: **+for/to/on** *We went away for the weekend.* **3** to disappear: *My headache still hasn't gone away.*

go back *phr v* **1** to return to a place: *We'd better go back.* | **+to/into/inside** *I'll never go back to my old school.* **2** to have started at some time in the past: *a tradition that goes back 200 years* | **+to** *The building goes back to Roman times.*

go back on sth *phr v* **go back on your word/promise/decision etc** to not do what you have promised or agreed to do

go back to sth *phr v* to start doing something again: *Go back to sleep!* | **go back to doing sth** *She went back to watching TV.*

go by *phr v* **1** if time goes by, it passes: *Two weeks went by before Tony called.* | *As the years went by, she forgot him.* **2 go by sth** to use information, rules etc to help you decide or judge something: *Going by her usual behaviour, she'll be back late.*

go down *phr v* **1** to become lower in level, amount etc: **+to/by/from** *The temperature went down to zero.* | **+in** *Computers have gone down in price.* **2 go down well/badly etc** to get a good or bad reaction from people: *His jokes didn't go down very well.* **3** if a ship goes down, it sinks **4** if a plane goes down, it crashes **5** if something such as a tyre goes down, air comes out of it and it becomes soft **6** if a computer goes down, it stops working **7** when the sun goes down, it goes below the HORIZON at the end of the day

go for sb/sth *phr v* **1** to try to get or win something: *We're going for the gold medal.* **2** *BrE* to attack or criticize someone: *She went for him with a knife.* **3** to choose or prefer something or someone: *I'll go for the soup.* **4 that goes for/the same goes for sb/sth** *spoken*

used to say that something is also true about someone or something else

go in for sth *phr v* **1** to take part in an examination or competition **2** to like doing something: *I've never gone in for gambling.*

go into sth *phr v* **1** to start working in a particular profession: *He wants to go into teaching.* **2** to be spent or used in doing something: *Years of research went into this book.* **3** to describe or explain something thoroughly: *I don't want to go into details right now.*

go off *phr v* **1** to leave in order to do something: *He went off to find Joe.* **2** to explode: *Suddenly a bomb went off.* **3** to make a loud noise: *My alarm clock didn't go off!* **4 go off sb/sth** *BrE* to stop liking someone or something: *I've gone off coffee.* **5** to stop working: *All the lights went off.* **6 go off well/badly/perfectly etc** to happen in a particular way

go off with sth *phr v* to leave with something that belongs to someone else: *She's gone off with my pen.*

go on *phr v* **1** to continue: *The meeting went on longer than expected.* | **go on doing sth** *We can't go on fighting like this!* | **+with** *He went on with his meal.* **2** to happen: *What's going on down there?* **3** to do something after finishing something else: **+to** *Shall we go on to the next topic?* | **go on to do sth** *She went on to become a successful surgeon.* **4** to continue speaking, after you have stopped for a while: *'But,' he went on, 'it's not that simple.'* **5** *spoken* used to encourage someone to do something: *Go on, have some more.* **6** if time goes on, it passes: *As time went on, it got easier.*

go out *phr v* **1** to leave your house, especially in order to enjoy yourself: *Are you going out tonight?* | **+for/to** *We went out for lunch.* **2** to have a romantic relationship with someone: *How long have you two been going out?* | **+with** *Lisa used to go out with Todd.* **3** to stop shining or burning: *All the lights went out.* → see box at **FIRE** **4** to be sent to a number of people: *A copy of the memo went out to all staff.* **5** to leave a competition because you have been defeated: *Our team went out in the first round.* **6** to stop being fashionable or used: *Hats like that went out years ago.* **7** when the TIDE goes out, the sea moves back from the land

go over sth *phr v* to look at or repeat something carefully so that it is all correct or clear: *Let's go over your speech one more time.*

go round *phr v BrE* → **GO AROUND**

go through *phr v* **1 go through sth** to have a difficult or upsetting experience: *She's just gone through a divorce.* **2 go through (sth)** if a deal, agreement, or law goes through, it is officially accepted: *My loan application has finally gone through.* | *The law went through Parliament last year.* **3 go through sth** to practise, read, or explain something carefully to make sure it is correct: *She went through my homework for me.* **4 go through sth** to search a container or place: *A customs man went through my bags.* → see box at **LOOK**

go through with sth *phr v* to do something you had planned or promised to do: *She couldn't go through with the wedding.*

go to sb/sth *phr v* to be given to someone: *The Oscar went to Nicole Kidman.*

go under *phr v* if a business goes under, it has serious problems and fails

go up *phr v* **1** to increase in number or amount: *Unemployment went up again.* | **+by/from/to** *Fares have gone up by almost 50%.* **2** to be built or put in place: *A lot of new houses have gone up.* **3** to explode or be destroyed by fire: *The entire factory went up in flames.*

go with sb/sth *phr v* **1** to be included as part of something: *The car goes with the job.* | **go with doing sth** *the responsibilities that go with having a family* **2** to accept someone's idea or plan: *Let's go with John's original idea.*

go without sth *phr v* **1 go without (sth)** to not have something that you usually have: *She went without food for several days.* **2 it goes without saying (that)** used to say that something is very obvious

go² *n* [C] plural **goes** **1** an attempt to do something: *'I can't get the lid off.' 'Here, let me have a go.'* | *Why not have a go at making your own pasta?* | **at/in one go** *She blew out all the candles in one go.* **2** especially *BrE* someone's turn to play in a game or to use something: *Whose go is it?* | *Can I have a go with the camera?* **3 make a go of sth** to make something succeed, especially a business or marriage **4 on the go a)** very busy **b)** being used or worked on: *I've got two projects on the go.* **5 have a go at sb** *BrE informal* to criticize someone

goad /gəʊd $ goʊd/ *v* [T] to make someone do something by annoying them until they do it: *Friends goaded him into asking her for a date.*

'go-ahead¹ *n* **give/get the go-ahead** to give or be given permission to start doing something: *We were given the go-ahead to start building.*

go-ahead² *adj BrE* a go-ahead company or person uses new methods and is eager to be successful

goal /gəʊl $ goʊl/ *n* [C]
1 something that you hope to achieve in the future [= aim]: *My goal is to study law.* | **achieve/reach a goal** *They achieved their goal of a 50% increase in sales.* → see box at **PURPOSE**
2 the area where a ball must go in order to score a point in games such as football or HOCKEY
3 the action of making the ball go into the goal, or the point scored by doing this: *Ramos scored two goals for the US.*
→ **OWN GOAL**

goalie /'gəʊli $ 'goʊ-/ *n* [C] *informal* a goalkeeper

goalkeeper /'gəʊlˌkiːpə $ 'goʊlˌkiːpər/ also **goaltender** /'gəʊlˌtendə $ 'goʊlˌtendər/ *AmE* *n* [C] the player in a sports team whose job is to stop the ball going into their team's goal

goalpost /'gəʊlpəʊst $ 'goʊlpoʊst/ *n* [C usually plural] one of the two posts with a bar between them that form the sides of a GOAL in games such as football or HOCKEY

goat /gəʊt $ goʊt/ *n* [C] an animal with horns which has long hair under its chin. Goats live on farms or wild in mountains. → see picture at **FARM¹**

goatee /gəʊ'tiː $ goʊ-/ *n* [C] a short BEARD on the end of a man's chin

gob /gɒb $ gɑːb/ *n* [C] *BrE informal* an impolite word for someone's mouth

gobble /'gɒbəl $ 'gɑː-/ also **gobble up/down** *v* [T] *informal* to eat something very quickly: *She gobbled up the whole pizza.* → see box at **EAT**

gobbledygook, **gobbledegook** /'gɒbəldiguːk $ 'gɑːbəldiguːk, -guːk/ *n* [U] *informal disapproving* complicated language, especially in official documents, that ordinary people cannot understand

'go-between *n* [C] someone who takes messages between people who cannot meet or do not want to meet

goblet /'gɒblɪ̩t $ 'gɑːb-/ *n* [C] a cup made of glass or metal, with a base and a stem but no handle

goblin /'gɒblɪ̩n $ 'gɑːb-/ *n* [C] a small ugly creature in children's stories who tricks people

gobsmacked /'gɒbsmækt $ 'gɑːb-/ *adj BrE spoken informal* very surprised → see box at **SURPRISED**

'go-cart *n* another spelling of GO-KART

God, god /gɒd $ gɑːd/ *n*
1 God the BEING who Christians, Jews, and Muslims pray to, and who they believe created everything: *Most Americans believe in God.* | *We asked God to protect us.*
2 [C] a male BEING who is believed to control some part of the world or to represent a particular quality [➔ **goddess**]: **+of** *Mars, the Roman god of war*
3 for God's sake *spoken* used to emphasize what you are saying, when you are angry: *For God's sake, shut up!*
4 God (only) knows *spoken* **a)** used to show that you are annoyed because you do not know or understand something: *God knows where she is now!* **b)** used to emphasize what you are saying: *God knows I've tried.*
5 God forbid *spoken* used to say that you hope that something does not happen: *God forbid that he should find out.*
6 I swear/hope/wish to God *spoken* used to emphasize a statement, hope, or wish: *I swear to God I didn't do it.*
7 sb thinks they're God's gift (to sb/sth) *disapproving* used to say that someone thinks they are perfect in some way
→ **thank God** at **THANK**

godchild /'gɒdtʃaɪld $ 'gɑːd-/ *n* [C] plural **godchildren** /-tʃɪldrən/ a child that a GODPARENT promises to help and to teach Christian values to

goddess /'gɒdɪ̩s $ 'gɑː-/ *n* [C] a female BEING who is believed to control some part of the world, or to represent a particular quality [➔ **god**]: **+of** *Venus, the Roman goddess of love*

godfather /'gɒdˌfɑːðə $ 'gɑːdˌfɑːðər/ *n* [C] a male GODPARENT

godforsaken /'gɒdfəseɪkən $ 'gɑːdfər-/ *adj* a godforsaken place is far from other places and has nothing interesting or cheerful in it

godmother /'gɒdˌmʌðə $ 'gɑːdˌmʌðər/ *n* [C] a female GODPARENT

godparent /'gɒdˌpeərənt $ 'gɑːdˌper-/ *n* [C] someone who promises at a BAPTISM ceremony to help a child and to teach Christian values

godsend /'gɒdsend $ 'gɑːd-/ *n* **be a godsend (for/to sb)** to be a good thing that happens when you really need it: *The rain has been a godsend for gardeners.*

,go-'getter / $ '. ,../ n [C] someone who is likely to be successful because they are very determined

,goggle-'eyed adj informal with your eyes wide open in surprise

goggles /ˈɡɒɡəlz $ ˈɡɑː-/ n [plural] a pair of glasses that protect your eyes, with an edge that fits against your skin: a pair of swimming goggles

goggles

swimming goggles

going[1] /ˈɡəʊɪŋ $ ˈɡoʊ-/ n [U]
1 informal the difficulty or speed with which something is done: **be good/hard/slow etc going** We got there in four hours, which is good going. | I'm finding this work hard going. **2 while the going's good** before a situation becomes difficult or impossible: Let's get out while the going's good.

going[2] adj **1 the going rate (for sth)** the usual amount you pay or receive for something: £25 an hour is the going rate for private lessons. **2** [not before noun] available: Are there any jobs going? | **the best/biggest etc going** We make the best computers going. **3 have a lot going for you** to have many advantages and good qualities **4 going concern** a successful business

,going-'over n [singular] **1** a thorough examination of something **2** when you clean something thoroughly: My car needs a good going-over with a vacuum.

,goings-'on n [plural] informal events or activities that are strange, interesting, or illegal

'go-kart, go-cart n [C] a small car made of an open frame on four wheels, used in races

gold[1] /ɡəʊld $ ɡoʊld/ n
1 [U] a valuable soft yellow metal, or things such as coins or jewellery made from this metal: **pure/solid gold** His watch was solid gold. | She was wearing lots of gold.
2 [C,U] the colour of gold: a room painted in cream and gold
3 [C,U] a GOLD MEDAL

gold[2] adj
1 made of gold: a gold necklace
2 having the colour of gold: a gold dress

golden /ˈɡəʊldən $ ˈɡoʊl-/ adj
1 having a bright yellow colour: golden hair
2 golden opportunity a rare chance to get something valuable or to be very successful: Don't miss this golden opportunity to make some cash.
3 golden age/years/days a time of great happiness or success: the golden age of film
4 golden anniversary, golden wedding BrE the date that is exactly 50 years after a wedding
5 golden boy/girl someone who is popular and successful
6 literary made of gold: a golden crown

goldfish /ˈɡəʊldfɪʃ $ ˈɡoʊld-/ n [C] plural **goldfish** a small orange fish often kept as a pet

,gold 'medal n [C] a prize, especially a round piece of gold, that is given to someone who wins a race or competition

goldmine /ˈɡəʊldmaɪn $ ˈɡoʊld-/ n [C]
1 informal a business or activity that produces large profits **2** a place where gold is dug out from under the ground

golf /ɡɒlf $ ɡɑːlf, ɡɔːlf/ n [U] a game in which players hit a small white ball into holes in the ground using a CLUB (=special stick): Do you **play golf**?
—**golfer** n [C]

'golf club n [C] **1** a long stick that you use to hit the ball in a game of golf **2** a place where people can go to play golf

'golf course n [C] an area of land that golf is played on

gone[1] /ɡɒn $ ɡɔːn/ the past participle of GO

gone[2] adj **be gone a)** to no longer be in a place: He waved and was gone. **b)** to be dead or no longer exist: The factory has gone now.

gone[3] prep BrE informal later than a particular time or older than a particular age: It's gone midnight. | He's gone 60.

gong /ɡɒŋ $ ɡɔːŋ/ n [C] a round piece of metal that you hit with a stick to make a loud sound

gonna /ˈɡɒnə, ɡənə $ ˈɡɔːnə, ɡənə/ informal a way of saying 'going to'. Some people consider this use to be incorrect: I'm gonna try it.

goo /ɡuː/ n [U] an unpleasantly sticky substance

good[1] /ɡʊd/ adj comparative **better** /ˈbetə $ -ər/ superlative **best** /best/
1 of a high standard or quality: a good hotel | good quality paint

G

THESAURUS

great especially spoken: We had a really great time in Ireland.
excellent: It was an excellent concert.
brilliant especially spoken: a brilliant match
outstanding: an outstanding achievement
exceptional: Ruth's an exceptional student.
first-class: This is a first-class wine.
ace informal: an ace guitarist
→ **BAD**
Use **good** to describe the quality of something or someone: a good teacher | Was the movie good?
Use **well** to talk about the way someone does something: He plays tennis very well.

---

2 able to do something well: a good builder | **+at** Gill's very good at sports. | She's good at swimming. | I'm not good enough to get into the team. | **+with** He's very good with animals (=able to deal with animals well).
3 pleasant or enjoyable: Did you have a good holiday? | We had a really good time. | It's good to see you. | That's good news!
4 likely to be successful: That's a good idea. | What's the best way to do this? | **best practice** (=the best way of performing a job or activity, that other people can copy in the future)
5 suitable or convenient: Is this a good time to talk? | **+for** The beach is good for families.
6 be good for sb/sth likely to improve someone's health or the condition of something: Exer-

cise is good for you. | products that are good for the environment

7 a good child behaves well: *Hurry up, be a good boy.*

8 not broken or damaged: *good strong boots* | *The car looks* **as good as new** (=in perfect condition).

9 kind and and nice: *He's a good man.* | *It was good of you to come.*

10 large in amount or size: *a good harvest*

11 complete or thorough: *The car needs a good wash.* | *Take a good look.*

12 as good as very nearly: *The job's as good as done.*

13 in good time *BrE* early enough to be ready for a particular time or event: *I arrived in good time.*

14 a good few/many quite a lot: *There were a good few people there.*

15 a good while quite a long time: *We had to wait a good while.*

16 good *spoken* used when you are pleased about something: *Good. I'm glad that's finished.* | *'Tom's here.' 'Oh, good.'*

17 (that's a) good idea/point/question *spoken* used to say that someone has just said or suggested something interesting or important

18 good luck *spoken* used to say that you hope that someone is successful

19 good grief/God/lord/heavens/gracious! *spoken* used to express surprise or anger

20 good for sb *spoken* used to say that you approve of something that someone has done: *'I'm getting married.' 'Good for you!'*

21 it's a good thing *spoken* also **it's a good job** *BrE* used when you are glad that something has happened: *It's a good thing I brought the map.*
→ **a good deal** at DEAL¹

good² *n* **1 no good/not much good/not any good a)** not useful or suitable: *One lesson's no good – you'll need more.* **b)** of a low standard or level of ability: *The movie wasn't much good.* | **no good at (doing) sth** *I'm no good at math.* **2 it's no good (doing sth)** used to say that an action will not achieve what you want: *It's no good crying.* **3 do some good/do sb good** to have a useful effect: *It won't do any good arguing.* | *A rest would do you good.* **4 what's the good of...?/what good is...?** used to say that it is not worth doing or having something in a particular situation: *What's the good of a car if you can't drive?* **5 for good** permanently: *Is he back home for good?* **6 for the good of sb/sth** in order to help someone or improve a situation: *working for the good of the community* | *I'm doing this for your own good!* **7** [U] behaviour, attitudes, forces etc that are morally right: *the battle between good and evil* → GOODS

good ,after'noon *spoken formal* used to say hello when greeting someone in the afternoon

goodbye /gʊd'baɪ/ used when you are leaving someone, or when they are leaving: *Goodbye, Jo.* | *I just want to* **say goodbye** *to Pete.* | *We* **said our goodbyes** (=said goodbye to everyone) *and left.*

saying goodbye

see you *informal*
take it easy *informal*

so long *informal*
have a nice day/have a good weekend/have a great time
(it was) nice to meet you
take care
→ HELLO

good 'evening *spoken formal* used to say hello when greeting someone in the evening [→ **good night**]

,good-for-'nothing *adj* lazy and useless —**good-for-nothing** *n* [C]

,good-'humoured *BrE*; **good-humored** *AmE adj* happy and friendly

goodie, goody /'gʊdi/ *n* [C] *BrE informal* a good person in a film or book [≠ **baddie**]

goodies /'gʊdiz/ *n* [plural] *informal* nice things, especially nice food: *a bag of goodies*

,good-'looking *adj* someone who is good-looking looks attractive → see box at ATTRACTIVE

,good 'looks *n* [plural] the attractive appearance of someone's face

good 'morning *spoken* used to say hello when greeting someone in the morning

good-natured /gʊd 'neɪtʃəd $ -ərd/ *adj* kind, helpful, and not easily made angry

goodness /'gʊdnəs/ *n* [U] **1 goodness (me)! /my goodness!** said when you are surprised **2 for goodness' sake** said when you are annoyed: *For goodness' sake stop arguing!* **3** when someone or something is morally good: *No one can doubt his moral goodness.*

good 'night *spoken* used to say goodbye at night, or when someone is going to bed [→ **good evening**]

goods /gʊdz/ *n* [plural]

1 things that are produced in order to be sold: *The shop sells a wide range of goods.* | *luxury goods*

2 stolen goods things that have been stolen

3 *BrE* things that are carried by road, train etc [= freight]: *a goods train*

4 come up with the goods/deliver the goods *informal* to do what is needed or expected

goodwill /ˌgʊd'wɪl◂/ *n* [U] kind feelings between people: *We invited the neighbours as a gesture of goodwill.*

'goody-,goody also **,goody-'two-shoes** *AmE n* [C] plural **goody-goodies** a child who tries too hard to be good and helpful, in a way that others think is annoying

gooey /'guːi/ *adj informal* sticky and soft: *gooey cakes*

goof¹ /guːf/ also **goof up** *v* [I] *AmE informal* to make a silly mistake

goof around *phr v AmE informal* to spend time doing silly things

goof off *phr v AmE informal* to waste time or avoid work

goof² *n* [C] *especially AmE informal* **1** a silly mistake **2** a silly person

goofy /'guːfi/ *adj informal* stupid or silly: *a goofy grin*

goop /guːp/ *n* [U] *AmE informal* a thick slightly sticky substance

goose /guːs/ *n* [C,U] plural **geese** /giːs/ a bird like a large duck, or the meat from this bird: *roast goose*

gooseberry /'gʊzbəri, 'guːz-, 'guːs- $ 'guːsberi/ *n* [C] plural **gooseberries** **1** a small round green fruit with a sour taste **2 play gooseberry** *BrE informal* to be with two people who want to be alone and romantic together

'goose ,pimples also **goose bumps** *especially AmE n* [plural] small raised spots on your skin that you get when you are cold or frightened

gore¹ /gɔː $ gɔːr/ *v* [T] if an animal gores someone, it wounds them with its horns

gore² *n* [U] *literary* thick dark blood from a wound

gorge¹ /gɔːdʒ $ gɔːrdʒ/ *n* [C] a deep narrow valley with steep sides

gorge² *v* **gorge yourself on sth** to eat something until you are too full to eat any more: *We gorged ourselves on cake.*

gorgeous /'gɔːdʒəs $ 'gɔːr-/ *adj informal* **1** very beautiful or attractive: *He's gorgeous!* | *a gorgeous sunny day* → see box at **ATTRACTIVE** **2** very pleasant or enjoyable

gorilla /gə'rɪlə/ *n* [C] the largest kind of APE (=animal like a large monkey)

gorse /gɔːs $ gɔːrs/ *n* [U] a bush with sharp points and yellow flowers

gory /'gɔːri/ *adj* involving a lot of violence and blood: *a gory film*

gosh /gɒʃ $ gɑːʃ/ *spoken informal* used when you are surprised

gosling /'gɒzlɪŋ $ 'gɑːz-, 'gɒːz-/ *n* [C] a very young GOOSE

gospel /'gɒspəl $ 'gɑːs-/ *n* **1** [C] one of the four books in the Bible that tell the story of Christ's life **2 the gospel** the life of Christ and the ideas that he taught: *He travelled around preaching the gospel* (=telling people about it). **3** also **gospel truth** [U] something that is completely true: *Don't take what she says as gospel.* **4** also **gospel music** [U] a type of Christian music

gossip¹ /'gɒsɪp $ 'gɑː-/ *n* **1** [U] informal talk about other people's behaviour and private lives: *She told me all the latest gossip.* **2** [C] *disapproving* someone who likes talking about other people's private lives

gossip² *v* [I] to talk about other people's behaviour and private lives: **+about** *People were gossiping about his wife.* → see box at **TALK**

'gossip ,column *n* [C] a regular article in a newspaper or magazine about the behaviour and private lives of famous people

got /gɒt $ gɑːt/ the past tense and a past participle of GET

gotta /'gɒtə $ 'gɑːtə/ *informal* a way of saying 'have got to', 'has got to', 'have got a', or 'has got a'. Some people consider this use to be incorrect: *I gotta go.*

gotten /'gɒtn $ 'gɑːtn/ *AmE* the past participle of GET

gouge /gaʊdʒ/ *v* [T] to make a deep hole or cut in the surface of something

gouge sth ⇔ **out** *phr v* to remove something by making a deep hole or cut

gourmet¹ /'gʊəmeɪ $ 'gʊr-, gʊr'meɪ/ *adj* [only before noun] relating to good food and drink: *a gourmet meal*

gourmet² *n* [C] someone who enjoys good food and wine

govern /'gʌvən $ -ərn/ *v*
1 [I,T] to legally control a country and make all the decisions about its laws, public services etc: *when the Belgians governed the Congo*
2 [T] if rules or principles govern a system or situation, they control how the system works or what happens: *the laws that govern the universe*

governess /'gʌvənɪs $ -ər-/ *n* [C] a female teacher in the past, who lived with a rich family and taught their children at home

government /'gʌvəmənt, 'gʌvənmənt $ 'gʌvərn-/ *n*
1 [C usually singular also + plural verb *BrE*] also **Government** the group of people who govern a country: *The Government is not doing enough.* | *The Government have promised to increase public expenditure.* | *the Chinese government* | *a government official* | *He criticized government policy on the environment.*

democracy – a political system in which everyone can vote to choose the government, or a country that has this system

republic – a country that has an elected government, and does not have a king or queen

monarchy – a country that has a king or queen as the head of state, and which may or may not also have an elected government

regime – a government, especially one that was not elected fairly or that you disapprove of: *a brutal military regime*

dictatorship – a political system in which a dictator (=a leader who has complete power and who has not been elected) controls a country, or a country that has this system

totalitarian country/state etc – a country in which the government has complete control over everything

police state – a country where the government strictly controls people's freedom, for example to travel or to talk about politics

2 [U] the process of governing a country: **in government** (=governing a country) *when the Conservatives were in government* | *the fight for democratic government*

governor, Governor /'gʌvənə $ -vərnər/ *n* [C] the person in charge of an organization or place: **+of** *the Governor of Texas*

gown /gaʊn/ *n* [C] **1** a long dress that a woman wears on very formal occasions: *a wedding gown* **2** a long loose piece of clothing that you wear for a special ceremony: *a graduation gown*

GP /,dʒiː 'piː/ *n* [C] *BrE* **general practitioner** a doctor who treats all kinds of patients when they first become ill, and sends them to special doctors in hospitals if they have a serious illness → see box at **DOCTOR**

GPA /ˌdʒiː piː 'eɪ/ n [C] *AmE* grade point average the average of a student's marks over a period of time

grab¹ /græb/ v [T] grabbed, grabbing

1 to take hold of someone or something suddenly or violently: *He grabbed my bag and ran.* → see box at **HOLD**

2 *informal* to get some food or sleep quickly because you are busy: *Let's grab some lunch.*

3 grab a chance/opportunity *informal* to quickly take advantage of an opportunity: *Grab the opportunity to travel while you can.*

4 to get someone's attention: *That should grab her attention.* | *a story which has grabbed the headlines* (=has been reported in the newspapers)

grab at/for sth *phr v* to suddenly put out your hand to try to take hold of something

grab² n **1 make a grab for/at sth** to suddenly try to take hold of something: *I made a grab for the gun.* **2 be up for grabs** *informal* if something is up for grabs, it is available for anyone who wants to try to get it

grace¹ /greɪs/ n [U] **1** a smooth way of moving that appears natural, relaxed, and attractive: *the grace of a dancer* **2** polite and pleasant behaviour: *At least he had the grace to apologize.* | *Len accepted his defeat with good grace* (=willingly and cheerfully). **3** more time that is allowed to someone to finish a piece of work, pay a debt etc: **a week's/month's etc grace** *I got a few days' grace to finish my essay.* **4** a short prayer that people say before a meal: *Who'll say grace?*

grace² v **1 grace sb with your presence** to agree to spend time with people although you think that you are better than them: *Perhaps Amy will grace us with her presence for once.* **2** [T] *formal* to make a place or an object look more attractive: *the pictures that grace the walls*

graceful /ˈgreɪsfəl/ adj

1 moving in a smooth and attractive way, or having an attractive shape: *a graceful movement* | *the graceful curve of the swan's neck* **2** behaving in a polite and pleasant way: *a graceful and quiet man*

—**gracefully** adv: *She rose gracefully to her feet.*

gracious /ˈgreɪʃəs/ adj **1** polite, kind, and generous: *a gracious host* **2** comfortable and wealthy: *a gracious country lifestyle* **3 gracious (me)!/good gracious!/goodness gracious!** *old-fashioned* used to express surprise —**graciously** adv

gradation /grəˈdeɪʃən/ n [C] *formal* a small change or difference between points on a scale: *gradations of colour*

grade¹ /greɪd/ n [C]

1 a level of quality that a product, material etc has: *different grades of wood* | **high/low grade** *low grade farmland*

2 a level of job: *He joined the company on the bottom grade.*

3 a letter or number given by a teacher to show how good a student's work is: *I got a grade A in maths.*

4 make the grade to succeed or reach the necessary standard: *players who fail to make the grade*

5 one of the 12 years students are at school in the US, or the students in a particular year: *He's in third grade.*

grade² v [T] **1** to say what level of a quality something has, or what standard it is: *All hotels are regularly checked and graded.* **2** *especially AmE* to give a mark to an examination paper or a piece of school work [= mark]: *The teacher hasn't graded the papers yet.*

'grade ˌcrossing n [C] *AmE* a place where a road and railway cross each other [= level crossing *BrE*]

'grade point ˌaverage n [C] *AmE* → **GPA**

'grade ˌschool n [C] *AmE* an ELEMENTARY SCHOOL

gradient /ˈgreɪdiənt/ n [C] a slope in a road or railway: *a steep gradient*

gradual /ˈgrædʒuəl/ adj happening slowly over a long period of time [≠ sudden]: *a gradual increase in price*

gradually /ˈgrædʒuəli/ adv slowly, over a long period of time [≠ suddenly]: *Gradually, she grew calmer.* | *The truth is gradually emerging.*

graduate¹ /ˈgrædʒuᵻt/ n [C]

1 someone who has completed a university degree [➔ undergraduate, postgraduate]: **+of** *a graduate of Leeds University* | *a history graduate* **2** *AmE* someone who has completed a course at a college, school etc: **high-school graduates**

graduate² /ˈgrædʒueɪt/ v [I]

1 to obtain a degree from a college or university: **+from** *He graduated from Harvard last year.* **2** *AmE* to complete your education at **HIGH SCHOOL**: **+from** *when I graduate from high school* **3 graduate (from sth) to sth** to start doing something better, more important, or more difficult: *She wants to graduate to serious drama.*

graduate³ /ˈgrædʒuᵻt/ adj [only before noun] *especially AmE* relating to or involved in studies done at a university after a first degree [= postgraduate *BrE*]: *a graduate student*

graduated /ˈgrædʒueɪtᵻd/ adj divided into different levels: *graduated rates of tax*

graduation /ˌgrædʒuˈeɪʃən/ n [U] when you complete a university degree or your education at an American **HIGH SCHOOL**: *After graduation, I left Cambridge.*

graffiti /græˈfiːti, grə-/ n [U] writing and pictures that are drawn illegally on the walls of buildings, trains etc

graffiti

graft¹ /grɑːft $ græft/ n **1** [C] a piece of skin or bone that is taken from a healthy part of someone's body and attached to a damaged part: *a skin graft* **2** [C] a piece cut from one plant and joined to another so that it grows there

3 [U] *especially BrE informal* hard work: *There's a lot of hard graft involved in getting a university degree.* **4** [U] *especially AmE* when someone deliberately uses their position to get money or advantages: *political graft and corruption*

graft² *v* [T] **1** to put a piece of skin or bone from a healthy part of someone's body onto a damaged part **2** to join a part of a plant or tree onto another plant or tree

grain /greɪn/ *n*

1 a) [U] the seeds of crops such as corn, wheat, or rice that are gathered for food, or these crops themselves: *sacks of grain* | *the grain harvest* b) [C] a single seed of corn, wheat etc: **+of** *a few grains of rice*

2 the grain the natural lines you can see in things such as wood, rock, or cloth: *Split the wood along the grain.*

3 [C] a very small piece or amount of something: **+of** *some grains of sand* | *There was a **grain of truth** in what he said.*

4 go against the grain if something goes against the grain, you do not like doing it because it is not what you would normally do: *It goes against the grain to throw food away.*

gram also **gramme** *BrE* /græm/ *n* [C] written abbreviation **g** or **gm** the basic unit for measuring weight in the METRIC system

grammar /ˈgræmə $ -ər/ *n*

1 [U] the rules by which words change their form and are combined into sentences: *English grammar* | *Check your spelling and grammar.*

2 [C] a book that describes grammar rules: *a Latin grammar*

'grammar ,school *n* [C] a school in Britain for children over the age of 11, who have to pass an examination to go there

grammatical /grəˈmætɪkəl/ *adj* **1** [only before noun] relating to grammar: *a grammatical error* **2** correct according to the rules of grammar: *a grammatical sentence* —**grammatically** /-kli/ *adv*

gramophone /ˈgræməfəʊn $ -foʊn/ *n* [C] *old-fashioned* a RECORD PLAYER

gran /græn/ *n* [C] *BrE informal* a GRANDMOTHER

granary /ˈgrænəri $ ˈgreɪ-, ˈgræ-/ *n* [C] plural **granaries** a place where grain, especially wheat, is stored

grand¹ /grænd/ *adj*

1 big and very impressive: *the grand hall* | *This was opera **on a grand scale**.*

2 intended to achieve something impressive: *a grand plan*

3 important and rich: *He thinks he's too grand to talk to us.*

4 a) used in the titles of buildings or places that are big and impressive: *the Grand Hotel* b) used in the titles of some people who belong to the highest social class: *the Grand Duke of Baden*

5 grand total the final total you get when you add up several numbers or amounts: **of** *We raised a grand total of £250,000.*

—**grandly** *adv*

grand² *n* [C] plural **grand** *informal* a thousand pounds or dollars: *The wedding cost ten grand.*

grandad, **granddad** /ˈgrændæd/ *n* [C] especially *BrE informal* a GRANDFATHER

grandchild /ˈgræntʃaɪld/ *n* [C] plural **grandchildren** /-tʃɪldrən/ the child of your son or daughter

granddaughter /ˈgræn,dɔːtə $ -,dɔːtər/ *n* [C] the daughter of your son or daughter

grandeur /ˈgrændʒə $ -ər/ *n* [U] impressive beauty, power, or size: *the grandeur of the mountains*

grandfather /ˈgræn,fɑːðə $ -ər/ *n* [C] the father of your mother or father → see box at **RELATIVE**

'grandfather ,clock *n* [C] an old-fashioned tall clock which stands on the floor

grandiose /ˈgrændiəʊs $ -oʊs/ *adj* grandiose plans sound very important or impressive, but are not practical

,grand 'jury *n* [C] *law* a group of people in the US who decide whether someone should be judged in a court of law

grandma /ˈgrænmɑː/ *n* [C] *informal* a GRANDMOTHER → see box at **RELATIVE**

grandmother /ˈgræn,mʌðə $ -ər/ *n* [C] the mother of your mother or father → see box at **RELATIVE**

grandpa /ˈgrænpɑː/ *n* [C] *informal* a GRANDFATHER → see box at **RELATIVE**

grandparent /ˈgræn,peərənt $ -,per-/ *n* [C usually plural] your grandparents are the parents of your mother or father: *My grandparents live in Kent.* → see box at **RELATIVE**

,grand pi'ano *n* [C] the type of large piano often used in concerts

grandson /ˈgrænsʌn/ *n* [C] the son of your son or daughter

grandstand

grandstand /ˈgrændstænd/ *n* [C] a large structure with rows of seats and a roof, where people sit to watch sports

granite /ˈgrænɪt/ *n* [U] a type of very hard grey rock, often used in building

granny /ˈgræni/ *n* [C] plural **grannies** *informal* a GRANDMOTHER

granola /grəˈnəʊlə $ -ˈnoʊ-/ *n* [U] *AmE* breakfast food made from nuts, grains, and seeds

grant¹ /grɑːnt $ grænt/ *v* [T] **1 take it for granted (that)** to believe that something is true without making sure: *He took it for granted that Claire would marry him.* **2 take sb/sth for granted** to expect that someone or something will always be there when you need them and never think how important or useful they are: *He spends all his time at work and takes his family for granted.* **3** *formal* to give someone something or allow them to have something that they have asked for: **grant sb sth** *Ms. Chung was granted American citizenship last year.* **4** to admit that something is true although it does

G

not make much difference to your opinion: *He's not a natural athlete,* **I grant you,** *but he does work hard.*

grant² *n* [C] an amount of money given to someone by an organization for a particular purpose: *a research grant*

granule /'grænjuːl/ *n* [C] a small hard piece of something: *instant coffee granules* —**granular** /-jŭlə $ -ər/ *adj* —**granulated** *adj*: *granulated sugar*

grape /greɪp/ *n* [C] one of a number of small round green or purple fruits that grow together on a VINE. Grapes are often used for making wine: *a bunch of grapes* → see picture at **FRUIT**

grapefruit /'greɪpfruːt/ *n* [C] a round yellow CITRUS fruit with a thick skin and a sour taste

grapevine /'greɪpvaɪn/ *n* **hear sth on/through the grapevine** to hear news because it has been passed from one person to another in conversation

graph /grɑːf $ græf/ *n* [C] a drawing that uses a line or lines to show how two or more sets of measurements are related to each other: *a sales graph*

graphic /'græfɪk/ *adj* **1** a graphic account or description of an event is very clear and gives a lot of details, especially unpleasant ones: *She gave a graphic account of her unhappy childhood.* **2** [only before noun] related to DRAWINGS, pictures etc: *graphic art* —**graphically** /-kli/ *adv*: *She described the scene graphically.*

,graphic de'sign *n* [U] the art of combining pictures and words in the production of books, magazines etc —**graphic designer** *n* [C]

graphics /'græfɪks/ *n* [plural] pictures or images, especially those produced on a computer

graphite /'græfaɪt/ *n* [U] a soft black substance that is a type of CARBON and is used in pencils

grapple /'græpəl/ *v* [I] to fight or struggle with someone, holding them tightly: **+with** *He tried to grapple with the guard.*

grapple with sth *phr v* to try hard to deal with or understand something difficult: *Molly's upstairs, grappling with her maths homework.*

grasp¹ /grɑːsp $ græsp/ *v* [T] **1** to take and hold something firmly in your hands: *Grasp the rope with both hands.* **2** to understand something completely: *At the time I didn't fully grasp what he meant.*

grasp at sth *phr v* to try to hold on to something

grasp² *n* [singular] **1** the ability to understand a subject or a situation completely: **+of** *Her grasp of the issues was impressive.* | **a good/ poor etc grasp of sth** *a good grasp of spoken English* **2** your ability to achieve or gain something: **within sb's grasp** *Eve felt that success was finally within her grasp.* | **beyond sb's grasp** *For many people, buying a house is beyond their grasp.* **3** the way you hold something or your ability to hold it: *The bottle slipped out of his grasp and smashed on the floor.*

grasping /'grɑːspɪŋ $ 'græs-/ *adj disapproving* very eager to get money and unwilling to give any of it away or spend it: *a hard, grasping man*

grass /grɑːs $ græs/ *n*

1 [U] a very common plant with thin leaves that covers the ground in fields and gardens and is often eaten by animals: *a lion lying in the long grass* | *Please keep off the grass.* | *a blade of grass* (=a single leaf)
2 [C] a particular kind of grass: *mountain grasses*
3 [U] *informal* MARIJUANA
—**grassy** *adj*: *a grassy bank*

grasshopper /'grɑːs,hɒpə $ 'græs,hɑːpər/ *n* [C] an insect that has long back legs for jumping and that makes short loud noises

grassland /'grɑːslænd $ 'græs-/ *n* [U] also **grasslands** [plural] a large area of land covered with wild grass

,grass 'roots *n* **the grass roots** the ordinary people in an organization, not the leaders —**grass-roots** *adj*: *grass-roots support*

grate¹ /greɪt/ *v* **1** [T] to rub cheese, vegetables etc against a GRATER (=a kitchen tool with a rough or sharp surface) in order to break them into small pieces: *grated carrot* → see box at **RECIPE** → see picture at **CUT¹** **2** [I] to annoy someone: **+on** *His voice grated on her ears.* **3** [I,T] to make an unpleasant sound by rubbing against something: *The stones beneath her shoes grated harshly.* —**grating** *adj*: *a loud grating laugh*

grate² *n* [C] the metal frame that holds wood, coal etc in a FIREPLACE

grateful /'greɪtfəl/ *adj*

1 feeling or showing thanks [≠ **ungrateful**]: **grateful (to sb) for sth** *Mona was very grateful to Peter for his advice.* | **+(that)** *I'm grateful that the kids help around the house.* | *Our grateful thanks go to all who participated.*
2 I would be grateful if you could/would ... *formal* used to ask something in a formal situation or a letter: *I would be grateful if you would allow me to visit your school.*
—**gratefully** *adv*: *We gratefully accepted their offer of help.*

grater /'greɪtə $ -ər/ *n* [C] a kitchen tool with a rough or sharp surface, used for grating food: *a cheese grater*

gratify /'grætɪfaɪ/ *v* [T] **gratified, gratifying, gratifies** *formal* to make someone pleased or satisfied: *She was gratified by the result.* —**gratifying** *adj*: *It was gratifying to know that I had won.* —**gratification** /,grætɪfɪ'keɪʃən/ *n* [U]

grating /'greɪtɪŋ/ *n* [C] a metal frame with bars across it, used to cover a window or hole

gratitude /'grætɪtjuːd $ -tuːd/ *n* [U] the feeling of being grateful [≠ **ingratitude**]: *Tears of gratitude filled her eyes.*

gratuitous /grə'tjuːɪtəs $ -'tuː-/ *adj* said or done without a good reason, in a way that offends someone [= **unnecessary**]: *gratuitous violence in films*

gratuity /grə'tjuːɪti $ -'tuː-/ *n* [C] plural **gratuities** *formal* a small gift of money given to someone for a service they provided [= **tip**]

grave¹ /greɪv/ *n* [C] the place where a dead body is buried: *We visited my grandfather's grave.*

grave² *adj* **1** very serious and worrying: *I have grave doubts about her ability.* | *His life is in grave danger.* **2** looking or sounding very serious: *Dr Fry looked grave. 'I have some bad news,' he said.* —**gravely** *adv*

gravel /ˈɡrævəl/ n [U] small stones used to make a surface for paths or roads —**gravelled** BrE; **graveled** AmE adj: a gravelled driveway

gravelly /ˈɡrævəli/ adj a gravelly voice sounds low and rough

gravestone /ˈɡreɪvstəʊn $ -stoʊn/ n [C] a stone on a GRAVE that shows the name of the person buried there and the dates when they were alive

graveyard /ˈɡreɪvjɑːd $ -jɑːrd/ n [C] an area of ground where people are buried, often near a church [➡ cemetery]

gravitate /ˈɡrævɪteɪt/ v [I] formal to be attracted to something and move towards it or become involved with it: +to/towards Students gravitate towards others with similar interests.

gravitational /ˌɡrævɪˈteɪʃənəl◂/ adj relating to gravity: the Earth's gravitational pull

gravity /ˈɡrævɪti/ n [U] **1** the force that makes objects fall to the ground: the laws of gravity **2** formal seriousness: +of We were soon made aware of the gravity of the situation.

gravy /ˈɡreɪvi/ n [U] a sauce made from the juice that comes from meat as it cooks, mixed with flour and water

gray /ɡreɪ/ adj, n the usual American spelling of GREY

graze¹ /ɡreɪz/ v **1** [I,T] if an animal grazes, it eats grass: cattle grazing in the field **2** [T] to break the surface of your skin by accidentally rubbing it against something rough: Billy grazed his knee when he fell. **3** [T] to touch something lightly while passing it: A bullet grazed his cheek.

graze² n [C] a slight wound that breaks the surface of your skin: minor cuts and grazes

grease¹ /ɡriːs/ n [U] **1** oil or fat from food that has been cooked **2** thick oil that you put on the moving parts of a machine to make them move smoothly

grease² v [T] put butter, grease etc on a pan etc to prevent food from sticking to it: Grease the tin lightly with butter.

greasy /ˈɡriːsi, -zi/ adj covered with or containing a lot of grease or oil: greasy food | a shampoo for greasy hair | greasy skin ➡ see box at DIRTY

great¹ /ɡreɪt/ adj

1 very large in amount or degree: We had great fun. | The great majority of people are against the war. | A great many people died in the flood. | **a great deal of sth** We spent a great deal of time and effort decorating the house.

2 spoken very good: It's great to see you again! | We had a great time in Rio. | **sound/taste/look/feel etc great** You look great in that dress. | +for Our holiday villas are great for families with children. ➡ see box at GOOD ➡ and NICE

3 [only before noun] very important, successful, or famous: the great civilizations of the past | the greatest movie star of them all | The play was a great success.

4 spoken used when you are disappointed or annoyed about something: 'Your car won't be ready until next week.' 'Oh, great!'

5 spoken **great big** very big: a great big fish

6 great-grandfather/great-aunt etc the grandfather, aunt etc of one of your parents

7 great-nephew/great-granddaughter etc the NEPHEW, GRANDDAUGHTER etc of your child

8 greater London/Boston etc used to talk about a large city, including all the parts on the edge

—**greatly** adv: Your chances of getting cancer are greatly increased if you smoke. —**greatness** n [U]

great² n [C usually plural] someone who is very successful in a particular sport, profession etc: Jack Nicklaus is one of golf's **all-time greats**.

greed /ɡriːd/ n [U] a strong desire for more food, money, power, possessions etc than you need: Burning the rainforest is motivated by greed.

greedy /ˈɡriːdi/ adj wanting more money, food, power, possessions etc than you need: a greedy and selfish society | +for They are greedy for profit.

—**greedily** adv —**greediness** n [U]

green¹ /ɡriːn/ adj

1 having the colour of grass: green eyes | a dark green dress ➡ see picture at PATTERN

2 covered with grass, trees, bushes etc: green fields

3 related to protecting the environment: green issues such as global warming

4 be green with envy to wish very much that you had something that someone else has

5 informal young and lacking experience: The trainees are still pretty green.

6 have green fingers BrE **have a green thumb** AmE to be good at making plants grow

7 give sb/get the green light if someone gives you the green light, they give permission for you to start a project, a new system etc

green² n

1 [C,U] the colour of grass: different shades of green

2 [C] the smooth flat area of grass around a hole on a golf course

3 [C] BrE an area of grass in the middle of a village: the village green

4 greens [plural] vegetables with large green leaves: Eat your greens.

greenback /ˈɡriːnbæk/ n [C] AmE informal an American BANK NOTE

'green belt n [C,U] an area of land around a city where building is not allowed, in order to protect fields and woods

green 'card n [C] a document that a foreigner must have in order to work legally in the US

greenery /ˈɡriːnəri/ n [U] green leaves and plants

greenfield site /ˈɡriːnfiːld ˌsaɪt/ n [C] BrE a piece of land that has never been built on before [➡ brownfield site]

greengrocer /ˈɡriːnˌɡrəʊsə $ -ˌɡroʊsər/ n [C] BrE **1** someone who owns or works in a shop selling fruit and vegetables **2 the greengrocer's** a greengrocer's shop ➡ see box at SHOP

greenhouse /ˈɡriːnhaʊs/ n [C] a glass building used for growing plants that need warmth, light, and protection

'greenhouse efˌfect n **the greenhouse effect** the warming of the air around the Earth as a result of the sun's heat being trapped by POLLUTION [➡ global warming] ➡ see box at ENVIRONMENT

G

Greenwich Mean Time /ˌgrenɪtʃ ˈmiːn taɪm, ˌgriː-, -nɪdʒ-/ n → **GMT**

greet /griːt/ v [T] **1** to say hello to someone or welcome them: *The children came rushing out to greet me.* **2** to react to something in a particular way: **be greeted with sth** *The speech was greeted with cheers and laughter.*

greeting /ˈgriːtɪŋ/ n [C,U] something you say or do when you meet someone: **in greeting** *She raised her hand in greeting.* | *The two cousins exchanged greetings* (=greeted each other).

gregarious /grɪˈgeəriəs $ -ˈger-/ adj someone who is gregarious enjoys being with other people [➔ **sociable**]

grenade /grɪˈneɪd/ n [C] a small bomb that can be thrown or fired from a gun: *a hand grenade*

grew /gruː/ v the past tense of **GROW**

grey¹ usually **gray** AmE /greɪ/ adj
1 having the colour of dark clouds, neither black nor white: *grey rain clouds* | *dark grey trousers*
2 having grey hair: *My father went grey in his forties.*
3 weather that is grey is dull and cloudy: *It was a grey Sunday morning.* → see box at **SUN**
4 boring and unattractive: *grey businessmen*
5 [only before noun] BrE relating to old people: *the grey vote*
6 grey area a part of a subject such as law or science that is hard to deal with because the rules are not clear

grey² usually **gray** AmE n [C,U] the colour of dark clouds, neither black nor white: *dull greys and browns*
—**greyness** n [U]

greyhound /ˈgreɪhaʊnd/ n [C] a type of thin dog that can run very fast and is used in races → see picture at **DOG¹**

greying¹ BrE; **graying** AmE /ˈgreɪ-ɪŋ/ adj greying hair is starting to become grey

greying² BrE; **graying** AmE n **the greying of sth** the situation in which the average age of a population increases, so that there are more old people than there were in the past

grid /grɪd/ n [C] **1** a pattern of straight lines that cross each other and form squares **2** the system of numbered squares printed on a map that helps you find exactly where something is **3** BrE a network of CABLES that supply an area with electricity

gridlock /ˈgrɪdlɒk $ -lɑːk/ n [U] when the main roads in a city have so many cars etc using them that the traffic stops moving —**gridlocked** adj

grief /griːf/ n [U] **1** extreme sadness, especially because someone you love has died: *His grief was obvious from the way he spoke.* | **+at/ over** *The grief she felt over Helen's death was almost unbearable.* **2 good grief!** spoken said when you are slightly surprised or annoyed **3 come to grief** to fail, or to be harmed or destroyed in an accident: *Their business came to grief after only six months.*

grievance /ˈgriːvəns/ n [C,U] a belief that you have been treated unfairly, or an unfair situation or event that affects and upsets you: **+against** *He has a grievance against his former employer.*

grieve /griːv/ v **1** [I,T] to feel extremely sad, especially because someone you love has died: **+over/for** *Sue's grieving over the death of her*

mother. | *She grieved over the loss of her only son.* **2** [T] if something grieves you, it makes you feel very unhappy: *My aunt, it grieves me to say, gets things confused.*

grievous /ˈgriːvəs/ adj formal very serious and causing great pain or suffering: *a grievous error* | *The death of his father was a grievous blow.* —**grievously** adv

grill¹ /grɪl/ v **1** [I,T] if you grill food, or if food grills, you cook it by putting it close to a strong heat coming from above [= **broil** AmE]: *Grill the bacon until crisp.* → see box at **COOK** **2** [T] informal to ask someone a lot of questions about something: *They let the man go after grilling him for several hours.*

grill² n [C] **1** BrE a part of a **COOKER** which cooks food on a metal shelf, using strong heat from above **2** a metal frame on which food can be cooked over a fire **3** also **grille** a frame with metal bars or wire across it that is put in front of a window or door for protection

grim /grɪm/ adj **1** making you feel worried and unhappy: *grim economic news* | *When he lost his job, his future looked grim.* **2** looking or sounding very serious: *a grim-faced judge* **3** BrE informal bad, ugly, or unpleasant: *grim industrial towns* —**grimly** adv —**grimness** n [U]

grimace /grɪˈmeɪs, ˈgrɪməs/ v [I] to twist your face in an ugly way because you feel pain or do not like something: **+at** *I grimaced at my reflection in the mirror.* —**grimace** n [C]

grime /graɪm/ n [U] a lot of dirt

grimy /ˈgraɪmi/ adj covered with dirt: *grimy windows*

grin /grɪn/ v [I] **grinned, grinning** to smile with a very wide smile: **+at** *Sally was grinning at me from across the room.* → see box at **SMILE** —**grin** n [C] *a friendly grin*

grind¹ /graɪnd/ v [T] past tense and past participle **ground** /graʊnd/ **1** to press and break something such as coffee beans into small pieces or powder: **grind sth into sth** *Grind the rice into a powder.* → see box at **PRESS** **2** to press and rub something onto a surface: *He ground his cigarette onto the floor.* **3** to make something such as a knife sharp by rubbing it against a rough hard surface **4 grind your teeth** to rub your upper and lower teeth together, making a noise **5 grind to a halt** if something grinds to a halt, it stops moving or making progress: *Traffic slowly ground to a halt.* | *After two days the talks had ground to a halt.*

grind sb ⇔ down phr v to treat someone in a cruel way for such a long time that they lose all courage and hope: *She had been ground down by years of poverty and hardship.*

grind² n [singular] informal something that is hard work and physically or mentally tiring: *It's Monday again – back to the grind.*

grinder /ˈgraɪndə $ -ər/ n [C] a machine for crushing coffee beans etc into powder: *a coffee grinder*

grinding /ˈgraɪndɪŋ/ adj **grinding poverty** extreme POVERTY

grip¹ /grɪp/ n
1 [singular] a tight hold on something, or your ability to hold it: *Don't loosen your grip on the rope or you'll fall.*

2 [singular] power and control over someone or something: **have/keep a (tight/firm etc) grip on sth** *Stalin's determination to keep an iron grip on Eastern Europe*
3 come/get to grips with sth to understand or deal with something difficult: *Have you got to grips with your new job yet?*
4 get/take a grip on yourself to start to control your emotions: *Stop being hysterical and get a grip on yourself.*
5 [singular, U] the ability of something to stay on a surface without slipping: *I want some tennis shoes with a good grip.*

grip[2] *v* [T] **gripped, gripping**
1 to hold something very tightly: *I gripped his hand in fear.* → see box at **HOLD**
2 to have a strong effect: *a country gripped by economic problems*
3 to keep your attention completely: *a story that really grips you*
4 if something grips a surface, it stays on it without slipping

gripe /graɪp/ *v* [I] *informal* to complain continuously —**gripe** *n* [C]

gripping /'grɪpɪŋ/ *adj* a gripping film, story etc is very exciting and interesting: *a gripping drama* → see box at **EXCITING**

grisly /'grɪzli/ *adj* extremely unpleasant because death or violence is involved: *a series of grisly murders*

gristle /'grɪsəl/ *n* [U] the part of a piece of meat that is not soft enough to eat —**gristly** *adj*

grit[1] /grɪt/ *n* [U] **1** very small pieces of stone or sand **2** *informal* determination and courage —**gritty** *adj*

grit[2] *v* [T] **gritted, gritting 1 grit your teeth** to use all your determination to continue in spite of difficulties **2** to put grit on a frozen road to make it less slippery

gritty /'grɪti/ *adj* **1** determined and brave **2** showing an unpleasant situation as it really is: *a gritty police drama* **3** containing or covered in sand

grizzled /'grɪzəld/ *adj literary* having grey hair

groan /grəʊn $ groʊn/ *v* [I] to make a long deep sound because you are in pain, or are not happy about something: *Captain Marsh was holding his arm and groaning.* | *The kids groaned when I turned off the television.* —**groan** *n* [C]

grocer /'grəʊsə $ 'groʊsər/ *n* [C] **1** someone who owns or works in a shop that sells food and other things used in the home **2 the grocer's** *BrE* a grocer's shop

grocery /'grəʊsəri $ 'groʊ-/ *n plural* **groceries**
1 groceries [plural] things that you buy in a grocer's shop or a SUPERMARKET **2** also **grocery store** *AmE* [C] a shop where you buy groceries

groggy /'grɒgi $ 'grɑːgi/ *adj* feeling weak and ill —**groggily** *adv*

groin /grɔɪn/ *n* [C] where your legs join at the front of your body

groom[1] /gruːm, grʊm/ *v* **1** [T] to train someone for an important job: **groom sb for sth** *Chris is being groomed for the job of manager.* **2** [T] to clean and brush the fur of an animal —**grooming** *n* [U]

groom[2] *n* [C] **1** also **bridegroom** a man who is getting married, or has just been married **2** someone whose job is to take care of horses

groove /gruːv/ *n* [C] a line cut into a surface

grope /grəʊp $ groʊp/ *v* **1** [I] to try to find something or go somewhere, using your hands because you cannot see: **+for/around** *He groped for the light switch.* | *I groped my way downstairs.* **2 grope for sth** to have difficulty in finding the right words to say or the right solution to a problem **3** [T] *informal* to touch someone sexually, when they do not want you to

gross[1] /grəʊs $ groʊs/ *adj* **1** [only before noun] a gross sum of money is the total amount before any tax or costs are taken away [➡ **net**]: *a gross profit of $5 million* **2** [only before noun] *formal* seriously wrong and unacceptable: *He was dismissed for gross misconduct.* **3** *spoken* very unpleasant: *There was one really gross part in the movie.* **4** *informal* very fat —**grossly** *adv*: *He's grossly overweight.* —**grossness** *n* [U]

gross[2] *v* [T] to gain an amount of money as a total profit, or earn it as a total amount, before tax is taken away
gross sb ⇔ **out** *phr v AmE spoken* if something grosses you out, it is so unpleasant that it makes you feel sick: *Dirty fingernails gross me out.*

,gross do,mestic 'product *n* [U] GDP

,gross ,national 'product *n* [U] GNP

grotesque /grəʊ'tesk $ groʊ-/ *adj* ugly in a strange frightening way —**grotesquely** *adv*

grotto /'grɒtəʊ $ 'grɑːtoʊ/ *n* [C] *plural* **grottos** or **grottoes** a small CAVE

grotty /'grɒti $ 'grɑːti/ *adj BrE informal* nasty, dirty, or unpleasant

grouch /graʊtʃ/ *n* [C] *informal* **1** someone who is always complaining **2** something unimportant that you complain about

grouchy /'graʊtʃi/ *adj informal* in a bad temper —**grouchiness** *n* [U]

ground[1] /graʊnd/ *n*

1 [singular, U] the surface of the earth: **on the ground** *She was lying asleep on the ground.* | *The ground was frozen solid.* | **above/below/under ground** *1000 feet below ground*

THESAURUS

The **ground** is the surface under your feet when you are outside: *There was snow on the ground.*
The **floor** is the surface under your feet when you are inside a building: *the kitchen floor*
Land is an area of ground that is owned or controlled by someone: *That land belongs to the farm.*
Earth or **soil** is the substance that plants grow in: *fertile soil*

2 a) [C] an area of land or water, especially one that is used for a special purpose: *These are safe breeding grounds for seals.* | *an expanse of **open ground** (=land with no houses, trees etc on it)* **b) grounds** [plural] the land or gardens surrounding a large building: *Smoking is not allowed on **school grounds**.*
3 grounds [plural] a good reason for doing something: **grounds for (doing) sth** *That's not grounds for divorce.* | **on moral/legal/medical etc grounds** *The proposal was rejected on environmental grounds.* | **on (the) grounds of sth** *discrimination on the grounds of race* | **on the**

G

grounds that *You can't fire a woman on the grounds that she's pregnant.*

4 [U] a subject or area of knowledge: *We keep going over the same ground* (=talking about the same things). | *The movie breaks new ground* (=introduces new and exciting ideas).

5 [U] a general opinion or set of attitudes: *Often parents and teenagers find they have little common ground* (=they do not share the same attitudes etc).

6 [C] a place where a sport is played: *a football ground* | *Old Trafford is Manchester United's home ground* (=the ground that belongs to them).

7 hold/stand your ground to refuse to move from where you are standing or to change your opinion, even though other people are trying to make you

8 get off the ground to start to be successful: *His new business is slow getting off the ground.*

9 gain/lose ground to become more or less successful than someone or something you are competing with: *The Democrats have gained ground since the last election.*

10 [singular] *AmE* a wire that connects a piece of electrical equipment to the ground for safety [= **earth** *BrE*]

→ BREEDING GROUND → **have/keep your feet on the ground** at FOOT[1] → **be thin on the ground** at THIN[1]

ground[2] *v* **1** [T] to stop an aircraft or pilot from flying: *All planes are grounded until the fog clears.* **2 be grounded in/on sth** to be based on something: *His ideas are grounded in his Christian faith.* **3** [T] *informal* to stop a child going out with their friends as a punishment: *If you stay out late again, you'll be grounded for a week.* **4** [T] *AmE* to make a piece of electrical equipment safe by connecting it to the ground with a wire [= **earth** *BrE*]

ground[3] *v* the past tense and past participle of GRIND

ground 'beef *n* [U] *AmE* BEEF that has been cut into very small pieces [= **mince** *BrE*]

groundbreaking /'graʊnd,breɪkɪŋ/ *adj* involving the use of new discoveries, new methods, or new ideas: *groundbreaking medical research*

ground 'floor *n* [C] the part of a building that is on the same level as the ground [= **first floor** *AmE*] → see box at FLOOR

grounding /'graʊndɪŋ/ *n* [singular] training in the basic parts of a subject or skill: +**in** *a basic grounding in maths*

groundless /'graʊndləs/ *adj* not based on facts or reason: *My suspicions proved groundless.*

'ground rules *n* [plural] the basic rules or principles on which future actions should be based: *There are a few ground rules you should follow.*

groundswell /'graʊndswel/ *n* **a groundswell of support/opinion/enthusiasm** a sudden increase in how strongly people feel about something

groundwork /'graʊndwɜːk $ -wɜːrk/ *n* [U] something that has to happen before an activity or plan can be successful: *His speech laid the groundwork for the peace talks.*

group[1] /gruːp/ *n* [C also + plural verb *BrE*]

1 several people or things that are together in

the same place: +**of** *a group of islands* | *Please get into groups of three* (=groups of three people).* | **in groups** *Dolphins travel in small groups.*

2 several people or things that are connected with each other: *a terrorist group* | +**of** *She is one of a group of women who have suffered side-effects from the drug.*

3 several musicians who play and sing popular music together [= **band**]: *a rock group* | *The group are currently on tour.*

4 several companies that all have the same owner: *the Savoy hotel group*

→ AGE GROUP, BLOOD GROUP, FOCUS GROUP, PRESSURE GROUP

group[2] *v* [I,T] to arrange things in a group: **group (sth) together/round/into etc** *Four men were grouped around a jeep.*

grouping /'gruːpɪŋ/ *n* [C] a set of people or things that have the same aims, qualities, or features: *political groupings*

grouse[1] /graʊs/ *n* [C,U] plural **grouse** a small fat bird that is hunted for food

grouse[2] *v* [I] *informal* to complain

grove /grəʊv $ groʊv/ *n* [C] an area of land where a particular type of tree grows: *a lemon grove*

grovel /'grɒvəl $ 'grɑː-, 'grʌ-/ *v* [I] grovelled, grovelling *BrE*; groveled, groveling *AmE* **1** to try very hard to please someone because you are frightened of them or you have upset them: *She's always grovelling to the boss.* **2** to move around on your hands and knees, looking for something: *I saw him grovelling in the road for his hat.*

grow /grəʊ $ groʊ/ *v* past tense **grew** /gruː/ past participle **grown** /grəʊn $ groʊn/

1 [I] to get bigger in size or amount: *Babies grow quickly in their first year.* | **+by** *Sales grew by 10%.* | *A growing number of people work from home.* | **grow rapidly/slowly/steadily** *The economy has grown steadily.* | **+in** *Skiing has grown in popularity.*

2 [I,T] if plants grow somewhere, or if you grow them there, they are alive in that place: *Weeds were growing everywhere.* | *We grow our own vegetables.*

3 [I,T] if your hair or nails grow, or if you grow them, they get longer because you do not cut them: *I've decided to grow my hair long.*

4 grow old/bored/strong etc to become old, bored etc: *He was growing old, and becoming forgetful.* | *We were lost, and it was growing dark.*

grow into sb/sth *v* **1** to develop and become a particular kind of person or thing: *Joe grew into a handsome young man.* **2** if children grow into clothes, they become big enough to wear them

grow on sb *phr v* if something grows on you, you gradually like it more and more: *The CD grows on you.*

grow out of sth *phr v* **1** if children grow out of clothes, they become too big to wear them **2** to stop doing something as you become older: *Sarah still sucks her thumb, but she'll grow out of it.*

grow up *phr v* **1** to gradually change from being a child to being an adult: *I grew up in Paris.* **2** to start to exist or develop gradually: *Villages grew up along the river.*

grower /'ɡrəʊə $ 'ɡrəʊər/ *n* [C] a person or company that grows fruit or vegetables in order to sell them

growl /ɡraʊl/ *v* [I] if a dog, bear etc growls, it makes a deep angry sound: **+at** *The dog growled at me.* —**growl** *n* [C]

grown[1] /ɡrəʊn $ ɡroʊn/ *v* the past participle of GROW

grown[2] *adj* **grown man/woman** an adult man or woman – used especially when you think someone is not behaving as an adult should: *Who ever heard of a grown man being afraid of the dark?*

'grown-up[1] *n* [C] an adult – used by or to children: *Ask a grown-up to help you.*

'grown-up[2] *adj* someone who is grown-up is an adult: *She has a grown-up son.*

growth /ɡrəʊθ $ ɡroʊθ/ *n* **1** [singular,U] when something gets bigger or develops: **+in/of** *the growth in population* | *the growth of television* | *economic growth* | *Vitamins are necessary for healthy growth.* | **growth area/industry** (=a business or activity that is growing) *Computing remains a growth area.* **2** [U] the development of someone's character: *personal growth* **3** [C] something that grows in your body or on your skin, caused by a disease **4** [C,U] something that has grown: *His chin bore a thick growth of stubble.*

grub /ɡrʌb/ *n* **1** [U] *informal* food **2** [C] a young insect in the form of a small white WORM → see picture on page A2

grubby /'ɡrʌbi/ *adj* dirty: *grubby hands* → see box at DIRTY

grudge[1] /ɡrʌdʒ/ *n* [C] an unfriendly feeling towards someone because of something they did in the past: **+against** *He has a grudge against her.*

grudge[2] *v* [T] to do or give something even though you do not want to: **grudge sb sth** *I don't grudge him his success.* —**grudging** *adj*: *a grudging apology* —**grudgingly** *adv*: *He grudgingly admitted his mistake.*

gruelling *BrE*; **grueling** *AmE* /'ɡruːəlɪŋ/ *adj* very difficult and tiring: *a gruelling journey*

gruesome /'ɡruːsəm/ *adj* relating to violence or death: *a gruesome murder*

gruff /ɡrʌf/ *adj* speaking in a rough unfriendly voice: *a gruff reply* —**gruffly** *adv*

grumble /'ɡrʌmbəl/ *v* [I] to complain: **+about** *He kept grumbling about the food.* —**grumble** *n* [C]

grumpy /'ɡrʌmpi/ *adj* slightly angry and easily annoyed: *She's always grumpy in the morning.* —**grumpily** *adv* —**grumpiness** *n* [U]

grunge /ɡrʌndʒ/ *n* [U] *AmE informal* unpleasant dirt [= grime] —**grungy** *adj*

grunt /ɡrʌnt/ *v* **1** [I,T] to make a short low sound to show that you are not interested in something: *I asked him, but he just grunted.* **2** [I] if a pig grunts, it makes a low rough sound —**grunt** *n* [C]

guarantee[1] /ˌɡærən'tiː/ *v* [T]

1 to promise something: **+(that)** *I guarantee you'll love this film.* → see box at PROMISE

2 to make a formal written promise to repair or replace a product if it breaks: *Our products are fully guaranteed.*

3 to make it certain that something will happen: *Talent doesn't always guarantee success.*

guarantee[2] *n* [C]

1 a formal written promise by a company to repair or replace a product if it breaks: *a two-year guarantee* | **under guarantee** *Is the TV still under guarantee?*

2 a formal promise that something will be done: **+that** *I can't give a guarantee that there'll be no redundancies.*

guard[1] /ɡɑːd $ ɡɑːrd/ *n*

1 [C] someone whose job is to protect a person or place, or to make sure that a person does not escape: *a security guard* | *a prison guard* | *regular patrols by armed guards*

2 [U] the act of protecting a place or person, or preventing a prisoner from escaping: **be on guard/stand guard** *Soldiers are on guard outside the palace.* | **keep/stand guard** *Gunmen stood guard at the camp entrance.* | **be (held/kept) under guard** *The men were under armed guard at a military camp.*

3 [singular] a group of soldiers who guard someone or something

4 [C] something that is used to protect someone or something from damage or injury: *a face guard* | *a fire guard*

5 [C] *BrE* someone whose job is to collect tickets on a train, help the passengers etc [= conductor *AmE*]

6 be on your guard (against something) to be very careful because you may have to deal with a bad situation: *These men are dangerous so you must be on your guard.*

G

7 catch/throw sb off guard to surprise someone by doing something that they were not expecting: *His question caught me off guard.*
→ COAST GUARD, LIFE GUARD

guard² *v* [T]

1 to watch someone or something so that they do not escape, or get damaged or stolen: *Two men were guarding the prisoner.* | **guard sb/sth against sth** *The village must be guarded against attack.*

2 to protect something such as a right or secret by preventing other people from taking it away, discovering it etc: *a closely guarded secret*

guard against sth *phr v* to try to prevent something from happening: *Exercise can guard against illness.*

guarded /ˈgɑːdɪd $ ˈgɑːr-/ *adj* careful not to give very much information or show your feelings: *The minister was very guarded in his comments.* | *He gave the idea a guarded welcome.*

guardian /ˈgɑːdiən $ ˈgɑːr-/ *n* [C] **1** a child's guardian is someone who is legally responsible for them, but who is not their parent: *His aunt is his legal guardian.* **2** *formal* someone who guards or protects something —**guardianship** *n* [U]

guardian 'angel *n* [C] a SPIRIT or person who looks after and protects someone

guerrilla /gəˈrɪlə/ *n* [C] a member of an unofficial army that is fighting for political reasons: *guerrilla warfare*

guess¹ /ges/ *v*

1 [I,T] to answer a question or decide something without being sure whether you are right: **guess right/correctly/wrong** *I guessed her age correctly.* | **guess how/what/whether/if etc** *Guess how much the dress cost.* | **+(that)** *The teacher guessed that the boys had been smoking.* | **+at** *I couldn't even guess at the cost.*

2 I guess *spoken* used when you think that something is true or likely: *His light's on, so I guess he's still up.* → see box at THINK

3 I guess so/not *spoken* to agree or disagree with a statement or question: *'I don't have any choice, do I?' 'I guess not.'* | *'Is her dad rich?' 'I guess so.'*

4 guess what/you'll never guess who/what etc *spoken* used to tell someone some surprising news: *Guess what! Dan's resigned.* | *You'll never guess who I saw today.*
→ SECOND-GUESS

guess² *n* [C]

1 an attempt to guess something: **make/have/take a guess (at sth)** *Have a guess where we're going tonight!* | *Make a guess if you don't know the answer.* | *I'd say she's about 35, but that's only a rough guess* (=one that is not exact). | **my guess is (that)** *My guess is that there won't be many people at the party.* | **at a guess** *spoken* (=used to say that what you are saying is just a guess) *At a guess, it would cost about £50.*

COLLOCATIONS

good guess – a guess that is likely to be right
educated guess – a guess that is likely to be correct because it is based on some information
wild guess – a guess that you make when you do not have any information, and that is likely to be wrong
lucky guess – a guess that is right, and that you made without very much information

2 be anyone's/anybody's guess *informal* to be something that no one can be certain about: *It's anyone's guess who'll win the match.*

3 your guess is as good as mine *spoken* used to tell someone that you do not know any more than they do about something

guesswork /ˈgeswɜːk $ -wɜːrk/ *n* [U] when you try to find the answer to something by guessing: *I got the right answer, but it was pure guesswork.*

guest /gest/ *n* [C]

1 someone who you invite to stay in your home or to go to an event: *How many guests are coming to your party?* | **as sb's guest** *You're here as my guests.*

2 someone who is staying in a hotel: *Use of the sauna is free to guests.* → see box at CUSTOMER

3 someone famous who is invited to take part in a television programme, concert etc: *He appeared as a guest on the show.* | *a guest appearance by Jack Nicholson* | **guest star/speaker etc**

4 be my guest *spoken* used to give someone permission: *'Could I use your phone?' 'Be my guest.'*

guesthouse /ˈgesthaʊs/ *n* [C] **1** *BrE* a small hotel that is also the hotel owner's private home **2** *AmE* a separate building next to someone's home, where visiting family or friends can stay → see box at ACCOMMODATION

guidance /ˈgaɪdəns/ *n* [U] helpful advice: *Your teacher can give you guidance on your career choice.*

guide¹ /gaɪd/ *n* [C]

1 something that helps you to make a decision: *As a rough guide, you need about 100 grams of meat per person.*

2 someone whose job is to show a place to tourists: *a tour guide*

3 a) a book that has information and advice on a particular subject: **+to** *a guide to African birds* **b)** a guidebook

4 *BrE* **a) the Guides** also **the Girl Guides** an organization that teaches girls practical skills such as camping, and teaches them to be good members of society **b)** a member of this organization [→ scout]

guide² *v* [T]

1 to help someone to go somewhere, for example by showing them the right direction: **guide sb to/through/across etc sth** *He took the old lady's arm and guided her across the road.* | *We were guided through the mountains by a local villager.*

2 to influence someone's behaviour or ideas: *Teenagers need adults to guide them.*

3 to show someone the right way to do something difficult or complicated: **guide sb through sth** *Guide your students through the program one section at a time.*

guidebook /ˈgaɪdbʊk/ *n* [C] a book that gives tourists information about a place

'guide dog n [C] BrE a specially trained dog that blind people use to help them to go to places [= **Seeing Eye dog** AmE]

guide dog BrE/
Seeing Eye dog AmE

guideline /'gaɪdlaɪn/ n [C usually plural] rules or advice about the best way to do something: **+on** guidelines on writing essays

guild /gɪld/ n [C] an organization of people who do the same job or have the same interests: the Writers' Guild

guile /gaɪl/ n [U] formal the use of clever but dishonest methods to deceive people

guillotine /'gɪlətiːn/ n [C] a piece of equipment used in the past to cut off criminals' heads —**guillotine** v [T]

guilt /gɪlt/ n [U]
1 a sad feeling you have when you have done something wrong: **feeling/sense of guilt** a terrible sense of guilt and shame
2 when someone has broken a law [≠ **innocence**]: The police couldn't prove his guilt.
3 when you are responsible for something bad that has happened

'guilt-,ridden adj feeling so guilty about something that you cannot think about anything else

guilty /'gɪlti/ adj
1 unhappy and ashamed because you have done something wrong: **+about/at** He felt guilty about stealing the pen. | You should have a guilty conscience!
2 having done something that is a crime [≠ **innocent**]: **+of** The jury found her guilty of murder. | He **pleaded guilty** to two charges of theft. → see box at **COURT**
—**guiltily** adv —**guiltiness** n [U]

'guinea pig n [C] **1** a small furry animal with no tail, that is often kept as a pet **2** informal someone who is used in a scientific test to see how successful or safe a new product, system etc is

guise /gaɪz/ n [C] formal the way someone or something appears to be: It's the same idea in a different guise.

guitar /gɪ'tɑː $ -'tɑːr/ n [C] a musical instrument with six strings that you play by pulling the strings → see picture on page A6 —**guitarist** n [C]

gulf /gʌlf/ n [C] **1** a large area of sea partly surrounded by land: the Gulf of Mexico **2 the Gulf** the Arabian Gulf and the countries next to it **3** a great difference and lack of understanding between two groups of people: **+between** the gulf between the rich and the poor

gull /gʌl/ n [C] a SEAGULL

gullible /'gʌlɪbəl/ adj disapproving a gullible person is easy to trick because they always believe what people say —**gullibility** /,gʌlɪ'bɪləti/ n [U]

gully /'gʌli/ n [C] plural **gullies** a small narrow valley

gulp /gʌlp/ v **1** also **gulp down** [T] to swallow food or drink quickly: Sip your drink – don't gulp it. → see box at **DRINK 2** [I] to swallow suddenly because you are surprised or nervous: I gulped when I saw the bill. **3** also **gulp in** [T] to breathe large amounts of air quickly: He gulped in the night air. —**gulp** n [C]

gum¹ /gʌm/ n **1** [C usually plural] the pink parts inside your mouth that your teeth grow out of **2** [U] CHEWING GUM

gum² v [T + adv/prep] **gummed, gumming** BrE old-fashioned to stick things together, using glue

gumption /'gʌmpʃən/ n [U] informal the ability and determination to decide what needs to be done and to do it: At least she had the gumption to phone.

gun¹ /gʌn/ n [C]
1 a weapon that fires bullets: **have/hold/carry a gun** | I've never **fired** a gun in my life.
2 a tool that forces out small objects or a liquid by pressure: a nail gun
→ **jump the gun** at **JUMP¹** → **MACHINE GUN**

gun² v **gunned, gunning 1 be gunning for sb** informal to be trying to find an opportunity to criticize or harm someone **2** [T] AmE informal to make a car go very fast by pressing the ACCELERATOR very hard
gun sb ⇔ down phr v to shoot someone, killing or injuring them badly: He was gunned down outside his home.

gunboat /'gʌnbəʊt $ -boʊt/ n [C] a small ship that carries several large guns → see box at **SHIP**

gunfire /'gʌnfaɪə $ -faɪr/ n [U] shots fired from a gun: the sound of gunfire

gunge /gʌndʒ/ n [U] BrE informal a dirty, sticky, or unpleasant substance —**gungy** adj

gunman /'gʌnmən/ n [C] plural **gunmen** /-mən/ a criminal who uses a gun

gunner /'gʌnə $ -ər/ n [C] a soldier or sailor whose job is to aim and fire a large gun

gunpoint /'gʌnpɔɪnt/ n [U] **at gunpoint** if someone does something to you at gunpoint, they do it while threatening to shoot you: We were held at gunpoint throughout the robbery.

gunpowder /'gʌn,paʊdə $ -ər/ n [U] an explosive substance

gunrunning /'gʌn,rʌnɪŋ/ n [U] when guns are taken into a country secretly and illegally —**gunrunner** n [C]

gunshot /'gʌnʃɒt $ -ʃɑːt/ n **1** [C] the sound made by a gun: We heard gunshots. **2** [U] the bullets fired from a gun: a **gunshot wound**

gun-toting /'gʌn ,təʊtɪŋ $ -,toʊ-/ adj [only before noun] carrying a gun: gun-toting street-gangs

gurgle /'gɜːɡəl $ 'gɜːr-/ v [I] to make a sound like flowing water: The baby gurgled with pleasure. —**gurgle** n [C]

guru /'gʊruː/ n [C] **1** informal someone that people respect because they are very wise or skilful in a particular subject: a management guru **2** a Hindu religious teacher

gush /gʌʃ/ v **1** [I] if a liquid gushes somewhere, a large amount of it flows there: **+out of/from etc** Water gushed out of the pipe. **2** [I,T] to express your praise or pleasure in a way that other people think is too strong: 'I love your dress,' she gushed. —**gush** n [C]

gust /gʌst/ n [C] a sudden strong movement of wind: **+of** *A gust of wind blew our tent over.* —**gust** v [I] *The forecast is for winds gusting at up to 45 miles per hour.* —**gusty** adj

gusto /'gʌstəʊ $ -toʊ/ n **with gusto** with a lot of energy and enjoyment

gut[1] /gʌt/ n **1 gut feeling/reaction/instinct** *informal* a feeling that you are sure is right, although you cannot give a reason for it: *I had a gut feeling that he was a dangerous man.* **2 guts** [plural] *informal* courage and determination to do something difficult: *It takes guts to leave a violent relationship.* **3 a)** [C] the tube in your body that food passes through **b) guts** [plural] all the organs inside your body → **hate sb's guts** at **HATE**[1]

gut[2] v [T] **gutted, gutting 1** to destroy the inside of a building completely: *The school was completely gutted by fire.* **2** to remove the organs from inside a fish or animal before cooking it

gutsy /'gʌtsi/ adj informal brave and determined

gutted /'gʌtɨd/ adj [not before noun] BrE informal very disappointed: *I was gutted when I lost my job.*

gutter /'gʌtə $ -ər/ n [C] the low part at the edge of a road, or a pipe fixed to a roof, which carries away water

guttering /'gʌtərɪŋ/ n [U] BrE pipes fixed to a roof to carry away rain water

guttural /'gʌtərəl/ adj a guttural sound is produced deep in your throat

guy /gaɪ/ n [C] informal
1 a man or a boy: *He's a really nice guy.* → see box at **MAN**
2 guys [plural] especially AmE informal people: *We'll see you guys Sunday, okay?*

guzzle /'gʌzəl/ v [I,T] informal to eat or drink a lot of something quickly: *They've been guzzling beer all evening.*

gym /dʒɪm/ n **1** [C] a large room that has equipment for doing physical exercise → see box at **EXERCISE** → and **SPORT 2** [U] sports and exercises that you do indoors: *a gym class*

gymnasium /dʒɪm'neɪziəm/ n [C] formal a GYM

gymnastics /dʒɪm'næstɪks/ n [U] a sport in which you do skilful physical exercises and movements, often in competitions: *a gymnastics display* —**gymnast** /'dʒɪmnæst, -nəst/ n [C] *She's an Olympic gymnast.*

gynaecology BrE; **gynecology** AmE /,gaɪnɨ'kɒlədʒi $ -'kɑː-/ n [U] the study and treatment of medical conditions that affect only women —**gynaecologist** n [C] —**gynaecological** /,gaɪnɨkə'lɒdʒɪkəl $ -'lɑː-/ adj

gypsy also **gipsy** BrE /'dʒɪpsi/ n [C] plural **gypsies** a member of a race of people who live and travel around in CARAVANS [→ **traveller**]

gyrate /dʒaɪ'reɪt $ 'dʒaɪreɪt/ v [I] to turn around fast in circles: *dancers gyrating wildly*

H, h

H, h /eɪtʃ/ n [C,U] plural **H's, h's** the eighth letter of the English alphabet

ha /hɑː/ *spoken* used to show that you are surprised or pleased about something: *Ha! I knew I was right.*

habit /'hæbᵻt/ n

1 [C,U] something that you do regularly or usually, often without thinking about it because you have done it so many times before: *Jeff was in the habit of taking a walk after dinner.* | *Try to get into the habit of taking regular exercise.* | *She has a habit of never finishing her sentences.* | **good/bad habit** *Biting your nails is a very bad habit.* | **out of habit/from habit** *After he left home, I was still cleaning his room out of habit.* | **break/kick the habit** (=stop a bad habit) *Brad's been smoking for 20 years and just can't kick the habit.*

THESAURUS

habit – something that you do regularly, often without thinking about it: *He has a habit of clearing his throat every time he speaks.*

custom – something that people in a particular society do because it is traditional, or something that people think is the normal and polite thing to do: *the Japanese custom of taking off your shoes when you enter a house*

tradition – a belief, custom, or way of doing something that has existed for a long time: *In many countries it's a tradition for the bride to wear white.* | *a family tradition*

---

2 [C] a strong physical need to keep taking a drug regularly: *His cocaine habit has ruined him.* → **force of habit** at FORCE¹

habitable /'hæbᵻtəbəl/ adj a place that is habitable is suitable for people to live in [≠ **uninhabitable**]

habitat /'hæbᵻtæt/ n [C] the natural environment in which a plant or animal lives: *It was great to see monkeys in their natural habitat.*

habitation /ˌhæbᵻ'teɪʃən/ n [U] when people live in a place: *There was no sign of habitation on the island.*

habitual /hə'bɪtʃuəl/ adj *formal* **1** [only before noun] usual or typical of someone: *Jane was in her habitual bad temper this morning.* **2** done as a habit that you cannot stop: *a habitual smoker*

hack¹ /hæk/ v [I,T] **1** to cut something into pieces roughly: *All of the victims had been hacked to death.* **2** to secretly find a way of getting information from someone else's computer or changing information on it: **+into** *Somebody hacked into the company's central database.*

hack² n [C] a writer who does a lot of low quality work, especially writing newspaper articles

hacker /'hækə $ -ər/ n [C] *informal* someone who secretly uses or changes the information in other people's computer systems —**hacking** n [U]

hackles /'hækəlz/ n [plural] **sb's hackles rise** if your hackles rise, you begin to feel very angry, because of what someone has said or done

hackneyed /'hæknid/ adj a hackneyed phrase does not have much meaning because it has been used so often

hacksaw /'hæksɔː $ -sɒː/ n [C] a cutting tool with small teeth on its blade, used for cutting metal

had¹ /d, əd, həd; *strong* hæd/ v the past tense and past participle of HAVE [➡ **-'d**]

had² /hæd/ adj *informal* **be had** to be tricked: *She had the feeling she'd been had.*

haddock /'hædək/ n [C,U] plural **haddock** a fish that lives in northern seas, and is caught for food

hadn't /'hædnt/ the short form of 'had not'

haemophilia *BrE*; **hemophilia** *AmE* /ˌhiːmə'fɪliə/ n [U] a serious disease in which the flow of blood from someone's body when they are injured cannot be stopped —**haemophiliac** /-liæk/ n [C]

haemorrhage *BrE*; **hemorrhage** *AmE* /'hemərɪdʒ/ n [C,U] a serious medical condition in which a person is injured inside their body and a lot of blood comes out

haemorrhoids *BrE*; **hemorrhoids** *AmE* /'hemərɔɪdz/ n [plural] *technical* painful swollen BLOOD VESSELS near a person's ANUS [= **piles**]

hag /hæg/ n [C] an ugly or unpleasant old woman

haggard /'hægəd $ -ərd/ adj looking tired, thin, and ill: *She arrived home looking pale and haggard.*

haggle /'hægəl/ v [I] to argue about the amount that you will pay for something: **+over** *We were haggling over the price for an hour.*

hah /hɑː/ another spelling of HA

ha 'ha used in writing to show that someone is laughing

hail¹ /heɪl/ v **1** [T] to describe someone or something as being very good: **hail sb/sth as sth** *Lang's first film was immediately hailed as a masterpiece.* **2** [T] to call or wave to someone: **hail a cab/taxi** (=wave at a taxi to make it stop) **3** [I] if it hails, frozen rain falls from the sky → see box at RAIN

hail from sth phr v *old-fashioned* to come from a particular place: *He hails from Massachusetts.*

hail² n **1** [U] small hard drops of frozen rain that fall from the sky → see box at RAIN → and SNOW **2 a hail of bullets/stones etc** a lot of bullets, stones etc that come through the air at the same time: *a hail of gunfire*

hailstone /'heɪlstəʊn $ -stoʊn/ n [C usually plural] a small hard drop of frozen rain → see box at RAIN → and SNOW

hair /heə $ her/ n

1 [U] the mass of things like thin threads that grows on your head: *Go and brush your hair.* | *a young woman with short blonde hair* | *a tall guy with dark hair* | **have/get your hair cut** *I must get my hair cut.* | *I want to grow my hair.* → see picture on page A3

H

COLLOCATIONS

short/long hair
shoulder-length hair
fair/blonde hair
dark/brown/black/grey hair
mousy hair – hair that is light brown
red/auburn hair also ginger hair *BrE*
straight/wavy/curly hair
frizzy hair – hair with many small curls in it
spiky hair – hair that sticks up from your head in thin stiff points
fine/thin/thick hair
dark-haired/fair-haired/long-haired etc (=used to describe someone)
cut/trim your hair
wash/shampoo your hair
dry your hair
blow dry your hair – to dry your hair, using an electric hairdryer
comb/brush your hair
style your hair – to arrange your hair in a particular way
dye your hair – to change the colour of your hair, using a dye
→ HEAD, SKIN

2 [C,U] one of the thin threads that grow on a person's or animal's skin [➡ fur]: *The sofa was covered in dog hairs.* | **long-haired/short-haired** *long-haired cats*
3 let your hair down *informal* to stop being serious and enjoy yourself
4 be pulling/tearing your hair out *informal* to be very worried
→ split hairs at SPLIT¹

hairbrush /ˈheəbrʌʃ $ ˈher-/ *n* [C] a brush that you use to make your hair tidy → see picture at BRUSH¹

haircut /ˈheəkʌt $ ˈher-/ *n* **1** [C usually singular] when you have your hair cut by someone: *I must have a haircut.* **2** [C] the style in which your hair has been cut: *I like your new haircut.*

hairdo /ˈheəduː $ ˈher-/ *n* [C] plural **hairdos** *informal* the style in which your hair is cut or shaped

hairdresser /ˈheəˌdresə $ ˈherˌdresər/ *n* [C]
1 a person who cuts and arranges people's hair in particular styles **2 the hairdresser's** a hairdresser's shop: *an appointment at the hairdresser's*

hairdryer /ˈheəˌdraɪə $ ˈherˌdraɪər/ *n* [C] a machine that blows out hot air for drying your hair

H

hair

spiky hair

short, curly hair

long, straight hair

moustache *BrE*/ mustache *AmE*

beard

long, curly hair

ponytail

braid *AmE*

long plaited hair

receding grey hair

fringe *BrE*/ bangs *AmE*

shoulder-length wavy hair

bobbed hair

hairgrip /'heəgrɪp $ 'her-/ n [C] BrE a small piece of metal that holds your hair in place [= **bobby pin** AmE]

hairline /'heəlaɪn $ 'her-/ n **1** [C] the place at the front of your head where your hair starts growing **2 hairline crack/fracture** a very thin crack: *a hairline fracture in the leg*

hairpin /'heəpɪn $ 'her-/ n [C] a U-shaped piece of metal that holds your hair in place

hairpin 'bend BrE; **hairpin 'turn** AmE n [C] a U-shaped bend on a steep road

'hair-,raising adj frightening in an exciting way: *hair-raising adventures*

hairstyle /'heəstaɪl $ 'her-/ n [C] the style in which your hair has been cut or shaped —**hairstylist** n [C]

hairy /'heəri $ 'heri/ adj **1** covered in hair: *a hairy chest* **2** *spoken* dangerous or frightening

halal /hɑː'lɑːl/ adj halal meat is meat from an animal that has been killed in a way that is approved by Muslim law

hale /heɪl/ adj **hale and hearty** *humorous* healthy and full of energy

half¹ /hɑːf $ hæf/ n [C,U] determiner plural **halves** /hɑːvz $ hævz/

1 one of two equal parts of something: *Two halves make a whole.* | *Over half the people in this area are unemployed.* | *Their son is two and a half.* | **+of** *I only saw the first half of the film.* | **half an hour/mile etc** *I got to work half an hour late.* | **in half** *Cut the tomatoes in half.* | **cut/reduce sth by half** (=make it 50% smaller) *Profits have been cut by half.* | **the first/second half** *Beckham scored in the first half of the match.*
2 the largest part of something: *She seems to be asleep half the time.*
3 not half as/so good/interesting etc (as sb/sth) much less good, interesting etc than someone or something else: *The movie wasn't half as good as the book.*
4 half (past) one/two/three etc *especially BrE* thirty minutes after one o'clock, two o'clock etc: *We're meeting at half past seven.* | *I phoned about half six.*
5 go halves (on sth) to share something, especially the cost of something, equally between two people: *Do you want to go halves on a pizza?*
6 half a dozen a) six: *half a dozen eggs* **b)** a few: *There were only half a dozen people there.*

half² adv partly but not completely: *He shouldn't be allowed to drive – he's half blind!* | *I half expected her to shout at me.* | *a half-empty bottle*

half-'baked adj informal a half-baked idea is not sensible and has not been thought about carefully

half 'board n [U] especially BrE the price of a room in a hotel including breakfast and dinner

'half-,brother n [C] a brother who is the child of only one of your parents

half-hearted /ˌhɑːf 'hɑːtɪ̣d◂ $ ˌhæf 'hɑːr-/ adj done without any real effort or interest: *He made a half-hearted attempt to tidy his room.* —**half-heartedly** adv

half-'hour, half hour n [C] a period of 30 minutes: *We waited for a good half-hour* (=at least 30 minutes, usually more). —**half-hour** adj: *a half-hour TV show*

half-'hourly adj, adv BrE done or happening every half-hour: *Trains depart at half-hourly intervals from 10.30 am until 4.00 pm.*

half-'mast adj **fly/be at half-mast** if a flag is flying at half-mast, it is lowered to the middle of its pole because someone important has died

'half-,sister n [C] a sister who is the child of only one of your parents

half 'term n [C,U] BrE a short holiday in the middle of a school TERM

half-'time n [U] a period when the players rest between two parts of a game such as football

halfway /ˌhɑːf'weɪ◂ $ ˌhæf-/ adj, adv at a middle point: **+between** *We live halfway between London and Manchester.* | **+through/down/up etc** *Halfway through the meal, Dan got up.* | *We had reached the halfway point of the walk.*

'half-wit n [C] a stupid person

hall /hɔːl $ hɒːl/ n [C]
1 the area just inside the door of a building, that leads to other rooms: *The bathroom's just down the hall on the right.*
2 a building or large room for public events such as meetings or dances: *a dance hall* | *Carnegie Hall*
→ **TOWN HALL**

hallmark /'hɔːlmɑːk $ 'hɒːlmɑːrk/ n [C]
1 something that is typical of a particular person or thing: **+of** *The explosion had all the hallmarks of a terrorist attack.* **2** a mark put on silver or gold that shows the quality of the metal, and where and when it was made

hallo /hə'ləʊ, hæ- $ -'loʊ/ a British spelling of HELLO

hall of 'residence n [C] BrE a college or university building where students live [= **dormitory** AmE]

hallowed /'hæləʊd $ -loʊd/ adj **1** respected and important: *the hallowed halls of government* **2** holy: *hallowed ground*

Halloween /ˌhæləʊ'iːn◂ $ -loʊ-/ n [U] the night of October 31, when children dress as WITCHES, GHOSTS etc

hallucinate /hə'luːsɪ̣neɪt/ v [I] to see, feel, or hear things that are not really there —**hallucination** /hə,luːsɪ̣'neɪʃən/ n [C,U] *The patients suffered hallucinations caused by the drug.* —**hallucinatory** /hə'luːsɪ̣nətəri $ -tɔːri/ adj: *hallucinatory drugs*

hallway /'hɔːlweɪ $ 'hɒːl-/ n [C] the area just inside the door of a building that leads to other rooms [= **hall**]

halo /'heɪləʊ $ -loʊ/ n [C] plural **halos** a golden circle that is shown in paintings above the head of a holy person

halt /hɔːlt $ hɒːlt/ n [singular] when something stops happening or moving for a period of time: **come/grind to a halt** *The bus slowly ground to a halt.* | *They decided to* **call a halt to** *the strike* (=make it stop). —**halt** v [I,T] formal: *The city council has halted repair work on the subways.*

halter /'hɔːltə $ 'hɒːltər/ n [C] a piece of rope or leather that is fastened around a horse's head to lead it along

halting /'hɔːltɪŋ $ 'hɒːl-/ adj stopping a lot when you move or speak, especially because you are nervous: *She spoke in a halting voice.*

H

hand

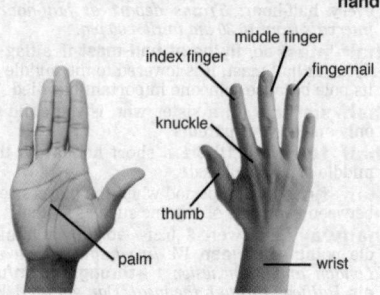

middle finger
index finger
fingernail
knuckle
thumb
palm
wrist

halve /hɑːv $ hæv/ v [T] **1** to reduce the amount of something by half: *Food production was almost halved during the war.* **2** to cut or divide something into two equal pieces: *Wash and halve the mushrooms.*

halves /hɑːvz $ hævz/ n the plural of HALF

ham /hæm/ n [C,U] preserved meat from a pig: *a slice of ham* | *a ham sandwich* → see box at MEAT

hamburger /'hæmbɜːgə $ -bɜːrgər/ n **1** [C] BEEF that is made into a round shape, cooked, and eaten inside a round piece of bread **2** [U] AmE BEEF that is cut into very small pieces [= mince BrE]

hamlet /'hæmlɪt/ n [C] a very small village

hammer[1] /'hæmə $ -ər/ n [C] a tool with a heavy metal part on a long handle, used for hitting nails into wood

hammer[2] v **1** [I,T] to hit something with a hammer **2** [I] to hit something several times, making a lot of noise: *Mike was hammering on the door with his fists.* → see box at KNOCK[1]

hammer sth into sb phr v to continue repeating something in order to force people to remember it: *Mom hammered the message into us: don't talk to strangers!*

hammer sth ⇔ **out** phr v to finally agree about the details of something: *It took several days to hammer out an agreement.*

hammering /'hæmərɪŋ/ n **1** [U] the sound of someone hitting something with a hammer or with their hands **2** [C] a very bad defeat

hammock /'hæmək/ n [C] a large piece of material used for sleeping on that hangs between two trees or poles

hamper[1] /'hæmpə $ -ər/ v [T] to make something difficult: *The search for the men was hampered by bad weather.*

hamper[2] n [C] a large basket for carrying food: *a picnic hamper*

hamster /'hæmstə $ -ər/ n [C] a small animal with soft fur and no tail that is often kept as a pet → see picture at PET[1]

hamstring[1] /'hæm,strɪŋ/ n [C] a TENDON behind your knee

hamstring[2] v [T] past tense and past participle **hamstrung** /-,strʌŋ/ to make it difficult for someone to do or achieve something

hand[1] /hænd/ n [C]

1 the part of your body at the end of your arm, including your fingers and thumb: *She writes with her left hand.* | *Tom stood in the doorway*

with his hands in his pockets. | **take sb's hand/take sb by the hand** *I took her hand and helped her down the stairs.* | *They sat there **holding hands** through the entire film.* | *The two leaders **shook hands** (=as a greeting).* | *They were cheering and **clapping** their **hands**.* | *He ripped the door open **with** his **bare hands** (=using only his hands).*

2 right-handed/left-handed always using the right hand or left hand to do things such as write, use tools etc

3 a hand help with something: **give/lend sb a hand** *Can you give me a hand moving this box?* | +with *Do you need a hand with the cooking?* → see box at HELP

4 one of the long things that point to the numbers on a clock → see picture at WATCH[2]

5 close/near at hand near: *Nurses are always close at hand in case of emergency.*

6 on hand/to hand close and ready to be used when needed: *Keep a supply of candles on hand in case of power cuts.*

7 at the hands of sb if you suffer at the hands of someone, they treat you badly

8 by hand using your hands, not a machine: *She does all her washing by hand.*

9 in hand being dealt with now: **job/task/matter in hand** *We need to discuss the most suitable working methods for the job in hand.*

10 in sb's hands/in the hands of sb being dealt with or cared for by someone: *The matter is in the hands of the police.*

11 get out of hand to become impossible to control: *Todd's behaviour is getting totally out of hand.*

12 get/lay your hands on sth to manage to get or find something: *I read every book I could get my hands on.*

13 hand in hand a) holding each other's hands: *They walked hand in hand through the park.* **b) go hand in hand** to be closely connected: *Wealth and power go hand in hand.*

14 hands off spoken used to warn someone not to touch something that is yours: *Hands off my cookies!*

15 have your hands full to be very busy: *You're going to have your hands full once you have the baby!*

16 on the one hand... on the other hand used when you are comparing two different facts or ideas: *On the one hand, they work slowly, but on the other hand they always finish the job.*

17 change hands if something changes hands, it is given or sold by one person to another person

18 have a hand in sth to influence or be involved in something: *He scored one goal and had a hand in two others.*

19 have sth/sb on your hands to have a difficult job, problem, situation etc to deal with: *I'm afraid we have a murder on our hands, Inspector.*

20 be an old hand (at sth) to have a lot of experience of doing something
→ LEFT-HAND, RIGHT-HAND

hand[2] v [T]

1 to give something to someone: **hand sth to sb** *She handed the letter to her father.* | **hand sb sth** *Can you hand me a towel?* → see box at GIVE

2 you have to hand it to sb *spoken* used to show that you admire someone: *You have to hand it to Liz – she's a great cook!*

hand sth ⇔ **around** also **hand** sth ⇔ **round** *BrE phr v* to offer something to each person in a group: *Could you hand the sandwiches around please, Mike?*

hand sth ⇔ **back** *phr v* to give something back to the person who gave it to you: **+to** *Mr Evans handed our essays back to us today.*

hand sth ⇔ **down** *phr v* to give something to a younger relation, or to people who live after you: *traditions that were handed down from generation to generation*

hand sth ⇔ **in** *phr v* to give something to someone in authority: *Please hand in your application by September 30.*

hand sth ⇔ **out** *phr v* to give something to each person in a group: *They were handing out free T-shirts at the club.*

hand sb/sth ⇔ **over** *phr v* to give someone or something to the person who wants to deal with them: **+to** *The thief was caught and handed over to the police.*

handbag /'hændbæg/ *n* [C] *especially BrE* a small bag that a woman uses to carry money and personal things [= purse *AmE*] → see picture at **BAG¹**

handbook /'hændbʊk/ *n* [C] a short book that gives information or instructions about something

handbrake /'hændbreɪk/ *n* [C] *BrE* a **BRAKE** in a car that you pull up with your hand to stop the car from moving when it is parked [= **emergency brake** *AmE*] → see picture on page A12

handcuffs /'hændkʌfs/ *n* [plural] a pair of metal rings that are put over a prisoner's wrists to hold their hands together —**handcuff** *v* [T]

handful /'hændfʊl/ *n* [C] **1** an amount that you can hold in your hand: **+of** *a handful of nuts* **2 a handful of sb/sth** a small number of people or things: *Only a handful of people came to the meeting.* **3 be a handful** *informal* if a child is a handful, they behave badly and are difficult to control

handgun /'hændgʌn/ *n* [C] a small gun you hold in one hand when you fire it

hand-'held *adj* a hand-held machine is small enough to hold in your hand when you use it: *a hand-held camera*

handicap /'hændikæp/ *n* [C] **1** *old-fashioned* if someone has a handicap, a part of their body or their mind has been permanently injured or damaged. Many people think that this word is offensive: *a child with a severe physical handicap* **2** something that makes it difficult for you to do or achieve something: *Not being able to speak French was a real handicap.*

handicapped /'hændikæpt/ *adj* if someone is handicapped, a part of their body or their mind has been permanently injured or damaged. Many people think that this word is offensive: *a mentally handicapped child*

handicraft /'hændikrɑːft $ -kræft/ *n* **1** [C] an activity in which you use your hands in a skilful way to make things **2 handicrafts** [plural] things that someone has made in a skilful way using their hands

handiwork /'hændiwɜːk $ -wɜːrk/ *n* [U] if something is your handiwork, you have done it or made it using your hands

handkerchief /'hæŋkətʃɪf $ -kər-/ *n* [C] a piece of cloth or paper that you use for drying your nose or eyes [= **hankie**]

handle¹ /'hændl/ *v* [T]

1 to deal with something: *Computers can handle huge amounts of data.* | *Ms Lee handled all of our travel arrangements.* | *The job was so stressful, he couldn't handle it any longer.* **2** to pick up or touch something: *Handle all packages with care.* **3** to buy or sell goods: *Upton was charged with handling stolen goods.*

handle² *n* [C] the part of something that you hold when you use it: *a pan with a broken handle* | *a door handle*

handlebars /'hændlbɑːz $ -bɑːrz/ *n* [plural] the bars above the front wheel of a bicycle or MOTOR-CYCLE, that you turn to control the direction you go in → see picture at **BICYCLE**

handler /'hændlə $ -ər/ *n* [C] someone whose job is to deal with or look after a particular kind of thing: *baggage handlers* | *a police dog and its handler*

'hand ,luggage *n* [U] small bags that you carry with you when you travel on a plane

handmade /,hænd'meɪd◂/ *adj* made by a person and not a machine: *handmade shoes*

handout /'hændaʊt/ *n* [C] **1** money or food that is given to someone because they are poor: *a cash handout* **2** a piece of paper with information on it that is given to people in a class or meeting

handover /'hændəʊvə $ -oʊvər/ *n* [singular] **1** the act of formally giving someone else control of a place or business: **+of** *Troops will stay in the country to ensure a smooth handover of power.* **2** the act of giving something to someone: **+of** *His lawyer demanded the immediate handover of all relevant documents.*

handpicked /,hænd'pɪkt◂/ *adj* carefully chosen: *a handpicked team*

handset /'hændset/ *n* [C] **1** the part of a telephone that you hold near your ear and mouth **2** the part of a MOBILE PHONE that you hold in your hand

hands-'free *adj* [only before noun] a hands-free machine is one that you can use without using your hands: *a hands-free phone*

handshake /'hændʃeɪk/ *n* [C] an action in which two people take each other's right hand when they meet or leave each other, or when they make an agreement: *He greeted me with a firm handshake.*

handsome /'hænsəm/ *adj*

1 a handsome man is attractive: *a tall handsome young officer* | *Sam was tall, dark, and hand-some.* → see box at **ATTRACTIVE** **2** [only before noun] a handsome amount of money is large: *He managed to make a hand-some profit out of the deal.*

'hands-on *adj* doing something yourself rather than just talking about it or telling other people to do it: *a chance to get some hands-on experi-ence of the job*

,**hand-to-'mouth** *adj, adv* if you have a hand-to-mouth existence, or if you live hand-to-mouth, you have only just enough money and food to live

handwash /'hændwɒʃ $ -wɒːʃ, -wɑːʃ/ *v* [T] if you handwash clothes, you wash them by hand, not in a washing machine

handwriting /'hænd,raɪtɪŋ/ *n* [U] the style of someone's writing: *She has very neat handwriting.*

handwritten /,hænd'rɪtn◂/ *adj* written by hand, not printed: *a handwritten letter*

handy /'hændi/ *adj* **1** useful: *a handy little tool* | *The extra key may* **come in handy** (=be useful in the future). **2** *informal* near and easy to reach: *Make sure you* **have** *your passport* **handy**. **3** **be handy with sth** to be good at using something, especially a tool: *Terry's very handy with a needle and thread.*

handyman /'hændimæn/ *n* [C] plural **handymen** /-men/ someone who is good at making and repairing things

hang[1] /hæŋ/ *v* past tense and past participle **hung** /hʌŋ/

1 also **hang up** [I,T] to put something somewhere so that its top part is fixed but its bottom part is free to move, or to be in this position: **hang sth above/on/over etc sth** *He hung his coat on the back of the door.* | **+from/on/over etc** *Her portrait was hanging on the wall.* | *The shirt hung down to his knees.* → see box at CLOTHES
2 [I,T] past tense and past participle **hanged** to kill someone by dropping them with a rope around their neck, or to die in this way, as a punishment for a crime: **be hanged for sth** *He was hanged for murder.* | *Corey hanged himself in his prison cell.*
3 [I] to stay in the air in the same place for a long time: *Dark clouds hung over the valley.*
4 hang your head to look ashamed and embarrassed: *Lewis hung his head and refused to answer.*
5 hang in the balance if something hangs in the balance, it is not certain what will happen to it: *Our whole future is hanging in the balance.*
6 leave sb/sth hanging to not finish something or not tell someone your decision about something: *The investigation should not be left hanging.*

hang around/round also **hang about** *BrE phr v informal* **1 hang around (sth)** to stay in one place without doing very much: *We hung around outside school for about an hour.* **2 hang around with sb** to spend a lot of time with someone: *I don't like the people she hangs around with.*

hang back *phr v* to not want to move forward or speak, often because you are shy: *Joe tends to hang back and let the others do the talking.*

hang on *phr v* **1 hang on!** *spoken* used to tell someone to wait for you: *Hang on, I'll be with you in a minute!* **2** *informal* to hold something tightly: *Hang on everybody, the road's pretty bumpy.*

hang onto sb/sth *phr v informal* to keep something: *Hang onto that letter – you might need it later.*

hang out *phr v informal* **1** to spend a lot of time at a particular place or with particular

people: *Where does he usually hang out?* **2 hang sth ⇔ out** to hang clothes outside in order to dry them

hang up *phr v* **1** to finish a telephone conversation by putting the telephone down: *She said good night and hung up.* | **+on** *Don't hang up on me!* (=put the phone down during a conversation because you are angry) → see box at TELEPHONE **2 hang sth ⇔ up** to hang clothes on a hook etc

hang[2] *n* **get the hang of (doing) sth** *informal* to learn how to do something: *You'll soon get the hang of using the computer.*

hangar /'hæŋə $ -ər/ *n* [C] a very large building where aircraft are kept

hanger /'hæŋə $ -ər/ also **coat hanger** *n* [C] a curved piece of plastic, wood, or metal with a hook on top, used for hanging clothes on

,**hanger-'on** *n* [C] plural **hangers-on** someone who spends a lot of time with important or rich people for their own advantage

'**hang ,glider** *n* [C] a large frame covered with cloth that you hold on to and fly slowly through the air on → see picture on page A9 —**hang gliding** *n* [U]

hangout /'hæŋaʊt/ *n* [C] *informal* a place that you often go to

hangover /'hæŋəʊvə $ -oʊvər/ *n* [C] an ill feeling that you have when you have drunk too much alcohol the evening before

'**hang-up** /'hæŋʌp/ *n* [C] *informal* if you have a hang-up about something, you feel worried or embarrassed about it: *Cindy has a hang-up about her nose.*

hanker /'hæŋkə $ -ər/ *v* **hanker after/for sth** *informal* to feel strongly that you want something: *She's always hankered after a place of her own.*

hankie, **hanky** /'hæŋki/ *n* [C] *informal* a HANDKERCHIEF

hanky-panky /,hæŋki 'pæŋki/ *n* [U] *informal humorous* sexual activity

Hanukkah /'hɑːnəkə $ 'kɑːnəkə, 'hɑː-/ *n* [C,U] an eight-day Jewish holiday in November or December

haphazard /,hæp'hæzəd◂ $ -ərd◂/ *adj* not planned or organized: *a haphazard way of working*

hapless /'hæpləs/ *adj literary* unlucky

happen /'hæpən/ *v* [I]

1 when something happens, there is an event, especially one that is not planned: *When did the accident happen?* | *Did anything exciting happen while I was away?* | *We waited for half an hour, but* **nothing happened**. | **Something** *terrible* **has happened**.

THESAURUS

Happen is mainly used to talk about things that have not been planned: *A funny thing happened on my way to work.* | *No one knows exactly what will happen.*
Take place is mainly used to talk about events that have been planned or that have already happened: *The next meeting will take place on Thursday.*
Occur is a formal word, used especially to say that something happens in a particular place or situation: *The accident occurred around 9 pm.*

H

2 happen to sb/sth to affect someone or something: *Strange things have been happening to me lately.* | *He should be here by now – something must have happened to him.*

3 happen to do sth to do something by chance: *I happened to see Hannah at the store today.*

4 as it happens/it (just) so happens used to tell someone something that is surprising, interesting, or useful: *It just so happened that Mike and I had been to the same school.*

happen on/upon sb/sth *phr v literary* to find something or meet someone by chance: *I happened on the restaurant by chance.*

happening /'hæpənɪŋ/ *n* [C] a strange or unusual event

happily /'hæpɪ̥li/ *adv* **1** in a happy way: *They're very happily married.* **2** fortunately: *Happily, no one was hurt in the fire.* **3** very willingly: *I'll happily look after the kids while you're out.*

happiness /'hæpin̥ɪs/ *n* [U] when someone is happy: *Her eyes shone with happiness.*

happy /'hæpi/ *adj*

1 feeling pleased and cheerful [≠ unhappy, sad]: *Sam's been looking very happy recently.* | **be happy to do sth** *John will be so happy to see you.* | **+for** *Congratulations! I'm very happy for you.* → see box at GLAD

2 a happy time or event is one that makes you feel happy: *Those were the happiest years of my life.* | *They have a very happy marriage.*

3 be happy to do sth to be willing to do something: *Our team of experts will be happy to answer any questions.*

4 [not before noun] satisfied: **+about** *I'm not very happy about this.* | **+with** *Are you happy with their decision?*

5 Happy Birthday/Happy New Year etc used as a way of greeting someone on a special occasion

happy-go-lucky *adj* not caring or worrying about what happens

harangue /həˈræŋ/ *v* [T] to speak angrily to someone, often for a long time, to try to persuade them that you are right

harass /'hærəs, həˈræs/ *v* [T] to deliberately annoy or threaten someone: *They claim that they are being harassed by the police.*

harassed /'hærəst, həˈræst/ *adj* anxious and tired: *He looked pale and harassed.*

harassment /'hærəsmənt, həˈræsmənt/ *n* [U] threatening or offensive behaviour: *racial harassment* | *Tina accused her boss of sexual harassment.*

harbour[1] *BrE*; **harbor** *AmE* /'hɑːbə $ 'hɑːrbər/ *n* [C] an area of water next to the land where ships can stay safely: *They sailed into Portsmouth Harbour.*

harbour[2] *BrE*; **harbor** *AmE v* [T] *formal* **1** to keep bad feelings or thoughts in your mind for a long time: *She began to harbour doubts over the wisdom of their journey.* **2** to protect someone by hiding them from the police: *She was accused of harbouring deserters.*

hard[1] /hɑːd $ hɑːrd/ *adj*

1 firm and stiff, and difficult to press down, cut, or break [≠ soft]: *a hard mattress* | *The plums are still too hard to eat.*

2 difficult to do or understand [≠ easy]: *The*

exam was quite hard. | **hard (for sb) to do sth** *Your question is hard for me to answer.* | *It's hard to say when Glenn will be back.*

3 involving a lot of physical or mental effort or suffering: *a long hard climb to the top of the hill* | *Poor Mary, she's had a hard life.* | *Bringing up children on your own is hard work.*

4 showing no kindness or sympathy: *Mr. Katz is a hard man to work for, but he's fair.* | **be hard on sb** *She's too hard on those kids.*

5 give sb a hard time *informal* to treat someone badly or criticize them a lot: *The guys were giving him a hard time about being late.*

6 do/learn sth the hard way to make a lot of mistakes or have a lot of difficulty before learning something: *I learned this lesson the hard way.*

7 no hard feelings *spoken* used to tell someone that you do not feel angry with them any more

8 hard facts/evidence facts etc that are true and can be proved

9 hard winter a very cold winter

10 hard cash paper money and coins

11 hard currency money from a country that has a strong ECONOMY, that is unlikely to lose its value

—**hardness** *n* [U]

hard[2] *adv*

1 using a lot of effort or force: *She'd been working hard all day.* | *Come on, push harder!*

2 be hard pressed/put/pushed to do sth to have difficulty doing something: *They'll be hard pushed to pay back the money.*

3 take sth hard to feel very upset about something: *Joe took the news very hard.*

hard-and-'fast *adj* hard-and-fast rules are clear and definite, and always used: *a hard-and-fast rule*

hardback /'hɑːdbæk $ 'hɑːrd-/ *n* [C] *BrE* a book that has a strong stiff cover [= hardcover *AmE*; → paperback] → see box at BOOK

hardball /'hɑːdbɔːl $ 'hɑːrdbɒːl/ *n AmE* **play hardball** *informal* to be very determined to get what you want, especially in business or politics

hardboard /'hɑːdbɔːd $ 'hɑːrdbɔːrd/ *n* [U] a kind of wood made out of smaller pieces of wood that have been pressed together

hard-'boiled *adj* a hard-boiled egg has been boiled until it becomes solid

'hard ˌcopy *n* [U] information from a computer that is printed onto paper

'hard core *n* [singular] *BrE* **1** the small group of people that are most active within a group or organization: *the hard core of the Communist Party* **2** a small group of people who refuse to change their behaviour or beliefs: *the hard core of drivers who carry on drinking and driving*

hardcore, **hard-core** /'hɑːdkɔː $ 'hɑːrdkɔːr/ *adj* [only before noun] **1** having very strong beliefs or opinions that are unlikely to change: *hardcore opposition to abortion* **2 hard-core pornography** pictures and films that show details of sexual behaviour, often in an unpleasant way

hardcover /'hɑːdkʌvə $ 'hɑːrdkʌvər/ *n* [C] *AmE* HARDBACK → see box at BOOK

hard 'disk *n* [C] a stiff DISK inside a computer that is used for permanently storing information

H

harden /ˈhɑːdn $ ˈhɑːrdn/ v [I,T] **1** to become firm or stiff, or to make something firm or stiff: *It will take about 24 hours for the glue to harden.* **2** if your attitude hardens, or if something hardens it, you become more strict and determined and less sympathetic: *Attitudes towards the terrorists have hardened even more since the attack.* —**hardened** *adj* [only before noun] *a hardened criminal*

ˌhard-ˈheaded *adj* able to make difficult decisions without being influenced by your emotions

hard-hearted /ˌhɑːd ˈhɑːtɪd $ ˌhɑːrd ˈhɑːr-/ *adj* not caring about other people's feelings

ˌhard-ˈhitting *adj* criticizing someone or something in a strong and effective way: *a hard-hitting TV documentary*

ˌhard-ˈline *adj* having extreme political beliefs, and refusing to change them: *hard-line conservatives* —**hard-liner** *n* [C]

hardly /ˈhɑːdli $ ˈhɑːrdli/ *adv* **1** almost not or almost none [➡ **barely**]: *I hardly know the people I'm working with* (=do not know them very well). | *I can hardly believe it.* | *We hardly ever* (=almost never) *go out in the evening.* | **hardly any/anything/anyone** (=almost nothing or no one) *She'd eaten anything all day.* → see box at **RARELY** **2** used to say that something is not at all true: *This is hardly the ideal time to buy a house.* **3** used to say that something has only just happened: *The serious building work has hardly begun.*

ˌhard-ˈnosed *adj* not affected by your emotions, and determined to get what you want: *a hard-nosed businessman*

ˌhard of ˈhearing *adj* unable to hear well [➡ **deaf**] → see box at **HEAR**

ˌhard-ˈpressed *adj* having a lot of problems and not much money or time: *help for hard-pressed families*

ˌhard ˈsell *n* [singular] when the person or company selling something puts a lot of pressure on people to buy it

hardship /ˈhɑːdʃɪp $ ˈhɑːrd-/ *n* [C,U] something that makes your life difficult, especially not having enough money: *Many families were suffering hardship.* | +**of** *the hardships of war*

ˌhard ˈshoulder *n* [singular] *BrE* the area at the side of a big road where you are allowed to stop if you have a problem with your car [= **shoulder** *AmE*]

ˌhard ˈup *adj informal* not having enough money: *I'm very hard up this month.* → see box at **POOR**

hardware /ˈhɑːdweə $ ˈhɑːrdwer/ *n* [U] **1** computer machinery and equipment [➡ **software**] **2** equipment and tools for your home and garden: *a hardware store*

ˌhard-ˈwearing *adj BrE* clothes and materials that are hard-wearing will stay in good condition for a long time [= **long-wearing** *AmE*]

hardwood /ˈhɑːdwʊd $ ˈhɑːrd-/ *n* [C,U] strong heavy wood used for making furniture

ˌhard-ˈworking *adj* working with a lot of effort: *a hard-working student*

hardy /ˈhɑːdi $ ˈhɑːrdi/ *adj* plants and animals that are hardy are strong and able to live in difficult conditions: *hardy mountain goats*

hare /heə $ her/ *n* [C] plural **hare** or **hares** an animal like a large rabbit, which can run very quickly

harem /ˈhɑːriːm, hɑːˈriːm $ ˈhɑːrəm, ˈher-/ *n* [C] the group of wives or women who lived with a rich or powerful man in some Muslim societies in the past

hark /hɑːk $ hɑːrk/ *v*
hark back to sth *phr v* to keep talking about things that happened in the past: *He's always harking back to his days in Hollywood.*

harlot /ˈhɑːlət $ ˈhɑːr-/ *n* [C] *literary* a PROSTITUTE

harm[1] /hɑːm $ hɑːrm/ *n*
1 [U] damage, hurt, or injury: *We must protect our children from harm.* | *I don't think a little wine does you any harm.* | *They got lost in the fog, but luckily they came to no harm* (=they were not hurt). | *Criticizing people's work often does more harm than good.* | *It was a silly thing to do, but don't worry. No harm done.* **2 there's no harm in doing sth** used to suggest that it might be useful to do something: *There's no harm in asking.* **3 not mean any harm/mean no harm** to have no intention of hurting or upsetting anyone: *I was only kidding – I didn't mean any harm.* **4 out of harm's way** in a safe place: *She was glad the children were at home, out of harm's way.*

harm[2] *v* [T] to damage or hurt someone or something: *Too much sun can harm your skin.*

harmful /ˈhɑːmfəl $ ˈhɑːrm-/ *adj* causing harm: *the harmful effects of smoking*

harmless /ˈhɑːmləs $ ˈhɑːrm-/ *adj* **1** unable or unlikely to cause any harm: *Their dog barks a lot but it's harmless.* **2** not likely to upset or offend anyone: *a bit of harmless fun* —**harmlessly** *adv*

harmonica /hɑːˈmɒnɪkə $ hɑːrˈmɑː-/ *n* [C] a small musical instrument that you hold to your mouth and blow into, moving it from side to side

harmonious /hɑːˈməʊniəs $ hɑːrˈmoʊ-/ *adj* **1** harmonious relationships are ones in which people are friendly and helpful to one another **2** sounds that are harmonious are very pleasant —**harmoniously** *adv*

harmonize also **-ise** *BrE* /ˈhɑːmənaɪz $ ˈhɑːr-/ *v* [I,T] **1** if two or more things harmonize, they work well together or look good together: +**with** *The new offices must harmonize with the other buildings in the area.* **2** to sing or play musical notes that make a pleasant sound with the main tune

harmony /ˈhɑːməni $ ˈhɑːr-/ *n* plural **harmonies** **1** [U] when people are not arguing, fighting, or disagreeing: *People of many races live here in harmony with each other.* **2** [C,U] notes of music combined together in a pleasant way: *in harmony a choir singing in perfect harmony*

harness[1] /ˈhɑːnɪs $ ˈhɑːr-/ *n* **1** [C,U] a set of leather bands used to fasten a horse to a vehicle so that it can pull it along **2** [C] a set of bands that you put round your body to hold you still or stop you falling: *a safety harness*

harness² *v* [T] **1** to control and use the natural power of something: *We can harness the power of the wind to generate electricity.* **2** to fasten two animals together, or to fasten an animal to a vehicle using a harness

harp¹ /hɑːp $ hɑːrp/ *n* [C] a large musical instrument with strings stretched across a frame with three corners, and that you play with your fingers → see picture on page A6 —**harpist** *n* [C]

harp² *v*

harp on *phr v informal disapproving* to talk about something all the time, in a way that is annoying or boring: **+about** *I wish they'd stop harping on about the fact they're vegetarians.*

harpoon /hɑːˈpuːn $ hɑːr-/ *n* [C] a weapon like a SPEAR used for hunting WHALES —**harpoon** *v* [T]

harrowing /ˈhærəʊɪŋ $ -roʊ-/ *adj* very shocking and upsetting: *a harrowing experience*

harry /ˈhæri/ *v* [T] **harried, harrying, harries 1** to keep attacking an enemy **2** to keep asking someone for something in a way that is upsetting or annoying —**harried** *adj*

harsh /hɑːʃ $ hɑːrʃ/ *adj* **1** harsh conditions are difficult to live in and are very uncomfortable: *The winters here are very harsh.* **2** unpleasantly bright, loud, or rough [≠ soft]: *harsh lighting* **3** unkind, cruel, or strict: *We need harsher laws to deal with drunk drivers.* | *a harsh regime* —**harshly** *adv*

harvest /ˈhɑːvɪst $ ˈhɑːr-/ *n* [C,U] the time when crops are gathered from the fields, or the crops that are gathered: *July is the time for the wheat harvest.* | *We've had a good harvest this year.* —**harvest** *v* [T]

has /z, əz, həz; *strong* hæz/ *v* the third person singular of the present tense of 'have'

'has-been *n* [C] *informal* someone who was important or popular in the past but who has now been forgotten

hash /hæʃ/ *n* [C] **1 make a hash of sth** *informal* to do something very badly: *I made a real hash of my exams.* **2** the symbol # **3** *informal* hashish

hashish /ˈhæʃiːʃ, -iːʃ/ *n* [U] an illegal drug that some people smoke

hasn't /ˈhæzənt/ *v* the short form of 'has not'

hassle¹ /ˈhæsəl/ *n* [C,U] *spoken* a situation that is annoying because it causes problems: *It's such a hassle not having a washing machine.* → see box at **PROBLEM**

hassle² *v* [T] *informal* to continuously ask someone to do something, in a way that is annoying: *Just stop hassling me, will you?*

haste /heɪst/ *n* [U] when you hurry to do something, because you do not have enough time: *In her haste, Pam forgot the tickets.*

hasten /ˈheɪsən/ *v* [T] *formal* **1** to make something happen faster or sooner [= hurry]: *Resting will hasten recovery.* **2 hasten to do sth** to do or say something quickly or without delay: *Gina hastened to assure him that everything was fine.*

hasty /ˈheɪsti/ *adj* if you are hasty, you do something quickly and not very carefully because you are in a hurry: *Don't be so hasty.* | *a hasty decision* —**hastily** *adv*: *A meeting was hastily organized.*

hats

top hat

woolly hat *BrE*/
wooly hat *AmE*

beret

cap

hard hat

hat /hæt/ *n* [C]

1 something that you wear to cover or protect your head: *a big straw hat* | **in a hat** *a man in a fur hat*
2 keep sth under your hat *informal* to keep something secret
→ **old hat** at **OLD**

hatch¹ /hætʃ/ *v* [I,T] **1** if an egg hatches, or if it is hatched, it breaks and a baby bird, fish, or insect comes out **2** also **hatch out** to break through an egg in order to be born: *All the chicks have hatched out.* **3 hatch a plot/plan/deal etc** to form a plan etc in secret

hatch² *n* [C] a small door on a ship or aircraft

hatchback /ˈhætʃbæk/ *n* [C] a car with a door at the back that opens upwards

hatchet /ˈhætʃɪt/ *n* [C] a small AXE with a short handle

hate¹ /heɪt/ *v* [T]

1 to dislike someone or something very much [≠ love]: *Mary really hated him after that.* | *I've always hated tomatoes.* | **hate doing sth** *Pam hates having her photo taken.* | **hate to do sth** *I hate to see you so unhappy.* | **hate sb's guts** *informal* (=hate someone very much)

THESAURUS

can't stand – to hate someone or something: *I can't stand being late.*
detest *formal* – to hate someone or something very much: *I was going out with a boy my mother detested.*
loathe – to hate something or someone very much: *I loathe my job.*
despise – to hate someone very much: *She despised her neighbours.*
abhor *formal* – to hate something because you think it is morally wrong: *He abhors violence of any kind.*
→ **LOVE**

2 I hate to think what/how *spoken* used when you feel sure that something would have a bad result: *I hate to think what Dad would say about this!*
3 I hate to do sth *spoken* used to say that you are sorry you have to do something: **I hate to**

H

say this/tell you ..., but *I hate to tell you this, but the match has been cancelled again.* | *I hate to ask, but could I borrow some money?*
—**hated** adj: *a hated dictator*

hate² n [U] an angry feeling that someone has when they dislike someone very much [≠ **love**]: *a look of hate*

hateful /'heɪtfəl/ adj very unpleasant or unkind: *What a hateful thing to say!*

hatred /'heɪtrɪd/ n [C,U] an angry feeling that someone has when they dislike someone or something very much [≠ **love**]: *eyes full of hatred* | **+of/for** *an intense hatred of authority*

'hat trick n [C] three successes coming one after the other, for example three GOALS by one player

haughty /'hɔːti $ 'hɒː-/ adj proud and unfriendly: *her haughty manner* —**haughtily** adv

haul¹ /hɔːl $ hɒːl/ v [I,T] to pull something heavy: *We managed to haul him out of the water.*
→ see box at PULL

haul² n [C] **1** a large amount of things that have been stolen, or found by the police: *a big drugs haul* **2 long haul** something that takes a lot of time and effort: *the long haul back to fitness* **3** the amount of fish caught in a net

haulage /'hɔːlɪdʒ $ 'hɒːl-/ n [U] the business of carrying things by road or railway

haunches /'hɔːntʃɪz $ 'hɒːn-/ n [plural] your bottom and the tops of your legs: *He sat on his haunches by the fire.*

haunt¹ /hɔːnt $ hɒːnt/ v [T] **1** if the SPIRIT of a dead person haunts a place, it appears there often: *His ghost still haunts the castle.* **2** if something unpleasant haunts you, you keep remembering it or being affected by it: *ex-soldiers still haunted by memories of the war*

haunt² n [C] a place that someone likes to go to often: *The café was a favourite haunt of artists.*

haunted /'hɔːntɪd $ 'hɒːn-/ adj a haunted building is believed to be visited regularly by the soul of a dead person

haunting /'hɔːntɪŋ $ 'hɒːn-/ adj beautiful, sad, and staying in your thoughts for a long time: *haunting landscapes* —**hauntingly** adv: *hauntingly beautiful music*

have¹ /v, əv, həv; *strong* hæv/ auxiliary verb past tense and past participle **had** /d, əd, həd; *strong* hæd/ present participle **having**, third person singular **has** /z, əz, həz; *strong* hæz/

1 used with the past participle of a verb to make perfect tenses: *Have you seen the new Disney movie?* | *She had lived in Peru for thirty years.* | *Julia hasn't skied before, has she?*
2 had better used to say what is the best thing to do: *You'd better take the cake out of the oven.* | *We'd better not tell Angela just yet.*

have² /hæv/ v [T not in passive] past tense and past participle **had**, present participle **having**, third person singular **has**

1 also **have got** used to say what someone or something looks like, or what features or qualities they possess: *He's got brown eyes and dark hair.* | *You need to have a lot of patience to be a teacher.* | *Japan has a population of over 120 million.*

2 also **have got** to own something, or be able to use something: *They've got a flat in the city centre.* | *Does she have a CD player?* | *I'd like to come, but I don't have the money.*
3 to experience or do something: **have problems/trouble etc** *I'm having problems using this fax machine.* | *Helen's had an accident at work.* | *The kids had great fun at the theme park.* | **have a meeting/party** *Let's have a party!* | **have a bath/wash etc** *I can't wait to get home and have a bath.* | **have sth stolen/taken etc** *She had all her jewellery stolen.*
4 to eat, drink, or smoke something: *Let's go and have a beer.* | *We're having steak tonight.* | **have lunch/breakfast etc** *What time do you usually have lunch?*
5 also **have got** to be carrying or holding something: *Watch out! He's got a gun!* | **have sth on/with you** *Do you have a pen on you?*
6 also **have got** to think of something or experience a feeling: **Have** *you got any* **ideas** *for presents for Tom?* | *I* **had** *the* **feeling** *I'd seen him before.*
7 BrE to receive something such as a letter, information, or advice: *Have you had any news from Michael?*
8 also **have got** to keep something in a particular position or state: **have sth open/closed/on etc** *He had his eyes closed.* | *You've always got the TV on so loud.*
9 may I have/can I have/I'll have spoken used when you are asking for something: *I'll have two hot dogs, please.*
10 have a friend/sister/uncle etc also **have got** to know or be related to someone: *Julie had six brothers.* | *I've got a friend who works for the UN.*
11 also **have got** if you have an amount of time to do something, it is available for you: *You have 30 minutes to finish the test.* | *I'm sorry, I haven't got time to stop now.*
12 also **have got** to be ill or injured in a particular way: *Sheila's had the flu for a week.* | *He's got a broken leg.*
13 have sth ready/done etc to make something ready, or finish something: *They promised to have the job done by Friday.*
14 have your hair cut/have your house painted etc to pay someone to cut your hair, paint your house etc
15 if a woman has a baby, she gives birth to it: *Sasha's had twins!*
16 also **have got** BrE to be visited by someone: *Sorry, I didn't realize you had guests.* | *We're having people to dinner.*
→ **be had** at HAD²

have (got) sth against sb/sth phr v to dislike someone or something for a particular reason: *I can't see what you've got against the idea.* | *I* **have nothing against** *Tim personally, but he's not right for the job.*

have sth/sb on phr v **1 have (got) sth** ⇔ **on** to be wearing something: *Mark had on a denim jacket.* **2 be having sb on** BrE to be trying to make someone believe something that is not true: *Are you having me on?*

have sth out phr v **1** to have something removed from your body by a medical operation: *She had her appendix out last year.* **2 have it out with sb** informal to talk to someone directly and honestly about something bad they have done: *I think it's time you had it out with Richard.*

have³, have (got) to do *modal verb*

1 if you have to do something, you must do it because someone makes you do it, or because it is necessary: *Susan hates having to get up early.* | *You don't have to answer all the questions.*

2 used to say that it is important that something happens: *You have to believe me!* | *There has to be an end to all this violence.*
3 used to tell someone how to do something: *First you have to take the wheel off.*
4 used to say that you are sure that something will happen or is true: *This has got to be a mistake.* | *Prices will have to come down eventually.*

haven /ˈheɪvən/ *n* [C] a safe or peaceful place: **+for** *The area is a haven for wildlife.*

haven't /ˈhævənt/ *v* the short form of 'have not'

havoc /ˈhævək/ *n* [U] a very confused situation in which there is a lot of damage: *The storm **caused havoc** everywhere.* | *The war will **wreak havoc on** the country's economy.*

hawk /hɔːk $ hɔːk/ *n* [C] a large wild bird that eats small birds and animals

hay /heɪ/ *n* [U] grass that has been cut and dried and is used as food for animals

'hay ˌfever *n* [U] a medical condition like a bad COLD, caused by breathing in dust from plants

haystack /ˈheɪstæk/ *n* [C] a large pile of stored hay

haywire /ˈheɪwaɪə $ -waɪr/ *adj* **go haywire** *informal* to start working in completely the wrong way: *My computer's going haywire again.*

hazard¹ /ˈhæzəd $ -ərd/ *n* [C] something that may be dangerous or cause accidents: **+to** *Plastic bags can be a hazard to wildlife.* | **health/ safety/fire hazard** *That old furniture is a fire hazard.*

hazard² *v* **hazard a guess** to say something that is only a guess: *I don't know how much he earns, but I could hazard a guess.*

hazardous /ˈhæzədəs $ -zər-/ *adj* dangerous or likely to cause accidents: **+to** *chemicals which may be hazardous to health* | *the disposal of **hazardous waste***

haze /heɪz/ *n* [singular,U] smoke, dust, or mist in the air: *a heat haze*

hazel¹ /ˈheɪzəl/ *adj* hazel eyes are light greenish-brown

hazel² *n* [C,U] a small tree that produces nuts

hazy /ˈheɪzi/ *adj* **1** air that is hazy is not clear because there is smoke, dust, or mist in it: *a*

hazy summer morning **2** not clear or exact: *My memories of that night are a little hazy.*

he /i, hi; *strong* hiː/ *pron* used to talk about a male person or animal that has already been mentioned: *'How's Josh?' 'Oh, he's fine.'*

head¹ /hed/ *n*

1 [C] the top part of your body that has your eyes, mouth, brain etc in it: *a severe **head injury*** | *He **turned** his **head** to look at her.* | *Alice smiled and **nodded** her **head** (=moved it up and down to show agreement).* | *'No,' I said, **shaking my head** (=moving it from side to side to show disagreement).* | **raise/lift/bow/lower your head** *She raised her head to see what was happening.* → see picture on page A3

COLLOCATIONS

Turn your **head** to look at something.
Shake your **head** (=move it from side to side) to disagree or say 'no'.
Nod your **head** (=move it up and down) to agree or say 'yes'.
Raise/lift your **head** to look up.
Bend/lower your **head** to look down.
Bow your **head** (=move it downwards) to show respect for someone.
Hang your **head** (=lower it and keep it lowered) if you are ashamed.
Scratch your **head** (=rub it with your fingers) if you are thinking hard.
→ HAIR

2 [C] your mind: *I just said the first thing that **came into** my **head** (=I thought of).* | *I wish I could **get** it **into** his **head** (=make him understand) that school is important.* | *Angela had **taken** it **into** her **head** (=suddenly decided) to go for a walk.* | **do sth in your head** (=calculate something in your mind) *You have to work out the answer in your head.*

3 [C] **a)** the leader or most important person in a group or organization: **+of** *the former head of the FBI* | *a meeting of **heads of state*** | **head waiter/chef/gardener etc b)** also **head teacher** *BrE* the person in charge of a school [= principal *AmE*]: *Any student caught smoking will have to see the head.*

4 keep/lose your head to behave in a sensible or stupid way in a difficult situation: *She had the ability to keep her head under pressure.*

5 [singular] the front or the most important position: **(at) the head of sth** *the man at the head of the queue*

6 [C] used in some expressions to say that someone is crazy or stupid: *He must **be off** his **head** to go out running in this weather.* | *That guy **needs** his **head examined**!*

7 have a (good) head for business/figures to be naturally good at business or calculations

8 keep your head down to try to avoid being noticed or getting involved

9 put your heads together to discuss a difficult problem together

10 go over sb's head to be too difficult for someone to understand: *I could see that the discussion was going over their heads.*

11 go to sb's head if success goes to someone's head, it makes them feel more important than they are

H

12 be banging your head against a brick wall to be making no progress at all when trying to do something

13 keep your head above water to succeed in continuing, even though you have a lot of problems with money

14 sb can't make head nor/or tail of sth used to say that someone cannot understand something at all: *I can't make head nor tail of these instructions.*

15 come to a head if a problem comes to a head, it becomes worse and you have to do something about it immediately: *The situation came to a head when the workers went on strike.*

16 a head/per head for each person: *The meal worked out at £15 a head.*

17 laugh/shout/scream your head off *informal* to laugh, shout etc a lot

18 heads [U] the side of a coin that has a picture of someone's head on it [≠ tails]

head² v

1 [I] to go in a particular direction: **+for/ towards/up etc** *a boat heading for the shore* | *It's time we headed home.*

2 [T] to be in charge of a government, organization, or group: *Most one-parent families are headed by women.*

3 be heading for sth also **be headed for sth** *AmE* if you are heading for a situation, it is likely to happen: *The company was heading for disaster.*

4 [T] to be at the top of a list, a page, or a group of words: *The longest list was headed 'Problems.'*

5 [T] to hit the ball with your head in football

  head sb/sth ⇔ off *phr v* **1** to stop someone moving in a particular direction by moving in front of them: *The police headed them off at the crossroads.* **2** to prevent something bad from happening

headache /'hedeɪk/ *n* [C]

1 a pain in your head: *I've got a splitting headache* (=very bad headache).

2 a serious problem that you worry about

'**head count** *n* [C] the act of counting how many people are present in a particular place at one time: *Teachers did a head count to check that none of the kids were missing.*

headdress /'hed-dres/ *n* [C] something that someone wears on their head for decoration at a ceremony or special occasion: *a feathered headdress*

head-first /ˌhed'fɜːst◂ $ -'fɜːrst◂/ *adv* with your head going first, before the rest of your body: *He dived head-first into the pool.*

headgear /'hedgɪə $ -gɪr/ *n* [U] hats and other things that you wear on your head: *Protective headgear must be worn.*

headhunter /'hed,hʌntə $ -ər/ *n* [C] someone whose job is to find people for particular jobs and persuade them to leave their present jobs —**headhunt** *v* [T]

heading /'hedɪŋ/ *n* [C] the title at the top of a piece of writing

headland /'hedlənd/ *n* [C] an area of land that sticks out into the sea

headlight /'hedlaɪt/   also   **headlamp** /'hedlæmp/ *n* [C] one of the large lights at the front of a vehicle → see picture on page A12

headline /'hedlaɪn/ *n* [C] **1** the title of a newspaper report, printed in large letters: *a front-page headline* → see box at **NEWSPAPER**
 2 the headlines the important news stories on radio or television, read out together before the rest of the program begins

headlong /'hedlɒŋ $ -lɔːŋ/ *adv* **1 rush headlong into sth** to do something important without thinking carefully about it first: *Fran isn't the type to rush headlong into marriage.* **2** with your head going first: *Ben went tumbling headlong down the hill.*

headmaster /ˌhed'mɑːstə $ 'hed,mæstər/ *n* [C] *BrE* a male teacher who is in charge of a school [= head teacher; = principal *AmE*]

headmistress /ˌhed'mɪstrɪs $ 'hed,mɪs-/ *n* [C] *BrE* a female teacher who is in charge of a school [= head teacher; = principal *AmE*]

,**head-'on** *adv* **1 meet/crash/hit head-on** if two vehicles meet head-on, the front part of one vehicle hits the front part of the other: *A car and a truck had collided head-on.* **2** if someone deals with a problem head-on, they deal with it in a direct way: *She decided to face her difficulties head-on.* —**head-on** *adj*: *a head-on collision*

headphones
/'hedfəʊnz $ -foʊnz/
n [plural] a piece of
equipment that you
wear over your ears to
listen to a radio, CD
PLAYER etc

headphones

headquarters
/'hed,kwɔːtəz,
ˌhed'kwɔːtəz
$ -ɔːrtərz/ *n* [plural],
HQ the main office of
a large company or
organization, or the place from which military action is controlled: **+of** *the headquarters of the UN*

headrest /'hed-rest/ *n* [C] the top part of a chair, that supports the back of your head

headroom /'hed-rʊm, -ruːm/ *n* [U] the amount of space above your head inside a car, or above a car when it is under a bridge

,**head 'start** *n* [C] an advantage that helps you to be successful: *His education gave him a head start.*

headstone /'hedstəʊn $ -stoʊn/ *n* [C] a piece of stone on a GRAVE, with the dead person's name on it

headstrong /'hedstrɒŋ $ -strɔːŋ/ *adj* very determined to do what you want [= stubborn]: *a headstrong child*

,**head 'teacher** *n* [C] *BrE* the teacher who is in charge of a school [= head *BrE*; = principal *AmE*]

,**head-to-'head** *adv, adj* competing directly with another person or group: *New courier companies will be going head-to-head with the Post Office.* | *a head-to-head contest*

headway /'hedweɪ/ *n* **make headway** to come closer to achieving something: **+towards/ with/in etc** *We have made little headway towards a solution.*

headwind /'hed,wɪnd/ *n* [C,U] a wind that blows directly towards you when you are moving

H

heady /'hedi/ *adj* making you feel excited, or as if you are drunk: *the heady days of their youth*

heal /hi:l/ also **heal up** *v* [I,T] if an injury or broken bone heals, or if someone heals it, it becomes healthy again: *The scratch on her finger healed quickly.* —**healer** *n* [C]

health /helθ/ *n* [U]

1 the general condition of your body, and how healthy you are: *Smoking can **damage** your health.* | *She has a lot of **health problems**.* | **in good/poor etc health** *Elsie's not in very good health.* | *Paul had to leave his job due to **ill health**.* | *doctors and other **health care** professionals*

2 how successful an economic system or organization is: *the health of the economy*

'health care *n* [U] the service that is responsible for looking after people's health: *the promise of free health care for everyone* | *health care workers*

'health ,centre *n* [C] *BrE* a place where there are several doctors and nurses, where you can go for medical treatment

'health food *n* [C,U] food that contains only natural substances: *a health food shop*

healthful /'helθfəl/ *adj AmE* good for your body: *healthful eating habits*

healthy /'helθi/ *adj*

1 strong and not likely to become ill [≠ **unhealthy**]: *a healthy baby girl* | *What do we need to stay healthy?*

2 good for your body or your mind [≠ **unhealthy**]: *a **healthy diet** | a campaign to encourage **healthy eating** | It's not healthy for her to depend on him like that.*

3 strong and successful: *The economy is in a healthy state.*

—**healthily** *adv*

heap¹ /hi:p/ *n* [C] **1** a large untidy pile of things: **+of** *a heap of newspapers* | **in a heap** *His clothes lay in a heap by the bed.* **2 heaps/a heap (of sth)** *informal* a lot of something: *We've got heaps of time.*

heap² *v* **1** also **heap up** [T] to put a lot of things on top of each other in an untidy way: *plates heaped with food* **2 heap praise/criticism/insults on sb** to praise, criticize etc someone a lot

heaped /hi:pt/ *adj* **heaped teaspoon/bowl/plate etc** *BrE* an amount of something that is as much as a spoon, plate etc can hold

hear /hɪə $ hɪr/ *v* [I,T] past tense and past participle **heard** /hɜːd $ hɜːrd/

1 to know that a sound is being made, using your ears: *Can you hear that noise?* | *She called his name but he didn't hear.* | **hear sb doing sth** *I thought I heard someone knocking.* | **hear sb do sth** *Did you hear them leave?*

THESAURUS

If a sound is **drowned out** by something, it prevents you from hearing the sound: *His voice was drowned out by the traffic.*

If you cannot hear someone because they are very far away from you, you can say that they are **out of earshot**: *'What are we going to do if you lose your job?' I asked John, as soon as the children were out of earshot.*

If someone is close enough to hear what you

say, they are **within earshot**.

If someone says something **under their breath**, they make a rude or angry statement very quietly because they do not want anyone to hear them: *'You rat,' he muttered under his breath.*

If someone is **inaudible**, they speak so quietly that you cannot hear them.

If someone is not able to hear very well because of a physical problem with their ears, you can say that they are **hard of hearing** or **hearing impaired**: *My grandmother's a little hard of hearing.*

If someone is **deaf**, they are not able to hear anything at all.

You **hear** a noise or something that someone says, often without trying to: *Did you hear that noise?* | *I could hear the phone ringing.*

If you **listen to** words, sounds, or music, you pay attention to them: *I enjoy watching movies and listening to music.* | *She listened carefully to his advice.*

→ **SEE**

2 to be told or to find out some information: **+(that)** *We were sorry to hear that you were ill.* | *You'll **be pleased to hear** that it's nearly finished.* | **+about/of** *Where did you hear about the job?* | *Have you **heard the news**?*

3 have heard of sb/sth to know that someone or something exists because you have been told about them: *Phil Merton? I've never heard of him.*

4 hear a case to listen to all the facts of a case in a court of law in order to make a legal decision [➤ **hearing**]: *The case will be heard on July 16th.*

5 (do) you hear (me)? *spoken* used to emphasize an order: *Be home by ten, you hear?*

6 won't hear of sth *spoken* used to say that someone will not allow something, especially because they want to help someone: *I offered to pay, but he wouldn't hear of it.*

hear from sb *phr v* to get news or information from someone, usually in a letter or by telephone: *Have you heard from Jane?* | *I look forward to hearing from you soon.*

hear sb **out** *phr v* to listen to someone's explanation for something, without interrupting: *I know you're angry, but just hear me out.*

hearing /'hɪərɪŋ $ 'hɪr-/ *n* **1** [U] the sense that you use to hear sounds: *My hearing's not as good as it used to be.* **2** [C] a meeting of a court or committee to find out the facts about something: *a court hearing* **3 a (fair) hearing** an opportunity for someone to explain their actions or ideas: *We must **give both sides a fair hearing**.*

'hearing aid *n* [C] a small thing that you put in your ear to make sounds louder if you cannot hear well

'hearing im,paired *adj* unable to hear well → see box at **HEAR**

hearsay /'hɪəseɪ $ 'hɪr-/ *n* [U] something that other people have told you but which may not be true [= **rumour**]: *Don't believe it – it's just hearsay.*

hearse /hɜːs $ hɜːrs/ *n* [C] a large car for carrying a dead body in a COFFIN at a funeral

H

heart /hɑːt $ hɑːrt/ *n* [C]

1 the organ inside your chest that pushes blood around your body: *Tom could feel his **heart beating** faster.* | *a severe **heart condition** (=something wrong with your heart)* | *His breathing and **heart rate** (=the number of times your heart beats per minute) were now normal.* → see picture on page A3

2 the part of you that feels emotions: *He's strict, but he has a kind heart.* | *It would **break her heart** (=make her very sad) if he left now.* | **in your heart** *I knew in my heart that he was right.* | *She wished **with all her heart** that she had never met him.* | *Michael was speaking **from the heart**.* | *She had **a heart of gold** (=a kind nature).* | **kind-hearted/cold-hearted/hard-hearted etc** (=having a kind, unkind, cruel etc nature)

3 a shape used to mean a heart or love

4 the heart of sth the centre or most important part of something: *deep in the heart of the countryside* | **the heart of the matter/problem etc** *Let's get to the heart of the matter.*

5 take/lose heart to begin to have more hope or to stop having hope: *I've failed my driving test so many times I'm beginning to lose heart.*

6 be sth at heart if you are a particular kind of person at heart, that is the kind of character you really have: *I'm just a kid at heart.*

7 have sb's interests at heart to want to do what is best for someone

8 take sth to heart to treat what someone says as important, especially when it upsets you: *Diana took the criticism to heart.*

9 close/dear to sb's heart very important to someone: *It was obviously a matter close to his heart.*

10 know/learn sth by heart to remember or learn all of a piece of writing: *We had to learn the poem by heart.*

11 sb's heart sinks used to say that someone suddenly becomes very sad or disappointed: *Bert's heart sank when he saw the mess.*

12 do sth to your heart's content to do something as much as you want to: *You can run around here to your heart's content.*

13 not have the heart to do sth *spoken* to not do something because you do not want to make someone unhappy: *I didn't have the heart to tell her the truth.*

14 sb's heart goes out to sb used to say that someone feels a lot of sympathy for someone

15 hearts [plural] in card games, the cards with red heart shapes on them: *the queen of hearts* → see picture at **PLAYING CARD**

→ **change of heart** at **CHANGE²**

heartache /ˈhɑːteɪk $ ˈhɑːrt-/ *n* [U] a feeling of great sadness

ˈheart atˌtack *n* [C] a serious medical condition in which your heart suddenly stops working normally: *He **had a heart attack** and was rushed to hospital.*

heartbeat /ˈhɑːtbiːt $ ˈhɑːrt-/ *n* [C,U] the action or the sound of your heart as it pushes blood around your body: *The doctor listened to the baby's heartbeat.*

heartbreak /ˈhɑːtbreɪk $ ˈhɑːrt-/ *n* [U] a strong feeling of sadness, especially about a person you love

heartbreaking /ˈhɑːtˌbreɪkɪŋ $ ˈhɑːrt-/ *adj* making you feel very sad: *heartbreaking pictures of starving children*

heartbroken /ˈhɑːtˌbrəʊkən $ ˈhɑːrtˈbroʊ-/ *adj* very sad because of something that has happened

heartburn /ˈhɑːtbɜːn $ ˈhɑːrtbɜːrn/ *n* [U] a burning feeling in your stomach or chest caused by acid from your stomach [➡ **indigestion**]

ˈheart disˌease *n* [U] a medical condition which prevents your heart from working normally

heartened /ˈhɑːtnd $ ˈhɑːr-/ *adj* feeling happier and more hopeful [≠ **disheartened**] —**hearten** *v* [T] —**heartening** *adj*: *heartening news*

ˈheart ˌfailure *n* [U] a serious medical condition in which your heart stops working

heartfelt /ˈhɑːtfelt $ ˈhɑːrt-/ *adj* felt very strongly and sincerely: *heartfelt thanks*

hearth /hɑːθ $ hɑːrθ/ *n* [C] the part of the floor around a FIREPLACE

heartily /ˈhɑːtɪli $ ˈhɑːr-/ *adv* **1** loudly and cheerfully [➡ **hearty**]: *He laughed heartily.* **2** very much or completely: *I'm heartily sick of hearing about her problems.*

heartland /ˈhɑːtlənd $ ˈhɑːrt-/ *n* [C] the part of a country where an activity or belief is based or is strongest: *the industrial heartland of England*

heartless /ˈhɑːtləs $ ˈhɑːrt-/ *adj* cruel or not feeling any sympathy: *How can you be so heartless?* —**heartlessly** *adv*

heartrending /ˈhɑːtˌrendɪŋ $ ˈhɑːrt-/ *adj literary* making you feel a lot of sympathy for someone: *a heartrending story*

ˈheart-ˌstopping *adj* very exciting or frightening

ˌheart-to-ˈheart *n* [C] a conversation in which two people say honestly what they think or feel: *It's time you and I **had a heart-to-heart**.* —**heart-to-heart** *adj*

heartwarming /ˈhɑːtˌwɔːmɪŋ $ ˈhɑːrtˌwɔːr-/ *adj* something that is heartwarming makes you feel happy: *a heartwarming story*

hearty /ˈhɑːti $ ˈhɑːrti/ *adj* **1** friendly and full of energy: *a hearty welcome* **2** a hearty meal is very large

heat¹ /hiːt/ *n*

1 [U] the quality of being warm or hot: **+of** *the heat of the sun* | *a material that withstands intense heat*

2 the heat very hot weather: *the summer heat*

3 [singular,U] the temperature used when cooking or heating something: **low/medium/high heat** *Melt the butter over a low heat.*

4 [U] strong feelings, especially anger or excitement: **In the heat of the moment** (=when feelings were strong), *I said things I didn't mean.*

5 [C] one part of a race or competition, which decides who will be in the next part

6 [U] *AmE* the system in a building that keeps it warm [= **heating** *BrE*]

→ **DEAD HEAT**

heat² also **heat up** *v* [I,T] to become warm or hot, or to make something warm or hot: *Let the oven heat up.* | *Heat the milk until it boils.*

heated /ˈhiːtɪd/ *adj* **1** made warm using a heater: *a heated swimming pool* **2** heated

debate/argument/discussion etc an argument etc in which people become very angry and excited

heater /'hiːtə $ -ər/ *n* [C] a machine for heating air or water

heath /hiːθ/ *n* [C] an area of wild land where grass and bushes grow

heathen /'hiːðən/ *adj old-fashioned disapproving* not belonging or relating to the Christian religion —**heathen** *n* [C]

heather /'heðə $ -ər/ *n* [U] a small plant with purple, pink, or white flowers that grows on hills

heating /'hiːtɪŋ/ *n* [U] *BrE* the system in a building that keeps it warm [= **heat** *AmE*]: *I've turned the heating up.*

heatwave /'hiːtweɪv/ *n* [C] a period of unusually hot weather

heave /hiːv/ *v* **1** [I,T] to pull or lift something heavy using a lot of effort: **heave sb/sth out of/onto etc sth** *He heaved himself out of the chair.* → see box at **PULL** **2** [I] to move up and down with strong regular movements: **+with** *His shoulders heaved with laughter.* **3 heave a sigh** to breathe out loudly: *Roz **heaved a sigh of relief** when he'd gone.* —**heave** *n* [C]

heaven /'hevən/ *n*

1 also **Heaven** the place where some people believe that good people go after they die [➡ **hell**]

2 [U] *informal* a very pleasant situation or experience: *It's **heaven** to lie back in a hot bath.*

3 for heaven's sake *spoken* used when you are annoyed or angry: *For heaven's sake, what do you want?*

4 (Good) Heavens! *spoken* used when you are surprised: *Good Heavens! What's happened?*

5 *spoken* used in some expressions to emphasize something you think or feel: **Heaven knows** (=I do not know) *how I would have coped without her.* | *Me, get married?* **Heaven forbid** (=I very much hope not)*!*

6 the heavens *literary* the sky

heavenly /'hevənli/ *adj* **1** [only before noun] *literary* relating to heaven or the sky: *God's heavenly kingdom* **2** *old-fashioned* very pleasant: *a heavenly smell*

heavily /'hevɪli/ *adv* **1** very much or a lot: *He became **heavily** involved in the project.* | *It rained **heavily** all night.* | **drink/smoke heavily** **2** slowly and in a way that shows you are sad or tired: *Emma sighed **heavily**.* **3 heavily-built** someone who is heavily-built has a large body that looks strong

heavy /'hevi/ *adj*

1 weighing a lot [≠ **light**]: *I can't lift this box – it's too heavy.* | *a heavy suitcase* | **How heavy is this parcel** (=how much does it weigh)? → see box at **FAT**

2 large in amount or degree: **Heavy traffic** *is causing delays.* | *There are reports of **heavy fighting** in the town.* | *the dangers of **heavy drinking*** | **heavy rain/snow** | **a heavy meal/lunch etc** (=making your stomach feel very full)

COLLOCATIONS

heavy smoker – someone who smokes a lot of cigarettes

heavy defeat *BrE* – used to say that a team has lost a sports competition by a large amount

heavy losses – used especially to say that a company has earned a lot less money than it spent

heavy casualties/losses – used to say that a lot of people have been injured or killed in a war, battle etc

heavy workload – used to say that you have a lot of work to do

heavy cold *BrE* – a bad cold

3 needing a lot of physical strength: *A gardener does the heavy work for me.*

4 difficult and serious: *Their relationship was **getting heavy**.* | *I found the course **heavy going*** (=difficult).

5 solid or thick: *heavy boots* | *heavy soil*

6 using or happening with a lot of force: *a heavy blow* | *heavy footsteps*

7 heavy day/schedule etc a day etc when you have a lot to do

8 make heavy weather of sth *BrE disapproving* to make something that you are doing seem more complicated than it really is

9 with a heavy heart feeling very sad

—**heaviness** *n* [U]

heavy-'duty *adj* heavy-duty materials, pieces of equipment etc are very strong and not easily damaged: *heavy-duty plastic*

heavy-'handed *adj* using too much force in the way you deal with people: *a heavy-handed style of management*

heavy 'metal *n* [U] a type of very loud modern music with a strong beat → see box at **MUSIC**

heavyweight /'heviweɪt/ *n* [C] **1** someone or something that has a lot of influence: *a **political heavyweight*** **2** a **BOXER** from the heaviest weight group —**heavyweight** *adj*

heck /hek/ *spoken informal* used when you are annoyed

heckle /'hekəl/ *v* [I,T] to shout at someone who is making a speech or performing, in order to embarrass them —**heckler** *n* [C] —**heckling** *n* [U]

hectare /'hektɑː, -teə $ -ter/ *n* [C] a unit for measuring an area of land, equal to 10,000 square metres

hectic /'hektɪk/ *adj* very busy, or full of activity: *a hectic day*

he'd /id, hid; *strong* hiːd/ the short form of 'he would' or 'he had': *I'm sure he'd help you.* | *He'd never liked her.*

hedge¹ /hedʒ/ *n* [C] a row of bushes that separates gardens or fields

hedge² *v* [I,T] **1** to avoid giving a direct answer: *'I'm not sure where she is,' he hedged.* **2 hedge your bets** to reduce your chances of failing by doing several different things: *I hedged my bets by applying to six colleges.*

hedgehog /'hedʒhɒg $ -hɑːg, -hɔːg/ *n* [C] a small animal with sharp points covering its body

hedgehog

hedgerow /'hedʒrəʊ $ -roʊ/ *n* [C] *BrE* a row of bushes along the edge of a field or road

H

hedonism /'hi:dənɪzəm/ n [U] the belief that pleasure is the most important thing —**hedonist** n [C]

heed[1] /hi:d/ v [T] formal to pay attention to someone's advice or warning: The company failed to **heed warnings** about safety.

heed[2] n **take heed of sth/pay heed to sth** formal to pay attention to something, especially something that someone says

heedless /'hi:dləs/ adj **heedless of sth** literary not paying attention to something

heel /hi:l/ n [C]
1 the back part of your foot [➡ toe]
2 the part under a shoe that makes it higher: boots with high heels | **high-heeled/low-heeled/flat-heeled** flat-heeled walking shoes → see picture at SHOE[1]

hefty /'hefti/ adj big, heavy, or strong: a tall hefty man | a **hefty fine**

heifer /'hefə $ -ər/ n [C] a young female cow

height /haɪt/ n
1 [C,U] how tall someone or something is: The boys are about the same height. | **6 feet/10metres etc in height** mountains over 300m in height | **a height of 6 feet/10metres etc** The plant grows to a height of 25cm.
2 [C,U] the distance something is above the ground: A fall from that height would kill you. | **a height of 2500 feet/10,000 metres etc** The aircraft was flying at a height of 10,000 metres. | **gain/lose height** (=move higher or lower in the sky) The plane was rapidly losing height.
3 [C] a high place or position: From a height, the town seemed to spread for miles. | She'd always been **scared of heights**.
4 new/great/dizzy heights extremely high levels: Prices had **reached** absurd **heights**.
5 [singular] the busiest, most successful etc time for something: It was the height of the tourist season. | Mini skirts were **the height of fashion** (=very fashionable). | **at its height** Demand for home computers was at its height.

heighten /'haɪtn/ v [I,T] if a feeling, effect etc heightens, or if something heightens it, it increases or becomes stronger: Television has **heightened awareness** of the issue. | The effect of the drug is heightened by alcohol.

heinous /'heɪnəs/ adj formal extremely shocking and bad: a **heinous crime**

heir /eə $ er/ n [C] someone who will receive money, property, or a title when another person dies: **+to** She was the heir to a fortune.

heiress /'eərɪs, 'eəres $ 'er-/ n [C] a woman who will receive money, property, or a title when someone dies

heirloom /'eəlu:m $ 'er-/ n [C] a valuable object that the same family has owned for many years: a **family heirloom**

held /held/ v the past tense and past participle of HOLD

helicopter /'helɪkɒptə $ -kɑːptər/ n [C] an aircraft with long metal parts on top which turn around very quickly to make it fly → see picture at TRANSPORT

helium /'hi:liəm/ n [U] a gas that is lighter than air

he'll /il, hil; strong hi:l/ the short form of 'he will' or 'he shall'

hell /hel/ n
1 also **Hell** [U] the place where some people believe bad people go when they die
2 [singular,U] a very difficult or unpleasant situation or experience: He **made** my **life hell**. | She's **been through hell** this last year.
3 spoken used when you are surprised or angry, or to emphasize what you are saying. Some people consider this use offensive: Oh hell! I've lost my keys. | **what/why/where etc the hell?** Where the hell have you been?
4 a/one hell of a sth informal used to emphasize that something or someone is very bad or good: The room was a hell of a mess. | It was one hell of a party!
5 like hell informal very much, very fast etc: It hurt like hell. | He ran like hell.
6 the sb/sth from hell informal used to say that someone or something is the worst you can imagine: the teenager from hell
7 (just) for the hell of it spoken for fun, not for any other reason: He stole things just for the hell of it.
8 all hell broke loose informal used to say that people suddenly became very noisy or angry

hell-'bent adj [not before noun] very determined to do something, especially something that other people do not approve of: **hell-bent on (doing) sth** young people who are hell-bent on having a good time

hellish /'helɪʃ/ adj informal extremely bad or difficult: I've had a hellish day at work. —**hellishly** adv

hello /hə'ləʊ, he- $ -'loʊ/ also **hallo, hullo** BrE
1 spoken used as a greeting when you meet someone or start speaking on the telephone: Hello, how are you? | Hello, can I speak to Paul please?

> **COMMUNICATION**
>
> **saying hello**
> **hi** informal
> **hiya** informal
> **how are you?/how's it going?**
> **good morning/afternoon/evening**
> **pleased/good/nice to meet you**
> **how do you do?** formal – only use this when you meet someone for the first time
> → GOODBYE, INTRODUCE

2 say hello to have a quick conversation with someone: I just called to say hello.

helm /helm/ n [C] **1 at the helm** in charge of something: There's a new manager at the helm. **2** the wheel or control that guides a boat

helmet /'helmɪt/ n [C] a hard hat that protects your head: a motorcycle helmet

help[1] /help/ v [I,T]
1 to make it easier for someone to do something, especially by doing something for them: How can I help? | **help sb (to) do sth** I helped him clear the table. | a course that helps students to develop confidence | **help sb with sth** Dad helped me with my homework. | **help (to) do sth** A good diet can help prevent heart disease. | **help sb up/across etc sth** (=help someone go somewhere) She helped her grandmother across the road.

give sb a hand (with sth) – to help someone, especially by carrying or lifting things: *Can you give me a hand moving these boxes?*
lend a hand (with sth) – to help someone, especially when there are not enough people to do something: *I went over to see if I could lend a hand.*

2 to improve a situation: *Crying won't help.* | **+to** *It helped to know that I had someone to talk to.*
3 sb can't help (doing) sth used to say that someone cannot stop doing or feeling something: *'Stop biting your nails.' 'I can't help it.'* | **can't help feeling/thinking/wondering** *I couldn't help feeling a bit jealous.*
4 help yourself (to sth) to take something when you want it, especially food that is offered to you: *Help yourself to more cake.*
5 Help! *spoken* used to call someone when you are in danger

help out *phr v* to help someone when they are busy or have problems: **+with** *My Mum helps out with the kids.* | **help sb ⇔ out** *Thanks for helping me out.*

help² *n*
1 [U] things someone does that make it easier for someone else: *Thanks for all your help.* | **+with** *Do you want any help with the cooking?* | *a place where students can* **get help**
2 [singular,U] someone or something that is useful and makes it easier for you to do something: *The instructions weren't much help.* | **with the help of sth** *We got there with the help of a map.* | **be a (great/big etc) help (to sb)** *Annie was a great help.* | **be of some/great/no etc help (to sb)** *Let me know if I can be of any help to you.*
→ SELF-HELP

helper /'helpə $ -ər/ *n* [C] someone who helps another person
helpful /'helpfəl/ *adj* **1** useful: *helpful advice* | *It's helpful to talk about it.* **2** willing to help: *The staff were very helpful.* —**helpfully** *adv* —**helpfulness** *n* [U]
helping /'helpɪŋ/ *n* [C] an amount of food for one person: *a generous helping of pasta*
'helping ,verb *n* [C] an AUXILIARY VERB
helpless /'helpləs/ *adj* unable to look after or defend yourself: *a helpless victim* —**helplessly** *adv* —**helplessness** *n* [U]
helpline /'helplaɪn/ *n* [C] a telephone number you can call for advice or information
hem¹ /hem/ *n* [C] the edge of a piece of clothing that is turned under and sewn down
hem² *v* **hemmed, hemming**
hem sb/sth ⇔ in *phr v* to surround someone or something closely: *a street hemmed in by tall buildings*
hemisphere /'hemɪsfɪə $ -fɪr/ *n* [C] one half of the Earth: *the northern hemisphere* → see picture at GLOBE
hemophilia /ˌhiːmə'fɪliə/ *n* the American spelling of HAEMOPHILIA
hemorrhage /'hemərɪdʒ/ *n* the American spelling of HAEMORRHAGE
hemorrhoids /'hemərɔɪdz/ *n* the American spelling of HAEMORRHOIDS
hemp /hemp/ *n* [U] a plant used to make rope and to produce the drug CANNABIS

hen /hen/ *n* [C] an adult female bird, especially a chicken
hence /hens/ *adv formal* **1** for this reason: *Her family are Welsh – hence the accent.* **2 two weeks/six months etc hence** two weeks, six months etc from now
henceforth /ˌhens'fɔːθ, 'hensfɔːθ $ -ɔːrθ/ also **henceforward** /-'fɔːwəd $ -'fɔːrwərd/ *adv formal* from this time
henchman /'hentʃmən/ *n* [C] plural **henchmen** /-mən/ someone who supports a powerful person and is willing to do illegal things for them
'hen ,party also **'hen night** *n* [C] *BrE informal* a party for women only, that happens before one of them gets married → see box at PARTY
henpecked /'henpekt/ *adj* a man who is henpecked is always being told what to do by his wife
hepatitis /ˌhepə'taɪtɪs/ *n* [U] a disease of the LIVER that makes your skin yellow
her /ə, hə; *strong* hɜː $ ər, hər; *strong* hɜːr/ *determiner, pron*
1 belonging or relating to a woman or girl who has already been mentioned: *That's her new car.* | *She makes all her own clothes.*
2 used when talking about a woman or girl who has already been mentioned: *Chris saw her last week.*
herald¹ /'herəld/ *v* [T] **1** to be a sign that something is going to happen soon: *flowers heralding the start of spring* **2** to publicly praise someone or something: *be heralded as sth The event was heralded as a great success.*
herald² *n* **herald of sth** *literary* a sign that something will happen soon: *dark clouds – the heralds of another storm*
herb /hɜːb $ ɜːrb, hɜːrb/ *n* [C] a plant used to improve the taste of food, or to make medicine —**herbal** *adj: herbal remedies*
herbivore /'hɜːbɪvɔː $ 'hɜːrbɪvɔːr, 'ɜːr-/ *n* [C] an animal that only eats plants [➡ carnivore] —**herbivorous** /hɜː'bɪvərəs $ hɜːr-, ɜːr-/ *adj*
herd¹ /hɜːd $ hɜːrd/ *n* [C] a large group of animals of one type: **+of** *a herd of cows* → see box at GROUP
herd² *v* [T] to make people or animals move somewhere in a large group: **herd sb into sth** *We were herded into a small room.*
here /hɪə $ hɪr/ *adv*
1 in, to, or from this place: *I've lived here all my life.* | *Come here, please.* | **up/down/in/out here** *It's very cold out here.* | **2 miles/6 kilometres etc from here** *The hospital's about 5 miles from here.*
2 used when you are giving or showing something to someone: *Here, have my chair.* | **here is/are sth** *Here's the money you lent me.* | *Here are some photos of John.* | **here you are/go** *'Here you go.' John handed her a drink.*
3 here and there in several different places: *He added a few details here and there.*
4 at this point in a process or discussion: *Spring will soon be here.* | *The subject is too difficult to explain here.*
5 used when you suddenly see or find someone or something: *Look, here's Jane!* | **here you are/here he is etc** *Here you are – where have you been?* | **here we are** (=used

H

when you finally arrive somewhere) *Here we are – home at last.*

6 here's to sb/sth *spoken* used to wish someone success, especially while you have a drink together: *Here's to your new job!*

7 here goes also **here we go** used when you are going to do something and are not sure whether you will succeed: *Ready? OK, here goes.*

hereabouts /ˌhɪərə'baʊts, 'hɪərəbaʊts $ 'hɪr,-'hɪr-/ *adv* near the place where you are: *We all live hereabouts.*

hereafter /ˌhɪər'ɑːftə $ ˌhɪr'æftər/ *adv formal* from this time

hereby /ˌhɪə'baɪ, 'hɪəbaɪ $ ˌhɪr-,'hɪr-/ *adv formal* as a result of this statement

hereditary /hɪ'redɪtəri $ -teri/ *adj* a hereditary quality or disease passes from a parent to a child before the child is born

heredity /hɪ'redɪti/ *n* [U] the process by which physical or mental qualities pass from a parent to a child

herein /ˌhɪər'ɪn $ ˌhɪr-/ *adv formal* in this place, situation, document etc

heresy /'herɪsi/ *n* [C,U] plural **heresies** a belief that is different from the official beliefs of a particular religion

heretic /'herɪtɪk/ *n* [C] someone who is considered immoral or evil because of their beliefs —**heretical** /hɪ'retɪkəl/ *adj*

heritage /'herɪtɪdʒ/ *n* [singular,U] the traditional customs, buildings, arts etc that are important to a country: *our national heritage*

hermit /'hɜːmɪt $ 'hɜːr-/ *n* [C] someone who prefers to live away from other people

hernia /'hɜːniə $ 'hɜːr-/ *n* [C] a medical condition in which an organ pushes through the muscles that should cover it

hero /'hɪərəʊ $ 'hɪroʊ/ *n* [C] plural **heroes**

1 a man who is admired for doing something very brave or good [➡ **heroine**]: **national/local hero** *He became the world champion and a national hero.* | **-of** *a hero of the Great War*

2 the man who is the main character in a book, film, play etc [➡ **heroine**]

heroic /hɪ'rəʊɪk $ -'roʊ-/ *adj* extremely brave or determined: *India's heroic effort against Australia*

heroics /hɪ'rəʊɪks $ -'roʊ-/ *n* [plural] brave actions or words, often intended to IMPRESS people

heroin /'herəʊɪn $ -roʊ-/ *n* [U] a very strong illegal drug: *heroin addicts*

heroine /'herəʊɪn $ -roʊ-/ *n* [C] **1** a woman who is admired for doing something very brave or good [➡ **hero**] **2** the woman who is the main character in a book, film, play etc [➡ **hero**]

heroism /'herəʊɪzəm $ -roʊ-/ *n* [U] great courage: *acts of heroism*

heron /'herən/ *n* [C] a large bird with long legs and a long beak, that lives near water

herring /'herɪŋ/ *n* [C,U] plural **herring** or **herrings** a small thin silver sea fish

hers /hɜːz $ hɜːrz/ *pron* the POSSESSIVE form of 'she': *That's my car. This is hers.* | **of hers** *Paul is a friend of hers.*

herself /ə'self, hə-; *strong* hɜː- $ ər-, hər-; *strong* hɜːr-/ *pron*

1 the REFLEXIVE form of 'she': *She cut herself on some glass.*

2 used to emphasize that you are talking about a particular woman or girl: *She's leaving – she told me so herself.*

3 (all) by herself alone or without help from anyone: *Katy lives by herself.* | *She painted the house all by herself.*

4 have sth (all) to herself to not have to share something: *Alison had the house to herself that night.*

5 not be/feel/seem herself to not feel well or not behave in the usual way

he's /iz, hiz; *strong* hiːz/ the short form of 'he is' or 'he has': *He's my brother.* | *He's lost his keys.*

hesitant /'hezɪtənt/ *adj* uncertain about what to do or say, for example because you are nervous: *a hesitant smile* | **hesitant about (doing) sth** *She was hesitant about joining the group.* —**hesitantly** *adv*

hesitate /'hezɪteɪt/ *v* [I]

1 to pause before doing or saying something because you are nervous or not sure: *She hesitated before answering.* | **+over/about** *He hesitated over whether to follow her.*

2 don't hesitate to do sth used to encourage someone to do something and not worry about offending anyone: *Don't hesitate to call if you need any help.*

hesitation /ˌhezɪ'teɪʃən/ *n* [C,U] when you hesitate: **without hesitation** *He agreed without hesitation.* | **I have no hesitation in** *recommending him for the job* (=I am very willing to recommend him).

heterogeneous /ˌhetərəʊ'dʒiːniəs $ -roʊ-/ also **heterogenous** /ˌhetə'rɒdʒənəs< $ -'rɑː-/ *adj formal* having parts or members that are very different from each other

heterosexual /ˌhetərə'sekʃuəl◁/ *adj* sexually attracted to people of the opposite sex [➡ **bisexual, homosexual**] —**heterosexual** *n* [C]

het up /ˌhet 'ʌp/ *adj* [not before noun] *BrE informal* anxious or upset: **+about/over** *There's no point in getting het up about it.*

hexagon /'heksəgən $ -gɑːn/ *n* [C] a flat shape with six sides —**hexagonal** /hek'sægənəl/ *adj*

hey /heɪ/ *spoken* used to get someone's attention or to show you are surprised or annoyed: *Hey! Look who's here!*

heyday /'heɪdeɪ/ *n* [C] the time when someone or something was most popular or successful: **in sb's/sth's heyday** *a photo of Greta Garbo in her heyday*

HGV /ˌeɪtʃ dʒiː 'viː/ *n* [C] *BrE* heavy goods vehicle a large truck

hi /haɪ/ *spoken informal* hello: *Hi! How are you?*

hiatus /haɪ'eɪtəs/ *n* [singular] *formal* a short pause

hibernate /'haɪbəneɪt $ -ər-/ *v* [I] if an animal hibernates, it sleeps through the winter —**hibernation** /ˌhaɪbə'neɪʃən $ -bər-/ *n* [U]

hiccup¹, hiccough /'hɪkʌp, -kəp/ *n* [C] **1** (usually plural) if you get hiccups, you make short sounds in your throat that you cannot control: *I've got the hiccups.* **2** a small problem: *a hiccup in the negotiations*

hiccup² *v* [I] **hiccupped, hiccupping** to have hiccups

hidden /'hɪdn/ adj difficult to see or find: *hidden cameras*

hide¹ /haɪd/ past tense **hid** /hɪd/ past participle **hidden** /'hɪdn/ present participle **hiding** v

hide

1 [T] to put something or someone in a place so that they are difficult to see: **hide sth in/under/behind etc** *Jane hid the presents under the bed.* | **hide sb/sth from sb** *She had to hide her children from the soldiers.* | *She keeps sweets hidden in her desk.*

2 [I] if you hide, you go to a place where no one can see you or find you [→ **hiding**]: **+in/under/behind etc** *The rebels hid in caves.* | **+from** *He was hiding from the police.*

3 [T] if you hide a fact or feeling, you keep it secret: *She laughed to hide her embarrassment.* | *He had **hidden the fact that** he was married.* | **hide sth from sb** *She tried to hide the truth from us.*

4 [T] to cover something so that it cannot be seen clearly: *Clouds hid the sun.*

hide² n **1** [C,U] the skin of an animal, used for making leather **2** [C] *BrE* a small building where you hide in order to watch wild animals [= **blind** *AmE*]

hide-and-'seek *BrE*; **hide-and-go-'seek** *AmE* n [U] a game in which a child tries to find other children who are hiding

hideaway /'haɪdəweɪ/ n [C] a place where you can go to be alone

hideous /'hɪdiəs/ adj very ugly or unpleasant: *a hideous building* —**hideously** adv

hideout /'haɪdaʊt/ n [C] a place where you can hide

hiding /'haɪdɪŋ/ n [U] if someone is in hiding, they are in a secret place because they do not want anyone to find them: *Some men **went into hiding** to avoid conscription.*

hierarchy /'haɪrɑːki $ -ɑːr-/ n plural **hierarchies** **1** [C,U] a system of organizing people or things according to their importance **2** [C] the most powerful members of an organization: *the church hierarchy* —**hierarchical** /haɪˈrɑːkɪkəl $ -ɑːr-/ adj

hieroglyphics /ˌhaɪrəˈɡlɪfɪks/ n [plural] a writing system that uses pictures to represent ideas

hi-fi /'haɪ faɪ, ˌhaɪ 'faɪ/ n [C] plural **hi-fis** *old-fashioned* a piece of equipment used to play recorded music [= **stereo**]

high¹ /haɪ/ adj

1 tall, or a long way above the ground [→ **tall**, **height**]: *a high mountain* | *high buildings* | *How high is the Eiffel tower?* | *Look how **high up** the windows are.* | **100 metres/30 ft etc high** *a wall 5 metres high* | **knee-/chest- etc high** (=reaching from the ground to your knees, chest etc) *The grass was **waist-high**.* | *a woman in*

high-heels (=shoes with high heels) → see box at **TALL**

2 greater than usual: *Petrol prices are quite high at the moment.* | *a **high temperature*** | *a **high speed** train* | *The caves are not safe at **high tide*** (=when the sea is at a high level). | *I have a **high opinion** of her* (=a good opinion). → see box at **EXPENSIVE**

3 of very good quality [≠ **low**]: *The standard of his work is very high.*

4 more advanced, powerful, or important than other people or things: *He rose to quite a high rank in the Navy.* | *Security is a high priority.*

5 a sound that is high is near the top of the range of sounds that humans can hear [≠ **low**]: *I couldn't sing the very high notes.* | *a **high-pitched** scream*

6 [not before noun] *informal* someone who is high is behaving strangely because they have taken drugs: **+on** *They were all high on cocaine.*

7 **high in sth** containing a lot of something: *foods that are high in fat*

8 **begin/end/finish on a high note** to begin, end etc very successfully

high² adv

1 at or to a level that is a long way from the ground [≠ **low**]: **+above/up** *I could see a plane high up in the sky.* | *She held the trophy high above her head.*

2 at or to a value, amount, or level that is above the normal one [≠ **low**]: *Prices are expected to go even higher.*

3 **high and low** everywhere: *I've **searched high and low** for my keys.*

high³ n [C] **1** the greatest price, level etc that has been recorded: *Last month temperatures reached **an all-time high*** (=the highest that has ever been known). **2** *informal* a feeling of great happiness: *She's **been on a high** since meeting Joe.* | *the **highs and lows** of a Hollywood career*

highbrow /'haɪbraʊ/ adj *a highbrow book, film etc is very serious and difficult to understand*

highchair /ˌhaɪˈtʃeə $ 'haɪtʃer/ n [C] a special tall chair for a young child to sit in while eating

high-'class adj of very good quality: *a high-class restaurant*

High 'Court n [singular] a court of law that can change the decisions made in a lower court

higher edu'cation n [U] education at a college or university rather than a school [→ **further education**]

high-'flyer n [C] someone who is very successful in their job or studies

high-'handed adj using your authority in an unreasonable way: *I didn't like her high-handed manner.*

'high jump n [singular] **1** a sport in which you jump over a high bar **2** **be for the high jump** *BrE informal* if someone is for the high jump, they will be punished for something that they have done

highlands /'haɪləndz/ n [plural] an area of a country where there are a lot of mountains: *the Scottish highlands*

high-'level adj [only before noun] involving people with a lot of power or importance: *high-level peace talks*

highlight¹ /'haɪlaɪt/ v [T] **1** to make a subject or problem noticeable so that people will pay attention to it: *The chief of police* **highlighted** *the* **problem** *of car theft.* **2** to mark words on paper or on a computer SCREEN, using a colour so that they are noticed more easily

highlight² *n* [C] **1** the most important, interesting, or enjoyable part of something: **+of** *the highlights of today's cricket* **2 highlights** [plural] parts of someone's hair that have been made a lighter colour than the rest

highlighter /'haɪlaɪtə $ -ər/ also **'highlighter pen** *n* [C] a thick coloured pen, used to mark words on paper

highly /'haɪli/ *adv*

1 very: *a highly successful businessman* | *a highly intelligent woman* | *It is highly unlikely that he will pass the test.*
2 to a very good level or standard: *a highly skilled builder* | *All our staff are highly trained.*
3 with approval or respect: *She speaks very* **highly of** *your work.*

highly-'strung *BrE*; **high-strung** *AmE adj* nervous and easily upset

Highness /'haɪnɪs/ *n* **Her/His/Your Highness** used to speak to or about a member of a royal family

high-per'formance *adj* [only before noun] a high-performance car, computer, aircraft etc is better and faster than normal ones

high-'pitched *adj* a high-pitched sound is very high

high-'powered *adj* **1** a high-powered machine or piece of equipment is very powerful **2** very important and successful: *a high-powered businessman*

high-'pressure *adj* [only before noun] **1** a high-pressure job or situation is one in which you must work very hard to succeed **2** using a lot of pressure: *a high-pressure water hose*

high-'profile *adj* [only before noun] attracting a lot of public attention: *a high-profile court case*

high-'ranking *adj* having a high position in an organization: *high-ranking officials* → see box at POSITION

'high-rise *adj* [only before noun] high-rise buildings are very tall

'high school *n* **1** [C,U] *AmE* a school in the US and Canada for students between the ages of 14 and 18: *high school graduates* **2** [singular] *BrE* used in the names of some schools for students between the ages of 11 and 18

high-'spirited *adj* having a lot of energy and a sense of fun: *John was in a high-spirited mood.*

'high street *n* [C] *BrE* the main street in a town where the shops and businesses are: **in/on the high street** *A new bookshop has opened on the high street.* | *the high street shops* | *your local high street bank* → see box at ROAD

high-'strung *adj AmE* HIGHLY-STRUNG

high-tech, **hi-tech** /ˌhaɪ 'tek◂ / *adj* using the most modern machines, equipment, and methods: *high-tech weapons* → see box at MODERN

highway /'haɪweɪ/ *n* [C] *AmE* a main road between two cities [➤ **freeway**, **motorway**]

hijack /'haɪdʒæk/ *v* [T] to use violence or threats to take control of a plane or vehicle: *Terrorists tried to hijack the plane in mid-flight.* —**hijacker** *n* [C] —**hijacking** *n* [C,U] *an attempted hijacking*

hike /haɪk/ *v* **1** [I,T] to go for a long walk in the countryside: *Utah is a great place to* **go hiking**. → see box at TRAVEL **2** also **hike up** [T] to increase prices, taxes etc by a large amount —**hike** *n* [C] *a hike across the Malvern Hills* | *4% hike in interest rates*

hiker /'haɪkə $ -ər/ *n* [C] someone who enjoys long walks in the countryside

hilarious /hɪ'leəriəs $ -'ler-/ *adj* very funny: *a hilarious comedy act* → see box at FUNNY —**hilariously** *adv*

hilarity /hɪ'lærᵻti/ *n* [U] *formal* laughter and fun

hill /hɪl/ *n*

1 [C] an area of high land, like a small mountain [➤ **uphill**, **downhill**]: *Their house is on a hill overlooking the sea.* | *We climbed to* **the top of** *the* **hill.** | *The village was on the top of* *a* **steep** *hill.*
2 over the hill *informal* someone who is over the hill is not young and attractive any more

hillside /'hɪlsaɪd/ *n* [C] the sloping part of a hill

hilly /'hɪli/ *adj* having many hills: *a hilly area*

hilt /hɪlt/ *n* **1** [C] the handle of a sword or knife **2 to the hilt** completely: *She'll defend him to the hilt.*

him /ɪm; *strong* hɪm/ *pron* the OBJECT form of 'he': *That's Alan. Do you know him?*

himself /ɪm'self; *strong* hɪm'self/ *pron*

1 the REFLEXIVE form of 'he': *Bill looked at himself in the mirror.* | *Did he enjoy himself at the party?* | **(all) by himself** (=alone or without help) *He lives by himself.* | **(all) to himself** (=for his own use) *At last he had some time to himself.*
2 used to emphasize that you are talking about a particular man or boy: *It was the King himself who opened the door.*
3 not be/feel/seem himself if a man is not himself, he is not behaving or feeling as he usually does

hind /haɪnd/ *adj* [only before noun] relating to the back part of an animal with four legs: *The dog stood up on its* **hind legs**. → see picture on page A2

hinder /'hɪndə $ -ər/ *v* [T] to make it difficult for something to happen: *The bad weather hindered our progress.*

hindrance /'hɪndrəns/ *n* [C] someone or something that makes it difficult for you to do something: **+to** *Marriage would be a hindrance to her career.*

hindsight /'haɪndsaɪt/ *n* [U] the ability to understand a situation only after it has happened: **with hindsight** *With hindsight, I should have warned you to expect trouble.*

Hindu /'hɪnduː, ˌhɪn'duː◂ / *n* [C] plural **Hindus** someone whose religion is Hinduism —**Hindu** *adj*: *a Hindu temple*

Hinduism /'hɪnduː-ɪzəm/ *n* [U] the main religion in India, which includes belief in REINCARNATION

hinge¹ /hɪndʒ/ *n* [C] a piece of metal fastened to a door, lid etc that allows it to swing open or shut

hinge² *v*

hinge on/upon sth *phr v* to depend on something: *The case against him hinged on Laura's evidence.*

hint¹ /hɪnt/ *n* [C] **1** something that you say or do to suggest something to someone without telling them directly: **+about** *Sue has been **dropping hints** about her birthday.* | *He **gave** me some strong **hints** about getting married.* | *If he won't **take a hint** (=understand a hint), you'll have to be honest.* | *Her remark was probably a **subtle hint** for us to leave.* **2** a small amount of something: **+of** *A hint of perfume drifted in the air.* **3** a useful piece of advice [**= tip**]: **+on/about** *He gave us a few **handy hints** (=useful hints) on gardening.*

hint² v [I,T] to suggest something to someone without saying it directly: **+at** *What are you hinting at?* | **+(that)** *Peg has been hinting she wants a baby.*

hinterland /'hɪntəlænd $ -ər-/ n [singular] an area of land that is far from the coast and not near any towns or cities

hip¹ /hɪp/ n [C] one of the two parts on each side of your body between the top of your legs and your waist: *a lady with a broken hip* → see picture on page A3

hip² adj informal modern and fashionable [**= cool**]

'hip-hop n [U] a type of modern popular music with a strong beat that people dance to → see box at MUSIC

hippie /'hɪpi/ n another spelling of HIPPY

hippo /'hɪpəʊ $ -poʊ/ n [C] plural **hippos** informal a hippopotamus

hippopotamus /ˌhɪpə'pɒtəməs $ -'pɑː-/ n [C] plural **hippopotamuses** or **hippopotami** /-maɪ/ a large grey African animal with a big head that lives near water

hippy, hippie /'hɪpi/ n [C] plural **hippies** someone who opposes violence and the values of western society, and believes in peace and love: *the hippies of the 1960s peace movement*

hire¹ /haɪə $ haɪr/ v [T]

1 *BrE* to pay money to borrow something for a short time [**= rent** *AmE*]: *It's best to hire a car when you arrive.*

2 a) to employ someone to do something for a period of time: **hire sb to do sth** *We've hired a childminder to look after Carole.* **b)** *AmE* to employ someone: *He couldn't find anyone who would hire him.*

hire sth ⇔ **out** phr v *BrE* to allow someone to borrow something in return for money: *His company hires out boats to tourists.*

hire² n [U] *BrE* an arrangement to borrow something in exchange for money: *a car hire company* | **for hire** *Are these fishing boats for hire?*

his /ɪz; strong hɪz/ determiner, pron the POSSESSIVE form of 'he': *Leo hates cleaning his room.* | *His own mother refused to see him.* | *Gary brought some friends of his.*

Hispanic /hɪ'spænɪk/ adj from or relating to Spain or Latin America, or the languages spoken there: *New York's Hispanic community* —**Hispanic** n [C]

hiss /hɪs/ v [I] **1** to make a noise that sounds like 'ssss': *Snakes only hiss at you when they're afraid.* → see picture on page A7 **2** to say something in a loud whisper: *'Get out!' she hissed furiously.* —**hiss** n [C]

'hissy ˌfit n [C] informal a sudden moment of unreasonable anger and annoyance

historian /hɪ'stɔːriən/ n [C] someone who studies history

historic /hɪ'stɒrɪk $ -'stɔː-, -'stɑː-/ adj a historic place or event is famous or important in history: *He told journalists it was a **historic** moment.* | *funds to restore Spain's historic monuments*

historical /hɪ'stɒrɪkəl $ -'stɔː-, -'stɑː-/ adj relating to people or things that happened or existed in the past: *a mixture of historical facts and fiction* | *a town of great **historical** interest* —**historically** /-kli/ adv: *a historically significant discovery*

history /'hɪstəri/ n plural **histories**

1 [U] the things that happened or existed in the past: **+of** *the history of post-war Europe* | *the early history of Peru* | **American/Chinese/European etc history** *The war was a turning point in Russian history.* | **recent/modern/ancient etc history** *He's very interested in ancient history.* | *Why don't you do a course on **local history** (=the history of the place where you live)?* | *She's studying **economic history** at university.* | *Venice is a city that **is steeped in history** (=has a long and interesting history).*

2 [singular] all the events in the development of a particular place, activity, institution etc: **+of** *the worst accident in the history of space travel* | *It is the first time this has happened in the college's 90-year history.*

3 [C] a written account of past events: **+of** *She has just written a history of Britain.*

4 [C,U] a record of something that someone has experienced in the past: *They asked about my **medical history**.* | *Does your family **have a history of** heart trouble?*

→ **NATURAL HISTORY**

hit¹ /hɪt/ v past tense and past participle **hit**, present participle **hitting**

1 [T] to touch something or someone roughly, using your hand, a stick etc: *Please don't hit me!* | **hit sb/sth with sth** *He used to hit the kids with a belt.* | *He **hit** the ball as **hard** as he could.* → see picture on page A11

punch – to hit someone hard with your closed hand, especially in a fight: *Steve punched him on the nose.*

slap/smack – to hit someone with the flat part of your hand, especially because you are angry with them: *I felt like slapping his face.* | *Do you agree with smacking children?*

bang/knock – to hit a door, in order to get attention: *Across the road, a policeman was banging on the door.*

2 [T] to move into or against someone or something quickly: **hit sth on/against sth** *I hit my knee on the desk.* | *He was hit in the chest by a stray bullet.*

3 [I,T] to affect someone badly: *His mother's death hit him very hard.* | *A lot of small companies have been hit by the rise in oil prices.*

4 [T] written to reach a particular number or level: *Unemployment hit 2 million last month.*

5 [T] if something hits you, you suddenly notice it or realize it: *The smell of smoke hit me as soon as I came in.* | *It hit me that he'd left me for good this time.*

H

6 [T] to experience a problem: *The business hit a bad patch in the '70s.*
7 hit the headlines to be reported in many newspapers, on television etc
8 hit it off (with sb) *informal* to like someone as soon as you meet them
9 hit the roof/ceiling *informal* to become very angry
10 hit the nail on the head *informal* if someone hits the nail on the head, what they have said is exactly right or true

hit back *phr v* to attack or criticize someone who has attacked or criticized you: **+at** *Yesterday the President hit back at his critics.*
hit on/upon sth *phr v* to suddenly have a good idea: *Phil has hit on a good way of raising money.*
hit out at/against sb/sth *phr v* to criticize someone or something

hit² *n* [C]
1 a very successful and popular film, song, play etc: *The show was a huge hit in London.* | *Which band had a hit with 'Bohemian Rhapsody'?* | *a hit musical* | *his first hit single* → see box at **POPULAR**
2 an occasion when something touches the thing it was aimed at: *The ship took a hit and sank.*
3 a visit to a website: *The site gets 20,000 hits a day.*

,hit-and-'miss also **,hit-or-'miss** *adj* done in a way that is not planned or organized
,hit-and-'run [only before noun] a hit-and-run accident is one in which a car hits someone and the driver does not stop to help
hitch¹ /hɪtʃ/ *v* **1** [I,T] *informal* if you hitch somewhere, you travel there without paying by asking people who are driving past to take you in their vehicle [= hitchhike]: **+across/around/to etc** *We hitched across Europe.* | *They hitched a lift to Paris.* **2** [T] to fasten one thing to another: **hitch sth to sth** *Dad hitched the boat to the car.* **3** also **hitch up** [T] to pull up a piece of clothing you are wearing: *She hitched her skirt above her knees.*
hitch² *n* [C] a small problem: *a couple of small technical hitches* | **without a hitch** *The concert went off without a hitch.* → see box at **PROBLEM**
hitchhike /'hɪtʃhaɪk/ *v* [I] to travel to places without paying by asking people who are driving past to take you in their vehicle [= hitch]: **+across/around etc** *They hitchhiked around France.* —**hitchhiker** *n* [C] *A hitchhiker raised his thumb as we approached.* —**hitchhiking** *n* [U]
hi-tech /ˌhaɪ'tek◂/ *adj* another spelling of HIGH-TECH → see box at **MODERN**
hitherto /ˌhɪðə'tuː◂ $ -ər-/ *adv formal* until now
'hit list *n* [C] *informal* a list of people or organizations that someone intends to harm: **on sb's hit list** *He says he's on the terrorists' hit list.*
'hit man *n* [C] *informal* a criminal who is employed to kill someone
HIV /ˌeɪtʃ aɪ 'viː◂/ *n* [U] a VIRUS that can develop into the disease AIDS
hive /haɪv/ *n* **1** also **beehive** [C] a wooden box where BEES are kept **2 a hive of activity/industry** *BrE* a place where everyone is busy
hiya /'haɪjə/ *spoken informal* used to say hello

h'm, hmm /m, hm/ a sound that expresses doubt or disagreement
HMS /ˌeɪtʃ em es/ *n* His/Her Majesty's Ship used before the name of a ship in the British navy: *HMS Sheffield*
hoard /hɔːd $ hɔːrd/ *n* [C] a set of things that someone hides so that they can use them later: **+of** *a hoard of gold* —**hoard** *v* [T] *She had hoarded the money she inherited.*
hoarding /'hɔːdɪŋ $ 'hɔːr-/ *n* [C] *BrE* a large board fixed to the side of a building, used to show advertisements [= billboard]
hoarse /hɔːs $ hɔːrs/ *adj* if you or your voice is hoarse, you speak in a low rough voice —**hoarsely** *adv*
hoax /həʊks $ hoʊks/ *n* [C] a false warning about something: *a bomb hoax* | *The police received over 300 hoax calls* (=telephone calls giving false warnings).
hob /hɒb $ hɑːb/ *n* [C] *BrE* the top of a COOKER → see picture at **KITCHEN**
hobble /'hɒbəl $ 'hɑː-/ *v* [I] to walk with difficulty: *He hobbled across the kitchen.*
hobby /'hɒbi $ 'hɑː-/ *n* [C] plural **hobbies** an activity that you enjoy in your free time: *My hobbies are gardening and reading.*
hobo /'həʊbəʊ $ 'hoʊboʊ/ *n* [C] plural **hobos** *AmE informal* someone without a home or job [= tramp *BrE*]
hockey /'hɒki $ 'hɑːki/ *n* [U] **1** *BrE* a game played on grass between two teams who use long curved sticks to hit a ball [= field hockey *AmE*] **2** *AmE* a game played on ice in which two teams use long sticks to hit a PUCK (=a hard flat object) [= ice hockey *BrE*]
hodgepodge /'hɒdʒpɒdʒ $ 'hɑːdʒpɑːdʒ/ *n* [singular] *AmE informal* a lot of different things mixed up together [= hotchpotch *BrE*]
hoe /həʊ $ hoʊ/ *n* [C] a garden tool with a long handle that you use to prepare soil before you plant things —**hoe** *v* [I,T]
hog¹ /hɒg $ hɑːg, hɔːg/ *n* **1** [C] *AmE* a large pig **2 go the whole hog** *informal* to do something very thoroughly: *Let's go the whole hog and have champagne.*
hog² *v* [T] **hogged, hogging** *informal* to use something yourself when you should share it: *How much longer are you going to hog the bathroom?*
hoist¹ /hɔɪst/ *n* [C] a piece of equipment used to lift heavy things [= crane]
hoist² *v* [T] to lift something heavy
hold¹ /həʊld $ hoʊld/ *v* past tense and past participle **held** /held/
1 [T] to have something in your hands: **hold sb/sth in your hands/arms** *She held a baby in her arms.* | *two lovers holding hands* (=holding each other's hands) | **hold sb/sth close/tightly etc** *He held her tightly.* → see picture on page A11

THESAURUS

grip: *I gripped the rail and tried not to look down.*
clutch: *a child clutching a bag of sweets*
catch/take/keep/get hold of sth – to take something in your hands and hold it tightly: *Catch hold of the rope and pull.*
grab (hold of sth)/seize – to take hold of

someone or something suddenly or violently: *He grabbed the bag and ran.*

2 [T] to make something stay in a particular position: **hold sth up/out etc** *He held out his hand in greeting.* | *The police tried to hold the crowd back.* | *We used a brick to **hold** the door open.* | *I used glue to **hold** the photos **in place**.*
3 [T] to have a meeting, ceremony, election etc: *The President will hold talks with the Russian leader.*
4 [T] to have or possess something: *Do you hold a British passport?* | *Sheila held the post of Director for three years.* | *Who holds the world record?*
5 [T] to keep something so that it can be used or made available later: *We can hold your flight reservations for three days.* | *Our records are held on computer.*
6 [T] to keep someone in a place so they cannot leave: **hold sb prisoner/hostage/captive** *A journalist is being held hostage.*
7 [T] to have enough space to contain a particular amount: *The hall holds up to 800 guests.*
8 [I,T] to be strong enough to support something: *The bridge might not hold our weight.*
9 hold an opinion/view *formal* to have an opinion: *I hold the view that all children should learn a foreign language.*
10 hold sb responsible/liable (for sth) to believe that someone is responsible for something: *The retailer will be held responsible for any faults in the product.*
11 hold it/hold on *spoken* used to tell someone to wait: *Hold on a minute, I'm just coming!*
12 [I] also **hold the line** if you ask someone on the telephone to hold, you are asking them to wait until the person they want to speak to is available
13 hold sb's attention/interest to make someone feel interested: *She didn't manage to hold the children's interest.*
14 [I] if something still holds, it is still true: *Does your invitation for lunch still hold?*
15 hold your breath to deliberately not breathe for a short time
16 hold your fire to not attack or criticize someone, when you had planned to
17 hold your own (against sb) to be as good at something as other people
18 not hold water if a reason or argument does not hold water, it does not seem true or reasonable
19 be left holding the baby *BrE* **be left holding the bag** *AmE* if you are left holding the baby, you have to deal with a difficult situation alone
→ **hold sb to ransom** at RANSOM

hold sth against sb *phr v* to not forgive someone for something they did in the past

hold sb/sth ⇔ **back** *phr v* **1** to stop yourself from showing a particular feeling: *She struggled to hold back the tears.* **2** to prevent someone from being successful or making progress

hold sth ⇔ **down** *phr v* **1** to keep something at a low level: *We are holding down prices until 2004.* **2 hold down a job** to manage to remain in a job for a period of time: *He's never held down a job for more than a month.*

hold off *phr v* **1** to delay doing something: **hold off doing sth** *We held off making a*

decision. **2 hold sb** ⇔ **off** to prevent someone from attacking you or coming near you: *Police held off reporters while the singer left the hall.*

hold on *phr v* **1** *spoken* to wait for a short time: *Hold on, I won't be long.* **2** to manage in a difficult or dangerous situation: *They had to hold on until the rescue team arrived.*

hold onto sth *phr v* to keep something and not give it to anyone: *Most investors are holding onto their shares.*

hold out *phr v* **1** to continue to defend yourself or refuse to do something: **+against** *The rebels held out against the army for three weeks.* **2** if a supply of something holds out, there is some left: *Water supplies won't hold out much longer.*

hold out for sth *phr v* to refuse to accept less than you asked for: *Workers are holding out for more money.*

hold over sb *phr v* to use secret information that you have about someone to control or threaten them

hold sb to sth *phr v* to make someone do what they promised: *He offered to help, and I'm going to hold him to it.*

hold together *phr v* if a group holds together, or if something holds it together, it stays strong and united: **hold sth** ⇔ **together** *It's the bad times that have held this family together.*

hold up sb/sth *phr v* **1 hold sb/sth** ⇔ **up** to delay someone or something: *Sorry we're late – we were held up in traffic.* **2** to try to steal money from a shop, bank etc by threatening someone: *The clerk is recovering after he was held up at gunpoint.*

hold² n

1 [singular,U] the action of holding something with your hand [= grip]: **+on/of** *I kept a tight hold on the fence.* | *Keep hold of my hand as we cross.* | *I took hold of her arm.*
2 get hold of sb/sth to find someone or get something: *I need to get hold of Graham quickly.* | *Drugs are easy to get hold of.*
3 [singular] control, power, or influence over someone or something: **+over** *He seemed to have a hold over her.* | *He had learned to keep a tight hold on his emotions.*
4 on hold a) if something is on hold, it is delayed and may not take place until later: *The project has been put on hold.* **b)** if you are on hold, you are waiting to speak to someone on the telephone: *I hate the music they play when they put you on hold.*
5 take (a) hold to start to have a definite effect: *Once the disease takes hold, it's difficult to treat.*
6 [C] the part of a ship or aircraft where goods are stored

holdall /ˈhəʊldɔːl $ ˈhoʊldɒːl/ *n* [C] *BrE* a bag for clothes, tools, or sports equipment [= carryall *AmE*] → see picture at BAG¹

holder /ˈhəʊldə $ ˈhoʊldər/ *n* [C] **1** someone who has something: **+of** *the holder of the world record* | *The concert is for ticket holders only.* **2** something that holds an object: *a candle holder*

holding /ˈhəʊldɪŋ $ ˈhoʊl-/ *n* [C] a part of a company that someone owns

H

holdover /ˈhəʊldˌəʊvə $ ˈhoʊldˌoʊvər/ *n* [C]
AmE an action, feeling, or idea that has continued from the past into the present [= **hang-over**]

'hold-up *n* [C] **1** a delay, especially one caused by traffic: *There was a hold-up on the way to the office.* **2** when people try to steal money from a shop or bank, using a gun

hole¹ /həʊl $ hoʊl/ *n* [C]

1 an empty space: **+in** *There's a hole in my shoe.* | *They climbed through a hole in the fence.* | *You'll need to* **dig** *a nice big* **hole.** | *These socks are* **full of holes.**
2 in golf, one of the holes that you try to hit the ball into
3 a hole in the ground that an animal lives in
4 if there is a hole in something, it is not right, usually because something or someone is missing: **+in** *His death left a big hole in her life.* | *Their theory is* **full of holes.**
5 *informal* an unpleasant place
6 *informal* a difficult situation: *We're in a bit of a hole now.*
7 make a big hole in sth *informal* to use a large part of something, especially money
8 hole in one when you get the golf ball into the hole with your first hit
➔ **BLACK HOLE**

hole² *v*
hole up also **be holed up** *phr v informal* to hide or be hiding somewhere

,hole-in-the-'wall *n* [C] *BrE informal* a machine from which you can obtain money, using a special card [= **ATM, cash machine**]

holiday¹ /ˈhɒlɪdi, -deɪ $ ˈhɑːlɪˌdeɪ/ *n*

1 [C,U] *BrE* also **holidays** a period when you rest and do not go to work or school [= **vacation** *AmE*]: *I really need a holiday.* | **on holiday** *I'm on holiday this week.* | *the* **school holidays**
2 [C,U] *BrE* also **holidays** a period when you travel to another place for pleasure [= **vacation** *AmE*]: *Did you enjoy your holidays?* | **on holiday** *They're on holiday in Greece.* | *We're* **going on holiday** *next week.* | *a camping holiday*
3 [C] a day on which people do not have to go to work or school: *Monday's a* **public holiday.**
➔ **BANK HOLIDAY, NATIONAL HOLIDAY**

holiday² *v* [I] *BrE* to go somewhere for a holiday [= **vacation** *AmE*]: *The couple are holidaying in Majorca.*

'holiday-,maker *n* [C] *BrE* someone who goes to a place for a holiday [= **vacationer** *AmE*]

holiness /ˈhəʊlinɪs $ ˈhoʊ-/ *n* [U] **1** the quality of being holy **2 Your/His Holiness** a title used for an important religious leader, especially the POPE

holistic /həʊˈlɪstɪk $ hoʊ-/ *adj* considering a person or thing as a whole, rather than as separate parts: *a holistic approach to treating illnesses*

holler /ˈhɒlə $ ˈhɑːlər/ *v* [I,T] *AmE informal* to shout loudly —**holler** *n* [C]

hollow

a hollow tree trunk

a solid rock

hollow¹ /ˈhɒləʊ $ ˈhɑː-/ *adj*

1 having an empty space inside: *a hollow tree* ➔ see box at **EMPTY**
2 having a surface that sinks inwards: *Tears ran down her* **hollow cheeks.**
3 without any meaning or emotion: *His words* **had a hollow ring.** | *They won, but it was a* **hollow victory.**

hollow² *n* [C] an area that is lower than the surrounding surface

hollow³ *v*
hollow sth ⇔ **out** *phr v* to remove the inside of something

holly /ˈhɒli $ ˈhɑːli/ *n* [U] a tree with sharp leaves and red BERRIES, used as a decoration at Christmas

holocaust /ˈhɒləkɔːst $ ˈhɑːləkɔːst/ *n* [C]
1 the Holocaust the killing of Jews and other people by the Nazis during the Second World War **2** a situation in which there is great destruction and death

hologram /ˈhɒləɡræm $ ˈhoʊl-, ˈhɑːl-/ *n* [C] a picture made with a LASER, which looks as if it is not flat

holster /ˈhəʊlstə $ ˈhoʊlstər/ *n* [C] a container for a gun that someone wears

holy /ˈhəʊli $ ˈhoʊ-/ *adj*
1 connected with God or religion: *the holy city of Jerusalem* | *a holy war*
2 very religious: *a holy man*

homage /ˈhɒmɪdʒ $ ˈhɑː-/ *n* [U] something you do or say to show respect for a person or achievement: *With this memorial, we* **pay homage to** *those who defended us.*

home¹ /həʊm $ hoʊm/ *n*

1 [C,U] the house or flat where you live: **at home** *I stayed at home all evening.* | **away from home** *He was away from home for six weeks.* | *He* **left home** (=stopped living with his family) *when he was 15.*
2 [C,U] the area or country that you come from or that you usually live in: *She's* **made** *Charleston her* **home.**
3 be/feel at home to feel comfortable somewhere, or feel confident doing something: *He seemed very at home using the computer.* | *They always try to* **make** *their guests* **feel at home.**
4 the home of sth the place where something comes from, or which is famous for something: *Chicago is known as the home of the blues.*
5 make yourself at home *spoken* used to tell someone to relax when they are visiting your home

6 [C] a place where people live and are looked after, for example old people or children who have no parents

7 at home a) at the place where a team usually plays [≠ **away**]: *Barcelona lost 2–0 at home.* **b)** in someone's own country, not in other countries: *He is popular at home and abroad.*

→ MOBILE HOME, NURSING HOME, REST HOME, STATELY HOME

home² *adv*

1 to or at the place where you live: *Mike got home* (=arrived home) *at five o'clock.* | *I want to go home.* | **+from** *Is Mum home from work?*
2 take home £120/$600 etc used to say how much someone earns, not counting the money which is kept for tax: *I take home about $200 a week.*
3 bring/drive sth home to make someone understand or realize something
4 be home and dry *BrE* to have succeeded in doing something

home³ *adj* [only before noun] **1** connected with your home or family: *Their home life isn't very good.* | *good old-fashioned home cooking* **2** playing at your team's own sports field [≠ **away**]: *The home team won.* | *They have won their last three home games.* **3** relating to a particular country, as opposed to foreign countries: *Most of their sales are in the home market.*
4 home truths unpleasant facts about someone or something

home⁴ *v*

home in on sth *phr v* **1** to move directly towards something **2** to give all your attention to something

homecoming /'həʊm,kʌmɪŋ $ 'hoʊm-/ *n* [C] when someone comes home after a long absence

home eco'nomics *n* [U] *old-fashioned* the study of cooking, sewing, and other skills used at home

homegrown /,həʊm'grəʊn‹ $,hoʊm'groʊn‹/ *adj* **1** from your own country or area: *home-grown rock stars* **2** grown in your own garden: *homegrown vegetables*

homeland /'həʊmlænd, -lənd $ 'hoʊm-/ *n* [C] **1** the country where you were born **2** an area with its own system of government

homeless /'həʊmləs $ 'hoʊm-/ *adj* **1** without a place to live: *Thousands of people were made homeless.* **2 the homeless** people who do not have a place to live —**homelessness** *n* [U]

homely /'həʊmli $ 'hoʊm-/ *adj* **1** *BrE* pleasant and ordinary in a comfortable way: *The hotel has a warm, homely atmosphere.* **2** *AmE* not very attractive [= **plain** *BrE*]: *his homely appearance*

homemade /,həʊm'meɪd‹ $,hoʊm-/ *adj* made at home: *homemade jam*

homemaker /'həʊm,meɪkə $ 'hoʊm,meɪkər/ *n* [C] *especially AmE* someone who works at home, cooking, cleaning, and looking after children

homeopathy /,həʊmi'ɒpəθi $,hoʊmi'ɑːp-/ *n* [U] a system of medicine in which someone is given very small amounts of a substance that causes their illness —**homeopathic** /,həʊmiə'pæθɪk‹ $,hoʊ-/ *adj* —**homeopath** /'həʊmiə'pæθ $ 'hoʊ-/ *n* [C]

homeowner /'həʊm,əʊnə $ 'hoʊm,oʊnər/ *n* [C] someone who owns their own home

'home-page *n* [C] the first page of a website

home 'run *n* [C] a long hit in baseball, from which you score a point

homesick /'həʊm,sɪk $ 'hoʊm-/ *adj* sad, because you are away from home → see box at SAD

homestead /'həʊmsted, -stᵻd $ 'hoʊm-/ *n* [C] a farm and the land around it

home 'town *especially BrE* also **hometown** /'həʊmtaʊn $ 'hoʊm-/ *especially AmE n* [C] the place where you were born or spent your childhood

homeward /'həʊmwəd $ 'hoʊmwərd/ also **homewards** *BrE adv* towards home: *He drove homewards.* —**homeward** *adj*: *the homeward journey*

homework /'həʊmwɜːk $ 'hoʊmwɜːrk/ *n* [U]
1 work for school that students do at home [→ **housework**]: *I've done all my homework.* | *French/biology/maths etc homework Have we got any maths homework?* → see box at SCHOOL
2 do your homework to prepare for something by getting information about it

homicidal /,hɒmᵻ'saɪdl‹ $,hɑː-/ *adj* likely to murder someone

homicide /'hɒmᵻsaɪd $ 'hɑː-/ *n* [C,U] the crime of killing someone

homogeneous /,həʊmə'dʒiːniəs‹ $,hoʊ-/ also **homogenous** /hə'mɒdʒᵻnəs $ -'mɑː-/ *adj formal* consisting of parts or members that are all the same [→ **heterogeneous**]: *a homogeneous group of students*

homophobia /,həʊmə'fəʊbiə $,hoʊmə'foʊ-/ *n* [U] hatred and fear of homosexuals —**homophobic** *adj*

homosexual /,həʊmə'sekʃuəl, ,hɒmə- $,hoʊ-/ *n* [C] someone who is sexually attracted to people of the same sex; GAY —**homosexual** *adj* —**homosexuality** /,həʊməsekʃu'ælᵻti, ,hɒ- $,hoʊ-/ *n* [U]

hone /həʊn $ hoʊn/ *v* [T] **1** to improve a skill **2** to make a knife or sword sharp

honest /'ɒnᵻst $ 'ɑːn-/ *adj*

1 someone who is honest does not lie, cheat, or steal [≠ **dishonest**]: *He seems a good, honest man.* **2** sincere or telling the true facts about something: *Give me an honest answer.* | *Do you want my honest opinion?* | **+with** *At least he was honest with you.* | **+about** *She was always honest about her feelings.*
3 to be honest (with you) *spoken* used when you are saying what you really think: *To be honest, I think she'll win.*

honestly¹ /'ɒnᵻstli $ 'ɑːn-/ *adv* **1** *spoken* used to emphasize that what you are saying is true: *I honestly don't know.* **2** in an honest way: *She spoke honestly about her problems.*

honestly² *spoken* used when you are surprised and annoyed: *Honestly! What a stupid thing to do!*

honesty /'ɒnᵻsti $ 'ɑːn-/ *n* [U] **1** when someone is honest [≠ **dishonesty**]: *We never doubted his honesty.* **2 in all honesty** *spoken* used to tell someone what you really think is true: *In all honesty, we did make mistakes.*

honey /'hʌni/ n [U] **1** a sweet substance made by BEES, used as food **2** spoken used to talk to someone you love: *Hi, honey!*

honeycomb /'hʌnikəʊm $ -koʊm/ n [C,U] the structure with many cells in which BEES store honey

honeymoon /'hʌnimuːn/ n [C] **1** a holiday after your wedding: **on a honeymoon** *We went to Italy on our honeymoon.* → see box at **WEDDING** **2** also **honeymoon period** a period at the start of a new job or situation, when everyone is happy —**honeymooner** n [C]

honk /hɒŋk $ hɑːŋk, hɔːŋk/ v [I,T] to make a noise using the horn of a car

honor /'ɒnə $ 'ɑːnər/ n the American spelling of HONOUR

honorable /'ɒnərəbəl $ 'ɑːn-/ adj the American spelling of HONOURABLE

honorary /'ɒnərəri $ 'ɑːnəreri/ adj an honorary title, rank, or university degree is given to show respect or admiration for someone

honour¹ BrE; **honor** AmE /'ɒnə $ 'ɑːnər/ n

1 [U] when someone is honest, and behaves in a way that makes people respect and trust them: *He was a **man of honour**.* | *He had a deep **sense of honor**.* | *He wished to protect his family's honour.*

2 [singular, U] something that makes you feel proud and glad: *It's a great **honour** to receive this award.* | *I **had the honour** of meeting the President.* | *Will you **do me the honour** of becoming my wife?*

3 in honour of sb/in sb's honour in order to show respect to someone: *a party given in honour of the prince*

4 in honour of sth in order to celebrate an event

5 [C,U] something that is given to a person to show that people respect them and admire their achievements: *The medal is the highest **honour** that the association can bestow* (=give).

6 Your Honour used to speak to a judge

7 honours [plural] BrE a university degree in which you achieve more than the most basic level: *He graduated with **first-class honours** (=the best possible degree).*

honour² BrE; **honor** AmE v [T] **1** to do what you have agreed or promised to do: *You must **honour** this **agreement**.* | *We intend to **honour** our **commitments**.* **2** to publicly praise someone, or to give them a special title or AWARD for their achievements: **honour sb with sth** *He was honoured with the Nobel Prize for Medicine.* | **honour sb for sth** *They have been honoured for their courage.* **3 be/feel honoured (to do sth)** to feel very proud and glad about something: *I'm very honoured to be here.* **4** to treat someone with special respect: *I was treated like an honored guest.*

honourable BrE; **honorable** AmE /'ɒnərəbəl $ 'ɑːn-/ adj **1** deserving respect: *an honourable tradition* **2** having high moral standards: *an honourable man* —**honourably** adv

hood /hʊd/ n [C] **1** the part of a coat or jacket that you pull up to cover your head **2** AmE the metal cover over the engine on a car [= bonnet BrE] → see picture on page A12 **3** informal especially AmE a HOODLUM

hooded /'hʊdɪd/ adj having or wearing a hood: *a hooded jacket*

hoodlum /'huːdləm/ n [C] especially AmE a violent criminal

hoodwink /'hʊd,wɪŋk/ v [T] to trick someone in a clever way

hoof /huːf $ hʊf, huːf/ n [C] plural **hoofs** or **hooves** /huːvz $ hʊvz, huːvz/ **1** the hard foot of an animal such as a horse or cow → see picture on page A2 **2 on the hoof** BrE if you do something on the hoof, you deal with it when it happens, without any preparation

hook¹ /hʊk/ n [C]

1 a curved piece of metal or plastic, used for hanging things on: *Tom hung his coat on the hook.*

2 a curved piece of metal, for example for catching fish

3 let/get sb off the hook to allow or help someone to get out of a difficult situation

4 off the hook if the telephone is off the hook, the part that you speak into is not in its correct position, and people cannot call you

5 a way of hitting your opponent in BOXING, with your elbow bent: **left/right hook**

hook² v [T] **1** to fasten or hang something onto or around something else: **hook sth onto/to etc sth** *Hook the bucket onto the rope and lower it down.* **2** to bend your finger, arm, or leg around something, so that you are holding or pulling it: **hook sth through/in/over etc sth** *Ruth hooked her arm through Tony's.* **3** to catch a fish: *He hooked a 20-lb salmon.*

hook up phr v **1 hook sb/sth** ⇔ **up** to connect someone or something to a machine or piece of equipment: **+to** *Millions of people are now hooked up to the Internet.* **2** AmE informal if people hook up, they meet, start having a relationship, or start working together: **+with** *He'd just hooked up with Angela.*

hooked /hʊkt/ adj [only before noun] **1** if you are hooked on something, you like it a lot and want to continue doing it: *children who are hooked on computer games* **2** if you are hooked on a drug, you cannot stop using it

hooker /'hʊkə $ -ər/ n [C] especially AmE informal a PROSTITUTE

hooky /'hʊki/ n **play hooky** AmE informal to stay away from school without permission

hooligan /'huːlɪɡən/ n [C] someone who is violent and noisy in public places —**hooliganism** n [U]

hoop /huːp $ hʊp, huːp/ n [C] **1** a large ring made of metal, plastic, or wood: *Throw the ball through the hoop.* **2 jump/go through hoops** to do difficult things before you can do what you want

hooray /hʊˈreɪ/ another spelling of HURRAY

hoot¹ /huːt/ n [C] **1** a shout or laugh that shows you think something is funny or stupid **2 be a hoot** to be very amusing **3 not give a hoot/two hoots** to not care about someone or something **4** the sound made by an OWL **5** the sound made by a vehicle's horn

hoot² v [I,T] **1** to laugh loudly: **+with** *He hooted with laughter.* **2** if an OWL hoots, it makes a loud noise **3** if a vehicle hoots, it makes a loud noise with its horn

Hoover /'huːvə $ -ər/ n [C] trademark BrE a VACUUM CLEANER

hoover v [I,T] BrE to clean the floor with a VACUUM CLEANER

hooves /huːvz $ hʊvz, huːvz/ n a plural of HOOF

hop¹ /hɒp $ hɑːp/ v [I] **hopped**, **hopping** **1** informal to move somewhere quickly: +**in/on etc** Hop in and I'll give you a ride. **2 a)** to jump or move on one leg: He hopped from one foot to the other. → see box at JUMP → see pictures at JUMP¹ → and on page A11 **b)** if a bird or animal hops, it moves by jumping along

hop² n [C] **1 catch sb on the hop** to do something when someone is not expecting it **2 a (short) hop** a short journey, especially by plane **3** a short jump, or a jump on one foot **4 hops** [plural] the flowers from which beer is made

hope¹ /həʊp $ hoʊp/ v [I,T]

1 to want something to happen or be true, and to believe that it is possible: +**(that)** I hope you feel better soon. | **hope to do sth** He's hoping to go to Africa next year. | +**for** We're hoping for better weather tomorrow.

2 I hope so spoken used to say that you hope something that has been mentioned happens or is true: 'Will Grandma be there?' 'I hope so.'

3 I hope not spoken used to say that you hope something that has been mentioned does not happen or is not true: 'Do you think it's going to rain?' 'I hope not.'

hope² n

1 [C,U] the feeling of wanting something to happen or be true, and believing that it is possible: +**of** There is no hope of a victory now. | We still **have hope** that he is alive. | a new treatment that has **given hope** to sufferers | We never **lost hope**. | We mustn't **give up hope** yet. | She came **in the hope of** seeing him. | They **have** very **high hopes** for their children.

2 [C,U] a chance that something will happen in the way that you want: **no/not much/little hope (of sth)** There's no hope of getting the money back. | +**that** There's a **faint hope** that he'll recover. | **sb's only/best/last hope** Please help me – you're my only hope.

3 [C] something that you hope will happen: We talked about her **hopes** and **fears** for the future.

hopeful¹ /'həʊpfəl $ 'hoʊp-/ adj **1** believing that something good is likely or possible: +**that** We're hopeful that we can find a solution. **2** making you feel that things will happen in the way that you want: Things don't look very hopeful. —**hopefulness** n [U]

hopeful² n [C usually plural] someone who is hoping to be successful, especially in acting, sports, politics etc

hopefully /'həʊpfəli $ 'hoʊp-/ adv

1 used when you are saying what you hope will happen: Hopefully, I'll be home on Monday.

2 in a hopeful way: 'Is there anything to eat?' he asked hopefully.

hopeless /'həʊpləs $ 'hoʊp-/ adj **1** if something you try to do is hopeless, it is certain to fail: It was a **hopeless task**. **2** very bad and not likely to get better: The situation seemed hopeless. **3** especially BrE informal very bad at doing something: +**at** I'm hopeless at spelling. |

+**with** He's hopeless with machinery. **4** feeling that you have no hope: a hopeless look on her face —**hopelessly** adv

horde /hɔːd $ hɔːrd/ n [C] a very large crowd of people: +**of** hordes of football fans

horizon /hə'raɪzən/ n **1 the horizon** the place where the land or sea seems to meet the sky: **on the horizon** We could see a ship on the horizon. | The sun dropped below the horizon. **2 be on the horizon** to be likely to happen soon **3 horizons** [plural] the limit of your ideas, knowledge, and experience: a trip that will **broaden** your **horizons**

horizontal /ˌhɒrɪ̯ˈzɒntl◂ $ ˌhɑːrɪ̯ˈzɑːntl◂/ adj a horizontal line remains the same distance from the ground or from the bottom of the page [➡ **vertical**] —**horizontally** adv

hormone /'hɔːməʊn $ 'hɔːrmoʊn/ n [C] a chemical in your body —**hormonal** /hɔːˈməʊnəl $ hɔːrˈmoʊ-/ adj

horn /hɔːn $ hɔːrn/ n **1 a)** [C] one of the two hard pointed parts on the heads of cows, goats etc [➡ **antler**] → see picture on page A2 **b)** [U] the substance that animals' horns are made of: ornaments made of rhino horn **2** [C] the thing in a vehicle that you use to make a sound as a warning or signal: He **sounded** his **horn** angrily. **3** [C] a musical instrument made of metal, that you play by blowing

horoscope /'hɒrəskəʊp $ 'hɑːrəskoʊp, 'hɔː-/ n [C] information about your life, according to the stars and PLANETS

horrendous /hɒ'rendəs, hə- $ hɑː-, hɔː-/ adj extremely bad → see box at BAD —**horrendously** adv

horrible /'hɒrɪ̯bəl $ 'hɔː-, 'hɑː-/ adj very unpleasant or upsetting: What a horrible thing to say! | a horrible smell

THESAURUS

Words to describe a horrible taste or smell
nasty: a nasty odour
disgusting: It tastes disgusting.
revolting: What's that revolting smell?
foul: Smoking leaves a foul taste in your mouth.

Words to describe a horrible experience, situation, or feeling
nasty: a nasty shock
terrible: I feel terrible.
awful: an awful headache
dreadful: What a dreadful thing to happen.
→ BAD, NICE

—**horribly** adv: The whole plan had gone horribly wrong.

horrid /'hɒrɪ̯d $ 'hɔː-, 'hɑː-/ adj horrible: Don't be so horrid to your sister. | a horrid smell

horrific /hɒ'rɪfɪk, hə- $ hɔː-, hɑː-/ adj very bad and shocking → see box at BAD —**horrifically** /-kli/ adv

horrified /'hɒrɪ̯faɪd $ 'hɔː-, 'hɑː-/ adj very shocked and upset: She was horrified to see that he was crying.

horrify /'hɒrɪ̯faɪ $ 'hɔː-, 'hɑː-/ v [T] **horrified**, **horrifying**, **horrifies** to make someone feel very shocked and upset —**horrifying** adj

H

horror /ˈhɒrə $ ˈhɔːrər, ˈhɑː-/ n

1 [U] a strong feeling of shock and worry: **in horror** *She stared at him in horror.* | **to sb's horror** *To my horror, I saw he was bleeding.*
2 [C,U] something that is very terrible, shocking, or frightening: +**of** *We soon realized the full horror of the attack.*
3 horror movie/film a film about strange and frightening things → see box at FILM

ˈhorror ˌstory n [C] **1** bad experiences or conditions that you hear about **2** a story about strange and frightening things

horse /hɔːs $ hɔːrs/ n [C] a large animal that people ride and use for pulling things [➡ **pony, equestrian**]: *I've never ridden a horse before.* → see picture at FARM¹ → **dark horse** at DARK¹

horseback /ˈhɔːsbæk $ ˈhɔːrs-/ n **1 on horseback** riding a horse **2 horseback riding** *AmE* the activity of riding a horse [= **horse-riding** *BrE*]

ˌhorse ˈchestnut / $ ˈ. ˌ.-/ n [C] a tree which has large round brown nuts, which cannot be eaten, inside cases with sharp points

ˈhorse-drawn adj pulled by a horse

horseman /ˈhɔːsmən $ ˈhɔːrs-/ n [C] plural **horsemen** /-mən/ a man who rides a horse

horseplay /ˈhɔːspleɪ $ ˈhɔːrs-/ n [U] rough noisy play, with a lot of hitting or pushing

horsepower /ˈhɔːsˌpaʊə $ ˈhɔːrsˌpaʊr/ n [C,U] plural **horsepower** abbreviation *hp* a unit for measuring the power of an engine

ˈhorse-riding n [U] *BrE* the activity of riding a horse [= **horseback riding** *AmE*]

horseshoe /ˈhɔːʃʃuː, ˈhɔːs- $ ˈhɔːr-/ n [C] a curved piece of metal fixed to a horse's foot

horsewoman /ˈhɔːsˌwʊmən $ ˈhɔːrs-/ n [C] plural **horsewomen** /-ˌwɪmɪn/ a woman who rides a horse

horticulture /ˈhɔːtɪ̆ˌkʌltʃə $ ˈhɔːrtɪ̆ˌkʌltʃər/ n [U] the activity or science of growing plants —**horticultural** /ˌhɔːtɪ̆ˈkʌltʃərəl◂ $ ˌhɔːr-/ adj —**horticulturalist** n [C]

hose¹ /həʊz $ hoʊz/ n **1** also **hosepipe** /ˈhəʊzpaɪp $ ˈhoʊz-/ [C,U] *BrE* a long rubber or plastic tube that you use to put water onto fires, gardens etc **2** [U] *AmE* PANTYHOSE

hose² v [T] to pour water over something or someone, using a hose: **hose sth/sb down** *Would you hose down the car for me?*

hosiery /ˈhəʊzjəri $ ˈhoʊʒəri/ n [U] a word for socks, TIGHTS, and STOCKINGS – used in shops

hospice /ˈhɒspɪ̆s $ ˈhɑː-/ n [C] a special hospital for people who are dying

hospitable /ˈhɒspɪtəbəl, hɒˈspɪ- $ hɑːˈspɪ-, ˈhɑːspɪ-/ adj friendly and welcoming to visitors [≠ **inhospitable**] —**hospitably** adv

hospital /ˈhɒspɪtl $ ˈhɑː-/ n [C,U] a building where sick or injured people receive medical treatment: **in hospital** *BrE*/**in the hospital** *AmE*: *Rick's dad is still in hospital.* | *She went to hospital for an X-ray.* | **be/come out of hospital** *Your mother should be out of hospital within three days.* | **be taken/admitted/rushed to hospital** *A man has been admitted to hospital with gunshot wounds.* | **be discharged/released from hospital** (=be allowed to leave hospital)

hospitality /ˌhɒspɪ̆ˈtælɪ̆ti $ ˌhɑː-/ n [U] friendly and welcoming behaviour towards visitors

hospitalize also **-ise** *BrE* /ˈhɒspɪtl-aɪz $ ˈhɑː-/ v **be hospitalized** if someone is hospitalized, they are taken into hospital for treatment

host /həʊst $ hoʊst/ n [C]

1 the person at a party, meal etc who organized it and invited the guests [➡ **hostess**]: *Our host greeted us at the door.*
2 someone who introduces the guests on a television or radio show: *a game show host*
3 a country, city, or organization that provides the space, equipment etc for a special event: **host country/government/city etc** *the host city for the next Olympic Games*
4 a (whole) host of people/things a large number of people or things: *a host of possibilities*
—**host** v [T] *Which country is hosting the next World Cup?*

hostage /ˈhɒstɪdʒ $ ˈhɑː-/ n [C] someone who is kept as a prisoner by an enemy, and may be hurt or killed in order to force other people to do something [➡ **kidnap**]: **take/hold sb hostage** *The group are holding two western tourists hostage.* | *Two days later, the hostages were freed.*

hostel /ˈhɒstl $ ˈhɑː-/ n [C] a cheap place for people to stay when they are away from home, or a place for people who have no home: *a student hostel*

hostess /ˈhəʊstɪ̆s $ ˈhoʊ-/ n [C] **1** the woman at a party, meal etc who organized it and invited the guests [➡ **host**] **2** a woman who introduces the guests on a television or radio show

hostile /ˈhɒstaɪl $ ˈhɑːstl, ˈhɑːstaɪl/ adj **1** unfriendly or angry, and opposed to someone or something: *a hostile crowd* | +**to** *Public opinion was hostile to the war.* **2** used to describe conditions that are difficult to live in: *animals that can survive in such a hostile environment* **3** belonging to an enemy: *hostile territory*

hostility /hɒˈstɪlɪ̆ti $ hɑː-/ n **1** [U] unfriendly feelings or behaviour: +**to/towards** *hostility towards foreigners* **2** [U] strong or angry opposition to something: +**to/towards** *local hostility to the scheme* **3 hostilities** [plural] *formal* fighting in a war: *efforts to end the hostilities in the region*

hot¹ /hɒt $ hɑːt/ adj

1 having a high temperature [≠ **cold**]: *The soup's really hot.* | *the hottest day of the year* | *I was hot and tired after the journey.* | *The bar serves hot food* (=rather than cold). | *a boiling hot day* | *It's hot in here – can I open a window?* | *people who live in hot countries* (=where the weather is very hot) | *The office gets unbearably hot in summer.*

THESAURUS

warm – a little hot, especially in a pleasant way: *a warm summer evening*
humid – having air that feels hot and wet rather than dry: *the humid heat of the Brazilian rainforest*
boiling/baking/scorching hot – extremely hot: *a baking hot weekend in August*
sweltering – hot in a very unpleasant,

uncomfortable way: *the sweltering heat of the desert*
→ COLD¹, WEATHER¹

2 having a burning taste [➡ spicy; ≠ mild]: *a hot curry* → see box at TASTE
3 *informal* very good, popular, exciting, or attractive: *a hot new band* | *His new film is hot stuff.* | *The boys all think she's really hot.* → see box at ATTRACTIVE
4 hot topic/issue a subject that a lot of people are discussing, especially one that causes a lot of disagreement: *Abortion is a hot topic in the US.*
5 hot potato *informal* a difficult subject or problem that no one wants to deal with
6 in the hot seat in an important position and responsible for making difficult decisions
7 hot favourite the person, party etc that most people expect to win
8 in hot pursuit following someone quickly and closely because you want to catch them
→ RED-HOT

hot² *v* hotted, hotting
   hot up *phr v especially BrE informal* if something hots up, there is more activity or excitement: *The election campaign is hotting up.*

hot 'air *n* [U] things that someone says that sound important, but are not sensible or true

hot 'air bal,loon *n* [C] a very large BALLOON that can carry people in the air

hotbed /ˈhɒtbed $ ˈhɑːt-/ *n* [C] a place where there is a lot of a particular kind of activity: +of *The university was a hotbed of protest.*

hotchpotch /ˈhɒtʃpɒtʃ $ ˈhɑːtʃpɑːtʃ/ *especially BrE*; **hodgepodge** *AmE n* [singular] *informal* a strange mixture of different things

hot 'dog / $ '. ./ *n* [C] a hot SAUSAGE, eaten in a long piece of bread

hotel /həʊˈtel $ hoʊ-/ *n* [C] a building where you pay to sleep and eat when you are travelling or on holiday: **stay in/at a hotel** *We'll be staying at the Hotel Ibis.* | **check into a hotel** also **book into a hotel** *BrE* (=go there to say you have arrived, leave your bags etc) *They checked into the Holiday Inn.* | *She watched TV in her hotel room.*

> **THESAURUS**
>
> **make a reservation/book a room** – to arrange to stay at a hotel
> **check into a hotel** also **book into a hotel** *BrE* – to go to the **reception desk** and say that you have arrived
> **call/ring room service** – to order food to be delivered to your room
> **check out of a hotel** – to pay the bill and leave a hotel
> → ACCOMMODATION

hotelier /həʊˈteliei, -liə $ ˌoʊtəlˈjeɪ, ˌhoʊ-/ *n* [C] someone who owns or manages a hotel

hothead /ˈhɒthed $ ˈhɑːt-/ *n* [C] someone who does things too quickly without thinking —**hotheaded** /ˌhɒtˈhedɪd◂ $ ˌhɑːt-/ *adj*

hotline /ˈhɒtlaɪn $ ˈhɑːt-/ *n* [C] a special telephone number that people can call for information or advice

hotly /ˈhɒtli $ ˈhɑːtli/ *adv* **1** in an excited or angry way: **hotly debated/disputed/denied etc** *a hotly debated issue* **2** done with a lot of energy and effort: *the hotly contested race for governor*

'hot spot *n* [C] **1** a place where there is likely to be a lot of activity or fighting: *Soldiers were moved to hot spots along the border.* **2** a part of a computer image on the screen that you CLICK on to make other pictures, words etc appear

hot-'tempered *adj* becoming angry very easily

hot-'water ,bottle *n* [C] a rubber container that you fill with hot water, used to make a bed warm

hot-water bottle

hound¹ /haʊnd/ *n* [C] a dog used for hunting

hound² *v* [T] to follow someone all the time and ask them questions in an annoying or threatening way: *She's constantly hounded by reporters.*

hour /aʊə $ aʊr/ *n*

1 [C] a period of 60 minutes: *The meeting lasted an hour.* | **in one/two/three etc hours** *I'll be home in two hours.* | **quarter of an hour/half an hour/three quarters of an hour** (=15, 30, 45 minutes) *He was quarter of an hour late.* | **+of** *The meeting ended after four hours of talks.* | *It's an hour's drive to the airport.* | *a top speed of 120 miles an hour* | **a two-hour/three-hour etc sth** *a five-hour delay*
2 [C] a fixed period of time in the day when a particular activity, business etc happens: **office/opening/working etc hours** *Our business hours are 9.00 to 5.00.* | *I could meet you in my lunch hour* (=when I stop working to have lunch). | *The key is kept with the caretaker after hours* (=after the time a company, shop etc closes).
3 hours [plural] *informal* a long time: *She spends hours on the phone.*
4 [C] a particular time during the day or night: *The buses don't run at this hour of the night.* | *The baby keeps them awake at all hours* (=at any time, even very late at night).
5 the hour the exact time when a new hour starts, for example one o'clock, two o'clock etc: **on the hour** *Classes begin on the hour.* | *Buses go at ten minutes past the hour.*
→ RUSH HOUR

hourglass /ˈaʊəglɑːs $ ˈaʊrglæs/ *n* [C] a glass container for measuring time, with sand moving slowly from the top half to the bottom in one hour

hourglass

hourly /ˈaʊəli $ ˈaʊrli/ *adj* **1** happening every hour: *an hourly news bulletin* → see box at REGULAR
2 for one hour: *I get an hourly rate of £8.*

H

house[1] /haʊs/ *n plural* **houses** /ˈhaʊzɪz/

1 [C] a building that you live in: *I'm going over to Dean's house.* | *a four-bedroom house* | **at sb's house** *She's staying at Alex's house.*

> **THESAURUS**
>
> **terraced house** *BrE*/**row house** *AmE* – one of a row of houses that are joined together
> **detached house** *BrE* – a house that is not joined to another house
> **semi-detached house** *BrE* – a house that is joined to another house on one side
> **cottage** – a small house in the country
> **bungalow** – a small house that is all on one level
> **duplex** *AmE* – a house that is divided into two separate homes
> **flat** *BrE*/**apartment** – a set of rooms that is part of a bigger building
> **country house** *BrE*/**mansion** – a very large house

2 [singular] all the people who live in a house: *Be quiet or you'll wake the whole house!*
3 [C] a building used for a particular purpose: *the Opera House* | *a hen house*
4 [C] a group of people who make the laws of a country: *The President will address both houses of Congress.* | *the House of Commons*
5 [C] a company involved in a particular area of business: *a famous Italian fashion house* | *a publishing house*
6 be on the house *spoken* if drinks or meals in a restaurant are on the house, they are free
7 [C] *BrE* one of the groups that the children in a school are put into, for the purposes of competing in sports etc
8 [U] HOUSE MUSIC

→ **FULL HOUSE, OPEN HOUSE, PUBLIC HOUSE**

house[2] /haʊz/ *v* [T] **1** to provide someone with a place to live: *a program to house the homeless* **2** if a building houses something, it is kept there: *The new building will house the art collection.*

'house ar,rest *n* **be under house arrest** to be kept as a prisoner by a government, inside your own house

houseboat /ˈhaʊsbəʊt $ -boʊt/ *n* [C] a river boat that you can live in

housebound /ˈhaʊsbaʊnd/ *adj* unable to leave your house because you are ill or old

household[1] /ˈhaʊshəʊld $ -hoʊld/ *adj* **1** [only before noun] relating to your home [= **domestic**]: *washing powder and other household products* | *household chores* **2 be a household name/word** to be very well-known

household[2] *n* [C] all the people who live together in one house: *Many households have at least one computer.* —**householder** *n* [C]

'house ,husband *n* [C] a married man who works at home doing the cooking, cleaning etc

housekeeper /ˈhaʊsˌkiːpə $ -ər/ *n* [C] someone whose job is to organize the cooking, cleaning etc in a house or hotel

housekeeping /ˈhaʊsˌkiːpɪŋ/ *n* [U] the work and organization involved in looking after a house, hotel etc, for example cooking and cleaning

houseman /ˈhaʊsmən/ *n* [C] *plural* **housemen** /-mən/ *BrE* someone who has almost finished training as a doctor and is working in a hospital [= **intern** *AmE*]

housemate /ˈhaʊsmeɪt/ *n* [C] *BrE* a person who you share a house with who is not a member of your family [→ **flatmate**; = **roommate** *AmE*]

'house ,music also **house** *n* [U] a popular type of dance music → see box at MUSIC

,House of 'Commons *n* **the House of Commons** the part of the British parliament whose members are elected by the people

,House of 'Lords *n* **the House of Lords** the part of the British parliament whose members have positions because of their rank or title

,House of Repre'sentatives *n* **the House of Representatives** the larger of the two parts of the US Congress or of the parliament of Australia or New Zealand [→ **senate**]

houseproud /ˈhaʊspraʊd/ *adj* someone who is houseproud spends a lot of time cleaning and taking care of their home

,Houses of 'Parliament *n* **the Houses of Parliament** the buildings where the British parliament meets, or the parliament itself

,house-to-'house *adj* **house-to-house collections/searches/inquiries etc** when people go to all the houses in an area to collect something or to find out about something

housewarming /ˈhaʊsˌwɔːmɪŋ $ -ɔːr-/ *n* [C] a party that you have to celebrate moving into a different house → see box at PARTY

housewife /ˈhaʊswaɪf/ *n* [C] *plural* **housewives** /-waɪvz/ a woman who stays at home doing the cooking, cleaning etc for her family, rather than doing a paid job [→ **homemaker**]

housework /ˈhaʊswɜːk $ -wɜːrk/ *n* [U] work that you do to look after a house, for example cleaning and washing

housing /ˈhaʊzɪŋ/ *n* [U] **1** the houses that people live in: *a shortage of good housing* **2** the work of providing houses for people to live in: *government housing policy*

'housing es,tate *BrE*; **'housing de,velopment** *AmE n* [C] a large number of similar houses that have been built together in the same place

hovel /ˈhɒvəl $ ˈhʌ-, ˈhɑː-/ *n* [C] a small dirty place where someone lives

hover /ˈhɒvə $ ˈhʌvər, ˈhɑː-/ *v* [I] **1** if a bird, insect, or HELICOPTER hovers, it stays in one place in the air: *A helicopter hovered above the crowd.* **2** to stay in one place, waiting for something: *Rick was hovering by the door, hoping to talk to me.*

hovercraft /ˈhɒvəkrɑːft $ ˈhʌvərkræft, ˈhɑː-/ *n* [C] *plural* **hovercraft** or **hovercrafts** a vehicle that travels over land or water on a strong current of air that the engines produce beneath it

how /haʊ/ *adv, linking word*

1 used to ask or talk about the way something happens or is done: *How do you spell your name?* | *He explained how the system worked.* | *We both work at the airport – that's how we met.* | **how to do sth** *Do you know how to get to her house?*
2 used to ask about amount, size, age etc: *How many children do you have?* | **how much?**

(=used to ask the price of something) *How much are those peaches?* | **How old** is Debbie? | **How long** have you been here?

3 a) used to ask about someone's health or happiness, especially when you meet them: *'Hi Laurie, how are you?' 'Fine, thanks.'* | *How's she feeling today?* **b)** used to ask someone for news about their life, work etc: *So how's it going at work?* | *How are you doing?*

4 used to ask someone their opinion: *'How do I look?' 'Great!'*

5 how about...? *spoken* used to suggest doing something: *How about a drink after work?*

6 used to emphasize the quality you are mentioning: **how good/well/hot/quickly etc** | *He was impressed at how well she could read.*

7 how do you do? *spoken formal* used when you meet someone new for the first time

8 how come? *spoken* used to ask why, especially when you are surprised about something: *How come Dave's home already?*
→ **KNOW-HOW**

however /haʊˈevə $ -ər/ *adv, linking word*

1 used to introduce an idea, fact etc that is surprising or unexpected after what you have just said: *It's an unpleasant disease. However, it's easy to treat.*

2 however difficult/expensive/hot etc used to say that even if something is very difficult etc, it does not change the situation: *We'll finish the job, however long it takes* (=even if it takes a very long time). | **however much/many** *I want that car, however much it costs.*

3 in any way: *You can travel however you like.*

howl /haʊl/ *v* [I] **1** if a dog or a WOLF howls, it makes a long crying sound **2** to cry very loudly **3** if the wind howls, it makes a loud high sound —**howl** *n* [C]

HQ /ˌeɪtʃ ˈkjuː/ *n* [C,U] the abbreviation of **headquarters**

hr the written abbreviation of **hour**

HRH the written abbreviation of **His Royal Highness** or **Her Royal Highness**

hub /hʌb/ *n* [C] **1** the central and most important part of an area, system etc [➡ **centre**]: **+of** *The local school was the hub of the community.* **2** the central part of a wheel

hubbub /ˈhʌbʌb/ *n* [singular, U] a lot of noise, excitement etc that you can hear: *the hubbub of the crowd*

hubcap /ˈhʌbkæp/ *n* [C] a metal cover for the centre of a wheel on a vehicle

huddle /ˈhʌdl/ also **huddle together/up** *v* [I] if a group of people huddle together, they stay very close to each other because they are cold or frightened: *We all huddled together for warmth.* —**huddle** *n* [C]

hue /hjuː/ *n* [C] *literary* a colour: *a golden hue*

huff¹ /hʌf/ *n* **in a huff** angry because someone has offended you: *Ray walked out in a huff.*

huff² *v* **huff and puff** to breathe in a noisy way, especially because you are doing something tiring

hug /hʌɡ/ *v* [T] **hugged**, **hugging 1** to put your arms around someone and hold them, because you like or love them: *We hugged and said goodnight.* **2** to move along the side, edge, top etc of something, staying very close to it: *The*

road to Barcelona hugs the Mediterranean coast. —**hug** *n* [C] *Give me a hug before you go.*

huge /hjuːdʒ/ *adj* very large [= **enormous**]: *Your room's huge compared to mine.* | *a huge dog* | *a* **huge amount/sum/quantity etc** *huge numbers of tourists* → see box at **BIG**

hugely /ˈhjuːdʒli/ *adv* extremely: *a hugely talented musician*

huh /hʌh, hʌ/ *spoken* used when you are asking a question or are slightly annoyed about something: *Not a bad restaurant, huh?*

hulk /hʌlk/ *n* [C] **1** a large heavy person or thing **2** an old ship, plane, or vehicle that is not used any more

hull /hʌl/ *n* [C] the main part of a ship that goes in the water

hullabaloo /ˌhʌləbəˈluː, ˈhʌləbəluː/ *n* [singular] *informal* a lot of noise or excitement: *There's been a big hullabaloo over his new book.*

hullo /hʌˈləʊ $ -loʊ/ a British spelling of HELLO

hum /hʌm/ *v* **hummed**, **humming 1** [I,T] to sing a tune by making a continuous sound with your lips closed: *If you don't know the words, just hum.* **2** [I] to make a low continuous sound: *insects humming in the sunshine* **3 be humming** *approving* if a place is humming, there is a lot of activity —**hum** *n* [singular] *the hum of traffic*

human¹ /ˈhjuːmən/ *adj*

1 belonging or relating to people: *the human body* | *the power of* **the human mind** | *The accident was a result of* **human error** (=a mistake made by a person, not a machine). | **human weakness/failing** (=a weakness that is typical of people) *Jealousy's one of the worst human failings.*

2 sb is only human used to say that someone should not be blamed for what they have done

3 human interest a quality that makes a story in a newspaper interesting because it is about someone's life, relationships etc

human² also **human 'being** *n* [C] a person

humane /hjuːˈmeɪn/ *adj* treating people or animals in a way that is not cruel or likely to cause suffering [≠ **inhumane**] —**humanely** *adv*

humanism /ˈhjuːmənɪzəm/ *n* [U] the belief that human problems can be solved through science rather than religion —**humanist** *n* [C] —**humanistic** /ˌhjuːməˈnɪstɪk/ *adj*

humanitarian /hjuːˌmænɪˈteəriən $ -ˈter-/ *adj* concerned with improving people's living conditions and preventing unfair treatment: *The UN sent humanitarian aid to help the refugees.* —**humanitarian** *n* [C]

humanity /hjuːˈmænɪti/ *n* [U] **1** kindness, respect, and sympathy towards other people [≠ **inhumanity**]: *a man of great humanity* **2** people in general, or the state of being human: *the importance of religion to humanity* **3 the humanities** subjects such as literature, history, and languages rather than mathematics and sciences

humankind /ˌhjuːmənˈkaɪnd/ *n* [U] people in general

humanly /ˈhjuːmənli/ *adv* **humanly possible** possible to do if you try very hard: *We'll finish it as fast as is humanly possible.*

human 'nature *n* [U] the qualities and behaviour that are natural to most people

,human 'race *n* **the human race** all people [➡ mankind] → see box at **PEOPLE**

,human re'sources / $,.. '.../ *n* [U] the department in a company that deals with employing, training, and helping people [= **personnel**]

,human 'rights *n* [plural] the basic rights that everyone have to say what they think, vote, be treated fairly etc

humble¹ /'hʌmbəl/ *adj* **1** *approving* not thinking yourself better or more important than other people [≠ **proud**] **2** having a low social class or position: *the senator's **humble beginnings** on a farm in Iowa* —**humbly** *adv*

humble² *v* [T usually passive] to make someone realize that they are not as important, good etc as they thought: *You are humbled when you enter this magnificent cathedral.* —**humbling** *adj*: *a humbling experience*

humdrum /'hʌmdrʌm/ *adj* boring and ordinary: *a humdrum job*

humid /'hjuːmɪd/ *adj* humid air, weather etc feels hot and wet: *the humid heat of a tropical forest* → see box at **DAMP** → and **HOT¹**

humidity /hjuːˈmɪdɪti/ *n* [U] the amount of water that is in the air: *The plants prefer **high humidity**.*

humiliate /hjuːˈmɪlieɪt/ *v* [T] to make someone feel ashamed or stupid: *She humiliated me in front of the whole class.* —**humiliating** *adj*: *a humiliating defeat* —**humiliated** *adj* —**humiliation** /hjuːˌmɪliˈeɪʃən/ *n* [C,U]

humility /hjuːˈmɪlɪti/ *n* [U] *approving* the quality of not being too proud of yourself [➡ **humble**]

humorous /'hjuːmərəs $ 'hjuː-, 'juː-/ *adj* funny and enjoyable: *a humorous story* → see box at **FUNNY** —**humorously** *adv*

humour¹ *BrE*; **humor** *AmE* /'hjuːmə $ 'hjuːmər, 'juː-/ *n* [U]
1 the ability to think that things are funny and to laugh: *I don't like her – she's got no **sense of humour**.*
2 the quality in something that makes it funny: *There's a lot of humour in his songs.*
3 good humour a cheerful friendly attitude: *his charm and good humour*

humour² *BrE*; **humor** *AmE v* [T] to do what someone wants or to pretend to agree with them so that they do not become upset: *'Of course,' he said, humouring her.*

humourless *BrE*; **humorless** *AmE* /'hjuːmələs $ 'hjuːmər-, 'juː-/ *adj* unable to laugh at things that are funny

hump¹ /hʌmp/ *n* [C] **1** a round raised area on the ground, a road etc: **speed/traffic humps** *BrE* (=a series of humps in the road to make traffic go more slowly) **2** a raised part on a CAMEL's back

hump² *v* [T] *BrE informal* to carry something heavy somewhere

hunch¹ /hʌntʃ/ *n* [C] a feeling you have that something is true or that something will happen, even if you have no information or proof: *I **had a hunch** you'd call today.*

hunch² *v* [I] to bend down and forward so that your back forms a curve: **hunched over sth** *He was sitting in his study, hunched over his books.* —**hunched** *adj*: *hunched shoulders*

hunchback /'hʌntʃbæk/ *n* [C] an offensive word for someone who cannot stand up straight and has a large raised part on their back

hundred /'hʌndrɪd/ *number* plural **hundred** or **hundreds**
1 the number 100: *The tree was probably a hundred years old.* | **two/three/four etc hundred** *I make six hundred pounds a week.* | **hundreds of pounds/dollars etc**
2 an extremely large number of things or people: **a hundred** *They've had this argument a hundred times before.* | **hundreds of sth** *He's had hundreds of girlfriends.*
—**hundredth** *adj*: *her hundredth birthday* —**hundredth** *n* [C] *four hundredths of a second*

hundredweight /'hʌndrɪdweɪt/ *n* [C] plural **hundredweight** written abbreviation **cwt** a unit for measuring weight equal to 112 pounds or 50.8 kilograms in Britain and 100 pounds or 45.36 kilograms in the US

hung /hʌŋ/ *v* the past tense and past participle of **HANG**

hunger /'hʌŋɡə $ -ər/ *n* [U]
1 the feeling you have when you need to eat: *The baby was crying with hunger.*
2 a severe lack of food, especially for a long period of time [➡ **thirst**]: *Hundreds of people are **dying of hunger** every day.*

'hunger strike *n* [C] when someone, especially a prisoner, refuses to eat as a way of protesting about something → see box at **PROTEST**

hungover /hʌŋˈəʊvə $ -ˈoʊvər/ *adj* feeling ill because you drank too much alcohol the day before

hungry /'hʌŋɡri/ *adj*
1 if you are hungry, you need to eat [➡ **thirsty**]: *I'm **getting hungry**, let's eat!*
2 ill or weak as a result of not having enough to eat for a long time: *We shouldn't waste food when half the world is hungry.* | *Many people in our city **go hungry** (=do not have enough food) every day.*
3 if you are hungry for something, you want it very much: **+for** *Rick was hungry for a chance to work.*
—**hungrily** *adv*

,hung-'up *adj informal* worrying too much about something

hunk /hʌŋk/ *n* [C] **1** a thick piece of something: **+of** *a hunk of bread* **2** *informal* an attractive man who has a strong body

hunker /'hʌŋkə $ -ər/ *v*
hunker down *phr v* to sit on your heels with your knees bent in front of you

hunt /hʌnt/ *v* [I,T]
1 to chase wild animals in order to catch or kill them: *These dogs have been trained to hunt.* | *They hunt rabbits and other wild animals.*
2 to look for someone or something very carefully [= **search**]: *The police are still hunting the killer.* | **+for** *Detectives are busy hunting for clues.* → see box at **LOOK**
—**hunt** *n* [C] *The hunt for the missing child continues today.*

hunt sb/sth ⇔ **down** *phr v* to search for a person or animal until you catch them, especially in order to punish or kill them: *These murderers will be hunted down and brought to justice.*

hunter /'hʌntə $ -ər/ *n* [C] someone who hunts wild animals

hunting /'hʌntɪŋ/ *n* [U] **1** chasing and killing animals for food or sport **2 job-hunting/ house-hunting etc** a search for a job, a house to live in etc

hurdle[1] /'hɜːdl $ 'hɜːr-/ *n* [C] **1** a problem or difficulty that you must deal with before you can achieve something: *Finding enough money for the project was the first hurdle.* **2** a small fence that a person or a horse jumps over during a race

hurdle

hurdling

hurdle[2] *v* [I,T] to jump over something while you are running —**hurdler** *n* [C]

hurl /hɜːl $ hɜːrl/ *v* [T] **1** to throw something with a lot of force: *Someone hurled a brick through the window.* → see box at THROW **2 hurl abuse/insults etc at sb** to shout angrily at someone

hurray, hooray /hʊˈreɪ/ *spoken* something that you shout when you are very glad about something

hurricane /'hʌrɪkən $ 'hɜːrɪkeɪn/ *n* [C] a violent storm with very strong fast winds [➔ tornado] → see box at WIND

hurry[1] /'hʌri $ 'hɜːri/ *v* hurried, hurrying, hurries
[I,T] to do something or go somewhere quickly, or to make someone do this: *If we hurry we'll be in time.* | *I hate having to hurry a meal.* | **+along/ across/down etc** *She hurried along as fast as she could.* | **hurry to do sth** *They were hurrying to catch their train.* | *Don't hurry me, I'm going as fast as I can.*
—**hurried** *adj*: *a hurried breakfast* —**hurriedly** *adv*

hurry up *phr v* **1 hurry up!** *spoken* used to tell someone to do something more quickly: *Hurry up! We're late.*

COMMUNICATION

come on *spoken*: *Come on, we've got to catch the next bus.*
get a move on *spoken*: *Let's get a move on or we'll be late.*

2 hurry sb/sth ⇔ **up** to make someone do something more quickly or make something happen more quickly: *Try to hurry the kids up or they'll be late for school.*

hurry[2] *n*
1 be in a hurry if you are in a hurry, you need to do things quickly because you do not have

much time: *I can't talk now – I'm in a hurry.* | **be in a hurry to do sth** *Why are you in such a hurry to leave?*
2 (there's) no hurry *spoken* used to tell someone that they do not have to do something immediately: *You can pay me back next week – there's no hurry.*
3 not be in any hurry/be in no hurry (to do sth) to be able to wait because you have a lot of time in which to do something: *Take your time, I'm not in any hurry.*

hurt[1] /hɜːt $ hɜːrt/ *v* past tense and past participle **hurt**

1 [T] to injure someone or make them feel pain: *Careful you don't hurt yourself with that knife.* | *She hurt her shoulder playing baseball.* | *Mind you don't hurt each other.* | *Ow, you're hurting me!*

THESAURUS

Hurt and **injure** can mean the same, but **hurt** is usually used when the damage to your body is not very great: *Alex fell and hurt his knee.*
Injure is used especially to say that someone has been hurt in an accident: *Three people were seriously injured in the crash.*
Wound is used to say that someone has been hurt by a weapon such as a gun or knife: *The gunman killed two people and wounded six others.*

2 [I,T] if a part of your body hurts, or if something hurts it, you can feel pain in it: *My feet really hurt after all that walking!* | *It hurts when I breathe.* | *The sun's hurting my eyes.*
3 [I,T] to make someone feel upset or unhappy: *His comments weren't true, but they hurt.* | *I'm sorry, I didn't mean to hurt your feelings.*
4 sth won't/doesn't hurt (sb) *informal* used when you think someone should do something: *It won't hurt him to make his own dinner for once.*

hurt[2] *adj* [not before noun]
1 suffering pain or injury: **badly/seriously/ slightly hurt** *Fortunately, no one was seriously hurt.*
2 very upset or offended: *I was very hurt by what you said.*
—**hurt** *n* [U]

hurtful /'hɜːtfəl $ 'hɜːrt-/ *adj* making you feel upset or offended [➔ **unkind**]: *a hurtful remark*

hurtle /'hɜːtl $ 'hɜːr-/ *v* [I] to move or fall very fast: **+down/along/through etc** *A huge rock came hurtling down the mountainside.*

husband /'hʌzbənd/ *n* [C] the man that a woman is married to [➔ **wife**]: *Have you met my husband Roy?*
→ HOUSE HUSBAND

hush[1] /hʌʃ/ *v* **hush** *spoken* used to tell someone to be quiet, or to comfort a child who is crying → see box at QUIET
hush sth ⇔ **up** *phr v* to prevent people from knowing about something dishonest or immoral: *The bank tried to hush the whole thing up.*

hush[2] *n* [singular] a peaceful silence

hushed /hʌʃt/ *adj* quiet because people are listening, waiting to hear something, or talking quietly: *The courtroom was hushed.* | *people speaking in hushed voices*

hush-'hush /$'. ./ adj informal secret: The project's very hush-hush.

husk /hʌsk/ n [C,U] the dry part that covers some grains or seeds

husky¹ /'hʌski/ adj **1** a husky voice is deep and sounds rough but attractive **2** AmE a husky man is big and strong —**huskily** adv

husky² n [C] plural **huskies** a large strong dog that is used for pulling SLEDGES over snow

hustle¹ /'hʌsəl/ v **1** [T] to make someone go somewhere by pushing them: Jackson was hustled into his car by bodyguards. **2** [I] AmE to hurry: We've got to hustle or we'll be late! **3** [I,T] AmE informal to buy or sell things illegally: Young boys were hustling stolen goods on the street.

hustle² n **hustle and bustle** busy and noisy activity

hustler /'hʌslə $ -ər/ n [C] especially AmE someone who tries to trick people into giving them money

hut /hʌt/ n [C] a small simple building with only one or two rooms: a wooden hut

hutch /hʌtʃ/ n [C] a wooden box that pet rabbits are kept in

hybrid /'haɪbrɪd/ n [C] **1** an animal or plant that is produced from two different types of animal or plant **2** something that is a mixture of two or more things —**hybrid** adj

hydrant /'haɪdrənt/ n [C] a FIRE HYDRANT

hydraulic /haɪ'drɒlɪk, -'drɔː- $ -'drɔː-/ adj a hydraulic machine or system works by the pressure of water or another liquid: hydraulic brakes

hydroelectric /ˌhaɪdrəʊɪ'lektrɪk◂ $ -droʊ-/ adj using water power to produce electricity: a hydroelectric dam

hydrogen /'haɪdrədʒən/ n [U] a gas that is lighter than air and that combines with oxygen to form water

hyena /haɪ'iːnə/ n [C] a wild animal like a dog that makes a loud laughing sound

hygiene /'haɪdʒiːn/ n [U] when you keep yourself and the things around you clean in order to prevent diseases: the importance of **personal hygiene** | We learnt the principles of **food hygiene**.

hygienic /haɪ'dʒiːnɪk $ -'dʒe-, -'dʒiː-/ adj clean and likely to prevent diseases from spreading: Food must be prepared in hygienic conditions.

hymn /hɪm/ n [C] a song sung in Christian churches

hype¹ /haɪp/ n [U] disapproving when something is talked about a lot on television, in the newspapers etc, to make it seem good or important: There's been a lot of **media hype** surrounding this movie.

hype² also **hype up** v [T] to try to make people think something is good or important by talking about it a lot on television, in the newspapers etc: The director is just using the controversy to hype his movie.

hyper /'haɪpə $ -ər/ adj informal too excited, or with too much energy

hyperactive /ˌhaɪpər'æktɪv◂/ adj a hyperactive child cannot keep still or quiet for very long —**hyperactivity** /ˌhaɪpəræk'tɪvᵻti/ n [U]

hyperbole /haɪ'pɜːbəli $ -ɜːr-/ n [U] a way of describing something by saying that it is much bigger, better, worse etc than it really is

hyperlink /'haɪpəlɪŋk $ -pər-/ n [C] a word or picture in a WEBSITE or computer document that will take you to another page or document if you CLICK on it

hypermarket /'haɪpəˌmɑːkᵻt $ -pərˌmɑːr-/ n [C] BrE a very large SUPERMARKET outside a town

hypersensitive /ˌhaɪpə'sensᵻtɪv◂ $ -pər-/ adj very easily offended or upset

hypertension /ˌhaɪpə'tenʃən $ -pər-/ n [U] technical a medical condition in which your BLOOD PRESSURE is too high

hypertext /'haɪpəˌtekst $ -pər-/ n [U] technical a way of writing computer documents that makes it possible to move from one document to another by CLICKing on words or pictures, especially on the Internet

hyphen /'haɪfən/ n [C] a short line (-) used to join parts of words together, or to show that a word has been divided and continues on the next line —**hyphenated** adj

hypnosis /hɪp'nəʊsᵻs $ -'noʊ-/ n [U] when someone is put into a state like a deep sleep, so that another person can control or influence their thoughts and actions: **under hypnosis** He remembered details of his childhood under hypnosis.

hypnotic /hɪp'nɒtɪk $ -'nɑː-/ adj **1** making you feel tired or unable to pay attention to anything else, especially because of a regularly repeated sound or movement: hypnotic music **2** relating to hypnosis: a hypnotic trance

hypnotize also **-ise** BrE /'hɪpnətaɪz/ v [T] to produce a sleep-like state in someone so that you can influence their thoughts and actions —**hypnotist** n [C] —**hypnotism** /-tɪzəm/ n [U]

hypochondriac /ˌhaɪpə'kɒndriæk $ -'kɑːn-/ n [C] someone who worries all the time about their health, even when they are not ill —**hypochondria** /-dria/ n [U]

hypocrisy /hɪ'pɒkrᵻsi $ -'pɑː-/ n [U] disapproving when someone pretends to be a good person and have moral beliefs that they do not really have [≠ sincerity] —**hypocrite** /'hɪpəkrɪt/ n [C]

hypocritical /ˌhɪpə'krɪtɪkəl◂/ adj pretending to be a good person and have moral beliefs that you do not really have [≠ sincere]: It would be **hypocritical** to get married in church when we don't believe in God.

hypodermic /ˌhaɪpə'dɜːmɪk◂ $ -ɜːr-/ n [C] a piece of medical equipment with a very thin hollow needle, used for putting drugs into someone's body through the skin [= syringe] —**hypodermic** adj

hypothermia /ˌhaɪpəʊ'θɜːmiə $ -poʊ'θɜːr-/ n [U] technical a serious medical condition in which a person's body becomes too cold

hypothesis /haɪ'pɒθᵻsᵻs $ -'pɑː-/ n [C] plural **hypotheses** /-siːz/ a suggested explanation for something which has not yet been proved [➡ theory]

hypothetical /ˌhaɪpə'θetɪkəl◂/ adj based on a situation that is not real but might happen: Students were given a hypothetical law case to discuss. | The question is purely hypothetical. —**hypothetically** /-kli/ adv

hysterectomy /ˌhɪstəˈrektəmi/ *n* [C,U] plural **hysterectomies** a medical operation to remove a woman's UTERUS

hysteria /hɪˈstɪəriə $ -ˈsteriə/ *n* [U] extreme excitement, anger, fear etc that you cannot control: *The incident provoked mass hysteria.*

hysterical /hɪˈsterɪkəl/ *adj* **1** unable to control your behaviour or emotions because you are very excited, angry, afraid etc: *When she heard the explosion she became hysterical.* **2** *informal* extremely funny: *a hysterical new comedy* → see box at **FUNNY** —**hysterically** /-kli/ *adv*

hysterics /hɪˈsterɪks/ *n* [plural] **1** when you cannot control your behaviour or emotions because you are very excited, angry, afraid etc **2 be in hysterics** *informal* to be laughing and not able to stop: *We were all in hysterics!*

H

I, i

I, i /aɪ/ n [C,U] plural **I's, i's** the ninth letter of the English alphabet

I /aɪ/ pron used by the person speaking or writing to refer to himself or herself: *I saw Mike yesterday.* | *My husband and I are going to Mexico.* | *I'm not late again, am I?*

ice¹ /aɪs/ n

1 [U] water that has frozen and become solid: *Do you want some ice in your drink?*

2 put something on ice to do nothing about a plan or suggestion for a period of time: *I'm putting my plans for a new car on ice until I finish college.*

→ **break the ice** at **BREAK¹**

ice² v [T] *BrE* to cover a cake with ICING [= **frost** *AmE*]

ice over/up phr v to become covered with ice: *The lake iced over during the night.*

iceberg /'aɪsbɜːg $ -bɜːrg/ n [C] a very large piece of ice floating in the sea

'ice cap n [C] an area of thick ice that permanently covers the North and South Poles

,ice-'cold adj very cold: *an ice-cold drink*

,ice 'cream / $ '. ./ n [C,U] a frozen sweet food with fruit, nuts, chocolate etc sometimes added to it: *strawberry ice cream*

'ice cube n [C] a small block of ice that you put in a drink to make it cold

'ice ,hockey n [U] *BrE* HOCKEY played on ice → see picture on page A9

'ice ,lolly n [C] *BrE* a piece of sweet tasting ice on a stick, that you suck [= **popsicle** *AmE*]

'ice pack n [C] a bag containing ice that is put on injured or painful parts of your body

'ice rink n [C] a specially prepared surface of ice inside a building where you can ICE SKATE

'ice skate¹ v [I] to slide on ice wearing ice SKATES —**ice skating** n [U] —**ice skater** n [C]

'ice skate² n [C] a special boot with thin metal blades on the bottom that allows you to move quickly on ice

icicle /'aɪsɪkəl/ n [C] a thin pointed piece of ice that hangs down, for example from a roof

icing /'aɪsɪŋ/ n [U] a sweet mixture of sugar, butter, etc that you use to cover a cake [= **frosting** *AmE*]

icon /'aɪkɒn $ -kɑːn/ n [C] **1** a small sign or picture on a computer screen that you choose when you want the computer to do something: *To send a*

icicle

icicles

fax, click on the telephone icon. **2** someone famous who is admired by many people and is thought to represent an important idea: *a feminist icon* **3** also **ikon** a picture or figure of a holy person —**iconic** /aɪˈkɒnɪk $ -ˈkɑː-/ adj

icy /'aɪsi/ adj comparative **icier**, superlative **iciest**
1 extremely cold: *an icy wind* → see box at **COLD**
2 covered in ice: *icy roads*

I'd /aɪd/ the short form of 'I had' or 'I would'

ID /ˌaɪ 'diː/ n [C,U] something official that shows your name, address etc, usually with a photograph [= **identification**]: *May I see some ID please?* | *You'll need to show your ID card at reception.*

idea /aɪˈdɪə/ n

1 [C] a plan or suggestion: **good/great etc idea** *What a good idea!* | *I knew it was a bad idea to leave him on his own.* | *I have an idea – let's go to the beach.* | **+for** *Where did you get the idea for the book?*

2 [singular, U] understanding or knowledge of something: **+of** *This book gives you an idea of what life was like during the war.* | *I want to get an idea of what the building will look like.* | *Give me a rough idea* (=not exact) *of how much it will cost.* | *Richard had no idea* (=he did not know at all) *where Celia had gone.* | *I don't have the faintest idea* (=I don't know at all) *what to get Rachel for her birthday.*

3 the idea of sth the aim or purpose of doing something: *The idea of the game is to hit the ball into the holes.*

4 [C] an opinion: **+about** *Bill has some strange ideas about women.*

ideal¹ /aɪˈdɪəl/ adj

1 the best that something could possibly be: *an ideal place for a picnic* | *an ideal opportunity* | **+for** *This film is ideal for young children.*

2 perfect, but not likely to exist: *In an ideal world there would be no war.*

ideal² n [C] **1** a standard that you would like to achieve: *We must work towards this ideal.* **2** a perfect example of something: **+of** *our ideals of beauty*

idealism /aɪˈdɪəlɪzəm/ n [U] the belief that you should live according to high standards or principles, even if it is difficult —**idealist** n [C] —**idealistic** /ˌaɪdɪəˈlɪstɪk/ adj: *an idealistic young doctor*

idealize also **-ise** *BrE* /aɪˈdɪəlaɪz/ v [T] to imagine that something is perfect or better than it really is: *an idealized view of marriage*

ideally /aɪˈdɪəli/ adv **1** used to say how you would like things to be, even if it is not possible: *Ideally, I'd like to live in the country.* **2** perfectly: *The hotel is ideally situated next to the beach.* | *He's ideally suited for the job.*

identical /aɪˈdentɪkəl/ adj exactly the same: *The two pictures looked identical.* | **+to** *Your shoes are identical to mine.* | **identical twins** (=two babies that are born together and look exactly the same) —**identically** /-kli/ adv

identifiable /aɪˈdentɪˌfaɪəbəl/ adj easy to recognize

identification /aɪˌdentɪfɪˈkeɪʃən/ n [U]
1 something official that shows your name, address etc, usually with a photograph [= **ID**]: *You can use a passport as identification.* **2** when

you say that you recognize someone or something: *The bodies are awaiting identification.*

identify /aɪˈdentɪfaɪ/ *v* [T] **identified, identifying, identifies**

1 to recognize someone or something and say correctly who or what they are: *She was unable to identify her attacker.*
2 to recognize something or discover exactly what it is: *Scientists have identified the gene that causes abnormal growth.*

identify with sb *phr v* to feel sympathy with someone or be able to share their feelings: *It was easy to identify with the novel's main character.*

identity /aɪˈdentɪti/ *n* plural **identities 1** [C,U] who someone is: *The identity of the killer is still unknown.* **2** [U] the qualities that someone has that make them different from other people: *our cultural identity* | *Many people's sense of identity comes from their job.*

ideology /ˌaɪdiˈɒlədʒi $ -ˈɑːl-/ *n* [C,U] plural **ideologies** a set of beliefs or ideas about politics: *Marxist ideology* —**ideological** /ˌaɪdiəˈlɒdʒɪkəl $ -ˈlɑː-/ *adj*: *They have ideological differences.*

idiocy /ˈɪdiəsi/ *n* [U] extremely stupid behaviour

idiom /ˈɪdiəm/ *n* [C] a group of words that have a different meaning from the usual meaning of the separate words. For example, 'under the weather' is an idiom meaning 'ill'. → see box at **PHRASE**

idiomatic /ˌɪdiəˈmætɪk◂/ *adj* **1** idiomatic language is typical of the way people usually talk and write **2 idiomatic expression/phrase** an idiom

idiosyncrasy /ˌɪdiəˈsɪŋkrəsi/ *n* [C] plural **idiosyncrasies** an unusual habit or way of behaving that a person has —**idiosyncratic** /ˌɪdiəsɪnˈkrætɪk◂/ *adj*

idiot /ˈɪdiət/ *n* [C] a stupid person: *Some idiot drove into the back of my car.* —**idiotic** /ˌɪdiˈɒtɪk◂/ *adj* —**idiotically** /-kli/ *adv*

idle¹ /ˈaɪdl/ *adj* **1** lazy: *That boy is bone idle* (=extremely lazy). **2** not working or being used: *The machines are now standing idle in the factory.* **3** not serious: *an idle threat* | *This is just idle gossip.* —**idleness** *n* [U] —**idly** *adv*

idle² *v* **1** [I] if an engine idles, it runs slowly while the vehicle is not moving **2** [I,T] to spend time doing nothing: *Don't just idle your time away.*

idol /ˈaɪdl/ *n* [C] **1** someone that you admire very much: *a pop idol* **2** a picture or object that people WORSHIP as a god

idolize also **-ise** *BrE* /ˈaɪdl-aɪz/ *v* [T] to admire someone so much that you think they are perfect: *They idolize their little boy.*

idyllic /ɪˈdɪlɪk, aɪ- $ aɪ-/ *adj* very pleasant and peaceful: *an idyllic country scene*

i.e. /ˌaɪ ˈiː/ written before a word or phrase that gives the exact meaning of something you have just written or said: *The movie is only for adults, i.e. those over 18.*

if /ɪf/ *linking word*

1 a) used to talk about something that might happen, or that might have happened: *If you finish first, you'll get a prize.* | *Add more salt if necessary.* | *I want to leave by 5 o'clock if possible.* | *I wouldn't tell you, even if I knew.* |

Are you coming to see us, and if so (=if you are coming), *when?* | *Does he know? If not, what shall I tell him?* **b)** used to talk about something that sometimes happens: *If I don't go to bed by 10, I'm exhausted the next day.*
2 used to mention a fact, situation, or event that someone asks about, or is not certain about: *He asked me if I was all right.* | *I wonder if John's home yet.* | *I'm not sure if she's coming.* | *I don't know if he's here or not.*
3 used to ask something politely: *I wonder if you could help me.* | *Would you mind if I open the window?*
4 used to add to what you have just said and make it stronger: *He rarely, if ever, swears.* | *The snow made it difficult, if not impossible, to go out.* | *He wasn't unpleasant - if anything* (=in fact), *he was nicer than before.*
5 if I were you used when giving someone advice: *I'd leave if I were you.*
6 if only used to express a strong wish: *If only he'd agree!*

iffy /ˈɪfi/ *adj informal* **1** *BrE* not good: *The weather looks a bit iffy.* **2** not certain or approving: *She sounded a bit iffy.*

igloo /ˈɪgluː/ *n* [C] a house made from blocks of snow or ice

ignite /ɪgˈnaɪt/ *v formal* **1** [I,T] to start burning, or to make something start burning **2** [T] to start a dangerous situation, angry argument etc: *actions that could ignite a war*

ignition /ɪgˈnɪʃən/ *n* [singular] the electrical part of a car engine that makes it start working: *Turn the key in the ignition.* → see box at **DRIVE** → see picture on page A12

ignominious /ˌɪgnəˈmɪniəs/ *adj formal* making you feel ashamed or embarrassed —**ignominiously** *adv*

ignorance /ˈɪgnərəns/ *n* [U] lack of knowledge or information: **+of** *Ignorance of the law is no excuse.* | **in ignorance** *She remained in blissful ignorance of the problem* (=was not worried because she did not know).

ignorant /ˈɪgnərənt/ *adj* not knowing facts or information: **+of** *We went on, ignorant of the dangers.* → see box at **IGNORE**

ignore /ɪgˈnɔː $ -ˈnɔːr/ *v* [T] to deliberately not pay attention to someone or something: *They can't ignore the fact that he's here.* | *She completely ignores her husband.* | **ignore sb's advice/warning**

USAGE

ignore – to know about something but deliberately not pay any attention to it: *You must not ignore other people's feelings.*
be ignorant of sth – to not know about something: *We were ignorant of the dangers involved.*

ikon /ˈaɪkɒn $ -kɑːn/ *n* another spelling of ICON

ill¹ /ɪl/ *adj*

1 suffering from a disease or not feeling well:: *Jenny can't come – she's ill.* | *I was feeling ill.* | *She was taken ill* (=became ill) *at school.* | *He's mentally ill.* | **terminally ill** *patients* (=patients who are going to die) | **seriously/critically ill**

feel sick – to feel ill in your stomach and as if you might vomit

be sick – to feel ill and vomit

sick *especially AmE* – ill: *Chris has been out sick all week* (=not at work because of an illness).

not very well: *You don't look very well* (=you look ill).

under the weather *spoken* – slightly ill: *I've been a bit under the weather lately.*

2 [only before noun] bad or harmful: *He was unable to attend because of* **ill health**. | *I ate the same thing, but suffered no* **ill effects**.

3 ill at ease nervous, uncomfortable, or embarrassed

ill² *adv* **1** badly: *We were* **ill prepared** *for the shock.* | **think/speak ill of sb** (=think or say bad things about someone) **2 sb can ill afford (to do) sth** used to say that an action or thing will make someone's situation worse

ill³ *n* **1 ills** [plural] problems: *a cure for the ills of old age* | **social/economic ills 2** [U] harm or bad luck: *She* **wished** *him no* **ill**.

ill- /ɪl/ *prefix* badly or bad: *ill-concealed boredom* | *They are ill-equipped to cope.* | *ill-mannered children*

I'll /aɪl/ the short form of 'I will' or 'I shall'

ill-ad'vised *adj* not sensible —**ill-advisedly** /-əd'vaɪzdᵈli/ *adv*

ill-con'ceived *adj* not planned well and not having an aim that is likely to be achieved: *The ill-conceived scheme was later abandoned.*

illegal /ɪ'liːgəl/ *adj* not allowed by law: *It's* **illegal** *to park here.* | **illegal drugs/substances** —**illegally** *adv*

il,legal 'immigrant also **il,legal 'alien** *AmE* *n* [C] someone who comes into a country to live or work without official permission

illegible /ɪ'ledʒᵻbəl/ *adj* impossible to read: *His handwriting's illegible.*

illegitimate /ˌɪlᵻ'dʒɪtᵻmᵻt◂/ *adj* **1** *old-fashioned* born to parents who are not married **2** not allowed or not acceptable: *an illegitimate use of public money* —**illegitimacy** *n* [U]

ill-'fated *adj* unlucky and resulting in serious problems or death: *an ill-fated venture*

ill-'fitting *adj* ill-fitting clothes do not fit the person who is wearing them: *ill-fitting shoes*

ill-gotten 'gains *n* [plural] money that is obtained in an unfair or dishonest way

illicit /ɪ'lɪsᵻt/ *adj* illegal or not approved of: *an illicit love affair* —**illicitly** *adv*

illiterate /ɪ'lɪtərᵻt/ *adj* unable to read or write —**illiteracy** *n* [U]

illness /'ɪlnᵻs/ *n* [C,U] a bad condition that affects your body or mind, or the state of having a condition like this [➡ **disease**]: **suffer from/ have an illness** *He's never had any serious illnesses.* | *She had* **recovered from** *her* **illness**. | *the treatment of* **mental illness** → see box at **DISEASE**

illogical /ɪ'lɒdʒɪkəl $ ɪ'lɑː-/ *adj* not sensible or reasonable: *illogical behaviour* —**illogically** /-kli/ *adv*

ill-'treat *v* [T] to be cruel to a person or animal —**ill-treatment** *n* [U]

illuminate /ɪ'luːmᵻneɪt, ɪ'ljuː- $ ɪ'luː-/ *v* [T] to make light shine on something or in something —**illumination** /ɪˌluːmᵻ'neɪʃən, ɪˌljuː- $ ɪˌluː-/ *n* [U]

illuminating /ɪ'luːmᵻneɪtɪŋ, ɪ'ljuː- $ ɪ'luː-/ *adj* making something easier to understand: *a very illuminating book*

illusion /ɪ'luːʒən/ *n* [C] **1** something that seems to be different from the way it really is: *The mirrors create an illusion of space.* **2** a false idea or belief: **be under an illusion** *Terry is under the illusion that all women love him.* | *We* **have no illusions about** *the hard work ahead.*

illusory /ɪ'luːsəri/ *adj formal* false, but seeming to be real or true

illustrate /'ɪləstreɪt/ *v* [T] **1** to make something clear by providing an example: *A chart might help to* **illustrate** *this point.* | **+how/what** *The following examples illustrate how the system works.* | **+that** *The dispute illustrates that the regime is deeply divided.* **2** to CREATE or provide pictures for a book

illustration /ˌɪlə'streɪʃən/ *n* **1** [C] a picture in a book → see box at **PICTURE** **2** [C,U] an example that helps you to understand something: **+of** *a vivid illustration of the problem*

illustrator /'ɪləstreɪtə $ -ər/ *n* [C] someone who draws pictures for books

illustrious /ɪ'lʌstriəs/ *adj formal* famous and admired: *her illustrious career*

ill 'will *n* [U] unfriendly feelings towards someone

im- /ɪm, ɪ/ *prefix* not – used before words beginning with 'm' or 'p': *immature* | *impossible*

I'm /aɪm/ the short form of 'I am'

image /'ɪmɪdʒ/ *n* [C]

1 the way that people consider someone or something to be: *The party is trying to* **improve** *its* **image**. | *It's important to* **project** *the right* **image**. | **+of** *the* **public image** *of the police*

2 a picture that you have in your mind: *She had a clear image of how he would look.*

3 a picture that you see through a camera, on a television or computer screen, in a mirror etc

4 a picture of a person or thing that is drawn, painted etc on a surface

5 be the (very/living/spitting) image of sb to look exactly like someone else
→ **SELF-IMAGE**

imagery /'ɪmɪdʒəri/ *n* [U] the use of words or pictures to describe ideas or actions in poems, books, films etc

imaginable /ɪ'mædʒᵻnəbəl/ *adj* used to emphasize what you are saying: *It was* **the most** *wonderful holiday* **imaginable**. | *They covered* **every imaginable** *subject.*

imaginary /ɪ'mædʒᵻnəri $ -neri/ *adj* not real, but imagined: *imaginary creatures*

imagination /ɪˌmædʒᵻ'neɪʃən/ *n* [C,U]

1 the ability to form pictures or ideas in your mind: *Art is all about* **using** *your* **imagination**. | *It doesn't take much imagination* (=it isn't difficult) *to appreciate the risks.* | **vivid/fertile/over-active imagination** *He has a very* **vivid imagination**. | *'Did you hear that noise?' 'No, it's* **your imagination** (=you imagined it).'

2 capture/catch sb's imagination to make someone feel interested or excited

imaginative /ɪˈmædʒɪnətɪv/ adj **1** good at thinking of interesting ideas **2** containing new and interesting ideas —**imaginatively** adv

imagine /ɪˈmædʒɪn/ v [T]
1 to think of what something would be like if it happened: +**(that)** Imagine you're lying on a beach. | +**what/how** Can you imagine what it's like?
2 to think that something is true when it is not: There's no one here – you're **imagining things**.
3 to think that something is probably true: +**(that)** I imagine Kathy will be there.
4 you can/can't imagine sth BrE spoken used to emphasize that something is very good, bad etc: You can imagine how peaceful it was.

imbalance /ɪmˈbæləns/ n [C,U] when two things are not equal in size, or not the right size in relation to each other

imbecile /ˈɪmbəsiːl $ -səl/ n [C] a very stupid person

imbibe /ɪmˈbaɪb/ v formal **1** [I,T] to drink something, especially alcohol **2** [T] to be influenced by ideas

imbue /ɪmˈbjuː/ v [T] formal to make someone have a feeling or quality

imitate /ˈɪmɪteɪt/ v [T] to copy the way that someone does something: Children often imitate their parents' behaviour. —**imitator** n [C]

imitation /ˌɪmɪˈteɪʃən◂/ n **1** [C,U] when you copy the way that someone talks, behaves etc: **by imitation** Children learn by imitation. | +**of** Harry can **do an excellent imitation** of Elvis. **2** [C] something that is a copy of something else **3 imitation leather/fur/pearls etc** something that is made to look like leather, fur etc

immaculate /ɪˈmækjʊlɪt/ adj extremely tidy and clean —**immaculately** adv: She was **immaculately dressed**.

immaterial /ˌɪməˈtɪəriəl◂ $ -ˈtɪr-/ adj formal not important: The details are immaterial.

immature /ˌɪməˈtʃʊə $ -ˈtʃʊr/ adj **1** disapproving behaving like a younger person: He's very immature. **2** not fully formed or developed: immature fish —**immaturity** n [U]

immeasurable /ɪˈmeʒərəbəl/ adj extremely great —**immeasurably** adv

immediacy /ɪˈmiːdiəsi/ n [U] formal when something seems important, urgent, or interesting because it is concerned with things happening now

immediate /ɪˈmiːdiət/ adj
1 happening or done without delay: **immediate action/response/reaction** a situation that requires immediate action
2 [only before noun] needing to be dealt with quickly: Our **immediate concern** was to stop the fire. | the most **immediate problem**
3 [only before noun] very near to a place: people living in the **immediate area**
4 happening just after or just before something else: plans for the **immediate future**
5 immediate family your parents, children, brothers, and sisters

immediately /ɪˈmiːdiətli/ adv
1 without delay: Open this door immediately!
2 immediately before/after/following sth

very soon before or after something: We spoke immediately after the meeting.
3 immediately behind/above/below etc sth in the closest position behind, above etc something: They live immediately above us.

immense /ɪˈmens/ adj extremely large or great: **immense amount/value/size** They do an immense amount of work. | **immense importance/power** —**immensity** n [U]

immensely /ɪˈmensli/ adv very much: He enjoyed it **immensely**. | She was **immensely popular**.

immerse /ɪˈmɜːs $ -ɜːrs/ v [T] **1 be immersed in sth** to be completely involved in something: He was immersed in his work. | **immerse yourself in sth** (=become completely involved) **2** to put something completely in a liquid —**immersion** /ɪˈmɜːʃən, -ʒən $ ɪˈmɜːrʒən/ n [U]

immigrant /ˈɪmɪɡrənt/ n [C] someone who comes to live in a country from another country

immigration /ˌɪmɪˈɡreɪʃən/ n [U] **1** when people come to a country in order to live there **2** the place where officials check your documents when you enter a country → see box at AIRPORT

imminent /ˈɪmɪnənt/ adj going to happen soon [➡ **eminent**] —**imminence** n [U] —**imminently** adv

immobile /ɪˈməʊbaɪl $ ɪˈməʊbəl/ adj not moving, or not able to move: Mark stood immobile. —**immobility** /ˌɪməˈbɪləti/ n [U]

immobilize also **-ise** BrE /ɪˈməʊbɪlaɪz $ ɪˈmoʊ-/ v [T] to stop someone or something from moving

immoral /ɪˈmɒrəl $ ɪˈmɔː-/ adj morally wrong: It's immoral to treat people like that. —**immorality** /ˌɪməˈræləti/ n [U]

immortal /ɪˈmɔːtl $ -ɔːr-/ adj **1** living or continuing for ever: Nobody is immortal. **2 the immortal words/line** used to refer to famous or amusing words said or sung by someone —**immortality** /ˌɪmɔːˈtæləti $ -ɔːr-/ n [U]

immortalize also **-ise** BrE /ɪˈmɔːtəlaɪz $ -ɔːr-/ v [T] to make someone or something famous for a long time by writing about them, painting them etc

immovable /ɪˈmuːvəbəl/ adj impossible to move or change

immune /ɪˈmjuːn/ adj [not before noun] **1** not affected or able to be affected by something unpleasant that affects other people: +**to** Their business seems to be immune to economic pressures. | +**from** He is immune from prosecution. **2** someone who is immune to a disease cannot get it

im'mune ˌsystem n [C] the system in your body that protects it against illness

immunity /ɪˈmjuːnəti/ n [U] **1** when people are protected from particular laws or from unpleasant things: +**from** They were **granted immunity** from prosecution. **2** when someone cannot get a disease: +**to** immunity to infection

immunize also **-ise** BrE /ˈɪmjʊnaɪz/ v [T] to give someone a substance that will prevent them from getting a disease [= **vaccinate, inoculate**]: Get your baby immunized against measles. —**immunization** /ˌɪmjʊnaɪˈzeɪʃən $ -nə-/ n [C,U]

immutable /ɪˈmjuːtəbəl/ adj formal never changing or impossible to change

imp /ɪmp/ *n* [C] a small creature in stories who has magic powers and behaves badly

impact¹ /'ɪmpækt/ *n* **1** [C,U] the effect or influence that something or someone has: **+of** *the environmental impact of car use* | **+on/upon** *He had a big impact on my life.* **2** [singular, U] the force of one object hitting another, or the moment when they touch: *The impact of the crash spun the car round.* | **on impact** *The plane's wing was damaged on impact.*

impact² /ɪm'pækt/ *v* [I,T] *especially AmE* to have an effect on someone or something: **+on/upon** *How will the changes impact on us?*

impair /ɪm'peə $ -'per/ *v* [T] *formal* to make something less good

impaired /ɪm'peəd $ -'perd/ *adj* **1** damaged or made weaker: *impaired vision* **2** **visually/ hearing impaired** used to describe people who cannot see or hear properly —**impairment** *n* [U]

impale /ɪm'peɪl/ *v* [T] to put a long pointed object through something

impart /ɪm'pɑːt $ -ɑːrt/ *v* [T] *formal* **1** to give information, knowledge etc to someone **2** to give a particular quality to something: *Garlic imparts a delicious flavour to the sauce.*

impartial /ɪm'pɑːʃəl $ -ɑːr-/ *adj* able to be fair, because of not being involved or having a particular opinion: *We offer impartial advice.* —**impartially** *adv* —**impartiality** /ɪm,pɑːʃi'æləti $ -ɑːr-/ *n* [U]

impassable /ɪm'pɑːsəbəl $ ɪm'pæ-/ *adj* impossible to travel along or through

impasse /æm'pɑːs $ 'ɪmpæs/ *n* [singular] when it is impossible to reach an agreement: *We were at an impasse.*

impassioned /ɪm'pæʃənd/ *adj* full of emotion: *an impassioned plea*

impassive /ɪm'pæsɪv/ *adj* not showing any emotion: *his impassive face* —**impassively** *adv*

impatient /ɪm'peɪʃənt/ *adj* **1** annoyed because of delays or mistakes that make you wait: *The passengers were becoming impatient.* | **+with** *He gets impatient with the kids.* → see box at CHARACTER **2** wanting to do something as soon as possible: **impatient to do sth** *Gary was impatient to leave.* —**impatience** *n* [U] —**impatiently** *adv*

impeach /ɪm'piːtʃ/ *v* [T] *law* if a government official is impeached, he or she is charged with a serious crime —**impeachment** *n* [U]

impeccable /ɪm'pekəbəl/ *adj* without any faults: *impeccable manners* —**impeccably** *adv*

impede /ɪm'piːd/ *v* [T] *formal* to make it difficult for something to happen: *problems that impede students' progress*

impediment /ɪm'pedɪmənt/ *n* [C] **1** a situation or event that makes it difficult or impossible for something to happen: **+to** *Debt has been an impediment to development.* **2** a physical problem that makes speaking, hearing, or moving difficult: *a speech impediment*

impel /ɪm'pel/ *v* [T] impelled, impelling *formal* to make you feel that you must do something

impending /ɪm'pendɪŋ/ *adj* [only before noun] going to happen soon: **impending danger/death/disaster etc**

impenetrable /ɪm'penɪtrəbəl/ *adj* **1** impossible to get through or see through: *impenetrable fog* **2** very difficult to understand: *impenetrable jargon*

imperative¹ /ɪm'perətɪv/ *adj* **1** *formal* extremely important: *It is imperative that you attend.* | *It was imperative to be prepared.* **2** in grammar, an imperative verb expresses an order

imperative² *n* [C] **1** something that must be done: *Reducing pollution has become an imperative.* **2** the form of a verb that expresses an order. In 'do it now', the verb 'do' is an imperative.

imperceptible /,ɪmpə'septɪbəl $ -pər-/ *adj* impossible to notice: *an almost imperceptible nod* —**imperceptibly** *adv*

imperfect¹ /ɪm'pɜːfɪkt $ -ɜːr-/ *adj* not perfect —**imperfection** /,ɪmpə'fekʃən $ -pər-/ *n* [C,U]

imperfect² *n* **the imperfect** the form of a verb that shows an incomplete action in the past. In 'We were walking home', the verb is in the imperfect.

imperial /ɪm'pɪəriəl $ -'pɪr-/ *adj* [only before noun] **1** relating to an EMPIRE or to its ruler **2** related to the system of weights and measurements based on INCHES, YARDS, MILES etc

imperialism /ɪm'pɪəriəlɪzəm $ -'pɪr-/ *n* [U] when one country rules a number of other countries, or has great influence over them —**imperialist** *n* [C] —**imperialist** *adj*

impersonal /ɪm'pɜːsənəl $ -ɜːr-/ *adj* not showing any sympathy, friendliness etc: *an impersonal letter* —**impersonally** *adv*

impersonate /ɪm'pɜːsəneɪt $ -ɜːr-/ *v* [T] to copy the way someone talks, behaves etc in order to pretend that you are that person, or to make people laugh —**impersonator** *n* [C] —**impersonation** /ɪm,pɜːsə'neɪʃən $ -ɜːr-/ *n* [C,U]

impertinent /ɪm'pɜːtɪnənt $ -ɜːr-/ *adj* not respectful [= **rude**] —**impertinently** *adv* —**impertinence** *n* [U]

impervious /ɪm'pɜːviəs $ -ɜːr-/ *adj formal* **1** not affected by something: **+to** *He seemed impervious to criticism.* **2** not allowing liquid to pass through: *impervious rock*

impetuous /ɪm'petʃuəs/ *adj* doing or saying things quickly, without thinking: *She was very impetuous in her youth.* —**impetuously** *adv*

impetus /'ɪmpɪtəs/ *n* [U] **1** an influence that makes something happen, or happen more quickly: **+for** *The report provided the impetus for reform.* **2** *technical* a force that makes an object start moving, or keeps it moving

impinge /ɪm'pɪndʒ/ *v*
impinge on/upon sb/sth *phr v formal* to have an effect, usually a bad effect, on something or someone

impish /'ɪmpɪʃ/ *adj* not showing enough respect or not being serious enough, but in a way that people find funny: *an impish grin*

implacable /ɪm'plækəbəl/ *adj* very determined to continue opposing something —**implacably** *adv*

implant¹ /ɪm'plɑːnt $ ɪm'plænt/ *v* [T] **1** to fix an idea in someone's mind so that they cannot forget it **2** to put something into someone's body —**implantation** /,ɪmplɑːn'teɪʃən $ -plæn-/ *n* [U]

implant[2] /'implɑːnt $ -plænt/ *n* [C] something artificial that has been put into someone's body: *breast implants*

implausible /ɪm'plɔːzɨbəl $ -'plɔː-/ *adj* not likely to be true: *an implausible excuse*
—**implausibly** *adv*

implement[1] /'implɨment/ *v* [T] if you implement a plan or process, you begin to make it happen: *Airlines were required to implement new safety recommendations.* —**implementation** /ˌimplɨmen'teɪʃən/ *n* [U]

implement[2] /'implɨmənt/ *n* [C] a tool: *farming implements*

implicate /'implɨkeɪt/ *v* [T] to suggest or show that someone or something is involved in something bad or illegal: **implicate sb in sth** *Two people have been implicated in the robbery.*

implication /ˌimplɨ'keɪʃən/ *n* **1** [C] something that may happen as a result of a plan, action etc: **+of** *the implications of the decision* | **+for** *This ruling will have implications for many people.* | **political/financial/social implications** **2** [C,U] something that you suggest is true, without saying it directly: **+that** *I resent your implication that I was lying.* | **by implication** *She blamed the hospital, and – by implication – the doctor who examined her son.*

implicit /ɪm'plɪsɨt/ *adj* **1** not stated directly [➙ **explicit**]: **implicit threat/criticism/ assumption** *There was implicit criticism in what she said.* **2** complete and containing no doubts: *He had implicit faith in me.* —**implicitly** *adv*

implode /ɪm'pləʊd $ -'ploʊd/ *v* [I] *formal* to explode inwards —**implosion** /ɪm'pləʊʒən $ -'ploʊ-/ *n* [C,U]

implore /ɪm'plɔː $ -ɔːr/ *v* [T] *formal* to ask someone in a very emotional way to do something [= **beg**]: **implore sb to do sth** *Jan implored him to stay.*

imply /ɪm'plaɪ/ *v* [T] **implied, implying, implies** to suggest that something is true without saying or showing it directly [➙ **infer**]: **+(that)** *He implied that the money had been stolen.* | *High profits do not necessarily imply efficiency.* → see box at **SAY**

impolite /ˌimpə'laɪt◂/ *adj formal* not polite → see box at **RUDE**

import[1] /'impɔːt $ -ɔːrt/ *n* [C,U] something that is brought into a country in order to be sold, or the process of doing this [≠ **export**]: *Car imports have risen.* | *the import of luxury goods* | **import restrictions/controls etc**

import[2] /ɪm'pɔːt $ -ɔːrt/ *v* [T]
1 to bring something into a country in order to sell it [≠ **export**]: **import sth from sth** *Oil was imported from the Middle East.*
2 to move information to your computer from another computer
—**importer** *n* [C] —**importation** /ˌimpɔː'teɪʃən $ -ɔːr-/ *n* [U]

importance /ɪm'pɔːtəns $ -ɔːr-/ *n* [U] the quality of being important: **+of** *She stresses the importance of exercise.* | *They attach great importance to family life.* | **of great/ paramount/particular importance** *Safety is of paramount importance.*

important /ɪm'pɔːtənt $ -ɔːr-/ *adj*

1 an important event, decision, or problem has a big effect or influence on people's lives: *It is*
important to write clearly. | *It's important that he understands.* | **important part/role/factor** *You play a very important role.* | *a very important meeting*

crucial: *The U.S. plays a crucial role in the region.*
vital: *vital information*
essential: *It's essential that you book tickets in advance.*

2 important people have a lot of power or influence: *an important customer* | *It makes them feel important.*

3 be important to sb if someone or something is important to you, you care a lot about them
—**importantly** *adv* → **SELF-IMPORTANT**

importantly /ɪm'pɔːtəntli $ -ɔːr-/ *adv* **more/ most importantly** used before mentioning something more important or the most important thing: *Ask them questions and, more importantly, listen to their answers.*

impose /ɪm'pəʊz $ -'poʊz/ *v* **1** [T] to force people to accept something: **impose sth on sb** *The government imposed a ban on all imports.* **2** [I] *formal* to expect or ask someone to do something for you when this is not convenient for them: **+on/upon** *I didn't want to impose on Martin.*

imposing /ɪm'pəʊzɪŋ $ -'poʊ-/ *adj* large and impressive: *an imposing building*

imposition /ˌimpə'zɪʃən/ *n* **1** [U] the introduction of a rule, punishment, tax etc: **of** *the imposition of VAT* **2** [C] *formal* something that someone expects you to do for them, which is not convenient for you

impossible /ɪm'pɒsɨbəl $ ɪm'pɑː-/ *adj*
1 something that is impossible cannot happen: *It is impossible to predict what will happen.* | *The noise made sleep impossible.* | **almost/ virtually/practically etc impossible** *It would be virtually impossible for us to win.*
2 an impossible situation is very difficult to deal with: *He's put me in an impossible position.*
3 the impossible something that cannot be done: *You can't do the impossible.* | *You're asking the impossible of me.*
4 someone who is impossible is unreasonable and very annoying: *You're impossible!*
—**impossibility** /ɪmˌpɒsɨ'bɪlɨti $ -ˌpɑː-/ *n* [C,U]

impossibly /ɪm'pɒsɨbli $ -'pɑː-/ *adv* extremely: *an impossibly difficult task*

impostor also **imposter** *AmE* /ɪm'pɒstə $ -'pɑːstər/ *n* [C] someone who pretends to be someone else in order to trick people

impotent /'impətənt/ *adj* **1** without enough power, strength, or control to influence a situation: *an impotent city council* **2** a man who is impotent cannot have sex because he cannot get an ERECTION —**impotence** *n* [U]

impound /ɪm'paʊnd/ *v* [T] *law* if the police or the courts impound something, they take it and keep it until they decide that its owner can have it back: *His car was impounded for four days.*

impoverished /ɪm'pɒvərɪʃt $ -'pɑː-/ *adj* very poor: *impoverished villages* → see box at **POOR**

impractical /ɪmˈpræktɪkəl/ *adj* impractical plans or ideas are unlikely to succeed: *The designs were totally impractical.*

imprecise /ˌɪmprɪˈsaɪs◂/ *adj* not exact: *She could only give a vague and imprecise description of her attacker.*

impregnable /ɪmˈpregnəbəl/ *adj* a place that is impregnable is so strong and well-protected that it cannot be entered by force: *an impregnable castle*

impregnate /ˈɪmpregneɪt $ ɪmˈpreg-/ *v* [T] **1** to make a substance spread completely through something: *The paper has been impregnated with perfume.* **2** *technical* to make a woman or female animal PREGNANT

impress /ɪmˈpres/ *v*

1 [I,T] to make someone feel admiration and respect: *He was trying to impress me.* | **be impressed with/by sth** *I was impressed by her singing.*

2 impress sth on sb to make someone realize that something is very important: *Dad always impressed on us the need to work hard.*

impression /ɪmˈpreʃən/ *n* [C]

1 the opinion or feeling you have about someone or something because of the way they seem: *I had the impression that she wasn't very happy.* | *What impression did you get of the new headmaster?* | *He gave the impression of being very shy.* | *Ruth was keen to make a good impression on us all.* | **be under the impression (that)** (=to believe that something is true when it is not) *Sorry, I was under the impression you were the manager.*

2 when someone copies the way a famous person talks or behaves, in order to make people laugh: *She does a great impression of Madonna.*

3 the mark left by pressing something into a soft surface

impressionable /ɪmˈpreʃənəbəl/ *adj* easy to influence: *an impressionable young child*

impressionistic /ɪmˌpreʃəˈnɪstɪk◂/ *adj* based on a general feeling of what something is like: *an impressionistic account of the war*

impressive /ɪmˈpresɪv/ *adj* something that is impressive makes you admire it because it is very good, big, important etc: *The view was impressive.* | *a very impressive achievement* —**impressively** *adv*: *an impressively tall oak*

imprint¹ /ˈɪmprɪnt/ *n* [C] the mark left by an object that has been pressed onto something: +**of** *the imprint of his hand on the clay*

imprint² /ɪmˈprɪnt/ *v* **1 be imprinted on your mind/memory/brain** if something is imprinted on your mind etc, you can never forget it **2** [T] to print or press a mark on something

imprison /ɪmˈprɪzən/ *v* [T] to put someone in prison or keep them in a place they cannot escape from: *He was imprisoned for 18 months.* —**imprisonment** *n* [U]

improbable /ɪmˈprɒbəbəl $ -ˈprɑː-/ *adj* not likely to happen or be true: *It is highly improbable that humans ever lived here.*

impromptu /ɪmˈprɒmptjuː $ ɪmˈprɑːmptuː/ *adj* done without preparation or planning: *He stood up and made an impromptu speech.*

improper /ɪmˈprɒpə $ -ˈprɑːpər/ *adj* **1** dishonest, illegal, or morally wrong: *Three police offic-ers have been accused of **improper conduct**.* **2** not sensible, right, or fair in a particular situation: *It would be improper to comment on the case until after the investigation.* **3** wrong or not correct: *improper labelling* —**improperly** *adv*: *improperly dressed*

impropriety /ˌɪmprəˈpraɪəti/ *n* [C,U] plural **improprieties** *formal* something that is unacceptable according to moral, social, or professional standards

improve /ɪmˈpruːv/ *v* [I,T] to become better, or to make something better: *Her German is improving.* | *The school needs to improve its exam results.* | **greatly/significantly/dramatically improve** *The situation improved dramatically.*—**improved** *adj*: *new improved materials*

improve on/upon sth *phr v* to do something better than before: *I improved on my 2:17:22 time from last year.*

improvement /ɪmˈpruːvmənt/ *n* [C,U] when something becomes better than it was: *There was a steady improvement in efficiency.* | **dramatic/significant improvement** *There has been a significant improvement in our profits.* | *Ben's schoolwork is showing **signs of improvement**.* | *The new version **is an improvement on** (=is better than) the old model.* | *His playing has made progress, but **there's** still **room for improvement** (=it could be even better).*

improvise /ˈɪmprəvaɪz/ *v* [I,T] to make or do something without any preparation, using things that are available: *I forgot to bring my notes, so I had to improvise.* —**improvisation** /ˌɪmprəvaɪˈzeɪʃən $ ɪmˌprɑːvə-/ *n* [C,U]

impudent /ˈɪmpjʊdənt/ *adj formal* behaving in a rude way and not showing respect —**impudence** *n* [U] —**impudently** *adv*

impulse /ˈɪmpʌls/ *n* **1** [C,U] a sudden desire to do something before thinking about whether it is sensible: **impulse to do sth** *I resisted the impulse to hit him.* | **on impulse** (=because of an impulse) *Don't buy things on impulse.* **2** [C] *technical* a short electrical signal that travels in one direction along a nerve or wire

impulsive /ɪmˈpʌlsɪv/ *adj* doing things without thinking about the possible dangers or problems: *an impulsive young man* —**impulsively** *adv*

impunity /ɪmˈpjuːnəti/ *n* [U] **with impunity** without risk of punishment: *Human rights were violated with impunity.*

impure /ɪmˈpjʊə $ -ˈpjʊr/ *adj* not pure or clean: *impure gold*

impurity /ɪmˈpjʊərəti $ -ˈpjʊr-/ *n* [C] plural **impurities** a part of an almost pure substance that is of a lower quality: *There were some impurities in the metal.*

in¹ /ɪn/ *prep*

1 used to say the place or container where someone or something is: *The cheese is in the fridge.* | *I live in Spain.* | *a hole in the ground* → see picture on page A8

2 into a container or place: *Lou looked in her bag.*

3 used to say how something is done: *She performed in a confident manner.* | *I write to Luca in Italian.* | *He spoke in a low voice.*

4 used with the names of months, years, seasons etc to say when something happens: *She* *retired in April.* | *Insects are most active in summer.*

5 during a period of time: *I earned £75 in a day.*
6 at the end of a period of time: *We'll be back in a week.*
7 doing a particular kind of job: *He's in marketing.*
8 wearing something: *a man in a suit* | *Lucy was dressed in black.*
9 used to describe the condition of something or someone: *The company was in trouble.* | *You may be in danger.*
10 arranged in a particular way: *We stood in a line.* | *Entries are in alphabetical order.*
11 used to say how common or how likely something is: *One in ten homes now has cable TV.*

in² *adv*
1 into or inside a container or place [≠ **out**]: *He walked to his car and got in.*
2 inside or into a building or room, especially the one where you live or work [≠ **out**]: *You're never in when I call.* | *Come in!*
3 if a train, plane, boat etc is in, it has arrived at the station, airport etc: *Our train's not in yet.*
4 received by a person or organization to be dealt with by them: *Applications must be in by June 1.*
5 be in for sth if someone is in for something unpleasant, it is going to happen to them: *Dana is in for a shock.*
6 be/get in on sth to be or become involved in something that is happening: *They were both in on the decision.*

in³ *adj informal* fashionable: *Long hair is in again.* | *Jeans are the in thing this year.*

in- /ɪn/ *prefix* not: *inactive* | *inattention* (=lack of attention)

inability /ˌɪnəˈbɪləti/ *n* [singular,U] when someone is unable to do something: *his inability to read*

inaccessible /ˌɪnəkˈsesəbəl/ *adj* impossible to reach: *In winter, the village is often inaccessible.*

inaccuracy /ɪnˈækjɒrəsi/ *n plural* **inaccuracies**
1 [C] a statement that is not completely correct: *The report contains several inaccuracies.* **2** [U] a lack of correctness: *the inaccuracy of the data*

inaccurate /ɪnˈækjɒrət/ *adj* not correct: *The figures were inaccurate.* → see box at **WRONG**
—**inaccurately** *adv*

inaction /ɪnˈækʃən/ *n* [U] the fact that someone is not doing anything: *The government was criticized for inaction.*

inactive /ɪnˈæktɪv/ *adj* not doing anything, not working, or not moving [≠ **active**]

inactivity /ˌɪnækˈtɪvəti/ *n* [U] when you are not doing anything, not moving, or not working [≠ **activity**]: *I was getting bored with all this inactivity.*

inadequacy /ɪnˈædɪkwəsi/ *n plural* **inadequacies 1** [U] a feeling that you are not as good, clever, skilled etc as other people: *He suffers from feelings of inadequacy.* **2** [U] when something is not good enough in quality, ability, size etc: +**of** *the inadequacy of public transport* **3** [C usually plural] a fault or weakness: *I am quite aware of my own inadequacies.*

inadequate /ɪnˈædɪkwət/ *adj* **1** not good enough, big enough, skilled enough etc: *The*

school has inadequate computer facilities.
2 someone who feels inadequate thinks other people are better, more skilful, more intelligent etc than they are —**inadequately** *adv*

inadmissible /ˌɪnədˈmɪsəbəl/ *adj law* inadmissible information cannot be used in a court of law: *The judge ruled that his evidence was inadmissible.*

inadvertently /ˌɪnədˈvɜːtəntli $ -ɜːr-/ *adv* without realizing what you are doing: *I inadvertently left without paying.* —**inadvertent** *adj*

inadvisable /ˌɪnədˈvaɪzəbəl/ *adj* not sensible: *Strong winds made driving inadvisable.*

inalienable /ɪnˈeɪliənəbəl/ *adj formal* an inalienable right cannot be taken away from you

inane /ɪˈneɪn/ *adj* very stupid or without much meaning: *the children's inane chatter*

inanimate /ɪnˈænɪmət/ *adj* not living: *an inanimate object*

inappropriate /ˌɪnəˈprəʊpriət $ -ˈproʊ-/ *adj* not suitable: *His behaviour was totally inappropriate.* —**inappropriately** *adv*

inarticulate /ˌɪnɑːˈtɪkjʊlət $ -ɑːr-/ *adj* not able to express yourself well when you speak

inasmuch as /ˌɪnəzˈmʌtʃ əz/ *linking word, formal* used to explain how what you are saying is true: *Ann is guilty, inasmuch as she knew what the others were planning.*

inaudible /ɪnˈɔːdəbəl $ -ˈdɒ-/ *adj* too quiet to be heard: *Her reply was inaudible.* → see box at **HEAR**

inaugurate /ɪˈnɔːgjʊreɪt $ -ˈnɒ-/ *v* [T] **1** to hold an official ceremony when someone starts doing an important job in government: *The President was inaugurated March 4.* **2** to open a building or start an organization, event etc for the first time: *The Turner Prize was inaugurated in 1984.* —**inaugural** *adj*: *the club's inaugural meeting* —**inauguration** /ɪˌnɔːgjʊˈreɪʃən $ ɪˌnɒ-/ *n* [C,U]

inauspicious /ˌɪnɔːˈspɪʃəs $ ˌɪnɒ-/ *adj formal* seeming to show that something will not be successful

inborn /ˌɪnˈbɔːn $ -ɔːrn/ *adj* an inborn quality is one that you have had since birth: *inborn instincts*

inbox /ˈɪnbɒks $ -bɑːks/ *n* [C] the place in a computer email program where new messages arrive

Inc. /ɪŋk/ the written abbreviation of **Incorporated**: *General Motors Inc.*

incalculable /ɪnˈkælkjʊləbəl/ *adj* too great to be calculated: *The scandal has done incalculable damage to her reputation.*

incandescent /ˌɪnkænˈdesənt $ -kən-/ *adj formal* **1** giving a bright light when heated **2** extremely angry —**incandescence** *n* [U]

incantation /ˌɪnkænˈteɪʃən/ *n* [C] a set of special words that are used in magic

incapable /ɪnˈkeɪpəbəl/ *adj* not able to do something: +**of** *He was incapable of controlling his temper.*

incapacitate /ˌɪnkəˈpæsɪteɪt/ *v* [T] to make you too ill or weak to live normally: *He was incapacitated by illness in 1993.*

incapacity /ˌɪnkəˈpæsɪti/ *n* [U] *formal* lack of ability or strength to do something, especially because you are ill

incarcerate /ɪnˈkɑːsəreɪt $ -ɑːr-/ v [T] formal to put someone in prison —**incarceration** /ɪnˌkɑːsəˈreɪʃən $ -ˌkɑːr-/ n [U]

incarnate /ɪnˈkɑːnət $ -ɑːr-/ adj **1 be beauty/ evil/greed etc incarnate** to be extremely beautiful, evil, etc: *She is patience incarnate.* **2** having taken human form: **God/the Devil etc incarnate** *the belief that Jesus was God incarnate*

incarnation /ˌɪnkɑːˈneɪʃən $ -ɑːr-/ n **1** [C] one of the different lives that, according to some religions, people have: *He felt he had met her before, in a previous incarnation.* **2 be the incarnation of goodness/evil etc** having a lot of goodness etc

incendiary /ɪnˈsendiəri $ -dieri/ adj **incendiary bomb/device etc** a bomb etc designed to cause a fire

incense /ˈɪnsens/ n [U] a substance that has a pleasant smell when you burn it

incensed /ɪnˈsenst/ adj very angry

incentive /ɪnˈsentɪv/ n [C,U] something that encourages you to work harder or to start a new activity: **incentive (for sb) to do sth** *an incentive for children to work hard*

inception /ɪnˈsepʃən/ n [singular] formal the start of an organization: *since the club's inception in 1905*

incessant /ɪnˈsesənt/ adj never stopping: *her incessant chatter* —**incessantly** adv

incest /ˈɪnsest/ n [U] illegal sex between people who are closely related, for example a brother and sister —**incestuous** /ɪnˈsestʃuəs/ adj

inch¹ /ɪntʃ/ n **1** [C] a unit for measuring length, equal to 2.54 centimetres: *The fish was 48 inches long.* | a **one/two etc inch sth** *a six-inch nail* **2 not give/budge an inch** to completely refuse to change your decision or opinion: *Neither side is prepared to give an inch.*

inch² v [I] to move very slowly and carefully: *I inched my way along the wall.*

incidence /ˈɪnsɪdəns/ n [singular] formal how often something happens: **+of** *The area has a high incidence of cancer.*

incident /ˈɪnsɪdənt/ n [C] an event, especially one that is unusual, important, or violent: *One man was arrested following the incident.*

incidental /ˌɪnsɪˈdentl◂/ adj happening or existing in connection with something else that is more important: **+to** *Where the story is set is incidental to the plot.*

incidentally /ˌɪnsɪˈdentli/ adv used to add more information to what you have just said, or to introduce a new subject that you have just thought of: *Incidentally, how old is Mary?*

incinerate /ɪnˈsɪnəreɪt/ v [T] to burn something in order to destroy it

incinerator /ɪnˈsɪnəreɪtə $ -ər/ n [C] a machine that burns things in order to destroy them

incipient /ɪnˈsɪpiənt/ adj [only before noun] formal just starting to happen or exist: *a sign of incipient illness*

incision /ɪnˈsɪʒən/ n [C] a neat cut made into something, especially during a medical operation

incisive /ɪnˈsaɪsɪv/ adj showing intelligence and a clear understanding of something: *He made some very incisive remarks.*

incite /ɪnˈsaɪt/ v [T] to deliberately encourage people to be violent, hate other people, or commit a crime: *He was accused of inciting racial hatred.* —**incitement** n [C,U]

inclement /ɪnˈklemənt/ adj formal inclement weather is unpleasantly cold and wet

inclination /ˌɪnklɪˈneɪʃən/ n [C,U] a feeling that makes you want to do something: **inclination to do sth** *He showed no inclination to leave.*

incline¹ /ɪnˈklaɪn/ v **1 incline sb to do sth** formal to influence someone or make them do something: *The accident inclined him to reconsider his career.* **2** [I] formal to think that a particular belief or opinion is probably right: **+to** *I incline to the view that the child was telling the truth.* **3** [I,T] to slope at a particular angle, or to make something do this: *The slope inclines at an angle of 36°.* **4 incline your head** formal to bend your neck so that your head is lowered

incline² /ˈɪnklaɪn/ n [C] a slope: *a steep incline*

inclined /ɪnˈklaɪnd/ adj **1 be inclined to agree/think/believe etc** to have a particular opinion, but not very strongly: *I'm inclined to think Ed is right.* **2 be inclined to do sth/be inclined to sth** to often do something: *Children are inclined to get lost.* **3 be/feel inclined (to do sth)** to want to do something, but without having a strong desire

include /ɪnˈkluːd/ v [T]

1 if one thing includes another, the second thing is part of the first: *The price includes lunch.* | **be included in sth** *Service is included in the bill.* → see box at **RESTAURANT**

2 to allow someone to be part of a group or activity [≠ **exclude**]: *The other children refused to include her in their games.*

including /ɪnˈkluːdɪŋ/ prep used to introduce someone or something that is part of the thing that you have just mentioned [≠ **excluding**]: *He trained many jockeys, including John Watts.* | *The price is £3, including postage.*

inclusion /ɪnˈkluːʒən/ n [C,U] when you include someone or something in a larger group or set: **+in** *I am surprised at his inclusion in the team.* | *Are there any new inclusions on the list?*

inclusive /ɪnˈkluːsɪv/ adj **1** an inclusive price or cost includes everything: **+of** *The cost is £200, inclusive of meals.* **2 Monday to Friday inclusive/15-20 inclusive etc** including Monday to Friday and all the days between them, 15 and 20 and all the numbers between them etc: *I will be away from 1–5 May inclusive.*

incognito /ˌɪnkɒɡˈniːtəʊ $ ˌɪnkɑːɡˈniːtoʊ/ adv hiding who you really are: *The prince travelled incognito.*

incoherent /ˌɪnkəʊˈhɪərənt◂ $ -koʊˈhɪr-/ adj confused and not expressing ideas clearly: *a rambling incoherent speech* —**incoherently** adv

income /ˈɪŋkʌm, ˈɪn-/ n [C,U] the money that you earn or receive regularly, for example from your work: *Their annual income is less than $24,000.* | **on a ... income** (=earning a particular amount) *families that are on a low income* | **high-income/low-income** *high-income households* | **+from** *He gets a small income from*

savings. | an elderly couple living on a **fixed income** (=an income that does not change or grow) → see box at **MONEY**
→ **DISPOSABLE INCOME**

'income tax n [U] tax that you pay on the money you earn

incoming /'ɪnkʌmɪŋ/ adj [only before noun]
1 arriving at or coming to a place [➡ **outgoing**]: incoming flights | incoming phone calls **2** an incoming president, government etc has just been elected or chosen [➡ **outgoing**]

incommunicado /ˌɪnkəmjuːnɪˈkɑːdəʊ $ -doʊ/ adj, adv if you are held incommunicado, you are kept in a place where other people cannot speak to you

incomparable /ɪnˈkɒmpərəbəl $ -ˈkɑːm-/ adj so impressive, beautiful etc that nothing or no one is better: an incomparable view

incompatible /ˌɪnkəmˈpætɪbəl◂/ adj too different to be used together or work or live together happily: two incompatible computer systems | Roy and I have always been incompatible. | +**with** Going to war is incompatible with his religious beliefs. —**incompatibility** /ˌɪnkəmpætɪˈbɪlɪti/ n [U]

incompetence /ɪnˈkɒmpɪtəns $ -ˈkɑːm-/ n [U] when someone does not do their job properly

incompetent /ɪnˈkɒmpɪtənt $ -ˈkɑːm-/ adj not doing your job properly: an incompetent teacher —**incompetently** adv

incomplete /ˌɪnkəmˈpliːt◂/ adj not having all its parts, or not finished: an incomplete sentence | The report is still incomplete. —**incompletely** adv

incomprehensible /ɪnˌkɒmprɪˈhensɪbəl $ -ˌkɑːm-/ adj impossible to understand: His speech was incomprehensible.

incomprehension /ɪnˌkɒmprɪˈhenʃən $ -ˌkɑːm-/ n [U] when you do not understand something: He gave me a look of complete incomprehension.

inconceivable /ˌɪnkənˈsiːvəbəl/ adj too strange to seem possible: It is inconceivable that her husband didn't know what she was doing.

inconclusive /ˌɪnkənˈkluːsɪv◂/ adj not leading to a clear decision or result: The evidence was inconclusive.

incongruous /ɪnˈkɒŋgruəs $ -ˈkɑːŋ-/ adj formal strange, unexpected, or unsuitable in a particular situation: He looked incongruous in his new suit.

inconsequential /ɪnˌkɒnsɪˈkwenʃəl◂ $ -ˌkɑːn-/ adj formal not important: the children's inconsequential chatter

inconsiderate /ˌɪnkənˈsɪdərɪt◂/ adj not caring about other people's needs or feelings [≠ **considerate**]: It was inconsiderate of you not to call.

inconsistency /ˌɪnkənˈsɪstənsi/ n plural **inconsistencies 1** [U] when someone keeps changing their behaviour, reactions etc so that other people become confused [≠ **consistency**] **2** [C,U] a situation in which two statements are different and cannot both be true: There are some inconsistencies in her statement.

inconsistent /ˌɪnkənˈsɪstənt◂/ adj **1** two statements that are inconsistent cannot both be true: +**with** His story was inconsistent with the evidence. **2** not right according to a set of prin-

ciples or standards: +**with** This approach is inconsistent with Section 38 of the Act. **3** inconsistent behaviour, work etc changes too often from good to bad: The team's performance has been very inconsistent this season.

inconsolable /ˌɪnkənˈsəʊləbəl $ -ˈsoʊ-/ adj so sad that you cannot be comforted: His widow was inconsolable.

inconspicuous /ˌɪnkənˈspɪkjuəs◂/ adj not easily noticed [≠ **conspicuous**]: She tried to look inconspicuous.

incontinent /ɪnˈkɒntɪnənt $ -ˈkɑːn-/ adj unable to control the passing of liquid or solid waste from your body —**incontinence** n [U]

incontrovertible /ɪnˌkɒntrəˈvɜːtɪbəl $ ɪnˌkɑːntrəˈvɜːr-/ adj formal facts that are incontrovertible are definitely true and cannot be proved false: The evidence against him is incontrovertible.

inconvenience¹ /ˌɪnkənˈviːniəns/ n **1** [U] when something causes problems for you: We apologise for the delay and any inconvenience caused. **2** [C] something or someone that causes you problems: His injury was an inconvenience rather than a disaster.

inconvenience² v [T] to cause problems for someone

inconvenient /ˌɪnkənˈviːniənt◂/ adj causing problems, often in a way that is annoying: Monday's a bit inconvenient. How about Tuesday? —**inconveniently** adv

incorporate /ɪnˈkɔːpəreɪt $ -ɔːr-/ v [T] to include something as part of a group, system, plan etc: **incorporate sth into/in sth** These exercises can easily be incorporated into your daily routine. —**incorporation** /ɪnˌkɔːpəˈreɪʃən $ -ɔːr-/ n [U]

Incorporated /ɪnˈkɔːpəreɪtɪd $ -ɔːr-/ adj written abbreviation **Inc** used after the name of a company to show that it is a CORPORATION

incorrect /ˌɪnkəˈrekt◂/ adj not correct: The advice given was incorrect. → see box at **WRONG** —**incorrectly** adv

incorrigible /ɪnˈkɒrɪdʒɪbəl $ -ˈkɔː-/ adj someone who is incorrigible has a fault that cannot be changed: He's an incorrigible liar.

increase¹ /ɪnˈkriːs/ v [I,T] if you increase something, or if it increases, it becomes bigger in amount, number, or degree [≠ **decrease, reduce**]: Regular exercise increases your chances of living longer. | The number of prisoners has **increased dramatically**. | **increase in value/price/ importance etc** The waves were increasing in size. | **increase (sth) by sth** Food prices increased by 3% last year.
—**increasing** adj: the increasing use of nuclear power —**increased** adj: an increased risk of cancer

increase² /'ɪnkriːs/ n [C,U] a rise in amount, number, or degree [≠ **decrease**]: +**in** There has been a massive increase in unemployment. | **tax/ wage/price etc increase** There may be further price increases later in the year. | Crime in the city **is on the increase** (=is increasing).

increasingly /ɪnˈkriːsɪŋli/ adv more and more: His music is becoming increasingly popular.

incredible /ɪnˈkredɪbəl/ adj
1 extremely good, large, or great: The view was incredible. | She moved with incredible speed.

2 too strange to be believed or very difficult to believe: *It's incredible that he survived the fall.* | *I find it almost incredible that no one noticed these errors.*

incredibly /ɪnˈkredɪbli/ *adv* **1** extremely: *Nicotine is incredibly addictive.* **2** in a way that is difficult to believe: *Incredibly, he was not injured.*

incredulous /ɪnˈkredjʊləs $ -dʒə-/ *adj* unable or unwilling to believe something: *She gave him an incredulous look.* —**incredulously** *adv*

increment /ˈɪŋkrɪmənt/ *n* [C] a regular increase in an amount: *an **annual** salary **increment** of 2%*

incriminate /ɪnˈkrɪmɪneɪt/ *v* [T] to make someone seem guilty of a crime: **incriminate yourself** *He refused to incriminate himself by answering questions.* —**incriminating** *adj*: *Police found some incriminating evidence at his home.*

incubate /ˈɪŋkjʊbeɪt/ *v* [I,T] if a bird incubates its eggs, or if the eggs incubate, they are kept warm until the birds are born —**incubation** /ˌɪŋkjʊˈbeɪʃən/ *n* [U]

incubator /ˈɪŋkjʊbeɪtə $ -ər/ *n* [C] **1** a machine used in hospitals for keeping very small babies alive **2** a machine for keeping eggs warm until the young birds come out

inculcate /ˈɪŋkʌlkeɪt $ ɪnˈkʌl-/ *v* [T] *formal* to fix an idea into someone's mind

incumbent¹ /ɪnˈkʌmbənt/ *n* [C] someone who has an official job for which they have been elected

incumbent² *adj formal* **it is incumbent on/upon sb to do sth** it is the duty or responsibility of someone to do something

incur /ɪnˈkɜː $ -ˈkɜːr/ *v* [T] **incurred, incurring** to experience something unpleasant: *We do not want to **incur** any further costs.* | *The company has **incurred** heavy financial **losses**.* | *I hope I won't **incur** his **anger**.*

incurable /ɪnˈkjʊərəbəl $ -ˈkjʊr-/ *adj* impossible to cure [≠ **curable**]: *an incurable disease*

incursion /ɪnˈkɜːʃən, -ʒən $ ɪnˈkɜːrʒən/ *n* [C] *formal* a sudden attack into an area that belongs to other people

indebted /ɪnˈdetɪd/ *adj* **be indebted to sb** *formal* to be very grateful to someone: *I am indebted to you for your help.*

indecent /ɪnˈdiːsənt/ *adj* likely to offend or shock people: *indecent photographs* —**indecency** *n* [C,U]

indecision /ˌɪndɪˈsɪʒən/ *n* [U] when you are unable to make a decision: *After a week of indecision, the jury finally gave its verdict.*

indecisive /ˌɪndɪˈsaɪsɪv/ *adj* unable to make decisions: *a weak indecisive leader*

indeed /ɪnˈdiːd/ *adv*
1 used to emphasize something that you are saying: *The test proved that Vince was indeed the father.* | *'Would it help if you had an assistant?' 'It would, indeed.'*
2 *formal* used to add something extra to support what you have said: *I didn't mind at all. Indeed, I was pleased.*
3 *especially BrE* used with 'very' to emphasize what you are saying: *The essay was very good indeed.* | *Thank you very much indeed.*
4 *especially BrE spoken* used to show that you

are surprised or annoyed by something: *'He said he was too busy to see you.' 'Did he indeed?'*

indefatigable /ˌɪndɪˈfætɪɡəbəl/ *adj formal* determined and never giving up

indefensible /ˌɪndɪˈfensɪbəl/ *adj* too bad to be excused: *indefensible behaviour*

indefinable /ˌɪndɪˈfaɪnəbəl/ *adj* difficult to describe or explain: *She felt a sudden indefinable sadness.*

indefinite /ɪnˈdefɪnɪt/ *adj* happening for a period of time that has no definite end: *He was away in Alaska for an indefinite period.*

in,definite 'article *n* [C] in grammar, the words 'a' or 'an' [➡ **definite article**]

indefinitely /ɪnˈdefɪnətli/ *adv* until a time in the future that has not yet been arranged: *The meeting has been postponed indefinitely.*

indelible /ɪnˈdelɪbəl/ *adj* impossible to forget or remove: *The film left an indelible impression on me.* | *indelible ink*

indelicate /ɪnˈdelɪkɪt/ *adj formal* slightly rude or offensive: *an indelicate question*

indemnity /ɪnˈdemnɪti/ *n* **plural indemnities** *law* **1** [U] protection that someone gives you by promising to pay for any damage or loss that you suffer **2** [C] a payment for the loss of money, goods etc

indent /ɪnˈdent/ *v* [T] if you indent a line when you are writing, you start it further into the page than the other lines

indentation /ˌɪndenˈteɪʃən/ *n* [C] a cut or small hole in the surface of something

independence /ˌɪndɪˈpendəns/ *n* [U]
1 political freedom from control by another country: **+from** *Nigeria **gained** independence from Britain in 1960.* | *the American **declaration** of independence*
2 the freedom and ability to make your own decisions in life, without having to ask other people for permission, help, or money: *Many old people want to maintain their independence.* | *Having a job gives you **financial** independence.*

independent /ˌɪndɪˈpendənt/ *adj*
1 not owned or controlled by another government or organization: *a small independent bookshop* | **+of** *a central bank that is independent of the government*
2 not involved in a particular situation, and therefore trusted to be fair in judging it: *an independent panel of scientists* | *Parents have called for an **independent inquiry** (=one organized by independent people).*
3 confident, free, and not needing to ask other people for help, money, or permission to do something: *Jo is an independent young woman.* | *He helps disabled people to lead independent lives.* —**independently** *adv*

'in-depth *adj* **in-depth study/report etc** a study, report etc that is thorough, complete, and considers all the details

indescribable /ˌɪndɪˈskraɪbəbəl/ *adj* something that is indescribable is so good, strange, frightening etc that it is hard to describe: *a feeling of indescribable joy*

indestructible /ˌɪndɪˈstrʌktɪbəl/ *adj* too strong to be destroyed: *an indestructible toy*

indeterminate /ˌɪndɪ'tɜːmɪnət $ -ɜːr-/ adj impossible to know exactly: *a woman of indeterminate age*

index¹ /'ɪndeks/ n [C] **1** plural **indexes** an alphabetical list of names, subjects etc at the back of a book, with the numbers of the pages where they can be found **2** plural **indexes** a set of cards or a DATABASE with information in alphabetical order **3** plural **indexes** or **indices** /'ɪndɪsiːz/ something you can use to compare prices, costs etc or to measure changes: *an index of economic growth*

index² v [T] to make an index for something

'index ˌfinger n [C] the finger next to your thumb [= **forefinger**] → see picture at **HAND¹**

Indian /'ɪndiən/ n [C] **1** someone from India **2** a NATIVE AMERICAN —**Indian** adj

ˌIndian 'summer n [C] a period of warm weather in the autumn

indicate /'ɪndɪkeɪt/ v **1** [T] to show that something exists or that it is likely to be true: **+(that)** *Research indicates that women live longer than men.* **2** [T] to say or do something that shows what you want or intend to do: **+(that)** *Ralph patted the sofa to indicate that she should join him.* **3** [T] to direct someone's attention to something or someone, for example by pointing: *'That's her,' he said, indicating a girl in a red skirt.* **4** [I,T] BrE to show which way you are going to turn in a vehicle [= **signal**]: *I indicated left.*

indication /ˌɪndɪ'keɪʃən/ n [C,U] a sign that something exists or is likely to be true: **+of** *Dark green leaves are an indication of healthy roots.*

indicative /ɪn'dɪkətɪv/ adj **1 be indicative of sth** to show that something exists or is likely to be true: *His reaction is indicative of how frightened he is.* **2** in grammar, an indicative verb expresses a statement

indicator /'ɪndɪkeɪtə $ -ər/ n [C] **1** something that can be regarded as a sign of something else: *The main economic indicators suggest that trade is improving.* **2** BrE one of the lights on a car which show which way it is going to turn [= **turn signal** AmE] → see picture on page A12

indices /'ɪndɪsiːz/ n a plural of INDEX

indict /ɪn'daɪt/ v [I,T] law especially AmE to officially charge someone with a crime: **+for** *He has been indicted for murder.* —**indictment** n [C,U] —**indictable** adj: *an indictable offense*

indie /'ɪndi/ adj used to refer to popular music that is produced by small independent companies: *an indie band*

indifference /ɪn'dɪfərəns/ n [U] lack of interest or concern: **+to** *his apparent indifference to material luxuries*

indifferent /ɪn'dɪfərənt/ adj **1** not interested in something, and not caring about it: **+to** *an industry that seems indifferent to environmental concerns* **2** not particularly good: *a rather indifferent meal*

indigenous /ɪn'dɪdʒənəs/ adj indigenous plants and animals grow or live naturally in a place

indigestible /ˌɪndɪ'dʒestɪbəl/ adj food that is indigestible is difficult for your stomach to deal with

indigestion /ˌɪndɪ'dʒestʃən/ n [U] pain that you get when your stomach can't break down food that you have eaten

indignant /ɪn'dɪgnənt/ adj angry because you feel insulted or unfairly treated: **+at/about** *Liz was indignant at the school's attitude.* —**indignantly** adv —**indignation** /ˌɪndɪg'neɪʃən/ n [U]

indignity /ɪn'dɪgnɪti/ n [C,U] plural **indignities** a situation that makes you feel ashamed and not respected: *Two diplomats suffered the indignity of being arrested.*

indirect /ˌɪndɪ'rekt/ adj **1** caused by something, but not in a direct or clear way: *the indirect effects of climate change* **2** an indirect way to a place is not the straightest way: *an indirect route* **3** not saying or showing something in a clear definite way —**indirectly** adv

ˌindirect 'object n [C] in grammar, the person that something is given to, said to, made for etc. For example, in the sentence 'I asked him a question', the indirect object is 'him'. [→ **direct object**]

ˌindirect 'speech n [U] REPORTED SPEECH

indiscreet /ˌɪndɪ'skriːt/ adj saying things in an open way when you should be more careful to keep them secret: *Try to stop him from saying something indiscreet.*

indiscretion /ˌɪndɪ'skreʃən/ n [C,U] behaviour that shows a lack of good judgment and often seems immoral to other people: *We can forgive him his youthful indiscretion.*

indiscriminate /ˌɪndɪ'skrɪmɪnət/ adj indiscriminate actions are done without considering what harm they might cause: *indiscriminate killings by terrorists* —**indiscriminately** adv

indispensable /ˌɪndɪ'spensəbəl/ adj someone or something that is indispensable is so important or useful that you cannot manage without them: **+to** *The book is indispensable to anyone learning maths.*

indisputable /ˌɪndɪ'spjuːtəbəl/ adj an indisputable fact is definitely true: *The evidence was indisputable.*

indistinct /ˌɪndɪ'stɪŋkt/ adj difficult to see, hear, or remember clearly: *She muttered something indistinct.* —**indistinctly** adv

indistinguishable /ˌɪndɪ'stɪŋgwɪʃəbəl/ adj if one thing is indistinguishable from another, it is so similar that you cannot see the difference: **+from** *This material is indistinguishable from real silk.*

individual¹ /ˌɪndɪ'vɪdʒuəl/ adj

1 [only before noun] an individual person or thing is just one, considered separately from other people or things: *Each individual drawing is slightly different.* | *We try to meet the needs of the individual customer.*
2 belonging to or intended for one person rather than a group: *The children get individual attention.* | *We divided the food into individual portions.*
3 an individual way of doing things is different from anyone else's: *She's got a very individual way of dressing.*

individual² n [C] one person, considered separately from the rest of the group or society that they live in: *the rights of the individual* | *dona-tions from **private** individuals* (=people not organizations)

individualism /ˌɪndɪˈvɪdʒuəlɪzəm/ *n* [U] when someone does things in their own way without being influenced by other people

individualist /ˌɪndɪˈvɪdʒuəlɪst/ *n* [C] someone who does things in their own way without being influenced by other people —**individualistic** /ˌɪndɪˌvɪdʒuəˈlɪstɪk/ *adj: a highly individualistic approach to life*

individuality /ˌɪndɪˌvɪdʒuˈælɪti/ *n* [U] the quality that makes someone different from everyone else: *work that allows children to express their individuality*

individually /ˌɪndɪˈvɪdʒuəli/ *adv* separately, not together in a group: *He thanked everyone individually.*

indoctrinate /ɪnˈdɒktrɪˌneɪt $ ɪnˈdɑːk-/ *v* [T] to train someone to accept one set of beliefs and not consider any others: *They were indoctrinated not to question their leaders.* —**indoctrination** /ɪnˌdɒktrɪˈneɪʃən $ ɪnˌdɑːk-/ *n* [U]

indomitable /ɪnˈdɒmɪtəbəl $ ɪnˈdɑː-/ *adj formal* very brave and determined

indoor /ˈɪndɔː $ -ɔːr/ *adj* [only before noun] used or happening inside a building [≠ **outdoor**]: *an indoor swimming pool* | *indoor plants*

indoors /ˌɪnˈdɔːz $ -ɔːrz/ *adv* inside a build-ing [≠ **outdoors**]: *It's raining – let's go indoors.* | *He stayed indoors all morning.*

induce /ɪnˈdjuːs $ ɪnˈduːs/ *v* [T] **1** *formal* to make someone decide to do something: **induce sb to do sth** *Nothing would induce me to vote for him again.* **2** to make a woman give birth to her baby by giving her a special drug **3** *formal* to cause a physical feeling or condition: *This drug may induce drowsiness.*

inducement /ɪnˈdjuːsmənt $ ɪnˈduːs-/ *n* [C,U] *formal* something that you are offered to per-suade you to do something

induct /ɪnˈdʌkt/ *v* [T] *especially AmE* to offi-cially introduce someone into a group or organi-zation

induction /ɪnˈdʌkʃən/ *n* [C,U] the process of officially introducing someone into a group or organization: *a two-day **induction course** for the new employees*

indulge /ɪnˈdʌldʒ/ *v* **1** [I,T] to let yourself do something that you enjoy, especially something that is considered bad for you: **+in** *From time to time we indulge in a little lunchtime drinking.* | **indulge yourself** *Go on, indulge yourself for a change!* **2** [T] to let someone do or have what-ever they want, even if it is bad for them: *Ralph indulges his children terribly.*

indulgence /ɪnˈdʌldʒəns/ *n* **1** [U] the habit of eating too much, drinking too much etc: *a life of indulgence* **2** [C] something that you do or have for pleasure, not because you need it: *Chocolate is my only indulgence.*

indulgent /ɪnˈdʌldʒənt/ *adj* willing to let someone have whatever they want, even if it is bad for them: *indulgent parents*

industrial /ɪnˈdʌstriəl/ *adj*

1 relating to industry or the people working in it: *industrial development* | *an industrial dispute* | *an industrial accident*

2 an industrial country or area has a lot of industries: *the industrial nations of the world* | *an industrial society*
—**industrially** *adv*

in,dustrial 'action *n* [U] *BrE* an action such as a STRIKE (=stopping work) taken by workers involved in a disagreement with their employer

in,dustrial es'tate *BrE*; **in,dustrial 'park** *AmE* /*n* [C] an area of land that has businesses and small factories on it

industrialist /ɪnˈdʌstriəlɪst/ *n* [C] someone who owns or runs a factory or industrial com-pany

industrialized also -**ised** *BrE* /ɪnˈdʌstriəlaɪzd/ an industrialized country or area has a lot of industry —**industrialization** /ɪnˌdʌstriəl-aɪˈzeɪʃən $ -lə-/ *n* [U]

in,dustrial re'lations *n* [plural] the relation-ship between workers and employers

industrious /ɪnˈdʌstriəs/ *adj formal* always working hard: *industrious young women* —**industriously** *adv*

industry /ˈɪndəstri/ *n plural* **industries**

1 [U] the production of goods: *the recent decline in **manufacturing industry*** | *The software is widely used in industry.* | **heavy/light industry** (=the production of large or small goods)

2 [C] all the companies that work in one particu-lar type of trade or service: *the coal industry* | *Italy's tourist industry*
→ COTTAGE INDUSTRY, SERVICE INDUSTRY

inebriated /ɪˈniːbrieɪtɪd/ *adj formal* drunk

inedible /ɪnˈedɪbəl/ *adj* something that is ined-ible cannot be eaten: *inedible mushrooms*

ineffective /ˌɪnɪˈfektɪv/ *adj* not achieving the correct effect or result: *The treatment was completely ineffective.*

ineffectual /ˌɪnɪˈfektʃuəl/ *adj* not having the ability, confidence, or personal authority to get things done: *an ineffectual leader*

inefficient /ˌɪnɪˈfɪʃənt/ *adj* not using time, money, energy etc in the best way: *an inefficient use of resources* —**inefficiently** *adv* —**inefficiency** *n* [C,U]

inelegant /ɪnˈelɪɡənt/ *adj* not graceful or attractive: *She was sitting in a rather inelegant position.*

ineligible /ɪnˈelɪdʒɪbəl/ *adj* not allowed to do or to have something: *People under 18 are ineligi-ble to vote.*

inept /ɪˈnept/ *adj* not good at doing something: *an inept driver* —**ineptly** *adv*

inequality /ˌɪnɪˈkwɒlɪti $ -ˈkwɑː-/ *n* [C,U] plu-ral **inequalities** an unfair situation, in which some groups in society have more money, opportuni-ties, power etc than others: **+in** *a new attempt to tackle inequalities in the education system* | **+of** *There is still inequality of opportunity.*

inequity /ɪnˈekwɪti/ *n* [C,U] plural **inequities** *formal* lack of fairness, or something that is unfair

inert /ɪˈnɜːt $ -ɜːrt/ *adj* **1** *technical* an inert substance does not produce a chemical reaction when it is combined with other substances: *an inert gas* **2** *formal* not moving: *He lay, inert, in his bed.*

inertia /ɪˈnɜːʃə $ -ɜːr-/ *n* [U] **1** when no one wants to do anything to change a situation: *There is a feeling of political inertia in the* *country.* **2** *technical* the force that keeps an object in the same position until it is moved, or that keeps it moving until it is stopped **3** a feeling that you have no energy and do not want to do anything

inescapable /ˌɪnɪˈskeɪpəbəl / *adj formal* an inescapable fact is one that cannot be ignored: *The inescapable conclusion is that Reynolds killed himself.*

inevitable /ɪˈnevɪ̩təbəl/ *adj* **1** if something is inevitable, it will definitely happen and you cannot avoid it: *Death is inevitable.* | *It is inevitable that you will be caught.* **2 the inevitable** something that will definitely happen: *Finally, the inevitable happened and he lost his job.* —**inevitably** *adv: Inevitably, his alcohol problem affected his work.* –**inevitability** /ɪˌnevɪ̩təˈbɪlɪ̩t / *n* [U]

inexact /ˌɪnɪɡˈzækt / *adj formal* not exact: *Psychology is an inexact science.*

inexcusable /ˌɪnɪkˈskjuːzəbəl / *adj* inexcusable behaviour is too bad to be excused

inexhaustible /ˌɪnɪɡˈzɔːstɪ̩bəl $ -ˈzɔːs-/ *adj* an inexhaustible amount of something is so large that it will never be finished or used up: *She has an **inexhaustible supply** of funny stories.*

inexorable /ɪnˈeksərəbəl/ *adj formal* an inexorable process cannot be stopped: *the seemingly inexorable rise in crime*

inexpensive /ˌɪnɪkˈspensɪv / *adj* cheap but good: *an inexpensive vacation* → see box at CHEAP —**inexpensively** *adv*

inexperienced /ˌɪnɪkˈspɪəriənst $ -ˈspɪr-/ *adj* not having very much experience or knowledge: *an inexperienced driver* —**inexperience** *n* [U]

inexplicable /ˌɪnɪkˈsplɪkəbəl $ ɪnˈeksplɪkəbəl, ˌɪnɪkˈsplɪk-/ *adj* something that is inexplicable is so unusual or strange that you cannot explain it: *the inexplicable disappearance of a young woman* —**inexplicably** *adv*

inextricably /ˌɪnɪkˈstrɪkəbli, ɪnˈekstrɪk-/ *adv formal* things that are inextricably connected cannot be separated from each other: *Poverty and bad health are inextricably linked.*

infallible /ɪnˈfæləbəl/ *adj* **1** always right and never making mistakes: *No expert is infallible.* **2** something that is infallible always works correctly: *an infallible cure for hiccups*

infamous /ˈɪnfəməs/ *adj* well known for being bad or evil: *an infamous killer* → see box at FAMOUS

infancy /ˈɪnfənsi/ *n* [U] **1** the period in a child's life before he or she can walk or talk: **in infancy** *Their son died in infancy* **2** the time when something is just starting to be developed: *Genetic engineering is still **in its infancy**.*

infant /ˈɪnfənt/ *n* [C] *formal* a baby or very young child → see box at BABY

infantile /ˈɪnfəntaɪl/ *adj formal* infantile behaviour seems silly in an adult because it is more suitable to a child: *infantile jokes*

infantry /ˈɪnfəntri/ *n* [U] soldiers who fight on foot

infatuated /ɪnˈfætʃueɪtɪ̩d/ *adj* having strong feelings of love for someone: +**with** *He's infatuated with her.* → see box at LOVE —**infatuation** /ɪnˌfætʃuˈeɪʃən/ *n* [C,U]

infect /ɪnˈfekt/ *v* [T] **1** to give someone a disease: *People can feel well but still infect others.* | **infect sb with sth** *Thousands of people have been infected with the virus.* **2** to make food, water etc likely to spread disease: *The eggs were infected with bacteria.* **3** if a feeling that you have infects other people, it makes them feel the same way: *His cynicism seems to have infected the whole team.*

infected /ɪnˈfektɪ̩d/ *adj* **1** a wound that is infected has harmful BACTERIA in it which prevent it from getting better **2** food, water etc that is infected contains BACTERIA that spread disease

infection /ɪnˈfekʃən/ *n* [C,U] a disease in part of your body, caused by BACTERIA or a VIRUS: *Wash the cut thoroughly to protect against infection.* | *an ear infection* | **bad/severe/nasty infection** *She's got a nasty infection in her throat.*

infectious /ɪnˈfekʃəs/ *adj*

1 an infectious disease can be passed from one person to another: *Flu is **highly infectious**.* **2** someone who is infectious has a disease that could be passed to other people: *Some people with HIV may feel well but will still be infectious.* **3** infectious feelings or laughter spread quickly from one person to another: *She's got an infectious smile.* | *his infectious enthusiasm*

infer /ɪnˈfɜː $ -ɜːr/ *v* [T] **inferred**, **inferring** *formal* to decide that something is probably true because of other information that you already have: **infer sth from sth** *I inferred from his letter that he was still angry with me.*

inference /ˈɪnfərəns/ *n* [C, U] *formal* a fact that you think is true, based on information that you already know, or the process of deciding this

inferior¹ /ɪnˈfɪəriə $ -ˈfɪriər/ *adj* not good, or not as good as someone or something else [➔ **superior**]: *wine of inferior quality* | +**to** *I always felt slightly inferior to her.* —**inferiority** /ɪnˌfɪəriˈɒrɪ̩ti $ ɪnˌfɪriˈɔːr-/ *n* [U] *She suffers from feelings of inferiority.*

inferior² *n* [C] someone who has a lower position or rank than you in an organization [➔ **superior**]

inferno /ɪnˈfɜːnəʊ $ -ɜːrnoʊ/ *n* [C] plural **infernos** *literary* a very large and dangerous fire: *a raging inferno* → see box at FIRE

infertile /ɪnˈfɜːtaɪl $ -ˈfɜːrtl/ *adj* **1** unable to have babies **2** infertile land is not good enough to grow plants in —**infertility** /ˌɪnfəˈtɪlɪ̩ti $ -fər-/ *n* [U]

infest /ɪnˈfest/ *v* [T] if insects, rats etc infest a place, there are a lot of them and they usually cause damage: **be infested with sth** *The kitchen was infested with cockroaches.* —**infestation** /ˌɪnfeˈsteɪʃən/ *n* [C,U] *an infestation of rats*

infidelity /ˌɪnfɪˈdelɪ̩ti/ *n* [C,U] plural **infidelities** when someone has sex with someone who is not their wife, husband, or partner

infighting /ˈɪnfaɪtɪŋ/ *n* [U] unfriendly disagreement between members of the same group or organization: *There has been a lot of political infighting in the party.*

infiltrate /ˈɪnfɪltreɪt $ ɪnˈfɪltreɪt, ˈɪnfɪl-/ *v* [I,T] to secretly join an organization to find out information about it: *police attempts to infiltrate neo-Nazi groups*

infinite /ˈɪnfₐnₐt/ *adj* **1** very great in amount or degree: *a teacher with infinite patience* **2** without limits in space or time: *an infinite universe*

infinitely /ˈɪnfₐnₐtli/ *adv* very much: *someone with infinitely more experience*

infinitesimal /ˌɪnfɪnₐˈtesₐməl/ *adj* extremely small: *infinitesimal changes in temperature*

infinitive /ɪnˈfɪnₐtɪv/ *n* [C] in grammar, the basic form of a verb, used with 'to'. In the sentence 'I forgot to buy milk', 'to buy' is an infinitive.

infinity /ɪnˈfɪnₐti/ *n* **1** [U] a space or distance without limits or an end **2** [singular, U] a number that is too large to be calculated

infirm /ɪnˈfɜːm $ -ɜːrm/ *adj* someone who is infirm is old, ill, and weak

infirmary /ɪnˈfɜːməri $ -ɜːr-/ *n* [C] plural **infirmaries** a hospital – used in the names of some hospitals

infirmity /ɪnˈfɜːmₐti $ -ɜːr-/ *n* [C,U] plural **infirmities** *formal* an illness

inflame /ɪnˈfleɪm/ *v* [T] to make someone's feelings of anger or excitement much stronger

inflamed /ɪnˈfleɪmd/ *adj* a part of your body that is inflamed is red and painful

inflammable /ɪnˈflæməbəl/ *adj* materials or substances that are inflammable burn very easily [= **flammable**; ≠ **non-flammable**]: *Petrol is highly inflammable*.

inflammation /ˌɪnfləˈmeɪʃən/ *n* [C,U] pain and swelling in a part of your body

inflammatory /ɪnˈflæmətəri $ -tɔːri/ *adj* formal an inflammatory speech or piece of writing is likely to make people angry

inflatable /ɪnˈfleɪtəbəl/ *adj* an inflatable object is one that you fill with air before you use it: *an inflatable boat*

inflate /ɪnˈfleɪt/ *v* **1** [I,T] to fill something such as a ball or tyre with air **2** [T] to make a price or number higher than it should be: *Hotels inflate prices at this time of year.*

inflated /ɪnˈfleɪtₐd/ *adj* **1** inflated prices or costs are higher than they should be: **grossly/vastly/hugely inflated** *hugely inflated prices for tickets* **2** filled with air: *an inflated life-jacket*

inflation /ɪnˈfleɪʃən/ *n* [U]
1 when the price of things you buy keeps increasing: **high/low inflation** *The 1990s was a period of high inflation.* | *What is the current* **rate of inflation**? | *the government's attempts to control inflation*
2 when you fill something with air

inflationary /ɪnˈfleɪʃənəri $ -ʃəneri/ *adj* causing prices to keep increasing

inflection, **inflexion** /ɪnˈflekʃən/ *n* [C,U]
1 *technical* the way the ending of a word changes to show that it is plural, in the past tense etc **2** the way the sound of your voice goes up and down when you are speaking

inflexible /ɪnˈfleksₐbəl/ *adj* **1** not willing to change your opinions or ideas **2** something that is inflexible is stiff and will not bend
—**inflexibility** /ɪnˌfleksₐˈbɪlₐti/ *n* [U]

inflict /ɪnˈflɪkt/ *v* [T] to make a person or place suffer something unpleasant: **inflict sth on/upon sb** *The earthquake inflicted a lot of damage on the area.*

'in-flight *adj* [only before noun] provided during a plane journey: *in-flight movies*

influence¹ /ˈɪnfluəns/ *n*
1 [C,U] if someone has influence, they have the power to change how things develop or how people behave: *The Queen has no political influence.* | *Kate used her influence to get her friend a job.* | **+on** *The food you eat* **has an** important **influence on** *your health.* | **under sb's/sth's influence/under the influence of sb/sth** *They had come under the influence of a religious sect.*
2 [C] someone or something that has an effect on other people or things: **bad/good etc influence (on sb)** *She was a bad influence on him.* | *The country remains untouched by* **outside influences**.
3 under the influence (of drink/alcohol/drugs etc) drunk, or feeling the effects of an illegal drug

influence² *v* [T] to change how something develops, or how someone behaves: *His advice* **strongly influenced** *my decision.*

influential /ˌɪnfluˈenʃəl/ *adj* able to influence what happens or what people think: *He has some very influential friends.*

influenza /ˌɪnfluˈenzə/ *n* [U] *technical* FLU

influx /ˈɪnflʌks/ *n* [C] the arrival of large numbers of people or things: **+of** *an influx of tourists*

info /ˈɪnfəʊ $ -foʊ/ *n* [U] *informal* information

inform /ɪnˈfɔːm $ -ɔːrm/ *v* [T] *formal* to formally tell someone about something: **inform sb about/of sth** *No one informed me about the change of plan.* | *She was informed of the accident by the police.* | **inform sb (that)** *The college informed me that I had been accepted.*

inform on/against sb *phr v* to secretly give information about someone to the police

informal /ɪnˈfɔːməl $ -ɔːr-/ *adj*
1 relaxed and friendly: *an informal party*
2 suitable for ordinary situations: *informal clothes*
—**informally** *adv* —**informality** /ˌɪnfɔːˈmælₐti $ -fɔːr-/ *n* [U]

informant /ɪnˈfɔːmənt $ -ɔːr-/ *n* [C] someone who secretly gives information about someone else to the police

information /ˌɪnfəˈmeɪʃən $ -fər-/ *n* [U] facts or details about a situation, person, or event: **+about/on** *The book contains information about many subjects.* | **bit/piece of information** *a useful bit of information* | **further/additional/more etc information** *For further information, call the number below.*

GRAMMAR

Information is a U noun and is never plural. Do not say 'an information' or 'some informations'. Say **some information**, **a lot of information**, or **a piece/bit of information**: *I'd like some information about train times, please.* | *That's a useful bit of information.*

information superhighway /ˌɪnfəmeɪʃən
ˌsuːpəˈhaɪweɪ $ -fərmeɪʃən ˌsuːpər-/ *n* **the information superhighway** the Internet

infor'mation tech,nology *n* [U] abbreviation *IT* the use of computers to store information and make it available

informative /ɪnˈfɔːmətɪv $ -ɔːr-/ *adj* providing useful information: *The lecture was very informative.*

informed /ɪnˈfɔːmd $ -ɔːr-/ *adj* having plenty of knowledge and information about something: **well-informed/ill-informed** *He's very well-informed about this subject.* | *I want to learn as much as I can so that I can make an **informed decision.***

informer /ɪnˈfɔːmə $ -ɔːrmər/ *n* [C] someone who secretly gives information about someone to the police

infraction /ɪnˈfrækʃən/ *n* [C,U] *formal* when someone breaks a rule or law

infra-red /ˌɪnfrə ˈred◂ / *adj* infra-red light gives out heat but cannot be seen

infrastructure /ˈɪnfrəˌstrʌktʃə $ -ər/ *n* [C,U] the basic systems and structures that a country or organization needs in order to work properly, for example roads, railways, banks etc

infrequent /ɪnˈfriːkwənt/ *adj* not often: *The buses into town are quite infrequent.* | *He was an infrequent visitor to our house.* —**infrequently** *adv*

infringe /ɪnˈfrɪndʒ/ *v* [T] to do something that is against the law or someone's legal rights: *Making photocopies of a book **infringes** the **copyright**.* —**infringement** *n* [C,U]
  infringe on/upon sth *phr v* to limit someone's freedom in some way: *The rule infringes our right to free speech.*

infuriate /ɪnˈfjʊərieɪt $ -ˈfjʊr-/ *v* [T] to make someone very angry: *His attitude infuriated me.*

infuriating /ɪnˈfjʊərieɪtɪŋ $ -ˈfjʊr-/ *adj* very annoying: *an infuriating delay*

infuse /ɪnˈfjuːz/ *v* **1** [T] *formal* to fill something or someone with a feeling or quality: **be infused with** sth *Her books are infused with humour.* **2** [I,T] if you infuse tea or HERBS, you leave them in very hot water while their taste passes into the water —**infusion** /-ˈfjuːʒən/ *n* [C,U]

ingenious /ɪnˈdʒiːniəs/ *adj* extremely clever: *an ingenious plan* | *an ingenious device for getting frost off your car window* | *He was an ingenious inventor.* —**ingeniously** *adv*

ingenuity /ˌɪndʒəˈnjuːɪti $ -ˈnuː-/ *n* [U] skill at inventing things and thinking of new ideas

ingest /ɪnˈdʒest/ *v* [T] *technical* to eat or drink something

ingrained /ɪnˈɡreɪnd/ *adj* **1** ingrained attitudes or behaviour are firmly established and difficult to change **2** ingrained dirt is under the surface of something and difficult to remove

ingratiate /ɪnˈɡreɪʃieɪt/ *v* **ingratiate yourself (with sb)** *disapproving* to try very hard to get someone's approval: *He tried to ingratiate himself with the boss.* —**ingratiating** *adj*

ingratitude /ɪnˈɡrætɪtjuːd $ -tuːd/ *n* [U] when someone is not grateful for something

recipe book
ingredient
ingredients for chocolate cake

ingredient /ɪnˈɡriːdiənt/ *n* [C] **1** one of the things you use to make a particular kind of food: *Mix the ingredients together in a bowl.* **2** one of the qualities that you need to achieve something: *Al **has** all **the ingredients of** a great player.*

inhabit /ɪnˈhæbɪt/ *v* [T] *formal* to live in a place: *The woods are inhabited by deer.*

inhabitant /ɪnˈhæbɪtənt/ *n* [C] *formal* the inhabitants of a place are the people who live there

inhale /ɪnˈheɪl/ *v* [I,T] *formal* to breathe in air, smoke, or gas: *Ed lit a cigarette and **inhaled deeply**.* —**inhalation** /ˌɪnhəˈleɪʃən/ *n* [U]

inhaler /ɪnˈheɪlə $ -ər/ *n* [C] a small plastic tube containing medicine that you breathe in if you suffer from ASTHMA

inherent /ɪnˈhɪərənt, -ˈher- $ -ˈhɪr-, -ˈher-/ *adj* a quality that is inherent in something is a natural part of it and cannot be separated from it: **+in** *The problem is inherent in our education system.* —**inherently** *adv*

inherit /ɪnˈherɪt/ *v* **1** [I,T] to receive money or property from someone when they die: **inherit sth from sb** *He inherited £10,000 from his aunt.* **2** [T] to have the same character or appearance as your parents: *I inherited my mother's curly hair.* **3** [T] if you inherit a difficult situation, you have to deal with problems that were caused by other people in the past: *The government inherited many problems.*

inheritance /ɪnˈherɪtəns/ *n* [C,U] money or property that you receive from someone when they die

inhibit /ɪnˈhɪbɪt/ *v* [T] **1** to prevent something from growing or developing well: *An unhappy family life may inhibit children's learning.* **2** to make someone feel embarrassed or nervous so that they cannot do or say what they want

inhibited /ɪnˈhɪbɪtɪd/ *adj* too embarrassed or nervous to do or say what you want

inhibition /ˌɪnhɪˈbɪʃən/ *n* [C,U] shyness or embarrassment that stops you doing or saying what you want: *He's got a lot of inhibitions.* | *People **lose** their **inhibitions** when they drink alcohol.*

inhospitable /ˌɪnhɒˈspɪtəbəl $ -hɑː-/ *adj* **1** an inhospitable place is unpleasant and difficult to live in **2** an inhospitable person is unfriendly to visitors

in-'house *adj, adv* within a company or organization: *in-house training*

inhuman /ɪnˈhjuːmən/ *adj* **1** very cruel and bad: *inhuman acts of terrorism* **2** lacking any human qualities in a way that seems strange or frightening: *a strange inhuman sound*

inhumane /ˌɪnhjuːˈmeɪn/ *adj* if you treat someone in an inhumane way, you are very cruel to them: *the inhumane treatment of prisoners* —**inhumanely** *adv*

inhumanity /ˌɪnhjuːˈmænəti/ *n* [U] very cruel behaviour: *man's inhumanity to man*

inimitable /ɪˈnɪmɪtəbəl/ *adj* too good or skilful for anyone else to copy with the same high standard: *the inimitable Elvis*

iniquity /ɪˈnɪkwəti/ *n* [C,U] plural **iniquities** *formal* something that is very unfair: +**of** *the iniquities of the tax system* —**iniquitous** *adj*

initial¹ /ɪˈnɪʃəl/ *adj* [only before noun] happening at the beginning: *an initial period of training* | *the initial stages of the disease* —**initially** *adv*: *Initially, I didn't like him.*

initial² *n* [C usually plural] the first letter of a name: *His initials are W.G. – for William Grout.*

initial³ *v* [T] **initialled, initialling** *BrE*; **initialed, initialing** *AmE* to write your initials on a document: *The two countries have initialled the agreement.*

initiate /ɪˈnɪʃieɪt/ *v* [T] **1** *formal* to arrange for something important to start: *He initiated legal proceedings against the newspaper.* **2** to tell someone about something or show them how to do something **3** to introduce someone into an organization, often with a special ceremony —**initiation** /ɪˌnɪʃiˈeɪʃən/ *n* [C,U]

initiative /ɪˈnɪʃətɪv/ *n* **1** [U] when you make decisions and do things without waiting for someone to tell you what to do: *You need to have a lot of initiative to do this job.* | *I wish he would show more initiative.* **2** [C] an important new plan or process to achieve an aim or solve a problem: *a new government initiative to reduce car crime* **3 the initiative** if you have or take the initiative, you are in a position to control a situation and decide what to do next

inject /ɪnˈdʒekt/ *v* [T] **1** to put a drug into someone's body by using a special needle: **inject sth into sb/sth** *The vaccine is injected into your arm.* **2** to improve something by adding excitement or interest to it: **inject sth into sth** *The company is injecting more fun into their designs.*

injection /ɪnˈdʒekʃən/ *n*
1 [C,U] when a drug is put into your body, using a special needle: *The nurse gave me an injection.* | +**of** *an injection of insulin*
2 [C] the addition of money to something in order to improve it: +**of** *The firm received a cash injection of $6 million.*

in-joke *n* [C] a joke that is only understood by a particular group of people

injunction /ɪnˈdʒʌŋkʃən/ *n* [C] *law* an order given by a court which tells someone not to do something

injure /ˈɪndʒə $ -ər/ *v* [T] to hurt someone or damage part of their body: *He injured his leg playing rugby.* | **be badly/seriously/critically injured** *She was badly injured in the accident.* → see box at **HURT**

injured /ˈɪndʒəd $ -ərd/ *adj* **1** an injured person or animal has been hurt: *The injured passengers were taken to hospital.* **2 the injured** people who have been hurt

injury /ˈɪndʒəri/ *n* [C,U] plural **injuries** physical harm that someone gets in an accident or attack: *She was taken to hospital with **serious** head injuries.* | *He **suffered** horrific **injuries** in the attack.* | *He was lucky to survive with only **minor injuries**.* | *Luckily, she **escaped injury** (=she was not injured).*

injustice /ɪnˈdʒʌstɪs/ *n* [C,U] when people are treated in a bad and unfair way: *There's so much injustice in the world.*

ink /ɪŋk/ *n* [C,U] a coloured liquid used for writing, printing, or drawing: **in ink** *a message written in black ink*

inkling /ˈɪŋklɪŋ/ *n* [C] a slight idea about something: *I had an inkling that she was pregnant.*

inland /ˈɪnlənd/ *adj, adv* away from the coast: *an inland village* | *Lake Sabaya lies six miles inland.*

'in-laws *n* [plural] *informal* the parents of your husband or wife

inlet /ˈɪnlet, ˈɪnlət/ *n* [C] **1** a narrow area of water that goes into the land from the sea or a lake **2** a tube through which liquid or gas flows into a machine

inmate /ˈɪnmeɪt/ *n* [C] someone who is kept in a prison

inn /ɪn/ *n* [C] a small hotel or PUB

innards /ˈɪnədz $ -ərdz/ *n* [plural] *informal* the parts inside your body

innate /ˌɪˈneɪt◂/ *adj* an innate quality or ability is something you are born with: *an innate ability to learn language* —**innately** *adv*

inner /ˈɪnə $ -ər/ *adj*
1 on the inside or near the centre of something: *the castle's inner walls*
2 inner thoughts or feelings are ones that you feel strongly but do not always show to other people

inner 'city *n* [C] the part of a city that is near the centre, especially the part where the buildings are in a bad condition and the people are poor: *the problem of crime in our inner cities* —**inner city** *adj*: *an inner city housing estate*

innermost /ˈɪnəməʊst $ -nərmoʊst/ *adj* [only before noun] **1** your innermost feelings, desires etc are your most personal and secret ones **2** *formal* furthest inside or nearest to the centre

inning /ˈɪnɪŋ/ *n* [C] one of the nine periods of play in a game of baseball

innings /ˈɪnɪŋz/ *n* [C] plural **innings** one of the periods of play in a game of CRICKET

innkeeper /ˈɪnˌkiːpə $ -ər/ *n* [C] *old-fashioned* someone who owns or manages an INN

innocence /ˈɪnəsəns/ *n* [U]
1 the fact that someone is not guilty of a crime [≠ guilt]: *Can you prove your innocence?*
2 when someone has not had much experience of life: *the innocence of a child*

innocent /ˈɪnəsənt/ *adj*
1 someone who is innocent has not done anything wrong [≠ guilty]: *Nobody believed that I was innocent.* | +**of** *He's innocent of the murder.* | *The court found him innocent.*
2 innocent victims/bystanders/people etc people who get hurt or killed in a war or crime although they are not directly involved in it: *Many innocent civilians were killed.*

3 done or said without intending to harm or offend anyone: *an innocent remark*
4 someone who is innocent does not know about the bad things in life: *an innocent child*
—**innocently** *adv*

innocuous /ɪ'nɒkjuəs $ ɪ'nɑːk-/ *adj* not likely to harm anyone or cause trouble: *an innocuous remark*

innovation /,ɪnə'veɪʃən/ *n* **1** [C] a new idea, method, or invention: **+in** *innovations in teaching* **2** [U] the introduction of new ideas or methods —**innovate** /'ɪnəveɪt/ *v* [I,T] —**innovative** *adj* —**innovator** *n* [C]

innuendo /,ɪnju'endəʊ $ -doʊ/ *n* [C,U] plural **innuendoes** or **innuendos** a remark that suggests something sexual or unpleasant without saying it directly

innumerable /ɪ'njuːmərəbəl $ ɪ'nuː-/ *adj* very many

inoculate /ɪ'nɒkjʊleɪt $ ɪ'nɑː-/ *v* [T] to protect someone against a disease by putting a weak form of the disease into their body using a needle [➔ **immunize, vaccinate**]: *Have you been inoculated against hepatitis?* —**inoculation** /ɪ,nɒkjʊ'leɪʃən $ ɪ,nɑːk-/ *n* [C,U]

inoffensive /,ɪnə'fensɪv◂/ *adj* unlikely to offend anyone: *an inoffensive little man*

inordinate /ɪ'nɔːdənət $ -ɔːr-/ *adj* far more than you would normally expect: *an inordinate amount of time* —**inordinately** *adv*

inorganic /,ɪnɔː'gænɪk◂ $ -ɔːr-/ *adj* not consisting of anything that is living or has lived in the past: *an inorganic fertilizer*

inpatient /'ɪn,peɪʃənt/ *n* [C] someone who stays in hospital while they receive treatment

input /'ɪnpʊt/ *n* **1** [U] information that is put into a computer **2** [C,U] the ideas and things that you do to make something succeed: *Teachers contributed most of the input into the survey.* **3** [C,U] *technical* electrical power that is put into a machine —**input** *v* [T]

inquest /'ɪnkwest/ *n* [C] an official process to discover why someone has died

inquire also **enquire** *BrE* /ɪn'kwaɪə $ -'kwaɪr/ *v* [I,T] *formal* to ask someone for information: *'Why are you doing that?' he inquired.* | **+about** *I am writing to inquire about your advertisement in The Times.* ➔ see box at **ASK**

   inquire into sth *phr v* to ask questions in order to get more information about something: *The investigation inquired into the company's financial dealings.*

inquiring also **enquiring** *BrE* /ɪn'kwaɪərɪŋ $ -'kwaɪr-/ *adj* **1** an inquiring look or expression shows that you want to ask about something **2 inquiring mind** someone who has an inquiring mind wants to learn new things —**inquiringly** *adv*

inquiry also **enquiry** *BrE* /ɪn'kwaɪəri $ ɪn'kwaɪri, 'ɪŋkwəri/ *n* [C] plural **inquiries**
1 a question you ask in order to get information: **+about** *We're getting a lot of inquiries about our new bus service.* | *I'll make some inquiries.*
2 an official process to discover why something bad happened: **+into** *a government inquiry into the causes of the disaster* | **launch/set up/hold an inquiry (into sb)** *The police have launched a murder inquiry.*

inquisition /,ɪnkwɪ'zɪʃən/ *n* [C] a series of questions that someone asks you in a threatening or unpleasant way

inquisitive /ɪn'kwɪzətɪv/ *adj* an inquisitive person or animal is very interested in everything: *Cats are inquisitive animals.* —**inquisitively** *adv*

inroads /'ɪnrəʊdz $ -roʊdz/ *n* **make inroads into/on sth** to start being more successful in something: *The company has made inroads into the European market.*

ins and 'outs *n* [plural] all the details of a complicated situation or problem: **+of** *the ins and outs of the matter*

insane /ɪn'seɪn/ *adj* **1** *informal* very stupid: *an insane idea* | *You're taking an insane risk.*
2 seriously mentally ill —**insanely** *adv*

insanity /ɪn'sænəti/ *n* [U] **1** when someone is seriously mentally ill **2** very stupid actions that may cause you serious harm

insatiable /ɪn'seɪʃəbəl/ *adj* always wanting more of something: *his insatiable appetite for power* | *an insatiable demand for new products*

inscribe /ɪn'skraɪb/ *v* [T] to write or cut words on something: **be inscribed in/on sth** *His name is inscribed on the trophy.* —**inscription** /-'skrɪpʃən/ *n* [C]

inscrutable /ɪn'skruːtəbəl/ *adj* someone who is inscrutable shows no emotion on their face so that it is impossible to know what they are thinking

insect /'ɪnsekt/ *n* [C] any small creature that has six legs, for example a fly

insecticide /ɪn'sektəsaɪd/ *n* [U] a chemical substance for killing insects

insecure /,ɪnsɪ'kjʊə◂ $ -'kjʊr◂/ *adj* **1** if you are insecure, you do not feel confident about yourself: **+about** *She's very insecure about her appearance.* ➔ see box at **CONFIDENT** **2** if something such as a job is insecure, it could be taken away or lost at any time —**insecurity** *n* [C,U]

insemination /ɪn,semə'neɪʃən/ *n* [U] *technical* the act of putting SPERM into a woman or female animal in order to make her have a baby: **artificial insemination** (=done by medical treatment, not sex)

insensitive /ɪn'sensətɪv/ *adj* **1** someone who is insensitive does not notice other people's feelings and often does or says things that upset them: *Sometimes he can be rather insensitive.* | *an insensitive remark* ➔ see box at **CHARACTER** **2** [not before noun] not affected by physical effects or changes —**insensitively** *adv* —**insensitivity** /ɪn,sensə'tɪvəti/ *n* [U]

inseparable /ɪn'sepərəbəl/ *adj* **1** people who are inseparable are always together and are very friendly with each other: *My brother and I were inseparable.* **2** *formal* things that are inseparable cannot be considered separately: **+from** *Britain's economic fortunes are inseparable from the world situation.*

insert¹ /ɪn'sɜːt $ -ɜːrt/ *v* [T] to put something inside something else: **insert sth in/into/between sth** *Insert the coins in the machine.*

insert² /'ɪnsɜːt $ -ɜːrt/ *n* [C] **1** printed pages that are put inside a newspaper or magazine in order to advertise something **2** something that is designed to be put inside something else: *Dave wore special inserts in his shoes to make him look taller.*

inside¹ /ɪn'saɪd/ *adv, prep*

1 in or into a container [≠ **outside**]: *Is there anything inside the box?*

2 in or into a building or room [≠ **outside**]: *The rooms inside the building have just been painted.* | *Let's go inside – it's cold.*

3 if someone is inside a group or organization, they are part of it [≠ **outside**]: *The information comes from sources inside the company.*

4 in a country or area [≠ **outside**]: *Little is known of events inside this mysterious country.*

5 if you have a feeling or thought inside your head, you feel or think it without telling anyone: *You just don't understand how I feel inside.* | *Joe's a strange guy – you never know what's going on inside his head.*

6 in less than a particular amount of time: *We'll be there inside an hour.*

inside² /ɪn'saɪd, 'ɪnsaɪd/ *n*

1 the inside the inner part of something [≠ **the outside**]: **+of** *The inside of the car was filthy.* | **on the inside** *The apple's rotten on the inside.*

2 inside out with the usual outside parts on the inside: *Your jumper's inside out.*

3 know sth inside out *BrE*; **know sth inside and out** *AmE* to know something in great detail: *She knows the business inside out.*

4 sb's inside/insides *informal* someone's stomach

inside³ /'ɪnsaɪd/ *adj* **1** on the inside of something: *the inside pages of the newspaper* | *the inside pocket of his jacket* **2 inside information/the inside story etc** information that is available only to people who are part of a group or organization

insider /ɪn'saɪdə $ -ər/ *n* [C] someone who knows a lot about an organization because they are part of it

insidious /ɪn'sɪdiəs/ *adj formal* happening gradually without being noticed, but causing a lot of harm: *the insidious effects of pollution* —**insidiously** *adv*

insight /'ɪnsaɪt/ *n* [C,U] a clear understanding of a complicated situation, idea etc: **+into** *The article gives us an insight into Chinese culture.*

insignia /ɪn'sɪgniə/ *n* [C] *plural* **insignia** a BADGE or sign that shows which organization someone belongs to, or the rank they have

insignificant /ˌɪnsɪg'nɪfɪkənt◂/ *adj* small and unimportant: *insignificant effects* —**insignificance** *n* [U]

insincere /ˌɪnsɪn'sɪə◂ $ -'sɪr◂/ *adj* pretending to feel or think something: *an insincere smile* —**insincerely** *adv* —**insincerity** /ˌɪnsɪn'serəti/ *n* [U]

insinuate /ɪn'sɪnjueɪt/ *v* [T] to suggest that something bad is true, without saying it directly: **+that** *He insinuated that she had lied.* —**insinuation** /ɪnˌsɪnju'eɪʃən/ *n* [C,U]

insipid /ɪn'sɪpd/ *adj* not strong or interesting: *insipid colors*

insist /ɪn'sɪst/ *v* [I,T]

1 to demand that something should happen: *I didn't want to go but Jane insisted.* | **insist on (doing) sth** *He insisted on paying the bill.* |

+(that) *I insisted that he leave.* | *I'll call her tomorrow if you insist.*

2 to say firmly and often that something is true, especially when other people do not believe you: **+(that)** *He insisted he had done nothing wrong.* | **+on** *She always insisted on her innocence.*

insistence /ɪn'sɪstəns/ *n* [U] **1** when you demand that something should happen: **+on** *an insistence on high standards* | **+that** *an insistence that safety checks should be done properly* **2** when you say firmly that something is true, especially when other people think it may not be true: **+that** *the government's insistence that the drug is safe*

insistent /ɪn'sɪstənt/ *adj* **1** saying firmly that something should happen or that something is true: *his father's insistent voice* | **+(that)** *He was insistent that I should come.* **2** continuing for a long time in a way that is difficult to ignore: *an insistent ringing sound* —**insistently** *adv*

insofar as, in so far as /ɪnsəʊ'fɑːr əz $ -soʊ-/ *linking word, formal* to the degree that: *The report was relevant only insofar as it provided financial information.*

insolent /'ɪnsələnt/ *adj formal* rude and not showing any respect: *an insolent stare* —**insolence** *n* [U] —**insolently** *adv*

insoluble /ɪn'sɒljəbəl $ ɪn'sɑːl-/ *also* **insolvable** /ɪn'sɒlvəbəl $ -'sɑːl-/ *AmE adj* **1** impossible to solve: *insoluble problems* **2** an insoluble substance does not DISSOLVE when you put it in liquid [≠ **soluble**]

insolvent /ɪn'sɒlvənt $ ɪn'sɑːl-/ *adj formal* not having enough money to pay what you owe [= **bankrupt**]

insomnia /ɪn'sɒmniə $ ɪn'sɑːm-/ *n* [U] the problem of not being able to sleep —**insomniac** *n* [C]

inspect /ɪn'spekt/ *v* [T]

1 to examine something carefully: **inspect sth carefully/closely** *She bent down to inspect the plant more closely.* | **inspect sth for sth** *He inspected the car for damage.*

2 to visit a building or organization officially in order to make sure everything is satisfactory and rules are being obeyed: *The building was inspected by fire officers.* —**inspection** /-'spekʃən/ *n* [C,U] *An inspection was carried out at the school.*

inspector /ɪn'spektə $ -ər/ *n* [C]

1 someone whose job is to check that something is satisfactory and that rules are being obeyed: *school inspectors*

2 a police officer of middle rank

inspiration /ˌɪnspʉ'reɪʃən/ *n* [C,U] **1** a good idea about what you should say, do, write etc, or the person or thing which gives you this: *an artist who* **drew inspiration from** *Monet's work* | **+for** *His time in Mexico* **provided** *the* **inspiration** *for this novel.* | *Libraries are a good* **source of inspiration.** **2 be an inspiration to sb** to be so good or successful that people admire you and want to achieve something themselves: *At 87, he's an inspiration to us all.* —**inspirational** *adj*

inspire /ɪn'spaɪə $ -'spaɪr/ *v* [T] **1** to encourage someone and make them want to do something: **inspire sb to do sth** *She inspired many young people to take up the sport.* **2** to make someone have a particular feeling or react in a particular way: **inspire sth in sb/inspire sb with sth** *A good teacher inspires confidence in students.* —inspiring *adj*

inspired /ɪnˈspaɪəd $ -ˈspaɪrd/ *adj* good and impressive: *It was an inspired choice.*

instability /ˌɪnstəˈbɪləti/ *n* [U] when a situation or someone's behaviour is likely to change suddenly [➔ **unstable**]: *political instability* | *mental instability*

install /ɪnˈstɔːl $ -ˈstɒːl/ *v* [T] **1** to put a piece of equipment somewhere and connect it so that you can use it: *The company has installed security cameras.* **2** to add new software to a computer **3** to give someone an important job or position: *She was installed as Chancellor of the university.* —**installation** /ˌɪnstəˈleɪʃən/ *n* [C,U]

instalment *BrE*; **installment** *AmE* /ɪnˈstɔːlmənt $ ɪnˈstɒːl-/ *n* [C] **1** a payment that you make every week, month etc in order to pay for something: *We're **paying** for the car by monthly **instalments**.* **2** one of several parts of a story that are PUBLISHED or shown at different times

instance /ˈɪnstəns/ *n* [C] **1 for instance** for example: *In many countries, for instance Japan, fish is an important part of the diet.* **2** an example of a particular kind of situation: **+of** *instances of violence* | *In this instance I think she was mistaken.*

instant[1] /ˈɪnstənt/ *adj* **1** happening immediately: *The band became an instant success.* **2** [only before noun] instant food can be prepared quickly by adding hot water: *instant coffee*

instant[2] *n* [singular] a moment: *He paused for an instant before replying.* | *He disappeared **in an instant** (=immediately).*

instantaneous /ˌɪnstənˈteɪniəs◂/ *adj* happening immediately: *an instantaneous reaction* —**instantaneously** *adv*

instantly /ˈɪnstəntli/ *adv* immediately: *Both victims died instantly.*

instant 'replay *n* [C] *AmE* an exciting moment in a sports game that is shown again on television immediately after it happens [= **action replay** *BrE*]

instead /ɪnˈsted/ *adv* used to say that something is done, used etc when something else is not done or used: *If Jane can't go, I'll go instead.* | **+of** *Can I have cheese instead of ham?*

instigate /ˈɪnstɪɡeɪt/ *v* [T] *formal* to make something start to happen: *The government instigated a programme of reforms.* —**instigator** *n* [C] —**instigation** /ˌɪnstɪˈɡeɪʃən/ *n* [U]

instil *BrE*; **instill** *AmE* /ɪnˈstɪl/ *v* [T] **instilled, instilling** to make someone think, feel, or behave in a particular way: **instil sth into sb** *Her parents had instilled a sense of duty into her.*

instinct /ˈɪnstɪŋkt/ *n* [C,U] a natural ability or feeling that makes people or animals know something or behave in a particular way: *Instinct told me something was wrong.* | **+for** *Animals have a natural instinct for survival.* | **instinct to do sth** *a cat's instinct to kill birds* —**instinctive** /ɪnˈstɪŋktɪv/ *adj: an instinctive reaction* —**instinctively** *adv*

institute[1] /ˈɪnstɪtjuːt $ -tuːt/ *n* [C] an organization that does scientific or educational work: *a research institute* | **+of/for** *the Institute for Space Studies*

institute[2] *v* [T] *formal* to start a system, rule, legal process etc: *New taxes have been instituted.*

institution /ˌɪnstɪˈtjuːʃən $ -ˈtuː-/ *n* [C] **1** a large important organization such as a university, church, or bank: **financial/political/educational etc institution** *banks and other financial institutions* ➔ see box at ORGANIZATION **2** an important custom that has existed for a long time: *social institutions such as the family and religion* | **+of** *the institution of marriage* **3** a place where people are sent to be looked after, for example old people or children with no parents

institutional /ˌɪnstɪˈtjuːʃənəl $ -ˈtuː-/ *adj* **1** relating to an institution: *institutional care* **2** institutionalized: *institutional racism*

institutionalized also **-ised** *BrE* /ˌɪnstɪˈtjuːʃənəlaɪzd $ -ˈtuː-/ *adj* institutionalized attitudes and behaviour have existed for so long in an organization that they seem normal even though they are bad: *institutionalized racism*

instruct /ɪnˈstrʌkt/ *v* [T] **1** to officially tell someone what to do: **instruct sb to do sth** *The doctor instructed me to change my diet.* **2** *formal* to teach someone something: **instruct sb in sth** *Greater effort is needed to instruct children in road safety.*

instruction /ɪnˈstrʌkʃən/ *n* **1 instructions** [plural] printed information that tells you how to do or use something: *Follow the **instructions** on the packet.* | **+on** *Are there any instructions on how to make the model?* | **+for** *The equipment comes with detailed instructions for use.* **2** [C usually plural] an order telling you what you must do: **instructions to do sth** *We were given strict instructions not to leave the building.* | **+that** *She left instructions that her paintings should not be sold.* **3** [U] *formal* training in a particular skill or subject: **+in** *The trainees were **given instruction** in the use of computers.* —**instructional** *adj*

instructive /ɪnˈstrʌktɪv/ *adj* giving useful information: *an instructive experience*

instructor /ɪnˈstrʌktə $ -ər/ *n* [C] someone who teaches a sport or activity: **driving/flying/ski etc instructor** ➔ see box at TEACHER

instrument /ˈɪnstrəmənt/ *n* [C] **1** a special tool or piece of equipment, especially one used in science or medicine: *scientific instruments* | *navigation instruments* **2** an object for producing music, such as a piano or VIOLIN: *Can you play any **musical instruments**?* | **wind/percussion/stringed instrument** **3** *formal* someone or something that is used to achieve a particular result: **+of** *an instrument of social change*

instrumental /ˌɪnstrəˈmentl◂/ *adj* **1 be instrumental in (doing) sth** *formal* to be important in making something happen: *He was*

instrumental in developing the program.
2 instrumental music is for instruments, not voices

insubordination /ˌɪnsəbɔːdɪˈneɪʃən $ -ˈbɔːrdnˈeɪ-/ *n* [U] *formal* when someone refuses to obey a person in authority —**insubordinate** /ˌɪnsəˈbɔːdɪnət $ -ˈbɔːr-/ *adj*

insubstantial /ˌɪnsəbˈstænʃəl/ *adj formal* not strong or large: *insubstantial changes*

insufferable /ɪnˈsʌfərəbəl/ *adj* very annoying

insufficient /ˌɪnsəˈfɪʃənt◂/ *adj* not enough: **+for** *Her salary was insufficient for their needs.* | **insufficient to do sth** *The heating was insufficient to kill the bacteria.* —**insufficiently** *adv* —**insufficiency** *n* [singular, U]

insular /ˈɪnsjʊlə $ ˈɪnsələr, ˈɪnʃə-/ *adj disapproving* not interested in other groups, countries, ways of life etc —**insularity** /ˌɪnsjʊˈlærəti $ -sə-, -ʃə-/ *n* [U]

insulate /ˈɪnsjʊleɪt $ ˈɪnsə-, ˈɪnʃə-/ *v* [T] to cover something with a material that stops electricity, sound, heat etc from getting in or out: *Insulate the pipes so they don't freeze.* —**insulation** /ˌɪnsjʊˈleɪʃən $ ˌɪnsə-/ *n* [U]

insulin /ˈɪnsjʊlɪn $ ˈɪnsə-/ *n* [U] a substance that controls the level of sugar in your blood

insult[1] /ˈɪnsʌlt/ *n* [C] a remark or action that is offensive or shows a lack of respect: *He started **shouting insults** at her.* | **+to** *The plan is an insult to teachers.*

insult[2] /ɪnˈsʌlt/ *v* [T] to say or do something that offends someone: *You should apologize for insulting her.* | *John would be insulted if we didn't go.* —**insulting** *adj*: *comments that are insulting to women* → see box at **RUDE**

insuperable /ɪnˈsjuːpərəbəl $ ɪnˈsuː-/ *adj formal* an insuperable difficulty or problem is impossible to solve

insurance /ɪnˈʃʊərəns $ -ˈʃʊr-/ *n* [U] an arrangement in which you pay a company money and they pay the costs if you become ill, have an accident etc: *an **insurance policy** | **insurance companies** | **+against** He took out insurance against unemployment.* | **health/car/ travel etc insurance** → LIFE INSURANCE

insure /ɪnˈʃʊə $ -ˈʃʊr/ *v* **1** [I,T] to buy or provide insurance: *Are the paintings insured?* | **insure (sb/sth) against/for sth** *Make sure you're insured against flood damage.* **2** an American spelling of ENSURE

insurmountable /ˌɪnsəˈmaʊntəbəl $ -sər-/ *adj formal* an insurmountable difficulty or problem is impossible to solve

insurrection /ˌɪnsəˈrekʃən/ *n* [C,U] *formal* a violent attempt by a group of people to take control of their country

intact /ɪnˈtækt/ *adj* [not before noun] not broken or damaged: *Fortunately, the glass **remained intact**.*

intake /ˈɪnteɪk/ *n* **1** [singular,U] the amount of food, drink etc that you take into your body: **+of** *Try to reduce your intake of fat.* | **food/alcohol/ calorie etc intake** **2** [C,U] the number of people who join a school, profession etc at a particular time: **+of** *a yearly intake of 300 students* **3 intake of breath** when you suddenly breathe in, especially when you are shocked

intangible /ɪnˈtændʒəbəl/ *adj* an intangible quality or feeling is difficult to describe exactly

integral /ˈɪntɪɡrəl/ *adj* forming part of something, especially a very important part: *Training is an **integral part** of any team's preparation.* | **+to** *Music is integral to the island's culture.* —**integrally** *adv*

integrate /ˈɪntɪɡreɪt/ *v* **1** [T] to combine things in a way that makes something more effective: **integrate sth with/into sth** *Pictures are integrated into the text.* **2** [I,T] to become part of a group or society, or to help someone do this: **integrate (sb) with/into sth** *Students with learning difficulties can be integrated into ordinary schools.* —**integrated** *adj* —**integration** /ˌɪntɪˈɡreɪʃən/ *n* [U]

integrity /ɪnˈteɡrəti/ *n* [U] the quality of being honest and having high moral standards: *a man of great professional integrity*

intellect /ˈɪntɪlekt/ *n* [C,U] the ability to understand things and think intelligently: *human intellect*

intellectual /ˌɪntɪˈlektʃuəl◂/ *adj* **1** relating to the ability to understand things and think intelligently: *children's intellectual development* → see box at **INTELLIGENT** **2** well-educated and interested in serious subjects and ideas —**intellectual** *n* [C] —**intellectually** *adv*

intelligence /ɪnˈtelɪdʒəns/ *n* [U]
1 the ability to learn and understand things: *You need a reasonable level of intelligence to be good at the game.* | **low/high intelligence** *a man of low intelligence*
2 information about the secret activities of criminals or foreign governments: *the British **intelligence services** | intelligence gathering* → **ARTIFICIAL INTELLIGENCE**

intelligent /ɪnˈtelɪdʒənt/ *adj* good at understanding ideas and thinking clearly, or showing this ability: **highly intelligent** *students* | *intelligent questions*

THESAURUS

clever *especially BrE*, **smart** *especially AmE* – intelligent: *clever students* | *smart kids*
bright – intelligent, used especially about children and young people: *a bright kid*
brilliant – extremely intelligent and good at the work you do: *a brilliant scientist*
wise – having a lot of experience and knowledge about people and the world: *a wise old man*
cunning/crafty *disapproving* – good at using your intelligence to trick people: *a cunning criminal*
intellectual – well-educated and interested in learning about art, science, literature etc
gifted – a gifted child is much more intelligent than most other children

—**intelligently** *adv*

intelligible /ɪnˈtelɪdʒəbəl/ *adj* clear enough to understand: **+to** *The instructions should be intelligible to users.* —**intelligibly** *adv*

intend /ɪnˈtend/ *v* [T]
1 to have something in your mind as a plan or purpose: *The work took longer than we intended.* | **intend to do sth** *I intend to move house next year.* | **intend doing sth** *I intended*

staying two nights. | **intend sth as sth** *It was intended as a joke.*

2 be intended for sb/sth to be provided or designed for a particular person or purpose: *a book intended for children aged 5–7*

intense /ɪnˈtens/ *adj* **1** extreme or very great: *Students are under intense pressure to succeed.* | *the intense heat of the desert* **2** *disapproving* someone who is intense is serious and has very strong feelings —**intensely** *adv* —**intensity** *n* [U]

intensify /ɪnˈtensɪfaɪ/ *v* [I,T] **intensified, intensifying, intensifies** to increase in degree or strength, or to make something do this: *The campaign has intensified.* —**intensification** /ɪnˌtensɪfɪˈkeɪʃən/ *n* [U]

intensive /ɪnˈtensɪv/ *adj* involving a lot of work or effort in a short time: *an intensive language course* —**intensively** *adv*

in,tensive 'care *n* [U] a hospital department for people who are very seriously ill or injured: *She died in intensive care.*

intent¹ /ɪnˈtent/ *adj* **1 be intent on (doing) sth** to be determined to do something: *She was intent on winning.* **2** giving careful attention to something: *an intent look*

intent² *n* [C,U] **1 to/for all intents and purposes** not exactly but in all the most important ways: *To all intents and purposes a baby is helpless.* **2** *formal or law* an intention: *the offence of possessing a firearm with intent to endanger life*

intention /ɪnˈtenʃən/ *n* [C,U] something you plan to do: **have no/every intention of doing sth** *I have no intention of getting married.* | *She went to the US* **with the intention of** *getting a job.* | **intention to do sth** *He announced his intention to resign.*

intentional /ɪnˈtenʃənəl/ *adj* done deliberately [= **deliberate**]: *I'm sorry I upset you – it wasn't intentional.* —**intentionally** *adv*

inter- /ɪntə $ -tər/ *prefix* between or involving two or more things or people: *intermarriage* (=marriage between people of different races, religions etc)

interact /ˌɪntərˈækt/ *v* [I] **1** if things interact, they have an effect on each other: **+with** *drugs that interact with each other* **2** to talk to people and do things with them: **+with** *the limited time teachers have to interact with each child* —**interaction** /-ˈækʃən/ *n* [C,U]

interactive /ˌɪntərˈæktɪv/ *adj* **1** involving communication between a computer, television etc and the person using it: *interactive software* **2** involving talking and working together —**interactively** *adv*

intercept /ˌɪntəˈsept $ -ər-/ *v* [T] to stop someone or something that is going from one place to another: *Police intercepted his letters.* —**interception** /-ˈsepʃən/ *n* [C,U]

interchangeable /ˌɪntəˈtʃeɪndʒəbəl $ -tər-/ *adj* things that are interchangeable can be used instead of each other: *interchangeable camera lenses* —**interchangeably** *adv*

intercom /ˈɪntəkɒm $ ˈɪntərkɑːm/ *n* [C] a system used for speaking to people in different parts of a building, aircraft etc

intercontinental /ˌɪntəkɒntɪˈnentl $ -tərkɑːn-/ *adj* going between or involving CONTINENTS: *an intercontinental flight*

intercourse /ˈɪntəkɔːs $ ˈɪntərkɔːrs/ *n* [U] *formal* when two people have sex

interdependent /ˌɪntədɪˈpendənt $ -tər-/ *adj* interdependent people or things depend on each other —**interdependence** *n* [U]

interest¹ /ˈɪntrɪst/ *n*

1 [singular, U] the feeling that you want to know more about something or someone: **+in** *We both* **have an interest** *in music.* | *He began to* **take an interest in** *politics.* | *She's never* **shown** *any* **interest** *in me.* | *After a while, I* **lost interest**.

have an/no/some/little interest in sth
show (an/no/some/little) interest in sth
express (an) interest in sth – to say that you are interested in something
attract/arouse interest – to make people interested
lack interest (in sth) – to not have much interest in something

2 [C] something you enjoy doing: *His main interests are reading and golf.*
3 [U] money charged or paid by a bank when you borrow or save money: **+on** *You pay 9% interest on the loan.* | *an* **interest-free** (=with no interest) *loan*
4 [U] the quality of being interesting: *museums, parks, and other places of interest* | *a book that will* **be of interest to** *parents*
5 [C,U] someone's success, happiness etc, which may be helped or harmed: *a policy designed to* **protect the interests of** *farmers* | **be in sb's (best) interest(s)** (=be the best thing for someone) *It's in your interests to provide the information.* | *changes that are in the public interest* (=will help the public)
6 in the interest(s) of justice/safety/efficiency etc in order to make something fair, safe etc: *The race was cancelled in the interests of safety.*
→ SELF-INTEREST, VESTED INTEREST

interest² *v* [T]
1 to make someone want to know more about something: *Here's a book that might interest you.* | *What interests me is the history of the place.*
2 can/could I interest you in sth? *spoken* used as a polite way of persuading someone to try or buy something: *Can I interest you in a cake?*

interested /ˈɪntrɪstɪd/ *adj*
1 [not before noun] wanting to find out more about something or give your attention to it [≠ **uninterested, bored**]: **+in** *She's very interested in computers.* | **be interested to hear/know/learn etc** *I'd be interested to know what you think about it.*
2 [not before noun] wanting to do or have something: **be interested in doing sth** *Would you be interested in coming to London with me?*
3 interested parties/groups the people or groups who will be affected by something [≠ **disinterested**]

interesting /ˈɪntrəstɪŋ/ *adj* unusual or exciting in a way that keeps your attention: *interesting people* | *I **found** the talk very **interesting**.* | ***It's interesting** to compare them.* | ***It's interesting that** she married someone similar to her father.*

THESAURUS

fascinating – very interesting: *He's had a fascinating life.*
intriguing – something that is intriguing is interesting because it is unusual or mysterious: *That raises some intriguing questions.*
absorbing – interesting and keeping your attention: *an absorbing read*
→ BORING

—**interestingly** *adv*

ˈinterest ˌrate *n* [C] the PERCENTAGE (=3%, 4% etc) charged by a bank when you borrow money or paid to you when you have money in an account there

interface /ˈɪntəfeɪs $ -ər-/ *n* [C] the way in which you see the information from a computer program on the screen, or how you type information into the program

interfere /ˌɪntəˈfɪə $ -tərˈfɪr/ *v* [I] to try to become involved in a situation when people do not want you to: **+in** *I wish he'd stop interfering in my life.*

interfere with sth *phr v* to prevent something from continuing or developing successfully: *Don't let sports interfere with your schoolwork.*

interference /ˌɪntəˈfɪərəns $ -tərˈfɪr-/ *n* [U] **1** when someone interferes in something: **+in** *I resented his interference in my work.* **2** unwanted noise on the radio, telephone etc, or faults in a television picture

interim¹ /ˈɪntərɪm/ *adj* temporary until something or someone final can be found or made: *an interim report*

interim² *n* **in the interim** in the period of time between two events

interior /ɪnˈtɪəriə $ -ˈtɪriər/ *n* [C] the inside part of something [≠ **exterior**]: *a car with a spacious interior* —**interior** *adj*

inˌterior deˈsign *n* [U] the job of choosing colours, materials, furniture etc for the inside of people's houses —**interior designer** *n* [C]

interject /ˌɪntəˈdʒekt $ -ər-/ *v* [I,T] *formal* to interrupt someone with a remark: *'I don't agree,' Kim interjected.*

interjection /ˌɪntəˈdʒekʃən $ -ər-/ *n* [C] in grammar, a word or phrase used to express surprise, shock, pain etc

interlude /ˈɪntəluːd $ -ər-/ *n* [C] a period of time between events or situations: *a brief interlude*

intermarriage /ˌɪntəˈmærɪdʒ $ -ər-/ *n* [U] marriage between people of different races, religions etc —**intermarry** *v* [I]

intermediary /ˌɪntəˈmiːdiəri $ ˌɪntərˈmiːdieri/ *n* [C] plural **intermediaries** someone who tries to help two people or groups to agree with each other

intermediate /ˌɪntəˈmiːdiət◂ $ -tər-/ *adj* **1** between the basic and advanced levels in a subject: *an intermediate English class* **2** between two stages, levels, places etc

interminable /ɪnˈtɜːmənəbəl $ -ɜːr-/ *adj* long and boring: *interminable speeches* —**interminably** *adv*

intermission /ˌɪntəˈmɪʃən $ -tər-/ *n* [C] *especially AmE* a short period between the parts of a play, concert etc [= **interval** *BrE*]

intermittent /ˌɪntəˈmɪtənt◂ $ -tər-/ *adj* happening sometimes but not continuously: *intermittent rain* —**intermittently** *adv*

intern¹ /ɪnˈtɜːn $ -ɜːrn/ *v* [T] to put someone in prison for political reasons —**internment** *n* [C,U]

intern² /ˈɪntɜːn $ -ɜːrn/ *n* [C] *AmE* **1** someone who has almost finished training as a doctor and is working in a hospital [= **houseman** *BrE*] **2** a student who does a job for a short time to get experience

internal /ɪnˈtɜːnl $ -ɜːr-/ *adj* inside something such as your body or a country [≠ **external**]: *internal bleeding* | *internal flights* —**internally** *adv*

international /ˌɪntəˈnæʃənəl◂ $ -tər-/ *adj* **1** relating to or involving more than one country [➡ **national**]: *international trade* **2 the international community** the powerful countries of the world and their government leaders —**internationally** *adv*

Internet, **internet** /ˈɪntənet $ -tər-/ *n* **the Internet** a system that allows people using computers around the world to exchange information [➡ **the Net, the Web**]: **on the Internet** *He spends hours on the internet.* | *internet businesses*

TOPIC

On the Internet, you can: **work online, email** people, or **visit websites** and **chatrooms**. If you spend a lot of time looking at websites, you can say that you are **surfing the net**.
→ EMAIL, COMPUTER

interpersonal /ˌɪntəˈpɜːsənəl◂ $ -tərˈpɜːr-/ *adj* involving relationships between people

interplay /ˈɪntəpleɪ $ -ər-/ *n* [U] the way that people or things affect each other: **+of** *the interplay of mental and physical factors*

interpret /ɪnˈtɜːprət $ -ɜːr-/ *v* **1** [T] to explain or decide what something means: **interpret sth as sth** *His silence was interpreted as guilt.* **2** [I,T] to translate spoken words into another language

interpretation /ɪnˌtɜːprəˈteɪʃən $ -ɜːr-/ *n* [C,U] **1** a way of explaining or understanding something: **+of** *a different interpretation of events* **2** the way someone performs a play, piece of music etc

interpreter /ɪnˈtɜːprətə $ -ˈtɜːrprətər/ *n* [C] someone who translates spoken words into another language

interrelated /ˌɪntərɪˈleɪtəd◂ / *adj* things that are interrelated are related and affect each other

interrogate /ɪnˈterəgeɪt/ *v* [T] to ask someone a lot of questions, often in a threatening way → see box at ASK —**interrogator** *n* [C] —**interrogation** /ɪnˌterəˈgeɪʃən/ *n* [C,U]

interrogative /ˌɪntəˈrɒgətɪv◂ $ -ˈrɑː-/ *n* [C] in grammar, a word or sentence that is used to ask a question —**interrogative** *adj*

interrupt /ˌɪntəˈrʌpt/ v

1 [I,T] to stop someone while they are speaking or doing something by suddenly speaking to them, making a noise etc: *Sorry to interrupt, but I need some help.* | *He was interrupted by the telephone.*

2 [T] to stop something happening for a short time: *His career was interrupted by the war.*
—**interruption** /-ˈrʌpʃən/ n [C,U]

intersect /ˌɪntəˈsekt $ -ər-/ v [I,T] if two lines, roads etc intersect, they meet or cross each other

intersection /ˌɪntəˈsekʃən, ˈɪntəsekʃən $ -tər-/ n [C] a place where two roads, lines etc meet or cross each other

interspersed /ˌɪntəˈspɜːst $ -tərˈspɜːrst/ adj **be interspersed with sth** if something is interspersed with something else, there is sometimes one thing and sometimes the other: *sunny periods interspersed with showers*

interstate[1] /ˈɪntəsteɪt $ -tər-/ n [C] *AmE* a wide road that goes between states, on which cars can travel very fast

interstate[2] adj [only before noun] involving different states, especially in the US: *interstate commerce*

intertwined /ˌɪntəˈtwaɪnd $ -tər-/ adj twisted together or closely related

interval /ˈɪntəvəl $ -tər-/ n [C] **1** a period of time between two events or activities: **+between** *the interval between arrival and departure* **2 at ... intervals a)** used to say how often something happens: *Payments are made at regular intervals.* | **at weekly/monthly etc intervals** *inspections at monthly intervals* **b)** used to talk about the distance between objects: **at regular/ 3m/5m etc intervals** *trees planted at regular intervals* **3** *BrE* a short period between the parts of a play, concert etc [= **intermission** *AmE*] → see box at **THEATRE**

intervene /ˌɪntəˈviːn $ -tər-/ v [I] **1** to do something to try to influence or stop an argument, problem, war etc: **+in** *He didn't want to intervene in the debate.* **2** to happen between two events, especially in a way that interrupts or prevents something: *They had planned to marry, but the war intervened.* —**intervention** /-ˈvenʃən/ n [C,U]

intervening /ˌɪntəˈviːnɪŋ $ -tər-/ adj **the intervening years/months/decades etc** the time between two events: *Not much has changed in the intervening years.*

interview[1] /ˈɪntəvjuː $ -ər-/ n [C]

1 a meeting in which someone asks you questions, especially to find out if you are suitable for a job: **+for** *She had an interview for a teaching job.* | *I'm going for a job interview tomorrow.* → see box at **JOB**

2 an occasion when someone famous is asked questions: **+with** *an exclusive interview with the President* | *He refused to give any interviews* (=he refused to answer any questions).

interview[2] v [T] to ask someone questions in an interview: *Police have named four suspects they want to interview.* | **interview sb for sth** *He was interviewed for the manager's job.*

interviewee /ˌɪntəvjuˈiː $ -tər-/ n [C] the person who answers the questions in an interview

interviewer /ˈɪntəvjuːə $ -tərvjuːər/ n [C] the person who asks the questions in an interview

intestine /ɪnˈtestɪn/ n [C] the tube in your body that carries food from your stomach → see picture on page A3 —**intestinal** adj

intimate[1] /ˈɪntɪmət/ adj **1** having a very close relationship: *They became intimate friends.* **2** very private or personal: *an interview revealing intimate details of his life* **3** private and friendly in a way that makes you feel comfortable: *a hotel with an intimate atmosphere* **4 intimate knowledge/understanding of sth** a knowledge or understanding of all the details of something: *She has an intimate knowledge of the business.* —**intimately** adv —**intimacy** n [U]

intimate[2] /ˈɪntɪmeɪt/ v [T] *formal* to make someone understand what you mean without saying it directly: **+that** *The President has strongly intimated that he will not sign the treaty.* —**intimation** /ˌɪntɪˈmeɪʃən/ n [C,U]

intimidate /ɪnˈtɪmɪdeɪt/ v [T] to frighten someone or make them feel nervous: *She refused to let him intimidate her.* —**intimidating** adj: *I found the interview quite intimidating.* —**intimidated** adj: *She felt intimidated by the crowd.* —**intimidation** /ɪnˌtɪmɪˈdeɪʃə/ n [U]

into /ˈɪntə; before vowels ˈɪntʊ; strong ˈɪntuː/ prep

1 towards the inside of a place or container: *He went back into the house.* | *Em got into bed.* → see picture on page A8

2 involved in a situation or activity: *He was always getting into trouble.* | *I'd like to go into teaching.*

3 making a shape: *She made the clay into a ball.* | *Cut the cake into pieces.*

4 moving towards something and hitting it: *The car ran into a wall.*

5 trying to find out information about something: *They are doing research into the causes of depression.*

6 be into sth *informal* to be interested in something: *Dave's really into music.*

intolerable /ɪnˈtɒlərəbəl $ -ˈtɑː-/ adj extremely bad, annoying, or painful: *The situation has become intolerable.* | *The exams will put intolerable pressure on students.*

intolerant /ɪnˈtɒlərənt $ -ˈtɑː-/ adj not willing to accept people who have different opinions or ways of behaving: **+of** *He's very intolerant of other people.* —**intolerance** n [U]

intonation /ˌɪntəˈneɪʃən/ n [C,U] the way in which the level of your voice changes as you speak

intoxicated /ɪnˈtɒksɪkeɪtɪd $ -ˈtɑːk-/ adj *formal* **1** drunk **2** very happy or excited: **+by/ with** *He was intoxicated by his own success.* —**intoxicating** adj

intractable /ɪnˈtræktəbəl/ adj *formal* very difficult to control or solve: *an intractable problem*

intranet /ˈɪntrənet/ n [C] a computer system for sending or looking at information within a company [➔ **Internet**]

intransigent /ɪnˈtrænsɪdʒənt/ adj *formal* not willing to change your opinions or behaviour —**intransigence** n [U]

intransitive /ɪnˈtrænsɪtɪv/ *adj* in grammar, an intransitive verb does not have an object. In the sentence, 'She cried', 'cry' is intransitive. [➡ **transitive**]

intravenous /ˌɪntrəˈviːnəs◂/ *adj* put into your VEINS: *an intravenous drug* —**intravenously** *adv*

intray /ˈɪntreɪ/ *n* [C] a container on your desk, containing work that you have to do

intrepid /ɪnˈtrepɪd/ *adj* willing to do dangerous things or go to dangerous places: *intrepid explorers*

intricate /ˈɪntrɪkɪt/ *adj* involving a lot of small parts or details: *an intricate pattern* —**intricacy** *n* [C,U] —**intricately** *adv*

intrigue[1] /ɪnˈtriːg/ *v* [T] if something intrigues you, it interests you a lot because it is unusual or mysterious: *He was intrigued by the woman next to him.*

intrigue[2] /ˈɪntriːg/ *n* [C,U] secret plans to harm or deceive someone: *political intrigue*

intriguing /ɪnˈtriːgɪŋ/ *adj* something that is intriguing is interesting because it is unusual or mysterious: *an intriguing story* → see box at INTERESTING

intrinsic /ɪnˈtrɪnsɪk, -zɪk/ *adj* part of the nature or character of something: *Steel is a useful material because of its intrinsic strength.* —**intrinsically** /-kli/ *adv*

intro /ˈɪntrəʊ $ -troʊ/ *n* [C] plural **intros** *informal* a short part at the beginning of a song, piece of writing etc [= **introduction**]

introduce /ˌɪntrəˈdjuːs $ -ˈduːs/ *v* [T]

1 to bring a system, plan, or product into use for the first time, or bring something such as an animal or plant to a place for the first time: *The store has introduced a new range of food.* | *A no-smoking policy was introduced last year.* | **introduce sth into sth** *The animal was introduced into Britain from Canada.*

2 if you introduce people who are meeting for the first time, you tell them each other's names: **introduce sb to sb** *Alice, let me introduce you to Jane.* | **introduce yourself** (=formally tell someone who you are) *Please allow me to introduce myself.*

introducing people

Alice, this is Megan.
Alice, have you met Megan?
Alice, I'd like you to meet Megan.
→ HELLO

3 introduce sb to sth to tell someone about something or give them an opportunity to try it for the first time: *Mary introduced us to Thai food.*

4 to announce who is going to speak or perform on a television or radio programme or at an event: *Jim Yeo will introduce the show.*

introduction /ˌɪntrəˈdʌkʃən/ *n*

1 [U] when people start using something for the first time or bring something to a place for the first time: **+of** *the recent introduction of new laws* | *the introduction of Buddhism to China*

2 [C] when you tell someone another person's name when they meet for the first time: *When everyone had arrived she **made the introductions**.*

3 [C] a short explanation at the beginning of a book or speech: *In the introduction she explains why she wrote the book.*

4 [C] something that explains the basic facts of something: **+to** *The book is a useful introduction to French history.*

5 [singular] your first experience of something: **+to** *My introduction to watersports came when we moved to Italy.*

introductory /ˌɪntrəˈdʌktəri◂/ *adj* [only before noun] **1** said or written at the beginning of a book or speech in order to explain what it is about: *a short introductory paragraph* **2** intended for people who have never done something before: *an **introductory course** in French* **3 introductory price/offer** a special low price that is intended to encourage people to buy a new product

introspective /ˌɪntrəˈspektɪv◂/ *adj* thinking a lot about your own thoughts and feelings

introvert /ˈɪntrəvɜːt $ -ɜːrt/ *n* [C] someone who is quiet and shy, and does not enjoy being with other people [≠ **extrovert**] —**introverted** *adj* → see box at CONFIDENT

intrude /ɪnˈtruːd/ *v* [I] to go into a place or become involved in a situation where you are not wanted: **+on/upon/into** *I'm sorry to intrude on your meal, but I need to talk to you.* —**intrusion** /-ˈtruːʒən/ *n* [C,U] —**intrusive** /-sɪv/ *adj*

intruder /ɪnˈtruːdə $ -ər/ *n* [C] someone who goes into a place where they should not be, especially in order to steal something

intuition /ˌɪntjuˈɪʃən $ -tuː-, -tjuː-/ *n* [C,U] the feeling that you know something is correct or true, although you do not know why: *Trust your intuition.*

intuitive /ɪnˈtjuːɪtɪv $ -ˈtuː-, -ˈtjuː-/ *adj* based on feelings rather than facts: *an intuitive judgment* —**intuitively** *adv*

Inuit /ˈɪnjuɪt, ˈɪnuɪt $ ˈɪnuːɪt/ *n* **the Inuit** a group of people who live in the very cold northern areas of North America —**Inuit** *adj*

inundate /ˈɪnʌndeɪt/ *v* [T] **be inundated (with/by sth)** to receive so much of something that you cannot easily deal with it all: *We were inundated with offers of help.*

invade /ɪnˈveɪd/ *v*

1 [I,T] to enter a place with an army, in order to take control of it: *The Romans invaded Britain.*

2 [T] to go into a place in large numbers, especially in a way that is not wanted: *Every summer the town is invaded by tourists.* —**invader** *n* [C] —**invasion** /-ˈveɪʒən/ *n* [C,U]

invalid[1] /ɪnˈvælɪd/ *adj* **1** not acceptable because of a law or rule: *The contract was invalid.* **2** not based on true facts or good judgment: *an invalid argument* **3** not recognized or accepted by a computer: *an invalid password* —**invalidity** /ˌɪnvəˈlɪdɪti/ *n* [U]

invalid[2] /ˈɪnvəliːd, -lɪd $ -lɪd/ *n* [C] someone who is ill and needs to be looked after

invaluable /ɪnˈvæljuəbəl, -jʊbəl $ -ˈvæljʊbəl/ *adj* extremely useful: *invaluable help* | **+for/to** *a service that's invaluable for elderly people*

invariably /ɪnˈveəriəbli $ -ˈver-/ *adv* always: *Visitors to the school invariably comment on its relaxed atmosphere.* —**invariable** *adj*

invent /ɪnˈvent/ v [T]

1 to make or design a new type of thing: *Alexander Bell invented the telephone.*

2 to think of an idea or story that is not true, usually in order to deceive someone: *You'll have to invent a better excuse!*

invention /ɪnˈvenʃən/ n

1 [C] a machine, tool, system etc that someone has invented: *The computer was one of the most important inventions of the twentieth century.*

2 [U] when someone invents something: **+of** *the invention of television*

3 [C,U] a story or explanation that is not true: *The story is just a media invention.*

inventive /ɪnˈventɪv/ adj using new and interesting ideas: *an inventive writer* | *inventive solutions to problems*

inventor /ɪnˈventə $ -ər/ n [C] someone who has invented something: *the inventor of the bicycle*

inventory /ˈɪnvəntri $ -tɔːri/ n [C] plural **inventories** a list of all the things in a place: **+of** *They made an inventory of the museum.*

invert /ɪnˈvɜːt $ -ɜːrt/ v [T] formal to put something in the opposite position to the one it was in before, especially by turning it upside down —**inversion** /-ˈvɜːʃən $ -ˈvɜːrʒən/ n [C,U]

in,verted 'commas n [plural] BrE QUOTATION MARKS

invest /ɪnˈvest/ v

1 [I,T] to buy shares, goods, or property because you hope you can make a profit: **invest (sth) in sth** *He made a lot of money investing in property.* | *She invested all her money in shares.*

2 [I,T] to spend money on something in order to improve it or make it succeed: **invest (sth) in sth** *The government needs to invest more in our schools.* | *The company invested £10 million in the project.*

3 [T] to use a lot of time, effort, or money to make something succeed: **invest sth in sth** *She invested all her energy in her job.*

—**investor** n [C]

invest in sth phr v to buy something because it will be useful: *I've invested in a new computer.*

investigate /ɪnˈvestɪɡeɪt/ v [I,T] to try to find out about something, especially a crime or accident: *The cause of the fire is being investigated.* → see box at POLICE

—**investigator** n [C] —**investigative** /-ɡətɪv $ -ɡeɪtɪv/ adj: *an investigative journalist*

investigation /ɪnˌvestɪˈɡeɪʃən/ n [C,U] an official attempt to find out about something, especially a crime or accident: *a murder investigation* | **+into** *Police have launched an investigation into the tragedy.* | **under investigation** (=being investigated) *The case is still under investigation.*

investment /ɪnˈvestmənt/ n **1** [C,U] the use of money to make a profit or make a business successful, or the money that is used: *a £50,000 investment* | **+in** *We have made a big investment in technology.* **2** [C] something that you buy because it will be useful: *A comfortable bed is a good investment.*

inveterate /ɪnˈvetərət/ adj [only before noun] doing something a lot, and not likely to stop doing it: *He's an inveterate traveller.*

invigorating /ɪnˈvɪɡəreɪtɪŋ/ adj making you feel more active and healthy: *an invigorating swim* —**invigorate** v [T]

invincible /ɪnˈvɪnsəbəl/ adj too strong to be defeated or destroyed

invisible /ɪnˈvɪzəbəl/ adj impossible to see: **+to** *a plane that's invisible to enemy radar* —**invisibility** /ɪnˌvɪzəˈbɪləti/ n [U]

invitation /ˌɪnvɪˈteɪʃən/ n

1 [C,U] a written or spoken request that invites someone to do something: **+to** *I've had an invitation to John's party.* | **invitation to do sth** *He accepted an invitation to speak at the conference.* | *Entry is by invitation only* (=only people who have been invited can go). | *He visited the country at the invitation of the President.*

2 [singular] a situation that encourages something else to happen, especially something unpleasant: **+to** *An unlocked door is an open invitation to thieves.*

invite¹ /ɪnˈvaɪt/ v [T]

1 to ask someone to come to a party, meal etc: **invite sb to (do) sth** *I was invited to their wedding.* | **invite sb for sth** *They've invited us for lunch.*

2 to officially ask someone to do something: **invite sb to do sth** *She was invited to give a speech.*

3 to encourage something bad to happen: *a policy that invites criticism*

invite sb along phr v to ask someone to come with you when you go somewhere: *Why don't we invite Jane along?*

invite sb in phr v to ask someone to come into your home

invite sb over also **invite sb round** BrE phr v to ask someone to come to your home: **+for** *Let's invite Rob over for a meal.*

invite² /ˈɪnvaɪt/ n [C] informal an invitation to a party, meal etc

inviting /ɪnˈvaɪtɪŋ/ adj something that is inviting is attractive and pleasant: *The room was warm and inviting.* —**invitingly** adv

invoice /ˈɪnvɔɪs/ n [C] a list of goods that have been supplied or work that has been done, and how much money you owe —**invoice** v [T]

invoke /ɪnˈvəʊk $ -ˈvoʊk/ v [T] formal to use a law or rule to support something that you are saying or doing

involuntary /ɪnˈvɒləntəri $ ɪnˈvɑːlənteri/ adj an involuntary movement is one you make suddenly in a way you cannot control: *She gave an involuntary gasp of surprise.* —**involuntarily** adv

involve /ɪnˈvɒlv $ ɪnˈvɑːlv/ v [T]

1 if an activity or situation involves something, that thing is a part of it: *The job involves a lot of travelling.* | **involve doing sth** *The project will involve working abroad.*

2 to include or affect someone or something: *an accident involving five cars*

3 to ask or allow someone to take part in something: **involve sb in (doing) sth** *Schools are trying to involve parents in their children's education.*

involved /ɪnˈvɒlvd $ ɪnˈvɑːlvd/ *adj* **1 be/get involved** to take part in something, or be related to it in some way: **+in** *Several companies were involved in the project.* | **+with** *If you'd like to get involved with the group, call this number.* | **closely/actively/heavily involved** *He was closely involved with training the team.* **2 be involved with sb** to have a relationship with someone, especially a romantic or sexual one: *She was involved with an older man.* **3** complicated: *a long involved story* —**involvement** *n* [U]

inward /ˈɪnwəd $ -wərd/ *adj* **1** [only before noun] an inward feeling or thought is one that you have but do not show to other people: *an inward feeling of despair* **2** towards the inside or centre of something —**inwardly** *adv*

inwards /ˈɪnwədz $ -wərdz/ *especially BrE*, **inward** *especially AmE adv* towards the inside of something [≠ **outwards**]: *The door opened inwards.*

in-your-'face *adj informal* intended to shock and insult: *in-your-face comedy*

iodine /ˈaɪədiːn $ -daɪn/ *n* [U] a chemical that is used on wounds to prevent infection

IOU /ˌaɪ əʊ ˈjuː $ -oʊ-/ *n* [C] *informal* a note you sign to say that you owe money to someone

IPA /ˌaɪ piː ˈeɪ◂/ *n* [singular] **International Phonetic Alphabet** a system of signs used to represent speech sounds

IQ /ˌaɪ ˈkjuː/ *n* [C] **Intelligence Quotient** your level of intelligence, measured by a special test: *She has an IQ of 120.*

ir- /ɪ/ *prefix* not – used before words beginning with 'r': *irregular* | *irreligious*

irate /ˌaɪˈreɪt◂/ *adj formal* very angry: *irate customers*

iris /ˈaɪərɪs $ ˈaɪrɪs/ *n* [C] **1** a tall plant with purple, yellow, or white flowers and long thin leaves **2** the coloured part of your eye

irk /ɜːk $ ɜːrk/ *v* [T] to annoy someone

iron[1] /ˈaɪən $ ˈaɪərn/ *n*

1 [U] a hard metal that is used to make steel, and is in food and blood in small quantities: *iron gates* | *I'm taking iron tablets.*

2 [C] a piece of equipment you use for making clothes smooth

iron[2] *v* [T] to make clothes smooth using an iron: *I need to iron my shirt.* → see box at **CLOTHES** —**ironing** *n* [U] *I hate doing the ironing.*

iron sth ⇔ **out** *phr v* to solve a small problem: *There are still a few problems to iron out.*

iron[3] *adj* very determined, strict, or severe: *He has an iron will.*

ironic /aɪˈrɒnɪk $ aɪˈrɑː-/ *adj* **1** an ironic situation is strange or amusing because it is completely different from what you expect: *It's ironic that your car was stolen outside the police station.* **2** saying the opposite of what you mean, especially in order to be funny: *I think he was being ironic.* —**ironically** /-kli/ *adv:* *Ironically, a lot of crimes are committed quite close to police stations.*

'ironing ,board *n* [C] a narrow table that you iron clothes on → see picture at **BOARD**

irony /ˈaɪərəni $ ˈaɪrə-/ *n* plural **ironies** **1** [C,U] a situation that is strange or amusing because it is completely different from what you expect: *The irony is that traffic congestion is worse despite new transport policies.* **2** [U] when you say the opposite of what you mean, especially in order to be amusing: *'You seem interested,' he said with a touch of irony.*

irrational /ɪˈræʃənəl/ *adj* not based on sensible reasons or thoughts: *irrational fears* —**irrationally** *adv*

irreconcilable /ɪˌrekənˈsaɪləbəl/ *adj formal* irreconcilable attitudes or opinions are so different that it is impossible to reach an agreement: *There are still some irreconcilable differences between them.*

irregular /ɪˈregjələ $ -ər/ *adj* **1** not happening at regular times: *an irregular heartbeat* | *He returned to Britain at irregular intervals.* **2** an irregular shape or surface is not smooth, even, or straight **3** not following the usual rules in grammar: *irregular verbs* **4** *formal* not obeying legal or moral rules: *financially irregular practices* —**irregularly** *adv* —**irregularity** /ɪˌregjʊˈlærəti/ *n* [C,U]

irrelevant /ɪˈreləvənt/ *adj* not useful or important in a particular situation: *I won't bore you with all the irrelevant details.* | *His age is completely irrelevant.* | **+to** *topics that are irrelevant to students* —**irrelevance** *n* [C,U]

irreparable /ɪˈrepərəbəl/ *adj* irreparable damage or harm is so bad that it can never be repaired or made better —**irreparably** *adv*

irreplaceable /ˌɪrɪˈpleɪsəbəl◂/ *adj* too valuable or rare to be replaced: *irreplaceable books*

irrepressible /ˌɪrɪˈpresəbəl◂/ *adj* always confident, happy, and full of energy

irreproachable /ˌɪrɪˈprəʊtʃəbəl $ -ˈproʊtʃ-/ *adj formal* very good and impossible to criticize: *His behaviour was irreproachable.*

irresistible /ˌɪrɪˈzɪstəbəl◂/ *adj* **1** if something is irresistible, it is so good or nice that you want it: **+to** *The offer of so much money would be irresistible to most people.* **2** too strong or powerful to be stopped: *I had an irresistible urge to laugh.*

irrespective /ˌɪrɪˈspektɪv/ *adv* **irrespective of sth** used to say that something does not affect a situation at all: *Anyone can join, irrespective of age.*

irresponsible /ˌɪrɪˈspɒnsəbəl◂ $ -ˈspɑːn-/ *adj* doing things that are not sensible, without thinking about the possible bad results: *He's got a very irresponsible attitude to his work.* | **highly/totally irresponsible** *He's unreliable and totally irresponsible.* —**irresponsibly** *adv*

irreverent /ɪˈrevərənt/ *adj* showing no respect for something that most people respect

irreversible /ˌɪrɪˈvɜːsəbəl◂ $ -ˈvɜːr-/ *adj* irreversible damage or change cannot be changed back to how it was before

irrevocable /ɪˈrevəkəbəl/ *adj formal* impossible to change or stop: *an irrevocable decision*

irrigate /ˈɪrɪgeɪt/ *v* [T] to supply land or crops with water —**irrigation** /ˌɪrɪˈgeɪʃən/ *n* [U]

island

a tropical island

irritable /ˈɪrɪtəbəl/ adj becoming annoyed very easily —**irritably** adv —**irritability** /ˌɪrɪtəˈbɪlɪti/ n [U]

irritant /ˈɪrɪtənt/ n [C] formal **1** something that annoys you: It was a minor irritant for the government. **2** something that makes part of your body painful and sore: a skin irritant

irritate /ˈɪrɪteɪt/ v [T] **1** to annoy someone: Her attitude irritated me. **2** to make a part of your body sore: Wool irritates my skin. —**irritated** adj: He was getting irritated. → see box at ANGRY —**irritating** adj: an irritating habit —**irritatingly** adv —**irritation** /ˌɪrɪˈteɪʃən/ n [C,U]

is /s, z, əz; strong ɪz/ the 3rd person singular of the present tense of BE

-ish /ɪʃ/ suffix **1** quite or fairly: youngish (=not very young, but not old either) | tallish | reddish hair **2** spoken about: We'll expect you eightish (=at about 8 o'clock). | He's fortyish (=about 40 years old).

Islam /ˈɪzlɑːm, ˈɪz-, ɪsˈlɑːm/ n [U] the religion that was started by Muhammad and whose holy book is the Koran —**Islamic** /ɪzˈlæmɪk, ɪs-/ adj

island /ˈaɪlənd/ n [C] a piece of land surrounded by water: the Greek island of Crete | the Cayman Islands
→ **DESERT ISLAND**

islander /ˈaɪləndə $ -ər/ n [C] someone who lives on an island

isle /aɪl/ n [C] island, used in poems or in names of islands

isn't /ˈɪzənt/ the short form of 'is not': He isn't here.

isolate /ˈaɪsəleɪt/ v [T] to separate one person or thing from other people or things: **isolate sb/sth from sb/sth** Presley's success isolated him from his friends.

isolated /ˈaɪsəleɪtɪd/ adj **1** far away from other places: an isolated farm **2** lonely and unable to meet other people: Young mothers often feel isolated. **3** happening only once, or existing in only one place: The violence was an isolated incident.

isolation /ˌaɪsəˈleɪʃən/ n [U] **1** when one person, place, or thing is separate from others: **geographical/political etc isolation** the island's geographical isolation | **in isolation (from sb/sth)** (=separately from other people or things) He works in complete isolation. | You

can't consider the facts in isolation from each other. **2** a feeling of being lonely: the isolation of old people

issue[1] /ˈɪʃuː, ˈɪsjuː $ ˈɪʃuː/ n [C]
1 a subject or problem that people discuss: This is a very important political issue. | **+of** We discussed the issue of teachers' pay. | I'd like to **raise the issue** (=start to discuss the issue) of safety. | **important/key/major issue** This is one of the key issues for the government.
2 a magazine or newspaper that is printed at one particular time: **+of** the latest issue of Vogue
3 take issue with sb/sth to disagree or argue with someone: He took issue with the decision.
4 make an issue of sth to start an argument or discussion about something that is not important

issue[2] v [T] **1** to officially make a statement or give an order, warning etc: The government has **issued a warning** to people travelling to this area. | a statement issued by the White House
2 to officially give people documents, equipment etc: Thousands of passports are issued each year. | **issue sb with sth** Staff are issued with special clothing.

it /ɪt/ pron
1 used to refer to something that has already been mentioned: 'Where's the bread?' 'It's on the shelf.' | Don't blame me. It wasn't my idea.
2 the situation that someone is in now: How's it going, Bob (=how are you?)? | I like it here in Rio.
3 used as the subject or object of a sentence when the real subject or object is later in the sentence: It costs less to drive than to take the bus.
4 used when talking about the weather, time, distance etc: It's raining. | What time is it?
5 used to emphasize a piece of information in a sentence: It's John you should talk to, not me.
6 used to say who a person is: 'Who's on the phone?' 'It's Jill.'

IT /ˌaɪ ˈtiː/ n [U] **information technology** the study or use of computers to store and manage information

italics /ɪˈtælɪks/ n [plural] a style of printed letters that slope to the right —**italic** adj

itch[1] /ɪtʃ/ v [I] **1** to have an unpleasant feeling on your skin that makes you want to rub it: Her leg was itching. **2 be itching to do sth, be itching for sth** informal to want to do something very much: He was itching to go home.

itch[2] n [singular] an unpleasant feeling on your skin that makes you want to rub it

itchy /ˈɪtʃi/ adj if part of your body is itchy, it feels unpleasant and you want to rub it: an itchy nose —**itchiness** n [U]

it'd /ˈɪtəd/ the short form of 'it would' or 'it had': It'd be nice to go to the beach. | It'd been raining all day.

item /ˈaɪtəm/ n [C]
1 a single thing of a particular type or in a set or list: **item of clothing/furniture/equipment etc** What was the last item of clothing you bought? | **item on a list/menu/agenda** the second item on my list
2 a piece of news in a newspaper or magazine, or on television: There was an item about the kidnapping in the paper. | a news item

itemize also **-ise** *BrE* /ˈaɪtəmaɪz/ *v* [T] to make a list with details about each thing on the list

itinerant /aɪˈtɪnərənt/ *adj formal* travelling from place to place: *an itinerant musician*

itinerary /aɪˈtɪnərəri $ -nəreri/ *n* [C] plural **itineraries** a plan or list of the places you will visit on a trip

it'll /ˈɪtl/ the short form of 'it will': *It'll never work.*

it's /ɪts/ the short form of 'it is' or 'it has': *It's snowing!* | *It's been a great year.* → see box at **ITS**

its /ɪts/ *determiner* the POSSESSIVE form of 'it': *The tree has lost all of its leaves.* | *The hotel has its own pool.*

GRAMMAR

Its is a possessive form and does not have (') before the 's' *Their dog's broken its leg.*
It's with (') before the 's' means 'it is' or 'it has' *It's been raining all day.*

itself /ɪtˈself/ *pron*

1 the REFLEXIVE form of 'it': *The cat was washing itself.*

2 in/of itself considered separately from other things or facts: *This might seem a small change in itself, but it is an important step.*

IV /ˌaɪ ˈviː/ *n* [C] *AmE* a piece of hospital equipment used for putting liquids directly into your blood [= **drip** *BrE*]

I've /aɪv/ the short form of 'I have': *I've seen you somewhere before.*

IVF /ˌaɪ viː ˈef/ *n* [U] *technical* in vitro fertilization a process in which a human egg is FERTILIZED outside the woman's body

ivory /ˈaɪvəri/ *n* [U] **1** the hard smooth yellow-white substance from the TUSK of an ELEPHANT **2** a pale yellow-white colour —**ivory** *adj*

ivy /ˈaɪvi/ *n* [U] a climbing plant with dark green shiny leaves

-ize also **-ise** *BrE* /aɪz/ *suffix* to change something: *We must modernize the system* (=make it modern). | *Divorce was legalized* (=made legal).

J, j

J, j /dʒeɪ/ *n* [C,U] plural **J's, j's** the tenth letter of the English alphabet

jab¹ /dʒæb/ *v* [I,T] **jabbed, jabbing** to push something into or towards something else with short quick movements: *He angrily jabbed a finger into my chest.*

jab² *n* [C] **1** a sudden hard push, especially with a pointed object **2** *BrE informal* an INJECTION: *a tetanus jab*

jabber /ˈdʒæbə $ -ər/ *v* [I] to talk quickly but not very clearly: *Franco jabbered away about football.*

jack¹ /dʒæk/ *n* [C] **1** a piece of equipment used for lifting something heavy, such as a car **2** a card used in card games which has a young man's picture on it: *the jack of hearts* → see picture at **PLAYING CARD**

jack² *v*

jack sth ⇔ **in** *phr v BrE informal* to stop doing something such as your job: *I'm seriously thinking about jacking it all in.*

jack sth ⇔ **up** *phr v* **1** to lift something heavy using a jack: *Dad jacked the car up so I could change the tyre.* **2** to increase prices, sales etc by a large amount: *Airlines always jack up fares at Christmas.*

jackal /ˈdʒækɔːl, -kəl $ -kəl/ *n* [C] a wild animal like a dog that lives in Africa and Asia

jacket /ˈdʒækɪt/ *n* [C] a short light coat: **denim/leather etc jacket** *He was wearing jeans and a leather jacket.* → see picture at **CLOTHES**
→ **DINNER JACKET, LIFE JACKET**

jacket po'tato *n* [C] *BrE* a potato baked with its skin on

'jack-knife *v* [I] if a large vehicle with two parts jack-knifes, the back part swings towards the front part because the driver cannot control it

jackpot /ˈdʒækpɒt $ -pɑːt/ *n* [C] **1** a large amount of money that you can win **2 hit the jackpot a)** to win a lot of money **b)** to be very successful or lucky: *The National Theatre hit the jackpot with its first musical.*

Jacuzzi /dʒəˈkuːzi/ *n* [C] *trademark* a large bath for one or more people with hot water full of bubbles

jade /dʒeɪd/ *n* [U] a hard green stone used for making jewellery

jaded /ˈdʒeɪdɪd/ *adj* no longer feeling interested or excited: *She seemed jaded and in need of a break.*

jagged /ˈdʒægɪd/ *adj* having a rough edge with sharp points: *jagged rocks* | *the jagged edge of an old tin can*

jaguar /ˈdʒægjuə $ ˈdʒæɡwɑːr/ *n* [C] a large wild cat with black spots that lives in Central and South America

jail¹ also **gaol** *BrE* /dʒeɪl/ *n* [C,U] a place where criminals are kept as a punishment [= **prison**]: **in**

jail *He was sentenced to six years in jail.* | **jail sentence/term** (=how long someone must spend in jail)

COLLOCATIONS

go to jail
put sb in jail
send sb to jail
spend time in jail
release sb from jail
get out of jail (=be released from jail)
escape from jail

jail² also **gaol** *BrE* *v* [T] to put someone in prison: *He was jailed for tax evasion.*

jailer also **gaoler** *BrE* /ˈdʒeɪlə $ -ər/ *n* [C] *old-fashioned* someone who guards prisoners in a prison

jam¹ /dʒæm/ *n*

1 [C,U] a thick sticky sweet food made from fruit: *raspberry jam* | *a jam sandwich*

2 [C] a situation in which it is difficult to move because there are too many people, cars etc → **TRAFFIC JAM**

jam² *v* **jammed, jamming** **1** [T] to push something somewhere using a lot of force until it cannot move any further: *I managed to jam everything into one suitcase.* | *A chair had been jammed up against the door.* **2** [I,T] if a machine, door etc jams, or if you jam it, it no longer works properly because something is stopping one of its parts from moving: *Every time I try to use the fax, it jams.* **3** [T] if a lot of people or things jam a place, they fill it so that no one or nothing can move: *Excited football fans jammed the streets.* **4** [I] to play music with other people in an informal way **5** [T] to deliberately block radio signals —**jammed** *adj*: *The door is jammed again.*

jamboree /ˌdʒæmbəˈriː/ *n* [C] a big noisy party or celebration

jam-'packed *adj informal* completely full of people or things: **+with** *The slopes were jam-packed with skiers.*

jangle /ˈdʒæŋɡəl/ *v* [I,T] if small metal objects jangle, they make a noise as they hit against each other: *Her jewellery jangled when she moved.* —**jangle** *n* [singular]

janitor /ˈdʒænɪtə $ -ər/ *n* [C] *especially AmE* someone whose job is to clean and look after a large building [= **caretaker** *BrE*]: *the school janitor*

January /ˈdʒænjuəri, -njuri $ -njueri/ *n* [C,U] plural **Januaries** written abbreviation **Jan.** the first month of the year, between December and February: **next/last January** *I haven't heard from him since last January.* | **in January** *My birthday's in January.* | **on January 6th** *The meeting will be on January 6th.* → see box at **MONTH**

jar¹ /dʒɑː $ dʒɑːr/ *n* [C] a round glass container with a lid, used for storing food: *a jam jar* | **+of** *a small jar of pickles* → see picture at **CONTAINER**

jar² *v* [I,T] **jarred, jarring** **1** to damage something by a sudden shock or pressure: *Alice landed badly and jarred her knee.* **2** to make someone feel uncomfortable or annoyed: *The noise of the drill was starting to jar on my nerves.*

jargon /ˈdʒɑːɡən $ ˈdʒɑːrɡən, -ɡɑːn/ *n* [U] words and phrases used by people in the same profession that are difficult for other people to understand: **technical/medical/legal etc jargon**

jaundice /'dʒɔːndɪs $ 'dʒɒːn-, 'dʒɑːn-/ n [U] an illness in which your skin becomes yellow

jaundiced /'dʒɔːndɪst $ 'dʒɒːn-, 'dʒɑːn-/ adj if you have a jaundiced attitude to something, you think it is bad because of your past experience: *a jaundiced view of the world*

jaunt /dʒɔːnt $ dʒɒːnt, dʒɑːnt/ n [C] a short journey for pleasure

jaunty /'dʒɔːnti $ 'dʒɒːnti, 'dʒɑːnti/ adj showing that you feel confident and happy: *his jaunty air of self-confidence* —**jauntily** adv

javelin /'dʒævəlɪn/ n [C] a long pointed stick thrown as a sport

jaw /dʒɔː $ dʒɒː/ n [C]

1 one of the two bones in your face that contain your teeth: *She suffered a broken jaw in the accident.* | **upper/lower jaw** → see picture on page A3
2 the bottom part of your face, below your mouth
3 sb's jaw dropped used to say that someone looked very surprised or shocked

jaywalking /'dʒeɪˌwɔːkɪŋ $ -ˌwɒː-/ n [U] when you walk across a street in a careless or dangerous way

jazz¹ /dʒæz/ n [U] a type of music with a strong beat, in which musicians often play in a way which is not planned: *modern jazz* | *a singer in a jazz band* → see box at **MUSIC**

jazz² v
jazz sth ⇔ up phr v to make something more exciting and interesting: *Jazz up your bathroom by replacing the tiles.*

jealous /'dʒeləs/ adj
1 feeling angry or unhappy because someone else has something that you wish you had: **+of** *You're just jealous of me because I got better grades.*
2 feeling angry or unhappy because someone you like or love is showing interest in another person: *I only went out with him to make Steve jealous.* | **jealous husband/lover/wife etc**

jealously /'dʒeləsli/ adv **1** if you jealously guard or protect something, you try very hard to keep or protect it: *a jealously guarded secret* **2** while feeling jealous

jealousy /'dʒeləsi/ n [C,U] plural **jealousies** the feeling you have when you are jealous: *She felt a stab* (=sudden strong feeling) *of jealousy.*

jeans /dʒiːnz/ n [plural] a popular type of trousers made from **DENIM**: *a new pair of jeans* → see picture at **CLOTHES**

Jeep /dʒiːp/ n [C] *trademark* a vehicle made for travelling over rough ground

jeer /dʒɪə $ dʒɪr/ v [I,T] to say rude things to someone or laugh at them: *Fans jeered at the referee.* —**jeer** n [C]

Jell-O, jello /'dʒeləʊ $ -loʊ/ n [U] *trademark AmE* **JELLY**

jelly /'dʒeli/ n plural **jellies 1** [C,U] *BrE* a sweet food made with fruit juice that is solid but shakes when you move it [= Jell-O *AmE*]: *strawberry jelly and ice cream* **2** [U] *especially AmE* a thick sweet food made from fruit [= jam *BrE*]: *a peanut butter and jelly sandwich*

jellyfish /'dʒeliˌfɪʃ/ n [C] plural **jellyfish** a transparent sea animal with long parts that hang down from its body

jeopardize also **-ise** *BrE* /'dʒepədaɪz $ -ər-/ v [T] to risk losing or destroying something valuable or important: *He didn't want to jeopardize his career by complaining about his boss.*

jeopardy /'dʒepədi $ -ər-/ n **in jeopardy** in danger of being lost or harmed: *The peace talks are in jeopardy.*

jerk¹ /dʒɜːk $ dʒɜːrk/ v [I,T] to move with a sudden quick movement, or to make something move this way: *Sara jerked her head up to look at him.* | *He suddenly jerked open the car door.*

jerk² n [C] **1** a sudden quick movement: *a jerk of her head* | *She sat up with a jerk.* **2** *AmE informal* someone who is stupid or very annoying

jerky /'dʒɜːki $ -ɜːr-/ adj jerky movements are rough, with many starts and stops: *The elevator's jerky movements alarmed me.* —**jerkily** adv

jersey /'dʒɜːzi $ -ɜːr-/ n **1** [C] a shirt made of soft material, worn for playing sports: *a football jersey* **2** [C] *BrE* a **SWEATER 3** [U] a soft material made of cotton or wool

jest /dʒest/ n **in jest** something you say in jest is meant to be funny, not serious —**jest** v [I]

jester /'dʒestə $ -ər/ n [C] a man employed in the past by a king to entertain people with jokes, stories etc

Jesus /'dʒiːzəs/ also **Jesus 'Christ** n the man who Christians believe was the son of God, and on whose life and ideas Christianity is based

jet¹ /dʒet/ n [C]
1 a very fast plane: *He travels in his own private jet.* | **jet fighter/aircraft**
2 a thin stream of gas, liquid etc that is forced out of a small hole: **+of** *a strong jet of water*
→ **JUMBO JET**

jet² v [I] **jetted, jetting** *informal* to travel somewhere by plane: **+off** *You could be jetting off for a week in the Caribbean.*

jet-'black adj very dark black: *jet-black hair*

jet 'engine n [C] a powerful engine used in planes

'jet lag n [U] the feeling of being very tired after a long journey in a plane —**jet-lagged** adj

jettison /'dʒetɪsən, -zən/ v [T] **1** to get rid of something that you do not need or want: *The scheme was jettisoned as it was too costly.* **2** to throw something away from a moving plane, ship, or vehicle

jetty /'dʒeti/ n [C] plural **jetties** a wide stone or wooden structure used for getting on and off boats

Jew /dʒuː/ n [C] someone whose religion is Judaism [➡ **Jewish**]

jewel /'dʒuːəl/ n [C] a valuable stone, such as a **DIAMOND**

jewelled *BrE*; **jeweled** *AmE* /'dʒuːəld/ adj decorated with valuable stones: *a jewelled box*

jeweller *BrE*; **jeweler** *AmE* /'dʒuːələ $ -ər/ n [C] someone who sells, makes, or repairs jewellery

jewellery *BrE*; **jewelry** *AmE* /'dʒuːəlri/ n [U] small things that you wear for decoration, such as rings and **NECKLACES**: *a piece of gold jewellery*

jewellery BrE/jewelry AmE

earrings — ring — necklace — bracelet

Jewish /ˈdʒuːɪʃ/ adj relating to Jews or Judaism

jibe, gibe /dʒaɪb/ n [C] something that you say to make someone else seem silly

jig /dʒɪg/ n [C] a type of quick dance, or the music for this dance

jiggle /ˈdʒɪgəl/ v [I,T] to move from side to side with short quick movements, or to make something move this way

jigsaw /ˈdʒɪgsɔː $ -sɒː/ also **'jigsaw ,puzzle** n [C] a picture that has been cut up into many small pieces that you try to fit together again

jilt /dʒɪlt/ v [T] old-fashioned to suddenly end a romantic relationship with someone

jingle¹ /ˈdʒɪŋgəl/ v [I,T] if small metal objects jingle, or if you jingle them, they make a noise when you shake them together: Tom nervously jingled the coins in his pocket.

jingle² n **1** [C] a short song used in television or radio advertisements **2** [singular] the sound of small metal objects being shaken together

jinx /dʒɪŋks/ n [singular] someone or something that brings bad luck: There's some kind of jinx on the team. —**jinxed** adj —**jinx** v [T]

jitters /ˈdʒɪtəz $ -ərz/ n [plural] a feeling of being nervous and anxious: her last-minute jitters before the wedding

jittery /ˈdʒɪtəri/ adj worried and nervous: She was so jittery about seeing him, she couldn't keep still.

Jnr BrE the written abbreviation of **Junior**, used after someone's name [= **Jr.** AmE]

job /dʒɒb $ dʒɑːb/ n [C]

1 work that you do regularly to earn money: **part-time/full-time job** Many students have part-time jobs. | **get/find a job** She hopes to get a job in television. | She **applied** for a job at a bank. | Things got worse after he **lost** his job. | **out of a job** (=unemployed) | We expect there to be some **job losses**. | I don't want to be stuck in a **dead-end job** (=a job with low pay from which you cannot progress).

THESAURUS

Your **job** is the particular work you do regularly to earn money.
Work is used in a more general way to talk about employment or the activities involved in it: I started work when I was 18.
Post and **position** are more formal words for a job in a particular organization, used especially in job advertisements: She's held the post since 1999.
Occupation is used mainly on official forms to mean your job: Please give your name, age, and occupation.
A **profession** is a job for which you need special education and training: the legal profession
Your **career** is the work you do or plan to do for most of your life: I'm interested in a career in journalism.
Do not say 'What is your job?' or 'What is your work?' Say **'What do you do?'**, **'What do you do for a living?'**, or **'What kind of work do you do?'**

TOPIC

Jobs are advertised in newspapers, magazines etc in **job ads/advertisements**. When you **apply** for a job, you **fill out/in** or **complete** an **application form**. You may have to send your **CV** BrE/**résumé** AmE (=a list describing your education, previous jobs etc), with a **covering letter** BrE/**cover letter** AmE. You will need to give a **reference** (=a letter saying that someone is suitable for a new job or the name of someone who will write this letter). If you are suitable, you are **invited to** an **interview**. If you are chosen, you will be **offered** the job.
→ **WORK**

2 something that needs doing: **the job of doing sth** Let's get on with the job of finding Jenny. | **difficult/easy etc job** It's not going to be an easy job. | I **do** some jobs around the house.

3 something that you are responsible for doing: **it is sb's job to do sth** It's my job to make sure everyone gets there on time.

4 **do a good/bad etc job (of sth)** also **make a good/bad etc job (of)** BrE to do something well or badly: They've done an excellent job of marketing the product.

5 **on the job** while doing work or at work: All our employees get **on the job** training.

6 **it's a good job (that)** BrE spoken used to say that it is lucky something happened: It's a good job you were wearing your seat belt.

7 **do the job** informal to have the effect or result you want: A little more glue should do the job.

8 **have a job doing/to do sth** spoken to have difficulty doing something: We had a job finding somewhere to park. | You'll have a job to see anything.

9 **be just the job** BrE spoken to be exactly what is needed or wanted

'job ,centre n [C] a place run by the British government where jobs are advertised and help is provided for people who are looking for work

'job de,scription n [C] an official list of the work and responsibilities that you have in your job

jobless /ˈdʒɒbləs $ ˈdʒɑːb-/ adj without a paid job [= **unemployed**]: 10% of the town's workers are jobless.

'job ,seeker n [C] BrE someone who does not have a job and is looking for one

jockey¹ /ˈdʒɒki $ ˈdʒɑːki/ n [C] someone who rides horses in races

jockey² v [I] to compete strongly to get into the best position or situation, or to get the most power: **+for** photographers jockeying for posi-

tion at the bar | *After the war, rival politicians began to jockey for power.*

jocular /ˈdʒɒkjʊlə $ ˈdʒɑːkjələr/ *adj formal* happy and making jokes

jog /dʒɒg $ dʒɑːg/ *v* **jogged, jogging** **1** [I,T] to run slowly, especially for exercise: *Julie jogs three miles every morning.* → see picture on page A11 **2 jog sb's memory** to make someone remember something: *This photo might jog your memory.* **3** [T] to knock or push something lightly by mistake: *Someone jogged her elbow, and she spilt her drink.* —**jog** *n* [singular]

jogging /ˈdʒɒgɪŋ $ ˈdʒɑː-/ *n* [U] the activity of running for exercise: *He goes jogging regularly.* → see box at **EXERCISE** —**jogger** *n* [C]

join¹ /dʒɔɪn/ *v*
1 [T] to become a member of an organization, society, or group: *Trevor joined the BBC in 1969.* | *Have you joined any clubs?*
2 [T] to begin to take part in an activity that other people are already doing: *Local people joined the hunt for the missing girl.*
3 [T] to go somewhere in order to be with someone else: *Shall we join the others in the garden?*
4 [I,T] to do something together with someone else: **join sb for sth** *Why don't you join us for dinner?* | **join (with) sb in doing sth** *Please join with me in welcoming tonight's speaker.*
5 [T] to connect or fasten things together: *Join the two pieces of wood with strong glue.* | **join sth together** *the corridor that joins the three buildings together* → see box at **FASTEN**
6 [I,T] if two roads, rivers etc join, they come together and are connected at a particular place: *the point where the two rivers join*
7 join hands if two people join hands, they hold each other's hands
8 join a queue/line to go and stand at the end of a line of people
  join in (sth) *phr v* to begin to take part in something that other people are doing: *The other children wouldn't let Sam join in.* | *Everyone joined in the conversation.*
  join up *phr v* **1** to combine or meet with other people to do something: *We can all join up for a drink later.* | **+with** *They've joined up with local environmentalists.* **2** *BrE* to become a member of the army, navy etc → see box at **ARMY**

join² *n* [C] a place where two parts of an object are connected or fastened together

joined-up *adj* [only before noun] *BrE* **1** joined-up writing has all the letters in each word connected to each other **2** *BrE* joined-up systems, institutions etc combine different groups, ideas, or parts in a way that works well: *joined-up government* | *the need for joined-up thinking between departments*

joiner /ˈdʒɔɪnə $ -ər/ *n* [C] *BrE* someone who makes wooden doors, window frames etc

joint¹ /dʒɔɪnt/ *adj* shared by or involving two or more people: *They have to reach a joint decision.* | *a joint bank account* | *The research was a joint effort by the two groups.*
—**jointly** *adv*: *Sam and I are jointly responsible for the project.*

joint² *n* [C]
1 a part of the body where two bones meet: **hip/knee/elbow etc joint**

2 a place where two things or parts of an object are joined together: *One of the joints between the pipes was leaking.*
3 *BrE* a large piece of meat with a bone in it: **+of** *a joint of beef*
4 *informal* a place such as a bar, club, or restaurant: *a fast-food joint*
5 *informal* a cigarette that contains CANNABIS

joint 'venture *n* [C] a business arrangement in which two or more companies work together

joke¹ /dʒəʊk $ dʒoʊk/ *n* [C]
1 something funny that you say or do to make people laugh: **+about** *kids' jokes about their teachers* | *I only did it as a joke.* | *Ed loves telling jokes.* | *He's always making silly jokes.* | *Come on – can't you take a joke* (=laugh at a joke about yourself)*?* | **get/see the joke** (=understand why a joke is funny) | **play a joke on sb** (=trick someone to make people laugh)

COLLOCATIONS

sick joke – a joke that is very unpleasant and is often about death or suffering
dirty joke – a joke that is about sex
practical joke – a trick that is intended to surprise someone or make other people laugh at them
tasteless joke – a joke that is slightly offensive
sexist/racist joke – a very offensive joke that makes fun of women or someone's race

2 be a joke *informal* to be completely useless, stupid, or unreasonable: *Public transport here is a joke.*
3 make a joke (out) of sth to treat something serious as if it were funny: *It was so bad, she tried to make a joke of it.*
4 be no joke used to emphasize that a situation is serious or difficult: *Looking after three kids on your own is no joke.*
5 get beyond a joke to become serious and worrying: *All this junk mail is getting beyond a joke.*
→ IN-JOKE, PRACTICAL JOKE

joke² *v* [I]
1 to say things that are funny or that you do not really mean: **+about** *The guys laughed and joked about it later.* | **+with** *He was relaxed, joking with the reporters.* | **+that** *His students joked that he should go into politics.* | *Hey, calm down – I'm only joking!*
2 you're joking/you must be joking *spoken* used when you are surprised by what someone has said because it seems strange or silly: *Buy a house on my salary? You must be joking!*
—**jokingly** *adv*

joker /ˈdʒəʊkə $ ˈdʒoʊkər/ *n* [C] **1** someone who likes to say or do funny things **2** a card used in some card games that has no fixed value

jolly¹ /ˈdʒɒli $ ˈdʒɑːli/ *adj* happy: *a jolly atmosphere*

jolly² *adv* *BrE spoken old-fashioned* very: *It's jolly cold outside!*

jolt¹ /dʒəʊlt $ dʒoʊlt/ *n* [C] **1** a sudden shock: *It gave me a jolt to see her looking so ill.* | *Sam woke with a jolt.* **2** a sudden strong movement: *There was a terrific jolt as the lift stopped.*

jolt² v [I,T] to move suddenly and strongly, or to make someone or something do this: *The train jolted to a halt.*

jostle /'dʒɒsəl $ 'dʒɑː-/ v [I,T] to push against other people in a crowd: **+for** *Spectators jostled for a better view.*

jot /dʒɒt $ dʒɑːt/ v **jotted, jotting**
 jot sth ⇔ **down** phr v to write something quickly on a piece of paper: *Let me jot down your phone number.* → see box at **WRITE**

journal /'dʒɜːnl $ -ɜːr-/ n [C] **1** a serious magazine about a particular subject: *a scientific journal* **2** a written account of the things that happen to you each day [**= diary**] → see box at **RECORD**

journalism /'dʒɜːnəl-ɪzəm $ -ɜːr-/ n [U] the job of writing reports for newspapers, magazines, television, or radio

journalist /'dʒɜːnəl-ɪst $ -ɜːr-/ n [C] someone who writes reports for newspapers, magazines, television, or radio [**➡ reporter**] → see box at **NEWSPAPER**

journey /'dʒɜːni $ -ɜːr-/ n [C] plural **journeys** *especially BrE* the time spent travelling from one place to another, especially over a long distance: **car/train/bus journey** *a long car journey* | **+to/ from/through** *My journey to work takes about an hour.* | **on a journey** *the people she met on her journey* | *They **made** the 180-mile **journey** to see her.*

THESAURUS

trip – a short journey to visit a place: *a trip to the seaside* | *a business trip*
voyage – a long journey over the sea: *the ship's maiden voyage* (=first journey)
crossing – a short journey over the sea, between two places that are not very far away from each other: *The crossing from Dover to Calais takes about 90 minutes.*
flight – a journey by air: *Please keep your seatbelts fastened during the flight.*
Do not use **travel** to mean a **journey**.
Travel is the general activity of moving from one place to another: *Her new job involves a lot of travel.*
A **journey** is the time spent travelling from one place to another: *the journey to work*

---

jovial /'dʒəuviəl $ 'dʒou-/ adj friendly and cheerful: *a jovial manner*

joy /dʒɔɪ/ n
1 [C,U] a feeling of great happiness and pleasure, or something that gives you this feeling: **for/with joy** *She cried with joy when she heard the news.* | **+of** *the joys of travel* | *The garden is her **pride and joy.*** | **be a joy to teach/watch** etc *The Jaguar's a joy to drive.*
2 **no/not any joy** *BrE spoken* if you have no joy, you do not succeed in getting something: *I've looked everywhere but I haven't **had any joy**.*

joyful /'dʒɔɪfəl/ also **joyous** /'dʒɔɪəs/ *literary* adj very happy, or making people very happy: *a joyful reunion* —**joyfully** adv

joyless /'dʒɔɪləs/ adj without any happiness: *a joyless childhood*

joyous /'dʒɔɪəs/ adj very happy, or making people very happy: *a joyous occasion* —**joyously** adv

joyriding /'dʒɔɪ,raɪdɪŋ/ n [U] the crime of stealing a car and driving it in a fast and dangerous way for fun —**joyride** v [I] —**joyrider** n [C]

joystick /'dʒɔɪstɪk/ n [C] a handle used to control an aircraft or a computer game

JP /,dʒeɪ 'piː/ n [C] a JUSTICE OF THE PEACE

Jr. *AmE* the written abbreviation of **Junior**, used after someone's name [**= Jnr** *BrE*]

jubilant /'dʒuːbɪlənt/ adj extremely happy because of a success: *a jubilant crowd* —**jubilation** /,dʒuːbɪ'leɪʃən/ n [U]

jubilee /'dʒuːbɪliː, ,dʒuːbɪ'liː/ n [C] a date that is celebrated because it is an exact number of years after an important event: **silver/golden/ diamond jubilee** (=25, 50, 60 years after something) | *Queen Victoria's diamond jubilee*

Judaism /'dʒuːdeɪ-ɪzəm, 'dʒuːdə- $ 'dʒuːdə-, 'dʒuːdi-/ n [U] the Jewish religion

judge¹ /dʒʌdʒ/ n
1 [C] the person who controls a court of law and decides how criminals should be punished: *the sentence imposed by the judge* | **federal/high court/district etc judge** (=a judge in a particular court) → see box at **COURT**
2 [C] someone who decides who has won a competition: *a panel* (=group) *of judges*
3 **a good/bad judge of sth** someone whose opinion of something is usually right or wrong: *She's a good judge of character.*

judge² v
1 [I,T] to form or give an opinion about someone or something using the information you have: **judge sb/sth on/by sth** *Never judge a person by their looks.* | *Employees should be judged on the quality of their work.* | **+whether/what/how** *It's difficult to judge whether he was telling the truth.* | **+that** *By then it was judged that the crisis was over.*
2 **judging by/from sth** used to give the reason why you think something is true: *Judging by his performance, he has a good chance of winning.*
3 [I,T] to decide who has won a competition: *Who's judging the talent contest?*
4 [I,T] to form an opinion about someone in a CRITICAL or unfair way: *You have no right to judge other people's lifestyles.*
5 [T] to decide in a court of law whether someone is guilty of a crime

judgment also **judgement** *BrE* /'dʒʌdʒmənt/ n
1 [C,U] your opinion about something, based on the information you have: *We must **make a judgment** about whether it's worth the risk.*
2 [U] the ability to make sensible decisions about situations or people: *I trust your **professional judgement**.* | *a serious **error of judgment***
3 [C,U] a legal decision made by a judge or a court of law

judgmental also **judgemental** *BrE* /dʒʌdʒ'mentl/ adj *disapproving* criticizing people unfairly

judicial /dʒuː'dɪʃəl/ adj relating to the law, judges etc: *the judicial system*

judiciary /dʒuː'dɪʃəri $ -ʃieri, -ʃəri/ n **the judiciary** *formal* all the judges in a country who, together, form part of the system of government

J

judicious /dʒuːˈdɪʃəs/ *adj formal* sensible and careful: *a judicious choice*

judo /ˈdʒuːdəʊ $ -doʊ/ *n* [U] a sport from Japan in which you try to throw your opponent onto the ground

jug /dʒʌɡ/ *n* [C] a container with an opening at the top and a handle, used for pouring or holding liquids

juggle /ˈdʒʌɡəl/ *v* **1** [I,T] to keep three or more balls, plates etc moving through the air by throwing and catching them very quickly **2** [T] to fit two or more activities into your life, especially with difficulty: **juggle sth and/with sth** *It's hard work trying to juggle family life and a career.*

juggler /ˈdʒʌɡlə $ -ər/ *n* [C] someone who juggles balls, plates etc to entertain people

juice /dʒuːs/ *n*
1 [C,U] the liquid from fruit or vegetables, or a drink made from this: *a carton of juice* | *an orange juice, please*
2 [C usually plural] the liquid that comes out of meat when it is cooked

juicy /ˈdʒuːsi/ *adj* **1** containing a lot of juice: *a juicy peach* **2 juicy gossip/details etc** *informal* interesting or shocking information about someone or something

jukebox /ˈdʒuːkbɒks $ -bɑːks/ *n* [C] a machine, usually in bars, that plays music when you put money in

July /dʒuˈlaɪ/ *n* [C usually singular,U] written abbreviation *Jul.* the seventh month of the year, between June and August: **next/last July** *She came over to England last July.* | **in July** *We usually go on holiday in July.* | **on July 6th** *The meeting will be on July 6th.* → see box at **MONTH**

jumble¹ /ˈdʒʌmbəl/ *n* **1** [singular] an untidy group of things: **+of** *a jumble of pots and pans* **2** [U] *BrE* things that are sold at a JUMBLE SALE

jumble² also **jumble up** *v* [T] to mix things together so that they become untidy: *Don't jumble all my papers up.*

'jumble sale *n* [C] *BrE* a sale of used clothes, books etc to get money for a local church, school etc [= rummage sale *AmE*]

jumbo /ˈdʒʌmbəʊ $ -boʊ/ *adj* [only before noun] *informal* larger than other things of the same type: *a jumbo sausage*

'jumbo jet also **jumbo** *n* [C] a very big plane that carries passengers

jump¹ /dʒʌmp/ *v*
1 [I,T] to push yourself up into the air, or over or off something using your legs: **+into/off/down etc** *Boys were jumping off the bridge into the river.* | *Fans were cheering and **jumping up and down**.* | *His horse jumped the final fence.* → see picture on page A11

jump

jump

hop

bounce

skip *BrE*/ skip rope *AmE*

2 [I] to move quickly or suddenly in a particular direction: **+up/into/out etc** *Paul jumped up to answer the door.* | *We all jumped in a taxi.* | *Robert **jumped** to his feet.*
3 [I] to make a sudden movement because you are surprised or frightened: *I didn't hear you come in – you **made** me **jump**!*
4 [I] to increase or improve suddenly and a lot: **+by** *Profits have jumped by 20%.* | **jump (from sth) to sth** *Norway jumped from ninth to third place.*
5 [I] to change quickly from one subject to another: **jump from sth to sth** *The story jumps from Tom's childhood to his wartime adventures.*
6 jump to conclusions to form an opinion about something before you have all the facts
7 jump the gun to start doing something too soon without thinking about it carefully
8 jump down sb's throat to suddenly speak angrily to someone
9 jump for joy to be extremely happy about something
10 jump the queue *BrE disapproving* to go ahead of other people who are already waiting in a line

jump at sth *phr v* to eagerly accept an opportunity to do something: *Ruth **jumped at the chance** to study in Paris.*

jump² *n*
1 [C] when you push yourself into the air using your legs, or let yourself drop from something: *the best jump of the competition* | **parachute/bungee jump** *I'd love to do a parachute jump.*
2 [singular] a sudden increase in an amount or value: **+in** *a big jump in house prices*
3 [C] something that a person or horse jumps over in a competition
→ **HIGH JUMP, LONG JUMP**

jumper /ˈdʒʌmpə $ -ər/ *n* [C] **1** *BrE* a piece of clothing made of wool that covers the upper part of your body and your arms [= sweater] → see picture at **CLOTHES** **2** *AmE* a dress without sleeves, usually worn over a shirt [= pinafore *BrE*]

'jump rope *n* [C] *AmE* a long piece of rope that children use for jumping over [= skipping rope *BrE*]

jumpy /'dʒʌmpi/ *adj informal* nervous or anxious

junction /'dʒʌŋkʃən/ *n* [C] a place where one road, railway line etc joins another: *the junction of Abbot Road and New Street*

juncture /'dʒʌŋktʃə $ -ər/ *n* [singular] *formal* a particular point in an activity or period of time: *At this juncture, we'll take a break.*

June /dʒuːn/ *n* [C,U] written abbreviation *Jun.* the sixth month of the year, between May and July: **next/last June** *He died last June.* | **in June** *My birthday's in June.* | **on June 6th** *We met on June 6th.* → see box at **MONTH**

jungle /'dʒʌŋɡəl/ *n* [C,U] a large tropical forest with trees and large plants growing very close together → see box at **TREE**

Junior /'dʒuːniə $ -ər/ written abbreviation *Jnr BrE Jr AmE* used after the name of a man who has the same name as his father: *John J. Wallace Junior*

junior¹ *adj*
1 having a low rank in an organization or profession [➡ **senior**]: *a junior executive* → see box at **POSITION**
2 for young people below a particular age: *the junior football club*

junior² *n* [C] **1** **be 10 years/6 months etc sb's junior** to be ten years, six months etc younger than someone: *His wife is ten years his junior.* **2** a young person who takes part in sport for people below a particular age **3** *especially BrE* someone who has a low rank in an organization or profession **4** *AmE* a student in the third year of HIGH SCHOOL or college **5** *BrE* a child at a junior school

junior 'college *n* [C,U] a college in the US and Canada where students do a course for two years

junior 'high school also **junior 'high** *n* [C,U] a school in the US and Canada for students between the ages of 12 and 14 or 15

'junior ,school *n* [C,U] a school in Britain for children aged 7 to 11 [➡ **primary school**]

junk /dʒʌŋk/ *n* [U] old or unwanted things that have no use or value: *a cupboard full of junk*

'junk food *n* [U] food that is not healthy because it contains a lot of fat or sugar → see box at **FOOD**

junkie /'dʒʌŋki/ *n* [C] *informal* **1** someone who takes dangerous drugs and is dependent on them **2** **TV/sports etc junkie** someone who likes something so much that they cannot stop doing it

'junk mail *n* [U] *disapproving* letters or emails, especially advertisements, sent to a large number of people → see box at **ADVERTISEMENT**

junta /'dʒʌntə, 'hʊntə/ *n* [C] a military government that has gained power by using force

Jupiter /'dʒuːpɪtə $ -ər/ *n* [singular] the fifth PLANET from the sun

jurisdiction /,dʒʊərɪs'dɪkʃən $,dʒʊr-/ *n* [U] the legal power to make decisions about something: *the court's jurisdiction*

juror /'dʒʊərə $ 'dʒʊrər/ *n* [C] a member of a jury

jury /'dʒʊəri $ 'dʒʊri/ *n* [C] plural **juries**
1 a group of twelve ordinary people in a court who decide whether someone is guilty: *the members of the jury* → see box at **COURT**
2 a group of people who choose the winner of a competition
→ **GRAND JURY**

just¹ /dʒəst; *strong* dʒʌst/ *adv*
1 exactly: *You look just like your dad.* | *The temperature was just right.* | *The phone rang just as* (=at the exact moment when) *we were leaving.* | *Just then* (=at exactly that moment) *Anne ran in from the garden.*
2 only: *'Who was there?' 'Just me and Elaine.'* | *It's not serious – just a small cut.* | *I just want to go to bed* (=that is all I want to do). | **just a minute/second** (=used to ask someone to wait for a short time)
3 only a short time ago: *She's just got married.* | *I've just had a really good idea.* → see box at **RECENTLY**
4 now or very soon: *Hang on, I'm just coming.* | *He's just leaving.* | **be just about to do sth** (=be going to do something very soon) *I was just about to phone you.*
5 **just before/after/outside/over etc sth** a small amount before, after, outside etc: *Lucy got home just after us.* | *They live just outside Paris.*
6 **(only) just** used to show that something happens with difficulty or almost does not happen: *They just managed to get to the station in time.* | *It only just fits through the door.* | *We had just enough* (=enough but no more) *money.*
7 **just as good/important/much etc** equally as good, important etc: *The $250 TV is just as good as the $300 one.*
8 *spoken* used to emphasize something you are saying: *I just couldn't believe the news.* | *That's just wonderful!* | *I didn't realise just how rich they were.*
9 *spoken* used to politely ask or tell someone something: *Could I just use your phone?*
10 **just about** almost: *We're just about finished.* | *Just about everyone replied.*
11 **just now** *spoken* **a)** a short time ago: *He was here just now.* **b)** at this moment: *I'm busy just now. Can I call you back?*
12 **just in case** *spoken* in order to be prepared for something that might happen: *I'll take my umbrella just in case.*
13 **it's just as well** *spoken* used to say that it is lucky that something happened: *It's just as well you were there to help.*

just² /dʒʌst/ *adj formal* morally right and fair [≠ **unjust**]: *a just punishment*

justice /'dʒʌstɪs/ *n* [U]
1 the system by which people are judged in courts of law and criminals are punished: *the criminal justice system* | *The killers must be **brought to justice*** (=caught and punished).
2 fairness in the way people are treated [≠ **injustice**]: *Children have a strong **sense of justice**.*
3 **do sb/sth justice** to show or talk about someone in a way that makes them seem as attractive, good etc as they really are: *This picture doesn't do you justice.*

Justice of the 'Peace *n* [C] abbreviation *JP* someone who decides whether a person is guilty of a crime in a small local court

justifiable /'dʒʌstɪ̯faɪəbəl/ *adj* done for good reasons: *a justifiable decision* —**justifiably** *adv*

justification /,dʒʌstɪ̯fɪ'keɪʃən/ *n* [C,U] a good reason for doing something: *There's no justification for upsetting her like that.*

justified /'dʒʌstɪ̯faɪd/ *adj* having an acceptable explanation or reason [≠ **unjustified**]: *Your complaints are certainly justified.*

justify /'dʒʌstɪ̯faɪ/ *v* [T] **justified, justifying, justifies** to give a good reason for doing something that other people think is unreasonable: **justify (doing) sth** *How can you justify spending so much money on a coat?*

jut /dʒʌt/ also **jut out** *v* [I] **jutted, jutting** to stick out further than the surrounding things: *a point of land that juts out into the ocean*

juvenile /'dʒuːvənaɪl $ -nəl, -naɪl/ *adj* **1** *law* relating to young people who are not yet adults: *juvenile crime* **2** *disapproving* silly and typical of a child rather than an adult: *a juvenile sense of humour* —**juvenile** *n* [C]

juvenile de'linquent *n* [C] *formal* a child or young person who behaves in a criminal way

juxtapose /,dʒʌkstə'pəʊz $ 'dʒʌkstəpoʊz/ *v* [T] *formal* to put together things that are very different, especially in order to compare them —**juxtaposition** /,dʒʌkstəpə'zɪʃən/ *n* [C,U]

K, k

K, k¹ /keɪ/ n [C,U] plural **K's, k's** the 11th letter of the English alphabet

K, k² **1** *informal* an abbreviation of **thousand**, used when talking about money: *He earns £50K a year.* **2** the written abbreviation of **kilobyte**

kaleidoscope /kə'laɪdəskəʊp $ -skoʊp/ n **1** [singular] a large number of very different things: **+of** *a kaleidoscope of cultures* **2** [C] a tube with mirrors and pieces of coloured glass at one end, that shows different coloured patterns when you turn it

kangaroo

kangaroo /ˌkæŋgə'ruː◂/ n [C] plural **kangaroos** a large Australian animal that jumps and carries its babies in a pocket on its stomach

karaoke /ˌkæri'əʊki $ ˌkɑːrɪ'oʊ-/ n [U] when someone sings popular songs while a machine plays the music, for entertainment

karat /'kærət/ n *AmE* a unit for measuring how pure a piece of gold is [= carat *BrE*]

karate /kə'rɑːti/ n [U] a sport from Japan in which you fight using your hands and feet

karma /'kɑːmə $ -ɑːr-/ n [U] the belief that the good and bad things you do in your life will affect you in the future, according to some religions

kayak /'kaɪæk/ n [C] a small boat, usually for one person [➡ canoe] → see picture on page A9

kebab /kɪ'bæb $ kɪ'bɑːb/ n [C] *BrE* **1** thin pieces of meat and pieces of vegetables wrapped in thin bread **2** small pieces of meat and vegetables, cooked on a stick → see picture on page A5

keel¹ /kiːl/ n [C] **1** a bar along the bottom of a boat that keeps it steady **2 on an even keel** continuing in a steady way: *I'd just got my life back on an even keel after the break-up.*

keel² v
keel over phr v to fall over suddenly: *Several soldiers keeled over in the heat.*

keen /kiːn/ adj
1 wanting to do something very much [= **eager**]: **keen to do sth** *US companies are keen to enter the Chinese market.* | **keen on doing sth** *They're*

keen on getting more young people to apply. | *The students all seem very keen* (=they want to learn).
2 *especially BrE* liking someone or something very much, or being very interested in them: **+on** *I'm not very keen on their music.* | *She takes* **a keen interest** *in politics.* | *a keen golfer*
3 a keen sense or feeling is very strong: *Sarah felt a* **keen sense** *of loss.* | *his* **keen eye** *for talent*
—**keenly** adj

keep¹ /kiːp/ v past tense and past participle **kept** /kept/
1 [linking verb, T] to stay in the same state or position, or to make someone or something do this: **keep (sb/sth) warm/safe/alive etc** *This blanket should help you keep warm.* | **keep (sb) awake/calm/happy etc** *activities to keep everyone happy* | **Keep still** *for a moment.* | *Try to* **keep** *the place tidy.* | **keep (sb/sth) away/back/out etc** *high fences to keep intruders out* | **keep sb busy/occupied/amused etc** *My work's been keeping me very busy.* | *They* **kept** *their plans secret.*
2 keep (on) doing sth to continue doing something, or to do the same thing many times: *Food prices keep on rising.* | **keep saying/telling/repeating etc** *I keep telling him, but he won't listen!* | **keep going** (=used to tell someone to continue doing something or going somewhere) *Keep going – we're nearly there.*
3 [T] to continue to have something and not give it back, sell it etc: *You can keep the book. I don't need it.* | *We've decided to keep this car for another year.*
4 [T] to store something in a particular place, so that you can find it: *Where do you keep your tea bags?* | **+in/on/under etc** *The information is kept on computer.*
5 [T] to make someone stay in prison, a hospital etc: *They kept him in jail for two weeks.*
6 [T] to delay someone: *I don't know what's keeping her. It's 8:00 already.* | *Sorry to* **keep you waiting** (=make you have to wait).
7 [T] to do something you have promised or arranged to do: *She had to rush off to* **keep an appointment.** | **keep your promise/word**
8 keep a secret to not tell anyone about a secret
9 keep a record/diary etc to regularly write down information about something: *Keep a record of what you spend.*
10 [T] to provide someone with the money, food etc they need: *I don't earn enough to keep a family.* | **keep sb going** (=to be enough for what is needed for a short time) *Have a biscuit to keep you going.*
11 [I] if food keeps, it stays fresh: *That yoghurt won't keep much longer.*
12 [T] to have animals and look after them: *We used to keep chickens.*

keep at sth phr v to continue to do something although it is difficult: *It's hard work but* **keep at it!**

keep sth ⇔ **back** phr v to not tell someone about something: *She was keeping something back from me.*

keep sth ⇔ **down** phr v to prevent something from increasing too much: *I hope they keep the rents down.* | *Please* **keep the noise down** (=be quieter)!

K

keep from sth *phr v* **1 keep sth from sb** to not tell someone about something: *He kept the news from his family for days.* **2 keep (sb/sth) from (doing) sth** to prevent someone from doing something or prevent something from happening: *Am I keeping you from your work?* | *I bit my lip to keep from crying.*

keep sb **in** *phr v* to make someone stay in hospital, or to make a child stay inside as a punishment

keep off *phr v* **1 keep sth off (sth)** to prevent something from touching or damaging something else: *A hat will keep the sun off your head.* **2 keep off sth** to avoid using, eating, touching etc something: *You should keep off alcohol.* | *Keep off the grass.*

keep on *phr v* **1 keep on doing sth** to continue doing something, or to do something many times: *Just keep on trying.* **2 keep sb on** to continue to employ someone: *If he's good they might keep him on.* **3** *informal disapproving* to talk about something a lot, or tell someone to do something many times, in an annoying way: **+about** *She kept on about the wedding all the time.* | **+at** *Don't keep on at me!*

keep out of sth *phr v* to not become involved with something: *You keep out of this, Campbell.*

keep to sth *phr v* **1** to do what you should do or agreed to do: *They failed to keep to the agreement.* **2** to stay on a particular road, path etc: *Keep to the main roads.* **3 keep sth to a minimum** to prevent the amount or level of something getting too high **4 keep sth to yourself** to not tell anyone about something: *Kim kept Gina's secret to herself.* **5 keep (yourself) to yourself** to live in a very quiet, private way

keep up *phr v* **1 keep sth ⇔ up** to continue doing something, or to make something continue: *Keep up the good work.* | *It's exhausting and I don't know how long she can keep it up.* **2** to do something as well as or as quickly as other people: **+with** *Dave isn't keeping up with the rest of the class.* **3** to move as quickly as someone: *Wait, I can't keep up!* **4** to know about the latest facts, information, and products in a particular area: **+with** *It's hard to keep up with all the changes in computer technology.* **5** if one process keeps up with another, it increases at the same speed and by the same amount: **+with** *Food production is not keeping up with population growth.* **6 keep sb up** to prevent someone from sleeping: *The baby kept us up all night.*

keep² *n* **1 earn your keep** to do enough work to pay for your food, clothes etc **2 for keeps** *informal* for ever: *It's yours for keeps.*

keeper /'ki:pə $ -ər/ *n* [C] **1** someone who looks after animals or a place and the things that are in it: *cattle keepers* | **+of** *the keeper of Egyptian Antiquities at the British Museum* **2** a GOALKEEPER → GAMEKEEPER, ZOO-KEEPER

,**keep 'fit** *n* [U] *BrE* a class in which you do exercises to keep yourself healthy → see box at EXERCISE

keeping /'ki:pɪŋ/ *n* **in keeping/out of keeping (with sth)** suitable or not suitable for a particular style or situation: *The modern furniture wasn't really in keeping with the rest of the house.* → SAFEKEEPING

keepsake /'ki:pseɪk/ *n* [C] a small object that you keep to remind you of someone

keg /keg/ *n* [C] a large container used for storing beer

kennel /'kenl/ *n* [C] **1** a small outdoor building for a dog to sleep in **2** also **kennels** *BrE* a place where dogs are looked after while their owners are not at home

kept /kept/ *v* the past tense and past participle of KEEP

kerb *BrE*; **curb** *AmE* /kɜːb $ kɜːrb/ *n* [C] the edge of the PAVEMENT at the side of the road

kernel /'kɜːnl $ 'kɜːr-/ *n* [C] the centre part of a nut or seed

kerosene /'kerəsiːn/ *n* [U] *especially AmE* a type of oil that is burned for heat and light [= paraffin *BrE*]

ketchup /'ketʃəp/ *n* [U] a cold red sauce made from tomatoes that you put on food

kettle /'ketl/ *n* [C] a container used for boiling water: *I'll put the kettle on for a cup of tea.* → see picture at KITCHEN

key¹ /kiː/ *n* [C]

1 something that you put into a lock in order to open a door, start a car etc: *house/car keys I lost my car keys.* | *A bunch of keys hung from his belt.* → see picture at PADLOCK

2 one of the things you press to produce letters and numbers on a computer, or sounds on a piano

3 the key (to sth) the part of a plan, action etc, that will make it possible for it to succeed: **+to** *Preparation is the key to success.* | *a discovery that may hold the key to our understanding of the universe*

4 a set of musical notes that is based on one particular note: *the key of C major*

5 a list of the signs, colours etc used on a map, technical drawing etc that explains what they mean

6 the printed answers to a test or set of questions in a book

key² *adj* [only before noun] very important or necessary: *a key witness* | *a key decision*

key³ *v*

key sth ⇔ **in** *phr v* to put information into a computer → see box at WRITE

keyboard /'kiːbɔːd $ -bɔːrd/ *n* [C] **1** a set of keys on a computer, a piano etc, which you press to produce letters or sounds **2** also **keyboards** [plural] an electric musical instrument similar to a piano that can make sounds like many different instruments

,**keyed 'up** *adj* [not before noun] worried or excited

keyhole /'kiːhəʊl $ -hoʊl/ *n* [C] the hole in a lock that you put the key in

keynote /'kiːnəʊt $ -noʊt/ *adj* **keynote speech/address/lecture** the most important speech etc at a formal meeting

keypad /'kiːpæd/ *n* [C] a small box with buttons on it that you press to put information into a computer, telephone etc

'**key ring** *n* [C] a metal ring that you keep keys on

keyword /'kiːwɜːd $ -wɜːrd/ *n* [C] a word that you type into a computer so that it will search for that word on the Internet: *You can find the site by entering the keyword 'Quark'.*

kg the written abbreviation of **kilogram**

khaki /'kɑːki $ 'kæki, 'kɑːki/ *n* [U] a dull green-brown or yellow-brown colour —**khaki** *adj*

kick[1] /kɪk/ *v*

1 [T] to hit or move something with your foot: **kick sth into/out of/around etc sth** *Billy was kicking a ball around the yard.* | **kick sth down** *The police kicked the door down.* → see picture on page A11

2 [I,T] to move your legs quickly forwards or backwards: *a baby kicking its legs* | *He kicked off his shoes and lay on the bed.*

3 kick yourself *spoken* to be annoyed with yourself because you have done something silly, made a mistake etc: *You'll kick yourself when I tell you the answer.*

4 kick the habit to stop doing something such as smoking, taking drugs etc: *smokers who want to kick the habit*

5 kick up a fuss *informal* to complain loudly about something

kick in *phr v informal* to begin to have an effect: *Those pills should kick in any time now.*

kick off *phr v informal* to start, or to make an event start: **+with** *The festivities will kick off with a barbecue dinner.*

kick sb ⇔ **out** *phr v informal* to make someone leave a place, job etc: **+of** *He was kicked out of college for taking cocaine.*

kick[2] *n* [C]

1 an action of hitting something with your foot: *Brazil scored with the last kick of the match.* | *If the gate won't open, just give it a good kick.*

2 *informal* a feeling of pleasure and excitement: *Alan gets a real kick out of skiing.* | **do sth for kicks** *She started stealing for kicks.*

→ **FREE KICK**

kickback /'kɪkbæk/ *n* [C,U] *informal* money that a person gets for secretly and dishonestly helping someone [= bribe]

kickoff /'kɪk-ɒf $ -ɒːf/ *n* [C,U] the time when a football game starts, or the first kick of the game: *Kickoff is at midday.*

'kick-start *v* [T] to do something to help a process or activity start or develop more quickly: *A cut in interest rates might kick-start the economy.*

kid[1] /kɪd/ *n*

1 [C] *informal* a child: *How many kids do you have?* | *when I was a **little kid*** → see box at CHILD

2 [C] *informal* a young person: *Kids these days spend a fortune on CDs.* | *college kids*

3 kid brother/sister *especially AmE informal* a younger brother or sister [= **little brother/sister** *BrE*]

4 [C,U] a young goat, or the leather made from its skin

kid[2] *v* **kidded, kidding** *informal* **1** [I,T] to make a joke, especially by saying something that is not true: *Don't worry, I was **just kidding**.* **2** [T] to make yourself or someone else believe something that is untrue or unlikely: **kid yourself (that)** *Don't kid yourself he'll ever change.* **3 no kidding/you're kidding** *spoken informal* said when you are surprised by what someone has said: *Carlotta's 39? No kidding!*

kidnap /'kɪdnæp/ *v* [T] **kidnapped, kidnapping** *BrE*; **kidnaped, kidnaping** *AmE* to take someone

somewhere by force, especially in order to get money for returning them —**kidnapper** *n* [C] —**kidnapping** also **kidnap** *n* [C,U]

kidney /'kɪdni/ *n* [C] one of the two organs in your lower back that separate waste liquid from blood → see picture on page A3

kill[1] /kɪl/ *v*

1 [I,T] to make a person or animal die: *He's in jail for killing a policeman.* | **kill yourself** *She tried to kill herself.* | *Smoking kills.*

murder – to deliberately kill someone
commit manslaughter – to kill someone without intending to
commit suicide – to deliberately cause your own death
assassinate – to deliberately kill an important person, especially a politician
slaughter/massacre – to kill a large number of people in a violent way
execute sb/put sb to death – to kill someone as a punishment for a crime

2 [T] to make something stop, or prevent it from happening: *They gave her drugs to kill the pain.*

3 sb will kill/could have killed sb *spoken* used to say that someone will be or was very angry with someone: *My wife will kill me if she finds out.*

4 my head/back etc is killing me *spoken* used to say that part of your body is hurting a lot: *I've walked miles and my feet are killing me.*

5 kill time/an hour etc *informal* to spend time doing something which is not important while you are waiting for something else to happen

6 kill two birds with one stone to achieve two things with one action

7 kill yourself laughing to laugh a lot about something

kill sb/sth ⇔ **off** *phr v* to stop someone or something from existing any more: *Pollution is rapidly killing off the plant life.*

kill[2] *n* [singular] **1** the act of killing a hunted animal **2 move in/close in for the kill** to get nearer to killing or defeating someone: *His opponent was moving in for the kill.*

killer /'kɪlə $ -ər/ *n* [C] a person, animal, or thing that kills: *The police are still looking for the girl's killer.* | *weed killer*

killing /'kɪlɪŋ/ *n* [C] **1** a murder: *a series of brutal killings* **2 make a killing** *informal* to make a lot of money very quickly

kiln /kɪln/ *n* [C] a special OVEN for baking clay pots, bricks etc

kilo /'kiːləʊ $ -loʊ/ *n* [C] plural **kilos** a kilogram: *I weigh 65 kilos.*

kilobyte /'kɪləbaɪt/ *n* [C] a unit for measuring computer information, equal to 1024 BYTES

kilogram, kilogramme /'kɪləɡræm/ also **kilo** *n* [C] written abbreviation *kg* a unit for measuring weight, equal to 1000 grams

kilometre *BrE*; **kilometer** *AmE* /'kɪlə,miːtə, kɪ'lɒmɪtə $ kɪ'lɑːmɪtər/ *n* [C] written abbreviation *km* a unit for measuring length, equal to 1000 metres

kilowatt /'kɪləwɒt $ -wɑːt/ *n* [C] written abbreviation *kw* a unit for measuring electrical power, equal to 1000 WATTS

K

kilt /kɪlt/ n [C] a skirt traditionally worn by Scottish men

kimono /kɪˈməʊnəʊ $ -ˈmoʊnoʊ/ n [C] plural **kimonos** a loose piece of clothing traditionally worn in Japan

kin /kɪn/ n **1** **next of kin** formal the person in your family who you are most closely related to **2** [plural] old-fashioned your family

kind¹ /kaɪnd/ n [C]

1 a type of person or thing [➡ sort]: +of What kind of pizza do you want? | We sell all kinds of hats. | I think they're having some kind of party upstairs. | of its kind The course is the only one of its kind. | Ted just isn't the marrying kind (=the type of person who gets married).
2 **kind of** spoken slightly or in some ways [= sort of; = kinda AmE]: He looks kind of weird to me. | I'm kind of glad I didn't win.
3 **a kind of (a) sth** spoken used to say that your description of something is not exact: a kind of reddish-brown colour
4 **one of a kind** the only one of a particular type of thing: Each vase is handmade and one of a kind.
5 **of a kind** disapproving used to say that something is not as good as it should be: I think it's chicken – of a kind.
6 **nothing/anything of the kind** spoken used to emphasize that what has been said is not true: I never said anything of the kind!

kind² adj

1 someone who is kind shows that they care about other people and wants to help them [≠ unkind]: She's a kind and generous person. | +to Everyone's been so kind to me. | Thank you for your kind offer. | **it's kind of sb (to do sth)** It was kind of him to call.

2 **kind regards** formal used to end a formal but friendly letter

kinda /ˈkaɪndə/ adv AmE spoken a way of writing or saying 'kind of', which many people think is incorrect [= slightly]: I'm kinda tired.

kindergarten /ˈkɪndəɡɑːtn $ -dərɡɑːrtn/ n [C,U] **a)** BrE a school for children aged two to five [= nursery school] **b)** AmE a school or class for children aged 5

kind-hearted /ˌkaɪnd ˈhɑːtɪd◂ $ -ɑːr-/ adj kind and generous

kindle /ˈkɪndl/ v [I,T] **1** if you kindle a fire, or if it kindles, it starts to burn **2** to make someone feel interested, excited, hopeful etc: **kindle sth in sb** A love of poetry was kindled in him by his mother.

kindling /ˈkɪndlɪŋ/ n [U] small pieces of dry wood, leaves etc that you use for starting a fire

kindly¹ /ˈkaɪndli/ adv **1** in a kind way: Miss Havisham looked kindly at Joe. | **kindly offer/agree/give etc** Dad's kindly offered to lend us his car. **2** spoken formal used to mean 'please', especially when you are annoyed: Kindly go

away. **3** **not take kindly to sth** to be unwilling to accept a situation because it annoys you: He didn't take kindly to being told what to do.

kindly² adj old-fashioned kind

kindness /ˈkaɪndnəs/ n [U] kind behaviour: Sam never forgot her kindness.

kindred /ˈkɪndrəd/ adj **kindred spirit** someone who thinks and feels the way you do

king /kɪŋ/ n [C]

1 a man from a royal family who rules a country [➡ queen]: +of the King of Spain | Leopold was crowned king in October.
2 **the king of sth** the most important or best person or thing in a particular area, activity etc: The lion is the king of the jungle.
3 the most important piece in a game of CHESS
4 a playing card with a picture of a king on it

kingdom /ˈkɪŋdəm/ n [C] **1** a country that is ruled by a king or queen: +of the Kingdom of Nepal **2** **the animal/plant kingdom** all animals or plants considered together as a group

kingfisher /ˈkɪŋˌfɪʃə $ -ər/ n [C] a small brightly coloured bird that catches fish in rivers

king-size also **king-sized** adj very big: a king-size bed

kink /kɪŋk/ n [C] a twist in something that is normally straight

kinky /ˈkɪŋki/ adj informal kinky sexual activities are strange and unusual: kinky sex videos

kinship /ˈkɪnʃɪp/ n **1** [U] literary family relationships **2** [singular, U] a strong connection between people: He felt a kinship with the only other American on the base.

kiosk /ˈkiːɒsk $ -ɑːsk/ n [C] a small building in the street where newspapers, sweets etc are sold

kip /kɪp/ n [singular, U] BrE informal a short period of sleep —**kip** v [T]

kipper /ˈkɪpə $ -ər/ n [C] a type of fish that has been preserved using smoke and salt

kiss¹ /kɪs/ v [I,T] to touch someone with your lips as a greeting or to show them love: **kiss sb on sth** She kissed me on the cheek. | Matt kissed her **goodnight** and left the room. | As they parted, John and Mary kissed.

kiss² n [C]

1 an act of kissing: a passionate kiss | Come here and **give me a kiss**.
2 **give sb the kiss of life** BrE to breathe air into someone's lungs in order to make them start breathing again

kit /kɪt/ n [C] **1** a set of tools, clothes etc that you use for a particular purpose or activity: a bike repair kit | my football kit **2** something that you buy in parts and put together yourself: I built the boat **from a kit**.

kitchen /ˈkɪtʃən/ n [C] the room where you prepare and cook food: She's in the kitchen making the dinner. | kitchen cupboards

kite /kaɪt/ n [C] a toy made of paper or cloth that flies in the air on the end of a long string

kitsch /kɪtʃ/ n [U] things such as decorations that are cheap, ugly, or unfashionable: Her house was full of 1970s kitsch.

kitten /ˈkɪtn/ n [C] a young cat

kitty /ˈkɪti/ n [C usually singular] plural **kitties** the money that people have collected for a particular purpose

kitchen

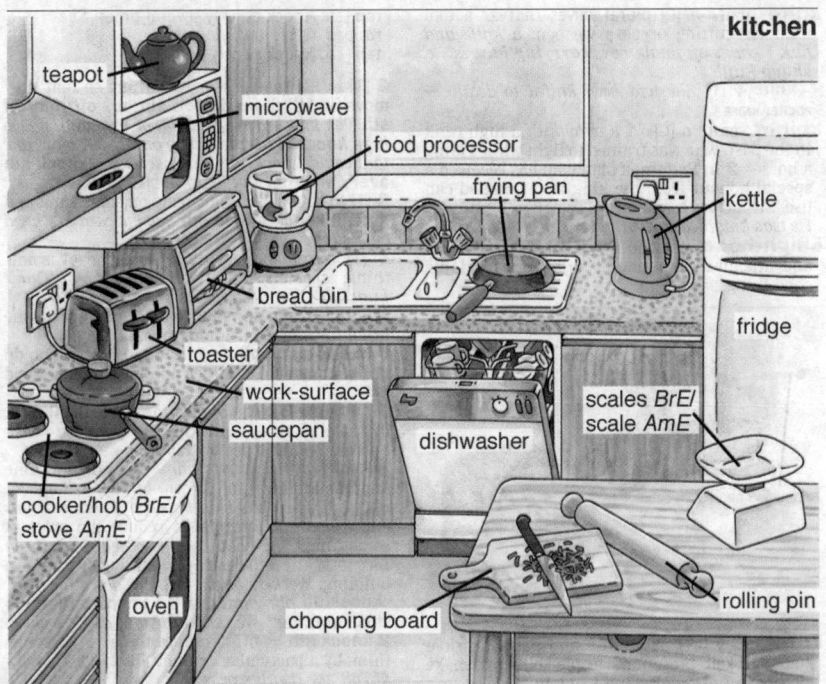

- teapot
- microwave
- food processor
- frying pan
- kettle
- bread bin
- toaster
- work-surface
- saucepan
- scales *BrE*/ scale *AmE*
- dishwasher
- cooker/hob *BrE*/ stove *AmE*
- oven
- chopping board
- rolling pin
- fridge

'kitty-,corner *adv AmE informal* on the opposite corner of a street from a particular place

kiwi fruit /'ki:wi: fru:t/ also **kiwi** *n* [C] a small brown fruit which is green inside with black seeds → see picture at **FRUIT**

Kleenex /'kli:neks/ *n* [C,U] plural **Kleenex** *trademark* a TISSUE

klutz /klʌts/ *n* [C] *AmE informal* someone who drops things or falls easily —**klutzy** *adj*

km the written abbreviation of **kilometre**

knack /næk/ *n* [singular] *informal* a natural skill or ability: **knack for/of doing sth** *Harry has the knack of making friends wherever he goes.*

knackered /'nækəd $ -ərd/ *adj* [not before noun] *BrE informal* extremely tired → see box at **TIRED**

knapsack /'næpsæk/ *n* [C] *AmE* a bag that you carry on your back [= **backpack**]

knead /ni:d/ *v* [T] to press a mixture of flour and water many times with your hands, for example to make bread: *Knead the dough for three minutes.* → see picture on page A4

knee /ni:/ *n* [C]

1 the middle part of your leg, where it bends: **on your knees** *She was on her knees, weeding the garden.* | *a painful knee injury* → see picture on page A3

2 the part of your trousers that covers your knees: *His jeans had holes in both knees.*

3 bring sb/sth to their knees to defeat or destroy someone or something, so that they cannot continue: *The recession brought many companies to their knees.*

kneecap /'ni:kæp/ *n* [C] the bone at the front of your knee → see picture on page A3

,knee-'deep *adj*

1 deep enough to reach your knees: *The snow was almost knee-deep.* **2** [not before noun] having a lot of something to deal with: **+in** *We ended up knee-deep in debt.*

,knee-'high *adj* tall enough to reach your knees: *knee-high grass*

'knee-jerk *adj* **knee-jerk reaction/ response** something you say or feel as an immediate reaction, without thinking about it

knee-deep

knee-deep in the snow

kneel /ni:l/ also **kneel down** *v* [I] past tense and past participle knelt /nelt/ also **kneeled** *AmE* to be in or move into a position where your body is resting on your knees: *She knelt down and began to pray.* → see picture on page A11

knew /nju: $ nu:/ *v* the past tense of **KNOW**

knickers /'nɪkəz $ -ərz/ *n* [plural] *BrE* women's underwear that covers the area between the waist and the top of the legs [= **panties** *AmE*]: *a pair of black knickers* → see picture at **CLOTHES**

knick-knack /'nɪk næk/ *n* [C] a small object used as a decoration

K

knife /naɪf/ n [C] plural **knives** /naɪvz/ a tool used for cutting or as a weapon: *a knife and fork* | *gangs of young boys **carrying knives*** | *a sharp knife*
—**knife** v [T] *She had been knifed to death.* →
POCKET KNIFE

knight /naɪt/ n [C] **1** a man with a high rank in the past, who was trained to fight while riding a horse **2** in Britain, a man who has received a special honour from the king or queen and can use 'Sir' before his name [➔ **dame**] —**knight** v [T] *He was knighted in 2001.*

knighthood /ˈnaɪthʊd/ n [C,U] a British rank and title given to a man as an honour for doing good things

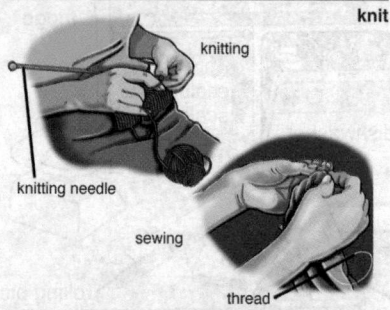

knit
knitting
knitting needle
sewing
thread

knit /nɪt/ v [I,T] past tense and past participle **knitted** or **knit**, present participle **knitting** to make clothes out of wool using two long needles or a special machine: *She's knitting a sweater.*
—**knitting** n [U]

ˈknitting ˌneedle n [C] one of the two long needles that you use to knit clothes out of wool → see picture at **KNIT**

knitwear /ˈnɪt-weə $ -wer/ n [U] knitted clothes such as SWEATERS sold in shops

knives /naɪvz/ n the plural of KNIFE

knob /nɒb $ nɑːb/ n [C] a round handle or button that you turn to open a door, turn on a radio etc

knobbly BrE /ˈnɒbli $ ˈnɑːbli/, **knobby** AmE /ˈnɒbi $ ˈnɑːbi/ adj not smooth, with hard parts sticking out from the surface: *knobbly knees*

knock¹ /nɒk $ nɑːk/ v
1 [I] to hit a door or window with your hand to attract the attention of people inside: +**on/at** *There's someone knocking on the front door.* → see box at **HIT**

knock

hammer – to hit something several times, making a lot of noise: *The police were hammering on his door last night.*
pound – to knock very hard, making a lot of noise: *Thomas pounded on the door with his fist.*

rap – to knock quickly several times: *She rapped on his window angrily.*
tap – to knock gently and quietly

2 [T] to hit someone or something so that they move or fall down: **knock sth out of/from/off sth** *Tim knocked the glass out of my hand.* | *Two boys **knocked** him **to the ground**.* | *A blow like that could **knock you unconscious**.* | **knock sth over** *I'm afraid I've knocked over a vase.*
3 [T] to hit part of your body on something and hurt it: **knock sth on sth** *She knocked her head on a stone.*
4 [T] *informal* to criticize someone or something, especially unfairly: *'I hate this job.' '**Don't knock it** – it could be worse!'*
5 knock some sense into sb to make someone learn to behave in a more sensible way
6 knock on wood AmE used to say that you do not want your good luck to end [= **touch wood** BrE]

knock sth ⇔ **back** phr v informal to drink a lot of alcohol very quickly: *We knocked back another bottle.* → see box at **DRINK**

knock sb/sth ⇔ **down** phr v **1** to hit someone and make them fall down to the ground: *A mother of two has been knocked down by a bus and killed.* **2** informal to reduce the price of something: *The chair was knocked down from $800 to $550.* **3** to destroy a building or part of a building: *Workers began to knock down the wall.*

knock off phr v informal **1 knock off (sth)** to stop working: *We knocked off at 5 o'clock.* **2 knock sth ⇔ off** to reduce the price of something by a particular amount: *I got him to knock $10 off the regular price.*

knock sb/sth ⇔ **out** phr v **1** to make someone become unconscious, especially by hitting them: *Ali knocked out his opponent in the fifth round.* **2** to defeat a person or team so that they cannot continue in a competition: *Indiana got knocked out in the first round.*

knock sb ⇔ **over** phr v to hit someone with a moving vehicle and hurt or kill them: *The elderly man was knocked over while crossing the road.*

knock sth ⇔ **up** phr v spoken to make something quickly and without using much effort: *I'm sure I can knock up some pasta.*

knock² n [C]
1 the sound of someone or something hitting a hard surface: *There was a **loud knock** at the door.*
2 the action of something hard hitting your body: +**on** *He got a knock on the head.*

knocker /ˈnɒkə $ ˈnɑːkər/ n [C] a piece of metal on a door that you use to knock on the door

ˈknock-on adj BrE **have a knock-on effect (on sth)** to start a process in which one thing that happens will have an effect on another thing: *The price rises will have a knock-on effect on the economy.*

knockout /ˈnɒk-aʊt $ ˈnɑːk-/ n [C] when a BOXER hits his opponent so hard that he falls down and cannot get up again

knot¹ /nɒt $ nɑːt/ n [C]
1 a place where pieces of string, rope, cloth etc have been tied together: *He put some string round the parcel and **tied a knot**.*
2 a unit for measuring the speed of a ship

K

3 a hard round place in a piece of wood where a branch once joined the tree

knot² *v* [T] **knotted, knotting** to fasten something by tying together pieces of rope, string etc

know¹ /nəʊ $ noʊ/ *v* past tense **knew** /njuː $ nuː/ past participle **known** /nəʊn $ noʊn/

1 [I,T] to have knowledge or information about something: *Who knows the answer?* | **know (something/nothing etc) about sth** *He knows a lot about cars.* | **know (something/nothing etc) of sth** *Do you know of any good restaurants in the area?* | **+(that)** *We know that greenhouse gases can affect the climate.* | **+how/what/where etc** *Nobody knows where she's gone.* | **know how to do sth** (=have learned how to do something) *Do you know how to make risotto?* | *Let me know* (=tell me) *what time you will arrive.*

2 [I,T] to be or feel sure about something: *'Are you seeing Jim tomorrow?' 'I don't know yet.'* | **+(that)** *I know I won't get the job.* | **+if/whether** *I don't know if I'll be able to come.* | *How do you know* (=what makes you sure) *he won't do it again?* | *Gail left at 6.00., as far as I know* (=I think, but I'm not sure).

3 [T] to be or become familiar with a person, place etc: *I knew Hilary in high school.* | *a chance for students to get to know each other* | *Jean knows Paris well.* | *Luckily, Jo knew the way to the hospital* (=knew how to get there). | *You should know the system inside out* (=be very familiar with it). | *I grew up here; I know the place like the back of my hand* (=know it very well).

4 [T] to realize or understand something: *She knew the risks involved.* | *'I felt so tired.' 'Yes, I know what you mean.'* | **+(that)** *Suddenly she knew that something was terribly wrong.*

5 [T] to have experience of something: *I don't think he ever knew true happiness.* | *I have never known a case quite like this one.*

6 know sb/sth as sth to think of someone as having particular qualities, or to give them a particular name: *I knew him as a hard-working and honest politician.* | *Diana became known as 'the people's Princess'.*

7 you know *spoken* **a)** used to emphasize a statement: *There's no excuse, you know.* **b)** used to make sure that someone understands what, who etc you are talking about: *I felt very upset, you know?* | *that girl, you know, with long blonde hair* **c)** used to pause while you think of what to say next: *Well, you know, that's not entirely true.* **d)** used to start talking about something or to make someone listen: *You know, he's going to be taller than his dad.*

8 I know a) used to agree with someone: *'We have to talk about it, Rob.' 'Yeah, I know.''* **b)** used when you suddenly think of an idea: *I know, let's ask Michael.*

9 you never know *spoken* used to say that something might happen, although it seems unlikely: *You never know. You might be lucky and win!*

10 Heaven/goodness/who knows *spoken* used to emphasize that you do not know something: *Who knows what will happen?*

11 know better (than to do sth) to be wise and experienced enough not to do something: *I thought you knew better than to tell Mum.*

know² *n* **in the know** having more information about something than most people: *People in the know go to beaches on the south of the island.*

'know-all *n* [C] *BrE disapproving* someone who behaves as if they know everything [= **know-it-all** *AmE*]

'know-how *n* [U] *informal* knowledge, practical ability, or skill: *technical know-how*

knowing /'nəʊɪŋ $ 'noʊ-/ *adj* [only before noun] showing that you know all about something, especially something secret: *He gave us a knowing look.*

knowingly /'nəʊɪŋli $ 'noʊ-/ *adv* **1** in a way that shows you know about something secret or embarrassing: *Brenda smiled knowingly at me.* **2** deliberately: *He'd never knowingly hurt you.*

'know-it-all *n* [C] *AmE disapproving* someone who behaves as if they know everything [= **know-all** *BrE*]

knowledge /'nɒlɪdʒ $ 'nɑː-/ *n* [U]

1 the information, skills, and understanding that you have got through learning or experience: *You don't need to have any special knowledge to do this job.* | **+of** *His knowledge of American history is impressive.* | **+about** *our knowledge about the functioning of the brain* | *a general knowledge quiz*

2 when you know about a particular situation or event, or the information you have about it: *Evans denied all knowledge of the robbery.* | **to (the best of) sb's knowledge** (=used to say that someone may not know all the facts) *To the best of my knowledge the new project will be starting in June.* | **without sb's knowledge** *The contract had been signed without his knowledge.*

→ **common knowledge** at **COMMON¹**

knowledgeable /'nɒlɪdʒəbəl $ 'nɑː-/ *adj* knowing a lot: **+about** *Steve's very knowledgeable about politics.*

known¹ /nəʊn $ noʊn/ *v* the past participle of KNOW

known² *adj* known about, especially by a lot of people [⇒ **well-known**]: *a known criminal* | **be known for sth** *The region is known for its fine wines.*

knuckle¹ /'nʌkəl/ *n* [C] the bones where your fingers join the rest of your hand → see picture at **HAND¹**

knuckle² *v*

knuckle down *phr v informal* to start working hard

knuckle under *phr v informal* to do what you are told to do, even though you do not want to

koala /kəʊˈɑːlə $ koʊ-/ *also* **ko,ala 'bear** / $.ˈ.. ./ *n* [C] an Australian animal like a small grey bear that climbs trees

Koran, Qur'an /kɔːˈrɑːn, kə- $ kəˈræn, -ˈrɑːn/ *n* **the Koran** the holy book of the Muslim religion

kosher /'kəʊʃə $ 'koʊʃər/ *adj* kosher food is prepared according to Jewish law

kowtow /ˌkaʊˈtaʊ/ *v* [I] to be very eager to obey or be polite to someone in authority: **+to** *I refuse to kowtow to that man.*

kph the written abbreviation of **kilometres per hour**

kudos /'kjuːdɒs $ 'kuːdɑːs/ *n* [U] admiration and respect that you get for something you do

kung fu /ˌkʌŋ 'fuː/ *n* [U] a Chinese sport in which people fight with their feet and hands

kw the written abbreviation of **kilowatt**

K

L, l

L, l /el/ n [C,U] plural **L's, l's** the 12th letter of the English alphabet

L 1 the written abbreviation of **large**, used on clothes to show the size **2** the written abbreviation of **lake**, used on maps **3** the written abbreviation of **learner**, used on cars to show that the driver is a learner **4** the written abbreviation of **litre → L-PLATE**

lab /læb/ n [C] informal a LABORATORY

label¹ /ˈleɪbəl/ n [C]

1 a piece of paper or cloth that is attached to something and gives information about it: **on a label** Always read the instructions on the label.
2 also **record label** a company that makes records: the EMI label
3 a word or phrase that is used to describe someone or something: She doesn't like being given the label 'feminist writer'.

label² v [T] **labelled, labelling** BrE; **labeled, labeling** AmE **1** to fasten a label to something, or write information on something to show what it is: Label the diagram clearly. | **label sth sth** The file was labelled 'Top Secret'. **2** to use a word or phrase to describe someone: **label sb/sth (as) sth** He was labelled a troublemaker.

labor /ˈleɪbə $ -ər/ n, v the American spelling of LABOUR

laboratory /ləˈbɒrətri $ ˈlæbrətɔːri/ n [C] plural **laboratories** a special room or building used for scientific work: a research laboratory

laborer /ˈleɪbərə $ -bərər/ n the American spelling of LABOURER

laborious /ləˈbɔːriəs/ adj taking a lot of time and effort: Sorting the books was a **laborious task**.

'labor ,union n [C] AmE an organization that represents workers who do the same kind of job [= trade union BrE]

Labour /ˈleɪbə $ -ər/ n the LABOUR PARTY: We've always voted Labour. | a Labour MP

labour¹ BrE; **labor** AmE n **1** [U] work, especially hard physical work: The job involves hard **manual labour** (=hard work that you do with your hands). **2** [U] people who work in an industry or country: There is a shortage of **skilled labour** (=trained workers). | These countries can provide **cheap labour**. | **labour force** (=all the people who work in a company or country) the number of women in the labour force | **labour-intensive** (=needing a lot of workers) labour-intensive farming methods **3** [singular,U] the process of giving birth to a baby: **in labour** Meg was in labour for six hours. **4 labour of love** something that you do because you enjoy it, not for money

labour² BrE; **labor** AmE v [I] **1** to work hard: Farmers were laboring in the fields. | **+over** I laboured over that report for days. **2** to move slowly and with difficulty: The bus was labouring up the steep, windy road.

laboured BrE; **labored** AmE /ˈleɪbəd $ -bərd/ adj done with difficulty: His breathing sounded rather laboured.

labourer BrE; **laborer** AmE /ˈleɪbərə $ -ər/ n [C] someone whose job involves hard physical work, especially outside: a farm labourer

'labour ,market BrE; **labor market** AmE n [C] used to talk about all the people looking for work and the jobs that are available: married women re-entering the labour market

'Labour ,Party n **the Labour Party** one of the main political parties in Britain

'labour-,saving BrE; **labor-saving** AmE adj [only before noun] labour-saving equipment makes it easier for you to do a job

labrador /ˈlæbrədɔː $ -ɔːr/ n [C] a large dog with short fur **→** see picture at **DOG¹**

labyrinth /ˈlæbərɪnθ/ n [C] a network of paths or passages from which it is difficult to find your way out [= maze]: **+of** a labyrinth of narrow streets

lace¹ /leɪs/ n **1** [U] a delicate cloth made with patterns of very small holes: lace curtains **2** [C] a string that is used to fasten a shoe [= shoelace] **→** see picture at **SHOE¹**

lace² also **lace up** v [T] to fasten clothes or shoes by tying the laces: Paul laced up his boots.

lack¹ /læk/ n [singular, U] when there is not enough of something [= shortage]: **+of** She suffers from a lack of confidence. | **for lack of sth** The museum may be forced to close for lack of funds.

lack² v [T] to not have something or not have enough of something: The only thing she lacks is experience.

lacking /ˈlækɪŋ/ adj [not before noun] **1** not having enough of something: **+in** He is completely lacking in confidence. **2** not existing or available: The information they need is lacking.

lacklustre /ˈlækˌlʌstə $ -ər/ adj not very good or exciting [= dull]: a lacklustre performance

laconic /ləˈkɒnɪk $ -ˈkɑː-/ adj using only a few words

lacquer /ˈlækə $ -ər/ n [U] a liquid painted on wood or metal to give it a hard shiny surface —lacquered adj

lacy /ˈleɪsi/ adj made of LACE, or looking like lace

lad /læd/ n [C] old-fashioned **1** a boy or young man **→** see box at **MAN 2 the lads** BrE spoken a group of male friends [**➡** the girls]: a night out with the lads

ladder /ˈlædə $ -ər/ n [C]

1 a piece of equipment used for climbing up to high places. A ladder has two long bars connected by RUNGS (=short bars that you use as steps).
2 a series of levels within an organization, profession, or society: Women have had to fight to **climb the career ladder**.
3 BrE a long hole in STOCKINGS or TIGHTS [= run AmE]

laden /ˈleɪdn/ adj heavily loaded with something, or containing a lot of something: **+with** The table was laden with food. | a fully-laden truck

'ladies' room n [C] AmE a women's toilet [= the ladies BrE]

L

ladle /'leɪdl/ n [C] a large round deep spoon with a long handle, used for serving soup —ladle also **ladle out** v [T] *He ladled soup into the bowls.*

lady /'leɪdi/ n [C] plural **ladies**
1 a polite word for a woman [➜ **gentleman**]: *Good afternoon, ladies.* | **young/old/elderly etc lady** *The young lady at reception sent me up here.* | *the ladies' hockey team* → see box at **WOMAN**
2 a woman who is polite and behaves well [➜ gentleman]: *A lady never swears.*
3 the ladies *BrE* a public toilet for women [= ladies' room *AmE*]
4 Lady a title used before the name of a British woman of high social rank: *Lady Helen Windsor*

ladybird *BrE* /'leɪdibɜːd $ -bɜːrd/, **ladybug** *AmE* /'leɪdibʌg/ n [C] a small insect that is red with black spots

ladylike /'leɪdilaɪk/ adj *old-fashioned* very polite or quiet in the way that people in the past thought was suitable for women: *ladylike behaviour*

lag¹ /læg/ v **lagged, lagging**
lag behind (sb) *phr v* to move or develop more slowly than others: *She stopped to wait for Ian who was lagging behind.*

lag² n [C] a delay between two events [= time lag]
→ JET LAG

lager /'lɑːgə $ -ər/ n [C,U] *BrE* a light beer, or a glass of this beer: *a glass of lager* | *Two lagers, please.*

lagoon /lə'guːn/ n [C] an area of sea water that is separated from the sea by sand, rocks etc

laid /leɪd/ v the past tense and past participle of LAY

laid-'back adj relaxed and not seeming to worry about anything: *He has a very laid-back approach to life.*

lain /leɪn/ v the past participle of LIE¹

lair /leə $ ler/ n [C] the place where a wild animal hides and sleeps [= den]

lake /leɪk/ n [C] a large area of water surrounded by land: *Lake Michigan* | **in a lake** *There were some boys swimming in the lake.* | **on a lake** *There were some small boats on the lake.*

lamb /læm/ n [C,U] a young sheep, or the meat of a young sheep [➜ mutton]: *roast lamb* → see box at MEAT

lambast /læm'bæst/ v [T] *formal* to criticize someone or something very severely, especially in public

lame /leɪm/ adj **1** unable to walk properly – used mainly about animals **2** a lame excuse or explanation is weak and difficult to believe: *She gave some lame excuse about missing the bus.*

lame 'duck n [C] **1** a person, business etc that is having problems and needs help **2 lame duck president/governor etc** *informal* a president etc with no real power because he or she will soon stop being president

lamely /'leɪmli/ adv if you say something lamely, you do not sound confident and other people find it difficult to believe you

lament /lə'ment/ v [I,T] *formal* to express feelings of sadness or disappointment about something —**lament** n [C]

lamentable /'læməntəbəl, lə'mentəbəl/ adj *formal* very unsatisfactory or disappointing

laminated /'læmɨneɪtɨd/ adj **1** laminated material is made stronger by joining several thin layers on top of each other: *laminated glass* **2** covered with a thin layer of plastic for protection: *a laminated ID card* —**laminate** /-nɨt/ n [C]

lamp /læmp/ n [C] an object that produces light by using electricity, oil, or gas: *a desk lamp* | *a bedside lamp* → see pictures at LIGHT¹ → and at BICYCLE

lampoon /læm'puːn/ v [T] to criticize someone such as a politician in a funny way that makes them seem stupid

'lamp-post /'læmp-pəʊst $ -poʊst/ n [C] a tall pole that supports a light over a street or public area

lampshade /'læmpʃeɪd/ n [C] a cover fixed over a light to make it less bright

land¹ /lænd/ n
1 [U] an area of ground: **agricultural/industrial etc land** *He owns 5000 acres of agricultural land.* | *They own a small piece of land.* → see box at GROUND
2 [U] the solid dry part of the Earth's surface [≠ sea]: **on land** *Frogs live on land and in the water.* | **by land** *They travelled by sea and by land.* | *They were glad to be back on dry land.*
3 [C] *literary* a country or area: **distant/foreign lands** *He had travelled to many foreign lands.* | *He longed to return to his native land* (=the land where he was born).

land

land

take off

land² v
1 [I,T] to come onto the ground after being in the air or on water: *Has her flight landed yet?* | *We will be landing in Rome in fifteen minutes.* | *One bird landed in front of us.* | **+in/on/under etc** *Chris slipped and landed on a nail.* | *The pilot managed to land the aircraft safely.* | *Two thousand troops were landed on the beach.*
2 [T] *informal* to succeed in getting an important job, contract, or deal: *Kelly's landed a job with a big law firm.*
3 land sb in/with sth to cause someone to be in a difficult situation or have serious problems: *She developed pneumonia which landed her in hospital.*
→ CRASH-LAND

landed /'lændɨd/ adj [only before noun] **1 landed gentry/family/nobility** a family or group that has owned a lot of land for a long time **2** including a lot of land: *farms and landed estates*

L

landfill /'lændfɪl/ n **1** [U] the practice of burying waste under the ground, or the waste buried in this way **2** [C] a place where waste is buried under the ground

landing /'lændɪŋ/ n **1** [C,U] the action of bringing a plane down to the ground after flying [→ take-off]: **emergency/forced/crash landing** *The pilot had to make an emergency landing.* **2** [C] the floor at the top of a set of stairs

landlady /'lænd,leɪdi/ n [C] plural **landladies 1** a woman that you rent a room or house from → see box at **RENT 2** *BrE* a woman who owns or manages a **PUB**

landlocked /'lændlɒkt $ -lɑːkt/ adj a land-locked country, state etc is surrounded by other countries and has no coast

landlord /'lændlɔːd $ -lɔːrd/ n [C] **1** a man that you rent a room or house from → see box at **RENT 2** *BrE* a man who owns or manages a **PUB**

landmark /'lændmɑːk $ -mɑːrk/ n [C] **1** something that helps you recognize where you are, such as a famous building **2** a very important event, change, or discovery in the development of something: **+in** *a landmark in the history of aviation*

landmass /'lændmæs/ n [C] *technical* a large area of land such as a **CONTINENT**

landmine /'lændmaɪn/ n [C] a bomb hidden in the ground that explodes when someone walks or drives over it

landowner /'lænd,əʊnə $ -,oʊnər/ n [C] someone who owns a large amount of land

landscape¹ /'lændskeɪp/ n [C] **1** a view across an area of land: **rural/industrial/urban landscape 2** a picture of an area of countryside: *a landscape painter* → see picture at **PAINTING**

landscape² v [T] to make an area of land look more attractive by changing its design and putting in new plants

landslide /'lændslaɪd/ n [C] **1** a victory in an election in which one person or party gets a lot more votes than all the others: *a landslide victory* **2** a sudden fall of a lot of earth or rocks down a hill, cliff, or mountain

lane /leɪn/ n [C] **1** a narrow road in the countryside: *a quiet country lane* → see box at **ROAD 2** a road in a town – used in the names of streets: *They live in Turnpike Lane.* **3** one of the parts of a road that vehicles travel along: **inside/middle/outside lane** *He was doing 100 mph in the outside lane.* **4** one of the narrow areas that a competitor in a race runs or swims along: *Radcliffe is running in lane eight.* **5** a course along which ships or aircraft regularly travel: *The accident happened in a busy shipping lane.*

language /'læŋgwɪdʒ/ n

1 [C] the words that people use to speak or write to each other: *Do you speak any foreign languages?* | *a language teacher* | **first/native language** (=the language you learn to speak as a child) *German is her first language.*

2 [U] the use of written or spoken words to communicate: *a new theory about the origins of language*

3 [U] the kind of words that a person uses, or that are used when talking or writing about a particular subject: **+of** *the language of business* | *He never used bad language* (=rude

words). | **legal/medical/scientific etc language**

4 [C,U] a system of instructions used in computer programs

5 [C,U] any system of signs, movements, or sounds that are used to express meanings or feelings: *the language of music* → **BODY LANGUAGE, SIGN LANGUAGE**

'language la,boratory / $ '.. ,..../ n [C] plural **language laboratories** a room in a school or college where you can practise a foreign language by listening to tapes and recording your own voice

languid /'læŋgwɪd/ adj *literary* moving or speaking slowly and with very little effort or energy

languish /'læŋgwɪʃ/ v [I] to remain in a difficult situation for a long time: **+in/at** *United are currently languishing at the bottom of the league.*

lanky /'læŋki/ adj very tall and thin

lantern /'læntən $ -ərn/ n [C] a type of lamp you can carry consisting of a glass or metal container with a light inside → see picture at **LIGHT¹**

lap¹ /læp/ n [C] **1** the upper part of your legs when you are sitting down: **on/in sb's lap** *Paul was sitting on his mother's lap.* **2** one journey around a race track or swimming pool: *Hill overtook Schumacher on the last lap.*

lap² v **lapped, lapping 1** [I,T] if water laps against something, it moves gently against it: **+against/at/over** *Waves were lapping against the shore.* **2** also **lap up** [T] if an animal laps a drink, it drinks with quick movements of its tongue: *The cat started to lap up the milk.*

lap sth ⇔ up phr v to accept something very eagerly in a way that shows you like it a lot: *She is lapping up all the attention.*

lapel /lə'pel/ n [C] the part at the front of a coat or **JACKET** that is joined to the collar and folds back on both sides

lapse¹ /læps/ n [C] **1** a short period of time during which you do not do something well or properly: **+of/in** *a brief lapse of concentration* **2** [usually singular] a period of time between two events: **+of** *They returned after a considerable lapse of time.*

lapse² v [I] if a contract or agreement lapses, it comes to an end: *Your membership of the tennis club has lapsed.*

lapse into sth phr v **1** to change into another state or condition, especially one that is worse or less active than before: *They lapsed into silence.* | *The Empire lapsed into chaos.* **2** to start behaving or speaking in a way that you did before: *Without thinking he lapsed into French.*

laptop /'læptɒp $ -tɑːp/ n [C] a small computer you can carry with you

laptop

lard /lɑːd $ lɑːrd/ n [U] thick white fat used in cooking

larder /'lɑːdə $ 'lɑːrdər/ n [C] a large cupboard or small room used for storing food

large /lɑːdʒ $ lɑːrdʒ/ *adj*

1 big in size, number, or amount [≠ **small**]: *a large pizza* | *Birmingham is the second largest city in Britain.* | **large number/amount/ quantity** *They spent large amounts of money on gambling.* | *The T-shirt comes in Small, Medium, and Large.* | *Frank was a very large man.* → see box at **BIG** → and **FAT**

2 be at large if a criminal or wild animal is at large, they have escaped from somewhere

3 the population/public etc at large people in general: *The population at large has become more mobile.*

4 larger than life more exciting or interesting than other people or things

5 by and large generally: *By and large, the show was a success.*

largely /ˈlɑːdʒli $ ˈlɑːr-/ *adv* mostly or mainly: *The delay was largely due to bad weather.*

large-ˈscale *adj* [only before noun] using or involving a lot of people or things [≠ **small-scale**]: *large-scale unemployment* | *a large-scale police operation*

lark /lɑːk $ lɑːrk/ *n* [C] a small brown bird that has a beautiful song

larva /ˈlɑːvə $ ˈlɑːrvə/ *n* [C] plural **larvae** /-viː/ a young insect with a soft body, before it becomes an adult → see picture on page A2

larynx /ˈlærɪŋks/ *n* [C] plural **larynges** /ləˈrɪndʒiːz/ or **larynxes** *technical* the part of your throat where your voice is produced

lasagne *BrE*; **lasagna** *AmE* /ləˈsænjə, -ˈzæn- $ -ˈzɑːn-/ *n* [C,U] a type of Italian food made with flat pieces of **PASTA**, meat or vegetables, and cheese → see picture on page A5

laser /ˈleɪzə $ -ər/ *n* [C] a piece of equipment that produces a powerful narrow beam of light, or the beam of light itself: *laser surgery*

lash¹ /læʃ/ *v* **1** [I,T] if rain, waves, or wind lash against something, they hit it hard or blow hard against it: **+against/down** *The rain was lashing down outside.* **2** [T] to hit someone very hard with a whip or stick [= **beat**] **3** [T] to tie something tightly to something else, using a rope: **lash sth to sth** *The oars were lashed to the sides of the boat.*

lash out *phr v* to suddenly attack someone or speak angrily to them: **+at** *Olson lashed out at the media.*

lash² *n* [C usually plural] **1** one of the hairs that grow along the edge of your eyes [= **eyelash**] **2** a hit with a whip as a punishment: *He was given fifty lashes.*

lass /læs/ *n* [C] *BrE* a girl or young woman – used in Scotland and the North of England

lasso /ləˈsuː, ˈlæsəʊ $ -soʊ/ *n* [C] plural **lassos** or **lassoes** a rope with one end tied in a circle, used for catching cattle and horses —**lasso** *v* [T]

last¹ /lɑːst $ læst/ *determiner, adj*

1 most recent: *My last boyfriend was crazy about football.* | *When was **the last time** you were here?* | **last night/week/Sunday etc** *Did you go out last night?* | **the last few months/10 years etc** (=the period until now) *The town has changed a lot in the last few years.*

one': *our last holiday in France* | *my last job*
Use **latest** to mean 'new and most recent': *the latest news* | *the latest Paris fashions*

2 happening or coming at the end, after all the others [≠ **first**]: *What time does the last bus leave?* | *the last chapter of the book* | **last but one/two etc** (=the one before the last one, two etc) *He escaped with his family on the last but one ship to leave.*

3 the last person or thing is the only one that remains: *Is it all right if I have the last piece of cake?* | *He was the last great explorer.*

4 the last minute/moment the latest possible time before something happens: *The concert was cancelled at the last minute.*

5 the last person/thing the person or thing you did not expect at all, or the one that you want least of all: *You're the last person I expected to see.* | *The last thing she wanted was to upset him.*

6 have the last word to say the last thing in a discussion or argument, or make the final decision about something

last² *adv*

1 most recently before now: *When did you last go shopping?*

2 after everything or everyone else [= **first**]: *Add the flour last.* | *Last of all, I'd like to thank you all for coming.*

3 last but not least used before mentioning the last person or thing in a list to emphasize that they are still important: *Last but not least, I'd like to thank my mother.*

last³ *n, pron*

1 the last the person or thing that comes after all the others [≠ **the first**]: **the last to do sth** *Lee was the last to go to bed.*

2 at (long) last used when something happens after people have waited a long time for it: *At last dinner was ready.* → see box at **LASTLY**

3 the day/week/year before last the day, week etc before the one that has just finished: *I saw her the night before last.*

4 the last of sth the only part of something that remains: *Is this the last of the bread?*

last⁴ *v* [I,T]

1 to continue for a particular length of time: **+for/until/through etc** *The hot weather lasted for two weeks.* | *The petrol should last until we get to London.* | **last an hour/ten minutes etc** *Each lesson lasts an hour.*

2 to continue to exist, be effective, or remain in good condition: *The batteries will last for up to 8 hours.* | **last (sb) two days/three weeks etc** *A good coat should last you ten years.*

3 to be enough for someone for a period of time: **last (sb) two days/three weeks etc** *We had $50 to last us the rest of the month.*

last-ˈditch *adj* **last-ditch effort/attempt etc** a final attempt to achieve something before it is too late: *a last-ditch effort to free the hostages*

lasting /ˈlɑːstɪŋ $ ˈlæs-/ *adj* continuing for a long time: *The incident made a **lasting impression** on me.*

lastly /ˈlɑːstli $ ˈlæst-/ *adv* used to say that the next thing you mention will be the last thing [≠ **firstly**]: *And lastly, I'd like to thank my producer.*

L

Use **lastly** or **finally** to introduce the last point, action, or instruction in a list: *Lastly, I'd like to say a big thank-you to you all.* | *Add flour, salt, and finally the milk.*
Use **finally** or **eventually** to say that something happens after a long time: *Finally we managed to get the car started.* | *She eventually apologized.*
Use **at last** to emphasize that you are glad when something happens, because you have been waiting a long time for it: *Spring's here at last!*
→ FIRST

,last-'minute *adj* [only before noun] happening or done as late as possible: *I was out doing some last-minute Christmas shopping.*

'last name *n* [C] a SURNAME → see box at NAME

latch¹ /lætʃ/ *n* [C] **1** a small metal bar used for fastening a door, gate, or window **2** a type of lock for a door, that needs a key when being opened from outside: *She left the door on the latch* (=closed but not locked).

latch² *v*
latch on to sth *phr v BrE informal* to become very interested in something

late /leɪt/ *adj, adv*
1 arriving, happening, or done after the expected time [≠ early]: *Sorry I'm late!* | *ten minutes/two hours etc late Our flight arrived two hours late.* | +**for** *Abi was late for school.*
2 too late after the time when something could have been done: *It's too late to change things now.*
3 near the end of a period of time [≠ early]: *We should be there by late afternoon.* | *music that was popular in the late 1970s* | *St Mary's church was built in the late 18th century.* | *He's in his late forties.* | +**in** *one day late in May*
4 near the end of the day [≠ early]: *It's getting late. We'd better go home.*
5 [only before noun] *formal* dead: *the late Sir William Russell*

latecomer /'leɪtˌkʌmə $ -ər/ *n* [C] someone who arrives late

lately /'leɪtli/ *adv* recently: *I've been feeling very tired lately.*

You must always use **lately** with the present perfect tense. It shows that the situation you are talking about is still continuing. You can use **recently** like this too: *I've been very busy lately.* | *There hasn't been much rain recently.*
You can also use **recently** with the simple past tense to talk about something that happened not long ago: *They recently got married.*

'late-night *adj* [only before noun] happening late at night, or later than usual: *late-night television* | *late-night shopping*

latent /'leɪtənt/ *adj formal* something that is latent is present but hidden, and may develop or become more noticeable in the future: *latent aggression*

later¹ /'leɪtə $ -ər/ also ,later 'on *adv* after the present time or a time you are talking about [≠ earlier]: *I'm going out – I'll see you later.* | *We can talk about that later on.* | **a year/three**

weeks etc later *He became senator two years later.* | **later that day/morning etc** *The baby died later that night.*

later² *adj* [only before noun] happening or coming in the future, or after something else [≠ earlier]: *The rules are dealt with in a later chapter.* | *The party was postponed to a later date.* | *Later models of the car are much improved.*

lateral /'lætərəl/ *adj formal* **1** relating to the sides of something: *The wall is weak and needs lateral support.* **2** relating to positions, jobs etc that are at the same rank: *Employees can expect lateral moves to different departments.* —**laterally** *adv*

latest¹ /'leɪtɪst/ *adj* [only before noun] the most recent or the newest: *all the latest gossip* → see box at LAST → , MODERN → and NEW

latest² *n* **1 the latest** the most recent or newest thing: +**in** *the latest in a series of meetings* **2 at the latest** no later than the time mentioned: *I'll be home by 11 o'clock at the latest.*

latex /'leɪteks/ *n* [U] a thick white liquid produced by some plants, used in making rubber, paint, glue etc

lather /'lɑːðə $ 'læðər/ *n* [singular, U] a white mass of bubbles produced by mixing soap in water

Latin¹ /'lætɪn $ 'lætn/ *n* [U] the language used in ancient Rome

Latin² *adj* **1** written in Latin **2** from or relating to a country whose language developed from Latin

,Latin A'merican *adj* relating to South or Central America

latitude /'lætɪˌtjuːd $ -tuːd/ *n* [C,U] *technical* the distance north or south of the EQUATOR, measured in degrees [⇒ longitude] → see picture at GLOBE

latter¹ /'lætə $ -ər/ *n* **the latter** *formal* the second of two people or things just mentioned [⇒ former]

latter² *adj* **1** being the second of two people or things [⇒ former] **2** the latter part of a period of time is nearest to the end of it: *the latter part of November*

latterly /'lætəli $ -ər-/ *adv BrE formal* recently

laudable /'lɔːdəbəl $ 'lɒːd-/ *adj formal* deserving praise

laugh¹ /lɑːf $ læf/ *v* [I] to make sounds with your voice because you think something is funny: +**at** *She was laughing at the memory.* | *Tony laughed so hard he nearly fell over.* | *Jill burst out* (=suddenly started) *laughing.*

giggle – to laugh quickly in a high voice, especially because you are nervous or embarrassed
chuckle – to laugh quietly
cackle – to laugh in an unpleasant loud way
snigger *BrE*/**snicker** *AmE* – to laugh quietly in an unkind way
→ CRY

laugh at sb/sth *phr v* to make unkind or funny remarks about someone, because you think they are stupid or look silly: *The other kids laughed at him when he didn't understand.*

laugh sth ⇔ **off** phr v to pretend that something is not very serious by joking about it: He laughed off suggestions that he would resign.

laugh² n [C]

1 the act of laughing or the sound you make when you laugh: a nervous laugh | **with a laugh** 'What a mess!' she said, with a laugh.

2 an enjoyable time: a great holiday with lots of laughs

3 be a (good) laugh BrE to be amusing

4 for a laugh BrE for fun

5 have the last laugh to be successful, after other people have criticized you or thought that you could not succeed

laughable /ˈlɑːfəbəl $ ˈlæ-/ adj something that is laughable is so bad, silly etc that you cannot be serious about it

'**laughing stock** n [singular] someone who has done something so silly that people have no respect for them

laughter /ˈlɑːftə $ ˈlæftər/ n [U] when people laugh, or the sound of people laughing: Tom **burst into laughter** (=started laughing). | The audience **roared with laughter**.

launch¹ /lɔːntʃ $ lɔːntʃ/ v [T] **1** to start something big or important: We have launched a campaign to raise $50,000. **2** to make a new product or book available to be sold: Jaguar is planning to launch a new sports car. **3** to put a boat into the water or to send a spacecraft into space

launch into sth phr v to suddenly start describing or criticizing something

launch² n [C] when something is launched

launder /ˈlɔːndə $ ˈlɔːndər/ v [T] to hide illegally obtained money by putting it into legal businesses

launderette BrE /ˌlɔːndəˈret $ ˌlɔːn-/, **Laundromat** /ˈlɔːndrəmæt $ ˈlɔːn-/ trademark AmE n [C] a place where you pay to wash your clothes in a machine

laundry /ˈlɔːndri $ ˈlɔːn-/ n plural **laundries**

1 [U] clothes, sheets etc that need to be washed, or that have been washed → see picture at **BATHROOM 2** [C] a place where clothes are washed

laurel /ˈlɒrəl $ ˈlɔː-, ˈlɑː-/ n [C,U] **1** a small tree with big smooth shiny leaves **2 rest on your laurels** to stop trying to achieve things, after achieving something good

lava /ˈlɑːvə/ n [U] hot melted rock that flows from a VOLCANO

lavatory /ˈlævətri $ -tɔːri/ n [C] plural **lavatories** formal a toilet

lavender /ˈlævɪndə $ -ər/ n [U] a plant that has purple flowers with a strong pleasant smell

lavish¹ /ˈlævɪʃ/ adj **1** expensive or impressive: a lavish lifestyle **2** very generous: **+with/in** Her mother was lavish with advice. —**lavishly** adv

lavish² v [T] to give someone a lot of love, praise, money etc: **lavish** sth **on** sb He lavished attention on her.

law /lɔː $ lɔː/ n

1 [U] the system of rules that people in a country or area must obey [→ **legal**]: **by law** By law, seatbelts must be worn by all passengers. | In Sweden, it **is against the law** to hit a child. | People are punished for **breaking the law**. | an interesting area of **criminal law** | I want to study law. | **law court/court of law**

2 [C] a rule that people in a country or place must obey: the anti-terrorism laws | **+against** The laws against drug use are severe. | **+on** European laws on equal opportunities

3 law and order when people obey the law, and crime is controlled by the police and the courts of law

4 the law the police: She may be in trouble with the law.

5 [C] something that always happens in nature or society, or a statement that describes this: the law of gravity

→ MARTIAL LAW

'**law-a,biding** adj obeying laws: a law-abiding citizen

lawful /ˈlɔːfəl $ ˈlɔː-/ adj formal allowed or recognized by law: a lawful arrest

lawless /ˈlɔːləs $ ˈlɔː-/ adj formal not obeying the law, or not controlled by law

lawn /lɔːn $ lɔːn/ n [C] an area of grass that is kept cut short

'**lawn ,mower** n [C] a machine used for cutting grass

lawsuit /ˈlɔːsuːt, -sjuːt $ ˈlɔːsuːt/ n [C] a problem or complaint that a person or organization brings to a court of law to be settled

lawyer /ˈlɔːjə $ ˈlɔːjər/ n [C] someone whose job is to advise people about the law or speak for them in court

lax /læks/ adj not strict: lax security

laxative /ˈlæksətɪv/ n [C] a medicine or something that you eat that makes your BOWELS empty easily —**laxative** adj

lay¹ /leɪ/ v the past tense of LIE¹

USAGE

Lay means to put something down in a flat position: She laid the newspaper down and picked up the phone.
Lie has two different meanings.
– to be in or move into a flat position on the floor, a bed etc: She was lying on the sofa. The past tense for this meaning of **lie** is **lay**: He lay on the bed.
– to say something that is not true: Why did you lie to me? The past tense for this meaning of **lie** is **lied**: The police think that he lied.

lay² v past tense and past participle **laid** /leɪd/

1 [T] to put something down in a flat position: **lay** sth **on** sth He laid his hand on my shoulder. | Lay the material **flat** on the table.

2 lay bricks/carpet/cables etc to put bricks, a CARPET etc in the correct place, especially on the ground or floor

3 [I,T] if a bird, insect etc lays eggs, it produces them from its body

4 lay the table/lay a place (for sb) BrE to put knives, forks, plates etc on a table before a meal

5 lay the foundations/groundwork/base to provide the conditions that make it possible for something to happen or be successful

6 lay (your) hands on sth to find something: I wish I could lay my hands on that book.

7 lay a hand/finger on sb to hurt someone by hitting them: If you lay a hand on her, I'll call the police.

L

8 lay sb open to sth to do something that makes it possible that someone will be blamed, criticized etc

9 lay a trap to prepare a trap to catch someone or something

10 lay claim to sth to say officially that something belongs to you

lay sth ⇔ **down** *phr v* **1** to say officially what rules or methods must be obeyed or used: *strict safety regulations laid down by the government* **2 lay down the law** to tell other people what to do in an unpleasant way

lay into sb *phr v informal* to attack or criticize someone: *Two men were laying into each other.*

lay off *phr v* **1 lay sb** ⇔ **off** to stop employing a worker because there is not enough work to do **2 lay off (sb/sth)** to stop doing or using something, or treating someone unkindly

lay sth ⇔ **on** *phr v* to provide food, entertainment etc: *Lola laid on a great meal for us.*

lay sth ⇔ **out** *phr v* **1** to spread something out: *Let's lay the map out on the table.* **2** to arrange a building, town, garden etc: *The gardens were attractively laid out.*

lay up *phr v* **be laid up** to have to stay in bed because you are ill or injured: **+with** *She's laid up with flu.*

lay³ *adj* [only before noun] **1** not having special training or knowledge: *lay witnesses* **2** not having an official position in the church: *a lay preacher*

layabout /ˈleɪəbaʊt/ *n* [C] *BrE informal* a lazy person who avoids work

'lay-by *n* [C] plural **lay-bys** *BrE* an area at the side of a road where vehicles can stop

layer /ˈleɪə $ -ər/ *n* [C]

1 an amount or piece of a substance that covers a surface or that is between two other things: **+of** *a layer of dust* | **thin/thick layer** | **top/ bottom layer**

2 one of several levels in a complicated system: **+of** *We have fewer layers of management.*
→ OZONE LAYER

layman /ˈleɪmən/ *n* [C] plural **laymen** /-mən/ someone who is not trained in a particular subject or type of work

'lay-off *n* [C usually plural] when a worker's job is stopped because there is not enough work

layout /ˈleɪaʊt/ *n* [C] the way in which the different parts of something are arranged: *He described the layout of the building.*

laze /leɪz/ *v* [I] to relax and not do very much: **+around/about** *We lazed around, gazing at the views.*

lazy /ˈleɪzi/ *adj*

1 someone who is lazy does not like working or doing things that need effort: *the laziest girl in the class* | *He felt too lazy to get out of bed.*

2 a lazy period of time is spent relaxing: *lazy summer afternoons*

lb. the written abbreviation of **pound**

lead¹ /liːd/ *v* past tense and past participle **led** /led/

1 [T] to take someone to a place by going with them or in front of them: *The manager led the way through the office.* | **lead sb to/into etc sth** *The horses were led to safety.*

2 [I,T] to go in front of a line of people or vehicles: *A jazz band was leading the parade.*

3 [T] to be in charge of something: *He has led the party for over twenty years.* | *Beckham led his team to victory.*

4 [I,T] to cause something to happen, or to cause someone to do something: **+to** *a degree that could lead to a career in journalism* | **lead sb to do sth** *He led everyone to believe that he was wealthy.*

5 [T] to be more successful than other people, companies, or countries: *US companies lead the world in biotechnology.*

6 [I,T] to be winning a game or competition: *At half-time, Brazil led 1–0.* → see box at WIN

7 [I] used to say where you can get to using a path, door etc: **+to/towards** *The path led down to a lake.*

8 lead a ... life to have a particular kind of life: *I lead a quiet life.*

9 lead sb astray to encourage someone to do bad or immoral things

lead off (sth) *phr v* if a road or room leads off a place, it is directly joined to that place: *A small track led off the main road.*

lead sb **on** *phr v* to make someone believe that you love them when you do not

lead up to sth *phr v* to come before something and often be a cause of it: *the events leading up to the trial*

lead² *n*

1 the lead the first position in a race or competition: **in/into the lead** *She was in the lead from start to finish.* | *The Canadians went into the lead immediately.* | *The Bears took the lead for the first time this season.*

2 [singular] the amount or distance by which one team or player is ahead of another: *Italy has a 2–0 lead.*

3 [singular] if someone follows someone's lead, they do the same as the other person has done: *Other countries are likely to follow Germany's lead.*

4 take the lead (in doing sth) to be the first, or the most active, in doing something: *The US took the lead in the war against terrorism.*

5 [C] a piece of information that may help you to solve a crime or problem: *The police have investigated several leads.*

6 also **lead role** [C] the main acting part in a play or film: *Brad Pitt will play the lead.*

7 lead singer/guitarist the main singer or GUITARIST in a group

8 [C] *BrE* a piece of rope, leather etc fastened to a dog's collar to control it

9 [C] *BrE* a wire used to connect a piece of electrical equipment to a power supply [= cord *AmE*]
→ see picture at ACOUSTIC

lead³ /led/ *n* **1** [U] a heavy soft grey metal **2** [C,U] the dark grey substance in the centre of a pencil

leader /ˈliːdə $ -ər/ *n* [C]

1 the person who is in charge of a group, organization, country etc: **+of** *leaders of the black community* | *a gathering of world leaders*

2 the person or group that is ahead of all the others in a race or competition

leadership /ˈliːdəʃɪp $ -ər-/ *n* **1** [U] when someone is the leader of a team, organization etc: **+of** *He took over the leadership of the Republican party.* **2** [U] the quality of being good at leading a team, organization, country etc: *someone with vision and leadership* **3** [singular] the people who are in charge of a country, organization etc

leading /'liːdɪŋ/ *adj* [only before noun]
1 best, most important, or most successful: *leading members of the government* | *He played a leading role in the development of radio.*
2 leading question a question that tricks someone into giving you the answer you want: *keen reporters asking leading questions*

leading edge /ˌliːdɪŋ 'edʒ/ *n* CUTTING EDGE

leaf¹ /liːf/ *n* [C] plural **leaves** /liːvz/
1 one of the flat green parts of a plant that are joined to its stem or branches → see picture at PLANT
2 take a leaf out of sb's book to behave like someone else who behaves well
3 turn over a new leaf to start to behave in a much better way

leaf² *v*
leaf through sth *phr v* to turn the pages of a book or magazine quickly, without reading it carefully

leaflet /'liːflɪt/ *n* [C] a piece of printed paper that gives information or advertises something

leafy /'liːfi/ *adj* **1** having a lot of leaves: *leafy vegetables* **2** having a lot of trees and plants: *a leafy suburb*

league /liːg/ *n* [C] **1** a group of sports teams or players who play games against each other: *the Football League* | **top/bottom of the league**
2 a group of people or countries that join together because they have similar aims or beliefs **3 not be in the same league (as sb/sth)** to be not nearly as good or important as someone or something else **4 be in league with sb** to be working with someone secretly, especially for a bad purpose: *He is suspected of being in league with terrorists.*

leak¹ /liːk/ *v*
1 [I,T] if a container, pipe, roof etc leaks, there is a small hole or crack in it that lets liquid or gas flow through: *The roof is leaking.* | *My car's leaking oil.* → see picture at FLOW²
2 [I] if a liquid or gas leaks somewhere, it gets through a hole in something: **+into/from/out** *Gas was leaking out of the pipes.*
3 [T] to deliberately give secret information to newspapers, television etc: *The report's findings had been leaked.* | **leak sth to sb** *She leaked information to the press.*
leak out *phr v* if secret information leaks out, a lot of people find out about it

leak² *n* [C]
1 a small hole that liquid or gas gets out through: *There's a leak in the roof.*
2 gas/oil/water etc leak when liquid or gas gets out through a hole: *The explosion was caused by a gas leak.*
3 when secret information is deliberately given to newspapers, television etc: *security leaks*

leakage /'liːkɪdʒ/ *n* [C,U] when liquid or gas gets out through a hole

leaky /'liːki/ *adj* having a hole or crack that liquid or gas can pass through: *a leaky roof*

lean¹ /liːn/ *v* past tense and past participle **leaned** or **leant** /lent/ *especially BrE*
1 [I] to move or bend your body in a particular position: **+forward/back/over etc** *Lean back and enjoy the ride.* | *She leant towards him and listened.* → see picture on page A11
2 [I,T] to be supported in a sloping position by a wall or surface, or to put something in this position: **lean (sth) on/against sth** *She was leaning on the fence.* | *He leant his bicycle against the wall.*
lean on sb *phr v* to depend on someone for support or encouragement

lean² *adj* **1** thin in a healthy and attractive way: *Mike was tall and lean.* **2** lean meat does not have much fat on it **3** not producing good results: *a lean year for small businesses*

leaning /'liːnɪŋ/ *n* [C] a tendency to agree with a particular set of ideas or beliefs: *his political leanings*

leap¹ /liːp/ *v* [I] past tense and past participle **leapt** /lept/ *especially BrE* or **leaped** *especially AmE* **1** to jump high into the air or over something: **+over/from/into etc** *She leapt over the fence.* → see box at JUMP **2** to move very quickly and with a lot of energy: **+up/out of etc** *He leapt up the stairs.* **3 leap at the opportunity/chance** to accept an opportunity very eagerly

leap² *n* [C] **1** a big jump **2** a large increase or change: *a leap in pre-tax profits* | *He improved in leaps and bounds* (=very much, very quickly).

leapfrog /'liːpfrɒg
$ -frɒːg, -frɑːg/ *n* [U]
a children's game in
which someone bends
over and someone else
jumps over them
—**leapfrog** *v* [I,T]

leapfrog

'leap year *n* [C] a
year when February
has 29 days instead of
28

learn /lɜːn $ lɜːrn/ *v*
past tense and past
participle **learned** or
learnt /lɜːnt $ lɜːrnt/
especially BrE
1 [I,T] to get knowledge of a subject or skill by studying, doing it, or being taught: *What's the best way to learn a language?* | **learn (how) to do sth** *I learned to drive when I was 17.* | **learn (sth) from sb/sth** *I learnt a lot from my father.* → see box at SCHOOL

USAGE

You **learn** a subject or skill when you study or practise it: *I'm thinking of learning Italian.* | *Jo's learning to drive.*
If you **teach** someone a subject or skill, you help them to learn it: *Dad taught me to play the guitar.* You cannot say 'Dad learned me to ...'

2 [I,T] *formal* to find out information or news by hearing it from someone or reading it: **+of/about** *He learned about his new job by telephone.* | **+(that)** *When did she learn that she was pregnant?* | **+whether/who/why** *I had yet to learn whether I had a college place.*

L

3 [T] to get to know something so well that you can easily remember it: *The actors are still learning their lines.*

4 [I,T] to gradually understand a situation and start behaving in the way that you should: **+(that)** *They have to learn that they can't do whatever they like.* | **learn to do sth** *These lads must learn to accept orders.* | *I think he's learned his lesson.*

—**learner** *n* [C] *a slow learner*

learned /'lɜːnɪd $ 'lɜːr-/ *adj formal* having a lot of knowledge because you have read and studied a lot

learning /'lɜːnɪŋ $ 'lɜːr-/ *n* [U] knowledge gained by reading and studying

learning curve *n* [C] the rate at which you learn a new skill: *Everyone in the centre has been through a steep learning curve* (=they had to learn very quickly).

learnt /lɜːnt $ lɜːrnt/ *v* a past tense and past participle of LEARN

lease /liːs/ *n* [C] **1** a legal agreement by which you pay rent in order to use a building, car etc for a period of time: *a two-year lease on the apartment* **2 a new lease of life** *BrE* **a new lease on life** *AmE* a further period of being useful or healthy, after becoming damaged, ill etc —**lease** *v* [T]

leash /liːʃ/ *n* [C] *especially AmE* a piece of rope or leather fastened to a dog's collar in order to control it [= lead *BrE*]

least¹ /liːst/ *determiner, pron*

1 at least a) not less than a particular number or amount: *It will take at least 20 minutes to get there.* | *He had at least $100,000 in savings.* **b)** even if something better is not true or is not done: *At least he didn't lie to me.* | *Well, at least the roof is fixed.* **c)** used before correcting or changing something that you have just said: *He's gone home – at least I think he has.*

2 the least the smallest amount: *Women get jobs which pay the least.* | *What would cause the least damage to the environment?*

3 not (in) the least (bit) not at all or none at all: *I wasn't in the least worried.*

4 to say the least used to show that something is worse or more serious than you are actually saying: *His teaching methods were strange, to say the least.*

least² *adv*

1 less that anything or anyone else [≠ most]: *It's amazing what happens when you least expect it.* | *He's my least favourite member of staff.*

2 not least *formal* used when mentioning an important example, reason etc: *Many other problems remain, not least the shortage of engineers.*

leather /'leðə $ -ər/ *n* [U] animal skin used for making shoes, bags etc: *a leather belt* → see picture at MATERIAL¹

leathery /'leðəri/ *adj* hard and stiff like leather, rather than soft or smooth: *leathery brown skin*

leave¹ /liːv/ *v* past tense and past participle left /left/

1 [I,T] to go away from a place or person: *Frances left work early to meet her mother.* | **+at** *The plane leaves at 12.30.* | **+for** *I'm sorry, he's already left for work.*

2 [I,T] if you leave your job, home, school etc, you permanently stop doing that job, living at home etc: *My daughter got a job as a hairdresser after she left school.* | *Next year the President leaves office.*

3 leave sb alone to stop annoying or upsetting someone: *Oh, just leave me alone, will you?*

4 leave sth alone to stop touching something: *Leave the joystick alone, you'll break it.*

5 [T] if you leave someone or something in a place when you go away, they remain there: **leave sth/sb in/on etc sth** *I left the car keys in the house* (=by accident). | *Just leave those letters on my desk, please.*

6 [T] to let something stay in a particular state or condition: **leave sth on/off/out etc** *You've left your lights on.* | **leave sth doing sth** *He'd left the tap running.*

7 [T] if an event leaves someone or something in a particular condition, they are in that condition because of it: **leave sb/sth with sth** *After the infection, she was left with a nasty cough.* | **leave sb doing sth** *The incident left her feeling confused and hurt.*

8 be left (over) to remain after everything else has gone, been taken away, or used: *There's never much money left over at the end of the week.* | *We don't have much time left.*

9 [T] to delay doing something: *Leave the dishes. I'll do them later.*

10 [T] to not eat or use part of something: *Hey – leave some cake for me!*

11 [T] to let someone decide something or be responsible for something: **leave sth to sb** *I'll leave it to you to decide.*

12 [I,T] to end a relationship with a husband, partner etc: **leave sb for sb** *He left his wife for a younger woman.*

13 [T] to give something to someone after you die: **leave sb sth** *Hugo left me his mother's ring.* → see box at GIVE

leave sb/sth ⇔ behind *phr v* **1** to not take something or someone with you when you leave a place **2** to make more progress than someone else

leave off *phr v informal* to stop doing something: *Let's start from where we left off yesterday.*

leave sb/sth ⇔ out *phr v* to not include someone or something: **+of** *Kidd has been left out of the team.*

leave² *n* [U] **1** time that you are allowed to spend away from your job: **on leave** *soldiers home on leave* | **sick/maternity leave** (=time away from work because you are ill or have had a baby) **2** *formal* permission

leaves /liːvz/ *n* the plural of LEAF

lecherous /'letʃərəs/ *adj* showing sexual desire in a way that is unpleasant or annoying —**lechery** *n* [U] —**lecher** *n* [C]

lectern /'lektən $ -ərn/ *n* [C] a high desk that you stand behind when you make a speech

lecture¹ /'lektʃə $ -ər/ *n* [C] **1** a long talk about a subject, especially a talk given by a teacher to college students: **+on/about** *He gave a series of lectures on French literature.* | **go to/attend a lecture** | **lecture hall/theatre/room** → see box at UNIVERSITY **2** a long serious talk that criticizes someone or warns them about something: **+on/about** *Dad gave me a long lecture about school.*

lecture² *v* **1** [T] to talk angrily to someone for a long time, criticizing them or warning them

about something: **lecture sb about/on sth** *He was lecturing us about making too much noise.*
2 [I] to teach a group of people about a subject, especially at a college —**lecturer** *n* [C] → see box at TEACHER → and UNIVERSITY

led /led/ *v* the past tense and past participle of LEAD

ledge /ledʒ/ *n* [C] a flat surface that sticks out from the side of a mountain or a wall

ledger /'ledʒə $ -ər/ *n* [C] a book in which the financial records of a company are kept → see box at RECORD

leech /liːtʃ/ *n* [C] a small creature that sticks to your skin and drinks your blood

leek /liːk/ *n* [C] a tall thin vegetable that tastes similar to an onion → see picture at VEGETABLE

leer /lɪə $ lɪr/ *v* [I] to look at someone in an unpleasant way that shows you think they are sexually attractive —**leer** *n* [C]

leeway /'liːweɪ/ *n* [U] freedom to do what you want: *We didn't give him much leeway.*

left¹ /left/ *adj* [only before noun]
1 on the side of your body that contains your heart [≠ right]: *the left side of his face* | **left leg/arm/knee etc** *Jim's broken his left leg.*
2 on the same side of something as your left side [≠ right]: *Take a left turn at the lights.*

left² *adv* towards the left side [≠ right]: *Turn left at the church.*

left³ *n*
1 [singular] the left side or direction [≠ right]: **on/to the/your left** *It's the second door on your left.* | *Also pictured are, from left to right, brothers Tom, Sam, and Jack.*
2 [singular] a left turn [≠ right]: *Take the next left.*
3 the left/the Left political parties or groups whose beliefs are typical of, or similar to, SOCIALISM

left⁴ *v* the past tense and past participle of LEAVE

left-'hand *adj* [only before noun] on the left side of something: *the top left-hand drawer*

left-'handed *adj* someone who is left-handed uses their left hand to write, throw etc

left 'luggage ,office *n* [C] *BrE* a place at a station, airport etc where you can pay to leave your bags and collect them later

leftovers /'leftəʊvəz $ -oʊvərz/ *n* [plural] food that has not been eaten during a meal —**leftover** *adj: leftover food*

left-'wing *adj* having beliefs that are typical of, or similar to, SOCIALISM: *a left-wing newspaper* —**left-winger** *n* [C] —**left wing** *n* [singular] *the left wing of the party*

leg /leg/ *n* [C]
1 one of the long parts of your body that your feet are joined to, or a similar part on an animal or insect
2 one of the parts that support a table, chair etc
3 the part of your trousers that covers your leg
4 one part of a journey, race, or competition: **+of** *the second leg of the World Championship*
5 not have a leg to stand on *informal* to be unable to prove or legally support something: *If you don't sign a contract, you won't have a leg to stand on.*

legacy /'legəsi/ *n* [C] plural **legacies** **1** a situation, especially a bad one, that exists as a result

of things that happened before: **+of** *the legacy of the war* **2** money or property that you receive from someone after they die [= inheritance]

legal /'liːgəl/ *adj*
1 allowed or done according to the law [≠ illegal]: *It's perfectly legal to charge a fee.* | *He had twice the legal limit of alcohol in his blood.*
2 relating to the law: *free legal advice* | *the Scottish legal system* | *She threatened to take legal action against them.*
—**legally** *adv* —**legality** /lɪ'gælɨti/ *n* [U]

legalize also **-ise** *BrE* /'liːgəlaɪz/ *v* [T] to make something legal: *a campaign to legalize cannabis* —**legalization** /ˌliːgəlaɪ'zeɪʃən $ -lə-/ *n* [U]

legend /'ledʒənd/ *n* **1** [C,U] an old well-known story about adventures or magical events: **+of** *the legend of King Arthur* | *According to legend, her tears formed a lake.* → see box at STORY
2 [C] someone who is famous for being very good at something: *He was a legend in his own lifetime.* **3** [C] a phrase or word written on a surface

legendary /'ledʒəndəri $ -deri/ *adj* **1** very famous and admired: *the legendary baseball player Babe Ruth* → see box at FAMOUS **2** [only before noun] appearing in legends

leggings /'legɪŋz/ *n* [plural] a piece of women's clothing that fits tightly around the legs

legible /'ledʒɨbəl/ *adj* written clearly enough to be read [≠ illegible] —**legibly** *adv*

legion¹ /'liːdʒən/ *n* [C] a large group of soldiers, especially in the ancient Roman army

legion² *adj* [not before noun] *formal* very many: *Examples of this are legion.*

legislate /'ledʒɨsleɪt/ *v* [I] to make a law about something: **+against/for/on** *The government has no plans to legislate against smoking in public.* —**legislator** *n* [C]

legislation /ˌledʒɨ'sleɪʃən/ *n* [U] a law or set of laws: **+on** *The government has introduced new legislation on taxation.*

legislative /'ledʒɨslətɪv $ -leɪtɪv/ *adj* relating to the making of laws: *legislative powers*

legislature /'ledʒɨsleɪtʃə, -lətʃə $ -lətʃər/ *n* [C] an institution that makes or changes laws

legitimate /lɨ'dʒɪtɨmɨt/ *adj* **1** reasonable: *a perfectly legitimate question* **2** not illegal: *legitimate business activities* —**legitimacy** *n* [U]

leisure /'leʒə $ 'liːʒər/ *n* **1** [U] time when you are not working and can do things you enjoy: *leisure activities such as sailing and swimming* | *They want better leisure facilities.*
2 at your leisure without hurrying or at a suitable time: *Read it at your leisure.*

'leisure ,centre *n* [C] *BrE* a place where you can do sports, exercise classes etc → see box at SPORT

leisurely /'leʒəli $ 'liːʒərli/ *adj* done in a slow relaxed way: *a leisurely walk around the park*

lemon /'lemən/ *n* [C,U] a yellow fruit that tastes sour: *a slice of lemon* | *lemon juice* → see picture at FRUIT

lemonade /ˌlemə'neɪd◂/ *n* [U] **1** *BrE* a sweet drink with bubbles that tastes of lemons **2** a drink made with lemon juice, sugar, and water

lend /lend/ *v* past tense and past participle **lent** /lent/

L

1 [T] to let someone borrow money or something that belongs to you: **lend sb sth** *Could you lend me £10?* | **lend sth to sb** *I've lent my bike to Tom.*

You **lend** something to someone when you give it to them so that they can use it for a short time: *I've lent that DVD to Rick.* | *Could you lend me some money?* You cannot say 'borrow me some money'.

You **borrow** something from someone when you use something that belongs to them for a short time, and then give it back: *Can I borrow your dictionary?* You cannot say 'can I lend your dictionary?'

2 [I,T] if a bank lends you money, it lets you have money which you must pay back with INTEREST
3 lend (sb) a hand to help someone do something → see box at HELP
4 lend itself to sth to be suitable for being used in a particular way
5 [T] *formal* to give something a particular quality: *The Prime Minister's presence lent a degree of importance to the occasion.*
6 lend (your) support (to sb/sth) *formal* to support someone or something
—**lender** *n* [C] —**lending** *n* [U]

length /leŋθ/ *n*

1 [C,U] the distance from one end of something to the other end [➔ **breadth, width**]: **+of** *What's the length of the room?* | **2 feet/8 metres etc in length** *The whale measured three metres in length.* | *She walked the full length of the train* (=all the way along the train).
2 [C,U] the amount of time that something continues for: **+of** *the average length of prison sentences*
3 go to great/some/any etc lengths (to do sth) to try very hard or to do whatever is necessary to achieve something: *She went to great lengths to help us.*
4 shoulder-length/knee-length etc reaching as far as your shoulders, knees etc: *knee-length shorts*
5 at length a) for a long time: *He spoke at length about his experiences.* **b)** *literary* after a long time: *'I think not,' he said at length.*
6 [C] a piece of something that is long and thin: **+of** *two lengths of rope*
→ **FULL-LENGTH**

lengthen /'leŋθən/ *v* [I,T] to become longer, or to make something longer
lengthwise /'leŋθwaɪz/ also **lengthways** *BrE* /-weɪz/ *adv* in the direction of the longest side: *Fold the cloth lengthwise.*
lengthy /'leŋθi/ *adj* continuing for a long time: *a lengthy process*
lenient /'liːniənt/ *adj* not strict when dealing with people: *The judge was too lenient.* —**leniency** *n* [U]
lens /lenz/ *n* [C] **1** a piece of glass or plastic that makes things look different, for example in a camera or pair of glasses **2** the part inside your eye that bends the light to produce an image → **CONTACT LENS**
lent /lent/ *v* the past tense and past participle of LEND
Lent *n* [U] the 40 days before Easter, when people sometimes stop eating some types of food

lentil /'lentl, -tļl/ *n* [C usually plural] a small round seed used as food
Leo /'liːəʊ $ 'liːoʊ/ *n* **1** [U] the sign of the Zodiac for people born between July 24 and August 23 **2** [C] someone who has this sign
leopard /'lepəd $ -ərd/ *n* [C] a large wild cat with yellow fur and black spots
leotard /'liːətɑːd $ -ɑːrd/ *n* [C] a tight piece of clothing which does not cover the arms or legs, worn for dancing
leper /'lepə $ -ər/ *n* [C] someone who has leprosy
leprosy /'leprəsi/ *n* [U] a serious disease in which the flesh is destroyed
lesbian /'lezbiən/ *n* [C] a woman who is sexually attracted to other women —**lesbian** *adj*
less¹ /les/ *adv* not so much, or to a smaller degree [≠ **more**]: *I definitely walk less since I've had the car.* | **less .... than ...** *The tickets were much less expensive than I expected.* | *Our trips became less and less frequent.*

less² *determiner, pron*

1 a smaller amount [≠ **more**]: *Most single parents earned £200 a week or less.* | *engines which use less fuel* | **+than** *I live less than a mile from here.* | **+of** *She spends less of her time abroad now.* | *We saw less and less of each other.*
2 no less used to emphasize that the person or thing you are talking about is impressive: *The award was presented by the mayor, no less.*
3 no less than sth used to emphasize that a number is surprisingly large: *The USA was importing no less than 45% of its oil.*

less, fewer
Use **less** before U nouns: *We've had less sunshine this year than last year.*
Use **fewer** before plural noun forms: *In those days there were fewer cars on the streets.*

-less /ləs/ *suffix* not having or doing something: *childless couples* | *a windowless room*
lessen /'lesən/ *v* [I,T] to become less, or to make something become less [= **reduce**]: *Exercise lessens the risk of heart disease.* —**lessening** *n* [singular]
lesser /'lesə $ -ər/ *adj* [only before noun] **1** *formal* not as large or important as something else: *a lesser sum* | *The major critics were Italy and, to a lesser extent, Germany.* **2 the lesser of two evils** the less unpleasant or harmful of two bad choices —**lesser** *adv*: *a lesser known French poet*
lesson /'lesən/ *n* [C]

1 a period of time in which someone is taught a subject or skill: **have/take lessons** *Hannah is taking guitar lessons.* | **+in/on** *lessons in First Aid*
2 *BrE* a period of time in which school students are taught a particular subject [= **class** *AmE*]: **French/physics/art etc lesson** → see box at SCHOOL
3 experience or information that you can use in the future: *Important lessons were learned from the accident.*

lest /lest/ *linking word, literary* in order to prevent something happening, or when it might happen: *He turned away lest his annoyance be seen.*

let /let/ *v* [T] past tense and past participle **let** present participle **letting**

1 to allow something to happen [➡ **permit**]: *I'll come if my dad lets me.* | **let sb do sth** '*Let him go,*' *said Ralph.* | **let sb in/through/out etc** *Let me through – I'm a doctor!* | **let yourself do sth** *She was afraid to let herself believe it.* | **let do sth** *She let the book fall.* → see box at ALLOW

2 let's *spoken* used to suggest to someone that you should do something together: *I'm hungry – let's eat.* | *Let's not argue.*

3 let's see *spoken* used when you are trying to remember or find something: *Now let's see, where did I put it?*

4 let go to stop holding someone or something: **+of** '*Let go of me!*' *Ben shouted.*

5 let sth go a) to not criticize or punish someone for something: *I'll let it go today, but don't be late again.* **b)** to stop worrying about something

6 let yourself go a) to relax completely and enjoy yourself **b)** to allow yourself to become unhealthy or unattractive

7 let sb know to tell someone something: *Let me know when you're ready.*

8 let me do sth *spoken* used when you are offering to help someone: *Let me carry that for you.*

9 let yourself in for sth to do something that will cause you trouble: *Now what's she let herself in for?*

10 let alone used to say that one thing is not true or does not happen, so another thing cannot possibly be true or happen: *The baby can't even crawl yet, let alone walk!*

11 also **let out** to allow someone to use a room or building in return for money: **let sth (out) to sb** *They let the flat to students.*

let sb/sth ⇔ down *phr v* to disappoint someone, especially by not doing what you promised: *You won't let me down, will you?*

let sb in on sth *phr v* to tell someone a secret

let sb off *phr v* to not punish someone or not make them do something: *I'll let you off this time, but don't be late again.*

let on *phr v* to show that you know a secret: **+(that)** *I won't let on I know anything.*

let out sth *phr v* **let out a scream/cry etc** to suddenly shout or make a noise

let up *phr v* to become less extreme or severe: *The rain never let up.*

letdown /'letdaʊn/ *n* [singular] *informal* something that disappoints you because it is not as good as you expected

lethal /'liːθəl/ *adj* able to cause death: *a lethal dose of the drug* | *a lethal weapon*

lethargic /lɪ'θɑːdʒɪk $ -'θɑːr-/ *adj* having no energy, so that you feel lazy or tired —**lethargy** /'leθədʒi $ -ər-/ *n* [U]

let's /lets/ the short form of 'let us'

letter /'letə $ -ər/ *n* [C]

1 a written message that you put into an envelope and send to someone: **+from/to** *The school had written several letters to his parents.* | *She*

sent me a lovely letter. | **get/receive/have a letter** | **post a letter** *BrE,* **mail a letter** *AmE*

Writing a letter

Ways of beginning a letter or an email
Dear...
Hi... *informal*

Ways of ending a letter or an email
Yours sincerely/sincerely (yours) *AmE*/Yours faithfully *BrE formal*
All the best/Best wishes
Take care *informal*
Love *informal*

2 a symbol using in writing to represent a sound: *the letter A*

3 follow/obey sth to the letter to do exactly what someone tells you to do: *He followed their instructions to the letter.*

4 the letter of the law the exact words of a law or agreement, rather than the intended or general meaning
→ COVERING LETTER

letterbox /'letəbɒks $ 'letərbɑːks/ *n* [C] *BrE*
1 a hole in a door through which letters are delivered [= **mailbox** *AmE*] **2** a box in a post office or in the street, where you post letters [= **postbox** *BrE*; = **mailbox** *AmE*]

lettering /'letərɪŋ/ *n* [U] letters that are written or drawn in a particular style: *ornate gold lettering*

lettuce /'letɪs/ *n* [C,U] a green vegetable with thin leaves, eaten raw in SALADS → see picture at VEGETABLE

letup /'letʌp/ *n* [singular, U] a pause or reduction in a difficult or unpleasant activity: *There has been no letup in the fighting.*

leukemia also **leukaemia** *BrE* /luː'kiːmiə/ *n* [U] a form of CANCER that affects the blood

level¹ /'levəl/ *n* [C]

1 an amount, degree, or number of something: **high/low level** *high levels of pollution* | *Try to reduce your* **stress levels**.

2 the height of something above or below something else: *The water level was rising.* | *The whole area is below ground level.* | **eye/knee/shoulder etc level** (=the same height as your eyes etc) *The picture was hung at eye level.*

3 a particular standard, for example in sport or education: **at ... level** *Few athletes compete at international level.* | *the advanced-level course*

4 a position or rank within an organization or system: *Employees at all levels were affected.*

5 a floor in a building that has several floors: *Her office is on Level 3.*

6 a way of considering something or of dealing with something: **On a personal level**, *I find this very upsetting.*
→ HIGH-LEVEL, LOW-LEVEL, SEA LEVEL

level² *adj*

1 flat, with no part higher than the rest: *The floor was not completely level.*

2 at the same height or in the same position as something else: **+with** *His face was level with hers.*

3 having the same number of points: *They finished level.*

4 a level playing field a situation in which different people, companies etc can compete fairly because no one has special advantages

level³ v **levelled, levelling** BrE; **leveled, leveling** AmE **1** also **level off** [T] to make a surface flat **2** [T] to knock something down to the ground and destroy it: *The earthquake leveled several buildings.* **3** [I,T] BrE to score a point in a competition, so that both sides are equal **4 level criticism/charges against/at sb** to say that you think someone has done something wrong

level off/out phr v to stop rising or falling, and continue at the same height or amount: *The plane levelled off at 30,000 feet.*

level with sb phr v informal to tell someone the truth or what you really think

,level 'crossing n [C] BrE a place where a railway crosses a road [= **grade crossing** AmE]

,level-'headed adj calm and sensible

lever¹ /'liːvə $ 'levər/ n [C] **1** a bar that you put under a heavy object in order to lift the object up **2** a handle on a machine that you move to make the machine work

lever² v [T] **1** to move something using a lever: *He levered the door open with a crowbar.* **2 lever yourself up/out of sth etc** to move your body by pushing on something with your arms

leverage /'liːvərɪdʒ $ 'le-, 'liː-/ n [U] **1** influence that you use to make people do what you want: *Small businesses have less leverage when dealing with banks.* **2** the action, use, or power of a lever

levitate /'levɪteɪt/ v [I] to rise and float in the air as if by magic —**levitation** /ˌlevɪ'teɪʃən/ n [U]

levy /'levi/ v **levied, levying, levies** **levy a tax/charge etc (on sth)** to officially make people pay a tax etc: *a tax levied on electrical goods* —**levy** n [C]

lewd /luːd/ adj using rude words or movements that make you think of sex: *lewd comments*

lexical /'leksɪkəl/ adj technical relating to words

lexicon /'leksɪkən $ -kaːn, -kən/ n [C] all the words used in a language or by a group of people

liability /ˌlaɪə'bɪlɪti/ n plural **liabilities** **1** [C,U] legal responsibility for something, especially for injury, damage, or a debt: **+for** *They have admitted liability for the accident.* **2** [singular] something that causes problems or is likely to be dangerous: *That car is a liability!*

liable /'laɪəbəl/ adj **1 be liable to do sth** to be likely to do something: *The car's liable to overheat.* **2** legally responsible for something: **+for** *The company is not liable for any damage.* **3 be liable to sth** to be likely to be affected by something bad

liaise /li'eɪz/ v [I] to work with other people and exchange information with them: **+with** *She liaises with local schools.*

liaison /li'eɪzən $ 'liːəzaːn, li'eɪ-/ n **1** [singular, U] the way two groups of people work together: **+between/with** *close liaison between the army and police* **2** [C] a sexual relationship, especially a secret one

liar /'laɪə $ -ər/ n [C] someone who tells lies

libel /'laɪbəl/ n [C,U] when someone writes or prints untrue statements about someone [➜ **slan-**

der]: *He sued the magazine for libel.* ➔ see box at LIE —**libel** v [T] —**libellous** BrE; **libelous** AmE adj

liberal¹ /'lɪbərəl/ adj **1** willing to understand or respect other people's ideas and behaviour: *a liberal attitude towards sex* **2** supporting changes in political, social, or religious systems that give people more freedom **3** giving or using a lot of something: *Don't be too liberal with the salt.*

liberal² n [C] someone with liberal opinions or principles

,Liberal 'Democrats n [plural] abbreviation **Lib Dem** a British political party —**Liberal Democrat** adj

liberalize also **-ise** BrE /'lɪbərəlaɪz/ v [T] to make a system, law, or attitude less strict —**liberalization** /ˌlɪbərəlaɪ'zeɪʃən $ -rələ-/ n [U]

liberally /'lɪbərəli/ adv in large amounts

liberate /'lɪbəreɪt/ v [T] to free someone or something from restrictions or someone's control: *The city was liberated by the Allies in 1944.* | **liberate sb from sth** *They need to liberate themselves from the past.* —**liberating** adj: *a very liberating experience* —**liberator** n [C] —**liberation** /ˌlɪbə'reɪʃən/ n [U]

liberated /'lɪbəreɪtɪd/ adj behaving in a free, modern way

liberty /'lɪbəti $ -ər-/ n plural **liberties** **1** [C,U] the freedom and the right to do whatever you want without asking permission or being afraid of authority: *principles of liberty and democracy* **2** [C] something that you do, although you do not have permission: *I took the liberty of inviting him to join us.* **3 be at liberty to do sth** formal to have permission to do something **4 at liberty** formal not in prison or not kept in an enclosed space [= **free**]

libido /lɪ'biːdəʊ $ -doʊ/ n [C,U] plural **libidos** sexual desire

Libra /'liːbrə/ n **1** [U] the sign of the Zodiac of people born between September 24 and October 23 **2** [C] someone who has this sign

librarian /laɪ'breəriən $ -'brer-/ n [C] someone who works in a library

library /'laɪbrəri, -bri $ -breri/ n plural **libraries**
1 a room or building containing books that can be looked at or borrowed: *a library book*
2 a group of books, CDs etc collected by one person

lice /laɪs/ n the plural of LOUSE

licence BrE; **license** AmE /'laɪsəns/ n
1 [C] an official document that gives you permission to do or own something: *a television licence* | *a driving licence* | **licence to do sth** *He has lost his licence to sell alcohol* (=had it taken away as a punishment).
2 under licence if a product is made or sold under licence, it is made or sold by a company that has an official agreement with the owner of the product that allows them to do this: *The car is built under licence in the UK.*
3 [U] formal freedom to do or say whatever you want
➔ **OFF-LICENCE**

license /'laɪsəns/ v [T] to give official permission for someone to do something: **be licensed**

to do sth *Is he licensed to carry a gun?*
—**licensed** *adj* [only before noun] *licensed drivers*

'license plate *n* [C] *AmE* a sign on the front and back of a car that shows its official number [= number plate *BrE*] → see picture on page A11

'licensing ,laws *n* [plural] the British laws that say when and where you can sell alcohol

lichen /'laɪkən, 'lɪtʃən/ *n* [C,U] a plant that spreads over the surface of stones and trees

lick¹ /lɪk/ *v* [T] to move your tongue across the surface of something: *The dog jumped up and licked her face.*

lick² *n* **1** [C usually singular] when you move your tongue across the surface of something **2 a lick of paint** *informal* some paint put on something to improve its appearance

licorice /'lɪkərɪs, -rɪʃ/ *n* the American spelling of LIQUORICE

lid /lɪd/ *n* [C]
1 a cover for a pot, box, or other container: *Put the lid on the pan.* → see box at COVER
2 an EYELID

lie¹ /laɪ/ *v* [I] past tense **lay** /leɪ/ past participle **lain** /leɪn/ present participle **lying**, third person singular **lies**
1 to be in a position in which your body is flat on the floor, a bed etc, or to put yourself in this position: +**on/in** *We lay on the beach all morning.* | +**back** *I love to lie back in a nice hot bath and relax.* | *My mom used to lie awake, worrying.* → see box at LAY
2 to be in a flat position on a surface: +**on/in etc** *His letter was lying on her desk.*
3 if a city, town etc lies in a particular position, it is in that position: *The town lies to the east of the lake.*
4 if a problem lies somewhere, it is caused by that thing, person, or situation: +**in/with etc** *The fault lies with the computer system.*
5 [linking verb] to be in a particular condition or state: *The boats in this once busy fishing village now lie idle* (=are not busy working). | *The city lay in ruins.*
6 if something lies in the future, it is going to happen to you in the future: *the difficulties that lie ahead for the refugees* | *Who knows what lies in store for any of us?*
7 lie low to remain hidden because someone is trying to find you
8 lie in wait (for sb/sth) to remain hidden in a place and wait for someone so that you can attack them

lie around also **lie about** *BrE phr v* **1 lie around (sth)** if something is lying around, it has been left somewhere in an untidy way, not in the place where it should be: *Stop leaving your clothes lying around.* **2** to spend time lying somewhere, not doing anything: *We just lay around on the beach the whole time.*

lie behind sth *phr v* to be the real reason for an action, even though this may be hidden: *What really lay behind her question?*

lie down *phr v* **1** to put yourself in a position in which your body is flat on the floor, a bed etc: *I'm going upstairs to lie down.* **2 not take sth lying down** *informal* to refuse to accept bad treatment without complaining

lie² *v* [I] **lied, lying, lies** to tell someone something that you know is not true: +**to** *I would never lie to you.* | +**about** *Have you ever lied about your age?* → see box at LAY

lie³ *n* [C] something that you say or write that you know is not true: *I always know when she's telling lies.* | *So you admit that it's a **blatant lie** (=an obvious and shocking lie).* | **white lie** (=a lie that is not serious)

THESAURUS

fib *informal* – a small, unimportant lie
falsehood *formal* – a statement that is not true
slander *law* – something untrue that is said about someone which could harm their reputation
libel *law* – something untrue that is written about someone which could harm their reputation

'lie de,tector *n* [C] a piece of equipment used to check whether someone is telling the truth or not, by measuring sudden changes in their heart rate

'lie-down *n* [singular] *BrE* a short rest: *I'm going to have a lie-down.*

'lie-in *n* [singular] *BrE* when you stay in bed longer than usual in the morning: *I always have a lie-in on a Sunday.*

lieu /ljuː, luː/ *n* **in lieu (of sth)** instead of something: *time off in lieu of payment*

lieutenant /lef'tenənt $ luː'ten-/ *n* [C] an officer with a fairly low rank in the army, navy, or AIR FORCE, or a fairly high rank in the US police

life /laɪf/ *n* plural **lives** /laɪvz/
1 [C,U] the period of time when you are alive: **sb's life** *This is the happiest day of my life.* | *He spent **the rest of** his life in France.* | *For the first time in my life, I felt old.*
2 [C,U] the state of being alive [➡ live, alive, dead, death]: *Wearing a seatbelt can **save your life**.* | *a plane crash involving great **loss of life*** | *She **took her own life** (=deliberately killed herself).* | *Cutting the hospital's funding will **cost lives** (=people will die).*
3 [C,U] all the experiences and activities that are typical of a particular job, situation, or activity [➡ lifestyle]: *Life in London is so hectic.* | **family/ home/married life** | **private/social/sex/love etc life** *I don't want any advice about my love life!* | *Having a baby **changes your life**.* | *the American way of life* | **a life of crime/poverty etc**
4 [U] living things such as people, animals, or plants: *Is there life on other planets?* | **plant/ animal/bird etc life** *the island's plant life*
5 [U] activity or movement: *She was so young and **full of** life.* | *There were no **signs of** life in the house.*
6 real life what really happens, rather than what happens in stories or in your imagination: **in real life** *Things like that don't happen in real life.* | *real life problems*
7 [C usually singular] the period of time that something continues to exist or be good enough to use [= lifespan]: +**of** *What's the average life of a family car?*

8 that's life *spoken humorous* said when something bad happens, to say that you accept it could happen to anyone

9 bring sth to life/come to life to make something more exciting, or to become more exciting: *The game really came to life in the second half.*

10 get a life *spoken* used to tell someone that they are boring and should find more exciting things to do

11 also **,life im'prisonment** [U] when someone is put in prison for the rest of their life: *I think murderers should get life.*

→ DOUBLE LIFE, STILL LIFE, WAY OF LIFE

lifebelt /'laɪfbelt/ *n* [C] **1** *BrE* a LIFEBUOY **2** *AmE* a special belt you wear in water to prevent you from sinking

lifeboat /'laɪfbəʊt $ -boʊt/ *n* [C] a boat that is used to help people who are in danger at sea

lifebuoy /'laɪfbɔɪ $ -buːi, -bɔɪ/ *n* [C] a large ring made from material that floats, which you throw to someone who has fallen in the water to prevent them from sinking

'life ,cycle *n* [C] the stages of development that a living thing goes through

,life ex'pectancy *n* [C,U] the length of time that someone is likely to live

'life guard *n* [C] someone whose job is to help swimmers who are in danger at a beach or swimming pool

'life in,surance *n* [U] a type of insurance that someone buys so that when they die their family will receive money

'life ,jacket *n* [C] a piece of clothing that you wear around your chest so that you will float if you fall into water

lifeless /'laɪfləs/ *adj* **1** *literary* dead or seeming to be dead **2** not at all interesting or exciting: *a lifeless performance*

lifelike /'laɪflaɪk/ *adj* a lifelike picture, model etc looks like a real person or thing: *a lifelike statue*

lifeline /'laɪflaɪn/ *n* [C] something that someone depends on completely: *The phone is her lifeline.*

lifelong /'laɪflɒŋ $ -lɔːŋ/ *adj* [only before noun] continuing all through your life: *a lifelong friend*

lifesaver /'laɪfseɪvə $ -ər/ *n* [C] someone or something that helps you in a very important way

life-saving¹ /'laɪf,seɪvɪŋ/ *adj* [only before noun] life-saving medical treatment or equipment is used to help save people's lives: *a life-saving heart operation*

life-saving² *n* [U] the skills necessary to save a person who cannot swim: *a life-saving certificate*

'life-size also **'life-sized** *adj* a life-size picture, model etc of something or someone is the same size as they really are

lifespan /'laɪfspæn/ *n* [C] the length of time that someone will live or something will work

lifestyle /'laɪfstaɪl/ *n* [C,U] the way that someone lives, including their work and activities, and what things they own: *Regular exercise is part of a healthy lifestyle.*

'life support ,system *n* [C] medical equipment that keeps someone alive when they are extremely ill

'life-,threatening *adj* a life-threatening illness, injury etc can kill you

lifetime /'laɪftaɪm/ *n* [C usually singular] the period of time during which someone is alive

'life vest *n* [C] *AmE* a LIFE JACKET

lift¹ /lɪft/ *v*

1 also **lift up** [I,T] to move something or someone to a higher position: *Can you help me lift this box?* | *He lifted his hand to wave.* | **lift sb/sth onto/into etc sth** *Dad lifted me onto his shoulders.* → see picture on page A11

2 [T] to remove a rule or law that stops something happening: *The US plans to lift its ban on Cuban cigars.*

3 [I] if cloud or MIST lifts, it starts to get sunny or bright

4 lift sb's spirits/sb's spirits lift to make someone feel happier, or to begin to feel happier

5 not lift a finger *informal* to do nothing to help

lift off *phr v* if a spacecraft lifts off, it leaves the ground and goes up into the air [➡ **take off**]

lift² *n* [C]

1 *BrE* a machine that takes you up and down between floors in a building; [= **elevator** *AmE*]: **take/use a lift**

2 *especially BrE* if you give someone a lift, you take them somewhere in your car: *Could anybody give Sue a lift home?* | *Do you want a lift?*

3 give sb/sth a lift to make someone more cheerful or confident: *A win would really give the team a lift.*

'lift-off *n* [C,U] the moment when a space vehicle leaves the ground

ligament /'lɪgəmənt/ *n* [C] a band of strong material in your body that joins bones together

light

candle

lantern

lamp

torch *BrE*/flashlight *AmE*

light¹ /laɪt/ *n*

1 [U] the energy from the sun, a lamp etc that allows you to see things: *Light poured in through the window.* | **good/strong/bright light** *The light in here isn't very good* (=not bright enough to see well). | **poor/dim etc light** | *We set out at first light* (=when it first gets light in the morning).

2 [C] something such as a lamp that produces light, using electricity: **turn/switch/put a light on/off** *Can you turn the light on, please?* | *The lights of the other traffic dazzled him.*

3 [C usually plural] a set of red, green, and yellow lights that control the movement of traffic [= **traffic lights**]: **at the lights** *Turn left at the lights.* | *Wait for the lights to change to green.*

4 a light something such as a match, used to light a cigarette: *Excuse me, do you have a light?*
5 come to light/be brought to light to become known: *The new evidence did not come to light until after the trial.*
6 shed/throw/cast light on sth to provide new information about something that makes it easier to understand
7 in the light of sth *BrE*; **in light of sth** *AmE* after considering something: *In light of the tragic events, tonight's concert has been cancelled.*
8 in a new/different/bad etc light if someone or something is seen or shown in a new, different, bad etc light, people have a new, different, bad etc opinion about them: *I suddenly saw my father in a different light.*
9 light at the end of the tunnel something that gives you hope that a bad situation will end soon
10 see the light to finally realize or understand something

light² *adj*

1 a light colour is pale, not dark [≠ **dark**]: **light blue/green/brown etc** *a light blue dress*
2 it is light used to say that there is enough light to see by [≠ **dark**]: *It was still light when we got home.*
3 if a room is light, a lot of light from the sun gets into it [≠ **dark**]: *The kitchen is light and roomy.*
4 not heavy: *Your bag's a lot lighter than mine.* | *It's as light as a feather* (=very light).
5 not having or using much force or power [= **gentle**]: *a light wind* | *a light tap on the door* | *Try some light exercise.*
6 light clothes are thin and not very warm: *a light sweater*
7 light food does not make you feel too full [≠ **rich**]: *a light snack*
8 not serious or difficult, and intended to entertain people: *It's the perfect book if you want some light reading.* | **light entertainment** (=programmes, shows etc that are very easy to watch or listen to, especially comedy)
9 small in amount: *Traffic is much lighter on Sundays.*
10 light sleep sleep from which you wake up easily
11 light sleeper someone who wakes up easily
12 make light of sth to joke about something or treat it as if it were not important
—**lightness** *n* [U]

light³ *v* past tense and past participle **lit** /lɪt/ or **lighted**

1 [I,T] to start to burn, or to make something start burning: *I lit another cigarette.* | *The fire won't light because the wood's wet.*
2 [T] to produce light in a room etc: *The room was warm and brightly lit.* | *well-lit streets*
　light up *phr v* **1 light sth** ⇔ **up** to make a place or thing become light or bright: *The fireworks lit up the sky.* | *The fountain is lit up at night.* **2** if someone's face or eyes light up, they suddenly look happy or excited **3** *informal* to light a cigarette

light⁴ *adv* **travel light** to not take too many clothes etc with you when you travel

'light bulb *n* [C] the glass part of an electric light, where the light shines from

lighted /'laɪtɪd/ *adj* **1** a lighted window, room etc has a light on inside **2** a lighted CANDLE, match etc is burning

lighten /'laɪtn/ *v* **1** [T] to reduce the amount of work, worry, debt etc that someone has: *The new computers should lighten our workload.* **2** [I,T] to become brighter, or to make something become brighter: *As the sky lightened, we could see where we were.*
　lighten up *phr v informal* to become less serious or strict

lighter /'laɪtə $ -ər/ *n* [C] a small object that produces a flame to light a cigarette

,light-'headed *adj* unable to think clearly or move steadily, for example because you are ill or have drunk some alcohol

light-hearted /,laɪt 'hɑːtɪd $ -ɑːr-/ *adj* **1** not intended to be serious: *a light-hearted remark* **2** cheerful and not worried

lighthouse /'laɪthaʊs/ *n* [C] a tower with a bright light that warns ships of danger

lighthouse

lighting /'laɪtɪŋ/ *n* [U] the lights in a place, or the quality of the light: *Better street lighting might help prevent crime.*

lightly /'laɪtli/ *adv* **1** with only a small amount of weight or force [= **gently**]: *He touched her lightly on the shoulder.* **2** using or having only a small amount of something: *a lightly greased pan* **3 take/treat/approach sth lightly** to do something without serious thought: *We did not take this decision lightly.* **4 get off lightly** also **be let off lightly** to be punished in a way that is less severe than you deserve

lightning

lightning¹ /'laɪtnɪŋ/ *n* [U] a bright flash of electrical light in the sky during a storm: *Several trees were struck* (=hit) *by lightning.* | *thunder and lightning*

lightning² *adj* [only before noun] very fast: *a lightning attack*

lightweight /'laɪt-weɪt/ *adj* weighing very little: *a lightweight jacket*

'light year *n* [C] **1** the distance that light travels in one year (about 9,460,000,000,000 kilometres), used for measuring distances between stars **2 light years ahead/better etc than sth**

L

informal much more advanced, better etc than someone or something else

likable /'laɪkəbəl/ *adj* another spelling of LIKE-ABLE

like¹ /laɪk/ *prep*
1 similar to something else, or happening in the same way: *Her hair is dark brown, like mine.* | **look/sound/feel etc like** *The garden looked like a jungle.* | *He's very like his brother.* | *Sometimes you sound just like* (=exactly like) *my Mum.* | *He looked nothing like* (=not at all like) *the man in the photo.*
2 what is sb/sth like? *spoken* used to ask someone to describe or give their opinion of a person or thing: *What's their house like inside?*
3 used to give an example of something: *Things like glass and paper can be recycled.*
4 typical of a person: *It's not like Dad to be late.*
5 like this/that/so *spoken* used when you are showing someone how to do something: *You have to fold the corners back, like this.*
6 just like that if you do something just like that, you do it without thinking about it or planning it carefully: *You can't give up your job just like that!*
7 something like not much more or less than a particular amount: *Seats cost something like $50 each.*
8 more like nearer to a particular amount: *The real figure may be more like ninety.*
9 nothing like *BrE* not at all: *This will be nothing like enough money.*

GRAMMAR

like, such as
Many teachers think that using **like** to give an example is wrong. It is better to use **such as**: *Games such as chess take a long time to learn.*

like² *v* [T]
1 to enjoy something or think that someone or something is nice, good, or right [≠ **dislike**]: *Do you like this colour?* | *I don't like it when you get angry.* | **like doing sth** *I don't like making speeches.* | **like to do sth** *I like to see people enjoying themselves.* | *I quite like their new CD.* | *We really liked the film.* | *She likes John very much.*
2 to prefer to do something or have something happen in a particular way: **like to do sth** *I like to get up early.* | **like sb to do sth** *We like our students to take part in sports.*
3 would like used to say what you want or to ask someone what they want: *I'd like a cheeseburger please.* | **would like to do sth** *I'd like to visit Australia some day.* | *I'd just like to say how grateful we are.* | *Would you like a drink?* | **would you like (sb) to do sth?** *Would you like to come with us?*
4 whatever/wherever/anything etc you like whatever thing you want, in whatever place you want etc: *You can sit wherever you like.*
5 as long/much etc as you like as long, as much etc as you want: *Take as many as you like.*
6 (whether you) like it or not used to emphasize that something will happen or is true and cannot be changed: *Like it or not, people are often judged by their appearance.*
7 I'd like to think/believe (that) used to say

that you wish or hope something is true, when you are not sure that it is: *I'd like to think that we offer a good service to everyone.*
8 if you like *spoken BrE* **a)** used to suggest or offer something: *We could watch a video this evening if you like.* **b)** used to agree to something: *'Shall we get a takeaway?' 'If you like.'*

GRAMMAR

Do not say 'I am liking it' or 'I am liking to do it'. Say *I like it* or *I like to do it.*
Do not say 'I am liking very much Anna'. Say *I like Anna very much.*

like³ *n* **1 sb's likes and dislikes** the things that someone likes and does not like **2 and the like** and similar things: *social problems such as poverty, unemployment, and the like* **3 the likes of sb** *spoken* used to talk about a particular type of person: *He thinks he's too good for the likes of us.*

like⁴ *adv spoken* **1** used while you are thinking what to say next: *The water was, like, really cold.* **2 I'm like/he's like etc** used to say what someone said: *I was like 'What?'*

like⁵ *linking word, spoken informal* **1** in the same way as someone or something: *No one can score goals like he can.* **2 like I say/said** used to repeat something that you have already said: *I'm sorry, but, like I say, she's not here right now.* **3** as if: *It looks like it's going to rain.*

-like /laɪk/ *suffix* similar to or typical of a thing or person: *a jelly-like substance* | *ladylike behaviour*

likeable, likable /'laɪkəbəl/ *adj* likeable people are nice and easy to like → see box at NICE

likelihood /'laɪklihʊd/ *n* **1** [singular, U] the degree to which something can be expected to happen: **+of** *Using a seatbelt reduces the likelihood of injury in a car accident.* **2 in all likelihood** almost certainly: *The president will, in all likelihood, have to resign.*

likely¹ /'laɪkli/ *adj* probably true or probably going to happen [≠ **unlikely**]: *Snow showers are likely tomorrow.* | *the most likely cause of the problem* | **likely to do/be sth** *Young drivers are more likely to have accidents than older drivers.* | *It is more than likely* (=almost certain) *the votes will have to be recounted.*

likely² *adv* **1** probably: **most/very likely** *I'd very likely have done the same thing.* **2 not likely** *especially BrE spoken* used to say that you definitely will not do something: *'Are you inviting Mary to the party?' 'Not likely!'*

like-'minded *adj* like-minded people have similar interests and opinions

liken /'laɪkən/ *v*
liken sb/sth to sb/sth *phr v* to say that two people or things are similar: *Critics likened the new theatre to a supermarket.*

likeness /'laɪknɪs/ *n* **1** [C,U] the quality of being similar in appearance to someone or something: **+to** *Hugh's likeness to his father* **2** [C] a picture of someone, especially one that looks very like them

likewise /'laɪk-waɪz/ *adv formal* in the same way: *The dinner was superb. Likewise, the concert.*

liking /ˈlaɪkɪŋ/ n **1 liking for sb/sth** *formal* when you like someone or something: *She had a liking for champagne.* **2 take a liking to sb/sth** to begin to like someone or something **3 be to sb's liking** *formal* to be just what someone wanted: *I hope everything was to your liking, Sir.* **4 too bright/strong/quiet etc for sb's liking** brighter, stronger etc than someone likes: *This weather's too hot for my liking.*

lilac /ˈlaɪlək/ n **1** [C,U] a small tree with pale purple or white flowers **2** [U] a pale purple colour —**lilac** *adj*

lilt /lɪlt/ n [singular] a pleasant pattern of rising and falling sound in someone's voice or in music —**lilting** *adj*

lily /ˈlɪli/ n [C] plural **lilies** a plant with large white or coloured flowers

limb /lɪm/ n [C] **1 out on a limb** alone and without help or support: *By voting for Wiesner we'd gone out on a limb.* **2** an arm or leg **3** a large branch of a tree

limbo /ˈlɪmbəʊ $ -boʊ/ n [singular, U] an uncertain situation in which you are waiting for something: **be in limbo** *I'm in limbo until I get my exam results.*

lime /laɪm/ n **1** [C,U] a bright green fruit with a sour taste, or the tree that this fruit grows on → see picture at **FRUIT** **2** [U] a white powdery substance used for making CEMENT

limelight /ˈlaɪmlaɪt/ n [singular, U] a situation in which someone has the attention of a lot of people: **in/out of the limelight** *Ted loves being in the limelight.*

limerick /ˈlɪmərɪk/ n [C] a short humorous poem with five lines

limestone /ˈlaɪmstəʊn $ -stoʊn/ n [U] a type of rock that contains CALCIUM

limit¹ /ˈlɪmɪt/ n [C]

1 the greatest or least amount, number etc that is allowed or possible: **+to/on** *There is a limit on the time you have to take the test.* | **We set a limit on our spending.** | **within a limit** *He finished within the **time limit**.* | *a 40 mph **speed limit** | There is no **age limit** for applicants.* | **+of** *the limits of human knowledge* | *He'd **reached the limit** of his patience.*

2 the border or edge of a place: *Los Angeles city* **limits**

3 off limits beyond the area where someone is allowed to go: *The beach is off limits after midnight.*

4 within limits within the time, level, amount etc considered acceptable: *You can come and go as you want – within limits.*

5 be over the limit to have drunk more than the legal amount of alcohol for driving

limit² v [T]

1 to stop something from increasing beyond a particular point: *a decision to limit imports of foreign cars* | **limit sth to sth** *Seating is limited to 500.*

2 to stop someone from doing something or developing: *A lack of education will limit your job opportunities.* | **limit yourself to sth** *I limit myself to two cups of coffee a day.*

3 be limited to sth to exist or happen only in a particular place, group etc: *The damage was limited to the roof.*
—**limiting** *adj*

limitation /ˌlɪmɪˈteɪʃən/ n **1** [C,U] when something is kept below a particular amount: *a nuclear limitation treaty* **2** [C usually plural] something that limits how good or effective someone or something can be: *It's a nice car, but it **has its limitations**.*

limited /ˈlɪmɪtɪd/ adj not much or not many: *My knowledge of the business is limited.*

limited ˈcompany n [C] a British company whose owners only have to pay a limited amount if the company gets into debt

limitless /ˈlɪmɪtləs/ adj without a limit or end

limousine /ˈlɪməziːn, ˌlɪməˈziːn/ also **limo** /ˈlɪməʊ $ -moʊ/ *informal* n [C] a large expensive comfortable car, driven by someone who is paid to drive

limp¹ /lɪmp/ adj not firm or strong: *a limp handshake* —**limply** *adv*

limp² v [I] to walk with difficulty because one leg is hurt: *He limped to the chair and sat down.* → see box at **WALK** —**limp** n [singular] *Brody walks with a limp.*

linchpin /ˈlɪntʃpɪn/ n **the linchpin of sth** the most important person or thing in a system or group, on which others depend: *My uncle was the linchpin of the family.*

line¹ /laɪn/ n [C]

1 a long thin mark on a surface: *Draw a **straight line** across the top of the page.* | *Marty raced towards **the finishing line**.* | *There were **fine lines** around her eyes.*

2 a row of people or things next to each other: **+of** *a line of trees at the side of the road* | *The men were **standing in a line**.*

3 *especially AmE* a number of people, cars etc that are waiting one behind the other [= queue *BrE*]: **+of** *a line of vehicles waiting to get into the car park* | **in line** *Three times a day we **stood in line** for food.*

4 the place where one area stops and another one starts: **state/county line** *AmE: He was born just across the state line.*

5 the direction in which something travels between two places: *Light travels **in a straight line.***

6 a telephone wire or connection: *I'm sorry, the **line is busy** (=someone is using it).* | **on the line** (=telephoning) *Harry is on the line from New York.* | *I **got on the line to** (=telephoned) the hospital this morning.* → see box at **TELEPHONE**

7 a track that a train travels along: *the London to Glasgow line* | **railway line** *BrE* /**railroad line** *AmE*

8 [usually singular] the point at which something becomes something else: **+between** *There is a **fine line** between religion and superstition.*

9 [usually plural] the outer shape of something long or tall: *the car's elegant lines*

10 a row of words in a poem, document etc: *the opening line of the song*

11 lines [plural] the words that someone learns and says in a play: *I haven't **learnt my lines** yet.*

12 a way of thinking about or doing something: **+on** *the government's line on immigration* | **take a tough/firm/hard line on sth** *The school takes a tough line on drugs.* | **line of argument/ reasoning/enquiry etc** *This line of questioning wasn't going to succeed.*

L

13 a piece of rope, string, or wire which has a particular purpose: *Could you hang the washing on the line?* | *a fishing line*

14 a type of goods for sale in a shop: *a line of low-priced computers*

15 along those/these lines similar to something else: *a trip to the beach or* **something along those lines**

16 on line connected to or using a computer system: *You can book tickets on line.*

17 be in line with sth to be what is expected or ordered, or to match something: *The figures were in line with economists' forecasts.*

18 be in line for sth to be likely to be given something: *He's in line for promotion.*

19 be/put sth on the line if something such as your job is on the line, you may lose it

20 be out of line *informal* to be behaving in a way that is not acceptable

21 drop sb a line *informal* to write a short letter or email to someone: *Drop me a line when you get there.*

→ ASSEMBLY LINE, DOTTED LINE, FRONT LINE, MAIN LINE → **somewhere along the line** at SOMEWHERE

line² v [T] **1** to sew a piece of material onto the inside or back of another piece: *a coat lined with silk* **2** to form rows along the edges of something: *Thousands of spectators lined the route.* | *a wide avenue lined with trees*

line up phr v **1** to stand in a row or line, or to make people do this: *Line up, everybody.* | **line sb ⇔ up** *He lined us up in the corridor.* **2 line sth ⇔ up** to arrange things in a row **3 line sb/sth ⇔ up** to arrange for something to happen, or for someone to be available: *We've lined up a good speaker for tonight.*

linear /'lɪniə $ -ər/ adj **1** consisting of lines, or in the form of a straight line: *a linear drawing* **2** involving a series of events, ideas etc that develop from one stage to the next

lined /laɪnd/ adj **1** a skirt, coat etc that is lined has a piece of material covering the inside: *a fur-lined coat* **2** lined paper has straight lines printed on it

'line ˌmanager n [C] BrE **sb's line manager** someone who has a higher rank than you in a company and is in charge of your work

linen /'lɪnᵻn/ n [U] **1** sheets, TABLECLOTHS etc: *bed linen* **2** a strong high-quality cloth

liner /'laɪnə $ -ər/ n [C] **1** a large ship for passengers: *an ocean liner* → see box at SHIP → see picture at TRANSPORT **2** a piece of material used inside something: *a dustbin liner*

linesman /'laɪnzmən/ n [C] plural **linesmen** /-mən/ an official in a sport who decides when a ball has gone out of the playing area

'line-up n [C usually singular] **1** the group of performers, players, or activities that will be part of an event **2** *especially AmE* a group of people arranged in a row by the police so that a person who saw a crime can try to recognize the criminal

linger /'lɪŋgə $ -ər/ v [I] **1** also **linger on** if a smell, memory etc lingers, it does not disappear for a long time: *a taste that lingers in your mouth* **2** to stay somewhere or continue something for longer than usual: **+over** *They lingered over their coffee.* —**lingering** adj

lingerie /'lænʒəri $ ˌlɑːnʒəˈreɪ, 'lænʒəri/ n [U] women's underwear

lingering /'lɪŋgərɪŋ/ adj continuing for a long time: *a lingering kiss*

lingo /'lɪŋgəʊ $ -goʊ/ n plural **lingos** *informal* **1** [C usually singular] a language **2** [singular, U] words and phrases used by a particular group of people: *medical lingo*

linguist /'lɪŋgwᵻst/ n [C] **1** someone who is good at languages **2** someone who studies linguistics

linguistic /lɪŋ'gwɪstɪk/ adj relating to language or linguistics: *a child's linguistic development*

linguistics /lɪŋ'gwɪstɪks/ n [U] the study of language and languages: *I did linguistics for two years at university.*

lining /'laɪnɪŋ/ n [C,U] a piece of material that covers the inside of something: *a jacket with a silk lining*

link¹ /lɪŋk/ v [T]

1 to make or show a connection between two or more situations, things, or people: **link sth to/with sth** *Lung cancer has been linked to cigarette smoking.*

2 be linked (to/with sth) if two things are linked, they are related in some way: *Are the deaths linked?*

3 to physically join two or more things or places: **link sth to/with sth** *A bridge links Venice to the mainland.*

link² n [C]

1 a relationship or connection between two or more events, people, or ideas: **+between** *the link between drug use and crime* | *the* **close links** *between students and teachers* | **+with** *The company has* **strong links** *with investors in France and Italy.*

2 rail/road/telephone etc link something that makes communication or travel between two places possible: *a direct computer link*

3 one of the rings that make up a chain

linkage /'lɪŋkɪdʒ/ n [C,U] *formal* a connection or relationship between two things

'linking ˌverb n [C] a verb that connects the subject of a sentence to its COMPLEMENT, for example 'seems' in the sentence 'The house seems big'

'linking ˌword n [C] a word such as 'but', 'and', or 'while' that connects phrases or parts of sentences [= conjunction]

'link-up n [C] a connection between two things, especially organizations or communication systems

linoleum /lᵻ'nəʊliəm $ -'noʊ-/, **lino** /'laɪnəʊ $ -noʊ/ n [U] a smooth material used to cover floors

lint /lɪnt/ n [U] *especially AmE* soft light pieces of thread or wool that come off a material [= fluff BrE]

lion

lion /'laɪən/ *n*
1 [C] a large brown wild cat from Africa or Asia. A male lion has a MANE (=long thick hair on its neck): *lion cubs* (=baby lions)
2 the lion's share (of sth) the largest share of something

lioness /'laɪənes, -nɪ̯s/ *n* [C] a female lion

lip /lɪp/ *n* [C]
1 the edge of your mouth where your skin is red or darker: *a kiss on the lips* | **top/bottom lip** *His bottom lip swelled up.* → see picture on page A3
2 [usually singular] the edge of a container used to hold or pour liquid

'lip balm also **'lip salve** *BrE n* [C,U] a soft substance, used to protect your lips

lippy /'lɪpi/ *adj BrE informal* not showing respect in the way that you speak to someone

lip-read /'lɪp riːd/ *v* [I,T] past tense and past participle **lip-read** /-red/ to understand what someone says by watching their lips move, especially because you cannot hear —**lip-reading** *n* [U]

'lip ,service *n* **pay lip service to sb/sth** to say that you support or agree with something without doing anything to prove it

lipstick /'lɪp,stɪk/ *n* [C,U] a substance you put on your lips to make them a different colour

liqueur /lɪ'kjʊə $ lɪ'kɜːr/ *n* [C,U] a strong sweet alcoholic drink

liquid /'lɪkwɪ̯d/ *n* [C,U] a substance that is not solid or a gas, such as water or milk: *Add a little more liquid to the sauce.*
—**liquid** *adj: liquid fuel*

liquidation /,lɪkwɪ̯'deɪʃən/ *n* [C,U] when a business is forced to close and sell everything in order to pay its debts: *The company has gone into liquidation.* —**liquidate** /'lɪkwɪ̯deɪt/ *v* [I,T]

liquidizer also **-iser** *BrE* /'lɪkwɪ̯daɪzə $ -ər/ *n* [C] a small electric machine that makes solid foods into liquids [= **blender**] —**liquidize** *v* [T]

liquor /'lɪkə $ -ər/ *n* [C,U] *especially AmE* a strong alcoholic drink such as WHISKY

liquorice *BrE*; **licorice** *AmE* /'lɪkərɪs, -rɪʃ/ *n* [U] a black substance with a strong taste, used in sweets

'liquor store *n* [C] *AmE* a shop where alcohol is sold [= **off-licence** *BrE*] → see box at SHOP

lisp /lɪsp/ *n* [C usually singular] a fault in the way someone speaks, which makes them pronounce 's' as 'th' —**lisp** *v* [I,T]

list /lɪst/ *n* [C] a number of things that you write down, one below the other: **+of** *a list of names* |

make/write a list *Make a list of the equipment you need.* | **on a list** *There are 30 people on the hospital waiting list.*

THESAURUS

shopping list *BrE*/**grocery list** *AmE* – a list of food you need to buy
price list – a printed list of a company's goods or services, and their prices
wine list – a list of the wines available in a restaurant
checklist – a list of things you need to check
waiting list – a list of people who want something but will have to wait for it
mailing list – a list of people that a company sends information to
guest list – a list of people invited somewhere

—**list** *v* [I,T] *The book lists more than 1000 hotels.*
→ HIT LIST, SHORT LIST

listen /'lɪsən/ *v* [I]
1 to pay attention to what someone is saying or to something you can hear: **+to** *What sort of music do you like listening to?* | **+for** *He stopped and listened carefully for any sound.* | *Listen Doug, I need your help.* → see box at HEAR
2 to accept advice from someone: **+to** *I wish I'd listened to Dad.* | *She refuses to listen to reason* (=accept sensible advice).

listen in *phr v* to listen secretly to someone's conversation [= **eavesdrop**]: **+on** *The kids listen in on our phone calls.*

listen out *phr v BrE informal* to listen carefully so that you will notice a particular sound

listen up *phr v especially AmE spoken* used to get people's attention before you say something

listener /'lɪsənə $ -ər/ *n* **1** [C] someone who listens to the radio **2 good listener** someone who listens carefully to other people's problems, stories etc

listing /'lɪstɪŋ/ *n* [C] an official or public list: *movie listings*

listless /'lɪstləs/ *adj* feeling tired and not interested in things —**listlessly** *adv*

lit /lɪt/ *v* the past tense and past participle of LIGHT

litany /'lɪtəni/ *n* [C] plural **litanies** *disapproving* a long list of problems, excuses, complaints etc

liter /'liːtə $ -ər/ *n* the American spelling of LITRE

literacy /'lɪtərəsi/ *n* [U] the ability to read and write

literal /'lɪtərəl/ *adj* the literal meaning of a word, phrase etc is its basic or original meaning [➡ **figurative**]: *a literal interpretation of the Bible*

literally /'lɪtərəli/ *adv* **1** according to the basic or original meaning of a word or phrase: *Your body is literally a 'machine'.* | **take sb/sth literally** (=believe the exact words someone says, rather than its general meaning) **2** used to emphasize that what you are saying is true: *We literally worked day and night.*

literary /'lɪtərəri $ 'lɪtəreri/ *adj* [only before noun] relating to literature: *a literary prize*

literate /'lɪtərɪ̯t/ *adj* **1** able to read and write [≠ **illiterate**] **2** well educated

literature /ˈlɪtərətʃə $ -tʃʊr/ n [U]

1 books, poems, plays etc that people think are good, serious, and important: *a major work of literature* | *a degree in English literature* → see box at BOOK

2 printed information about something: *+on government literature on energy conservation*

lithe /laɪð/ adj able to move your body easily and gracefully

litigation /ˌlɪtɪˈɡeɪʃən/ n [U] law the process of taking legal action in a court of law

litre BrE; **liter** AmE /ˈliːtə $ -ər/ n [C] written abbreviation *l* a unit for measuring liquid in the METRIC system: *a litre of water* | **litre bottle/container etc** *a 3-litre oil drum*

litter¹ /ˈlɪtə $ -ər/ n **1** [U] paper, bottles, cans etc that people do not want and have left on the ground in a public place [➡ garbage]: *Anyone caught dropping litter is fined.* → see box at RUBBISH **2** [C] a group of baby animals born from the same mother at the same time: *+of a litter of kittens* → see box at GROUP

litter² v [T] if things litter a place, they are spread over it in an untidy way: **litter sth with sth** *His desk was littered with papers.*

little¹ /ˈlɪtl/ adj

1 small in size: *The little shop was very crowded.* | *a tiny little baby* | **a little bit (of sth)** (=a small amount of something) *Add a little bit of milk to the sauce.* → see box at SMALL

2 [only before noun] spoken used after an adjective to emphasize that you like or dislike something: *a nice little town* | *What a horrid little man!*

3 [only before noun] short in time or distance: *He arrived a little while ago.* | *Let's walk a little way together.*

4 young or still a child: *two little girls* | *Were you naughty when you were little?* | **little brother/sister** BrE (=a younger brother or sister) → see box at YOUNG

5 [only before noun] not important: *You worry too much about little things.*

little² determiner, pron

1 not much or not enough [➡ less]: *Little is known about his life.* | *She had very little money.*

2 a little a small amount: *'More coffee?' 'Just a little.'* | **a little more/less** *Let's have a little less noise please.* | **as little as £5/3 months etc** (=used to emphasize how small an amount is) *Insurance can cost as little as £2 a week.*

GRAMMAR

little, a little

Use **little** when you mean 'not much': *I've got very little money left.*

Use **a little** when you mean 'a small amount': *I'm afraid I've spilt a little wine on the carpet.*

Little and **a little** are always used with U nouns.

→ FEW

---

little³ adv

1 a little slightly or to a small degree [= a bit]: *She trembled a little as she spoke.* | **a little more/better/further etc** *Move your chair a little closer.*

2 not much: *She goes out very little.* | **little**

more/better (than sth) *His voice was little more than a whisper.* | **a little known fact** (=known by only a few people)

3 little by little gradually: *Little by little she gained confidence.*

little 'finger n [C] the smallest finger on your hand

live¹ /lɪv/ v

1 [I] if you live in a place, your home is there: **+in/at/near etc** *Matt lives in Boston.* | *She lived next door to me.* | *Sam is 25 but he still lives at home* (=with his parents). | **live here/there** *Does Paul live here?*

2 [I] to be alive or to continue to stay alive: **+in/before/at** *He lived in the eighteenth century.* | *Plants can't live without light.* | *People are living longer than ever.* | **live to (be) 80/90 etc** *My grandma lived to be 84.*

3 [I,T] to have a particular kind of life, or to live in a particular way: **live in peace/poverty etc** *We live in fear of crime.* | **live peacefully/quietly etc** *Mark likes living dangerously.* | **live a quiet/active/healthy etc life** *She lives a busy life.*

4 [I] to have an exciting life: *I want to live a little before I settle down.*

5 live it up informal to spend a lot of money doing things that you enjoy

live sth ⇔ down phr v to be able to stop people reminding you about something embarrassing that you did: *I'll never live it down if the boys find out.*

live for sb/sth phr v if you live for something, it is the most important thing in your life: *She lives for her children.*

live in phr v BrE to live in the place where you work or study: *Many students live in during the first year.*

live off sb/sth phr v to depend on someone or something for money, food etc: *Older people do not want to live off their savings.*

live on phr v **1** to continue to exist: *Her memory will live on* (=people will remember her). **2 live on sth a)** to have a particular amount of money to buy what you need: *I don't know how you live on only £80 a week.* **b)** to eat a lot of a particular kind of food: *Kids these days live on burgers and fries.*

live through sth phr v to experience a difficult or dangerous situation: *She has lived through two wars.*

live together phr v if two people live together, they share a house and have a sexual relationship but they are not married [= live with] → see box at MARRIED

live up to sth phr v to be as good as someone expects: *Did the game live up to your expectations?*

live with sb/sth phr v **1** to accept a difficult situation that will probably continue: *I've learned to live with stress.* **2** to live in the same house as someone and have a sexual relationship with them, without being married [= live together]

live² /laɪv/ adj, adv

1 [only before noun] alive, not dead [= living; ≠ dead]: *experiments on live animals*

2 a live television or radio programme is seen or heard by people while it is happening: *a live*

broadcast of the World Cup Final | *live TV coverage* | **broadcast/show sth live** *The funeral will be shown live on TV.*
3 live music, theatre etc is performed for people who are watching in the same place: **live music/jazz/performance etc** *We have live bands on Saturdays.* | **perform/play live** *Grandad saw the Beatles play live.*
4 a live wire has electricity flowing through it
5 a live bomb, bullet etc has not yet exploded: *a live landmine*
6 go live if a project or system goes live, people use it for the first time

livelihood /ˈlaɪvlihʊd/ *n* [C,U] the way you earn money in order to live: *Farming is their livelihood.*

lively /ˈlaɪvli/ *adj* **1** happy and active: *a lively child* **2** interesting and exciting: *a lively debate* | *the city's lively nightlife* —**liveliness** *n* [U]

liven /ˈlaɪvən/ *v*
liven up *phr v* to become more exciting or interesting, or to make something do this: **liven sth ⇔ up** *Better music would have livened the party up.*

liver /ˈlɪvə $ -ər/ *n* **1** [C] the organ inside your body that cleans your blood → see picture on page A3 **2** [C,U] the liver of an animal, used as food

lives /laɪvz/ *n* the plural of LIFE

livestock /ˈlaɪvstɒk $ -staːk/ *n* [U] animals that are kept on a farm

livid /ˈlɪvɪd/ *adj* very angry [= furious] → see box at ANGRY

living¹ /ˈlɪvɪŋ/ *adj* **1** alive now [≠ dead]: *one of our greatest living writers* | *All living things* (=people, animals, and plants) *are made of cells.* **2** still used or done now: *a living language* (=one that people still use) | *the worst disaster in living memory* (=that people can still remember)

living² *n*
1 [C usually singular] the money that you earn from working: *What do you do for a living* (=what is your job)*?* | **earn/make a living** *It's hard to make a living as an actor.*
2 [U] the way that someone lives their life: *a guide to healthy living*
3 the living all the people who are alive, not dead [≠ the dead]
→ **the cost of living** at COST¹ → STANDARD OF LIVING

ˈliving room also **sitting room** BrE *n* [C] the main room in a house, where you relax, watch television etc [= lounge]

lizard /ˈlɪzəd $ -ərd/ *n* [C] a small animal with thick skin and a long tail that lives in hot countries

-'ll /l/ the short form of 'will' or 'shall': *He'll be here soon.*

load¹ /ləʊd $ loʊd/ *n* [C]
1 a large quantity of something that a vehicle, person etc is carrying: **+of** *a ship with a full load of fuel* | **bus load/car load** (=the amount that a bus or car can carry) *a bus load of tourists*
2 a load of sth/loads of sth BrE *informal* a lot of something: *Don't worry, we have loads of time.* | **loads to do/see/eat etc** *There's loads to do in Tokyo.*
3 the amount of work that a person or a

machine has to do: *a **heavy work load** *(=large amount of work)
4 a load of rubbish/nonsense BrE *spoken* used to say that you think something is very stupid or bad

load² *v*
1 also **load up** [I,T] to put a large quantity of something into a vehicle or container [≠ unload]: *Have you finished loading the dishwasher?* | **load sth into/onto sth** *They loaded their baggage into the car.*
2 [T] to put something into a machine in order to use it or make it work: **load sth with sth** *Did you load the camera with 400mm film?*
3 [I,T] if you load a program onto a computer, or if it loads, you put it into the computer [➔ download]
load sb/sth ⇔ down *phr v* if you are loaded down with something, you have too much of it to do, carry etc: **+with** *I was loaded down with shopping.*

loaded /ˈləʊdɪd $ ˈloʊ-/ *adj* **1** a loaded gun has bullets in it **2** containing or carrying a lot of things: *a loaded truck* | **+with** *a table loaded with delicious desserts* **3** [not before noun] *informal* very rich → see box at RICH **4 loaded question** *disapproving* a question that is unfair because it is meant to make you say something that you do not want to say

loaf /ləʊf $ loʊf/ *n* [C] plural **loaves** /ləʊvz $ loʊvz/ bread that is baked in one large piece: *a loaf of bread* → see picture at BREAD

loan¹ /ləʊn $ loʊn/ *n*
1 [C] an amount of money that you borrow: **+of** *a loan of $6,000* | *a $25,000 **bank loan*** (=from a bank) | **business/student/personal loan** (=money you borrow for business, university, or personal costs) *We took out a personal loan to pay for our holiday.* | **pay off/repay/pay back a loan** (=give back money you have borrowed)
2 [singular] when you lend something to someone: **+of** *Thanks for the loan of that book.*
3 on loan (from sb/sth) if something is on loan, it has been borrowed: *The paintings are on loan from other galleries.*

loan² *v* [T] to lend something to someone: **loan sb sth** *Can you loan me $20?*

ˈloan shark *n* [C] *disapproving* someone who lends money at a very high rate of INTEREST

loath /ləʊθ $ loʊθ/ *adj* **be loath to do sth** *formal* to be unwilling to do something [= reluctant]

loathe /ləʊð $ loʊð/ *v* [T] to hate someone or something very much → see box at HATE —**loathing** *n* [C,U]

loathsome /ˈləʊðsəm $ ˈloʊθ-/ *adj* very unpleasant or cruel

loaves /ləʊvz $ loʊvz/ *n* the plural of LOAF

lob /lɒb $ laːb/ *v* [T] **lobbed, lobbing** to throw or hit something high into the air: **lob sth at/over etc sth** *kids lobbing stones at cars* —**lob** *n* [C]

lobby¹ /ˈlɒbi $ ˈlaːbi/ *n* [C] plural **lobbies** **1** a large area inside the entrance of a public building: *the hotel lobby* → see box at FLOOR **2** a group of people who try to persuade a government to change a particular law or situation: *the anti-war lobby*

L

lobby[2] *v* [I,T] lobbied, lobbying, lobbies to try to persuade a government to do something: **+for/against** *The group is lobbying for a change in the law.* —**lobbyist** *n* [C]

lobe /ləʊb $ loʊb/ *n* [C] **1** an EARLOBE **2** *technical* a round part of your brain or lung

lobster /'lɒbstə $ 'lɑːbstər/ *n* [C,U] a sea animal with eight legs, a shell, and large CLAWS, or the meat of this animal as food

local[1] /'ləʊkəl $ 'loʊ-/ *adj*

1 relating to a particular area, especially the area you live in: *Our kids go to the local school.* | *the local newspaper* | *local residents* | **local government** also **local authority** *BrE* (=the government of a particular area or city) → see box at NEAR

2 affecting only part of your body: *Local anaesthetic is used for tooth extractions.*

local[2] *n* [C] **1** someone who lives in the place that you are talking about: *I asked one of the locals for directions.* **2** sb's local *BrE informal* the PUB nearest someone's home, where they usually go **3** *AmE* a bus or train that stops at all the stopping places

locality /ləʊ'kæləti $ loʊ-/ *n* [C] plural localities *formal* a small area of a country, city etc

localized also **-ised** *BrE* /'ləʊkəlaɪzd $ 'loʊ-/ *adj formal* happening within a small area: *localized flooding*

locally /'ləʊkəli $ 'loʊ-/ *adv* in the area where you are or the area you are talking about: *Do you live locally?*

THESAURUS

nearby: *Do you live nearby?*
close by/close to here: *My folks live close by.*
around here also **round here** *BrE*: *Is there a bank around here?*
in the neighbourhood *BrE*/**in the neighborhood** *AmE*: *Is there a good Chinese restaurant in the neighborhood?*
→ NEAR

local time *n* [U] the time of day in a particular part of the world: *We arrived in Boston at 16.40 local time.*

locate /ləʊ'keɪt $ 'loʊkeɪt/ *v* **1** [T] to find the exact position of something: *Divers have located the shipwreck.* **2** be located in/near etc sth to be in a particular place or position: *The town is located on the shores of a lake.* **3** [I,T] to build or move a company's offices somewhere: **locate (sth) in/at etc sth** *Big retail stores are not prepared to locate in poor areas.*

location /ləʊ'keɪʃən $ loʊ-/ *n* **1** [C] a particular place or position: **+of** *Draw a map showing the precise location of the accident.* | *the town's geographical location* → see box at PLACE **2** [C,U] a place where a film is made, away from the usual building: **on location** *The scene was shot on location in Montana.*

loch /lɒx, lɒk $ lɑːk, lɑːx/ *n* [C] a word for a lake in Scotland: *Loch Garten*

lock[1] /lɒk $ lɑːk/ *v*

1 [I,T] to fasten something with a key, or to fasten with a key [≠ unlock]: *Did you lock the car?* | *The window won't lock.*

2 [T] to put someone or something in a place and fasten the door, lid etc with a key: **lock sth in sth** *He locked the money in a drawer.* | **lock sth away** *The documents were locked away in a safe.*

3 [I,T] to become fixed in one position and impossible to move: *The wheels locked and we skidded.*

lock sb in/out *phr v* to prevent someone from entering or leaving a place by locking the door: *I turned the handle but we were locked in.*

lock up *phr v* **1** to make a building safe by fastening the doors with a key: **lock sth ⇔ up** *I'll lock up the garage.* **2** lock sb ⇔ up to put someone in prison: *Too many kids are being locked up.*

lock[2] *n* [C]

1 something you use to fasten a door, drawer etc and that you usually open with a key: *I put my key in the lock.* | *a bicycle lock* | *Dad keeps his cigars under lock and key* (=somewhere fastened with a lock).

2 a group of hairs growing together on your head: **+of** *a lock of hair*

3 a part of a river or CANAL that you close with gates to raise or lower the level of the water

4 lock, stock, and barrel including every part of something
→ COMBINATION LOCK

locker /'lɒkə $ 'lɑːkər/ *n* [C] a small cupboard that locks, used to store books, clothes etc safely in a building such as a college or office

locker room *n* [C] a room in a sports building, school etc where people change their clothes and leave them in lockers

locket /'lɒkɪt $ 'lɑː-/ *n* [C] a piece of jewellery that you wear on a chain around your neck, with a small box that can contain a picture, piece of hair etc

locksmith /'lɒksmɪθ $ 'lɑːk-/ *n* [C] someone who makes and repairs locks

locomotive /ˌləʊkə'məʊtɪv $ ˌloʊkə'moʊ-/ *n* [C] *technical* a train engine

locust /'ləʊkəst $ 'loʊ-/ *n* [C] an insect from Africa or Asia that flies in a large group, eating and destroying crops: *a swarm of locusts*

lodge[1] /lɒdʒ $ lɑːdʒ/ *v* **1** [I,T] to become stuck somewhere, or make something become stuck: **+in** *A fishbone lodged in his throat.* | **be lodged in/between/behind etc sth** *A bullet was lodged behind his heart.* **2** lodge a complaint/protest/appeal *BrE* to make a formal complaint, protest etc: **+with/against** *Do you wish to lodge a complaint against the club?* **3** [I + adv/prep] *old-fashioned* to pay to live in someone's house

lodge[2] *n* [C] **1** a small building or room at the entrance to a building: *the porter's lodge* **2** a small house in the country, especially one at the entrance to a very large house

lodger /'lɒdʒə $ 'lɑːdʒər/ *n* [C] *BrE* someone who pays to live in someone's house [= boarder *AmE*]

lodging /'lɒdʒɪŋ $ 'lɑː-/ *n* [C,U] a place where you pay to live: *I pay £90 a week for board and lodging* (=meals and a room).

loft /lɒft $ lɔːft/ *n* [C] **1** *BrE* a room or space under the roof of a house [= attic] **2** *AmE* a raised area above the main part of a room

lofty /'lɒfti $ 'lɔː-/ *adj* very high and impressive: *the lofty heights of Ben Nevis*

log¹ /lɒg $ lɔːg, lɑːg/ *n* [C]   **1** a thick piece of wood from a tree   **2** an official record of events: **+of** *The captain keeps a log of incidents.* → see box at **RECORD**

log² *v* [T] **logged**, **logging**   to make an official record of events

log in/on *phr v* to do the actions on a computer that will allow you to start using it: **+to** *Log on to your home page.* → see box at **COMPUTER**

log out/off *phr v* to stop using a computer by doing particular actions → see box at **COMPUTER**

logarithm /ˈlɒgərɪðəm $ ˈlɔː-, ˈlɑː-/ *n* [C] one of a set of numbers that you use to solve some mathematical problems

loggerheads /ˈlɒgəhedz $ ˈlɔːgər-, ˈlɑː-/ *n* **be at loggerheads (with sb)** to disagree very strongly with someone: *The two families have been at loggerheads for years.*

logging /ˈlɒgɪŋ $ ˈlɔː-, ˈlɑː-/ *n* [U] the activity of cutting down trees in order to sell the wood

logic /ˈlɒdʒɪk $ ˈlɑː-/ *n* [U]   **1** a sensible reason or way of thinking: *There is no logic in releasing criminals just because prisons are crowded.* | **+of** *the logic of my argument*   **2** a formal method of reasoning, in which ideas are based on previous ideas

logical /ˈlɒdʒɪkəl $ ˈlɑː-/ *adj*   **1** reasonable and sensible [≠ **illogical**]: *He seems the logical choice for the job.* | *There's only one logical conclusion.*   **2** based on the rules of logic: *logical analysis* —**logically** /-kli/ *adv*

logistics /ləˈdʒɪstɪks $ loʊ-/ *n* [plural] the practical arrangements that are necessary to make a complicated plan or activity succeed: **+of** *the logistics of organizing an international music festival* —**logistical** *adj* —**logistically** /-kli/ *adv*

logo /ˈləʊgəʊ $ ˈloʊgoʊ/ *n* [C] a design that is the official sign of a company or organization

loins /lɔɪnz/ *n* [plural] *literary* the part of your body below your waist, where the sex organs are

loiter /ˈlɔɪtə $ -ər/ *v* [I] to stand or wait somewhere, especially in a public place, without any clear reason

loll /lɒl $ lɑːl/ *v* [I] to sit or lie in a lazy or relaxed way: **+around/in etc** *He lolled back in his chair.*

lollipop /ˈlɒlipɒp $ ˈlɑːlipɑːp/ also **lolly** *BrE* /ˈlɒli $ ˈlɑː-/ *n* [C] a hard sweet on a stick

lone /ləʊn $ loʊn/ *adj* [only before noun] used to talk about the only person in a place, or the only person that does something: *a lone gunman* | *the lone survivor of a shipwreck* | **a lone parent** (=someone who lives alone with their children)

lonely /ˈləʊnli $ ˈloʊn-/ *adj*

1 unhappy because you are alone [= **lonesome** *AmE*]: *Don't you get lonely living on your own?* | *a lonely old man*

2 a lonely place is a long way from where people live: *a lonely country road* —**loneliness** *n* [U]

lonely ˈhearts *n* **lonely hearts club/ column/ad** *BrE* a club or an advertisement page in a newspaper used by people who want to meet someone and have a romantic relationship with them

loner /ˈləʊnə $ ˈloʊnər/ *n* [C] someone who likes to be alone

lonesome /ˈləʊnsəm $ ˈloʊn-/ *adj AmE* LONELY

long¹ /lɒŋ $ lɔːŋ/ *adj*

1 measuring a large distance from one end to the other [≠ **short**]: **long hair** | *It's a long walk home from here.* | *My parents live quite* **a long way** *away.*

2 continuing for a large amount of time [≠ **short**]: *a long, boring meeting* | **a long period of time** | *It took a long time for the little girl to start to relax.* | **a long day/week** (=a boring or tiring day or week) | *I work very* **long hours** (=more working hours than usual).

3 used to talk or ask about the distance between the ends of something, or the time between the beginning and the end of something: *The snake was at least 3 feet long.* | *His speech was 20 minutes long.* | *How long is your garden?*

4 in the long run *informal* in the future, not immediately: *All our hard work will be worth it in the long run.*

5 long shot someone or something with very little chance of success

6 a) a long book has a lot of pages **b)** a long list has a lot of things on it

long² *adv*

1 a great amount of time: *This won't take long.* | *Have you been* **waiting long**? | **for long** *Have you known the Garretts for long?* | **long before/after/ago** *The farm was sold long before you were born.* | **long-awaited/long-lasting/ long-established etc** *a long-forgotten argument*

2 as/so long as on the condition that: *You can go as long as you're back by four o'clock.*

3 no longer/not any longer used to show that something happened in the past, but does not happen now: *Mr. Allen no longer works for the company.*

4 before long soon: *It will be Christmas before long.* → see box at **SOON**

long³ *v* [I] *formal* to want something very much: **+for** *I used to long for a baby sister.* | **long to do sth** *The children longed to get outside.* —**longing** *n* [singular, U] *She had a great longing for her home country.* —**longingly** *adv*

long-ˈdistance *adj* involving places that are a long distance apart: *long-distance flights* | *a long-distance phone call* —**long-distance** *adv*

longevity /lɒnˈdʒevɪti $ lɑːn-, lɔːn-/ *n* [U] *formal* long life

longhand /ˈlɒŋhænd $ ˈlɔːŋ-/ *n* [U] writing by hand rather than using a machine such as a computer

ˈlong-haul *adj* [only before noun] **long-haul flight/route/destination etc** a long-haul flight etc is over a very long distance

longing /ˈlɒŋɪŋ $ ˈlɔːŋɪŋ/ *n* [singular, U] a strong feeling of wanting something or someone: *She had a great longing for her home country.* —**longingly** *adv*

longitude /ˈlɒndʒɪtjuːd $ ˈlɑːndʒətuːd/ *n* [C,U] a position on the Earth measured in degrees east or west of an imaginary line from the top of the Earth to the bottom [➡ **latitude**] → see picture at **GLOBE** —**longitudinal** /ˌlɒndʒɪˈtjuːdɪnəl◂ $ ˌlɑːndʒɪˈtuː-/ *adj*

ˈlong jump *n* **the long jump** a sport in which you jump as far as possible

ˌlong-ˈlife *adj*   **1** long-life products continue working longer than ordinary ones: *long-life*

batteries **2** *BrE* long-life foods stay fresh longer than ordinary ones: *long-life milk*

long-lived /ˌlɒŋ ˈlɪvd◂ $ ˌlɔːŋ ˈlaɪvd/ *adj* living or existing for a long time

ˌlong-ˈlost *adj* **long-lost friend/cousin/brother etc** a friend etc that you have not seen for a very long time: *He greeted me like a long-lost friend.*

ˌlong-ˈrange *adj* [only before noun] **1** able to hit something that is a long way away [≠ short-range]: *a long-range missile* **2** relating to a time that continues far into the future: *a long-range weather forecast*

ˌlong-ˈrunning *adj* [only before noun] used about something that has been continuing for a long time: *their long-running legal battle*

longshoreman /ˈlɒŋʃɔːmən $ ˈlɔːŋʃɔːr-/ *n* [C] plural **longshoremen** /-mən/ *AmE* someone whose job is to load and unload ships at a DOCK [= **docker** *BrE*]

longsighted /ˌlɒŋˈsaɪtᵻd◂ $ ˌlɔːŋ-/ *adj BrE* able to see or read things clearly only when they are far from your eyes [= **far-sighted** *AmE*; ≠ **short-sighted**]

ˌlong-ˈstanding *adj* having continued or existed for a long time: *a long-standing agreement between the two countries*

ˌlong-ˈsuffering *adj* patient in spite of problems or other people's annoying behaviour: *his long-suffering wife*

ˌlong-ˈterm *adj* continuing for a long period of time into the future [➦ **short-term**]: *the long-term effects of smoking* ➔ **in the long/short term** at **TERM¹**

ˈlong-time *adj* [only before noun] having existed or continued to be a particular thing for a long time: *a long-time ambition* | *a long-time friend of the family*

ˈlong ˌwave *n* [U] written abbreviation *LW* radio broadcasting using radio WAVES of 1000 metres or more in length [➦ **medium wave**, **short wave**, **FM**]

long-winded /ˌlɒŋ ˈwɪndᵻd◂ $ ˌlɔːŋ-/ *adj* talking for too long in a way that is boring: *a long-winded speech*

loo /luː/ *n* [C] plural **loos** *BrE informal* a toilet

look¹ /lʊk/ *v*

1 [I] to turn your eyes towards something or someone so that you can see them: *I didn't see it. I wasn't looking.* | **+at** *'It's time to go,' said Patrick, looking at his watch.* | **+down/away/over etc** *I looked down the road but she'd gone.* ➔ see box at **SEE**
2 [I] to try to find someone or something: **+for** *Brad was looking for you last night.* | **+in/under/between etc** *Try looking under the bed.*

search/hunt for sb/sth – to look carefully for someone or something: *a mouse searching for food* | *The police are still hunting for clues.*
try to find sb/sth – to look for someone or something that is hard to find: *I've been trying to find my car keys.*
have a look for sb/sth *spoken* – to look quickly for someone or something: *I've had a quick look for her upstairs, but she's not there.*
seek – to look for someone or something that you are trying hard to find: *The police issued a picture of the man they are seeking.*

go through sth – to examine something very thoroughly when looking for something: *Security officers went through our bags.*

3 [linking verb] to seem or appear: *You look nice in that dress.* | **look tired/happy/worried etc** | **look good/bad etc** *The future's looking good.* | **what does sb/sth look like?** (=describe their appearance) | **+as if/as though/like** *He looked as if he hadn't washed for a week.* | *It looks like she's not coming back.* | **strange-looking/dirty-looking etc** *healthy-looking children*
4 **look** *spoken* **a)** used to make someone notice something: *Look! There's a fox!* **b)** used to draw attention to what you are saying, especially when you are annoyed: *Look, I've had enough of this. I'm going home.*
5 **look out!** *spoken* used to warn someone of danger: *Look out! There's a car coming.*
6 [I] if a building looks in a particular direction, it faces that direction: *Our room looks over the harbour.*
7 **be looking to do sth** to want or be planning to do something
8 **forward-looking/backward-looking** modern or old-fashioned in your ideas, methods etc
9 **look to sb for sth/to do sth** to depend on someone to provide help, advice etc: *He looks to me for advice.*
10 **look sb in the eye** to look directly at someone when you are speaking to them, especially to show that you are not afraid of them or that you are telling the truth: *Owen didn't dare look his father in the eye.*

look after sb/sth *phr v* to take care of someone or something: *We look after Rodney's kids until he gets home from work.*

look ahead *phr v* to think about and plan for what might happen in the future

look around also **look round** *BrE phr v* **1** to try to find something: **+for** *I'm looking around for a new job.* **2** **look around/round (sth)** to look at what is in a place such as a building, shop, town etc, especially when you are walking: *We have three hours to look around the city.*

look at sb/sth *phr v* **1** to read something quickly, but not thoroughly: *Jane was looking at a magazine while she waited.* **2** to examine something and try to find out what is wrong with it: *You should get a doctor to look at that cut.* **3** to study and think carefully about something: *The government will look at the report this week.* **4** **look at sb/sth** *spoken* used to mention someone or something as an example: *You can get a good job without a degree – just look at your Uncle Ron.* **5** to think about something in a particular way: *It all depends how you look at the situation.*

look back *phr v* to think about something that happened in the past: **+on** *Looking back on it, I think I was wrong to leave when I did.*

look down on sb *phr v* to think that you are better than someone else

look forward to sth *phr v* to be excited and happy about something that is going to happen: **look forward to doing sth** *I'm really looking forward to going to Japan.* ➔ see box at **WAIT**

look into sth *phr v* to try to find out the truth about a problem, crime etc: *We are looking into the cause of the fire.*

L

look on phr v **1** to watch something, without being involved in it: *The crowd looked on as the two men fought.* **2 look on/upon sb/sth** to think about someone or something in a particular way: **+as** *I look on him as a good friend.*

look out for sb/sth phr v to try to notice someone or something: *Look out for Jane at the conference.*

look sth ⇔ **over** phr v to examine something quickly: *Can you look this letter over for me before I send it?*

look round phr v BrE → **LOOK AROUND**

look through sth phr v **1** to look for something in a pile of papers, a drawer, someone's pockets etc: *Look through your pockets and see if you can find the receipt.* **2** to read something carefully

look up phr v **1** if a situation is looking up, it is getting better: *Things are looking up since I found a job.* **2 look** sth ⇔ **up** to find information in a book, on a computer etc: *If you don't know the word, look it up in the dictionary.* **3 look** sb ⇔ **up** to visit someone you have not seen for quite a long time: *Don't forget to look me up when you come to Atlanta.*

look up to sb phr v to admire and respect someone: *He looks up to his older brother.*

look² n

1 [C usually singular] when you look at something: **have/take a look (at sb/sth)** *Let me have a look at that map again.* **2** [singular] an attempt to find something: **+for** *He's had a look for the file but he hasn't found it.* **3** [C] **a)** an expression on someone's face: *He had a worried look on his face.* **b)** when someone looks at you with a particular expression on their face: *She gave me an angry look.* **4** [singular] an act of examining something and thinking about it: **+at** *This month, take a long hard look at where your money is going.* **5** [C usually singular] the appearance of someone or something: *I don't like the look of those rain clouds.* **6** [C] a particular fashion or style: *the nautical look* **7 looks** [plural] physical attractiveness: *Stop worrying about your looks.*

lookalike /ˈlʊkəlaɪk/ n [C] informal someone who looks very similar to a famous person: *a Madonna lookalike*

'look-in n **get a look-in** BrE informal to have a chance to take part in or succeed in something: *The rest of us didn't get a look-in.*

lookout /ˈlʊkaʊt/ n **1 be on the lookout (for sb/sth)** to pay attention to the things around you in order to find something you want or to avoid something: *Be on the lookout for snakes!* **2** [C] someone who watches carefully for danger, or the place where they do this

loom¹ /luːm/ v [I] **1** to appear as a large, unclear, often frightening shape: **+ahead/up etc** *The mountain loomed in front of us.* **2** if a problem or difficulty looms, it is likely to happen very soon: *My exams are looming.*

loom² n [C] a machine used for weaving cloth

loony /ˈluːni/ n [C] informal plural **loonies** someone who behaves in a crazy or strange way —**loony** adj: *He's full of loony ideas.*

loop¹ /luːp/ n **1** [C] a shape like a circle in a piece of wire, string etc: *A loop of wire held the gate shut.* **2 be out of the loop** AmE to not be part of a group of people that make decisions: *Gaynor says he was out of the loop when the order was given.*

loop² v **loop sth over/around etc sth** to make a loop or to tie something with a loop

loophole /ˈluːphəʊl $ -hoʊl/ n [C] a small mistake in a law that makes it possible to legally avoid doing what the law says: *tax loopholes*

loose¹ /luːs/ adj

1 not firmly fixed in place: *a loose tooth* | *The screw has come loose.* **2** not fastened together or kept together in a container: *She had left her hair loose.* | *The potatoes are sold loose.* **3** loose clothes are big and do not fit tightly → see box at **CLOTHES** **4** free, not controlled, tied up, or kept in a prison, cage etc: *Two of the prisoners broke loose from the guards.* | **let/turn/set sb loose** *He threatened to let his dogs loose.* **5** not exact: *a loose translation* **6 loose ends** parts of something that have not been completed or correctly done: *We've nearly finished, but there are still a few loose ends to be tied up* (=dealt with or completed). **7 be at a loose end** to have nothing to do **8 loose change** coins that you have —**loosely** adv

loose² n **be on the loose** if a criminal or animal is on the loose, they have escaped

loosen /ˈluːsən/ v [I,T] to become or to make something less tight or less firmly fastened: *The screws holding the shelf had loosened.* | *He loosened his tie.*

loosen up phr v to become more relaxed: *Claire loosened up after a few drinks.*

loot¹ /luːt/ v [I,T] to steal things during a war or RIOT: *Shops were looted and burned down.* —**looting** n [U] —**looter** n [C]

loot² n [U] things that have been stolen

lop /lɒp $ lɑːp/ v lopped, lopping **lop** sth ⇔ **off** phr v to cut part of something off, especially a branch from a tree

lope /ləʊp $ loʊp/ also **lope off** v [I] to run or walk with long slow steps: *He loped off down the corridor.* —**lope** n [singular]

lopsided /ˌlɒpˈsaɪdɪd $ ˌlɑːp-/ adj having one side that is heavier or lower than the other: *a lopsided grin*

Lord /lɔːd $ lɔːrd/ n [C] **1** a man in the highest social class, especially in Britain [➡ **Lady**]: *Lord Mountbatten* **2 the/our Lord** a title for God or Jesus Christ **3 the Lords** the HOUSE OF LORDS [➡ **the Commons**]

lore /lɔː $ lɔːr/ n [U] traditional stories, history, or knowledge about magic, nature etc

lorry /ˈlɒri $ ˈlɔːri, ˈlɑːri/ n [C] BrE plural **lorries** a large vehicle used for carrying goods [= **truck**] → see picture at **TRANSPORT**

lose /luːz/ v past tense and past participle **lost** /lɒst $ lɔːst/

1 [T] to stop having something that is important to you or that you need [➡ **loss**]: *Tom lost his job.* | *Drunk drivers should lose their licence.* | **lose an arm/leg/eye etc** *He lost his leg in a*

motorcycle accident. | *He's lost a lot of blood.* | *I lost a lot of money when the stock market crashed.*
2 [T] to stop having a particular attitude, quality, ability etc, or to gradually have less of it [➡ **loss**]: *You're looking slim. Have you **lost weight**?* | **lose your sight/hearing/voice/balance etc** *Jim lost his balance and fell.* | **lose confidence/interest/hope etc** *Carol lost interest in ballet in her teens.* | *Try not to **lose heart** (=become sad and hopeless) – there are plenty of other jobs.* | *We must never **lose sight of** (=forget) our goals.*
3 [T] to become unable to find someone or something: *Danny's always losing his keys.*
4 [I,T] to fail to win a game, argument, war etc [≠ **win**; ➡ **defeat**]: *They played so badly they deserved to lose.* | **+by** *The Democrat candidate lost by 8000 votes.* | **+to** *Liverpool lost to AC Milan.*
5 a) lose your life to die: *5000 soldiers lost their lives.* **b)** if you lose a relative or friend, that person dies
6 [T] *spoken informal* to confuse someone when you are trying to explain something to them: *Explain it again – you've lost me already.*
7 [T] to waste time or an opportunity: *You lost your chance!* | *There's **no time to lose**!*
8 lose your temper/cool to become angry: **+with** *Diana was determined not to lose her temper with him.*
9 have nothing to lose if you have nothing to lose, it is worth taking a risk because you cannot make your situation any worse
10 lose your way/bearings to stop knowing where you are or which direction you should go in
11 lose it *informal* to become angry, confused, upset etc
lose out *phr v* to not get something good, valuable etc because someone else gets it instead: **+to/in/on** *She lost out to Nicole Kidman for the lead role.*

loser /ˈluːzə $ -ər/ *n* [C] **1** someone who has lost a competition, game etc: **good/bad loser** (=someone who behaves well or badly when they lose) **2** *informal* someone who is never successful in life, work, or relationships: *Pam's boyfriend is such a loser!*

loss /lɒs $ lɒːs/ *n*
1 [C,U] when you do not have something any longer, or when you have less of it: **+of** *The loss of their home was a shock to the family.* | *a temporary loss of memory* | *severe weight loss* | *There may be job losses.*

COLLOCATIONS

loss of confidence – when you stop believing in your ability to do things well
loss of appetite – when you do not get hungry, for example because you are ill
loss of memory also **memory loss** – when you cannot remember things well
loss of blood also **blood loss** – when you bleed a lot, for example after an accident
weight loss – when you become a lot thinner
hearing loss also **loss of hearing** – when you cannot hear as well as you could before
job losses – when a number of people lose their jobs in a company, industry etc

2 [C,U] if a company makes a loss, it earns less money than it spends [≠ **profit**]: *The company **made a loss** of $250,000 last year.*

3 [C,U] the death of a person: *After **heavy losses** (=many deaths), they were forced to surrender.* | *The floods caused great damage and **loss of life**.*
4 [U] a feeling of sadness because someone or something is not there any more: *She felt a great **sense of loss** when her son left home.*
5 [singular] a disadvantage caused by someone leaving or something being taken away: **+to** *If she leaves, it will be a great loss to the company.*
6 be at a loss to be confused or uncertain about what to do or say: *Local people are at a loss to know how to deal with the problem.*
→ **cut your losses** at CUT[1]

lost[1] /lɒst $ lɒːst/ *adj*
1 not knowing where you are or how to find your way: *We **got lost** driving around the city.* | *a lost child*
2 if something is lost, you cannot find it: *two boys searching for a lost ball* | *My passport **got lost** in the post.*
3 be/feel lost to not feel confident or happy
4 get lost! *spoken* used to tell someone rudely to go away
5 be lost on sb if something such as a joke is lost on someone, they cannot understand it
6 be lost for words to be so shocked, IMPRESSED etc that you cannot think what to say
7 lost cause something that will definitely not be successful: *It looked like the match was a lost cause.*
→ **LONG-LOST**

lost[2] *v* the past tense and past participle of LOSE

,lost 'property *n* [U] things that people have accidentally left in a public place, which are kept until the owner collects them

lot /lɒt $ lɑːt/ *n*
1 a lot also **lots** *informal* a large amount, quantity, or number of something: **+of** *There were a lot of people at the concert last night.* | *She's got lots of money.* | *'How many CDs have you got?' 'Lots.'* | **a lot to do/see etc** *There's a lot to see in London.*
2 a lot a) used to say that something happens to a great degree or often: *Things have changed a lot since I was a child.* → see box at OFTEN **b)** if someone or something is a lot better, faster etc, they are much better, faster etc: *You'll get there a lot faster if you drive.*
3 [C] *BrE informal* a group of people or things considered together: *I need to take this lot to the post office.* | **+of** *There's another lot of students starting next week.*
4 the lot *especially BrE* the whole of something: *He bought a huge bar of chocolate and ate the lot.*
5 [C] *AmE* an area of land used for a particular purpose: *a parking lot*
6 [C] something being sold at an AUCTION
7 [singular] the kind of life you have: *She seems happy enough with her lot.*

GRAMMAR

a lot of, much, many
In negative sentences, you can use **much** or **many** instead of **a lot of**.
Much is used with U nouns: *There isn't much wine left.*
Many is used with plural noun forms: *I didn't see many people there that I knew.*

A lot of can be used with both types of noun: *I don't have a lot of money.* | *She doesn't have a lot of friends.*

lotion /ˈləʊʃən $ ˈloʊ-/ *n* [C,U] a liquid mixture that you put on your skin or hair to clean, SOFTEN, or protect it: *suntan lotion*

lottery /ˈlɒtəri $ ˈlɑː-/ *n* [C] plural **lotteries** a competition in which people choose a set of numbers and win money if they have chosen the winning numbers

lotto /ˈlɒtəʊ $ ˈlɑːtoʊ/ *n* [C] a game used to make money, in which people buy tickets with a series of numbers on them. If their number is picked by chance, they win money or a prize.

loud¹ /laʊd/ *adj*

1 making a lot of noise: *The TV's too loud!* | *a loud bang*

THESAURUS

noisy – making a lot of noise, or full of noise: *a classroom full of noisy kids* | *a noisy bar*
rowdy – behaving in a noisy and uncontrolled way: *rowdy football fans*
thunderous – extremely loud: *thunderous applause*
deafening – very loud, so that you cannot hear anything else: *a deafening roar*
ear-splitting – painfully loud
→ QUIET

2 loud clothes are very brightly coloured
—**loudly** *adv*

loud² *adv* **1** in a way that makes a lot of noise [= loudly]: *You'll have to speak a bit louder.* **2** out loud in a way that people can hear: *Read it out loud, so we can all hear.*

loudspeaker /ˌlaʊdˈspiːkə, ˈlaʊdˌspiːkə $ -ər/ *n* [C] a piece of equipment that makes sounds louder

lounge¹ /laʊndʒ/ *n* [C]

1 a room in a hotel or airport, where people can sit and relax: *the **departure lounge***
2 *BrE* the room in your house where you sit and relax

lounge² *v* [I] to stand or sit somewhere in a relaxed way: *We were lounging by the pool.*
lounge about/around *phr v BrE* to spend time relaxing and doing nothing

louse /laʊs/ *n* [C] plural **lice** /laɪs/ a very small insect that lives on the skin or hair of animals and people

lousy /ˈlaʊzi/ *adj informal* very bad: *a lousy film*
→ see box at BAD

lout /laʊt/ *n* [C] a loud, violent man

lovable, loveable /ˈlʌvəbəl/ *adj* easy to love: *a lovable child*

love¹ /lʌv/ *v* [T]

1 to like someone in a romantic or sexual way: *I love you.* | *the first boy I ever really loved*

THESAURUS

If you **are infatuated with** someone, you have unreasonably strong feelings of love for them.
If you **have a crush on** someone, you have a strong feeling of love for them, but it usually only lasts for a short time: *Carrie has a crush on her art teacher.*

If you **are crazy about** someone, you love them very much, especially in a way that you cannot control.
If you **are devoted to** someone, you love them and are loyal to them: *He has always been devoted to his wife.*
→ HATE

2 to care about someone a lot, especially a member of your family or a close friend: *I love my Mom.* | *It can be hard to cope with the death of a loved one* (=person you care about).
3 to like something very much, or enjoy doing something very much: *I love chocolate.* | **love doing sth** *Tom loves going to the cinema.* | **love to do sth** *He loved to spend time there.*
4 I'd love to (do sth) *spoken* used to say that you want to do something very much: *I'd love to go to Egypt one day.* | *'Do you want to come?' 'I'd love to.'*

love² *n*

1 [U] a strong romantic feeling for someone: **+for** *their love for each other* | **be/fall in love (with sb)** *She fell **madly** in love with him.* | *Do you believe in **love at first sight** (=when you love someone as soon as you meet them)?* | *a love song* | *I've kept all his old **love letters**.*
2 [U] when you care very much about someone, especially a member of your family or a close friend: **+for** *a mother's love for her son*
3 [C] someone who you love: *You were my **first love**.*
4 [C,U] a strong feeling of liking or enjoying something very much, or something that gives you this feeling: **+of** *his love of the countryside* | *She **has** a great **love of** music.* | *His greatest love is football.*
5 make love (to/with sb) to have sex with someone
6 (with) love (from) sb used at the end of a friendly letter: *With love from Peter.* | *Hope to see you soon. Lots of love, Chris.*
7 send/give your love (to sb) to ask someone to give your friendly greetings to someone else: *Your father sends his love.*
8 *BrE spoken informal* **a)** used when talking to someone who you love: *Are you OK, love?* **b)** used when talking in a friendly way to someone you do not know, especially a woman

ˈlove afˌfair *n* [C] a romantic sexual relationship

lovely /ˈlʌvli/ *adj*

1 beautiful: *You look lovely in that dress.* | *What a lovely garden!*
2 *especially BrE* very pleasant or enjoyable: *Thanks for a lovely evening.* | *The food was lovely.* → see box at NICE

lover /ˈlʌvə $ -ər/ *n* [C] **1** someone you have a sexual relationship with, especially who you are not married to: *They became lovers soon after they met.* **2** someone who enjoys something very much: **music/art/animal lover**

loving /ˈlʌvɪŋ/ *adj* behaving in a gentle, kind way that shows you love someone: *a wonderful, loving husband* —**lovingly** *adv*

low¹ /ləʊ $ loʊ/ *adj*

1 not far above the ground [≠ high]: *a low ceiling* | *low clouds* | *Put it on the lowest shelf.*

L

2 small in amount, value etc [≠ **high**]: *Tempera-tures will be lower than yesterday.* | *We try to keep our prices as low as possible.* | *families on low incomes* | **low-fat/low-salt etc** (=with very little fat, salt etc) *low-alcohol beer*
3 below an acceptable standard [≠ **high**]: *She got a very low grade in English.* | *low quality goods*
4 [not before noun] unhappy: *Kerry's been pretty low lately.* → see box at **SAD**
5 a low voice or sound is quiet or deep [≠ **high**]
6 lights that are low are not bright

low² *adv* in a low position or at a low level [≠ **high**]: *The sun sank low on the horizon.* | *low-flying aircraft* | **low-paid workers** (=who do not earn much money)

low³ *n* [C] a low price, level etc [≠ **high**]: *Oil prices have dropped to an all-time low* (=the lowest they have ever been). | *Tomorrow's low will be 8°C.*

lowbrow /'ləʊbraʊ $ 'loʊ-/ *adj disapproving* a lowbrow newspaper, book etc is easy to under-stand and not very serious [≠ **highbrow**]

low-'cut *adj* low-cut clothes show the top of a woman's chest: *a tight low-cut dress*

lowdown /'ləʊdaʊn $ 'loʊ-/ *n* **the lowdown (on sb/sth)** the important facts about someone or something: *Give me the lowdown on what happened then.*

lower¹ /'ləʊə $ 'loʊər/ *adj* [only before noun]
1 below something else, or at the bottom of something [≠ **upper**]: *I injured my lower back.* | *the lower floors of the building*
2 less important than other things [≠ **higher**]: *the lower levels of management*

lower² *v* [T] **1** to reduce something in amount, strength etc: *We're lowering prices on all our products!* | *Helen lowered her voice* (=spoke more quietly). **2** to move something down [≠ **raise**]: *The flag was lowered at sunset.*

lower 'case *n* [U] letters written in their small form, for example a, b, c [➡ **upper case, capital**]

low-'key *adj* done in a way that will not attract a lot of attention: *The reception was very low-key.*

lowlands /'ləʊləndz $ 'loʊ-/ *n* [plural] an area of land that is lower than the land around it [➡ **highlands**]: *the Scottish lowlands* —**lowland** *adj* [only before noun]

low-'level *adj* **1** close to the ground: *low-level bombing attacks* **2** used about positions or jobs that are not very important [≠ **high-level**]: *rou-tine, low-level, clerical tasks*

lowly /'ləʊli $ 'loʊ-/ *adj literary* low in rank or importance: *He had a very lowly job.*

low-'lying *adj* low-lying land is not much higher than the level of the sea

low-rise *adj* [only before noun] a low-rise building does not have many levels [➡ **high-rise**]

low-tech /,ləʊ 'tek◄ $,loʊ-/ *adj* not using the most modern machines or methods [≠ **high-tech**]

loyal /'lɔɪəl/ *adj* always supporting your friends, beliefs, country etc [≠ **disloyal**]: *a loyal friend* | *his loyal supporters* | **+to** *soldiers who remain loyal to the president* → see box at **CHARAC-TER**

loyalist /'lɔɪəlᵻst/ *n* [C] someone who continues to support a government or country, especially during a period of change: *loyalist troops* —**loyalist** *adj*

loyalty /'lɔɪəlti/ *n plural* **loyalties 1** [U] when someone always supports someone or some-thing: *The company demands loyalty from its workers.* **2** [C usually plural] a feeling of sup-port for someone or something: *My loyalties lie with my family.* | *I wasn't sure where his politi-cal loyalties lay.*

lozenge /'lɒzᵻndʒ $ 'lɑː-/ *n* [C] a small SWEET containing medicine

LP /,el 'piː/ *n* [C] *old-fashioned* **long playing record** a record that plays for about 25 minutes on each side [= **album**]

L-plate /'el pleɪt/ *n* [C] a red letter 'L' put on a car in Britain to show that the driver is learning to drive

LSD /,el es 'diː/ *n* [U] an illegal drug that makes people see things that are not really there

Ltd the written abbreviation of **limited company**, used after the names of companies [➡ **plc**]: *Bark-ers Tools Ltd*

lubricant /'luːbrᵻkənt/ *n* [C,U] a substance such as oil that is put on things that rub together, making them move more smoothly

lubricate /'luːbrᵻkeɪt/ *v* [T] to put a substance such as oil on something so that it will move more smoothly

lucid /'luːsᵻd/ *adj* **1** clear and easy to under-stand: *a lucid and interesting article* **2** able to think clearly

luck /lʌk/ *n* [U]

1 good things that happen by chance: *Have you had any luck finding a job?* | *I'm not having much luck with this.* | *a combination of hard work and good luck* | **bit/piece/stroke of luck** *We had an unexpected stroke of luck.* | **with (any/a bit of) luck** *With any luck, he won't be home yet.* | *Wish me luck for the exam.*

You can use **have** with **luck** only when luck has something before it such as 'bad', 'good', 'any', 'a bit of' etc: *I've had a bit of luck today!*
Or you can use **be** with **lucky**: *You're lucky to live by the sea.*
You cannot say you 'have luck to do something'.
Never say 'a luck'. You must say a **bit/piece/stroke of luck**: *What a piece of luck!*

2 bad/terrible/rotten etc luck bad things that happen to someone by chance: *He's had terrible luck with injuries this season.* | *They believe it brings bad luck.*
3 the way in which good or bad things happen to people by chance: *It's just a matter of luck, there's nothing we can do.*
4 good luck/best of luck *spoken* used to say that you hope someone is successful: **+with** *Good luck with the competition!*
5 be in/out of luck to be lucky or unlucky: *You're in luck – there's one ticket left.*
6 bad/hard/tough luck *spoken* used to express sympathy for someone when something bad has happened

lucky /'lʌki/ *adj* someone who is lucky has good luck, and something that is lucky happens because of good luck [= **fortunate**; ≠ **unlucky**]: *'I just got the last bus.' 'That was lucky!'* | **be lucky**

to be/do/have sth *You're lucky to have such a caring husband.* | *We're lucky to still be alive!* | *I was* **lucky enough** *to see them live in concert.* | **+if** *You'll be lucky if you get that far.* | *The boys* **had a lucky escape** (=were fortunate that nothing bad happened to them). | *the* **lucky winner** *of $10,000* → see box at **LUCK**
—**luckily** *adv: Luckily, I had my keys with me.*

lucrative /'lu:krətɪv/ *adj formal* a lucrative job or activity is one that you earn a lot of money from

ludicrous /'lu:dɪkrəs/ *adj* stupid, wrong, and unreasonable [= **ridiculous**]: *a ludicrous suggestion* —**ludicrously** *adv*

lug /lʌg/ *v* [T] **lugged, lugging** *informal* to pull or carry something heavy: *We lugged our suitcases up to our room.*

luggage /'lʌgɪdʒ/ *n* [U] the bags that you carry when you are travelling [= **baggage** *AmE*]

> **GRAMMAR**
>
> **Luggage** does not have a plural form. You can say **some luggage**, **any luggage**, or **pieces of luggage**: *Do you have any more luggage?*

'luggage rack *n* [C] **1** a shelf in a train, bus etc for putting luggage on **2** *AmE* a special frame on top of a car that you tie luggage on [= **roof rack** *BrE*]

lugubrious /lu:'gu:briəs/ *adj literary* very sad and serious

lukewarm /ˌlu:k'wɔ:m◂ $ -'wɔ:rm◂/ *adj* **1** a liquid that is lukewarm is only slightly warm: *lukewarm water* **2** not showing very much interest or excitement: *a lukewarm response*

lull¹ /lʌl/ *v* [T] **1** to make someone feel calm and SLEEPY: *Singing softly, she lulled us to sleep.* **2** to make someone feel safe so that they can easily be tricked: **lull sb into (doing) sth** *She was lulled into believing that there was no danger.*

lull² *n* [C] a short period when there is less activity or noise than usual: *a lull in the conversation*

lullaby /'lʌləbaɪ/ *n* [C] plural **lullabies** a song that you sing to children to make them sleep

lumber¹ /'lʌmbə $ -ər/ *v* **1** [I] to move slowly and heavily: **+along/towards etc** *The bear lumbered towards us.* **2 get/be lumbered with sth** to be given a job or responsibility that you do not want: *I got lumbered with looking after my brother.*

lumber² *n* [U] *especially AmE* wood that is used for building

luminous /'lu:mɪnəs/ *adj* able to shine in the dark

lump¹ /lʌmp/ *n* [C]

1 a small irregular piece of something: **+of** *a lump of mud* | *a huge lump of cheese* → see picture at **PIECE**
2 a hard swelling on someone's skin or in their body: *She found a lump in her breast.*
3 a lump in your throat a feeling that you want to cry

lump² *v* [T] to put two or more different people or things together and consider them as a single group: **lump sth together/with sth** *All the costs have been lumped together.*

lump 'sum *n* [C] an amount of money given in a single payment: *You'll receive a lump sum of £50,000.*

lumpy /'lʌmpi/ *adj* with a lot of lumps: *a lumpy mattress*

lunacy /'lu:nəsi/ *n* [U] behaviour that seems completely crazy: *It would be* **sheer lunacy** *to give up college now.*

lunar /'lu:nə $ -ər/ *adj* relating to the moon [→ **solar**]: *a lunar eclipse*

lunatic /'lu:nətɪk/ *n* [C] someone who behaves in a stupid or crazy way that can be dangerous —**lunatic** *adj*

lunch¹ /lʌntʃ/ *n* [C,U] a meal that you eat in the middle of the day: *We* **had lunch** *before we left.* | *Thank you for the delicious lunch.* | **for lunch** *What's for lunch?* | **at lunch** *I think she's at lunch right now.* | **lunch break/hour** (=a time when you stop working or studying to have lunch)

> **COLLOCATIONS**
>
> **have/eat lunch**
> **have sth for lunch** – to eat a particular food for lunch
> **go out for lunch** – to go to eat lunch in a restaurant, bar etc
> **take sb out to lunch** – to take someone to a restaurant, bar etc for lunch and pay the bill
> **be at lunch** – not to be working, because you are having lunch
> **break for lunch** – to stop working in order to eat lunch
> **packed lunch** *BrE*, **bag lunch** *AmE* – food that you take to work, school etc for lunch, for example sandwiches
> **light lunch** – a small meal for lunch
> **working lunch** – lunch that you eat while you are working with other people
> → **MEAL**

lunch² *v* [I] *formal* to eat lunch

luncheon /'lʌntʃən/ *n* [C,U] *formal* lunch

lunchtime /'lʌntʃtaɪm/ *n* [C,U] the time in the middle of the day when people usually eat lunch: *I'll give you a call at lunchtime.*

lung /lʌŋ/ *n* [C] one of two organs in your body that you use for breathing → see picture on page A3

lunge /lʌndʒ/ *v* [I] to make a sudden movement towards someone or something, often to attack them: **+forward/at/towards** *Greg lunged forward to grab her arm.* —**lunge** *n* [C]

lurch¹ /lɜ:tʃ $ lɜ:rtʃ/ *v* [I] to move in an unsteady or uncontrolled way: **+across/along etc** *He lurched drunkenly towards us.*

lurch² *n* **1 leave sb in the lurch** to leave someone in a very difficult situation **2** [singular] when something or someone moves in an unsteady or uncontrolled way

lure¹ /lʊə, ljʊə $ lʊr/ *v* [T] to persuade or trick someone into doing something by making it seem attractive or exciting: *Salesmen who lure people into spending large amounts of money.*

lure² *n* [singular] when something attracts people: *the lure of huge profits*

lurid /'lʊərɪd, 'ljʊərɪd $ 'lʊrɪd/ *adj* **1** deliberately shocking and involving sex or violence: *a*

L

lurid description of the murder **2** too brightly coloured: *a lurid green dress*

lurk /lɜːk $ lɜːrk/ *v* [I] to wait somewhere secretly, usually before doing something bad: *I was scared that someone might be lurking in the bushes.*

luscious /'lʌʃəs/ *adj* very good to eat or drink: *luscious ripe strawberries*

lush /lʌʃ/ *adj* having a lot of green and healthy plants or leaves: *lush green fields*

lust[1] /lʌst/ *n* [U] **1** a very strong feeling of sexual desire **2** strong desire to have something, such as power or money: **+for** *his lust for glory* **3 lust for life** when someone has a lot of energy and seems to enjoy life very much

lust[2] *v* [I] **1 lust after sb** to have a strong feeling of sexual desire for someone **2 lust after/for sth** to want something very much: *politicians who lust after power*

lustre *BrE*; **luster** *AmE* /'lʌstə $ -ər/ *n* [singular, U] an attractive shiny appearance

lusty /'lʌsti/ *adj* strong and healthy

luxuriant /lʌg'zjʊəriənt, ləg'ʒʊəriənt $ ləg'ʒʊriənt/ *adj formal* hair that is or plants that are luxuriant are growing thickly and strongly

luxurious /lʌg'zjʊəriəs, ləg'ʒʊəriəs $ ləg'ʒʊriəs/ *adj* very comfortable, beautiful, and expensive: *a luxurious hotel*

luxury /'lʌkʃəri/ *n plural* **luxuries**
1 [U] great comfort and pleasure, especially from beautiful or expensive things: *They lived a life of luxury.* | **in luxury** *They now live in luxury in Switzerland.* | *We never had much money for luxury goods.* | **luxury car/home/hotel etc** (=large and expensive)
2 [C] something expensive that you want but do not need [≠ **necessity**]: *luxuries like chocolate and perfume* | *A holiday is a luxury we can't afford.*
3 afford/have/enjoy the luxury of sth to have or do something pleasant: *They don't have the luxury of choosing where to live.*

-ly /li/ *suffix* in a particular way: *She dressed quickly.* | *He is financially dependent on his parents.*

Lycra /'laɪkrə/ *n* [U] *trademark* a material that is used especially for making sports clothes that fit tightly, because it moves with your body

lying /'laɪ-ɪŋ/ *v* the present participle of LIE

lynch /lɪntʃ/ *v* [T] if a crowd of people lynches someone they think is guilty of a crime, they kill them without a TRIAL —**lynching** *n* [C]

lyrical /'lɪrɪkəl/ *adj* expressing feelings in a beautiful way: *lyrical poetry*

lyrics /'lɪrɪks/ *n* [plural] the words of a song: *a simple melody and great lyrics*

L

PICTURE DICTIONARY

LEARNER'S HANDBOOK

tail feathers

beak

webbed foot

throat

breast

claw

talon

antler

whiskers

fang

horn

fur

front leg

hind leg

paw

claw

tusk

trunk

pouch

hooves

antenna

wing

tail

scales

fin

chrysalis

gill

larva/grub

eggs

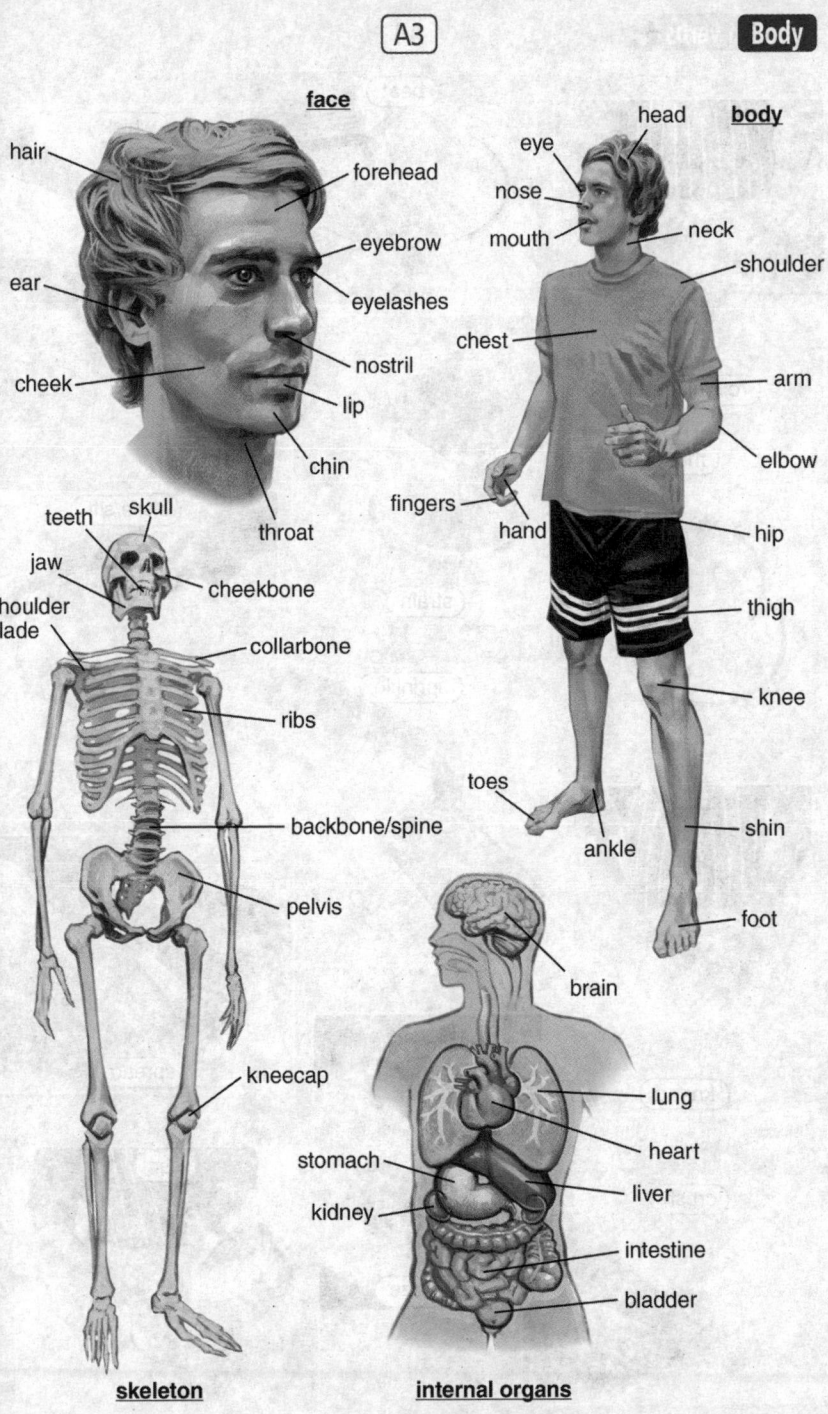

face

hair
forehead
eyebrow
eyelashes
ear
nostril
cheek
lip
chin
throat

body

head
eye
nose
mouth
neck
shoulder
chest
arm
elbow
fingers
hand
hip
thigh
knee
toes
ankle
shin
foot

skeleton

teeth
skull
jaw
cheekbone
shoulder blade
collarbone
ribs
backbone/spine
pelvis
kneecap

internal organs

brain
lung
heart
stomach
liver
kidney
intestine
bladder

Kitchen verbs

beat

whisk

roll/roll out

mix

strain

sieve/sift

sprinkle

spread

knead

squeeze

crush

stir

kebabs *BrE*/kabobs *AmE*

salad

popcorn

chilli

lasagne *BrE*/lasagna *AmE*

soup

roast chicken

lemon tart

macaroni cheese

muffins

souffle

spaghetti

biscuits *BrE*/cookies *AmE*

pancakes

stir-fry

quiche

waffles

pork chop

barbecued steak

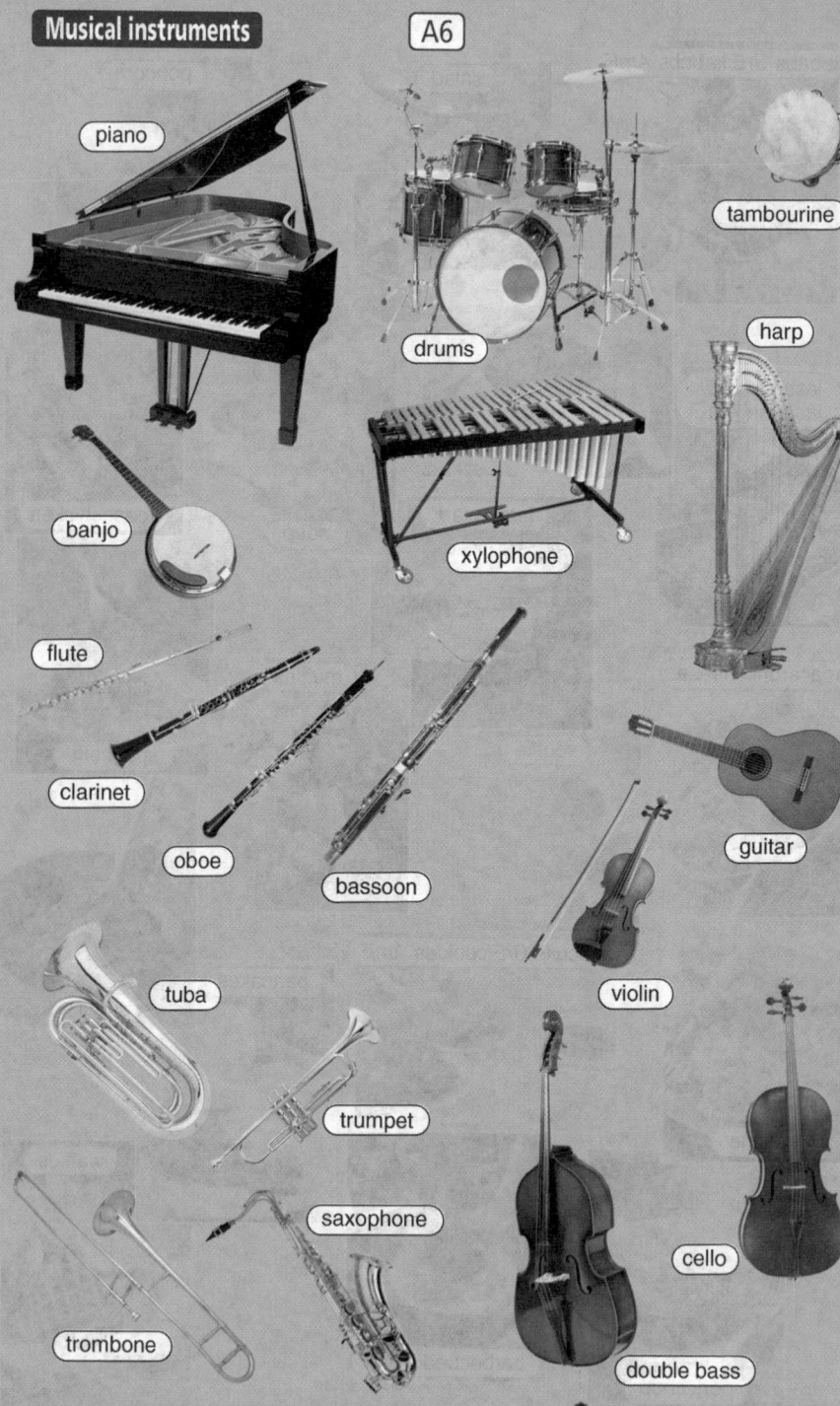

Musical instruments

A6

piano

drums

tambourine

harp

banjo

xylophone

flute

clarinet

oboe

bassoon

guitar

violin

tuba

trumpet

saxophone

cello

double bass

trombone

ring

tick

crash

squeak

creak

bang

splash

buzz

rustle

rattle

crunch

click

fizz

sizzle

hiss

crackle

1. A girl is walking **towards** the fountain.
2. There's a boy walking **across** the street.
3. There's a girl **inside** the telephone box.
4. The car park (parking lot *AmE*) is **behind** the fire station.
5. Some children are **in front of** the bakery.
6. A little boy is standing **beside** his mother.
7. A boy is walking **down** the steps of the library.
8. The bank is **opposite** the department store.
9. There's an ambulance **outside** the hospital.
10. The mechanic is **under** the car.

11. A man is going **into** the CD shop.
12. A boy is leaning **against** a wall.
13. The post office is **next to** the chemist's (drugstore *AmE*).
14. There's a motorbike **between** two parked cars.
15. The window cleaner is climbing **up** the ladder.
16. Pigeons are perched **on** a lamp-post.
17. A car is going **over** the bridge.
18. A car is going **round** the roundabout (traffic circle *AmE*).
19. There's a restaurant **above** the florist's.
    The florist's is **below** the restaurant.
20. A bus is going **through** the tunnel.

surfing

sailing

kayaking

windsurfing

rowing

hang gliding

parachuting

mountain biking

gliding

scuba diving

climbing

cycling

swimming

skiing

ice hockey

speed skating

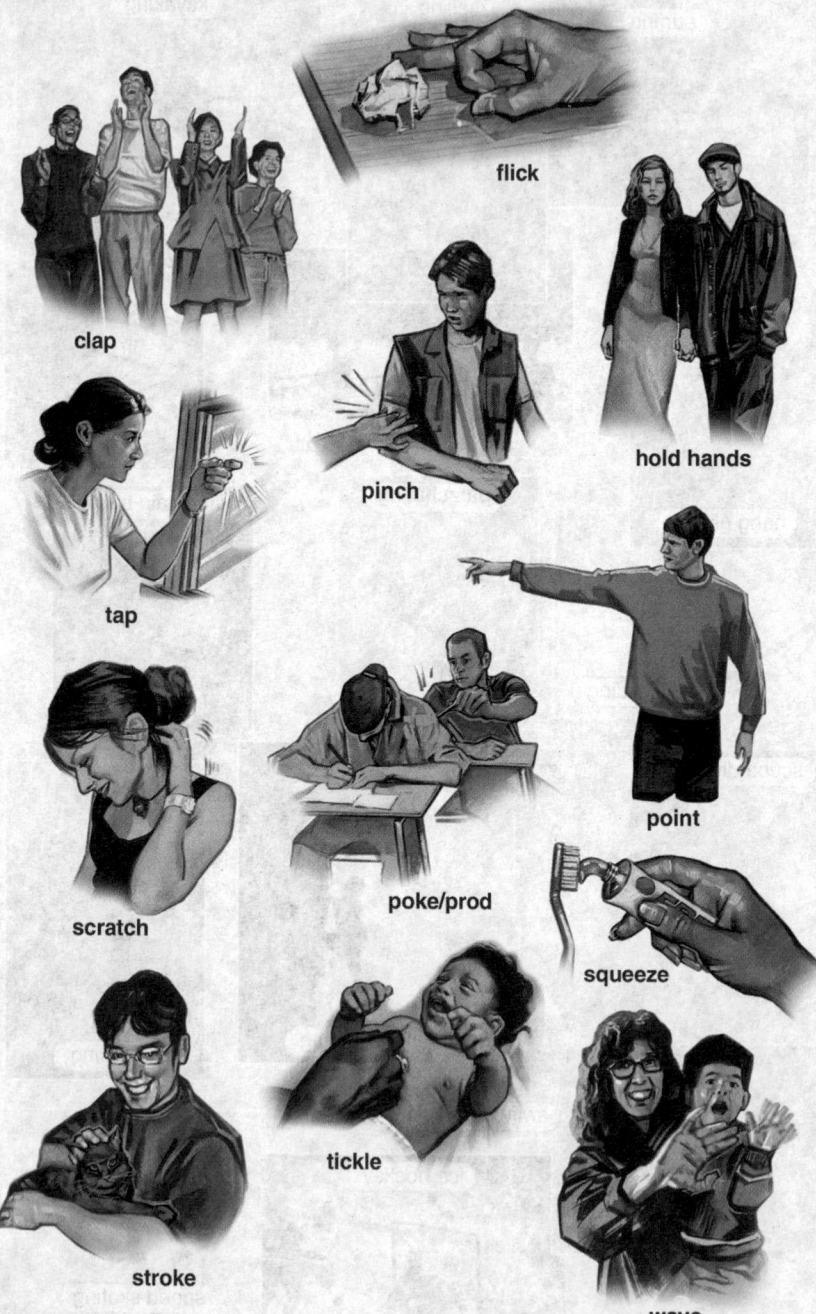

flick

clap

pinch

hold hands

tap

scratch

poke/prod

point

squeeze

stroke

tickle

wave

Verbs of movement (body)

pick up

put down

lift

carry

hold

stretch

bend

squat

kneel

hop

skip

jump

lean

crouch

drag

push

pull

drop

climb

fall

jog

walk

march

sit

crawl

tiptoe

run

throw

kick

hit

punch

catch

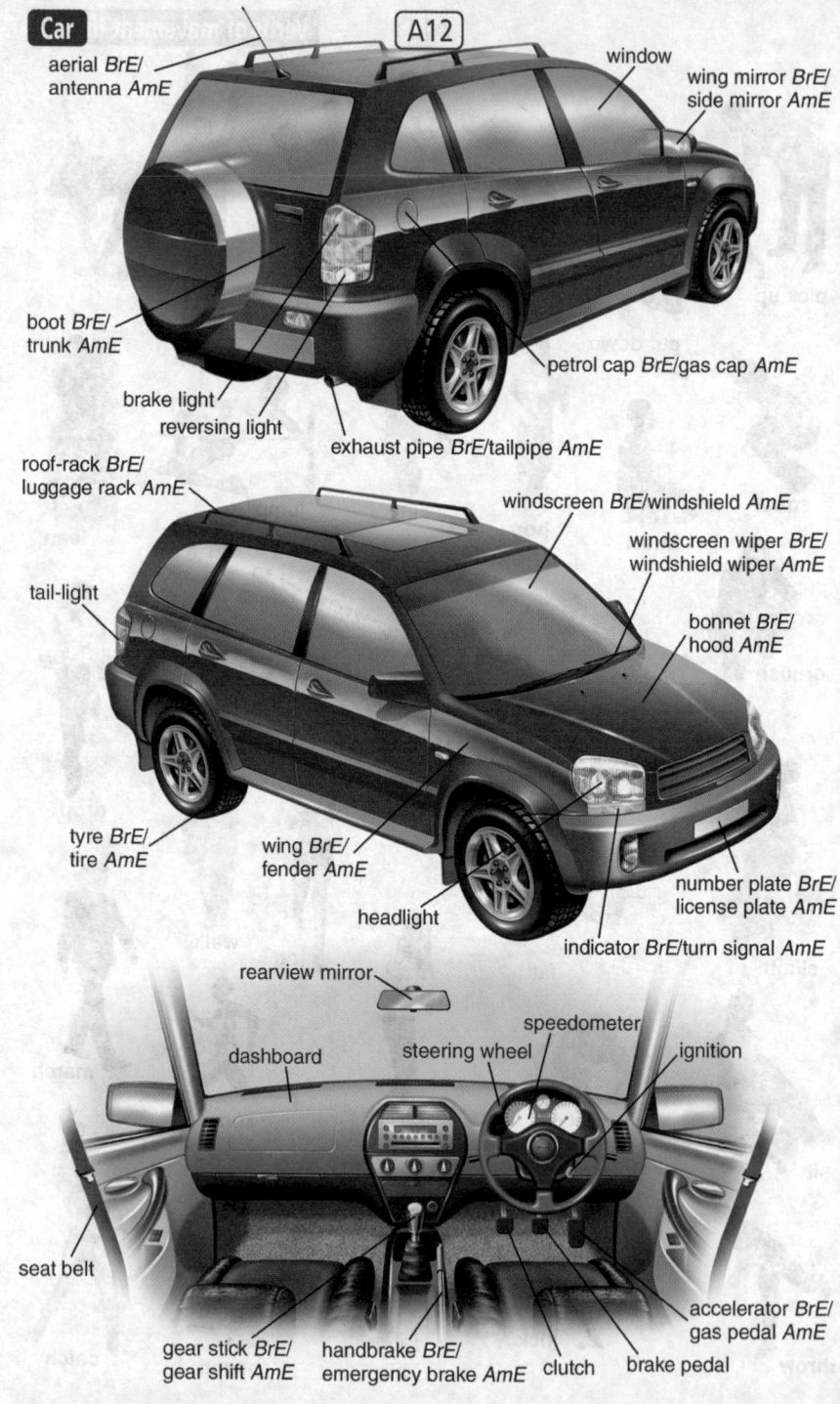

Car A12

aerial *BrE*/antenna *AmE*

window

wing mirror *BrE*/side mirror *AmE*

boot *BrE*/trunk *AmE*

brake light

reversing light

petrol cap *BrE*/gas cap *AmE*

exhaust pipe *BrE*/tailpipe *AmE*

roof-rack *BrE*/luggage rack *AmE*

windscreen *BrE*/windshield *AmE*

windscreen wiper *BrE*/windshield wiper *AmE*

tail-light

bonnet *BrE*/hood *AmE*

tyre *BrE*/tire *AmE*

wing *BrE*/fender *AmE*

headlight

number plate *BrE*/license plate *AmE*

indicator *BrE*/turn signal *AmE*

rearview mirror

speedometer

steering wheel

ignition

dashboard

seat belt

gear stick *BrE*/gear shift *AmE*

handbrake *BrE*/emergency brake *AmE*

clutch

brake pedal

accelerator *BrE*/gas pedal *AmE*

WORKBOOK

Finding words in the dictionary

Exercise 1

To find a word in the dictionary, you will need to know the correct spelling, especially the first two or three letters. If you can't find a word, you may have got the spelling wrong. Think what other spellings may be possible.

These words all contain spelling mistakes in the first two or three letters. What are the correct spellings?

1 fotograph   3 rinkle   5 yuseless   7 shugar
2 sissors   4 nitwear   6 fewtile   8 enyway

Exercise 2

The dictionary lists words in alphabetical order. Write these groups of words in alphabetical order.

1 foggy `1`   nose `4`   unless `6`   kind `3`   guess `2`   skinny `5`
2 vote ☐   scrap ☐   develop ☐   tense ☐   forget ☐   slap ☐
3 trunk ☐   trip ☐   trinket ☐   thread ☐   turtle ☐   trestle ☐
4 feisty ☐   flutter ☐   flashy ☐   freckle ☐   fluff ☐   florid ☐

Exercise 3

Some words are made from other words. For example, the adjective motivated comes from the verb motivate, so it appears in the same entry.

The following words do not have separate entries in this dictionary. Which main entry would you go to to find them?

1 greatness   _great_   5 poisoner   ....
2 genuinely   ....   6 transparently ....
3 impatience   ....   7 uncertainly   ....
4 encouragement ....   8 critically   ....

Active words

Exercise 4

Some entries begin with a word that is red. These are the *Active words*. They are the most important words to learn and remember.

In the following groups of words, one word is *not* an Active word and is less frequently used than the other words. Circle the word which is not an active word.

1 ask explore [seek] search   3 part piece section segment
2 beautiful stunning handsome lovely   4 belief creed opinion view

Checking spellings

Exercise 5

Use the dictionary to check words if you are unsure of their spelling.

Each of the following words has one letter missing. Correct the spelling. Look the words up in the dictionary if necessary.

1 bound^ary   _boundary_   5 accomodation ....
2 frige ....   6 relable ....
3 matress ....   7 disatisfied ....
4 forsee ....   8 forteen ....

Word classes

Exercise 6

The dictionary tells you the grammatical function of each word. These functions are called 'word classes' or 'parts of speech'.

What word classes do the following words belong to?

1 an   _noun_
2 soccer   _pronoun_
3 hot   _verb_
4 slowly   _preposition_
5 us   _determiner_
6 however   _adverb_
7 speak   _adjective_
8 into   _linking word_

Exercise 7

Sometimes the same word may have more than one part of speech. There is an entry for each different grammatical function of the same word. If you see a small raised number after the main word that begins an entry (crisp¹), it means there is more than one entry for this word.

Read the sentences and circle the correct word class for the word in bold type.

1 I'm sorry, but your new Picasso is actually a fake.   _noun_ / verb
2 The police found fake passports and identity papers.   adjective / verb
3 Crocodiles can run incredibly fast.   adjective / adverb
4 She's a fast runner.   noun / adjective
5 We need to map out the various options.   noun / verb
6 The man in the tourist office gave us a map.   noun / adjective
7 Will you clear away all this rubbish, please?   verb / adjective
8 He doesn't like children. He's made that perfectly clear.   noun / adjective
9 They put some chemical in to kill the bacteria.   noun / adjective
10 A chemical reaction occurs when the two substances are mixed. verb / adjective

11 We've had to put poison down for the rats. *noun / adjective*
12 I thought he was trying to poison us with his home-made wine. *verb / noun*

13 Buying that puppy was a big mistake. *adjective / noun*
14 People often mistake me for my brother. *verb / adjective*

15 The exchange rate has reached an all-time low. *noun / verb*
16 He crouched down low so no one would see him. *adjective / adverb*

Irregular verbs

Exercise 8

For all irregular verbs, the dictionary gives the past tense, the past participle and the present participle (see the irregular verbs table on page 867).

Complete this chart of irregular verbs. If necessary, check the verbs in the dictionary by looking up the infinitive form.

Infinitive	Past tense	Past participle	Present participle
bring	brought	brought	bringing
draw	drew	drawn	1 ...drawing...
feed	2	fed	feeding
forget	3	4	forgetting
shine	shone	5	shining
6	swept	swept	sweeping

Pronunciation

Exercise 9

Learning to read the International Phonetic Alphabet (IPA) will help you with pronunciation, since the normal spellings of English words do not always show you how to say them. Pronunciations are given in IPA at the beginning of each dictionary entry. The pronunciation table can be found on the inside back cover of this dictionary.

Can you read these words?

1 'sɪnᵻmə ...cinema...
2 naɪf ....
3 streɪndʒ ....
4 kjuːt ....
5 'kwɪkli ....
6 fəˈnetɪks ....

Exercise 10

Circle the correct pronunciation of these six words.

1 chips tʃɪps / tʃɪpz
2 useful 'uːsfel / 'juːsfəl
3 blue bloʊ / bluː
4 gorgeous 'ɡɔːdʒəs / 'ɡɔːdʒəz
5 houses 'haʊzᵻz / 'haʊsᵻz
6 sword swɔːrd / sɔːd

Exercise 11

There are many irregularities in English spelling. Words can sound the same yet be spelled differently. Find the pairs of rhyming words in these lists.

1 ball — straight
2 bread — drum
3 drain — fed
4 laughter — sneeze
5 night — crawl
6 plate — white
7 tease — after
8 thumb — plane

Stress

Exercise 12

If a word has two or more syllables we put a stress on one of the syllables. The phonetics in this dictionary show you which syllable is stressed. The symbol /'/ appears before the stressed syllable. For example, the phonetic transcription of *discuss*, [dɪ'skʌs], shows that the second syllable is stressed.

Circle the stressed syllable in the following words.

1 de(cide)
2 difficulty
3 embarrass
4 explode
5 marvellous
6 responsible
7 retrospect
8 underestimate

Exercise 13

Words may change their stress when they are used for different grammatical functions. Read these sentences and circle the correct stress pattern for the words in bold type.

1 These T-shirts are cheap because they are rejects.   reJECTS / REjects
2 The body may reject the transplanted organ.   REject / reJECT
3 The weather was perfect.   perFECT / PERfect
4 They have perfected a technique for recycling plastic. perFECted / PERfected
5 There has been a sharp increase in car thefts.   inCREASE / INcrease
6 Unless we increase profitability, the company will not survive. INcrease / inCREASE
7 You need a special permit to park here.   PERmit / perMIT
8 Foreign travel was only permitted under certain circumstances. perMITted / PERmitted

Countable and uncountable nouns

Exercise 14

Most English nouns (like *chair*, *house* and *computer*) have plural forms (*chairs*, *houses*, *computers*). These are called *countables* and are marked [C] in this dictionary. Nouns that don't have plurals (*laughter*, *money*, *information*) are *uncountables* and are marked [U].

Is the noun in red type countable or uncountable? Write [C] or [U].

1 Why do you have so many keys?   C

2 I need your advice.   ☐

3 Have you had any news from Jeremy?   ☐

4 What an extraordinary coincidence!   ☐

5 I'm having trouble with my car.   ☐

6 We need to buy more bread.   ☐

7 Shall we have pizza tonight?   ☐

8 I'd like three pizzas to take away.   ☐

Irregular plurals

Exercise 15

To form the plural of nouns in English, we usually add -s or -es to the singular form.
A few nouns have irregular plurals. These irregular forms are always shown in the
dictionary at the beginning of the entry.

Here are eight irregular plural nouns. What are their singular forms?

1 men ....*man*........   5 mice ....

2 feet ....   6 knives ....

3 fish ....   7 children ....

4 teeth ....   8 sheep ....

British English and American English

Exercise 16

People in Britain may not understand you if you use the word *faucet*. *Faucet* is only
used in American English. In Britain, people call a 'faucet' a *tap*. Words which are used
only in British English or in American English are marked *BrE* and *AmE* in this dictionary.

In the lists below, match the *AmE* words with their *BrE* equivalents.

AmE	BrE
1 faucet	petrol
2 freeway	diaper
3 gas	tap
4 movie theater	roundabout
5 pants	motorway
6 baby carriage	pram
7 traffic circle	trousers
8 nappy	cinema

Exercise 17

There are small differences between *AmE* and *BrE* spelling. In your written English, try to be consistent and always use either British or American spellings.

These eight words are all *AmE* spellings. How are the *BrE* spellings different?

1 center   *centre*   5 glamor   ....
2 colorful   ....   6 centimeter   ....
3 favorite   ....   7 traveled   ....
4 fulfill   ....   8 TV program   ....

Understanding definitions

Exercise 18

The definitions in this dictionary use a selected vocabulary of 2000 words. This means that even definitions of difficult words are easy to understand.

The following verbs all describe ways of walking. Try and match them to the definitions below.

| creep | rush | skip | sprint | stagger | stride | stroll |

1 to walk with quick long steps   *stride*
2 to move very quietly so that no one will notice you   ....
3 to walk in a slow relaxed way   ....
4 to walk or move in an unsteady way, almost falling over   ....
5 to move forwards with little jumps between your steps   ....
6 to move or go somewhere quickly   ....

Words with more than one meaning

Exercise 19

Many words in English have more than one meaning. Different meanings are listed separately in the entry, each preceded by a number in bold type: **1, 2, 3** ...

When a word has more than one word class, you will find completely separate entries for each function.

Read the following pairs of definitions. Each pair refers to the same word, but used in different meanings. What is the word?

| fair | fine | flat | fly | last | park | star | sweet |

1 *n* a small insect with two wings
  v to travel somewhere by plane   } 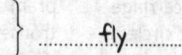 *fly*

2   *n BrE* a set of rooms for someone to live in
      that is part of a larger building
   adj smooth and level, without any raised
      parts
           ....

3   *n* a large ball of burning gas in space that you
      can see as a point of light in the night sky
   n a famous actor, singer, sports player, etc.
           ....

4   *adj* kind, gentle and friendly
   adj having a taste like sugar
           ....

5   *n* a large area with grass and trees in a town, where
      people walk, play games, etc.
   v to put your car somewhere for a period of time
           ....

6   *n* money that you pay as a punishment for breaking
      a law or rule
   adj satisfactory or acceptable
           ....

7   *n* a form of outdoor entertainment where you can ride
      on exciting machines and play games to win prizes
   adj reasonable, right, and accepted by most people
           ....

8   *adj* most recent
   v to continue for a particular length of time
           ....

Exercise 20

The different meanings of words are listed in order of frequency. The first definition shows the most frequently used meaning of the word, but read all the meanings to make sure you have found the right one.

Read these pairs of sentences. Tick the sentence which illustrates the more frequent use of the word in **bold** type.

1 a Most schools do not place enough **emphasis** on health education. ✔

   b The **emphasis** should go on the word "would". ☐

2 a 'Air France flight 519 is now boarding at **Gate** 15.' ☐

   b Fred left the **gate** open and the dog ran off. ☐

3 a He was wearing a **light** blue shirt. ☐

   b I'll only want a **light** meal. ☐

4 a I plan to study **medicine**. ☐

   b Don't forget to take your **medicine**. ☐

5 a **Pick** a card but don't show it to me. ☐

   b He **picked** all the cherries off the cake. ☐

6 a **Selling** the idea to the boss could be difficult. ☐

   b I **sold** my scooter to a girl in my class. ☐

Vocabulary building (Thesaurus boxes)

Exercise 21

The Thesaurus boxes in this dictionary help students to build their vocabulary by grouping together words on a particular topic or which are similar in meaning.

Go to the Thesaurus box at the word group, read the definitions for the various nouns, then look at the exercise below without referring to the Thesaurus box.

| gang   flock   bunch   crowd |

Fill in the gaps with a suitable noun from the list above.

1 A .... of seagulls followed the fishing boat back to the shore.
2 A huge .... gathered in the main city square protesting against the war.
3 Violence between .... is one of the main reasons for such high crime levels.
4 I'll send her a .... of roses to say thank you.

Exercise 22

This time go to the Thesaurus box at the word bad, read the definitions for the various adjectives then look at the exercise below without referring to the Thesaurus box.

| horrific   atrocious   lousy   abysmal |

Fill in the gaps with a suitable noun from the list above.

1 It was a .... book, a real disappointment in fact.
2 I'm staying at home today, the weather is .... outside.
3 Unemployment figures were released today and they are really ....
4 There was a .... accident on the motorway this morning.

Word combinations (Collocation boxes)

Exercise 23

Collocations are pairs or groups of words that are frequently used together. For example the verb commit is often used with the noun crime. You can find collocation boxes throughout the dictionary that give important information to learn in order to sound natural in English.

verbs and nouns

The words in red below have their own Collocation box in the dictionary. Study the relevant Collocation boxes then choose a verb from the box below and use it in the correct form to complete these sentences.

| nod | rent | go | study | call | send out | receive | have |

1 We're leaving soon. Can you .... a cab?
2 I am expecting to .... an **email** with the details of the meeting.
3 They .... to **jail** for burglary and fraud.
4 If we .... the **map** carefully we should find our way back to the campsite.
5 I'm going to .... a **video** and have a quiet night in.
6 They .... over fifty **invitations** for their party.
7 She .... her **head** to show that she understood the question.
8 Have you already .... **lunch**?

Exercise 24

adjectives and nouns
The words in red below have their own Collocation box in the dictionary. Fill in the gaps with suitable adjectives from the Collocation boxes.

1 I really regret leaving my job now. I think it was a .... **opportunity**.
2 Inflation and unemployment are both high. The .... **situation** is very poor.
3 I am sure that this young couple will have a very .... **marriage**.
4 I take a .... **lunch** to school with me every day.
5 It isn't so difficult. It's a fairly .... **task**.
6 There are only four of us in my .... **family**.
7 His car wasn't outside – a .... **sign** that he'd already left.
8 I felt a .... **pain** and knew immediately that my leg was broken.

Prepositions

Exercise 25

The dictionary shows many examples of the way prepositions are used. Choose the correct preposition for these sentences. Compare your answers to the examples given in the dictionary.

| after | at | behind | by | in | in front of | through | under |

1 Have you read any books ......**by**...... Charles Dickens?
2 She smiled .... me.
3 We crouched .... a wall to avoid the gunfire.
4 She walked out halfway .... the film.
5 I couldn't see because a tall man was standing .... me.

6 He was driving _____ the influence of alcohol.

7 She's been _____ a bad mood all day.

8 I don't like walking home _____ dark.

Modal verbs

Exercise 26

Write the correct modal in these sentences.

can	could	may	must	shall	should	will	would

1 _____Could_____ you help me move this wardrobe?

2 They're both excellent players. It _____ be a good match.

3 We _____ not have time to go to the museum.

4 He _____ be very obstinate, I find.

5 You _____ be tired after that long journey.

6 I'm sure she _____ love your present.

7 I _____ love to see the inside of Buckingham Palace.

8 _____ we take a picnic?

Phrasal verbs

Exercise 27

At the end of the entries for many verbs, phrasal verbs are given with their definitions. Try keeping your own lists of phrasal verbs. You will be surprised how soon you start to meet verbs from your lists in different contexts.

Complete the sentences.

broke	feel	fell	run	stand	take	throw	touched

1 What does BBC _____stand_____ for?

2 John's got two exams on the same day. I really _____ for him.

3 We planned to go to Nepal but it all _____ through.

4 These eggs are six weeks old. We'd better _____ them away.

5 We need to buy some soap. And we've nearly _____ out of toilet paper.

6 I _____ after my father. We both get seasick.

7 Our bus _____ down just outside Madrid. We were stuck there for ages.

8 The plane _____ down at 12:45 – right on time!

Exercise 28

Match the definition to the phrasal verbs which appear in the previous exercise.

1 to feel sympathy for someone   *feel for*
2 to stop working   ....
3 to get rid of something that you do not want or need   ....
4 to be a short form of a word or phrase   ....
5 to look or behave like an older member of your family   ....
6 to use all of something, so that there is none left   ....
7 to fail to happen or be completed   ....
8 to land on the ground at an airport   ....

Idioms

Exercise 29

An idiom is an expression which means something different from the meanings of the separate words.

Look at these idioms. The words in red type show you where you can find the idiom. What do they mean?

1 in small **doses**
2 be up to your **eyes** in something
3 come out of your **shell**
4 on the **trot**
5 **stand** on your own two feet
6 like a **shot**
7 till the **cows** come home
8 the **slippery** slope

Which idioms can be used in the sentences below? Write the number in the box at the end of the sentence.

a I'm .... work at the moment.   `2`
b It's about time you learned to ....   ☐
c She's on .... to a life of crime.   ☐
d If I was offered the job I would take it ....   ☐
e You can argue .... , I won't change my mind.   ☐
f Manchester United won five games ....   ☐
g You need to .... and talk more about how you feel.   ☐
h Robert's funny but I can only take him ....   ☐

Transitive and intransitive verbs

Exercise 30

Many verbs normally have an object (noun or pronoun or clause). These are called 'transitive' verbs and are marked [T] in this dictionary. Examples of these verbs include *hit, see, enjoy, contain, need*.

> We can't say *Did you see?* We can say *Did you see the game yesterday?*

Many verbs do not normally have an object. These are called 'intransitive' verbs and are marked [I] in this dictionary. Examples of these verbs include *happen, wait, snow, scream, sleep, arrive, rain*.

> We can't say *Look, it's snowing* (+ object). We can only say *Look, it's snowing*.

Some verbs can be used transitively and intransitively. They are marked [I,T] in this dictionary. Examples of these verbs include *begin, drop, open, win, ring*.

> We can say *Williams won the game* (transitive) or *Williams won* (intransitive).

Put an object (noun or pronoun) after these verbs wherever possible. Which sentences include verbs that are transitive or intransitive?

1 We need ....

2 The girl screamed ....

3 I really enjoyed ....

4 I began ....

5 It's raining ....

6 Did you see .... ?

7 Has he won .... ?

8 The bag contains ....

Compound nouns

Exercise 31

Look through the dictionary and you will notice two-word entries, for example *foul play*. This is because compounds are nouns in their own right.

How many of these compounds do you recognize and understand? Try and match them to the definitions listed below.

| alarm clock | barbed wire | game show | global warming |
| hit man | old age | middle name | theme park |

1 a television programme in which people play games in order to win prizes
   game show

2 an increase in world temperatures, caused by an increase in carbon dioxide around the Earth
   ....

3 the time in your life when you are old ....

4 a criminal who is employed to kill someone ....

5 a place where you can have fun riding on big machines, which are all based on one subject such as water or space travel ....

6 the name that is between your first name and your family name ....

7 a clock that makes a noise to wake you up ....

8 wire with sharp points on it, used to stop people getting into a place

....

Interjections

Exercise 32

An interjection is a word that is used to express surprise, pleasure, pain, etc. or to attract people's attention. Do you recognize the interjections in this list? Which interjection would you use in each of the situations described below?

| er   hey   phew   shh   whoops   wow   yuck   yum |

1 You think something tastes good. ....yum.........

2 You are not sure what to say next. ....

3 You feel tired, hot or relieved. ....

4 You are telling someone to be quiet. ....

5 You've made a small mistake or you've dropped something. ....

6 You see something very impressive or surprising. ....

7 You want to get your friend's attention. ....

8 You think something is unpleasant. ....

Recording and learning vocabulary

Exercise 33

Make your own lists of words that you think will be useful or words that interest you. Organize your word lists under headings, such as

• family • sport • describing people • the street

Don't only list single words. Include

• phrasal verbs, for example take after
• adjective + noun combinations, for example (he's a) bad loser
• verb + object combinations, for example find fault (with)

List these words under the following headings: *Ways of talking*, *Personalities*, *The cinema*

| chat   confident   cult film   director   extrovert   interrupt   laid-back   multiplex   mumble   obnoxious   praise   shout   shy   special effects   subtitled   touchy   trailer   whisper |

ANSWER KEY

Exercise 1
1 photograph 2 scissors 3 wrinkle
4 knitwear 5 useless 6 futile
7 sugar 8 anyway

Exercise 2
1 foggy 1 nose 4 unless 6
kind 3 guess 2 skinny 5
2 vote 6 scrap 3 develop 1
tense 5 forget 2 slap 4
3 trunk 5 trip 4 trinket 3
thread 1 turtle 4 trestle 2
4 feisty 1 flutter 5 flashy 2
freckle 6 fluff 4 florid 3

Exercise 3
1 great 2 genuine 3 impatient
4 encourage 5 poison
6 transparent 7 uncertain
8 critical

Exercise 4
1 seek 2 stunning 3 segment
4 creed

Exercise 5
1 boundary 2 fridge 3 mattress
4 foresee 5 accommodation
6 reliable 7 dissatisfied
8 fourteen

Exercise 6
1 an – determiner 2 soccer – noun
3 hot – adjective
4 slowly – adverb 5 us – pronoun
6 however – linking word
7 speak – verb
8 into – preposition

Exercise 7
1 noun 2 adjective 3 adverb
4 adjective 5 verb 6 noun 7 verb
8 adjective 9 noun 10 adjective
11 noun 12 verb 13 noun
14 verb 15 noun 16 adverb

Exercise 8
1 drawing 2 fed 3 forgot
4 forgotten 5 shone 6 sweep

Exercise 9
1 cinema 2 knife 3 strange
4 cute 5 quickly 6 phonetics

Exercise 10
1 tʃɪps 2 ˈjuːsfəl 3 bluː
4 ˈɡɔːdʒəs 5 ˈhauzɨz 6 sɔːd

Exercise 11
1 ball – crawl 2 bread – fed
3 drain – plane 4 laughter – after
5 night – white 6 plate – straight
7 tease – sneeze 8 thumb – drum

Exercise 12
1 deCIDE 2 DIfficulty 3 emBArrass
4 exPLODE 5 MARvellous
6 resPONsible 7 RETrospect
8 underEStimate

Exercise 13
1 REjects 2 reJECT 3 PERfect
4 perFECted 5 INcrease
6 inCREASE 7 PERmit
8 perMITted

Exercise 14
1 [C] 2 [U] 3 [U] 4 [C] 5 [U] 6 [U]
7 [U] 8 [C]

Exercise 15
1 man 2 foot 3 fish 4 tooth
5 mouse 6 knife 7 child 8 sheep

Exercise 16
1 faucet – tap
2 freeway – motorway
3 gas – petrol
4 movie theater – cinema
5 pants – trousers
6 baby carriage – pram
7 traffic circle – roundabout
8 nappy – diaper

Exercise 17
1 centre 2 colourful 3 favourite
4 fulfil 5 glamour 6 centimetre
7 travelled 8 TV programme

Exercise 18
1 stride 2 creep 3 stroll 4 stagger
5 skip 6 rush

Exercise 19
1 fly 2 flat 3 star 4 sweet 5 park
6 fine 7 fair 8 last

Exercise 20
1 a 2 b 3 a 4 b 5 a 6 b

Exercise 21
1 flock 2 crowd 3 gangs 4 bunch

Exercise 22
1 lousy 2 atrocious 3 abysmal
4 horrific

Exercise 23
1 call 2 receive 3 went 4 study
5 rent 6 sent out 7 nodded
8 had

Exercise 24
1 wasted, lost, missed
2 economic, political
3 happy 4 packed, bag
5 easy, simple, straightforward
6 immediate 7 sure
8 severe, terrible, intense,
unbearable

Exercise 25
1 by 2 at 3 behind 4 through
5 in front of 6 under 7 in 8 after

Exercise 26
1 Could 2 should 3 may 4 can
5 must 6 will 7 would 8 Shall

Exercise 27
1 stand 2 feel 3 fell 4 throw
5 run 6 take 7 broke 8 touched

Exercise 28
1 feel for 2 break down
3 throw away 4 stand for
5 take after 6 run out
7 fall through 8 touch down

Exercise 29
a up to my eyes in (2)
b stand on your own two feet (5)
c the slippery slope (8)
d like a shot (6)
e till the cows come home (7)
f on the trot (4)
g come out of your shell (3)
h in small doses (1)

Exercise 30
1 [T] 2 [I] 3 [T] 4 [I,T] 5 [I] 6 [T]
7 [I,T] 8 [T]

Exercise 31
1 game show 2 global warming
3 old age 4 hit man 5 theme park
6 middle name 7 alarm clock
8 barbed wire

Exercise 32
1 yum 2 er 3 phew 4 shh
5 whoops 6 wow 7 hey 8 yuck

Exercise 33
Ways of talking: chat, interrupt,
mumble, praise, shout, whisper
Personalities: confident, extrovert,
laid-back, obnoxious, shy, touchy
The cinema: cult film, director,
multiplex, special effects,
subtitled, trailer

LANGUAGE NOTES

Articles

The articles in English are a or an, and the. Which article you choose depends on what you are talking about.

When to use *the*

- When it is clear what you are talking about:
  I cannot go to the party. (= the person you are talking to knows about the party)

- When you refer to a particular thing or when there is only one thing of this kind:
  I live in the house with the blue door. (= there is only one house like this)
  The sun shone all day. (= there is only one sun)

When to use *a or an*

- When you refer to something for the first time and when it may not be clear what you are talking about:
  Would you like to go to a party? (= the person you are talking to does not know about the party yet)

- When you are talking about one of several things in a general way:
  I live in a house with a blue door. (= there is more than one house like this)

- When you talk about a particular type of thing or person:
  My mother is a doctor.　　*I need a new umbrella.*

a or an?

- You use an instead of a before a word which starts with a vowel:
  - ✗ I saw a̶ elephant.　　　✗ I saw a̶n̶ big elephant.
  - ✔ I saw an elephant.　　　✔ I saw a big elephant.

- Because whether you choose a or an depends on pronunciation, not spelling, a also changes to an before a consonant which is pronounced as a vowel:
  - ✗ I arrived a̶ hour early.　　✔ I arrived an hour early.

- When a word begins with 'u', whether you use a or an depends on how the 'u' is pronounced. If the 'u' is pronounced /juː/, like in 'you', you do not change the a to an:
  - ✗ A̶ unfinished essay　　✗ A̶n̶ university professor
  - ✔ An unfinished essay　　✔ A university professor

REMEMBER

1 Use *an*, not *a*, before a word that begins with a vowel sound: *an apple*
2 Do not use *a/an* before an adjective unless it is followed by a noun: *a green apple*
3 Do not use *a/an/the* before uncountable nouns: *a glass of milk, She's learning French.*
4 Always use an article before the name of a job or profession: *He's a banker.*
5 Do not use *a/an* before a plural noun: *the dogs/some dogs*

→ You can Test Yourself on a or an by doing the exercises on the CD-ROM
　See also **Language note** on **Countable and uncountable nouns**.

Countable and uncountable nouns

Countable nouns

Things that you can count are called **countable nouns**. These are often (but not always) objects such as *apple* and *house*:

an apple   two apples   a house   six houses

In this dictionary, countable nouns appear with a label like this: **[C]**

REMEMBER

1 Countable nouns can be both singular (*chair*) and plural (*chairs*).
2 A countable noun in the singular is almost always used with a determiner (a word like *a*, *another*, *the*).
3 A plural countable noun is not always used with a determiner. For example, when you are talking in general about something, *the* is not used: *Boys are noisier than girls.*
4 When the noun is singular, the following verb is also singular: *A chair has four legs.* When the noun is plural, the following verb is also plural: *Chairs have four legs.*

Uncountable nouns

Things that you cannot count are called **uncountable nouns**. Uncountable nouns are usually the names of substances (such as *water*, *grass*), qualities (such as *happiness*), collections (such as *furniture*, *money*) and other things which we do not see as individual objects (such as *electricity*).

In this dictionary, uncountable nouns appear with a label like this: **[U]**

Common mistakes with uncountable nouns

Here are some common mistakes that students make with uncountable nouns:

✗ I want to give you ~~an~~ advice.
✓ I want to give you a piece of advice.

✗ I need to buy new ~~furnitures~~ for my home.
✓ I need to buy new furniture for my home.

✗ They have ~~many~~ furniture in their house.
✓ They have a lot of furniture in their house.

REMEMBER

1 Uncountable nouns never have a plural form. You say *some furniture* (not *some furnitures*).
2 Uncountable nouns are not usually used with words like *a*, *an* or *another* in the singular, or with words like *many*, *these* or *three* in the plural.
3 Uncountable nouns can be preceded by *the* when you are referring to something in particular. You say *The weather was lovely* (not *Weather was lovely*), or *They gave me the information I needed* (not *They gave me information I needed*).
4 The verb that follows an uncountable noun is always singular. You say *The music was beautiful* (not *The music were beautiful*).

Note that some nouns which are **countable** in your language may be **uncountable** in English. The nouns in the list below are all uncountable nouns in English.

advice, equipment, furniture, hardware, homework, housework, information, knowledge, machinery, money, scenery, stuff, traffic, weather

A piece of ...

If you want to talk about one or more individual examples of an uncountable noun, you cannot use *a* or *an*. For example, you cannot say *an advice*, you have to say *a piece of advice*. Here are some more uncountable nouns which can be used with *a piece of*:

information	An interesting *piece of* information
furniture	Some new *pieces of* furniture
equipment	A useful *piece of* equipment
rubbish	I found a *piece of* rubbish under the sofa.
homework	I have to do a difficult *piece of* homework.
bread	Would you like a *piece of* bread?
research	An interesting *piece of* research

Nouns that are countable AND uncountable

Some nouns can have both a countable [C] and an uncountable [U] meaning. This often happens with the names of animals that are also a type of food:

> **fish¹** /fɪʃ/ *n* plural **fish** or **fishes**
> **1** [C] an animal that lives, breathes, and swims in water: *How many fish did you catch?*
> **2** [U] the flesh of a fish used as food: *We had fish for dinner.*

Some nouns are countable and uncountable in the same meaning. These are often things we eat and drink. You can talk about an amount of the food or drink (uncountable), or about different types of the food or drink (countable). In this dictionary, these nouns appear with a label like this: **[C/U]**.

Quantities and amounts

As we have already seen, you use different words and expressions in English to describe *quantities* of countable nouns and *amounts* of uncountable nouns. The table below will help you to learn and remember the correct way to describe these two types of nouns:

countable nouns	uncountable nouns
How many apples?	How much luggage?
an apple	luggage, a piece of luggage
some / several / a few / not many apples	some / a little / not much luggage
fewer apples	less luggage
not ... any / no apples	not ... any / no luggage
none	none

Collocations: choosing the right word

When you learn a new noun, make a note of the verbs and the adjectives that are often used with it.

Words that belong together are called *collocations*. The more of these that you can learn and use, the more natural your English will sound.

Verbs that go with nouns

Some words sound right when they are used together and others do not. For example, you cannot say *do a mistake*. You have to say *make a mistake*. If you say *do a mistake*, people will understand what you mean, but your English will sound unnatural.

Common mistakes with verb + noun collocations

✗ She is in prison because she ~~did~~ a serious crime.
✔ She is in prison because she committed a serious crime.

✗ He ~~did~~ a long speech about the environment.
✔ He made a long speech about the environment.

✗ She ~~said~~ a remark about my new trousers.
✔ She made a remark about my new trousers.

This dictionary will tell you which verbs are used with which nouns. Here is the entry for mistake:

> **mistake¹** /mɪˈsteɪk/ *n*
> **1** [C] something that is wrong or has been done in the wrong way [➜ **error**]: *Ivan's work is full of* ***spelling mistakes****. | We may have **made a mistake** in our calculations.*
> **2** [C] something you do that is not sensible or has a bad result: *It's your decision, but I warn you – you're **making a mistake***. *| I **made the mistake** of giving him my phone number. | Marrying Julie was a **big mistake**. | It would **be a mistake** to underestimate Moya's ability.*
> **3 by mistake** without intending to do something [= **accidentally**; ≠ **on purpose**]: *Someone must have left the door open by mistake.*

make and *do, have* and *take*

Learning verb + noun combinations will improve your English and make it sound more correct and natural.

Look at the following table. It shows collocations for *make, do, have* and *take*. Using a table like this is one way in which you can make a note of collocations. The first few collocations have been recorded. Look up the nouns in this dictionary and complete the rest of the table.

	make	do	have	take		make	do	have	take
preparations	✔				a photograph				
damage		✔			a test				
a bath			✔BrE	✔AmE	a promise				
research		✔			a complaint				
lessons			✔	✔	justice				
an exam				✔	breakfast				
an operation					progress				
a decision					fun				
a discovery					an effort				
a phone call					harm				
a look					a comment				
a baby					a break				
a party					a suggestion				
a noise					a wash				

Adjectives that go with nouns

If you want to describe a noun, there are many adjectives to choose from. Some adjectives are always used with particular nouns. Somebody who eats a lot is a *big* eater, but somebody who smokes a lot is a *heavy* smoker (NOT a *big* smoker).

When you look up a noun in the dictionary, the entry tells you if there are adjectives which often go with it. Here is the entry for situation:

> **situation** /ˌsɪtʃuˈeɪʃən/ *n* [C]
> **1** the things that are happening at a particular time somewhere, or are happening to a particular person: **in a ... situation** *She's in a very difficult situation.* | **economic/political/financial etc situation** *Things are very difficult for farmers given the current economic situation.* | *Little is being done to try and **improve** the **situation**.*

Nouns that go with nouns

Sometimes, when two or more nouns often appear together, they only sound correct in English if they are used in a particular order. For example, you always say fish and chips. If you say chips and fish it sounds very strange.

Here are examples of nouns matched with their correct partners (look them up in the dictionary if you are not sure what they mean):

knife and fork   bed and breakfast   board and lodging   dos and don'ts   law and order
hustle and bustle   ins and outs   pros and cons   salt and pepper   bread and butter

→ See also **Language notes** on **Intensifying adjectives and adverbs**

Intensifying adjectives and adverbs

Intensifying adjectives

You can make your English sound more natural and interesting by using a wider variety of adjectives and adverbs to emphasize what you are saying. Instead of saying that something is a big problem or a big surprise, you can say that it is a serious problem or a total surprise.

Common mistakes with intensifying adjectives

Sometimes it is hard to choose the correct adjective. For example, you can say that something is great fun, but you can't say that it is big fun.

- ✗ of big importance
- ✔ of great importance

- ✗ of utter importance
- ✔ of utmost importance

- ✗ a big interest in something
- ✔ a great interest in something

- ✗ a strong illness/infection/disease
- ✔ a serious illness/infection/disease

The box below shows you some of the different adjectives that are used to emphasize some common nouns:

	big	complete	total	serious	great	strong	distinct	huge
difficulty				✔	✔			✔
problem	✔			✔				✔
mistake	✔			✔	✔			
possibility						✔	✔	
disaster		✔	✔					
difference	✔				✔			✔
surprise	✔	✔	✔		✔			✔
fun					✔			
importance					✔			✔
lack (of)	✔	✔	✔				✔	

Intensifying adverbs

Instead of saying that something is very difficult or that somebody is very intelligent, you can say extremely difficult, or highly intelligent.

Common mistakes with intensifying adverbs.

Sometimes it is hard to choose the correct adverb. For example, you can say highly intelligent, but NOT highly clever (you have to say very clever).

✗ strongly sure	✗ absolutely different	✗ highly sure/certain
✔ absolutely sure	✔ completely different	✔ absolutely sure/certain
✗ completely hungry	✗ strongly disappointed	
✔ very hungry	✔ deeply disappointed	

The box below shows you some of the different adverbs that are used to emphasize some common adjectives:

	very	highly	completely	totally	seriously	terribly	absolutely	really
difficult	✔				✔	✔		✔
interesting	✔					✔		✔
important	✔	✔			✔	✔		✔
funny	✔					✔		✔
exhausted			✔	✔		✔	✔	✔
sorry	✔					✔		✔
upset	✔				✔	✔		✔
successful	✔	✔	✔	✔		✔		✔
ill					✔	✔		✔
different	✔		✔	✔				✔
impossible			✔	✔			✔	

This dictionary gives a lot of useful information to help you learn which adverbs and adjectives to use to add emphasis. Look at the entry for highly:

> **highly** /'haɪli/ adv
> **1** very: *a highly successful businessman | a highly intelligent woman | It is highly unlikely that he will pass the test.*
> **2** to a very good level or standard: *a highly skilled builder | All our staff are highly trained.*
> **3** with approval or respect: *She **speaks** very **highly** of your work.*

NOTE

Often, different meanings of a word will collocate with different intensifying adjectives and adverbs. So you say:

• She was *badly/seriously* hurt (= injured) in the accident.

but

• I was *deeply/very* hurt (= upset) by their unfriendly attitude.

→ See also **Language notes** on **Collocations**

Verb patterns

STUDY TIP

Whenever you learn a new verb, look it up in the dictionary and study the patterns that can follow it. Use the example sentences in the dictionary to help you to learn these patterns.

When one verb follows another in a sentence, there are many grammatical patterns that can follow it. Read the passage below:

> Michael wanted to buy a present for his mother. He finished doing his homework and asked his friend to come with him to help him decide what to buy. He thought about buying a vase, but he couldn't afford it, so in the end his friend advised him to buy some flowers.

The patterns for the verbs in this passage are:

want to do sth   finish doing sth   ask sb to do sth   help (sb) decide sth
think about doing sth   (can't) afford to do sth   advise sb to do sth

Common mistakes with verb patterns

✗ I want ~~that you come~~ to my party.
✔ I want you to come to my party.

✗ You can ~~to~~ go there by bus.
✔ You can go there by bus.

✗ I am ~~waiting a letter~~ from the hospital.
✔ I am waiting for a letter from the hospital.

The box below gives important information about the different verb patterns that verbs follow:

Types of verb pattern	Examples	In the dictionary, the verb patterns look like this
Verb + -ing	I enjoy studying He denies eating the cakes. He keeps forgetting.	**enjoy doing sth** **deny doing sth** **keep (on) doing sth**
Verb + infinitive with to	I want to go home. He needs to study. She always forgets to close the door.	**want to do sth** **need to do sth** **forget to do sth**
Verb + direct object + infinitive with to	The doctor advised me to rest. I asked him to go with me.	**advise sb to do sth** **ask sb to do sth**
Verb + direct object + infinitive without to (+ object)	She let me drive her car home. He watched her dance. I saw her leave the cinema early.	**let sb do sth** **watch sb do sth** **see sb do sth**
Verb (+ direct object) + preposition + -ing	He thought about going to the cinema. He prevented me from falling.	**think about doing sth** **prevent sb from doing sth**

Adjective patterns

Choosing the right preposition or pattern

When you use an adjective such as **interested**, you need to know which preposition to use with it. Do you say *interested about* something or *interested in* something? You also need to know which verb pattern to use. Do you say *interested to do* something or *interested in doing* something?

This dictionary shows you clearly which words and patterns to use. Here is the entry for interested:

> **interested** /ˈɪntrɪˌstɪd/ *adj*
> **1** [not before noun] wanting to find out more about something or give your attention to it [≠ **uninterested, bored**]: **+in** *She's very interested in computers.* | **be interested to hear/know/ learn etc** *I'd be interested to know what you think about it.*
> **2** [not before noun] wanting to do or have something: **be interested in doing sth** *Would you be interested in coming to London with me?*
> **3 interested parties/groups** the people or groups who will be affected by something [≠ **disinterested**]

As you can see, the usual preposition to use with interested is in. The verb pattern that you choose depends on the meaning of interested. If you want to talk about 'wanting to know about something', you say interested to hear/know/learn. If you want to talk about 'wanting to do something', you say interested in doing something.

Common mistakes with adjectives

- ✗ She is good ~~in~~ maths.
- ✓ She is good at maths.
- ✗ I'm tired ~~to wait~~ for the bus.
- ✓ I'm tired of waiting for the bus.
- ✗ Are you interested ~~about~~ politics?
- ✓ Are you interested in politics?

- ✗ He is good ~~with~~ teaching.
- ✓ He's good at teaching.
- ✗ She's bored ~~about~~ him.
- ✓ She's bored with him.
- ✗ I'm frightened ~~of to swim~~ in the sea.
- ✓ I'm frightened of swimming in the sea.

Choosing the right pattern

Here is a list of common adjectives and the verb patterns that can follow them:

Verb -*ing*	Infinitive verb forms	+ *that*
bored with working all the time	pleased to hear the news	surprised (that) he didn't know
upset about/at being forgotten	keen to have a party	pleased (that) she had remembered
keen on going to the cinema	unable to come to the lesson	sure (that) she would arrive soon
tired of waiting for the bus	reluctant to give the answer	determined (that) he would go
proud of being the winner	determined to go to Paris	aware (that) she was uncomfortable
fond of dancing	proud to be the winner	
	surprised to learn the truth	

Phrasal verbs

What is a phrasal verb?

Read the passage below:

> As soon as the alarm went off, I woke up, jumped out of bed, threw on my dressing gown, and rushed to the bathroom to get ready. I needed to hurry up if I wanted to get to the exam on time.

In this passage go off, wake up, throw on and hurry up are phrasal verbs, but _jump out of_, _rush to_, and _get to_ are not. Why?

A phrasal verb is a verb that is made up of two or three words. The first word is a verb, and the second word (and the third, if there is one) is a *particle*. A particle can be an adverb or a preposition.

In some verbs such as fall over, the particle does not change the meaning of the main verb. In phrasal verbs the addition of the particle creates a completely new meaning. The phrasal verb get up to (which means 'to do something that might be slightly bad') is not connected with the usual meanings of the words get + up + to. It is often difficult to guess the meaning of a phrasal verb.

NOTE

If a verb is followed by a preposition but keeps its ordinary meaning, it is *not* a phrasal verb. This is why *jump out of*, *rush to*, and *get to* in the passage above are not phrasal verbs.

In this dictionary, phrasal verbs are labelled *phr v* and appear in blue at the end of the main verb entry. With different types of phrasal verb, the particles and objects can appear in different places.

Different types of phrasal verb	
Phrasal verbs which do not have an object	get up *phr v* **1** to wake up and get out of bed: *Rory likes to have a coffee before he **gets up**.* *He **got up** and went downstairs for breakfast.*
Phrasal verbs which must have an object The **Longman Active Study Dictionary** uses a special symbol ↔ between the verb and the particle which shows you that the verb is separable.	**1** The object can come *either* before *or* after the particle. put sb/sth ↔ up *phr v* **1** to build or make an upright structure: *The kids were **putting** a tent **up** in the garden.* You can also say: *The kids were **putting up** a tent in the garden.* **Note:** If the object is a <u>pronoun</u> (it/them/her/him etc), the pronoun <u>must</u> always come <u>before</u> the particle: *They **put it up**.* **NOT** *They **put up** it.*

2 The object must <u>always</u> come *between* the verb and the particle.

get sb/sth down *phr v*
1 *informal* to make someone feel unhappy:
*Her illness **gets** her **down**.*

3 With non-separable phrasal verbs, the object must <u>always</u> come *after* the particle.

get through *phr v*
1 *informal* get through **sth**
to use or deal with a particular amount of something:
*I **get through** about 20 cigarettes a day. | I've **got through** a lot of work this month.*

Phrasal verbs with two objects	**4** With phrasal verbs that have two objects, one object is used <u>after the verb</u> and the other is used <u>after the particle</u>. get out of sth *phr v* **2** get sth out of sb to persuade someone to tell or give you something **3** get sth out of sth to enjoy an activity and feel you have gained something from it: get sth out of doing sth *Do you get a lot out of playing the violin?*

Expand your vocabulary

Often there is a single word that has a similar meaning to a particular phrasal verb. For example, the single word distribute means the same as the phrasal verb hand out (they both mean 'to give something to everyone in a group'). However, you should be careful when you use a single-word verb because they are often more formal or more technical than the equivalent phrasal verb. Always check whether a verb is formal or informal, so that you use words that are appropriate for the situation.

Here are some verbs that you can use when talking about telephoning someone, ending a telephone call, etc.

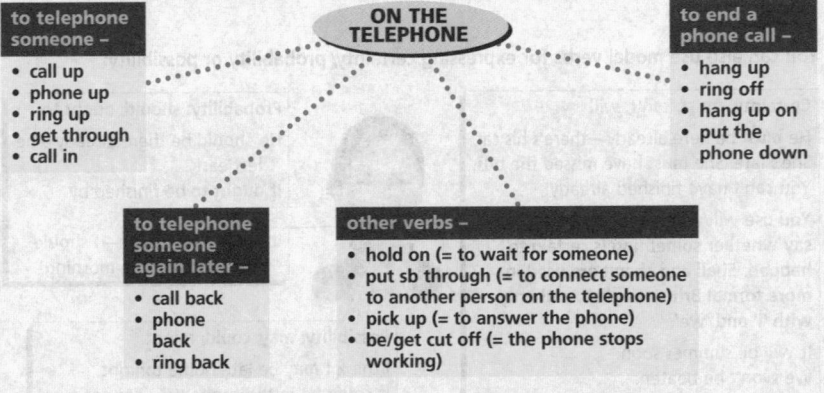

to telephone someone –
- call up
- phone up
- ring up
- get through
- call in

ON THE TELEPHONE

to end a phone call –
- hang up
- ring off
- hang up on
- put the phone down

to telephone someone again later –
- call back
- phone back
- ring back

other verbs –
- hold on (= to wait for someone)
- put sb through (= to connect someone to another person on the telephone)
- pick up (= to answer the phone)
- be/get cut off (= the phone stops working)

→ If you want more information on phrasal verbs, the *Longman Phrasal Verbs Dictionary* explains the meaning of 5,000 phrasal verbs and shows how to use them.

Modal verbs

The modal verbs in English are can, could, must, will, would, should, may, shall, and might. These verbs are used before an infinitive verb without *to*. They are used to give extra information about the main verb. Need (to), ought to, have to and have got to are also often used in similar ways.

Modal verbs are often contracted (=shortened), especially in speech and informal writing. So we say *I can't* rather than *I cannot*, *you mustn't* rather than *you must not*, *they wouldn't* rather than *they would not*.

You can use modal verbs for offering help, advice or suggestions, and for asking for and giving permission:

Making requests: can, will, could, would

Can you help me, please?
Will you close the door?
Could you tell me the time, please?
Would you pass me the salt, please?

Note: could and would are more formal and polite.

Offering to help: can, may (more formal), shall, will

Can I give you a hand?
May I help you?
Shall I carry your bag?
I'll show you the way.

Asking for and giving permission: can, could, may

You can borrow my car.
Can I have some more soup?
Could I speak to the manager, please?
May I go to the cinema tonight?

Note: could is more polite than can, and may is used in more formal English.

Making suggestions and giving advice: should, ought to, shall, must

You should take more exercise.
You ought to go to the dentist's.
Shall we try again?
You must try this cake – it's delicious!

You can also use modal verbs for expressing certainty, probability or possibility:

Certainty: must, can't, will

He must be here already – there's his car.
She's late. She must have missed the bus.
You can't have finished already!

You use will/won't and shall/shan't to say whether something is certain to happen. Shall and shan't are used in more formal British English, and only with 'I' and 'we'.

It will be summer soon.
We won't be beaten.

We shall succeed
I shan't forget you.

Probability: should, ought to

He should be there already – he left early.
It ought to be finished by tonight.
It's only a headache – I should feel better in the morning.

Possibility: may, could, might

I think I may be late home tonight.
It could be in the cupboard – I'm not sure.
I might have left it on the bus – I can't remember.

Or for talking about somebody's abilities or about necessity and obligations:

> **Talking about ability: can, could**
>
> She **can** swim.
> **Can** you see the sea from here?
> I **can't** afford to go.
> **Could** you understand what he was saying?
> I **could** hear the traffic in the street.

> **Talking about necessity and obligation:**
> **must, need to, have to, have got to (BrE)**
>
> I **must** do my homework before I go out.
> It's getting late. I really **must** go home.
> I**'ve got to** get up early in the morning.
>
> **You use will have to or will need to to say that it is necessary to do something in the future.**
>
> You**'ll have to** help me carry my bag – it's too heavy.
> It's too far to walk. They**'ll need to** get the bus.

Common mistakes with modal verbs

Modal verbs are followed by a verb in the infinitive, without 'to':

✗ I must ~~to do~~ my homework.
✔ I must **do** my homework.

They do not take 's' in the 3rd person singular:

✗ He ~~musts~~ do his homework.
✔ He must do his homework.

They cannot follow another verb. If you want to talk about the future, use 'will have to':

✗ I will ~~must~~ do my homework.
✔ I will **have to** do my homework.

STUDY TIP

Avoid repetition by using different modal verbs to express the same meaning. For example, you can say: Tonight **I have to** do my homework, then **I must** write to Sally, and then **I've got to** go to bed early.

Idioms

STUDY TIP

1 Always look idioms up in the dictionary and make sure you have understood their meaning.
2 Check if the idiom is informal or slang. If it is, use it with care.
3 Remember that you cannot usually translate idioms directly from one language into another.
4 Learning and using idioms can be fun, but remember not to use too many idioms together, as this can sound strange or unnatural.

What is an idiom?

An idiom is a group of two or more words which have a special meaning. This meaning is different from the meanings of the individual words when they are used separately.

For example, if you are told that somebody is in hot water, you cannot guess the meaning from the usual meanings of in + hot + water. This idiom actually means 'in a lot of trouble'.

In this dictionary, each idiom is shown in **bold** at the beginning of a new sense. For example, the entry for cold shows these four idioms:

> **4 get/have cold feet** *informal* to start to feel that you are not brave enough to do something: *She was getting cold feet about getting married.*
> **5 leave sb cold** if something leaves you cold, you are not at all interested in it: *Most poetry leaves me cold.*
> **6 in cold blood** in a cruel and deliberate way: *innocent civilians murdered in cold blood*
> **7 give sb the cold shoulder** *informal* to deliberately ignore someone or be unfriendly to them, especially because they have upset or offended you

Idiom meanings

We saw above that in hot water means 'in a lot of trouble'. There are many idioms which people use to talk about problems and difficulties. The table below shows just a few of them. Look up the words in **bold** in the dictionary to find out exactly what they mean.

PROBLEMS AND DIFFICULTIES

in a difficult situation –
- be in the **doghouse**
- be up the **creek** (without a paddle)
- be in hot/deep **water**
- be in a **fix**
- hit/reach **rock bottom**
- in dire **straits**
- **come up against** sth/sb
- not have a **leg** to stand on
- be **bogged** down

cause problems for others or for yourself –
- **rock** the boat
- **deal** a blow (to sb)
- put your **foot** in it
- **stick** your neck out

a problem –
- a stumbling **block**
- a **thorny** question/problem/issue
- **teething** troubles/problems
- a **sticky** situation

When you learn a new idiom it is very important to make sure that you understand what it means. Do you know the difference between being bogged down and being up the creek? The dictionary will make it clear.

Metaphor in idioms

If we say that someone is in hot water, we do not mean that they are literally in some water that is hot. In hot water has a metaphorical meaning – it is understood as a difficult situation to be in. A metaphor is a way of describing something by comparing it to something else that has similar qualities. Many idioms use metaphor in this way.

For example, words related to explosions and being hot are often used as a metaphor for anger:

- hit the roof
- go ballistic
- get steamed up
- lose your cool

Similarly, cold is associated with other types of emotion:

- give sb the cold shoulder
- have/get cold feet
- be left out in the cold
- keep your cool
- break the ice (see entry at break)

Metaphorical actions

Many idioms describe an action, but the meaning of the idiom is not the same as the meaning of the action. It can be very difficult to guess what these idioms mean. For example, show somebody the ropes means 'to show someone how to do a job'.

Sometimes, two of these 'action' idioms can look very similar but have very different meanings. For example:

- bite the bullet means 'to start dealing with an unpleasant situation because you can no longer avoid it'.
- bite the dust means 'to die, fail or be defeated'.

Sometimes several different idioms can mean the same thing. For example:

- spill the beans
- let the cat out of the bag
- give the game away
- let sth slip

These idioms all describe a situation where someone reveals a secret.

→ If you want more information on idioms, the **Longman Idioms Dictionary** and the **Longman American Idioms Dictionary** show clearly the meaning and use of thousands of spoken and written idioms.

Writing essays

WRITING TIPS

- Give your essay a clear structure with a beginning (introduction), middle and end (conclusion).
- Remember to check your punctuation. Use the punctuation guide below.
- Do not use contracted forms such as *don't* and *can't*. These are used in spoken and informal English.

Essay questions usually ask you to do one of three things:

1. Compare two or more things and decide which is best
2. Discuss the advantages and disadvantages of doing something
3. Discuss a problem and suggest a solution

Organizing your essays

You need to present your ideas in a clear and organized way. It is helpful to organize your essay like this:

1. Introduce the subject by describing the things you want to discuss. Say why the subject is important.
2. Describe the main points of the situation or problem in a sensible order. Organize your discussion into paragraphs. Each main point should have its own paragraph.
3. Always use clear, short sentences. Use common words that you know well but avoid very informal words.
4. Give a summary of the points you have made and present your conclusion.

Punctuation

Always use capital letters at the start of:

- Every sentence (and always end the sentence with a full stop)
- Names of places, people, organisations, languages, religions and nationalities, e.g. Japanese
- Names of days of the week and months of the year, e.g. April
- Titles and ranks used with people's names, e.g. Professor Smith

Use commas (,):

- To show a pause which separates the parts of a sentence
- To separate spoken words from the rest of the sentence: e.g. "Hello", he said.
- After sentence connectors: e.g. *For example, However, Furthermore*, etc.

Use a colon (:):

- To start a list, e.g. *You will need: oranges, peaches, grapes, and a banana.*

Use a semi-colon (;):

- To separate two parts of a sentence: e.g. *The exam was easy; I'm sure I will pass.*

Use an apostrophe ('):

- To represent missing letters, e.g. *can't, haven't, I'll, there's*
- To show a possessive, e.g. *Rory's computer*

Use inverted commas or quotation marks (" "):

- To show words which are spoken: e.g. *"I'm sorry I'm late", she said.*

Useful phrases

If you understand and learn these useful phrases, it will help you to organize your essay and make your argument clear.

Introduce the subject	*It is a well-known fact that ...*
	Many people believe that ...
	It is often claimed that ...
	By way of introduction, I would like to point out that ...
	There are several ways of looking at the problem of ...
	One of the most important issues in society today is ...
Start the discussion	*First of all, / Firstly, / To begin with, / In the first place, ...*
	(**NOT** *Firstly of all*)
	Let us begin by looking at ...
	First of all, let us consider ...
	The first thing that should be noted is ...
	It is worth stating from the outset that ...
Continue the discussion	**If you want to continue discussing one side of the question:**
	Secondly, (**NOT** *Second* or *Secondly of all*)
	As far as ... is concerned / As regards / As for ...
	This brings us to the question of (whether/how/who etc.)
	It should also be noted/stressed that ...
	if you want to show the other side of the question
	However / Nevertheless, ...
	The opposite may also be true.
	There is more than one way of looking at this problem.
Present a conclusion or a solution to the problem	*Lastly, / Finally,* (**NOT** *In the last / final place*)
	On balance, ...
	To sum up, / In summary / conclusion, it would seem that ...
	This brings us to the conclusion that ...
	To conclude, it seems likely that ...
Express your personal opinion	*In my opinion, ...* (do **NOT** write *I think* after this phrase)
	My personal opinion is that ...
	My own view of this is that ...
	It is my opinion that ...

Link your ideas

You can link your ideas by using these words at the start of each sentence:
Firstly, ... Secondly, ... Thirdly, ...

Remember that it sounds unnatural to do this more than three times. Do not use *fourthly* and *fifthly*.

If you use *On the one hand ...* , you should also use *On the other hand ...* in the following sentence or paragraph.

Try not to use these words or phrases more than once in the same essay. Find words or phrases which have a similar meaning. For example, here are some other ways to say *also*: *furthermore, moreover, what is more, besides, in addition*. Use these at the start of a sentence.

Writing letters and emails

WRITING TIPS

- Choose the correct level of formality and make sure that you use the same level of formality from the beginning to the end. Use the boxes below to guide you.
- For a formal style, do not use contractions like *I'm*, *I've*, or *you'd*, and avoid abbreviations like *etc.* and *e.g.*
- Make sure you use punctuation consistently. If you have used a comma after *Dear Sir/Madam,* at the beginning of your letter, put a comma after *Yours faithfully,* at the end.
- Use paragraphs to organize the main points in your letter.

Writing letters

You use different styles for different kinds of letter. The box below will help you to decide how to start and finish your letter.

	Formal letters	Informal letters
Ways of beginning a letter	**Dear Mr/Mrs/Miss/Ms** + family name (you can use **Ms** as the title for a woman whether she is married or not) **Dear Dr/Professor** + family name (do **NOT** use the person's first name with **Dear Dr/Professor**) **Dear Sir or Madam** *or* **Dear Sir/Madam** *or* **Dear Sirs** (use this when you do not know whether you are writing to a man or a woman) **Dear Madam** (use this when you do not know the woman's name) **Dear Sir** (use this when you do not know the man's name) **To whom it may concern** (use this when you do not know the person's name and the letter is very formal)	**Dear** + first name (use this when you know the person well enough to use their first name only) **Hi/Hello** (+ first name) (use this in letters to friends and people that you know well)
Ways of ending a letter	**Yours sincerely** (use this in British English when you have used the person's family name at the start) **Yours faithfully** (use this in British English when you have **NOT** used the person's family name at the start) **Yours truly** (use this in American English)	**Lots of love/Love (from)** (use this in letters to your close friends and family) **All the best/Best wishes** **Take care** **Regards/Kind regards** (use this in letters to people you work with or do not know very well)

Formal letters	Informal letters
Further to my letter of 20th July ...	I was really pleased to get your letter.
I am writing to enquire about ...	It was great to see you/hear from you.
I am writing to apply for the position of ... advertised in ...	Sorry it's been so long since I last wrote/Sorry I haven't written for so long.
I am writing in response to your advertisement in ...	Thanks for your letter.
I am writing to inform you that ...	I hope you are well/How are you?/How's things?
I would be most grateful if you could ...	Just a quick note to let you know ...
Please accept my apologies for ...	Let me know when you are free so we can get together.
Please find enclosed ...	It would be great to have your news.
Please do not hesitate to contact me if you require any further information.	Give me a ring and let me know whether you can make it.
I can be contacted at the address above or on 0204 639 8756.	Hope to see you soon/Really looking forward to seeing you soon.
I look forward to hearing from you.	Write soon/Keep in touch.
Thank you for your kind attention.	Do drop me a line when you have a moment.
Thank you in advance for ...	Give my love/regards to ...

Writing emails

Emails to companies and organizations are usually formal, and you can use the same beginnings and endings as in a formal letter. Emails to friends and colleagues are usually written in a very brief and informal style:

Informal emails:

You can start the email with: Hi

               Hi + first name

               Dear + first name (*slightly more formal*)

               first name only

               no name and no greeting

You can end the email with: All the best/Best

               Best wishes

               Regards (*slightly more formal*)

               Love (*only to friends and family*)

               your first name

               the first letter of your first name only (*informal*)

Word building

Prefixes and suffixes

A prefix is a short group of letters found at the beginning of some words, which gives the word a particular meaning. For example, un- is a prefix that means *not*, as in unhealthy (= not healthy) or unhelpful (= not helpful).

A suffix is a short group of letters found at the end of some words which gives the word a particular meaning. A common suffix is -less, meaning *without*, as in painless (= without any pain) or hopeless (= without any hope).

Some words contain both a *prefix* and a *suffix*. For example, unrecognizable contains both the prefix un- (= *not*), and the suffix -able (= able to be ...), giving the meaning 'not able to be recognized'.

Often the suffix makes a word change its part of speech. For example, the noun realization contains the verb realize and the suffix -ation (= the act of ...), giving the meaning 'the act of realizing that something is true'. The adverb easily contains the adjective easy and the suffix -ly (= in a ... way), giving the meaning 'in an easy way'.

Word formation using prefixes and suffixes

The tables below show you how new meanings and new parts of speech can be created using prefixes and suffixes.

Noun formation

Noun beginnings (Prefixes)	Meaning	Examples
anti-	used to prevent something	antifreeze, antiseptic
bio-	relating to life and living things	biology, biochemistry
co-	with or together	co-worker, co-author
eco-	relating to the environment	ecology, ecosystem
ex-	former, in the past	ex-husband, ex-girlfriend
inter-	between or among	intersection, interference
mid-	middle	midday, midnight, midweek
mis-	bad or wrong	misspelling, mismanagement
non-	not	non-smoker, nonsense
over-	too much	overgrowth, overpopulation
psycho-	relating to the mind	psychology, psychotherapy
self-	of or by yourself	self-confidence, self-control
semi-	half	semi-circle, semi-detached
sub-	1 under 2 less important or smaller	submarine, subconscious, subway subcommittee, subsection

Noun endings (Suffixes)	Meaning	Examples
-ability, -ibility	when sth is possible (*makes nouns from adjectives*)	reliability, flexibility, responsibility
-al	used to say that sb/sth does sth or sth happens (*makes nouns from verbs*)	arrival, refusal, denial
-an **-ian**	a particular person, place or subject (*makes nouns from names*)	American, Christian, historian
-ation	when sb does sth or sth happens (*makes nouns from verbs*)	creation, confirmation, hesitation, exploration
-ator	sb or sth that does or makes something (*makes nouns from verbs*)	creator, generator, administrator, investigator
-cy	used in the names of qualities	fluency, accuracy, decency
-er, -or, -ar, -r	1 a person who does an activity 2 a person who lives in a place 3 a thing that does something	footballer, actor, liar Londoner, New Zealander heater, cooler, computer
-ful	the amount that a container holds	spoonful, cupful, handful
-ist	1 sb who supports a particular set of ideas or beliefs 2 sb who plays a particular musical instrument 3 sb who does a particular activity or type of work	idealist, communist, leftist, environmentalist violinist, pianist, cellist, guitarist novelist, journalist, geologist, motorist, cyclist
-ity **-ty**	used in the names of qualities or types of behaviour (*makes nouns from adjectives*)	stupidity, brutality, cruelty, beauty, anxiety
-let	a small kind of a particular thing	piglet, booklet
-ment	1 an activity or way of doing sth 2 a particular quality (*makes nouns from verbs*)	development, entertainment embarrassment, amusement, contentment
-ness	used in the names of qualities (*makes nouns from adjectives*)	happiness, goodness, loudness, quietness
-ology	the science or study of sth	psychology, sociology, biology
-ship	1 a situation between people or organisations 2 a skill or ability to do sth well	friendship, partnership, relationship craftsmanship, musicianship
-ware	used in the names of particular kinds of goods	hardware, software, glassware, silverware
-y	used in the names of feelings	jealousy, sympathy

Adjective formation

Adjective beginnings (Prefixes)	Meaning	Examples
anti-	1 opposed to 2 opposite to	antinuclear anticlockwise
cross-	going across or between	cross-country, cross-cultural
dis-	not	discontented, disapproving
eco-	relating to the environment	ecofriendly
extra-	beyond or outside, or not included in something	extracurricular, extramarital, extraordinary
in- **im-** before b, m, p **il-** before l **ir-** before r	not	inexact, incorrect impossible, imprecise illegal, illegible irregular, irresponsible
inter-	between or among	international, interpersonal
multi-	having many of something	multinational, multimedia
non-	not	nonstop, non-smoking
over-	1 too much 2 across or above	overexcited, overemotional overland, overseas, overhead
post-	after or later than	postwar, postgraduate
pre-	before or earlier than	pre-existing, prehistoric
trans-	across or on the other side of	transatlantic
ultra-	1 very, extremely sth 2 beyond	ultramodern ultrasonic
un-	not	uncomfortable, unhappy

Adjective endings (Suffixes)	Meaning	Examples
-able **-ible**	1 able to be (broken, drunk, washed etc.) 2 having a particular quality	breakable, drinkable, washable reasonable, responsible (*makes adjectives from verbs*)
-al **-ial**	relating to something	political, ceremonial, facial
-an **-ian**	relating to a particular person, place or subject	American, Christian, civilian, reptilian
-ed	1 having a particular thing 2 having a particular quality	bearded, armed big-headed, bored
-en	made of something	wooden, golden, silken

Adjective endings (Suffixes)	Meaning	Examples
-er	makes the comparative of short adjectives	hotter, cooler, nearer, bigger, safer
-est	makes the superlative of short adjectives	hottest, coolest, nearest, biggest
-ish	1 relating to a country, its language or its people	British, Spanish, Swedish
	2 like or typical of	childish, impish, boyish
	3 quite or slightly	smallish, greenish
	4 approximately, about	sixish, fortyish
-ive	used to say that sb or sth does or is able to do sth (*makes adjectives from verbs*)	creative, communicative, cooperative, supportive
-less	without	hopeless, childless, painless
-like	like or typical of (*makes adjectives from nouns*)	childlike, lifelike, godlike
-ly	1 behaving in a way that is typical of a particular kind of person	friendly, motherly, fatherly
	2 happening regularly	hourly, weekly, monthly
-most	makes the superlative of some adjectives	topmost, northernmost, uppermost
-ous	having a particular quality	dangerous, spacious, envious
-th	makes adjectives from numbers (apart from numbers which end in 1, 2, 3)	sixth, hundredth, ninth, fortieth
-y	covered in sth or having a lot of sth, or having a particular quality	dirty, dusty, cloudy, rainy, noisy, windy, smelly, greedy

Verb formation

Verb beginnings (Prefixes)	Meaning	Examples
de-	to remove or reduce sth	decaffeinate, devalue
dis-	1 to not do sth	disagree, disapprove, disobey
	2 to remove sth	disconnect, disinfect
mis-	to do sth badly or wrongly	misunderstand, misinterpret
re-	to make or do sth again	rethink, remake, redo, reinvent
trans-	1 to change sth completely	translate, transform
	2 to move sth to a new place	transfer, transport
un-	to remove or unfasten sth	undress, unlock, untie

Verb endings (Suffixes)	Meaning	Examples
-en	to become or make sth become	darken, soften, lighten
-ize, -ise (*BrE*) -ize (*AmE*)	to become or make sth become	popularize, legalize, modernize, harmonize
-ify	to give sth a particular quality	solidify, simplify, purify

Adverb formation

Because most adverbs are formed from adjectives, they can take the same beginnings as adjectives.

Adverb endings (Suffixes)	Meaning	Examples
-er, -r	makes the comparative of adverbs	later, sooner, farther
-est, -st	makes the superlative of adverbs	latest, soonest, farthest
-ly	1 in a particular way (*makes adverbs from adjectives*) 2 happening regularly (*makes adverbs from nouns*)	carefully, slowly, easily, fully, freely, impatiently hourly, daily, weekly
-ward, -wards	in a particular direction	northward(s), backward(s)

Note that there are a small number of adverbs which do not have the same meaning as the adjectives they were formed from. You should look these up in the dictionary and learn them:

awfully ≠ awful + ly   lately ≠ late + ly   terribly ≠ terrible + ly
barely ≠ bare + ly   shortly ≠ short + ly   scarcely ≠ scarce + ly
hardly ≠ hard + ly

NOTE

You can also refer to word building exercises on the CD-ROM in the exam practice and vocabulary sections.

M, m

m **1** the written abbreviation of **metre** **2** the written abbreviation of **medium**, used on clothes to show the size **3** the written abbreviation of **mile** **4** the written abbreviation of **million**

M, m /em/ n [C,U] plural **M's, m's** the 13th letter of the English alphabet

MA, M.A. /ˌem ˈeɪ/ n Master of Arts a higher university degree [➡ MSc]

ma'am /mæm, mɑːm, məm $ mæm/ n AmE spoken a polite word you use to talk to a woman you do not know

mac /mæk/ n [C] BrE a coat you wear to keep out the rain [= mackintosh]

macabre /məˈkɑːbrə, -bə $ -brə, -bər/ adj strange and frightening

macaroni /ˌmækəˈrəʊni $ -ˈroʊ-/ n [U] a type of PASTA in the shape of small tubes → see picture on page A5

machete /məˈʃeti, məˈtʃeti/ n [C] a large knife with a wide heavy blade

machine /məˈʃiːn/ n [C] a piece of equipment that uses power such as electricity to do a job: **washing/sewing etc machine** (=a machine that washes, sews, etc) | There was a message on the **answering machine** (=for taking telephone messages). | **+for** a machine for sorting the mail | Some of these new computers are very powerful machines. | **by machine** The cloth is cut by machine.
→ CASH MACHINE, SLOT MACHINE, VENDING MACHINE

ma'chine gun n [C] a gun that fires a lot of bullets very quickly

machinery /məˈʃiːnəri/ n [U] **1** large machines: agricultural machinery **2** a system for doing something: the machinery of the government

macho /ˈmætʃəʊ $ ˈmɑːtʃoʊ/ adj informal behaving in a way which is typical of men, for example being strong or brave, or not showing your feelings

mackintosh /ˈmækɪntɒʃ $ -tɑːʃ/ n [C] BrE old-fashioned a coat you wear to keep out the rain; [= mac]

macro /ˈmækrəʊ $ -roʊ/ n [C] plural macros a set of instructions for a computer, stored and used as a unit

macrocosm /ˈmækrəʊˌkɒzəm $ -kroʊ,kɑː-/ n [C] a large group or system, considered as a single unit [≠ microcosm]

mad /mæd/ adj

1 informal angry: You **make** me so **mad**! | **+at** Lisa was really mad at me for telling Dad. | **go mad** BrE (=become very angry) Mum will go mad when she finds out. → see box at ANGRY

2 BrE informal stupid: You're mad to get involved with someone like him!

3 a) not able to think clearly: I began to wonder if I was **going mad**. **b)** old-fashioned mentally ill

4 be mad about sb/sth BrE informal to like someone or something very much: The kids are mad about football.

5 drive sb mad if something or someone drives you mad, you find them very annoying: The flies are driving me mad.

6 behaving in an excited or uncontrolled way: The crowd **went mad** when Liverpool scored.

7 like mad informal very quickly: everyone was working like mad.

8 a mad dash/rush/panic informal when you try to do something very quickly because you do not have much time: It was a mad rush to get ready on time.

madam /ˈmædəm/ n **1** a polite word used to talk to a woman who is a customer in your shop, restaurant etc [➡ sir]: Can I help you, madam? **2 Dear Madam** used to begin a formal letter to a woman whose name you do not know

mad 'cow disease n [U] informal BSE

madden /ˈmædn/ v [T] to make someone very angry —**maddening** adj: Things moved with maddening slowness.

made¹ /meɪd/ v the past tense and past participle of MAKE

made² adj

1 be made (out) of/from sth to be built from something or consist of something: The frame is made of silver. | a shelter made out of old wooden boxes

> **USAGE**
>
> Use made of when you can clearly see what material has been used to make something: a table made of wood | a handbag made of leather
> Use made from when the materials have been completely changed in the process of making something: Paper is made from wood. | soap made from the finest ingredients
> Use made by to talk about the person or company that has made something: furniture made by craftsmen

2 be made for sth/sb to be perfectly suitable for a person, group, or situation: I think Anna and Juan were **made for each other**.

3 have (got) it made informal to have everything you need to be happy or successful: If you can get this job, you've got it made.
→ MAN-MADE, READY-MADE

madhouse /ˈmædhaʊs/ n [C] a place that is very busy and noisy

madly /ˈmædli/ adv **1** in a wild, uncontrolled way: Allen was beating madly on the door. **2 madly in love** very much in love

madman /ˈmædmən/ n [C] plural madmen /-mən/ **1** a man who behaves in a very dangerous or stupid way: He drives **like a madman**. **2** old-fashioned a man who is mentally ill

madness /ˈmædnɪs/ n [U] **1** very stupid and often dangerous behaviour: It would be madness to go cycling in this weather. **2** BrE old-fashioned severe mental illness [= insanity]

maestro /ˈmaɪstrəʊ $ -roʊ/ n [C] plural maestros someone who can do something very well, especially a musician

mafia /'mæfiə $ 'mɑː-, 'mæ-/ *n* **the Mafia** a large organization of criminals

magazine /ˌmægə'ziːn $ 'mægəziːn/ *n* [C]
1 a large thin book with a paper cover, which is sold every week or every month: **in a magazine** | *an article in a women's magazine* | *a fashion magazine*
2 the part of a gun that holds the bullets

maggot /'mægət/ *n* [C] a young insect with a soft body that grows into a FLY

magic¹ /'mædʒɪk/ *n* [U]
1 a special power that can make strange or impossible things happen in stories: *Do you believe in magic?*
2 when someone does tricks which look like magic: *a magic show*
3 a special attractive quality: **+of** *the magic of the East*
→ **BLACK MAGIC**

magic² *adj* [only before noun] having magic powers or used in magic: *magic spells* | *a magic carpet*

magical /'mædʒɪkəl/ *adj* **1** very enjoyable and exciting, in a strange or special way: *a magical evening beneath the stars* **2** having magic powers or done using magic —**magically** /-kli/ *adv*

magician /mə'dʒɪʃən/ *n* [C] **1** someone who does magic tricks to entertain people **2** a man in stories who has magic powers

magistrate /'mædʒɪˌstreɪt, -strɪt/ *n* [C] someone who decides if people are guilty of less serious crimes in a court of law

magnanimous /mæg'nænɪməs/ *adj formal* kind and generous towards other people, especially someone you have just defeated

magnate /'mægneɪt, -nɪt/ *n* [C] **steel/oil/shipping etc magnate** a rich and powerful person who owns a company that produces steel, oil etc

magnesium /mæg'niːziəm/ *n* [U] a silver-white metal that burns with a bright white flame

magnet /'mægnɪt/ *n* [C] **1** a piece of iron or steel that makes other metal objects move towards it **2** a person or place that attracts a lot of people: *Darlington has recently become a magnet for new companies.* —**magnetize** also **-ise** *BrE v* [T]

magnetic /mæg'netɪk/ *adj* **1** something that is magnetic has the power of a magnet **2** **magnetic tape/disks/media** tape or DISKS on which sound, pictures, or computer information are recorded **3** making you feel attracted to someone or something: *He's got a magnetic personality.*

magnetism /'mægnɪˌtɪzəm/ *n* [U] **1** the power that a magnet has to attract things **2** a quality that makes people feel attracted to someone

magnificent /mæg'nɪfɪsənt/ *adj* very good or beautiful, and very impressive: *He gave a magnificent performance.*

magnify /'mægnɪfaɪ/ *v* [T] **magnified, magnifying, magnifies 1** to make something appear bigger **2** to make something become, or seem, more important or serious: *The report magnifies the risks.*
—**magnification** /ˌmægnɪfɪ'keɪʃən/ *n* [C,U]

magnify
magnifying glass

'magnifying ˌglass *n* [C] a round piece of glass with a handle, that makes things look bigger when you look through it → see picture at **MAGNIFY**

magnitude /'mægnɪtjuːd $ -tuːd/ *n* [U] how large or important something is: **the magnitude of sth** *He was surprised by the magnitude of the task.*

magnolia /mæg'nəʊliə $ -'noʊ-/ *n* [C] a bush with large white or pink flowers

magpie /'mægpaɪ/ *n* [C] a black and white bird with a long tail

mahogany /mə'hɒgəni $ mə'hɑː-/ *n* [U] a hard dark wood, often used for making furniture

maid /meɪd/ *n* [C] **1** a female servant, especially in a large house **2** *literary* a maiden

maiden¹ /'meɪdn/ *n* [C] *literary* a girl or young woman who is not married

maiden² *adj* **maiden flight/voyage** the first trip that a plane or ship makes

'maiden ˌname *n* [C] a woman's family name before she gets married → see box at **NAME**

mail¹ /meɪl/ *n* [U]
1 the letters and packages that are delivered to you [= **post** *BrE*]: *What time does the mail come?* | *They promised to forward my mail to my new address.*
2 **the mail** *especially AmE* the system of collecting and delivering letters and packages [= **post** *BrE*]: **in the mail** *I just put the letter in the mail.*
3 messages that are sent and received on a computer [= **email**]: *Check your mail every day.*
4 **hate mail** letters that say bad things about the person they are sent to
→ **JUNK MAIL**

mail² *v* [T]
1 to send a message or document to someone using a computer [= **email**]: **mail sth to sb** *Did you mail those pictures to me?* | *I'll mail you.*
2 *especially AmE* to send a letter or package to someone [= **post** *BrE*]: *I'll mail it to you tomorrow.*

mailbox /'meɪlbɒks $ -bɑːks/ *n* [C] **1** a box, usually outside your house, where your letters are delivered or collected **2** a container where you post letters [= **postbox** *BrE*] **3** in a computer, the part where email messages are stored

'mailing ˌlist *n* [C] a list of names and addresses, used by an organization when it sends information to people → see box at **LIST**

mailman /'meɪlmæn/ *n* [C] *plural* **mailmen** /-men/ *AmE* a man who delivers letters and packages to people's houses [= **postman** *BrE*]

,mail 'order n [U] a system of buying goods in which you choose them at home and they are delivered to you

maim /meɪm/ v [T] to wound or injure someone very seriously and often permanently: *Landmines continue to kill and maim people.*

main¹ /meɪn/ adj [only before noun]

1 bigger or more important than other things: *the main meal of the day | The main problem is the cost. | the main reason for his decision*

2 the main thing *spoken* used to say that something is the most important thing in a situation: *You're safe, that's the main thing.*

main² n [C] **1** a large pipe carrying water or gas, which is connected to people's houses by smaller pipes: *a water main* **2 the mains** *BrE* **a)** the place on a wall where you connect equipment to the electricity supply **b)** electricity that is supplied through wires, or water or gas that is supplied through pipes: **mains electricity/water/gas** *Some of the older houses do not have mains electricity.* **3 in the main** *spoken* generally: *The weather was very good in the main.*

,main 'clause n [C] in grammar, a group of words that can stand alone as a complete sentence [➡ subordinate clause]

,main 'course n [C] the main part of a meal → see box at RESTAURANT

mainframe /ˈmeɪnfreɪm/ n [C] a large computer that can work very fast and that a lot of people can use at the same time

mainland /ˈmeɪnlənd, -lænd/ n **the mainland** the main part of an area of land, not the islands that are near it —**mainland** adj: *mainland Europe*

,main 'line n [C] an important railway that connects two cities: *the main line between Belfast and Dublin*

mainly /ˈmeɪnli/ adv used to mention the main part of something: *The workforce consists mainly of women. | I don't go out much, mainly because of the kids.*

mainstay /ˈmeɪnsteɪ/ n [C] the most important part of something, which allows it to continue or succeed: **+of** *Farming was the mainstay of the economy.*

mainstream /ˈmeɪnstriːm/ n **the mainstream** the most usual ideas or ways of doing something which are accepted by most people: **+of** *the mainstream of religious opinion* —**mainstream** adj: *mainstream education*

'Main Street n [C] *AmE* the most important street in a town, with many shops and businesses on it [= high street *BrE*] → see box at ROAD

maintain /meɪnˈteɪn, mən-/ v [T]

1 to make something continue in the same way or at the same standard as before: *We need to maintain good relations with our customers. | It is important to maintain a reasonable level of fitness.*

2 to keep something in good condition by taking care of it: *It costs a lot of money to maintain a big house.*

3 to say that you are sure that something is true: **+that** *She always maintained that her son was alive. | He has always maintained his innocence* (=said that he is innocent).

maintenance /ˈmeɪntənəns/ n [U] **1** the work that is necessary to keep something in good condition: *He was carrying out routine maintenance work.* **2** when people make a situation continue: **+of** *the maintenance of international peace and security* **3** *BrE* payments that are made to a former wife or husband after a marriage ends

maisonette /ˌmeɪzəˈnet/ n [C] *BrE* an apartment that is part of a building like a large house

maize /meɪz/ n [U] *BrE* a tall plant with yellow seeds that are used for food [= corn *AmE*]

majestic /məˈdʒestɪk/ adj very big, impressive, or beautiful: *majestic mountain scenery*

majesty /ˈmædʒəsti/ n [U] **1 Your/Her/His Majesty** used when talking to or about a king or queen **2** *formal* when something is powerful, impressive, or beautiful: *the majesty of the hills*

major¹ /ˈmeɪdʒə $ -ər/ adj

1 very large or important [➡ minor]: *Traffic is a major problem. | He played a major part in the negotiations.*

2 a major key is one of the two main sets of musical notes [➡ minor]: *a symphony in A major*

major² n [C] **1** also **Major** an officer of middle rank in the army **2** *AmE* **a)** the main subject that you study at college or university **b) English/history etc major** a student at college or university whose main subject is English, history etc

major³ v

major in sth *phr v AmE* to study something as your main subject at college or university [➡ minor]

majority /məˈdʒɒrəti $ məˈdʒɔː-, məˈdʒɑː-/ n plural **majorities**

1 [singular also + plural verb *BrE*] most of the people or things in a group [➡ minority]: **+of** *Money is a problem for the majority of students. | The majority of people support the idea.* | **great/ vast/overwhelming majority** (=almost all of a group) *In the vast majority of cases the disease is fatal.* | **be in the majority** (=form the largest group) *Boys were in the majority.* | **majority vote/decision/verdict etc** (=when more people vote for something than against it) *He was found guilty by majority verdict.*

2 [C usually singular] if one person or group wins a majority in an election, they win more votes than other people or groups: **+of** *He won by a majority of 500.* | **clear/overall/absolute majority** (=when one party wins more votes than all the others)

make¹ /meɪk/ v past tense and past participle **made** /meɪd/

1 [T] to produce or build something: *She makes all her own clothes. | The furniture was made by a Swedish firm.* | **make sth from/out of sth** *She made the skirt out of some old fabric.* | **be made from/of/out of sth** *Paper is made from wood.* | **make sb sth** *He made me a beautiful card.*

2 [T] used with some nouns to say that someone does something: *You've made a mistake. | Could I make a suggestion?*

3 [T] to cook something: *I've made a cake. | She made lunch for everyone.*

4 [T] to cause something to happen: **make sb/sth do sth** *Sarah always makes me laugh.* | **make sb sad/happy/excited etc** *He's made me*

M

M

so happy. | **make sth difficult/easy/possible etc** *Heavy rain made driving very difficult.*
5 [T] to cause something to appear: *Make a hole in the paper.*
6 [T] to force someone to do something: **make sb do sth** *He made me stand against the wall.*
7 [T] to give someone a particular job or title: **make sb sth** *They made her the manager.*
8 [T] to earn or get money: *Irene makes about $60,000 a year.*
9 [linking verb] to be a particular number or amount when added together: *2 and 2 make 4.*
10 [T] used to say what you have calculated a number to be: *I make that 54.*
11 [T] to succeed in achieving something: *He didn't make the team* (=he wasn't good enough to be in the team). | *The story made the front page of the newspapers.*
12 make it a) to succeed in arriving somewhere: *We made it to the station just in time.* **b)** to achieve a high level of success, for example in your work: *He really felt he'd made it.* **c)** to continue to live after being ill or after a difficult experience: *They didn't think he'd make it.* **d)** if you make it a particular time, your watch says that time: *I make it ten past two.*
13 [T] *informal* to be able to go to something that has been arranged: *I'm afraid I **can't make** the meeting next week.*
14 make it Friday/10 o'clock etc *spoken* used to arrange a day or time to meet someone: *Let's make it Saturday morning.*
15 [linking verb] to be suitable for a job or purpose, because you have the right qualities: *John will make a good father.*
16 that makes two of us *spoken informal* used to say that you feel the same as someone else: *'I'm so tired!' 'Yeah, that makes two of us.'*
17 make or break sth to make someone or something be very successful, or make them fail completely
18 make do to use the things you have, although you really want other things: **+with** *You'll have to make do with some toast.*

make for sth *phr v* **1** to go towards a place: *He made for the door.* **2** to have a particular result or effect: *It should make for an interesting day.* → **be made for sth/sb** at **MADE²**

make sth **into** sth *phr v* to change something into something else: *We made his room into a study.*

make sth **of** sb/sth *phr v* **1** to have a particular opinion or understanding of something: *What do you make of this letter?* | *I **don't know what to make of her.*** **2 make too much of sth** to treat something as if it is more important than it really is **3 make sth of your life/of yourself** to use the opportunities that you have to become successful

make off with sth *phr v* to steal something

make out *phr v* **1 make sth** ⇔ **out** to be able to hear, see, or understand something: *He could just make out a dark shape.* | **+what/who etc** *I can't make out what the sign says.* → see box at **SEE** **2 make a cheque out (to sb)** to write a cheque so that money is paid to someone **3 make out sth** *informal* to say that something is true when it is not: **+(that)** *Brian was making out he'd won.* **4** *AmE informal* to kiss and touch in a sexual way

make up *phr v* **1 make sth** ⇔ **up** to invent a story or an excuse: *Ron made up an excuse.* **2 make up sth** to combine together to form something: *the rocks and minerals that make up the Earth's outer layer* **3 make it up to sb** to do something good for someone because you feel responsible for something bad that happened to them **4** to become friends with someone again, after an argument **5 make sb** ⇔ **up** to put coloured substances on someone's face, in order to improve or change their appearance

make up for sth *phr v* **1** to replace something that is lost or missing, or to make a bad situation seem better: *He ate a big lunch, to make up for missing breakfast.* **2** to have so much of one quality that it does not matter that you do not have others: *Jay lacks experience, but he makes up for it with hard work.* **3 make up for lost time** to do something quickly because you started late or worked too slowly

make² *n* [C] **1** a type of product made by a company: **+of** *a very popular make of washing machine* | *What make is your car?* **2 be on the make** *disapproving* to try to get money or power for yourself

'make-be,lieve *n* [U] when you imagine or pretend that something is real

makeover /'meɪkəʊvə $ -oʊvər/ *n* [C] **1** when you change the way you look completely by buying new clothes, getting your hair cut etc **2** when you change the way a building, room etc looks: *Let's **give** this room a **makeover**.*

maker /'meɪkə $ -ər/ *n* [C] **1** a person or company that produces something: **+of** *the makers of the car* | *the film maker Steven Spielberg* **2** a piece of equipment that makes something: *a bread maker* **3 decision/policy etc maker** someone who makes decisions etc

makeshift /'meɪkʃɪft/ *adj* [only before noun] made to be used for a short time only, when nothing better is available: *They slept in makeshift tents.*

'make-up, makeup /'meɪkʌp/ *n* **1** [U] coloured substances that you put on your face to improve or change your appearance: *I don't wear much **make-up**. It always takes her ages to **put on** her **make-up**.* **2** [singular] the combination of different people in a group: **+of** *I don't think we should change the make-up of the team.* **3** [singular, U] the different qualities that make someone or something the way they are: *They have the same **genetic make-up**.*

making /'meɪkɪŋ/ *n* **1** [U] the process or business of making something: *the art of rug making* | *the people involved in decision making* | *a book that was ten years **in the making*** (=took ten years to make) **2 in the making** a person or thing that will develop into something: *He is certainly a star in the making.* **3 be the making of sb** to make someone a better or more successful person: *This job will be the making of him.* **4 have the makings of sth** to have the qualities needed to become a particular kind of person or thing: *Sandy has the makings of a good doctor.* **5 of your own making** done or caused by you, and not by anyone else: *These problems are all of his own making.*

malaise /mə'leɪz, mæ-/ n [singular, U] *formal* a problem or illness that is difficult to describe exactly: *the general economic malaise*

malaria /mə'leəriə $ -'ler-/ n [U] a serious tropical disease that is spread by MOSQUITOES

male¹ /meɪl/ *adj*
1 belonging to the sex that cannot have babies [≠ **female**; ➡ **masculine**]: *a male lion*
2 typical of this sex [≠ **female**]: *a male voice*

male² n [C] a male person or animal [≠ **female**]

,male 'chauvinist n [C] a man who has fixed, traditional ideas about the position of women in society, and thinks that men are better or more important than women —**male chauvinism** n [U]

malevolent /mə'levələnt/ *adj formal* wanting to cause harm to someone

malfunction /mæl'fʌŋkʃən/ n [C] a fault in the way something works —**malfunction** v [I]

malice /'mælɪs/ n [U] when you want to hurt, upset, or embarrass someone: *He didn't do it out of malice.*

malicious /mə'lɪʃəs/ *adj* intended to hurt, upset, or embarrass someone: *malicious gossip* —**maliciously** *adv*

malign¹ /mə'laɪn/ v [T] *formal* to say or write unpleasant and untrue things about someone: *He was much maligned by the press.*

malign² *adj formal* harmful [≠ **benign**]: *He is a malign influence on the children.*

malignant /mə'lɪgnənt/ *adj* containing CANCER cells [➡ **benign**]: *a malignant tumour*

mall /mɔːl, mæl $ mɒːl/ n [C] a large covered area containing a lot of shops: *a shopping mall*

malleable /'mæliəbəl/ *adj*   **1** easy to press or bend into a new shape: *Clay is a malleable material.*   **2** *formal* someone who is malleable is easy to influence

mallet /'mælɪt/ n [C] a wooden hammer

malnourished /ˌmæl'nʌrɪʃt◂ $ -'nɜː-, -'nʌ-/ *adj* ill or weak because of not eating enough good food

malnutrition /ˌmælnjuː'trɪʃən $ -nuː-/ n [U] a serious medical condition caused by not eating enough good food

malpractice /mæl'præktɪs/ n [C,U] when someone such as a doctor or lawyer does not do his or her job properly

malt /mɔːlt $ mɒːlt/ n   **1** [U] grain, usually BARLEY, that is used for making beer, WHISKY etc   **2** [C] *AmE* a drink made from milk, malt, and ICE CREAM

maltreatment /mæl'triːtmənt/ n [U] *formal* when someone is treated cruelly —**maltreat** v [T]

mama /'mɑːmə/ n [C] *AmE* mother – used by or to children

mammal /'mæməl/ n [C] an animal that can feed its young with milk from its body, for example a dog, cow, or human

mammoth¹ /'mæməθ/ *adj* extremely large: *a mammoth task*

mammoth² n [C] a creature like an ELEPHANT that existed a long time ago

man¹ /mæn/ n plural **men** /men/
1 [C] an adult male person: *This rule applies to both men and women.* | *a middle-aged man*

guy *informal*/**chap** *BrE informal*/**bloke** *BrE informal*
gentleman – a polite word for a man, often used in formal situations
boy – a young male person, usually a child or a teenager
lad *old-fashioned* – a boy or young man
the lads *BrE spoken* – a group of male friends
youth – a teenage boy or young man, used especially in news reports: *The gang of youths terrorised the local community.*
→ **WOMAN**

2 [C] *old-fashioned* a person, either male or female: *All men are equal.*
3 [U] people as a group: *This is one of the worst diseases known to man.*
4 the man in the street ordinary people
→ **BEST MAN, HIT MAN, RIGHT-HAND MAN, STUNT MAN**

man² v [T] **manned, manning** to work with a machine or system, or to work in a place: *The phones were manned by volunteers.* —**manned** *adj*: *a manned rocket*

man³ *especially AmE spoken informal* used to emphasize what you are saying: *Man! Was she angry!*

manage /'mænɪdʒ/ v
1 [I,T] to succeed in doing something difficult or in dealing with problems: **manage to do sth** *I finally managed to open the door.* | *How do you manage to stay so slim?* | *I don't know how I'll manage it, but I'll be there.* | +**without** *How do you manage without a washing machine?* | **Can you manage** *that suitcase* (=can you carry it)?
2 [I] to succeed in buying the things that you need, even though you do not have much money: *I don't know how we'll manage now you've lost your job.*
3 [T] to be in charge of a business: *The hotel has been owned and managed by the same family for 200 years.*
4 [T] to use time, money, or other things sensibly, without wasting them: *You need to learn to manage your time more effectively.*

manageable /'mænɪdʒəbəl/ *adj* easy to control or deal with: *Divide the task into manageable sections.*

management /'mænɪdʒmənt/ n
1 [U] the job of controlling and organizing the work of a company or organization: *I don't enjoy management.* | **in management** *He works in management.* | *She's a* **management consultant.** | *You will need to learn* **management skills.**
2 [singular, U] the people who are in charge of controlling and organizing a company or organization: *Management will discuss this issue next week.* | *The factory is* **under new management.** | **senior/middle management**
3 [U] the way that a situation or event is controlled or organized: +**of** *careful management of the economy*

manager /'mænɪdʒə $ -ər/ n [C]
1 someone who is in charge of a business or of part of a business: +**of** *the manager of the factory* | *our new* **sales manager** | *the* **general manager**

M

2 someone who is in charge of training and organizing a sports team: *the England manager* | **+of** *the manager of Lazio*
3 someone who is in charge of the business affairs of a singer, actor etc
→ **LINE MANAGER, STAGE MANAGER**

manageress /ˌmænɪdʒəˈres $ ˈmænɪdʒərəs/ *n* [C] *BrE old-fashioned* a woman who is in charge of a shop, restaurant etc

M **managerial** /ˌmænəˈdʒɪəriəl $ -ˈdʒɪr-/ *adj* connected to the job of a manager: *She's got good managerial skills.*

managing di'rector *n* [C] *BrE* a person who is in charge of a large company

mandate¹ /ˈmændeɪt/ *n* [C] **1** the authority to do something, because people have voted for it: **mandate to do sth** *The President has a clear mandate to tackle crime.* | **+for** *a mandate for reform* **2** *formal* an official instruction

mandate² /mænˈdeɪt/ *v* [T] *especially AmE formal* to officially order or allow someone to do something: *Teachers are mandated by law to give this information.*

mandatory /ˈmændətəri $ -tɔːri/ *adj formal* something that is mandatory must be done because of a rule or law: *mandatory safety inspections* → see box at **NECESSARY**

mane /meɪn/ *n* [C] the long hair on the neck of a horse or lion

maneuver /məˈnuːvə $ -ər/ *n, v* the American spelling of MANOEUVRE

maneuverable /məˈnuːvərəbəl/ *adj* the American spelling of MANOEUVRABLE

manger /ˈmeɪndʒə $ -ər/ *n* [C] a container from which horses and cattle eat

mangled /ˈmæŋɡəld/ *adj* twisted and crushed: *the mangled remains of the vehicle*

mango /ˈmæŋɡəʊ $ -ɡoʊ/ *n* [C] plural **mangos** a tropical fruit with sweet yellow flesh → see picture at **FRUIT**

manhandle /ˈmænhændl/ *v* [T] to move someone or something roughly, using force: *They manhandled him out of the house.*

manhole /ˈmænhəʊl $ -hoʊl/ *n* [C] a covered hole on the surface of a road, which people go down to check pipes, wires etc

manhood /ˈmænhʊd/ *n* [U] being a man: *He had not yet **reached manhood**.* | *He felt he had to prove his **manhood**.*

manhunt /ˈmænhʌnt/ *n* [C] an organized search for a criminal

mania /ˈmeɪniə/ *n* [C,U] **1** a very strong interest in something: **+for** *her mania for cleanliness* **2** *technical* a mental illness which makes someone extremely excited or violent

maniac /ˈmeɪniæk/ *n* [C] *informal* someone who behaves in a stupid or dangerous way: *He drives like a maniac.*

manic /ˈmænɪk/ *adj* behaving in a very excited way: *He seemed full of manic energy.* | *She suffers from **manic depression** (=a mental illness in which you are sometimes very excited and sometimes very sad).*

manicure /ˈmænɪkjʊə $ -kjʊr/ *n* [C,U] a treatment in which someone cuts and shapes your finger nails —**manicure** *v* [T]

manifest¹ /ˈmænəˌfest/ *v* [T] *formal* to show something or be seen clearly: **manifest itself** *The disease manifests itself in many ways.*

manifest² *adj formal* easy to see: *his manifest reluctance to discuss the matter* —**manifestly** *adv*

manifestation /ˌmænəfeˈsteɪʃən $ -fə-/ *n* [C,U] *formal* a sign that something happens or that something exists: **+of** *a manifestation of the greenhouse effect*

manifesto /ˌmænəˈfestəʊ $ -toʊ/ *n* [C] plural **manifestos** a written statement by a political group, saying what they intend to do: *the party's election manifesto*

manipulate /məˈnɪpjʊleɪt/ *v* [T] **1** to make someone do what you want by skilfully influencing them: *Don't try to manipulate me!* **2** to skilfully control or move something: *You can manipulate the graphic images.* —**manipulation** /məˌnɪpjʊˈleɪʃən/ *n* [U]

manipulative /məˈnɪpjʊlətɪv $ -leɪ-/ *adj disapproving* clever at influencing people to get what you want

mankind /ˌmænˈkaɪnd/ *n* [U] all humans, considered as a group [= humankind]: *the evolution of mankind* → see box at **PEOPLE**

manly /ˈmænli/ *adj* having qualities that people expect and admire in a man: *a deep manly voice* —**manliness** *n* [U]

man-'made *adj* not made naturally, or not made of natural materials: **man-made fabrics** | *a man-made lake* → see box at **NATURAL**

mannequin /ˈmænəkɪn/ *n* [C] a model of the human body used for showing clothes

manner /ˈmænə $ -ər/ *n*
1 [singular] *formal* the way in which something is done or happens: **the manner of (doing) sth** *The manner of his death was surprising.* | **in a manner** *It will be decided in a manner that is fair.*
2 [singular] the way in which someone behaves with other people: *She has a calm relaxed manner.* | **+towards** *Beth's manner towards him had changed.*
3 manners [plural] polite ways of behaving in social situations: **good/bad manners** *Her children all **had good manners**.* | *Dad gave us a lecture about **table manners**.*
4 in a manner of speaking in some ways, though not exactly: *I'm in charge here now, in a manner of speaking.*
5 all manner of sth *formal* many different kinds of things or people: *We discussed all manner of subjects.*

mannered /ˈmænəd $ -ərd/ *adj* **well-mannered/bad-mannered/mild-mannered etc** polite, impolite etc in the way you behave → see box at **RUDE**

mannerism /ˈmænərɪzəm/ *n* [C,U] a way of speaking or behaving that is typical of a particular person: *He has the same mannerisms as his father.*

manoeuvrable *BrE*; **maneuverable** *AmE* /məˈnuːvərəbəl/ *adj* easy to move or turn

manoeuvre¹ *BrE*; **maneuver** *AmE* /məˈnuːvə $ -ər/ *n* [C] **1** a movement that needs skill or care: *a complicated manoeuvre* **2** a clever action done to get an advantage for yourself:

political maneuvers **3 manoeuvres** [plural] military activities which are done as practice or training

manoeuvre² *BrE*; **maneuver** *AmE v* [I,T] to move or to move something into a different position, especially something heavy: *Small boats are easier to manoeuvre.*

manor /'mænə $ -ər/ *also* '**manor house** *n* [C] a big old house with a large area of land around it

manpower /'mæn,paʊə $ ‚-paʊr/ *n* [U] all the people available to do a particular kind of work: *a lack of trained manpower*

mansion /'mænʃən/ *n* [C] a very large house → see box at HOUSE

manslaughter /'mæn,slɔːtə $ -,slɔːtər/ *n* [U] *law* the crime of killing someone, but without intending to kill them [➡ **murder**] → see box at KILL

mantelpiece /'mæntlpiːs/ *also* **mantel** /'mæntl/ *AmE n* [C] the shelf above a FIREPLACE

mantle /'mæntl/ *n formal* **take on/assume/wear the mantle of sth** to accept or have an important job or position: *Callaghan took on the mantle of party leader.*

mantra /'mæntrə/ *n* [C] a word or phrase that is repeated many times, for example while praying

manual¹ /'mænjuəl/ *adj* **1** manual work involves using your hands or physical strength: *manual jobs* | *manual workers* **2** operated or done by hand: *a manual typewriter* —**manually** *adv*

manual² *n* [C] a book that tells you how to do something, especially use a machine: *a computer manual*

manufacture /ˌmænjᵿˈfæktʃə $ -ər/ *v* [T] to use machines to make goods, usually in large numbers or amounts: *The company manufactures chemicals.* | *manufactured goods* —**manufacture** *n* [U] *the manufacture of high technology equipment*

manufacturer /ˌmænjᵿˈfæktʃərə $ -ər/ *n* [C] a company that makes goods: *a paint manufacturer*

manufacturing /ˌmænjᵿˈfæktʃərɪŋ/ *n* [U] the business of producing goods in factories: *the manufacturing industry*

manure /mə'njʊə $ mə'nʊr/ *n* [U] solid waste from animals, put into the soil to improve it and help plants grow

manuscript /'mænjᵿskrɪpt/ *n* [C] **1** a book or piece of writing before it is printed **2** an old book or document written by hand: *a medieval manuscript*

many /'meni/ *determiner, pron, adj*

1 a large number of people or things – used especially in negative sentences or questions [≠ **few**]: *I don't have many friends.* | *Were there many people at the party?* | *Some of the houses have bathrooms but many do not.* | **+of** *Many of our staff work part-time.* | *There are so many I want.* | *You've been reading too many romantic novels* (=more than you should). | **a great many/a good many/very many** (=a very large number) *It happened a good many years ago.*

2 how many used to ask or talk about how large a number is: *How many sisters do you have?* | *I don't know how many tickets to buy.*

3 as many used to talk about a number of people or things compared to another number: **as many ... as** *I don't have as many lessons as I did last year.* | **twice/three times etc as many** *They now employ twice as many women as men.*

4 as many as 50/100 etc used to emphasize that a number is surprisingly large: *As many as 2000 jobs could disappear.*

5 many a sth *formal or old-fashioned* a large number of people or things: *I've sat here **many a time** (=often) and wondered about it.*

6 many thanks *written* used in letters to thank someone for something

M

many, a lot of
In sentences that are not negative and not questions, it is more usual to say **a lot of** rather than **many**, especially in spoken English: *She has a lot of friends.*
→ LOT

Maori /'maʊri/ *n* [C] someone who belongs to the race of people that first lived in New Zealand —**Maori** *adj*

map¹ /mæp/ *n* [C] a drawing of a particular area that shows its roads, rivers, mountains etc: **+of** *a street map of Mexico City* | *I'll draw a map of where we live.* | **on a map** *I'm trying to find Vancouver on the map.* | *Are you any good at reading a map?*

COLLOCATIONS

You **look at** a map when you are trying to find your way to or around a place.
If you look very carefully at a map, you can say that you **study** the map.
If you can **read** a map, you can understand the information on a map.
If something is **on the map**, the map shows it: *I can't find Church Street on the map.*
A **detailed map** is one which includes a lot of information: *a detailed map of Edinburgh*

map² *v* [T] **mapped, mapping** to make a map of an area
map sth ⇔ out *phr v* to plan carefully how something will happen: *Her parents had already mapped out her future.*

maple /'meɪpəl/ *n* [C,U] a tree with leaves that have five points and that turn red or gold in autumn

mar /maː $ maːr/ *v* [T] **marred, marring** to make something less attractive or enjoyable [= **spoil**]: *The election day was marred by violence.*

marathon /'mærəθən $ -θɑːn/ *n* [C] **1** a race in which people run about 26 miles or 42 kilometres **2** an activity that continues for a long time and needs determination or patience: *a marathon journey lasting 56 hours*

marauding /mə'rɔːdɪŋ $ -'rɒː-/ *adj* [only before noun] *written* searching for something to kill, steal, or destroy: *marauding gangs*

marble /'maːbəl $ 'maːr-/ *n* **1** [U] a type of hard rock that becomes smooth when polished, used for making buildings, STATUES etc **2** [C] a small coloured glass ball, used to play a children's game

M

march¹ /mɑːtʃ $ mɑːrtʃ/ v [I]
1 if soldiers march, they walk with firm regular steps: **+across/along/past etc** *Troops marched into the capital.* → see box at **WALK** → see picture on page A11
2 to walk together in a large group to protest about something: **+along/down/through etc** *5,000 demonstrators marched through the city.* → see box at **PROTEST**
3 to walk quickly because you are angry or determined: **+off/out etc** *He marched out of the room without a word.*

march² n [C]
1 an organized event in which a lot of people walk together to protest about something: *a peace march* (=demanding peace not war) → see box at **PROTEST**
2 a journey made by soldiers who are walking from one place to another: *the long march south*
3 a piece of music with a regular beat for people to march to

March n [C,U] written abbreviation **Mar.** the third month of the year, between February and April: **next/last March** *She started work here last March.* | **in March** *The theater opened in March.* | **on March 6th** *There's a meeting on March 6th.* → see box at **MONTH**

mare /meə $ mer/ n [C] a female horse

margarine /ˌmɑːdʒəˈriːn, ˌmɑːgə- $ ˈmɑːrdʒ-ərᵻn/ n [U] a food used instead of butter, made from animal or vegetable fat

margin /ˈmɑːdʒᵻn $ ˈmɑːr-/ n [C] **1** the empty space at the side of a page: **in the margin** *Write your marks in the margin.* **2** the difference between the number of votes, points etc that the winners and the losers get in an election or competition: *They won by a wide margin* (=by a lot of votes etc). **3** technical the difference between what it costs a business to buy or produce something and how much they sell it for: *a profit margin of 30%* **4 margin of error** the degree to which a calculation might or can be wrong

marginal /ˈmɑːdʒᵻnəl $ ˈmɑːr-/ adj very small or unimportant: *a marginal improvement*

marginalize also **ise** BrE /ˈmɑːdʒᵻnəlaɪz $ ˈmɑːr-/ v [T] to make a person or group unimportant and powerless in an unfair way: *Some employees complained of being marginalized.*

marginally /ˈmɑːdʒᵻnəli $ ˈmɑːr-/ adv very slightly: *The other car was marginally cheaper.*

marijuana /ˌmærᵻˈwɑːnə, -ˈhwɑːnə/ n [U] an illegal drug that is smoked [= cannabis]

marina /məˈriːnə/ n [C] a small area of water where people keep boats used for pleasure

marinate /ˈmærᵻneɪt/ also **marinade** /ˌmærᵻˈneɪd/ v [T] to put food into a mixture of oil and spices before you cook it —**marinade** n [C,U]

marine /məˈriːn/ adj [only before noun] **1** relating to the sea and the creatures that live there: *marine life* **2** relating to ships or the navy

Marine n [C] a soldier who serves on a ship, especially a member of the Royal Marines or the US Marine Corps

mariner /ˈmærᵻnə $ -ər/ n [C] literary a SAILOR

marital /ˈmærᵻtl/ adj [only before noun] relating to marriage: *marital problems* | *your marital status* (=whether you are married or not)

maritime /ˈmærᵻtaɪm/ adj [only before noun] relating to the sea or ships

mark¹ $ mɑːk $ mɑːrk/ n [C]
1 a small area of dirt or damage on something: **+on** *His feet left dirty marks on the carpet.* | **burn/scratch/bite etc mark** *burn marks on the kitchen table*

THESAURUS

blemish – a mark on your skin that spoils its appearance
bruise – a purple or brown mark on your skin that you get because you have fallen or been hit
scar – a permanent mark on your skin, caused by a cut or by something that burns you
spot BrE/**pimple/zit** AmE informal – a small raised red mark or lump on your skin
wart – a small hard raised mark on your skin caused by a virus
blister – a small area of skin that is swollen and full of liquid because it has been rubbed or burned
freckle – one of several small light brown marks on someone's skin

2 a small area of different colour on a person's skin or an animal's fur [➡ birthmark]: *a black cat with a white mark on its chest*
3 a sign or shape that is written or printed: *Make a mark in the centre of the circle.* | *punctuation marks*
4 a particular level, number etc that something reaches: *Unemployment passed the one million mark.* | *The temperature should reach the 20 degree mark tomorrow.*
5 especially BrE a letter or number given by a teacher to show how good a student's work is [= grade AmE]: **good/high/top mark** *She always gets good marks.* | **pass mark** (=the mark needed to pass an exam) | **get full marks** (=get everything correct)
6 make/leave your mark to become successful or famous: **+as** *Dorsey made his mark as a pianist.*
7 off the mark/wide of the mark not correct: *Our estimate was way off the mark* (=completely wrong).
8 a mark of sth a sign of a particular quality or feeling: *The 2 minute silence was a mark of respect for the dead.*
9 be quick/slow etc off the mark to be quick, slow etc to understand or react to something
10 on your marks, get set, go! spoken said in order to start a race

mark² v [T]
1 to write or draw on something, for someone else to see: **mark sth on sth** *The price is marked on the bottom.* | **mark sth personal/fragile/urgent etc** *a document marked 'private and confidential'*
2 to leave an area of dirt or damage on something: *The front of the car was marked where a truck had hit it.*
3 to celebrate an important event: **mark sth with sth** *They're planning to mark their anniver-*

sary with a big party. | *She was given a gold watch to* **mark the occasion.**
4 to show where something is: *He marked the route on the map in red.*
5 to be a sign of an important change or development: *The move* **marks a change** *in government policy.* | *These elections* **mark the end** *of an era.*
6 *especially BrE* to read a piece of a student's work and give a number or letter which shows how good it is [= **grade** *AmE*]
7 *especially BrE* to stay close to someone from the opposing team in a sports game [= **guard** *AmE*]

mark sth ⇔ **down** *phr v* **1** to write something on paper, usually in order to keep a record: **+as** *The teacher marked him down as absent.*
2 to reduce the price of something: **+from/to** *Coats have been marked down from $80 to $50.*

mark sth ⇔ **out** *phr v* to show the shape or position of something by drawing lines around it: *A volleyball court was marked out on the grass.*

mark sth ⇔ **up** *phr v* to increase the price of something: *CDs may be marked up as much as 80%.*

marked /mɑːkt $ mɑːrkt/ *adj* very easy to notice: *a marked lack of enthusiasm* —**markedly** /ˈmɑːk$dli $ ˈmɑːr-/ *adv*

marker /ˈmɑːkə $ ˈmɑːrkər/ *n* [C] **1** an object, sign etc that shows the position of something **2** also **'marker pen** *BrE* a large pen with a thick point → see picture at CLASSROOM

market¹ /ˈmɑːk$t $ ˈmɑːr-/ *n*

fruit and vegetable market

1 [C] an outside area or large building where people buy and sell goods, food etc: *We buy all our vegetables from the market.* | **fish/fruit and vegetable/flower etc market** *an antiques market* | *a* **street market** (=where people sell things from tables in the street) | *a* **market stall** (=big table on which you put things you want to sell)
2 the market the STOCK MARKET: *Analysts are forecasting a downturn in the market.*
3 [C] business or trade in a particular type of goods or service: *The company has 50% of the market.* | **the housing/property etc market** *the European car market*
4 on the market available for people to buy: *The new game will be on the market in May.* | *We're* **putting** *our house* **on the market** (=offering it for sale).
5 [C] a country or area where a company sells its goods: *Our main overseas market is Japan.*
6 [singular] the number of people who want to buy something: **+for** *The market for academic books is small.*
→ **BLACK MARKET, FLEA MARKET, FREE MARKET, LABOUR MARKET**

market² *v* [T] to advertise something in a particular way in order to sell it: **market sth as sth** *The book is being marketed as a sophisticated comedy.*

marketable /ˈmɑːk$təbəl $ ˈmɑːr/ *adj* marketable goods or skills are easy to sell

,market e'conomy *n* [C] an economic system in which companies are not controlled by the government

,market 'forces *n* [plural] the way things affect the levels of prices and wages, for example how many people want to buy a particular product and how much is available

marketing /ˈmɑːk$tɪŋ $ ˈmɑːr-/ *n* [U] the activity of deciding how to advertise a product, what price to charge for it etc: *He works in* **sales and marketing.** | *a* **marketing campaign**

marketplace /ˈmɑːk$tpleɪs $ ˈmɑːr-/ *n* [C]
1 the marketplace the business of competing with other companies to buy and sell goods
2 an area in a town where there is a market

,market re'search *n* [U] the business activity of finding out what goods people buy and why they buy them

marking /ˈmɑːkɪŋ $ ˈmɑːr-/ *n* [C usually plural] things painted or written on something, or the colours and patterns on something such as an animal's fur: *strange markings on the walls of the cave*

marksman /ˈmɑːksmən $ ˈmɑːrks-/ *n* [C] plural **marksmen** /-mən/ someone who can shoot a gun very well

'mark-up *n* [C] the amount by which a shop increases the price of its goods from what they paid for them to what they sell them for: *The usual mark-up is 20%.*

marmalade /ˈmɑːməleɪd $ ˈmɑːr-/ *n* [U] a JAM made from fruit such as oranges or LEMONS

maroon¹ /məˈruːn/ *n* [U] a dark brownish red colour —**maroon** *adj*

maroon² *v* **be marooned** to be left somewhere in a difficult situation, where there is no one to help you: *The car broke down and we were marooned.*

marquee /mɑːˈkiː $ mɑːr-/ *n* [C] **1** *BrE* a large tent used at an outdoor event or for a party **2** *AmE* a large sign above the door of a theatre or cinema which gives the name of the play or film

marriage /ˈmærɪdʒ/ *n*
1 [C,U] a relationship between two people who are married, or the state of being married: *They have a very* **happy marriage.** | **+to** *his marriage to Marilyn Monroe*

M

COLLOCATIONS

happy marriage
unhappy/troubled/failed/loveless marriage
marriage breaks down – a marriage ends because of problems and disagreement
breakdown/breakup of your/sb's marriage – the end of a marriage
your/sb's marriage ends in divorce
proposal of marriage when someone asks you to marry them
mixed marriage – a marriage between people of different races
arranged marriage – when your parents choose the person you marry

2 [C] a wedding ceremony: *The **marriage took place** at St John's Church.*

married /'mærɪd/ *adj* having a husband or a wife: *Are you married or single?* | **+to** *Nicole is married to my brother.* | *We're **getting married** next month.*

THESAURUS

If someone is **single**, they are not married.
If someone is **engaged**, they have formally agreed to marry someone in the future.
If a husband and wife are **separated**, they are living apart because they are having problems in their marriage.
If a husband and wife get **divorced**, they officially end their marriage.
If a couple is **living together**, they are in a romantic relationship and share a home together, but are not married.
If someone is **widowed**, their husband or wife has died.
→ WEDDING

---

marrow /'mærəʊ $ -roʊ/ *n* **1** [U] the soft substance in the middle of bones **2** [C] *BrE* a large long green vegetable

marry /'mæri/ *v* **married, marrying, marries**

1 [I,T] if you marry someone, you become their husband or wife [➡ **married**]: *I've asked her to marry me.* | *She **married young** (=at a young age).* | *They **got married** last year.*

2 [T] to officially make two people husband and wife at a special ceremony

Mars /mɑːz $ mɑːrz/ *n* [singular] a small red PLANET, fourth from the sun

marsh /mɑːʃ $ mɑːrʃ/ *n* [C,U] an area of soft wet land —**marshy** *adj*

marshal[1] /'mɑːʃəl $ 'mɑːr-/ *n* [C] **1** an officer of the highest rank in the army or air force of some countries **2** someone who helps to organize or control a large public event

marshal[2] *v* [T] **marshalled, marshalling** *BrE*; **marshaled, marshaling** *AmE* to organize something so that you can use it in an effective way: *She paused a moment to **marshal** her thoughts.*

marshmallow /ˌmɑːʃˈmæləʊ $ 'mɑːrʃmeloʊ/ *n* [C,U] a soft white or pink sweet made of sugar

marsupial /mɑːˈsuːpiəl $ mɑːr-/ *n* [C] an animal such as a KANGAROO that carries its babies in a pocket of skin on its body

mart /mɑːt $ mɑːrt/ *n* [C] *AmE* a place where goods are sold

martial /'mɑːʃəl $ 'mɑːr-/ *adj* [only before noun] relating to war or fighting

martial 'art *n* [C] a sport such as KARATE in which you fight using your hands and feet

martial 'law *n* [U] a situation in which the army controls a city, country etc

Martian /'mɑːʃən $ 'mɑːr-/ *n* [C] an imaginary creature from the PLANET Mars —**Martian** *adj*

martyr /'mɑːtə $ 'mɑːrtər/ *n* [C] **1** someone who dies for their religious or political beliefs **2** someone who tries to get other people's sympathy by complaining about their life —**martyrdom** *n* [U]

marvel[1] /'mɑːvəl $ 'mɑːr-/ *v* [I,T] **marvelled, marvelling** *BrE*; **marveled, marveling** *AmE* to feel or express great surprise or admiration for something: **+at** *I marvelled at her ingenuity.*

marvel[2] *n* [C] something or someone that is extremely good or skilful: **+of** *the marvels of modern science*

marvellous *BrE*; **marvelous** *AmE* /'mɑːvələs $ 'mɑːr-/ *adj* extremely good or enjoyable: *a marvellous book*

Marxism /'mɑːksɪzəm $ 'mɑːr-/ *n* [U] a system of political ideas based on the writings of Karl Marx

Marxist /'mɑːksɪst $ 'mɑːr-/ *adj* relating to Marxism —**Marxist** *n* [C]

marzipan /'mɑːzɪˌpæn $ 'mɑːrts\tfrac{1}{2}-, 'mɑːrz\tfrac{1}{2}-/ *n* [U] a sweet food made with ALMONDS and used to cover cakes

mascara /mæˈskɑːrə $ mæˈskærə/ *n* [U] something you can put on your EYELASHES to make them look darker and longer

mascot /'mæskət, -kɒt $ -kɑːt/ *n* [C] an animal, toy etc that a team or organization thinks will bring them good luck

masculine /'mæskjÜlɪn/ *adj*

1 having qualities that people think are typical of men: *a masculine voice*

2 in some languages, belonging to a group of nouns, PRONOUNS etc that is different from the FEMININE and NEUTER groups [➡ **feminine**]

masculinity /ˌmæskjÜˈlɪnɪti/ *n* [U] the qualities that are considered to be typical of men [➡ **femininity**]

mash /mæʃ/ *v* [T] to crush food until it is soft: *Mash the potatoes in a bowl.* → see box at PRESS → see picture at POTATO —**mashed** *adj*

mask[1] /mɑːsk $ mæsk/ *n* [C] something that covers all or part of your face in order to protect or hide it: *He was robbed by two men **wearing masks**.*

mask[2] *v* [T] to prevent a smell, taste, sound etc from being noticed: *The sugar masks the taste of the medicine.*

masked /mɑːskt $ mæskt/ *adj* wearing a mask

'masking tape *n* [U] paper that is sticky on one side, used to protect the edge of an area you are painting

masochism /'mæsəkɪzəm/ *n* [U] when someone gets pleasure from being hurt, for example sexual pleasure —**masochist** *n* [U] —**masochistic** /ˌmæsəˈkɪstɪk◀/ *adj*

mason /'meɪsən/ *n* [C] **1** a person who makes things using stone **2** a FREEMASON

masonry /'meɪsənri/ *n* [U] bricks or stones that a building or wall is made from

masquerade /ˌmæskəˈreɪd/ *v* [I] to pretend to be someone or something different: **+as** *He masqueraded as a doctor.*

mass[1] /mæs/ *n*

1 [C usually singular] a large amount or number of something all together: **a great/solid/dense etc mass (of sth)** *a dense mass of forest* | *a seething mass of people* → see box at GROUP

2 masses (of sth) *BrE informal* a lot of something: *I've got masses of homework.*

3 the masses all the ordinary people in a society

4 also **Mass** [C,U] the main religious ceremony in the Roman Catholic Church and some other Christian churches

5 [U] *technical* the amount of material in something – used in physics: **+of** *the mass of the sun*

mass² *adj* involving a large number of people: *mass communication* | *weapons of mass destruction*

mass³ *v* [I,T] to come together, or to make people or things come together, in a large group: *Troops are massing at the border.*

massacre /'mæsəkə $ -ər/ *n* [C,U] when a lot of INNOCENT people are killed violently: *the massacre of women and children* —**massacre** *v* [T] → see box at KILL

massage /'mæsɑːʒ $ mə'sɑːʒ/ *n* [C,U] when you press and rub someone's body to reduce pain or help them relax: *He gave me a back massage.* —**massage** *v* [T]

masseur /mæ'sɜː $ -'sɜːr/ *n* [C] someone who gives massages

masseuse /mæ'sɜːz $ mæ'suːz/ *n* [C] a woman who gives massages

massive /'mæsɪv/ *adj* very big: *a massive dog* | *He had a massive heart attack.*

'mass-,market *adj* [only before noun] designed to be bought by a very large number of people: *mass-market paperbacks*

,mass 'media *n* **the mass media** television, radio, and newspapers

,mass 'murderer *n* [C] someone who has murdered a lot of people

,mass-pro'duced *adj* things that are mass-produced are made cheaply and in large numbers, using machines: *mass-produced cars* —**mass production** *n* [C]

mast /mɑːst $ mæst/ *n* [C] **1** a tall pole used to hold up the sails of a ship **2** *BrE* a metal pole that sends out radio signals

master¹ /'mɑːstə $ 'mæstər/ *n* [C] **1** someone who is very skilled at something: *a master of kung fu* **2** *old-fashioned* the man who has control over servants, animals, or workers [➙ **mistress**] **3** a document or recording that you use to make copies **4 Master of Arts/Science etc** a QUALIFICATION that you study at university after you have got your first DEGREE **5** *BrE old-fashioned* a male teacher

master² *v* [T] **1** to learn a subject or skill very well: *I never mastered the violin.* **2** to learn to control a feeling or situation: *I finally mastered my fear of water.*

master³ *adj* [only before noun] a master document or recording is the one you use to make copies

masterful /'mɑːstəfəl $ 'mæstər-/ *adj* done with great skill: *a masterful performance*

mastermind /'mɑːstəmaɪnd $ 'mæstər-/ *n* [C usually singular] someone who organizes a complicated plan, especially a criminal plan: **+behind** *the mastermind behind the hijacking* —**mastermind** *v* [T]

masterpiece /'mɑːstəpiːs $ 'mæstər-/ *n* [C] a very good work of art or piece of writing

'master's de,gree also **master's** *informal n* [C] a QUALIFICATION that you study at university after you have got your first DEGREE

mastery /'mɑːstəri $ 'mæ-/ *n* [U] **1** great skill or understanding of something: *a pianist with total mastery of her instrument* **2** complete control over someone or something: **+of/over** *They fought for mastery of the area.*

masturbate /'mæstəbeɪt $ -tər-/ *v* [I,T] to rub your sex organs for sexual pleasure —**masturbation** /,mæstə'beɪʃən $ -tər-/ *n* [U]

mat¹ /mæt/ *n* [C] **1** a piece of thick material that covers part of a floor: *a prayer mat* (=used to kneel on to pray) → see picture at BATHROOM **2** a small piece of thick material that you put on a table: *Put that hot dish on a mat.* | *a mouse mat* (=used with a computer mouse)

mat² *adj* another spelling of MATT

match¹ /mætʃ/ *n*

1 [C] *especially BrE* a game or sports event between two teams or players: **+against/ between/with** *Did you watch the match between Kenya and Ireland?* | **tennis/cricket/football match** *Who won the football match?* | **boxing/ wrestling match**

2 [C] a small wooden stick with a coloured substance at one end that produces a flame when you rub it quickly against something rough: **strike/light a match** *He lit a match so we could see.* | *a box of matches*

3 [singular] something that is the same colour or pattern as something else, or looks attractive with it: **+for** *These shoes are a perfect match for your bag.*

4 [singular] someone who is as strong, as clever, as fast etc as an opponent: **+for** *I don't think he'll be a match for the champion.*

match² *v*

1 [I,T] if one thing matches another, or if two things match, they look good together because they are the same or similar: *The carpet matches the curtains.* | *Your socks don't match.*

2 [I,T] if two pieces of information match, or if one matches the other, they are connected and are not different from each other: *The suspect matches the eye-witness description.*

3 [T] to put two people or things together because they are similar, connected, or suitable for each other: **match sth to/with sth** *Match the celebrities to their pets.* | *accommodation that matches your needs*

4 [T] to be as good as someone or something else: *No one can match his speed on the field.* | **equally/evenly matched** *The two candidates are evenly matched.*

match up *phr v* **1 match sb/sth ⇔ up** to put people or things together because they are connected or suitable for each other: *We match up graduates and employers.* | **+with** *Annie tried to match me up with her cousin.* **2** if two pieces of information match up, they are the same: **+with** *The evidence does not match up with his statement.* **3 match up to sb's expectations/ hopes etc** to be as good as someone expected, wanted etc

matchbox /'mætʃbɒks $ -bɑːks/ *n* [C] a small box containing matches

matching /'mætʃɪŋ/ *adj* [only before noun] in the same colour, style, pattern etc as something else: *a necklace with matching earrings*

matchless /'mætʃləs/ *adj literary* better than anything else

mate¹ /meɪt/ *n* [C] **1** someone that you do things with, such as a job or sport: *His team mates congratulated him.* | *an evening out with her work mates* | *her school mates* **2** *BrE*

M

informal a friend **3** the sexual PARTNER of an animal **4** an officer on a ship → **CLASSMATE, ROOMMATE**

mate² *v* [I] when animals mate, they have sex to produce babies: **+with** *The male mates with several females.*

materials

silver bracelet

woolly glove *BrE*/
wooly glove *AmE*

concrete block

wooden barrel

rubber boots

leather belt

glass jar

plastic mixing bowl

material¹ /mə'tɪəriəl $ -'tɪr-/ *n*
1 [C,U] cloth used to make clothes, curtains etc [= **fabric**]: *a dress made of light cotton material* | *a selection of woollen materials*
2 [C,U] a solid substance that you can use to make things: *They sell all sorts of building materials.* | *Most of our raw materials* (=natural materials that have not been changed) *are imported.* | *a lorry transporting radioactive material*
3 [U] information or ideas that are used in books, films etc: *Does his book contain any new material?*

material² *adj* **1** relating to money or possessions, rather than religion, moral beliefs etc [≠ **spiritual**]: *We are not interested in material wealth.* **2** *formal* important and having an effect on a result: *No material evidence was presented in court.*

materialism /mə'tɪəriəlɪzəm $ -'tɪr-/ *n* [U] *disapproving* the belief that money and posses-

sions are more important than religion, moral beliefs etc —**materialistic** /mə,tɪəriə'lɪstɪk◂ $ -,tɪr-/ *adj*

materialize also **-ise** *BrE v* [I] if a possible event or plan materializes, it happens: *His dream failed to materialize.*

maternal /mə'tɜːnl $ -ɜːr-/ *adj* **1** typical of the way a good mother behaves: *Looking after the twins awakened her maternal instincts.* **2** [only before noun] *technical* relating to your mother [↔ **paternal**]: *my maternal grandfather*

maternity /mə'tɜːnᵻti $ -ɜːr-/ *adj* [only before noun] relating to a woman who is going to have a baby soon [↔ **paternity**]: *maternity clothes* | *maternity leave* (=time that a woman has away from her job because she has just had a baby)

math /mæθ/ *n* [U] *AmE* mathematics [= **maths** *BrE*]

mathematical /,mæθᵻ'mætɪkəl◂/ *adj* connected with mathematics: *a mathematical equation*

mathematician /,mæθᵻmə'tɪʃən/ *n* [C] someone who studies or teaches mathematics

mathematics /,mæθᵻ'mætɪks/ *n* [U] the science of numbers and shapes

maths /mæθs/ *n* [U] *BrE* mathematics [= **math** *AmE*]

matinée /'mætᵻneɪ $,mætn'eɪ/ *n* [C] a performance of a play or film in the afternoon

matriarch /'meɪtriɑːk $ -ɑːrk/ *n* [C] an older woman who has the most power and influence in her family

matrimony /'mætrᵻməni $ -mouni/ *n* [U] *formal* being married —**matrimonial** /,mætrᵻ'mouniəl $ -'mou-/ *adj*

matron /'meɪtrən/ *n* [U] *BrE old-fashioned* a nurse who is in charge of other nurses in a hospital

matt, matte, mat /mæt/ *adj* a matt paint, colour, or photograph is not shiny [≠ **gloss**]

matted /'mætᵻd/ *adj* matted hair or fur is twisted and stuck together

matter¹ /'mætə $ -ər/ *n*
1 [C] a subject or situation that you must deal with: *We have some important matters to discuss.* | *Don't laugh, it's a serious matter.* | *This is a personal matter.* | *It's a matter for you to decide.* | *If you say anything, it will make matters worse.*
2 as a matter of fact *spoken* used to add details to something you have just said, especially when these are surprising or unexpected: *'Do you know Liz?' 'As a matter of fact we were in school together.'*
3 the matter *spoken* used in phrases when you are saying that there is a problem of some sort: *What's the matter? You look upset.* | *Is there something the matter with Jane?* | *Nothing's the matter, leave me alone.* | *There's something the matter with my computer* (=it isn't working properly). → see box at **PROBLEM**
4 no matter how/where/what etc *spoken* used to say that a situation stays the same whatever happens: *No matter how hard she tried, she couldn't open it.*
5 [U] **a)** *technical* the material that everything in the universe is made of **b)** *formal* a particular substance or type of thing: **waste/solid/ organic etc matter** *The insects eat vegetable*

matter. | **reading/printed etc matter** *Take some reading matter for the trip.*

6 be a matter of (doing) sth used to say what something involves: *Driving is just a matter of practising.* | *Whether he has any talent is a matter of opinion* (=it depends on your views). | *Fitting a smoke alarm could be a matter of life or death* (=it could involve very serious consequences).

7 a matter of seconds/days/inches etc only a few seconds, days etc: *An ambulance came in a matter of minutes.*

8 as a matter of sth because of a particular belief or quality: *As a matter of interest* (=because I am interested), *where are you from?*

9 as a matter of course as part of the normal process or system: *They checked the rest of the house as a matter of course.*

10 for that matter used to say that what is true about one thing is also true of another: *I don't like him, or his sister for that matter!*

→ SUBJECT MATTER

matter² *v* [I] to be important: **it doesn't/won't etc matter if** *It doesn't matter if you're late.* | **matter what/which/how** *I don't think it matters what you do.* | **+that** *Does it matter that the covers don't match?* | **+to** *Money is the only thing that matters to him.* | *The environment really matters* (=it matters a lot). | *Age doesn't matter much in this job.*

matter-of-'fact *adj* showing no emotion when you talk about something: **+about** *Jan was matter-of-fact about her divorce.*

matting /'mætɪŋ/ *n* [U] strong rough material

mattress /'mætrɨs/ *n* [C] the soft thick part of a bed that you lie on: *I sleep better on a firm mattress.* | *a soft mattress*

mature /mə'tʃʊə $ -'tʃʊr/ *adj* **1** behaving in a reasonable way like an adult [≠ **immature**]: *She's very mature for her age.* **2** fully grown or developed: *a mature cherry tree* | *Cats are sexually mature at a young age.* **3** [only before noun] a polite way of referring to someone who is older than other people who are doing the same thing: *fashions for mature brides* | **mature student** *BrE* (=a student who is over 25 years old) **4** mature cheese or wine tastes strong because it has developed for a long time —**mature** *v* [I,T] *Pat's matured since going to college.* | *Mature the wine in a cool place.*

maturity /mə'tʃʊərɨti $ -'tʃʊr-/ *n* [U] **1** when someone behaves sensibly and like an adult [≠ **immaturity**]: *He showed a lack of maturity for his age.* **2** the time when someone or something is fully developed: *Rabbits reach maturity in only five weeks.*

maudlin /'mɔːdlɨn $ 'mɒː-/ *adj* talking in a sad and silly way: *He gets maudlin after a few drinks.*

maul /mɔːl $ mɒːl/ *v* [T] **1** if an animal mauls someone, it injures them by tearing their flesh: *He was mauled by a lion.* **2** *disapproving* to touch someone in a rough sexual way

mausoleum /ˌmɔːsə'liːəm $ ˌmɒː-/ *n* [C] a stone building containing the dead bodies of important people

mauve /məʊv $ moʊv/ *n* [U] a pale purple colour —**mauve** *adj*

maverick /'mævərɪk/ *n* [C] someone whose ideas or opinions are different from those of most people: *a political maverick*

max /mæks/ *adj* the abbreviation of **maximum** —**max** *adv*: *It'll cost $50 max.* —**max** *n* [singular]

maxim /'mæksɨm/ *n* [C] a phrase that gives advice on sensible behaviour

maximize also **-ise** *BrE* /'mæksɨmaɪz/ *v* [T] to increase something as much as possible [≠ **minimize**]: *Reduce costs and maximize profits.*

maximum /'mæksɨməm/ *adj* [only before noun] the maximum amount, speed, number etc is the biggest that is possible [≠ **minimum**]: *a maximum speed limit of 70 mph* —**maximum** *n* [C usually singular] *He now faces a maximum of 10 years in jail.* —**maximum** *adv*

may /meɪ/ *modal verb*

1 if something may happen, it is possible that it will happen, but not certain [➡ **might, can**]: *Your job may involve travel.* | *I may not have enough money.*

2 *formal* used to say that someone is allowed to do something: *Students may borrow CDs from the library.*

3 *spoken* used to ask or suggest something politely: *May I ask your name?*

4 used to say that you accept that one thing is true but that something else connected to it is more important: *Exercise may be dull but we all need it.*

5 may as well *spoken* used to say that someone should do something because there is no reason not to [= **might as well**]: *We may as well go to bed.*

GRAMMAR

May is not used in questions about possible events or situations. Use might instead: *Might there be problems?*

May *n* [C,U] the fifth month of the year, between April and June: **next/last May** *I haven't heard from her since last May.* | **in May** *The work began in May.* | **on May 6th** *We don't have any meetings on May 6th, do we?* → see box at MONTH

maybe /'meɪbi/ *adv*

1 used to say that something could be true or could happen, but you are not sure [= **perhaps**]: *Maybe Ann has already left.* | *Maybe you're right and maybe not.*

2 *spoken* used to answer a question when you are not sure whether to answer yes or no: *'Are you going to accept?' 'I don't know. Maybe.'*

3 used to make a suggestion: *Maybe you should complain.*

4 used to show that you are not sure about a number or amount: *He was 30, maybe 35 years old.*

mayday /'meɪdeɪ/ *n* [singular] a radio signal that a ship or plane uses to ask for help [➡ **SOS**]

mayhem /'meɪhem/ *n* [U] a very confused situation in which people are frightened or excited: *A scene of complete mayhem followed the blast.*

mayonnaise /ˌmeɪə'neɪz $ 'meɪəneɪz/ *n* [U] a thick cold white SAUCE made with eggs and oil

mayor /meə $ 'meɪər/ *n* [C] **1** the person who is elected to lead the government of a town or city **2** *BrE* someone who is chosen to represent a town or city at official ceremonies

M

maze /meɪz/ *n* [C] a complicated system of roads or paths where you might get lost: **+of** *a maze of corridors*

MB /ˌem 'biː/, **Mb** the written abbreviation of **megabyte**

MBA also **M.B.A.** *AmE* /ˌem biː 'eɪ/ *n* [C] **Master of Business Administration** a university degree in the skills needed to be in charge of a business that you can get after your first degree

McCoy /məˈkɔɪ/ *n* **the real McCoy** *informal* something that is real, not a copy

MD *BrE*; **M.D.** *AmE* /ˌem 'diː/ *n* **1** Doctor of Medicine a university degree in medicine that you can get after your first degree **2** [C] *BrE* a MANAGING DIRECTOR

me /mi; *strong* miː/ *pron*
1 the object form of 'I': *Give me a kiss.* | *'Who's that in the photo?' 'It's me!'*
2 me too *spoken* used to agree with someone: *'I'm hungry!' 'Me too.'*
3 me neither also **nor me** *spoken* used to agree with a negative statement: *'I don't like coffee.' 'Nor me.'*

meadow /ˈmedəʊ $ -doʊ/ *n* [C] a field with wild grass and flowers

meagre *BrE*; **meager** *AmE* /ˈmiːɡə $ -ər/ *adj* very small in amount: *his meagre wages* | *a school with meagre resources*

meal /miːl/ *n* [C] when you sit down to eat food, or the food that you eat: *When did you last eat a proper meal?* | *We had a delicious four-course meal.* | *Shall we go for a meal?*

COLLOCATIONS

evening/midday meal
the main meal of the day
three/four/five-course meal – a large meal that has three etc courses (=separate parts of a meal)
light/quick meal – a small meal
decent/proper/solid meal – a large meal with good food
have/eat a meal
cook/prepare/make a meal
go (out) for a meal – to go to a restaurant, bar etc to eat
ask sb out for a meal also take sb out for a meal – to ask someone to come to a restaurant with you to eat, or to take someone there

THESAURUS

breakfast – a meal that you eat in the morning
brunch – a meal that you eat in the late morning, instead of breakfast or lunch
lunch – a meal that you eat in the middle of the day
dinner – the main meal of the day, which most people eat in the evening
supper – a meal that you eat in the evening
tea – a meal that you eat in the afternoon or evening
picnic – a meal that you eat outdoors, consisting of food that you cook or prepare earlier
barbecue – a meal that you cook and eat outdoors
→ LUNCH

mealtime /ˈmiːltaɪm/ *n* [C] the usual time that you eat a meal: **at mealtimes** *I only see my boys at mealtimes.*

mealy-'mouthed *adj* not brave or honest enough to say what you really think

mean¹ /miːn/ *v* [T] past tense and past participle **meant** /ment/
1 to have a particular meaning or idea: *What does that word mean?* | **+(that)** *The red light means the battery is flat.*
2 to intend to express a particular idea or feeling when you say something: **+(that)** *I meant we'd be coming later.* | *I don't quite see what you mean* (=I don't understand what you are trying to say). | **(do) you mean...?** (=used to check that you understand what someone intended to say) *Do you mean I should go?* | *He didn't really mean it when he said he loved me.* | *I meant what I said.* | *Julie seems rude but she means well* (=intends to be kind and helpful).
3 to intend to do something or make something happen: **mean to do sth** *I've been meaning to call you.* | *She didn't mean to upset you.* | **mean sb/sth to do sth** *I never meant this to happen.* | *It was meant to be a joke.* | **mean (for) sb to do sth** *especially AmE: I didn't mean for her to get hurt.*
4 to cause something or make it likely to happen: **+(that)** *Those clouds mean that it will snow.* | **mean doing sth** *The job will mean travelling.*
5 used to say how important something is to you: **mean sth to sb** *That medal meant a lot to Dad.*
6 be meant for sb/sth to be intended for a particular person or purpose: *The chocolate was meant for Mum.*
7 be meant to do sth if you are meant to do something, you should do it: *The police are meant to protect us.* | *You're meant to inform the school if you change your address.*
8 be meant to be sth if something is meant to be good, exciting etc, people say that it is good, exciting etc: *His latest book is meant to be really good.*
9 I mean *spoken* used to correct or explain more about something you have just said: *She plays the violin, I mean the viola.* | *She's just so nice. I mean, she's a kind person.*
10 mean business *informal* if you mean business, you are very determined to do something
11 what do you mean...? *spoken* **a)** used when you do not understand what someone is trying to say **b)** used when you are surprised and annoyed by what someone has just said: *What do you mean, you sold the car?*

mean² *adj*
1 cruel and not kind: **+to** *Don't be so mean to your sister.* | *It was mean of you not to ask her.* → see box at UNKIND
2 *BrE* not willing to spend money [= cheap *AmE*; = stingy *BrE*]: *He's too mean to offer us a lift.* | **+with** *She's very mean with money.*
3 a mean sth *informal* used to say that something is very good: *Ray plays a mean game of tennis.*
4 no mean achievement/performance/feat used to say that what someone has done is very impressive: *Winning was no mean feat.*

5 [only before noun] *technical* average: *What is the mean annual rainfall of Brazil?*

mean³ *n* [C usually singular] *technical* an average amount, figure, or value

meander /miːˈændə $ -ər/ *v* [I] to move slowly and not in a straight line: *a meandering stream*

meaning /ˈmiːnɪŋ/ *n*
1 [C,U] the idea that is expressed or represented by something you read, see, or hear: **+of** *What's the meaning of this word?* | **+behind** *I guessed the meaning behind his speech.* | *a poem with a hidden meaning*
2 [U] the importance or purpose something has: **+of** *the meaning of life* | *After his death, my work had no meaning.*

meaningful /ˈmiːnɪŋfəl/ *adj* **1** having a clear meaning that people can understand: *data that is meaningful only to scientists* **2 meaningful look/smile etc** a look etc that clearly expresses the way someone feels: *We exchanged meaningful glances.* **3** serious, useful, or important: *I want to do something meaningful with my life.*

meaningless /ˈmiːnɪŋləs/ *adj* without purpose or meaning: *Life felt meaningless.*

means /miːnz/ *n* plural **means**
1 [C] a way of doing something: **+of** *The window is the only means of escape.* | **means of communication/transport** *Email is the best means of communication.* | **a means of doing sth** *I had no means of getting home.*
2 by all means used to agree or give permission [= of course]: *'Can I bring Alan?' 'By all means!'*
3 by no means/not by any means not at all: *He was not rich by any means.*
4 a means to an end something that you do only to achieve a particular result: *My job is just a means to an end.*
5 [plural] the money or income you have: **have the means to do sth** *We don't have the means to pay for private education.* | *A holiday is beyond my means* (=I cannot afford it).

'means-,tested *adj* means-tested income is money you can only receive from the government after an official check has proved that you need it

meant /ment/ *v* the past tense and past participle of MEAN

meantime /ˈmiːntaɪm/ *n* **in the meantime** until something happens, or in the time between two events: *Dinner's nearly ready. Would you like a drink in the meantime?*

meanwhile /ˈmiːnwaɪl/ *adv* while something else is happening, or in the time between two events: *Bill took the dogs out. Meanwhile, I fed the cats.*

measles /ˈmiːzəlz/ *n* [U] an infectious illness which produces a fever and small red spots on your body

measly /ˈmiːzli/ *adj informal* very small and disappointing in size or amount: *a measly gift*

measurable /ˈmeʒərəbəl/ *adj* big enough to be measured or have an effect: *There has been a measurable improvement in your work.* —**measurably** *adv*

measure¹ /ˈmeʒə $ -ər/ *v*

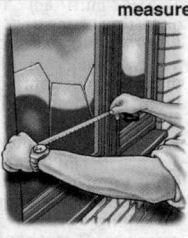
measure

1 [I,T] to find out the size, weight, or quantity of something: **measure sth with sth** *I measured it with a ruler.* | **measure sth in inches/kilos etc** *The instrument measures depth in metres.* | **measure the height/weight/amount etc of sth** *How can we measure the amount of rainfall?*
2 [linking verb] to be a particular size, length, or amount: *The room measures 4 metres by 6 metres.* | *The earthquake measured 6.5 on the Richter scale.*
3 [T] to decide how important or good something is: **measure sth by sth** *Success is not only measured by exams.*
measure sth/sb against sb/sth *phr v* to judge someone or something by comparing them with another person or thing
measure up *phr v* to be good enough for a particular job or to reach a particular standard: **+to** *Does college measure up to your expectations?*

measure² *n*
1 [C, usually plural] an official action that is meant to deal with a problem: *New safety measures are needed.* | *The government must take measures to reduce crime.*
2 half measures things done to deal with a problem that are not firm or effective enough
3 be a measure of sth *formal* to be a sign of how important something is: *It's a measure of our trust that we let you go.*
4 a measure of sth *formal* a reasonable amount of something: *He achieved a measure of success with his first book.*
5 [C,U] an amount or unit in a measuring system: *a table of **weights and measures***
6 for good measure in addition to what has already been done: *Add a bit more salt for good measure.*
→ TAPE MEASURE

measurement /ˈmeʒəmənt $ -ʒər-/ *n*
1 [C] the length, height, level etc of something, or the process of measuring it: *What's your chest measurement?* | *Do you know the measurements of the room?* | *I need to take a few measurements.*
2 [U] when you measure something: *After careful measurement, we felt sure the furniture would fit in.*

meat /miːt/ *n* [U] the flesh of animals and birds that people eat: *I don't eat meat.* | *a meat pie* | **red meat** (=dark meat, such as beef) | **white meat** (=pale meat, such as chicken)

THESAURUS

beef – meat from a cow
veal – meat from a young cow
pork/ham/bacon – meat from a pig
lamb – meat from a lamb (=young sheep)
mutton – meat from a sheep
venison – meat from a deer
game – meat from wild animals and birds

M

meaty /'miːti/ *adj* **1** containing a lot of meat, or tasting of meat **2** interesting or important: *his first meaty role as an actor*

mecca /'mekə/ *n* [singular] **1** a place that many people want to visit because they are interested in something: **+for** *The island is a mecca for windsurfers.* **2 Mecca** a city in Saudi Arabia which is a holy place for Muslims

mechanic /mɪ'kænɪk/ *n* **1** [C] someone whose job is to repair vehicles and machinery **2 the mechanics of (doing) sth** the way in which something works or is done: *the mechanics of grammar* **3 mechanics** [U] the science of how forces affect objects

mechanical /mɪ'kænɪkəl/ *adj* **1** relating to machines, or using power from a machine: *Mechanical failure caused the accident.* | *mechanical toys* **2** saying or doing something without thinking, because you have said or done it so often before: *a mechanical smile* —**mechanically** /-kli/ *adv*

mechanism /'mekənɪzəm/ *n* [C] **1** the part of a machine that does a particular job: *the brake mechanism* **2** a system for doing something: **mechanism for (doing) sth** *We need an effective mechanism for dealing with enquiries.*

mechanized also **-ised** *BrE* /'mekənaɪzd/ *adj* using machines instead of people: *mechanized farming*

medal /'medl/ *n* [C] a round flat piece of metal given to someone who has been successful in a competition or done something brave: **gold/ silver/bronze medal** *She won a gold medal at the Olympics.*

medallion /mɪ'dæliən/ *n* [C] a piece of metal like a large coin, worn on a chain around someone's neck

medallist *BrE*; **medalist** *AmE* /'medl-ɪst/ *n* [C] someone who has won a medal in a competition: **gold/silver/bronze medallist** *an Olympic silver medallist*

meddle /'medl/ *v* [I] to try to influence a situation that does not involve you or that you do not understand: **+in** *I don't want him meddling in our affairs.*

media /'miːdiə/ *n* **1 the media** television, radio, newspapers, and magazines: **in the media** *The story was reported in the media.* | **media coverage/attention/ interest** *The trial created huge media interest.* → see box at **NEWSPAPER** **2** the plural of **MEDIUM** → **MASS MEDIA**

mediaeval /ˌmedi'iːvəl $ ˌmiː-/ *adj* a British spelling of **MEDIEVAL**

median /'miːdiən/ *n* [C] *AmE* a narrow piece of land that separates the two sides of a big road [= **central reservation** *BrE*]

mediate /'miːdieɪt/ *v* [I,T] to try to end an argument between people: **+between** *UN officials mediated between the two countries.* —**mediator** *n* [C] —**mediation** /ˌmiːdi'eɪʃən/ *n* [U]

medic /'medɪk/ *n* [C] *informal* **1** *BrE* a doctor or medical student **2** *AmE* someone in the army who is trained to give medical treatment

medical[1] /'medɪkəl/ *adj* relating to medicine and the treatment of diseases or injuries: *medi-cal treatment* | *medical students* | **the medical profession** (=doctors, nurses etc) —**medically** /-kli/ *adv*

medical[2] *n* [C] *BrE* an examination by a doctor to see if you are healthy [= **physical** *AmE*]

medicated /'medɪkeɪtɪd/ *adj* containing a substance that helps skin or hair problems: *medicated shampoo*

medication /ˌmedɪ'keɪʃən/ *n* [C,U] drugs given to people who are ill: **be on medication (for sth)** *He's on medication for depression.*

medicinal /mɪ'dɪsɪnəl/ *adj* used for treating illnesses: *plants with medicinal properties* (=containing things that can cure illnesses)

medicine /'medsən $ 'medɪsən/ *n*

1 [C,U] a substance for treating an illness, especially one that you drink: *Have you taken your medicine?* | *a medicine bottle* | *cough medicine*

pill/tablet/capsule – a small tablet or tube of medicine that you swallow
eye/ear drops – liquid medicine that you put into your eye or ear
drug – a medicine or a substance for making medicines
dosage – the amount of medicine that you should take

2 [U] the treatment and study of illnesses and injuries: *Sarah is studying medicine.* | **alternative/traditional/modern medicine** *advances in modern medicine* → **COMPLEMENTARY MEDICINE**

medieval also **mediaeval** *BrE* /ˌmedi'iːvəl $ ˌmiː-/ *adj* relating to the MIDDLE AGES (=the time between about AD 1100 and 1500): *a medieval castle*

mediocre /ˌmiːdi'əʊkə $ -'əʊkər/ *adj* not very good: *a mediocre performance*

meditate /'medɪteɪt/ *v* [I] **1** to be silent and calm for a period of time as part of your religion or to help you relax **2** *formal* to think seriously about something: **+on** *She sat meditating on the day's events.* —**meditation** /ˌmedɪ'teɪʃən/ *n* [U]

Mediterranean /ˌmedɪtə'reɪniən/ *n* **the Mediterranean** the sea that has the countries of southern Europe, North Africa, and the Middle East around it, or the area of southern Europe around this sea —**Mediterranean** *adj*

medium[1] /'miːdiəm/ *adj* of middle size or amount: *What size do you want – small, medium, or large?* | **(of) medium height/length/size etc** *a man of medium height*

medium[2] *n* [C] **1** plural **media** /-diə/ or **mediums** a way of communicating information or ideas [➞ **media**]: *Advertising is a powerful medium.* | **+of** *Language is a medium of communication.* | **+for** *Sport is the perfect medium for publicity.* **2** plural **mediums** someone who says they receive messages from dead people

'medium-sized also **'medium-size** *adj* not small or large: *a medium-size business*

'medium ˌwave *n* [U] written abbreviation **MW** radio broadcasting using radio WAVES between 100 and 1000 metres in length [➞ **long wave, short wave, FM**]

medley /'medli/ *n* [C] **1** a piece of music with several different songs in it: **+of** *a medley of Beatles songs* **2** a mixture of different things: **+of** *a medley of smells*

meek /mi:k/ *adj* very quiet and always doing what other people want —**meekly** *adv*

meet /mi:t/ *v* past tense and past participle **met** /met/

1 [I,T] to be at the same place as someone else because you have arranged it: *I'll meet you at 8 o'clock.* | *We'll meet at the theatre.* | **meet (sb) for sth** *Let's meet for lunch.*
2 [I,T] to see and speak to someone without planning it: *Guess who I just met?* | *We met while we were both shopping in town, and decided to go for a coffee.*
3 [I,T] to see and talk to someone for the first time: *We first met at a party.* | *I met my husband at school.* | **nice/pleased to meet you** *spoken* (=used when you meet someone for the first time) *'This is my sister, Jane.' 'Pleased to meet you.'*
4 [T] to be waiting for someone when they arrive at an airport, station etc: *Dad came to meet us at the station.* | **meet sb off a train/plane etc** *A friend's meeting her off the boat.*
5 [I,T] if two things meet, they join or touch: *the place where the path meets the road* | *His eyebrows meet in the middle.*
6 [I] if a group of people meet, they come together to do something: *The chess club meets every Tuesday.*
7 [I,T] to play against someone in a competition: *Leeds will meet Liverpool on Saturday.* | *The two teams haven't met since last season.*
8 meet a need/demand/requirement etc to be good enough to do what someone needs, wants, or expects: *She didn't meet the requirements for the job.* | *beaches that* **meet** *European* **standards** *of cleanliness*
9 meet a cost/expense etc to provide the money for something: *Many families have difficulty meeting the cost of university education.*

meet up *phr v* to meet someone in order to do something together: *Let's meet up later.* | **+with** *I'm planning to meet up with my brother.*
meet with *sb/sth phr v* **1** to have a meeting with someone: *The President met with European leaders today.* **2** to get a particular reaction or result: *The plans have met with widespread opposition.* | *Our efforts have so far met with little success.*

meeting /'mi:tɪŋ/ *n* [C]
1 an event where people meet to discuss something: *I've* **got** *an important* **meeting** *this afternoon.* | *We* **had** *a* **meeting** *yesterday.* | *They decided to* **hold** *a* **meeting** *to discuss the problem.* | **at/in a meeting** *She's in a meeting at the moment.* | **+with** *a meeting with my tutor* | *a committee meeting*
2 when you meet someone: *She had disliked him since their first meeting.* | *A* **chance meeting** (=a meeting that was not planned) *in 1985 changed his life.*

mega /'megə/ *adj informal* very big and impressive: *Their first single was a mega hit.*

megabyte /'megəbaɪt/ *n* [C] written abbreviation *Mb* a unit for measuring computer information, equal to just over a million BYTES

megalomania /ˌmegələʊ'meɪniə $ -loʊ-/ *n* [U] when someone wants a lot of power and enjoys controlling people —**megalomaniac** /-niæk/ *n* [C]

megaphone /'megəfəʊn $ -foʊn/ *n* [C] a piece of equipment you talk through to make your voice louder when speaking to a crowd

melancholy /'melənkəli $ -ka:li/ *n* [U] *formal* a feeling of sadness

melee /'meleɪ $ 'meɪleɪ, meɪ'leɪ/ *n* [C] a confusing and noisy situation involving a lot of people

mellow¹ /'meləʊ $ -loʊ/ *adj* **1** pleasant and not too loud, bright, strong etc: *mellow music* | *a mellow flavor* **2** calm, relaxed, and gentle: *He was in a mellow mood.*

mellow² *v* [I,T] if you mellow, or something mellows you, you become more gentle and sympathetic: *Age had not mellowed her.*

melodic /mɪ'lɒdɪk $ -'la:-/ also **melodious** /mɪ'ləʊdiəs $ -'loʊ-/ *adj* pleasant to listen to: *a melodic voice*

melodrama /'melədra:mə $ -dra:mə, -dræmə/ *n* [C,U] a story or play in which a lot of exciting things happen, and the characters show a lot of strong feelings

melodramatic /ˌmelədrə'mætɪk◂/ *adj* behaving in a way that makes a situation seem much worse or much more important than it really is

melody /'melədi/ *n* [C,U] plural **melodies** a tune

melon /'melən/ *n* [C,U] a large sweet fruit with yellow or green skin and a lot of flat seeds

melt

frozen | melted

melt /melt/ *v*
1 [I,T] to change from solid to liquid, or to make something do this by heating it [➡ **freeze, thaw**]: *The snow's melting.* | *Melt the chocolate in a pan.* → see box at RECIPE
2 also **melt away** [I] to gradually disappear: *His anger slowly melted away.*
3 [I,T] to suddenly feel love or sympathy: *My heart melted when I saw her crying.*

melt sth ⇔ **down** *phr v* to heat a metal object until it becomes liquid

meltdown /'meltdaʊn/ *n* [C,U] an accident in which material inside a NUCLEAR REACTOR melts and burns through its container

'melting pot *n* [singular] a place where people from different races, countries, or social classes come to live together

member /'membə $ -ər/ *n* [C]
1 someone who belongs to a group or organization [➡ **charter member, founder member**]: **+of** *He's a member of the tennis club.* | *The building is open to* **members of the public.** | *one of his fellow* **team members**

M

committee/party/union/team etc member
staff member also member of staff BrE
member of sb's family
member of the public
member of society
leading member – one of the most important members
active member – one who does a lot to support the club, organization etc

2 something that is part of a group: *Cats and tigers are members of the same species.*
→ FOUNDER MEMBER

Member of 'Parliament *n* [C] plural **Members of Parliament** an MP → see box at GOVERNMENT

membership /'membəʃɪp $ -ər-/ *n* **1** [U] when someone is a member of a group or organization: **+of** *Greece applied for membership of the EU in 1975.* | **+in** AmE: *I renewed my membership in the club.* | *membership fees* | *a membership card* **2** [singular, U] the members of an organization, or the total number of members: *There has been an increase in membership this year.* | *The membership voted to change the rules.*

membrane /'membreɪn/ *n* [C,U] a thin piece of skin that covers or connects parts of your body

memento /mɪ'mentəʊ $ -toʊ/ *n* [C] plural **mementos** a small thing that you keep to remind you of someone or something [= **souvenir**]: **+of** *I kept the photos as a memento of our trip.*

memo /'meməʊ $ -moʊ/ *n* [C] plural **memos** a short official note to someone in the same company: **+to/from** *a memo from the manager*

memoirs /'memwɑːz $ -wɑːrz/ *n* [plural] a book that someone writes about their life and experiences

memorabilia /ˌmemərə'bɪliə/ *n* [plural] things that you collect because they relate to a famous person or a subject you are interested in: *soccer memorabilia*

memorable /'memərəbəl/ *adj* good or enjoyable and likely to be remembered: *a memorable day*

memorandum /ˌmemə'rændəm/ *n* [C] plural **memoranda** /-də/ or **memorandums** formal a MEMO

memorial¹ /mɪ'mɔːriəl/ *adj* [only before noun] done to remind people of someone who has died: *a memorial service for people who died in the fire*

memorial² *n* [C] something that is built to remind people of someone who has died: **+to** *The stone is a permanent memorial to the victims of war.* | *a war memorial*

memorize also **-ise** BrE /'meməraɪz/ *v* [T] to learn words, music etc so you remember them perfectly

memory /'meməri/ *n* plural **memories**

1 [C,U] the ability to remember things: *She has a very good memory.* | **+for** *My memory for names is terrible.* | **from memory** (=using your memory and not notes) *He recited the list from memory.*

2 [C usually plural] something that you remember from the past: **+of** *I have happy memories of that summer.* | *My most vivid memory is the silence after the accident.* | *The smell brought back memories of childhood.*

3 [C,U] the part of a computer where information is stored: *128 megabytes of memory*

4 in/within memory during the time that people can remember: *the worst floods in living memory* (=that anyone can remember)

5 in memory of sb in order to remind people of someone who has died: *a garden created in memory of the princess*
→ refresh sb's memory at REFRESH

men /men/ *n* the plural of MAN

menace¹ /'menəs/ *n* **1** [C] something or someone that is dangerous: **+of** *the growing menace of oil pollution at sea* | **+to** *He's a menace to society.* **2** [U] a threatening quality or feeling: *There was menace in her voice.*

menace² *v* [T] formal to threaten someone

menacing /'menəsɪŋ/ *adj* making you expect something unpleasant [= **threatening**]: *a menacing look* —**menacingly** *adv*

menagerie /mɪ'nædʒəri/ *n* [C] a group of wild animals that someone keeps

mend¹ /mend/ *v* [T] to repair something that is broken or damaged [= **fix**]: *We need someone to mend the roof.* → see box at REPAIR

mend

mend² *n* **be on the mend** to be getting better after an illness

menial /'miːniəl/ *adj* menial work is boring and needs no skill

meningitis /ˌmenɪn'dʒaɪtɪs/ *n* [U] a serious infectious disease that affects the brain

menopause /'menəpɔːz $ -pɔːz/ *n* **the menopause** the time when a woman stops menstruating, which usually happens around the age of 50

'men's room *n* [C] especially AmE a toilet for men [= **gents** BrE]

menstruate /'menstrueɪt/ *v* [I] technical when a woman menstruates every month, blood flows from her body —**menstrual** *adj* —**menstruation** /ˌmenstru'eɪʃən/ *n* [U]

mental /'mentl/ *adj* [only before noun] relating to the mind, or happening in the mind: *Stress affects physical and mental health.* | *mental illness* | *a child's mental development* | *mental arithmetic* | *He made a mental note* (=made a special effort to remember) *to call her.*
—**mentally** *adv*: *mentally ill*

mentality /men'tæləti/ *n* [C] plural **mentalities** a particular attitude or way of thinking: *I can't understand his middle-class mentality.*

mention¹ /'menʃən/ *v* [T]

1 to talk or write about something without giving many details: *Your name was mentioned in the book.* | **mention sth to sb** *I'll mention it to Jo and see what she says.* | **+(that)** *He did mention he was having problems.* → see box at SAY

2 don't mention it spoken used to say politely that someone does not need to thank you: *'Thanks for the meal.' 'Don't mention it.'*

3 not to mention sth used to add something even more surprising: *He already owns several cars, not to mention the boat.*

mention² *n* [singular, U] when you mention someone or something in a conversation or piece of writing: **+of** *There was no mention of money.* | *He made no mention of his wife.* | *At the mention of ice cream, the child became excited.*

mentor /'mentɔː $ -tɔːr/ *n* [C] someone who advises and helps a less experienced person —**mentoring** *n* [U]

menu /'menjuː/ *n* [C]
1 a list of all the food you can choose in a restaurant: *Could we see the menu, please?* | **on the menu** *Is there any fish on the menu?* → see box at RESTAURANT
2 a list of things on a computer screen that you can ask the computer to do: *Select 'Print' from the main menu.*
→ **DROP-DOWN MENU**

meow /mi'aʊ/ *n, v* the usual American spelling of MIAOW

MEP /ˌem iː 'piː/ *n* [C] Member of the European Parliament someone who has been elected as a member of the Parliament of the European Union

mercenary¹ /'mɜːsənəri $ 'mɜːrsəneri/ *n* [C] plural **mercenaries** a soldier who will fight for any country for money

mercenary² *adj* only interested in getting money for yourself

merchandise /'mɜːtʃəndaɪz, -daɪs $ 'mɜːr-/ *n* [U] *formal* goods that are being sold

merchandising /'mɜːtʃəndaɪzɪŋ $ 'mɜːr-/ *n* [U] products you can buy relating to a popular film, sports team, singer etc

merchant¹ /'mɜːtʃənt $ 'mɜːr-/ *n* [C] someone whose job is to buy and sell large amounts of something: *a wine merchant*

merchant² *adj* [only before noun] merchant ships are used for trade, not for war

merciful /'mɜːsɪfəl $ 'mɜːr-/ *adj* **1** kind and forgiving someone **2** a merciful death seems fortunate because it ends someone's suffering

mercifully /'mɜːsɪfəli $ 'mɜːr-/ *adv* fortunately, because a situation could have been much worse: *The trip was mercifully short.*

merciless /'mɜːsɪləs $ 'mɜːr-/ *adj* cruel and not caring if people suffer: *a merciless attack*

mercury /'mɜːkjʊ̩ri $ 'mɜːr-/ *n* [U] a silver-coloured liquid metal, used in THERMOMETERS
Mercury *n* the PLANET that is nearest the sun

mercy /'mɜːsi $ 'mɜːrsi/ *n* [U]
1 kindness and willingness to forgive someone: *He showed no mercy to anyone.*
2 at the mercy of sb/sth unable to do anything to protect yourself from someone or something: *We were at the mercy of the weather.*

mere /mɪə $ mɪr/ *adj* [only before noun] used to emphasize how small or unimportant something is: *She won by a mere two points.* | *The mere thought made her furious.* | *The merest noise makes him nervous.*

merely /'mɪəli $ 'mɪrli/ *adv* **1** used to emphasize that you are talking about only one thing and nothing else: *I called merely to say that I won't be able to come tomorrow.* **2** used to

emphasize that something is very small or unimportant: *It was not a big problem, merely an inconvenience.*

merge /mɜːdʒ $ mɜːrdʒ/ *v* [I,T] to combine, or to join things together to form one thing: *a computer program that makes it easy to merge text and graphics* | **+with** *The company merged with a German electronics firm.* | **+into** *The village seems to merge into the landscape.* | **merge sth into sth** *The two magazines were merged into a single publication.*

merger /'mɜːdʒə $ 'mɜːrdʒər/ *n* [C] when two companies join to form one larger one: **+of/between** *a proposed merger between two banks* | **+with** *a merger with another hotel group*

meridian /mə'rɪdiən/ *n* [C] one of the imaginary lines drawn from the North Pole to the South Pole on a map

meringue /mə'ræŋ/ *n* [C,U] a light sweet food made by baking a mixture of sugar and the white part of eggs

merit¹ /'merɪt/ *n* [C,U] a good quality or feature: *The new scheme has several merits.* | **+of** *The book has the merit of being short yet informative.* | *There is some merit in this argument.* | **on merit** *Students are selected on merit* (=because they are good). | **of great/considerable/outstanding merit** *a poet of considerable merit*

merit² *v* [T] *formal* to deserve something: *an interesting question which merits attention*

mermaid /'mɜːmeɪd $ 'mɜːr-/ *n* [C] in stories, a woman who has a fish's tail instead of legs, and lives in the sea

merry /'meri/ *adj* **1 Merry Christmas!** used to greet someone at Christmas **2** *literary* happy: *a merry tune* —**merrily** *adv*

'merry-go-ˌround *n* [C] a machine that turns around and around and has model cars or animals for children to sit on [= **roundabout** *BrE*; = **carousel** *AmE*]

mesh¹ /meʃ/ *n* [C,U] material made of threads or wires that have been fastened together like a net: *a wire mesh fence*

mesh² *v* [I] if two ideas or things mesh, they fit well together: **+with** *His ideas didn't mesh with the views of the party.*

mesmerize also **-ise** *BrE* /'mezməraɪz/ *v* [T] if you are mesmerized by someone or something, you cannot stop looking at them or listening to them because they are so attractive or interesting: *He was mesmerized by her beauty.* —**mesmerizing** *adj*

mess¹ /mes/ *n* **1** [singular, U] when a place or person looks dirty and untidy: *The house was a complete mess.* | **in a mess** *BrE: He left the room in a terrible mess.* | *Try not to make a mess while you're cooking.* → see box at ORGANIZED
2 [singular] *informal* a situation in which there are a lot of problems: **in a mess** *The whole system is in a mess.* | *She felt she'd made a mess of her life.*

mess² *v*

mess around also **mess about** *BrE phr v informal* **1** to do things that are silly or not useful: *Come on, we haven't time to mess around.* **2 mess sb around** to treat someone badly, especially by changing your mind or not being honest: *I won't let him mess me around.*

M

mess around with sb/sth also **mess about with sb/sth** BrE phr v informal **1** to play with something or make small changes to it, especially in a way that annoys someone: *Who's been messing around with my camera?* **2** to have a sexual relationship with someone, which people do not approve of

mess up phr v informal **1 mess sth ⇔ up** to spoil something: *I hope I haven't messed up your plans.* **2 mess sth ⇔ up** to make something dirty or untidy: *Who messed up the kitchen?* **3** to make a mistake and do something badly: *I messed up on the last question.* | **mess sth ⇔ up** *I think I messed up the test.*

mess with sb/sth phr v informal to get involved with someone or something that is dangerous or could cause problems: *Don't mess with this guy.*

message /'mesɪdʒ/ n [C]

1 a piece of information that you tell someone, send to them, or leave for them: *Did you get my message?* | *I left a message on her voicemail.* | *Sorry, she's not home yet, can I take a message?* | *An error message came up on the computer screen.*

THESAURUS

telephone/phone message
email/mail message
fax message
text message – a written message on a mobile phone
error message – a message on a computer screen, saying that the computer cannot do what you want it to do
message of thanks/congratulations/support/sympathy

---

2 [usually singular] the main idea that someone is trying to communicate in a film, book, speech etc: *The film sends a clear message about the horrors of war.* | *an effective way of getting your message across* (=communicating what you want to say)
3 get the message informal to understand what someone is trying to tell you: *OK, I get the message – I'm going.*

messenger /'mesɪndʒə, -sən- $ -ər/ n [C] someone who takes messages to other people

messiah /mɪ'saɪə/ n **the Messiah** the person who some religions believe will be sent by God to save the world

Messrs the written plural of MR

messy /'mesi/ adj **1** dirty or untidy: *a messy room* **2** a messy job or activity involves making a lot of mess **3** a messy situation is complicated and unpleasant: *a messy divorce*

met /met/ v the past tense and past participle of MEET

metabolism /mɪ'tæbəlɪzəm/ n [C,U] the chemical processes in your body that change food into energy

metal /'metl/ n [C,U] a hard substance such as iron, gold, or steel: *It's made of metal.* | *a metal box*

metal detector n [C] a machine used for finding metal objects

metallic /mɪ'tælɪk/ adj containing metal, or tasting, sounding, or shining like metal: *metallic blue paint*

metamorphosis /ˌmetə'mɔːfəsɪs $ -'mɔːr-/ n [C,U] plural **metamorphoses** /-siːz/ formal when something changes into something completely different: *the country's metamorphosis into a modern, industrialized nation*

metaphor /'metəfə, -fɔː $ -fɔːr/ n [C,U] a way of describing something by referring to it as something else [➔ **simile**]: *'A river of tears' is a metaphor.* —**metaphorical** /ˌmetə'fɒrɪkəl $ -'fɔː- -'fɑː-/ adj —**metaphorically** /-kli/ adv

metaphysical /ˌmetə'fɪzɪkəl◂/ adj concerned with the nature of truth, life, and reality

mete /miːt/ v
mete sth ⇔ out phr v formal to give a punishment to someone

meteor /'miːtiə $ -ər/ n [C] a small piece of rock or metal that is moving through space ➔ see box at **SPACE**

meteoric /ˌmiːti'ɒrɪk◂ $ -'ɔːrɪk, -'ɑːrɪk/ adj happening very suddenly and quickly: *his meteoric rise to fame*

meteorite /'miːtiəraɪt/ n [C] a piece of rock or metal that has come from space and landed on Earth

meteorology /ˌmiːtiə'rɒlədʒi $ -'rɑː-/ n [U] the scientific study of weather —**meteorologist** n [C]

meter /'miːtə $ -ər/ n [C] **1** a piece of equipment that measures the amount of gas, electricity, water etc you have used: *A man came to read the electricity meter.* | *a parking meter* (=one that measures how long you have parked somewhere) **2** the American spelling of 'metre'

methadone /'meθədəʊn $ -doʊn/ n [U] technical a drug that is often given to people who are trying to stop taking HEROIN

methane /'miːθeɪn $ 'me-/ n [U] a gas with no colour or smell

method /'meθəd/ n [C] a way of doing something, especially one that a lot of people know about and use: *traditional teaching methods* | **method of/for (doing) sth** *This is the simplest method of payment.*

methodical /mɪ'θɒdɪkəl $ -'θɑː-/ adj careful and well-organized —**methodically** /-kli/ adv

Methodist /'meθədɪst/ n [C] someone who belongs to a Christian religious group that follows the ideas of John Wesley —**Methodist** adj

methodology /ˌmeθə'dɒlədʒi $ -'dɑː-/ n [C,U] plural **methodologies** the set of methods used to do a job or study something

meticulous /mɪ'tɪkjʊləs/ adj very careful about details, with everything done correctly: *They keep meticulous records.* —**meticulously** adv

metre BrE; **meter** AmE /'miːtə $ -ər/ n
1 [C] written abbreviation **m** a unit for measuring length equal to 100 centimetres
2 [C,U] the regular pattern of sounds made by the words of a poem

metric /'metrɪk/ adj using the system of weights and measures based on grams, metres, and litres [➔ **imperial**]

metro /'metrəʊ $ -troʊ/ n [singular] a railway system running under the ground in a city [= **underground** BrE; = **subway** AmE]: *the Paris Metro*

M

metropolis /mə'trɒpəlɪs $ -'trɑː-/ n [C] a very large city, or the most important city of a country —**metropolitan** /ˌmetrə'pɒlɪtən $ -'pɑː-/ adj [only before noun]

mettle /'metl/ n [U] courage and determination to do something even when it is very difficult

mews /mjuːz/ n [plural] BrE a small street or area in a city where horses used to be kept, but where people now live

mg the written abbreviation of **milligram**

miaow BrE, **meow** AmE /mi'aʊ/ v [I] if a cat miaows, it makes a crying sound —**miaow** n [C]

mice /maɪs/ n the plural of MOUSE

mickey /'mɪki/ also **mick** /mɪk/ n **take the mickey (out of sb)** BrE informal to make someone seem silly, for example by making jokes about them or copying them [➡ **tease**]

micro- /maɪkrəʊ, -krə $ -kroʊ, -krə/ prefix very small, or relating to very small things: microcomputers | a microscope (=for looking at very small things)

microbe /'maɪkrəʊb $ -kroʊb/ n [C] an extremely small living thing that you cannot see without a MICROSCOPE

microbiology /ˌmaɪkrəʊbaɪ'ɒlədʒi $ -kroʊbaɪ'ɑːl-/ n [U] the scientific study of very small living things —**microbiologist** n [C]

microchip /'maɪkrəʊˌtʃɪp $ -kroʊ-/ n [C] a very small piece of SILICON containing electronic parts, used in computers and other machines

microcosm /'maɪkrəʊkɒzəm $ -kroʊkɑː-/ n [C] a small group that has the same qualities or features as a much larger one [➡ **macrocosm**]: New York's mix of people is a microcosm of America.

microorganism /ˌmaɪkrəʊ'ɔːgənɪzəm $ -kroʊ-'ɔːr-/ n [C] an extremely small living thing that you cannot see without a MICROSCOPE

microphone /'maɪkrəfəʊn $ -foʊn/ n [C] a piece of equipment that you use to record sounds or to make sounds louder

microprocessor /'maɪkrəʊˌprəʊsesə $ -kroʊ-ˌprɑːsesər/ n [C] the main MICROCHIP in a computer, which controls most of its operations

microscope /'maɪkrəskəʊp $ -skoʊp/ n [C] a scientific instrument that makes very small things look larger

microscope

microscopic /ˌmaɪkrə'skɒpɪk $ -'skɑː-/ adj extremely small: microscopic organisms

microsurgery /'maɪkrəʊˌsɜːdʒəri $ -kroʊˌsɜːr-/ n [U] medical treatment in which part of someone's body is repaired or removed using very small medical instruments

microwave /'maɪkrəweɪv/ also **microwave 'oven** n [C] a machine that cooks food very quickly, using electric waves instead of heat ➜ see picture at **KITCHEN** —**microwave** v [T]

microwave

mid- /mɪd/ prefix middle: She's in her mid-20s. | in mid-July

midair /ˌmɪd'eə◂ $ -'er◂/ n **in midair** in the air or sky: The plane exploded in midair. —**midair** adj [only before noun]

midday /ˌmɪd'deɪ◂ $ 'mɪd-deɪ/ n [U] twelve o'clock in the middle of the day [= noon; ➡ midnight]: **at/around/by midday** I met him at midday.

middle¹ /'mɪdl/ n

1 the middle the centre part of something, or the part between the beginning and end of something: **+of** We rowed out to the middle of the lake. | Go back to sleep – it's the middle of the night! | **in the middle** Look at this old photo – that's me in the middle. | Someone fainted in the middle of the ceremony.

2 be in the middle of (doing) sth to be busy doing something: Can I call you back? I'm in the middle of cooking dinner.

3 sb's middle informal someone's waist

4 in the middle of nowhere a long way from a town: The house was in the middle of nowhere.

middle² adj [only before noun]

1 nearest the centre: Shall we sit in the middle row? | The middle lane was blocked because of an accident. ➜ see picture at **HAND¹**

2 half of the way through an event or period of time: the middle part of the day

3 between high and low, big and small etc: a car in the middle price range

4 middle ground opinions or ideas that are not extreme, and that people can agree about

middle-'aged adj between the ages of about 40 and 60 years old: a middle-aged businessman —**middle age** n [U]

Middle 'Ages n **the Middle Ages** the period in European history between about 1100 and 1500 AD

middle 'class n [C] the social class that includes people who are educated and work in professional jobs, for example teachers or managers —**middle-class** adj: middle-class families

Middle 'East n **the Middle East** the area including Iran and Egypt and the countries between them

middleman /'mɪdlmæn/ n [C] plural **middlemen** /-men/ someone who buys things to sell to someone else, or who arranges a business deal between two other people

middle 'name n [C] the name that is between your first name and your family name ➜ see box at **NAME**

middle-of-the-'road adj middle-of-the-road opinions are not extreme or likely to cause disagreement

M

'middle school n [C] a school in Britain for children between the ages of 8 and 12, and in the US for children between 11 and 14

midfield /'mɪdfiːld/ n [U] the middle part of the area where a game such as football is played —**midfielder** n [C]

midget /'mɪdʒɪt/ n [C] an offensive word for a very small person

Midlands /'mɪdləndz/ n **the Midlands** the central area of England, around Birmingham

midlife crisis /ˌmɪdlaɪf 'kraɪsɪs/ n [singular] a period of worry and doubt about your life that some people experience when they are about 40 and 50 years old

midnight /'mɪdnaɪt/ n [U] 12 o'clock at night [➞ midday]: **at/around/by midnight** We close at midnight.

midriff /'mɪdrɪf/ n [C] the part of your body between your chest and your waist

midst /mɪdst/ n [U] the middle of an event, situation, place, or group: The government is **in the midst** of a major crisis.

midsummer /ˌmɪd'sʌmə $ -ər / n [U] the middle of summer: a lovely midsummer day

midterm /'mɪdtɜːm $ -tɜːrm/ adj [only before noun] in the middle of one of the main periods of the school year, or in the middle of an elected government's time in power: midterm tests | midterm elections

midway /ˌmɪd'weɪ $ 'mɪdweɪ/ adj, adv at the middle point between two places, or between the beginning and end of something: **midway between sth and sth** There's a gas station midway between here and Fresno. | **+through** He collapsed midway through the performance.

midweek /ˌmɪd'wiːk $ 'mɪdwiːk/ adj, adv on one of the middle days of the week: a midweek match against Liverpool | I'll be seeing him midweek.

Midwest /ˌmɪd'west/ n **the Midwest** the central area of the US —**Midwestern** adj

midwife /'mɪdwaɪf/ n [C] plural **midwives** /-waɪvz/ a nurse who has been trained to help women when they are having a baby

midwinter /ˌmɪd'wɪntə $ -ər/ n [U] the middle of winter

miffed /mɪft/ adj informal slightly annoyed

might¹ /maɪt/ modal verb

1 if something might happen or might be true, it is possible, but you are not certain: I might be able to go. | I think he might be French. | Do you think she might have missed the train?
2 might have used to say that something was a possibility in the past although it did not actually happen: The tiger might have killed you!
3 especially BrE formal used to politely ask for something [= may]: Might I have some water?
4 used to suggest politely what someone should do: You might try phoning her at home.
→ **may/might as well** at WELL¹

might² n [U] literary great strength and power: She pushed **with all her might**.

mightn't /'maɪtənt/ especially BrE informal the short form of 'might not'

might've /'maɪtəv/ informal the short form of 'might have'

mighty¹ /'maɪti/ adj literary very strong, big, and powerful: the mighty Mississippi river

mighty² adv AmE informal very: That chicken smells mighty good.

migraine /'miːgreɪn, 'maɪ- $ 'maɪ-/ n [C] an extremely bad HEADACHE

migrant /'maɪgrənt/ n [C] **1** someone who goes to live in another area or country, especially to find work [➞ emigrant, immigrant]: the flow of economic migrants | migrant workers **2** a bird or animal that migrates

migrate /maɪ'greɪt $ 'maɪgreɪt/ v [I] **1** if birds or animals migrate, they travel from one part of the world to another at the same time each year **2** to go to live in another area or country, especially to find work [➞ emigrate] —**migration** /maɪ'greɪʃən/ n [C,U] —**migratory** /'maɪgreɪtəri, 'maɪgrətəri $ 'maɪgrətɔːri/ adj

mike /maɪk/ n [C] informal a MICROPHONE

mild /maɪld/ adj
1 quite warm: a mild climate
2 not too severe, strong, or serious: a mild case of flu | mild criticism | The previous recession was **relatively mild**.
3 not having a strong taste: mild cheddar cheese

mildew /'mɪldjuː $ -duː/ n [U] a substance that grows on walls or other surfaces in wet, slightly warm places —**mildewed** adj

mildly /'maɪldli/ adv **1** slightly: She seemed mildly amused. **2 to put it mildly** spoken used to say that you could use much stronger words, but are being polite: He's not very pleased with you, to put it mildly.

mile /maɪl/ n
1 [C] written abbreviation **m** a unit for measuring distance, equal to 1760 yards or 1609 metres: My house is about 15 miles north of here. | Mark walks at least five miles a day. | He was driving at 70 **miles per hour**.
2 miles [plural] informal a very long distance: **for miles** We walked for miles without seeing anyone.

mileage /'maɪlɪdʒ/ n [singular,U] the number of miles that a vehicle has travelled since it was new: a used car with a **low mileage**

milestone /'maɪlstəʊn $ -stoʊn/ n [C] a very important event in the development of something: **+in** an important milestone in South African history

milieu /'miːljɜː $ miːr'ljɜː, -'ljuː/ n [C,U] plural **milieux** /-ljɜː, -ljɜːz $ -'ljuːz, -'ljɜː, -'ljuː/ or **milieus** formal the things and people that surround you and influence the way you live and think

militant /'mɪlɪtənt/ adj willing to use strong or violent action in order to achieve political or social change: a militant protest group —**militant** n [C] —**militancy** n [U]

militarism /'mɪlɪtərɪzəm/ n [U] the belief that a country should increase its army, navy etc and use them to get what it wants

military¹ /'mɪlɪtəri $ -teri/ adj used by or relating to the army, navy, or airforce: military aircraft | **military forces** | All young men had to **do military service** (=spend a period of time in the army, navy, or air force).

military² n **the military** the military forces of a country [= the forces]: My father is in the military.
→ see box at ARMY

militia /mɪˈlɪʃə/ *n* [C] a group of trained soldiers who are not part of an official army

milk¹ /mɪlk/ *n* [U] a white liquid produced by female animals and drunk by people, or produced by women and animals to feed their babies: *a glass of milk* | *Would you like milk in your coffee?* | **Breast milk** *is best for babies.*

> **THESAURUS**
>
> **skimmed milk** *BrE*/**skim milk** *AmE* – milk that has had all the fat removed from it
> **low-fat/semi-skimmed milk** – milk that has had some of the fat removed from it
> **full fat milk/whole milk** – milk that has not had any fat removed from it

milk² *v* [T]
1 to take milk from a cow or goat.
2 milk sb/sth for sth to get all the money, advantages etc that you can from a person or situation.

milkman /ˈmɪlkmən/ *n* [C] plural **milkmen** /-mən/ someone in Britain who delivers milk to houses

milk'shake / $ '. ./ *n* [C,U] a cold drink made from milk mixed with fruit or chocolate

milky /ˈmɪlki/ *adj* containing a lot of milk, or similar to milk: *milky coffee* | *a sweet milky flavour*

Milky 'Way *n* **the Milky Way** the pale white band of stars that can be seen across the sky at night

mill¹ /mɪl/ *n* [C] **1** a building containing a large machine for crushing grain into flour, or the machine itself **2** a factory that produces materials such as cotton, cloth, or steel: *an old cotton mill* **3 coffee/pepper mill** a small machine for crushing coffee or pepper

mill² *v* [T] to crush grain, pepper etc in a mill: *freshly milled black pepper*
mill around/about (**sth**) *phr v informal* if a lot of people are milling around, they move around a place without a particular purpose: *Crowds of students were milling around in the streets.*

millennium /mɪˈleniəm/ *n* [C] plural **millennia** /-niə/ a period of 1000 years, or the time when a new 1000-year period begins: *How did you celebrate* **the millennium** (=when the year 1999 became 2000)?

milligram /ˈmɪlɪɡræm/ *n* [C] written abbreviation **mg** a unit for measuring weight. There are 1000 milligrams in one gram.

millilitre *BrE*; **milliliter** *AmE* /ˈmɪlɪˌliːtə $ -ər/ *n* [C] written abbreviation **ml** a unit for measuring liquids. There are 1000 millilitres in one litre.

millimetre *BrE*; **millimeter** *AmE* /ˈmɪlɪˌmiːtə $ -ər/ *n* [C] written abbreviation **mm** a unit for measuring length. There are 1000 millimetres in one metre.

million /ˈmɪljən/ *number* plural **million** or **millions**
1 the number 1,000,000: **two/three/four etc million** *six million people* | **millions of pounds/dollars etc**
2 an extremely large number of people or things: **a million** *I've got a million ideas.* | **millions of sth** *She seems to have millions of friends.*

—**millionth** *adj*: *The park has just received its millionth visitor.* —**millionth** *n* [C]

millionaire /ˌmɪljəˈneə $ -ˈner/ *n* [C] someone who is very rich and has at least one million dollars or pounds

millisecond /ˈmɪlɪˌsekənd/ *n* [C] a unit for measuring time. There are 1000 milliseconds in one second.

mime /maɪm/ *n* [C,U] the use of movements to tell a story, without any words —**mime** *v* [I,T]

mimic¹ /ˈmɪmɪk/ *v* [T] **mimicked, mimicking** to copy the way someone speaks or behaves, especially to make people laugh: *Some of the boys were mimicking the teacher.* —**mimic** *n* [C] *He's a good mimic.* —**mimicry** *n* [U]

min. **1** the written abbreviation of **minimum** **2** the written abbreviation of **minute**

mince¹ /mɪns/ *v* [T] to cut food into extremely small pieces, using a machine: *minced beef*

mince² *n* [U] *BrE* meat that has been cut into very small pieces in a machine [= **ground beef** *AmE*]

mincemeat /ˈmɪnsˌmiːt/ *n* [U] a mixture of dried fruits and nuts, used to make cakes etc

mince 'pie *n* [C] a small PIE filled with mincemeat, traditionally eaten at Christmas

mind¹ /maɪnd/ *n* [C,U]
1 your thoughts or your ability to think, feel, and imagine things [➔ **brain**]: *Relaxation is good for mind and body.* | *the complex nature of* **the human mind** | **in sb's mind** *I keep going over the problem in my mind.*
2 make up your mind to decide something: *Have you made up your mind which college to go to?*
3 have sth in mind to be planning to do something: *What changes do you have in mind?*
4 keep/bear sth in mind to remember something that may be useful in the future: *It's a good idea – I'll keep it in mind.*
5 with sb/sth in mind considering someone or something when doing something: *cities designed with wildlife in mind*
6 on your mind if something is on your mind, you are thinking or worrying about it a lot: *Dad seems to* **have something on** *his* **mind.**
7 cross/enter your mind if a particular idea crosses your mind, you think of it: *It never crossed my mind that she was lying.*
8 come/spring to mind if something comes to mind, you suddenly think of it: *A memory of last night came to mind, and he smiled.*
9 take sb's mind off sth to make someone stop thinking and worrying about something
10 go/be out of your mind *informal* to be stupid or crazy: *Marry him? She must be out of her mind!*
11 to my mind in my opinion: *To my mind, they are the better team.*
12 get/put sb/sth out of your mind to stop yourself thinking about someone or something: *I just couldn't get her out of my mind.*
13 put your mind to sth to decide that you want to achieve something and try very hard to do it: *Anyone can lose weight if they put their mind to it.*
14 put/set sb's mind at rest to make someone feel less worried about something: *See a doctor to put your mind at rest.*

M

M

15 independently-minded/politically-minded etc having a particular attitude or interested in a particular thing: *scientifically-minded students* → **at/in the back of your mind** at BACK¹ → **cast your mind back** at CAST¹ → **change your mind** at CHANGE¹ → **frame of mind** at FRAME¹ → **have an open mind** at OPEN¹ → **give sb a piece of your mind** at PIECE¹ → **slip your mind** at SLIP¹ → **speak your mind** at SPEAK → STATE OF MIND

mind² *v*

1 [I,T] to feel annoyed or upset about something: *It was raining, but we didn't mind.* | *Do you think she'd mind if we didn't come?* | **mind (sb) doing sth** *Do you mind having to work so late?*

2 I don't mind *especially BrE* used to say that you are happy to accept whatever someone else decides: *'Orange or apple juice?' 'I don't mind.'* | +**what/who/where** *I don't mind where we go.*

3 not mind doing sth to be willing to do something: *I don't mind driving if you're tired.*

4 do/would you mind? *spoken* used to ask politely if you can do something, or if someone will do something: *Do you mind if I use your phone?* | *Would you mind waiting a moment?*

5 never mind *spoken* used to tell someone not to worry, or that something is not important: *'I'm sorry I'm so late.' 'Never mind.'*

6 I wouldn't mind... *spoken* used to say that you would like something: *I wouldn't mind another cup of coffee.*

7 mind you used to add more information to what you have just said: *It's a beautiful house. Mind you, it cost enough.*

8 mind your own business *spoken* to not ask questions about a situation that does not involve you: *'So did he kiss you?' 'Mind your own business!'*

9 [T] to look after someone or something for a short time: *Could you mind my bag?*

10 Mind! *BrE spoken* used to warn someone to be careful of something: *Mind the step!* | *Mind you don't hit your head.*

mind out *phr v BrE spoken* used to warn someone to move out of the way

'mind-,blowing *adj informal* very exciting or strange

'mind-,boggling *adj informal* very difficult to imagine because of being so big, strange, complicated etc: *the mind-boggling distances in space*

minder /ˈmaɪndə $ -ər/ *n* [C] *BrE* someone who is employed to protect another person

mindful /ˈmaɪndfəl/ *adj formal* **mindful of sth** remembering a particular rule or fact when you are making decisions about what to do: *Mindful of the guide's warning, they returned before dark.*

mindless /ˈmaɪndləs/ *adj* **1** stupid and without any purpose: *mindless vandalism* **2** able to be done without using your mind: *a mindless job*

mindset /ˈmaɪndset/ *n* [C] the attitude and way of thinking that someone has: *a very old-fashioned mindset*

mine¹ /maɪn/ *pron* the POSSESSIVE form of 'I': *'Whose coat is this?' 'It's mine.'* | *His English is better than mine.* | **of mine** *He's an old friend of mine.*

mine² *n* [C]

1 a deep hole or holes in the ground that people dig to remove coal, gold etc: *a coal mine*

2 a bomb that is hidden under the ground or under water, that explodes when it is touched

mine³ *v* **1** [I,T] to dig into the ground to get gold, coal etc **2** [T] to put bombs under the ground or in the sea

minefield /ˈmaɪnfiːld/ *n* **1** [C] an area of land or sea where bombs have been hidden **2** [singular] a situation in which there are many hidden difficulties and dangers: *Choosing the right school can be a minefield.*

miner /ˈmaɪnə $ -ər/ *n* [C] someone who works in a mine

mineral /ˈmɪnərəl/ *n* [C]

1 a substance that is formed naturally in the earth, such as coal, salt, stone, or gold: *The area is very rich in minerals.*

2 a natural substance such as iron that is in some foods and is important for good health: *Milk is full of vitamins and minerals.*

'mineral ,water *n* [C,U] water that comes from under the ground and contains minerals that are good for you

mingle /ˈmɪŋɡəl/ *v* **1** [I,T] if smells, sounds, or feelings mingle, they mix together: *Add the wine and allow the flavours to mingle.* **2** [I] to meet and talk to a lot of different people at an event: +**with** *Diana enjoyed mingling with the crowds.*

mini- /mɪni/ *prefix* very small or short: *a minibreak* (=a short holiday)

miniature¹ /ˈmɪnət̬ʃə $ ˈmɪniətʃər/ *adj* [only before noun] much smaller than normal: *a miniature railway* | *miniature roses*

miniature² *n* [C] **1** a very small painting, especially of a person **2 in miniature** exactly like someone or something else, but much smaller: *She's her mother in miniature.*

minibus /ˈmɪnibʌs/ *n* [C] *BrE* a small bus for about 12 people → see picture at TRANSPORT

minicab /ˈmɪnikæb/ *n* [C] *BrE* a taxi that you have to order by telephone, not one that you can stop in the street

minimal /ˈmɪnɪməl/ *adj* very small in degree or amount: *The storm caused only minimal damage.* —**minimally** *adv*

minimalism /ˈmɪnɪməlɪzəm/ *n* [U] a style of art, design, music etc that is very simple and uses only basic shapes, colours etc —**minimalist** *adj*

minimize also **-ise** *BrE* /ˈmɪnɪmaɪz/ *v* [T] **1** to make the amount of something dangerous or unpleasant as small as possible: *To minimize the risk of getting heart disease, exercise daily.* **2** to make a document or program on your computer very small while you are not using it [≠ maximize]

minimum¹ /ˈmɪnɪməm/ *adj* the minimum number or amount is the smallest that is possible or needed [≠ maximum]: *The minimum age for retirement is 55.* | *the national minimum wage*

—**minimum** *adv*

minimum² *n* [singular] the smallest number or amount that is possible or needed [≠ maximum]: **a minimum of sth** *Having a horse costs a minimum of £2000 a year.* | *Costs were kept to a minimum.*

mining /ˈmaɪnɪŋ/ *n* [U] the job or industry of digging gold, coal etc out of the ground

miniscule /'mɪnɪˌskjuːl/ *adj* another spelling of
MINUSCULE

miniskirt /'mɪnɪskɜːt $ -skɜːrt/ *n* [C] a very
short skirt

minister[1] /'mɪnɪstə $ -ər/ *n* [C]

1 a politician who is in charge of a government
department: **+of** *the Minister of Education* → see
box at GOVERNMENT

2 a priest in some Christian churches

minister[2] *v*

minister to sb/sth *phr v formal* to give help to
someone, especially someone sick or old: *doctors*
ministering to the needs *of their patients*

ministerial /ˌmɪnɪ'stɪəriəl◂ $ -'stɪr-/ *adj* [only
before noun] relating to government ministers:
ministerial decisions

ministry /'mɪnɪstri/ *n* [C] plural **ministries** a
government department: *the Defence Ministry* |
the Ministry of Agriculture

mink /mɪŋk/ *n* [C,U] plural **mink** or **minks** a small
animal with soft brown fur, or the valuable fur
from this animal: *a mink coat*

minnow /'mɪnəʊ $ -noʊ/ *n* [C] a very small fish

minor[1] /'maɪnə $ -ər/ *adj*

1 small and not very important or serious [➡
major]: *We made a few minor changes to the
plan.* | *a minor road* | **minor injury/surgery/**
illness *He escaped with only minor injuries.*

2 based on a particular type of musical SCALE [➡
major]: *Mahler's Symphony No. 3 in D minor*

minor[2] *n* [C] *law* someone who is below the age
at which they become legally responsible for
their actions

minor[3] *v*

minor in sth *phr v AmE* to study a second
subject as part of your university degree [➡
major]: *I'm minoring in African Studies.*

minority /maɪ'nɒrəti $ mɪ'nɔː-, mɪ'nɑː-/ *n* plu-
ral **minorities**

1 [singular] a small part of a larger group of
people or things [➡ **majority**]: **+of** *Only a minority
of students get a first-class degree.*

2 [C usually plural] plural **minorities** a group of
people of a different race or religion than most
people in a country: *children from* **ethnic**
minorities | *language classes for* **minority**
groups | *the teaching of* **minority languages** *in
schools*

3 be in the/a minority to form less than half of
a larger group: *Boys are very much in the minority in the dance class.*

mint[1] /mɪnt/ *n* **1** [U] a plant with leaves that
have a strong fresh taste, used in cooking: *mint
tea* **2** [C] a sweet with the strong fresh taste of
PEPPERMINT **3** [C] a place where coins are officially made —**minty** *adj*: *a minty taste*

mint[2] *v* [T] to make a coin

minus[1] /'maɪnəs/ *prep* **1** used to show that
one number is being taken away from another
[➡ **plus**]: *17 minus five is 12 (17 – 5 = 12).* → see
box at CALCULATE **2** a minus number is below
zero: *Temperatures tonight will fall to minus 8.*
3 without something that would normally be
there: *He came back minus a couple of front teeth.*

minus[2] *n* [C] something bad about a situation
[➡ **plus**]: *There are* **pluses and minuses** *of living
in a big city.* | **On the minus side**, *there is no free
back-up service if things go wrong.*

minuscule, **miniscule** /'mɪnɪˌskjuːl/ *adj* very
small: *a minuscule amount of food*

'minus ˌsign also **minus** *n* [C] the sign (-) used
to show that a number is less than zero, or that
one number is taken away from another

minute[1] /'mɪnɪt/ *n* [C]

1 a period of time equal to 60 seconds. There are
60 minutes in one hour: *Clare's train arrives in
15 minutes.* | *It's three minutes to ten.* | *a ten
minute bus ride* | *He called 20 minutes ago.*

2 a minute a very short period of time: *It'll only
take me a minute to do this.* | *He was there a
minute ago.*

3 in a minute very soon: *I'll do it in a minute.* →
see box at SOON

4 last minute done at the last possible time, just
before it is too late: *He cancelled his trip* **at the
last minute.** | *a few last-minute arrangements*

5 wait/just a minute *spoken* **a)** used to ask
someone to wait a short period of time: *'Are you
coming with us?' 'Yes, just a minute.'* **b)** used
when you do not agree with someone: *Wait a
minute – that can't be right!*

6 the minute (that) as soon as: *I knew it was Jill
the minute I heard her voice.*

7 (at) any minute (now) very soon: *She should
get here any minute now.*

8 this minute immediately: *Come here, this
minute!*

9 by the minute used to say that something is
happening more and more: *She was getting
angrier by the minute.*

10 minutes [plural] an official written record of
the things that were said during a meeting: *the
minutes of the last meeting* | *Is someone* **taking**
the minutes?

minute[2] /maɪ'njuːt $ -'nuːt/ *adj* **1** extremely
small: *minute handwriting* → see box at SMALL
2 very careful and thorough: *John explained the
plan in minute detail.*

miracle /'mɪrəkəl/ *n* [C] **1** something very
lucky or very good that you did not expect to
happen or did not think was possible: *It's a
miracle that no one was hurt.* | *The builders
have* **worked miracles** *in finishing the job so
quickly.* **2 miracle cure/drug** a very effective
medical treatment that cures even serious diseases: *There is no miracle cure for diabetes.*
3 something that seems impossible and is
thought to be caused by God

miraculous /mɪ'rækjʊləs/ *adj* very lucky and
completely unexpected: *a miraculous recovery*
—**miraculously** *adv*

mirage /'mɪrɑːʒ $ mɪ'rɑːʒ/ *n* [C] when the hot
air in a desert makes you see water that is not
really there

mirror[1] /'mɪrə $ -ər/ *n* [C] a piece of special
glass made so that when you look at it you see
yourself: **in a mirror** *He glanced at his reflection
in the mirror.* → see picture at BATHROOM

mirror[2] *v* [T] to be very similar to something or
to show clearly what it is like: *The excitement of
the 1960s is mirrored in its music.*

mirth /mɜːθ $ mɜːrθ/ *n* [U] *formal* laughter and
happiness

mis- /mɪs/ *prefix* bad or wrong, or badly or
wrongly: *Don't misbehave.* | *economic
mismanagement* | *You misunderstand me.*

M

misapprehension /ˌmɪsæprɪˈhenʃən/ n [C,U] *formal* a mistaken belief: **under a misapprehension** *I was under the misapprehension that Eric was still working in Germany.*

misappropriate /ˌmɪsəˈprəʊprɪeɪt $ -ˈproʊ-/ v [T] *formal* to dishonestly take money that you are responsible for —**misappropriation** /ˌmɪsəprəʊprɪˈeɪʃən $ -proʊ-/ n [U] *the misappropriation of funds*

misbehave /ˌmɪsbɪˈheɪv/ v [I] to behave badly [≠ **behave**] —**misbehaviour** *BrE*; **misbehavior** *AmE* /-ˈheɪvjə $ -ər/ n [U]

miscalculate /mɪsˈkælkjʊleɪt/ v [I,T] **1** to make a mistake when you are calculating something: *We miscalculated how long it would take to get there.* **2** to make a wrong judgment about a situation: *The Government has miscalculated public opinion.* —**miscalculation** /mɪsˌkælkjʊˈleɪʃən/ n [C,U]

miscarriage /ˌmɪsˈkærɪdʒ, ˈmɪskærɪdʒ/ n **1** [C,U] if a woman has a miscarriage, her baby is born much too early and it dies [➡ **abortion**] **2 miscarriage of justice** when someone is wrongly punished by a court of law for something they did not do

miscarry /mɪsˈkæri/ v **miscarried, miscarrying, miscarries 1** [I,T] to give birth to a baby too early so that it dies **2** [I] *formal* to not be successful: *All our careful plans had miscarried.*

miscellaneous /ˌmɪsəˈleɪniəs/ adj of many different kinds: *a miscellaneous assortment of books*

mischief /ˈmɪstʃɪf/ n [U] bad behaviour by children, that is annoying but causes no serious harm: *He was a lively child, and full of mischief.*

mischievous /ˈmɪstʃɪvəs/ adj a mischievous child behaves badly, but in a way that is not serious: *a mischievous little girl* —**mischievously** adv

misconception /ˌmɪskənˈsepʃən/ n [C,U] an idea that is wrong or untrue, but which people still believe: **+that** *the misconception that only gay people can get AIDS*

misconduct /ˌmɪsˈkɒndʌkt $ -ˈkɑːn-/ n [U] *formal* bad or dishonest behaviour by someone in a position of authority: *Dr Patton was found guilty of serious professional misconduct.*

misdeeds /ˈmɪsdiːdz/ n [plural] *literary* wrong or illegal actions

misdemeanour *BrE*; **misdemeanor** *AmE* /ˌmɪsdɪˈmiːnə $ -ər/ n [C] *formal* a crime that is not very serious

miser /ˈmaɪzə $ -ər/ n [C] someone who is not generous and does not like spending money

miserable /ˈmɪzərəbəl/ adj **1** very unhappy: *I felt miserable.* | *Why are you looking so miserable?* ➔ see box at **SAD 2** unpleasant: *The weather's been pretty miserable all summer.* | *They lead miserable lives.* **3** very small in amount, or very bad in quality: *Nurses tend to earn a miserable salary.* —**miserably** adv

misery /ˈmɪzəri/ n [C,U] plural **miseries 1** when someone is very unhappy or is suffering badly: **+of** *the misery of life in the refugee camps* | *the miseries of war* **2 put sb/sth out of their misery a)** *informal* to make someone stop feeling worried, especially by telling them something they are waiting to hear: *Come on, put us out of our misery and tell us what happened.* **b)** to kill an animal that is old or ill so that it does not suffer any more

misfire /ˌmɪsˈfaɪə $ -ˈfaɪr/ v [I] **1** to not have the result that you intended: *His attempt at a joke misfired.* **2** if a gun misfires, the bullet does not come out

misfit /ˈmɪsˌfɪt/ n [C] someone who seems strange because they are different from the other people in a group: *I was always a bit of a misfit at school.*

misfortune /mɪsˈfɔːtʃən $ -ɔːr-/ n [C,U] bad luck, or something that happens to you as a result of bad luck: *They had the misfortune to be in the wrong country when the war broke out.*

misgiving /mɪsˈɡɪvɪŋ/ n [C,U] a feeling of doubt or worry about something: *Opponents of nuclear energy have deep misgivings about its safety.*

misguided /mɪsˈɡaɪdɪd/ adj based on an idea or opinion that is wrong: *the misguided belief that it would be easier to find work in London*

mishandle /ˌmɪsˈhændl/ v [T] to deal with something in the wrong way: *The investigation was seriously mishandled by the police.*

mishap /ˈmɪshæp/ n [C,U] a small accident or mistake

mishear /ˌmɪsˈhɪə $ -ˈhɪr/ v [I,T] past tense and past participle **misheard** /-ˈhɜːd $ -ˈhɜːrd/ not to hear properly what someone says, so that you think they said something different

mishmash /ˈmɪʃmæʃ/ n [singular] *informal disapproving* a mixture of a lot of very different things

misinform /ˌmɪsɪnˈfɔːm $ -ɔːrm/ v [T] to give someone information that is incorrect or untrue: *I'm afraid you've been misinformed – she doesn't live here any more.*

misinterpret /ˌmɪsɪnˈtɜːprət $ -ɜːr-/ v [T] to understand something wrongly: *She had misinterpreted his silence as anger.*

misjudge /ˌmɪsˈdʒʌdʒ/ v [T] **1** to form a wrong or unfair opinion about a person or a situation: *The President had badly misjudged the mood of the voters.* **2** to guess an amount or distance wrongly: *I misjudged the speed of the car coming towards me.* —**misjudgement, misjudgment** n [C,U]

mislay /ˌmɪsˈleɪ/ v [T] past tense and past participle **mislaid** /-ˈleɪd/ to put something somewhere and then forget where you put it: *I seem to have mislaid my gloves.*

mislead /ˌmɪsˈliːd/ v [T] past tense and past participle **misled** /-ˈled/ to deliberately tell someone something that is not true: *Wiggins has admitted trying to mislead the police.* ➔ see box at **WRONG**

misleading /mɪsˈliːdɪŋ/ adj likely to make someone believe something that is not true: *Statistics can be very misleading.*

mismanagement /mɪsˈmænɪdʒmənt/ n [U] when someone manages a company or organization badly or illegally: *He has been accused of mismanagement.* —**mismanage** v [T]

mismatch /ˈmɪsmætʃ/ n [C] a combination of things or people that do not work well together or are not suitable for each other: **+between** *There was a huge mismatch between supply and demand.*

misnomer /mɪsˈnəʊmə $ -ˈnoʊmər/ n [C] a wrong or unsuitable name: *'Silent movie' is a misnomer since the movies usually had a musical accompaniment.*

misogynist /mɪˈsɒdʒɪnɪst $ mɪˈsɑː-/ n [C] a man who hates women —**misogyny** n [U]

misplaced /ˌmɪsˈpleɪst◂/ adj misplaced feelings of trust, love etc are wrong and unsuitable, because the person that you have these feelings for does not deserve them

misprint /ˈmɪs-prɪnt/ n [C] a small spelling mistake in a book, magazine etc

mispronounce /ˌmɪsprəˈnaʊns/ v [T] to pronounce a word wrongly

misquote /ˌmɪsˈkwəʊt$ -ˈkwoʊt/ v [T] to make a mistake when you are reporting what someone else has said or written: *They insisted that the Governor had been misquoted.*

misread /ˌmɪsˈriːd/ v [T] past tense and past participle **misread** /-ˈred/ **1** to make a wrong judgment about a situation: *The UN misread the situation.* **2** to read something wrongly: *I must have misread the date on the letter.*

misrepresent /ˌmɪsreprɪˈzent/ v [T] to deliberately give a wrong description of someone's opinions or of a situation → see box at **CHANGE** —**misrepresentation** /ˌmɪsreprɪzenˈteɪʃən/ n [C,U]

Miss /mɪs/ n

1 used in front of the name of a girl or a woman who is not married [➡ **Mrs, Ms, Mr**]: *Miss Jones will see you now.*

2 *spoken* used as a polite way of talking to a young woman when you do not know her name [➡ **madam, sir**]: *Excuse me Miss, you've dropped your umbrella.*

3 *BrE spoken* used by children when talking to a female teacher, whether she is married or not: *I know the answer, Miss.*

miss¹ v

1 [T] to feel sad because you cannot be with someone that you like, or cannot do something that you enjoy: *I really missed Paula after she'd left.* | *What do you most miss about life in Canada?* | **miss doing sth** *I really miss talking to him on the phone.*

2 [T] to not go somewhere or do something, especially when you want to but cannot: *Vialli will miss tonight's game because of a knee injury.* | *She was upset at missing all the excitement.* | **miss a chance/an opportunity** *I'd hate to miss the chance of meeting him.*

3 [T] to be too late for something: *By the time we got there, we'd missed the beginning of the movie.* | **miss a bus/train/plane etc** *Hurry up or we'll miss the train!*

4 [I,T] to not succeed in hitting or catching something: *She fired at the target but missed.* | *Jackson missed an easy catch.*

5 [T] to not see, hear, or notice something: *Jody found an error that everyone else had missed.* | *Maeve's sharp eyes missed nothing.* | *It's a huge hotel on the corner. You can't miss it.*

6 miss the point to not understand the most important fact about something: *I'm sorry, I think you're missing the point completely.*

7 miss the boat/bus *informal* to not use an opportunity to do something

miss out *phr v* **1** to not have the chance to do something that you would enjoy: *Some children miss out because their parents can't afford to pay for school trips.* **2 miss sb/sth** ⇔ **out** *BrE* to not include someone or something: *I hope we haven't missed any names out from the list.*

miss² n **1** [C] when you fail to hit, catch, or hold something: *The players are still talking about the penalty miss in the second half.* **2 give sth a miss** *BrE informal* to decide not to do something: *As the tickets were so expensive, we decided to give the concert a miss.*

misshapen /ˌmɪsˈʃeɪpən, mɪˈʃeɪ-/ adj not the normal or natural shape

missile /ˈmɪsaɪl $ ˈmɪsəl/ n [C] **1** a weapon that can fly over long distances and that explodes when it hits the thing it has been aimed at: *a nuclear missile* **2** an object that someone throws at a person in order to hurt them

missing

one shirt button is missing

missing /ˈmɪsɪŋ/ adj

1 lost, or not in the usual or expected place: *Police are still searching for the missing child.* | *Two crew members survived, but two are still missing.* | +**from** *There's a button missing from this shirt.* | *The scissors have gone missing again.*

2 not included: +**from** *Why is my name missing from the list?*

mission /ˈmɪʃən/ n [C] **1** an important job that someone has been sent to a place to do: *Our mission was to find out everything about their plans.* | *a bombing mission* | *a peacekeeping mission* **2** a group of important people who are sent by their government to another country to discuss something or collect information: *a Canadian trade mission to Japan* **3** something that you feel you must do because it is your duty: *His mission was to help young people in his local community.*

missionary /ˈmɪʃənəri $ -neri/ n [C] plural **missionaries** someone who goes to a foreign country in order to teach people about Christianity

misspell /ˌmɪsˈspel/ v [T] past tense and past participle **misspelt** /-ˈspelt/ or **misspelled** to spell a word wrongly —**misspelling** n [C,U]

misstep /ˈmɪs-step/ n [C] *AmE* a mistake, especially one that is caused by not understanding a situation correctly: *A misstep here could cost millions of dollars.*

mist¹ /mɪst/ n [C,U] a layer of cloud close to the ground that makes it difficult for you to see very far [➡ **fog**]: *The mist was starting to clear.*

mist² also **mist over/up** *v* [I,T] to become covered with very small drops of water, or to make something do this: *All the windows had misted over.*

mistake¹ /mɪˈsteɪk/ *n*

1 [C] something that is wrong or has been done in the wrong way [➜ **error**]: *Ivan's work is full of spelling mistakes.* | *We may have made a mistake in our calculations.*

2 [C] something you do that is not sensible or has a bad result: *It's your decision, but I warn you – you're making a mistake.* | *I made the mistake of giving him my phone number.* | *Marrying Julie was a big mistake.* | *It would be a mistake to underestimate Moya's ability.*

3 by mistake without intending to do something [= **accidentally**; ≠ **on purpose**]: *Someone must have left the door open by mistake.*

mistake² *v* [T] past tense **mistook** /-ˈstʊk/ past participle **mistaken** /-ˈsteɪkən/ **1** to understand something wrongly: *I must have mistaken what he said.* **2 there's no mistaking sb/sth** used to say that you are certain about something: *There was no mistaking the anger in her voice.* **3 mistake sb/sth for sb/sth** to wrongly think that one person or thing is someone or something else: *I mistook him for his brother.*

mistaken /mɪˈsteɪkən/ *adj* if you are mistaken, you are wrong about something: *I thought he said 12 o'clock, but I might have been mistaken.* | *We bought the rug in Turkey, if I'm not mistaken.* ➜ see box at **WRONG** —**mistakenly** *adv*

Mister /ˈmɪstə $ -ər/ *n* the full form of **MR**

mister *n AmE spoken informal* used to talk to a man whose name you do not know: *Hey mister, is this your wallet?*

mistletoe /ˈmɪsəltəʊ $ -toʊ/ *n* [U] a plant with small round white fruit that is often used as a decoration at Christmas

mistook /mɪˈstʊk/ *v* the past tense of **MISTAKE**

mistreat /ˌmɪsˈtriːt/ *v* [T] to treat a person or animal cruelly: *The hostages said they had not been mistreated.* —**mistreatment** *n* [U]

mistress /ˈmɪstrɪs/ *n* [C] a married man's secret lover

mistrust /mɪsˈtrʌst/ *n* [U] the feeling that you cannot trust someone or something: *He had a deep mistrust of politicians.* —**mistrust** *v* [T] —**mistrustful** *adj*

misty /ˈmɪsti/ *adj* misty weather is weather with a lot of mist: *a cold, misty morning*

misunderstand /ˌmɪsʌndəˈstænd $ -ər-/ *v* past tense and past participle **misunderstood** /-ˈstʊd/ [I,T] to not understand something correctly: *I think you misunderstand my question.*

misunderstanding /ˌmɪsʌndəˈstændɪŋ $ -ər-/ *n* **1** [C,U] a problem caused by someone not understanding a question, situation, or instruction correctly: *There must have been some misunderstanding. I didn't order this.* **2** [C] a small argument or disagreement

misunderstood /ˌmɪsʌndəˈstʊd $ -ər-/ *adj* if someone is misunderstood, people do not like them because they do not know them or understand them

misuse /ˌmɪsˈjuːz/ *v* [T] to use something in the wrong way or for the wrong purpose: *The chair-*

man was accused of misusing club funds. —**misuse** /-ˈjuːs/ *n* [C,U] *a misuse of power*

mite /maɪt/ *n* [C] **1** a very small insect that lives in plants, animals' fur, stored food etc **2** a small child, especially one you feel sorry for **3 a mite** *informal* slightly: *She's a mite shy.*

mitigate /ˈmɪtɪɡeɪt/ *v* [T] *formal* to make something less harmful or less serious —**mitigation** /ˌmɪtɪˈɡeɪʃən/ *n* [U]

mitigating /ˈmɪtɪɡeɪtɪŋ/ *adj* **mitigating circumstances/factors** facts that make a crime or mistake seem less serious

mitt /mɪt/ *n* [C] **1** a type of leather **GLOVE** used for catching a ball in **BASEBALL** **2** a thick **GLOVE** that you wear to protect your hand: *an oven mitt*

mitten /ˈmɪtn/ *n* [C] a type of **GLOVE** that does not have separate parts for each finger

mix¹ /mɪks/ *v*

1 [I,T] if you mix two or more substances or if they mix, they combine to become a single substance: *Oil and water don't mix.* | **mix sth and sth** *You can make green by mixing blue and yellow paint.* | **mix sth with sth** *Shake the bottle well to mix the oil with the vinegar.* | **mix sth together** *First mix the butter and sugar together, then add the milk.* → see box at **RECIPE** → see picture on page A4

2 [I,T] to combine two or more different activities, ideas, styles etc: **mix sth and sth** *Glennie's latest CD mixes classical music and rock 'n' roll.* | **mix sth with sth** *I don't like to mix business with pleasure.*

3 [I] to enjoy talking to other people and meeting new people: **+with** *Charlie doesn't mix well with the other children.*

mix sb/sth ⇔ up *phr v* **1** to think that one person or thing is someone or something else: *I'm always mixing up the kids' names.* **2** to change the order in which things have been arranged: *Whatever you do, try not to mix those papers up.*

mix² *n* **1** [singular] a combination of different things or people: **+of** *There was a good mix of people at the party.* | *a complicated mix of colours and textures* **2** [C,U] a powder that is added to liquid to make something: *cake mix* **3** [C] a particular arrangement of sounds, instruments, and voices in a piece of music

mixed /mɪkst/ *adj*

1 consisting of a lot of different types of things, people, ideas etc: *mixed herbs* | *We had **mixed feelings** (=feelings of happiness and sadness at the same time) about moving so far away.*

2 mixed reaction/response/reviews etc if something gets a mixed reaction etc, some people say they like it, but others dislike it: *The film has had mixed reviews from the critics.*

3 a mixed blessing something that is good in some ways but bad in others: *Living so near my parents was a mixed blessing.*

4 *BrE* for both males and females [➜ **co-ed**]: *a mixed school*

5 (of) mixed race a person of mixed race has parents of different races

mixed 'marriage *n* [C] a marriage between people from different races or religions

mixed 'up *adj* **1 be/get mixed up in sth** to be involved in an illegal or dishonest activity: *He was only 14 when he got mixed up in*

M

drug-dealing. **2** also **mixed-up** confused and suffering from emotional problems: *a lonely mixed-up adolescent* **3** confused, for example because you have too many different details to remember or think about: *I got a little mixed up and went to the wrong restaurant.*

mixer /ˈmɪksə $ -ər/ *n* [C] **1** a piece of equipment used for mixing things together: *a food mixer* **2** a drink that can be mixed with alcohol: *There are some mixers in the fridge.*

mixture /ˈmɪkstʃə $ -ər/ *n*

1 [C,U] a liquid or other substance that is made by mixing several substances together, especially in cooking: *cake mixture* | *Pour the mixture into four small dishes.*
2 [C] a combination of two or more different things: **+of** *The town is a mixture of the old and the new.* | *a mixture of emotions*

'mix-up *n* [C] *informal* a situation in which people are confused or make mistakes about arrangements: *There was a mix-up at the station and Eddie got on the wrong bus.* | **+over** *There was a mix-up over the hotel booking.*

ml the written abbreviation of **millilitre**

mm the written abbreviation of **millimetre**

moan /məʊn $ moʊn/ *v* [I] **1** to make a long low sound expressing pain or unhappiness: *She lay on the bed moaning with pain.* **2** to complain about something in an annoying way: *I wish you'd stop moaning all the time.* —**moan** *n* [C] *There was a moan of pain from the injured man.*

moat /məʊt $ moʊt/ *n* [C] a deep wide hole that is dug around a castle to defend it

mob¹ /mɒb $ mɑːb/ *n* [C] a large noisy crowd, especially one that is angry and violent

mob² *v* [T] **mobbed, mobbing** if people mob a famous person, they rush to get near them and form a crowd around them: *Wherever she went, she was mobbed by fans.*

mobile¹ /ˈməʊbaɪl $ ˈmoʊbəl, -biːl/ *adj* **1** able to move to or be moved quickly and easily: *She's 83 and not very mobile.* | *mobile missile systems* **2** able to move from one job, area, or social class to another: *an increasingly mobile population* **3 mobile shop/library/clinic etc** *BrE* a shop etc in a vehicle which is driven from place to place

mobile² /ˈməʊbaɪl $ ˈmoʊbiːl/ *n* [C] **1** a MOBILE PHONE **2** a decoration made of small objects that hang down on wires or strings and move when air blows around them

mobile 'home *n* [C] **1** *BrE* a large CARAVAN which always stays in the same place and is used as a house **2** *AmE* a type of house made of metal, that can be pulled by a vehicle and moved to another place

mobile 'phone *n* [C] *BrE* a telephone that you can carry with you and use anywhere [= **cell phone** *AmE*]

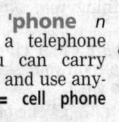

mobile phone *BrE/* **cell phone** *AmE*

To use a mobile phone, you first **switch** it **on**. Then you can either **call** someone or **listen** to

messages that people have left you on your **voicemail**. You can also read **text messages** (=written messages) or **text** someone (=send them a text message).
→ **TELEPHONE**

mobility /məʊˈbɪləti $ moʊ-/ *n* [U] **1** the ability to move easily from one job, area, or social class to another: *social mobility* **2** the ability to move easily: *elderly people with limited mobility*

mobilize also **-ise** *BrE* /ˈməʊbɪlaɪz $ ˈmoʊ-/ *v* **1** [T] to encourage people to support something in an active way: *a campaign to mobilize support for the strike* **2** [I,T] if a country mobilizes, or mobilizes its army, it prepares to fight a war —**mobilization** /ˌməʊbɪlaɪˈzeɪʃən $ ˌmoʊbələ-/ *n* [C,U]

mobster /ˈmɒbstə $ ˈmɑːbstər/ *n* [C] *especially AmE* a member of a criminal group

mock¹ /mɒk $ mɑːk/ *v* [I,T] to try to make someone seem stupid, for example by copying them or saying unkind things about them: *'Are you afraid?' he mocked.* —**mockingly** *adv*

mock² *adj* [only before noun] not real, but intended to be very similar to something real: *a mock interview* | **mock surprise/horror etc** *She shook her head in mock disgust.*

mock³ *n* [C] *BrE* a school examination taken as practice for an official examination

mockery /ˈmɒkəri $ ˈmɑː-/ *n* **1 make a mockery of sth** to make a plan, system, organization etc seem useless or stupid: *His release makes a mockery of the law.* **2** [U] when someone laughs at someone or something or tries to make them seem stupid

'mock-up *n* [C] a model of something, made before the real thing is built, or made for a film, show etc

modal verb /ˌməʊdl ˈvɜːb $ ˌmoʊdl ˈvɜːrb/ also **modal** *n* [C] *technical* a verb such as 'can', 'might', or 'must' that is used with other verbs to show ideas such as possibility, permission, or intention

mode /məʊd $ moʊd/ *n* [C] *formal* a particular way of behaving, living, or doing something: **+of** *different modes of transport*

model¹ /ˈmɒdl $ ˈmɑːdl/ *n* [C]

1 a small copy of a building, vehicle, machine etc, especially one that can be made from separate parts: **+of** *a model of the Eiffel Tower* | *Simon spends hours making models.* | *a working model* (=one with parts that move) *of a steam engine*
2 someone whose job is to show clothes, hair styles etc by wearing them at fashion shows or for photographs: *a fashion model*
3 a particular type or design of a vehicle or machine: *the latest* (=newest) *model from BMW*
4 a computer representation or scientific description of something: **+of** *computer models of climate change*
5 someone or something which people want to copy because they are successful or have good qualities: **+for** *This approach may serve as a model* (=be used as a model) *for projects in other cities.*

6 someone who is employed by an artist or photographer to be painted or photographed → ROLE MODEL

model² *adj* [only before noun] **1 model aeroplane/train/car etc** a small copy of a plane, train etc, especially one that you can make **2** a model student, wife etc does everything exactly as they should: *a model employee*

model³ *v* modelled, modelling *BrE*; modeled, modeling *AmE* **1** [I,T] to wear clothes at a fashion show or in magazine photographs in order to show them to people: *She models for Elle magazine.* **2 model yourself on sb** *BrE*; **model yourself after sb** *AmE* to try to be like someone because you admire them: *Pete models himself on Elvis Presley.* **3 be modelled on sth** to be designed in a way that copies another system or way of doing something: *a constitution modelled on the French system*

modelling *BrE*; **modeling** *AmE* /'mɒdl-ɪŋ $ 'mɑː-/ *n* [U] the work of a fashion model: *a career in modelling*

modem /'məʊdəm, -dem $ 'moʊ-/ *n* [C] a piece of electronic equipment used for sending information along telephone wires from one computer to another

moderate¹ /'mɒdərᵻt $ 'mɑː-/ *adj* **1** not very big or very small, very hot or very cold, very fast or very slow etc: *Cook over a moderate heat.* **2** having opinions or beliefs, especially about politics, that are not extreme: *moderate Republicans* —**moderately** *adv*

moderate² /'mɒdəreɪt $ 'mɑː-/ *v* [I,T] *formal* to make something less extreme, or to become less extreme: *The students moderated their demands.*

moderate³ /'mɒdərᵻt $ 'mɑː-/ *n* [C] someone whose opinions or beliefs, especially about politics, are not extreme

moderation /ˌmɒdə'reɪʃən $ ˌmɑː-/ *n* **1 in moderation** if you do something in moderation, you do not do it too much: *He drinks only in moderation.* **2** [U] *formal* sensible control of your behaviour and ideas

modern /'mɒdn $ 'mɑːdərn/ *adj*

1 [only before noun] belonging to the present time or most recent time [= contemporary]: *in the modern world | people in modern society | one of the greatest events of modern times*

2 using the most recent designs, methods, ideas etc: *the use of modern technology | advances in modern medicine | The school is very modern in its approach to sex education.*

THESAURUS

the latest: *the very latest mobile phones | the latest summer fashions*
up-to-date – used about modern equipment or methods: *up-to-date training methods*
advanced – used about modern weapons, machines, and systems: *an advanced security system*
high-tech/hi-tech – using very modern electronic equipment and machines, especially computers: *high-tech graphics*
→ NEW

3 [only before noun] modern art, music, literature etc uses styles that are very different from traditional styles: *modern dance*

—**modernity** /mɒ'dɜːnᵻti $ mə'dɜːr-/ *n* [U] *a conflict between tradition and modernity*

'modern-day *adj* [only before noun] existing now, not in the past: *modern-day Egypt*

modernize also **-ise** *BrE* /'mɒdənaɪz $ 'mɑːder-/ *v* [I,T] to make something more modern, or to become more modern: *plans to modernize the factory* —**modernization** /ˌmɒdənaɪ'zeɪʃən $ ˌmɑːdərnə-/ *n* [C,U]

ˌmodern 'languages *n* [plural] *BrE* languages that are spoken now such as French or German, studied as a subject at school or university

modest /'mɒdᵻst $ 'mɑː-/ *adj* **1** *approving* someone who is modest does not talk in a proud way about their abilities or achievements: *a quiet modest man* **2** not very big in size, amount, value etc: *a modest increase* —**modestly** *adv*

modesty /'mɒdᵻsti $ 'mɑː-/ *n* [U] the quality of not talking in a proud way about your achievements, abilities etc

modicum /'mɒdɪkəm $ 'mɑː-/ *n* **a modicum of sth** *formal* a small amount of something, especially something good: *a modicum of success*

modification /ˌmɒdᵻfᵻ'keɪʃən $ ˌmɑː-/ *n* [C,U] a small change to something, or the process of changing something: *+to We've made a few modifications to the design.*

modifier /'mɒdᵻfaɪə $ 'mɑːdᵻfaɪər/ *n* [C] *technical* an adjective, adverb, or phrase that gives additional information about another word

modify /'mɒdᵻfaɪ $ 'mɑː-/ *v* [T] modified, modifying, modifies **1** to make small changes to something in order to make it better or more suitable: *The course will have to be modified for younger students.* → see box at CHANGE **2** *technical* if an adjective, adverb etc modifies another word, it gives more information about it

module /'mɒdjuːl $ 'mɑːdʒuːl/ *n* [C] **1** especially *BrE* one of the parts of a course of study: *You can choose five modules in the first year.* **2** a part of a spacecraft that can separate from the main part and be used for a particular purpose —**modular** /'mɒdjᵿlə $ 'mɑːdʒələr/ *adj*

mogul /'məʊgəl $ 'moʊ-/ *n* [C] **movie/media etc mogul** someone who has great power and influence in a particular industry

mohair /'məʊheə $ 'moʊher/ *n* [U] expensive wool made from the hair of a type of goat

Mohammed /məʊ'hæmᵻd, mə- $ moʊ-/ *n* another spelling of MUHAMMAD

moist /mɔɪst/ *adj* slightly wet, especially in a pleasant way: *a moist chocolate cake | Make sure the soil is moist.* → see box at DAMP

moisten /'mɔɪsən/ *v* [T] to make something slightly wet

moisture /'mɔɪstʃə $ -ər/ *n* [U] small amounts of water in or on something: *your skin's natural moisture*

moisturizer also **-iser** *BrE* /'mɔɪstʃəraɪzə $ -ər/ *n* [C,U] liquid that you put on your skin to make it less dry —**moisturize** *v* [I,T]

molar /'məʊlə $ 'moʊlər/ *n* [C] one of the large teeth at the back of your mouth

molasses /mə'læsᵻz/ *n* [U] *AmE* a thick sweet black liquid that is obtained from the sugar plant and used in cooking [= treacle *BrE*]

mold /məʊld $ moʊld/ *n, v* the American spelling of MOULD

molding /'məʊldɪŋ $ 'moʊl-/ *n* the American spelling of MOULDING

moldy /'məʊldi $ 'moʊl-/ *adj* the American spelling of MOULDY

mole /məʊl $ moʊl/ *n* [C] **1** a small dark furry animal which is almost blind. Moles live under the ground. **2** a small dark brown mark on your skin **3** someone who works for an organization while secretly giving information to its enemies

molecule /'mɒlɪkjuːl $ 'mɑː-/ *n* [C] the smallest unit into which a substance can be divided without losing its own chemical nature: *Water molecules are made of one hydrogen and two oxygen atoms.* —**molecular** /mə'lekjələ $ -ər/ *adj*

molest /mə'lest/ *v* [T] to attack or harm someone, especially a child, by touching them in a sexual way or trying to have sex with them: *He was accused of molesting a 14-year-old boy.* —**molester** *n* [C] *a child molester* —**molestation** /ˌməʊle'steɪʃən $ ˌmoʊ-/ *n* [U]

mollify /'mɒlɪfaɪ $ 'mɑː-/ *v* [T] **mollified, mollifying, mollifies** *formal* to make someone feel less angry

mollusc *BrE*; **mollusk** *AmE* /'mɒləsk $ 'mɑː-/ *n* [C] a type of sea or land animal that has a soft body covered by a hard shell: *snails and other molluscs*

mollycoddle /'mɒliˌkɒdl $ 'mɑːliˌkɑːdl/ *v* [T] *disapproving* to treat someone too kindly and protect them from anything unpleasant

molt /məʊlt $ moʊlt/ *v* the American spelling of MOULT

molten /'məʊltən $ 'moʊl-/ *adj* molten metal or rock is liquid because it is very hot

mom /mɒm $ mɑːm/ *n* [C] *AmE informal* mother [= mum *BrE*]: *Mom, can we go swimming? | My mom's a secretary.* → see box at RELATIVE

moment /'məʊmənt $ 'moʊ-/ *n* [C]

1 a particular point in time: *It was one of the most exciting moments in his life.* | **at that/this moment** (=exactly then/now) *At that moment there was a knock on the door.* | *Do you remember the moment when we first met?*
2 a very short period of time: *He was here a moment ago.* | *A few moments later the phone rang.* | *Would you mind waiting a moment?* | **in a moment** (=very soon) *I'll bring you some tea in a moment.* | **for a moment** *She was silent for a moment.*
3 at the moment now: *We're very busy at the moment.* → see box at NOW
4 for the moment used to say that something is happening or is true now but may change in the future: *For the moment we're just friends.*
5 the moment (that) ... as soon as someone does something or something happens: *I'll call you the moment I hear anything.*
6 (at) any moment very soon: *It could start to rain at any moment.*
7 the last moment at the latest possible time: *As usual, she arrived at the last moment.*
→ **on the spur of the moment** at SPUR[1]

momentarily /'məʊməntərəli $ ˌmoʊmən'terəli/ *adv* **1** for a very short time [= briefly]: *Jim paused momentarily.* **2** *AmE* very soon: *I'll be with you momentarily.*

momentary /'məʊməntəri $ 'moʊmənteri/ *adj* happening for a very short time [= brief]: *There was a momentary silence.*

momentous /məʊ'mentəs, mə- $ moʊ-, mə-/ *adj* a momentous event, change, or decision is very important: *the momentous events at the end of the century*

momentum /məʊ'mentəm, mə- $ moʊ-, mə-/ *n* [U] **1** when something continues to increase, develop, or become more successful: **gain/gather momentum** *The campaign continued to gather momentum.* **2** the force that makes a moving object continue to move: **gain/gather momentum** (=move faster and faster) *The wheel rolled downhill, gathering momentum.*

momma /'mɒmə $ 'mɑːmə/ *n AmE* another form of MAMA

mommy /'mɒmi $ 'mɑːmi/ *n* [C] plural **mommies** *AmE* mother – used by or to young children [= mummy *BrE*] → see box at RELATIVE

Mon. also **Mon** *BrE* the written abbreviation of Monday

monarch /'mɒnək $ 'mɑːnərk, -ɑːrk/ *n* [C] a king or queen

monarchy /'mɒnəki $ 'mɑːnərki/ *n* plural **monarchies** **1** [U] the system in which a country is ruled by a king or queen **2** [C] a country that is ruled by a king or queen [→ republic]

monastery /'mɒnəstri $ 'mɑːnəsteri/ *n* [C] plural **monasteries** a place where MONKS live [→ convent]

monastic /mə'næstɪk/ *adj* relating to MONKS or a monastery

Monday /'mʌndi, -deɪ/ *n* [C,U] written abbreviation **Mon.** the day between Sunday and Tuesday: **on Monday** *It was raining on Monday.* | **Monday morning/afternoon etc** *Let's go out for a meal on Monday night.* | **last Monday** *They arrived last Monday.* | **next Monday** (=Monday of next week) *Shall we meet next Monday?* | **this Monday** *The UK office will open for business this Monday.* | **a Monday** (=one of the Mondays in the year) *My birthday is on a Monday this year.* → see box at DAY

monetary /'mʌnɪtəri $ 'mʌnɪteri/ *adj* [only before noun] relating to money, especially all the money in a particular country: *the government's monetary policy*

money /'mʌni/ *n* [U]

1 what you earn by working and use to buy things, often in the form of coins, paper notes etc [→ monies]: *I spend a lot of money on clothes.* | *He doesn't earn much money.* | *She put the money in her purse.* | **a large sum** (=amount) **of money** | **make money** (=earn money or make a profit) *The company is making a lot of money.* | *The repairs will cost a lot of money.* | *I'm trying to save money for a holiday.* | *It's an absolute waste of money.* | **lend/borrow/owe money** *Could you lend me some money?*

THESAURUS

Types of money
note *BrE*/**bill** *AmE* – paper money: *a £20 note*
coin – metal money: *Roman coins*
ten-pence/fifty-cent piece – a coin worth a particular amount
cash – money in the form of coins and notes: *The restaurant accepts cash only* (=it does not

M

accept cheques or credit cards). | *We paid in cash.*

change – money in the form of coins: *Do you have any change for the phone?*

currency – the money used in a particular country: *You'll need about £500 worth of Japanese currency.*

Money that you earn or receive

income – all the money that you earn or receive regularly from your job, from the government etc: *a regular monthly income*

pay – a general word for money that you are given for working: *The pay in her new job isn't very good.*

salary – the money that someone receives every month as payment for working

wage/wages – the money that someone receives every day or week as payment for working

benefit – money that you get from the government when you are ill or do not have a job

→ PAY

2 sb's money all someone's money and the things they own: *The family made their money in the woollen trade.*

3 the money *informal* the amount of money that you earn for doing a job [= the salary]: *The money's terrible.*

4 get your money's worth to get enough for the price that you paid: *We stayed right to the end, to get our money's worth.*

→ POCKET MONEY → be rolling in money at ROLL¹ → SPENDING MONEY

'**money ,market** *n* [C] all the banks and other institutions that buy, sell, lend, or borrow money in order to make a profit

'**money ,order** *n* [C] *especially AmE* an official document that you buy in a post office or bank and send to someone so that they can exchange it for money in a bank [= postal order *BrE*]

mongrel /'mʌŋgrəl $ 'mɑːŋ-, 'mʌŋ-/ *n* [C] a dog that is a mix of different breeds

monies, moneys /'mʌniz/ *n* [plural] *law* money: *a refund of all monies paid*

monitor¹ /'mɒnɪtə $ 'mɑːnɪ̯tər/ *v* [T] to carefully watch or measure something to see how it changes over a period of time: *Your manager will closely monitor your progress.*

monitor² *n* [C] **1** the part of a computer with a screen, or a television screen: *the information displayed on the computer monitor* **2** a piece of equipment that measures and shows the level, speed etc of something: *a heart monitor*

monk /mʌŋk/ *n* [C] a member of a religious group of men who live together in a MONASTERY [→ nun]

monkey /'mʌŋki/ *n* [C]

1 a small brown animal with a long tail, which uses its hands to climb trees and lives in hot countries

2 monkey business *informal* bad or dishonest behaviour

'**monkey wrench** *n* [C] *especially AmE* a tool used for holding or turning things

mono /'mɒnəʊ $ 'mɑːnoʊ/ *n* [U] *AmE informal* an infectious illness that makes you feel weak and tired for a long time [= glandular fever *BrE*]

mono- /mɒnəʊ, -nə $ -noʊ, -nə/ *prefix* one: *a monolingual dictionary* (=using only one language)

monochrome /'mɒnəkrəʊm $ 'mɑːnəkroʊm/ *adj* consisting only of the colours black, white, and grey: *a monochrome image*

monogamy /məˈnɒgəmi $ məˈnɑː-/ *n* [U] when people have only one husband or wife or only one sexual partner —**monogamous** *adj*: *We live in a monogamous society.*

monogram /'mɒnəgræm $ 'mɑː-/ *n* [C] a design that is made using the first letters of someone's names, and is put on clothes and other possessions —**monogrammed** *adj*

monolingual /ˌmɒnəʊˈlɪŋgwəl◂ $ ˌmɑːnə-/ *adj* speaking or using only one language [→ bilingual, multilingual]: *a monolingual dictionary*

monolithic /ˌmɒnəˈlɪθɪk $ ˌmɑː-/ *adj* a monolithic organization, political system etc is large, powerful, and difficult to change —**monolith** /'mɒnəlɪθ $ 'mɑː-/ *n* [C]

monologue also **monolog** *AmE* /'mɒnəlɒg $ 'mɑːnl-ɒːg, -ɑːg/ *n* [C] a long speech by one person [→ dialogue]

monopolize also **-ise** *BrE* /məˈnɒpəlaɪz $ -ˈnɑː-/ *v* [T] to control a situation completely so that other people cannot share it or take part in it: *The company has monopolized the drinks market.* | *He monopolized the conversation all evening.* —**monopolization** /məˌnɒpəlaɪˈzeɪʃən $ -ˌnɑːpələ-/ *n* [U]

monopoly /məˈnɒpəli $ məˈnɑː-/ *n* plural **monopolies** **1** [C usually singular] the complete control of an area of business or industry by a company or government, which makes it impossible for other organizations to compete: +**of** *the state monopoly of television* | +**on** *The company used to have a monopoly on telephone services.* **2** [C] a large company that controls all or most of a business activity **3** [singular] if someone has a monopoly on something, no one else can have it, share it etc: +**on** *No religion has a monopoly on truth.*

monosyllabic /ˌmɒnəsɪˈlæbɪk◂ $ ˌmɑː-/ *adj* **1** someone who is monosyllabic does not say very much and does not try to be friendly **2** a monosyllabic word has only one SYLLABLE

monosyllable /'mɒnə,sɪləbəl $ 'mɑː-/ *n* [C] a word with only one SYLLABLE, for example 'no'

monotone /'mɒnətəʊn $ 'mɑːnətoʊn/ *n* [singular] a way of speaking that sounds boring because your voice never changes: *He continued talking in a slow monotone.*

monotonous /məˈnɒtənəs $ məˈnɑː-/ *adj* boring and always the same: *monotonous work* | *He won every game with monotonous regularity.* —**monotony** *n* [U] —**monotonously** *adv*

monsoon /mɒnˈsuːn $ mɑːn-/ *n* [C] the time when it rains a lot in India and other southern Asian countries

monster¹ /'mɒnstə $ 'mɑːnstər/ *n* [C] **1** a large ugly frightening creature in stories: *a sea monster* **2** someone who is very cruel and evil: *Only a monster could kill an innocent child.*

monster² *adj* [only before noun] *informal* unusually big

monstrosity /mɒnˈstrɒsɪ̯ti $ mɑːnˈstrɑː-/ *n* [C] plural **monstrosities** something that is large and ugly, especially a building

monstrous /'mɒnstrəs $ 'mɑːn-/ adj **1** very wrong, immoral, or unfair: *a monstrous crime* **2** very large and often frightening: *monstrous waves* —**monstrously** adv

montage /'mɒntɑːʒ $ mɑːn'tɑːʒ/ n [C,U] a picture, piece of music etc made by combining parts of different pictures, pieces of music etc, or the process of making it

month /mʌnθ/ n [C]
1 one of the twelve periods of time that a year is divided into: **this/last/next month** *She'll be ten this month.* | *The work should be finished by the end of the month.* | *She earns £1000 a month* (=each month).
2 a period of time of about four weeks: *We'll be away for four months.* | *We have an eight-month-old daughter.*
3 months a long time, especially several months: *Painting the house took months.*

GRAMMAR

Talking about months
Use **in** to talk about a month but not about a particular date in that month: *He was born in February.*
Use **on** to talk about a particular date in a month: *He was born on February 20th.* | *She finishes school on the nineteenth of July.*
Use **next** to talk about a month after the present one: *They're getting married next June.*
Use **last** to talk about a month before the present one: *He died last October.*

monthly /'mʌnθli/ adj happening or produced once a month: *monthly meetings* | *a monthly magazine* | *a monthly salary of $2000.* → see box at **REGULAR** —**monthly** adv: *All employees are paid monthly.*

monument /'mɒnjᵘmənt $ 'mɑː-/ n [C] **1** something that is built to remind people of an important event or famous person: **+to** *The cross is a monument to the men who died in battle.* **2** an old building or place that is important in history: *ancient monuments* **3 be a monument to sth** to show clearly the result of someone's qualities, beliefs, actions etc: *The company is a monument to his energy and determination.*

monumental /ˌmɒnjᵘ'mentl◂ $ ˌmɑː-/ adj extremely large, bad, impressive, important etc: *a monumental task* | *a monumental error* | *Darwin's monumental work on evolution*

moo /muː/ v [I] to make the sound that a cow makes —**moo** n [C]

mood /muːd/ n [C]
1 the way someone feels at a particular time: **be in a good/bad/relaxed etc mood** (=be happy, annoyed etc) *You're certainly in a good mood today!* | *The players are in a confident mood.* | *His mood suddenly changed.* | *The government has misjudged the public mood.*
2 be in a mood to feel unhappy or angry
3 be/feel in the mood to feel that you want to do something: **+for** *We were all in the mood for a party.* | **be in no mood for sth/be in no mood to do sth** (=not want to do something) *He was obviously in no mood for talking.*
4 technical one of the sets of verb forms in

grammar such as the INDICATIVE (=expressing a fact or action) or the IMPERATIVE (=expressing a command) etc

moody /'muːdi/ adj often becoming angry or unhappy: *a moody teenager* → see box at **CHARACTER** —**moodily** adv —**moodiness** n [U]

moon /muːn/ n
1 the moon/Moon the round object that moves around the Earth and shines in the sky at night: *the first person to land on the moon* → see box at **SPACE**
2 [singular] the shape of the moon at a particular time of the month: *There's no moon tonight* (=it cannot be seen). | **full/half moon** (=when the moon is a complete/half circle)
3 [C] a round object that moves around another PLANET: *How many moons does Jupiter have?*
4 over the moon BrE informal very happy: *She's over the moon about her new job.*
→ **once in a blue moon** at ONCE¹

moonbeam /'muːnbiːm/ n [C] a line of light from the moon

moonlight¹ /'muːnlaɪt/ n [U] the light that comes from the moon: **in the moonlight** *The pool glistened in the moonlight.*

moonlight² v [I] informal to have a second job in addition to your main job: *He's been moonlighting as a DJ.*

moonlit /'muːnˌlɪt/ adj lit by the moon: *a beautiful moonlit night*

moor¹ /mʊə $ mʊr/ n [C usually plural] especially BrE a wild area of high land covered with rough grass or low bushes: *the North Yorkshire Moors*

moor² v [I,T] to fasten a boat to land or to the bottom of the sea

mooring /'mʊərɪŋ $ 'mʊr-/ n [C] **1** the place where a ship or boat is fastened to land **2 moorings** [plural] the ropes, chains etc used to fasten a ship or boat to the land

moose /muːs/ n [C] plural **moose** a large wild animal like a DEER with large flat horns

moot¹ /muːt/ adj **1 a moot point/question** something that has not yet been decided or agreed, and that people have different ideas about: *Whether she was to blame or not is a moot point.* **2** AmE no longer likely to happen or exist: *The proposal is moot because of a lack of funds.*

moot² v **be mooted** to be suggested for people to consider

mop¹ /mɒp $ mɑːp/ n **1** [C] a thing for washing floors consisting of a long stick with a soft end **2** [singular] informal a large amount of thick untidy hair: **+of** *a mop of black curly hair*

mop² v [T] **mopped, mopping 1** to wash a floor with a mop **2** to dry your face or remove liquid from something using a cloth [= **wipe**]: **mop sth from sth** *He mopped the sweat from his face.*
mop sth ⇔ up phr v to remove liquid from a surface, using a mop or cloth: *Can you mop up the milk you've spilled?*

mope /məʊp $ moʊp/ also **mope around** v [I] to spend time feeling unhappy and doing very little

moped /'məʊped $ 'moʊ-/ n [C] a vehicle like a bicycle with a small engine

moral¹ /'mɒrəl $ 'mɔː-/ adj

1 [only before noun] based on principles of what is right and wrong [➡ ethical; ≠ immoral]: *This is a moral issue, not a political one.* | **moral values/standards/principles** *an emphasis on traditional moral values* | **moral obligation/duty/responsibility** *We have a moral duty to help the poor.* | *This presented him with a moral dilemma.*
2 moral support help and encouragement that you give to someone: *I went along to offer moral support.*
3 moral victory when you show that your beliefs are right and fair even if you do not win the argument, game etc
4 a moral person has high standards of behaviour based on principles of what is right and wrong [≠ immoral, amoral]: *a man of high moral integrity*
—**morally** adv: *Slavery is morally wrong.*

moral² n [C] **1 morals** [plural] principles or standards of good behaviour [➡ ethics]: *He has no morals!* **2** something you learn from a story: **+of** *The moral of the story is that crime doesn't pay.*

morale /mə'rɑːl $ mə'ræl/ n [U] the level of confidence and positive feelings that a person or group feels: *Talk of job losses is bad for morale.* | *Morale in the team is quite low.*

moralistic /ˌmɒrə'lɪstɪk◂ $ ˌmɔː-/ adj with strong beliefs about what is right and wrong and about how people should behave —**moralist** /'mɒrəl̪st $ 'mɔː-/ n [C]

morality /mə'ræl̪ti/ n [U] ideas about what is right and wrong: *Are standards of morality declining?* | **+of** *a discussion on the morality of abortion*

moralize also **-ise** BrE /'mɒrəlaɪz $ 'mɔː-/ v [I] to tell people what is the right or wrong way to behave, especially when they think this is annoying

moratorium /ˌmɒrə'tɔːriəm $ ˌmɔː-/ n [singular] when an activity is officially stopped for a period of time: *a moratorium on arms sales*

morbid /'mɔːb̪d $ 'mɔːr-/ adj with a strong interest in unpleasant subjects, especially death: *a morbid fascination with murder stories*

more¹ /mɔː $ mɔːr/ adv

1 [used before an adjective or adverb to form a comparative] used to say that someone or something has a greater amount of a quality [≠ less]: *You'll have to be more careful next time.* | **more ... than** *My meal was more expensive than Dan's.* | *That's much more interesting!* | *She's far more intelligent than I am.* | *He seems a lot more cheerful these days.*
2 used to say that something happens a greater number of times or for longer than before [≠ less]: *I promised I'd help more with the housework.* | *We see our grandchildren more than we used to.* | *She goes out a lot more now that she has a car.* | *I miss him much more than I used to.*
3 used to say that something happens to a greater degree [≠ less]: *She cares more about her dogs than she does about me!*
4 more and more used to say that a situation

gradually increases: *She finds getting about more and more difficult.*
5 more or less almost: *It looks more or less flat.*
6 not any more no longer happening or true [➡ any more]: *Sarah doesn't live here any more.*
→ **once more** at ONCE¹

more² determiner, pron

1 a greater amount or number [≠ less, fewer]: **more ... than** *There's more advertising than there used to be.* | *Orange juice costs more than beer in some bars.*
2 an additional number or amount: *Would you like some more coffee?* | **some/a few more** *I have to make a few more phone calls.* | **10/20 etc more** *We need five more chairs.*
3 more and more an increasing number of something: *These days, more and more people travel long distances to work.*
4 more or less almost: *The article says more or less the same thing as the other one.*

moreover /mɔːr'əʊvə $ -'oʊvər/ adv formal used to introduce information which adds to or supports something you have just said: *The new design is not very good. Moreover, it is very expensive.*

mores /'mɔːreɪz/ n [plural] formal the customs, social behaviour, and moral values of a particular group

morgue /mɔːg $ mɔːrg/ n [C] a room or building where dead bodies are kept before they are buried or burned [= mortuary]

morning /'mɔːnɪŋ $ 'mɔːr-/ n [C,U]

1 the early part of the day, from when the sun rises until the middle of the day: *I got a letter from Jack this morning.* | **yesterday/tomorrow morning** *I'll see you tomorrow morning.* | **in the morning** *I'll deal with it in the morning* (=tomorrow morning). | *Classes start at nine in the morning* (=every morning). | **on Monday/Friday etc morning** *He sleeps late on Sunday mornings.*
2 the part of the night that is after MIDNIGHT: *The phone rang at three o'clock in the morning.*
3 (Good) Morning spoken used when you meet someone in the morning

'morning ˌsickness n [U] a feeling of sickness that some women have during the morning when they are PREGNANT, usually in the early months

moron /'mɔːrɒn $ -rɑːn/ n [C] informal an offensive word for someone who you think is very stupid —**moronic** /mə'rɒnɪk $ -'rɑː-/ adj

morose /mə'rəʊs $ -'roʊs/ adj unhappy, bad-tempered, and silent

morphine /'mɔːfiːn $ 'mɔːr-/ n [U] a powerful drug used to stop pain

morsel /'mɔːsəl $ 'mɔːr-/ n [C] literary a small piece of food: *a morsel of bread*

mortal¹ /'mɔːtl $ 'mɔːrtl/ adj **1** not able to live for ever [≠ immortal]: *All men are mortal.* **2** causing death [= fatal]: *a mortal wound* **3 mortal fear/terror/danger etc** extreme fear, danger etc: *He lived in mortal fear of being attacked.* —**mortally** adv: *He was mortally wounded.*

mortal² n **1 lesser/ordinary/mere mortals** ordinary people, when compared with people who are more important or powerful **2** [C] literary a human being

mortality /mɔːˈtæləti $ mɔːr-/ n [U] **1** also **mor'tality rate** the number of deaths during a particular period of time or from a particular cause: *a rise in the infant mortality rate* **2** the fact that you will die one day [≠ **immortality**]: *The heart attack reminded me of my own mortality.*

mortar /ˈmɔːtə $ ˈmɔːrtər/ n **1** [U] a mixture of CEMENT, sand, and water, used in building for joining bricks or stones together **2** [C] a heavy gun that fires EXPLOSIVES high into the air

mortgage /ˈmɔːɡɪdʒ $ ˈmɔːr-/ n [C] money that you borrow in order to buy a house, and pay back over a large number of years: *They're finding it difficult to pay their mortgage.* —**mortgage** v [T]

mortician /mɔːˈtɪʃən $ mɔːr-/ n [C] *AmE* someone whose job is to arrange funerals and prepare bodies to be buried [= **undertaker** *BrE*]

mortified /ˈmɔːtəˌfaɪd $ ˈmɔːr-/ adj extremely embarrassed or ashamed: *Pete was mortified to learn of his mistake.*

mortuary /ˈmɔːtʃuəri $ ˈmɔːrtʃueri/ n [C] plural **mortuaries** a building or room where dead bodies are kept before they are buried or burned [= **morgue**]

mosaic /məʊˈzeɪ-ɪk $ moʊ-/ n [C,U] a pattern or picture made from small pieces of coloured stone or glass

Moslem /ˈmɒzlɪm $ ˈmɑːz-/ n [C] another spelling of MUSLIM —**Moslem** adj

mosque /mɒsk $ mɑːsk/ n [C] a building where Muslims go to pray

mosquito /məˈskiːtəʊ $ -toʊ/ n [C] plural **mosquitoes** or **mosquitos** a small flying insect that bites and sucks blood

moss /mɒs $ mɒːs/ n [U] a very small green plant that grows in a thick, soft mass on trees and rocks —**mossy** adj

most¹ /məʊst $ moʊst/ adv

1 [used before an adjective or adverb to form a superlative] used to say that someone or something has the greatest amount of a quality [≠ **least**]: *Anna is one of the most beautiful women I know.* | *I forgot to tell you the most important thing!* | *easily the most popular sport in schools*

2 more than anything or anyone else: *She liked the dark beer most.* | *The weaker students will benefit most of all.*

3 *AmE spoken* almost: *We eat at Joe's most every weekend.*

4 *formal* very: *It was a most pleasant evening.*

most² determiner, pron

1 almost all: *Most computers have a disk drive.* | +*of Most of the kids in the team live near here.* | *Most of the time* (=usually) *he's no trouble.*

2 more than anyone or anything else: **the most** *Which class has the most children?* | *Whoever scores most will win.*

3 the largest number or amount that is possible: **the most** *How can we get the most power from the engine?* | *The most I can give you is $100.*

4 at (the) most used to say that a number or amount will not be larger than you say: *The book should cost $10 at the most.*

5 for the most part usually or generally, but not always or not completely [= **mostly**]: *Things, for the most part, had gone smoothly.*

6 make the most of sth to get the greatest advantage you can from a situation: *Go out and make the most of the sunshine.*

mostly /ˈməʊstli $ ˈmoʊst-/ adv in most cases or most of the time: *Mostly, he travels by car.* | *The room was full of sports people, mostly footballers.*

MOT /ˌem əʊ ˈtiː $ -oʊ-/ also **MOT test** n [C] a test in Britain that all cars more than three years old must pass every year in order to show that they are still safe to be driven

motel /məʊˈtel $ moʊ-/ n [C] a hotel for people travelling by car → see box at ACCOMMODATION

moth /mɒθ $ mɒːθ/ n [C] an insect similar to a BUTTERFLY that usually flies at night

mother¹ /ˈmʌðə $ -ər/ n [C]

1 a) your female parent, or any woman who is a parent: *My mother said I have to be home by 9:00.* | **mother of two/three etc** (=with two, three etc children) *a 34-year-old mother of four* → see box at RELATIVE **b)** an animal's female parent **2 the mother of all sths** *informal* an extremely bad or severe example of something: *I woke up with the mother of all hangovers.*

mother² v [T] to take care of someone as if they were a child

motherhood /ˈmʌðəhʊd $ -ðər-/ n [U] being a mother

'mother-in-ˌlaw n [C] plural **mothers-in-law** the mother of your husband or wife

motherly /ˈmʌðəli $ -ðər-/ adj a motherly woman is loving and kind

ˌmother-of-ˈpearl n [U] a smooth shiny substance on the inside of some shells, used for making buttons, jewellery etc

'Mother's Day n [singular] a day when people give cards and gifts to their mothers [➡ **Father's Day**]

ˌmother 'tongue n [C] the first language that you learn as a child [= **native language**]

motif /məʊˈtiːf $ moʊ-/ n [C] **1** an idea or subject that is regularly repeated and developed in a book, film etc **2** a small picture used to decorate something: *a T-shirt with a butterfly motif*

motion¹ /ˈməʊʃən $ ˈmoʊ-/ n **1** [U] the process of moving, or the way that someone or something moves: +*of the rolling motion of the ship* **2** [C] a single movement of your head or hand: *He made a motion with his hand, to tell me to keep back.* **3** [C] a suggestion that is made formally at a meeting and then decided on by voting: *I'd like to propose a motion to change our working hours.* | *Most people opposed the motion he had put forward.* | *The motion was carried unanimously.* | *I think the motion will be defeated.* **4 put/set sth in motion** to start a process **5 go through the motions (of doing**

sth) to do something because you have to do it, without being very interested → **SLOW MOTION**

motion² *v* [I,T] to tell someone to do something by moving your head or hand: **motion (for) sb to do sth** *She motioned for him to sit down.*

motionless /ˈməʊʃənləs $ ˈmoʊ-/ *adj* not moving at all: *He stood motionless in the doorway.*

,motion ˈpicture *n* [C] *AmE* a film made for cinema [= **movie**]

motivate /ˈməʊtɪ̯veɪt $ ˈmoʊ-/ *v* [T]   **1** to be the reason why someone does something: *I can't understand what motivates him to do such terrible things.*   **2** to make someone want to achieve something, especially by encouraging them to work harder: **motivate sb to do sth** *managers who motivate their staff to achieve targets* —**motivated** *adj*: *a racially motivated attack* | *highly motivated students* (=students who are eager to work hard)

motivation /ˌməʊtɪ̯ˈveɪʃən $ ˌmoʊ-/ *n*   **1** [U] when you are keen and willing to do something: *Jack is smart, but he lacks motivation.*   **2** [C] the reason why you want to do something: **+for** *What was your motivation for writing the book?*

motivational /ˌməʊtɪ̯ˈveɪʃənəl $ ˌmoʊ-/ *adj* [only before noun] motivational speeches, books etc are intended to make people eager to do something

motive /ˈməʊtɪv $ ˈmoʊ-/ *n* [C] the reason why someone does something, especially something wrong or bad: **+for** *Jealousy was the motive for the murder.* → see box at **REASON**

motley /ˈmɒtli $ ˈmɑːtli/ *adj* **motley crew/ collection etc** a group of people or things that do not seem to belong together

motor¹ /ˈməʊtə $ ˈmoʊtər/ *n* [C] the part of a machine that uses electricity, petrol etc to make it move: *an electric motor*

motor² *adj* [only before noun]   **1** using power from an engine: *a motor vehicle*   **2** *BrE* relating to cars [= **auto** *AmE*]: *the motor industry*

motorbike /ˈməʊtəbaɪk $ ˈmoʊtər-/ *n* [C] especially *BrE* a **MOTORCYCLE** → see picture at **TRANSPORT**

motorboat /ˈməʊtəbəʊt $ ˈmoʊtərboʊt/ *n* [C] a small fast boat with an engine → see picture at **TRANSPORT**

motorcade /ˈməʊtəkeɪd $ ˈmoʊtər-/ *n* [C] a group of cars that surround an important person's car to protect it

ˈmotor car *n* [C] *formal* a car

motorcycle /ˈməʊtəˌsaɪkəl $ ˈmoʊtər-/ *n* [C] a vehicle with two wheels and an engine [= **motorbike**]

motorcyclist /ˈməʊtəˌsaɪklɪst $ ˈmoʊtər-/ *n* [C] someone who rides a **MOTORCYCLE**

motoring /ˈməʊtərɪŋ $ ˈmoʊ-/ *adj* [only before noun] *BrE* relating to cars and driving: *a motoring holiday*

motorist /ˈməʊtərɪ̯st/ *n* [C] someone who drives a car [= **driver**]

motorized also **-ised** *BrE* /ˈməʊtəraɪzd $ ˈmoʊ-/ *adj* having a motor: *a motorized wheelchair*

ˈmotor ˌvehicle *n* [C] *formal* a car, bus etc

motorway /ˈməʊtəweɪ $ ˈmoʊtər-/ *n* [C] *BrE* a wide road for driving fast over long distances [= **freeway** *AmE*; → **expressway, highway**]: **on a motorway** *We broke down on the motorway.* → see box at **ROAD**

mottled /ˈmɒtld $ ˈmɑː-/ *adj* covered with patterns of light and dark colours: *the kitten's mottled grey fur*

motto /ˈmɒtəʊ $ ˈmɑːtoʊ/ *n* [C] plural **mottos** or **mottoes** a short statement that expresses someone's aims or principles

mould¹ *BrE*; **mold** *AmE* /məʊld $ moʊld/ *n*   **1** [C] a container that you pour liquid into so that the liquid will take its shape when it becomes solid: *a chocolate mould*   **2** [U] a green or black substance that grows on old food or on wet things: *a piece of old cheese covered in mould*

mould² *BrE*; **mold** *AmE v*   **1** [T] to shape a soft substance by pressing it or rolling it   **2** [T] to influence the way someone's character or attitudes develop: *an attempt to mould public opinion*

moulding *BrE*; **molding** *AmE* /ˈməʊldɪŋ $ ˈmoʊl-/ *n* [C,U] a piece of wood, stone etc put around the edge of something as a decoration

mouldy *BrE*; **moldy** *AmE* /ˈməʊldi $ ˈmoʊl-/ *adj* covered with mould: *mouldy cheese* | *Some of the vegetables had gone mouldy.*

moult *BrE*; **molt** *AmE* /məʊlt $ moʊlt/ *v* [I] when an animal or bird moults, it loses hair or feathers so that new ones can grow

mound /maʊnd/ *n* [C]   **1** a pile of earth that looks like a small hill   **2** a large pile of something: **+of** *a mound of papers*

Mount /maʊnt/ *n* used in the names of mountains written abbreviation **Mt**: *Mount Everest*

mount *v*   **1** [T] to organize and begin an event or course of action: *The museum is mounting an exhibition of students' art.* | **mount a campaign/challenge/attack** *They are mounting a campaign to stop the school closing.*   **2** also **mount up** [I] to gradually increase [→ **mounting**]: *His debts continued to mount up.* | *Tensions in the region are mounting.*   **3** [I,T] *formal* to get on a horse or bicycle [≠ **dismount**]   **4** [T] *formal* to go up something such as stairs or a step: *He mounted the steps to the stage.*   **5** [T] to fix something onto a surface: *a metal box mounted on the wall*

mountain

mountain /ˈmaʊntn̩ $ ˈmaʊntən/ *n* [C]   **1** a very high hill: *She is the first woman to climb this mountain.* | *the Himalaya mountain range* (=line of mountains) | **in the mountains** *We went hiking up in the mountains.*

The highest part of a mountain is called the **peak** or **summit**.
The bottom of a mountain is called **the foot of** the mountain.
A group or line of mountains is called a **range**.
A **valley** is a low area between two lines of mountains.

2 *informal* a large amount of something: **+of** *I've got a mountain of ironing to do.*
3 make a mountain out of a molehill to treat a small problem as if it were very serious

'mountain ,bike *n* [C] a strong bicycle with wide TYRES designed for riding on rough ground → see picture on page A9

mountaineering /ˌmaʊntɪˈnɪərɪŋ $ ˌmaʊntənˈɪrɪŋ/ *n* [U] the sport of climbing mountains —**mountaineer** *n* [C]

mountainous /ˈmaʊntɪnəs $ ˈmaʊntənəs/ *adj* a mountainous area has a lot of mountains

mountainside /ˈmaʊntɪnsaɪd $ ˈmaʊntən-/ *n* [C] the side of a mountain: *They walked down the mountainside.*

mounting /ˈmaʊntɪŋ/ *adj* [only before noun] increasing: *The government has come under mounting criticism.* | *the company's mounting debts*

mourn /mɔːn $ mɔːrn/ *v* **1** [I,T] to feel very sad because someone has died: *She is still mourning her son's death.* | **+for** *mourning for her child* **2** [T] to feel sad because something no longer exists

mourner /ˈmɔːnə $ ˈmɔːrnər/ *n* [C] someone who is at a FUNERAL

mournful /ˈmɔːnfəl $ ˈmɔːrn-/ *adj* very sad: *slow, mournful music* —**mournfully** *adv*

mourning /ˈmɔːnɪŋ $ ˈmɔːr-/ *n* [U] feelings of great sadness because someone has died: *a day of national mourning for victims of the earthquake* | **in mourning** (=feeling great sadness) *She is still in mourning for her husband.*

mouse /maʊs/ *n* [C]
1 plural **mice** /maɪs/ a small furry animal with a long tail and a pointed nose
2 plural **mouses** a small object connected to a computer that you move with your hand to give instructions to the computer

mousse /muːs/ *n* [C,U] **1** a cold sweet food made from cream, eggs, and fruit or chocolate **2** a substance that you put in your hair to hold it in position

moustache also **mustache** *AmE* /məˈstɑːʃ $ ˈmʌstæʃ/ *n* [C] hair a man grows on his upper lip → see picture at HAIR

mousy, mousey /ˈmaʊsi/ *adj* mousy hair is light brown

mouth[1] /maʊθ/ *n* [C] plural **mouths** /maʊðz/
1 the part of your face that you use for speaking and eating: *She put her hand over her mouth.* | **in/into your mouth** *The sweet left a strange taste in my mouth.* | **I opened my mouth to say something.** | **(with) your mouth open/shut** *He was fast asleep with his mouth wide open.* | *Don't talk* **with your mouth full** (=with food in your mouth.) | *a cigarette hung out of the* **corner of** *his* **mouth** → see picture on page A3

2 keep your mouth shut *informal* to not talk about something, especially a secret: *The party's a surprise, so keep your mouth shut about it.*
3 the entrance to a CAVE or large hole: **+of** *the mouth of the tunnel*
4 the part of a river where it joins the sea
5 the open part at the top of a container: **+of** *the mouth of a jar*
6 big/loud mouth *informal* someone who often says things that they should not say or who says things in a loud way
7 make your mouth water if food makes your mouth water, it looks so good you want to eat it immediately [→ **mouth-watering**]

mouth[2] /maʊð/ *v* [T] to move your lips as if you are saying words, but without making any sound: *Karen was mouthing the answer to me behind the teacher's back.*
mouth off *phr v informal* to talk angrily or rudely to someone: *Mick was suspended for mouthing off to teachers.*

mouthful /ˈmaʊθfʊl/ *n* **1** [C] an amount of food or drink that you put into your mouth at one time: *He took a big mouthful of cake.* **2 a mouthful** *informal* a long word or phrase that is difficult to say: *Her real name is quite a mouthful, so we just call her Dee.*

'mouth ,organ *n* [C] a HARMONICA

mouthpiece /ˈmaʊθpiːs/ *n* [C] **1** the part of a musical instrument, telephone etc that you put in or next to your mouth **2** [usually singular] a person or newspaper that expresses the opinions of a government or political group: *Pravda used to be the mouthpiece of the Communist Party.*

mouthwash /ˈmaʊθwɒʃ $ -wɒːʃ, -wɑːʃ/ *n* [C,U] a liquid that you use to clean your mouth and make your breath smell fresh

'mouth-,watering *adj* mouth-watering food looks or smells extremely good

movable /ˈmuːvəbəl/ *adj* something that is movable can be moved: *toy soldiers with movable arms and legs*

move[1] /muːv/ *v*
1 [I,T] to change from one place or position to another, or to make something do this: **move (sth) away/back/forward etc** *Move away from the door!* | *He moved the chair into the corner of the room.* | **+about/around** *She could hear someone moving around downstairs.* | *The traffic was still moving slowly.*
2 also **move away** [I] to go to a new place to live or work: *Henry moved away after college.* | **+to/into/from** *They moved to Birmingham in May.* | **move house** *BrE* (=go to live in a different house) *We're moving house next week.*
3 [I] to make progress or changes: *Things are moving fast now we've got a new manager.* | *You need to move quickly to take advantage of this opportunity.*
4 [T] to make someone feel a strong emotion, especially sadness or sympathy [→ **moving**]: *The story* **moved us to tears** (=made us cry). | *Harry was genuinely moved by what he saw.*
5 [T] to change the time or order of something: **move sth from/to sth** *The meeting's been moved from Wednesday to Thursday.*
6 get moving *spoken* used to tell someone they need to hurry: *If you don't get moving, you'll miss the bus.*

M

move in phr v **1** to start living in a new house: *When are you moving in?* **2** to start living with someone in the same house: **+with** *Steve's moving in with his girlfriend.* | **+together** *We're thinking about moving in together.*

move off phr v if a car, train etc moves off, it moves forward to start its journey

move on phr v **1** to stop doing or dealing with one thing, and start doing or dealing with something else: *I enjoyed my job, but it was time to move on.* | **+to** *I'd like to move on now to the subject of education.* **2** to leave a place where you have been staying and continue on your journey: *After three days we decided it was time to move on.* **3** to develop, improve, or become more modern: *Her ideas have hardly moved on since the thirties.*

move out phr v to permanently leave the house where you are living: *We have to move out by next Friday.*

move over phr v to change position so that there is more space for other people or things: *Move over so Jim can sit down.*

move up phr v **1** to change to a higher job, group, level etc: **+to** *He's moved up to tenth in the world rankings.* **2** BrE to change position so that there is more space for other people or things: *If everyone moves up a bit, you can sit here.*

move² n [C]

1 something that you decide to do in order to achieve something: *She wondered what her next move should be.* | *Hiring Peter was definitely a* **good move** (=a good decision). | **+to/towards** *The talks are a definite move towards peace.*

2 a movement in a particular direction: *Arnison* **made a move** *for the door.* | *I knew he was* **watching** *my every* **move**.

3 be on the move to be travelling to different places all the time

4 make a move BrE spoken to leave a place: *It's late, we'd better be making a move.*

5 get a move on spoken used to tell someone to hurry: *Get a move on, or we'll be late!*

6 when you go to live or work in a new place: *How did the move go?*

7 when you change the position of one of the pieces in a game such as CHESS: *It's your move.*

movement /'muːvmənt/ n

1 [C] a group of people who have the same beliefs and work together to achieve a particular aim: **civil rights/peace etc movement** *the civil rights movement of the 1960s* | **+for** *the movement for independence*

2 [C,U] a change of position, or when someone or something moves or is moved: *Any movement caused him a lot of pain.* | *She was neat and quick in all her movements.* | **+of** *I noticed a* **slight movement** *of the curtain.*

3 [C] a gradual change in a situation or in people's attitudes or opinions: **+away/towards** *a movement away from traditional values*

4 sb's movements the places where someone goes and the things they do during a particular time: *Police are trying to trace his movements over the last 48 hours.*

5 [C] one of the parts that a piece of CLASSICAL music is divided into

mover /'muːvə $ -ər/ n [C] **1** especially AmE someone whose job is to move people's furniture from one house to another **2** someone or something that moves in a particular way

movie /'muːvi/ n [C]

1 especially AmE a film that is shown at a cinema or on television [= film BrE]: **see/watch a movie** *Do you want to see a movie tonight?* | *the movie industry* | **horror/disaster/action etc movie** → see box at FILM

2 the movies AmE the cinema: *How often do you go to the movies?*

moviegoer /'muːvi,ɡəʊə $ -,ɡoʊər/ n [C] especially AmE someone who goes to see films at the cinema, especially regularly

'movie ,theater n [C] AmE a building where you go to see films [= cinema BrE]

moving /'muːvɪŋ/ adj **1** making you feel strong emotions, especially sadness or sympathy: **deeply/profoundly moving** *a deeply moving experience* **2** [only before noun] changing from one position to another: *the effects of moving light* | **fast-moving/slow-moving** *fast-moving traffic* —**movingly** adv: *He spoke movingly about his experiences.*

mow /məʊ $ moʊ/ v [I,T] past tense **mowed**, past participle **mowed** or **mown** /məʊn $ moʊn/ to cut grass with a machine: *Dan was* **mowing** *the lawn.* → see box at CUT

mow sb ⇔ down phr v informal to kill someone by shooting them or driving into them very fast: *A driver was jailed for mowing down a nine-year-old girl.*

mower /'məʊə $ 'moʊər/ n [C] a machine for cutting grass [= lawn mower]

MP /,em 'piː/ n [C] Member of Parliament someone who has been elected to a parliament to represent people from a particular area: **+for** *She's the MP for Liverpool North.* → see box at GOVERNMENT

,MP'3 ,player n [C] a machine or computer program that plays music which has been DOWN-LOADED from the Internet

mpg /,em piː 'dʒiː/ miles per gallon used to describe the amount of petrol a car uses

mph /,em piː 'eɪtʃ/ miles per hour used to describe the speed of a vehicle or the wind: *a speed of 180 mph*

Mr BrE; **Mr.** AmE /'mɪstə $ -ər/ a title used before a man's family name: *Mr Smith is the headteacher.*

Mrs BrE; **Mrs.** AmE /'mɪsɪz/ a title used before a married woman's family name [→ Ms, Miss, Mr]: *Mrs Smith*

Ms BrE; **Ms.** AmE /mɪz, məz/ a title used before the family name of a married or unmarried woman [→ Miss, Mrs, Mr]

MS /,em 'es/ n [U] multiple sclerosis a serious illness that affects your nerves, and gradually makes you weak and unable to move

MSc BrE; **M.Sc.** AmE /,em es 'siː/ n [C] a higher university degree in a science subject [→ MA]

Mt. the written abbreviation of Mount: *Mt. Everest*

much¹ /mʌtʃ/ adv

1 a lot: **much better/easier/higher etc** *I'm feeling much better now.* | *This test was much more difficult.* | **much too young/big/fast etc** *He was driving much too fast.* | *'Did you enjoy it?'*

'No, *not much* (=not a lot) '. | *Thank you very much.* → see box at **VERY**

2 so much, how much used to emphasize the amount or degree of something: *I know how much he likes Ann.* | *He'd changed so much I didn't recognize him.*

3 much like sth also **much (the same) as …** very similar to something: *It tastes much like butter.* | *The house was much as I remembered it.*

4 not much good (at sth) not good at doing something: *I'm not much good at cooking.*

much² *determiner, pron*

1 a large amount of something: *Was there much traffic?* | *We don't have much time.* | *You haven't eaten much.* | **+of** *Much of the city was destroyed.* | **(far/much) too much** *There was much too much work for one person.* | *There's so much I need to do.* | *How much is that shirt?*

2 how much used to talk or ask about the amount or cost of something: *How much milk do we need?* | *How much is that shirt?*

3 not be much of a sth to not be a good example of something, or to not be good at something: *He wasn't much of a father.*

4 be too much for sb to be too difficult or unpleasant for someone: *The shock was too much for him.*

5 not be up to much *BrE informal* to be of bad quality: *The hotel food wasn't up to much.*

GRAMMAR

much, a lot of
In sentences that are not negative and not questions, use **a lot of** rather than **much**: *There was a lot of traffic.* Do not say 'There was much traffic'.
→ **LOT**

---

muck¹ /mʌk/ *n* [U] **1** dirt or mud: *His hands were covered in muck.* **2** *BrE* solid waste from animals: *dog muck*

muck² *v*
 muck about/around *phr v BrE informal* **1** to behave in a silly way, especially when you should be working: *Stop mucking about and do your homework.* **2 muck sb about/around** to cause trouble for someone by changing your mind a lot or not doing what you promised to do
 muck in *phr v BrE informal* to work together with other people in order to get a job done: *If we all muck in, we should finish the painting tomorrow.*
 muck sth ⇔ up *phr v BrE informal* to spoil something, or do something badly: *I don't want to muck up my chances of success.*

mucky /ˈmʌki/ *adj informal* dirty: *mucky hands* → see box at **DIRTY**

mucus /ˈmjuːkəs/ *n* [U] a thick liquid produced in your nose

mud /mʌd/ *n* [U] soft wet earth: *a vehicle that can drive through mud and water* | **covered/ caked with mud** *boots caked with mud*

muddle¹ /ˈmʌdl/ *n* [C,U] a situation when people are confused about something, especially with the result that they make mistakes: *The ceremony was an embarrassing muddle.* | **be/get in a muddle** (=be or get confused) *I was in such*

a muddle I forgot the meeting was today. | **+over/ about** *There was some muddle over our hotel reservation.*

muddle² also **muddle up** *v* [T] *especially BrE*
 1 to put things in the wrong order: *The papers had all been muddled up.* **2** to wrongly think that one person or thing is someone or something else: *The twins are so alike that it's easy to get them **muddled up**.* **3** to confuse someone, especially so that they make a mistake: *I've got a bit **muddled**. What date are we leaving?*
 muddle through/along *phr v* to continue doing something even though it is difficult or you feel unsure about it: *The students were often left to muddle along without help.*

muddled /ˈmʌdld/ *adj* confused: *muddled thinking*

muddy¹ /ˈmʌdi/ *adj* covered with mud or containing mud: *muddy boots* | *muddy water* → see box at **DIRTY**

muddy² *v* [T] **muddied, muddying, muddies 1** to make something dirty with mud: *Try not to muddy your shoes.* **2 muddy the waters/the issue** to make a situation more complicated or confusing than it was before

mudguard /ˈmʌdgɑːd $ -gɑːrd/ *n* [C] *BrE* a curved piece of metal or plastic that covers the wheel of a bicycle or MOTORBIKE → see picture at **BICYCLE**

muesli /ˈmjuːzli/ *n* [U] grain, nuts, and dried fruit that you eat with milk for breakfast

muffin /ˈmʌfɪn/ *n* [C] **1** a small cake: *a blueberry muffin* → see picture on page A5 **2** a small round type of bread that you eat hot with butter

muffle /ˈmʌfəl/ *v* [T] to make a sound less loud or clear: *Snow muffled the sound of the traffic.* —**muffled** *adj*: *I heard muffled voices downstairs.* → see box at **QUIET**

muffler /ˈmʌflə $ -ər/ *n* [C] **1** *old-fashioned* a SCARF **2** *AmE* a piece of equipment that makes a vehicle's engine sound quieter [= **silencer** *BrE*]

mug¹ /mʌg/ *n* [C]
1 a large cup with straight sides, or the liquid inside it: *a coffee mug* | **a mug of sth** *He was drinking a mug of tea.* **2** *BrE informal* someone who is stupid and easy to deceive

mug

mug² *v* [T] **mugged, mugging** to attack and rob someone in a public place: *He was mugged outside the bank.* → see box at **ATTACK** → and **STEAL** —**mugger** *n* [C] —**mugging** *n* [C,U]

muggy /ˈmʌgi/ *adj informal* muggy weather is unpleasant because it is too warm and the air is wet [= **humid**]

mugshot /ˈmʌgʃɒt $ -ʃɑːt/ *n* [C] *informal* a photograph of someone's face, especially a criminal's

Muhammad, Mohammed /mʊˈhæmɪd, mə-/ the holy man whose life and teaching the religion of Islam is based on

mulch /mʌltʃ/ *n* [singular, U] decaying leaves that you put on soil to improve its quality

M

mule /mjuːl/ *n* [C] an animal that has a DONKEY and a horse as parents

mull /mʌl/ *v*

mull sth ⇔ over *phr v* to think about something carefully: *She had plenty of time to* **mull things over**.

mullah /'mʌlə, 'mʊlə/ *n* [C] a Muslim teacher of law and religion

multi- /mʌlti, mʌlti/ *prefix* many: *multicoloured posters*

multicultural /ˌmʌlti'kʌltʃərəl/ *adj* involving people or ideas from many different countries, races, or religions: *a multicultural society*

multilateral /ˌmʌltɪ'lætərəl/ *adj* involving several different countries or groups [➔ **bilateral, unilateral**]: *multilateral peace talks*

multilingual /ˌmʌltɪ'lɪŋgwəl/ *adj* using or speaking several different languages [➔ **bilingual, monolingual**]: *multilingual communities*

multimedia /ˌmʌlti'miːdiə/ *adj* [only before noun] using a mixture of sounds, pictures etc to give information, especially on a computer: *multimedia software* —**multimedia** *n* [U]

multinational[1] /ˌmʌltɪ'næʃənəl/ *adj* based or working in many countries: *multinational companies* | *multinational workforces*

multinational[2] *n* [C] a large company that has offices in many different countries ➔ see box at **COMPANY**

multiple[1] /'mʌltɪpəl/ *adj* [only before noun] many, or involving many things or people: *He suffered multiple injuries.* | *a multiple murderer*

multiple[2] *n* [C] a number that contains a smaller number an exact number of times: *20 is a multiple of 5.*

multiple 'choice *adj* a multiple choice examination or question shows several different answers, and you must choose the correct one

multiple sclerosis /ˌmʌltɪpəl sklɪ'rəʊsɪs $ -'roʊ-/ *n* [U] written abbreviation **MS** a serious illness that affects your nerves, and gradually makes you weak and unable to move

multiplex /'mʌltɪpleks/ *n* [C] a large cinema with several rooms in which films are shown

multiplication /ˌmʌltɪplɪ'keɪʃən/ *n* [U] when you calculate something by adding the same number to itself a particular number of times [➔ **division**]

multiplicity /ˌmʌltɪ'plɪsɪti/ *n* [C,U] *formal* a large number or great variety of things

multiply /'mʌltɪplaɪ/ *v* [I,T] **multiplied, multiplying, multiplies 1** to do a calculation in which you add one number to itself a particular number of times [➔ **divide**]: **multiply sth by sth** *Four multiplied by five is 20.* ➔ see box at **CALCULATE 2** to increase by a large amount or number, or to make something do this: *Smoking multiplies the risk of having a heart attack.*

multipurpose /ˌmʌlti'pɜːpəs $ -'pɜːr-/ *adj* having many different uses: *a multipurpose tool*

multiracial /ˌmʌlti'reɪʃəl/ *adj* including or involving many different races of people: *a multiracial society*

multi-'storey *adj* [only before noun] *BrE* a multi-storey building has many levels: *a multi-storey car park*

multitasking /'mʌlti,tɑːskɪŋ $ -,tæs-/ *n* [U] when a person or computer does more than one thing at the same time

multitude /'mʌltɪtjuːd $ -tuːd/ *n* **a multitude of sb/sth** *formal* a very large number of things or people: *a multitude of possibilities*

mum /mʌm/ *n* [C] *BrE* mother [= **mom** *AmE*]: *Mum, can I borrow some money?* | *My mum's a teacher.* ➔ see box at **RELATIVE**

mumble /'mʌmbəl/ *v* [I,T] to say something very quietly, so that it is difficult to understand you: *Micky mumbled an apology.* ➔ see box at **SAY**

mumbo-jumbo /ˌmʌmbəʊ 'dʒʌmbəʊ $ -boʊ 'dʒʌmboʊ/ *n* [U] *informal* ideas or words that you think are stupid or have no meaning

mummy /'mʌmi/ *n* [C] plural **mummies 1** *BrE* mother – used especially by or to young children [= **mommy** *AmE*]: *Go and ask Mummy for a drink.* ➔ see box at **RELATIVE 2** a dead body that has been preserved by wrapping it in cloth, especially in ancient Egypt

mumps /mʌmps/ *n* [U] an infectious illness which makes your neck swell and become painful

munch /mʌntʃ/ *v* [I,T] to eat something in a noisy way: **+on** *Anna sat munching on her toast.*

mundane /mʌn'deɪn/ *adj* ordinary and boring: *a mundane job*

municipal /mjuː'nɪsɪpəl $ mjʊ-/ *adj* relating to the government of a town or city: *municipal elections*

munitions /mjuː'nɪʃənz $ mjʊ-/ *n* [plural] military supplies such as bombs and guns

mural /'mjʊərəl $ 'mjʊrəl/ *n* [C] a picture painted on a wall

murder[1] /'mɜːdə $ 'mɜːrdər/ *n*

1 [C,U] the crime of killing someone deliberately [➔ **manslaughter**]: *Police believe the murders were committed by the same person.* | **+of** *He was charged with the murder of his wife.* | *The murder weapon was believed to be an axe.* | *the murder victim*

2 get away with murder *informal* to do anything you want, even bad things, without being punished: *She lets the children get away with murder.*

3 sth is murder *spoken* used to say something is very difficult or unpleasant: *The traffic was murder this morning.*

murder[2] *v* [T] to kill someone deliberately: *He denies murdering the teenager.* ➔ see box at **CRIME** ➔ and **KILL**
—**murderer** *n* [C]

murderous /'mɜːdərəs $ 'mɜːr-/ *adj* dangerous and likely to kill people: *a murderous attack*

murky /'mɜːki $ 'mɜːr-/ *adj* **1** dark and difficult to see through: *murky water* **2** involving dishonest or illegal behaviour: *a man with a murky past*

murmur /'mɜːmə $ 'mɜːrmər/ *n* [C] a soft quiet sound, especially one made by someone's voice: *She answered in a low murmur.* | *the murmur of voices* | **murmur of agreement/surprise etc** (=one that expresses a particular feeling) —**murmur** *v* [I,T] *He softly murmured her name.* ➔ see box at **SAY**

muscle¹ /'mʌsəl/ n

1 [C,U] one of the pieces of flesh inside your body that you use in order to move: **leg/neck/ stomach etc muscles** *exercises to strengthen your leg muscles* | **pull/strain a muscle** (=injure a muscle)

2 [U] power or influence: *financial muscle*

muscle² v

muscle in *phr v disapproving* to use your power to get involved in something that someone else was doing, especially in business

muscular /'mʌskjŭlə $ -ər/ *adj* **1** having large strong muscles: *strong muscular arms* **2** relating to the muscles: *a muscular disease*

muse /mju:z/ v [I] *formal* to think about something for a long time

museum /mju:'ziəm $ mju-/ n [C] a building where people can go and see important objects relating to art, history, science etc: *the Museum of Modern Art* | *a military museum*

mush /mʌʃ/ n [singular, U] an unpleasant soft substance, especially food —**mushy** *adj*

mushroom¹ /'mʌʃru:m, -rŭm/ n [C] one of several types of FUNGUS with a stem and a round top. Some types can be eaten [➙ toadstool]: *mushroom soup* → see picture at VEGETABLE

mushroom² v [I] to increase or develop very quickly: *Sales began to mushroom.*

music /'mju:zɪk/ n [U]

1 a pattern of sounds made by people playing musical instruments or singing: **pop/classical/ dance/rock etc music** *I prefer pop music.* | *He enjoys* **listening to music.** | **write/compose music** *Who wrote the music for the film?* | *What's your favourite* **piece of music**? | *a music teacher*

THESAURUS

pop (music), rock (music), rock 'n' roll, heavy metal, reggae, house (music), hip-hop, jazz, classical music, country (music), folk (music)

2 a set of written marks representing musical sounds, or paper with these marks on it: *Can you read music?*
→ **face the music** at FACE²

musical¹ /'mju:zɪkəl/ *adj* **1** [only before noun] relating to music: *a musical instrument* (=piano, GUITAR *etc*) **2** good at playing or singing music: *I'm not very musical.* —**musically** /-kli/ *adv*

musical² n [C] a play or film that includes singing and dancing → see box at THEATRE

musician /mju:'zɪʃən $ mju-/ n [C] someone who plays a musical instrument, especially as a job: *a talented musician* | *jazz musicians*

musket /'mʌskɪt/ n [C] a type of gun used in the past

Muslim /'mʊzlɪm, 'mʌz-, 'mʊs-/ n [C] someone whose religion is Islam —**Muslim** *adj*

muslin /'mʌzlɪn/ n [U] very thin cotton cloth

mussel /'mʌsəl/ n [C] a small sea animal with a black shell and a soft body that you can eat

must¹ /məst; *strong* mʌst/ *modal verb* negative short form **mustn't**

1 used to say that it is necessary for something to happen or not happen: *All passengers must wear seatbelts.* | *This book must not be removed from the library* (=do not remove it). | *It's getting late, I really must go.* → see box at HAVE

2 used to say that you think something is very likely to be true: *George must be almost eighty now.* | *You must have been very upset.*

3 *spoken* used to suggest that someone should do something: *You must come and visit us sometime.*

must² /mʌst/ n [C usually singular] something that you must do or have: *Warm clothes are a must in the mountains.*

mustache /məˈstɑːʃ $ 'mʌstæʃ/ n the usual American spelling of MOUSTACHE

mustard /'mʌstəd $ -ərd/ n [U] a yellow sauce with a strong taste, usually eaten with meat

muster /'mʌstə $ -ər/ also **muster up** v [T] to get enough confidence, courage etc to do something difficult: **muster (up) the support/ courage/energy etc to do sth** *Finally she mustered the courage to call him.* | *He hit the ball with as much strength as he could muster.*

mustn't /'mʌsənt/ the short form of 'must not': *You mustn't tell him what I said.*

must've /'mʌstəv/ the short form of 'must have': *He must've been tired.*

musty /'mʌsti/ *adj* having an unpleasant, old, or wet smell: *the musty smell of old books*

mutant /'mju:tənt/ n [C] an animal or plant that is different from others of the same kind because of a change in its GENES —**mutant** *adj*

mutate /mju:'teɪt $ 'mju:teɪt/ v [I] if an animal or plant mutates, it becomes different from others of the same kind because of a change in its GENES —**mutation** /mju:'teɪʃən/ n [C,U] *genetic mutation*

mute¹ /mju:t/ *adj written* not saying anything: *She stayed mute and defiant.*

mute² n [C] *old-fashioned* someone who cannot speak

muted /'mju:tɪd/ *adj* **1** quieter than usual: *the sound of muted voices* **2** not expressing strong feelings: *The proposal received a muted response.* **3** a muted colour is not very bright

mutilate /'mju:tɪleɪt/ v [T] to violently damage someone's body, especially by cutting off part of it: *Many of the bodies had been mutilated.* —**mutilation** /ˌmju:tɪˈleɪʃən/ n [C,U]

mutineer /ˌmju:tɪˈnɪə $ ˌmju:tɪnˈɪr/ n [C] someone who is involved in a mutiny

mutinous /'mju:tɪnəs $ -tn-əs/ *adj formal* refusing to obey someone: *mutinous soldiers*

mutiny /'mju:tɪni $ -tn-i/ n [C,U] plural **mutinies** when a group of people, especially soldiers or SAILORS, refuse to obey the person who is in charge, and try to take control themselves —**mutiny** v [I]

mutt /mʌt/ n [C] *informal* a dog that is a mixture of different breeds

mutter /'mʌtə $ -ər/ v [I,T] to say something quietly, especially because you are annoyed or do not want someone to hear you: *'Stupid fool,'* *he muttered.* → see box at SAY —**mutter** n [singular] *'I don't know,' he said in a low mutter.*

mutton /'mʌtn/ n [U] the meat from an adult sheep [➙ lamb] → see box at MEAT

mutual /'mju:tʃuəl/ *adj* **1** mutual feelings are when two or more people have the same feelings about each other: *Mutual trust is important in a marriage.* | *I didn't like Dev and the feeling was mutual.* | *The relationship ended by mutual*

M

M

agreement (=they both agreed to it).   **2** [only before noun] mutual support, help etc is support that two or more people give each other: *the mutual support you get in a small community*   **3** a mutual friend or interest is one that two people both have —**mutually** *adv*: *a mutually beneficial arrangement*

muzzle[1] /ˈmʌzəl/ *n* [C]   **1** the nose and mouth of an animal, especially a dog or horse   **2** a cover you put over a dog's mouth to stop it biting people   **3** the open end of a gun where the bullets come out

muzzle[2] *v* [T]   **1** to put a muzzle over a dog's mouth so that it cannot bite people   **2** to prevent someone from saying what they think in public

my /maɪ/ *determiner* belonging or relating to me: *My mother's a doctor.* | *I tried not to let my feelings show.* | *It was my own idea.*

myriad /ˈmɪriəd/ *n* [C] *written* **myriad of sth** a large number of things: *a myriad of colours* —**myriad** *adj*: *Florida's myriad attractions*

myself /maɪˈself/ *pron*

1 the REFLEXIVE form of 'I': *I made myself a cup of coffee.* | *I went over to Jane and introduced myself.*

2 used to emphasize 'I': *Why do I have to do everything myself?* | *I myself have never been there.*

3 (all) by myself alone or without anyone else's help: *I went to the movie by myself.* | *I painted the house all by myself.*

4 have sth (all) to myself to not have to share something with anyone else: *I've got the house to myself this weekend.*

mysterious /mɪˈstɪəriəs $ -ˈstɪr-/ *adj*

1 strange or difficult to explain or understand: *mysterious deaths* | *She disappeared in mysterious circumstances.* | *my mysterious new neighbour* → see box at **STRANGE**

2 not saying much about something, in a way that makes people want to know more: **+about** *He's being very mysterious about his new girlfriend.*

—**mysteriously** *adv*: *He had mysteriously disappeared.*

mystery[1] /ˈmɪstəri/ *n plural* **mysteries**

1 [C] something that is difficult to explain or understand: *There's still much about the disease that remains a mystery.* | *The way her mind worked was a mystery to him.* | *The police never solved the mystery of his death.*

2 [U] a quality that makes someone or something seem strange, interesting, or difficult to understand: *the mystery surrounding his disappearance* | *The dark glasses gave her an air of mystery.*

3 also **'murder ,mystery** [C] a story about a murder, in which you are not told who the murderer is until the end: *an Agatha Christie mystery*

mystery[2] *adj* [only before noun] used to describe something or someone that people do not have full information about: *a mystery illness*

mystic /ˈmɪstɪk/ *n* [C] someone who tries to discover religious truth through long periods of prayer, thought etc

mystical /ˈmɪstɪkəl/ also **mystic** *adj* relating to religious or magic powers that people cannot understand: *a mystical experience* —**mystically** /-kli/ *adv*

mysticism /ˈmɪstɪsɪzəm/ *n* [U] when people try to discover religious truth through long periods of prayer, thought etc

mystify /ˈmɪstɪfaɪ/ *v* [T] **mystified, mystifying, mystifies** if something mystifies you, it is so strange or confusing that you cannot understand or explain it: *Her disappearance has mystified her family.* —**mystifying** *adj*

mystique /mɪˈstiːk/ *n* [U] the quality that makes someone or something seem mysterious, special, or exciting: *the mystique surrounding showbusiness*

myth /mɪθ/ *n* [C,U]   **1** an idea that many people believe, but which is not true: **+of** *the myth of male superiority* | **+that** *the myth that the disease only affects older people*   **2** an ancient story that explains a natural or historical event → see box at **STORY**

mythical /ˈmɪθɪkəl/ *adj*   **1** existing only in an ancient story: *mythical creatures*   **2** imagined, but not real or true

mythology /mɪˈθɒlədʒi $ -ˈθɑː-/ *n* [U] ancient stories and the beliefs they represent: *Greek mythology* —**mythological** /ˌmɪθəˈlɒdʒɪkəl $ -ˈlɑː-/ *adj*

N, n

N, n /en/ *n* [C,U] plural **N's, n's** the 14th letter of the English alphabet

N the written abbreviation of **north** or **northern**

n. also **n** *BrE* the written abbreviation of **noun**

'n' /n, ən/ *informal* a short form of 'and': *rock 'n' roll*

N/A not applicable written on a form to show that you do not need to answer a particular question

nab /næb/ *v* [T] **nabbed, nabbing** *informal* to catch someone who is doing something wrong: *The police nabbed him for speeding.*

naff /næf/ *adj BrE informal* silly and unfashionable: *a naff film*

nag /næg/ *v* [I,T] **nagged, nagging** to keep asking someone to do something in an annoying way: *She keeps nagging me to fix the lamp.*

nagging /'nægɪŋ/ *adj* [only before noun] making you worry or feel pain all the time: *a nagging doubt*

nail¹ /neɪl/ *n* [C]

1 a thin pointed piece of metal with a flat end that you hit with a hammer: **hammer/drive a nail** *She hammered a nail into the wall.*

2 the thin hard parts on the ends of your fingers and toes: *Stop biting your nails!*

nail² *v* [T] to fasten something to something else with nails: *The windows were nailed shut.*

nail sth ⇔ **down** *phr v* to reach a definite agreement about something: *They nailed down the details of the deal.*

'nail-,biting *adj* very exciting: *a nail-biting finish to the race* → see box at **EXCITING**

nailbrush /'neɪlbrʌʃ/ *n* [C] a small brush for cleaning your nails

'nail file *n* [C] a thin piece of metal with a rough surface used for shaping your nails

'nail ,polish also **'nail ,varnish** *BrE n* [U] coloured liquid that women put on their nails

naive /naɪ'iːv/ *adj* if someone is naive, they believe that people are nicer and that things will be easier than they really are, because they have not had much experience of life: *a naive young girl* —**naively** *adv* —**naivety** /naɪ'iːvəti/ *n* [U]

naked /'neɪkɪd/ *adj*

1 not wearing any clothes [= **nude**; ➝ **bare**]: *a naked man* | **stark naked** (=completely naked)

2 with/to the naked eye if you can see something with the naked eye, you can see it without the help of an instrument such as a MICROSCOPE: *These tiny creatures are barely visible to the naked eye.*

3 [only before noun] naked emotions are not hidden and are shocking: *naked aggression*

4 naked flame/light a flame or light that is not covered

—**nakedness** *n* [U]

name¹ /neɪm/ *n*

1 [C] what someone or something is called: *Her name is Jo Wilson.* | *What's your name?* | *Hello, my name's Ian.* | **last name/family name** | *She called him by his first name* (=she used his first name when talking to him). | *your full name* (=complete name) *and address* | *She didn't give* (=say) *her name.* | **+of** *What's the name of the street?* | **+for** *Edo was the ancient name for Tokyo.*

2 [singular] the opinion that people have about a person or organization [= **reputation**]: *the good name of the company* | *This kind of incident gives football a bad name.* | **make your name/make a name for yourself** (=become famous for something) *He made a name for himself as a painter.*

3 big/famous/household name *informal* a famous person, company, or product: *the biggest names in show business*

4 call sb names to insult someone by using unpleasant words to describe them

5 be in sb's name/in the name of sb to legally belong to someone: *The house is in my husband's name.*

6 in the name of religion/freedom/science etc using religion, freedom etc as the reason why something is done: *experiments done in the name of science*

→ **BIG NAME, BRAND NAME, PLACE NAME, TRADE NAME, USER NAME**

name² *v* [T] **1** to give someone or something a name [➝ **call**]: **name sb John/Ann etc** *We named our daughter Sarah.* | **name sb/sth after sb/sth** *BrE/***name sb/sth for sb/sth** *AmE* (=give them the same name as another person or thing) *He was named after his grandfather.* **2** to say what the name of someone or something is, especially officially: *The murder victims have not yet been named.* | **name sb as sth** *The woman who was shot has been named as Mary Grey.* **3** to say that someone has been chosen for an important job or prize: **name sb/sth (as) sth**

Quinn was named as the new manager. **4 you name it(, they've got it)** *spoken* used after a list of things to mean that there are many more you could mention: *Beer, whisky, wine – you name it, we've got it!* **5 name your price** *spoken* to say how much you are willing to pay or sell something for

'**name-check** *n* [C] when the name of a famous person, product, organization etc is mentioned in something such as an advertisement —**name-check** *v* [T]

namedropping /'neɪm,drɒpɪŋ $ -,drɑː-/ *n* [U] when someone mentions the name of a famous person to make it seem that they know them personally

nameless /'neɪmləs/ *adj* **1 who shall remain nameless** *spoken* used when you want to say that someone has done something wrong, but without mentioning their name: *Someone, who shall remain nameless, forgot to lock the door.* **2** a nameless person is someone whose name is not known: *pictures by a nameless artist*

namely /'neɪmli/ *adv* used to add more information about the people or things that you have just mentioned: *He was arrested for possessing a weapon, namely a knife.*

namesake /'neɪmseɪk/ *n* **sb's namesake** someone who has the same name as someone else

nan /næn/ also **nanna** /'nænə/ *n* [C] *BrE informal* grandmother – used especially by children

nanny /'næni/ *n* [C] plural **nannies** a woman whose job is to take care of a family's children, usually in their own home

nanotechnology /,nænəʊtek'nɒlədʒi $ -noʊtek'nɑː-/ *n* [U] *technical* the science of developing and making extremely small but powerful machines

nap[1] /næp/ *n* [C] a short sleep during the day: **take/have a nap** *He's having his afternoon nap.*

nap[2] *v* [I] napped, napping **1 be caught napping** *informal* to not be ready when something happens **2** to sleep for a short time during the day

napalm /'neɪpɑːm $ -pɑːm, -pɑːlm/ *n* [U] a substance used as a weapon to burn people or things

nape /neɪp/ *n* [singular] *literary* the back of your neck

napkin /'næpkɪn/ *n* [C] a square of cloth or paper that you use at meals to keep your clothes, hands, and mouth clean

nappy /'næpi/ *n* [C] plural **nappies** *BrE* a piece of cloth or paper that a baby wears on its bottom [= diaper *AmE*]: *His **nappy** needs **changing**.*

narcissism /'nɑːsɪsɪzəm $ 'nɑːr-/ *n* [U] *disapproving* when someone spends too much time thinking about and admiring their own appearance or abilities —**narcissistic** /,nɑːsɪ'sɪstɪk $ 'nɑːr-/ *adj*

narcotic /nɑː'kɒtɪk $ nɑːr'kɑː-/ *n* [C] a strong drug such as HEROIN that stops pain and makes people sleep —**narcotic** *adj*

narrate /nə'reɪt $ 'næreɪt, næ'reɪt, nə-/ *v* [T] *formal* to tell a story or explain what is happening in a film, television programme etc —**narration** /nə'reɪʃən/ *n* [C,U]

narrative /'nærətɪv/ *n* [C,U] the description of events in a story —**narrative** *adj*

narrator /nə'reɪtə $ 'næreɪtər, næ'reɪtər, nə-/ *n* [C] someone who tells a story or explains what is happening in a film, television programme etc

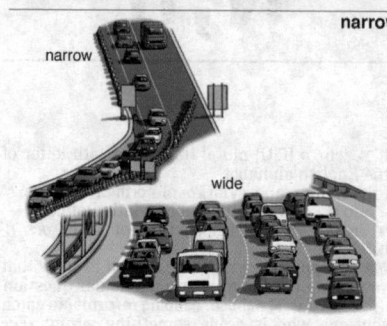

narrow

narrow[1] /'nærəʊ $ -roʊ/ *adj*

1 something that is narrow measures a short distance from one side to the other [≠ **wide**; → **broad**]: *the **narrow** streets* | *his **narrow** bed* | *The stairs were very narrow.*

2 narrow escape when you only just avoid danger or trouble: *We had a **narrow escape** when a bus hit the car.*

3 narrow victory/defeat etc when someone wins or loses by only a small amount

4 limited: *a **narrow** view of life* —**narrowness** *n* [U]

narrow[2] *v* [I,T] to become narrower, or to make something narrower: *The road narrows here.*

narrow sth ⇔ down *phr v* to reduce the number of people or things that you can choose from: **+to** *We've narrowed down the number of candidates to two.*

narrowly /'nærəʊli $ -roʊ-/ *adv* by only a small amount: *He **narrowly avoided** being killed.*

,**narrow-'minded** / $ '.. ,../ *adj* not willing to accept ideas that are new and different from your own

nasal /'neɪzəl/ *adj* **1** [only before noun] relating to the nose: *the nasal passage* **2** a nasal sound or voice comes mainly through your nose

nasty /'nɑːsti $ 'næsti/ *adj* unpleasant or unkind: *a **nasty** accident* | *a **nasty** shock* | *Drivers have a **nasty habit** of driving too close to cyclists.* | *What a **nasty** thing to say!* | **+to** *Don't be so **nasty** to your sister* (=treat her unkindly). | **get/turn nasty** *especially BrE* (=suddenly start behaving in a threatening way) *When Tim refused, Dan turned nasty.* → see box at **HORRIBLE** → and **UNKIND**
—**nastiness** *n* [U] —**nastily** *adv*

nation /'neɪʃən/ *n* [C] a country and its people: *the world's leading industrial nations* | *the President's speech to the nation*

national[1] /'næʃənəl/ *adj*

1 relating to the whole of a nation, not just part of it [→ **local**]: *Drugs are a **national** problem.* | *national elections* | *an issue of national importance*

2 relating to or typical of a particular nation [→ **international**]: *national dress*

3 owned or controlled by the government of a country: *Spain's national airline*

→ **GROSS NATIONAL PRODUCT**

national[2] n [C] *formal* a citizen of a particular country who is living in another country: *Turkish nationals*

,**national 'anthem** n [C] a country's official song

,**National 'Health ,Service** n **the National Health Service** , **the NHS**

,**national 'holiday** n [C] *AmE* a day when people in a country do not work and the shops are closed [= **public holiday** *BrE*]

nationalise /'næʃənəlaɪz/ v a British spelling of NATIONALIZE

nationalism /'næʃənəlɪzəm/ n [U] **1** when a group of people want to have their own government and be independent of another country: *Scottish nationalism* **2** the feeling of being proud of your country and believing that it is better than other countries

nationalist /'næʃənəlɪst/ n [C] **1** someone who wants their country to be politically independent from another country: *Welsh nationalists* **2** someone who is very proud of their country and believes that it is better than other countries —**nationalist** *adj*

nationalistic /,næʃənə'lɪstɪk◂/ *adj disapproving* believing that your country is much better than other countries: *a nationalistic speech*

nationality /,næʃə'nælɪti/ n [C,U] plural **nationalities** when you are legally a citizen of a country: *He has British nationality.*

nationalize also **-ise** *BrE* /'næʃənəlaɪz/ v [T] if a government nationalizes an organization, it takes control of it [≠ **privatize**] —**nationalization** /,næʃənəlaɪ'zeɪʃən $ -nələ-/ n [C,U]

nationally /'næʃənəli/ *adv* throughout a country: *nationally recognized qualifications*

,**national 'monument** n [C] a building, area of land etc that is protected by the government for people to visit

,**national 'park** n [C] beautiful land which is protected by the government for people to visit

,**national se'curity** n [U] the ways a country protects its citizens by keeping its secrets safe and its army strong

,**national 'service** n [U] the system of making all adults spend a period of time in the army, navy, or air force

,**nation 'state** n [C] a politically independent country

nationwide /,neɪʃən'waɪd◂ , 'neɪʃənwaɪd/ *adv, adj* in every part of a country: *a nationwide search for the missing girl* | *It's available in department stores nationwide.*

native[1] /'neɪtɪv/ *adj* **1** [only before noun] relating to the place where you were born or have always lived: *He returned to his native Poland.* | **native Californian/New Yorker etc** | **native language/tongue** (=the language you first learned to speak) **2** a native plant or animal grows or lives naturally somewhere, and was not brought there from somewhere else: *native species of trees*

native[2] n [C] **1** someone who was born in a particular country: **+of** *a native of Brazil* **2** [usually plural] *old-fashioned* a word used in the past to refer to the people who lived in Africa, America etc before Europeans arrived. Many people now consider this use to be offensive.

,**Native A'merican** n [C] someone who belongs to one of the races that lived in North America before Europeans arrived

,**native 'speaker** n [C] someone who learned a particular language as their first language when they were a baby

NATO /'neɪtəʊ $ -toʊ/ n **North Atlantic Treaty Organization** a group of countries in North America and Europe that give military help to each other

natter /'nætə $ -ər/ v [I] *BrE informal* to talk about unimportant things [➔ **chat**] —**natter** n [singular]

natural[1] /'nætʃərəl/ *adj*

1 natural things are found in nature rather than being made by humans: *earthquakes and other natural disasters* | *the natural world* (=trees, rivers, animals, plants etc) | *death from natural causes* (=because of illness or old age)

THESAURUS

wild – used about flowers, plants, and animals that are not controlled by people: *Wild dogs roamed the streets.*
pure – used about food or drink that has not had anything added to it: *pure orange juice*
organic – used about fruit, vegetables, meat etc that is produced without using chemicals: *organic tomatoes*

(antonyms)

artificial – not made of natural materials or substances, but made to be like something natural: *The drink contains artificial colouring.*
processed – used about food that has been treated with chemicals to make it stay fresh or look good: *processed cheese*
synthetic – used about cloth or substances made by a chemical process: *nylon, polyester, and other synthetic materials*
man-made – made by people, but similar to something natural: *a man-made lake*

2 normal or usual in a particular situation [≠ **unnatural, abnormal**]: **it is natural (for sb) to do sth** *It's not natural for a child of his age to be so quiet.* | **It's only natural that** *he's worried.* | *Babies have a natural fear of falling.*

3 having a skill or ability which you were born with, rather than one you had to learn: *a natural athlete* —**naturalness** n [U]

natural[2] n **be a natural** to be very good at doing something without being taught

,**natural 'gas** n [U] gas used for cooking or heating that is taken from under the ground

,**natural 'history** n [U] the study of plants and animals

naturalist /'nætʃərəlɪst/ n [C] someone who studies plants and animals

naturalize also **-ise** *BrE* /'nætʃərəlaɪz/ v **be naturalized** to be officially given the right to live in a country where you were not born —**naturalization** /,nætʃərəlaɪ'zeɪʃən $ -lə-/ n [U]

naturally /'nætʃərəli $ -tʃərəli, -tʃərli/ *adv*

1 used to say that something is normal and not surprising: *Naturally, we wanted to win.* | *Naturally enough, she wanted promotion.*

2 in a way that is the result of nature, not of someone's actions: *My hair is naturally curly.* | *a naturally gifted soccer player* | *The tomatoes are left to dry naturally in the sun.*
3 in a relaxed and normal way: *Try to act naturally.*

,natural re'sources / $,... '.../ *n* [plural] things that exist in nature and can be used by people, for example oil, trees etc

,natural se'lection *n* [U] *technical* the process by which only plants and animals that are suitable for life in their environment will continue to exist

nature /'neɪtʃə $ -tʃər/ *n*

1 [U] everything in the world that is not made or controlled by humans, such as animals, plants, and the weather: *the forces of nature* | **in nature** *substances that are not found in nature*
2 [C,U] someone's character, or what something is like: *a child with a happy nature* | **sb's nature** (=used to say that you do not think someone would behave in that way) *It's not in Jane's nature to lie.* | **by nature** *She was by nature a friendly person.* | *Of course she's jealous – it's only human nature* (=the feelings and ways of behaving that all people have). | **+of** *The exact nature of the problem is not clear.* | **of this/that nature** *I never trouble myself with questions of that nature.* | *The support being given is of a practical nature.* | *Any government funding would be temporary in nature.*
→ GOOD-NATURED, HUMAN NATURE

'nature re,serve *n* [C] an area of land where animals and plants are protected

naught /nɔːt $ nɒːt/ *n* [U] a word meaning 'nothing', which was used in the past: *Our plans came to naught* (=failed).

naughty /'nɔːti $ 'nɒːti, 'nɑːti/ *adj* a naughty child behaves badly —**naughtiness** *n* [U] —**naughtily** *adv*

nausea /'nɔːziə, -siə $ 'nɒːziə, -ʃə/ *n* [U] *formal* the feeling that you have when you are going to VOMIT

nauseate /'nɔːzieɪt, -si- $ 'nɒːzi-, -ʃi-/ *v* [T] to cause someone to feel that they are going to VOMIT

nauseating /'nɔːzieɪtɪŋ, -si- $ 'nɒːzi-, -ʃi-/ *adj*
1 making you feel annoyed or offended: *nauseating racist remarks* **2** making you want to VOMIT: *a nauseating smell* —**nauseatingly** *adv*

nauseous /'nɔːziəs, -siəs $ 'nɒːziəs, -ʃəs/ *adj* feeling that you are going to VOMIT, or making you feel this way [= **sick**]: *I felt slightly nauseous.* | *a nauseous smell*

nautical /'nɔːtɪkəl $ 'nɒː-/ *adj* relating to ships or sailing —**nautically** /-kli/ *adv*

naval /'neɪvəl/ *adj* [only before noun] relating to the navy: *a naval battle*

navel /'neɪvəl/ *n* [C] the small hole in your stomach [= **belly button**]

navigable /'nævɨɡəbəl/ *adj* a river, lake etc that is navigable is deep and wide enough for ships to travel on

navigate /'nævɨɡeɪt/ *v* **1** [I,T] to decide which way a car or ship should go, using maps: *I'll drive, you take the map and navigate.* **2** [T] to sail across or along an area of water

navigation /,nævɨ'ɡeɪʃən/ *n* [U] when you decide which direction your car or ship should go —**navigational** *adj*

navigator /'nævɨɡeɪtə $ -tər/ *n* [C] a person on a ship or plane whose job is to plan the direction it should be travelling

navy /'neɪvi/ *n* plural **navies** **1** [C] the people and ships that a country has for fighting a war at sea: **in the navy** *Is he still in the navy?* | *Join the navy and see the world.* **2** [U] a very dark blue colour —**navy** *adj*

,navy 'blue also **navy** *adj* very dark blue

Nazi /'nɑːtsi/ *n* [C] a member of the National Socialist Party which controlled Germany from 1933 to 1945 —**Nazi** *adj* —**Nazism** *n* [U]

N.B. also **NB** *written* **nota bene** used to make a reader pay attention to important information

NCO /,en si: 'əʊ $ -'oʊ/ *n* [C] **non-commissioned officer** an officer of low rank in the British army

NE the written abbreviation of **northeast** or **northeastern**

near¹ /nɪə $ nɪr/ *adv, prep*

1 a short distance away from someone or something: *They live near Osaka.* | *Is there a bank near here?* | *They moved house to be nearer the school.* | **+to** *a hotel near to the beach*

THESAURUS

close: *He sat close to his mom.*
not far (away): *The station's not far away.*
nearby – near here or near a particular place: *Do you live nearby?* | *a nearby farm*
within walking distance (of sth) – easy to walk to from somewhere: *The sea's within walking distance of the hotel.*
local – used about shops, schools etc that are in the area where you live: *your local library*
neighbouring – used about towns, countries etc that are very near a particular place: *discussions between Egypt and neighbouring states*

Near and **close** are both used to talk about short distances between things.
Near can be followed directly by a noun: *Is the hotel near the beach?*
Close cannot be followed directly by a noun.
Close must be followed by the preposition 'to' and then a noun: *They live close to the station.*

2 soon before a particular time or event: *near the end of the week* | **+to** *nearer to Christmas*
3 almost doing something or almost in a particular state: *The work is near completion.* | *a near impossible task* | *We're no nearer an agreement.* | **+to** *People fleeing the building were near to panic.* | **come/be near to doing sth** *She came near to hitting him.*

near² *adj*

1 only a short distance away from someone or something: *It's very near.* | *The nearest* (=closest) *beach is only a mile away.*
2 near disaster/collapse etc almost a DISASTER, COLLAPSE etc: *The election was a near disaster for the party.*
3 in the near future soon: *The school hopes to open in the near future.*
4 near miss when a bomb, plane, car etc nearly hits something but does not: *a near miss between two aircraft*
5 near relative/relation a relative who is very closely related to you, such as a parent

near

far

near

essential – important and necessary
vital – extremely important or necessary
mandatory – if something is mandatory, it must be done because of a rule or law
compulsory – if something is compulsory, you must do it
→ NEED

2 necessary evil something unpleasant that you have to accept in order to achieve what you want: *He regarded work as a necessary evil.*

necessitate /nəˈsesɪteɪt/ *v* [T] *formal* to make something necessary: *His injuries may necessitate long-term treatment.*

necessity /nəˈsesəti/ *n* plural **necessities** **1** [C] something you need: **+for** *A car is an absolute necessity for this job.* | **+of** *Water is a basic necessity of life.* **2** [U] when you must do something: **necessity to do sth** *There's no necessity to pay now* (=you do not need to pay now). | **through/out of necessity** (=because you must do it) *They did it out of necessity.*

neck¹ /nek/ *n* [C]

1 the part of your body that joins your head to your shoulders: **around sb's neck** *She wore a gold chain around her neck.* → see picture on page A3
2 the part of a piece of clothing that goes around your neck: **V-necked/open-necked etc** *a V-necked sweater*
3 the narrow part near the top or end of something such as a bottle
4 be up to your neck in sth *informal* **a)** to have too much work to do: *She's up to her neck in work.* **b)** to be in a very difficult situation: *He's up to his neck in debt.*
5 neck and neck if two people, teams etc are neck and neck during a race or competition, they are level with each other
6 in this/sb's neck of the woods *informal* in a particular area or part of the country: *What are you doing in this neck of the woods?*
→ POLO NECK, V-NECK

neck² *v* **be necking** *old-fashioned* to be kissing in a sexual way

necklace /ˈnek-ləs/ *n* [C] a piece of jewellery that you wear around your neck: *a diamond necklace* → see picture at JEWELLERY

neckline /ˈnek-laɪn/ *n* [C] the edge of a piece of woman's clothing around the neck

necktie /ˈnektaɪ/ *n* [C] *AmE formal* a TIE

nectar /ˈnektə $ -ər/ *n* [U] the sweet liquid that BEES collect from flowers

nectarine /ˈnektəriːn $ ˌnektəˈriːn/ *n* [C] a juicy fruit like a PEACH

née /neɪ/ *adj* used to say what a married woman's family name was when she was born. 'Née' is put after her married name and before her old name: *Jo Lee, née Jones*

need¹ /niːd/ *v* [T]

1 if you need something, you must have it: *These plants need plenty of light and water.* | *I live in the city, so I don't really need a car.* | *How much money do you need?* | **need sth for sth** *I need glasses for reading.* | **need sb to do sth** *I need you to help me with the cooking.* | *Food and medicines are urgently needed.* | *This job needs a lot of patience.*

near³ *v* [T] to come closer to a particular place, time, or state [= approach]: *Jo began to feel nervous as she neared the house.* | *employees nearing retirement*

nearby¹ /ˈnɪəbaɪ $ ˈnɪr-/ *adj* not far away: *a nearby lake*

nearby² /nɪəˈbaɪ $ nɪr-/ *Do you live nearby?* → see box at LOCALLY → and NEAR

nearly /ˈnɪəli $ ˈnɪrli/ *adv*

1 *especially BrE* almost: *We've nearly finished.* | *It's nearly seven years since I last saw him.* | *He's nearly as tall as me.* | *He very nearly died.*
2 not nearly used to say that something is definitely not true: *He's not nearly as nice as his brother.*

nearsighted /ˌnɪəˈsaɪtɪd◂ $ ˈnɪrsaɪtɪd/ *adj* unable to see things clearly unless they are close to you [= shortsighted *BrE*]

neat /niːt/ *adj*

1 arranged in a tidy and careful way: *neat handwriting* | *His clothes were always neat and clean.* | *Her room was neat and tidy.*
2 someone who is neat likes to keep things tidy
3 *AmE spoken informal* very good or enjoyable: *That's a neat idea!*
4 simple and effective: *a neat solution to the problem*
5 *especially BrE* a neat alcoholic drink has no ice or water or any other liquid added [= straight]
—**neatly** *adv*: *It fits neatly into the corner.* | *The clothes were neatly folded.* —**neatness** *n* [U]

necessarily /ˈnesəsərəli, ˌnesəˈserəli $ ˌnesəˈserəli/ *adv* **not necessarily** used to say that something may not be true, or may not always happen: *Expensive restaurants do not necessarily have the best food.*

necessary /ˈnesəsəri $ -seri/ *adj*

1 if something is necessary, you must do it or have it to make a situation possible: *'Do I need to bring any money with me?' 'No, that won't be necessary.'* | *The booklet provides all the necessary information.* | *The police are advising motorists to travel only if their journey is absolutely necessary.* | **it is necessary (for sb) to do sth** *It may be necessary for me to have an operation.* | **make it necessary (for sb) to do sth** *The rise in costs made it necessary to increase prices.* | **necessary for (doing) sth** *A good diet is necessary for maintaining a healthy body.* | **if/when/where necessary** *You can take the test again if necessary.*

N

THESAURUS

could do with sth/could use sth *spoken*: *Shall we stop? I could do with a rest.*

be desperate for sth – to need something urgently: *Liz was desperate for a cigarette.*

can't do without sth – to be unable to manage without something: *A lot of people can't do without their mobile phones.*

be dependent on sth/sb – to be unable to live or continue normally without something or someone: *The refugees are dependent on outside food supplies.*

require *formal*: *Children require a lot of attention.*

2 to feel that you want something very much: *I need a drink.*

3 need to do sth used to say that an action or situation is necessary: *He needs to see a doctor.* | *She didn't need to think about her decision.* | **needn't do sth** *I needn't take up any more of your time.*

USAGE

Compare don't need to, needn't, must not

If an action is not necessary, you can say that you **don't need to** do it or **needn't** do it: *I don't need to leave until 10.* | *You needn't apologize.*

Do not use these expressions to mean **must not** (=should not or are not allowed to): *You mustn't take any sharp objects on the plane.*

Compare needn't have, didn't need to, didn't have to

Use **needn't have** to say that it was not necessary for someone to do something that they have done: *We needn't have ordered so much food.*

If you want to say that something was not necessary and was not done, use **didn't need to** or **didn't have to**: *I didn't need/have to tell him who I was – he already knew.*

4 used to say that something should have something done to it: **sth needs painting/cleaning/cutting etc** *The house needs painting.* | **sth needs to be ...** *The car needs to be repaired.* | **need a (good) wash/clean/cut etc** *His hair needs a wash.*

5 you don't need to/you needn't used to give someone permission not to do something: *You don't need to wait for me.*

need² *n*

1 [singular,U] a situation in which something is necessary: **+for** *an urgent need for more nurses* | **need to do sth** *the need to have better trained staff* | **feel the need (to do sth)** *He did not feel the need to complain.* | *I'll work all night* **if need be** (=if it is necessary).

2 [C usually plural] something you must have in order to have a normal life: **sb's needs** *a family's basic needs* | **meet/satisfy a need** (=provide something that people want or need) *Schools must satisfy the needs of their pupils.*

3 there's no need (for sb) to do sth a) used to say that someone does not have to do something: *There's no need to come if you don't want*

to. **b)** *spoken* used to tell someone to stop doing something: *There's no need to shout; I'm not deaf.*
4 be in need of sth to need something: *We're* **in** *urgent need of help.*
5 in need not having enough food or money: *families in need*
→ **SPECIAL NEEDS**

needle¹ /'niːdl/ *n* [C]

1 a) a small thin piece of metal that you use for sewing, with a point at one end and a hole at the other end [➡ **pin**]: *a needle and thread* → see picture at **KNIT b)** a KNITTING NEEDLE
2 a very thin piece of metal on the end of a SYRINGE (=hollow tube), used to put medicine or drugs into your body, or to take blood out
3 a part on a piece of equipment which points to measurements or directions: *a compass needle*
4 a small thin pointed leaf, especially from a PINE tree → see picture at **PLANT**
5 the very small part in a RECORD PLAYER that touches the record in order to play it
6 be like looking for a needle in a haystack *informal* used to say that something is almost impossible to find
→ **PINE NEEDLE, PINS AND NEEDLES**

needle² *v* [T] *informal* to deliberately annoy someone, often in a joking way [= **tease**]: *She's always needling Jim about his weight.*

needless /'niːdləs/ *adj* **1 needless to say** used when you are telling someone something that you expect they will already know: *Needless to say, with four children we're always busy.*
2 not necessary, and easy to avoid: *needless suffering* —**needlessly** *adv*

needlework /'niːdlwɜːk $ -wɜːrk/ *n* [U] sewing, or things that you make by sewing

needn't /'niːdnt/ *especially BrE spoken* the short form of 'do not need to'

needy /'niːdi/ *adj* **1 a)** having very little food or money: *a needy family* **b) the needy** people who do not have enough food or money
2 someone who is needy needs a lot of love and attention

negate /nɪˈɡeɪt/ *v* [T] *formal* to prevent something from having any effect: *The increase in the price of oil was negated by the fall in the value of the dollar.* —**negation** /-ˈɡeɪʃən/ *n* [U]

negative¹ /'neɡətɪv/ *adj*

1 bad or harmful [≠ **positive**]: *Late nights were starting to have a* **negative effect** *on my work.* | *Technological innovation also has a* **negative side**.
2 thinking only about the bad things about a situation, person etc [≠ **positive**]: *teenagers with a* **negative attitude** *towards authority* | **+about** *She's been very negative about school lately.*
3 a) a negative answer or reply means 'no' [≠ **affirmative**]: *We were puzzled by their negative response to our request.* **b)** a negative sentence or phrase contains a word such as 'no', 'not', or 'nothing'
4 a scientific test that is negative shows that a particular chemical or medical condition has not been found [≠ **positive**]: *The pregnancy test was negative.*
5 less than zero: *negative numbers*
6 *technical* a negative electrical current is carried by ELECTRONS [≠ **positive**]
—**negatively** *adv*

negative² *n* [C] **1** a word or phrase that means 'no' **2** a camera film from which you can print a photograph. A negative shows dark areas as light, and light areas as dark. → see box at CAMERA

neglect¹ /nɪˈglekt/ *v* [T] **1** to not pay enough attention to someone or something, or not take care of them: *You mustn't neglect your family.* | *The building has been badly neglected.* **2 neglect to do sth** to not do something that you should do: *The company neglected to pay according to the contract.* —**neglected** *adj* —**neglectful** *adj*

neglect² *n* [U] when something or someone is not looked after well: *children suffering from neglect*

negligence /ˈneglɪdʒəns/ *n* [U] when someone does not do something that they are responsible for doing, with the result that something bad happens: *The boy's parents are suing the hospital for negligence.*

negligent /ˈneglɪdʒənt/ *adj* not doing something that you are responsible for doing, with the result that something bad happens

negligible /ˈneglɪdʒɪbəl/ *adj* very small and unimportant: *The damage was negligible.*

negotiable /nɪˈgəʊʃiəbəl, -ʃə- $ -ˈgoʊ-/ *adj* prices, amounts etc that are negotiable can be discussed and changed

negotiate /nɪˈgəʊʃieɪt $ -ˈgoʊ-/ *v* **1** [I,T] to discuss something in order to make an agreement, especially in business or politics: **+with** *The government refuses to negotiate with terrorists.* | *UN representatives are trying to negotiate a ceasefire.* **2** [T] to succeed in going past or over a difficult place on a road, path etc: *She slowed down to negotiate the corner.* —**negotiator** *n* [C]

negotiation /nɪˌgəʊʃiˈeɪʃən $ -ˌgoʊ-/ *n* [C usually plural, U] official discussions between two groups who are trying to make an agreement: **peace/trade/wage negotiations** *Employers are facing another **round of wage negotiations**.* | **+with** *We refuse to enter into negotiations with the rebels.*

Negro /ˈniːgrəʊ $ -groʊ/ *n* [C] plural **Negroes** *old-fashioned* a word meaning a black person, which some people now consider offensive

neigh /neɪ/ *v* [I] if a horse neighs, it makes a loud noise —**neigh** *n* [C]

neighbour *BrE*; **neighbor** *AmE* /ˈneɪbə $ -bər/ *n* [C]

1 someone who lives next to you or near you: **sb's neighbours** *My neighbours often look after the kids after school.* | **next-door neighbours** (=the people who live in the house next to yours) *Our next-door neighbours complained about the noise.*

2 a person or country that is next to another person or country: **sb's/sth's neighbour** *You'll have to share a book with your neighbor.* | *Germany's neighbours*

neighbourhood *BrE*; **neighborhood** *AmE* /ˈneɪbəhʊd $ -ər-/ *n* [C] an area of a town, and the people who live there: *He grew up in a tough neighbourhood.* | *a neighborhood school* → see box at AREA → and LOCALLY

neighbouring *BrE*; **neighboring** *AmE* /ˈneɪbərɪŋ/ *adj* [only before noun] near the place you are talking about: *neighbouring towns* → see box at NEAR

neighbourly *BrE*; **neighborly** *AmE* /ˈneɪbəli $ -ər-/ *adj* friendly and helpful to people who live near you: *a neighbourly visit* —**neighbourliness** *n* [U]

neither¹ /ˈnaɪðə $ ˈniːðər/ *determiner, pron* not one and not the other of two people or things [→ **either, both**]: *It was a boring game and neither team played well.* | **+of** *Neither of them can drive.*

neither, neither of

Neither is used with a singular noun form and a singular verb: *Neither answer is right.*

Neither of is used with a plural noun form or pronoun, and the verb can be singular or plural: *Neither of us has/have ever been to America before.*

neither² *adv* used to show that a negative statement is also true about another person or thing [→ **either**]: **neither does/can/will etc sb** *'I didn't like sport at school.' 'Neither did I.'* | *'Tom can't swim yet.' 'Neither can Sam.'* | *'I haven't seen Greg in a long time.' 'Me neither* (=and I have not seen him).*'

neither³ *linking word* **neither ... nor ...** used when mentioning two things that are not true or do not happen: *Neither his mother nor his father spoke English.* | *The equipment is neither accurate nor safe.*

neo- /niːəʊ, niːə $ niːoʊ, niːə/ *prefix* used to say that a style, belief etc is similar to one that existed in the past: *a neo-classical palace*

neon /ˈniːɒn $ -ɑːn/ *n* [U] a gas that is used in tubes in electric lights and signs: *neon lights*

nephew /ˈnefjuː, ˈnev- $ ˈnef-/ *n* [C] the son of your brother or sister, or the son of your husband's or wife's brother or sister [→ **niece**] → see box at RELATIVE

nepotism /ˈnepətɪzəm/ *n* [U] when people use their power in an unfair way by giving the best jobs to their family or friends

Neptune /ˈneptjuːn $ -tuːn/ *n* the PLANET that is eighth in order from the sun

nerd /nɜːd $ nɜːrd/ *n* [C] *informal* someone who is unfashionable and interested in boring things —**nerdy** *adj*

nerve /nɜːv $ nɜːrv/ *n*

1 nerves [plural] the feeling of being worried or a little frightened: *A lot of people **suffer from nerves** before going on stage.* | **calm/steady your nerves** (=stop yourself feeling worried or frightened) *I drank a glass of brandy to calm my nerves.* | **Exam nerves** *are part of student life.* | **be a bundle/bag of nerves** (=be very nervous)

2 [C] a thing in your body that sends information to and from your brain, for example when you feel pain, or when you want to move: *damage to the optic nerves*

3 [U] courage and confidence in a dangerous or difficult situation: **the nerve to do sth** *I didn't have the nerve to ask for a pay rise.* | *It takes nerve to stand up for what you believe like that.* | *I was going to jump, but I **lost my nerve** (=became nervous and unable to do what you had intended).*

N

4 get on sb's nerves *informal* to annoy someone, especially by doing a particular thing a lot: *Her voice was starting to get on my nerves.*
5 [singular] *informal disapproving* a way of behaving that does not seem polite or sensitive: *'She didn't even say sorry.' 'What a nerve!'* | **have the nerve to do sth** *And then he had the nerve to criticize my cooking!*
6 touch/hit a (raw) nerve to say something that upsets someone

nerve-racking, nerve-wracking /'nɜːv ˌrækɪŋ $ 'nɜːrv-/ *adj* very worrying or frightening: *Giving a speech is a nerve-racking experience.*

nervous /'nɜːvəs $ 'nɜːr-/ *adj*
1 worried or frightened about something, and unable to relax [➔ **anxious**]: **+about** *Sam's very nervous about his driving test.* | *Stop watching me. You're making me nervous.* | *Most people get nervous before an interview.* | *By the end of the journey, I was a nervous wreck* (=extremely nervous and frightened). | **a nervous smile/laugh/look etc**

> ### USAGE
> Use **nervous** about someone who feels worried or a little frightened: *Katie gets very nervous before exams.*
> Use **annoyed** about someone who feels a little angry about something: *Everyone was annoyed that he was late again.*
> ➔ **WORRIED**

2 a nervous person becomes worried, frightened, or upset easily: *a nervous child*
3 [only before noun] a nervous illness is related to the nerves in your body
—**nervously** *adv* —**nervousness** *n* [U]

nervous 'breakdown *n* [C] a mental illness in which someone becomes very worried and unhappy, and cannot live a normal life

'nervous ˌsystem *n* [C] the nerves in your body, together with your brain, which allow you to feel pain, heat etc, and which control your movements

-ness /nɪs/ *suffix* used to form nouns that refer to a quality or state: *happiness* | *effectiveness*

nest /nest/ *n* [C] **1** a place that a bird makes to lay its eggs in: *a bird's nest* | *Crows build their nests high in the trees.* **2** a place where insects or small animals live: *a wasps' nest* —**nest** *v* [I]

'nest egg *n* [C] an amount of money that you have saved

nestle /'nesəl/ *v* [I,T] to be in or move into a comfortable or pleasant position, surrounded by something soft or protecting: **+in/among/between etc** *a village nestling among the hills* | *The little cat nestled its head in my arms.*

net¹ /net/ *n*
1 the Net also **the net** the system that allows computer users around the world to exchange information [= the Internet, the Web]: **on the Net** *I saw the advertisement on the net.*
2 [C] the thing that you hit the ball into in sports such as football, or that you hit the ball over in tennis [➔ **goal**]: **into the net** *The ball bounced off the post and into the net.*
3 [C] something that you use for catching fish, animals etc, made of pieces of string or wire joined together with spaces between them: *a fishing net*

4 [C, U] material made from very fine threads with small spaces between them, or something made from this material: *net curtains* | *a mosquito net*
→ **SAFETY NET** → **surf the net** at **SURF¹**

net² *v* [T] **netted, netting 1** to get a particular amount of money as profit **2** to kick the ball into the net in football [➔ **score**] **3** to catch a fish in a net

net³ also **nett** *BrE adj* **1** a net amount of money is the amount that remains after tax etc has been taken away [➔ **gross**]: *a net profit of $500,000*
2 net weight the weight of something without its container

netball /'netbɔːl $ -bɒːl/ *n* [U] a game in which two teams, usually girls or women, try to win points by throwing a ball to each other and through a high net [➔ **basketball**]

netting /'netɪŋ/ *n* [U] material made from pieces of string, wire etc joined together with spaces between [➔ **net**]

nettle /'netl/ *n* [C] a wild plant with leaves that sting your skin if you touch them

network¹ /'netwɜːk $ -wɜːrk/ *n* [C] **1** a system of things that are connected with each other: *a high-speed European rail network* | *a mobile phone network* **2** a number of computers that are connected to each other so that they can share information: *the university computer network* **3** a large number of people, organizations etc that know and help each other, or work together: **+of** *Tim had a strong network of contacts in Europe.* | *the importance of the family network* **4** a group of radio or television companies that broadcast the same programmes in different parts of a country

network² *v* **1** [I] to talk to other people who do the same type of work in order to share information, help each other etc **2** [T] to connect several computers together so that they can share information —**networking** *n* [U]

neural /'njʊərəl $ 'nʊr-/ *adj technical* relating to a nerve or the NERVOUS SYSTEM

neurology /njʊ'rɒlədʒi $ nʊ'rɑː-/ *n* [U] the scientific study of the NERVOUS SYSTEM and the diseases relating to it —**neurologist** *n* [C] —**neurological** /ˌnjʊərə'lɒdʒɪkəl◂ $ ˌnʊrə'lɑː-/ *adj*

neurosis /njʊ'rəusɪs $ nʊ'rou-/ *n* [C,U] plural **neuroses** /-siːz/ a mental illness that makes someone very worried or frightened

neurotic /njʊ'rɒtɪk $ nʊ'rɑː-/ *adj* very worried or frightened about something in a way that is not normal: *She's neurotic about her health.* —**neurotic** *n* [C]

neuter¹ /'njuːtə $ 'nuːtər/ *adj* used to describe the nouns, adjectives etc in some languages that do not belong to the FEMININE or MASCULINE groups

neuter² *v* [T] to remove part of an animal's sex organs so that it cannot produce baby animals

neutral¹ /'njuːtrəl $ 'nuː-/ *adj* **1** not supporting any of the countries, groups, or people in a war, argument etc: *Switzerland remained neutral during World War II.* **2** not showing any strong feelings or opinions: *'I see,' she said in a neutral tone.* **3** a neutral colour is not strong or bright, for example grey

neutral² n [U] the position of the GEARS of a car when the engine does not turn the wheels: *Start the car in neutral.*

neutrality /njuːˈtrælɨti $ nuː-/ n [U] when a country or person does not support any of the people or groups involved in a war, argument etc

neutralize also **-ise** *BrE* /ˈnjuːtrəlaɪz $ ˈnuː-/ v [T] to prevent something from having any effect: *a substance that neutralized the smell*

neutron /ˈnjuːtrɒn $ ˈnuːtrɑːn/ n [C] a part of an atom that has no electrical CHARGE

never /ˈnevə $ -ər/ adv

1 not at any time, or not once: *He never saw her again.* | *I've never been to Hawaii.* | *I'll never forgive him.*

THESAURUS

never ever *spoken* – used to emphasize that you mean never: *I'll never ever forget him.*
not in a million years *spoken* – used to say that something is completely impossible: *She wouldn't go without me – not in a million years!*
not once – used to express surprise or annoyance: *Craig didn't phone all week – not once!*
→ **RARELY, OFTEN, SOMETIMES**

---

2 used to make a strong negative statement about the past: *She never even knew he was married!*

3 never mind *spoken* used to tell someone that they do not need to worry about something: *'We've missed the bus.' 'Never mind, there's another one in ten minutes.'*

4 you never know *spoken* used to say that something that seems unlikely may happen: *You never know, you might be lucky.*

5 Never! *BrE spoken* used when you are very surprised about something: *'He's sixty now, you know.' 'Never!'*

GRAMMAR

Use **never** before a verb, unless the verb is 'be': *He never listens to me.* | *Her father was never angry.*
If there are two or more verbs together, **never** comes after the first one: *I have never read any of her books.*

---

never-'ending adj disapproving seeming to continue for a very long time [= endless]: *The journey was never-ending.*

nevertheless /ˌnevəðəˈles $ -vər-/ adv formal in spite of what has just been mentioned: *He's friendly enough, but nevertheless I don't trust him.*

new /njuː $ nuː/ adj

1 recently made, built, or developed [≠ old]: *Have you got their new album?* | *a new leisure centre* | *technology that is completely new*

THESAURUS

recent – used about something that was new or that happened a short time ago: *recent news reports*
modern – used about things that are different from earlier things of the same kind: *modern technology*
original – completely new and different from

---

anything that has been done or thought of before: *original ideas*
fresh – used about food that was made, picked etc only a short time ago: *fresh bread*
latest – used about a film, book, fashion etc that is the newest one: *his latest movie*
→ **OLD**

---

2 recently bought: *Do you like my new shoes?*
3 not used or owned by anyone before: *New and second-hand books for sale.* | *a **brand new** (=completely new) car*
4 different or changed from what you had or experienced before [≠ old]: *Is your new teacher OK?* | **+to** *a lifestyle that was completely new to me*
5 someone who is new in a place, job etc has recently arrived or started there: *information for new students* | *Are you new here?*
6 recently discovered: *a new planet* | *important new evidence*
—**newness** n [U]

New 'Age adj New Age SPIRITUAL beliefs, medicines etc are not based on traditional Western ideas

newborn /ˈnjuːbɔːn $ ˈnuːbɔːrn/ adj a newborn baby or animal has just been born
—**newborn** n [C]

newcomer /ˈnjuːkʌmə $ ˈnuːkʌmər/ n [C] someone who has recently arrived somewhere or recently started doing an activity: **+to** *a newcomer to teaching*

newfangled /ˌnjuːˈfæŋɡəld◂ $ ˌnuː-/ adj disapproving newfangled ideas, machines etc are new or modern

'new-found adj [only before noun] recently obtained, found, or achieved: *He enjoyed his new-found freedom.*

newly /ˈnjuːli $ ˈnuːli/ adv **newly built/married/qualified etc** very recently built, married etc → see box at **RECENTLY**

newlyweds /ˈnjuːliwedz $ ˈnuː-/ n [plural] a man and a woman who have recently got married

news /njuːz $ nuːz/ n [U]

1 information about something that has happened recently: *an interesting **piece of news*** | **good/bad etc news** *I have some good news for you!* | *Have you **heard** any news from Emma yet?* | *Sit down and **tell** me all your news.* | **+of/about** *Everyone was shocked by the news of the arrests.* | **break the news (to sb)** (=tell someone about something bad that has happened) *A policewoman broke the news to the family.*
2 reports of recent events in the newspapers, on the radio, or on television: *Here's the sports news from Jane Murray.* | **+of** *news of an explosion in the city* | **news story/report/programme etc** *a news broadcast*
3 the news a regular television or radio programme that gives you reports of recent events: *the ten o'clock news* | **on the news** *I heard it on the news last night.* | **watch/listen to the news** *Shall we watch the news?* → see box at **TELEVISION**
4 that's news to me *spoken* used when you are surprised or annoyed because you have not been told something earlier: *He's married? That's news to me.*

News is always followed by a singular verb: *The news was very exciting.* You can say **some news**, **any news** etc, or **a piece of news**: *Is there any interesting news in the paper?*

'news ,agency *n* [C] a company that supplies news stories to newspapers, radio, and television

newsagent /'nju:z,eɪdʒənt $ 'nu:z-/ *n* [C] *BrE* **1 newsagent's** a shop that sells newspapers and magazines → see box at **SHOP** **2** someone who owns or works in a shop selling newspapers and magazines

N **'news ,bulletin** *n* [C] **1** *BrE* a short news programme on radio or television **2** *AmE* a short news report about something important that has just happened, given suddenly in the middle of a television or radio programme [= **newsflash** *BrE*]

newscast /'nju:zkɑ:st $ 'nu:zkæst/ *n* [C] *AmE* a news programme on television

newscaster /'nju:z,kɑ:stə $ 'nu:z,kæstər/ *n* [C] someone who reads the news on television

newsflash /'nju:zflæʃ $ 'nu:z-/ *n* [C] *BrE* a very short news report about something important that has just happened, given suddenly in the middle of a television or radio programme [= **news bulletin** *AmE*]

newsgroup /'nju:zgru:p $ 'nu:z-/ *n* [C] a discussion group on the Internet, with a place where people who share an interest can exchange messages

newsletter /'nju:z,letə $ 'nu:z,letər/ *n* [C] a printed report with news about an organization, sent regularly to its members: *our church newsletter*

newspaper /'nju:s,peɪpə $ 'nu:z,peɪpər/ *n*
1 [C] a set of folded pieces of paper printed with news, advertisements etc and sold daily or weekly [= **paper**]: **in the newspaper** *I saw his picture in the newspaper.* | **local/national newspaper** | *a newspaper article*

Types of newspaper
tabloid – a newspaper that has small pages, a lot of photographs, and not very much serious news
broadsheet – a serious newspaper that has large pages

Newspapers in general
the papers, the press, the media (=newspapers, TV, radio etc)

Parts of a newspaper
front/back page, sports/TV/arts etc page, headlines, article, column

People who write newspapers
editor, reporter, journalist, columnist

2 [C] a company that produces a newspaper [= **paper**]
3 [U] pieces of paper from old newspapers: *plates wrapped in newspaper*

newsprint /'nju:z,prɪnt $ 'nu:z-/ *n* [U] the paper and ink that is used to print newspapers

newsreader /'nju:z,ri:də $ 'nu:z,ri:dər/ *n* [C] *BrE* someone who reads the news on television or radio [= **anchor** *AmE*]

newsstand /'nju:zstænd $ 'nu:z-/ *n* [C] a place on a street where newspapers are sold

newsworthy /'nju:z,wɜ:ði $ 'nu:z,wɜ:rði/ *adj* important or interesting enough to be reported as news: *newsworthy events*

newt /nju:t $ nu:t/ *n* [C] a small animal with a long body, four legs, and a tail, which lives in water and on land

,New 'Testament *n* **the New Testament** the part of the Bible that describes the life of Jesus Christ [➞ **Old Testament**]

,new 'wave *n* [singular] people who try to introduce new ideas in music, films, art, politics etc: *the new wave of British cinema* —**new wave** *adj*

,New 'World *n* **the New World** North, Central, and South America

,New 'Year *n* [U] the time when you celebrate the beginning of the year: *Happy New Year!*

new year *n* **the new year** the first few weeks of a year: **in the new year** *Let's meet up in the new year.*

,New Year's 'Day *n* [singular,U] January 1st, the first day of the year in Western countries

,New Year's 'Eve *n* [singular,U] December 31st, the last day of the year in Western countries

next¹ /nekst/ *adj, determiner*
1 the next day, time, event etc is the one that happens after the present one: *They returned to New York the next day.* | *The next flight leaves in 45 minutes.* | *Next time* (=when something happens again)*, be more careful!* | **next Monday/May/year/summer etc** *See you next week.* | **the next thing sb knew** (=used when something surprising happens suddenly) *The next thing I knew I was lying face down on the table.*
2 the next place is the one closest to where you are now: *Turn left at the next corner.* | *the people at the next table*
3 the next person or thing in a list, series etc is the one after the present one: *Who will be the next President?* | *Read the next chapter by Friday.* | **the next biggest/largest etc** *Jo's the next oldest in the family.*
4 the next best thing something that is almost as good as what you really want: *Talking on the phone is the next best thing to being together.*

next² *adv*
1 immediately afterwards: *What shall we do next?* | *Next, write your name at the top of the page.*
2 next to sb/sth a) beside someone or something: *I sat next to a really nice guy on the plane.* → see picture on page A8 **b)** used to give a list of things you like, hate etc, when you want to say which you like, hate etc most: *Next to soccer, I like tennis best.*
3 on the next occasion: *When I next saw her, she ignored me.*
4 next to nothing very little: *I bought the car for next to nothing!*

next³ *pron*
1 the person or thing in a list, series etc that comes after the one you are dealing with now: *What's next on the shopping list?* | **the next to do sth** *Who's next to see the doctor?*
2 the week/year etc after next the week, year etc that follows the next one: *Let's meet some time the week after next.*

,next 'door *adv* **1** in the building that is nearest to your home: *The Simpsons live next door.* |

+to *Who's next door to you?* **2 next door to sth** in the building that is nearest to another building: *The post office is next door to the supermarket.* —**'next-door** *adj*: *my* **next-door neighbour**

,next of 'kin *n* [C] plural **next of kin** *formal* the person who has the closest family relationship to you, for example your husband, wife, or mother

NHS /,en eɪtʃ 'es/ *n* **the NHS** the National Health Service the British system that provides free medical treatment for everyone, paid for by taxes

nib /nɪb/ *n* [C] the part of a pen that puts the ink on the page

nibble /'nɪbəl/ *v* [I,T] to eat a small amount of food with very small bites → see box at EAT —**nibble** *n* [C]

nice /naɪs/ *adj*

1 pleasant, attractive, or enjoyable: *Did you have a nice time?* | *That's a nice sweater.* | **look/taste/ smell nice** *You look nice in that suit.* | **nice and warm/cool/sweet etc** *It's nice and warm in here.* | **a nice big/new/long etc sth** *a nice long holiday* | **It would be nice** *to go to Spain.*

THESAURUS

Words to describe a nice person
pleasant, friendly, kind, likeable, lovely, sweet, great

Words to describe something you do that is nice
enjoyable, great, fantastic, wonderful, brilliant
→ BAD, CHARACTER, HORRIBLE

2 friendly or kind: *They're all really nice people.* | **+to** *Everyone's been very nice to us since we arrived.* | **+about** *I said sorry and he was quite nice about it.* | **it is nice of sb (to do sth)** *It was nice of you to come.* → see box at KIND

3 (it's) nice to meet you also **nice meeting you** *spoken* used when you meet someone for the first time

,nice-'looking *adj* attractive: *a nice-looking guy*

nicely /'naɪsli/ *adv* **1** in a good, satisfactory, or attractive way: *'How's your love life going?' 'Very nicely, thanks!'* | *a* **nicely-dressed** *young man* **2** in a polite or pleasant way: *Don't forget to ask nicely.*

nicety /'naɪsəti/ *n* [C usually plural] plural **niceties** a small detail that is the difference between the correct and the incorrect way of doing something: *the niceties of the law*

niche /niːʃ, nɪtʃ $ nɪtʃ, niːʃ/ *n* [C] **1** a job or activity that is perfect for someone's abilities and character: *She found her niche as a fashion designer.* **2 niche market** *technical* a small group of people with particular needs or interests, that companies try to sell specific products to **3** a hollow place in a wall, often made to hold a STATUE

nick¹ /nɪk/ *n* [C] **1 in the nick of time** at the last moment before it is too late to do something: *The doctor arrived in the nick of time.* **2** a very small cut on the surface or edge of something **3 in good/bad nick** *BrE informal* in good or bad condition: *Our car's old but it's in good nick.*

nick² *v* [T] **1** to accidentally make a small cut on the surface or edge of something: *I nicked my*

chin when I was shaving. **2** *BrE informal* to steal something → see box at STEAL

nickel /'nɪkəl/ *n* **1** [U] a hard silver-white metal that is an ELEMENT and is used for making other metals **2** [C] a coin used in the US and Canada that is worth 5 cents

nickname /'nɪkneɪm/ *n* [C] a short or friendly name for someone that is used by their friends or family: *His nickname was 'Curly' because of his hair.* → see box at NAME —**nickname** *v* [T] *The puppy was soon nicknamed 'Trouble'.*

nicotine /'nɪkətiːn/ *n* [U] the substance in tobacco that makes you want to continue smoking

niece /niːs/ *n* [C] the daughter of your brother or sister, or the daughter of your husband's or wife's brother or sister [➙ **nephew**] → see box at RELATIVE

nifty /'nɪfti/ *adj informal* something that is nifty is good because it is effective or fast: *a nifty little gadget*

niggle /'nɪgəl/ *v* [T] to annoy or worry someone slightly: *Something's been niggling her all day.*

niggling /'nɪgəlɪŋ/ *adj* **niggling doubt/injury/ problem etc** a slight doubt, injury etc that does not go away

nigh /naɪ/ *adv* **1** *literary* near **2 well nigh/ nigh on** *old-fashioned* almost

night /naɪt/ *n* [C,U]

1 the time when it is dark, when people usually sleep [≠ **day**]: *I woke up in the middle of the night.* | *She works three nights a week.* | **at night** *It's very cold here at night.* | *The party went on* **all night.** | **in the night** *Did you hear the storm in the night?* | *He* **stayed the night** (=spent the night) *at a friend's house.* | **a late/early night** (=when you go to bed later or earlier than usual) *I'm tired. I think I'll have an early night.* | *What you need is* **a good night's sleep** (=a night when you sleep very well).

2 the evening: **last/tomorrow night** *Did you go out last night?* | *He goes out* **every night.** | **on Monday/Saturday etc night** *There's a party on Friday night.* | *We had a really good* **night out** (=an evening when you go to a restaurant, party etc). | *The park is open until* **late at night.**

3 night and day/day and night all the time: *The prisoners were guarded day and night.*

→ GOOD NIGHT, STAG NIGHT

nightclub /'naɪtklʌb/ *n* [C] a place where people go late in the evening to drink and dance

nightdress /'naɪtdres/ *n* [C] a piece of clothing, like a dress, that women wear in bed

'night ,duty *n* [U] work that is done during the night, as part of someone's job: *There are three nurses on night duty each night.*

nightfall /'naɪtfɔːl $ -fɔːl/ *n* [U] *literary* the time in the evening when it starts to get dark [= **dusk**]

nightgown /'naɪtgaʊn/ *n* [C] *old-fashioned* a nightdress

nightie /'naɪti/ *n* [C] *informal* a nightdress

nightingale /'naɪtɪŋgeɪl/ *n* [C] a small bird that sings beautifully, especially at night

nightlife /'naɪtlaɪf/ *n* [U] bars, clubs, restaurants etc that people can go to in the evening in a town or city: *Las Vegas is famous for its nightlife.*

nightlight /'naɪtlaɪt/ *n* [C] a small light that you put in a child's room at night

nightly /'naɪtli/ *adj, adv* happening every night: *a nightly news broadcast* | *The hotel has live music nightly.*

nightmare /'naɪtmeə $ -mer/ *n* [C] **1** a very frightening dream: **+about** *I still have nightmares about the accident.* **2** [usually singular] a very unpleasant or difficult experience: *The trip was an absolute nightmare.* | *It was every teacher's worst nightmare* (=the worst thing that could have happened). | *a nightmare journey* —**nightmarish** *adj*

'night school *n* [U] classes that you go to in the evening: *I'm studying Spanish at night school.*

'night shift *n* [C,U] a period of time at night when people regularly work: **work/do a night shift** *Doctors often have to work night shifts.* | **on (the) night shift** *Lee's on night shift this week.*

nightshirt /'naɪt-ʃɜːt $ -ʃɜːrt/ *n* [C] a long loose shirt that someone, especially a man, wears in bed

nightstand /'naɪtstænd/ *n* [C] *AmE* a small table beside a bed

nightstick /'naɪt,stɪk/ *n* [C] *AmE* a short stick carried as a weapon by police officers [= **truncheon** *BrE*]

'night-time *n* [U] the time during the night when it is dark: **at night-time** *It's quite noisy here at night-time.*

,night 'watchman *n* [C] someone whose job is to guard a building at night

nil /nɪl/ *n* [U] nothing or zero: *The score was seven nil.* | *His chances of winning are almost nil.* → see box at **ZERO**

nimble /'nɪmbəl/ *adj* able to move quickly and skilfully: *nimble fingers* —**nimbly** *adv*

nine /naɪn/ *number* the number 9: *He's only been in this job for nine months.* | *We open at nine* (=nine o'clock). | *Tim learnt to swim when he was nine* (=nine years old).

nineteen /,naɪn'tiːn◂/ *number*

1 the number 19: *It was nineteen minutes past seven.* | *I was only nineteen* (=19 years old).

2 nineteen to the dozen if someone talks nineteen to the dozen, they talk very quickly without stopping

—**nineteenth** *adj, pron*: *her nineteenth birthday* | *I'm planning to leave on the nineteenth* (=the 19th day of the month).

,nine-to-'five *adj* nine-to-five jobs or hours involve working between 9 o'clock in the morning and 5 o'clock in the afternoon: *Being a chef is not a nine-to-five job.* —**nine-to-five** *adv*: *If you want to work nine-to-five, don't become a nurse.*

ninety /'naɪnti/ *number*

1 the number 90

2 the nineties also **the '90s, the 1990s** [plural] the years from 1990 to 1999: **the early/mid/late nineties** *The industry received a lot bad publicity in the early nineties.*

3 be in your nineties to be aged between 90 and 99: **early/mid/late nineties** *He was in his late nineties when he died.*

4 in the nineties if the temperature is in the nineties, it is between 90 degrees and 99 degrees F

—**ninetieth** *adj*: *her ninetieth birthday*

ninth¹ /naɪnθ/ *adj* coming after eight other things in a series: *her ninth birthday* —**ninth** *pron*: *I'm planning to leave on the ninth* (=ninth day of the month).

ninth² *n* [C] one of nine equal parts of something

nip¹ /nɪp/ nipped, nipping *v* **1** [I] *BrE informal* to go somewhere quickly or for a short time: **+into/to etc** *I've got to nip into town.* **2** [I,T] to bite someone or something slightly: *The dog nipped her on the leg.* **3 nip sth in the bud** to prevent something from becoming a problem by stopping it as soon as it starts

nip² *n* [C] a slight bite

nipple /'nɪpəl/ *n* [C] **1** one of the two dark raised circles on your chest. Babies suck their mother's nipple to get milk. **2** *AmE* the piece of rubber that a baby sucks to get milk from a bottle [= **teat** *BrE*]

nippy /'nɪpi/ *adj informal* **1** weather that is nippy is cold **2** *BrE* able to move quickly: *a nippy little car*

nirvana /nɪə'vɑːnə, nɜː- $ nɪr-, nɜːr-/ *n* [U] the final state of complete knowledge and understanding that believers in Buddhism try to achieve

'nit-,picking *n* [U] when someone argues about small details or criticizes small mistakes in a way that annoys you —**nit-picking** *adj*

nitrate /'naɪtreɪt, -trət/ *n* [C,U] a chemical used on soil in order to make crops grow better

nitrogen /'naɪtrədʒən/ *n* [U] a gas that is the main part of the Earth's air

nits /nɪts/ *n* [plural] the eggs of a small insect that are sometimes found in people's hair

nitty-gritty /,nɪti 'grɪti/ *n* **the nitty-gritty** *informal* the basic and practical facts and details of something: **+of** *the nitty-gritty of finding a job* | *Let's get down to the nitty-gritty and work out costs.*

no¹ /nəʊ $ noʊ/ *spoken*

1 used to give a negative reply to a question, offer, or request [≠ **yes**]: *'Are you Spanish?' 'No, Italian.'* | *'Do you want some more coffee?' 'No thanks.'* | *I asked Dad if I could have a dog but he said no.* | *'Do you see her often?' 'Oh no, only about once a year.'*

2 used when you disagree with a statement: *'Gary's strange.' 'No, he's just shy.'*

3 used when you agree with a negative statement: *'He shouldn't drive so fast.' 'No, it's really dangerous.'*

4 used when you do not want someone to do something: *No, Jan, don't touch that switch.*

5 used when you are surprised, shocked, or annoyed by something: *Oh no, I've lost my keys!*

no² *determiner*

1 not any: *I'm sorry, there are no tickets left.* | *a house with no garage* | *'There's no need to explain,' he said.*

2 used on a sign to show that something is not allowed: *No smoking.*

no³ *adv* not any – used before a COMPARATIVE form: *We're inviting no more than thirty people.* | *I'll be back no later than 10 o'clock.*

no⁴ *n* [C] plural **noes** a negative answer or decision: *Her answer was a definite no.*

no. plural **nos.** the written abbreviation of **number**

nobility /nəʊ'bɪləti, nə- $ noʊ-, nə-/ *n* **1 the nobility** the group of people in some countries who have the highest social rank **2** [U] the quality of being morally good or generous

noble[1] /'nəʊbəl $ 'noʊ-/ adj **1** morally good or generous: *a noble ideal* **2** belonging to the nobility: *noble families* —**nobly** adv

noble[2] also **nobleman** /'nəʊbəlmən $ 'noʊ-/, **noblewoman** /'nəʊbəl,wʊmən $ 'noʊ-/ n [C] someone of the highest social rank

nobody[1] /'nəʊbədi $ 'noʊbɑːdi, -bədi/ pron NO ONE: *Nobody knows what will happen.* | *I'll have the cake if nobody else wants it.*

nobody[2] n [C] plural **nobodies** someone who is not important, successful, or famous: *I don't know why he's interested in a nobody like me.*

nocturnal /nɒk'tɜːnl $ nɑːk'tɜːr-/ adj **1** nocturnal animals are active at night and sleep during the day **2** formal happening at night

nod /nɒd $ nɑːd/ v [I,T] **nodded, nodding**

1 to move your head up and down, especially to say yes or to show that you understand something [➡ **shake**]: *'Are you Jill?' he asked. She smiled and nodded.* | *She nodded her head sympathetically.*

2 to move your head up and down once, in order to greet someone or to give them a sign: **+to/at/towards** *I nodded to the waiter.* | *'Sally's in there,' he said, nodding towards the kitchen.*

—**nod** n [C] *He gave a nod of agreement.*

nod off phr v informal to begin to sleep, often without intending to: *I kept nodding off during the lecture.*

nodule /'nɒdjuːl $ 'nɑːdʒuːl/ n [C] a small round raised part, especially a small swelling on a plant or someone's body

no-'frills adj having only features that are basic and necessary: *a no-frills airline*

no-'go ,area n [C] an area of a city where it is not safe for people to go because of the crime or violence there

noise /nɔɪz/ n [C,U] a sound, especially one that is unpleasant or loud: **+of** *the noise of traffic* | *The computer is making a strange noise.* | *He heard a whistling noise outside.* | *People living near the airport have complained about noise levels.*

THESAURUS

A **sound** is anything that you can hear: *the sound of voices*
A **noise** is usually a loud, unpleasant, or unexpected sound: *the deafening noise of overhead planes*

noiselessly /'nɔɪzləsli/ adv written without making any sound: *Adam crept noiselessly around the house.*

'noise pol,lution n [U] loud or continuous noise that is unpleasant and annoying

noisy /'nɔɪzi/ adj making a lot of noise, or full of noise [≠ **quiet**]: *noisy children* | *The bar was too noisy.* ➔ see box at **LOUD**
—**noisily** adv

nomad /'nəʊmæd $ 'noʊ-/ n [C] a member of a tribe that does not live in one place, but travels from place to place, usually in order to find grass for their animals —**nomadic** /nəʊ'mædɪk $ noʊ-/ adj

'no-man's ,land n [singular, U] land that no one owns or controls, especially an area between two opposing armies

nominal /'nɒmɪnəl $ 'nɑː-/ adj **1 nominal sum/charge/fee etc** a small amount of money, not what something would usually cost: *A nominal charge is made for use of the tennis court.* **2** officially described as something, when this is not really true: *He was the nominal leader of the campaign.*

nominally /'nɒmɪnəli $ 'nɑː-/ adv officially described as something, when this is not really true: *a nominally independent country*

nominate /'nɒmɪneɪt $ 'nɑː-/ v [T] to officially suggest that someone or something should be given an important position or prize: **nominate sb/sth for sth** *The film was nominated for an award.* | **nominate sb/sth as sth** *The party nominated him as presidential candidate.*
—**nomination** /,nɒmɪ'neɪʃən $,nɑː-/ n [C,U]

nominee /,nɒmɪ'niː $,nɑː-/ n [C] someone who has been nominated for something: *the Democratic Party's presidential nominee*

non- /nɒn $ nɑːn/ prefix not: *non-British visitors* | *non-smokers* (=people who do not smoke)

,non-ag'gression n [U] when a country or government does not use military force or threats against another

,non-alco'holic adj a non-alcoholic drink does not have any alcohol in it

nonchalant /'nɒnʃələnt $,nɑːnʃə'lɑːnt/ adj not seeming worried or interested: *'Will John be at the party?' she asked, trying to sound nonchalant.* | *a nonchalant shrug*
—**nonchalance** n [U] —**nonchalantly** adv

,non-'combatant / $,. .'../ n [C] a member of an army who does not fight, for example an army doctor

,non-com'mittal adj not giving a definite answer, or not showing what your intentions are: *a noncommittal reply* —**noncommittally** adv

nonconformist /,nɒnkən'fɔːmɪst◂ $,nɑːnkən 'fɔːr-/ adj having different beliefs or different ways of doing something from most other people: *nonconformist writers* —**nonconformist** n [C]

nondescript /'nɒndɪ,skrɪpt $,nɑːndɪ'skrɪpt/ adj disapproving not having any noticeable or interesting qualities: *a nondescript brown suit*

none[1] /nʌn/ pron not any of something, or not one person or thing: *'Can I have some more coffee?' 'Sorry, there's none left.'* | **+of** *None of the money was missing.* | *None of us really knew him.* | *Small improvements are better than none at all.*

GRAMMAR

When you use **none** with a U noun, the verb is singular: *None of the food was left.*
When you use **none** with a plural noun form, the verb can be singular or plural: *None of my friends was/were there.*

none[2] adv **1 none too** not at all: *He's none too happy with the situation.* | *She put the glass down none too gently.* **2 none the worse/wiser** not any worse than before, or not knowing any more than before: **+for** *She seems none the worse for her terrible experience.*

nonentity /nɒ'nentɪti $ nɑː-/ n [C] plural **nonentities** someone who is not important or special in any way

nonetheless /ˌnʌnðəˈles/ adv formal in spite of what has just been mentioned [= **nevertheless**]: *The information was complicated but nonetheless helpful.*

ˌnon-eˈvent n [C usually singular] informal an event that is much less exciting or interesting than you expected: *My 21st birthday was a complete non-event.*

nonexistent /ˌnɒnɪɡˈzɪstənt◂ $ ˌnɑːn-/ adj not existing at all: **almost/virtually/practically nonexistent** *Industry in the area is virtually nonexistent.*

ˌnon-ˈfiction n [U] books about real facts or events [≠ fiction] → see box at **BOOK**

ˌnon-ˈflammable adj materials or substances that are non-flammable do not burn easily or do not burn at all [≠ flammable, inflammable]

ˌnon-interˈvention n [U] when a government of a powerful country does not get involved in the affairs of other countries

ˈno-no n [singular] informal something that you must not do because people think it is unacceptable: *At that time, wearing a short skirt was a definite no-no.*

ˌno-ˈnonsense adj [only before noun] very practical and sensible: *a no-nonsense attitude to work*

nonpayment /ˌnɒnˈpeɪmənt $ ˌnɒːn-/ n [U] when you do not pay money that you owe: **+of** *nonpayment of rent*

nonplussed /nɒnˈplʌst $ nɑːn-/ adj [not before noun] not knowing what to do or say because you are so surprised: *He was a little nonplussed by the question.* → see box at **SURPRISED**

ˌnon-ˈprofit also **ˌnon-ˈprofitmaking** BrE adj a non-profit organization uses the money it earns to help people instead of making a profit

ˌnon-prolifeˈration n [U] the POLICY of limiting the number of NUCLEAR or chemical weapons in the world

ˌnon-reˈnewable adj non-renewable types of energy such as coal or gas cannot be replaced after they have been used

ˌnon-ˈresident n [C] **1** someone who does not live permanently in a particular country **2** BrE someone who is not staying in a particular hotel: *The hotel restaurant is open to non-residents.*

nonsense /ˈnɒnsəns $ ˈnɑːnsens/ n [U]

1 statements or opinions that are not true or seem very stupid [= rubbish BrE]: **absolute/complete/utter nonsense** *He described the rumours as 'absolute nonsense'.* | **+about** *Do you believe all this nonsense about ghosts?* | *Now you're **talking nonsense**.* | *I've never heard such **a load of nonsense** (=a lot of nonsense).* | **it is nonsense to do sth** *It's nonsense to say that mistakes are never made.*

2 stupid and annoying behaviour: *I'm not putting up with any more of this nonsense!*

3 speech or writing that you cannot understand because it has no meaning

—**nonsensical** /nɒnˈsensɪkəl $ nɑːn-/ adj

ˌnon-ˈsmoker n [C] someone who does not smoke

ˌnon-ˈsmoking adj a non-smoking area or building is one where smoking is not allowed

ˌnon-ˈstandard adj **1** non-standard ways of speaking are considered to be incorrect by a lot of people **2** not the usual type or size: *a non-standard size*

ˌnon-ˈstarter n [C usually singular] informal something or someone that is very unlikely to succeed: *The idea is a complete non-starter.*

nonstick /ˌnɒnˈstɪk◂ $ ˌnɑːn-/ adj a nonstick pan has a special surface that food will not stick to

nonstop /ˌnɒnˈstɒp◂ $ ˌnɑːnˈstɑːp◂/ adj, adv without stopping: *Dan worked nonstop for 12 hours.* | *a nonstop flight from Vancouver to London*

nonviolence /ˌnɒnˈvaɪələns $ ˌnɑːn-/ n [U] when people try to make political or social changes without using violence: *a policy of non-violence* —**nonviolent** adj

noodles /ˈnuːdlz/ n [plural] long thin pieces of food made from flour, water, and eggs, usually cooked in boiling water

nook /nʊk/ n **1** [C] literary a small quiet place: *a shady nook* **2 every nook and cranny** every part of a place: *We searched every nook and cranny.*

noon /nuːn/ n [U] 12 o'clock in the middle of the day [= midday]: **at/by/before noon** *They left at noon.* | *The wedding is at 12 noon.*

ˈno one also **nobody** pron not anyone: *No one saw him arrive.* | *She whispered so that **no one else** could hear.*

noose /nuːs/ n [C] a circle of rope that can be pulled tight to catch animals or hang someone

nope /nəʊp $ noʊp/ adv spoken informal used to say 'no' when you answer someone: *'Hungry?' 'Nope, I just ate.'*

ˈno place adv especially AmE informal nowhere: *There's no place left to hide.*

nor /nɔː $ nɔːr/ linking word, adv

1 neither ... nor used to show that two things are not true or do not happen: *Julie was neither shocked nor surprised by the news.* | *They can neither read nor write.*

2 formal used after a negative statement and before another negative statement: *She didn't reply, nor did she look at him.*

3 nor can I/nor did he etc used after a negative statement to say that the same thing is true for someone or something else: *'I don't want to go.' 'Nor do I.'*

norm /nɔːm $ nɔːrm/ n **1 the norm** what is usual or normal: *a country where disease and poverty are the norm* **2 norms** [plural] the usual and acceptable ways of behaving: *cultural and social norms*

normal /ˈnɔːməl $ ˈnɔːr-/ adj

1 usual, typical, or expected [➡ abnormal]: *He just wanted a normal life.* | *I'll be glad when things get **back to normal**.* | *The test was done **in the normal way**.* | *It's normal to feel nervous before an operation.* | **quite/perfectly normal** *His voice sounded perfectly normal.*

THESAURUS

ordinary – not special or unusual: *an ordinary day*

average – typical of a normal person or thing: *the average family*

standard – used about products or methods that are the most usual type: *We only sell shoes in standard sizes.*

routine – used about something that is done regularly and is part of a normal system: *a routine check of the plane*

conventional – used when comparing a piece of equipment, method etc that has been used for a long time with something that is new and different: *microwaves and conventional ovens*
→ **NATURAL**

2 someone who is normal is mentally and physically healthy and behaves like most other people: *a perfectly normal little boy*

normality /nɔːˈmælɪ̩ti $ nɔːr-/ also **normalcy** /ˈnɔːrməlsi $ ˈnɔːr-/ *AmE n* [U] a situation in which everything happens in the usual way: *a return to normality after years of war*

normalize also **-ise** *BrE* /ˈnɔːrməlaɪz $ ˈnɔːr-/ *v* [I,T] to become normal again, or to make a situation become normal again: *The two countries are working to* ***normalize*** *relations.* —**normalization** /ˌnɔːrməlaɪˈzeɪʃən $ ˌnɔːrmələ-/ *n* [U]

normally /ˈnɔːrməli $ ˈnɔːr-/ *adv*
1 usually: *I normally cycle to college.*
2 in the usual or expected way: *Try to relax and breathe normally.*

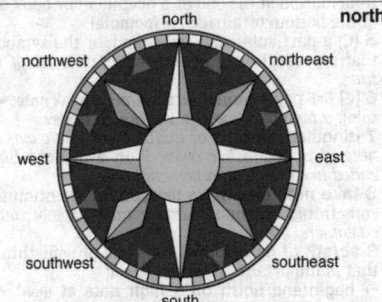

north | **north**
northwest | northeast
west | east
southwest | southeast
south

north¹, **North** /nɔːrθ $ nɔːrθ/ *n* [singular,U] written abbreviation **N**
1 the direction towards the top of a map: *Which way is north?* | **from/towards the north** *The army is approaching from the north.* | **to the north (of sth)** *Santorini is about 110km to the north of Crete.*
2 the north the northern part of a country or area: *The north will be dry and bright.* | **+of** *the north of France*

north², **North** *adj* [only before noun] written abbreviation **N**
1 in the north or facing the north: *the north side of the building* | *He lives in North Wales.*
2 a north wind comes from the north

north³ *adv* written abbreviation **N**
1 towards the north: *The birds fly north in the summer.* | **+of** *Chicago is four hours north of Indianapolis.*
2 up north *informal* to or in the north of the country: *They've moved up north.*

northbound /ˈnɔːrθbaʊnd $ ˈnɔːrθ-/ *adj* travelling or leading towards the north: *northbound traffic*

northeast¹, **Northeast** /ˌnɔːrθˈiːst $ ˌnɔːrθ-/ *n* [U] written abbreviation **NE** **1** the direction that is exactly between north and east → see picture at **NORTH¹** **2 the northeast** the northeastern part of a country —**northeast** *adv*: *He headed northeast across the open sea.*

northeast², **Northeast** *adj* written abbreviation **NE** **1** a northeast wind comes from the northeast **2** in the northeast of a place: *the northeast outskirts of Las Vegas*

northeasterly /ˌnɔːrθˈiːstəli $ ˌnɔːrθˈiːstərli/ *adj* **1** towards or in the northeast: *They set off in a northeasterly direction.* **2** a northeasterly wind comes from the northeast

northeastern /ˌnɔːrθˈiːstən $ ˌnɔːrθˈiːstərn/ *adj* written abbreviation **NE** in or from the northeast part of a country or area: *the northeastern states of the US*

northerly /ˈnɔːrðəli $ ˈnɔːrðərli/ *adj* **1** towards or in the north: *We set off in a northerly direction.* **2** a northerly wind comes from the north

northern, **Northern** /ˈnɔːrðən $ ˈnɔːrðərn/ *adj* written abbreviation **N** in or from the north of a country or area: *a man with a northern accent* | *northern Europe*

northerner, **Northerner** /ˈnɔːrðənə $ ˈnɔːrðərnər/ *n* [C] someone from the northern part of a country

northernmost /ˈnɔːrðənməʊst $ ˈnɔːrðərnmoʊst/ *adj* furthest north: *the northernmost tip of the island*

North ˈPole *n* **the North Pole** the most northern point on the surface of the Earth → see picture at **GLOBE**

northwards /ˈnɔːrθwədz $ ˈnɔːrθwərdz/ also **northward** *adv* towards the north: *We sailed northwards.* —**northward** *adj*: *the northward journey*

northwest¹, **Northwest** /ˌnɔːrθˈwest‹ $ ˌnɔːrθ-/ *n* [U] written abbreviation **NW** **1** the direction that is exactly between north and west → see picture at **NORTH¹** **2 the northwest** the northwestern part of a country —**northwest** *adv*: *She rode northwest toward Boulder.*

northwest², **Northwest** *adj* written abbreviation **NW** **1** a northwest wind comes from the northwest **2** in the northwest of a place: *the northwest suburbs of the city*

northwesterly /ˌnɔːrθˈwestəli $ ˌnɔːrθˈwestərli/ *adj* **1** towards or in the northwest: *They set off in a northwesterly direction.* **2** a northwesterly wind comes from the northwest

northwestern /ˌnɔːrθˈwestən $ ˈnɔːrθˈwestərn/ *adj* written abbreviation **NW** in or from the northwest part of a country or area: *a town in northwestern Canada*

nose¹ /nəʊz $ noʊz/ *n* [C]
1 the part of your face that you use for smelling and breathing [→ **nasal, nostril**]: *a broken nose* | *He had a long nose.* | *He took out a tissue and* ***blew his nose*** (=cleared his nose by blowing). | *I had a sore throat and* ***runny nose*** (=liquid was coming out of it). | **red-nosed/long-nosed etc** → see picture on page A3
2 (right) under sb's nose so close to someone that they should notice, but do not: *The crime was committed right under the nose of a police officer.*
3 stick/poke your nose into sth *informal* to be too interested in a situation that should not involve you, in a way that annoys people: *I wish he'd stop poking his nose into my business.*
4 keep your nose out (of sth) *informal* to avoid

N

becoming involved in a situation that should not involve you

5 get up sb's nose *informal* to annoy someone

6 turn your nose up at sth to refuse to accept something because you do not think it is good enough for you: *Shoppers are turning their noses up at cheap cuts of meat.*

7 look down your nose at sb to think you are much better than someone else

8 the front end of a plane, ROCKET etc

nose² *v* [I] if a vehicle noses forward, it moves forward slowly and carefully [= edge]: **+forward/ out etc** *The taxi nosed out into the traffic.*

nose around (sth) also **nose about (sth)** *BrE* *phr v* to look around a place in order to find something where no one else is there: *I don't like the idea of someone nosing around my house.*

nosebleed /'nəʊzbliːd $ 'noʊz-/ *n* [C] if you have a nosebleed, blood comes out of your nose

nosedive /'nəʊzdaɪv $ 'noʊz-/ *n* [C] **1** a sudden big fall in the price, value, or amount of something: *Profits took a nosedive last year.* **2** a sudden steep drop by a plane, with its front end pointing towards the ground —**nosedive** *v* [I]

nosey /'nəʊzi $ 'noʊ-/ *adj* another spelling of NOSY

nostalgia /nɒ'stældʒə $ nɑː-/ *n* [singular, U] the slightly sad feeling you have when you think about nice things that happened in the past: **+for** *He felt a brief nostalgia for his life on the farm.* —**nostalgic** *adj* —**nostalgically** /-kli/ *adv*

nostril /'nɒstrəl $ 'nɑː-/ *n* [C] one of the two holes at the bottom end of your nose, which you breathe through → see picture on page A3

nosy, nosey /'nəʊzi $ 'noʊ-/ *adj* always trying to find out private information about someone: *Our neighbours are really nosy.* —**nosiness** *n* [U]

not /nɒt $ nɑːt/ *adv*

1 used to make a word or statement negative [➡ no]: *Most stores are not open on Sundays.* | *He does not speak English.* | *There were not many people there.* | **not at all/not ... at all** (=used to emphasize what you are saying) *I was not at all surprised to see her.* | *I did not like her at all.* | **not a lot/not much** (=little) *Not much is known about the disease.*

2 used in order to make a word or expression have the opposite meaning: *Edinburgh is not far now.* | *The food is not very good here.* | *Not many people* (=only a few) *have read the report.* | *Most of the hotels are not that cheap* (=they are expensive).

3 used instead of a whole phrase to mean the opposite of what has been mentioned before it [➡ so]: *No one knows if the story is true or not.* | *'Is Mark still ill?' 'I hope not'.*

4 not only in addition to being or doing something: **not only ... (but) also** *She's not only funny, she's also clever.*

5 not a/not one not any person or thing; none: *Not one of the students knew the answer.* | *There wasn't a cloud in the sky.*

notable /'nəʊtəbəl $ 'noʊ-/ *adj* important, interesting, or unusual enough to be noticed: **+for** *an area notable for its forests*

notably /'nəʊtəbli/ *adv* especially; particularly: *Some politicians, most notably the President, refused to comment.*

notation /nəʊ'teɪʃən $ noʊ-/ *n* [C,U] a system of marks and signs to show musical sounds, numbers etc

notch¹ /nɒtʃ $ nɑːtʃ/ *n* [C] **1** a level of something, for example quality or achievement: *Her new book is several notches above anything else she has written.* **2** a V-shaped cut in a surface or edge

notch² *v*

notch sth ⇔ up *phr v* to achieve a victory or a particular total: *He has notched up four goals in four games.*

note¹ /nəʊt $ noʊt/ *n*

1 [C] something that you write down in order to remember something: *I'll just make a note of your new address.* | *Keep a note of any problems that you have.* → see box at WRITE

2 notes [plural] information that a student writes down in a lesson or from a book: *Did you take notes during the lecture?* | *lecture notes*

3 [C] a short informal letter: *I wrote Jane a short note to thank her for the meal.* | *This is just a quick note to let you know that I can't come.*

4 [C] a short piece of writing that gives extra information at the end of a document or book or at the bottom of a page [➡ footnote]

5 [C] a particular musical sound, or the symbol that represents it: *He hummed a few notes of a tune.*

6 [C] *BrE* paper money [= bill *AmE*; = bank note; ➡ coin]: *a ten-pound note* → see box at MONEY

7 [singular] a feeling or quality: **+of** *There was a note of doubt in her voice.* | **on a ... note** *She ended her speech on a personal note.*

8 take note (of sth) to pay careful attention to something: *We must always take note of our customers' views.*

9 sb/sth of note *formal* someone or something that is important: *a writer of note*

→ **begin/end/finish on a high note** at HIGH¹ → **compare notes (with sb)** at COMPARE → **note of caution** at CAUTION¹

note² *v* [T] **1** to notice or pay careful attention to something: **+that** *Please note that the museum is closed on Mondays.* **2** also **note down** to write something down so that you will remember it: *He noted down my name.*

notebook /'nəʊtbʊk $ 'noʊt-/ *n* [C] **1** a book in which you can write notes → see picture at CLASSROOM **2** a small computer that is about the size of a book

noted /'nəʊtᵻd $ 'noʊ-/ *adj* well-known or famous: *a noted author* | **+for** *an area noted for its cheeses*

notepad /'nəʊtpæd $ 'noʊt-/ *n* [C] a group of sheets of paper fastened together at the top, used for writing notes

notepaper /'nəʊt,peɪpə $ 'noʊt,peɪpər/ *n* [U] paper used for writing letters

noteworthy /'nəʊt,wɜːði $ 'noʊt,wɜːr-/ *adj* *formal* important or interesting enough to deserve attention: *a noteworthy event*

nothing¹ /'nʌθɪŋ/ *pron*

1 not anything: *There's nothing in the bag.* | *There was nothing else we could do.* | *He had nothing more to say.* | *We know nothing about her family.* | *I couldn't just do nothing.*

2 nothing but only: *We've had nothing but rain for two weeks.*

3 have nothing against sb/sth if you have

nothing against someone or something, they do not annoy or offend you: *I have nothing against him personally.*

4 not anything that you consider to be important or interesting: *There's nothing on television tonight.* | *'What did you say?' 'Oh, nothing.'*

5 zero, or zero points [= nil *BrE*]: *The Red Sox won the game three nothing.* → see box at ZERO

6 have/be nothing to do with sb/sth to not be connected or involved with someone or something: *I had nothing to do with the decision.* | *It's got nothing to do with you.*

7 for nothing without any result or payment: *I did all that work for nothing.*

8 there's nothing like sth used to say that something is very good: *There's nothing like a hot bath at the end of a tiring day.*

9 there's nothing in/to sth used to say that what people are saying about someone or something is not true: *It seems there's nothing in the rumours that she is going to leave.*

10 if nothing else used to emphasize that there is one good quality or feature, although it may be the only one: *If nothing else, Jack is good at making decisions.*

nothing[2] *adv* **be nothing like sb/sth** to have no qualities that are similar to someone or something: *She's nothing like her brother.*

nothingness /'nʌθɪŋnɪ̣s/ *n* [U] a state of complete emptiness, where nothing exists

notice[1] /'nəʊtɪ̣s $ 'noʊ-/ *v* [I,T] to see, feel, or hear someone or something: *I said 'hello,' but she didn't notice.* | +**(that)** *Max noticed that her hands were shaking.* | +**who/what/how etc** *She hadn't noticed before how tired he looked.* | **notice sb/sth doing sth** *Did you notice him leaving the party early?* → see box at SEE

notice[2] *n*

1 [U] when you notice or pay attention to someone or something: *Don't take any notice of her, she's just annoyed.* | *I waved but she took no notice.* | *It came to the notice of the committee* (=they noticed) *that many members had not paid their fees.*

2 [C] a written or printed statement that gives information or a warning to people [→ sign]: *The notice said 'No Entry'.* | *I'll put up a notice about the meeting.*

3 [U] information or a warning about something that will happen: *You must give the bank three days' notice before closing your account.*

4 until further notice from now until another change is announced: *The store will be closed until further notice.*

5 hand in your notice/give (your) notice to tell your employer that you will soon be leaving your job [→ resign]

6 at short notice *BrE*; **on short notice** *AmE* if you do something at short notice, you do not have much time to prepare for it: *Thanks for agreeing to see me at such short notice.*

noticeable /'nəʊtɪ̣səbəl $ 'noʊ-/ *adj* easy to notice: *There's been a noticeable improvement in your work.*

THESAURUS

clear: *a clear difference in meaning*
obvious: *an obvious mistake*
conspicuous – too noticeable: *I felt conspicuous in my red coat.*

eye-catching – noticeable and attractive: *an attractive eye-catching design*

—**noticeably** *adv*

noticeboard /'nəʊtɪ̣s,bɔːd $ 'noʊtɪ̣s,bɔːrd/ *n* [C] *BrE* a board on a wall that notices can be fixed to [= **bulletin board** *AmE*] → see picture at CLASSROOM

notify /'nəʊtɪ̣faɪ $ 'noʊ-/ *v* [T] **notified, notifying, notifies** *formal* to tell someone something officially [= **inform**]: *Have you notified the police?*
—**notification** /,nəʊtɪ̣fɪ̣'keɪʃən $,noʊ-/ *n* [C,U]

notion /'nəʊʃən $ 'noʊ-/ *n* [C] an idea, belief, or opinion about something, especially one that is wrong: *Where did you get the notion that I was leaving?*

notoriety /,nəʊtə'raɪəti $,noʊ-/ *n* [U] when someone is famous for doing something bad

notorious /nəʊ'tɔːriəs, nə- $ noʊ-, nə-/ *adj* famous for something bad: +**for** *The city is notorious for its rainy weather.* → see box at FAMOUS
—**notoriously** *adv*

notwithstanding /,nɒtwɪθ'stændɪŋ, -wɪð- $,nɑːt-/ *prep, adv formal* in spite of something: *The team has continued to be successful notwithstanding recent criticism.*

nought /nɔːt $ nɒːt/ *number BrE* the number 0 [= zero]: *A billion is 1 with 9 noughts after it.* | **nought point one/two/three etc** (=0.1, 0.2, 0.3 etc) → see box at ZERO

noun /naʊn/ *n* [C] in grammar, a word that is the name of a person (such as 'Michael' or 'teacher'), place (such as 'France' or 'school'), thing or activity (such as 'coffee' or 'football'), or quality or idea (such as 'danger' or 'happiness') → PROPER NOUN

nourish /'nʌrɪʃ $ 'nɜːrɪʃ, 'nʌ-/ *v* [T] to give a person, animal, or plant the food they need in order to live and grow: *healthy well-nourished children*

nourishing /'nʌrɪʃɪŋ $ 'nɜː-, 'nʌ-/ *adj* nourishing food makes you strong and healthy: *nourishing soup* → see box at FOOD

nourishment /'nʌrɪʃmənt $ 'nɜː-, 'nʌ-/ *n* [U] *formal* food that is needed to live, grow, and be healthy

novel[1] /'nɒvəl $ 'nɑː-/ *n* [C] a long written story about characters and events that are not real [→ fiction]: *the novels of Jane Austen* | *He's written several novels.* → see box at BOOK

novel[2] *adj* new, different, and unusual: *What a novel idea!*

novelist /'nɒvəlɪ̣st $ 'nɑː-/ *n* [C] someone who writes novels

novelty /'nɒvəlti $ 'nɑː-/ *n plural* **novelties**
1 [C] something that is new and unusual: *In the 1950s, television was still a novelty.* **2** [U] the quality of being new, different, and unusual: *the novelty of using the new type of mobile phone*
3 [C] a small cheap object often given as a present

November /nəʊ'vembə, nə- $ noʊ'vembər, nə-/ *n* [C,U] *written abbreviation* **Nov.** the 11th month of the year, between October and December: **next/last November** *We met last November.* | **in November** *It snowed in early November.* | **on November 6th** *The match will take place on November 6th.* → see box at MONTH

novice /'nɒvɪ̣s $ 'nɑː-/ *n* [C] someone who has just begun learning a skill or activity: *a novice at chess*

now¹ /naʊ/ *adv*

1 at the present time: *Jean and her husband are now living in Canada.* | **right now/just now** (=at the time of speaking) *Right now, we're not really ready to decide.* | **by/before now** (=before the present time) *Steve should be home by now.* | **from now on** (=starting now) *Meetings will be held on Friday from now on.* | **for now** (=for a short time) *You can leave your bags in the hall for now.*

THESAURUS

at present, at/for the moment, presently *AmE*, currently

2 immediately: *The bell has rung – stop writing now.* | *If we leave now, we'll be there before dark.*
3 3 weeks/2 years etc now used when saying how long ago something started: *It's been over a year now since I started working here.*
4 (every) now and then/now and again sometimes: *He sees her every now and then at the college.*
5 *spoken* used to get someone's attention, when you are going to ask for information, or when you pause: *Now, let's discuss payment.* | *Now what did you say your name was?*

now² also **'now then** *linking word* because of something or as a result of something: *Now that the kids have left home, the house feels empty.* | *I'm going to relax now the school year is over.*

nowadays /'naʊədeɪz/ *adv* now, compared to what happened in the past: *People live longer nowadays.*

,no 'way *adv spoken* used to emphasize that you will not agree or be able to do something: *'Are you going to work over the weekend?' 'No way!'* | *No way will we be finished by five o'clock.* | *There's no way I'm going to pay £300 just for a weekend in Paris.*

nowhere /'nəʊweə $ 'noʊwer/ *adv*

1 not in or to any place: **nowhere to go/live/sit etc** *He's got nowhere to sleep tonight.* | *There's nowhere to put anything in our new apartment.*
2 get nowhere to have no success, or to make no progress: **+with** *He was getting nowhere with his new play.* | *A negative attitude will get you nowhere.*
3 nowhere near a) far from a particular place: *Buffalo is nowhere near New York City.* **b)** not at all: *The building's nowhere near finished.*
4 nowhere to be seen/found also **nowhere in sight** not in a particular place: *Her husband was nowhere to be seen.*
5 from nowhere happening or appearing suddenly and without warning: *The policeman appeared as if from nowhere.*

no-'win situ,ation *n* [C] a situation which will end badly whatever you decide to do

noxious /'nɒkʃəs $ 'nɑːk-/ *adj formal* harmful or poisonous: *noxious chemicals*

nozzle /'nɒzəl $ 'nɑː-/ *n* [C] a short tube on the end of a pipe or HOSE that controls the amount of liquid coming out

nr *BrE* the written abbreviation of **near**

n't /nt/ the short form of 'not': *He isn't* (=is not) *here.* | *She can't* (=cannot) *see him.* | *I didn't* (=did not) *do it.*

nuance /'njuːɑːns $ 'nuː-/ *n* [C,U] a very small difference in meaning, colour, or feeling

nuclear /'njuːkliə $ 'nuːkliər/ *adj*

1 relating to or involving the NUCLEUS (=central part) of an atom, or the energy produced when the nucleus of an atom is either split or joined with the nucleus of another atom: *a nuclear power station* | *France relies on **nuclear energy**.* | *nuclear physics*
2 relating to or involving the use of weapons that use nuclear energy: *a nuclear war* | *nuclear weapons* | *a nuclear bomb*

,nuclear dis'armament *n* [U] when a country or government gets rid of its NUCLEAR weapons

,nuclear 'family *n* [C] a family that consists of a father, mother, and children

,nuclear re'actor *n* [C] a large machine that produces nuclear energy

nucleus /'njuːkliəs $ 'nuː-/ *n* [C] plural **nuclei** /-kliaɪ/ **1** the central part of an atom or cell **2 the nucleus of sth** the most important part of something: *Photographs by Weston form the nucleus of the collection.*

nude¹ /njuːd $ nuːd/ *adj* not wearing any clothes [= **naked**] —**nudity** *n* [U]

nude² *n* **1** [C] a painting, photograph etc of someone who is not wearing clothes **2 in the nude** not wearing any clothes

nudge /nʌdʒ/ *v* [T] to push someone or something gently with your elbow: *Ken nudged me and said, 'Look!'* → see box at **PUSH** —**nudge** *n* [C]

nudist /'njuːdɪst $ 'nuː-/ *n* [C] someone who believes it is good for you to wear no clothes —**nudist** *adj*: *a nudist beach* —**nudism** *n* [U]

nudity /'njuːdɪ̥ti $ 'nuː-/ *n* [U] when people are not wearing any clothes: *There are scenes of nudity in the play.*

nugget /'nʌgɪ̥t/ *n* [C] a small rough piece of a valuable metal: *a gold nugget*

nuisance /'njuːsəns $ 'nuː-/ *n* [C usually singular] someone or something that annoys you or causes problems: *Sorry to be a nuisance, but could I use your phone?* | **what a nuisance** *BrE spoken*: *What a nuisance! I've forgotten my keys.*

nuke¹ /njuːk $ nuːk/ *v* [T] *informal* to attack a place using NUCLEAR weapons

nuke² *n* [C] *informal* a NUCLEAR weapon

null and void /,nʌl ənd 'vɔɪd/ *adj law* having no legal authority: *The court declared the contract to be null and void.*

nullify /'nʌlɪ̥faɪ/ *v* [T] **nullified, nullifying, nullifies 1** *law* to state officially that something has no legal force: *The Senate has voted to nullify the decree.* **2** *formal* to make something less powerful or effective: *Recent wage increases have been nullified by inflation.*

numb¹ /nʌm/ *adj* **1** not able to feel anything: *My feet were numb with cold.* **2** very shocked and unable to think or speak: *We all felt numb when we heard the news.* —**numbness** *n* [U] —**numbly** *adv*

numb² *v* [T] **1** to make a part of your body unable to feel anything: *The cold wind numbed my face.* **2** to make someone unable to think, feel, or react in a normal way

number¹ /'nʌmbə $ -bər/ *n*

1 [C] a word or sign that shows an amount or quantity [→ **figure**]: *Add the numbers 7, 4, and 3.* | *Five was her lucky number.* | **an odd number** (=1, 3, 5, 7, 9 etc) | **an even number** (=2, 4, 6, 8, 10 etc)

2 [C] a telephone number: *My new number is 502–6155.* | *Sorry, you have the **wrong number**.*

3 [C] a number used to show the position of something in a set or list: *Look at question number 5.* | *a number 17 bus*

4 [C] a set of numbers used to recognize something: *What's your credit card number?*

5 [C,U] an amount of something that can be counted: **the number of sth** *an increase in the number of cars on the roads* | **a number of sth** (=several) *We received a number of complaints.* | **a large/small/ significant/growing etc number of sth** *a small number of people affected* | *Young people have been leaving the countryside for the towns **in large numbers**.* | *What sort of numbers (=how many people) are you expecting at the party?*

6 [C] a single piece of popular music out of several performed together

→ CARDINAL NUMBER, ORDINAL NUMBER, REGISTRATION NUMBER, SERIAL NUMBER, WHOLE NUMBER

number² *v* **1** [T] to give a number to something that is part of a set or list: *Number the items from one to ten.* **2** [linking verb] if people or things number a particular amount, that is how many there are in: *The crowd numbered around 20,000.*

'number ,plate *n* [C] *BrE* the sign on the front and back of a vehicle that shows its official number [= license plate *AmE*] → see picture on page A12

numeracy /'njuːmərəsi $ 'nuː-/ *n* [U] the ability to do calculations and understand simple mathematics [➔ literacy]: *numeracy skills*

numeral /'njuːmərəl $ 'nuː-/ *n* [C] a written sign such as 5 or 22 used to show a number: *Roman numerals* —**numeral** *adj*

numerate /'njuːmərɨt $ 'nuː-/ *adj* able to understand basic mathematics

numerical /njuː'merɪkəl $ nuː-/ *adj* expressed in numbers, or relating to numbers: **in numerical order** (=numbered 1, 2, 3 etc) *The pages should be in numerical order.* —**numerically** /-kli/ *adv*

numerous /'njuːmərəs $ 'nuː-/ *adj formal* many: *We've discussed this before on **numerous occasions**.*

nun /nʌn/ *n* [C] a member of a group of religious women that lives apart from other people in a CONVENT [➔ monk]

nurse¹ /nɜːs $ nɜːrs/ *n* [C] someone whose job is to look after people who are ill or injured: *a male nurse* | *the school nurse* | *a student nurse* (=someone who is learning to be a nurse)

nurse² *v* **1** [T] to look after someone who is ill or injured **2** [T] to rest when you have an injury so that it will get better: *Blake is nursing an ankle injury.* **3** [I, T] to BREAST-FEED a baby **4** [T] to have an idea or feeling in your mind for a long time: *Tom had always nursed an ambition to be a pilot.*

nursery /'nɜːsəri $ 'nɜːr-/ *n plural* **nurseries** **1** [C] a place where young children are looked after during the day [= day care centre] **2** [C] a place where plants and trees are grown and sold → see box at SHOP

'nursery rhyme *n* [C] a short song or poem for children

'nursery ,school *n* [C] a school for children between three and five years old

nursing /'nɜːsɪŋ $ 'nɜːr-/ *n* [U] the job of looking after people who are ill, injured, or very old: *the nursing profession*

'nursing home *n* [C] a small hospital for people who are too old or ill to take care of themselves

nurture /'nɜːtʃə $ 'nɜːrtʃər/ *v* [T] *formal* **1** to help a plan, feeling etc develop: *We will nurture closer relationships with companies abroad.* **2** to feed and look after a child, plant etc while it is growing: *children nurtured by loving parents*

nut /nʌt/ *n* [C]

1 a large seed that you can eat, that usually grows in a hard brown shell: *a cashew nut*

2 a small piece of metal with a hole in the middle that is screwed onto a BOLT to fasten things together

3 *informal* someone who is crazy or behaves strangely

4 **golf/opera etc nut** *informal* someone who is very interested in golf etc [➔ fanatic]

nutcracker /'nʌt,krækə $ -ər/ *n* [C] also **nutcrackers** [plural] *BrE* the thing you use for breaking the shells of nuts

nutrient /'njuːtriənt $ 'nuː-/ *n* [C] a chemical or food that helps plants, animals, or people to live and grow: *Plants absorb nutrients from the soil.* —**nutrient** *adj*

nutrition /njuː'trɪʃən $ nuː-/ *n* [U] the kind of food you eat and the way it affects your health: *Good nutrition is vital.* —**nutritional** *adj*: *the nutritional content of foods* —**nutritionally** *adv*

nutritionist /nju'trɪʃənɨst $ nuː-/ *n* [C] someone who has EXPERT knowledge about nutrition

nutritious /njuː'trɪʃəs $ nuː-/ *adj* food that is nutritious contains the substances that your body needs: *a simple but **highly nutritious** meal* → see box at FOOD

nuts /nʌts/ *adj informal* crazy, silly, or angry: *I'll **go nuts** if I have to wait any longer.* | *That noise is **driving me nuts**.*

nutshell /'nʌtʃel/ *n* **(to put it) in a nutshell** *spoken* used when you are explaining only the main facts or details about something: *The problem, in a nutshell, was money.*

nutter /'nʌtə $ -ər/ *n* [C] *BrE informal* a crazy person: *That woman's a complete nutter!*

nutty /'nʌti/ *adj* **1** *informal* crazy **2** tasting like nuts

nuzzle /'nʌzəl/ *v* [I,T] to gently rub your head or nose against someone to show that you like them: *The dog nuzzled its head against her knees.*

NW the written abbreviation of **northwest** or **northwestern**

nylon /'naɪlɒn $ -lɑːn/ *n* [U] a strong artificial material used for making clothes, plastic, rope etc: *nylon stockings* | *a carpet made of 80% wool and 20% nylon*

nymph /nɪmf/ *n* [C] one of the SPIRITS of nature who appears as a young girl in ancient Greek and Roman stories

N

O, o

O, o /əʊ $ oʊ/ *n* [C,U] plural **O's, o's** **1** the 15th letter of the English alphabet **2** *spoken* a zero

oaf /əʊf $ oʊf/ *n* [C] a man who is stupid or rude

oak /əʊk $ oʊk/ *n* [C,U] a large tree that is common in northern countries, or the hard wood from this tree

OAP /ˌəʊ eɪ ˈpiː $ ˌoʊ-/ *n* [C] *BrE* an OLD AGE PENSIONER

oar /ɔː $ ɔːr/ *n* [C] a long pole that is wide at one end, used for rowing a boat

oasis /əʊˈeɪsɪs $ oʊ-/ *n* [C] plural **oases** /-siːz/ **1** a place in a desert where there are trees and water **2** somewhere that is more pleasant and peaceful than the area that surrounds it: *The park was an oasis of peace.*

oath /əʊθ $ oʊθ/ *n* plural **oaths** /əʊðz $ oʊðz/ **1** [C] a formal promise: **swear/take an oath** *He swore an oath to support the Constitution.* → see box at PROMISE **2** [singular U] *law* a formal promise to tell the truth in a court of law: **on/under oath** (=having promised to tell the truth) *The evidence was given under oath.*

oatmeal /ˈəʊtmiːl $ ˈoʊt-/ *n* [U] crushed oats used for making cakes or PORRIDGE

oats /əʊts $ oʊts/ *n* [plural] a grain that is eaten by people and animals

obedient /əˈbiːdiənt/ *adj* someone who is obedient does what a person, law, or rule tells them to do [≠ **disobedient**]: *a quiet and obedient child* —**obedience** *n* [U] *absolute obedience to the King* —**obediently** *adv*

obese /əʊˈbiːs $ oʊ-/ *adj* much too fat, in a way that is dangerous to your health → see box at FAT —**obesity** *n* [U]

obey /əˈbeɪ, ə- $ oʊ-, ə-/ *v* [I,T] to do what a person, law, or rule tells you to do [≠ **disobey**]: *Most dogs will obey simple commands.* | *He refused to obey his father.*

THESAURUS

do what sb says
do as you are told
follow sb's orders/instructions
respect sb's authority

obituary /əˈbɪtʃuəri $ -tʃueri/ *n* [C] plural **obituaries** a report of someone's death in a newspaper

object¹ /ˈɒbdʒɪkt $ ˈɑːb-/ *n*

1 [C] a thing that you can see, hold, or touch: *a small silver object* | *an everyday object*

2 [singular] the purpose of a plan, activity etc [➡ **aim, goal**]: **+of** *The object of the game is to improve children's skills.*

3 an object of desire/pity etc someone or something that you want to have, feel sorry for etc

4 [C] in grammar, a noun or phrase that describes the person or thing that is affected by an action [➡ **subject**]
→ DIRECT OBJECT, INDIRECT OBJECT

object² /əbˈdʒekt/ *v* [I,T] to say that you do not like or approve of something: *If no one objects, I would like to be present.* | **+to** *I objected to having to rewrite the article.* —**objector** *n* [C]

objection /əbˈdʒekʃən/ *n* [C] a reason you have for opposing something: **have no/any objection** *I have no objection to her being invited.* | **raise/make an objection** (=say you oppose something) *I don't think my boss will raise any objections.* | **+to** *He had moral objections to killing animals for food.*

COLLOCATIONS

raise an objection
make an objection
state an objection
voice an objection
lodge/register *formal* an objection

objectionable /əbˈdʒekʃənəbəl/ *adj* unpleasant and likely to offend people [= **offensive**]: *an objectionable remark*

objective¹ /əbˈdʒektɪv/ *n* [C] something that you are working hard to achieve: *Our main objective is to raise money.* → see box at PURPOSE

objective² *adj* not influenced by your own feelings or opinions [≠ **subjective**]: *It's hard to give an objective opinion about your own children.* —**objectively** *adv* —**objectivity** /ˌɒbdʒekˈtɪvəti $ ˌɑːb-/ *n* [U]

obligated /ˈɒblɪɡeɪtɪd $ ˈɑːb-/ *adj* **be/feel obligated to sb** *especially AmE* to feel that it is your duty to do something for someone

obligation /ˌɒblɪˈɡeɪʃən $ ˌɑːb-/ *n* [C,U] a moral or legal duty to do something: **an obligation to do sth** *Employers have an obligation to provide a safe working environment.* | **be under an/no obligation to do sth** *People entering the shop are under no obligation to buy.*

obligatory /əˈblɪɡətəri $ -tɔːri/ *adj formal* something that is obligatory has to be done because of a law, rule etc [= **compulsory**]

oblige /əˈblaɪdʒ/ *v* **1** [T] *formal* if you are obliged to do something, you have to do it because the situation, the law etc makes it necessary: **be obliged to do sth** *Doctors are obliged to keep all medical records secret.* **2** [I,T] to do something that someone has asked you to do: *Whenever we needed help, Ed was always **happy to oblige**.*

obliged /əˈblaɪdʒd/ *adj* **1 feel obliged to do sth** to feel that you must do something: *I felt obliged to tell her the truth.* **2 (I'm) much obliged (to you)** *spoken old-fashioned* used to thank someone very politely

obliging /əˈblaɪdʒɪŋ/ *adj* always ready to help other people —**obligingly** *adv*

oblique /əˈbliːk/ *adj* not said or written in a direct way: *an **oblique reference** to his drinking problem*

obliterate /əˈblɪtəreɪt/ *v* [T] to destroy something completely: *Large areas of the city were obliterated.* —**obliteration** /əˌblɪtəˈreɪʃən/ *n* [U]

oblivion /əˈblɪviən/ *n* [U] **1** when someone or something is completely forgotten: *old movie stars who have faded into oblivion* **2** when someone does not notice what is happening around them: *He drank himself into oblivion.*

oblivious /ə'blɪvɪəs/ *adj* not noticing or not knowing about something [= **unaware**]: **+to/of** *Max was fast asleep, completely oblivious to the noise outside.*

oblong /'ɒblɒŋ $ 'ɑːblɔːŋ/ *n* [C] a shape that has four straight sides, two of which are longer than the other two, and four angles of 90 degrees [➡ **rectangle**] ➔ see box at **SHAPE** —**oblong** *adj*: *an oblong box*

obnoxious /əb'nɒkʃəs $ -'nɑːk-/ *adj* extremely unpleasant or rude: *What an obnoxious man!*

oboe /'əʊbəʊ $ 'oʊboʊ/ *n* [C] a wooden musical instrument like a narrow tube that you play by blowing into it ➔ see picture on page A6 —**oboist** *n* [C]

obscene /əb'siːn/ *adj* **1** offensive and shocking in a sexual way: *obscene phone calls* | *He made an obscene gesture.* **2** extremely immoral or unfair, in a way that makes you angry: *obscene pay increases* —**obscenely** *adv*

obscenity /əb'senɪti/ *n plural* **obscenities** **1** [C usually plural] a sexually offensive word or phrase: *kids shouting obscenities* **2** [U] sexually offensive words, pictures, or actions, especially in a book, play etc: *laws against obscenity*

obscure¹ /əb'skjʊə $ -'skjʊr/ *adj* **1** difficult to understand: *Jarrett didn't like the plan, for some obscure reason.* **2** not famous: *an obscure poet*

obscure² *v* [T] **1** to make something difficult to know or understand: *Recent successes have obscured the fact that the company is still in trouble.* **2** to prevent something from being seen: *The top of the hill was obscured by clouds.*

obscurity /əb'skjʊərɪti $ -'skjʊr-/ *n* [U] when someone is not known or remembered: *O'Brien retired from politics and died in obscurity.*

observance /əb'zɜːvəns $ -ɜːr-/ *n* [U] *formal* when people obey a law, or do something because it is part of a religious custom: **+of** *strict observance of religious law*

observant /əb'zɜːvənt $ -ɜːr-/ *adj* good at noticing things: *The bomb was spotted by an observant member of the public.*

observation /ˌɒbzə'veɪʃən $ ˌɑːbzər-/ *n* **1** [U] when you watch someone or something carefully: **+of** *careful observation of the animal's behaviour* | **under observation** (=being watched carefully) *He was kept under observation in the hospital.* **2** [C] a spoken or written remark: *I would like to make an observation* (=say something about what is being discussed).

observatory /əb'zɜːvətəri $ əb'zɜːrvətɔːri/ *n* [C] *plural* **observatories** a special building from which scientists watch the sky

observe /əb'zɜːv $ -ɜːrv/ *v* [T] **1** to watch someone or something carefully: *psychologists observing child behaviour* **2** *formal* to see or notice something: *I observed the suspect entering the house.* **3** *formal* to say something: *'We're already late,' Hendry observed.* **4** to obey a law, agreement, or religious custom: *Both sides are observing the ceasefire.*

observer /əb'zɜːvə $ -ɜːrvər/ *n* [C] **1** someone who goes to a meeting, class, event etc to officially watch or check what is happening: *a group of UN observers in Bosnia* **2** someone who watches or notices something

obsessed /əb'sest/ *adj* if you are obsessed with something, you think about it all the time and cannot think of anything else: **+with/about** *William is obsessed with making money.*

obsession /əb'seʃən/ *n* [C,U] when you are obsessed with something, or the thing you are obsessed with: **+with** *an obsession with sex* —**obsessional** *adj*

obsessive /əb'sesɪv/ *adj* thinking about something all the time: **+about** *She's obsessive about her weight.* —**obsessively** *adv*

obsolete /'ɒbsəliːt $ ˌɑːbsə'liːt/ *adj* no longer used or useful, because something newer or better is now available: *Our computer system will soon be obsolete.* —**obsolescence** /ˌɒbsə'lesəns $ ˌɑːb-/ *n* [U]

obstacle /'ɒbstəkəl $ 'ɑːb-/ *n* [C] **1** something that makes it difficult to do something: **+to** *Lack of confidence can be a big obstacle to success.* **2** something that blocks a road, path etc ➔ see picture at **BARRIER**

obstetrician /ˌɒbstə'trɪʃən $ ˌɑːb-/ *n* [C] a doctor who deals with the birth of children

obstinate /'ɒbstɪnət $ 'ɑːb-/ *adj* refusing to change your opinions or behaviour [= **stubborn**] —**obstinately** *adv* —**obstinacy** *n* [U]

obstruct /əb'strʌkt/ *v* [T] **1** to block a road, path etc: *A van was obstructing traffic.* **2** to try to prevent something from happening by making it difficult: *Maya was charged with obstructing the investigation.* —**obstructive** *adj*

obstruction /əb'strʌkʃən/ *n* **1** [C, U] when something blocks a road, tube etc, or the thing which blocks it: *The accident caused an obstruction on the freeway.* ➔ see picture at **BARRIER** **2** [U] when someone tries to prevent a legal or political process: *obstruction of justice*

obtain /əb'teɪn/ *v* [T] *formal* to get something: *Maps can be obtained at the tourist office.* | **obtain sth from sth/sb** *You will need to obtain permission from the principal.* —**obtainable** *adj*

obtrusive /əb'truːsɪv/ *adj disapproving* too noticeable [≠ **unobtrusive**]: *obtrusive lighting*

obtuse /əb'tjuːs $ -'tuːs/ *adj formal* slow to understand something

obvious /'ɒbvɪəs $ 'ɑːb-/ *adj* easy to notice or understand: *an obvious mistake* | *It was obvious that Gina was lying.* | **+to** *It might be obvious to you but it isn't to me.* | *Thornton seemed the obvious choice for the job.* | *The obvious thing to do* (=clearly the best thing to do) *was to ring the school.* ➔ see box at **NOTICEABLE** —**obviously** *adv*: *She obviously didn't want to go.*

occasion /ə'keɪʒən/ *n*

1 a) [C] a time when something happens: **on ... occasion** *They had met on several occasions.* **b)** [singular] a suitable time or a reason to do something: *Christmas is an occasion to see old friends.* **2** [C] an important event: *We're saving the champagne for a special occasion.*

3 on occasion(s) sometimes but not often: *She can be very rude on occasion.*

occasional /ə'keɪʒənəl/ *adj* happening sometimes but not often: *Tomorrow will be warm with occasional showers.* | **the occasional trip/ letter/game etc** (=a few trips, letters etc, not happening or coming regularly) *I still get the occasional letter from him.*

O

occasionally /ə'keɪʒənəli/ adv sometimes but not often: *We occasionally meet for a drink.* | *The birds are seen only very occasionally* (=rarely) *in this country now.* → see box at **SOMETIMES**

occult /'ɒkʌlt, ə'kʌlt $ ə'kʌlt, 'ɑːkʌlt/ n **the occult** things relating to magic, SPIRITS etc —**occult** adj

occupant /'ɒkjᵿpənt $,ɑːk-/ n [C] formal someone who lives in a building, room etc, or who is in it

occupation /,ɒkjᵿ'peɪʃən $ 'ɑːk-/ n
1 [C] formal a job or profession: *Please state your name and occupation.* → see box at **JOB**
2 [U] when an army goes into another country and takes control of it using force: *the occupation of Poland*
3 [C] formal a way of spending your time

occupational /,ɒkjᵿ'peɪʃənəl◂ $,ɑːk-/ adj relating to your job: **occupational hazard** (=a risk of a particular job)

occupied /'ɒkjᵿpaɪd $ 'ɑːk-/ adj [not before noun] **1** a room, bed, seat etc that is occupied is being used: *All the apartments on the first floor are occupied.* **2** busy doing something: *I brought along some toys to keep the kids occupied.*

occupier /'ɒkjᵿpaɪə $ 'ɑːkjᵿpaɪər/ n [C] BrE formal someone who lives in or uses a place

occupy /'ɒkjᵿpaɪ $ 'ɑːk-/ v [T] occupied, occupying, occupies **1** to be living, working, or staying in a place: *The seventh floor of the building is occupied by Salem Press.* **2** if something occupies you or your time, you are busy doing it: *Sport occupies most of his spare time.* | **occupy yourself** (=keep busy) *How do you occupy yourself now that you're retired?* **3** to go into a place and take control of it, using military force: *Rebel forces occupied the city.* **4** if something occupies a space, it fills it: *A painting occupied the entire wall.* **5** formal to have a particular job or position: *Few women occupy senior positions.*

occur to sb phr v to come into someone's mind: *It occurred to me today that no one has told John yet.* | *Did it never occur to you to phone?*

occurrence /ə'kʌrəns $ ə'kɜː-/ n [C] something that happens: *Stress-related illness is now a fairly common occurrence.*

ocean /'əʊʃən $ 'oʊ-/ n
1 the ocean the large area of salt water that covers most of the Earth's surface
2 [C] one of the five very large areas of water in the world: *the Indian Ocean*
—**oceanic** /,əʊʃi'ænɪk◂ $,oʊ-/ adj

o'clock /ə'klɒk $ ə'klɑːk/ adv **one/two/three etc o'clock** one of the times when the clock shows the exact hour as a number from 1 to 12: **at ... o'clock** *We got up at six o'clock.* | *'What time is it?' 'It's almost four o'clock.'*

octagon /'ɒktəgən $ 'ɑːktəgɑːn/ n [C] a flat shape that has eight sides —**octagonal** /ɒk'tægənəl $ ɑːk-/ adj

octave /'ɒktɪv, -teɪv $ 'ɑːk-/ n [C] the set of eight musical notes between the first and last note of a SCALE

October /ɒk'təʊbə $ ɑːk'toʊbər/ n [C,U] written abbreviation *Oct.* the tenth month of the year, between September and November: **next/ last October** *We moved in last October.* | **in October** *His birthday's in October.* | **on October 6th** *We arrived on October 6th.* → see box at **MONTH**

octopus /'ɒktəpəs $ 'ɑːk-/ n [C] plural **octopuses** or **octopi** a sea creature with a soft body and eight TENTACLES (=arms)

odd /ɒd $ ɑːd/ adj
1 strange or different from what you expect: *Jake's an odd guy.* | **The odd thing was that** *he didn't seem to mind.* | **It's odd that** *she hasn't phoned.* → see box at **STRANGE**
2 odd numbers cannot be divided exactly by two [≠ even]
3 the odd drink/game/occasion etc spoken a few drinks, games etc, but not happening regularly: *I still enjoy the odd game of tennis.*
4 odd jobs small practical jobs of different kinds
5 20-odd/30-odd etc spoken a little more than 20, 30 etc: *He must have worked here twenty-odd years.*
6 [only before noun] separated from its pair or set: *an odd sock*
7 the odd man/one out someone or something that is different from the other people or things in a group

oddity /'ɒdᵻti $ 'ɑː-/ n [C] plural **oddities** a strange or unusual person or thing

oddly /'ɒdli $ 'ɑːdli/ adv **1** in a strange or unusual way: *Roger's been behaving very oddly.* **2 oddly enough** used when something seems strange or surprising: *Oddly enough, she didn't seem offended.*

odds /ɒdz $ ɑːdz/ n [plural] **1** how likely it is that something will or will not happen: **+of** *The odds of winning the lottery are about 14 million to 1.* | **The odds are** (=probably) *you won't need it, but you never know.* **2** difficulties that make a good result seem very unlikely: *He recovered from his injury **against all the odds** (=in spite of it seeming very unlikely).* **3 at odds (with sb)** disagreeing with someone: *Britain was at odds with France on the subject of nuclear testing.*

odds and 'ends n [plural] informal small things that are not important or valuable

ode /əʊd $ oʊd/ n [C] a poem written to or about a person or thing

odour BrE; **odor** AmE /'əʊdə $ 'oʊdər/ n [C] a smell, especially an unpleasant one → see box at **SMELL**

odyssey /'ɒdᵻsi $ 'ɑː-/ n [C] literary a long journey involving a series of experiences

oestrogen BrE; **estrogen** AmE /'iːstrədʒən $ 'es-/ n [U] a chemical substance produced by a woman's body

of /əv, ə; strong ɒv $ əv, ə; strong ɑːv/ prep
1 used to show what or who something belongs to or relates to: *the colour of his eyes* | *a friend of Sam's* | *the first part of the story*

2 used when talking about amounts or groups: *two kilos of sugar | a cup of coffee | a herd of elephants*

3 used to show the size or age of something: *a rise of 9% | a child of eight*

4 used in dates: *the 23rd of January, 1998*

5 used to mention a particular thing, after describing it as something: *the city of New Orleans | the problem of unemployment*

6 used to say what something shows: *a photo of Paula's baby*

7 used to show direction: *I live just north of here.*

8 used after nouns describing an action to show who or what it is done to or who did it: *the testing of river water for chemicals | the arrival of British troops*

9 written, made, produced etc by someone: *the novels of Charles Dickens*

10 used to say when something happened: *the floods of 1997*

11 used to show the cause of someone's death: *She died of cancer.*

→ **of course** at **COURSE**[1]

off /ɒf $ ɒːf/ *adv, adj, prep*

1 away from something: *She waved goodbye as she drove off. | Turn off the motorway at junction 11.*

2 not on something, or removed from something: *A button's come off my shirt. | Take your coat off. | Keep off the grass!*

3 out of a bus, train, plane etc [≠ **on**]: *I'll get off at the next stop.*

4 not working or being used [≠ **on**]: *All the lights were off. | Remember to switch the computer off.*

5 not at work or school because you are ill or on holiday: *He's been off work for six weeks. | I'm **taking** the **day off** tomorrow.*

6 used to say how far away something is in distance or time: *Spring is still a long way off. | the mountains off in the distance*

7 **a)** a short distance from a place: *an island off the coast of Florida | a hotel just off the main square* **b)** joined to a room, area, building etc: *There's a small bathroom off the main bedroom.*

8 used to talk about a reduction in price: *You get 15% off if you buy $100 worth of groceries.*

9 if an event that was arranged is off, it will not now happen [≠ **on**]: *The wedding's off!*

10 **be off** to have started a journey: *At last, we're off!*

11 **off and on/on and off** for short periods of time, but not regularly: *I worked as a secretary off and on for three years.*

12 **have an off day** *spoken* to have a day when you are not doing something as well as you usually do

13 *especially BrE* food or drink that is off is no longer fresh [➡ **rotten, sour**]: *This milk smells off.*

14 not correct: *His calculations are off by 20%.*

→ **BETTER OFF**

offal /ˈɒfəl $ ˈɒː-, ˈɑː-/ *n* [U] the KIDNEYS, LIVER etc of an animal, used as food

offbeat /ˌɒfˈbiːt◂ $ ˌɒːf-/ *adj informal* unusual, especially in an interesting way: *offbeat humour*

off-'centre *BrE*; **off-center** *AmE adv, adj* not exactly in the centre of something

'off-chance *n* **on the off-chance** if you do something on the off-chance, you do it hoping that something will happen, although it is unlikely: **+(that)** *He only went to the party on the off-chance that Pippa might be there.*

off-'colour *adj BrE* [not before noun] slightly ill

offence *BrE*; **offense** *AmE* /əˈfens/ *n*

1 [C] a crime: *Possession of stolen goods is a **criminal offence**. | If you lie to the police, you are **committing** an **offence**.*

2 [U] when you upset or offend someone by something you say or do: **cause/give offence** *The problem was how to say 'no' without causing offence. | A lot of women **took offence** (=felt offended) at Rawling's speech. | **no offence (meant)** spoken* (=used to tell someone that you hope what you are going to say will not upset them) *No offence, John, but I'd rather get a professional opinion.*

offend /əˈfend/ *v*

1 [T] to make someone angry or upset, by doing or saying something which they think is rude, unkind, or unacceptable: *I'm sorry, I didn't mean to offend you. | Anna was **deeply offended** by such a personal question.*

2 [I] *formal* to commit a crime

offender /əˈfendə $ -ər/ *n* [C] someone who has committed a crime: *an institution for **young offenders*** → see box at **CRIME**

offense[1] /əˈfens/ *n* the American spelling of OFFENCE

offense[2] /əˈfens ˈɒːfens, ˈɑː-/ *n* [C,U] *AmE* the players in a game such as football who try to get points [≠ **defense**]

offensive[1] /əˈfensɪv/ *adj* **1** likely to upset or offend people [≠ **inoffensive**]: *Some people found the song **offensive**.* → see box at **RUDE** **2** used or intended for attacking [≠ **defensive**]: *an offensive weapon*

offensive[2] *n* **1** [C] an attack on a place by an army **2** **be/go on the offensive** to attack or criticize people

offer[1] /ˈɒfə $ ˈɒːfər, ˈɑː-/ *v*

1 [T] to ask someone if they would like something, or to hold something out for them to take: **offer sb sth** *Can I offer you a drink?* | **offer sth to sb** *Simon lit a cigarette then offered one to Ben.*

COMMUNICATION

offering

Have sth *informal: Have a biscuit.*
Would you like sth?: *Would you like some wine?*
Can I offer you sth?: *Can I offer you a lift into town?*
Help yourself to sth (=take something, especially food, whenever you want it): *Help yourself to fruit.*

2 [I,T] to say that you are willing to do something: **offer to do sth** *Carol didn't even offer to help.*

3 [T] to provide something that people want or need: *We offer a wide range of services. | **offer advice/help/support etc** Your doctor should be able to offer you advice on diet.*

4 [T] to say that you will pay a particular amount of money for something: **offer sb sth** *They've offered us £170,000 for the house.*

offer² n [C]

1 when you say that you will give something to someone or do something for them: *He's had a number of job offers.* | **+of** *Thanks for your offer of help.*

COLLOCATIONS

make someone an **offer**
have/receive an **offer** from someone
consider an **offer** – to think about an offer carefully before making a decision
accept/take up an **offer** – to say yes
refuse/reject an **offer** or **turn** it **down** – to say no
→ ACCEPT, REFUSE

2 an amount of money that someone says they will pay for something: *He made me an offer of $50 for the bike.*
3 when something is sold at a lower price than usual [➡ discount]: *Don't miss our special offer – two videos for the price of one.*
4 on offer *BrE* **a)** available to buy, use, or do: *Activities on offer include windsurfing and water-skiing.* **b)** being sold at a price that is lower than usual

offering /'ɒfərɪŋ $ 'ɒː-, 'ɑː-/ n [C] something that you give to someone, especially to God

offhand¹ /ˌɒf'hænd◂ $ ˌɒːf-/ adj seeming not friendly or interested: *an offhand voice*

offhand² adv immediately, without time to think: *I can't tell you offhand – I'll have to check.*

office /'ɒfɪs $ 'ɒː-, 'ɑː-/ n

1 [C] a building that belongs to an organization, where people work: *Are you going to the office today?* | **main/head office** (=most important office) | **office worker**
2 [C] a room where you work that has a desk, telephone etc: *the manager's office*

TOPIC

Many modern offices are **open plan** (=not divided into separate rooms). People sit at **desks**. On your **desk** is a **computer/PC** . Somewhere in the office there is a **printer**, a **photocopier**, a **fax (machine)** and **filing cabinets**. The office building may have several **floors**. There is often a **canteen/cafeteria** where you can eat.

3 office hours the time between about 9.00 in the morning and 5.00 in the afternoon, when people in offices are working: *He can be contacted during normal office hours.*
4 [C,U] an important job or position: **in office** *The president died after only fifteen months in office.* | *Watson held office* (=had an important job) *as finance minister.*
→ BOOKING OFFICE, BOX OFFICE, POST OFFICE, REGISTER OFFICE, REGISTRY OFFICE

officer /'ɒfɪsə $ 'ɒːfɪsər, 'ɑː-/ n [C]

1 someone who has a position of authority in the army, navy etc: **army/naval/military officer**
2 someone who has a position of authority in an organization: *a local government officer*
3 a policeman or policewoman [= police officer]
→ COMMANDING OFFICER, PROBATION OFFICER

official¹ /ə'fɪʃəl/ adj

1 approved of or done by someone in authority, especially the government: *an official inquiry*

into the plane crash | *You will have to get official permission.*
2 relating to a position of authority: *Her official title is Public Safety Adviser.* | *The President began a four-day official visit to France.*
3 official reasons, information etc are what people are told, although they may not be true: *The official reason for his resignation was ill health.*

official² n [C] someone who has a position of authority in an organization, especially a government: *US Administration officials*

officially /ə'fɪʃəli/ adv

1 in an official or formal way: *The new bridge was officially opened this morning.*
2 according to the reason or information that has been given, which may not be true: *The meeting was cancelled, officially because of bad weather.*

officiate /ə'fɪʃieɪt/ v [I] formal to do official duties at a ceremony or important event

officious /ə'fɪʃəs/ adj disapproving too eager to tell people what to do: *officious bureaucrats*

offing /'ɒfɪŋ $ 'ɒː-, 'ɑː-/ n **be in the offing** to be going to happen soon: *Big changes are in the offing.*

off-'key adj sung or played slightly too high or too low [➡ in tune] —**off-key** adv: *He sang off-key.*

'off-licence n [C] *BrE* a shop that sells alcohol [= liquor store *AmE*] → see box at SHOP

offline /ˌɒf'laɪn◂ $ ˌɒːf-/, **off-line** adj, adv if your computer is offline, it is not connected to the Internet [≠ online]: *I work offline most of the day.*

off-'message adj if a politician is off-message, he or she says things that do not follow the ideas of their political party [➡ on-message]

off-'peak adj, adv *BrE* off-peak travel, electricity etc is cheaper because it is done or used at less busy times: *off-peak rail services*

off-'putting adj *BrE* if a feature of something is off-putting, it makes you not want to do or have it: *I found the style of the book very off-putting.*

off-ramp n [C] *AmE* a road for driving off a HIGHWAY or FREEWAY [≠ on-ramp]

offset /'ɒfset, ˌɒf'set $ 'ɒːfset, ˌɒːf'set/ v [T] past tense and past participle **offset** present participle **offsetting** if one thing offsets another, it has an opposite effect so that the final result is less expensive, less noticeable etc: *The cost of the flight was offset by the cheapness of the hotel.*

offshoot /'ɒfʃuːt $ 'ɒːf-/ n [C] something that has developed from something bigger: *The company was an offshoot of Bell Telephones.*

offshore /ˌɒf'ʃɔː◂ $ ˌɒːf'ʃɔːr◂/ adj **1** in the sea, not far from the coast: *America's offshore oil reserves* **2 offshore bank/account/company** a bank, bank account etc that is not in your home country but in another country where you pay less tax

offside /ˌɒf'saɪd◂ $ ˌɒːf-/ adj, adv in a position in FOOTBALL or HOCKEY where you are not allowed to touch the ball

offspring /ˈɒfˌsprɪŋ $ ˈɒːf-/ *n* [C] plural **offspring** someone's child

offstage /ˌɒfˈsteɪdʒ $ ˌɒːf-/ *adj, adv* just behind or at the side of a stage in a theatre: *There was a loud crash offstage.*

off-the-'wall *adj informal* very strange

off-'white *adj* greyish-white or yellowish-white

often /ˈɒfən, ˈɒftən $ ˈɒːf-/ *adv*
1 many times or regularly: *I often work at the weekend.* | *We should go out more often.* | *How often do you see your parents?* | *She's quite often late for school.* | *This kind of accident happens all too often.*

THESAURUS

a lot *informal*, **frequently**, **regularly**, **repeatedly**, **constantly**, **continuously**
→ **NEVER, RARELY, SOMETIMES**

2 in many situations or at many times: *Headaches are often caused by stress.*
3 every so often sometimes but not very frequently: *I see him every so often.*

GRAMMAR

often, very often
Use **often** before a verb, unless the verb is 'be': *Dad often gets home late.* | *This is often not possible.*
If there are two or more verbs together, **often** comes after the first one: *I don't often go to the cinema.*
Very often is used at the end of a negative sentence: *He doesn't telephone very often.*

ogle /ˈəʊgəl $ ˈoʊ-/ *v* [I,T] to look at someone in a way that shows you think they are sexually attractive

ogre /ˈəʊgə $ ˈoʊgər/ *n* [C] **1** someone who is cruel and frightening **2** a large, ugly man in children's stories

oh /əʊ $ oʊ/ *spoken* **1** used before saying something, or replying to a question: *Oh, hello.* | *'What time did he leave?' 'Oh, about ten.'* **2** used to express a strong emotion or to emphasize your opinion: *Oh, how annoying!* | *Oh good, Ted's here.*

ohm /əʊm $ oʊm/ *n* [C] a unit for measuring electrical RESISTANCE

oil¹ /ɔɪl/ *n* [U]
1 a thick dark liquid from under the ground, used to make petrol: *the price of oil* | *oil companies*
2 a thick liquid used to make the parts of machines move more easily: *engine oil*
3 a liquid that comes from plants or animals, used especially in cooking: *cooking oil* | **vegetable/olive/sunflower oil** *tuna in olive oil*
→ **CRUDE OIL, ESSENTIAL OIL**

oil² *v* [T] to put oil onto something

oilfield /ˈɔɪlfiːld/ *n* [C] an area of land or sea under which there is oil

'oil ,painting *n* [C] a picture painted with paint that contains oil

'oil rig *n* [C] a large structure with equipment for getting oil out of the ground

'oil slick *n* [C] a large area of oil floating on the sea or a river

'oil well *n* [C] a deep hole made to get oil out of the ground

oily /ˈɔɪli/ *adj* **1** covered with oil, or containing a lot of oil: *oily fish* **2** similar to oil: *an oily substance*

ointment /ˈɔɪntmənt/ *n* [C,U] a substance that you rub into your skin as a medical treatment

oil rig

0

OK¹, okay /ˌəʊˈkeɪ $ ˌoʊ-/ *spoken*
1 used to say that you agree, or to ask someone if they agree: *'Can I borrow your bike?' 'Okay.'* | *We have to leave early, OK?*
2 used when you start talking, or continue to talk after a pause: *OK, any questions?*

OK², okay *adj spoken*
1 if you are OK, you are not ill, injured, or sad [= all right]: *Is everybody OK?* | *Do you feel OK now?*
2 something that is OK is acceptable: *Does my hair look OK?* | *'Sorry I'm late.' 'That's OK.'* | *Is it OK if Lisa comes?*
3 not bad, but not very good: *'Was the food good?' 'It was OK.'*
—**OK** *adv*: *Is your computer working OK?*

OK³, okay *v* [T] **OK'd, OK'ing, OK's** *informal* to agree to allow something to happen: *His parents okayed the plan.*

OK⁴, okay *n* **give/get the OK** *informal* to give or get permission to do something

old /əʊld $ oʊld/ *adj*
1 a) someone or something that is old has lived or existed for a long time [≠ young, new]: *an old man* | *Her car is really old.* | *Wear old clothes for exercising.* | *one of the oldest houses in the village* **b) the old** old people

THESAURUS

ancient – used about buildings, cities, languages etc that existed long ago
antique – used about furniture, jewellery etc that is old and valuable
vintage – used about things that are old but of high quality: *vintage cars*
secondhand – used about books, clothes, cars etc that were owned by someone else and then sold
used – used about cars or other products which are being sold that are not new: *a used car dealer*
elderly – a polite word to say that someone is old
stale – used about bread, cakes etc that are no longer fresh
rotten – used about food, especially fruit or eggs, that is no longer good to eat
→ **NEW, YOUNG**

2 used to talk about the age of someone or something: **be three/50/300 etc years old** *Our dog is three years old.* | *How old are you?* | *My sister is older than me.* | **ten-year-old/six-week-old etc** *a ten-year-old boy*

3 [only before noun] your old house, job, car etc is one that you had before but do not have now [= former]: *one of her old boyfriends*

4 [only before noun] old things are familiar because you have experienced or heard them many times before: *He always gives the same old excuse.*

5 old friend/enemy/colleague etc someone who has been your friend, enemy etc for a long time: *He's an old friend of my father's.*

6 the old days times in the past

7 any old thing/place/way etc *spoken* used to say that it does not matter which thing, place etc you choose: *Do it any old way you like.*

8 good/poor/silly old etc *spoken* used to talk about someone you like: *Good old Liz! She's so smart.*

9 old hat not new or interesting

old 'age *n* [U] the time in your life when you are old

old age 'pensioner *n* [C] *BrE* abbreviation **OAP** an old person who does not work any more and receives a PENSION (=money from a company or from the government)

olden /'əʊldən $ 'oʊld-/ *adj* **in the olden days/in olden times** a long time ago

old-'fashioned *adj* not modern or not fashionable any more: *old-fashioned ideas about women* | *All her clothes look old-fashioned.*

THESAURUS

out-of-date, outdated, dated

old 'flame *n* [C] *informal* someone who was your boyfriend or girlfriend in the past

oldie /'əʊldi $ 'oʊldi-/ *n* [C] *informal* an old thing or person, especially a song or film

old 'man *BrE spoken informal* **1** your husband **2** your father

Old 'Testament *n* **the Old Testament** the part of the Bible that is about the time before the birth of Christ [➔ New Testament]

old-time *adj* [only before noun] of the sort that used to exist or be done in the past: *old-time remedies*

old 'wives' tale *n* [C] an old belief that is now considered to be untrue

Old 'World *n* **the Old World** Europe, Asia, and Africa

olive /'ɒlɪv $ 'ɑː-/ *n* **1** [C] a small black or green fruit, used as food or for making oil: *olive oil* **2** also **olive green** [U] a pale green colour —**olive** *adj*

Olympic Games /ə,lɪmpɪk 'geɪmz/ also **Olympics** *n* **the Olympic Games/the Olympics** an international sports event held every four years —**Olympic** *adj*

ombudsman /'ɒmbʊdzmən $ 'ɑːm-/ *n* plural **ombudsmen** someone who deals with complaints made by ordinary people against companies, newspapers, the government etc

omelette *BrE*; **omelet** *AmE* /'ɒmlɪt $ 'ɑːm-/ *n* [C] eggs mixed together and cooked in hot fat: *a cheese omelette*

omen /'əʊmən $ 'oʊ-/ *n* [C] a sign of what will happen in the future: *a good/bad omen*

ominous /'ɒmɪnəs $ 'ɑː-/ *adj* making you feel that something bad is going to happen: *ominous black clouds* —**ominously** *adv*

omission /əʊ'mɪʃən, ə- $ oʊ-, ə-/ *n* [C,U] when something is not included or not done: *the omission of his name from the report*

omit /əʊ'mɪt, ə- $ oʊ-, ə-/ *v* [T] **omitted, omitting 1** to not include something [= leave out]: *Important details had been omitted.* **2 omit to do sth** *formal* to not do something: *She omitted to tell me she was married.*

omnipotent /ɒm'nɪpətənt $ ɑːm-/ *adj formal* powerful enough to be able to do anything —**omnipotence** *n* [U]

on¹ /ɒn $ ɑːn, ɒːn/ *prep*

1 touching something or being supported by something: *She sat on the bed.* | *the picture on the wall* | *You've got mud on your face.* ➔ see picture on page A8

2 in a place or position: *Henry grew up on a farm.* | *a restaurant on Main Street* | **on the left/right** *That's Jill on the left.*

3 written, shown, or broadcast somewhere: *the picture on page 25* | **on television/TV/the radio** *Is there anything good on TV?*

4 during a particular day: *See you on Monday.* | *I was born on June 15th.*

5 using a machine, instrument, or piece of equipment: *Did you do this on a computer?* | *Anna's on the phone.* | **on the piano/violin etc** *Play me something on the piano.*

6 about a subject: *a book on China* | *information on hotels*

7 used to say that a person or thing is affected by something: *a tax on cigarettes*

8 travelling using something: **on a bus/plane/train/boat** *I came on the bus.* | **on a bike/horse** *He likes riding around on his bike.*

9 used for saying how information is stored or recorded: **on disk/tape/video/DVD** *Keep a back-up copy on disk.*

10 taking a medicine or drugs: *She's on antibiotics.*

11 on a trip/vacation/holiday etc during a trip, holiday etc: *They met on a trip to Spain.*

12 included in a group or a list: *You're on my team.*

13 immediately after something happens: *Go to the Reception desk on arrival.*

14 have sth on you to have something with you now: *Do you have a pen on you?*

on² *adj, adv*

1 used to say that someone continues to do something, or that something continues to happen: *The meeting went on for hours.* | *Let's drive on a little further.* | *He talked on and on about his job.*

2 if a machine is on, it is operating or working [≠ off]: *The lights are still on in her office.* | *How do you switch the computer on?*

3 if you have a piece of clothing on, you are wearing it: *Put your coat on, it's cold.*

4 into a bus, plane, train, or ship: *I got on at Vine Street.*

5 attached to something: *Put the lid on properly.* | *a box with a label on*

6 from then on/from that day on after that time into the future: *From that day on they were friends.*

7 being broadcast or shown: *The news will be on in a minute.* | *What's on at the cinema?*

8 if an event is on, it has been planned and is happening: *There's a festival on this weekend.*

9 have sth on *informal* to have something that you must do: *I've got a lot on at the moment.*
→ **off and on/on and off and off** at **OFF**

once¹ /wʌns/ *adv*

1 one time: *We only met once.* | *I've been here once before.* | **once a week/year etc** (=one time every week, year etc) *She goes to the gym once a week.*

2 in the past, but not now: *They were once close friends.*

3 at once a) at the same time: *I can't do two things at once!* **b)** immediately: *I recognised him at once.*

4 (every) once in a while sometimes, but not often: *I see my ex-boyfriend every once in a while.*

5 once again/more a) again, after happening several times before: *He asked the question once more.* **b)** used to say that a situation returns to a previous state: *Everything was peaceful once again.*

6 all at once *literary* suddenly: *All at once, there was a loud bang.*

7 for once *spoken* used to say that something should happen more often: *Will you listen for once?*

8 once and for all definitely and finally: *Let's settle this once and for all.*

9 once upon a time a long time ago – used in children's stories

10 once in a blue moon very rarely

once² *linking word* from the time something happens: *Once she started crying, she couldn't stop.*

oncoming /ˈɒnˌkʌmɪŋ $ ˈɑːn-, ˈɔːn-/ *adj* oncoming cars are coming towards you

one¹ /wʌn/ *number*

1 the number 1: *They have one child.* | *one hundred and twenty-one pounds* | *Come back at one* (=one o'clock). | *Katie's about one* (=one year old).

2 one or two a small number of people or things [= a few]: *We've made one or two changes.*

one² *pron plural* **ones**

1 used when you are talking about someone or something of the kind that has already been mentioned: *'Do you have a DVD player?' 'No, but I'm getting one.'* | *He ate his sandwich and took another one.* | *That winter was a cold one.*

2 used to talk about a particular person or thing from a group: *He has two sisters. One is a doctor.* | *I'm the one on the left of the picture.* | **+of** *One of my CDs is missing.* | **this/that one** *I like that one best.*

3 one by one if people do something one by one, first one person does it, then the next etc: *One by one, people sat down.*

4 one after the other/one after another happening without much time in between: *He scored three goals, one after another.*

5 (all) in one if something is several different things all in one, it is all of those things: *a garage and workshop in one*

6 *formal* used to mean people in general, including yourself: *One never knows what may happen.*
→ **NO ONE**

one³ *determiner, adj*

1 used to emphasize a particular person or thing: *One person she really likes is Kim.* | *I know one thing for sure – he's lying.*

2 one day/morning etc a) on a particular day etc in the past: *I saw him one day in town.* **b)** at some time in the future: *Let's go out one evening.*

3 only: *Our one worry is, it's very expensive.*

4 for one thing *spoken* used when giving a reason: *You can't go. You're not old enough, for one thing.*

one anˈother *pron* each other: *They shook hands with one another.*

one-ˈliner *n* [C] a very short joke or funny remark

ˈone-man, ˈone-person *adj* [only before noun] performed or controlled by one person: *a one-man show*

one-night ˈstand *n* [C] *informal* an occasion when two people have sex, but do not meet again

one-ˈoff *adj* [only before noun] happening only once: *a one-off payment* —**one-off** *n* [C]

onerous /ˈɒnərəs, ˈəʊ- $ ˈɑː-, ˈoʊ-/ *adj formal* difficult and tiring: *onerous duties*

oneself /wʌnˈself/ *pron formal* the REFLEXIVE form of 'one', used when you are talking about people in general, including yourself

one-ˈsided *adj* **1** *disapproving* considering or showing only one opinion in an argument, in a way that is unfair: *a one-sided view of the problem* **2** a one-sided competition is not equal because one team is much stronger

ˈone-time *adj* [only before noun] former: *the one-time captain of the US team*

one-to-ˈone *adj* between only two people: *tuition on a one-to-one basis*

one-track ˈmind *n* [C] if you have a one-track mind, you are always thinking about one thing, especially sex

one-upmanship /wʌnˈʌpmənʃɪp/ *n* [U] attempts to make yourself seem better than other people

one-ˈway *adj* **1** a one-way street is one on which cars can only travel in one direction **2** a one-way ticket is for travelling to a place, but not for coming back [= single *BrE*; ≠ return, round trip]
→ see box at **TICKET**

ˈone-woman *adj* [only before noun] performed by one woman: *a one-woman show*

ongoing /ˈɒnˌɡəʊɪŋ $ ˈɑːnˌɡoʊɪŋ, ˈɔːn-/ *adj* continuing to happen: *ongoing discussions*

onion /ˈʌnjən/ *n* [C,U] a round white vegetable, usually with brown skin, which has a strong smell and taste: *Chop the onions finely.* | *onion soup* → see picture at **VEGETABLE**
→ **SPRING ONION**

online /ˌɒnˈlaɪn◂ $ ˌɑːn-, ˌɔːn-/, **on-line** *adj, adv* connected to or using a computer or network of computers [≠ offline]: *online banking facilities* (=available using the Internet) | *Our* *school* **went online** (=started to be online) *this year.* → see box at **INTERNET**

onlooker /'ɒn,lʊkə $ 'ɑːn-, 'ɒːn-/ *n* [C] someone who watches something happening without being involved in it

only¹ /'əʊnli $ 'oʊn-/ *adv*

1 not more than a particular amount, number etc: *Tina left home when she was only 16.* | *He only has one pair of shoes.* | *It took only a few minutes.*

2 not anyone or anything else: *Only you know the truth.* | *Parking is for customers only.* | *We can only hope* (=all we can do is hope) *she never finds out.*

3 not in any other situation, or not for any other reason: *You can only get to the beach by boat.* | *You can come, but only if you don't interfere.* | *I only invited him because I felt sorry for him.*

4 used to say that someone or something is not important: *It's only a piece of paper.*

5 used to say that something happened very recently: **only last week/last year/yesterday** *I saw him only yesterday and he looked fine.*

6 only just **a)** a very short time ago: *They only just left.* **b)** almost not [= **barely**]: *I only just finished in time.*

7 if only used to say that you wish something was true: *If only I'd brought my camera.* | *If only she would listen!*

8 not only ... (but) used to say that one thing is true, and another thing is also true: *He's not only great-looking, he's also a nice guy.*

9 only too very: *She was only too glad to help.*

only² *adj*

1 used to say that there are no other people or things of the same kind: *She's the only girl in the class.* | *I was the only one who disagreed.*

2 an only child a child with no brothers or sisters

3 the only thing is ... *spoken* used when you are going to mention a problem: *I'd like to come – the only thing is I've got a lot of homework.*

only³ *linking word* used to mean 'but' when you are giving the reason why something did not or will not happen: *I would help you, only I'm too busy.*

,on-'message *adj* if a politician is on-message, he or she says things that agree with the ideas of their political party [➦ **off-message**]

,on-'off *adj* [only before noun] happening sometimes and not at other times: *an on-off romantic relationship*

'on-ramp *n* [C] *AmE* a road for driving onto a HIGHWAY or FREEWAY [≠ **off-ramp**]

'on-screen *adj* shown on a computer screen, or on a television or cinema screen: *Click 'Yes', then follow the on-screen instructions.*

onset /'ɒnset $ 'ɑːn-, 'ɒːn-/ *n* **the onset of sth** the beginning of something: *the onset of winter*

onslaught /'ɒnslɔːt $ 'ɑːnslɔːt, 'ɒːn-/ *n* [C] a very strong attack or criticism

onto /'ɒntə; *before vowels* 'ɒntʊ; *strong* 'ɒntuː $ 'ɑːn-, 'ɒːn-/ *prep*

1 used to say that someone or something moves to a position on a surface: *The cat jumped onto the table.* | **get onto a bus/plane/train** (=get into it) *Two girls got onto the bus.*

2 be onto sb *informal* to know who did something wrong or illegal: *The police are onto him.*

3 be onto sth *informal* to have discovered or

produced something important or interesting: *He seems to be onto something with his latest ideas.*

onus /'əʊnəs $ 'oʊ-/ *n* **the onus is on sb to do sth** it is someone's responsibility to do something: *The onus is on you to check the equipment is safe.*

onward /'ɒnwəd $ 'ɑːnwərd, 'ɒːn-/ *adj* [only before noun] moving forward or continuing: *the onward journey*

onwards /'ɒnwədz $ 'ɑːnwərdz, 'ɒːn-/ *especially BrE*, **onward** *especially AmE adv* **from ... onwards** starting at a particular time and continuing: *The cafeteria is open from 8.30 onwards.*

oops /ʊps/ *spoken* used when you have made a small mistake, dropped something etc: *Oops, sorry about that!*

ooze /uːz/ *v* **1** [I,T] to flow slowly from somewhere: *Blood oozed from the wound.* **2** [T] *informal* to show a lot of a particular quality: *He oozes charm.*

opal /'əʊpəl $ 'oʊ-/ *n* [C,U] a white stone used in jewellery

opaque /əʊ'peɪk $ oʊ-/ *adj* **1** difficult or impossible to see through [≠ **transparent**]: *opaque glass* **2** *formal* hard to understand

open¹ /'əʊpən $ 'oʊ-/ *adj*

1 if something is open, it has been moved so that there is a space between different parts of it [≠ **closed, shut**]: *Come in – the door's open.* | *I could barely* **keep** *my eyes open.* | *A book lay* **open** *on the table.* | *All the windows were* **wide open.** | *His shirt was open at the neck.*

2 ready for business and allowing customers, visitors etc to enter [≠ **closed**]: *We're open until six.* | *When will the new library be open?* | *The firm will be* **open for business** *next week.*

3 available for anyone to do or take part in: +**to** *Few jobs were open to women in those days.* | *an open competition*

4 not surrounded by buildings, walls etc: *the open countryside*

5 not covered: *an open fire*

6 honest and not keeping anything secret [➦ **openly, openness**]: *We try to be open with each other.*

7 keep/have an open mind (about/on sth) to not decide about something until you have found out more

8 keep your eyes/ears open *spoken* to keep looking or listening carefully so that you notice anything that may be important

9 be open to question/criticism/doubt etc to be likely or able to be questioned, criticized etc: *His analysis is open to question.*

10 open hostility/impatience/curiosity etc hostility, impatience etc that is not hidden or secret: *open hostility between the two nations*

11 be open to sth to be willing to consider or accept something new: *The committee is open to suggestions.*

12 in the open air outside

13 welcome/greet sb/sth with open arms to be very pleased to see someone or something

open² *v*

1 [I,T] to become open, or to make something open [≠ **shut**]: *The doors open automatically.* | *Can you open the window?* | *She opened her eyes.* | *Louise opened a bottle of wine.*

THESAURUS

unlock – to open a door, drawer etc with a key
unscrew – to open a lid on a bottle, container etc by turning it
unwrap – to open a package by removing the paper that covers it
unfold – to open a piece of paper, a cloth etc that was folded
unfasten/undo – to open something that is fastened or tied, for example a seat belt or a piece of clothing
→ CLOSE
Do not use **open** and **close** to talk about things that use electricity, or things that provide water or gas. Use **turn on/off** instead: *Can you turn off the taps?* | *I've turned on the TV.*
For things that use electricity, you can also use **switch on/off**: *Don't forget to switch off the lights.*

2 [I] if a shop, bank etc opens at a particular time, people can use it after that time: *What time does the bookstore open on Sundays?*
3 [I,T] if a film, play, public building etc opens, or if it is opened, people can start to see it or use it: *A new play opens next week on Broadway.* | *The restaurant first opened in 1986.* | *Parts of the White House will be opened to the public.*
4 [I,T] to spread something out, or to become spread out: *I can't open my umbrella.* | *The flowers are starting to open.*
5 [T] to make a computer program ready to use
→ see box at COMPUTER
6 open fire (on sb/sth) to start shooting at someone or something: *Troops opened fire on the protesters.*
7 open an account if you open a bank account, you arrange for it to start
open into/onto sth *phr v* to lead directly into a place: *The kitchen opens onto the back yard.*
open up *phr v* **1** to become available or possible, or to make something available or possible: *New business opportunities are opening up all the time.* | **open sth ⇔ up** *They decided to open up their home to young people.* **2** to stop being shy and say what you really think: *It takes a long time for him to open up.*

open³ *n* **out in the open a)** outdoors: *It's fun to eat out in the open.* **b)** not hidden or secret: *The truth is finally out in the open.*

,open-'air *adj* not inside a building: *open-air concerts*

'open day *n* [C] *BrE* a day when people can visit a school, company etc and see what is done there [= **open house** *AmE*]

,open-'ended *adj* without a fixed ending time: *an open-ended contract*

opener /'əʊpənə $ 'oʊpənər/ *n* [C] **can/tin/bottle opener** something you use to open cans or bottles

,open-heart 'surgery *n* [U] when doctors cut open someone's chest to do an operation on their heart

,open 'house *n* [C] *AmE* a time when people can visit a school, company etc and see what is done there [= **open day** *BrE*]

an open-air concert

opening¹ /'əʊpənɪŋ $ 'oʊ-/ *n* [C] **1** a ceremony to celebrate the first time that a new public building, road etc is available for people to use: *the opening of the new art gallery* **2** the beginning of something: *a speech at the opening of the conference* **3** a job or opportunity that is available: *Are there any openings for gardeners?* **4** a hole or space in something: *an opening in the fence*

opening² *adj* [only before noun] **1** first or happening at the beginning of something: *the President's opening remarks* | *the opening match of the season* | **opening night** (=the first night of a new play, film etc) **2 opening hours** the time each day when a shop, library etc is open

openly /'əʊpənli $ 'oʊ-/ *adv* honestly and without keeping anything secret: *a chance to talk openly about your problems*

,open-'minded *adj* willing to consider new ideas, opinions, or ways of doing things: *their sympathetic, open-minded attitudes to young people* —**open-mindedness** *n* [U]

,open-'mouthed *adj, adv* with your mouth wide open, because you are surprised or shocked: *We **stared open-mouthed** at the images on the screen.*

openness /'əʊpənn̩s $ 'oʊ-/ *n* [U] when someone is honest and does not keep things secret

'open ,plan *adj* an open plan office, school etc does not have walls dividing it into separate rooms → see box at OFFICE

opera /'ɒpərə $ 'ɑː-/ *n* [C,U] a musical play in which all of the words are sung: *an opera singer* —**operatic** /,ɒpə'rætɪk $,ɑː-/ *adj* → SOAP OPERA

operate /'ɒpəreɪt $ 'ɑːp-/ *v*

1 [I,T] to work, or to make something work: *The machine seems to be operating smoothly.* | *He doesn't know how to operate the equipment.* | *Most freezers operate at below –18°C.*
2 [I] to cut into someone's body in order to remove or repair a part that is damaged: *Doctors had to operate to remove the bullet.* | **+on** *Surgeons operated on him for eight hours.*
3 [I,T] to do business, or to manage and control something: *She operated her business from a large house in Brighton.* | *The bakery operates all day.* | *Volunteers are operating an emergency hospital.*
4 [I] to have a particular effect: **+as** *The foam operates as a filter.*

O

'operating room n [C] *AmE* a part of a hospital where doctors do operations [= **operating theatre** *BrE*]

'operating ,system n [C] a system in a computer that helps all the programs to work

'operating ,theatre n [C] *BrE* a part of a hospital where doctors do operations [= **operating room** *AmE*]

operation /ˌɒpəˈreɪʃən $ ˌɑːp-/ n
1 [C] when doctors cut into someone's body to repair or remove a part that is damaged: *She's **having** her **operation** today.* | **+on** *He's recovering from an operation on his shoulder.* | *a heart operation*
2 [C] when people work together in a planned way in order to do something: *a rescue operation*
3 [C,U] the work of a business or organization, or one of the parts of a company or organization: *Many small businesses fail in the first year of operation.* | *the company's property development operation*
4 [U] the way in which something works, or when someone makes something work: *The job involves the operation of heavy machinery.*
5 in/into operation if a system or machine is in operation, it is working: *Video cameras were in operation.* | *The new system **came into operation** in 1999.*
6 [C] *technical* an action done by a computer

operational /ˌɒpəˈreɪʃənəl $ ˌɑːp-/ adj
1 working and ready to be used: *The new airport will soon be operational.* **2** relating to the work of a business, government etc: *operational costs*

operative /ˈɒpərətɪv $ ˈɑːpərə-, -ˈɑːpəreɪ-/ adj formal working and able to be used: *The law will become operative in a month.*

operator /ˈɒpəreɪtə $ ˈɑːpəreɪtər/ n [C]
1 someone who works on a telephone SWITCHBOARD: *Ask the operator to help you with the call.*
2 someone whose job is to use a machine or piece of equipment: *a crane operator* **3** a company that does a particular type of business: *a tour operator*

opinion /əˈpɪnjən/ n [C,U] what you think about a subject or situation: **+on/of/about** *We have very different opinions on education.* | *What is your **opinion** of the band?* | **In my opinion** (=I think) *he made the right decision.* | **have a high/low/good etc opinion of sth** (=think that something is good, bad etc) *Her boss has a high opinion of her work.* | **be of the opinion that** formal: *Otto is of the opinion that you are honest.* | *He doesn't seem to care about **public opinion** (=what most people in a country think).* | **Contrary to popular opinion,** *chocolate is good for you* (=most people think it is not). | *My doctor says I need an operation, but I've asked for a **second opinion** (=advice from a second doctor).* → **difference of opinion** at DIFFERENCE

opinionated /əˈpɪnjəneɪtɪd/ adj disapproving an opinionated person has very strong opinions: *an opinionated old fool*

o'pinion poll n [C] when a lot of people are asked what they think about a subject, especially about politics

opium /ˈəʊpiəm $ ˈoʊ-/ n [U] a very strong illegal drug made from POPPY seeds

opponent /əˈpəʊnənt $ əˈpoʊ-/ n [C]
1 someone who is competing against you in a sport or competition: *His opponent is twice as big as he is.*
2 someone who disagrees with a plan, idea etc: **+of** *opponents of Darwin's theory*

opportune /ˈɒpətjuːn $ ˌɑːpərˈtuːn/ adj formal **an opportune moment/time etc** a good time for doing something

opportunist /ˌɒpəˈtjuːnɪst $ ˌɑːpərˈtuː-/ n [C] someone who uses every chance to get power or advantages —**opportunism** n [U] —**opportunist** also **opportunistic** /ˌɒpətjuːˈnɪstɪk $ ˌɑːpərtuː-/ adj

opportunity /ˌɒpəˈtjuːnɪti $ ˌɑːpərˈtuː-/ n [C,U] plural **opportunities** a chance to do something: **opportunity to do sth** *He wasn't given the opportunity to defend himself.* | *I would like to **take this opportunity** to thank you.* | *job opportunities* | *an equal opportunities policy* | *I left school **at the earliest opportunity**.*
→ **PHOTO OPPORTUNITY**

oppose /əˈpəʊz $ əˈpoʊz/ v [T] to disagree with something and try to change or stop it: *They oppose any changes to the present system.*

opposed /əˈpəʊzd $ əˈpoʊzd/ adj
1 be opposed to sth to believe that something is wrong and should not be allowed: *Most people are opposed to the death penalty.*
2 as opposed to sth used when mentioning two different things, when only one is involved, acceptable etc: *Students discuss ideas, as opposed to just copying from books.*

opposing /əˈpəʊzɪŋ $ əˈpoʊ-/ adj [only before noun] **1** opposing teams, groups etc are competing or arguing with each other **2** opposing ideas, opinions etc are completely different from each other

opposite¹ /'ɒpəzɪt $ 'ɑːp-/ *adj*

1 completely different: *I thought the music would relax me, but it had the opposite effect.*
2 facing something, or directly across from something: *a building on the opposite side of the river* → see box at **FRONT**
3 the opposite sex people who are of a different sex: *She finds it hard to talk to members of the opposite sex.*
4 your opposite number someone who does the same job as you for a different organization, a different country etc: *a speech by his opposite number in the Labour party*

opposite² *prep, adv* if one thing or person is opposite another, they are facing each other: *Put the piano opposite the sofa.* | *He's moved into the house opposite.* → see picture on page A8

opposite³ *n* [C] something that is completely different from something else: *I didn't feel sleepy; just the opposite.* | *'What is the opposite of happiness?' 'Sadness.'*

Opposition /ˌɒpə'zɪʃən $ ˌɑːp-/ *n* **the Opposition** in some countries such as Britain, the main political party in the parliament that is not part of the government: *the leader of the Opposition*

opposition *n*

1 [U] when people disagree strongly with something: **+to** *opposition to the war* | **strong/fierce/stiff opposition** *The proposals met with strong opposition.* | **in opposition to sb/sth** *They were united in opposition to a common enemy.*
2 [C,U also + plural verb *BrE*] the person, team, company etc that you are competing against: *They played well against good opposition.* | *The opposition were beginning to dominate the game.*

oppress /ə'pres/ *v* [T] to treat people in an unfair and cruel way —**oppressed** *adj*: *an oppressed minority* —**oppression** /ə'preʃən/ *n* [U]

oppressive /ə'presɪv/ *adj* **1** cruel and unfair: *an oppressive military government* **2** making you feel uncomfortable: *oppressive heat*

oppressor /ə'presə $ -ər/ *n* [C] a person or group that treats people in a cruel and unfair way

opt /ɒpt $ ɑːpt/ *v* **opt for sth/to do sth** to choose one thing instead of another: *We've opted for a smaller car.* | *More students are opting to go to college.* → see box at **CHOOSE**

opt out *phr v* to choose not to join in a group or system: **+of** *Several countries may opt out of the agreement.*

optic /'ɒptɪk $ 'ɑːp-/ *adj technical* relating to the eyes: *the optic nerve*

optical /'ɒptɪkəl $ 'ɑːp-/ *adj* **1** relating to the way light is seen, or relating to the eyes: *an optical instrument* **2** using light to record and store information, especially in computer systems —**optically** /-kli/ *adv*

optical il'lusion *n* [C] a picture or image that tricks your eyes and makes you see something that is not actually there

optician /ɒp'tɪʃən $ ɑːp-/ *n* [C] **1** *BrE* someone who tests people's eyes and sells them glasses in a shop **2** *AmE* someone who makes glasses

optimal /'ɒptɪməl $ 'ɑːp-/ *adj formal* OPTIMUM

optimism /'ɒptɪmɪzəm $ 'ɑːp-/ *n* [U] the belief that good things will happen [≠ **pessimism**]: *optimism about the country's economic future*

optimist /'ɒptɪmɪst $ 'ɑːp-/ *n* [C] someone who believes that good things will happen [≠ **pessimist**]

optimistic /ˌɒptɪ'mɪstɪk◂ $ ˌɑːp-/ *adj* believing that good things will happen in the future [≠ **pessimistic**]: **+about** *Tom's optimistic about finding a job.* | **+that** *I'm optimistic that things will improve.* → see box at **CHARACTER**
—**optimistically** /-kli/ *adv*

optimize also **-ise** *BrE* /'ɒptɪmaɪz $ 'ɑːp-/ *v* [T] to do or use something in a way that is as effective as possible

optimum /'ɒptɪməm $ 'ɑːp-/ *adj* [only before noun] *formal* best or most suitable for a particular purpose: *optimum use of space*

option /'ɒpʃən $ 'ɑːp-/ *n* [C] **1** something that you can choose to do [= **choice**]: *It's the only option we have left.* | *You have the option of walking or going on the bus.* **2 have no option (but to do sth)** to have to do something, especially when you do not want to do it: *They had no option but to cut jobs.* **3 keep/leave your options open** to not make a definite decision so that you have more possibilities to choose from: *Leave your options open until you have the results of the test.*

optional /'ɒpʃənəl $ 'ɑːp-/ *adj* if something is optional, it is available but you do not have to choose it [≠ **compulsory**]: *The sunroof is optional.*

optometrist /ɒp'tɒmɪtrɪst $ ɑːp'tɑː-/ *n* [C] someone who examines people's eyes and orders glasses for them —**optometry** *n* [U]

opulent /'ɒpjʊlənt $ 'ɑːp-/ *adj* decorated in an expensive way: *an opulent hotel* —**opulence** *n* [U] —**opulently** *adv*

or /ə; *strong* ɔː $ ər; *strong* ɔːr/ *linking word*

1 used between two possibilities, or before the last in a series of possibilities [➦ **either**]: *Coffee or tea?* | *You can go by bus, by train, or by plane.*
2 used after a negative verb when you mean not one thing and not another thing: *They don't eat meat or fish.*
3 also **or 'else** used to warn someone that something bad will happen if they do not do something: *Hurry, or you'll miss your plane.*
4 two or three/20 or 30 etc about or between the numbers you mention: *'How many people were there?' 'Oh, 30 or 40.'*
5 or so used after a number, time, distance etc to show that it is not exact: *There's a gas station a mile or so down the road.*
6 or anything/something *spoken* used to talk or ask about something similar to the thing you have just mentioned: *Do you want to go out for a drink or something?*
7 used to further explain something that you have just said: *biology, or the study of living things*

oral¹ /'ɔːrəl/ *adj*

1 spoken, not written: *an oral report*
2 relating to the mouth: *oral hygiene*
—**orally** *adv*

oral² *n* [C] a test in which questions and answers are spoken rather than written

orange /'prɪ̯ndʒ $ 'ɔː-, 'ɑː-/ *n*

1 [C] a juicy round fruit with a thick skin that is a colour between red and yellow → see picture at **FRUIT**
2 [U] a colour that is between red and yellow → see picture at **PATTERN**
—**orange** *adj: an orange shirt*

orangutang /ɔː'ræŋuːˌtæŋ $ əˈræŋətæŋ/, **orangutan** /-tæn/ *n* [C] a large animal like a monkey that has long arms and long orange hair

orator /'prətə $ 'ɔːrətər, 'ɑː-/ *n* [C] someone who is good at making political speeches

orbit¹ /'ɔːbɪ̯t $ 'ɔːr-/ *n* [C] the circle that something moves in when it is going around the Earth, the sun etc

orbit² *v* [I,T] to travel in space around a larger object such as the Earth, the sun etc: *a satellite that orbits the Earth*

orchard /'ɔːtʃəd $ 'ɔːrtʃərd/ *n* [C] a place where fruit trees are grown

orchestra /'ɔːkₐstrə $ 'ɔːr-/ *n* [C also + plural verb *BrE*] a large group of musicians who play CLASSICAL music together

TOPIC

the wind section – the instruments made mostly of wood that you blow through
the strings/the string section – the instruments that have strings
the brass (section) – the instruments made of metal that you blow through
the percussion (section) – the instruments such as drums and bells
conductor – the person who directs the music and musicians

—**orchestral** /ɔː'kestrəl $ -ɔːr-/ *adj*

orchestrate /'ɔːkₐstreɪt $ 'ɔːr-/ *v* [T] to organize an important event or a complicated plan, especially secretly: *a carefully orchestrated campaign*

orchid /'ɔːkₐd $ 'ɔːr-/ *n* [C] a flower which is often very beautiful and unusual

ordain /ɔː'deɪn $ ɔːr-/ *v* [T] to officially make someone a priest [➜ **ordination**]

ordeal /ɔː'diːl, 'ɔːdiːl $ ɔːr'diːl, 'ɔːrdiːl/ *n* [C] a very unpleasant experience: *School can be an ordeal for some children.*

order¹ /'ɔːdə $ 'ɔːrdər/ *n*

1 in order so that something can happen, or so that someone can do something: **in order (for sb/sth) to do sth** *Plants need light in order to live.* | *In order for the company to remain competitive, jobs must be shed.* | **+that** *I must have it in writing in order that I know exactly what is happening.*
2 [C,U] the way that several things are arranged in relation to each other [➜ **sequence**]: **in the right/wrong/same order** *Can you keep the pictures in the same order?* | **in order/out of order** *Are all the slides in order?* | *The names were written in alphabetical order* (=with 'a' names first, then 'b' names etc). | *State the main points in order of importance.*
3 [C] when a customer asks for a particular kind of food or drink in a restaurant: *Can I take your order* (=write down what you want to eat)?
4 [C] when a customer asks a company to make or send goods: **+for** *The school has just put in an*

order for 10 new computers. | **on order** *Hundreds of the aircraft are on order.*
5 [C] an official instruction from someone in authority that must be obeyed: **order (for sb) to do sth** *Captain Smith gave the order to advance.* | *You have to obey orders.*
6 out of order **a)** if a machine is out of order, it has stopped working: *The photocopier is out of order again.* **b)** *BrE informal* used to say that someone's behaviour is rude or unacceptable: *That remark was out of order!*
7 in order legally or officially correct: *Your passport seems to be in order.*
8 [U] when people obey laws or rules, and do not cause trouble: *Police are working hard to maintain law and order.* | *Order has now been restored in the capital city.*
→ **MAIL ORDER, MONEY ORDER, POSTAL ORDER, STANDING ORDER**

order² *v*

1 [I,T] to ask for food or drink in a restaurant, bar etc: *He sat down and ordered a beer.* | *Are you ready to order?* → see box at **ASK**
2 [T] to ask a company to make or send something: *I've ordered a new computer from the supplier.* | **order sb sth** *I'll order you a taxi.*
3 [T] to officially tell someone that they must do something: *'Stay right there,' she ordered.* | **order sb to do sth** *Her doctor ordered her to rest for a week.* | **+that** *He ordered that his daughters be brought up as Christians.*
4 [T] to arrange something in a particular way: *The names are ordered alphabetically.*

order sb about/around *phr v BrE* to give someone orders in an annoying or threatening way: *How dare he order her about like that?*

orderly¹ /'ɔːdəli $ 'ɔːrdərli/ *adj* well-organized or tidily arranged: *an orderly desk*

orderly² *n* [C] plural **orderlies** someone who does jobs in a hospital which do not need any special training

ordinal number /ˌɔːdₐnəl 'nʌmbə $ ˌɔːrdənəl 'nʌmbər/ *n* [C] a number such as first, second, or third [➜ **cardinal number**]

ordinarily /'ɔːdₐnərₐli, ˌɔːdən'eərₐli $ ˌɔːrdən'erₐli/ *adv* especially *AmE* usually: *I don't ordinarily go to movies in the afternoon.*

ordinary /'ɔːdₐnəri $ 'ɔːrdəneri/ *adj*

1 average, common, or usual, not different or special: *It's just an ordinary camera.* | *The book is about ordinary people.* → see box at **NORMAL**
2 not particularly good or impressive: *I thought the paintings were pretty ordinary.*
3 out of the ordinary very different from what usually happens: *Anything out of the ordinary made her nervous.*

ordination /ˌɔːdₐ'neɪʃən $ ˌɔːr-/ *n* [C,U] the ceremony in which someone is ORDAINED (=officially made a priest)

ore /ɔː $ ɔːr/ *n* [C,U] rock or earth from which metal can be obtained

organ /'ɔːgən $ 'ɔːr-/ *n* [C]

1 part of the body of a human, animal, or plant that has a particular purpose: *the liver and other internal organs* | **sexual/reproductive organs** | **organ transplant** (=when an organ is put into the body of another person) | **organ donor** (=the person from whose body an organ is taken to be transplanted) → see picture on page A3

2 a) a musical instrument like a piano with large pipes that produce the sound, played especially in churches [➥ **organist**] **b)** an electronic instrument with a KEYBOARD like a piano → MOUTH ORGAN

organic /ɔːˈgænɪk $ ɔːr-/ *adj*
1 relating to farming or gardening without using chemicals that are harmful to the environment: *organic food/vegetables/milk etc* → see box at FOOD, ENVIRONMENT → and NATURAL
2 related to or produced by living things [≠ **inorganic**]: *organic matter*
—**organically** /-kli/ *adv*

organism /ˈɔːgənɪzəm $ ˈɔːr-/ *n* [C] a living thing, usually a very small one: *a microscopic organism*

organist /ˈɔːgənɪst $ ˈɔːr-/ *n* [C] someone who plays the ORGAN

organization also **-isation** *BrE* /ˌɔːgənaɪˈzeɪʃən $ ˌɔːrgənə-/ *n*
1 [C] a group such as a club or business that has formed for a particular purpose: *the human rights organization Amnesty International* | *international organizations such as the UN* | *a charity organization*

> **THESAURUS**
>
> **institution** – a large, important organization such as a bank, church, or university
> **association** – an organization for people who do the same kind of work or have the same interests
> **party** – an organization of people with the same political aims
> **club/society** – an organization for people who share an interest
> **union** – an organization formed by workers in order to protect their rights

2 [U] the way in which something is organized, or the activity of organizing something: *He was responsible for the organization of the party's election campaign.*
—**organizational** *adj*

organize also **-ise** *BrE* /ˈɔːgənaɪz $ ˈɔːr-/ *v* [T] to plan or arrange something: *Who's organizing the New Year's party?*
—**organizer** *n* [C]

organized also **-ised** *BrE* /ˈɔːgənaɪzd $ ˈɔːr-/ *adj* **1 well/badly organized a)** planned and arranged well or badly: *The exhibition wasn't very well organized.* **b)** good or bad at planning the things that you have to do and doing them at the right time: *She's really badly organized.* → see box at CHARACTER

> **THESAURUS**
>
> **efficient** – working well, without wasting time or energy: *an efficient boiler*
> **well run** – organized efficiently: *a well-run hotel*
> **businesslike** – sensible and practical in the way you do things: *a businesslike attitude*
> **be a mess, be a shambles, be in chaos**

2 involving many people doing something in a planned way: *organized sports*

organized 'crime *n* [U] crimes committed by a large and organized group of powerful criminals

orgasm /ˈɔːgæzəm $ ˈɔːr-/ *n* [C,U] the moment when you have the greatest sexual pleasure during sex

orgy /ˈɔːdʒi $ ˈɔːr-/ *n* [C] plural **orgies 1** a party at which people behave in an uncontrolled way, for example drinking a lot of alcohol and having sex **2 an orgy of sth** when people do something a lot, especially something bad: *an orgy of violence*

Orient /ˈɔːriənt, ˈɒ- $ ˈɔːr-/ *n* **the Orient** old-fashioned the eastern part of the world, especially China and Japan

Oriental /ˌɔːriˈentl◂, ˌɒri- $ ˌɔːr-/ *adj* old-fashioned relating to Asia, especially China and Japan: *Oriental culture*

orientation /ˌɔːriənˈteɪʃən, ˌɒri- $ ˌɔːr-/ *n*
1 [C,U] the kind of beliefs and ideas that a group or person has: **political/religious orientation** *the group's right-wing political orientation*
2 sexual orientation whether someone is HETEROSEXUAL or HOMOSEXUAL

oriented /ˈɔːrientɪd, ˈɒri- $ ˈɔː-/ also **orientated** /ˈɔːriənteɪtɪd, ˈɒri- $ ˈɔː-/ *BrE adj* mainly concerned with or aimed at a particular thing or group of people: *complaints that the magazine has become too politically oriented* | **market-oriented/export-oriented etc**

origin /ˈɒrɪdʒɪn $ ˈɔː-, ˈɑː-/ *n* [C,U]
1 where, when, or how something began: **+of** *the origin of life on Earth* | **of Latin/German etc origin** *The word is of Latin origin.* | **in origin** *Some field boundaries are medieval in origin.* | *The company had its origins in France.*
2 the country, race, or social class from which someone comes: *He's proud of his Italian origins.* | **ethnic/racial/social origin** | *She could never forget her humble origins* (=the low social class she came from). | *They will be sent back to their country of origin.*

original¹ /əˈrɪdʒɪnəl, -dʒənəl/ *adj*
1 [only before noun] existing first, before any changes were made: *The house still has its original stone floor.* | *Our original plan was too expensive.*
2 completely new and different: *a highly original style of painting* → see box at NEW
3 [only before noun] an original painting, drawing etc is not a copy: *Is that an original Matisse* (=painting by Matisse)?

original² *n* [C] a painting, document etc that is not a copy

originality /əˌrɪdʒɪˈnæləti/ *n* [U] the quality of being completely new and different: *The design is good but lacks originality.*

originally /əˈrɪdʒɪnəli, -dʒənəli/ *adv* in the beginning: *Her family originally came from Thailand.* | *We had originally intended to go by car, but in the end we took the train.*

originate /əˈrɪdʒɪneɪt/ *v formal* **1** [I] to start to develop in a particular place or at a particular time: **+in** *The custom of having a Christmas tree originated in Germany.* **2** [T] to have the idea for something and start it: *the man who originated this technique* —**originator** *n* [C]

ornament /ˈɔːnəmənt $ ˈɔːr-/ *n* [C] an object that you keep in your house as a decoration: *china ornaments*

ornamental /ˌɔːnəˈmentl◂ $ ˌɔːr-/ adj
intended to be attractive rather than useful:
ornamental plants

ornate /ɔːˈneɪt $ ɔːr-/ adj having a lot of deco-
ration: *ornate furniture* —**ornately** adv

ornithology /ˌɔːnɪˈθɒlədʒi $ ˌɔːrnəˈθɑː-/ n [U]
the study of birds —**ornithologist** n [C]

orphan¹ /ˈɔːfən $ ˈɔːr-/ n [C] a child whose
parents are dead

orphan² v **be orphaned** if a child is orphaned,
both its parents die or its only remaining parent
dies

orphanage /ˈɔːfənɪdʒ $ ˈɔːr-/ n [C] a place for
orphans to live in, especially in past times

orthodox /ˈɔːθədɒks $ ˈɔːrθədɑːks/ adj
1 orthodox ideas or methods are traditional
ones that most people think are right or normal:
orthodox methods of treating disease **2** having
traditional religious beliefs and practices: *an
orthodox Jew* —**orthodoxy** n [C,U]

orthopedic also **orthopaedic** BrE
/ˌɔːθəˈpiːdɪk◂ $ ˌɔːr-/ adj relating to the medical
treatment of problems that affect people's bones
or muscles

Oscar /ˈɒskə $ ˈɑːskər/ n [C] *trademark* a prize
that is given each year in the US for the best
film, performance in a film etc

oscillate /ˈɒsəleɪt $ ˈɑː-/ v [I] *formal* to keep
changing between two things, amounts, or directions

osmosis /ɒzˈməʊsəs $ ɑːzˈmoʊ-/ n [U] if you
learn facts or ideas by osmosis, you gradually
learn them by hearing them often

ostensible /ɒˈstensəbəl $ ɑː-/ adj [only before
noun] an ostensible reason, aim etc is one that
seems or is said to be the real one, but is not
—**ostensibly** adv: *She moved away, ostensibly to
examine a photo on the wall.*

ostentatious /ˌɒstənˈteɪʃəs◂, -ten- $ ˌɑː-/ adj
done, worn etc in order to make other people
notice and admire you: *an ostentatious display of
wealth* —**ostentatiously** adv —**ostentation** n
[U]

osteopath /ˈɒstiəpæθ $ ˈɑː-/ n [C] someone
who treats medical problems such as back pain
by moving and pressing the muscles and bones

ostracize also **-ise** BrE /ˈɒstrəsaɪz $ ˈɑː-/ v [T] if
people ostracize a member of their group, they
start treating them in an unfriendly way: *There
was a time when criminals would be ostracized by
the whole village.* —**ostracism** /-sɪzəm/ n [U]

ostrich /ˈɒstrɪtʃ $ ˈɒː-, ˈɑː-/ n [C] a big African
bird with long legs that cannot fly

other /ˈʌðə $ ˈʌðər/ determiner, adj, pron
1 used to refer to the rest of a group or the
second thing of a pair: *Anna has a job, but the
other girls are still at school.* | *The other students
are about the same age as me.* | *Here's one sock –
where's the other one?* | *We ate one of the pizzas
and froze the other.* | *Can I stay here until the
others come back?*
2 used to refer to additional things or people of
the same kind [➔ another]: *Have you any other
questions?*
3 used to refer to a different person or thing
from the one you have just mentioned or from
this one [➔ another]: *Can we meet some other time
– I'm busy right now.* | *Their cottage is on the
other side of the lake.* | *I do not deny that some
schools are better than others.*
4 the other day/morning etc *spoken* recently: *I
was talking to Ted the other day.*

5 other than except: *She has no one to talk to
other than her family.*
6 every other day/week etc one day, week etc
in every two: *Her husband cooks dinner every
other day.*
7 someone/something etc or other used when
you are not certain about the person, thing etc
you are referring to: *We'll get the money somehow or other.*
➔ EACH OTHER

GRAMMAR

Do not use **other** after 'an'. Use **another**:
There must be another way of doing it.

otherwise /ˈʌðəwaɪz $ ˈʌðər-/ adv
1 a) used to say what will happen if something
else does not happen first, usually when it is
bad: *You'd better go now, otherwise you'll be
late.* **b)** used to say what would or might have
happened if the situation had been different: *We
had no phone then, otherwise we would have rung
the police.*
2 except for what has just been mentioned: *The
sleeves are a bit long, but otherwise the dress fits
fine.* | *The weather spoiled an otherwise perfect
day.*
3 think/decide etc otherwise to think or
decide the opposite of what someone else thinks
or decides
4 or otherwise or not: *respect for all creatures,
human or otherwise*

otter /ˈɒtə $ ˈɑːtər/ n [C] a small animal with
brown fur that swims and eats fish

ouch /aʊtʃ/ *spoken* said when you suddenly feel
pain: *Ouch! That hurt!*

oughtn't /ˈɔːtnt $ ˈɒː-/ the short form of 'ought
not'

ought to /ˈɔːt tuː $ ˈɒːt-/ *modal verb*
1 used to say that someone should do something
[= should]: *You ought to take a day off.* | *I ought
not to be telling you this.* | *We ought to have
invited them back with us* (=but we didn't).
2 used to say that you expect something to happen or be true: *The weather ought to be nice in
August.*

ounce /aʊns/ n [C] written abbreviation **oz** **1** a
unit for measuring weight, equal to 1/16 of a
pound or 28.35 grams **2 an ounce of sth** even a
small amount of something: *If you had an ounce
of sense, you'd leave him.*

our /aʊə $ aʊr/ determiner belonging to or relat-
ing to us: *Our daughter is at college.*

ours /aʊəz $ aʊrz/ pron the POSSESSIVE form of
'we': *'Whose car is that?' 'It's ours.'* | *They have
their tickets, but ours haven't come yet.*

ourselves /aʊəˈselvz $ aʊr-/ pron
1 the REFLEXIVE form of 'we': *It was strange
seeing ourselves on television.*
2 used to emphasize the word 'we': *We started
this business ourselves.*
3 (all) by ourselves alone or without help: *We
found our way here all by ourselves.*
4 have sth (all) to ourselves to not have to
share something with other people: *We'll have
the house to ourselves next week.*

oust /aʊst/ v [T] to force someone out of a
position of power: *an attempt to oust the commu-
nists from power*

out¹ /aʊt/ adv, adj
1 a) from inside a place or container [≠ in]:

Close the door on your way out. | **+of** *She tipped cereal out of the packet into her bowl.* **b)** no longer inside a place or container [≠ **in**]: *The kids are out in the back garden.* | *Ms Jackson is out right now* (=not at home or not in her office). | **+of** *He was thrilled to be out of hospital.*

THESAURUS

out – away from the building where you live or work: *Tom's out. He should be back soon.*

outside – not in a room or building but near it: *I'll wait for you outside.*

outdoors or **out of doors** – not inside a building: *We spent most of the summer outdoors.*

outdoor (without an -s) – used to describe things that are outside, or that happen outside: *an outdoor swimming pool* | *outdoor sports*

---

2 in or to a place far away: *The family are due to fly out to America shortly.*
3 a light or fire that is out is no longer shining or burning: *Turn the lights out when you go to bed.*
4 8 out of 10/19 out of 20 etc used to say how many people or things in a group do something or are something: *Eight out of ten teachers* (=80 per cent of teachers) *say they have too much paperwork to do.*
5 be out of sth to have none of something left: *We're almost out of gas.*
6 available to be bought: *Morrison has a new book out this month.*
7 *spoken* not possible: *Skiing's out because it costs too much.*
8 not fashionable now [≠ **in**]: *Bright lipstick shades are out.*
9 be out for sth/be out to do sth *informal* to intend to get or do something: *He's just out to get attention.*
10 if a number obtained by calculating is out, it is wrong: *Their forecast of population increase was out by 5%.*
11 out of curiosity/fear/pity etc because of curiosity, fear etc: *She gave him the job out of pity.*
12 out of trouble/danger/office etc not in trouble, danger etc: *Keep out of trouble.* | *The patient is now out of danger.*
13 not allowed to continue playing a game, according to its rules
14 if flowers on a plant are out, they have opened
15 if the sun or stars are out, they can be seen in the sky
16 if a secret is out, it has become known
17 if the TIDE is out, the sea is at its lowest level

out² *v* [T] to publicly say that someone is HOMO-SEXUAL when they do not want that fact known

out-and-'out *adj* [only before noun] used to emphasize your description of someone or something: *an out-and-out lie*

outback /'aʊtbæk/ *n* **the outback** the part of Australia far away from cities, where not many people live

outbid /aʊt'bɪd/ *v* [T] past tense and past participle **outbid** present participle **outbidding** to offer more money for something than someone else

outbreak /'aʊtbreɪk/ *n* [C] when something bad such as a serious disease or a war starts: **+of** *an outbreak of malaria*

outburst /'aʊtbɜːst $ -bɜːrst/ *n* [C] when someone suddenly shows a strong emotion, especially anger: *an angry outburst*

outcast /'aʊtkɑːst $ -kæst/ *n* [C] someone who is not accepted by other people: *a social outcast*

outclass /aʊt'klɑːs $ -'klæs/ *v* [T] to be much better than someone at doing something

outcome /'aʊtkʌm/ *n* [singular] the final result of a meeting, process etc: **+of** *the outcome of the election* → see box at **RESULT**

outcrop /'aʊtkrɒp $ -krɑːp/ also **outcropping** *AmE* /-'kəʊtrɒpɪŋ $ -krɑː-/ *n* [C] a large piece of rock that is not covered by earth

outcry /'aʊtkraɪ/ *n* [singular] an angry protest by a lot of people: **+against** *a public outcry against nuclear weapons testing*

outdated /ˌaʊt'deɪtɪd◂/ *adj* no longer useful or modern: *factories full of outdated machinery* → see box at **OLD-FASHIONED**

outdo /aʊt'duː/ *v* [T] past tense **outdid** /-'dɪd/ past participle **outdone** /-'dʌn/ third person singular **outdoes** /-'dʌz/ to be better or more successful than someone else: *two brothers trying to outdo each other* | *Not to be outdone, Robson made the score 2–0 just before half-time* (=he did as well as the other player who scored).

outdoor /ˌaʊt'dɔː◂ $ -'dɔːr◂/ *adj* [only before noun] existing, happening, or used outside, not inside a building [≠ **indoor**]: *an outdoor swimming pool* → see box at **OUT**

outdoors¹ /ˌaʊt'dɔːz $ -'dɔːrz/ *adv* not in a building [= **outside**; ≠ **indoors**]: *I prefer working outdoors.* → see box at **OUT**

outdoors² *n* **the (great) outdoors** the countryside

outer /'aʊtə $ -ər/ *adj* [only before noun] on or near the outside of something [≠ **inner**]: *Remove the tough outer leaves.*

outermost /'aʊtəməʊst $ -tərmoʊst/ *adj* [only before noun] furthest from the middle of something [≠ **innermost**]: *the outermost planets*

outer 'space *n* [U] the area outside the Earth's air where the stars and PLANETS are

outfit /'aʊtfɪt/ *n* [C] a set of clothes that you wear together: *She was wearing her usual outfit of white blouse and black skirt.*

outflank /aʊt'flæŋk/ *v* [T] to gain an advantage over an opponent, especially in politics

outgoing /ˌaʊt'ɡəʊɪŋ◂ $ -'ɡoʊ-/ *adj* **1** someone who is outgoing enjoys meeting and talking to people **2 the outgoing president/ government etc** a person or group that is finishing a job as president, government etc **3** [only before noun] going away from a place: *outgoing phone calls*

outgoings /'aʊtˌɡəʊɪŋz $ -'ɡoʊ-/ *n* [plural] *BrE* the money that you spend on rent, food etc

outgrow /aʊt'ɡrəʊ $ -'ɡroʊ/ *v* [T] past tense **outgrew** /-'ɡruː/ past participle **outgrown** /-'ɡrəʊn $ -'ɡroʊn/ to become too big or too old for something: *Kara's already outgrown her shoes.* | *She had outgrown her passion for horses.*

outing /'aʊtɪŋ/ *n* [C] a short trip for a group of people: *We're going on a family outing.*

outlandish /aʊt'lændɪʃ/ *adj* strange and unusual: *outlandish clothes*

outlast /aʊt'lɑːst $ -'læst/ *v* [T] to continue for longer than someone or something else: *The whole point of the game is to outlast your opponent.*

outlaw¹ /ˈaʊtlɔː $ -lɒː/ v [T] to officially say that something is illegal: *Gambling was outlawed here in 1980.*

outlaw² n [C] *old-fashioned* someone who is hiding from law officers

outlay /ˈaʊtleɪ/ n [C,U] an amount of money that you spend to start a new business, activity etc: *a huge initial outlay*

outlet /ˈaʊtlet, -lɪt/ n [C] **1** a way of expressing or getting rid of strong feelings: *I use judo as an outlet for stress.* **2** a place where gas or liquid can flow out of something **3** *formal* a shop that sells a company's products

outline¹ /ˈaʊtlaɪn/ n **1** [singular] the main ideas or facts about something: +**of** *an outline of the company's plan* **2** [C] a line around the edge of something that shows its shape

outline² v [T] to describe the main ideas or facts about something: *a speech outlining his work in refugee camps*

outlive /aʊtˈlɪv/ v [T] to live longer than someone else: *She outlived her husband by 10 years.*

outlook /ˈaʊtlʊk/ n [C] **1** your general attitude to life and the world: +**on** *a positive outlook on life* **2** what is expected to happen in the future: +**for** *The long-term outlook for the industry is worrying.*

outlying /ˈaʊtˌlaɪ-ɪŋ/ adj [only before noun] a long way from other places: *Outlying villages had been attacked.*

outmanoeuvre *BrE*; **outmaneuver** *AmE* /ˌaʊtməˈnuːvə $ -ər/ v [T] to cleverly achieve something when someone else does not want you to achieve it: *Alan had outmanoeuvred her with ease.*

outmoded /aʊtˈməʊdɪd $ -ˈmoʊ-/ adj OUT-DATED

outnumber /aʊtˈnʌmbə $ -ər/ v [T] to be greater in number than another group: *Women outnumber men in the nursing profession.*

out-of-'date adj OUTDATED → see box at OLD-FASHIONED

out-of-the-'way adj a long way from other places

out-of-'town adj [only before noun] **1** to, from, or in another town **2** *BrE* on the edge of a town: *out-of-town shopping centres*

outpace /aʊtˈpeɪs/ v [T] to go faster, work better, or develop faster than other people or things

outpatient /ˈaʊtˌpeɪʃənt/ n [C] someone who goes to a hospital for treatment but does not stay there all night

outperform /ˌaʊtpəˈfɔːm $ -pərˈfɔːrm/ v [T] to do something better than other things or people: *Mart Stores continued to outperform other retailers.*

outplay /aʊtˈpleɪ/ v [T] to play better than your opponent in a game

outpost /ˈaʊtpəʊst $ -poʊst/ n [C] a small town or group of buildings a long way from other places

outpouring /ˈaʊtpɔːrɪŋ/ n [C] when a lot of people suddenly start expressing an emotion: +**of** *the public outpouring of grief following the Princess's death*

output¹ /ˈaʊtpʊt/ n [C,U] the amount of goods, energy etc that someone or something produces [➙ **input**]: *Economic output is down by 10% this year.*

output² v [T] past tense and past participle **output** present participle **outputting** if a computer outputs information, it produces it

outrage¹ /ˈaʊtreɪdʒ/ n **1** [U] a feeling of extreme anger or shock: *public outrage at the scandal* **2** [C] something that causes extreme anger or shock: *This is an outrage!* | *terrorist outrages*

outrage² v [T] to make someone feel very angry or shocked —**outraged** adj

outrageous /aʊtˈreɪdʒəs/ adj very shocking or bad: *the outrageous cost of school uniform* —**outrageously** adv

outright¹ /ˈaʊtraɪt/ adj [only before noun] **1** complete and total: *outright victory* | *an outright ban on handguns* **2** said clearly and directly: *an outright refusal*

outright² /aʊtˈraɪt/ adv **1** clearly and directly: *Should I ask Margaret outright?* **2 be killed outright** to be killed immediately in an accident **3** completely: *They haven't rejected the plan outright.*

outrun /aʊtˈrʌn/ v [T] past tense **outran** /-ˈræn/ past participle **outrun** present participle **outrunning** **1** to run faster or further than someone **2** to develop more quickly than something else

outset /ˈaʊtset/ n **at/from the outset** at or from the beginning: *I warned you at the outset that this wouldn't be easy.*

outshine /aʊtˈʃaɪn/ v [T] past tense and past participle **outshone** /aʊtˈʃɒn $ -ˈʃoʊn/ to be much better at something than someone else

outside¹ /aʊtˈsaɪd, ˈaʊtsaɪd/ prep, adv

1 not inside a building or room, but near it [≠ **inside**]: *Can I go and play outside, Dad?* | *Wait outside, I want to talk to him alone.* | *He left an envelope outside my door.* → see box at OUT → see picture on page A8

2 further than the edge of a city, town etc: *We live just outside Leeds.* | +**of** *especially AmE*: *a field outside of Roswell*

3 further than the limits of a situation, activity etc: *Teachers can't control what students do outside school.* | +**of** *especially AmE*: *I have a lot of interests outside of football.*

outside² /aʊtˈsaɪd, ˈaʊtsaɪd/ n **1 the outside** the part of something that is furthest from the centre [≠ **the inside**]: *The outside of the building is pink.* **2 on the outside** used when describing the way someone or something seems to be: *Their marriage seemed so perfect on the outside.*

outside³ /ˈaʊtsaɪd/ adj [only before noun] **1** an outside wall, toilet etc is not inside a building **2** involving someone who does not belong to your group or organization: *We need some outside help.* **3 the outside world** the rest of the world: *The city is cut off from the outside world by floods.* **4 outside interests** things you do or are interested in that are not connected with your work

outsider /aʊtˈsaɪdə $ -ər/ n [C] someone who does not belong to a particular group or organization: *Sometimes I feel like an outsider in my own family.*

outsize /ˈaʊtsaɪz/ also **outsized** /ˈaʊtsaɪzd/ adj [only before noun] larger than normal: *her outsize handbag*

outskirts /'aʊtskɜ:ts $ -ɜ:r-/ n **the outskirts** the parts of a city or town that are furthest from the centre: **on the outskirts (of sth)** *They have an apartment on the outskirts of Geneva.*

outspoken /aʊt'spəʊkən $ -'spoʊ-/ adj someone who is outspoken says what they think even though it may shock or offend people: *an outspoken critic of the government*

outstanding /aʊt'stændɪŋ/ adj **1** excellent and impressive: *an outstanding performance →* see box at **GOOD 2** not yet done or paid: *an outstanding debt* —**outstandingly** adv: *The business has been outstandingly successful.*

outstay /aʊt'steɪ/ v → outstay your welcome at **WELCOME⁴**

outstretched /ˌaʊt'stretʃt◄/ adj if your arms or legs are outstretched, they are stretched out as far as possible: *I took hold of his outstretched arm.*

outstrip /aʊt'strɪp/ v [T] **outstripped, outstripping** to be larger or better than someone or something else: *His qualifications far outstripped those of the other candidates.*

outward /'aʊtwəd $ -wərd/ adj **1** relating to how someone or something seems to be: *Amy answered with outward composure.* | *the car's* **outward appearance 2** going away from a place or towards the outside: *an outward flight*

outwardly /'aʊtwədli $ -wərd-/ adv used when saying how someone or something seems to be, rather than how they really are: *outwardly confident people*

outwards /'aʊtwədz $ -wərdz/ *especially BrE*; **outward** *especially AmE* adv away from the centre of something [≠ **inwards**]: *Lie on your tummy with your elbows pointing outwards.*

outweigh /aʊt'weɪ/ v [T] to be more important than something else: *The benefits outweigh the costs.*

outwit /aʊt'wɪt/ v [T] **outwitted, outwitting** to use tricks or clever plans to defeat someone, escape from them etc: *He outwitted his pursuers by suddenly changing direction.*

oval /'əʊvəl $ 'oʊ-/ n [C] a shape that is like a circle, but longer than it is wide → see box at **SHAPE** → see picture at **SHAPE¹** —**oval** adj

ovary /'əʊvəri $ 'oʊ-/ n [C] plural **ovaries** the part of a female person or animal that produces eggs

ovation /əʊ'veɪʃən $ oʊ-/ n [C] if people give someone an ovation, they CLAP their hands to show their approval: **standing ovation** (=when people stand and clap)

oven /'ʌvən/ n [C] a piece of equipment that you cook food inside, usually a metal box with a door [➡ **cooker, stove**]: *Bake in a hot oven for ten minutes.* | **gas/electric/microwave oven** → see picture at **KITCHEN**

over¹ /'əʊvə $ 'oʊvər/ prep

1 going from one side of something to the other, especially by jumping, climbing, or flying [➡ **across**]: *I jumped over the wall and ran along the bank.* | *They had to climb over piles of rubble to reach him.* | *the next bridge over the river →* see picture on page A8

2 above or higher than something [≠ **under**]: *The sign over the door said 'No Exit.'*

3 **over the road/street/river etc** on the opposite side of the road, street etc: *There's a supermarket over the road.*

4 on something or covering it [≠ **under**]: *Put this blanket over him.*

5 more than a particular amount, number, or age: *It cost over £1000.* | **the over-30s/over-50s etc** (=people who are more than a particular age)

6 during: *I saw Julie over the summer.* | **over the past/next few months/years etc** *The situation has improved over the past ten years.*

7 down from the edge of something: *The car fell over a cliff.*

8 **be/get over sth** to feel better after being ill or upset [➡ **recover**]: *I still haven't got over this flu.*

9 about: *an argument over some jewellery*

10 used to say who or what is controlled, influenced, or defeated: *the period in which Spain ruled over Portugal* | *their 2–1 victory over Leeds*

11 using the telephone or a radio: *The salesman explained it to me over the phone.*

over² adv, adj

1 down from an upright position: *Kate fell over and hurt her ankle.* | *I saw him push the bike over.*

2 to a particular place: *Come over tomorrow and we'll go shopping.*

3 to or in a place on the other side of something: *I'm flying over to Sweden next week.* | *He strolled over to the window.* | **over here/there** *I'm over here!*

4 finished: *The game was nearly over.*

5 **(all) over again** once more from the beginning: *The computer lost all my work, and I had to do it all over again.*

6 **over and over (again)** many times: *He made us sing the song over and over until we got it right.*

7 **get sth over with** to do something unpleasant so that you do not have to worry about it any more: *Call her and get it over with.*

8 **roll/turn/flip etc (sth) over** to move, or to move something, so that another side can be seen: *He rolled over and went to sleep.*

9 above or higher than something: *You can't hear anything when the planes fly over.*

10 more than a particular amount, number, or age: *a game for children aged 6 and over*

11 **over to sb** used to say that it is now someone else's turn to do something: *We've raised the issue – now it's over to the government.*

over- /əʊvə $ oʊvər/ prefix too much: *You're overqualified.* | *overcrowded prisons* | *people who overeat*

overall¹ /ˌəʊvər'ɔːl◄ $ ˌoʊvər'ɔːl◄/ adj, adv considering or including everything: *The overall cost of the trip is $500.* | *Overall, the situation looks good.*

overall² /'əʊvərɔːl $ 'oʊvərɔːl/ n **1** [C] *BrE* a loose-fitting piece of clothing like a coat that is worn over clothes to keep them clean when you are working **2** **overalls** [plural] *BrE* a piece of clothing like a shirt and trousers joined together, that you wear over your clothes to keep them clean when you are working **3** **overalls** [plural] *AmE* trousers with a piece that covers your chest, held up by two bands that go over your shoulders [= **dungarees** *BrE*] → see picture at **CLOTHES**

overate /ˌəʊvər'et, -'eɪt $ ˌoʊvər'eɪt/ *v* the past tense of OVEREAT

overawed /ˌəʊvər'ɔːd $ ˌoʊvər'ɒːd/ *adj* if you are overawed by someone or something, they IMPRESS you a lot and make you feel nervous or slightly frightened: *Our players were overawed by the large crowd.*

overbearing /ˌəʊvə'beərɪŋ $ ˌoʊvər'ber-/ *adj* always trying to control other people without considering their feelings: *an overbearing father*

overboard /'əʊvəbɔːd $ 'oʊvərbɔːrd/ *adv* **1** over the side of a ship into the water: *He fell overboard into the icy water.* **2 go overboard** *informal* to do something in a way that is too extreme, for example to praise or thank someone too much: *'That was absolutely amazing!' 'OK, there's no need to go overboard.'*

overburdened /ˌəʊvə'bɜːdnd $ ˌoʊvər'bɜːrdnd/ *adj* having too much work to do, or too many problems: *teachers overburdened with work*

overcame /ˌəʊvə'keɪm $ ˌoʊvər-/ *v* the past tense of OVERCOME

overcast /ˌəʊvə'kɑːst $ ˌoʊvər'kæst◂/ *adj* a sky that is overcast is dark and cloudy → see box at SUN

overcharge /ˌəʊvə'tʃɑːdʒ $ ˌoʊvər'tʃɑːrdʒ/ *v* [I,T] to ask someone for too much money for something you are selling

overcoat /'əʊvəkəʊt $ 'oʊvərkoʊt/ *n* [C] a long thick warm coat

overcome /ˌəʊvə'kʌm $ ˌoʊvər-/ *v* [T] past tense **overcame** /-'keɪm/ past participle **overcome** **1** to succeed in controlling a feeling or solving a problem: *I'm trying to overcome my fear of flying.* **2 be overcome (by sth)** to be so strongly affected by an emotion that you become weak or unable to control your feelings: *Alice tried to speak but she was overcome by tears.* **3 be overcome by fumes/smoke/gas** to become seriously ill or unconscious because of breathing smoke or gas **4** to fight against someone or something and win

overcrowded /ˌəʊvə'kraʊdɪd◂ $ ˌoʊvər-/ *adj* a place that is overcrowded has too many people in it: *overcrowded prisons* —**overcrowding** *n* [U]

overdo /ˌəʊvə'duː $ ˌoʊvər-/ *v* [T] past tense **overdid** /-'dɪd/ past participle **overdone** /-'dʌn/ third person singular **overdoes** /-'dʌz/ to do or use too much of something: *Don't overdo it.*

overdone /ˌəʊvə'dʌn◂ $ ˌoʊvər-/ *adj* cooked for too long: *This steak is overdone.*

overdose /'əʊvədəʊs $ 'oʊvərdoʊs/ *n* [C] too much of a drug taken at one time: **+of** *She took an overdose of painkillers.* —**overdose** /ˌəʊvə'dəʊs $ ˌoʊvər'doʊs/ *v* [I]

overdraft /'əʊvədrɑːft $ 'oʊvərdræft/ *n* [C] an arrangement with your bank that allows you to spend more money than you have in your account: *a £200 overdraft* → see box at OWE

overdrawn /ˌəʊvə'drɔːn $ ˌoʊvər'drɒːn/ *adj* **be/go overdrawn** to have spent more money than the amount you have in your bank account → see box at ACCOUNT → and OWE

overdue /ˌəʊvə'djuː◂ $ ˌoʊvər'duː◂/ *adj* late in arriving or being done: *Her baby's ten days overdue.* | *an overdue gas bill*

overeat /ˌəʊvər'iːt $ ˌoʊ-/ *v* [I] past tense **overate** /-'et, -'eɪt $ -'eɪt/ past participle **overeaten** /-'iːtn/ to eat too much

overestimate /ˌəʊvər'estɪmeɪt $ ˌoʊ-/ *v* [I,T] to think that someone or something is bigger, more important etc than they really are [≠ **underestimate**]: *The company overestimated demand for their new product.* —**overestimate** /-mɪt/ *n* [C]

overflow /ˌəʊvə'fləʊ $ ˌoʊvər'floʊ/ *v* **1** [I,T] if a container or the liquid in it overflows, the liquid goes over the edges of the container **2** [I] if a place overflows with people or things, there are too many of them to fit into it

overflow

overgrown /ˌəʊvə'grəʊn $ ˌoʊvər'groʊn◂/ *adj* covered with plants that have grown in an untidy way

overhang /ˌəʊvə'hæŋ $ ˌoʊvər-/ *v* [I,T] past tense and past participle **overhung** /-'hʌŋ/ to hang over something: *branches overhanging the path*

overhaul /ˌəʊvə'hɔːl $ ˌoʊvər'hɒːl/ *v* [T] to examine all the parts of a machine, system etc and repair or change them if necessary —**overhaul** /'əʊvəhɔːl $ 'oʊvərhɒːl/ *n* [C]

overhead /ˌəʊvə'hed◂ $ ˌoʊvər-/ *adj, adv* above your head: *overhead lights* | *A plane flew overhead.*

overheads /'əʊvəhedz $ 'oʊvər-/ *BrE* [plural] **overhead** *AmE* [U] *n* money that a business has to spend on rent, electricity etc

overhear /ˌəʊvə'hɪə $ ˌoʊvər'hɪr/ *v* [T] past tense and past participle **overheard** /-'hɜːd $ -'hɜːrd/ to hear what people are saying when they are talking to each other and do not know you are listening: *I couldn't help overhearing bits of their conversation.*

overheat /ˌəʊvə'hiːt $ ˌoʊvər-/ *v* [I,T] to become too hot, or to make something too hot

overhung /ˌəʊvə'hʌŋ $ ˌoʊvər-/ *v* the past tense and past participle of OVERHANG

overjoyed /ˌəʊvə'dʒɔɪd $ ˌoʊvər-/ *adj* extremely happy

overkill /'əʊvəkɪl $ 'oʊvər-/ *n* [U] when there is more of something than is necessary or wanted: *More television coverage of the election would be overkill.*

overland /ˌəʊvə'lænd◂ $ ˌoʊvər-/ *adj, adv* across land, not by sea or air: *They are travelling overland to China.* | *an overland route*

overlap /ˌəʊvə'læp $ ˌoʊvər-/ *v* [I,T] **overlapped**, **overlapping** **1** if two things overlap, part of one thing covers part of the other: *Roof tiles must overlap.* **2** if two subjects, activities, ideas etc overlap, they include some but not all of the same things: *Our jobs overlap in certain areas.* —**overlap** /'əʊvəlæp $ 'oʊvər-/ *n* [C,U]

overleaf /ˌəʊvə'liːf $ 'oʊvərliːf/ *adv* on the other side of a page: *See the chart overleaf.*

overload /ˌəʊvə'ləʊd $ ˌoʊvər'loʊd/ *v* [T] past participle **overloaded** or **overladen** /-'leɪdn/ **1** to put too many things or people on or into something: *The boat was overloaded and began to* *sink.* **2** to give someone too much work to do or information to deal with **3** to put too much electricity through an electrical system or piece of equipment —**overload** /ˈəʊvələʊd $ ˈoʊvərloʊd/ *n* [U]

overlook /ˌəʊvəˈlʊk $ ˌoʊvər-/ *v* [T] **1** to not notice something or to not realize how important it is: *The police overlooked a key piece of evidence.* **2** if a building, room, window etc overlooks something, you can see that thing from the building, room etc: *a room overlooking the beach* **3** *formal* to forgive someone for a mistake, bad behaviour etc: *I am willing to overlook what you said this time.*

overly /ˈəʊvəli $ ˈoʊvər-/ *adv* too: *I think Kane is being overly optimistic.*

overnight /ˌəʊvəˈnaɪt $ ˌoʊvər-/ *adv, adj* **1** for or during the night: *She's staying overnight at a friend's house.* | *an overnight flight to Boston* **2** if something happens overnight, it happens quickly: *You can't expect to lose weight overnight.* | *The play was an overnight success.*

overpass /ˈəʊvəpɑːs $ ˈoʊvərpæs/ *n* [C] *AmE* a structure like a bridge that allows one road to go over another road [= **flyover** *BrE*]

overpopulated /ˌəʊvəˈpɒpjˈ∗leɪtˈ∗d $ ˌoʊvərˈpɑːp-/ *adj* a country or city that is overpopulated has too many people —**overpopulation** /ˌəʊvəpɒpjˈ∗leɪʃən $ ˌoʊvərpɑːp-/ *n* [U]

overpower /ˌəʊvəˈpaʊə $ ˌoʊvərˈpaʊr/ *v* [T] to defeat someone because you are stronger

overpowering /ˌəʊvəˈpaʊərɪŋ $ ˌoʊvərˈpaʊr-/ *adj* an overpowering feeling, need, smell etc is very strong: *The smell of gas was overpowering.*

overpriced /ˌəʊvəˈpraɪstˈ∗ $ ˌoʊvər-/ *adj* too expensive: *overpriced restaurants* → see box at **EXPENSIVE**

overran /ˌəʊvəˈræn $ ˌoʊ-/ *v* the past tense of **OVERRUN**

overrated /ˌəʊvəˈreɪtˈ∗dˈ∗ $ ˌoʊ-/ *adj* not as good or important as some people think: *We thought the play was overrated.*

overreact /ˌəʊvəriˈækt $ ˌoʊ-/ *v* [I] to be more angry, afraid, worried etc than you should be —**overreaction** /-riˈækʃən/ *n* [C,U]

override /ˌəʊvəˈraɪd $ ˌoʊ-/ *v* [T] past tense **overrode** /-ˈrəʊd $ -ˈroʊd/ past participle **overridden** /-ˈrɪdn/ **1** to use your power to change someone else's decision: *Congress has overridden the President's veto.* **2** to be stronger or more important than something else: *The economy often seems to override other political issues.*

overriding /ˌəʊvəˈraɪdɪŋˈ∗ $ ˌoʊ-/ *adj* [only before noun] more important than anything else: *Crime seems to be the overriding concern of voters.*

overrule /ˌəʊvəˈruːl $ ˌoʊ-/ *v* [T] to change an order or decision that you think is wrong, using your official power

overrun /ˌəʊvəˈrʌn $ ˌoʊ-/ *v* past tense **overran** /-ˈræn/ past participle **overrun** present participle **overrunning** **1** [T] if unwanted things or people overrun a place, they spread over it in great numbers: *The town is being overrun by rats.* **2** [I] to take more time or money than intended: *The meeting overran by half an hour.*

overseas /ˌəʊvəˈsiːzˈ∗ $ ˌoʊvər-/ *adj, adv* to, in, or from a foreign country that is across the sea: *overseas students* | *My wife is working overseas.*

oversee /ˌəʊvəˈsiː $ ˌoʊvər-/ *v* [T] past tense **oversaw** /-ˈsɔː $ -ˈsɒː/ past participle **overseen** /-ˈsiːn/ to be in charge of a group of workers and check that work is done correctly

overshadow /ˌəʊvəˈʃædəʊ $ ˌoʊvərˈʃædoʊ/ *v* [T] **1** to make something less enjoyable or happy: *The film festival was overshadowed by the news of the actor's death.* **2** to make someone or something else seem less important or successful: *He felt constantly overshadowed by his older brother.*

overshoot /ˌəʊvəˈʃuːt $ ˌoʊvər-/ *v* [I,T] past tense and past participle **overshot** /-ˈʃɒt $ -ˈʃɑːt/ to accidentally go a little further than you intended

oversight /ˈəʊvəsaɪt $ ˈoʊvər-/ *n* [C,U] a mistake that is caused by someone forgetting to do something or not noticing something

oversimplify /ˌəʊvəˈsɪmplˈ∗faɪ $ ˌoʊvər-/ *v* [I,T] **oversimplified, oversimplifying, oversimplifies** *disapproving* to make something seem simpler than it really is by ignoring many important facts —**oversimplification** /ˌəʊvəsɪmplˈ∗fˈ∗ˈkeɪʃən $ ˌoʊvər-/ *n* [C,U] *a gross oversimplification*

oversized /ˌəʊvəˈsaɪzdˈ∗ $ ˌoʊvər-/ *adj* bigger than usual, or too big

oversleep /ˌəʊvəˈsliːp $ ˌoʊvər-/ *v* [I] past tense and past participle **overslept** /-ˈslept/ to sleep for longer than you intended

overspend /ˌəʊvəˈspend $ ˌoʊvər-/ *v* [I,T] past tense and past participle **overspent** /-ˈspent/ to spend more money than you can afford: *The hospital has overspent its budget.*

overstate /ˌəʊvəˈsteɪt $ ˌoʊvər-/ *v* [T] to talk about something in a way that makes it seem more important, serious etc than it really is

overstep /ˌəʊvəˈstep $ ˌoʊvər-/ *v* [T] **overstepped, overstepping** to behave in a way that is not acceptable or allowed: *Wilson has clearly overstepped his authority.* | **overstep the limits/bounds/boundary (of sth)** | **overstep the mark/line**

overstretch /ˌəʊvəˈstretʃ $ ˌoʊvər-/ *v* [T] to try to do more than you can in the time or money that you have available

overt /ˈəʊvɜːt, əʊˈvɜːt $ ˈoʊvɜːrt, oʊˈvɜːrt/ *adj* done publicly, without trying to hide anything [≠ **covert**]: *overt discrimination* —**overtly** *adv*

overtake

overtake /ˌəʊvəˈteɪk $ ˌoʊvər-/ *v* past tense **overtook** /-ˈtʊk/ past participle **overtaken** /-ˈteɪkən/

1 [I,T] to go past a moving vehicle or person because you are going faster than them: *The accident happened as he was overtaking a bus.*

2 [T] *literary* if something bad overtakes you, it happens suddenly and affects you strongly [➡ **overcome**]: *She was overtaken by exhaustion.*

3 [T] to develop and become more successful, important, or advanced than someone or something else: *Television soon overtook the cinema in popularity.*

‚over-the-'counter *adj* over-the-counter drugs can be obtained without a PRESCRIPTION (=a written order) from a doctor

overthrow /‚əʊvə'θrəʊ $ ‚oʊvər'θroʊ/ *v* [T] past tense **overthrew** /-'θruː/ past participle **overthrown** /-'θrəʊn $ -'θroʊn/ to remove a leader or government from power by using force

overtime /'əʊvətaɪm $ 'oʊvər-/ *n* [U] time that you spend working in your job in addition to your normal working hours → see box at PAY

overtones /'əʊvətəʊnz $ 'oʊvərtoʊnz/ *n* [plural] if something has overtones, an emotion, attitude etc is involved but not expressed directly: **political/racial/emotional etc overtones** *the murder's political overtones*

overtook /‚əʊvə'tʊk $ ‚oʊvər-/ *v* the past tense of OVERTAKE

overture /'əʊvətjʊə, -tʃʊə, -tʃə $ 'oʊvərtʃʊr, -tʃʊr, -tʃər/ *n* [C] a piece of music that comes before a longer musical piece, especially an OPERA

overturn /‚əʊvə't3ːn $ ‚oʊvər't3ːrn/ *v* **1** [I,T] if something overturns, or if you overturn it, it turns upside down or falls over on its side: *The car overturned on a country road.* **2** [T] to officially change a decision made by a court: *The appeal court overturned the decision.*

overview /'əʊvəvjuː $ 'oʊvər-/ *n* [C] a short description of a subject or situation, giving its main features but not all the details

overweight /‚əʊvə'weɪt◂ $ ‚oʊvər-/ *adj* too heavy or too fat: *I'm ten pounds overweight.* → see box at FAT

overwhelm /‚əʊvə'welm $ ‚oʊvər-/ *v* [T] if a feeling overwhelms you, you feel it so strongly that you cannot think clearly: *Josh was overwhelmed with guilt.* | *She was overwhelmed by emotion when she heard the news.*

overwhelming /‚əʊvə'welmɪŋ $ ‚oʊvər-/ *adj* **1** very big in amount or number: *overwhelming evidence that smoking damages your health* **2** affecting you very strongly: *an overwhelming urge to cry* —**overwhelmingly** *adv*

overworked /‚əʊvə'w3ːkt◂ $ ‚oʊvər'w3ːrkt◂/ *adj* made to work too much or too hard: *overworked nurses* —**overwork** *n* [U]

overwrite /‚əʊvə'raɪt $ ‚oʊvər-/ *v* [T] to replace a computer FILE with another of the same name

overwrought /‚əʊvə'rɔːt◂ $ ‚oʊvə'rɔːt◂/ *adj* very upset, nervous, and worried

ow /aʊ/ *spoken* used when you suddenly feel pain: *Ow! That hurt!*

owe /əʊ $ oʊ/ *v* [T]

1 if you owe someone money, you have to pay them money that they lent to you, or give them money for something that they have done for you or sold to you [➡ **borrow, lend**]: **owe sb money/£10 etc** *Bob owes me $20.* | **owe sth to sb** *We owe money to the bank.* | **owe sb for sth** *I still owe Conrad for dinner.* | *How much do I owe you* (=used when you want to pay for something)?

owe money to your bank
be in the red – to have spent more money than you have

2 to feel that you should do something for someone or give someone something, for example because they have done something for you: **owe sb sth** *I owe you an apology.* | *Gary owes me a favour.*

3 to have something or have achieved something because of what someone else has done: **owe sth to sb** *I owe it all to my parents*

'owing to *prep* because of: *Work on the building has stopped, owing to lack of money.*

owl /aʊl/ *n* [C] a bird that hunts at night and has large eyes and a loud call

own¹ /əʊn $ oʊn/ *determiner, pron*

1 belonging to you and no one else: *She wants her own room.* | **sth of your own** *He decided to start a business of his own.* | *I can't afford a place of my own* (=my own home).

2 done by a particular person without the help of anyone else: *Luis has started writing his own songs.* | *You have to learn to make your own decisions.*

3 (all) on your own **a)** alone: *Rick lives on his own.* **b)** without anyone's help: *Martha raised six children all on her own.*

4 get your own back (on sb) *informal* to do something bad to someone because they have done something bad to you

own² *v* [T] if you own something, it belongs to you legally, especially because you bought it or were given it [➡ **possess**]: *Duane and his wife own a restaurant in Atlanta.*

own up *phr v* to admit that you have done something wrong: **own up to (doing) sth** *No one owned up to breaking the window.*

owner /'əʊnə $ 'oʊnər/ *n* [C] someone who owns something: *a dog owner* | **+of** *the owner of the local hotel* —**ownership** *n* [U]

‚own 'goal *n* [C] *BrE* **1** a GOAL that you accidentally score against your own team **2** *informal* something you do that has bad results for you or the group you belong to

ox /ɒks $ ɑːks/ *n* [C] plural **oxen** /'ɒksən $ 'ɑːk-/ a large type of BULL (=male cow). In the past, oxen were used to pull heavy loads, especially on farms.

oxygen /'ɒksɪdʒən $ 'ɑːk-/ *n* [U] a gas in the air that all living things need

oyster /'ɔɪstə $ -ər/ *n* [C,U] a small sea animal that has a shell and makes a jewel called a PEARL

oz the written abbreviation of **ounce**

ozone layer /'əʊzəʊn ‚leɪə $ 'oʊzoʊn ‚leɪər/ *n* [singular] a layer of gases around the Earth that stops harmful RADIATION from the sun from reaching the Earth

P, p

P, p /piː/ *n* [C,U] plural **P's, p's** the 16th letter of the English alphabet

p. also **p** *BrE n* **1** the written abbreviation of **page** **2** *BrE* the abbreviation of **penny** or **pence**

p & p *BrE* the written abbreviation of **postage and packing**

p.a. the written abbreviation of **per annum**

PA /ˌpiː ˈeɪ/ *n* [C] **1** *BrE* **personal assistant** a secretary who works for one person **2 public address system** electronic equipment that makes someone's voice loud enough to be heard by large groups of people

pace¹ /peɪs/ *n* **1** [singular] the speed at which something happens, or at which someone moves, works etc: *She heard someone behind her and quickened her pace.* | **+of** *the relaxed pace of life in Italy*

COLLOCATIONS

pace of life – how busy people are, how quickly things are done etc
pace of change/reform/growth – how quickly change etc happens
at your own pace – at the pace that suits you
at a rapid/slower/steady etc pace
at a snail's pace – very slowly

2 keep pace (with sb/sth) to change as fast as something else, or to move as fast as someone else: *Supply has to keep pace with increasing demand.* **3** [C] a single step: *He took a pace towards the door.*

pace² *v* **1** [I,T] to walk first in one direction and then in the other many times, especially because you are worried: **+around/up and down** *He paced up and down the hospital corridor.* **2 pace yourself** to do something at a steady speed so that you do not get tired too quickly

pacemaker /ˈpeɪsˌmeɪkə $ -ər/ *n* [C] a small machine that is put inside someone's chest to help their heart beat regularly

pacifier /ˈpæsɪˌfaɪə $ -faɪər/ *n* [C] *AmE* a rubber object that a baby sucks so that he or she does not cry [= **dummy** *BrE*]

pacifist /ˈpæsɪfɪst/ *n* [C] someone who believes that wars are wrong and who refuses to fight in them —**pacifism** *n* [U]

pacify /ˈpæsɪfaɪ/ *v* [T] **pacified, pacifying, pacifies** to make someone calm and quiet after they have been angry or upset

pack¹ /pæk/ *v*

1 also **pack up** [I,T] to put things into cases, bags etc ready for a journey: *Have you finished packing up yet?* | *Don't forget to pack a warm coat.*

2 [T] to put something into a container so that it can be moved, sold, or stored: *Glass must be packed carefully.* | **pack sth in/into sth** *The fish are packed in ice at sea.*

3 [I,T] to go in large numbers into a place, or to make people or animals do this, until the place is too full [➡ **packed**]: **+into/in/onto** *Thousands of people packed into the stadium.* | *chickens packed together in tiny cages*

pack sth ⇔ **in** *phr v* **1** also **pack sth into sth** to do a lot of things in a short time: *I don't know how we packed so much activity into one weekend.* **2** *BrE informal* to stop doing a job or activity, especially because you do not enjoy it: *Sometimes I feel like packing my job in.*

pack sb **off** *phr v informal* to send someone to stay somewhere: *We were packed off to camp every summer.*

pack up *phr v* **1** *informal* to finish work: *I think I'll pack up and go home early.* **2** *BrE informal* if a machine packs up, it stops working because something is wrong with it: *The television's packed up again.*

pack² *n* [C]

1 several similar things wrapped or packed together in order to sell them or send them to someone: **+of** *a pack of three T-shirts* | *Send for your free information pack.*

2 *AmE* a small container made of paper or plastic that something is sold in [= **packet** *BrE*]: **+of** *a pack of cigarettes* → see picture at **CONTAINER**

3 a group of wild animals that hunt together: **+of** *a pack of dogs* → see box at **GROUP**

4 a bag for equipment, clothes etc that you carry on your back, especially when climbing or walking [= **backpack**; = **rucksack** *BrE*]

5 a group of the same type of people, especially a group who you do not approve of: **+of** *a pack of thieves*

6 a set of playing cards [= **deck** *AmE*]

→ **ICE PACK**

package¹ /ˈpækɪdʒ/ *n* [C]

1 something that has been packed in a box or wrapped in paper, and then sent by mail or delivered [= **parcel** *BrE*]

2 *AmE* the box, bag etc that food or other goods are sold in [= **packet** *BrE*]: *a package of cookies*

3 a set of related programs sold together for use on a computer: *a new software package*

package² *v* [T] **1** to put food or goods in a box, bag etc ready to be sold: *food packaged in cartons* **2** to make something seem attractive so that people will become interested in it or buy it: *The band was packaged to appeal to young girls.*

package tour also **package ˌholiday** *BrE n* [C] a holiday arranged by a company for a fixed price that includes the cost of your hotel and travel

packaging /ˈpækɪdʒɪŋ/ *n* [U] the bags, boxes etc that a product is sold in

packed /pækt/ *adj* full of people: **+with** *The island was packed with tourists.*

ˌpacked 'lunch *n* [C] *BrE* food such as sandwiches and fruit that you take to eat at work, school etc

packet /ˈpækɪt/ *n* [C] *BrE* a small container made of paper or plastic that something is sold in [= **pack** *AmE*]: **+of** *a packet of biscuits* → see picture at **CONTAINER**

packing /ˈpækɪŋ/ *n* [U] **1** when you put things into cases or boxes in order to send or take them somewhere: *I can do my packing on Friday night.* **2** the material used for packing things so that they can be sent somewhere

pact /pækt/ n [C] a formal agreement between two countries, groups, or people

pad¹ /pæd/ n [C] **1** a thick piece of soft material used to protect something or make it more comfortable: +**of** *a pad of cotton wool* | **knee/elbow/shin etc pad** (=worn to protect part of your body when playing a sport) **2** several sheets of paper fastened together, used for writing or drawing: *a sketch pad*

pad² v **padded, padding 1** [I + adv/prep] to walk somewhere quietly **2** also **pad out** [T] to make a piece of writing longer by adding unnecessary words or information

padded /ˈpædɪd/ adj covered or filled with soft material in order to protect something or make something more comfortable: *a padded envelope* | *padded boots*

padding /ˈpædɪŋ/ n [U] material used to protect something or make it feel softer

paddle¹ /ˈpædl/ n [C] **1** a short pole with a wide flat end, used for moving a small boat in water [→ **oar**] **2** [usually singular] BrE when you take off your shoes and socks and walk in water: *Let's go for a paddle.*

paddle² v **1** [I,T] to move a small boat in water, using a paddle [→ **row**] **2** [I] BrE to walk without shoes or socks in water: +**in** *children paddling in the stream*

paddock /ˈpædək/ n [C] a small field where horses are kept

paddy field /ˈpædi fiːld/ n [C] a field where rice is grown

padlock /ˈpædlɒk $ -lɑːk/ n [C] a small lock that you put on a door, bicycle etc —**padlock** v [T]

padlock

padlock

key

paediatrician BrE; **pediatrician** AmE /ˌpiːdiəˈtrɪʃən/ n [C] a doctor who deals with children

paediatrics BrE; **pediatrics** AmE /ˌpiːdiˈætrɪks/ n [U] the area of medicine relating to children and their illnesses —**paediatric** adj

paedophile BrE; **pedophile** AmE /ˈpiːdəfaɪl/ n [C] someone who is sexually attracted to children

pagan /ˈpeɪɡən/ adj not belonging to any of the main world religions – used about very old religious beliefs and customs: *pagan festivals* —**pagan** n [C]

page¹ /peɪdʒ/ n [C] a piece of paper in a book, newspaper etc, or one side of it: **on page 2/14/80 etc** *The test questions start on page 2.* | *Jane quickly turned the page.* | *the front page of the newspaper* | *The report was 50 pages long.* | *There's one page missing.*
→ **TITLE PAGE, WEB PAGE**

page² v [T] **1** to call someone's name in a public place using a LOUDSPEAKER **2** to call someone using a PAGER (=small machine that receives messages)

pageant /ˈpædʒənt/ n [C] a public show that usually tells a historical or religious story: *the annual Christmas pageant*

pageantry /ˈpædʒəntri/ n [U] impressive ceremonies or events, involving many people wearing special clothes: *the splendour of royal pageantry*

pager /ˈpeɪdʒə $ -ər/ n [C] a small machine you can carry that receives telephone messages and makes a noise when one is waiting for you

paid¹ /peɪd/ v the past tense and past participle of PAY

paid² adj **1** paid work is work that you receive money for doing: *paid employment* | **highly/poorly paid** *a highly paid job* **2** used to talk about a period of time when your employer pays you even though you are not working: *paid holidays*

paid-'up adj [only before noun] BrE someone who has paid the money needed to be a member of a club, political party etc: *a paid-up member of the union*

pail /peɪl/ n [C] especially AmE a BUCKET

pain¹ /peɪn/ n

1 [C,U] the feeling you have when part of your body hurts: **chest/back/neck etc pain** *I woke up with terrible stomach pains.* | **in pain** *Cassie lay groaning in pain on the bed.* | +**in** *I have a pain in my lower back.* | *Aspirin is used to relieve pain* (=make it less bad).

COLLOCATIONS

If you **have** a **pain in** your stomach, chest etc, you can call it a **stomach/chest etc pain**.
A **pain** that is very bad is **terrible**, **severe**, **intense** or **unbearable**.
A **sharp pain** is short but severe.
A **dull pain** is not severe but it continues for a long time.
Another word for a **pain** that continues but is not very strong is an **ache**.
If you are **in pain**, you take **medicine** or **painkillers** to **lessen/ease/relieve/soothe/kill** the **pain**.

2 a pain (in the neck) spoken someone or something that is very annoying: *I find the paperwork a pain.*
3 [U] sadness and unhappiness: *the pain children feel when their parents divorce*
4 be at pains to do sth/take pains to do sth to make a special effort to do something: *He was at pains to emphasize the advantages of the new system.*

pain² v **it pains sb to do sth** formal used to say that it is difficult and unpleasant for someone to have to do something

pained /peɪnd/ adj upset or slightly annoyed: *a pained expression*

painful /ˈpeɪnfəl/ adj

1 making you feel very unhappy or upset: *painful memories of the war* | **it is painful to do sth** *It was painful to leave the house where I was born.* | +**for** *The divorce was painful for the children.*
2 making you feel physical pain: *Her ankle was swollen and painful.* | *a painful blow on the head*

painfully /ˈpeɪnfəli/ adv **1** very – used to emphasize a bad quality, or something that is unpleasant and upsetting: *She was painfully shy as a child.* | **painfully clear/obvious/apparent** *It was painfully obvious that he was lying.* **2** in a way that makes you feel physical pain: *Bill walked slowly and painfully to the door.*

painkiller /'peɪn,kɪlə $ -ər/ *n* [C] a medicine that reduces pain

painless /'peɪnləs/ *adj* causing no pain: *a painless death*

painstaking /'peɪnz,teɪkɪŋ/ *adj* very careful and thorough: *painstaking research* —**painstakingly** *adv*

paint¹ /peɪnt/ *n*
1 [C,U] a liquid that you put on walls and other surfaces using a brush to make the surface a particular colour: *a can of yellow paint* | *The kitchen needs a fresh coat of paint* (=layer of paint).
2 paints [plural] a set of small tubes or blocks of paint, used for painting pictures: *oil paints*

paint² *v* [I,T]
1 to put paint on a surface: *What color are you painting the house?* | **paint sth (in) blue/red/green etc** *I'm painting my bedroom yellow.*
2 to make a picture of someone or something, using paint: *He's just finished painting his wife's portrait.*

paintbox /'peɪntbɒks $ -bɑːks/ *n* [C] a small box containing blocks of coloured paints

paintbrush /'peɪntbrʌʃ/ *n* [C] a brush used to paint pictures or walls → see picture at BRUSH¹

painter /'peɪntə $ -ər/ *n* [C]
1 someone who paints pictures [= artist]: *a landscape painter* → see box at ART
2 someone whose job is painting houses, rooms etc: *a painter and decorator*

---

painting

still life

abstract

landscape

portrait

painting /'peɪntɪŋ/ *n*
1 [C] a painted picture: *an exhibition of paintings and sculptures*
2 [U] the process of painting: *Van Gogh's style of painting* → see box at ART
→ **OIL PAINTING**

paintwork /'peɪntwɜːk $ -wɜːrk/ *n* [U] paint on a car, house etc

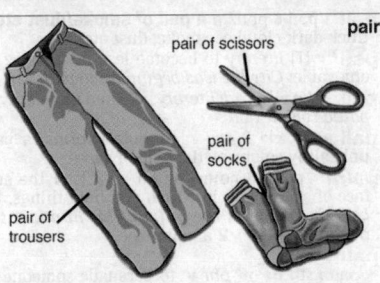
pair
pair of scissors
pair of socks
pair of trousers

pair¹ /peə $ per/ *n* [C]
1 something made of two similar parts that are joined together: **pair of trousers/scissors/glasses etc** *a pair of jeans*
2 two things of the same type that are used together: **pair of socks/earrings/shoes etc** *a new pair of gloves* → see box at TWO
3 two people who do something together or who know each other well [→ **couple**]: *a pair of dancers* | **Work in pairs** *on the next exercise.*
→ **AU PAIR**

pair² *v*
pair off *phr v* if two people pair off or someone pairs them off, they come together, especially to start a romantic relationship: *The guests paired off for the first dance.* | **pair sb ⇔ off (with sb)** *She tried to pair me off with her son.*
pair up *phr v* if two people pair up or someone pairs them up, they work together or do something together: **+with** *I paired up with Mike for the quiz.* | **pair sb ⇔ up** *The children were paired up.*

pajamas /pə'dʒɑːməz $ -'dʒæ-, -'dʒɑː-/ *n* the American spelling of PYJAMAS

pal /pæl/ *n* [C] *informal* a friend: *a college pal*

palace /'pæləs/ *n* [C] a large house where a king or queen lives: *Buckingham Palace*

palatable /'pælətəbəl/ *adj* **1** palatable food or drink tastes quite pleasant: *a very palatable wine*
2 an idea, suggestion etc that is palatable is acceptable: *The idea was more palatable to Washington than London.*

palate /'pælət/ *n* [C] **1** the top inside part of your mouth **2** your sense of taste

palatial /pə'leɪʃəl/ *adj* a palatial building is big and beautifully decorated: *a palatial hotel*

pale¹ /peɪl/ *adj*
1 having a skin colour that is whiter than usual, especially because you are ill or frightened: *Jan looked tired and pale.* | **turn/go pale** *He suddenly went pale.*
2 a pale colour is a light form of a colour [= light; ≠ dark]: *pale green walls*

pale² *v* [I] **1** to seem unimportant, unattractive etc compared to something else: *Once you've experienced sailing, other sports **pale in comparison.*** **2** if you pale, your face becomes whiter than usual, especially because you are ill or frightened: *Hettie paled when she heard the news.*

palette /'pælət/ *n* [C] a board that an artist uses for mixing paints

pall¹ /pɔːl $ pɒːl/ n **a pall of smoke/dust etc** a thick dark cloud of smoke, dust etc

pall² v [T] *literary* to become less interesting or enjoyable: *City life was beginning to pall.*

pallid /'pælɪd/ adj *literary* pale and unhealthy: *a pallid complexion*

pallor /'pælə $ -ər/ n [singular] *formal* a pale unhealthy colour of the skin or face

palm¹ /pɑːm $ pɑːm, pɑːlm/ n [C] **1** the surface of your hand in which you hold things: *He held the pebble **in the palm of his hand.*** → see picture at HAND¹ **2** a palm tree

palm² v
  palm sth ⇔ off *phr v* to persuade someone to take or buy something that is not of good quality or is not what they really want: **+on/onto** *My brother's always trying to palm his old clothes off on me.*
  palm sb off with sth *phr v* to give someone an explanation that is not true but that you hope they will accept: *She's always palming me off with excuses.*

palmtop /'pɑːmtɒp $ 'pɑːmtɑːp, 'pɑːlm-/ n [C] a very small computer that you can hold in your hand

'palm tree n [C] a tall tree with large pointed leaves at the top that grows near beaches or in deserts

palpable /'pælpəbəl/ adj easy to notice: *a palpable sense of relief* —**palpably** adv

palpitations /ˌpælpɪ'teɪʃənz/ n [plural] when your heart beats in a fast irregular way, especially because you are ill or very anxious

paltry /'pɔːltri $ 'pɒːl-/ adj too small to be useful or important: *a paltry pay increase*

pamper /'pæmpə $ -ər/ v [T] to give someone a lot of care and attention

pamphlet /'pæmflɪt/ n [C] a thin paper book containing information about something

pan¹ /pæn/ n [C] a metal container that you use for cooking, usually with a long handle [➙ **saucepan**]: *Melt the butter in a pan.* | *a frying pan* | *pots and pans*

pan² v **panned, panning** **1** [T] *informal* to strongly criticize a film, play etc in a newspaper or on television or radio: *His latest movie has been panned by the critics.* **2** [I] if a film or television camera pans in a particular direction, it moves in that direction: **+across/back etc** *The camera panned across the crowd.*
  pan out *phr v informal* to happen or develop in a particular way: *Let's wait and see how things pan out.*

panacea /ˌpænə'sɪə/ n [C] something that people think will solve all their problems

panache /pə'næʃ, pæ-/ n [U] a way of doing something that people admire because it makes it seem easy: **with panache** *He played with skill and panache.*

pancake /'pænkeɪk/ n [C] a thin flat food made from flour, milk, and eggs that is cooked in a pan and eaten hot → see picture on page A5

panda /'pændə/ n [C] a large black and white animal that is similar to a bear and lives in China

pandemonium /ˌpændɪ'məʊniəm $ -'moʊ-/ n [U] when there is a lot of noise and activity because people are angry, excited etc

pander /'pændə $ -ər/ v
  pander to sb/sth *phr v* to give someone anything they want in order to please them, even when it is unreasonable or unnecessary

pane /peɪn/ n [C] a piece of glass in a window or door: *a window pane*

panel /'pænl/ n [C] **1** a piece of wood, glass etc that is part of a door, wall, or ceiling: *an oak door with three panels* **2** a group of people who are chosen to discuss something or answer questions: **+of** *a panel of experts* | **on a panel** *There were several professors on the panel.* **3** **instrument/control panel** the part in a car, plane, boat etc that has the controls on it

panelled *BrE*; **paneled** *AmE* /'pænld/ adj covered with flat pieces of wood: *a panelled door*

panelling *BrE*; **paneling** *AmE* /'pænəl-ɪŋ/ n [U] flat pieces of wood, used to decorate walls: *oak panelling*

panellist *BrE*; **panelist** *AmE* /'pænəlɪst/ n [C] one of a group of people who answer questions on a radio or television programme

pang /pæŋ/ n [C] a sudden strong feeling of pain, sadness etc: **hunger pangs** | **+of** *She was having pangs of guilt about Pete.*

panhandle /'pæn,hændl/ v [I] *AmE informal* to ask for money in the streets [= **beg**] —**panhandler** n [C]

panic¹ /'pænɪk/ n [C,U] a sudden strong feeling of fear or anxiety that makes you do things without thinking carefully: *Stephen had a sudden feeling of panic.* | **in (a) panic** *People ran into the streets in a panic after the explosion.* | *There was panic on Wall Street as prices fell.*

panic² v [I,T] **panicked, panicking** to feel so frightened that you cannot think clearly or behave sensibly, or to make someone feel like this: *Stay where you are and don't panic!* —**panicky** adj

'panic-,stricken adj very frightened and unable to think clearly or behave sensibly

panorama /ˌpænə'rɑːmə $ -'ræmə/ n [C] a view over a wide area of land —**panoramic** /ˌpænə'ræmɪk◂/ adj: *a panoramic view of Hong Kong*

pansy /'pænzi/ n [C] plural **pansies** a small brightly coloured garden flower

pant /pænt/ v [I] to breathe quickly with short noisy breaths, especially after exercising or because it is hot → see box at BREATHE

panther /'pænθə $ -ər/ n [C] a large black wild animal that is a type of cat

panties /'pæntiz/ n [plural] *especially AmE* a piece of women's underwear that covers the area between the waist and the top of the legs [= **knickers** *BrE*] → see picture at CLOTHES

pantomime /'pæntəmaɪm/ n [C,U] **1** also **panto** /'pæntəʊ $ -toʊ/ *BrE informal* a type of play for children that is performed in Britain around Christmas, with a traditional story, jokes, and songs **2** *AmE* a method of performing using only actions and not words, or a play performed using this method [= **mime**]

pantry /'pæntri/ n [C] plural **pantries** a small room near or in a kitchen where food is kept

pants[1] /pænts/ *n* [plural]

1 *BrE* a piece of underwear that covers the area between your waist and the top of your legs [= **underpants** *AmE*; ➡ **boxer shorts, knickers**]

2 *especially AmE* a piece of clothing that covers you from your waist to your feet and has a separate part for each leg [= **trousers** *BrE*]: *young men in baggy pants* ➔ see picture at **CLOTHES**

pants[2] *adj* [not before noun] *BrE spoken informal* very bad: *The concert was pants.*

pantsuit /'pæntsu:t, -sju:t $ -su:t/ *n* [C] *AmE* a suit for women, which consists of a jacket and trousers [= **trouser suit** *BrE*]

pantyhose /'pæntihəʊz $ -hoʊz/ *n* [plural] *AmE* a piece of women's clothing made of very thin material that covers the legs from the feet to the waist, usually worn under dresses or skirts [= **tights** *BrE*]

papacy /'peɪpəsi/ *n* **the papacy** the position and authority of the **POPE**

papal /'peɪpəl/ *adj* relating to the **POPE**

paparazzi /ˌpæpə'rætsi $ ˌpɑːpə'rɑː/ *n* [plural] photographers who follow famous people in order to take photographs they can sell to newspapers

paper[1] /'peɪpə $ -ər/ *n*

1 [U] thin material used for writing on, drawing on, wrapping things etc: **piece/sheet of paper** *He wrote her number down on a piece of paper.* | *Have you got any coloured paper?*

2 [C] a newspaper: *I read about it in yesterday's paper.* | a **local paper** (=the newspaper for the area you live in) ➔ see box at **NEWSPAPER**

3 papers [plural] important or official documents or letters: *There are several papers for you to sign.*

4 [C] a piece of writing or a talk on a particular subject by someone who has studied it: **+on** *She's giving a paper on classical architecture.*

5 on paper a) if you put ideas or information on paper, you write them down: *You need to get some of your thoughts down on paper.* **b)** if an idea seems good on paper, it is good as an idea, but probably not in a real situation: *It looks good on paper, but I still don't think it will work.*

6 [C] an examination on a particular subject done as part of a course at school or university: *The history paper was really easy.*

➔ **BLOTTING PAPER, TOILET PAPER, WRAPPING PAPER**

paper[2] *v* [T] to cover the walls of a room with **WALLPAPER**

paperback /'peɪpəbæk $ -ər-/ *n* [C] a book with a fairly stiff paper cover [➡ **hardback**]: **in paperback** *His novel is now available in paperback.* ➔ see box at **BOOK**

'paper boy *n* [C] a boy who delivers newspapers to people's houses

paperclip /'peɪpəklɪp $ -ər-/ *n* [C] a small piece of curved wire used for holding sheets of paper together

'paper girl *n* [C] a girl who delivers newspapers to people's houses

paperweight /'peɪpəweɪt $ -ər-/ *n* [C] a small heavy object that you put on top of pieces of paper to keep them in that place

paperwork /'peɪpəwɜːk $ -pɔːrwɜːrk/ *n* [U]

1 work such as writing letters or reports: *The job involves a lot of paperwork.* **2** the docu-

ments that you need for a business deal, journey etc: *I've left all the paperwork in the office.*

par /pɑː $ pɑːr/ *n* **1 be on a par (with sth)** to be at the same level or standard: *Technological developments in the US are on a par with those in Japan.* **2 be below par/not be up to par** to be not as good as the usual or expected standard: *Italy's performance in the Championships wasn't up to par.*

parable /'pærəbəl/ *n* [C] a short story that teaches a moral or religious lesson, especially one from the Bible

paracetamol /ˌpærə'siːtəmɒl, -'set- $ -mɑːl, -mɒːl/ *n* [C,U] plural **paracetamol** or **paracetamols** *BrE* a common drug used to reduce pain which does not contain **ASPIRIN**

parachute[1] /'pærəʃuːt/ *n* [C] a piece of equipment worn by people who jump out of planes, to make them fall slowly and safely to the ground

parachute

parachute[2] *v* [I + adv/prep] to jump from a plane using a parachute ➔ see picture on page A9

parade[1] /pə'reɪd/ *n* [C] **1** a public celebration when musical bands, decorated vehicles etc move down the street: *a victory parade* **2** a military ceremony in which soldiers stand or march together so that important people can examine them: **on parade** *The soldiers were on parade.*

parade[2] *v* **1** [I] to walk in a large group to celebrate or protest about something: **+through/around etc** *Peace demonstrators paraded through the town.* **2** [T] to show your skill, knowledge, possessions etc in order to make people admire you: *He loves parading his wealth in front of people.*

paradigm /'pærədaɪm/ *n* [C] *formal* a very clear or typical example of something —**paradigmatic** /ˌpærədɪg'mætɪk/ *adj*

paradise /'pærədaɪs/ *n* **1 Paradise** the place where some people think good people go after they die [= **heaven**] **2** [singular, U] a place or situation that you like very much or that is very beautiful: **+for** *Hawaii is a paradise for wind surfers.* | a **walker's/shopper's etc paradise**

paradox /'pærədɒks $ -dɑːks/ *n* [C] a situation or statement that seems strange because it involves two ideas or qualities that are very different: *It's a paradox that so many poor people are living in such a rich country.* —**paradoxical** /ˌpærə'dɒksɪkəl $ -'dɑːk-/ *adj* —**paradoxically** /-kli/ *adv*

paraffin /'pærəfɪn/ *n* [U] *BrE* oil used for heating and in lamps, made from **PETROLEUM** or coal [= **kerosene** *AmE*]

paragon /'pærəgən $ -gɑːn/ *n* [C] someone who is perfect or extremely brave, good etc: **+of** *He expects me to be a paragon of virtue* (=perfectly good, honest etc).

P

paragraph /'pærəgrɑːf $ -græf/ *n* [C] a part of a piece of writing that starts on a new line

parallel[1] /'pærəlel/ *adj* **1** two lines, roads etc that are parallel go in the same direction and are the same distance apart all the way: **+to/with** *The street runs parallel to the railroad.* **2** similar and happening at the same time: *The British and French police are conducting parallel investigations.*

parallel[2] *n* [C] a relationship or similarity between two things: **+between** *books that attempt to draw parallels between brains and computers* (=show how they are similar).

parallel[3] *v* [T] *formal* to be similar to something else, or to happen at the same time as something else: *Symptoms of depression often parallel those of more severe mental illnesses.*

paralyse *BrE*; **paralyze** *AmE* /'pærəlaɪz/ *v* [T] **1** [usually passive] to make someone lose the ability to move their body or part of their body **2** to make a system or organization unable to work or continue normally: *Heavy snow has paralyzed transport in several cities.* —**paralysed** *adj*: *The stroke left him paralyzed.*

paralysis /pə'ræləsəs/ *n* [U] when you lose the ability to move your body or part of your body

paramedic /ˌpærə'medɪk/ *n* [C] someone who usually works in an AMBULANCE and is trained to help ill or injured people, but is not a doctor or nurse

parameter /pə'ræmətə $ -ər/ *n* [C usually plural] a fixed limit that controls the way that something should be done: *Congress will decide on parameters for the investigation.*

paramilitary /ˌpærə'mɪlətəri◂ $ -teri◂/ *adj* a paramilitary organization is an illegal group that is organized like an army: *paramilitary forces* —**paramilitaries** *n* [plural]

paramount /'pærəmaʊnt/ *adj* *formal* more important than anything else: *Safety is paramount.* | *Good education is of paramount importance.*

paranoia /ˌpærə'nɔɪə/ *n* [U] an unreasonable belief that you cannot trust people or that they are trying to harm you

paranoid /'pærənɔɪd/ *adj* feeling anxious and worried that you cannot trust people or that they are trying to harm you: **+about** *She's paranoid about going out at night alone.*

paranormal /ˌpærə'nɔːməl◂ $ -'nɔːr-/ *adj* paranormal events cannot be explained by science and seem strange and mysterious: *ghosts and other paranormal phenomena*

parapet /'pærəpət, -pet/ *n* [C] **1** a low wall at the edge of a high roof, bridge etc **2** put/stick your head above the parapet *BrE* to take a risk

paraphernalia /ˌpærəfə'neɪliə $ -fər-/ *n* [U] the things that are used for a particular activity: *photographic paraphernalia*

paraphrase /'pærəfreɪz/ *v* [T] to express what someone says or writes in a shorter and clearer way —**paraphrase** *n* [C]

paraplegic /ˌpærə'pliːdʒɪk◂/ *n* [C] someone who is unable to move the lower part of their body

parasite /'pærəsaɪt/ *n* [C] a plant or animal that lives on or in another plant or animal and gets food from it

parasol /'pærəsɒl $ -sɒːl, -sɑːl/ *n* [C] a type of UMBRELLA used for protection from the sun

paratrooper /'pærəˌtruːpə $ -ər/ *n* [C] a soldier who is trained to jump out of planes using a PARACHUTE

paratroops /'pærətruːps/ *n* [plural] a group of paratroopers that fights together as a military unit

parcel /'pɑːsəl $ 'pɑːr-/ *n* [C] *especially BrE* something that has been packed in a box or wrapped in paper, and then sent by mail or delivered [= package]

parched /pɑːtʃt $ pɑːrtʃt/ *adj* **1** *spoken* very thirsty **2** parched land is very dry

parchment /'pɑːtʃmənt $ 'pɑːr-/ *n* [U] thick yellow-white writing paper used in the past

pardon[1] /'pɑːdn $ 'pɑːrdn/ *spoken*

1 *especially BrE* also **pardon me** *AmE* used to politely ask someone to repeat something because you did not hear it: *'Your shoes are in the bedroom.' 'Pardon?' 'I said your shoes are in the bedroom.'*

2 pardon me a) used to say 'sorry' when you have done something that is considered rude [= excuse me] **b)** *AmE* used to politely get someone's attention in order to ask them a question [= excuse me]: *Pardon me, is this the way to City Hall?*

pardon[2] *v* [T] to officially allow someone who is guilty of a crime to go free: *Over 250 political prisoners were pardoned.*

pardon[3] *n* [C] an official order allowing someone who is guilty of a crime to go free: *Tyler was later given a pardon.* → **I beg your pardon** at BEG

pare /peə $ per/ *v* [T] to cut off the outer layer of something, especially the skin of a fruit: *Pare the apples and slice them into chunks.*

pare sth ⇔ down *phr v* to gradually reduce an amount or number: *Production costs have had to be pared down.*

parent /'peərənt $ 'per-/ *n* [C] someone's father or mother: *My parents are coming to visit next week.* → see box at RELATIVE
→ **SINGLE PARENT** —**parental** /pə'rentl/ *adj*: *parental concern*

parentage /'peərəntɪdʒ $ 'per-/ *n* [U] used to talk about your parents, especially the country where they were born, their social class, or their religion: *an English-born man with Irish parentage*

parent company *n* [C] a company that controls a smaller company or organization

parenthesis /pə'renθəsəs/ *n* [C usually plural] plural **parentheses** /-siːz/ one of the pair of signs ( ) put around words to show additional information [= bracket]: **in parentheses** *The numbers in parentheses refer to page numbers.*

parenthood /'peərənthʊd $ 'per-/ *n* [U] when someone is a parent

parenting /'peərəntɪŋ $ 'per-/ *n* [U] the skill or activity of looking after your own children: *the importance of good parenting skills*

parish /'pærɪʃ/ *n* [C] an area that has its own church

parishioner /pə'rɪʃənə $ -ər/ *n* [C] someone who lives in a parish, especially someone who regularly goes to church there

parity /'pærᵻti/ n [U] *formal* the state of being equal, especially having equal pay, rights, or power [= equality]: **+with** *Prison workers are demanding **pay parity** with the police force.*

park¹ /pɑːk $ pɑːrk/ n [C]
1 a large area with grass and trees in a town, where people walk, play games etc
2 a large area of land in the country which has been kept in its natural state to protect the plants and animals there: **national/state/ county park**
→ AMUSEMENT PARK, CAR PARK, NATIONAL PARK, THEME PARK, TRAILER PARK

park² v [I,T] to put your car somewhere for a period of time: *We couldn't find anywhere to park.* | *Tony parked the car and got out.*

parking /'pɑːkɪŋ $ 'pɑːr-/ n [U] when you park a car somewhere, or the space where you can park it: *No Parking.* | *Free parking is available at the hotel.* | **parking space/place/spot** *Are there any parking spaces left?*

'parking lot n [C] *AmE* an open area where people can park their cars [= car park *BrE*]

'parking ˌmeter n [C] a machine at the side of a road which you put money into when you park your car beside it

'parking ˌticket n [C] an official piece of paper that is put on your car telling you to pay money because you have parked illegally

parliament /'pɑːləmənt $ 'pɑːr-/ n
1 also **Parliament** [C also + plural verb *BrE*] the group of people who are elected to make a country's laws and discuss important affairs [➜ government, MP]: *the Russian parliament*
2 Parliament [U also + plural verb *BrE*] the parliament of the United Kingdom: *He **entered Parliament** (=was elected to Parliament) in 1979.* | **in Parliament** *decisions taken in Parliament*

parliamentary /ˌpɑːlə'mentəri◂ $ ˌpɑːr-/ adj [only before noun] relating to or governed by a parliament: *a parliamentary democracy*

parlour *BrE*; **parlor** *AmE* /'pɑːlə $ 'pɑːrlər/ n [C] **massage/ice cream/funeral etc parlour** a shop or business that provides a particular service

parochial /pə'rəʊkiəl $ -'roʊ-/ adj *disapproving* only interested in things that affect your local area: *Local newspapers are very parochial.*

parody¹ /'pærədi/ n [C,U] plural **parodies** a piece of writing, music etc or an action that copies someone or something in an amusing way: **+of** *a parody of a Texas accent*

parody² v [T] **parodied, parodying, parodies** to copy someone or something in an amusing way

parole¹ /pə'rəʊl $ -'roʊl/ n [U] when someone is allowed to leave prison early, but they will have to return if they do not behave well: **on parole** *He was **released on parole**.*

parole² v [T] to allow someone to leave prison on parole

parrot /'pærət/ n [C] a tropical bird with brightly coloured feathers that you can teach to copy human speech

'parrot ˌfashion adv *BrE disapproving* if you learn something parrot fashion, you repeat what someone has just said without understanding it

parsley /'pɑːsli $ 'pɑːr-/ n [U] a herb with curly leaves

parsnip /'pɑːsnɪp $ 'pɑːr-/ n [C,U] a white or yellow vegetable that is the root of a plant

part¹ /pɑːt $ pɑːrt/ n
1 [C] one of the pieces, areas, times etc that together form the whole of something: **+of** *the upper part of the body* | *people in other parts of the country* | *the early part of the 19th century* | *The book is divided into three parts.*

bit *BrE spoken* – a small part of something: *I liked the first bit of the film.*
piece – one of several different parts that you join together to make something: *One of the pieces of the jigsaw puzzle was missing.*
section – one of several parts that a place, shop, container etc is divided into: *the non-smoking section of the plane*
chapter – one of the parts that a book is divided into: *I've read the first two chapters.*
scene – one of the parts that a play or film is divided into: *the opening scene* | *a love scene*
department – one part of a large organization, which is responsible for a particular kind of work: *the marketing department*

2 [C usually plural] a piece used to make a machine or vehicle: *a shortage of **spare parts** (=parts used to replace broken or old ones)* | *a car parts factory*
3 part of sth some, but not all, of a particular thing: *Part of the problem is that we're just too busy.* | *As part of my job I visit local schools.*
4 take part to be involved in an activity, sport, event etc with other people: **+in** *About 400 students took part in the protest.*
5 play a part (in sth) to be involved in something and affect the way it happens or develops: **+in** *Luck certainly played a part in their success.* | **play a major/important/big etc part** *Music has always played an important part in my life.*
6 have a part to play to have a particular job or be responsible for something: **+in** *We all have a part to play in making a better world.*
7 in part partly but not completely: *The accident was due in part to bad weather.*
8 on sb's part/on the part of sb used when describing a particular person's actions or feelings: *It was a mistake on her part.* | *There has never been any jealousy on my part.*
9 [C] the words and actions of a particular character in a play or film [= role]: *Sara **played the part** of Cinderella.*
10 [C] *AmE* the line on your head made by dividing your hair with a comb [= parting *BrE*]
11 for the most part mostly or usually: *For the most part, residents were thankful.*
12 for my/his etc part *formal* used when saying what a particular person thinks or does: *David, for his part, was very worried.*
13 the best/better part of sth nearly all of something, especially a period of time: *We waited for the best part of an hour.*
14 be part and parcel of sth to be a part of an activity, job etc that cannot be avoided: *Working long hours is part and parcel of being a journalist.*

P

part² v **1** also **,part 'company** [I] **a)** to end a romantic or working relationship with someone [➞ **separate**]: +**from** *Ben parted from his wife last year.* | *Not long after, the Beatles parted company.* **b)** to say goodbye and go in different directions: *They parted at Baker Street.* **2** [I,T] to move apart, or to make two things move apart: *Her lips parted slightly.* | *I parted the curtains and looked out.* **3 be parted from sb/sth** to be separated from someone or something that you love: *She couldn't bear to be parted from her son.* **4** [T] to separate your hair into two parts, using a comb

part with sth *phr v* to give or sell something to someone, although you do not want to: *I was reluctant to part with the painting.*

part³ *adv* partly one thing and partly another: *The exam is part written, part spoken.*

,part ex'change *n* [C,U] *BrE* a way of buying a new car, television etc in which you give your old car, television etc as part of the payment

partial /'pɑːʃəl $ 'pɑːr-/ *adj* **1** not complete: *The exhibition was only a partial success.* **2 be partial to sth** to like something very much: *I'm very partial to fish.*

partially /'pɑːʃəli $ 'pɑːr-/ *adv* not completely [= **partly**]: *The operation was partially successful.* | *partially-sighted people* (=who cannot see well)

participant /pɑːˈtɪsɪ̣pənt $ pɑːr-/ *n* [C] someone who takes part in an activity or event

participate /pɑːˈtɪsɪ̣peɪt $ pɑːr-/ *v* [I] to take part in an activity or event: +**in** *Eight schools participated in the project.* —**participation** /pɑːˌtɪsɪ̣ˈpeɪʃən $ pɑːr-/ *n* [U] *Participation in sport is encouraged.*

participle /'pɑːtɪ̣sɪpəl, pɑːˈtɪsɪ̣pəl $ 'pɑːr-/ *n* [C] the form of a verb, usually ending in '-ing' or '-ed', that is used to form verb tenses or adjectives → **PAST PARTICIPLE, PRESENT PARTICIPLE**

particle /'pɑːtɪkəl $ 'pɑːr-/ *n* [C] a very small piece of something: *dust particles*

particular¹ /pəˈtɪkjɡ̊lə $ pərˈtɪkjɡ̊lər/ *adj* **1** [only before noun] a particular thing, person, or time is the one that you are talking about, and not any other [= **specific**]: *In this particular case, no one was injured.* | *Each writer has his own particular style.* | *I was very busy at that particular time.* **2** [only before noun] special or great: *Pay particular attention to your brakes.* | *The video is of particular interest to teachers.* | *There's no particular reason to worry.* **3** very careful about choosing exactly what you like, and not easily satisfied [= **fussy**]: +**about** *He's very particular about his food.*

particular² *n* **1 in particular** especially: *I liked Venice in particular.* | *anything/anyone/anywhere in particular Is there anything in particular you'd like to see?* **2 particulars** [plural] details about something, especially a job, property, or legal case: *Further particulars may be obtained from Dr Evans.*

particularly /pəˈtɪkjɡ̊ləli $ pərˈtɪkjɡ̊lərli/ *adv* **1** more than usual, or more than other people or things [= **especially**]: *It was particularly hot that day.* | *He's particularly popular with the students.*

2 not particularly not very or not very much: *I'm not particularly religious.* | *'Are you hungry?' 'Not particularly.'*

parting¹ /'pɑːtɪŋ $ 'pɑːr-/ *n* **1** [C,U] *formal* an occasion when two people leave each other: *an emotional parting* **2** [C] *BrE* the line on your head made by dividing your hair with a comb [= **part** *AmE*]

parting² *adj* **1 parting kiss/gift/glance etc** a kiss etc that you give someone as you leave **2 parting shot** an unpleasant remark that you make just as you are leaving, especially at the end of an argument

partisan /ˌpɑːtɪˈzæn $ 'pɑːrtɪ̣zən, -sən/ *adj* strongly supporting one political party, plan, or leader, especially without enough thought: *a fiercely partisan crowd* —**partisan** *n* [C]

partition¹ /pɑːˈtɪʃən $ pər-, pɑːr-/ *n* **1** [C] a thin wall that separates one part of a room from another **2** [U] when a country is divided into two or more separate countries: +**of** *the partition of India*

partition² *v* [T] to divide a country, building, or room into two or more parts

partition sth ⇔ **off** *phr v* to divide part of a room from the rest, using a partition

partly /'pɑːtli $ 'pɑːr-/ *adv* to some degree, but not completely: *They moved to France, partly to be nearer their daughter.* | *I was partly to blame.*

partner¹ /'pɑːtnə $ 'pɑːrtnər/ *n* [C]
1 the person that you are married to, or that you live with as if you were married [➞ **husband, wife**]: *She lives with her partner Tom.*
2 one of the owners of a business: +**in** *He's a partner in a law firm.*
3 someone that you do an activity with, for example dancing or playing a game against two other people: *my tennis partner*
4 a country or organization that has an agreement with another: *Germany's trading partners*

partner² *v* [T] to be someone's partner in a dance, game etc

partnership /'pɑːtnəʃɪp $ 'pɑːrtnər-/ *n*
1 [C,U] a relationship between two or more people, organizations, or countries: *Marriage is a partnership.* | **in partnership with sb** *We work in partnership with other schools.* **2** [U] when you are a partner in a business: *He went into partnership with John Kent.* **3** [C] a business owned by two or more people

,part of 'speech *n* [C] plural **parts of speech** *technical* one of the groups into which words are divided in grammar, for example noun, verb, or adjective

,part-'time *adj, adv* for only a part of the normal working day or week [➞ **full-time**]: *a part-time job* | *I work part-time.*

party¹ /'pɑːti $ 'pɑːrti/ *n* [C] plural **parties**
1 a social event when a lot of people meet to eat, drink, dance etc: **have/throw/give a party** *We're having a party on Friday. Come over.* | **birthday/Christmas/farewell etc party** *Are you going to Amy's birthday party?* | *Sam's a real party animal* (=someone who goes to a lot of parties).

get-together – a small informal party
a do/sb's do *informal* – a party
bash *informal* – a party
dinner party – a party where people are invited to someone's house for an evening meal
house-warming party – a party that you have when you move into a new house
drinks party *BrE*/**cocktail party** – a party that people go to in order to talk and have a drink together for a few hours
fancy-dress party – a party where people dress in special clothes, for example to look like a famous person or a character in a story
hen party *especially BrE* – a social event that is just for women, which happens before a wedding
stag night *BrE*/**bachelor party** *AmE* – a social event that is just for men, which happens before a wedding
baby/wedding shower *AmE* – an event at which people give presents to a woman who is going to have a baby or get married
reception – a large formal party, for example after a wedding
celebration – a party that is organized in order to celebrate something

2 [also + plural verb *BrE*] a political organization with particular ideas and aims that you can vote for in elections: **the Labour/Communist/ Democratic etc Party** *The Labour Party are demanding a change in the law.* | *the country's two main* **political parties** | *members of the* **ruling party** (=the party in power) | *the* **opposition party** (=the party that is not in power) → see box at **ORGANIZATION**

3 [also + plural verb *BrE*] a group of people who are travelling or working together: **+of** *a party of schoolchildren* | *No one in our party spoke French.* → see box at **GROUP**

4 one of the people or groups who are involved in a legal argument or agreement
→ **SEARCH PARTY, THIRD PARTY**

party² *v* [I] **partied, partying, parties** *informal* to enjoy yourself with a group of other people by eating, drinking, dancing etc: *He likes to party.*

pass¹ /pɑːs $ pæs/ *v*

1 also **pass by** [I,T] to move past someone or something: *We used to pass the shop every day.* | *Luke stepped aside to let me pass.* | *A plane passed overhead.*

Passed is the past tense of the verb 'pass': *We've just passed Tim's house.*
Past is an adjective or noun which is used to talk about a period of time before now: *The past year has been very difficult.* | *things that happened in the past*
Past is also an adverb and a preposition used to describe something's movement or position in relation to other things: *She cycled past us on her way to work.* | *The hotel is just past the church.*

2 [I,T] to go through, across, around etc something, or to make something do this: **+through/ across/around etc** *We passed through the gate*

into the yard. | *The road passes through the town centre.* | *Pass the rope around the post.*
3 [T] to give something to someone else, especially by putting it in their hand: **pass sb sth/ pass sth to sb** *Could you pass me the salt, please?* | *I passed the letter back to her.* | *I'll pass the information to our sales department.*
4 a) [I,T] to succeed in an examination or test [≠ **fail**]: *Did you pass all your exams?* | *I passed my driving test!* | *She* **passed with flying colours** (=got very high marks). **b)** [T] to officially decide that someone has succeeded in an examination or test [≠ **fail**]
5 [I,T] to kick, throw, or hit a ball to another member of your team: **+to** *Why didn't he pass to Mark?* → see box at **THROW**
6 a) [I] if time passes, it goes by: *The days passed slowly.* **b)** [T] to spend time, especially when you are waiting for something or are bored: *We played cards* **to pass the time** (=help us stop feeling bored).
7 [T] to officially accept a law or suggestion, especially by voting: *The Act was passed in 1993.*
8 pass sentence to officially decide how a criminal will be punished
9 pass judgment (on sb/sth) to give your opinion about someone or something: *I'm here to help, not to pass judgement.*
10 [I] *formal* to change from being owned or controlled by one person to another person: **+to** *The land will pass to my son when I die.*
11 [I] to end: *The storm soon passed.*
12 let sth pass to deliberately not say anything when someone says or does something that you do not like: *He was very rude, but I decided to* **let it pass.**
13 pass water to **URINATE**

pass sth ⇔ **around** also **pass sth** ⇔ **round** *BrE phr v* to offer or show something to each person in a group: *Pass the cakes around, Roy.*
pass away *phr v* to die – use is you want to avoid saying the word 'die'
pass by (sb/sth) *phr v* to go past someone or something: *He waited until the doctor had passed by.* | *You'll pass by the Hotel Bern.*
pass sth ⇔ **down** *phr v* [usually passive] to give or teach something to people who are younger than you or live after you: *The skill was passed down from father to son.*
pass for sb/sth *phr v* to be thought to be something that you are not: *She could easily pass for a boy.*
pass sb/sth off as sth *phr v* to make people think that a person or thing is something that they are not: *He passed himself off as a doctor.*
pass sth ⇔ **on** *phr v* to give someone something, especially information that someone else has given you: **+to** *Can you pass the message on to Bob?*
pass out *phr v* to suddenly become unconscious [= **faint**]
pass sth ⇔ **up** *phr v* to not use a chance to do something: **pass up a chance/opportunity/ offer etc** *You shouldn't pass up the chance to go to university.*

pass² *n* [C] **1** an official piece of paper that shows that you are allowed to enter a building or travel on a bus or train without paying: *The guard checked our passes.* | *a bus pass* **2** a successful result in an examination [≠ **fail**]: **+in**

an A-level pass in English | *The **pass mark*** (=mark you need to be successful) *is 55%.* **3** an action of kicking, throwing, or hitting a ball to another member of your team: *a brilliant pass* **4** a road or path through or over mountains: *a narrow **mountain pass***

passable /ˈpɑːsəbəl $ ˈpæ-/ *adj* **1** fairly good, but not excellent: *The beer was passable.* **2** a road or river that is passable is not blocked, so you can travel along or across it [≠ **impassable**]

passage /ˈpæsɪdʒ/ *n*

1 also **passageway** /ˈpæsɪdʒweɪ/ [C] a long narrow area with walls on either side which connects one room or place to another [➥ **corridor**]: *My office is just along the passage.* | *an underground passage*
2 [C] a short part of a book, poem, speech, piece of music etc: +**from/of** *a passage from the Koran*
3 [U] movement or progress from one place or stage to another: *Thousands of people have been offered **free passage** out of the war zone.*
4 [C] a tube in your body that air or liquid can pass through: *nasal passages*
5 the passage of time *literary* the passing of time

passé /ˈpæseɪ, ˈpɑː- $ pæˈseɪ/ *adj* no longer modern or fashionable

passenger /ˈpæsɪndʒə, -sən- $ -ər/ *n* [C] someone who is travelling in a car, plane, train etc, but is not driving it or working on it: *Rail passengers are facing even longer delays.* → see box at TRAVEL

passerby /ˌpɑːsəˈbaɪ $ ˌpæsər-/ *n* [C] plural **passersby** someone who is walking past a place: *His shouts were heard by a passerby.*

passing¹ /ˈpɑːsɪŋ $ ˈpæ-/ *adj* [only before noun] **1** a passing thought or feeling is short and not very serious: *a passing interest in golf* **2** going past: *A passing car stopped to help.*

passing² *n* **1 in passing** if you say something in passing, you mention it while you are talking about something else: *He did **mention** Jean, but only **in passing**.* **2 the passing of time** the process of time going by

passion /ˈpæʃən/ *n* **1** [C,U] a very strong feeling of love or sexual desire: *His eyes were burning with passion.* **2** [C,U] a very strong belief or feeling about something: *She writes with passion and humour.* **3** [C] a very strong liking for something: +**for** *Lucy's passion for music*

passionate /ˈpæʃənɪ̥t/ *adj* **1** showing or involving very strong feelings of love or sexual desire: *a passionate kiss* **2** showing very strong feelings or ideas about something: *a passionate speech* —**passionately** *adv*

passive¹ /ˈpæsɪv/ *adj*

1 someone who is passive accepts what happens or what people say without trying to change or influence it [≠ **active**]: *their passive acceptance of their fate*
2 *technical* used to describe a verb or sentence in which the subject of the verb is affected by the action rather than doing the action. In the sentence 'I was invited to the party', the verb is passive. [≠ **active**]
—**passively** *adv* —**passivity** /pæˈsɪvɪ̥ti/ *n* [U]

passive² *n* **the passive (voice)** *technical* the passive form of a verb

passive 'smoking *n* [U] when you breathe in smoke from other people's cigarettes

Passover /ˈpɑːsəʊvə $ ˈpæsoʊvər/ also **the Passover** *n* [U] the Jewish holiday that celebrates the Jewish escape from ancient Egypt

passport /ˈpɑːspɔːt $ ˈpæspɔːrt/ *n* [C]

1 an official document with your photograph and details about you inside it that you need when you travel to other countries: **American/British etc passport** *My son holds* (=has) *an American **passport**.*

You **apply for** a passport at the **passport office**.
A **passport holder** is the person who a passport belongs to.
If you travel to a foreign country, you must **show** your passport at **passport control** when you enter the country and may **have/get** your passport stamped.
A **valid passport** is officially acceptable.
A **passport** that has **expired** is too old to be acceptable.
→ AIRPORT, TRAVEL

2 passport to success/happiness etc something that makes success, happiness etc easy to achieve: *Money is not always a passport to happiness.*

'passport con,trol *n* [U] the place where your passport is checked when you leave or enter a country

password /ˈpɑːswɜːd $ ˈpæswɜːrd/ *n* [C] a secret word that you must use before you can use a computer system or enter a place: *Type in your password.*

past¹ /pɑːst $ pæst/ *adj*

1 [only before noun] done, used, or experienced in a time before now: *Hopefully, I have learned from past mistakes.* | *He knew from **past experience** that Maria had a bad temper.* → see box at PASS
2 [only before noun] used to talk about a period of time that has just finished: *the events of the past year* | *Tim's been in Rome for the past week.*
3 finished or having come to an end: *By mid-June the danger was past.*
4 past leader/president/champion etc a leader etc in the past
5 the past tense *technical* the form of a verb that is used to show a past action or state

past² *prep, adv*

1 later than a particular time: *It's ten past nine* (=ten minutes after nine). | *It was already past midnight.*
2 go/walk/drive etc past (sb/sth) to move towards and then beyond a person or place, without stopping: *He walked past me as though I didn't exist.* | *We drove past slowly.*
3 further than a particular place: *Our house is just past* (=a little further than) *the bridge.*
4 beyond a particular limit, stage, or age: *This yoghurt's **past its sell-by date**.* | *I'm past the age for romance.*
5 if a period of time goes past, it passes: *Weeks went past without any news.*
6 I wouldn't put it past sb (to do sth) *spoken* used to say that you would not be surprised if

someone did something bad or unusual because it is typical of them: *I wouldn't put it past Neil to be violent.*

7 past it *BrE spoken* too old to do something or be useful

past³ *n*

1 the past a) the time that existed before the present: **in the past** *People travel more now than in the past.* | *Good manners have become a thing of the past* (=no longer exist). **b)** the form of a verb that is used to show past action or state **2** [C] all the things that have happened in a person's life or in a particular place: *She never talks about her past.*

pasta /'pæstə $ 'pɑː-/ *n* [U] an Italian food made from flour, eggs, and water and cut into various shapes and cooked

paste¹ /peɪst/ *n* [C,U] **1 meat/fish/tomato etc paste** a soft smooth food made from crushed meat, fish etc **2** a soft wet mixture that can be easily spread **3** a type of thick glue that is used for sticking paper: *wallpaper paste*

paste² *v* **1** [T] to stick paper to a surface, using glue **2** [I,T] to move or copy words, pictures etc from one computer document to another

pastel¹ /'pæstl $ pæ'stel/ *adj* [only before noun] pastel colours are light and pale

pastel² *n* **1** [C,U] a small coloured stick used for drawing **2** [C usually plural] a picture drawn with pastels **3** [C usually plural] a light colour

pasteurized also **-ised** *BrE* /'pɑːstʃəraɪz, -stə- $ 'pæs-/ *adj* pasteurized milk has been specially heated to kill any BACTERIA in it

pastime /'pɑːstaɪm $ 'pæs-/ *n* [C] something that you enjoy doing when you are not working [= hobby]

pastor /'pɑːstə $ 'pæstər/ *n* [C] a priest in some Protestant churches

pastoral /'pɑːstərəl $ 'pæ-/ *adj* **1** relating to the work of a priest or teacher in helping people with personal matters: *Pastoral care at the school is excellent.* **2** *literary* typical of peaceful country life: *pastoral scenes*

past participle *n* [C] the form of a verb used in PERFECT tenses (for example 'eaten' in 'I have eaten'), or in the PASSIVE (for example 'changed' in 'it was changed'), or sometimes as an adjective (for example 'broken' in 'a broken leg')

past perfect *n* **the past perfect** the form of a verb that shows that an action was completed before another event happened. In the sentence 'After I had finished my meal, I went upstairs', 'had finished' is in the past perfect.

pastry /'peɪstri/ *n plural* **pastries 1** [U] a mixture of flour, fat, and water that you roll flat then fill with other food and bake **2** [C] a small cake made with pastry

pasture /'pɑːstʃə $ 'pæstʃər/ *n* [C,U] land that is covered with grass and used for cows, sheep etc to feed on

pasty¹ /'peɪsti/ *adj* a pasty face looks pale and unhealthy

pasty² /'pæsti/ *n* [C] *plural* **pasties** *BrE* a type of food with meat or vegetables in the middle and pastry all around the outside

pat¹ /pæt/ *v* [T] **patted, patting 1** to touch someone or something lightly with your flat hand, in a friendly way: *She patted me on the shoulder.*

2 pat sb on the back to praise someone when they have done something well

pat² *n* [C] **1** a way of touching someone or something lightly with your flat hand, in a friendly way: *He gave the dog a friendly pat.* **2 a pat on the back** praise for something you have done well

pat³ *adj* [only before noun] *disapproving* a pat answer seems too quick and simple, as though it has been used many times

patch¹ /pætʃ/ *n* [C] **1** a small area of something: **+of** *a patch of grass* | *a black cat with white patches* | *icy patches on the road* | *He wore a hat to cover his bald patch.* **2** a small piece of material that you use to cover a hole in your clothes: *old trousers with patches on the knees* **3** a small area of land where you grow fruit or vegetables: *a vegetable patch* **4** a small piece of material that you use to cover one eye when it is injured **5 a bad/rough patch** *informal especially BrE* a difficult or unhappy time: *I've been going through a bad patch recently.* **6 not be a patch on sb/sth** *BrE informal* to be much less good, attractive etc than someone or something else: *His second book isn't a patch on his first.*

patch² also **patch up** *v* [T] to repair a hole in something by putting a small piece of material over it: *a pair of old patched jeans*
    patch sth/sb ⇔ up *phr v* **1** to end an argument and become friendly with someone again: *He's patched things up with his girlfriend now.* **2** to give quick and basic medical treatment to someone who is injured: *They patched him up and sent him back to work.*

patchwork /'pætʃwɜːk $ -wɜːrk/ *n* [U] a type of sewing in which you sew a lot of different coloured pieces of cloth together to make a large piece of cloth: *a patchwork quilt*

patchy /'pætʃi/ *adj* **1** happening in some places but not everywhere: *patchy fog* **2** good in some ways but not in others: *My French is quite patchy.*

pâté /'pæteɪ $ pɑː'teɪ, pæ-/ *n* [U] a smooth mixture made from meat, fish, or vegetables, that you spread on bread: *smoked salmon pâté*

patent¹ /'peɪtnt, 'pæ-/ *n* [C] an official document that gives one person or company the right to make and sell a new product, and no one else is allowed to copy it

patent² *v* [T] to get a patent for something

patent³ *adj* [only before noun] *formal* **a patent lie/patent nonsense etc** something that is clearly not true or not sensible

patent leather /ˌpeɪtnt 'leðə◂ $ ˌpætnt 'leðər/ *n* [U] very shiny leather

patently /'peɪtntli $ 'pæ-/ *adv* in a way that is very clear and easy to see: *This is patently untrue.* | *It's patently obvious that she's lying.*

paternal /pə'tɜːnl $ -ɜːr-/ *adj* **1** paternal feelings or behaviour are like those of a good father [➡ maternal]: *Dad gave me some paternal advice.* **2 paternal grandfather/uncle etc** your father's father, brother etc

paternity /pə'tɜːnɪ̩ti $ -ɜːr-/ *n* [U] *law* when someone is a father or becomes a father: *paternity leave*

path /pɑːθ $ pæθ/ *n* [C] plural **paths** /pɑːðz $ pæðz/
1 a narrow track that people walk along: *a path through the woods* | *Follow this **path** down to the river.* | *a **garden path***
2 the direction or line along which someone or something is moving: **+of** *He walked straight into the path of a lorry.* | *The plane had strayed off its **flight path**.*
3 a plan or series of actions that will lead to achieving something: **+to** *the path to economic recovery*

pathetic /pəˈθetɪk/ *adj* **1** very bad, useless, or weak: *a pathetic excuse* | *Stop being so pathetic!*
2 making you feel sadness and sympathy: *The boy looked small and pathetic.*

pathological /ˌpæθəˈlɒdʒɪkəl◂ $ -ˈlɑː-/ *adj*
1 pathological behaviour or feelings are extreme and unreasonable, and you cannot control them: *He's a **pathological liar**.* **2** *technical* relating to pathology

pathologist /pəˈθɒlədʒɪ̩st $ -ˈθɑː-/ *n* [C] a doctor who has studied pathology, especially one who tries to find out the causes of death

pathology /pəˈθɒlədʒi $ -ˈθɑː-/ *n* [U] the study of diseases and causes of death

pathos /ˈpeɪθɒs $ -θɑːs/ *n* [U] *literary* the quality in a person or a situation that makes you feel sympathy for them

pathway /ˈpɑːθweɪ $ ˈpæθ-/ *n* [C] a PATH

patience /ˈpeɪʃəns/ *n* [U]
1 the ability to stay calm and not get angry when you are waiting for something or doing something difficult [≠ **impatience**]: *I don't **have the patience** to be a teacher.* | **+with** *She's got no patience with children.* | *I finally **lost my patience** and shouted at her.* | *He was **running out of patience**.*
2 *BrE* a game of cards played by one person [= **solitaire** *AmE*]

patient[1] /ˈpeɪʃənt/ *n* [C] someone who is getting medical treatment from a doctor or in hospital: *Dr Ross is very popular with his patients.*

patient[2] *adj* able to stay calm and not become angry when you are waiting for something or doing something difficult [≠ **impatient**]: *Just be patient and wait.* | **+with** *She's always very patient with her students.* → see box at **CHARACTER**
—**patiently** *adv*: *He waited patiently to speak.*

patio /ˈpætiəʊ $ -oʊ/ *n* [C] plural **patios** a flat hard area near a house where people sit outside: *We'll eat on the patio.*

patriarchal /ˌpeɪtriˈɑːkəl◂ $ -ˈɑːr-/ *adj* a patriarchal society is ruled or controlled only by men

patriot /ˈpætriət, -triɒt, ˈpeɪ- $ ˈpeɪtriət, -triɑːt/ *n* [C] someone who loves their country and is willing to fight to defend it

patriotic /ˌpætriˈɒtɪk◂, ˌpeɪ- $ ˌpeɪtriˈɑːtɪk◂/ *adj* having or showing great love for your country: *patriotic songs* —**patriotism** /ˈpætriətɪzəm, ˈpeɪ- $ ˈpeɪ-/ *n* [U]

patrol[1] /pəˈtrəʊl $ -ˈtroʊl/ *n* **a)** [C,U] when police, guards, or soldiers go regularly around a building or area to check that there is no trouble

or danger: **on patrol** *a police officer on patrol* **b)** [C] a group of police, guards, or soldiers that regularly check a particular area: *the US border patrol* | *a police **patrol car***

patrol[2] *v* [I,T] **patrolled, patrolling** to regularly go around a building or area to check that there is no trouble or danger: *Officers patrol the area regularly.*

patrolman /pəˈtrəʊlmən $ -ˈtroʊl-/ *n* [C] plural **patrolmen** /-mən/ *AmE* a police officer who patrols a particular area

patron /ˈpeɪtrən/ *n* [C] **1** someone who supports or gives money to an organization, artist, writer, or musical performer: **+of** *a patron of the arts* **2** *formal* someone who uses a particular shop, restaurant, or hotel

patronage /ˈpætrənɪdʒ $ ˈpeɪ-, ˈpæ-/ *n* [U] the support or money that a patron gives: *artists who enjoyed the Prince's patronage*

patronize also **-ise** *BrE* /ˈpætrənaɪz $ ˈpeɪ-, ˈpæ-/ *v* [T] **1** to talk to someone in a way that shows you think you are better than they are or know more than they do: *It's important not to patronize children.* | *Don't patronize me.* **2** *formal* to regularly go to a particular shop, restaurant etc

patronizing also **-ising** *BrE* /ˈpætrənaɪzɪŋ $ ˈpeɪ-, ˈpæ-/ *adj* someone who is patronizing talks to you in a way that shows they think they are better than you or know more than you do: *patronizing remarks*

ˌpatron ˈsaint *n* [C] a Christian holy person who is believed to protect a particular place or particular people

patter /ˈpætə $ -ər/ *n* [singular] **1** the gentle sound made by light quick steps or rain hitting a surface: **+of** *the patter of rain on the roof* **2** a way of talking that is fast and continuous: *a car salesman's patter* —**patter** *v* [I]

pattern /ˈpætən $ ˈpætərn/ *n* [C]
1 the regular way in which something happens: *Weather patterns have changed in recent years.* | **+of** *changing patterns of behaviour among students* | *Children's development does not **follow a set pattern*** (=always happen in the same way).
2 a regular design of shapes, colours, and lines: *a pattern of small red and white squares*
3 a shape that you copy onto cloth or paper when you are making something, especially clothes: *a skirt pattern*

patterned /ˈpætənd $ -ərnd/ *adj* decorated with a pattern: *a patterned carpet* → see picture at **PATTERN**

paunch /pɔːntʃ $ pɒːntʃ/ *n* [C] a man's fat stomach

pauper /ˈpɔːpə $ ˈpɒːpər/ *n* [C] *old-fashioned* someone who is very poor

pause[1] /pɔːz $ pɒːz/ *v* [I] to stop doing something for a short time before you start again: **+for** *She paused for a moment before replying.* | *He paused for breath halfway up the stairs.*

pause[2] *n* [C]
1 a short time when you stop speaking or doing something: *'Yes,' she said, after a brief pause.* | **+in** *There was a pause in the conversation.*
2 give sb pause for thought to make someone think seriously and carefully about something

patterns

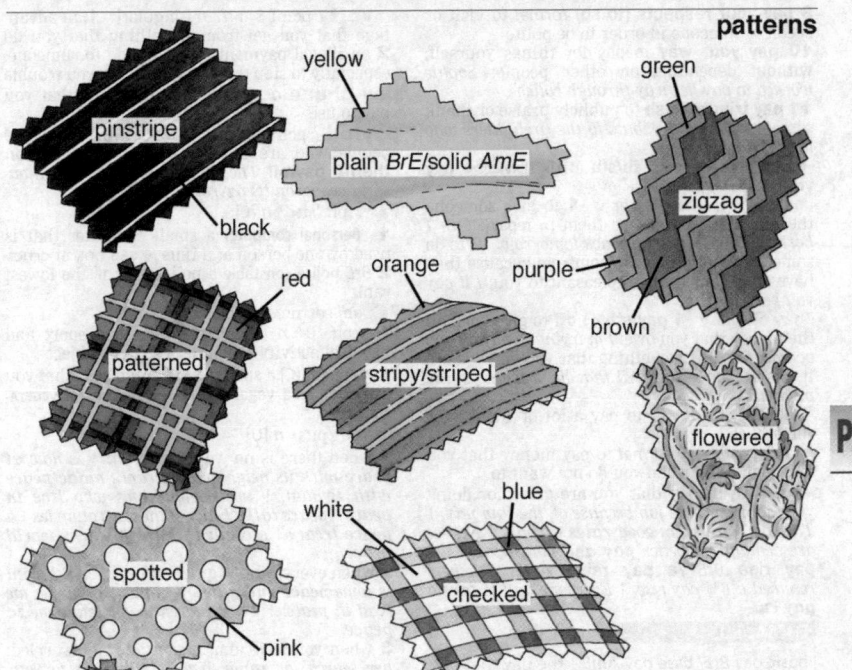

pinstripe
black
yellow
plain *BrE*/solid *AmE*
green
zigzag
purple
brown
red
orange
patterned
stripy/striped
flowered
white
blue
spotted
checked
pink

pave /peɪv/ v [T usually passive] **1** to cover a path, road etc with a hard surface, especially of large flat stones: *a paved courtyard* **2 pave the way for sth** to make it possible for something to happen in the future: *The talks could pave the way for a ceasefire agreement.*

pavement /'peɪvmənt/ n

1 [C] *BrE* the path you walk on at the side of a road [= **sidewalk** *AmE*]: *A policeman was standing on the pavement outside the bank.*
2 [U] *AmE* the hard surface of a road

pavilion /pə'vɪljən/ n [C] **1** a temporary building or tent that is used for public shows or other events **2** *BrE* a building at a sports field where players can change their clothes

'paving stone n [C] a flat piece of stone – used with other pieces to make a hard surface to walk on

paw[1] /pɔː $ pɒː/ n [C] the foot of an animal such as a dog, cat, or lion → see picture on page A2

paw[2] v [I,T] if an animal paws something, it touches it several times with its paw: **+at** *The dog whined and pawed at the door.*

pawn[1] /pɔːn $ pɒːn/ n [C] **1** a piece in a game of CHESS that can move forward one square at a time **2** a weak person who is used or controlled by a much more powerful person

pawn[2] v [T] to leave something valuable with a pawnbroker in order to borrow money from them: *She pawned her wedding ring.*

pawnbroker /'pɔːnˌbrəʊkə $ 'pɒːnˌbroʊkər/ n [C] someone who lends money to people. You leave something valuable with a pawnbroker, who sells it if you do not pay back the money.

pay[1] /peɪ/ v past tense and past participle **paid** /peɪd/

1 [I,T] to give someone money for something you buy or for a service: **+for** *Who's going to pay for all this?* | **pay sth for sth** *I paid £25 for that watch.* | **pay sb for sth** *I've paid him for the lessons in advance.* | *Can you* **pay cash**? | *I'll* **pay by cheque**.
2 [I,T] to give someone money for the job that they do: *They only pay £4 an hour.* | **pay sb sth** *I pay him $20 a day.* | *He gets paid £500 a week.* | **well/badly paid** *a well paid job*
3 [T] to give money that you owe to a person, organization etc: *Don't forget to* **pay** *the electricity* **bill**. | *Can I pay you the rest next week?* | **pay a fine/pay damages/pay costs** (=give money to someone because the law says you must)
4 pay attention (to sb/sth) to listen to or watch someone or something carefully: *Always pay attention to the car in front.*
5 pay sb a visit/pay a visit to sb/sth to go to see a person or place: *I'll pay you a visit when I'm in town.* | *We paid a visit to the art gallery.*
6 [I] if something pays, it is worth doing because you get an advantage from it: *Crime doesn't pay.*
7 [I,T] to suffer or be punished for something wrong you have done: **+for** *You'll pay for this one day!* | **pay the penalty/price** *He's paying the price for not working hard enough at school.*
8 pay sb a compliment to tell someone that you think they are nice, attractive, intelligent etc

9 pay your respects (to sb) *formal* to visit or speak to someone in order to be polite

10 pay your way to pay for things yourself, without depending on other people: *Sophie worked to pay her way through college.*

11 pay tribute to sb to publicly praise or thank someone: *He paid tribute to the firefighters who fought the blaze.*

→ **pay lip service to sb/sth** at LIP SERVICE → **pay your respects** at RESPECT¹

pay sb/sth ⇔ back *phr v* **1** to give someone the money that you owe them [= repay]: *Can I borrow $10? I'll pay you back tomorrow.* **2** to do something unpleasant to someone because they have done something unpleasant to you: *I'll pay you back for this!*

pay off *phr v* **1 pay sth ⇔ off** to give back all the money that you owe: *I'm trying to pay off my overdraft.* **2** if something that you do pays off, it has a good result: *All that hard work finally paid off.*

pay out sth *phr v* to pay a lot of money for something

pay up *phr v informal* to pay money that you owe, especially when you do not want to

pay² *n* [U] money that you are given for doing your job: *I left the job because of the low pay.* | *The company offers good rates of pay.* | *Nurses are demanding better pay and conditions.* | **a pay rise** *BrE* /**a pay raise** *AmE*: *Teachers received a 6% pay rise.* | *Everyone had to take a pay cut.*

THESAURUS

basic pay *BrE*/ **base** pay *AmE* – the pay that you always receive, without payment for any extra hours

overtime pay – payment for extra hours that you work

take-home pay – the money you receive after tax etc has been taken away

holiday pay *BrE*/**vacation** pay *AmE* – payment for the time when you are on holiday

sick pay – payment for the times when you are ill

maternity pay – pay a woman receives when she stops working to have a baby

→ MONEY, PENSION

---

payable /ˈpeɪəbəl/ *adj* **1** a bill or debt etc that is payable must be paid: *The rent is payable on the first day of the month.* **2 payable to sb** a cheque that is payable to someone has their name written on it and the money must be paid to them: *Cheques should be made payable to Granada TV.*

'pay cheque *BrE*; **paycheck** *AmE* /ˈpeɪtʃek/ *n* [C] a cheque that you get each week or each month for doing your job

payday /ˈpeɪdeɪ/ *n* [U] the day each week or month when you are paid for doing your job

payee /peɪˈiː/ *n* [C] the person that a cheque must be paid to

payer /ˈpeɪə $ -ər/ *n* [C] someone who pays something: *tax payers*

payment /ˈpeɪmənt/ *n* [C,U] an amount of money that is paid: *You can make payments in cash or by cheque.* | *Do you accept payment by credit card?* | *I received a payment of £200.*

→ BALANCE OF PAYMENTS, DOWN PAYMENT

payoff /ˈpeɪɒf $ -ɒːf/ *n* [singular] **1** an advantage that you get from something that you do **2** an illegal payment that is made to someone, especially to stop them from causing you trouble

'pay phone *n* [C] a public telephone that you pay to use

payroll /ˈpeɪrəʊl $ -roʊl/ *n* [C] a list of all the people who are employed by a company: **on the/its payroll** *The company has over a thousand people on its payroll.*

PC¹ /ˌpiː ˈsiː◂ / *n* [C]

1 personal computer a small computer that is used by one person at a time → see box at OFFICE **2** *BrE* **police constable** a policeman of the lowest rank

PC² *adj* POLITICALLY CORRECT

PE /ˌpiː ˈiː/ *n* [U] **physical education** sport and physical activity taught as a school subject

pea /piː/ *n* [C] a small round green seed that you can cook as a vegetable → see picture at VEGETABLE

peace /piːs/ *n* [U]

1 when there is no war: *The country is now at peace with its neighbour.* | *France made peace with Britain.* | *two communities who live in peace* | *peace talks between the two countries* | *a peace treaty* | *a conflict which threatens world peace*

2 when everything is quiet and calm: *All I want is some peace and quiet.* | **in peace** *Just let me read in peace.* | *The children won't leave me in peace.*

3 when you feel calm, happy, and not worried: *her search for inner peace* | *Talking to your doctor will give you peace of mind.*

peaceable /ˈpiːsəbəl/ *adj* not wanting to argue or fight

peaceful /ˈpiːsfəl/ *adv*

1 quiet and calm: *The wood was cool and peaceful.* | *a peaceful afternoon* → see box at QUIET **2** not involving war or violence: *a peaceful demonstration* | *a peaceful solution to the conflict* —**peacefully** *adv*: *She was sleeping peacefully.* —**peacefulness** *n* [U]

peacekeeping /ˈpiːsˌkiːpɪŋ/ *adj* **peacekeeping troops/forces etc** soldiers who are sent to a place to stop people from fighting each other —**peacekeeper** *n* [C]

peacetime /ˈpiːstaɪm/ *n* [U] when a country is not fighting a war

peach /piːtʃ/ *n* [C] a round juicy fruit with a soft yellow and red skin and a large seed inside → see picture at FRUIT

peacock /ˈpiːkɒk $ -kɑːk/ *n* [C] a large bird. The male has long blue and green tail feathers that it can lift and spread out.

peak¹ /piːk/ *n* [C] **1** the time when someone or something is best, highest, or most successful: *The holiday season is now at its peak.* | *Profits this month have reached a new peak.* | *At 40 many people are at the peak of their careers.* **2** a mountain or the pointed top of a mountain: *the snow-covered peaks of the Alps* | *a mountain peak* → see box at MOUNTAIN **3** *BrE* the flat curved part of a hat that covers your eyes [= visor *AmE*]

peak² *v* [I] to reach the highest point or level: *Sales peaked in July.*

peak³ *adj* **1** highest or best: *Prices hit their peak level last year.* | *a new shampoo that will keep your hair in peak condition* **2** *BrE* peak times are when the largest number of people are travelling or doing something: *There are extra buses during peak times.* | *the peak holiday periods*

peal /piːl/ *n* [C] a loud long sound of laughter, THUNDER, or bells ringing: +**of** *peals of laughter* | *a sudden peal of thunder*

peanut /ˈpiːnʌt/ *n* [C] **1** a small nut in a light brown shell which grows under the ground: *a packet of salted peanuts* **2 peanuts** *informal* a very small amount of money: *He gets paid peanuts!*

,peanut 'butter / $ '.. ,../ *n* [U] a soft food made from crushed peanuts that you spread on bread

pear /peə $ per/ *n* [C] a sweet juicy fruit that is round at the bottom and thinner at the top → see picture at FRUIT

pearl /pɜːl $ pɜːrl/ *n* [C] a small white round object that forms inside an OYSTER and is a valuable jewel

'pear-shaped *adj* **go pear-shaped** *informal* if something you are doing goes pear-shaped, it fails completely

peasant /ˈpezənt/ *n* [C] a poor farmer who owns or rents a small amount of land, either in the past or in poor countries

peat /piːt/ *n* [U] a black substance formed in the ground from decaying plants that you can use to help plants grow or burn instead of coal

pebble /ˈpebəl/ *n* [C] a small smooth stone that you find in a river or on a beach

peck¹ /pek/ *v* [I,T] **1** if a bird pecks something, it hits or bites it with its beak: +**at** *pigeons pecking at breadcrumbs* **2 peck sb on the cheek/forehead etc** to kiss someone quickly and gently

peck² *n* [C] **1** a quick kiss: *He gave her a quick peck on the cheek.* **2** the action of a bird pecking something with its beak

peculiar /pɪˈkjuːliə $ -ər/ *adj* **1** strange and surprising: *a peculiar smell* | *He's a rather peculiar boy.* → see box at STRANGE **2 be peculiar to sb/sth** if something is peculiar to one place, person etc, only that place or person has it: *a building style peculiar to this area*

peculiarity /pɪˌkjuːliˈærəti/ *n* plural **peculiarities 1** [C] an unusual feature or habit that only one particular person, thing, or place has: *a peculiarity of the British legal system* **2** [U] the quality of being strange or unusual: +**of** *the peculiarity of her situation*

peculiarly /pɪˈkjuːliəli $ -ər-/ *adv* **1 peculiarly British/male etc** typical only of British people, men etc: *a peculiarly American attitude* **2** in a strange or unusual way: *He was behaving very peculiarly.*

pedagogical /ˌpedəˈɡɒdʒɪkəl $ -ˈɡɑː-/ *adj formal* pedagogical ideas and methods are about the different ways of teaching things to people

pedal¹ /ˈpedl/ *n* [C] **1** the part of a bicycle that you push round with your foot to make it move forward → see picture at BICYCLE **2** the part of a car or machine that you press with your foot to make it move or work: **brake/clutch pedal** | **accelerator pedal** *BrE* /**gas pedal** *AmE*

pedal² *v* [I] **pedalled, pedalling** *BrE*; **pedaled, pedaling** *AmE* to ride a bicycle by pushing the pedals with your feet: *He pedalled along the road.*

pedantic /pɪˈdæntɪk/ *adj disapproving* paying too much attention to small unimportant details or rules

peddle /ˈpedl/ *v* [T] to try to sell things to people, especially illegal drugs or other things that people disapprove of: *He was accused of peddling drugs.* | *The pictures were peddled around to various dealers.*

peddler /ˈpedlə $ -ər/ *n* [C] **1** *AmE* someone who walked from place to place in the past selling things [= **pedlar** *BrE*] **2** *old-fashioned* someone who sells illegal drugs [= **dealer**]

pedestal /ˈpedɪstəl/ *n* [C] **1** the base that a STATUE stands on **2 put sb on a pedestal** to admire someone very much

pedestrian¹ /pɪˈdestriən/ *n* [C] someone who is walking, especially along a street where there are cars

pedestrian² *adj* **1** ordinary, and not very interesting or exciting: *The whole ceremony was rather pedestrian.* **2** [only before noun] used by pedestrians: *a pedestrian precinct* (=a shopping area where cars cannot go)

pe,destrian 'crossing *n* [C] *BrE* a marked place on the road where people who are walking can safely cross [= **crosswalk** *AmE*]

pediatrician /ˌpiːdiəˈtrɪʃən/ *n* the American spelling of PAEDIATRICIAN

pediatrics /ˌpiːdiˈætrɪks/ *n* the American spelling of PAEDIATRICS

pedicure /ˈpedɪkjʊə $ -kjʊr/ *n* [C] a treatment for feet and toenails, to make them more comfortable or beautiful —**pedicurist** *n* [C]

pedigree¹ /ˈpedɪɡriː/ *n* [C,U] **1** the parents and other past family members of a person or animal, or an official written record of this: *a horse with a good pedigree* **2** all the things that a person or organization has achieved: *a young writer with an impressive pedigree*

pedigree² *adj* [only before noun] a pedigree animal has parents and grandparents from the same special BREED: *a pedigree Alsatian*

pedlar /ˈpedlə $ -ər/ *n* [C] *BrE* someone who walked from place to place in the past selling things [= **peddler** *AmE*]

pedophile /ˈpiːdəfaɪl/ *n* the American spelling of PAEDOPHILE

pee /piː/ *n* [singular] *informal* when you go for a pee, you URINATE —**pee** *v* [I]

peek /piːk/ *v* [I] to look at something quickly, especially when you should not: *The door was open, so I peeked into the room.* —**peek** *n* [C]

peel¹ /piːl/ *v* **1** [T] to remove the skin of a fruit or vegetable: *Will you peel the potatoes, please?* → see box at CUT **2** also **peel off** [I] if skin, paint, or paper peels, it comes off, usually in small pieces: *My skin always peels when I've been in the sun.* | *The paint was beginning to peel off.* → **keep your eyes peeled** at EYE¹

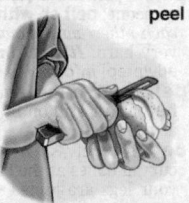

peel

peeling a potato

peel sth ⇔ **off** *phr v* **1** to remove a layer from the surface of something else: *Peel off the label.* **2** to take your clothes off: *Tom peeled off his wet shorts.*

peel² *n* [U] the skin of a fruit or vegetable that you remove before eating it: *orange peel | potato peel* → see picture at **FRUIT**

peep¹ /pi:p/ *v* [I] **1** to look at something quickly and secretly: **+through/out/at etc** *I saw Joe peeping through the curtains.* **2** if something peeps from somewhere, you can just see a small amount of it: **+out/above/through etc** *The sun finally peeped out from behind the clouds.*

peep² *n* [C usually singular] **1** a quick or secret look at something: **+at/into** *She took a peep at the answers in the back of the book.* **2** *informal* a sound that someone makes: *There has **not** been **a peep out of** the children.*

peer¹ /pɪə $ pɪr/ *n* [C] **1** [usually plural] *formal* also **peer group** your peers or peer group are people who are the same age as you or who have the same type of job or social position: *Teenagers usually prefer to spend their time with their peers. | Kids may take drugs because of **peer pressure** (=because they feel they must do the same as other people of their age).* **2** someone who belongs to a family of high social rank in Britain, for example a lord

peer² *v* [I] to look very carefully, especially because it is difficult for you to see something clearly: **+at/into/through etc** *Someone was peering through the window.*

peerage /ˈpɪərɪdʒ $ ˈpɪr-/ *n* [U] the rank of a British peer

peeved /piːvd/ *adj informal* annoyed: *Peeved at his silence, she left.*

peg¹ /peg/ *n* [C] **1** a short object that is fastened to a wall, used for hanging things on: *a coat peg* **2** *BrE* a small plastic or wooden object used to fasten wet clothes to a thin rope to dry [= **clothes peg**; = **clothes pin** *AmE*] **3** also **tent peg** a pointed piece of wood or metal that you push into the ground to keep a tent in the correct position

peg² *v* [T] **pegged, pegging** **1** to fasten wet clothes to a rope with pegs: *Peg the clothes on the washing line.* **2** to keep prices, wages etc at a particular level or value: *a currency pegged to the American dollar*

pelican /ˈpelɪkən/ *n* [C] a large water bird that catches fish and stores them in a deep bag of skin under its beak

pellet /ˈpelət/ *n* [C] a small hard ball made from paper, metal etc: *shotgun pellets*

pelt¹ /pelt/ *v* **1** [T] to throw a lot of things at someone: **pelt sb with sth** *Two kids were pelting each other with snowballs.* **2** [I] to be raining very hard: *It's **pelting down** out there.* **3** [I + adv/prep] *informal* to run somewhere very fast

pelt² *n* [C] **1** the skin of a dead animal with the fur or hair still on it **2 (at) full pelt** *BrE* as fast as possible

pelvis /ˈpelvɪs/ *n* [C] the set of large wide curved bones at the base of your SPINE, to which your legs are joined → see picture on page A3 —**pelvic** *adj*

pen¹ /pen/ *n* [C,U] **1** a thing that you use for writing and drawing in ink: *a ballpoint pen | a felt-tip pen |* **in pen** *Please fill out the form in pen.* → see picture at **CLASSROOM** **2** a small area surrounded by a fence, used for keeping farm animals in → **FOUNTAIN PEN**

pen² *v* [T] **penned, penning** *literary* to write a letter, note, poem etc with a pen

penal /ˈpiːnl/ *adj* [only before noun] relating to the legal punishment of criminals: *the penal system*

penalize also **-ise** *BrE* /ˈpiːnəl-aɪz $ ˈpiː-, ˈpe-/ *v* [T] **1** to punish someone or treat them unfairly: *Two students were penalized very differently for the same offence.* **2** to punish a team or player in sports by giving an advantage to the other team: *Our team was penalized for wasting time.*

penalty /ˈpenlti/ *n* [C] plural **penalties** **1** a punishment for not obeying a law, rule, or legal agreement: *There's a penalty of £50 for not paying your bus fare. | I'm against **the death penalty** (=the punishment of being killed).* → see box at **PUNISHMENT** **2** something bad that happens to you because of something you have done or because of the situation you are in: *One of the penalties of being famous is the loss of privacy.* **3** a disadvantage in sports given to a team or player for not obeying a rule: *Woodson received a penalty.* **4** a chance to kick the ball into the GOAL in a game of football, given because the other team has not obeyed a rule

penance /ˈpenəns/ *n* [C,U] something you must do to show that you are sorry for something wrong you have done, especially in some religions

pence /pens/ *BrE* abbreviation **P** a plural of **PENNY**

penchant /ˈpɒnʃɒn, ˈpentʃənt $ ˈpentʃənt/ *n* **a penchant for sth** if you have a penchant for something, you like it very much: *He has a penchant for fast cars.*

pencil¹ /ˈpensəl/ *n* [C,U] a thing that you use for writing and drawing using the black or coloured substance in the middle: *a sharp pencil | Remember to bring a pencil and paper. |* **in pencil** *The note was written in pencil.* → see picture at **CLASSROOM**

pencil² *v* [T] **pencilled, pencilling** *BrE*; **penciled, penciling** *AmE* to write or draw something using a pencil

pencil sth/sb ⇔ **in** *phr v* to make an arrangement to meet someone or do something, although it is not very definite: *I've pencilled you in for next Tuesday.*

pencil case *n* [C] a bag or box used for keeping pens, pencils etc in

pencil sharpener *n* [C] a thing you use for making pencils sharp → see picture at **CLASSROOM**

pendant /ˈpendənt/ *n* [C] a piece of jewellery that hangs from a chain around your neck

pending¹ /ˈpendɪŋ/ *prep formal* while waiting for something, or until something happens: *The decision has been delayed pending further medical tests.*

pending² *adj formal* not yet decided, agreed on, or finished: *Their divorce is still pending.*

pendulum /ˈpendjʊləm $ -dʒə-/ n [C] a long metal stick with a heavy part at the bottom that swings regularly from side to side to control the working of a clock

penetrate /ˈpenɪtreɪt/ v [I,T] to enter something or pass through it, especially when this is difficult: *bullets that can penetrate metal* | *Sunlight barely penetrated the dirty windows.* —**penetration** /ˌpenɪˈtreɪʃən/ n [U]

penetrating /ˈpenɪtreɪtɪŋ/ adj **1 penetrating look/stare etc** a look etc that makes you feel uncomfortable and seems to see inside your mind **2** showing an ability to understand things quickly and well: *They asked a number of penetrating questions.* **3** a penetrating sound is very loud and clear: *a high penetrating voice*

ˈpen friend n [C] BrE a PEN PAL

penguin /ˈpeŋgwɪn/ n [C] a large black and white Antarctic sea bird, which cannot fly but uses its wings for swimming

penicillin /ˌpenɪˈsɪlɪn/ n [U] a type of medicine used to treat infections caused by BACTERIA

peninsula /pəˈnɪnsjʊlə $ -sələ/ n [C] a piece of land that is almost completely surrounded by water but is joined to a larger area of land: *the Malay peninsula*

penis /ˈpiːnɪs/ n [C] the male sex organ

penitent /ˈpenɪtənt/ adj formal feeling sorry because you have done something bad, and intending not to do it again [= **repentant**] —**penitence** n [U]

penitentiary /ˌpenɪˈtenʃəri/ n [C] plural penitentiaries a prison in the US

penknife /ˈpen-naɪf/ n [C] plural penknives /-naɪvz/ a small knife with blades that fold into the handle, usually carried in your pocket

ˈpen name n [C] a name used by a writer instead of his or her real name → see box at NAME

pennant /ˈpenənt/ n [C] a long pointed flag

penniless /ˈpeniləs/ adj having no money

penny /ˈpeni/ n [C] abbreviation **P 1** plural **pence** or **pennies** a coin worth 1/100 of a pound **2** plural **pennies** a coin worth 1/100 of a dollar [➡ **cent**] **3 every penny** all of an amount of money **4 not a penny** no money at all: *It won't cost you a penny!*

ˈpen pal n [C] someone you become friendly with by writing letters, especially someone who lives in another country and who you have never met

pension /ˈpenʃən/ n [C] money that the government or a company pays regularly to someone who does not work any more because they are old or ill: *She was receiving a **state pension**.* | *a company **pension** scheme*

state pension also **old age pension** BrE/**public pension** AmE – one that the government pays
company pension also **occupational pension** BrE – one that your employer pays
private pension also **personal pension** BrE – one organized by a private pension company
take out a pension BrE/**set up a pension plan** AmE – to arrange with a company to start saving money towards your pension
pay into a pension BrE/**contribute to a pension** especially AmE – to pay money

regularly so that you can have a pension when you are older
get/receive/draw/collect a pension – to receive regular amounts of money from your pension
→ **PAY**[1], **RETIRE**

pensioner /ˈpenʃənə $ -ər/ n [C] BrE an old person who receives a pension

pensive /ˈpensɪv/ adj thinking about something and seeming slightly worried or sad: *a pensive expression* —**pensively** adv

Pentagon /ˈpentəgən $ -gɑːn/ n **the Pentagon** the building in Washington DC from which the US army, navy etc are controlled, or the people who work there

pentagon n [C] a flat shape with five sides and five angles

pentathlon /penˈtæθlən/ n [C] a sports competition in which you have to do five different sports

penthouse /ˈpenthaʊs/ n [C] an expensive apartment on the top floor of a tall building

pent-up /ˌpent ˈʌp◂/ adj pent-up emotions are emotions that you have stopped yourself from showing for a long time: *pent-up anger*

penultimate /peˈnʌltɪmət, pə-/ adj [only before noun] not the last, but immediately before the last: *the penultimate chapter of the book*

people[1] /ˈpiːpəl/ n

1 [plural] men, women, or children. 'People' is the usual plural of 'person': *I like the people I work with.* | *How many people were at the party?* | *I don't care what people think.*

the public – ordinary people, not people who belong to the government or other special organizations: *It's the job of the media to inform the public.*
society – all the people who live in a country: *responsible members of society*
the human race/mankind – all the people in the world, considered as a group: *the origins of the human race*
→ **GROUP**

2 the people all the ordinary people in a country or place who do not have important jobs or high social positions [➡ **population**]: *Rice was the main food of the **common people**.*

3 [C also + plural verb] formal a race or nation: **+of** *the peoples of Asia* | *the American people*

4 of all people spoken used to emphasize that you are very surprised that a particular person did or did not do something: *Why did he, of all people, get promotion?*

people[2] v **be peopled with/by sb** literary if a country or area is peopled by people of a particular type, they live there

pepper[1] /ˈpepə $ -ər/ n

1 [U] a powder that is used to add a hot taste to food: *salt and pepper*

2 [C] a hollow red, yellow, or green vegetable: *green peppers* → see picture at VEGETABLE

pepper[2] v **be peppered with sth** to contain a lot of things of a particular type: *The article is peppered with mistakes.*

peppermint /'pepə,mɪnt $ -ər-/ n **1** [U] a plant with a strong taste and smell, often used in sweets **2** [C] a sweet with the taste of peppermint

'pep talk /'pep tɔːk $ -tɒːk/ n [C] informal a short speech intended to encourage people to work harder, win a game etc: The coach **gave the team a pep talk**.

per /pə; strong pɜː $ pər; strong pɜːr/ prep for each: How much are bananas per pound? | He charges £20 per lesson.

per annum /pər ˈænəm/ adv formal written abbreviation **p.a.** for each year: a salary of $40,000 per annum

per capita /pə ˈkæpɪtə $ pər-/ adj, adv formal used to describe the average amount of something in a particular place, calculated according to the number of people who live there: the country's per capita income

perceive /pə'siːv $ pər-/ v [T] formal **1** to understand or think about something or someone in a particular way [➡ perception]: **perceive sth/sb as sth** Even as a young woman she was perceived as a future leader. **2** to notice, hear, or see something: Cats are not able to perceive colour.

percent /pə'sent $ pər-/ also **per 'cent** BrE n, adj, adv

1 5 per cent (5%)/10 per cent (10%) etc an amount equal to five, ten etc parts out of a total of a hundred parts: Inflation is down 2%. | There's a 10% service charge. | **+of** Only 50% of the people voted. | **go up/down (by) 5%/10% etc** Sales have gone up by 20%. | an interest rate of 5%
2 a/one hundred per cent completely: I agree with you a hundred per cent.

percentage /pə'sentɪdʒ $ pər-/ n [C usually singular] an amount that is expressed as if it is a part of a total that is 100: **+of** What percentage of the workers are women? | **a high/low/small percentage of sth**

perceptible /pə'septɪbəl $ pər-/ adj formal something that is perceptible can be noticed, although it is small [≠ imperceptible]: perceptible changes in temperature —**perceptibly** adv

perception /pə'sepʃən $ pər-/ n **1** [C] the way you think about something and your idea of what it is like: children's perceptions of the world **2** [U] the way you notice things with your senses: drugs that alter perception **3** [U] the ability to understand or notice things quickly: She shows unusual perception for a child of her age.

perceptive /pə'septɪv $ pər-/ adj someone who is perceptive notices things quickly and understands situations, people's feelings etc well: a perceptive young man —**perceptively** adv

perch¹ /pɜːtʃ $ pɜːrtʃ/ n [C] a branch or stick where a bird sits

perch² v [I,T] **1 be perched on/above etc sth** to be in a position on top of something or on the edge of something: The hotel was perched high on a cliff above the bay. **2** to sit on the edge of something: She perched herself on the bar stool.

percussion /pə'kʌʃən $ pər-/ n [U] drums and other musical instruments which you play by hitting them → see box at ORCHESTRA

perennial /pə'reniəl/ adj continuing or existing for a long time, or happening again and again: the **perennial problem** of poverty

perfect¹ /'pɜːfɪkt $ 'pɜːr-/ adj
1 not having any mistakes, faults, or damage [≠ imperfect]: a car in perfect condition | Her Spanish is perfect.
2 very good: John was in perfect health. | The jeans were a perfect fit.
3 exactly right for a particular purpose [= ideal]: **+for** This rug's perfect for the living room. | a perfect day for a picnic
4 used to emphasize what you are saying [= complete, total]: I felt a perfect fool! | It **makes perfect sense.** | a perfect stranger

perfect² /pə'fekt $ pər-/ v [T] to make something perfect: He was trying to perfect his guitar technique.

perfect³ /'pɜːfɪkt $ 'pɜːr-/ n **the perfect (tense)** the form of a verb which is used when talking about some time up to and including the present. In English this is formed with 'have' and the past participle, for example 'someone has stolen my car'. [= present perfect] → FUTURE PERFECT, PAST PERFECT

perfection /pə'fekʃən $ pər-/ n [U] when something is perfect: I'll do my best, but don't expect perfection. | **to perfection** The beef was cooked to perfection.

perfectionist /pə'fekʃənɪst $ pər-/ n [C] someone who is not satisfied with anything unless it is completely perfect

perfectly /'pɜːfɪktli $ 'pɜːr-/ adv
1 used to emphasize what you are saying: The sale was perfectly legal. | You know perfectly well what I mean!
2 in a perfect way: She speaks English perfectly.

perforated /'pɜːfəreɪtɪd $ 'pɜːr-/ adj something that is perforated has a hole or holes in it: Store the fruit in perforated polythene bags. | a **perforated eardrum** (=damaged by having a hole in it)

perform /pə'fɔːm $ pər'fɔːrm/ v
1 [I,T] to do something to entertain people such as acting a play or playing music: We performed 'Hamlet' last year.
2 [T] to do something such as a job or piece of work: Surgeons performed an emergency operation. | **perform a function/role** software that performs a specific function
3 perform well/badly etc to work or do something well, badly etc: The car performs well on mountain roads.

performance /pə'fɔːməns $ pər'fɔːr-/ n
1 [C] an occasion when someone entertains people by performing a play or a piece of music: a brilliant performance of Beethoven's Fifth Symphony | The next performance is at 8 o'clock. | a **live performance** by a local band
2 [C,U] how well or badly someone or something does something: the country's economic performance | The car's performance on mountain roads was impressive.
3 [U] when someone does their job: the performance of his official duties

performer /pə'fɔːmə $ pər'fɔːrmər/ n [C] an actor, musician etc who performs to entertain people: a circus performer

per,forming 'arts *n* **the performing arts** arts such as dance, music, or DRAMA

perfume /'pɜːfjuːm $ 'pɜːr-/ *n* [C,U]
1 a liquid with a strong pleasant smell, which you put on your skin [= scent]: *She never wears perfume.* → see box at SMELL
2 *literary* a pleasant smell
—**perfumed** *adj: perfumed soap*

perhaps /pəˈhæps, præps $ pər-, præps/ *adv*
1 used to say that something may be true, but you are not sure [= maybe]: *Sarah's late – perhaps she missed the bus.* | *'Are you sure he knows?' 'Perhaps not.'*
2 *spoken* used to politely ask or suggest something: *Perhaps you'd like to join us?*
3 used to say that a number is only a guess: *Perhaps 200 people were there.*
4 used to give your opinion, when you do not want to be too definite: *This is perhaps her best novel yet.*

peril /'perəl/ *n* [C, U] *formal* great danger: **in peril** *Our soldiers were in great peril.* | *the perils of taking drugs*

perilous /'perələs/ *adj literary* very dangerous: *a perilous journey* —**perilously** *adv*

perimeter /pəˈrɪmɪtə $ -ər/ *n* [C] the edge that surrounds an area of land or a shape: **+of** *the perimeter of the airfield* | *Calculate the perimeter of the triangle* (=the total length of its sides).

period¹ /'pɪəriəd $ 'pɪr-/ *n* [C]
1 a length of time: **+of** *a period of six weeks* | *the period from Christmas until New Year* | *We've been studying the Civil War period.*
2 the flow of blood that comes from a woman's body each month
3 *AmE* the mark (.) used in a piece of writing to show the end of a sentence or an abbreviation [= full stop *BrE*]
4 one of the equal parts that the school day is divided into [= lesson *BrE*]: *The first period on Tuesday is history.*

period² *adj* **period costume/furniture** clothes or furniture in the style of a particular time in history

periodic /ˌpɪəriˈɒdɪk◂ $ ˌpɪriˈɑː-/ also **periodical** *adj* happening a number of times but not frequently: *periodic attacks of flu* —**periodically** /-kli/ *adv: The river floods periodically.*

periodical /ˌpɪəriˈɒdɪkəl $ ˌpɪriˈɑː-/ *n* [C] a magazine, especially one about a technical subject

peripheral¹ /pəˈrɪfərəl/ *adj formal* less important or less central than other facts, places, jobs etc: *peripheral information*

peripheral² *n* [C] a piece of equipment that is connected to a computer, for example a PRINTER

periphery /pəˈrɪfəri/ *n* [C usually singular] plural **peripheries** the outside area or edge of something: *an industrial site on the periphery of the city*

perish /'perɪʃ/ *v* [I] *literary* to die: *Hundreds perished when the ship sank.*

perishable /'perɪʃəbəl/ *adj* food that is perishable can quickly become bad to eat: *milk and other perishable items*

perjury /'pɜːdʒəri $ 'pɜːr-/ *n* [U] the crime of not telling the truth in a law court —**perjurer** *n* [C]

perk¹ /pɜːk $ pɜːrk/ *n* [C usually plural] something that your employer gives you in addition to your pay, such as free meals or a car: *Free travel is one of the perks of the job.*

perk² *v*
perk up *phr v* to become happier and more interested in what is happening around you, or to make someone feel this way: *Meg soon perked up when his letter arrived.* | **perk sb ⇔ up** *A cup of tea should perk you up.*

perky /'pɜːki $ 'pɜːrki/ *adj informal* confident, happy, and active: *a perky salesgirl* —**perkily** *adv* —**perkiness** *n* [U]

perm /pɜːm $ pɜːrm/ *n* [C] a way of putting curls into straight hair, using chemicals: *I've decided to have a perm.* —**perm** *v* [T]

permanent /'pɜːmənənt $ 'pɜːr-/ *adj* continuing to exist for a long time or for all future time [≠ temporary]: *a permanent job* | *an illness that causes permanent loss of sight* —**permanence** *n* [U]

permanently /'pɜːmənəntli $ 'pɜːr-/ *adv* always, or for a very long time: *The accident left him permanently disabled.* → see box at ALWAYS

permeate /'pɜːmieɪt $ 'pɜːr-/ *v* [I,T] *formal* to spread through every part of something, or to be present in every part: *Water had permeated through the wall.* | *A feeling of sadness permeates his music.*

permissible /pəˈmɪsɪbəl $ pər-/ *adj formal* allowed by law or by the rules: *permissible levels of pollution*

permission /pəˈmɪʃən $ pər-/ *n* [U] if you have permission to do something, someone in authority allows you to do it: *You have to ask permission if you want to leave early.* | **permission to do sth** *Did your father give you permission to use his car?* | **without permission** *Don't take food from the fridge without permission.* | **+for** *The Department of transport finally granted permission for the scheme.*

COMMUNICATION

asking for permission

Can I ...?: *'Can I borrow your book?' 'Sure.'*
Could I/May I ...? *more formal: 'May I use your phone?' 'Of course - go ahead.'*
Do you mind if I ...?: *'Do you mind if I open the window?' 'No, that's fine.'*
Is it all right if I .../Would it be all right if I ...?: *'Is it all right if I leave a bit early?' 'Of course you can.'*
Would it be possible to ...?: *'Would it be possible to borrow more?' 'I don't see why not.'*

permissive /pəˈmɪsɪv $ pər-/ *adj* not strict, and allowing behaviour that many people disapprove of: *the permissive society of the 1970s*

permit¹ /pəˈmɪt $ pər-/ *v* [T] **permitted, permitting** *formal* **1** to allow something to happen or someone to do something: *Smoking is not permitted inside the building.* | **permit sb to do sth** *The visa permits you to stay for three weeks.* → see box at ALLOW **2 weather permitting** if the weather is good enough: *We'll probably go to the beach, weather permitting.*

permit² /'pɜːmɪt $ 'pɜːr-, pərˈmɪt/ *n* [C] an official written statement allowing you to do something: *You can't park here without a permit.* | *a work permit*

permutation /ˌpɜːmjʊˈteɪʃən $ ˌpɜːr-/ *n* [C] one of the different ways in which a number of things can be arranged: *We tried various permutations of the colours.*

pernicious /pəˈnɪʃəs $ pər-/ *adj formal* very harmful or evil: *the pernicious influence of TV violence*

perpendicular /ˌpɜːpənˈdɪkjələ◂ $ ˌpɜːrpənˈdɪkjələr◂/ *adj* at an angle of 90 degrees to something, especially the ground [➔ **vertical**]: *a perpendicular line*

perpetrate /ˈpɜːpətreɪt $ ˈpɜːr-/ *v* [T] *formal* to do something that is wrong or illegal —**perpetrator** *n* [C]

perpetual /pəˈpetʃuəl $ pər-/ *adj* continuing all the time without changing or stopping: *the perpetual noise of the machines* —**perpetually** *adv*

perpetuate /pəˈpetʃueɪt $ pər-/ *v* [T] *formal* to make a situation, attitude etc continue to exist for a long time, especially one that is bad: *The prison system seems designed to perpetuate crime, not prevent it.*

perplexed /pəˈplekst $ pər-/ *adj* confused by something that you do not understand [= **puzzled**]: *The child looked totally perplexed.* —**perplex** *v* [T]

persecute /ˈpɜːsɪkjuːt $ ˈpɜːr-/ *v* [T] to treat someone cruelly and unfairly, especially because of their beliefs: *Christians were persecuted by the Emperor Nero.* —**persecutor** *n* [C] —**persecution** /ˌpɜːsɪˈkjuːʃən $ ˌpɜːr-/ *n* [U]

perseverance /ˌpɜːsɪˈvɪərəns $ ˌpɜːrsɪˈvɪr-/ *n* [U] determination to keep trying to do something difficult: *I admire her perseverance.*

persevere /ˌpɜːsɪˈvɪə $ ˌpɜːrsɪˈvɪr/ *v* [I] to continue trying to do something difficult in a determined way: **+with** *I'm not enjoying the course, but I'll persevere with it.*

persist /pəˈsɪst $ pər-/ *v* [I] **1** to continue to do something, even though it is difficult or other people do not approve of it: **persist in (doing) sth** *He persisted in denying the charges against him.* **2** if something bad persists, it continues to exist or happen: *If the pain persists, see a doctor.*

persistent /pəˈsɪstənt $ pər-/ *adj* **1** continuing for a long time or happening often, especially in a way that is unpleasant or annoying: *a persistent cough* | *persistent problems* **2** continuing to do something even when it is difficult or people tell you not to do it: *You have to be persistent if you want to get a job.* | *penalties for* **persistent offenders** —**persistently** *adv* —**persistence** *n* [U]

person /ˈpɜːsən $ ˈpɜːr-/ *n plural* **people** /ˈpiːpəl/ **1** [C] a man, woman, or child: *She's a very generous person.* | *Dan was the first person I met when I arrived.* | **the sort/kind/type of person** *I'm not the sort of person who watches TV all day.* | **a city/outdoor/cat etc person** (=someone who likes cities, outdoor activities etc) **2 in person** if you do something in person, you do it by going somewhere yourself rather than sending someone else or writing a letter etc: *You*

can reserve tickets either in person or by telephone.
➔ **FIRST PERSON, SECOND PERSON, THIRD PERSON**

persona /pəˈsəʊnə $ pərˈsoʊ-/ *n* [C] plural **personas** or **personae** /-niː/ the way you behave when you are with other people or in a particular situation: *His **public persona** is very different from the one his family sees.*

personable /ˈpɜːsənəbəl $ ˈpɜːr-/ *adj* someone who is personable is attractive and pleasant

personal /ˈpɜːsənəl $ ˈpɜːr-/ *adj* **1** [only before noun] belonging or relating to one particular person: *books, clothes, and other personal belongings* | *I know from personal experience how difficult it is to write a book.* | *a matter of personal choice* **2** relating to the private parts of your life such as your feelings, health, relationships etc: *I don't answer questions about my personal life.* | *She has a few personal problems.* | *Can I ask you a personal question?* **3** criticizing someone in a rude way: *personal remarks* | *There's no need to get personal.* | *It's nothing personal* (=I am not trying to offend you), *I just need some time alone.* **4** involving doing something yourself rather than asking someone else to do it: *The President made a personal visit to the scene of the accident.* **5** [only before noun] relating to your body or the way you look: *personal hygiene*

ˌpersonal asˈsistant *n* [C] a PA

ˌpersonal comˈputer *n* [C] a PC

personality /ˌpɜːsəˈnælɪti $ ˌpɜːr-/ *n plural* **personalities**
1 [C,U] someone's character, especially the way they behave towards other people: *She's an ambitious woman with a strong personality.* | *Childhood experiences can affect personality.* **2** [C] a famous person, especially in sport, television, films etc [= **celebrity**]: *a TV personality* **3** [U] the qualities that make someone interesting to be with: *You need personality rather than qualifications to do this job.*

personalize also **-ise** *BrE* /ˈpɜːsənəlaɪz $ ˈpɜːr-/ *v* [T] **1** to put your name or INITIALS on something or decorate it in your own way to show that it belongs to you: *You can personalize the T-shirts with your own pictures.* **2** to design or change something so that is is suitable for a particular person: *We provide a complete beauty programme personalized to you.* —**personalized** *adj*: *personalized number plates*

personally /ˈpɜːsənəli $ ˈpɜːr-/ *adv*
1 *spoken* used to emphasize that you are giving your own opinion: *Personally, I think it's a bad idea.* **2** doing something yourself rather than getting someone else to do it: *I delivered the letter personally.* | *The manager has personally overseen the design of the rooms.* | *Students are personally responsible for the payment of their fees.* **3** as a friend or as someone you have met: *I don't know her personally but I like her work.* **4 take sth personally** to get upset because you think someone's remarks or behaviour are directed at you

,personal 'organizer n [C] a small book with loose pages, or a very small computer, for recording addresses, meetings etc

,personal 'pronoun n [C] a PRONOUN such as 'I', 'you', or 'they'

,personal 'stereo n [C] a small machine that plays CASSETTES or CDs, which you carry around with you and listen to with HEADPHONES

,personal 'trainer n [C] someone whose job is to help people decide what type of exercise is best for them and show them how to do it

personify /pəˈsɒnɪfaɪ $ pərˈsɑː-/ v [T] personi-fied, personifying, personifies **1** to be a typical example of something or have a lot of a particular quality: *He personifies the English gentleman.* | **be kindness/charm/courage etc personified** *Mr Rowley was diplomacy personified.* **2** to think of or represent something as a person: **personify sth as sb** *Time is often personified as an old man.* —personification /pəˌsɒnɪfɪˈkeɪʃən $ pər,sɑː-/ n [C, U]

personnel /ˌpɜːsəˈnel $,pɜːr-/ n **1** [plural] the people who work in a company or organization [➔ staff]: *military personnel* **2** [U] the department in a company that chooses people for jobs, deals with their problems etc [= human resources]: *a personnel manager*

perspective /pəˈspektɪv $ pər-/ n **1** [C] a way of thinking about something: **+on** *Working abroad gives you a whole new perspective on life.* | **from a ... perspective** *Try and approach the problem from a different perspective.* **2** [U] a sensible way of thinking about something so that you do not imagine that something is more serious than it is: **get/keep/put sth in per-spective** *It's important to put things in perspective.* | *We must keep a sense of perspec-tive about this.* **3** [U] a method of drawing a picture which makes objects look solid and makes some things look further away than others

perspiration /ˌpɜːspəˈreɪʃən $,pɜːr-/ n [U] formal SWEAT

perspire /pəˈspaɪə $ pərˈspaɪr/ v [I] formal to SWEAT

persuade /pəˈsweɪd $ pər-/ v [T]
1 to make someone decide to do something by telling them why it is a good idea: **persuade sb to do sth** *John was trying to persuade me to stay.* **2** to make someone believe something [= con-vince]: **+(that)** *She'll only take me back if I can persuade her that I've changed.* | **persuade sb of sth** *We must persuade people of the impor-tance of protecting the environment.*

persuasion /pəˈsweɪʒən $ pər-/ n **1** [U] when you persuade someone to do something: *After a little gentle persuasion, Debbie agreed to come.* | *It took all his powers of persuasion* (=skill at persuading people) *to convince her.* **2** [C,U] for-mal a particular belief that you have: **political/ religious persuasion** *people of all kinds of religious persuasion*

persuasive /pəˈsweɪsɪv $ pər-/ adj able to make people do or believe something: *He can be very persuasive.* | *persuasive evidence* —persuasively adv

pertain /pəˈteɪn $ pər-/ v

pertain to sth phr v formal to relate directly to something

pertinent /ˈpɜːtɪnənt $ ˈpɜːr-/ adj formal directly relating to something that is being con-sidered [= relevant]: *He asked a lot of very perti-nent questions.*

perturbed /pəˈtɜːbd $ pərˈtɜːrbd/ adj formal worried or upset: **+by/at/about** *He didn't seem at all perturbed by the news of his father's death.* —perturb v [T]

peruse /pəˈruːz/ v [T] formal to read or look at something carefully

pervade /pəˈveɪd $ pər-/ v [T] formal if a feel-ing, idea, or smell pervades a place, it is in every part of the place: *A feeling of hopelessness per-vaded the country.* | *The smell of tobacco per-vaded the room.*

pervasive /pəˈveɪsɪv $ pər-/ adj existing every-where: *the pervasive influence of television*

perverse /pəˈvɜːs $ pərˈvɜːrs/ adj strange or unreasonable, and not what people expect: *He takes perverse pleasure in arguing with everyone.* —perversely adv

perversion /pəˈvɜːʃən, -ʒən $ pərˈvɜːrʒən/ n [C,U] sexual behaviour that is considered strange and unacceptable

pervert[1] /ˈpɜːvɜːt $ ˈpɜːrvɜːrt/ n [C] someone whose sexual behaviour is considered strange and unacceptable

pervert[2] /pəˈvɜːt $ pərˈvɜːrt/ v [T] to change someone or something in a harmful way: *Violent images may pervert the minds of young children.*

perverted /pəˈvɜːtɪd $ pərˈvɜːr-/ adj strange and unacceptable, often in a sexual way: *per-verted desires*

pessimism /ˈpesɪmɪzəm/ n [U] the feeling that things will happen in a bad or unsuccessful way [≠ optimism]: **+about/over** *There is widespread pessimism over the future of the Middle East peace talks.*

pessimist /ˈpesɪmɪst/ n [C] someone who always expects that bad things will happen [≠ optimist]

pessimistic /ˌpesɪˈmɪstɪk◂/ adj expecting that bad things will happen [≠ optimistic]: *a pessimis-tic view of life* | **+about** *She was very pessimistic about the future.* → see box at CHARACTER

pest /pest/ n [C] **1** a small animal or insect that destroys crops or food **2** informal an annoying person

pester /ˈpestə $ -ər/ v [I,T] to annoy someone, especially by asking them many times to do something: **pester sb to do sth** *He keeps pester-ing me to buy him a new bike.* | **pester sb for sth** *Tourists are likely to be pestered for money.*

pesticide /ˈpestɪsaɪd/ n [C,U] a chemical used to kill insects that damage crops

pets

rabbit

cat

dog

hamster

pet¹ /pet/ n [C]
1 an animal that you keep at home: *Cats are popular pets.* | *a pet shop* | **pet rabbit/bird/snake etc**
2 pet name a short friendly name for someone that is used especially by their friends and family [= nickname]
→ TEACHER'S PET

pet² adj **1 pet project/subject/theory etc** a plan, subject, or idea that you particularly like or are interested in **2 pet hate** BrE **pet peeve** AmE something that you particularly dislike

pet³ v [T] **petted, petting** to touch and move your hand gently over someone, especially an animal or a child [= stroke]: *Our cat loves being petted.*

petal /'petl/ n [C] one of the coloured parts of a flower: *rose petals* → see picture at PLANT

peter /'piːtə $ -ər/ v
peter out phr v to gradually become smaller, quieter, less etc and then stop: *The road finally petered out.*

petite /pə'tiːt/ adj a woman who is petite is small and attractively thin

petition¹ /pə'tɪʃən/ n [C] a piece of paper that a lot of people have signed, asking someone in authority to do or change something: **+for/against** *More than 1000 people signed a petition against experiments on animals.*

petition² v [I,T] to officially ask someone in authority to do something, especially by giving them a petition: **+for/against** *Residents are petitioning against the new road.* | **petition sb to do sth** *Many people have petitioned the government to intervene.*

petrified /'petrɪfaɪd/ adj very frightened: *I'm absolutely petrified of dogs.* → see box at FRIGHTENED —**petrify** v [T]

petrol /'petrəl/ n [U] BrE a liquid that you put in a vehicle to make the engine work [= gas AmE]: *How much petrol did you put in?* | *petrol prices*

petroleum /pə'trəʊliəm $ -'troʊ-/ n [U] oil from under the ground that is used to make petrol and other substances

'petrol ,station n [C] BrE a place where you buy petrol for your car [= gas station AmE]

petticoat /'petikəʊt $ -koʊt/ n [C] BrE a piece of women's underwear like a thin dress or skirt [= slip]

petty /'peti/ adj **1** not serious or important: *petty problems* | **petty crime/theft 2** caring too much about unimportant things, especially in an unkind way: *He can be very petty.* —**pettiness** n [U]

petulant /'petʃələnt/ adj behaving in an impatient and angry way, like a child —**petulance** n [U] —**petulantly** adv

pew /pjuː/ n [C] a long wooden seat in a church

pewter /'pjuːtə $ -ər/ n [U] a grey metal made by mixing LEAD and TIN

phantom¹ /'fæntəm/ n [C] literary a GHOST

phantom² adj [only before noun] imaginary and not real

pharaoh /'feərəʊ $ 'feroʊ/ n [C] a ruler of ancient Egypt

pharmaceutical /ˌfɑːmə'sjuːtɪkəl◂ $ ˌfɑːrmə'suː-/ adj relating to the production of drugs and medicines: *pharmaceutical companies*

pharmacist /'fɑːməsɪst $ 'fɑːr-/ n [C] someone whose job is to prepare medicines in a shop or hospital

pharmacy /'fɑːməsi $ 'fɑːr-/ n plural **pharmacies 1** [C] a shop or a part of a shop where you can get medicines [= chemist] **2** [U] the study or preparation of medicines and drugs

phase¹ /feɪz/ n [C] one part of a process: **+of** *the first phase of the project* | *The new drug is still in the experimental phase.*

phase² v
phase sth ⇔ in phr v to gradually start using a new system, law etc: *Regular homework is phased in as children approach high school age.*
phase sth ⇔ out phr v to gradually stop using or providing something: *All tax relief on company cars will be phased out.*

PhD /ˌpiː eɪtʃ 'diː/ n [C] **Doctor of Philosophy** the highest university DEGREE, or someone who has this degree

pheasant /'fezənt/ n [C,U] a large bird with a long tail, often shot for food, or the meat from this bird

phenomenal /fɪ'nɒmɪnəl $ -'nɑː-/ adj very great or impressive: *the phenomenal success of computer games* | *a phenomenal growth in population* —**phenomenally** adv

phenomenon /fɪ'nɒmɪnən $ fɪ'nɑːmɪnɑːn, -nən/ n [C] plural **phenomena** /-nə/ something that happens or exists, especially something that is unusual or difficult to understand: **+of** *The phenomenon of laughter is unknown in animals.* | **social/natural/cultural etc phenomena** *earthquakes and other natural phenomena*

phew /fjuː/ spoken used when you feel tired, hot, or happy to have avoided a difficult or unpleasant situation

philanthropist /fɪ'lænθrəpɪst/ n [C] a rich person who gives a lot of money to help people —**philanthropic** /ˌfɪlən'θrɒpɪk◂ $ -'θrɑː-/ adj

philistine /'fɪlɪstaɪn $ -stiːn/ n [C] someone who does not like or understand art, literature, music etc —**philistine** adj

philosopher /fɪ'lɒsəfə $ -'lɑːsəfər/ *n* [C] someone who studies and develops ideas about life, thought, or behaviour

philosophical /ˌfɪlə'sɒfɪkəl◂ $ -'sɑː-/ also **philosophic** /-'sɒfɪk $ -'sɑː-/ *adj* **1** relating to philosophy: *a philosophical discussion* **2** calmly accepting a difficult or unpleasant situation that you cannot change: **+about** *He was philosophical about losing.* —**philosophically** /-kli/ *adv*

philosophy /fɪ'lɒsəfi $ -'lɑː-/ *n* plural **philosophies** **1** [C,U] the study of ideas about life, thought, and behaviour: *She's studying philosophy at university.* | *the philosophy of Aristotle* **2** [C] a belief about how you should live your life, do your job etc: *My philosophy is enjoy life while you can!*

phlegm /flem/ *n* [U] a thick substance produced in your nose and throat when you have a cold

phlegmatic /fleg'mætɪk/ *adj formal* calm and not easily excited or worried

phobia /'fəʊbiə $ 'foʊ-/ *n* [C] a strong unreasonable fear of something: **+about** *He has a phobia about birds.* —**phobic** *adj*

phone¹ /fəʊn $ foʊn/ *n* [C] a telephone: *What's your phone number?* | *The phone rang while I was in the shower.* | *He rushed to answer the phone.* | *Greg said goodbye and put the phone down* (=ended the telephone conversation). | **on the phone** (=talking to someone using a telephone) *Could you turn the TV down? I'm on the phone.* | **by phone** *You can reserve tickets by phone.* → see box at TELEPHONE
→ CELL PHONE, MOBILE PHONE, PAY PHONE

phone² also **phone up** *v* [I,T] to speak to someone using a telephone [= call]: *Carla phoned me in the middle of the night.* | *I'll phone up and find out what time the museum opens.* | *For more information, phone 0296 333444.* | *I'm busy but I'll phone you back* (=phone again) *later.*

THESAURUS

Phone, **ring**, **call** and **telephone** all mean 'to use the telephone to speak to someone'.
Phone and **ring** are the usual words in British English.
Call is the usual word in American English.
Telephone is only used in fairly formal situations.

'phone book *n* [C] a book containing the names, addresses, and telephone numbers of people in an area [= **telephone directory**]

'phone booth also **'phone box** *BrE n* [C] a structure containing a public telephone

'phone call *n* [C] a situation when you telephone someone, or they telephone you: *I need to make a phone call.* | *There's a phone call for you.*

'phone card *n* [C] a plastic card that can be used in some public telephones instead of money

'phone-in *n* [C] a radio or television programme in which you hear people asking questions and expressing their opinions on the telephone

phonetic /fə'netɪk/ *adj technical* relating to the sounds of human speech —**phonetically** /-kli/ *adv*

phonetics /fə'netɪks/ *n* [U] the study of speech sounds

phoney also **phony** *AmE* /'fəʊni $ 'foʊ-/ *adj* **1** not real, or intended to deceive someone [= fake]: *a phoney American accent* → see box at FAKE **2** *disapproving* pretending to be something you are not —**phoney** *n* [C]

phosphate /'fɒsfeɪt $ 'fɑːs-/ *n* [C,U] a chemical used in industry and farming

photo /'fəʊtəʊ $ 'foʊtoʊ/ *n* [C] plural **photos** *informal* a photograph: **+of** *Will you take a photo of me and Anna together?* | **in the photo** *The boy in the photo is my brother.*

photocopier /'fəʊtəʊˌkɒpiə $ 'foʊtəˌkɑːpiər/ *n* [C] a machine that makes copies of documents → see box at OFFICE

photocopy¹ /'fəʊtəʊˌkɒpi $ 'foʊtəˌkɑːpi/ *n* [C] plural **photocopies** a copy of a document made by a photocopier: **+of** *She made a photocopy of the map.*

photocopy² *v* [T] **photocopied**, **photocopying**, **photocopies** to make a copy of a document using a photocopier → see box at COPY

photo 'finish *n* [C] the end of a race in which the runners finish very close together, so that a photograph has to be looked at to decide who won

photogenic /ˌfəʊtə'dʒenɪk◂ , ˌfəʊtəʊ- $ ˌfoʊtə-/ *adj* someone who is photogenic always looks attractive in photographs

photograph¹ /'fəʊtəɡrɑːf $ 'foʊtəɡræf/ also **photo** *informal n* [C] a picture that you make using a camera: *She showed me a photograph of her son.* | *I like taking photographs.* → see box at CAMERA

photograph² *v* [T] to make a picture of someone or something using a camera

photographer /fə'tɒɡrəfə $ -'tɑːɡrəfər/ *n* [C] someone who takes photographs, especially as a job → see box at ART

photographic /ˌfəʊtə'ɡræfɪk◂ , ˌfoʊ-/ *adj* relating to photographs and photography: *photographic equipment*

photography /fə'tɒɡrəfi $ -'tɑː-/ *n* [U] the skill or process of taking photographs → see box at ART

'photo oppor,tunity *n* [C] a chance for someone such as a politician to be photographed for a newspaper in a way that will make them look good

,phrasal 'verb *n* [C] a verb with an adverb or PREPOSITION after it, which has a different meaning from the verb used alone. 'Set off', 'look after', and 'put up with' are all phrasal verbs.

phrase¹ /freɪz/ *n* [C]

1 a group of words that together have a particular meaning: *Darwin's famous phrase 'the survival of the fittest'*

THESAURUS

expression/idiom – a group of words that have a different meaning from the usual meaning of the separate words
cliché – a phrase that has been repeated so often that it is not interesting
saying/proverb – a well-known phrase that people use to give advice

2 *technical* a group of words without a main verb, used to form part of a sentence, for example 'a piece of bread'

phrase² *v* [T] to express something in a particular way: *Ben tried to think how to phrase his next question.*

'phrase book *n* [C] a book that contains useful words and phrases in a foreign language that you use when you are travelling

physical¹ /'fɪzɪkəl/ *adj*

1 relating to your body rather than your mind [➡ **mental, emotional**]: *physical strength* | *people with mental and physical disabilities* | **Physical appearance** *(=the way you look) is very important to young people.* | *My attraction to him was totally physical.*

2 relating to real things you can see and touch: *ways to improve the physical environment in our cities*

3 physical science is related to PHYSICS: *physical chemistry*
—**physically** /-kli/ *adv*: *Try to keep physically fit.*

physical² *n* [C] *especially AmE* an examination of your body by a doctor to check that you are healthy

,physical edu'cation *n* [U] abbreviation **PE** sport and physical exercise that are taught as a school subject

physician /fɪ'zɪʃən/ *n* [C] *especially AmE formal* a doctor ➜ see box at **DOCTOR**

physics /'fɪzɪks/ *n* [U] the science that involves the study of natural forces such as light, heat, and movement
—**physicist** // *n* [C]

physiology /,fɪzi'ɒlədʒi $ -'ɑː-/ *n* [U] the science that studies the way that the bodies of living things work —**physiological** /,fɪziə'lɒdʒɪkəl◄ $ -'lɑː-/ *adj*

physiotherapy /,fɪziəʊ'θerəpi $ -ziou-/ *n* [U] a way of treating injuries and medical conditions using special exercises, heat etc
—**physiotherapist** *n* [C]

physique /fɪ'ziːk/ *n* [C] the shape and size of your body: *a man with a muscular physique*

pianist /'piːənɪst $ pi'ænɪst, 'piːə-/ *n* [C] someone who plays the piano

piano /pi'ænəʊ $ -noʊ/ *n* [C] plural **pianos** a large musical instrument that you play by pressing down black and white KEYS [➡ **pianist**]: *I'm learning to **play the piano**.* | *piano music* | *piano lessons* ➜ see picture on page A6
➜ **GRAND PIANO**

pick¹ /pɪk/ *v* [T]

1 to choose something or someone: *Students have to pick three courses.* | **pick sb for sth** *Have you been picked for the volleyball team?* ➜ see box at **CHOOSE**

2 to remove a flower or fruit from a plant or tree: *Amy picked a bunch of wild flowers.* | **freshly picked** *strawberries*

3 to remove something carefully from a place, especially something small: **pick sth off (sth)** *She sat nervously picking bits of fluff off her sweater.*

4 pick your way through/across/along etc sth to walk carefully, choosing exactly where to put your feet: *Ella picked her way carefully over the rocks.*

5 pick and choose to choose only the things or people that you like very much: *I don't have enough money to pick and choose.*

6 pick a fight/argument/quarrel (with sb) to deliberately start an argument or fight with someone

7 pick sb's brain(s) to ask someone for information or advice about something: *I've come to pick your brains.*

8 pick a lock to open a lock using something such as a piece of wire, not a key

9 pick sb's pocket to steal something from someone's pocket [➡ **pickpocket**]

pick at sth *phr v* **1** to eat only a small amount of food because you are not hungry or do not like the food: *I was so nervous I could only pick at my lunch.* → see box at **EAT** → see picture on page A11 **2** to pull something slightly several times with your fingers: *She was picking nervously at her skirt.*

pick on sb *phr v* to criticize or blame someone in an unfair way: *The teacher's always picking on me!*

pick sb/sth ⇔ out *phr v* **1** to choose someone or something from a group: *His story was picked out as the best.* **2** to recognize someone from a group of people: *The woman was able to pick out her attacker.*

pick up *phr v* **1 pick sb/sth ⇔ up** to lift someone or something: *Pick me up, Daddy!* | *I picked up the phone just as it stopped ringing.* **2 pick sth ⇔ up** to get something: *He's already picked up three prizes this year.* **3 pick sb/sth ⇔ up** to collect someone or something from a place, especially in the car: *What time should we pick you up at the airport?* **4** if a situation picks up, it improves: *Business will pick up soon.* **5** if the wind picks up, it becomes stronger **6 pick sth ⇔ up** to learn something by listening to or watching other people: *I picked up a few words of French while I was in France.* **7 pick sth ⇔ up** to notice something that is not easy to notice: *The dogs were able to pick up the scent.* **8 pick sth ⇔ up** if a machine picks up a sound or a signal, it receives it: *We can pick up French radio stations from here.* **9 pick sth ⇔ up** to get an illness: *I picked up a virus while I was in England.* **10 pick sb ⇔ up** if the police pick someone up, they take them somewhere to answer questions **11 pick sb ⇔ up** to talk to someone and try to begin a sexual relationship with them

pick² *n* **1 take/have your pick** if you can take or have your pick of different things, you can choose which one you want: *Take your pick from a choice of hot or cold dishes.* | *She could take her pick of any of the men in the office.* **2 the pick of sth** *informal* the best of a group of things or people: *We'll be reviewing the pick of this month's new movies.* | *All the wines were good but this was **the pick of the bunch**.* **3** [C] a pickaxe

pickaxe *BrE*; **pickax** *AmE* /'pɪk-æks/ *n* [C] a large tool used for breaking up rocks or hard ground. It has a long handle with a curved iron bar.

picker /'pɪkə $ -ər/ *n* **apple/cotton/mushroom etc picker** a person or machine that picks fruit or vegetables

picket[1] /'pɪkɪ̨t/ *n* [C] **a)** when a group of people stand outside a building in order to protest about something or to stop people entering during a STRIKE: *There were* **mass pickets** (=involving a lot of people) *at the factory gates.* **b)** a person or group of people involved in a picket

picket[2] *v* [I,T] to stand in front of a building in order to protest about something or to stop people entering during a STRIKE: *Demonstrators picketed the US Embassy.*

'picket ,fence *n* [C] *AmE* a fence made of a line of pointed sticks fixed into the ground

pickle[1] /'pɪkəl/ *n* **1** [C,U] *BrE* a thick cold sauce made from pieces of vegetables preserved in VINEGAR **2** [C] *especially AmE* a CUCUMBER that has been preserved in VINEGAR or salt water

pickle[2] *v* [T] to preserve food in VINEGAR and salt

pickled /'pɪkəld/ *adj* pickled vegetables, eggs etc have been preserved in VINEGAR

'pick-me-up *n* [C] *informal* a drink or medicine that makes you feel happier and gives you more energy

pickpocket /'pɪk,pɒkɪ̨t $ -,pɑːk-/ *n* [C] someone who steals things from people's pockets or bags in public places → see box at STEAL

pickup /'pɪkʌp/ also **'pickup ,truck** *n* [C] a vehicle with a large open part at the back, used for carrying goods

picky /'pɪki/ *adj informal* someone who is picky only likes a small number of things [= fussy]: *a picky eater*

picnic[1] /'pɪknɪk/ *n* [C] if you have a picnic, you take food somewhere and eat it outdoors, especially in the country: *We decided to* **have a picnic** *down by the lake.* | *Shall we* **take** *a picnic with us?* | **go on/for a picnic**

picnic[2] *v* [I] picnicked, picnicking to have a picnic

pictorial /pɪk'tɔːriəl/ *adj formal* relating to or using pictures

picture[1] /'pɪktʃə $ -ər/ *n*

1 [C] a painting, drawing, or photograph: *a book with pictures in it* | **+of** *She has a picture of her boyfriend by her bed.* | **draw/paint a picture** *Draw a picture of your house.* | *Do you mind if I* **take** *a picture* (=take a photograph) *of you?* | **sb's picture** (=a photograph of someone) *Leo's picture was in the paper yesterday.* | **wedding/ holiday etc pictures** (=photographs of a wedding, holiday etc)

> **THESAURUS**
>
> **sketch** – a picture that is drawn quickly
> **snap/snapshot** – a photograph that is taken quickly
> **portrait** – a picture of a person
> **cartoon** – a funny drawing in a newspaper or magazine that tells a story or a joke
> **caricature** – a funny drawing of someone that exaggerates a particular feature of their face or body (=makes it look bigger, worse etc than it really is)
> **illustration** – a picture in a book
> **poster** – a large picture printed on paper that you stick to a wall as decoration
> → CAMERA

2 [C] an image on a television or film screen: *dramatic pictures of the floods in Eastern Europe*

3 [C usually singular] a description or idea of what something is like: **+of** *The report gives a* **clear picture** *of life in the army.* | **overall/ complete/accurate picture** *It is difficult to get a complete picture of what happened.* | **give/ paint a ... picture** *He painted a depressing picture of life in the city.*

4 [singular] the general situation in a place, organization etc: *The political picture has changed greatly.* | **the big/bigger/wider picture** (=a situation considered as a whole) *We need to step back and look at the bigger picture.*

5 put/keep sb in the picture *informal* to give someone the information they need to understand a situation

6 out of/not in the picture *informal* if someone is out of the picture, they are no longer involved in a situation: *With his brother out of the picture, Alex was getting all the attention.*

7 get the picture *spoken* to understand something: *Yeah, okay. I get the picture.*

8 a) [C] a film **b) the pictures** *BrE* the cinema: *Do you want to go to the pictures on Saturday?*
→ MOTION PICTURE

picture[2] *v* [T] **1** to imagine something clearly: *She pictured him opening the letter and reading it.* **2** to show something or someone in a photograph, painting, or drawing: *The prince is pictured on every front page today.*

picturesque /,pɪktʃə'resk◂/ *adj* a picturesque place is pretty in an old-fashioned way

pie /paɪ/ *n* [C,U]

1 a) fruit baked inside PASTRY: *an apple pie* **b)** *BrE* meat, fish, or vegetables baked inside PASTRY or with potato on top: *chicken and mushroom pie*

2 pie in the sky *informal* something that someone says will happen but which you think is very unlikely
→ MINCE PIE

piece[1] /piːs/ *n* [C]

1 a part of something that has been cut, broken, or separated from the rest of it: **+of** *Do you want a piece of bread?* | *You'll need several small pieces of string.* | **in pieces** (=broken into many parts) *The vase lay in pieces on the floor.* | *shelves that* **come to pieces** (=separate into parts) *for easy transport* | *He had to* **take the clock to pieces** (=separate it into parts) *to repair it.* | *All my clothes are* **falling to pieces** (=are old and in bad condition). | **smash/tear/rip sth to pieces** (=break something into many parts, especially violently) → see box at PART

2 a single thing of a particular type, or one part of a set of things: **+of** *a beautiful* **piece of furniture** | *I wrote the address down on a* **piece of paper.** | *valuable* **pieces of equipment** | *a chess piece*

3 a piece of advice/information/luck etc a small amount of advice, information etc: *Let me give you a piece of advice.* | *I've had a rather surprising piece of news.*

4 go to pieces to become so upset or nervous that you cannot think or behave normally: *After his wife left, he went to pieces.*

5 (all) in one piece not damaged or injured: *Ring Mum and let her know you got here in one piece* (=arrived safely).

6 give sb a piece of your mind *informal* to tell someone that you are very angry with them: *If I see her, I'll give her a piece of my mind!*
7 be a piece of cake *informal* to be very easy to do
8 something that has been written or made by an artist, musician, or writer: **+of** *a beautiful piece of music | Robert wrote a short piece on the festival for the local paper.*
9 a coin that is worth a particular amount: *a 50p piece* → see box at **MONEY**

piece² v

piece sth ⇔ **together** *phr v* **1** to use all the information you have about a situation to discover the truth about it: *Police are trying to piece together exactly what happened.* **2** to put all the parts of something into their correct position

piecemeal /'piːsmiːl/ *adj* happening or done slowly and not in a planned way: *a piecemeal approach to the problem* —**piecemeal** *adv*: *The changes were introduced piecemeal.*

piecework /'piːswɜːk $ -wɜːrk/ *n* [U] work for which you are paid for the amount you produce rather than for the number of hours you work

'pie ,chart *n* [C] a circle divided into parts by lines coming from the centre to show how big the different parts of a total amount are

pier /pɪə $ pɪr/ *n* [C] a structure that is built out into the sea so that boats can stop next to it or people can walk along it

pierce /pɪəs $ pɪrs/ *v* [T] **1** to make a hole in or through something using an object with a sharp point: *A bullet pierced his body. | I'm getting my*

ears pierced (=having holes for jewellery made in my ears). **2** *literary* if a bright light or a loud sound pierces something, you suddenly see it or hear it: *The lights from the boat pierced the fog.*

piercing /'pɪəsɪŋ $ 'pɪr-/ *adj* **1** a piercing sound is very loud, high, and unpleasant: *a piercing scream* **2** a piercing wind is strong and cold **3** *literary* someone with piercing eyes is looking at you and seems to know what you are thinking

piety /'paɪəti/ *n* [U] behaviour that shows respect for God and religion

pig¹ /pɪg/ *n* [C]

1 a farm animal with short legs, a fat body, and a curled tail [= hog *AmE*]
2 *spoken* someone who eats too much, or who is dirty or unpleasant: *You ate all the pizza, you pig.*
→ **GUINEA PIG**

pig² *v* **pigged, pigging**

pig out *phr v informal* to eat too much food all at one time: **+on** *We pigged out on ice cream last night.*

pigeon /'pɪdʒən/ *n* [C] a grey bird with short legs that is common in cities

pigeonhole¹ /'pɪdʒənhəʊl $ -hoʊl/ *n* [C] one of a set of small open boxes fixed to a wall. You leave letters, messages etc for particular people in the boxes.

pigeonhole² *v* [T] to decide unfairly that someone or something belongs to a particular group or type

pieces

sheet (of paper)

lump (of coal)

block (of concrete)

bunch (of flowers)

(ice) cubes

bar (of soap)

dollop (of cream)

chunk (of cheese)

slice (of bread)

wad (of bank notes)

pigeon-'toed *adj* someone who is pigeon-toed has feet that turn towards each other as they walk

piggyback /'pɪgibæk/ *n* [C] if you give a child a piggyback, you carry them on your back —**piggyback** *adv*

piggy bank /'pɪgi bæŋk/ *n* [C] a small container used by children for saving coins, often in the shape of a pig

pigheaded /ˌpɪg'hedɪd◂/ *adj* determined to do things a particular way even when there are good reasons not to

piglet /'pɪglɪt/ *n* [C] a young pig

pigment /'pɪgmənt/ *n* [C,U] *technical* a substance that makes skin, hair, plants etc a particular colour

pigmentation /ˌpɪgmən'teɪʃən/ *n* [U] *technical* the natural colour of living things

pigsty /'pɪgstaɪ/ also **pigpen** *AmE* /'pɪgpen/ *n* [C] plural **pigsties** **1** a place on a farm where pigs are kept **2** *informal* a very dirty or untidy place

pigtail /'pɪgteɪl/ *n* [C] long hair that is twisted together [= plait *BrE*; = braid *AmE*; ➡ ponytail]

pike /paɪk/ *n* plural **pike** a large fish that eats other fish and lives in rivers and lakes

pile¹ /paɪl/ *n* [C]

1 a lot of similar things put one on top of the other: **+of** *a pile of folded clothes* | *She tidied up the books and* **put them in piles**.

2 a large amount of something arranged in a shape like a small hill: **+of** *a huge pile of rubbish* | *piles of snow by the side of the road*

3 **piles of sth/a pile of sth** *informal* a lot of something: *I've piles of work to do tonight.*

4 **piles** [plural] *informal* painfully swollen BLOOD VESSELS near a person's ANUS [= haemorrhoids]

pile² also **pile up** *v* [T] to make a pile of things somewhere: *They piled the boxes up in a corner of the garage.* | **+with** *a plate* **piled high** *with spaghetti*

pile into/out of sth *phr v informal* if people pile into or out of a place or vehicle, they go in or out quickly in no particular order: *We all piled into the car.*

pile up *phr v* to become larger in quantity or amount: *Debts from the business were piling up quickly.*

'pile-up *n* [C] *informal* a traffic accident involving several vehicles: *a 16-car pile-up* ➡ see box at ACCIDENT

pilfer /'pɪlfə $ -ər/ *v* [I,T] to steal a small amount of money or things that are not worth much

pilgrim /'pɪlgrɪm/ *n* [C] someone who travels to a holy place for a religious reason

pilgrimage /'pɪlgrɪmɪdʒ/ *n* [C,U] a trip to a holy place for a religious reason

pill /pɪl/ *n* [C]

1 a small solid piece of medicine that you swallow: *He has to* **take pills** *to control his blood pressure.* | *a bottle of* **sleeping pills** ➡ see box at MEDICINE

2 **the Pill** a pill that some women take to prevent them from having a baby: **on the Pill** *My doctor advised me to go on the Pill* (=take the Pill).

pillage /'pɪlɪdʒ/ *v* [I,T] if soldiers pillage a place in a war, they steal things from it and cause damage

pillar /'pɪlə $ -ər/ *n* **1** [C] a tall solid piece of stone, wood etc used to support part of a building **2** **pillar of the community/church etc** someone who is an active and important member of a group or organization

pillion /'pɪljən/ *n* [C] the seat for a passenger on a MOTORCYCLE —**pillion** *adv*

pillow /'pɪləʊ $ -loʊ/ *n* [C] the soft object you rest your head on when you sleep ➡ see picture at BED

pillowcase /'pɪləʊkeɪs $ -loʊ-/ *n* [C] a cover for a pillow

pilot /'paɪlət/ *n* [C]

1 someone who flies a plane: *an* **airline pilot**

2 someone who guides a ship through a difficult area of water

3 **pilot study/programme etc** a study etc that is done to test whether people like an idea, product etc

—**pilot** *v* [T]

pimp /pɪmp/ *n* [C] a man who controls PROSTITUTES and takes the money that they earn

pimple /'pɪmpəl/ *n* [C] a small raised red spot on your skin ➡ see box at MARK —**pimply** *adj*

pin¹ /pɪn/ *n* [C]

1 **a)** a short thin piece of metal with a sharp point at one end, used especially for holding pieces of cloth together **b)** a thin piece of metal used to fasten things together, especially broken bones

2 *AmE* a piece of jewellery fastened to your clothes by a pin [= brooch *BrE*]

➡ BOBBY PIN, DRAWING PIN, PINS AND NEEDLES, ROLLING PIN, SAFETY PIN

pin² *v* [T] **pinned, pinning** **1** to fasten something with a pin: **pin sth to/on etc sth** *There was a note pinned to the door.* | *Pin your name tag on your jacket.* | **pin sth up** *I'll pin these photos up on the notice board.* **2** **pin your hopes on sth** to hope that something will happen or be successful, because all your plans depend on it: *She's pinned all her hopes on winning.* **3** **pin the blame on sb** to blame someone for something, often unfairly **4** to prevent someone from moving because of pressure or weight: **pin sb to/against/under etc sth** *He was pinned under the car.*

pin sb/sth down *phr v* **1** to make someone decide something, or tell you what their decision is: *I couldn't pin him down to a definite date.* **2** **pin sth ⇔ down** to discover exactly what something is: *Scientists may have pinned down the cause of the disease.*

PIN /pɪn/ also **'pin ˌnumber** *n* [C] **personal identification number** a number you use to take money from a machine using a plastic card

pinafore /'pɪnəfɔː $ -fɔːr/ *n* [C] *BrE* a dress that does not cover your arms, usually worn over a shirt

pinball /'pɪnbɔːl $ -bɒːl/ *n* [U] a game played on a machine in which you push buttons to try to stop a ball rolling off a sloping board

pincer /'pɪnsə $ -ər/ *n* [C] one of the pair of CLAWS (=sharp curved nails) that some insects and SHELLFISH have

pinch¹ /pɪntʃ/ *v* [T] **1** to press a part of someone's skin tightly between your finger and thumb: *He pinched her arm playfully.* ➡ see pic-

P

ture on page A10 **2** *informal* to steal something: *Someone's pinched my pen!* → see box at STEAL

pinch² *n* **1 a pinch of salt/pepper etc** a small amount of salt, pepper etc that you can hold between your finger and thumb **2** [C] when you press someone's skin between your finger and thumb: *She gave him a playful pinch.* **3 at a pinch** *BrE* **in a pinch** *AmE* used to say that you could probably do something difficult if it was really necessary or urgent: *I could get $300, maybe $400 in a pinch.* **4 take sth with a pinch of salt** to not completely believe what someone says to you **5 feel the pinch** to have financial difficulties because you do not have enough money: *Small businesses are feeling the pinch.*

pinched /pɪntʃt/ *adj* a pinched face looks thin and unhealthy

pincushion /'pɪn,kʊʃən/ *n* [C] something soft that you stick pins in until you need them

pine¹ /paɪn/ *n* **1** also **'pine tree** [C,U] a tall tree with long leaves shaped like needles **2** [U] the pale wood of pine trees

pine² *v* [I] to feel sad and not enjoy your life, especially because you are away from a person or place you love: **+for** *Karen was still pining for her friends back home.*

pineapple /'paɪnæpəl/ *n* [C,U] a large yellow-brown tropical fruit or its sweet yellow flesh → see picture at FRUIT

'pine cone *n* [C] a thing that grows on the branches of pine trees and contains the seeds of the tree

'pine ,needle *n* [C] a leaf of the PINE tree, which is thin and sharp like a needle

ping /pɪŋ/ *v* [I] if a bell, machine, or metal object pings, it makes a short high sound —**ping** *n* [C]

'ping-pong *n* [U] *informal* TABLE TENNIS

pink /pɪŋk/ *adj* pale red: *a bright pink dress* → see picture at PATTERN —**pink** *n* [C,U]

pinkie, pinky /'pɪŋki/ *n* [C] *AmE informal* the smallest finger on your hand

pinnacle /'pɪnəkəl/ *n* **1** [singular] the most successful part of something: **+of** *She reached the pinnacle of her career at the age of 45.* **2** [C] *literary* a high mountain top

pinpoint¹ /'pɪnpɔɪnt/ *v* [T] to say exactly where something is or what something is: **+what/how/why etc** *I'm trying to pinpoint where we are on the map.*

pinpoint² *adj* **with pinpoint accuracy** very exactly: *Today's planes can drop bombs with pinpoint accuracy.*

pinprick /'pɪn,prɪk/ *n* [C] a very small area or hole: *pinpricks of light*

,pins and 'needles *n* [U] an uncomfortable feeling, especially in your foot or leg, that you get when you have not moved part of your body for a long time

pinstripe /'pɪnstraɪp/ *n* [U] dark cloth with thin light lines on it: *a blue pinstripe suit* → see picture at PATTERN

pint /paɪnt/ *n* [C] a unit for measuring liquid, equal to 0.473 litres in the US or 0.568 litres in Britain: **+of** *a pint of milk*

'pin-up *n* [C] a picture of someone famous or attractive, often not wearing many clothes

pioneer¹ /,paɪə'nɪə $ -'nɪr/ *n* [C] **1** one of the first people to do something, whose work or ideas are later developed by other people: **+of** *the pioneers of cinema* **2** one of the first people to travel to an unknown place and begin living there

pioneer² *v* [T] to be the first person to do, invent, or use something new: *a technique pioneered by the Cambridge team*

pioneering /,paɪə'nɪərɪŋ◂ $ -'nɪr-/ *adj* [only before noun] introducing new or better ideas or methods for the first time: **pioneering work/research/efforts etc** *the pioneering work of NASA scientists*

pious /'paɪəs/ *adj* having strong religious beliefs, and showing this in the way you behave [➙ piety] —**piously** *adv*

pip¹ /pɪp/ *n* [C] *BrE* a small seed from a fruit such as an apple or orange → see picture at FRUIT

pip² *v* [T] **pipped, pipping** *BrE* to beat someone by a small amount or at the last moment in a race or competition: **pip sb to/for sth** *Jackson just pipped him for the gold medal.* | *The Maclaren team were pipped at the post* (=beaten at the last moment) *by Ferrari.*

pipe¹ /paɪp/ *n* [C]

1 a tube that liquid or gas flows through: *a water pipe* | *A pipe had burst in the kitchen, flooding the floor.*
2 a thing used for smoking tobacco, consisting of a small tube with a container shaped like a bowl at one end: *My grandad used to smoke a pipe.*
3 a simple musical instrument like a tube that you blow through
4 pipe dream an idea, plan etc that will probably never happen

pipe² *v* [T] to send a liquid or gas through a pipe to another place: **pipe sth into/from/out of etc sth** *The oil is piped from Alaska.*

pipe up *phr v informal* to suddenly start speaking: *Then Dennis piped up, saying he didn't agree.*

pipeline /'paɪp-laɪn/ *n* **1** [C] a line of pipes used to carry gas, oil etc over long distances **2 be in the pipeline** if a change, idea, or event is in the pipeline, it is being planned and will happen soon

piping¹ /'paɪpɪŋ/ *n* [U] the pipes used to carry liquid or gas in or out of a building

piping² *adv* **piping hot** very hot – used about food or drinks: *piping hot soup*

piquant /'pi:kənt/ *adj formal* having a pleasantly spicy taste: *a piquant sauce*

pique¹ /pi:k/ *v* [T] **1** [usually passive] to make someone feel annoyed or upset: *Privately, Zach was piqued not to get the job.* **2 pique sb's interest/curiosity** to make someone interested in something

pique² *n* [U] *formal* a feeling of being annoyed or upset: *Greta left in a fit of pique.*

piracy /'paɪərəsi $ 'paɪrə-/ *n* [U] **1** the crime of attacking and stealing from ships **2** the crime of illegally copying and selling books, videos, computer programs etc: *software piracy*

piranha /pɪˈrɑːnə $ -ˈrɑːnjə, -ˈrænə/ n [C] a South American fish with sharp teeth that lives in rivers and eats flesh

pirate¹ /ˈpaɪərət $ ˈpaɪrət/ n [C] **1** someone on a ship who attacks other boats and steals things from them **2** someone who illegally copies and sells another person's work: *video pirates*

pirate² v [T] to illegally copy and sell someone else's work → see box at COPY

Pisces /ˈpaɪsiːz/ n **1** [U] the sign of the Zodiac of people born between February 20 and March 20 **2** [C] someone who has this sign

pistachio /pɪˈstɑːʃiəʊ $ pɪˈstæʃioʊ/ n [C] plural **pistachios** a small green nut you can eat

piste /piːst/ n [C] *BrE* a slope covered in snow which is prepared for people to SKI on

pistol /ˈpɪstl/ n [C] a small gun you hold in one hand

piston /ˈpɪstən/ n [C] a part of an engine that moves up and down to make the other parts move

pit¹ /pɪt/ n [C] **1** a hole that has been dug in the ground: *a deep pit* **2** a coal mine **3 be the pits** *informal* to be very bad: *This place is the pits!* **4 in the pit of your stomach** if you have a feeling in the pit of your stomach, you feel very nervous, afraid etc, especially in a way that makes you feel sick **5** *AmE* the large hard seed in some fruits [= stone *BrE*]: *a peach pit* → see picture at FRUIT **6 the pits** *BrE* **the pit** *AmE* the place beside a race track where race cars come for petrol, new tyres etc

pit² v [T] **pitted, pitting** *AmE* to take out the large hard seed inside some types of fruit

pit sb/sth against sb/sth *phr v* to test someone's strength, ability etc against someone or something else in a competition or fight: *This week's big game pits Houston against Miami.*

pitch¹ /pɪtʃ/ n **1** [C] *BrE* an area of ground used for playing a sport [= field]: **football/cricket/rugby etc pitch** *the Wembley soccer pitch* → see box at SPORT **2** [singular,U] a strong level of feeling about something: *Their excitement rose to fever pitch* (=a very excited level). **3** [singular U] how high or low a note or other sound is **4** [C] *informal* an attempt to persuade someone to buy something or do something: *an aggressive sales pitch* **5** [C] a throw of the ball in a game of baseball

pitch² v **1** [T] to set a speech, examination etc at a particular level of difficulty: +**at** *The questions were pitched at a very high level.* **2** [T] to throw something with a lot of force: **pitch sth over/into etc sth** *Carl tore up the letter and pitched it into the fire.* **3** [I,T] to aim and throw the ball in a game of baseball: *Who's pitching for the Red Sox today?* → see box at THROW **4** [I,T] to fall suddenly and heavily in a particular direction, or to make someone or something fall in this way: +**into/forward etc** *She slipped and pitched forward onto the ground.* **5** [T] to aim a product at a particular group of people: **pitch sth at sb/sth** *Their new range of PCs is pitched at the home user.* **6** [I,T] to try to persuade someone to do business with you: +**for** *Several*

companies are pitching for the contract. **7** [T] to make a sound at a particular level: *Her voice was pitched low and soft.* **8 pitch a tent/pitch camp** to put up a tent

pitch in *phr v informal* to join others and help with an activity: *If we all pitch in, we'll finish in no time.*

pitch 'black also **pitch 'dark** *adj* completely black or dark: *It was pitch black in the basement.*

pitcher /ˈpɪtʃə $ -ər/ n [C] **1** the player in baseball who throws the ball **2** *AmE* a container used for holding and pouring liquids [= jug *BrE*]

pitchfork /ˈpɪtʃfɔːk $ -fɔːrk/ n [C] a farm tool with a long handle and two long metal points

piteous /ˈpɪtiəs/ *adj literary* making you feel pity for someone: *a piteous cry* —**piteously** *adv*

pitfall /ˈpɪtfɔːl $ -fɒːl/ n [C usually plural] a problem or difficulty that is likely to happen in a particular situation: +**of** *the pitfalls of buying an old car*

pith /pɪθ/ n [U] the white substance just under the skin of fruit such as oranges

pithy /ˈpɪθi/ *adj* spoken or written in clear language, without using too many words: *pithy comments*

pitiful /ˈpɪtɪfəl/ *adj* **1** making you feel sadness and pity: *a pitiful sight* **2** extremely bad: *His performance last night was pitiful.* —**pitifully** *adv*

pitiless /ˈpɪtɪləs/ *adj* showing no pity for people who are suffering

pittance /ˈpɪtəns/ n [singular] a very small amount of money: *She earns a pittance.*

pitted /ˈpɪtɪd/ *adj* a pitted surface is covered in small marks or holes: *a road pitted with potholes*

pity¹ /ˈpɪti/ n

1 a pity *spoken* used when you are disappointed about a situation and wish it was different [= shame]: **it's a pity (that)** *It's a pity you can't come.* | **what a pity/that's a pity** *'We're leaving tomorrow.' 'What a pity!'*
2 [U] sadness that you feel for someone who is suffering or unhappy [➔ pitiful, pitiless]: *I listened to Jason's story with pity.* | **take/have pity on sb** (=feel sympathy for someone and try to help them) *Anna looked so upset that Jean took pity on her.*

pity² v [T] **pitied, pitying, pities** to feel sympathy for someone who is in a bad situation: *Sam pitied his grandmother, living there all alone.*

pivot /ˈpɪvət/ n [C] **1** a fixed central point or pin that something balances or turns on **2** the most important thing about a situation which other things depend on —**pivot** v [I,T]

pivotal /ˈpɪvətəl/ *adj* having a very important effect on a situation, system etc: *Japan has a pivotal role in the world economy.*

pixel /ˈpɪksəl/ n [C] *technical* the smallest unit of an image on a computer screen

pixie /ˈpɪksi/ n [C] a small imaginary creature that looks like a person and has magic powers

pizza /ˈpiːtsə/ n [C,U] a food made of thin flat round bread, baked with tomato, cheese, and sometimes vegetables or meat on top

pizzeria /ˌpiːtsəˈriːə/ n [C] a restaurant that serves pizza

pl. also **pl** *BrE* the written abbreviation of **plural**

placard /ˈplækɑːd $ -ərd/ *n* [C] a large notice or advertisement on a piece of card, which is put up or carried in a public place

placate /pləˈkeɪt $ ˈpleɪkeɪt/ *v* [T] *formal* to make someone stop feeling angry

place¹ /pleɪs/ *n* [C]
1 any space, building, area, or position: *He showed me the place where the accident happened.* | **in a ... place** *Keep your passport in a safe place.* | *The place was full of screaming children.* | *Paint is coming off the wall* **in places** (=in some areas). | **+for** *Portugal is a great place for a holiday.* | **a place to do sth** *I couldn't find a place to park.* | *Are there any good places to eat round here?*

THESAURUS

position – the exact place where someone or something is: *We need to know the enemy's position.*
spot *informal* – a place, especially a pleasant one: *It's a favourite spot for picnics.*
location – the place where a hotel, shop, office etc is built, or where a film is made: *The apartment's in an ideal location.*
site – a place where something is going to be built, or where something important happened: *the site for the new airport* | *an archaeological site*
point – an exact place, for example on a map: *At this point the path gets narrower.*
Space and **room** can both be used to talk about the size of an area that is empty or available to be used: *a bigger house with lots of space* | *There's enough room for us all in the car.*
Place cannot be used like this. Do not say 'There's enough place for us all.'

---

2 *informal* a house or apartment where someone lives: **sb's place** *Shall we go back to my place for coffee?* | *They've got a big place in the country.*
3 **take place** to happen: *When did the robbery take place?* → see box at **HAPPEN**
4 a space where you can sit, or a space where you can put something: *I might be late, so can you save me a place?* | *Put the CDs back in their place.*
5 an opportunity to go somewhere or join in an activity: **+on** *There are a few places left on the German course.* | **+in** *If you don't come, you might lose your place in the team.*
6 the importance or position that someone or something has: **+in** *Work has an important place in all our lives.* | *Boston's got a special place in my heart.*
7 the right occasion or situation for something: *This isn't the place to discuss money.*
8 the point that you have reached in a book or a speech: *You made me lose my place* (=forget the point that I had reached).
9 **in place a)** in the correct position: *The chairs for the concert were nearly all in place.* **b)** existing and ready to be used: *By then the new system will be in place.*
10 **in place of sb/sth** instead of someone or something else: *There's football on in place of the normal programmes.*
11 **take the place of sb/sth** to exist to be used

instead of someone or something else [= **replace**]: *Could computers ever take the place of teachers?*
12 **in sb's place** used when talking about what you would do if you were in someone else's situation: *What would you do in my place?*
13 **first/second/third etc place** first, second etc position in a race or competition: *Jerry finished in fifth place.* | *Italy took second place.* → see box at **WIN**
14 **all over the place** *informal* everywhere: *There were policemen all over the place!*
15 **out of place** not suitable for or comfortable in a particular situation: *He always felt out of place at parties.*
16 **put sb in their place** to show someone that they are not as important or intelligent as they think they are
17 **fall into place** if things fall into place in your mind, you suddenly understand what is really happening
→ **NO PLACE** → **in the first place** at **FIRST¹**

place² *v* [T] **1** to put something carefully somewhere [= put]: **place sth in/on etc sth** *She placed the bowl on the top shelf.* **2** to put someone or something in a particular situation [= put]: *This places me in an embarrassing position.* **3** to consider that something has a particular level of importance: *Most people* **place a high value on** *friendship.* **4 can't place sb** to be unable to remember who someone is or where you have met them: *He looks familiar, but I can't place him.* **5** to arrange for something to be done: *You can* **place orders** *by telephone.* | *We* **placed an advertisement** *in the local paper.*

placebo /pləˈsiːbəʊ $ -boʊ/ *n* [C] plural **placebos** a harmless substance given to a sick person instead of medicine, without telling them it is not real

placement /ˈpleɪsmənt/ *n* **1** [C] a job that is found for someone, especially to give them experience of work: *a work experience placement* **2** [singular, U] when you find a place for someone to live, work, or study: *the placement of children in special schools*

ˈplace name *n* [C] the name of a particular place, such as a town, mountain etc

placid /ˈplæsɪd/ *adj* not getting angry or upset easily: *a placid baby* —**placidly** *adv*

plagiarism /ˈpleɪdʒərɪzəm/ *n* [U] when someone uses another person's ideas or work and pretends it is their own: *She was accused of plagiarism in her thesis.* —**plagiarist** *n* [C]

plagiarize also **-ise** *BrE* /ˈpleɪdʒəraɪz/ *v* [I,T] to use another person's ideas or words, and pretend they are yours

plague¹ /pleɪɡ/ *n* **1** [C,U] a disease that spreads quickly and kills a lot of people **2 a plague of sth** a sudden large increase in the numbers of a particular animal or insect that is difficult to control: *a plague of rats*

plague² *v* [T] to cause pain or trouble to someone for a long time: *Renee had always been plagued by ill health.*

plaice /pleɪs/ *n* [C,U] plural **plaice** a flat sea fish that people eat

plaid /plæd/ *n* [U] a pattern of crossed lines and squares, especially on cloth [= **tartan**]

plain¹ /pleɪn/ adj

1 easy to understand or recognize [= **obvious**]: *It's plain that he doesn't agree.* | *They made it plain* (=said clearly) *that they did not want us there.*

2 without anything added or without decoration [= **simple**]: *plain food* | *a plain white shirt* | *a sheet of plain paper* (=paper with no lines on it) → see picture at **PATTERN**

3 saying what you think honestly and in clear simple language: *The plain fact is that we can't afford it.* | *The document is written in plain English.*

4 a plain person is not attractive

plain² n [C] a large area of flat dry land

plain³ adv informal used to emphasize some adjectives: *They're just plain lazy.*

plain-'clothes adj plain-clothes police wear ordinary clothes so that they can work without being recognized → see box at **POLICE**

plainly /'pleɪnli/ adv **1** in a way that is easy to see or understand [= **clearly**]: *Mrs Gorman was plainly delighted.* | *She told him plainly that she wouldn't marry him.* **2** simply or without decoration: *a plainly furnished room*

plaintiff /'pleɪntɪf/ n [C] law someone who brings a legal action against another person in a court of law [→ **defendant**]

plaintive /'pleɪntɪv/ adj sounding sad: *plaintive cries*

plait /plæt $ pleɪt, plæt/ v [T] BrE to twist three long pieces of hair, rope etc over and under each other to make one long piece [= **braid** AmE] → see picture at **HAIR** —**plait** n [C]

plan¹ /plæn/ n [C]

1 something you have decided to do, or an idea for doing something in an organized way: **plan to do sth** *The company has plans to create 30 more jobs.* | *There's been a slight change of plan.* | **+for** *the government's plans for economic recovery* | *Helen's busy making plans for her wedding.* | *If things go according to plan* (=happen in the way we expect), *we'll leave on Monday.*

THESAURUS

plot/conspiracy – a secret plan to do something bad or illegal, especially one that involves a lot of people: *a plot to assassinate the President*

scheme BrE – an official plan that is intended to help people: *a new scheme to help young people find work*

strategy – a careful plan aimed at achieving something difficult: *the government's economic strategy*

schedule – a plan of what someone has to do, showing when they have to do it: *The President's schedule looks pretty busy.*

timetable – a plan that shows the exact times when something should happen: *the school timetable* (=when lessons are planned to start and end)

2 a drawing of a building, room, or machine as you would see it from above, showing its shape and measurements: *An architect is drawing up some plans for us.*

3 a map showing roads, towns, and buildings: **+of** *a street plan of London*

4 **Plan A** your first plan, which you will use if things happen the way you expect

5 **Plan B** your second plan, which you can use if things do not happen the way you expect
→ **FLOOR PLAN, GAME PLAN, OPEN PLAN**

plan² v planned, planning

1 [I,T] to think about something you want to do, and decide how you will do it: *We've been planning our trip for months.* | *You need to plan ahead to make the best use of your money.* | **+for** *Talks are planned for next week.*

2 [T] to intend to do something: **plan on doing sth** *How long do you plan on staying?* | **plan to do sth** *Where do you plan to go next year?*

3 [T] to think about something you are going to make, and decide what it will be like [→ **design**]: *We spent ages planning the garden.*
—**planning** n [U]

plane /pleɪn/ n [C]

1 a vehicle with wings and an engine, which can fly: **by plane** *It's much quicker to go by plane.* | *The plane will take off in twenty minutes.* | *Our plane landed in Chicago.* | *a plane crash*

2 a level of thought or activity: **on a different/higher plane** *Creative people live on a different plane.*

3 a tool used for making wooden surfaces smooth

planet /'plænɪt/ n [C]

1 a very large round object in space that moves around the sun or another star: *Mercury is the smallest planet.* → see box at **SPACE**

2 **the planet** the world: *the environmental future of the planet*
—**planetary** adj

planetarium /ˌplænɪ'teəriəm $ -'ter-/ n [C] a building where lights on a curved ceiling show the movements of planets and stars

plank /plæŋk/ n [C] a long flat piece of wood

plankton /'plæŋktən/ n [U] extremely small plants and animals that live in water and are eaten by fish

planner /'plænə $ -ər/ n [C] someone whose job is to plan something, especially the way towns develop

plant¹ /plɑːnt $ plænt/ n [C]

1 a living thing that has leaves and roots and grows in earth: *Don't forget to water the plants.* | *a tomato plant* → **LOG, SAPLING**

2 a factory and all its equipment: *a chemical plant*

plant² v [T] **1** to put plants or seeds in the ground to grow: *I planted the rose bush last year.* | **plant a field/an area etc with sth** *a hillside planted with pine trees* **2** informal to hide stolen or illegal goods in someone's bags, room etc in order to make that person seem guilty: **plant sth on sb** *Someone must have planted the drugs on her.* **3** to put something firmly in or on something else: **plant sth in/on etc sth** *He planted a kiss on her cheek.* **4 plant a bomb** to put a bomb somewhere

plantation /plæn'teɪʃən, plɑːn- $ plæn-/ n [C]

1 a large area of land in a hot country where crops such as tea, cotton, or sugar are grown: *a*

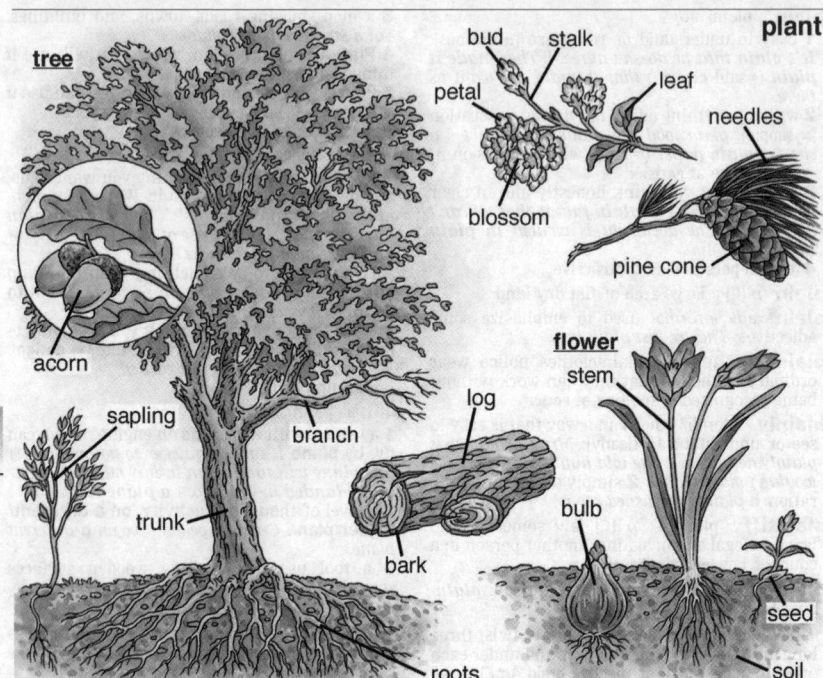

tree

acorn
sapling
branch
trunk
bark
roots
log

plant
bud
stalk
petal
leaf
needles
blossom
pine cone

flower
stem
bulb
seed
soil

rubber plantation **2** a large group of trees that are grown to produce wood

plaque /plɑːk, plæk $ plæk/ *n* **1** [C] a piece of flat metal or stone with writing on it, attached to a building to remind people of a famous event or person: *The plaque read: Samuel Johnson was born here.* **2** [U] a harmful substance that forms on your teeth

plasma /ˈplæzmə/ *n* [U] the liquid part of your blood that contains the blood cells

'plasma screen *n* [C] a special very thin television or computer screen

plaster¹ /ˈplɑːstə $ ˈplæstər/ *n* **1** [U] a substance used to cover walls and ceilings and give them a smooth surface **2** [C] *BrE* a piece of special material that you stick on your skin to cover small wounds [= **Band-Aid** *AmE*] **3 in plaster** *BrE* if your leg, arm etc is in plaster, it has a PLASTER CAST around it because a bone is broken

plaster² *v* [T] **1** to completely cover a surface with something: **plaster sth with sth** *The walls were plastered with posters.* **2** [usually passive] to make your hair lie flat or stick to your head: **plaster sth to sth** *His hair was plastered to his forehead with sweat.* **3** to put plaster on a wall or ceiling in order to make it smooth

'plaster cast *n* [C] a cover made from plaster, used to protect a broken bone

plaster of Paris /ˌplɑːstər əv ˈpærɪs $ ˌplæs-/ *n* [U] a mixture of white powder and water, used especially for making plaster casts

plastic¹ /ˈplæstɪk/ *n* [C,U] a cheap light material that is produced by a chemical process and used for making many different objects: *toys made of plastic*

plastic² *adj* made of plastic: *a plastic bag* | *plastic spoons* → see picture at **MATERIAL¹**

plasticity /plæˈstɪsɪti/ *n* [U] *technical* the quality of being easily made into any shape

,plastic 'surgery *n* [U] medical treatment that changes someone's appearance, either to make them more attractive or to repair injuries —**plastic surgeon** *n* [C]

,plastic 'wrap *n* [U] *AmE* thin transparent plastic used to cover food to keep it fresh [= **Saran wrap**; = **Clingfilm** *BrE*]

plate /pleɪt/ *n* [C]

1 a) a flat dish that you use for eating or serving food: *Take a plate and help yourself.* | *a dinner plate* (=a large round plate) **b)** also **plateful** the amount of food that is on a plate: **+of** *I've already had a huge plate of spaghetti.*

2 a flat piece of metal with words or numbers on it: **number/license/registration plate** (=on a car) *a car with French number plates*

3 gold/silver plate metal with a thin covering of gold or silver

4 a picture in a book, printed on good quality paper

5 the plate the place where the person hitting the ball stands in baseball

plateau /ˈplætəʊ $ plæˈtoʊ/ *n* [C] plural **plateaus** or **plateaux** /-təʊz $ -ˈtoʊz/ **1** a large area of flat land that is higher than the land around it **2** a period when the level of something does not change: *Inflation has **reached a plateau**.*

plated /'pleɪtɨd/ *adj* **gold-plated/silver-plated** covered with a thin layer of gold or silver: *a silver-plated spoon*

plateful /'pleɪtfʊl/ *n* [C] all the food that is on a plate: **+of** *a plateful of toast*

plate 'glass *n* [U] glass made in large thick sheets, used especially in shop windows

platform /'plætfɔːrm $ -fɔːrm/ *n* [C]

1 *especially BrE* the area at a station where you get on and off a train: *The Edinburgh train will depart from platform six.* → see box at **TRAIN**

2 a raised structure for people to stand on when they are speaking or performing [➡ **stage**]: *He climbed onto the platform and began to address the crowd.*

3 a) the main ideas and aims of a political party, especially the ones that they state just before an election: **+of** *The government was elected on a platform of reform.* **b)** a chance for someone to express their opinions, especially political opinions: **+for** *He used the interview as a platform for his views on education.*

4 a tall structure that people can stand or work on: *an oil exploration platform*

5 the type of computer system or software that someone uses: *a multimedia platform*

platinum /'plætɨnəm/ *n* [U] a silver-grey metal that is used to make expensive jewellery and in industry

platitude /'plætɨtjuːd $ -tuːd/ *n* [C] *disapproving* a statement that has been made many times before and is not interesting: *a speech full of platitudes*

platonic /plə'tɒnɪk $ -'tɑː-/ *adj* a platonic relationship is friendly and not sexual

platoon /plə'tuːn/ *n* [C] a small group of soldiers

platter /'plætə $ -ər/ *n* [C] *especially AmE* a large plate used for serving food

plaudits /'plɔːdɨts $ 'plɒː-/ *n* [plural] *formal* praise

plausible /'plɔːzɨbəl $ 'plɒː-/ *adj* a plausible story, reason etc seems likely to be true [≠ **implausible**]: *a plausible explanation*

play¹ /pleɪ/ *v*

1 [I,T] when children play, they do things that they enjoy, often with other people or with toys: *Kids were playing outside in the street.* | **+with** *Why don't you go and play with your friends?* | *The children were playing cowboys and Indians.*

2 [I,T] to take part in a sport or game: *The guys are playing basketball.* | *Do you know how to play chess?* | **+against** *Manchester United are playing against Liverpool on Saturday.* | *Who is she playing* (=playing against) *in the final?* | **play for sth** (=play in a particular team) *Garcia plays for the Hornets.* | *Scholes is injured and won't play.* | *The game will be played at Shea stadium.*

3 [I,T] to use a musical instrument to produce music: *I'm learning to play the piano.* | *You play very well.*

4 [I,T] if a CD, radio etc plays, or if you play it, it produces music or sounds: *A radio was playing softly.* | **play sb sth** *Let me play you my new CD.*

5 [T] to act the part of a particular character in a film, play etc: *The hero is played by Sean Penn.* | **play a role/part/character** *Josie Lawrence plays the part of Lottie.*

6 play a part/role to have an effect on something: *A good diet plays an important part in keeping healthy.*

7 play a trick/joke on sb to do something to surprise or trick someone

8 [I,T] to behave in a particular way: *I wish he'd stop **playing the fool** (=behaving in a silly way).* | *Always **play safe** (=avoid risks) by telling someone where you are going.*

9 play games *disapproving* to cause problems or annoy people by not being completely honest with them

10 play ball a) to play with a ball: *Don't play ball in the house.* **b)** *informal* to agree to do what someone wants you to do: *Do you think he'll play ball?*

11 play it by ear to wait until you know more about a situation before you make any definite plans: *'Shall we take a picnic?' 'Well, let's play it by ear.'*

12 play the game to do things in the usual or expected way: *If you don't play the game, you won't survive.*

→ **play hooky** at **HOOKY** → **play truant** at **TRUANT**

GRAMMAR

Do not use a preposition or 'the' after **play** when you are talking about playing a game or sport. Say *They're playing football.*
Do not say *'They're playing at football'* or *'They're playing the football'*.
Always use 'the' after the verb **play** and before the names of musical instruments: *Anna plays the piano.*

play around also **play about** *BrE phr v*
1 *informal* to have a sexual relationship with someone who is not your husband or wife **2** to try doing something in different ways to see which is best: **+with** *Play around with the images until you are satisfied.* **3** to behave in a silly way: *I wish those kids would stop playing around outside our house.*

play around with sth also **play about with sth** *BrE phr v* to keep touching or moving something [= **fiddle with**]: *Stop playing around with the remote control!*

play at sth *phr v* **1** to do something without being serious about it or doing it properly: *He's just playing at being an artist.* **2 what is sb playing at?** *BrE spoken* used when you do not understand what someone is doing or why they are doing it, and you are annoyed with them: *What do you think you're playing at?*

play sth ⇔ **back** *phr v* to play something that has been recorded on a machine so that you can listen to it or watch it

play sth ⇔ **down** *phr v* to try to make something seem less important or bad than it really is: *The government was anxious to play down the latest unemployment figures.*

play sb **off against** sb *phr v* to encourage two people or groups to argue or compete with each other, in order to get advantages for yourself

play on sth *phr v* to use someone's fears or weaknesses in order to get what you want: *The film plays on people's fears and prejudices.*

play up *phr v* **1 play** sth ⇔ **up** to make something seem better, more important etc than it really is: *He was obviously keen to play up his* *relationship with her.* **2 play (sb) up** *BrE informal* if children play up, they behave badly

play with sth *phr v* to keep touching or moving something: *Stop playing with the light switch!*

play² *n*

1 [C] a story that is written to be performed by actors, especially in a theatre: *We went to see a new play by Tom Stoppard.* | *He wrote the play in 1964.* | **put on/perform a play** *The play was put on by a local school.* → see box at THEATRE

2 [U] things that people, especially children, do to enjoy themselves: *a play area with slides and swings* | **at play** *the sounds of children at play* (=playing)

3 [U] the activity of playing a game or sport: *Rain stopped play.*

4 come into play/be brought into play to affect or influence a situation: *Many different factors may come into play.*

5 a play on words a use of a word or phrase that is interesting or amusing because it can have two meanings [➡ pun]

→ FAIR PLAY, FOUL PLAY

'play-,acting *n* [U] when someone pretends to be serious or sincere, but is not

playboy /'pleɪbɔɪ/ *n* [C] a rich man who spends his time enjoying himself

player /'pleɪə $ -ər/ *n* [C]

1 someone who plays a game or sport: *a football player*

2 someone who plays a musical instrument: *a piano player*

3 one of the people, countries etc that are involved in a situation: **a major/key etc player** *a major player in the UN peace talks*

→ CASSETTE PLAYER, CD PLAYER, MP3 PLAYER, RECORD PLAYER

playful /'pleɪfəl/ *adj* **1** intended to be fun rather than serious: *playful teasing* **2** very active and happy: *a playful little kitten* —**playfully** *adv* —**playfulness** *n* [U]

playground /'pleɪɡraʊnd/ *n* [C] an outdoor area where children can play, especially while they are at school

playgroup /'pleɪɡruːp/ *n* [C] *BrE* an organized group where small children go to play, learn etc in the years before they go to school

playhouse /'pleɪhaʊs/ *n* [C] **1** a theatre – used especially in the names of theatres: *the Oxford Playhouse* **2** a small house or tent that children can play in

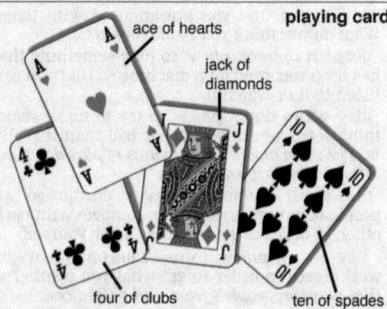

playing card

ace of hearts

jack of diamonds

four of clubs

ten of spades

'playing card *n* [C] one of a set of 52 cards that is used for playing games

'playing field *n* [C] an area of ground used for playing football, baseball etc → **a level playing field** at LEVEL²

playmate /'pleɪmeɪt/ *n* [C] a friend that a child plays with

'play-off *n* [C] a game between the best teams or players in a competition, played in order to choose the final winner

playpen /'pleɪpen/ *n* [C] a thing that you put young children in to play safely, surrounded by wooden bars or a net

playroom /'pleɪruːm, -ruːm/ *n* [C] a room for children to play in

plaything /'pleɪ,θɪŋ/ *n* [C] **1** *formal* a toy **2** a person that you use for your own amusement or advantage, without caring about them

playtime /'pleɪtaɪm/ *n* [C] a period of time when children can play, especially at school

playwright /'pleɪraɪt/ *n* [C] someone who writes plays

plc /,piː el 'siː/ *n* [C] *BrE* **Public Limited Company** used after the name of a big company in Britain which has SHARES that you can buy: *British Telecom plc*

plea /pliː/ *n* [C] **1** a request that is urgent or full of emotion: **+for** *Her mother ignored her pleas for help.* **2** *law* a statement by someone in a court of law saying whether they are guilty or not guilty

'plea-,bargaining *n* [U] when someone agrees to admit in court that they are guilty of one crime if another crime that they are connected with is not mentioned

plead /pliːd/ *v* past tense and past participle **pleaded** also **pled** *AmE* /pled/ **1** [I] to ask for something in an urgent and anxious way: **plead with sb (to do sth)** *Amy pleaded with him to stay.* **2 plead ignorance/illness/insanity etc** to give a particular excuse for your actions: *She stayed home from work, pleading illness.* **3** [I,T] *law* to state in a court of law whether or not you are guilty of a crime: **plead guilty/not guilty/innocent** *The defendant pleaded not guilty.* —**pleadingly** *adv*

pleasant /'plezənt/ *adj* enjoyable, nice, or friendly [≠ unpleasant; ➡ pleasure]: *They spent a pleasant evening together.* | *a pleasant young man* | *Kate! What a **pleasant surprise!*** | **+to** *He's always been very pleasant to me.* → see box at NICE —**pleasantly** *adv*: *She smiled pleasantly.*

pleasantries /'plezəntriz/ *n* [plural] *formal* polite things that you say when you meet someone

please¹ /pliːz/

1 used when you are politely asking for something: *Please could I have a glass of water?* | *Can you all sit down, please?* | *Please be quiet!*

2 yes please *spoken* used to politely accept something that someone offers you: *'More coffee?' 'Yes, please!'*

3 *spoken* used when you think someone has said something silly or unreasonable

please² *v* **1** [I,T] to make someone feel happy or satisfied: **be hard/easy/impossible etc to please** *She's hard to please. Everything has to be perfect.* **2** used in some phrases to show that someone can do or have anything they want: **whatever/however etc you please** *He can buy*

P

whatever he pleases. | She does **what she pleases**.
3 please yourself spoken used when telling someone to do whatever they like, even though you think they are making the wrong choice: 'I don't want any dinner.' 'OK, please yourself.'

pleased /pli:zd/ adj
1 happy about something or satisfied with something: **+with/about** Are you pleased with the result? | **+for** That's wonderful. I'm really pleased for you. | **+(that)** I was pleased that he agreed to see me. | **pleased to hear/see/know etc sth** You'll be pleased to hear that you've got the job. → see box at GLAD
2 pleased with yourself disapproving feeling proud and satisfied because you think you have done something clever: She's a bit too pleased with herself.
3 (I'm) pleased to meet you spoken a polite expression used when you meet someone for the first time

pleasing /ˈpli:zɪŋ/ adj giving pleasure, enjoyment, or satisfaction: a pleasing view —**pleasingly** adv

pleasurable /ˈpleʒərəbəl/ adj formal enjoyable: a pleasurable experience

pleasure /ˈpleʒə $ -ər/ n
1 [U] a feeling of happiness, satisfaction, or enjoyment [➔ pleasant]: **with pleasure** She sipped her drink with pleasure. | **for pleasure** I often read for pleasure. | She took great **pleasure in** telling him that he was wrong. | The garden has **given pleasure** to many people.
2 [C] an experience or activity that you enjoy very much: the simple pleasures of life | **a pleasure (to do)** My new car is an absolute pleasure to drive. | It's a **pleasure** to do business with you.
3 my pleasure/it's a pleasure spoken used when someone has thanked you for doing something, and you want to say that you were glad to do it: 'Thanks for your help.' 'My pleasure.'

pleat /pli:t/ n [C] a flat fold in a skirt, pair of trousers, dress etc

pleated /ˈpli:tɪd/ adj a pleated skirt, dress etc has a number of flat narrow folds

pleb /pleb/ n [C usually plural] informal humorous someone who belongs to a low social class

plebiscite /ˈplebɪsɪt $ -saɪt/ n [C,U] formal a system by which everyone in a country votes on an important decision that affects the whole country [➔ referendum]

pled /pled/ v AmE a past tense and past participle of PLEAD

pledge[1] /pledʒ/ n [C] a serious or public promise: a pledge of support | **pledge to do sth** the president's pledge to end the war | a Labour election pledge

pledge[2] v [T] **1** to make a formal, usually public, promise to do or give something: **pledge (yourself) to do sth** They have pledged to cut inflation. **2** to make someone formally promise something: We were all pledged to secrecy.

plentiful /ˈplentɪfəl/ adj more than enough in quantity: a plentiful supply of fruit and vegetables —**plentifully** adv

plenty /ˈplenti/ pron, adv
1 a large quantity that is enough or more than enough: **+of** We have plenty of time to get to the airport. | **plenty to do** There's plenty to see in New York. | If you need more wine, we've **plenty more** in here.
2 AmE very: By then Ronah was plenty scared.

plethora /ˈpleθərə/ n **a plethora of sth** formal a very large number of things: a plethora of complaints

pliable /ˈplaɪəbəl/ adj **1** able to bend easily without breaking or cracking **2** easily influenced by other people

pliers /ˈplaɪəz $ -ərz/ n [plural] a tool for cutting wire or pulling nails out of wood: a **pair of pliers**

plight /plaɪt/ n [singular] a very bad situation that someone is in: **+of** the plight of the refugees

plimsoll /ˈplɪmsəl, -səʊl $ -səl, -səʊl/ n [C] BrE a cotton shoe with a flat rubber SOLE [= sneaker AmE]

plod /plɒd $ plɑːd/ v [I] plodded, plodding **1** to walk along slowly, especially when this is difficult: **+on/along/up etc** The old dog plodded along behind him. **2** to work slowly or make slow progress: **+on/along/through** He plodded along in the same boring job for years.

plonk[1] /plɒŋk $ plɑːŋk, plɔːŋk/ also **plonk down** v [T] especially BrE informal to put something down somewhere, especially in a careless way: **plonk sth on/onto/beside etc sth** He plonked a mug of coffee down beside me.

plonk[2] n [U] BrE informal cheap wine

plop[1] /plɒp $ plɑːp/ v [I,T] plopped, plopping **1** to fall or drop something somewhere, making a sound like something dropping in water: **+into/out of etc** The frog plopped back into the pond. **2 plop (yourself) down** to sit down heavily: She plopped down onto the sofa.

plop[2] n [C] the sound made by something when it falls or is dropped in liquid

plot[1] /plɒt $ plɑːt/ n [C] **1** a secret plan to do something illegal or harmful: **plot to do sth** a plot to kill the king → see box at PLAN **2** the events that form the main story of a book, film, or play: I didn't really understand the plot. **3** a small piece of land for building or growing things on: a vegetable plot

plot[2] v plotted, plotting **1** [I,T] to make a secret plan to harm someone or do something illegal: **plot to do sth** He denied plotting to kidnap the girl. | **+against** The army were secretly plotting against him. **2** also **plot out** [T] to draw marks or a line to represent facts, numbers etc: We plotted a graph to show the increase in profits.

plough[1] BrE; **plow** AmE / plaʊ/ n [C] a large piece of farm equipment used to turn over the earth so that seeds can be planted

plough[2] BrE; **plow** AmE v **1** [I,T] to turn over the earth using a plough so that seeds can be planted: newly **ploughed fields 2** [I] to hit or move through something with a lot of force: **+into/through etc** A truck ploughed into the back of my car.
plough sth ⇔ back phr v to use money that you have earned from a business to make the business bigger and more successful: **+into** We ploughed the profits back into the business.
plough on phr v to continue doing something, even though it is difficult or boring

plough through sth *phr v* to read all of something even though it is difficult or boring → see box at **READ**

ploy /plɔɪ/ *n* [C] a clever way of getting what you want, especially by deceiving someone: *His usual ploy is to pretend he's ill.*

pluck¹ /plʌk/ *v* [T] **1** to quickly pull something or someone from the place where they are: **+from/off etc** *She plucked an apple off the tree.* | *Three yachtsmen were plucked from the Atlantic yesterday.* **2 pluck up (the) courage (to do sth)** to make yourself be brave and do something difficult or unpleasant: *I finally plucked up the courage to ask for a raise.* **3** to pull the feathers off a dead bird before cooking it **4** to play a musical instrument by pulling the strings with your fingers

pluck at sth *phr v* to pull something quickly several times with your fingers, especially to attract attention: *The little boy plucked at her sleeve.*

pluck² *n* [U] courage and determination —**plucky** *adj*

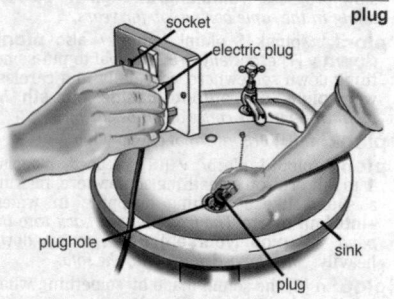

plug

socket

electric plug

plughole

sink

plug

plug¹ /plʌg/ *n* [C]

1 the thing that you push into a wall to connect a piece of electrical equipment to the electricity supply: *an electric plug*
2 a round flat piece of rubber used for blocking the hole in a bath or SINK: *the bath plug*
3 *informal* a way of advertising a book, film etc by mentioning it publicly, especially on television or radio: **put/get in a plug (for sth)** *During the show she managed to put in a plug for her new book.*
→ **SPARK PLUG**

plug² *v* [T] plugged, plugging **1** also **plug up** to fill or block a hole **2** *informal* to advertise a book, film etc by mentioning it on television or radio

plug away *phr v informal* to continue working hard at something: *He's been plugging away at his essay all week.*

plug sth ⇔ **in** *phr v* to connect a piece of electrical equipment to the electricity supply, or to another piece of equipment [≠ unplug]: *Is the TV plugged in?*

plughole /ˈplʌɡhəʊl $ -hoʊl/ *n* [C] *BrE* a hole in a bath or SINK, where the water flows out → see picture at **PLUG**

plum /plʌm/ *n* [C] a soft round fruit which is purple, red, or yellow → see picture at **FRUIT**

plumage /ˈpluːmɪdʒ/ *n* [U] a bird's feathers

plumber /ˈplʌmə $ -ər/ *n* [C] someone whose job is to repair water pipes, baths, toilets etc

plumbing /ˈplʌmɪŋ/ *n* [U] **1** the pipes that water flows through in a building **2** the work of fitting and repairing water pipes, baths, toilets etc

plume /pluːm/ *n* [C] **1** a cloud of smoke, dust etc which rises up into the air: *a plume of smoke* **2** a large feather

plummet /ˈplʌmɪt/ *v* [I] **1** to suddenly and quickly decrease in value or amount: *House prices have plummeted over the past year.* **2** to fall quickly from a very high place → see box at **FALL**

plump¹ /plʌmp/ *adj* slightly fat or round: *a cheerful plump woman* | *plump juicy strawberries* → see box at **FAT**

plump² also **plump up** *v* [T] to make PILLOWS, CUSHIONS etc rounder and softer by shaking or hitting them

plump for sth *phr v informal* to choose something after thinking carefully about it: *In the end I plumped for the tuna steak.*

plunder¹ /ˈplʌndə $ -ər/ *v* **1** [I,T] to steal large amounts of money or property from somewhere, especially during a war: *The city was plundered by invaders in 1793.* **2** [T] to use up all or most of a supply of something in a careless way: *We cannot continue to plunder the Earth's resources.*

plunder² *n* [U] *literary* the act of stealing things, or the things that someone steals, especially during a war

plunge¹ /plʌndʒ/ *v* **1** [I] to fall forwards and DOWNWARDS, especially into water: **+into/off etc** *The van plunged into the river.* **2** [T] to push something into another thing using a lot of force: **plunge sth into sth** *He plunged the knife into the man's chest.* **3** [I] to suddenly decrease by a large amount: *Oil prices have plunged to a new low.*

plunge (sb/sth) into sth *phr v* to suddenly experience a difficult or unpleasant situation, or to make someone suddenly do this: *A strike would plunge the country into chaos.*

plunge² *n* **1 take the plunge** to decide to do something important and risky, especially after thinking about it carefully **2** [singular] a sudden large decrease in the price, value etc of something: *a plunge in house prices*

plunger /ˈplʌndʒə $ -ər/ *n* [C] a tool for clearing waste that is blocking a kitchen or bathroom pipe

pluperfect /pluːˈpɜːfɪkt $ -ɜːr-/ *n* **the pluperfect** the PAST PERFECT

plural /ˈplʊərəl $ ˈplʊr-/ *n* [C] the form of a word that shows you are talking about more than one person, thing etc. For example, 'dogs' is the plural of 'dog'. —**plural** *adj*

plus¹ /plʌs/ *prep, linking word*

1 used to show that one number or amount is added to another [≠ minus]: *Three plus six equals nine (3+6=9).* | *The jacket costs $49.95 plus tax.* → see box at **CALCULATE**
2 and also: *There are numerous clubs plus a casino.*
3 plus or minus used to say that a number may be more or less by a particular amount: *The final cost may be plus or minus 5%.*

plus² *adj* **1** [only before noun] used to talk about something that is good about a thing or situation: *One of the hotel's **plus points** is that it's right in the middle of town.* **2** more than a particular amount: *She makes $50,000 a year plus.* | *a temperature of plus 12°* (=more than 12 degrees above zero)

plus³ *n* [C] **1** something that is good about something: *The restaurant's location is a real plus.* **2** a plus sign [≠ **minus**]

plush /plʌʃ/ *adj* comfortable, expensive, and of good quality: *a large plush office*

'plus sign also **plus** *n* [C] the sign (+), used to show that two or more numbers or amounts are added together

Pluto /'pluːtəʊ $ -toʊ/ *n* the small PLANET that is furthest from the sun

plutonium /pluː'təʊniəm $ -'toʊ-/ *n* [U] a metal used to produce NUCLEAR power

ply /plaɪ/ *v* **plied, plying, plies ply your trade** *literary* to do your usual work, especially by trying to sell things to people
ply sb with sth *phr v* to give someone large amounts of food or drink

plywood /'plaɪwʊd/ *n* [U] a material made from several thin layers of wood stuck together

p.m. also **pm** *BrE* /ˌpiː 'em/ used after numbers expressing time, to show that it is between NOON and MIDNIGHT [➔ **am**]: *I leave work at 5.30 p.m.*

PM /ˌpiː 'em/ *n* [C] *BrE informal* the PRIME MINISTER

PMS /ˌpiː em 'es/ also **PMT** *BrE* /ˌpiː em 'tiː/ *n* [U] **premenstrual syndrome/tension** the unpleasant physical and emotional feelings that many women have before their PERIOD

pneumatic /njuː'mætɪk $ nʊ-/ *adj* **1** *technical* filled with air: *a pneumatic tyre* **2** worked by air pressure: *a pneumatic drill*

pneumonia /njuː'məʊniə $ nʊ'moʊ-/ *n* [U] a serious disease of the lungs

poach /pəʊtʃ $ poʊtʃ/ *v* **1** [T] to cook food, especially eggs, in gently boiling liquid **2** [I,T] to illegally catch or hunt animals or fish on someone else's private land **3** [T] to take and use someone else's ideas unfairly or illegally

poacher /'pəʊtʃə $ 'poʊtʃər/ *n* [C] someone who illegally catches or hunts animals or fish on private land

PO Box /ˌpiː əʊ bɒks $ -oʊ bɑːks/ *n* [C] **Post Office Box** used before a number as an address at a post office where letters to you can be sent: *Write to PO Box 714, Accra, Ghana.*

pocket¹ /'pɒkɪt $ 'pɑː-/ *n* [C]

1 a small cloth bag sewn into or onto a piece of clothing, that you put your money, keys etc in: **shirt/trouser etc pocket** *There's some money in my jacket pocket.* | *Luke came in with his hands in his pockets.*

2 a small bag or piece of material fastened to something so that you can put things into it: *Please read the air safety card in the pocket of the seat in front.*

3 the amount of money that you have to spend: *There are eight hotels, with a price range to suit every pocket.* | **from/out of/into your own pocket** *He had to pay for the repairs out of his own pocket.*

4 a small area or amount of something that is

different from what surrounds it: **+of** *pockets of resistance* | *pockets of air*

5 out of pocket if you are out of pocket, you have less money than usual because you have made a mistake or been unlucky
➔ **pick sb's pocket** at PICK¹

pocket² *v* [T] **1** to put something in your pocket: *He locked the door and pocketed the keys.* **2** to get an amount of money, especially in a way that is illegal or seems very easy: *Baines pocketed $2,500 in prize money.*

pocket³ also **'pocket-sized** *adj* small enough to fit in a pocket: *a pocket calculator*

pocketbook /'pɒkɪtbʊk $ 'pɑː-/ *n* [C] *AmE old-fashioned* a HANDBAG or WALLET

pocketful /'pɒkɪtfʊl $ 'pɑː-/ *n* [C] the amount that can fit in a pocket: **+of** *a pocketful of coins*

'pocket knife *n* [C] a small knife with a blade that you can fold into its handle

'pocket ˌmoney *n* [U] *BrE* a small amount of money that parents give regularly to their children, usually every week or month [= **allowance** *AmE*]: *How much pocket money do you get?*

pockmarked /'pɒkmɑːkt $ 'pɑːkmɑːrkt/ *adj* covered with hollow marks or holes

pod /pɒd $ pɑːd/ *n* [C] the long green part of plants such as beans and PEAS which the seeds grow in: *a pea pod*

podiatrist /pə'daɪətrɪst/ *n* [C] *AmE* a doctor who takes care of people's feet and treats foot diseases [= **chiropodist** *BrE*] —**podiatry** *n* [U]

podium /'pəʊdiəm $ 'poʊ-/ *n* [C] a small raised area for a performer, speaker etc to stand on, sometimes with a high surface to put a book or notes on

poem /'pəʊɪm $ 'poʊ-/ *n* [C] a piece of writing that is written in short lines, especially using words that RHYME (=have similar sounds at the end) [➔ **poetry**]: *a famous poem by Wordsworth*

poet /'pəʊɪt $ 'poʊ-/ *n* [C] someone who writes poems [➔ **poetry**]

poetic /pəʊ'etɪk $ poʊ-/ *adj* relating to poetry or typical of poetry: *poetic language* —**poetically** /-kli/ *adv*

po,etic 'justice *n* [U] a situation in which someone suffers, and you think they deserve it because they did something bad

po,etic 'licence *BrE*; **poetic license** *AmE n* [U] the freedom that poets and other artists have to change facts because what they are making is poetry or art

poetry /'pəʊɪtri $ 'poʊ-/ *n* [U] poems in general, or the art of writing poems [➔ **poet, prose**]: *Shelley's poetry* | *a poetry class* | *a poetry reading* (=when someone reads poetry to an audience)

poignant /'pɔɪnjənt/ *adj* making you have strong feelings of sadness or sympathy: *a poignant scene near the end of the film* —**poignancy** *n* [U] —**poignantly** *adv*

point¹ /pɔɪnt/ *n*

1 [C] a single fact, idea, or opinion that is part of an argument or discussion: *I'd like to **make** one final point before I stop.* | *That's a **good point**.* | *'Have you spoken to Alan?' '**That's a point** (=a good thing to mention)! I completely forgot to tell him.'* | *You **have a point** there* (=I agree with your idea or opinion). | *I can **see your point** (=I understand it) and I agree with you.*

2 the point the most important fact, idea, or part of a situation: *The point is we just don't have enough money.* | *I wish she'd hurry up and get to the point* (=talk about the most important thing). | **that's not/beside the point** (=that's not really important) *'But I gave you the money back.' 'That's not the point; you shouldn't have taken it.'*

3 also **the point** [U] the purpose or reason for doing something: **+of** *What's the point of this meeting anyway?* | *The whole point of travelling is to experience new things.* | **There's no point in** going now – we're already too late.

4 [C] a particular position or place: *the point where two lines cross each other* | *Dover is a major point of entry into Britain.* → see box at **PLACE**

5 [C] a time or part of a process when something happens: *At that point I began to get seriously worried.* | *I will probably sell the car at some point in the future.* | **high/low point** (=the best or worst part of something) *the high point of his career* | **reach/get to a point** *It got to the point where we both wanted a divorce.*

6 [C] a particular quality, ability, or feature that someone or something has: **sb's/sth's good/bad points** *He has his good points.* | *The low price was one of its selling points* (=features that will help to sell it). | *Driving is not one of my strong points.*

7 [C] a unit used for showing the score in a game or competition: *He is now only three points behind the leader.* | **score/lose a point** *You lose a point if you do not finish on time.*

8 [C] the sharp end of something: *the point of a needle*

9 boiling/freezing/melting point the temperature at which something boils, freezes, or melts: *Heat the water until it reaches boiling point.*

10 to the point of sth so much that something almost happens or is almost true: *The bird has been hunted to the point of extinction.*

11 up to a point partly, but not completely: *He's right, but only up to a point.*

12 make a point of doing sth to do something deliberately, even when it involves making a special effort: *I always make a point of being early.*

13 in point of fact *formal* used when emphasizing, correcting, or adding something: *They said that the prisoner was being well treated. In point of fact, he looked sick and hungry.*

14 to the point mentioning only the most important things: *Her next letter was short and to the point.*

15 be on the point of (doing) sth to be going to do something very soon, when something happens: *I was just on the point of leaving for work when the phone rang.*

16 the point of no return the time when it becomes impossible to stop something from happening: *I knew that we had passed the point of no return.*

17 [C] a mark or measure on a scale: *Stocks were down 12 points today at 4,298.*

18 [C] the sign (.) used for separating a whole number from the DECIMALS that follow it

19 the points of the compass directions such as north, south, east, and west

20 [C] a long thin piece of land that stretches out into the sea

21 [C] a very small spot: *a tiny point of light*

→ **BREAKING POINT, DECIMAL POINT, POINT OF VIEW, STARTING POINT, TURNING POINT**

point² v

1 [I,T] to show something to someone by holding up one of your fingers or a thin object towards it: **+to/at/towards etc** *John pointed to a chair. 'Please sit down.'* | *'That's my car,' she said, pointing at a white Ford.* | *He pointed his finger at me.* → see picture on page A10

2 [T] to hold something so that it is aimed towards a person or thing: **point sth at sth** *He pointed a gun at the old man's head.*

3 [I] to face or be aimed in a particular direction: **+to/towards/at etc** *Hold the bat so that your fingers point towards the end.* | *The hands of the clock pointed to one o'clock.*

4 [T] to show someone which direction to go: *There should be signs pointing the way to her house.*

5 point the/a finger at sb *informal* to blame someone [= accuse]: *I knew that they would point the finger at me.*

point sth ⇔ out *phr v* **1** to tell someone something that they did not already know or had not thought about: *He was always keen to point out my mistakes.* | **+that** *He pointed out that we did not have enough money to buy the house.* | **+to** *Thank you for pointing this out to me.* → see box at **SAY** **2** to show a person or thing clearly to someone by pointing at them: **+to** *I'll point him out to you next time we see him.*

point to sb/sth *phr v* to show that something is probably true: *The study points to stress as a cause of heart disease.*

point-'blank *adj, adv* **1** if you say something point-blank, you say it in a direct way and without explaining your reasons: *She refused point-blank to help.* **2 at point-blank range** from an extremely close position: *The victim was shot at point-blank range.*

pointed /'pɔɪntɪd/ *adj*

1 a pointed object has a point at the end: *pointed teeth*

2 criticizing in an indirect way: *a pointed remark*

pointedly /'pɔɪntɪdli/ *adv* in a way that shows clearly that you disapprove of something or that you are annoyed: *She pointedly ignored him.*

pointer /'pɔɪntə $ -ər/ *n* [C] **1** a useful piece of advice or information that helps you to do or understand something [= tip]: **+on** *Ruth can give you a few pointers on using the equipment.* **2** a small symbol such as an ARROW that you use to point to a place, for example on a computer screen

pointless /'pɔɪntləs/ *adj* without any useful purpose or effect: *a pointless argument* | *It is pointless trying to explain it to him.*

point of 'view *n* [C] plural **points of view**
1 one way of thinking about a situation: *From a financial point of view, this is a good idea.*
2 someone's personal opinion or attitude in a situation: *Try to see it from my point of view.* → see box at **OPINION**

pointy /'pɔɪnti/ *adj informal* a pointy object has a point at the end

poise /pɔɪz/ n [U] **1** calm, confident behaviour: *She showed great poise in an awkward situation.* **2** a graceful way of moving or standing: *the poise of a ballet dancer*

poised /pɔɪzd/ adj **1** ready to do something or to move soon: *The army was poised to attack.* **2** behaving in a calm, confident way

poison[1] /ˈpɔɪzən/ n [C,U] a substance that can kill or harm you if you eat it, drink it etc: *Arsenic is a **deadly poison**.*

poison[2] v [T] **1** to try to kill someone by giving them poison, especially by adding it to their food or drink: *He tried to poison his parents.* | *She killed him by poisoning his tea.* **2** to make water, air, land etc dangerous by adding harmful chemicals to it: *Pesticides are poisoning our rivers.* **3** to have a very harmful and unpleasant effect on something: *The quarrel had poisoned their relationship.* | *He tried to **poison** their **minds against** their mother.* —**poisoned** adj —**poisoner** n [C]

poisoning /ˈpɔɪzənɪŋ/ n [C,U] an illness that is caused by swallowing, touching, or breathing a poisonous substance: *lead poisoning*

poisonous /ˈpɔɪzənəs/ adj **1** containing poison or producing poison: *Many household chemicals are poisonous.* | *a poisonous snake* **2** full of very unpleasant and unfriendly feelings: *the poisonous atmosphere in the office*

poke /pəʊk $ poʊk/ v **1** [I,T] to push your finger or an object into something: *Stop poking me!* | **+at** *He poked at the ground with a stick.* → see box at **PUSH** → see picture on page A10 **2** [T] to push something through a space or opening: **poke sth into/through/out of etc sth** *Dave poked his head around the door.* **3** [I] to appear through a hole or opening: **+up/through/out etc** *Weeds poked through cracks in the ground.* **4 poke fun at sb/sth** to joke about someone in an unkind way —**poke** n [C] → **poke your nose into sth** at **NOSE**[1]

poker /ˈpəʊkə $ ˈpoʊkər/ n **1** [U] a card game that people usually play for money **2** [C] a metal stick used for moving coal or wood in a fire

poker-'faced adj showing no expression or emotion on your face

poky, pokey /ˈpəʊki $ ˈpoʊ-/ adj BrE informal disapproving a poky place is too small: *a poky apartment* → see box at **SMALL**

polar /ˈpəʊlə $ ˈpoʊlər/ adj relating to the North or South Pole: *polar ice caps*

,polar 'bear / $ ˈ.. ./ n [C] a large white bear that lives near the North Pole

polarize also **-ise** BrE /ˈpəʊləraɪz $ ˈpoʊ-/ v [I,T] formal to make people divide into two groups with completely opposite opinions: *The war polarized public opinion.* —**polarization** /ˌpəʊləraɪˈzeɪʃən $ ˌpoʊlərə-/ n [U]

Polaroid /ˈpəʊlərɔɪd $ ˈpoʊ-/ n [C,U] trademark a camera that uses a special film to produce a photograph very quickly, or a picture taken using this camera

pole /pəʊl $ poʊl/ n [C]

1 a long piece of wood or metal: *tent poles*

2 North/South Pole the most northern and southern point on Earth: *an expedition to the North Pole*

3 be poles apart to be completely different: *Their political views are poles apart.* → **TELEGRAPH POLE**

polemic /pəˈlemɪk/ n [C,U] strong arguments that criticize or defend an idea —**polemical** adj

'pole vault n **the pole vault** a sport in which you jump over a high bar using a special long pole

police[1] /pəˈliːs/ n [plural]

1 the police the official organization whose job is to catch criminals and make sure that people obey the law: *The police are looking for him.* | *If you see anything suspicious, **call the police**.* | *She **reported** the incident **to the police**.* | *a police car*

2 members of the police: *Police surrounded the building.* | *Several police were hurt.* → **SECRET POLICE**

police[2] v [T] to make sure that laws or rules are obeyed in an area or activity: *an agency that polices the nuclear power industry*

po,lice 'constable n [C] BrE formal abbreviation *PC* a police officer of the lowest rank

po'lice de,partment n [C] AmE the official police organization in an area or city

po'lice force n [C] the official police organization in a country or area

policeman /pəˈliːsmən/ n [C] plural **policemen** /-mən/ a male police officer

po'lice ,officer n [C] a member of the police

po'lice state n [C] disapproving a country where the government strictly controls people's freedom, for example to travel or to talk about politics → see box at **GOVERNMENT**

po'lice ,station n [C] a local office of the police

policewoman /pəˈliːsˌwʊmən/ n [C] plural **policewomen** /-ˌwɪmɪn/ a female police officer

policy /ˈpɒlɪsi $ ˈpɑː-/ plural **policies** n

1 [C,U] a way of dealing with something, especially one that has been officially decided by a political party or an organization: **foreign/economic/social etc policy** *a foreign policy adviser to the government* | **+on** *What is the school's policy on bullying?* | *The company operates a strict no-smoking policy.* | **it is sb's policy to do sth** *It was her policy not to lend money to friends.*

2 [C] a written agreement with an insurance company: *a life insurance policy*

polio /'pəʊliəʊ $ 'poʊlioʊ/ *n* [U] a serious disease that can make you unable to move your muscles

polish[1] /'pɒlɪʃ $ 'pɑː-/ *v* [T] to make something clean and shiny by rubbing it: *Dad polished his glasses.* —**polishing** *n* [U]

polish sth ⇔ **off** *phr v informal* to quickly eat or finish all of something: *Who polished off the pizza?*

polish sth ⇔ **up** *phr v* to improve a skill by practising it: *I need to polish up my French.*

polish[2] *n* **1** [C,U] a substance used for polishing things: *shoe polish* **2** [singular] if you give something a polish, you polish it → NAIL POLISH

polished /'pɒlɪʃt $ 'pɑː-/ *adj* **1** shiny because of being rubbed with polish: *polished shoes* **2** done with a lot of skill and with no mistakes: *a polished performance*

polite /pə'laɪt/ *adj* speaking or behaving in a way that shows respect for other people [≠ impolite, rude]: *He was always very polite.* | *a polite question* | *It is polite to cover your mouth when you yawn.* —**politely** *adv*: *'It's very nice,' she said politely.* —**politeness** *n* [U]

political /pə'lɪtɪkəl/ *adj*
1 relating to the government, politics, and public affairs of a country: *a time of great political change* | *The US has two main political parties.* | *People want a new political system.*
2 interested in or involved in politics: *I'm not very political.* —**politically** /-kli/ *adv*

po,litical a'sylum *n* [U] the right to stay in another country because the political situation in your own country makes it dangerous for you to live there

po,litically cor'rect *adj* abbreviation PC politically correct language or behaviour is carefully chosen so that it does not offend or insult anyone —**political correctness** *n* [U]

po,litical 'prisoner *n* [C] someone who is put in prison because of their political activities or opinions

politician /,pɒlɪ'tɪʃən $,pɑː-/ *n* [C] someone who works in politics, especially someone who is elected → see box at GOVERNMENT

politicize also **-ise** *BrE* /pə'lɪtɪsaɪz/ *v* [T] to involve politics in a situation, or to make a person more involved in politics: *He does not believe in politicizing sport.* —**politicized** *adj*

politics /'pɒlɪtɪks $ 'pɑː-/ *n*
1 [U also + plural verb *BrE*] ideas and activities relating to how a place is governed and who has power [→ political, politician]: *Are you interested in politics?* | *modern American politics* | *Politics have always interested Anita.*
2 [U] the job of being a politician: *She retired from politics at the age of 70.*
3 [plural] the activities of people in a group who are trying to get advantages for themselves: *I try not to get involved with office politics.*
4 [plural] someone's political beliefs: *Anna's politics are pretty left-wing.*

polka /'pɒlkə, 'pəʊlkə $ 'poʊlkə/ *n* [C] a kind of dance, or the music for this dance

poll[1] /pəʊl $ poʊl/ *n* [C] **1** the process of finding out what most people think about something by asking a lot of people the same questions [= opinion poll]: *Polls show that most people support the President.* **2 the polls** [plural] the place where you go to vote in an election: *The polls have now closed and the results are being counted.* | *Tomorrow UK voters will go to the polls* (=vote).

poll[2] *v* [T] **1** to try to find out what people think about a subject by asking a lot of people the same questions: *Most of the teachers we polled support the changes.* **2** to get a particular number of votes in an election: *The Conservatives polled 35% of the vote.*

pollen /'pɒlən $ 'pɑː-/ *n* [U] a powder produced by flowers, which is carried by the wind or insects to make other flowers produce seeds

'pollen count *n* [C] a measurement of the amount of pollen in the air

pollinate /'pɒlɪneɪt $ 'pɑː-/ *v* [T] to make a flower produce seeds by giving it pollen —**pollination** /,pɒlɪ'neɪʃən $,pɑː-/ *n* [U]

'polling day *n* [U] *BrE* the day when people vote in an election

'polling ,station *BrE*; **'polling place** *AmE n* [C] the place where you vote in an election

pollster /'pəʊlstə $ 'poʊlstər/ *n* [C] a person or company that carries out POLLS to find out what people think about a subject

pollutant /pə'luːtənt/ *n* [C] a substance that pollutes the air, water etc

pollute /pə'luːt/ *v* [T] to make air, water, soil etc dirty or dangerous: *companies that pollute the environment* | *The beach was polluted by an oil spill.* —**polluter** *n* [C]

polluted /pə'luːtɪd/ *adj* full of pollution: **heavily/seriously/severely polluted** *The rivers are heavily polluted.*

pollution /pə'luːʃən/ *n* [U] damage caused to air, water, soil etc by harmful chemicals and waste: *tough laws to reduce pollution* | *The public are in danger from industrial pollution.* | **air/water pollution** → see box at ENVIRONMENT → NOISE POLLUTION

pollution
the result of pollution

polo /'pəʊləʊ $ 'poʊloʊ/ *n* [U] a game played between two teams riding horses, who hit a small ball with long wooden hammers

'polo neck *n* [C] *BrE* a SWEATER with a high collar that fits closely around your neck and folds over [= turtleneck *AmE*]

poltergeist /'pɒltəgaɪst $ 'poʊltər-/ *n* [C] a GHOST that moves objects around, often noisily

polyester /,pɒliestə, ,pɒli'estə $ 'pɑːliestər/ *n* [U] an artificial material used to make cloth

polyethylene /,pɒli'eθəliːn $,pɑː-/ *n* [U] *AmE* POLYTHENE

polygamy /pə'lɪgəmi/ *n* [U] the custom of having more than one wife or husband at the same time —**polygamous** *adj*

polystyrene /ˌpɒlɪˈstaɪriːn‹ $ ˌpɑː-/ *n* [U] *BrE* a soft light plastic material, used especially to make containers [= **Styrofoam** *AmE*]

polytechnic /ˌpɒlɪˈteknɪk $ ˌpɑː-/ *n* [C] a college in Britain where students could study for a degree, which existed until 1993

polythene /ˈpɒlɪθiːn $ ˈpɑː-/ *n* [U] *BrE* a thin plastic material, used especially to make bags [= **polyethylene** *AmE*]

pomp /pɒmp $ pɑːmp/ *n* [U] *formal* the impressive clothes, decorations, music etc at an important official ceremony

pompous /ˈpɒmpəs $ ˈpɑːm-/ *adj disapproving* someone who is pompous tries to make people think they are important, especially by using formal language: *He's a pompous idiot.* —**pompously** *adv* —**pomposity** /pɒmˈpɒsɨti $ pɑːmˈpɑː-/ *n* [U]

pond /pɒnd $ pɑːnd/ *n* [C] a small area of water, especially one that is made in a field or garden

ponder /ˈpɒndə $ ˈpɑːndər/ *v* [I,T] *formal* to think carefully and seriously about something: *She pondered her answer for a long time.*

ponderous /ˈpɒndərəs $ ˈpɑːn-/ *adj formal*
1 boring and too serious: *a long, ponderous explanation* **2** slow and awkward because of being big and heavy: *an elephant's ponderous walk*

pong /pɒŋ $ pɑːŋ/ *n* [C] *BrE informal* an unpleasant smell → see box at **SMELL** —**pong** *v* [I]

pontificate /pɒnˈtɪfɨkeɪt $ pɑːn-/ *v* [I] *disapproving* to give your opinion about something in a way that shows you think you are always right: *She's always pontificating about moral values.*

pony /ˈpəʊni $ ˈpoʊ-/ *n* [C] plural **ponies** a small horse

ponytail /ˈpəʊniteɪl $ ˈpoʊ-/ *n* [C] hair tied at the back of your head so that it hangs down like a horse's tail: *She had her hair in a ponytail.* → see picture at **HAIR**

poodle /ˈpuːdl/ *n* [C] a type of dog with thick curly hair → see picture at **DOG**[1]

pooh-pooh /ˌpuː ˈpuː/ *v* [T] *informal* to say that you think an idea is silly or useless: *He pooh-poohs everything I say.*

pool[1] /puːl/ *n*
1 [C] a place that has been made for people to swim in [= **swimming pool**]: *Does the hotel have a pool?*
2 [U] a game in which you use a long stick to hit balls into holes at the edge of a table
3 [C] a small area of water or another liquid on a surface: *Pools had formed among the rocks.* | **pool of water/blood/oil etc** *She was lying in a pool of blood.*
4 [C] a quantity of money or things that is available for a group of people to use: *the company car pool*
5 the pools a game in Britain in which people try to win money by guessing the results of football games

pool[2] *v* [T] if people pool their money, knowledge etc, they combine it so that they can all use it: *a meeting to pool ideas*

poor /pɔː $ pʊr/ *adj*
1 a) someone who is poor has very little money and not many possessions [≠ **rich**]: *Her family were very poor.* | *a poor country* **b) the poor** people who are poor: *a charity that helps the poor*

2 not as good as it should be or could be: *Her health is poor.* | **poor quality/standard** *The work was of a very poor standard.* | *the team's poor performance*
3 [only before noun] *spoken* used to show that you feel sorry for someone: *Poor Kate was sick.* | *Oh, you poor thing!*
4 not good at doing something: *a poor swimmer* | **+at** *He's always been poor at languages.*

poorly[1] /ˈpɔːli $ ˈpʊrli/ *adv* badly: *a poorly paid job*

poorly[2] *adj BrE informal* ill: *I felt poorly.*

pop[1] /pɒp $ pɑːp/ *v* **popped, popping 1** [I] to suddenly come off or out of something: **+off/out/up etc** *The button popped off my skirt.* | **out/up popped sth** *The egg cracked and out popped a chick.* **2** [I] *spoken* to go somewhere for a short time: **+in/out/along etc** *I'm just popping out to get a newspaper.* | *Pop round and see me later.* **3** [T] *BrE spoken* to put something somewhere: **pop sth in/on/into etc sth** *I'll just pop the chicken in the oven.* **4** [I,T] to make a sound like a small explosion, for example by bursting: *A balloon popped.* **5** [I] if your ears pop, you feel the pressure in them suddenly change, for example when you go up or down in a plane **6 sb's eyes pop (out)** *informal* used to say that someone looks very surprised and excited **7 sth pops into your mind/head** used to say that you suddenly think of something

  pop up *phr v* to appear suddenly or unexpectedly: *Click here, and a list of options pops up.*

pop[2] *n* **1** also **'pop ,music** [U] modern music that is popular with young people: *Their music is a mixture of jazz and pop.* | **pop group/singer/concert etc** *Which pop bands do you like?* → see box at **MUSIC** **2** [C] a sudden short sound like a small explosion: *The balloon went pop* (=burst with a pop). **3** [U] *informal* a sweet drink with bubbles in it [= **soda** *AmE*]

popcorn /ˈpɒpkɔːn $ ˈpɑːpkɔːrn/ *n* [U] corn that is heated until it swells. You eat it with salt or sugar. → see picture on page A5

Pope /pəʊp $ poʊp/ *n* [C] the leader of the Roman Catholic Church: *the Pope's recent visit* | *Pope John Paul II*

poppy /ˈpɒpi $ ˈpɑː-/ *n* [C] plural **poppies** a bright red flower with small black seeds

Popsicle /ˈpɒpsɨkəl $ ˈpɑːp-/ *n* [C] *AmE* trademark frozen fruit juice on a stick

populace /ˈpɒpjɨləs $ ˈpɑː-/ *n* **the populace** *formal* the ordinary people of a country

popular /ˈpɒpjʊlə $ ˈpɑːpjʊlər/ *adj*

1 liked by a lot of people [≠ **unpopular**]: *Is Ben popular at school?* | *the most popular team in the country* | **+with** *a cafe popular with teenagers* | *a hugely popular novel*

THESAURUS

bestseller – a book that a lot of people buy
blockbuster – a film that a lot of people watch, especially an exciting film
hit – a record, song, or play that a lot of people buy or pay to watch
craze/fad – a fashion, game etc that is very popular for a short time
cult – a film, group of musicians etc that has become very popular among a group of people: *a cult TV programme*

2 popular belief/opinion/view etc a belief etc that a lot of people have: *The government cannot ignore popular opinion.* | **Contrary to popular belief,** *many cats dislike milk.*

3 for ordinary people: *the popular press* | *She knows nothing about popular culture* (=TV, pop music etc).

popularity /ˌpɒpjʊˈlærəti $ ˌpɑː-/ *n* [U] when someone or something is liked by a lot of people: *The popularity of the Internet has grown dramatically.*

popularize also **-ise** *BrE* /ˈpɒpjʊləraɪz $ ˈpɑː-/ *v* [T] to make something known and liked or understood by a lot of people: *He popularized reggae music.*

popularly /ˈpɒpjʊləli $ ˈpɑːpjʊlər-/ *adv* **popularly believed/called/known etc** believed, called something etc by many people: *It's popularly believed that people need eight hours sleep a night.*

populate /ˈpɒpjʊleɪt $ ˈpɑː-/ *v* **be populated** if an area is populated by a group of people, they live there: *a region populated mainly by farmers* | **densely/heavily populated** (=a lot of people live there) | **sparsely/thinly populated** (=very few people live there)

population /ˌpɒpjʊˈleɪʃən $ ˌpɑː-/ *n* [C]

1 the number of people living in an area, a country etc: **+of** *What's the population of Tokyo?* | *India has a population of over 1 billion.* | **population growth/density** *a declining rate of population growth*

2 all of the people who live in an area: *Most of the world's population live in poverty.* | **the male/adult/Jewish etc population** (=people in an area who are male, adult etc) *Only 30% of the male population have jobs.*

populist /ˈpɒpjʊlɪst $ ˈpɑː-/ *adj* relating to or representing ordinary people, rather than rich or very highly educated people: *a populist campaign* —**populist** *n* [C]

populous /ˈpɒpjʊləs $ ˈpɑː-/ *adj formal* a populous area has a large population: *the most populous part of Germany*

porcelain /ˈpɔːslɪn $ ˈpɔːrsələn/ *n* [U] a hard white substance made by baking clay: *a priceless porcelain vase*

porch /pɔːtʃ $ pɔːrtʃ/ *n* [C] **1** *BrE* an entrance covered by a roof built onto a house or church **2** *AmE* a structure built onto the front or back of a house, with a floor and roof but no walls

porcupine /ˈpɔːkjʊpaɪn $ ˈpɔːr-/ *n* [C] an animal with long pointed parts on its back and sides

pore¹ /pɔː $ pɔːr/ *n* [C] one of the small holes in your skin that SWEAT can pass through

pore² *v*

pore over sth *phr v* to read or look at something very carefully for a long time: *I spent days poring over old photos.* → see box at **READ**

pork /pɔːk $ pɔːrk/ *n* [U] meat from pigs: *roast pork* | *pork chops* → see box at **MEAT**

pornography /pɔːˈnɒgrəfi $ pɔːrˈnɑːg-/ also **porn** /pɔːn $ pɔːrn/ *n* [U] magazines, films etc that are intended to make people feel sexually excited —**pornographic** /ˌpɔːnəˈgræfɪk $ ˌpɔːr-/ also **porn** *adj*: *porn videos*

porous /ˈpɔːrəs/ *adj* porous material allows liquid or gas to pass through it slowly: *porous rock*

porpoise /ˈpɔːpəs $ ˈpɔːr-/ *n* [C] a sea animal that looks similar to a DOLPHIN

porridge /ˈpɒrɪdʒ $ ˈpɑː-, ˈpɔː-/ *n* [U] OATS that are cooked in milk or water and eaten hot for breakfast

port /pɔːt $ pɔːrt/ *n*

1 [C,U] a place where ships arrive and leave from: *a fishing port* | **in port** *The ship was back in port.*

2 [U] a strong sweet Portuguese wine

3 [U] the left side of a ship or aircraft when you are looking towards the front [≠ **starboard**]

4 port of call *informal* one of the places that you visit

portable /ˈpɔːtəbəl $ ˈpɔːr-/ *adj* easy to carry: *a portable television* —**portable** *n* [C]

portal /ˈpɔːtl $ ˈpɔːrtl/ *n* [C] a website that helps you find other websites

porter /ˈpɔːtə $ ˈpɔːrtər/ *n* [C] someone whose job is to carry bags at airports, stations, hotels etc

portfolio /pɔːtˈfəʊliəʊ $ pɔːrtˈfoʊlioʊ/ *n* [C] plural **portfolios** a set of pictures that an artist, photographer etc uses as examples of his or her work

portable

portable TV

porthole /ˈpɔːthəʊl $ ˈpɔːrthoʊl/ *n* [C] a small round window in a ship

portion /ˈpɔːʃən $ ˈpɔːr-/ *n* [C] **1** a part of something: **+of** *The return portion of the plane ticket can be used at any time.* | **large/substantial/significant portion** *A large portion of the money has been spent on advertising.* **2** an amount of food for one person: **+of** *a small portion of icecream*

portly /ˈpɔːtli $ ˈpɔːr-/ *adj* fat

portrait /ˈpɔːtrət $ ˈpɔːr-/ *n* [C] **1** a painting, drawing, or photograph of a person: **+of** *a portrait of a young woman* → see box at **PICTURE** → see picture at **PAINTING** **2** a description of someone or something in a book, film etc: **+of** *The novel is a portrait of life in Harlem in the 1940s.*

portray /pɔːˈtreɪ $ pɔːr-/ *v* [T] **1** to describe or show something or someone in a story, film etc: *a film that portrays the life of Charlie Chaplin* |

portray sb/sth as sth *The incident was portrayed as a defeat for the President.* **2** to act the part of a character in a play, film etc [= **play**]: *In 'Out of It' he portrayed a high-school football hero.* —**portrayal** n [C,U]

pose¹ /pəʊz $ poʊz/ v **1 pose a threat/problem/risk/danger etc** to cause a problem, danger etc: *Officials claim the chemical poses no threat to health.* **2** [I] to sit or stand in a particular position in order to be photographed or painted: +**for** *The winning team posed for photographs.* **3 pose a question** *formal* to ask a difficult question: *Her book poses several interesting questions about the relationship between mental and physical health.*

pose as sb *phr v* to pretend to be someone else in order to deceive people: *He obtained the drugs by posing as a doctor.*

pose² n **1** [C] the position in which someone stands or sits, especially in a photograph or painting: *She stood in an aggressive pose with one hand on her hip.* **2** [singular] when someone pretends to have a quality or opinion that they do not really have: *He looked confident but she knew it was a pose.*

posh /pɒʃ $ pɑːʃ/ *adj informal* **1** expensive and used by rich people: *a posh hotel* → see box at **EXPENSIVE** **2** *BrE* relating to people from a high social class: *a posh voice*

position¹ /pəˈzɪʃən/ n

1 [C usually singular] the situation that someone is in: **in a position** *He's in a difficult position.* | *changes in the company's financial position* | **be in a position to do sth** (=be able to do something) *I'm afraid I'm not in a position to advise you.*

2 [C] the way someone is standing, sitting, or lying, or the direction that an object is pointing in: **in a position** *Lie in a comfortable position.* | *Make sure the switch is in the 'off' position.*

3 [C] the place where someone or something is, in relation to other things: *The position of the hotel makes it popular with young families.* → see box at **PLACE**

4 [C,U] the place where someone or something should be: **into/in position** *The lid was put into position and screwed down.* | **out of position** *Some of the tiles had slipped out of position.*

5 [C] someone's level or importance in a society or organization: *Women's position in society has changed.* | **position of power/authority** *Voters are in a position of power.*

THESAURUS

senior – used about someone who has an important position: *a senior executive*
chief – used about someone who has the most important or one of the most important positions in a company or organization, used especially in job titles: *the company's chief financial officer*
high-ranking – used about someone who has a high position in an organization such as the police, the army, or the government: *high-ranking military officers*
top – used about someone who is very good, important, or successful in their job: *a top lawyer*
junior – used about someone who does not have an important position: *a junior clerk*

assistant – an assistant manager, director, editor etc has a position just below a manager etc: *the store's assistant manager*

6 [C] the opinion that someone has, especially the opinion of a government or organization: +**on** *the US government's position on global warming* → see box at **OPINION**

7 [C] *formal* a job in a particular organization: *He became president of the club in 1952 and held the position for over 30 years.* | +**of** *Hart will shortly take up the position of marketing director.* → see box at **JOB**

8 [C] the place where you play in relation to other players in a sports team: *'What position do you play?' 'Goalkeeper.'*

9 [C] your place in a race or competition in relation to other people: **(in) 2nd/3rd/4th etc position** *Alesi finished in third position.*

position² v [T] to put something or someone in a particular position: **position sth on/against/above etc sth** *He positioned the hat carefully on his head.* | **position yourself** *Two guards positioned themselves at the door.*

positive /ˈpɒzɪtɪv $ ˈpɑː-/ adj

1 hopeful and confident [≠ **negative**]: *You should try and be more positive.* | **positive attitude/approach** *a positive attitude to life*

2 good or useful [≠ **negative**]: *Reducing stress has a positive effect on health.* | *The school has made a positive contribution to the community.* | *I wanted to do something positive to help him.*

3 expressing support, agreement, or approval [≠ **negative**]: *We've had a positive response to our suggestions.*

4 showing that you definitely want to achieve something: *The situation requires positive action by the government.* | *We're taking positive steps to ensure that it doesn't happen again.*

5 [not before noun] very sure that something is true [= **certain**]: *'Are you sure you don't want a drink?' 'Positive.'* | +**(that)** *I'm absolutely positive I locked the door.*

6 showing that there can be no doubt that something is true: *the first positive evidence that life exists on other planets*

7 a scientific test that is positive shows that a chemical or medical condition is present [≠ **negative**]: *He tested positive for drugs.*

8 *technical* a positive number is higher than zero

9 *technical* having the type of electrical charge that is carried by **PROTONS**

positively /ˈpɒzɪtɪvli $ ˈpɑː-/ adv **1** *spoken* used to emphasize what you are saying, especially when it is surprising: *Some of these diets for losing weight are positively dangerous.* **2** in a way that shows you agree with or approve of something: *Local people have responded positively to the news.* **3** in a way that shows you are thinking about the good parts of a situation rather than the bad parts: *Try and think more positively.*

possess /pəˈzes/ v [T] **1** *formal* to own or have something: *The fire destroyed everything he possessed.* | *She possesses considerable skill.* **2 what possessed you/him etc?** *spoken* used when someone has done something stupid and

you cannot understand why: *What possessed you to ask a question like that?* —**possessor** *n* [C]
possessed /pə'zest/ *adj* controlled by an evil SPIRIT
possession /pə'zeʃən/ *n*
1 [C usually plural] something that you own [= **belongings**]: *Prisoners were allowed no **personal possessions**.* | **treasured/prized possession** (=one that is very important to you) *One of my most treasured possessions is a book my grandfather gave me.* → see box at OWN
2 [U] *formal* when you have or own something: **in sb's possession** *The land remained in the duke's possession for many years.* | **be in possession of sth** *He was found in possession of a stolen car.* | *How did the books **come into your possession**?* | *The court has **taken possession of** the documents.*
possessive /pə'zesɪv/ *adj* **1** wanting someone to love and spend time with you and no one else: *a possessive husband* | **+of/about** *She's very possessive of her children.* **2** not wanting other people to use your things **3** *technical* used in grammar to describe words that show who something belongs to: *'Ours' and 'mine' are possessive pronouns.* —**possessiveness** *n* [U]
possibility /ˌpɒsə'bɪləti $ ˌpɑː-/ *n* plural **possibilities**
1 [C,U] something that may happen or may be true: **+of** *the possibility of an enemy attack* | **+(that)** *She refused to consider the possibility that he was lying to her.* | **a real/distinct/strong possibility** (=something that is likely to happen or be true) *There's a distinct possibility that the victim knew her killer.*
2 [C] one of the things that you could do: *I'm not sure what I want to study but French is one possibility.* | **+of** *We're **exploring the possibilities** of opening a club in the city.*
possible /'pɒsəbəl $ 'pɑː-/ *adj*
1 if something is possible, it can be done [≠ **impossible**]: *Is it possible to get tickets for the game?* | *Computer technology **makes it possible** for many people to work from home.* | *I want to get back by 5 o'clock if possible.* | **as soon/quickly/much etc as possible** (=as soon etc as you can) *Please reply to the invitation as soon as possible.* | **wherever/whenever possible** *Get fresh air and some exercise whenever possible.*
2 something that is possible may happen or may be true, but is not certain: *It's possible that we might be late.* | *There seem to be only two **possible explanations**.* | *the **possible causes** of rising crime*
3 **the best/worst/greatest etc possible** the best, worst etc that can exist or be achieved: *She was determined to get the best possible price for her paintings.*
possibly /'pɒsəbli $ 'pɑː-/ *adv*
1 used to say that something may be true or likely, but you are not sure [= **perhaps, maybe**]: *The journey will take three hours – possibly more.* | *'Are you going to have a picnic?' 'Possibly. It depends on the weather.'*
2 **could/can you possibly** *spoken* used to make a polite request: *Could you possibly open the window for me?*
3 used to emphasize that something is impossible or very surprising: *I couldn't possibly eat all that!* | *How could anyone possibly find out?*

post¹ /pəʊst $ poʊst/ *n*
1 [U] *BrE* the official system for sending letters, packages etc [= **mail**]: **in the post** *The letter's in the post.* | **by post** *He sent it by post.*
2 [U] *BrE* letters or packages that are delivered to your house [= **mail**]: *Is there any post for me?*
3 [C] *formal* a job in a particular organization [→ **position**]: *She has **held the post** (=had the job) since 1999.* | **+of** *She **applied for the post** of senior lecturer.* → see box at JOB
4 [C] an upright piece of wood or metal that is fixed into the ground
5 [C] the place where a soldier or guard stands to do their job
post² *v* [T]

post

1 *BrE* to send a letter or package by post [= **mail**]: *She posted the letter on her way to work.* | **post sth (off) to sb** *Did you remember to post the card to your Dad?*
2 to send someone to a place to work: **post sb to London/Germany etc** *He joined the army and was posted to Corsica.*
3 also **post up** to put a notice about something on a wall or board: *The students' test results were posted on the board.*

posting a letter

4 keep sb posted to regularly tell someone the most recent news about something: *You will keep me posted, won't you?*
post- /pəʊst $ poʊst/ *prefix* after: *the post-election period*
postage /'pəʊstɪdʒ $ 'poʊs-/ *n* [U] the money charged for sending a letter or package by post
postal /'pəʊstl $ 'poʊs-/ *adj* [only before noun] relating to the official system for sending letters, packages etc: *the postal service*
'postal ˌorder *n* [C] *BrE* an official document that you buy at a post office and send to someone so they can exchange it for money
postbox /'pəʊstbɒks $ 'poʊstbɑːks/ *n* [C] *BrE* a box in a public place where you put letters that you want to send [= **mailbox** *AmE*]
postcard /'pəʊstkɑːd $ 'poʊstkɑːrd/ *n* [C] a card that you can send by post without an envelope, often one with a picture on it: **+of** *a postcard of Paris*
postcode /'pəʊstkəʊd $ 'poʊstkoʊd/ *n* [C] *BrE* a group of letters and numbers that you write at the end of an address [= **zip code** *AmE*]
poster /'pəʊstə $ 'poʊstər/ *n* [C] a large notice, picture etc used to advertise something or as a decoration: *She was **putting up posters** in her bedroom.* | **+of** *posters of movie stars*
posterity /pɒ'sterəti $ pɑː-/ *n* [U] the people who will live after you are dead: **for posterity** *I'm saving these pictures for posterity.*
postgraduate /ˌpəʊst'grædʒuət $ ˌpoʊst'grædʒuət/ *n* [C] *BrE* someone who is studying at a university to get a MASTER'S DEGREE or PHD [= **graduate student** *AmE*] —**postgraduate** *adj*
posthumous /'pɒstjəməs $ 'pɑːstʃə-/ *adj* happening after someone's death: *a posthumous collection of his articles* —**posthumously** *adv*

posting /'pəustɪŋ $ 'pous-/ n [C] *especially BrE*
1 a job in a foreign country that your employer sends you to do: **+to** *His first posting was to Jedda.* **2** a message sent to an Internet discussion group

postman /'pəustmən $ 'poust-/ n [C] plural **postmen** /-mən/ *BrE* someone whose job is to collect and deliver letters [= **mailman** *AmE*]

postmark /'pəustmɑːk $ 'poustmɑːrk/ n [C] a mark on an envelope, package etc that shows the place and time it was posted —**postmark** v [T]

post-mortem /,pəust'mɔːtəm $,poust'mɔːr-/ n [C] an official examination of a dead body to discover why the person died

postnatal /,pəust'neɪtl◂ $,poust-/ adj relating to the time after a baby is born: *postnatal care*

'post ,office n [C] a place where you can buy stamps, and send letters and packages

postpone /pəus'pəun $ pous'poun/ v [T] to change the date or time of an event to a later one: *The meeting has been postponed until July.* —**postponement** n [C,U]

postscript /'pəus,skrɪpt $ 'pous-/ n [C] a PS

posture /'pɒstʃə $ 'paːstʃər/ n [C,U] the way that you sit or stand: **good/bad posture** *Bad posture can cause back problems.*

postwar /,pəust'wɔːr◂ $,poust'wɔːr◂/ adj after a war, especially World War II

posy /'pəuzi $ 'pou-/ n [C] plural **posies** a small BUNCH of flowers

pot¹ /pɒt $ paːt/ n [C]
1 a round container, especially one used for cooking or storing food [→ **saucepan, flowerpot, jar**]: *pots and pans* | *a plant growing in a pot* | **+of** *a pot of honey* → see picture at CONTAINER
2 a container used to make tea or coffee. It has a handle, and a tube for pouring: **+of** *I'll make a pot of tea.*
→ MELTING POT

pot² v [T] **potted, potting** to put a plant in a pot filled with soil

potato
mashed potatoes
roast potatoes
fried potatoes
boiled potatoes

potato /pə'teɪtəu $ -tou/ n [C,U] plural **potatoes** a round white vegetable with a brown or pale yellow skin that grows under the ground: **mashed/roast/boiled potato** | **baked/jacket potato** (=cooked with its skin on) | *I'll peel the potatoes.*
→ COUCH POTATO, SWEET POTATO

po'tato chips n [plural] *AmE* very thin pieces of potato cooked in oil and eaten cold [= **crisps** *BrE*]

potent /'pəutənt $ 'pou-/ adj powerful and effective: *potent drugs* | *a potent influence* —**potency** n [U]

potential¹ /pə'tenʃəl/ adj [only before noun] likely to become a particular type of person or thing in the future: **potential customers/buyers/clients etc** *The salesmen were eager to impress potential customers.* | *Potential buyers have expressed interest in the building.* | **potential problem/danger/threat etc** *a potential threat to international peace* —**potentially** adv: *a potentially dangerous situation*

potential² n **1** [singular, U] the possibility that something will develop in a particular way or do something: **+for** *There is still considerable potential for development.* | **+of** *the potential of the Internet to create jobs* **2** [U] abilities or qualities that may make someone or something very successful in the future: **+as** *She was told she had great potential as a singer.* | **achieve/realize your (full) potential** (=become as successful as you can): *She wanted to achieve her full potential in her new job.*

pothole /'pɒthəul $ 'paːthoul/ n [C] a hole in the surface of a road

potholing /'pɒt,həulɪŋ $ 'paːt,houl-/ n [U] the sport of climbing down into CAVES in the ground

potion /'pəuʃən $ 'pou-/ n [C] *literary* a magic drink

,pot 'luck *BrE*; **potluck** *AmE* /,pɒt'lʌk◂ $,paːt-/ n **take pot luck** to choose something without knowing very much about it, and hope that it will be what you want: *We hadn't booked a hotel so we had to take pot luck.*

potted /'pɒtɪd $ 'paː-/ adj [only before noun] **1** a potted plant is grown in a pot indoors **2** **potted history/biography/version** *BrE* a short account of something

potter¹ /'pɒtə $ 'paːtər/ n [C] someone who makes pottery → see box at ART

potter² also **potter around/about** v [I] *BrE* to spend time slowly doing pleasant things: *I was just pottering in the garden.*

pottery /'pɒtəri $ 'paː-/ n [U] **1** pots, dishes etc made out of baked clay **2** the activity of making objects out of baked clay

potty¹ /'pɒti $ 'paːti/ n [C] plural **potties** a container used by very young children as a toilet

potty² adj *BrE informal* crazy or silly

pouch /pautʃ/ n [C] **1** a small leather or cloth bag **2** a pocket of skin that animals such as KANGAROOS carry their babies in → see picture on page A2

poultry /'pəultri $ 'poul-/ n [plural] birds such as chickens and ducks that are kept for their meat and eggs

pounce /paʊns/ v [I]
to suddenly move for-
ward and attack or
catch someone or
something: **+on** *Police
are hunting an
attacker who pounced
on a young woman.*

pounce

pounce on sb/sth
phr v **1** to criticize
someone's mistakes
or ideas quickly and
eagerly **2** to accept
or take something
quickly and eagerly:
*She pounced on the
opportunity to work in
the Paris office.*

pound¹ /paʊnd/ n [C]
1 written abbreviation **lb** a unit for measuring
weight, equal to 16 OUNCES or 453.6 grams: **+of** *a
pound of apples* | *Mary weighs 130 pounds.*
2 the standard unit of money in Britain and
some other countries; £: *The dress cost £50.* | *a
pound coin* | *a ten pound note*

pound² v **1** [I,T] to hit something hard many
times, making a lot of noise: **+on** *She pounded
on the door with both hands.* → see box at KNOCK
2 [I] if your heart pounds, it beats very quickly
3 [I] to walk or run quickly with heavy steps:
+up/along etc *He pounded up the stairs.*

pour /pɔː $ pɔːr/ v
1 [T] to make a liquid flow out of a container:
pour sth into/over etc sth *Pour the milk into a
jug.* | **pour sb sth** *He poured himself a drink.*
2 [I] to flow or come out quickly and in large
amounts: **+out of/from etc** *Tears poured down
her cheeks.* | *Smoke was pouring from the engine.*
→ see picture at FLOW²
3 also **pour down** [I] to rain heavily: *It poured
with rain all afternoon.* → see box at RAIN → and
WEATHER
4 [I] if people or things pour into or out of a
place, a lot of them arrive or leave at the same
time: **+in/out of** *Letters of complaint poured in.*
pour sth ⇔ out *phr v* to tell someone all your
unhappy thoughts or feelings: *Sonia poured out
her grief in a letter to her sister.* | *I ended up
pouring my heart out to a stranger.*

pout /paʊt/ v [I] to push out your lower lip
because you are annoyed, or in order to look
sexually attractive —**pout** n [C]

poverty /ˈpɒvəti $ ˈpɑːvərti/ n [U] **1** when
people are extremely poor: *Poverty and unem-
ployment are increasing.* | **in poverty** *families
living in extreme poverty* **2** **the poverty line**
also **the poverty level** *AmE* the income below
which someone is officially considered to be
very poor and in need of help

'poverty line n **the poverty line** the lowest
level of income that is considered acceptable:
*60% of the population were living below the
poverty line.*

'poverty-,stricken adj extremely poor → see
box at POOR

POW /ˌpiː əʊ ˈdʌbəljuː $ -oʊ-/ n [C] a PRISONER OF
WAR

powder¹ /ˈpaʊdə $ -ər/ n [C,U] a dry substance
in the form of very small grains: *soap powder* |
curry powder
→ TALCUM POWDER, WASHING POWDER —**powdery** adj:
powdery snow

powder² v [T] to put powder on your skin,
usually in order to make it look better

powdered /ˈpaʊdəd $ -ərd/ adj in the form of
powder: *powdered milk*

power¹ /ˈpaʊə $ paʊr/ n
1 [U] the ability to control people or events [➡
powerful, powerless]: *the power of the media* |
+over *People want to feel they have some power
over their future.* | **political/economic power**
Workers had little political power.
2 [U] the position of having political control of a
country: **in power** *The Socialist Party were in
power for five years.* | *De Gaulle came to power*
(=began to control his country) *in 1958.* | **power
base** (=an area or group of people whose support makes a politician or leader powerful) *His
strongest power base was in the northern state of
Havana.*
3 [C,U] the legal right or authority to do something: **power to do sth** *The police have the
power to stop and search people.* | **be in/within
sb's power** (=be legally possible for someone)
*It's within the power of the council to make this
payment.* | *The ambassador promised to **do
everything in** his **power** to get the hostages
released.*
4 [U] energy that is used to make a machine
work or produce light, heat etc: *nuclear power* |
wind power | **power failure/cut** (=a time when
the supply of electricity stops) *The storm caused
a power cut.*
5 [C] a country that has a lot of influence over
other countries: *a meeting of world powers*
6 [U] force or physical strength: *the power of the
explosion*
7 [C,U] a natural or special ability to do something: *After the accident he lost the **power of
speech** (=ability to speak).* | **powers of
observation/concentration/persuasion** *Her
powers of concentration were not helped by the
noise.*
8 **the powers that be** the people who have
positions of authority
→ BALANCE OF POWER, WORLD POWER

power² v [T] to supply power to a machine: *The
camera is powered by a small battery.* | **battery-
powered/solar-powered etc** (=made to work
by a particular type of power)

'power ,broker n [C] a person or country that
has a lot of political influence and power

powerful /ˈpaʊəfəl $ ˈpaʊr-/ adj
1 able to control and influence people and
events [≠ **powerless**]: *the most powerful man in
Hollywood* | *rich and powerful nations*
2 having a lot of physical power, strength, or
force: *The engine is extremely powerful.* | *power-
ful weapons* | *a powerful voice*
3 having a strong effect: *a powerful argument* | *a
powerful influence* | *powerful drugs*
—**powerfully** adv

powerless /ˈpaʊələs $ ˈpaʊr-/ adj unable to
stop or control something: **powerless to do sth**
The police were powerless to stop last night's

shootings. | **+against** *Local people were powerless against the rising flood water.* —**powerlessness** *n* [U]

'power ,station also **'power plant** *n* [C] a building where electricity is made

'power tool *n* [C] a tool that works by electricity

pp. also **pp** *BrE* the written abbreviation of **pages**: *Read pp 20–35.*

PR /,pi: 'ɑː $ -'ɑːr/ *n* [U] PUBLIC RELATIONS: *a PR company*

practicable /'præktɪkəbəl/ *adj formal* possible in a particular situation: *It's not practicable to publish all the results.*

practical[1] /'præktɪkəl/ *adj*

1 relating to real situations and events rather than ideas [➡ **theoretical**]: *He's had no practical experience of teaching.* | *the practical problems of old age* | *The charity offers practical help to homeless people.*
2 likely to succeed or be effective [≠ **impractical**]: *A practical solution has to be found.*
3 useful and suitable for a particular purpose [≠ **impractical**]: *Remember to wear practical shoes and warm clothing.*
4 good at planning and making decisions [≠ **impractical**]
5 good at repairing or making things: *I'm not very practical – I can't even change a lightbulb.*

practical[2] *n* [C] *BrE* a lesson or test where you do or make something rather than writing

practicality /,præktɪ'kæləti/ *n* **1 practicalities** [plural] the real facts of a situation, rather than ideas about how it might be: **+of** *the practicalities of the job* **2** [U] how suitable something is, or whether it will be effective: *I'm not sure about the practicality of the idea.*

,practical 'joke *n* [C] a trick that is intended to surprise someone and make other people laugh at them

practically /'præktɪkli/ *adv*

1 almost: **practically all/every/no etc** *That's practically everyone we know!* | *The theatre was practically empty.*
2 in a sensible way

practice /'præktɪs/ *n*

1 [U] **a)** when you do something regularly to improve your skill: *It takes a lot of practice to be a good piano player.* **b)** a regular occasion when people meet to improve their skill at doing something: **football/rugby/choir etc practice**
2 [C,U] something that people do often, especially in a particular way: *dangerous working practices* | **common/standard/normal practice** (=the usual way of doing something) *The use of chemical sprays has become common practice.* | **the practice of doing sth** *the widespread practice of dumping waste in the sea*
3 in practice used to say what really happens, instead of what people think may happen: *It looks difficult to make, but in practice it's quite easy.*
4 [C] the work of a doctor or lawyer, or the place where they work: **private practice** (=the business of a professional person that is independent of a bigger or government-controlled organization) | **legal/medical practice**
5 put sth into practice to start using an idea,

plan etc: *It gave him the chance to put his ideas into practice.*
6 be out of practice to be unable to do something well because you have not done it for a long time: *I'd like to sing with you, but I'm so out of practice.*

practise *BrE*; **practice** *AmE* /'præktɪs/ *v*

1 [I,T] to do something regularly to improve your skill or ability: **practise doing sth** *Today we're going to practise parking.* | **+for** *He's practicing for his driving test.* | **practise sth on sb** *Everyone wants to practise their English on me.*

THESAURUS

train – to practise a physical activity for a race or game
rehearse – to practise a play, speech, or concert

2 [I,T] to work as a doctor or lawyer: *He has been practising law for 15 years.* | **+as** *Gemma is now practising as a dentist.*
3 [T] to use a particular method or custom: *a technique not widely practised in Europe*
4 practise what you preach to do what you always say other people should do

practised *BrE*; **practiced** *AmE* /'præktɪst/ *adj* good at doing something because you have done it many times before: *a practised performer* | **practised in (doing) sth** *He was well practised in giving speeches.*

practising *BrE*; **practicing** *AmE* /'præktɪsɪŋ/ *adj* **practising Catholic/Jew/Muslim etc** someone who follows the rules and customs of a particular religion

practitioner /præk'tɪʃənə $ -ər/ *n* [C] *formal* someone who works as a doctor or lawyer: **medical/legal practitioner** → GENERAL PRACTITIONER

pragmatic /præg'mætɪk/ *adj* dealing with problems in a sensible and practical way rather than following a set of ideas: *a pragmatic approach to education* —**pragmatism** /'prægmətɪzəm/ *n* [U] —**pragmatist** *n* [C]

prairie /'preəri $ 'preri/ *n* [C] a large area of flat land in North America that is covered in grass

praise[1] /preɪz/ *v* [T] to say that someone has done something well or that you admire them [≠ **criticize**]: **praise sb for (doing) sth** *The Mayor praised the rescue team for their courage.* | *a highly praised novel*

THESAURUS

congratulate – to tell someone that you are happy that they have achieved something
flatter – to say nice things about someone, sometimes when you do not really mean it in order to get something from them
compliment also **pay sb a compliment** – to say something nice to someone in order to praise them

praise[2] *n* [U] things you say to praise someone or something: *Most parents are full of praise for the school* (=praise it a lot). | **in praise of sth** *a poem in praise of freedom*

praiseworthy /'preɪzwɜːði $ -ɜːr-/ *adj formal* something that is praiseworthy deserves praise

pram /præm/ *n* [C] *BrE* a thing on wheels that a baby can lie in and be pushed along [= **baby carriage** *AmE*] → see box at BABY

prance /prɑːns $ præns/ v [I] **1** to walk or dance around in a way that makes people notice you: **+around** *He started prancing around in front of the cameras.* **2** if a horse prances, it moves with high steps

prank /præŋk/ n [C] a trick that is intended to make someone look silly: *a childish prank*

prat /præt/ n [C] *BrE informal* a stupid person: *Of course it's not, you prat!*

prattle /'prætl/ v [I] to talk continuously about silly or unimportant things —**prattle** n [U]

prawn /prɔːn $ prɒːn/ n [C] a small pink sea animal that you can eat

pray /preɪ/ v [I,T]
1 to speak to God in order to ask for something or give thanks: **+for** *Let us pray for peace.* | **+to** *He prayed to God for forgiveness.*
2 to hope for something very strongly: **+for** *We're praying for good weather for the wedding.* | **+(that)** *Paul was praying that no one had noticed.*

prayer /preə $ prer/ n
1 [C] words that you say to God: *The children knelt down to say their prayers.* | **+for** *a prayer for the dead* | *a prayer book*
2 [U] when someone prays: *the power of prayer* | **in prayer** *They bowed their heads in prayer.*
3 **prayers** [plural] when people pray together at an arranged time: *morning prayers*

pre- /priː/ *prefix* before: *the prewar period* | *pre-school children*

preach /priːtʃ/ v [I,T] **1** to give a speech about a religious subject, usually in a church: *The pastor preached a sermon on forgiveness.* **2** to try to persuade other people to do, support, or believe something, often in an annoying way: *politicians who preach fairness and equality*

preacher /'priːtʃə $ -ər/ n [C] someone who gives talks at religious meetings

preamble /pri'æmbəl $ 'priːæmbəl/ n [C] *formal* a statement at the beginning of a book or speech, explaining what it is about

prearranged /ˌpriːə'reɪndʒd/ adj planned or decided before: *At a prearranged signal, everyone stood up.*

precarious /prɪ'keəriəs $ -'ker-/ adj **1** a precarious situation may easily or quickly become worse: *The club is in a precarious financial position.* **2** not held in place firmly and likely to fall —**precariously** adv

precaution /prɪ'kɔːʃən $ -'kɒː-/ n [C] something that you do to prevent something bad or dangerous from happening: *fire precautions* | **+against** *precautions against theft* | **as a precaution** *She was taken to hospital as a precaution.* | *I took the precaution of insuring my camera.* —**precautionary** adj: *Residents were evacuated as a precautionary measure.*

precede /prɪ'siːd/ v [T] *formal* to happen or exist before something else [≠ **follow**]: *The fire was preceded by a loud explosion.* —**preceding** adj [only before noun] *an increase of 18% on the preceding year*

precedence /'presɪdəns/ n **take/have precedence (over sth)** to be considered more important or urgent than something else: *This project takes precedence over everything else.*

precedent /'presɪdənt/ n [C,U] an action or official decision that is used as an example for

similar actions or decisions taken in the future: *The trial set a precedent for civil rights.*

precinct /'priːsɪŋkt/ n [C] **1** **shopping/pedestrian precinct** *BrE* an area of a town where cars are not allowed and where people can walk and shop **2** *AmE* a part of a city that has its own police force, local government etc: *the 12th precinct* **3** **precincts** [plural] the area around an important building: *the precincts of the cathedral*

precious¹ /'preʃəs/ adj **1** something that is precious is valuable or important and should not be wasted: **precious seconds/minutes/time etc** *We cannot afford to waste precious time.* | *the planet's precious resources* **2** precious memories or possessions are very important to you because they remind you of people or events in your life: **+to** *I know it's old, but it's very precious to me.* **3** valuable because of being rare: **precious metal** (=a metal such as gold or silver) | **precious stone** (=a jewel such as a diamond or ruby)

precious² adv **precious little/few** *informal* very little or very few: *We had precious little time left.*

precipice /'presɪpɪs/ n [C] a very steep side of a mountain or cliff

precipitate /prɪ'sɪpɪteɪt/ v [T] *formal* to make something happen suddenly: *The President's death precipitated a political crisis.*

precipitation /prɪˌsɪpɪ'teɪʃən/ n [U] *formal* rain or snow

precipitous /prɪ'sɪpɪtəs/ adj *formal* **1** dangerously steep or high: *precipitous cliffs* **2** very sudden: *a precipitous decline in profit*

précis /'preɪsiː $ preɪ'siː/ n [C] plural **précis** *formal* a piece of writing giving only the main ideas of a longer piece of writing, speech etc

precise /prɪ'saɪs/ adj **1** precise information, details etc are exact, clear, and correct: *We don't yet have precise details of the agreement.* **2 to be precise** used to add exact details about something: *It's 9 o'clock, or 9.02 to be precise.* **3** [only before noun] used to emphasize that you are talking about an exact thing: *No one seems to know the precise cause of the illness.* | *At that precise moment, her husband walked in.*

precisely /prɪ'saɪsli/ adv **1** exactly: **+what/how/why etc** *That's precisely what I mean.* | *at precisely 4 o'clock* **2** used to emphasize that something is completely correct or true: *The photos are fascinating precisely because they are of such ordinary situations.* **3** *spoken* used to say that you agree completely with someone: *'So you want them to give it all back.' 'Precisely.'*

precision /prɪ'sɪʒən/ n [U] when something is done in a very exact way: **with precision** *Some animals can find their way in the dark with great precision.*

preclude /prɪ'kluːd/ v [T] *formal* to make it impossible for something to happen: **preclude sb from (doing) sth** *Bad eyesight may preclude you from driving.*

precocious /prɪ'kəʊʃəs $ -'koʊ-/ adj a precocious child shows skill or intelligence at a young age, or behaves in an adult way —**precociously** adv

preconceived /ˌpriːkən'siːvd/ adj [only before noun] preconceived ideas are formed before you know what something is really like: *He has a lot of preconceived ideas about life in America.*

preconception /ˌpriːkənˈsepʃən/ n [C] an idea that is formed before you know what something is really like

precondition /ˌpriːkənˈdɪʃən/ n [C] something that must happen before something else can happen: **+for/of** *An end to the fighting is a precondition for talks.*

precursor /prɪˈkɜːsə $ -ˈkɜːrsər/ n [C] *formal* something that existed or happened before something else and influenced its development: **+of** *a machine that was the precursor of the computer*

predate /priːˈdeɪt/ v [T] to happen or exist before something else: *Many of the changes predate the 1981 reforms.*

predator /ˈpredətə $ -ər/ n [C] an animal that kills and eats other animals

predatory /ˈpredətəri $ -tɔːri/ adj **1** predatory animals kill and eat other animals **2** *disapproving* trying to use someone's weakness to get an advantage for yourself

predecessor /ˈpriːdɪˌsesə $ ˈpredɪˌsesər/ n [C] **1** the person who had a job before the person who has it now: *My predecessor worked here for ten years.* **2** a machine, system etc that existed before another one

predetermined /ˌpriːdɪˈtɜːmɪnd $ -ɜːr-/ adj *formal* already decided or arranged: *Schools cannot exceed a predetermined level of spending.*

predicament /prɪˈdɪkəmənt/ n [C] a difficult situation when you do not know what is the best thing to do: **in a predicament** *Many other young couples are in a similar predicament.*

predicate /ˈpredɪkət/ n [C] the part of a sentence that gives information about the subject. In the sentence 'He ran out of the house', 'ran out of the house' is the predicate. [➡ **subject**]

predicative /prɪˈdɪkətɪv $ ˈpredɪkeɪ-/ adj a predicative adjective comes after a verb and describes the subject, for example 'sad' in 'She is sad' [➡ **attributive**]

predict /prɪˈdɪkt/ v [T] to say that something will happen, before it happens [➡ **prediction**]: *Organisers are predicting a close race.* | **+(that)** *We predict that student numbers will double in the next ten years.* | **+what/how/whether etc** *It's difficult to predict exactly what the effects will be.*

predictable /prɪˈdɪktəbəl/ adj behaving or happening in the way that you expect, and not different or interesting: *an entertaining but predictable film* —**predictably** adv: *Predictably, they rejected the plan.* —**predictability** /prɪˌdɪktəˈbɪləti/ n [U]

prediction /prɪˈdɪkʃən/ n [C,U] when you say what you think will happen in the future: *It's hard to **make** a **prediction** about who'll win the championship this year.* | **+of** *predictions of climate change*

predilection /ˌpriːdɪˈlekʃən $ ˌpredl̩ˈek-/ n [C] *formal* a strong liking for something: **+for** *a predilection for chocolate*

predisposed /ˌpriːdɪsˈpəʊzd $ -ˈpoʊzd/ adj **be predisposed to/towards sth** to be likely to

behave in a particular way or have particular problems: *Some people are predisposed to depression.*

predisposition /ˌpriːdɪspəˈzɪʃən/ n [C] a tendency to behave in a particular way, or to have particular problems: **+to/towards** *a predisposition to violence*

predominance /prɪˈdɒmɪnəns $ -ˈdɑː-/ n **1** [singular] when there is more of one type of thing or person in a group than of any other type: **+of** *the predominance of boys in the class* **2** [U] the most power or importance in a place or situation: *rival supermarkets fighting to achieve predominance*

predominant /prɪˈdɒmɪnənt $ -ˈdɑː-/ adj more powerful or common than other people or things: *In this painting, the predominant colour is black.*

predominantly /prɪˈdɒmɪnəntli $ -ˈdɑː-/ adv mostly or mainly: *a college in a predominantly working class area*

predominate /prɪˈdɒmɪneɪt $ -ˈdɑː-/ v [I] *formal* if something predominates in a group or area, it is more important or more common than other things: *areas where industries such as mining predominate*

pre-eminent /priˈemɪnənt/ adj much more important or powerful than other people or things of the same kind: *a pre-eminent expert in cancer treatment* —**pre-eminence** n [U]

pre-empt /priˈempt/ v [T] to make what someone has planned to do unnecessary or not effective by doing something first: *The deal pre-empted a strike by rail workers.* —**pre-emptive** adj: *a pre-emptive attack*

preen /priːn/ v **1 preen yourself** to spend a lot of time making yourself look attractive: *He's always preening himself in the mirror.* **2** [I,T] if a bird preens, or preens itself, it makes its feathers clean and smooth

pre-existing /ˌpriːɪɡˈzɪstɪŋ◂/ adj existing already, or before something else: *a pre-existing arrangement*

prefabricated /priːˈfæbrɪkeɪtɪd/ adj a prefabricated building is built by putting together large parts which have already been made

preface /ˈprefəs/ n [C] an introduction at the beginning of a book

prefect /ˈpriːfekt/ n [C] *BrE* an older student in a school who has special powers and duties

prefer /prɪˈfɜː $ -ˈfɜːr/ v [T] preferred, preferring **1** to like or want someone or something more than someone or something else [➡ **preference**]: *Would you prefer a hot or a cold drink?* | **prefer sb/sth to sb/sth** *She prefers walking to driving.* | **prefer to do sth** *I'd prefer not to talk about it at the moment.* | **prefer doing sth** *Most kids prefer wearing casual clothes.* | *Or, if you prefer, you can email us.* | **+(that)** *formal: The firm would prefer that the details were not made public.*

2 I would prefer it if *spoken* used to tell someone politely not to do something: *I'd prefer it if you didn't smoke in the house.*

preferable /ˈprefərəbəl/ adj better or more suitable: **+to** *Anything is preferable to war.*

preferably /ˈprefərəbli/ adv used to show which person, thing, place etc would be the best or most suitable: *You'll need some form of identification, preferably a passport.*

preference /'prefərəns/ *n* **1** [C,U] when someone likes something more than something else: *Which style you choose is just a matter of* **personal preference**. | **+for** *Some parents have a* **strong preference** *for one school or another.* | **in preference to sth** *He drinks coffee in preference to tea.* | *You can list up to five choices,* **in order of preference**. **2 give/show preference (to sb)** to treat someone better or give them an advantage over other people: *Preference will be given to candidates who speak foreign languages.*

preferential /ˌprefə'renʃəl◂/ *adj* if you are given preferential treatment, you are treated better than another person, and have an advantage over them: *Why should she get preferential treatment?*

prefix /'priːfɪks/ *n* [C] a group of letters added to the beginning of a word to make a new word [➔ **affix, suffix**]

pregnancy /'pregnənsi/ *n* [C,U] plural **pregnancies** when a woman is pregnant: *You should try to avoid alcohol during pregnancy.* | *a* **pregnancy test**

pregnant /'pregnənt/ *adj*
1 if a woman or female animal is pregnant, she has an unborn baby growing in her body [➔ **pregnancy**]: *a pregnant woman* | *She's three months pregnant.* | *I* **got pregnant** *when I was only 16.* | **+with** *Maria was pregnant with her second child.*
2 pregnant silence/pause a silence or pause which is full of meaning or emotion

preheat /ˌpriː'hiːt/ *v* [T] to heat an oven to a particular temperature before it is used to cook something: *Preheat the oven to 375 degrees.*

prehistoric /ˌpriːhɪ'stɒrɪk◂ $ -'stɔː-, -'stɑː-/ *adj* relating to the time in history before anything was written down: *prehistoric cave drawings*

prejudge /ˌpriː'dʒʌdʒ/ *v* [T] *disapproving* to form an opinion about someone or something before you know or have considered all the facts

prejudice¹ /'predʒədɪs/ *n* [C,U] *disapproving* when people do not like or trust someone because they are of a different race, sex, religion etc: **+against** *There's still a lot of prejudice against gay men in employment.* | *the problem of* **racial prejudice** *in the police force*

prejudice² *v* [T] **1** to influence someone so that they have an unfair opinion about someone or something: **prejudice sb against sth** *I didn't want to say anything that might prejudice him against her.* **2** to have a bad effect on someone's opportunities or chances of success: *Stories in the newspapers are prejudicing their chances of a fair trial.*

prejudiced /'predʒədɪst/ *adj* having an unfair dislike of someone or something, especially because they belong to a particular group: **+against** *He's prejudiced against anyone who doesn't have a degree.*

prejudicial /ˌpredʒə'dɪʃəl◂/ *adj formal* having a bad effect on someone or something

preliminary¹ /prɪ'lɪmɪnəri $ -neri/ *adj* [only before noun] happening before something that is more important, often in order to prepare for

it: *European leaders meet tomorrow for preliminary talks.* | *the* **preliminary stages** *of the competition*

preliminary² *n* [C usually plural] plural **preliminaries** something that is done or said to introduce or prepare for something else later: *the preliminaries of the competition*

prelude /'preljuːd/ *n* **1 be a prelude to sth** to happen just before something else, often as an introduction to it: *The attack may be a prelude to full-scale war.* **2** [C] a short piece of music that comes before a longer musical piece

premature /'premətʃə, -tʃʊə, ˌpremə'tʃʊə $ ˌpriːmə'tʃʊr◂/ *adj* **1** happening too early or before the usual time: *Smoking is one of the major causes of premature death.* **2** a premature baby is born too early and is small or weak: *The baby was six weeks premature.* —**prematurely** *adv*: *The sun causes your skin to age prematurely.*

premeditated /priː'medɪteɪtɪd $ prɪ-/ *adj* a premeditated attack or crime is planned before it happens: *a premeditated murder* —**premeditation** /priːˌmedɪ'teɪʃən $ prɪ-/ *n* [U]

premenstrual /priː'menstruəl/ *adj* happening or relating to the time just before a woman's period (=the time each month when blood flows from her body)

premier¹ /'premiə $ prɪ'mɪr/ *n* [C] the leader of a government: *the Chinese premier*

premier² *adj* [only before noun] best or most important: *one of Dublin's premier hotels* | *football's Premier League*

premiere /'premiə $ prɪ'mɪr/ *n* [C] the first public performance of a film or play: *a movie premiere* —**premiere** *v* [I,T]

premiership /'premiəʃɪp $ prɪ'mɪrʃɪp/ *n* [C,U] the period when someone is the leader of a government

premise /'premɪs/ *n* **1 premises** [plural] the buildings and land that a shop, company etc uses: **on/off the premises** *No smoking is allowed on the premises.* **2** [C] *formal* a statement or idea that you consider to be true and use to develop other ideas: **+that** *The argument is based on the premise that men and women are equal.*

premium¹ /'priːmiəm/ *n* [C] **1** an amount of money that you pay for insurance: *health insurance premiums* **2** an additional amount of money above the usual rate or amount: *The shares are being sold at a premium.* **3 be at a premium** to be difficult to get because there is only a limited amount available: *Parking space is at a premium in most cities.* **4 put/place a premium on sth** to think that one quality or type of thing is much more important than others: *schools that put a premium on exam results*

premium² *adj* **1** of very high quality: *consumer demand for premium products* **2 premium price/rate** premium prices and rates are higher than the usual ones: *premium rate phone calls*

premonition /ˌpremə'nɪʃən, ˌpriː-/ *n* [C] a feeling that something bad is going to happen: **+of/that** *She had a premonition that her daughter was in danger.*

prenatal /ˌpriːˈneɪtl◂ / *adj* prenatal care is the medical care given to a woman who is going to have a baby [= antenatal *BrE*; ➡ postnatal]

preoccupation /priːˌɒkjʊˈpeɪʃən $ -ˌɑːk-/ *n*
1 [singular,U] when you think or worry about something all the time: **+with** *the artist's preoccupation with death* **2** [C] something that you give all your attention to: *Their **main preoccupation** was how to feed their families.*

preoccupied /priːˈɒkjʊpaɪd $ -ˈɑːk-/ *adj* thinking or worrying about something a lot, so that you do not pay attention to other things: **+with** *I was too preoccupied with my own problems to notice.* —**preoccupy** *v* [T]

prep. also **prep** *BrE* the written abbreviation of **preposition**

prepaid /ˌpriːˈpeɪd◂ / *adj* if something is prepaid, it is paid for before it is needed or used: *a prepaid envelope*

preparation /ˌprepəˈreɪʃən/ *n*
1 [U] the work of preparing something or preparing for something: **+for** *The England team have begun their preparation for next week's game.* | **in preparation for sth** *We've had extra training sessions in preparation for the tests.* | **+of** *the preparation of the report*
2 preparations [plural] arrangements for something that is going to happen: **+for** *preparations for the wedding* | *Preparations are being made for the President's visit.* → see box at PREPARE

preparatory /prɪˈpærətəri $ -tɔːri/ *adj* done in order to get ready for something: *a preparatory meeting*

prepare /prɪˈpeə $ -ˈper/ *v*
1 [T] to make something ready to be used: **prepare sth for sth/sb** *Carol was upstairs preparing a room for the guests.*

THESAURUS

get sth ready: *I've been getting everything ready for the party.*
set sth up – to make a piece of equipment ready to be used: *Kim's setting up the computer in the meeting room.*
make preparations – to prepare for an important event: *They spent six months making preparations for the journey.*
It is quite formal to say that someone **prepares** a meal. It is more usual to say that they **make** or **cook** a meal, or that they are **getting a meal ready**: *Bella was making dinner.* | *Shall I get lunch ready?*

2 [I,T] to make plans or arrangements for something that will happen soon, or to get yourself ready for it: **+for** *I haven't even begun to prepare for tomorrow's test.* | **prepare yourself (for sth)** *Prepare yourself for a shock.* | **prepare to do sth** *Just as we were preparing to leave, the phone rang.*
3 [T] to give someone the training or skills that they need to do something: **prepare sb for sth** *The course prepares students for a career in business.*
4 [T] to make a meal or substance: *This dish can be prepared the day before.* | *Anna was in the kitchen preparing vegetables.*
5 [T] to write a document: *The inspector will prepare a report for the minister.*

prepared /prɪˈpeəd $ -ˈperd/ *adj* **1** [not before noun] ready to deal with a situation: **+for** *He wasn't really prepared for all their questions.*
2 be prepared to do sth to be willing to do something, especially something difficult or unpleasant: *You have to be prepared to take risks in this kind of work.* **3** [only before noun] already planned, written etc and ready to be used: *His lawyer read out a **prepared statement**.* —**preparedness** /prɪˈpeədnɪs, -ˈpeərɪd- $ -ˈperɪd-, -ˈperd-/ *n* [U]

preponderance /prɪˈpɒndərəns $ -ˈpɑːn-/ *n* [singular] *formal* when there is more of one type of person or thing in a group than any other: **+of** *There was a preponderance of students in the audience.*

preposition /ˌprepəˈzɪʃən/ *n* [C] a word or phrase used before a noun or PRONOUN to show place, time, direction etc. 'At', 'with', and 'into' are all prepositions.

preposterous /prɪˈpɒstərəs $ -ˈpɑːs-/ *adj* completely unreasonable or silly [= absurd]: *That's a preposterous suggestion!*

'prep school *n* [C,U] **1** a private school in Britain for children between 7 and 13 **2** a private school in the US that prepares students for college

prequel /ˈpriːkwəl/ *n* [C] a book, film etc that tells you what happened before the story told in a previous popular book or film [➡ sequel]

prerequisite /priːˈrekwɪzɪt/ *n* [C] *formal* something that is necessary before another thing can happen or be done: **+for/of/to** *A degree in French is a prerequisite for the job.*

prerogative /prɪˈrɒɡətɪv $ -ˈrɑː-/ *n* [C usually singular] *formal* a special right that someone has: **+of** *Owning a motor car used to be the prerogative of the rich.*

presage /ˈpresɪdʒ, prɪˈseɪdʒ/ *v* [T] *formal* to be a sign that something bad is going to happen: *Heavy clouds presaged the coming of snow.*

'pre-school *adj* relating to the time in a child's life before they are old enough to go to school: *a pre-school playgroup*

preschool /ˈpriːskuːl/ *n* [C] *AmE* a school for children between two and five

prescribe /prɪˈskraɪb/ *v* [T] **1** to say what medicine or treatment an ill person should have: **prescribe sb sth** *The doctor prescribed him tranquilizers.* **2** *formal* to state officially what must be done in a situation: *a punishment prescribed by the law*

prescription /prɪˈskrɪpʃən/ *n* **1** [C] a piece of paper on which a doctor writes what medicine a sick person should have, or the medicine itself: **+for** *a prescription for painkillers* **2 on prescription** *BrE* **by prescription** *AmE* a drug that is only available on prescription can only be obtained with a written order from a doctor [➡ over-the-counter]

prescriptive /prɪˈskrɪptɪv/ *adj formal* saying how something should be done

presence /ˈprezəns/ *n* **1** [singular] when someone or something is somewhere at a particular time, or a group of people who are somewhere at a particular time [≠ absence]: **in sb's presence** *The document should be signed in the presence of a witness.* | **+of** *Tests revealed the presence of drugs in his blood.* | *A heavy **police***

P

presence (=group of police sent to a place to control a situation) *prevented further trouble.*
2 presence of mind the ability to deal with a dangerous or difficult situation quickly and calmly: **have the presence of mind to do sth** *Luckily, she had the presence of mind to phone for an ambulance.* **3 make your presence felt** to have a strong effect on a situation or the people you are with: *Hanley has certainly made his presence felt since joining the company.*

present¹ /'prezənt/ *adj*
1 [not before noun] in a particular place [≠ absent]: **+in/at** *How many people were present at the meeting?*
2 [only before noun] happening or existing now: *This is the best we have* **at the present time.** | *Many people are unhappy with* **the present situation.**
3 the present day the time now, or modern times: *a collection of musical instruments from the sixteenth century to the present day*
4 the present tense the form of a verb that you use to talk about what exists or is happening now

present² /prɪ'zent/ *v* [T] **1** to give something to someone, especially at an official occasion: **present sb with sth** *She was presented with an award by the mayor.* | **present sth to sb** *We will present a cheque for £5000 to the winner.* **2** to give or show information in a particular way: *The evidence was presented to the court by Conor's lawyer.* **3 present yourself** the way you present yourself is the way you look and behave when you meet new people: *She presents herself as willing and efficient.* **4 present a problem/threat etc** to cause a problem, threat etc: *Heavy rain has presented a new difficulty for tournament organisers.* **5** to organize or make a play, film, show, or programme: *The Lyric Theatre is presenting a brand new production of 'Hamlet'.* **6** *especially BrE* to introduce a television or radio programme [= **host** *AmE*]: *Tonight's show will be presented by Jay Williams.* **7** to introduce someone formally to someone else: *May I present my parents, Mr and Mrs Benning.* **8 sth presents itself** if an opportunity or situation presents itself, it suddenly starts to exist: *If the opportunity ever presented itself, I'd love to go and work abroad.*

present³ /'prezənt/ *n*
1 [C] something that you give to someone, for example at Christmas or to say thank you [= **gift**]: *He got the computer as a* **birthday present.** | *He didn't even give me a* **present.**
2 the present the time that is happening now: *Live in the present – don't worry about the past!*
3 at present at this time [= **now**]: *We have no plans at present for closing the factory.* → see box at **NOW**
4 for the present if something is true or happening for the present, it is true now, but may change in the future: *She tried to put it out of her mind, for the present anyway.*

presentable /prɪ'zentəbəl/ *adj* looking clean and tidy enough to be seen by other people: *Do I look presentable?* | *We need to* **make the house presentable.**

presentation /ˌprezən'teɪʃən $ ˌpriːzen-, -zən-/ *n* **1** [C] when someone is given a prize or

present at a formal ceremony: **+of** *the presentation of the awards* | *a presentation ceremony*
2 [C] an event at which someone describes and explains a new product or idea: *The managing director gave a short presentation.* **3** [U] the way something looks because of how it has been arranged: *You need to improve the presentation of your work.*

'present-day *adj* [only before noun] existing now, not in the past: *present-day technology*

presenter /prɪ'zentə $ -ər/ *n* [C] someone who introduces a television or radio programme

presently /'prezəntli/ *adv formal* **1** soon: *The doctor will be here presently.* **2** now: *He's presently living in London.* → see box at **NOW**

ˌpresent 'participle *n* [C] the form of a verb that ends in '-ing'

ˌpresent 'perfect *n* **the present perfect** the verb tense that you use to talk about a time up to and including the present. It is formed with 'have' and the PAST PARTICIPLE, as in 'he has gone'.

preservation /ˌprezə'veɪʃən $ -zər-/ *n* [U] when you prevent something from being harmed or damaged: **+of** *the preservation of the environment*

preservative /prɪ'zɜːvətɪv $ -ɜːr-/ *n* [C,U] a substance that is added to food to keep it in good condition: *foods that contain artificial preservatives*

preserve¹ /prɪ'zɜːv $ -ɜːrv/ *v* [T]
1 to stop something from being harmed, damaged, or destroyed [➔ **preservation**]: *It is important to preserve the rainforests.* | *The college wants to preserve its independence.*
2 to add something to food so that it will stay in good condition: *fruit preserved in alcohol*

preserve² *n* **1** [C] a food that is made by cooking fruit or vegetables with sugar, salt, or other substances so that they will remain in good condition: *jams and other fruit preserves*
2 [singular] if an activity is the preserve of one group of people, only that group does it: *Politics is no longer a* **male preserve.** | **+of** *a sport which used to be the preserve of the middle classes*
3 [C] an area of land or water that is kept for private hunting or fishing

preside /prɪ'zaɪd/ *v* [I] to be in charge of a formal meeting or ceremony: **+at** *He agreed to preside at the meeting.* | **+over** *the judge who will preside over this trial*
preside over sth *phr v* to be in control of a country at a time when something is happening in the country: *This government has presided over two major recessions.*

presidency /'prezɪdənsi/ *n* [C] plural **presidencies** the job of being a president, or the period of time when someone is a president: *his first attempt to win the presidency* | *the economic problems that developed during his presidency*

president, President /'prezɪdənt/ *n* [C]
1 the official leader of a country that does not have a king or queen: *President Lincoln* | *the US President* | **+of** *the President of France* → see box at **GOVERNMENT**
2 someone who is in charge of a large organization: **+of** *the President of the Royal Geographical Society*
→ **VICE PRESIDENT**

presidential /ˌprezₔ¹denʃəlₔ / adj [only before noun] relating to the president of a country: *a presidential election* | *the party's presidential candidate*

press¹ /pres/ v

1 [I,T] to push something firmly: *What happens if I press this button?* | **+down** *Press down with your left foot and pull back the lever.* | **press sth into/against/to sth** *He pressed some money into her hand.* | *Their faces were pressed against the window.*

2 [I,T] to try very hard to persuade someone to do something: **+for** *Nurses are pressing for a pay rise.* | **press sb to do sth** *He pressed me to accept the job.* | **press sb for sth** *I pressed her for an answer.* | *workers who are **pressing** their **claim** for more money* (=trying to persuade their employers to give them more money)

3 [I] to move forward by pushing against other people: **+forward** *The crowd continued to press forward.*

4 press charges to say officially that someone has done something illegal and must go to a court of law: *The police have decided not to press charges against him.*

5 [T] to use something heavy to crush something or make it flat: *a machine for pressing grapes*

> **THESAURUS**
>
> **squash** – to press something and damage it by making it flat: *Put the tomatoes where they won't get squashed.*
>
> **crush** – to press something very hard so that it is broken or destroyed: *His leg was crushed in the accident.*
>
> **mash** – to press fruit or cooked vegetables until they are soft and smooth: *Mash the potatoes well.*
>
> **grind** – to press something into powder using a special machine: *Can you grind the coffee beans?*
>
> **squeeze** – to press something from both sides, usually with your fingers: *Squeeze the toothpaste tube from the bottom.* | *freshly-squeezed orange juice*

press on/ahead phr v to continue doing something in a determined way: *Shall we press on?* | **+with** *Let's press ahead with the meeting.*

press² n

1 the press [also + plural verb BrE] newspapers and magazines, and the people who write for them: *He agreed to give an interview to the press.* | *The press have been very nasty about him.* | *a press report about the tragedy* | **the national/local press** *I read about it in the local press.* | **the gutter press** BrE disapproving (=newspapers that like to print shocking and frightening stories) *fears stirred up by the gutter press* → see box at **NEWSPAPER**

2 get a good/bad press to be praised or criticized in newspapers and on radio or television: *The government has been getting a bad press recently.*

3 go to press when a newspaper or book goes to press, it is printed: *The story came out just as the newspaper was going to press.*

4 [C] a piece of equipment used to crush something or make it flat: *a trouser press*

5 [C] a machine used for printing books or newspapers
→ PRINTING PRESS

ˈpress ˌconference n [C] a meeting at which someone answers questions asked by people from newspapers, television etc: *The police will hold a press conference later today.*

pressed /prest/ adj **be pressed for time/ money** informal to not have enough time or money

pressing /ˈpresɪŋ/ adj a pressing problem needs to be dealt with very soon: *one of the country's most pressing problems*

ˈpress ˌoffice n [C] the office of an organization or government department which gives information to the newspapers, radio, or television —**press officer** n [C]

ˈpress reˌlease n [C] an official statement giving information to newspapers, radio, television etc

ˈpress-up n [C] BrE an exercise in which you lie facing the ground and push your body up using your arms [= push-up AmE]: *He does fifty press-ups every morning.*

pressure¹ /ˈpreʃə $ -ər/ n

1 [U] attempts to make someone do something by threatening them or making them believe that they should do it: *Her family are **putting pressure on** her to stay at home.* | **be/come under pressure to do sth** *The director is now under pressure to resign.* | **+from** *The school agreed to the changes after pressure from parents.* | **+on** *There is pressure on the government to increase spending on health.*

2 [C,U] conditions in your life that make you feel worried because you have too much to do or think that you must do well: **+of** *the pressures of modern life* | **+on** *There is a lot of pressure on children these days.* | *I've been **under a lot of pressure** at work recently.*

3 [C,U] conditions that cause something to change or fail, especially in business or politics: *in response to **commercial pressures***

4 [C,U] the force that a gas or liquid has when it is pushed and held inside a container: *The air pressure in the tyres was too high.*

5 [U] the force or weight that is produced by pressing against something: *the pressure of the water against the sea walls*
→ BLOOD PRESSURE

pressure² v [T] especially AmE to try to make someone do something by threatening them or making them believe that they should do it [= pressurize BrE] —**pressured** adj

ˈpressure group n [C] a group of people who try to influence public opinion and persuade the government to do something: *an environmental pressure group*

pressurize also **-ise** BrE /ˈpreʃəraɪz/ v [T] to try to make someone do something by threatening them or making them believe that they should do it: *I was pressurized into lending him the money.*

pressurized also **-ised** BrE /ˈpreʃəraɪzd/ adj if a place is pressurized, the air inside it is kept at a controlled pressure: *a pressurized aircraft cabin*

P

prestige /preˈstiːʒ/ n [U] if you have prestige, you are respected and admired because of your job or something that you have achieved

prestigious /preˈstɪdʒəs $ -ˈstiː-, -ˈstɪ-/ adj a prestigious job or prize is one that people admire and respect a lot: a prestigious literary award

presumably /prɪˈzjuːməbli $ -ˈzuː-/ adv used to say that you think something is probably true: Presumably, the match will be cancelled.

presume /prɪˈzjuːm $ -ˈzuːm/ v **1** [T] to think that something is true, although you do not know for certain: **+(that)** I presume you'll be there. | The three soldiers are missing and presumed dead. **2** [I] formal to behave rudely by doing something that you have no right to do: **presume to do sth** I would never presume to tell you what to do.

presumption /prɪˈzʌmpʃən/ n formal **1** [C] something that you suppose is true because it seems very likely, although you do not know for certain: There is a general presumption that he is guilty. **2** [U] rude behaviour in which you do something that you have no right to do

presumptuous /prɪˈzʌmptʃuəs/ adj formal doing something that you have no right to do, in a way that seems rude

presuppose /ˌpriːsəˈpəʊz $ -ˈpoʊz/ v [T] formal to accept as a fact that something is true or will happen, even though this might not really be true: **+that** The sales projections presuppose that the economy will continue to grow.

pre-tax /ˌpriː ˈtæks◂/ adj pre-tax profits or losses are the profits or losses of a company before tax has been taken away

preteen /ˌpriːˈtiːn◂/ adj relating to or made for children who are 11 or 12 years old: preteen clothing —preteen /ˈpriːtiːn/ n [C]

pretence BrE; **pretense** AmE /prɪˈtens $ ˈpriːtens/ n **1** [C usually singular, U] when you pretend that something is true: We had to keep up the pretence that we were married. | She made no pretence of being surprised (=she did not pretend to be surprised). **2** under false pretences if you do something under false pretences, you do it by telling people things that are not true: You brought me here under false pretences.

pretend¹ /prɪˈtend/ v [I,T] to behave as if something is true when you know it is not: He's not really angry – he's just pretending. | **+(that)** She pretended that she hadn't seen me. | Let's pretend we're soldiers. | **pretend to do sth** He was only pretending to be asleep.

pretend² adj imaginary or not real – used especially by children: We sang songs around a pretend campfire.

pretense /prɪˈtens $ ˈpriːtens/ n the American spelling of PRETENCE

pretension /prɪˈtenʃən/ n [C usually plural, U] when someone tries to seem more important or more intelligent than they really are: his honesty and lack of pretension

pretentious /prɪˈtenʃəs/ adj trying to seem more important or more intelligent than you really are: a pretentious young man | a pretentious film

pretext /ˈpriːtekst/ n [C] a false reason for doing something, which you give in order to

hide the real reason: **+for** The terrorist attack gave them a pretext for war. | **on a pretext** He left immediately on the pretext that he had to catch a train.

pretty¹ /ˈprɪti/ adv
1 spoken fairly or quite: She looks pretty miserable. | I'm pretty sure he'll agree. → see box at RATHER
2 pretty much/pretty well almost completely: The streets were pretty well empty. | They all look pretty much the same.

pretty² adj
1 a woman or girl who is pretty is attractive: a very pretty girl | You look really pretty with your hair long. → see box at ATTRACTIVE
2 attractive to look at or pleasant to listen to: a pretty vase | a pretty tune
3 not a pretty sight very unpleasant to look at: His face was covered in spots and he was not a pretty sight!
—prettily adv

prevail /prɪˈveɪl/ v [I] formal **1** if a belief or opinion prevails, it is common among a group of people: the beliefs which still prevail in our society **2** if something prevails, it is successful after a struggle: Justice prevailed in the end.

prevail on/upon sb phr v formal to persuade someone to do something: **prevail on/upon sb to do sth** He prevailed upon the committee to reconsider its decision.

prevailing /prɪˈveɪlɪŋ/ adj **1** [only before noun] most common or accepted at a particular time: the prevailing views on education **2** the prevailing wind the wind that usually blows over a particular area

prevalent /ˈprevələnt/ adj very common in a particular place or among a particular group of people: **+in** a problem that is prevalent in Britain | **+among** a disease that is prevalent among young people —prevalence n [U]

prevaricate /prɪˈværɪkeɪt/ v [I] formal to hide the truth by not answering questions directly: Stop prevaricating and tell me what you know.

prevent /prɪˈvent/ v [T] to stop something from happening, or stop someone from doing something: an accident that could have been prevented | **prevent sb from doing sth** A knee injury prevented him from playing. | We were prevented from entering the building.
—preventable adj: preventable diseases

preventative /prɪˈventətɪv/ adj PREVENTIVE

prevention /prɪˈvenʃən/ n [U] when something is prevented: **+of** the prevention of accidents | crime prevention

preventive /prɪˈventɪv/ also **preventative** adj intended to prevent something bad from happening: preventive medicine (=actions that prevent people from becoming ill)

preview /ˈpriːvjuː/ n [C] **1** an occasion when you see a film, play, or painting before it is shown to the public **2** an advertisement for a film or television programme that shows short parts from it

previous /ˈpriːviəs/ adj [only before noun] happening or existing before now or before a particular time or thing: She has two children from a previous marriage. | I had seen him on the previous day (=the day before that day).

previously /'pri:viəsli/ *adv* before now or before a time in the past: *She had previously lived in Cambridge.*

prewar /ˌpri:'wɔː◂ $ -'wɔːr◂/ *adj* before a war, especially World War II: *life in prewar Britain*

prey[1] /preɪ/ *n* **1** [U] an animal that is hunted and eaten by another animal: *a tiger stalking its prey* **2 fall prey to sth** to be harmed by something: *More and more teenagers are falling prey to drugs.* → BIRD OF PREY

prey[2] *v*

prey on sb/sth *phr v* **1** if an animal preys on another type of animal, it hunts it and eats it **2** to deceive or harm someone who is not as clever or experienced as you are: *drug dealers who prey on young people* **3 prey on sb's mind** if something preys on your mind, it worries you a lot

price[1] /praɪs/ *n*

1 [C,U] the amount of money you have to pay for something: +**of** *the price of oil* | **high/low price** *They charge quite high prices.* | *House prices have gone up again.* | *The price of fuel has come down.* | *They're selling computers at half price.* → see box at COST

COLLOCATIONS

go up/rise/increase – to become higher
go down/fall/drop – to become lower
rocket/soar – to suddenly become much higher
tumble/plummet – to suddenly become much lower
fluctuate – to keep becoming higher and then lower
put up *BrE*/**increase/raise prices** – to make them higher
cut/lower/slash prices – to make them lower

2 [singular] something unpleasant that you must suffer in order to have something: *Being followed around by the press is the price you have to pay for success.* | *This was a small price to pay for his freedom.* | *She was determined to have a child at any price* (=even if there were a lot of difficulties).

price[2] *v* [T] to say how much something you are selling costs: *Tickets are priced at $25.*

priceless /'praɪsləs/ *adj* **1** worth a lot of money: *priceless antiques* **2** very important or useful: *a priceless asset*

pricey, pricy /'praɪsi/ *adj informal* expensive: *The food's a bit pricey.* → see box at EXPENSIVE

prick[1] /prɪk/ *v* [T] **1** to make a small hole in the surface of something, using a sharp point: *Prick the sausages with a fork before cooking them.* | *I pricked my finger on a pin.* **2** if tears prick your eyes, your eyes sting slightly because you are going to cry **3 prick (up) its ears** if an animal pricks up its ears, it lifts them up so that it can listen **4 prick up your ears** to start listening to what someone is saying because it is interesting

prick[2] *n* [C] a slight pain you feel when something sharp goes into your skin: *I just felt a slight prick as the needle went into my arm.*

prickle[1] /'prɪkəl/ *n* [C] a sharp point on the skin of an animal or the surface of a plant

prickle[2] *v* [I,T] if your skin prickles, you feel slight stinging pains: *My skin prickled with tension.*

prickly /'prɪkli/ *adj* **1** covered with thin sharp points: *prickly bushes* **2** making your skin sting slightly: *a prickly woollen sweater* **3** *informal* someone who is prickly gets annoyed or offended easily

pricy /'praɪsi/ *adj* another spelling of PRICEY

pride[1] /praɪd/ *n* [U]

1 the feeling you have when you are proud of something that you or someone connected with you has achieved [→ **proud**]: *His father smiled with pride.* | +**in** *They have a strong sense of pride in their country.* | *She takes great pride in her work* (=she is very proud of it).

2 the feeling that you like and respect yourself and want other people to respect you: *Losing his job really hurt his pride.*

3 the feeling that you are better or more important than other people and do not need their help: *I had too much pride to ask for money.* | *In the end I had to swallow my pride* (=forget about my pride) *and apologize.*

4 sb's pride and joy a person or thing that someone is very proud of: *His garden is his pride and joy.*

5 have/take pride of place to be in the best place for people to see: *A family photograph took pride of place on the wall.*

6 the pride of sth something that people in a place are very proud of: *The football team is the pride of the town.*

pride[2] *v* **pride yourself on (doing) sth** to be very proud of something that you can do well: *a restaurant that prides itself on serving top quality food*

priest /priːst/ *n* [C] someone who performs religious duties and ceremonies in some religions

priestess /'priːstes/ *n* [C] a woman who performs religious ceremonies in some religions

priesthood /'priːsthʊd/ *n* **the priesthood** the job of being a Christian priest: *his decision to enter the priesthood*

prim /prɪm/ *adj* always behaving in a polite and formal way, and easily shocked by anything rude: *a very prim and proper young lady* —**primly** *adv*

primacy /'praɪməsi/ *n* [U] *formal* when something is considered to be more important than anything else: *We must give primacy to education.*

prima donna /ˌpriːmə 'dɒnə $ -'dɑːnə/ *n* [C] someone who thinks that they are very important, and so expects other people to admire and praise them even when they behave badly

primal /'praɪməl/ *adj formal* primal feelings are basic and seem to come from ancient times when humans were more like animals: *primal fears*

primarily /'praɪmərəli $ praɪ'merəli/ *adv* mainly: *an advertisement that is aimed primarily at children*

primary[1] /'praɪməri $ -meri/ *adj* [only before noun] **1** most important: *Our primary concern is the safety of the children.* **2** *especially BrE* primary education is for children between 5 and 11 years old [= **elementary** *AmE*]: *a good primary school*

primary² also **‚primary e'lection** n [C] plural **primaries** an election in the US when people vote to decide who will be their political party's CAN-DIDATE in the main election

‚primary 'colour n [C] one of the three colours, red, yellow, and blue, that you can mix together to make any other colour

'primary ‚school n [C,U] a school in Britain for children aged 5 to 11 [➧ **junior school**]

primate /'praɪmeɪt/ n [C] a member of the group of animals that includes monkeys and humans

prime¹ /praɪm/ adj [only before noun] **1** most important: *Smoking is the prime cause of lung disease.* | *the prime suspect in the police investigation* **2** very good: *a house in a prime location* | *This is a prime example of this government's incompetence.*

prime² n **be in your prime/be in the prime of life** to be at the time in your life when you are strongest and most active

prime³ v [T] to prepare someone for a situation so that they know what to do: *He was well primed for the interview.*

‚prime 'minister, **Prime Minister** n [C] the leader of the government in some countries with a PARLIAMENT → see box at **GOVERNMENT**

primer /'praɪmə $ -ər/ n **1** [C,U] paint that you put on the surface of unpainted wood, metal etc before you put on the main layer of paint **2** [C] *AmE* a book that contains basic information about something

'prime ‚time n [U] the time in the evening when the largest number of people watch television: *a prime-time TV show*

primeval /praɪ'miːvəl/ adj belonging to a very early time in the history of the world: *primeval forests*

primitive /'prɪmətɪv/ adj **1** having a simple way of life without modern machines: *a primitive society* | *the tools used by primitive people* **2** very simple, old-fashioned, and uncomfortable: *The living conditions were a bit primitive.*

primrose /'prɪmrəʊz $ -roʊz/ n [C] a small wild plant with pale yellow flowers

prince, **Prince** /prɪns/ n [C] **1** the son of a king or queen: *Prince William* **2** the male ruler of a small country: *Prince Rainier of Monaco*

princely /'prɪnsli/ adj **princely sum** a large amount of money – often used humorously to mean a very small amount of money: *We now have the princely sum of £26.*

princess, **Princess** /ˌprɪn'ses◂ $ 'prɪnsəs/ n [C] **1** the daughter of a king or queen: *Princess Anne* **2** the wife of a prince

principal¹ /'prɪnsəpəl/ adj [only before noun] most important [= **main**]: *the principal character in the book* | *our principal reason for making this journey*

principal² n [C] *AmE* the person in charge of a school or college [= **head teacher** *BrE*]

principality /ˌprɪnsə'pæləti/ n [C] plural **principalities** a country that is ruled by a prince

principally /'prɪnsəpli/ adv mainly: *It's principally a language college, but they do teach some other subjects.*

principle /'prɪnsəpəl/ n

1 [C,U] a moral rule that you believe is right, and you use to guide the way you behave: *the need to teach children moral principles* | **be against sb's principles** *It's against my principles to eat meat.* | *She refused to accept the money as a matter of principle.* | **on principle** *He wouldn't pay the fine on principle* (=because he thought it was wrong).

2 [C] a basic rule or idea that controls or explains the way something works or is organized: *the principles of economics* | **general/basic principle** *The general principle is that education should be available to all children equally.* | **on the principle that** *The machine works on the principle that air will expand when heated.*

3 in principle a) if something is possible in principle, there is no reason why it should not happen, but it has not actually happened yet: *In principle, the new computer system should make our job easier.* **b)** if you agree in principle, you agree with the main parts of a plan before you know the details: *They have accepted the idea in principle.*

principled /'prɪnsəpəld/ adj someone who is principled has strong beliefs about what is morally right and wrong

print¹ /prɪnt/ v

1 [T] to produce words or pictures on paper, using a machine: *I'm printing the document now.* | *a notice printed on bright blue paper*

2 [T] to produce copies of a book, newspaper etc: *The book was first printed in 1879.*

3 [T] to include a piece of writing in a newspaper or magazine [= **publish**]: *The magazine should never have printed this article.*

4 [I,T] to write words by hand without joining the letters: *Please print your name clearly at the top of the page.*

print sth ⇔ off/out *phr v* to produce a printed copy of a computer document: *I'll print out a copy of the letter for you.*

print² n **1** [U] writing that has been printed in books or newspapers: *I can't read small print without my glasses.* | **in print** *It was really exciting to see my name in print.* **2 be in print/be out of print** if a book is in print, it is still being printed and you can buy new copies of it. If it is out of print, it is no longer being printed. **3** [C] a picture or copy of a painting that has been printed onto paper **4** [C] a photograph: *an extra set of prints free.* → see box at **CAMERA** **5** [C] a mark that is left on a surface when something is pressed onto it [➧ **fingerprint**, **footprint**]: *His feet left prints in the snow.* → FINE PRINT, SMALL PRINT

printer /'prɪntə $ -ər/ n [C]

1 a machine that prints documents from a computer onto paper: *a laser printer* → see box at **OFFICE**

2 a person or company whose work is printing books, magazines etc

printing /'prɪntɪŋ/ n [U] the process of making a book, magazine etc, using a machine

'printing press n [C] a machine used for printing newspapers, books etc

printout /'prɪntˌaʊt/ n [C,U] a piece of paper containing information printed from a computer

prior /'praɪə $ praɪr/ adj formal **1** [only before noun] a prior arrangement, agreement etc was planned or made earlier: *He is unable to attend due to a **prior engagement**.* **2 prior to sth** before: *the weeks prior to the election*

prioritize also **-ise** *BrE* /praɪˈɒrɪtaɪz $ -ˈɔːr-/ v [I,T] to put several things in order of importance, so that you can do the most important first: *Try to prioritize your work.*

priority /praɪˈɒrɪti $ -ˈɔːr-/ n plural **priorities**
1 [C] the thing that you think is most important and that needs your attention first: **(sb's) top/ first/main priority** *The government's top priority is education.* | **high/low priority** (=something that is considered very important or not very important) *Road repairs are a low priority.*
2 [U] when something is given or should be given more attention than other people or things: **have/take priority (over sth/sb)** *Your family should take priority over your job.* | *Security is **given** high **priority** in military establishments.*

prise /praɪz/ v [T] *BrE* to force something open or away from something else [= pry *AmE*]: **prise sth off/open etc** *I managed to prise the lid open.*

prism /ˈprɪzəm/ n [C] a block of glass with three sides that separates white light into different colours

prison /ˈprɪzən/ n [C,U] a building where criminals are kept as a punishment [= jail]: *a women's prison* | **in prison** *He spent two years in prison.* | *He attacked two **prison officers**.* | *a five-year **prison sentence***

COLLOCATIONS

go to prison
put sb in prison
send sb to prison
spend time in prison (=be there for committing a crime)
release sb from prison
get out of prison (=be released from prison)

prisoner /ˈprɪzənə $ -ər/ n [C]
1 someone who is kept in a prison as a punishment
2 someone who is kept somewhere by force, for example during a war: **hold/keep sb prisoner** *The rebels kept him prisoner for three months.* | *Hundreds of soldiers were **taken prisoner**.*
→ POLITICAL PRISONER

prisoner of 'war n [C] abbreviation *POW* a soldier etc who is caught by an enemy during a war and kept as a prisoner

pristine /ˈprɪstiːn/ adj extremely clean and looking as good as when new: *a 1973 Volkswagen in **pristine condition***

privacy /ˈprɪvəsi, ˈpraɪ- $ ˈpraɪ-/ n [U] when you are alone and not seen or heard by other people: *Teenagers need some privacy.* | *I read the letter **in the privacy of** my own room.*

private¹ /ˈpraɪvət/ adj
1 for only one person or group to use, not for everyone [≠ public]: *a room with a private bath* | *A sign said 'Private property. Keep out.'*
2 not owned or paid for by the government: *a private company* | *private health care*
3 a private meeting, conversation etc is for a few particular people, and nobody else: *Heads of state met for **private talks**.*
4 private feelings, information etc are secret or

personal and not for other people to know about: *Don't read that – it's private.* | *'What are you laughing at?' 'It's **a private joke** (=a joke that only a few particular people will understand).'*
5 not related to your work: *The president made a private visit to Mexico.* | *He's had some problems in his **private life** (=his life with family and friends).*
6 used to describe someone who is not publicly known, or does something for themselves rather than for the government or another organization: *donations from **private individuals*** | *The painting was sold to a **private collector**.*
7 quiet and without other people there: *a private corner of the garden*
—**privately** adv

private² n **1 in private** without other people listening or watching: *Can I speak to you in private?* **2** also **Private** [C] a soldier of the lowest rank in the army

private de'tective also **private in'vestigator** n [C] someone who can be employed to look for information or missing people, or to follow people and report on what they do

private 'enterprise n [U] when private businesses are allowed to compete freely with each other, and the government does not own or control them

'private school n [C] a school that is not supported by government money, where education must be paid for by the children's parents

privatize also **-ise** *BrE* /ˈpraɪvətaɪz/ v [T] to sell an organization, industry etc that was previously owned by a government [≠ nationalize]
—**privatization** /ˌpraɪvətaɪˈzeɪʃən $ -tə-/ n [U]

privet /ˈprɪvɪt/ n [U] a bush with leaves that stay green all year, often grown to form a HEDGE

privilege /ˈprɪvəlɪdʒ/ n **1** [C,U] a special advantage that only one person or group has: *Leisure travel used to be a privilege for the rich.* | *positions of privilege and power* **2** [singular] something that you are lucky to have as a chance to do: *It's **been a privilege** to meet you, sir.*
—**privileged** adj: *students from **privileged** backgrounds*

privy /ˈprɪvi/ adj **be privy to sth** *formal* to know about something that is secret: *Only Colby was privy to the deal.*

prize¹ /praɪz/ n [C] something that is given to someone who is successful in a competition, race etc: *He won **a prize** of £3000.* | **first/ second/third etc prize** *First prize was a weekend for two in Paris.*
→ BOOBY PRIZE

prize² adj [only before noun] good enough to win a prize: *prize cattle*

prize³ v [T] to think that something is very important or valuable: *These coins are prized by collectors.* —**prized** adj: *our most **prized** possession*

pro /prəʊ $ proʊ/ n [C] plural **pros 1** *informal* someone who earns money by playing a sport: *a tennis pro* **2 the pros and cons (of sth)** the advantages and disadvantages of something

pro- /prəʊ $ proʊ/ prefix supporting or approving of something or someone [≠ anti-]: *pro-government troops*

proactive /prəʊˈæktɪv $ proʊ-/ *adj* proactive actions are done to make something happen or change, not as a reaction to an event: *Banks need to take a more proactive approach to fraud.*

probability /ˌprɒbəˈbɪlɪti $ ˌprɑː-/ *n* plural **probabilities** **1** [C,U] how likely it is that something will happen: *There's a high probability of success.* | **+(that)** *What's the probability that she will inherit the disease?* **2 in all probability** very probably: *In all probability, he's missed the bus.* **3** [singular] something that is likely to happen or exist: *War is a real probability now.*

probable /ˈprɒbəbəl $ ˈprɑː-/ *adj* likely to happen or be true: *The probable cause of the crash was engine failure.* | *It's probable that more people will be infected.*

probably /ˈprɒbəbli $ ˈprɑː-/ *adv* used to say that something is likely to happen or be true: *We'll probably go to France next year.* | *'Are you going to come?' 'Yes, probably.'*

probation /prəˈbeɪʃən $ proʊ-/ *n* [U] **1** a system that allows some criminals not to go to prison if they behave well and see a probation officer regularly: **on probation** *He's on probation for theft.* **2** a period of time when someone starts a new job, when they must show that they are suitable for that job —**probationary** *adj*

proˈbation ˌofficer *n* [C] someone whose job is to help criminals who are on probation, and check that they are behaving well

probe[1] /prəʊb $ proʊb/ *v* [I,T] **1** to ask questions in order to get secret or personal information: **+into** *She didn't want him probing into her past.* **2** to look for or examine something, using a long thin object —**probing** *adj*

probe[2] *n* [C] **1** a long thin tool that doctors and scientists use to examine parts of someone's body **2** a spacecraft without people in it, sent into space to collect information → see box at **SPACE** **3** a process of getting information by asking a lot of questions

problem /ˈprɒbləm $ ˈprɑː-/ *n* [C] **1** a situation that is bad or causes difficulties: **+of** *the problem of unemployment* | **have a problem (with sth)** *I've been having a few problems with the kids.* | **deal with/solve/tackle a problem** *Do you need advice on how to deal with the problem?* | **drug/crime etc problem** *an area with a huge crime problem* | *Smoking causes health problems.* | **the (only) problem is (that)** spoken (=used before saying what the main difficulty is) *The problem is, there isn't enough time.*

THESAURUS

setback – a problem that stops you from making progress
snag *informal* – a problem, especially one that you had not expected
hitch – a small problem that delays or prevents something
trouble – when something does not work properly: *The plane developed engine trouble.*
hassle *spoken* – a situation that is annoying because it causes problems

COMMUNICATION

Asking someone what the problem is
What's the matter?
What's the problem?
What's wrong?
What's up? *informal*

2 a question for which you must find the right answer: *a mathematical problem* | *Can you solve this problem?*
3 that's your/his etc problem spoken used to say that someone else is responsible for dealing with a situation, not you: *If you're late, that's your problem.*

problematic /ˌprɒbləˈmætɪk◂ $ ˌprɑː-/ also **problematical** /-tɪkəl/ *adj* full of problems, or causing problems: *a problematic relationship*

procedure /prəˈsiːdʒə $ -ər/ *n* [C,U] the correct or normal way of doing something: **+for** *the procedure for getting a visa* —**procedural** *adj*

proceed /prəˈsiːd/ *v* [I] *formal* **1** to continue to do something or happen: **+with** *The company decided to proceed with the project.* | *Talks are proceeding smoothly.* **2 proceed to do sth** to do something after you have done something else: *He stood up and proceeded to give an embarrassed speech.*

proceedings /prəˈsiːdɪŋz/ *n* [plural] **1** a series of events: *We watched the proceedings from the window.* **2** legal actions in a law court: *divorce proceedings*

proceeds /ˈprəʊsiːdz $ ˈproʊ-/ *n* [plural] the money that you get from selling something or from an organized event: *The proceeds from the concert will go to charity.*

process[1] /ˈprəʊses $ ˈprɑː-/ *n* [C]
1 a series of things you do in order to achieve a particular result or to produce something: **+of** *the process of learning a language* | *the Israeli-Egyptian peace process* | *the car production process*
2 a series of events or changes that happen naturally: **+of** *the natural process of evolution*
3 be in the process of (doing) sth to have started doing something and not yet finished: *We're in the process of buying a house.*
4 in the process while you are doing something else, or while something else is happening: *I ran, twisting my ankle in the process.*

process[2] *v* [T] **1** to add chemicals to a substance or food in order to give it colour, keep it fresh etc: *processed cheese* **2** to deal with an official document, information etc by putting it through a system or into a computer: *Your application is still being processed.* **3** to print a photograph or film —**processing** *n* [U]

processed /ˈprəʊsest $ ˈprɑː-/ *adj* [only before noun] processed food has substances added to it before it is sold in order to preserve it, improve its colour etc → see box at **NATURAL**

procession /prəˈseʃən/ *n* [C] **1** a line of people or vehicles moving slowly as part of a ceremony [➡ **parade**]: *a funeral procession* **2** many people or things of the same kind, appearing or happening one after the other: **+of** *an endless procession of visitors*

processor /ˈprəʊsesə $ ˈprɑːsesər/ *n* [C] the part of a computer that deals with information → **FOOD PROCESSOR**

proclaim /prəˈkleɪm $ proʊ-/ *v* [T] *formal* to officially tell people something important: *The* new government proclaimed independence immediately. —**proclamation** /ˌprɒkləˈmeɪʃən $ ˈprɑː-/ n [C]

procrastinate /prəˈkræstˌneɪt/ v [I] formal to delay doing something that you ought to do: The government cannot procrastinate any longer on this issue. —**procrastination** /prəˌkræstˌˈneɪʃən/ n [U]

procreate /ˈprəʊkrieɪt $ ˈprəʊ-/ v [I,T] formal to produce children or baby animals [= reproduce] —**procreation** /ˌprəʊkriˈeɪʃən $ ˌprəʊ-/ n [U]

procure /prəˈkjʊə $ prəʊˈkjʊr/ v [T] formal to get something, especially something that is difficult to get: Clark had been procuring guns for the rebels.

prod /prɒd $ prɑːd/ v [I,T] **prodded, prodding** **1** to push someone or something with your finger or a pointed object: He prodded the snake with a stick. → see picture on page A10 **2** to persuade or remind someone to do something that they are not eager to do: We had to prod Ed into applying for the job. —**prod** n [C] a cattle prod

prodigious /prəˈdɪdʒəs/ adj formal very large or impressive: a prodigious amount of money —**prodigiously** adv

prodigy /ˈprɒdɪdʒi $ ˈprɑː-/ n [C] plural **prodigies** a young person who is extremely good at doing something [→ genius]: Mozart was a child prodigy.

produce[1] /prəˈdjuːs $ -ˈduːs/ v [T] **1** to cause a particular thing to happen: Research in the US produced similar results. | The drug can produce serious side effects. **2** to make something using a particular process or skill [→ product, production]: The factory produces 100 cars an hour. | wine produced in California | The children produced some wonderful paintings. **3** to make or grow something naturally: Plants produce oxygen. | a snake that produces a deadly poison **4** to bring out or show something so that someone can see it: He suddenly produced a gun. **5** to control how a film, play, record etc is made [→ producer]: James Cameron produced Terminator 2.

produce[2] /ˈprɒdjuːs $ ˈprəʊduːs/ n [U] food that is grown in large quantities to be sold: dairy produce

producer /prəˈdjuːsə $ -ˈduːsər/ n [C] **1** someone who controls the making of a film, play, record etc: Hollywood producers → see box at FILM **2** a company or country that makes or grows something: +of Spain is a large producer of olive oil.

product /ˈprɒdʌkt $ ˈprɑː-/ n [C] **1** something that is made in a factory or grown to be sold: **agricultural/dairy/software etc products** a list of new food products **2 be the product of sth** to be the result of something: The system is the product of two years' development.

production /prəˈdʌkʃən/ n **1** [U] the process of growing things or making them in factories, or the amount that is produced [→ produce, product]: The production of consumer goods | **food/oil/milk etc production** Industrial production rose by 0.1%. | **in produc-**

tion (=being produced) The old model was in production for about 30 years. | production costs **2** [U] when something is produced through a natural process: **+of** the body's production of red blood cells **3** [C,U] a film, play etc, or the process of producing it: a modern production of Romeo and Juliet | video production

proˈduction ˌline n [C] a line of machines and workers in a factory, each doing one job in the process of making a product before passing it to the next machine or worker

productive /prəˈdʌktɪv/ adj producing or achieving a lot: a productive meeting —**productively** adv

productivity /ˌprɒdʌkˈtɪvˌti, -dək- $ ˌprɑː-/ n [U] the speed at which goods are produced, and the amount that is produced: ways to **increase productivity**

Prof. the written abbreviation of Professor

profane /prəˈfeɪn/ adj formal showing a lack of respect for God or holy things: profane language

profess /prəˈfes/ v [T] formal to say something about yourself, especially when it is not true: He professes to love her.

profession /prəˈfeʃən/ n **1** [C] a job that needs special education and training: **the legal/medical/teaching etc profession** I spent most of my life in the teaching profession. | **enter/go into/join a profession** My father wanted me to go into the legal profession. | **by profession** He's an architect by profession. → see box at JOB **2** [singular also + plural verb BrE] all the people in a particular profession: the nursing profession

professional[1] /prəˈfeʃənəl/ adj **1** [only before noun] relating to a job that needs special education and training: You'll need professional legal advice. | professional qualifications | We rented the house to a professional couple. **2** showing that someone has been well trained and is good at their work: Your report looks very professional. | a professional approach to the job **3** doing a sport or activity as your job: a professional tennis player | In 1990 he **turned professional** (=started to do a sport etc as a job). **4** [only before noun] professional sports are played by people who are paid [→ amateur]: a professional golf championship —**professionally** adv

professional[2] n [C] **1** someone who works in a job that needs special education and training: a health care professional **2** someone who earns money by doing a sport or activity that other people do for enjoyment [→ amateur]

professionalism /prəˈfeʃənəlɪzəm/ n [U] the skill and high standards that a professional person is expected to have

professor /prəˈfesə $ -ər/ n [C] **1** BrE a teacher at the highest level in a university department **2** AmE a teacher at a university or college → see box at TEACHER → and UNIVERSITY

proffer /ˈprɒfə $ ˈprɑːfər/ v [T] formal to offer something to someone

proficient /prəˈfɪʃənt/ adj able to do something very skilfully: **+in/at** Gwen is proficient in three languages. —**proficiency** n [U] Nick's proficiency with computers —**proficiently** adv

profile¹ /'prəʊfaɪl $ 'prou-/ n [C] **1** a view of someone's head from the side, not the front: **in profile** *a drawing of her in profile* **2** a short description that gives the main details of what someone or something is like: **+of** *a profile of the singer* | *a job profile* **3 a high profile** if something or someone has a high profile, the public are very interested in them: *Drugs education has a high profile right now.* **4 keep a low profile** to avoid doing things that will make people notice you → HIGH-PROFILE

profile² v [T] to write or give a short description of someone or something

profit¹ /'prɒfɪt $ 'prɑː-/ n [C,U] the money that you get when you sell something for more than you paid for it, especially in business [≠ **loss**]: *The company made a huge profit on the deal.* | **at a profit** *They sold the house at a big profit.* | *Marston's profits rose last year to $17 million.* | *That left my client with a handsome profit* (=a large one).

profit² v [I,T] formal to get something good or useful from a situation: **+by/from** *Wealthy people will profit from the new tax laws.*

profitability /ˌprɒfɪtə'bɪlɪti $ ˌprɑː-/ n [U] the amount of profit that a business makes

profitable /'prɒfɪtəbəl $ 'prɑː-/ adj producing a profit or a useful result: *profitable investments* —**profitably** adv

profiteering /ˌprɒfɪ'tɪərɪŋ $ ˌprɑː'tɪr-/ n [U] when a person or company makes a large profit by selling something that is difficult to obtain at an unfairly high price —**profiteer** n [C]

'profit-ˌmaking adj a profit-making organization or business makes a profit

profound /prə'faʊnd/ adj **1** a profound effect, feeling etc is very great or serious: *The story had a profound effect on me.* | *Her death was a profound shock.* **2** showing a lot of knowledge and understanding: *a profound remark* —**profoundly** adv

profuse /prə'fjuːs/ adj produced or present in large amounts: *Moira phoned with profuse apologies.* —**profusion** /prə'fjuːʒən/ n [U] *Wildlife is here in profusion.* —**profusely** adv

prognosis /prɒg'nəʊsɪs $ prɑːg'nou-/ n [C] plural **prognoses** /-siːz/ formal the way something, especially an illness, seems likely to develop in the future: *With some cancers the prognosis is good.*

program¹ /'prəʊgræm $ 'prou-/ n [C]

1 a set of instructions given to a computer to make it do something: *The students learnt how to write a computer program.* | *a graphics program* | *The program will run on Windows.* **2** the American spelling of PROGRAMME

program² v [T] **programmed, programming** to give a set of instructions to a computer to make it do something —**programming** n [U]

programme¹ BrE; **program** AmE /'prəʊgræm $ 'prou-/ n [C]

1 a series of planned actions that are intended to develop or improve something: **training/investment/building etc programme** *the US space program* | *my new fitness programme* | **+of** *our programme of reforms* | **programme to do sth** *a programme to improve living conditions in the region*

2 a show on television or radio: *What's your favourite TV programme?* | **+on/about** *I watched a programme on killer whales.*

3 a series of activities or events for people to enjoy or take part in: *Tomorrow's programme includes drama, music, and dance.* | **+of** *a programme of exhibitions*

4 a small book or piece of paper that you get at a concert, play etc which tells you about the performance: *a theatre programme* → see box at THEATRE

5 AmE a course of study: *Stanford's MBA program*

programme² BrE; **program** AmE v [T] **1** to give a set of instructions to a machine to make it do something: *I've programmed the video to record tonight's movie.* **2 be programmed to do sth** to naturally behave or think in a particular way: *Cats are programmed to hunt.* **3** to arrange for something to happen at a particular time: *The festival is programmed for later this year.*

programmer /'prəʊgræmə $ 'prougræmər/ n [C] someone whose job is to write programs for computers

progress¹ /'prəʊgres $ 'prɑː-/ n [U]

1 the process of getting better at doing something, or getting closer to finishing or achieving something: *Nick has made a lot of progress at school.* | **+of** *Millions of people watched the progress of the trial on TV.* | **+towards** *There's been steady progress towards a peace settlement.* | **slow/good etc progress**

2 useful change or improvement in society: *Do we need all this technology? Is it really progress?* | **social/technological/economic etc progress**

3 in progress formal happening now: *The class was already in progress.*

progress² /prə'gres/ v [I] **1** to develop and move to a further stage: *He soon progressed to more difficult exercises.* **2** to continue or move forward slowly: *As the meeting progressed, I became bored.*

progression /prə'greʃən/ n [C,U] change or development: *the rapid progression of the disease*

progressive¹ /prə'gresɪv/ adj **1** supporting or using modern ideas and methods: *progressive teaching methods* **2** a progressive change happens gradually over a period of time: *the progressive increase in air travel* —**progressively** adv

progressive² n **the progressive** the form of a verb that shows that an action is continuing to happen. In English, it has the verb 'be' followed by the PRESENT PARTICIPLE, for example, 'I was waiting for a bus'.

prohibit /prə'hɪbɪt $ prou-/ v [T] formal to say that something is not allowed because of a rule or law [= **forbid**]: *Smoking is prohibited in the building.* | **prohibit sb from doing sth** *In some communities, women were prohibited from remarrying.* —**prohibition** /ˌprəʊhɪ'bɪʃən $ ˌprou-/ n [U]

prohibitive /prə'hɪbɪtɪv $ prou-/ adj prohibitive prices are very high and prevent people from buying or doing something —**prohibitively** adv

project¹ /'prɒdʒekt $ 'prɑː-/ n [C]

1 a piece of work that is carefully planned and

done over a period of time: *a three-year **research project*** | **project to do sth** *a project to build new houses* | *a **project manager***

2 a piece of school work for which students have to collect information about a subject over a period of time: *a geography project* | **+on** *a project on pollution*

project² /prəˈdʒekt/ *v* **1** [T usually passive] to plan or calculate what will probably happen in the future: *The President's visit is projected for March.* | *Inflation was projected to rise to 8.9%.* **2** [I] *formal* to stick out beyond an edge or surface [= **protrude**]: *The roof projects over the driveway.* **3** [T] to make a picture, film etc appear on a large screen, using light

projectile /prəˈdʒektaɪl $ -tl/ *n* [C] *formal* an object that is thrown at someone, or fired from a weapon

projection /prəˈdʒekʃən/ *n* **1** [C] a statement about what is likely to happen, using information you have now: *projections of an increase of 3%* **2** [C] something that sticks out beyond an edge or surface **3** [U] the use of light to make a picture, film etc appear on a large screen

projector /prəˈdʒektə $ -ər/ *n* [C] a piece of equipment that uses light to make a picture, film etc appear on a large screen

proliferate /prəˈlɪfəreɪt/ *v* [I] *formal* to increase very quickly in number —**proliferation** /prəˌlɪfəˈreɪʃən/ *n* [U] *the proliferation of shopping centres*

prolific /prəˈlɪfɪk/ *adj* producing a lot of something: *a prolific writer* —**prolifically** /-kli/ *adv*

prologue /ˈprəʊlɒɡ $ ˈproʊlɔːɡ, -lɑːɡ/ *n* [C] the introduction to a book, film, or play → **EPILOGUE**

prolong /prəˈlɒŋ $ -ˈlɔːŋ/ *v* [T] to make something continue for longer: *There was no point in prolonging the conversation.*

prolonged /prəˈlɒŋd $ -ˈlɔːŋd/ *adj* continuing for a long time: *a prolonged illness*

prom /prɒm $ prɑːm/ *n* [C] a formal dance party for HIGH SCHOOL students in the US

promenade /ˌprɒməˈnɑːd‹, ˈprɒmənɑːd $ ˌprɑːməˈneɪd‹/ *n* [C] *BrE* a wide path next to the sea where people walk for pleasure

prominence /ˈprɒmɪnəns $ ˈprɑː-/ *n* [U] when someone or something is important and wellknown: **come to/rise to prominence (as sth)** *She came to prominence as an artist in 1993.*

prominent /ˈprɒmɪnənt $ ˈprɑː-/ *adj* **1** wellknown or important: *a prominent politician* **2** easy to see or notice: *a prominent nose* —**prominently** *adv*

promiscuous /prəˈmɪskjuəs/ *adj* having many sexual partners: *promiscuous sexual behaviour* —**promiscuity** /ˌprɒmɪˈskjuːɪti $ ˌprɑː-/ *n* [U]

promise¹ /ˈprɒmɪs $ ˈprɑː-/ *v* [I,T]

1 to say that you will definitely do something or that something will definitely happen: **promise to do sth** *She promised to write to me.* | **+(that)** *Hurry up – we promised that we wouldn't be late.* | **promise sb (that)** *He promised me the car would be ready by then.* | **promise sb sth** *The company promised us a bonus.* | **promise sth to sb** *I've promised that book to Ian.*

THESAURUS

swear – to make a very serious promise: *He had sworn not to reveal her secret.*

take/swear an oath – to make a very serious promise in public: *You must take an oath of loyalty to your country.*

vow – to make a serious promise, often to yourself: *She vowed that she would never drink alcohol again.*

guarantee – to promise something that you feel very sure about: *I can guarantee you a month's work on the project.*

give sb your word – to promise someone very sincerely that you will do something: *I'll be there – I give you my word.*

2 to seem likely to be something in the future: **promise to be sth** *The meeting promises to be difficult.*

promise² *n*

1 [C] a statement that you will definitely do something or that something will definitely happen: **+of** *a promise of help* | **+to** *his promise to me* | **promise to do sth** *She made a promise to visit them.* | **+that** *his promise that the job would be mine* | **keep/break a promise** (=do or fail to do something you promised) *Anna kept her promise to be back early.*

2 [U] signs that something or someone will be good or successful: *He **shows** a lot of **promise** as a writer.*

promising /ˈprɒmɪsɪŋ $ ˈprɑː-/ *adj* likely to be good or successful: *a promising young actor* —**promisingly** *adv*

promo /ˈprəʊməʊ $ ˈproʊmoʊ/ *n* [C] plural **promos** *informal* a short film that advertises an event or product

promontory /ˈprɒməntəri $ ˈprɑːməntɔːri/ *n* [C] plural **promontories** a long narrow piece of land which goes out into the sea

promote /prəˈməʊt $ -ˈmoʊt/ *v* [T] **1** to help something happen or be successful [= **encourage**]: *a meeting to promote trade between Taiwan and the UK* **2** to give someone a higher job: **promote sb to sth** *Helen was promoted to manager.* **3** to help sell a new product, film etc, especially by advertising it: *She's in London to promote her new book.* **4** [usually passive] *BrE* if a sports team is promoted, they play in a better group of teams the next year

promoter /prəˈməʊtə $ -ˈmoʊtər/ *n* [C] **1** someone who arranges and advertises concerts or sports events **2** someone who tries to persuade people to support or use something: *promoters of organic farming*

promotion /prəˈməʊʃən $ -ˈmoʊ-/ *n* **1** [C,U] when you are given a higher job: *his promotion to manager* **2** [C,U] an advertisement or special attempt to sell something: *a sales promotion* **3** [U] when you help something happen or try to persuade people to support something: **+of** *the promotion of equal rights* **4** [U] *BrE* if a sports team gets promotion, they play in a better group of teams the next season

promotional /prəˈməʊʃənəl $ -ˈmoʊ-/ *adj* promotional films, events etc advertise something

prompt¹ /prɒmpt $ prɑːmpt/ *v* [T] **1** to make someone decide to do something: **prompt sb to do sth** *What prompted you to buy that suit?* | *The accident prompted an investigation into rail safety.* **2** to remind someone, especially an actor, of what they should say next

prompt² adj **1** done quickly or immediately: *Prompt action must be taken.* **2** someone who is prompt is not late: *The meeting starts at 11, so please be prompt.* —**promptly** also **prompt** BrE informal adv

prompt³ n [C] **1** a word or words said to actors to help them remember what to say **2** a sign on a computer screen that shows the computer is ready for the next instruction

pron. also **pron** BrE the written abbreviation of pronoun

prone /prəʊn $ proʊn/ adj **1** likely to do something bad, or likely to suffer from something: **+to** *Some plants are very prone to disease.* | **prone to do sth** *She's prone to eat too much.* | **accident-prone/injury-prone etc** *He's always been accident-prone.* **2** formal lying with the front of your body facing down

prong /prɒŋ $ prɔːŋ/ n [C] **1** one of the thin sharp parts of something such as a fork **2** one of two or three ways of achieving something which are used at the same time: **two-pronged/three-pronged** *a two-pronged attack*

pronoun /'prəʊnaʊn $ 'proʊ-/ n [C] a word such as 'he' or 'themselves' that is used instead of a noun
→ PERSONAL PRONOUN, RELATIVE PRONOUN

pronounce /prə'naʊns/ v [T]
1 to make the sound of a word [**→ pronunciation**]: *How do you pronounce your name?*
2 formal to state something officially: **pronounce sb/sth sth** *The doctor pronounced him dead.*
3 formal to give a judgment or opinion: *The scheme was pronounced a failure.*

pronounced /prə'naʊnst/ adj very noticeable: *He walks with a pronounced limp.*

pronouncement /prə'naʊnsmənt/ n [C] formal an official statement

pronunciation /prə,nʌnsi'eɪʃən/ n [C,U] the way in which a language or word is pronounced: **+of** *What's the correct pronunciation of this word?* | *His pronunciation is poor.*

proof /pruːf/ n
1 [C,U] something that proves something is true: **+of** *proof of the existence of life on other planets* | **proof of purchase/ownership/identity** *Do you have any proof of purchase* (=something to prove that you have paid for something)? | **+(that)** *This letter is proof that he knew about the robbery.*
2 [C usually plural] technical a first copy of a printed page that you correct mistakes on

-proof /pruːf/ suffix not able to be harmed or damaged by something, or not letting something through: *a waterproof jacket* | *a bulletproof car*

proofread /'pruːfriːd/ v [I,T] past tense and past participle **proofread** /-red/ to read something in order to correct mistakes in it —**proofreader** n [C]

prop¹ /prɒp $ prɑːp/ v [T] **propped, propping** to support something and make it stay in a particular position: **prop sth against/on sth** *He propped his bike against the tree.*

prop sth ⇔ up phr v **1** to prevent something from falling by putting something against it or under it: *We propped the fence up with old bits of wood.* **2** to help an economy, industry, or government to continue to exist, especially by giving money: *government measures to prop up the stock market*

prop² n [C] **1** an object that you put under or against something to hold it in position **2** an object used in a play or film

propaganda /,prɒpə'gændə $,prɑː-/ n [U] false information that a political organization gives to the public to influence them

propagate /'prɒpəgeɪt $ 'prɑː-/ v **1** [T] formal to spread your ideas or beliefs to many people: *The group uses its website to propagate its ideas.* **2** [I,T] technical if you propagate plants, or if they propagate, new plants are produced —**propagation** /,prɒpə'geɪʃən $,prɑː-/ n [U]

propel /prə'pel/ v [T] **propelled, propelling 1** to move or push something forwards [**→ propulsion**]: *a boat propelled by a small motor* **2** to move someone into a new situation or make them do something: *The film propelled her to stardom.*

propeller /prə'pelə $ -ər/ n [C] the part of a boat or plane that spins around and makes it move

propensity /prə'pensₔti/ n [C] plural **propensities** formal a natural tendency to behave in a particular way: *his propensity to argue*

proper /'prɒpə $ 'prɑːpər/ adj
1 [only before noun] right, suitable, or correct: *Everything was in its proper place.* | *the proper way to clean your teeth*
2 [only before noun] BrE spoken real, or of a good and generally accepted standard: *a proper job* | *a proper meal*
3 socially correct and acceptable [≠ improper]: *It wouldn't be proper for me to ask her.*
4 [only after noun] used to describe the main part of something: *a friendly chat before the interview proper* | *the city centre proper*

properly /'prɒpəli $ 'prɑːpərli/ adv especially BrE correctly or in a way that is considered right [= right AmE]: *I can't see properly without my glasses.* | *The brakes aren't working properly.* | *properly trained staff*

,proper 'noun also **,proper 'name** n [C] a noun such as 'Mike' or 'Paris' that is the name of a person, place, or thing and is spelled with a capital letter

property /'prɒpəti $ 'prɑːpər-/ n plural **properties**
1 [U] something that someone owns: *Police recovered some of the stolen property.* | *his personal property* **→** see box at OWN
2 [C,U] a building or piece of land: *property prices*
3 [C] a natural quality that something has [**→ characteristic, quality**]: *herbs with healing properties* | **physical/chemical etc properties** *the chemical properties of a substance*
→ LOST PROPERTY

prophecy /'prɒfₔsi $ 'prɑː-/ n [C,U] plural **prophecies** a statement saying what you believe will happen in the future —**prophesy** /-fₔsaɪ/ v [I,T]

prophet /'prɒfₔt $ 'prɑː-/ n [C] someone who people believe God has chosen to be a religious leader or teacher

prophetic /prə'fetɪk/ adj correctly saying what will happen in the future: *His warnings proved prophetic.*

propitious /prə'pɪʃəs/ adj formal likely to bring good results: *a propitious time to attack*

proponent /prə'pəʊnənt $ -'poʊ-/ n [C] formal someone who supports something or persuades people to do something: *a proponent of women's rights*

proportion /prə'pɔːʃən $ -'pɔːr-/ n **1** [C usually singular] a part of an amount or group: **+of** *The proportion of adults who smoke is decreasing.* | *a large proportion of the population* **2** [C,U] the relationship between two amounts: **proportion of sth to sth** *What's the proportion of boys to girls in your class?* | **in proportion to sth** *Taxes rise in proportion to the amount you earn.* **3** **out of/in proportion (with sth)** when the size of one part of something looks wrong or right in relation to other parts: *The porch is out of proportion with the rest of the house.* **4** **proportions** [plural] the size or importance of something: *a disaster of enormous proportions* **5** **out of (all) proportion (to sth)** too big or strong in relation to something: *Fear of violent crime is out of proportion to the actual risk.* | **get/blow sth out of proportion** (=treat something as more serious than it really is) **6** **keep sth in proportion** to react to a situation sensibly, and not think that it is worse than it really is **7** **sense of proportion** the ability to judge what is most important in a situation

proportional /prə'pɔːʃənəl $ -'pɔːr-/ also **proportionate** /-ʃənɪt/ adj if something is proportional to something else, its size, amount, importance etc is related to another amount: **+to** *The punishment should be proportional to the crime.*

proposal /prə'pəʊzəl $ -'poʊ-/ n [C] **1** a suggested plan: **+for** *his proposal for a change in the law* | **proposal to do sth** *a proposal to build a new road* **2** when you ask someone to marry you: *Did you accept his proposal?*

propose /prə'pəʊz $ -'poʊz/ v
1 [T] to officially suggest a plan [➡ **proposal**]: *The President proposed a 5% cut in tax.* | **+(that)** *I propose that we discuss this at a later meeting.* | **propose doing sth** *The report proposed extending the motorway.*
2 [I] to ask someone to marry you: **+to** *Tom proposed to me.*
3 [T] formal to intend to do something: **propose to do sth** *What do you propose to do?*
4 [T] to formally suggest someone for an official position: **propose sb for sth** *He proposed Jill for the position of Treasurer.*

proposition[1] /ˌprɒpə'zɪʃən $ ˌprɑː-/ n [C] **1** an offer or suggestion, especially in business or politics: *They came to me with a business proposition.* **2** **be a ... proposition** used to give your opinion about a possible activity: *Setting up your own business is a very attractive proposition.* **3** formal a statement in which you express an idea or opinion

proposition[2] v [T] formal to suggest to someone that they have sex with you

proprietor /prə'praɪətə $ -ər/ n [C] formal the owner of a business

propriety /prə'praɪəti/ n [U] formal correct social or moral behaviour

propulsion /prə'pʌlʃən/ n [U] technical the force that moves a vehicle forward: *jet propulsion*

pro rata /ˌprəʊ 'rɑːtə $ ˌproʊ 'reɪtə/ adj, adv technical a pro rata payment is calculated according to how much of something is used, how much work is done etc

prosaic /prəʊ'zeɪɪk, prə- $ proʊ-, prə-/ adj formal boring or ordinary —**prosaically** /-kli/ adv

proscribe /prəʊ'skraɪb $ proʊ-/ v [T] formal to officially say that something is not allowed: *Child labor is proscribed by law.* —**proscription** /-'skrɪpʃən/ n [C,U]

prose /prəʊz $ proʊz/ n [U] ordinary written language, not poetry

prosecute /'prɒsɪkjuːt $ 'prɑː-/ v [I,T] to say officially that you think someone is guilty of a crime and must be judged by a court of law: **prosecute sb for (doing) sth** *The police prosecuted him for theft.*

prosecution /ˌprɒsɪ'kjuːʃən $ ˌprɑː-/ n **1** [C,U] when someone is charged with a crime and judged in a court of law **2** **the prosecution** the lawyers who are trying to prove that someone is guilty of a crime in a court of law [≠ **defence**]: *The prosecution have a good case.* → see box at **COURT**

prosecutor /'prɒsɪkjuːtə $ 'prɑːsɪkjuːtər/ n [C] a lawyer who is trying to prove in a court of law that someone is guilty of a crime

prospect[1] /'prɒspekt $ 'prɑː-/ n **1** [C,U] the possibility that something will happen: **+of** *I see no prospect of things improving.* | **+for** *good prospects for increasing profits* **2** [singular] an event which will probably or definitely happen in the future – used when you say how you feel about it: **+of** *The prospect of marriage terrified Alice.* | *It's an exciting prospect.* **3** **prospects** [plural] chances of future success: *His job prospects are not good.*

prospect[2] /prə'spekt $ 'prɑːspekt/ v [I] to look for things such as gold or oil in the ground or under the sea —**prospector** n [C]

prospective /prə'spektɪv/ adj **prospective buyer/husband/employer etc** someone who is likely to do or be something

prospectus /prə'spektəs/ n [C] a small book that advertises a school, college, business etc

prosper /'prɒspə $ 'prɑːspər/ v [I] to be successful, especially financially: *Businesses are prospering.*

prosperity /prɒ'sperəti $ prɑː-/ n [U] when people have a lot of money

prosperous /'prɒspərəs $ 'prɑː-/ adj formal rich and successful: *a prosperous farmer* → see box at **RICH**

prostitute /'prɒstɪtjuːt $ 'prɑːstɪtuːt/ n [C] someone who earns money by having sex with people

prostitution /ˌprɒstɪ'tjuːʃən $ ˌprɑːstɪ'tuːʃən/ n [U] the work of prostitutes

prostrate /'prɒstreɪt $ 'prɑː-/ adj lying on your front with your face towards the ground

protagonist /prəʊ'tægənɪst $ proʊ-/ n [C] formal the main character in a play, film, or story

protect /prə'tekt/ v [I,T] to prevent someone or something from being harmed or damaged [➡ **protection**, **protective**]: *laws to protect the environment* | **protect sb/sth from sth** *The*

cover *protects the machine from dust.* | **protect (sb/sth) against sth** *a cream to protect your skin against sunburn*
—**protected** *adj: Owls are a protected species.*
—**protector** *n* [C]

protection /prə'tekʃən/ *n* [singular,U] when someone or something is protected, or something that protects you: **+of** *the protection of the environment* | **+against/from** *Vitamin C gives* **protection** *against cancer.* | **+for** *This law pro-* **vides protection** *for threatened animals.* | **as (a) protection (against sth)** *He pulled up his collar as protection against the wind.*

protective /prə'tektɪv/ *adj* **1** [only before noun] used to protect someone or something from damage: *protective clothing* **2** wanting to protect someone from harm: *She is very protective towards her children.*

protégé /'prɒtəʒeɪ $ 'proʊ-/ *n* [C] a young person who is taught and helped by an older and more experienced person

protein /'prəʊtiːn $ 'proʊ-/ *n* [C,U] a substance in food such as meat and eggs which helps your body to grow and be healthy

protest¹ /'prəʊtest $ 'proʊ-/ *n* [C,U]
1 when you do something to show publicly that you think something is wrong: **+against/over** *protests against the war* | **in protest (at/against sth)** *She resigned in protest at this behaviour.* | *Demonstrators* **staged** *a* **protest** *outside UN headquarters.*
2 words or actions which show that you do not want someone to do something, or that you dislike a situation very much: **+from** *I turned off the TV, despite* **loud protests** *from the kids.* | *He* **ignored** *her* **protests.** | **do sth under protest** *She paid the bill under protest* (=while making it clear that she did not want to pay).

protest² /prə'test/ *v* [I,T]
1 if people protest against something, they show publicly that they think it is wrong: **+against/at/about** *a group protesting against the war* | **protest sth** *AmE: Students protested the decision.*

2 to say that you strongly disagree with or are angry about something because it is wrong or unfair: *'Why should I take the blame for this!' she protested.*
3 protest your innocence to say strongly that you are not guilty

Protestant /'prɒtɪstənt $ 'prɑː-/ *n* [C] a Christian who is not a Roman Catholic —**Protestant** *adj* —**Protestantism** *n* [U]

protestation /ˌprɒtɪ'steɪʃən ˌprəʊ- $ ˌprɑː-, ˌproʊ-/ *n* [C] *formal* a strong statement saying that something is true or not true, when other people believe the opposite

protester, protestor /prə'testə $ -ər/ *n* [C] one of a group of people who are showing publicly that they think something is wrong or unfair: *anti-war protesters*

protocol /'prəʊtəkɒl $ 'proʊtəkɔːl, -kɑːl/ *n* [U] rules about the correct way to behave on official occasions

proton /'prəʊtɒn $ 'proʊtɑːn/ *n* [C] *technical* a part of the NUCLEUS of an atom which carries positive electricity

prototype /'prəʊtətaɪp $ 'proʊ-/ *n* [C] the first form of a new car, machine etc, which is used to test the design before it is made in large numbers

protracted /prə'træktɪd/ *adj* continuing for a long time, usually longer than necessary: *protracted negotiations*

protractor /prə'træktə $ proʊ'træktər/ *n* [C] a flat object shaped like a half-circle, used for measuring and drawing angles

protrude /prə'truːd $ proʊ-/ *v* [I] *formal* to stick out from somewhere: *a rock protruding from the water* —**protrusion** /prə'truːʒən $ proʊ-/ *n* [C]

proud /praʊd/ *adj*
1 feeling pleased because you think that something you have achieved or are connected with is very good [➔ **pride**]: **+of** *Her parents are very proud of her.* | **proud to do/be sth** *I'm proud to receive this award.* | **+(that)** *She was proud that her book was going to be published.* | **proudest moment/achievement/possession** *His proudest moment* (=the one he is most proud of) *was winning the cup final.*
2 having respect for yourself, so that you are embarrassed to ask for help when you are in a difficult situation: *She was too proud to ask him for money.*
3 *disapproving* thinking that you are better, more important etc than other people

4 do sb proud to make people feel proud of you by doing something well: *The team did their fans proud.*
—**proudly** *adv*

prove /pruːv/ *v* past tense **proved**, past participle **proved** or **proven** *especially AmE* /'pruːvən/
1 [T] to show that something is definitely true [➔ **proof**]: *You're wrong and I can prove it.* |

+(that) *Tests have proved that the system works.* | **prove sth to sb** *I knew she had done it, but I couldn't prove it to Joe.* | **prove sb's guilt/innocence** *evidence that proves his guilt* | **prove sb right/wrong** *They said I was too old, but I proved them wrong.* | *To* **prove** *his* **point** (=show that he was right), *he showed me the results.*
2 [linking verb] if something proves useful, difficult etc, it is found to be useful, difficult etc: *Getting a job proved difficult.* | **prove to be sth** *The design proved to be a success.*
3 prove yourself/prove something (to sb) to show that you can do something well: *When I first started this job, I felt I had to prove myself.*

proven /'pruːvən, 'prəʊvən $ 'pruːvən, 'pruːvən/ *adj* shown to be good or true: *a player of proven ability*

proverb /'prɒvɜːb $ 'prɑːvɜːrb/ *n* [C] a short well-known sentence that tells you something about life, such as 'Many hands make light work'
→ see box at **PHRASE**

proverbial /prə'vɜːbiəl $ -ɜːr-/ *adj* [only before noun] used when you use all or part of a well-known expression: *There is little sign of light at the end of the proverbial tunnel.* —**proverbially** *adv*

provide /prə'vaɪd/ *v* [T] to give someone something they need [➡ **provision**]: *Tea and biscuits will be provided.* | **provide sth for sb** *The hotel provides a shoe-cleaning service for guests.* | **provide sb with sth** *I can provide you with a place to stay.*—**provider** *n* [C] *an Internet service provider*

provide for sb/sth *phr v* **1** to give someone the things they need to live, such as money, food etc: *He has to provide for a family of five.* **2** *formal* if a law, rule, or plan provides for something, it makes it possible for it to be done or dealt with

provided /prə'vaɪdɪd/ also **provided that** *linking word* used to say that something will happen only if another thing happens: *You will get good marks, provided you do the work.*

Providence, providence /'prɒvɪdəns $ 'prɑː-/ *n* [U] *literary* a force which some people believe controls our lives and protects us

providing /prə'vaɪdɪŋ/ also **providing that** *linking word* used to say that something will happen only if another thing happens [= **provided**]

province /'prɒvɪns $ 'prɑː-/ *n* [C] **1** one of the large areas into which some countries are divided: *a Chinese province* **2 the provinces** the parts of a country that are not near the capital

provincial /prə'vɪnʃəl/ *adj* **1** relating to a province or the provinces: *the provincial capital* **2** someone who is provincial is not modern or fashionable, because they do not live in a large city

provision /prə'vɪʒən/ *n* **1** [C usually singular, U] when you provide something that someone needs: *the provision of childcare facilities* **2 make provision for sb/sth** to make arrangements for someone or something: *He made provision for his wife in his will* (=arranged for her to have money etc when he dies). **3 provisions** [plural] food supplies: *We had enough provisions*

for a week. **4** [C] a part of an agreement or law: *the provisions of the treaty*

provisional /prə'vɪʒənəl/ *adj* likely or able to be changed in the future: *a provisional government* —**provisionally** *adv*

proviso /prə'vaɪzəʊ $ -zoʊ/ *n* [C] plural **provisos** *formal* something that you say must happen before you allow another thing to happen

provocation /ˌprɒvə'keɪʃən $ ˌprɑː-/ *n* [C,U] an action that makes someone angry or upset, or is intended to do this: *He attacked me totally without provocation.*

provocative /prə'vɒkətɪv $ -'vɑː-/ *adj* **1** intended to make someone angry or upset, or to cause a lot of discussion: *a provocative comment* **2** intended to make someone sexually excited: *provocative images of young women* —**provocatively** *adv*

provoke /prə'vəʊk $ -'voʊk/ *v* [T] **1** to cause a reaction or feeling: *The plan provoked widespread criticism.* **2** to deliberately make someone angry: *The dog wouldn't have attacked him if it hadn't been provoked.*

provost, Provost /'prɒvəst $ 'proʊvoʊst/ *n* [C] an important official at a university

prow /praʊ/ *n* [C] the front part of a ship or boat

prowess /'praʊɪs/ *n* [U] *formal* great skill at doing something: *athletic prowess*

prowl¹ /praʊl/ *v* [I,T] to move around an area quietly, especially when hunting: *a tiger prowling through the jungle*

prowl² *n* **be on the prowl** to be moving around quietly, hunting for another animal, or looking for someone to attack

prowler /'praʊlə $ -ər/ *n* [C] someone who moves around quietly at night, especially in order to steal things or attack someone

proximity /prɒk'sɪməti $ prɑːk-/ *n* [U] *formal* closeness to something: **+to** *We chose this house because of its proximity to the school.*

proxy /'prɒksi $ 'prɑːksi/ *n* **by proxy** if you do something by proxy, you arrange for someone else to do it for you

prude /pruːd/ *n* [C] *disapproving* someone who is easily shocked by anything relating to sex —**prudish** *adj* —**prudishness, prudery** *n* [U]

prudent /'pruːdənt/ *adj* sensible and careful: *prudent use of resources* —**prudence** *n* [U]

prune¹ /pruːn/ also **prune back** *v* [T] to cut branches off a tree or bush

prune² *n* [C] a dried **PLUM**

prurient /'prʊəriənt $ 'prʊr-/ *adj* *formal disapproving* showing too much interest in sex —**prurience** *n* [U]

pry /praɪ/ *v* **pried, prying, pries** **1** [I] to try to find out about someone's private life in an impolite way: *I don't want to pry, but are you still seeing Tom?* **2** [T] *especially AmE* to force something open or away from something else [= **prise**]: **pry sth open/off etc** *I used a screwdriver to pry off the lid.*

PS /ˌpiː 'es/ *n* [C] **postscript** a note added to the end of a letter: *PS I love you*

psalm /sɑːm $ sɑːm, sɑːlm/ *n* [C] a song in the Bible praising God

pseudo- /sjuːdəʊ $ suːdoʊ/ *prefix* not real: *pseudoscience*

pseudonym /'sju:dənɪm $ 'su:-/ n [C] a name used by a writer, artist etc instead of his or her real name → see box at NAME

psych /saɪk/ v

psych yourself up phr v informal to prepare for something difficult by telling yourself that you can do it —**psyched up** adj

psyche /'saɪki/ n [C] your mind and deepest feelings: the human psyche

psychedelic /ˌsaɪkᵻ'delɪk◂/ adj producing or having bright colours and strange patterns

psychiatrist /saɪˈkaɪətrᵻst $ sə-/ n [C] a doctor who treats people who have a mental illness [➡ **psychologist**] → see box at DOCTOR

psychiatry /saɪˈkaɪətri $ sə-/ n [U] the study and treatment of mental illness —**psychiatric** /ˌsaɪki'ætrɪk◂/ adj: a psychiatric hospital

psychic¹ /'saɪkɪk/ adj related to strange events or things that cannot be explained by science: **psychic phenomena** | She claims to have **psychic powers**.

psychic² n [C] someone with special powers, such as knowing what people are thinking

psycho /'saɪkəʊ $ -koʊ/ n [C] plural **psychos** informal a crazy person who is violent and dangerous

psychoanalysis /ˌsaɪkəʊ-ə'nælᵻsᵻs $ -koʊ-/ n [U] a treatment for mental illness that involves talking to the patient about their life, dreams, feelings etc

psychoanalyst /ˌsaɪkəʊ'ænəl-ᵻst $ -koʊ-/ n [C] someone who treats mental illness using psychoanalysis → see box at DOCTOR

psychological /ˌsaɪkə'lɒdʒɪkəl◂ $ -'lɑː-/ adj relating to your mind, or the study of people's minds: psychological problems —**psychologically** /-kli/ adv

psychologist /saɪˈkɒlədʒᵻst $ -'kɑː-/ n [C] someone who studies the way people's minds work [➡ **psychiatrist**]

psychology /saɪˈkɒlədʒi $ -'kɑː-/ n plural **psychologies** **1** [U] the study of the way people's minds work **2** [C,U] the way that a particular kind of person thinks and behaves: the psychology of child killers

psychopath /'saɪkəpæθ/ n [C] someone who has a mental illness that makes them violent and dangerous —**psychopathic** /ˌsaɪkə'pæθɪk◂/ adj

psychosis /saɪˈkəʊsᵻs $ -'koʊ-/ n [C,U] plural **psychoses** /-siːz/ a serious mental illness

psychosomatic /ˌsaɪkəʊsə'mætɪk◂ $ -kəsə-/ adj technical a psychosomatic illness is caused by your mind, not by a real physical problem

psychotherapy /ˌsaɪkəʊ'θerəpi $ -koʊ-/ n [U] the treatment of mental illness by talking to someone about their problems, rather than using drugs —**psychotherapist** n [C] → see box at DOCTOR

psychotic /saɪˈkɒtɪk $ -'kɑː-/ adj relating to serious mental illness: psychotic behaviour

pt. the written abbreviation of **part**, the written abbreviation of **pint**

PTA /ˌpiː tiː 'eɪ/ n [C] BrE Parent Teacher Association an organization of the teachers and parents of children at a school [= **PTO** AmE]

PTO¹ /ˌpiː tiː 'əʊ $ -'oʊ/ **please turn over** used at the bottom of a page

PTO² AmE **Parent-Teacher Organization** an organization of the teachers and parents of children at a school [= **PTA** BrE]

pub /pʌb/ n [C] BrE a building where you can buy and drink beer, wine etc, and where meals are often served [= **bar**]: Are you **going to the pub**? | He'd been **in the pub** (=drinking in a pub) all day. | a pub lunch

puberty /'pjuːbəti $ -ər-/ n [U] the time when your body changes from being a child to being an adult

pubic /'pjuːbɪk/ adj relating to the sex organs: pubic hair

public¹ /'pʌblɪk/ adj

1 relating to the ordinary people in a country: **Public opinion** is in favor of the war. | **public health** risks | Can you prove your actions were **in the public interest** (=useful or helpful to ordinary people)?

2 available for anyone to use [≠ **private**]: a public telephone | public toilets | a ban on smoking in **public places** | damage to **public property**

3 relating to the government and the services it provides: cuts in **public spending** | She was elected to **public office** (=an important government job).

4 known, seen, or talked about by most people: There is to be a **public inquiry** into the incident. | We need a wider **public debate** on gay issues. | His job puts him **in the public eye** (=people know about what he does). | **go public/make sth public** (=tell people something that was secret) The name of the killer was made public.

—**publicly** adv: The matter was never discussed publicly.

public² n

1 the public [also + plural verb BrE] people in general: The museum is open to the public every day. | Police appealed to **members of the public** for help. | They are not yet on sale to the general **public** (=ordinary people). | The public are fed up with the Government's feeble excuses. | **the travelling/viewing/record-buying etc public** (=people who travel, watch television etc) a campaign aimed at the record-buying public → see box at PEOPLE

2 in public if you do something in public, you do it where other people can see you: I hate having rows in public.

public ad'dress ˌsystem n [C] a PA

publican /'pʌblɪkən/ n [C] someone who owns or manages a PUB

publication /ˌpʌblᵻ'keɪʃən/ n **1** [U] the process of printing a book, magazine etc and offering it for sale [➡ **publish**]: +of the publication of her latest novel | His article was accepted for publication. **2** [U] when information is made available to people: +of the publication of exam results on the Web **3** [C] formal a book, magazine etc that is printed and sold: a monthly publication | scientific publications

public 'figure n [C] someone who is often on television, in newspapers and magazines etc

public 'holiday n [C] BrE a day when people do not work and many shops are closed [= **national holiday** AmE]

public 'house n [C] BrE formal a PUB

P

publicist /'pʌblɪˌsɪst/ n [C] someone whose job is to make sure that people know about a new film, book, event etc

publicity /pʌ'blɪsɪti/ n [U]
1 attention that someone or something gets from newspapers, television etc: **good/bad etc publicity** *They had hoped to **avoid bad publicity**.* | **attract/receive publicity** *The trial received **widespread publicity**.*
2 the business of making sure that people know about a new film, book, event etc: *We launched a **publicity campaign** for the new range of sports shoe.* | **advance publicity** | *The fight was just a **publicity stunt** (=something only done to get publicity).*

publicize also **-ise** BrE /'pʌblɪˌsaɪz/ v [T] to tell people about a new film, book, event etc: **well/ highly publicized** *His visit has been highly publicized.*

public re'lations n abbreviation **PR 1** [U] the work of explaining to people what an organization does, so that they will understand and approve of it **2** [plural] the relationship between an organization and ordinary people

public 'school n [C] **1** in Britain, an expensive private school for children aged between 13 and 18 **2** in the US, a school that the government pays for

public-'spirited adj willing to help people and society in general

public 'television n [U] a television service in the US that the government, large companies, and ordinary people pay for

public 'transport BrE; **public transpor'tation** AmE n [U] trains, buses etc that are available for everyone to use

publish /'pʌblɪʃ/ v
1 [I,T] to print a book, magazine etc and offer it for sale [➔ **publication**]: *The book was published in 1968.*
2 [T] if a newspaper, magazine etc publishes a story, photograph etc, it prints it: *We publish as many of your letters as we can.*
3 [T] to make information available: *The results will be published this week.*
4 [I,T] if a writer, musician etc publishes his or her work, their work is printed in a book, magazine etc: *She's published a few short stories.*

publisher /'pʌblɪʃə $ -ər/ n [C] a person or company that produces books, magazines etc and offers them for sale

publishing /'pʌblɪʃɪŋ/ n [U] the business of producing books, magazines etc and offering them for sale

puck /pʌk/ n [C] the hard flat piece of rubber used in the game of ICE HOCKEY

pudding /'pʊdɪŋ/ n [C,U]
1 a sweet food made with milk, eggs, sugar, flour etc: *chocolate pudding*
2 BrE sweet food eaten at the end of a meal: *What's for pudding?*

puddle /'pʌdl/ n [C] a small pool of liquid, especially rain water: *children splashing through the puddles*

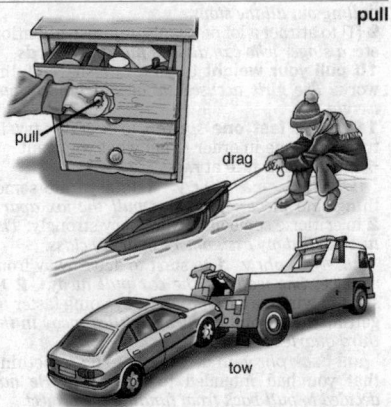
puddle

pudgy /'pʌdʒi/ adj disapproving fat

puff¹ /pʌf/ v **1** [I] to breathe quickly after running, carrying something heavy etc: *George **puffed and panted** as he ran.*
2 [I,T] to smoke a cigarette, pipe etc: **+at/on** *He puffed thoughtfully on his pipe.* **3** [I,T] if something puffs smoke, steam etc, small amounts of smoke, steam etc keep coming out of it: *a chimney puffing out black smoke*
puff sth ⇔ **out** phr v to make your cheeks or chest bigger by filling them with air
puff up phr v if part of your body puffs up, it becomes swollen: *His ankle had started to puff up.*

puff² n [C] **1** when you breathe smoke in and out: *He took a puff on his cigar.* **2** a small amount of air, smoke, wind etc: *puffs of smoke*

puffy /'pʌfi/ adj if part of your body is puffy, it is swollen: *Her eyes were red and puffy from crying.* —**puffiness** n [U]

pugnacious /pʌg'neɪʃəs/ adj formal very eager to argue or fight with people

puke /pjuːk/ v [I,T] informal to VOMIT —**puke** n [U]

pull

pull¹ /pʊl/ v
1 [I,T] to make something move in a particular direction, especially towards you, by holding it and using force in that direction [≠ push]: *He pulled her close and kissed her.* | **pull sb/sth out/from/away etc** *A motorist stopped and helped to pull him from the water.* | *Some kids had pulled up all the flowers.* | *Pulling on her coat, she ran outside.* | **pull sth open/shut** *Pull the door shut behind you.* | **pull the curtains/ blinds etc** (=open or close them) ➔ see picture on page A11

tug – to pull something suddenly, especially several times: *The little boy was tugging at her sleeve.*

drag – to pull something somewhere, usually along the ground: *I dragged the chair upstairs.*

haul – to pull something heavy, often using a rope: *fishermen hauling in their nets*

tow – to pull another vehicle or boat: *cars towing caravans*

heave – to pull or lift something very heavy, especially with one movement: *We managed to heave the piano into position.*
→ PUSH

2 [T] to move while attached to something so that it moves along behind you: *a car pulling a trailer*
3 [I,T] to move away from someone or something: **pull (sth) away/free** *He struggled to pull free.* | **pull sth out of/from sth** *She pulled her arm from his grasp.* | **+back** *As he moved, she pulled back.*
4 pull a muscle to injure a muscle by stretching it: *Paul pulled a muscle in training.*
5 pull a knife/gun (on sb) to take out a weapon and threaten someone with it
6 pull sb's leg to tell someone something that is untrue, as a joke: *Don't worry – I'm only pulling your leg.*
7 pull strings to secretly use your influence with important people to get what you want
8 pull out all the stops to do everything you can to make something succeed: *The doctors are pulling out all the stops.*
9 [T] to attract a lot of people, interest, attention etc: *a singer who can always **pull the crowds***
10 pull your weight to do a fair share of the work: *The girls accused us of not pulling our weight.*
11 pull a fast one *spoken* to secretly try to trick someone in order to get what you want
→ **make/pull a face** at FACE¹

pull sth ⇔ **apart** *phr v* **1** to separate something into pieces: *The dogs pull the fox apart.* **2** to criticize someone's work very strongly: *The tutor pulled my assignment apart in class.*

pull away *phr v* **1** to start to drive away from a place: *She watched the car pull away.* **2** to start to win in a race or game, by going faster or getting more points: *Chicago pulled away in the third quarter to win 107–76.*

pull back *phr v* to decide not to do something that you had intended to do: **+from** *He has decided to pull back from funding the project.*

pull sth ⇔ **down** *phr v* to destroy a building, wall etc: *My old school was pulled down.*

pull in *phr v* **1** to drive to the side of the road and stop: *A police car pulled in behind me.* **2** if a train pulls in, it arrives at a station

pull off *phr v* **1 pull sth** ⇔ **off** to succeed in doing something difficult: *The goalkeeper pulled off six terrific saves.* **2 pull off (sth)** to drive a car off the road you are on so that you can stop, change direction etc: *Shall we pull off at the next junction?*

pull out *phr v* **1** if a car pulls out, it moves away from the side of a road into a line of traffic: *Some idiot pulled out in front of me.* → see

box at DRIVE **2** if a train pulls out, it starts to leave a station **3** to not be involved in something that you had agreed to do: **+of** *The injury may force him to pull out of the championship.* **4** to leave a place or situation: **+of** *The country is just pulling out of a bad year.* | **pull sb/sth** ⇔ **out** *US troops were pulled out on Sunday.*

pull (sb/sth) over *phr v* if a car pulls over, it moves to the side of the road and stops: *The cops pulled him over for speeding.*

pull through *phr v informal* to stay alive after you have been very ill or badly injured: *Do the doctors think he'll pull through?*

pull together *phr v* **1** if a group of people pull together, they work hard together to succeed: *If we all pull together, we can win.* **2 pull yourself together** *informal* to force yourself to be calm and stop behaving in an uncontrolled way: *Pull yourself together, man!*

pull up *phr v* if a car pulls up, it stops: *A red Buick pulled up at the lights.*

pull² *n* **1** [C] the movement you make when you pull something towards you [≠ push]: **Give the rope a pull.** **2** [singular] a force such as GRAVITY that makes things move in a particular direction: *the gravitational pull of the moon*

pulley /ˈpʊli/ *n* [C] a piece of equipment used for lifting things, which has a rope and a wheel

pullout /ˈpʊlaʊt/, **ˈpull-out** *n* [C] **1** when an army, organization etc leaves a place: *the pullout of troops* **2** part of a book or magazine that you take out and read separately

pullover /ˈpʊlˌəʊvə $ -ˌoʊvər/ *n* [C] a SWEATER

pulp /pʌlp/ *n* [U] **1** a soft wet substance made by crushing something: *wood pulp* **2** the soft part inside fruit or vegetables [= flesh]

pulpit /ˈpʊlpɪt/ *n* [C] a high place where the priest in a church stands to speak to the people

pulsate /pʌlˈseɪt $ ˈpʌlseɪt/ *v* [I] to move, change, or make sounds in a strong regular way: *pulsating lights* —**pulsation** /pʌlˈseɪʃən/ *n* [C,U]

pulse¹ /pʌls/ *n* **1** [C usually singular] the regular beat that your heart makes as it pumps blood around your body: *a fast **pulse rate*** | **take sb's pulse** (=touch someone's wrist or neck to check how fast their heart is beating) **2** [C usually plural] seeds such as beans and LENTILS that you can eat

pulse² *v* [I] to move quickly with a strong regular beat or sound: *the blood pulsing through his veins*

pulverize also **-ise** *BrE* /ˈpʌlvəraɪz/ *v* [T] **1** to crush something into powder: *a machine that pulverizes rocks* **2** *informal* to defeat someone completely

pummel /ˈpʌməl/ *v* [T] **pummelled, pummelling** *BrE*; **pummeled, pummeling** *AmE* to hit someone or something many times with your FISTS (=closed hands)

pump¹ /pʌmp/ *n* [C] **1** a machine that forces liquid or gas into or out of something: **water/ fuel/air etc pump** → see picture at BICYCLE **2** a type of plain light shoe: *a pair of black pumps*

pump²
1 [I,T] if liquid or gas pumps somewhere, or if you pump it, it is forced to move in a particular direction: **+from/out of** *Blood was pumping from the wound.* | **pump sth into/out of etc sth** *Fire crews will pump the water out of the flooded*

homes. | *Your heart pumps blood around your body.* | **pump gas** *AmE* (=put gasoline in a car)
2 [T] *informal* if you pump someone for information, you ask them lots of questions: **pump sb for sth** *Laura began to pump Ben for more details.*
3 [I] to move quickly up and down or in and out: *His legs pumped harder as he cycled up the hill.*
   pump sth into sth *phr v* if you pump money into a business or project, you spend a lot of money on it: *The government has pumped millions into the space project.*
   pump sth ⇔ out *phr v* to keep producing a lot of something: *bands that pump out three new records a month*
   pump sth ⇔ up *phr v* **1** to fill a tyre, ball etc with air [= inflate]: *Pump up the tyres before a long journey.* **2** to increase the value, amount, or level of something: *Nick pumped up the volume on the stereo.*

pumpkin /'pʌmpkɪn/ *n* [C,U] a large round orange vegetable that grows on the ground: *pumpkin pie*

pun /pʌn/ *n* [C] a joke that is funny because it uses two words that sound the same but have different meanings

punch¹ /pʌntʃ/ *v* [T]
1 to hit someone or something hard with your FIST (=closed hand): **punch sb on/in sth** *He punched me in the face.* → see box at HIT → see picture on page A11
2 to make a hole in something, using a sharp tool: *The inspector punched our tickets.* | *These bullets can punch a hole through 20mm steel.*
3 punch the air to move your FIST up quickly above your head, to show that you are pleased

punch² *n* **1** [C] when you hit someone once with your FIST (=closed hand): *a punch in the stomach* **2** [U] a drink made from fruit juice, sugar, and alcohol **3** [C] a sharp tool used to make a hole in something

'punch bag *BrE*; **'punching bag** *AmE n* [C] a heavy leather bag that BOXERS hit when they are training

punchline /'pʌntʃlaɪn/, **'punch line** *n* [C] the last few words of a joke or story, which make it funny or clever: *Jake had forgotten the punchline.*

'punch-up *n* [C] *BrE informal* a fight

punctual /'pʌŋktʃuəl/ *adj* arriving at exactly the time that has been arranged: *Ted's always very punctual.* —**punctually** *adv* —**punctuality** /ˌpʌŋktʃu'æləti/ *n* [U]

punctuate /'pʌŋktʃueɪt/ *v* [T] **1** to divide writing into sentences, phrases etc, using COMMAS (,), FULL STOPS (.) etc **2 be punctuated by/with sth** to be interrupted by something several times: *silence punctuated by cries*

punctuation /ˌpʌŋktʃu'eɪʃən/ *n* [U] the use of COMMAS (,), FULL STOPS (.) etc in writing: *The punctuation in this essay is awful.*

ˌpunctu'ation mark *n* [C] a sign, such as a COMMA (,) or a FULL STOP (.), used to divide writing into sentences, phrases etc

puncture¹ /'pʌŋktʃə $ -ər/ *n* [C] **1** a small hole made by a sharp point **2** *BrE* a hole in a tyre [= flat *AmE*]

puncture² *v* [I,T] if you puncture something, or if it punctures, a small hole appears in it

pundit /'pʌndɪt/ *n* [C] a person who often gives their opinion about something on television or in newspapers: *political pundits*

pungent /'pʌndʒənt/ *adj* having a strong taste or smell: *the pungent smell of garlic* —**pungency** *n* [U]

punish /'pʌnɪʃ/ *v* [T]
1 to do something unpleasant to someone because they have done something wrong [➡ punishment]: **punish sb for (doing) sth** *He was severely punished for lying to his father.* | *She deserves to be punished for her crimes.* | **punish sb by doing sth** *The class was punished by being given extra work.*
2 if a crime is punished in a particular way, anyone who is guilty of it receives that punishment: *Drug smuggling is punished by death.*

punishable /'pʌnɪʃəbəl/ *adj* a crime that is punishable by death, prison etc is punished in that way

punishing /'pʌnɪʃɪŋ/ *adj* difficult to do and making you tired: *a punishing schedule*

punishment /'pʌnɪʃmənt/ *n* [C,U] something that is done to punish someone [➡ punitive]: *tougher punishments for sex offenders* | *They had to stay late after school as a punishment.* | +**for** *the punishment for stealing*

sentence – a punishment given by a judge in a court: *a prison sentence*
fine – an amount of money that you must pay as a punishment: *I got a fine for speeding.*
penalty – a general word for a punishment given to someone who has broken a law, rule, or agreement: *Drug dealers face severe penalties.*
death sentence/penalty also **capital punishment** – when someone is killed as punishment for a crime: *The UK no longer has the death penalty.*
community service – unpaid work helping other people that someone does as punishment for a crime: *He was ordered to do 60 hours community service.*
corporal punishment – when someone punishes a child by hitting them: *Corporal punishment is illegal in schools.*

punitive /'pjuːnɪtɪv/ *adj* done to punish someone, or like a punishment: *punitive action* | *punitive price rises* —**punitively** *adv*

punk /pʌŋk/ *n* **1** [U] a type of loud music and strange fashions that were popular in the 1970s and 1980s: *punk music* **2** [C] *AmE informal* a young man who fights and breaks the law

punnet /'pʌnɪt/ *n* [C] *BrE* a small box in which small fruit is sold

punt /pʌnt/ *n* [C] a long narrow boat that you move by pushing a long pole against the bottom of the river —**punt** *v* [T]

punter /'pʌntə $ -ər/ *n* [C] *BrE informal* **1** someone who buys something [= customer] **2** someone who makes a BET on the result of a race, game etc

puny /'pjuːni/ *adj* small, thin, and weak: *a puny little kid*

pup /pʌp/ *n* [C] a PUPPY

pupil /'pjuːpəl/ *n* [C]
1 *BrE* a child in a school: *the star pupil* (=the best)
2 someone who learns from an experienced musician, artist etc: *a pupil of Yehudi Menuhin*
3 the round black part in the middle of your eye [➔ **iris**]

puppet

puppet

hand/glove puppet

puppet /'pʌpɪt/ *n* [C] **1** a model of a person or animal that you move by putting your hand inside it or by pulling strings attached to it: *a puppet show* **2** *disapproving* a person or organization that allows other people to control them and make their decisions: *a puppet leader*

puppy /'pʌpi/ *n* [C] plural **puppies** a young dog

purchase¹ /'pɜːtʃəs $ 'pɜːr-/ *v* [T] *formal* to buy something: *Where did you purchase the car?* —**purchaser** *n* [C]

purchase² *n* [C,U] *formal* something you buy, or the act of buying something: +**of** *money for the purchase of new equipment* | *Every time you* **make** *a* **purchase***, you pay tax.*

pure /pjʊə $ pjʊr/ *adj*
1 not mixed with anything else [≠ **impure**]: *pure gold* | **pure cotton/wool/silk etc** *pure wool blankets* ➔ see box at **NATURAL**
2 complete and total [= **sheer**]: *We met by* **pure chance***.* | *a smile of* **pure joy**
3 clean and not containing anything harmful or unhealthy: **pure drinking water** | *In the mountains, the air is* **pure***.*
4 *literary* without any sexual experience or evil thoughts: *a pure young girl*
5 [only before noun] work in science etc that increases our knowledge of the subject rather than using it for practical purposes [➔ **applied**]: *pure mathematics*

puree /'pjʊəreɪ $ pjʊ'reɪ/ *n* [C,U] food that has been boiled or crushed until it is almost a liquid: *tomato puree* —**puree** *v* [T]

purely /'pjʊəli $ 'pjʊrli/ *adv* completely and only: *He did it for* **purely** *selfish reasons.* | *It happened* **purely by chance***.*

Purgatory /'pɜːɡətəri $ 'pɜːrɡətɔːri/ *n* in Roman Catholic belief, a place where the souls of dead people suffer until they are pure enough to enter heaven

purge /pɜːdʒ $ pɜːrdʒ/ *v* [T] to remove unwanted people or things from something: **purge sth of sb/sth** *Local languages were purged of Russian words.* —**purge** *n* [C] *a purge of the army*

purify /'pjʊərɪfaɪ $ 'pjʊr-/ *v* [T] **purified, purifying, purifies** to remove dirty or unwanted parts from something: *purified water* —**purification** /ˌpjʊərɪfɪ'keɪʃən $ ˌpjʊr-/ *n* [U]

purist /'pjʊərɪst $ 'pjʊr-/ *n* [C] someone who has very strict ideas about the correct way to do something

puritanical /ˌpjʊərɪ'tænɪkəl◂ $ ˌpjʊr-/ *adj disapproving* very strict about moral matters, especially sex: *Her parents had very puritanical views.* —**puritan** *n* [C]

purity /'pjʊərɪti $ 'pjʊr-/ *n* [U] the quality of being pure: *the purity of our water* | *moral purity*

purple /'pɜːpəl $ 'pɜːr-/ *n* [U] a dark colour made from red mixed with blue ➔ see picture at **PATTERN**
—**purple** *adj*: *a purple shirt*

purport /pɜː'pɔːt $ pɜːr'pɔːrt/ *v* [T] *formal* to claim to be or do something, even if this is not true: *a man purporting to be a police officer* —**purportedly** *adv*

purpose /'pɜːpəs $ 'pɜːr-/ *n*
1 [C] the purpose of something is what it is intended to achieve: **the purpose of (doing) sth** *What is the purpose of your visit to England?* | *The purpose of running a business is to make money.*

aim – something that you want to achieve: *Our main aim is to find the child before dark.*
goal – something that you hope to achieve in the future: *Athletes set themselves personal goals.*
objective – something that you are working hard to achieve: *The major objectives have been achieved.*

2 on purpose deliberately [≠ **by accident**]: *I'm sorry. I didn't hurt you on purpose.*
3 [C usually plural] what something is used for: *The planes may be used for military purposes.*
4 [U] determination to succeed in what you want to do: *She went back to her work with a new* **sense of purpose***.*
➔ **to/for all intents and purposes** at **INTENT²**

purpose-'built *adj BrE* designed and made for a particular purpose: *purpose-built toilets for disabled people*

purposeful /'pɜːpəsfəl $ 'pɜːr-/ *adj* having a clear aim or purpose [= **determined**]: *He picked up his toolbox in a purposeful manner.* —**purposefully** *adv*

purposely /'pɜːpəsli $ 'pɜːr-/ *adv* deliberately [= **on purpose**]: *They purposely left him out of the discussion.*

purr /pɜː $ pɜːr/ *v* [I] if a cat purrs, it makes a soft, low sound in its throat to show that it is pleased —**purr** *n* [C]

purse¹ /pɜːs $ pɜːrs/ *n*
1 [C] *BrE* a small container used for carrying money, especially by women [= **wallet** *AmE*]: *I opened my handbag and took out my purse.*
2 [C] *AmE* a bag used by women to carry money and personal things [= **handbag** *BrE*] ➔ see picture at **BAG¹**

3 [singular] *formal* the amount of money that a person, organization, or country has available to spend: *demands on the public purse*
4 the purse strings used to refer to the control of spending in a family, company, country etc: *She holds the purse strings.*

purse² *v* **purse your lips** to bring your lips together tightly, especially to show that you do not like or do not agree with something

pursue /pəˈsjuː $ pərˈsuː/ *v* [T] **1** to continue doing something, or to try to achieve something over a long period of time: *He hoped to pursue a career in film-making.* **2 pursue the matter/question** to continue trying to find out about a particular subject or persuade someone: *Janet did not dare pursue the matter further.* **3** to chase someone or something in order to catch them: *The stolen car was pursued by police for several miles.* —**pursuer** *n* [C]

pursuit /pəˈsjuːt $ pərˈsuːt/ *n* **1** [U] when someone chases or follows someone else: *There were four police cars **in hot pursuit** (=following closely behind).* **2** [U] when someone tries to achieve something or get something: **in (the) pursuit of sth** *He left his home town in pursuit of work.* **3 pursuits** [plural] *formal* things that you spend time doing, especially to enjoy yourself: *outdoor pursuits*

purveyor /pɜːˈveɪə $ pɜːrˈveɪər/ *n* [C] *formal* a shop or company that sells or provides something: *purveyors of fine cheeses*

pus /pʌs/ *n* [U] yellow liquid produced in an infected part of your body

push¹ /pʊʃ/ *v*

1 [I,T] to make something move away from you by putting your hand on it and using force [≠ **pull**]: *It didn't move, so she pushed harder.* | **push sth/sb down/into etc sth** *Lisa pushed Amy into the pool.* | **push sth/sb away/back/aside etc** *She pushed him away.* | **push sth open/shut** *I slowly pushed the door open.* | *Push the green button to start the engine.* → see picture on page A11

THESAURUS

poke – to push someone or something with your finger or something sharp: *Jill poked the fish to see if it was alive.*
shove – to push someone or something roughly: *He shoved her against a wall.*
nudge – to push someone gently with your elbow to get their attention: *'Move up,' she said, nudging my arm.*
roll – to push a round object so that it moves forward: *He rolled the wheel over to the car.*
→ **PULL**

2 [I,T] to move forward, using your hands to move people or things away from you: *Don't push. Everyone will get a turn.* | **push (your) way past/through/into etc sth** *Heather pushed past us without speaking.* | *She pushed her way to the front of the crowd.*
3 [T] to encourage or force someone to do something or to work hard: **push sb into (doing) sth** *My parents pushed me into going to college.* | **push yourself** *Mike has been **pushing** himself too hard lately.*
4 [I,T] to try to persuade people to accept your ideas, opinions etc in order to achieve something: **+for** *He was **pushing hard** for changes in education.*
5 [T] to try to sell more of a product by advertising it a lot
6 [T] to make a number, amount, price etc greater or less: **push sth up/down** *The new tax will push up the price of consumer goods.*
7 [T] *informal* to sell illegal drugs [= **deal**]
8 push your luck *informal* to do something or ask for something when this is likely to annoy someone or involve a risk: *Don't push your luck.*
9 be pushing 40/50 etc *informal* to be nearly 40, 50 etc years old

push ahead *phr v* to continue trying to do something you have planned to do: **+with** *He has promised to push ahead with reform.*
push sb around also **push sb about** *BrE phr v informal* to tell someone what to do in a rude or threatening way
push in *phr v BrE informal* to go in front of other people who are waiting for something, instead of joining the end of the line: *Don't push in!*
push off *phr v BrE spoken* used to rudely tell someone to go away
push on *phr v* to continue travelling somewhere or trying to achieve something: *The others stopped for a rest, but I pushed on to the top.*
push sb/sth ⇔ over *phr v* to make someone or something fall to the ground by pushing them: *He went wild, pushing over tables and chairs.*
push sth ⇔ through *phr v* to get a plan, law etc officially accepted, especially quickly

push² *n* [C usually singular] **1** when someone pushes something [≠ **pull**]: *If the door's stuck, give it a push.* **2** when people try very hard to achieve something: *part of the party's final push for victory* **3 give sb the push** *BrE informal* **a)** to end a relationship with someone: *She gave her boyfriend the push.* **b)** to make someone leave their job **4 at a push** *BrE informal* used to say that something can be done if necessary, but it will be difficult: *We have room for five people, six at a push.* **5 when/if push comes to shove** if a situation becomes very difficult or action needs to be taken: *If push comes to shove, I can always rent out the house.*

pushbike /ˈpʊʃbaɪk/ *n* [C] *BrE* a bicycle
'push-button *adj* [only before noun] operated by pressing a button with your finger: *a push-button telephone*
pushchair /ˈpʊʃ-tʃeə $ -tʃer/ *n* [C] *BrE* a chair on wheels, used for pushing young children in [= **stroller** *AmE*]
pusher /ˈpʊʃə $ -ər/ *n* [C] *informal* someone who sells illegal drugs
pushover /ˈpʊʃˌəʊvə $ -ˌoʊvər/ *n* **be a pushover** *informal* **a)** to be easy to persuade, influence, or defeat: *The team is no pushover.* **b)** *BrE* to be easy to do or win: *The exam was a pushover.*
'push-up *n* [C] *AmE* an exercise in which you lie on the floor and push yourself up with your arms [= **press-up** *BrE*]
pushy /ˈpʊʃi/ *adj disapproving* someone who is pushy does everything they can to get what they want from other people: *pushy salespeople*

pussycat /'pʊsikæt/ also **puss** /pʊs/, **pussy** /'pʊsi/ n [C] BrE informal a cat – used especially by children

pussyfoot /'pʊsifʊt/ also **pussyfoot around/about** v [I] informal to be too careful and afraid to deal with a situation firmly

put

put on   take off

put /pʊt/ v [T] past tense and past participle **put** present participle **putting**

1 to move something to or into a place or position: **put sth in/on etc sth** Just put the bags on the table. | Where did you put the newspaper?

2 to change someone's situation or the way they feel: **put sb in a good/bad mood** The long delay had put us all in a bad mood. | Politics **puts** me to **sleep**.

3 to write or print something: **put sth in/on/ under etc sth** Put your name at the top of each answer sheet.

4 to say something in a particular way: It was an accident, an 'act of God' if you want to **put it like that**. | It is hard to **put into words** how I feel now. | He's not very musical, **to put it mildly** (=he's not musical at all).

5 to arrange for someone to go to a place, or to make them go there: I don't want to put my dad into hospital. | I'll **put the kids to bed**. | They **put** him **in prison** for life.

6 to ask a question or make a suggestion, especially in order to get someone's opinion or agreement: Can I **put a question** to you?

7 **put an end/a stop to** to stop an activity that is harmful or unacceptable: We must put an end to their threats.

8 **put sth into action/effect/practice** to start using a plan, idea, knowledge etc: James was keen to put the things he had learned into practice.

9 **put sth to use** to use something: We can put this money to use immediately.

10 **put sb to work** to make someone work

11 **put sth behind you** to stop thinking about a bad experience or a mistake in the past

12 **I wouldn't put it past sb (to do sth)** used to say that you think someone might do something wrong or illegal: I wouldn't put it past him to blackmail them.

13 **put sth right** to make a situation better, especially after someone has made a mistake or behaved badly

put sth ⇔ **across** phr v to explain your ideas, beliefs etc in a way that people can understand: She's good at putting her ideas across.

put sth ⇔ **aside** phr v to save money regularly in order to use it later: We're trying to put some money aside for a new car.

put sth ⇔ **away** phr v to put something in the place where it is usually kept: Those kids never put anything away!

put sth ⇔ **back** phr v **1** to return something to its place: I put the letter back in the envelope. **2** to delay something: The publication date has been put back by three months. **3** **put a clock/ watch back** to make a clock or watch show an earlier time

put sb/sth ⇔ **down** phr v **1** to put something onto a surface such as a table or the floor: She put down her knitting. **2** to criticize someone and make them feel silly or stupid: She's always putting him down. **3** to write something on a piece of paper: Put down your name and address. **4** to kill an animal because it is old or ill **5** **put down a revolution/revolt/rebellion etc** to stop a REVOLUTION etc by using force

put sth **down to** sth phr v to think that something is caused by something else: She put her illness down to stress.

put sb/sth ⇔ **forward** phr v **1** to suggest a plan or idea, or suggest someone for a job or position: Milne has put his name forward as a candidate at the next election. **2** **put a clock/watch forward** to make a clock or watch show a later time

put sth ⇔ **in** phr v **1** to add or replace equipment in your home [= install]: They're having a new bathroom put in. **2** to officially ask for something: She put in an insurance claim. **3** to spend time or effort doing something: Doug's been putting in a lot of hours at work recently. **4** **put in an appearance** to go to a social event, meeting etc for a short time

put sth **into** sth phr v to spend time, effort, or money doing something: We must put more money into education. | I put a lot of effort into writing that essay.

put sb/sth ⇔ **off** phr v **1** to delay doing something [= postpone]: You can't keep putting the decision off. **2** to tell someone that you cannot do something that you had agreed to do: I managed to put him off by promising to pay next week. **3** BrE to make it difficult for someone to do something by preventing them from thinking clearly about what they are doing: Stop laughing – you're putting me off! **4** BrE to make you dislike something or not want to do something: Don't be put off by the title – it's a really good book.

put sth ⇔ **on** phr v **1** to put clothes on your body [≠ take off]: Put your coat on – it's cold. → see picture on page A11 **2** to put MAKE-UP, cream etc on your skin: I need to put on some more lipstick. **3** to make a machine or a piece of equipment start working [= turn on]: Is it all right if I put the fire on? **4** to put a record, video etc into a machine and start playing it: Let's put some music on. **5** **put on weight/5 pounds/2 kg etc** to become heavier [→ gain] **6** to arrange or perform a concert, play etc: They're putting

on a concert to raise money for landmine victims.
7 to pretend to feel or believe something that you do not really feel or believe: *Don't take any notice of her – she's just **putting it on**. | I was trying to **put on a brave face** (=not show that I was sad or worried).*

put sb/sth ⇔ **out** *phr v* **1** to make a fire or cigarette stop burning [= **extinguish**] **2** to make an electric light stop working by pressing a button: *Don't forget to put out the lights when you leave.* **3** to produce a book, record, film etc: *They're putting out a new album in the fall.* **4** to make extra work or problems for someone: *Will it put you out if I bring an extra guest?*

put sb **through** *phr v* **1 put sb through sth** to make someone experience something unpleasant: *She was put through a lot during her first marriage, so I'm glad she's happy now.* **2** to connect someone to someone else on the telephone

put sth ⇔ **together** *phr v* **1** to make a machine or model by joining the different parts [= **assemble**]: *It took us all day to put the table together.* **2** to prepare or produce something by collecting information, ideas etc: *The band are currently putting a new album together.* **3 more/louder etc than ... put together** used to say that an amount is greater than a combined total: *Italy scored more points than the rest of the group put together.*

put sb/sth ⇔ **up** *phr v* **1** to build or make an upright structure [= **erect**]: *The kids were putting a tent up in the garden.* **2** to put a picture, sign etc on a wall so that people can see it: *Posters advertising the concert were put up on all the notice boards.* **3** to increase the cost of something [= **raise**]: *Our landlord keeps putting the rent up.* **4 put up money/£500/$3 million etc** to provide the money that is needed to do something: *Firth put up $42,000 in prize money for the contest.* **5** to let someone stay in your house for a short time: *Yeah, we can put you up for the night.* **6 put up resistance/a fight/a struggle** to argue against something or fight against someone in a determined way: *The rebels have put up fierce resistance.*

put sb **up to** sth *phr v* to encourage someone to do something stupid or dangerous: *It's not like Martha to steal – someone must have put her up to it.*

put up with sth *phr v* to accept a bad situation without complaining: *I don't know how you put up with all this noise.*

'put-down *n* [C] *informal* something someone says that is intended to make you feel stupid or unimportant

,put 'out *adj* [not before noun] *BrE informal* upset and offended: *Of course she feels put out when you don't ask what she wants to do.*

putrid /'pju:trɪd/ *adj* dead animals, plants etc that are putrid are decaying and smell very bad: *a putrid odour*

putt /pʌt/ *v* [I,T] to hit a golf ball lightly a short distance along the ground towards the hole
—**putt** *n* [C]

putty /'pʌti/ *n* [U] a soft substance used for fixing glass into window frames

puzzle[1] /'pʌzəl/ *n*

1 [C] a game or toy that you have to think about carefully in order to solve it or put it together [➡ **jigsaw**]: *a crossword puzzle | a jigsaw puzzle*

2 [usually singular] something that is difficult to understand or explain: **+of** *the puzzle of how the sun works | He thought he had solved the puzzle.*

puzzle
crossword puzzle

puzzle[2] *v* [T] if something puzzles you, you feel confused because you do not understand it: *What puzzles me is why he never mentioned this before.*

puzzle sth ⇔ **out** *phr v* to solve a confusing or difficult problem by thinking about it carefully: *I'm trying hard to puzzle things out.*

puzzle over sth *phr v* to think about something for a long time in order to understand it: *Joe sat puzzling over the map.*

puzzled /'pʌzəld/ *adj* confused and unable to understand something: **puzzled look/ expression/frown etc** *Dan had a puzzled expression on his face.*

puzzling /'pʌzlɪŋ/ *adj* difficult to understand or explain: *The results of the survey were a little puzzling.*

PVC /ˌpiː viː 'siː◂/ *n* [U] a type of plastic, used to make pipes, window frames, clothes etc

pyjamas *BrE*; **pajamas** *AmE* /pə'dʒɑːməz $ -'dʒæ-, -'dʒɑː-/ *n* [plural] light trousers and a shirt that you wear in bed

pylon /'paɪlən $ -lɑːn, -lən/ *n* [C] a tall metal structure that supports electric wires high above the ground

pyramid /'pɪrəmɪd/ *n* [C] a shape with a flat base and four sides in the shape of TRIANGLES that slope to a point at the top → see picture at **SHAPE**[1]

pyre /paɪə $ paɪr/ *n* [C] a high pile of wood on which a dead body is burned at a funeral ceremony: *a funeral pyre*

pylon

python /'paɪθən $ -θɑːn, -θən/ *n* [C] a large tropical snake that kills animals for food by crushing them

P

Q, q

Q, q /kjuː/ *n* [C,U] plural **Q's, q's** the 17th letter of the English alphabet

quack¹ /kwæk/ *v* [I] if a duck quacks, it makes a loud noise from its throat

quack² *n* [C] **1** the sound a duck makes **2** *informal disapproving* someone who pretends to be a doctor **3** *humorous* a doctor

quad /kwɒd/ *n* [C] *also* **quadrangle** /'kwɒdræŋgəl $ 'kwɑː-/ *n* [C] a square area with buildings all around it in a school or college

quadruple /'kwɒdrʊpəl, kwɒ'druː- $ kwɑː'druː-/ *v* [I,T] if you quadruple an amount, or if an amount quadruples, it becomes four times as big: *The number of car owners has quadrupled in the last twenty years.*

quagmire /'kwæɡmaɪə, 'kwɒɡ- $ 'kwæɡmaɪr/ *n* [C] **1** an area of soft wet muddy ground **2** a very difficult or complicated situation: *a legal quagmire*

quail¹ /kweɪl/ *n* [C,U] a small bird that is hunted for food and sport, or this bird as food

quail² *v* [I] *literary* to feel afraid: *Our troops quailed at the size of his army.*

quaint /kweɪnt/ *adj* attractive in an old-fashioned way: *quaint narrow streets*

quake¹ /kweɪk/ *v* [I] *formal* to shake because you are afraid: **+with** *Kate stood in the doorway **quaking with fear**.*

quake² *n* [C] *informal* an EARTHQUAKE

qualification /ˌkwɒlɪfɪ'keɪʃən $ ˌkwɑː-/ *n*

1 *especially BrE* [C usually plural] if you have a qualification, you have passed an examination or course to show you have a particular level of skill or knowledge in a subject: *He left school without any qualifications.* | *Applicants should **have** a teaching **qualification** and a year's experience.*

THESAURUS

educational/academic qualification – one relating to your school or university work and the examinations you passed

vocational qualification – one relating to skills you have been taught that will be useful in a job

professional qualification – one relating to the examinations you have passed in a particular type of professional work

certificate – an official document showing that you have passed an examination: *Keep all your examination certificates carefully.*

diploma – what you get when you successfully complete a course of study or training: *a diploma in nursing*

degree *BrE/*college diploma/degree *AmE* – what you get when you successfully complete a course of study at a university or college: *a degree in Modern Languages*

2 [C] a skill or quality that you need to do a job: **+for** *The mayor criticized his opponent's qualifications for the job.*
3 [U] when you achieve the necessary standard to work in a profession, enter a sports competition etc: **+for** *Portugal's qualification for the European Championships*
4 [C,U] something that you add to a statement to limit its effect or meaning [= **reservation**]: *He welcomed the proposal **without qualification**.*

qualified /'kwɒlɪfaɪd $ 'kwɑː-/ *adj* **1** having suitable knowledge, experience, or skills, especially for a particular job: **+for** *Gibbons is **highly qualified** for the job.* | **qualified to do sth** *He's not really **well qualified** to judge.* **2** having passed an official examination that shows you are trained to do a particular job: *a qualified teacher*

qualifier /'kwɒlɪfaɪə $ 'kwɑːlɪfaɪər/ *n* [C] **1** a game that you have to win to take part in a sports competition: *a World Cup qualifier* **2** a person or team who achieves the standard that is needed to enter a sports competition: *Bronson was the fastest qualifier at the US Olympic Trials.*

qualify /'kwɒlɪfaɪ $ 'kwɑː-/ *v* **qualified, qualifying, qualifies** **1** [I] to pass an examination that shows you are trained to do a particular job: **+as** *Sue qualified as a solicitor last year.* **2** [I] to be successful at one stage of a sports competition so that you can continue to the next stage: **+for** *The US beat Nigeria to qualify for the finals.* **3** [I,T] to have the right to do something, or to give someone the right to do something: **+for** *Members qualify for a 20% discount.* **4** [T] to add information to something you have already said in order to limit its meaning or effect: *Let me qualify that statement.*

qualitative /'kwɒlɪtətɪv $ 'kwɑːlɪteɪ-/ *adj* *formal* relating to the quality of something rather than to the amount or number [➡ **quantitative**]: *a qualitative study of the health care program*

quality¹ /'kwɒlɪti $ 'kwɑː-/ *n* plural **qualities**

1 [U] how good or bad something is: *the decline in air quality in our cities* | **poor/good/high etc quality** *good quality shoes* | *Much of the land was of poor **quality**.* | **top quality** (=highest quality) *products*
2 [U] a high standard: **+of** *I've been impressed by the quality of his work.*
3 [C usually plural] a good or bad part of someone's character [➡ **characteristic**]: **+of** *Stacy has all the qualities of a natural leader.*
4 [C] something that is typical of a person or thing: *Atkinson's novels all have a humorous quality.*

quality² *adj* [only before noun] very good: *We sell quality clothing at a price you can afford.*

qualm /kwɑːm $ kwɑːm, kwɑːlm/ *n* [C] a worry or doubt because you are not sure what you are doing is right: *She **had no qualms** whatsoever **about** firing people.*

quandary /'kwɒndəri $ 'kwɑːn-/ *n* [C] plural **quandaries** a difficult situation in which you cannot decide what to do: **in a quandary** *Ian's in a quandary about whether to accept their offer.*

quantifier /'kwɒntɪfaɪə $ 'kwɑːntɪfaɪər/ *n* [C] a word or phrase such as 'much', 'few', or 'a lot of' which is used with a noun to show an amount

quantify /'kwɒntᵻfaɪ $ 'kwɑːn-/ v [T] **quantified, quantifying, quantifies** to measure something and show it as a number: *These kinds of improvement are hard to quantify.* —**quantifiable** *adj*

quantitative /'kwɒntᵻtətɪv $ 'kwɑːntᵻteɪ-/ *adj formal* relating to amounts [➡ **qualitative**]: *a quantitative analysis*

quantity /'kwɒntᵻti $ 'kwɑːn-/ *n* plural **quantities**

1 [C,U] an amount of something that you can measure or count: **+of** *Police found a quantity of drugs hidden in their bags.* | **large quantities** of money | **in quantity** *It's cheaper buying goods in quantity* (=in large amounts).
2 [U] the amount of something that is produced: *It's quality that's important, not quantity.*

quantum leap /,kwɒntəm 'liːp $,kwɑːn-/ *n* [C usually singular] a very big and important improvement: *a quantum leap in medical science*

quarantine /'kwɒrəntiːn $ 'kwɔː-/ *n* [U] when a person or animal with a disease is kept apart from other people or animals so that they do not get the disease too: **in quarantine** *Animals coming into Britain must be kept in quarantine.* —**quarantine** *v* [T]

quarrel[1] /'kwɒrəl $ 'kwɔː-, 'kwɑː-/ *n* [C]

1 an angry argument: **+with** *We've had a quarrel with our neighbours.* | **+about/over** *They had a quarrel about some girl.*
2 *formal* a reason to disagree with something or argue with someone: **+with** *We have no quarrel with the court's decision.*

quarrel[2] *v* [I] **quarrelled, quarrelling** *BrE*; **quarreled, quarreling** *AmE* to have an angry argument: **+with** *She's always quarrelling with her sister.* → see box at ARGUE

quarrelsome /'kwɒrəlsəm $ 'kwɔː-, 'kwɑː-/ *adj* a quarrelsome person is always quarrelling with other people

quarry[1] /'kwɒri $ 'kwɔː-, 'kwɑː-/ *n* [C] plural **quarries** **1** a place where stone or sand are dug out of the ground **2** a person or animal that is being hunted

quarry[2] *v* [I] **quarried, quarrying, quarries** to dig stone or sand from a quarry

quart /kwɔːt $ kwɔːrt/ *n* [C] written abbreviation *qt* a unit for measuring liquid, equal to two PINTS

quarter /'kwɔːtə $ 'kwɔːrtər/ *n* [C]

1 one of four equal parts that you can divide something into: *She cut the cake into quarters.* | **+of** *A quarter of Canada's population is French-speaking.* | **three quarters (of sth)** (=75%) *The house is about three quarters of a mile from the road.*
2 15 minutes: *Can you be ready in **a quarter of an hour**?* | **(a) quarter to (sth)** also **(a) quarter of (sth)** *AmE* (=15 minutes before the hour) *It's quarter to five.* | **(a) quarter past (sth)** also **(a) quarter after (sth)** *AmE* (=15 minutes after the hour) *It's a quarter past five.* | *The bus leaves at quarter after.*
3 a period of three months: *Profits increased in the first quarter.*
4 a coin in the US and Canada worth 25 cents
5 *AmE* one of the four periods into which a year at school or college is divided [➡ **semester**]

6 *AmE* one of the four equal periods of time into which some sports games are divided
7 **in/from...quarters** among or from different people: *He received help from several quarters.*
8 an area of a town where a particular group of people live: *the Latin quarter*
9 **quarters** [plural] rooms that are given to someone to live in as part of their job: *the kitchen staff's **living quarters***

quarterback /'kwɔːtəbæk $ 'kwɔːrtər-/ *n* [C] the player in American football who directs the team's attacking play, especially by throwing the ball

quarterfinal /,kwɔːtə'faɪnl $,kwɔːrtər-/ *n* [C] one of four games near the end of a competition. The winners play in the two SEMI-FINALS.

quarterly /'kwɔːtəli $ 'kwɔːrtər-/ *adj* produced or happening four times a year: *a quarterly report* —**quarterly** *adv*: *The magazine is published quarterly.*

quartet /kwɔː'tet $ kwɔːr-/ *n* [C] four singers or musicians who sing or play together [➡ **trio, quintet**]: *a string quartet*

quartz /kwɔːts $ kwɔːrts/ *n* [U] a type of hard rock used for making electronic clocks

quash /kwɒʃ $ kwɑːʃ, kwɒʃ/ *v* [T] *formal* **1** to officially say that a decision is not legal or correct any more: *The Court of Appeal quashed Maloney's conviction.* **2** to use force to stop fighting or protests: *Troops loyal to the President quickly quashed the rebellion.*

quaver /'kweɪvə $ -ər/ *v* [I] *literary* if your voice quavers, it shakes as you speak because you are nervous or upset

quay /kiː $ keɪ, kiː/ *n* [C] a place beside the sea or a big river for loading or unloading boats

queasy /'kwiːzi/ *adj* if you feel queasy, you feel as if you are going to be sick: *The sea got rougher, and I began to **feel queasy**.*

queen /kwiːn/ *n* [C]

1 **Queen** the female ruler of a country, or the wife of a king [➡ **king**]: *Queen Elizabeth II*
2 a playing card with a picture of a queen on it: *the queen of clubs*
3 a large female BEE that lays the eggs for a whole group

queen-size *adj* a queen-size bed, sheet etc is a bed for two people that is larger than the standard size

queer /kwɪə $ kwɪr/ *adj* strange and not normal: *There's something a bit queer about him.*

quell /kwel/ *v* [T] *formal* to stop something: *Troops were called in to quell the riots.* | *Police tried to quell public fear about the murders.*

quench /kwentʃ/ *v* [T] **quench your thirst** to drink something so that you no longer feel thirsty

query /'kwɪəri $ 'kwɪri/ *n* [C] plural **queries** a question asking for more information: *Staff are always available to **answer your queries**.* —**query** *v* [T] *formal*

quest /kwest/ *n* [C] *formal* a long and difficult search: **+for** *a quest for knowledge*

question[1] /'kwestʃən/ *n*

1 [C] something you say or write when you are asking for information [≠ **answer**]: *I couldn't answer some of the questions.* | *Do you mind if I **ask** you a personal **question**?* | *You never* *answered my question.* | **+about/on** *I have one or two* **questions** *about the timetable.*

ask a question
answer a question
have a question – to want to ask one
put a question to sb – to ask someone a question in a formal situation
pose a question – to ask a difficult question
bombard sb with questions – to ask someone a lot of questions
rephrase a question – to ask it in a different way
avoid/evade/sidestep a question – to avoid giving a direct answer
set a question *BrE* – to include it in a test

2 [C] a subject that needs to be discussed or a problem that needs to be solved [= **issue**]: *Dunn's murder* **raises the question** *of whether more police should carry guns.*
3 [C,U] a feeling of doubt about something: *We've played poorly this season* — **there's no question about it** (=it is very certain). | *Her honesty is* **beyond question** (=certainly true). | **call/bring/throw sth into question** (=make people doubt something) *Recent events have called into question the wisdom of the government's decision.*
4 without question a) without complaining or asking why: *Soldiers must follow orders without question.* **b)** used to say that something is definitely true: *It is without question the best show on television.*
5 there's no question of sth used to emphasize that something will definitely not happen: *There's no question of Shearer leaving the team.*
6 in question the person or thing in question is the person or thing that is being discussed: *Where were you on the evening in question?*
7 be out of the question used to emphasize that something is not possible or not allowed: *A new washing machine is out of the question at the moment.*
8 (that's a) good question *spoken* used as a way of saying that you do not know the answer to a question: *'How can we afford this?' 'Good question!'*
→ **TRICK QUESTION**

question² *v* [T]
1 to ask someone questions about something [➡ **interrogate**]: *Two men are being questioned by police.* | **question sb about sth** *Nelson was questioned about his activities on the night of the robbery.* → see box at **ASK**
2 to say that you have doubts about something: *Are you questioning my honesty?*
—**questioning** *n* [U] *The four men were* **held for questioning** *but later released.*

questionable /'kwestʃənəbəl/ *adj* something that is questionable does not seem to be completely true, correct, or honest: *Her motives are highly questionable.* | **It's questionable whether** *this research is actually useful.*

'question mark *n* [C] the sign (?) that you write at the end of a question

questionnaire /ˌkwestʃə'neə, ˌkes- $ -'ner/ *n* [C] a set of written questions that you answer in

order to give information about something: *Students were asked to* **fill out a questionnaire** (=answer it).

'question tag *n* [C] a phrase such as 'isn't it?' or 'does she?' that you add to the end of a sentence to make it a question or check that someone agrees with you

queue¹ /kjuː/ *n* [C] *BrE* a line of people or vehicles that are waiting for something [= **line**]: *There was a long queue outside the cinema.* | **be/stand/wait in a queue** *We stood in a queue for half an hour.* | *We* **joined the queue** *at the ticket counter.*

queue² also **queue up** *v* [I] *BrE* to wait in a line of people [= **line up**]: **+for** *We had to queue for over an hour to get tickets.*

quibble /'kwɪbəl/ *v* [I] to argue about something that is not very important: **+about/over/with** *Let's stop quibbling over small details.*

quiche /kiːʃ/ *n* [C,U] a PIE without a top, filled with a mixture of eggs, cheese, vegetables etc → see picture on page A5

quick¹ /kwɪk/ *adj*
1 taking only a very short time [➡ **fast**]: *I'll just have a quick shower first.* | *The journey is much quicker by train.* | *What's the quickest way to the airport?* | *She felt she had to make a quick decision.*
2 moving or happening fast: *She walked with short, quick steps.*
3 able to learn things fast: *Carolyn's a* **quick learner**.
4 be quick to do sth to react quickly to something someone says or does: *The President was quick to deny the rumours.*

quick² *adv informal* quickly. Some people think that this use is not correct English: *Come quick! There's been an accident.*

quicken /'kwɪkən/ *v* [I,T] to become quicker, or to make something quicker: *Her heartbeat quickened when she saw him.*

quickie /'kwɪki/ *n* [C] *informal* something that you can do quickly and easily: *I've got a question for you - it's just a quickie.* —**quickie** *adj*: *a quickie divorce*

quickly /'kwɪkli/ *adv* fast, or done in a short amount of time: *He quickly put the money back in the box.* | *Get over here as quickly as you can.* → see box at **FAST**

quicksand

quicksand /'kwɪksænd/ *n* [U] wet sand that is dangerous to walk on because you sink into it

quid /kwɪd/ *n* [C] plural **quid** *BrE informal* a pound in British money: *You owe me fifty quid.*

quiet¹ /'kwaɪət/ *adj*

1 not making a lot of noise [≠ **loud, noisy**]: *We'll have to be quiet – we don't want to wake your parents.* | **(be) quiet!** *spoken* (=used to tell someone to stop talking or making noise) *Be quiet! I've got a headache.*

THESAURUS

Words to describe a quiet voice or sound
low, soft, muffled, hushed, subdued
Ways of telling someone to be quiet
Be quiet!, sh/ssh, shut up *informal not polite*,
keep it down *informal*, **hush** (=used especially when talking to a child who is crying)
→ LOUD

THESAURUS

Words to describe a quiet place
peaceful, calm, tranquil, sleepy (=quiet with very little happening)

---

2 without much activity or without many people: *The shop has been really quiet this morning.* | *They live in a quiet part of town.*
3 not speaking or not likely to say much: *Sam's a quiet hardworking boy.* | *You're awfully quiet today, Tania.*
4 keep sth quiet/keep quiet (about sth) to not talk about something: *I have something to tell you, but you have to keep it quiet.*

quiet² *n* [U] **1** when there is not very much noise and not many things are happening: *All I want is some* **peace and quiet.** **2 on the quiet** *BrE* secretly: *He was doing some freelance work on the quiet.*

quieten /'kwaɪətn/ *BrE*; **quiet** *AmE* also **quieten down, quiet down** *v* [I,T] to become quiet after making a lot of noise: *After a while the children quietened down.*

quietly /'kwaɪətli/ *adv*
1 without making much noise: *Ron shut the door quietly.* | *'I'm sorry,' he said quietly.*
2 in a way that does not attract attention: *He quietly got on with his work.*

quilt /kwɪlt/ *n* [C] a cover for a bed that is filled with soft warm material

quilted /'kwɪltɪd/ *adj* quilted clothing has a thick layer of material sewn into it: *a quilted jacket*

quintessential /ˌkwɪntɪ'senʃəl◂/ *adj* being a perfect example of a particular type of person or thing: *New York is the quintessential big city.*

quintet /kwɪn'tet/ *n* [C] five singers or musicians who perform together [➡ **trio, quartet**]

quip /kwɪp/ *v* [I,T] **quipped, quipping** to say something clever and amusing —**quip** *n* [C]

quirk /kwɜːk $ kwɜːrk/ *n* [C] **1** a strange habit or feature that someone or something has: *one of her annoying little quirks* **2** something strange that happens by chance: **+of** *By a quirk of fate, I met him again the following day.*

quirky /'kwɜːki $ -ɜːr-/ *adj* slightly strange: *a quirky sense of humour*

quit /kwɪt/ *v* [I,T] past tense and past participle **quit** also **quitted** *BrE* present participle **quitting** *informal*

1 to leave a job or school permanently: *I'm thinking about quitting school.* | *People are now calling on the chairman to quit.*
2 *especially AmE* to stop doing something bad or annoying [➡ **give up**]: *He quit smoking three years ago.* | *Quit complaining and get to work!*
3 to close a computer PROGRAM

quite /kwaɪt/ *adv*
1 *especially BrE* fairly or very, but not extremely [= **pretty**]: *She's quite tall for her age.* | *The food in the canteen is usually quite good.* | *Butch is out of the hospital and doing quite well.* | **quite sth** *They live quite a long way from the nearest town.* | **quite like/enjoy** *BrE: I quite enjoyed that film.* **→** see box at **RATHER**
2 *especially BrE* completely: *Although they're sisters, they're quite different.* | *I'm afraid that's* **quite impossible.** | *I think you've had* **quite enough** *to drink already!*
3 not quite almost, but not completely or not exactly: *I'm not quite sure how much it costs.* | *Lewis isn't quite as fast as he used to be.* | *I'm not quite finished.*
4 quite a lot/bit/few a fairly large number or amount: *They've had quite a bit of snow this year.* | *This painting is worth quite a lot of money.*
5 quite a sth/quite some sth used to emphasize that something is especially good, bad etc: *He certainly made quite an impression on the kids.* | *Brad's quite some musician.*

quiver /'kwɪvə $ -ər/ *v* [I] to shake slightly, especially because you are angry, upset, or nervous: **+with** *His voice was quivering with rage.*

quiz¹ /kwɪz/ *n* [C] plural **quizzes**
1 a competition in which you have to answer questions: *a quiz show*
2 *AmE* a short test that a teacher gives to a class: *a math quiz*

quiz² *v* [T] **quizzed, quizzing** to ask someone a lot of questions [= **question**]: *Reporters quizzed Harvey about his plans for the future.*

quizzical /'kwɪzɪkəl/ *adj* a quizzical look, smile etc shows that you do not understand something

quorum /'kwɔːrəm/ *n* [singular] the smallest number of people that must be at a meeting in order for official decisions to be made

quota /'kwəʊtə $ 'kwoʊ-/ *n* [C] an amount of something that someone is allowed to have: **+on** *a strict quota on imports*

quotation /kwəʊ'teɪʃən $ kwoʊ-/ *n* [C]
1 words that come from a book, poem etc: **+from** *a quotation from the Bible* **2** a statement showing how much it will cost to do something: *Ask the builder to* **give** *you a written* **quotation** *for the job.*

quo'tation ˌmark *n* [C usually plural] a sign ("") that you write before and after someone's speech

quote¹ /kwəʊt $ kwoʊt/ *v* **1** [I,T] to repeat exactly what someone else has said or written: **+from** *She quoted from a newspaper article.* | *A company spokesman was* **quoted as saying** *that 2000 people may lose their jobs.* **2** [T] to mention something as an example to support what you are saying: *Wilkins quoted several cases where errors had occurred.* **3** [T] to tell a customer the price you will charge them for something

quote² *n* [C] a QUOTATION

Q

R, r

R, r /ɑː $ ɑːr/ n [C,U] plural **R's, r's** the 18th letter of the English alphabet

rabbi /'ræbaɪ/ n [C] a Jewish religious leader

rabbit

rabbit /'ræbət/ n [C] a small animal with long ears and soft fur that lives in holes in the ground → see picture at **PET¹**

rabble /'ræbəl/ n [singular] a noisy crowd of people who are behaving badly: **+of** *a rabble of angry youths* → see box at **GROUP**

rabid /'ræbəd, 'reɪ-/ adj **1** *disapproving* having extreme opinions: *rabid right-wing fanatics* **2** a rabid animal has rabies

rabies /'reɪbiːz/ n [U] a disease that can kill animals and people that are bitten by an infected animal

raccoon /rə'kuːn, ræ- $ ræ-/ n [C] an animal with black fur around its eyes and black and white rings on its tail

race

race¹ /reɪs/ n

1 [C] a competition in which people, animals, cars etc try to go faster than each other: *Hill won the race easily.* | **in a race** *Over 80 bikes took part in the race.*

2 [C,U] one of the main groups into which people are divided according to the colour of their skin and physical appearance: *The school welcomes children of all races.* | *people of mixed race*

3 [C] a situation in which people compete with

each other to obtain a position of power: *Davis has decided to enter the presidential race.* | **+for** *the race for city council*

4 [singular] a situation in which one group of people tries to obtain or achieve something before another group: **+for** *the race for the final playoff position* | **the race to do sth** *the race to find a cure for cancer*

5 a race against time when you must finish doing something in a short period of time

6 the races an event at which horses race against each other

→ ARMS RACE, HUMAN RACE, RAT RACE

race² v **1 a)** [I,T] to compete against someone or something in a race: **+against** *She will be racing against some of the world's top athletes.* **b)** [T] to use an animal or a vehicle to compete in a race: *My father has raced horses since he was 18.* **2** [I,T] to go somewhere very quickly, or to move someone or something quickly: **+across/back/down** *I raced down the stairs to answer the phone.* | **race sb to sth** *The crash victims were raced to Pacific Hospital.* **3** [I] if your heart or mind races, it works harder and faster than usual, for example because you are afraid or excited

racecourse /'reɪs-kɔːs $ -kɔːrs/ n [C] a place where horses compete in races

racehorse /'reɪshɔːs $ -hɔːrs/ n [C] a horse that competes in races

'race re,lations n [plural] the relationship that exists between people from different countries, religions etc who are now living in the same place

racetrack /'reɪs-træk/ n [C] a track on which runners, cars etc race

racial /'reɪʃəl/ adj relating to someone's race or to the relationships between people of different races: *different **racial groups*** | **racial discrimination/prejudice** | *a rise in racial tension* —**racially** adv: *a racially motivated attack*

racing /'reɪsɪŋ/ n [U] the sport of racing horses, cars, dogs etc: **horse/motor/greyhound etc racing** | *a racing driver*

racism /'reɪsɪzəm/ n [U] when someone believes that people of their own race are better than people of other races, and they treat other races unfairly: **the struggle/fight against racism**

racist /'reɪsəst/ n [C] someone who believes that people of their own race are better than people of other races, and who treats other races unfairly —**racist** adj: *racist views*

rack¹ /ræk/ n [C] a frame or shelf with bars, where you can put or keep things: *a **luggage rack*** | *a **vegetable rack*** | *a **roof rack** (=for carrying luggage on top of a car)

rack² v **1 be racked with/by sth** if you are racked with pain or an emotion, it is causing you a lot of suffering: *Liza was **racked with guilt**.* **2 rack your brain(s)** to try very hard to remember something or think of something: *I racked my brains to remember her name.*

racket /'rækət/ n **1** also **racquet** [C] a piece of equipment that you use for hitting the ball in games such as tennis **2** [C] *informal* an illegal way of making a lot of money: *a drugs racket* **3** [singular] *informal* a loud unpleasant noise: *Who's **making that racket**?*

racy /'reɪsi/ *adj* racy writing is exciting and entertaining and often about sex

radar /'reɪdɑː $ -ɑːr/ *n* [C,U] a method of finding the position of things such as planes and ships using radio waves, or the equipment that does this

radiance /'reɪdiəns/ *n* [U] *literary* **1** happiness that shows in someone's face and makes them look attractive **2** a soft gentle light

radiant /'reɪdiənt/ *adj* **1** very happy and attractive: *The bride looked radiant.* | *a radiant smile* **2** [only before noun] *literary* very bright: *radiant light* —**radiantly** *adv*

radiate /'reɪdieɪt/ *v* **1** [I,T] if you radiate a feeling or quality, or if it radiates from you, people can see it very easily: *She radiated an air of calm.* **2** [I,T] to send out light or heat in all directions **3** [I] to spread out in different directions from a central point: **+(out) from** *Tiny lines radiated out from the corners of his eyes.*

radiation /,reɪdi'eɪʃn/ *n* [U] **1** a form of energy that comes especially from NUCLEAR reactions, which in large amounts can harm or kill people: *radiation sickness* **2** energy in the form of heat or light that is sent out as waves that you cannot see: *ultraviolet radiation from the sun*

radiator /'reɪdieɪtə $ -ər/ *n* [C] **1** a piece of equipment, usually fastened to a wall, that heats a room. It consists of a metal container that fills up with hot water. **2** the part of a car that stops the engine from getting too hot

radical[1] /'rædɪkəl/ *adj* **1** a radical change or difference is very big and important: *radical economic reforms* **2** if someone is radical, or if they have radical ideas, their ideas are very new and extreme: *radical feminists* —**radically** /-kli/ *adv*: *Life suddenly changed radically.*

radical[2] *n* [C] someone who has new and extreme ideas, especially someone who wants complete social and political change —**radicalism** *n* [U]

radio[1] /'reɪdiəʊ $ -dioʊ/ *n*

1 a) [C] a piece of equipment that you use to listen to programmes that are broadcast, such as music and news: **put/switch/turn the radio on b)** [U] programmes that you can listen to using a radio: *Do you listen to the radio much?* | **on the radio** *I heard about it on the radio.* | *a radio station* | **local/national radio**
2 a) [C] a piece of electrical equipment, for example on a plane or ship, which can send and receive spoken messages through the air **b)** [U] the method of sending and receiving messages in this way: **by radio** *We communicated by radio.* | *Suddenly they lost radio contact* (=could no longer send or receive messages).

radio[2] *v* [I,T] to send a message using a radio: **+for** *The pilot radioed for help.*

radioactive /,reɪdiəʊ'æktɪv◂ $ -dioʊ-/ *adj* a radioactive substance sends out RADIATION (=a form of energy that can harm or kill people): *radioactive waste* —**radioactivity** /,reɪdiəʊæk'tɪvɪti $ -dioʊ-/ *n* [U] *high levels of radioactivity*

radiography /,reɪdi'ɒɡrəfi $ -'ɑːɡ-/ *n* [U] the process of taking X-RAY photographs of people's bodies for medical purposes

radiotherapy /,reɪdiəʊ'θerəpi $ -dioʊ-/ *n* [U] the treatment of illnesses using RADIATION

radish /'rædɪʃ/ *n* [C] a small round red vegetable that has a strong spicy taste and is eaten raw

radius /'reɪdiəs/ *n* [C] plural **radii** /-diaɪ/ **1** the distance from the centre to the edge of a circle **2 within a 10 mile/200 metre etc radius** within a distance of 10 miles etc from a place in any direction

RAF /,ɑːr eɪ 'ef, ræf/ *n* **the RAF** the Royal Air Force the British AIR FORCE

raffle /'ræfəl/ *n* [C] a competition in which you buy a ticket with a number on it and win a prize if your number is chosen: *a raffle ticket*

raft

raft /rɑːft $ ræft/ *n* [C] **1** a flat structure that is used to travel on water. It is made from long pieces of wood tied together. **2 a raft of sth** a large number of people or things: *a raft of new taxes*

rafter /'rɑːftə $ 'ræftər/ *n* [C usually plural] a sloping piece of wood that supports a roof

rafting /'rɑːftɪŋ $ 'ræf-/ *n* [U] the activity of travelling on a raft, especially as a sport: **white-water rafting** (=rafting where the water is flowing very fast)

rag /ræɡ/ *n*

1 [C,U] a piece of old cloth that you use to clean things
2 rags [plural] old torn clothes: **in rags** *children dressed in rags*
3 from rags to riches becoming very rich after starting your life very poor: *his rise from rags to riches*

rage[1] /reɪdʒ/ *n* [C,U] **1** a feeling of uncontrollable anger: *He was trembling with rage.* | *Sally flew into a rage* (=suddenly become very angry). **2 be all the rage** *informal* to be very popular and fashionable

rage[2] *v* [I] **1** to speak or behave in a way that shows you are extremely angry: **+at/against** *She raged at them in Arabic.* **2** to continue with great force: *The storm was still raging.* | *The battle raged on.* → see box at **FIRE**

ragged /'ræɡɪd/ *adj* **1 a)** old and torn: *ragged clothes* **b)** wearing clothes that are old and torn: *ragged children* **2** having a rough uneven edge: **ragged hole/edge/line**

raging /'reɪdʒɪŋ/ *adj* [only before noun] **1** very great or severe: *a raging appetite* | *The show was a raging success.* | *Nick had a raging headache.* **2** continuing with a lot of force or violence: *a raging blaze* | *a raging storm*

raid /reɪd/ *n* [C] **1** a short surprise military attack on a place: **air/bombing raid** | **+on**

R

America's raid on Libya → see box at ATTACK **2** a surprise visit by the police to look for illegal goods or criminals: *a police raid* | *Uniformed police carried out the raid.* **3** a surprise attack on a bank, shop etc to steal things: *a bank raid* | *an armed raid* (=using guns) —raid *v* [T]

raider /'reɪdə $ -ər/ *n* [C] someone who attacks a place or steals things: *armed raiders*

rail¹ /reɪl/ *n* **1** [U] the railway system: *the UK rail network* | **by rail** *people who travel by rail* **2** [C usually plural] one of the two long metal tracks that trains move along **3** [C] a bar along or around something, usually to stop you falling **4** [C] a bar that you use to hang things on: *a towel rail*

rail² *v* [I] *formal* to complain angrily

railcard /'reɪlkɑːd $ -kɑːrd/ *n* [C] *BrE* a small card that allows you to travel by train at a lower price than usual

railing /'reɪlɪŋ/ *n* [C] also **railings** [plural] a fence consisting of upright metal bars

railroad¹ /'reɪlrəʊd $ -roʊd/ *n* [C] *AmE* **1** a system of tracks along which trains run, or a system of trains [= railway *BrE*] **2 railroad track** one of the two metal tracks fixed to the ground that trains move along

railroad² *v* [T] to force or persuade someone to do something without giving them enough time to think about it

railway /'reɪlweɪ/ *n* [C] *BrE*
1 a system of tracks along which trains run, or a system of trains [= railroad *AmE*]: *the main East Coast railway* | *Mick met me at the railway station.* | *He worked on the railways.*
2 railway line one of the two metal tracks fixed to the ground that trains move along

rain¹ /reɪn/ *n*
1 [U] water that falls in small drops from clouds in the sky [➔ rainy]: *There's been no rain for weeks.* | **in the rain** *You can't go out in the rain.* | *The rain fell steadily.* | *It was pouring with rain* (=there was a lot of rain). | **heavy/pouring/torrential rain** (=a lot of rain)

light/heavy rain
drizzle – light rain with very small drops of water: *a fine drizzle*
shower – a short period of rain: *a light shower*
downpour – when it suddenly rains very hard for a short period of time: *a heavy downpour*
storm – very bad weather with a lot of wind and rain: *violent storms* | *a tropical storm*
hail – frozen rain that falls in the form of **hailstones** (=small balls of ice): *We sheltered from the hail storm.*
sleet – a mixture of snow and rain: *sleet and snow showers*
→ SNOW, SUN, WEATHER, WIND

2 the rains [plural] heavy rain that falls during a particular period in the year in tropical countries: *The rains came on time.*
→ ACID RAIN

rain² *v* **it rains** if it rains, drops of water fall from clouds in the sky: *Is it still raining?* | *It started to rain.* | *It rained heavily* (=there was a lot of rain).

It's raining hard/heavily – a lot of water is falling
It's pouring (down) *BrE*/**It's pouring (rain)** *AmE* – it's raining very heavily
It's drizzling – a small amount of water is falling
It's sleeting – it's raining and snowing at the same time
It's hailing – small balls of ice are falling
→ WEATHER

rain down *phr v* to fall in large quantities: +**on** *Bombs rained down on the city.*

be rained off *BrE*; **be rained out** *AmE phr v* if an event or activity is rained off, it has to stop because there is too much rain

rainbow /'reɪnbəʊ $ -boʊ/ *n* [C] a large curve of different colours in the sky that is caused by the sun shining through rain

'rain check *n* **I'll take a rain check** *spoken* used to say that you cannot accept an offer or an invitation now but you would like to at a later time

raincoat /'reɪnkəʊt $ -koʊt/ *n* [C] a coat that you wear when it rains

raindrop /'reɪndrɒp $ -drɑːp/ *n* [C] a single drop of rain

rainfall /'reɪnfɔːl $ -fɒːl/ *n* [C,U] the amount of rain that falls on an area in a particular period of time: *The annual rainfall is about 70 cm.*

'rain ,forest *n* [C,U] tropical forest with tall trees that are very close together, growing in an area where it rains a lot → see box at TREE

rainstorm /'reɪnstɔːm $ -ɔːrm/ *n* [C] a storm with a lot of rain

rainwater /'reɪnwɔːtə $ -wɒːtər, -wɑː-/ *n* [U] water that has fallen as rain

rainy /'reɪni/ *adj* **1** a rainy period of time is one when it rains a lot: *a rainy evening* → see box at WEATHER **2 save sth for a rainy day** to keep something, especially money, until a time when you will need it

raise¹ /reɪz/ *v* [T]
1 to move something to a higher position or into an upright position [≠ lower]: *Raise your hand if you know the answer.* | *I raised the lid.* | **raise your head/eyes/face** (=move your head, eyes etc so that you are looking up) | **raise yourself (up)** *I raised myself up on one elbow.* → see box at RISE
2 to increase an amount, number, or level [≠ lower]: *We had to raise our prices.* | *plans to raise taxes* | *an attempt to raise standards in primary schools* | **raise your voice** (=to speak loudly or shout because you are angry)
3 to get people to give money that will be used to help other people or to do a particular job: *The event will raise money for charity.* | *We raised £900.*
4 raise a question/issue/subject etc to mention a question etc, or to bring something to someone's attention, so that it can be discussed or dealt with [= bring up]: *I plan to raise the issue with him face-to-face.* | *Thank you for raising that point.*
5 raise hopes/doubts/fears etc to cause a particular emotion or reaction: *This attack*

raises fears of increased violence against foreigners.

6 *especially AmE* to look after a child until he or she grows up [= **bring up**]: *His mother had raised five children by herself.*

7 to keep animals or grow crops to sell or eat: *They used to* **raise cattle**.

8 raise the alarm to tell people there is a dangerous situation: *The alarm was raised by a passerby.*

9 raise your eyebrows/an eyebrow to show surprise, doubt, or disapproval by moving your EYEBROWS upwards

raise² *n* [C] *AmE* an increase in the money you earn [= **rise** *BrE*]: *It would be nice to* **get a raise**.

raisin /ˈreɪzən/ *n* [C] a dried GRAPE

rake¹ /reɪk/ *n* [C] a gardening tool with a row of metal teeth at the end of a long handle, used for gathering up dead leaves etc

rake² *v* [I,T] if you rake soil or dead leaves, you smooth the soil or gather the leaves with a rake
  rake sth ⇔ **in** *phr v informal* to earn a lot of money very easily: *He's absolutely* **raking it in**.

rally¹ /ˈræli/ *n* [C] plural **rallies** **1** a large public meeting that is held in support of something such as a political idea: *About 1,000 people attended the rally in Hyde Park.* **2** a car race on public roads

rally² *v* rallied, rallying, rallies **1** [I,T] to come together, or to bring people together, to support an idea, a political party etc: +**to** *Fellow Republicans rallied to his defence.* | *attempts to* **rally support** *for his regime* **2** [I] to become stronger or higher again: *Share prices have rallied.*
  rally around (sb); **rally round** (sb) *BrE phr v informal* if a group of people rally around, they all try to help you when you are in a difficult situation: *My friends all rallied round when Mom died.*

ram¹ /ræm/ *v* rammed, ramming **1** [I,T] if one vehicle rams another, or rams into another, it crashes into it with a lot of force: *Thieves used his van to ram a police car.* **2** [T] to push something somewhere using great force: *I rammed my foot down on the brake.* **3 ram sth down sb's throat** *informal* to try to force someone to accept an idea or opinion

ram² *n* [C] a male sheep

RAM /ræm/ *n* [U] *technical* **Random Access Memory** the part of a computer that keeps information temporarily so that it can be used immediately [➙ **ROM**]

Ramadan /ˈræmədæn, -dɑːn, ˌræməˈdɑːn, -ˈdæn/ *n* [U] the ninth month of the Muslim year, when Muslims do not eat or drink during the day

ramble¹ /ˈræmbəl/ *v* [I] **1** to talk for a long time in a confused and often boring way: *Sorry, I'm rambling.* | +**about** *Uncle Sid was always rambling on about the old days.* **2** to go for a walk in the countryside for pleasure

ramble² *n* [C] a walk in the countryside for pleasure

rambler /ˈræmblə $ -ər/ *n* [C] someone who walks in the countryside for pleasure

rambling /ˈræmblɪŋ/ *adj* **1** a rambling building has an irregular shape and covers a large area **2** rambling speech or writing is very long

and does not seem to have any clear organization or purpose: *a long rambling letter*

ramifications /ˌræmɪfɪˈkeɪʃənz/ *n* [plural] the additional results of something you do, which may not have been clear when you first decided to do it: +**of** *the ramifications of the new legislation*

ramp /ræmp/ *n* [C] **1** a slope that has been built to connect two places that are at different levels: *ramps for wheelchair users* **2** *AmE* a road for driving onto or off a large main road [= **slip road** *BrE*]

rampage¹ /ræmˈpeɪdʒ, ˈræmpeɪdʒ/ *v* [I] to rush about in groups, acting in a wild or violent way: +**through** *rioters rampaging through the streets*

rampage² *n* **on the rampage** rushing about in a wild and violent way: *gangs on the rampage*

rampant /ˈræmpənt/ *adj* if something bad is rampant, there is a lot of it and it is very difficult to control: **rampant inflation**

rampart /ˈræmpɑːt $ -ɑːrt/ *n* [C usually plural] a wide pile of earth or a stone wall built to protect a castle or city

ramshackle /ˈræmʃækəl/ *adj* a ramshackle building is in very bad condition: *a ramshackle old farm house*

ran /ræn/ *v* the past tense of RUN

ranch /rɑːntʃ $ ræntʃ/ *n* [C] a large farm in the US or Canada where cattle, sheep, or horses are kept —**rancher** *n* [C]

rancid /ˈrænsɪd/ *adj* oily or fatty food that is rancid smells or tastes unpleasant because it is no longer fresh: **rancid butter**

rancour *BrE*; **rancor** *AmE* /ˈræŋkə $ -ər/ *n* [U] *formal* an angry feeling towards someone when you hate them and cannot forgive them

random /ˈrændəm/ *adj* happening or chosen without any definite plan, aim, or pattern: *a* **random sample** *of 120 families* **2 at random** without any definite plan, aim, or pattern: **choose/select/pick sth at random** *Participants were chosen at random.* —**randomly** *adv*

randy /ˈrændi/ *adj BrE informal* full of sexual desire

rang /ræŋ/ *v* the past tense of RING

range¹ /reɪndʒ/ *n*

1 [C] **a)** a group of things that are different, but belong to the same general type: +**of** *The Centre provides a range of services for the elderly.* | **wide/whole/full etc range of sth** (=lots of very different things) *A wide range of subjects are on offer.* **b)** a set of similar products made by a particular company or available in a particular shop: +**of** *a new range of tennis clothing*

2 [C usually singular] the limits within which amounts, quantities, ages etc vary: **age/price/temperature etc range** *The age range of the patients was 39–97 years.* | **within/in your price range** (=that you can afford)

3 [singular,U] the distance over which a weapon can hit things, or the distance within which something can be seen or heard: +**of** *missiles with a range of 3000 km* | **within range (of sth)** *We waited until the enemy was within range* (=near enough to be hit). | **out of range (of sth)** *Charles moved swiftly out of range.* | **at close range** (=very close to something) *We saw dozens of animals at close range.*

R

4 [C] a line of mountains or hills: *high mountain ranges* | **range of mountains/hills** → see box at MOUNTAIN

5 [C] an area where you can practise shooting: **rifle/firing/shooting range**

range² *v* [I] **1** to include the two things mentioned and other things in between them: **range from sth to sth** *issues ranging from abortion to taxes* | *Toys range in price from $5 to $25.* **2** to deal with a large number of different subjects or ideas in a book, speech, conversation etc: **+over** *The conversation ranged over a variety of topics.*

ranger /ˈreɪndʒə $ -ər/ *n* [C] someone whose job is to look after a forest or area of public land

rank¹ /ræŋk/ *n*

1 [C,U] the position or level that someone has in an organization such as the police or army, or in society: **+of** *She held* (=had) *the rank of Inspector.* | **high/senior/low/junior rank** *an officer of junior rank* | *people of all ranks in society*

2 ranks [plural] the ranks of a large organization or group are the people who belong to it: *The Democrats now face opposition from within their own ranks.* | **+of** *I joined the ranks of* (=became one of) *the unemployed.*

3 the ranks [plural] the ordinary members of an organization, for example soldiers who are not officers

4 the rank and file [plural] the ordinary members of an organization rather than the leaders: *the Party's rank and file*

5 break ranks to behave in a way which is different from other members of a group, especially when they expect your support: **+with** *In an angry speech, the senator broke ranks with the rest of his party.*

6 [C] a line of people or things: *a taxi rank* (=taxis waiting in a line to be hired)

rank² *v* [I,T] to have a particular position in a list that shows how good or important people or things are, or to decide someone's or something's position in a list like this: **+as/among** *The lake must rank as one of the most beautiful in Europe.* | *The England team is ranked fourth in the world.*

ranking /ˈræŋkɪŋ/ *n* [C] a position on a list that shows how good someone or something is compared with others

rankle /ˈræŋkəl/ *v* [I,T] if something rankles, it continues to make you angry a long time after it happens: *an insult that still rankles*

ransack /ˈrænsæk/ *v* [T] **1** to go through a place stealing things and causing damage: *The whole house had been ransacked.* **2** to search a place very thoroughly

ransom /ˈrænsəm/ *n* [C,U] **1** the money paid to free someone who is being kept as a prisoner: *The kidnappers demanded a ransom of $50,000.* **2 hold sb to ransom a)** to try to force someone to do what you want by threatening to do something if they do not do it **b)** to keep someone as a prisoner until money is paid to you

rant /rænt/ *v* [I] *disapproving* to talk in a loud, excited, and angry way: **+about** *She was still ranting on about the unfairness of it all.* | **rant and rave** (=talk or complain very loudly and angrily)

rap¹ /ræp/ *n* **1** [C,U] a type of popular music in which the words are not sung but are spoken in time to music with a steady beat **2** [C] a series of quick sharp hits or knocks: *There was a rap on the door.* **3 take the rap (for sth)** *informal* to be blamed or punished for a mistake or crime, especially unfairly

rap² *v* **rapped**, **rapping** **1** [I,T] to hit or knock something quickly several times: **+on/at** *Angrily, she rapped on the door.* → see box at KNOCK **2** [T] *informal* to publicly criticize someone: *a film rapped by critics for its excessive violence*

rape¹ /reɪp/ *v* [T] to force someone to have sex, especially by using violence: *She had been raped and stabbed.*

rape² *n* [C,U] the crime of forcing someone to have sex, especially by using violence: *a rape victim* | **date rape** (=when the people involved have just spent time together socially) → see box at CRIME

rapid /ˈræpɪd/ *adj* done or happening very quickly [= **fast, quick**]: *rapid economic growth* → see box at FAST —**rapidly** *adv* —**rapidity** /rəˈpɪdəti/ *n* [U]

rapids /ˈræpɪdz/ *n* [plural] a part of a river where the water looks white because it is moving very fast over rocks

rapist /ˈreɪpɪst/ *n* [C] someone who forces someone else to have sex when they do not want to

rapper /ˈræpə $ -ər/ *n* [C] someone who sings RAP songs

rapport /ræˈpɔː $ -ɔːr/ *n* [singular,U] friendly understanding and agreement between people: **+with** *She quickly established a rapport with her students.*

rapt /ræpt/ *adj* so interested in something that you do not notice anything else

rapture /ˈræptʃə $ -ər/ *n* [U] *literary* great excitement, pleasure, and happiness: *a look of rapture on her face*

rare /reə $ rer/ *adj*

1 not happening often, or not common [≠ **common**]: *a disease that is very rare among children* | *rare plants such as orchids* | **it is rare (for sb/sth) to do sth** *It is very rare for her to miss a day at school.*

2 meat that is rare has only been cooked for a short time and is still red

rarely /ˈreəli $ ˈrerli/ *adv* not often: *She rarely goes out after dark.*

raring /ˈreərɪŋ $ ˈrer-/ *adj* **raring to do sth** *informal* very eager to do something: *We woke up early and were raring to go.*

rarity /ˈreərəti $ ˈrer-/ *n* **be a rarity** to not happen or exist very often: *Old cars in good condition are a rarity.*

rascal /ˈrɑːskəl $ ˈræs-/ *n* [C] a child who behaves badly but whom you still like

rash[1] /ræʃ/ n **1** [C] a lot of small red spots on someone's skin: **come/break out in a rash** *The baby broke out in a rash.* **2 a rash of sth** *informal* a lot of unpleasant things that suddenly start happening: *a rash of shootings*

rash[2] *adj* doing something too quickly, without thinking carefully first: *a **rash decision*** —**rashly** *adv*

rasher /ˈræʃə $ -er/ n [C] *BrE* a thin piece of BACON

rasp /rɑːsp $ ræsp/ v [I] to make a rough unpleasant sound: *Her breath rasped in her throat.* —**rasp** n [singular]

raspberry /ˈrɑːzbəri $ ˈræzberi/ n [C] plural **raspberries** a small soft sweet red fruit that grows on bushes → see picture at FRUIT

rat[1] /ræt/ n [C] an animal like a large mouse

rat[2] v [I] **ratted, ratting** *informal* if someone rats on you, they tell someone in authority about something wrong that you have done: **+on** *They'll kill you if they find out you've ratted on them!*

rate[1] /reɪt/ n [C]

1 the number of times something happens over a period of time: **birth/unemployment/crime etc rate** *a country with a low birth rate*

2 a charge or payment that is set according to a standard scale: *Workers are demanding higher **rates of pay**.* | *What's **the going rate** (=the usual amount paid) for a piano teacher?* | *high **interest rates***

3 the speed at which something happens: *Our money was running out **at an alarming rate** (=very quickly).*

4 at any rate *spoken* **a)** used when you are stating one definite fact in a situation that you are not certain about [= anyway]: *He's planning to come. At any rate, I think that's what he said.* **b)** used to introduce a statement that is more important than what was said before [= anyway]: *Well, at any rate, the next meeting will be on Wednesday.*

5 at this rate *spoken* used to say what will happen if things continue in the same way: *At this rate, we'll never finish on time.*

6 first-rate/second-rate/third-rate of good, bad, or very bad quality: *a third-rate movie*
→ EXCHANGE RATE

rate[2] v **1** [T] to think that someone or something is good, bad etc: *Johnson is rated one of the best basketball players in the world.* **2** [I] to be considered good, bad etc: **+as** *That rates as one of the best meals I've ever had.*

rather /ˈrɑːðə $ ˈræðər/ adv

1 a little or fairly: *I think she was rather upset last night.* | *It's a rather difficult problem.* | *I'm rather surprised to hear you say that.*

quite *especially BrE*: *It's quite late.* | *That's quite a difficult problem.*
fairly: *The test was fairly easy.* | *It's a fairly long way.*
pretty *spoken*: *Her French is pretty good.* | *It's pretty tough work.*

2 rather than instead of something else: *We decided to have the wedding in the summer rather than in the spring.*

3 would rather if you would rather do or have

something, you would prefer to do or have it: *I hate sitting doing nothing – I'd rather be working.*

4 or rather *spoken* used to give more correct or exact information about what you have said: *Mr Dewey, or rather his secretary, asked me to come to the meeting.*

ratify /ˈrætɪfaɪ/ v [T] **ratified, ratifying, ratifies** to make a written agreement official: *Both nations **ratified the treaty**.* —**ratification** /ˌrætɪfɪˈkeɪʃən/ n [U]

rating /ˈreɪtɪŋ/ n **1** [C] a measurement of how popular, good, important etc someone or something is: *The president's popularity rating has fallen.* **2 the ratings** a list that shows which films, television programmes etc are the most popular

ratio /ˈreɪʃiəʊ $ ˈreɪʃoʊ/ n [C] plural **ratios** a relationship between two amounts, written as two numbers that show how much bigger one amount is than the other: **the ratio of sth to sth** *a school where the ratio of students to teachers is about 5:1* (=five students for every teacher)

ration[1] /ˈræʃən $ ˈræ-, ˈreɪ-/ n [C] a limited amount of something such as food that you are allowed to have when there is not much available: *the weekly meat ration*

ration[2] v [T] to control the supply of something by allowing people to have only a limited amount of it: *Coffee was rationed during the war.* —**rationing** n [U]

rational /ˈræʃənəl/ adj **1** based on real facts or scientific knowledge, and not influenced by feelings: *There must be a **rational explanation** for their disappearance.* **2** able to make decisions based on the facts of a situation, and not influenced too much by feelings [≠ irrational]: *Let's try to discuss this like rational human beings.* —**rationally** *adv*

rationale /ˌræʃəˈnɑːl $ -ˈnæl/ n [C,U] *formal* the reasons for a decision: **+behind/for** *What's the rationale behind the President's decision?*

rationalize also **-ise** *BrE* /ˈræʃənəlaɪz/ v [I,T] to think of reasons to explain your behaviour, especially when you have done something wrong: *He always finds a way to rationalize what he's done.* —**rationalization** /ˌræʃənəlaɪˈzeɪʃən $ -lə-/ n [C,U]

'rat race n **the rat race** *informal* the unpleasant situation in business, politics etc in which people are always competing against each other

rattle[1] /ˈrætl/ v **1** [I,T] if something rattles, or if you rattle it, it makes a noise because it keeps shaking and hitting against something else: *The wind was rattling the windows.* → see box at SHAKE **2** [T] *informal* to make someone lose their confidence and become nervous: *Keep calm – don't let yourself get rattled.*

rattle sth ⇔ **off** *phr v* to say something very quickly and easily from your memory: *She rattled off the names of all the American states.*

rattle[2] n [C] **1** a baby's toy that makes a noise when it is shaken **2** a short repeated sound, made when something shakes: **+of** *the rattle of chains* → see picture on page A7

rattlesnake /ˈrætlsneɪk/ n [C] a poisonous American snake that makes a noise with its tail

raucous /'rɔːkəs $ 'rɒː-/ *adj* a raucous voice or noise is very loud and unpleasant: *a raucous laugh*

raunchy /'rɔːntʃi $ 'rɒː-/ *adj informal* sexually exciting, often in a way that is shocking: *a raunchy movie*

ravage /'rævɪdʒ/ *v* [T] to destroy or damage something very badly: *The forest was ravaged by fire.*

ravages /'rævɪdʒz/ *n literary* **the ravages of sth** damage or destruction caused by something such as war, disease, or time

rave¹ /reɪv/ *n* [C] a large party where young people dance to electronic music

rave² *v* [I] **1** to talk in an excited way about something because you think it is very good: **+about** *Everybody raved about the movie, but I hated it.* **2** to talk in an angry and uncontrolled way → **rant and rave** at **RANT**

rave³ *adj* **rave reviews** strong praise for a new film, book, play etc

raven /'reɪvən/ *n* [C] a large black bird

ravenous /'rævənəs/ *adj* extremely hungry —**ravenously** *adv*

ravine /rə'viːn/ *n* [C] a deep narrow valley with steep sides

raving /'reɪvɪŋ/ also **,raving 'mad** *adj informal* completely crazy: *a raving lunatic*

ravings /'reɪvɪŋz/ *n* [plural] crazy things that someone says

ravishing /'rævɪʃɪŋ/ *adj* very beautiful

raw /rɔː $ rɒː/ *adj*
1 not cooked: *raw onions*
2 raw cotton, sugar, and other materials are still in their natural state, and have not been prepared for people to use [➡ **refined**]: *raw materials such as coal and iron*
3 skin that is raw is red and sore
4 not experienced, fully trained, or completely developed: *raw recruits in the army* (=people who have just joined the army) | *This idea was the raw material* (=an idea that is not developed) *for his new play.*
5 hit/touch a raw nerve to accidentally upset or annoy someone by something you say: *I think I hit a raw nerve by asking him about his wife.*
6 a raw deal unfair treatment: *She deserved a raise; I think she's getting a raw deal.*

ray /reɪ/ *n* [C] **1** a narrow beam of light or energy from the sun, a lamp etc: *the rays of the sun* **2 ray of hope/comfort etc** something that gives you a small amount of hope, happiness etc

rayon /'reɪɒn $ -ɑːn/ *n* [U] a smooth material like silk used for making clothes

raze /reɪz/ *v* [T] to destroy a city, building etc completely: *Their headquarters have been razed to the ground.*

razor /'reɪzə $ -ər/ *n* [C] a sharp instrument for removing hair from the body [➡ **shaver**]

'razor blade *n* [C] a small, flat, very sharp blade that is put inside a razor

Rd., Rd the written abbreviation of **Road**: *5007 Rowan Rd.*

re /riː/ *prep written formal* used in business letters to introduce the subject: *Dear sirs, re your enquiry of 19 October*

re- /riː/ *prefix* again: *plans to remake 'The Graduate'* | *We'll have to rethink our plans.*

're /ə $ ər/ the short form of 'are': *We're* (=we are) *ready now.*

reach¹ /riːtʃ/ *v*

reach

1 [T] to arrive at a place: *It took four days for the letter to reach me.*
2 [I,T] to move your hand or arm in order to touch, hold, or pick up something: **+for** *He reached for his knife.* | **+out** *Mike reached out and took her hand.*
3 [T] to increase, decrease, or develop to a particular level or standard over time: *Temperatures will reach 95° today.* | *I had reached the point where I was getting a good salary.*
4 [I,T] to be big enough, long enough etc to get to a particular level or point: *I can't reach the top shelf.* | *Will the ladder reach the roof?*
5 [T] to successfully agree with people about something: *We have finally reached a decision.*
6 [T] to speak to someone, especially by telephone [= **contact**]: *I wasn't able to reach him yesterday.*

reach² *n* [singular, U] **1** the distance that you can stretch out your arm to touch something: **out of/beyond (sb's) reach** *The box was just out of her reach.* | **within reach (of sb)** *Keep a glass of water within reach.* **2 within (easy) reach of sth** close to a place: *The train is within easy reach of the hotel.* **3** the limit of someone's power or ability to do something: *He lives in Paraguay, well beyond the reach of the British authorities.*

react /ri'ækt/ *v* [I]

1 to behave in a particular way because of what someone has done or said to you, or because of the situation you are in [➡ **respond**]: **react by doing sth** *The audience reacted by shouting and booing.* | **react to sth** *How did she react to the news?*
2 to become ill when a chemical or drug goes into your body, or when you eat a particular kind of food: *Quite a lot of children react badly to antibiotics.*
3 *technical* to change when mixed with another substance

react against sth *phr v* to show that you do not like someone else's rules or ideas by deliberately doing the opposite: *Many teenagers react against their parents.*

reaction /ri'ækʃən/ *n*

1 [C,U] something that you feel or do because of what has happened to you or been said to you [➡ **response**]: **+to** *What was his reaction to the question?* | *The news brought an angry reaction from the unions.* | *My first reaction was to run away.*
2 [C] a bad effect, such as an illness from food that you have eaten or from a drug that you have taken: *Some people have a very bad reaction to peanuts* (=peanuts make them ill). | **+to** *She had a severe allergic reaction to the drug.*

3 reactions [plural] *BrE* the ability to move quickly when something dangerous happens suddenly [= **reflexes**]: *a driver with **quick reactions***
4 [singular] a change in people's attitudes, behaviour etc that happens because they disapprove of the way in which things were done in the past: **+against** *a reaction against his strict upbringing*
5 [C,U] *technical* a change that happens when two or more chemical substances are mixed together
→ CHAIN REACTION → **gut reaction** at GUT¹

reactionary /ri'ækʃənəri $ -ʃəneri/ *adj disapproving* strongly opposed to any social or political change —**reactionary** *n* [C]

reactor /ri'æktə $ -ər/ *n* [C] a NUCLEAR REACTOR

read¹ /riːd/ *v* past tense and past participle **read** /red/

1 [I,T] to look at written words, numbers, or signs and understand what they mean: *Can Billy read yet?* | *She sat reading a magazine.* | *I can't actually read music, but I can play the guitar.* | **+about** *I read about the accident in the paper.* | **+that** *I read that the new drug is available now.* | *Her books are quite **widely read** (=read by a lot of people).*

> **THESAURUS**
>
> **flick through sth** – to look at parts of a book, magazine etc quickly
> **browse through sth** – to look at parts of a book, magazine etc slowly
> **skim/scan (through) sth** – to read something quickly to get the main ideas
> **pore over sth** – to read something very carefully for a long time
> **devour sth** – to read something quickly and eagerly
> **plough/wade through sth** – to read something long and boring
> → WRITE

2 [I,T] to say the words written in a book, newspaper etc so that other people can hear you: *John read his report **out loud**.* | **read to sb/read sb a story** *Our mother used to read to us every evening.*
3 read sb's mind/thoughts to guess what someone is thinking: *'Want some coffee?' 'You read my mind.'*
4 read between the lines to guess what someone really feels or means, even when their words do not show it
5 [T] if a measuring instrument reads a particular number, it shows that number: *The thermometer read 100°.*
6 [T] to understand a remark, situation etc in a particular way: *The poem can be read as a protest against war.*
7 [T] *technical* if a computer reads a DISK, it takes the information that is on the disk and puts it into its memory
8 [T] to study a subject at university: *He read chemistry at Oxford.* → see box at UNIVERSITY

read sth **into** sth *phr v* to think that a situation, action etc means more than it really does: *You shouldn't read so much into what she says.*

read sth ⇔ **out** *phr v* to say the words you are reading to someone else: *He read out the names on the list.*
read sth ⇔ **through/over** *phr v* to read something carefully from beginning to end: *Read the contract over carefully before you sign it.*
read up on sth *phr v* to read a lot about something because you will need to know about it: *We need to read up on the new tax laws.*

read² *n* **a good read** something that you enjoy reading: *I thought his last book was a really good read.*

readable /'riːdəbəl/ *adj* **1** interesting and enjoyable to read: *a very readable history of Western Philosophy* **2** clear and able to be read [= **legible**]

reader /'riːdə $ -ər/ *n* [C] **1** someone who reads books, or who reads in a particular way: *I've always been an **avid reader** (=someone who likes to read a lot).* | **a fast/slow reader** **2** someone who reads a particular newspaper or magazine regularly: *Many of our readers wrote in to complain about the article.* **3** an easy book for children who are learning to read or for people who are learning a foreign language

readership /'riːdəʃɪp $ -ər-/ *n* [singular] the people who read a newspaper, magazine etc

readily /'redɨli/ *adv* **1** quickly and easily: *The information is **readily available** on computer.* **2** quickly, willingly, and without complaining: *He readily agreed to help.*

readiness /'redɨnɨs/ *n* [U] **1** willingness to do something: **readiness to do sth** *I admire his readiness to help people.* **2** when someone is prepared and ready for something that might happen: **in readiness (for sth)** *The army was standing by in readiness for an attack.*

reading /'riːdɪŋ/ *n*

1 [singular,U] the activity of looking at and understanding written words: *I enjoy reading in bed.* | *a careful reading of the contract*
2 [U] the books, articles etc that you read: *Her main reading seems to be romantic novels.* | *It's **light reading** (=easy to read and not very serious).*
3 [C] your way of understanding what a particular statement, situation, event etc means [= **interpretation**]: **+of** *What's your reading of the situation, Herb* (=what do you think has caused the situation, or what might happen)?
4 [C] a number or amount shown on a measuring instrument: *The man came to **take** a **reading** from the electric meter.*
5 [C] an occasion when something is read to people: *a poetry reading*

readjust /ˌriːə'dʒʌst/ *v* **1** [I] to get used to a new job, situation, or way of life: **+to** *After the war, I needed time to readjust to life at home.* **2** [T] to make a small change to something, or move something to a new position: *She readjusted the microphone and began to sing.* —**readjustment** *n* [C,U]

readout /'riːdaʊt/ *n* [C] information produced by a computer that is shown on a screen or in print

ready /'redi/ *adj* [not before noun]

1 someone who is ready is prepared or able to do something: *Go and get ready for bed.* | **ready to**

do sth *We're just about ready to eat.* | **+for** *I don't think he's ready for marriage yet.*
2 something that is ready has been prepared and can be used, eaten etc immediately: *Is supper ready?* | *The computer is now set up and ready to use.* | **+for** *Is everything ready for the party?* | *I've got to get a room **ready** for our guests.* | *Have your passport **ready** for when we go through immigration.* → see box at PREPARE
3 willing or likely to do something: **ready to do sth** *She's always ready to help in a crisis.*

ready-'made *adj* already made or provided and ready for you to use: *a ready-made cake*

real¹ /rɪəl/ *adj*
1 actually existing and not just imagined: *The new system has real advantages.* | *Do your kids still think Santa Claus is a real person?* | *This kind of thing only happens in films, not **in real life**.*
2 true and not pretended: *What's the real reason you were late?* | *Jack isn't his real name.*
3 not false or artificial [≠ fake]: *real leather* | *I don't want a plastic Christmas tree – I want the real thing.*
4 a real thing has all the qualities you expect something of that type to have: *I remember my first real job.* | *Simon was her first real boyfriend.*
5 used to emphasize what you are saying: *It's a real pleasure to meet you.*
6 for real seriously, not just pretending: *After two trial runs we did it for real.*

real² *adv AmE spoken* very: *I'm real sorry!*

'real es,tate *n* [U] *especially AmE* property such as houses or land

'real estate ,agent *n* [C] *AmE* someone whose job is to sell houses or land [= estate agent *BrE*]

realism /'rɪəlɪzəm/ *n* [U] the ability to deal with situations in a practical or sensible way

realist /'rɪəlɪ̧st/ *n* [C] someone who is realistic

realistic /rɪə'lɪstɪk/ *adj* **1** someone who is realistic accepts the facts about a situation and realizes what is possible and what is not possible: **+about** *You need to be realistic about your chances of winning.* **2** showing things as they really are: *a very realistic TV drama* —**realistically** /-kli/ *adv*: *We can't realistically hope for any improvement this year.*

reality /ri'æļti/ *n* plural **realities**
1 [C,U] what actually happens or is true, not what is imagined or thought: **+of** *Crime is one of the realities of living in the city.* | *She refuses to **face reality**.* | **the harsh/tough realities** (=unpleasant things that are real) *the harsh realities of unemployment*
2 in reality used to say that something is different from what seems to be true: *He said he'd retired, but in reality he was fired.*
3 become a reality/make sth a reality to begin to exist or happen, or to make something do this: *Her dream had become a reality.*

realization also **-isation** *BrE* /ˌrɪəlaɪ'zeɪʃən $ -lə-/ *n* [singular, U] **1** when you understand something that you had not understood before: **+that** *She finally came to the realization that Jeff had been lying all the time.* **2** *formal* when you achieve something you had planned or hoped for: **+of** *the realization of a lifelong ambition.*

realize also **-ise** *BrE* /'rɪəlaɪz/ *v* [T]
1 to know and understand something, or suddenly begin to understand it: *He obviously didn't realize the dangers involved.* | **+(that)** *I'm sorry, I didn't realize that it was so late.*
2 realize a hope/goal/dream etc to achieve something you have been hoping to achieve
3 sb's (worst) fears were realized used to say that the thing that you were most afraid of has actually happened

really¹ /'rɪəli/ *adv*
1 very or very much [= extremely]: *Yeah, he's a really nice guy.* | *I really like this place.* → see box at VERY
2 used to make a negative statement less strong: *I don't really think it matters.*
3 if something is really true or really happens, it is true or it does happen: *Oliver's not really her cousin.* | *Now tell us what really happened.*

really² *spoken* **1 really?** used when you are surprised about or interested in what someone has said: *'Jay's getting married.' 'Really? When?'*
2 not really used to say no, especially when something is not completely true: *'Is it cold outside?' 'Not really.'*

realm /relm/ *n* [C] **1** *formal* an area of knowledge, interest, or thought: *new discoveries in the realm of science* **2** *literary* a country ruled over by a king or queen

'real-time *adj* [only before noun] *technical* a real-time computer system deals with information as fast as it receives it —**real time** *n* [U]

Realtor /'rɪəltə, -tɔː $ -ər, -ɔːr/ *n* [C] *trademark AmE* a REAL ESTATE AGENT

reams /riːmz/ *n* **reams of sth** a lot of something: *She took reams of notes in class.*

reap /riːp/ *v* **1** [T] to get something good because of the hard work you have done: *It will be some time before you **reap the benefits** of your hard work.* **2** [I,T] *old-fashioned* to cut and gather a crop of grain

reappear /ˌriːə'pɪə $ -'pɪr/ *v* [I] to appear again after not being seen for some time: *Many of these ideas reappear in later books.* —**reappearance** *n* [C,U]

reappraisal /ˌriːə'preɪzəl/ *n* [C,U] *formal* when you think carefully about something again in order to decide whether you should change your opinion of it

rear¹ /rɪə $ rɪr/ *n* **1 the rear** the back part of an object, vehicle, building etc: **at the rear** *There are more seats at the rear of the hall.*
2 also **rear end** [C] the part of your body which you sit on **3 bring up the rear** to be at the back of a line of people or a group of people in a race —**rear** *adj*: *a rear window*

rear² *v* **1** [T] to look after a person or animal until they are fully grown [= raise]: *She reared seven children by herself.* **2** also **rear up** [I] if an animal rears, it rises up on its back legs: *The horse reared and threw me off.* **3 rear its ugly head** if a problem or something bad rears its ugly head, it appears or happens: *We must fight racism wherever it rears its ugly head.*

rearrange /ˌriːə'reɪndʒ/ *v* [T] **1** to change the position or order of things: *Let's rearrange the furniture.* **2** to change the time of a meeting or event: *I can rearrange the appointment.* —**rearrangement** *n* [C,U]

reason[1] /'riːzən/ *n*

1 [C] a fact that explains why something happens or why someone does something: **+why** *There are several reasons why the treatment didn't work.* | **+for** *He wouldn't give the reasons for his decision.* | **+(that)** *The reason I'm calling is to see if you're free on Monday.* | **For some reason** (=for a reason you do not know), *I didn't believe her.* | *The bridge was closed for safety reasons.*

THESAURUS

explanation – a reason why something happens which is given or guessed: *Is there any explanation for his behaviour?*

excuse – a reason that you give for why you did something bad: *I hope she has a good excuse for being late again.*

motive – a reason that makes someone do something, especially something bad: *The police have found no motive for the attack.*

---

2 [C,U] a fact that makes it right or fair to do something: **(no) reason to do sth** *There is no reason to panic.* | *I have no reason to believe that he's lying.* | *You had every reason* (=very good reasons) *to be suspicious.*
3 [U] sensible ideas or advice: *He won't listen to reason* (=be persuaded by sensible advice). | *He is the voice of reason.*
4 [U] the ability to think, understand, and make good judgments: *our powers of reason*
5 within reason within reasonable limits: *You can go anywhere you want, within reason.*

reason[2] *v* **1** [T] to decide that something is true by thinking carefully about the facts: **+that** *The jury reasoned that he could not have committed the crimes.* **2** [I] to think and make judgments: *the ability to reason*
reason with sb *phr v* to talk to someone in order to persuade them to be more sensible: *I tried to reason with her.*

reasonable /'riːzənəbəl/ *adj*

1 fair and sensible [≠ **unreasonable**]: *a reasonable excuse* | *a reasonable man* | *a **perfectly reasonable** (=completely reasonable) suggestion* | *It's reasonable to assume he must have known about this.*
2 reasonable prices are not too high [= **fair**]: *good furniture at very reasonable prices* → see box at **CHEAP**
3 quite big, good etc but not very big, good etc [= **average**]: *a reasonable amount of money* | *a reasonable standard of work*
—**reasonableness** *n* [U]

reasonably /'riːzənəbli/ *adv* **1** quite but not very: *I think I did reasonably well on the test.*
2 in a way that is fair or sensible: *You can't reasonably expect people to work for such low wages.*

reasoned /'riːzənd/ *adj* [only before noun] based on careful thought [= **logical**]: *a reasoned argument*

reasoning /'riːzənɪŋ/ *n* [U] the process of thinking carefully about something in order to form an opinion or make a decision: *scientific reasoning*

reassurance /ˌriːə'ʃʊərəns $ -'ʃʊr-/ *n* [C,U] something that you say or do to make someone feel less worried: **+that** *Many patients need reassurance that their condition will improve.*

reassure /ˌriːə'ʃʊə $ -'ʃʊr/ *v* [T] to make someone feel less worried about something: **reassure sb (that)** *Police have reassured the public that the area is now perfectly safe.*

reassuring /ˌriːə'ʃʊərɪŋ◂ $ -'ʃʊr-/ *adj* making you feel less worried: *a reassuring smile*
—**reassuringly** *adv*

rebate /'riːbeɪt/ *n* [C] an amount of money that is paid back to you because you have paid too much rent, tax etc: *a tax rebate*

rebel[1] /'rebəl/ *n* [C] someone who opposes or fights against people in authority: *rebel soldiers*

rebel[2] /rɪ'bel/ *v* [I] **rebelled, rebelling** to oppose or fight against a person in authority, a law, an idea etc: **+against** *Teenagers often rebel against their parents.*

rebellion /rɪ'beljən/ *n* [C,U] **1** when a group of people use violence to try to change the government: **+against** *an armed rebellion against the government* → see box at **REVOLUTION** **2** when someone opposes ideas, rules, or people in authority: *teenage rebellion* | **+against** *a rebellion against middle-class values*

rebellious /rɪ'beljəs/ *adj* opposing someone in authority or the rules of society: *young people with a **rebellious streak** (=a tendency to rebel)*

rebirth /ˌriːˈbɜːθ $ -ɜːrθ/ *n* [singular] when something becomes popular, important, or effective again: **+of** *the rebirth of British rock music*

reboot /ˌriːˈbuːt/ *v* [I,T] if you reboot a computer, you start it again after it has stopped working → see box at **COMPUTER**

rebound[1] /rɪ'baʊnd/ *v* [I] to move quickly backwards after hitting a surface: **+off** *The ball rebounded off the wall.*
rebound on sb *phr v* if a situation or something you have done rebounds on you, it has a bad effect on you

rebound[2] /'riːbaʊnd/ *n* **1 on the rebound** feeling sad because your romantic relationship has ended, and looking for a new relationship in order to forget the old one **2** [C] a ball that has hit something and is moving back through the air

rebuff /rɪ'bʌf/ *n* [C] *formal* an unfriendly answer to a suggestion or offer —**rebuff** *v* [T]

rebuild /ˌriːˈbɪld/ *v* [T] past tense and past participle **rebuilt** /-'bɪlt/ **1** to build something again, after it has been damaged or destroyed: *The church was completely rebuilt in the last century.* **2** to make something strong and successful again: *We try to help drug addicts rebuild their lives.*

rebuke /rɪ'bjuːk/ *v* [T] *formal* to speak angrily to someone because they have done something wrong —**rebuke** *n* [C,U]

rebut /rɪ'bʌt/ *v* [T] **rebutted, rebutting** *formal* to say or prove that a statement is not true —**rebuttal** *n* [C,U]

recalcitrant /rɪ'kælsɪ̩trənt/ *adj* *formal* refusing to obey rules or orders, even after being punished —**recalcitrance** *n* [U]

recall /rɪ'kɔːl $ 'riːkɒːl/ *v* [T] **1** to remember something: **+(that)** *I seem to recall we had problems finding the place.* | *I don't recall meeting him.* **2** to officially order that something is returned or that someone should go back to a

R

place: *The cars have been recalled because of a fault with the brakes.* —**recall** /rɪˈkɔːl, ˈriːkɔːl $ -ɒːl/ *n* [C,U]

recap /ˈriːkæp, riːˈkæp/ *v* [I,T] **recapped, recapping** to repeat the main points of something that has just been said —**recap** /ˈriːkæp/ *n* [C]

recapture /riːˈkæptʃə $ -ər/ *v* [T] **1** to make someone experience or feel something again: *a movie that recaptures the innocence of childhood* **2** to catch a prisoner or animal that has escaped

recede /rɪˈsiːd/ *v* [I] **1** to move further and further away and gradually stop being heard or seen: *The sound of the engines receded into the distance.* **2** to become less likely or less strong: *Hopes of finding the girls alive are receding.* **3** if your hair recedes, you gradually lose the hair from the front of your head: *his receding hairline*

receipt /rɪˈsiːt/ *n* **1** [C] a piece of paper that shows you have paid for something: **+for** *Always keep the receipt.* **2** [U] *formal* when someone receives something: **+of** *Please acknowledge receipt of the letter.* | **on/upon receipt of sth** (=when something is received) *The fee will be paid on receipt of an invoice.*

receive /rɪˈsiːv/ *v* [T]

1 to get or be given something [= **get**]: **receive sth from sb** *She received a letter from her mother.* | *The school receives strong support from parents.* | *She received an award for bravery.*

2 to react to something in a particular way [➡ **reception**]: *The speech was **well received** (=people said it was good).*

3 be on/at the receiving end (of sth) to be the person who is affected by something, usually in an unpleasant way: *I would not want to be on the receiving end of his bad temper.*

4 *formal* to accept or welcome someone officially as a guest: *Perez was formally received at the White House.*

receiver /rɪˈsiːvə $ -ər/ *n* [C] **1** the part of a telephone that you hold next to your mouth and ear **2** someone who officially takes control of a business that is BANKRUPT (=does not have enough money to pay its debts) **3** a piece of equipment that receives television, radio, or other electronic signals

receivership /rɪˈsiːvəʃɪp $ -vər-/ *n* [U] if a business is in receivership, a receiver takes control of it because it has no money

recent /ˈriːsənt/ *adj* having happened or been done only a short time ago: *a recent photo* | **in recent years/months/weeks** *Cases of skin cancer have increased in recent years.* ➔ see box at **NEW**

recently /ˈriːsəntli/ *adv* not long ago: *They recently moved from South Africa.* | *Have you seen Anna recently?* | *He worked as a teacher **until recently**.*

just – only a few minutes, hours, or days ago: *The film's just started.* | *They've just got back from France.*
a short/little while ago – only a few minutes, hours, or days ago: *Ned phoned a short while ago.*
lately – in the recent past: *I haven't been to the cinema lately.*
freshly – used to say that something was

recently made, picked etc: *freshly baked bread* | *freshly cut flowers*
newly – used to say that something was recently built, done etc: *a newly married couple*
➔ **LATELY**

receptacle /rɪˈseptəkəl/ *n* [C] *formal* a container

reception /rɪˈsepʃən/ *n*

1 [C usually singular] a particular type of reaction or welcome that someone gets [➡ **receive**]: *The audience gave her an enthusiastic reception.* | *His paintings received a **mixed reception** (=some people liked them and some people did not).*

2 [U] the place where you go when you arrive at a hotel or large organization: *the reception desk* ➔ see box at **HOTEL**

3 [C] a big formal party to celebrate something or to welcome someone: *a wedding reception* | *a civic reception for the US visitors* ➔ see box at **PARTY** ➔ and **WEDDING**

4 [U] the quality of radio, television, or other electronic signals: *complaints of poor reception from mobile phone users*

receptionist /rɪˈsepʃənɪst/ *n* [C] someone whose job is to welcome and help people when they arrive at a hotel, office building etc

receptive /rɪˈseptɪv/ *adj* willing to consider new ideas and suggestions: *a receptive audience* | **+to** *Young people are usually very receptive to new ideas.*

recess /rɪˈses, ˈriːses $ ˈriːses, rɪˈses/ *n* **1** [C,U] a time when no work is done in a law court, parliament etc: *Parliament's summer recess* **2** [U] *AmE* a short period of free time between lessons at school [= **break** *BrE*] **3** [C] a space in a room, where part of the wall is further back than the rest

recession /rɪˈseʃən/ *n* [C,U] a time when there is much less trade and business activity than usual in a country: **out of/into recession** *ways to pull the country out of recession* | *the economic recession of the 1970s* | *a deep recession* (=one that lasts a long time)

recharge /ˌriːˈtʃɑːdʒ $ -ɑːr-/ *v* **1** [T] to put a new supply of electricity into a BATTERY **2 recharge your batteries** *informal* to get back your strength and energy again —**rechargeable** *adj*: *rechargeable batteries*

recipe /ˈresɪpi/ *n* [C]

1 a set of instructions that tells you how to cook something: **+for** *a recipe for chocolate cake* | *a recipe book* ➔ see picture at **INGREDIENT**

chop – to cut something into small pieces: *First chop the garlic.*
slice – to cut something into thin pieces
grate – to make something into small pieces by rubbing it against a special tool: *Grate the cheese.*
melt – to make butter, chocolate etc become liquid
fry – to cook in fat in a pan: *Fry the meat.*
add – to put into other food that you already have: *Season the meat by adding salt and pepper.*

sieve *BrE*/**sift** *especially AmE* – to put flour or other powders through a sieve (=tool like a net made of wire)
mix – to combine the different foods together: *Mix the sauce with the spices.*
stir – to turn food around with a spoon: *Add the milk and stir.*
beat/whisk – to mix food together quickly with a fork or other tool: *Beat the eggs.*
serve – to put different foods together as part of a meal: *Serve with rice and a salad.*
→ **COOK**

2 be a recipe for sth to be very likely to cause a particular result: *Driving for too long without a break is a **recipe for disaster**.*

recipient /rɪˈsɪpiənt/ *n* [C] *formal* someone who receives something: **+of** *the recipient of the Nobel Peace Prize*

reciprocal /rɪˈsɪprəkəl/ *adj* a reciprocal arrangement, relationship etc is one in which two people or groups do or give the same things to each other —**reciprocally** /-kli/ *adv*

reciprocate /rɪˈsɪprəkeɪt/ *v* [I,T] *formal* to do or give something because something similar has been done or given to you

recital /rɪˈsaɪtl/ *n* [C] a performance of music or poetry, usually given by one person: *a piano recital*

recite /rɪˈsaɪt/ *v* [I,T] to say something that you have learned, for example a poem or list of facts —**recitation** /ˌresəˈteɪʃən/ *n* [C,U]

reckless /ˈrekləs/ *adj* not caring about the possible bad effects of what you are doing: *reckless driving* —**recklessly** *adv* —**recklessness** *n* [U]

reckon /ˈrekən/ *v* [T]
1 *spoken* to think that something is true: *We've done all we can, I reckon.* | **+(that)** *I reckon he'll win.* | *Do you reckon you'll be able to come?* | *Moving house is reckoned to be one of the most stressful things you can do.* → see box at **THINK**
2 to guess a number or amount without calculating it exactly: **+(that)** *Experts reckon profits will be around £280 million.* | *The car's speed was reckoned to be 180kph when it left the road.*
reckon on sth *phr v* to expect something to happen and base your plans on it: *They had reckoned on profits of over a million dollars.* | **reckon on doing sth** *You can reckon on paying about £250,000 for a decent house in this area.*
reckon with sb/sth *phr v* **1** **sb/sth to be reckoned with** someone or something that will not be easy to defeat or deal with: *He's a real force to be reckoned with.* **2** **not reckon with sb/sth** to not consider a possible problem when you are making plans: *I hadn't reckoned with the fact that the roads would be very busy.*

reckoning /ˈrekənɪŋ/ *n* [U] a calculation that is not exact: *By my reckoning, they should be here soon.*

reclaim /rɪˈkleɪm/ *v* [T] **1** to get back something you have lost or money you have paid: *Any lost property that is not reclaimed will be destroyed or sold.* **2** to make an area of land suitable for farming or building: *Large areas of derelict land have been reclaimed.* —**reclamation** /ˌrekləˈmeɪʃən/ *n* [U]

recline
reclining

recline /rɪˈklaɪn/ *v* **1** [I] *formal* to lie back in a relaxed way **2** [I,T] if a seat reclines, you can move the back of the seat to a lower position so you can lean back in it: *a reclining chair*

recluse /rɪˈkluːs $ ˈrekluːs/ *n* [C] someone who lives alone and avoids other people —**reclusive** /rɪˈkluːsɪv/ *adj*

recognition /ˌrekəɡˈnɪʃən/ *n* **1** [singular, U] when you realize that something is important or true: **+of** *a growing recognition of the problems of homelessness* | **+that** *a general recognition that many prisons are failing* **2** [U] public respect or thanks for someone's work or achievements: *He **gained** international **recognition** after winning the competition.* | **in recognition of sth** *She was given the award in recognition of her work with animals.* **3** [U] when you know someone or something because you have seen them before: *He looked past me with no sign of recognition.*

recognize also **-ise** *BrE* /ˈrekəɡnaɪz, ˈrekən-/ *v* [T]
1 to know someone or something because you have seen them before and remember them: *He'd lost so much weight I hardly recognized him!* | *It can be difficult for doctors to recognize the symptoms of the disease.*
2 to accept officially that an organization, government, document etc is legal: *The UN refused to recognize the new government.*
3 to accept that something is true: **+that** *It's important to recognize that stress can affect your health.*
4 to realize that someone or something that they have done is good and to show approval: *His contribution to medical science should be recognized.* —**recognizable** /ˈrekəɡnaɪzəbəl, -kən-ˌrekəɡˈnaɪ-/ *adj* —**recognizably** *adv*

recoil /rɪˈkɔɪl/ *v* [I] to move back suddenly from something that you do not like or find frightening: **+from/at** *She recoiled in horror from his touch.*

recollect /ˌrekəˈlekt/ *v* [T] *formal* to remember something: *I don't recollect her name.*

recollection /ˌrekəˈlekʃən/ *n* [C,U] when you remember something from the past, or something you remember: **+of** *He had no **recollection** of the accident.*

R

recommend /ˌrekəˈmend/ v [T]
1 to advise someone to do something: **+(that)**
Dentists **strongly recommend** *that you change your toothbrush every few months.*
2 to say that someone or something is good: *Can you recommend a local restaurant?* | **recommend sth to sb** *I recommend this book to anyone who enjoys adventure stories.*

recommendation /ˌrekəmenˈdeɪʃən/ n
1 [C] an official statement advising people what to do about something: *The committee* **made** *detailed* **recommendations** *to the school.* | **+that** *the recommendation that babies should be laid to sleep on their backs* **2** [C,U] when you suggest that someone should choose a person or thing because they are very good: **on sb's recommendation** *We took the tour on a friend's recommendation.* **3** [C] *especially AmE* a letter or statement saying that someone is suitable for a job, course etc

recompense /ˈrekəmpens/ n [singular, U] *formal* something you give to someone for trouble or loss that you have caused them or as a reward for their help —**recompense** v [T]

reconcile /ˈrekənsaɪl/ v [T] **1** to find a way in which two different ideas, needs, situations etc can both happen or be true: **reconcile sth with sth** *difficulties in reconciling demands for leisure facilities with environment protection* **2** **be reconciled (with sb)** to have a good relationship with someone again after arguing with them: *The couple are now reconciled.* —**reconciliation** /ˌrekənsɪliˈeɪʃən/ n [singular, U]

reconcile sb to sth *phr v* to make someone accept an unpleasant situation: **reconcile yourself to sth** *He couldn't reconcile himself to the fact that his marriage was over.*

reconnaissance /rɪˈkɒnɪsəns $ rɪˈkɑː-/ n [C,U] when aircraft and soldiers are sent somewhere in order to get information about the enemy

reconsider /ˌriːkənˈsɪdə $ -ər/ v [I,T] to think again about something in order to decide whether you should change your opinion: *Please reconsider your decision.* —**reconsideration** /ˌriːkənsɪdəˈreɪʃən/ n [U]

reconstitute /riːˈkɒnstɪtjuːt $ riːˈkɑːnstɪtuːt/ v [T] to change something so that it exists in a different form

reconstruct /ˌriːkənˈstrʌkt/ v [T] **1** to produce a description or copy of an event, using the information you have: *Police were reconstructing the movements of the murdered couple.* **2** to build something again after it has been destroyed —**reconstruction** /-ˈstrʌkʃən/ n [U] *the post-war reconstruction of Europe*

record¹ /ˈrekɔːd $ -ərd/ n
1 [C,U] information that is written down or stored on computer so that it can be looked at in the future: *medical records* | **+of** *Keep a record of everything you spend.* | **on record** (=that has been recorded) *This month has been the wettest on record.*

THESAURUS

diary/journal – a book in which you write down the things that have happened to you
file – a set of written records, or information stored on a computer under a particular name

accounts – an exact record of the money that a company has received and spent
books – written records of a company's financial accounts
ledger – a book in which a company's financial records are kept
register – an official list of names, for example of the people attending a school
log (book) – an official record of events, especially on a ship or plane

2 [C] the fastest speed, longest distance, highest or lowest level etc that has ever been achieved: **+for** *He* **holds** *the world* **record** *for the 400m.* | *The movie* **broke** *all box office* **records**. | *We've had a* **record number** *of enquiries.*
3 [C] the facts about how good, bad etc someone or something has been in the past: *an airline with a good safety record* | **+on** *The government has a poor record on environmental issues.* | *He has a criminal record.*
4 [C] a round flat piece of plastic that music is stored on: *a large record collection*
5 **off the record** used to say that what you are saying is not official and you do not want someone to tell other people
6 **for the record** used to tell someone that what you are saying should be remembered
7 **set/put the record straight** to tell someone the truth about something because you think they have false information
→ **TRACK RECORD**

record² /rɪˈkɔːd $ -ɔːrd/ v
1 [T] to write down information or store it in a computer so that it can be looked at in the future: *All the events were recorded in a diary.*
2 [I,T] to store films, events, music etc on TAPE or DISCS so that you can watch or listen to them again: *The interview will be recorded.* | *The band has just finished recording their third album.*

ˈrecord-ˌbreaking *adj* [only before noun] better, higher, faster etc than anything done before: *a record-breaking victory*

recorder /rɪˈkɔːdə $ -ˈkɔːrdər/ n [C]
1 **tape/video/cassette etc recorder** a piece of equipment that records sound or pictures **2** a musical instrument like a tube with holes that you play by blowing into it

recording /rɪˈkɔːdɪŋ $ -ɔːr-/ n [C,U] something that has been recorded on TAPE or DISC, or the process of recording something: **+of** *a recording of Mozart's Requiem*

ˈrecord ˌlabel n [C] a company that records and produces music on DISCS or TAPES

ˈrecord ˌplayer n [C] a piece of equipment for playing records

recount¹ /rɪˈkaʊnt/ v [T] *formal* to tell a story or describe events

recount² /ˈriːkaʊnt/ n [C] the process of counting votes again

recoup /rɪˈkuːp/ v [T] to get back money that you have lost or spent

recourse /rɪˈkɔːs $ ˈriːkɔːrs/ n [U] *formal* something you can do or use to help you in a difficult situation: **have recourse to sth** *Did you have recourse to the data?* | **without recourse to sth** *a way of solving disputes without recourse to courts of law*

recover /rɪ'kʌvə $ -ər/ v

1 [I] to get better after an illness, injury, shock etc: **+from** *My uncle is recovering from a heart attack.*

2 [I] to return to a normal condition after a period of trouble or difficulty: *The economy will take years to recover.*

3 [T] to get back something that was lost, taken etc: *The police managed to recover the stolen goods.*

4 [T] to get back control over your feelings, your movements etc [= **regain**]: *He never recovered the use of his arm.*

recovery /rɪ'kʌvəri/ n **1** [singular, U] the process of getting better after an illness, injury etc: **+from** *He has **made** a remarkable **recovery** from the operation.* | **full/complete recovery** *Doctors expect her to make a full recovery.* **2** [singular, U] the process of returning to a normal condition after a period of trouble or difficulty: *economic recovery* **3** [U] when you get back something that has been taken or lost

recreate /ˌriːkri'eɪt/ v [T] to make something like it was in the past or like something in another place: *The zoo tries to recreate the animals' natural habitats.*

recreation /ˌrekri'eɪʃən/ n [C,U] something you do for pleasure or fun: *outdoor recreation* —**recreational** adj

recrimination /rɪˌkrɪmɪ'neɪʃən/ n [C usually plural, U] when people blame and criticize each other: *bitter recriminations*

recruit¹ /rɪ'kruːt/ v [I,T] to find new people to work in a company, join an organization, do a job etc: *It's not easy to recruit well-qualified people.* —**recruitment** n [U]

recruit² n [C] someone who has recently joined a company or an organization

rectangle /'rektæŋgəl/ n [C] a shape with four straight sides and four angles of 90 degrees [**→ oblong**] **→** see box at **SHAPE → see** picture at **SHAPE** —**rectangular** /rek'tæŋgjᵿlə $ -ər/ adj

rectify /'rektᵻfaɪ/ v [T] **rectified, rectifying, rectifies** *formal* to correct something that is wrong: *efforts to rectify the problem*

rector /'rektə $ -ər/ n [C] a priest in some Christian churches

rectum /'rektəm/ n [C] *technical* the lowest part of your **BOWEL** —**rectal** adj

recuperate /rɪ'kjuːpəreɪt, -'kuː-/ v [I] to spend time getting better after an illness, injury etc: **+from** *people recuperating from major operations* —**recuperation** /rɪˌkjuːpə'reɪʃən, -ˌkuː-/ n [U]

recur /rɪ'kɜː $ -ɜːr/ v [I] **recurred, recurring** to happen again: *a recurring dream* —**recurrence** /-'kʌrəns $ -'kɜːr-/ n [C,U] —**recurrent** adj

recycle /ˌriː'saɪkəl/ v [I,T] to put glass, paper etc through a special process so that it can be used again: *Glass bottles can be recycled.* **→** see box at **ENVIRONMENT →** and **RUBBISH** —**recycled** adj: *recycled paper* —**recycling** n [U] —**recyclable** adj: *recyclable plastics* (=that can be recycled)

red¹ /red/ adj

1 having the colour of blood: *a red dress* **→** see picture at **PATTERN**

2 red hair is an orange-brown colour

3 if you go red, your face becomes pink because you are embarrassed, angry etc —**redness** n [U]

red² n [C,U]

1 the colour of blood

2 be in the red to owe more money than you have [**≠ be in the black; → overdrawn**] **→** see box at **OWE**

3 see red to become very angry

red 'carpet n **the red carpet** special treatment that you give to someone important who is visiting you

redden /'redn/ v [I,T] to become red, or to make something do this

redeem /rɪ'diːm/ v [T] **1** to make something less bad: *Smith redeemed a poor game with a brilliant last-minute goal.* **2 redeem yourself** to do something that improves what other people think of you, after you have done something bad —**redeemable** adj

redemption /rɪ'dempʃən/ n [U] **1 past/ beyond redemption** too bad to be saved or improved **2** when someone is saved from the power of evil, especially according to the Christian religion

redeploy /ˌriːdɪ'plɔɪ/ v [T] to move soldiers, workers, equipment etc to a different place or use them in a more effective way —**redeployment** n [U]

redevelop /ˌriːdɪ'veləp/ v [T] to make an area more modern by putting in new buildings and businesses or improving old ones —**redevelopment** n [C,U]

ˌred-'handed adj **catch sb red-handed** *informal* to catch someone at the moment when they are doing something wrong

redhead /'redhed/ n [C] someone who has red hair

ˌred 'herring n [C] a fact or idea that is not important but takes your attention away from something that is important

ˌred-'hot adj extremely hot: *red-hot metal*

redid /riː'dɪd/ v the past tense of **REDO**

redirect, re-direct /ˌriːdaɪ'rekt, -dᵻ-/ v [T] **1** to send something in a different direction **2** to use something for a different purpose: *She needs to redirect her energy into something more useful.*

redistribute /ˌriːdɪ'strɪbjuːt/ v [T] to share something between people in a different way from before —**redistribution** /ˌriːdɪstrᵻ'bjuːʃən/ n [U]

ˌred-'light ˌdistrict n [C] the area of a city where there is a lot of **PROSTITUTION**

ˌred 'meat n [U] dark coloured meat such as **BEEF** [**→ white meat**]

redneck /'rednek/ n [C] *AmE informal* a man who lives in a country area who is not educated and who has strong unreasonable opinions

redo /riː'duː/ v [T] past tense **redid** /-'dɪd/ past participle **redone** /-'dʌn/ third person singular **redoes** /-'dʌz/ to do something again: *You'll have to redo this essay.*

redouble /riː'dʌbəl/ v **redouble your efforts** to greatly increase your efforts to do something

redress /rɪ'dres/ v [T] *formal* to correct something that is wrong, not equal, or unfair —**redress** /rɪ'dres $ 'riːdres/ n [U]

R

,red 'tape *n* [U] official rules that seem unnecessary and prevent things from being done quickly

reduce /rɪˈdjuːs $ rɪˈduːs/ *v* [T] to make something become less in size, amount, price etc [= cut; ➙ reduction]: **reduce the number/amount/level etc of sth** *They're trying to reduce the number of students in the college.* | *attempts to reduce unemployment* | **reduce sth (from sth) to sth** *The jacket was reduced from £75 to £35.*

reduce sb/sth **to** sth *phr v* **1 reduce sb to tears** to make someone cry: *Many staff were reduced to tears by the tragedy.* **2 reduce sb to doing sth** to make someone do something which they would prefer not to, especially when it is worse than what they did before: *They were reduced to begging on the streets.* **3 reduce sth to rubble/ashes/ruins** to destroy something, especially a building or city, completely

reduction /rɪˈdʌkʃən/ *n* [C,U] a decrease in the size, amount, or price of something, or when something is decreased: **+in** *a reduction in the number of students choosing science* | **+of** *targets for the reduction of pollution* | **+on** *There are 40% reductions on winter shoes.*

redundancy /rɪˈdʌndənsi/ *n* plural **redundancies 1** [C,U] *BrE* when someone has to leave their job because there is not enough work: **compulsory/voluntary redundancy** *The company hopes that many staff will take voluntary redundancy.* | *Part-time workers may not be entitled to **redundancy payments**.* **2** [U] when something is not used or needed because something else does the same thing

redundant /rɪˈdʌndənt/ *adj* **1** *BrE* if you are made redundant, you have to leave your job because there is not enough work: *Over 1000 workers were **made redundant**.* **2** something that is redundant is no longer needed because something else does the same thing

reed /riːd/ *n* [C] **1** a tall plant like grass that grows near water **2** a thin piece of wood in some musical instruments that produces a sound when you blow air over it

reef /riːf/ *n* [C] a line of sharp rocks or a raised area near the surface of the sea, often made of CORAL

reek /riːk/ *v* [I] to smell of something unpleasant: *His breath reeked of garlic.* —**reek** *n* [singular]

reel¹ /riːl/ *n* [C] a round object that things such as thread or film can be wound onto

reel² *v* [I] **1** to walk in an unsteady way, almost falling over, as if you are drunk: *A guy came reeling down the hallway.* **2** to feel very shocked or confused: *The party is still reeling from its defeat in the election.*

reel sth ⇔ **off** *phr v* to repeat a lot of information quickly and easily: *Andy can reel off the names of all the state capitals.*

re-elect /ˌriː ɪˈlekt/ *v* [T] to elect someone again —**re-election** /-ˈlekʃən/ *n* [C,U]

re-entry /riˈentri/ *n* [C,U] plural **re-entries** when someone or something enters a place again: *The shuttle made a successful re-entry into the Earth's atmosphere.*

ref /ref/ *n* [C] *spoken* a REFEREE

refer /rɪˈfɜː $ -ɜːr/ *v* **referred, referring**

refer to sb/sth *phr v* **1** to mention someone or something: *He referred to her several times.* | **+as** *Some people refer to them as 'gangsters'.* **2** to look at a book, map, piece of paper etc for information: *Refer to page 14 for instructions.* **3 refer sb to sb/sth** to send someone to another place or person for information, advice etc: *Professor Harris referred me to an article she had written.* | *My doctor referred me to an eye specialist.*

referee¹ /ˌrefəˈriː/ *n* [C] **1** someone who makes sure that the rules are followed during a sports game

2 *BrE* someone who writes a letter saying that you are suitable for a job, course etc → see box at **JOB**

referee² *v* [I,T] **refereed, refereeing** to be the referee for a game

reference /ˈrefərəns/ *n*

1 [C,U] something you say or write that mentions another person or thing: **+to** *Her writings contain references to members of her family.* | *In his letter, Sam **made no reference** to his illness.*
2 [C,U] when you look at something for information, or the place you get information from: *Keep this dictionary on your desk **for reference**.* | *The conversations are recorded **for future reference** (=so that they can be looked at in the future).*
3 [C] **a)** a letter saying that someone is suitable for a new job, course etc **b)** the person who writes a letter saying that someone is suitable for a new job or course [= referee]

'reference book *n* [C] a book, for example a dictionary, that you look at to find information → see box at **BOOK**

referendum /ˌrefəˈrendəm/ *n* [C,U] plural **referenda** /-də/ or **referendums** when people vote to make a decision on a particular subject, rather than for a person: **+on** *a referendum on independence* | *The assembly has agreed to **hold a referendum** on the issue.*

refill /ˌriːˈfɪl/ *v* [T] to fill something again: *A waiter refilled our glasses.* —**refill** /ˈriːfɪl/ *n*: *He held out his glass for a refill.*

refine /rɪˈfaɪn/ *v* [T] **1** to use an industrial process to make a natural substance more pure: *The sugar is refined and then shipped abroad.* **2** to improve a method, plan, system etc by making small changes to it —**refinement** *n* [U]

refined /rɪˈfaɪnd/ *adj* **1** a refined substance has been made more pure using an industrial process [≠ unrefined]: **refined sugar/oil/petroleum 2** a method or process that is refined is improved and made more effective: *a more refined technique* **3** someone who is refined is polite and seems to be well educated: *a refined accent*

refinery /rɪˈfaɪnəri/ *n* [C] plural **refineries** a factory where something such as oil, sugar, or metal is refined

reflect /rɪˈflekt/ v **1** [I,T] if something such as a mirror or water reflects something, you can see the image of that thing in the mirror or water: **be reflected in sth** *She could see the truck behind reflected in her wing mirror.* **2** [T] if a surface reflects heat, light, sound etc, it sends back the light, heat, or sound that reaches it: *White clothes reflect more heat than dark ones.* **3** [T] to show or be a sign of something: *The new law reflects social changes in attitudes to marriage.* **4** [I] formal to think carefully: **+on** *Take some time to reflect on what I've said.*

reflect on sb/sth phr v to influence people's opinion about someone or something, especially in a bad way: *Behaviour like that always **reflects** very **badly on** the school.*

reflection

reflection /rɪˈflekʃən/ n **1** [C] an image that is reflected in a mirror or a similar surface: **+in** *We looked at our reflections in the pool.* **2** [U] when an image, light, sound etc is reflected **3** [C,U] careful and serious thought: *She paused for a moment's reflection.* **4** [singular] something that shows what something else is like, or is a sign of a particular situation: **+of** *The increase in ticket sales is a reflection of the popularity of the competition.* | **be a reflection on** **sb/sth** (=to show how good or bad someone or something is) *To some extent, students' grades are a reflection on the teacher.*

reflective /rɪˈflektɪv/ adj **1** reflective things reflect light: *reflective clothing* **2** thinking quietly: *a reflective mood*

reflector /rɪˈflektə $ -ər/ n [C] a piece of plastic that reflects light

reflex /ˈriːfleks/ n [C] a quick physical reaction that your body makes without you thinking about it: *Tennis players need to have quick reflexes.* | *Her reflex action was to pull her hand away.*

reflexive /rɪˈfleksɪv/ adj a reflexive verb or PRONOUN shows that an action affects the person or thing that does the action. In the sentence 'He cut himself', 'himself' is a reflexive pronoun. —**reflexive** n [C]

reform[1] /rɪˈfɔːm $ -ɔːrm/ v **1** [T] to change a law, system, or organization so that it is fairer or more effective: *plans to reform the voting system* → see box at **CHANGE** **2** [I,T] to change your behaviour and become a better person, or to make someone do this: *a reformed criminal* | *He doesn't drink any more – he's a reformed character.*

reform[2] n [C,U] a change that is made to a political or legal system in order to make it fairer or more effective: **+of** *the reform of local government* | **economic/political/educational reform**

reformer /rɪˈfɔːmə $ -ɔːrmər/ n [C] someone who works to improve laws or society

refrain /rɪˈfreɪn/ v [I] formal to not do something that you want to do: **+from** *Please refrain from smoking.*

refresh /rɪˈfreʃ/ v **1** [T] to make someone feel less tired or hot: *A shower will refresh you.* **2 refresh sb's memory** to make someone remember something **3** [I,T] to make a computer screen show new information that has arrived since you began looking at it —**refreshed** adj

refreshing /rɪˈfreʃɪŋ/ adj **1** making you feel less tired or less hot: *a refreshing drink* **2** pleasantly different and interesting: *The film made a refreshing change from the usual Hollywood blockbusters.* —**refreshingly** adv

refreshments /rɪˈfreʃmənts/ n [plural] food and drinks that are provided at a meeting, party, sports event etc: *Refreshments will be served at the interval.*

refrigerate /rɪˈfrɪdʒəreɪt/ v [T] to make food or drink cold so that it stays fresh for longer: *Cover the dish and refrigerate overnight.* —**refrigeration** /rɪˌfrɪdʒəˈreɪʃən/ n [U]

refrigerated /rɪˈfrɪdʒəreɪt̬ɪd/ adj **1** a refrigerated container, vehicle, ship etc keeps the food it contains cold **2** refrigerated food or drink has been kept cold in a refrigerator

refrigerator /rɪˈfrɪdʒəreɪtə $ -ər/ n [C] a piece of kitchen equipment like a cupboard that keeps food cold so that it stays fresh for longer [= **fridge**; → **freezer**]

refuel /ˌriːˈfjuːəl/ v [I,T] **refuelled, refuelling** BrE; **refueled, refueling** AmE to fill a vehicle or plane with FUEL before continuing a journey

refuge /ˈrefjuːdʒ/ n **1** [U] protection from danger, bad weather, trouble etc: **take/seek refuge** *A number of women and children took refuge in the French Embassy.* **2** [C] a place that provides protection from danger: **+for** *a refuge for abused women*

refugee /ˌrefjʊˈdʒiː/ n [C] someone who has had to leave their country to escape from danger or war: *a refugee camp near the border*

refund[1] /ˈriːfʌnd/ n [C] money that is given back to you in a shop, restaurant etc, for example, because you are not satisfied with what you bought: *If you're not completely satisfied, we'll give you a refund.* —**refund** /rɪˈfʌnd/ v [T]

refurbish /ˌriːˈfɜːbɪʃ $ -ɜːr-/ v [T] to repair and improve a building —**refurbishment** n [C,U]

refusal /rɪˈfjuːzəl/ n [C,U] when someone refuses to do, accept, or allow something: **refusal to do sth** *His refusal to pay the fine means he may go to prison.*

refuse[1] /rɪˈfjuːz/ v

1 [I,T] to say firmly that you will not do or accept something: *I asked her to marry me, but she refused.* | **refuse to do sth** *Cindy refuses to go to school.* | **flatly refuse/refuse point blank (to do sth)** (=refuse completely) *Mother flatly refused to go back into hospital.* | *The offer seemed too good to refuse.*

R

refusing

No, thanks: *'Would you like a lift?' 'No, thanks.'*
Thanks, but ...: *'How about lunch on Sunday?' 'Thanks, but I've promised to meet Mum.'*
I won't, thanks: *'Chocolate?' 'I won't, thanks.'*
I'd love to, but ...: *'Why don't you stay another day?' 'I'd love to, but I've got to get back.'*
I can't ...: *'Are you coming to the party?' 'I can't ... exams tomorrow.'*
I'd better not: *'Another drink?' 'I'd better not, I'm driving.'*
→ ACCEPT, AGREE

2 [T] to not give or allow someone something that they want: **refuse sb sth** *We were refused permission to enter the country.*
refuse² /'refjuːs/ *n* [U] *formal* waste material [= rubbish]: *refuse collection* | **domestic/ household refuse** → see box at RUBBISH
refute /rɪ'fjuːt/ *v* [T] *formal* **1** to prove that a statement or idea is not correct: **refute an idea/ hypothesis etc** **2** to say that a statement is wrong or unfair: **refute an allegation/a charge etc**
regain /rɪ'geɪn/ *v* [T] to get something back: *The army has regained control of the area.* | *When he regained consciousness he was in hospital.*
regal /'riːɡəl/ *adj* typical of a king or queen and therefore very impressive —**regally** *adv*
regard¹ /rɪ'ɡɑːd $ -ɑːrd/ *n* **1** [U] when you respect or consider someone or something: *Doctors are held in high regard* (=respected a lot) *by society.* | *She has no regard for* (=does not consider) *other people's feelings.* **2 with/in regard to sth** *formal* used to say what subject you are talking or writing about: *Several changes have been made with regard to security.* **3 regards** [plural] used to send good wishes to someone in a polite and slightly formal way: *Give my regards to your aunt.* | **(with) kind/best regards** (=used at the end of a letter or message)
regard² *v* [T] **1** to think about someone or something in a particular way: **regard sb as sth** *I've always regarded you as my friend.* **2** *formal* to look at someone or something: *She regarded him thoughtfully.*
regarding /rɪ'ɡɑːdɪŋ $ -ɑːr-/ *prep formal* a word used especially in business letters to introduce the subject you are writing about: *Regarding your recent inquiry, I've enclosed a copy of our new brochure.*
regardless /rɪ'ɡɑːdləs $ -ɑːr-/ *adv* **1 regardless of sth** in spite of something: *He'll sign that contract regardless of what anyone says!* **2** if you continue doing something regardless, you do it in spite of problems or difficulties: *You get a lot of criticism but you just have to carry on regardless.*
regatta /rɪ'ɡætə/ *n* [C] a sports event in which there are boat races
regeneration /rɪˌdʒenə'reɪʃən/ *n* [U] when a thing or place is developed, improved, or grows strong again: *inner city regeneration* —**regenerate** /rɪ'dʒenəreɪt/ *v* [T]
reggae /'reɡeɪ/ *n* [U] a type of popular music from Jamaica with a strong regular beat → see box at MUSIC

regime /reɪ'ʒiːm/ *n* [C] a government, especially one that was not elected fairly or that you disapprove of: *a brutal military regime* → see box at GOVERNMENT
regiment /'redʒɪmənt/ *n* [C] a large group of soldiers consisting of several BATTALIONS —**regimental** /ˌredʒɪ'mentl◂/ *adj*
regimented /'redʒɪmentɪd/ *adj* strictly controlled —**regiment** *v* [T]
region /'riːdʒən/ *n* [C]
1 a large area of a country or of the world, usually without exact limits: **+of** *the north-eastern region of Russia* | **central/border etc region** *Snow is expected in mountain regions.* → see box at AREA
2 an area of your body: *pain in the lower back region*
3 (somewhere) in the region of sth used to describe an amount without being exact: *It will cost in the region of $750.*
—**regional** *adj*: *a regional accent* —**regionally** *adv*
register¹ /'redʒɪstə $ -ər/ *n* **1** [C] an official list or record of something: **+of** *the register of births, marriages, and deaths* → see box at RECORD **2** [C,U] a way of speaking or writing that is formal, informal, humorous etc which you use when you are in a particular situation → CASH REGISTER
register² *v* **1** [I,T] to put the name of someone or something on an official list: **+with** *You need to register with a doctor.* | **+for** *How many students have registered for the course so far?* | *Is the car registered in your name?* **2** [T] *formal* to state an opinion or show a feeling: *The club has registered a formal protest about the decision.* **3** [I,T] if something registers, or you register it, you notice or realize it: *Then I remembered something that hadn't registered at the time.* **4** [I,T] if an instrument registers an amount, or an amount registers on it, it shows that amount: *The thermometer registered 74°F.*
'register ˌoffice *n* [C] a REGISTRY OFFICE
registrar /ˌredʒɪ'strɑː◂ $ 'redʒɪstrɑːr/ *n* [C] **1** someone who is in charge of official records of births, marriages, and deaths **2** *BrE* a hospital doctor
registration /ˌredʒɪ'streɪʃən/ *n* [U] when names and details are recorded on an official list, or when you add your name to an official list
regi'stration ˌnumber *n* [C] *BrE* the numbers and letters on a car's NUMBER PLATE
registry /'redʒɪstri/ *n* [C] plural **registries** a place where official records are kept
'registry ˌoffice also **'register ˌoffice** *n* [C] a place in Britain where you can get married and where records of marriages, births, and deaths are kept
regress /rɪ'ɡres/ *v* [I] *formal* to go back to an earlier, less developed state [→ progress] —**regression** /-'ɡreʃən/ *n* [U]
regret¹ /rɪ'ɡret/ *v* [T] regretted, regretting
1 to feel sorry about something you have done and wish you had not done it: **regret doing sth** *We've always regretted selling that car.* | **+(that)** *He regrets that he never went to college.* | **bitterly/deeply/greatly regret** *It was a stupid thing to do and I bitterly regret it.* | *If we don't*

*deal with the problem now, we'll **live to regret it*** (=will regret it in the future).

2 *formal* to be sorry and sad about a situation: +**(that)** *Miss Otis regrets she's unable to attend today.*

regret² *n* [C,U] sadness that you feel about something because you wish it had not happened: *Carl said he **had** no **regrets about** his decision.* | *The company **expressed** deep **regret** at the accident.* —**regretfully** *adv* —**regretful** *adj*

regrettable /rɪ'gretəbəl/ *adj* something regrettable is something you wish had not happened: *a regrettable mistake* —**regrettably** *adv*

regular¹ /'regjʊlə $ -ər/ *adj*

1 happening every hour, every week, every month etc, usually with the same amount of time in between [≠ **irregular**]: *regular meetings* | *His heartbeat became slow and regular.* | *We hear from him **on a regular basis**.* | *War planes were taking off **at regular intervals**.* | *He already has a **regular job** (=one he does every week).*

> **THESAURUS**
>
> hourly, daily, weekly, monthly, yearly/annually

2 happening or doing something very often [≠ **irregular**]: *He's one of our regular customers.* | *Regular exercise helps keep your weight down.*
3 normal or usual: *She's not our regular babysitter.*
4 with the same amount of space between one thing and the next [≠ **irregular**]: *The markers are spaced at regular intervals.*
5 of a normal or standard size: *fries and a regular coke*
6 *especially AmE* ordinary or normal and not special or different: *He's just **a regular guy**.*
7 evenly shaped with parts or sides of equal size
8 a regular verb or noun changes its forms in the same way as most verbs or nouns. The verb 'walk' is regular, but 'be' is not [≠ **irregular**] —**regularity** /ˌregjʊ'lærɪ̯ti/ *n* [U]

regular² *n* **1** [C] *informal* a customer who goes to the same shop, restaurant etc very often **2** [U] *AmE* petrol that contains LEAD [➔ **unleaded**]

regularly /'regjʊ̯ləli $ -ərli/ *adv*
1 often: *He visits the old man regularly.* ➔ see box at **OFTEN**
2 at the same time every day, week, or month: *They are checked regularly, once a week.*
3 evenly arranged or shaped: *The plants are regularly spaced.*

regulate /'regjʊ̯leɪt/ *v* [T] **1** to control an activity or process, especially by having rules: *rules regulating the use of chemicals in food* **2** to keep something at a particular speed, temperature etc

regulation /ˌregjʊ̯'leɪʃən/ *n* **1** [C] an official rule or order: *There seem to be so many **rules and regulations**.* **2** [U] when a system or process is controlled: +**of** *government regulation of arms sales*

regulator /'regjʊ̯leɪtə $ -ər/ *n* [C] **1** an instrument which controls the temperature, speed etc of something **2** someone who makes sure that a system works properly or fairly —**regulatory** /ˌregjʊ̯'leɪtəri $ 'regjʊ̯lətɔːri/ *adj*

rehab /'riːhæb/ *n* [U] *informal* treatment to help someone who takes drugs or drinks too much alcohol: *Frank's **been in rehab** for six weeks.*

rehabilitate /ˌriːhə'bɪlɪ̯teɪt/ *v* [T] **1** to help someone to live a healthy or useful life again after they have been ill or in prison: *special help to rehabilitate stroke patients* **2** to improve a building, business, or area —**rehabilitation** /ˌriːhəbɪlɪ̯'teɪʃən/ *n* [U] *a project for the rehabilitation of drug addicts*

rehash /riː'hæʃ/ *v* [T] *informal* to use the same ideas again in a way that is not really different or better: *He keeps rehashing the same old speech.* —**rehash** /'riːhæʃ/ *n* [C]

rehearsal /rɪ'hɜːsəl $ -ɜːr-/ *n* [C,U] a time when all the people in a play, concert etc practise it before giving a public performance: *rehearsals for 'Romeo and Juliet'*

rehearse /rɪ'hɜːs $ -ɜːrs/ *v* [I,T] to practise or make people practise something such as a play or concert before giving a public performance ➔ see box at **PRACTISE**

rehouse /ˌriː'haʊz/ *v* [T] to provide someone with a new or better home

reign¹ /reɪn/ *n* **1** [C] a period of time during which someone, especially a king or queen, rules a country: +**of** *the reign of Queen Anne* **2** [singular] a period of time during which someone is in control of an organization, business etc: *his 4-year reign as team coach* **3 reign of terror** when a government, army etc uses violence to control people

reign² *v* [I] **1** to be the ruler of a country **2 the reigning champion** the most recent winner of a competition **3** *literary* to be the main feature or feeling of a situation: *For a few moments confusion reigned.*

reimburse /ˌriːɪ̯m'bɜːs $ -ɜːrs/ *v* [T] *formal* to pay money back to someone: **reimburse sb for sth** *The company will reimburse you for your travel expenses.* —**reimbursement** *n* [U]

rein /reɪn/ *n* **1** [C usually plural] a long narrow band of leather that is fastened around a horse's head in order to control it **2 give sb (a) free rein** to give someone complete freedom to say or do things the way they want to **3 keep a tight rein on sb/sth** to strictly control someone or something: *They've promised to keep a tight rein on spending.*

reincarnate /ˌriːɪn'kɑːneɪt $ -ɑːr-/ *v* **be reincarnated** to be born again in another body after you have died

reincarnation /ˌriːɪnkɑː'neɪʃən $ -ɑːr-/ *n* **1** [U] the belief that people return to life in another body after they have died **2** [C] the person or animal that a person becomes when they return to life after they have died

reindeer /'reɪndɪə $ -dɪr/ *n* [C] plural **reindeer** a type of DEER with long horns that lives in very cold places

reinforce /ˌriːɪn'fɔːs $ -'fɔːrs/ *v* **1** to support an opinion, feeling, system etc and make it stronger: *The minister's speech served to reinforce the government's policy on the environment.* **2** to make something such as a part of a building, a piece of clothing etc stronger —**reinforced** *adj*: *reinforced concrete*

R

reinforcements /ˌriːɪnˈfɔːsmənts $ -ˈfɔːrs-/ n [plural] more soldiers or police who are sent to help make a group stronger

reinstate /ˌriːɪnˈsteɪt/ v [T] to give someone their job back after they have lost it —**reinstatement** n [C,U]

reinvent /ˌriːɪnˈvent/ v **1 reinvent yourself** to completely change your appearance and image: *Pop stars constantly need to reinvent themselves.* **2 reinvent the wheel** *informal* to waste time trying to find a way of doing something, when everyone already knows how to do it

reiterate /riːˈɪtəreɪt/ v [T] *formal* to say something important again

reject¹ /rɪˈdʒekt/ v [T]

1 to not accept something or someone [≠ **accept**]: *Your application has been rejected.* | *He flatly rejected* (=completely rejected) *our offers of help.* | *I had expected my idea to be rejected outright* (=without even being considered). | **reject sth as sth** *The meat was rejected as unfit to eat.* | *Doctors say her body may reject the new kidney.*
2 to not give someone love or attention: *She felt rejected by her parents.*

reject² /ˈriːdʒekt/ n [C] a product that is damaged: *cheap rejects*

rejection /rɪˈdʒekʃən/ n **1** [C,U] when someone does not accept something: +**of** *his rejection of his parents' values* | *She received many rejections before the novel was published.* **2** [U] when someone stops giving someone love or attention: *fear of rejection*

rejoice /rɪˈdʒɔɪs/ v [I] *literary* to be very happy because of something that has happened —**rejoicing** n [U]

rejoin /ˌriːˈdʒɔɪn/ v [T] to return to a group or person

rejuvenate /rɪˈdʒuːvəneɪt/ v [T] to make someone feel young and strong again: *I returned from holiday refreshed and rejuvenated.*

rekindle /riːˈkɪndl/ v [T] to make someone have feelings that they had a long time ago

relapse /rɪˈlæps $ ˈriːlæps/ n [C,U] when someone becomes ill or worse after seeming to improve: **have/suffer a relapse** *He had a relapse and went back in hospital.* —**relapse** /rɪˈlæps/ v [I]

relate /rɪˈleɪt/ v **1** [T] if you relate two things, you show how they are connected: **relate sth to/with sth** *The report relates health with standards of living.* **2** [I] if one thing relates to another, it is connected with it in some way: +**to** *I collect anything that relates to baseball.* | *The doctor will ask some questions relating to your lifestyle.* **3** [T] *formal* to tell someone about something that has happened: **relate sth to sb** *He later related the whole story to us.*
relate to sb/sth *phr v* to understand how someone feels: *I find it hard to relate to kids.*

related /rɪˈleɪtɪd/ adj

1 things that are related are connected: *Police believe the murders are related.* | +**to** *diseases related to smoking* | **closely/directly related** *Sunbathing is directly related to skin cancer.* | **stress-related/drug-related etc** *stress-related illness*

2 belonging to the same family or group: +**to** *Are you related to Paula?* | *Dogs and wolves are closely related.*

relation /rɪˈleɪʃən/ n

1 relations [plural] official connections and attitudes between countries, organizations, groups etc: +**with** *Relations with the next village gradually worsened.* | +**between** *Are the relations between the staff and students good?* | **diplomatic/international relations** *Britain broke off* (=ended) *diplomatic relations.* | *East-West relations* (=between countries in the East and the West)
2 in relation to sb/sth a) compared with something or someone else: *Women's earnings are still low in relation to men's.* **b)** about a particular thing or person: *Is your enquiry in relation to an advertisement?*
3 [C,U] a connection between things [= **relationship**]: +**between** *the relation between drugs and mental illness* | *His statement bore no relation to the truth* (=it was not true at all).
4 [C] a member of your family [= **relative**]: +**of** *a distant relation of the Royal Family* | +**to** *What relation are you to John?* | *He's no relation to the film star Michael Douglas.*
→ **INDUSTRIAL RELATIONS, PUBLIC RELATIONS, RACE RELATIONS**

relationship /rɪˈleɪʃənʃɪp/ n

1 [C] the attitude that two people or groups show towards each other: +**with** *I had a close relationship with my father.* | +**between** *the special relationship between the US and Britain*
2 [C] a situation in which two people have sexual or romantic feelings for each other: +**with** *Do you remember when I was having a relationship with Anna?* | *a sexual relationship*
3 [C,U] the way that things or people are connected: +**between** *the relationship between smoking and cancer* | +**to** *'What's your relationship to Sue?' 'She's my cousin.'*

relative¹ /ˈrelətɪv/ n [C] your relatives are the other members of your family [= **relation**]: *He's staying with relatives.* | *an elderly relative* | **close/distant relative** *She has no close relatives.*

THESAURUS

parents
father/mother
dad/daddy *informal*/mum/mummy *BrE*
informal/mom/mommy *AmE* *informal*
brother/sister
grandparents
grandfather/grandmother
grandpa/grandma *informal*
great-grandparents
uncle/aunt
nephew/niece
cousin

---

relative² adj **1** having a particular quality when compared with similar things: *a period of relative peace* **2 relative to sth** *formal* compared with something else

relative 'clause n [C] a part of a sentence which contains a verb and adds information about the person or thing you are talking about

relatively /ˈrelətɪvli/ adv quite, when compared with other things: *Food is relatively cheap in the US.*

relative 'pronoun n [C] a PRONOUN such as 'who', 'which', or 'that' which connects a relative clause to the rest of a sentence

relativity /ˌreləˈtɪvɪti/ n [U] the relationship between time, space, and speed: *Einstein's theory of relativity*

relax /rɪˈlæks/ v

1 [I] to rest or do something you enjoy, especially after working: *What do you do to relax?*
2 [I,T] to feel calmer and less worried, or to make someone do this: *Sit down and relax!* | *The music will help relax you.*
3 [I,T] if you relax part of your body, or if it relaxes, it becomes less stiff: *Let your muscles relax.*
4 [T] to make rules, laws etc less strict: *plans to relax immigration controls*

relaxation /ˌriːlækˈseɪʃən/ n [U] **1** a way of resting and enjoying yourself: **for relaxation** *I swim for relaxation.* **2** when rules, laws etc are made less strict: **+of** *the relaxation of drug laws*

relaxed /rɪˈlækst/ adj

1 calm and not worried or angry: *Gail was lying in the sun, looking happy and relaxed.*
2 a situation or attitude that is relaxed is informal and not strict: *There's a relaxed atmosphere in school.*

relaxing /rɪˈlæksɪŋ/ adj making you feel calm: *a relaxing bath*

relay[1] /ˈriːleɪ $ rɪˈleɪ, ˈriːleɪ/ v [T] to pass a message or signal from one person or place to another: *broadcasts relayed by satellite*

relay[2] /ˈriːleɪ/ also **'relay race** n [C] a running or swimming race between two or more teams, each of which has several people in it. When one person finishes their part of the race, the next person starts and the race is over when everyone has finished.

release[1] /rɪˈliːs/ v [T]

1 to allow someone to be free after you have kept them somewhere [➡ discharge, free]: *The hostages were released this morning.* | **release sb from sth** *He was released from hospital this morning.*
2 to give news or information to people after it has been secret: *The name of the victim has not been released.*
3 to make a film, record etc available for people to buy or see: *The film is released in May.*
4 to stop holding something: **release your grip/hold** *A sudden noise made him release his grip.*

release[2] n **1** [singular] when someone is allowed to be free after they have been a prisoner: *the release of political prisoners* **2** [C] a new film or record that is available to see or buy: *her latest release* **3** **be on general release** if a film is on general release, it is being shown at most cinemas → PRESS RELEASE

relegate /ˈrelɪɡeɪt/ v [T] **1** to put someone or something in a less important position: **relegate sb to sth** *He was relegated to the role of assistant.* **2** *BrE* if a sports team is relegated, it is moved to a lower group of teams because it has won fewer games than the other teams in that group: **relegate sb/sth to sth** *We were relegated to the Third Division last year.* —**relegation** /ˌrelɪˈɡeɪʃən/ n [U]

relent /rɪˈlent/ v [I] to be less strict and allow something that you did not allow before

relentless /rɪˈlentləs/ adj not stopping or changing: *relentless pressure* —**relentlessly** adv

relevant /ˈreləvənt/ adj **1** directly relating to the thing that is being discussed [≠ irrelevant]: **+to** *Are your qualifications relevant to the job?* **2** important and useful: *The teachings of Jesus are still relevant today.* —**relevance** also **relevancy** n [U]

reliable /rɪˈlaɪəbəl/ adj if someone or something is reliable, you can trust and depend on them [≠ unreliable; ➡ rely]: *Rick is hard-working and very reliable.* | *a reliable computer* | *a reliable witness* —**reliably** adv —**reliability** /rɪˌlaɪəˈbɪlɪti/ n [U]

reliance /rɪˈlaɪəns/ n [U] when someone or something depends on another thing [➡ rely]: **+on/upon** *our reliance on imported oil*

reliant /rɪˈlaɪənt/ adj if you are reliant on someone, you depend on them [➡ rely]: *She's still reliant on her parents for money.*

relic /ˈrelɪk/ n [C] something from the past that still exists: **+of** *a relic of ancient times*

relief /rɪˈliːf/ n

1 [singular, U] the happy feeling you have when you are no longer worried or frightened [➡ relieved]: *a tremendous feeling of relief* | *It was a relief to be alone.* | **with/in relief** *I saw with relief that he wasn't hurt.* | **to sb's relief** *To my relief, she spoke English.* | *The news will come as a great relief to his family.* | *The car halted and I breathed a sigh of relief.*
2 [U] when pain or suffering is made less severe or stops for a time [➡ relieve]: *drugs for pain relief* | **+of** *the relief of suffering* | **+from** *relief from the intense heat*
3 [U] money, food, clothes etc given to people who need them: **famine/disaster/flood etc relief** | *Relief workers distributed rice.*
4 **in relief** a decoration that is in relief is higher than the surface around it

relieve /rɪˈliːv/ v [T] to reduce pain, suffering, a bad feeling etc: *Exercise can help relieve stress.*
relieve sb of sth phr v formal to take something from someone

relieved /rɪˈliːvd/ adj happy because you are no longer worried or frightened: **relieved to do sth** *I was relieved to be back home.* | **+(that)** *I felt relieved that Ben would be there to help.*

religion /rɪˈlɪdʒən/ n [C,U] a system of belief in one or more gods: *the study of religion* | *people of different religions*

religious /rɪˈlɪdʒəs/ adj

1 relating to religion: *We don't share the same religious beliefs.*
2 having very strong religious beliefs: *a deeply religious woman*

religiously /rɪˈlɪdʒəsli/ adv if you do something religiously, you are always careful to make sure that you do it: *He phones her religiously every evening.*

relinquish /rɪˈlɪŋkwɪʃ/ v [T] formal to give your position, power, rights etc to someone else

relish[1] /ˈrelɪʃ/ v [T] to enjoy the thought that something good is going to happen: *Jamie didn't relish* (=did not like) *the idea of getting up so early.*

relish[2] n **1** [U] great enjoyment **2** [C,U] a thick cold spicy sauce, usually eaten with meat

R

relive /ˌriːˈlɪv/ v [T] to remember something so well that it seems to be happening again: *We spent the morning reliving our schooldays.*

reload /ˌriːˈləʊd $ -ˈloʊd/ v [I,T] **1** to put more bullets into a gun **2** to make a computer give you information again

relocate /ˌriːləʊˈkeɪt $ riːˈloʊkeɪt/ v [I,T] *formal* to move to a new place: +**to** *Our company relocated to the West Coast.* —**relocation** /ˌriːləʊˈkeɪʃən $ -loʊ-/ n [U]

reluctant /rɪˈlʌktənt/ adj unwilling to do something: *a reluctant smile* | **reluctant to do sth** *She was very reluctant to ask for help.* —**reluctance** n [U] —**reluctantly** adv

rely /rɪˈlaɪ/ v relied, relying, relies
rely on sb/sth *phr v* to trust or depend on someone or something [➡ **reliable**]: *I knew I could rely on you.* | **rely on sb to do sth** *Can I rely on you to carry out my instructions?* | +**for** *He relies on the Web for the latest score.*

remain /rɪˈmeɪn/ v
1 [I, linking verb] to stay in the same place or condition: +**at/in/with** *The others left while I remained at home.* | *The Communist Party remained in power for years.* | **remain standing/ seated etc** *Please remain seated until the train stops.* | *The boy remained silent.*
2 [I] to be left after other people, things, or parts have gone: *A pile of bricks was all that remained of our home.*
3 [I] if something remains to be done, said etc, it still needs to be done, said etc: **It remains to be seen** *whether the operation has been a success* (=we do not know yet whether it has succeeded).

remainder /rɪˈmeɪndə $ -ər/ n **the remainder** the part of something that is left after everything else has gone: +**of** *The remainder of the class stayed behind.*

remaining /rɪˈmeɪnɪŋ/ adj [only before noun] left when other things or people have gone

remains /rɪˈmeɪnz/ n [plural] the parts of something that are left after the rest has been destroyed: +**of** *the remains of a temple*

remake /ˈriːmeɪk/ n [C] a film that has the same story as one that was made before: +**of** *a remake of 'The Wizard of Oz'* —**remake** /riːˈmeɪk/ v [T]

remand[1] /rɪˈmɑːnd $ rɪˈmænd/ v [T] *BrE* to send someone away from a court of law to wait for their TRIAL: *Smith was remanded in custody* (=sent to prison) *until Tuesday.*

remand[2] n [U] *BrE* the period of time that someone spends in prison before their TRIAL: **on remand** *He committed suicide while on remand.*

remark[1] /rɪˈmɑːk $ -ɑːrk/ n [C] something that you say to express your opinion [= **comment**]: +**about** *Carl made a spiteful remark about her hair.*

remark[2] v [T] to say something that expresses your opinion: +**that** *One woman remarked that he was very handsome.* | *'It must be a very old house,' John remarked.* | +**on/upon** *Several people remarked on the poor service.*

remarkable /rɪˈmɑːkəbəl $ -ɑːr-/ adj excellent and unusual: *a remarkable achievement*

remarkably /rɪˈmɑːkəbli $ -ɑːr-/ adv in a way that is surprising: *Jane and her cousin look remarkably similar.*

remarry /ˌriːˈmæri/ v [I,T] remarried, remarrying, remarries to marry again —**remarriage** /riːˈmærɪdʒ/ n [C,U]

remaster /riːˈmɑːstə $ -ˈmæstər/ v [T] to improve the quality of a film or musical recording, using a computer

remedial /rɪˈmiːdiəl/ adj intended to help, improve, or correct something: *a remedial class for students with learning difficulties*

remedy[1] /ˈremɪdi/ n [C] plural **remedies** **1** a successful way of improving a situation or solving a problem: +**for** *the remedy for rising crime rates* **2** a simple medicine to cure an illness that is not very bad: *cold and flu remedies*

remedy[2] v [T] remedied, remedying, remedies to improve a bad situation: *To remedy the situation, we need more teachers.*

remember /rɪˈmembə $ -ər/ v
1 [I,T] if you remember a fact or something from the past, it comes back into your mind [➡ **forget**]: +**(that)** *She suddenly remembered that she had an appointment.* | +**what/why/how etc** *Can you remember when you last saw him?* | **remember (sb) doing sth** *He couldn't even remember getting home.* | *Remember, you should never speak to strangers.* | **distinctly/clearly remember** *I distinctly remember reading about it in the paper.*
2 [I,T] to not forget something that you should do, get, or bring: **remember to do sth** *Did you remember to phone Nicky?*
3 [T] to think about and show respect for someone who has died: *a ceremony to remember those who died*

remembrance /rɪˈmembrəns/ n [U] when you think about and show respect for someone who has died: **in remembrance of sb/sth** *a tree planted in remembrance of her husband*

remind /rɪˈmaɪnd/ v [T] if you remind someone about something, you make them remember it or remember to do it: **remind sb to do sth** *Remind me to go to the bank.* | **remind sb about sth** *Thanks for reminding me about tonight's party.* | **remind sb that** *I had to remind her that we still had a lot of work to do.* | **remind sb of sth** *I reminded him of his promise.* | **that reminds me** *spoken* (=said when something makes you remember something) *Oh, that reminds me, we've run out of milk.*

remind sb of sb/sth *phr v* if someone or something reminds you of another person or place, they make you think of that person or place because they are similar: *She reminds me of my mother.*

reminder /rɪˈmaɪndə $ -ər/ n [C] something that makes you remember something else: +**of** *a painful reminder of the war* | *I received a reminder to return my library books* (=a message reminding me to return them).

reminisce /ˌremɪˈnɪs/ v [I] to talk or think about pleasant events in your past: +**about** *We were reminiscing about our college days.* —**reminiscence** n [C,U]

reminiscent /ˌremɪˈnɪsənt/ adj **be reminiscent of sth** making you think of something similar: *a scene reminiscent of a Hollywood movie*

remission /rɪˈmɪʃən/ n [C,U] a period of time when an illness improves: **in remission** *Her cancer is in remission.*

R

remit /'ri:mɪt $ rɪ'mɪt, 'ri:mɪt/ *n* [singular] *BrE* the work that you are responsible for in your job

remittance /rɪ'mɪtəns/ *n* [C] *formal* a payment for something

remnant /'remnənt/ *n* [C] a small part of something that is left after the rest has gone: +**of** *the remnants of our meal*

remodel /ˌriː'mɒdl $ -'mɑːdl/ *v* [I,T] remodelled, remodelling *BrE*; remodeled, remodeling *AmE* to change the shape or appearance of something, especially a building: *The airport terminals have been remodelled.*

remonstrate /'remənstreɪt $ rɪ'mɑːn-/ *v* [I] *formal* if you remonstrate with someone, you tell them that you strongly disapprove of what they have done

remorse /rɪ'mɔːs $ -ɔːrs/ *n* [U] a feeling of being sorry because you have done something bad: +**for** *Keating showed no remorse for his crime.* | *Poor Dorothy was filled with remorse.* —**remorseful** *adj*

remorseless /rɪ'mɔːsləs $ -'mɔːr-/ *adj* **1** not stopping **2** very cruel or strict —**remorselessly** *adv*

remote /rɪ'məʊt $ -'moʊt/ *adj* **1** far away: *a remote village* | *in the remote past* **2** very slight or small: *The prospects for peace seem very remote.* **3** not friendly

re,mote con'trol *n* **1** also **remote** [C] a piece of equipment that you use to control a television, VIDEO etc from a distance **2** [U] a system for controlling something from a distance

remotely /rɪ'məʊtli $ -'moʊt-/ *adv* even to a very small degree: *He didn't sound remotely interested.*

removable /rɪ'muːvəbəl/ *adj* able to be removed: *seats with removable covers*

removal /rɪ'muːvəl/ *n* [C,U] **1** when something is taken away or someone gets rid of it: +**of** *the removal of rubbish* **2 removal firm/ van/men etc** *BrE* a company, vehicle etc that is used to move all your furniture from your old house to a new house

remove /rɪ'muːv/ *v* [T]

1 to take something away from the place where it is: *The police will remove any illegally parked cars.* | **remove sth from sth** *Dictionaries may not be removed from the library.*

THESAURUS

take off – to remove clothing: *She began to take off her clothes.*

tear off – to remove part of a piece of paper or cloth by tearing it: *Tear off the attached form and send it to us.*

break off – to remove a part of something by breaking it: *Ted broke off a piece of chocolate.*

scrape off – to remove something, using a knife or sharp tool: *We began by scraping off the wallpaper.*

wipe off/up – to remove dirt, liquid etc with a cloth: *He wiped the sweat off his forehead.* | *Julie wiped up the milk she had spilled.*

rub off – to remove dirt, marks etc with a cloth or brush: *She tried to rub the paint off her jeans.*

---

2 to get rid of something so that it no longer exists: *This will remove the risk of infection.*

3 *formal* to force someone to leave their job: **remove sb from sth** *The college board has the power to remove a teacher from his post.*
4 far removed from sth very different from something

remover /rɪ'muːvə $ -ər/ *n* [C,U] **paint remover/stain remover etc** a substance used to remove paint, dirt etc

remuneration /rɪˌmjuːnə'reɪʃən/ *n* [C,U] *formal* payment for a job, service etc

renaissance /rɪ'neɪsəns $ ˌrenə'sɑːns/ *n* [U] when something becomes popular or successful again

Renaissance *n* **the Renaissance** an important time in Europe between the 14th and 17th centuries when art, literature, music etc became very different from what they had been before

rename /ˌriː'neɪm/ *v* [T] to give something a new name

render /'rendə $ -ər/ *v* [T] *formal* to cause someone or something to be in a particular condition: *The blow to his head rendered him unconscious.*

rendering /'rendərɪŋ/ *n* [C] someone's performance of a poem, play, piece of music etc

rendezvous /'rɒndɪvuː, -deɪ- $ 'rɑːndeɪ-/ *n* [C] plural **rendezvous** /-vuːz/ **1** an arrangement to meet someone at a particular time and place, especially secretly: +**with** *a midnight rendezvous with her lover* **2** a place where people arrange to meet: *a popular London rendezvous* —**rendezvous** *v* [I]

rendition /ren'dɪʃən/ *n* [C] someone's performance of a play, piece of music etc

renegade /'renɪgeɪd/ *n* [C] *formal* someone who joins the opposing side in a war, argument etc: *a political renegade*

renege /rɪ'niːg, rɪ'neɪg $ rɪ'nɪg, rɪ'niːg/ *v* [I] *formal* to not do something that you promised to do: *He reneged on that promise.*

renew /rɪ'njuː $ rɪ'nuː/ *v* [T] **1** to arrange for an agreement or arrangement to continue: *You can renew your library books on the Internet.* **2** to begin to do something again: *The search will be renewed in the morning.* **3** to replace something that is old or broken —**renewal** *n* [C,U]

renewable /rɪ'njuːəbəl $ rɪ'nuː-/ *adj* **1** renewable energy can be replaced as quickly as it is used **2** a renewable agreement or document is one that you can continue after it EXPIRES (=the time limit is reached)

renewed /rɪ'njuːd $ -'nuːd/ *adj* starting again with greater energy or strength: *renewed efforts to tackle poverty*

renounce /rɪ'naʊns/ *v* [T] **1** to say publicly that you no longer believe in or support an idea: *They must renounce violence if the talks are to continue.* **2** to say publicly that you no longer have a right to something

renovate /'renəveɪt/ *v* [T] to repair a building or furniture so that it is in good condition again → see box at REPAIR —**renovation** /ˌrenə'veɪʃən/ *n* [C,U]

renown /rɪ'naʊn/ *n* [U] *formal* fame and respect that you get for something you have done

renowned /rɪ'naʊnd/ *adj* famous and admired: +**for** *an island renowned for its beauty*

R

rent¹ /rent/ v

1 [I,T] if you rent a house, flat etc, you pay money regularly to the owner so that you can live there: **rent sth from sb** I rented a room from friends while I looked for work. | a rented apartment

TOPIC

When you rent a house or apartment, you are called the **tenant**. You usually have to **pay a deposit** before moving in. After that you **pay the rent** every month to the **landlord/landlady** (=owner). If you do not pay the rent or behave properly, the landlord can **evict** you (=force you to leave).

2 [T] to pay money for the use of something for a short time [= **hire** BrE]: Will you rent a car while you're in Spain?

3 also **rent out** [T] to let someone live in a place that you own in return for money [= **let** BrE]: **rent sth (out) to sb** They've rented out their house to tourists this summer.
—**rented** adj [only before noun] rented accommodation —**renter** n [C] AmE

rent² n [C,U] money that you pay for the use of a house, room, car etc that belongs to someone else: I pay my **rent** at the beginning of the month. | How much do you pay in rent? | **for rent** (=available to rent) houses for rent → see box at **COST**

rental /'rentl/ n **1** [C,U] money that you pay to use a car, television etc for a period of time: Ski rental is $14. **2** [C] AmE something that you rent, such as a house or car

renunciation /rɪ,nʌnsi'eɪʃən/ n [U] formal when someone makes a decision to stop doing something, stop believing in something etc

reopen /ri'əʊpən $ -'oʊ-/ v [I,T] if a place reopens, it opens again after a period when it was closed

reorganize also **-ise** BrE /riː'ɔːɡənaɪz $ -'ɔːr-/ v [I,T] to organize something in a new and better way: The office needs reorganizing. —**reorganization** /riː,ɔːɡənaɪ'zeɪʃən $ -,ɔːrɡənə-/ n [U]

rep /rep/ n [C] informal someone who sells things for a company

repaid /rɪ'peɪd/ v [C] the past tense and past participle of REPAY

repair¹ /rɪ'peə $ -'per/ v [T]

1 to make something that is broken or damaged satisfactory again: How much will it cost to repair the car? | Your shoes **need repairing**. | I must **get** the roof **repaired** (=arrange for someone to fix it).

THESAURUS

fix especially AmE/**mend** BrE: Someone's coming to fix the washing machine.
mend AmE – to repair a hole in something: Can you mend the hole in this sweater?
service – to check a vehicle or machine and repair it if necessary: Have your car serviced regularly.
renovate – to repair a building or furniture so that it is in good condition again: They're renovating a cottage in Wales.
restore – to repair something so that it looks new: The church was carefully restored after

the war.

2 to do something to remove the harm that you have done: The government was left trying to **repair the damage**.

repair² n **1** [C,U] something you do to fix something that is broken or damaged: **make/do repairs** They're doing repairs on the bridge. | **+to** repairs to the road | The roof is badly **in need of repair**. | **be under repair** (=being repaired) **2 in good/bad repair** formal in good or bad condition

reparation /,repə'reɪʃən/ n **1 reparations** [plural] money paid by a country that loses in a war for the deaths, damage etc it has caused **2** [U] formal when you do something good for someone because you have done something bad to them in the past: Offenders must **make reparation** for their crimes.

repatriate /riː'pætrieɪt $ riː'peɪ-/ v [T] to send someone back to the country that they came from —**repatriation** /riː,pætri'eɪʃən $ riː,peɪ-/ n [U]

repay /rɪ'peɪ/ v [T] past tense and past participle **repaid** /-'peɪd/ **1** to pay back money that you have borrowed: How long will it take to repay the loan? **2** to reward someone for helping you: How can I ever repay you? —**repayment** n [C,U] —**repayable** adj

repeal /rɪ'piːl/ v [T] to officially end a law: plans to repeal anti-immigration laws —**repeal** n [U]

repeat¹ /rɪ'piːt/ v [T]

1 to say or do something again: Sally kept repeating, 'It wasn't me, it wasn't me.' | You'll have to repeat the course. | **repeat yourself** (=say something that you have said before, usually by mistake) Elderly people tend to repeat themselves.

COMMUNICATION

asking someone to repeat what they said

Sorry?/Pardon?/Excuse me?
What? informal
I didn't quite catch that.
Could you repeat that?/Would you mind repeating that? formal

2 to say something that you have heard someone else say: **repeat sth to sb** Please don't repeat this to anyone.

repeat² n **1** [singular] a situation or event that has happened before [➜ **repetition**]: **+of** Are you expecting a repeat of last year's trouble? | It was a terrible journey – I hope we don't have a **repeat performance** (=have the same thing happen again) on the way home. **2** [C] especially BrE a television or radio programme that has been broadcast before [= **rerun** AmE]

repeated /rɪ'piːtɪd/ adj [only before noun] done or happening several times: repeated attempts to kill him —**repeatedly** adv. Graham was repeatedly warned not to work so hard. → see box at **OFTEN**

repel /rɪ'pel/ v [T] **repelled, repelling 1** to force someone to go away or to stop attacking you: Tear gas was used to repel the rioters. **2** if something repels you, you dislike it very much

repellent[1] /rɪ'pelənt/ n [C,U] a substance that keeps something, especially insects, away: *mosquito repellent*

repellent[2] adj extremely unpleasant: *The sight of blood is repellent to some people.*

repent /rɪ'pent/ v [I,T] formal to be sorry for something bad that you have done —**repentance** n [U] —**repentant** adj

repercussions /ˌriːpə'kʌʃənz $ -pər-/ n [plural] unpleasant effects or results of something that you do: *The collapse of the company will have repercussions for the whole industry.*

repertoire /'repətwɑː $ -pərtwɑːr/ n [C] the plays, songs, jokes etc that a performer knows and can perform: +**of** *a wide repertoire of songs*

repetition /ˌrepɪ'tɪʃən/ n [C,U] when something happens again or is done again many times: +**of** *We don't want a repetition of this disaster.*

repetitive /rɪ'petɪtɪv/ also **repetitious** /ˌrepɪ'tɪʃəs◂/ adj done many times in the same way and boring: *repetitive exercises*

rephrase /ˌriː'freɪz/ v [T] to say or write something in different words so that its meaning is clearer: *OK, let me rephrase the question.*

replace /rɪ'pleɪs/ v [T]
1 to start doing something instead of another person, or start being used instead of another thing: *I'm replacing Sue on the team.*
2 to remove someone from their job or something from its place, and put a new person or thing there: *Two of the tyres had to be replaced.* | **replace sth with sth** *They replaced thousands of permanent staff with part-timers.*
3 to put something back where it was before: *Please replace the books when you are finished.*
4 if you replace something that has been broken, stolen etc, you get a new one

replacement /rɪ'pleɪsmənt/ n **1** [C] someone or something that replaces another person or thing: *We're waiting for Mr Dunley's replacement.* **2** [U] when something is replaced: *the replacement of worn-out equipment*

replay /'riːpleɪ/ n [C] **1** BrE a sports game that is played again because neither team won the first time: *The replay will be on Thursday.* **2** something that happens in a sports game on television that is immediately shown again [➡ **action replay**] —**replay** /ˌriː'pleɪ/ v [T]

replenish /rɪ'plenɪʃ/ v [T] formal to make something full or complete again —**replenishment** n [U]

replica /'replɪkə/ n [C] an exact copy of something: *replica guns*

replicate /'replɪkeɪt/ v [T] formal if you replicate someone's work, a scientific study etc, you do it again, or try to get the same result again

reply[1] /rɪ'plaɪ/ v [I,T] **replied, replying, replies** to answer: *'Of course,' she replied.* | +**to** *I haven't replied to his letter yet.* | +**that** *When asked, she replied that he hadn't seen her.*

reply[2] n [C,U] plural **replies** something that is said, written, or done as a way of answering [= **answer**]: *Stephen made no reply.* | +**to** *There have been no replies to our ad.* | **in reply (to sth)** *Marcy said nothing in reply.*

report[1] /rɪ'pɔːt $ -ɔːrt/ n [C]
1 a written or spoken description of a situation or event: +**on/of/about** *Martens gave a report on his sales trip to Korea.* | *a police report on the accident* | *a weather report* | *a news report*
2 BrE a written statement by teachers about a child's progress at school [= **report card** AmE]

report[2] v
1 [I,T] to tell people about an event or situation, especially in newspapers, on television, or on the radio [➡ **reporter**]: *We aim to report the news as fairly as possible.* | +**on** *She was sent to report on the floods in Bangladesh.* | +**that** *The newspaper wrongly reported that he had died.*
2 [T] **a)** to tell someone in authority that a crime or accident has happened: *Who reported the fire?* **b)** to officially complain about someone: *Somebody reported Kyle for smoking in school.*
3 be reported to be/do sth used to say that a statement has been made about someone or something, but you do not know if it is true: *The stolen necklace is reported to be worth $57,000.*
4 [I] to go somewhere and officially state that you have arrived: +**to** *Visitors must report to the main reception desk.*

reportedly /rɪ'pɔːtɪdli $ -ɔːr-/ adv according to what people say: *She's reportedly one of the richest women in Europe.*

re,ported 'speech n [U] the style of speech or writing that is used for reporting what someone says, without repeating the actual words

reporter /rɪ'pɔːtə $ -'pɔːrtər/ n [C] someone whose job is to write about news events for a newspaper, or to tell people about them on television or on the radio [➡ **journalist**] → see box at **NEWSPAPER**

reporting /rɪ'pɔːtɪŋ $ -ɔːr-/ n [U] the activity of telling people about events in newspapers, on television, or on the radio: *news reporting*

repose /rɪ'pəʊz $ -'poʊz/ v [I + adv/prep] literary to have been put somewhere, or to lie or rest somewhere —**repose** n [U]

repossess /ˌriːpə'zes/ v [T] to take back something that someone has partly paid for, because they cannot pay the rest of the money they owe —**repossession** /-'zeʃən/ n [C,U]

reprehensible /ˌreprɪ'hensɪbəl/ adj formal reprehensible behaviour is very bad

represent /ˌreprɪ'zent/ v [T]
1 to speak and do things for someone else because they have asked you to: *Craig hired a lawyer to represent him.*
2 if you represent a country, school etc in a competition, you compete in it for the country, school etc
3 to be a sign or mark that means something: *The green triangles on the map represent campgrounds.*
4 to form or be something: *This figure represents a 25% increase in wages.*
5 to describe someone or something in a particular way [= **portray**]: *The article represents the millionaire as a simple family man.*

representation /ˌreprɪzen'teɪʃən/ n **1** [U] when you have someone to speak, vote, or make decisions for you: *Minority groups need more effective parliamentary representation.* **2** [C,U] the way that something is described or shown: +**of** *the representation of women in literature*

R

representative¹ /ˌreprɪˈzentətɪv◂/ n [C] someone who has been chosen to speak, vote, or make decisions for someone else

representative² adj typical of the people or things in a particular group: *a representative sample of New York residents* | **+of** *I don't claim to be representative of the majority of young people.*

repress /rɪˈpres/ v [T] **1** to stop yourself from expressing what you really feel: *It's not healthy to repress your emotions.* | *I repressed a smile.* **2** to control people by force —**repression** /-ˈpreʃən/ n [U]

repressed /rɪˈprest/ adj having feelings or needs that you do not express

repressive /rɪˈpresɪv/ adj cruel and very strict: *a repressive political system*

reprieve /rɪˈpriːv/ n [C] **1** an official order stopping a prisoner from being killed as a punishment **2** a delay before something bad happens or continues to happen: *a temporary reprieve* —**reprieve** v [T]

reprimand /ˈreprɪmaːnd $ -mænd/ v [T] to tell someone officially that they have done something wrong —**reprimand** n [C]

reprint /ˈriːprɪnt/ n [C] **1** a book that has been printed again **2** an occasion when more copies of a book are printed because all the other copies have been sold —**reprint** /ˌriːˈprɪnt/ v [T]

reprisal /rɪˈpraɪzəl/ n [C,U] something that is done unofficially to punish someone: *They didn't tell the police for fear of reprisal.*

reproach¹ /rɪˈprəʊtʃ $ -ˈprəʊtʃ/ n [C,U] **1** blame or criticism: *His mother gave him a look of reproach.* **2 above/beyond reproach** impossible to criticize: *The police should be above reproach.* —**reproachful** adj —**reproachfully** adv

reproach² v [T] to blame someone and try to make them sorry for something they have done: **reproach sb for/with sth** *She reproached her son for his bad behaviour.*

reproduce /ˌriːprəˈdjuːs $ -ˈduːs/ v **1** [T] to make a copy of something or do it again in the same way: *an attempt by scientists to reproduce conditions on Mars* **2** [I] to produce babies, eggs etc: *Most birds and fish reproduce by laying eggs.*

reproduction /ˌriːprəˈdʌkʃən◂/ n **1** [U] the process of producing babies, eggs etc: *human reproduction* **2** [C] a copy of something, especially a work of art or piece of expensive furniture

reproductive /ˌriːprəˈdʌktɪv◂/ adj relating to reproduction: *the reproductive organs*

reprove /rɪˈpruːv/ v [T] formal to angrily criticize someone for doing something bad —**reproof** /rɪˈpruːf/ n [C,U]

reptile /ˈreptaɪl $ ˈreptl/ n [C] an animal such as a snake or LIZARD that lays eggs, and whose blood changes temperature with the temperature around it —**reptilian** /repˈtɪliən/ adj

republic /rɪˈpʌblɪk/ n [C] a country that has an elected government, and does not have a king or queen [➡ **monarchy**] → see box at **GOVERNMENT**

Republican /rɪˈpʌblɪkən/ n [C] a member or supporter of the Republican Party in the US [➡ **Democrat**] —**Republican** adj [only before noun] *a Republican candidate for the Senate*

republican n [C] someone who believes in government by elected representatives only, with no king or queen —**republican** adj: *the spread of republican ideas*

Republican ˌParty n **the Republican Party** one of the two main political parties of the US [➡ **the Democratic Party**]

repudiate /rɪˈpjuːdieɪt/ v [T] formal to refuse to accept something: *He repudiated all offers of friendship.*

repugnance /rɪˈpʌgnəns/ n [U] formal a strong feeling of dislike for something [➡ **disgust**]

repugnant /rɪˈpʌgnənt/ adj formal very unpleasant and offensive: *morally repugnant behaviour*

repulse /rɪˈpʌls/ v [T] **1** if something or someone repulses you, you think that they are extremely unpleasant **2** to defeat a military attack: *Enemy forces were repulsed with the help of French troops.* —**repulsion** /-ˈpʌlʃən/ n [singular, U]

repulsive /rɪˈpʌlsɪv/ adj extremely unpleasant: *What a repulsive man!*

reputable /ˈrepjʊtəbəl/ adj respected for being honest or for doing good work [≠ **disreputable**]: *a reputable company*

reputation /ˌrepjʊˈteɪʃən/ n [C] the opinion that people have of a person, product, company etc: **good/bad etc reputation** *The neighbourhood used to have a very bad reputation.* | **+for** *a man with a reputation for honesty*

repute /rɪˈpjuːt/ n **of good/bad etc repute** formal having a good, bad etc reputation

reputed /rɪˈpjuːtɪd/ adj formal **be reputed to be/do sth** if something is reputed to be true, people say it is true but it is not definitely true: *He is reputed to be a millionaire.* —**reputedly** adv

request¹ /rɪˈkwest/ n **1** [C,U] when someone politely or formally asks for something: **+for** *We've made a request for new equipment.* | **on request** (=if you ask) *Drinks are available on request.* | **at sb's request** (=because someone asked for it to be done) *The study was done at the request of the Chairman.* **2** [C] a piece of music that someone asks to be played

request² v [T] to ask for something officially or formally: *The pilot requested permission to land.* | **+that** *We request that everyone remain quiet.* | **request sb to do sth** *All club members are requested to attend the annual meeting.* → see box at **ASK**

requiem /ˈrekwiəm, -em/ n [C,U] a Christian ceremony of prayers for someone who has died, or music written for this ceremony

require /rɪˈkwaɪə $ -ˈkwaɪr/ v [T]
1 to need something: *Pets require a lot of care.* → see box at **NEED**
2 formal to officially demand that someone does something: **be required to do sth** *All passengers are required to show their tickets.*

requirement /rɪˈkwaɪəmənt $ -ˈkwaɪr-/ n [C] something that is needed or asked for: *The refugees' main requirements are food and water.*

requisite /ˈrekwɪzɪt/ adj [only before noun] formal needed for a particular purpose: *He lacks the requisite qualifications.*

requisition /ˌrekwᵻˈzɪʃən/ v [T] *formal* if someone in authority, especially a soldier, requisitions something owned by someone else, they demand to use it

re-release /ˌriːrɪˈliːs/ v [T] to produce a CD, record, or film for a second time and to sell or show it again —**re-release** /ˈriːrɪliːs/ n [C]

rerun /ˈriːrʌn/ n [C] *especially AmE* a television programme that is shown again [= **repeat** *BrE*]

resat /riːˈsæt/ v the past tense and past participle of RESIT

reschedule /ˌriːˈʃedjuːl $ -ˈskedʒʊl, -dʒəl/ v [T] to arrange for something to happen at a different time from the one that was planned: **reschedule sth for sth** *The conference had to be rescheduled for March 19.*

rescue

a mountain rescue

rescue¹ /ˈreskjuː/ v [T] to save someone from harm or danger: **rescue sb from sth** *He rescued two people from the fire.* | *Survivors of the crash were rescued by helicopter.*
—**rescuer** n [C]

rescue² n [C,U] when someone is saved from harm or danger: *his attempted rescue of a drowning man* | *A lifeboat **came to** our **rescue*** (=rescued us). | **rescue team/workers/boat etc**

research¹ /rɪˈsɜːtʃ, ˈriːsɜːtʃ $ -ɜːr-/ n [U] serious and detailed study of a subject in order to find out new information: *the latest **medical** research* | +**on/into** *scientific research into heart disease* | *He is **doing** research for a book on the Middle Ages.*
→ **MARKET RESEARCH**

research² /rɪˈsɜːtʃ $ -ɜːr-/ v [I,T] to study a subject in detail so you can discover new facts about it: *Conner spent eight years researching the history of the group.* | *His book has been very well researched.* —**researcher** n [C]

resemblance /rɪˈzembləns/ n [C,U] a similarity between two people or things: +**between** *There's a slight resemblance between Mike and his cousin.*

resemble /rɪˈzembəl/ v [T] to be similar to someone or something: *She resembles her mother in many ways.*

resent /rɪˈzent/ v [T] to feel angry and upset about a situation or action: *I've always resented my father for leaving the family.* | **resent doing sth** *I resent having to work such long hours.*
—**resentful** *adj*: *a resentful look* —**resentfully** *adv* —**resentment** n [U] *a feeling of resentment*

reservation /ˌrezəˈveɪʃən $ -zər-/ n **1** [C] an arrangement you make so that a place in a hotel,

on a plane etc is kept for you to use: *Have you **made reservations** at the restaurant yet?* → see box at **HOTEL** **2** [C,U] a feeling of doubt because you do not completely agree with a plan, idea etc: *I still **have reservations** about promoting her.*

reserve¹ /rɪˈzɜːv $ -ɜːrv/ v [T]
1 to arrange for a place in a hotel, on a plane etc to be kept for you to use [= **book**]: *Do you have to reserve tickets in advance?* | *I'd like to reserve a table for two.*
2 to keep something separate so that it can be used for a particular purpose: **reserve sth for sb/sth** *a parking space reserved for the disabled*

reserve² n **1** [C usually plural] a supply of something that is kept to be used at a time when it is needed: *Water reserves are dangerously low.*
2 in reserve ready to be used if needed: *We always **keep** some money **in reserve**, just in case.*
3 [U] when someone does not show or talk about their thoughts and feelings: *She found it difficult to overcome her **natural reserve**.* **4** [C] an area of land where wild animals, plants etc are protected: *a nature reserve* **5** [C] an extra player who plays in a team if one of the other players is injured or ill [➡ **substitute**]

reserved /rɪˈzɜːvd $ -ɜːr-/ *adj* unwilling to show or talk about your thoughts and feelings

reservoir /ˈrezəvwɑː $ -ərvwɑːr, -vɔːr/ n [C]
1 an artificial lake where water is stored before it is supplied to people's houses **2 reservoir of sth** a supply of something that can be used if it is needed

reset /ˌriːˈset/ v [T] past tense and past participle **reset** present participle **resetting** to press the switches on a clock or other machine, so that it will work at a different time or in a different way, or so that it is ready to be used again: *I've reset the alarm for 7 o'clock.*

reshuffle /riːˈʃʌfəl, ˈriːʃʌfəl/ n [C] *especially BrE* when the jobs of people who work in an organization are changed around, especially in a government: *a Cabinet reshuffle*

reside /rɪˈzaɪd/ v [I + adv/prep] *formal* to live or be somewhere

residence /ˈrezᵻdəns/ n *formal* **1** [C] a house, apartment etc where someone lives: *a private residence* **2** [U] when someone lives in a particular place: *He left home and took up residence in London.* | **in residence** *The emperor was in residence at his summer palace.*

residency /ˈrezᵻdənsi/ n [U] **1** legal permission to live in a country for a certain period of time **2** *formal* when someone lives or works in a particular place

resident /ˈrezᵻdənt/ n [C] **1** someone who lives in a house, apartment, area etc: *a park for local residents* **2** *AmE* a doctor working at a hospital where he or she is being trained
—**resident** *adj*

residential /ˌrezᵻˈdenʃəl/ *adj* a residential area consists of houses, not offices or factories

residual /rɪˈzɪdʒuəl/ *adj* [only before noun] *formal* remaining after a process, event etc has finished: *the residual effects of exposure to radiation*

residue /ˈrezᵻdjuː $ -duː/ n [C] a substance that remains after something else has disappeared or been removed: *an oily residue*

R

resign /rɪˈzaɪn/ v [I,T]
1 to officially tell your employer that you are going to leave your job: **+from** *Burton resigned from the company yesterday.* | **+as** *He resigned as chairman in October.*
2 resign yourself to (doing) sth to accept a situation that you do not like but cannot change: *I've resigned myself to living in the city for a while.*

resignation /ˌrezɪɡˈneɪʃ*ə*n/ n **1** [C,U] when someone officially tells their employer that they are going to leave their job: *I'm planning to* **hand in** *my* **resignation.** **2** [U] when you accept a situation that you cannot change although you do not like it

resigned /rɪˈzaɪnd/ adj willing to accept a situation you do not like —**resignedly** /rɪˈzaɪn*ɪ̬*dli/ adv

resilient /rɪˈzɪliənt/ adj **1** strong enough to get better quickly after problems, illness, damage etc: *Small babies can be remarkably resilient.* **2** a resilient substance will not break or get damaged easily —**resilience** n [U]

resin /ˈrez*ɪ̬*n/ n **1** [U] a thick sticky liquid produced by some trees **2** [C,U] a type of plastic

resist /rɪˈzɪst/ v [I,T] **1** to try to prevent yourself from doing something that you should not do, even though you want to: **cannot resist (doing) sth** *I just can't resist chocolate.* **2** to oppose or fight against someone or something: *British troops could not resist the attack any longer.* | *Residents were ordered to leave the area, but they resisted.*

resistance /rɪˈzɪst*ə*ns/ n [U] **1** when people oppose or fight against someone or something: **+to** *There is strong public resistance to the new taxes.* | *The rebels* **put up fierce resistance** *against the army.* **2** the natural ability of a person, animal, or plant to stop diseases or difficult conditions from harming them: **+to** *resistance to disease*

resistant /rɪˈzɪst*ə*nt/ adj **1** not easily harmed or damaged by something: *a water-resistant watch* **2** unwilling to accept new ideas or changes: **+to** *people who are resistant to change*

resit /ˌriːˈsɪt/ v [T] past tense and past participle **resat** /-ˈsæt/ present participle **resitting** *especially BrE* to take an examination again —**resit** /ˈriːsɪt/ n [C]

resolute /ˈrezəluːt/ adj *formal* determined not to change what you are doing because you are sure that you are right [≠ **irresolute**]: *resolute leadership* —**resolutely** adv

resolution /ˌrezəˈluːʃ*ə*n/ n **1** [C] an official decision by a group or organization, especially after a vote: *a United Nations resolution* **2** [singular, U] a solution to a difficult situation: *a peaceful resolution to the crisis* **3** [C] a promise that you make to yourself to do something: *I made a New Year's resolution to stop smoking.* **4** [U] *formal* determination

resolve¹ /rɪˈzɒlv $ rɪˈzɑːlv, rɪˈzɔːlv/ v **1** [T] to find a way of dealing with a problem or of ending a disagreement: *efforts to resolve the conflict in the Middle East* **2** [I,T] *formal* to make a definite decision to do something: **resolve to do sth** *He resolved to leave the country as soon as possible.*

resolve² n [U] *formal* determination

resonant /ˈrezənənt/ adj having a loud, pleasant, strong sound: *a resonant voice* —**resonance** n [U]

resonate /ˈrezəneɪt/ v [I] to make a loud strong sound

resort¹ /rɪˈzɔːt $ -ɔːrt/ n **1** [C] a place where a lot of people go for a holiday: *a beach resort* **2 as a last resort** if everything else fails: *I could borrow the money off my parents, but only as a last resort.*

resort² v
resort to sth phr v to do something that you do not want to do, in order to try to achieve something: *They may have to resort to court action.*

resound /rɪˈzaʊnd/ v [I] to make a loud sound, or be full of a loud sound: *His voice resounded throughout the house.*

resounding /rɪˈzaʊndɪŋ/ adj **1 a resounding success/victory/defeat etc** a great success, victory etc **2** very loud: *a resounding crash*

resource /rɪˈzɔːs, -ˈsɔːs $ ˈriːsɔːrs/ n [C usually plural] something that a country, organization, person etc has which they can use: *South Africa's vast* **natural resources**

resourceful /rɪˈzɔːsf*ə*l, -ˈsɔːs- $ -ɔːr-/ adj good at finding ways to deal with problems effectively —**resourcefulness** n [U]

respect¹ /rɪˈspekt/ n [U]
1 when you admire someone, especially for their personal qualities [➜ **admiration**]: **+for** *I have great respect for her as a writer.*
2 when you treat someone in a polite way, especially because they are older or more important than you [≠ **disrespect**]: **+for** *He ought to show more respect for authority* (=for his parents, teachers, managers etc).
3 when you show by your behaviour that you think something is important: *countries where there is no respect for basic human rights*
4 in one respect/in many respects etc used to say that something is true in one way, in many ways etc: *In some respects, José is right.*
5 with (all due) respect *spoken formal* used before you say something to disagree with someone: *With all due respect, that is not the point.*
6 with respect to sth/in respect of sth *formal* concerning a particular thing [= **regarding**]: *With respect to your question about jobs, all our positions are filled.*
7 pay your (last) respects to go to someone's funeral
8 pay your respects *formal* to visit someone

respect² v [T]
1 to admire someone, especially for their personal qualities: *The students like and respect him.*
2 if you respect someone's wishes, rights, customs etc, you are careful not to do anything that they do not want, or that they think is wrong: *I would like you to respect my privacy.* | *the need to respect human rights*
3 if you respect the law or the rules, you obey them ➔ see box at **OBEY**

respectable /rɪˈspektəb*ə*l/ adj **1** someone who is respectable behaves in a way that is socially acceptable: *a respectable middle-aged lady* | *Try and make yourself look respectable.*

2 good or satisfactory: *We made quite a respectable profit.* —**respectability** /rɪ,spektə'bɪləti/ *n* [U]

respected /rɪ'spektɪd/ *adj* admired by many people because of things you have achieved: *a **highly respected** journalist*

respectful /rɪ'spektfəl/ *adj* showing respect for someone or something [≠ **disrespectful**]: *The interviewer was very respectful.* —**respectfully** *adv*

respective /rɪ'spektɪv/ *adj* [only before noun] used to talk about things that belong to each of the people or things you have mentioned: *They all went back to their respective homes.*

respectively /rɪ'spektɪvli/ *adv* in the same order as the things you have just mentioned: *They've got two children, Sam and Ben, who are eight and ten respectively.*

respiration /,respə'reɪʃən/ *n* [U] *technical* the process of breathing → **ARTIFICIAL RESPIRATION**

respirator /'respəreɪtə $ -ər/ *n* [C] a piece of equipment that helps you to breathe, for example if you are very ill or in a place where there is smoke or gas

respiratory /'respɪrətəri, 'respəreɪtəri, rɪ'spaɪərə- $ 'respərətɔːri, rɪ'spaɪrə-/ *adj* technical relating to breathing: *a respiratory illness*

respite /'respɪt, -paɪt $ -pɪt/ *n* [singular, U] a short period of time when something unpleasant stops happening: **+from** *The weekend away gave me a **brief respite** from the pressures of work.*

resplendent /rɪ'splendənt/ *adj* formal looking very attractive and impressive: **+in** *The guards looked resplendent in their uniforms.*

respond /rɪ'spɒnd $ rɪ'spɑːnd/ *v* [I] **1** to do something because of something that has happened: **+to** *How will the government respond to this latest development?* | **respond by doing sth** *The United Nations responded by sending troops to the area.* **2** to answer: *I called her name, but she didn't respond.* | **+to** *He didn't respond to my email.* **3** to improve as a result of a medical treatment: **+to** *She is responding well to the drugs.*

respondent /rɪ'spɒndənt $ rɪ'spɑːn-/ *n* [C] formal someone who answers questions in a SURVEY

response /rɪ'spɒns $ rɪ'spɑːns/ *n* [C,U] a reply or reaction to something: *I knocked on the door but there was no response.* | **+to** *the government's response to the economic crisis* | **in response to sth** *I am writing in response to your advertisement.*

responsibility /rɪ,spɒnsə'bɪləti $ rɪ,spɑːn-/ *n* plural **responsibilities**
1 [C,U] if something is your responsibility, it is your job or duty to do it: *He showed me round the office and explained what my responsibilities would be.* | *a job with a lot of responsibility* | *The committee will **have responsibility for** the budget.* | **be sb's responsibility** *It's your responsibility to pay the bills on time.*
2 [U] the fact that you were the person who made something bad happen: **+for** *No one is willing to **accept responsibility** for the accident.* | *A terrorist group has **claimed responsibility** for the bombing.*

responsible /rɪ'spɒnsəbəl $ rɪ'spɑːn-/ *adj*
1 [not before noun] if you are responsible for something bad that has happened, you caused it and you are the person who should be blamed: **+for** *a man who is responsible for the deaths of fifteen people* | *If anything goes wrong, I will **hold you responsible** (=blame you).*
2 [not before noun] if you are responsible for something, you are in charge of it or it is your job to do it: **+for** *Local authorities are responsible for the schools in their area.* | *You will be responsible for training new staff.*
3 someone who is responsible is sensible and can be trusted [≠ **irresponsible**; ➡ **reliable**]: *a responsible young man*
4 **responsible job/position** a job in which you have to make important decisions
5 **be responsible to sb** if you are responsible to someone in your job, they tell you what to do and check your work

responsibly /rɪ'spɒnsəbli $ rɪ'spɑːn-/ *adv* in a sensible way: *Can I trust you to **behave responsibly** while I'm away?*

responsive /rɪ'spɒnsɪv $ rɪ'spɑːn-/ *adj* someone who is responsive does what people want or need, or replies to them: **+to** *We must be responsive to the needs of our customers.* | *I tried talking to him, but he wasn't very responsive.*

rest[1] /rest/ *n*
1 **the rest** the part of something that still remains, or the people or things that still remain: **+of** *What shall I do with the rest of the pizza?* | *We spent the rest of the day at home.* | *There were a few people in the kitchen and the rest were in the garden.*
2 [C,U] a period of time when you relax or sleep: *You can **have a rest** later.* | *Sit down if you **need a rest**.* | *I need to **get some rest**.*
3 **put/set sb's mind at rest** to stop someone from feeling worried
4 **come to rest** to stop moving: *The truck came to rest at the bottom of the hill.*
5 **at rest** formal resting or not moving

rest[2] *v*
1 [I,T] to stop working or moving and relax for a period of time: *We can stop for a minute if you need to rest.* | **rest your legs/feet/eyes** *I sat down to rest my feet.*
2 [I,T] to put something in a position where it is supported by something else, or to be in this position [➡ **lean**]: **rest (sth) on/against sth** *I rested my head on his shoulder.* | *Her head was resting against his chest.* | *She rested her bike against the wall.*
3 **rest assured (that)** formal used to tell someone not to worry: *Rest assured that everything will be ready on time.*
4 **rest on your laurels** to be satisfied with your achievements and not try hard to succeed any more
5 **let sth rest** to stop talking about something: *He wouldn't let the matter rest.*

rest on/upon sth *phr v* formal to depend on something or be based on something: *The whole case rests on his evidence.*

rest with sb *phr v* formal if a decision rests with someone, they must make it: *The final decision rests with the chairman.*

R

restart /ˌriːˈstɑːt $ -ˈstɑːrt/ v [I,T] if something restarts, or if you restart it, it starts again: *new efforts to restart the peace process*

restate /ˌriːˈsteɪt/ v [T] to say something again: *He restated his support for military action.*

restaurant /ˈrestərɒnt $ -rənt, -rɑːnt/ n [C] a place where you can buy and eat a meal: **French/Italian/Indian etc restaurant** *a very good Chinese restaurant* | **in/at a restaurant** *We had dinner in an Italian restaurant.*

> **TOPIC**
>
> The **waiter** or **waitress** brings you the **menu** and you choose what you want to eat. The menu may be divided into **starters** *especially BrE*/**appetizers** (=first courses), **main courses**/**entrees** *AmE*, and **desserts/sweets** *BrE* (=sweet food eaten at the end). When you have finished your meal, you ask for the **bill** *BrE*/**check** *AmE*. Waiter **service** may be **included** in the cost. If it is not, people usually **leave a tip**.

> **THESAURUS**
>
> **cafe/coffee shop/tea shop** – a place where you can get drinks, cakes, and small meals
> **fast food restaurant** – one where you can get meals such as hamburgers, french fries and so on
> **self-service restaurant** – one where you collect the food yourself
> **diner** *AmE* – a restaurant where you can eat cheap and simple food
> **canteen** *BrE*/**cafeteria** *AmE* – a place at work or school where you can collect and eat meals

rested /ˈrestɪd/ adj [not before noun] feeling healthier, stronger etc because you have had time to relax

restful /ˈrestfəl/ adj peaceful and quiet: *restful music* | *a restful weekend*

'rest home n [C] a place where people who are old or ill can be cared for

restive /ˈrestɪv/ adj formal bored or unhappy with your situation and wanting it to change

restless /ˈrestləs/ adj **1** unable to relax and keep still, especially because you are bored: *The children were getting restless.* **2** not satisfied with your situation and wanting new experiences: *After three years at college I started to get restless.* —**restlessly** adv —**restlessness** n [U]

restore /rɪˈstɔː $ -ɔːr/ v [T] **1** to make a situation, feeling etc exist again: **restore peace/order** *The police were called in to restore order.* | *the need to restore public confidence in the legal system* | **restore sth to sth** *an attempt to restore the company to profitability* **2** to repair something so that it looks new: *He spends hours restoring old cars.* | **restore sth to sth** *The clock has been restored to full working order.* → see box at REPAIR **3** formal to give something back to someone: **restore sth to sb** *The goods have now been restored to their rightful owner.* —**restoration** /ˌrestəˈreɪʃən/ n [C,U] *an old building in need of restoration* | *the restoration of the death penalty*

restrain /rɪˈstreɪn/ v [T] **1** to prevent someone from doing something: *We had to restrain him*

physically. | *I had to restrain myself from running after her.* **2** to control something: *efforts to restrain inflation*

restrained /rɪˈstreɪnd/ adj calm and controlled: *She was quite restrained, although she was obviously angry.*

restraint /rɪˈstreɪnt/ n **1** [U] when you behave in a calm way, even though you are angry, excited, or frightened: *The police showed great restraint.* **2** [C,U] something that limits what you can do: *new restraints on public spending*

restrict /rɪˈstrɪkt/ v [T] to limit something: *laws that restrict people's freedom* | **restrict sth to sth** *The sale of alcohol is restricted to people over the age of 18.* | **restrict yourself to sth** *I usually restrict myself to one glass of wine.*

restricted /rɪˈstrɪktɪd/ adj limited or controlled: *He has a very restricted diet.*

restriction /rɪˈstrɪkʃən/ n [C,U] a rule or law that limits what you are allowed to do: **+on** *new restrictions on the sale of guns* | *a 50 mph* **speed restriction**

restrictive /rɪˈstrɪktɪv/ adj something that is restrictive limits people too much

restroom /ˈrestrʊm, -ruːm/ n [C] *AmE* a room with a toilet, in a place such as a restaurant or theatre [= **toilet** *BrE*]

restructure /ˌriːˈstrʌktʃə $ -ər/ v [T] to change the way in which a company, government, or system is organized —**restructuring** n [U]

result[1] /rɪˈzʌlt/ n

1 [C,U] something that happens or exists because of something else: **+of** *The present crisis is a result of the government's incompetence.* | *High unemployment is the direct result of the recession.* | **as a result (of sth)** *Did she die as a result of the doctor's mistake?* | **with the result that** *The crops failed, with the result that thousands of people starved.*

> **THESAURUS**
>
> **consequences** – the things that happen as a result of an action, event etc: *the tragic consequences of the accident*
> **effect** – a change that is the result of something: *the harmful effects of pollution*
> **outcome** – the final result of a meeting, election, war etc: *the final outcome of the talks*
> **upshot** – the final result of a situation: *What was the upshot of it all?*

2 [C] the number of points or votes that each person or team has at the end of a game, competition, or election: **+of** *What was the result of the England-Italy game?* | *the election results* | *a good result for the Democrats*
3 [C] the information that you get from a scientific study or test: *The study has produced some very interesting results.* | **+of** *When will I get the results of my blood test?*
4 [C] *especially BrE* a number or letter that shows how well you have done in an examination [= **score** *AmE*]: *The exam results come out in August.*
5 [C] something good that you achieve: *We need a sales team that will* **get results** (=achieve a lot).
→ **END RESULT**

result² /v [I] to happen or exist because of something: **+from** *His illness resulted from excessive drinking.* | *He has coped well with his disability and the resulting loss of freedom.*

result in sth *phr v* to make something happen [= **cause**]: *a fire that resulted in the death of two children*

resultant /rɪˈzʌltənt/ *adj* [only before noun] *formal* happening or existing because of something else: *damage caused by the heavy rain and resultant flooding*

resumé, résumé /ˈrezjʊmeɪ, ˈreɪ- $ ˌrezʊˈmeɪ/ *n* [C] *AmE* a short list of your education and previous jobs, which you send to employers when you are looking for a new job [= **CV** *BrE*] → see box at **JOB**

resume /rɪˈzjuːm $ rɪˈzuːm/ *v* [I,T] *formal* if something resumes, or if you resume it, it starts again: *The meeting will resume after lunch.* | *She'll resume work on Monday.* —**resumption** /rɪˈzʌmpʃən/ *n* [singular, U] *the resumption of the war*

resurface /ˌriːˈsɜːfɪs $ -ɜːr-/ *v* **1** [I] to appear again: *a problem which is likely to resurface* **2** [T] to put a new surface on a road **3** [I] to come back up to the surface of water

resurgence /rɪˈsɜːdʒəns $ -ɜːr-/ *n* [singular, U] when something starts to happen again: *a resurgence of racial violence*

resurrect /ˌrezəˈrekt/ *v* [T] to bring back something that has not existed or been used for a long time: *an attempt to resurrect his singing career*

Resurrection /ˌrezəˈrekʃən/ *n* **the Resurrection** when Jesus Christ started to live again after his death, according to the Christian religion

resuscitate /rɪˈsʌsɪteɪt/ *v* [T] to make someone start breathing again: *Doctors managed to resuscitate her.* —**resuscitation** /rɪˌsʌsɪˈteɪʃən/ *n* [U]

retail¹ /ˈriːteɪl/ also **retailing** /ˈriːteɪlɪŋ/ *n* [U] the business of selling things in shops [➡ **wholesale**]: *a career in retail* | *retail profits*

retail² *v* [I] *technical* to be sold for a particular price in shops: **+at/for** *wine which retails at £4.50 a bottle*

retailer /ˈriːteɪlə $ -ər/ *n* [C] a person or company that sells things to people in shops

retain /rɪˈteɪn/ *v* [T] *formal* to keep something and not lose it or give it away [➡ **retention**]: *He wants to retain control of the business.*

retainer /rɪˈteɪnə $ -ər/ *n* [C] **1** an amount of money that you pay to someone so that they will continue to work for you when you need them **2** *AmE* something that you wear inside your mouth to keep your teeth straight [= **brace** *BrE*]

retake /ˌriːˈteɪk/ *v* [T] past tense **retook** /-ˈtʊk/ past participle **retaken** /-ˈteɪkən/ **1** to get control of a place again during a war: *Government forces have retaken the city.* **2** *BrE* to take an examination again because you failed it the first time

retaliate /rɪˈtælieɪt/ *v* [I] to do something bad to someone because they have done something bad to you: *The demonstrators threw stones and the police retaliated by firing into the crowd.* —**retaliation** /rɪˌtæliˈeɪʃən/ *n* [U] *an attack in retaliation for last week's bombing*

retard /rɪˈtɑːd $ -ɑːrd/ *v* [T] *formal* to delay something or make it happen more slowly than usual: *Cold weather can retard the plants' growth.*

retarded /rɪˈtɑːdɪd $ -ɑːr-/ *adj old-fashioned* less mentally developed than other people. Many people think that this use is rude and offensive.

retch /retʃ/ *v* [I] to almost VOMIT: *The smell made me retch.*

retention /rɪˈtenʃən/ *n* [U] *formal* when you keep something [➡ **retain**]: *the recruitment and retention of staff*

rethink /riːˈθɪŋk/ *v* [I,T] past tense and past participle **rethought** /-ˈθɔːt $ -ˈθɒːt/ to think about a plan or idea again and decide what changes should be made: *The government needs to rethink its economic policy.* —**rethink** /ˈriːθɪŋk/ *n* [singular] *a complete rethink of our strategy*

reticent /ˈretɪsənt/ *adj* not wanting to talk about something: **+about** *He was very reticent about his childhood.* —**reticence** *n* [U]

retina /ˈretɪnə/ *n* [C] the area at the back of your eye that receives light and sends messages to your brain

retinue /ˈretɪnju $ -nuː/ *n* [C] a group of helpers who travel with a famous person: *the star's retinue of security guards*

retire /rɪˈtaɪə $ -ˈtaɪr/ *v* [I]

R

1 to stop working because you are old: **+at** *He retired at 65.* | **+from** *She retired from teaching last year.* | *She had to **retire early** because of poor health.*

2 *formal* to go away to a quiet place: **+to** *He retired to his room.*
—**retired** *adj*: *a retired police officer*

retirement /rɪˈtaɪəmənt $ -ˈtaɪr-/ *n* [C,U] when you stop working or have stopped working because you are old: *a party to celebrate her retirement* | **+from** *He has announced his retirement from politics.* | *She **took early retirement** because of her health.* | *I hope you enjoy a long and happy retirement.*

retiring /rɪˈtaɪərɪŋ $ -ˈtaɪrɪŋ/ *adj* shy

retook /riːˈtʊk/ *v* the past tense of RETAKE

retort /rɪˈtɔːt $ -ɔːrt/ *v* [T] to answer someone quickly in an angry or amusing way: *'It's easy for you to say that !' he retorted.* —**retort** *n* [C] *a clever retort*

retrace /rɪˈtreɪs, riː-/ *v* [T] **1 retrace your steps/path** to go back exactly the same way as you came: *We retraced our steps to the car.* **2** to repeat a journey made by someone else: *They will be retracing the route taken by Captain Cook.*

retract /rɪˈtrækt/ *v* [T] *formal* to say that something you said before is not true: *He later retracted his confession.*

retractable /rɪˈtræktəbəl/ *adj* a retractable part of something can be pulled back into the main part: *a knife with a retractable blade*

retraining /ˌriːˈtreɪnɪŋ/ n [U] when someone learns new skills so that they can do a different job —**retrain** v [I,T]

retreat[1] /rɪˈtriːt/ v [I] **1** if an army retreats, it moves back to avoid fighting [≠ **advance**]: *The British army was forced to retreat.* | *They retreated to the hills behind the city.* **2** to move away to a safe or quiet place: +**to/into** *She retreated into the kitchen.* | +**from** *He retreated from the busy office.*

retreat[2] n **1** [C,U] when an army moves back to avoid fighting: +**from** *the British retreat from Paris* **2 beat a retreat** *informal* to leave a place quickly: *We saw the teacher coming and beat a hasty retreat.* **3** [C] a quiet place where you can go to rest or spend time alone: *a weekend retreat in the country*

retrial /ˌriːˈtraɪəl, ˈriːtraɪəl $ ˌriːˈtraɪəl/ n [C] when a law case is judged for a second time in a court: *The judge ordered a retrial.*

retribution /ˌretrɪˈbjuːʃən/ n [singular, U] when someone is punished for something bad that they have done: *The victims are demanding retribution.*

retrieve /rɪˈtriːv/ v [T] to find something and bring it back: **retrieve sth from sth** *I retrieved my suitcase from the hall cupboard.* | *ways of retrieving information from the computer* —**retrieval** n [U] *the storage and retrieval of data*

retriever /rɪˈtriːvə $ -ər/ n [C] a type of dog

retro /ˈretrəʊ $ -troʊ/ adj based on a style from the past: *clothes with a retro look*

retrospect /ˈretrəspekt/ n **in retrospect** when you think about something that happened in the past, knowing more about it now than you knew then: *In retrospect, I shouldn't have given him the money.*

retrospective[1] /ˌretrəˈspektɪv◂/ adj a law or decision that is retrospective is made now but will affect earlier things

retrospective[2] n [C] a show of the past work of an artist

retry /ˌriːˈtraɪ/ v [T] **retried, retrying, retries 1** to judge a person or a law case again in court, for example because the original TRIAL was unfair in some way [➡ **retrial**] **2** to try to do an action on a computer again

return[1] /rɪˈtɜːn $ -ɜːrn/ v

1 [I] to come back or go back to a place: *She didn't return until late.* | +**to** *I hope to return to Italy soon.* | +**from** *He had just returned from work.* | *We decided to return home.*
2 [T] to give, put, or send something back where it came from: **return sth to sb/sth** *I returned the books to the library.* | *The letter was returned unopened.* | *He returned the ball beautifully* (=hit it back to his opponent).
3 [I] to start to happen again: *Next morning, the pain had returned.*
4 [T] to do something to someone, after they have done the same thing to you: *He smiled warmly, and she returned his smile.* | *I phoned and left a message, but she hasn't returned my call.*
5 return a verdict when a JURY returns a verdict, they say whether someone is guilty or not

return to sth phr v **1** to change back to a previous state: *After a couple of weeks things*

had returned to normal. **2** to start doing something again: *When will you return to work?*

return[2] n **1** [singular] when someone comes back or goes back to a place: +**to** *I was looking forward to my return to college.* | **on your return (to/from sth)** *He was arrested on his return to England.* **2** [singular] when something is given back, put back, or sent back: +**of** *a reward for the return of the stolen necklace* | *He hit a brilliant return* (=a ball back to his opponent). **3** [singular] when someone starts doing something again: *her return to work* **4** [singular] when something starts to happen again: *the return of high unemployment* | *a return to normal* **5** [C,U] the amount of profit that you get from something: *a big return on our investment* **6** [U] a button that you press on a computer at the end of an instruction or to move to a new line **7** [C] *BrE* a ticket for a journey to a place and back again [= **round trip** *AmE*; ➡ **single**] → see box at TICKET **8 in return (for sth)** as a payment or reward for something: *What does he expect in return for his help?* **9 many happy returns** *BrE* used to wish someone a happy BIRTHDAY → DAY RETURN, TAX RETURN

return[3] adj [only before noun] **1** relating to a journey to a place and back again [= **round trip** *AmE*; ➡ **single**]: *a return ticket* | *The price includes a return flight.* → see box at TICKET **2** a return game, match etc is the second one played between two people or teams

reunification /ˌriːˌjuːnɪf̬ɪˈkeɪʃən/ n [U] when different parts of a country are joined together again and become one nation: *the reunification of Germany*

reunion /riːˈjuːnjən/ n [C] a meeting of people who have not met for a long time: *a college reunion* | *a family reunion* | *He had an emotional reunion with his son.*

reunite /ˌriːjuːˈnaɪt/ v [T] to bring people together again: **reunite sb with sb** *He was at last reunited with his children.*

reuse /ˌriːˈjuːz/ v [T] to use something again: *The bottles may be reused up to 20 times.* —**reusable** adj: *reusable containers* —**reuse** /ˌriːˈjuːs/ n [U]

Rev. the written abbreviation of **Reverend**

rev /rev/ also **rev up** v [I,T] **revved, revving** if an engine revs, or if you rev it, it works faster and makes a loud noise

revamp /riːˈvæmp/ v [T] to change something in order to improve it and make it more modern

reveal /rɪˈviːl/ v [T] **1** to tell people something that was secret: *The information was first revealed in a Sunday newspaper.* | +**that** *He revealed that he had spent five years in prison.* **2** to show something that people could not see before: *The curtains opened to reveal a large stage.*

revealing /rɪˈviːlɪŋ/ adj **1** telling people information that they did not know before, especially about a person's character or feelings: *Some of the answers he gave were very revealing.* **2** revealing clothes show parts of your body that are usually kept covered: *a very revealing nightdress*

revel /ˈrevəl/ v **revelled, revelling** *BrE*; **reveled, reveling** *AmE*

revel in sth *phr v* to enjoy something very much: *He was secretly revelling in his new fame.*

revelation /ˌrevəˈleɪʃən/ *n* **1** [C] a surprising fact that was secret and has now been told to people: *revelations about the Prime Minister's private life* **2 be a revelation** to be surprisingly good: *Her first book was a revelation to me.*

reveller *BrE*; **reveler** *AmE* /ˈrevələ $ -lər/ *n* [C] someone who is having fun singing, drinking etc in a noisy way

revelry /ˈrevəlri/ *n* [U] wild noisy dancing, eating, drinking etc

revenge[1] /rɪˈvendʒ/ *n* [U] when you hurt or punish someone because they have done something bad to you: *She was determined to get revenge.* | *He later took revenge on his employers.* | *an act of revenge* | **in revenge for** sth *The bombing was in revenge for the killing of two students by soldiers.*

revenge[2] *v* [T] *formal* to punish someone who has harmed you or someone else: **revenge yourself on sb** *He vowed to revenge himself on his attackers.*

revenue /ˈrevɪnjuː $ -nuː/ *n* [U] also **revenues** [plural] money that a business or the government receives: *Most of the theatre's revenue comes from ticket sales.* | *an increase in tax revenues*

reverberate /rɪˈvɜːbəreɪt $ -ɜːr-/ *v* [I] if a sound reverberates, you hear it many times in a place as it comes back off different surfaces: *Her voice reverberated around the empty warehouse.*

revere /rɪˈvɪə $ -ˈvɪr/ *v* [T] *formal* to respect and admire someone or something a lot —**revered** *adj*: *Ireland's most revered poet*

reverence /ˈrevərəns/ *n* [U] *formal* a great respect and admiration for someone

Reverend /ˈrevərənd/ used in the title of a Christian priest: *Reverend Larson*

reverent /ˈrevərənt/ also **reverential** /ˌrevəˈrenʃəl/ *adj formal* showing great respect for someone —**reverently** *adv*

reverie /ˈrevəri/ *n* [C,U] *literary* when you are thinking about pleasant things and not noticing what is around you

reversal /rɪˈvɜːsəl $ -ɜːr-/ *n* [C] a change so that something becomes the opposite of what it was before: *a sudden reversal of government policy*

reverse[1] /rɪˈvɜːs $ -ɜːrs/ *v* **1** [T] to change something completely so that it is the opposite of what it was before: *The decision was later reversed by the Appeal Court.* | *Our roles have now been reversed.* **2** [I,T] if you reverse a car, or if it reverses, it moves backwards: *I reversed the car into a parking space.* | *She reversed into a side street.* | *The lorry was reversing.* **3 reverse the charges** *BrE* to make a telephone call which is paid for by the person you are telephoning [= **call collect** *AmE*]

reverse[2] *n* **1 the reverse** the complete opposite: *I wasn't disappointed by the film, quite the reverse.* **2 in reverse** in the opposite way or the opposite order: *They're taking the same route, but in reverse.* **3** also **reverse gear** [U] if a car is in reverse, the controls are arranged so that it is ready to drive backwards: *Put the car in reverse.*

reverse[3] *adj* [only before noun] opposite to what is usual or expected: *The names were read out in reverse order.*

reversible /rɪˈvɜːsɪbəl $ -ɜːr-/ *adj* **1** something that is reversible can be changed back: *This decision is not reversible.* **2** a reversible piece of clothing can be worn with the inside part on the outside: *a reversible jacket*

revert /rɪˈvɜːt $ -ɜːrt/ *v*
revert to sb/sth *phr v* to change back to a previous thing or situation: *The city reverted to its former name of St Petersburg.* —**reversion** /rɪˈvɜːʃən $ -ˈvɜːrʒən/ *n* [singular,U]

review[1] /rɪˈvjuː/ *n*
1 [C,U] when someone examines something carefully in order to see if changes are necessary: **+of** *a review of training methods* | **carry out/conduct/undertake a review** *They're conducting a review of their safety procedures.* | **under review** *We're keeping this policy under review.*
2 [C] a report about a new book, film, or television show: *a film review* | **+of** *The paper published a review of her book.* | **good/bad review** *The band's new CD has had very good reviews.*
3 [C] a report on a series of events or a period of time that mentions the most important parts: **+of** *a review of the year*

review[2] *v* **1** [T] to examine something carefully in order to see if changes are necessary: *The school is reviewing its policy on homework.* **2** [T] to write a report about a new book, film, or television show **3** [I,T] *AmE* to prepare for a test by studying books and notes from your lessons [= **revise** *BrE*]

reviewer /rɪˈvjuːə $ -ər/ *n* [C] someone who writes about new books, films etc

revile /rɪˈvaɪl/ *v* [T] *formal* to express hatred of someone or something

revise /rɪˈvaɪz/ *v* **1** [T] to change something in order to improve it: *We need to revise our plans.* | *the revised edition of the book* **2** [I] *BrE* to prepare for a test by studying books and notes from your lessons [= **review** *AmE*]: **+for** *She's revising for her history exam.* → see box at **SCHOOL**

revision /rɪˈvɪʒən/ *n* **1** [C,U] when you change something in order to improve it **2** [U] *BrE* when you prepare for a test by studying books and notes from your lessons

revitalize also **-ise** *BrE* /riːˈvaɪtəlaɪz/ *v* [T] to put new strength or power into something: *an attempt to revitalize the economy* —**revitalization** /riːˌvaɪtəlaɪˈzeɪʃən $ -tl-ə-/ *n* [U]

revival /rɪˈvaɪvəl/ *n* **1** [C,U] when something becomes popular or successful again: *economic revival* | **+of/in** *a revival of interest in Picasso's work* **2** [C] a new performance of a play that has not been performed for a long time: *a revival of 'Oklahoma!'*

revive /rɪˈvaɪv/ *v* **1** [T] to make something popular or used again: *This centuries-old tradition is being revived.* **2** [I,T] to become healthy and strong again, or to make someone or something healthy and strong again: *The economy is beginning to revive.* | *The doctors were unable to revive him* (=they couldn't make him conscious again).

R

revoke /rɪˈvəʊk $ -ˈvoʊk/ v [T] *formal* to officially end a law or agreement, or change a decision

revolt[1] /rɪˈvəʊlt $ -ˈvoʊlt/ v **1** [I] if people revolt, they take strong and often violent action against their government in order to change it: **+against** *The army revolted against the government.* **2** [T usually passive] if you are revolted by something, you feel sick and shocked because it is very unpleasant: *He was revolted by the smell.*

revolt[2] n [C,U] when people try to change the government, often by using violence, or refuse to obey someone in authority: *the Paris student revolt of May 1968* → see box at **REVOLUTION**

revolting /rɪˈvəʊltɪŋ $ -ˈvoʊl-/ adj very unpleasant: *The food was revolting.* → see box at **HORRIBLE**

revolution /ˌrevəˈluːʃən/ n

1 [C] a complete change in the way people think or do something: **+in** *a revolution in scientific thinking* | **social/cultural/sexual etc revolution** *the sexual revolution of the 1960s*

2 [C,U] when the people of a country change the political system completely, using force: *the French Revolution*

> **THESAURUS**
>
> **revolt/rebellion/uprising** – an attempt at revolution: *Troops loyal to the President crushed the revolt.* | *an armed rebellion* | *a popular uprising* (=involving ordinary people, not the army)
> **coup** – when a group of people, especially soldiers, suddenly take control of their country: *The President was deposed in a violent military coup.*

3 [C,U] a circular movement around something [➔ **revolve**]: *a speed of 100 revolutions per minute*

revolutionary[1] /ˌrevəˈluːʃənəri $ -ʃəneri/ adj **1** completely new and different: *a revolutionary new product* **2** [only before noun] relating to a political revolution: *a revolutionary leader*

revolutionary[2] n [C] plural **revolutionaries** someone who takes part in a political revolution

revolutionize also **-ise** *BrE* /ˌrevəˈluːʃənaɪz/ v [T] to completely change the way people think or do something: *The Internet has revolutionized the way people work.* → see box at **CHANGE**

revolve /rɪˈvɒlv $ rɪˈvɑːlv/ v [I] to move around in a circle: *The wheel began to revolve.* | *a revolving door*
   revolve around sb/sth *phr v* to have something as the most important part: *Jane's life revolves around her children.*

revolver /rɪˈvɒlvə $ rɪˈvɑːlvər/ n [C] a small gun

revue /rɪˈvjuː/ n [C] a show in a theatre that includes singing, dancing, and jokes

revulsion /rɪˈvʌlʃən/ n [U] the feeling you have when you are very shocked by something unpleasant

reward[1] /rɪˈwɔːd $ -ˈwɔːrd/ n [C,U] something, especially money, that is given to someone to thank them for doing something: *She offered a £20 reward to anyone who could find her cat.* |

reward for (doing) sth *Some parents give their children rewards for passing exams.*

reward[2] v [T] if you are rewarded for something you have done, something good happens to you or is given to you: **reward sb for (doing) sth** *He was rewarded for all his hard work.* | **reward sb with sth** *They rewarded him with a free ticket.*

rewarding /rɪˈwɔːdɪŋ $ -ɔːr-/ adj making you feel happy and satisfied: *a rewarding job*

rewind /riːˈwaɪnd/ v [I,T] past tense and past participle **rewound** /-ˈwaʊnd/ to make a tape go back towards the beginning

rework /ˌriːˈwɜːk $ -ˈwɜːrk/ v [T] to make changes to something such as a piece of writing in order to improve it

rewrite /ˌriːˈraɪt/ v [T] past tense **rewrote** /-ˈrəʊt $ -ˈroʊt/ past participle **rewritten** /-ˈrɪtn/ to write something again in a different way —**rewrite** /ˈriːraɪt/ n [C]

rhapsody /ˈræpsədi/ n [C] plural **rhapsodies** a piece of music that is written to express emotion, and does not have a regular form

rhetoric /ˈretərɪk/ n [U] **1** words that sound impressive, but are not sincere: *political rhetoric* **2** the skill of using words effectively to influence people

rhetorical /rɪˈtɒrɪkəl $ -ˈtɔː-, -ˈtɑː-/ adj **1** a rhetorical question is one that you ask as a way of making a statement, without expecting an answer **2** used in rhetoric —**rhetorically** /-kli/ adv

rheumatism /ˈruːmətɪzəm/ n [U] a disease that makes your muscles and joints painful and difficult to move

rhinestone /ˈraɪnstəʊn $ -stoʊn/ n [C] a jewel made from glass or a rock that is intended to look like a DIAMOND

rhinoceros /raɪˈnɒsərəs $ -ˈnɑː-/ also **rhino** /ˈraɪnəʊ $ -noʊ/ n [C] plural **rhinoceros** or **rhinoceroses** a large heavy African or Asian animal with thick skin and a horn on its nose

rhododendron /ˌrəʊdəˈdendrən $ ˌroʊ-/ n [C] a large bush with bright flowers

rhubarb /ˈruːbɑːb $ -ɑːrb/ n [U] a plant with red stems that are cooked and eaten as fruit

rhyme[1] /raɪm/ v [I] if two words or lines of poetry rhyme, they end with the same sound: **+with** *'Hat' rhymes with 'cat'.*

rhyme[2] n **1** [C] a short poem or song using words that rhyme **2** [U] when you use words that rhyme → **NURSERY RHYME**

rhythm /ˈrɪðəm/ n [C,U]

1 a regular repeated pattern of sounds or movements: *Drums are basic to African rhythm.* | **+of** *the rhythm of the music*

2 a regular pattern of changes: *the body's natural rhythms*

—**rhythmic** /ˈrɪðmɪk/ adj —**rhythmically** /-kli/ adv

rib /rɪb/ n [C] one of the curved bones in your chest → see picture on page A3

ribald /ˈrɪbəld/ adj ribald humour is about sex in a rude way

ribbed /rɪbd/ adj something that is ribbed has raised lines on it: *a ribbed sweater*

ribbon /ˈrɪbən/ n [C,U] a narrow piece of attractive cloth that you use, for example, to tie your hair or hold things together

'rib cage *n* [C] the structure of RIBS in your chest

rice /raɪs/ *n* [U] food that consists of small white or brown grains that are cooked in water, or the plant that produces it: *We had chicken with* **boiled rice**. | *a few* **grains of rice**

rich /rɪtʃ/ *adj*

1 a) someone who is rich has a lot of money and valuable things [≠ **poor**]: *He's one of the richest people in the world.* | *She found herself a rich husband.* | *an easy way to* **get rich** (=become rich) **b) the rich** [plural] people who are rich

---

THESAURUS

well-off – fairly rich, so that you can live very comfortably
wealthy – used especially about people whose families have been rich for a long time
prosperous *formal* – rich and successful
well-to-do – rich and having a high position in society
loaded/rolling in it *informal* – extremely rich
→ **POOR**

---

2 containing a lot of something good: +**in** *Citrus fruits are rich in vitamin C.* | **oxygen-rich/ nutrient-rich/protein-rich etc** *nutrient-rich soil* | *Red meat is a* **rich source** *of iron.*
3 rich food contains a lot of butter, cream, or eggs and makes you feel full very quickly: *a rich fruit cake* | *The sauce was very rich.*
4 a rich smell, taste, or colour is strong and pleasant: *the rich smell of fresh coffee* | *a rich dark brown colour*
5 rich soil is good for growing plants in

riches /'rɪtʃɪz/ *n* [plural] *literary* a lot of money or valuable things [= **wealth**]

richly /'rɪtʃli/ *adv* **1** in a beautiful and expensive way: *The room was richly decorated in marble.* **2 richly coloured/flavoured/scented** having a strong pleasant colour, taste, or smell **3 richly deserve sth** to completely deserve something: *They got the punishment they so richly deserved.*

richness /'rɪtʃnɪs/ *n* [U] **1** when something contains a lot of interesting things: *the richness and diversity of the Amazonian rain forests* **2** the richness of a colour, taste, or smell is its quality of being strong and pleasant

rickety /'rɪkɪti/ *adj* in a bad condition and likely to break: *a rickety old chair*

rickshaw /'rɪkʃɔː $ -ʃɔː/ *n* [C] a small vehicle used in South East Asia for carrying one or two passengers. It is pulled by someone walking or riding a bicycle.

ricochet /'rɪkəʃeɪ/ *v* [I] if a bullet or stone ricochets off a surface, it hits it and moves away in a different direction —**ricochet** *n* [C]

rid¹ /rɪd/ *adj*

1 get rid of sth a) to throw away, sell, or destroy something you do not want any more: *I got rid of all those old toys.* **b)** to make something that you do not want go away: *We couldn't get rid of the smell in the house.* | *I can't get rid of this cough.*
2 get rid of sb to make someone leave a place or job: *Most people were glad to get rid of the old president.* | *Andy stayed for hours – we couldn't get rid of him!*

3 be rid of sb/sth to have got rid of someone or something: *To be honest, I'm glad to be rid of him.*

rid² *v* past tense and past participle **rid**, present participle **ridding**
  rid sb/sth of sth *phr v* to remove something bad: *a promise to rid the country of nuclear weapons* | **rid yourself of sth** (=stop having a feeling or problem) *He managed to rid himself of his fears.*

riddance /'rɪdns/ *n* **good riddance (to sb/sth)** *spoken* a rude way of saying you are glad that an annoying person or thing has gone away

-ridden /rɪdn/ *suffix* having a lot of something unpleasant: *disease-ridden slums* | *a debt-ridden company*

riddle /'rɪdl/ *n* [C] **1** a joke or question that you try to guess the answer to for fun **2** something that you cannot understand or explain: *the riddle of Len's death*

riddled /'rɪdld/ *adj* **riddled with sth** containing a lot of something bad: *His essay was riddled with mistakes.*

ride
riding a bicycle
driving a car

ride¹ /raɪd/ *v* [I,T] past tense **rode** /rəʊd $ roʊd/ past participle **ridden** /'rɪdn/

1 to move along on a horse or bicycle: *She learned to ride when she was five.* | *Can you ride a bicycle?* | +**away/across/through etc** *Paul jumped on his bike and rode off.*
2 *AmE* to travel in a bus, car etc: *We got onto the bus and rode into San Francisco.* | *Ann rides the subway to work.*
  ride on sth *phr v* if one thing is riding on another, it depends on it for success: *There's a lot riding on this match.*
  ride sth ⇔ **out** *phr v* to come out of a difficult situation without being badly harmed by it: *He managed to ride out the scandal.*

ride² *n* [C] **1** a trip in a car, bus etc, or on a bicycle or horse: *a trip in a car, bus etc, or on a bicycle or horse: +**on** *Can I have a ride on your bike?* | **a car/bus/train etc ride** *a fifteen minute taxi ride* | **a smooth/comfortable/bumpy etc ride**
2 a large moving machine that people go on for fun: *children's fairground rides* **3 rough/easy ride** *informal* if people give someone, especially someone in authority, a rough or easy ride, they make a situation difficult or easy for them
4 take sb for a ride *spoken* to trick someone, especially in order to get money from them

rider /'raɪdə $ -ər/ *n* [C] someone who rides a horse, bicycle, or MOTORCYCLE

R

ridge /rɪdʒ/ *n* [C] **1** a long narrow area of high land along the top of a mountain: *We could see climbers on the ridge.* **2** a raised line on a surface: *the ridges on the soles of her shoes*

ridicule[1] /'rɪdɨkjuːl/ *n* [U] *formal* when people laugh and say unkind things about someone or something: *She became an **object of ridicule** (=people laughed at her).*

ridicule[2] *v* [T] to laugh and say unkind things about someone or something: *His ideas were ridiculed.*

ridiculous /rɪ'dɪkjɨləs/ *adj* very silly: *That's a ridiculous idea!* —**ridiculously** *adv*

riding /'raɪdɪŋ/ *n* [U] the sport of riding horses

rife /raɪf/ *adj* [not before noun] if something bad is rife, it is very common: *Burglary is rife in large cities.*

riff-raff /'rɪf ræf/ *n* [U] an insulting word for people who are noisy or behave badly, or are of low social class

rifle[1] /'raɪfəl/ *n* [C] a long gun that you hold against your shoulder to shoot

rifle[2] also **rifle through** *v* [T] to search a place quickly, especially in order to steal something: *Somebody has been rifling through my desk.*

rift /rɪft/ *n* [C] **1** a serious disagreement: **+between** *a rift between the two men* **2** a crack in the ground, a mountain etc

rig[1] /rɪg/ *v* [T] **rigged, rigging** to make an election or competition have the result you want by doing something dishonest: *The election was rigged.*

rig sth ⇔ up *phr v informal* to make something quickly from materials you can find easily: *We rigged up a shelter using a piece of plastic sheeting.*

rig[2] *n* [C] **1** a large structure used for getting oil or gas from under the bottom of the sea **2** *AmE informal* a large truck

rigging /'rɪgɪŋ/ *n* [U] the ropes and chains that support a ship's sails

right[1] /raɪt/ *adj*

1 correct or true [≠ **wrong**]: *Yes, that's the **right answer**.* | *Is that the **right time**?* | *I got most of the questions **right**.* | **+about** *You were right about Geoff getting married. Lisa told me the news yesterday.* | *'You live in London, don't you?' 'Yes, **that's right**.'*

2 suitable [≠ **wrong**]: *She is the **right person** for the job.*
3 your right side is the side with the hand that most people write with [≠ **left**]: *He had a knife in his **right** hand.* | *a scar on the **right side** of her face* | *Take the next **right** turn.*
4 something that is not right is not in the state it should be in: *The engine's not quite right.* | *If*

*anything goes wrong, the technicians are here to **put it right** (=correct it).*
5 fair or morally good [≠ **wrong**]: **right to do sth** *I think you were absolutely right to report them to the police.*
6 [only before noun] *BrE spoken* used to emphasize how bad someone or something is [= **total, complete**]: *He made me feel a **right idiot**.*
7 (as) right as rain *spoken* completely healthy, especially after an illness
→ **ALL RIGHT**

right[2] *adv*

1 exactly in a particular position: **+in/in front of/by etc** *She was standing **right in** the middle of the room.* | **+here/there** *I left my bags **right here**.*
2 immediately: **+after** *The show is on **right after** the news.* | **right now/away** (=now or immediately) *I'll phone him **right away**.* | *I'm sorry, I can't talk to you **right now**.* | **I'll be right with you/right there/right back** (=used to ask someone to wait for a short time)
3 towards the side nearest your right hand [≠ **left**]: *Turn **right** at the traffic lights.*
4 *informal* in a good or satisfactory way [= **well**]: *Everything's **going right** for him.*
5 correctly [≠ **wrong**]: *They didn't spell my name **right**.*
6 right along/through/round etc all the way along, through etc: *Go **right** to the end of the road.* | *The bullet went **right** through the car door.*

right[3] *spoken* **1** used to show that you have understood or agree with what someone has just said: *'You need to be there by ten o'clock.' 'Right.'* **2** used to ask if what you have said was correct: *You wanted to go to the show, right?* **3** *BrE* used when you want to make someone listen or get ready to do something: *Right, everyone! It's time to go!*

right[4] *n*

1 [C] something that you are legally or morally allowed to do: **+of** *the rights and duties of citizens* | *the struggle for **women's rights*** | *equal rights for gay men* | **+to** *All children have the **right to** free education.* | **right to do sth** *You have the right to consult a lawyer.* | **within your rights** (=legally or morally allowed) *You're within your rights to ask for your money back.*
2 have a right to be angry/upset etc to have a good reason to be angry, upset etc: *You had **every right** to be angry with them.*
3 have no right to do sth used to say that someone's behaviour is completely unreasonable or unfair: *You had **no right** to take money from my purse!*
4 the right/sb's right the side with the hand that most people write with [≠ **left**]: **on/to the right (of sth)** *Our car is just to the **right** of that white van.* | **on/to sb's right** *The school is on your right as you come into the village.*
5 the right/the Right political groups that believe that the government should not own any business or try to control business by making too many rules: **extreme/far right** *politicians on the extreme right*
6 [U] behaviour that is morally good and correct: *It's important to teach kids the difference between **right and wrong**.*

7 rights [plural] if someone has the rights to a book, film etc, they are allowed to sell it or show it: **+to** *They paid £2 million for the **film rights** to the book.*

8 by rights *spoken* used to describe what should happen if things are done fairly or correctly: *By rights, the house should be mine now.*

9 be in the right to have the best reasons, arguments etc in a disagreement: *Both sides are convinced that they are in the right.*

10 in your own right without depending on anyone else: *She's a very wealthy woman in her own right.*
→ CIVIL RIGHTS, HUMAN RIGHTS

right⁵ *v* [T] **1 right a wrong** to do something to stop an unfair situation from continuing **2** to put something, especially a boat, back into its correct upright position: *I managed to right the canoe.*

'right ,angle *n* [C] an angle of 90°, like the angles at the corners of a square —**right-angled** *adj*

righteous /'raɪtʃəs/ *adj* **1 righteous indignation/anger etc** strong feelings of anger when you think something is not morally right or fair **2** morally good —**righteousness** *n* [U]

rightful /'raɪtfəl/ *adj* [only before noun] according to what is legally and morally correct: *He is the rightful owner of the house.* —**rightfully** *adv*

'right-hand *adj* [only before noun] on the right side of something: *the **right-hand side** of his body*

,right-'handed *adj* someone who is right-handed uses their right hand rather than their left hand to do most things

,right-hand 'man *n* [C] the person who supports and helps you the most, especially in your job

rightly /'raɪtli/ *adv* correctly or for a good reason: *Her father **quite rightly** said that she was too young to drive.*

,right of 'way *n* plural **rights of way** **1** [U] the right to drive into or across a road before other vehicles **2** [C] *BrE* **a)** the right to walk across someone else's land **b)** a path that people have the right to use

,right-'wing *adj* a right-wing person or group does not like changes in society, and supports CAPITALISM rather than SOCIALISM: *right-wing parties* —**right-winger** *n* [C] —**right wing** *n* [singular]

rigid /'rɪdʒɪd/ *adj* **1** rules or ideas that are rigid are strict and difficult to change: *a society with rigid traditions* **2** very unwilling to change your ideas **3** stiff and not moving or bending: *rigid plastic* —**rigidly** *adv*: *The laws were rigidly enforced.* —**rigidity** /rɪ'dʒɪdɪti/ *n* [U]

rigmarole /'rɪgmərəʊl $ -roʊl/ also **rigamarole** /'rɪgəmərəʊl $ -roʊl/ *AmE n* [singular,U] a long confusing process or description: *I don't want to **go through the rigmarole** of taking him to court.*

rigorous /'rɪgərəs/ *adj* careful and thorough: *rigorous safety checks* —**rigorously** *adv*

rigour *BrE*; **rigor** *AmE* /'rɪgə $ -ər/ *n* **1 the rigours of sth** the problems and difficulties of a situation: *the rigors of a Canadian winter* **2** [U]

great care and thoroughness in making sure that something is correct: *Their research is lacking in rigour.*

rile /raɪl/ *v* [T] *informal* to make someone very angry: *Don't let him rile you.*

rim /rɪm/ *n* [C] the outside edge of something round, such as a glass or wheel: **steel-rimmed/ red-rimmed etc** *gold-rimmed glasses*

rind /raɪnd/ *n* [C,U] the thick skin on the outside of some foods, such as BACON or cheese

ring¹ /rɪŋ/ *n* [C]

1 a circle of silver, gold etc that you wear on your finger: *a wedding ring* | *a diamond ring*
→ see picture at JEWELLERY

2 an object in the shape of a circle: *a key ring* | *a rubber ring for children to go swimming with*

3 a group of people or things arranged in a circle: *A ring of armed troops surrounded the building.*

4 give sb a ring *BrE informal* to telephone someone: *I'll give you a ring at the weekend.*

5 the sound made by a bell: *a ring at the doorbell*
→ see picture on page A7

6 a group of people who illegally control a business or criminal activity: *a drugs ring*

7 have the/a ring of sth if what someone says has a ring of truth, confidence etc, it seems to have this quality

8 *BrE* one of the circular areas on top of a COOKER that is heated by gas or electricity [= burner *AmE*; ➡ hob]

9 a square or circular area surrounded by seats where BOXING or a CIRCUS takes place: *a boxing ring*

10 ring finger the finger next to the smallest finger on your hand, that you usually wear your wedding ring on

ring² *v* past tense **rang** /ræŋ/ past participle **rung** /rʌŋ/

1 [I] if a bell or telephone rings, it makes a sound: *I heard the church bells ringing.* | *The phone hasn't stopped ringing all day.* → see box at PHONE ➡ and TELEPHONE

2 [I,T] if you ring a bell, you make it make a sound: *I rang the doorbell, but no one came.* | **+for** *The sign said 'Ring for service'.*

3 also **ring up** [I,T] *BrE* to telephone someone [= phone, call]: *I rang you yesterday, but you weren't in.* | *I rang up and made an appointment.* | **+for** *Sally rang for a taxi.* → see box at PHONE

4 [I] if your ears ring, they are filled with a continuous sound after hearing something loud: *The explosion made our ears ring.*

5 ring a bell *informal* if something rings a bell, it seems familiar but you cannot remember exact details about it: *Her name rings a bell, but I can't remember her face.*

6 not ring true if something does not ring true, you do not believe it: *His excuse didn't ring true.*

ring sb back *phr v BrE* to telephone someone later [= call back]: *I'm busy at the moment. Can I ring you back?*

ring off *phr v BrE* to end a telephone call: *He rang off without giving his name.*

ring out *phr v written* to make a loud and clear sound: *The sound of a shot rang out.*

ring³ v [T] past tense and past participle **ringed**
1 to surround something: *The police ringed the building.* **2** *BrE* to draw a circular mark around something [= circle]: *Ring the mistakes in red.*

ringleader /'rɪŋ,liːdə $ -ər/ n [C] someone who leads a group that is doing something wrong: *Police caught three of the gang, but the ring-leader escaped.*

ringlet /'rɪŋlɪt/ n [C] a long curl of hair

'**ring road** n [C] *BrE* a road that goes around a large town to keep traffic away from the centre
→ see box at ROAD

rink /rɪŋk/ n [C] an area where you can ICE SKATE or ROLLER SKATE

rinse /rɪns/ v [T] to wash something in clean water in order to remove soap or dirt from it: *Rinse the lettuce in cold water.* | **rinse sth out** *He rinsed out a glass and poured himself a whisky.* —**rinse** n [C] *I'll just give this shirt a quick rinse.*

riot¹ /'raɪət/ n [C] **1** when a crowd of people behave violently in a public place: *His death triggered race riots.* **2 run riot** to become impossible to control: *parents who let their children run riot*

riot² v [I] if a crowd of people riot, they behave violently in a public place → see box at PROTEST —**rioter** n [C] —**rioting** n [U] *Rioting broke out in the city late last night.*

riotous /'raɪətəs/ adj **1** noisy, excited, and enjoyable in an uncontrolled way: *riotous celebrations* **2** noisy and violent in an uncontrolled way: *riotous crowds*

rip¹ /rɪp/ v ripped, ripping **1** [I,T] to tear something, or become torn: *Her clothes had all been ripped.* | *Don't pull the curtain too hard or it'll rip.* | *Sue ripped the letter open.* **2** [T] to remove something quickly and violently, using your hands: **rip sth out/off/away/down** *He ripped off his clothes and jumped into the pool.*
  rip sb/sth ⇔ off phr v informal **1** to charge someone too much money for something: *Banks have been ripping people off for years.* **2** to steal something: *Somebody had come in and ripped off the TV and stereo.*
  rip sth ⇔ up phr v to tear something into a lot of pieces: *She ripped his photo up into tiny bits.*

rip² n [C] a hole in a piece of clothing or material where it has torn

ripe /raɪp/ adj
1 fruit that is ripe is ready to eat: *Those peaches don't look ripe yet.* | *ripe tomatoes*
2 be ripe for sth to be ready for a change to happen, especially when it should have happened sooner: *The former dock area is ripe for development.* | *The time is ripe* (=it is the right time) *for trade talks.*
—**ripen** v [I,T] *The apples were ripened to perfection.*

ripoff /'rɪpɒf $ -ɒːf/ n [C] informal something that is much too expensive: *The drinks in the hotel bar are a ripoff!* → see box at EXPENSIVE

ripples

ripple /'rɪpəl/ n [C] **1** a small wave: *A gentle breeze made ripples on the lake.* **2** a feeling or sound that spreads from one person to another: **+of** *A ripple of laughter ran through the audience.* —**ripple** v [I,T] *a flag rippling in the wind*

rise¹ /raɪz/ v [I] past tense **rose** /rəʊz $ roʊz/ past participle **risen** /'rɪzən/

1 if an amount rises, it increases [= go up; ≠ fall]: *World oil prices are rising.* | *The population has risen steadily since the 1950s.* | **+by** *Salaries rose by 10% last year.* | **+to/from** *The research budget rose to £22.5 million.* | **rise from sth to sth** *The cost has risen from $100 to $200.*
2 also **rise up** to move upwards: *Flood waters are still rising in parts of Missouri.* | **+from** *Smoke rose from the chimney.*

USAGE

Rise is not followed by an object: *The balloon rose high into the air.*
Raise is always followed by an object: *Raise your hand if you know the answer.*

3 to stand up: *Everyone rose as the judge entered the courtroom.* | **+from** *Suddenly, Holmes rose from his chair and began shouting.* | *Thornton rose to his feet and turned to speak to them.*
4 to become important, powerful, successful, or rich [≠ fall]: **+to** *Mussolini rose to power in Italy in 1922.*
5 if a feeling or emotion rises, you begin to notice and feel it more and more strongly: *You could feel the excitement rising as we waited.*
6 if the sun or moon rises, it appears in the sky [≠ set]: *The sun rises at around 6 am.*
7 also **rise up** written if a mountain, building, tree etc rises, it is taller than anything else around it: *They could see Mount Shasta rising in the distance.*
8 rise to the occasion/challenge to deal successfully with a difficult situation, especially by working harder or performing better than usual
9 written also **rise up** if a large group of people rise, they try to defeat the government, army etc that is controlling them: **+against** *In 1917 the Russian people rose against the Czar.*
  rise above sth phr v to not let a bad situation affect you: *The President needs to rise above criticism of his administration.*

rise² n **1** [C] an increase [≠ fall]: *a tax rise* | **+in** *a sudden rise in temperature* | **+of** *a rent rise of more than 15%* **2** [C] *BrE* an increase in wages [= raise *AmE*]: *a pay rise* | *We got a 4% rise last year.* **3** [singular] when someone or something becomes more important, more successful, or

more powerful [≠ fall]: **+to** *Stalin's rise to power*
4 [C] a slope that goes up: *a slight rise in the road*
5 give rise to sth *formal* to be the reason why something happens, especially something bad

riser /'raɪzə $ -ər/ *n* **early/late riser** someone who usually gets up early or late in the morning

risk¹ /rɪsk/ *n*

1 [C,U] a possibility that something bad or dangerous may happen [➡ **danger, chance**]: *risks involved in starting a small business* | **+of** *There is a slight risk of infection.* | *the risk of serious injury* | *There is a real risk that the wheat crop may be lost.* | **+to** *Scientists believe there is no risk to public health.* | **increase/reduce the risk of sth** *Healthy eating can reduce the risk of heart disease.* | *Nothing is **worth the risk** of losing your life.*
2 take a risk to do something even though you know it is dangerous or you may not succeed: *Are you **willing** to take the risk?* | **take the risk of doing sth** *I couldn't take the risk of leaving him alone.*
3 run the risk to be in a situation where there is a possibility that something bad could happen to you: **run the risk of doing sth** *Travellers without passports run the risk of being arrested.*
4 at risk in a situation where you may suffer or be harmed: **+from** *people at risk from AIDS* | **+of** *Many high school boys are at risk of joining gangs.* | *The smallest mistake could **put** patients **at risk**.*
5 at your own risk if you do something at your own risk, you have been warned about the possible dangers and you understand that no one else is responsible if something bad happens: *Cars are left at your own risk.*
6 [C] something or someone that is likely to be dangerous: **+to** *Heart disease is the greatest **health risk** (=something likely to harm people's health) to women over 50.* | *The tire dump is a major **fire risk** (=something that could cause a fire).*

risk² *v* [T]

1 if you risk your life, money etc, you do something which may make you lose it: *He **risked** his life helping others to escape.* | **risk sth to do sth** *He had a dream and was willing to risk everything to follow it.* | **risk sth on sth** *You'd be crazy to risk your money on an investment like that!*
2 to do something that may be dangerous or may cause something bad to happen: **risk doing sth** *I wasn't prepared to risk losing my business.* | *You could slip out of school between classes, but I wouldn't **risk it**.*
3 risk death/punishment/defeat etc to do something which could result in your being killed, punished etc: *She was willing to risk arrest in order to protect her children.*

risky /'rɪski/ *adj* involving a risk that something bad or dangerous will happen: *a risky financial investment*

risqué /'rɪskeɪ $ rɪ'skeɪ/ *adj* a joke, remark etc that is risqué is slightly shocking because it is about sex

rite /raɪt/ *n* [C] a ceremony that is always performed in the same way, especially for religious purposes: *funeral rites*

ritual /'rɪtʃuəl/ *n* [C,U] a ceremony or set of actions that is always done in the same way: *church rituals* —**ritual** *adj*: *a ritual dance* —**ritually** *adv*

rival¹ /'raɪvəl/ *n* [C] a person or group that you compete with: *The two teams had always been rivals.* —**rival** *adj*: *rival gangs*

rival² *v* [T] rivalled, rivalling *BrE*; rivaled, rivaling *AmE* if one thing rivals another, it is as good as the other thing: *The college's facilities rival those of Yale or Harvard.*

rivalry /'raɪvəlri/ *n* [C,U] plural rivalries when people or groups try to show that they are better than each other: *There is a **friendly rivalry** between the two teams.*

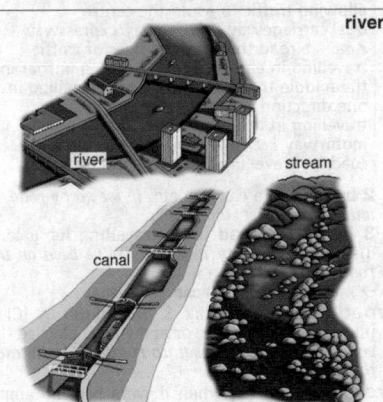

river

river *stream* *canal*

river /'rɪvə $ -ər/ *n* [C] a long area of water that flows into a sea [➡ **stream**]: *the River Thames* | *I went for a walk **along** the river.* | *We saw a group of boats sailing **on** the river.*

riverside /'rɪvəsaɪd $ -ər-/ *n* [singular] the land along the sides of a river: *riverside apartments*

rivet¹ /'rɪvɪt/ *v* **be riveted** if you are riveted by something, you cannot stop looking at it or listening to it because it is very interesting: *People sat riveted to their TVs during the trial.* —**riveting** *adj*: *a riveting movie*

rivet² *n* [C] a metal pin used to fasten pieces of metal together

roach /rəʊtʃ $ roʊtʃ/ *n* [C] *AmE* a COCKROACH

road /rəʊd $ roʊd/ *n* [C,U]

1 a hard surface that cars and other vehicles travel on: *Her address is 25 Park Road.* | *Is this **the road** to Stratford?* | **on/in the road** *There were loads of cars parked on the road.* | *Take the **main road** and turn left at the first light.* | **up/down the road** *The boys go to the school down the road.* | *An old man cycled **along the road**.* | *We stopped and had something to eat **by the side of the road**.* | *There's a tire **in the middle of the road**.* | *I saw some bushes on the **other side of the road**.* | *Look both ways before you **cross the road** (=walk across the road).*

R

THESAURUS

street – a road in a town, with houses or shops on each side
high street *BrE*/**main street** *AmE* – a road in the middle of a town where most of the shops, offices etc are
avenue – a road in a town, often with trees on each side
lane – a narrow road in the country
track – a narrow road in the country, usually without a hard surface
main road – a large and important road
the main drag *especially AmE informal* – the main road through a town
ring road *BrE* – a road that goes around a town
bypass – a road that goes past a town, allowing traffic to avoid the centre
dual carriageway *BrE*/**freeway**/**expressway** *AmE* – a road that has two lines of traffic travelling in each direction. It has a barrier in the middle that keeps the lanes travelling in one direction separate from the lanes travelling in the other direction.
motorway *BrE*/**highway** *AmE* – a very wide road for travelling fast over long distances

2 by road in a car, bus etc: *If we go by road, it will take at least eight hours.*
3 be on the road to be travelling for a long distance, especially in a car: *We've been on the road since 7:00 a.m.*
→ A-ROAD, B-ROAD, SLIP ROAD, TRUNK ROAD

roadblock /'rəʊdblɒk $ 'roʊdblɑːk/ *n* [C] a place where the police or army have blocked the road: *The police have* **set up roadblocks** *to catch the two men.*

'road rage *n* [U] when drivers become angry and start shouting at or attacking other drivers

roadside /'rəʊdsaɪd $ 'roʊd-/ *n* [singular] the land at the edge of a road: *a roadside café*

roadway /'rəʊdweɪ $ 'roʊd-/ *n* [C] the part of the road used by vehicles

roadworks /'rəʊdwɜːks $ 'roʊdwɜːrks/ *n* [plural] *BrE* work that is being done to repair a road

roadworthy /'rəʊd,wɜːði $ 'roʊd,wɜːr-/ *adj* a vehicle that is roadworthy is in good condition and safe enough to drive

roam /rəʊm $ roʊm/ *v* [I,T] to walk or travel all over a place: *Teenage gangs* **roamed the streets.** | **+around/over/through etc** *bears roaming through the forest*

roar /rɔː $ rɔːr/ *v* **1** [I] to make a deep very loud noise: *We heard a lion roar.* | *The wind roared as she opened the front door.* **2** [I] if a vehicle roars somewhere, it moves very quickly and noisily: **+past/off etc** *A truck roared past.* **3** [I,T] to shout with a deep loud voice: *'Get out of here now!' he roared.* —**roar** *n* [C] *a roar of laughter*

roaring /'rɔːrɪŋ/ *adj* **1** [only before noun] making a deep, very loud, continuous noise: *roaring floodwaters* **2 roaring fire** a fire that burns with a lot of flames and heat **3** extremely successful: *The souvenir shops* **do a roaring trade.** | *The show was* **a roaring success.**

roast¹ /rəʊst $ roʊst/ *v* [I,T] to cook meat or vegetables in an OVEN or over a fire → see box at COOK → see picture at POTATO

roast² *n* [C] **1** a large piece of roasted meat **2** *AmE* an outdoor party where you cook food on an open fire: *a pig roast* —**roast** *adj* [only before noun] *roast beef*

rob /rɒb $ rɑːb/ *v* [T] **robbed**, **robbing**
1 to steal money or other things from a bank, shop, or person [→ **burgle**, **steal**]: *The two men were jailed for robbing a bank.* | **rob sb of sth** *Thieves robbed the woman of $70,000 in jewelry.* → see box at STEAL
2 rob sb/sth of sth to take away an important quality, ability etc from someone or something: *The disease has robbed him of his ability to speak.*

robber /'rɒbə $ 'rɑːbər/ *n* [C] someone who steals money or other things from a bank, shop etc: *a bank robber* → see box at STEAL

robbery /'rɒbəri $ 'rɑː-/ *n* [C,U] plural **robberies** the crime of stealing money or other things from a bank, shop etc: *They're in prison for* **armed robbery** (=robbery with a gun). → see box at CRIME

robe /rəʊb $ roʊb/ *n* [C] **1** a long loose piece of clothing that people wear especially for formal ceremonies: *a judge's robe* **2** *AmE* a DRESSING GOWN

robin /'rɒbɪn $ 'rɑː-/ *n* [C] a small brown bird with a red chest

robot /'rəʊbɒt $ 'roʊbɑːt, -bət/ *n* [C] a machine that can move and do jobs like a person: *cars built by robots* —**robotic** /rəʊ'bɒtɪk $ roʊ'bɑː-/ *adj*

robust /rə'bʌst, 'rəʊbʌst $ rə'bʌst, 'roʊ-/ *adj* strong and not likely to become ill or be damaged: *a surprisingly robust 70-year-old* | *a robust structure*

rock¹ /rɒk $ rɑːk/ *n*
1 [U] the hard substance in the Earth's surface that cliffs and mountains are made of [→ **stone**]: *Pluto is made of ice and rock.* | *a tunnel cut through* **solid rock**
2 [C] a large piece of stone: *Jack stood on a rock for a better view.* | *The storm drove their ship onto* **the rocks** (=a line of rocks under or next to the sea).
3 also **'rock music** [U] a type of popular modern music with a strong loud beat: *a rock band* | *a rock concert* | *Their music is a mixture of rock and disco.* → see box at MUSIC
4 be on the rocks a relationship or business that is on the rocks is having a lot of problems and will probably fail soon: *I'm afraid Tim's* **marriage is on the rocks.**

rock² *v* **1** [I,T] if something rocks, or if you rock it, it moves gently from side to side [→ **sway**]: *Jane sat rocking the baby.* | *The boat rocked slowly.* **2** [T] *written* to shock and frighten a large number of people: *a city rocked by violence* **3 rock the boat** *informal* to upset people in a group by criticizing or trying to change something that everyone else is satisfied with

rock and 'roll *n* [U] ROCK 'N' ROLL

rock 'bottom *n* **hit/reach rock bottom** *informal* to become as bad as it is possible to be: *By June, their marriage had hit rock bottom.*

rock-bottom *adj informal* rock-bottom prices are as low as they can be

rocker /'rɒkə $ 'rɑːkər/ *n* [C] *AmE* a ROCKING CHAIR

rocket[1] /'rɒkɪt $ 'rɑː-/ *n* [C] **1** a long thin vehicle that carries people or scientific equipment into space: *a Soviet space rocket* → see box at SPACE **2** a long thin weapon that carries a bomb and is fired from a plane, ship etc: *anti-tank rockets* **3** a FIREWORK that goes high into the air and explodes

rocket[2] *v* [I] *informal* to increase very quickly: *The price of coffee has rocketed.*

'rocking chair *n* [C] a chair with curved pieces of wood on the bottom that allow it to move backwards and forwards when you sit on it → see picture at SEAT[1]

rock 'n' roll /ˌrɒk ən 'rəʊl $ ˌrɑːk ən 'roʊl/ [U] a type of music with a strong loud beat for dancing → see box at MUSIC

rocky /'rɒki $ 'rɑːki/ *adj* covered with rocks or made of rock: *the rocky coast of Maine*

rod /rɒd $ rɑːd/ *n* [C] a long thin pole or stick: *a fishing rod*

rode /rəʊd $ roʊd/ *v* the past tense of RIDE

rodent /'rəʊdənt $ 'roʊ-/ *n* [C] an animal such as a rat or a rabbit that has long sharp front teeth

rodeo /'rəʊdiəʊ, rəʊ'deɪ-əʊ $ 'roʊdioʊ, roʊ'deɪoʊ/ *n* [C] plural **rodeos** a show in which COWBOYS ride wild horses and catch cattle with ropes

roe /rəʊ $ roʊ/ *n* [C,U] fish eggs

rogue[1] /rəʊg $ roʊg/ *n* [C] *old-fashioned* a man or boy who behaves badly or is not honest

rogue[2] *adj* [only before noun] not behaving in the usual or accepted way and often causing trouble: *rogue regimes that may have nuclear weapons*

role /rəʊl $ roʊl/ *n* [C]

1 the way in which someone or something is involved in an activity or situation: +**of** *What is the role of the sales manager?* | +**in** *the diet's role in the prevention of disease* | *The company **plays a** major **role** in the world's economy.*

2 a character in a play or film: +**of** *Brendan will **play the role** of Romeo.*

'role ˌmodel *n* [C] someone you admire and try to copy: *I try to be a **positive role model** for my kids.*

'role-play *n* [C,U] a training activity in which you pretend to be in a particular situation, especially to help you learn a language —**role-playing** *n* [U]

roll[1] /rəʊl $ roʊl/ *v*

1 [I,T] to move somewhere smoothly by turning over many times like a ball, or to make something move this way: +**down/into/through etc** *The ball rolled across the lawn.* | **roll sth along/in/onto etc sth** *Roll the chicken breasts in flour and spices.* → see box at PUSH

2 also **roll over** [I,T] to turn your body over when you are lying down, or to turn someone else's body over: +**down/onto/off etc** *Beth's dog had been rolling in the mud.* | **roll sb onto/off sth** *We rolled him onto his back to see if he was still breathing.*

3 **a)** [I] if a vehicle rolls, it moves on its own, with no one driving it: +**into/forwards/past etc** *The car was starting to roll down the hill.* **b)** [T] to make something that has wheels move: **roll sth to/around etc sth** *The waitress rolled the dessert trolley over to our table.*

4 [I] if a drop of liquid rolls down, off etc something, it moves over a surface smoothly without stopping: +**down/off/onto etc** *Tears rolled down his cheeks.*

5 [T] to make something into the shape of a tube or ball: *Bob rolled another cigarette.*

6 also **roll out** [T] to make something flat by moving a round and heavy object over it [➡ **rolling pin**]: *Roll the pastry out.* → see picture on page A4

7 **be rolling in it/money** *informal* to be very rich → see box at RICH

8 **(all) rolled into one** if something or someone is several different things all rolled into one, they include qualities of all those things: *While making the film, he was the producer, director, and writer all rolled into one.*

roll in *phr v informal* to begin to arrive in large amounts: *The money soon came rolling in.*

roll up *phr v* **1 roll sth ⇔ up** to bend something so that it is in the shape of a ball or a tube: *Painters arrived and rolled up the carpet.* | *a rolled-up newspaper* **2 roll your sleeves up** to start doing a difficult or unpleasant job **3** *informal* to arrive late: *David rolled up after everyone else had left.*

roll[2] *n* [C] **1** a piece of paper, plastic etc that has been curled into the shape of a tube: +**of** *a roll of toilet paper* | *rolls of film* **2** a small round LOAF of bread for one person [➡ **bun**] **3** an official list of names [= **register**]: *the union membership roll* **4** **be on a roll** *informal* to be having a lot of success with what you are doing **5** **roll of fat** a layer of skin or fat around your waist → ROCK 'N' ROLL, SAUSAGE ROLL, TOILET ROLL

'roll call *n* [C,U] when someone reads out all the names on a list to check who is there

roller /'rəʊlə $ 'roʊlər/ *n* [C] **1** a tube-shaped piece of wood, metal etc that can be rolled over and over, used for painting, crushing etc: *a paint roller* **2** a small plastic or metal tube used for making hair curl

Rollerblade /'rəʊləbleɪd $ 'roʊlər-/ *n* [C] *trademark* a boot with a single row of wheels fixed under it that you wear for SKATING [➡ **roller skate**] —**rollerblade** *v* [I] —**rollerblading** *n* [U]

'roller ˌcoaster *n* [C] a small railway which carries people up and down a steep track very fast for fun

'roller skate *n* [C] a boot with four wheels fixed under it that you wear for SKATING —**roller skate** *v* [I] —**roller skating** *n* [U]

rolling /'rəʊlɪŋ $ 'roʊ-/ *adj* [only before noun] rolling hills have long gentle slopes

'rolling pin *n* [C] a long tube-shaped piece of wood used for making PASTRY flat and thin before you cook it → see picture at KITCHEN

ROM /rɒm $ rɑːm/ *n* [U] *technical* read-only memory the part of a computer where permanent instructions and information are stored [➡ RAM]

Roman[1] /'rəʊmən $ 'roʊ-/ *adj* relating to ancient Rome: *the Roman Empire*

Roman[2] *n* [C] the Romans were the people of ancient Rome

R

,Roman 'Catholic *adj* belonging or relating to the part of the Christian religion whose leader is the Pope —**Roman Catholic** *n* [C] —,Roman Ca'tholicism *n* [U]

romance /rəʊˈmæns, ˈrəʊmæns $ roʊˈmæns, ˈroʊ-/ *n* **1** [C,U] an exciting relationship between two people who love each other: *a summer romance* **2** [C] a story or film about two people who love each other **3** [U] the feeling of excitement and adventure that is related to a particular place, activity etc: **+of** *the romance of travelling to distant places*

,Roman 'numeral *n* [C] a number in a system that was used in ancient Rome, for example I, II, III, IV etc instead of 1, 2, 3, 4 etc

romantic¹ /rəʊˈmæntɪk, rə- $ roʊ-, rə-/ *adj*
1 related to love and with treating the person you love in a special way: *I wish my boyfriend was more romantic.* | *She enjoys romantic movies.*
2 based too much on the way you would like things to be, rather than on the way they really are [≠ realistic]: **romantic notion/view/idea etc** *her romantic dreams of becoming a famous writer*
—**romantically** /-kli/ *adv*

romantic² *n* [C] someone who is not practical and thinks that things are better than they really are [≠ realist]: *an incurable romantic*

romanticize also **-ise** *BrE* /rəʊˈmæntɪsaɪz, rə- $ roʊ-, rə-/ *v* [I,T] to talk or think about things in a way that makes them seem more attractive than they really are: *a romanticized idea of country life*

romp /rɒmp $ rɑːmp/ *v* [I] **1** to play in a noisy way, especially by running, jumping etc: **+around/about** *They could hear the children romping around upstairs.* **2** to win a race, competition, election etc very easily: *Miano romped to an easy victory.* —**romp** *n* [C] *the Yankees 12–1 romp over the Red Sox*

roof /ruːf $ ruːf, rʊf/ *n* [C]
1 the part of a building or vehicle that covers the top of it: *He installed a satellite dish on the roof.* | **+of** *She had to jump from the roof of the building to escape.* | **flat/sloping/pitched roof**
2 the top of a PASSAGE under the ground: *The roof of the tunnel suddenly collapsed.*
3 the roof of your mouth the top part of the inside of your mouth
4 a roof over your head somewhere to live: *I may not have a job, but at least I've got a roof over my head.*
5 hit the roof/go through the roof *spoken informal* to become very angry: *My wife is going to hit the roof when she finds out.*
6 under one roof/under the same roof in the same building or house: *If we're going to live under the same roof, we need to get along.*

roofing /ˈruːfɪŋ $ ˈruːf-, ˈrʊf-/ *n* [U] material used for roofs

'roof-rack *n* [C] *BrE* a metal frame fixed to the top of a car, used to carry bags etc [= luggage rack *AmE*] → see picture on page A12

rooftop /ˈruːftɒp $ ˈruːftɑːp, ˈrʊf-/ *n* [C] the top surface of a roof: *flying over the rooftops*

rooftops

rook /rʊk/ *n* [C] a large black bird

rookie /ˈrʊki/ *n* [C] *AmE* someone who has just started doing a job or playing a sport: *rookie cops*

room¹ /ruːm, rʊm/ *n*
1 [C] a space in a building that is separated from the rest by walls and a door: *a hotel room* | *My brother is in the next room* (=the one beside the one you are in). | **sb's room** (=a room that someone uses regularly) *Which is Derek's room?* | **living/dining/meeting etc room** *the doctor's waiting room* | **single/double room** (=a hotel room for one person or for two) | **one room(ed)/two-room(ed) etc** *a three-room apartment*
2 [U] enough space for something or someone: **+in** *I hope there's room in the fridge.* | **+for** *Have you enough room for your legs?* | **room to do sth** *A bush needs plenty of room to grow.* | **make/leave room (for sb/sth)** (=move so that there is enough space) *Leave room for people to pass.* | *This desk takes up too much room* (=there is not enough space for it). | **leg/head room** (=space for your legs or head in a vehicle) → see box at PLACE
3 [U] the possibility that something can happen or exist: **+for** *I always try to make room for meditation in my day.* | *The curriculum gives teachers little room for manoeuvre* (=opportunity to change something). | *Good work is being done, but there's room for improvement* (=possibility of doing better).
4 [singular] all the people in a room: *The whole room fell silent as he entered.*
→ CHAT ROOM, DRAWING ROOM, DRESSING ROOM, OPERATING ROOM, UTILITY ROOM

room² *v* **room with sb** *AmE* to share a bedroom with someone who is not in your family, for example at college

roomful /ˈruːmfʊl, ˈrʊm-/ *n* [C] a large number of people or things in a room: **+of** *a roomful of reporters*

roommate /ˈruːmmeɪt, ˈrʊm-/ *n* [C] someone who is not in your family who shares a bedroom with you, for example at college

'room ,service *n* [U] a service that a hotel provides to bring food, drinks etc to your room

roomy /ˈruːmi/ *adj* with plenty of space inside: *a roomy car*

roost /ruːst/ *n* [C] **1** a place where birds sleep **2 rule the roost** to be the most powerful and important person in a place —**roost** *v* [I]

rooster /ˈruːstə $ -ər/ *n* [C] a male chicken

root¹ /ruːt/ *n* [C]
1 the part of a plant that grows under the ground and gets water from the soil: *tree roots* | *Be careful not to break the roots.* → see picture at PLANT

2 roots [plural] the place where someone or something began: +**in** *Jazz has roots in slave songs.* | **sb's roots** (=the connection someone feels with the place where their family came from) *She's very proud of her Jamaican roots.* | *He enjoys returning to his roots.*
3 the basic cause of a problem: **at/to the root of sth** *Religion lies at the root of the conflict.* | *A good mechanic will get to the root of the problem.* | *the root causes of crime*
4 take root if something takes root, it starts to exist: *Orthodox Judaism took root after the war.*
5 the part of a tooth, hair etc that is under the skin
→ **GRASS ROOTS, SQUARE ROOT**

root² v [I] **1** to search for something by moving things [= rummage]: +**around/through/among** etc *She rooted in her bag for a pen.* **2 be rooted in sth** to have developed from something and to be strongly influenced by it: *feelings rooted in childhood* **3 rooted to the spot** so shocked or frightened that you cannot move: *She stood rooted to the spot, staring in disbelief.*
   root for sb *phr v informal* to support and encourage someone to succeed
   root sth ⇔ **out** *phr v* to completely remove a problem: *We must root out bullying in schools.*

rope¹ /rəʊp $ roʊp/ n
1 [C,U] very strong thick string: *a skipping rope* | *pieces of rope tied to a tree*
2 the ropes [plural] the things someone needs to know in order to do a job: *I spent the first month learning the ropes.* | *Miss McGinley will show you the ropes.*
3 on the ropes *informal* if you are on the ropes, you are likely to fail or be defeated
4 be at/near the end of your rope *AmE* to have no more strength or ability to deal with a difficult situation: *With three kids and no money, I'm at the end of my rope.*

rope² v [T] to tie things or people together, using rope: **rope sth to sth** | **rope sth together** *The climbers were roped together for safety.*
   rope sb ⇔ **in** *phr v informal* to persuade someone to help you: **rope sb in to do sth** *I've been roped in to help.*

ropey, ropy /'rəʊpi $ 'roʊ-/ *adj BrE informal* not in good condition or not good quality

rosary /'rəʊzəri $ 'roʊ-/ n [C] plural **rosaries** a string of BEADS (=small round balls), used by Roman Catholics when they pray

rose¹ /rəʊz $ roʊz/ n [C] a beautiful sweet-smelling flower that grows on a bush with sharp THORNS

rose² v the past tense of RISE

rosé /'rəʊzeɪ $ roʊ'zeɪ/ n [U] pink wine

rosette /rəʊ'zet $ roʊ-/ n [C] a circular decoration made of coloured silk that you wear to show you have won a prize or to show that you support a particular political party

roster /'rɒstə $ 'rɑːstər/ n [C] *AmE* a list of names showing the jobs that each person on the list must do and when they must do them [= rota *BrE*]

rostrum /'rɒstrəm $ 'rɑː-/ n [C] a small raised area that someone stands on, for example to make a speech

rosy /'rəʊzi $ 'roʊ-/ adj **1** showing hope of success or happiness: *The company has a rosy future.* **2** pink and healthy looking: *children with rosy cheeks*

rot¹ /rɒt $ rɑːt/ v **rotted, rotting** [I,T] if something rots, or if something rots it, it goes bad and breaks into pieces because it is old, wet etc [= decay]: *rotting vegetables* | *Sugary drinks rot your teeth.* | *The wooden stairs had rotted away.*

rot² n [U] **1** the natural process that happens when something gets older and begins to go bad [= decay]: *a tree full of rot* **2 the rot** *informal* a bad situation that is getting worse: *how to stop the rot* | **the rot set in** (=a situation started to get worse) *After he left, the rot started to set in.*

rota /'rəʊtə $ 'roʊ-/ n [C] *BrE* a list of names showing the jobs that each person on the list must do and when they must do them [= roster *AmE*]

rotary /'rəʊtəri $ 'roʊ-/ adj turning in a circle from a fixed point

rotate /rəʊ'teɪt $ 'roʊteɪt/ v [I,T] **1** to turn around from a fixed point, or to make something do this: *The Earth rotates on its axis.* | **rotate sth to/towards/away from etc sth** *Rotate the handle to the right.* **2** to change the use or position that things or people have, following a regular pattern: *The presidency rotates yearly.* | *Rotating the type of crops you grow will improve the soil.* —**rotation** /rəʊ'teɪʃən $ roʊ-/ n [C,U] *We work nights in rotation.*

rote /rəʊt $ roʊt/ n [U] **learn sth by rote** to learn something by repeating it but not really understanding it

rotor /'rəʊtə $ 'roʊtər/ n [C] a part of a machine that turns around from a fixed point

rotten /'rɒtn $ 'rɑːtn/ adj **1** rotten food or wood is in bad condition because it is old [= decayed]: *rotten apples* **2** *informal* old-fashioned unkind or unfair

rottweiler /'rɒtvaɪlə, -waɪlə $ 'rɑːtwaɪlər/ n [C] a type of large strong dog

rotund /rəʊ'tʌnd $ roʊ-/ adj *formal* having a fat round body

rouge /ruːʒ/ n [U] *old-fashioned* a red substance that women put on their cheeks to make them pink [= blusher]

rough¹ /rʌf/ adj
1 not smooth or even [≠ smooth]: *rough ground* | *rough skin* | *his rough voice*
2 a rough description or idea is not exact and has few details [➝ approximate]: *Can you give us a rough idea of the cost?* | *a rough draft of an essay*
3 if your life or a period of time is rough, it is difficult and unpleasant [= tough]: *Sounds like you had a rough day at work.* | *We've seen some rough times together.* | *My boyfriend and I hit a rough patch.* | *Did you have a rough night* (=did you sleep badly)?
4 violent, dangerous, or using too much force: *Ice hockey is a rough sport.* | *a rough part of town* | *Don't be so rough with her.* | *A truck can withstand rough treatment.* | *The boat sank in rough seas.*
5 unfair or unkind: **be rough on sb** *I think you were a bit rough on her.* | **rough justice** (=unfair or illegal punishment) *rough justice handed out by street gangs*

R

6 simple or not very well made: *a rough wooden table* | **rough and ready** (=not perfect, but good enough to use)
7 *BrE informal* ill, untidy, or dirty: **feel/look rough** *The next morning I felt pretty rough.*
—**roughness** *n* [U]

rough² *n* **1 the rough** uneven ground with long grass on a golf course [➡ green] **2 take the rough with the smooth** to accept the bad things in life as well as the good

rough³ *v* **rough it** to live for a short time in uncomfortable conditions: *She wasn't used to roughing it.*
　rough sb ⇔ **up** *phr v informal* to attack and hurt someone by hitting them

rough⁴ *adv* **sleep/live rough** *BrE* to live outdoors because you have no home

roughage /'rʌfɪdʒ/ *n* [U] a substance in some foods that helps your BOWELS to work [= fibre]

,rough-and-'tumble *n* [U] **1** noisy and violent play **2** a situation or activity that is busy and sometimes unpleasant for the people who are involved in it: **+of** *the rough-and-tumble of political life*

roughen /'rʌfən/ *v* [I,T] to make something uneven or not smooth

roughly /'rʌfli/ *adv*
1 not exactly [= about, approximately]: *roughly 100 people* | *I worked out the cost roughly.*
2 violently or using force: *She pushed him away roughly.*

roughshod /'rʌfʃɒd $ -ʃɑːd/ *adv disapproving* **ride roughshod over sb/sth** to ignore other people's feelings or opinions

roulette /ruːˈlet/ *n* [U] a game in which you spin a ball on a moving wheel and people try to win money by guessing where the ball will stop

round¹ /raʊnd/ *adj*
1 shaped like a circle: *a round table* | *big round eyes* | *Cut a 2 cm round hole in the top.*
2 a round number is a whole number, often ending in 0: *Let's make it a round number, say $50?* | **in round figures** (=given as the nearest number to 10, 100, 1000 etc) *In round figures, there are 30,000 students.*
—**roundness** *n* [U]

round² *especially BrE* also **around** *adv, prep*
1 surrounding something: *We sat round the fire.* | *the path round the lake* | **Gather round** *for a story.* | *He put his arm round her waist.*
2 moving to face the opposite direction: **look/turn etc round** *I looked round to see who had come in.* | *Turn the picture* **the other way round.**
3 moving in a circle: *Bikes raced round and* **round.** | *fish swimming round in circles* → see picture on page A8
4 to different parts of a place: **go/travel etc round** *She spent her gap year travelling round Europe.* | **show sb round (sth)** (=show someone the different parts of a place) *A tour guide showed us round.*
5 on or to the other side of something: **+to** *She moved round to his side of the desk.* | *The two boys disappeared* **round the corner.**
6 to other people or positions: *Three men were* **passing** *a bottle* **round.**
7 if there is a way round a problem, there is a way to avoid it: *Somehow, the burglars had* **found a way round** *the alarm.*

8 *spoken* to someone's home: **come/go round** *What time are you coming round?* | *We've been invited round for dinner.*
9 *spoken* in a particular area: *Do you* **live round** *here?* → see box at LOCALLY
10 *spoken informal* **round about sth** nearly but not exactly: *I heard a scream round about midnight.*
→ AROUND

round³ *n* [C] **1** a set of related events that are part of a longer process: **+of** *the latest round of peace talks* | *endless rounds of meetings* **2** a separate part of a sports competition [➡ heat, stage]: **first/final/next etc round** *She made it to the second round.* | **+of** *the final round of the championship* **3 a round of applause** when people CLAP at the end of a speech, performance etc: *Let's give them* **a round of applause.** **4** if you buy a round of drinks in a bar, you buy a drink for each person in your group: **sb's round** (=when it is someone's turn to buy a round) *Whose round is it?* **5** a complete game of golf: *We played* **a round of golf** *on Sunday.* **6** a bullet: *He let off* **a round of ammunition.**

round⁴ *v* [T] to go around a bend, corner, piece of furniture etc: *The car* **rounded the bend** *at 75 mph.*
　round sth ⇔ **down** *phr v* to reduce a figure to the nearest whole number: **+to** *It cost £21.70 so we rounded it down to £20.*
　round sth ⇔ **off** *phr v* to end something in a pleasant or suitable way: *Why not round off your visit at a nightclub?*
　round on sb *phr v* to suddenly attack or criticize someone when they do not expect it: *After Miss Evans had left, Edward rounded on him angrily.*
　round sb/sth ⇔ **up** *phr v* **1** to find and bring together a group of people: *The police rounded 20 people up for questioning.* **2** to increase a figure to the nearest whole number

roundabout¹ /'raʊndəbaʊt/ *n* [C] *BrE* **1** a circular area where roads meet and which cars must drive around [= traffic circle *AmE*]: *Turn left at the next roundabout.* **2** a round structure in a park that children sit on while it turns

roundabout² *adj* [only before noun] a roundabout way of saying or doing something is not clear, simple, or direct

rounded /'raʊndɪd/ *adj* curved

rounders /'raʊndəz $ -ərz/ *n* [U] a British ball game that is similar to baseball

roundly /'raʊndli/ *adv* if someone criticizes you roundly, they criticize you very strongly: *The administration has been* **roundly condemned** *for allowing it to happen.*

,round-the-'clock *adj* happening all the time: *round-the-clock care*

,round 'trip *n* [C] a journey to a place and back again —**round-trip** *adj AmE: a round-trip ticket* → see box at TICKET

roundup /'raʊndʌp/ *n* [C] **1** a short description of the main news on radio or television: **+of** *First, here's a roundup of the local news.* **2** when a lot of people or animals are brought together by force: **+of** *a roundup of criminal suspects*

rouse /raʊz/ v [T]　**1** to make someone want to do something: *The speech roused King's supporters to action.*　**2** *formal* to wake someone

rousing /'raʊzɪŋ/ adj making people excited and eager to do something: *a rousing speech*

rout /raʊt/ v [T] to defeat someone completely

route[1] /ruːt $ ruːt, raʊt/ n [C]

1 the roads, paths etc that you follow to get from one place to another: **+to/from** *What's the quickest route to the station?* | *the most **direct route** home* | **bus/shipping etc route** *a map of local bus routes* | **take/follow a route** *Which is the best route to take?* | *Cheering crowds **lined the route** (=stood in a line along a road being used for a race, march etc).*

2 a way of achieving something: **+to** *Money is not always the route to happiness.*

→ EN ROUTE

route[2] v [T] to send something or someone by a particular route: *Flights were routed through Paris because of the snow.*

routine[1] /ruː'tiːn/ n　**1** [C,U] the usual way that you do things or the things you do regularly: **daily/normal/usual routine** *Making the beds was part of her usual routine.* | *Try to **get into a routine.***　**2** [C] a series of movements or other actions that are performed regularly: *my **exercise routine***

routine[2] /ˌruː'tiːn◂/ adj happening as part of a normal and regular process: *a routine medical test* | *routine jobs around the house* → see box at NORMAL —**routinely** adv

roving /'rəʊvɪŋ $ 'roʊ-/ adj [only before noun] travelling or moving from one place to another as part of your job: *roving reporters*

row[1] /rəʊ $ roʊ/ n [C]

1 a line of things or people next to each other: **+of** *a row of houses* | *children standing **in a row***　**2** a line of seats in a theatre, cinema etc　**3 twice/three times/4 days etc in a row** if something happens twice, three times etc in a row, it happens twice, three times etc, and each occasion is straight after the one before: *She's lost three times in a row.*

→ DEATH ROW

row[2] v [I,T] to make a boat move across water, using OARS (=long poles): *They rowed across the lake.* → see picture on page A9 —**rowing** n [U]

row[3] /raʊ/ n *BrE*　**1** [C] an argument [= quarrel]: *Anna and her boyfriend are **having another row.*** → see box at ARGUE　**2** [C] a situation in which people disagree strongly about important public affairs [= controversy]: **+over** *a row over government cuts*　**3** [singular] an annoying loud noise [= racket, din]

row[4] /raʊ/ v [I] *BrE* to argue in an angry way [= quarrel]: **+about** *They rowed about money all the time.*

rowdy /'raʊdi/ adj behaving in a noisy and uncontrolled way: *rowdy children* → see box at LOUD

row house /'rəʊ haʊs $ 'roʊ-/ n [C] *AmE* a house that is joined to other houses on both sides [= terraced house *BrE*] → see box at HOUSE

rowing boat /'rəʊɪŋ bəʊt $ 'roʊɪŋ boʊt/ *BrE*; **rowboat** /'rəʊbəʊt $ 'roʊboʊt/ *AmE* n [C] a

small boat that you move across water using OARS (=long poles) → see picture at TRANSPORT

royal[1] /'rɔɪəl/ adj belonging to or connected with a king or queen [➡ regal]: *the royal family* | *the Royal Navy*

royal[2] n [C] a member of a royal family

,royal 'blue n [U] a strong bright blue colour —**royal blue** adj

royalist /'rɔɪəlɪst/ n [C] someone who supports the idea that a king or queen should rule their country [≠ republican]

royalty /'rɔɪəlti/ n plural **royalties**　**1** [U] members of a royal family　**2 royalties** [plural] payment made to the writer of a book or piece of music: *How much did he get **in royalties?***

rpm /ˌɑː piː 'em $ ˌɑːr-/ **revolutions per minute** used to describe how fast something such as an engine or motor turns: *1200 rpm*

RSI /ˌɑːr es 'aɪ/ n [U] *technical* **repetitive strain injury** pains in your hands, arms etc caused by doing the same movements many times, especially when using a computer

RSVP /ˌɑːr es viː 'piː/ used on invitations to ask someone to reply

rub[1] /rʌb/ v [I,T] **rubbed, rubbing**

1 to move your hand, a cloth etc quickly backwards and forwards over a surface: **rub sth with sth** *She rubbed her hair with a towel.* | **rub sth into/onto etc sth** *Make sure you rub sunscreen into baby's delicate skin.* | **Rub a bit harder** (=with more force). | **rub (sth) out/off** (=remove something by rubbing) *Don't worry, the marks will rub off.* | **rub sth down** (=rub something to make it dry, clean etc) *Rub the wood down with sandpaper.* → see box at REMOVE

2 to press against something and move backwards and forwards: *Are your shoes rubbing?* | *He smiled, rubbing his hands at the prospect of a sale.* | **rub (sth) against/on sth** *The cat rubbed against her legs, purring.*

3 rub shoulders with sb, rub elbows with sb *AmE informal* to spend time with important or famous people

4 rub sb's nose in it/in the dirt *informal* to keep reminding someone about something bad they have done in order to punish or embarrass them

5 rub sb up the wrong way *informal* to annoy someone by saying and doing things that make them cross

6 rub salt into the wound to make a bad situation even worse for someone

　rub sth ⇔ in *phr v* to upset or annoy someone by reminding them about something when you know that they want to forget it: *Ok, there's no need to **rub it in!***

　rub off *phr v* if a person's behaviour rubs off on you, you start to behave in the same way as them because you are spending time together: **+on** *Her positive attitude rubs off on everyone.*

rub[2] n **give sth a rub** to rub something for a short time

rubber[1] /'rʌbə $ -ər/ n

1 [U] a strong substance used to make tyres, boots etc that is made from the juice of a tropical tree or chemicals: *The seal is **made of rubber.***

2 [C] *BrE*　**a)** a small piece of rubber used to remove pencil marks from paper [= eraser *AmE*]

R

→ see picture at CLASSROOM **b)** a piece of wood or plastic with soft material on one side used to remove marks from a BLACKBOARD [= eraser AmE]
3 [C] *informal* a CONDOM

rubber² *adj* made of rubber: *rubber gloves* | *a rubber ball* → see picture at MATERIAL¹

,rubber 'band *n* [C] a small thin circle of rubber, used to hold things together [= elastic band]

,rubber-'stamp *v* [T] *disapproving* to officially approve a plan or decision without considering it carefully

rubbery /'rʌbəri/ *adj disapproving* looking or feeling like rubber: *rubbery eggs*

rubbish /'rʌbɪʃ/ *n* [U] *BrE*
1 things such as paper, old food, empty bottles etc that you do not need and that you can throw away [= garbage AmE]: *household rubbish* | *a rubbish bin* | *a pile of rubbish* | **rubbish dump/tip** (=a place to take rubbish)

THESAURUS

litter – empty bottles, pieces of paper etc that people have dropped carelessly on the street
refuse *formal* – things that people have thrown away
waste – materials, substances etc that need to be thrown away after they have been used or after an industrial process
garbage/trash *AmE*

COLLOCATIONS

throw rubbish away – to get rid of rubbish – by putting it in a
bin/wastepaper basket *BrE*/**wastebasket** *AmE* or a
dustbin *BrE*/**garbage can** *AmE*
throw rubbish out – to get rid of rubbish – by putting it in a
dustbin *BrE*/**garbage can** *AmE*
dump – to get rid of something unwanted in a careless way
recycle – to put glass, paper etc through a special process so that it can be used again

2 *informal* something you think is silly, wrong, or bad quality: *You do talk rubbish sometimes.* | *What a load of rubbish!*

rubble /'rʌbəl/ *n* [U] broken stones, bricks etc from a building that has been destroyed: *a pile of rubble*

rubella /ruːˈbelə/ *n* [U] an infectious disease that makes red spots appear on your body [= German measles]

rubric /'ruːbrɪk/ *n* [C] an explanation or set of instructions on an examination paper or in a book

ruby /'ruːbi/ *n* [C,U] plural **rubies** a valuable dark red jewel —**ruby** *adj*

rucksack /'rʌksæk/ *n* [C] *BrE* a bag you carry on your back [= backpack] → see picture at BAG¹

rudder /'rʌdə $ -ər/ *n* [C] a flat part at the back of a boat or plane you turn in order to change direction

ruddy /'rʌdi/ *adj* a ruddy face looks pink and healthy

rude /ruːd/ *adj*
1 speaking or behaving in a way that is not polite [= impolite]: **rude remark/comment** *The boys were making rude remarks about the teacher.* | **+to** *Don't be so rude to your mother!* | *It's rude to stare.*

THESAURUS

impolite *formal*
bad-mannered – behaving in a rude way
cheeky *BrE* – showing no respect, sometimes in an amusing way: *a cheeky grin*
insulting – saying or doing something that insults someone: *comments that are insulting to women*
tactless – carelessly saying or doing things that are likely to upset someone: *a tactless remark*
offensive – likely to upset or offend people: *His remarks are offensive to African Americans.*

2 rude words, jokes, songs etc are about sex [= dirty]
—**rudely** *adv* —**rudeness** *n* [U]

rudimentary /ˌruːdɪˈmentəri◂/ *adj formal* very simple and basic: *a rudimentary knowledge of Chinese*

rudiments /'ruːdɪmənts/ *n* [plural] *formal* the most basic parts of a subject: **+of** *the rudiments of grammar*

rueful /'ruːfəl/ *adj* showing that you wish something had not happened but that you accept it: *a rueful smile* —**ruefully** *adv*

ruffle¹ /'rʌfəl/ *v* [T] **1** to make a smooth surface uneven: *The wind ruffled his hair.* **2** to offend, annoy, or upset someone: *Don't let yourself get ruffled.* | *I don't want to ruffle his feathers* (=upset him).

ruffle² *n* [C] cloth sewn in folds as a decoration around the edges of a shirt, skirt etc

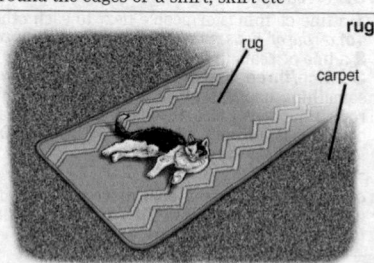

rug

carpet

rug /rʌg/ *n* [C] **1** a piece of thick cloth or wool that is put on the floor as a decoration [→ carpet] **2** *BrE* a type of BLANKET

rugby /'rʌgbi/ *n* [U] a game in which two teams carry, kick, or throw an OVAL ball

rugged /'rʌgɪd/ *adj* **1** land that is rugged is rough and uneven: *a rugged coastline* **2** a man who is rugged is attractive with strong features, which may not be perfect: *his rugged good looks* **3** a vehicle or piece of equipment that is rugged is strongly built

ruin¹ /'ruːɪn/ *v* [T]
1 to spoil or destroy something completely: *This new road will ruin the countryside.* | *One stupid comment had ruined everything.*
2 to make someone lose all their money: *Jefferson was ruined by the court case against him.*

ruin[2] *n* **1** [U] a situation in which someone loses their social position or money, especially because of a business failure: *small businesses facing **financial ruin*** **2** [C] also **ruins** [plural] the part of a building that is left after the rest has been destroyed: **+of** *the ruins of the temple* **3 be in ruins** to be badly damaged: *The country's economy is in ruins.* **4 fall/crumble into ruin** if a building has fallen into ruin, it is in a bad condition because it has not been looked after

ruinous /'ru:nəs/ *adj* extremely damaging: *a ruinous decision*

rule[1] /ru:l/ *n*

1 [C] an official instruction about what is allowed, especially in a game, organization, or job [➡ **law, regulation**]: **+of** *Do you know the rules of the game?* | **strict rules** *about what you can wear* | *Well, that's what happens if you **break** the school **rules** (=disobey the rules).* | **follow/obey/ observe the rules** *If you follow the rules, you won't get into trouble.* | **against the rules** *It's against the rules to pick up the ball* (=it's not allowed). | **bend the rules** (=allow something that is usually not allowed) *Can't we bend the rules just this once?*
2 [C] what you should do in a particular situation: ***The rule is:*** *if you feel any pain, you should stop exercising.* | ***The golden rule*** (=the most important thing to remember) *in interviews is to listen carefully to the question.* | **+of** *the two basic rules of survival*
3 [singular] something that is normal or usually true: *I don't drink alcohol **as a rule** (=usually).* | *As **a general rule** vegetable oils are much better for you than animal fats.* | *Not having a television **is the exception rather than the rule** (=unusual).*
4 [U] the government or control of a country: **under ... rule** (=controlled by that country or group) *At that time Vietnam was under French rule.* | **colonial/military rule** *the end of British colonial rule*
5 [C] a statement of the correct way of doing something in a language, area of science etc: **+of** *the rules of grammar*
6 rule of thumb a general principle or method for calculating something: *As a rule of thumb, plant tall hedge plants two feet apart.*
→ GROUND RULES

rule[2] *v* **1** [I,T] to have the official power to control a country [➡ **govern**]: *The King ruled for 30 years.* **2** [T] if a feeling or desire rules someone, it has a powerful influence in their life: *Don't let your job **rule** your life.* **3** [I,T] to make an official decision about something such as a legal problem: **+that** *The judge ruled that the baby should live with his father.*

rule sth/sb ⇔ **out** *phr v* to decide that something or someone is not possible or suitable: *We can't **rule out the possibility** that he may have left the country.*

ruled /ru:ld/ *adj* ruled paper has lines printed across it

ruler /'ru:lə $ -ər/ *n* [C]

1 someone such as a king who has official power over a country
2 a flat narrow piece of plastic, wood, or metal that you use for measuring things and drawing straight lines → see picture at **CLASSROOM**

ruling[1] /'ru:lɪŋ/ *n* [C] an official decision, especially by a law court: **+on** *the Supreme Court's ruling on the case*

ruling[2] *adj* [only before noun] the ruling group in a country or organization is the group that controls it: *the **ruling classes***

rum /rʌm/ *n* [C,U] a strong alcoholic drink made from sugar

rumble /'rʌmbəl/ *v* [I] **1** to make a continuous low sound: *Thunder rumbled in the distance.* **2** if your stomach rumbles, it makes a noise because you are hungry —**rumble** *n* [singular]

rumbling /'rʌmblɪŋ/ *n* **1 rumblings** [plural] remarks that show people are starting to become annoyed or that a difficult situation is developing: **+of** *rumblings of discontent* **2** [C usually singular] a long low sound

ruminate /'ru:mɪ̣neɪt/ *v* [I] *formal* to think about something carefully

rummage /'rʌmɪdʒ/ *v* [I] to search for something by moving things around: **+in/through** *Kerry was rummaging through a drawer looking for a pen.*

rummage sale *n* [C] *AmE* an event at which old clothes, furniture, toys etc are sold [= **jumble sale** *BrE*]

rumour *BrE*; **rumor** *AmE* /'ru:mə $ -ər/ *n* [C,U] information that is passed from one person to another and may not be true: **+that** *rumors that the President may have to resign* | **+about** *I heard a rumour about him and Sylvia.* | ***Rumour has it*** (=people are saying) *that Jean's getting married again.*

rumoured *BrE*; **rumored** *AmE* /'ru:məd $ -ərd/ *adj* if something is rumoured to be true, people are saying that it may be true but no one is sure: *It was rumoured that a magazine offered £10,000 for her story.* | **rumoured to be/have done sth** *The actress is rumoured to be pregnant again.*

rump /rʌmp/ *n* [C,U] the part of an animal that is just above its back legs

rumpled /'rʌmpəld/ *adj* rumpled hair, clothes etc are untidy

run[1] /rʌn/ *v* past tense **ran** /ræn/ past participle **run**, present participle **running**

1 [I] to move very quickly, moving your legs faster than when you walk: **+down/up/to/ towards etc** *Some kids were running down the street.* | *The boys ran off into the crowd.* | *Stephen **came running** down the stairs.* → see picture on page A11

dash/tear – to run very fast in a hurried way
sprint – to run as fast as you can for a short distance
jog/go jogging – to run quite slowly for exercise over a long distance
→ WALK

2 [I,T] to run in a race: *The horse ran a superb race.* | *He's training to run the marathon.*
3 [T] to control, organize, or operate a business, organization, activity etc: *My parents **run** their own **business**.* | *They run full-time and part-time*

R

courses of study. | **well/badly run** *The hotel is well-run and extremely popular.*
4 [I,T] if a machine, engine, or other piece of equipment runs, or if someone runs it, it is working: *Dad left the engine running.* | **run on coal/petrol/batteries etc** (=use coal, petrol etc to work) | *She didn't realise the tape was still running* (=recording).
5 [I,T] if something long, such as a road or wire, runs in a particular direction, that is its position: **+along/through/past etc** *The road runs along the coast.* | *a shelf that **runs the length of** one wall*
6 [T] to move your fingers or an object through or over something: *She ran her fingers through her hair.*
7 [I,T] to flow or to produce a stream of water etc: *Tears ran down her face.* | *Who **left the tap running?*** | *I'm just **running a bath** (=filling it with water).* | **sb's nose is running** (=liquid is coming out)
8 [I] to happen in a particular way or for a particular time: *The tour guide helps to keep things **running smoothly**.* | *Trains run every 10 minutes.* | **+for** *The play ran for two years* (=was performed for two years).
9 be running late to be doing things late: *Sorry you had to wait – I've been running late all day.*
10 [T] to start or use a computer program: *You can run this software on any PC.*
11 [I,T] to print or broadcast a story, piece of news etc: *They ran the item on the 6 o'clock news.*
12 [I] to try to get elected: **+for** *He is running for President.*
13 [T] to own and use a vehicle: *I can't afford to run a car.*
14 [T] to drive someone somewhere: *I'll run you home if you like.*
15 [I] to be at a particular level, amount, or price: **+at** *Inflation was running at 20% a year.* | **+to/into** *The bill could run to thousands of pounds.*
16 be running short (of sth) to have little of something left: *I'm running short of money.*
17 run a check/test/experiment etc to arrange for someone or something to be checked or tested: *My GP ran a test to check my blood sugar levels.*
18 [I] if a colour runs, it spreads to other parts of a piece of material when it is washed
19 run in the family if something such as a quality, disease, or skill runs in the family, many people in that family have it

run across sb/sth *phr v* to meet or find someone or something by chance: *I ran across my old school photos the other day.*

run after sb/sth *phr v* to chase someone or something: *She started to leave, but Smith ran after her.*

run away *phr v* to leave a place in order to escape from someone or something: **+from** *Kathy ran away from home at the age of 16.*

run sth **by** sb *phr v informal* to tell someone about something so that they can give you their opinion about it: *Can you run that by me again?*

run sb/sth ⇔ **down** *phr v* **1** to hit a person or animal with a car and kill or injure them: *As he was cycling into school a car ran him down.* **2** to criticize someone or something: *Her boyfriend's always running her down.*

run into sb/sth *phr v* **1** *informal* to meet someone by chance: *I ran into him the other day in town.* **2 run into trouble/problems/debt etc** to begin to have trouble, problems etc: *She ran into trouble when she couldn't get a work permit.* **3** to hit someone or something with a car: *He lost control and ran into another car.*

run off *phr v* **1** to leave a place or person when you should not: *Our dog keeps running off.* **2 run off a copy** to quickly print a copy of something: *I'll need to run off a few more copies before the meeting.*

run off with sb/sth *phr v* **1** *disapproving* to go away with someone to marry them or to live with them: *Her husband ran off with his secretary.* **2** to take or steal something: *A thief ran off with her mobile phone.*

run out *phr v* **1 a)** to use all of something, so that there is none left: **+of** *We've run out of sugar.* | *I'm running out of ideas.* **b)** if something is running out, there will soon be none left: *We'll have to make a decision soon – **time is running out.*** **2** if an official document, contract etc runs out, the period of time for which it is legal or you can use it ends: *My membership runs out in September.*

run sb/sth ⇔ **over** *phr v* to hit someone or something with your car, and drive over them: *I think you just ran over some broken glass.*

run through sth *phr v* **1** to read, check, or practise something quickly: *I'd like to run through the questions again before you start.* **2** if a quality or feature runs through something, it exists in all parts of it: *a theme which runs through the book*

run up sth *phr v* if you run up a bill, debt etc, you then owe a lot of money: *We ran up a huge phone bill.*

run up against sth *phr v* to suddenly have to deal with something difficult: *The team ran up against tough opposition.*

run² *n* [C]
1 when someone runs, or the distance that someone runs: *He usually **goes for** a **run** before breakfast.* | *a five-mile run.*
2 in the short/long run in the near future, or later in the future: *Wood is more expensive, but in the long run it's better value.*
3 [usually singular] a series of good or bad things which happen to you: **run of good/bad luck** *She has had a run of bad luck recently.* | **unbeaten/winning run** *an unbeaten run of 19 games*
4 the usual/normal/general run of sth the usual type of something: *It was just a bit different from the usual run of city centre bars.*
5 a point in a game such as BASEBALL or CRICKET: *He scored 218 runs.*
6 be on the run to be trying to escape from someone, especially the police: **+from** *a criminal on the run from the police*
7 make a run for it to try to escape by suddenly running away
8 a period of time during which a play, film, or television show is shown or performed regularly: *The play starts an 8-week run on Friday.*
9 a run on sth when a lot of people suddenly buy something at the same time: *There is a run on swimwear in hot weather.*

10 have the run of sth to be allowed to use the whole of a place: *We had the run of the house for the weekend.*

→ HOME RUN, TEST RUN, TRIAL RUN

runaway[1] /'rʌnəweɪ/ *adj* [only before noun] **1** a runaway vehicle is out of control **2** happening quickly and suddenly: *The film was a runaway success.*

runaway[2] *n* [C] someone, especially a child, who has left their home, school etc secretly

run-'down *adj* **1** if a building or area is run-down, it is in bad condition because it has not been looked after: *a run-down apartment block* **2** [not before noun] if a person is run-down, they feel tired and ill: *He's been feeling run-down lately.*

rundown /'rʌndaʊn/ *n* [singular] a quick report or explanation of a situation or idea: **+on** *Can you give me a rundown on what happened while I was away?*

rung[1] /rʌŋ/ *v* the past participle of RING

rung[2] *n* [C] **1** one of the steps of a LADDER **2** *informal* a particular level or position in an organization: **first/lowest/bottom rung** *I started on the bottom rung in the company.*

'run-in *n* [C] an argument with someone in authority: **+with** *He had a run-in with his boss.*

runner /'rʌnə $ -ər/ *n* [C] **1** someone who runs as a sport, or a horse that runs in a race: *a long-distance runner* **2 gun/drug runner** someone who illegally takes guns or drugs from one country to another

runner-'up *n* [C] plural **runners-up** the person or team that finishes second in a competition

running[1] /'rʌnɪŋ/ *n* [U] **1** the activity or sport of running: *a running track* | *Do you want to go running?* **2 the running of sth** the process of managing a business, organization etc: *the day-to-day running of the company* **3 be in/out of the running** to have some chance or no chance of winning or being successful: **+for** *Is Sam still in the running for the swimming team?*

running[2] *adj* **1 running water** water that flows from a TAP: *hot and cold running water* **2 running battle** an argument that continues or is repeated over a long period of time **3 running commentary** a spoken description of an event while it is happening **4 running total** a total that gets bigger as new amounts are added to it

running[3] *adv* **three years/five times etc running** for three years, five times etc without a change: *This is the fourth day running that it has rained.*

'running costs *n* [plural] the amount of money you have to pay to operate something

runny /'rʌni/ *adj informal* **1** if you have a runny nose, liquid is coming out of your nose because you are ill **2** food that is runny is not as thick as normal or as you want: *The sauce is far too runny.*

run-of-the-'mill *adj* not special or interesting: *a run-of-the-mill performance*

'run-up *n* **the run-up to sth** the period just before an important event: *political campaigning in the run-up to the election*

runway /'rʌnweɪ/ *n* [C] a long wide road that planes land on and take off from → see box at AIRPORT

rupture /'rʌptʃə $ -ər/ *v* [I,T] to break or burst open violently: *An oil pipeline ruptured.* —**rupture** *n* [C,U]

rural /'rʊərəl $ 'rʊr-/ *adj* relating to or happening in the country rather than in the city [→ **urban**]: *a peaceful rural setting* | *a rural community*

ruse /ruːz $ ruːs, ruːz/ *n* [C] a clever trick

rush[1] /rʌʃ/ *v*

1 [I] to move or go somewhere quickly [= **hurry**]: *There's no need to rush – we have plenty of time.* | **+into/along/from etc** *David rushed into the bathroom.*

2 rush to do sth to do something eagerly and without delay: *People are rushing to buy shares in the company.*

3 [I,T] to do or decide something too quickly, especially without being careful or thinking about it: **rush into (doing) sth** *I don't want to just rush into buying the first house we see.* | *Take your time, don't rush it.*

4 [T] to take or send a person or thing somewhere very quickly: **rush sb/sth to sth** *We had to rush Helen to the hospital.*

5 [T] to try to make someone do something more quickly than they want to: *Don't rush me – let me think.* | **rush sb into (doing) sth** *I don't want to rush you into anything.*

rush around *phr v* to go to a lot of places or do a lot of things in a short period of time

rush[2] *n*

1 [singular] a sudden fast movement of things or people: **rush of air/water/wind** *She felt a cold rush of air as she wound down her window.* | **in a rush** *Her words came out in a rush.* | **+for** *There was a rush for the door.*

2 [singular, U] a situation in which you need to hurry: *We have plenty of time. There's no rush.* | **in a rush** *I can't stop – I'm in a rush.* | **rush to do sth** *There's a big rush to get tickets.*

3 the rush the time when a lot of people are doing something, for example travelling or shopping: *the Christmas rush*

4 [singular] a sudden strong feeling: **+of** *a sudden rush of emotion* | *Mark felt a rush of anger.*

5 rushes [plural] tall plants that grow near rivers and are used to make baskets etc

rushed /rʌʃt/ *adj* **1** if you are rushed, you are very busy because you have a lot to do quickly: *I've been rushed off my feet* (=extremely busy) *all day.* **2** done too quickly: *a rushed meeting*

'rush hour *n* [C,U] the time of day when there is a lot of traffic because people are going to and from work

rust[1] /rʌst/ *n* [U] the reddish-brown substance that forms on iron, steel etc when it gets wet

rust[2] *v* [I,T] to become covered with rust, or to make rust form on something

rustic /'rʌstɪk/ *adj* simple and old-fashioned in a way that is attractive and typical of the country: *The village has a certain rustic charm.*

rustle /'rʌsəl/ *v* [I,T] if papers, leaves etc rustle, or if you rustle them, they make a noise as they move against each other: *the sound of kids rustling ice-cream wrappers* → see picture on page A7 —**rustle** *n* [singular]

rustle sth ⇔ up *phr v informal* to make something quickly, especially a meal

rusty /'rʌsti/ *adj* **1** covered with rust: *rusty nails* **2** if a skill is rusty, you are not as good at doing something as you were, because you have not practised: *My tennis is a little rusty.*

rut /rʌt/ *n* **1 in a rut** *informal* living or working in a boring situation that you cannot easily change: *Margaret felt she was **stuck in a rut**.* **2** [C] a deep narrow track left in the ground by a wheel

rutabaga /ˌruːtə'beɪgə/ *n* [C,U] *AmE* a round yellow vegetable that grows under the ground [= **swede** *BrE*]

ruthless /'ruːθləs/ *adj* not caring if you have to harm other people to get what you want: *a ruthless dictator* —**ruthlessly** *adv* —**ruthlessness** *n* [U]

rye /raɪ/ *n* [U] a type of grain that is used for making bread and WHISKY

R

S, s

S, s /es/ n [C,U] plural S's, s's the 19th letter of the English alphabet

S the written abbreviation of **south** or **southern**

-'s /z, s/ **1** the short form of 'is' or 'has': *What's that?* | *He's gone out.* **2** used to make the POSSESSIVE form of nouns: *Bill is one of Jason's friends.*

Sabbath /'sæbəθ/ n **the Sabbath** a day of the week for resting and praying, which is Sunday for Christians and Saturday for Jews

sabbatical /sə'bætɪkəl/ n [C,U] a period when someone, especially a university teacher, stops doing their usual work to travel or study: **on sabbatical** *Professor Burton is on sabbatical for two months.*

saber /'seɪbə $ -ər/ n the American spelling of SABRE

sabotage /'sæbətɑːʒ/ v [T] **1** to secretly damage or destroy something so that an enemy cannot use it: *The plane had been sabotaged and exploded in mid-air.* **2** to secretly spoil someone's plans because you do not want them to succeed: *He denied he was trying to sabotage the talks.* —sabotage n [U] *deliberate acts of sabotage*

saboteur /ˌsæbə'tɜː $ -'tɜːr/ n [C] someone who deliberately damages, destroys, or spoils someone else's property or activities, in order to prevent them from doing something: *Saboteurs could have been on the train.*

sabre BrE; saber AmE /'seɪbə $ -ər/ n [C] **1** a thin pointed sword used in the sport of FENCING **2** a heavy sword with a curved blade

saccharin /'sækərɪn/ n [U] a sweet chemical that is used in food instead of sugar

sachet /'sæʃeɪ $ sæ'ʃeɪ/ n [C] a small bag containing a liquid or powder: +**of** *a sachet of shampoo*

sack¹ /sæk/ n [C]

1 a large bag made of strong cloth, plastic, or paper in which you carry or store things: +**of** *a sack of potatoes*

2 get the sack/give sb the sack BrE informal to be told to leave your job or to tell someone to leave their job: *If someone complains to my manager about it, I could get the sack.*

sack² v [T] BrE to tell someone to leave their job [= **fire**]: *Campbell was sacked for coming in drunk.*

sacrament /'sækrəmənt/ n [C] an important Christian ceremony such as marriage or COMMUNION

sacred /'seɪkrɪd/ adj **1** relating to a god or religion, and believed to be holy: *sacred texts* | +**to** *The site is sacred to Muslims.* **2** very important: *Human life is sacred.* **3 sacred cow** something that is very important to some people, and which they will not change or allow anyone to criticize

sacrifice¹ /'sækrɪfaɪs/ n [C,U] **1** when you give up something important or valuable in order to get something that is more important: *Her parents made a lot of sacrifices to give her a good education.* **2** when something is offered to a god in a ceremony, especially an animal that is killed —sacrificial /ˌsækrɪ'fɪʃəl/ adj

sacrifice² v **1** [T] to give up something important or valuable in order to get something else: **sacrifice sth for sth** *It's not worth sacrificing your health for your job.* **2** [I,T] to offer something, especially an animal, to a god in a ceremony, often by killing it

sacrilege /'sækrɪlɪdʒ/ n [C,U] when something holy or important is treated in a way that does not show respect: *It would be sacrilege to demolish such a beautiful building.* —sacrilegious /ˌsækrɪ'lɪdʒəs/ adj

sacrosanct /'sækrəʊsæŋkt $ -roʊ-/ adj too important to be changed or criticized in any way: *Our time spent together as a family is sacrosanct.*

sad /sæd/ adj

1 unhappy, especially because something unpleasant has happened to you [≠ **happy**]: *Linda looks very sad today.* | +**about** *I was sad about the friends that I was leaving behind.* | +**that** *I am sad that you do not believe me.* | **sad to do sth** *I was sad to hear that he had died.*

THESAURUS

unhappy
miserable – very sad
upset – sad because something unpleasant or disappointing has happened
depressed – sad for a long time because things are wrong in your life
down/low informal – a little sad about things in your life
homesick – sad because you are away from your home, family, and friends
gloomy – sad because you think a situation will not improve
glum – used especially to say that someone looks sad

2 a sad event, story etc makes you feel unhappy: *Have you heard the sad news about Mrs. Winters?* | *It's just so sad.* | **sad story/song/film etc** *a story with a sad ending* **3** very bad or unacceptable: *It's a sad state of affairs* (=bad situation) *when a person isn't safe in her own home.* **4** informal boring or not deserving any respect: *Stay in on a Saturday night? What a sad idea!* —sadness n [U]

sadden /'sædn/ v [T] formal to make someone feel sad or disappointed: *They were shocked and saddened by his death.*

saddle¹ /'sædl/ n [C] **1** a seat made of leather that is put on a horse's back so that you can ride it **2** a seat on a bicycle or a MOTORCYCLE → see picture at BICYCLE

saddle² also **saddle up** v [I,T] to put a saddle on a horse

saddle sb with sth phr v to make someone have a job or problem that is difficult or boring and that they do not want: *I've been saddled with organizing the whole party!*

S

sadism /'seɪdɪzəm/ n [U] when someone gets enjoyment or sexual pleasure from being cruel or violent [➡ **masochism**] —**sadist** n [C] —**sadistic** /sə'dɪstɪk/ adj: a sadistic boss

sadly /'sædli/ adv

1 in a sad way: Jimmy nodded sadly.

2 unfortunately: Sadly, the concert was cancelled.

3 in a way that seems wrong or bad: Politeness is sadly lacking these days. | You're sadly mistaken if you think Anne will help.

sae /ˌes eɪ 'iː/ n [C] BrE stamped addressed envelope an envelope that you put your name and address and a stamp on, so that someone can send you something in it

safari /sə'fɑːri/ n [C,U] a trip through the country areas of Africa in order to watch wild animals: **on safari** We'll be going on safari in Kenya.

safe¹ /seɪf/ adj

1 not likely to cause injury or harm: Women are safer drivers than men. | Don't go near the edge – it isn't safe. | **Is it safe to** swim here? | **a safe trip/drive/journey** Have a safe trip! | **safe to use/drink etc** Is the water safe to drink?

2 [not before noun] not in danger of being lost, harmed, or stolen: She doesn't feel safe in the house on her own. | **+from** The city is now safe from further attack. | Both children were found **safe and sound** (=unharmed).

3 safe place a place where something is not likely to be stolen or lost: Keep your passport **in a safe place**.

4 not likely to be wrong or to fail: Gold is a safe investment. | I think **it's safe to say** that everyone is happy with the arrangement.

5 just to be safe/to be on the safe side in order to avoid a possible bad situation: Take some extra money with you, just to be on the safe side.

6 be in safe hands to be with someone who will look after you very well

—**safely** adv: Drive safely! | Did the package arrive safely?

safe² n [C] a strong metal box or cupboard with a lock on it, where you keep money and valuable things

safeguard /'seɪfgɑːd $ -gɑːrd/ n [C] a law, agreement or action that protects someone or something: **+against** Copy the data as a safeguard against loss or damage. —**safeguard** v [T] laws to safeguard endangered animals

safe 'haven n [C] a place where someone can go to escape from danger

safekeeping /ˌseɪf'kiːpɪŋ/ n **for safekeeping** if you put something somewhere for safekeeping, you put it in a place where it will not get damaged, lost, or stolen

safety /'seɪfti/ n [U]

1 the state of being safe from danger or harm: Some students are concerned about safety on campus. | **For your own safety**, please do not smoke inside the plane. | road safety (=being safe on roads) | **+of** There are fears for the safety of the hostages.

2 how safe something is to use, do etc: **+of** doubts about the safety of the drug | **safety standards/regulations/precautions etc** (=things that are done in order to make sure that something is safe) The device meets safety standards.

'safety belt n [C] a SEAT BELT

'safety net n [C] **1** a system that helps people when they are too ill, poor etc to help themselves: the safety net of unemployment pay and pensions **2** a large net that will catch an ACROBAT if they fall from a high place

'safety pin n [C] a wire pin with a cover that its point fits into

'safety valve n [C] **1** something that prevents a dangerous situation developing **2** a part of a machine that allows gas, steam etc to be let out when the pressure is too high

sag /sæg/ v [I] **sagged, sagging** to sink or bend down: The branches sagged under the weight of the snow.

saga /'sɑːgə/ n [C] a long story or a description of a long series of events

sage¹ /seɪdʒ/ n **1** [U] a plant used to give a special taste to food **2** [C] literary someone who is very wise

sage² adj literary very wise —**sagely** adv

Sagittarius /ˌsædʒɪ'teəriəs $ -'ter-/ n **1** [U] the sign of the Zodiac of people born between November 23 and December 21 **2** [C] someone who has this sign

said /sed/ v the past tense and past participle of SAY

sail¹ /seɪl/ v

1 [I] to travel across water in a boat or ship: **+across/into/out of etc** We sailed along the coast of Alaska. → see box at TRAVEL

2 [I,T] to control the movement of a boat or ship: The captain sailed the ship safely past the rocks. | I'd like to learn how to sail.

3 [I] to start a trip by boat or ship: What time do we sail?

4 [I] to move quickly and gracefully, especially through the air: **+into/out of/past etc** The ball sailed past the goalkeeper into the back of the net.

sail through sth phr v to succeed very easily in a test, examination etc: Adam sailed through his final exams.

sail² n **1** [C] a large piece of strong cloth fixed onto a boat, so that the wind will push the boat along: a yacht with white sails **2 set sail** to begin a trip by boat or ship: The ship set sail at dawn.

sailboat /'seɪlbəʊt $ -boʊt/ AmE; **'sailing boat** BrE n [C] a small boat with one or more sails

sailing /'seɪlɪŋ/ n [U] the activity of sailing in boats: They've invited us to **go sailing** this weekend. → see picture on page A9

sailor /'seɪlə $ -ər/ n [C] someone who sails on boats or ships, especially as a job [➡ **seaman**] → see picture at ARMED FORCES

saint /seɪnt/ n [C] **1** someone who is given the title 'saint' by the Christian church after they have died, because they have been very good and holy: Saint Patrick **2** spoken someone who is very good, kind, or patient: You're a real saint to help us like this.

saintly /'seɪntli/ adj very good, kind, and patient

sake /seɪk/ n **1 for the sake of sth** in order to help or improve a situation: Both sides are willing to take risks for the sake of peace. **2 for sb's sake** in order to help or please someone: She *only stays with her husband for the children's sake.* **3 for goodness'/Pete's/heaven's etc sake** *spoken* used to emphasize what you are saying, especially when you are annoyed: *Why didn't you tell me, for heaven's sake?*

salad /ˈsæləd/ *n* [C,U] a mixture of vegetables eaten cold and usually RAW: *a salad of lettuce, tomatoes, and cucumber* | *a large mixed salad* → see picture on page A5

salami /səˈlɑːmi/ *n* [C,U] a large SAUSAGE with a strong taste which is eaten cold in thin pieces

salary /ˈsæləri/ *n* [C,U] plural **salaries** money that you receive every month as payment from the organization you work for [→ **pay, wage**]: *The average salary is $39,000 a year.* | *people with **high salaries*** → see box at **MONEY**
—**salaried** *adj: salaried workers*

sale /seɪl/ *n*
1 [C,U] an act of selling something, or when something is sold: **+of** *The sale of alcohol to under-18s is forbidden.* | *John showed the customer several jackets, trying to **make a sale** (=sell something).*
2 for sale available to be bought: *Is this table for sale?* | *They had to **put** their home **up for sale** (=make it available to be bought).*
3 sales a) [plural] the total number of products that are sold during a particular period of time: **+of** *Sales of automobiles are up this year.* **b)** [U] the part of a company that deals with selling products: *Sally got a job as sales manager.*
4 [C] a time when a shop sells its goods at lower prices than usual: *There's a great sale on at Macy's now.* | *I bought it in a sale.*
5 on sale a) available to be bought: *Tickets will go on sale tomorrow.* **b)** *especially AmE* available to be bought at a lower price than usual: *Don's found a really good CD player on sale.*
→ **CAR BOOT SALE, JUMBLE SALE, RUMMAGE SALE**

saleable also **salable** *AmE* /ˈseɪləbəl/ *adj* something that is saleable can be sold, or is easy to sell: *salable products*

ˈsales asˌsistant *n* [C] *BrE* someone who sells things in a shop [= **shop assistant** *BrE*] → see box at **SHOP**

salesclerk /ˈseɪlzklɑːk $ -klɜːrk/ *n* [C] *AmE* someone who serves customers in a shop [= **shop assistant** *BrE*]

salesman /ˈseɪlzmən/ *n* [C] plural **salesmen** /-mən/ a man whose job is to sell things: *a car salesman*

salesperson /ˈseɪlzˌpɜːsən $ -ˌpɜːr-/ *n* [C] plural **salespeople** /-ˌpiːpəl/ someone whose job is to sell things

ˈsales repreˌsentative also **ˈsales rep** *n* [C] someone who travels around an area selling their company's products

saleswoman /ˈseɪlzˌwʊmən/ *n* [C] plural **saleswomen** /-ˌwɪmɪn/ a woman whose job is to sell things

salient /ˈseɪliənt/ *adj formal* the salient points or features of something are the most noticeable or important ones —**salience** *n* [U]

saline /ˈseɪlaɪn/ *adj* containing salt: *a saline solution* (=liquid with salt in it)

saliva /səˈlaɪvə/ *n* [U] the liquid that is produced naturally in your mouth

salivate /ˈsælɪveɪt/ *v* [I] to produce more saliva in your mouth than usual, especially because you see or smell food

sallow /ˈsæləʊ $ -loʊ/ *adj* sallow skin looks slightly yellow and unhealthy

salmon /ˈsæmən/ *n* [C,U] a large fish with silver skin and pink flesh: *smoked salmon*

salmonella /ˌsælməˈnelə/ *n* [U] a kind of BACTERIA in food that makes you ill

salon /ˈsælɒn $ səˈlɑːn/ *n* [C] a place where you can get your hair cut, have BEAUTY TREATMENTS etc: *a beauty salon*

saloon /səˈluːn/ *n* [C] **1** a place where alcoholic drinks were sold and drunk in the US in the 19th century **2** *BrE* a car that has a separate enclosed space for bags, cases etc [= **sedan** *AmE*]: *a four-door saloon*

salsa /ˈsælsə $ ˈsɑːl-/ *n* [U] **1** a hot-tasting SAUCE **2** a type of Latin American dance music

salt¹ /sɔːlt $ sɒːlt/ *n*
1 [U] a natural white mineral that is added to food to make it taste better: *Add a **pinch of salt** (=a small amount) to the mixture.* | *This might need some **salt and pepper**.* | *salt water* (=water that contains salt)
2 take sth with a pinch/grain of salt to not completely believe what someone tells you because you have reason to think that it might not be true

salt² *v* [T] to add salt to food: *salted peanuts*

ˈsalt ˌcellar *BrE*; **ˈsalt ˌshaker** *AmE n* [C] a small container for salt

saltwater /ˈsɔːltˌwɔːtə $ -ˌwɒːtər, -ˌwɑː-/ *adj* living in salty water: *saltwater fish*

salty /ˈsɔːlti $ ˈsɒːlti/ *adj* tasting of or containing salt → see box at **TASTE** —**saltiness** *n* [U]

salutary /ˈsæljʊtəri $ -teri/ *adj formal* a salutary experience is unpleasant but teaches you something

salute¹ /səˈluːt/ *v* [I,T] to move your right hand to your head to show respect to an officer in the army, navy etc

salute² *n* [C] **1** when someone salutes a person of higher rank: *As they left, the Corporal gave them a respectful **salute**.* **2** when guns are fired into the air as part of a military ceremony: *a 21-gun salute*

salvage /ˈsælvɪdʒ/ *v* [T] to save something from a situation in which other things have already been damaged, destroyed, or lost: **salvage sth from sth** *They managed to salvage only a few of their belongings from the fire.* —**salvage** *n* [U] *a salvage operation*

salvation /sælˈveɪʃən/ *n* [U] **1** the state of being saved from evil by God, according to the Christian religion **2** something that prevents danger, loss, or failure: *Donations of food and clothing have been the salvation of the refugees.*

salve /sælv, sɑːv $ sæv/ *v* [T] **salve your conscience** to make yourself feel less guilty about something you have done wrong

salvo /ˈsælvəʊ $ -voʊ/ *n* [C usually singular] plural **salvos** or **salvoes** *formal* **1** when several guns are fired during a battle or as part of a ceremony **2 opening/first salvo** the first in a series of things that you say or do to try to win an argument, competition etc

S

same¹ /seɪm/ *adj*

1 the same a) the same person, place, thing etc is one particular person etc and not a different one: *They go to the same place for their vacation every summer.* | *Kim's birthday and Roger's are on the same day.* **b)** used to say that two or more people, things, events etc are exactly like each other: *The same thing could happen again.* | *That's funny, Simon said exactly the same thing.* | **+as** *She does the same job as I do, but in a bigger company.*
2 at the same time a) if two things happen at the same time, they happen together: *How can you type and talk at the same time?* **b)** used when you want to say that something else is also true: *She was a little suspicious of him, but at the same time she liked him.*
3 the same old story/excuse etc *informal* something that you have heard many times before: *It's the same old story – his wife didn't understand him.*

GRAMMAR

Do not say 'a same'. Say **the same sort of**: *I'd like the same sort of car as that.*

same² *pron* **1 the same a)** used to say that two or more people, actions, or things are exactly like each other: **look/sound/taste etc the same** *The houses may look the same, but one's slightly larger.* **b)** used to say that a particular person or thing does not change: *'How's Danny?' 'Oh, he's the same as ever.'* **2 (and the) same to you!** *spoken* used as a reply to a greeting or as an angry reply to a rude remark: *'Have a good weekend!' 'Thanks, same to you!'*
3 all/just the same in spite of what has just been mentioned: *I realise she can be very annoying, but I think you should apologise all the same.*
4 same here *spoken* used to say that you feel the same way as someone else: *'I hate shopping malls.' 'Same here.'*

same³ *adv* **the same (as sth)** in the same way: *'Rain' and 'reign' are pronounced the same even though they are spelt differently.*

sample¹ /ˈsɑːmpəl $ ˈsæm-/ *n* [C] a small part or amount of something that is examined or tried to find out what the rest is like: **+of** *free samples of a new shampoo* | *Doctors take a **blood sample** to test for HIV.* | *The questionnaire was given to a **random sample** of students.*

sample² *v* [T] **1** to taste food or drink to see what it is like: *We sampled several local cheeses.* **2** to do something for the first time to see what it is like: *Win a chance to sample the exotic nightlife of Paris!*

sanatorium /ˌsænəˈtɔːriəm/ also **sanitarium** /ˌsænɪˈteəriəm $ -ˈter-/ *AmE n* [C] *old-fashioned* a hospital for people who are getting better but still need rest and care

sanctify /ˈsæŋktɪfaɪ/ *v* [T] **sanctified, sanctifying, sanctifies** to make something holy

sanctimonious /ˌsæŋktɪˈməʊniəs◂ $ -ˈmoʊ-/ *adj* behaving as if you are morally better than other people: *a long and sanctimonious speech*

sanction¹ /ˈsæŋkʃən/ *n* **1 sanctions** [plural] official orders or laws stopping trade, communication etc with another country, as a way of forcing its leaders to make political changes: **+against** *US sanctions against Cuba* **2** [U] *formal* official permission or approval: *The protest march was held without government sanction.* **3** [C] *formal* something such as a punishment that makes people obey a rule or law: *severe sanctions against those who avoid paying taxes*

sanction² *v* [T] *formal* to officially approve of or allow something: *The UN refused to sanction the use of force.*

sanctity /ˈsæŋktɪti/ *n* **the sanctity of sth** the fact that something is very important and must be respected and preserved: *the sanctity of marriage*

sanctuary /ˈsæŋktʃuəri, -tʃəri $ -tʃueri/ *n* plural **sanctuaries 1** [C,U] a peaceful place that is safe and provides protection, especially for people who are in danger: **seek/find sanctuary** *The refugees were seeking sanctuary in Australia.* **2** [C] an area for birds or animals where they are protected and cannot be hunted: **+for** *a sanctuary for tigers*

sanctum /ˈsæŋktəm/ *n* **the inner sanctum** *humorous* a place that only a few important people are allowed to enter: *We were only allowed into the director's inner sanctum for a few minutes.*

sand¹ /sænd/ *n*

1 [U] the substance that forms deserts and BEACHES, which consists of many very small pieces of rock: *a **grain of sand***
2 sands [plural] a large area of sand

sand² *v* [T] to make a surface smooth by rubbing it with SANDPAPER

sandal /ˈsændl/ *n* [C] a light open shoe that you wear in warm weather: *a pair of leather sandals* → see picture at **SHOE**¹

sandbag /ˈsændbæg/ *n* [C] a bag filled with sand, used for protection against floods, explosions etc

sandbank /ˈsændbæŋk/ *n* [C] a raised area of sand in a river, sea etc

sandbox /ˈsændbɒks $ -bɑːks/ *n* [C] *AmE* a SANDPIT

sandcastle /ˈsænd,kɑːsəl $ -,kæ-/ *n* [C] a small model of a castle made out of sand, usually by children on a BEACH

ˈsand dune *n* [C] a DUNE

sandpaper /ˈsænd,peɪpə $ -ər/ *n* [U] strong paper covered with a rough substance, used for rubbing wood in order to make it smooth

sandpit /ˈsænd,pɪt/ *BrE*; **sandbox** *AmE n* [C] an enclosed area of sand for children to play in

sandstone /ˈsændstəʊn $ -stoʊn/ *n* [U] a type of rock formed from sand

sandtrap /ˈsændtræp/ *n* [C] *AmE* a wide hole on a GOLF COURSE filled with sand [= bunker *BrE*]

sandwich¹ /ˈsænwɪdʒ $ ˈsændwɪtʃ, ˈsænwɪtʃ/ *n* [C] two pieces of bread with cheese, meat, egg etc between them: *chicken sandwiches*

sandwich² *v* **be sandwiched between sth** to be in a very small space between two other things: *a motorcycle sandwiched between two vans*

sandy /ˈsændi/ *adj* covered with or containing sand: *a sandy beach* | *sandy soil*

sane /seɪn/ adj **1** not mentally ill [≠ insane]: *He seems **perfectly** sane* (=completely sane) *to me.* **2** reasonable and sensible: *a sane solution to a difficult problem*

sang /sæŋ/ v the past tense of SING

sanguine /'sæŋgwɪn/ adj formal happy and hopeful about the future

sanitarium /ˌsænɪ'teəriəm $ -'ter-/ n [C] AmE a SANATORIUM

sanitary /'sænɪtəri $ -teri/ adj **1** [only before noun] relating to health, especially to the removal of dirt, infection, or human waste: *Workers complained about sanitary arrangements at the factory.* **2** clean and not involving any danger to your health: *All food is stored under sanitary conditions.*

'sanitary ˌtowel BrE; **'sanitary ˌnapkin** AmE n [C] a piece of soft material that a woman wears when she has her PERIOD, to take up the blood

sanitation /ˌsænɪ'teɪʃən/ n [U] the protection of public health by removing and treating waste, dirty water etc

sanitize also **-ise** BrE /'sænɪtaɪz/ v [T] to make news, literature etc less offensive or shocking by taking out anything unpleasant

sanity /'sænɪti/ n [U] **1** the quality of being reasonable and sensible **2** the condition of being mentally healthy [≠ insanity]: *He lost his sanity after his children were killed.*

sank /sæŋk/ v the past tense of SINK

Santa Claus /'sæntə klɔːz $ 'sænti klɔːz, 'sæntə-/, **Santa** n an imaginary old man with red clothes and a long white BEARD, who children believe brings them presents at Christmas [= Father Christmas BrE]

sap¹ /sæp/ n [U] the liquid that carries food through a plant

sap² v sapped, sapping **sap sb's/sth's strength/energy/confidence etc** to gradually make someone or something weaker, less confident etc: *The illness sapped her strength.*

sapling /'sæplɪŋ/ n [C] a young tree

sapphire /'sæfaɪə $ -faɪr/ n [C,U] a bright blue jewel

sappy /'sæpi/ adj AmE expressing love and emotions too strongly [= soppy BrE]

Saran Wrap /sə'ræn ræp/ n [U] trademark AmE thin transparent plastic used to wrap food [= clingfilm BrE]

sarcasm /'sɑːkæzəm $ 'sɑːr-/ n [U] when you say the opposite of what you mean in order to make an unkind joke or to show that you are annoyed: *There was a touch of sarcasm in her voice as she thanked him.*

sarcastic /sɑː'kæstɪk $ sɑːr-/ adj saying the opposite of what you mean in order to make an unkind joke or to show that you are annoyed: *a sarcastic comment* —**sarcastically** /-kli/ adv

sardine /ˌsɑː'diːn◂ $ ˌsɑːr-/ n [C,U] a small silver fish, often sold in cans

sardonic /sɑː'dɒnɪk $ sɑːr'dɑː-/ adj showing that you do not respect someone: *a sardonic smile*

sari /'sɑːri/ n [C] a long piece of cloth that you wrap around your body like a dress, worn especially by women from India

SARS /sɑːz $ sɑːrz/ n [U] **severe acute respiratory syndrome** a very serious illness that affects your lungs, that can develop into PNEUMONIA

sash /sæʃ/ n [C] a long piece of cloth that you wear around your waist or over one shoulder

sass /sæs/ v [T] AmE informal to talk in a rude way to someone you should respect

sassy /'sæsi/ adj especially AmE **1** a sassy child is rude to someone they should respect [= cheeky BrE] **2** confident and full of energy: *a sassy young woman | sassy music*

sat /sæt/ v the past tense and past participle of SIT

Sat. also **Sat** BrE the written abbreviation of **Saturday**

Satan /'seɪtn/ n [singular] a name for the Devil

satanic /sə'tænɪk/ adj relating to practices that treat the Devil like a god: *satanic rituals* —**satanism** /'seɪtənɪzəm/ n [U]

satchel /'sætʃəl/ n [C] a leather bag that children in the past used for carrying their books to school

satellite
a satellite photo

satellite /'sætɪlaɪt/ n [C] **1** a machine that is sent into space and travels around the Earth, moon etc. Satellites are used to send radio or television signals, or for other forms of communication: **by/via satellite** *This broadcast comes live via satellite from New York.* → see box at SPACE **2** a natural object such as a moon that moves around a PLANET

'satellite ˌdish n [C] a large circular piece of metal that is attached to a building and receives the SIGNALS for satellite television

ˌsatellite 'television also **ˌsatellite T'V** n [U] television programmes that are broadcast using satellites in space

satin /'sætɪn $ 'sætn/ n [U] a smooth, shiny cloth

satire /'sætaɪə $ -taɪr/ n **1** [U] using jokes to make a person or political party seem silly so that people will see their faults: *political satire* **2** [C] a play or story that uses satire: **+on** *a satire on political corruption* —**satirical** /sə'tɪrɪkəl/ adj

satirist /'sætɪrɪst/ n [C] someone who writes satire

satirize also **-ise** BrE /'sætɪraɪz/ v [T] to use jokes to make a person or political party seem silly so that people will see their faults

satisfaction /ˌsætɪs'fækʃən/ n **1** [C,U] a feeling of happiness or pleasure because you have achieved something or got what you wanted

S

[≠ **dissatisfaction**]: *She gets great satisfaction from her job.* | **with satisfaction** *Jo looked around the room with satisfaction.* **2** to **sb's satisfaction** as well or completely as someone wants: *I'm not sure I can answer that question to your satisfaction.*

satisfactory /ˌsætɪsˈfæktəriˎ/ *adj* good enough [≠ **unsatisfactory**; = **acceptable**]: *Your work this term has been satisfactory.* | **+to/for** *an agreement that is satisfactory to both sides* | **satisfactory explanation/solution/answer** *There seems to be no satisfactory explanation.* | **satisfactory result/outcome** *We managed to achieve a satisfactory result.*
—**satisfactorily** *adv*

satisfied /ˈsætɪsfaɪd/ *adj*

1 pleased because something has happened in the way that you want, or because you have achieved something [≠ **dissatisfied**]: **+with** *I'm not really satisfied with the way he cut my hair.* | *We have thousands of satisfied customers.*
2 feeling sure that something is right or true: **+(that)** *I'm satisfied that he's telling the truth.*

satisfy /ˈsætɪsfaɪ/ *v* [T] **satisfied**, **satisfying**, **satisfies** **1** to make someone happy by doing what they want: *I felt that nothing I did would ever satisfy my father.* **2** if you satisfy someone's needs or demands, you provide what they need or want: **satisfy sb's needs/requirements/demands** *We aim to satisfy the needs of our customers.* | **satisfy sb's hunger/appetite/thirst** *A salad won't be enough to satisfy your hunger.* **3** *formal* to make someone believe that something is true or right: **satisfy sb/yourself (that)** *I want to satisfy myself that everything's OK.*

satisfying /ˈsætɪsfaɪ-ɪŋ/ *adj* making you feel pleased and happy, especially because you have achieved something: *a satisfying job*

saturate /ˈsætʃəreɪt/ *v* [T] **1** to make something completely wet [= **soak**]: *Rain had saturated the ground.* **2** to fill a place with a lot of things, so there is no space for any more: **saturate with sth** *The market is saturated with cheap imports.* —**saturation** /ˌsætʃəˈreɪʃən/ *n* [U]

ˌsaturated ˈfat *n* [C,U] a kind of fat from meat and milk products

satuˈration ˌpoint *n* [singular] a situation in which no more people or things can be added because there are already too many: *The number of tourists has now reached saturation point.*

Saturday /ˈsætədi, -deɪ $ -ər-/ *n* [C,U] written abbreviation **Sat.** the day between Friday and Sunday
→ see examples at **MONDAY** → see box at **DAY**

Saturn /ˈsætən $ -ərn/ *n* the second largest PLANET, sixth from the sun

sauce /sɔːs $ sɒːs/ *n* [C,U] a thick liquid that is served with food to give it a nice taste: **tomato/wine/cheese etc sauce** *spaghetti with tomato sauce*
→ **SOY SAUCE**

saucepan /ˈsɔːspən $ ˈsɒːspæn/ *n* [C] a round metal container with a handle that you use for cooking → see picture at **KITCHEN**

saucer /ˈsɔːsə $ ˈsɒːsər/ *n* [C] a small round plate that you put under a cup: *a china cup and saucer*
→ **FLYING SAUCER**

saucy /ˈsɔːsi $ ˈsɒːsi/ *adj* about sex in a way that is amusing but not shocking: *saucy pictures*

sauna /ˈsɔːnə $ ˈsɒːnə, ˈsaʊnə/ *n* [C] **1** a room that is heated to a very high temperature, where people sit and relax **2** when you have a sauna, you spend time in a sauna

saunter /ˈsɔːntə $ ˈsɒːntər/ *v* [I] to walk in a slow relaxed way

sausage /ˈsɒsɪdʒ $ ˈsɒː-/ *n* [C,U] a mixture of meat and spices that is put into a small tube of skin and cooked: *beef sausages*

ˌsausage ˈroll *n* [C] a piece of sausage meat wrapped in PASTRY

sauté /ˈsəʊteɪ $ soʊˈteɪ/ *v* [T] to cook something quickly in a little hot oil or fat → see Thesaurus note at **COOK**

savage[1] /ˈsævɪdʒ/ *adj* **1** very cruel or violent: *a savage murder* **2** very severe: *a savage attack on the government* | *savage cuts in public spending* —**savagely** *adv* —**savagery** *n* [U]

savage[2] *v* [T] **1** if an animal savages someone, it attacks them and seriously injures them **2** to criticize someone or something very severely: *The movie was savaged by the critics.*

savage[3] *n* [C] *old-fashioned* an offensive word for someone who does not live in a modern society

save[1] /seɪv/ *v*

1 [T] to make someone or something safe from danger or harm [➡ **rescue**]: *The new speed limit could save many lives.* | **save sb/sth from sth** *Only three people were saved from the fire.* | *a campaign to save the old theatre*
2 also **save up** [I,T] to keep money so that you can use it later: *I've saved $600 so far.* | **+for** *We're saving up for a new car.*
3 also **save on** [T] to use less time, money, energy etc, so that you do not waste any [≠ **waste**]: *We'll save time if we take a taxi.* | *There are many ways to save on energy costs.*
4 [T] also **save sth ⇔ up** to keep something so that you can use or enjoy it in the future: *You can save up the vouchers and get free airline tickets.* | **save sth for sth** *We'd been saving the champagne for a special occasion.*
5 [T] to help someone by making it unnecessary for them to do something unpleasant or inconvenient: **save sb (doing) sth** *If you get some bread, it will save me a trip to the shops.* | *I'll give you a lift to save you waiting at the bus stop.*
6 [T] to stop people from using something, so that it is available for someone else [= **keep**]: **save sth for sb** *We'll save some dinner for you.* | **save sb sth** *Will you save me a seat?*
7 [T] to make a computer keep the work that you have done on it: *Don't forget to save the changes that you made.* → see box at **COMPUTER**
8 [I,T] to stop someone from scoring in games such as football: *The goalkeeper saved the shot.*
9 saving grace the one good thing that makes someone or something acceptable when everything else about them is bad: *His sense of humour was his only saving grace.*
→ **save face** at **FACE**[1]

save[2] *n* [C] when a player in a game such as football prevents the other team from scoring: *Martin made a brilliant save.*

saver /'seɪvə $ -ər/ n [C] someone who saves money in a bank

saving /'seɪvɪŋ/ n **1 savings** [plural] money that you have saved, usually in a bank: *He has savings of over $150,000.* | *a savings account* → see box at ACCOUNT **2** [C] an amount of money that you have not spent or an amount of something that you have not used: **+of** *a saving of 25%* | **+in** *savings in fuel consumption*

,savings and 'loan associ,ation n [C] AmE a business, similar to a bank, where you can save money or borrow money to buy a house [= building society BrE]

saviour BrE; **savior** AmE /'seɪvjə $ -ər/ n **1** [C] someone who saves you from a difficult or dangerous situation: **+of** *He was seen as the saviour of his people.* **2 the/our Saviour** in the Christian religion, Jesus Christ

savour BrE; **savor** AmE /'seɪvə $ -ər/ v [T] to make something last as long as possible, because you are enjoying it so much: *Drink it slowly and savour every drop.*

savoury BrE; **savory** AmE /'seɪvəri/ adj savoury food has a salty or spicy taste: *a savoury snack*

savvy /'sævi/ n [U] informal practical knowledge and ability: *political savvy*

saw[1] /sɔː $ sɒː/ v the past tense of SEE

saw[2] n [C] a tool that you use for cutting wood. It has a flat blade with a row of sharp points.

saw[3] v [I,T] past participle **sawed** or **sawn** /sɔːn $ sɒːn/ to cut something using a saw: *Dad was outside sawing logs.* → see box at CUT

sawdust /'sɔːdʌst $ 'sɒː-/ n [U] very small pieces of wood that are left when you cut wood with a saw

sawmill /'sɔːmɪl $ 'sɒː-/ n [C] a factory where trees are cut into boards

saxophone /'sæksəfəʊn $ -foʊn/ also **sax** /sæks/ informal n [C] a curved musical instrument made of metal that you play by blowing into it and pressing buttons, used especially in JAZZ → see picture on page A6

say[1] /seɪ/ v past tense and past participle **said** /sed/ third person singular **says** /sez/

1 [I,T] to express a thought or feeling in words: *'I'm so tired,' she said.* | *I'm sorry, I didn't hear what you said.* | **+(that)** *Dave said he'd call back.* | *He didn't seem to understand a word I said* (=anything I said). | **say how/why/who etc** *Did she say what happened?* | **say sth to sb** *What did you say to them?* | **say hello/goodbye/ thank you etc** *They left without saying goodbye.* | **say sorry/say you're sorry** (=apologize) *I've said I'm sorry, what more do you want?* | **a nice/nasty/silly etc thing to say** *That's a pretty mean thing to say.*

THESAURUS

mention – to say something but without giving many details: *He mentioned something about a party.*

add – to say something more about something: *Is there anything you'd like to add?*

express – to say how you feel about something: *It's hard to express how I felt.*

point out – to say something that other people had not noticed or thought of: *'It's upside down,' Liz pointed out.*

suggest/imply – to say something in an indirect way, especially something unpleasant: *He seemed to be suggesting that I'd stolen it!*

whisper – to say something very quietly: *'Is the baby asleep?' she whispered.*

mumble/mutter/murmur – to say something quietly so that your words are not clear: *He mumbled something about working late.* | *'It's not fair,' she muttered.*

USAGE

' Say ' cannot have a person as its object. Do not use 'say me'. Use 'tell me' instead. Compare these sentences: *He said that he was tired.* | *He told me that he was tired.*

2 [T] to give information in writing, pictures, or numbers: *The clock said nine thirty.* | *What do the instructions say?* | **+(that)** *He received a letter saying the appointment had been cancelled.* | **It says here** *the concert starts at 8.*

3 [T] to talk about what someone means: *What do you think the writer is* **trying to say?** | **be saying (that)** *Are you saying I'm fat?*

4 [T] used when talking about something that people think is true: **they say/people say/it is said (that)** *They say she's the richest woman in the world.*

5 [I,T] to express something without using words: *Your clothes* **say a lot about** *the kind of person you are.*

6 (let's) say spoken used when suggesting or imagining something: *Say you were going to an interview. What would you wear?*

7 say to yourself to think something: *I was worried about it, but I said to myself, 'You can do this.'*

8 I must say/I have to say spoken used to emphasize what you are saying: *That cake does look good, I must say.*

9 I would say spoken used for giving your opinion: *I'd say he's jealous.*

10 you can say that again spoken used to say that you agree with someone very strongly

11 it/that goes without saying used to say that the thing you have just mentioned is so clear that it really did not need to be said: *It goes without saying it will be a very difficult job.*

12 having said that spoken used when you are adding a different opinion to the one you have just expressed: *This isn't really a brilliant movie, but having said that, the kids should enjoy it.*

13 you don't say! spoken used to say that you are not at all surprised by what someone has told you

14 say when spoken used when you are pouring a drink for someone and you want them to tell you when there is enough in their glass

say[2] n [singular,U] **1** the right to help decide something: **have some/no/little say in sth** *Members felt that they had no say in the proposed changes.* | *Who has* **the final say** (=the final decision)? **2 have your say** to give your opinion on something: *You'll all have the chance to have your say.*

saying /'seɪ-ɪŋ/ n [C] a well-known phrase that people use to give advice [= proverb] → see box at PHRASE

S

scab /skæb/ n [C] a hard layer of dried blood that forms over a wound

scaffold /'skæfəld, -fəʊld $ -fəld, -foʊld/ n [C] **1** a structure of poles and boards that is built next to a building for people to stand on while they work on the building **2** a wooden frame on which criminals were killed in the past by being hanged

scaffolding /'skæfəldɪŋ/ n [U] poles and boards that are made into a structure for workers to stand on when they are working on a building

scaffolding

scald /skɔːld $ skɒːld/ v [T] to burn someone with hot liquid or steam: *The coffee scalded his tongue.* —**scald** n [C]

scalding /'skɔːldɪŋ $ skɒːl-/ also ,**scalding** 'hot adj extremely hot: *scalding tea*

scale[1] /skeɪl/ n

1 [singular, U] how big or important something is: **large-/small-scale** *a large-scale development project* | *The house is built on a grand scale.* | *People underestimated the sheer scale* (=very big size) *of the problem.*

2 [singular] the full range of different types of people or things: *One-third of the group had no qualifications at all while,* **at the other end of the scale**, *six were qualified teachers.* | *They came from opposite ends of the social scale.*

3 [C usually singular] a system for measuring how strong, fast, or good something is: **on a scale** *The earthquake measured 5.8 on the Richter scale.* | *Your papers will be marked on a scale of one to ten.*

4 scales [plural] BrE **scale** AmE a piece of equipment for weighing people or objects: *kitchen scales* | *a set of bathroom scales* (=for weighing people) → see picture at WEIGH

5 [C] a set of marks with regular spaces between them on a tool that is used for measuring things: *a ruler with a metric scale*

6 [C,U] the relationship between the size of a map, drawing, or model and the actual size of the place or thing that it shows: *a scale of 1 inch to the mile*

7 [C] a series of musical notes with a fixed distance between them that become gradually higher or lower

8 [C usually plural] the scales on a fish or snake are the small flat pieces of hard skin that cover its body → see picture on page A2

scale[2] v [T] to climb to the top of something that is high: *They scaled a 40-foot wall and escaped.*

scale sth ⇔ **back/down** phr v to reduce the size or effectiveness of something [➡ **decrease**]: *Military operations in the area have been scaled down.*

scale sth ⇔ **up** phr v to increase the size or effectiveness of something: *Production at the factory is being scaled up.*

scallop /'skɒləp, 'skæ- $ 'skɑː-/ n [C] a small sea creature that has a shell and can be eaten

scalloped /'skɒləpt, 'skæ- $ 'skɑː-/ adj scalloped edges are cut in a series of small curves

scalp[1] /skælp/ n [C] the skin on the top of your head

scalp[2] v [T] **1** to cut the scalp off a dead enemy as a sign of victory **2** AmE informal to buy tickets for an event and sell them again at a much higher price [= **tout** BrE]

scalpel /'skælpəl/ n [C] a small, very sharp knife that is used by doctors during operations

scalper /'skælpə $ -ər/ n [C] AmE someone who buys tickets for a concert, sports match etc and sells them at a higher price [= **tout** BrE]

scaly /'skeɪli/ adj **1** an animal that is scaly is covered with small flat pieces of hard skin called SCALES **2** scaly skin is dry and rough

scam /skæm/ n [C] informal a clever but dishonest way to get money

scamper /'skæmpə $ -ər/ v [I] to run with short quick steps, like a small animal: **+off/up/ through etc** *The boy scampered up the steps.*

scampi /'skæmpi/ n [plural] BrE PRAWNS covered in bread CRUMBS and cooked in oil

scan[1] /skæn/ v [T] scanned, scanning **1** to examine an area carefully, because you are looking for a particular person or thing: **scan sth for sth** *Lookouts were scanning the sky for enemy planes.* **2** also **scan through** to read something quickly: *I scanned through the report on the plane.* → see box at READ **3** if a machine scans something, it produces a picture of what is inside it: *All luggage has to be scanned at the airport.* **4** to copy a picture or piece of writing onto a computer by putting it into a machine attached to the computer: *You can scan the photos onto your PC.*

scan[2] n [C] a medical test in which a machine produces a picture of the inside of your body: *a brain scan*

scandal /'skændl/ n **1** [C] something dishonest or immoral that a famous or important person does which shocks a lot of people: **financial/ political/sexual etc scandal** *He was involved in a major financial scandal.* **2** [U] talk about dishonest or immoral things that famous or important people are believed to have done: *The magazine is full of gossip and scandal.*

scandalize also -ise BrE /'skændəlaɪz/ v [T] to make people feel very shocked

scandalous /'skændələs/ adj very bad or wrong: *scandalous mismanagement*

scanner /'skænə $ -ər/ n [C] **1** a machine that passes electronic waves through something in order to produce a picture of what is inside it **2** a machine that copies a picture or piece of writing from paper onto a computer

scant /skænt/ adj very little: *The story has received scant attention in the press.*

scanty /'skænti/ adj **1** very little: *They had obtained only scanty information.* **2** scanty clothes are very small and do not cover much of your body: *a scanty bikini* —**scantily** adv: *scantily dressed*

scapegoat /'skeɪpɡəʊt $ -ɡoʊt/ n [C] someone who is blamed for something bad that happens, even if it is not their fault: *Our department has been made a scapegoat for the company's difficulties.* —**scapegoat** v [T]

scar[1] /skɑː $ skɑːr/ n [C] **1** a permanent mark on someone's skin from a cut or wound: *The cut will leave a permanent scar.* → see box at MARK **2** a feeling of fear and sadness that stays with a person after a bad experience: *The community still bears the scars of the conflict.*

scar² /skɑː $ skɑːr/ *v* [T] **scarred, scarring** **1** if a wound or cut scars you, it leaves a permanent mark on your skin: *The fire had left him **scarred for life** (=for ever).* **2** if a bad experience scars you, it leaves you with a feeling of sadness and fear that continues for a long time: *She was deeply scarred by her father's suicide.*

scarce /skeəs $ skers/ *adj* if something is scarce, there is not enough of it available: *Food was often scarce in the winter.*

scarcely /'skeəsli $ 'sker-/ *adv* **1** hardly any at all: *The city had scarcely changed since we were last there.* | *The country has **scarcely any** industry.* → see box at **RARELY** **2** definitely not: *Owen is really angry, and you can scarcely blame him.*

scarcity /'skeəsɪti $ 'sker-/ *n* [singular] when there is not enough of something: **+of** *a scarcity of clean water*

scare¹ /skeə $ sker/ *v* [T]

1 to make someone feel frightened [= **frighten**]: *The fireworks will scare the animals.* | **scare the life/living daylights/hell etc out of sb** (=scare someone very much) *The alarm scared the life out of me.*
2 scare easily to easily become frightened: *I don't scare easily, you know.*

scare sb/sth ⇔ **off/away** *phr v* **1** to make someone or something go away by frightening them: *Move quietly or you'll scare the birds away.* **2** to make someone worried, so that they do not do something they were going to do: *Customers are being scared off by high prices.*

scare² *n* **1** [singular] a sudden feeling of fear: *You really **gave us a scare**.* **2** [C] a situation in which a lot of people become frightened about something: *a bomb scare*

scarecrow /'skeəkrəʊ $ 'skerkroʊ/ *n* [C] an object made to look like a person that is put in a field to frighten birds away

scarecrow

scared /skeəd $ skerd/ *adj* frightened or nervous about something [= **afraid**]: **+(that)** *We were scared that something terrible might happen.* | **scared of (doing) sth** *She's always been scared of flying.* | **scared stiff/scared to death** (=very frightened) *I'm scared stiff of spiders.* → see box at **FRIGHTENED**

scarf /skɑːf $ skɑːrf/ *n* [C] plural **scarves** /skɑːvz $ skɑːrvz/ or **scarfs** a piece of material that you wear around your neck, head, or shoulders → see picture at **CLOTHES**

scarlet /'skɑːlɪt $ -ɑːr-/ *n* [U] a bright red colour —**scarlet** *adj*

scary /'skeəri $ 'skeri/ *adj informal* frightening: *a scary movie*

scathing /'skeɪðɪŋ/ *adj* criticizing someone or something very strongly: *a **scathing attack** on the government*

scatter /'skætə $ -ər/ *v* **1** [T] to throw or drop things over a wide area: **scatter (sth) over/around/across etc sth** *Scatter the seeds over the*

ground. **2** [I,T] if people or animals scatter, or if something scatters them, they move quickly in different directions: *Guns started firing, and the crowd scattered in terror.*

scattered /'skætəd $ -ərd/ *adj* spread over a wide area or over a long period of time: *a scattered population* | *The weather forecast is for **scattered showers** (=short periods of rain).*

scattering /'skætərɪŋ/ *n* **a scattering of sth** *written* a small number of things or people spread out over a large area: *a scattering of isolated farms*

scavenge /'skævɪndʒ/ *v* [I,T] to search for food or useful objects among things that have been thrown away: **+for** *Children were scavenging for food.* —**scavenger** *n* [C]

scenario /sɔ'nɑːriəʊ $ -'nærioʊ, -'ner-/ *n* [C] plural **scenarios** a situation that could possibly happen: **worst-case/nightmare scenario** *The worst-case scenario would be if the college had to close.*

scene /siːn/ *n*

1 [C] a short part of a play or film, when the events happen in one place: *the opening scene of the film* | *a love scene*
2 [singular] a set of activities and the people who are involved in them: **the music/fashion/political etc scene** *The London music scene* | *I'm not into the **club scene** (=going to nightclubs) at all.*
3 [singular] the place where an accident or crime happened: **at the scene** *Firefighters arrived at the scene within minutes.* | **+of** *the scene of the crime*
4 [C] a view or picture of a place: *a peaceful country scene*
5 [C] a loud angry argument in a public place: *Sit down and stop **making a scene!***
6 behind the scenes working secretly, while other things are happening publicly: *People are working hard behind the scenes.*
7 set the scene a) to provide the conditions in which an event can happen: **+for** *This agreement sets the scene for democratic elections.* **b)** to describe the situation before you tell a story

scenery /'siːnəri/ *n* [U]

1 the natural features of a place, such as the mountains, forests etc: **beautiful/spectacular/dramatic etc scenery** *Alaska's magnificent scenery* | *It's an area of wild **mountain scenery** and unspoilt villages.* → see box at **VIEW**
2 the large pictures of buildings, countryside etc used at the back of a theatre stage

scenic /'siːnɪk/ *adj* a scenic place or road has beautiful views of the countryside: *Let's take the **scenic coastal route**.*

scent¹ /sent/ *n* **1** [C] a pleasant smell: **+of** *the scent of roses* **2** [C] the smell that an animal or person leaves behind them: *The dogs soon **picked up** the fox's **scent** (=were able to follow the smell).* **3** [C,U] *especially BrE* a liquid with a pleasant smell that you put on your skin [= **perfume**] → see box at **SMELL**

scent² *v* [T] **1** if an animal scents another animal or a person, it knows that they are near because it can smell them **2** *written* to suddenly think that something is going to happen or exists: *We **scented danger** and decided to leave.*

S

scented /'sentɨd/ *adj* having a pleasant smell: *scented soap*

sceptic *BrE*; **skeptic** *AmE* /'skeptɪk/ *n* [C] someone who doubts whether something is true or right

sceptical *BrE*; **skeptical** *AmE* /'skeptɪkəl/ *adj* doubting whether something is true or right: **+about/of** *I'm highly sceptical about what I read in the press.*

scepticism *BrE*; **skepticism** *AmE* /'skeptɨsɪzəm/ *n* [U] when someone doubts whether something is true or right

schedule[1] /'ʃedjuːl, 'ske- $ 'skedʒʊl, -dʒəl/ *n*
1 [C,U] a plan of what someone is going to do, or when work is to be done: **on schedule** (=at the planned time) *The project looks like finishing on schedule.* | **ahead of/behind schedule** (=earlier or later than the planned time) *Meg's book was written well ahead of schedule.* | **busy/tight schedule** (=a plan that includes a lot of things to be done in a short time) *I have a busy schedule this week.* | **+of** *a schedule of meetings* → see box at PLAN
2 [C] *AmE* a list that shows the times that buses, trains etc leave or arrive [= **timetable** *BrE*]
3 [C] a formal written list: **+of** *a schedule of postal charges*

schedule[2] *v* [T usually passive] to arrange that something will happen at a particular time: **schedule sth for sth** *The meeting has been scheduled for Friday.* | **scheduled flight/service** (=a plane service that flies at the same time every day or every week) *daily scheduled flights to Paris*

scheme[1] /skiːm/ *n* [C]
1 *BrE* an official plan that is intended to help people or to achieve something [= **program** *AmE*]: **+for** *a government training scheme for young people* | *a pension scheme* | **scheme to do sth** *schemes to encourage people to recycle waste* → see box at PLAN
2 an idea or plan that someone has, especially a slightly dishonest or stupid one: *a crazy scheme for making money*

scheme[2] *v* [I] to make secret plans to get or achieve something, often dishonestly: **scheme to do sth** *politicians scheming to win votes* —**schemer** *n* [C]

schizophrenia /ˌskɪtsəʊˈfriːniə, -sə- $ -soʊ-, -sə-/ *n* [U] a serious mental illness in which someone thinks that imaginary events, conversations, ideas etc are really happening or true —**schizophrenic** /-ˈfrenɪk◂/ *adj, n* [C]

scholar /'skɒlə $ 'skɑːlər/ *n* [C] someone who studies a subject and knows a lot about it: *a Latin scholar*

scholarly /'skɒləli $ 'skɑːlərli/ *adj* relating to or involved with the serious study of a subject: *a scholarly journal*

scholarship /'skɒləʃɪp $ 'skɑːlər-/ *n* **1** [C] an amount of money given to someone by an organization to help pay for their education
2 [U] the knowledge, work, or methods used in serious studying

school /skuːl/ *n*
1 [C,U] a place where children are taught: *I went to school* (=attended a school) *in London.* | *Lizzie's starting a new school* (=different school) *in*

September. | *a school trip to the sea* | **at school** *BrE*/**in school** *AmE* (=in the school building) *I work while the kids are at school.*

COLLOCATIONS

school children/pupils/teachers
school uniform
school curriculum – the subjects that are taught at school –
school playground/library/bus
school meal/school dinner *BrE*/**school lunch** *AmE*
school holiday(s) *BrE*

TOPIC

What you do at school
At school, you **study/learn** a range of subjects. You have **classes** or **lessons** *BrE* with a **teacher**. After school, you have to **do homework**. Before you **take exams**, you have to **revise/do revision** *BrE*.
→ UNIVERSITY

2 [U] **a)** the day's work at school: *School begins at 9 o'clock.* | *I'll meet you after school.* **b)** the time in your life that you spend at school: *She started school when she was four.* | **at school** *BrE* (=attending a school, not at university, doing a job etc) *John's only 14, so he's still at school.* | *What do you want to do when you leave school?*
3 [singular] all the students and teachers at a school: *The whole school was sorry when she left.*
4 [C,U] *AmE* a university or college: *She was going to school in Boston.* | **in school** (=attending a university or school rather than having a job) *Are your boys still in school?*
5 [C,U] a college or a department at a university that teaches a particular subject: **law/business/medical school** *If I pass my exams, I'll go to medical school.* | *the London School of Economics*
6 riding/driving/language etc school an organization that teaches a particular skill or subject: *an English language school* | *the Amwell School of Motoring*
7 [C] a group of painters or writers whose style of work is similar: *the Dutch school of painting*
8 school of thought an opinion that is shared by a group of people: *One school of thought is that red wine is good for you.*
9 [C] a large group of fish etc swimming together: **+of** *a school of dolphins* → see box at GROUP
10 of the old school of the kind that used to exist or be typical: *a soldier of the old school*
→ COMPREHENSIVE SCHOOL, HIGH SCHOOL, NURSERY SCHOOL, PRIVATE SCHOOL, PUBLIC SCHOOL

GRAMMAR

Do not use 'the' before **school** when you are talking about someone studying or teaching there: *What time do you leave for school in the morning?*
Use 'the' before **school** if someone goes there for some other reason, not to study or teach: *We all went to see the play at the school.*
You must also use 'the' if you describe exactly which school you are talking about: *the local school.*

S

schoolboy /'sku:lbɔɪ/ *n* [C] *especially BrE* a boy who goes to school

schoolchild /'sku:l.tʃaɪld/ *n* [C] plural **schoolchildren** /-.tʃɪldrən/ a child who goes to school

schooldays /'sku:ldeɪz/ *n* [plural] the time in your life when you go to school

schoolgirl /'sku:lɡɜ:l $ -ɡɜ:rl/ *n* [C] *especially BrE* a girl who goes to school

schooling /'sku:lɪŋ/ *n* [U] education at school

'school-,leaver *n* [C] *BrE* someone who has just finished their education at school

schoolteacher /'sku:l.ti:tʃə $ -ər/ *n* [C] a teacher in a school

science /'saɪəns/ *n*

1 [C,U] knowledge about the physical world based on testing and proving facts, or work that results in this knowledge: *the teaching of science in schools* | *the **physical sciences** (=subjects such as physics and chemistry)* | *developments in **science and technology*** | *the advances of **medical science***

2 [C,U] the study of a particular type of human behaviour: *political science*

→ **EARTH SCIENCE, SOCIAL SCIENCE**

,science 'fiction *n* [U] books and stories about the future, for example about travelling in time and space → see box at **BOOK** → and **FILM**

scientific /,saɪən'tɪfɪk◂/ *adj*

1 relating to science: *scientific discoveries* | *a **scientific experiment*** | *advances in **scientific research***

2 using an organized system: *We keep records, but we're not very scientific about it.*
—**scientifically** /-kli/ *adv*

scientist /'saɪəntɪst/ *n* [C] someone who studies or works in science

sci-fi /,saɪ 'faɪ◂/ *n* [U] *informal* SCIENCE FICTION

scintillating /'sɪntɪleɪtɪŋ/ *adj* very exciting, impressive, or interesting: *a scintillating speech*

scissors /'sɪzəz $ -ərz/ *n* [plural] a tool for cutting paper or cloth, with two sharp blades that are joined together, and handles with holes for your finger and thumb: *a **pair of scissors*** → see picture at CLASSROOM

scoff /skɒf $ skɒ:f, skɑ:f/ *v* [I] **1** to laugh at a person or idea and talk about them in a way that shows that you think they are stupid: **+at** *David scoffed at my fears.* **2** *BrE informal* to eat a lot of something quickly

scold /skəʊld $ skoʊld/ *v* [I,T] to tell someone in an angry way that they have done something wrong: **scold sb for sth** *Her father scolded her for upsetting her mother.* —**scolding** *n* [C,U]

scone /skɒn, skəʊn $ skoʊn, skɑ:n/ *n* [C] a small round cake that you eat with butter or cream and JAM

scoop¹ /sku:p/ *n* [C] **1** a deep spoon for serving food, or the amount that a scoop contains: *two scoops of ice-cream* **2** an exciting news story that is reported by one newspaper, television station etc before any of the others know about it

scoop² *v* [T] to remove or lift something with a spoon or with your curved hand: **scoop sth out/up** *Cut the melon and scoop out the seeds.*

scoot /sku:t/ *v* [I] *informal* to leave a place quickly: *You kids, get out of here – scoot!*

scooter /'sku:tə $ -ər/ *n* [C] **1** a small two-wheeled vehicle with an engine **2** a board on wheels with an upright handle. You stand on it with one foot and push against the ground with the other to make it move along. → see picture at TRANSPORT

scope /skəʊp $ skoʊp/ *n* **1** [singular] the range of things that a subject, book, activity etc deals with: **within/beyond/outside the scope of sth** *Such questions are beyond the scope of this book.* **2** [U] the opportunity to do or develop something: **+for** *a house with scope for improvement*

scorch /skɔːtʃ $ skɔːrtʃ/ *v* [I,T] if you scorch something, or if it scorches, its surface burns slightly and becomes brown: *Even the walls were scorched by the fire.* —**scorch** *n* [C] *scorch marks from the iron*

scorching /'skɔːtʃɪŋ $ 'skɔːr-/ *adj informal* scorching weather is very hot: *the **scorching heat** of an Australian summer* → see box at HOT

score¹ /skɔː $ skɔːr/ *n* [C]

1 the number of points that each team or player has won in a game or competition: **+of** *a score of 3–2* | *What's the score?* | *The **final score** was 35 to 17.*

2 the number of points that one person or group gets in a test [= mark]: **+of** *Sammy got a **top score** of 90%.* | *research based on children's **test scores***

3 know the score to know the facts about a person or situation, including any unpleasant ones: *You knew the score when you married him.*

4 a printed copy of a piece of music

5 scores of sth a large number of people or things: *Scores of buildings were damaged in the blast.*

6 on that score *spoken* concerning the thing you have just mentioned: *As for the cost – don't worry on that score.*

7 settle a score to do something to harm someone who has harmed you in the past

score² *v*

1 [I,T] to get points in a game, competition, or test: *Dallas scored in the final minute of the game.* | **score a goal/point/run etc** *How many goals has he scored this year?* | *She scored 75% in the exam.*

2 [T] to give a particular number of points in a game, competition, or test [= mark]: *Teachers score the answers on a scale of 1 to 6.*

3 [I,T] *informal* to be successful or succeed in getting something you want: *Barnes has scored again with another popular book.* | *The JET project scored a major success.*

4 score points (off/over sb) also **score off sb** *BrE* to try to prove that you are better or cleverer than someone else: *The two guys were trying to score points off each other in front of her.*

5 [T] to mark a line on a piece of paper, wood etc with something sharp

scoreboard /'skɔːbɔːd $ 'skɔːrbɔːrd/ *n* [C] a large board on which the score of a game is shown

scorer /'skɔːrə $ -ər/ *n* [C] **1** someone who scores a GOAL, point etc in a game **2** someone who officially records the number of points won in a game

scorn¹ /skɔːn $ skɔːrn/ *n* [U] complete lack of respect for someone or something because you think they are stupid or not good: **with scorn**

S

*Scientists **treated** the findings **with scorn**.* | *Critics **poured scorn on** the idea* (=criticized it strongly). —**scornful** *adj* —**scornfully** *adv*

scorn² *v* [T] *formal* to show that you think that a person, idea, or suggestion is stupid or not worth considering: *young people who scorn the attitudes of their parents*

Scorpio /ˈskɔːpiəʊ $ ˈskɔːrpioʊ/ *n* plural **Scorpios** **1** [U] the sign of the Zodiac of people born between October 24 and November 22 **2** [C] someone who has this sign

scorpion /ˈskɔːpiən $ -ɔːr-/ *n* [C] a creature like a large insect with a curved tail which has a poisonous sting

Scotch /skɒtʃ $ skɑːtʃ/ *n* [C,U] a strong alcoholic drink made in Scotland, or a glass of this drink [= **whisky**]

ˌScotch ˈtape *n* [U] *trademark AmE* thin clear TAPE used for sticking things together [= **Sellotape** *BrE*] → see picture at **CLASSROOM**

scoundrel /ˈskaʊndrəl/ *n* [C] *old-fashioned* a bad or dishonest man or boy

scour /skaʊə $ skaʊr/ *v* [T] **1** to search somewhere for something very carefully: **scour sth for sth** *I've scoured the whole area for a suitable house.* **2** to clean something by rubbing it with something rough

scourge /skɜːdʒ $ skɜːrdʒ/ *n* [C] *formal* something that causes a lot of harm or suffering: **+of** *the scourge of war*

scout¹ /skaʊt/ *n* [C] **1 a) the Scouts** an organization that teaches young people practical skills and good behaviour **b)** also **Boy Scout, Girl Scout** a boy or girl who is a member of this organization [→ **guide**] **2** a soldier who is sent in front of an army to search an area and get information

scout² *v* [I] to look for something in an area: **+for** *I'll scout around for a place to eat.*

scowl /skaʊl/ *v* [I] to look at someone in an angry way: **+at** *Don't scowl at me!* —**scowl** *n* [C]

scrabble /ˈskræbəl/ *v* [I] to quickly feel around with your fingers in order to find something: **+for** *She scrabbled around for the light.*

scramble /ˈskræmbəl/ *v* [I] **1** to quickly climb up or over something difficult, using your hands to help you: **+up/down/over etc** *The kids were scrambling over the rocks.* **2** to move somewhere quickly, especially in order to compete with other people to get something: *Mick scrambled to his feet* (=stood up very quickly). | **+for** *Everyone was scrambling for shelter.* —**scramble** *n* [singular] *It was a tough scramble to the top.* | *the usual scramble for the bathroom*

ˌscrambled ˈegg *n* [C,U] one or more eggs which are mixed together and cooked

scrap¹ /skræp/ *n* **1** [C] a small piece of paper, cloth etc: **+of** *He wrote his address on a scrap of paper.* **2** [C] a small amount of information, truth etc: **+of** *There isn't a scrap of evidence against him.* **3** [U] metal and parts from old or damaged cars and machines, which can be used again in another way: *Scrap metal fetched high prices after the War.* | *You'd better **sell** the car for **scrap** – it's not worth fixing.* **4** [C] *informal* a short fight or argument: *He had a scrap with one of the boys at school.* → see box at **FIGHT** **5 scraps** [plural] pieces of food that are left after you have finished eating: *scraps for the dog*

scrap² *v* [T] **scrapped, scrapping** *informal* to decide not to do something or keep something: *We've scrapped the idea of renting a car.*

scrapbook /ˈskræpbʊk/ *n* [C] a book with empty pages where you can stick pictures, newspaper articles, or other things you want to keep

scrape¹ /skreɪp/ *v* **1** [T] to remove something from a surface using the edge of a knife, stick etc: **scrape sth away/off** *Scraping away the sand, they found a hidden entrance.* | **scrape sth off/into etc sth** *Scrape some of the mud off your boots.* → see box at **REMOVE** **2** [T] to damage something slightly by rubbing it against a rough surface: *She fell and scraped her knee.* | **scrape sth against/on sth** *Careful! You nearly scraped the car on the wall!* **3** [I,T] to make an unpleasant noise by rubbing against a surface: *Chairs scraped loudly as they stood up.*

scrape by *phr v* to have enough money to live, but only with difficulty: *They have to scrape by on her tiny salary.*

scrape through (sth) *phr v* to succeed in passing an examination, competition etc, but only with difficulty: *Nick just managed to scrape through his degree course.*

scrape sth ⇔ **together/up** *phr v* to get enough money for something with difficulty: *We're trying to scrape together enough money for a vacation.*

scrape² *n* [C] **1** slight damage or injury caused by rubbing against a rough surface [= **graze**]: *She wasn't badly hurt – only a few **cuts and scrapes**.* **2** *informal* a situation in which you are in trouble or have difficulties: *He got **into** all sorts of scrapes as a boy.* **3** the unpleasant noise of one surface rubbing roughly against another: **+of** *the scrape of chalk on the blackboard*

scrapheap /ˈskræphiːp/ *n* **on the scrapheap** no longer wanted or considered useful: *When I lost my job, I felt I was on the scrapheap.*

scrappy /ˈskræpi/ *adj* **1** *BrE* untidy or badly organized: *a scrappy, badly written report* **2** *AmE informal* determined and always willing to compete, argue, or fight: *a scrappy team*

scratch¹ /skrætʃ/ *v* [I,T] **1** to rub your skin with your nails to stop it feeling uncomfortable: *Try not to scratch those mosquito bites.* → see picture on page A10 **2** to make a long thin cut on someone's skin with your nails, or a mark on something with a sharp object: *She bit him and scratched his face.* | *I'm afraid I've scratched your car.* **3** if an animal scratches, it rubs its foot against something, making a noise: **+at** *My dog scratches at the door when it wants to come in.* **4** to remove something from a surface using something sharp: **scratch sth off/away etc** *I managed to scratch off the paint.* **5 scratch the surface** to deal with only a very small part of a problem: *Our aid can only scratch the surface of the problem.*

scratch² *n* **1** [C] a long thin cut or mark on something: *Her face was covered in scratches.* **2 from scratch** if you do something from scratch, you start it from the beginning, sometimes for the second time: *I deleted the file by mistake and had to start again from scratch.* **3 up to scratch** *BrE informal* good enough: *Some of your work isn't up to scratch.* **4** [singular] especially *BrE* when you rub your skin with your nails: *Can you give my back **a scratch**?*

scratchcard /'skrætʃkɑːd $ -kɑːrd/ n [C] BrE a card that you can buy which gives you a chance of winning money or a prize. You rub off the surface to see whether you have won.

scrawl /skrɔːl $ skrɒːl/ v [T] to write something in a careless or untidy way: *Charlie scrawled his name on the wall.* —**scrawl** n [C,U] *The letter finished in a scrawl.*

scrawny /'skrɔːni $ 'skrɒː-/ adj thin and weak: *a scrawny little kid*

scream¹ /skriːm/ v

1 [I] to make a loud high noise because you are hurt, frightened, angry, or excited: *There was a bang and people started screaming.* | **+with/in** *She jumped up screaming in terror.* | *kids in the playground screaming with laughter*

2 also **scream out** [I,T] to shout something in a very loud high voice because you are afraid or angry [= yell]: +**for** *I screamed out for help.* | *'Get out!' she screamed.* → see box at SHOUT

scream² n [C]

1 a loud high noise that you make when you are hurt, frightened, angry, or excited: +**of** *a scream of rage* | *She saw the knife and let out a scream.*

COLLOCATIONS

shrill/piercing – very loud, high, and unpleasant
high-pitched – very high
ear-splitting – very loud
bloodcurdling – very frightening
terrible – very frightening or upsetting
→ SHOUT

2 be a scream informal to be very funny: *The play was a scream!*

screech /skriːtʃ/ v **1** [I,T] to shout loudly in an unpleasant high voice: *'Get out of my way!' she screeched.* **2** [I] if a vehicle screeches, its wheels makes a high unpleasant noise as it moves along or stops: *A police car sped round the corner, tyres screeching.* | *The train screeched to a halt.* —**screech** n [C]

screen¹ /skriːn/ n

1 [C] the part of a television or computer where the picture or information appears [→ monitor]: *a computer with an 18-inch screen* | **on (the) screen** *the flickering images on the screen* | *You can edit the text on screen.*

2 [C] a large white surface that a film is shown on in a cinema: *The town has nine cinema screens and over 300 restaurants.*

3 [singular,U] films in general: **on screen** *his first appearance on screen* | *The play is being adapted for the big screen* (=the cinema).

4 [C] an upright piece of furniture like a thin wall, used for dividing one part of a room from another

5 [C] something that hides a place or thing: +**of** *a house hidden behind a screen of trees*

screen² v [T] **1** to do medical tests on people to find out whether they have a particular illness: **screen sb for sth** *All women over 50 are screened for breast cancer.* **2** to find out information about people in order to decide whether they can be trusted in a particular job: *People wanting to work with children are thoroughly screened.* **3** also **screen off** to hide something, or separate it from another area, by putting

something in front of it: *The garden is screened by tall hedges.* **4** to show a film or television programme

screenplay /'skriːnpleɪ/ n [C] a story written for film or television

'screen ˌsaver n [C] a moving picture that appears on a computer screen while you are not using the computer

screenwriter /'skriːnˌraɪtə $ -ər/ n [C] someone who writes plays for film or television

screw¹ /skruː/ n [C] a thin pointed piece of metal that you push and turn to fasten pieces of wood, metal etc together [→ nail]

screw² v **1** [T] to fasten one thing to another, using a screw: **screw sth into/onto/to sth** *Screw the shelf to the wall.* **2** [I,T] to fasten or close something by twisting it around until it is tight [≠ unscrew]: **screw sth on/onto sth** *Don't forget to screw the lid on.* **3** also **screw up** [T] to twist paper or cloth into a small round shape: *She screwed the letter up and flung it in the bin.*

screw up phr v **1** informal to spoil something or to make a bad mistake [= mess up]: *You'd better not screw up again!* | **screw sth ⇔ up** *The bad weather screwed up our holiday plans.* **2 screw up your eyes/face** to make your eyes become narrow by changing the expression on your face

screwdriver /'skruːˌdraɪvə $ -ər/ n [C] a tool that you use for turning screws

ˌscrewed 'up adj informal very unhappy or anxious because you have had a lot of bad experiences

scribble /'skrɪbəl/ v **1** also **scribble down** [T] to write something quickly in an untidy way: *I scribbled his number on my hand.* → see box at WRITE **2** [I] to draw marks that do not mean anything —**scribble** n [C,U]

script /skrɪpt/ n **1** [C] the written form of a speech, play, film etc **2** [C,U] the letters used in writing a language: *Arabic script*

scripted /'skrɪptɪd/ adj a scripted speech or broadcast has been planned and written down before it is read

scripture /'skrɪptʃə $ -ər/ n [U] also **the Scriptures** the holy books of a religion, for example the Bible

scriptwriter /'skrɪptˌraɪtə $ -ər/ n [C] someone who writes the stories and words for films or television programmes

scroll¹ /skrəʊl $ skroʊl/ n [C] a long document that is rolled up

scroll² v [I,T] to move information up or down a computer screen so that you can read it

scrooge /skruːdʒ/ n [C] informal someone who hates spending money

scrounge /skraʊndʒ/ v [T] to get money or something you want by asking other people for it: **scrounge sth off/from sb** *I'll try to scrounge some money off my dad.* —**scrounger** n [C]

scrub¹ /skrʌb/ v [I,T] **scrubbed, scrubbing** to clean something by rubbing it hard, especially with a brush: *Tom was on his knees, scrubbing the floor.*

scrub² n **1** [U] low bushes and trees growing in a dry place **2** [singular] if you give something a scrub, you clean it by rubbing it hard

scruff /skrʌf/ n **by the scruff of the/your neck** by the back of a person's or animal's neck: *She grabbed him by the scruff of the neck.*

S

scruffy /'skrʌfi/ *adj* dirty and untidy: *a scruffy pair of jeans* | *a scruffy kid* → see box at CLOTHES

scrum /skrʌm/ *n* [C] when players in a game of RUGBY form a tight circle and push against each other, with their heads down, to try to get the ball

scrunch /skrʌntʃ/ *v*
scrunch sth ⇔ **up** *phr v* to twist and press a piece of paper into a ball: *He scrunched up the letter and threw it in the bin.*

scruples /'skru:pəlz/ *n* [plural] a belief that something is wrong, which stops you from doing it: *He has no scruples about lying.*

scrupulous /'skru:pjələs/ *adj* **1** always careful to be honest and fair: *Not all car dealers are scrupulous.* **2** if you do something in a scrupulous way, you do it very carefully and well: *The names are all checked with scrupulous attention to detail.* —**scrupulously** *adv*: *The kitchen must be scrupulously clean.*

scrutinize also **-ise** *BrE* /'skru:tɪnaɪz/ *v* [T] to examine something very carefully: *He scrutinized the document closely.*

scrutiny /'skru:tɪni/ *n* [U] when people examine or watch something very carefully: *Her marriage has come under public scrutiny recently.*

scuba diving /'sku:bə ˌdaɪvɪŋ/ *n* [U] the sport of swimming under water using a container of air on your back to help you breathe → see picture on page A9

scuff /skʌf/ *v* [T] if you scuff your shoes, you accidentally rub them against something rough and leave a mark on them

scuffle /'skʌfəl/ *n* [C] a short fight: *A scuffle broke out between demonstrators and the police.* → see box at FIGHT —**scuffle** *v* [I] *Demonstrators scuffled with the police.*

sculptor /'skʌlptə $ -ər/ *n* [C] someone who makes sculptures

sculpture /'skʌlptʃə $ -ər/ *n* **1** [C,U] a work of art made from stone, wood, clay etc: *a bronze sculpture of a horse* | *an exhibition of modern sculpture* **2** [U] the art of making objects out of stone, wood, clay etc: *She teaches painting and sculpture.* → see box at ART

scum /skʌm/ *n* **1** [U] an unpleasant dirty layer that sometimes forms on the surface of a liquid: *a pond covered with green scum* **2** [plural] *informal* nasty, unpleasant people: *Scum like that should be locked away!*

scurrilous /'skʌrɪləs $ 'skɜ:r-/ *adj* scurrilous remarks say unpleasant, untrue things about a person

scurry /'skʌri $ 'skɜ:ri/ *v* [I] **scurried, scurrying**, **scurries** to move very quickly with small steps: **+away/along/across etc** *The mouse scurried away.* | *She scurried off to work.*

scuttle /'skʌtl/ *v* [I] to move quickly with small steps: **+across/away/off etc** *The spider scuttled away.*

scythe /saɪð/ *n* [C] a tool with a long curved blade that is used for cutting long grass or grain

SE the written abbreviation of **southeast** or **south-eastern**

sea /si:/ *n* [C,U]
1 a large area of salty water [➡ **ocean**]: *the Mediterranean Sea* | *The sea was lovely and calm.* | *The sea was too rough for sailing.* | *swimming in the sea* | *I've always wanted to live by the sea.* | **at sea** *We spent the next six weeks at sea.* | **by sea** *It's cheaper to send goods by sea than by air.* | **out to sea** *The small boat drifted out to sea.* | **the high seas** (=the areas of sea that are not near any country) | *The boat sank in heavy seas* (=when the sea was rough).
2 a sea of sth a very large number of people or things: *He stared at the sea of faces in front of him.*

seabed /'si:bed/, **'sea bed** *n* **the seabed** the land at the bottom of the sea

'sea change *n* [C] a very big change in something: *There's been a sea change in his attitude.*

seafood /'si:fu:d/ *n* [U] fish and animals from the sea that you can eat

seafront /'si:frʌnt/ *n* [C usually singular] a part of a town next to the sea: *a hotel on the seafront*

seagull /'si:gʌl/ also **gull** *n* [C] a common grey and white bird that lives near the sea

seal¹ /si:l/ *n* [C] **1** a large sea animal that eats fish and lives by the sea in cold areas **2** a piece of paper or plastic that you break to open a container: *Do not use this product if the seal on the bottle is broken.* **3** a mark that has a special design and is put on documents to show that they are legal or official: *The letter had the seal of the Department of Justice at the top.* **4** a piece of rubber or plastic that keeps air or water out of something or inside something: *One of the seals was broken and oil was leaking out.*

seal² *v* [T] **1** also **seal up** to close something very firmly so that people or things cannot get in or out: *The windows were sealed shut.* **2** to close an envelope and fasten the edges in place: *He sealed the envelope and handed it to me.* **3 seal a deal/agreement etc** to make an agreement definite and official —**sealed** *adj*: *a sealed envelope*
seal sth ⇔ **in** *phr v* to stop something that is inside something else from getting out: *Fry the meat quickly to seal in the flavour.*
seal sth ⇔ **off** *phr v* to stop people entering an area or building, because it is dangerous: *Police have sealed off the city centre.*

'sea ˌlevel *n* [U] the average level of the sea, used as a standard for measuring the height of an area of land: *a village 200 feet above sea level*

'sea ˌlion *n* [C] a type of large SEAL

seam /si:m/ *n* [C] **1** a line where two pieces of cloth have been sewn together: *an old jacket that was coming apart at the seams* **2** a layer of coal under the ground

seaman /'si:mən/ *n* [C] plural **seamen** /-mən/ a sailor

seamless /'si:mləs/ *adj* happening so smoothly that you cannot tell where one thing stops and the next thing begins: *The show is a seamless blend of song, dance, and storytelling.*

seamy /'si:mi/ *adj* involving bad things such as crime or violence: *the seamy side of life in the city*

seance /'seɪɒns, -ɒns $ -ɑːns/ *n* [C] a meeting where people try to talk to the SPIRITS of dead people

sear /sɪə $ sɪr/ *v* [T] *literary* to burn something with a sudden powerful heat [➡ **searing**]

search¹ /sɜːtʃ $ sɜːrtʃ/ n

1 [C usually singular] an attempt to find someone or something: **+for** *The police are continuing their search for the missing girl.* | **+of** *We have* **carried out** *a search of the whole area.* | *After three days the search was* **called off**. | *We set off* **in search** *of somewhere to eat.*

2 an attempt to find information using a computer: *I* **did** *a search and found 16 websites.* | *an online search*

3 [singular] an attempt to find the explanation of a difficult problem: *the search for the meaning of life*

search² v

1 [I,T] to look carefully for someone or something: **+for** *Police are still searching for the missing children.* | *We searched the house from top to bottom.* | **search sth for sth** *Detectives were searching nearby woods for evidence.* | **+through** *I searched through the papers on my desk.* → see box at **LOOK**

2 [I,T] to use a computer to find information: **+for** *Try searching for information on the Internet.* | *searching the Web*

3 [T] if the police search someone, they look in their clothes or bags for weapons, drugs etc: *We were all searched before we were allowed to leave.*

4 [I] to try to find an answer or explanation for a difficult problem: **+for** *Scientists are still searching for a cure for this disease.*

'search ,engine n [C] a computer program that helps you find information on the Internet

searching /'sɜːtʃɪŋ $ 'sɜːr-/ adj a searching question or look is intended to discover the truth about something: *She asked some very searching questions.*

searchlight /'sɜːtʃlaɪt $ 'sɜːrtʃ-/ n [C] a very large bright light that can be turned in different directions to find things or people at night

'search ,party n [C] a group of people who look for someone who is missing or lost

'search ,warrant n [C] a legal document that gives the police permission to search a building

searing /'sɪərɪŋ $ 'sɪr-/ adj **1** searing heat is very hot: *the searing heat of the desert* **2** a searing pain is very painful **3** searing words criticize someone very strongly: *a searing attack on the government*

seashell /'siːʃel/ n [C] the empty shell of a small sea animal

seashore /'siːʃɔː $ -ʃɔːr/ n **the seashore** the sand and rocks along the edge of the sea

seasick /'siː,sɪk/ adj if you feel seasick, you feel ill because of the way a boat or ship is moving

seaside /'siːsaɪd/ n **the seaside** *BrE* a place next to the sea where people go to enjoy themselves: *a day* **at the seaside** | *Shall we go* **to the** *seaside?* | *a seaside town* → see box at **SHORE**

season¹ /'siːzən/ n [C]

1 one of the main periods into which a year is divided. In Europe, the four seasons are winter, spring, summer, and autumn: *Autumn is my favourite season.* | *the rainy season*

2 a period of time in a year when something usually happens: **the football/baseball etc season** *The cricket season starts in April.*

3 the time of year when a lot of people take their holiday: **the holiday/tourist season** *It*

gets very busy here during the holiday season. | **the high/low season** (=the busiest or least busy time) *Prices go up in the high season.* | **the festive season** *BrE* (=Christmas and New year)

4 be in season a) if vegetables or fruit are in season, they are ready to pick and eat and so are available to buy **b)** if a female animal is in season, she is ready to **MATE**

5 out of season a) if vegetables or fruit are out of season, they are not ready to pick and eat and so are not available to buy **b)** if you go somewhere out of season, you go when there are not many people there on holiday: *It's quite cheap if you go out of season.*

season² v [T] to add salt, pepper, or spices to food when you are cooking it: *Season the meat with salt and pepper.*

seasonal /'siːzənəl/ adj happening or available only during one particular season: *You might be able to get seasonal work in the summer.*

seasoned /'siːzənd/ adj [only before noun] with a lot of experience of doing something: *a seasoned traveller* | *seasoned musicians*

seasoning /'siːzənɪŋ/ n [C,U] salt, pepper, and spices that you add to food when you are cooking it

'season ,ticket n [C] a ticket that you can use for several journeys or events during a fixed period of time, without having to pay for each one → see box at **TICKET**

seats

deckchair

rocking chair

stool

chair

armchair

seat¹ /siːt/ n [C]

1 something that you can sit on, for example a chair: *I asked for a seat by the window.* | *We had very good seats right at the front of the hall.* | **have/take a seat** (=sit down) *Come in and take a seat.* | **front/back/passenger seat** *Jo was driving and I was sitting in the back seat.*

COLLOCATIONS

back/rear/front seat – the back or front seat in a car
driver's seat – where the driver sits
passenger seat – the seat next to the driver's
empty/vacant seat – one that is not being used

window/aisle seat – a seat next to the window or aisle on a plane
front row seat – a seat in a theatre, sports ground etc that is closest to the stage, field etc
good seat – one in a theatre or cinema from which you can see well
book/reserve a seat – to arrange to have a seat in a theatre, on a plane etc at a particular time in the future

2 the part of a chair, bicycle etc that you sit on: *a bike with a comfortable seat*
3 a place on a plane, train etc or a chair in a cinema etc that you pay to sit in: *I've booked two seats for Saturday's concert.*
4 a position as a member of a government or an official group: **+in** *a seat in the House of Commons* | **+on** *a seat on the company's board* | **win/lose** a seat (=gain or lose a position as member of a government) *She lost her seat at the last election.*

seat² *v* [T] **1** if a place seats a particular number of people, it has enough seats for that number: *The new Olympic stadium seats over 70,000.* **2** *formal* if you seat yourself somewhere, you sit there: *He seated himself by the fire.*

seat belt *n* [C] a strong belt that holds you safely in your seat in a car or plane → see picture on page A12

seated /ˈsiːtɪd/ *adj formal* **1** if someone is seated, they are sitting down: *He was seated by the window.* **2** **be seated** used to ask people politely to sit down: *Please be seated.*

seating /ˈsiːtɪŋ/ *n* [U] the seats or chairs in a place, or the way that they are arranged: *a restaurant with seating for 40 customers* | *How shall we arrange the seating?*

seaweed /ˈsiːwiːd/ *n* [U] a plant that grows in the sea

sec /sek/ *n* [C] *spoken informal* a very short time: *Wait a sec – I'm coming too!* | *I'll be with you in a sec.*

secede /sɪˈsiːd/ *v* [I] *formal* if a country secedes from another country, it officially becomes independent from it

secluded /sɪˈkluːdɪd/ *adj* a secluded place is very quiet and private: *a secluded beach* | *a secluded corner of the garden*

seclusion /sɪˈkluːʒən/ *n* [U] when someone lives alone, away from other people: *I needed a few days of peace and seclusion.* | *He prefers to live in seclusion.*

second¹ /ˈsekənd/ *adj*

1 the second person or thing is the one that is after the first one: *Joanna's in her second year at university.* | *We only saw the second half of the match.* | *He won second prize.* | *She came second in the 100 metres.*
2 **be second to none** to be better than any others: *The food in this hotel is second to none.*
3 **have second thoughts** to have doubts about whether you have made the right decision about something: *I was having second thoughts about the whole idea.*
4 **on second thoughts** *BrE* **on second thought** *AmE spoken* used to say that you have just

changed your mind about something: *On second thoughts, I will have a glass of wine.*
5 **be second nature to sb** if something is second nature to you, you have done it so often that you do it without thinking about it
6 **not give sth a second thought/do sth without giving it a second thought** to do something without worrying about it: *I used to stay out all night without giving it a second thought.*
7 **your second wind** if you get your second wind, you suddenly feel less tired and have the energy to continue doing something
—**second** *pron: the second of August*

second² *n* [C]

1 a very short period of time. There are 60 seconds in a minute: *It takes about 30 seconds for the computer to start up.*
2 a very short period of time: *Can you just wait a second?* | *I'll be with you in a second.* | *Hang on just a second while I make a quick phone call.*
3 something that is sold more cheaply than other goods because it is not quite perfect: *Most of the clothes they sell are seconds.*
→ **SPLIT SECOND**

second³ *v* [T] to formally support a suggestion that someone else has made at a meeting: **second a motion/proposal/amendment** *Sarah has proposed this motion – do we have someone who will second it?*

second⁴ /sɪˈkɒnd $ -ˈkɑːnd/ *v* [T] *BrE* to send someone to do someone else's job for a short time: *Jill's been seconded to the marketing department for six months.*

secondary /ˈsekəndəri $ -deri/ *adj* **1** [only before noun] secondary education is for children between 11 and 18 years old: *He's at secondary school.* | *a secondary teacher* **2** not as important as something else: *Work was always of secondary importance to him.* **3** a secondary problem or illness develops from another one: *She developed a secondary infection.*

second best *adj* not quite best, but next best: *I'm the second best runner in the school.*

second class *n* [U] **1** a way of travelling that is cheaper but not as comfortable as FIRST CLASS **2** a way of sending letters that is cheaper but slower than FIRST CLASS —**second class** *adv: to travel second class* | *I sent the letters second class.*

second-class *adj* [only before noun] **1** less important than other people or things, or not as good as them: *They treated us like second-class citizens.* | *We didn't want our children to have a second-class education.* **2** a second-class service costs less than a FIRST-CLASS one, but is not quite as good or as fast: *second-class post* | *a second-class train ticket*

second-guess *v* [T] **1** to try to say what will happen or what someone will do: *I'm not going to try and second-guess her decision.* **2** *AmE* to criticize something after it has already happened: *The decision has been made – there's no point in second-guessing it now.*

secondhand /ˌsekənd'hænd◂/ *adj* **1** something that is secondhand is not new but has already been owned by someone else when you buy it: *We bought a cheap secondhand car.* | *shops selling secondhand clothes* → see box at **OLD**

2 secondhand information is told to you by someone who did not do, say, or see something themselves but got the information from another person [≠ **firsthand**]: *We only have secondhand accounts of the attack.* —**secondhand** *adv*: *We bought it secondhand.*

,second 'language *n* [C] a language that you speak in addition to the language that you learned as a child

secondly /'sekəndli/ *adv* used to introduce the second fact or reason that you want to talk about: *Firstly, the cars are expensive to make and secondly, they are not very good.*

,second 'person *n* the form of a verb that you use with 'you' [➜ **first person, third person**]

,second-'rate *adj* not very good: *a second-rate school*

secrecy /'si:krəsi/ *n* [U] when something is kept secret: *The operation was carried out in total secrecy.* | *We were all sworn to secrecy* (=made to promise that we would keep something secret).

secret[1] /'si:krɪt/ *adj*

1 if something is secret, only a few people know about it [➜ **secrecy**]: *a secret plan* | *a secret meeting* | *You must keep this secret* (=not tell anyone). | *He kept his marriage secret from his parents* (=he did not tell his parents about it).
2 [only before noun] doing something without telling anyone, because you do not want other people to know about it: *I think he's a secret gambler.* | *You've got a secret admirer* (=someone who likes you romantically without telling you).
—**secretly** *adv*: *I secretly recorded our conversation.*

secret[2] *n*

1 [C] something that is only told to a few people [➜ **secrecy**]: *I can't tell you his name. It's a secret.* | *Can you keep a secret* (=not tell it to anyone)? | *She wanted to tell everyone her secret.*
2 in secret without other people knowing: *The meeting was held in secret.*
3 the secret the best way to achieve something: **the secret to doing sth** *the secret to making good pastry* | **+of** *What's the secret of your success?*

,secret 'agent *n* [C] a SPY

secretary /'sekrₐtəri $ -teri/ *n* [C] plural **secretaries**

1 someone whose job is to write letters, arrange meetings, answer telephone calls etc in an office: *Please make an appointment with my secretary.*
2 also **Secretary** an official who is in charge of a large government department: *the Secretary of Education*
—**secretarial** /ˌsekrₐ'teəriəl◂ $ -'ter-/ *adj*: *secretarial work*

secrete /sɪ'kri:t/ *v* [T] if a plant or animal secretes a liquid, it produces it: *The leaves secrete a mild poison.* —**secretion** /-'kri:ʃən/ *n* [C,U]

secretive /'si:krₐtɪv, sɪ'kri:tɪv/ *adj* unwilling to tell people things: *Why are you being so secretive about your job?* —**secretively** *adv*

,secret po'lice *n* **the secret police** a police force controlled by a government, that secretly tries to defeat the political enemies of the government

,secret 'service *n* [singular] **1** a country's secret service is the government department that tries to discover secret information from other countries **2** a US government department that does special police work and protects the President

sect /sekt/ *n* [C] a group of people with their own religious or political beliefs that have become separate from a larger group

sectarian /sek'teəriən $ -'ter-/ *adj* sectarian problems or fighting take place between people from different religious groups: *sectarian violence* | *a sectarian murder*

section /'sekʃən/ *n* [C] one of the parts that something is divided into: **+of** *Some sections of the motorway are very busy.* | *One section of the bridge has collapsed.* | *the sports section of the newspaper* | *The rocket is built in sections and fitted together later.* → see box at **PART**
→ **CROSS SECTION**

sector /'sektə $ -ər/ *n* [C] **1** one part of a country's ECONOMY: *the public sector* (=businesses controlled by the government) | *the private sector* (=businesses controlled by private companies) **2** one of the parts that an area is divided into: *the northern sector of the city*

secular /'sekjₐlə $ -ər/ *adj* not religious or not controlled by a religious authority: *secular education* | *a secular society*

secure[1] /sɪ'kʊə $ -'kjʊr/ *adj* **1** not likely to change or fail: *a secure job* | *Does the company now have a secure future?* **2** a place that is secure is locked so that people cannot get in or out: *Make sure the house is secure before you leave.* **3** if you feel secure, you feel safe, confident, and free from worries: *Children need to feel secure.* **4** firmly fastened and not likely to fall: *That mirror doesn't look very secure.* —**securely** *adv*: *Are the doors securely locked?*

secure[2] *v* [T] **1** to get something important, especially after a lot of effort: *an attempt to secure the release of the hostages* **2** to make something safe from being attacked or harmed: *to secure the building against attack* **3** to fasten or tie something firmly: *We secured the boat with a rope.*

security /sɪ'kjʊərₐti $ -'kjʊr-/ *n* [U] **1** the things you do to keep someone or something safe from danger or crime: *the man in charge of airport security* | **Security** *around the President has been tightened.* | *security cameras* **2** when you are not likely to lose something, or something is not likely to fail: *People want job security.* | *financial security* **3** a feeling of being safe, confident, and free from worries: *Children need a sense of security.* **4** something valuable that you promise to give to someone if you fail to pay back money you have borrowed: *You can use your house as security for the loan.*

se'curity ,service *n* [C] a government organization that protects a country's secrets or government against enemies

sedan /sɪ'dæn/ *n* [C] *AmE* a large car that has four doors and a separate part at the back for bags and cases [= **saloon** *BrE*]

sedate[1] /sɪ'deɪt/ *adj* calm and formal

sedate² v [T] to give someone a drug to make them feel calm or ready to sleep: *He was still sedated after his operation.* —**sedation** /-'deɪʃən/ n [U]

sedative /'sedətɪv/ n [C] a drug that doctors give you to make you feel calm or ready to sleep

sedentary /'sedəntəri $ -teri/ adj a sedentary job or life involves sitting down a lot rather than moving around

sediment /'sedⁱmənt/ n [singular, U] a solid substance that forms a layer at the bottom of a liquid

sedition /sɪ'dɪʃən/ n [U] formal when you do or say things that encourage people to disobey a government —**seditious** adj

seduce /sɪ'djuːs $ -'duːs/ v [T] **1** to persuade someone to have sex with you, especially someone young **2** to persuade someone to do something by making it seem very attractive or interesting: *people who were seduced into investing in the company* —**seduction** /-'dʌkʃən/ n [C,U]

seductive /sɪ'dʌktɪv/ adj **1** sexually attractive **2** making something very attractive and interesting to you: *highly seductive advertising*

see /siː/ v past tense **saw** /sɔː $ sɒː/ past participle **seen** /siːn/

1 [I,T] to use your eyes to look at and notice people or things: *Can you see that car over there?* | *I can't see without my glasses.* | +(that) *I could see that she looked upset.* | +who/what/where etc *I didn't see who she was with.* | **see sb do sth** *I saw a man come out of the building.* | **see sb doing sth** *I saw her walking towards the library.*

THESAURUS

notice – to see something interesting or unusual: *I noticed a police car outside their house.*

spot – to suddenly see something, especially something you are looking for: *Nick spotted the advertisement in the paper.*

catch sight of sb/sth – to suddenly see someone or something: *She caught sight of Alec, waiting in a doorway.*

catch a glimpse of sth – to see something but only for a short time: *I caught a glimpse of his face as he ran past the window.*

make out – to see something, but only with difficulty: *Ahead, I could just make out the figure of a woman.*

witness – to see something happen, especially an accident or a crime: *Several people witnessed the attack.*

→ **HEAR**

You **see** something without planning to: *Two people saw him take the bag.*

You **look at** a picture, person, thing etc because you want to: *Hey, look at these jeans.*

You **watch** TV, a film, or something that happens for a period of time: *Did you watch the football match last night?* | *The kids are watching TV.*

You can also say that you saw a film, a programme etc, but you cannot say 'see television': *I saw a great film on TV last night.*

2 [I,T] to understand or realize something: *I can*

see why he's angry. | Oh, **I see**, the water goes in here. | I can't **see the point** of doing extra homework. | It looks broken, do you **see what I mean** (=understand what I am saying)? | I **see what you mean** about George now.

3 [T] to watch a film, television programme etc: *Have you seen any good films lately?* | *I didn't see last week's episode.*

4 [T] to visit or meet someone: *I saw Helen in town.* | *You should see a doctor.* → see box at **VISIT**

5 [T] to discover or learn something: **see what/whether/if etc** *Let's phone him and see what he says.* | *I'll see what time the train leaves.*

6 [T] to think about someone or something in a particular way: **see sb/sth as sth** *Fighting on TV can make children see violence as normal.* | *He sees himself as a failure.*

7 [T] to be the time when or the place where something happens: *The 20th century saw huge social changes.*

8 [T] if you can see something happening, you can imagine it and think that it will happen: *I can't see people accepting a cut in pay.*

9 [T] to make sure that something is done correctly: +(that) *Please see that everything is put back in the right place.*

10 [T] to go with someone to a place, usually to make sure they get there safely: **see sb to/into etc** *He saw me to my room.* | *I'll see you home.*

11 be seeing sb to be having a romantic relationship with someone: *I'm not seeing anyone at the moment.*

12 see eye to eye (with sb) to agree with someone: *Those two don't always see eye to eye.*

13 see you spoken used to say goodbye to someone: *See you, Ben.* | *I'll see you later.*

14 let's see/let me see spoken used when you are trying to remember something or are thinking about something: *Let's see. When did you send it?*

15 I'll/we'll see spoken used when you do not want to make a decision immediately: *'Can I have an ice cream?' 'We'll see.'*

see about sth phr v to make arrangements or deal with something: *Fran went to see about her passport.*

see sb ⇔ **off** phr v to go to an airport, train station etc to say goodbye to someone who is leaving: *We saw her off from the airport.*

see sb **out** phr v to go with someone to the door when they leave: *It's OK, I can see myself out.*

see through phr v **1 see through sb/sth** to know that someone is not telling you the truth: *Can't you see through his lies?* **2 see sth through** to continue doing something difficult until it is finished: *Miller is determined to see the project through.*

see to sth phr v to deal with something: *I must go and see to the food.*

seed¹ /siːd/ n [C,U] plural **seed** or **seeds**

1 a small hard thing produced by a plant, from which a new plant will grow: *sunflower seeds* | **plant/sow seeds** (=put them in the ground) *Sow the seeds one inch deep in the soil.* → see picture at **PLANT**

2 seeds of sth something that makes a new situation start to develop: *the seeds of change in Eastern Europe* | *Something Lucy said began to sow seeds of doubt in his mind.*

seed² v [T usually passive] to remove seeds from a fruit or vegetable

seedless /ˈsiːdləs/ adj seedless fruit has no seeds in it: *seedless grapes*

seedling /ˈsiːdlɪŋ/ n [C] a young plant grown from a seed

seedy /ˈsiːdi/ adj informal a seedy person or place looks dirty and poor, and is often connected with illegal or immoral activity: *a seedy nightclub*

Seeing 'Eye ˌdog n [C] trademark AmE a specially trained dog that blind people use to help them go to places [= **guide dog** BrE]

seek /siːk/ v past tense and past participle **sought** /sɔːt $ sɒːt/ **1** [T] to try to find or get something: *The UN is seeking a political solution.* | **seek refuge/asylum/shelter etc** *People were crossing the border, seeking refuge from the war.* → see box at **LOOK** **2 seek (sb's) advice/help/assistance etc** to ask someone for advice or help: *You should seek advice from a lawyer.* **3** [I,T] to try to do something: *Do you think the President will seek re-election?* | **seek to do sth** *We're always seeking to improve our results.*

seem /siːm/ v [linking verb] how something seems is how it appears to you: *The house seemed very quiet after he'd left.* | **seem to be** *She seemed to be upset.* | **seem to do sth** *He seemed to hesitate before answering.* | **seem important/right/strange etc to sb** *Doesn't that seem strange to you?* | **it seems to sb (that)** *It seems to me that we're lost.* | **it seems (that)** *It seems that he forgot to tell her.* | **seem as if/as though/like** *York seems like a nice place to live.*

seemingly /ˈsiːmɪŋli/ adv used to say that something seems true, but is actually not true: *a seemingly endless list of jobs*

seen /siːn/ v the past participle of **SEE**

seep /siːp/ v [I] if a liquid seeps somewhere, it flows there slowly through small holes: *Water was seeping into the boat.*

seesaw¹ /ˈsiːsɔː $ -sɒː/ n [C] a piece of equipment which children play on outdoors. It is made of a board that is balanced in the middle so that when one end goes up, the other end goes down.

seesaw² v [I] written to move from one state or condition to another and back again many times

seethe /siːð/ v [I] to be very angry, but not show it: *He was seething with anger.*

segment /ˈsegmənt/ n [C] one of the parts that something is divided into: *a large segment of the population* | *Cut the orange into segments.*

segmented /segˈmentɪd/ adj divided into separate parts

segregate /ˈsegrɪgeɪt/ v [T usually passive] to separate one group of people from others: *They were segregated from the other prisoners.* —**segregation** /ˌsegrɪˈgeɪʃən/ n [U] *racial segregation*

segregated /ˈsegrɪgeɪtɪd/ adj a segregated school or other institution can only be used by members of one particular race, sex, religion etc

seismic /ˈsaɪzmɪk/ adj technical relating to EARTHQUAKES

seize /siːz/ v [T] **1** to take something in your hand and roughly: *He suddenly seized the gun from her.* → see box at **HOLD** **2** if some-

one seizes power or control, they take it, using force: *The rebels have seized power.* **3** if the police or government officers seize illegal things such as drugs or guns, they take them away: *Police seized 10 kilos of cocaine.*

seize on/upon sth phr v to suddenly become interested in an idea, what someone says etc: *His remarks were seized on by the press.*

seize up phr v **a)** if a machine seizes up, it stops working, for example because of lack of oil **b)** if part of your body seizes up, you cannot move it and it is very painful

seizure /ˈsiːʒə $ -ər/ n **1** [C,U] when someone suddenly takes control of something, especially by force: *the Fascist seizure of power* **2** [C,U] when the police or government officers take away illegal goods such as drugs or guns: *drugs seizures* **3** [C] a sudden attack of an illness: *a heart seizure*

seldom /ˈseldəm/ adv not very often: *He seldom goes out.* → see box at **RARELY**

select¹ /sɪˈlekt/ v [T] to choose something or someone: *He wasn't selected for the team.* → see box at **CHOOSE**

select² adj formal a select group is a small group of carefully chosen people: *a select group of students* | *Only a select few were invited.*

selection /sɪˈlekʃən/ n **1** [U] when something or someone is chosen: +**of** *the selection of a new leader* **2** [C] a group of things that someone has chosen: *a selection of his favourite poems* **3** [C] a group of things that you can choose from: +**of** *The shop has a wide selection of books.*

selective /sɪˈlektɪv/ adj **1** careful about the things you choose: *Be selective when you're shopping.* **2** relating to only a few specially chosen people or things: *children attending selective schools*

selector /sɪˈlektə $ -ər/ n [C] BrE a member of a committee that chooses the best people for something such as a sports team

self /self/ n [C,U] plural **selves** /selvz/ your nature and character: *sb's usual/normal self Sid was not his usual smiling self.* | **be/look/feel (like) your old self** (=be the way you usually are again) *You'll soon be back to your old self.*

self-ap'pointed adj disapproving giving yourself a responsibility or job without the agreement of other people, especially those you claim to represent

self-as'sured adj confident about what you are doing —**self-assurance** n [U]

self-'catering adj BrE a self-catering holiday is one in which you stay in a place where you can cook your own food: *a self-catering apartment* → see box at **ACCOMMODATION**

self-'centred BrE; **self-centered** AmE adj disapproving only interested in yourself [= **selfish**]

self-'confident adj feeling sure that you can do things successfully —**self-confidence** n [U]

self-'conscious adj uncomfortable and worried about what other people think about you or your appearance: *He felt self-conscious in his new suit.* —**self-consciously** adv —**self-consciousness** n [U]

self-con'tained adj **1** something that is self-contained is complete and does not need other things to make it work **2** BrE a self-contained **FLAT** has its own kitchen and bathroom

S

self-con'trol n [U] the ability to behave calmly and sensibly even when you are angry, excited, or upset

self-de'fence BrE; **self-defense** AmE n [U] the use of force to protect yourself when you are attacked: **in self-defence** She shot the man in self-defence.

self-destruct /ˌself dɪˈstrʌkt◂/ v [I] if something such as a bomb self-destructs, it destroys itself

self-de'structive adj deliberately doing things that are likely to seriously harm or kill yourself

self-determi'nation n [U] the right of the people of a particular country to choose their own government or system of government

self-'discipline n [U] the ability to make yourself do the things you should do —**self-disciplined** adj

self-ef'facing adj not wanting to attract attention to yourself or your achievements [= modest]: her honesty and self-effacing modesty —**self-effacement** n [U]

self-em'ployed adj someone who is self-employed has their own business rather than being employed by a company

self-es'teem n [U] how you feel about yourself and whether, for example, you feel that you are a nice or successful person: **low/high self-esteem**

self-'evident adj clearly true and needing no more proof [= obvious]

self-ex'planatory adj clear and easy to understand, and needing no more explanation

self-'help adj [only before noun] solving your problems by yourself, instead of depending on other people: self-help books

self-'image n [C] your opinions about yourself

self-im'portant adj disapproving behaving in a way that shows you think you are more important than other people —**self-importance** n [U]

self-im'posed adj a self-imposed rule, duty etc is one that you have made for yourself

self-in'dulgent adj disapproving allowing yourself to have or do things that you enjoy but do not need —**self-indulgence** n [C,U]

self-in'flicted adj a self-inflicted injury or problem is one that you have caused yourself

self-'interest n [U] when you only care about what is best for you, and not for other people

selfish /ˈselfɪʃ/ adj disapproving caring only about yourself and not about other people [≠ unselfish]: That was a very selfish thing to do. | selfish behaviour
—**selfishness** n [U] —**selfishly** adv

selfless /ˈselfləs/ adj approving caring about other people more than about yourself

self-'made adj a self-made man or woman has become rich and successful by working hard: a self-made millionaire

self-'pity n [U] disapproving when you feel sorry for yourself, but without a good reason

self-'portrait n [C] a picture of yourself, done by you

self-pos'sessed adj approving calm, confident, and in control of your feelings

self-preser'vation n [U] when you protect your own life in a threatening or dangerous situation

self-re'liant adj able to do things by yourself without depending on other people

self-re'spect n [U] a feeling of respect for yourself —**self-respecting** adj: No self-respecting person would do that.

self-'righteous adj disapproving too sure that your moral behaviour or beliefs are right, in a way that annoys other people

self-'sacrifice n [U] when you decide not to have something in order to help someone else —**self-sacrificing** adj

self-'satisfied adj disapproving too pleased with yourself

self-'service adj a self-service restaurant, shop, garage etc is one where you get food, petrol etc for yourself before paying for it

'self-styled adj [only before noun] disapproving having given yourself a title or position without having a right to it

self-suf'ficient adj able to provide for all your own needs without help from other people: Australia is 65% self-sufficient in oil. —**self-sufficiency** n [U]

sell /sel/ v past tense and past participle **sold** /səʊld $ soʊld/

1 [I,T] to give something to someone and accept money from them for it [➞ buy]: **sell sth for £100/$50/30p etc** He sold his car for £5000. | **sell sth to sb** I sold a ticket to Mary. | **sell sb sth** Sally's going to sell me her bike.

2 [T] to offer something for people to buy: Do you sell stamps? | **sell at/for £100/$50/30p etc** The T-shirts sell at £10 each.

3 [T] to make someone want to buy something: Scandal sells newspapers.

4 [I,T] to be bought by people: Her book sold millions of copies. | **sell well/badly** These cakes are selling well.

5 [T] to try to persuade someone to accept a new plan or idea: **sell sth to sb** We have to sell the idea to the viewers.

6 sell yourself to make yourself seem impressive to other people: If you want promotion, you've got to sell yourself better.

➔ **HARD SELL**

sell sth ⇔ **off** phr v to sell goods quickly and cheaply: The library is selling off some of its old books.

sell out phr v **1** if a shop sells out of something, or if something sells out, the shop sells all of it and there is none left: **have/be sold out** Tickets for the show have sold out. | **+of** We've sold out of bread. **2** informal disapproving to do something against your beliefs in order to get money or some other advantage: ex-hippies who've sold out and become respectable businessmen

sell up phr v to sell your house or your business: Liz decided to sell up and move abroad.

'sell-by date n [C] BrE the date printed on a food product, after which a shop should not sell it

seller /ˈselə $ -ər/ n [C] **1** someone who sells something [➞ buyer] **2 good/bad/poor seller** a product that is popular or not popular etc with customers: *The album remains one of the biggest sellers of all time.*

'sell-off *n* [C] *BrE* the sale of a company or part of a company

Sellotape /'seləteɪp, -loʊ- $ -lə-, -loʊ-/ *n* [U] *trademark BrE* tape that you use for sticking pieces of paper or card together [= **Scotch tape** *AmE*] → see picture at **CLASSROOM**

sellout /'selaʊt/ *n* [singular] a performance, sports event etc for which all the tickets have been sold

selves /selvz/ *n* the plural of SELF

semantic /sɪ'mæntɪk/ *adj formal* relating to the meaning of words —**semantically** /-kli/ *adv*

semblance /'sembləns/ *n* **a/some semblance of sth** a situation that is slightly similar to another one: *After the war, life returned to a semblance of normality.*

semen /'siːmən/ *n* [U] the liquid containing SPERM (=substance produced by the male sex organs)

semester /sɪ'mestə $ -ər/ *n* [C] *AmE* one of two periods into which the school or college year is divided

semi- /semi/ *prefix* **1** partly but not completely: *semi-skilled labour* | *semi-automatic weapons* | *semi-darkness* **2** exactly half: *a semi-circle*

'semi-ˌcircle *n* [C] half a circle: *The children sat in a semicircle.* → see box at **SHAPE** —ˌsemi-'circular *adj*

semicolon /ˌsemi'kəʊlən $ 'semi,koʊlən/ *n* [C] the mark (;) that you use in writing to separate different parts of a sentence or list

ˌsemi-de'tached *adj BrE* a semi-detached house is joined on one side to another house → see box at **HOUSE**

ˌsemi-'final *BrE*; **semifinal** /ˌsemi'faɪnl/ *AmE n* [C] the two games that are played in a competition before the last game. The winners of the two semi-finals play each other in the final game to find the winner.

seminar /'semɪnɑː $ -nɑːr/ *n* [C] a meeting in which a group of people discuss a subject → see box at **UNIVERSITY**

seminary /'semɪnəri $ -neri/ *n* [C] plural **seminaries** a college for training priests

senate, **Senate** /'senɪt/ *n* **the Senate** the smaller of the two parts of government in countries such as the US and Australia [➡ **House of Representatives**]

senator, **Senator** /'senətə $ -tər/ *n* [C] a member of a senate: *Senator Dole* → see box at **GOVERNMENT**

send /send/ *v* [T] past tense and past participle **sent** /sent/

1 to arrange for something to go to a place or person: *He sent the cheque last week.* | **send sb sth** *I'll send you an email confirming the date.* | **send sth to sb/sth** *I need to send some money to my family.* | **send sth back/up/over etc** *She signed the form and sent it back.* | **send sth by post/sea/air etc** *It's quicker to send parcels by air.* | **send sth off** *She sent the letter off this morning.*

2 to make someone go somewhere: *The U.N. is sending troops.* | **send sb to sth** *Al was sent to*

prison for stealing. | **send sb back/away/over/ home etc** *The refugees were sent back to Vietnam.* | **send sb to do sth** *I sent Joe to buy some food.*

3 send your love/regards/best wishes etc *spoken* to ask someone to give your greetings, good wishes etc to someone else: *Mother sends her love.*

4 to cause someone or something to be in a particular state: *His lectures send me to sleep.* | **send sb/sth into sth** *The tail broke off, sending the plane into a dive.*

send away/off for sth *phr v* to send a letter to an organization asking them to post something to you: *Send away for a free recipe booklet.*

send for sb/sth *phr v* to ask for someone or something to come to you: *We sent for an ambulance.*

send sb/sth ⇔ **in** *phr v* **1** to send something, usually by post, to a place where it can be dealt with: *Did you send in your application?* **2** to send soldiers, police etc somewhere to deal with a dangerous situation: *British troops were sent in as part of the peace-keeping force.*

send sb ⇔ **off** *phr v BrE* to order a sports player to leave a game because they have behaved badly

send sth ⇔ **out** *phr v* **1** to send things to several people so that they receive one each: *I sent out all the party invitations.* | *The school is sending a letter out to all the parents.* **2** if a machine sends out light, sound etc, it produces it: *The ship's radio sends out a powerful signal.*

send sb/sth ⇔ **up** *phr v BrE informal* to make someone or something look silly by copying them in a funny way: *The film sends up Hollywood disaster movies.*

sender /'sendə $ -ər/ *n* [C] the person who sent a particular letter, package, message etc

'send-off *n* [C] *informal* an occasion when a group of people say goodbye to someone who is leaving: *They gave her a good send-off when she retired.*

senile /'siːnaɪl/ *adj* mentally confused because of old age —**senility** /sɪ'nɪlɪti/ *n* [U]

senior¹ /'siːniə $ -ər/ *adj* a senior person has an important position or rank [➡ **junior**]: *senior management* | **+to** *She's senior to me* (=she has a higher position than me). → see box at **POSITION**

senior² *n* [C] **1** *AmE* a student in the last year of HIGH SCHOOL or college [➡ **junior, freshman**] **2** *AmE* a senior citizen **3 be two/five/ten etc years sb's senior** to be two, five, ten etc years older than someone

Senior written abbreviation **Snr** *BrE* **Sr.** *AmE* used after the name of a man who has the same name as his son

ˌsenior 'citizen *n* [C] someone who is over the age of 65

seniority /ˌsiːni'ɒrɪti $ -'ɔː-, -'ɑː-/ *n* [U] when you are older or higher in rank than someone else: *a position of seniority*

sensation /sen'seɪʃən/ *n* **1** [C,U] a feeling that you get from one of your five senses: *She had a tingling sensation in her hands.* **2** [C] a feeling caused by a particular experience, which you cannot describe: *Carol had the sensation that she* *was being watched.* **3** [singular] extreme excitement or interest, or something that causes this: *The film caused a sensation.*

sensational /sen'seɪʃənəl/ *adj* **1** very interesting, exciting, or good: *a sensational discovery* | *She looked sensational.* **2** *disapproving* intended to interest, excite, or shock people: *sensational newspaper stories* —**sensationally** *adv*

sensationalism /sen'seɪʃənəlɪzəm/ *n* [U] *disapproving* a way of reporting events that makes them seem as strange, exciting, or shocking as possible

sense¹ /sens/ *n*

1 [singular] a feeling about something: **+of** *I felt a great sense of relief.* | *She has a strong sense of loyalty.*
2 [singular] the ability to judge or understand something: **sense of humour** *BrE*/**sense of humor** *AmE* (=the ability to understand and enjoy things that are funny) *She has a really good sense of humour.* | **sense of direction** (=the ability to judge which way you should be going) *It was dark and he had completely lost his sense of direction.* | *She has excellent business sense.* | **dress/clothes sense** (=the ability to judge what clothes look good)
3 [C] one of the five physical abilities of sight, hearing, touch, taste, and smell: **sense of smell/taste/touch etc** *Dogs have a good sense of smell.*
4 [U] when someone makes sensible or practical decisions, or behaves in a sensible, practical way: **have the sense to do sth** (=do the thing that is most sensible) *She had the sense to call the police.* | **Have some sense** (=be sensible). *We can't possibly have a picnic in this rain.* | **there is no sense in (doing) sth** *spoken* (=it is not sensible to do something) *There's no sense in getting upset.*
5 make sense a) to have a clear meaning and be easy to understand: *Read this and tell me if it makes sense.* **b)** to be a sensible thing to do: **it makes sense (for sb) to do sth** *It would make sense to leave early, so that we miss the traffic.* **c)** if something makes sense, there seems to be a good reason for it: *Why did she do a thing like that? It doesn't make sense.*
6 make (some) sense of sth to understand something difficult: *Can you make sense of the instructions?*
7 [C] the meaning of a word, phrase, sentence etc: *The word 'bank' has two main senses.*
8 [C] a way in which something can be true or real: *What he says is right in a sense* (=in one way, but not every way).
9 come to your senses to start to think clearly and behave sensibly: *One day he'll come to his senses and realize what a fool he's been.*
→ **COMMON SENSE, SIXTH SENSE**

sense² *v* [T] to feel or know something without being told: *I could sense that something was wrong.* | *Cats can sense danger.*

senseless /'sensləs/ *adj* **1** a senseless action is bad and will not achieve anything: *senseless violence* | *The destruction of the rainforest is senseless.* **2** if someone is beaten senseless, they are hit until they are not conscious

sensibility /ˌsensɪ'bɪlɪti/ *n* [C,U] plural **sensibilities** *formal* the way that someone reacts to particular subjects or types of behaviour: *Avoid using words that might offend someone's religious sensibilities.*

sensible /'sensɪbəl/ *adj*

1 someone who is sensible is able to make good decisions: *She's a very sensible girl.*
2 something that is sensible is a good idea: *He gave me some sensible advice.* | **It's sensible to** *keep a note of your passport number.* | *Moving house seemed like the sensible thing to do.*
—**sensibly** *adv*: *If you won't behave sensibly, you must leave.*

sensitive /'sensɪtɪv/ *adj*

1 a sensitive person thinks of how other people will feel about something [≠ **insensitive**]: **+to** *He was very sensitive to other people's needs.*
2 easily offended or upset: *a sensitive child* | **+about** *She's sensitive about her weight.*
3 easily affected or damaged by something such as a substance or temperature: *sensitive skin* | **+to** *Older people tend to be very sensitive to cold.*
4 a situation or subject that is sensitive needs to be dealt with very carefully because it is secret or because it may offend people: *Abortion is a politically sensitive issue.* | *highly sensitive information*
5 reacting to very small changes in light, temperature, position etc: *a highly sensitive electronic camera*
—**sensitively** *adv*: *an issue which needs to be handled sensitively* —**sensitivity** /ˌsensɪ'tɪvɪti/ *n* [C,U] *His comments show a lack of sensitivity.*

sensor /'sensə $ -ər/ *n* [C] a piece of equipment that is used to find light, heat, movement etc, even in very small amounts

sensory /'sensəri/ *adj* relating to your senses of sight, hearing, smell, taste, or touch

sensual /'senʃuəl/ *adj* relating to physical pleasure: *sensual pleasures such as massage* —**sensuality** /ˌsenʃuˈælɪti/ *n* [U]

sensuous /'senʃuəs/ *adj* making you feel physical pleasure: *the sensuous feel of silk*

sent /sent/ *v* the past tense and past participle of SEND

sentence¹ /'sentəns/ *n* [C]

1 a group of words that are written with a capital letter at the beginning and a FULL STOP at the end
2 a punishment that a judge gives to someone who is guilty of a crime: *She received an eight-year prison sentence.* | *He's serving a life sentence for murder.* | *The crime carries an automatic death sentence.* → see box at **PUNISHMENT**

sentence² *v* [T] when a judge sentences someone, he or she gives them a punishment for a crime: *He was sentenced to six years in prison.*

sentiment /'sentɪmənt/ *n* **1** [C,U] *formal* an opinion or feeling you have about something: *Similar sentiments were expressed by many politicians.* **2** [U] feelings of pity, love, or sadness that are often considered to be unsuitable for a particular situation: *There's no room for sentiment in business.*

sentimental /ˌsentɪ'mentl◂/ *adj* **1** showing emotions such as love, pity, and sadness too strongly or in a silly way: *sentimental love songs* | **+about** *People can be very sentimental about animals.* **2** relating to your feelings rather than practical reasons: *The ring has sentimental value.* —**sentimentality** /ˌsentɪmenˈtælɪti/ *n* [U]

sentry /'sentri/ *n* [C] plural **sentries** a soldier who stands outside a building and guards it

separable /'sepərəbəl/ *adj* two things that are separable can be separated [≠ **inseparable**]

separate¹ /'sepərɪt/ *adj*

1 separate things are different ones, not the same ones: *The sisters have separate bedrooms.* | *That's a separate issue.* | **+from** *I keep my work separate from my home life.*

2 not joined to or touching another thing: *The library is in a separate building.* | **+from** *Keep raw meat separate from cooked meat.*

—**separately** *adv*: *His parents arrived separately.*

separate² /'sepəreɪt/ *v*

1 [I,T] to divide or split something into different parts: **separate sth into sth** *The class was separated into four groups.* | **separate sth from sth** *Separate the urgent letters from the rest.*

2 [T] to be between two things so that they cannot touch each other: **separate sth from sth** *A screen separates the dining area from the kitchen.* | *The two parts of the park are separated by a busy road.*

3 [I,T] to make people move apart, or to move apart: *A teacher separated the two boys.* | **separate sb** *I got separated from my friends in the crowd.*

4 [I] to start to live apart from your husband, wife, or partner: *Her parents separated last year.*

—**separated** *adj* → see box at **MARRIED**

separation /ˌsepəˈreɪʃən/ *n* **1** [U] when two things are different or are split into different parts: *There can be no separation of politics from morality.* **2** [C,U] when people spend time apart from each other: *a long separation from his mother* **3** [C] an agreement between a husband and wife to live apart

separatist /'sepərətɪst/ *n* [C] someone who wants part of a country to become separate and form a new country with its own government

September /sep'tembə $ -ər/ *n* [C,U] written abbreviation **Sept.** or **Sep.** the ninth month of the year, between August and October: **next/last September** *He starts college next September.* | **in September** *He came here in September.* | **on September 6th** *My birthday is on September 6th.* → see box at **MONTH**

septic /'septɪk/ *adj especially BrE* infected with BACTERIA: *The wound went septic.*

sequel /'si:kwəl/ *n* [C] a film, book etc that continues the story of an earlier one: **+to** *the sequel to 'Silence of the Lambs'*

sequence /'si:kwəns/ *n* **1** [C,U] the order that something happens or exists in: **in a ... sequence** *Ask the questions in a logical sequence.* | **in/out of sequence** (=in or not in the right order) *Read the chapters in sequence.* **2** [C] a series of events, numbers, letters etc that have a particular order: **+of** *a sequence of numbers* | *the sequence of events that led to war*

sequin /'si:kwɪn/ *n* [C] a small shiny piece of metal that is sewn on clothes for decoration

serenade /ˌserəˈneɪd/ *n* [C] a song, especially a love song —**serenade** *v* [T]

serene /sɪˈriːn/ *adj* very calm and peaceful: *Her face was serene.* | *a serene mountain lake* —**serenity** /sɪˈrenɪti/ *n* [U]

sergeant /'sɑːdʒənt $ 'sɑːr-/ *n* [C] an officer of low rank in the army, air force, or police

serial¹ /'sɪəriəl $ 'sɪr-/ *n* [C] a story that is broadcast or printed in several separate parts

serial² *adj* **serial killer/murderer/rapist etc** someone who commits the same crime several times

'serial ˌnumber *n* [C] a number put on things that are produced in large quantities, so that each one has its own number

series /'sɪəriːz $ 'sɪr-/ *n* [C] plural **series**

1 a series of sth several events or actions of the same kind that happen one after the other: *series of accidents* | *He was found guilty of a whole series of crimes.*

2 a set of television or radio programmes with the same characters or on the same subject: *a new comedy series*

serious /'sɪəriəs $ 'sɪr-/ *adj*

1 a serious problem, situation etc is very bad and worrying: *Drugs are a serious problem here.* | *The damage was not serious.* | **serious illness/injury/accident etc**

2 be serious to really mean something that you say, and not be joking or pretending: *Are you serious about becoming a model?*

3 something that is serious is important and should not be laughed at: *Be quiet. This is serious.* | *Bullying is a serious matter.* | **serious thought/discussion etc** *We need to have a serious talk about your future.*

4 a serious person is always quiet and sensible and does not often laugh

—**seriousness** *n* [U]

seriously /'sɪəriəsli $ 'sɪr-/ *adv*

1 very much or very badly: **seriously ill/ injured/damaged etc** *Nobody was seriously hurt in the accident.* | *I'm seriously worried about Ben.*

2 in a way that is not joking, because something is important: *I'm thinking seriously about leaving my job.* | **take sb/sth seriously** (=think they are very important) *You shouldn't take what he says seriously.*

3 *spoken* used to say that you are not joking, or to ask whether someone is joking: *Seriously, he likes you.*

sermon /'sɜːmən $ 'sɜːr-/ *n* [C] a talk given as part of a Christian church service

serpent /'sɜːpənt $ 'sɜːr-/ *n* [C] *literary* a snake

serrated /sɪˈreɪtɪd, se-/ *adj* a serrated knife has a sharp edge made from a row of V-shaped points

serum /'sɪərəm $ 'sɪr-/ *n* [C,U] *technical* a liquid containing substances that fight infection [➡ **vaccine**]

servant /'sɜːvənt $ 'sɜːr-/ *n* [C] someone, especially in the past, who was paid to do jobs such as cleaning and cooking in another person's house → **CIVIL SERVANT**

S

serve¹ /sɜːv $ sɜːrv/ *v*

1 [I,T] to give someone food or drinks as part of a meal: *Dinner is served at eight.* | **serve sth with sth** *Serve the soup with crusty bread.* | **serve two/four etc** (=be enough for two people, four people etc) *The recipe serves six.* → see box at RECIPE

2 [I,T] to help the customers in a shop: *There was only one girl serving customers.* | *Are you being served?*

3 [I,T] to be useful or suitable for a particular purpose: *The sofa also serves as a bed.* | **serve to do sth** *The incident served to emphasize the importance of security.*

4 [I,T] to spend time in the army or in an organization doing useful work: **serve in the army/navy/air force etc** *They served in the same regiment.* | **+on** *She serves on the student committee.*

5 [T] to spend time in prison: *He served two years for theft.*

6 [I,T] to start playing in a game such as tennis, by throwing the ball in the air and hitting it over the net

7 it serves sb right *spoken* used to say that someone deserves something bad, because they have done something wrong: *If you fail your exam it will serve you right.*

serve² *n* [C] the action in a game such as tennis in which you throw the ball in the air and hit it over the net

server /ˈsɜːvə $ ˈsɜːrvər/ *n* [C] the main computer on a network that controls all the others

service¹ /ˈsɜːvɪs $ ˈsɜːr-/ *n*

1 [C] the official system or organization that provides something, especially something that everyone needs: **the health/prison/postal etc service** *She works for the health service.* | **emergency/essential services** (=medical help, fire service, water supply etc)

2 [C] help or work that a business provides for customers, rather than goods produced by a business: **provide/offer a service** *We offer a free information service.* | **insurance and other financial services**

3 [U] the help that people who work in a restaurant, shop etc give you: **good/poor/slow etc service** *The food is OK but the service is terrible.* | *Service is included in your bill.* | *We are proud of our customer service.* → see box at RESTAURANT

4 [U] also **services** [plural] work that you do for a person or organization: *He retired after 20 years of service.* | **+as** *You could offer your services as an English teacher.*

5 in service/out of service available or not available for people to use: *Sorry, this bus is out of service.*

6 the services *BrE* **the service** *AmE* a country's military forces → see box at ARMY

7 [singular, U] *formal* help that you give someone: *Our trained assistants are at your service* (=available to help). | *Can I be of service* (=help)?

8 [C] a formal religious ceremony, especially in a church: *the evening service at St Marks*

9 [C] a regular examination of a machine or car to make sure it works correctly: *My car needs a service.*

10 [C] an act of hitting the ball over the net to start a game of tennis etc

11 services [C] *BrE* a place where you can stop to buy petrol, food etc on a MOTORWAY [= **service station**]

→ CIVIL SERVICE, COMMUNITY SERVICE, FIRE SERVICE, LIP SERVICE, NATIONAL SERVICE

service² *v* [T] to examine a machine or vehicle and fix it if necessary: *I'm having the car serviced next week.* → see box at REPAIR

ˈservice ˌcharge *n* [C] *BrE* an amount that is added to a bill as a charge for the waiters that serve you

ˈservice ˌindustry *n* [C,U] an industry that provides a service rather than a product, for example insurance or travel

serviceman /ˈsɜːvɪsmən $ ˈsɜːr-/ *n* [C] plural **servicemen** /-mən/ a man who is a member of the military

ˈservice ˌstation *n* [C] a place that sells petrol, food, and other goods [= **gas station** *AmE*]

servicewoman /ˈsɜːvɪsˌwʊmən $ ˈsɜːr-/ *n* [C] plural **servicewomen** /-ˌwɪmɪn/ a woman who is a member of the military

serviette /ˌsɜːviˈet $ ˌsɜːr-/ *n* [C] *BrE* a NAPKIN

servile /ˈsɜːvaɪl $ ˈsɜːrvəl, -vaɪl/ *adj disapproving* very eager to obey and please someone

serving /ˈsɜːvɪŋ $ ˈsɜːr-/ *n* [C] an amount of food that is enough for one person [= **helping**]

session /ˈseʃən/ *n* [C] **1** a period of time used for a particular activity, especially by a group of people: *We run training sessions.* | *There will be a question-and-answer session later.* **2** a formal meeting, or group of meetings, of a law court or parliament: **+of** *a new session of Parliament* | **in session** (=meeting) *The court is now in session.*

set¹ /set/ *v* past tense and past participle **set** present participle **setting**

1 [T] *written* to carefully put something somewhere: **set sth down** *He brought in a jug and set it down.* | **set sth on sth** *She set the tray on the bed.*

2 [T] if a story, film etc is set in a place or at a particular time, the events in it happen in that place or at that time: **set sth in sth** *The film is set in Hong Kong.*

3 [T] to decide or establish what something should be: **set a date/time** *Have they set a date for the wedding?* | **set a target/limit/standard etc** *The target that was set was much too high.* | **set a pattern/trend etc** *Their computers set the trend for user-friendly graphics.* | *He set a new world record for the 100 metres.* | *I expect you to set an example* (=show good behaviour for others to copy).

4 [T] to consider something in relation to other things: **set sth against/beside sth** *The number of accidents is small when set against the number of cars on the road.*

serve

5 [T] to start something happening: **set sth in motion/progress** *An inquiry into the incident was set in motion.* | **set sth on fire/alight/ablaze** also **set fire to sth** *Rioters set cars on fire.* | **set sb doing sth** *What she said has set me thinking.*

6 [T] to move the switch on a machine, clock etc so that it will work in the way that you want: *Can you set the video recorder?* | *I forgot to set the alarm.* | **set sth to/on/at sth** *Set the oven to 180°.*

7 [I] if a liquid mixture sets, it becomes hard and solid: *The concrete has set.*

8 [I] when the sun sets, it moves lower in the sky until it disappears [≠ **rise**]

9 [T] *BrE* to give a student a piece of work or a test to do: **set sb sth** *Did he set you any homework?*

10 set (sb) to work to start doing something, or make someone start doing something: *I set to work clearing up.*

11 set your heart/sights/mind on also **have your heart/sights/mind set on sth** to want very much to achieve or get something: *I've set my heart on that pair of boots.* | *We now have our sights set on winning the championship.*

12 set the table to arrange plates, knives etc on a table so that it is ready for a meal

13 set a trap a) to make a trap to catch an animal **b)** to invent a plan to catch someone

14 set sb free/loose to allow a person or animal to be free: *The hostages were finally set free.*

15 set foot in sth to go into a place: *I had never set foot in a pub before.*

→ **set sb's mind at rest** at REST¹ → **set sail** at SAIL²
→ **set the ball rolling** at BALL

set about sth *phr v* **set about doing sth** to start doing something: *How do you set about getting a job?*

set sb against sb *phr v* to make someone argue or fight with someone else: *The civil war set brother against brother.*

set sth ⇔ **apart** *phr v* to make someone or something different from or better than other people or things: **+from** *His intelligence set him apart from the other students.*

set sth ⇔ **aside** *phr v* **1** to keep something for a special purpose: *I set aside a little money every week.* | **+for** *a room that had been set aside for visitors* **2** to decide not to consider a problem or feeling: *Let's set aside the question of payment for now.* | **set aside your differences** (=agree to stop arguing)

set sb/sth **back** *phr v* **1 set sb/sth** ⇔ **back** to delay something, or delay someone in doing something: *Her resignation set back the project.* | *I hurt my leg, which set me back a few days.* **2** to cost someone a lot of money: *Dinner set us back $300.*

set sth ⇔ **down** *phr v* to write something, especially in an official document: *We have set down clear guidelines.*

set forth *phr v* **1 set sth** ⇔ **forth** to explain something clearly in writing or speech [= **set out**]: *The book sets forth her views on childcare.* **2** *literary* to start a journey

set in *phr v* if something unpleasant sets in, it begins and is likely to continue: *Winter was setting in.*

set off *phr v* **1** to leave and start going somewhere: *We'd better set off before it gets dark.* | **+for** *What time do you have to set off for the airport?* **2 set sth** ⇔ **off** to make something start happening: *The news set off widespread panic.* **3 set sth** ⇔ **off** to make something explode or make a loud noise: *Some kids were setting off fireworks.*

set out *phr v* **1** to start a long journey: **+for** *They set out for the border at dawn.* **2** to intend and try to achieve a particular result: **set out to do sth** *He set out to prove his innocence.* | **set sth** ⇔ **out** to explain something clearly in writing or speech: *She set out her reasons for resigning in a letter.*

set up *phr v* **1** to start a company or organization [= **establish**]: **set sth** ⇔ **up** *She left the company to set up her own business.* | **set (yourself) up as sth** *John set himself up as a consultant.* **2 set sth** ⇔ **up** to make arrangements for something to happen: *Do you want me to set up a meeting?* **3** to get equipment ready to be used: *The DJ was still setting up when we arrived.* | **set sth** ⇔ **up** *He had set up a computer in the classroom.* → see box at PREPARE **4 set sth** ⇔ **up** to place or build something somewhere, especially something that is not permanent: *The police set up roadblocks around the city.* **5 set sb** ⇔ **up** to deliberately make other people think that someone has done something wrong: *He believes his partner set him up.*

set² *n* [C]

1 a group of things that belong together or are related: **+of** *a set of tools* | *You need a different set of skills.* | *a chess set* → see picture at COLLECTION

2 a television or radio: **a TV/television set**

3 a) a place where a film or programme is filmed: *He met her on the set of his latest movie* (=while filming it). **b)** the furniture, scenery etc used in a film or television programme, or on stage in a play

4 one part of a game of tennis: *Sampras won the set 6-4.*

5 a performance by a band, singer, or DJ: *They played a 90-minute set.*

set³ *adj* **1** in a particular place or position: **+on/in/among etc** *a village set high on a hill* | *The house is set back from the road.* **2** [only before noun] fixed and not changing: *You are given a set amount to spend.* | *We eat at a set time every day.* | *He has rather set ideas about religion.* **3** [not before noun] *informal* ready to do something: **+for** *Are you all set for your trip?* | *Get set for a fun evening!* **4 set on/upon/against sth** determined about something: *Tina is set on becoming a teacher.* | *His parents were dead set against the marriage.* **5 set to do sth** likely to do something: *The hot weather is set to continue.* **6 be set in your ways** to be used to doing things in the same way and not want to change

setback /'setbæk/ *n* [C] a problem that stops you from making progress: **+for** *Today's result was a major setback for the team.* → see box at PROBLEM

settee /se'tiː/ *n* [C] *BrE* a comfortable seat for two or three people [= **sofa**]

setting /'setɪŋ/ *n* [C usually singular] **1** the place where something is or happens, and the things that surround it: *a farmhouse in a beautiful setting* **2** the place or time in which the events in a book, film etc happen: **+for** *Ireland is the setting for his latest movie.* **3** a position in which you put the controls on a machine: *Turn the oven to its highest setting.*

settle /'setl/ v **1** [I,T] to end an argument or disagreement: **settle a dispute/lawsuit/conflict/argument etc** *a meeting to settle a pay dispute* | *I hope they can settle their differences* (=agree to stop arguing). **2** [T usually passive] to decide or arrange the details of something: *We need to agree a date so we can get things settled.* | *That settles it* (=helps to make a definite decision) – *I'm not going.* **3** [I] to start living in a place where you intend to live for a long time: **+in** *He finally settled in Madrid.* | *Many German families settled here in the 19th century.* **4** [I,T] to move into a comfortable position: **+back/on/in etc** *I settled back against my pillows.* | **settle yourself back/into etc** *Settle yourself down here and I'll bring you a drink.* **5** [I] to move or fall down and stay there: **+on** *Snow had settled on the roofs.* **6** [I,T] to pay money that you owe: **settle a bill/account/claim** *Please settle your account within 30 days.* | *He managed to settle with his creditors.* **7 settle a score** to do something bad to someone because they have done something bad to you

settle down *phr v* **1 settle (sb) down** to become calm and quiet, or to make someone calm and quiet: *Settle down, class.* | *Laura is upstairs settling the baby down.* **2** to start living a quiet life in one place, especially when you get married: *I want to settle down and have children.*

settle for sth *phr v* to accept something that is not as much or as good as you wanted: *We had to settle for a smaller car.*

settle in *phr v* to start to feel happy in a new house, job, or school: *Adam seems to have settled in at his new school.*

settle on/upon sth *phr v* to decide or agree on something: *Have you settled on a title for the book?*

settle up *phr v* to pay money that you owe

settled /'setld/ *adj* **1 feel/be settled** to feel happy and comfortable in a situation because it is no longer completely new: *I still don't feel settled in my new job.* **2** not changing, and not likely to change: *a period of more settled weather*

settlement /'setlmənt/ *n* [C] **1** an official agreement that ends an argument or fighting: **a political/peace/peaceful settlement** *We still hope to reach a peaceful settlement.* **2** a group of buildings or houses where people live or lived: *a Stone Age settlement*

settler /'setlə $ -ər/ *n* [C] someone who goes to live permanently in an area where not many people have lived before: *the early settlers in the American West*

'set-top ,box *n* [C] *BrE* a piece of electronic equipment that is connected to your television, that allows it to receive DIGITAL signals

'set-up *n informal* **1** [C] the way that something is organized or arranged: *We have a new set-up at work.* **2** [C] a dishonest plan that is intended to trick someone: *I realized that the whole thing was a set-up.* **3** [U] the act of organizing a new business or computer system: *Our IT department will help with installation and setup.*

seven /'sevən/ *number* the number 7: *We need seven chairs.* | *I got up at seven* (=seven o'clock). | *He's seven* (=7 years old).
→ **TWENTY-FOUR SEVEN**

seventeen /,sevən'ti:n◂/ *number* the number 17: *a group of seventeen soldiers* | *I'm nearly seventeen* (=17 years old).
—**seventeenth** *adj, pron: her seventeenth birthday* | *I'm planning to leave on the seventeenth* (=the 17th day of the month).

seventh¹ /'sevənθ/ *adj* coming after six other things in a series: *his seventh birthday*
—**seventh** *pron: I'm planning to leave on the seventh* (=the seventh day of the month).

seventh² *n* [C] one of seven equal parts of something

seventy /'sevənti/ *number*
1 the number 70
2 the seventies also **the '70s, the 1970s** [plural] the years from 1970 to 1979: **the early/mid/late seventies** *In the early seventies, Sag Harbor was still a peaceful village.*
3 be in your seventies to be aged between 70 and 79: **early/mid/late seventies** *Bill must be in his mid seventies now.*
4 in the seventies if the temperature is in the seventies, it is between 70 degrees and 79 degrees F
—**seventieth** *adj: her seventieth birthday*

sever /'sevə $ -ər/ *v* [T] *formal* **1** to cut through something completely: *His finger was severed in the accident.* **2** to completely end a relationship or connection: *He severed all ties with his father.*

several /'sevərəl/ *determiner, pron* more than a few, but not a lot [➡ **few**]: *I called her several times.* | *Several people offered to help.* | **several hundred/thousand etc** *A computer costs several hundred pounds.* | **+of** *Several of his students complained.*

severe /sɪ'vɪə $ -'vɪr/ *adj*
1 a severe problem, injury etc is very bad: *severe head injuries* | *The damage to the building was severe.*
2 severe weather is very extreme, for example very cold: *severe storms and gales*
3 severe punishment or criticism is very extreme or strict: *Drug smugglers face severe punishment.*
4 someone who is severe seems strict and not at all friendly [= **stern**]: *her severe expression*
—**severity** /sɪ'verɪti/ *n* [C,U]

severely /sɪ'vɪəli $ -'vɪr-/ *adv*
1 very badly: *She was severely injured.*
2 in a very strict way: *Those who disobeyed were severely punished.*

sew /səu $ sou/ *v* [I,T] past tense **sewed** past participle **sewn** /səun $ soun/ or **sewed**
to use a needle and thread to make or repair clothes: *My mother taught me to sew.* | **sew sth on sth** *Will you sew a button on my shirt?* → see picture at **KNIT**

sew sth ⇔ **up** *phr v* **1** [usually passive] to arrange or control something so that you get the result you want: *I've just sewn up a deal on a new account.* | *He has this election sewn up* (=is certain to win). **2** to close or repair something by sewing it

sewage /'sjuːɪdʒ, 'suː- $ 'suː-/ n [U] waste from the human body and used water that is carried away from buildings through pipes

sewer /'sjuːə,'suːə $ 'suːər/ n [C] a pipe under the ground that carries away sewage

sewing /'səʊɪŋ $ 'soʊ-/ n [U] **1** the activity of sewing **2** something that you have been sewing

'sewing ma,chine n [C] a machine for sewing cloth together

sewn /səʊn $ soʊn/ v a past participle of SEW

sex /seks/ n

1 [U] the physical activity that two people do together to produce babies or for pleasure: **+with** *He had sex with his sister's friend.* | **sex education** (=when young people are taught about sex) | **safe sex** (=when people use something that will protect them from sexual diseases)

2 [U] whether someone is male or female: *We don't want to know the sex of the baby before it's born.*

3 [C] all women considered as a group, or all men considered as a group: *people of **both sexes** (=men and women)* | *He doesn't have much success with **the opposite sex** (=people that are not his own sex).*

'sex ap,peal n [U] the quality of being sexually attractive

sexism /'seksɪzəm/ n [U] when someone is treated unfairly because of the sex that they are: *sexism in education* —**sexist** adj: *sexist attitudes*

'sex life n [C] someone's sexual activities

'sex of,fender n [C] someone who is guilty of a sexual crime such as RAPE

'sex ,symbol n [C] a famous person who a lot of people think is very sexually attractive

sexual /'sekʃuəl/ adj

1 relating to the physical activity of sex: *sexual abuse* | *sexual partners*

2 relating to differences between men and women: *sexual stereotypes*
—**sexually** adv: *He was sexually assaulted.*

,sexual 'harassment n [U] when someone makes sexual remarks to a person they work with, or touches them, when that person does not want them to

,sexual 'intercourse n [U] *formal* the activity of having sex

sexuality /,sekʃu'ælɪti/ n [U] someone's sexual feelings and activities

sexy /'seksi/ adj comparative **sexier**, superlative **sexiest** sexually attractive or exciting: *sexy underwear* | *a sexy man*

Sgt. the written abbreviation of **Sergeant**

sh, shh /ʃ/ *spoken* used to tell someone to be quiet → see box at QUIET

shabby /'ʃæbi/ adj **1** old and in bad condition: *a shabby old coat* **2** unfair or slightly dishonest: *shabby treatment* —**shabbily** adv —**shabbiness** n [U]

shack¹ /ʃæk/ n [C] a small simple building made of wood or metal

shack² v
shack up with sb phr v *informal* to start living with someone you have sex with, without marrying them

shackle /'ʃækəl/ v [T] **1** *literary* to prevent someone from being able to do what they want:

The government is opposed to shackling the media with privacy laws. **2** to put shackles on someone

shackles /'ʃækəlz/ n [plural] **1** *literary* limits that something puts on your freedom: **+of** *the shackles of the past* **2** two metal rings joined by a chain, used to keep a prisoner's hands or feet together

shade¹ /ʃeɪd/ n

1 [U] an area that is cooler because the light of the sun cannot reach it: *a plant that needs shade* | **in the shade** *Let's find a table in the shade.* → see box at SHADOW

2 [C] something used for reducing or keeping out light: *a lamp shade*

3 [C] a particular type of a colour: **+of** *a room painted in shades of blue*

4 shades [plural] *informal* SUNGLASSES

5 a shade very slightly: *The jacket was a shade too small.* | **a shade under/over/higher etc** *It weighed a shade over 5 kg.*

6 shade of meaning/opinion etc a meaning or opinion that is slightly different from others: *All shades of opinion are represented.*

7 put sb/sth in the shade *informal* to be much better than someone or something else

shade² v [T] to protect something from light: *She lifted her hand to shade her eyes.* | *a courtyard shaded by trees*

shadow¹ /'ʃædəʊ $ -doʊ/ n

1 [C] a dark shape on a surface, caused by a person or object being between the light and the surface: *the long shadow of a tree* | *The lamp **cast shadows** (=made shadows) around the room.*

USAGE

A **shadow** is a dark shape made by something that blocks the sun or a light: *She saw his shadow on the wall.*
Shade is a cool dark area where the sun does not reach: *We ate our lunch in the shade.*

2 [U] also **shadows** a part of an area that is dark, because light cannot reach it: **in shadow** *Most of the room was in shadow.* | **in the shadows** *He waited in the shadows.*

3 [singular] a bad effect or influence that something has: **under the shadow of sth** *families living under the shadow of unemployment* | *The financial problems will **cast a shadow over** the future of the project* (=make it less good).

4 without/beyond a shadow of (a) doubt used to say you are certain about something: *She knew without a shadow of doubt that he was lying to her.*

shadow² v [T] to follow someone in order to watch what they are doing

shadow³, Shadow adj [only before noun] having a particular job in the main party in the British parliament that is not in government: *the Shadow Chancellor*

shadowy /'ʃædəʊi $ -doʊi/ adj **1** difficult to see because of shadows, or full of shadows: *a shadowy corner* | *a shadowy figure* **2** mysterious or unknown: *the shadowy forces of evil*

shady /'ʃeɪdi/ adj **1** protected from the sun: *a shady corner* **2** slightly dishonest or illegal: *a shady character*

S

shaft /ʃɑːft $ ʃæft/ *n* [C] **1** a passage that goes down through a building or down into the ground: *a mine shaft* **2** a long handle on a tool or weapon **3** a narrow beam of light

shaggy /'ʃægi/ *adj* shaggy hair or fur is long and untidy

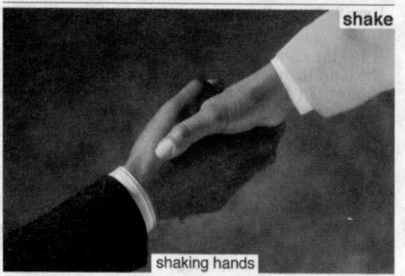

shake

shaking hands

shake¹ /ʃeɪk/ *v past tense* **shook** /ʃʊk/ *past participle* **shaken** /'ʃeɪkən/

1 [I,T] to move up and down or from side to side with quick movements, or to make something do this: *His hands were shaking.* | *Shake the bottle before use.*

THESAURUS

tremble – to shake because you are frightened or upset: *The dog was trembling with fear.*
shiver – to shake because you are very cold: *I jumped up and down to stop myself shivering.*
wobble – to shake from side to side: *The pile of books wobbled and fell.*
vibrate – to shake continuously with small fast movements: *The music was so loud that the whole room vibrated.*
rattle – to shake and make a noise: *The windows rattled in the wind.*

2 shake your head to move your head from side to side as a way of saying no [➡ **nod**]
3 shake hands (with sb) to hold someone's hand and move it up and down, as a greeting or when you have made an agreement: *We shook hands and said goodbye.*
4 [T] to make someone feel shocked and upset: *Mark was clearly shaken by the news.* | *terrorist attacks that shook the whole world*
5 [I] if your voice is shaking, it is unsteady and you sound nervous or angry
6 shake sb's confidence/faith/belief to make someone feel less confident, or less sure about their beliefs

shake sb ⇔ **down** *phr v AmE informal* to get money from someone by using threats
shake sb/sth ⇔ **off** *phr v* **1** to get rid of an illness or problem: *I can't shake off this cold.* **2** to escape from someone who is chasing you
shake sth ⇔ **out** *phr v* to shake something so that small pieces of dirt, dust etc come off it: *He shook out the blanket.*
shake sb/sth ⇔ **up** *phr v* **1** to make someone feel shocked or upset: *She was badly shaken up by the accident.* **2** to make changes to an organization so it is more effective: *plans to shake up the legal profession* → **SHAKE-UP**

shake² *n* [C] **1** when someone shakes something: *He gave the bottle a shake.* **2** a MILKSHAKE

shakedown /'ʃeɪkdaʊn/ *n* [C] *AmE informal* when someone gets money from another person by using threats

'shake-up *n* [C] when big changes are made to the way something is organized

shaky /'ʃeɪki/ *adj* **1** weak and unsteady because you are ill or old, or have had a shock: *My legs felt shaky.* **2** not very good and likely to fail: *a shaky economy* | *The team got off to a shaky start.* **3** not firm or steady: *a dangerously shaky elevator*

shall /ʃəl; *strong* ʃæl/ *modal verb especially BrE* negative short form **shan't**

1 I/we shall used to say what you are going to do: *We shall be away next week.*

USAGE

You can use both **shall** and **will** to say what you are going to do, but **will** or the short form **'ll** is usually used in ordinary speech and shall is more formal.

2 shall I/we? used to make a suggestion or ask someone to decide about what to do: *Shall I make some coffee?* | *Where shall we meet?*

shallow

shallow

deep

shallow /'ʃæləʊ $ -loʊ/ *adj*

1 not deep [≠ **deep**]: *a shallow pool* | *a shallow bowl*
2 not showing any serious or careful thought [≠ **deep**]: *a shallow argument*

shallows /'ʃæləʊz $ -loʊz/ *n* **the shallows** a part of a river, lake etc which is not deep

sham /ʃæm/ *n* [singular] something that is not what it seems to be and is intended to deceive people: *Their marriage was a sham.* —**sham** *adj*

shamble /'ʃæmbəl/ *v* [I + adv/prep] to walk slowly and awkwardly because you are weak or lazy

shambles /'ʃæmbəlz/ *n* [singular] *informal* something that is very badly organized or very untidy: *The project was a complete shambles.* → see box at **ORGANIZED**

shame¹ /ʃeɪm/ *n*

1 it's a shame/what a shame *spoken* used to say that a situation is disappointing and you wish that it was different: **+(that)** *It's a shame you can't come.* | *It's a great shame to be indoors on such a nice day.*
2 [U] the feeling that you have when you know that you have behaved badly or have lost other people's respect [➡ **ashamed**]: *a deep sense of*

shame | He's **brought shame** on the whole family. | *Have you **no shame**?*
3 put sb/sth to shame to be much better than someone or something else

shame² v [T] to make someone feel ashamed

shamefaced /ˌʃeɪmˈfeɪst◂/ adj looking ashamed or embarrassed

shameful /ˈʃeɪmfəl/ adj so bad that someone should be ashamed: *a shameful waste of money* —**shamefully** adv

shameless /ˈʃeɪmləs/ adj behaving badly and not caring whether other people disapprove: *a shameless deception* —**shamelessly** adv

shampoo¹ /ʃæmˈpuː/ n [C,U] liquid soap for washing your hair

shampoo² v [T] to wash something with shampoo

shandy /ˈʃændi/ n [C,U] plural **shandies** a drink made of beer mixed with LEMONADE

shan't /ʃɑːnt $ ʃænt/ BrE the short form of 'shall not'

shanty town /ˈʃænti taʊn/ n [C] an area where very poor people live in small houses made from pieces of metal, wood etc

---

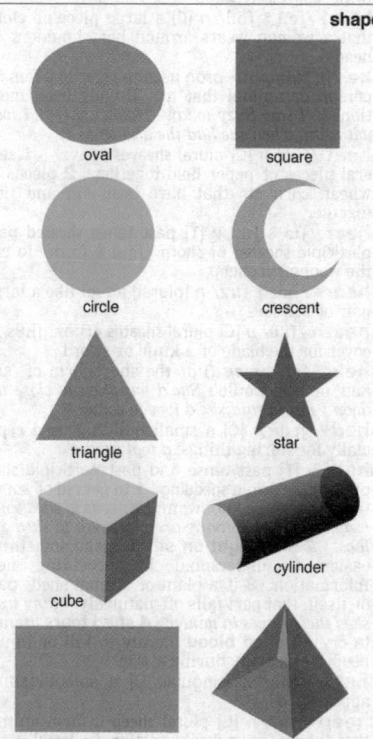

shape

oval   square

circle   crescent

triangle   star

cube   cylinder

rectangle   pyramid

---

shape¹ /ʃeɪp/ n
1 [C,U] the form that something has, for example round, square etc: **in the shape of sth** *a card in*

the shape of a heart | **in shape** *The room was square in shape.* | **heart-shaped/oval-shaped etc**

Types of shape

square – a shape with four straight sides that are equal in length and four angles of 90 degrees
circle – a round shape that is like an O
semi-circle – half a circle
triangle – a shape with three straight sides and three angles
rectangle – a shape with four straight sides and four angles of 90 degrees
oblong – a rectangle with four straight sides, two of which are longer than the other two
oval – a shape like a circle, but which is longer than it is wide
cylinder – an object in the shape of a tube

Adjectives to describe different shapes

square – shaped like a square: *a square box*
circular – shaped like a circle: *a circular table*
semi-circular – shaped like a semi-circle: *a semi-circular arch above the door*
triangular – shaped like a triangle: *a triangular pattern*
rectangular – shaped like a rectangle: *a simple rectangular building*
oblong – shaped like an oblong: *an oblong courtyard*
oval – shaped like an oval: *a large oval mirror*
cylindrical – shaped like a cylinder: *The statue is on top of a tall cylindrical column.*

S

2 [U] the health or condition that someone or something is in: **in good/poor etc shape** *The business is in good shape.* | *How do you **keep in shape** (=stay healthy)?* | **out of shape** (=not healthy) *I'm out of shape these days.* → see box at **EXERCISE**
3 take shape to develop into a clear and definite form: *A plan was beginning to take shape in his mind.*

shape² v [T] **1** to influence something and make it develop in a particular way: *an event that will shape the country's future* **2** to make something have a particular shape: **shape sth into sth** *Shape the clay into small balls.*
shape up phr v informal to develop or improve: *The day was shaping up well.*

shapeless /ˈʃeɪpləs/ adj not having a clear or definite shape

shapely /ˈʃeɪpli/ adj having an attractive shape: *shapely legs*

shard /ʃɑːd $ ʃɑːrd/ also **sherd** n [C] a sharp piece of broken glass, metal etc: **+of** *a shard of pottery*

share¹ /ʃeə $ ʃer/ v
1 [I,T] to have or use something with other people: **share sth with sb** *I shared a room with her when I was at college.* | *You'll have to share if there aren't enough books.*
2 also **share out** [T] to divide something between two or more people: **share sth between/among sb** *We shared the cake between us.* → see box at **GIVE**
3 [T] to have the same interests, opinion etc as

someone else: *She didn't share my point of view.* | *a feeling shared by many people*
4 [I,T] to tell someone else about an idea, secret, problem etc: *The Internet allows people to share information.*

share[2] *n*
1 [singular] a part of something which has been divided between two or more people: **+of** *I paid my share of the bill and left.*
2 [C] one of the equal parts into which the value of a company is divided, which people can buy and sell [➡ **stock**]: **+in** *A lot of people are **buying shares** in the company.*
3 have your (fair) share of sth to have quite a lot of something such as trouble or success: *I've had my share of bad luck this year.*
shareholder /'ʃeə,həʊldə $ 'ʃer,hoʊldər/ *n* [C] someone who owns shares in a company
shark /ʃɑːk $ ʃɑːrk/ *n* [C] a large sea fish with very sharp teeth
sharp[1] /ʃɑːp $ ʃɑːrp/ *adj*

sharp

blunt

1 something that is sharp has a very thin edge or narrow point that can cut things easily [≠ **blunt**]: *a sharp knife* | **razor sharp** (=very sharp)
2 a sharp turn, bend, corner etc changes direction very suddenly
3 a sharp increase, decrease etc is big and sudden [= **steep**]: *a sharp rise in profits*
4 sharp differences are very easy to notice: *There's a **sharp contrast** between his home and work life.*
5 good at noticing things or thinking very quickly [≠ **slow**]: *a sharp mind*
6 a sharp voice, remark, expression etc shows that you are annoyed or being unkind: *His tone was sharp.* | *He gave her a sharp look.* | *She **has** a very **sharp tongue** (=often says unkind things).*
7 a sharp pain is sudden and bad [≠ **dull**]: *He felt a sharp pain in his chest.*
8 wearing clothes that are attractive and fashionable [= **smart** *BrE*]: *She was a sharp dresser.*
9 a sharp image is clear and you can see all the details in it
10 a sharp taste is slightly bitter [≠ **mild**]
11 a sharp sound is sudden and loud: *a sharp cry*
12 F sharp/C sharp etc the musical note that is slightly higher than F, C etc [➡ **flat**]
13 a musical note that is sharp is played or sung slightly higher than it should be [➡ **flat**]
—**sharply** *adv* —**sharpness** *n* [U]
sharp[2] *adv* **1 at 8 o'clock/two-thirty etc sharp** at exactly 8.00, 2.30 etc **2 sharp left/right** *BrE* if you turn sharp left or right, you change direction suddenly to the left or right
sharp[3] *n* [C] a musical note that is slightly higher than a particular note, shown by the sign (#) in written music [➡ **flat**]
sharpen /'ʃɑːpən $ 'ʃɑːr-/ *v* [T] to make something sharp: *She sharpened all her pencils.*
,**sharp-'eyed** *adj* good at noticing things

shatter /'ʃætə $ -ər/ *v* **1** [I,T] to break suddenly into very small pieces, or to make something do this: **+into** *The plate hit the floor and shattered into tiny pieces.* ➜ see box at **BREAK** **2** [T] to destroy something completely, especially someone's hopes or beliefs: *An injury shattered his hopes of a baseball career.*
shattered /'ʃætəd $ -ərd/ *adj* **1** very shocked and upset **2** *BrE informal* very tired ➜ see box at **TIRED**
shattering /'ʃætərɪŋ/ *adj* very shocking or upsetting: *a shattering experience*
shave[1] /ʃeɪv/ *v* [I,T] to cut off hair from the skin on your face, legs etc, using a razor: *He washed and shaved.* | **shave sth off** *I've decided to shave off my beard.*
—**shaven** *adj*: *his shaven head*
shave[2] *n* **1** [C usually singular] if a man has a shave, he shaves the hair growing on his face **2 a close shave** a situation in which you only just avoid an accident or something bad
shaver /'ʃeɪvə $ -ər/ *n* [C] a piece of electrical equipment used for shaving [➡ **razor**]
shavings /'ʃeɪvɪŋz/ *n* [plural] very thin pieces that have been cut from the surface of something, especially wood
shawl /ʃɔːl $ ʃɒːl/ *n* [C] a large piece of cloth that a woman wears around her shoulders or head
she /ʃi; *strong* ʃiː/ *pron* used to refer to a female person or animal that has already been mentioned: *'I saw Suzy today.' 'How is she?'* | *I was with Ann when she had the accident.*
sheaf /ʃiːf/ *n* [C] plural **sheaves** /ʃiːvz/ **1** several pieces of paper held together **2** pieces of wheat, corn etc that have been cut and tied together
shear /ʃɪə $ ʃɪr/ *v* [T] past tense **sheared** past participle **sheared** or **shorn** /ʃɔːn $ ʃɔːrn/ to cut the wool off of a sheep
shears /ʃɪəz $ ʃɪrz/ *n* [plural] a tool like a large pair of scissors
sheath /ʃiːθ/ *n* [C] plural **sheaths** /ʃiːðz, ʃiːθs/ a cover for the blade of a knife or sword
she'd /ʃid; *strong* ʃiːd/ the short form of 'she had' or 'she would': *She'd forgotten to close the door.* | *Paula said she'd love to come.*
shed[1] /ʃed/ *n* [C] a small building used especially for storing things: *a tool shed*
shed[2] *v* [T] past tense and past participle **shed** present participle **shedding** **1** to get rid of something that you do not want: *He needs to shed some weight.* | *The company are planning to shed 200 jobs.* **2 shed light on sth** to make something easier to understand by providing new information **3** if a plant or animal sheds part of itself, that part falls off naturally: *Many trees shed their leaves in winter.* **4 shed tears** *literary* to cry **5 shed blood** *literary* to kill or injure people, especially during a war
sheen /ʃiːn/ *n* [singular, U] a smooth shiny appearance
sheep /ʃiːp/ *n* [C] plural **sheep** a farm animal that is kept for its wool and meat [➡ **lamb**] ➜ see picture at **FARM**[1]
➜ **BLACK SHEEP**
sheepish /'ʃiːpɪʃ/ *adj* slightly embarrassed because you have done something silly or wrong: *a sheepish smile* —**sheepishly** *adv*

S

sheepskin /'ʃiːp,skɪn/ *n* [C,U] the skin of a sheep with the wool still on it: *a sheepskin coat*

sheer /ʃɪə $ ʃɪr/ *adj* **1** [only before noun] used to emphasize the amount, size, or degree of something: **the sheer size/weight/volume etc** *The sheer size of some files caused problems.* | **sheer delight/joy/luck etc** *She giggled with sheer delight.* **2** extremely steep: *a sheer drop*

sheet /ʃiːt/ *n* [C]
1 a large piece of thin cloth that you put on a bed [➡ **blanket, duvet**]: *Have you changed the sheets* (=put clean sheets on the bed)? → see picture at **BED**
2 a piece of paper, glass, or metal: **+of** *a sheet of paper with names on it* → see picture at **PIECE**
→ **BALANCE SHEET**

sheikh, **sheik** /ʃeɪk $ ʃiːk/ *n* [C] an Arab leader or prince

shelf /ʃelf/ *n* [C] plural **shelves** /ʃelvz/ a long flat board fixed to a wall or in a cupboard, used for putting things on: **top/bottom shelf** *Put the book back on the top shelf.* | *shelves of books* | *supermarket shelves*

she'll /ʃɪl; *strong* ʃiːl/ the short form of 'she will': *She'll be here soon.*

shell[1] /ʃel/ *n* [C]

shell

1 a) the hard outside part of a nut, egg, or seed **b)** the hard outside part that covers some animals, for example SNAILS and CRABS
2 a metal container filled with an explosive substance, which is fired from a large gun [= **cartridge**]
3 the outside structure of something such as a building or vehicle: *the concrete shell of the building*
4 come out of/go into your shell to become less shy or become shyer

shell[2] *v* [T] **1** to fire at something with shells from a gun **2** to remove the shell from something
   shell out (sth) *phr v informal* to pay a lot of money for something

shellfish /'ʃel,fɪʃ/ *n* [C,U] plural **shellfish** an animal that lives in water, has a shell, and is eaten as food

shelter[1] /'ʃeltə $ -ər/ *n*
1 [U] protection from danger or from the weather: **in/under the shelter of sth** *He was standing in the shelter of a doorway.* | *They took shelter under a tree.*
2 [C] a small building or covered place that protects you from bad weather or from attack: *an air-raid shelter* | *a bus shelter* (=where people wait for buses)
3 [C] a place where people or animals can stay if they do not have a home or are in danger: *an animal shelter* | *a shelter for homeless people*

shelter[2] *v* **1** [I] to stay somewhere in order to be protected from danger or the weather: **+from** *People were in doorways, sheltering from the rain.* **2** [T] to provide a place where someone or something is protected from danger or the

weather: *people who shelter criminals* | **shelter sb/sth from sth** *The trees shelter you from the sun.*

sheltered /'ʃeltəd $ -ərd/ *adj* **1** protected from extreme weather conditions: *a sheltered bay* **2** someone who has had a sheltered life has not experienced many things: *Gina had a sheltered childhood.*

shelve /ʃelv/ *v* [T] to decide not to continue with a plan, although you might continue with it later: *Plans to build a new airport have been shelved.*

shelves /ʃelvz/ *n* the plural of SHELF

shelving /'ʃelvɪŋ/ *n* [U] a set of shelves

shepherd[1] /'ʃepəd $ -ərd/ *n* [C] someone whose job is to take care of sheep

shepherd[2] *v* [T] to lead someone somewhere and make sure they go where you want them to: **shepherd sb out of/into etc sth** *He took her arm and shepherded her to the taxi.*

sherd /ʃɜːd $ ʃɜːrd/ *n* another spelling of SHARD

sheriff /'ʃerɪf/ *n* [C] an elected law officer in a US COUNTY

sherry /'ʃeri/ *n* [C,U] plural **sherries** a strong Spanish wine

she's /ʃiz; *strong* ʃiːz/ *spoken* the short form of 'she is' or 'she has': *She's called Ruth.* | *She's arrived!*

shh /ʃ/ another spelling of SH

shield[1] /ʃiːld/ *n* [C] a piece of metal or plastic that you hold in front of your body to protect yourself in a fight or battle: *The police were carrying riot shields.*

shield[2] *v* [T] to protect someone or something from being hurt or damaged: *I tried to shield my eyes from the sun.*

shift[1] /ʃɪft/ *v* **1** [I,T] to move from one place or position to another, or to make something do this: *Paul shifted uncomfortably in his seat.* | *We'll have to shift the furniture.* **2** [I] if your opinions or beliefs shift, they change **3 shift the blame/responsibility** to say that someone else is responsible for something, especially something bad

shift[2] *n* [C] **1** a change in the way people think about something, or in the way something is done: **+in** *a shift in public opinion* **2** one of the periods during each day and night when workers in a factory, hospital etc do their work: *the night shift*

shifty /'ʃɪfti/ *adj* someone who is shifty looks dishonest

shilling /'ʃɪlɪŋ/ *n* [C] a British coin used in the past

shimmer /'ʃɪmə $ -ər/ *v* [I] to shine with a soft light that seems to shake slightly: *The sea shimmered in the sunlight.*

shin /ʃɪn/ *n* [C] the front part of your leg between your knee and your foot → see picture on page A3

shine[1] /ʃaɪn/ *v* past tense and past participle **shone** /ʃɒn $ ʃoʊn/
1 [I] to produce bright light: *The sun was shining.*

THESAURUS

flash – to shine brightly for a very short time: *Lightning flashed across the sky.*

flicker – to shine with an unsteady light: *The candle flickered and went out.*

twinkle – to shine in the dark but not very brightly or continuously: *stars twinkling in the sky*

glow – to shine with a warm soft light: *The evening sun glowed in the sky.*

sparkle – to shine with many small bright points of light: *diamonds sparkling in the light*

2 [T] to point a light in a particular direction: **shine sth on/at/around etc sth** *He shone his torch around the room.*
3 [I] to look bright and smooth: *her long shining hair*
4 [I] if your eyes are shining, they are very bright because you are happy or excited
5 [I] if you shine at an activity, you do it very well: **+at** *She shines at most sports.*

shine² *n* [singular,U] **1** the brightness that something has when light shines on it: *hair with lots of shine* **2 take a shine to sb** *informal* to like someone and be attracted to them when you have only just met them

shingle /ˈʃɪŋɡəl/ *n* [U] small round pieces of stone on a beach

shiny /ˈʃaɪni/ *adj* smooth and bright: *shiny black shoes* | *shiny hair*

ship¹ /ʃɪp/ *n* [C] a large boat used for carrying people or things across the sea: **cruise/cargo/supply etc ship** | **by ship** *Supplies came by ship.*

THESAURUS

Ships that carry people
passenger ship, cruise ship, liner, ferry
Ships that carry goods
cargo ship, merchant ship, freighter, oil tanker, barge
Fighting ships
aircraft carrier, battleship, cruiser, destroyer, frigate, gunboat, submarine, warship

ship² *v* [T] **shipped, shipping** to send goods somewhere

shipment /ˈʃɪpmənt/ *n* [C,U] a load of goods sent by sea, road, or air, or the act of sending them: **+of** *a shipment of grain* | *The goods are ready for shipment.*

shipping /ˈʃɪpɪŋ/ *n* [U] **1** ships: *The port is closed to all shipping.* **2** the sending of goods from one place to another, especially by ship: *a shipping company*

shipwreck¹ /ˈʃɪp-rek/ *n* [C,U] an accident in which a ship is destroyed at sea

shipwreck² *v* **be shipwrecked** if you are shipwrecked, the ship you are travelling on is destroyed in an accident at sea

shipyard /ˈʃɪp-jɑːd $ -jɑːrd/ *n* [C] a place where ships are built or repaired

shirk /ʃɜːk $ ʃɜːrk/ *v* [I,T] to deliberately avoid working: *He was accused of shirking his duties.* —**shirker** *n* [C]

shirt /ʃɜːt $ ʃɜːrt/ *n* [C] a piece of clothing for the upper part of your body and your arms that usually has a collar and has buttons down the front [➡ **blouse**] → see picture at **CLOTHES**
→ **TEE SHIRT, T-SHIRT**

shiver /ˈʃɪvə $ -ər/ *v* [I] if you shiver, your body shakes slightly because you are cold or frightened [= **tremble**]: *Come inside, you're shivering.* | **shiver with cold/fear/delight etc** → see box at **SHAKE** —**shiver** *n* [C] *His words sent a shiver down her spine.* —**shivery** *adj*

shoal /ʃəʊl $ ʃoʊl/ *n* [C] a large group of fish swimming together → see box at **GROUP**

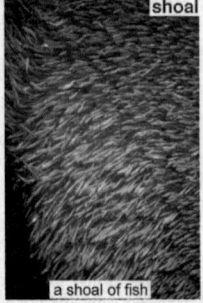
a shoal of fish

shock¹ /ʃɒk $ ʃɑːk/ *n*
1 [C usually singular] if something is a shock, or if it gives you a shock, you did not expect it, and it makes you feel very surprised, and usually upset: *I got a terrible shock when I saw the bill.* | *The sudden noise gave me a shock.* | *Tom's death came as a complete shock* (=was a complete shock) *to us all.* | **be a shock to discover/find/realize etc (that)** *It was a shock to hear that she was leaving.* | **+of** *I'm still recovering from the shock of his death.*
2 [C] an **ELECTRIC SHOCK**
3 [U] a medical condition in which someone looks pale and their heart and lungs are not working correctly, usually after a sudden very unpleasant experience: *I was taken to hospital suffering from shock.* | *She's still in a state of shock.*
4 [C,U] violent shaking caused by an explosion, a crash etc: *The rubber supports are designed to absorb shock.*
→ **CULTURE SHOCK**

shock² *v*
1 [T] to make someone feel very surprised and upset: *I was shocked by his arrogance.* | **be shocked to hear/learn/discover etc sth** *They were shocked to hear of his arrest.*
2 [I,T] to make someone feel very offended, by talking or behaving in an immoral or socially unacceptable way: *The play shocked audiences all over the country.* | *Ken loved to shock.*
—**shocked** *adj*: *We are deeply shocked by what happened.*

shocking /ˈʃɒkɪŋ $ ˈʃɑːk-/ *adj* very upsetting, wrong, or immoral: *a shocking waste of money*

'shock wave *n* [C] **1** a very strong wave of air pressure or heat from an explosion, **EARTHQUAKE** etc **2 shock waves** strong feelings of shock that people feel when something bad happens unexpectedly – used especially in news reports: *His murder sent shock waves through the city.*

shod¹ /ʃɒd $ ʃɑːd/ *adj literary* wearing shoes of the type mentioned

shoddy /ˈʃɒdi $ ˈʃɑːdi/ *adj* **1** badly or cheaply made: *shoddy goods* **2** unfair and dishonest: *He treated me in a pretty shoddy way.* —**shoddily** *adv*

shoe¹ /ʃuː/ *n* [C]
1 something that you wear to cover your feet, made of leather or other strong material: *a pair of shoes* | *running shoes*

shoot² n [C] **1** a new part of a plant **2** an occasion when someone takes photographs or makes a film: *a photo shoot*

shooting /'ʃuːtɪŋ/ n **1** [C] a situation in which someone is injured or killed by a gun **2** [U] the sport of killing animals and birds with guns

,shooting 'star n [C] a piece of rock or metal from space that burns brightly as it falls towards the Earth

'shoot-out n [C] a fight using guns: *a shoot-out with police*

shop¹ /ʃɒp $ ʃɑːp/ n

1 [C] *especially BrE* a building where you can buy things [= store *AmE*]: **toy/pet/shoe/gift etc shop** | *a shop window* | *I'm just going to the shops.* | **coffee/tea shop** (=where you can buy and drink coffee or tea)

shoes   shoe

heel

laces

sole

slippers

boots

sandals

stilettos

clogs

2 be in sb's shoes to be in the situation that someone else is in: *I wouldn't like to be in your shoes when Kate gets home.*

shoe² v [T] past tense and past participle **shod** /ʃɒd $ ʃɑːd/ present participle **shoeing** to put HORSESHOES (=curved pieces of metal) on a horse's feet

shoelace /'ʃuːleɪs/ n [C] a thin piece of string or leather used to fasten a shoe [= lace]

shoestring /'ʃuːˌstrɪŋ/ n **on a shoestring** using very little money: *a movie made on a shoestring*

shone /ʃɒn $ ʃoʊn/ v the past tense and past participle of SHINE

shoo /ʃuː/ *spoken* used to tell a person or an animal to go away —**shoo** v [T] *Gran shooed us back upstairs.*

shook /ʃʊk/ v the past tense of SHAKE

shoot¹ /ʃuːt/ v past tense and past participle **shot** /ʃɒt $ ʃɑːt/

1 [I,T] to fire a gun at someone, or kill or injure someone with a gun: *She pulled out a gun and shot him.* | *Don't shoot!* | **+at** *Someone on the roof was shooting at her.* | *Three people were **shot dead** by police.* | **shoot yourself** *Finally, he shot himself.*

2 [I,T] to move quickly in a particular direction, or to make something move in this way: **+out/ through/into etc** *I shot out of bed.* | **shoot sth out/into etc** *Most fountains shoot water into the air.*

3 [I,T] to take photographs or make a film of something: *The movie was shot in Rome.*

4 [I] to kick or throw a ball towards the place in a sports game where you can make points: *Giggs shot from outside the penalty box.*

shoot sb/sth ⇔ **down** phr v **1** to make an enemy plane crash to the ground, by firing weapons at it: *His plane was shot down over Russia.* **2** to tell someone that what they are saying or suggesting is wrong or stupid: *Whenever I suggest anything, I get **shot down in flames.***

shoot up phr v to increase very quickly: *Prices shot up by 60%.*

Small shops

bakery/baker's *BrE* – a shop selling bread and cakes

butcher's – a shop selling meat

greengrocer's *BrE* – a shop selling fruit and vegetables

delicatessen – a shop selling special foods, cheeses, cooked meats etc

off licence *BrE*/**liquor store** *AmE* – a shop selling wine, beer etc

newsagent's *BrE*/**newsstand** *especially AmE* – a shop selling newspapers, magazines, cigarettes, sweets

chemist's *BrE*/**drugstore** *AmE* – a shop selling medicines, bath and beauty products etc

convenience store – a shop selling food, alcohol, magazines etc, especially one that is open 24 hours a day

Big shops

supermarket – a big shop that sells food, alcohol, cleaning materials, and other things for the house

department store – a very big shop with one part for clothes, one for furniture, one for the kitchen etc

superstore – a very big modern shop, especially one built outside the centre of a city

DIY store *BrE* – a very large shop that sells equipment for repairing and decorating your home

garden centre *BrE*/**garden center** *AmE* – a place that sells plants and garden equipment

People who use or work in shops

customer – someone who buys the things sold in a shop

sales assistant, shop assistant *BrE*/**sales clerk** *AmE* – someone whose job it is to help customers to buy things

→ CUSTOMER

2 [U] *AmE* a subject taught in schools that shows students how to use tools and machinery to make or repair things

→ BETTING SHOP, CHARITY SHOP, CORNER SHOP, THRIFT SHOP

shop² v [I] **shopped, shopping** to go to a shop to buy things: *Zoe wanted to go shopping.* | **+for** *I was out shopping for food.* | **+at** *I usually shop at Tesco's.*—**shopper** n [C] → see box at CUSTOMER

S

shop around *phr v* to compare the price and quality of different things before you decide which to buy

shopaholic /ˌʃɒpəˈhɒlɪk $ ˌʃɑːpəˈhɒː-/ *n* [C] *informal* someone who likes to go shopping a lot, and often buys things that they do not really need

'shop as,sistant *n* [C] *BrE* someone who serves customers in a shop [= **sales clerk** *AmE*]

,shop 'floor *n* [singular] the part of a factory where goods are made, or the people who work there

shopkeeper /'ʃɒpˌkiːpə $ 'ʃɑːpˌkiːpər/ *n* [C] *especially BrE* someone who owns or is in charge of a small shop [= **storekeeper** *AmE*]

shoplifting /'ʃɒpˌlɪftɪŋ $ 'ʃɑːp-/ *n* [U] the crime of taking things from shops without paying for them: *She was arrested for shoplifting.* → see box at STEAL —**shoplifter** *n* [C] —**shoplift** *v* [I]

shopping /'ʃɒpɪŋ $ 'ʃɑː-/ *n* [U]

1 the activity of going to shops to buy things: *late-night shopping* | *I hate doing the shopping* (=buying the food and other things you regularly need). | **shopping trolley/cart/basket** | *a shopping list* (=list of the things you need to buy).

2 *BrE* the things that you have just bought from a shop: *Shall I help you carry the shopping in?* → WINDOW SHOPPING

'shopping ,centre *BrE*; **shopping center** *AmE* *n* [C] a group of shops together in one area

'shopping mall *n* [C] a MALL

shore¹ /ʃɔː $ ʃɔːr/ *n* [C,U] the land along the edge of an ocean, sea, or lake: *We were still about a mile from shore.* | *Only a few survivors reached the shore.* | **on the shore(s) of sth** *a town on the shores of Lake Garda*

THESAURUS

coast – the land next to the sea
beach – an area of sand or small stones at the edge of the sea
seaside *BrE* – the areas or towns next to the sea where people go to enjoy themselves

shore² *v*

shore sth ⇔ **up** *phr v* **1** to support a wall with pieces of wood or metal to stop it from falling down **2** to help or support something that is likely to fail or is not working well: *attempts to shore up the struggling economy*

shoreline /'ʃɔːlaɪn $ 'ʃɔːr-/ *n* [C,U] the land along the edge of a large area of water such as an ocean or lake: *I stood silently on the shoreline.* | *the bay's 13000 km of shoreline*

shorn /ʃɔːn $ ʃɔːrn/ *v* the past participle of SHEAR

short¹ /ʃɔːt $ ʃɔːrt/ *adj*

1 happening for only a little time [≠ **long**]: *a short meeting* | *I've only lived here a short time.* | *Life is short.* | *People have short memories* (=they soon forget things that have happened).

2 not very long in length or far in distance [≠ **long**]: *a short skirt* | *His hair was very short.* | *a short distance from the sea*

3 not very tall [≠ **tall**]: *a short fat man*

4 a) if you are short of something, you do not have enough of it: **+of** *Are you short of money?* | *I'm a bit short of time.* | **be 5p/$10**

etc short | *Do you want to join our team? We're one short.* **b)** if something is short, there is not enough of it: *Money was short.* | *Water was in short supply* (=not enough was available).

5 at short notice *BrE* **on short notice** *AmE* with very little warning that something is going to happen: *The party was arranged at short notice.*

6 in the short term/run having an effect for only a short time, not very far into the future [≠ **short-term**]: *The problem has been solved, at least in the short term.*

7 be short for sth to be a shorter way of saying a name: *Her name's Jo, short for Joanne.*

8 be short with sb to speak to someone using very few words, in a way that seems rude or unfriendly: *Sorry I was so short with you.*

9 have a short temper someone who has a short temper gets angry very easily —**shortness** *n* [U]

short² *adv* **short of doing sth** except for doing something: *They've done everything short of cancelling the project.* → **cut sth short** at CUT¹ → **fall short** at FALL¹ → **be running short (of sth)** at RUN¹ → **stop short of (doing) sth** at STOP¹

short³ *n* **1 shorts** [plural] **a)** short trousers ending at the knees: *a pair of shorts* | *a boy in shorts* | **running/cycling/tennis etc shorts** → see picture at CLOTHES **b)** *especially AmE* men's underwear with short legs **2 in short** used when you want to say the most important point in a few words: *In short, the answer is no.* **3 for short** used as a shorter way of saying a name: *His name's Maximilian, or Max for short.* **4** [C] *BrE* a glass of a strong alcoholic drink such as WHISKY [= **shot** *AmE*] → BOXER SHORTS

shortage /'ʃɔːtɪdʒ $ 'ʃɔːr-/ *n* [C,U] a situation in which there is not enough of something: **+of** *a shortage of skilled labour* | *food shortages*

shortbread /'ʃɔːtbred $ 'ʃɔːrt-/ *n* [U] a hard sweet BISCUIT made with a lot of butter

,short-'change *v* [T] **1** to treat someone unfairly by not giving them what they deserve: *Is society short-changing older people?* **2** to give back too little money to a customer who has paid for something

,short 'circuit *n* [C] a failure of an electrical system, caused by a fault in the wires —**short circuit** *v* [I,T]

shortcoming /'ʃɔːtˌkʌmɪŋ $ 'ʃɔːrt-/ *n* [C usually plural] a fault in someone or something that makes them less effective: **+of/in** *the shortcomings of the political system*

,short 'cut /ˌ$ ˈ. ./ *n* [C] a quicker and more direct way of getting somewhere or achieving something: *He took a short cut across the fields.* | **+to** *There are no short cuts to becoming an actor.*

shorten /'ʃɔːtn $ 'ʃɔːrtn/ *v* [I,T] to become shorter, or to make something shorter: *Smoking shortens your life.*

shortfall /'ʃɔːtfɔːl $ 'ʃɔːrtfɒːl/ *n* [C] if there is a shortfall in something, there is not enough of it: **+in** *a $2.5 billion shortfall in funds*

shorthand /'ʃɔːthænd $ 'ʃɔːrt-/ *n* [U] a fast method of writing using special signs and short forms of words

S

'short list *n* [C] *BrE* a list of people or things that have been chosen from a larger group to be considered for a job or prize

short-list *v* **be short-listed** *BrE* to be put on a short list

short-lived /ˌʃɔːt ˈlɪvd◂ $ ˌʃɔːrt ˈlaɪvd◂ / *adj* existing or happening for only a short time: *His success was short-lived.*

shortly /'ʃɔːtli $ 'ʃɔːrt-/ *adv* **1** soon: *The report will be published shortly.* | *We left shortly after two.* → see box at **SOON** **2** speaking impatiently: *'I know that,' he replied shortly.*

,short-'range *adj* [only before noun] short-range weapons are designed to travel or be used over a short distance

shortsighted /ˌʃɔːtˈsaɪtᵻd◂ $ ˌʃɔːrt-/, **,short-'sighted** *adj* **1** *especially BrE* if you are short-sighted, you cannot see objects clearly unless they are close to you [= **nearsighted** *AmE*] **2** if a decision or action is shortsighted, it is not sensible because it does not consider the future effects of something: *short-sighted economic policies*

,short 'story *n* [C] a short written story

,short-'term *adj* continuing for only a short time: *short-term benefits*

'short wave *n* [U] a range of short radio waves used for broadcasting [➜ **medium wave, long wave, FM**]

shot¹ /ʃɒt $ ʃɑːt/ *n* [C]

1 when someone fires a gun, or the sound that this makes: *The gunman **fired** three **shots**.* | *We **heard** a **shot**.* | *He's a very **good shot** (=he can fire a gun well).*

2 an attempt in sport to throw, kick, or hit the ball towards the place where you can get a point: **Good shot!** | **+at** *We only had one **shot at goal** in the whole match.*

3 a photograph, or a picture of something in a film: **+of** *I got a lovely **shot** of John.* | **opening/closing/final shot** *the opening shots of the movie*

4 *informal* an attempt to do something: *I'm going to **have a shot at** decorating the house myself.* | *I'll **give it** my best **shot** (=try as hard as possible).*

5 like a shot very quickly and eagerly: *I'd marry Pete **like a shot**.*

6 a small amount of a strong alcoholic drink: **+of** *a shot of whisky*

7 *especially AmE* when a doctor puts medicine into your body using a needle [= **injection, jab** *BrE*]: *Have you **had** your typhoid **shot**?* | **+of** *The doctor gave me a shot of antibiotics.*

8 a shot in the arm something that makes you more confident or successful: *Being chosen was a real shot in the arm for Mike.*
→ **call the shots** at **CALL¹** → **long shot** at **LONG¹**

shot² *v* the past tense and past participle of **SHOOT**

shotgun /'ʃɒtɡʌn $ 'ʃɑːt-/ *n* [C] a long gun, used especially for shooting animals and birds

should /ʃəd; *strong* ʃʊd/ *modal verb* negative short form **shouldn't**

1 used to say what is the right or sensible thing to do: *You **should** see a doctor.* | *Children **shouldn't** be outside this late.* | *They **should have** called the police (=it would have been sensible, but they did not do it).*

2 used to give or ask for advice: *You **should** read

his new book – it's fascinating.* | *Should I wear my black dress?*

3 used to say that you expect something to happen or be true: *Your Dad **should** be back soon.* | *It **should** be a nice day tomorrow.* | *It was an easy test and he **should have** passed (=he was expected to pass, but he did not).*

4 *formal* used to talk about something that may possibly be true: *Should you (=if you) wish to complain, please use this leaflet.*

5 *especially BrE formal* used to ask politely for something, offer to do something, or say that you want to do something: *I **should be grateful if you would** send a receipt.*

6 *spoken* **I should think/imagine/hope** used to say that you think or hope something is true, when you are not certain: *'Is that enough?' 'I should think so.'*

shoulder¹ /'ʃəʊldə $ 'ʃoʊldər/ *n* [C]

1 one of the two parts of your body at each side of your neck where your arm is connected: *She rested her head on my shoulder.* | *When we asked what was wrong, she just **shrugged** her **shoulders** (=raised them to show that she did not know or care).* | **look/glance over your shoulder** (=to look behind you) *I looked over my shoulder to see if anyone was following me.* → see picture on page A3

2 the part of a piece of clothing that covers your shoulders: *a jacket with **padded shoulders***

3 a shoulder to cry on someone who gives you sympathy: *Chris was always there when I **needed a shoulder to cry on**.*

4 on sb's shoulders if blame or a difficult job falls on someone's shoulders, they have to accept it or do it
→ **HARD SHOULDER**

shoulder² *v* [T] **1 shoulder the responsibility/blame/cost etc** to accept a difficult or unpleasant responsibility, duty etc: *Residents are being asked to shoulder the costs of the repairs.* **2** to lift something onto your shoulder to carry it

'shoulder bag *n* [C] a bag that hangs from your shoulder

'shoulder blade *n* [C] one of the two flat bones just below your shoulders on your back → see picture on page A3

shouldn't /'ʃʊdnt/ the short form of 'should not'

should've /'ʃʊdəv/ the short form of 'should have'

shout¹ /ʃaʊt/ *v*

[I,T] to say something very loudly: *There's no need to shout.* | *'Over here!' he shouted.* | **+at** *I wish he'd stop shouting at the children.* | **+for** *They shouted for help.*

THESAURUS

call (out) – to shout in order to get someone's attention
scream – to shout with a high voice because you are frightened, angry, excited etc
yell – to shout because you are angry, excited etc, or to make someone hear you
cry (out) – to shout something loudly
raise your voice – to say something more loudly than normal in order to make sure people can hear you

cheer – to shout to show that you like a team, performance etc
→ SCREAM

shout sb ⇔ **down** *phr v* to shout so that someone who is speaking cannot be heard: *She tried to argue, but was quickly shouted down.*

shout sth ⇔ **out** *phr v* to say something suddenly in a loud voice: *Don't shout out the answer.*

shout² *n* [C]

1 something that someone says very loudly: *She heard a shout.* | **+of** *He gave a shout of pain.*

2 give sb a shout *spoken* to go and find someone and tell them something: *Give me a shout if you need any help.*

shove /ʃʌv/ *v* **1** [I,T] to push someone or something in a rough or careless way: *He shoved her towards the car.* → see box at PUSH **2** [T] to put something somewhere carelessly or without thinking much: **shove sth into/in etc sth** *She shoved the books into her briefcase.* —**shove** *n* [C]

shovel¹ /ˈʃʌvəl/ *n* [C] a tool with a rounded blade and a long handle used for moving earth, stones etc

shovel² *v* [I,T] shovelled, shovelling *BrE*; shoveled, shoveling *AmE* **1** to move earth, stones etc with a shovel **2 shovel sth into/onto sth** to put something, usually food, somewhere quickly: *He sat shovelling his dinner into his mouth.*

show¹ /ʃəʊ $ ʃoʊ/ *v* past tense **showed** past participle **shown** /ʃəʊn $ ʃoʊn/

1 [T] to let someone see something: **show sb sth** *She showed me her photos.* | **show sth to sb** *I showed the letter to Ruth.*

2 [T] if you show someone how to do something, you do it and they watch, so that they learn how to do it: **show sb how/what etc** *Could you show me how to turn the oven on?* | *I'll show you what to do.*

3 [T] to make it clear that something is true or exists, by providing facts or information: **+(that)** *This study shows that poverty is increasing.* | **show how/what etc** *We wanted to show how united we were.*

4 [T] if you show your feelings, other people can see how you feel by the way that you look or behave: *Alan tried not to show his disappointment.*

5 [I,T] if something shows, people can see or notice it easily: *His anger showed on his face.* | *Ellie was tired, and it showed.* | *Light-coloured clothes tend to show the dirt.*

6 [T] to go with someone and guide them to a place: **show sb to/into sth** *Jill showed me to my room.* | *Did Rachel show you where to leave your coat?* | *I'll show you the way.*

7 [T] if a picture, map etc shows something, you can see it on the picture, map etc

8 [I,T] when a film or television programme is shown, people are able to see it in a cinema or on television: *The film will be shown on Channel 4.*

9 [T] if someone or something shows a particular quality, that quality can be seen: *The economy was showing signs of recovery.* | **show yourself (to be) sth** *Mr Peters has shown himself to be a fine teacher.*

10 have something/nothing to show for sth to have achieved something or nothing as a result of your efforts: *By the end of the day I was exhausted, but had nothing to show for all my work.*

show sb **around** (sth) *phr v* to go with someone around a place and show them what is important, interesting etc: *His wife showed us around the house.*

show off *phr v* **1** to try to make people admire you and think you are attractive, clever, funny, or important, in a way that is annoying other people: *Ignore him. He's just showing off.* **2 show** sth ⇔ **off** to show something to someone because you are very proud of it: *Jen proudly showed off her engagement ring.*

show up *phr v* **1** *informal* to arrive somewhere, especially when someone is waiting for you [= turn up]: *It was 9.20 when he finally showed up.* **2** to be easy to see or notice: *The bacteria showed up under the microscope.* **3 show** sb ⇔ **up** to make someone feel embarrassed by behaving in a stupid or unacceptable way when you are with them: *She showed me up in front of my friends.*

show² *n*

1 [C] a performance for the public, especially one that includes singing, dancing, or jokes: *The show starts at 7:30 pm.* | *a Broadway show*

2 [C] a programme on television or on the radio: *a TV show*

3 [C] an occasion when a group of things are brought together for people to look at: *the Chelsea Flower Show*

4 on show being shown to the public: *The photographs will be on show until May 4.*

5 a show of sth an occasion when someone deliberately shows a particular feeling, attitude, or quality: *a show of force by the police*

6 [singular,U] something that you do to pretend to other people that something is true, or to make them think you are attractive or impressive: **+of** *Lucy put on a show of indignation.* | **for show** *Critics say such efforts are just for show.*

→ CHAT SHOW, GAME SHOW, TALK SHOW

'show ˌbusiness also **show biz** /ˈʃəʊ bɪz $ ˈʃoʊ-/ *informal n* [U] the industry that makes money by entertaining people in films, the theatre etc: *a career in show business*

showcase /ˈʃəʊkeɪs $ ˈʃoʊ-/ *n* [C] an event that is designed to show the best qualities someone or something has: *a showcase for new musical talent*

showdown /ˈʃəʊdaʊn $ ˈʃoʊ-/ *n* [C] a final argument that will end a long disagreement: *a showdown between managers and staff*

shower¹ /ˈʃaʊə $ ˈʃaʊr/ *n* [C]

1 a piece of equipment that sends out water and that you stand under to wash yourself: *Are you in the shower?* | *a shower cubicle* → see picture at BATHROOM

2 when you wash your body under a shower: **have a shower** *BrE* /**take a shower** *AmE*: *Have I time to take a shower?*

3 a short period of rain: *a heavy shower* → see box at RAIN

4 many small things that fall through the air together: **+of** *a shower of sparks*

5 *AmE* a party for a woman who is going to have a baby or get married → see box at PARTY

shower² v

1 [I] to wash yourself by standing under a shower: *Tom showered and changed.*

2 [I,T] to cover a person or place with a lot of small things: **shower sb/sth with sth** *Bystanders were showered with broken glass.*

3 [T] to give someone a lot of something: **shower sb with sth** *Mother showered us with gifts.*

showery /'ʃaʊəri $ 'ʃaʊri/ *adj* with short periods of rain: *a showery afternoon*

showing /'ʃəʊɪŋ $ 'ʃoʊ-/ n **1** [C] an occasion when a film is shown or a television programme is broadcast: *a second showing of this popular programme* **2** [singular] something that shows the level of your success: *He **made** a strong **showing** in his last race.*

showjumping /'ʃəʊ,dʒʌmpɪŋ $ 'ʃoʊ-/ n [U] a sport in which horses with riders jump over fences

showman /'ʃəʊmən $ 'ʃoʊ-/ n [C] plural **showmen** /-mən/ someone who is good at entertaining people

shown /ʃəʊn $ ʃoʊn/ v the past participle of SHOW

'show-off n [C] *disapproving* someone who likes to show how clever, funny, or attractive they are

showpiece /'ʃəʊpiːs $ 'ʃoʊ-/ n [C] something that an organization is proud of because it is a good example of its work

showroom /'ʃəʊrʊm, -ruːm $ 'ʃoʊ-/ n [C] a room where you can look at things that are for sale: **car/furniture showroom**

showy /'ʃəʊi $ 'ʃoʊi/ *adj* very big, bright, or expensive in a way that gets your attention

shrank /ʃræŋk/ v the past tense of SHRINK

shrapnel /'ʃræpnəl/ n [U] small pieces of metal from a bomb or bullet that has exploded: *shrapnel wounds*

shred¹ /ʃred/ n **1** [C usually plural] a small thin piece that has been torn from something: **+of** *a shred of paper* | **rip/tear sth to shreds** *The puppy had ripped my shoes to shreds.* | **in shreds** *His shirt was in shreds.* **2** **not a shred of sth** not even a small amount of something: *There is not a shred of evidence against him.*

shred² v [T] **shredded, shredding** to cut or tear something into small pieces → see picture at CUT¹ —**shredder** n [C] *a paper shredder*

shrewd /ʃruːd/ *adj* good at understanding situations and making clever decisions: *a shrewd businesswoman*

shriek /ʃriːk/ v [I,T] to shout in a high voice [= scream]: *'Stop it!' she shrieked.* | **+with** *students shrieking with laughter* —**shriek** n [C]

shrill /ʃrɪl/ *adj* a shrill sound is high and unpleasant: *shrill voices*

shrimp /ʃrɪmp/ n [C,U] plural **shrimp** or **shrimps** a small pink sea creature that you eat

shrine /ʃraɪn/ n [C] a place that people visit for religious reasons or because it is connected with a special event or person: **+of/to** *the shrine of St John*

shrink¹ /ʃrɪŋk/ v past tense **shrank** /ʃræŋk/ past participle **shrunk** /ʃrʌŋk/

1 [I,T] if something shrinks, or if you shrink it, it becomes smaller: *Families have been shrink-*

ing since the 1970s. | **shrink (sth) to sth** *Global warming has shrunk the ice cap to 13 km.*

2 [I] to move away because you are afraid: **+back/away from** *She shrank back in fright.*

shrink from sth *phr v* to avoid doing something difficult or unpleasant: **shrink from doing sth** *She never shrank from doing her duty.*

shrink² n [C] *informal humorous* a PSYCHOANALYST or PSYCHIATRIST

,shrink-'wrapped *adj* wrapped tightly in thin plastic

shrivel /'ʃrɪvəl/ also **shrivel up** v [I,T] **shrivelled, shrivelling** *BrE*, **shriveled, shriveling** *AmE* if something shrivels, or if it is shrivelled, it becomes smaller and covered in lines because it is dry or old: *The flowers had shrivelled up.* | *her shriveled hands*

shroud¹ /ʃraʊd/ n [C] **1** a cloth that is wrapped around the body of a dead person before it is buried **2** *literary* something that hides or covers something: *a shroud of fog*

shroud² v *formal* **1** **be shrouded in sth** to be hidden by something: *The hill was shrouded in mist.* **2** **be shrouded in mystery/secrecy** to be difficult to understand or explain: *His death was shrouded in mystery.*

shrub /ʃrʌb/ n [C] a small bush

shrubbery /'ʃrʌbəri/ n [C] plural **shrubberies** part of a garden where many small bushes have been planted

shrug /ʃrʌg/ v [I,T] **shrugged, shrugging** to raise and lower your shoulders to show that you do not know or care about something: *Dan shrugged and returned to his book.* | *Melanie shrugged her shoulders.* —**shrug** n [C]

shrug sth ⇔ **off** *phr v* to treat something as unimportant and not worry about it: *Mary tried to shrug off her failure.*

shrunk /ʃrʌŋk/ v the past participle of SHRINK

shrunken /'ʃrʌŋkən/ *adj* something that is shrunken has become smaller: *a shrunken old woman*

shuck /ʃʌk/ v [T] *AmE* to remove the outer part of a vegetable such as corn or PEAS

shudder /'ʃʌdə $ -ər/ v [I] **1** to shake because you are afraid or cold, or because you think something is unpleasant: **+at** *She shuddered at the thought.* | **+with** *Gwen shuddered with embarrassment.* **2** if a vehicle or machine shudders, it shakes —**shudder** n [C]

shuffle /'ʃʌfəl/ v **1** [I] to walk slowly and without lifting your feet up properly: **+across/away/into etc** *The old man shuffled across the room.* **2** [T] to move papers, cards etc into a different position or order: *Joe **shuffled the pack** (=of playing cards) and dealt.* **3** [I,T] to keep moving slightly when you are sitting down because you are bored, nervous, or embarrassed: *He **shuffled** his feet nervously.*

shun /ʃʌn/ v [T] **shunned, shunning** to deliberately avoid someone or something: *She **shunned** publicity.*

shunt /ʃʌnt/ v [T] **1** to move someone or something to another place or position in a way that seems unfair: *She was tired of being shunted to and fro.* **2** to push a vehicle from behind so that it is in a different position

shush /ʃʊʃ/ *spoken* used to tell someone to be quiet

S

shut¹ /ʃʌt/ v [I,T] past tense and past participle **shut** present participle **shutting**

1 if you shut something, or if it shuts, it closes: *Would you mind shutting the window?* | *I heard the door shut with a bang.* | *Shut your eyes and go to sleep.* | **shut sth/sb in (sth)** (=close a door etc so that someone or something cannot get out) *Are the dogs shut in?* | *He shut his finger in the door.* | **shut sb/sth out** (=close a door etc so that someone or something cannot get in) *Close the curtains to shut out the noise.*

2 *BrE* if a shop, bank etc shuts, it stops being open to people [= **close**]: *What time does the bank shut?*

shut sb/sth away *phr v* to put someone or something in a place where other people cannot see them: *He shut himself away in his office.*

shut down *phr v* if a company, factory, machine etc shuts down, or if you shut it down, it stops operating: *Hundreds of local post offices have shut down.* | **shut sth ⇔ down** *Did you shut the computer down?* → see box at **COMPUTER**

shut off *phr v* **1** to stop a machine or supply of something from working, or to stop working [= **turn off**]: **shut sth ⇔ off** *Don't forget to shut the gas off.* **2 shut yourself off** to deliberately avoid other people: **+from** *After her death, he shut himself off from the world.*

shut (sb) up *phr v informal* to stop talking, or to make someone stop talking: *Shut up a minute!* | *The chairman tried to shut us up.* → see box at **QUIET**

shut² *adj* [not before noun]

1 not open [= **closed**]: *Is the door shut?* | *Keep the windows shut.* | **slam/swing etc shut** *The gates swung shut behind him.*

2 *BrE* if a shop, bar etc is shut, it is not open for people to use

shutdown /ˈʃʌtdaʊn/ n [C] when a factory, business, or machine stops working

shutter /ˈʃʌtə $ -ər/ n [C] **1** a wooden or metal cover for a window: *a pair of wooden shutters* **2** a part of a camera that lets light in

shuttered /ˈʃʌtəd $ -ərd/ adj a shuttered window or building has closed shutters

shuttle¹ /ˈʃʌtl/ n [C] **1** a plane, bus, or train that makes regular trips between two places: *the Washington-New York shuttle service* | *a shuttle bus* **2** a spacecraft that goes into space and returns more than once

shuttle² v [I,T] to travel or move people regularly between two places: **+between/to and from** *Graham shuttles between Rotterdam and Rome.* | *Guests are shuttled to and from the hotel by bus.*

shuttlecock /ˈʃʌtlkɒk $ -kɑːk/ n [C] a small light object with feathers attached that you hit across a net in **BADMINTON** [= **birdie** *AmE*]

shy¹ /ʃaɪ/ adj

1 nervous and embarrassed about meeting or talking to other people: **+with** *She's painfully shy with strangers.* | *He's too shy to speak up for himself.* → see box at **CONFIDENT**

2 unwilling to do or get involved in something: **not be shy about (doing) sth** *John has strong views, and he's not shy about voicing them.* |

publicity **shy/camera-shy** *He's publicity shy and rarely gives interviews.*

—**shyly** *adv* —**shyness** n [U] *I gradually overcame my shyness.*

shy² v [I] **shied, shying, shies** if a horse shies, it suddenly moves away from something because it is frightened

shy away from sth *phr v* to avoid doing something because you are nervous or lack confidence: *He shies away from any sort of responsibility.*

shyster /ˈʃaɪstə $ -ər/ n [C] *AmE informal* a dishonest lawyer or politician

sibling /ˈsɪblɪŋ/ n [C] *formal* a brother or sister

sic /sɪk/ adv written (**sic**) used after a mistake to show that you know it is not correct

sick¹ /sɪk/ adj

1 feel sick to feel ill in your stomach and as if you might **VOMIT** [➔ **carsick, seasick**]: *I felt really sick.* | *Coffee makes me feel sick.* | **+with** *Anna felt sick with fear.* → see box at **ILL**

2 be sick if you are sick, food comes up from your stomach and out through your mouth [= **vomit**]: *The baby had been violently sick down her sweater.*

3 ill: *a hospital for sick children* | **off sick** *BrE*; **out sick** *AmE* (=not at work because you are ill) *Steve's been off sick all week.* | **call in/ring in/phone in sick** (=telephone to say you are not coming to work because you are ill) *John called in sick this morning.* | *Mr Smith is on sick leave* (=allowed to stay off work because of illness). → see box at **ILL**

4 laughing about death and suffering in a cruel way: *a sick joke*

5 be sick of sb/sth to be annoyed and bored with a person or situation: **be sick of doing sth** *I'm sick and tired of waiting.*

6 be worried sick to be very worried: *Why didn't you ring? I was worried sick!*

7 make sb sick *spoken* if something makes you sick, it makes you very angry: *Cruelty to animals makes me sick.*

8 *formal* **the sick** people who are ill

sick² n [U] *BrE* food that has come out of your mouth from your stomach [= **vomit**]

'sick bay n [C] a room on a ship or in a building with beds for people who are ill

sicken /ˈsɪkən/ v [T] if something sickens you, it makes you feel shocked and angry: *men who were sickened by the war* —**sickening** *adj*: *a sickening waste of life*

sickle /ˈsɪkəl/ n [C] a cutting tool with a curved blade for cutting long grass or grain crops

sickly /ˈsɪkli/ adj **1** weak and unhealthy **2** a sickly smell, taste, or colour is very unpleasant

sickness /ˈsɪknəs/ n [U] **1** when you **VOMIT** (=bring food up from your stomach through your mouth) [➔ **morning sickness**]: *sickness and diarrhoea* | **travel/motion/sea sickness** (=caused by travel, movement etc) **2** the state of being ill [= **illness**]: *people suffering from radiation sickness*

side¹ /saɪd/ n [C]

1 one part or area of something: **+of** *Stop when you reach the other side of the field.* | **on this/ that side** *the people on this side of the room* | **the left/right-hand etc side** *Keep to the left-hand* side of the stream. | **the right/wrong side** *driving on the wrong side of the road* | **the east/ north etc side** *the east side of the city* | **on/from all sides** (=on or from all directions) *We're surrounded on all sides.*

2 a position directly next to someone or something: **+of** *a house by the side of a lake* | **by/at sb's side** (=close to someone) *She stayed by his side throughout.*

3 the part of something that is furthest from the middle [= **edge**]: **+of** *She sat on the side of the bed.* | *Pull in at the side of the road.*

4 a part of something that is not the front, back, top, or bottom: **+of** *the side of the house* | *One of the carriages was lying on its side.*

5 one of the two surfaces of a thin object: **+of** *Use both sides of the paper.*

6 your sides are the parts of your body on your left and your right from your shoulders to the tops of your legs: *Turn over and lie on your right side.*

7 from side to side moving left to right, then from right to left: *The lamp swung from side to side.*

8 side by side a) next to each other: *two cars parked side by side* **b)** if people work or live side by side, they work or live close to each other peacefully

9 one of the flat surfaces something has: **six-sided/three-sided etc** *a six-sided shape*

10 the sloping part of a hill or valley

11 one separate part of a subject, problem, or situation: *the social side of the job* | *Can't you see the funny side* (=the parts of a situation that are funny rather than serious)? | *Always look on the bright side* (=the good things about a situation).

12 one person, group, or team in an argument, war, competition etc: **on sb's side** *Are you on our side?* | **the winning/losing side** *No one likes to be on the losing side.* | *Teachers should never take sides* (=support just one person, group etc).

13 one person's opinion [= **point of view**]: **sb's side of sth** *You never see my side of the story* (=my opinion or account of an event).

14 a part of someone's character: **+of** *a side of Karen I hadn't seen before* | **practical/emotional etc side** *All men have a feminine side.*

15 the part of your family that is related to either your mother or your father: **mother's/ father's side** *There's a history of heart disease on my father's side.*

16 on the side secretly or dishonestly: *He was seeing another woman on the side.*

17 get on the right/wrong side of sb *informal* to make someone pleased or angry with you

18 put/leave/set sth to one side to save something for later: *Put some money to one side each week.*

→ **FLIP SIDE**

side² *adj* [only before noun]

1 in or on the side of something: **side door/exit** *The Prince left by a side door.* | *side pockets* | *a side view of the statue*

2 side street/road a small street or road that is attached to a main street: *a quiet side street*

3 side order/dish food that is served separately as part of a meal

side³ *v*

side with sb *phr v* to support someone in an argument: **+against** *Germany has sided with France against the other states.*

sideboard /'saɪdbɔːd $ -bɔːrd/ *n* [C] a long low piece of furniture, used for storing plates, glasses etc

sideburns /'saɪdbɜːnz $ -bɜːrnz/ *n* [plural] hair that has grown down in front of a man's ears

sidecar /'saɪdkɑː $ -kɑːr/ *n* [C] a small vehicle for a passenger that is attached to a MOTORCYCLE

'side ef‚fect *n* [C] **1** an additional effect that a drug has on your body as well as treating illness or pain: *a drug with harmful side effects* **2** an unexpected result: **+of** *one side effect of the economic crisis*

sidekick /'saɪd‚kɪk/ *n* [C] *informal* someone's sidekick is a friend or helper who is not as important as they are

sidelight /'saɪdlaɪt/ *n* [C] one of the two small lights beside the main lights on a car

sideline¹ /'saɪdlaɪn/ *n* **1** [C] something that you do to earn money in addition to your main job: *Mark does translations as a sideline.* **2 on the sidelines** not taking part in an activity, even though you want to or should: *Alison had had enough of standing on the sidelines.* **3 the sidelines** [plural] the area just outside the lines around the edge of a sports field

sideline² *v* [T] if you are sidelined, you are prevented from taking part in something: *Their quarterback was sidelined with an injury.*

sidelong /'saɪdlɒŋ $ -lɒːŋ/ *adj* **sidelong look/ glance** a way of looking at someone by only moving your eyes, not your head, to show that you do not trust or believe them: *He gave me a sidelong glance.* —**sidelong** *adv*

sideshow /'saɪdʃəʊ $ -ʃoʊ/ *n* [C] part of an event or activity that is smaller, less important, or less serious than the thing it is connected with

sidestep /'saɪdstep/ *v* [T] **sidestepped, sidestepping** to avoid a difficult question or decision: *The report sidesteps the environmental issues.*

sideswipe /'saɪdswaɪp/ *v* [T] *AmE* to hit the side of another vehicle with your car

sidetrack /'saɪdtræk/ *v* [T] if you sidetrack someone, you make them forget about doing what they should be doing by getting them interested in something else: *Don't get sidetracked by the audience's questions.*

sidewalk /'saɪdwɔːk $ -wɒːk/ *n* [C] *AmE* the hard surface beside the road that people walk on [= **pavement** *BrE*]

sideways /'saɪdweɪz/ *adv* **1** towards one side: *She moved her legs sideways to let him pass.* **2** with the side rather than the front or back facing forwards: *Mel's car slid sideways across the road.* —**sideways** *adj*

siding /'saɪdɪŋ/ *n* **1** [C] *BrE* a short railway track next to a main track, where trains stay when they are not being used **2** [U] *AmE* long narrow pieces of metal or wood, used for covering the outside walls of a house

sidle /'saɪdl/ *v* [I] to walk towards someone or something slowly because you do not want to be noticed: **+up/over etc** *Tom sidled up, looking embarrassed.*

S

siege /siːdʒ/ n [C,U] a situation in which the army, police, or a crowd of people surround a place to get control of it or to force people to come out: **+of** *the siege of Vienna* | **under siege (by/from sb)** *His apartment was under siege from journalists.* | **lay siege to sb/sth** *The army laid siege to the town.*

siesta /siˈestə/ n [C] a short sleep in the afternoon, often taken by people in warm countries: **take/have a siesta**

sieve /sɪv/ n [C] a tool made of a wire net and a handle that you use to separate solid things and liquids, or small things from larger things → see picture on page A4 —**sieve** v [T] → see box at RECIPE

sift /sɪft/ v [T] **1** also **sift through** to examine a lot of documents or information carefully: *Investigators are still sifting through the evidence.* **2** to put flour or sugar through a SIEVE → see picture on page A4

sigh /saɪ/ v [I] to take a deep breath and breathe out slowly and loudly because you are annoyed or unhappy: *Phil sighed heavily and shook his head.* | *'I'm so sorry,' she sighed.* —**sigh** n [C] *a deep sigh of relief*

sight¹ /saɪt/ n

1 [U] the ability to see [= eyesight, vision]: *She is losing her sight* (=becoming blind).
2 [singular,U] when you see something: **+of** *The sight of him made me tremble.* | *I caught sight of* (=saw) *a man in the garden.* | *They drove on ahead and we lost sight of* (=could no longer see) *them.* | *I can't stand the sight of blood.* | **on sight** (=as soon as you see something) *Rebel soldiers were shot on sight.*
3 [U] if something is in sight, you can see it. If it is out of sight, you cannot see it: **in/within sight (of sth)** *There was no one in sight.* | **out of sight (of sth)** *We parked out of sight of the house.* | *We waved until the train disappeared from sight.*
4 [C] something that you can see: **a common/rare/strange etc sight** *Street dentists are a common sight here.*
5 the sights the interesting places to visit in a town or city: *I hope we get a chance to see the sights.*
6 in/within sight likely to happen: *Peace is in sight.*
7 lose sight of sth to forget an important part of something because you are too concerned about the details: *We have lost sight of the fact that a computer is only a tool.*
8 set your sights on (doing) sth to decide that you definitely want something: *She had set her sights on becoming a star.*
9 not let sb out of your sight to make sure that someone stays near you: *Since the accident, she hasn't let the kids out of her sight.*
10 sights [plural] the parts of a gun that you look into to help you aim it
→ **at first sight** at FIRST¹

sight² v [T] to see something that is far away or something you have been searching for: *The missing child was sighted in Manchester.*

sighted /ˈsaɪtɪd/ adj able to see: *a school for blind and partially sighted children*

sighting /ˈsaɪtɪŋ/ n [C] an occasion when someone sees something unusual or rare: **+of** *a sighting of a rare bird* | *UFO sightings*

sightseeing /ˈsaɪtˌsiːɪŋ/ n [U] when you visit the famous or interesting places in a town or city: *In the afternoon, we went sightseeing.* → see box at VISIT —**sightseer** n [C]

sign¹ /saɪn/ n [C]

1 a piece of wood, metal, plastic etc with words or pictures on it to give people information: *a 'No Smoking' sign* | **road signs** | *Follow the signs to Birmingham.* | *What does that sign say* (=what words are written on it)?
2 an event or fact that shows that something exists or will happen: **+of** *Headaches are a sign of stress.* | *We searched, but there was no sign of them.* | **+that** *The marks are a sign that a tiger is close by.* | *She's smiling, which is a good sign.* | *a sure sign* (=clear proof) *of guilt* | **show signs of (doing) sth/show no sign of (doing) sth** *Auntie Meg showed no sign of leaving.*

COLLOCATIONS

clear/obvious sign – one that you can clearly see
outward/visible sign – one that you can clearly see
good/positive/encouraging sign – one that tells you something good might happen
bad/warning sign – one that tells you something bad might happen
sure sign – one that proves that something is true

3 a picture or shape that has a particular meaning [= symbol]: *a dollar sign*
4 a movement or sound made in order to tell someone something [= signal]: **give/make a sign** *He made a sign for me to follow him into the kitchen.* | **sign for sb to do sth** *The whistle was the sign for us to begin.*
→ EQUALS SIGN, MINUS SIGN, PLUS SIGN, STAR SIGN

sign² v [I,T]

1 to write your name on a letter, document etc to show that you wrote it or agree with it [➔ signature]: *Sign your name here please.* | *You forgot to sign the cheque.* | *a signed photo* | **sign a contract/treaty/agreement** (=make it legal by signing it) *France and Italy have signed a trade agreement.* → see picture at CHEQUE
2 also **sign up** if a sports team or record company signs a player or musician, it gives the player or musician a job by signing a contract with them: *Virgin Records signed the band back in 1998.* | **+to/with** *He has signed up with Milan.*

sign sth ⇔ **away** phr v to sign an official document that gives your property or rights to someone else

sign for sth phr v to sign a document to prove you have received something

sign in phr v to sign your name in a book when you enter a building, club etc: *Delegates must sign in at reception.* | **sign sb** ⇔ **in** *I'll sign you in as my guest.*

sign on phr v **1** to sign a document to say that you agree to work for someone, do a course etc: **+for/with** *I signed on with an IT agency.* **2** BrE to sign an official document to say that you have no job and can receive money from the government

sign out phr v to sign your name in a book when you leave a building, club etc: **sign sb** ⇔ **out** *I'll sign you out.*

sign sth ⇔ **over** phr v to sign an official document that gives your property or rights to someone else: +**to** He signed the property over to his daughter.

sign up phr v **1 sign sb** ⇔ **up** to agree to give someone a job, for example in a sports team: The Yankees signed him up when he finished college. **2** to put your name on a list because you want to do something: +**for** Ten people signed up for the trip to Paris.

signal[1] /'sɪgnəl/ n [C]

1 a sound or something that you do to give information or to tell someone to do something: **signal (for sb) to do sth** That was the signal for me to switch out the lights. | The headmaster **gave** the **signal** to start.
2 something which shows what someone feels, what exists, or what is likely to happen: +**that** The result is a **clear signal** that voters are not happy. | This will **send** the wrong **signal** to potential investors.
3 a series of light waves, sound waves etc that carry information to a radio, television etc: **send/transmit/emit a signal** Signals are sent via satellite. | **receive/pick up/detect a signal** a small antenna which receives radio signals
4 a piece of equipment that tells a train driver whether to go or stop
→ TURN SIGNAL

signal[2] v signalled, signalling BrE; signaled, signaling AmE **1** [I,T] to move your hand, head etc as a way of telling someone something: +**to/for** Tom signalled for the bill. | **signal (to) sb to do sth** She signalled to the children to come inside. **2** [T] to be a sign or proof of something happening: The elections signalled the end of a nine-year civil war. **3** [T] to make something clear by what you say or do: Carter has signalled his intention to resign.

signatory /'sɪgnətəri $ -tɔːri/ n [C] plural **signatories** formal a person or country that signs a formal agreement

signature /'sɪgnətʃə $ -ər/ n [C] your name written the way you usually write it, for example at the end of a letter or on a cheque [➡ sign]

significance /sɪg'nɪfɪkəns/ n [U] the importance of something, especially something that might affect you in the future: +**of** What is the significance of this new evidence? | **of great/some/major etc significance** a political agreement of some significance

significant /sɪg'nɪfɪkənt/ adj **1** noticeable or important [≠ insignificant]: **significant change/difference/increase etc** significant changes in the exam system **2** a significant smile, look etc has a special meaning: He gave me a significant look. —**significantly** adv: Her work has been significantly better this year.

signify /'sɪgnɪfaɪ/ v [T] **signified**, **signifying**, **signifies** to mean or be a sign of something: Does this signify a change in policy?

signing /'saɪnɪŋ/ n **1** [U] when you write your name at the end of document to show that you agree with it: +**of** the signing of the ceasefire agreement **2** [C,U] someone who has just signed a contract to join a sports team or work with a record company, or the act of doing this: +**of**

Birmingham City have completed the signing of Doug Bell from Shrewsbury Town. **3** [U] the use of sign language

'sign ˌlanguage n [C,U] a language that uses hand movements instead of spoken words, used by people who cannot hear

signpost[1] /'saɪnpəʊst $ -poʊst/ n [C] a sign on a road that shows directions and distances

signpost[2] v **be signposted** BrE to have signposts showing you which way to go: The village isn't very well signposted.

Sikh /siːk/ n [C] a member of an Indian religious group that developed from Hinduism —**Sikh** adj

silence[1] /'saɪləns/ n

1 [C,U] when there is no sound or nobody is talking: **complete/total/dead silence** There was a loud bang, then complete silence. | **in silence** The two men sat in silence. | +**of** the silence of the night
2 [U] when someone refuses to talk about something: +**on** So far, he has maintained his silence on the subject.

silence[2] v [T] **1** to make someone stop criticizing or giving their opinions: Critics of the system were quickly silenced. **2** to stop someone from talking, or to stop something from making a noise

silencer /'saɪlənsə $ -ər/ n [C] **1** a thing that is put on the end of a gun so that it makes less noise **2** BrE a piece of equipment that makes an engine quieter [= muffler AmE]

silent /'saɪlənt/ adj

1 not saying anything: **keep/remain/stay silent** They both remained silent, just looking at her.
2 without any sound, or not making any sound: The whole room **fell silent** (=became silent). —**silently** adv

silhouette /ˌsɪluːˈet/ n [C] a dark shape seen against a light background —**silhouetted** adj: tall chimneys silhouetted against the sunset

silicon /'sɪlɪkən/ n [U] an ELEMENT that is used for making glass, bricks, and computer parts: a silicon chip

silk /sɪlk/ n [C,U] soft cloth made from the threads produced by a type of CATERPILLAR: a silk shirt

silken /'sɪlkən/ adj literary soft and smooth like silk, or made of silk: her silken hair

silky /'sɪlki/ adj soft and smooth like silk: silky fur

sill /sɪl/ n [C] a WINDOWSILL

silly /'sɪli/ adj stupid or not sensible: What a silly question! | That was a **silly thing to do**, wasn't it? | **Don't be silly** – it's only a spider. | She makes a fuss about such **silly little** (=unimportant) things. —**silliness** n [U]

silo /'saɪləʊ $ -loʊ/ n [C] plural **silos 1** a tall building on a farm, used for storing grain **2** a structure under the ground, from which a MISSILE can be fired

silt /sɪlt/ n [U] sand or mud in a river

silver¹ /'sɪlvə $ -ər/ n [U]
1 a valuable shiny white metal, used for making jewellery, spoons etc: *a tiny figure made of solid silver*
2 things that are made of silver [= silverware]

silver² adj
1 made of silver: *a silver spoon* → see picture at **MATERIAL¹**
2 having the colour of silver: *a shimmering silver dress*
3 silver wedding/anniversary/jubilee the date that is 25 years after something began

silver 'medal n [C] a prize, especially a round piece of silver, that is given to someone who comes second in a race or competition

silverware /'sɪlvəweə $ -vərwer/ n [U]
1 things that are made of silver **2** AmE metal knives, forks, and spoons

silvery /'sɪlvəri/ adj shining like silver

similar /'sɪmələ, 'sɪmɪlə $ -ər/ adj almost the same [≠ different; ➡ alike]: *They came from similar backgrounds.* | *The two brothers do look quite similar.* | *This one works in a similar way.* | +to *Your shoes are similar to mine.* | +in *All the apartments are similar in size.*

similarity /ˌsɪmə'lærəti/ n [C,U] plural **similarities** when people or things are similar, or a way in which they are similar: +between *There is some similarity between the styles of the two authors.* | +with/to *English has many similarities with German.*

similarly /'sɪmələli $ -ərli/ adv in a similar way

simile /'sɪmɪli/ n [C] an expression that describes something by comparing it with something else using the word 'like' or 'as', for example 'as red as blood'

simmer /'sɪmə $ -ər/ v [I,T] to cook food by boiling it very gently: *Let the soup simmer for 5 minutes.*

simper /'sɪmpə $ -ər/ v [I] literary to smile in a way that is silly and annoying —**simper** n [C]

simple /'sɪmpəl/ adj
1 not difficult or complicated: *a simple solution to the problem* | **simple to use/make/operate etc** *Modern cameras are very simple to use.* | *When planning what to cook, it's best to keep it simple.*
2 made in a plain style, without unnecessary decorations or things added: *a simple white dress*
3 used to emphasize that something is the only reason, fact etc involved: *She didn't answer for the simple reason that she couldn't think what to say.* | *It was a business decision, pure and simple.*
4 ordinary and not special in any way: *a simple country existence*
5 simple past/present a tense of a verb in English that is not formed with an AUXILIARY such as 'have' or 'be'

simplicity /sɪm'plɪsəti/ n [U] when something is simple: +of *the simplicity and effectiveness of the technique*

simplify /'sɪmpləfaɪ/ v [T] **simplified, simplifying, simplifies** to make something easier to do or understand: *an attempt to simplify the tax system* —**simplification** /ˌsɪmpləfə'keɪʃən/ n [U]

simplistic /sɪm'plɪstɪk/ adj disapproving making something seem less complicated than it really is: *a rather simplistic view of life*

simply /'sɪmpli/ adv
1 used to emphasize what you are saying: *But that simply isn't true!* | *His performance was quite simply dazzling.*
2 only: *Some students lose marks simply because they don't read the question properly.*
3 in a way that is easy to understand: **To put it simply,** *the bank won't lend us the money.*
4 used to emphasize how easy it is to do something: *Simply fill in the form and take it to the post office.*
5 in a plain and ordinary way: *a simply decorated room*

simulate /'sɪmjʊleɪt/ v [T] to make or do something that seems like the real thing but is not: *an experiment to simulate the effects of being weightless* —**simulator** n [C] *a flight simulator*

simulation /ˌsɪmjʊ'leɪʃən/ n [C,U] something you do or produce in order to study or test what happens in a real situation: +of *a computer simulation of an emergency landing*

simultaneous /ˌsɪməl'teɪniəs $ ˌsaɪ-/ adj happening or done at the same time as something else: *a simultaneous broadcast on TV and radio* —**simultaneously** adv

sin¹ /sɪn/ n **1** [C,U] something that is against religious laws: +of *the sin of greed* | *He knew he'd committed a terrible sin.* **2** a sin informal something that you think is very wrong: *It's a sin to waste good food.*

sin² v [I] **sinned, sinning** to do something that is against religious laws —**sinner** n [C]

since /sɪns/ linking word, prep, adv
1 from a particular time or event in the past until now, or in that period of time: *I haven't seen him since we left school.* | *Jim's been working at Citibank since last April.* | *She phoned last week, but I haven't heard from her since.* | *He left the US in 1995 and since then he's lived in London.* | *We've had problems with the system* **ever since** (=for all the time since) *it was introduced.*
2 used to give a reason or explanation for something: *I'll do it myself since you're obviously not going to help.*
3 since when spoken used in questions to show that you are annoyed or surprised about something: *Since when have you been such a computer expert?* → see box at **AGO**

sincere /sɪn'sɪə $ -'sɪr/ adj honest and really meaning what you say [≠ insincere]: **sincere thanks/apology/sympathy etc** *Please accept my sincere apologies.* | *a sincere and loyal friend* —**sincerity** /sɪn'serəti/ n [U]

sincerely /sɪn'sɪəli $ -'sɪr-/ adv **1** in a sincere way: *I sincerely hope we meet again.* **2** Yours **sincerely** BrE **Sincerely (yours)** AmE something you write at the end of a formal letter before you sign your name

sinew /'sɪnjuː/ n [C,U] a part of the body that connects a muscle to a bone —**sinewy** adj

sinful /'sɪnfəl/ adj morally bad or wrong

sing /sɪŋ/ v [I,T] past tense **sang** /sæŋ/ past participle **sung** /sʌŋ/ to produce musical sounds with your voice: *Sophie sings in a choir.* | *They* sang *a beautiful* song. | +to *a mother singing to her baby*

—singing *n* [U]

sing. the written abbreviation of **singular**

singe /sɪndʒ/ *v* [T] **singed, singeing** to burn something slightly on its surface or edge: *I singed my hair on a candle.*

singer /ˈsɪŋə $ -ər/ *n* [C] someone who sings, especially as a job: *an opera singer*

single¹ /ˈsɪŋɡəl/ *adj*

1 [only before noun] only one: *We lost the game by a single point.* | *a single-sex* (=for only girls or only boys) *school*

2 every single used to emphasize that you are talking about every person or thing: *My dad has every single Beatles album.*

3 the single biggest/greatest etc used to emphasize that you are talking about the biggest, greatest etc thing of its kind: *The single biggest problem is lack of money.*

4 not a single no people or things at all: *We didn't get a single reply to the advert.*

5 not married, or not involved in a romantic relationship: *Terry is 34 and still single.* → see box at **MARRIED**

6 single bed/room etc a bed, room etc to be used by only one person [➡ **double**] → see picture at **BED**

7 single figures *BrE* **,single 'digits** *AmE* the numbers from 1 to 9 [➡ **double figures**]

single² *n* **1** [C] a record or CD with only one song on it, or the song itself: *Madonna's new single* **2 singles** [U] a game, especially tennis, played by one person against another person [➡ **doubles**]: *the women's singles final* **3** [C] *BrE* a ticket to go from one place to another but not back again [➡ **return**]: *a single to Liverpool* → see box at **TICKET** **4 singles bar/club/night etc** a bar, club etc for people who are not married

single³ *v*

single *sb/sth* ⇔ **out** *phr v* to choose someone or something from a group, especially in order to praise or criticize them: **+for** *The school was singled out for its excellent academic results.*

,single-'handedly, **,single-'handed** *adv* if one person does something single-handedly, they do it without help from anyone else: *She's brought up four kids single-handedly.* —**'single-handed** *adj* [only before noun]

,single-'minded *adj* having one aim and working hard to achieve it: *a single-minded determination to succeed* —**single-mindedness** *n* [U]

,single 'parent *n* [C] a mother or father who looks after her or his children alone

singly /ˈsɪŋɡli/ *adv* separately or one at a time: *The animals live singly or in small groups.*

'sing-song *n* [C] *BrE* when people sing songs together for fun, for example at a party

singular¹ /ˈsɪŋɡjʊlə $ -ər/ *adj*

1 the singular form of a word is used when you are talking or writing about one person or thing [➡ **plural**]

2 *formal* very great or noticeable: *singular beauty*

singular² *n* **the singular** the form of a word that you use when you are talking or writing about one person or thing

singularly /ˈsɪŋɡjʊləli $ -lərli/ *adv formal* very: *a singularly unattractive building*

sinister /ˈsɪnɪstə $ -ər/ *adj* making you feel that something bad or evil is happening: *There's something sinister about the whole thing.*

sink¹ /sɪŋk/ *v* past tense **sank** /sæŋk/ past participle **sunk** /sʌŋk/

1 [I,T] to go down, or make something go down, below the surface of water [≠ **float**]: *The boat sank after hitting a rock.* | *He watched his keys sink to the bottom* of the river. → see picture at **FLOAT¹**

2 [I] to fall or sit down heavily, because you are weak or tired: **+into/down etc** *Lee sank into a chair and went to sleep.*

3 [I] to move to a lower level [= **drop**; ≠ **rise**]: *The sun sank beneath the horizon.*

4 your heart sinks/your spirits sink used to say that you lose hope or confidence [➡ **sinking**]: *Her heart sank as she read the results.*

sink in *phr v* if information, news etc sinks in, you gradually understand it or realize the effect it will have: *He paused for a moment for his words to sink in.*

sink into sth *phr v* **1** to gradually get into a worse state: *She could see him sinking into depression.* **2 sink sth into sth** to spend a lot of money on a business, in order to make more money: *They had sunk thousands into the business.* **3 sink your teeth/a knife etc into sth** to put your teeth or something sharp into someone's flesh, into food etc

sink² *n* [C] a piece of furniture in a kitchen or bathroom that you fill with water to wash dishes, your hands etc [➡ **basin**] → see picture at **BATHROOM**

sinking /ˈsɪŋkɪŋ/ *adj* **a sinking feeling** a feeling you get when you realize that something bad is going to happen

sinus /ˈsaɪnəs/ *n* [C] your sinuses are the hollow areas in the bones connected to your nose

sip /sɪp/ *v* [I,T] **sipped, sipping** to drink something slowly, taking only small amounts: *She sipped her tea.* → see box at **DRINK** —**sip** *n* [C] *He took a sip of coffee.*

siphon¹ also **syphon** *BrE* /ˈsaɪfən/ *n* [C] a tube that you use to take liquid out of a container

siphon² also **syphon** *BrE* *v* [T] **1** to remove liquid from a container using a siphon **2** also **siphon off** to secretly take money from an organization over a period of time: *He had been siphoning money from his employer's account.*

sir /sə; *strong* sɜː $ sər; *strong* sɜːr/ *n*

1 *spoken* **a)** used when speaking politely to a man, for example a customer in a shop: *Can I help you, sir?* **b)** *especially AmE* used to get the attention of a man whose name you do not know: *Sir! You dropped your wallet!*

2 Dear Sir used at the beginning of a business letter to a man when you do not know his name

3 Sir used before the name of a KNIGHT: *Sir James*

siren /ˈsaɪərən $ ˈsaɪr-/ *n* [C] a piece of equipment that makes loud warning sounds: *the wail of police sirens*

sissy, cissy /ˈsɪsi/ *n* [C] plural **sissies** *informal disapproving* a boy who is thought to be weak or not brave, or like a girl —**sissy** *adj*

S

sister /ˈsɪstə $ -ər/ n [C]
1 a girl or woman who has the same parents as you [➡ **brother**]: *He's got two sisters.* | **older/big sister** *My older sister is a nurse.* | **younger/little sister** *I had to look after my little sister.* → see box at RELATIVE
2 Sister a title given to a NUN: *Sister Frances*
3 Sister *BrE* a nurse who is in charge of a hospital WARD
4 sister company/organization/paper etc a company, newspaper etc that belongs to the same group or organization: *We have a sister company in the United States.*
5 a woman who belongs to the same race, religion, or organization as you
—**sisterly** *adj*

ˈsister-in-ˌlaw n [C] plural **sisters-in-law** **1** the sister of your husband or wife **2** the wife of your brother

sisterly /ˈsɪstəli $ -ər-/ *adj* typical of a loving sister: *a sisterly kiss*

sit /sɪt/ v past tense and past participle **sat** /sæt/ present participle **sitting**
1 a) [I] to be on a chair, on the ground etc with the top half of your body upright and your weight resting on your bottom: **+on/in/by etc** *The children were sitting on the floor.* | **sit at a desk/table etc** *I don't want to sit at a desk all day.* | *Sit still* (=sit without moving) *and let me fix your hair.* | *I spent half the morning sitting in a traffic jam.* → see picture on page A11 **b)** also **sit down** [I] to move to a sitting position after you have been standing: **+by/beside etc** *Come and sit by me.* **c)** [T] to make or help someone sit somewhere: **sit sb in/on sth** *She sat the boy in the corner.*
2 [I] to be in a particular position, especially not being used: **+on/in etc** *My walking boots were still sitting unused in the cupboard.*
3 sit tight to stay in the same place or situation and not do anything: *Investors should sit tight and see what happens in a few days.*
4 [T] *BrE* to take an examination: *Anna's sitting her final exams this year.*
5 [I] if a committee, court, or parliament sits, it does its work in an official meeting: *The court sits once a month.*
6 sit on the fence to avoid saying which side of an argument you support or what you think is the best thing to do

sit around also **sit about** *BrE phr v* to sit and not do very much: *Dan just sits around watching TV all day.*

sit back *phr v* to let someone else do something or let something happen, without taking any action yourself: *You can't just sit back and wait for business to come to you.*

sit down *phr v* to move into a sitting position after you have been standing: *Do sit down.*

sit in for sb *phr v* to do a job instead of the person who usually does it

sit in on sth *phr v* to watch a meeting or activity but not get involved in it: *Do you mind if I sit in on your class?*

sit sth ⇔ **out** *phr v* to stay where you are until something finishes and not get involved in it: *I'll sit this dance out.*

sit through sth *phr v* to stay until a meeting, performance etc finishes, even if it is very long or boring: *We had to sit through a three-hour class this morning.*

sit up *phr v* **1** to move to a sitting position after you have been lying down: *He sat up and rubbed his eyes.* **2** to stay awake and not go to bed: *We sat up all night talking.*

sitcom /ˈsɪtkɒm $ -kɑːm/ n [C,U] a funny television programme that has the same characters every week in a different story → see box at TELEVISION

site[1] /saɪt/ n [C] **1** a place where something important or interesting happened: **+of** *the site of the battle* → see box at PLACE **2** an area where something is being built, or was or will be built: *a construction site* | *an archaeological site* **3** a WEBSITE

site[2] v **be sited** *formal* to be put or built in a particular place

ˈsit-in n [C] a protest in which people refuse to leave a place until they get what they want → see box at PROTEST

sitter /ˈsɪtə $ -ər/ n [C] *especially AmE spoken* a BABYSITTER

sitting /ˈsɪtɪŋ/ n [C] one of the times when a meal is served when it is not possible for everyone to eat at the same time

ˈsitting room n [C] *BrE* a LIVING ROOM

situated /ˈsɪtʃueɪtᵻd/ *adj* **be situated** *formal* to be in a particular place: *The hotel is situated on the lakeside.*

situation /ˌsɪtʃuˈeɪʃən/ n [C]
1 the things that are happening at a particular time somewhere, or are happening to a particular person: **in a ... situation** *She's in a very difficult situation.* | **economic/political/financial etc situation** *Things are very difficult for farmers given the current economic situation.* | *Little is being done to try and improve the situation.*

COLLOCATIONS
difficult/dangerous/tricky situation – one that is bad and difficult to deal with
impossible situation – one that is very difficult to deal with
economic/political/financial situation
present/current situation – one that exists now
If a situation **arises**, it happens
If a situation **improves/worsens/deteriorates**, it becomes better or worse

2 *formal* the position of a building or a town → NO-WIN SITUATION

ˈsit-up n [C usually plural] an exercise in which you sit up from a lying position while keeping your feet on the floor

six /sɪks/ *number* the number 6: *six months ago* | *She arrived just after six* (=six o'clock). | *He learnt to play the violin when he was six* (=six years old).

sixteen /ˌsɪkˈstiːn◂/ *number* the number 16: *sixteen years later* | *He moved to London when he was sixteen* (=16 years old).
—**sixteenth** *adj, pron: her sixteenth birthday* | *Let's have dinner on the sixteenth* (=the 16th day of the month).

sixteenth /ˌsɪk'stiːnθ◂/ n [C] one of sixteen equal parts of something

sixth¹ /sɪksθ/ adj coming after five other things in a series: *his sixth birthday* —**sixth** pron: *Let's have dinner on **the sixth** (*=the sixth day of the month).

sixth² n [C] one of six equal parts of something

'**sixth form** n [C] the classes of school students between the ages of 16 and 18 in Britain —**sixth former** n [C]

ˌsixth 'sense n [singular] a special ability to know something without using any of your five usual senses such as hearing or sight

sixty /'sɪksti/ number

1 the number 60: *sixty years ago*

2 the sixties also **the '60s, the 1960s** [plural] the years from 1960 to 1969: **the early/mid/late sixties** *the student riots in Paris in the late sixties*

3 be in your sixties to be aged between 60 and 69: **early/mid/late sixties** *She's in her late sixties.*

4 in the sixties if the temperature is in the sixties, it is between 60 degrees and 69 degrees F —**sixtieth** adj: *her sixtieth birthday*

sizable /'saɪzəbəl/ adj another spelling of SIZE-ABLE

size¹ /saɪz/ n

1 [C,U] how big or small something is: *A diamond's value depends on its size.* | *The Jensens' house is about **the same size** as ours.* | **+of** *plans to reduce the size of the army* | *I saw a spider the size of* (=as big as) *my hand in the backyard.* | **medium-sized/normal-sized etc** *a medium-sized car* | *Cut the chicken into **bite-sized** pieces* (=pieces that will fit in your mouth).

2 [C] a measurement for clothes, shoes etc: *These shoes are one size too big.* | *What size do you take?*

size² v

size sb/sth ⇔ **up** phr v to look at a person or think about a situation and make a judgment: *It only took a few seconds for her to size up the situation.*

sizeable, sizable /'saɪzəbəl/ adj fairly large: *a sizeable amount of money*

sizzle /'sɪzəl/ v [I] to make a sound like water falling on hot metal: *bacon sizzling in the pan* → see picture on page A7

skate¹ /skeɪt/ n **1** [C] an ICE SKATE or ROLLER SKATE **2** [C,U] a large flat sea fish

skate² v [I] to move around on skates: *I never learned how to skate.* —**skating** n [U] *Let's go skating.* —**skater** n [C]

skateboard /'skeɪtbɔːd $ -bɔːrd/ n [C] a board with wheels on the bottom that you stand on and ride on → see picture at **BOARD** —**skateboarding** n [U]

skeleton /'skelɨtən/ n [C] **1** all the bones in a human or animal body: *We found the skeleton of a cat.* | *the human skeleton* → see picture on page A3 **2 have a skeleton in the closet/cupboard** to have a secret about something embarrassing or unpleasant that you did in the past **3 skeleton staff/crew/service** only just enough people to keep an organization working: *We will be working with a skeleton staff during the Christmas period.* —**skeletal** adj technical: *skeletal remains*

skeptic /'skeptɪk/ the American spelling of SCEPTIC

skeptical /'skeptɪkəl/ the American spelling of SCEPTICAL

skepticism /'skeptɨsɪzəm/ the American spelling of SCEPTICISM

sketch¹ /sketʃ/ n [C] **1** a drawing that you do quickly and without a lot of details: **+of** *Cantor drew a **rough sketch** of his apartment.* → see box at **PICTURE** **2** a short humorous scene that is part of a longer performance: *a comic sketch* **3** a short description of something

sketch² v [I,T] to draw a sketch of something

sketch sth ⇔ **out** phr v to describe something giving only the basic details: *Barry sketched out a plan for next year's campaign.*

sketch sth in phr v to add more information or details: *I'll try to sketch in the historical background.*

sketchy /'sketʃi/ adj a sketchy account or description has very few details: **Details** *of the accident are still **sketchy**.*

skewed /skjuːd/ adj if information is skewed, it contains only one opinion or point of view and so is not fair: *The media's coverage of the election has been skewed.*

skewer /'skjuːə $ -ər/ n [C] a metal or wooden stick that you put through pieces of food that you want to cook —**skewer** v [T]

ski¹ /skiː/ n [C] plural **skis** skis are long narrow pieces of wood or plastic that you fasten to boots so you can move across snow

ski² v [I] skied, skiing, skis to move over snow on skis: *Can you ski?* → see picture on page A9 —**skier** n [C] —**skiing** n [U] *We're going skiing in Colorado.*

skid /skɪd/ v [I] skidded, skidding if a vehicle skids, it suddenly slides sideways and you cannot control it: *The car skidded on ice.* → see picture at **SLIDE¹** —**skid** n [C]

skilful BrE; **skillful** AmE /'skɪlfəl/ adj

1 good at doing something that you have learned and practised: *a skilful photographer*

2 done very well: *the skilful use of sound effects* —**skilfully** adv

skill /skɪl/ n [C,U] an ability to do something well after you have learned it and practised it [➔ **talent**]: *a course that teaches basic computer skills* | *As a footballer he shows great skill.* | *You have to be able to **learn new skills** quickly.*

skilled /skɪld/ adj having the ability and experience needed to do something well [≠ **unskilled**]: *a skilled carpenter* | **highly skilled** *workers* | **+at/in** *She's very skilled in dealing with these kind of problems.*

skillet /'skɪlɨt/ n [C] a heavy cooking pan made of iron

skillful /'skɪlfəl/ adj the American spelling of SKILFUL

skim /skɪm/ v skimmed, skimming **1** [T] to remove something that is floating on the surface of a liquid: **skim sth off/from sth** *Skim the fat off the soup.* **2** also **skim through** [I,T] to read something quickly to find the main facts or ideas in it: *She skimmed through that morning's headlines.* → see box at **READ** **3** [I,T] to move along quickly, nearly touching the surface of something: *a plane skimming the tops of the trees*

,skimmed 'milk *BrE;* **'skim milk** *AmE n* [U] milk that has had most of the fat removed from it → see box at **MILK**

skimp /skɪmp/ *v* [I] to try to use or spend less than you really need to: **+on** *They try to save money by skimping on staff.*

skimpy /'skɪmpi/ *adj* skimpy clothes do not cover much of your body: *a skimpy little dress* → see box at **CLOTHES**

skin¹ /skɪn/ *n* [C,U]

1 the outside part of a human's or animal's body: *My skin is quite sensitive.* | *Tom has really bad skin* (=unhealthy looking skin). | *a skin disease* | **dark-skinned/smooth-skinned etc** *If you are fair-skinned, you should try to stay out of the sun.*

COLLOCATIONS

fair/pale skin
dark/olive skin
dark-skinned/fair-skinned
dry/oily/greasy/sensitive skin
smooth/soft skin
rough/leathery skin
good/bad skin – healthy or unhealthy skin
→ **HAIR**

2 the skin of an animal used as leather, fur etc: *a tiger skin rug*

3 the outside part of a fruit or vegetable [= peel]: *banana skins* → see picture at **FRUIT**

4 a thin solid layer that forms on the top of a liquid, especially when it gets cold: *Cover the soup to stop a skin from forming.*

5 do sth by the skin of your teeth *informal* to only just succeed in doing something: *He escaped by the skin of his teeth.*

6 have (a) thin/thick skin to be easily upset or not easily upset by criticism

skin² *v* [T] **skinned, skinning** to remove the skin from an animal, fruit, or vegetable

skinhead /'skɪnhed/ *n* [C] a young white person who has hair that is cut very short, especially one who behaves violently

skinny /'skɪni/ *adj* a skinny person is very thin → see box at **THIN**

skint /skɪnt/ *adj* [not before noun] *BrE informal* having no money: *I'm skint at the moment.* → see box at **POOR**

skip¹ /skɪp/ *v* **skipped, skipping** **1** [I] to move forwards with little jumps between your steps: **+down/along etc** *children skipping down the street* → see box at **JUMP** **2** [I] *also* **skip rope** *AmE* to move a rope over your head and under your feet, jumping as it goes under your feet → see picture at **JUMP¹** **3** [I,T] to avoid something or not do something: *You shouldn't skip breakfast.* | *Let's skip the next question.* | **+over** *I'll skip over the details.*

skip² *n* [C] **1** a quick light stepping and jumping movement **2** *BrE* a large container where you put waste such as bricks and broken furniture [= **Dumpster** *AmE*]

skipper /'skɪpə $ -ər/ *n* [C] *informal* a CAPTAIN of a ship or of a sports team

'skipping ,rope *n* [C] *BrE* a long piece of rope with handles that children use for jumping over [= **jump rope** *AmE*]

skirmish /'skɜːmɪʃ $ 'skɜːr-/ *n* [C] a fight between small groups of people or soldiers

skirt¹ /skɜːt $ skɜːrt/ *n* [C] a piece of clothing for girls and women that fits around the waist and hangs down like a dress → see picture at **CLOTHES**

skirt² *also* **skirt around** *v* [T] **1** to go around the outside edge of a place: *The train skirted around the lake.* **2** to avoid talking directly about a subject: *We cannot **skirt around** these issues.*

skit /skɪt/ *n* [C] a short performance or piece of writing that uses humour to criticize someone or something

skittle /'skɪtl/ *n* **1 skittles** [U] a British game in which you roll a ball to try to knock down skittles **2** [C] an object shaped like a bottle that you try to knock down with a ball

skive /skaɪv/ *also* **skive off** *v* [I] *BrE informal* to not go to school or work when you should do: *He skived off work and went fishing.* —**skiver** *n* [C]

skulk /skʌlk/ *v* [I] to hide or move around quietly because you do not want people to see you: **+in/behind etc** *Two men were skulking in the shadows.*

skull /skʌl/ *n* [C] the bones of a person's or animal's head → see picture on page A3

'skull cap *n* [C] a small cap that some men wear for religious reasons

skunk /skʌŋk/ *n* [C] a small black and white animal that produces an unpleasant smell if it is attacked

sky /skaɪ/ *n plural* **skies**

1 [singular, U] the space above the earth where the sun, clouds, and stars are: **clear/cloudy/dark etc sky** *a clear blue sky* | **in the sky** *There wasn't a cloud in the sky.*

2 skies [plural] the sky – used especially to describe the weather: *Tomorrow there will be clear skies and some sunshine.* | **clear/cloudy skies**

3 the sky's the limit *spoken* used to say that there is no limit to what someone can achieve or spend

skydiving /'skaɪ,daɪvɪŋ/ *n* [U] the sport of jumping from a plane with a PARACHUTE

skylight /'skaɪlaɪt/ *n* [C] a window in the roof of a building

skyline /'skaɪlaɪn/ *n* [C] the shape made by tall buildings or hills against the sky: *the famous New York skyline*

skyscraper /'skaɪ,skreɪpə $ -ər/ *n* [C] a very tall building

skyscrapers

slab /slæb/ *n* [C] a thick flat piece of something: *a concrete slab*

slack¹ /slæk/ *adj* **1** loose and not pulled tight: *a slack rope* **2** with less business activity than usual: *Trade is slack at the moment.* **3** not taking enough care to do things correctly: *slack safety procedures* | *I've been slack about getting this work done.*

slack² n **1 take up/pick up the slack a)** to do extra work because someone else is not doing it: *With McGill gone, I expect the rest of you to pick up the slack.* **b)** to pull a rope so that it is tight and not loose **2 slacks** [plural] trousers

slack³ also **slack off** v [I] to not work as quickly as you should: *Don't let me see you slacking off!* —**slacker** n [C]

slacken /'slækən/ v [I,T] **1** also **slacken off** to gradually become slower, weaker, or less active, or to make something do this: *He slackened his pace so I could catch up.* **2** to make something looser, or to become looser: *Slacken the screw a little.*

slag¹ /slæg/ n [U] waste material that is left when metal has been taken from rock

slag² v slagged, slagging
slag sb ⇔ off phr v BrE informal to criticize someone to another person

slain /sleɪn/ v the past participle of SLAY

slalom /'slɑːləm/ n [C,U] a race on SKIS or in CANOES in which people move down a curving course marked by flags

slam¹ /slæm/ v slammed, slamming **1** [I,T] if a door, gate etc slams, or if someone slams it, it shuts loudly and quickly: *He slammed the door shut.* **2** [T] to put something somewhere roughly or violently: **slam sth down/against/ onto** *Andy slammed the phone down angrily.*

slam² n [C usually singular] the action of hitting or closing something noisily or violently: *She shut the door with a slam.*

slander /'slɑːndə $ 'slændər/ n [C,U] a spoken statement about someone that is not true and is intended to damage the good opinion that people have of that person [➔ **libel**] ➔ see box at LIE —**slander** v [T] —**slanderous** adj

slang /slæŋ/ n [U] very informal language that uses new or rude words instead of the usual words for something
—**slangy** adj

slant¹ /slɑːnt $ slænt/ v [I] to slope, or move in a sloping line

slant² n [singular] **1** a way of writing about a subject that shows support for a particular set of ideas: **+on** *Each article has a slightly different slant on the situation.* **2** a sloping position or angle: **at/on a slant** *The pole was set at a slant.*

slanted /'slɑːntᵻd $ 'slæn-/ adj **1** disapproving unfairly supporting only one person, opinion, or argument [= biased]: *a process heavily slanted towards the banks* **2** sloping: *slightly slanted eyes*

slap¹ /slæp/ v [T] slapped, slapping to hit someone with the flat part of your hand: *She slapped him across the face.* ➔ see box at HIT
slap sth ⇔ on phr v informal to put or spread something quickly onto a surface: *Just slap some paint on and it'll look a bit better.*

slap² n **1** [C] a hit with the flat part of your hand **2 a slap in the face** something someone does that makes you feel shocked and offended

slapdash /'slæpdæʃ/ adj done quickly and carelessly: *slapdash work*

slapstick /'slæp,stɪk/ n [U] humorous acting in which the actors fall over and throw things at each other

'slap-up adj **slap-up meal/dinner etc** BrE informal a big and good meal

slash¹ /slæʃ/ v [T] **1** to cut something violently, making a long deep cut: *He tried to kill himself by slashing his wrists.* **2** informal to reduce something by a lot: *Many companies are slashing prices.*

slash² n [C] **1** a long deep cut **2** also **'slash mark** a line (/) used in writing to separate words or numbers

slat /slæt/ n [C] a thin flat piece of wood, plastic etc, used especially in furniture —**slatted** adj

slate¹ /sleɪt/ n **1** [U] a dark grey rock that can be split into thin flat pieces **2** [C] a piece of slate used as a roof covering ➔ **clean slate** at CLEAN¹

slate² v [T] **1 be slated to do sth/be slated for sth** AmE if something is slated to happen, it is planned to happen in the future: *He is slated to appear at the jazz festival next year.* **2** BrE to criticize someone or something severely: *Leconte's latest film has been slated by the critics.*

slaughter /'slɔːtə $ 'slɔːtər/ v [T] **1** to kill an animal for its meat **2** to kill a lot of people in a violent way: *Hundreds of people were slaughtered.* ➔ see box at KILL —**slaughter** n [U]

slaughterhouse /'slɔːtəhaʊs $ 'slɔːtər-/ n [C] a building where animals are killed for their meat [= abattoir]

slave¹ /sleɪv/ n [C] **1** someone who is owned by another person and must work for them without any pay **2 be a slave to/of sth** to be influenced too much by something: *She's a slave to fashion.*

slave² also **slave away** v [I] to work very hard: *Michael's been slaving away in the kitchen all day.*

,slave 'labour BrE; **slave labor** AmE n [U] **1** informal work for which you are very badly paid: *£2.00 an hour? That's slave labour!* **2** work done by slaves, or the slaves that do this work

slavery /'sleɪvəri/ n [U] the system of using slaves or the condition of being a slave: *Slavery was abolished* (=officially ended) *after the Civil War.*

slavish /'sleɪvɪʃ/ adj disapproving obeying or copying someone completely, without thinking: *slavish devotion to duty*

slay /sleɪ/ v [T] past tense **slew** /sluː/ past participle **slain** /sleɪn/ literary to kill someone violently —**slaying** n [C]

sleaze /sliːz/ n [U] immoral behaviour in business or politics

sleazy /'sliːzi/ adj low in quality, immoral, and unpleasant: *a sleazy nightclub*

sledge /sledʒ/ BrE; **sled** /sled/ AmE n [C] a vehicle used for travelling on snow —**sledge** v [I]

'sledge ,hammer n [C] a large heavy hammer

sleek /sliːk/ adj **1** sleek hair or fur is smooth and shiny **2** a sleek car is attractive and expensive

sleep¹ /sliːp/ v [I] past tense and past participle **slept** /slept/

1 to rest your mind and body, usually at night when you are lying in bed with your eyes closed: **sleep well/soundly/badly etc** *Did you sleep well?* | *I normally sleep on my back.* | *We usually sleep late* (=not get up until late in the morning) *on Sundays.* | *Good night, sleep tight* (=sleep well).

S

COLLOCATIONS

sleep well/soundly/deeply/peacefully
sleep badly
sleep lightly – to wake up very easily if there is a sound
sleep late/in – deliberately to sleep – later than usual in the morning
sleep like a log *informal* – to sleep – very well
not sleep a wink – not to sleep – at all
sleep fitfully *literary* – to keep waking up while you are sleeping –

THESAURUS

doze – to sleep lightly, for example in a chair
have/take a nap – to sleep for a short time during the day
oversleep – to sleep for too long, so that you are late
Use **sleep** when you are giving more information, for example how long someone sleeps, or where they sleep: *Most people sleep for about eight hours.* | *He slept downstairs.*
Do not use **sleep** to talk about starting to sleep. Use **fall asleep** or **go to sleep**: *Children often fall asleep during a car journey.*

2 sleep on it *spoken* not to make a decision about something important until the next day: *Sleep on it, and we'll discuss it tomorrow.*
3 sleep rough *BrE* to sleep outdoors because you have no home
4 sleep two/four/six etc to have enough beds for a particular number of people: *The cottage will sleep four easily.*

sleep around *phr v informal disapproving* to have sex with a lot of different people

sleep in *phr v* to wake up later than usual in the morning: *I slept in till 10:00 on Saturday.*

sleep sth ⇔ **off** *phr v* to sleep until you do not feel ill or drunk any more

sleep through sth *phr v* to continue to sleep while something is happening: *Amazingly, Jim had slept through the storm.*

sleep together *phr v informal* if people sleep together, they have sex with each other

sleep with sb *phr v informal* to have sex with someone: *Everyone knows he's sleeping with Diana.*

sleep² *n* [singular, U]
1 a time when you are sleeping: *We didn't get much sleep last night.* | *Her eyes were red through lack of sleep.* | **in sb's sleep** *Ed sometimes talks in his sleep.* | *What you need is a good night's sleep* (=a night when you sleep well).
2 go to sleep a) to start sleeping: *Be quiet and go to sleep!* | *I went to sleep at 9 o'clock and woke up at 6.* | *It's nothing, just go back to sleep* (=sleep again after waking up). **b)** *informal* if a part of your body goes to sleep, you cannot feel it for a short time, because it has not been getting enough blood
3 not lose (any) sleep over sth *spoken* to not worry about something
4 put sth **to sleep** to give an animal drugs so that it dies without pain

sleeper /'sliːpə $ -ər/ *n* [C] **1 a light/heavy sleeper** someone who wakes up easily or does not wake up easily from sleep **2** *BrE* a train with beds for passengers to sleep on

'sleeping bag *n* [C] a large warm bag for sleeping in

'sleeping pill *n* [C] a drug that helps you to sleep

sleepless /'sliːpləs/ *adj* unable to sleep: *He spent a sleepless night* (=a night when you do not sleep) *worrying about what to do.* —**sleeplessness** *n* [U]

sleepover /'sliːpəʊvə $ -oʊvər/ *n* [C] a party for children in which they stay the night at someone's house

sleepwalk /'sliːp,wɔːk $ -,wɒːk/ *v* [I] to get out of bed and walk around while you are asleep —**sleepwalker** *n* [C]

sleepy /'sliːpi/ *adj* **1** tired and ready to sleep: *I felt really sleepy after lunch.* **2** a sleepy town or village is very quiet → see box at **QUIET** —**sleepily** *adv* —**sleepiness** *n* [U]

sleet /sliːt/ *n* [U] a mixture of rain and snow → see box at **RAIN** → and **SNOW** —**sleet** *v* [I]

sleeve /sliːv/ *n*
1 [C] the part of a piece of clothing that covers your arm: *a blouse with short sleeves*
2 long-sleeved/short-sleeved with long or short sleeves: *a long-sleeved sweater*
3 have sth **up your sleeve** *informal* to have a secret plan that you are going to use later: *Jansen usually has a few surprises up his sleeve.*
4 [C] *BrE* a cover for a record [= **jacket** *AmE*]

sleeveless /'sliːvləs/ *adj* without sleeves: *a sleeveless dress*

sleigh /sleɪ/ *n* [C] a large vehicle that is pulled by animals, used for travelling on snow

sleight of hand /,slaɪt əv 'hænd/ *n* [U] **1** *disapproving* the use of skilful tricks and lies in order to deceive someone **2** quick and skilful movements with your hands when doing a magic trick

slender /'slendə $ -ər/ *adj* thin in an attractive way: *long slender fingers* → see box at **THIN**

slept /slept/ *v* the past tense and past participle of **SLEEP**

sleuth /sluːθ/ *n* [C] *literary* a **DETECTIVE**

slew¹ /sluː/ *n* *AmE informal* **a slew of** sth a large number of things: *A whole slew of coffee bars are opening up downtown.*

slew² *v* the past tense and past participle of **SLAY**

slice¹ /slaɪs/ *n* [C]
1 a thin piece of bread, meat etc that you cut from a larger piece: **+of** *a slice of bread* | **thin/thick slice** *Cut the tomato into thin slices.* → see picture at **PIECE**
2 a slice of sth a share of something: *Everyone wants a slice of the profits.*

slice² *v*
1 also **slice up** [T] to cut meat, bread etc into thin pieces [➜ **chop**]: *Could you slice the bread?* | *Slice up the onions and add them to the meat.* → see box at **CUT** → see picture at **CUT¹**
2 [I,T] to cut through something quickly and easily: **+through/into** *The knife is so sharp it can slice through bone.* | **slice** sth **in two/half** *Slice the lemon in half.* | **slice** sth **off** *She sliced off the top of her finger with a bread knife.*

slick¹ /slɪk/ *adj* **1** good at persuading people, often in a way that does not seem honest: *a slick salesman* **2** if something is slick, it is done in a skilful and attractive way, but is not important or interesting: *a slick Hollywood production*

slick² n [C] an OIL SLICK

slide

slide

slip

skid

slide¹ /slaɪd/ v [I,T] past tense and past participle **slid** /slɪd/

1 to move smoothly over a surface, or to make something move in this way: **+along/around/down etc** *The children were sliding along the ice.* | **slide sth across/along etc sth** *She slid my drink along the bar.*

2 to move somewhere quietly and smoothly, or to move something in this way: **+into/out of etc** *Daniel slid out of the room when no one was looking.* | **slide sth into/out of etc sth** *He slid the gun into his pocket.*

slide² n **1** [C] a photograph in a frame. You shine light through it to show the photograph on a screen: *a **slide show*** **2** [C] a long metal slope with steps at one end, that children can climb up and slide down **3** [singular] a decrease in the price, level, standard etc of something: **+in** *a slide in profits* **4** [C] a piece of thin glass used for holding something under a MICROSCOPE

slight¹ /slaɪt/ adj

1 small in amount or degree: *a slight improvement* | *I have a slight headache.* | *There has been a slight change of plan.*

2 not the slightest chance/doubt/difference etc no doubt, chance etc at all: *I don't have the slightest idea where she is.*

3 not in the slightest *spoken* not at all: *'You're not worried, are you?' 'Not in the slightest.'*

4 someone who is slight is thin and delicate [≠ stocky]

slight² n [C] a remark or action that offends someone: **+on/to** *a slight to his authority*

slighted /ˈslaɪtᵻd/ adj offended because you feel that someone has treated you rudely or without respect: *Meg **felt slighted** at not being invited to the party.*

slightly /ˈslaɪtli/ adv a little: *Each painting is **slightly different**.* | *Women make up **slightly more** than half the population.* | **slightly higher/lower/better/larger etc** *She's slightly older than I am.* | *We know each other slightly.* | *He leaned forward **ever so slightly**.*

slim¹ /slɪm/ adj

1 someone who is slim is thin in an attractive

way [= slender]: *You're looking a lot slimmer – have you lost weight?* | *a slim waist* → see box at THIN

2 very small in amount or degree: *Doctors say she has only a **slim chance** of recovery.* | *a slim margin of profit*

slim² also **slim down** v [I] **slimmed, slimming** to make yourself thinner by eating less or by exercising [➞ diet]: *After he quit drinking, he slimmed to 210 pounds.* —**slimming** n [U]

  slim sth ⇔ down *phr v* to reduce the size or number of something: *Apex Co. is slimming down its workforce to cut costs.*

slime /slaɪm/ n [U] a thick sticky liquid that looks or smells unpleasant

slimy /ˈslaɪmi/ adj **1** covered with slime: *slimy rocks* **2** *informal* friendly in a way that is not sincere: *slimy politicians*

sling¹ /slɪŋ/ v [T] past tense and past participle **slung** /slʌŋ/ **1** to throw or put something somewhere carelessly: *Duncan slung his suitcase onto the bed.* **2** to put something somewhere so that it hangs loosely: *Dave wore a tool belt slung around his waist.*

sling² n [C] **1** a piece of cloth that is put under your arm and then tied around your neck to support your arm or hand when it is injured **2** ropes or strong pieces of cloth used for lifting or carrying heavy objects: *a baby sling*

slingshot /ˈslɪŋʃɒt $ -ʃɑːt/ n [C] *AmE* a small Y-shaped stick with a thin band of rubber across the top, used to throw stones [= catapult *BrE*]

slink /slɪŋk/ v [I] past tense and past participle **slunk** /slʌŋk/ to move somewhere quietly and secretly: *The cat slunk behind the chair.*

slip¹ /slɪp/ v **slipped, slipping**

1 [I] if you slip, your feet move accidentally and you fall or almost fall: *Be careful not to slip — I just mopped the floor.* | **+on** *Joan slipped on the ice and broke her ankle.* → see box at FALL → see picture at SLIDE¹

2 [I] to go somewhere quickly and quietly: **+out of/away/through etc** *Ben slipped quietly out of the room while his father was asleep.* | *No one saw Bill slip away when the police arrived.*

3 [T] to put something quietly or secretly [= slide]: **slip sth into/around etc sth** *Ann slipped the book into her bag.* | *He slipped his arm around her waist and kissed her.*

4 [I] if something slips, it accidentally moves or falls: *The knife slipped as he cut into the wood.* | **+off/down/from etc** *The ring had slipped off Julia's finger.*

5 [I,T] to put on a piece of clothing or take it off quickly and easily: **slip sth off/on** *Ken sat on the couch and slipped off his shoes.* | **+into/out of** *She slipped into her pyjamas.*

6 slip your mind *spoken* if something slips your mind, you forget about it: *I was supposed to meet her for lunch, but it completely slipped my mind.*

7 [I] to become worse or lower than before [= fall]: *Standards in our schools have been slipping.* | *The mayor's popularity is slipping.*

8 let sth slip *informal* to say something that is supposed to be a secret without intending to: *Don't let it slip that I'm in town.*

  slip away *phr v* if an opportunity to do something slips away, the situation changes and the

S

opportunity no longer exists: *This time, Radford did not let her chance slip away.*

slip out *phr v* if something slips out, you say it without intending to: *Sorry, I shouldn't have said that – it just slipped out.*

slip up *phr v* to make a mistake: *He can't afford to slip up again or he'll be fired.*

slip² n [C] 1 a small piece of paper: *He wrote his address on a slip of paper.* **2** a small mistake: *Molly knew she could not afford to **make a single slip**.* **3** a piece of clothing worn by women under a dress or skirt **4** an act of sliding accidentally so that you fall or almost fall **5 a slip of the tongue/pen** something that you say or write by accident, when you meant to say or write something else **6 give sb the slip** *informal* to escape from someone who is chasing you: *Palmer gave them the slip in the hotel lobby.*

slipper /'slɪpə $ -ər/ *n* [C usually plural] a light soft shoe that you wear indoors → see picture at **SHOE¹**

slippery /'slɪpəri/ *adj*

1 something that is slippery is difficult to walk on or hold because it is wet, oily, or covered in ice: *a slippery mountain path* | *Harry's palms were slippery with sweat.*
2 a/the slippery slope a process or habit that is difficult to stop and which will develop into something dangerous or harmful: **+to/towards** *He is on the slippery slope to a life in crime.*

'slip road *n* [C] *BrE* a road used when you drive onto or off a MOTORWAY

slit¹ /slɪt/ *n* [C] a long narrow cut or opening: *a slit in the curtains*

slit² *v* [T] past tense and past participle **slit**, present participle **slitting** to make a long narrow cut in something: *Guy **slit open** the envelope.*

slither /'slɪðə $ -ər/ *v* [I] **1** to slide somewhere: *He slithered down the muddy bank.* **2** if a snake slithers somewhere, it moves there

sliver /'slɪvə $ -ər/ *n* [C] a small thin pointed piece that has been cut or broken off something: **+of** *a sliver of glass*

slob /slɒb $ slɑːb/ *n* [C] *informal* someone who is lazy, dirty, or untidy

slobber /'slɒbə $ 'slɑːbər/ *v* [I] to let SALIVA (=the liquid produced in your mouth) come out of your mouth and run down: *That dog slobbers everywhere.*

slog /slɒg $ slɑːg/ *v* [I] **slogged**, **slogging** *informal* **1** to make a long hard journey somewhere, especially by walking: *We had to slog through mud and dirt to get to the farm.* **2** also **slog away** to work hard at something without stopping, especially when the work is difficult or boring: *I don't want to slog away in a factory for the rest of my life.* —**slog** *n* [singular, U] *The second day was a hard slog.*

slogan /'sləʊgən $ 'sloʊ-/ *n* [C] a short phrase that is easy to remember and is used in advertising or politics

slop /slɒp $ slɑːp/ *v* **slopped**, **slopping** [I,T] if liquid slops, or if you slop it, it moves around or over the edge of a container: *Water was slopping over the side of the bath.*

slope¹ /sləʊp $ sloʊp/ *n* [C] a piece of ground or a surface that is higher at one end than at the other: *The house was built on a slope.* | *a steep slope* | *a gentle* (=not steep) *slope* | *a ski slope*

slope² *v* [I] if something slopes, it is higher at one end than at the other: **+up/down/away etc** *The front yard slopes down to the street.* | *a sloping ceiling*

sloppy /'slɒpi $ 'slɑːpi/ *adj* **1** not tidy or careful: *sloppy work* **2** sloppy clothes are large, loose, and not neat: *a sloppy sweater* —**sloppily** *adv* —**sloppiness** *n* [U]

slosh /slɒʃ $ slɑːʃ/ *v* [I] if liquid in a container sloshes, it moves against or over the sides of the container: **+around/about** *Water was sloshing around in the bottom of the boat.*

slot¹ /slɒt $ slɑːt/ *n* [C] **1** a long narrow hole in something, especially one for putting coins in: *Put 20p in the slot and see how much you weigh.* **2** a period of time allowed for one particular event: *I was offered a slot on a local radio station.*

slot² *v* [I,T] **slotted**, **slotting** to put something into a slot, or to go into a slot: *The cassette slots in here.* | *The instructions tell you how to slot the shelf together.*

'slot ma,chine *n* [C] a machine that you put coins into to play a game and try to win money

slouch /slaʊtʃ/ *v* [I] to stand, sit, or walk in a lazy way, with your shoulders bent forward: **+back/against/in etc** *Jimmy slouched back in his chair.* —**slouch** *n* [singular]

slovenly /'slʌvənli/ *adj written* dirty, untidy, and careless

slow¹ /sləʊ $ sloʊ/ *adj, adv*

1 not moving or happening quickly [≠ **fast**]: *The slowest runners started at the back.* | *It's a very slow process.* | *My computer's very slow today.* | *Go slower.*
2 slow to do sth/slow in doing sth if you are slow to do something, you do not do it as soon as you can or should: *We were slow to realize what was happening.* | *New ideas have been slow in coming.*
3 a clock that is slow shows a time earlier than the true time [≠ **fast**]: *My watch is a few minutes slow.*
4 if business is slow, there are not many customers: *Business is usually slow this time of year.*
5 someone who is slow does not understand things very quickly or easily: *The school gives extra help for slower students.*

slow² also **slow down** *v* [I,T] to become slower, or to make something slower: *The traffic slowed to a crawl.* | *The ice on the road slowed us down.*

slowdown /'sləʊdaʊn $ 'sloʊ-/ *n* [C] when an activity takes place more slowly than it did before: **+in** *a slowdown in the tourist trade*

slowly /'sləʊli $ 'sloʊ-/ *adv* at a slow speed [≠ **quickly**]: *White clouds drifted slowly across the sky.* | *His voice became lower and he spoke more slowly.*

,slow 'motion *n* [U] if part of a film or television programme is shown in slow motion, it is shown at a slower speed than the real speed: *Let's look at that goal in slow motion.*

sludge /slʌdʒ/ *n* [U] a soft thick unpleasant substance

slug¹ /slʌg/ *n* [C] a small soft creature with no legs that moves very slowly along the ground [➜ **snail**]

slug² *v* [T] **slugged**, **slugging 1 slug it out** to argue or fight until someone wins: *The two sides* *are slugging it out in court.* **2** *informal* to hit someone hard with your closed hand

sluggish /'slʌgɪʃ/ *adj* moving or reacting more slowly than usual: *Alex woke late feeling tired and sluggish.*

slum /slʌm/ *n* [C] a house or an area of a city that is in very bad condition, where many poor people live: *He had grown up in the slums of Chicago.* → see box at **AREA**

slumber /'slʌmbə $ -ər/ *n* [singular, U] also **slumbers** [plural] *literary* sleep: *She awoke from her slumbers.* —**slumber** *v* [I]

slump¹ /slʌmp/ *v* [I] **1** if a price or amount slumps, it suddenly becomes less: *Car sales have slumped recently.* **2** to fall or lean heavily against something because you are tired, ill, unhappy etc: **+against/over/back etc** *Carol slumped back in her chair, defeated.* | *He was found slumped over the steering wheel of his car.*

slump² *n* [C] **1** a sudden decrease in prices, sales, profits etc: **+in** *a slump in profits* **2** a period when there is a reduction in business and many people lose their jobs: *The war was followed by an economic slump.*

slung /slʌŋ/ *v* the past tense and past participle of SLING

slunk /slʌŋk/ *v* the past tense and past participle of SLINK

slur¹ /slɜː $ slɜːr/ *v* [I,T] **slurred**, **slurring** to speak in an unclear way without separating your words or sounds correctly: **slur your speech/ words** *After a few drinks, he started to slur his words.*

slur² *n* [C] an unfair criticism that is intended to make people dislike someone or something: **+on/against** *a slur on his character* | *a racist slur*

slurp /slɜːp $ slɜːrp/ *v* [I,T] *informal* to drink in a noisy way → see box at **DRINK** —**slurp** *n* [C]

slush /slʌʃ/ *n* [U] snow on the ground that has partly melted → see box at **SNOW**

sly /slaɪ/ *adj* **1** someone who is sly tries to get what they want by not being completely honest [= **cunning**] **2** showing that you know something that others do not know: *a sly smile* **3 on the sly** *informal* secretly —**slyly** *adv*

smack¹ /smæk/ *v* [T] **1** to hit someone, especially a child, with your open hand in order to punish them → see box at **HIT** **2 smack your lips** to make a short noise with your lips to show that you like a drink or some food **3** to hit something: *The waves smacked against my knees.* —**smack** *n* [C] *a smack on the head*

  smack of sth *phr v* if a situation smacks of something unpleasant, it seems to involve that thing: *a policy that smacks of sex discrimination*

smack² *adv informal* **1** exactly in a place: *an old building smack in the middle of campus* **2** with a lot of force: *The van ran smack into a wall.*

small /smɔːl $ smɒːl/ *adj*

1 not big: *She comes from a small town.* | *Smaller cars use less gas.* | *These shoes are too small.* | *Only a small number of people were affected.* | *Police found a small amount of drugs in the car.*

little – small in size: *a little house* also used after another adjective when you want to show how you feel about someone or something small: *Poor little dog!*
tiny – very small: *a tiny baby*
minute – extremely small: *The glass broke into hundreds of minute pieces.*
poky *especially BrE* – used about a room, house etc that is too small: *a poky flat near the station*
cramped – used about a space that is too small: *cramped working conditions*

2 unimportant or easy to deal with [= **minor**]: *a small problem* | *We may have to make a few small changes.*

3 a small child is young: *She has two small children.* → see box at **YOUNG**

4 feel/look small to feel or look stupid or unimportant: *She was always trying to **make** me **look small**.*

5 the small hours the early morning hours, between about one and four o'clock: *The party went on until the small hours.*

'small ad *n* [C] *BrE* an advertisement put in a newspaper by someone who wants to sell something, buy something etc → see box at **ADVERTISEMENT**

,small 'change *n* [U] coins of low value: *I didn't have any small change for the parking meter.*

'small fry *n* [U] *informal* people or things that are not important when compared to other people or things: *They're small fry compared to the real criminals.*

smallholding /'smɔːl,həʊldɪŋ $ 'smɒːl,hoʊld-/ *n* [C] *BrE* a small farm

smallpox /'smɔːlpɒks $ 'smɒːlpɑːks/ *n* [U] a serious disease that killed a lot of people in the past

'small ,print also **fine print** *n* [U] all the rules and details relating to a contract or agreement: *Make sure you **read the small print** before you sign anything.*

,small-'scale *adj* not very big, or not involving a lot of people: *small-scale enterprises*

'small talk *n* [U] polite friendly conversation about unimportant subjects: *He's not very good at **making small talk**.*

'small-time *adj* a small-time criminal or BUSINESSMAN is not very important or successful

smart¹ /smɑːt $ smɑːrt/ *adj*

1 intelligent [= **clever**; ≠ **stupid**]: *Jill's a smart kid.* | *Kelly didn't think she was smart enough to go to law school.* → see box at **INTELLIGENT**

2 *BrE* **a)** someone who looks smart is wearing attractive clothes and looks very neat [= **sharp** *AmE*; ≠ **scruffy**] **b)** smart clothes, buildings etc are clean, tidy, and attractive [= **sharp** *AmE*; ≠ **scruffy**]: *a smart black suit* | *smart new offices* → see box at **CLOTHES**

3 *BrE* fashionable, or used by fashionable people: *one of London's smartest restaurants*

4 someone who is smart tries to be funny or clever in a way that is rude and does not show respect towards someone else: *Don't **get smart with me**, young lady!* | *He made some smart remark.*

5 smart machines, weapons etc are controlled by computers
—**smartly** adv

smart² v [I] **1** to be upset because someone has offended you: **+from** *He's still smarting from the insult.* **2** if a part of your body smarts, it hurts with a stinging pain

smarten /'smɑːtn $ 'smɑːr-/ v
   smarten sb/sth ⇔ **up** phr v to make a person or place look neater and more attractive: *You'd better smarten yourself up.*

smash¹ /smæʃ/ v [I,T]

1 to break into a lot of small pieces, or to make something break in this way: *The plates smashed on the floor.* | *Rioters smashed store windows.* | *The boat was **smashed to pieces** on the rocks.* → see box at **BREAK**
2 to hit an object or surface violently, or to make something do this: *Murray smashed his fist against the wall.* | **+against/down/into etc** *A stolen car smashed into the bus.*
   smash sth ⇔ **in** phr v to hit something so violently that you break it and make a hole in it: *Pete's window was smashed in by another driver.*
   smash sth ⇔ **up** phr v to deliberately destroy something by hitting it: *A group of young men started smashing the place up.*

smash² also **,smash 'hit** n [C] a very successful new song, film, play etc: *The song became a smash hit.*

smashing /'smæʃɪŋ/ adj BrE old-fashioned very good: *We had a smashing holiday.*

smattering /'smætərɪŋ/ n [singular] a small number or amount of something: **+of** *a smattering of applause*

smear¹ /smɪə $ smɪr/ v [T] **1** to spread a liquid or soft substance on a surface: **smear sth on/over etc sb** *Jill smeared lotion on Rick's back.* | **smear sth with sth** *His face was smeared with mud.* **2** to tell an untrue story about someone important in order to harm them – used especially in newspapers: *an attempt to smear the party leadership*

smear² n [C] **1** a dirty mark made by a small amount of something spread on a surface: *It left a black smear on his forehead.* **2** an untrue story about someone important that is meant to harm them – used especially in newspapers

smell¹ /smel/ v past tense and past participle **smelled** or **smelt** /smelt/

1 [I] to have a particular smell: *The stew **smelled delicious.*** | **+like** *It smells like rotten eggs.* | **+of** BrE: *My clothes smelled of smoke.*
2 [I] to have an unpleasant smell: *Your feet smell!*
3 [I,T] to notice or recognize a smell: *I can smell something burning!*
4 [T] to put your nose near something in order to discover what kind of smell it has: *Come and smell these roses.*

smell² n

1 [C] a quality that you recognize using your nose: *What a lovely smell!* | **+of** *the smell of fresh bread* | **strong/pungent smell** *a strong smell of paint* | *The smell's getting worse.*

THESAURUS

A good smell
aroma – used especially about food: *the*

aroma of fresh coffee
perfume/fragrance/scent: *She's wearing a new perfume.*

A bad smell
stink: *the stink of rotting fish*
stench: *the stench of burning rubber*
odour BrE/**odor** AmE: *stale odours*
pong BrE: *an awful pong*

2 [U] the ability to notice or recognize smells: *Dogs have a good **sense of smell**.*

smelly /'smeli/ adj having a strong unpleasant smell

smidgen /'smɪdʒən/ also **smidge** /smɪdʒ/ n [singular] spoken informal a very small amount of something

smile¹ /smaɪl/ v

1 [I] to have a happy expression on your face, with your mouth curving: *She came in, smiling.* | **+at** *Keith smiled sweetly at me.*

THESAURUS

grin – to give a big happy smile
beam – to smile because you are very pleased about something: *Jenny ran across the room, beaming with pleasure.*
smirk – to smile in an unpleasant way, for example because you are pleased about someone else's bad luck

2 [T] to say or express something with a smile: *'Thanks,' she smiled.*

smile² n [C] a happy expression on your face, with your mouth curving: *'Hello,' she said with a smile.* | **broad/big smile** *A broad smile spread over Lucy's face.* | **little/faint smile** *He managed a faint smile.*

smirk /smɜːk $ smɜːrk/ v [I] to smile in a satisfied and annoying way → see box at **SMILE**
—**smirk** n [C]

smithereens /ˌsmɪðəˈriːnz/ n **smash/blow sth to smithereens** to destroy something or break it into very small pieces

smitten /'smɪtn/ adj [not before noun] loving someone very much: **+with/by** *He's absolutely smitten with her.*

smock /smɒk $ smɑːk/ n [C] a long loose shirt or a loose dress

smog /smɒg $ smɑːg, smɔːg/ n [U] unhealthy air in cities that contains a lot of smoke

smoke¹ /sməʊk $ smoʊk/ n

1 [U] the white, grey, or black gas that is produced by something burning: *Clouds of black smoke billowed out.* | *cigarette smoke*
2 [singular] when someone smokes a cigarette
3 go up in smoke informal **a)** if your plans go up in smoke, they fail **b)** to be destroyed by burning

smoke² v

1 [I,T] to suck smoke from a cigarette or pipe: *I don't smoke any more.* | *He smokes a pipe.*
2 [I] to be producing smoke: *a smoking chimney*
3 [T] to prepare food by hanging it in smoke: *smoked salmon*
—**smoking** n [U]

smoker /'sməʊkə $ 'smoʊkər/ n [C] someone who smokes [≠ **non-smoker**]: *He's a **heavy smoker** (=he smokes a lot).*

smokescreen /'sməʊkskriːn $ 'smoʊk-/ n [C] something that you do or say to hide your real plans or actions

smoky /'sməʊki $ 'smoʊ-/ adj **1** containing or producing smoke: *a smoky room* | *a smoky fire* **2** having the taste, smell, or appearance of smoke: *smoky cheese*

smolder /'sməʊldə $ 'smoʊldər/ v the American spelling of SMOULDER

smooch /smuːtʃ/ v [I] *informal* if two people smooch, they kiss and hold each other in a romantic way, especially while dancing —**smooch** n [singular]

smooth¹ /smuːð/ adj

1 having an even surface [≠ rough]: *The road was wide and smooth.* | *She had lovely smooth skin.* | *The stone steps had been worn smooth.* → see picture at BUMPY

2 a substance that is smooth has no big pieces in it [≠ lumpy]: *Beat all the ingredients together until smooth.*

3 graceful or comfortable, with no sudden movements: *Swing the racket in one smooth motion.* | *It wasn't a very smooth ride.*

4 happening or continuing without problems: *Sarah ensures the smooth running of the sales department.* | *a smooth transition from school to university*

5 polite and confident in a way that people do not trust: *a smooth talker*

—**smoothly** adv —**smoothness** n [U]

smooth² v [T] **1** to make something flat by moving your hands across it: *Tanya sat down, smoothing her skirt.* | **smooth sth back/down** *She smoothed back her hair.* **2** to take away the roughness from a surface: *a face cream that smooths your skin*

     smooth sth ⇔ **out** phr v to make something such as paper or cloth flat by moving your hands across it: *She smoothed out the newspaper.*

     smooth sth ⇔ **over** phr v to end an unpleasant situation by talking to the people involved: *He depended on Nancy to smooth over any troubles.*

smoothie /'smuːði/ n [C] a thick drink made from fruit

smother /'smʌðə $ -ər/ v [T] **1** to cover someone's face so that they cannot breathe and they die **2** to put a large amount of a substance onto something: **smother sth in/with sth** *cakes smothered in chocolate* **3** to make someone unhappy by giving them more attention than they want **4** to stop yourself from having or expressing a feeling: *They tried to smother their giggles.* **5** to make a fire stop burning by preventing air from reaching it

smoulder BrE; **smolder** AmE /'sməʊldə $ 'smoʊldər/ v [I] **1** if a fire is smouldering, it is burning slowly without flames → see box at FIRE **2** to have strong feelings which you are trying to hide: *Underneath he was smouldering with rage.*

smudge¹ /smʌdʒ/ n [C] a dirty mark where something has been touched

smudge² v [I,T] if ink, paint etc on a surface smudges, or if you smudge it, its appearance is spoiled because it has been touched

smug /smʌg/ adj very satisfied with your situation, in a way that annoys other people: *a smug smile* —**smugly** adv

smuggle /'smʌgəl/ v [T] to take something illegally from one place to another: *The guns were smuggled across the border.* —**smuggler** n [C] —**smuggling** n [U]

smutty /'smʌti/ adj referring to sex in an unpleasant or silly way: *smutty jokes*

snack¹ /snæk/ n [C] food that you eat between meals or instead of a large meal: *The cafe serves drinks, snacks, and meals.* → see picture at DINE

snack² v [I] to eat small amounts of food between main meals or instead of a meal

'snack bar n [C] a place where you can buy snacks

snag¹ /snæg/ n [C] *informal* a difficulty or problem: *The only snag is lack of money.* → see box at PROBLEM

snag² v [I,T] **snagged, snagging** to damage something by getting it stuck on something sharp

snail /sneɪl/ n

1 [C] a small creature with a long soft body and a round shell on its back

2 at a snail's pace extremely slowly: *Traffic was moving at a snail's pace.*

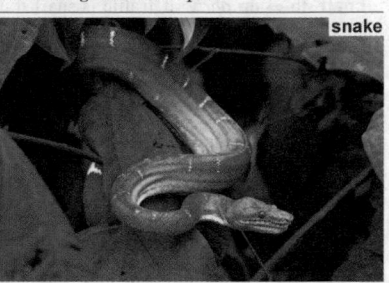

snake

snake¹ /sneɪk/ n [C] a long thin animal that slides across the ground: *A snake slithered across the path.* | **poisonous/venomous snake**

snake² v [I] *written* to move in long curves or have long curves: **+through/across etc** *The convoy snaked through the city.* | *She saw the river snaking its way through the gorge.*

snap¹ /snæp/ v **snapped, snapping** **1** [I,T] if something snaps, or if you snap it, it breaks with a short loud noise: *Dry branches snapped under their feet.* | **snap (sth) in half/two** *He snapped the chalk in two.* → see box at BREAK **2** [I,T] to move into a position with a short loud noise, or to make something do this: **snap (sth) together/open/shut** *She snapped her briefcase shut.* **3** [I,T] to speak suddenly in an angry way: **+at** *I'm sorry I snapped at you.* | *'What?' she snapped.* **4** [I] if a dog snaps at you, it tries to bite you **5** [I] to be suddenly unable to control your anger: *He just snapped.* **6** [I,T] to take a photograph **7 snap your fingers** to make a short loud noise with your finger and thumb

     snap out of sth phr v *informal* to stop being sad or upset: *Jane's still depressed — I wish she'd snap out of it.*

     snap sth ⇔ **up** phr v quickly to take an opportunity to get something: *At that price, they'll be snapped up in no time.*

snap² n **1** [singular] a sudden short loud noise, especially of something breaking or closing: *He shut the book with a snap.* **2 be a snap** AmE

S

informal to be very easy   **3** [C] a photograph that is taken quickly: *holiday snaps*   **4** [U] a card game in which you say 'snap" when two cards are the same

snap[3] *adj* **snap judgment/decision** a judgment or decision made very quickly, without thought or discussion

snappy /'snæpi/ *adj*   **1 make it snappy** *spoken* used to tell someone to hurry   **2** a snappy phrase is short, clear, and often funny

snapshot /'snæpʃɒt $ -ʃɑːt/ *n* [C]   **1** a photograph that is taken quickly [= **snap**]   **2** information that quickly gives an idea of a situation: **+of** *a snapshot of life during that time*

snare[1] /sneə $ sner/ *n* [C] a trap for catching birds or small animals

snare[2] *v* [T]   **1** to catch an animal using a snare   **2** to catch someone, especially by tricking them

snarl /snɑːl $ snɑːrl/ *v*   **1** [I,T] to say something in a nasty angry way: *'Shut up!' he snarled.*   **2** [I] if an animal snarls, it makes a low angry sound and shows its teeth: *The dog growled and snarled at me.* —**snarl** *n* [C]

snarl sth ⇔ **up** *phr v* if traffic is snarled up, vehicles are not able to move

snatch[1] /snætʃ/ *v* [T]   **1** to take something from someone with a sudden movement: **snatch sth from sb** *The boy snatched the note from her hand.*   **2** to quickly do something or get something, when you have a short amount of time: *I managed to snatch an hour's sleep on the train.*

snatch at sth *phr v* to quickly put out your hand to try to take or hold something: *Jessie snatched at the bag.*

snatch[2] *n* **a snatch of conversation/song etc** a short part of a conversation, song etc that you hear

snazzy /'snæzi/ *adj informal* bright, fashionable, and attractive: *a snazzy jacket*

sneak[1] /sniːk/ *v* past tense and past participle **sneaked** or **snuck** /snʌk/   **1** [I] to go somewhere quietly and secretly: **+out/past/off etc** *We managed to sneak past the guard.* → see box at **WALK**   **2** [T] to take something somewhere secretly: *I'll sneak his present upstairs.*   **3 sneak a look/ glance at sth** to look at something quickly and secretly: *She sneaked a look at the diary.*

sneak up *phr v* to come close to someone very quietly, so that they do not notice you: **+on/ behind** *Don't sneak up on me like that!*

sneak[2] *n* [C] *BrE informal disapproving* a child who tells adults when other children have done something wrong

sneaker /'sniːkə $ -ər/ *n* [C] *especially AmE* a soft sports shoe

sneaking /'sniːkɪŋ/ *adj*   **1 have a sneaking suspicion/feeling (that)** to think you know something without being sure: *I've a sneaking feeling this won't work.*   **2 have a sneaking admiration for sb** to like someone, although you do not want to admit it

sneaky /'sniːki/ *adj* done in a clever, but unfair, way: *a sneaky trick*

sneer /snɪə $ snɪr/ *v* [I,T] to smile or speak in a nasty unkind way: **+at** *She sneered at his taste in music.* | *'What happened to you?' he sneered.* —**sneer** *n* [C]

sneeze /sniːz/ *v* [I] when you sneeze, air suddenly comes out of your nose and mouth in a noisy and uncontrollable way: *The dust is mak-ing me sneeze.* —**sneeze** *n* [C]

snicker /'snɪkə $ -ər/ *v* [I] *AmE* to laugh quietly in an unkind way [= **snigger** *BrE*] → see box at **LAUGH** —**snicker** *n* [C]

snide /snaɪd/ *adj* a snide remark criticizes someone in a way that is unkind, although it may be clever: **snide comment/remark** *She started making snide remarks about him.*

sniff /snɪf/ *v*

1 [I] to breathe air into your nose noisily, for example when you are crying or have a cold: *Stop sniffing and blow your nose.*

2 [I,T] to breathe in through your nose in order to smell something: *'What's this?' he asked, sniffing it suspiciously.* | **+at** *The dog was sniffing at the carpet.*

3 not to be sniffed at *especially BrE spoken* worth considering or accepting: *An 8% salary increase is not to be sniffed at.*

—**sniff** *n* [C]

'sniffer dog *n* [C] *BrE* a dog that has been trained to find drugs or explosives

sniffle /'snɪfəl/ *v* [I] to sniff a lot, especially when you are crying or ill —**sniffle** *n* [C]

snigger /'snɪgə $ -ər/ *v* [I] *BrE* to laugh quietly in an unkind way [= **snicker** *AmE*] → see box at **LAUGH** —**snigger** *n* [C]

snip[1] /snɪp/ *v* [I,T] **snipped, snipping** to cut something with quick small cuts, using scissors → see box at **CUT**

snip[2] *n* [C]   **1** a quick small cut with scissors   **2 be a snip** *BrE informal* to be surprisingly cheap

snipe /snaɪp/ *v* [I]   **1** to criticize someone in an unkind way: *I wish you two would stop sniping at each other.*   **2** to shoot at people from a hidden position —**sniping** *n* [U]

sniper /'snaɪpə $ -ər/ *n* [C] someone who shoots at people from a hidden position

snippet /'snɪpət/ *n* [C] a small piece of news, information, or conversation: **+of** *The book contains some fascinating snippets of information.*

snivel /'snɪvəl/ *v* [I] **snivelled, snivelling** *BrE*; **sniveled, sniveling** *AmE* to cry and behave in a weak complaining way: *Stop snivelling!*

snob /snɒb $ snɑːb/ *n* [C] *disapproving* someone who thinks they are better than people from a lower social class

snobbery /'snɒbəri $ 'snɑː-/ *n* [U] the attitudes and behaviour of snobs

snobbish /'snɒbɪʃ $ 'snɑː-/ also **snobby** /'snɒbi $ 'snɑːbi/ *adj* behaving like a snob

snog /snɒg $ snɑːg/ *v* [I,T] **snogged, snogging** *BrE informal* to kiss someone in a sexual way —**snog** *n* [singular]

snook /snuːk $ snʊk, snuːk/ *n* → **cock a snook at sb/sth** at **COCK**[2]

snooker /'snuːkə $ 'snʊkər/ *n* [U] a game played on a special table with long sticks, one white ball, and a set of coloured balls

snoop /snuːp/ *v* [I] to try to find out about someone's activities by secretly watching them or looking at their things: **+on** *He got a detective to snoop on her.* | **+around** *I caught him snooping around outside.* —**snooper** *n* [C]

snooty /'snuːti/ *adj* rude and unfriendly, because you think you are better than other people

snooze /snuːz/ *v* [I] *informal* to sleep lightly for a short time [= **doze**] —**snooze** *n* [C]

snore /snɔː $ snɔːr/ *v* [I] to make a loud noise each time you breathe while you are asleep —**snoring** *n* [U] —**snore** *n* [C]

snorkel[1] /'snɔːkəl $ 'snɔːr-/ *n* [C] a tube that you breathe through while swimming with your face under water

snorkel[2] *v* [I] **snorkelled, snorkelling** *BrE*; **snorkeled, snorkeling** *AmE* to swim using a snorkel —**snorkelling** *n* [U]

snort /snɔːt $ snɔːrt/ *v* [I,T] to make a noise by forcing air out through your nose, especially to express impatience or amusement: *She snorted with laughter.* —**snort** *n* [C]

snot /snɒt $ snɑːt/ *n* [U] *informal* the substance produced in your nose

snotty /'snɒti $ 'snɑːti/ *adj informal* **1** rude and believing you are better than other people **2** having snot on your nose

snout /snaʊt/ *n* [C] the long nose of a pig or other animal

snow[1] /snəʊ $ snoʊ/ *n* [U] soft white pieces of frozen water that fall like rain: *Snow was falling heavily.* | *The roads were blocked by deep snow.* | *The snow was already melting.*

THESAURUS

light/heavy snow
snowflakes – pieces of falling snow
sleet – a mixture of snow and rain
slush – snow on the road that has partly melted and is very wet
blizzard – a storm with a lot of snow and a strong wind
frost – white powder that covers the ground when it is cold
hail – drops of rain that fall as ice, which are called **hailstones**
→ **RAIN, SUN, WEATHER, WIND**

---

snow[2] *v*

1 it snows when it snows, snow falls from the sky: *Look, it's snowing!* | *It snowed throughout the night.* → see box at **WEATHER**

2 be snowed in to be unable to leave a place because so much snow has fallen: *We were snowed in for a week.*

3 be snowed under (with sth) to have too much work, so that you cannot deal with anything else

snowball[1] /'snəʊbɔːl $ 'snoʊbɒːl/ *n* [C] a ball made out of snow that children throw at each other

snowball[2] *v* [I] if a plan, problem, or activity snowballs, it develops or grows very quickly

snowboarding /'snəʊbɔːdɪŋ $ 'snoʊbɔːrd-/ *n* [U] the sport of coming down snowy mountains standing on a board —**snowboarder** *n* [C]

snowbound /'snəʊbaʊnd $ 'snoʊ-/ *adj* unable to leave a place because there is too much snow

snowdrift /'snəʊˌdrɪft $ 'snoʊ-/ *n* [C] a deep pile of snow formed by the wind

snowdrop /'snəʊdrɒp $ 'snoʊdrɑːp/ *n* [C] a plant with a small white flower that appears in early spring

snowfall /'snəʊfɔːl $ 'snoʊfɒːl/ *n* [C,U] when snow falls, or the amount that falls

snowflake /'snəʊfleɪk $ 'snoʊ-/ *n* [C] a piece of falling snow → see box at **SNOW**

snowman /'snəʊmæn $ 'snoʊ-/ *n* [C] plural **snowmen** /-men/ a figure of a person made of snow

snowplough *BrE*; **snowplow** *AmE* /'snəʊplaʊ $ 'snoʊ-/ *n* [C] a vehicle for pushing snow off roads

snowstorm /'snəʊstɔːm $ 'snoʊstɔːrm/ *n* [C] a storm with a lot of snow

snowy /'snəʊi $ 'snoʊi/ *adj* if it is snowy, the ground is covered with snow or snow is falling

Snr *BrE* the written abbreviation of **Senior**, used after someone's name: *James Taylor, Snr*

snub /snʌb/ *v* [T] **snubbed, snubbing** to be rude to someone, especially by ignoring them —**snub** *n* [C]

snuck /snʌk/ *v* a past tense and past participle of SNEAK

snuff[1] /snʌf/ *v* **snuff it** *BrE informal* to die
snuff sth ⇔ **out** *phr v* **1** to end something in a sudden way: *the violence which snuffed out his life* **2** to stop a CANDLE burning

snuff[2] *n* [U] **1** tobacco powder, which some people breathe in through their noses **2 not be up to snuff** *AmE informal* not to be good enough

snuffle /'snʌfəl/ *v* [I] to breathe noisily in and out through your nose

snug /snʌg/ *adj* **1** warm and comfortable: *It's nice and snug in here.* **2** snug clothes fit tightly —**snugly** *adv*

snuggle /'snʌgəl/ *v* [I] if you snuggle into a comfortable position, you get into that position: **+up/down/into etc** *We snuggled up together on the sofa.*

so[1] /səʊ $ soʊ/ *adv*

1 used before an adjective or adverb to emphasize what you are saying: *It was so embarrassing – everyone was looking at us!* | *She works so hard!* | **so much/many** *I've never seen so many people in one place before!* | **so ... (that)** (=used to mention a result) *He was so fat that he couldn't get through the door.*

2 used to refer back to something that has just been mentioned: *'Has she gone?' 'I believe so.'* (=I believe she has gone) | *'Will I need my coat?' 'I don't think so.'* | *Are you going into town? If so, can I come?*

3 so do I/so is he/so would Peter etc used to say that something is also true about someone else: *She's been ill, and so has her husband.* | *If you're going to have a drink then so will I.*

4 so she is/so there are etc *especially BrE spoken* used to agree with something that has just been mentioned: *'Look, she's wearing a hat like yours.' 'So she is.'*

5 *spoken* used to introduce the next part of what you are saying: *So anyway, he finally arrived.*

6 *spoken informal* definitely: *He is so not the right man for her.* | *I am so going to enjoy this.*

7 used with a movement of your hand to show how big, tall etc something or someone is, or how to do something: *It was about so big.* | *Then you fold the paper like so.*

8 be so to be true or correct: *People say that exams are easier now, but it isn't so!*

9 or so used when you cannot be exact about a

number, amount, or period of time: *He left a week or so ago.*

10 and so on/forth used after a list to show that there are other similar things that could be mentioned: *a room full of old furniture, paintings, and so forth*

11 so?/so what? used to say that you do not think that something is important, especially in a way that seems impolite: *Yes, I'm late. So what?*

12 so much for sb/sth *spoken* used to say that an action, idea, statement etc was not useful: *He's late again. So much for good intentions!*

13 only so much/many only a limited quantity: *Only so many people are allowed in at a time.*

14 not so big/good/bad etc not very big, good etc: *The news is not so good.*

15 so long! *spoken* used to say goodbye
→ see box at **SUCH**

so² *linking word*

1 used to say that someone does something because of the reason just stated: *I heard a noise so I got out of bed.*

2 so (that) a) in order to make something happen, or to make something possible: *I put your keys in the drawer so that they wouldn't get lost.* **b)** with the result that: *The groups are small, so everyone knows each other.*

3 so as to do sth *formal* in order to do something: *I drove at a steady 50 mph so as to save fuel.*

soak /səʊk $ soʊk/ *v* [I,T]

1 if you soak something, or if you let it soak, you cover it with liquid and leave it: *Soak the beans overnight.* | *Leave the dishes soaking.*

2 if water soaks somewhere, or if it soaks something, it makes something wet: +**into/through** *Sweat soaked into his collar.* | *The rain had soaked her shoes.*

soak sth ⇔ **up** *phr v* **1** if something soaks up a liquid, it takes the liquid into itself [= absorb]: *The bread will soak up the milk.* **2** to let yourself experience or enjoy something: *Sit outside a cafe and soak up the atmosphere.* | *I just wanted to soak up the sun.*

soaked /səʊkt $ soʊkt/ *adj* very wet: *I'm soaked through* (=completely wet).

soaking /ˈsəʊkɪŋ $ ˈsoʊ-/ also **,soaking 'wet** *adj* completely wet

'so-and-so *n* plural **so-and-so's** **1** [U] used to refer to someone or something without saying who or what they are: *People ask, 'Where's Mrs So-and-So?'.* **2** [C] *spoken* an unpleasant person

soap¹ /səʊp $ soʊp/ *n*

1 [U] a substance that you use to wash yourself with: *a bar of soap* | *Wash your hands with soap and water.* → see picture at **BATHROOM**

2 also **soap opera** [C] a television story about the ordinary lives of a group of people: *I don't watch any of the soaps.*

soap² *v* [T] to rub soap on someone or something

soapbox /ˈsəʊpbɒks $ ˈsoʊpbɑːks/ *n* **be/get on your soapbox** to talk about your opinion in a way that is boring and annoying for other people

'soap ,opera *n* [C] a television **SOAP** → see box at **TELEVISION**

'soap ,powder *n* [C,U] *BrE* a powder that is made from soap and other chemicals, used for washing clothes

soapy /ˈsəʊpi $ ˈsoʊpi/ *adj* soapy water has soap in it

soar /sɔː $ sɔːr/ *v* [I] **1** to increase quickly to a high level: *The temperature soared to 32°.* **2** to fly fast and high: *Above her, an eagle soared.* **3** buildings or cliffs that soar are very high: *The cliffs soar 500 feet above the sea.*

sob /sɒb $ sɑːb/ *v* [I,T] **sobbed, sobbing** to cry noisily while taking short breaths: *She began to sob uncontrollably.* → see box at **CRY** —**sob** *n* [C]

sober¹ /ˈsəʊbə $ ˈsoʊbər/ *adj* **1** not drunk **2** serious and calm: *a sober, hard-working man* **3** making you feel very serious: *a sober reminder of our duties* **4** plain and not brightly coloured: *a sober grey suit* —**soberly** *adv*

sober² *v*

sober up *phr v* to become less drunk, or to make someone become less drunk: **sober sb** ⇔ **up** *A cup of coffee soon sobered him up.*

sobering /ˈsəʊbərɪŋ $ ˈsoʊ-/ *adj* making you feel very serious: **a sobering experience/thought**

'sob ,story *n* [C] *informal* a story that someone tells you to get sympathy

'so-called *adj* [only before noun] **1** used when you think the word used to describe something is wrong: *The so-called experts were no help.* **2** used to show that you are using a word that is new or that has a special meaning: *He was a victim of so-called 'Mad Cow Disease'.*

soccer /ˈsɒkə $ ˈsɑːkər/ *n* [U] a game in which two teams try to kick a ball into a net at each end of a field [= football *BrE*]: *the soccer team* | **soccer stars/players** | **soccer fans**

sociable /ˈsəʊʃəbəl $ ˈsoʊ-/ *adj* someone who is sociable is friendly and enjoys being with other people

social /ˈsəʊʃəl $ ˈsoʊ-/ *adj*

1 relating to human society and the way it is organized: *social issues such as unemployment and homelessness* | *people from different social backgrounds*

2 social activities are ones in which you talk to other people and do things with them for enjoyment: *The social life at college is brilliant.* | *a range of social events for employees*

3 having the ability or opportunity to behave and speak properly with other people: *He has absolutely no social skills.* | *There were few opportunities for social interaction.*

4 social animals live together in groups [≠ solitary]

—**socially** *adv*: *behaviour that is socially acceptable*

socialism /ˈsəʊʃəl-ɪzəm $ ˈsoʊ-/ *n* [U] a political system that tries to give equal opportunities to all people, and in which many industries belong to the government [➡ capitalism, communism] —**socialist** *adj, n* [C]

socialite /ˈsəʊʃəl-aɪt $ ˈsoʊ-/ *n* [C] a rich person who enjoys going to fashionable parties

socialize also **-ise** *BrE* /ˈsəʊʃəl-aɪz $ ˈsoʊ-/ *v* [I] to spend time with other people for enjoyment: *I don't socialize with him.*

,social 'science *n* [C,U] subjects such as history, politics, and **ECONOMICS**, or one of these subjects

,social se'curity n [U] a system run by the government to provide money for people when they are old, ill, or cannot work [= welfare AmE]

'social ,studies n [plural] → SOCIAL SCIENCE

'social ,worker n [C] someone whose job is to help people who are having difficulties with money or their family —social work n [U]

society /sə'saɪəti/ n plural societies

1 [C,U] all the people who live in the same country and share the same laws and customs: *They are valued members of society.* | *important changes in the structure of society* | *a modern industrial society* → see box at PEOPLE

2 [C] an organization or club with members who have similar interests: *I joined the school film society.* → see box at ORGANIZATION

3 [U] the rich, fashionable people within a country: *a society wedding*
→ BUILDING SOCIETY

socioeconomic /,səʊsiəʊekə'nɒmɪk, ,səʊʃiəʊ-, -i:kə- $,soʊsioʊekə'nɑː-, ,soʊʃioʊ-, -i:kə-/ adj relating to social and economic conditions

sociology /,səʊsi'ɒlədʒi, ,səʊʃi- $,soʊsi'ɑːl-/ n [U] the study of society and the way people behave towards each other —sociologist n [C]

sock¹ /sɒk $ sɑːk/ n [C]

1 a piece of clothing that you wear on your foot: *Put your socks and shoes on.* | *a pair of socks* → see picture at CLOTHES

2 knock/blow sb's socks off informal to surprise and excite someone a lot

3 pull your socks up especially BrE to make an effort to improve your behaviour or your work

sock² v [T] informal to hit someone hard [= thump]: *Someone socked him in the mouth.*

socket /'sɒkᵻt $ 'sɑː-/ n [C] **1** a place in a wall where you connect electrical equipment to the supply of electricity → see picture at PLUG¹ **2** the place on a piece of electrical equipment where you can connect another piece of equipment **3** a place where one thing fits into another

soda /'səʊdə $ 'soʊ-/ n [C,U] **1** also 'soda water water that contains bubbles and is added to other drinks **2** also 'soda pop AmE a sweet drink containing bubbles [= pop BrE]

sodden /'sɒdn $ 'sɑːdn/ adj very wet: *His clothes were sodden.*

sodium /'səʊdiəm $ 'soʊ-/ n [U] a silver-white metal that produces salt when mixed with CHLORINE

sofa /'səʊfə $ 'soʊ-/ n [C] a comfortable seat with arms and a back, wide enough for two or three people [= couch; = settee BrE]: *She sat down on the sofa.*

soft /sɒft $ sɒːft/ adj

1 not hard, firm, or stiff, but easy to press [≠ hard]: *a soft pillow*

2 gentle: *She gave him a soft kiss.*

3 smooth and pleasant to touch [≠ rough]: *soft skin* | *a cat with lovely soft fur*

4 soft sounds are quiet [≠ loud, harsh]: *Her voice was softer now.* → see box at QUIET

5 soft colours or lights are not too bright [≠ bright]: *Soft lighting is much more romantic.*

6 soft drugs are illegal drugs that are considered to be less harmful than some other drugs

7 informal a soft job or punishment does not involve hard work or difficulties: *Some people see this course as a soft option.*

8 informal someone who is soft does not treat people severely enough when they have done something wrong [≠ strict, tough]: +on *The government does not want to seem soft on crime.*

9 BrE informal stupid or silly: *Don't be so soft!*

10 soft water makes a lot of bubbles when you use soap

11 have a soft spot for sb informal to like someone: *She's always had a soft spot for Chris.*

12 a soft touch informal someone whom you can easily persuade, especially someone from whom you can easily get money
—softness n [U]

softball /'sɒftbɔːl $ 'sɒːftbɒːl/ n [C,U] a game like baseball, played with a larger and softer ball, or the ball used for this game

'soft drink n [C] a cold drink that does not contain alcohol

soften /'sɒfən $ 'sɒː-/ v [I,T] **1** to become softer, or to make something softer [≠ harden]: *Cook the onion until it has softened.* **2** to become less severe and more gentle, or to make something do this [≠ harden]: *The government has softened its stance on this.* | sb's face/voice softens *His voice softened as he spoke to her.* **3** soften the blow to make something seem less unpleasant

soften sb ⇔ up phr v to be nice to someone so that they will do something for you

softhearted /,sɒft'hɑːtᵻd◂ $,sɒːft'hɑːr-/ adj kind and sympathetic

softie, softy /'sɒfti $ 'sɒːf-/ n [C] informal someone who is very kind, or who is easily persuaded: *He's just a big softie really.*

softly /'sɒftli $ 'sɒːftli/ adv quietly or gently: *She spoke softly, so that the baby did not wake.*

,soft-'spoken adj especially AmE also ,softly 'spoken BrE having a quiet pleasant voice

software /'sɒftweə $ 'sɒːftwer/ n [U] computer programs [➡ hardware]: *a piece of software* | software companies/development/packages etc

softy /'sɒfti $ 'sɒːf-/ n plural softies another spelling of SOFTIE

soggy /'sɒgi $ 'sɑːgi/ adj wet, soft, and unpleasant: *The pie was all soggy.*

soil¹ /sɔɪl/ n [C,U]

1 the earth in which plants grow [= earth]: *The soil here is very poor.* | *rich, fertile soil* | *plants that grow in sandy soil* → see box at GROUND → see picture at PLANT

2 on American/French/foreign etc soil in America, France, etc: *She stood on Irish soil for the first time.*

soil² v [T] formal to make something dirty —soiled adj: *soiled diapers*

solace /'sɒlᵻs $ 'sɑː-/ n [U] formal comfort or happiness after you have been very sad or upset: *After the death of her son, Val found solace in the church.* | *Mary was a great solace to me after Arthur died.*

S

solar panels

solar /'səʊlə $ 'soʊlər/ *adj* **1** relating to the sun [➡ lunar]: *a solar eclipse* **2** relating to energy obtained from sunlight: **solar energy/power** | **solar panels** (=equipment that gets energy from sunlight)

'solar ,system *n* **the solar system** the sun and all the PLANETS that move around it

sold /səʊld $ soʊld/ *v* the past tense and past participle of SELL

solder /'sɒldə, 'səʊl- $ 'sɑːdər/ *v* [T] to join metal surfaces together using melted metal

soldier¹ /'səʊldʒə $ 'soʊldʒər/ *n* [C] a member of the army, especially someone who is not an officer [➡ troop] → see box at ARMY → see picture at ARMED FORCES

soldier² *v*
soldier on *phr v* to continue doing something in spite of difficulties: *He wasn't enjoying the course, but he soldiered on.*

,sold 'out *adj* if a concert, film etc is sold out, all the tickets have been sold

sole¹ /səʊl $ soʊl/ *adj* [not before noun] **1** only: *He was the sole survivor of the crash.* | *The story was published for the sole purpose of selling newspapers.* **2** not shared with anyone else: *The women were forced to take sole responsibility for their children.*

sole² *n* **1** [C] the bottom surface of your foot or shoe → see picture at SHOE¹ **2** [C,U] a flat fish that you can eat

solely /'səʊl-li $ 'soʊl-/ *adv* only: *Grants are awarded solely on the basis of need.*

solemn /'sɒləm $ 'sɑː-/ *adj* **1** serious and slightly sad: *His face grew solemn.* | *a solemn ceremony* | *solemn music* **2** [only before noun] a solemn promise is a promise that you will definitely keep —**solemnly** *adv*

solicit /sə'lɪsɪt/ *v formal* **1** [I,T] to ask someone for money, help, or information **2** [I] to offer to have sex with someone for money: *She was arrested for soliciting.*

solicitor /sə'lɪsɪtə $ -ər/ *n* [C] a lawyer in Britain who gives legal advice and works in the lower law courts [➡ barrister, lawyer]

solicitous /sə'lɪsɪtəs/ *adj formal* careful to make someone happy or comfortable

solid¹ /'sɒlɪd $ 'sɑː-/ *adj*
1 hard or firm, with a fixed shape, and not hollow: *solid rock* | *The milk was frozen solid.*
2 strong and well-made: *a good, solid chair*
3 solid gold/silver/oak etc completely made of gold etc [➡ pure]: *a solid gold necklace*
4 continuous, without any spaces or pauses: *a solid white line* | *She didn't talk to me for three solid weeks.*
5 solid information is definitely correct: *We need solid evidence.*
6 someone who is solid is honest and can be trusted to do the right thing: *a firm with a solid reputation*
7 a solid achievement or performance is very good: *It was a solid performance.*
8 on solid ground not likely to be criticized, damaged, or upset: *Legally the company is on solid ground.*
—**solidly** *adv*

solid² *n* [C] **1** an object or substance that has a firm shape: *Water is a liquid and wood is a solid.* **2** solids [plural] food that is not liquid: *He's still too ill to eat solids.* **3** *technical* a shape that has length, width, and height

solidarity /ˌsɒlɪ'dærɪti $ ˌsɑː-/ *n* [U] support and agreement among people who share the same aim or opinions: *We are striking to show solidarity with the nurses.*

solidify /sə'lɪdɪfaɪ/ *v* [I,T] solidified, solidifying, solidifies to become solid, or to make a substance become solid

soliloquy /sə'lɪləkwi/ *n* [C] plural soliloquies a long speech made by an actor who is alone on the stage

solitaire /ˌsɒlɪ'teə $ ˌsɑːlɪ'ter/ *n* [U] **1** a single jewel, or a piece of jewellery with a single jewel in it **2** *AmE* a card game for one player [= patience *BrE*] **3** a game for one player, in which you move small pieces around a board

solitary /'sɒlɪtəri $ 'sɑːlɪteri/ *adj* **1** [only before noun] a solitary person or thing is the only one: *A solitary tree grew on the hilltop.* **2** a solitary activity is something that you do alone: *a long solitary walk* **3** solitary people and animals spend a lot of time alone

,solitary con'finement *n* [U] a punishment in which a prisoner is kept alone

solitude /'sɒlɪtjuːd $ 'sɑːlɪtuːd/ *n* [U] when you are alone, especially if you enjoy it: *She enjoyed the silence and solitude.*

solo¹ /'səʊləʊ $ 'soʊloʊ/ *adj* **1** performed by one musician, rather than by a group: *I don't really like his solo album.* **2** done alone, without anyone else helping you: *his first solo flight* —**solo** *adv*

solo² *n* [C] plural solos a piece of music for one performer

soloist /'səʊləʊɪst $ 'soʊloʊ-/ *n* [C] a musician who performs a solo

solstice /'sɒlstɪs $ 'sɑːl-/ *n* [C] the longest or the shortest day of the year: **the summer/ winter solstice**

soluble /'sɒljʊbəl $ 'sɑː-/ *adj* a soluble substance can DISSOLVE in liquid

solution /sə'luːʃən/ *n* [C]
1 a way of solving a problem or dealing with a difficult situation [= answer; ➡ solve]: +to *the perfect solution to all our problems* | *It was the ideal solution.* | *The only solution was to move into a quieter apartment.*
2 the correct answer to a question [➡ solve]: *The solution to the puzzle is on page 14.*
3 a liquid in which a solid or a gas has been DISSOLVED: *a weak sugar solution*

S

solve /sɒlv $ saːlv/ v [T]
1 to find a way of dealing with a problem [➡ solution]: *Charlie thinks money will solve all his problems.*
2 to find the correct answer to a problem or the explanation for something that is difficult to understand [➡ solution]: **solve a mystery/ crime/case** *Police are under great pressure to solve the case quickly.* | **solve an equation/ puzzle/riddle**

solvent¹ /'sɒlvənt $ 'saːl-/ adj someone who is solvent has enough money to pay their debts [≠ insolvent] —**solvency** n [U]

solvent² n [C,U] a chemical that is used to DISSOLVE another substance

'solvent a.buse n [U] when someone deliberately breathes in dangerous gases from glue or other substances for pleasure

sombre BrE; **somber** AmE /'sɒmbə $ 'saːmbər/ adj **1** sad and serious: *a sombre mood* **2** dark or without any bright colours: *a somber room*

some¹ /səm; *strong* sʌm/ determiner, pron
1 an amount of something or a number of things, when you are not saying how much or how many: *Do you want some coffee?* | *I've made a cake; would you like some?* | *There were some children playing in the street.*
2 a number of people or things, but not most or all of them: *Most of the children enjoyed the film, but some didn't.* | *Some days, I just can't get out of bed.* | **+of** *Some of the roads were closed because of snow.*
3 **some time/days/weeks etc** quite a long time: *It was some time before the police finally arrived.*
4 used to talk about a person or thing without being specific: *I read about it in some magazine.* | *For some reason or other* (=it is not certain why) *he wasn't at work that day..*

GRAMMAR

Use **some** in questions when you think the answer will be 'yes' *Would you like some coffee?*
Use **any** when you do not know what the answer will be *Were there any letters for me?*

some² adv **1** **some 10 people/some 50%/ some $600** about 10 people, about 50% etc: *Some 700 homes were damaged by the storm.*
2 **some more** an additional number or amount of something: *Would you like some more cake?*
3 AmE spoken a little: *'Are you feeling better today?' 'Some, I guess.'*

somebody /'sʌmbɒdi, -bədi $ -baːdi, -bədi/ used to mention a person without saying who the person is [= someone; ➡ anybody]: *I want somebody who can help me.* | *She told me to ask somebody else.*

someday /'sʌmdeɪ/ adv at an unknown time in the future: *Maybe someday I'll be rich!*

somehow /'sʌmhaʊ/ adv
1 in some way, although you do not know how: *Somehow, he managed to escape.* | *We'll get there somehow.* | *Maybe we could mend it somehow or other* (=in some way).
2 for some reason, but you are not sure why: *Somehow it seemed the right thing to do.* | *I don't trust him somehow.*

someone /'sʌmwʌn/ pron used to mention a person without saying who the person is [= somebody; ➡ anyone]: *I want someone who can help me.* | *She told me to ask someone else.*

GRAMMAR

someone, anyone
In questions and negative sentences, we usually use **anyone** and not **someone**: *Have you told anyone about this?* | *I didn't see anyone there.*

someplace /'sʌmpleɪs/ adv AmE SOMEWHERE: *Let's go someplace else.*

somersault /'sʌməsɔːlt $ -ərsɒːlt/ n [C] a movement in which you roll and your feet go over your head before you stand up again —**somersault** v [I]

something /'sʌmθɪŋ/ pron
1 used to mention a thing without saying what it is [➡ anything]: *She said something that I found very interesting.* | *Would you like something to drink?* | *There's something else I wanted to talk to you about.* | *I was afraid something like this would happen.* | *He said something about a party.* | *There was something wrong.* | *Can't you do something about that noise?*
2 **have/be something to do with** to be connected with a person, thing, or activity in a way that you are not sure about: *High-fat diets may have something to do with the disease.*
3 **...or something** informal used when you cannot remember or cannot be sure: *Maybe I cooked it too long or something.*
4 **there's something in...** used to admit that an idea is worth considering: *There's something in what you say.*
5 **that's something** spoken used to say that there is one thing that you should be glad about, even if everything else is wrong: *At least we've got some money left – that's something.*
6 **be (really) something** used to say that a thing, action, person etc is impressive or unusual: *It's really something to see all those jets taking off together.*
7 **something like** used when giving a number or amount that is not exact: *It will take something like four hours.*

GRAMMAR

something, anything
In questions and negative sentences, we usually use **anything** and not **something**, but if you are offering someone some food, a drink etc, it sounds more polite to use **something**: *Would you like something to eat?*

sometime¹ /'sʌmtaɪm/ adv at an unknown time in the past or future: *I'll call you sometime next week.* | **+in/during/after etc** *Work will start sometime in July.*

sometime² adj [only before noun] **1** formal former: *a former governor and sometime presidential candidate* **2** AmE used to say that someone does something part of the time, but not always: *a gifted writer who has been my friend and sometime co-author for many years*

S

sometimes /ˈsʌmtaɪmz/ adv on some occasions, but not always: *Sometimes I don't get home until 9:00 at night.* | *'Do you miss your old school?' 'Sometimes.'*

> **THESAURUS**
>
> **occasionally** – sometimes but not often: *We see each other occasionally for a meal.*
> **(every) now and then/every so often** – sometimes but not regularly: *He phones me every now and then.*
> **from time to time** – sometimes but not often or regularly: *A situation like this arises from time to time.*
> → OFTEN, NEVER, RARELY

somewhat /ˈsʌmwɒt $ -wɑːt/ adv slightly, but not very much: *I was somewhat annoyed.* | *Things have changed somewhat.*

somewhere /ˈsʌmweə $ -wer/ also **someplace** AmE adv
1 in or to a place, although you do not say exactly where [➡ **anywhere**]: *Go and play somewhere else – I'm trying to work.* | *The hotel's around here somewhere.* | *Let's find somewhere to eat.*
2 somewhere around/between etc sth used when stating an amount which is not exact [= approximately]: *It cost somewhere around $500.*
3 be getting somewhere to be making progress: *At last we're getting somewhere!*
4 somewhere along the line/way at some time: *Somewhere along the line they lost control.*

> **GRAMMAR**
>
> **somewhere, anywhere**
> In questions and negative sentences, we usually use **anywhere** and not **somewhere**: *I haven't seen it anywhere.*

son /sʌn/ n [C]
1 someone's male child [➡ **daughter**]: **his/my etc son** *Her son was born in 1990.* | **the son of** *He was the son of a Welsh farmer.* | *She had two daughters and one son.*
2 used by an older person when they are speaking to a boy in a friendly way: *What's your name, son?*

sonata /səˈnɑːtə/ n [C] a piece of music written for a piano or for another instrument with a piano

song /sɒŋ $ sɒːŋ/ n
1 [C] a short piece of music with words: *She sang a song.* | **pop/folk/love etc song** | *He suddenly burst into song* (=started singing).
2 [U] songs in general: *a celebration of music, song and dance*
3 [C,U] the musical sounds made by birds: *the song of the blackbird*
4 make a song and dance (about sth) if you make a song and dance about something, you say that it is very serious when it is not

songwriter /ˈsɒŋˌraɪtə $ ˈsɒːŋˌraɪtər/ n [C] a person who writes songs

sonic /ˈsɒnɪk $ ˈsɑː-/ adj technical relating to sound

'son-in-law n [C] plural **sons-in-law** your daughter's husband

sonnet /ˈsɒnɪt $ ˈsɑː-/ n [C] a poem with 14 lines that RHYME with each other in a fixed pattern

sonorous /ˈsɒnərəs, səˈnɔːrəs $ səˈnɔːrəs, ˈsɑːnərəs/ adj a sonorous voice is deep and pleasantly loud

soon /suːn/ adv
1 in a short time from now, or after a short time: *It will be dark soon.* | **Soon afterwards** *he realized his mistake.* | *I'll get it fixed* **as soon as possible**. | *How soon can you get here?*

> **THESAURUS**
>
> **in a minute** spoken: *I'll be ready in a minute.*
> **any minute now** spoken – used when something exciting or important will happen soon: *The train should be here any minute now.*
> **before long**: *I think they'll open another shop before long.*
> **shortly** formal: *We will shortly be landing at Heathrow.*
> **in the near future** – in the next few weeks or months: *They promised to contact us again in the near future.*

2 as soon as immediately after something has happened: *I came as soon as I heard the news.*
3 the sooner (...) the better used to say that something should happen as quickly as possible: *The sooner we get this job finished the better.*
4 sooner or later used to say that something will definitely happen but you are not sure when: *He's bound to find out sooner or later.*
5 no sooner had ... than used to say that something happened immediately after something else: *No sooner had I stepped in the shower than the phone rang.*
6 too soon too early: *It's too soon to say what will happen.*
7 I would sooner/I would just as soon... used when you are saying what you would prefer to happen: *I'd just as soon stay in and watch TV.*

soot /sʊt/ n [U] black powder that is produced when something burns —**sooty** adj

soothe /suːð/ v [T] **1** to make someone feel calmer and less worried or upset: *He poured himself a drink to soothe his nerves.* **2** to make something less painful: *bath oil to soothe aching muscles* —**soothing** adj: *her soothing voice*

sophisticated /səˈfɪstɪkeɪtɪd/ adj **1** having a lot of experience of life, or knowledge about a subject: *a play for a sophisticated audience* | *today's more sophisticated investors* **2** a sophisticated machine or system is designed in a very clever way: **highly sophisticated** *weapons* —**sophistication** /səˌfɪstɪˈkeɪʃən/ n [U]

sophomore /ˈsɒfəmɔː $ ˈsɑːfəmɔːr/ n [C] AmE a student in the second year of HIGH SCHOOL or college

soporific /ˌsɒpəˈrɪfɪk◂ $ ˌsɑː-/ adj formal making you feel ready to sleep

sopping /ˈsɒpɪŋ $ ˈsɑː-/ also **,sopping 'wet** adj very wet

soppy /ˈsɒpi $ ˈsɑːpi/ adj BrE informal expressing sadness or love in a way that seems silly [= sappy AmE]: *a soppy film*

soprano /səˈprɑːnəʊ $ -ˈprænoʊ/ n [C] plural **sopranos** a woman, girl, or young boy singer with a very high voice

sorbet /'sɔːbeɪ $ 'sɔːrbət/ n [C,U] a sweet frozen food made from fruit juice, sugar, and water

sorcerer /'sɔːsərə $ 'sɔːrsərər/ n [C] a person in stories who uses magic [= **wizard**]

sorcery /'sɔːsəri $ 'sɔːr-/ n [U] magic, especially evil magic

sordid /'sɔːdᵻd $ 'sɔːr-/ adj **1** involving dishonest behaviour: *all the **sordid** details of the scandal* **2** a sordid place is dirty and unpleasant: *a sordid hotel room*

sore¹ /sɔː $ sɔːr/ adj

1 a part of your body that is sore is painful: *I've got a **sore throat** (=usually because of an illness).* | +**from** *Her fingers were sore from the cold.*

2 sore point/spot (with sb) something that is likely to make someone upset or angry: *Don't mention marriage – it's a sore point with him.*

3 stand/stick out like a sore thumb to be very noticeable because of being very different from everyone or everything else
—**soreness** n [U]

sore² n [C] a painful place on your body where your skin or a cut is infected

sorely /'sɔːli $ 'sɔːrli/ adv very much: **sorely missed/needed/tempted** *I was sorely tempted to hit him.*

sorority /sə'rɒrᵻti $ sə'rɔːr-/ n [C] plural **sororities** a club for women students at some American colleges and universities [➡ **fraternity**]

sorrow /'sɒrəʊ $ 'saːroʊ, 'sɔː-/ n [C,U] a feeling of great sadness, or an event that makes you feel very sad: *a time of **great sorrow*** | *the joys and sorrows of family life* —**sorrowful** adj

sorry /'sɒri $ 'saːri, 'sɔːri/ adj

1 sorry/I'm sorry spoken **a)** used to tell someone that you feel bad about doing something that has upset them, annoyed them etc: *I'm sorry if I was rude.* | +**about** *Sorry about the mess!* | +**(that)** *I'm sorry I'm late.* | **sorry for (doing) sth** *Sorry for waking you up.* | *Sorry to bother you, but what's the address again?* **b)** used when politely saying something disappointing, or disagreeing with someone: *I'm sorry, but all the flights are booked.* | *'Can I borrow the car?' 'Sorry, I'm using it myself.'* | *I'm sorry, I think you're wrong.* **c)** used when correcting what you have just said: *Turn right – sorry, left.*

2 [not before noun] feeling sad about a situation and wishing it was different: +**for** *She was sorry for what she had done.* | +**(that)** *Casey was sorry he'd been so angry with the kids.* | **sorry to do sth** *I was very sorry to hear about your accident.*

3 be/feel sorry for sb to feel sadness and sympathy for someone who has problems: *He was lonely and I felt sorry for him.* | *Stop feeling sorry for yourself and do something!*

4 [only before noun] bad: *The old house was in a sorry state.*

5 sorry? especially BrE used to ask someone to repeat what they have just said because you did not hear it properly [= **pardon**]

sort¹ /sɔːt $ sɔːrt/ n

1 [C] a type or kind of something: +**of** *What sort of work does he do?* | *There are many **different sorts** of mushrooms.* | **all sorts (of sth)** (=a lot of different types) *I like rock, jazz – all sorts of*

music. | *On expeditions **of this sort** you must be well prepared.*

2 sort of spoken used when what you are saying or describing is not very definite or exact: *'Do you like him then?' 'Sort of.'* | *The walls are sort of greeny-blue.* | *It was sort of a shock when I found out.*

3 of sorts/of a sort disapproving used to say that something is not very good: *He's written an essay – of sorts.*

4 [singular] if a computer does a sort, it arranges a list of things in order

sort² v [T]

1 to put things in a particular order, or arrange them into groups: *Eggs are **sorted according to** size.* | **sort sth into sth** *Our names were sorted into alphabetical order.*

2 BrE spoken to deal with a situation so there are no more problems and everything is organized: *Don't worry, Jim'll **sort** it.* | *I want to **get** everything **sorted** before I go.*

sort sth ⇔ **out** phr v **1** to organize something that is untidy or in the wrong order: *I must **sort** out my desk.* **2** if you sort out a problem, you deal with it: *It's a mistake – I'll sort it out and call you back.*

sort through sth phr v to look at a lot of things in order to find something or arrange things in order: *We sorted through all his papers after he died.*

sortie /'sɔːti $ 'sɔːrti/ n [C] a short trip to find out what a place is like or to make an attack: *The Tornado crashed on a sortie over Iraq.*

SOS /ˌes əʊ 'es $ -oʊ-/ n [singular] a signal used to call for help when a ship, plane, or person is in danger

'so-so adj, adv spoken not very good

soufflé /'suːfleɪ $ suːˈfleɪ/ n [C,U] a light food made from the white part of an egg and baked ➔ see picture on page A5

sought /sɔːt $ sɔːt/ v the past tense and past participle of SEEK

'sought-ˌafter adj wanted by a lot of people, but difficult to get: *Her paintings are **highly sought-after**.*

soul /səʊl $ soʊl/ n **1** [C] the part of a person which many people believe continues to exist after you die [= **spirit**]: *the inner areas of the **mind and soul*** **2** [C] a person: **not a soul** (=no one) *Don't tell a soul!* **3** also **soul music** [U] a type of popular music which often expresses strong emotions, usually performed by black singers and musicians

soulful /'səʊlfəl $ 'soʊl-/ adj expressing strong sad emotions: *a soulful song*

soulless /'səʊl-ləs $ 'soʊl-/ adj a soulless place has no interesting or attractive qualities

'soul-ˌsearching n [U] careful thought about your feelings when you are not sure what is the right thing to do: *After much soul-searching, I decided to resign.*

sound¹ /saʊnd/ n

1 [C,U] something that you can hear: +**of** *She could **hear the sound** of voices.* | *Light travels faster than sound.* | **banging/rattling/tearing etc sound** *What's that clicking sound?* ➔ see box at NOISE

2 [U] the voices, music etc that come from a television, radio, film etc: **good/poor sound**

S

quality (=clear or unclear sound) *A hi-fi like this gives better sound quality.* | **turn the sound down/up** (=make it quieter or louder)
3 by/from the sound of it/things *spoken* judging from what you have been told or have read about something: *It's a computer error, by the sound of it.*
4 not like the sound of sth to be worried about something that you have heard or read: *A teachers' strike? I don't like the sound of that.*

sound² *v*
1 [linking verb] if someone or something sounds strange, interesting etc, they seem like that to you from what you have been told: *Your holiday sounds great.* | **+like** *Lou sounds like a nice guy.* | **it sounds as if/as though/like** *It sounds as if he's doing well at school.*
2 [linking verb] if someone sounds tired, upset etc, or if something sounds loud, strange etc, they seem like that to you when you hear them: *You sound tired. Are you OK?* | *Her breathing sounded steady.* | **sound as if/as though/like** *The noise sounded as if it was coming from next door.*
3 [I,T] if something such as a bell sounds, or if you sound it, it makes a noise as a signal: **+for** *A whistle sounded for half time.*
  sound off *phr v* to complain angrily about something: **+about** *She was sounding off about the poor rail service.*
  sound sb ⇔ **out** *phr v* to talk to someone in order to find out what they think about a plan or idea: *Why don't you sound her out about the job?*

sound³ *adj* **1** sensible and likely to produce good results: *Our helpline offers sound advice to new parents.* **2** complete and thorough: *a sound knowledge of English* **3** in good condition: *The roof leaks, but the floors are sound.*

sound⁴ *adv* **be sound asleep** to be completely asleep

'sound ,barrier *n* **the sound barrier** the point at which an aircraft reaches the speed of sound

'sound bite *n* [C] a short phrase that is easy to remember, especially one said by a politician

'sound ef,fects *n* [plural] the sounds produced artificially for a film, radio programme etc

soundings /'saʊndɪŋz/ *n* **take soundings** to ask what people's opinion of something is, in a private and unofficial way

soundly /'saʊndli/ *adv* **1** completely or severely: *Our team was soundly defeated.* **2 sleep soundly** to sleep well without waking up **3** in a strong way: *Their relationship is soundly based.*

soundproof /'saʊndpruːf/ *adj* a soundproof wall, room etc does not allow sound to pass through it or into it —**soundproof** *v* [T]

'sound ,system *n* [C] a piece of equipment for playing music

soundtrack /'saʊndtræk/ *n* [C] the recorded music from a film

soup /suːp/ *n* [C,U] liquid food that usually has pieces of meat or vegetables in it: *tomato soup* → see picture on page A5

'soup ,kitchen *n* [C] a place where poor people are given free food

sour /saʊə $ saʊr/ *adj*
1 having an acid taste, like the taste of a LEMON

[≠ **sweet**; ➡ **bitter**]: *sour green apples* → see box at TASTE
2 milk or other food that is sour is not fresh and has a bad taste and smell: *The milk has gone sour.* → see box at FOOD
3 looking unfriendly and angry: **sour look/ face/smile etc** *The waiter had a really sour expression.*
4 go/turn sour *informal* if a relationship or situation goes sour, it becomes less enjoyable or is no longer what you want: *As time went on, their marriage turned sour.*
5 sour grapes *disapproving* used to say that someone is only pretending to dislike something because they cannot have it
—**sourly** *adv* —**sour** *v* [I,T]

source¹ /sɔːs $ sɔːrs/ *n* [C] **1** the thing, place, or person that you get something from: **+of** *Tourism is our main source of income.* | **energy/ information/food source** *a new energy source*
2 the cause of a problem, or the place where it starts: **+of** *Engineers have found the source of the trouble.* **3** a person, book, or document that you get information from: *Reliable sources say the company's in trouble.* **4** the place where a stream or river starts

source² *v* [T] *technical* if something is sourced from a particular place, it is obtained from that place

south¹, **South** /saʊθ/ *written abbreviation* **S** *n* [singular,U]
1 the direction towards the bottom of a map: *Which way is south?* | **from/towards the south** *The army was approaching from the south.* | **to the south (of sth)** *Sandy beaches lie to the south.* → see picture at NORTH¹
2 the south the southern part of a country or area: **+of** *the south of France*

south², **South** *written abbreviation* **S** *adj* [only before noun]
1 in the south or facing the south: *a village on the south coast* | *south Texas*
2 a south wind comes from the south

south³ *written abbreviation* **S** *adv*
1 towards the south: *Most of the birds had already flown south.* | **+of** *a town 20 km south of London*
2 down south a) *BrE informal* in or to the southern part of England: *They live down south near Brighton.* **b)** *AmE* also **down South** in or to the southern US states: *His sister lives down south.*

southbound /'saʊθbaʊnd/ *adj* travelling or leading towards the south: *southbound traffic*

southeast¹, **Southeast** /ˌsaʊθ'iːst◂/ *written abbreviation* **SE** *n* [U] **1** the direction that is exactly between south and east → see picture at NORTH¹ **2 the southeast** the southeastern part of a country —**southeast** *adv*: *We continued southeast to Kells.*

southeast², **Southeast** *written abbreviation* **SE** *adj* **1** a southeast wind comes from the southeast **2** in the southeast of a place: *the southeast quarter of the city*

southeasterly /ˌsaʊθ'iːstəli $ -ər-/ *adj* **1** towards or in the southeast: *They set off in a southeasterly direction.* **2** a southeasterly wind comes from the southeast

southeastern /ˌsaʊθˈiːstən $ -ərn/ *adj* written abbreviation *SE* in or from the southeast part of a country or area: *southeastern Europe*

southerly /ˈsʌðəli $ -ər-/ *adj* **1** towards or in the south: *Keep going in **a southerly direction**.* **2** a southerly wind comes from the south

southern, Southern /ˈsʌðən $ -ərn/ written abbreviation *S adj* in or from the south of a country or area: *Southern Italy* | *a southern accent*

southerner, Southerner /ˈsʌðənə $ -ərnər/ *n* [C] someone from the southern part of a country

southernmost /ˈsʌðənməʊst $ -ərnmoʊst/ *adj* furthest south: *the southernmost tip of India*

South 'Pole *n* **the South Pole** the most southern point on the surface of the Earth [➡ **North Pole**] → see picture at **GLOBE**

southwards /ˈsaʊθwədz $ -wərdz/ also **southward** /ˈsaʊθwəd $ -wərd/ *adv* towards the south: *We followed the coast southwards.* —**southward** *adj*: *the southward route to Charlestown*

southwest¹, Southwest /ˌsaʊθˈwest◂/ written abbreviation *SW n* [U] **1** the direction that is exactly between south and west → see picture at **NORTH¹** **2 the southwest** the southwestern part of a country —**southwest** *adv*: *The plane flew southwest toward Egypt.*

southwest², Southwest written abbreviation *SW adj* **1** a southwest wind comes from the southwest **2** in the southwest of a place: *the southwest corner of France*

southwesterly /ˌsaʊθˈwestəli $ -ərli/ *adj* **1** towards or in the southwest: *They set off in a southwesterly direction.* **2** a southwesterly wind comes from the southwest

southwestern /ˌsaʊθˈwestən $ -ərn/ written abbreviation *SW adj* in or from the southwest part of a country or area: *southwestern Colorado*

souvenir /ˌsuːvəˈnɪə, ˈsuːvənɪə $ -nɪr/ *n* [C] an object that you keep to remind yourself of a special occasion or place that you have visited [= **memento**]: **+of** *a souvenir of Paris*

sovereign¹ /ˈsɒvrɪn $ ˈsɑːv-/ *adj* a sovereign country or state is independent and governs itself —**sovereignty** *n* [U]

sovereign² *n* [C] *formal* a king or queen

Soviet /ˈsəʊviət, ˈsɒ- $ ˈsoʊ-, ˈsɑː-/ *adj* relating to the former USSR (Soviet Union)

sow¹ /səʊ $ soʊ/ *v* [I,T] past tense **sowed**, past participle **sown** /səʊn $ soʊn/ or **sowed** to plant seeds in the ground: *Sow the seeds in early spring.*

sow² /saʊ/ *n* [C] a female pig

'soya bean /ˈsɔɪə biːn/ also **soybean** /ˈsɔɪbiːn/ *n* [C] a bean that is often used in making other foods

ˌsoy 'sauce /ˌsɔɪ ˈsɔːs $ ˈsɔɪ sɔːs/ *n* [U] a dark brown sauce used especially in Chinese cooking

spa /spɑː/ *n* [C] a place where people go to improve their health, especially because the water has special minerals in it

space¹ /speɪs/ *n*

1 a) [C] an area that is empty or available to be used: **+for** *There's a space for the table here.* | *Write your name in this space.* | *a plan for 700 more **parking spaces*** | *the city's **open spaces*** **b)** [U] the amount of an area that is empty or available to be used [= **room**]: *Is there any more space in the car?* | *How much space is there on the disk?* | *The cupboard **takes up** too much **space**.* | **storage/cupboard/shelf etc space** *6,900 square feet of office space* → see box at **PLACE**

2 [U] the area beyond the Earth where the stars and PLANETS are: **in/into space** *Who was the first American in space?* | **space travel/research/ exploration etc** *the US space programme*

3 [C usually singular] a period of time: **in the space of an hour/two weeks etc** *All this happened in the space of a few weeks.* | *There's been a lot of rain in **a short space of time**.* **4** [U] time and freedom to do what you want: *She needed space to sort out her life.* → **BREATHING SPACE, OUTER SPACE**

space² also **space out** *v* [T] to arrange objects, events etc so that they have an equal amount of space or time between them: *Space the plants four feet apart.*

spacecraft /ˈspeɪskrɑːft $ -kræft/ also **spaceship** /ˈspeɪsʃɪp/ *n* [C] a vehicle that can travel in space → see box at **SPACE**

'space ˌshuttle *n* [C] a spacecraft that can go into space and return to Earth several times → see box at **SPACE**

spacious /ˈspeɪʃəs/ *adj* a spacious room, house etc is large inside

spade /speɪd/ *n* [C]
1 a tool that you use for digging, with a long handle and a wide flat part at the end [➡ **shovel**] **2 spades** [plural] in card games, the cards with black shapes like pointed leaves on them: *the queen of spades* → see picture at **PLAYING CARD**

spaghetti /spəˈɡeti/ *n* [U] long thin pieces of PASTA that look like strings → see picture on page A5

spam /spæm/ *n* [U] unwanted email messages, especially emails that advertise something → see box at **ADVERTISEMENT**

span¹ /spæn/ *n* [C] **1** a length of time in which something happens or continues: **within/in/ over a span (of sth)** *Can the project be completed within that **time span**?* | *The mayfly has a two-day **life span** (=lives for two days).* | **attention/ concentration span** (=how long you can pay attention to something) **2** the distance from one side of something to the other: *a bird with a large **wing span***

span² *v* [T] **spanned, spanning** **1** to include all of a period of time: *a career which spanned 45 years* **2** to go from one side of something to the other: *a bridge spanning the river*

spank /spæŋk/ *v* [T] to hit a child on the bottom with your open hand

spanner /'spænə $ -ər/ *n* [C] *BrE* a tool used for turning NUTS (=small metal rings that fasten things together) [= **wrench** *AmE*]

spare¹ /speə $ sper/ *adj*

1 spare key/tyre etc an extra key, tyre etc that you have so that it is available if it is needed: *Leave a spare key with a neighbour.* | *Don't forget to take spare clothes.*

2 not being used and therefore available: *We haven't much spare cash for holidays.* | *the spare bedroom*

3 spare time/moment/hour etc time when you are not working: *I play tennis in my spare time.*

spare² *v* [T] **1** to let someone have or use something, because you do not need it: **spare sb sth** *Can you spare me £5?* | *I'm sorry, I can't spare the time* (=have not enough time to do something). **2** to prevent someone from having to do something difficult or unpleasant: **spare sb the trouble/difficulty/pain etc (of doing sth)** *I wanted to spare you the trouble of picking me up.* **3 money/time etc to spare** if you have money, time etc to spare, you have plenty or enough of it: *We need volunteers with a few hours to spare each week.* **4 spare no expense/effort** to spend a lot of money, time etc on something in order to make it a success: *No effort was spared to find them.* **5** not to damage or harm someone or something: *The children's lives were spared.*

spare³ *n* [C] an extra key, tyre etc that you have so that it is available if it is needed

sparingly /'speərɪŋli $ 'sper-/ *adv* if you use something sparingly, you use only a little of it —**sparing** *adj*

spark¹ /spɑːk $ spɑːrk/ *n* [C] **1** a very small piece of burning material, especially from a fire **2** a flash of light caused by electricity **3 spark of interest/intelligence/humour etc** a small amount of a good feeling or quality

spark² also **spark off** *v* [T] to make something start happening: *The speech sparked off riots.*

sparkle /'spɑːkəl $ 'spɑːr-/ *v* [I] to shine with small bright flashes → see box at **SHINE** —**sparkle** *n* [C,U]

sparkling /'spɑːklɪŋ $ 'spɑːr-/ *adj* a sparkling drink has bubbles of gas in it [= **fizzy**]: *sparkling wine*

'spark plug *n* [C] a part in a car engine that makes the petrol start burning

sparrow /'spærəʊ $ -roʊ/ *n* [C] a common small brown or grey bird

sparse /spɑːs $ spɑːrs/ *adj* existing only in small amounts, and often spread over a large area: *sparse vegetation* —**sparsely** *adv*

spartan /'spɑːtn $ -ɑːr-/ *adj* very simple and often uncomfortable: *spartan living conditions*

spasm /'spæzəm/ *n* [C,U] a movement that you cannot control in which your muscles suddenly become tight and painful: *back spasms*

spasmodic /spæz'mɒdɪk $ -'mɑː-/ *adj* happening for short periods of time but not regularly or continuously: *spasmodic efforts to stop smoking* —**spasmodically** /-kli/ *adv*

spat /spæt/ *v* the past tense and past participle of SPIT

spate /speɪt/ *n* **a spate of sth** a large number of similar, usually bad things that happen in a short period of time: *a spate of burglaries*

spatial /'speɪʃəl/ *adj technical* relating to the position, size, or shape of things

spatter /'spætə $ -ər/ *v* [I,T] if a liquid spatters or if it is spattered somewhere, drops of it fall all over a surface: **spatter sb/sth with sth** *The walls were spattered with blood.*

spawn¹ /spɔːn $ spɒːn/ *v* **1** [T] to make a series of things happen or start to exist: *The book 'Dracula' has spawned several movies.* **2** [I,T] if a fish or FROG spawns, it lays a lot of eggs

spawn² *n* [U] the eggs of a fish or FROG

speak /spiːk/ *v* past tense **spoke** /spəʊk $ spoʊk/ past participle **spoken** /'spəʊkən $ 'spoʊ-/

1 [I] to say something or talk to someone about something: *For a minute, nobody spoke.* | **+to** *I'll speak to you tomorrow.* | *'Can I speak to Mr Hunt, please?' 'Yes, speaking* (=used on the telephone).*'* | **+about** *Have you spoken to Mike about this?* | **+with** *especially AmE: Who did you speak with?* | **+of** *formal: He never spoke of his first wife.*

2 [T] to be able to talk in a particular language: **speak English/French/Spanish etc** *Do you speak Italian?* | **French-speaking/Spanish-speaking etc** (=using French, Spanish etc as a language) *French-speaking countries*

3 [I] to make a formal speech to a group of people: *I get nervous if I have to speak in public.* | **+on/about** *The Prime Minister was speaking on education.*

4 [I] to say something that expresses your ideas and opinions: **speaking as a parent/teacher/friend etc** *He was speaking as a policeman with 20 years' experience.* | **generally/technically etc speaking** *Generally speaking, boys are noisier than girls.*

5 be speaking (to sb) also **be on speaking terms (with sb)** to be willing to talk to someone again after an argument: *I'm surprised she's speaking to you after that.* | *Dan and Jo still aren't on speaking terms.*

6 so to speak *spoken* used to say that the expression you have used does not have its most basic meaning: *My parents live on our doorstep* (=very close), *so to speak.*

7 speaking of ... *spoken* used when you want to say more about someone or something that has just been mentioned: *Speaking of birthdays, when's yours?*

8 speak your mind to say exactly what you think

9 no ... to speak of very little of something: *They've no money to speak of.*

speak for sb/sth *phr v* **1** to express the feelings, thoughts etc of a person or group of people: *You'll be missed, and I know I'm speaking for all of us.* **2 speak for yourself** *spoken* used to tell someone that something that may be true for them is not true for you: *'I think we're too old now.' 'Speak for yourself!'* **3 speak for itself** to show something very clearly: *A school's exam results speak for themselves.* **4 be spoken for** to be promised to someone else: *The puppies are already spoken for.*

speak out *phr v* to say publicly what you think about something, especially as a protest: **+against** *People are afraid to speak out against the government.*

speak up *phr v* **1** *spoken* used to ask someone to speak more loudly: *Could you speak up, please?* **2** to say publicly what you think about something: *If we don't speak up, nothing will be done.*

speaker /'spiːkə $ -ər/ *n* [C] **1** someone who makes a speech **2** someone who speaks a language: **French/German etc speaker 3** the part of a radio or other machine where the sound comes out

spear[1] /spɪə $ spɪr/ *n* [C] a long pointed weapon that you can throw

spear[2] *v* [T] to push something pointed such as a spear or fork into something: *He speared a piece of meat with his fork.*

spearhead /'spɪəhed $ 'spɪr-/ *v* [T] to lead an attack or an organized action: *an anti-smoking campaign spearheaded by the government*

spearmint /'spɪəˌmɪnt $ 'spɪr-/ *n* [U] a strong, fresh taste used in sweets and TOOTHPASTE

special[1] /'speʃəl/ *adj* different from other things or people in some way and often better or more important: *a special friend* | *special facilities for disabled students* | **anything/something/nothing special** *I want to do something special for my birthday.* | *Tonight is a very special occasion.* | *This plant needs special attention.* | *He's got his own special chair.* | *We try to make every child feel special.*

special[2] *n* [C] **1** a single special television programme: *a two-hour special on the election campaign* **2** a meal or cheaper price that a restaurant offers for one day only: *today's special*

ˌspecial efˈfects *n* [plural] pictures and sounds that are made for a film or television programme to make it seem as if something exciting or impossible is really happening

specialist /'speʃəlɪst/ *n* [C] someone who knows a lot about a subject: *a cancer specialist* | **+in** *a specialist in international banking* → see box at EXPERT

speciality /ˌspeʃiˈælɪti/ *BrE*; **specialty** /'speʃəlti/ *AmE n* [C] plural **specialities 1** a type of food that is made in a particular restaurant or area and is always very good there: *Fish is our speciality.* | **+of** *a speciality of this region* **2** a subject that you know a lot about: *His speciality is American literature.*

specialize also **-ise** *BrE* /'speʃəlaɪz/ *v* [I] to study mainly one subject or do mainly one activity: **+in** *a lawyer who specializes in divorce* —**specialization** /ˌspeʃəlaɪˈzeɪʃən $ -lə-/ *n* [C,U]

specialized also **-ised** *BrE* /'speʃəlaɪzd/ *adj* used or made for doing one particular thing: *specialized equipment*

specially /'speʃəli/ *adv*

1 for one particular purpose or person: **specially made/designed/built** *a plane that is specially designed for speed* | **+for** *I bought this specially for you.*

2 *spoken* much more than usual, or much more than other people or things [= **especially**]: *I specially liked the ice cream.* | *I got up specially early.*

ˌspecial ˈneeds *n* [plural] needs that someone has because they have mental or physical problems: *children with special needs*

ˌspecial ˈoffer *n* [C] a special low price that is charged for something for a short period of time

specialty /'speʃəlti/ *n* [C] plural **specialties** *AmE* a SPECIALITY

species /'spiːʃiːz/ *n* [C] plural **species** a group of animals or plants of the same kind: **+of** *Three different species of deer live in the forest.*

specific /spəˈsɪfɪk/ *adj* **1** [only before noun] a specific thing or person is one particular thing or person: *toys and games for this specific age group* | *Do you have any specific problems?* **2** detailed and exact: *He gave us specific instructions.* | **+about** *Can you be more specific about what you're looking for?*

specifically /spəˈsɪfɪkli/ *adv* **1** for one particular type of person or thing: *a campaign specifically aimed at young mothers* **2** if you specifically say something, you say it clearly because it is important: *I specifically told you to be here at two o'clock!*

specification /ˌspesɪfɪˈkeɪʃən/ *n* [C usually plural] a detailed instruction about how something should be made or built: *furniture that is made to your own specifications*

specifics /spəˈsɪfɪks/ *n* [plural] exact details: **+of** *We can discuss the specifics of the deal later.*

specify /'spesɪfaɪ/ *v* [T] **specified, specifying, specifies** to give information or instructions in an exact and detailed way: **+that** *The rules specify that competitors must be under 18 years of age.* | **+what/how etc** *He did not specify how this could be achieved.*

specimen /'spesəmən/ *n* [C] **1** a small amount of something that you take so that you can test or examine it: *a blood specimen* | **+of** *a specimen of her clothing* **2** a single example of something

speck /spek/ *n* [C] a very small spot, or a very small piece of something: *The plane was just a tiny speck in the sky.* | **+of** *a speck of dirt*

speckled /'spekəld/ *adj* covered with a lot of small spots: *a speckled egg*

specs /speks/ *n* [plural] *informal* GLASSES

spectacle /'spektəkəl/ *n* [C] **1** something that is unusual or exciting to see: *the magnificent spectacle of a herd of elephants* **2** **spectacles** *old-fashioned* GLASSES

spectacular[1] /spekˈtækjʊlə $ -ər/ *adj* very impressive: *a spectacular view of the Grand Canyon* —**spectacularly** *adv*: *spectacularly beautiful scenery*

spectacular[2] *n* [C] a very big and impressive show or event

spectator /spekˈteɪtə $ 'spekteɪtər/ *n* [C] someone who watches an event, especially a sports event

spectre *BrE*; **specter** *AmE* /'spektə $ -ər/ *n* [C] **1** **the spectre of sth** something frightening that people think might happen: *the spectre of war* **2** *literary* a GHOST

spectrum /'spektrəm/ *n* [C] plural **spectra** /-trə/ **1** all the different ideas, opinions, or situations that are possible: *They have support from right across the political spectrum.* **2** the set of different colours that light can be separated into: *all the colours of the spectrum*

speculate /'spekjʊleɪt/ *v* **1** [I,T] to guess why something happened or what will happen next without knowing all the facts: **+on/about** *He refused to speculate on the cause of the accident.* |

+that *Some economists have speculated that inflation will increase next year.* **2** [I] to buy things because you think you will make a profit when you sell them later —**speculator** *n* [C] —**speculation** /ˌspekjʊ̩ˈleɪʃən/ *n* [U] *There has been a lot of speculation about his future.*

speculative /ˈspekjʊ̩lətɪv $ -leɪ-/ *adj* involving guessing —**speculatively** *adv*

sped /sped/ *v* the past tense and past participle of SPEED

speech /spiːtʃ/ *n*
1 [C] a talk that someone gives to a group of people: **+to** *The President will give a speech to Congress later today.* | *Her father made a long speech.* | **+about/on** *a speech on the environment*
2 [U] when someone speaks, or the way that they speak: *words that are used in speech as well as in writing* | *Her speech was slow and rather slurred.*
3 freedom of speech/free speech the right to say or print whatever you want
→ DIRECT SPEECH, FIGURE OF SPEECH, INDIRECT SPEECH, PART OF SPEECH, REPORTED SPEECH

speechless /ˈspiːtʃləs/ *adj* unable to speak because you are so angry, shocked, or upset: *His answer left me speechless.*

'speech marks *n* [plural] the marks (" ") or (' ') that you use in writing to show when someone starts and stops speaking [= quotation marks]

speed¹ /spiːd/ *n*
1 [C,U] how fast something moves: *What speed were you travelling at?* | **at a speed of 30 mph/100 kph etc** *driving along at a speed of 60 mph* | *trains travelling at high speeds* | *We drove off at top speed* (=as fast as possible). | *Motorists are being encouraged to reduce their speed.*

COLLOCATIONS
at high/low speed
at great speed
at top/full speed
at lightning speed – extremely fast
at breakneck speed – dangerously fast
at the speed of light

2 [U] the rate at which something happens: **+of** *the speed of change within the car industry*
3 [U] the quality of being fast: *She acted with speed and efficiency.* | *The train began to pick up speed* (=gradually move faster).

speed² *v* past tense and past participle **sped** /sped/ **1** [I] to move quickly: *The bus sped along the motorway.* **2 be speeding** to be driving faster than the legal limit —**speeding** *n* [U]
speed up *phr v* past tense and past participle **speeded 1** to move faster [≠ slow down] **2** to happen more quickly, or to make something happen more quickly [≠ slow down]: **speed sth ⇔ up** *an attempt to speed up production at the factory*

speedboat /ˈspiːdbəʊt $ -boʊt/ *n* [C] a small fast boat with a powerful engine

'speed ˌlimit *n* [C] the fastest speed that you are legally allowed to drive at: *a 40 mph speed limit* | *motorists who break the speed limit* (=go faster than the speed limit)

speedometer /spɪˈdɒmɪ̩tə, spiː- $ -ˈdɑːmɪ̩tər/ *n* [C] an instrument in a car that shows how fast it is going → see picture on page A12

speedy /ˈspiːdi/ *adj* happening quickly, without a delay: *He made a speedy recovery.* —**speedily** *adv* → see box at FAST

spell¹ /spel/ *v* past tense and past participle **spelt** /spelt/ *especially BrE;* **spelled** *especially AmE*
1 [I,T] to form a word by writing or saying the letters in the correct order: *How do you spell 'necessary'?* | *I've never been able to spell.* | *They've spelled my name wrong.*
2 [T] if letters spell a word, they form it
3 spell trouble/defeat/danger etc if a situation spells trouble etc, it makes you expect trouble: *weather that could spell disaster for farmers*
spell sth ⇔ out *phr v* to explain something in great detail: *Do I have to spell everything out for you?*

spell² *n* [C] **1** a piece of magic, or the special words that make magic happen: **cast/put a spell on sb** *They say that a witch cast a spell on her.* **2** a short period of time: **brief/short spell** *a short spell in jail* | **+of** *a spell of bad luck*

spellbound /ˈspelbaʊnd/ *adj* extremely interested in something you are listening to or watching: *The children listened spellbound to his story.* —**spellbinding** /-baɪndɪŋ/ *adj*: *a spellbinding story*

spelling /ˈspelɪŋ/ *n*
1 [U] the ability to spell words correctly: *Your spelling has improved.* | *a spelling mistake*
2 [C] the way that a word is spelled: *Who can give me the correct spelling?*

spelt /spelt/ *v especially BrE* a past tense and past participle of SPELL

spend /spend/ *v* [T] past tense and past participle **spent** /spent/
1 to use your money to pay for something: *I've spent all my money.* | **spend sth on sth** *I spent $40 on these shoes.*
2 to use time doing something: *I want to spend more time with my family.* | *We spent two weeks in London.* | **spend sth doing sth** *I spent the morning working.*

spending /ˈspendɪŋ/ *n* [U] the amount of money that an organization or the government spends: **+on** *an increase in government spending on education*

'spending ˌmoney *n* [U] money that you can spend on the things you want rather than things such as food or rent

spendthrift /ˈspend̩θrɪft/ *n* [C] someone who spends a lot of money in a careless way

spent /spent/ *adj* **1** already used and now empty or useless: *spent cartridges* **2** extremely tired

sperm /spɜːm $ spɜːrm/ *n* plural **sperm** or **sperms 1** [C] a cell produced by the male sex organ that can join with an egg to produce new life **2** [U] the liquid from the male sex organ that contains sperm cells

spew /spjuː/ *v* [I,T] **1** also **spew out** if gas or liquid spews out of something, or if something spews gas or liquid, a large amount of liquid or gas flows out of it: *Smoke and gas were spewing out of the volcano.* **2** also **spew up** *informal* to VOMIT

sphere /sfɪə $ sfɪr/ n [C] **1** the shape of a ball **2** an area of work, interest, knowledge etc: *in the sphere of international politics*

spherical /ˈsferɪkəl/ adj shaped like a ball

spice¹ /spaɪs/ n **1** [C,U] a seed or powder from a plant which you add to food to give it a special taste: *herbs and spices* **2** [U] something that makes a situation or activity more interesting or exciting: *The argument added a bit of spice to the evening.* —**spiced** adj: *a dish of spiced plums*

spice² v
spice sth ⇔ **up** phr v to make something more interesting or exciting: *I need a few jokes to spice up my speech.*

spick and span /ˌspɪk ən ˈspæn/ adj very clean and neat

spicy /ˈspaɪsi/ adj spicy food has a strong taste because it contains a lot of spices → see box at **TASTE**

spider /ˈspaɪdə $ -ər/ n [C] a small creature with eight legs that makes nets of sticky threads to catch insects: *a spider's web*

spidery /ˈspaɪdəri/ adj spidery writing is untidy and uses a lot of long thin lines

spiel /ʃpiːl, spiːl/ n [C] *informal* a speech that someone makes to try to persuade people to buy something

spike¹ /spaɪk/ n [C] a long thin piece of metal, wood etc with a sharp point

spike² v [T] to add alcohol or a drug to someone's drink without telling them

spiky /ˈspaɪki/ adj something that is spiky has a lot of thin points sticking out from it: *spiky hair* → see picture at **HAIR**

spill /spɪl/ v past tense and past participle **spilt** /spɪlt/ *especially BrE*; **spilled** *especially AmE*
1 [I,T] if a liquid spills or if you spill it, it flows over the edge of a container by accident [➡ **pour**]: **spill (sth) on/over sth** *I spilled coffee on my shirt.* | **+out** *Some water had spilled out onto the floor.*
2 [I] if people spill out of a place, a lot of them leave at the same time [= **pour**]: **+out/onto/into etc** *The doors opened and people spilled out into the street.*
3 spill the beans *informal* to tell something that other people wanted you to keep secret —**spill** n [C] *a huge oil spill in the Atlantic*
spill over phr v if a problem spills over, it begins to affect other places, people etc: **+into** *There's a danger that the fighting will spill over into other countries.*

spillage /ˈspɪlɪdʒ/ n [C,U] a spill

spin¹ /spɪn/ v past tense and past participle **spun** /spʌn/ present participle **spinning**
1 [I,T] to turn around very quickly, or to make something do this: **spin (sb/sth) round/around** *She spun round to face him.* | *He spun the rope around over his head.*

2 [I,T] to make cotton, wool etc into thread by twisting it together
3 [T] to get water out of wet clothes by making them turn round and round very quickly in a washing machine
4 [T] if an insect spins a WEB or a COCOON, it produces the thread to make it
spin sth ⇔ **out** phr v to make something last as long as possible

spin² n **1** [C,U] when something turns round and round very quickly: *The plane went into a spin.* **2** [C] *informal* a short trip in a car for pleasure [= **drive**]: *Shall we go for a spin?* **3** [singular, U] when someone talks about something in a way that makes it seem better than it really is, especially in politics: *He tried to put a positive spin on the situation.*

spinach /ˈspɪnɪdʒ, -ɪtʃ/ n [U] a vegetable with large dark green leaves

spinal /ˈspaɪnl/ adj relating to your **SPINE**: *a spinal injury*

ˈspinal cord n [C] the long string of nerves that goes from your brain down to the bottom of your back

spindly /ˈspɪndli/ adj long, thin, and not very strong: *spindly legs*

ˈspin ˌdoctor n [C] *informal* someone whose job is to make the public have a good opinion of an organization or politician, especially when there is a problem

spine /spaɪn/ n [C] **1** the row of bones down the centre of your back → see picture on page A3 **2** a stiff sharp point on an animal or plant: *the spines of a hedgehog*

spineless /ˈspaɪnləs/ adj not brave

ˈspin-off n [C] something that develops from something else, especially in an unexpected way

spinster /ˈspɪnstə $ -ər/ n [C] *old-fashioned* an old woman who has never been married

spiral¹ /ˈspaɪərəl $ ˈspaɪr-/ n [C] **1** a curve that goes round and round as it goes up or down **2** a situation in which something gets worse and worse in a way that cannot be controlled: *a spiral of hatred and violence* —**spiral** adj: *a spiral staircase*

spiral² v [I] **spiralled, spiralling** *BrE*; **spiraled, spiraling** *AmE* **1** to move up or down in the shape of a spiral: **+to** *The plane spiralled to the ground.* **2** to become worse and worse in a way that cannot be controlled: *Crime is spiralling out of control.*

spire /spaɪə $ spaɪr/ n [C] a tall pointed tower on a church

spirit¹ /ˈspɪrɪt/ n
1 [C,U] a person's mind, including their thoughts and feelings: **in spirit** *I'm 85, but I still feel young in spirit.*
2 spirits [plural] the way you are feeling, for example whether you are happy or sad [➡ **mood**]: *The children were all in high spirits* (=very happy). | *We were all tired, and our spirits were low.* | *The warm sun lifted our spirits* (=made us feel happy).
3 [C] a dead person or a creature that is thought to exist in a form that is not physical [➡ **ghost, soul**]
4 [U] courage and determination: *You've got to admire her spirit.*

spider
web

5 [singular] the attitude that you have towards something: **+of** *a spirit of cooperation* | *Everyone played the game* **in the right spirit.** | *Some people didn't* **enter into the spirit** *of the occasion* (=have the right attitude towards it).

6 team/community/public spirit the strong feeling that you belong to a particular group and want to help them

7 [C usually plural] a strong alcoholic drink such as BRANDY

8 the spirit of the law/an agreement etc the effect a law or agreement was intended to have, even though this may be different from its written details

spirit² *v*
  spirit sb/sth ⇔ **away** *phr v* to take someone or something away secretly

spirited /'spɪrɪ̥tɪ̥d/ *adj* full of courage and determination: *a spirited performance by the team*

spiritual /'spɪrɪ̥tʃuəl/ *adj* **1** relating to your mind, thoughts, and feelings, rather than your body and the things that you own: *your spiritual needs* **2** relating to religion: *their spiritual leader* —**spiritually** *adv* —**spirituality** /ˌspɪrɪ̥tʃu'æli̥ti/ *n* [U]

spiritualism /'spɪrɪ̥tʃʊlɪzəm/ *n* [C] the belief that dead people can send messages to living people —**spiritualist** *n* [C]

spit¹ /spɪt/ *v* past tense and past participle **spat** /spæt/ also **spit** *AmE* present participle **spitting** **1** [I,T] to push liquid or food out of your mouth: **+at/on** *That boy spat at me!* | **spit sth out** *He tasted the wine and then spat it out.* **2 spit it out** *spoken* used to tell someone to say something they do not want to say: *Come on, spit it out.* **3 it is spitting** used to say it is raining very lightly

spit² *n* **1** [U] the liquid that is produced in your mouth **2** [C] a stick that you put through meat to cook it over a fire

spite¹ /spaɪt/ *n*
1 in spite of sth although something exists or is true [= **despite**]: *We enjoyed ourselves in spite of the rain.* | *She stayed with him* **in spite of the fact that** *he had beaten her up.* **2** [U] the feeling of wanting to annoy or upset someone: **out of spite** *She burned the letters out of spite.* | *an act of* **pure spite**

spite² *v* **do sth to spite sb** to annoy or upset someone deliberately

spiteful /'spaɪtfəl/ *adj* deliberately wanting to annoy or upset someone: *a spiteful remark* —**spitefully** *adv*

splash¹ /splæʃ/ *v* [I,T] if a liquid splashes, or if you splash it, it falls on something or hits it: **splash sth on/over sth** *He splashed water on his face.* | **+against/on/over** *The waves splashed against the side of the boat.* | **+in/through/around** *children splashing through the puddles*
  splash out *phr v* to spend a lot of money on something that you do not really need: **+on** *We've splashed out on a new kitchen.*

splash² *n* [C] **1** the sound that water makes when something hits it: *Jerry jumped into the water with a loud splash.* → see picture on page A7 **2** a small amount of a liquid that falls onto something: *splashes of paint on the floorboards* **3 splash of colour** a small area of bright colour

4 make a splash *informal* to do something that gets a lot of public attention

splatter /'splætə $ -ər/ *v* [I,T] if a liquid splatters, or if you splatter it, drops of it fall onto something: *Blood splattered everywhere.*

splay /spleɪ/ *v* [T] to spread your fingers, arms, or legs wide apart

splendid /'splendɪd/ *adj old-fashioned* very good: *a splendid idea*

splendour *BrE*; **splendor** *AmE* /'splendə $ -ər/ *n* [U] very impressive beauty: *the splendour of the scenery*

splice /splaɪs/ *v* [T] to join the ends of two pieces of film, rope etc so they form one continuous piece

splint /splɪnt/ *n* [C] a flat piece of wood or plastic that stops a broken bone from moving while it mends

splinter¹ /'splɪntə $ -ər/ *n* [C] a small sharp piece of wood, glass, or metal: *I've got a splinter in my finger.* | *splinters of glass*

splinter² *v* [I] to break into a lot of thin sharp pieces

'splinter group *n* [C] a group of people who have separated from a larger political or religious group because they have different ideas

split¹ /splɪt/ *v* past tense and past participle **split**, present participle **splitting**

1 [I,T] if a group of people splits, or if something splits them, they disagree very strongly about something and divide into smaller groups: *an issue that could split the church* | **be split on/over sth** *The government is split over the question of immigration.* | **+from** *their decision to split from the Labour Party*
2 also **split up** [I,T] to divide or separate something into different parts, or to be divided or separated in this way: **split (sth) into sth** *I'm going to split the class into three groups.*
3 [T] to share something between different people: **split sth between sb** *We decided to split the money between us.* | **split sth with sb** *He promised to split the profit with me.*
4 [I,T] if you split something, or if it splits, it tears or breaks into separate pieces: *He split the logs in half.* | *One of the bags had split.*
5 split hairs to argue about small unimportant details
  split up *phr v* if people split up, they end their marriage or relationship: *My parents split up when I was three.*

split² *n* [C] **1** a long cut or hole in something: **+in** *a split in the curtain* **2** a serious disagreement that divides an organization or group [= **rift**]: **+in** *a split in the Republican Party*

ˌsplit-'level *adj* a split-level house or room has floors at different heights in different parts

ˌsplit 'second *n* [singular] an extremely short period of time: *He hesitated for a split second.* —**split-second** *adj*

splitting /'splɪtɪŋ/ *adj* **splitting headache** a very bad HEADACHE

splutter /'splʌtə $ -ər/ *v* [I,T] to speak in a confused way because you are surprised, angry, or guilty

spoil /spɔɪl/ *v* past tense and past participle **spoiled** or **spoilt** /spɔɪlt/

1 [T] to make something less good or enjoyable [= ruin]: *I'm not going to let him spoil my day.* | *She didn't want anything to spoil the look of the garden.*
2 [T] to let a child have or do whatever they want, with the result that they behave badly
3 [T] to treat someone in a way that is kind or too kind: *All these chocolates – you're spoiling me.* | **spoil yourself** *Go on, spoil yourself. Have another cake.*
4 [I] if food spoils, it starts to decay

spoiled /spɔɪld/ also **spoilt** /spɔɪlt/ *BrE adj* someone who is spoiled behaves badly because they have always been allowed to have or do whatever they want

spoils /spɔɪlz/ *n* [plural] *formal* things that have been taken by thieves or by an army that has won a war

spoilsport /'spɔɪlspɔːt $ -spɔːrt/ *n* [C] *informal* someone who spoils other people's fun: *Come and play, don't be such a spoilsport.*

spoke[1] /spəʊk $ spoʊk/ *v* the past tense of SPEAK
spoke[2] *n* [C] one of the thin metal bars which connect the centre of a wheel to the outside edge
→ see picture at BICYCLE

spoken[1] /'spəʊkən $ 'spoʊ-/ *v* the past participle of SPEAK

spoken[2] *adj* **1 spoken English/language** the form of language that you speak rather than write **2 softly-spoken/well-spoken etc** speaking quietly, in an educated way etc

spokesperson /'spəʊks,pɜːsən $ 'spoʊks-,pɜːr-/, **spokesman** /'spəʊksmən $ 'spoʊks-/, **spokeswoman** /'spəʊks,wʊmən $ 'spoʊks-/ *n* [C] someone who has been chosen to speak officially for a group, organization, or government

sponge[1] /spʌndʒ/ *n* [C,U] **1** a soft object full of small holes that takes in and holds water, and is used for washing things **2** *BrE* a sponge cake → **throw in the sponge** at THROW[1]

sponge[2] *v* **1** also **sponge down** [T] to wash something with a wet cloth or sponge **2** [I] *informal disapproving* to get money, food etc from someone without doing anything to help them: **+off** *He's always sponging off his friends.*

'**sponge bag** *n* [C] *BrE* a small bag for carrying soap, a TOOTHBRUSH etc when you are travelling

'**sponge cake** *n* [C,U] a light cake

spongy /'spʌndʒi/ *adj* soft and full of air or liquid like a SPONGE: *the soft, spongy earth*

sponsor[1] /'spɒnsə $ 'spɑːnsər/ *v* [T] **1** to give money to an event or institution, especially in exchange for the right to advertise: *a competition sponsored by British Airways* **2** to agree to give someone money for a CHARITY if they do something difficult, for example walk a long way: *a sponsored walk* —**sponsorship** *n* [U]

sponsor[2] *n* [C] a person or company that pays for a show, sports event etc, especially in exchange for the right to advertise

spontaneous /spɒn'teɪniəs $ spɑːn-/ *adj* something that is spontaneous happens without being planned: *a spontaneous reaction* | *spontaneous applause* —**spontaneously** *adv* —**spontaneity** /,spɒntə'niːɪti, -'neɪ‖ti $,spɑːn-/ *n* [U]

spoof /spuːf/ *n* [C] a funny book, film etc that copies a serious one and makes it seem silly: **+on/of** *a spoof on one of Shakespeare's plays*

spooky /'spuːki/ *adj informal* strange and frightening: *a spooky house*

spool /spuːl/ *n* [C] an object shaped like a small wheel that you wind thread, wire, film etc around

spoon[1] /spuːn/ *n* [C] something that you use for eating and serving food. It has a small bowl-shaped part and a handle.

spoon[2] *v* [T] to move food with a spoon: **spoon sth into/onto/over sth** *Spoon the sauce over the fish.*

'**spoon-feed** *v* [T] past tense and past participle **spoon-fed** *disapproving* to give someone too much help and information: *I don't believe in spoon-feeding students.*

spoonful /'spuːnfʊl/ *n* [C] the amount that a spoon can hold: **+of** *a spoonful of sugar*

sporadic /spə'rædɪk/ *adj* not happening regularly, or happening only in a few places: *sporadic fighting* —**sporadically** /-kli/ *adv*

sport[1] /spɔːt $ spɔːrt/ *n* **a)** [C] a game or physical activity that you do for enjoyment or in order to compete against other people: *Swimming is a very popular sport.* | *sports facilities* | *winter sports* **b)** [U] *BrE* sports in general: *I always hated sport at school.*
→ **BLOOD SPORT**

sport[2] *v* **be sporting sth** to be wearing something, especially something unusual or something that you seem proud of: *He walked in sporting an orange tie.*

sporting /'spɔːtɪŋ $ 'spɔːr-/ *adj* [only before noun] relating to sports: *sporting events*

'**sports car** *n* [C] a low fast car, often with a roof that can be folded back

sportscast /'spɔːtskɑːst $ 'spɔːrtskæst/ *n* [C] *AmE* a television broadcast of a sports game

'**sports ,centre** *BrE*; **sports center** *AmE n* [C] a building where you can do different sports → see box at SPORT

sportsman /'spɔːtsmən $ 'spɔːrts-/ *n* [C] plural **sportsmen** /-mən/ a man who plays sports: *Stuart is a keen sportsman.*

sportsmanlike /'spɔːtsmənlaɪk $ 'spɔːrts-/ *adj* behaving fairly and honestly in a game or competition

S

sportsmanship /'spɔːtsmənʃɪp $ 'spɔːrts-/ n [U] behaviour that is fair and honest in a game or competition

sportswear /'spɔːtsweə $ 'spɔːrtswer/ n [U] clothes that you wear to play sports

sportswoman /'spɔːts,wʊmən $ 'spɔːrts-/ n [C] plural **sportswomen** /-,wɪmɪn/ a woman who plays sports: *a great all-round sportswoman*

sporty /'spɔːti $ 'spɔːrti/ adj **1** a sporty car is designed to look attractive and go fast **2** BrE good at sport

spot[1] /spɒt $ spɑːt/ n [C]

1 a place: *This is the spot where the accident happened.* | **+for** *a great spot for a picnic* | **in a spot** *a plant that will flourish in a sunny spot* → see box at **PLACE**

2 a small round area on a surface, that is a different colour from the rest [= patch]: *a white dog with black spots*

3 a small mark on something: *grease spots* | **+of** *a few spots of blood* → see box at **MARK**

4 BrE a small red mark on someone's skin [= pimple]: *Many teenagers get spots.*

5 on the spot a) immediately: *He had to make a decision on the spot.* **b)** at the place where something is happening: *Our reporter is on the spot.*

6 put sb on the spot to ask someone a difficult or embarrassing question

7 a short time that is available for something on television or radio: *an advertising spot*

8 a spot of sth BrE spoken informal a small amount of something: **a spot of bother/trouble** *I've been having a spot of trouble with the car.*
→ **BEAUTY SPOT, BLIND SPOT, HOT SPOT, TROUBLE SPOT**

spot[2] v [T] **spotted, spotting** to notice someone or something: *A pilot spotted the wreckage.* | *His talent was spotted at an early age.* → see box at **SEE**

spot 'check n [C] a check that is done without warning, in order to make sure everything is being done correctly or legally: **+on** *Police are doing spot checks on cars.*

spotless /'spɒtləs $ 'spɑːt-/ adj completely clean: *The kitchen was spotless.* —**spotlessly** adv: *Her house is always spotlessly clean.*

spotlight[1] /'spɒtlaɪt $ 'spɑːt-/ n **1** [C] a light with a very bright beam that can be directed at someone or something **2 the spotlight** a lot of attention from newspapers, television etc: **in/under the spotlight** *Education is once again under the spotlight.*

spotlight[2] v [T] past tense and past participle **spotlighted** or **spotlit** to put attention on someone or something: *The program spotlights the problems of the homeless.*

spot-'on adj BrE informal exactly right: *Her prediction was spot-on.* → see box at **RIGHT**

spotted /'spɒtɪd $ 'spɑː-/ adj covered in small round marks, especially in a way that forms a pattern: *a red and white spotted dress* → see picture at **PATTERN**

spotty /'spɒti $ 'spɑːti/ adj **1** BrE having a lot of raised red marks on your skin: *spotty schoolboys* **2** AmE good in some parts but not in other parts [= patchy BrE]

spouse /spaʊs, spaʊz/ n [C] formal your spouse is your husband or wife

spout[1] /spaʊt/ n [C] a part on the side of a container that you pour liquid out through: *The spout of the jug was broken.*

spout[2] v **1** [I,T] if a liquid spouts, or if something spouts a liquid, the liquid comes out of it very quickly with a lot of force: **+from** *Blood was spouting from her leg.* | *a whale spouting water* **2** [I] informal also **spout off** to talk a lot in a boring way: **+about** *He's always spouting off about politics.*

sprain /spreɪn/ v [T] to injure your wrist, knee etc by suddenly twisting it: *I fell and sprained my ankle.* —**sprain** n [C]

sprang /spræŋ/ v the past tense of SPRING

sprawl /sprɔːl $ sprɒːl/ v [I,T] **1** if you sprawl or are sprawled somewhere, you lie or sit with your arms and legs stretched out: **+on/in etc** *Ian was sprawled on the sofa.* **2** if a building or town sprawls, it spreads out over a wide area —**sprawl** n [singular, U] *miles and miles of urban sprawl*

spray[1] /spreɪ/ v

1 [T] to force liquid out of a container in a stream of very small drops: **spray sb/sth with sth** *She sprayed herself with perfume before going to the party.* | **spray sth on/onto/over sth** *Farmers were spraying chemicals onto crops.* → see picture at **SQUIRT**

2 [I] to scatter in small pieces or drops through the air: *The glass shattered and sprayed everywhere.*

spray[2] n [C,U] very small drops of liquid floating in the air: *spray blowing off the sea* | *hair spray*

spread[1] /spred/ v past tense and past participle **spread**

1 [I,T] to move and affect a larger area or more people, or to make something do this: **+through** *Fire spread quickly through the building.* | **+to** *The cancer had spread to her liver.* | *Rats often spread disease.*

2 [I,T] to tell a lot of people about something, or to become known by a lot of people: **spread lies/rumours/gossip** *She's been spreading lies about me.* | *News of his arrest spread quickly.* | *The news **spread like wildfire** (=became known very quickly).*

3 also **spread out** [T] to open something or arrange a group of things so that they cover a flat surface: **spread sth over/across/on sth** *Spread the map out on the floor.* | *Books and papers were spread all over the table.*

4 [T] to put a soft substance onto a surface: **spread sth on/over sth** *Spread the cream over the top of the cake.* | **spread sth with sth** *She spread the bread with butter.* → see picture on page A4

5 also **spread out** [T] if you spread your hands, arms, legs, or fingers, you move them wide apart: *He spread his hands in a gesture of confusion.*

6 also **spread out** [T] to do something over a period of time rather than at one time: **spread sth over sth** *You can spread the payments over a year.*

spread out *phr v* if a group of people spread out, they move apart from each other so that they cover a larger area: *They spread out to search the forest.*

spread² *n* **1** [singular] when something increases and affects a larger area or more people [➡ **increase**]: **+of** *the spread of disease* **2** [C,U] a soft food that you put on bread: *cheese spread* **3** [singular] a range of people or things: **wide/broad/good spread of sth** *books on a wide spread of subjects* **4** [C] a special article or advertisement that covers more than one page in a newspaper or magazine: *a two-page spread* | *a fashion spread*

spreadsheet /'spredʃiːt/ *n* [C] a computer program that can show and calculate financial information

spree /spriː/ *n* [C] a short period of time when you do a lot of something you enjoy: *He went on a shopping spree.* | **a shopping/spending/drinking spree**

sprig /sprɪɡ/ *n* [C] a small stem with leaves or flowers on it: **+of** *a sprig of parsley*

sprightly /'spraɪtli/ *adj* an old person who is sprightly is active and full of energy

spring¹ /sprɪŋ/ *n*
1 [C,U] the season between winter and summer: **in spring/in the spring** *The park is full of daffodils in spring.* | *spring flowers*
2 [C] a place where water comes up naturally from the ground: *hot springs*
3 [C] a twisted piece of metal that will return to its original shape after you have pressed or pulled it: *bed springs*
4 [C] a sudden quick movement or jump

spring² *v* [I] past tense **sprang** /spræŋ/ also **sprung** /sprʌŋ/ *AmE* past participle **sprung 1** to move or jump suddenly and quickly [= leap]: **+out/at/back etc** *He sprang out of bed.* | *She sprang to her feet* (=stood up suddenly). | **spring open/shut** (=open or shut suddenly) **2 spring to (sb's) mind** if something springs to mind, you immediately think of it: *Two questions spring to mind.* **3 spring into life/action** suddenly to become active or start doing something: *He sprang into action when he heard their screams.* **4 tears spring to sb's eyes** *written* if tears spring to someone's eyes, they are almost crying

spring from sth *phr v* to be caused by something: *problems springing from childhood experiences*

spring sth **on** sb *phr v informal* to tell someone something or ask them to do something that they are not expecting: *It's not fair to spring this on her now.*

spring up *phr v* to suddenly appear or start to exist: *Hotels are springing up all over the city.*

springboard /'sprɪŋbɔːd $ -bɔːrd/ *n* [C] **1** something that helps you start doing something or helps something happen: **+for/to** *He hoped the course would be a springboard to success.* **2** a strong board, used to help you jump high, for example when you are jumping into water

spring-'clean *v* [T] to clean a place thoroughly —**spring-cleaning** *n* [U]

spring 'onion *n* [C] *BrE* a small white onion with a long green stem

springtime /'sprɪŋtaɪm/ *n* [U] the time of the year when it is spring

springy /'sprɪŋi/ *adj* something that is springy is soft and comes back to its usual shape after it has been pressed: *springy grass*

sprinkle /'sprɪŋkəl/ *v* [T] **1** to scatter small drops of liquid or small pieces of something onto something else: **sprinkle sth over/on sth** *Sprinkle the cheese over the salad.* | **sprinkle sth with sth** *a cake sprinkled with sugar* → see picture on page A4 **2 it is sprinkling** *AmE* if it is sprinkling, it is raining slightly —**sprinkle** *n* [C]

sprinkler /'sprɪŋklə $ -ər/ *n* [C] a piece of equipment that scatters water over an area

sprinkling /'sprɪŋklɪŋ/ *n* [singular] a small amount of something, especially something scattered over an area: **+of** *a sprinkling of snow on the hills*

sprint /sprɪnt/ *v* [I] to run very fast for a short distance: **+up/across etc** *He sprinted up the stairs.* → see box at **RUN** —**sprinter** *n* [C] —**sprint** *n* [C]

sprout¹ /spraʊt/ *v* **1** [I,T] to start to grow or produce new flowers, leaves etc **2** also **sprout up** [I] to appear suddenly and quickly: *Office blocks seem to be sprouting up everywhere.*

sprout² *n* [C] **1** a new stem or leaf that is starting to grow on a plant **2** also **brussels sprout** a green vegetable like a very small CABBAGE

spruce¹ /spruːs/ *n* [C,U] a tree with leaves shaped like needles

spruce² *v*
spruce up *phr v* to make yourself or something look cleaner and neater: *I want to spruce up before dinner.* | **spruce sb/sth ⇔ up** *Sarah had spruced herself up.*

sprung /sprʌŋ/ *v* the past participle of SPRING

spry /spraɪ/ *adj* an old person who is spry is active and has a lot of energy

spud /spʌd/ *n* [C] *informal* a POTATO

spun /spʌn/ *v* the past tense and past participle of SPIN

spur¹ /spɜː $ spɜːr/ *n* [C] **1** a fact or event that encourages you to do something: **+to** *Ill health is often the spur to lifestyle changes.* **2 on the spur of the moment** suddenly and without any planning: *We decided to go to Paris on the spur of the moment.*

spur² *v* [T] **spurred, spurring 1** also **spur on** to encourage someone and make them want to do something: *The band were spurred on by the success of their last CD.* **2** to make an improvement or change happen faster: *The growth of the city was spurred by cheap housing.*

spurious /'spjʊəriəs $ 'spjʊr-/ *adj formal* based on incorrect facts and reasons: *spurious arguments*

spurn /spɜːn $ spɜːrn/ *v* [T] *literary* to refuse an offer or someone's love: *a spurned lover*

spurt¹ /spɜːt $ spɜːrt/ *v* **1** [I,T] if liquid spurts from something, or if something spurts a liquid, the liquid flows out quickly and with a lot of force: **+from/out of** *Blood spurted from his arm.*

S

2 [I] to suddenly start moving more quickly: **+to/along/past etc** *The Ferrari spurted to the top of the ramp.*

spurt² *n* [C] **1** when a liquid comes out of something quickly and with a lot of force: **+of** *a spurt of blood* | **in spurts** (=a small amount at a time) *Water was coming out in spurts.* **2** a short sudden increase in activity, effort, or speed: **+of** *a spurt of energy* | *a **growth spurt*** (=when a child suddenly grows quickly)

sputter /'spʌtə $ -ər/ *v* **1** [I] to make sounds like a lot of small explosions: *The engine sputtered and stopped.* **2** [I,T] to talk with difficulty because you are so angry or shocked: *'What do you mean?' he sputtered.*

spy¹ /spaɪ/ *n* [C] plural **spies** someone whose job is to find out secret information about a country or organization

spy² *v* **spied, spying, spies 1** [I] secretly to get information for a government or organization **2** [T] *literary* suddenly to see someone or something: *Ellen spied her friend in the crowd.* —**spying** *n* [U] *He was arrested for spying.*
spy on sb *phr v* to secretly watch someone

sq. the written abbreviation of **square**

squabble /'skwɒbəl $ 'skwɑ:-/ *v* [I] to argue about something unimportant: **+about/over** *What are you two squabbling about?* → see box at **ARGUE** —**squabble** *n* [C]

squad /skwɒd $ skwɑ:d/ *n* [C] **1** a team of police officers or soldiers who do a particular type of job: *the police bomb squad* **2** the group of people that a sports team is chosen from

'squad car *n* [C] a car used by police

squadron /'skwɒdrən $ 'skwɑ:-/ *n* [C] a group of military aircraft or ships

squalid /'skwɒlɪ̯d $ 'skwɑ:-/ *adj* **1** dirty and unpleasant: *squalid living conditions* **2** dishonest or immoral: *a squalid affair*

squall /skwɔ:l $ skwɒl/ *n* [C] a sudden strong wind with rain or snow

squalor /'skwɒlə $ 'skwɑ:lər, 'skwɒ:-/ *n* [U] when a place is extremely dirty and unpleasant: **in squalor** *people living in squalor*

squander /'skwɒndə $ 'skwɑ:ndər/ *v* [T] to waste money, time, or opportunities: **squander sth on sth** *They squandered their money on expensive cars.*

square¹ /skweə $ skwer/ *adj*
1 something that is square has four straight sides of equal length and four angles of 90 degrees: *a square room* | **2 metres/5 feet etc square** *The room is four metres square.* → see box at **SHAPE**
2 square metre/mile etc a measurement of an area equal to a square with sides a metre, mile etc long: *two square acres of land*
3 if part of someone's body is square, it is broad and strong: *a square jaw*
4 a square meal a big healthy meal
5 a square deal honest and fair treatment, especially in business: *We want our customers to have a square deal.*
6 (all) square a) if two people are square, they do not owe each other any money: *Here's your $20 so we're square.* **b)** *BrE* having the same

number of points as your opponent in a game: *The teams were all square at 2–2.*

square² *n* [C]
1 a shape with four straight sides that are equal in length and four angles of 90 degrees [➡ **rectangle**] → see box at **SHAPE** → see picture at **SHAPE¹**
2 an open area with buildings around it in the middle of a town: *Trafalgar Square* | *a market square*
3 square one the situation from which you started to do something: **back to/back @ square one** *He had spent all the money and was back to square one.* | **from square one** *The rehearsals went well from square one.*
4 the result of multiplying a number by itself [➡ **square root**]: **+of** *The square of 5 is 25.*

square³ *v* [T] to multiply a number by itself
square up *phr v* to pay money that you owe: *I'll get the drinks, and you can square up later.*
square with sth *phr v* **1 square (sth) with sth** if you square two ideas, facts etc with each other, or if they square with each other, they agree: *evidence that doesn't square with the facts* **2 square sth with sb** *BrE* to persuade someone to allow something: *I don't know if I can come. I'll have to square it with my Dad first.*

squarely /'skweəli $ 'skwer-/ *adv* **1** exactly or completely: *The report puts the blame squarely on senior managers.* **2** also **square** directly: *He looked her squarely in the eye.*

,square 'root *n* [C] the number that produces another number when multiplied by itself: **+of** *The square root of nine is three.*

squash¹ /skwɒʃ $ skwɑ:ʃ, skwɔ:ʃ/ *v*
1 [T] to damage something by pressing it until it is flat [➡ **flatten**]: *My hat got squashed on the bus.* → see box at **PRESS**
2 [I,T] to push yourself or something into a space that is too small [= **squeeze**]: **+into** *Seven of us squashed into the car.*

squash² *n* **1** [U] a game played by two people who hit a small rubber ball against the four walls of an indoor court **2 it's a squash** *spoken* used to say that there is not enough space for everyone to fit in comfortably **3** [C,U] *AmE* a type of big hard fruit, such as a **PUMPKIN**, that you cook and eat as a vegetable **4** [C,U] *BrE* a drink made from fruit juice, sugar, and water: *a glass of orange squash*

squat¹ /skwɒt $ skwɑ:t/ *v* [I] **squatted, squatting 1** also **squat down** to balance on your feet with your knees bent and your bottom close to the ground: *He squatted down next to the child.* → see picture on page A11 **2** to live somewhere without permission and without paying rent —**squatter** *n* [C]

squat² *adj* short and wide: *small squat houses*

squat³ *n* [singular] *BrE* a home that people are living in without permission and without paying rent

squawk /skwɔ:k $ skwɒk/ *v* [I] if a bird squawks, it makes a loud angry sound —**squawk** *n* [C]

squeak /skwi:k/ *v* [I] to make a very high sound: *Is that your chair squeaking?* → see picture on page A7 —**squeak** *n* [C]

squirt

squirt

spray

squeaky /'skwiːki/ *adj* **1** a squeaky sound or voice is very high **2 squeaky clean** *informal* never having done anything morally wrong

squeal /skwiːl/ *v* [I] to make a long loud high sound: *children squealing with excitement* —**squeal** *n* [C] *squeals of delight*

squeamish /'skwiːmɪʃ/ *adj* easily upset by seeing unpleasant things: *I couldn't be a nurse – I'm too squeamish.*

squeeze¹ /skwiːz/ *v*
1 [T] to press something from both sides, usually with your fingers: *She squeezed his hand reassuringly.* ➔ see box at **PRESS** ➔ see picture on page A10
2 [T] to twist or press something in order to get liquid out of it: **squeeze sth out** *Can you squeeze a bit more juice out?* ➔ see picture on page A4
3 [I,T] to try to make yourself or a thing fit into a small space [= squash]: **+in/into/through etc** *Can you squeeze in next to Rick?*

squeeze² *n* **1 a (tight) squeeze** when there is only just enough room for a group of people or things: *It'll be a tight squeeze with 14 of us at the table.* **2** [C] when you press something firmly with your hand: *Laurie gave his hand a little squeeze.*

squelch /skweltʃ/ *v* [I] to make a sucking sound by moving through something soft and wet, such as mud

squid /skwɪd/ *n* [C] plural **squid** or **squids** a sea creature with a soft body and ten long TENTACLES (=arms)

squiggle /'skwɪɡəl/ *n* [C] a short line that curls and twists —**squiggly** *adj*

squint¹ /skwɪnt/ *v* [I] **1** to look at something with your eyes partly closed in order to see better: *He squinted in the bright sunlight.* | **+at** *Stop squinting at the screen – put your glasses on.* **2** to have a condition in which each of your eyes looks in a different direction

squint² *n* [singular] a condition that makes each eye look in a different direction

squire /skwaɪə $ skwaɪr/ *n* [C] a wealthy man who, in the past, owned a lot of land in the countryside

squirm /skwɜːm $ skwɜːrm/ *v* [I] to twist your body from side to side because you are uncomfortable or nervous: *I was squirming with embarrassment.*

squirrel /'skwɪrəl $ 'skwɜːrəl/ *n* [C] a small animal with a big tail that lives in trees and eats nuts

squirt /skwɜːt $ skwɜːrt/ *v* [I,T] if you squirt liquid or if it squirts, it is forced out of a narrow hole in a thin fast stream: **+out/from/into** *Water suddenly squirted out of a hole.* | **squirt sb/sth with sth** *He squirted me with water.* —**squirt** *n* [C]

squish /skwɪʃ/ *v* [I,T] *informal* to SQUASH something

squishy /'skwɪʃi/ *adj* something that is squishy feels soft when you press it

Sr. *AmE* the written abbreviation of **Senior**, used after someone's name: *Douglas Fairbanks, Sr.*

St., St 1 the written abbreviation of **Street**: *Oxford St.* **2** the written abbreviation of **Saint**: *St. John's church*

stab¹ /stæb/ *v* [T] **stabbed, stabbing 1** to push a knife into someone: *He was stabbed to death in a fight.* | **stab sb in the arm/chest etc** *The man had been stabbed several times in the stomach.* **2 stab sb in the back** *informal* to do something bad to someone who likes and trusts you

stab² *n* **1** [C] when someone stabs someone else with a knife: *severe stab wounds* **2 a stab at (doing) sth** *informal* an attempt to do something difficult: *Always have a stab at answering the questions.* **3 a stab of pain/guilt/regret etc** *literary* a sudden feeling of pain etc: *Monique felt a stab of regret.*

stabbing¹ /'stæbɪŋ/ *n* [C] a crime in which someone is stabbed

stabbing² *adj* [only before noun] a stabbing pain is very sudden and strong

stability /stə'bɪləti/ *n* [U] when a situation is steady and does not change [≠ instability]: *a long period of political stability*

stabilize also **-ise** *BrE* /'steɪbɪlaɪz/ *v* [I,T] to stop changing and to become steady, or to make something do this [≠ destabilize]: *The patient's condition has now stabilized.* —**stabilization** /ˌsteɪbɪlaɪ'zeɪʃən $ -lə-/ *n* [U]

stable¹ /'steɪbəl/ *adj* **1** not likely to change suddenly [≠ unstable]: *a stable marriage* | *He's in a stable condition in hospital.* **2** in a firm position and not likely to move [≠ unstable]: *Make sure the ladder is stable.* **3** calm, reasonable, and not likely to be upset easily [≠ unstable]

stable² *n* [C] a building where horses are kept

stack¹ /stæk/ *n* [C] **1** a neat pile of things: **+of** *a stack of magazines* **2 stacks of sth** *BrE informal* a lot of something: *I've got stacks of work to do.*

stack² *v* **1** also **stack up** [I,T] to make a neat pile: *Just stack the dishes in the sink.* | *chairs designed to stack easily* **2** [T] to put piles of things in a place: *Al has a job stacking shelves in the supermarket.*

stadium /'steɪdiəm/ *n* [C] plural **stadiums** or **stadia** /-diə/ a large area for playing sports, surrounded by a building that has rows of seats: *a football stadium* ➔ see box at **SPORT**

staff¹ /stɑːf $ stæf/ *n* [singular,U also + plural verb *BrE*] the group of people who work for an organization: *Lisa's the only female member of staff.* | *The staff were* (=each member was) *very*

S

helpful. | **medical/academic/library etc staff** *a strike by hospital staff* → see box at **WORK**

staff² *v* [T] to provide the workers for an organization: *a hospital staffed by experienced nurses*

staffer /ˈstɑːfə $ ˈstæfər/ *n* [C] *AmE* one of the people who works for an organization: *a Mercury News staffer*

stag /stæg/ *n* [C] an adult male DEER

stage¹ /steɪdʒ/ *n*

1 [C] one part of a process or one time in the development of something [➜ **phase**]: **+of** *the first stage of the project* | *the early stages of the disease* | *They have now **reached** the halfway **stage** of the course.* | *the teams that **get to** the second **stage** of the competition* | *Children **go through** various **stages** of development.* | **at some/this/one stage** *At this stage, I'm not sure what the result will be.*

2 [C,U] the raised floor in a theatre where actors perform a play [➜ **backstage**]: **on stage** *I get very nervous before I go on stage.* → see box at **THEATRE**

3 the stage the profession of acting: *I've always wanted to **go on the stage** (=become an actor).*

stage² *v* [T] to organize an event or performance: *They're staging a rock concert in the park.*

ˈstage ˌfright *n* [U] the nervous feeling some people, especially actors, have before they perform in front of a lot of people

ˈstage ˌmanager *n* [C] a person in charge of what happens on the stage during a performance

stagger /ˈstægə $ -ər/ *v* **1** [I] to walk or move in an unsteady way, almost falling over: **+along/back/down etc** *Tom staggered drunkenly into the kitchen.* **2** [T] to make someone feel very surprised or shocked **3** [T] to arrange the time when things happen so that they do not all happen at the same time: *Student registration will be staggered to avoid delays.*

staggered /ˈstægəd $ -ərd/ *adj* [not before noun] very shocked or surprised: *I was staggered by the size of the bill.* → see box at **SURPRISED**

staggering /ˈstægərɪŋ/ *adj* very surprising or shocking: *She spent a staggering £2000 on a new dress.* → see box at **SURPRISING**

stagnant /ˈstægnənt/ *adj* **1** stagnant water or air does not move and often smells bad **2** not changing or improving: *a stagnant economy*

stagnate /stægˈneɪt $ ˈstægneɪt/ *v* [I] to stop developing or improving: *fears that the economy might stagnate* —**stagnation** /stægˈneɪʃən/ *n* [U]

ˈstag ˌnight also **ˈstag ˌparty** *n* [C] a social occasion when a man goes out with his male friends just before his wedding → see box at **PARTY**

staid /steɪd/ *adj* serious, old-fashioned, and boring: *a staid old bachelor*

stain¹ /steɪn/ *v* **1** [I,T] to accidentally make a mark on something, especially one that is difficult to remove, or to be marked in this way: *The carpet stains easily.* | **be stained with sth** *The tablecloth was stained with wine.* **2** [T] to paint wood with a stain

stain² *n* **1** [C] a mark that is difficult to remove: **+on** *coffee stains on the carpet* **2** [C,U] a kind of paint used to colour wood and protect it

ˌstained ˈglass *n* [U] coloured glass that is used to make pictures and patterns in windows

stained glass
stained glass window

ˌstainless ˈsteel *n* [U] a type of steel that does not RUST

stair /steə $ ster/ *n*

1 stairs a set of steps that you use to go from one level of a building to another: **up/down the stairs** *Kim ran up the stairs.* | *The office is up two **flights of stairs**.*

2 [C] one of the steps in a set of stairs: *Jane sat on the bottom stair.*

→ **DOWNSTAIRS, UPSTAIRS**

staircase /ˈsteəkeɪs $ ˈster-/ also **stairway** /ˈsteəweɪ $ ˈster-/ *n* [C] a set of stairs inside a building

stake¹ /steɪk/ *n* **1 be at stake** if something is at stake, you will lose it if a plan or action is not successful: *We need this contract – hundreds of jobs are at stake.* **2 a stake in sth a)** a part or share in a business, plan etc: *She has a 5% stake in the company.* **b)** if you have a stake in something, you will get advantages if it is successful, and so you feel an important connection to it: *Many young people don't feel they have a stake in the country's future.* **3 stakes** the things you could lose in a game or uncertain situation: *I don't think you should get involved – the **stakes** are too **high** (=you could lose a lot).* **4** [C] a long sharp piece of wood or metal that you push into the ground to mark something or to support a plant **5** [C] money risked on the result of a game, race etc [= **bet**]: *a £10 stake*

stake² *v* [T] **1** to risk something on the result of a situation or competition: **stake sth on sth** *The President is staking his reputation on the peace plan.* **2 stake a claim** to say that you think you have a right to have something

stake sth ⇔ **out** *phr v informal* to watch a place secretly: *The police have been staking out the club for weeks.*

stale /steɪl/ *adj* **1** no longer fresh: *This bread's gone stale.* | *the smell of stale smoke* → see box at **FOOD** **2** no longer interesting: *stale news* **3** someone who is stale has no new ideas because they have been doing something for too long: *I was getting stale in my old job.*

stalemate /ˈsteɪlmeɪt/ *n* [C,U] a situation when neither side in an argument, battle, or game can make progress or win: *The discussions ended in stalemate.*

stalk¹ /stɔːk $ stɒːk/ *n* [C] the main stem of a plant → see picture at **FRUIT**

stalk² *v* **1** [T] to follow a person or animal in order to watch or attack them: *a tiger stalking its prey* **2** [I] to walk in a stiff, proud, or angry way: **+off/out etc** *She rose from her chair and stalked out of the room.*

stalker /ˈstɔːkə $ ˈstɒːkər/ *n* [C] a person who follows and watches someone for a long time in a way that annoys or frightens them —**stalking** *n* [U]

stall[1] /stɔːl $ stɒːl/ *n* [C] **1** a large table on which you put things you want to sell: *a market stall* **2 the stalls** the seats on the lowest floor nearest to the stage in a theatre → see box at **THEATRE** **3** *AmE* a small enclosed area for washing or using the toilet: *a shower stall*

stall[2] *v* [I,T] **1** if an engine stalls, or if you stall it, it suddenly stops working: *The car stalled at the junction.* **2** *informal* to deliberately delay doing something, or to make someone else delay: *Quit stalling and answer my question!*

stallion /ˈstæljən/ *n* [C] an adult male horse

stalwart /ˈstɔːlwət $ ˈstɒːlwərt/ *n* [C] someone who is very loyal in their support for an organization: *Labour Party stalwarts*

stamina /ˈstæmɪnə/ *n* [U] physical or mental strength that lets you continue doing something for a long time: *exercises to improve speed and stamina*

stammer /ˈstæmə $ -ər/ *v* [I,T] to repeat the first sound of a word when you speak: *'N-n-no,' he stammered.* —**stammer** *n* [singular] *She has a bad stammer.*

stamp[1] /stæmp/ *n* [C]

1 also **postage stamp** a small piece of paper that you buy and stick on a letter before you post it: *a first-class stamp* | *Don't forget to put a stamp on the letter.*

2 a) an official mark that has been printed on a document using a tool covered with ink: *a stamp in my passport* **b)** the tool that you press onto paper to make a mark

3 have/bear the stamp of sth to clearly have a particular quality: *a speech that definitely bore the stamp of authority*

→ **FOOD STAMP**

stamp[2] *v*

1 [I,T] to put your foot down very hard on the ground, or to walk in this way: **+in/out/through etc** *She stamped out of the room.* | *She was stamping her feet to keep warm.*

2 [T] to print an official mark on a document by pressing a tool covered with ink onto it: *Did they stamp your passport?*

stamp sth ⇔ **out** *phr v* to end something bad completely: *efforts to stamp out drug abuse*

stampede /stæmˈpiːd/ *n* [C] **1** when a large number of animals suddenly start running together **2** when a lot of people suddenly want to do the same thing or go to the same place —**stampede** *v* [I]

stance /stɑːns $ stæns/ *n* [C] **1** an opinion that someone states publicly: **+on** *Senator, what is your stance on nuclear tests?* **2** *formal* a way of standing

stand[1] /stænd/ *v* past tense and past participle **stood** /stʊd/

1 [I] to be on your feet with your body in an upright position: **+in/by etc** *Anna was standing in front of me.* | *Jo stood still* (=stood without moving) *and listened.* | **stand doing sth** *Hundreds of people stood watching.* | *Don't just stand there* (=stand doing nothing) *– help me!* | **stand back/aside** (=move and stand further away) *A policeman told everyone to stand back.*

2 also **stand up** [I] to rise onto your feet after you have been sitting, bending, or lying down: *She finished her drink and stood to leave.* | *She stood up and put her coat on.*

3 [I,T] to be in a place or position, or to put something in a place or position: **+in/on/by etc** *Their house stood on a corner near the park.* | **stand sth in/on sth** *We stood the lamp in the corner.* | *Few buildings were left standing after the explosion.*

4 can't stand *spoken* to hate someone or something: *Dave can't stand dogs.* | **can't stand (sb) doing sth** *I can't stand being late.* | *I know he can't stand the sight of me* (=really hates me). → see box at **HATE**

5 [T] to be able to accept or deal with something unpleasant or difficult [= **tolerate**]: *She couldn't stand the pain any longer.* | **stand (sb) doing sth** *How can she stand him treating her like that?*

6 [linking verb] to be in a particular state or condition: *The kitchen door stood open.* | *old houses standing empty* | *I'm not happy with the way things stand* (=the situation) *at the moment.* | *Your proposal, as it stands, is not acceptable.*

7 [T] to be good enough or strong enough not to be damaged or destroyed by something: *jeans that can stand the rough wear kids give them* | *Their marriage has certainly stood the test of time* (=stayed strong).

8 stand to do sth to be likely to get something: **stand to gain/lose/make/win** *They stand to make more than £12 million if the deal is successful.*

9 [linking verb] to be at a particular level or amount: **+at** *The unemployment rate stands at 8%.*

10 [linking verb] *formal* to have a particular height: *The Eiffel Tower stands 300 metres high.* | *John stood 6 feet tall.*

11 [I] *BrE* to try to be elected [= **run** *AmE*]: **+for** *He stood for parliament in 1959.* | **+against** *She stood against John Woodford for the party leadership.*

12 [I] if an offer still stands, it is still available for someone to accept

13 where/how you stand (on sth) what your opinion about something is: *Where do you stand on the issue of immigration?*

14 know where you stand (with sb) to know what someone's feelings or intentions towards you are: *You never know where you stand with Debbie.*

15 stand a chance (of doing sth) to be likely to succeed in doing something: *You don't stand a chance of winning.* | **stand a better/a good/ little/no chance (of doing sth)** *Short letters stand a better chance of publication.*

16 stand in the way/stand in sb's way to prevent someone from doing something, or prevent something from happening: *There are a few problems that stand in the way of the agreement.*

17 stand on your own two feet to be independent and not need help from other people: *It's about time you learned to stand on your own two feet.*

18 it stands to reason (that) used to say that something is clearly true: *It stands to reason that children will want to do what their friends do.*

19 stand trial if you stand trial for a crime,

S

people try to prove that you are guilty of the crime in a court of law
→ **stand guard** at GUARD[1]

stand around *phr v* to stand somewhere and not do anything: *Everybody was just standing around waiting.*

stand by *phr v* **1 stand by sth** if you stand by something, you still believe it and say that it is true: *I stand by what I said earlier.* **2 stand by sb** to stay loyal to someone and support them in a difficult situation: *Matt's parents have stood by him throughout his drug treatments.* **3** to be ready to do something [➡ **standby**]: *Fire crews are now standing by.* **4** to allow something bad to happen by doing nothing: *People just stood by and watched him being attacked.*

stand down *phr v* *BrE* to leave an important job or position [= **step down** *AmE*]: *The chairman stood down last month.*

stand for sth *phr v* **1** to be a short form of a word or phrase: *What does ATM stand for?* **2** to support an idea, principle etc: *I don't like her, or what she stands for.* **3 not stand for sth** *BrE* not to allow something to happen or continue: *I won't stand for this behaviour.*

stand in for sb *phr v* to do someone else's job while they are away [➡ **stand-in**]: *Lyn stood in for me while I was ill.*

stand out *phr v* **1** to be clearly better than other things or people: **+as** *Morrison stands out as the most experienced candidate.* **2** to be very easy to see or notice: *She really stood out in her bright green dress.*

stand up *phr v* **1** to be on your feet, or to rise to your feet: *I've been standing up all day.* | *I stood up when the judge came in.* | *Stand up straight and put your shoulders back.* **2** to be proved to be true, useful, or strong when tested: *The accusations will never stand up in court.* **3 stand sb up** to not meet someone when you have promised to meet them: *Tom stood me up last night.*

stand up for sb/sth *phr v* to defend a person or idea when they are being criticized or attacked: *Why didn't you stand up for me?*

stand up to sb *phr v* to refuse to accept unfair treatment from someone: *He became a hero for standing up to the local gangs.*

stand[2] *n* [C] **1** a piece of furniture or equipment for supporting something: *a music stand* **2** a table used for selling or showing things to people [= **stall** *BrE*]: *a hotdog stand* **3** an opinion that you state publicly: *The prime minister took a firm stand on the issue of import controls.* **4** a strong attempt to defend yourself or to oppose something: **make/take a stand (against sth)** *We have to take a stand against racism.* **5 the stands** a building where people sit or stand to watch a game in a sports ground [➡ **grandstand**] **6 the stand** *AmE* the place in a court of law where someone sits when the lawyer asks them questions → ONE-NIGHT STAND, WITNESS STAND

standard[1] /'stændəd $ -ərd/ *n*

1 [C,U] a level that measures how good something is or how well someone does something: **+of** *We must improve standards of food hygiene.* | **high/low standard** *a high standard of service* | *This work does not meet the standard we require.* | *We set very high standards in this school.* | *There's been a great improvement in*

living standards (=the level of comfort and amount of money that people have). | **safety/ quality/environmental etc standards** *national health and safety standards* | **up to/below standard** (=good enough or not good enough) *Her work was not up to standard.*

2 by ... standards compared to the normal or expected level of something else: **by modern/ today's standards** *By today's standards, I earned very little.* | *Prices are low by Western standards.*

3 standards [plural] moral principles about what is acceptable: *He has very high moral standards.*
→ DOUBLE STANDARD

standard[2] *adj* normal or usual [➡ **non-standard**]: *The shoes are available in all standard sizes.* | **standard practice/procedure** *Security checks are now standard procedure.* → see box at NORMAL

standardize also **-ise** *BrE* /'stændədaɪz $ -ər-/ *v* [T] to change things so that they are all the same as each other: *an attempt to standardize the tests* —**standardization** /ˌstændədaɪˈzeɪʃən $ -dərdə-/ *n* [U]

standard of 'living *n* [C] the amount of money that people have to spend, and how comfortable their life is: *Japan has a very high standard of living.*

standby /'stændbaɪ/ *n* plural **standbys** **1** [C] something that is ready to be used if needed: *a standby generator* **2 on standby a)** ready to be used if needed: *The police have been kept on standby in case of trouble.* **b)** if you are on standby for a plane ticket, you will be allowed to travel if there are any seats that are not being used.

'stand-in *n* [C] someone who does another person's job or does something instead of them for a short time

standing[1] /'stændɪŋ/ *n* [U] the opinion that people have about someone, and how good and important they are: **+in** *This has improved the president's standing in the opinion polls.*

standing[2] *adj* **1 standing invitation** when someone has invited you to come whenever you want **2 standing ovation** when people stand up to CLAP after a performance because they think it is very good: *He was given a standing ovation.* **3 standing joke** something that happens often and that people make jokes about

standing 'order *n* [C] an arrangement in which your bank pays a fixed amount of money to someone regularly from your account [➡ direct debit]

'stand-off *n* [C] a situation in which a fight or battle stops because neither side can win

standpoint /'stændpɔɪnt/ *n* [C] one way of thinking about a situation [= **point of view**]: *Let's look at this from a practical standpoint.*

standstill /'stænd,stɪl/ *n* [singular] a situation in which nothing is moving or happening: *The funeral brought the city to a standstill.* | *The traffic came to a standstill.*

'stand-up *adj* [only before noun] a stand-up COMEDIAN stands alone in front of a group of people and tells jokes

stank /stæŋk/ *v* the past tense of STINK

stanza /'stænzə/ *n* [C] a group of lines that forms part of a poem [= **verse**]

staple[1] /'steɪpəl/ n [C] **1** a small piece of thin wire used to fasten pieces of paper together **2** a food that people use all the time: *staples like flour and rice* —**staple** v [T] *Staple the pages together.* → see box at **FASTEN**

staple[2] adj [only before noun] staple foods are very important and used all the time: *staple foods like potatoes* | *a staple diet of* (=consisting mainly of) *rice*

stapler /'steɪplə $ -ər/ n [C] a machine that puts staples through paper

star[1] /staː $ staːr/ n [C]

1 a large ball of burning gas in space that you can see as a point of light in the night sky: *The stars were out* (=shining). → see box at **SPACE**
2 a famous actor, singer, sports player etc: *movie/film/Hollywood star photographs of movie stars* | **pop/rock star**
3 someone who has one of the main parts in a film, show, or play: +**of** *Tom Kay, star of the TV comedy 'Tom's World'*
4 the best in a group of players, students etc: **star player/student/performer etc** *Jim is one of our star salesmen.* | *Louise was the star of the show* (=gave the best performance).
5 a shape with five or six points: *paper decorated with silver stars* → see picture at **SHAPE**[1]
6 **two-star/four-star etc** a mark used in a system for showing how good a hotel or restaurant is: *a three-star hotel*
7 **the stars** *BrE* the way that some people believe that your life is affected by the position of the stars when you were born
→ **SHOOTING STAR**

star[2] v [I,T] **starred, starring** if a film, play etc stars someone, or if someone stars in a film, play etc, they have one of the main parts in it: *a movie starring Mel Gibson* | +**in** *She starred in her own TV series.* | +**as** *Nicole Kidman stars as Emma.* | **star sb as sb** *The film starred Hugh Grant as Will.*

starboard /'staːbəd $ 'staːrbərd/ n [U] the right side of a ship or aircraft when you are facing the front [≠ **port**]

starch /staːtʃ $ staːrtʃ/ n **1** [C,U] a substance in foods such as bread, rice, and potatoes **2** [U] a substance used for making cloth stiff

starchy /'staːtʃi $ 'staːr-/ adj starchy foods contain a lot of starch

stardom /'staːdəm $ 'staːr-/ n [U] when someone is a very famous performer: *He rose to stardom.*

stare /steə $ ster/ v [I] to look at someone or something for a long time: +**at** *She stared at me in horror.* | *He sat there bored, staring into space* (=looking at nothing).
—**stare** n [C] *She gave him a hard stare.*

stark[1] /staːk $ staːrk/ adj **1** very plain in appearance, with no decoration: *the stark beauty of the desert* **2** unpleasantly clear and impossible to avoid: *a stark choice between life and death*
—**starkly** adv

stark[2] adv **stark naked** not wearing any clothes

starlight /'staːlaɪt $ 'staːr-/ n [U] the light that comes from stars at night —**starlit** /-lɪt/ adj: *a starlit sky*

starry /'staːri/ adj a starry sky has a lot of stars

,starry-'eyed adj hopeful about things in a way that is silly or unreasonable, especially because you are young: *a starry-eyed teenager*

,Stars and 'Stripes n **the Stars and Stripes** the national flag of the US

'star sign n [C] one of the 12 signs of the ZODIAC (=a system based on the belief that the time you were born affects what will happen to you)

'star-,studded adj including many famous performers: *The film has a star-studded cast.*

start[1] /staːt $ staːrt/ v

1 [I,T] to begin doing something: *Now you're here, we can start.* | *When does she start college?* | **start doing sth** *He started laughing.* | **start to do sth** *It's started to rain.* | **start by doing sth** *I'll start by introducing myself.* | *I did it wrong, so I had to start again.* | *It's late, we should get started.* | +**on** *I'd better start on my homework.*
2 also **start off** [I,T] to begin happening or existing, or to make something begin happening: *The show starts soon.* | *The fire was started by a candle.* | **Starting from** *tomorrow, this will be your room.* | **start (sth) with sth** *The meal started with soup.* | *He always starts off the lesson with a test.* | **start by doing sth** *Let's start off by saying why we're here.* | +**as** *The website started as a school project.*
3 also **start up** [T] to form a new business or organization: *We started our own record company.*
4 also **start up** [I,T] if you start an engine or machine, or if it starts, it begins to work: *The car wouldn't start this morning.*
5 **start at/from etc sth** if prices start at or from an amount, that is the lowest amount that you can pay to get something: *Tickets start from £12.*
6 **to start with** *spoken* **a)** at the beginning of a situation: *You'll need some help to start with.* **b)** used to emphasize the first of a list of things you want to mention: *I can't join the police – to start with, I'm too short.*

start sb off phr v to make someone begin doing something: **start sb off doing sth** *That started me off crying.*

start out phr v to begin life, existence, work etc in a particular way or form: *When we started out, my bedroom was our office.* | +**as** *The book started out as a short article.*

start over phr v *AmE* to start doing something again from the beginning

start[2] n

1 [C] the beginning of something: +**of** *Hurry, or we'll miss the start of the show.* | *She came here at the start of 2001.* | *The project has had problems from the start.* | **get off to a good/bad start** (=start well/badly) *The year got off to a good start.*
2 **make a start** to begin doing something: +**on** *I'll make a start on the cleaning.*
3 [singular] a sudden movement of your body, caused by fear or surprise: *Ed woke with a start.*
4 **the start** the place where a race or game begins
5 [C usually singular] an advantage you have when you start something before other people: **give sb/have a start** *He had a 100 metre start on his pursuers.*

S

6 for a start *BrE spoken* used to emphasize the first of several reasons or other things you want to mention: *I hated it. The food was awful, for a start.*

7 be a start used to say that something may not be impressive, but it will help: *I go to the gym once a week, which is a start.*

→ HEAD START

starter /'stɑːtə $ 'stɑːrtər/ *n* [C] **1** *BrE* **appetizer** *AmE* a small amount of food that you eat as the first part of a meal **2** a person, horse, car etc that is in a race when it begins **3** someone who gives the signal for a race to begin **4 for starters** *spoken* used to emphasize the first thing in a list: *You've spelled the title wrong, for starters.*

'starting ,point *n* [C] something from which a discussion or situation can develop: **+for** *The article is a good starting point for debate.*

startle /'stɑːtl $ 'stɑːrtl/ *v* [T] to make someone suddenly feel surprised or slightly shocked: *Sorry, I didn't mean to startle you.* —**startled** *adj*: *a startled expression*

'start-up[1] *adj* [only before noun] connected with starting a new business: *start-up costs*

start-up[2] *n* [C] a new small company: *an Internet start-up*

starvation /stɑːˈveɪʃən $ stɑːr-/ *n* [U] suffering or death caused by lack of food: *people dying of starvation*

starve /stɑːv $ stɑːrv/ *v* [I,T] to suffer or die because you do not have enough to eat, or to make someone do this: *Thousands of people could starve to death.* | *starving refugees*

  starve sb/sth of sth *phr v* not to give something that is needed: *Schools have been starved of funding.*

starving /'stɑːvɪŋ $ 'stɑːr-/ *adj*
1 someone who is starving has not had enough food for a long time and could die: *starving children*
2 *BrE spoken* **starved** /stɑːvd $ stɑːrvd/ *AmE* very hungry: *Let's have lunch – I'm starving.*

stash[1] /stæʃ/ *v* [T] *informal* to store something secretly somewhere: **stash sth away** *The money is stashed away in a bank account.*

stash[2] *n* [C] *informal* an amount of something, especially drugs or money, that is kept in a secret place

state[1] /steɪt/ *n*
1 [C] the condition that someone or something is in: **+of** *We are concerned about the state of the economy.* | *The house was in a terrible state.* | *They found him in a state of shock.* | *You are in no fit state to drive.*
2 the state also **the State** the government of a country: *the power of the state* | **state-owned/state-funded etc** *state-owned industries*
3 also **State** [C] one of the parts that the US and some other countries are divided into, which each have their own government: *the state of Texas*
4 also **State** [C,U] a country considered as a political organization: *EU* **member states** | *a meeting between* **heads of state** (=leaders of countries)
5 the States *spoken* the US: *Have you been to the States?*

6 be in/get into a state *BrE informal* to be or become very nervous or upset
7 state visit/ceremony/opening etc an important official visit, ceremony etc involving governments or rulers

→ NATION STATE, POLICE STATE, WELFARE STATE

state[2] *v* [T] *formal* to say something publicly or officially: *Please state your name.* | **+(that)** *The rules state that contestants must be over 18.*

stately /'steɪtli/ *adj* formal and impressive: *a stately mansion*

,stately 'home *n* [C] a large old house in the countryside in Britain, especially one that is open to the public

statement /'steɪtmənt/ *n* [C]
1 something that you say or write publicly or officially: **+on/about** *the President's statements on the economy* | *The minister will* **make a statement** *later today.* | *He* **gave a statement** *to the police.*
2 a list showing amounts of money that have been paid and received: *According to my* **bank statement***, I haven't been paid.*

,state of a'ffairs *n* [C] a situation

,state of e'mergency *n* [C] plural **states of emergency** a situation in which a government uses special powers to limit people's freedom

,state of 'mind *n* [C] someone's feelings, for example whether they are happy or upset

,state-of-the-'art *adj* using the newest methods, materials, or knowledge: *state-of-the-art technology*

'state ,school *n* [C] *BrE* a school which provides free education and is paid for by the government

statesman /'steɪtsmən/ *n* [C] plural **statesmen** /-mən/ a political leader, especially one who is respected and admired —**statesmanship** *n* [U]

static[1] /'stætɪk/ *adj* not changing or moving: *Prices have remained static.*

static[2] *n* [U] **1** noise caused by electricity in the air that spoils the sound on the radio or television **2** also **,static elec'tricity** electricity that collects on an object and gives you a small electric shock when you touch it

station[1] /'steɪʃən/ *n* [C]
1 a building where trains or buses stop so that passengers can get on and off: **at a station** *We get off at the next station.* | **bus station/train station/railway station** *BrE*
2 a building where a service or activity is based: **police/fire station** *He was interviewed at the police station.* | **petrol station** *BrE* **/gas station** *AmE* (=where petrol is sold)
3 a company that broadcasts on radio or television: *a country music station* | **radio/TV station**

→ FILLING STATION, POLLING STATION, POWER STATION, SERVICE STATION

station[2] *v* [T usually passive] to send a soldier to a place as part of their duty: *He was stationed in Germany.*

stationary /'steɪʃənəri $ -neri/ *adj* not moving: *a stationary vehicle*

stationer's /'steɪʃənəz $ -ərz/ *n* [C] *BrE* a shop that sells stationery

stationery /'steɪʃənəri $ -neri/ *n* [U] things such as paper or pens that you use for writing

'station ,wagon *n* [C] *AmE* a large car with extra space at the back [**= estate car** *BrE*]

statistic /stə'tɪstɪk/ *n* **1 statistics a)** [plural] a set of numbers which represent facts or measurements: *the government's official crime statistics* | **Statistics show** *that 15% of students do not complete their courses.* **b)** [U] the science of collecting and studying such numbers: *an expert in statistics* **2** [singular] a single number which represents a fact: *1 in 3 people get cancer – a frightening statistic.* —**statistical** *adj*: *statistical analysis* —**statistically** /-kli/ *adv*

statistician /ˌstætəˈstɪʃən/ *n* [C] someone who works with statistics

statue

statue /'stætʃuː/ *n* [C] a large image of a person or animal made of stone, wood, or metal [**➡ sculpture**]: **+of** *a statue of Queen Victoria*

stature /'stætʃə $ -ər/ *n* [U] *formal* **1** when someone is important and well respected: *a musician of great stature* **2** someone's height

status /'steɪtəs $ 'steɪtəs, 'stæ-/ *n* [U]

1 the official or legal importance that someone or something has: *the status of women in society* | *This document has no* **legal status** *the UK.* | *your name, age, and* **marital status** (=whether you are married or not)

2 respect or importance that is given to someone or something: *Caring for children should have more status.*

status quo /ˌsteɪtəs ˈkwəʊ $ ˌsteɪtəs ˈkwoʊ, ˌstæ-/ **the status quo** the situation that exists at a particular time

'status ,symbol *n* [C] something that you own that suggests you are rich or important

statute /'stætʃuːt/ *n* [C] *formal* a law or rule

statutory /'stætʃətəri $ -tɔːri/ *adj formal* fixed or controlled by law: *your statutory rights*

staunch[1] /stɔːntʃ $ stɒːntʃ, stɑːntʃ/ *adj* very loyal: *a staunch supporter of the Liberal Party* —**staunchly** *adv*

staunch[2] also **stanch** *AmE v* [T] to stop a flow of blood from a wound

stave /steɪv/ *v* past tense and past participle **staved** or **stove** /stəʊv $ stoʊv/

stave sth ⇔ off *phr v* to stop something unpleasant from happening for a short time: *She ate an apple to stave off hunger.*

stay[1] /steɪ/ *v*

1 [I] to remain in the same place, job, school etc, and not leave: *He came to see me and stayed all day.* | **+at/in** *I stayed at school late.* | *He stayed in his job for 10 years.* | **stay at home** *BrE* /**stay home** *AmE*: *She decided to stay home.* | **stay here/there** *Stay here in case anybody calls.* |

stay and do sth *I want to stay and help.* | **stay for dinner/lunch etc** *Why don't you stay for tea?*

2 [I, linking verb] to continue to be in a particular state, and not change: *It was hard to* **stay awake.** | *Try to* **stay calm.** | *This town has* **stayed the same** *for centuries.* | *I hope we can* **stay friends.**

3 [I] to live in a place for a short time as a visitor or guest: **+at/in** *They're staying at her mother's.* | *How long are you staying in Paris?* | **+with** *We're going to stay with friends this weekend.*

4 stay put *informal* to remain in one place and not move

stay away *phr v* not to go near someone or something: **+from** *Stay away from my sister!*

stay behind *phr v* to stay in a place after the other people have left: *I had to stay behind after school.*

stay in *phr v* to stay in your home and not go out: *Let's stay in and watch TV.*

stay on *phr v* to continue to do a job or to study after the time when people can leave: *Rachel is staying on for another year in college.*

stay out *phr v* **1** to remain away from home during the evening or night: *She stayed out till midnight.* **2 stay out of sth** *spoken* to not get involved in an argument: *He told me to stay out of it.*

stay up *phr v* not to go to bed: *We* **stayed up** *late last night.*

stay[2] *n* [C] a short period of time that you spend somewhere: *We hope you enjoy your stay.* | **+in/at** *a short stay in hospital*

stead /sted/ *n* **1 stand sb in good stead** to be very useful for someone in the future: *Her training stood her in good stead.* **2 do sth in sb's stead** *formal* to do something instead of someone else

steadfast /'stedfɑːst $ -fæst/ *adj literary* refusing to change your opinion or your support for someone

steady[1] /'stedi/ *adj*

1 continuing or developing at the same rate, without stopping or changing: *He has made steady progress.* | *a steady speed of 50 mph* | **hold/remain steady** *Inflation held steady at 3%.*

2 not moving or shaking [**➡ stable**]: *Keep the ladder steady.* | *Her voice remained steady.*

3 a steady job a job you get paid regularly for, and is likely to continue for a long time

4 steady boyfriend/girlfriend someone that you have had a romantic relationship with for a long time

—**steadily** *adv* —**steadiness** *n* [U]

steady[2] *v* **steadied, steadying, steadies** [I,T] to control someone or something so that they do not shake or fall, or to become controlled like this: **steady yourself** *He put out his hand to steady himself.* | *The ship steadied.*

steak /steɪk/ *n* [C,U] a large thick piece of meat or fish ➡ see picture on page A5

steal /stiːl/ *v* past tense **stole** /stəʊl $ stoʊl/ past participle **stolen** /'stəʊlən $ 'stoʊ-/

1 [I,T] to take something that does not belong to you: *Someone stole my passport.* | **steal (sth) from sb/sth** *He even stole from his friends.* | *Money was stolen from her purse.* | *a stolen car*

S

THESAURUS

burgle – to go into someone's home and steal things: *Their house was burgled while they were away.*

rob – to steal money or other things from a bank, shop, or person: *The post office has been broken into and robbed.*

mug – to attack someone in the street and steal something from them: *An elderly lady was mugged in the centre of Oxford.*

shoplift – to steal things from a shop while it is open

nick *especially BrE*/**pinch** – an informal way of saying that something has been stolen: *Someone nicked my wallet while I was out of the office for a moment.*

People who steal
thief, burglar, robber, mugger, shoplifter, pickpocket

Steal and rob
Use **steal** to talk about the things that were taken: *Matt's bike was stolen yesterday.* | *He was arrested trying to steal some cigarettes.*
Use **rob** to talk about the person that money is taken from, or the place, especially a bank: *Someone robbed the bank last night.* | *You'll only get robbed if you carry all that money.*
→ CRIME

2 [I,T] to use someone else's ideas and pretend that they are yours: *She accused him of stealing her invention.*
3 [I] to move secretly and quietly: **+away/ across/into etc** *Silently she stole away.*

stealth /stelθ/ *n* [U] when you do something secretly or quietly —**stealthy** *adj*

steam¹ /stiːm/ *n* [U]
1 the mist that hot water produces: *The kitchen was full of steam.* | **steam engine/boat/train etc** (=that uses power from steam) **2 let off steam** to get rid of your anger or energy by doing something active **3 under your own steam** without help from anyone else

steam

steam

kettle

steam² *v* **1** [I] to produce steam: *a cup of steaming coffee* **2** [T] to cook something in steam [➡ **boil**]: *Steam the vegetables.* → see box at **COOK**

,steamed 'up *adj* **1** covered with steam: *My glasses were all steamed up.* **2** *informal* angry or worried

steamer /'stiːmə $ -ər/ *n* [C] **1** a ship that uses steam power **2** a pan in which you cook food by steaming it

steamroller¹ /'stiːmˌrəʊlə $ -ˌroʊlər/ *v* [T] *informal* to defeat someone or force someone to do something by using all your power

steamroller² *n* [C] a heavy vehicle used for making road surfaces flat

steamy /'stiːmi/ *adj* **1** full of steam or covered in steam: *steamy windows* **2** sexually exciting: *a steamy love scene*

steed /stiːd/ *n* [C] *literary* a horse

steel¹ /stiːl/ *n* [U] a strong metal that can be shaped easily and is used for making knives etc: *cutlery made of **stainless steel*** (=steel that remains shiny for a long time) | *a steel factory*

steel² *v* **steel yourself** to prepare yourself to do something unpleasant

steelworks /'stiːlwɜːks $ -wɜːrks/ *n* [C] plural **steelworks** a factory where steel is made

steely /'stiːli/ *adj* very determined and strong: *his steely determination*

steep¹ /stiːp/ *adj*
1 a steep road or hill goes down or up at a sharp angle: *a steep mountain track*
2 a steep increase or decrease is large: *a steep rise in profits*
3 *informal* very expensive
—**steeply** *adv* —**steepness** *n* [U]

steep² *v* [T] **1 be steeped in history/tradition etc** to contain a lot of a particular quality **2** to put food in a liquid and leave it for some time

steeple /'stiːpəl/ *n* [C] a tall pointed tower on a church

steer¹ /stɪə $ stɪr/ *v*
1 [I,T] to control the direction a vehicle is going: **+for/towards etc** *I steered for the harbour.* | **steer sth towards/away from etc** *He steered the van through the traffic.*
2 [T] to influence someone's behaviour or the way a situation develops: **steer sb/sth towards/away from sth** *She steered me towards a medical career.* | *Helen tried to **steer** the conversation away from school.*
3 steer clear of sb/sth *informal* to try to avoid someone or something: *I steer clear of talking about politics.*

steer² *n* [C] a young male cow

steering /'stɪərɪŋ $ 'stɪr-/ *n* [U] the parts of a car, boat etc that control its direction: *power steering*

'steering wheel *n* [C] a wheel that you turn to control the direction of a car → see picture on page A12

stem¹ /stem/ *n* [C] the long thin part of a plant that grows up out of the ground → see picture at **PLANT**

stem² *v* [T] **stemmed, stemming** to stop something from spreading or growing: **stem the tide/ flood/flow of sth** *an effort to stem the rising tide of crime*

stem from sth *phr v* to develop as a result of something

stench /stentʃ/ *n* [C] a very strong unpleasant smell [= **stink**] → see box at **SMELL**

stencil /'stensəl/ *n* [C] a piece of paper or plastic with patterns or letters cut out of it, which you use for painting patterns or letters onto a surface —**stencil** *v* [T]

step¹ /step/ *n* [C]
1 the movement you make when you put one foot in front of the other when walking: *He took a few steps, then stopped.* | **+forwards/back/ towards etc** *Jamie took a step back and shook his head.*
2 one of a series of things that you do in order to deal with a problem or achieve something: **+towards** *an important step towards peace* | *We must **take steps** to make sure it never happens*

again. | *Environmentalists called the change* **a step in the right direction** (=a good thing to do).

3 a flat narrow piece of wood or stone that you put your foot on when you are going up or down, especially outside a building: *Jenny sat on the step in front of the house, waiting.* | *We walked down a short* **flight of steps** (=set of steps) *to the car park.*

4 one of the movements you make with your feet when you are doing a dance

5 in step a) thinking or behaving in the same way as other people: **+with** *The party needs to get in step with the voters.* **b)** moving your feet at the same time as people you are walking with

6 out of step a) thinking or behaving in a different way from other people: **+with** *Katy felt a little out of step with her schoolmates.* **b)** moving your feet in a different way from people you are walking with

7 watch your step *BrE* to be careful about what you say and how you behave

→ FOOTSTEP, STEP-BY-STEP

step² v [I] **stepped, stepping**

1 to move somewhere by putting one foot down in front of the other: **+back/forward etc** *Everyone stepped back to let the doctor through.* | *I opened the door and* **stepped outside**.

2 *BrE* to put your foot on or in something [= **tread** *BrE*]: **+in/on etc** *Sorry, I didn't mean to step on your foot.*

3 step out of line to break the rules, or not do what you have been told to do

step down/aside *phr v* to leave an important job or official position

step forward *phr v* to offer help [= **come forward**]: *Several volunteers have kindly stepped forward.*

step in *phr v* to become involved in a situation, especially to stop trouble [= **intervene**]: *The police stepped in and stopped the fight.*

step sth ⇔ **up** *phr v* to increase the amount of an activity or the speed of a process: *Airlines are stepping up security checks.*

stepbrother /'stepbrʌðə $ -ər/ n [C] the son of someone who has married one of your parents

,step-by-'step *adj* a step-by-step plan, method etc deals with things carefully and in a fixed order: **step-by-step guide/instructions** *a step-by-step guide to buying a house* —**step by step** *adv*

stepchild /'steptʃaɪld/ *n* [C] plural **stepchildren** /-,tʃɪldrən/ a STEPDAUGHTER or STEPSON

stepdaughter /'stepdɔːtə $ -dɔːtər/ *n* [C] a daughter that your husband or wife has from a previous marriage

stepfather /'stepfɑːðə $ -ər/ *n* [C] a man who is married to your mother, but who is not your father

stepladder /'step,lædə $ -ər/ *n* [C] a LADDER with two sloping parts that are joined at the top so that it can stand without support

stepmother /'stepmʌðə $ -ər/ *n* [C] a woman who is married to your father, but who is not your mother

'stepping-,stone *n* [C] **1** something that will help you to achieve something else: *a stepping-stone to a better job* **2 stepping-stones** [plural] a row of stones that you walk on to get across a stream

stepsister /'stepsɪstə $ -ər/ *n* [C] the daughter of someone who has married one of your parents

stepson /'stepsʌn/ *n* [C] a son that your husband or wife has from a previous marriage

stereo /'steriəʊ, 'stɪər- $ 'steriou, 'stɪr-/ *n* plural **stereos 1** [C] a machine for playing records, CDs etc that produces sound from two SPEAKERS **2** [U] a system for playing music or speech through two SPEAKERS

stereotype /'steriətaɪp, 'stɪər- $ 'ster-, 'stɪr-/ *n* [C] an idea of what a type of person is like, especially one which is wrong or unfair: **racial/ sexual/cultural etc stereotype** —**stereotype** *v* [T] —**stereotypical** /,steriə'tɪpɪkəl, ,stɪər- $,ster-, ,stɪr-/ *adj*: *stereotypical images of women*

sterile /'steraɪl $ -rəl/ *adj* **1** unable to have children [= **infertile**; ≠ **fertile**] **2** completely clean and not containing any BACTERIA: *a sterile bandage* | **sterile equipment/needles/ dressings etc 3** lacking new ideas or interest: **sterile debate/argument** —**sterility** /stə'rɪlゝti/ *n* [U]

sterilize also **-ise** *BrE* /'sterゝlaɪz/ *v* [T] **1** to make something completely clean and kill any BACTERIA in it: *a sterilized needle* **2** if someone is sterilized, they have an operation that makes them unable to have children —**sterilization** /,sterゝlaɪ'zeɪʃən $ -lə-/ *n* [C,U]

sterling¹ /'stɜːlɪŋ $ 'stɜːr-/ *n* [U] the standard unit of money in the United Kingdom, based on the pound

sterling² *adj* [only before noun] very good: **sterling work/service**

stern¹ /stɜːn $ stɜːrn/ *adj* **1** very strict and severe: **stern voice/look/face etc** | *He was fined and given a stern warning.* **2 be made of stern stuff** to have a strong character and be determined to succeed: *Ann was made of sterner stuff than me.* —**sternly** *adv*

stern² *n* [C] the back part of a ship [→ **bow**]

steroid /'stɪərɔɪd, 'ste- $ 'stɪr-/ *n* [C] a chemical that is produced by the body or made as a drug. People sometimes use steroids illegally in sport to improve their performance.

stethoscope /'steθəskəʊp $ -skoup/ *n* [C] a piece of equipment that doctors use to listen to your heart or breathing

stew¹ /stjuː $ stuː/ *n* [C,U] a meal made by cooking meat or fish and vegetables together slowly for a long time [= **casserole**]: *beef stew*

stew² *v* [T] to cook something slowly in liquid: *stewed apples*

steward /'stjuːəd $ 'stuːərd/ *n* [C] **1** a man who serves food and drinks to people on a plane or a ship **2** *BrE* someone who helps to organize a race

stewardess /'stjuːədゝs $ 'stuːərd-/ *n* [C] *old-fashioned* a woman who serves food and drinks to people on a plane [= **flight attendant**]

stick¹ /stɪk/ *v* past tense and past participle **stuck** /stʌk/

1 [I,T] to join something to something else using a substance such as glue, or to become joined to

something: **stick sth on/to/in etc sth** *Did you remember to stick a stamp on the envelope?* | *The pages were all stuck together.* | *Put a drop of oil in the water to stop the pasta from sticking.*
2 [I,T] if a pointed object sticks into something, or if you stick it there, it is pushed into it: **stick sth in/into/through sth** *The nurse stuck a needle in my arm.*
3 [T] *informal* to put something somewhere [= put]: *Just stick your coat on that chair.* | *Clara stuck her head round the door to see who was there.*
4 [I] if something sticks, it becomes fixed in one position and is difficult to move: *The door's stuck.*
5 stick in sb's mind if something sticks in your mind, you remember it well because it was surprising, interesting etc
6 stick your neck out *informal* to take the risk of saying or doing something that may be wrong, or that other people may disagree with
7 [T] *BrE spoken* if you cannot stick someone or something, you feel you cannot deal with them any more [= stand]: *I can't stick ironing.* | *I don't know how she sticks him.*

stick around *phr v informal* to remain in a place, waiting for something to happen or someone to arrive

stick at sth *phr v* to continue working hard in order to achieve something

stick by sb *phr v informal* **1** to help and support someone who is in a difficult situation: *Laura has always stuck by me.* **2** not to change what you have decided to do, or not change what you have said: *The paper is sticking by its original story.*

stick out *phr v* **1** if a part of something sticks out, it comes out much further than the rest of a surface: *Paul's legs were sticking out from under the car.* **2 stick sth ⇔ out** to deliberately make something come forward or out: *Don't stick your tongue out at me!* **3 stick it out** *informal* to continue doing something that is difficult, boring etc **4** *informal* to be easily noticed because of being very different from everyone or everything else: *Here, any stranger sticks out like a sore thumb.*

stick to sth *phr v* **1** to do what you said you would do, even when it is difficult [= keep to]: *We decided to stick to our original plan.* **2 stick to your guns** to refuse to change your mind, even though other people say that you are wrong

stick together *phr v informal* if people stick together, they continue to support each other when they have problems

stick up *phr v* if a part of something sticks up, it is pointing up above a surface

stick up for sb *phr v informal* to defend someone who is being criticized: **stick up for yourself** *You'll have to learn to stick up for yourself.*

stick with sb/sth *phr v informal* to continue doing something or supporting someone: *He stuck with his job at the zoo.*

stick² n [C]
1 a long thin piece of wood, especially one that has fallen from a tree [→ branch, twig]
2 a long thin piece of wood, plastic etc that you use for a particular purpose: *Grandad walks with a stick* (=uses a stick to help him walk).

3 a long thin piece of something: **+of** *a stick of chewing gum*
4 a long thin piece of wood, plastic etc that you use in some sports to hit a ball: *a hockey stick*
5 (out) in the sticks a long way from a town or city: *Living out in the sticks, a car is a necessity.*
→ **GEAR STICK**, **WALKING STICK** → **get (hold of) the wrong end of the stick** at **WRONG¹**

sticker /ˈstɪkə $ -ər/ n [C] a small piece of paper or plastic with a picture or writing on it, that you can put onto something

stickler /ˈstɪklə $ -ər/ n [C] someone who is very strict about rules or small details: **+for** *She's a stickler for accuracy.*

ˈstick shift n [C] *AmE* a piece of equipment in a car that you move with your hand to control its GEARS [→ automatic]

sticky /ˈstɪki/ adj
1 made of or covered with a substance that sticks to surfaces: *sticky cakes* | *Your hands are all sticky.* | **sticky tape/label etc** *BrE* (=tape etc that is made so it will stick to surfaces)
2 a sticky situation or problem is difficult to deal with
3 sticky weather is hot and damp, and makes you feel uncomfortable [= humid]
—**stickiness** n [U]

stiff¹ /stɪf/ adj
1 if someone or a part of their body is stiff, their muscles hurt and it is difficult to move: *I've got a stiff neck.* | **+with** *Her fingers were stiff with cold.*
2 hard and difficult to bend or move: *stiff cardboard*
3 a stiff mixture is thick and almost solid: *Beat the egg whites until stiff.*
4 very strict, severe, or difficult: **a stiff penalty/fine/sentence** | *Graduates face stiff competition in getting jobs.*
5 behaving in a formal and not very friendly way: *a stiff smile*
6 a stiff wind/breeze a fairly strong wind or BREEZE
7 a stiff drink a large amount of a strong alcoholic drink
—**stiffly** adv —**stiffness** n [U]

stiff² adv **bored/worried/scared stiff** *informal* extremely bored, worried, or frightened

stiffen /ˈstɪfən/ v [I] to suddenly stop moving, especially because you are frightened or worried [≠ relax]

stifle /ˈstaɪfəl/ v [T] to stop something from happening or developing: **stifle a yawn/cry/grin etc** | *laws that stifle competition*

stifling /ˈstaɪflɪŋ/ adj a room or weather that is stifling is very hot and makes you feel uncomfortable

stigma /ˈstɪɡmə/ n [singular, U] a strong feeling in society that being in a particular situation or having a particular illness is something to be ashamed of: *the stigma of mental illness* —**stigmatize** /-mətaɪz/ v [T]

stile /staɪl/ n [C] a set of steps that helps people climb over a fence in the countryside

stiletto /stɪˈletəʊ $ -toʊ/ n [C] plural **stilettos** or **stilettoes** a woman's shoe with a high thin heel, or the heel of this kind of shoe → see picture at **SHOE¹**

still[1] /stɪl/ adv

1 up to a particular point in time and continuing at that moment: *Andy's still asleep.* | *I still haven't finished my homework.*

Still is used to say that a situation that began in the past has not changed and is continuing: *He still lives with his parents.* **Always** means 'all the time' or 'every time': *Her house was always clean and tidy.* | *I always see him on Tuesdays.*

2 in spite of what has just been said or done: *Clare didn't study much, but she still passed the exam.* | *The hotel was terrible. Still, the weather was OK.*

3 used to say that something continues to be possible: *We could still catch the bus if we hurry.*
4 colder/harder/better etc still even colder, harder etc than something else: *Dan found biology difficult, and physics harder still.*

GRAMMAR

Use **still** before a verb unless the verb is 'be': *She still calls me regularly.* | *It was still dark outside.*
If there are two or more verbs together, **still** comes after the first one: *I can still remember them.*
Still usually comes before any negative word: *She still isn't ready.*

still[2] adj

1 not moving: **keep/stay/stand still** *The children wouldn't keep still.*
2 quiet and calm: *The forest was completely still.*
3 BrE a still drink does not contain gas [≠ fizzy]: *still lemonade*
—**stillness** n [U]

still[3] n [C] a photograph of a scene from a film

stillborn /'stɪlbɔːn, ˌstɪl'bɔːn $ -ɔːrn/ adj born dead

,still 'life n [C,U] plural **still lifes** a picture of objects, especially flowers or fruit → see picture at **PAINTING**

stilted /'stɪltɪd/ adj a stilted style of writing or speaking is formal and not natural

stilts /stɪlts/ n [plural] a pair of poles you can stand on, used for walking high above the ground

stimulant /'stɪmjələnt/ n [C] a drug or substance that makes you feel more active: *Caffeine is a stimulant.*

stimulate /'stɪmjəleɪt/ v [T] **1** to encourage an activity to grow and develop: *These measures are designed to stimulate the economy.* **2** to make someone interested and excited about something: *We hope the project will stimulate students' interest in science.* —**stimulation** /ˌstɪmjəˈleɪʃən/ n [U]

stimulating /'stɪmjəleɪtɪŋ/ adj interesting and full of new ideas: *a stimulating conversation*

stimulus /'stɪmjələs/ n plural **stimuli** /-laɪ/ [C, U] something that causes a development or reaction: **+to/for** *a stimulus to industrial development* | *visual stimuli*

sting[1] /stɪŋ/ v [I,T] past tense and past participle **stung** /stʌŋ/

1 if an insect, animal, or plant stings you, it hurts you by putting poison into your skin: *Jamie got stung by a bee.*
2 to feel a sudden sharp pain, or to make someone feel this: *The antiseptic might sting a little.*
3 if you are stung by something someone says, it makes you feel upset: *She was stung by his criticism.*

sting[2] n [C] **1** a wound that is made when an insect, plant etc stings you: *a bee sting* **2** a pain that you feel in your eyes, throat, or on your skin **3** BrE the sharp part of an insect's or animal's body, with which it stings you [= **stinger** AmE]

stinger /'stɪŋə $ -ər/ n [C] AmE the sharp part of an insect's or animal's body, with which it stings you [= **sting** BrE]

stinging /'stɪŋɪŋ/ adj criticizing someone very severely: *a stinging attack*

stingy /'stɪndʒi/ adj not generous, especially with money [= **mean**]

stink[1] /stɪŋk/ v [I] past tense **stank** /stæŋk/ past participle **stunk** /stʌŋk/ **1** to have a very strong and unpleasant smell: **+of** *The room stank of cigar smoke.* **2** spoken used to say that something is very bad, unpleasant, or unfair: *I think the whole thing stinks.*

stink[2] n [C] **1** a very bad smell → see box at **SMELL** **2 make/cause/kick up a stink** to complain very strongly about something

stint /stɪnt/ n [C] a period of time that you spend doing something: **+in/at** *a five-year stint in the army*

stipulate /'stɪpjəleɪt/ v [T] formal if an agreement, law, or rule stipulates something, it must be done [= **state**]: **+that** *The regulations stipulate that safety standards must be observed.* —**stipulation** /ˌstɪpjəˈleɪʃən/ n [C]

stir[1] /stɜː $ stɜːr/ v stirred, stirring

1 [T] to mix a liquid or food by moving a spoon around in it: *Add milk, then stir for 5 minutes.* | **stir sth into sth** *Stir the flour into the mixture.* → see box at **RECIPE** → see picture on page A4
2 [I,T] to move slightly, or to make someone or something do this: *A gentle breeze stirred the curtains.* | *He hadn't stirred from his chair all morning.*
3 [T] to make someone feel an emotion: *The music stirred childhood memories.*
stir sth ⇔ up phr v to deliberately cause problems or arguments: *John was always stirring up trouble.*

stir[2] n [C, usually singular] **1** a feeling of excitement or annoyance: **create/cause a stir** *The movie caused quite a stir.* **2** when you stir something: *Give the soup a stir.*

'stir-fry v [T] stir-fried, stir-frying, stir-fries to cook vegetables or meat quickly in a little hot oil → see picture on page A5 —**stir-fry** n [C]

stirring /'stɜːrɪŋ/ adj making people feel very excited or proud: *a stirring speech*

stirrup /'stɪrəp $ 'stɜː-/ n [C] one of the two metal rings that you put your feet in when you are riding a horse

stitch[1] /stɪtʃ/ n

1 [C] a line of thread that has been sewn in a piece of cloth

2 [C] a piece of thread that a doctor uses to sew together a cut or wound: *Tony needed five stitches in his head.*
3 [C] one of the small circles of wool that you put round a needle when you are KNITTING
4 [singular] a pain that you get in the side of your body when you run too fast
5 in stitches laughing so much that you cannot stop: *Her jokes had us all in stitches.*

stitch² v [T] to sew two things together, or to sew something onto a piece of cloth

stock¹ /stɒk $ stɑːk/ n **1** [C] a supply of something that you keep so you can use it when you need it: *How long will the country's coal stocks last?* | **+of** *She kept a stock of candles in the cupboard.* **2** [C,U] a supply of a particular type of thing that a shop has available to sell: *Hurry – buy now while stocks last!* | **in stock/out of stock** (=available or unavailable to be sold) *Their new album is now in stock.* **3** [C,U] a SHARE or SHARES in a company **4** [C,U] a liquid made from boiling meat, bones, or vegetables, used to make soup: *chicken stock* **5 take stock (of sth)** to think carefully about a situation so that you can decide what to do next: *We need to take stock of the situation.*

stock² v [T] **1** to have something available for people to buy: *Do you stock camping equipment?* **2** to fill something with a supply of something [➔ **well-stocked**]: **stock sth with sth** *The fridge was stocked with food.*
stock up phr v to buy a lot of something in order to keep it for when you need to use it later: **+on** *I need to stock up on groceries.*

stock³ adj **stock answer/remark etc** something that people usually say, but which is not interesting or original

stockade /stɒˈkeɪd $ stɑː-/ n [C] a fence built to defend a place, made from large pieces of wood

stockbroker /ˈstɒkˌbrəʊkə $ ˈstɑːkˌbroʊkər/ n [C] someone whose job is to buy and sell SHARES, STOCKS, and BONDS for other people —**stockbroking** n [U]

'stock ex,change n [C usually singular] **1** the business of buying and selling STOCKS and SHARES **2** a place where STOCKS and SHARES are bought and sold [= **stock market**]

stocking /ˈstɒkɪŋ $ ˈstɑː-/ n [C] a very thin piece of clothing that fits closely over a woman's foot and leg: *a pair of silk stockings*

stockist /ˈstɒkɪ�ბst $ ˈstɑː-/ n [C] BrE a shop that sells the products of a particular company: *Telephone for details of your nearest stockist.*

'stock ,market n [C usually singular] **1** the business of buying and selling STOCKS and SHARES **2** a place where STOCKS and SHARES are bought and sold [= **stock exchange**]

stockpile /ˈstɒkpaɪl $ ˈstɑːk-/ v [T] to collect a large supply of something to use in the future: *Rebel troops have been stockpiling food and weapons.* —**stockpile** n [C]

stocktaking /ˈstɒkˌteɪkɪŋ $ ˈstɑːk-/ n [U] BrE when people in a shop or business check what goods they have [= **inventory** AmE]

stocky /ˈstɒki $ ˈstɑː-/ adj a stocky person is short and heavy and looks strong: *a stocky man with red hair*

stodgy /ˈstɒdʒi $ ˈstɑː-/ adj BrE disapproving stodgy food is heavy and makes you feel full very quickly [≠ **light**]: *a stodgy pudding*

stoic /ˈstəʊɪk $ ˈstoʊ-/ also **stoical** /ˈstəʊɪkəl $ ˈstoʊ-/ adj formal not complaining when something bad happens to you: *a look of stoic resignation* —**stoicism** /-ɪsɪzəm/ n [U] —**stoically** /-kli/ adv

stoke /stəʊk $ stoʊk/ v [T] **1** to add more coal or wood to a fire **2** also **stoke up** to cause something to increase, especially something bad: *Rising oil prices stoked inflation.*

stole¹ /stəʊl $ stoʊl/ v the past tense of STEAL

stole² n [C] a long straight piece of cloth or fur that is worn over the shoulders

stolen /ˈstəʊlən $ ˈstoʊ-/ v the past participle of STEAL

stolid /ˈstɒlɪ̐d $ ˈstɑː-/ adj disapproving not showing your emotions or becoming excited easily —**stolidly** adv

stomach¹ /ˈstʌmək/ n [C]
1 the part of your body where food goes when you have eaten it: *a stomach upset* (=pain and illness after eating something bad) | *a stomach bug* (=illness that you get from someone else) | *It was a long walk, especially on an empty stomach* (=when you have not eaten). | *The smell turned my stomach* (=made me feel ill). → see picture on page A3
2 the front part of your body, below your chest: *He punched Carlos in the stomach.*
3 have little/no stomach for sth used to emphasize that someone does not want to do something: *Their soldiers had no stomach for a fight.*

stomach² v [T] **can't stomach sth** to be unable to look at, accept etc something unpleasant [➔ **bear**]: *He couldn't stomach the sight of blood.*

'stomach-ache n [C] a pain in your stomach

stomp /stɒmp $ stɑːmp/ v [I] to walk with heavy steps, especially because you are angry: **+off/out/through etc** *She stomped out, slamming the door.*

stone¹ /stəʊn $ stoʊn/ n
1 [U] a hard solid mineral substance: *a stone wall* | *The house is built of stone.*
2 [C] a small piece of rock found on the ground: *Those boys threw stones at me.*
3 [C] a jewel
4 [C] plural **stone** written abbreviation **st** a British unit for measuring weight, equal to 14 pounds or 6.35 kilograms: *He weighs about 12 stone.*
5 [C] BrE the large hard part at the centre of some fruits, containing the seed [= **pit** AmE] → see picture at **FRUIT**
6 a stone's throw from sth/away (from sth) very near to a place: *The beach is only a stone's throw away from the hotel.*
7 stone cold very cold: *This coffee's stone cold!* → **PAVING STONE**

stone² v [T] to throw stones at someone or something: *Christian martyrs who were stoned to death*

'Stone Age n **the Stone Age** a very early time in human history, when only stone was used for making tools and weapons

stoned /stəʊnd $ stoʊnd/ *adj informal* **1** very relaxed or excited because you have used an illegal drug: *Everyone got completely stoned.* **2** very drunk

stonework /'stəʊnwɜːk $ 'stoʊnwɜːrk/ *n* [U] the parts of a building made of or decorated with stone

stony /'stəʊni $ 'stoʊ-/ *adj* **1** stony ground is covered with stones or contains stones: *stony soil* **2** not friendly or sympathetic: *They listened to him in **stony silence**.* | *The judge was **stony-faced**.*

stood /stʊd/ *v* the past tense and past participle of STAND

stool /stuːl/ *n* [C] a seat with three or four legs but no back or arms: *He was **perched on** a bar stool* (=sitting on it). | *a piano stool* → see picture at SEAT

stoop /stuːp/ also **stoop down** *v* [I] to bend your body forward and down: *Dave stooped to pick up a pencil.* —**stoop** *n* [singular]

 stoop to sth *phr v* to do something bad or wrong, which you would not normally do: **not stoop to doing sth** *I wouldn't stoop to taking money from a kid.*

stop¹ /stɒp $ staːp/ *v* **stopped, stopping**

 1 [I,T] not to walk or move any more, or to make someone or something do this: *Stop, come back!* | *We were stopped at the gate by security guards.* | **+at/outside/in etc** *Our driver stopped the car outside the hotel.* | **watch/clock has stopped** (=is not working)

 2 [I,T] not to continue, or to make someone or something not continue: *Has the rain stopped yet?* | *What time do you **stop work** (=finish working at the end of the day)?* | *The referee stopped the fight.* | **stop doing sth** (=not do something any more) *Everyone stopped talking when she came in.* | **stop sb doing sth** *I couldn't stop her crying.* | **stop it/that** *spoken* (=used to tell someone to stop doing something annoying) *Stop it! You're hurting me.*

 3 [I] to pause in order to do something before you continue: **+for** *Do we need to stop for petrol?* | *I worked for three hours before stopping for a break.* | **stop to do sth** *She stopped to light a cigarette.* | **stop and do sth** *Let's stop and look at the view.* | **a bus/train etc stops** (=stops so that you can get off) *Does this train stop at Reading?*

THESAURUS
have/take a break – to stop doing something for a short time in order to rest: *Feeling tired? Take a break.*
break – to stop for a short time in order to rest or eat something: *Shall we break for lunch?*

 4 [T] to prevent someone from doing something, or something from happening: *efforts to stop the spread of AIDS* | *He's decided to go and you can't stop him.* | **stop sb/sth (from) doing sth** *With small kids you can't stop the place from being untidy.* | **stop yourself (from) doing sth** *I couldn't stop myself laughing.*

 5 [T] if you stop an amount of money, you prevent it from being paid to someone: *I've asked the bank to **stop the cheque** (=not pay a cheque that I had written).*

 6 will/would stop at nothing (to do sth) to be ready to do anything to achieve something that is important to you, even if it is dangerous or illegal: *We will stop at nothing in our fight against terrorism.*

 7 stop short of (doing) sth to decide not to do something, although you almost do it: *Tom stopped short of calling her a liar.*

 stop by sb/sth *phr v* to make a short visit to a friend: *It was nice of Judy to stop by.* → see box at VISIT

 stop off *phr v* to make a short visit to a place while you are going somewhere else: **+at/in** *We stopped off at the supermarket on the way home.*

 stop over *phr v* to stop somewhere and stay there for a short time before continuing a long journey: **+at/in** *The plane stopped over in Dubai.*

stop² *n*

 1 [singular] if a vehicle comes to a stop, or you bring it to a stop, it stops moving: *Our taxi came to a stop outside his house.* | *The driver brought the truck to a sudden stop.*

 2 [singular] if an activity comes to a stop, or you bring it to a stop, it stops happening: *Work on the project has come to a stop.* | *efforts to bring the war to a stop*

 3 [C] a place where you stop during a trip, or the short time you spend there: *Our first stop is Brussels.* | *The trip includes an **overnight stop** in London.*

 4 [C] a place where a bus or train regularly stops for people to get on and off: *I get off at **the next stop**.* | **sb's stop** (=the place where someone usually gets off) *This is your stop, isn't it?*

 5 put a stop to sth to prevent something from continuing or happening: *They tried to put a stop to the rumour.*

 → BUS STOP, FULL STOP → **pull out all the stops** at PULL¹

stopgap /'stɒpgæp $ 'staːp-/ *n* [C] something you use or do for a short time until you can find something better: *a **stopgap measure** to deal with the parking problem*

stoplight /'stɒplaɪt $ 'staːp-/ *n* [C] *AmE* a set of red, yellow, and green lights, used for controlling traffic [= traffic lights]

stopover /'stɒp,əʊvə $ 'staːp,oʊvər/ *n* [C] a stop or short stay somewhere during a long plane journey: *a three-hour stopover in Atlanta*

stoppage /'stɒpɪdʒ $ 'staːp-/ *n* [C] when people stop working as a protest [= strike]

stopper /'stɒpə $ 'staːpər/ *n* [C] the thing that you put in the top of a bottle to close it [= cork]

stopwatch /'stɒpwɒtʃ $ 'staːpwaːtʃ, -wɒːtʃ/ *n* [C] a watch used for measuring the exact time it takes to do something, especially to finish a race → see picture at WATCH²

storage /'stɔːrɪdʒ/ *n* [U] when things are kept in a special place until they are needed: **+of** *a shed for the storage of tools* | *There's plenty of **storage space** in the attic.* | **in storage** (=in a place where you pay to store things) *Our furniture's in storage until we find a new house.*

store¹ /stɔː $ stɔːr/ *n* [C]

 1 a place where goods are sold to the public. In British English, a store is a large shop. In American English, a store is any kind of shop: **high street stores** *BrE*: *It costs £10.99 from leading high street stores* | *company-owned **retail***

stores | **shoe/clothing/grocery etc store** *especially AmE* (=shop that sells one type of goods) *She worked in a book store during college.* | *out-of-town furniture stores* | **go to the store** *AmE* (=go to a shop that sells food) *I'm going to the store for some milk.*
2 a supply of something that you keep to use later: **+of** *a store of wood for the winter*
3 in store (for sb) to be going to happen to someone in the future: *There's a surprise in store for you tomorrow!* | *We began to wonder what the future had in store.*
→ CHAIN STORE, CONVENIENCE STORE, DEPARTMENT STORE

store² *v* [T]

1 to put things in a special place and keep them there: *All my old clothes are stored away in the loft.* | *The data is stored on a disk.* | **store sth up** (=keep a supply of something for the future) *animals that store up food for the winter*
2 store up trouble/problems etc to do something that will cause trouble for you later

storekeeper /'stɔːˌkiːpə $ 'stɔːrˌkiːpər/ *n* [C] *AmE* someone who owns or is in charge of a shop [= shopkeeper *BrE*]

storeroom /'stɔːrʊm, -ruːm/ *n* [C] a room for storing things

storey *BrE*; **story** *AmE* /'stɔːri/ *n* [C] plural **storeys** *BrE*, plural **stories** *AmE* a level of a building: *stairs leading to the upper storey* | **two-storey/three-storey etc** *a four-storey house*

stork /stɔːk $ stɔːrk/ *n* [C] a tall white water bird with long legs and a long beak

storm¹ /stɔːm $ stɔːrm/ *n*

1 [C] very bad weather with a lot of wind, rain, or snow etc: *There was a terrible storm in the night.* | **rain/snow/thunder storm** *Suddenly a violent thunder storm broke* (=started). | **dust/sand storm** *The plane crashed when a sand storm blew up* (=started). | *Tropical storms struck the whole region.* → see box at RAIN
2 [C,U] a situation in which people disagree strongly with something and express very strong feelings about it: **a storm of protest/criticism/disapproval etc** *There was a storm of protest over the government's decision.* | **cause/create/provoke etc a storm** *The scandal provoked a political storm.*
3 take sth by storm to be very successful in a particular place: *The show took Broadway by storm.*

storm² *v* **1** [T] to attack and enter a place: *Enemy troops stormed the city.* **2** [I] to walk somewhere in a very angry way: **+out of/off/past etc** *She stormed out of the meeting.*

stormy /'stɔːmi $ 'stɔːr-/ *adj* **1** with strong winds, heavy rain, and dark clouds: *stormy weather* | *a stormy night* **2** a stormy relationship, meeting etc is one in which people argue a lot and have strong feelings

story /'stɔːri/ *n* [C] plural **stories**

1 a description of imaginary events and people, which is intended to entertain people: **+of** *the story of Romeo and Juliet* | **+about** *It's a story about a princess.* | **fairy/ghost/love etc story** *a detective story* | **tell/read sb a story** *Grandma told us stories every night.* | *a book of short stories*

tale – a story about things that happened long ago, or things that may not have really happened: *tales of adventure*
myth – a very old story about gods, magical creatures etc: *myths about giants and dragons*
legend – an old story about brave people or magical events: *the legend of King Arthur*

2 an account of events that have really happened: *The film was based on a true story.* | *He's writing his life story.*
3 a report in a newspaper or news programme about something that has happened: *a front-page story in the Times*
4 an explanation of how or why something has happened, which may be untrue: *Do you believe his story?* | *What's your side of the story* (=your personal explanation)? | **the full/whole story** (=all the facts) *I don't think you're telling us the whole story.*
5 the American spelling of STOREY
6 it's a long story *spoken* used to say that something will take too long to explain: *It's a long story – I'll tell you later.*
7 to cut a long story short *spoken* used when you want to finish explaining something quickly: *To cut a long story short, she's leaving him.*
→ HORROR STORY, SHORT STORY, SOB STORY

storyteller /'stɔːriˌtelə $ -ər/ *n* [C] someone who tells stories

stout¹ /staʊt/ *adj* **1** rather fat: *a stout middle-aged man* **2** strong and thick: *a stout pair of shoes*

stout² *n* [U] a strong dark beer

stove /stəʊv $ stoʊv/ *n* [C]

1 *AmE* a piece of kitchen equipment that you cook on [= cooker *BrE*]: *There's some soup on the stove.* → see picture at KITCHEN
2 a thing used for heating a room, which burns gas, wood, coal etc

stow /stəʊ $ stoʊ/ also **stow away** *v* [T] to put something in a particular space until you need it: *Please stow your bags under your seat.*

stowaway /'stəʊəweɪ $ 'stoʊ-/ *n* [C] someone who hides on a ship or plane in order to travel without paying

straddle /'strædl/ *v* [T] **1** to sit or stand with your legs on either side of something: *He sat straddling the fence.* **2** to be on either side of a place: *The town straddles the River Oder.*

straggle /'strægəl/ *v* [I] to move more slowly than the other people in a group, so that you are behind them: *Ali straggled behind, carrying the shopping.*

straggly /'strægəli/ *adj* growing or spreading out in an untidy way: *a straggly moustache*

straight¹ /streɪt/ *adj*

1 not bent or curved: *a straight road* | *The children stood in a straight line.* | *Keep your back straight.* | *My sister has straight hair* (=without curls). → see picture at HAIR
2 level or upright, and not leaning to one side: *Is my tie straight?* | *straight teeth*
3 honest and direct: *Just give me a straight answer, please.* | **be straight with sb** *I don't think he's being straight with me.*

4 [only before noun] happening one after the other: *The Australian team had three* **straight wins.**
5 [not before noun] clean and tidy: *It took hours to get the house* **straight.**
6 get sth straight *spoken* to understand completely the true facts about a situation: *Let's get this straight. You don't want to get married?*
7 a straight face if you have a straight face, you are not laughing or smiling, although you would like to: *It was hard to keep a straight face.*
8 *informal* someone who is straight is attracted to people of the opposite sex [= **heterosexual;** ≠ **gay**]
9 a straight alcoholic drink has no ice, water etc added to it: *a straight Scotch*
10 [only before noun] involving only two choices, people, or things: *It was a* **straight choice** *between my career and my family.*
11 get straight A's to get 'A' (=the highest possible mark) in all your examinations or school subjects
→ **set/put the record straight** at **RECORD**¹

straight² *adv*
1 in a straight line, not curved or bent: **+at/down/forwards etc** *The truck was coming straight towards me.* | *She kept staring* **straight ahead.** | *Go* **straight on** *to the roundabout.* | **sit up/stand up straight** (=with your back straight, not curved)
2 immediately, without stopping to do something first: **+to/back/past etc** *Why didn't you go* **straight** *to the police?* | *Come* **straight back.** | **+after** *There's a meeting straight after lunch.*
3 straight away also **straightaway** if you do something straight away, you do it immediately or without delay: *I phoned the hospital straight away.*
4 tell sb straight/straight out to tell someone something in an honest and direct way: *I told him straight that I wouldn't do it.*
5 go straight to stop being a criminal
6 not see/think straight to be unable to see or think clearly: *It was so noisy I couldn't think straight.*

straighten /'streɪtn/ also **straighten out** *v* **1** [I,T] to become straight, or to make something straight: *He straightened his tie.* | *The road straightened out.*
2 also **straighten up** [T] *especially AmE* to make something tidy: *Straighten your room!*
straighten sth ⇔ **out** *phr v* to deal with a problem or difficult situation: *I'll see if I can straighten things out.*

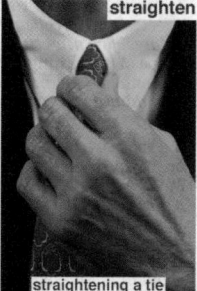
straighten

straightening a tie

straighten up *phr v* to stand with your back straight

straightforward /ˌstreɪtˈfɔːwəd◂ $ -ˈfɔːrwərd◂/ *adj* **1** simple to do or easy to understand: *The questions seemed* **straightforward.** **2** honest and not hiding what you think: *Is he being straightforward?*

straightjacket /'streɪtˌdʒækɪt/ *n* another spelling of **STRAITJACKET**

strain¹ /streɪn/ *n* **1** [C,U] the pressure or worry that is caused by a difficult situation, job, or problem: **the strain of sth** *He couldn't cope with the strain of being a teacher.* | **under (a) strain** *She's been under a lot of strain recently.* | **put a strain on sb/sth** (=cause them to be in a difficult situation) *The flu epidemic has put a huge strain on the health service.* | **break/crack/collapse etc under the strain** *Their relationship was cracking under the strain.* **2** [U] when something is pulled or stretched very tightly or has to carry a lot of weight: **under the strain** (=because of the strain) *The rope snapped under the strain.* **3** [C,U] an injury caused by using part of your body too much: *eye strain* **4** [C] a type of plant, animal, or disease: **+of** *a new strain of the virus*

strain² *v* **1** [T] to injure part of your body by stretching it too much: *Kevin* **strained a muscle** *in his neck.* **2** [I,T] to try very hard to do something: **strain to do sth** *She moved closer, straining to hear what they said.* **3** [T] to separate solid things from a liquid by pouring the mixture through a strainer → see picture on page A4 **4** [T] to make a situation or relationship more difficult: *It's an issue that's* **straining relations** *between the countries.*

strained /streɪnd/ *adj* **1** not relaxed or friendly: *a strained conversation* **2** worried and tired: *Alex looks strained.*

strainer /'streɪnə $ -ər/ *n* [C] a kitchen tool used for separating solid food from liquid

strait /streɪt/ *n* [C usually plural] **1** a narrow area of sea that joins two larger areas of sea: *the Straits of Gibraltar* **2 be in dire straits** to be in a very difficult situation

straitjacket, straightjacket /'streɪtˌdʒækɪt/ *n* [C] a special piece of clothing that is used to prevent someone who is violent from moving their arms

strand /strænd/ *n* [C] **1** a single thin piece of thread, hair, wire etc **2** one part of a story, problem, idea etc

stranded /'strændɪd/ *adj* unable to get away from a place: *Bad weather* **left** *travellers* **stranded.**

strange /streɪndʒ/ *adj*
1 unusual or surprising, in a way that is difficult to understand or explain: *I had a strange dream last night.* | *What's that strange noise?* | *It's strange that Brad isn't here yet.* | **+about** *There was something strange about him.* | *That's strange – I thought I left my keys on the table.*

THESAURUS

funny/odd – a little strange in a way that makes you slightly worried: *a funny noise downstairs*
peculiar – strange in a slightly unpleasant way: *a peculiar taste*
mysterious – strange in a way that is hard to explain or understand: *his mysterious disappearance*
weird – strange and different from what you

are used to: *a weird experience* | *weird clothes*
eccentric – an eccentric person is strange and
different in a way that people think is slightly
amusing: *an eccentric old man*

2 not familiar or known to you: *I was alone in a
strange country.* | *Never speak to strange men.*
—**strangely** *adv*: *She was looking at me very
strangely.* —**strangeness** *n* [U]

stranger /'streɪndʒə $ -ər/ *n* [C]
1 someone you do not know: *Don't get in a car
with a stranger.* | **perfect/complete/total
stranger** (=used to emphasize that you do not
know them) *I didn't want to kiss a complete
stranger.*
2 someone in a new and unfamiliar place: +**to**
He was a stranger to New York.

strangle /'stræŋgəl/ *v* [T] to kill someone by
pressing their throat with your hands, a rope etc

stranglehold /'stræŋgəlhəʊld $ -hoʊld/ *n* [C]
complete control over a situation, organization
etc: +**on** *The government had a stranglehold on
the media.*

strap[1] /stræp/ *n* [C] a strong band of cloth or
leather used to keep something in position or to
carry something: *a watch strap* | *She slipped
the strap of her bag over her shoulder.* → see
picture at **WATCH**[2]

strap[2] *v* [T] **strapped, strapping** to fasten something in place using a strap: *Make sure your
backpack is strapped on tightly.* | **be strapped in**
(=have a belt fastened around you in a car) *Are
the kids strapped in?*

strapped /stræpt/ *adj* **be strapped (for cash)**
informal to have very little money to spend

strata /'strɑːtə $ 'streɪtə/ *n* the plural of STRA-
TUM

stratagem /'strætədʒəm/ *n* [C] *formal* a plan
or idea for defeating an enemy or gaining an
advantage

strategic /strə'tiːdʒɪk/ *adj* **1** done as part of a
plan, especially in business, politics, or war: *a
strategic decision to sell off part of the
company* **2** relating to fighting wars: *strategic
weapons* (=powerful weapons for attacking
other countries from your own) **3** a strategic
position is good for a particular purpose: *He
placed himself in a strategic position next to the
door.* —**strategically** /-kli/ *adv*

strategy /'strætⁱdʒi/ *n* plural **strategies 1** [C] a
plan used to achieve something: **business/
political etc strategy** *the long-term economic
strategy* → see box at **PLAN 2** [U] the skill of
making plans so that you are successful, especially in war: *an expert in military strategy*
—**strategist** *n* [C]

stratum /'strɑːtəm $ 'streɪ-/ *n* [C] plural **strata**
/-tə/ **1** *technical* a layer of rock or soil **2** *formal* a social class in society

straw /strɔː $ strɒː/ *n*
1 [C,U] the dried stems of plants such as wheat,
used for animals to sleep on or to make things
such as baskets (➙ **hay**]: *a straw hat*
2 [C] a thin tube of plastic or paper, used for
sucking a drink from a bottle or cup
3 the last/final straw the last in a series of
problems or bad events that finally makes you
give up or become angry

strawberry /'strɔːbəri $ 'strɒːberi, -bəri/ *n* [C]
plural **strawberries** a small red juicy fruit that
grows on plants near the ground: *strawberries
and cream* → see picture at **FRUIT**

stray[1] /streɪ/ *v* [I] to move away from the safe
place where you should be: *Some of the kids had
strayed into the woods.*

stray[2] *adj* **1** a stray animal is lost or has no
home: *a stray dog* **2** stray things have become
separated from others of the same kind: *a few
stray hairs*

stray[3] *n* [C] an animal that is lost or has no
home

streak[1] /striːk/ *n* [C] **1** a thin coloured line or
mark: **grey/blond etc streak** *a few grey streaks
in her hair* **2** a part of someone's character
that is surprising, especially because it seems a
little bad: **stubborn/mean/nasty etc streak**
Richard has a wild streak in him. **3 a winning/
losing streak** a period when you are always
successful or unsuccessful: *Our team was on a
winning streak.*

streak[2] *v* **1** [I] to move or run very quickly: *A
fighter jet streaked across the sky.* **2 be
streaked with sth** to be covered with thin lines
of a colour, liquid etc: *Marcia's face was streaked
with sweat.*

stream[1] /striːm/ *n* [C]
1 a very small river: *a mountain stream* → see
picture at **RIVER**
2 a long series of people, vehicles, ideas etc
coming continuously or one after another: +**of**
stream of traffic | *the stream of refugees cross-
ing the border* | **endless/constant/steady etc
stream** *an endless stream of questions*
3 a flow of liquid, gas, smoke etc: +**of** *A stream
of cold air rushed in.*

stream[2] *v* [I] to move or flow continuously in
one direction, especially in large amounts
[= **pour**]: +**out/past/through etc** | *Tears were
streaming down his cheeks.* | *People streamed
through the gates.*

streamer /'striːmə $ -ər/ *n* [C] a long piece of
coloured paper used to decorate a building for a
special occasion

streamline /'striːmlaɪn/ *v* [T] **1** to organize
something so that it happens more quickly and
effectively: *The college has streamlined entry pro-
cedures for new students.* **2** to improve the
shape of something so that it moves more easily
through the air or water —**streamlined** *adj*: *a
streamlined sports car*

street /striːt/ *n* [C]
1 a road in a town or city with houses and shops
on it: *24, West Street* | **on a street** *We live on
Main Street.* | **up/down/along the street** *We
walked down the street.* | **across the street** *They
live just across the street.* | *a street map* → see
box at **ROAD**
2 the streets the busy part of a city: *She
shouldn't be out walking the streets after
dark.* | *young people who live on the streets*
(=have no home and sleep outside)
3 right up your street *BrE informal* exactly
right for you
4 streets ahead *BrE informal* much better than
other people or things: *He's streets ahead of the
other children.*
→ **HIGH STREET**

streetcar /'striːtkɑː $ -kɑːr/ *n* [C] *AmE* an electric bus that goes along metal tracks in the road [= **tram** *BrE*]

'street light, streetlight /'striːtlaɪt/ also **'street lamp** *n* [C] a light on a long pole in a street

streetwise /'striːtwaɪz/ *adj* able to deal with the situations and people that you meet in a big city: *streetwise kids*

strength /streŋθ, strenθ/ *n*

1 [U] physical power and energy [≠ **weakness**]: *a job which requires a lot of strength* | *They pushed with all their strength.* | **have the strength to do sth** *I didn't have the strength to lift it.*
2 [U] determination to do something difficult: **have the strength to do sth** *She didn't have the strength to leave him.* | **strength of mind/ character** *It took great strength of character to carry on.*
3 [U] how strong a feeling or belief is: *We hadn't realized the **strength of feeling** among parents about this issue.*
4 [U] how strong or powerful something is: *US military strength* | **+of** *the strength of the economy*
5 [U] the value of a country's CURRENCY (=the money used there) compared to other currencies: **+of** *the strength of the euro against the pound*
6 [C] your strengths are the good things about you, or the things you are good at: *We have all got **strengths and weaknesses**.*
7 [C,U] how strong a liquid is: *extra-strength beers*
8 go from strength to strength to become more and more successful: *The company has gone from strength to strength.*
9 on the strength of sth because of information or advice that you have
10 at full strength/below strength with all the people that you need, or with fewer people than you need: *The French team is at full strength.*

strengthen /'streŋθən, 'strenθən/ *v* [I,T] to make something stronger, or to become stronger: *an exercise to strengthen your arms* | *We may need to strengthen the bridge.* | *government measures to strengthen the economy* | *The euro has strengthened against the dollar.*

strenuous /'strenjuəs/ *adj* using a lot of effort: *He is supposed to avoid **strenuous exercise**.* | *He's been making a **strenuous effort** to lose weight.*

stress[1] /stres/ *n*

1 [C,U] a strong feeling of worry that prevents you from relaxing [➡ **strain**]: *a headache caused by stress* | *ways of coping with stress at work* | **under stress** *I've been under a lot of stress lately.* | *the **stresses and strains** of a doctor's life* | *a **stress-related** illness* (=one caused by stress)
2 [U] special importance that is given to something [= **emphasis**]: **lay/put stress on sth** *He lays particular stress on discipline in schools.*
3 [C,U] physical force or pressure on something: *Some sports **put a lot of stress on** joints.*
4 [C,U] the stress on a word is the way you say one part more loudly than the rest: *The stress is on the last syllable.*

stress[2] *v* [T] **1** to say that something is very important: *She **stressed the need for** more money for the project.* | **+that** *He stressed that the plan must be kept secret.* **2** to say one word or part of a word more loudly than others

stressed /strest/ also **,stressed 'out** *adj* [not before noun] so worried and tired that you cannot relax: *I was feeling really stressed out.* ➔ see box at **WORRIED**

stressful /'stresfəl/ *adj* a stressful job or situation makes you feel very worried and unable to relax

stretch[1] /stretʃ/ *v*

1 [I,T] to make something bigger or looser by pulling it, or to become bigger or looser in this way: *Don't stretch my jumper!* | *Stretch the canvas so that it covers the whole frame.* | *Trainers tend to stretch when you wear them.* ➔ see picture on page A11
2 [I,T] to push your arms, legs, or another part of your body as far as they can go: *He sat up in bed and stretched.* | *an exercise to stretch the leg muscles* | **+over/across/out/up** *She stretched over and picked up the phone.* ➔ see box at **EXERCISE**
3 [I] to cover a large area of land: **+away/to** *The lake stretched away into the distance.*
4 [I] to continue for a long period of time: **+into/to** *The project will probably stretch into next year.*
5 [T] to give someone difficult work so that they have to use all their intelligence and ability to do it: *It's important to stretch students.*
6 stretch your legs *informal* to go for a walk
7 be stretched (to the limit) not to have enough money, time etc: *We're really stretched for money at the moment.*

stretch[2] *n* [C] **1** an area of land or water: **+of** *a beautiful stretch of coastline* | *a dangerous stretch of road* **2** a continuous period of time: **+of** *a long stretch of dry weather* | *We worked for ten hours **at a stretch** (=without stopping).* **3** an action in which you stretch part of your body: *I stood up and **had a stretch**.* | *I usually do a few stretches before the game.* **4 (not) by any stretch (of the imagination)** *spoken* used to say that something is definitely not true: *She isn't fat, not by any stretch of the imagination.*

stretcher /'stretʃə $ -ər/ *n* [C] a type of bed on which you carry someone who is injured

stretchy /'stretʃi/ *adj* material that is stretchy will stretch when you pull it

strew /struː/ *v* [T] past participle **strewn** /struːn/ or **strewed** to drop a lot of things over an area in an untidy way: **be strewn over/ across sth** *Papers were strewn all over the floor.* | **be strewn with sth** *The streets were strewn with rubbish.*

stricken /'strɪkən/ *adj* *formal* suffering from something very badly: **+with/by** *Half the class were stricken with flu.* | *a country stricken by economic problems* ➔ **POVERTY-STRICKEN**

strict /strɪkt/ *adj*

1 a strict person makes sure that people always obey rules and behave well [≠ **lenient**]: *a strict teacher* | **+with** *She's very strict with her children.*
2 a strict rule or order must be obeyed completely: *I have **strict instructions** not to let any-*

S

one leave. | He's under **strict orders** to be home before dark.

3 always behaving according to a set of rules or religious beliefs: *a strict Muslim* | *a strict vegetarian*

4 [only before noun] the strict meaning of a word is its exact meaning

strictly /ˈstrɪktli/ *adv* **1 strictly prohibited/ forbidden** definitely not allowed: *Smoking is strictly forbidden.* **2** in a strict way: *The children were brought up very strictly.* **3** exactly and correctly: *That's **not strictly true**.* | **strictly speaking** (=used when you are explaining something in a very exact way) *Strictly speaking, spiders are not insects.* **4** only for one purpose or one person: *Our meeting was strictly for business.*

stride¹ /straɪd/ *v* [I] past tense **strode** /strəʊd $ stroʊd/ past participle **stridden** /ˈstrɪdn/ to walk with quick long steps: **+into/across/out of etc** *He strode across the room.* → see box at **WALK**

stride² *n* [C] **1** a long step that you take when you are walking: *He was getting further away from me with every stride.* **2 make great strides** to make a lot of progress: *We have made great strides in reducing poverty.* **3 get into your stride** *BrE* **hit your stride** *AmE* to start doing something confidently and well **4 take sth in your stride** *BrE* **take sth in stride** *AmE* to deal with a situation calmly without becoming annoyed or upset

strident /ˈstraɪdənt/ *adj* **1** expressing opinions in a strong and determined way: *a strident critic of the reforms* **2** a strident voice is loud and unpleasant

strife /straɪf/ *n* [U] *formal* trouble or disagreement between people

strike¹ /straɪk/ *v* past tense and past participle **struck** /strʌk/

1 [T] to hit someone or something: *The car struck a tree.* | *She struck him across the face.* | *He was struck on the head by a falling rock.* | *The church tower was **struck by lightning**.*
2 [T] if a thought strikes you, you think of it: *The first thing that struck me was how few people were there.* | **it strikes sb that** *It suddenly struck me that we might lose the company.* | **be struck by sth** *I was struck by the friendliness of the local people.*
3 [T] the way that something strikes you is the way it seems to you: **strike sb as (being) sth** *His behaviour struck me as odd.* | *He strikes me as being very intelligent.*
4 [I] if people strike, they stop working for a period of time because they want better pay or working conditions: *Teachers will vote today on whether to strike.* | **+for** *Nurses are striking for a shorter working week.*
5 [I] to attack someone: *The police fear that the killer will strike again.*
6 [I,T] if something bad strikes, it happens suddenly: *Later that evening **disaster struck**.* | *The hurricane struck the town just after dark.*
7 strike a balance to give the right amount of importance to two different things: *It's never easy to strike a balance between work and family.*
8 strike a bargain/deal if two people strike a deal, they each promise to do something for the

other: *The company has struck a deal with the union.*
9 strike a match to make a match start burning
10 strike oil/gold etc to discover oil, gold etc under the ground
11 [I,T] if a clock strikes, its bell makes a number of sounds to show the time: **strike two/ three/four etc** *The clock struck four.*
12 be within striking distance (of sth) to be close enough to a place to reach it easily

strike back *phr v* to attack someone after they have attacked you

strike out *phr v* **1 strike sth ⇔ out** to draw a line through part of a piece of writing **2 strike out for sth** to try to reach a place: *They struck out for the coast.* **3 strike out on your own** to start doing something new without other people's help **4** in the game of BASEBALL, to not hit the ball three times so that you are not allowed to continue, or to make someone do this: **strike sb ⇔ out** *The first batter was struck out.*

strike up *phr v* **strike up a conversation/ friendship** to begin a conversation, friendship etc with someone

strike² *n* [C]

1 when a group of workers stop working for a period of time because they want better pay or better working conditions: *Bus drivers are threatening to **go on strike**.* | *Workers at the factory have **been out on strike** for two months.* | **+over** *a strike over pay*
2 a military attack: **+on/against** *an air strike against military targets*
3 in the game of BASEBALL, an attempt to hit the ball that fails

→ GENERAL STRIKE, HUNGER STRIKE

striker /ˈstraɪkə $ -ər/ *n* [C] **1** someone who has stopped working because they want better pay or working conditions **2** a football player whose main job is to try to get GOALS

striking /ˈstraɪkɪŋ/ *adj* **1** unusual and noticeable: *There's a striking similarity between the two girls.* **2** very attractive: *a very striking woman*

string¹ /strɪŋ/ *n*

1 [C,U] a strong thread that you use for tying or fastening things [➜ rope]: *The package was tied up with string.* | *a piece of string* | *a ball of string*
2 [C] a number of similar things that happen one after the other [= series]: **+of** *She's had a string of hit singles.*
3 [C] a set of things that are joined together on a thread: *a string of beads* | *a string of onions*
4 a) [C] the strings on a musical instrument are the pieces of wire that produce sound **b) the strings** [plural] the musicians in a group who play musical instruments with strings → see box at ORCHESTRA
5 (with) no strings attached with no special conditions or limits: *The policy offers a high rate of interest with no strings attached.*
→ **pull strings** at PULL¹

string² *v* [T] past tense and past participle **strung** /strʌŋ/ to hang things up in a line, using string: *Dad was busy stringing up the Christmas lights.*

string sb along *phr v informal* to keep promising that you will do something for someone when you do not intend to do it: *I think he's just stringing you along.*

string sth ⇔ **out** *phr v* to do something very slowly so that it takes longer than it should

string sth ⇔ **together** *phr v* **string words/a sentence together** to form words into a sentence so that people can understand it: *He was so drunk he could hardly string a sentence together.*

‚stringed 'instrument *n* [C] a musical instrument that produces sound from strings, for example a VIOLIN

stringent /'strɪndʒənt/ *adj* stringent rules or laws are very strict and must be obeyed: *stringent new laws on gun ownership*

strip¹ /strɪp/ *v* **stripped, stripping 1** also **strip off** [I,T] to take off your clothes, or take someone else's clothes off: *I stripped and got into the shower.* | *He was stripped and beaten.* | *She stripped off her sweater.* | *The men were all stripped to the waist.* **2** also **strip off** [T] to remove something that is covering the surface of something else: *I've stripped the old paint off the door.* | *We'll need to strip off the old wallpaper first.* **3 strip sb of sth** to take property or rights away from someone: *If the drugs test proves positive, he could be stripped of his title.*

strip² *n* **1** [C] a long narrow piece of something: *Tear the paper into one-inch strips.* | **+of** *a narrow strip of land* **2** [singular] when someone takes their clothes off to entertain other people: *She did a strip.* | *a strip show*

stripe /straɪp/ *n* [C] a narrow line of colour: *a shirt with blue and white stripes*

striped /straɪpt/ *adj* something that is striped has a pattern of stripes on it: *a red and white striped dress* → see picture at **PATTERN**

stripey /'straɪpi/ *adj* STRIPY

stripper /'strɪpə $ -ər/ *n* [C] someone who is paid to take off their clothes to entertain other people

striptease /'strɪptiːz, ‚strɪp'tiːz/ *n* [C,U] a performance in which someone takes off their clothes

stripy, stripey /'straɪpi/ *adj* something that is stripy has a pattern of stripes on it: *stripy socks*

strive /straɪv/ *v* [I] past tense **strove** /strəʊv $ stroʊv/ past participle **striven** /'strɪvən/ *formal* to try very hard to do something: **+for** *Don't always strive for perfection.* | *We are always striving to improve our efficiency.*

strode /strəʊd $ stroʊd/ *v* the past tense of STRIDE

stroke¹ /strəʊk $ stroʊk/ *n* **1** [C] an illness in which your brain becomes damaged and you are unable to move part of your body: *He had a stroke last year.* **2** [C,U] a movement with your arms when you are swimming, often used after another noun to talk about a particular way of swimming: *backstroke* | *breaststroke* **3** [C] a way of hitting the ball in a game such as tennis: *He played some beautiful strokes.* **4** [C] a single movement of a pen or brush when you are writing or drawing **5 at a stroke/at one stroke** with one single sudden action: *This would solve the problem at one stroke.* **6 a stroke of luck** something lucky that happens to you: *Finding the key was a real stroke of luck.* **7 not do a stroke (of work)** *informal* to not do any work at all

stroke² *v* [T] to move your hand gently over something: *He was stroking the cat.* | *She stroked his face gently.* → see picture on page A10

stroll /strəʊl $ stroʊl/ *v* [I] to walk in a slow relaxed way: **+along/down/across etc** *We strolled along the beach.* → see box at **WALK** —**stroll** *n* [C]

stroller /'strəʊlə $ 'stroʊlər/ *n* [C] *AmE* a chair on wheels in which a small child can be pushed along [= **buggy** *BrE*] → see box at **BABY**

strong /strɒŋ $ strɔːŋ/ *adj*

1 someone who is strong has big muscles and can lift heavy things, and is not weak or ill [➡ **strength**]: *a strong man* | **strong hands/arms/ muscles etc**

2 something that is strong cannot be broken or damaged easily: *a strong rope* | *Is that branch strong enough to hold your weight?*

3 powerful and determined: *a strong leader* | *We will take strong action against terrorists.*

4 strong feelings and beliefs are ones that you feel or believe a lot: *a strong belief in God* | *a strong desire for power*

5 something that is strong is good, or has good qualities: *a strong economy* | *They have a very strong relationship.* | *There's strong evidence to suggest he was innocent.* | *There is now a strong case for a change in the law.*

6 someone who is strong can deal with problems without becoming too upset or worried: *You have to be strong to cope with the death of a child.*

7 a strong taste or smell is one that you notice easily: *a strong smell of onions*

8 a strong CURRENCY (=the money used in a country) is worth a lot compared to others: *The dollar is quite strong at the moment.*

9 a strong drink contains a lot of alcohol, coffee, or tea

10 a strong wind, current, or sun has a lot of force or power

11 strong language rude words that some people may find offensive

12 strong point a good quality that someone has, or something that they can do well: *Science is not my strong point.*

13 500/10,000 etc strong having 500, 10,000 etc people: *The crowd was over 100,000 strong.*

14 be still going strong to still be working or living successfully: *a pop group that is still going strong*

stronghold /'strɒŋhəʊld $ 'strɔːŋhoʊld/ *n* [C] **1** an area where there is a lot of support for a particular idea or political party: *a Conservative stronghold* **2** an area that is strongly defended: *a rebel stronghold*

strongly /'strɒŋli $ 'strɔːŋ-/ *adv* **1** if you feel or believe something strongly, you think it is important or care a lot about it: *He is strongly in favour of capital punishment.* **2** tasting or smelling of something a lot: *The house smelled strongly of gas.* **3** if you say something strongly, you say it in a way that tries to persuade someone else: **strongly suggest/advise/ recommend** *I strongly advise you to see a doctor.*

‚strong-'willed *adj* determined to do what you want, even though other people tell you not to do it

stroppy /'strɒpi $ 'strɑːpi/ *adj BrE informal* bad-tempered or easily annoyed

S

strove /strəʊv $ stroʊv/ v the past tense of STRIVE

struck /strʌk/ v the past tense of STRIKE

structural /ˈstrʌktʃərəl/ adj relating to the structure of something: *structural damage*

structure[1] /ˈstrʌktʃə $ -ər/ n

1 [C,U] the way in which the parts of something are put together or organized: +**of** *the structure of society* | *the structure of the company* | *the structure of an atom*
2 [C] something that has been built: *a large wooden structure*

structure[2] v [T] to arrange something in a clear organized way [= organize]: *Students learn how to structure their essays.*

struggle[1] /ˈstrʌɡəl/ v [I] **1** to try very hard to achieve something difficult: **struggle to do sth** *parents who struggle to bring up children on a low income* | +**with** *I really struggled with that homework.* **2** to fight someone who is attacking or holding you: +**with** *She struggled with her attacker.* **3** to move somewhere with a lot of difficulty: +**up/down/along etc** *He struggled up the stairs with the luggage.*
  struggle on phr v to continue doing something, even though it is difficult

struggle[2] n [C] **1** when someone tries hard for a long time to achieve something: +**for** *their struggle for survival* **2** a fight between two people

strum /strʌm/ v [I,T] **strummed, strumming** to play an instrument such as a GUITAR by moving your fingers across the strings

strung /strʌŋ/ v the past tense and past participle of STRING

strut[1] /strʌt/ v [I] **strutted, strutting** to walk in a proud and annoying way

strut[2] n [C] a long piece of metal or wood that supports something

stub[1] /stʌb/ n [C] the part of a cigarette that is left after the rest has been used

stub[2] v **stubbed, stubbing** **stub your toe** to hurt your toe by hitting it against something
  stub sth ⇔ **out** phr v to stop a cigarette burning by pressing it against something

stubble /ˈstʌbəl/ n [U] **1** the very short hairs on a man's face when he has not SHAVED → see picture at CLEAN-SHAVEN **2** short pieces of corn or wheat that are left in a field after it has been cut —**stubbly** adj: *his stubbly chin*

stubborn /ˈstʌbən $ -ərn/ adj refusing to change your mind even when other people criticize you or try to persuade you: *Steve can be very stubborn sometimes.*
—**stubbornly** adv: *He stubbornly refused to join in.* —**stubbornness** n [U]

stubby /ˈstʌbi/ adj short and thick or fat: *stubby fingers*

stuck[1] /stʌk/ v the past tense and past participle of STICK

stuck[2] adj [not before noun] **1** if something is stuck, it cannot move: *I tried to open the window but it was stuck.* | *The car got stuck in the mud.* **2** if you are stuck, you cannot get away from a boring or unpleasant situation: +**at/in** *I was stuck at home with a cold.* **3** informal if you are stuck, you cannot continue with something because it is too difficult: *Can you help me with this? I'm stuck.* **4 be stuck with sth** informal to have to have something that you do not want: *It's an awful building but we're stuck with it.*

stud /stʌd/ n **1** [C] a small round piece of metal that is stuck into the surface of something as a decoration: *a leather jacket with silver studs* **2** [C] a horse that is used for breeding, or a place where these horses are kept **3** [C] a small round EARRING

studded /ˈstʌdɪd/ adj decorated with a lot of studs or jewels: *a diamond-studded watch* → STAR-STUDDED

student /ˈstjuːdənt $ ˈstuː-/ n [C] someone who studies at a school or university [➞ **pupil**]: *a first year student at London University* | **law/medical/engineering etc student** → see box at UNIVERSITY

studio /ˈstjuːdiəʊ $ ˈstuːdioʊ/ n [C] plural **studios 1** a room where a painter or photographer works: *an art studio* **2** a room where television and radio programmes are made **3** a film company, or the place where films are made: *the big Hollywood studios*

studious /ˈstjuːdiəs $ ˈstuː-/ adj someone who is studious spends a lot of time reading and studying: *a quiet, studious young man*

studiously /ˈstjuːdiəsli $ ˈstuː-/ adv very carefully

study[1] /ˈstʌdi/ n plural **studies**

1 [C] a piece of work that someone does to find out more about something: *They are carrying out a study of the kinds of food that children eat.* | +**of** *a study of teenagers' language*
2 [U] when you spend time learning: *a period of study*
3 studies [plural] **a)** the subjects that you study: *a degree in Business Studies* **b)** the work you do as a student: *He went on to continue his studies at Harvard.*
4 [C] a room in your house where you read, write, or study [➞ **office**]
→ CASE STUDY

study[2] v **studied, studying, studies**

1 [I,T] to spend time reading, going to classes etc in order to learn about a subject: *Her son's at university studying medicine.* | **study to be sth** *She's studying to be a lawyer.* → see box at SCHOOL → and UNIVERSITY
2 [T] to look at something carefully to find out more about it: *He studied the document carefully.* | **study how/when/why etc** *a way of studying how genes affect development*

stuff[1] /stʌf/ n [U] informal

1 a substance or material of any sort: *What's that blue stuff on the floor?* | *Where's all the camping stuff?*
2 information, ideas, or activities of any sort: *He taught us all kinds of stuff.* | *I've got a lot of stuff to do this weekend.* | *He does skiing and stuff like that.*
3 sb's stuff the things that belong to someone [= **things** BrE]: *I need a place to store my stuff for a while.* → see box at OWN
4 know your stuff to know a lot about a subject: *He really knows his stuff.*

stuff[2] v [T] **1** to push things into a small space [= **shovel**]: **stuff sth in/into sth** *She stuffed some clothes in a bag and left.* **2** to fill something until it is full: **be stuffed with sth** *a pillow* stuffed with feathers | boxes **stuffed full** of papers **3 stuff yourself** informal to eat a lot of food: The kids have been stuffing themselves all afternoon. **4** to fill a chicken, vegetable etc with a mixture of food before cooking it: stuffed tomatoes **5** to fill the skin of a dead animal in order to make the animal look still alive: a stuffed owl

stuffing /'stʌfɪŋ/ n [U] **1** a mixture of food that you put inside a chicken etc before you cook it: lemon and herb stuffing **2** soft material that is used to fill a piece of furniture, a toy, or a CUSHION

stuffy /'stʌfi/ adj **1** a room or building that is stuffy does not have enough fresh air in it **2** disapproving people who are stuffy are formal and old-fashioned: Rob's family is really stuffy.

stumble /'stʌmbəl/ v [I] **1** to almost fall while you are walking: **+over/on** Vic stumbled over the step as he came in. → see box at FALL **2** to stop or make a mistake when you are speaking: **+over** I hope I don't stumble over any of the long words.

stumble on/across sb/sth phr v to find something or someone by chance: While clearing out a cupboard, she stumbled across one of her old diaries.

'stumbling ,block n [C] a problem that stops you achieving something: **+to** The question of disarmament is still the main stumbling block to peace.

stump[1] /stʌmp/ n [C] the part of something that is left when the rest has been cut off: an old tree stump

stump[2] v **1** [T] if you are stumped by a question or problem, you are unable to find an answer to it: The police are stumped by this case. **2** [I] to walk with very firm heavy steps: **+off/out etc** He nodded and stumped off.

stump up (sth) phr v BrE informal to pay money, especially when you do not want to: We stumped up eight pounds each.

stun /stʌn/ v [T] **stunned, stunning 1** to surprise or shock someone very much: Everyone was stunned by Betty's answer. **2** to make someone unconscious for a short time

stung /stʌŋ/ v the past tense and past participle of STING

stunk /stʌŋk/ v the past participle of STINK

stunning /'stʌnɪŋ/ adj **1** extremely beautiful: You look stunning in that dress. → see box at ATTRACTIVE **2** very surprising or shocking: stunning news → see box at SURPRISING

stunt[1] /stʌnt/ n [C] **1** something dangerous that a person does to entertain people, especially in a film: an actor who does all his own stunts **2** something that is done to get people's attention: a **publicity stunt**

stunt[2] v [T] to stop something or someone from growing or developing properly: Lack of sunlight will stunt the plant's growth.

'stunt man n [C] a man who is employed to do the dangerous things in a film, instead of an actor

stupefied /'stjuːpɪfaɪd $ 'stuː-/ adj so surprised or tired that you cannot think clearly —**stupefy** v [T] —**stupefying** adj

stupendous /stjuː'pendəs $ stuː-/ adj extremely large or impressive: a stupendous achievement

stupid /'stjuːpɪd $ 'stuː-/ adj

1 not very clever or intelligent [➡ **silly**]: Don't be so stupid! | He understands – he's not stupid. | **It was stupid of me** to lose my temper. | a stupid mistake

2 [only before noun] spoken used to talk about someone or something that annoys you: I can't get this stupid door open! | What is that stupid idiot doing?

—**stupidly** adv —**stupidity** /stjuː'pɪdɪti $ stuː-/ n [C,U]

stupor /'stjuːpə $ 'stuːpər/ n [C,U] when you are almost unconscious and cannot think clearly, especially because you have drunk too much alcohol: a drunken stupor

sturdy /'stɜːdi $ 'stɜːr-/ adj strong and not likely to break or be hurt: sturdy shoes | sturdy legs —**sturdily** adv

stutter /'stʌtə $ -ər/ v [I,T] to repeat the first sound of a word when you speak: 'I'm D-d-david,' he stuttered. —**stutter** n [singular]

sty /staɪ/ n [C] plural **sties 1** a place where pigs are kept [= **pigsty**] **2** also **stye** an infection at the side of your eye

style[1] /staɪl/ n

1 [C] the way in which a person or group of people typically does something: He's trying to copy Picasso's style of painting. | architecture in the Gothic style | The dinner will be served buffet style.

2 [C] the particular way in which someone usually behaves or works: **+of** Children have different styles of learning. | his own personal style of management

3 a) [C] a particular design or fashion for something such as clothes, hair, or furniture: Shoes are available in several styles. | His hair was cut in a very strange style. **b)** [U] the quality of being fashionable: **in/out of style** Long skirts are back in style.

4 [U] a quality that people admire or think is attractive: You may not like him, but you have to admit he **has style**.

style[2] v [T] to design clothing, furniture, or the shape of someone's hair in a particular way

stylish /'staɪlɪʃ/ adj attractive and fashionable: stylish clothes | a very stylish woman —**stylishly** adv

stylistic /staɪ'lɪstɪk/ adj relating to the style of a piece of writing, music, or art: I've made a few stylistic changes to your report.

stylized also **-ised** BrE /'staɪlaɪzd/ adj done in a style that does not look natural or like real life: a very stylized painting

Styrofoam /'staɪrəfəʊm $ 'staɪrəfoʊm/ n [U] AmE trademark a soft light plastic material, used especially to make containers [= **polystyrene** BrE]

suave /swɑːv/ adj polite, attractive, and confident, especially in a way that is not sincere

sub /sʌb/ n [C] **1** a SUBMARINE **2** a SUBSTITUTE **3** AmE a long thin sandwich

sub- /sʌb/ prefix **1** under or below: subzero temperatures **2** smaller or less important: a subcommittee

subconscious[1] /sʌb'kɒnʃəs $ -'kɑːn-/ adj subconscious feelings affect your behaviour

S

although you do not realize that they exist: *her subconscious fear of failure* —**subconsciously** *adv*

subconscious[2] *n* [singular] the part of your mind that can affect the way you behave without you realizing it

subcontinent /ˌsʌbˈkɒntɪnənt $ -ˈkɑːn-/ *n* [C] a large area of land that is part of a CONTINENT: *the Indian subcontinent*

subcontract /ˌsʌbkənˈtrækt $ -ˈkɑːntrækt/ *v* [T] if a company subcontracts work, they pay other people to do part of the work for them: *Some of the work will be subcontracted to another company.* —**subcontractor** *n* [C] —**subcontract** /sʌbˈkɒntrækt $ -ˈkɑːn-/ *n* [C]

subculture /ˈsʌbˌkʌltʃə $ -ər/ *n* [C] a particular group of people within a society who have their own beliefs and ways of behaving

subdivide /ˌsʌbdɪˈvaɪd/ *v* [I,T] to divide something into smaller parts —**subdivision** /-ˈvɪʒən/ *n* [C,U]

subdue /səbˈdjuː $ -ˈduː/ *v* [T] to stop someone from behaving violently, especially by using force: *Police managed to subdue the angry crowd.*

subdued /səbˈdjuːd $ -ˈduːd/ *adj* **1** someone who is subdued is quiet because they are sad or worried: *her sad face and subdued manner* **2** not as bright or loud as usual: *subdued lighting* | *She spoke in a subdued voice.* → see box at QUIET

subject[1] /ˈsʌbdʒɪkt/ *n* [C]
1 something that you are talking or writing about: +**of** *I don't want to talk about the subject of death.* | **on/about a subject** *She's written several books on this subject.* | *Stop trying to change the subject* (=start talking about something different)! | *Can we just drop the subject* (=stop talking about something) *now, please.*
2 something that you study at a school or university: *'What's your favourite subject?' 'Science.'* → see box at SCHOOL → and UNIVERSITY
3 the word that usually comes before the verb in a sentence and shows who is doing the action of the verb. In the sentence 'Jean loves cats', 'Jean' is the subject. [➔ object]
4 a person or animal that is used in a test or EXPERIMENT
5 someone who is from a country that has a king or queen: *a British subject*

subject[2] *adj* **subject to sth a)** likely to be affected by something: *All prices are subject to change.* **b)** only happening if something else happens: *We're going to build a garage, subject to planning permission.*

subject[3] /səbˈdʒekt/ *v*
subject sb/sth to sth *phr v* to make someone or something experience something unpleasant: *The victim was subjected to a terrifying ordeal.*

subjective /səbˈdʒektɪv/ *adj* influenced by your own opinions and feelings rather than facts [≠ **objective**]: *Try not to be too subjective when you write about the film.* —**subjectively** *adv*

'subject ˌmatter *n* [U] the subject that is being discussed

subjugate /ˈsʌbdʒʊɡeɪt/ *v* [T] *formal* to force a person or group to obey you —**subjugation** /ˌsʌbdʒʊˈɡeɪʃən/ *n* [U]

subjunctive /səbˈdʒʌŋktɪv/ *n* [singular] a verb form used to express doubt, possibility, or a

wish. In the sentence 'I suggested that Peter come with us', 'come' is in the subjunctive.

sublime /səˈblaɪm/ *adj* extremely beautiful: *a sublime view of the mountains* —**sublimely** *adv*

submarine /ˈsʌbməriːn, ˌsʌbməˈriːn/ *n* [C] a ship that can travel under water → see box at SHIP

submerge /səbˈmɜːdʒ $ -ˈmɜːrdʒ/ *v* [I,T] to go or put something below the surface of water: *Whole villages were submerged by the flood.* —**submerged** *adj* —**submersion** /-ˈmɜːʃən $ -ˈmɜːrʒən/ *n* [U]

submission /səbˈmɪʃən/ *n* **1** [U] when someone obeys a person or group and is completely controlled by them: **into submission** *The prisoners were starved into submission.* **2** [C,U] when you give a document such as a legal contract to someone so that they can consider it, or the document itself

submissive /səbˈmɪsɪv/ *adj* ready to obey other people and do whatever they want

submit /səbˈmɪt/ *v* **submitted, submitting** **1** [T] to give a plan or piece of writing to someone in authority so that they can consider it: *They submitted a report calling for changes in the law.* **2** [I,T] to agree to obey a person, group, set of rules, especially when you have no choice: +**to** *They were forced to submit to the kidnappers' demands.*

subordinate[1] /səˈbɔːdɪnət $ -ˈbɔːr-/ *n* [C] *formal* someone who has a less important job than someone else in an organization

subordinate[2] *adj formal* **1** in a less important position than someone else: +**to** *Women were subordinate to men.* **2** less important than something else: +**to** *These aims were subordinate to the aims of the mission.*

subordinate[3] /səˈbɔːdɪneɪt $ -ˈbɔːr-/ *v* [T] *formal* to put someone or something in a less important position —**subordination** /səˌbɔːdɪˈneɪʃən $ -ˌbɔːr-/ *n* [U]

suˌbordinate 'clause *n* [C] in grammar, a part of a sentence that begins with a word such as 'when' or 'because' and adds information to the main part

subpoena /səˈpiːnə, səb-/ *n* [C] *law* a legal document that orders someone to attend a TRIAL in a law court

subscribe /səbˈskraɪb/ *v* [I] to pay money so that a newspaper or magazine is regularly sent to you: +**to** *What magazines do you subscribe to?* —**subscriber** *n* [C]
subscribe to sth *phr v formal* to agree with an idea or opinion

subscription /səbˈskrɪpʃən/ *n* [C] an amount of money that you pay to receive a newspaper or magazine regularly, or to belong to an organization

subsequent /ˈsʌbsɪkwənt/ *adj* [only before noun] *formal* happening or coming after something else: *These skills were passed on to subsequent generations.* —**subsequently** *adv*

subservient /səbˈsɜːviənt $ -ˈsɜːr-/ *adj* too willing to obey other people in a way that makes you seem weak —**subservience** *n* [U]

subset /ˈsʌbset/ *n* [C] a small group of people or things that is part of a larger group

subside /səbˈsaɪd/ *v* [I] to become calmer or quieter: *The storm subsided around dawn.*

subsidence /səb'saɪdəns, 'sʌbsɪdəns/ n [U] when the ground sinks to a lower level, especially when this causes damage to buildings

subsidiary[1] /səb'sɪdiəri $ -dieri/ n [C] plural **subsidiaries** a company that is owned or controlled by a larger company: **+of** *a subsidiary of a large American firm* → see box at **COMPANY**

subsidiary[2] adj relating to, but less important than, something else

subsidize also **-ise** BrE /'sʌbsɪdaɪz/ v [T] to pay part of the cost of something: *Farming is heavily subsidized by the government.*

subsidy /'sʌbsɪdi/ n [C] plural **subsidies** money that a government or organization pays to help with the cost of something

subsist /səb'sɪst/ v [I] formal to stay alive using only small amounts of food or money: **+on** *The prisoners subsisted on rice and water.* —**subsistence** n [U]

substance /'sʌbstəns/ n

1 [C] any type of solid, liquid, or gas: *The bag was covered with a sticky substance.* | *a poisonous substance*

2 [singular, U] the most important ideas in a speech or piece of writing: **+of** *The news report said little about the substance of the peace talks.* | **in substance** *What she said, in substance, was that the mayor should resign.*

3 [U] formal if something has substance, it is true: *There's no substance to the rumour.* | **without substance** *His remarks are completely without substance.*

substandard /ˌsʌb'stændəd◂ $ -ərd◂ / adj not as good as the usual standard: *substandard health care*

substantial /səb'stænʃəl/ adj **1** large in amount or number: *a substantial salary* | *a substantial breakfast* **2** large and strongly made: *a substantial piece of furniture*

substantially /səb'stænʃəli/ adv very much: *Prices have increased substantially.*

substantiate /səb'stænʃieɪt/ v [T] formal to prove that something someone has said is true: *Can he substantiate his claims?*

substitute[1] /'sʌbstɪtjuːt $ -tuːt/ n [C] a person or thing that takes the place of another: *a substitute teacher* | *a sugar substitute* | **+for** *You can use oil as a substitute for butter.*

substitute[2] v **1** [T] to use something new or different instead of something else: **substitute sth for sth** *You can substitute olive oil for butter in the recipe.* **2** [I] to do someone's job for a short time until they are able to do it again: **+for** *I substituted for John when he was sick.* —**substitution** /ˌsʌbstɪ'tjuːʃən $ -'tuː-/ n [C,U]

subsume /səb'sjuːm $ -'suːm/ v [T] formal to include someone or something in a group or type

subterfuge /'sʌbtəfjuːdʒ $ -ər-/ n [C,U] formal a trick or dishonest way of doing something, or behaviour in which someone does this

subterranean /ˌsʌbtə'reɪniən◂ / adj formal under the surface of the earth: *a subterranean lake*

subtitles /'sʌbˌtaɪtlz/ n [plural] the words printed over a film in a foreign language to translate what the actors are saying —**subtitled** adj

subtle /'sʌtl/ adj **1** not easy to notice or understand: *subtle changes in climate* | *subtle humour* | *a subtle form of racism* **2** a subtle taste, smell, sound, or colour is pleasant and delicate: *the subtle scent of mint in the air* **3** clever in a way that does not attract attention: *I think we need a more subtle approach.* —**subtlety** n [C,U] —**subtly** adv

subtract /səb'trækt/ v [T] to take one number away from another number [≠ add]: **subtract sth from sth** *If you subtract 15 from 25 you get 10.* → see box at **CALCULATE** —**subtraction** /-'trækʃən/ n [C,U]

suburb /'sʌbɜːb $ -ɜːrb/ n [C] an area where people live which is on the edge of a city: **+of** *a suburb of Chicago* → see box at **AREA**

suburban /sə'bɜːbən $ -'bɜːr-/ adj **1** relating to a suburb: *a quiet suburban street* **2** boring and ordinary: *suburban attitudes*

suburbia /sə'bɜːbiə $ -'bɜːr-/ n [U] suburbs in general

subversive /səb'vɜːsɪv $ -'vɜːr-/ adj subversive ideas or activities are secret and intended to damage or destroy a government or an established system —**subversive** n [C]

subvert /səb'vɜːt $ -'vɜːrt/ v [T] formal to try to destroy the power and influence of a government or the established system

subway /'sʌbweɪ/ n [C] **1** BrE a path for people to walk under a road or railway [= underpass] **2** AmE a railway that runs under the ground in a big city [= metro; = underground BrE] → see picture at **TRANSPORT**

succeed /sək'siːd/ v

1 [I] to do what you tried or wanted to do [≠ fail]: *I was determined to succeed.* | **succeed in doing sth** *Did you succeed in finding a place to stay?*

2 [I] to reach a high position in something such as your job [≠ fail]: **+as** *She gave herself one year to succeed as a writer.*

3 [I] to have the result or effect that was intended [≠ fail]: *The negotiations are unlikely to succeed.*

4 [I,T] to take a position or do a job after someone else: **succeed sb as sth** *Mr Harvey will succeed Mrs Lincoln as chairman.*

succeeding /sək'siːdɪŋ/ adj coming after something else: *Sales improved in succeeding years.* | *succeeding generations*

success /sək'ses/ n

1 [U] when you achieve what you want to achieve [≠ failure]: *Her success is due to hard work.* | **without success** *I tried to contact him, but without success.* | **success in doing sth** *Did you have any success in persuading Alan to come?* | *What's the secret of your success?*

2 [C] something that a lot of people like or buy [≠ failure]: *The party was a great success.* | *This product has been a huge success.*

successful /sək'sesfəl/ adj

1 having the result or effect that you intended [≠ unsuccessful]: *If the operation is successful, you should make a full recovery.* | *a successful attempt to sail around the world*

2 a successful person earns a lot of money or is very well known and respected [≠ unsuccessful]: *a successful businesswoman*

S

3 a successful business, film, or product makes a lot of money [≠ **unsuccessful**]: *a highly successful product* | *The film was hugely successful.* —**successfully** *adv*

succession /sək'seʃən/ *n* **1** [singular, U] a number of things that happen one after the other: +**of** *She's had a succession of failed marriages.* | **in succession** *United have won four championships in succession.* **2** [U] when someone takes a position or job after someone else

successive /sək'sesɪv/ *adj* happening one after the other: *The team had three successive victories.* —**successively** *adv*

successor /sək'sesə $ -ər/ *n* [C] someone's successor is the person who has their job after they leave: *No one was certain who her successor would be.*

succinct /sək'sɪŋkt/ *adj* approving clearly expressed in a few words: *a succinct description* —**succinctly** *adv*

succulent /'sʌkjʊlənt/ *adj* juicy and good to eat: *a succulent steak* —**succulence** *n* [U]

succumb /sə'kʌm/ *v* [I] formal **1** to stop opposing someone or something that is stronger than you, and allow them to take control: +**to** *Eventually, she succumbed to his charms.* **2** to become ill or die from an illness

such /sʌtʃ/ *determiner, pron*
1 similar to the thing or person which has already been mentioned: *What would you do in such a situation?* | *Such behaviour is not acceptable here.* | *'You said you'd come.' 'I said **no such thing!**'*
2 **such as** used to give an example of something: *big cities such as New York*
3 used to emphasize your description of someone or something: *He's such an idiot.* | *It's such a long way from here.*
4 **such ... that** used to say what the result of something is: *The animal was such a nuisance that we had to get rid of it.*
5 **not ... as such** spoken used to say that the word you are using to describe something is not exactly correct: *There isn't a garden as such, just a little vegetable patch.*
6 **there's no such thing/person (as sb/sth)** used to say that something or someone does not exist: *There's no such thing as a perfect marriage.*

GRAMMAR

such, so

Use **such** and **so** to emphasize a quality that someone or something has.

Use **so** before an adjective or an adverb: *Your dress is so pretty.* | *Some people are so rude.* | *He talks so loudly.*

Use **such** before a noun, or before an adjective and noun: *It was such a shock.* | *Mark is such a good swimmer.* | *She has such beautiful eyes.*

'such and ,such *determiner, pron* spoken used to talk about a certain thing, time, amount etc without saying exactly what it is: *They will ask you to come on such and such a day, at such and such a time.*

suck[1] /sʌk/ *v* [I,T]
1 to hold something in your mouth and pull on it

with your tongue and lips: *Don't suck your thumb, Katie.* | +**on** *Barry was sucking on a candy bar.*
2 to take air or liquid into your mouth by making your lips form a small hole and then pulling it in: +**up** *She sucked up the last of her lemonade with a straw.*
3 to pull someone or something with a lot of force: **suck sb under/down** *The river sucked him under.*
4 **be sucked into (doing) sth** to become involved in something unpleasant without wanting to: *He was quickly sucked into a life of crime.*

suck[2] *n* [C] an act of sucking

sucker /'sʌkə $ -ər/ *n* [C] spoken someone who is easily tricked: *Ellen always was a sucker.*

suction /'sʌkʃən/ *n* [U] the process of sucking air or liquid from a container or space

sudden /'sʌdn/ *adj*
1 happening quickly, when you are not expecting it: *a sudden change in the weather* | *She felt a sudden rush of anger.*
2 **all of a sudden** suddenly: *All of a sudden, the lights went out.*
—**suddenness** *n* [U]

suddenly /'sʌdnli/ *adv* if something happens suddenly, it happens quickly, when you are not expecting it: *I suddenly realized that someone was following me.* | *George died very suddenly.*

suds /sʌdz/ *n* [plural] the BUBBLES produced when soap and water are mixed together

sue /sju: $ su:/ *v* [I,T] to start a legal process to get money from someone who has harmed you in some way: *She plans to sue the company for $1 million.*

suede /sweɪd/ *n* [U] soft leather with a slightly rough surface

suffer /'sʌfə $ -ər/ *v*
1 [I,T] to experience physical or emotional pain: *She's suffering a lot of pain.* | *He died in his sleep and didn't suffer.* | +**from** *David is suffering from a knee injury.*
2 [I,T] to experience and be badly affected by something [≠ **benefit**]: *Small businesses suffered financially because of the crisis.* | *He is suffering from financial problems.* | *We are suffering the consequences of other people's bad decisions.* | *In 1667 England suffered a defeat by the Dutch* (=they lost a battle to the Dutch).
3 [I] to become worse in quality because of something: *Safety will suffer if costs are cut.* —**sufferer** *n* [C] —**suffering** *n* [C,U]

suffice /sə'faɪs/ *v* [I] formal to be enough: *A light lunch will suffice.*

sufficient /sə'fɪʃənt/ *adj* as much as you need for a particular purpose [= **enough**; ≠ **insufficient**]: *The police have sufficient evidence to charge him with murder.* —**sufficiently** *adv*

suffix /'sʌfɪks/ *n* [C] a letter or letters added to the end of a word to make a new word, for example 'ness' at the end of 'kindness' [➡ **affix**, **prefix**]

suffocate /'sʌfəkeɪt/ *v* [I,T] to die because there is not enough air, or to kill someone by preventing them from breathing —**suffocation** /ˌsʌfə'keɪʃən/ *n* [U]

suffocating /'sʌfəkeɪtɪŋ/ *adj* so hot that you have difficulty breathing: *the suffocating heat of the studio lights*

suffrage /'sʌfrɪdʒ/ *n* [U] *formal* the right to vote

sugar /'ʃʊgə $ -ər/ *n*
1 [U] a sweet substance obtained from plants and used for making food and drinks sweet: *Do you take sugar in your tea?* | *a bag of sugar* → see picture at **INGREDIENT**
2 [C] *BrE* the amount of sugar that a small spoon can hold: *How many sugars do you want in your coffee?*
—**sugar** *v* [T]

sugary /'ʃʊgəri/ *adj* containing sugar or tasting like sugar: *sugary drinks*

suggest /sə'dʒest $ səg'dʒest/ *v* [T]
1 to tell someone your ideas about what should be done [➡ **propose**]: *My doctor suggested a week off work.* | **+(that)** *I suggest that you phone before you go over there.* | **suggest doing sth** *Joan suggested asking her father for his opinion.* | **+how/where/what** etc *The teacher suggested how Andy could research the project.*

suggesting

let's ...: *Let's meet up at the weekend.*
shall we ...?: *Shall we go into town this afternoon?*
do you want to ...?: *Do you want to go out for a meal?*
how/what about ...?: *How about a weekend in London?* | *What about asking Tim over?*
why don't we ...?: *Why don't we have a cycling holiday this year?*
do you fancy ...? *BrE*: *Do you fancy a trip to the sea?*
may/can I suggest (that) ... *formal*, **I suggest** *formal*: *May I suggest you try the fish, sir.*
→ **ACCEPT, AGREE**

2 to show that something might be true: **evidence/results/data etc suggest(s) that** *The evidence suggests that single fathers are more likely to work than single mothers.*
3 to say something in an indirect way: **+(that)** *Are you suggesting I'm too fat?* → see box at **SAY**
4 to say that someone or something would be suitable for a particular job or activity: **suggest sb/sth for sth** *John Roberts has been suggested for the post of manager.*

suggestion /sə'dʒestʃən $ səg-/ *n*
1 [C] an idea, plan, or possibility that someone suggests: *May I make a suggestion?* | *Do you have any suggestions about what we can do in New York?* | **+that** *the suggestion that we could go to war*
2 [singular, U] a sign or possibility of something: **+of** *There was never any suggestion of criminal activity.* | **+that** *There's some suggestion that he was the person that killed Angie.*
3 a suggestion of sth a slight amount of something: *There was just a suggestion of a smile on her face.*

suggestive /sə'dʒestɪv $ səg-/ *adj* **1 suggestive of sth** similar to something: *Her symptoms are suggestive of an anxiety disorder.* **2** making you think of sex: *a suggestive remark*

suicidal /ˌsuːɪˈsaɪdl◂ , ˌsjuː- $ ˌsuː-/ *adj*
1 someone who is suicidal feels so unhappy that he or she wants to kill himself or herself: *She admits that she sometimes had suicidal thoughts.*
2 very dangerous or likely to have a very bad result: *It would be suicidal to attack in daylight.*

suicide /'suːɪsaɪd, 'sjuː- $ 'suː-/ *n* [C,U]
1 when someone deliberately kills himself or herself: *There's been a rise in the number of suicides among young men.* | *Her brother com-**mitted suicide** last year.* | *She left a **suicide note**.*
2 political/economic suicide something that you do that ruins your good position in politics or the ECONOMY: *It would be political suicide to hold an election now.*
3 suicide bombing/attack/mission an attack in which someone deliberately kills himself or herself in the act of killing other people

suit¹ /suːt, sjuːt $ suːt/ *n* [C]
1 a jacket and trousers or a skirt that are made of the same material and are worn together: *a light-weight suit* | *I wear a suit to work.*
2 bathing/jogging etc suit a piece of clothing or a set of clothes that you wear for swimming, running etc: *a ski suit*
3 a LAWSUIT: *a civil suit*
4 one of the four types of playing cards in a set of playing cards
→ **BOILER SUIT, TROUSER SUIT, WET SUIT**

suit² *v* [T]
1 to be acceptable, right, or suitable for someone: *It's difficult to find a date that **suits** everyone.* | *There's a range of restaurants to **suit all tastes** (=the different things that people like).* | *Either steak or chicken would **suit** me fine.*
2 clothes, colours etc that suit you make you look attractive: *I don't think that new hairstyle really suits her.* → see box at **CLOTHES**
3 best/well/ideally etc suited to/for sth to have the right qualities to do something: *Lucy's ideally suited for the job.*
4 suit yourself used to tell someone they can do whatever they want, even though it annoys you

suitable /'suːtəbəl, 'sjuː- $ 'suː-/ *adj* having the right qualities for a particular person, purpose, or situation [≠ **unsuitable**]: *We are hoping to find a suitable school.* | **+for** *The film isn't suitable for young children.*
—**suitably** *adv* —**suitability** /ˌsuːtə'bɪlɪti, ˌsjuː- $ ˌsuː-/ *n* [U]

suitcase /'suːtkeɪs, 'sjuːt- $ 'suːt-/ *n* [C] a case with a handle, used for carrying clothes and possessions when you travel → see picture at **CASE**

suite /swiːt/ *n* [C] **1** *especially BrE* a set of matching furniture for a room: *a living-room suite* **2** a set of expensive rooms in a hotel: *the honeymoon suite*

suitor /'suːtə, 'sjuː- $ 'suːtər/ *n* [C] *old-fashioned* a woman's suitor is the man who wants to marry her

sulfur /'sʌlfə $ -ər/ *n* the American spelling of SULPHUR

sulk /sʌlk/ *v* [I] to show that you are annoyed by being silent and looking unhappy: *Stop sulking – you can go out and play later.* —**sulk** *n* [C] —**sulky** *adj*

sullen /'sʌlən/ *adj* being and looking angry but not saying anything: *a sullen expression* —**sullenly** *adv*

sulphur *especially BrE*, **sulfur** *AmE* /'sʌlfə $ -fər/ *n* [U] a yellow chemical powder that smells unpleasant —**sulphurous** *adj*

sultan /'sʌltən/ *n* [C] a ruler in some Muslim countries

sultana /sʌl'tɑːnə $ -'tænə/ *n* [C] *BrE* a dried white GRAPE, used in cooking

sultry /'sʌltri/ *adj* **1** sultry weather is hot with no wind **2** a woman who is sultry makes other people feel strong sexual attraction to her

sum¹ /sʌm/ *n* [C] **1** an amount of money: *The city has spent a large sum of money on parks.* **2 the sum of sth** the total when you add two or more numbers together: *The sum of 4 and 5 is 9.* **3** *BrE* a simple calculation such as adding or dividing numbers

sum² *v* **summed, summing**
sum up *phr v* **1** to end a discussion or speech by giving the main information about it in a short statement: *So, to sum up, we need to organize our time better.* | **sum sth ⇔ up** *You should sum up your argument in the final paragraph.* **2 sum sth ⇔ up** to form an opinion about someone or something: *Pat summed up the situation at a glance.* —**summing-up** *n* [C]

summarize also **-ise** *BrE* /'sʌməraɪz/ *v* [I,T] to give only the main information about something without the details

summary¹ /'sʌməri/ *n* [C] plural **summaries** a short statement that gives the main information about something: *I've given a brief summary on a separate sheet.*

summary² *adj* [only before noun] *formal* done immediately, without following the usual processes or rules: *summary executions*

summer /'sʌmə $ -ər/ *n* [C,U] the season between spring and autumn, when the weather is hottest: *Are you going away this summer?* | **in (the) summer** *Miriam likes to relax in the garden in summer.*
→ **INDIAN SUMMER** —**summery** *adj*

summertime /'sʌmətaɪm $ -ər-/ *n* [U] the time of year when it is summer: *It's really hot here in the summertime.*

summit /'sʌmɪt/ *n* [C] **1** a meeting between the leaders of several governments: *an economic summit* **2** the top of a mountain → see box at **MOUNTAIN**

summon /'sʌmən/ *v* [T] *formal* **1** to officially order someone to come to a particular place: **summon sb to sth** *I was summoned to the principal's office.* **2** also **summon up** if you summon your courage, strength etc, you try to be brave, strong etc even though it is difficult: *Tom summoned up the courage to ask Kay to marry him.*

summons /'sʌmənz/ *n* [C] plural **summonses** an official letter that says you must go to a court of law —**summons** *v* [T]

sumptuous /'sʌmptʃuəs/ *adj* very impressive and expensive: *a sumptuous meal* —**sumptuously** *adv*

sun¹ /sʌn/ *n*
1 [singular] the large bright object in the sky that gives us light and heat, and which the Earth moves around: *The sky was blue and the sun was shining.* → see box at **SPACE**
2 [singular,U] the heat and light that come from the sun: **in the sun** *We sat in the sun, eating ice cream.* | *the warmth of the afternoon sun*

sun² *v* **sunned, sunning sun yourself** to sit or lie outside when the sun is shining

Sun. also **Sun** *BrE* the written abbreviation of **Sunday**

sunbathe /'sʌnbeɪð/ *v* [I] to sit or lie outside in the sun in order to become brown —**sunbathing** *n* [U]

sunbeam /'sʌnbiːm/ *n* [C] a line of light shining down from the sun

sunbed /'sʌnbed/ *n* [C] a piece of equipment with special lights, that you lie on to make your skin brown

'sun block *n* [C,U] SUNSCREEN

sunburn /'sʌnbɜːn $ -bɜːrn/ *n* [U] when your skin is red and sore from spending too much time in the sun —**sunburned, sunburnt** *adj*

'sun cream *n* [C,U] SUNSCREEN

sundae /'sʌndeɪ $ -di/ *n* [C] a dish made from ICE CREAM, fruit, nuts etc

Sunday /'sʌndi, -deɪ/ *n* [C,U] written abbreviation *Sun.* the day between Saturday and Monday → see examples at **MONDAY** → see box at **DAY**

sundial /'sʌndaɪəl/ *n* [C] an object that shows the time by using the shadow made on it by the sun

sundown /'sʌndaʊn/ *n* [U] *old-fashioned* SUNSET

sundry /'sʌndri/ *adj* *formal* **1 all and sundry** everyone, not just a few carefully chosen people: *I don't want all and sundry coming into our garden.* **2** [only before noun] sundry people or things are all different, and cannot be considered as a group [= **various**]

sunflower

sunflower /'sʌn,flaʊə $ -,flaʊər/ *n* [C] a tall plant with a large yellow flower and seeds that you can eat

sung /sʌŋ/ *v* the past participle of SING

sunglasses /'sʌn,glɑːsɪz $ -,glæ-/ *n* [plural] dark glasses that you wear to protect your eyes from the sun

sunk /sʌŋk/ *v* the past tense and past participle of SINK

sunken /'sʌŋkən/ *adj* [only before noun] **1** built or put at a lower level than the surrounding area: *a sunken garden* **2** having fallen to the bottom of the sea: *sunken treasure* **3** sunken cheeks or eyes have fallen inwards, making someone look ill

sunlight /'sʌnlaɪt/ *n* [U] natural light that comes from the sun: *He stepped out into strong sunlight.*

sunlit /'sʌnlɪt/ *adj* made brighter by light from the sun: *a sunlit kitchen*

sunny /'sʌni/ *adj* full of light from the sun [➡ **bright**]: *a warm sunny day* | *I hope it's sunny tomorrow.* → see box at **WEATHER**

THESAURUS

It's sunny/fine/lovely.
It's a nice/lovely/glorious day.
It's bright/a bright day – used especially in weather reports.
There isn't a cloud in the sky.
It's cloudy/grey/dull.
It's a grey/dull/miserable day.
It's overcast – very dark and likely to rain.
→ RAIN, SNOW, WEATHER, WIND

sunrise /'sʌnraɪz/ *n* **1** [U] the time when the sun first appears in the morning: **at sunrise** *In the summer we start work at sunrise and finish at sunset.* **2** [C] the coloured part of the sky where the sun first appears

sunroof /'sʌnruːf/ *n* [C] a part of the roof of a car that you can open to let in air and light

sunscreen /'sʌnskriːn/ *n* [C,U] a skin cream to stop the sun from burning you [= **sun block, sun cream**]

sunset /'sʌnset/ *n* **1** [U] the time when the sun disappears and night begins: **at sunset** *In the summer we start work at sunrise and finish at sunset.* **2** [C] the coloured part of the sky where the sun disappears

sunshine /'sʌnʃaɪn/ *n* [U] the light and heat that comes from the sun: *Let's go out and enjoy the sunshine.* | *After a week of sunshine, it started to rain.*

sunstroke /'sʌnstrəʊk $ -stroʊk/ *n* [U] an illness caused by being in the sun too long

suntan /'sʌntæn/ also **tan** *n* [C] when your skin goes brown from being in the sun —**suntanned** *adj*

sunup /'sʌnʌp/ *n* [U] *old-fashioned* SUNRISE

super[1] /'suːpə $ -pər/ *adj informal* extremely good: *a super idea*

super[2] *adv spoken* extremely: *a super expensive restaurant*

super- /suːpə $ -pər/ *prefix* extremely or extreme: *the super-rich* | *a super-efficient secretary* | *a superhero*

superb /sjuː'pɜːb, suː- $ su'pɜːrb/ *adj* very good: *a superb cook* —**superbly** *adv*

superficial /ˌsuːpə'fɪʃəl◂ $ -pər-/ *adj* **1** not studying or looking at something carefully and only seeing the most noticeable things: *a superficial knowledge of the culture* **2** seeming to have a particular quality, although this is not true or real: *The two animals have a **superficial resemblance** but they are actually different breeds.* **3** superficial damage, injury etc only affects the skin or the outside of something and is not serious: *superficial cuts* —**superficially** *adv*

superfluous /suː'pɜːfluəs $ -'pɜːr-/ *adj formal* not necessary, or more than is needed: *superfluous details*

superhuman /ˌsuːpə'hjuːmən◂ $ -pər'hjuː-, -'juː-/ *adj* using powers that are much greater

than those of ordinary people: *It will take a superhuman effort to rebuild the country.*

superimpose /ˌsuːpərɪm'pəʊz $ -'poʊz/ *v* [T] to put a picture, photograph etc on top of another one so that both of them can be seen

superintendent /ˌsuːpərɪn'tendənt/ *n* [C] **1** a British police officer who has a fairly high rank **2** someone who is officially responsible for a building or place

superior[1] /suː'pɪəriər $ su'pɪriər/ *adj* **1** better than something or someone else [≠ **inferior**]: **+to** *Today's computers are superior to those we had ten years ago.* | *a **vastly superior** (=very much better) army* **2** *disapproving* showing that you think you are better than other people: *his superior attitude*

superior[2] *n* [C] someone who has a higher position than you at work: *I'll have to discuss this with my superiors.*

superiority /suːˌpɪəri'ɒrɪti $ su,pɪri'ɔ:-, -'ɑ:-/ *n* [U] **1** the quality of being better than other things: **+of** *the superiority of modern telecommunications* **2** *disapproving* when you show that you think you are better than other people: *She spoke with an air of superiority.*

superlative[1] /suː'pɜːlətɪv, sjuː- $ su'pɜːr-/ *adj* extremely good: *a superlative actor*

superlative[2] *n* **the superlative** the form of an adjective or adverb that you use when saying that someone or something is the biggest, best, worst etc. For example 'fastest' is the superlative of 'fast', and 'most expensive' is the superlative of 'expensive'. [➡ **comparative**]

supermarket /'suːpəˌmɑːkɪ̥t $ -pərˌmɑːr-/ *n* [C] a large shop that sells food, drink, products for cleaning the house etc → see box at **SHOP**

supermodel /'suːpəˌmɒdl $ -pərˌmɑːdl/ *n* [C] a very famous fashion MODEL

supernatural /ˌsuːpə'nætʃərəl◂ $ -pər-/ *n* **the supernatural** events, powers, or creatures that are impossible to explain by science or natural causes —**supernatural** *adj*: *supernatural powers*

superpower /'suːpəˌpaʊə $ -pərˌpaʊr/ *n* [C] a country that has a lot of military and political power

supersede /ˌsuːpə'siːd $ -pər-/ *v* [T] if a new product, idea, method etc supersedes another one, people start to use the new one because it is better: *TV had superseded radio by the 1960s.*

supersonic /ˌsuːpə'sɒnɪk◂ $ -pər'sɑː-/ *adj* faster than the speed of sound: *supersonic jets*

superstar /'suːpəstɑː $ -pərstɑːr/ *n* [C] an extremely famous actor, singer etc

superstition /ˌsuːpə'stɪʃən $ -pər-/ *n* [C,U] a belief that some objects or actions are lucky or unlucky: *the old superstition that the number 13 is unlucky*

superstitious /ˌsuːpə'stɪʃəs◂ $ -pər-/ *adj* believing that some objects or actions are lucky or unlucky: *Are you superstitious?*

superstore /'suːpəstɔː $ -pərstɔːr/ *n* [C] *BrE* a very large shop that sells many different types of goods: *a DIY superstore* → see box at **SHOP**

supervise /'suːpəvaɪz $ -pər-/ *v* [I,T] to be in charge of an activity or person, making sure that work is done properly or people behave correctly: *The engineer supervises all the construction work.* —**supervisor** *n* [C]

S

—**supervisory** /'suːpəvaɪzəri / ,suːpər'vaɪzəri/ *adj*: *The mayor has a supervisory role.*

supervision /,suːpə'vɪʒən $ -pər-/ *n* [U] when you supervise someone or something

supper /'sʌpə $ -ər/ *n* [C] a meal that you eat in the evening [= **dinner**]: *We had supper in an Italian restaurant.* | *Have you eaten supper?*

supplant /sə'plɑːnt $ sə'plænt/ *v* [T] *formal* to take the place of another person or thing: *Smith was soon supplanted as party leader.*

supple /'sʌpəl/ *adj* able to bend and move easily: *supple leather*

supplement /'sʌplɪmənt/ *n* [C] something that you add to something else to improve it: *You may need vitamin supplements.* —**supplement** /'sʌplɪment/ *v* [T] *I supplement my income by teaching Italian at weekends.*

supplementary /,sʌplɪ'mentəri◂ / *adj* added to something, or provided as well as something: *supplementary vitamins*

supplier /sə'plaɪə $ -ər/ *n* [C] a company that provides goods for shops and businesses: *medical suppliers*

supply¹ /sə'plaɪ/ *n* plural **supplies**

1 [C,U] an amount of something that can be used, or the process of providing this: **+of** *a week's supply of fresh meat* | *the supply of oxygen to the brain*

2 supplies [plural] food, clothes, and other things that are needed for an activity, journey etc: *emergency medical supplies*

3 water/electricity/power/gas supply a system of providing water, electricity etc

supply² *v* [T] **supplied, supplying, supplies** to provide people with something that they need, especially regularly over a period of time: **supply sb with sth** *Drivers are supplied with a uniform.* | **supply sth to sb** *He supplies information to the police.*

support¹ /sə'pɔːt $ -ɔːrt/ *v* [T]

1 to say that you agree with an idea, group, or person and want them to succeed: *I don't support any one political party.* | **support sb in (doing) sth** *We need to support teachers in their aims.*

2 to help and encourage someone or something: *My parents have always supported my decision to be an actor.*

3 to provide enough money for someone to have all the things they need: *I have a wife and two children to support.* | **support himself/herself etc** *You've got to learn to support yourself.*

4 to give money to a group or organization or for an event: *Which charities do you support?*

5 to be under something, holding it up and preventing it from falling: *The bridge is supported by two columns.*

6 to help to show that something is true: *The results support our original theory.*

7 *BrE* to like a particular sports team and want them to win: *Which team do you support?*

support² *n*

1 [U] encouragement and help that you give to someone or something: *Many people have given us support in our campaign.* | **+for** *There was widespread support for the war.* | **the support of sb** *The board do not have the support of the shareholders.*

2 [U] sympathy and help that you give to someone: *I needed the support of my boyfriend.*

3 [U] money that provides help for people: *We will provide financial support for the trip.*

4 [C,U] something that holds someone or something up, stopping them from falling: *supports for the roof* | *He leant against the wall for support.*

→ **CHILD SUPPORT, LIFE SUPPORT SYSTEM**

supporter /sə'pɔːtə $ -ɔːrtər/ *n* [C] **1** someone who supports a person, group, or plan **2** *especially BrE* someone who likes a particular team and wants them to win: *Manchester United supporters*

supporting /sə'pɔːtɪŋ $ -ɔːr-/ *adj* **1 supporting part/role/actor etc** a small part in a play or film, not one of the main characters **2 supporting wall** a wall that supports the weight of something

supportive /sə'pɔːtɪv $ -ɔːr-/ *adj* giving help or encouragement: *Mark and Sally are very supportive of each other.*

suppose /sə'pəʊz $ -'poʊz/ *v* [T]

1 I suppose a) used to say you think something is true, although you are not sure: **+(that)** *I suppose you're right.* | *'Aren't you pleased?' 'Yes, I suppose so.'* **b)** used when agreeing to let someone do something, especially when you do not want to: *'Can we come with you?' 'Oh, I suppose so.'* **c)** used when you are angry with someone: **+(that)** *I suppose you thought that was funny!*

2 I don't suppose (that) used to ask a question in an indirect or polite way: *I don't suppose you know where my pen is?*

3 do you suppose (that) ...? used to ask someone their opinion or guess: *Do you suppose he was hurt?*

4 suppose/supposing (that) used when imagining a possible situation or condition: *Suppose you lost your job. What would you do?*

5 be supposed a) used to say what someone should or should not do, according to rules or what someone has said: *You're not supposed to smoke in here.* **b)** used to say what is expected or intended to happen, especially when it did not happen: *The new laws are supposed to prevent crime.* **c)** if something is supposed to be true, many people believe it is true: *Mrs Carver is supposed to have a lot of money.*

supposed /sə'pəʊzd, sə'pəʊzɪd $ -'poʊzd, -'poʊzɪd/ *adj* [only before noun] used to say that what you are talking about is believed to be true, but that you do not believe or agree with it yourself: *the supposed link between violent movies and crime*

supposedly /sə'pəʊzɪdli $ -'poʊ-/ *adv* used to say that you do not believe what you are saying about the thing or person you are describing, even though other people think it is true: *How can a supposedly intelligent person make so many mistakes?* | *He's quite well paid, supposedly.*

supposition /,sʌpə'zɪʃən/ *n* [C,U] *formal* something that someone believes is true even though they cannot prove it

suppress /sə'pres/ *v* [T] **1** to stop people from opposing the government, especially by using force: *The army was called in to suppress the revolt.* **2** to prevent important information or opinions from becoming known: *His lawyer illegally suppressed evidence.* **3** to control a feeling, so that you do not show it or it does not affect you: *Andy could barely suppress his anger.* —**suppression** /sə'preʃən/ *n* [U]

supremacy /sʊ'preməsi, sju:- $ sʊ-, su:-/ *n* [U] when someone is more powerful or advanced than other people

supreme /sʊ'pri:m, sju:- $ sʊ-, su:-/ *adj*
1 having the highest position of authority or power: *the Supreme Commander of the UN forces*
2 the greatest possible: *He made a supreme effort.* | *a matter of supreme importance*

Su,preme 'Court *n* [singular] the most important court of law in some countries or some states of the US

supremely /sʊ'pri:mli, sju:- $ sʊ-, su:-/ *adv* extremely: *a supremely confident athlete*

surcharge /'sɜ:tʃɑːdʒ $ 'sɜːrtʃɑːrdʒ/ *n* [C] money that you have to pay in addition to the basic price of something

sure /ʃɔː $ ʃʊr/ *adj, adv*
1 [not before noun] certain about something: **+(that)** *Are you sure you've had enough?* | **+about** *Are you quite sure* (=completely sure) *about this?* | **+of** *He wasn't sure of her name.* | *He felt sure he knew her.* | **not sure what/where/ why etc** *I'm not sure what happened.* | **not sure if/whether...** *I'm not sure if he's coming.*
2 **make sure (that)-** **a)** to check that something is true or that something has been done: *Can you make sure the door's locked?* **b)** to do something so that you can be certain of the result: *Make sure you get there early.*
3 certain to happen or be true: *This one's a sure winner.* | *Those clouds are a sure sign of rain.* | **sure to do sth** *He's sure to say something stupid.*
4 **be sure of sth** to be certain to get something or certain that something will happen: *You're sure of a warm welcome at Liz's.*
5 **sure of yourself** confident about your own abilities and opinions
6 **be sure to do sth** *spoken* used to tell someone to remember to do something: *Be sure to write!*
7 **sure thing** *AmE spoken* used to agree to something: *'See you Friday.' 'Yeah, sure thing.'*
8 **for sure** *informal* if you know something for sure, you are certain about it: *I think Jack's married, but I don't know for sure.*
9 **that's for sure** used to emphasize that something is true: *It's a lot better than it was, that's for sure.*
10 *spoken* used to say yes to someone: *'Can I read your paper?' 'Sure.'*
11 **sure enough** *informal* used to say that something happened that you expected to happen: *Sure enough, we got lost.*
12 *informal* used to admit that something is true, before you say something very different: *Sure, he's attractive, but I'm not interested.*

'sure-fire *adj* [only before noun] *informal* certain to succeed: *a sure-fire way to make money*

surely /'ʃɔːli $ 'ʃʊrli/ *adv*
1 used to show that you are surprised at something: *Surely you're not leaving so soon?*
2 used to show that you think something must be true: *This will surely result in more problems.*

surf¹ /sɜːf $ sɜːrf/ *v* [I,T] **1** to ride on ocean waves standing on a board: *Matt goes surfing every day.* → see picture on page A9 **2 surf the**

Internet/net/Web to look for information on the INTERNET → see box at **INTERNET** —**surfer** *n* [C] —**surfing** *n* [U]

surf² *n* [U] the white part that forms on the top of waves

surface¹ /'sɜːf‚ɪs $ 'sɜːr-/ *n*
1 [C] the outside or top layer of something: **+of** *the surface of the vase* | *the Earth's surface*
2 **the surface** **a)** the top of an area of water: *The diver swam to the surface.* | **+of** *the surface of the lake* **b)** the way that someone or something seems to be, when their real qualities are hidden: **on the surface** *On the surface she seems happy enough.* | **below/beneath/under the surface** *I sensed a lot of tension beneath the surface.*
3 [C] a flat area, for example on top of a cupboard, on which you can work: *Keep kitchen surfaces clean and tidy.*

surface² *v* **1** [I] to rise to the surface of water: *Whales were surfacing near the boat.* **2** [I] to become known: *Rumours have begun to surface in the press.* | *No major problems have surfaced.*
3 [I] to appear again after being hidden or absent: *Three years later he surfaced again.*
4 [T] to put the surface on a road

surfboard /'sɜːfbɔːd $ 'sɜːrfbɔːrd/ *n* [C] a plastic board that you stand on to ride on ocean waves

surfeit /'sɜːf‚ɪt $ 'sɜːr-/ *n* [singular] too much of something: **+of** *a surfeit of alcohol*

surge¹ /sɜːdʒ $ sɜːrdʒ/ *v* [I] **1** to suddenly move very quickly in a particular direction: **+forward/through/ahead** *The crowd surged forward.* **2** if a price or level surges, it suddenly becomes much higher **3** also **surge up** if a feeling surges in you, you suddenly feel it very strongly: *Rage surged up inside her.*

surge² *n* [C] **1 a surge of anger/fear/ excitement etc** a sudden and very strong emotion **2** a sudden increase: *a surge in oil prices* | *a new surge of interest* **3** a sudden movement of a lot of people

surgeon /'sɜːdʒən $ 'sɜːr-/ *n* [C] a doctor who does operations in a hospital → see box at **DOCTOR**

surgery /'sɜːdʒəri $ 'sɜːr-/ *n* plural **surgeries**
1 [U] medical treatment in which a doctor cuts open your body to repair or remove something: *heart surgery* | **in surgery** (=having/doing an operation) *He was in surgery for three hours.*
2 [C] *BrE* a place where you go to see a doctor or DENTIST

surgical /'sɜːdʒɪkəl $ 'sɜːr-/ *adj* relating to or used for medical operations: *surgical gloves* —**surgically** /-kli/ *adv*

surly /'sɜːli $ 'sɜːrli/ *adj* unfriendly and rude

surmise /sə'maɪz $ sər-/ *v* [T] *formal* to guess something, using the information that you have: *One can only surmise that she disagreed.*

surmount /sə'maʊnt $ sər-/ *v* [T] *formal* to deal successfully with a problem or difficulty [= **overcome**]

surname /'sɜːneɪm $ 'sɜːr-/ *n* [C] your family name [= **last name, family name**] → see box at **NAME**

surpass /sə'pɑːs $ sər'pæs/ *v* [T] *formal* to be better than someone or something else: *He had surpassed all our expectations.*

surplus¹ /'sɜːpləs $ 'sɜːr-/ n [C,U] more of something than is needed or used: **+of** the country's huge surplus of grain

surplus² adj more than what is needed or used: surplus land | They said he was **surplus to requirements** (=not needed).

surprise¹ /sə'praɪz $ sər-/ n
1 [U] the feeling you have when something unexpected or unusual happens: **in surprise** Bill looked at him in surprise. | **To my surprise**, she agreed. | It came as no surprise when he left.
2 [C,U] something that is unexpected or unusual [➡ shock]: I've got a surprise for you! | We had a surprise visit from our grandson. | a surprise party
3 take/catch sb by surprise to happen in an unexpected way: The snow caught everyone by surprise.

surprise² v [T] **1** to make someone feel surprise [➡ shock]: Her reaction surprised me. | It wouldn't surprise me if they got married. **2** to catch or attack someone when they do not expect it: A security guard surprised the robber.

surprised /sə'praɪzd $ sər-/ adj
1 having a feeling of surprise: **+(that)** We were surprised Tom wasn't there. | **+at/by** She was surprised at his attitude. | **surprised to hear/ see/find sth** I'm surprised to hear you say that. | Jane looked surprised.

THESAURUS
amazed, astonished, astounded, staggered, flabbergasted, dumbfounded, nonplussed, gobsmacked BrE informal

2 I'm surprised at you/him etc spoken used to say that you are disappointed by someone's behaviour

surprising /sə'praɪzɪŋ $ sər-/ adj unexpected or unusual: It's hardly surprising that they lost the game. | It's surprising how well it works. | A surprising number of people came.

THESAURUS
extraordinary, amazing, astonishing, astounding, staggering, stunning, unbelievable

—**surprisingly** adv: The test was surprisingly easy.

surreal /sə'rɪəl/ also **surrealistic** /sə,rɪə'lɪstɪk◂/ adj very strange, like something from a dream

surrender /sə'rendə $ -ər/ v **1** [I] to stop fighting or trying to escape, because you cannot win or escape: **surrender to sb** The man finally surrendered to police. | The rebel forces have surrendered. **2** [T] formal to give something to someone in authority, for example weapons or official documents: They had to **surrender their passports**. —**surrender** n [U] their unconditional surrender to the Allied forces

surreptitious /,sʌrəp'tɪʃəs◂ $,sɜː-/ adj done secretly so that other people do not notice: She cast surreptitious glances backwards. —**surreptitiously** adv

surrogate /'sʌrəgeɪt, -gət $ 'sɜːr-/ adj [only before noun] taking the place of someone or something else: a surrogate mother (=woman who has a baby for another woman) —**surrogate** n [C]

surround /sə'raʊnd/ v
1 [T] to be or go all around someone or something: **be surrounded by sth** The lake was surrounded by trees. | The police surrounded the house.
2 be surrounded by sb/sth to have a lot of a particular kind of people or things near you: She is surrounded by friends. | **surround yourself with sb/sth** He surrounds himself with exquisite objects.
3 [T] to be closely related to a situation or event: Some of the issues surrounding alcohol abuse are very complex.
—**surrounding** adj: the surrounding countryside

surroundings /sə'raʊndɪŋz/ n [plural] the place where you are and all the things in it: I soon got used to my new surroundings.

surveillance /sə'veɪləns $ sər-/ n [U] when someone is being watched, for example by the police or by doctors: **under surveillance** Police have the man under surveillance.

survey¹ /'sɜːveɪ $ 'sɜːr-/ n [C]
1 a set of questions that you ask a lot of people in order to find out about their opinions or behaviour: **+of** We conducted a survey of people's eating habits. | The survey showed that 61% backed the President.
2 an examination of an area or building

survey² /sə'veɪ $ sər-/ v [T] **1** to ask a lot of people questions in order to find out about their opinions or behaviour: More than 50% of those surveyed agreed. **2** to look at someone or something carefully: I surveyed the damage to the car. **3** to examine and measure land or a building

surveyor /sə'veɪə $ sər'veɪər/ n [C] someone whose job is to examine and measure land or buildings

survival /sə'vaɪvəl $ sər-/ n [U] when someone continues to live or exist, especially after a difficult or dangerous situation: The operation will increase his **chances of survival**. | It's been a case of **survival of the fittest**.

survive /sə'vaɪv $ sər-/ v [I,T]
1 to continue to live after an accident, war, illness etc: She survived the war. | They may not survive the winter. | Only one person survived.
2 to continue to live normally or to exist in spite of problems: A lot of firms did not survive the recession. | People are struggling to survive. | **+on** How do you survive on such a low salary? | I've had a tough few months, but I'll survive.
3 to continue to exist after a very long time: **+from** Several buildings have survived from medieval times.

survivor /sə'vaɪvə $ sər'vaɪvər/ n [C] **1** someone who continues to live after an accident, illness etc: There were no survivors. **2** someone who will not fail or stop trying, even when life is difficult: He's a survivor.

susceptible /sə'septɪbəl/ adj likely to be affected by an illness or problem: **+to** I've always been very susceptible to colds. —**susceptibility** /sə,septɪ'bɪlɪti/ n [U]

sushi /'suːʃi/ n [U] Japanese food containing raw fish

suspect¹ /'sʌspekt/ n [C] someone who may be guilty of a crime: **main/prime/chief suspect**

suspect² /sə'spekt/ v [T] **1** to think that some-one may be guilty of a crime: **suspect sb of sth** *She is suspected of murder.* **2** to think that something is true, may happen, or has happened: **+(that)** *I suspected that she would leave.* | *I strongly suspected he was lying.* → see box at THINK **3** to think that something is not honest or true: *She suspected his motives.*

suspect³ /'sʌspekt/ adj difficult to believe or trust: *Her methods were highly suspect.*

suspend /sə'spend/ v [T] **1** to stop or delay something: *The talks have been suspended.* | *He decided to suspend judgement.* **2 suspend sb's sentence** to say that someone will go to prison for a crime, if they commit another crime within a specific period **3** to officially make someone leave their school or job for a short time, after something bad has happened **4** if something is suspended somewhere, it is hanging or floating there: *A light was suspended from the ceiling.*

suspenders /sə'spendəz $ -ərz/ n [plural] **1** *BrE* pieces of ELASTIC fixed to a woman's underwear and to her STOCKINGS to hold them up [= garters AmE] **2** *AmE* bands of cloth that hold up your trousers, worn over your shoulders [= braces BrE]

suspense /sə'spens/ n [U] the feeling you have when waiting for something exciting to happen: *Don't keep us in suspense. What happened?*

suspension /sə'spenʃən/ n **1** [U] when someone stops or delays something for a period of time **2** [C,U] when someone is removed from a school or job for a short time as a punishment **3** [U] equipment fixed to the wheels of a vehicle to make it comfortable to ride in

sus'pension ˌbridge n [C] a bridge that has no supports under it, but is hung from strong steel ropes fixed to towers

suspicion /sə'spɪʃən/ n **1** [C,U] a feeling that someone has done something wrong: *He was arrested on suspicion of robbery.* | **under suspicion** (=thought to have done something wrong) *He felt he was still under suspicion.* **2** [C] a feeling that something may be true: *She had a suspicion that Steve might be right.*

suspicious /sə'spɪʃəs/ adj **1** something that is suspicious appears to involve a crime: *a suspicious package* | *the suspicious circumstances surrounding his death* **2** if you are suspicious of someone, you do not trust them: *His behaviour made me suspicious.* —**suspiciously** adv: *They were acting suspiciously.*

suss /sʌs/ also **suss out** v [T] *BrE informal* to discover something about someone or something: *He finally sussed out the truth.*

sustain /sə'steɪn/ v [T] **1** to make something continue: *a strategy that would sustain economic growth* **2** to keep someone strong or healthy: *A good breakfast will sustain you through the morning.* **3** *formal* to suffer injury, damage, or loss: *Two people sustained minor injuries.*

sustainable /sə'steɪnəbəl/ adj able to continue, especially without destroying the environment: *sustainable rural development*

sustained /sə'steɪnd/ adj continuing without becoming weaker: *A sustained effort is needed.* | *sustained economic growth*

sustenance /'sʌstənəns/ n [U] *formal* food that you need in order to live

svelte /svelt/ adj thin and graceful

SW the written abbreviation of **southwest** or **southwestern**

swab /swɒb $ swɑːb/ n [C] a small piece of material, used to clean wounds or do medical tests

swagger /'swægə $ -ər/ v [I] to walk with a swinging movement, in a way that seems too proud and confident —**swagger** n [singular]

swallow¹ /'swɒləʊ $ 'swɑːloʊ/ v **1** [I,T] to make food or drink go down your throat: *He swallowed a mouthful of coffee.* **2** [I] to make a movement in your throat, because you are nervous: *Lee swallowed hard and walked in.* **3** [T] *informal* to believe that something is true, especially when it is not true: *I found his story a bit hard to swallow.* **4** [T] to stop yourself from having or showing a feeling: *I swallowed my pride and phoned him.* **swallow sth ⇔ up** phr v to make something disappear or become part of something else: *As the city grew, nearby villages were swallowed up.*

swallow² n [C] **1** when you make food or drink go down your throat **2** a common small bird with pointed wings and a tail with two points

swam /swæm/ v the past tense of SWIM

swamp¹ /swɒmp $ swɑːmp/ n [C,U] land that is always very wet or covered with water —**swampy** adj: *swampy ground*

swamp² v [T] **1** to suddenly give someone more work or problems than they can deal with: *We've been swamped with phone calls.* **2** to suddenly cover something with a lot of water: *Huge waves swamped the town.*

swan /swɒn $ swɑːn/ n [C] a large white bird with a long neck that lives on lakes and rivers

swanky /'swæŋki/ adj *informal* very fashionable or expensive: *a swanky hotel*

swansong /'swɒnsɒŋ $ 'swɑːnsɔːŋ/ n [C] the last piece of work that an artist or writer produces, or the last time someone gives a performance: *This concert will be her swansong.*

swap, swop /swɒp $ swɑːp/ v [I,T] swapped, swapping to exchange something you have for something that someone else has: **swap (sth) with sb** *Can I swap seats with you?* | **swap sth for sth** *I'll swap my red T-shirt for your green one.* —**swap** n [C] *Shall we do a swap?*

swarm¹ /swɔːm $ swɔːrm/ v [I + adv/prep] if people swarm somewhere, they quickly move there together **swarm with sth** phr v if a place is swarming with people or things, many people or things are moving around there: *The beach was swarming with people.*

swarm² n [C] a large group of insects that move together: **+of** *a swarm of bees*

swarthy /'swɔːði $ -ɔːr-/ adj *written* someone who is swarthy has dark skin

swat /swɒt $ swɑːt/ v [T] swatted, swatting to hit an insect to try to kill it

swathe¹ /sweɪð $ swɑːð, swɒð, sweɪð/ n [C] **1** a long thin area of something, especially land

2 cut a swathe through sth to destroy a large amount or part of something

swathe² v [T usually passive] to wrap or cover something: *women swathed in expensive furs*

sway¹ /sweɪ/ v **1** [I] to move slowly from one side to another: *Trees swayed gently in the breeze.* **2** [T] to make someone change their opinion: *Nothing you say will sway her.*

sway² n [U] formal **hold sway** to have power or influence

swear /sweə $ swer/ v past tense **swore** /swɔː $ swɔːr/ past participle **sworn** /swɔːn $ swɔːrn/

1 [I] to use rude or offensive language: *She doesn't smoke, drink, or swear.* | **+at** *He swore at me.*

2 [T] to promise that you will do something: **swear to do sth** *Do you swear to tell the truth?* | **+(that)** *I swear I'll never leave you.* → see box at PROMISE

3 [T] to say very strongly that what you are saying is true: **+(that)** *She swore that she had never seen him before.* | *I never touched your purse, I swear.*

4 I could have sworn (that) spoken used to say that you were sure about something: *I could have sworn I left my keys here.*

swear by sth phr v informal to strongly believe that something is effective: *Heidi swears by aromatherapy.*

swear sb ⇔ in phr v if someone is sworn in, they make a public promise before beginning an important job or before speaking in court: *She was sworn in as president.*

swearing /'sweərɪŋ $ 'swer-/ n [U] when people use rude or offensive language

swear word n [C] a word that is considered rude or shocking

sweat¹ /swet/ v

1 [I] if you sweat, liquid comes out through your skin [= perspire]: *The heat was making us sweat.* | **sweat profusely/heavily**

2 [I,T] informal to work hard: *I sweated blood* (=worked extremely hard) *to get that report finished.*

sweat sth ⇔ out phr v to continue in an unpleasant situation and wait anxiously for it to end: *We had to sweat it out until they arrived.*

sweat² n [singular, U]

1 liquid that comes out through your skin, especially when you are hot or nervous [= perspiration]: *Beads of sweat appeared on his forehead.* | *He broke out into a sweat* (=began to sweat). | *She had worked up quite a sweat* (=started sweating because of working hard).

2 a cold sweat a state of fear or nervousness, in which you start to sweat even though you are not hot

3 no sweat spoken informal used to say that you can do something easily: *'Can you give me a ride home?' 'Yeah, no sweat!'*

sweater /'swetə $ -ər/ n [C] a piece of clothing with long sleeves and no buttons for the top half of your body [= jumper BrE]

sweatshirt /'swet-ʃɜːt $ -ʃɜːrt/ n [C] a thick soft cotton shirt with long sleeves, no collar, and no buttons → see picture at CLOTHES

sweatshop /'swet-ʃɒp $ -ʃɑːp/ n [C] a factory where people work in bad conditions for very little money

sweaty /'sweti/ adj covered with SWEAT, or smelling of sweat

swede /swiːd/ n [C,U] BrE a round vegetable that grows under the ground [= rutabaga AmE]

sweep¹ /swiːp/ v past tense and past participle **swept** /swept/

1 [I,T] to clean a floor or the ground, using a brush [➡ brush]: *I've just swept the kitchen floor.*

2 [I] if a crowd of people sweeps somewhere, it moves there quickly: **+through/across etc** *The crowd swept through the gates.*

3 [I,T] if a feeling, idea, or type of weather sweeps an area, it spreads quickly across it: **sweep the country/nation** *the latest fitness craze to sweep the nation* | *Storms swept through the mountains.*

4 [I] to move quickly in a way that shows you are very confident or annoyed: *She swept into the room.*

5 [T] to move someone or something quickly in a particular direction: **sweep sb/sth into/out/along etc** *I swept the papers quickly into the drawer.* | *Jessie was swept along by the angry crowd.* | *He swept his hair back with his hand.*

6 sweep sb off their feet to make someone feel very attracted to you romantically, in a short time

7 sweep sth under the carpet especially BrE also **sweep sth under the rug** especially AmE to try to hide something bad that has happened

sweep sth ⇔ away phr v to completely destroy something or make something disappear: *Many houses were swept away by the floods.*

sweep up phr v to remove dirt from the floor or ground using a brush: **sweep sth ⇔ up** *Could you sweep up the leaves?*

sweep² n **1** [C usually singular] a long, swinging movement: *She spoke with a sweep of her arm.* **2** [singular] a long curved line or area of land: *the sweep of the bay* **3** [C] someone whose job is to clean CHIMNEYS

sweeping /'swiːpɪŋ/ adj **1** affecting many things, or affecting one thing very much: *sweeping changes* **2** **sweeping statement/generalization** disapproving a statement that is too general and does not consider all the facts: *sweeping generalizations about women drivers*

sweepstake /'swiːpsteɪk/ n [C] a type of GAMBLING in which the winner gets all the money

sweet¹ /swiːt/ adj

1 having a taste like sugar [➡ sour, bitter]: *a cup of sweet tea* | *a sweet, sticky chocolate cake* → see box at TASTE

2 having a pleasant smell or sound: *a sweet-smelling rose* | *the sweet sounds of the cello*

3 kind, gentle, and friendly: **be sweet of sb** *It was sweet of you to help.* | *She's a sweet girl.* → see box at NICE

4 making you feel pleased or happy: *Goodnight, darling – sweet dreams.* | *Winning the match was sweet revenge.*

5 especially BrE pretty and pleasant – used when you are talking about children or small things [= cute]: *Her baby is so sweet!*

6 have a sweet tooth to like to eat sweet foods

7 Sweet! *spoken informal* used to show that you think something is very good: *'I got those tickets.' 'Sweet!'*
—**sweetly** *adv*: *She smiled sweetly.* —**sweetness** *n* [U]

sweet² *n BrE*
1 [C] a small piece of sweet food made of sugar or chocolate [= **candy** *AmE*]: *Don't eat too many sweets.*
2 [C,U] sweet food served after the meat and vegetables during a meal [= **dessert**] → see box at **RESTAURANT**

sweetcorn /'swiːtkɔːn $ -kɔːrn/ *n* [U] *BrE* soft yellow seeds from **MAIZE**, cooked as a vegetable [= **corn** *AmE*] → see picture at **VEGETABLE**

sweeten /'swiːtn/ *v* [T] **1** to make something sweeter **2** also **sweeten up** to try to persuade someone to do something by giving them presents or being nice to them

sweetener /'swiːtnə $ -ər/ *n* **1** [C,U] a substance used instead of sugar to make food or drinks taste sweeter **2** [C] something that you give to someone to persuade them to do something: *The tax cut is just a sweetener.*

sweetheart /'swiːthɑːt $ -hɑːrt/ *n* [C] **1** a way of speaking to someone you love: *Good night, sweetheart.* **2** *old-fashioned* the person you love romantically: *He married his childhood sweetheart.*

sweetie /'swiːti/ *n* [C] **1** *BrE* a **SWEET** used by children **2** someone who is easy to love: *He's such a sweetie.* **3** a way of speaking to someone that you love

sweet po'tato *n* [C] a root that looks like a long red potato, cooked as a vegetable

swell¹ /swel/ *v* past tense **swelled** past participle **swollen** /'swəʊlən $ 'swoʊ-/ **1** also **swell up** [I] to increase in size: *My ankle swelled up like a balloon.* **2** [I,T] to increase to a much bigger amount or number: *The city's population has swollen to 2 million.*

swell² *n* [singular] the movement of the sea as waves go up and down

swelling /'swelɪŋ/ *n* [C,U] an area on your body that becomes bigger than usual because of injury or illness: *This should reduce the swelling.*

sweltering /'sweltərɪŋ/ *adj* unpleasantly hot: *sweltering heat* → see box at **HOT**

swept /swept/ *v* the past tense and past participle of **SWEEP**

swerve /swɜːv $ swɜːrv/ *v* [I] to suddenly move to the left or right while you are driving: *She swerved but too late.* | **+across/off/into etc** *The car suddenly swerved off the road.*

swift /swɪft/ *adj* happening or moving quickly: *a swift recovery from illness* | *swift, agile movements* —**swiftly** *adv* → see box at **FAST**

swig /swɪɡ/ *v* [T] **swigged, swigging** *informal* to drink something by taking large amounts into your mouth → see box at **DRINK** —**swig** *n* [C]

swill /swɪl/ *v* **1** [T] to wash something by pouring a lot of water over or into it: *He swilled the yard down with water.* **2** [I,T] to make a liquid move around in a container: *He swilled the whisky round in his glass.* **3** also **swill down** [T] *informal* to drink a lot of something, especially beer

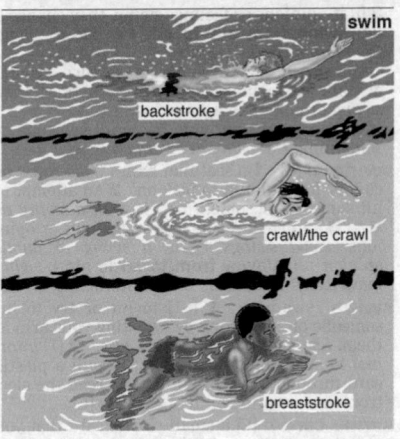

swim

backstroke

crawl/the crawl

breaststroke

swim¹ /swɪm/ *v* past tense **swam** /swæm/ past participle **swum** /swʌm/ present participle **swimming**
1 [I,T] to move through water, using your arms and legs: *Can Lucy swim?* | *Let's go swimming.* | *She swims 20 lengths every day.* | **+in** *We used to swim in the lake.* | **+across/back/out etc** *We swam across the bay.*
2 [I] if your head swims, you feel confused or as if everything is spinning around
3 [I] if something swims, it seems to be moving or turning, because you are ill, tired, drunk etc: *The room swam around her.*
4 be swimming in/with sth to be covered by a lot of liquid: *potatoes swimming in gravy*
—**swimming** *n* [U] *Let's all go swimming this afternoon.* —**swimmer** *n* [C]

swim² *n* [C] a time when you swim: *I went for a swim after school.*

'swimming ,costume *n* [C] *BrE* a swimsuit

'swimming pool *n* [C] a structure that has been built for people to swim in [= **pool**] → see box at **SPORT**

'swimming trunks *n* [plural] a piece of clothing that boys and men wear for swimming

swimsuit /'swɪmsuːt, -sjuːt $ -suːt/ *n* [C] a piece of clothing that girls and women wear for swimming

swindle /'swɪndl/ *v* [T] to get money from someone by tricking them —**swindle** *n* [C] —**swindler** *n* [C]

swine /swaɪn/ *n* [C] **1** *informal* someone who behaves very badly **2** *old-fashioned* a pig

swing¹ /swɪŋ/ *v* past tense and past participle **swung** /swʌŋ/
1 [I,T] to move backwards and forwards while hanging from something, or to make something do this: *a sign swinging in the wind* | *They walked along, swinging their arms.*
2 [I,T] to move smoothly in a curved direction, or to make something move this way: **+into/out of etc** *A car swung into the drive.* | **swing sth into/out of etc sth** *Kate swung her legs out of bed.* | **swing open/shut** *The door swung shut.*

S

3 [I] if opinions or feelings swing, they change a lot: **swing from sth to sth** *Her mood swung from happiness to despair.*

swing around/round *phr v* to turn around quickly, or to make something do this: *Mike swung around to look at me.*

swing at sb/sth *phr v* to try to hit someone or something: *He swung at me and missed.*

swing² *n* [C] **1** a seat that hangs from ropes or chains, for children to play on **2** an attempt to hit someone or something: *He took a swing at me.* **3** a fairly large change in feelings or opinions: *mood swings* | +**in** *a swing in public opinion* | +**to/away from/towards etc** *a swing towards left-wing ideas* → **be in full swing** at FULL¹

swipe /swaɪp/ *v* **1** [I,T] to hit or try to hit someone or something by swinging your arm at them: *She swiped me across the face.* **2** [T] *informal* to steal something **3** [T] to pull a plastic card through a machine that can read the electronic information on it —**swipe** *n* [C]

'swipe card *n* [C] a small plastic card that you pull through a machine in order to open a door

swirl /swɜːl $ swɜːrl/ *v* [I,T] to move around and around in a circular movement: +**around/round** *Smoke swirled around her.* —**swirl** *n* [C]

swish /swɪʃ/ *v* [I,T] to move or make something move through the air with a soft sound: *horses swishing their tails* —**swish** *n* [C]

switch¹ /swɪtʃ/ *v* [I,T]

1 to change from one thing to another thing [= change]: +**to** *If you switch to a low-fat diet, your health will improve.* | **switch from sth to sth** *He kept switching from one subject to another.* | +**between** *It is possible to switch between courses.* | *soldiers who switch sides*

2 to exchange things, or replace one thing with another thing [= change]: **switch sth for sth** *I'm going to switch it for something newer.*

switch off *phr v* to turn off a machine, light etc, using a switch: **switch sth ⇔ off** *My mobile phone was switched off.* | *Switch off the lights before you leave.*

switch on *phr v* to turn on a machine, light etc using a switch: **switch sth ⇔ on** *Switch the radio on.* | *The video will switch on automatically.* → see box at OPEN

switch over *phr v* **1** to change to a different television CHANNEL **2** to start using a different product, system etc: +**to** *More and more people are switching over to internet banking.*

switch² *n* [C]

1 the thing you press to make a machine, light etc start or stop working: *a light switch*

2 a change from one thing to another: +**to** *Shoppers are making the switch to organic food.* | +**in** *a switch in emphasis*

switchboard /'swɪtʃbɔːd $ -bɔːrd/ *n* [C] a system used to connect telephone calls in an office building, hotel etc

swivel /'swɪvəl/ also **swivel around** *v* [I,T] **swivelled, swivelling** *BrE*; **swiveled, swiveling** *AmE* to turn around quickly, or to make something do this: *He swivelled his chair to face her.*

swollen¹ /'swəʊlən $ 'swoʊ-/ *v* the past participle of SWELL

swollen² *adj* **1** a part of your body that is swollen is bigger than usual, especially because

you are ill or injured: *swollen glands* **2** a swollen river has more water in it than usual

swoop /swuːp/ *v* [I] **1** to move down suddenly through the air, especially to attack something: +**down/over/across etc** *The birds swooped down.* **2** if soldiers or the police swoop on a place, they go there quickly and without warning in order to find someone or something —**swoop** *n* [C]

swop /swɒp $ swɑːp/ *v, n* another spelling of SWAP

sword /sɔːd $ sɔːrd/ *n* [C] a weapon with a long sharp blade and a handle

swordfish /'sɔːd,fɪʃ $ 'sɔːrd-/ *n* [C] plural **swordfish** a large fish with a long pointed upper jaw

swore /swɔː $ swɔːr/ *v* the past tense of SWEAR

sworn¹ /swɔːn $ swɔːrn/ *v* the past participle of SWEAR

sworn² *adj* **1 sworn statement/evidence etc** a statement etc that you officially say is true **2 sworn enemies** two people or groups who hate each other

swot¹ /swɒt $ swɑːt/ *n* [C] *BrE informal disapproving* someone who studies too much

swot² *v* [I] **swotted, swotting** *BrE informal* to study hard, especially for an examination

swot up *phr v* to learn as much as you can about something: +**on** *Swot up on the company before your interview.*

swum /swʌm/ *v* the past participle of SWIM

swung /swʌŋ/ *v* the past tense and past participle of SWING

sycamore /'sɪkəmɔː $ -mɔːr/ *n* [C,U] a tree with seeds shaped like two wings, or the wood from this tree

sycophant /'sɪkəfənt/ *n* [C] *formal disapproving* someone who always praises an important person, but not in an honest way —**sycophantic** /ˌsɪkə'fæntɪk/ *adj*

syllable /'sɪləbəl/ *n* [C] a part of a word that contains a single vowel sound. 'Cat' has one syllable, and 'butter' has two.

syllabus /'sɪləbəs/ *n* [C] a plan of what students should learn in a particular subject

symbol /'sɪmbəl/ *n* [C]

1 a picture, shape, letter etc that has a particular meaning or represents a particular chemical, amount etc [➡ sign]: *a symbol showing that the product is fire resistant* | +**for** *Fe is the chemical symbol for iron.*

2 someone or something that represents a particular quality or idea: +**of** *A suntan is not a symbol of fitness and health.*

→ **SEX SYMBOL, STATUS SYMBOL**

symbolic /sɪm'bɒlɪk $ -'bɑː-/ *adj* **1** representing a particular idea or quality: +**of** *The fighting is symbolic of the chaos in the country.* **2** important but not having any real effect: *a symbolic victory* —**symbolically** /-kli/ *adv*

symbolism /'sɪmbəlɪzəm/ *n* [U] the use of symbols to represent ideas or qualities: *religious symbolism*

symbolize also **-ise** *BrE* /'sɪmbəlaɪz/ *v* [T] to represent a particular quality or feeling: *Crime often symbolizes a wider social problem.*

symmetrical /sɪˈmetrɪkəl/ also **symmetric** /sɪˈmetrɪk/ adj having two halves that are exactly the same size and shape [≠ **asymmetrical**]

symmetry /ˈsɪmɪtri/ n [U] when both halves of something are exactly the same size and shape

sympathetic /ˌsɪmpəˈθetɪk◂/ adj
1 showing that you understand and care about someone's problems [≠ **unsympathetic**]: *a sympathetic attitude* | **+towards/to** *Parents aren't always very sympathetic towards their children.*
2 [not before noun] willing to support someone's ideas or actions: **+to/towards** *He wanted someone who was sympathetic to his views.*
—**sympathetically** /-kli/ adv

sympathize also **-ise** BrE /ˈsɪmpəθaɪz/ v [I]
1 to show that you understand and care about someone's problems: **+with** *I can sympathize with the way you're feeling.* **2** to support someone's ideas or actions: **+with** *I don't sympathize with the party's views.*

sympathizer also **-iser** BrE /ˈsɪmpəθaɪzə $ -ər/ n [C] someone who supports the aims of an organization or political party

sympathy /ˈsɪmpəθi/ n [U] also **sympathies** [plural]
1 the feeling you have when you understand why someone is unhappy and want to help them feel better: **+for** *I have a lot of **sympathy** for her.* | *My **sympathies are with** the victims' families.*
2 belief in or support for an idea or action: **+with** *I do **have some sympathy** with their aims.* | **in sympathy with sth** *He is in sympathy with many Green Party policies.* | **liberal/left-wing/Republican etc sympathies**

symphony /ˈsɪmfəni/ n [C] plural **symphonies** a long piece of music written for an ORCHESTRA

symptom /ˈsɪmptəm/ n [C] **1** something that shows you have an illness: **+of** *Chest pain can be a symptom of heart disease.* **2** a sign that a serious problem exists: **+of** *Crime is often seen as a symptom of the breakdown in society.*

symptomatic /ˌsɪmptəˈmætɪk◂/ adj formal showing that a serious problem exists: **+of** *The rise in unemployment is symptomatic of problems in the economy.*

synagogue /ˈsɪnəɡɒɡ $ -ɡɔːɡ/ n [C] a building for Jewish religious meetings

sync /sɪŋk/ n informal **1** **out of sync** working at a different time or speed or in a different way **2** **in sync** working together at the same time or speed or in the same way

synchronize also **-ise** BrE /ˈsɪŋkrənaɪz/ v [T] to make two or more things happen at the same time —**synchronization** /ˌsɪŋkrənaɪˈzeɪʃən $ -nə-/ n [U]

syndicate /ˈsɪndɪkət/ n [C] a group of people or companies that work together to achieve something: **+of** *a syndicate of banks*

syndrome /ˈsɪndrəʊm $ -droʊm/ n [C] **1** a medical condition that consists of a particular set of problems: *irritable bowel syndrome* **2** a set of feelings, qualities etc that are typical of a particular problem

synonym /ˈsɪnənɪm/ n [C] a word with the same meaning as another word in the same language [≠ **antonym**]

synonymous /sɪˈnɒnɪməs $ -ˈnɑː-/ adj **1** so closely related to something else that when you think of one thing you also think of the other thing: **+with** *His name has become synonymous with success.* **2** if two words are synonymous, they have the same meaning

synopsis /sɪˈnɒpsɪs $ -ˈnɑːp-/ n [C] plural **synopses** /-siːz/ a short description of the main parts of a story

syntax /ˈsɪntæks/ n [U] technical the way words are arranged to form sentences or phrases

synthesis /ˈsɪnθɪsɪs/ n [C,U] plural **syntheses** /-siːz/ formal when several things are combined to form something

synthesize also **-ise** BrE /ˈsɪnθɪsaɪz/ v [T] to combine different things in order to produce something: *Plants synthesize energy from sunlight.*

synthesizer also **-iser** BrE /ˈsɪnθɪsaɪzə $ -ər/ n [C] an electronic instrument that can produce the sounds of various musical instruments

synthetic /sɪnˈθetɪk/ adj made from artificial substances, not natural ones: *synthetic fabrics* → see box at **NATURAL**

syphilis /ˈsɪfəlɪs/ n [U] a very serious disease that can be passed from one person to another during sex

syphon /ˈsaɪfən/ n a British spelling of SIPHON

syringe /sɪˈrɪndʒ/ n [C] a tube and needle used for removing blood from your body, or for putting drugs into it

syrup /ˈsɪrəp $ ˈsɜː-, ˈsɪ-/ n [U] thick sticky liquid made from sugar —**syrupy** adj

system /ˈsɪstɪm/ n [C]
1 a group of things or parts that work together: *an alarm system* | *your body's digestive system* | *our new computer system* | *the building's heating system*
2 a way of organizing or doing something: **+of** *a system of government* | **system for doing sth** *the system for electing a leader* | **political/legal/education system**
3 **get sth out of your system** informal to do something that gets rid of an unpleasant emotion
4 **the system** informal the rules and powerful organizations that restrict what you do
→ **IMMUNE SYSTEM, NERVOUS SYSTEM, OPERATING SYSTEM, SOLAR SYSTEM, SOUND SYSTEM**

systematic /ˌsɪstɪˈmætɪk◂/ adj organized carefully and done thoroughly: *a **systematic approach** to training* —**systematically** /-kli/ adv

T, t

T, t /tiː/ n [C,U] plural **T's, t's** the 20th letter of the English alphabet

ta /tɑː/ BrE spoken informal thank you

tab /tæb/ n **1 pick up the tab** to pay for something, especially a meal in a restaurant **2 keep (close) tabs on sb/sth** informal to watch someone or something carefully to check what they are doing **3** [C] a small piece of metal, plastic, paper etc that is attached to something so that you can open it or find it easily

tabby /'tæbi/ n [C] plural **tabbies** a cat with light and dark lines on its fur

table¹ /'teɪbəl/ n [C]
1 a piece of furniture which has a flat top resting on legs: *Otto sat at the kitchen table reading a newspaper.* | *a coffee table* | **lay the table** BrE; **set the table** AmE (=to put knives, forks, dishes etc on a table, ready for a meal)
2 a table in a restaurant that you arrange to use at a particular time: **book/reserve a table**.*I've booked a table for 8 o'clock.*
3 snooker/billiard/ping-pong etc table a special table, used for playing a particular game
4 a set of numbers or facts that are arranged in rows
5 the table of contents a list of the parts of a book and the pages they are on
6 turn the tables (on sb) to change a situation completely so that someone loses an advantage and you gain one: *The tables were turned when she married a younger man.*
→ **DRESSING TABLE**

table² v [T] **1 table a proposal/question etc** BrE to formally suggest something to be discussed at a meeting **2 table an offer/idea etc** AmE to decide to wait until a later time to discuss an offer, idea etc

tablecloth /'teɪbəlklɒθ $ -klɔːθ/ n [C] a cloth for covering a table

tablespoon /'teɪbəlspuːn/ n [C] a large spoon, or the amount it holds

tablet /'tæbl̩t/ n [C] a small round piece of medicine that you swallow [= pill]: *She took a couple of sleeping tablets.* → see box at **MEDICINE**

'table ,tennis n [U] a game in which people hit a ball to each other over a net that is stretched across a table [= ping-pong]

tableware /'teɪbəlweə $ -wer/ n [U] formal the plates, glasses, knives etc used when eating a meal

tabloid /'tæblɔɪd/ n [C] a newspaper that has small pages, a lot of photographs, and not very much serious news → see box at **NEWSPAPER**

taboo /tə'buː, tæ-/ n [C,U] plural **taboos** something that you must not do or talk about because it offends or embarrasses people —**taboo** adj: *Sex is a taboo subject in many homes.*

tacit /'tæsɪ̩t/ adj tacit agreement, approval, or support is given without anything actually being said

taciturn /'tæsɪ̩tɜːn $ -ɜːrn/ adj a taciturn person does not talk a lot, and seems unfriendly

tack¹ /tæk/ n **1** [C] a small nail with a sharp point and a flat top **2** [C] AmE a short pin with a large round flat top, for attaching notices to boards, walls etc [= thumbtack AmE; = drawing pin BrE] **3** [C,U] a method that you use to achieve something: *If polite requests don't work, you'll have to try a different tack.*

tack² v [T] to attach something to a wall, board etc using a tack
tack sth ⇔ on phr v to add something new to something that is already complete: *a small porch tacked on to the front of the house*

tackle¹ /'tækəl/ v [T] **1** to deal with a difficult problem: *a new attempt to tackle the problem of homelessness* | *Firemen tackled the blaze at the factory.* **2 a)** to try to take the ball away from someone in a game such as football **b)** to force someone to the ground so that they stop running, in a game such as American football **3** to talk to someone about a difficult subject or something that they have done: **tackle sb about sth** *When I tackled her about it, she admitted that she had lied.*

tackle² n **1** [C] **a)** an attempt to take the ball away from another player in a game such as football **b)** an attempt to stop an opponent by forcing them to the ground, in a game such as American football **2** [U] the equipment used in some sports, especially FISHING

tacky /'tæki/ adj **1** cheap and badly made: *tacky furniture* **2** slightly sticky

tact /tækt/ n [U] the ability to be careful not to say or do things that will upset other people

tactful /'tæktfəl/ adj careful not to say or do something that will upset someone [≠ tactless] —**tactfully** adv

tactic /'tæktɪk/ n [C usually plural] a method that you use to achieve what you want: *aggressive business tactics*

tactical /'tæktɪkəl/ adj relating to what you do to achieve what you want: *For tactical reasons we won't ask for help.* | **tactical voting** (=voting in any way that will prevent a particular party from winning an election) —**tactically** /-kli/ adv

tactless /'tæktləs/ adj carelessly saying or doing things that are likely to upset someone [≠ tactful] → see box at **RUDE**

tad /tæd/ n spoken **a tad a)** a small amount: *'Would you like some milk?' 'Just a tad.'* **b)** slightly: *She looks a tad nervous.*

tadpole /'tædpəʊl $ -poʊl/ n [C] a small creature that will become a FROG or TOAD → see picture at **FROG**

taffeta /'tæfɪ̩tə/ n [U] a shiny stiff cloth made from silk or NYLON: *a taffeta dress*

tag¹ /tæg/ n [C] a small piece of paper, plastic etc that is fastened to something and gives information about it: *I can't find the price tag on these jeans.* → **QUESTION TAG**

tag² v [T] **tagged, tagging** to attach a tag to something
tag along phr v informal to go somewhere with someone, especially when they have not asked you to go with them: *Is it all right if I tag along?*

tail¹ /teɪl/ n [C]

1 the long thin part on the back end of an animal's body: *The dog was **wagging** its **tail**.* → see picture on page A2
2 the back part of a plane → see picture at
AEROPLANE
3 the tail end of sth the last part of something: *the tail end of the century*
4 tails a) [U] the side of a coin that does not have a picture of someone's head on it [≠ **heads**] **b)** [plural] a man's suit coat with two long parts that hang down the back, worn to very formal events

tail² v [T] *informal* to secretly follow someone and watch what they do, where they go etc
  tail off *phr v* to become gradually quieter, smaller, less etc, and often stop or disappear completely: *His voice tailed off as he saw his father approaching.*

tailback /'teɪlbæk/ n [C] *BrE* a line of cars on a road that are moving very slowly or not moving at all

'tail-light, 'tail light n [C] one of the two red lights at the back of a vehicle → see picture on page A12

tailor¹ /'teɪlə $ -ər/ n [C] someone whose job is to make men's clothes that are measured to fit each customer exactly

tailor² v [T] to make something so that it is exactly what someone wants or needs: *Courses are specially tailored to the needs of each student.*

tailored /'teɪləd $ -ərd/ adj a piece of clothing that is tailored is made to fit very well: *a tailored suit*

tailoring /'teɪlərɪŋ/ n [U] the way that clothes are made, or the job of making them

,tailor-'made adj very suitable for someone or something: *The job's tailor-made for you.*

tailpipe /'teɪlpaɪp/ n [C] *AmE* an **EXHAUST** pipe → see picture on page A12

taint /teɪnt/ v [T usually passive] **1** if something bad taints a situation or person, it makes the person or situation seem bad: *Baker argues that his trial was tainted by negative publicity.* **2** to damage something by adding an unwanted substance to it: *hamburger meat tainted with harmful bacteria* —**taint** n [singular]

take¹ /teɪk/ v [T] past tense **took** /tʊk/ past participle **taken** /'teɪkən/

1 to move something from one place to another, or help someone go from one place to another: **take sb/sth to/into etc sth** *Take this note to Dr Mason.* | *The policeman took him into a tiny room.* | **take sth off/from etc sth** *Take your feet off the seats.* | **take sb/sth with you** *His wife went to Spain, taking the children with her.* | **take sb to do sth** *Howard took me to meet his parents.* → see box at **BRING**
2 to steal something or borrow it without permission: *Did you take my soda?*
3 to carry something or have it with you when you go somewhere: *Make sure you take an umbrella when you leave.*
4 used with some nouns instead of using a verb to say that someone does something, or that something happens: *Here, take a look.* | *I took a shower and got ready to go out.* | **take a holiday/break/rest etc** *Let's take a short break and meet here in ten minutes.* | **take a picture/**

photograph/photo (=use a camera to make a picture)
5 also **take out** to go with someone to a restaurant, film etc and pay for them or be responsible for them: *I'm taking her to a movie.*
6 to hold something: *Let me take your coat.* | *She took his arm.*
7 if something takes a particular amount of time, money, effort etc, you need that amount of time etc for it to happen or succeed: *Looking after children takes hard work.* | *It took a few minutes for his eyes to adjust to the dark.* | **take (sb) ages/forever** *informal: The drive to the airport took forever.* | **take courage/guts** *Starting your own business takes a lot of guts.* | *They can still win, but it'll **take some doing** (=be difficult and take a lot of effort).*
8 to accept something that is offered or given to you: *Are you going to take the job?* | *Jim took all the credit, even though he didn't do much of the work.* | **take credit cards/a cheque etc** (=accept them as a way of paying) *Do you take American Express?*
9 take a test/exam to do a test or examination [= **sit** *BrE*]: *I'm taking my driving test next week.*
10 to study a particular subject in school or college: *Are you taking French next year?*
11 to swallow or use a medicine or drug: *A lot of kids start **taking drugs** (=using illegal drugs) when they're 14 or 15.*
12 to use a car, bus, train etc to go somewhere, or to travel using a particular road: *Let's take the bus.* | *Take the M6 to Junction 19.* → see box at
TRAVEL
13 to accept an unpleasant situation [= **stand**]: *I can't take any more of her complaining.*
14 to have a particular feeling about something: **take pleasure/pride/an interest etc in (doing) sth** *You should take pride in your work.* | **take pity on sb** (=help someone because you feel sorry for them) *Howard took pity on the man and gave him food.*
15 to think about someone or something in a particular way, or react to them in this way: **take sth badly/personally/seriously etc** *Try not to take his criticism personally.* | **take sb seriously** *I was joking but he took me seriously.* | **take sth as sth** *I shall take that as a compliment.*
16 to be a suitable size, type etc for a particular person or thing: *Our car can take up to six people.* | *What size shoe do you take?*
17 to choose to buy something: *We'll take a pound of ham and a half pound of cheese.* | *'It's $50.' 'OK, I'll take it.'*
18 to get possession or control of something: *Rebel forces have taken the airport.* | **take control/charge/power** *Republicans hope to take control of Congress this fall.* | *Six soldiers were taken prisoner* (=captured by an enemy).
19 to use something such as sugar, milk, salt etc in your food or drinks: *Do you take milk and sugar in your coffee?*
20 to make a number smaller by a particular amount [= **subtract**]: **take sth away/take sth (away) from sth** *Take 2 from 9 and you get 7.* → see box at **CALCULATE**
21 take a lot out of you to make you very tired: *My job takes a lot out of me.*
22 take sb's word for it/take it from sb

spoken used to tell someone to accept that what someone says is true: *He'll be there on time tomorrow, take my word for it.*

23 I take it (that) *spoken* used to check with someone that something is true or has been done: *I take it you two have already met.*

24 to write down information: *Sue offered to take notes.* | *He's not here right now — can I take a message* (=write down information from someone on the telephone and give the information to someone else)?

25 to measure the amount, level, rate etc of something: *The doctor took her blood pressure.*

take after sb *phr v* to look or behave like an older member of your family: *Jenny takes after her dad.*

take sth ⇔ **apart** *phr v* to separate something into all its different parts: *Jim took apart the faucet and put in a new washer.*

take sb/sth ⇔ **away** *phr v* to remove something or someone from a place: *Hyde was taken away in handcuffs.*

take sth ⇔ **back** *phr v* **1** to return something to the place or person it came from: *If the shirt doesn't fit, take it back to the shop.* **2** to admit that you were wrong to say something: *All right, I'm sorry, I take it back.*

take sth ⇔ **down** *phr v* **1** to remove something that is attached to a wall: *Our teacher made us take down all the posters.* **2** to separate something into all its different parts and move it to a different place: *Would you help me take down the tent?* **3** to write information on a piece of paper: *The receptionist took down his name.* → see box at **WRITE**

take sb/sth ⇔ **in** *phr v* **1** to understand and remember new facts and information: *There was so much happening in the film, it was difficult to take it all in.* **2 be taken in (by sb/sth)** to be deceived by someone or something: *The bank had been taken in by the forged receipts.* **3** to let someone stay in your house because they have nowhere else to stay: *The Humane Society took in almost 38,000 cats and dogs last year.* **4** to make a piece of clothing narrower, so that it fits you

take off *phr v* **1 take** sth ⇔ **off** to remove something [≠ **put on**]: *He took off his shoes.* → see box at **REMOVE** → see picture at **PUT (ON)** **2** if an aircraft takes off, it leaves the ground and goes up into the air [≠ **land**] → see box at **AIRPORT** → see picture at **LAND**² **3 take some time/a day/a week etc off** to not go to work for a period of time **4** *informal* to leave somewhere quickly and suddenly: *We packed everything in the car and took off.* **5** to suddenly start being successful: *The song became a surprise hit and his career suddenly took off.*

take sb/sth ⇔ **on** *phr v* **1** to compete or fight against someone, especially someone bigger or better than you: *The winner of this game will take on Miami.* **2** to start doing some work or start being responsible for something: *I've taken on far too much work lately.* **3** to start to employ someone: *We're taking on 50 new staff this year.*

take sb/sth **out** *phr v* **1 take** sth ⇔ **out** to remove something from inside a building, your body etc: *The dentist says she may have to take out one of my back teeth.* **2** to go with someone to a restaurant, film etc, and pay for them: **+for** *Rich wants to take me out for Chinese food.*

3 take sth ⇔ **out** to officially arrange to get something from a bank, insurance company etc: **take out a policy/loan etc** *The couple took out a £20,000 loan.* **4 take** sth ⇔ **out** to borrow books from a library: *You can take out six books at a time.*

take sth **out on** sb *phr v* to treat someone badly when you are angry, tired etc, even though it is not their fault: *Don't take it out on me just because you've had a bad day.*

take over *phr v* to take control of something [→ **takeover**]: **take** sth ⇔ **over** *His son will take over the business.*

take to sb/sth *phr v* **1** to start to like someone or something: *We took to each other right away.* **2 take to doing sth** to begin doing something regularly: *Sandra has taken to getting up early to go jogging.*

take up sth *phr v* **1 take** sth ⇔ **up** to start doing a new job or activity: *I've just taken up golf.* **2** to use or fill an amount of time or space: *The program takes up a lot of memory on the hard drive.*

take sb **up on** sth *phr v* to accept an invitation or suggestion: *Thanks for the offer. I might take you up on it.*

take sth **up with** sb *phr v* to discuss something with someone, especially a complaint or problem: *If you're unhappy, you should take it up with your supervisor.*

take² *n* **1** [C] an occasion when a scene from a film or a song is recorded: *We had to do six takes for this particular scene.* **2** [singular] *AmE informal* an American word for TAKINGS → **DOUBLE TAKE, GIVE AND TAKE**

takeaway /'teɪkəweɪ/ *n* [C] *BrE* a meal that you buy from a restaurant to eat at home, or a restaurant that sells this food [= **takeout** *AmE*]: *a Chinese takeaway* —**take-away** *adj*

'take-home ,pay *n* [U] the amount of money that you receive from your job after taxes etc have been taken out → see box at **PAY**

taken /'teɪkən/ *v* **1** the past participle of TAKE **2 be taken with sb/sth** to like someone or something very much: *Chris was very taken with her.*

'take-off, takeoff /'teɪkɒf $ -ɒːf/ *n* [C,U] when a plane moves off the ground into the air

takeout /'teɪk-aʊt/ *n* [C] *AmE* a TAKEAWAY —**take-out** *adj*

takeover /'teɪk,əʊvə $ -,oʊvər/ *n* [C] **1** when a company gets control of another company by buying over half of the SHARES: *The takeover bid was rejected by shareholders.* **2** the act of getting control of a country or political organization, using force

takings /'teɪkɪŋz/ *n* [plural] the amount of money that a shop, bar etc gets from selling things over a particular period of time: *the day's takings*

talcum powder /'tælkəm ,paʊdə $ -dər/ also **talc** /tælk/ *n* [U] a powder with a nice smell that you put on your skin after washing

tale /teɪl/ *n* [C] a story about things that happened long ago, or things that may not have really happened: *a book of fairy tales* (=children's stories in which magical things happen) | *old Japanese folk tales* (=traditional stories from a country) | **+of/about** *Roger was always*

telling tales about life in the army. → see box at
STORY
→ OLD WIVES' TALE

talent /'tælənt/ *n* [C,U] a natural ability to do
something well: *Turner has more talent than
any other player on the team.* | **+for** *Lee has
always had a natural talent for public speaking.*

talented /'tæləntɪd/ *adj* having a natural ability to do something well: *a talented musician*

talisman /'tælɪzmən/ *n* [C] plural **talismans** an
object that is believed to have magic powers to
protect the person who owns it

talk¹ /tɔːk $ tɒːk/ *v*

1 [I] to say things to someone as part of a
conversation: *I could hear Sarah and Andrew
talking in the next room.* | **+to/with** *Tara's talk-
ing with a customer.* | *She's very easy to talk to.* |
+about *Grandpa never talks much about the
war.* | *Sue and Bob still aren't talking* (=are
refusing to talk to each other).

THESAURUS

chat (to sb) – to talk to someone in a friendly
way about things that are not very important
converse *formal* – to have a conversation with
someone
visit with sb *AmE informal* – to have a
conversation with someone
discuss – to talk seriously about ideas or plans
gossip – to talk about other people's private
lives when they are not there
whisper – to talk quietly, usually because you
do not want other people to hear what you
are saying

---

2 [I,T] to discuss something serious or important
with someone: *Joe, we need to talk.* | **+to/with** *I'd
like to talk with you in private.* | **+about** *My wife
and I are talking about buying a new car.* | **talk
sport/politics/dinner etc** *Casey likes to drink
beer and talk politics.*
3 [I] to use your voice to say words [= speak]:
How old are babies when they start to talk? | *She
was talking so fast I could hardly understand her.*
4 [I] to tell someone secret information because
they force you to: *They threatened to shoot him,
but he still refused to talk.*
5 talk your way out of sth *informal* to avoid an
unpleasant situation by giving an explanation or
excuse: *He usually manages to talk his way out
of trouble.*
6 what are you talking about? *spoken* used
when you think someone has said something
stupid or wrong: *What are you talking about? I
gave you the money weeks ago.*
7 talk to yourself to say your thoughts out loud
8 talk about lazy/cheap/lucky etc *spoken
informal* used to emphasize that someone is very
lazy, cheap, lucky etc: *Talk about annoying! I
thought she was never going to shut up.*
9 talk sense/nonsense/rubbish etc used to
say that you think someone is saying something
sensible or stupid
10 talk (some) sense into sb to talk to someone and make them start behaving in a sensible
way: *She hoped Father McCormack would be able
to talk some sense into her son.*
11 know what you are talking about *spoken*
to know a lot about a particular subject

talk back *phr v* if a child talks back to an
adult, they answer the adult rudely: **+to** *Don't
talk back to your father!*
talk down to sb *phr v* to talk to someone in a
way that shows you think they are not important or not intelligent: *The teachers talked down
to us and treated us like children.*
talk sb into sth *phr v* to persuade someone to
do something that they do not really want to do:
*I didn't want to go, but my friends talked me into
it.*
talk sb out of sth *phr v* to persuade someone
not to do something that they wanted to do: *No
one could talk Luis out of joining the army.*
talk sth ⇔ over *phr v* to discuss a problem
with someone before deciding what to do: **+with**
*I'm going to have to talk it over with your father
first.*

talk² *n*
1 [C] when people talk to each other about a
subject: **+about** *We must have a talk about
money.* | **+with** *After a long talk with her hus-
band, Teri decided to get a divorce.*
2 [C] a speech on a particular subject: **+on/
about** *Professor Mason will be giving a talk on
the Civil War.*
3 [U] when people say that something may be
true or may happen: **+of** *Tickets sold so quickly
there's talk of a second concert.*
4 talks [plural] formal discussions between different countries, organizations, leaders etc: *the
latest trade talks*
→ PEP TALK, SMALL TALK

talkative /'tɔːkətɪv $ 'tɒːk-/ *adj* a talkative
person talks a lot
talker /'tɔːkə $ 'tɒːkər/ *n* [C] *informal* someone
who talks a lot or talks in a particular way:
Will's a fast talker.
'talk show *n* [C] *AmE* a television or radio show
in which people answer questions about themselves [= chat show *BrE*] → see box at TELEVISION
tall /tɔːl $ tɒːl/ *adj*
1 a tall person, building, tree etc is a greater
height than normal [≠ small]: *the tallest boy in
the class* | *a house surrounded by tall trees*

THESAURUS

Use **tall** to talk about the height of people
and trees: *She's only five feet tall.* | *a road
with tall trees on either side*
Use **tall** to talk about other narrow objects:
an old house with tall chimneys | *the tall mast
of a ship*
Use **high** to talk about mountains, walls,
fences etc: *the highest mountain in the world* |
How high is that hedge?
Use **high** to talk about how far something is
from the ground: *The shelf's too high for the
kids to reach.*
You can use both **tall** and **high** to talk about
buildings: *the tallest building in Toronto* | *I
often worry when I'm in a high building.*

---

2 used to talk about the height of someone or
something: **5ft/2m/12 inches etc tall** *My broth-
er's almost 6 feet tall.* | *How tall is that book-
case?*

tally¹ /'tæli/ *n* [C] plural **tallies** a record of how
much you have won, spent, used etc by a particular point in time

tally² also **tally up** v tallied, tallying, tallies **1** [I] if numbers or statements tally, they match each other: *The witnesses' statements didn't tally.* **2** [T] to calculate the total number of something

talon /'tælən/ n [C] a bird's CLAW → see picture on page A2

tambourine /ˌtæmbə'riːn/ n [C] a small drum that you hold in your hand and play by hitting or shaking it → see picture on page A6

tame¹ /teɪm/ adj **1** a tame animal is not wild any more because it has been trained to obey people and not to fear them **2** disappointing and not exciting

tame² v [T] to train a wild animal to obey people

tamper /'tæmpə $ -ər/ v

tamper with sth phr v to change something without permission: *Someone had tampered with the switches.*

tampon /'tæmpɒn $ -pɑːn/ n [C] a tube-shaped piece of cotton that a woman uses to collect the blood during her PERIOD (=monthly flow of blood)

tan¹ /tæn/ n

1 [C] if you have a tan, your skin is darker than usual because you have spent time in the sun [= suntan]

2 [U] a pale yellow-brown colour

tan² v [I,T] tanned, tanning to get darker skin by spending time in the sun: *I don't tan easily.* —tanned adj

tan³ adj **1** pale yellow-brown in colour **2** AmE having darker skin after spending time in the sun [= tanned BrE]

tandem /'tændəm/ n [C] **1** a bicycle for two people **2** in tandem (with sb/sth) doing something at the same time as someone or something else

tangent /'tændʒənt/ n [C] go off on a tangent to suddenly start talking about something completely different

tangerine /ˌtændʒə'riːn/ n [C] a small sweet orange

tangible /'tændʒɪbəl/ adj definite and able to be seen or touched [≠ intangible]: *tangible proof*

tangle¹ /'tæŋgəl/ n [C] a mass of hair, wires etc that are twisted together: +of *a tangle of cables*

tangle² also **tangle up** v [I,T] if hair, wires, string etc tangle, or if you tangle them, they become twisted together untidily: *Don't tangle all the electrical wires.* —tangled adj: *tangled hair*

tangle

tangled telephone cord

tangle with sb/sth phr v informal to argue or fight with someone

tango /'tæŋgəʊ $ -goʊ/ n [C] plural **tangos** a fast dance from South America, or music for this dance —tango v [I]

tangy /'tæŋi/ adj having a pleasantly sour taste or smell

tank¹ /tæŋk/ n [C]

1 a large container for liquid or gas: +of *a tank*

of water | *The plane's fuel tanks were full.* | a storage tank | **petrol tank** BrE; **gas tank** AmE (=a tank in a vehicle to hold petrol)

2 a large military vehicle that has a big gun and moves on metal belts that fit over the wheels → THINK TANK

tank² v

tank sth ⇔ up phr v AmE to fill a car's tank with petrol [= fill up BrE]

tankard /'tæŋkəd $ -ərd/ n [C] a large metal cup

tanker /'tæŋkə $ -ər/ n [C] a ship or vehicle used for carrying liquid or gas: *an oil tanker*

tannoy /'tænɔɪ/ n [singular] trademark BrE a system of LOUDSPEAKERS: **over the tannoy** *We heard an announcement over the tannoy.*

tantalizing also **-ising** BrE /'tæntəl-aɪzɪŋ/ adj making you want something: *the tantalizing smell of fresh coffee* —tantalizingly adv

tantamount /'tæntəmaʊnt/ adj **be tantamount to sth** if something is tantamount to a bad or harmful action, it has the same effect or is equally bad

tantrum /'tæntrəm/ n [C] a short period when a child becomes very angry: **have/throw a tantrum** *Jenny threw one of her temper tantrums.*

tap¹ /tæp/ v tapped, tapping

1 [I,T] to gently hit something, often making a slight noise: **tap (sb/sth) on sth** *I tapped him on the shoulder.* | *Carol tapped her foot in time to the music.* → see box at KNOCK → see picture on page A10

2 also **tap into** [T] to use or take what you need from a supply of something: *Youngsters tap the knowledge of more experienced players.*

3 [T] to use special equipment to listen secretly to a telephone conversation from a distance: *They've probably tapped our phone.*

tap sth ⇔ in also **tap sth into sth** phr v BrE to put information into a computer or machine by pressing buttons

tap² n [C]

1 especially BrE a piece of equipment that you turn to control the flow of a liquid or gas [= faucet AmE]: **turn a tap on/off** *You forgot to turn off the tap.* | **hot/cold (water) tap** | **kitchen/bath/garden tap** | *The tap's dripping* (=letting out drops of water continuously). | **tap water** (=water that comes out through a tap) → see picture at BATHROOM

2 when you hit something gently, especially to get someone's attention: +on/at *a tap on my shoulder*

3 on tap available for use: *Cash for disabled sport is rarely on tap.*

'tap ,dancing n [U] dancing in which you move your feet very quickly and wear shoes with metal pieces on the bottom that make a noise as you move —tap dancer n [C] —tap dance v [I]

tape¹ /teɪp/ n

1 [C,U] a thin band of plastic used to record sounds or pictures, or the plastic box that contains it [= cassette; → videotape]: +of *a tape of African music* | **on tape** *I've got that film on tape.* | *Have you any blank tapes* (=tapes with nothing recorded on them)?

2 [U] a band of sticky material that you use to fasten things together [= Sellotape BrE; = Scotch tape AmE]

3 [C,U] a long thin piece of material, used to mark out an area or show where a race ends
→ **MASKING TAPE, RED TAPE**

tape² v [I,T] **1** to record sounds or pictures on a tape [→ **videotape**]: *Are you taping this movie?* **2** to fasten or cover something using tape → see box at **FASTEN**

'tape deck n [C] the part of a STEREO on which you can record and play music tapes

'tape ,measure n [C] a long thin piece of cloth or plastic marked with centimetres, metres etc that you use to measure things

taper¹ /'teɪpə $ -ər/ v [I,T] to become gradually narrower at one end —**tapered** adj
  taper off phr v to decrease gradually: *The rain had tapered off.*

taper² n [C] a long thin CANDLE, used to light lamps, fires etc

'tape re,corder n [C] a piece of equipment on which you can record and play sounds on a TAPE —**tape recording** n [U]

tapestry /'tæpɨstri/ n [C,U] plural **tapestries** a piece of heavy cloth that is woven with coloured threads to make a picture

tar /tɑː $ tɑːr/ n [U]
1 a black sticky substance that is used to cover roads and roofs
2 a harmful sticky substance that gets into the lungs of people who smoke
—**tar** v [T]

target¹ /'tɑːɡɨt $ 'tɑːr-/ n [C]
1 a person or place that people attack or criticize: **+for/of** *Airports are prime targets* (=very likely targets) *for terrorist attacks.* | *His country has recently been the target of criticism.* | **easy/ soft target** *Tourists are an easy target for thieves.*
2 the people that someone is trying to influence: *Who is the target audience for this show?*
3 an amount, level, or result that you try to achieve [= **goal**]: *I didn't meet* (=achieve) *my sales targets last month.* | *Set realistic targets for yourself.* | **+of** *a target of three batches per week* | **on target** *We're on target to finish by 2004.*
4 something that you shoot, throw, or kick something at: *The arrow missed the target.*
5 target language the language you are learning or translating into

target² v [T] **1** to aim something at someone or something: **target sth at sth** *fears that they might target missiles at major cities* **2** to choose a particular person or place to attack: *The bombers are targeting tourist resorts.* **3** to offer something to a particular group because you want them to buy or accept it: **target sth at sb** *a magazine targeted at teenagers*

tariff /'tærɨf/ n [C] **1** a tax on goods coming into a country **2** BrE a list or system of prices for a particular service: *mobile phone tariffs*

Tarmac /'tɑːmæk $ 'tɑːr-/ n trademark
1 BrE a mixture of TAR and small stones, used to cover the surface of roads [= **blacktop** AmE]
2 the tarmac the large area at an airport where planes land and take off

tarnish /'tɑːnɪʃ $ 'tɑːr-/ v **1** [T] to damage the opinion people have of someone or something: *The scandal tarnished his reputation forever.*
2 [I] if metal tarnishes, it becomes dull

tarot /'tærəʊ $ -roʊ/ n [singular,U] a set of 78 cards that some people use to find out what will happen in the future

tarpaulin /tɑːˈpɔːlɨn $ tɑːrˈpɒː-/ n [C,U] a large WATERPROOF cloth, used to protect things from the rain

tart¹ /tɑːt $ tɑːrt/ n [C] **1** a food with PASTRY on the bottom and a filling on the top: *jam tarts* → see picture on page A5 **2** an offensive word for a woman who you think has sex with a lot of men

tart² v
  tart sth ⇔ up phr v BrE informal to try to make something old or ugly look more attractive

tart³ adj food that is tart has a sour taste

tartan /'tɑːtn $ 'tɑːrtn/ n [C,U] a traditional Scottish pattern with coloured squares and lines

task /tɑːsk $ tæsk/ n
1 [C] a piece of work you must do: **the task of doing sth** *I was given the task of handing out the cups.* | *Our tutor sets some tough tasks.* | **do/carry out/perform a task** *She couldn't perform even simple tasks on her own.*

COLLOCATIONS

easy/simple/straightforward task
difficult/impossible/daunting task

2 take sb to task (for/over sth) to criticize someone angrily

'task force n [C] a group of people who work together for a short time to solve a particular problem

tassel /'tæsəl/ n [C] a decoration made of a lot of threads tied together at one end

taste¹ /teɪst/ n
1 [C,U] the taste of food or drink is what it is like when you put it in your mouth, for example how sweet or salty it is [= **flavour**]: **the taste of sth** *I don't like the taste of garlic.* | **sweet/sour/ sharp/bitter taste** *The soup had a slightly sweet taste.* | *He's got a good sense of taste* (=an ability to recognize different tastes).

THESAURUS

delicious – very good
disgusting – very bad
sweet – like sugar
tasty – having a pleasant taste, but not sweet
sour – like a lemon
salty – containing a lot of salt
spicy – containing lots of spices
hot – containing spices that give you the feeling that your mouth is burning
bland – not having an interesting taste

2 [C] a small amount of something that you put in your mouth to see what it is like: *Can I have a taste of your ice cream?*
3 [C,U] the kind of things that you like: **+in** *We had similar tastes in music.*
4 a taste for sth if you have a taste for something, you like it: *a young man with a taste for adventure*
5 [U] the ability to judge what is attractive, suitable, good quality etc: *'You've got good taste'* said Eva, looking round the flat. | **be in good/ bad taste** (=used to say how nice or acceptable something is) *Her dress was in very bad taste for a funeral.*

6 [singular] a short experience of something new: **+of** *The weekend gave us a taste of university life.*

taste² v

1 [linking verb] food that tastes sweet, sour etc has that quality when you put it in your mouth: *The soup tasted lovely.* | **taste good/sweet/sour etc** *This milk tastes sour.* | **+of** *The stew tasted of garlic.* | **taste like sth** *What does the soup taste like?* | **sweet-tasting/strong-tasting etc**

2 [T] to recognize what something is when you put it in your mouth: *You can taste the spices in this curry.*

3 [T] to eat or drink a small amount of something, to find out what it is like: *Have you tasted the wine?*

4 taste success/freedom/victory etc to experience success etc for a short time

'taste bud n [C usually plural] the part of your tongue that can taste things

tasteful /'teɪstfəl/ adj attractive and of good quality: *tasteful Christmas decorations* —**tastefully** adv: *tastefully furnished apartments*

tasteless /'teɪstləs/ adj **1** clothes, furniture etc that are tasteless are unattractive and show that the person who chose them has bad judgment: *tasteless ornaments* **2** slightly offensive: *a tasteless joke* **3** tasteless food is unpleasant because it does not have a strong taste

taster /'teɪstə $ -ər/ n [C] **1** someone whose job is to judge the quality of food or drink by tasting it: *wine tasters* **2** a small example of something that you try to see whether you like it: *college taster courses*

tasty /'teɪsti/ adj food that is tasty has a nice taste, but is not sweet → see box at **TASTE**

tattered /'tætəd $ -ərd/ adj old and torn

tatters /'tætəz $ -ərz/ n **in tatters** very badly damaged or spoiled: *Her self-confidence was in tatters.*

tattoo /tə'tuː, tæ'tuː/ n [C] plural tattoos a picture or writing that is permanently marked on your skin, using a needle and ink —**tattooed** adj —**tattoo** v [T] —**tattooist** n [C]

tattoo

tatty /'tæti/ adj BrE informal in bad condition

taught /tɔːt $ tɒːt/ v the past tense and past participle of TEACH

taunt /tɔːnt $ tɒːnt/ v [T] to try to upset someone by continuously saying unkind things about them: **taunt sb about sth** *The other kids taunted him about his weight.* —**taunt** n [C]

Taurus /'tɔːrəs/ n **1** [U] the sign of the Zodiac of people born between April 21 and May 21 **2** [C] someone who has this sign

taut /tɔːt $ tɒːt/ adj **1** stretched tight: *a taut rope* **2** showing signs of anxiety: *a taut smile* —**tautly** adv

tavern /'tævən $ -ərn/ n [C] old-fashioned a PUB

tawdry /'tɔːdri $ 'tɒː-/ adj cheap or badly made: *tawdry jewels*

tawny /'tɔːni $ 'tɒː-/ adj yellowish brown in colour: *tawny fur*

tax /tæks/ n [C,U] money that you pay to the government and that is used to provide public services: *How much tax do you pay?* | **+on** *plans to increase the tax on alcohol* | *The government has promised tax cuts after the next election.* | *a huge tax increase* | **income tax** (=tax paid on money you receive) | *a tax-free salary* (=with no tax to pay) | **before/after tax** *She earns about $50,000 a year, after tax.*
—**tax** v [T] *Cigarettes are heavily taxed.*

taxable /'tæksəbəl/ adj if something is taxable, you must pay tax on it

taxation /tæk'seɪʃən/ n [U] the system of charging taxes, or the money that is collected

taxi¹ /'tæksi/ also **taxicab** /'tæksikæb/ n [C] a car with a driver that you pay to take you somewhere [= cab]: **by taxi** *We went by taxi.* | **take/get a taxi** *We'll get a taxi to the airport.* | *a taxi driver* | *How much was the taxi fare?* → see picture at **TRANSPORT**

COLLOCATIONS

call a taxi – to telephone and ask a taxi to come to where you are
call sb a taxi – to telephone a taxi for someone else
hail a taxi – to stand outside and raise your arm so that a taxi will stop for you

---

taxi² v [I] taxied, taxiing, taxies or taxis if a plane taxis, it moves slowly along the ground

taxing /'tæksɪŋ/ adj needing a lot of effort: *a taxing job*

'taxi rank BrE; **'taxi-stand** AmE n [C] BrE a place where taxis wait

taxpayer /'tæks,peɪə $ -ər/ n [C] **1** someone who pays taxes: *It will cost taxpayers 1.3 million.* **2 the taxpayer** all the people who pay taxes

'tax re,turn n [C] an official form that you fill in to say how much you have earned so that the amount of tax you must pay can be calculated

TB /,tiː 'biː/ n [U] the abbreviation of **tuberculosis**

tba written to be announced used to say that the time or place of an event will be given at a later date

tbsp the written abbreviation of **tablespoon**: *1 tbsp sugar*

tea /tiː/ n [C,U]

1 a drink made by pouring boiling water onto dried leaves, or the leaves used to make this drink: *a cup of tea* | *Are you making tea?* | *I don't like strong tea.* | *herbal teas*

2 BrE a meal eaten in the afternoon or early evening

teabag /'tiːbæg/ n [C] a small paper bag containing dried leaves, used to make tea

teach /tiːtʃ/ v past tense and past participle taught /tɔːt $ tɒːt/

1 [I,T] to give classes or instructions in a particular subject: **teach (sb) sth** *He taught physics for 15 years.* | *the woman who taught us French* | **teach sth to sb** *I taught English to Italian students.* | **teach sb (sth) about sth** *They teach us about all the different religions.* | **+at** *She teaches at the Institute of Technology.* | **teach school/college etc** AmE (=teach in a school etc) → see box at **LEARN**

2 [T] to tell or show someone how to do something: **teach sb (how) to do sth** *We kids were taught to behave politely.* | **teach sb what/where etc** *Will you teach me what to do?* | **teach sb sth** *My grandfather tried to teach me chess.*

3 [T] if an experience teaches you something, it helps you understand something about life: **teach sb that** *It taught me that money can't buy happiness.*

teacher /'tiːtʃə $ -ər/ *n* [C] someone whose job is to teach: **history/physics/English etc teacher** *Mr Paulin is my history teacher.*
→ HEAD TEACHER

> **THESAURUS**
>
> A **teacher** usually works in a school.
> A **lecturer** or **professor** teaches in a university or college.
> An **instructor** teaches a sport or practical skill such as swimming or driving: *a driving instructor*
> A **coach** helps a person or team improve in a sport: *the football coach*
> → SCHOOL, UNIVERSITY

teacher's 'pet *n* [singular] *informal* a child who other students do not like because they think he or she is the teacher's favourite student

teaching /'tiːtʃɪŋ/ *n* **1** [U] the work or job of being a teacher: *I decided to go into teaching* (=become a teacher). | *the teaching profession* | **language/science/English etc teaching** **2 teachings** [plural] the important moral, political, or religious ideas of a famous person: **+of** *the teachings of Marx*

teacup /'tiːkʌp/ *n* [C] a small cup used for drinking tea

teak /tiːk/ *n* [C,U] a type of wood, used to make expensive furniture

team¹ /tiːm/ *n* [C also + plural verb BrE]

1 a group of people who play a sport or game against another group: **football/basketball etc team** *the school netball team* | *The best team won.* | *Which football team do you support?* | **in/on a team** *Do you want to be on our team?* | *The team are* (=each member is) *confident.*
2 a group of people who work together: **+of** *a team of doctors* | *the team leader* | **sales/design/management etc team** *a member of the sales team* → see box at GROUP

team² *v*

team up *phr v* to join another person, company etc in order to work together: **+with** *Can I team up with you?*

teammate /'tiːmmeɪt/ *n* [C] someone who is in your team in a game

'team ,player *n* [C] an office worker who works well as part of a team

teamwork /'tiːmwɜːk $ -wɜːrk/ *n* [U] the ability of a group to work well together

teapot /'tiːpɒt $ -pɑːt/ *n* [C] a container used for making and serving tea, which has a handle and a **spout** → see picture at KITCHEN

tear¹ /teə $ ter/ *v* past tense **tore** /tɔː $ tɔːr/ past participle **torn** /tɔːn $ tɔːrn/ present participle **tearing**

1 [T] if you tear paper, cloth etc, or if it tears, you make a hole in it or it breaks into small pieces [➡ **rip**]: *Be careful the bag doesn't tear.* |

I've torn my trousers. | **tear sth off** *Tear off the slip at the bottom of the page.* | **tear sth out (of sth)** *Someone had torn the last two pages out of the book.* | **tear sth to pieces/shreds** *She tore his letter to pieces.* → see box at BREAK → and REMOVE

2 [I] to move quickly in a dangerous or careless way: **+around/into/out of etc** *The kids were tearing round the house.* → see box at RUN

3 be torn if you are torn, you cannot decide which of two things you should do: **+between** *Anne was torn between her love for Alex and her duty.*

4 be tearing your hair out *informal* to feel very anxious or upset

tear sb/sth apart *phr v* to make people argue or fight with each other: *a country torn apart by civil war*

tear sb away *phr v* to force yourself or someone else to leave a place: *I was having so much fun I could hardly tear myself away.*

tear sth ⇔ down *phr v* to deliberately destroy a building: *The old school has been torn down.*

tear sth ⇔ off *phr v* to remove something roughly: *He tore off his wet clothes.*

tear into sb *phr v informal* to criticize someone strongly

tear sth ⇔ up *phr v* **1** to tear paper into a lot of small pieces **2** if you tear up an agreement, contract etc, you refuse to accept it

tear² /tɪə $ tɪr/ *n* [C usually plural] a drop of liquid that falls from your eye when you cry: *She had tears in her eyes.* | *The children were in tears* (=crying). | *Brian burst into tears* (=started to cry). | *He was close to tears* (=almost crying). | *We all shed a few tears.*

tear³ /teə $ ter/ *n* [C] a hole in a piece of cloth or paper where it has torn: **+in** *There was a big tear in the sheet.*

tearaway /'teərəweɪ $ 'ter-/ *n* [C] a young person who is often in trouble because they behave badly

teardrop /'tɪədrɒp $ 'tɪrdrɑːp/ *n* [C] a single drop of liquid that falls from your eye when you cry

tearful /'tɪəfəl $ 'tɪr-/ *adj* crying or almost crying —**tearfully** *adv*

teargas /'tɪəgæs $ 'tɪr-/ *n* [U] a gas that hurts your eyes, used by the police to control violent crowds

tease /tiːz/ *v* [I,T] if you tease someone, you say amusing or slightly unkind things to them about their appearance, behaviour etc: *Don't cry, I was only teasing.* | **tease sb about sth** *The other kids teased her about her hair.*—**teasingly** *adv*

tease sth ⇔ out *phr v* to carefully separate thread, hair etc that is stuck together: *She carefully teased the knots out of his hair.*

teaspoon /'tiːspuːn/ *n* [C] **1** a small spoon that you use for mixing sugar into tea, coffee etc **2** also **teaspoonful** /'tiːspuːnfʊl/ the amount this spoon can hold

teat /tiːt/ *n* [C] **1** the small red part on the breast of a female animal which their babies suck to get milk [= **nipple**] **2** *BrE* the soft rubber part attached to a baby's bottle [= **nipple** *AmE*]

teatime /'tiːtaɪm/ *n* [U] *BrE* a time in the afternoon or early evening when people have a meal

'tea ,towel n [C] *BrE* a cloth that you use to dry cups, plates etc [= **dish towel** *AmE*]

techie /'teki/ n [C] *informal* someone who knows a lot about computers

technical /'teknɪkəl/ *adj*

1 connected to machines and methods that are used in science or industry: *a **technical** problem* | *We provide **technical** training for our staff.* | ***technical** support for Internet subscribers*

2 relating to a particular subject or profession: *a document full of **technical** terms* | *The language is very **technical**.*

technicality /,teknᵻ'kælᵻti/ n [C] plural **technicalities 1 technicalities** [plural] the small details of how something works **2** one small detail in a law or agreement

technically /'teknɪkli/ *adv* **1** according to the exact details of a rule or law: *What you have done is technically illegal.* **2** relating to the way machines are used in science and industry: *methods which are technically quite advanced*

technician /tek'nɪʃən/ n [C] someone whose job involves practical work relating to science or technology

technique /tek'niːk/ n [C,U] a special skill or way of doing something: *guitar-playing techniques* | **+of** *techniques of problem solving* | **technique for doing sth** *a new technique for dealing with air pollution*

techno /'teknəʊ $ -noʊ/ n [U] a type of popular electronic dance music with a fast strong beat

technology /tek'nɒlədʒi $ -'nɑː-/ n [C,U] plural **technologies** modern machines and equipment: *the use of new computer technology* | *the achievements of modern technology*

→ INFORMATION TECHNOLOGY —**technological** /,teknə'lɒdʒɪkəl◂ $ -'lɑː-/ *adj*: *technological advances*

teddy bear /'tedi beə $ -ber/ also **teddy** *BrE* n [C] a soft toy shaped like a bear

tedious /'tiːdiəs/ *adj* very boring: *a tedious discussion* → see box at BORING —**tediously** *adv*

tee /tiː/ n [C] a small object used for holding a GOLF ball on the ground before you hit it

teem /tiːm/ v **be teeming with sth** to be full of people or animals that are all moving around: *The lake was teeming with fish.* —**teeming** *adj*: *the teeming streets of Cairo*

teen /tiːn/ n [C] *AmE informal* a teenager

teenage /'tiːneɪdʒ/ also **teenaged** /'tiːneɪdʒd/ *adj* [only before noun] aged between 13 and 19, or suitable for people between 13 and 19: *She's got two teenage sons.* | *teenage fashion* → see box at YOUNG

teenager /'tiːneɪdʒə $ -ər/ n [C] someone who is between 13 and 19 years old [➡ **adolescent**]: *a TV series aimed at teenagers* → see box at CHILD

teens /tiːnz/ n [plural] the time in your life when you are aged between 13 and 19: **be in your teens** *She got married when she was still in her teens.*

teeny /'tiːni/ also **teeny-weeny** /,tiːni 'wiːni◂/ *adj informal* very small: *I was just a teeny bit disappointed.*

'tee shirt n [C] a T-SHIRT

teeter /'tiːtə $ -ər/ v **1** [I] to stand or walk moving from side to side, as if you are going to

fall: *She teetered along in her high-heeled shoes.* **2 be teetering on the brink/edge of sth** to be close to a very bad situation: *The country teetered on the brink of war.*

teeth /tiːθ/ n the plural of TOOTH

teethe /tiːð/ v [I] **1** if a baby is teething, his or her teeth are starting to grow **2 teething troubles/problems** *BrE* small problems that you have when you first start doing a new job or using a new system

teetotaller *BrE*; **teetotaler** *AmE* /tiː'təʊtələ $ -'təʊtələr/ n [C] someone who never drinks alcohol —**teetotal** *adj*

TEFL /'tefəl/ n [U] Teaching English as a Foreign Language

tel. the written abbreviation of **telephone number**

telecommunications /,telikəmjuːnᵻ'keɪʃənz/ also **telecoms** /'telikɒmz $ -kɑːmz/ n [plural] the sending and receiving of messages by telephone, radio, television etc

teleconference /'teli,kɒnfərəns $ -,kɑːn-/ n [C] a discussion in which people in different places talk to each other using telephones or video equipment —**teleconference** v [I]

telegram /'telᵻgræm/ n [C] a message sent by telegraph

telegraph /'telᵻgrɑːf $ -græf/ n [U] an old-fashioned method of sending messages using radio or electrical signals

'telegraph ,pole n [C] *BrE* a tall wooden pole for supporting telephone wires

telepathy /tᵻ'lepəθi/ n [U] the ability to communicate your thoughts directly to someone else's mind without speaking or writing —**telepathic** /,telᵻ'pæθɪk◂/ *adj*

telephone¹ /'telᵻfəun $ -foʊn/ also **phone** n [C]

1 the system of communication that you use to have a conversation with someone in another place: *a telephone call* | **by telephone** *Reservations can be made by telephone.* | **on the telephone** *I spoke to him on the telephone.*

When you want to make a phone call, **lift/pick up** the **receiver** (=part you speak into) and **dial** the **number** you want. If the telephone **rings**, someone·may **answer** it, or there may be **no answer**. If the number is **engaged** *BrE*/**busy** *AmE*, someone is already speaking on that **line**, and you cannot **get through**. If you **get the wrong number** by mistake, try **dialling** again. When you finish speaking on the phone **hang up** (=put the receiver down).
→ MOBILE PHONE

2 the piece of equipment that you use when you are talking to someone by telephone: *The telephone rang just as I was leaving.* | *Could you answer the telephone?* | *Do you know her telephone number?*

telephone² v [I,T] *formal* to talk to someone by telephone [= **call**] → see box at PHONE

'telephone ,box *BrE*; **'telephone ,booth** *AmE* n [C] a structure containing a public telephone

'telephone di,rectory n [C] a book containing a list of the names, addresses, and telephone numbers of all the people in a particular area [= phone book]

'telephone ex,change n [C] an office where telephone calls are connected so that people can talk to each other

telesales /'teliseɪlz/ also. **telemarketing** /'teli,mɑːkɪtɪŋ $ -ɑːr-/ n [U] selling things by telephone

telescope /'telɪ̩skəʊp $ -skoʊp/ n [C] a piece of scientific equipment shaped like a tube that you look through to make distant objects look larger and closer

Teletext /'telitekst/ n [U] trademark a service that provides news and other information in written form on television

televise /'telɪ̩vaɪz/ v [T] to broadcast something on television: Is the game going to be televised?

television /'telɪ̩ˌvɪʒən, ˌtelɪ̩'vɪʒən/ n

1 also **tele'vision ,set** [C] a thing shaped like a box with a screen, which you use to watch programmes [= TV]: We need a new television. | **turn/switch a television on/off** Turn the television off!

TOPIC

film/movie: There's a film starting on BBC1 at 9:00.

soap opera – a programme that is on TV regularly about the same group of people

sitcom – a funny TV programme which has the same people in it every week in a different story

game show – a programme in which people play games in order to try and win prizes

talk show AmE/**chat show** BrE – a programme in which people answer questions about themselves

cartoon – a film that uses characters that are drawn and not real

drama series: a new drama series for Saturday nights

documentary – a programme that gives information about a subject

the news: the 6 o'clock news | the news headlines (=the main news stories, read at the beginning of a news programme)

Check **what's on TV** (=look through a list of TV programmes). **Switch/turn the TV on**.

Change channels (=television stations) to find the programme you want.

2 [U] the programmes that you can watch on a television: He's been **watching television** all day. | **on television** What's on television tonight?
3 [U] the business of making and broadcasting programmes for television: a job in television
→ CABLE TELEVISION, CLOSED CIRCUIT TELEVISION, PUBLIC TELEVISION, SATELLITE TELEVISION

teleworker /'teliwɜːkə $ -wɜːrkər/ n [C] someone who works from home and communicates with their employer, customers etc using a computer or telephone —**teleworking** n [U]

tell /tel/ v past tense and past participle **told** /təʊld $ toʊld/

1 [T] to give someone facts or information by speaking to them: **tell sb about sth** Have you told John about the party? | **tell sb sth** Tell me your phone number again. | **tell sb (that)** She told me she can't come on Friday. | **tell sb how/ where/when etc** Could you tell me when he left? | **tell (sb) a story/joke/secret/lie** She's been telling lies again. → see box at SAY

2 can/could tell to know that something is true because you can see it, hear it etc: **can tell (that)** I could tell that Jo was in a bad mood. | Can you **tell the difference** between the twins?

3 [T] to say that someone should or must do something: **tell sb to do sth** He told me to come in and sit down. | **tell sb (that)** His doctor told him he should take more exercise. | **tell yourself sth** I keep telling myself not to worry.

4 [T] to give information in a way that does not use speech or writing: **tell sb (that)** The machine's red light tells you it's recording. | **tell sb how/where/who etc** The survey tells us how young people spend their money.

5 [I,T] spoken informal to tell a teacher, parent etc about something wrong that someone else has done: **+on** Please don't tell on me! | I'll tell Dad if you do that again!

6 tell the time BrE **tell time** AmE to be able to know what time it is by looking at a clock

7 there's no telling what/how/whether etc spoken used to say that it is impossible to know what will happen: There's just no telling what he'll say next.

8 tell the truth to say what really happened

9 (I'll) tell you what spoken used to suggest something: Tell you what, call me on Friday.

10 I tell you/I'm telling you spoken used to emphasize something: I'm telling you, the food was unbelievable!

11 I told you (so) spoken used when someone does something you have warned them not to do, and it has had a bad result: I told you so – I told you it wouldn't work.

12 you never can tell/you can never tell spoken used to say that you can never be certain about what will happen in the future: They're not likely to win, but you never can tell.

tell sb/sth **apart** phr v to be able to see the difference between two people or things, even though they are similar: It's difficult to tell them apart.

tell sb ⇔ **off** phr v informal to talk angrily to someone because they have done something wrong: **be/get told off** Sean's always getting told off at school.

teller /'telə $ -ər/ n [C] especially AmE someone whose job is to take and pay out money in a bank

telling /'telɪŋ/ adj showing what someone really thinks or what a situation is really like: a telling remark

telltale /'telteɪl/ adj clearly showing something that is unpleasant or supposed to be secret: the telltale signs of drug addiction

telly /'teli/ n [C] plural **tellies** BrE informal a television

temp¹ /temp/ n [C] someone who works in an office for a short time, doing someone else's job while they are away

temp² v [I] to work as a temp: Anne's temping until she can find another job.

temper[1] /'tempə $ -ər/ n

1 [C,U] a tendency to become suddenly angry: *Mark needs to learn to **control** his temper.* | *Robin **has** quite **a temper**.* | *I lost my temper and shouted at them.* | *As a teacher, you have to be able to **keep** your temper* (=not get angry).

2 [singular,U] the angry or happy way that you feel: *be in a bad/foul/good temper You're certainly in a foul temper this morning.*

3 in a temper very angry: *He was in a terrible temper.*

→ BAD-TEMPERED

temper[2] v [T] *formal* to make something less severe or extreme

temperament /'tempərəmənt/ n [C,U] your character, or the type of person that you are: *He hasn't got the right temperament to work with children.*

temperamental /ˌtempərə'mentl◂/ adj *disapproving* someone who is temperamental changes suddenly from being happy to being sad, angry etc

temperate /'tempərɪt/ adj temperate weather is never very hot or very cold: *a temperate climate*

temperature /'temprətʃə $ -ər/ n

1 [C,U] how hot or cold something is: +**of** *Check the temperature of the water.* | *a temperature of 100°C*

2 sb's temperature the temperature of your body, used as a sign of whether you are ill: *The nurse took my temperature.*

3 have a temperature to be hot because you are ill: *Susie has a temperature and has gone to bed.*

tempest /'tempɪst/ n [C] *literary* a storm

tempestuous /tem'pestʃuəs/ adj full of anger and strong emotions: *a tempestuous relationship*

template /'templeɪt, -plɪt/ n [C] **1** a piece of paper, plastic etc that you use to help you cut other materials in the same shape **2** *technical* a computer document that you use as a model for producing many similar documents

temple /'tempəl/ n [C]

1 a building where people in some religions go to pray

2 the area on the side of your head, between your eye and your ear

tempo /'tempəʊ $ -poʊ/ n [C, U] plural **tempos**
1 the speed at which something happens: *the tempo of city life* **2** the speed at which music is played

temporary /'tempərəri, -pəri $ -pəreri/ adj existing or happening only for a short time [≠ **permanent**]: *a temporary job* | *She was employed **on a temporary basis**.*
—**temporarily** /'tempərərɪli $ ˌtempə'rerɪli/ adv: *The library is temporarily closed.*

tempt /tempt/ v **1** [T] to make someone want to do something: *He was tempted by the big profits of the drugs trade.* | **tempt sb to do sth** *They're offering free gifts to tempt people to join.*
2 be tempted to do sth to feel you would like to do something: *I was tempted to tell him the whole truth.* —**tempting** adj: *a tempting offer*

temptation /temp'teɪʃən/ n **1** [C,U] a strong feeling that you want to have or do something, although you know you should not: *I had to **resist the temptation** to slap him.* | *I finally*

gave in to temptation and had a cigarette.
2 [C] something that you want to have or do, even though you know you should not: *Having chocolate in the house is a great temptation!*

ten /ten/ number the number 10: *Snow had been falling steadily for ten days.* | *I need to be home by ten* (=ten o'clock). | *She's about ten* (=ten years old).

tenacious /tɪ'neɪʃəs/ adj very determined to do something, even when it is difficult
—**tenaciously** adv —**tenacity** /tɪ'næsɪti/ n [U]

tenancy /'tenənsi/ n [C,U] plural **tenancies** the period of time that someone rents a house or piece of land

tenant /'tenənt/ n [C] someone who pays rent to live in a room or house → see box at RENT

tend /tend/ v

1 tend to do sth to usually do something: *My car tends to overheat.* | *People tend to need less sleep as they get older.*

2 also **tend to sth** [T] *formal* to take care of someone or something: *farmers tending their cattle*

tendency /'tendənsi/ n [C] plural **tendencies**
1 if someone or something has a tendency to do something, they are likely to do it: **tendency to do sth** *He has a tendency to talk too much.* | +**towards** *Some people may inherit a tendency towards alcoholism.* **2** a general change or development in a particular direction: *There is an increasing **tendency** for women to have children later in life.*

tender[1] /'tendə $ -ər/ adj **1** tender food is soft and easy to cut and eat [≠ **tough**] **2** a tender part of your body is painful if someone touches it **3** gentle in a way that shows love: *a tender look* **4 at a tender age** young and without much experience of life: *He lost his father at the tender age of seven.* —**tenderly** adv
—**tenderness** n [U]

tender[2] v **1** [T] *formal* to formally offer something to someone: *Maria has **tendered** her **resignation*** (=said formally that she will leave her job). **2** [I] *BrE* to make a formal offer to do a job or provide goods and services

tender-hearted /ˌtendə 'hɑːtɪd◂ $ -dər 'hɑːr-/ adj very kind and gentle

tendon /'tendən/ n [C] a thick strong part inside your body that connects a muscle to a bone

tenement /'tenəmənt/ n [C] a large building divided into apartments, especially in a poor area of a city

tenet /'tenɪt/ n [C] a principle or belief: *the tenets of Buddhism*

tenner /'tenə $ -ər/ n [C] *BrE spoken* £10 or a ten pound note: *Can you lend me a tenner?*

tennis /'tenɪs/ n [U] a game for two people or two pairs of people who use RACKETS to hit a small ball to each other over a net: *Let's **have a game** of tennis.*
→ TABLE TENNIS

tenor /'tenə $ -ər/ n **1** [C] a male singer with a high voice **2 the tenor of sth** *formal* the general meaning or attitude behind something: *the tenor of her argument*

tenpin bowling /ˌtenpɪn 'bəʊlɪŋ $ -'boʊ-/ n [U] *BrE* an indoor sport in which you roll a heavy ball along a floor to knock down bottle-shaped wooden objects [= **bowling** *AmE*]

tense[1] /tens/ *adj*

1 nervous and anxious [➟ **tension**]: *You seem really tense – what's wrong? | This has been a tense two weeks.*

2 tense muscles feel tight and stiff [➟ **tension**]: *Massage helps to relax tense neck muscles.*

tense[2] also **tense up** *v* [I,T] to become tight and stiff, or to make your muscles do this

tense[3] *n* [C,U] a form of a verb that shows whether something happens in the past, the present, or the future

tension /'tenʃən/ *n* **1** [C,U] the feeling that exists when people do not trust each other and may suddenly attack each other: *an effort to calm racial tensions in the city* **2** [U] a nervous and anxious feeling: *The tension as we waited for the news was unbearable.* **3** [U] tightness or stiffness in a wire, rope, muscle etc: *Muscle tension can be a sign of stress.*

tent /tent/ *n* [C] a shelter consisting of a sheet of cloth supported by poles and ropes, used especially for camping: *We looked for a place to **put up** our tent.*

tentacle /'tentɪkəl/ *n* [C] one of the long parts like arms of a sea creature such as an OCTOPUS

tentative /'tentətɪv/ *adj* **1** a tentative idea or plan is not definite or certain **2** done without confidence: *a tentative smile* —**tentatively** *adv*

tenterhooks /'tentəhʊks $ -ər-/ *n* **be on tenterhooks** to feel nervous and excited because you are waiting for something to happen

tenth[1] /tenθ/ *adj* coming after nine other things in a series: *her tenth birthday* —**tenth** *pron*: *I'm planning to leave on the tenth* (=the tenth day of the month).

tenth[2] *n* [C] one of ten equal parts of something

tenuous /'tenjuəs/ *adj* a situation or relationship that is uncertain or weak: *There is only a **tenuous connection** between the two events.* —**tenuously** *adv*

tenure /'tenjə, -jʊə $ -jər/ *n* [U] **1** the legal right to use land or buildings for a period of time **2** the period of time when someone has an important job: *during his tenure as chairman*

tepid /'tepɪd/ *adj* tepid liquid is slightly warm

tequila /tɪ'kiːlə/ *n* [U] a strong alcoholic drink made in Mexico

term[1] /tɜːm $ tɜːrm/ *n* [C]

1 in terms of sth used when you are talking about something from one particular point of view: *In terms of profits, the project was a disaster.* | **in financial/artistic etc terms** *A million years isn't a very long time in geological terms.* | **in general/broad/simple etc terms** *What do these statistics mean in simple terms?*

2 a word or phrase that has a particular technical or scientific meaning: **legal/medical/technical term** *I don't understand all the legal terms.*

3 terms [plural] the rules of an agreement: *Sign here to say you agree to the terms and conditions.*

4 a fixed period of time during which someone does something or something happens: *The President hopes to be elected for a second term.* | **+of** *the maximum term of imprisonment*

5 *BrE* one of the periods of time that a school or university year is divided into

6 come to terms with sth to understand and deal with a difficult situation: *It was hard to come to terms with Marie's death.*

7 be on good/bad/friendly etc terms (with sb) to have a good, bad etc relationship with someone: *We're on good terms with our neighbours.*

8 be on speaking terms to be able to talk to someone and have a friendly relationship with them: *We're barely on speaking terms now.*

9 in the long/short/medium term during a long, short, or middle-sized period from now [➟ **long-term, short-term**]: *Things don't look good in the short term.*

10 in no uncertain terms in a direct and often angry way: *I told him to leave in no uncertain terms.*

→ **HALF TERM**

term[2] *v* [T usually passive] *formal* to use a particular word or expression to describe something: *The meeting could hardly be termed a success.*

terminal[1] /'tɜːmɪnəl $ 'tɜːr-/ *n* [C] **1** a building where you get onto planes, buses, or ships: *They're building a new terminal at the airport.* → see box at **AIRPORT** **2** a KEYBOARD and screen connected to a computer

terminal[2] *adj* a terminal disease cannot be cured, and causes death: *terminal cancer* —**terminally** *adv*: *terminally ill*

terminate /'tɜːmɪneɪt $ 'tɜːr-/ *v* [I,T] *formal* if something terminates, or if you terminate it, it ends —**termination** /ˌtɜːmɪ'neɪʃən $ ˌtɜːr-/ *n* [C,U]

terminology /ˌtɜːmɪ'nɒlədʒi $ ˌtɜːrmɪ'nɑː-/ *n* [C,U] plural **terminologies** the technical words that are used in a subject: *computer terminology*

terminus /'tɜːmɪnəs $ 'tɜːr-/ *n* [C] plural **termini** /-naɪ/ the station or stop at the end of a railway line or bus service

termite /'tɜːmaɪt $ 'tɜːr-/ *n* [C] an insect that eats and destroys wood from trees and buildings

terrace /'terəs/ *n* [C] **1** a flat area next to a building or on a roof, where you can sit **2** *BrE* a row of houses that are joined to each other

terraced 'house *n* [C] *BrE* a house that is one of a row of houses joined together → see box at **HOUSE**

terracotta /ˌterə'kɒtə $ -'kɑː-/ *n* [U] hard red-brown baked clay: *a terracotta pot*

terrain /te'reɪn, tɪ-/ *n* [C,U] a particular type of land: *mountainous terrain*

terrestrial /tɪ'restriəl/ *adj technical* **1** relating to the earth rather than space: *terrestrial TV* (=TV broadcast from the earth, not through space using a SATELLITE) **2** living on or relating to land rather than water

terrible /'terəbəl/ *adj* very bad [= **awful**]: *The food at the hotel was terrible.* | *a terrible accident* | *You're making a terrible mistake.* → see box at **BAD** → and **HORRIBLE**

terribly /'terəbli/ *adv* **1** very badly: *He missed his mother terribly.* **2** *BrE* extremely: *I'm terribly sorry.*

terrier /'teriə $ -ər/ *n* [C] a type of small dog → see picture at **DOG**[1]

terrific /təˈrɪfɪk/ *adj informal* **1** very good: *a terrific opportunity* | *She looked terrific.* **2** very big: *Losing his job was a terrific shock.* —**terrifically** /-kli/ *adv*

terrified /ˈterɪfaɪd/ *adj* very frightened: **+of** *I'm absolutely terrified of spiders.* | **terrified to do sth** *He was terrified to stay in the house alone.* → see box at FRIGHTENED

terrify /ˈterɪfaɪ/ *v* [T] **terrified, terrifying, terrifies** to make someone extremely frightened: *That dog terrifies me.* —**terrifying** *adj*

territorial /ˌterɪˈtɔːriəl◂/ *adj* [only before noun] relating to land that is owned or controlled by a particular country: *US territorial waters*

territory /ˈterɪtəri $ -tɔːri/ *n plural* **territories**
1 [C,U] land that a particular country owns and controls: *Canadian territory* | *The plane was flying over **enemy territory**.*
2 [U] an area of business, experience, or knowledge: *We are moving into **unfamiliar territory** with the new software.*
3 [C,U] the area that an animal thinks is its own

terror /ˈterə $ -ər/ *n* [U] a feeling of extreme fear: *She screamed in terror.*

terrorism /ˈterərɪzəm/ *n* [U] the use of bombs and violence, especially against ordinary people, to try to force a government to do something

terrorist /ˈterərɪst/ *n* [C] someone who uses bombs and violence, usually against ordinary people, to try to force a government to do something [➡ **freedom fighter**]

terrorize also **-ise** *BrE* /ˈterəraɪz/ *v* [T] to deliberately frighten people by threatening them with violence: *Gangs have been terrorizing the community.*

terse /tɜːs $ tɜːrs/ *adj* said with few words, often in an unfriendly way: *a terse answer* —**tersely** *adv*

tertiary /ˈtɜːʃəri $ ˈtɜːrʃieri, -ʃəri/ *adj technical* third in place, degree, or order

test¹ /test/ *n* [C]
1 a set of questions or exercises to measure someone's skill or knowledge: *I've got a history test tomorrow.* | **pass/fail a test** *I failed my driving test twice.* | **do/take a test** *The children are doing a French test today.*
2 a medical check on part of your body: *an eye test* | *a blood test*
3 a process used to find out whether something works, whether it is safe etc: *safety tests on diving equipment*
4 a situation that shows how good, bad etc something is: **+of** *Today's race is a real test of skill.*

test² *v* [T]
1 to measure someone's skill or knowledge by giving them questions or activities to do: **test sb on sth** *We're being tested on grammar tomorrow.*
2 to use or check something to find out whether it works or is successful: *None of our products are tested on animals.* | *It's time to test our theory.*
3 to do a medical check on part of someone's body: *You need to get your eyes tested.*
4 to show how good or strong something is: *The next six months will test her powers of leadership.*

testament /ˈtestəmənt/ *n formal* **a testament to sth** something that shows or proves something else very clearly: *His latest CD is a testament to his growing musical abilities.*

'**test case** *n* [C] a legal CASE that makes a principle of law clear and is used to judge future cases

testicle /ˈtestɪkəl/ *n* [C] plural **testicles** or **testes** /-tiːz/ a man's testicles are the two round organs below his PENIS

testify /ˈtestɪfaɪ/ *v* [I,T] **testified, testifying, testifies** to make a statement in a law court: **+that** *He testified that he saw the two men fighting.* | **+against** *She refused to testify against her husband.*

testimonial /ˌtestɪˈməʊniəl $ -ˈmoʊ-/ *n* [C] a written statement about someone's character and abilities

testimony /ˈtestɪməni $ -moʊni/ *n* [C,U] plural **testimonies 1** a formal statement that someone makes in a law court → see box at COURT **2 a testimony to sth** something that shows or proves that something is true: *This achievement is a testimony to your hard work.*

testosterone /teˈstɒstərəʊn $ -ˈstɑːstəroʊn/ *n* [U] the HORMONE in men that gives them their male qualities

'**test run** *n* [C] when you do a particular thing or use a machine before you really need to, in order to make sure that everything works properly

'**test tube** *n* [C] a small glass container shaped like a tube that is used in scientific tests

testy /ˈtesti/ *adj* impatient and easily annoyed

tetanus /ˈtetənəs/ *n* [U] a serious disease that you can get when dirt gets into a cut on your body

tether /ˈteðə $ -ər/ *n* [C] **1 be at/reach the end of your tether** to feel that you cannot deal with your problems any more **2** a rope or chain used to tie an animal to something —**tether** *v* [T] *a dog tethered to a post*

text¹ /tekst/ *n*
1 [U] words or writing: *a disk that can store huge quantities of text* | *a book with pictures but no text*
2 [C] a work of literature that you study at school or college: *There are three **set texts** this year.*
3 the text of sth the exact words of a speech: *Some newspapers printed the full text of the speech.*

text² *v* [T] to send someone a TEXT MESSAGE: *I'll text you later.* → see box at MOBILE PHONE

textbook¹ /ˈtekstbʊk/ *n* [C] a book about a subject which students use: *a history textbook* → see box at BOOK → see picture at CLASSROOM

textbook² *adj* **textbook example/case of sth** something that happens or is done in exactly the way that you would expect

textile /ˈtekstaɪl/ *n* [C] any cloth that is made by weaving threads together: *colourful textiles* | *the textile industry*

'**text ˌmessage** *n* [C] a written message that you send to someone using a MOBILE PHONE → see box at MOBILE PHONE —**text message** *v* [T] —**text messaging** *n* [U]

texture /ˈtekstʃə $ -ər/ *n* [C,U] the way that something feels when you touch it: *the smooth texture of silk*

textured /ˈtekstʃəd $ -ərd/ *adj* having a surface that is not smooth

than /ðən; *strong* ðæn/ *linking word, prep* used to compare two things or people: *She's taller* *than her sister.* | *a car that costs less than £5000* | *He earns more than I do.*

thank /θæŋk/ *v* [T]

1 to tell someone that you are grateful for something that they have given you or done for you: **thank sb for (doing) sth** *I thanked him for the flowers.* | *They thanked us for helping them.*

2 thank God/goodness/heavens *spoken* used to say that you are very glad about something: *Thank God no one was hurt!* | *+for 'We're nearly there.' 'Thank goodness for that!'*

thankful /'θæŋkfəl/ *adj* [not before noun] glad that something good has happened: *+for I was thankful for a chance to rest.* | *+that I'm just thankful that no one was hurt.*

thankfully /'θæŋkfəli/ *adv* used to say that you are glad that something good has happened: *Thankfully, they all got home safely.*

thankless /'θæŋkləs/ *adj* a thankless job is difficult and you do not get much praise for doing it: *Cleaning is always a thankless task.*

thanks¹ /θæŋks/ *informal*

1 used to tell someone that you are grateful for something they have given you or done for you [= thank you]: *Can I borrow your pen? Thanks.* | *The flowers are lovely. Thanks very much.* | *+for Thanks for the drink.* | **thanks for doing sth** *Thanks for helping out.*

2 *spoken* used when answering someone's question politely: *'How are you?' 'Fine, thanks.'*

3 no thanks *spoken* used to say politely that you do not want something: *'Would you like a drink?' 'No, thanks.'*

thanks² *n* [plural]

1 something that you say or do to show that you are grateful to someone: *I did all that tidying up, but I didn't get any thanks.* | *He left without a word of thanks.*

2 thanks to sb/sth because of someone or something: *The church now has a new clock, thanks to the generosity of local people.* | *It's ruined now, thanks to you!*

Thanksgiving /θæŋks'gɪvɪŋ/ *n* [U] a holiday in the US and Canada in November, when families have a large meal together

'thank you

1 used to tell someone that you are grateful for something they have given you or done for you: *I really liked the book. Thank you.* | *Thank you very much.* | *+for Thank you for the perfume.* | **thank you for doing sth** *Thank you for coming today.*

COMMUNICATION

saying thank you

thanks: *Pass the salt, please ... thanks.*

thanks a lot: *'Would you like a drink?' 'Yes, thanks a lot.'*

thank you very much/thanks very much: *Thanks very much for all your help.*

cheers *BrE spoken informal*: *'Here's that £10 I owe you.' 'Cheers.'*

many thanks *especially written*: *Many thanks for your letter of the 19th.*

thank you so much *formal*: *Thank you so much for coming.*

2 *spoken* used when answering someone's ques-

tion politely: *'Did you have a nice holiday?' 'Yes, thank you.'*

3 no, thank you *spoken* used to say politely that you do not want something: *'Would you like another piece of cake?' 'No, thank you.'*

'thank-you *n* [C] something that you say or do to thank someone for something: *+for They bought me some flowers as a thank-you for looking after the children.* | *I want to say a big thank-you to everyone who helped organize this event.*

that¹ /ðæt/ *determiner, pron* plural **those** /ðəuz $ ðouz/

1 used to talk about someone or something that is a distance away from you [➝ this]: *My office is in that building.* | *What's that?* | *Who are those boys over there?*

2 used to talk about someone or something that has already been mentioned [➝ this]: *I've never seen that film.* | *We met for coffee later that day.* | *Who told you that?* | *Those were her exact words.*

3 used as a RELATIVE PRONOUN instead of 'which' or 'who': *the books that I bought yesterday* | *the man that I spoke to on the phone*

4 that is (to say) used to correct something you have just said: *Everyone was there – everyone, that is, except Paul.*

5 that's it *spoken* **a)** used to say that something is completely finished: *That's it, then. We can go home.* **b)** used to tell someone that they are doing something correctly: *Turn the wheel to the left, yes, that's it.*

6 that's that *spoken* used to tell someone that a situation will not change: *I'm not going and that's that!*

GRAMMAR

The relative pronoun **that** is often left out when it is the object of a verb *She's the woman (that) I love.*

You can use **that** instead of **which** or **who** when you are saying which thing or person you mean *This is the man that/who told the police.*

You cannot use **that** instead of **which** or **who** if you are simply adding information *This is my father, who lives in Dublin. She owns an old Rolls Royce, which she bought in 1954.*

that² /ðət; *strong* ðæt/ *linking word*

1 used after some verbs, adjectives, and nouns to start a new CLAUSE: *He promised that he would be here.* | *Is it true that you're leaving?* | *There is no proof that he stole the money.*

2 used after a phrase with 'so' or 'such' to say what the result of something is: *I was so tired that I could hardly walk.* | *They were making such a noise that I didn't hear the phone.*

that³ /ðæt/ *adv*

1 that long/much/big etc used when you are talking about the size of something and showing it with your hands: *It's about that long.*

2 that good/bad/difficult etc as good, bad etc as someone has already mentioned: *I didn't realize things were that bad.*

3 not (all) that much/long/big etc not very much, long, big etc: *It won't cost all that much.*

thatch /θætʃ/ *n* [C,U] dried STRAW used for making roofs —**thatched** *adj*: *a thatched cottage*

T

thaw /θɔː $ θɒː/ v **1** also **thaw out** [I,T] if something frozen thaws, or if heat thaws it, it becomes warmer and softer: *The snow was beginning to thaw.* | *Is the meat properly thawed?* **2** [I] to become more friendly or less formal: *Relations between the two countries are beginning to thaw.* —**thaw** n [singular] *a thaw in relations*

the /ðə; *before vowels* ði; *strong* ðiː/ *determiner*

1 used before nouns when you are talking about a person or thing that has already been mentioned or is already known about, or that is the only one [➡ **a**]: *the shop next to our school* | *the woman I saw yesterday*
2 used as part of the names of some countries, rivers, oceans etc: *the United States* | *the Pacific Ocean*
3 used before an adjective to make it into a noun that refers to a particular group of people: *a hotel with facilities for the disabled* | *shelter for the homeless*
4 used before a singular noun to show that you are talking about that thing in general: *The computer has changed our lives.*
5 each or every: *He's paid by the hour.* | *There are 9 francs to the pound.*
6 used before the names of musical instruments: *I enjoy playing the piano.*
7 used to talk about a part of the body: *The ball hit him right in the eye!*
8 used before a particular date or period of time: *the third of April* | *the 1960s*
9 the ... the ... used to show that two things happen together and depend on each other: *The more you practise, the better you'll play.*

GRAMMAR

Do not use **the** when you are talking about something in general using a U noun or a plural noun form: *I like ice cream.* | *Cats often hunt at night.*
Use **the** when you are talking about a particular thing: *I like the ice cream you bought.* | *The cats on our street make a lot of noise.*
Do not use **the** before the names of airports, railway stations, or streets: *We arrived at Gatwick Airport.* | *The train leaves from Euston Station.* | *She lives in Spencer Road.*
Use **the** when you are talking about a particular airport, station, or street without naming it: *We arrived at the airport.* | *The train was just leaving the station.* | *She lives in the same street as me.*

theatre *BrE*; **theater** *AmE* /'θɪətə $ -ər/ n

1 [C] a building with a stage where plays are performed: *Shall we go to the theatre this evening?* | **at a theatre** *There's a good play on at the Apollo Theatre.*

TOPIC

You go to the **theatre** to **see** a **play**, **musical**, **opera** or **ballet**. The place that you pay to sit in is called a **seat**. You have seats in **the stalls** *BrE* or on **the floor** *AmE* (=lowest level) or in the **circle** *BrE*/**balcony** *AmE* (=highest level). You can buy a **programme** *BrE*/**program** *AmE* (=small book telling you about the play, the actors etc). In front of the **audience**

(=people watching), there may be an **orchestra** (=group of musicians) below the **stage**. During the play there is usually an **interval** *BrE*/**intermission** *AmE* (=when the performance stops for a short time and people can have a drink). Before you go to the theatre, you can **reserve**/**book tickets** at the **box office**.

2 [U] writing or performing plays as entertainment: *a study of modern Russian theatre*
3 [C] *AmE* a building where you go to see films [= **cinema** *BrE*]
4 [C,U] *BrE* the room in a hospital where doctors do operations [= **operating room** *AmE*]: **in theatre** *The patient is in theatre now.*
→ **OPERATING THEATRE**

theatrical /θi'ætrɪkəl/ *adj* **1** relating to the theatre and the performing of plays: *a theatrical production* **2** speaking or moving in a way that is intended to make people notice you: *He let out a theatrical sigh.*

theft /θeft/ *n* [C,U] the crime of stealing something: *Car theft is on the increase in this area.* | **+of** *the theft of two valuable paintings* → see box at **CRIME**

their /ðə; *strong* ðeə $ ðər; *strong* ðer/ *adj*

1 relating to or belonging to the people or things that have already been mentioned: *The children closed their eyes.* | *Their daughter is a teacher.*
2 used instead of 'his' or 'her' after words such as someone, anyone etc: *Everybody brought their own wine to the party.*

theirs /ðeəz $ ðerz/ *pron*

1 the POSSESSIVE form of 'they': *When our computer broke Tom and Sue let us use theirs.*
2 used instead of 'his' or 'hers' after words such as someone, anyone etc: *There's a coat left. Someone must have forgotten theirs.*

them /ðəm; *strong* ðem/ *pron*

1 the object form of 'they' – the people, animals, or things that have already been mentioned: *Has anybody seen my keys? I can't find them.* | *My friends want me to go out with them tonight.*
2 the object form of 'they' – used instead of 'him' or 'her': *If anyone phones, can you tell them to call back later?*

theme /θiːm/ *n* [C]

1 the main subject or idea in a book, film, discussion etc: **+of** *Love is the main theme of the book.* | *Education has become a central theme of this election campaign.*
2 theme music/song/tune music that is always played with a particular television or radio programme

'theme park *n* [C] a place where you can have fun riding on big machines, which are all based on one subject such as water or space travel

themselves /ðəm'selvz/ *pron*

1 the REFLEXIVE form of 'they': *People usually like to talk about themselves.*
2 used to emphasize a plural subject or object of a sentence: *Doctors themselves admit that the treatment does not always work.*
3 (all) by themselves a) alone: *Many old people live by themselves.* **b)** without help from other people: *The kids made the cake all by themselves.*

then¹ /ðen/ adv

1 at a particular time in the past or future: *I was still at university then.* | **by/until/since then** *He's coming at eight, but I'll have left by then.* | *Just then* (=at that exact moment) *I heard the door open.*

2 used to say what happens next: *We had lunch and then went shopping.*

3 used to say what the result of something will be: *Have something to eat now, then you won't be hungry later.* | *If the others want to go, then I'll go too.*

4 *spoken* used when you are adding something to what has been said before: *He's in bed? Is he not very well then?* | *If you can't come on Friday, then how about Saturday?*

5 now/OK/right then *spoken* used when you have finished talking about one subject and want to end the conversation or talk about something else: *Right then, shall we go?* | *OK then, I'll see you tomorrow.*

6 then and there/there and then immediately: *He demanded the money there and then.*

→ **but then (again)** at BUT¹ → **(every) now and then** at NOW¹

then² *adj* [only before noun] used when talking about someone who did a job at a particular time in the past: *George Bush, the then president of the US*

thence /ðens/ adv formal from that place: *They travelled to Paris, and thence by train to Rome.*

theology /θiˈɒlədʒi $ θiˈɑː-/ n [U] plural **theologies** the study of religion —**theological** /ˌθiːəˈlɒdʒɪkəl $ -ˈlɑː-/ adj: *theological arguments*

theorem /ˈθɪərəm $ ˈθiːə-/ n [C] technical a statement that you can prove is true, especially in mathematics

theoretical /θɪəˈretɪkəl $ ˌθiːə-/ adj **1** relating to scientific ideas rather than practical situations: *a good theoretical understanding of physics* **2** a theoretical situation could exist but does not exist yet: *There is a theoretical risk of an explosion.*

theoretically /θɪəˈretɪkli $ ˌθiːə-/ adv if something is theoretically possible, it could happen but has not happened yet

theorist /ˈθɪərɪst $ ˈθiːə-/ n [C] someone who develops ideas that explain why particular things happen

theorize also **-ise** BrE /ˈθɪəraɪz $ ˈθiːə-/ v [I,T] to think of a possible explanation or reason for something: **+about** *We can only theorize about the cause of the fire.*

theory /ˈθɪəri $ ˈθiːəri/ n plural **theories**

1 [C] an idea that tries to explain something [→ **theoretical**]: **+of** *Darwin's theory of evolution* | **+about** *different theories about how the brain works* | *One theory is that he was killed by members of a rival gang.*

2 in theory something that is true in theory should be true, but may not actually be true: *In theory, I don't work on Saturdays.*

3 [U] the general principles of a subject: *studying economic theory*

therapeutic /ˌθerəˈpjuːtɪk◄/ adj **1** making you feel calm and relaxed: *I find walking very therapeutic.* **2** [only before noun] relating to the treatment of diseases: *therapeutic drugs*

therapy /ˈθerəpi/ n [C,U] plural **therapies** the treatment of a mental or physical illness over a long period of time, especially without using drugs or operations: *He's having therapy to help with alcohol addiction.* —**therapist** n [C] *She's been seeing a therapist to help her get over the death of her child.*

there¹ /ðeə, ðə $ ðer, ðər/ pron **there is/are/ was/were etc** used to say that something exists or happens: *There's a bank just round the corner.* | *There are two biscuits left.* | *Is there a telephone here?* | *Suddenly, there was a loud crash.*

there² /ðeə $ ðer/ adv

1 in or to another place, not the place where you are [→ **here**]: *I know Edinburgh well because I used to live there.* | **in/out/over/under there** *It's raining out there.* | *Look at that man over there.*

2 at a particular point in time or in a situation: *We'll stop there for today.* | *She left her husband, but her troubles didn't end there.*

3 if something is there, it exists: *The next morning the pain was still there.* | *The money's there if you need it.*

4 there it is/there you are etc *spoken* used when you have found someone or something that you were looking for: *I'm sure I put my keys here somewhere – oh there they are.* | *There he is, over by the bar.*

5 there is/are *spoken* used when you have just seen something or someone: *Oh look, there's Kate.*

6 there you are *spoken* used when you are giving something to someone or when you have done something for them: *I'll just get you the key – there you are.*

7 be there for sb to be ready to help someone when they need help: *You know I'll always be there for you.*

8 there and then/then and there immediately: *They offered me the job there and then.*

→ **here and there** at HERE

there³ /ðeə $ ðer/ *spoken* used when you have finished something: *There, that's done.*

thereabouts /ˌðeərəˈbaʊts $ ˌðer-/ adv near a particular number, amount, or time, but not exactly: *We'll arrive at 10 o'clock, or thereabouts.*

thereafter /ðeərˈɑːftə $ ðerˈæftər/ adv formal after a particular event or time: *He became ill in May and died shortly thereafter.*

thereby /ðeəˈbaɪ, ˈðeəbaɪ $ ðerˈbaɪ, ˈðer-/ adv formal with the result that something happens: *Expenses were cut 12%, thereby increasing efficiency.*

therefore /ˈðeəfɔː $ ˈðerfɔːr/ adv for the reason that has just been mentioned: *The car is smaller and therefore cheaper to run.*

therein /ðeərˈɪn $ ðer-/ adv formal **1** in that place, or in that piece of writing: *We have studied the report and the information contained therein.* **2 therein lies sth** used in order to say what the cause of something is: *The two sides will not talk to each other, and therein lies the problem.*

thereupon /ˌðeərəˈpɒn, ˈðeərəpɒn $ ˌðerəˈpɒːn, -ˈpɑːn, ˈðer-/ adv formal immediately after something happens and as a result of it

thermal /ˈθɜːməl $ ˈθɜːr-/ adj **1** relating to heat or caused by heat: *thermal energy* **2** thermal clothes are made of a special cloth to keep you warm

thermometer /θəˈmɒmɪtə $ θərˈmɑːmɪtər/ n [C] a piece of equipment that measures the temperature of something, for example of your body

Thermos /ˈθɜːməs $ ˈθɜːr-/ also **'Thermos flask** n [C] *trademark* a container like a bottle that keeps drinks hot or cold

thermostat /ˈθɜːməstæt $ ˈθɜːr-/ n [C] a piece of equipment that keeps a room or machine at a particular temperature

thesaurus /θɪˈsɔːrəs/ n [C] plural **thesauruses** or **thesauri** /-raɪ/ a book that contains lists of words with similar meanings

these /ðiːz/ *determiner, pron* the plural form of THIS

thesis /ˈθiːsɪs/ n [C] plural **theses** /-siːz/ **1** a long piece of writing that you do for a university degree: **+on** *He wrote a thesis on children's literature.* **2** *formal* an idea that tries to explain why something happens

they /ðeɪ/ *pron*
1 the people or things that have already been mentioned or that are already known about: *Ken gave me some flowers, aren't they beautiful? | I called on my parents, but they weren't in.*
2 the group of people who organize something or are in charge of something: *They're going to build a new road round the town centre.*
3 they say/think used to say what people in general say or think: *Nowadays, they say it's wrong to be too strict with children.*
4 used instead of 'he' or 'she' after words such as someone, everyone etc: *Someone at work said they saw you at the party.*

they'd /ðeɪd/ **1** the short form of 'they had': *They'd been missing for three days.* **2** the short form of 'they would': *They'd like to visit us.*

they'll /ðeɪl/ the short form of 'they will': *They'll have to wait.*

they're /ðə; *strong* ðeə, ðeɪə $ ðər; *strong* ðer, ðeɪər/ the short form of 'they are': *They're very nice people.*

they've /ðeɪv/ the short form of 'they have': *They've been here before.*

thick¹ /θɪk/ adj
1 something that is thick is wide and not thin [≠ thin]: *a thick slice of bread | thick stone walls | thick woollen material | a thick layer of paint →* see picture at THIN¹
2 5cm/1m etc thick used to say exactly how thick something is: *The walls are 30 cm thick.*
3 a thick liquid does not have much water in it: *a thick sauce*
4 difficult to see through: *driving through thick fog*
5 growing close together with not much space in between: *a thick forest | his thick black hair*
6 *BrE informal* stupid: *Don't be so thick!*
—**thickly** adv: *She sliced the bread thickly.*

thick² n **1 be in the thick of sth** to be in the busiest or most dangerous part of a situation: *US troops are right in the thick of the action.* **2 through thick and thin** in spite of any difficulties or problems: *The family has stuck together through thick and thin.*

thick³ adv **thick and fast** happening quickly, one after the other: *Letters have been coming in thick and fast.*

thicken /ˈθɪkən/ v [I,T] to become thick, or to make something thick: *The fog was beginning to thicken. | Thicken the soup with flour.*

thicket /ˈθɪkɪt/ n [C] a group of bushes or small trees growing close together

thickness /ˈθɪknəs/ n [C,U] how thick something is: *the different thicknesses of the old stone walls*

thick-'skinned adj not easily upset by criticism or insults

thief /θiːf/ n [C] plural **thieves** /θiːvz/ someone who steals things: *Thieves broke in and stole some valuable jewellery. | a car thief | a petty thief* (=someone who steals things that are not valuable) → see box at STEAL

thigh /θaɪ/ n [C] the top part of your leg above your knee → see picture on page A3

thimble /ˈθɪmbəl/ n [C] a small hard cap that you put over the end of your finger to protect it when you are sewing

thin

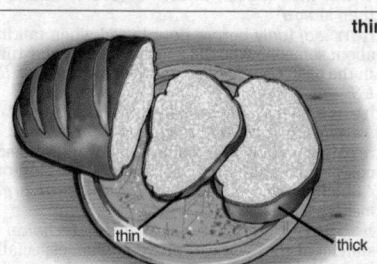

thin¹ /θɪn/ adj
1 something that is thin is not very wide or thick [≠ thick]: *a thin slice of bread | a thin layer of paint | a thin summer jacket* (=one made of light material)
2 someone who is thin does not have very much fat on their body [≠ fat]: *He was tall and thin. | a long, thin face*

THESAURUS

slim and **slender** – used about someone who is thin in an attractive way
skinny – used about someone who is very thin in a way that is not attractive
underweight – used, especially by doctors, about someone who is too thin, in a way that is not healthy
emaciated – used about someone who is extremely thin and weak because of illness or not eating
→ FAT

3 if someone has thin hair, they do not have very much hair [≠ thick]: *His hair's getting a bit thin on top.*
4 the thin end of the wedge *BrE informal* the first stage of something that will get much worse later: *Are these job cuts the thin end of the wedge?*
5 vanish/disappear into thin air to disappear suddenly completely in a mysterious way

6 be thin on the ground *informal* to be very few: *Good restaurants are very thin on the ground here.*

7 thin air is difficult to breathe because there is little OXYGEN in it

8 a thin liquid has a lot of water in it [≠ thick]: *thin soup*

—**thinness** *n* [U]

thin² *v* thinned, thinning **1** also **thin down** [T] to make a liquid weaker by adding water or another liquid: *You need to thin the paint down a little bit.* **2** also **thin out** [I] to become fewer in number: *The crowd was beginning to thin out.*

thing /θɪŋ/ *n* [C]

1 something that happens, or something that someone says or does: *A funny thing happened last week.* | *She did a very stupid thing.* | *That was a terrible thing to say.*

2 an object: *What's that thing on the kitchen table?*

3 sb's things *especially BrE* someone's clothes or possessions [= stuff *AmE*]: *Pack your things – we have to leave right now.* → see box at **own**

4 things [plural] the situation that exists in your life: *How are things?* | *Things have improved a lot since I last saw you.*

5 not see/hear/feel etc a thing not see, hear etc anything at all: *It was so dark I couldn't see a thing.*

6 silly/poor etc thing used to talk about a person or animal: *You look tired, you poor thing.*

7 for one thing *spoken* used to give one of the reasons why you think something is true: *I don't think she'll get the job – for one thing she can't drive!*

8 the thing is *spoken* used to explain what a particular problem is: *I'd like to come, but the thing is, I promised to see Jim tonight.*

9 first thing *informal* at the beginning of the day: *I'll call you first thing tomorrow, OK?*

10 not sb's thing *informal* not something that a person enjoys: *I'm afraid sport's not really my thing.*

11 do your own thing *informal* to do what you want, and not what other people tell you to do

thingy /'θɪŋi/ *n* [C] plural **thingies** *spoken* **1** used when you cannot remember or do not know the name of something you want to mention: *What are those plastic thingies for?* **2** *BrE* used when you cannot remember or do not know the name of someone you want to mention: *Is thingy coming?*

think¹ /θɪŋk/ *v* past tense and past participle **thought** /θɔːt $ θɒːt/

1 [T] to have an opinion about someone or something: **+(that)** *I think it's a brilliant film.* | *I don't think the food here is very good* (=I think it is not very good). | *What do you think of my new hairstyle?* | **think well/highly/a lot of sb** (=have a good opinion of someone) *His teachers seem to think highly of him.* | *The hotel was OK, but I **didn't think much of** the food* (=I didn't think it was very good).

believe sth – to think that it is true
suspect sth – to think that something, especially something unpleasant, is true but not be sure

consider a plan/choice etc – to think about it carefully before deciding what to do
reckon/figure sth *AmE* – used to say what your opinion is: *I reckon he's at least 19.*
guess – to think that something is true, but not be certain

giving your opinion

I think (that) ...: *I think you should apologize.*
If you ask me ...: *If you ask me, he should apologize.*
It seems to me ...: *It seems to me there isn't enough time.*
In my opinion/view ...: *In my opinion, you should accept the offer.*
personally: *Personally, I really like the idea.*

2 [T] to believe that something is true, although you are not sure: **+(that)** *I think they've gone home.* | *'Is David still here?' ' I think so.'*

3 [I] to use your mind to imagine or remember something, or to solve a problem: **+about/of** *What are you thinking about?* | *I couldn't think of anything to say.* | *I'll be thinking of you tomorrow.* | **Think hard** (=think a lot) *before you make a decision.*

4 think of/about doing sth to consider the idea of doing something: *We are thinking of moving to the countryside.*

5 think of/about sb to consider the feelings and wishes of another person, rather than just doing what you want to do: *You never think about other people!*

6 think twice to think carefully before deciding to do something that may cause problems for you: *You should think twice before signing the contract.*

7 think nothing of doing sth to do something often or easily, even though other people think it is very difficult: *He thinks nothing of driving two hours to work every day.*

8 think better of it to decide not to do something that you had intended to do: *He reached for a cigar, but then thought better of it.*

think back *phr v* to remember something from the past: **+to** *I thought back to the years I spent in London.*

think sth ⇔ **out** *phr v* to plan all the details of something very carefully: *Everything has been really well thought out.*

think sth ⇔ **over** *phr v* to consider something carefully before making a decision: *I'll need to think it over for a couple of days.*

think sth ⇔ **through** *phr v* to think carefully about the possible results of doing something: *It sounds like a good idea, but I don't think they've really thought it through.*

think sth ⇔ **up** *phr v* to produce a new idea: *It's a great idea. I wonder who first thought it up.*

think² *n* **have a think** to think carefully about something: *I need to have a think about this.*

thinker /'θɪŋkə $ -ər/ *n* [C] **1** someone who is famous for the work they have done in a subject such as science or PHILOSOPHY **2 an independent/positive/free etc thinker** a person who thinks in a particular way

thinking /'θɪŋkɪŋ/ *n* [U] **1** someone's opinions and ideas about a subject: *His thinking on the*

T

issue has changed. **2** when you think about something: *Lance's quick thinking had saved her life.* → WISHFUL THINKING

'think tank *n* [C] a group of people with special skills or experience in a particular subject that an organization or government employs to give advice and suggest new ideas

thinly /'θɪnli/ *adv* **1** if something is cut thinly, it is cut into thin pieces: *thinly sliced ham* **2** with only a small number of people or things spread over a large area: *a thinly populated area*

thinning /'θɪnɪŋ/ *adj* if your hair is thinning, some of it has fallen out

third[1] /θɜːd $ θɜːrd/ *adj* coming after two other things in a series: *her third birthday*
—**third** *pron*: *I'm planning to leave on the third* (=the third day of the month). —**thirdly** *adv*

third[2] *n* [C] one of three equal parts of something: *Divide it into thirds.* | **+of** *A third of these jobs are held by women.* | **one-third/two-thirds** *Two-thirds of the profits are given to charity.*

third 'party *n* [singular] someone who is not one of the two main people involved in something, but who is involved in it or affected by it

third 'person *n* **the third person** a form of a verb that you use with 'he', 'she', 'it', or 'they' [→ **first person, second person**]

third-'rate *adj* of very bad quality

Third 'World *n* **the Third World** the poorer countries of the world that are not industrially developed. Some people now consider this expression offensive. —**Third World** *adj*: *Third World debt*

thirst /θɜːst $ θɜːrst/ *n*
1 [singular] the feeling of wanting or needing a drink [→ **hunger**]: *a drink to quench your thirst* (=get rid of it)
2 [U] the state of not having enough to drink: *Many of the animals had died of thirst.*
3 [singular,U] a strong need or desire for something: **+for** *a thirst for knowledge*

thirsty /'θɜːsti $ 'θɜːr-/ *adj* if you are thirsty, you want or need to drink something [→ **hungry**]: *I'm thirsty – can I have a glass of water?* | *All this digging is thirsty work.*
—**thirstily** *adv*

thirteen /ˌθɜːˈtiːn◂ $ ˌθɜːr-/ *number* the number 13: *They've only sold thirteen tickets so far.* | *When it happened, I was thirteen* (=13 years old).
—**thirteenth** *adj, pron*: *his thirteenth birthday* | *I'm planning to leave on the thirteenth* (=the 13th day of the month).

thirty /'θɜːti $ 'θɜːrti/ *number*
1 the number 30
2 **the thirties** also **the '30s, the 1930s** [plural] the years from 1930 to 1939: **the early/mid/late thirties** *The house was built in the early thirties.*
3 **be in your thirties** to be aged between 30 and 39: **early/mid/late thirties** *a good-looking guy in his early thirties*
4 **in the thirties** if the temperature is in the thirties, it is between 30 degrees and 39 degrees
—**thirtieth** *adj, pron*: *her thirtieth birthday* | *I'm planning to leave on the thirtieth* (=the 30th day of the month).

this[1] /ðɪs/ *determiner, pron* plural **these** /ðiːz/
1 used to talk about something or someone that is near to you: *My mother gave me this necklace.* | *Where did you get this from?*
2 used to talk about something that has just been mentioned or that is already known about: *I'm going to make sure this doesn't happen again.*
3 used to talk about the present time or a time that is close to the present: *What are you doing this week?* | *We'll be seeing Malcolm this Friday* (=on Friday of the present week).
4 **this is ...** *spoken* used to introduce someone to a person they do not know: *Nancy, this is my wife, Elaine.*

this[2] *adv* as much as this: *I've never stayed up this late before.*

thistle /'θɪsəl/ *n* [C] a wild plant with leaves that have sharp points and purple flowers

thorn /θɔːn $ θɔːrn/ *n* [C] a sharp pointed part on the stem of a plant such as a rose

thorny /'θɔːni $ 'θɔːrni/ *adj* **1** **thorny question/ problem/issue etc** a difficult question, problem etc **2** having a lot of thorns

thorough /'θʌrə $ 'θʌroʊ, 'θʌrə/ *adj* careful to check every part of something, or doing something carefully so that you do not make mistakes [→ **thoroughly**]: *The police carried out a thorough search of the house.* | *As a scientist, Madison is methodical and thorough.*
—**thoroughness** *n* [U]

thoroughbred /'θʌrəbred $ 'θʌroʊ-, 'θʌrə-/ *n* [C] a horse that has parents of the same very good BREED

thoroughfare /'θʌrəfeə $ 'θʌroʊfer, 'θʌrə-/ *n* [C] a main road through a city

thoroughly /'θʌrəli $ 'θʌroʊli, 'θʌrə-/ *adv* **1** very or very much: *Thanks for the meal. I thoroughly enjoyed it.* **2** carefully and completely: *Rinse the vegetables thoroughly.*

those /ðəʊz $ ðoʊz/ *determiner, pron* the plural of THAT

thou /ðaʊ/ *pron* a word meaning 'you' which was used in the past

though /ðəʊ $ ðoʊ/ *linking word, adv*
1 used in order to introduce a statement that is surprising, unexpected, or different from your other statements [→ **although**]: *Though Beattie is almost 40, she still plans to compete.* | *I seem to keep gaining weight even though I'm exercising regularly.* | *It looks like fun. Isn't it risky, though?*
2 used before you add something that makes what you have just said seem less strong or important [= **but**]: *I thought he'd been drinking though I wasn't completely sure.*
3 **as though** used to say how something seems [= **as if**]: *She was staring at me as though she knew me.*

thought[1] /θɔːt $ θɒːt/ *v* the past tense and past participle of THINK

thought[2] *n*
1 [C] something that you think of, remember, or realize [= **idea**]: *I've just had a thought. I'll ask Terry to come.* | *The thought that it might be illegal didn't worry him.* | *She hated the thought of leaving her son.*
2 **thoughts** [plural] a person's ideas or opinions about something: **+on** *What are your thoughts on the subject?*

3 [U] when you think about something: *I've been* **giving** *your proposal some* **thought** (=thinking about it). | **lost/deep in thought** (=thinking so much about something that you do not notice what is happening around you) *She was staring out of the window, lost in thought.*

4 [C,U] a feeling of worrying or caring about something: **+for** *He acted without any thought for his own safety.* | *You are always* **in my thoughts** (=used to tell someone that you think and care about them a lot).

5 [U] the ideas that people have about a subject: *modern scientific thought*

thoughtful /ˈθɔːtfəl $ ˈθɒːt-/ *adj* **1** serious and quiet because you are thinking about something: *a thoughtful expression on his face* **2** kind and always thinking of things you can do to make other people happy: *It's very thoughtful of you to visit me.* → see box at **KIND** —**thoughtfully** *adv* —**thoughtfulness** *n* [U]

thoughtless /ˈθɔːtləs $ ˈθɒːt-/ *adj* not thinking about other people or how your actions or words will affect them: *a thoughtless remark* → see box at **UNKIND** —**thoughtlessly** *adv* —**thoughtlessness** *n* [U]

'thought-pro,voking *adj* a thought-provoking film, book etc makes you think deeply about the subject of the film, book etc

thousand /ˈθaʊzənd/ *number* plural **thousand** or **thousands**

1 the number 1000: *a journey of almost a thousand miles* | **two/three/four etc thousand** *The company employs 30 thousand people.* | **thousands of pounds/dollars etc**

2 an extremely large number of things or people: **a thousand** *I've been this route a thousand times before.* | **thousands of sth** *There are thousands of things I want to do.* —**thousandth** *n* [C] *ten thousandths of a second* —**thousandth** *adj*

thrash /θræʃ/ *v* **1** [T] to hit someone violently, usually as a punishment **2** [I] to move violently from side to side: *a fish thrashing around in the net* —**thrashing** *n* [C,U]

thrash sth ⇔ out *phr v* to discuss something thoroughly until you reach an agreement: *Officials are still trying to thrash out an agreement.*

thread¹ /θred/ *n*

1 [C,U] a long thin string of cotton, silk etc, used to sew cloth: *a needle and thread* → see picture at **KNIT**

2 [singular] an idea, feeling, or feature that forms the connection between the different parts of an explanation, story etc: *There's a* **common thread** *linking the different chapters of the book.* | *Halfway through the film I started to* **lose the thread** (=not understand the story).

thread² *v* [T] **1** to put thread, string etc through a hole: *Will you thread the needle for me?* **2 thread your way through/along etc** to move through a place by carefully going around things and people: *He threaded his way through the traffic.*

threadbare /ˈθredbeə $ -ber/ *adj* threadbare clothes, CARPETS etc are thin and in bad condition because they have been used a lot

threat /θret/ *n*

1 [C,U] an occasion when someone says they will hurt or cause problems, especially if you do not do what they tell you to do: *Threats were* **made against** *his life.* | **+of** *threats of violence* | *Nichols never* **carried out** *his* **threat** *to sue.* | **death threats** | *a bomb threat*

2 [C usually singular] someone or something that may cause damage or harm to another person or thing: **+to** *Pollution in the river* **poses a threat** *to fish.*

3 [C usually singular] the possibility that something bad will happen: **+of** *the threat of famine* | **under threat** *The countryside is under threat from a massive increase in traffic.*

threaten /ˈθretn/ *v*

1 [T] if someone threatens you, they say that they will hurt you or cause problems, especially if you do not do what they tell you to do: **threaten to do sth** *The hijackers threatened to shoot him.* | **threaten sb with sth** *I was threatened with jail if I published the story.*

2 [T] to be likely to harm or destroy something: *Illegal hunting threatens the survival of the white rhino.* | **be threatened with sth** *The rainforest is threatened with extinction.*

3 [I] if something unpleasant threatens to happen, it seems likely to happen: **threaten to do sth** *The fighting threatens to turn into a major civil war.* —**threatening** *adj*: *a threatening letter* —**threateningly** *adv*

three /θriː/ *number* the number 3: *They've won their last three games.* | *We'd better go. It's almost* **three** (=three o'clock). | *My little sister's only* **three** (=three years old).

,three-di'mensional also **3-D** /ˌθriː ˈdiː◂/ *adj* having or seeming to have length, depth, and height: *a 3-D movie*

threefold /ˈθriːfəʊld $ -foʊld/ *adj* three times as much or as many: *a threefold increase in price* —**threefold** *adv*

three-'quarters *n* [plural] an amount equal to three of the four equal parts that make up a whole: **+of** *three-quarters of an hour*

threshold /ˈθreʃhəʊld, -ʃəʊld $ -oʊld/ *n* [C] **1** the floor of the entrance to a room or building **2** the level at which something starts to happen or have an effect: *I have a* **high pain threshold** (=am able to suffer a lot of pain before reacting to it). **3** the beginning of a new and important event or period: *We're* **on the threshold** *of a new era in telecommunications.*

threw /θruː/ *v* the past tense of **THROW**

thrift /θrɪft/ *n* [U] wise and careful use of money —**thrifty** *adj*: *thrifty shoppers*

'thrift shop *n* [C] *AmE* a shop that sells used things, especially clothes, in order to make money for a CHARITY [= **charity shop** *BrE*]

thrill¹ /θrɪl/ *n* [C] a strong feeling of excitement and pleasure, or something that makes you feel this: **the thrill of (doing) sth** *the thrill of driving a fast car*

thrill² *v* [T] to make someone very excited and pleased: *His music continues to thrill audiences.* —**thrilled** *adj*: *We're thrilled with the results.* —**thrilling** *adj*: *a thrilling game* → see box at **EXCITING**

thriller /ˈθrɪlə $ -ər/ *n* [C] an exciting film or book about murder or a crime → see box at **FILM**

thrive /θraɪv/ *v* [I] past tense **thrived** or **throve** /θrəʊv $ θroʊv/ past participle **thrived** to become very successful or very strong and healthy: *a plant that is able to thrive in dry conditions* —**thriving** *adj*: *a thriving business*

throat /θrəʊt $ θroʊt/ *n* [C]
1 the back part of your mouth and the tubes that go down the inside of your neck: *I have a sore throat.* → see picture on page A3
2 the front of your neck: *His attacker held him by the throat.*
→ **clear your throat** at CLEAR²

throaty /'θrəʊti $ 'θroʊ-/ *adj* a throaty sound is low and rough: *a throaty whisper*

throb /θrɒb $ θrɑːb/ *v* [I] **throbbed, throbbing**
1 if a part of your body throbs, you get a regular feeling of pain in it: **+with** *My head was throbbing with pain.* **2** to beat strongly and regularly: *the throbbing sound of the engines* —**throb** *n* [C] *the low throb of distant war drums*

throes /θrəʊz $ θroʊz/ *n formal* **in the throes of sth** in the middle of a very difficult situation: *Nigeria was in the throes of a bloody civil war.*

thrombosis /θrɒmˈbəʊsɪs $ θrɑːmˈboʊ-/ *n* [C,U] plural **thromboses** /-siːz/ *technical* a serious medical problem caused by a CLOT forming in your blood that prevents it from flowing normally

throne /θrəʊn $ θroʊn/ *n* **1** [C] the chair that a king or queen sits on **2 the throne** the position and power of being king or queen

throng¹ /θrɒŋ $ θrɒːŋ/ *n* [C] *literary* a crowd of people

throng² *v* [I,T] *literary* if people throng a place, they go there in large numbers: *crowds thronging St. Peter's Square*

throttle¹ /'θrɒtl $ 'θrɑːtl/ *v* [T] to hold someone's throat tightly, stopping them from breathing [= **strangle**]

throttle² *n* [C] a part of a vehicle or machine that controls the speed of an engine by controlling the amount of FUEL that flows into it

through¹ /θruː/ *adv, prep*
1 from one side or end of something to the other: *The train went through the tunnel.* | *I pushed my way through the crowd.* | *We found a gap in the fence and climbed through.* → see picture on page A8
2 from the beginning to the end, including all parts of something: *She slept through the film.* | *I've searched through all the papers but I can't find your certificate.* | **read/think etc sth through** *Make sure to read the contract through before you sign it.*
3 if you see or hear something through a window, wall etc, the window, wall etc is between you and it: *I could see him through the window.*
4 because of something or with the help of something or someone: *She succeeded through sheer hard work.* | *I got the job through an employment agency.*
5 past one stage in a competition to the next stage: **+to** *This is the first time they've ever made it through to the final.*
6 Friday through Sunday/March through May etc *AmE* from Friday until the end of Sunday, from March until the end of May etc
7 *BrE* connected to someone by telephone: *Please hold the line and I'll* **put** *you* **through.**
8 through and through completely: *a typical Englishman through and through*

through² *adj* **1 be through with sth** *informal* to have finished using something, doing something etc.: *Can I borrow the book when you're through with it?* **2 be through (with sb)** *informal* to no longer have a relationship: *That's it. Steve and I are through!* **3 through train/road** a train or road that goes all the way to another place

throughout /θruːˈaʊt/ *adv, prep*
1 in every part of a place: *Thanksgiving is celebrated throughout the US.*
2 during all of an event or a period of time: *She was calm throughout the interview.*

throve /θrəʊv $ θroʊv/ *v* a past tense of THRIVE

throw¹ /θrəʊ $ θroʊ/ *v* [T] past tense **threw** /θruː/ past participle **thrown** /θrəʊn $ θroʊn/
1 to make an object such as a ball move quickly through the air by pushing your hand forward quickly and letting the object go: **throw sth to sb** *Throw the ball to Daddy.* | **throw sth at sb/sth** *Demonstrators began throwing rocks at the police.* | **throw sb sth** *Throw me a towel, would you.* → see picture on page A11

THESAURUS

toss – to throw something, especially in a careless way: *She tossed her coat onto the bed.*
chuck *informal*: *Kids were chucking snowballs at passing cars.*
hurl – to throw something with a lot of force: *They hurled a brick through his window.*
fling – to throw something somewhere with a lot of force, often in a careless way: *He flung her keys into the river.*

To throw a ball in sport
pass – to throw, kick, or hit a ball to another member of your team
pitch – to throw the ball to the person who is batting in a game of baseball
bowl – to throw the ball towards the person who is batting in a game of cricket

---

2 to put something somewhere quickly and carelessly: *Just throw your coat on the bed.*
3 to push someone or something suddenly and violently, or make them fall down: *The bus stopped suddenly and we were all thrown forward.* | *They were* **thrown to the ground** *by the force of the explosion.*
4 to suddenly move your body somewhere, or part of your body into another position: *She threw her arms around him.* | **throw yourself down/onto/into etc sth** *When he got home, he threw himself into an armchair.*
5 throw sb in jail/prison *informal* to put someone in prison
6 throw yourself into sth to start doing an activity eagerly
7 throw a party to organize a party
8 throw in the towel/sponge to admit that you have been defeated
9 *informal* to make someone feel very confused: *Her question* **threw** *me* **completely** *for a moment.* | *Everyone was thrown into confusion by this news.*

throw sth ⇔ **away** *phr v* **1** to get rid of something that you do not want or need: *Can I throw those boxes away?* → see box at RUBBISH **2** to waste a chance, advantage etc: *He had everything – a good job, a beautiful wife – but he threw it all away.*

throw sth ⇔ **in** phr v informal to include something extra in something you are selling, without increasing the price: *The computer is going for only £900 with a free software package thrown in.*

throw sth ⇔ **on** phr v to put on a piece of clothing quickly

throw sth/sb ⇔ **out** phr v **1** to get rid of something: *The meat smells bad – you'd better throw it out.* → see box at RUBBISH **2** to make someone leave: **+of** *Jim got thrown out of the Navy for taking drugs.*

throw up phr v **1** informal to make food come out of your mouth from your stomach because you are ill [= vomit] **2 throw** sth ⇔ **up** to make something fly up into the air: *Passing trucks threw up clouds of dust.*

throw² n [C] an action in which you throw something

throwback /ˈθrəʊbæk $ ˈθroʊ-/ n [C] something that is like another thing that existed in the past: *His music is a throwback to the 1970s.*

thrown /θrəʊn $ θroʊn/ v the past participle of THROW

thru /θruː/ adv, prep, adj AmE a way of saying or writing 'through'. Some people consider this use to be incorrect.

thrush /θrʌʃ/ n [C] a brown bird with spots on its front

thrust¹ /θrʌst/ v [T] past tense and past participle **thrust** to push something somewhere suddenly or with a lot of force: *Dean thrust his hands in his pockets.*

thrust² n **1** [C,U] when something is pushed forward with force or the power used to push something forward **2 the thrust of** sth the main meaning of what someone says or does: *What was the main thrust of his argument?*

thud /θʌd/ n [C] the low sound made when something heavy falls or hits another thing: *He hit the floor with a thud.* —**thud** v [I]

thug /θʌɡ/ n [C] a violent person who may attack people

thumb¹ /θʌm/ n [C]

1 the short thick finger on the side of your hand which helps you to hold things → see picture at HAND¹

2 be under sb's thumb if you are under someone's thumb, they control everything you do

3 give sth the thumbs up/down to say you approve or disapprove of something

thumb² v

thumb through sth phr v to quickly look at each page of a book, magazine etc

thumbnail¹ /ˈθʌmneɪl/ adj **thumbnail sketch/ portrait** a short description that gives only the main facts about a person, thing, or event

thumbnail² n [C] **1** the nail on your thumb **2** a small picture of a document on a computer screen

thumbtack /ˈθʌmtæk/ n [C] AmE a short pin with a wide flat top, used for fastening notices to walls [= drawing pin BrE]

thump /θʌmp/ v **1** [T] informal to hit someone or something hard with your hand closed: *I'm going to thump you if you don't shut up!* **2** [I,T] to make a repeated low sound by beating or by hitting a surface: *I could hear my heart thumping.* —**thump** n [C]

thunder¹ /ˈθʌndə $ -ər/ n [U] the loud noise that you hear during a storm after a flash of LIGHTNING: *a huge storm with **thunder and lightning*** | **a clap/crack of thunder** (=one sudden noise of thunder)
—**thundery** adj

thunder² v **1 it thunders** if it thunders, a loud noise comes from the sky after LIGHTNING **2** [I] to make a very deep loud sound: *The guns thundered in the distance.*

thunderbolt /ˈθʌndəbəʊlt $ -dərboʊlt/ n [C] **1** a flash of LIGHTNING that hits something **2** something that shocks you

thunderous /ˈθʌndərəs/ adj extremely loud: *thunderous applause* → see box at LOUD

thunderstorm /ˈθʌndəstɔːm $ -dərstɔːrm/ n [C] a storm with THUNDER and LIGHTNING

Thursday /ˈθɜːzdi, -deɪ $ ˈθɜːrz-/ n [C,U] written abbreviation **Thurs.** or **Thur.** the day between Wednesday and Friday
→ see examples at MONDAY → see box at DAY

thus /ðʌs/ adv formal **1** as a result of something that you have just mentioned [= so]: *Traffic will become heavier, thus increasing pollution.* **2** in this way or like this: *Thus began one of the darkest periods in the country's history.*

thwart /θwɔːt $ θwɔːrt/ v [T] to prevent someone from doing what they are trying to do: *His plans had been thwarted.*

thy /ðaɪ/ determiner a word meaning 'your' which was used in the past

thyme /taɪm/ n [U] a plant used for giving a special taste to food

tiara /tiˈɑːrə/ n [C] a piece of jewellery like a small CROWN

tic /tɪk/ n [C] a sudden uncontrolled movement of a muscle in your face

tick¹ /tɪk/ n [C] **1** the sound that a clock or watch makes every second → see picture on page A7 **2** BrE a mark (✔) used to show that something is correct or has been done [= check AmE] **3** BrE spoken a moment: *I'll be back in a tick.* **4** a small creature that sticks to animals and sucks their blood

tick² v **1** [I] if a clock or watch ticks, it makes a short sound every second **2** [T] BrE to mark something with a tick **3 what makes sb tick** informal the thoughts, feelings, opinions etc that make someone behave in a particular way: *I can't figure out what makes him tick.*

tick away/by phr v if time ticks away or by, it passes

tick sb/sth ⇔ **off** phr v **1** BrE informal to tell someone angrily that you are annoyed with them **2** AmE informal to annoy someone: *Her attitude is really ticking me off.* **3** BrE to put a tick next to something on a list to show that it has been done

tick over phr v BrE to continue working at a slow steady rate without producing much: *We kept the business just ticking over until new orders arrived.*

ticket /ˈtɪkɪt/ n [C]

1 a printed piece of paper that shows that you have paid to do something, for example travel on a train or watch a film: **+for** *How much are tickets for the concert?* | **+to** *He bought a ticket to London.* | **train/bus/theatre etc ticket** *Have* *you **booked*** (=arranged to buy) *your plane ticket?* | **ticket to do sth** *I've got two tickets to see Madonna.*

single/one-way ticket – a ticket that lets you go to a place but not back again
return (ticket) *BrE*/**round trip ticket** *AmE* – a ticket that lets you go to a place and back again
cheap day return *BrE* – a return ticket that is cheaper than the usual price because you must return on the same day and cannot use it at the busiest times
season ticket – a ticket that lets you make the same journey every day for a fixed period of time
e-ticket – a ticket that you buy over the Internet, which you print from your computer or which you collect when you arrive at the airport to go on your journey

2 a printed note that orders you to pay money because you have done something illegal while driving or parking your car: **speeding/parking ticket**
→ SEASON TICKET

tickle /'tɪkəl/ v **1** [T] to move your fingers gently over someone's body in order to make them laugh: *Stop tickling me!* → see picture on page A10 **2** [I,T] if something touching your body tickles, it is uncomfortable in a way that makes you want to rub your body: *Your hair is tickling me.* **3** [T] to amuse someone: *I was really tickled by what she said.* —**tickle** n [C]

tidal /'taɪdl/ *adj* relating to the regular rising and falling of the sea: *tidal forces*

'tidal wave n [C] a very large wave that flows over the land, destroying things

tidbit /'tɪd,bɪt/ n [C] *AmE* a TITBIT

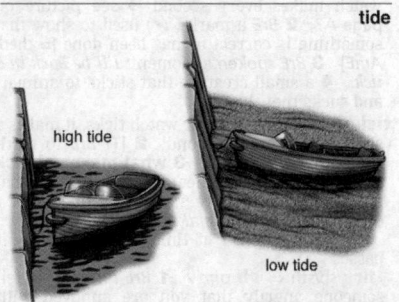

tide

high tide

low tide

tide¹ /taɪd/ n **1** [C] the regular rising and falling of the level of the sea: **the tide is in/out** (=the sea is high/low) | **high/low tide** (=when the sea is high/low) **2** [C] the way that events or people's opinions are developing: **+of** *The tide of public opinion* **turned** *against him.* | *the* **rising tide** *of crime*

tide² v
tide sb **over** *phr v* to help someone through a difficult period, especially by lending them money: *I'll lend you $50 to tide you over.*

tidy¹ /'taɪdi/ *adj especially BrE*
1 a tidy place is neatly arranged with every-

thing in the right place [➡ neat; ≠ untidy, messy]: *a tidy desk* | *Try to* **keep** *your room* **tidy.**
2 a tidy person keeps their things neat and clean [= neat *AmE*]: *I'm not very tidy.*
—**tidily** *adv* —**tidiness** n [U]

tidy² also **tidy up** v [I,T] **tidied, tidying, tidies**
to make a place look tidy: *Tidy up after you've finished.*
tidy sth ⇔ **away** *phr v BrE* to put things back in the place where they should be: *Please tidy your toys away.*

tie¹ /taɪ/ v **tied, tying, ties**
1 [T] **a)** to fasten something by making a knot in a piece of string, rope etc [≠ untie]: **tie sth to/onto/around etc sth** *Tie this label to your suitcase.* | *She tied a scarf around her head.* | **tie sth with sth** *a parcel tied with string* | **tie sb to sth** *They tied him to a chair.* | **tie sb's hands/feet b)** to make a knot in a rope, string etc [≠ untie]: *Can he tie his shoelaces?* | **tie a knot/bow** *She put a ribbon round it and tied a bow.* → see box at FASTEN
2 [I] also **be tied** to have the same number of points in a competition: **+with** *San Diego are tied with Denver Broncos.* | **+for** *Jones and Beale tied for second place.*
3 be tied to sth to be dependent on something or restricted by a particular situation: *Salary increases are tied to inflation.* | **be tied to doing sth** *I don't want to be tied to doing paperwork all day.*
4 tie the knot *informal* to get married
tie sb **down** *phr v* to stop someone from being free to do what they want to do: *I'm not ready to be tied down at my age.*
tie in with sth *phr v* to be similar to or related to another thing: *How does the new job tie in with your long-term plans?*
tie sb/sth ⇔ **up** *phr v* **1** to tie someone's arms, legs etc so that they cannot move **2** to fasten something together using string or rope **3** to use something continuously, stopping other people from using it: *Don't tie up the phone with personal calls.* **4 be tied up** to be very busy: *I'll be tied up all day.*

tie² n [C]
1 a long narrow piece of cloth that a man wears around his neck with a shirt: *He wore a suit and tie.* → see picture at CLOTHES
2 [usually plural] a relationship between two people, groups, or countries: **close/strong ties** *close family ties* | **+between/with** *economic ties between the two countries*
3 the result of a game, competition etc when two people or teams get the same number of points [= draw *BrE*]: *There was a tie for first place.*
→ BLACK TIE, BOW TIE

tiebreaker /'taɪbreɪkə $ -ər/ n [C] **1** an extra question in a game or QUIZ, used to decide who will win when two people have the same number of points **2** also **tiebreak** /'taɪbreɪk/ the final game of a SET in tennis, played when each player has won six games

'tie-in n [C] a product such as a record, book, or toy that is related to a new film, TV show etc

tier /tɪə $ tɪr/ n [C] **1** one of several levels or layers, each one higher than the one in front: *the* lower tier of seats **2** one of several levels in an organization or system: *the senior tier of management*

tiff /tɪf/ *n* [C] a small argument between two people who know each other well: *a **lover's tiff***

tiger

tiger /'taɪgə $ -ər/ *n* [C] a large wild cat with yellow and black lines on its fur

tight¹ /taɪt/ *adj*

1 fitting part of your body very closely [≠ **loose**]: *tight jeans* | *These shoes feel too tight.* → see box at **CLOTHES**

2 attached or pulled very firmly, so that nothing can move [≠ **loose**]: *Make sure the screws are tight.* | *She put a belt on and **pulled** it **tight***. | *He had a **tight grip** on her arm.*

3 strictly controlled: *We have to **keep a tight grip** on spending.* | *Security is **tight** for the Pope's visit.*

4 with hardly enough time, money, or space: **a tight schedule/deadline/budget etc** *We are working to a tight schedule.* | **a tight squeeze/fit** *Six in the car will be a tight squeeze.* | **money/time etc is tight** *Money's a bit tight this month.* —**tightly** *adv*

tight² *adv* firmly or closely: *Hold **tight** to the rail.* | *I kept my eyes **tight shut**.*

tighten /'taɪtn/ *v* [I,T] to become tighter, or to make something tighter: *Richard's grip tightened on her arm.* | *How do I tighten my seat belt?*
tighten sth ⇔ **up** also **tighten up on sth** *phr v* to make something stricter or more strictly controlled: *We need to tighten up the rules.*

tight-'knit *adj* a tight-knit group of people have a strong close relationship with each other: *a tight-knit island community*

tight-lipped /ˌtaɪt 'lɪpt◂ / *adj* unwilling to talk about something

tightrope /'taɪt-rəʊp $ -roʊp/ *n* [C] **walk a tightrope** to be in a difficult situation in which you have to be careful about what you say or do

tights /taɪts/ *n* [plural] a piece of women's clothing that fits closely around the feet and legs and up to the waist [= **pantyhose** *AmE*]

tile /taɪl/ *n* [C] a flat square piece of clay or other material, used for covering roofs, floors etc → see picture at **BATHROOM**
—**tile** *v* [T]

till¹ /tɪl, tl/ *prep, linking word* until: *Let's wait till tomorrow.* | *Don't move till I tell you.* → see box at **UNTIL**

till² /tɪl/ *n* [C] a machine used in a shop to show how much you have to pay, and to keep money in [= **cash register**]

tilt /tɪlt/ *v* [I,T] to move or make something move into a position where one side is higher than the other: *She tilted her head.* | *His chair tilted back.*
—**tilt** *n* [C]

timber /'tɪmbə $ -ər/ *n* **1** [U] *BrE* wood used for building or making things [= **lumber** *AmE*] **2** [C] a wooden beam that forms part of a structure

time¹ /taɪm/ *n*

1 [U] the thing that is measured in minutes, hours, years etc, using clocks: *measurements of space and time* | **period/amount of time** *We only have a short amount of time.* | **time passes/goes by** *Time went by so quickly.* | **with/over time** (=as time passes) *The landscape changes over time.*

2 [C,U] a particular point in time, shown on a clock in hours and minutes: *a list giving the times of the exams* | **what time is it?/do you have the time?** *'What time is it?' 'It's five o'clock.'* | **What time** *does school start?* | *Josh is learning to **tell the time** (=see what time it is, using a clock).*

3 [C] an occasion when something happens or when you do something: *How many **times** have you been there?* | **the first/second/last etc time** *That was the last time I saw him.* | *Tim failed his exam for the second time.* | **last/next time** *Next time we go to the cinema, I'll pay.*

4 [singular,U] an amount of time: **a long/short time** *It happened **a long time** ago.* | *I want to **spend** more **time** at home.* | *Making friends **takes time**.* | *Don't **waste time** talking about it.*

5 [C,U] the particular time when something happens: **at the time/at that time** (=a time in the past when something happened) *I was living in Mexico at that time.* | **a good/bad/suitable etc time** *Is this a convenient time to talk?* | **dinner time/bed time etc** *7 o'clock is the children's bath time.* | **it's time for sth/to do sth** *Come on, it's time for lunch.* | **at one time** (=in the past) *At one time they were friends.*

6 [U] time that is available to do something: **time to do sth** *I don't have time to talk now.* | **+for** *There was no time for questions.* | **waste/save time** *I'll go on my bike to save time.*

7 by the time when: *By the time I arrived, he had left.*

8 all the time continuously or very often: *He's getting better all the time.*

9 most of the time very often or almost always: *Most of the time I'm right.*

10 at times sometimes: *At times I wish I didn't live here.*

11 from time to time sometimes, but not often: *We see each other from time to time.* → see box at **SOMETIMES**

12 for the time being for a short period of time, but not permanently: *You can stay here for the time being.*

13 in 2 days'/5 years' etc time two days, five years etc from now: *Call back in ten minutes' time.*

14 in time early enough, before something happens: **+for** *She arrived in time for dinner.*

15 five/ten/many times bigger/more etc used to say how much bigger, more etc one thing is than another: *He earns three times as much as I do.*

16 take your time to do something without hurrying: *We took our time walking to school.*

T

17 one/two etc at a time one, two etc at the same time: *I'll answer questions one at a time.*

18 on time at the correct time or the time that was arranged: *You must get to work on time.* | *At least the trains run on time.*

19 (it's) about time *spoken* used to say that something should already have happened: *It's about time you got a job!*

20 the best/biggest etc of all time *spoken* the best, biggest etc that has ever existed: *What do you think is the best film of all time?*

21 in no time very soon or quickly: *We'll be there in no time.*

22 any time (now) *spoken* very soon: *She should be here any time now.*

23 have a good/great time to enjoy yourself

24 time after time again and again

25 [C] the amount of time taken by someone in a race: *The winner's time was 2 hours 6 minutes.*

26 [U] the time in a particular part of the world: *The plane arrived at 5.30 local time.*

→ at the same time at SAME¹ → BIG TIME, GREENWICH MEAN TIME, LOCAL TIME, PRIME TIME

time² *v* [T] **1** to arrange that something will happen at a particular time: *She timed her arrival perfectly.* | **be timed to do sth** *The book was timed to coincide with a new movie.* | **well-timed** (=said or done at a very suitable time) *a well-timed remark* **2** to measure the time taken to do something: *We timed our journey.*

'time bomb *n* [C] **1** a bomb that is set to explode at a particular time **2** a situation that is likely to become a very serious problem: *the population time bomb*

'time-con,suming *adj* taking a long time to do

'time frame *n* [C] the period of time during which you expect or agree that something will happen or be done

'time-,honoured *BrE*; **time-honored** *AmE adj* a time-honoured method is one that has been used for a long time

'time lag also **'time lapse** *n* [C] the period of time between two connected events

timeless /'taɪmləs/ *adj* always remaining beautiful, attractive etc

'time ,limit *n* [C] the longest time in which you are allowed to do something: *The time limit for the exam is three hours.*

timely /'taɪmli/ *adj* done or happening at exactly the right time

,time 'off *n* [U] time when you are allowed not to be at work or studying: **take/have/get time off** *Can you get some time off for the funeral?*

,time 'out *n* **1 take time out** to rest or do something different from your usual job or activities **2** [C] a short period during a sports match when the team can rest

timer /'taɪmə $ -ər/ *n* [C] an instrument on a machine, used to measure, for example, how long food should be cooked in an OVEN

times /taɪmz/ *prep* multiplied by: *Two times two equals four.*

timescale /'taɪmskeɪl/ *n* [C] the period of time in which something will or should happen: *The timescale for the project is 6 months.*

timetable /'taɪm,teɪbəl/ *n* [C]

1 *BrE* a list of the times of buses, trains etc [= **schedule** *AmE*]

2 a list of times of classes in a school or college → see picture at CLASSROOM
—**timetable** *v* [T]

'time zone *n* [C] one of the 24 areas that the world is divided into, each of which has its own time

timid /'tɪmɪd/ *adj* shy and not showing courage or confidence → see box at CONFIDENT —**timidly** *adv* —**timidity** /tɪ'mɪdəti/ *n* [U]

timing /'taɪmɪŋ/ *n* [U] **1** the time when someone does something or when something happens: *the timing of the election* **2** the skill of doing something at exactly the right time: *Comedy depends on timing.*

tin /tɪn/

1 [U] a soft light metal that is often mixed with other metals: *a tin can*

2 [C] *BrE* a small metal container in which food is sold [= **can** *AmE*]: *a tin of tuna* → see picture at CONTAINER

3 [C] a metal container in which food is stored or cooked: *a biscuit tin*

tinfoil /'tɪnfɔɪl/ *n* [U] thin shiny metal that bends like paper, used for covering food

tinge /tɪndʒ/ *n* [C] a very small amount of a feeling or colour: **+of** *There was a tinge of sadness in her voice.* —**tinged** *adj*: *white tinged with pink*

tingle /'tɪŋgəl/ *v* [I] if your skin tingles, you feel a slight stinging in it: *a tingling sensation in my arm* —**tingle** *n* [C]

tinker /'tɪŋkə $ -ər/ *v* [I] to try and improve something by making small changes to it: *Joe was tinkering with his bike.*

tinkle /'tɪŋkəl/ *v* [I] to make quick high ringing sounds —**tinkle** *n* [C]

tinned /tɪnd/ *adj BrE* tinned food is sold in small metal containers [= **canned**]: *tinned tomatoes* → see box at FOOD

tinny /'tɪni/ *adj* a tinny sound is weak, unpleasant, and sounds like it comes from inside a metal container

'tin ,opener *n* [C] *BrE* a tool for opening TINS [= **can opener**]

tinsel /'tɪnsəl/ *n* [U] thin strings of shiny paper, used as Christmas decorations

tint¹ /tɪnt/ *n* [C] a small amount of colour

tint² *v* [T] to change parts of your hair to a slightly different colour, in order to make it look more attractive

tinted /'tɪntɪd/ *adj* tinted glass is coloured, so that less light goes through it

tiny /'taɪni/ *adj* extremely small: *tiny fish* | *The increase was tiny.* | *I felt a tiny bit sad.* → see box at SMALL

tip¹ /tɪp/ *n* [C]

1 the narrow or pointed end of something: **+of** *the tip of her nose*

2 an additional amount of money that you give to someone such as a WAITER or taxi driver: **give sb/leave sb a tip** *I left a big tip.* → see box at RESTAURANT

3 a helpful piece of advice: **+on/for** *He gave me some tips on travelling alone.*

4 the tip of the iceberg a small sign of a much larger problem

5 on the tip of your tongue if a word or phrase is on the tip of your tongue, you nearly say it but do not, because you cannot remember it or because you decide not to say it

6 *BrE* an area where unwanted waste is taken and left [= **dump**]: *a rubbish tip*

7 *BrE informal* a very dirty or untidy place: *This place is an **absolute tip**!*
→ **FELT TIP PEN**

tip² *v* **tipped, tipping**

1 [I,T] to move something so that one side is higher than the other, or to move in this way [= **tilt**]: **tip sth forward/back etc** *She tipped her hat forward over her eyes.* | **+forward/back etc** *The seat tips back.*

2 [T] to pour something out of a container: **tip sth onto/into etc sth** *Tip the mixture into a dish.* | **tip sth out** *He grabbed her bag and tipped everything out.*

3 [I,T] to give a small additional amount of money to a WAITER, taxi driver etc

4 be tipped to do sth to be thought most likely to succeed in doing something

tip sb ⇔ off *phr v informal* to give someone such as the police a secret warning or piece of information: **+about/that** *The police had been tipped off about the robbery.*

tip over *phr v* to fall or turn over, or to make something do this: *A bucket had tipped over.* | **tip sth ⇔ over** *A large wave tipped the boat over.*

'tip-off *n* [C] *informal* a secret warning or piece of information, especially one given to the police about illegal activities

tipsy /'tɪpsi/ *adj* slightly drunk

tiptoe /'tɪptəʊ $ -toʊ/ *n* **on tiptoe** standing on your toes, with the rest of your feet above the ground → see picture on page A11 —**tiptoe** *v* [I] *They tiptoed silently out.*

tirade /taɪ'reɪd, tɪ- $ 'taɪreɪd, tə'reɪd/ *n* [C] a long angry speech criticizing someone or something

tire¹ /taɪə $ taɪr/ *n* [C] the American spelling of TYRE → see picture on page A12

tire² *v* [I,T] to make someone feel tired, or to become tired: *Even short walks tire her.*

tire of sb/sth *phr v* to become bored with someone or something: *She soon tired of him.*

tire sb ⇔ out *phr v* to make someone very tired: *Those kids tire me out.*

tired /taɪəd $ taɪrd/ *adj*

1 feeling that you want to sleep or rest: *You look tired.* | *The children were **tired out** (=very tired).* | *I'm **too tired to** go out tonight.*

THESAURUS

exhausted, worn out, shattered *BrE*, **beat** *AmE informal*, **knackered** *BrE spoken informal*

---

2 tired of (doing) sth bored or annoyed with something: *I'm tired of her criticisms.*

tireless /'taɪələs $ 'taɪr-/ *adj* working very hard and not stopping —**tirelessly** *adv*

tiresome /'taɪəsəm $ 'taɪr-/ *adj* annoying or boring

tiring /'taɪərɪŋ $ 'taɪr-/ *adj* making you feel tired: *a long, tiring journey*

tissue /'tɪʃuː, -sjuː $ -ʃuː/ *n* **1** [C] a piece of soft thin paper, used for cleaning your nose: *a box of tissues* **2** also **'tissue ,paper** [U] soft

thin paper used for wrapping and packing things **3** [U] the material forming animal or plant cells

titbit /'tɪt,bɪt/ *n* [C] *BrE* a small piece of food or interesting information [= **tidbit** *AmE*]

tit for tat /,tɪt fə 'tæt $ -fər-/ *n* [U] *informal* when you do something unpleasant to someone because they have done something unpleasant to you

titillate /'tɪtɪleɪt/ *v* [T] to make someone feel sexually excited —**titillation** /,tɪtɪ'leɪʃən/ *n* [U]

title /'taɪtl/ *n* [C]

1 the name given to a book, painting, play etc: **+of** *The title of her novel is 'Zoo'.*

2 a book: *They publish thousands of titles.*

3 a word such as Mr, Mrs, Dr, or Sir, that is used before someone's name

4 the official name of someone's job: *Her title is editorial manager.*

5 the position of being the winner of an important sports competition: *He won the world heavyweight title.*

titled /'taɪtld/ *adj* **1** a titled person is a member of the ARISTOCRACY and has a title such as 'lord' **2** used to say what the name of a book, play etc is: *a book titled 'A History of America'*

'title-,holder *n* [C] the person or team that has won an important sports competition

'title page *n* [C] the page near the front of a book that shows the book's title and the writer's name

'title role *n* [C] the main acting part in a film or play, which has the same name as the film or play

'title track *n* [C] the song on a CD, CASSETTE etc that has the same title as the whole CD etc

titter /'tɪtə $ -ər/ *v* [I] to laugh quietly, especially in a nervous way —**titter** *n* [C]

T-junction /'tiː ,dʒʌŋkʃən/ *n* [C] *BrE* a place where two roads meet and form the shape of the letter T

TNT /,tiː en 'tiː/ *n* [U] a powerful explosive

to¹ /tə; *before vowels* tʊ; *strong* tuː/

1 used before the basic form of a verb to show that it is in the INFINITIVE: *I want to go home.* | *They decided to wait.* | **how/where/whether etc to do sth** *Show me how to print things.*

2 used to show a purpose or intention [= **in order to**]: *I left early to catch the first train.*

to² *prep*

1 used to say the place or direction where someone or something goes: *She walked to the door.* | *He flew to Florida.* | *We're going to a party.* | *Which is **the way to** the station?* | **to the left/right/north etc** *Can you move a little to the left?*

2 used to say who receives something or is told or shown something: **say/call/whisper etc sth to sb** *Did Liz say hello to you?* | **give/pass/show etc sth to sb** *Show your ticket to the inspector.*

3 used to say where something is touching, facing, or connected: *She held her finger to her lips.* | *He stood with his back to me.* | **tie/stick/fasten etc sth to sth** *Stick the label to the package.*

4 a) as far as a particular point or limit: **from ... to ...** *It's 30 miles from here to Toronto.* | *books on everything from cooking to camping* | *The water came up to our knees.* | *Read to page*

T

45. b) until and including a particular time or date: **from ... to ...** *The banks are open from 9.30 to 3.00.* | *I work from Monday to Thursday.*
5 used to say what something is connected with: *the key to the front door* | *I don't know the answer to that question.* | *a danger to health*
6 used to say who has a particular attitude or opinion: *To some people, £20 is a lot of money.* | *It looks a bit strange to me.*
7 used to compare two things or numbers: *I prefer New York to LA.* | *Brazil won by 2 goals to 1.*
8 used to say what state something is in as a result of an action or change: **turn/change to sth** *Wait until the light turns to green.* | *Mix the ingredients to a smooth paste.*
9 used to say how much time is left before a particular time or event: *It's only two weeks to Christmas.* | **ten to four/quarter to six etc** *School starts at five to nine.*
10 to sb's surprise/horror/relief etc used to say what someone's reaction is to something: *To her surprise, they offered her the job.*

to³ /tu:/ *adv* **1** if you push a door to, you close or almost close it **2 to and fro** moving in one direction and then in the other

toad /təʊd $ toʊd/ *n* [C] a brown animal like a large FROG → see picture at FROG

toadstool /'təʊdstu:l $ -toʊd-/ *n* [C] a wild plant like a MUSHROOM, which is often poisonous

toast¹ /təʊst $ toʊst/ *n* **1** [U] bread that has been heated until it is brown: **piece/slice of toast** → see picture at BREAD **2** [C] when people lift their glasses and drink because they want to thank someone, wish someone luck etc: *I'd like to propose a toast to the happy couple.*

toast² *v* [T] **1** to make bread turn brown by heating it **2** to lift your glass and drink with other people because you want to thank someone, wish someone luck etc

toaster /'təʊstə $ 'toʊstər/ *n* [C] a machine you use for making toast → see picture at KITCHEN

tobacco /tə'bækəʊ $ -koʊ/ *n* [U] the dried brown leaves that are smoked in cigarettes, pipes etc

tobacconist /tə'bækənⁱst/ *n* [C] **1** also **tobacconist's** a small shop that sells cigarettes, sweets etc **2** someone who owns or works in a small shop that sells cigarettes, sweets etc

toboggan /tə'bɒgən $ -'bɑ:-/ *n* [C] a curved wooden board, used for sliding down hills that are covered in snow [= sledge] —**tobogganing** *n* [U]

today /tə'deɪ/ *adv, n* [U]
1 this day [➡ **yesterday, tomorrow**]: *Today is Wednesday.* | *Can we go to the park today?* | *today's newspaper* | *We're leaving a week today* (=on this day next week).
2 the present period of time: *today's athletic superstars* | *Today more and more girls are taking up smoking.*

toddle /'tɒdl $ 'tɑ:dl/ *v* [I + adv/prep] *informal* to walk somewhere

toddler /'tɒdlə $ 'tɑ:dlər/ *n* [C] a young child who has just learned to walk → see box at CHILD

toe¹ /təʊ $ toʊ/ *n* [C]
1 one of the five parts at the end of your foot [➡ **finger**]: **your big/little toe** (=your largest/

smallest toe) | *I just stubbed my toe* (=hurt it by kicking against something).
2 keep sb on their toes to make sure that someone is ready for anything that might happen: *They do random checks to keep workers on their toes.*

toe² *v* ▸ **toe the line** to do what people in authority tell you to do, whether you agree or not

toenail /'təʊneɪl $ 'toʊ-/ *n* [C] the hard part that covers the top of each of your toes

toffee /'tɒfi $ 'tɑ:fi/ *n* [C,U] a sticky brown sweet food made from sugar and butter

together¹ /tə'geðə $ -ər/ *adv*
1 if people do something together, they do it with each other [➡ **alone, separately**]: *Kevin and I went to school together.* | *Together they went back into the house.*
2 if you put things together, you join them into one thing: *Mix the flour and the sugar together.* | *Glue the broken pieces together.*
3 if people or things are together, they are next to each other: *The children were all sitting together in a group.*
4 if you keep things together, you keep them in one place: *Keep all your important documents together.*
5 at the same time: *Why do all the bills seem to come together?*
6 together with sth in addition to something else: *Bring it back to the store together with your receipt.*

together² *adj informal approving* someone who is together is good at organizing his or her life: *Carla seems really together.*

togetherness /tə'geðənⁱs $ -ðər-/ *n* [U] a feeling that you have when you have a close relationship with other people

toggle /'tɒgəl $ 'tɑ:-/ *n* [C] a small piece of wood or plastic that is used like a button to fasten coats, bags etc

toil /tɔɪl/ *v* [I] *literary* to work very hard for a long period of time —**toil** *n* [U]

toilet /'tɔɪlⁱt/ *n* [C]
1 a large bowl that you sit on to get rid of waste substances from your body: *I need to use the toilet before we leave.* → see picture at BATHROOM
2 *BrE* a room with a toilet: *the men's toilet*
3 go to the toilet *BrE* to use the toilet

'toilet bag *n* [C] a small bag in which you carry soap, TOOTHPASTE etc when you are travelling

'toilet ,paper *n* [U] soft thin paper used for cleaning yourself after you have used the toilet

toiletries /'tɔɪlⁱtriz/ *n* [plural] things such as soap that you use when you wash yourself

'toilet roll *n* [C] toilet paper that is wound around a small tube → see picture at BATHROOM

token¹ /'təʊkən $ 'toʊ-/ *n* [C] **1** *formal* something that is intended to show your intentions or feelings: **+of** *He gave her the ring as a token of his love.* **2** a piece of metal or plastic, used instead of money in some machines **3 book/ record/gift token** *BrE* a piece of paper that you can exchange for a book, record etc in a shop, given to someone as a present [= gift certificate *AmE*]

token² *adj* [only before noun] **1 token woman/black etc** someone who is included in a group to make everyone think that the group has all types of people in it, when this is not really true **2** a token action, change etc is small and not very important, and is usually only done so that someone can pretend that they are dealing with a problem

told /təʊld $ toʊld/ v the past tense and past participle of TELL

tolerable /ˈtɒlərəbəl $ ˈtɑː-/ adj something that is tolerable is acceptable but not very good [≠ **intolerable**]: *tolerable levels of pollution* —**tolerably** adv

tolerant /ˈtɒlərənt $ ˈtɑː-/ adj allowing other people to do or say what they want, without criticizing them or punishing them [≠ **intolerant**]: *a tolerant society* —**tolerance** n [U] *religious tolerance*

tolerate /ˈtɒləreɪt $ ˈtɑː-/ v [T] **1** to accept or allow something, especially something that you do not like or approve of [➡ **stand**]: *I will not tolerate this sort of behaviour.* **2** to not be harmed by something: *plants that will tolerate all kinds of weather conditions* —**toleration** /ˌtɒləˈreɪʃən $ ˌtɑː-/ n [U]

toll¹ /təʊl $ toʊl/ n **1** [singular] the number of people killed or injured by something: *The death toll has risen to 83.* **2 take its toll (on sb/sth)** to have a bad effect on someone or something over a long period of time: *Years of smoking have taken their toll on his health.* **3** [C] money you pay to use a road, bridge etc: *toll roads*

toll² v [I,T] if a bell tolls, it rings slowly

toll-'free adv, adj if you telephone a number toll-free, you do not have to pay for the call

tomato /təˈmɑːtəʊ $ -ˈmeɪtoʊ/ n [C] plural **tomatoes** a round soft red fruit eaten raw or cooked as a vegetable ➔ see picture at VEGETABLE

tomb /tuːm/ n [C] a place above or below the ground in which a dead person is buried

tomboy /ˈtɒmbɔɪ $ ˈtɑːm-/ n [C] a girl who likes to play the same games as boys

tombstone /ˈtuːmstəʊn $ -stoʊn/ n [C] a stone on a GRAVE, showing the name of the dead person

tomcat /ˈtɒmkæt $ ˈtɑːm-/ n [C] a male cat

tome /təʊm $ toʊm/ n [C] formal a large heavy book

tomorrow /təˈmɒrəʊ $ -ˈmɔːroʊ, -ˈmɑː-/ adv, n [U]

1 the day after this day [➡ **today**, **yesterday**]: *Tomorrow is Thursday.* | *What are you doing tomorrow?* | **tomorrow morning/night etc** *We're meeting for dinner tomorrow evening.* **2** the future: *the computers of tomorrow*

ton /tʌn/ n [C]

1 a unit for measuring weight, equal to 2240 pounds or 1016 kilos in Britain, and 2000 pounds in the US [➡ **tonne**]
2 tons of sth informal a lot: *tons of letters* | *I've got tons of work to do.*
3 weigh a ton informal to be very heavy: *Your bag weighs a ton!*

tone¹ /təʊn $ toʊn/ n

1 [C,U] the way your voice sounds, which shows how you are feeling or what you mean: **in a ... tone** *'Hello,' she said in a welcoming tone.* | *He spoke in an angry tone of voice.*

2 [singular, U] the general feeling of something: **+of** *The tone of her letter was rather unfriendly.*
3 [C] a sound made by a piece of electronic equipment, especially a telephone: *Please leave a message after the tone.* | **dialling tone** BrE; **dial tone** AmE (=the sound you hear from a telephone before you dial)
4 [C] one of the many types of a particular colour, which are lighter or darker [= **shade**]

tone² also **tone up** v [T] to improve the strength and firmness of your muscles, skin etc: *I'm trying to tone up my stomach.*

tone sth ⇔ down phr v to reduce the effect of something such as a speech or piece of writing, so that people will not be offended

,tone-'deaf adj unable to hear the difference between different musical notes

toner /ˈtəʊnə $ ˈtoʊnər/ n [C] **1** a type of ink that is used in machines that print or copy documents **2** a liquid that you put on your face to make your skin feel soft and smooth

tongs /tɒŋz $ tɑːŋz, tɔːŋz/ n [plural] a tool for picking up small things. It has two movable bars that are joined together at one end.

tongue /tʌŋ/ n

1 [C] the soft part inside your mouth that you move and use for tasting and speaking: *the taste of chocolate on her tongue* | *The girl* **stuck out her tongue** (=put her tongue outside her mouth as a rude sign) *at me.*
2 [C] a language: **mother/native tongue** (=the first language you learned as a child)
3 [C,U] the tongue of a cow or sheep, cooked and eaten cold
➔ **on the tip of your tongue** at TIP¹ ➔ **a slip of the tongue** at SLIP²

,tongue-in-'cheek adj, adv said or done as a joke, although you pretend to be serious

'tongue-tied adj unable to speak because you are nervous

'tongue-,twister n [C] a phrase or sentence with many similar sounds, which is difficult to say quickly

tonic /ˈtɒnɪk $ ˈtɑː-/ n **1** also **tonic ,water** [C,U] a clear bitter-tasting drink that you can mix with alcoholic drinks such as GIN **2** [singular] something that makes you healthier, happier, or have more energy

tonight /təˈnaɪt/ adv, n [U] this evening or night: *Tonight should be fun.* | *Do you want to go out tonight?* | *We're meeting at nine o'clock tonight.*

tonnage /ˈtʌnɪdʒ/ n [U] the total weight or amount of something, measured in TONS

tonne /tʌn/ n [C] plural **tonnes** or **tonne** a unit for measuring weight, equal to 1000 kilograms [➡ **ton**]

tonsil /ˈtɒnsəl $ ˈtɑːn-/ n [C] your tonsils are the two small round pieces of flesh at the sides of your throat

tonsillitis /ˌtɒnsəˈlaɪtəs $ ˌtɑːn-/ n [U] an infection of the tonsils

too /tuː/ adv

1 more than is acceptable or possible: *He was driving too fast.* | *It's too hot!* | **too ... for sb/sth** *This dress is* **much too** *small for me.* | **too ... to**

do sth *He was too ill to travel.* | **too much/many** *$200 for a room? That's far too much.* | *I drank too many cups of coffee.*

2 also: *Sheila wants to come too.* | *'I'm really hungry.' 'Me too!'* → see box at **ALSO**
3 not too *spoken* not very: *He wasn't too pleased when I told him I was leaving.*
4 all too/only too used to emphasize that a particular situation exists when you wish it did not exist: *This kind of attack happens all too often these days.*
5 be too much for sb used to say that something is so difficult, tiring, upsetting etc that someone cannot do it or bear it: *The shock was too much for him.*

took /tʊk/ *v* the past tense of TAKE
tool /tuːl/ *n* [C]
1 something such as a hammer that you hold in your hand and use to do a particular job: *gardening tools* | *a tool kit* (=a set of tools) → see picture at **BOX¹**
2 something that can be used for a particular purpose: *Computers can be used as a tool for learning.*
→ **POWER TOOL**

toolbar /ˈtuːlbɑː $ -bɑːr/ *n* [C] a row of small pictures at the top of a computer screen that allow you to do particular things in a document
toot /tuːt/ *v* [I,T] if you toot the horn in your car, or if it toots, it makes a short sound —**toot** *n* [C]
tooth /tuːθ/ *n* [C] plural **teeth** /tiːθ/
1 one of the hard white things in your mouth, used for biting food: *She had white, even teeth.* | *Did you remember to brush your teeth?* | *Dentists recommend that you floss your teeth* (=use a thin piece of string between your teeth to clean them). → see picture on page A3
2 one of the long narrow pointed parts of a , comb, SAW etc
→ **have a sweet tooth** at **SWEET¹** → **WISDOM TOOTH**
toothache /ˈtuːθ-eɪk/ *n* [C] a pain in a tooth
toothbrush /ˈtuːθbrʌʃ/ *n* [C] a small brush for cleaning your teeth → see picture at **BATHROOM**
toothpaste /ˈtuːθpeɪst/ *n* [U] a substance used for cleaning your teeth → see picture at **BATHROOM**
toothpick /ˈtuːθ-pɪk/ *n* [C] a small pointed piece of wood, used for removing pieces of food from between your teeth
top¹ /tɒp $ tɑːp/ *n* [C]
1 the highest part of something [≠ bottom]: +**of** *Write your name at the top of the page.* | **on top (of sth)** *ice cream with chocolate sauce on top* | **at the top (of sth)** *He waited at the top of the stairs.* | **to the top** *I filled the glass right to the top.*
2 the flat upper surface of an object [≠ bottom]: *The table has a glass top.* | +**of** *the top of my desk*
3 on top of sth a) in addition to something: *On top of everything else, I need $700 to fix my*

car! **b)** completely able to deal with a job or situation: *Don't worry, I'm back on top of things now.*
4 at the top (of sth) in the most successful or important position in a company or competition [≠ bottom]: *United are at the top of the league.*
5 on top winning: *Australia were on top throughout the game.*
6 the lid or cover for a pen, container etc → see box at **COVER**
7 on top of sb very near you: *The truck was almost on top of us.*
8 a piece of clothing that you wear on the upper part of your body: *She was wearing a yellow top.*
9 off the top of your head *informal* when you give an answer or opinion immediately, without checking that you are right: *Off the top of my head I'd say there were about 50.*
10 shout/scream etc at the top of your voice to shout etc as loudly as you can
11 a toy that spins and balances on its point
12 on top of the world *informal* extremely happy
13 from top to bottom completely and thoroughly: *They searched the house from top to bottom.*
14 get on top of sb if your work or a problem gets on top of you, it begins to make you feel unhappy and upset
15 over the top too extreme and therefore unacceptable

top² *adj*
1 [only before noun] best or most successful: *the world's top tennis players* | *She got top marks.* → see box at **POSITION**
2 [only before noun] nearest to the top of something [≠ bottom]: *the top floor of the building* | *the top button of my shirt* | *the top drawer of the desk*
3 winning in a game or competition: +**of** *Barcelona are top of the league.*
4 top speed the fastest speed a vehicle can move at: *a sports car with a top speed of 155 mph*
5 top dog *informal* the most powerful or important person in a group
top³ *v* [T] **topped, topping 1** to be more than a particular amount: *Their profits have topped $9 million this year.* **2** to be in the highest position in a list of the most successful people or things: *Their single topped the charts for two weeks.* **3** if something is topped with another thing, it is covered with it: *ice cream topped with maple syrup*
top sth ⇔ **off** *phr v* *informal* to finish something successfully by doing one last thing: *We topped off the evening with a visit to a local bar.*
top sth ⇔ **up** *phr v* to fill something that is partly empty: *Let me top up your glass.*
,top 'brass *n* [plural] the people of highest rank in a company, the army etc
,top 'hat *n* [C] a tall hat with a flat top, worn by men on very formal occasions → see picture at **HAT**
,top-'heavy *adj* too heavy at the top and therefore likely to fall over
topic /ˈtɒpɪk $ ˈtɑː-/ *n* [C] a subject that people talk or write about: +**of** *Jackie's engagement was the main topic of conversation.* | *a wide range of topics*

topical /'tɒpɪkəl $ 'tɑː-/ *adj* relating to something that is important at the present time: *topical issues*

topless /'tɒpləs $ 'tɑːp-/ *adj* a woman who is topless is not wearing any clothes on the upper part of her body

topmost /'tɒpməʊst $ 'tɑːpmoʊst/ *adj* highest: *the topmost branches*

top-'notch *adj informal* something that is top-notch is of the highest quality or standard

topography /tə'pɒgrəfi $ -'pɑː-/ *n* [U] the shape of an area of land, including its hills, valleys etc —**topographical** /ˌtɒpə'græfɪkəl◂ $ ˌtɑː-, ˌtoʊ-/ *adj*

topping /'tɒpɪŋ $ 'tɑː-/ *n* [C,U] food that you put on top of other food to make it taste better: *pizza with extra toppings*

topple /'tɒpəl $ 'tɑː-/ *v* **1** [I] to fall over: **+over** *Several trees toppled over in the storm.* **2** [T] to take power away from a leader or government: *The scandal could topple the government.*

top-'secret *adj* top secret documents or information must be kept completely secret

topsy-turvy /ˌtɒpsi 'tɜːvi◂ $ ˌtɑːpsi 'tɜːrvi◂ / *adj* in a state of complete disorder or confusion

torch¹ /tɔːtʃ $ tɔːrtʃ/ *n* [C] **1** *BrE* a small electric lamp that you carry in your hand [= flashlight *AmE*] → see picture at **LIGHT**¹ **2** a long stick with burning material at one end that produces light: *the Olympic torch*

torch² *v* [T] *informal* to start a fire deliberately in order to destroy something: *Rioters had torched several cars.*

tore /tɔː $ tɔːr/ *v* the past tense of **TEAR**

torment¹ /'tɔːment $ 'tɔːr-/ *v* [T] **1** if you are tormented by something, it makes you feel very worried and unhappy: *He was tormented by feelings of guilt.* **2** to be deliberately cruel to someone, and try to hurt them —**tormentor** *n* [C]

torment² /'tɔːment $ 'tɔːr-/ *n* [C,U] great pain and suffering, or something that causes this

torn /tɔːn $ tɔːrn/ *v* the past participle of **TEAR**

tornado /tɔː'neɪdəʊ $ tɔːr'neɪdoʊ/ *n* [C] plural **tornadoes** or **tornados** an extremely violent storm consisting of air that spins very quickly and causes a lot of damage → see box at **WIND**

torpedo /tɔː'piːdəʊ $ tɔːr'piːdoʊ/ *n* [C] plural **torpedoes** a long narrow weapon that is fired under the surface of the sea and explodes when it hits something —**torpedo** *v* [T]

torrent

torrential rain

torrent /'tɒrənt $ 'tɔː-, 'tɑː-/ *n* **1** [singular] **a torrent of sth** a lot of something: **+of** *He answered with a **torrent of abuse**.* **2** [C] a large

amount of water moving very quickly in a particular direction —**torrential** /tə'renʃəl/ *adj*: *torrential rain*

torrid /'tɒrɪd $ 'tɔː-, 'tɑː-/ *adj* **1** involving strong emotions, especially of sexual love: *a torrid love affair* **2** *literary* torrid weather is very hot

torso /'tɔːsəʊ $ 'tɔːrsoʊ/ *n* [C] plural **torsos** the main part of your body, not including your arms, legs, or head

tortoise /'tɔːtəs $ 'tɔːr-/ *n* [C] a slow-moving land animal that can pull its head and legs into the shell that covers its body

tortuous /'tɔːtʃuəs $ 'tɔːr-/ *adj* **1** very long, complicated, and difficult: *a tortuous process* **2** a tortuous road or path has a lot of turns and is very difficult to travel along

torture¹ /'tɔːtʃə $ 'tɔːrtʃər/ *v* [T] to hurt someone deliberately in order to force them to give you information, to punish them, or to be cruel: *Resistance leaders were **tortured to death** in prison.* —**torturer** *n* [C]

torture² *n* [C,U] **1** when someone is tortured: *the torture of innocent civilians* | **under torture** *He confessed under torture.* **2** severe physical or mental suffering

Tory /'tɔːri/ *n* [C] plural **Tories** someone who belongs to or votes for the Conservative Party in Britain

tosh /tɒʃ $ tɑːʃ/ *n* [U] *BrE spoken informal* nonsense, used when you believe that something is not true or correct: *What a load of tosh!*

toss¹ /tɒs $ tɑːs/ *v* **1** [T] to throw something, especially in a careless way: **toss sth into/on/ onto etc sth** *He tossed his jacket on the bed.* | **toss sb sth** *Frank tossed her the newspaper.* | **toss sth to sb** *'Catch,' said Tom, tossing his bag to her.* → see box at **THROW** **2** also **toss up** [I,T] *especially BrE* to throw a coin in the air, and then make a decision according to the side that faces upwards when it comes down [= flip *AmE*]: *Let's toss up to see who goes first.* **3 toss and turn** to change your position a lot in bed because you cannot sleep **4 toss your head (back)** *written* to move your head back quickly

toss² *n* **1 a toss of a coin** when you throw a coin in the air and then make a decision according to the side that faces upwards when it comes down **2 a toss of his/her head** when someone moves their head backwards quickly and suddenly

tot /tɒt $ tɑːt/ *n* [C] *informal* **1** a small child **2** *especially BrE* a small amount of an alcoholic drink

total¹ /'təʊtl $ 'toʊ-/ *adj*

1 [only before noun] including everything: *His farm has a **total** area of 100 acres.* | *The **total** cost of the building will be $6 million.*

2 complete, or as great as is possible: *The sales campaign was a **total disaster**.* | *a **total ban** on cigarette advertising*

total² *n* [C] the final number or amount of things, people etc when everything has been counted: **a total of sth** *The city spent a total of two million dollars on the library.* | **in total** (=including everything) *In total, I spent £100.*

total³ *v* [T] **totalled, totalling** *BrE*; **totaled, totaling** *AmE* **1** to add up to a particular amount: *Sales* *totalled nearly $700,000 last year.* **2** *AmE informal* to damage a car so badly that it cannot be repaired

totalitarian /təʊˌtælɪ̩'teəriən $ toʊˌtælɪ̩'ter-/ *adj* based on a political system in which the government has complete control over everything → see box at GOVERNMENT —**totalitarianism** *n* [U]

totally /'təʊtl-i $ 'toʊ-/ *adv* completely: *I totally agree.* | *The system was totally unfair.* → see box at COMPLETELY

totter /'tɒtə $ 'tɑːtər/ *v* [I] to walk or move in an unsteady way

touch[1] /tʌtʃ/ *v*

1 [T] to put your hand or finger on something: *Don't touch the paint – it's wet!* | **touch sb on the arm/leg etc** *Ricky touched her on the shoulder.*
2 [I,T] if two things touch, or one thing touches another, they come together physically: *Their lips touched* (=they kissed). | *He sat on the table, his feet not touching the ground.*
3 [T] to make someone feel sad, sympathetic, or grateful [➜ **touched, touching**]: *The refugees' plight has **touched the hearts** of us all.* | *She knew that he cared and it touched her.*
4 not touch sth a) to not use, eat, or drink something: *He never touches alcohol.* **b)** to not deal with or become involved with something or someone: *Several lawyers refused to touch the case.*
5 not touch sb/sth to not hurt someone or damage something: *I didn't touch the kid!*
6 there's no one/nothing to touch sb/sth *also* **no one/nothing can touch sb/sth** *spoken* used to say that someone or something is the best
7 touch wood *BrE spoken* said when you do not want your good luck to end [= **knock on wood** *AmE*]

touch down *phr v* when a plane touches down, it lands on the ground

touch sth ⇔ **off** *phr v* to make a difficult situation or violent events begin: *The story touched off an international scandal.*

touch on/upon sth *phr v* to mention something when you are talking or writing: *I'll be touching on that subject later.*

touch[2] *n*

1 [C usually singular] the action of putting your hand, finger etc on someone or something: **+of** *Rita felt the touch of his hand on her arm.*
2 [U] the sense that you use to feel something, by putting your finger, hand etc on it: *the **sense of touch*** | **firm/warm/soft etc to the touch** *The cake should be golden and firm to the touch.*
3 in touch (with sb) if you are in touch with someone, you speak or write to them regularly: *Are you still **in touch** with John?* | **keep/stay in touch** *Bye, Jane! Don't forget to stay in touch.* | *We'll **get in touch** (=phone or write to you) when we know the results of the test.*
4 lose touch (with sb) to stop seeing, telephoning, or writing to someone you used to know: *I lost touch with Julie after we moved.*
5 in touch/out of touch (with sth) knowing or not knowing the most recent information about something, or what people think about something at the moment: *The government was*

accused of being out of touch. | *I try to **keep in touch** with how the kids today feel.*
6 [C] a small detail or change that improves something: **the final/finishing touches** *Becky **put the finishing touches** to the cake.* | *The flowers in the room were **a nice touch**.*
7 [singular] a particular way of doing something: *I like a hotel with a **personal touch**.*
8 a touch a small amount: **+of** *the touch of sadness in her voice*
→ **a soft touch** at SOFT

,touch-and-'go *adj informal* if a situation is touch-and-go, there is a risk that something bad could happen

touchdown /'tʌtʃdaʊn/ *n* [C] **1** the moment when a plane or spacecraft lands on the ground **2** when a player scores by moving the ball across the opposing team's GOAL line in American football or RUGBY

touched /tʌtʃt/ *adj* feeling happy and grateful because of what someone has done: **+by** *She was **deeply touched** by his kindness.*

touching /'tʌtʃɪŋ/ *adj* making you feel sad, sympathetic, or grateful: *a touching story*

touchline /'tʌtʃlaɪn/ *n* [C] one of the two lines that mark the longer sides of a sports playing area, especially in football

touchstone /'tʌtʃstəʊn $ -stoʊn/ *n* [C] something used as a test for whether something is good or not

touchy /'tʌtʃi/ *adj* **1** easily upset or annoyed: *Don't be so touchy!* **2 touchy subject/question etc** a subject that might upset someone, so you should be careful when you talk about it

tough /tʌf/ *adj*

1 difficult or involving problems: *It was a tough job.* | *They asked some **tough questions**.* | *Recently she's **had a tough time**.* | *It's tough being married to a cop.* | **be tough on sb** (=make things difficult for someone) *The divorce was tough on the kids.*
2 a tough person is strong or determined, and not easily upset: *Bruce Willis plays the part of a tough cop.* | *a gang of teenage boys, trying to look tough* | *a tough businesswoman*
3 tough material is not easily broken or damaged: *a tough waterproof jacket*
4 very strict: **+on/with** *The government said it was going to **get tough on** crime.* | *tough immigration laws*
5 tough food, especially meat, is difficult to cut and eat [≠ **tender**]: *The steak was a bit tough.*
6 tough!/tough luck! *spoken* used when a bad situation affecting someone cannot or will not be changed, and you do not care: *If you don't like it, tough.*
—**toughness** *n* [U]

toughen /'tʌfən/ *also* **toughen up** *v* [I,T] to become stronger, or to make someone or something stronger: *The army toughened him up.*

toupee /'tuːpeɪ $ tuː'peɪ/ *n* [C] a small WIG

tour[1] /tʊə $ tʊr/ *n* [C]

1 a journey for pleasure in which you visit several different towns, areas etc: **+of/around/round** *We went on a 14-day tour of Egypt.* | *a* **walking/cycling/sightseeing etc tour** *a coach tour of Italy*
2 a short trip around a place to see it: **+of/around/round** *Shall I give you **a tour** of the*

house? | **a guided tour** (=when someone shows you around a place and tells you about it) *We had a guided tour of the cathedral.*
3 a journey made by musicians, a sports team etc to perform or play in different places: **+of** *the cricket team's tour of India* | **on tour** *The group went on tour in America.*
→ **PACKAGE TOUR**

tour² *v* [I,T] to travel around an area to visit it or perform in different places there: *A few of us decided to tour the Greek islands.*

tourism /'tʊərɪzəm $ 'tʊr-/ *n* [U] the business of providing people who are on holiday with places to stay, things to do etc: *The island depends on tourism for most of its income.* | *Morocco is still unspoilt by* **mass tourism** (=large numbers of tourists).

tourist /'tʊərɪ̜st $ 'tʊr-/ *n* [C] someone who is visiting a country or place for pleasure: *Oxford's full of tourists in the summer.* | *the* **tourist industry** | *Italy has so many* **tourist attractions** (=things that tourists want to see). → see box at **TRAVEL**

tournament /'tʊənəmənt, 'tɔː- $ 'tɜːr-, 'tʊr-/ *n* [C] a competition in which many players compete against each other until there is one winner: *a tennis tournament*

tourniquet /'tʊənɪkeɪ, 'tɔː- $ 'tɜːrnɪkɪ̜t, 'tʊr-/ *n* [C] a band of cloth that you twist tightly around an injured arm or leg to make it stop BLEEDing

tousled /'taʊzəld/ *adj* tousled hair looks untidy

tout¹ /taʊt/ *v* [T] to praise something or someone in order to persuade people that they are good: **be touted as sth** *He is being touted as a possible future Wimbledon champion.*

tout² also **'ticket tout** *n* [C] *BrE* someone who buys tickets for a concert, sports match etc and sells them at a higher price, usually on the street near a sports ground, theatre etc [= **scalper** *AmE*]

tow¹ /təʊ $ toʊ/ *v* [T] if one vehicle or ship tows another one, it pulls the other one along behind it: *Our car had to be towed away.* → see picture at **PULL¹**

tow² *n* [singular, U] **1** when a vehicle or ship is pulled somewhere by another vehicle or ship **2 in tow** following closely behind someone: *Mattie arrived with her children in tow.*

towards *especially BrE*; /tə'wɔːdz $ tɔːrdz, twɔːrdz/, **toward** *especially AmE* /tə'wɔːd $ tɔːrd, twɔːrd/ *prep*
1 moving, facing, or pointing in a particular direction: *I saw Tim coming towards me.* | *She stood with her back towards me.* → see picture on page A8
2 used to say that someone is involved in a process that will lead to something: *Britain was moving towards war.* | *the first steps towards an agreement*
3 your attitude towards something or someone is how you feel about them or treat them: *Attitudes towards divorce have changed.* | *They were very sympathetic towards me at work.*
4 in order to help pay for something: *Mum gave me £500 towards a car.* | *The money from the sale went towards new computers.*
5 near a particular time or place: *I often feel tired toward 5 o'clock.* | *It's cooler towards the coast.*

towel /'taʊəl/ *n* [C] a piece of cloth used for drying your skin: *She rubbed herself dry with a towel.* | **bath/beach/hand towel** → see picture at BATHROOM
→ **SANITARY TOWEL, TEA TOWEL** → **throw in the towel** at THROW¹

tower¹ /'taʊə $ -ər/ *n* [C]
1 a tall narrow building, or a tall narrow part of a castle, church etc: *the Eiffel Tower* | *a castle with four towers* | *a* **church tower**
2 a tower of strength someone who gives you a lot of help, sympathy etc when you are in a difficult situation

tower² *v* [I] to be much taller than someone or something else that is near: **+over/above** *The teacher towered above him.* | *the towering cliffs*

'tower block *n* [C] *BrE* a tall building that contains apartments or offices [= **high-rise** *AmE*]

town /taʊn/ *n*
1 [C,U] a place that has many houses, shops, and offices but is smaller than a city: *a lovely town on the coast* | **+of** *the town of Bridgwater* | **in/into town** (=in or into the centre of a town, where the shops, restaurants etc are) *We had lunch in town.* | *He's buried in his* **home town** (=the town where he was born).
2 [singular] all the people who live in a town: *The whole town watched the procession.*
3 [U] *especially AmE* the town or city where you live: *Jodie's in town this week.* | *He* **left town** *yesterday.*
4 go to town (on sth) *informal* to spend a lot of money, time, or effort on something: *They really went to town on the decorations.*
5 on the town *informal* if you go out on the town, you go to a restaurant, bar, theatre etc and enjoy yourself
→ **GHOST TOWN, SHANTY TOWN**

town 'hall *n* [C] a public building used for a town's local government

townspeople /'taʊnzpiːpəl/ also **townsfolk** /-'taʊnzfəʊk $ -foʊk/ *n* [plural] all the people who live in a particular town

toxic /'tɒksɪk $ 'tɑːk-/ *adj* poisonous: **toxic chemicals/substances/gases etc** | *toxic waste* (=from industry)

toxin /'tɒksɪ̜n $ 'tɑːk-/ *n* [C] *technical* a poisonous substance

toy¹ /tɔɪ/ *n* [C] a thing for children to play with: *Anna was* **playing with her toys.** | **toy gun/soldier/truck etc** *a new toy car* | **soft/cuddly toy** *BrE* (=a toy that is like an animal, covered with fur)

toy² *v*
toy with sth *phr v* **1** to think about an idea, but not very seriously: *She had* **toyed with the idea** *of becoming an actress.* **2** to move an object or food around rather than using it or eating it: *Roy toyed with his pen before he spoke.*

'toy boy *n* [C] *informal humorous* a woman's boyfriend who is much younger than she is

trace¹ /treɪs/ *v* [T] **1** to find someone or something that has disappeared by searching for them carefully: *Police are trying to trace her husband.* **2** to find out where and when something began or how something has developed: **trace sth (back) to sth** *He traced his family history back to the 17th century.* | *The book* **traces the development** *of trade.* **3** to copy something by putting thin paper over it and drawing the lines that you can see through the paper

trace² *n* **1** [C,U] a small sign that shows that someone or something has been in a place: **+of** *We found **no trace** of them on the island.* | **disappear/vanish without (a) trace** (=disappear completely) *The plane vanished without a trace.* **2** [C] a very small amount of something, which is difficult to notice: **+of** *Traces of the drug were found in his body.*

track¹ /træk/ *n*

1 [C] a narrow road or path with a rough surface: *a steep mountain track* → see box at ROAD
2 tracks [plural] marks on the ground made by a moving animal, person, or vehicle: *Ned followed the tracks of the fox in the snow.*
3 [C] a circular path or road used by people, cars etc for races
4 [C] the two metal lines that a train travels on [= railway line]: *Never try to cross the track.*
5 be on the right/wrong track to be doing something in a way that is likely to be successful or unsuccessful: *Our profits are up, so we're on the right track.*
6 be on track to be developing in the right way and likely to be successful: *I want to get my career back on track.*
7 keep/lose track of sth to know or not know the present state or position of something, when it keeps changing: *I can never keep track of how old their kids are.* | *I'm sorry I'm late. I lost track of the time.*
8 [C] one of the songs or pieces of music on a record, CD etc: *the best track on the album*
9 [U] *especially AmE* the sport of running on a race track: **track events**
→ FAST TRACK, TITLE TRACK

track² *v* [T] to follow someone or something by looking for signs of their movement, or by using special electronic equipment: *The whales were tracked across the Atlantic.*
 track sb/sth ⇔ **down** *phr v* to find someone or something by searching for a long time: *Detectives finally tracked her down.*

,track and 'field *n* [U] *especially AmE* all sports that involve running races, jumping, and throwing things [= athletics *BrE*]

'track ,record *n* [singular] the things that a person, organization etc has done in the past which show how good they are at doing something

tracksuit /'træksuːt, -sjuːt $ -suːt/ *n* [C] *BrE* loose trousers and a matching jacket or SWEATER, worn especially for sport → see picture at CLOTHES

tract /trækt/ *n* [C] a large area of land

traction /'trækʃən/ *n* [U] **1** the type of power needed to make a vehicle move, or to pull a heavy load **2** the force that prevents a wheel sliding on a surface **3** the process of treating a broken bone with special medical equipment that pulls it

tractor /'træktə $ -ər/ *n* [C] a strong vehicle with large wheels, used for pulling farm equipment

trade¹ /treɪd/ *n*
1 [U] the activity of buying and selling goods, especially from or to another country [➡ business, commerce]: **+with/between** *They hope to*

increase trade with China.* | *trade between the two countries* | **+in** *the trade in cotton, sugar, and tobacco* | **international trade** | *The local shop doesn't seem to **do** much **trade*** (=do much business).
2 the hotel/retail/motor etc trade a particular kind of business [➡ industry]: *My first job was in the motor trade.*
3 [C,U] a particular job, especially one needing skill with your hands: *All my sons **learnt a trade**.* | **by trade** *Jo's a plumber by trade* (=that is his job).
→ FREE TRADE

trade² *v* [I,T]
1 to buy or sell goods or services: **+with** *Then India began trading with Europe.* | **+in** *The company traded in silk and tea.* | *Over a million shares were traded during the day.*
2 *AmE* to exchange something you have for something another person has [= swap *BrE*]: *We traded necklaces.* | **trade sth for sth** *He traded the cigarettes for food.*
 —trading *n* [U] *the Christmas trading period*
 trade sth ⇔ **in** *phr v* to give something that you own as part of the payment when you buy something new: **+for** *I traded my Chevy in for a Honda.*

'trade-in *n* [C] *AmE* a used car, piece of equipment etc that you give to the company from which you buy a new one, as part of the payment

trademark /'treɪdmɑːk $ -mɑːrk/ *n* [C] a special name, mark, or word on a product that shows it is made by a particular company

'trade name *n* [C] a name given to a particular product, that helps you recognize it from other similar products [= brand name]

'trade-off *n* [C] a balance between two very different things: **+between** *There is a trade-off between the risks and the benefits involved.*

trader /'treɪdə $ -ər/ *n* [C] someone who buys and sells goods, or STOCKS and SHARES

tradesman /'treɪdzmən/ *n* [C] plural **tradesmen** /-mən/ *BrE* someone who brings goods to people's houses to sell, or who has a shop

,trade 'union *n* [C] *BrE* an organization that represents the workers in a particular job, especially in meetings with employers [= union]

tradition /trə'dɪʃən/ *n* [C,U] a custom, belief, or way of doing something that has existed for a long time: **+of** *The country has a **long tradition** of state control.* | *the **old tradition** of hospitality* | **by tradition** *By tradition, the oldest son inherited everything.* → see box at HABIT

traditional /trə'dɪʃənəl/ *adj* relating to the traditions of a country or group of people: *traditional Italian cooking* | *a **traditional way of life*** | *It's **traditional** to have a party after the wedding.*
 —traditionally *adv*

traditionalist /trə'dɪʃənəlɪ̩st/ *n* [C] someone who likes traditional ways of doing things and does not like modern ones

traffic /'træfɪk/ *n* [U]
1 the vehicles moving along a road: *There was **heavy traffic*** (=a lot of vehicles) *on the motorway.* | *We left early to **avoid the traffic*** (=not meet a lot of other vehicles). | *I **get caught/stuck in traffic*** (=be delayed by a lot of vehicles on the road) | *a **traffic accident***

2 the movement of planes, ships etc from one place to another: *air traffic control*
3 the buying and selling of illegal drugs, weapons etc

'traffic ,circle *n* [C] *AmE* a circular area where several roads meet, which all traffic must drive around [= **roundabout** *BrE*]

'traffic ,jam *n* [C] a long line of vehicles on the road that cannot move, or that move very slowly: *We were **stuck in a traffic jam** for hours.*

trafficking /'træfɪkɪŋ/ *n* [U] the buying and selling of illegal goods, especially drugs —**traffic** *v* [T] —**trafficker** *n* [C]

'traffic ,lights *n* [plural] a set of red, yellow, and green lights that control the movement of traffic

'traffic ,warden *n* [C] *BrE* someone who checks that people's cars are parked legally

tragedy /'trædʒɪdi/ *n* plural **tragedies**
1 [C,U] a very sad event or situation, especially one involving death: *The evening **ended in tragedy**.* | *This tragedy could have been avoided.*
2 [singular] *informal* something that seems sad to you [= **pity**]: *It's a tragedy that this match wasn't shown on TV.*
3 [C,U] a serious play that ends sadly [➡ **comedy**]: *Shakespeare's tragedies*

tragic /'trædʒɪk/ *adj* a tragic event, situation, or story is very sad, especially because it involves death: *the **tragic death** of their only child* | *the tragic story of Romeo and Juliet* —**tragically** /-kli/ *adv*

trail¹ /treɪl/ *n* [C] **1** a rough path across countryside or through a forest: *a woodland trail*
2 a series of marks or signs that are left behind by someone or something as they move: **+of** *a trail of blood* **3 be on sb/sth's trail** to be trying to find someone or something by getting information about them

trail² *v* **1** [I,T] to pull something behind you as you move along, or to be pulled in this way: *Her long dress trailed on the ground behind her.* **2** [I] to walk slowly, usually behind someone, because you are tired or bored: **+behind/around** *Sue trailed along behind her parents.* **3** [I,T] to be losing a game, competition, or election: *The Cowboys were trailing in the third quarter.* **4** [I] to hang down or lie across something: *a **trailing plant*** | **+across/along/down** *Wires trailed across the floor.* **5** [T] to follow someone to see where they go
trail away/off *phr v* if someone's voice trails away or off, it gradually becomes quieter and then stops

trailer /'treɪlə $ -ər/ *n* [C] **1** a container on wheels that can be pulled behind a vehicle, used for carrying things **2** *AmE* a vehicle that can be pulled behind a car, used for living and sleeping in during a holiday [= **caravan** *BrE*] **3** a short part of a film or television programme, shown to advertise it

'trailer ,park *n* [C] *AmE* an area where trailers are parked and used as people's homes

train¹ /treɪn/ *n* [C]
1 a long vehicle which travels along a railway carrying people or goods. It consists of a line of carriages pulled by an engine: **+to** *What time's*

the next train to Birmingham? | **by train** *We decided to go by train.* | **catch/take/get a train** *I caught the 7 o'clock train to London.* | *Hurry up or we'll **miss the train**.* | *a train journey* | *I always do my homework on the train.* → see picture at **TRANSPORT**

TOPIC

You **decide** which **train** you are going to **get/catch**. You buy your ticket at the **ticket office**. You look at the **departures board** to check which **platform/track** *AmE* your train **leaves from**. Sometimes the train is **on time** but sometimes it is **running late** or **delayed**. When your train **arrives**, you **get on** and find a **seat** in one of the **carriages** *BrE*/**cars** *AmE* (=one of the connected parts of a train). You can usually get a drink or small meal in the **buffet/dining car**.

2 train of thought/events a series of thoughts or events that are related to each other: *The phone rang and interrupted my train of thought.*

train² *v*
1 [I] to learn the skills needed in a particular job: **+as** *She trained as a nurse for four years.* | **train to be sth** *You could train to be a policeman.*
2 [T usually passive] to teach someone how to do something, especially the skills they need to do a job: **train sb in sth** *Staff are trained in sales techniques.* | **train sb to do sth** *All teachers are trained to deal with minor accidents.* | *a **highly trained** pilot*
3 [I,T] to prepare for a sports event by practising and exercising, or to help someone to do this: **+for** *He's training for the Olympics.*
4 [T] to teach an animal to do something or to behave correctly
train sth on sb/sth *phr v* to aim something such as a gun or camera at someone or something

trainee /ˌtreɪˈniː◂/ *n* [C] someone who is being taught to do a job: *a trainee teacher*

trainer /'treɪnə $ -ər/ *n* [C] **1** someone whose job is to train people or animals to do something **2** *BrE* a type of shoe that you wear for sport or with informal clothes

training /'treɪnɪŋ/ *n* [U]
1 the process of teaching or learning the skills for a particular job or activity [➡ **train**]: **+in** *We all received training in First Aid.* | *a staff training course* | *an international teacher training college*
2 physical exercises that you do to stay healthy or prepare for a sports event [➡ **train**]: **be in training for sth** *She's in training for the Olympics.*
→ **WEIGHT TRAINING**

trait /treɪ, treɪt $ treɪt/ *n* [C] a quality that is part of someone's character

traitor /'treɪtə $ -ər/ *n* [C] someone who is not loyal to their country, friends etc

trajectory /trəˈdʒektəri/ *n* [C] plural **trajectories** *technical* the direction or line along which something moves when it goes through the air

T

tram *BrE*/**streetcar** *AmE*

tram /træm/ *n* [C] *especially BrE* a type of bus which carries passengers along the street on metal tracks [= **streetcar** *AmE*]

tramp[1] /træmp/ *n* [C] someone who has no home or job and moves from place to place

tramp[2] *v* [I,T] to walk slowly with heavy steps: **+through/across etc** *They tramped through the snow.*

trample /'træmpəl/ *v* [I,T] to step heavily on something and damage it with your feet: **+on/over/through etc** *Don't trample on my flowers!*

trampoline /'træmpəli:n/ *n* [C] a piece of equipment that you jump up and down on for sport or fun. It is made of a piece of material stretched across a metal frame.

trance /trɑ:ns $ træns/ *n* [C] a state in which you seem to be asleep, but can still hear and understand what is said

tranquil /'træŋkwɪl/ *adj* calm and peaceful: *a tranquil little town* → see box at QUIET —**tranquillity** /træŋ'kwɪləti/ *n* [U]

tranquillizer also **-iser** *BrE*; /'træŋkwəlaɪzə $ -ar/ *n* [C] a drug used to make someone calm or unconscious —**tranquillize** *v* [T]

trans- /træns, trænz/ *prefix* across or between: *a transatlantic flight* | *transcontinental travel*

transaction /træn'zækʃən/ *n* [C] *formal* a business deal, such as buying or selling something: *financial transactions*

transatlantic /ˌtrænzət'læntɪk◂ / *adj* crossing the Atlantic Ocean, or involving countries on both sides of the Atlantic: *a transatlantic flight*

transcend /træn'send/ *v* [T] *formal* to not be limited by something: *the need to transcend barriers of race and religion*

transcribe /træn'skraɪb/ *v* [T] to write down the words that someone has said, or the notes of a piece of music

transcript /'trænskrɪpt/ *n* [C] a written copy of a speech, conversation etc

transfer[1] /træns'fɜ: $ -'fɜ:r/ *v* [I,T] **transferred**, **transferring** to move from one place, part of an organization etc to another, or to make someone or something do this: **+to** *Stella's transferred to head office.* | **transfer sb to sth** *You will be transferred to your hotel by coach.* | **transfer sth to/into sth** *I'd like to transfer some money into my savings account.* —**transferable** *adj*

transfer[2] /'trænsfɜ: $ -fɜ:r/ *n* [C,U] when someone or something is moved from one place, part of an organization etc to another: **+of** *the transfer of electronic data* | **+to** *He's applied for a transfer to Hong Kong.*

transfixed /træns'fɪkst/ *adj* so shocked, interested, frightened etc by something that you cannot move: *She stood transfixed, unable to look away.*

transform /træns'fɔ:m $ -'fɔ:rm/ *v* [T] to change something or someone completely, especially in a way that improves them: **transform sb/sth (from sth) into sth** *The movie transformed Amy from an unknown schoolgirl into a star.* → see box at CHANGE —**transformation** /ˌtrænsfə'meɪʃən $ -fər-/ *n* [C,U] *The city has undergone a total transformation* (=it has changed completely).

transformer /træns'fɔ:mə $ -'fɔ:rmər/ *n* [C] a piece of electrical equipment that changes electricity from one VOLTAGE to another

transfusion /træns'fju:ʒən/ *n* [C,U] if you have a blood transfusion, doctors put blood into your body

transgress /trænz'gres $ træns-/ *v* [I,T] *formal* to break a rule —**transgression** /-'greʃən/ *n* [C,U]

transient[1] /'trænziənt $ 'trænʃənt/ *adj formal* **1** continuing or existing for only a short time: *transient fashions* **2** working or staying somewhere for only a short time

transient[2] *n* [C] *AmE* someone who has no home and moves from place to place

transistor /træn'zɪstə, -'sɪstə $ -ər/ *n* [C] a small piece of electronic equipment in radios, televisions etc that controls the flow of electricity

transit /'trænsɪt, -zɪt/ *n* [U] when goods or people are moved from one place to another: *Goods often get lost in transit.*

transition /træn'zɪʃən, -'sɪ-/ *n* [C,U] *formal* when something changes from one form or state to another: **transition from sth to sth** *the smooth transition from work to retirement* —**transitional** *adj: a two year transitional period*

transitive /'trænsətɪv, -zə-/ *adj* in grammar, a transitive verb is followed by an object. In the sentence 'He hit the ball', 'hit' is transitive and 'the ball' is the object. [➔ **intransitive**]

transitory /'trænsətəri $ -tɔ:ri/ *adj formal* existing for only a short time

translate /træns'leɪt, trænz-/ *v* [I,T] **1** to change written or spoken words from one language to another [➔ **interpret**]: **translate sth (from sth) into sth** *I am translating the book into English.* **2** if one thing translates into another, the second thing happens as a result of the first: **translate (sth) into sth** *A rise in public spending could translate into a rise in taxation.*

translation /træns'leɪʃən, trænz-/ *n* [C,U] when you translate something, or something that has been translated: **+of** *a new translation of the Bible* | **+from** *a translation from Arabic*

translator /træns'leɪtə, trænz- $ -ər/ *n* [C] someone who changes written or spoken words into a different language

translucent /trænz'lu:sənt $ træns-/ *adj* clear enough to allow light to pass through, but not transparent —**translucence** *n* [U]

transmission /trænz'mɪʃən $ træns-/ *n* **1** [C,U] the process of broadcasting radio or television programmes, or a television or radio programme **2** [U] *formal* when something is sent or passed from one place, person etc to another: *the transmission of diseases* **3** [C,U] the system of GEARS in a car: *automatic transmission*

transmit /trænz'mɪt $ træns-/ *v* [T] **transmitted**, **transmitting 1** to send out electronic signals, messages etc using radio, television, or similar equipment **2** *formal* to send or pass something from one place, person etc to another: *The virus is transmitted through sexual contact.*

transmitter /trænz'mɪtə $ træns'mɪtər/ *n* [C] a piece of equipment that sends out radio or television signals

transparency /træn'spærənsi, -'speər- $ -'spær-,'sper- / *n* [C] plural **transparencies** a piece of plastic or film through which light can be shone to show a picture on a large screen

transparent /træn'spærənt, -'speər- $ -'spær-, -'sper-/ *adj* **1** clear and able to be seen through [➜ **opaque, translucent**]: *transparent plastic* **2** easy to recognize or understand —**transparently** *adv*

transpire /træn'spaɪə $ -'spaɪr/ *v* [I] *formal* **1** if it transpires that something is true, you discover that it is true **2** to happen

transplant¹ /'trænsplɑːnt $ -plænt/ *n* [C,U] a medical operation in which part of someone's body is put into the body of another person: **heart/liver/kidney transplant**

transplant² /træns'plɑːnt $ -'plænt/ *v* [T] **1** to remove part of someone's body and put it into the body of another person **2** to move something to another place

transport¹ /'trænspɔːt $ -ɔːrt/ *n* [U] **1** *BrE* **transportation** *AmE* a system or method for carrying passengers or goods from one place to another: **air/rail/road transport** *We need improved rail transport.* | *commuters who travel on **public** transport* (=buses, trains etc) | **means/form/mode of transport** *cars and other forms of transport* | *Do you have your own transport* (=car, bicycle etc)? **2** *especially BrE* also **transportation** /ˌtrænspɔː'teɪʃən $ -spər-/ *AmE* when people, goods etc are moved from one place to another: **+of** *the transport of goods*

transport² /træn'spɔːt $ -ɔːrt/ *v* [T] to move goods, people etc from one place to another in a vehicle

transport *BrE*/ transportation *AmE*

aeroplane *BrE*/ airplane *AmE*

helicopter

train

lorry/truck

minibus

bus

scooter

car

motorbike

taxi

bicycle

liner

underground train *BrE*/ subway train *AmE*

ferry

yacht

rowing boat *BrE*/rowboat *AmE*

motorboat

transsexual /træn'sekʃuəl $ træns'sek-/ *n* [C]
someone who has changed their sex or wants to
be a different sex

transvestite /trænz'vestaɪt $ træns-/ *n* [C]
someone who enjoys dressing like a person of
the opposite sex

trap¹ /træp/ *n*

1 [C] a piece of equipment for catching animals:
*You should **set a trap** to catch mice.*

2 [singular] a trick that is intended to make
someone do something that they do not want to
do: **fall/walk into a trap** *Mr Smith had fallen
into a **trap** set by the opposition.*

3 [singular] an unpleasant situation from which
it is difficult to escape: *the **poverty trap** | the
unemployment trap*
→ BOOBY TRAP, DEATH TRAP

trap² *v* [T] **trapped, trapping**

1 [usually passive] if you are trapped in a dangerous place or a bad situation, there is something preventing you from escaping: *Two people
were trapped in the burning building.* | *Ann **felt
trapped** in her marriage.*

2 to catch an animal in a trap

3 to catch someone by forcing them into a place
from which they cannot escape

4 to trick someone in order to make them do or
say something that they do not want to: *a series
of questions intended to trap him* | **trap sb into
(doing) sth** *He was trapped into signing a confession.*

5 to prevent something such as gas or water
from getting away: *solar panels that trap the
sun's heat*

trapdoor /'træpdɔː $ -dɔːr/ *n* [C] a small door
that covers an opening in a floor or roof

trapeze /trə'piːz $ træ-/ *n* [C] a short bar hang-
ing from two ropes high above the ground, used
by ACROBATS

trappings /'træpɪŋz/ *n* [plural] the things that
someone gets because of their position, especially because they are rich, famous, successful
etc: **+of** *the trappings of stardom*

trash¹ /træʃ/ *n* [U]

1 *AmE* waste material such as old food or paper
that is thrown away [= **rubbish** *BrE*] → see box at
RUBBISH

2 *informal* something that is of very poor quality: *There's so much trash on TV these days.*

trash² *v* [T] *informal* to destroy something completely

trashcan /'træʃkæn/ *n* [C] *AmE* a large container for keeping waste material in [= **dustbin**
BrE] → see box at BIN → and RUBBISH

trashy /'træʃi/ *adj* of extremely bad quality:
trashy novels

trauma /'trɔːmə, 'traʊmə $ 'traʊmə, 'trɔː-/ *n*
[C,U] the shock caused by an unpleasant and
upsetting experience, or an experience that
causes this feeling: *the trauma of divorce*

traumatic /trɔː'mætɪk $ trɔ-/ *adj* very shock-
ing and upsetting: *a traumatic experience*

traumatized also **-ised** *BrE* /'trɔːmətaɪzd,
'traʊ- $ 'traʊ-, 'trɔː-/ *adj* so badly shocked by
something that you cannot forget it or have a
normal life

travel¹ /'trævəl/ *v* **travelled, travelling** *BrE*;
traveled, traveling *AmE*

1 [I,T] to go to one place from another, or to
several places: *Martha would like to **travel
abroad.*** | **+to/across/through/around etc**
*Jack spent the summer travelling around
Europe.* | **travel widely/extensively** *He has
travelled widely in China.* | **travel by train/car/
air etc** *I usually travel to work by car.*

THESAURUS

drive or **go by car**
fly or **go by plane**
sail or **go by boat/ship**
take a train/bus/taxi/cab or **go by train/bus
etc**
walk/hike or **go on foot**
cycle or **go by bike**
traveller – any person who is travelling
passenger – someone who is travelling in a
car, bus, train, plane etc
tourist – someone who is travelling
somewhere for a holiday
→ AIRPORT, JOURNEY, PASSPORT

2 [I,T] to move along, especially at a particular
speed: **+at** *The train was travelling at 100 mph.* |
shock waves travelling through the earth

travel² *n*

1 [U] the activity of travelling: **air/rail/road
travel** *Heavy rain is making road travel difficult.*
→ see box at JOURNEY

2 travels [plural] journeys to places that are far
away, usually for pleasure: **on your travels** *We
met some interesting people on our travels.*

'travel ,agency also **'travel ,agent's** *n* [C] a
shop or company that makes arrangements for
people to travel or have holidays

'travel ,agent *n* [C] someone who works in a
travel agency

traveller *BrE*; **traveler** *AmE* /'trævələ $ -ər/ *n*
[C] someone who is on a journey or who travels a
lot

'traveller's ,cheque *BrE*; **traveler's check**
AmE *n* [C] a special cheque that can be
exchanged for the money of a foreign country

traverse /'trævɜːs $ trə'vɜːrs/ *v* [T] *formal* to go
across or over something

travesty /'trævɪsti/ *n* [singular] plural **travesties**
if something is a travesty, it is very bad and not
what it is claimed to be: **+of** *The trial was a
travesty of justice.*

trawl /trɔːl $ trɔːl/ *v*
trawl through sth *phr v* to search through
things in order to find something —**trawl** *n* [C]

trawler /'trɔːlə $ 'trɔːlər/ *n* [C] a large fishing
boat that pulls a big net along the sea bottom

tray /treɪ/ *n* [C] a flat piece of plastic, wood etc
with raised edges, used for carrying plates, food
etc

treacherous /'tretʃərəs/ *adj* **1** someone who
is treacherous cannot be trusted because they
secretly intend to harm you **2** very dangerous
because you cannot see the dangers easily:
treacherous mountain roads

treachery /'tretʃəri/ *n* [U] when someone does
something that harms someone they should
have been loyal to

treacle /'triːkəl/ *n* [U] *BrE* a dark sweet sticky
liquid made from sugar plants [= **molasses** *AmE*]

tread¹ /tred/ *v* past tense **trod** /trɒd $ trɑːd/ past participle **trodden** /'trɒdn $ 'trɑːdn/

1 [I,T] *especially BrE* to put your foot on something [➜ **step**]: **+on/in** *Sorry, did I tread on your foot?* | *He trod the narrow path between the trees.*
2 tread carefully/warily/cautiously etc to be very careful about what you say or do
3 [T] to press something into the ground with your feet: *Look – you've trodden mud into the carpet.*

tread² *n* **1** [C,U] the pattern of deep lines on the surface of a tyre **2** [singular] the sound that someone makes when they walk: *She heard her father's **heavy tread** on the stair.*

treadmill /'tred.mɪl/ *n* **1** [C] a piece of exercise equipment that you walk or run on **2** [singular] a job or situation that seems very boring because you always have to do the same thing

treason /'triːzən/ *n* [U] the crime of doing something that could cause great harm to your country or government, especially by helping its enemies

treasure¹ /'treʒə $ -ər/ *n*
1 [U] a group of valuable things such as gold, silver, jewels etc: **buried/hidden/sunken treasure**
2 [C] a very valuable and important object such as a painting: *the **art treasures** of the Uffizi Gallery*

treasure² *v* [T] to keep and care for something that is very special or important: *one of his most treasured memories*

treasurer /'treʒərə $ -ər/ *n* [C] someone who takes care of the money for an organization

Treasury /'treʒəri/ *n* **the Treasury** the government department that controls a country's money

treat¹ /triːt/ *v* [T]
1 to behave towards someone in a particular way [➜ **treatment**]: *She treats me like one of the family.* | **well/badly treated** *Tracy felt she had been badly treated.* | **treat sb with respect/contempt/courtesy etc** *Children must treat teachers with respect.*
2 to deal with or consider something in a particular way [➜ **treatment**]: **treat sth as sth** *Please treat this information as confidential.*
3 to give someone medical treatment for an illness or injury [➜ **treatment**]: **treat sb for sth** *Eleven people were treated for minor injuries.* | *Malaria can be treated with drugs.*
4 to buy or arrange something special for someone: **treat sb/yourself to sth** *We're treating Jill to dinner for her birthday.* | *I thought I'd treat myself to a new dress.*
5 to put a special substance on something or use a chemical process in order to protect it or clean it: *The metal has been treated against rust.*

treat² *n*
1 [C] something special that you give someone or do for them: **as a treat** *Stephen took his son to Disneyland as a treat.*
2 [singular] an event that gives you a lot of pleasure: *Getting your letter was a **real treat**.*
3 my treat *spoken* used to tell someone that you will pay for something, especially a meal
➜ **TRICK OR TREAT**

treatise /'triːtɪs, -tɪz/ *n* [C] a serious book or article about a subject: **+on** *a treatise on political philosophy*

treatment /'triːtmənt/ *n*
1 [C,U] something that is done to try to cure someone who is injured or ill: *She was **given** emergency **treatment**.* | *hospital treatment*
2 [U] a way of behaving towards someone or of dealing with them: *complaints about the treatment of prisoners*

treaty /'triːti/ *n* [C] plural **treaties** a formal written agreement between two or more countries: *a **peace treaty***

treble¹ /'trebəl/ *determiner BrE* three times as big, as much, or as many as something else [= **triple**]: *They sold the house for treble the amount they paid for it.*

treble² *v* [I,T] to become three times as much, or to make something do this [= **triple**]

treble³ *n* [U] the upper half of the whole range of musical notes

tree /triː/ *n* [C] a very tall plant that has branches and leaves: **cherry/peach/apple etc tree** *He has three apple trees in his garden.* | *the **trunk** (=main central part) of an old oak tree* ➜ see picture at **PLANT**
➜ **CHRISTMAS TREE, FAMILY TREE, PALM TREE**

THESAURUS

copse – a small group of trees
wood – a large area with many trees
forest – a very large area with a lot of trees growing closely together
rain forest – a tropical forest with tall trees, in an area where it rains a lot
jungle – a tropical forest with trees and large plants

trek /trek/ *v* [I] **trekked, trekking** to make a long and difficult journey on foot —**trek** *n* [C]

trellis /'trelɪs/ *n* [C] a wooden frame for supporting climbing plants

tremble /'trembəl/ *v* [I] to shake slightly because you are afraid, worried, or excited: *Her voice trembled as she spoke.* | **tremble with anger/fear etc** *John was trembling with rage.* ➜ see box at **SHAKE**

tremendous /trɪ'mendəs/ *adj* **1** very great: *I have tremendous respect for her.* **2** excellent —**tremendously** *adv*: *It was tremendously exciting.*

tremor /'tremə $ -ər/ *n* [C] **1** a small EARTHQUAKE **2** a slight shaking movement that you cannot control

trench /trentʃ/ *n* [C] a long narrow hole that is dug in the ground

trenchant /'trentʃənt/ *adj* very firm and clear: *a trenchant critic of big business*

trenchcoat /'trentʃkəut $ -kout/ *n* [C] a long RAINCOAT with a belt

trend /trend/ *n* [C] **1** the way a situation is generally developing or changing: *There's a trend toward more part-time employment.* | *the latest fashion trends* **2 set the trend** to start doing something that other people copy

trendy /'trendi/ *adj* modern and fashionable: *a trendy bar*

trepidation /ˌtrepɪˈdeɪʃən/ n [U] *formal* anxiety or fear about something that is going to happen

trespass /ˈtrespəs $ -pəs, -pæs/ v [I] to go onto someone's land without permission —**trespasser** n [C]

trestle /ˈtresəl/ n [C] a wooden support under a table

tri- /traɪ/ *prefix* three: *She's trilingual* (=able to speak three languages).

trial /ˈtraɪəl/ n
1 [C,U] a legal process in which a court of law decides whether or not someone is guilty of a crime [➡ try]: *a murder trial* | **on trial (for sth)** (=being judged in a court) *He is on trial for armed robbery.* | *She is due to* **stand trial** (=be judged in a court) *on a drugs charge.* | *He claimed he would not receive a fair trial.*
2 [C,U] when something or someone is tested to find out how good, effective etc they are [➡ try]: *The drug is undergoing* **clinical trials** (=tests involving sick people).
3 trial and error when you test different methods or answers in order to find the most suitable one: *Students learn through a process of trial and error.*
4 trial basis/period if you use something or someone on a trial basis or for a trial period, you use them for a short period to find out whether they are satisfactory
5 [C usually plural] something that is difficult or unpleasant to deal with [➡ trying]: *the trials and tribulations of running a business*
6 trials [plural] *BrE* a sports competition that tests the ability of people who want to be included in a team [= **tryout** *AmE*]

trial 'run n [C] when something new is tested to see if it works

triangle /ˈtraɪæŋɡəl/ n [C]
1 a flat shape with three straight sides and three angles → see box at **SHAPE** → see picture at **SHAPE**[1]
2 a small musical instrument shaped like a triangle. You hit it with a metal stick.
—**triangular** /traɪˈæŋɡjələ $ -ər/ adj

triathlon /traɪˈæθlən/ n [C] a sports competition in which competitors run, swim, and cycle long distances

tribe /traɪb/ n [C] a group of people of the same race with the same language and customs, who usually live together in the same area —**tribal** adj: *tribal art*

tribulation /ˌtrɪbjʊˈleɪʃən/ n [C,U] a problem in your life or work: *the trials and tribulations of married life*

tribunal /traɪˈbjuːnl/ n [C] a type of court that has official authority to deal with a particular situation or problem: *a war crimes tribunal* | *He took his case to an* **industrial tribunal** (=one that judges disagreements between workers and employers).

tributary /ˈtrɪbjʊtəri $ -teri/ n [C] plural **tributaries** a river or stream that flows into a larger river

tribute /ˈtrɪbjuːt/ n **1** [C,U] something that you say or do to show how much you admire and respect someone: *The concert was held as a tribute to Bob Dylan.* | *Today she* **paid tribute to the** *hospital staff who had treated her.* **2 be a trib-**

ute to sb/sth to be a sign of how good, effective etc someone or something is

trick[1] /trɪk/ n [C]
1 something you do in order to deceive someone, or as a joke to make people laugh at someone: *The phone call was just a trick to get him out of the office.* | *The girls were always* **playing tricks** *on their teacher.*
2 something that seems like magic which is done in order to entertain people: *a card trick*
3 do the trick *spoken* if something does the trick, it helps you to succeed in doing what you want: *A little salt should do the trick.*
4 a clever and effective way of doing something: *The trick is to keep your design simple.*
5 it was a trick of the light used to say that something appeared to be different from the way it really is
→ **HAT TRICK**

trick[2] v [T] to deceive someone in order to get something from them, or to make them do something: **trick sb into doing sth** *He was tricked into carrying drugs.*

trickery /ˈtrɪkəri/ n [U] the use of tricks to deceive or cheat people

trickle /ˈtrɪkəl/ v [I] **1** if liquid trickles somewhere, it flows slowly in drops or in a thin stream: **+down/from etc** *Sweat trickled down his face.* **2** if people or things trickle somewhere, they move there slowly in small groups or amounts —**trickle** n [C] *a trickle of blood*

trick or 'treat v **go trick or treating** if children go trick or treating, they go to people's houses on HALLOWEEN (October 31) and say 'trick or treat' in order to get sweets and other small presents

trick 'question n [C] a question that seems easy, but which is intended to deceive you

tricky /ˈtrɪki/ adj difficult to do or deal with: *It was a tricky decision.*

tricycle /ˈtraɪsɪkəl/ n [C] a bicycle with three wheels

tried[1] /traɪd/ v the past tense and past participle of TRY

tried[2] adj **tried and tested/trusted** used successfully many times

trifle /ˈtraɪfəl/ n **1 a trifle** slightly: *He looked a trifle unhappy.* **2** [C,U] a cold DESSERT made of layers of cake, fruit, CUSTARD etc

trifling /ˈtraɪflɪŋ/ adj small or unimportant

trigger[1] /ˈtrɪɡə $ -ər/ n [C] the part of a gun that you pull with your finger to fire it: *He pointed the gun and pulled the trigger.*

trigger[2] also **trigger off** v [T] to make something start to happen: *Heavy rain may trigger mudslides.*

trillion /ˈtrɪljən/ number plural **trillion** or **trillions** **1** the number 1,000,000,000,000: **two/three/four etc trillion** *$5.3 trillion* | **trillions of pounds/dollars etc** **2** an extremely large number of people or things: **a trillion** *a shirt with a trillion holes in it.* | **trillions of sth** *We've made this mistake trillions of times before.* —**trillionth** adj —**trillionth** n [C]

trilogy /ˈtrɪlədʒi/ n [C] plural **trilogies** a series of three books, plays, films etc, which have the same subject or characters

trim[1] /trɪm/ v [T] **trimmed, trimming** **1** to cut a small amount off something to make it look neater: *Get your hair trimmed regularly.* → see box at CUT **2** to reduce the size or amount of something: *We need to **trim costs**.* **3** to decorate something by adding something attractive: **be trimmed with sth** *The sleeves were trimmed with velvet.*

trim[2] *adj* **1** thin and healthy looking [= slim]: *a trim figure* **2** neat and attractive

trim[3] *n* **1** [singular] when something is cut to make it look neater: *Your beard needs a trim.* **2** [singular, U] the decoration on something such as a piece of clothing **3 in trim** in good physical condition

trimester /trɪˈmestə $ traɪˈmestər/ *n* [C] *AmE* one of three periods that a year at school or college is divided into

trimming /ˈtrɪmɪŋ/ *n* **1** [C,U] decoration on the edge of a piece of clothing **2 with all the trimmings** with all the other types of food that are traditionally served with the main dish of a meal: *a turkey dinner with all the trimmings*

Trinity /ˈtrɪnɪti/ *n* **the Trinity** the three forms of God in the Christian religion, which are the Father, the Son, and the Holy Spirit

trinket /ˈtrɪŋkɪt/ *n* [C] a piece of jewellery or a small pretty object that is not worth much money

trio /ˈtriːəʊ $ ˈtriːoʊ/ *n* [C] plural **trios** a group of three people, especially a group of three musicians who play together

trip[1] /trɪp/ *n* [C] a visit to a place that involves a journey: **+to** *Did you enjoy your trip to Disneyland?* | *His wife was away on a **business trip**.* | **boat/coach/bus trip** | *a **day trip** to Brighton* → see box at JOURNEY
→ FIELD TRIP, ROUND TRIP

trip[2] *v* **tripped, tripping**
1 [I] to hit something with your foot while you are walking or running so that you fall or almost fall [➝ **stumble**]: *He tripped and fell.* | **+on/over** *I tripped over a chair.* → see box at FALL
2 also **trip up** [T] to make someone fall by putting your foot in front of them: *Baggio was tripped inside the penalty area.*
  trip up *phr v* to make a mistake, or to make someone make a mistake: **trip sb** ⇔ **up** *The interviewer tried to trip her up with a tricky question.*

triple[1] /ˈtrɪpəl/ *adj* [only before noun] consisting of three things or parts of the same kind, or doing something three times: *a triple gold medal winner*

triple[2] *v* [I,T] to become three times as big or as many, or to make something do this: *The population may triple in 20 years.*

triple[3] *determiner* three times as big, as much, or as many as something else: *The rail system has triple the average number of accidents.*

triplet /ˈtrɪplɪt/ *n* [C] one of three children born at the same time to the same mother

tripod /ˈtraɪpɒd $ -pɑːd/ *n* [C] a piece of equipment with three legs, used for supporting something such as a camera

trite /traɪt/ *adj* a trite remark or idea has been used so much that it does not seem sincere or interesting

triumph[1] /ˈtraɪəmf/ *n*
1 [C] an important success or victory: **+for** *It was a diplomatic triumph for France.* | **+over** *the team's 5–2 triumph over England* | *Winning the championship was a great **personal triumph**.*
2 [U] the feeling of pleasure you get from victory or success: *a look of triumph* | **in triumph** *She smiled in triumph.*
—**triumphal** /traɪˈʌmfəl/ *adj*

triumph[2] *v* [I] to win a victory or be successful: **+over** *people who've triumphed over pain and disability*

triumphant /traɪˈʌmfənt/ *adj* pleased because you have succeeded or won: *a triumphant smile*
—**triumphantly** *adv*

trivia /ˈtrɪviə/ *n* [plural] unimportant details or facts: *We chatted about trivia.* | *a quiz of sporting trivia*

trivial /ˈtrɪviəl/ *adj* not serious or important: *a trivial matter* —**triviality** /ˌtrɪviˈælɪti/ *n* [C,U]

trivialize also **-ise** *BrE* /ˈtrɪviəlaɪz/ *v* [T] to make something seem less important or serious than it really is

trod /trɒd $ trɑːd/ *v* the past tense of TREAD

trodden /ˈtrɒdn $ ˈtrɑːdn/ *v* the past participle of TREAD

trolley /ˈtrɒli $ ˈtrɑːli/ *n* [C] **1** *BrE* a container on wheels, that you use for carrying things, for example in a SUPERMARKET [= cart *AmE*] **2** a small table on wheels, used for carrying food and drinks **3** *AmE* an electric vehicle that moves along the street on tracks [= tram *BrE*]

trombone /trɒmˈbəʊn $ trɑːmˈboʊn/ *n* [C] a large metal musical instrument that you play by blowing into it and sliding a long tube in and out → see picture on page A6 —**trombonist** *n* [C]

troop[1] /truːp/ *n* [C] **1 troops** [plural] soldiers: *Troops have been sent to the area to keep the peace.* → see box at ARMY **2** a large group of people or animals —**troop** *adj* [only before noun] *troop movements*

troop[2] *v* [I] to walk somewhere in a group: **+into/out of etc** *We all trooped out of the classroom.*

trooper /ˈtruːpə $ -ər/ *n* [C] **1** a soldier **2** a member of a state police force in the US

trophy /ˈtrəʊfi $ ˈtroʊ-/ *n* [C] plural **trophies** an object such as a silver cup that you get for winning a race or competition

tropical /ˈtrɒpɪkəl $ ˈtrɑː-/ *adj* in or from the hottest parts of the world: *tropical rain forests* | *tropical fish*

tropics /ˈtrɒpɪks $ ˈtrɑː-/ *n* **the tropics** the hottest parts of the world, which are near the EQUATOR

trot[1] /trɒt $ trɑːt/ *v* [I] **trotted, trotting** to walk or run with quick short steps: **+off/along/up etc** *A group of horses trotted past.* | *He trotted along behind his parents.*
  trot sth ⇔ **out** *phr v* informal disapproving to give an opinion or idea that has been used too many times before: *They always trot out the same old excuses.*

trot[2] *n* [singular] **1 on the trot** happening one after the other: *The team have won five games on the trot.* **2** a speed that is slightly faster than walking

T

trouble¹ /'trʌbəl/ *n*

1 [C,U] problems or difficulties: **+with** *We've been **having trouble** with the new computer system.* | **have trouble doing sth** *We had no trouble getting here.* | *Leaving the door unlocked is **asking for trouble*** (=is stupid and likely to cause problems). | *It's good to be able to talk to someone about your troubles.*

2 [singular] the thing that is causing a problem, or the thing that is bad about someone or something: *I'd love to come but **the trouble is** I can't afford it.* | ***The trouble with** you is that you don't listen.*

3 in/into trouble a) in a situation with a lot of problems: **get/run into trouble** *The project has already run into trouble.* | **in serious/deep trouble** *The company was in deep financial trouble.* **b)** if someone is in trouble, they have done something wrong which they will be punished for: **+with** *He's been in trouble with the police.* | *I was always **getting into trouble** at school.*

4 [U] time and effort that is needed to do something: *It was a lovely meal. They'd obviously **gone to a lot of trouble**.* | *He'd **taken the trouble** to learn all our names.* | *Doing the course over the Internet **saves you the trouble of** attending classes.*

5 [C,U] a situation in which people fight or argue with each other: *crowd trouble* | **cause/ make trouble** *English fans have a reputation for causing trouble.*

6 [U] problems with part of your body or part of a machine: *heart trouble* | *engine trouble* → see box at **PROBLEM**

trouble² *v* [T] **1** if something troubles you, it makes you feel worried or upset: *She was troubled by feelings of guilt.* **2** *formal* to cause someone a slight problem by asking them to do something, used especially when making a polite request [= **bother**]: *I'm sorry to trouble you, but could you open the door for me?*

troubled /'trʌbəld/ *adj* **1** worried: *a troubled expression* **2** having many problems: *a troubled marriage*

troublemaker /'trʌbəl,meɪkə $ -ər/ *n* [C] someone who deliberately causes problems

troubleshooter /'trʌbəl,ʃuːtə $ -ər/ *n* [C] someone whose job is to solve problems that an organization is having —**troubleshooting** *n* [U]

troublesome /'trʌbəlsəm/ *adj* causing problems: *troublesome symptoms*

'trouble ˌspot *n* [C] a place where there is likely to be fighting or trouble: *Tourists have been warned to stay away from trouble spots.*

trough /trɒf $ trɔːf/ *n* [C] **1** a long container for animals to drink or eat from **2** a period when prices or economic activity are low

trounce /traʊns/ *v* [T] to defeat someone easily: *We trounced them 58–7.*

troupe /truːp/ *n* [C] a group of singers, actors, dancers etc who work together

trousers /'traʊzəz $ -ərz/ *n* [plural] a piece of clothing that covers the lower part of your body, with a separate part for each leg [= **pants** AmE]: *a pair of trousers* → see picture at **CLOTHES** —**trouser** *adj* [only before noun] *The tickets are in my trouser pocket.*

'trouser ˌsuit *n* [C] BrE a woman's suit that consists of a jacket and trousers [= **pant suit** AmE]

trout /traʊt/ *n* [C,U] plural **trout** a fish that lives in rivers and can be eaten

trowel /'traʊəl/ *n* [C] **1** a small garden tool used for digging small holes **2** a small tool used for spreading CEMENT on bricks

truant /'truːənt/ *n* [C] **1** a student who stays away from school without permission **2 play truant** BrE to stay away from school without permission [= **play hooky** AmE] —**truancy** *n* [U]

truce /truːs/ *n* [C] an agreement to stop fighting or arguing for a short time: *They agreed to **call a truce**.*

truck /trʌk/ *n* [C] a large road vehicle used for carrying goods [= **lorry** BrE]: *a truck driver* → see picture at **TRANSPORT**
→ **FIRE TRUCK**

trucker /'trʌkə $ -ər/ *n* [C] especially AmE someone who drives a truck

trucking /'trʌkɪŋ/ *n* [U] AmE the business of taking goods from one place to another by truck

truckload /'trʌkləʊd $ -loʊd/ *n* [C] the amount that fills a truck: **+of** *a truckload of oranges*

truculent /'trʌkjələnt/ *adj* formal bad-tempered and often arguing with people

trudge /trʌdʒ/ *v* [I] to walk with slow heavy steps, especially because you are tired: **+through/up/off etc** *He trudged up the stairs.* → see box at **WALK**

true /truː/ *adj*

1 correct and based on facts, not invented [≠ **false**; ➡ **truth**]: **it is true (that)** *Is it true that you're moving to Denver?* | *a true story* | *The results appear to **hold true*** (=still be correct) *for other countries too.*

2 [only before noun] real: *He's a **true friend**.* | *Is this **true love**? | *The house was sold for a fraction of its **true value**.* | *the **true cost** of the holiday* | *the **true meaning** of the word*

3 come true if a dream, wish, or statement about the future comes true, the thing that someone thought or spoke about happens: *My dream of living in the country had finally come true.*

4 *spoken* used to admit that something is correct, especially when saying that something else is also correct: *True, he has a college degree, but he doesn't have enough experience.*

5 true to sb/sth faithful and loyal, or doing what you have promised to do: *She remained true to him all her life.* | *He was **true to** his **word** and said nothing to anyone.*

6 true to form/type used to say that someone is behaving exactly as they always do: *True to form, he disagreed with everything I said.*

7 true to life a book, film etc that is true to life seems similar to what really happens in people's lives [= **realistic**]

truffle /'trʌfəl/ *n* [C] **1** a soft sweet made with chocolate **2** a FUNGUS you can eat that grows under the ground

truism /'truːɪzəm/ *n* [C] a statement that is clearly true, so that there is no need to say it

truly /'truːli/ *adv* **1** used to emphasize that the way you are describing something is really true: *a truly remarkable man* | *By now we were well* *and truly* (=completely) *lost.* **2** sincerely: *She truly believed he was innocent.* → **yours truly** at YOURS

trump /trʌmp/ *n* [C] **1** a card that has a higher value than the other cards in some card games, for example BRIDGE **2 come/turn up trumps** to provide what is needed, especially when you do not expect it: *The school came up trumps and said we could use the school hall.*

'trump card *n* [C] something you can do or use in a situation which will give you an advantage

trumped-'up *adj* using false information to make someone seem guilty of doing something wrong: *He was sent to prison on trumped-up charges.*

trumpet /'trʌmpᵻt/ *n* [C] a metal musical instrument that you blow into, with three buttons that you press to change the notes → see picture on page A6 —**trumpeter** *n* [C]

truncate /trʌŋ'keɪt $ 'trʌŋkeɪt/ *v* [T] *formal* to make something shorter: *a truncated version of the report*

truncheon /'trʌnʃən/ *n* [C] *BrE* a short stick that police officers carry as a weapon [= **nightstick** *AmE*]

trundle /'trʌndl/ *v* [I,T] to move slowly on wheels, or to make something do this by pushing or pulling it: **trundle (sth) along/out etc** *We trundled the luggage trolley onto the platform.*

trunk /trʌŋk/ *n* [C]

1 the thick main part of a tree, which the branches grow from: *a tree trunk* → see picture at PLANT

2 *AmE* the space at the back of a car where you can put things [= **boot** *BrE*] → see picture on page A12

3 the long nose of an ELEPHANT → see picture on page A2

4 a large box used for storing or carrying things

5 trunks also **swimming trunks** [plural] a piece of clothing that men wear for swimming

6 *technical* the main part of your body, not including your head, arms, or legs: *He had bruises all over his chest and trunk.*

'trunk road *n* [C] *BrE* a main road between towns

trust¹ /trʌst/ *n*

1 [U] the belief that someone or something is honest or good: *There's a **lack of trust** between teachers and the government.* | *I had **put my trust in** the doctor.*

2 [C] an organization that controls how money will be used to help someone else: *a charitable trust*

3 [C,U] an arrangement in which someone legally controls your money or property, usually until you are old enough to have it: *The money is being **held in trust** until she's 21.*

4 take sth on trust to believe that something is true without having any proof

trust² *v* [T]

1 to believe that someone is honest and will not do anything bad or wrong [≠ **distrust, mistrust**]: *I don't trust her at all.*

2 trust sb to do sth to believe that someone will definitely do something: *I know I can trust you to keep this secret.*

3 to be sure that something is correct or right: *I'm not sure if I trust his judgment.*

4 trust you/him etc (to do sth)! *spoken* used to say that it is typical of someone to do something silly or bad: *Trust you to be late!*

5 I trust (that) *formal* used to say that you hope something is true: *I trust that these arrangements are satisfactory.*

trust sb with sth *phr v* to let someone have or control something because you believe they will be careful with it: *I wouldn't trust him with the keys.*

trustee /ˌtrʌ'stiː◂/ *n* [C] a person or company that legally controls someone else's property or money

'trust fund *n* [C] money belonging to someone that is controlled for them by a trustee

trusting /'trʌstɪŋ/ *adj* believing that other people are good and honest: *a trusting young girl*

trustworthy /'trʌst,wɜːði $ -ɜːr-/ *adj* if someone is trustworthy, you can trust them completely

trusty /'trʌsti/ *adj* [only before noun] *old-fashioned* a trusty person or object is one you can depend on

truth /truːθ/ *n*

1 the truth the true facts about something [➜ lie]: *The truth is I don't know what will happen.* | *I'm sure she's **telling the truth**.* | *Her view is that consumers should be told **the whole truth**.* | **the simple/plain truth** *The plain truth is that there are no easy answers.*

2 [U] if there is truth in something, it is true: **+in** *Do you think there's any truth in these accusations?*

3 [C] *formal* an important fact or idea that people accept is true: *scientific truths*

4 to tell (you) the truth *spoken* used when giving your opinion or admitting something: *To tell you the truth, I've never really liked him.*

truthful /'truːθfəl/ *adj* honest and saying things that are true: *a truthful answer* | *a truthful witness* —**truthfully** *adv*

try¹ /traɪ/ *v* tried, trying, tries

1 [I,T] to attempt to do something: **try to do sth** *I'm trying to find out what happened.* | **try and do sth** *Try and take some exercise each day.* | *I **tried hard** not to smile.*

2 [T] to do, use, or taste something in order to find out if you like it or it is good: *You must try some of this cake!* | **try doing sth** *Try walking to work instead of driving.*

3 [T] to examine facts in a law court in order to decide if someone is guilty [➜ trial]: **try sb for sth** *Three men were tried for murder.*

4 try your hand at sth to try a new activity: *He was keen to try his hand at painting.*

try sth ⇔ on *phr v* to put on a piece of clothing to find out if it fits or if you like it: *Can I try these jeans on, please?* → see box at CLOTHES

try sth ⇔ out *phr v* to test something to find out if it is effective or works properly: *I want to try out my new camera.*

try² *n* [C] plural **tries** **1** an attempt to do something: *He succeeded on his first try.* | *I don't know if I can do it but I'll **have a try**.* **2** a test of something to see if it is suitable or successful: *I decided to **give the job a try**.* **3** when a team gets points in RUGBY by putting the ball down behind the other team's goal line

trying /'traɪ-ɪŋ/ *adj* annoying or difficult: *I've had a very trying day.*

tsar, tzar, czar /zɑː, tsɑː $ zɑːr, tsɑːr/ *n* [C] a ruler of Russia before 1917

T-shirt /'tiː ʃɜːt $ -ʃɜːrt/ *n* [C] a soft shirt with short SLEEVES and no collar → see picture at CLOTHES

tsp. the written abbreviation of **teaspoon**

tub /tʌb/ *n* [C]

1 a container with a lid, in which food is sold: +**of** *a tub of margarine* → see picture at CONTAINER **2** a deep round container: *flowers growing in tubs* **3** *AmE* a container in which you sit to wash yourself [= **bath** *BrE*]

tuba /'tjuːbə $ 'tuːbə/ *n* [C] a large metal musical instrument that consists of a curved tube and produces very low notes → see picture on page A6

tubby /'tʌbi/ *adj informal* slightly fat

tube /tjuːb $ tuːb/ *n* [C]

1 a pipe made of glass, rubber, metal etc that liquids or gases go through: *He had to be fed through a tube because he was so weak.* **2** a container for a soft substance that you press between your fingers to make the substance come out: +**of** *a tube of toothpaste* → see picture at CONTAINER **3** a long round hollow object: *a cardboard tube* **4 the Tube** the railway system under the ground in London [= **subway** *AmE*]: *He took the tube to Embankment.* | *Which is the nearest tube station?*

→ TEST TUBE

tuberculosis /tjuː,bɜːkjʊ'ləʊsəs $ tuː,bɜːrkjʊ'loʊ-/ also **TB** *n* [U] a serious infectious disease that affects your lungs

tubing /'tjuːbɪŋ $ 'tuː-/ *n* [U] tubes, usually connected together in a system: *copper tubing*

tubular /'tjuːbjʊlə $ 'tuːbjʊlər/ *adj* made of tubes or shaped like a tube

tuck /tʌk/ *v* [T] **1** to push the end of a shirt, sheet etc somewhere so that it looks tidy: **tuck sth in** *John tucked his shirt in.* | **tuck sth into/under/behind sth** *I tucked my T-shirt into my shorts.* | *She tucked a curl of hair behind her ear.* **2** to put something in a small space, especially so that it is safe or comfortable: **tuck sth into/under/behind sth** *She tucked the money into her pocket.*

tuck sth ⇔ **away** *phr v* **1** to put something in a safe place: *He tucked the letter away in a drawer.* **2 be tucked away** to be in a place that is far away or difficult to find: *a little village tucked away in the mountains*

tuck in *phr v* **1 tuck sb** ⇔ **in/up** to make someone comfortable in bed by arranging the sheets around them **2** also **tuck into sth** *BrE informal* to eat something eagerly: *Come on, tuck in!*

tuck sb ⇔ **up** *phr v* **1 be tucked up (in bed)** to be sitting or lying in bed **2** → TUCK SB IN

Tuesday /'tjuːzdi, -deɪ $ 'tuːz-/ *n* [C,U] written abbreviation **Tues.** or **Tue.** the day between Monday and Wednesday

→ see examples at MONDAY → see box at DAY

tuft /tʌft/ *n* [C] a bunch of hairs, grass etc growing together: *a tuft of hair*

tug¹ /tʌɡ/ *v* [I,T] **tugged, tugging** to pull something suddenly and hard: +**at/on** *Alice tugged at my hand.* → see box at PULL

tug² *n* [C] **1** also **'tug boat** a boat used for pulling ships **2** a strong pull: *I gave the handle a tug.*

tug-of-'war *n* [singular] a competition in which two teams pull on the opposite ends of a rope

tuition /tjuː'ɪʃən $ tuː-/ *n* [U] **1** teaching, especially in small groups: +**in** *I had private tuition in English.* **2** *AmE* **tu'ition fees** *BrE* the money you pay for being taught: *Tuition went up to $3000 last semester.*

tulip /'tjuːlɪp $ 'tuː-/ *n* [C] a flower that is shaped like a cup and grows from a BULB in spring.

tumble /'tʌmbəl/ *v* [I] **1** to fall somewhere suddenly: +**down/into etc** *She lost her balance and tumbled backwards.* **2** to move somewhere in an uncontrolled way: +**into/out etc** *The door opened and a group of students tumbled out.* **3** if prices tumble, they suddenly become much lower: *Share prices tumbled yesterday.* —**tumble** *n* [C]

tumble 'dryer, tumble drier *n* [C] *BrE* a machine for drying clothes

tumbler /'tʌmblə $ -ər/ *n* [C] a glass with no handle or STEM

tummy /'tʌmi/ *n* [C] plural **tummies** *informal* your stomach

tumour *BrE*; **tumor** *AmE* /'tjuːmə $ 'tuːmər/ *n* [C] a group of diseased cells in someone's body that grow too quickly: *He died of a brain tumor.*

tumult /'tjuːmʌlt $ 'tuː-/ *n* [C,U] *formal* a situation in which there is a lot of noise, confusion, or excitement

tumultuous /tjuː'mʌltʃuəs $ tuː-/ *adj* **1** very noisy because people are excited: *They received a tumultuous welcome from the crowd.* **2** full of activity, confusion, or violence: *the tumultuous years of the Civil War*

tuna /'tjuːnə $ 'tuːnə/ *n* [C,U] plural **tuna** a large sea fish that can be eaten

tundra /'tʌndrə/ *n* [U] large flat areas of land in the north of Russia, Canada etc, where it is very cold and there are no trees

tune¹ /tjuːn $ tuːn/ *n* [C]

1 a series of musical notes that are nice to listen to: *He started to play a tune on the piano.* **2 in tune** playing or singing the correct musical notes [≠ off-key] **3 out of tune** playing or singing notes that are too high or low **4 be in tune with sb/sth** to understand or realize what someone wants **5 be out of tune with sb/sth** to not understand or realize what someone wants: *a party that is out of tune with the people of this country*

→ change your tune at CHANGE¹

tune² *v* [T] **1** to make changes to a musical instrument so that it plays the correct musical notes: *The piano needs tuning.* **2** to make a television or radio receive broadcasts from a particular place: **be tuned to sth** *You're tuned to ABC Radio.* | *Stay tuned* (=keep listening or watching) *for more great music.* **3** also **tune up** to make small changes to a car engine so that it works better

tune in *phr v* to watch a television programme or listen to a radio programme: **+to** *Over 3 million viewers tuned in to the show.*

tune up *phr v* when musicians tune up, they prepare their instruments so they will play the correct notes: *They're still tuning up.* | **tune sth ⇔ up** *He was tuning up his violin.*

tuneful /ˈtjuːnfəl $ ˈtuːn-/ *adj* music that is tuneful is pleasant to listen to

tungsten /ˈtʌŋstən/ *n* [U] a hard metal used in some lights

tunic /ˈtjuːnɪk $ ˈtuː-/ *n* [C] a long loose piece of clothing, usually without sleeves, that covers the top part of your body

tunnel¹ /ˈtʌnl/ *n* [C] a passage that has been dug under the ground, especially for cars or trains to go through

tunnel² *v* [I,T] **tunnelled, tunnelling** *BrE*; **tunneled, tunneling** *AmE* to dig a tunnel: **+under/through etc** *They managed to tunnel under the fence.*

tunnel

railway tunnel

ˌtunnel ˈvision *n* [U] *disapproving* the tendency to think about only one part of something such as a problem or plan, instead of considering all the parts of it

turban /ˈtɜːbən $ ˈtɜːr-/ *n* [C] a long piece of cloth that you wind tightly around your head, often for religious reasons

turbine /ˈtɜːbaɪn $ ˈtɜːrbən, -baɪn/ *n* [C] an engine or motor which gets power from the pressure of a liquid or gas moving a wheel around

turbulent /ˈtɜːbjʊlənt $ ˈtɜːr-/ *adj* **1** a turbulent period or situation is one in which there are a lot of changes: *a turbulent time in European history* **2** turbulent air or water moves suddenly and violently —**turbulence** *n* [U] *There was a lot of turbulence during the flight.*

tureen /tjʊˈriːn $ təˈriːn/ *n* [C] a large dish with a lid, used for serving soup or vegetables

turf¹ /tɜːf $ tɜːrf/ *n* [U] **1** thick short grass and the soil under it **2** *informal* someone's turf is the area that they control or that they know well: *She felt he was intruding on her turf.*

turf² *v*
turf sb ⇔ out *phr v BrE informal* to force someone to leave a place or organization

turkey /ˈtɜːki $ ˈtɜːrki/ *n* [C,U] a bird that is like a chicken but larger, or the meat from this bird

turmoil /ˈtɜːmɔɪl $ ˈtɜːr-/ *n* [singular, U] a situation in which there is a lot of trouble or confusion: **in turmoil** *In 1968 the country was in turmoil.*

turn¹ /tɜːn $ tɜːrn/ *v*

1 [I,T] to move your body so that you are looking in a different direction: *Ricky turned and walked away.* | *Ida turned her head slowly.* | **+around/round/away** *He turned around to look at Kim.* | **+to/towards** *Alison turned towards us.*
2 [T] to move something so that it is facing in a new direction: *Turn the plant so it's facing the sun.* | **turn sth around/over/upside down etc** *You may turn over your exam papers.*
3 [I,T] to start going in a new direction, or to make the vehicle you are using do this: *The car turned a corner.* | **turn left/right** *Turn right at the next stop light.* | **+into/onto/down etc** *We turned onto a bumpy road.*
4 [I,T] to move around in a circle, or to make something move in this way: *The wheels turned slowly.* | **turn a handle/knob/key/tap etc** *She gently turned the handle of the door.*
5 [linking verb, T] to become different, or to make something become different: *Helen turned bright red.* | *The weather will turn colder tonight.* | *Police are worried that the situation could turn violent.* | **turn (sth) into/to sth** *His disappointment turned to joy.* | *Hollywood discovered her and turned her into a star.*
6 [T] **a)** to become a particular age: *She's just turned 40.* **b)** *BrE* to reach and pass a particular time: *'What time is it?' 'It's just turned 3.00.'*
7 [T] to move a page in a book or magazine so that you can see the next one
8 turn your back on sb/sth to refuse to help or be involved with someone or something: *She turned her back on all her old friends.*
9 [I,T] if your thoughts, attention etc turn to something, you direct your attention to that thing instead of what you were thinking about or doing before: **turn your attention/thoughts/efforts etc to sth** *Brian looked up, then turned his attention back to the book he was reading.* | **+to/towards** *As usual, the conversation turned to her children.*

turn (sb) against sb/sth *phr v* to stop liking or agreeing with someone or something, or to make someone do this: *Many people had turned against the war.*

turn sth ⇔ around also **turn sth ⇔ round** *BrE phr v* to make a company, business etc become successful again: *Gibson believes he can turn the struggling company around quickly.*

turn sb ⇔ away *phr v* **1** to not allow someone to enter a place: *Hundreds of fans were turned away at the door.* **2** to refuse to help someone: *Anyone who comes to us will not be turned away.*

turn back *phr v* to go back in the direction you came from, or to make someone do this: *It's getting late – maybe we should turn back.* | **turn sb ⇔ back** *Journalists are being turned back at the border.*

turn sb/sth **⇔ down** *phr v* **1** to make a machine produce less sound, heat etc, using its controls [≠ **turn up**]: *Can you turn the radio down? I'm trying to work.* **2** to say no when someone offers you something: *She was offered a job there, but she turned it down.*

turn in *phr v* **1 turn sb ⇔ in** to tell the police where a person who is believed to be a criminal is: *Morris finally agreed to turn himself in.* **2** *informal* to go to bed **3 turn sth ⇔ in** *AmE* to give a piece of work you have done to a teacher, your employer etc: *Has everyone turned in last night's homework?*

turn off *phr v* **1 turn sth ⇔ off** to use the controls on something to make it stop working, or to make a supply of water, gas etc stop flowing [≠ **turn on**]: *She turned off the computer and went to bed.* **2 turn off (sth)** to leave the road you are travelling on and start travelling on a different road: *Turn off at the next light.*

turn on sb/sth *phr v* **1 turn sth ⇔ on** to use the controls on something to make it start working, or to make a supply of water, gas etc start flowing [≠ **turn off**]: *Could you turn on the TV?* | *He turned on the tap and washed the mugs.* → see box at OPEN **2** to criticize or physically attack someone suddenly: *All of a sudden, the dog turned on him and bit him.*

turn out *phr v* **1** to happen in a particular way or to be found to be something: *Joanna wished things had turned out differently.* | **turn out well/badly/fine etc** *I'm confident things will turn out all right in the end.* | **turn out to be sth** *The car turned out to be more expensive than we thought.* **2 turn sth ⇔ out** to make a light stop working by pressing a button, pulling a string etc [≠ **turn on**]: *Don't forget to turn out the lights when you leave.* **3** if people turn out for something, they go to watch it or be involved in it [➡ **turnout**]: **+for** *Only about 30 people turned out for the show.*

turn over *phr v* **1 turn sb over to sb** to take someone who is believed to be a criminal to the police or another official organization: *Benson was turned over to the FBI yesterday.* **2 turn sth over to sb** to give someone the right to own or be responsible for something: *He'll turn the shop over to his son when he retires.* **3** *BrE* to change to a different CHANNEL on your television

turn to sb/sth *phr v* **1** to ask someone for help or sympathy: **+for** *He still turns to us for advice.* **2** to look at a particular page in a book, magazine etc: *Turn to page 45 in your history book.* **3** to start to do or use something new, especially as a way of solving a problem: *Many consumers are turning to the Internet for their shopping needs.* | **turn to drugs/crime/drink etc** *Bored teenagers are more likely to turn to crime.*

turn up *phr v* **1 turn sth ⇔ up** to make a machine produce more sound, heat etc, using its controls [≠ **turn down**]: *If you're cold, I can turn the heat up.* **2** if something turns up after you have been looking for it, you suddenly find it: *Eventually my watch turned up in a coat pocket.* **3** to arrive: **turn up late/early/on time etc** *Danny turned up late as usual.*

turn² *n* [C]

1 if it is your turn to do something, it is the time when you can or should do it, not anyone else [= **go** *BrE*]: *It's your turn. Roll the dice.* | **Whose turn is it** to walk the dog? | *You'll just have to **wait your turn** (=wait until it is your turn).*

2 take turns, take it in turns *BrE* if a group of people take turns doing something, first one person does it, then another: **take turns doing sth** *They took turns caring for their mother.* | **take turns to do sth** *We took it in turns to do the driving.*

3 in turn one after another: *He spoke to each of the students in turn.*

4 a change in the direction you are moving in: **left/right turn** *The car made a left turn at the lights.*

5 a) a road that joins the road you are on [= **turning**]: *Take the first turn on your left.* **b)** a curve in a road, river etc: *There's a sharp turn coming up ahead.*

6 when you turn something completely around a fixed point: *Give the wheel another turn.*

7 the turn of the century the beginning of a new century: *My ancestors moved to America at the turn of the century.*

8 a sudden or unexpected change that makes a situation develop in a different way: *this new turn of events* | **take a turn for the better/worse** *Two days after the operation, Dad took a turn for the worse.*

9 good turn something that someone does that is helpful to someone else: *He certainly did Patrick a good turn.*

turnaround /ˈtɜːnəraʊnd $ ˈtɜːrn-/ *n* [C] a complete change from a bad situation to a good one: **+in** *a turnaround in the team's fortunes*

turning /ˈtɜːnɪŋ $ ˈtɜːr-/ *n* [C] *BrE* a road that joins the road you are on [= **turn**]: *Take the next turning on the left.*

'turning point *n* [C] the time when an important change starts to happen: **+in** *The film marked a turning point in Kubrick's career.*

turnip /ˈtɜːnɪp $ ˈtɜːr-/ *n* [C,U] a round white vegetable that grows under the ground

'turn-off *n* [C] a place where you can leave a main road to go onto a smaller one

turnout /ˈtɜːnaʊt $ ˈtɜːr-/ *n* [singular] the number of people who go to an event such as a party, meeting, or election: **low/high turnout** *the low turnout in the elections*

turnover /ˈtɜːnəʊvə $ ˈtɜːrnˌoʊvər/ *n* **1** [singular,U] the amount of money a business earns during a particular period **2** [U] the rate at which people leave an organization and are replaced by others: **+of** *The company has a high turnover of staff.* **3** [C] a small fruit PIE

turnpike /ˈtɜːnpaɪk $ ˈtɜːrn-/ *n* [C] *especially AmE* a large road that drivers have to pay to use

turnround /ˈtɜːnraʊnd $ ˈtɜːrn-/ *n* [C] *BrE* a TURNAROUND

'turn ˌsignal *n* [C] *AmE* one of the lights on a car that flash to show which way the car is going to turn [= **indicator** *BrE*] → see picture on page A12

turnstile /ˈtɜːnstaɪl $ ˈtɜːrn-/ *n* [C] a small gate that spins around and only lets one person at a time go through an entrance

turntable /ˈtɜːnˌteɪbəl $ ˈtɜːrn-/ *n* [C] a piece of equipment used for playing RECORDS

turpentine /ˈtɜːpəntaɪn $ ˈtɜːr-/ also **turps** *BrE* /tɜːps $ tɜːrps/ *n* [U] a strong-smelling type of oil used for removing paint

turquoise /ˈtɜːkwɔɪz, -kwɑːz $ ˈtɜːrkwɔɪz/ *n* [U] a greenish-blue colour —**turquoise** *adj*

turret /ˈtʌrɪt/ *n* [C] a small tower on a large building, especially a castle

turtle /ˈtɜːtl $ ˈtɜːrtl/ *n* [C] an animal that lives mainly in water and has a hard flat shell

turtleneck /ˈtɜːtlnek $ ˈtɜːr-/ *n* [C] *AmE* a type of SWEATER or shirt with a collar that covers most of your neck [= **polo neck** *BrE*]

tusk /tʌsk/ *n* [C] one of the two long pointed teeth that grow outside the mouth of some animals, such as ELEPHANTS → see picture on page A2

tussle /ˈtʌsəl/ *n* [C] a struggle or fight —**tussle** *v* [I]

tut /tʌt/ also **tut-'tut** a sound you make with your tongue to show disapproval —**tut** v [I]

tutor /'tjuːtə $ 'tuːtər/ n [C] **1** someone who teaches one person or a small group of people: *a private tutor* **2** a teacher at a British university —**tutor** v [T]

tutorial /tjuːˈtɔːriəl $ tuː-/ n [C] a class, especially at a British university, in which a small group of students discuss a subject with their tutor → see box at **UNIVERSITY**

tuxedo /tʌkˈsiːdəʊ $ -doʊ/ also **tux** /tʌks/ *informal* n [C] plural **tuxedos** a type of man's suit or jacket, usually black, that is worn on very formal occasions

TV /ˌtiː ˈviː◂/ n [C,U] television: **on TV** *What's on TV tonight?* → see box at **TELEVISION**

ˌTV 'dinner n [C] a meal that is sold already prepared, so that you just need to heat it before eating it

twang /twæŋ/ n [C] **1** a way of speaking in which the sound seems to come from your nose as well as your mouth **2** a quick ringing sound like the one made by pulling a very tight wire and then suddenly letting it go —**twang** v [I,T]

tweak /twiːk/ v [T] **1** to pull or twist something suddenly: *Grandpa tweaked my nose and laughed.* **2** to make small changes to something in order to improve it —**tweak** n [C]

tweed /twiːd/ n [U] a thick wool cloth used especially for making jackets

tweezers /'twiːzəz $ -ərz/ n [plural] a small tool consisting of two thin pieces of metal joined at one end. You use tweezers to pull out hairs or pick up small things.

twelfth /twelfθ/ n [C] one of twelve equal parts of something

twelve /twelv/ *number* the number 12: *He received a twelve-month jail sentence.* | *Come at twelve* (=12 o'clock). | *Their son Dylan is twelve* (=12 years old).
—**twelfth** *adj, pron*: *her twelfth birthday* | *I'm planning to leave on **the twelfth*** (=the 12th day of the month).

twenty /'twenti/ *number*
1 the number 20: *a small village twenty miles from Nairobi* | *I'm nearly twenty* (=20 years old).
2 the twenties also **the '20s, the 1920s** [plural] the years from 1920 to 1929: **the early/mid/late twenties** *The photograph was taken in the late twenties.*
3 be in your twenties to be aged between 20 and 29: **early/mid/late twenties** *She was in her late twenties.*
4 in the twenties if the temperature is in the twenties, it is between 20 degrees and 29 degrees —**twentieth** *adj, pron*: *her twentieth birthday* | *I'm leaving on **the twentieth*** (=the 20th day of the month).

ˌtwenty-four 'seven, **24–7** *adv informal* if something happens twenty-four seven, it happens all the time, every day

twice /twaɪs/ *adv* two times: *I've seen that movie twice already.*

twiddle /'twɪdl/ v [I,T] **1** to move or turn something around with your fingers many times, especially because you are nervous or bored **2 twiddle your thumbs** to do nothing while you are waiting

twig /twɪg/ n [C] a very thin branch that grows on a larger branch of a tree

twilight /'twaɪlaɪt/ n [U] the time when day is just starting to become night, or the small amount of light at this time

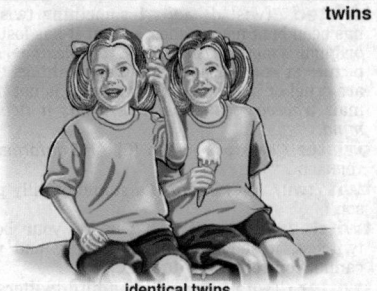

twins

identical twins

twin¹ /twɪn/ n [C] one of two children who are born at the same time and have the same mother: *My sister and I are **identical twins*** (=twins that look exactly the same).

twin² *adj* [only before noun] **1** used to describe a child who is a twin: **twin sister/brother 2** used to talk about two things of the same kind that are together or connected: *twin beds* **3** a twin room has two beds in it

twine /twaɪn/ n [U] thick strong string

twinge /twɪndʒ/ n [C] **1** a sudden slight pain **2 twinge of guilt/sadness/jealousy etc** a sudden slight feeling of guilt etc

twinkle /'twɪŋkəl/ v [I] **1** if a star or light twinkles, it shines very brightly, but not continuously → see box at **SHINE 2** if someone's eyes twinkle, they look happy —**twinkle** n [C]

twinned /twɪnd/ *adj* **be twinned with sth** if a town in one country is twinned with a town in another country, an official relationship exists between them —**twinning** n [C,U]

twirl /twɜːl $ twɜːrl/ v [I,T] to turn around and around, or to make something do this: *Elaine twirled across the dance floor.* —**twirl** n [C]

twist¹ /twɪst/ v

1 [T] to bend or turn something around several times and change its shape: *He rolled up the paper and began twisting the ends.* | **twist sth into/in/around sth** *Her hair was twisted in a bun.*
2 [I,T] to turn a part of your body around or change your position by turning: **+around/round** *He twisted around in order to get a better look.*
3 twist your knee/ankle to hurt your knee or ankle by suddenly turning it
4 [T] to turn something in a circle using your hand: **twist sth off (sth)** *Jack twisted the cap off the bottle.*
5 [T] to change the meaning of what someone says, especially in order to get some advantage for yourself: *Davis accused reporters of **twisting his words**.* → see box at **CHANGE**
6 [I] if a road, river etc twists, it has a lot of curves in it
7 twist sb's arm to persuade someone to do something they do not want to do

twist² n [C] **1** a sudden change in a story or situation that you did not expect: *Her disappearance added a new twist to the story.* **2** a small piece of something that is twisted into a particular shape: +of *a twist of lemon* **3** a bend in a river or road

twisted /'twɪst½d/ adj **1** something twisted has been bent many times, so that it has lost its original shape: *twisted pieces of metal* → see picture at **BENT²** **2** seeming to enjoy things that are cruel or shocking, in a way that is not normal: *Whoever sent those letters has a twisted mind.*

twister /'twɪstə $ -ər/ n [C] AmE informal a TORNADO

twit /twɪt/ n [C] informal a stupid or silly person

twitch /twɪtʃ/ v [I] if a part of your body twitches, it suddenly moves slightly and you cannot control it —**twitch** n [C]

twitter /'twɪtə $ -ər/ v [I] if a bird twitters, it makes a lot of short high sounds —**twitter** n [singular]

two /tuː/ number the number 2: *I'll be away for almost two weeks.* | *We have to be there by two* (=two o'clock). | *His family moved to Australia when he was two* (=two years old).

THESAURUS

a pair (of sth) – two things of the same type that you use together: *a pair of shoes*
a couple (of sth) – two things of the same type: *a couple of stamps*
a couple – two people who are married or have a romantic relationship: *a married couple*
twins – two children who were born on the same day to the same mother
double room/bed etc – a room, bed etc for two people
twice – two times: *I phoned her twice yesterday.*
for two – for two people: *A table for two, please.*

'two-bit adj AmE informal not very good or important: *a two-bit actor*

,two-di'mensional adj flat: *a two-dimensional shape*

,two-'faced adj disapproving someone who is two-faced is not honest or sincere because they say different things about something to different people

twofold /'tuːfəʊld $ -foʊld/ adj two times as much or as many: *a twofold increase in price* —**twofold** adv

'two-time v [T] informal if you two-time your boyfriend or girlfriend, you secretly have a sexual relationship with someone else

'two-tone adj having two colours: *two-tone shoes*

,two-'way adj **1** moving in two opposite directions: *two-way traffic* **2** a two-way radio sends and receives messages

tycoon /taɪˈkuːn/ n [C] someone who is very successful in business and has a lot of money

tying /'taɪ-ɪŋ/ v the present participle of TIE

type¹ /taɪp/ n

1 [C] a group of people or things that are similar to each other in some way [➡ **kind**]: +of *What type of food do you like?* | **a particular/certain/different etc type** *To run this program you need a special type of software.* | **of this/that/each etc type** *Accidents of this type are very common.*
2 [C usually singular] someone with particular qualities or interests: *He's not really the athletic type.*
3 be sb's type spoken to be the kind of person that someone is attracted to: *Alex is OK – but he's not really my type.*
4 [U] printed letters: *italic type*
→ **BLOOD TYPE**

type² v [I,T] to write something using a computer or typewriter: *Cindy can type 50 words a minute.*

typecast /'taɪpkɑːst $ -kæst/ v [T usually passive] past tense and past participle **typecast** if an actor is typecast, he or she is always given the same kind of characters to play: *In the early days of Hollywood, black actors were often typecast as servants.*

typeface /'taɪpfeɪs/ n [C] letters, numbers etc of a particular style and size, used in printing

typewriter /'taɪp.raɪtə $ -ər/ n [C] a machine that prints letters, numbers etc on paper when you press its keys

typewritten /'taɪp.rɪtn/ adj written using a typewriter

typhoid /'taɪfɔɪd/ also **,typhoid 'fever** n [U] a serious infectious disease that is caused by dirty food or drink

typhoon /ˌtaɪˈfuːn◂/ n [C] a tropical storm with very strong winds

typical /'tɪpɪkəl/ adj

1 having the usual features or qualities of a particular group or thing: *a typical American family* | +of *This painting is typical of his early work.*
2 happening in the usual way: *On a typical day I wake up at 6.*

typically /'tɪpɪkli/ adv **1** used to say what usually happens: *Prices typically start at around $600.* **2** used to say that something is typical of a person, thing, or group: *Typically, Lenny said nothing, keeping his feelings to himself.* | *a typically Japanese dish*

typify /'tɪp½faɪ/ v [T] **typified, typifying, typifies** to be a typical example or feature of something

typing /'taɪpɪŋ/ n [U] writing that you do using a TYPEWRITER or computer

typist /'taɪp½st/ n [C] someone whose job is to type letters and other documents in an office

tyranny /'tɪrəni/ n [U] when a government, leader etc uses their power in a cruel and unfair way —**tyrannical** /tɪˈrænɪkəl/ adj

tyrant /'taɪərənt $ 'taɪr-/ n [C] someone who uses their power in a cruel and unfair way: *Despite his friendly appearance, her father was a real tyrant.*

tyre BrE; **tire** AmE /taɪə $ taɪr/ n [C] the round piece of rubber that fits around a wheel of a car, bicycle etc and is filled with air: *I had a flat tyre* (=all the air went out of it) *on the way home.* → see picture on page A12

tzar /zɑː, tsɑː $ zɑːr, tsɑːr/ n another spelling of TSAR

U, u

U, u /juː/ *n* [C,U] plural **U's, u's** the 21st letter of the English alphabet

ubiquitous /juːˈbɪkwɪtəs/ *adj formal* seeming to be everywhere

udder /ˈʌdə $ -ər/ *n* [C] the part of a cow, goat etc that hangs below its body and produces milk

UFO /ˈjuːfəʊ, ˌjuː ef ˈəʊ $ -foʊ, -ˈoʊ/ *n* [C] **Unidentified Flying Object** a moving object in the sky that some people believe could be carrying creatures from another world

ugh /ʊx, ʌɡ/ *spoken* the sound that people make when something is extremely unpleasant: *Ugh! This tastes foul!*

ugly /ˈʌɡli/ *adj*
1 very unattractive or unpleasant to look at [≠ **beautiful**; ➡ **hideous**]: *ugly modern buildings* | *She's not pretty, but she's not ugly either.*
2 unpleasant and violent: *There were **ugly scenes** at the England-Italy game.*
—**ugliness** *n* [U]

uh huh /ʌ ˈhʌ, ˈʌ hʌ/ *spoken informal* a sound that you make to say 'yes', or when you want someone to continue what they are saying: *'Can I sit here?' 'Uh huh.'*

uh-oh /ˈʌ əʊ $ -oʊ/ *spoken informal* a sound that you make when you have made a mistake, or when something bad is going to happen: *Uh-oh, I've deleted the wrong file.* | *Uh-oh! Here she comes.*

uh-uh /ˈʌ ʌ/ *spoken informal* a sound that you make to say 'no': *'Is Paul here yet?' 'Uh-uh.'*

ulcer /ˈʌlsə $ -ər/ *n* [C] a sore area on or inside your body, which may BLEED: *a stomach ulcer*

ulterior /ʌlˈtɪəriə $ -ˈtɪriər/ *adj* **ulterior motive** a secret reason for doing something

ultimate¹ /ˈʌltɪmɪt/ *adj* [only before noun]
1 better or greater than all other things or people of the same kind: *the ultimate rock and roll band* | *the ultimate disgrace* **2** final or coming at the end: *their ultimate objective* | *the ultimate failure of the project*

ultimate² *n* **the ultimate in sth** the best example or highest level of something: *Guy's home is **the ultimate in luxury**.*

ultimately /ˈʌltɪmɪtli/ *adv* finally, after everything else has been done or considered: *Their efforts ultimately resulted in his release from prison.* | *Ultimately it's your decision.*

ultimatum /ˌʌltɪˈmeɪtəm/ *n* [C] a threat saying that if someone does not do what you want by a particular time, you will do something they do not want: **issue/give sb an ultimatum** *The government issued an ultimatum to the rebels to surrender.*

ultra- /ʌltrə/ *prefix* extremely: *an ultra-modern kitchen*

ultrasonic /ˌʌltrəˈsɒnɪk $ -ˈsɑː-/ *adj technical* ultrasonic sounds are too high for humans to hear

ultrasound /ˈʌltrəsaʊnd/ *n* [C,U] a medical process that produces an image of something inside your body

ultraviolet /ˌʌltrəˈvaɪələt $ / *adj* ultraviolet light cannot be seen but makes your skin become darker when you are in the sun [➡ **infra-red**]

um /ʌm, əm/ *spoken* used when you cannot immediately decide what to say next: *Um, yeah, I guess so.*

umbilical cord /ʌmˈbɪlɪkəl ˌkɔːd $ -ˌkɔːrd/ *n* [C] the tube that connects a baby to its mother before it is born

umbrage /ˈʌmbrɪdʒ/ *n* **take umbrage (at sth)** *old-fashioned* to be offended by something, often without a good reason

umbrella /ʌmˈbrelə/ *n* [C]
1 a thing that you hold above your head to protect yourself from the rain [➡ **parasol**]: *It started to rain so I **put up my umbrella**.*
2 **umbrella organization/group etc** an organization that includes several smaller groups

umbrella

umpire /ˈʌmpaɪə $ -paɪr/ *n* [C] the person who makes sure that the players of a sports game obey the rules → see box at **REFEREE** —**umpire** *v* [I,T]

umpteen /ˌʌmpˈtiːn $ / *determiner informal* very many – used especially when you are annoyed there are so many: *umpteen reasons* —**umpteenth** /ˌʌmpˈtiːnθ $ / *adj*: *For the umpteenth time he checked his watch.*

UN, U.N. /ˌjuː ˈen/ *n* **the UN** the United Nations

un- /ʌn/ *prefix* **1** not: *unhappy* | *unexpected* **2** used to talk about the opposite of an action: *I undressed quickly* (=took my clothes off). | *You can unfasten your seat belt now.*

unabashed /ˌʌnəˈbæʃt $ / *adj written* not ashamed or embarrassed: *She stared at him with unabashed curiosity.*

unabated /ˌʌnəˈbeɪtɪd $ / *adj, adv* if something continues unabated, it does not stop or become weaker: *The storm continued unabated.*

unable /ʌnˈeɪbəl/ *adj* **be unable to do sth** not to be able to do something [➡ **inability**]: *She was unable to sleep.* | *I'm sorry; I'm unable to help you.*

unacceptable /ˌʌnəkˈseptəbəl $ / *adj* something that is unacceptable is wrong or bad and should not be allowed to continue: *Your behaviour is totally unacceptable.* —**unacceptably** *adv*

unaccompanied /ˌʌnəˈkʌmpənid $ / *adj, adv* **1** if you go somewhere unaccompanied, you go there alone **2** if you sing or play a musical instrument unaccompanied, no one plays with you

unaccountable /ˌʌnəˈkaʊntəbəl $ / *adj* **1** very surprising and difficult to explain: *For some **unaccountable reason** he's moving to New*

York. **2** not having to explain your actions or decisions to anyone else —**unaccountably** *adv*

unadulterated /ˌʌnəˈdʌltəreɪtᵻd◂/ *adj* complete or pure: *sheer unadulterated pleasure*

unaffected /ˌʌnəˈfektᵻd/ *adj* not changed or harmed by something: *Parts of the city remained unaffected by the fire.*

unaided /ʌnˈeɪdᵻd/ *adv* without help: *She can no longer walk unaided.*

unanimous /juːˈnænᵻməs/ *adj* a unanimous decision, vote etc is one in which everyone agrees —**unanimously** *adv* —**unanimity** /ˌjuːnəˈnɪmᵻti/ *n* [U]

unannounced /ˌʌnəˈnaʊnst◂/ *adj, adv* if you arrive somewhere unannounced, your arrival was not expected

unanswered /ʌnˈɑːnsəd $ -ˈænsərd/ *adj* an unanswered letter, question etc has not been answered: *Many **questions remain unanswered.***

unapproachable /ˌʌnəˈprəʊtʃəbəl◂ $ -ˈproʊ-/ *adj* not friendly and not easy to talk to

unarmed /ˌʌnˈɑːmd◂ $ -ˈɑːrmd◂/ *adj, adv* not carrying any weapons: *the killing of unarmed civilians*

unashamedly /ˌʌnəˈʃeɪmᵻdli/ *adv* used to say that someone is not embarrassed or worried that other people will disapprove of what they are doing: *Their latest record is unashamedly commercial.* —**unashamed** /-ˈʃeɪmd◂/ *adj*

unassailable /ˌʌnəˈseɪləbəl◂/ *adj formal* impossible to be criticized or beaten: *The win gave the Yankees an **unassailable lead.***

unassuming /ˌʌnəˈsjuːmɪŋ◂ , -ˈsuː- $ -ˈsuː-/ *adj* not trying to be noticed or given special treatment [= modest]: *a quiet unassuming man*

unattached /ˌʌnəˈtætʃt◂/ *adj* not married or involved in a romantic relationship [→ single]

unattended /ˌʌnəˈtendᵻd◂/ *adj, adv formal* left alone without being watched or looked after: *Please do not **leave** your bags **unattended**.* | *an unattended vehicle*

unattractive /ˌʌnəˈtræktɪv◂/ *adj* **1** not pleasant to look at **2** not good enough to be wanted

unauthorized also **-ised** *BrE* /ʌnˈɔːθəraɪzd $ -ˈɒː-/ *adj* done without official permission: *the unauthorized use of government funds*

unavailable /ˌʌnəˈveɪləbəl/ *adj* **1** not able to be bought, obtained, or used: *an album previously unavailable on CD* **2** not able to be spoken to: *I'm afraid she's unavailable at the moment.* | +**for** *Officials were **unavailable for comment*** (=not able or willing to talk to reporters).

unavoidable /ˌʌnəˈvɔɪdəbəl/ *adj* impossible to prevent: *an unavoidable delay* —**unavoidably** *adv*

unaware /ˌʌnəˈweə $ -ˈwer/ *adj* [not before noun] not noticing or realizing what is happening: +**of** *She seemed completely unaware of what was happening.*

unawares /ˌʌnəˈweəz $ -ˈwerz/ *adv* **catch/ take sb unawares** if something catches you unawares, it happens when you are not expecting it: *The enemy had been caught unawares.*

unbalanced /ʌnˈbælənst/ *adj* **1** slightly crazy: *He's obviously mentally unbalanced.* **2** unfair or unequal: *unbalanced reporting*

unbearable /ʌnˈbeərəbəl $ -ˈber-/ *adj* too painful, unpleasant etc for you to accept or deal with [= intolerable]: *The pain was **unbearable**.* —**unbearably** *adv*: *an unbearably hot day*

unbeatable /ʌnˈbiːtəbəl/ *adj* something that is unbeatable is the best of its kind: *Their prices are unbeatable.*

unbeaten /ˌʌnˈbiːtn◂/ *adj* a team, player etc that is unbeaten has not been defeated

unbelievable /ˌʌnbᵻˈliːvəbəl◂/ *adj* **1** extremely bad, impressive, or surprising [= incredible]: *The noise was unbelievable.* | *an unbelievable amount of money* → see box at **SURPRISING** **2** very difficult to believe and therefore probably untrue: *His story sounded completely unbelievable.* —**unbelievably** *adv*

unbending /ʌnˈbendɪŋ/ *adj disapproving* unwilling to change your opinions, decisions etc

unborn /ˌʌnˈbɔːn◂ $ -ˈɔːrn◂/ *adj* not yet born: *an unborn child*

unbridled /ʌnˈbraɪdld/ *adj literary disapproving* extreme and not controlled: *unbridled passion*

unbroken /ʌnˈbrəʊkən $ -ˈbroʊ-/ *adj* continuing without being interrupted: *unbroken peace*

unbutton /ʌnˈbʌtn/ *v* [T] to unfasten the buttons on a piece of clothing → see box at **FASTEN**

uncalled for /ʌnˈkɔːld fɔː $ -ˈkɒːld fɔːr/ behaviour or remarks that are uncalled for are not fair or suitable

uncanny /ʌnˈkæni/ *adj* very strange and difficult to explain: *an uncanny coincidence* —**uncannily** *adv*

uncaring /ʌnˈkeərɪŋ $ -ˈker-/ *adj* not caring about other people's feelings

unceremoniously /ˌʌnserəˈməʊniəsli $ -ˈmoʊ-/ *adv* in a way that shows no care or respect: *She dumped the flowers unceremoniously in the bin.*

uncertain /ʌnˈsɜːtn $ -ɜːr-/ *adj*

1 [not before noun] feeling doubt about something [= unsure]: +**whether/how/what etc** *She was uncertain whether she would recognize him.* | +**about/of** *I was uncertain about what to do next.*

2 not clear, definite, or decided [= unclear]: *His future with the company is uncertain.*

3 in no uncertain terms if you tell someone something in no uncertain terms, you tell them very clearly without trying to be polite —**uncertainty** *n* [C,U] —**uncertainly** *adv*

unchanged /ʌnˈtʃeɪndʒd◂/ *adj* the same as before

unchanging /ʌnˈtʃeɪndʒɪŋ/ *adj* always staying the same

uncharacteristic /ˌʌnˌkærᵻktəˈrɪstɪk◂/ *adj* not typical of someone or something —**uncharacteristically** /-kli/ *adv*

uncharted /ʌnˈtʃɑːtᵻd $ -ɑːr-/ *adj* **uncharted territory/waters** a situation or activity that you have never experienced before

unchecked /ʌnˈtʃekt◂/ *adj, adv* if something bad continues unchecked, it is not stopped

uncle /ˈʌŋkəl/ *n* [C] the brother of your mother or father, or the husband of your AUNT → see box at **RELATIVE**

unclear /ʌnˈklɪə◂ $ -ˈklɪr◂/ *adj* **1** difficult to understand or be sure about: *The law is unclear* *on this issue.* **2 be unclear about sth** to not understand something clearly: *I'm a little unclear about what they mean.*

uncomfortable /ʌnˈkʌmftəbəl, -ˈkʌmfət- $ -ˈkʌmfərt-, -ˈkʌmft-/ *adj*

1 not feeling physically relaxed, or not making you feel physically relaxed: *The heat made her feel uncomfortable.* | *an uncomfortable chair*
2 embarrassed or worried, or making you feel embarrassed and worried [= **awkward**]: *There was an uncomfortable silence.* | **+about** *She felt uncomfortable about being photographed.*
—**uncomfortably** *adv*

uncommon /ʌnˈkɒmən $ -ˈkɑː-/ *adj* rare or unusual: *It is not uncommon for patients to have to wait five hours to see a doctor.*
—**uncommonly** *adv*

uncompromising /ʌnˈkɒmprəmaɪzɪŋ $ -ˈkɑː-/ *adj* unwilling to change your opinions or intentions: *an uncompromising opponent of democratic reform*

unconcerned /ˌʌnkənˈsɜːnd $ -ɜːrnd◂/ *adj* not worried about or interested in something: *Her parents seemed unconcerned by her absence.*

unconditional /ˌʌnkənˈdɪʃənəl◂/ *adj* not limited by or depending on any conditions: *unconditional surrender* —**unconditionally** *adv*

unconfirmed /ˌʌnkənˈfɜːmd◂ $ -ˈfɜːrmd◂/ *adj* if a report or story is unconfirmed, there is no definite proof that it is true

unconnected /ˌʌnkəˈnektɪd◂/ *adj* not related in any way: *The murders are probably unconnected.*

unconscious¹ /ʌnˈkɒnʃəs $ -ˈkɑːn-/ *adj*

1 unable to see, move, feel etc, especially because you have had an accident, been given drugs etc: *She was found alive but unconscious.* | *The driver was knocked unconscious.*
2 be unconscious of sth to not notice something or realize what is happening
3 an unconscious feeling is one that you do not realize that you have [➡ **subconscious**]: *an unconscious desire*
—**unconsciously** *adv* —**unconsciousness** *n* [U]

unconscious² *n* **the/sb's unconscious** the part of your mind in which there are ideas and feelings that you do not realize you have [➡ **subconscious**]

unconstitutional /ˌʌnkɒnstɪˈtjuːʃənəl $ -kɑːnstɪˈtuː-/ *adj* not allowed by the rules of a country or organization

uncontrollable /ˌʌnkənˈtrəʊləbəl◂ $ -ˈtroʊl-/ *adj* something that is uncontrollable cannot be controlled or stopped: *uncontrollable rage*

unconventional /ˌʌnkənˈvenʃənəl◂/ *adj* very different from the kind that most people have, use etc: *unconventional teaching methods*

uncool /ˌʌnˈkuːl◂/ *adj informal* not fashionable or acceptable

uncountable /ʌnˈkaʊntəbəl/ *adj* an uncountable noun has no plural form, for example 'money', 'happiness', or 'furniture'

uncouth /ʌnˈkuːθ/ *adj* behaving or speaking in a rude, unpleasant way

uncover /ʌnˈkʌvə $ -ər/ *v* [T] **1** to find out about something that has been kept secret: *They uncovered a plot to kill the president.* **2** to remove the cover from something

undaunted /ʌnˈdɔːntɪd $ -ˈdɒːn-/ *adj, adv* not afraid to continue doing something, in spite of difficulties or danger: **+by** *Fisher was undaunted by their opposition.*

undecided /ˌʌndɪˈsaɪdɪd◂/ *adj* [not before noun] not having made a decision: **+about** *Many people are still undecided about how they will vote.*

undeniable /ˌʌndɪˈnaɪəbəl◂/ *adj* definitely true or certain —**undeniably** *adv*

under /ˈʌndə $ -ər/ *prep, adv*

1 below or at a lower level than something, or covered by something [≠ **over**]: *The cat was asleep under a chair.* | *She kept her head under the blankets.* | *We sailed under the Golden Gate Bridge.* | *He dived into the water and stayed under for over a minute.* → see picture on page A8
2 less than a particular number, amount, age, or price: *You can buy a good computer for under $1,000.* | *children aged 16 and under*
3 governed or controlled by a leader, political party etc: *Would things have been different under a Conservative government?*
4 used to say what is being done to something or how it is being dealt with: *The tunnel is still under construction.* | *We're under attack!* | **under discussion/consideration/review etc**
5 under .... conditions/circumstances when particular conditions exist: *I wish I'd met him under different circumstances.*
6 under way if something is under way, it is being done or happening: *Important changes are now under way.*
7 affected by a particular condition, influence, or situation: *She performs well under pressure.* | **under the influence of sth** *He was accused of driving while under the influence of alcohol.* | *I've got everything under control.*
8 if you are under someone, they are in charge of you: *She has a team of researchers under her.*
9 according to a law, agreement, system etc: *The trade is illegal under international law.*
10 used to say in which part of a book, list, or system something can be found: *You'll find her books under 'Modern Fiction'.*
11 using a particular name: *He writes under the name of Taki.*

under- /ˈʌndə $ -dər/ *prefix* **1** not enough: *undercooked cabbage* | *undernourished children* **2** beneath something else: *underwear* | *undersea exploration* **3** less important or lower in rank: *an under-secretary*

under-'age *adj* too young to legally buy alcohol, drive a car etc: *under-age drinking*

underarm /ˈʌndərɑːm $ -ɑːrm/ *n* [C] the area under your arm, where it joins your body [= **armpit**]

undercarriage /ˈʌndəˌkærɪdʒ $ -ər-/ *n* [C] the wheels of an aircraft or train and the structure that holds them

underclass /ˈʌndəklɑːs $ -dərklæs/ *n* [singular] a group of people in society who are very poor and cannot change the situation they are in

underclothes /ˈʌndəkləʊðz -kləʊz $ -dərkloʊðz, -kloʊz/ *n* [plural] *old-fashioned* clothes that you wear next to your body, under your other clothes [= **underwear**]

U

undercover /ˌʌndəˈkʌvə◂ $ -dərˈkʌvər◂ / adj, adv working secretly in order to find out information for the government or the police: an undercover agent

undercurrent /ˈʌndəˌkʌrənt $ -dər,kɜːr- / n [C] a feeling, especially of anger or dissatisfaction, that people do not express openly: +of an undercurrent of racism

undercut /ˌʌndəˈkʌt $ -ər- / v [T] past tense and past participle **undercut** present participle **undercutting** to sell something more cheaply than someone else: We've undercut our competitors by 15%.

underdog /ˈʌndədɒg $ ˈʌndərdɔːg/ n [C] the person or team in a game or competition that is not expected to win

underestimate /ˌʌndərˈestɪˌmeɪt/ v [T] **1** to think that something is smaller than it really is [≠ **overestimate**]: They underestimated the size of the problem. **2** to think that someone is less skilful, intelligent etc than they really are [≠ **overestimate**]: Never underestimate your opponent. —**underestimate** /-mɪt/ n [C]

underfoot /ˌʌndəˈfʊt $ -ər- / adv under your feet when you are walking: It's very wet underfoot.

undergo /ˌʌndəˈgəʊ $ ˌʌndərˈgoʊ/ v [T] past tense **underwent** /-ˈwent/ past participle **undergone** /-ˈgɒn $ -ˈgɔːn/ third person singular **undergoes** /-ˈgəʊz $ -ˈgoʊz/ if you undergo a change, an unpleasant experience etc, it happens to you or is done to you: He had to undergo major heart surgery.

undergraduate /ˌʌndəˈgrædʒuˌɪt◂ $ -ər- / n [C] a student who is doing their first degree at university [➝ **postgraduate**] —**undergraduate** adj

underground¹ /ˌʌndəˈgraʊnd◂ $ -ər- / adj, adv **1** under the surface of the ground: underground streams | an underground car park | animals that live underground **2** [only before noun] an underground political organization is secret and illegal: an underground resistance movement

underground² /ˈʌndəgraʊnd $ -ər- / n [singular] BrE a railway system under a city [= **metro**; = **subway** AmE]: the London Underground ➝ see picture at **TRANSPORT**

undergrowth /ˈʌndəgrəʊθ $ -dərgroʊθ/ n [U] bushes and plants that grow around bigger trees

underhand /ˌʌndəˈhænd◂ $ ˈʌndərhænd◂ also **underhanded** /ˌʌndəˈhændɪ̯d◂ $ ˈʌndərhændɪ̯d/ adj disapproving dishonest or done secretly: underhand tactics

underlie /ˌʌndəˈlaɪ $ -ər- / v [T] past tense **underlay** /-ˈleɪ/ past participle **underlain** /-ˈleɪn/ present participle **underlying** formal to be the basic cause of something, or the basic thing from which something develops: the principle which underlies the party's policies —**underlying** adj: the underlying cause of the disease

underline /ˌʌndəˈlaɪn $ -ər- / v [T] **1** to draw a line under a word to show that it is important **2** to show or emphasize that something is important: This tragic incident underlines the need for immediate action.

undermine /ˌʌndəˈmaɪn $ -ər- / v [T] to gradually make someone or something less strong or effective: She totally undermined his self-confidence.

underneath¹ /ˌʌndəˈniːθ $ -ər- / prep, adv **1** directly under another object or covered by it: I found the keys underneath a cushion. | She was wearing a jacket with a T-shirt underneath. **2** on the lower surface of something: The car was rusty underneath. **3** used to say what someone is really like, when their behaviour does not show this: I think he's a nice person underneath.

underneath² n **the underneath** the bottom surface of something

underpaid /ˌʌndəˈpeɪd◂ $ -ər- / adj earning less money than you should

underpants /ˈʌndəpænts $ -ər- / n [plural] a piece of clothing that men wear under their trousers ➝ see picture at **CLOTHES**

underpass /ˈʌndəpɑːs $ ˈʌndərpæs/ n [C] a road or path that goes under another road or a railway

underpin /ˌʌndəˈpɪn $ -ər- / v [T] **underpinned**, **underpinning** to give strength or support to something

underprivileged /ˌʌndəˈprɪvɪ̯lɪdʒd◂ $ -dər- / adj poor and having no advantages in society: underprivileged children

underrated /ˌʌndəˈreɪtɪ̯d◂ / adj better than people think or say: an underrated player —**underrate** v [T]

underscore /ˌʌndəˈskɔː $ -dərˈskɔːr/ v [T] especially AmE to emphasize that something is important [= **underline**]

undershirt /ˈʌndəʃɜːt $ ˈʌndərʃɜːrt/ n [C] a piece of underwear worn under a shirt

underside /ˈʌndəsaɪd $ -ər- / n **the underside (of sth)** the bottom surface of something: white spots on the underside of the leaves

understaffed /ˌʌndəˈstɑːft◂ $ ˌʌndərˈstæft◂ / adj not having enough workers

understand /ˌʌndəˈstænd $ -ər- / v [I,T] past tense and past participle **understood** /-ˈstʊd/ **1** to know the meaning of what someone is telling you, or the language that they speak [≠ **misunderstand**]: She spoke clearly, so that everyone could understand. | Most people there understand English. **2** **make yourself understood** to explain or say something in a way that people find easy to understand: I'm not very good at German, but I can make myself understood. **3** to know how something works, or why something happens: Scientists still don't really understand this phenomenon. | +how/why/where etc You don't need to understand how computers work to be able to use them. **4** to know how someone feels and why they behave in the way they do: Believe me, John – I understand how you feel. | My parents don't understand me. **5** to believe or think that something is true because you have heard it or read it: +(that) I *understand that you want to buy a painting.* | *It is understood that she is going to resign.*

understandable /ˌʌndəˈstændəbəl $ -dər-/ *adj* understandable behaviour etc seems reasonable because of the situation: *Of course she's upset. It's a perfectly understandable reaction.* —**understandably** *adv*

understanding¹ /ˌʌndəˈstændɪŋ $ -ər-/ *n* **1** [U] knowledge about something based on learning or experience: **+of** *major advances in our understanding of the brain* **2** [U] the ability to think or learn about something: *a concept that is beyond the understanding of a four-year-old* **3** [singular] an unofficial or informal agreement: *I thought we* **had an understanding** *about the price.* **4** [U] sympathy towards someone: *Harry thanked us for our understanding.*

understanding² *adj* showing sympathy towards someone who has problems: *an understanding boss*

understated /ˌʌndəˈsteɪtɪd◂ $ -dər-/ *adj approving* simple in style: *the understated elegance of her dress*

understatement /ˌʌndəˈsteɪtmənt $ -dər-/ *n* [C,U] a statement that is not strong enough to express how good, bad, impressive etc something really is: *To say the movie is bad is an understatement.*

understood /ˌʌndəˈstʊd $ -ər-/ *v* the past tense and past participle of UNDERSTAND

understudy /ˈʌndəˌstʌdi $ -ər-/ *n* [C] plural **understudies** an actor who learns the words of a character in a play so that they can perform if the usual actor is ill

undertake /ˌʌndəˈteɪk $ -dər-/ *v* [T] past tense **undertook** /-ˈtʊk/ past participle **undertaken** /-ˈteɪkən/ *formal* **1** to start to do a piece of work, especially one that is long and difficult: *Baker undertook the task of writing the report.* **2 undertake to do sth** to promise or agree to do something: *He undertook to pay the money back in six months.*

undertaker /ˈʌndəteɪkə $ -dərteɪkər/ *n* [C] someone whose job is to arrange funerals

undertaking /ˌʌndəˈteɪkɪŋ $ ˈʌndərteɪ-/ *n* [C usually singular] **1** an important or difficult piece of work: *Starting a new business can be a risky undertaking.* **2** a legal or official promise to do something

undertone /ˈʌndətəʊn $ -dərtoʊn/ *n* [C] **1** a feeling or quality that exists but is not very easy to recognize: *the political undertones of Sartre's work* **2 in an undertone** in a low quiet voice

undertook /ˌʌndəˈtʊk $ -ər-/ *v* the past tense of UNDERTAKE

undervalue /ˌʌndəˈvælju: $ -ər-/ *v* [T] to think that someone or something is less important or valuable than they really are

undervalued /ˌʌndəˈvælju:d◂ $ -ər-/ *adj* more important or valuable than people think

swimming underwater

underwater /ˌʌndəˈwɔːtə $ ˌʌndərˈwɒːtər◂, -ˈwɑː-/ *adj, adv* below the surface of the water: *underwater photography* | *He dived underwater and swam away.*

underway /ˌʌndəˈweɪ $ -ər-/ *adj* if something is underway, it is being done or happening: *The game was already* **well underway**.

underwear /ˈʌndəweə $ -dərwer/ *n* [U] clothes that you wear next to your body under your other clothes

underweight /ˌʌndəˈweɪt $ -ər-/ *adj* below the normal weight [≠ **overweight**]: *an underweight baby* → see box at THIN

underwent /ˌʌndəˈwent $ -ər-/ *v* the past tense of UNDERGO

underworld /ˈʌndəwɜːld $ ˈʌndərwɜːrld/ *n* [singular] **1** the criminals in a place and the activities they are involved in: *the London underworld of the 1960s* **2** the home of the dead, in ancient Greek stories

undesirable /ˌʌndɪˈzaɪərəbəl $ -ˈzaɪr-/ *adj formal* something that is undesirable is not wanted because it may have a bad effect: *The treatment has no undesirable side-effects.*

undid /ʌnˈdɪd/ *v* the past tense of UNDO

undies /ˈʌndiːz/ *n* [plural] *informal* underwear

undisclosed /ˌʌndɪsˈkləʊzd $ -ˈkloʊzd◂/ *adj* not known publicly: *They bought the company for an undisclosed sum.*

undisguised /ˌʌndɪsˈɡaɪzd◂ / *adj* an undisguised feeling is clearly shown and not hidden: *She looked at me with undisguised hatred.*

undisputed /ˌʌndɪˈspjuːtɪd◂ / *adj* **undisputed leader/champion/master etc** someone who everyone agrees is the leader etc

undisturbed /ˌʌndɪˈstɜːbd $ -ɜːr-/ *adj, adv* not interrupted, moved, or changed: *I was able to work undisturbed.*

undivided /ˌʌndɪˈvaɪdɪd◂ / *adj* complete: *I need your* **undivided attention** (=full attention).

undo /ʌnˈduː/ *v* [T] past tense **undid** /-ˈdɪd/ past participle **undone** /-ˈdʌn/ third person singular **undoes** /-ˈdʌz/
1 to open something that is tied, fastened, or wrapped: *He undid his shoelaces.* | *Have you undone all the screws?* → see box at FASTEN → and OPEN
2 to remove the bad effects of something: *There's no way of undoing the damage done to his reputation.*

undoing /ʌnˈduːɪŋ/ *n* **be sb's undoing** to cause someone's failure: *His overconfidence proved to be his undoing.*

U

undone /ˌʌnˈdʌn◂/ *adj* **1** not tied or fastened: *Your shirt button has come undone*. **2** not finished: *Much of the repair work has been left undone*.

undoubtedly /ʌnˈdaʊtɪdli/ *adv* used to emphasize that something is definitely true: *Amis is undoubtedly one of the best writers of his generation.* —**undoubted** *adj*: *his undoubted talent*

undress /ʌnˈdres/ *v* [I,T] to take your clothes off, or to take someone else's clothes off: *He started to get undressed.* —**undressed** *adj*

undue /ˌʌnˈdjuː◂ $ -ˈduː◂/ *adj formal* more than is reasonable or necessary: *We don't want to cause undue distress to the animals.*

undulating /ˈʌndjʊleɪtɪŋ $ -dʒə-/ *adj* land that is undulating has gentle slopes and hills

unduly /ʌnˈdjuːli $ -ˈduː-/ *adv formal* more than is normal or reasonable: *Helen didn't seem unduly worried.*

undying /ʌnˈdaɪ-ɪŋ/ *adj literary* continuing for ever: *undying love*

unearth /ʌnˈɜːθ $ -ˈɜːrθ/ *v* [T] **1** to find something that was buried in the ground: *They unearthed a collection of Roman coins.* **2** to find something that has been hidden or secret: *New evidence has been unearthed that connects them to the crime.*

unearthly /ʌnˈɜːθli $ -ˈɜːr-/ *adj* very strange and not seeming natural: *an unearthly sound*

unease /ʌnˈiːz/ *n* [U] a feeling of worry or slight fear

uneasy /ʌnˈiːzi/ *adj* worried because you think something bad may happen: *We felt uneasy about his decision.* → see box at **WORRIED** —**uneasiness** *n* [U] —**uneasily** *adv*

uneconomical /ˌʌniːkəˈnɒmɪkəl, ˌʌnekə- $ -ˈnɑː-/ *adj* costing too much money to use or operate: *an old, uneconomical coal mine*

unemployed /ˌʌnɪmˈplɔɪd◂/ *adj*
1 without a job [= out of work]: *an unemployed teacher*
2 the unemployed people who do not have jobs

unemployment /ˌʌnɪmˈplɔɪmənt/ *n* [U] when someone does not have a job, or the number of people who do not have a job: *Many workers now face unemployment.* | *a city with a high unemployment rate* | *a time of high unemployment* (=when a lot of people do not have a job)

unending /ʌnˈendɪŋ/ *adj* something that is unending seems as if it will continue for ever: *an unending stream of people*

unequal /ʌnˈiːkwəl/ *adj* **1** unfair because people are treated differently and do not have the same rights or the same amount of power: *the unequal distribution of wealth* **2** not the same in size, amount, or level —**unequally** *adv*

unequivocal /ˌʌnɪˈkwɪvəkəl◂/ *adj formal* completely clear and definite: *unequivocal proof* —**unequivocally** /-kli/ *adv*

unerring /ʌnˈɜːrɪŋ/ *adj* completely right or always right: *He hit the target with unerring accuracy.*

unethical /ʌnˈeθɪkəl/ *adj* morally wrong

uneven /ʌnˈiːvən/ *adj* **1** not flat, smooth, or level: *uneven ground* **2** not equal, balanced, or regular: *Her breathing became slow and uneven.* —**unevenly** *adv*

unexpected /ˌʌnɪkˈspektɪd◂/ *adj* something that is unexpected is surprising because you did not expect it to happen —**unexpectedly** *adv*

unfailing /ʌnˈfeɪlɪŋ/ *adj* always there, even in times of difficulty or trouble: *Thank you for your unfailing support.*

unfair /ˌʌnˈfeə◂ $ -ˈfer◂/ *adj* not right or fair: *The other team had an unfair advantage.* | +to *Jenny was really being very unfair to him.* —**unfairly** *adv*: *He felt he had been treated unfairly.* —**unfairness** *n* [U]

unfaithful /ʌnˈfeɪθfəl/ *adj* someone who is unfaithful has sex with someone who is not their wife, husband, or usual partner: +to *He had been unfaithful to his wife.*

unfamiliar /ˌʌnfəˈmɪliə◂ $ -ər◂/ *adj* **1** not known to you: +to *Some of the vocabulary was unfamiliar to me.* **2 be unfamiliar with sth** not to have any experience of something: *I am unfamiliar with his work.*

unfashionable /ʌnˈfæʃənəbəl/ *adj* not popular or fashionable

unfasten /ʌnˈfɑːsən $ -ˈfæsən/ *v* [T] to undo something that is fastened or tied: *Don't unfasten your seat belt yet.* → see box at **FASTEN** → and **OPEN**

unfathomable /ʌnˈfæðəməbəl/ *adj literary* too strange or mysterious to be understood

unfavourable *BrE*; **unfavorable** *AmE* /ʌnˈfeɪvərəbəl/ *adj* **1** not good and likely to cause problems for you: *unfavorable weather conditions* **2** showing that you do not like someone or something: *The play received unfavourable reviews.*

unfeeling /ʌnˈfiːlɪŋ/ *adj* not showing that you care about other people

unfinished /ʌnˈfɪnɪʃt/ *adj* not finished

unfit /ʌnˈfɪt/ *adj* **1** not in a good physical condition: *He's still unfit after his injury.* **2** not suitable or good enough to do something or be used for something: *meat that is unfit for human consumption* (=not suitable to eat)

unfold /ʌnˈfəʊld $ -ˈfoʊld/ *v* **1** [I] if a story or event unfolds, it becomes clearer and you understand it: *The case began to slowly unfold in court.* **2** [T] to open something that is folded: *She unfolded the map.* → see box at **OPEN**

unforeseen /ˌʌnfɔːˈsiːn◂ $ -fɔːr-/ *adj* an unforeseen situation is one that you did not expect to happen: *unforeseen problems*

unforgettable /ˌʌnfəˈgetəbəl◂ $ -fər-/ *adj* something that is unforgettable is extremely good or exciting and you will remember it for a long time

unforgivable /ˌʌnfəˈgɪvəbəl◂ $ -fər-/ *adj* an unforgivable action is so bad that you cannot forgive the person who did it: *His behaviour was unforgivable.*

unfortunate /ʌnˈfɔːtʃənət $ -ˈfɔːr-/ *adj*
1 not lucky: *The teacher was yelling at some unfortunate student.* | *an unfortunate accident*
2 used to say that you wish something had not happened or was not true: **it is unfortunate (that)** *It is unfortunate that so few people seem*

willing to help. | *It's most unfortunate* (=very unfortunate) *that your father can't be here.*

unfortunately /ʌnˈfɔːtʃənətli $ -ˈfɔːr-/ *adv* used to say that you wish that something had not happened or was not true: *Unfortunately, the show had to be cancelled.*

unfounded /ʌnˈfaʊndɪd/ *adj* not true and not based on facts: *unfounded allegations*

unfriendly /ʌnˈfrendli/ *adj* not friendly: *I don't know why he was so unfriendly.* | **+to/towards** *The villagers were really quite unfriendly towards us.*
—**unfriendliness** *n* [U]

unfurl /ʌnˈfɜːl $ -ɜːrl/ *v* [I,T] *literary* if a flag or sail unfurls, or if someone unfurls it, it unrolls and opens

unfurnished /ʌnˈfɜːnɪʃt $ -ɜːr-/ *adj* an unfurnished room, house etc has no furniture in it

ungainly /ʌnˈɡeɪnli/ *adj* moving in a way that is not graceful: *an ungainly teenager*

ungracious /ʌnˈɡreɪʃəs/ *adj* not polite or friendly —**ungraciously** *adv*

ungrammatical /ˌʌnɡrəˈmætɪkəl◂/ *adj* wrong according to the rules of grammar

ungrateful /ʌnˈɡreɪtfəl/ *adj* not thanking someone for something they have given to you or done for you —**ungratefully** *adv*

unhappy /ʌnˈhæpi/ *adj*
1 not happy: *If you're so unhappy, why don't you change jobs?* | *an unhappy childhood* → see box at **SAD**
2 feeling worried or annoyed because you do not like what is happening in a situation: **+with/about** *O'Neill was unhappy with his team's performance.* | *I'm slightly unhappy about you using my car.*
—**unhappiness** *n* [U] —**unhappily** *adv*

unharmed /ʌnˈhɑːmd $ -ɑːr-/ *adj* [not before noun] *adv* not hurt or harmed

unhealthy /ʌnˈhelθi/ *adj* **1** likely to make you ill: *an unhealthy diet* | *an unhealthy lifestyle* **2** not healthy: *a rather unhealthy-looking child* **3** not normal or natural and likely to be harmful: *an unhealthy obsession with sex*

unheard-of /ʌnˈhɜːd ɒv $ -ˈhɜːrd ɑːv/ *adj* something that is unheard-of has never happened before and seems surprising: *Women pilots were practically unheard-of twenty years ago.*

unhelpful /ʌnˈhelpfəl/ *adj* not helping in a situation and sometimes making it worse: *The staff were unfriendly and unhelpful.*

unholy /ʌnˈhəʊli $ -ˈhoʊ-/ *adj* **1** *informal* **unholy alliance** an agreement between people or groups who do not usually work together, for bad purposes **2** [only before noun] very great and very bad: *an unholy row between the two families* | *an unholy mess* **3** not holy or not respecting what is holy

unhurt /ʌnˈhɜːt $ -ɜːrt/ *adj* [not before noun] *adv* not injured

unicorn /ˈjuːnɪkɔːn $ -ɔːrn/ *n* [C] an imaginary animal like a white horse with one long straight horn on its head

unidentified /ˌʌnaɪˈdentɪfaɪd◂/ *adj* an unidentified person or thing is one that you do not know the name of

unification /ˌjuːnɪfɪˈkeɪʃən/ *n* [U] when two or more countries or groups join together to form a single group or country: *the unification of Germany*

uniform[1] /ˈjuːnɪfɔːm $ -ɔːrm/ *n* [C,U] a type of clothing worn by all the members of an organization, or all the children at a school: **school/army/police etc uniform** *Do you like the new school uniform?* | *He wasn't wearing his uniform.* | **in uniform** *a police officer in uniform* —**uniformed** *adj*: *a uniformed police officer*

uniform[2] *adj* things that are uniform are all the same size, shape etc —**uniformly** *adv* —**uniformity** /ˌjuːnɪˈfɔːmɪti $ -ɔːr-/ *n* [U]

unify /ˈjuːnɪfaɪ/ *v* [T] **unified, unifying, unifies** to join the parts of a country or organization together to make a single country or organization [➙ **unification**]: *Spain was unified in the 16th century.* —**unified** *adj*

unilateral /ˌjuːnɪˈlætərəl◂/ *adj formal* a unilateral action or decision is taken by only one of the groups that is involved in a situation, without the agreement of the other groups: *The UN urged Washington not to take unilateral action.* —**unilaterally** *adv*

unimaginable /ˌʌnɪˈmædʒɪnəbəl◂/ *adj* very difficult to imagine: *unimaginable wealth*

unimportant /ˌʌnɪmˈpɔːtənt◂ $ -ɔːr-/ *adj* not important

unimpressed /ˌʌnɪmˈprest/ *adj* if you are unimpressed with something, you do not think it is very good

uninhabitable /ˌʌnɪnˈhæbɪtəbəl◂/ *adj* a place that is uninhabitable is impossible to live in

uninhabited /ˌʌnɪnˈhæbɪtɪd◂/ *adj* a place that is uninhabited has no one living there → see box at **EMPTY**

uninhibited /ˌʌnɪnˈhɪbɪtɪd◂/ *adj* feeling free to behave how you want, without worrying about what other people think

unintelligible /ˌʌnɪnˈtelɪdʒɪbəl◂/ *adj* impossible to understand

unintentional /ˌʌnɪnˈtenʃənəl◂/ *adj* not done deliberately —**unintentionally** *adv*

uninterested /ʌnˈɪntrɪstɪd/ *adj* not interested [➙ **disinterested**]

uninterrupted /ˌʌnɪntəˈrʌptɪd◂/ *adj* continuing without stopping or being interrupted: *All I want is two hours of uninterrupted work.*

union /ˈjuːnjən/ *n*
1 [C] also **trade union** *BrE*; **labor union** *AmE* [C] an organization that is formed by workers in order to protect their rights: *the car workers' union* | **+of** *the National Union of Teachers* | *Are you planning to join the union?* → see box at **ORGANIZATION**
2 [singular, U] *formal* when two countries or organizations join together: **+of** *the union of East and West Germany*
3 [singular] a group of countries or states with the same central government: *the European Union*

Union 'Jack *n* [C] the national flag of the United Kingdom

unique /juːˈniːk/ *adj*
1 something that is unique is the only one of its kind: *Every house we build is unique.*

2 *informal* unusually good and special: *a unique opportunity to study with an artist*
3 unique to sb/sth existing only in a particular place, group etc: *animals that are unique to Australia*
—**uniquely** *adv* —**uniqueness** *n* [U]

unisex /'juːnɪseks/ *adj* intended for both men and women: *a unisex jacket*

unison /'juːnɪsən, -zən/ *n* **in unison** if a group of people do something in unison, they all do it at the same time

unit /'juːnɪt/ *n* [C]
1 one part of something that is whole or complete in itself but is also part of the bigger thing: *the emergency unit at the hospital* | *The apartment building is split into eight units.* | *The book is divided into eight units.* | *The engine's cooling unit is broken.*
2 an amount or quantity of something that is used as a standard of measurement: **+of** *The dollar is the basic unit of money in the US.*
3 a piece of furniture, especially one that can be fitted to others of the same type: *a storage unit*

unite /juːˈnaɪt/ *v* [I,T] to join together as a group, or to make people join together: *Germany was united in 1990.* | **+behind** *Congress united behind the President.*

united /juːˈnaɪtɪd/ *adj* **1** if people are united, they all want to stay together, or they all agree with each other: *the Democrats are united on this issue* **2** a united country has been formed by two or more countries or states joining together: *a united Europe*

U,nited 'Nations, the UN *n* **the United Nations** the international organization that most countries belong to, which tries to find peaceful solutions to world problems

unity /'juːnɪti/ *n* [singular, U] when everyone in a group, country etc wants to stay together, or they all agree with each other: *We must try to preserve party unity.*

universal /ˌjuːnɪˈvɜːsəl $ -ɜːr-/ *adj* **1** involving everyone in the world, or everyone in a group: *a universal ban on nuclear weapons* | *There was almost universal agreement.* **2** true or suitable in every situation: *a universal truth*
—**universally** *adv*

universe /'juːnɪvɜːs $ -ɜːrs/ *n* **the universe** all the stars and PLANETS and all of space

university /ˌjuːnɪˈvɜːsɪti $ -ɜːr-/ *n* [C,U] plural **universities** a place where students study a subject at a high level in order to get a DEGREE: *Do you want to go to university when you leave school?* | **at university** *He's studying geography at university.* | *a university professor*

TOPIC

People who **go to university** *BrE*/**go to a university** *AmE* to **study** a subject are called **students**. They study an **arts subject** *BrE*/**liberal arts subject** *AmE* (=English, History etc) or a **science subject**. During their 3 or 4-year **course**, students **go to/attend lectures/classes** *AmE*/**tutorials** *BrE* and seminars. They are taught by **professors** and **lecturers**. They are asked to do regular **essays** or **assignments**. At the end of their **course**, they **sit** *BrE*/**take** examinations called **finals**. If they pass, they

get a degree (=document showing that they have graduated).
→ SCHOOL

GRAMMAR

In British English, do not use 'a' or 'the' before **university** when you are talking about the time when someone is studying there: *His daughter is away at university.*

unjust /ˌʌnˈdʒʌst◂/ *adj* not fair or reasonable: *unjust laws* —**unjustly** *adv*

unjustified /ʌnˈdʒʌstɪfaɪd/ *adj* happening without any good reason: *Our fears were unjustified.*

unkempt /ˌʌnˈkempt◂/ *adj* not neat or tidy: *His hair looked dirty and unkempt.*

unkind /ˌʌnˈkaɪnd◂/ *adj* nasty, unpleasant, or cruel: *an unkind remark* | **+to** *Her husband is very unkind to her.*

THESAURUS

mean – behaving towards other people in a way that is not nice: *That was a mean thing to do.*
nasty – unpleasant or unkind: *Don't be nasty to your sister.*
cruel – making people or animals suffer, often by hurting them: *You say such cruel things sometimes.*
thoughtless – not caring about people's feelings or how your actions will affect them: *a thoughtless remark*

—**unkindly** *adv* —**unkindness** *n* [U]

unknowingly /ʌnˈnəʊɪŋli $ -ˈnoʊ-/ *adv* without realizing what you are doing or what is happening

unknown¹ /ˌʌnˈnəʊn◂ $ -ˈnoʊn◂/ *adj* **1** not known: *The number of people injured is still unknown.* | **+to** *His criminal history was unknown to us.* **2** not famous: *an unknown actor*

unknown² *n* **1 the unknown** things that you know nothing about and have never experienced before: *a fear of the unknown* **2** [C] someone who is not famous

unlawful /ʌnˈlɔːfəl $ -ˈlɒː-/ *adj formal* not legal: *an unlawful act* —**unlawfully** *adv*

unleaded /ʌnˈledɪd/ *adj* unleaded petrol does not contain any LEAD

unleash /ʌnˈliːʃ/ *v* [T] to suddenly make something start happening which has a great effect: *The decision unleashed a storm of protest.*

unless /ʌnˈles, ən-/ *linking word* used to say that something will only happen if something else happens: *He won't go to sleep unless you tell him a story.*

unlike /ʌnˈlaɪk/ *prep*
1 completely different from another person or thing: *Unlike me, she's very intelligent.*
2 not typical of the way someone usually behaves: *It's unlike Judy to leave without telling anyone.*

unlikely /ʌnˈlaɪkli/ *adj* not likely to happen or to be true: **it is unlikely (that)** *It's very unlikely that they'll win.* | *an unlikely explanation*

unlimited /ʌnˈlɪmɪtɪd/ *adj* without a fixed limit: *They seem to have unlimited funds.*

U

unlit /ˌʌnˈlɪt◂/ *adj* dark because there are no lights

unload /ʌnˈləʊd $ -ˈloʊd/ *v* **1** [T] to remove things from a vehicle or large container: *Can you unload the dishwasher for me?* | **unload sth from sth** *The driver unloaded some boxes from the back of the truck.* **2** [T] *informal* to get rid of something that you do not want by giving it to someone else: **unload sth on/onto sb** *Ben has a habit of unloading his work on others.*

unlock /ʌnˈlɒk $ -ˈlɑːk/ *v* [T] to open something by unfastening the lock on it → see box at OPEN

unlucky /ʌnˈlʌki/ *adj*
1 having bad luck: **+with** *We were unlucky with the weather this weekend.* | *The German team was unlucky not to win.*
2 happening because of bad luck: *an unlucky accident*
3 something that is unlucky is believed to make you have bad luck: *13 is an unlucky number.*
—**unluckily** *adv*

unmanned /ˌʌnˈmænd◂/ *adj* an unmanned vehicle or building does not have anyone in it

unmarked /ˌʌnˈmɑːkt◂ $ -ˈmɑːrkt◂/ *adj* something that is unmarked has no words or signs on it to show what it is: *an unmarked police car*

unmarried /ˌʌnˈmærid◂/ *adj* not married [= single]

unmistakable /ˌʌnməˈsteɪkəbəl◂/ *adj* if something is unmistakable, you know immediately what it is: *the unmistakable taste of garlic*

unmitigated /ʌnˈmɪtɪɡeɪtɪd/ *adj* used to emphasize how bad something is: *an unmitigated disaster*

unmoved /ʌnˈmuːvd/ *adj* not feeling any sympathy, excitement, worry etc because of something

unnamed /ˌʌnˈneɪmd◂/ *adj* an unnamed person or thing is one whose name is not mentioned

unnatural /ʌnˈnætʃərəl/ *adj* different from normal, in a way that seems strange or wrong: *It's unnatural for a child to spend so much time alone.* —**unnaturally** *adv*

unnecessary /ʌnˈnesəsəri $ -seri/ *adj* not needed: *the unnecessary use of drugs* | *an unnecessary expense*
—**unnecessarily** /ʌnˈnesəsərəli $ ˌʌnnesəˈserⁱli/ *adv*: *We don't want to take risks unnecessarily.*

unnerve /ʌnˈnɜːv $ -ɜːrv/ *v* [T] to make someone frightened or nervous: *I was slightly unnerved by his behaviour.* —**unnerving** *adj*: *an unnerving experience*

unnoticed /ʌnˈnəʊtⁱst $ -ˈnoʊ-/ *adj, adv* without being noticed: *She sat unnoticed at the back of the room.* | *His remark went unnoticed by everyone except me.*

unobserved /ˌʌnəbˈzɜːvd $ -ɜːrvd/ *adj, adv* without being seen

unobtrusive /ˌʌnəbˈtruːsɪv◂/ *adj formal* not attracting attention and not likely to be noticed

unoccupied /ʌnˈɒkjⁱpaɪd $ -ˈɑːk-/ *adj* a seat, house, room etc that is unoccupied has no one in it

unofficial /ˌʌnəˈfɪʃəl◂/ *adj* **1** done or produced without formal approval or permission: *an unofficial biography* **2** not done as part of

someone's official duties: *The Senator is in Berlin on an unofficial visit.* —**unofficially** *adv*

unorthodox /ʌnˈɔːθədɒks $ ʌnˈɔːrθədɑːks/ *adj* unusual and different from most people's ideas or ways of doing things: *her unorthodox lifestyle*

unpack /ʌnˈpæk/ *v* [I,T] to take everything out of a box or bag: *I unpacked my suitcase.*

unpaid /ˌʌnˈpeɪd◂/ *adj* **1** an unpaid bill or debt has not been paid **2** working without receiving any money: *unpaid workers* | *unpaid work*

unparalleled /ʌnˈpærəleld/ *adj formal* much greater or better than anything else: *an unparalleled success*

unpleasant /ʌnˈplezənt/ *adj*
1 not pleasant or enjoyable [≠ nice]: *an unpleasant surprise*
2 unkind or rude [≠ nice]: *What an unpleasant man!* | **+to** *She was rather unpleasant to me on the phone.*
—**unpleasantly** *adv*

unplug /ʌnˈplʌg/ *v* [T] **unplugged, unplugging** to disconnect a piece of electrical equipment by taking its PLUG out of a SOCKET

unpopular /ʌnˈpɒpjⁱlə $ -ˈpɑːpjⁱlər/ *adj* not liked by most people: *an unpopular decision* | **+with** *He was unpopular with many of his colleagues.*
—**unpopularity** /ʌnˌpɒpjⁱˈlærⁱti $ -ˌpɑːp-/ *n* [U]

unprecedented /ʌnˈpresⁱdentⁱd/ *adj* something that is unprecedented has never happened before: *an unprecedented achievement*

unpredictable /ˌʌnprɪˈdɪktəbəl◂/ *adj* changing so much that you do not know what to expect: *unpredictable weather*

unprofessional /ˌʌnprəˈfeʃənəl◂/ *adj* not behaving in the way that people doing a particular job should behave: *His behaviour was extremely unprofessional.*

unprovoked /ˌʌnprəˈvəʊkt◂ $ -ˈvoʊkt◂/ *adj* unprovoked anger, attacks etc are directed at someone who has not done anything to deserve them

unqualified /ʌnˈkwɒlⁱfaɪd $ -ˈkwɑː-/ *adj*
1 not having the right knowledge, experience, or QUALIFICATIONS to do something: **+for** *She was totally unqualified for the job.* **2** completely and in every way: *The festival was an **unqualified success**.*

unquestionably /ʌnˈkwestʃənəbli/ *adv* used to emphasize that something is certainly true: *He is unquestionably the world's greatest living composer.* —**unquestionable** *adj*

unravel /ʌnˈrævəl/ *v* [I,T] **unravelled, unravelling** *BrE*; **unraveled, unraveling** *AmE* **1** if you unravel a complicated situation, or if it unravels, it becomes clear and you start to understand it: *Detectives are trying to unravel the mystery surrounding his death.* **2** if you unravel threads, or if they unravel, they stop being twisted together

unreal /ˌʌnˈrɪəl◂/ *adj* **1** something that is unreal seems so strange that you think you must be imagining it: *The whole situation was completely unreal.* **2** not related to real things that happen: *Many people go into marriage with unreal expectations.* —**unreality** /ˌʌnriˈælⁱti/ *n* [U]

U

unrealistic /ˌʌnrɪəˈlɪstɪk◂/ adj unrealistic ideas are not sensible or based on what is really likely to happen: *She had rather **unrealistic expectations** of marriage.* | *It is unrealistic to expect children to carry heavy equipment.*

unreasonable /ʌnˈriːzənəbəl/ adj **1** not fair or sensible about what you expect: *Do you think I'm being unreasonable?* **2** unreasonable prices, costs etc are too high —**unreasonably** adv

unrecognizable also **-isable** BrE /ʌnˈrekəɡnaɪzəbəl, -ˈrekə-/ adj looking completely different and difficult to recognize

unrelated /ˌʌnrɪˈleɪtɪd◂/ adj events, situations etc that are unrelated are not connected with each other: *The police think the attacks are unrelated.*

unrelenting /ˌʌnrɪˈlentɪŋ◂/ adj formal continuing without stopping and without becoming less unpleasant or difficult: *the unrelenting pressures of the job*

unreliable /ˌʌnrɪˈlaɪəbəl◂/ adj if someone or something is unreliable, you cannot trust them: *The buses here are often unreliable.*

unremarkable /ˌʌnrɪˈmɑːkəbəl◂ $ -ɑːr-/ adj ordinary and not very interesting

unremitting /ˌʌnrɪˈmɪtɪŋ◂/ adj formal never stopping, and never becoming less difficult or unpleasant: *Life here is an **unremitting struggle**.*

unrepentant /ˌʌnrɪˈpentənt◂/ adj not ashamed of your behaviour or beliefs, even though other people disapprove

unrequited /ˌʌnrɪˈkwaɪtɪd◂/ adj **unrequited love** literary when you love someone, but they do not love you

unreservedly /ˌʌnrɪˈzɜːvɪdli $ -ɜːr-/ adv completely: *He **apologized unreservedly**.* —**unreserved** /-ˈzɜːvd◂ $ -ˈzɜːrvd◂/ adj

unresolved /ˌʌnrɪˈzɒlvd◂ $ -ˈzɑːlvd◂, -ˈzɒːlvd◂/ adj an unresolved problem or question has not yet been solved or dealt with: *an unresolved dispute*

unresponsive /ˌʌnrɪˈspɒnsɪv◂ $ -ˈspɑːn-/ adj not reacting to something or not affected by it: *His manner was cold and unresponsive.* | **-to** an illness that is unresponsive to drug treatment

unrest /ʌnˈrest/ n [U] when the people in a country feel angry about something and protest about it, often violently: **political/social/civil unrest** *a period of social unrest* | *the **growing** student **unrest** before the election*

unrestrained /ˌʌnrɪˈstreɪnd◂/ adj not controlled or limited: *unrestrained power*

unrivalled BrE; **unrivaled** AmE /ʌnˈraɪvəld/ adj better than any other: *an unrivaled collection of Chinese art*

unroll /ʌnˈrəʊl $ -ˈroʊl/ v [I,T] to open something that is in the shape of a tube or ball and make it flat, or to become open in this way: *He unrolled his sleeping bag.*

unruffled /ʌnˈrʌfəld/ adj calm and not upset by a difficult situation

unruly /ʌnˈruːli/ adj behaving badly and difficult to control: *unruly schoolchildren*

unsafe /ˌʌnˈseɪf◂/ adj **1** dangerous or likely to cause harm: *The river is unsafe to swim in.* **2** likely to be harmed: *Many people feel **unsafe** in the streets at night.*

unsaid /ʌnˈsed/ adj **be left unsaid** if something is left unsaid, you do not say it although you think it

unsatisfactory /ˌʌnˌsætɪsˈfæktəri/ adj not good enough or not acceptable

unsavoury BrE; **unsavory** AmE /ʌnˈseɪvəri/ adj unpleasant or dishonest: *The bar was full of **unsavoury characters*** (=people).

unscathed /ʌnˈskeɪðd/ adj [not before noun] adv not injured or harmed: *No one **escaped unscathed** from the accident.*

unscrew /ʌnˈskruː/ v [T] to remove or open something by twisting it round: *She unscrewed the light bulb.* → see box at OPEN

unscrupulous /ʌnˈskruːpjələs/ adj behaving in a dishonest way in order to get what you want

unseat /ʌnˈsiːt/ v [T] to remove someone from a powerful position

unseemly /ʌnˈsiːmli/ adj formal unseemly behaviour is not polite or not acceptable in a particular situation

unseen /ˌʌnˈsiːn◂/ adj, adv formal not noticed or seen: *She left the building unseen.*

unselfish /ʌnˈselfɪʃ/ adj caring about other people and thinking about them rather than yourself

unsettled /ʌnˈsetld/ adj **1** an unsettled political or social situation is one in which no one is sure what will happen next: *the unsettled financial markets* **2** worried, upset, or nervous: *Children often **feel unsettled** by moving home.* **3** still continuing without reaching any agreement: *The dispute **remains unsettled**.* **4** if the weather is unsettled, it keeps changing and there is a lot of rain: *Tomorrow will be cloudy and unsettled.* —**unsettle** v [T]

unsettling /ʌnˈsetlɪŋ/ adj making you feel nervous or worried: *It was slightly unsettling seeing so many people watching me.*

unshaven /ʌnˈʃeɪvən/ adj a man who is unshaven has short hairs growing on his face because he has not SHAVEd → see picture at CLEAN-SHAVEN

unsightly /ʌnˈsaɪtli/ adj something that is unsightly is ugly or unpleasant to look at

unskilled /ˌʌnˈskɪld◂/ adj **1** an unskilled worker does not have any special training for a job: *companies employing **unskilled labour*** (=people with no training) **2** unskilled work does not need people with special training

unsocial /ˌʌnˈsəʊʃəl◂ $ -ˈsoʊ-/ also **unsociable** /ʌnˈsəʊʃəbəl $ -ˈsoʊ-/ adj **unsocial hours** when someone has to work very late at night or early in the morning, when most people do not work

unsolicited /ˌʌnsəˈlɪsɪtɪd◂/ adj formal not asked for and not wanted: *unsolicited advice*

unsolved /ˌʌnˈsɒlvd◂ $ -ˈsɑːlvd◂, -ˈsɒːlvd◂/ adj an unsolved problem, mystery etc does not have an answer or explanation yet: *unsolved crimes*

unsophisticated /ˌʌnsəˈfɪstɪkeɪtɪd◂/ adj **1** having little knowledge or experience of life or of things like art, fashion etc: *She was eighteen and quite unsophisticated.* **2** unsophisticated equipment, methods etc are very simple

unsound /ˌʌnˈsaʊnd◂/ adj **1** based on ideas or reasons that are wrong: **scientifically/**

politically etc unsound *The method was educationally unsound.* **2** in bad condition and likely to fall down: *buildings that are **structurally unsound***

unspeakable /ʌnˈspiːkəbəl/ *adj* extremely bad: *unspeakable crimes*

unspecified /ʌnˈspesₗfaɪd/ *adj* not known or not yet announced: *The painting was sold for an unspecified amount.*

unspoiled /ˌʌnˈspɔɪld◂/ also **unspoilt** *BrE* /ˌʌnˈspɔɪlt◂/ *adj* an unspoiled place is beautiful because it has not changed and there are no buildings on it: *unspoiled countryside*

unspoken /ʌnˈspəʊkən $ -ˈspoʊ-/ *adj* not said or discussed with other people: *She nodded in answer to his unspoken question.* | *my unspoken fears*

unstable /ʌnˈsteɪbəl/ *adj* **1** likely to change suddenly and become worse: *The political situation is still very unstable.* **2** someone who is unstable is not always in control of their feelings or behaviour, especially because there is something wrong with them mentally **3** likely to fall over: *an unstable wall*

unsteady /ʌnˈstedi/ *adj* **1** shaking when you walk or hold something, or when you speak, in a way that you cannot control: *I felt hot and **unsteady on my feet** (=as though I might fall over).* | *Her voice was unsteady.* **2** an unsteady object is not firmly in position and might fall

unstoppable /ʌnˈstɒpəbəl $ -ˈstɑːp-/ *adj* not possible to stop or beat: *The team seems unstoppable this year.*

unstuck /ʌnˈstʌk◂/ *adj* **come unstuck a)** *BrE* to fail or start to go wrong: *Our plans came unstuck.* **b)** if something comes unstuck, it becomes separated from the surface that it was stuck to

unsubstantiated /ˌʌnsəbˈstænʃieɪtₗd/ *adj* unsubstantiated reports, stories etc have not been proved to be true

unsuccessful /ˌʌnsəkˈsesfəl◂/ *adj* not achieving what you wanted to achieve: *an **unsuccessful attempt** to climb Everest* —**unsuccessfully** *adv*

unsuitable /ʌnˈsuːtəbəl, -ˈsjuː- $ -ˈsuː-/ *adj* not having the right qualities for a particular person, situation etc: **+for** *The movie is unsuitable for young children.*

unsung /ˌʌnˈsʌŋ◂/ *adj* [only before noun] not praised or famous for something you have done, although you deserve to be: *the **unsung heroes** of the revolution*

unsure /ˌʌnˈʃɔː◂ $ -ˈʃʊr◂/ *adj* **1** not certain about something: **+of/about** *If you are unsure about anything, just ask.* | **unsure what/ whether etc** *I was unsure what reaction I would get.* **2 unsure of yourself** not having very much confidence in yourself → see box at **CONFIDENT**

unsurpassed /ˌʌnsəˈpɑːst◂ $ -sərˈpæst◂/ *adj* better than anyone or anything else

unsuspecting /ˌʌnsəˈspektɪŋ◂/ *adj* not knowing about something that is happening or going to happen: *He would creep up from behind on his **unsuspecting victims**.*

unsweetened /ʌnˈswiːtnd/ *adj* unsweetened food or drink has not had sugar added to it: *unsweetened orange juice*

unswerving /ʌnˈswɜːvɪŋ $ -ˈɜːr-/ *adj* an unswerving belief or attitude is very strong and never changes: *his unswerving loyalty*

unsympathetic /ˌʌnsɪmpəˈθetɪk◂/ *adj* **1** not kind or helpful to someone who is having problems: *Dad was cold and unsympathetic.* **2** not supporting or approving of an idea, aim etc: **+to/towards** *The new committee was unsympathetic to these views.* **3** an unsympathetic character in a book, film etc is unpleasant and difficult to like

untangle /ˌʌnˈtæŋɡəl/ *v* [T] **1** to separate pieces of string, wire etc that are twisted together **2** to understand something that is very complicated

untapped /ˌʌnˈtæpt◂/ *adj* an untapped supply of something has not yet been used: *huge **untapped reserves** of oil and coal*

untenable /ʌnˈtenəbəl/ *adj formal* an untenable position or idea no longer seems right and is impossible to continue with: *His position as chairman proved to be untenable.*

unthinkable /ʌnˈθɪŋkəbəl/ *adj* impossible to imagine or accept: *It is **unthinkable that** a mistake like that could happen.*

untidy /ʌnˈtaɪdi/ *adj especially BrE*
1 not neat [= **messy**]: *an untidy room* | *untidy hair* | *Why's your desk always so untidy?*
2 an untidy person does not keep their house, clothes, hair etc neat [= **messy**]: *Most teenagers are pretty untidy.*

untie /ʌnˈtaɪ/ *v* [T] **untied, untying, unties** to unfasten something that has been tied in a knot: *Can you help me untie the rope?* → see box at **FASTEN**

until /ʌnˈtɪl, ən-/ also **till** *prep, linking word*
1 if something happens until a time, it continues and then stops at that time: *The banks are open until 3.30.* | *He waited until she had finished speaking.*

THESAURUS

Until and **till** are used to talk about the time when something stops: *They stayed until/till after midnight.*
As far as is used to talk about the place where something stops: *Does the bus go as far as the station?*
Up to is used mainly to talk about the final number or the biggest possible number: *The children had to count up to fifty.*

2 not until used to say that something will not happen before a particular time: *The movie doesn't start until 8.* | *We won't start until everyone's here.*

untimely /ʌnˈtaɪmli/ *adj* happening too soon: *her **untimely death***

untold /ˌʌnˈtəʊld◂ $ -ˈtoʊld◂/ *adj* [only before noun] very bad or very great: *The floods caused **untold damage**.*

untouched /ˌʌnˈtʌtʃt◂/ *adj* **1** not changed, affected, or damaged in any way: **+by** *an area untouched by human activity* **2** food or drink that is untouched has not been eaten or drunk

untoward /ˌʌntəˈwɔːd $ ʌnˈtɔːrd/ *adj* unpleasant or unacceptable: **nothing/anything untoward** *Nothing untoward happened.*

U

untrained /ˌʌnˈtreɪnd◂/ *adj* **1** not trained to do a job: *untrained staff* **2 to the untrained eye/ear** to someone who does not know a lot about something: *To the untrained eye, the painting looks like a Van Gogh.*

untreated /ʌnˈtriːtᵻd/ *adj* **1** an untreated illness has not had medical treatment **2** an untreated substance has not been made safe: *untreated water*

untried /ˌʌnˈtraɪd◂/ *adj* new and not yet tested or proved to be good: *a young untried actress*

untrue /ʌnˈtruː/ *adj* not true: *Most of what she said was untrue.*

untruth /ʌnˈtruːθ, ˈʌntruːθ/ *n* [C] *formal* something that is not true [= lie]

untruthful /ʌnˈtruːθfəl/ *adj* saying things that are untrue

untying /ʌnˈtaɪ-ɪŋ/ *v* the present participle of UNTIE

unused¹ /ˌʌnˈjuːzd◂/ *adj* not being used at the moment, or never used: *unused land*

unused² /ʌnˈjuːst/ *adj* **unused to (doing) sth** not having any experience of something: *She's unused to driving at night.* | *I was unused to the hot climate.*

unusual /ʌnˈjuːʒuəl, -ʒəl/ *adj* different from what is usual or normal: *a very unusual situation* | **be unusual for sb/sth** *He seemed sad, which was unusual for him.* | **it is unusual for sb to do sth** *It's unusual for Paul to be late.* | **it is unusual to do sth** *It's unusual to have snow in April.*

unusually /ʌnˈjuːʒuəli, -ʒəli/ *adv* **1 unusually hot/big/quiet etc** hotter, bigger etc than is usual: *That winter was unusually cold.* **2** in a way that is different from usual: +**for** *Unusually for Michael, he arrived on time.*

unveil /ʌnˈveɪl/ *v* [T] to show the public something for the first time, or tell them about a new plan, product etc: *He unveiled a painting of the princess in a pink gown.* | *The chairman unveiled plans for a £100 million stadium.*

unwanted /ʌnˈwɒntᵻd $ -ˈwɒːnt-, -ˈwɑːnt-/ *adj* not wanted: *an unwanted gift* | *an unwanted pregnancy*

unwarranted /ʌnˈwɒrəntᵻd $ -ˈwɔː-, -ˈwɑː-/ *adj formal* done without any good reason: *unwarranted demands for further payment*

unwary /ʌnˈweəri $ -ˈweri/ *adj* not knowing about possible problems or dangers and easy to harm or deceive: *unwary tourists*

unwelcome /ʌnˈwelkəm/ *adj* not wanted: *unwelcome changes* | *an unwelcome visitor*

unwell /ʌnˈwel/ *adj* [not before noun] *formal* ill: *Anna's feeling unwell today.*

unwieldy /ʌnˈwiːldi/ *adj* difficult to move or use: *a large, unwieldy shopping trolley*

unwilling /ʌnˈwɪlɪŋ/ *adj* not wanting to do something, or refusing to do it: **unwilling to do sth** *He's unwilling to admit he was wrong.* —**unwillingly** *adv* —**unwillingness** *n* [U]

unwind /ʌnˈwaɪnd/ *v* past tense and past participle **unwound** /-ˈwaʊnd/ **1** [I] to relax and stop thinking about your work or problems: *Swimming helps me unwind.* **2** [I,T] to undo something that has been wrapped around something else, or to come undone: *He unwound the rope.* | *The snake slowly unwound.*

unwise /ˌʌnˈwaɪz◂/ *adj* not sensible and likely to cause problems: *an unwise decision* | *It's unwise to drink before driving.* —**unwisely** *adv*

unwittingly /ʌnˈwɪtɪŋli/ *adv* without knowing or realizing something: *Seb had unwittingly broken the law.* —**unwitting** *adj*

unworkable /ʌnˈwɜːkəbəl $ -ɜːr-/ *adj* a plan, idea etc that is unworkable cannot succeed

unwound /ʌnˈwaʊnd/ *v* the past tense and past participle of UNWIND

unwrap

unwrapping a present

unwrap /ʌnˈræp/ *v* [T] **unwrapped, unwrapping** to remove the paper that is covering something: *Sally was unwrapping her birthday presents.* → see box at OPEN

unwritten /ʌnˈrɪtn/ *adj* an unwritten rule or law is one that everyone knows about although it is not official

unyielding /ʌnˈjiːldɪŋ/ *adj* refusing to change what you believe or what you want: *The terrorists were unyielding in their demands.*

unzip /ʌnˈzɪp/ *v* [T] **unzipped, unzipping** to open something by undoing the ZIP on it → see box at FASTEN

up¹ /ʌp/ *adv, prep*
1 towards or in a higher place [≠ **down**]: *They began walking up the hill.* | *Can you move the picture up a little higher?* | *Dave's up in his room.* → see picture on page A8
2 into an upright position: **get/sit/stand up** *The children stood up to sing.* | *He turned up the collar of his coat.*
3 further along something: **up the street/road/river etc** *She lives just up the street.* | *Can you move up* (=move along) *a little?*
4 if the amount or level of something is up, it has increased: +**by** *Inflation is up by 2%.* | *Violent crime went up last year.*
5 walk/go/come etc up to move towards someone or something until you are very near them: *A man came up and asked me for a cigarette.* | +**to** *She drove right up to the door.*
6 in or towards the north: *His relatives live up in Scotland.*
7 not in bed: *We were up all night.* | *They stayed up to watch the game.* | *He's up and about* (=well and not in bed) *again after his illness.*
8 beating your opponent by a particular number of points: **two goals/three points etc up** *United were two goals up at half time.*
9 up and down a) backwards and forwards: *He walked up and down, thinking carefully.* **b)** to a higher position and then a lower one, several times: *The kids were jumping up and down on the bed.*

10 up to sth a) as much or as many as a particular number or amount: *I can get up to six people in the car.* → see box at **UNTIL** **b)** also **up until** until a particular date or time: *The offer is valid up to December 15.* **c)** as good as a particular level or standard: *This essay isn't up to your usual standard.* **d)** well enough to do something, or good enough to do a particular job: *Do you feel up to a walk?* | *He isn't really up to the job.* **e)** doing something secret or something that you should not be doing: *I think Nick's up to something.*

11 it's up to sb used to say that someone has to decide about something: *'Should I go?' 'It's up to you.'*

12 be up against sth to have to compete against a very difficult opponent, or deal with a very difficult situation: *We're up against some of the biggest companies in the world.*

13 *spoken* if a period of time is up, it has finished: *She left when two weeks were up.*

14 be up for sale/discussion etc to be available to be sold, discussed etc: *Their house is up for sale.*

15 if a computer system is up, it is working: *Are the computers up and running yet?*
→ **UPS AND DOWNS**

up² *v* [T] **upped, upping** to increase the amount or level of something: **up sth to/by sth** *They've upped her salary to £35,000.*

,up-and-'coming *adj* likely to become successful: *an up-and-coming actor*

upbeat /'ʌpbiːt/ *adj* cheerful and making you feel that good things will happen: *a movie with an upbeat ending*

upbringing /'ʌp,brɪŋɪŋ/ *n* [singular] the way that your parents care for you and teach you to behave when you are a child: *He had a very strict upbringing.*

upcoming /'ʌp,kʌmɪŋ/ *adj* [only before noun] happening soon: *the upcoming elections*

update¹ /ʌp'deɪt/ *v* [T] to add the most recent information to something, or to make something more modern: *We need to update some of the older files.*

update² /'ʌpdeɪt/ *n* [C] the most recent information about a news story: **+on** *an update on the earthquake*

upend /ʌp'end/ *v* [T] to turn something over so that it is upside down

upfront¹ /,ʌp'frʌnt◂/ *adv* if you pay someone upfront, you pay them before they do any work for you

upfront² *adj spoken* behaving or talking in an honest and open way about something: **+about** *He was quite upfront about his feelings.*

upgrade /ʌp'greɪd/ *v* [T] to improve something, or change it for something better: *We need to upgrade our computer.* —**upgrade** /'ʌpgreɪd/ *n* [C]

upheaval /ʌp'hiːvəl/ *n* [C,U] a very big change, especially one that causes problems: *Moving house is a major upheaval.*

uphill /,ʌp'hɪl◂/ *adj, adv* **1** towards the top of a hill [≠ **downhill**]: *an uphill climb* **2 an uphill struggle/battle/task etc** something that is difficult to do and needs a lot of effort

uphold /ʌp'həʊld $ -'hoʊld/ *v* [T] past tense and past participle **upheld** /-'held/ *formal* to support a law or decision: *The job of the police is to uphold law and order.*

upholstery /ʌp'həʊlstəri $ -'hoʊl-/ *n* [U] material used to cover chairs: *leather upholstery*

upkeep /'ʌpkiːp/ *n* [U] the process and cost of keeping something in good condition, or looking after a child or animal: **+of** *The money went towards the upkeep of the church.*

uplands /'ʌpləndz/ *n* [plural] high areas of land —**upland** *adj*

uplifting /ʌp'lɪftɪŋ/ *adj* making you feel happier and more hopeful: *an uplifting experience*

upmarket /,ʌp'mɑːkɪt◂ $ -ɑːr-/ *adj* especially *BrE* intended for or used by people who are rich and like expensive things: *an upmarket restaurant*

upon /ə'pɒn $ ə'pɑːn/ *prep formal* on: *The trip was dependent upon the weather.* | *a vicious attack upon the government*

upper /'ʌpə $ -ər/ *adj* [only before noun]
1 in a higher position than another part of something [≠ **lower**]: *the upper jaw* | *the upper floors of the building*
2 more important than other parts in an organization, system etc: *the upper job levels in the company* | *areas at the upper end of the housing market*
3 have/get/gain the upper hand to have more power than someone else, so that you are able to control a situation: *The Republicans seem to have the upper hand.*
4 upper limit the most, highest etc that is possible or allowed: **+of** *a short story with an upper limit of 5000 words*

,upper 'case *n* [U] CAPITAL LETTERS (A, B, C etc not a, b, c etc) [➡ **lower case**]

,upper 'class *n* **the upper class/classes** the group of people who belong to the highest social class

uppermost /'ʌpəməʊst $ -pərmoʊst/ *adj*
1 be uppermost in sb's mind to be the thing that someone is thinking about most of all: *Exams were uppermost in my mind.* **2** [only before noun] highest: *the uppermost branches of the tree*

upright /'ʌpraɪt/ *adj, adv*
1 standing, sitting, or pointing straight up: **sit/ stand/walk upright** *When did man first walk upright?* | *Please put your seat in an upright position.*
2 always behaving in an honest way: *upright citizens*

uprising /'ʌp,raɪzɪŋ/ *n* [C] an attempt by people in a country to change their government by force: *an armed uprising* (=using weapons) → see box at **REVOLUTION**

upriver /,ʌp'rɪvə $ -ər/ *adv* in the opposite direction to the way the river is flowing

uproar /'ʌp-rɔː $ -rɔːr/ *n* [singular, U] a lot of noise, shouting, or angry protest about something: *The announcement caused an uproar.* | **in (an) uproar** *The whole class was in uproar.*

uproot /ʌp'ruːt/ *v* [T] **1** to pull a plant and its roots out of the ground **2** to make someone leave their home and move to a new place: *If I take the job, I'll have to uproot the whole family.*

U

,ups and 'downs n [plural] the good and bad things that happen in life, business etc: *Every marriage has its ups and downs.*

upscale /ˌʌpˈskeɪl/ adj AmE used by rich people from a high social class [= **upmarket** BrE]: *upscale housing*

upset¹ /ˌʌpˈset◂/ adj
1 unhappy because something unpleasant or disappointing has happened: **+about/at** *She's still very upset about her father's death.* | **+that** *He was upset that Helen had lied to him.* | *When I told him he'd failed, he got very upset.* → see box at SAD
2 upset stomach/tummy when an illness affects your stomach

upset² /ʌpˈset/ v [T] past tense and past participle **upset** present participle **upsetting 1** to make someone feel unhappy or angry: *Kopp's comments upset many of his listeners.* **2** to change something in a way that causes problems: *I hope I haven't upset all your plans.* **3** to push something over, usually accidentally: *He upset the table and everything on it.*

upset³ /ˈʌpset/ n **1** [C,U] unhappiness, or something that causes it: *His decision caused great upset.* **2** [C] when a player or team unexpectedly wins: *There's been a big upset in the French Open tennis.* **3** [C] an unexpected problem **4 stomach upset** when your stomach is affected by an illness

upsetting /ʌpˈsetɪŋ/ adj something that is upsetting makes you feel shocked and unhappy: *an upsetting experience*

upshot /ˈʌpʃɒt $ -ʃɑːt/ n **the upshot (of sth)** the final result of a situation: *The upshot is that she's decided to take the job.* → see box at RESULT

upside /ˈʌpsaɪd/ n [singular] the good part of a situation: **+of** *The upside is that we got a free trip to Jamaica.*

,upside 'down, upside-down adj, adv
1 with the top at the bottom and the bottom at the top: *Isn't that picture upside down?* | *an upside-down U shape*
2 turn sth upside down a) to move a lot of things and make a place untidy because you are looking for something: *The police turned the place upside down.* **b)** to change something completely: *Her life had been turned upside down by the accident.*

upstage /ʌpˈsteɪdʒ/ v [T] to do something that takes people's attention away from a more important person or event

upstairs /ˌʌpˈsteəz◂ $ -ˈsterz◂/ adj, adv on or towards a higher floor of a building [≠ **downstairs**]: *The kids went upstairs to bed.* | *Her office is upstairs on your right.* | *an upstairs window*

upstart /ˈʌpstɑːt $ -ɑːrt/ n [C] disapproving someone who has recently become involved in something or become more powerful, and who is thought to be too confident about themselves

upstate /ˈʌpsteɪt/ adj, adv AmE in or towards the northern part of a state: *She lives upstate.*

upstream /ˌʌpˈstriːm◂/ adv along a river in the opposite direction from the way the water is flowing

upsurge /ˈʌpsɜːdʒ $ -sɜːrdʒ/ n [C] a sudden increase: **+in/of** *the recent upsurge in crime*

uptake /ˈʌpteɪk/ n **be slow/quick on the uptake** informal to be slow or fast at understanding or learning things

uptight /ˌʌptaɪt, ˌʌpˈtaɪt/ adj informal behaving in an angry way because you are nervous and worried: *You shouldn't get so uptight about it.*

,up-to-'date adj
1 up-to-date information includes the most recent facts available: *access to up-to-date medical information* | **keep (sb) up-to-date (with/on sth)** *Keep me up-to-date with the latest developments.*
2 modern: *the most up-to-date technology* | *The design has been brought bang up-to-date* (=made very modern). → see box at MODERN

,up-to-the-'minute adj including the most recent information, details etc: *a service that provides up-to-the-minute information on share prices*

uptown /ˌʌpˈtaʊn◂/ adj, adv AmE to or in the northern area of a city or town, or the area where richer people live [➡ **downtown**]: *The Parkers live uptown.*

upturn /ˈʌptɜːn $ -tɜːrn/ n [C] when economic conditions improve and business activity increases: *an upturn in the economy*

upturned /ˌʌpˈtɜːnd◂ $ -ˈtɜːr-/ adj **1** pointing or facing upwards: *an upturned nose* **2** turned upside down: *I sat on an upturned box.*

upward /ˈʌpwəd $ -wərd/ adj [only before noun] **1** towards a higher position [≠ **downward**]: *an upward movement of his hand* **2** increasing to a higher level [≠ **downward**]: *the recent upward trend in house prices*

upwards /ˈʌpwədz $ -wərdz/ also **upward** especially AmE adv
1 towards a higher position [≠ **downwards**]: *Billy pointed upward at the clouds.*
2 increasing to a higher level [≠ **downwards**]: *Salaries have been moving steadily upwards.*
3 upwards of sth more than an amount: *paintings valued at upwards of $100 million*

uranium /juˈreɪniəm/ n [U] a RADIOACTIVE metal used to produce NUCLEAR power and weapons

Uranus /ˈjʊərənəs, jʊˈreɪnəs $ ˈjʊr-, jʊˈreɪ-/ n the seventh PLANET from the sun

urban /ˈɜːbən $ ˈɜːr-/ adj in or relating to a town or city [➡ **rural**]: *urban areas*

urbane /ɜːˈbeɪn $ ɜːr-/ adj behaving in a relaxed and confident way in social situations

urge¹ /ɜːdʒ $ ɜːrdʒ/ v [T] to strongly suggest that someone do something: **urge sb to do sth** *Her friends urged her to go to France.* | **+that** *The report urged that there should be no further cuts.*
urge sb ⇔ on phr v to encourage someone to try harder, go faster etc: *Urged on by the crowd, they scored two more goals.*

urge² n [C] a strong wish or need: *sexual urges* | **urge to do sth** *I felt a sudden urge to hit him.*

urgent /ˈɜːdʒənt $ ˈɜːr-/ adj if something is urgent, it is very important and needs to be dealt with immediately: *an urgent message* | *She's in urgent need of medical attention.* | *calls for urgent action to tackle the situation*
—**urgency** n [U] *a matter of great urgency*
—**urgently** adv. *Help is urgently needed.*

urinal /'juər̯nəl, juˈraɪ- $ 'jurl̩-/ n [C] a toilet where men urinate

urinate /'juər̯neɪt $ 'jur-/ v [I] *technical* to make urine flow out of your body

urine /'juər̯n $ 'jur-/ n [U] liquid waste that comes out of your body when you go to the toilet

urn /ɜːn $ ɜːrn/ n [C] **1** a large container in which tea or coffee is made **2** a decorated container, especially one that is used for holding the ASHES of a dead person

us /əs, s; *strong* ʌs/ *pron* the object form of 'we': *I'm sure he didn't see us.* | *You four go in the car and the rest of us can get a taxi.* | *an issue affecting us all*

usable /'juːzəbəl/ adj something that is usable is in a good enough condition to be used

usage /'juːsɪdʒ, 'juːz-/ n **1** [C,U] the way that words are used in a language: *a book on modern English usage* **2** [U] the way in which something is used, or the amount that it is used: *Car usage has increased dramatically.*

use¹ /juːz/ v [T]

1 if you use something, you do something with it for a particular purpose: *Can I use your phone?* | **use sth to do sth** *Use a food processor to grate the vegetables.* | *The system is easy to use.*

2 to need or take an amount of electricity, petrol, food etc [= **consume**]: *These light bulbs use less electricity.* | *Our car's using too much oil.*

3 to treat someone in an unkind and unfair way in order to get something that you want: *Can't you see that Andy is just using you?*

4 to say or write a particular word or phrase: *Why did you use the word 'if'?* | *Don't use bad language.*

use sth ⇔ **up** *phr v* to use all of something: *Who used up the toothpaste?*

use² /juːs/ n

1 [U] when people use something to do something: **+of** *Are you in favour of the use of animals for research?* | *an exit for emergency use*

2 [C] a purpose for which something can be used: *The drug has many uses.*

3 **make use of sth** to use something that is available: *Try to make good use of your time.*

4 **the use of sth** the right or ability to use something: *Joe's given me the use of his office.* | *She lost the use of both legs.*

5 **be (of) no use (to sb)** to not be useful to someone: *The ticket's of no use to me now.*

6 **it's no use (doing sth)** also **what's the use (of doing sth)** *spoken* used to say that something will not have any effect: *It's no use arguing with her. She just won't listen.*

7 **put sth to good use** to use your knowledge, skills etc well: *a chance to put your medical training to good use*

8 **in use** being used: *The meeting room is in use all morning.*

9 [C] one of the meanings of a word or phrase, or a way in which it is used [➡ **usage**]: *an interesting use of the word 'brave'*

used¹ /juːst/ adj **be used to (doing) sth** if you are used to something, you have experienced it many times before and it no longer seems surprising, difficult etc: *He's used to getting up early.* | *I soon got used to the Japanese way of life.* → see box at USED TO

used² /juːzd/ adj used cars, clothes etc have already been owned by someone and are then sold [= **secondhand**] → see box at OLD

used to /'juːst tuː/ *modal verb* if something used to happen, it happened often or regularly in the past but does not happen now: *We used to go to the movies every week.* | *'Didn't you used to smoke?' 'Yes, but I quit.'*

USAGE

Used to is used to talk about something that someone did regularly in the past: *I used to play tennis twice a week, but I don't have time now.*
Be used to and **get used to** are used to talk about being or becoming more comfortable with a situation or activity, so that it does not seem surprising, difficult etc: *Are you used to the cold winters yet?* | *I can't get used to living in a big city.*

---

useful /'juːsfəl/ adj something that is useful helps you to do or get what you want [≠ **useless**]: *a useful book for travellers* | **+for** *Trade fairs are useful for meeting new clients.* | *It's useful to make a list before you start.* | *His knowledge of Italian was to come in useful* (=be useful) *later on.*

—**usefully** adv —**usefulness** n [U]

useless /'juːsləs/ adj

1 not useful or effective at all [≠ **useful**]: *useless information* | **virtually/completely/totally etc useless** *These scissors are completely useless.* | **+for** *The land is useless for growing crops.* | **it is useless doing sth/to do sth** *It's useless trying to talk to her.*

2 *informal* very bad at doing something: **+at** *I'm useless at golf.*

user /'juːzə $ -ər/ n [C] someone who uses a product, service etc: *computer users*

user-'friendly adj something that is user-friendly is designed so that it is easy to use

'user name n [C] a name or word that you use to enter a computer system or use the Internet

usher¹ /'ʌʃə $ -ər/ v [T] to take someone into or out of a room or building: *His secretary ushered us into his office.*

usher in sth *phr v* to make something new start happening: *Gorbachev ushered in a new era of reform.*

usher² n [C] someone who shows people to their seats in a theatre, at a wedding etc

usual /'juːʒuəl, 'juːʒəl/ adj

1 the same as what happens most of the time or in most situations [➡ **unusual**]: *Plant the bulbs in the usual way.* | *Let's meet at the usual place.* | **longer/bigger/worse etc than usual** *The food was even worse than usual.* | *It was usual for young mothers to stay at home.*

2 **as usual** in the way that happens on most occasions or most of the time: *They were late, as usual.*

usually /'juːʒuəli, 'juːʒəli/ adv used to say what happens on most occasions or in most situations: *We usually go out for dinner on Saturday.* | *I usually walk to work.*

usurp /juːˈzɜːp $ -ˈsɜːrp/ v [T] *formal* to take someone else's power, position, or job

U

utensil /juːˈtensəl/ n [C] formal a tool or object that you use for doing something, especially for cooking: *kitchen utensils*

uterus /ˈjuːtərəs/ n [C] plural **uteruses** technical the part of a woman or female MAMMAL where babies develop [= **womb**]

utilities /juːˈtɪlɨtiz/ n [plural] services such as gas or electricity provided for people to use: *Does the rent include utilities?*

u'tility ˌroom n [C] a room in a house where you can have your washing machine, FREEZER etc

utilize also **-ise** BrE /ˈjuːtɨlaɪz/ v [T] formal to use something —**utilization** /ˌjuːtɨlaɪˈzeɪʃən $ -lə-/ n [U]

utmost[1] /ˈʌtməʊst $ -moʊst/ adj **the utmost importance/care etc** the greatest possible importance, care etc: *a matter of the utmost importance*

utmost[2] n [singular] the most that can be done: *The team **did** their **utmost** (=tried as hard as possible) to have it finished on time.* | *The course challenges drivers **to the utmost**.*

utopia /juːˈtəʊpiə $ -ˈtoʊ-/ n [C,U] an imaginary perfect world —**utopian** adj: *a utopian society*

utter[1] /ˈʌtə $ -ər/ adj complete or extreme: *That's **utter nonsense!*** | *We watched in **utter** amazement.* | *It was a **complete and utter** failure.* —**utterly** adv: *That's **utterly ridiculous!*** → see box at COMPLETELY

utter[2] v [T] literary to say something: *No one uttered a word.* —**utterance** n [C]

U-turn /ˈjuː tɜːn $ ˌjuː ˈtɜːrn/ n [C] **1** if a driver does a U-turn, they turn their car around in the road and go back in the direction they came from **2** a complete change of ideas, plans etc: **+on/over** *a government U-turn on economic policy*

V, v

V, v /viː/ n [C,U] plural **V's, v's** the 22nd letter of the English alphabet

v. also **v** BrE **1** the written abbreviation of **verb 2** BrE informal the written abbreviation of **very 3** a written abbreviation of **versus 4** the written abbreviation of **volt**

vacancy /ˈveɪkənsi/ n [C] plural **vacancies 1** a job that is available for someone to start doing: *information about **job vacancies*** | **+for** *Are there any vacancies for cooks?* **2** a room that is available in a hotel

vacant /ˈveɪkənt/ adj **1** empty and available for someone to use: *vacant apartments* **2** if a position in an organization is vacant, the job is

available because no one is doing it: *The post of Director became vacant.* **3** if someone has a vacant expression, they do not seem to be thinking about anything —**vacantly** adv

vacate /vəˈkeɪt, veɪ- $ ˈveɪkeɪt/ v [T] formal to leave a seat, room etc so that someone else can use it: *Guests must vacate their rooms by noon.*

vacation[1] /vəˈkeɪʃən $ veɪ-/ n [C,U]

1 AmE a period of time that you spend in another place for enjoyment [= **holiday** BrE]: *We're thinking of **taking a vacation** in the Virgin Islands.* | **on vacation** *I went there once on vacation.*

2 especially AmE a period of time when you do not have to work or go to school [= **holiday** BrE]: *the summer vacation* | **on vacation** *They're on vacation for the next two weeks.* | *Contractors aren't entitled to paid **vacation time**.*

vacation[2] v [I] AmE to go somewhere for a holiday [= **holiday** BrE] —**vacationer** n [C]

vaccinate /ˈvæksɨneɪt/ v [T] to give someone a vaccine to protect them from a disease: *The children should all be vaccinated against measles.*

vaccination /ˌvæksɨˈneɪʃən/ n [C,U] when someone is given a vaccine to protect them from a disease: *a vaccination against measles*

vaccine /ˈvæksiːn $ vækˈsiːn/ n [C,U] a substance used to protect people against a disease which contains a weak form of the VIRUS that causes the disease

vacuum[1] /ˈvækjuəm, -kjʊm/ n **1** [C] a vacuum cleaner **2** [C] a space that is completely empty of all air or gas **3** [singular] a situation in which someone or something is missing or lacking: *His death left a vacuum in her life.*

vacuum[2] v [I,T] to clean a place using a vacuum cleaner

'vacuum ˌcleaner n [C] a machine that cleans floors by sucking up the dirt from them

'vacuum ˌflask n [C] BrE a container like a bottle that keeps drinks hot or cold

vagaries /ˈveɪɡəriz/ n [plural] formal changes and events that cannot be controlled: *the vagaries of fashion*

vagina /vəˈdʒaɪnə/ n [C] the part that connects a woman's outer sexual organs to her UTERUS —**vaginal** /vəˈdʒaɪnəl $ ˈvædʒɨnəl/ adj

vagrant /ˈveɪɡrənt/ n [C] formal someone who has no home or work

vague /veɪɡ/ adj not clear or certain: **+about** *She's been a bit vague about her plans for the summer.* | **have a vague idea/feeling etc** *I had only a vague idea where the house was.* | *Looking closely, he could just see the vague outline of her face.*

vaguely /ˈveɪɡli/ adv **1** slightly: *The woman's face looked vaguely familiar.* **2** in a way that is not clear or exact [≠ **clearly**]: *a vaguely worded statement* **3** in a way that shows you are not thinking about what you are doing: *He smiled vaguely.*

vain /veɪn/ adj **1** disapproving too proud of yourself, especially of your appearance [➔ **vanity**]: *Men can be so vain.* → see box at PROUD **2 in vain** without success: *Doctors tried in vain to save his life.* **3 vain attempt/hope etc** a vain hope or attempt is not successful —**vainly** adv

Valentine /'væləntaɪn/ also **'Valentine's ,card** n [C] a card that you send to someone you love on Valentine's Day (February 14)

valet /'vælɪt, 'væleɪ $ væ'leɪ/ n [C] **1** a male servant who takes care of a man's clothes, serves his meals etc **2** *AmE* someone who parks your car for you at a hotel or restaurant

valiant /'væliənt/ adj *formal* very brave: *a valiant rescue attempt* —**valiantly** adv

valid /'vælɪd/ adj **1** a valid ticket, document, or agreement is legally or officially acceptable [≠ **invalid**]: *a valid passport* | *Your return ticket is valid for three months.* **2** a valid reason, argument etc is based on something reasonable or sensible: *a valid criticism* —**validity** /və'lɪdɪti/ n [U]

validate /'vælɪdeɪt/ v [T] *formal* to show that something is true or correct

valley /'væli/ n [C] an area of lower land between two lines of hills or mountains: *a village in the Loire valley* → see box at **MOUNTAIN**

valour *BrE*; **valor** *AmE* /'vælə $ -ər/ n [U] *literary* great courage, especially in war

valuable /'væljuəbəl, -jʊbəl $ 'væljʊbəl/ adj
1 worth a lot of money [≠ **worthless**]: *a valuable ring*
2 help, advice etc that is valuable is very useful [➡ **invaluable**]: *volunteers who have made a valuable contribution to our work*

valuables /'væljuəbəlz, -jʊbəlz $ -jʊbəlz/ n [plural] things that you own that are worth a lot of money, such as jewellery or cameras: *Put your valuables in the hotel safe.* → see box at **OWN**

valuation /,væljuˈeɪʃən/ n [C,U] when people decide how much something is worth

value[1] /'væljuː/ n
1 [C,U] the amount of money that something is worth: +**of** *the value of the house* | **increase/go up/fall etc in value** *The dollar has been steadily increasing in value.* | *Did the thieves take anything of value* (=worth a lot of money)?
2 [U] the importance or usefulness of something: +**of** *the value of direct personal experience* | **of great/little value** *His research was of great value to doctors working with the disease.*
3 good/excellent etc value used to say that something is worth the amount you pay for it: *At only $45 a night, it's great value for your money.* → see box at **CHEAP**
4 values [plural] your beliefs about what is right and wrong, or about what is important in life: *traditional family values*
→ **FACE VALUE**

value[2] v [T] **1** to think that something is important and worth having: *I always value your advice.* **2** to say how much something is worth: *a painting valued at $5 million*

valve /vælv/ n [C] a part of a tube that opens and closes to control the flow of liquid, air etc passing through: *the valves of the heart* → see picture at **BICYCLE**

vampire /'væmpaɪə $ -paɪr/ n [C] in stories, a dead person who bites people's necks and sucks their blood

van /væn/ n [C] a vehicle used for carrying goods which is smaller than a truck, and which has a roof and metal sides: *a delivery van*

vandal /'vændl/ n [C] someone who deliberately damages things, especially public property

vandalize also **-ise** *BrE* /'vændəl-aɪz/ v [T] to deliberately damage things, especially public property —**vandalism** /-lɪzəm/ n [U]

vanguard /'vænɡɑːd $ -ɡɑːrd/ n **in the vanguard (of sth)** involved in the greatest way in something, especially in developing something new: *a group in the vanguard of political reform*

vanilla /və'nɪlə/ n [U] a substance with a slightly sweet taste, used in ICE CREAM and other foods

vanish /'vænɪʃ/ v [I] to disappear suddenly, especially in a way that cannot be easily explained: *When I looked again, he'd vanished.* | +**from** *The bird vanished from sight.* | *The smile vanished from her face.* | *The ship vanished without trace* (=disappeared, leaving no sign of what had happened to it).

vanity /'vænɪti/ n [U] *disapproving* when someone is too proud of their appearance or their abilities [➡ **vain**]

vanquish /'væŋkwɪʃ/ v [T] *literary* to defeat someone or something completely

vantage point /'vɑːntɪdʒ pɔɪnt $ 'væn-/ n [C] a good position from which you can look at something

vaporize also **-ise** *BrE* /'veɪpəraɪz/ v [I,T] to be changed into a vapour, or to change a liquid into a vapour

vapour *BrE*; **vapor** *AmE* /'veɪpə $ -ər/ n [C,U] many small drops of liquid that float in the air: *water vapour*

variable[1] /'veəriəbəl $ 'ver-/ adj likely to change often or to be different [➡ **vary**]: *a variable rate of interest* | *Hospital food is highly variable in quality.* —**variability** /,veəriə'bɪlɪti $,ver-/ n [U]

variable[2] n [C] something that may be different in different situations: *economic variables*

variance /'veəriəns $ 'ver-/ n **be at variance (with sth/sb)** *formal* if two things or people are at variance with each other, they are very different or do not agree

variant /'veəriənt $ 'ver-/ n [C] something that is slightly different from the usual form of something: *a spelling variant* —**variant** adj

variation /,veəri'eɪʃən $,ver-/ n **1** [C,U] a difference between similar things, or a change from the usual amount or form of something [➡ **vary**]: +**in** *variations in price from store to store* | +**between/within/among** *There is considerable variation between different areas.* **2** [C] something that is done in a slightly different way to normal: *This is the traditional recipe, but of course there are many variations.*

varicose veins /,værɪkəʊs 'veɪnz $ -koʊs-/ n [plural] a medical condition in which the VEINS in your leg become swollen and painful

varied /'veərid $ 'ver-/ adj including many different types of things: *a varied diet*

variety /və'raɪəti/ n plural **varieties**
1 a variety of sth a lot of different types of things or people: *The college offers a wide variety of language courses.* | *Potatoes can be cooked in a variety of ways.*
2 [U] the different things or activities which

V

something involves and which make it interesting: *I wanted a job with plenty of variety.*
3 [C] a type of something: **+of** *different varieties of lettuce*

various /'veəriəs $ 'ver-/ *adj* several different: *The coat is available in various colours.* | *He decided to leave school for various reasons.*

variously /'veəriəsli $ 'ver-/ *adv* in many different ways: *He's been variously called a genius and a madman.*

varnish[1] /'vɑːnɪʃ $ 'vɑːr-/ *n* [C,U] a clear liquid that is painted onto wood to protect it and give it a shiny surface

varnish[2] *v* [T] to paint something with VARNISH

vary /'veəri $ 'veri/ *v* **varied, varying, varies**
1 [I] if things vary, they are all different from each other: **vary from sth to sth** *Prices vary from £15 to £25.* | **+in** *The flowers vary in colour and size.*
2 [I] to change: **+according to** *His moods seem to vary according to the weather.* | *'What do you wear when you go out?' 'Well it varies.'*
3 [T] to regularly change what you do or the way that you do it: *You need to vary your diet.*
—**varying** *adj: varying degrees of success*

vase /vɑːz $ veɪs, veɪz/ *n* [C] a container used for putting flowers in

vasectomy /və'sektəmi/ *n* [C] plural **vasectomies** a medical operation to prevent a man from having children

vast /vɑːst $ væst/ *adj*
1 extremely large [= huge]: *vast areas of rainforest* | *Refugees crossed the border in vast numbers.* → see box at BIG
2 the vast majority almost all of a group of people or things

vastly /'vɑːstli $ 'væstli/ *adv formal* very much: *The two books are vastly different.*

vat /væt/ *n* [C] a very large container for keeping liquids in

VAT /ˌviː eɪ 'tiː, væt/ *n* [U] **value added tax** a tax on goods and services in Britain and Europe

vault[1] /vɔːlt $ vɒːlt/ *n* [C] **1** a room in a bank with thick walls and a strong door, used for keeping money, jewels etc safely **2** a room where people from the same family are buried

vault[2] *v* [I,T] to jump over something in one movement, using your hands or a pole to help you: **+over** *He vaulted over the fence and ran off.* → see box at JUMP

VCR /ˌviː siː 'ɑː $ -'ɑːr/ *n* [C] **video cassette recorder** a machine used for recording television programmes or playing videos

VD /ˌviː 'diː/ *n* [U] **venereal disease** a disease that is passed from one person to another during sex

VDU /ˌviː diː 'juː/ *n* [C] **visual display unit** a computer screen [= monitor]

-'ve /v, əv/ the short form of 'have': *We've finished.*

veal /viːl/ *n* [U] meat from a CALF (=very young cow) → see box at MEAT

veer /vɪə $ vɪr/ *v* [I] to change direction suddenly: *The car veered sharply to the left.*

veg[1] /vedʒ/ *n* [C,U] plural **veg** *BrE informal* vegetables

veg[2] *v* **vegged, vegging**
veg out *phr v informal* to relax and not do anything

vegan /'viːgən $ 'viː-, 'vedʒən/ *n* [C] someone who does not eat meat, fish, eggs, or milk products

vegetable /'vedʒtəbəl/ *n* [C] a plant such as a CARROT, CABBAGE, or potato, which you can eat

vegetarian /ˌvedʒə'teəriən◂ $ -'ter-/ *n* [C] someone who does not eat meat or fish
—**vegetarian** *adj: More and more people are becoming vegetarian.* → see box at FOOD

vegetation /ˌvedʒə'teɪʃən/ *n* [U] the plants, flowers, trees etc that grow in a particular area: *dense vegetation*

veggie /'vedʒi/ *n* [C] **1** a VEGETARIAN **2** *AmE* a vegetable —**veggie** *adj*

vehement /'viːəmənt/ *adj* having very strong feelings or opinions about something: *his vehement opposition to the plan* —**vehemently** *adv*

vehicle /'viːɪkəl/ *n* [C]
1 *formal* something such as a car or bus that is used for carrying people or things from one place to another: *a stolen vehicle*
2 a vehicle for (doing) sth something that you use as a way of spreading ideas, opinions etc: *The newspaper is a vehicle for government propaganda.*
→ MOTOR VEHICLE

veil /veɪl/ *n* **1** [C] a thin piece of material that women wear to cover their faces: *a bridal veil*
2 draw a veil over sth *formal* to avoid talking about something because it is unpleasant or embarrassing

veiled /veɪld/ *adj* veiled criticisms or threats are not said directly

vein /veɪn/ *n* [C]
1 one of the tubes through which blood flows to your heart from other parts of your body [→ artery]
2 one of the thin lines on a leaf or on the wing of an insect
3 a thin layer of coal, gold etc in rock
4 in a ... vein in a particular style of speaking or writing: *She went on in the same vein for several minutes.*

Velcro /'velkrəʊ $ -kroʊ/ *n* [U] *trademark* a material used for fastening shoes, clothes etc, made from two special pieces of material that stick to each other

velocity /vɪˈlɒsɪti $ -'lɑː-/ *n* [C,U] plural **velocities** *technical* the speed at which something moves in a particular direction: *the velocity of light*

velvet /'velvɪt/ *n* [U] cloth with a soft thick surface on one side: *velvet curtains* | *a velvet dress*

velvety /'velvɪti/ *adj* pleasantly smooth and soft: *the cat's velvety fur*

vendetta /ven'detə/ *n* [C] when one person tries to harm another, or two people argue violently, over a long period of time

vending machine /'vendɪŋ məˌʃiːn/ *n* [C] a machine that sells cigarettes, drinks etc

vendor /'vendə $ -ər/ *n* [C] someone who sells something, especially on the street: *street vendors*

veneer /vɪˈnɪə $ -'nɪr/ *n* **1** [C,U] a thin layer of wood that covers the outside of something that is made of a cheaper material: *oak veneer* **2** a

vegetables

aubergine *BrE*/eggplant *AmE*

Brussels sprouts

cucumber

sweetcorn *BrE*/corn *AmE*

mushroom

cabbage

lettuce

leek

potatoes

courgettes *BrE*/zucchini *AmE*

pepper

broccoli

onion

tomatoes

celery

cauliflower

peas

carrots

veneer of sth behaviour that hides someone's real feelings or character: *a veneer of politeness*

venerable /ˈvenərəbəl/ *adj formal* a venerable person or organization is very old and respected: *venerable institutions*

venerate /ˈvenəreɪt/ *v* [T] *formal* to honour or respect someone or something because they are old or holy

venereal disease /vəˈnɪəriəl dɪˌziːz $ -ˈnɪr-/ *n* [C,U] VD

venetian blind /vəˌniːʃən ˈblaɪnd/ *n* [C] a covering for a window made of bars of wood or plastic that can be raised or lowered to let in light

vengeance /ˈvendʒəns/ *n* **1** [U] a violent or harmful action that someone does to punish someone for harming them or their family: *his desire for vengeance* **2 with a vengeance** with great force or a lot of effort: *The hot weather is back with a vengeance.*

vengeful /ˈvendʒfəl/ *adj literary* very eager to punish someone who has done something bad

venison /ˈvenɪzən, -sən/ *n* [U] meat from a DEER → see box at MEAT

venom /ˈvenəm/ *n* [U] **1** great anger or hatred: *a speech full of venom* **2** poison produced by some snakes, insects etc —**venomous** *adj*: *a venomous snake*

vent¹ /vent/ *n* [C] **1** a special hole through which smoke or dirty air can go out, or fresh air can come in **2 give vent to sth** *formal* to do something that shows how angry, annoyed etc you feel

vent² *v* [T] to express strong feelings of anger, hatred etc: *She was venting her frustration by banging the pots.*

ventilate /ˈventɪleɪt $ -tleɪt/ *v* [T] to let fresh air into a room or building —**ventilation** /ˌventɪˈleɪʃən $ -tlˈeɪ-/ *n* [U] *the ventilation system*

ventilator /ˈventɪleɪtə $ -tl-eɪtər/ *n* [C] a piece of equipment that pumps air into and out of someone's lungs so that they can breathe

ventriloquist /venˈtrɪləkwɪst/ *n* [C] someone who speaks without moving their lips, in a way that makes the sound seem to come from somewhere else, especially from a PUPPET —**ventriloquism** *n* [U]

venture¹ /ˈventʃə $ -ər/ *n* [C] a new activity that involves taking risks, especially in business: *The new venture was not a success.* → JOINT VENTURE

venture² *v formal* **1** [I] to go somewhere that could be dangerous: **+into/out etc** *Kate rarely ventured beyond her nearest town.* **2** [T] to say or do something in an uncertain way because you are afraid it is wrong or will seem stupid: *No one else ventured an opinion.*

venue /ˈvenjuː/ *n* [C] a place where a concert, sports game etc takes place: *a popular jazz venue*

Venus /ˈviːnəs/ *n* [singular] the second PLANET from the sun

veracity /vəˈræsɪti/ *n* [U] *formal* the quality of being true

V

veranda, **verandah** /vəˈrændə/ n [C] an open area with a floor and a roof that is built on the side of a house

verb /vɜːb $ vɜːrb/ n [C] a word used to say what someone does or what happens, for example 'go', 'eat', or 'finish'
→ AUXILIARY VERB, HELPING VERB, LINKING VERB, MODAL VERB, PHRASAL VERB

verbal /ˈvɜːbəl $ ˈvɜːr-/ adj **1** spoken, not written: *a verbal agreement* **2** relating to words or using words: *verbal skills* —**verbally** adv

verbatim /vɜːˈbeɪtɪ̯m $ vɜːr-/ adj, adv repeating the actual words that were spoken or written

verbose /vɜːˈbəʊs $ vɜːrˈboʊs/ adj formal using too many words

verdict /ˈvɜːdɪkt $ ˈvɜːr-/ n [C] **1** an official decision in a court of law about whether someone is guilty or how someone died: *Has the jury reached a verdict?* → see box at COURT **2** an official decision about something or someone's opinion about something: +**on** *What's your verdict on the movie?*

verge[1] /vɜːdʒ $ vɜːrdʒ/ n [C] **1 be on the verge of sth** to be about to do something: *Helen was on the verge of tears.* **2** BrE a narrow area of grass at the side of a road

verge[2] v
 verge on/upon sth phr v to be very close to a harmful or extreme state: *Their behaviour sometimes verged on insanity.*

verify /ˈverɪ̯faɪ/ v [T] **verified, verifying, verifies** to check or prove that something is true or correct: *There's no way of verifying his story.* —**verification** /ˌverɪ̯fɪ̯ˈkeɪʃən/ n [U]

veritable /ˈverɪ̯təbəl/ adj formal used to emphasize your description of someone or something: *a veritable masterpiece*

vermin /ˈvɜːmɪ̯n $ ˈvɜːr-/ n [plural] small animals, birds, and insects that are harmful because they destroy crops, spoil food, or spread disease

vernacular /vəˈnækjʊ̯lə $ vərˈnækjʊ̯lər/ n [singular] a form of a language that ordinary people use, especially one that is not the official language

versatile /ˈvɜːsətaɪl $ ˈvɜːrsətl/ adj **1** someone who is versatile has many different skills: *a versatile actor* **2** having many different uses: *a versatile computer system* —**versatility** /ˌvɜːsəˈtɪlɪ̯ti $ ˌvɜːr-/ n [U]

verse /vɜːs $ vɜːrs/ n **1** [C] a set of lines that forms one part of a song or poem: *the last verse of the poem* **2** [U] words arranged in the form of poetry: *a book of verse*

versed /vɜːst $ vɜːrst/ adj **be (well) versed in** formal to know a lot about a subject: *lawyers who are well-versed in these matters*

version /ˈvɜːʃən $ ˈvɜːrʒən/ n [C]

1 one form of something that is slightly different from all other forms: +**of** *the original version of the film* | *a new version of an old Beatles song* | **English/German/electronic/film etc version** (=presented in a different language or form) *I think I preferred the television version.*
2 someone's version of an event is their description of it, when this is different from the description given by another person: +**of** *The*

newspapers all gave different versions of the story. | *the official version of events*
→ COVER VERSION

versus /ˈvɜːsəs $ ˈvɜːr-/ prep written abbreviation **v, vs 1** used to say that two people or teams are playing against each other in a game or fighting a court case: *Connors versus McEnroe* **2** used when comparing the advantages of two different things or ideas: *It's a question of quantity versus quality.*

vertebra /ˈvɜːtɪ̯brə $ ˈvɜːr-/ n [C] plural **vertebrae** /-briː, -breɪ/ one of the small hollow bones down the centre of your back

vertical /ˈvɜːtɪkəl $ ˈvɜːr-/ adj pointing straight upwards [► horizontal]: *a vertical line* | **vertical cliff/climb/rock etc** (=one that is very deep) *a vertical rock face* —**vertically** /-kli/ adv

vertigo /ˈvɜːtɪgəʊ $ ˈvɜːrtɪgoʊ/ n [U] a feeling of sickness and DIZZINESS that you get when you look down from a high place

verve /vɜːv $ vɜːrv/ n [U] literary if someone does something with verve, they do it with energy, excitement, or great pleasure

very[1] /ˈveri/ adv

1 used to emphasize an adjective, adverb, or phrase: *It's a very good book.* | *John gets embarrassed very easily.* | *I miss her very much.* | *I'm very, very pleased you could come.* | *My sister and I were married on the very same* (=exactly the same) *day.*

USAGE

Do not use **very** with adjectives and adverbs that already have a strong meaning, for example 'huge' or 'terrible'. Say: *a terrible war* not 'a very terrible war'. You can use **really** instead: *a really awful film*
Do not use **very** with the comparative form of adjectives. Use **much** instead: *This school's much better.* Do not say 'This school's very better'.
→ TOO

2 not very good/difficult/far etc not good, difficult, far etc at all: *I'm not very good at spelling.* | *'Was the talk interesting?' 'Not very* (=only slightly).'
3 your very own used to emphasize the fact that something belongs to one particular person and to no one else: **of your very own** *At last, a home of her very own.*

very[2] adj used to emphasize that you are talking exactly about one particular thing or person: *He died in this very room.*

vessel /ˈvesəl/ n [C] formal a ship or large boat
→ BLOOD VESSEL

vest /vest/ n [C] **1** BrE a piece of underwear that you wear under a shirt [= undershirt AmE] **2** a special piece of clothing without SLEEVES that you wear to protect your body: *a bulletproof vest* **3** AmE a piece of clothing without SLEEVES and with buttons down the front that you wear as part of a suit [= waistcoat BrE]

vested interest /ˌvestɪ̯d ˈɪntrɪ̯st/ n [C] if you have a vested interest in something happening, you have a strong reason for wanting it to happen because you will get money or advantages from it

vestibule /'vestɪbjuːl/ *n* [C] *formal* a wide PAS-SAGE or small room inside the front door of a public building

vestige /'vestɪdʒ/ *n* [C] a small part or amount of something that still remains, when most of it no longer exists: **+of** *the last vestiges of the British Empire*

vet[1] /vet/ *n* [C] *especially BrE*
1 also **veterinary surgeon** *BrE formal* someone who is trained to give medical care and treatment to sick animals [= **veterinarian** *AmE*]: *We had to take our cat to the vet.*
2 *AmE informal* a veteran from a war: *Vietnam vets*

vet[2] *v* [T] **vetted, vetting** *BrE* to check details about a person in order to make sure they are suitable for a particular job: *All staff are vetted for security purposes.*

veteran /'vetərən/ *n* [C] **1** someone who has been a soldier, sailor etc in a war **2** someone who has had a lot of experience of doing something: *veteran Hollywood entertainer Bob Hope*

veterinarian /ˌvetərɪ'neəriən $ -'ner-/ *n* [C] *AmE* someone who is trained to give medical care and treatment to sick animals [= **vet** *BrE*]

veterinary /'vetərɪnəri $ -neri/ *adj technical* relating to the medical care and treatment of sick animals

'veterinary ˌsurgeon *n* [C] a VET[1]

veto[1] /'viːtəʊ $ -toʊ/ *v* [T] past tense and past participle **vetoed** present participle **vetoing** third person singular **vetoes** to officially refuse to allow something to happen, especially something that other people or organizations have agreed: *The President vetoed the bill.*

veto[2] *n* [C,U] plural **vetoes** when someone officially refuses to allow something to happen: *The chairman can use his veto to stop the deal.*

vex /veks/ *v* [T] *old-fashioned* to make someone feel annoyed or worried

vexed /vekst/ *adj* **1 vexed question/issue/problem etc** a question or problem that is difficult to deal with and causes a lot of problems or discussion **2** *old-fashioned* worried or annoyed

via /'vaɪə, 'viːə/ *prep* **1** travelling through a place when you are going to another place: *We're flying to Denver via Chicago.* **2** using a particular machine, system, person etc to send, receive, or broadcast something: *The concert was broadcast around the world via satellite.*

viable /'vaɪəbəl/ *adj* something that is viable is able to exist or succeed: *a viable alternative to the petrol engine* | *At twenty-eight weeks, the foetus is viable.* —**viability** /ˌvaɪə'bɪlɪti/ *n* [U]

viaduct /'vaɪədʌkt/ *n* [C] a long high bridge across a valley

vibe /vaɪb/ *n* [C usually plural] a general feeling that you get from a person or a place: *I get bad vibes from that guy.*

vibes /vaɪbz/ *n* [plural] *informal* the feelings that you get from a person, group, or situation

vibrant /'vaɪbrənt/ *adj* **1** full of activity or energy in a way that is exciting and attractive: *a vibrant personality* **2** a vibrant colour is bright and strong

vibrate /vaɪ'breɪt $ 'vaɪbreɪt/ *v* [I,T] to shake with small fast movements, or to make some-

thing shake in this way: *The vocal chords vibrate as air passes over them.* → see box at SHAKE

vibration /vaɪ'breɪʃən/ *n* [C,U] a continuous slight shaking movement: *vibration caused by passing traffic*

vicar /'vɪkə $ -ər/ *n* [C] a priest in the Church of England

vicarage /'vɪkərɪdʒ/ *n* [C] the house where a vicar lives

vicarious /vɪ'keəriəs $ vaɪ'ker-/ *adj* [only before noun] vicarious feelings are feelings that you get by watching or reading about someone else doing something rather than doing it yourself

vice /vaɪs/ *n* **1** [U] criminal activities that involve sex or drugs **2** [C] a bad habit or a bad part of someone's character: *Smoking is my only vice.* **3** *BrE* [C] a tool used to hold something firmly while you work on it, for example to hold a piece of wood while you cut it [= **vise** *AmE*]

ˌvice 'president *n* [C] **1** the person who is next in rank to the president of a country **2** *AmE* someone who is responsible for one part of a company: *the vice president for marketing*

ˌvice 'versa /ˌvaɪs 'vɜːsə, ˌvaɪsi- $ -ɜːr-/ *adv* used to say that the opposite of a situation you have just described is also true: *The boys may refuse to play with the girls, and vice versa.*

vicinity /vɪ'sɪnɪti/ *n* **in the vicinity (of sth)** *formal* in the area near or around a place: *The stolen car was found in the vicinity of the station.*

vicious /'vɪʃəs/ *adj* **1** violent, cruel, and likely to harm someone: *a vicious attack* **2** cruel in a way that is intended to hurt someone's feelings or make their character seem bad: *a vicious rumour* —**viciously** *adv* —**viciousness** *n* [U]

ˌvicious 'circle *n* [singular] a situation in which one problem causes another problem which then causes the first problem again

victim /'vɪktɪm/ *n* [C] someone who has been hurt, attacked, or killed because of something bad: **+of** *victims of crime* | **rape/murder etc victims** *Most homicide victims are under 30.* | *an aid programme for the famine victims*

victimize also **-ise** *BrE* /'vɪktɪmaɪz/ *v* [T] to deliberately treat someone unfairly: *People with AIDS have been victimized at work.* —**victimization** /ˌvɪktɪmaɪ'zeɪʃən $ -mə-/ *n* [U]

victor /'vɪktə $ -ər/ *n* [C] *formal* the winner of a battle or competition

Victorian /vɪk'tɔːriən/ *adj* connected with the period in British history between 1837 and 1901: *Victorian buildings* —**Victorian** *n* [C]

victorious /vɪk'tɔːriəs/ *adj* successful in a battle or competition

victory /'vɪktəri/ *n* [C,U] plural **victories** the success you achieve when you win a battle, game, election etc [≠ **defeat**]: *Napoleon's military victories* | **+over/against** *Poland's victory over France in the World Cup* | *The government has won an important victory.* | *He led his troops to victory.* | **+for** *This ruling represents a victory for all women.*

video[1] /'vɪdiəʊ $ -dioʊ/ *n* plural **videos**
1 [C,U] a copy of a film or television programme, or a film of an event, recorded on VIDEOTAPE: *Do you want to watch a video*

V

tonight? | **on video** *I've got the whole ceremony on video.* | *The movie has just been **released on video**.*

COLLOCATIONS

go to a **video shop** *BrE*/**video store** *AmE*
get/rent/hire *BrE* a **video**
watch a **video**
rewind a **video** – to press a button to go back to an earlier part
fast forward a **video** – to press a button to go to a later part
pause a **video** – to stop the video for a short time
make a **video** – to use a video camera to film someone or something, for example a **home video** (=of your family, a holiday etc), or a **promotional video** (=one intended to help sell a product)

2 [C] *BrE* a video cassette recorder: *Could you set the video to record the football match?*

video² *v* [T] past tense and past participle **videoed**, present participle **videoing**, third person singular **videos** *BrE* to record a television programme, film, or event on a video: *A friend videoed our wedding.* | *Are you going to video that film on TV tonight?*

video cas'sette re,corder also **'video ,recorder, VCR** *n* [C] a machine used for recording television programmes or showing videos

'video ,game *n* [C] a game in which you move images on a screen using electronic controls

videophone /'vɪdiəʊfəʊn $ -diəʊfoʊn/ *n* [C] a type of telephone that allows you to see the person you are talking to on a screen

videotape¹ /'vɪdiəʊteɪp $ -dioʊ-/ *n* [C] a long narrow band of MAGNETIC material in a plastic container, on which films, television programmes etc can be recorded

videotape² *v* [T] to record a television programme, film, or event using a video

vie /vaɪ/ *v* [I] **vied, vying, vies** to compete with another person, company etc in order to get something: **+for** *The brothers vied for her attention.*

view¹ /vjuː/ *n*

1 [C] your opinion about something: **+about** *He has strong views about politics.* | **+on** *What's your view on this matter?* | *Everyone at the meeting **had different views**.* | *Not all her friends **shared** her **views**.* | **In my view** *the government is wrong.* | *The **general view** was that it was a good idea.* → see box at OPINION
2 [C,U] your view is what you can see, or how well you can see things: **+of** *We had a really good view of the stage.* | **be in view/come into view** *Suddenly the pyramids were in view.* | **disappear/hide/vanish from view** *The gun had disappeared from view.* | *Fran hit him **in full view of** all the guests* (=where they could see him clearly). | *When we reached the top, we had a **bird's eye view** (=a view of an area from high up) of the city.*
3 [C] everything that you can see from a place: **+of** *There was a beautiful view of the mountains from our hotel room.*

THESAURUS

View is used to talk about all the things you can see from a place: *We had a fabulous view of St Mark's Square from our hotel.* | *spectacular views*
Scenery is used to talk about the natural features that you can see around you, such as mountains, forests etc: *the beautiful river and forest scenery*
You cannot say 'sceneries'.

4 [C] a photograph or picture that shows a beautiful or interesting place: **+of** *postcards showing views of New York*
5 on view being shown to the public: *The painting is currently on view at the Museum of Modern Art.*
6 in view of sth *formal* because of something: *In view of his behaviour the club has decided to suspend him.*
7 with a view to (doing) sth because you are planning to do something in the future: *We bought the house with a view to retiring there.*
→ POINT OF VIEW

view² *v* [T] *formal* **1** to think of someone or something in a particular way [= see]: **view sb/sth as sth** *Women were viewed as sex objects.*
2 to look at or watch something: *The scenery was spectacular, especially when viewed from high ground.*

viewer /'vjuːə $ -ər/ *n* [C] someone who watches a television programme: *The series is watched by millions of viewers.*

viewfinder /'vjuː,faɪndə $ -ər/ *n* [C] the small square of glass on a camera that you look through when you are taking a photograph

viewing /'vjuːɪŋ/ *n* [C,U] **1** the activity of watching a television programme or a film: *young people's **television viewing** habits* **2** the activity of going to look at something, or an occasion when people can do this: *The palace is now open for **public viewing**.* | *a **private viewing** of the paintings*

viewpoint /'vjuːpɔɪnt/ *n* [C] a particular way of thinking about a problem or subject [= point of view]: *Try and think of it from the child's viewpoint.*

vigil /'vɪdʒɪl/ *n* [C,U] a period of time when you stay quietly somewhere, especially in order to protest, pray, or be with someone who is ill: *Protesters **held a vigil** outside the embassy.*

vigilant /'vɪdʒɪlənt/ *adj* watching carefully what happens, so that you notice anything dangerous or illegal: *People should **remain vigilant** at all times and report suspicious packages to the police.* —**vigilance** *n* [C]

vigilante /,vɪdʒɪ'lænti/ *n* [C] someone who tries to catch and punish criminals without having any legal authority to do so

vigor /'vɪgə $ -ər/ *n* the American spelling of VIGOUR

vigorous /'vɪgərəs/ *adj* using a lot of energy and strength or determination: *vigorous exercise* | *a vigorous campaign against dumping nuclear waste* —**vigorously** *adv*

vigour *BrE*; **vigor** *AmE* /'vɪgə $ -ər/ *n* [U] physical or mental energy and determination

vile /vaɪl/ *adj* very unpleasant: *The food **tasted vile**.*

vilify /ˈvɪlɪ̩faɪ/ v [T] *formal* **vilified, vilifying, vilifies** to say or write bad things about someone: *He was vilified by the press.*

villa /ˈvɪlə/ n [C] a house with a garden in the countryside or near the sea, used especially for holidays → see box at **ACCOMMODATION**

village /ˈvɪlɪdʒ/ n [C] a group of houses usually with a church, shop etc in the countryside: *a fishing village* | **village school/shop/church etc** *The children go to the village school.*

villager /ˈvɪlɪdʒə $ -ər/ n [C] someone who lives in a village

villain /ˈvɪlən/ n [C] **1** the main bad character in a story, film etc **2** *BrE informal* a criminal

vindicate /ˈvɪndɪ̩keɪt/ v [T] *formal* to prove what someone said or did was right, even though many people believed that they were wrong —**vindication** /ˌvɪndɪ̩ˈkeɪʃən/ n [singular, U]

vindictive /vɪnˈdɪktɪv/ *adj* deliberately cruel and unfair —**vindictively** *adv* —**vindictiveness** n [U]

vine /vaɪn/ n [C] a climbing plant, especially one that produces **GRAPES**

vinegar /ˈvɪnɪgə $ -ər/ n [U] a sour-tasting liquid made from **MALT** or wine that is used to improve the taste of food or preserve it

vineyard /ˈvɪnjəd $ -jərd/ n [C] an area of land where **GRAPES** are grown to make wine

vintage¹ /ˈvɪntɪdʒ/ *adj* [only before noun] **1** vintage wine is good quality wine that is made in a particular year **2** old but of high quality: *vintage cars* → see box at **OLD** **3** showing all the best or most typical qualities of something: *a vintage performance by the champion*

vintage² n [C] the wine made in a particular year

vinyl /ˈvaɪnl̩/ n [U] a type of strong plastic

viola /viˈəʊlə $ -ˈoʊ-/ n [C] a wooden musical instrument like a **VIOLIN** but larger and with a lower sound

violate /ˈvaɪəleɪt/ v [T] *formal* **1** to do something against an official law, principle, agreement etc **2** to do something that makes someone feel that they have been attacked or have suffered a great loss of respect —**violation** /ˌvaɪəˈleɪʃən/ n [C,U] *human rights violations*

violence /ˈvaɪələns/ n [U]
1 behaviour that is intended to hurt other people physically: *There's too much violence on TV these days.* | +**against** *violence against women* | *We condemn any act of violence.*
2 extreme force: *the violence of a tornado*

violent /ˈvaɪələnt/ *adj*
1 involving actions that are intended to injure or kill people, or are likely to hurt or kill someone: *an increase in violent crime* | *violent clashes between police and demonstrators* | *Arthur was a violent and dangerous man.*
2 showing very strong angry emotions that are difficult to control: **violent quarrel/argument/row etc** | *his violent temper*
3 a physical feeling or reaction that is painful or difficult to control: *a violent headache*
4 **violent film/play/drama** a film etc that contains a lot of violence
5 **violent storm/earthquake/explosion etc** a storm etc that happens with a lot of force —**violently** *adv*

violet /ˈvaɪələt/ n **1** [C] a small sweet-smelling dark purple flower **2** [U] a purple colour —**violet** *adj*

violin /ˌvaɪəˈlɪn/ n [C] a wooden musical instrument that you hold under your chin and play by pulling a **BOW** (=special stick) across the strings → see picture on page A6 —**violinist** n [C]

VIP /ˌviː aɪ ˈpiː/ n [C] **very important person** someone who is famous or powerful and receives special treatment

viper /ˈvaɪpə $ -ər/ n [C] a small poisonous snake

viral /ˈvaɪərəl $ ˈvaɪrəl/ *adj* related to or caused by a **VIRUS**

virgin¹ /ˈvɜːdʒɪ̩n $ ˈvɜːr-/ n [C] someone who has never had sex

virgin² *adj* virgin land, forest etc is still in its natural condition and has not been used or spoiled by people

virginity /vɜːˈdʒɪnɪti $ vɜːr-/ n **lose your virginity** to have sex for the first time

Virgo /ˈvɜːgəʊ $ ˈvɜːrgoʊ/ n plural **Virgos 1** [U] the sign of the Zodiac of people born between August 24 and September 23 **2** [C] someone who has this sign

virile /ˈvɪraɪl $ ˈvɪrəl/ *adj approving* a man who is virile is strong in a sexually attractive way —**virility** /vɪˈrɪlɪti/ n [U]

virtual /ˈvɜːtʃuəl $ ˈvɜːr-/ *adj* **1** very nearly a particular thing: *He became a virtual prisoner in his own home.* **2** made, done, seen etc on the Internet or on a computer, rather than in the real world: *a virtual library*

virtually /ˈvɜːtʃuəli $ ˈvɜːr-/ *adv* almost [= practically]: *The town was virtually destroyed.* | *He was virtually unknown before running for office.*

virtual re'ality n [U] when a computer makes you feel as though you are in a real situation by showing images and sounds

virtue /ˈvɜːtʃuː $ ˈvɜːr-/ n **1** [C,U] behaviour that is morally good, or a good quality in someone's character: *a life of virtue* | *Stella has many virtues.* **2** [C,U] an advantage that makes something better or more useful than other things: *the virtues of organic farming* **3 by virtue of sth** *formal* by means of, or as a result of something: *people who get promoted by virtue of their age*

virtuoso /ˌvɜːtʃuˈəʊsəʊ $ ˌvɜːrtʃuˈoʊsoʊ/ n [C] plural **virtuosos** someone who is a very skilful performer, especially in music: *a piano virtuoso* —**virtuoso** *adj*: *a virtuoso performance*

virtuous /ˈvɜːtʃuəs $ ˈvɜːr-/ *adj* behaving in a way that is morally good

virulent /ˈvɪrↄlənt/ *adj* **1** a virulent poison or disease is very dangerous and affects people very quickly **2** *formal disapproving* full of hatred for something, or expressing this in a strong way: *virulent anti-Semitism*

virus /ˈvaɪərəs $ ˈvaɪrəs/ n [C]
1 a very small living thing that causes diseases, or an illness caused by this: *the common cold virus*
2 a set of instructions secretly put into a computer that can destroy information stored in the computer

V

visa /ˈviːzə/ n [C] an official mark that is put on your PASSPORT that allows you to enter or leave another country: *She's here on a student visa.*

vis-à-vis /ˌviːz ɑː ˈviː, ˌviːz ə-/ prep formal concerning or compared with: *Where do we stand vis-à-vis last week's change in the law?*

viscous /ˈvɪskəs/ adj technical a viscous liquid is thick and does not flow easily —**viscosity** /vɪˈskɒsɪti $ -ˈskɑː-/ n [U]

vise /vaɪs/ n [C] AmE a tool used to hold something firmly while you work on it, for example to hold a piece of wood while you cut it [= vice BrE]

visibility /ˌvɪzɪˈbɪlɪti/ n [U] the distance that you can see, especially when this is affected by the weather conditions: *Dense fog led to poor visibility in many areas.*

visible /ˈvɪzɪbəl/ adj something that is visible can be seen or noticed [≠ invisible]: *The lights of the city were clearly visible below them.* | *a visible change in her attitude* —**visibly** adv: *She was visibly shocked by the news.*

vision /ˈvɪʒən/ n

1 [U] the ability to see [= sight]: *Will the operation improve my vision?* | **good/normal/poor etc vision** *children who are born with poor vision*

2 [U] the area that you can see, especially without turning your head: *a figure at the edge of her vision*

3 [C] an idea about something: **+of** *He had a clear vision of how he wanted the company to develop.* | **+for** *The President outlined his vision for the future* (=what he wanted to happen in the future). | *I had visions of* (=imagined) *the children getting hurt.*

4 [C] something you seem to see as part of a powerful religious experience

5 [U] the knowledge and imagination that are needed in planning for the future with a clear purpose: *We need a leader with vision.*
→ TUNNEL VISION

visionary /ˈvɪʒənəri $ -neri/ adj approving having clear ideas of what the world should be like in the future —**visionary** n [C]

visit¹ /ˈvɪzɪt/ v

1 [I,T] to go and spend time in a place or with someone: *My aunt is coming to visit us next week.* | *Which cities did you visit in Spain?* | *She doesn't visit very often.*

THESAURUS

You **go to** a museum, theatre, cinema etc.
You **go to see/go and see** a person or place.
If you **go sightseeing**, you visit places of interest in a country.
If someone **comes around/by/over**, they visit you informally in your home.
If someone **calls** AmE or **calls in/by** BrE, **drops in/by**, or **stops by**, they visit you in your home, especially on their way to another place.

---

2 [T] if someone visits a place, they go to examine something there as part of their job: *The building inspector will visit the site next week.*

3 [T] to look at a WEBSITE on the Internet: *Over 1000 people visit our site each week.* → see box at INTERNET

4 [I] AmE informal to have a conversation with someone: **+with** *We watched TV while Mom visited with Mrs. Levison.* → see box at TALK

visit² n

1 [C] when someone visits a place or person: **+to** *a visit to Chicago* | **on a visit** *We're only here on a flying visit* (=a very short visit). | *I decided to pay Grandad a visit.*

2 [singular] AmE informal a conversation with someone: *Barbara and I had a nice long visit.*

visitation /ˌvɪzɪˈteɪʃən/ n **1** [C,U] formal an official visit to a place or person **2** [C] an occasion when God or a SPIRIT is believed to appear to someone on earth

visitor /ˈvɪzɪtə $ -ər/ n [C] someone who visits a place or person: **+to** *visitors to Mexico City* | **+from** *visitors from overseas*

visor /ˈvaɪzə $ -ər/ n [C] **1** the part of a HELMET (=a hard hat) that can be lowered to protect your face **2** AmE the curved part of a cap that sticks out in front above your eyes **3** a flat object fixed above the front window of a car that you pull down to keep the sun out of your eyes

vista /ˈvɪstə/ n [C] literary a beautiful view of a large area of land

visual¹ /ˈvɪʒuəl/ adj relating to seeing: *The movie has a strong visual impact.* | **the visual arts** (=art such as painting that you look at) —**visually** adv

visual² n [C usually plural] a picture or the part of a film, video etc that you can see, rather than the parts that you hear: *the film's stunning visuals*

visual 'aid n [C] something such as a picture, film etc that is used to help people learn

visualize also **-ise** BrE /ˈvɪʒuəlaɪz/ v [T] to form a picture of someone or something in your mind [= imagine]: *I tried to visualize the house as she had described it.* —**visualization** /ˌvɪʒuəlaɪˈzeɪʃən $ -lə-/ n [U]

vital /ˈvaɪtl/ adj

1 extremely important or necessary: **+to** *His evidence was vital to the defence case.* | *The work she does is absolutely vital.* → see box at IMPORTANT

2 full of energy, in a way that seems attractive —**vitally** adv: *The work is vitally important.*

vitality /vaɪˈtælɪti/ n [U] energy and eagerness to do things

vitamin /ˈvɪtəmɪn, ˈvaɪ- $ ˈvaɪ-/ n [C] a chemical substance found in food that is necessary for good health

vitriolic /ˌvɪtriˈɒlɪk $ -ˈɑːlɪk/ adj formal disapproving vitriolic language or actions are full of anger and intended to hurt someone: *a vitriolic attack*

vivacious /vɪˈveɪʃəs $ vɪ-, vaɪ-/ adj someone, especially a woman, who is vivacious has a lot of energy and a happy attractive way of behaving

vivid /ˈvɪvɪd/ adj **1** vivid descriptions, memories, dreams etc are so clear that they seem real: *a vivid description of her childhood in Cornwall* | *She has a vivid imagination* (=she can imagine things clearly and easily). **2** vivid colours are very bright —**vividly** adv

vivisection /ˌvɪvɪˈsekʃən/ n [U] when scientists operate on living animals in order to do scientific tests

vixen /ˈvɪksən/ n [C] a female FOX

V-neck /'viː nek/ n [C] **1** an opening for the neck in a piece of clothing, shaped like the letter V: *a V-neck sweater* **2** a piece of clothing with a V-neck —**V-necked** /-nekt/ adj

vocab /'vəʊkæb $ 'voʊ-/ n [U] informal VOCABULARY

vocabulary /və'kæbjələri, vəʊ- $ -leri, voʊ-/ n plural **vocabularies**
1 [C,U] all the words that someone knows or uses: *Reading helps to improve your vocabulary.* | *He has a wide vocabulary.*
2 [singular] all the words in a language or all the words that are used in a type of language: *new words coming into the vocabulary of English* | *a specialized vocabulary*

vocal /'vəʊkəl $ 'voʊ-/ adj **1** expressing strong opinions publicly: *Mary was a vocal opponent of the plan.* **2** relating to the human voice, especially in singing: *vocal music* —**vocally** adv

'vocal cords n [plural] thin pieces of muscle in your throat that produce sound when you speak or sing

vocalist /'vəʊkəlɪst $ 'voʊ-/ n [C] someone who sings popular songs, especially with a band

vocals /'vəʊkəlz $ 'voʊ-/ n [plural] the part of a piece of music that is sung rather than played on an instrument: **on vocals** *The song features Elton John on vocals.*

vocation /vəʊ'keɪʃən $ voʊ-/ n [C,U] when you feel that the purpose of your life is to do a particular kind of work, or a job that gives you this feeling: *Teaching isn't just a job to her – it's her vocation.*

vocational /vəʊ'keɪʃənəl $ voʊ-/ adj relating to, or teaching, the skills needed to do a job: *vocational training* → see box at QUALIFICATION

vociferous /və'sɪfərəs, vəʊ- $ voʊ-/ adj formal expressing your opinions loudly and strongly: *a vociferous opponent of the plan* —**vociferously** adv

vodka /'vɒdkə $ 'vɑːdkə/ n [U] a strong alcoholic drink originally from Russia

vogue /vəʊg $ voʊg/ n [singular,U] when something is fashionable and popular: **be in vogue** *Japanese food is in vogue these days.*

voice¹ /vɔɪs/ n
1 [C,U] the sounds you make when you speak or sing, or the ability to make these sounds: *He called out in a loud voice.* | *He never raises his voice* (=speaks more loudly). | *She lowered her voice so Alex couldn't hear.* | *Keep your voice down* (=speak quietly) – *the baby's asleep.* | *Jack's got a cold and he's lost his voice* (=can't speak properly).
2 [C,U] someone's opinion, or the right to express an opinion or influence decisions: *Parents should have a voice in deciding how their children are educated.*
3 speak with one voice if people speak with one voice, they all express the same opinion
4 [singular] a person, organization, newspaper etc that says publicly what a group of people think or want: **+of** *Dr King become the voice of the Civil Rights Movement.*
5 the voice of reason/experience etc when someone speaks in a way that seems sensible, that shows they have had a lot of experience of doing something etc

voice² v [T] formal to tell people your opinions or feelings about something

ˌvoice-'activated adj a voice-activated piece of equipment starts working at the sound of someone's voice

'voice box n [C] the part of your throat where your voice is produced

voicemail /'vɔɪs,meɪl/ n [U] a system that records telephone calls so that you can listen to them later → see box at MOBILE PHONE

void¹ /vɔɪd/ n [singular] **1** a feeling of great sadness that you have when someone you love dies or when something is taken from you: *Work helped to fill the void after his wife died.* **2** a situation where something is needed or wanted but does not exist

void² adj **1** an agreement, result, or ticket that is void is not legally or officially acceptable **2 be void of sth** literary to be completely without something → NULL AND VOID

vol. the written abbreviation of **volume**

volatile /'vɒlətaɪl $ 'vɑːlətl/ adj **1** a volatile situation is likely to change suddenly and become worse **2** someone who is volatile can suddenly become angry or violent —**volatility** /,vɒlə'tɪləti $,vɑː-/ n [U]

volcano /vɒl'keɪnəʊ $ vɑːl'keɪnoʊ/ n [C] plural **volcanoes** or **volcanos** a mountain with a large hole at the top, through which LAVA (=very hot liquid rock) is sometimes forced out: *The island has several active volcanoes.* —**volcanic** /-'kænɪk/ adj: *volcanic rocks*

volcano

volcanic eruption

volition /və'lɪʃən $ voʊ-, və-/ n [U] formal **of your own volition** because you want to do something and not because you are forced to do it: *She left the company of her own volition.*

volley /'vɒli $ 'vɑːli/ n [C] **1** a large number of bullets, rocks etc fired or thrown at the same time: *a volley of shots* **2 a volley of questions/ abuse etc** a lot of questions, INSULTS etc that are all said at the same time **3** a hit in tennis, or a kick in football etc in which a player hits or kicks a ball before it touches the ground —**volley** v [I,T]

volleyball /'vɒlibɔːl $ 'vɑːlibɒːl/ n [U] a game in which two teams hit a ball to each other across a net with their hands and try not to let it touch the ground

volt /vəʊlt $ voʊlt/ n [C] a unit for measuring the force of an electric current

voltage /'vəʊltɪdʒ $ 'voʊl-/ n [C,U] the force of an electric current measured in volts

volume /'vɒljuːm $ 'vɑːljəm/ n
1 [U] the amount of sound produced by a television, radio etc: **turn the volume up/down** *Can you turn down the volume on the TV?*
2 [C,U] the total amount of something: **+of** *an increase in the volume of traffic*
3 [U] the amount of space that an object con-

V

tains or that a substance fills: **+of** *an instrument for measuring the volume of a gas*

4 [C] a book, especially one that is part of a series of books: *a 12-volume set of poetry*

voluminous /və'lu:mᵻnəs, və'lju:- $ və'lu:-/ *adj formal* very large: *a voluminous cloak*

voluntary /'vɒləntəri $ 'vɑ:lənteri/ *adj*

1 working without being paid, especially to help people: **voluntary organization/association/ agency etc** *a voluntary organization providing help for the elderly* | *She does voluntary work for the Red Cross.*

2 done willingly and without being forced [➡ **compulsory**]: *voluntary redundancy*

—**voluntarily** /'vɒləntər‿əli, ˌvɒlən'ter‿əli $ ˌvɑ:lən'ter‿əli/ *adv*

volunteer¹ /ˌvɒlən'tɪə $ ˌvɑ:lən'tɪr/ *n* [C]

1 someone who does work without being paid: *The helplines are manned by volunteers.*

2 someone who offers to do something without being told that they must do it: *I need someone to help me with the barbecue. Any volunteers?*

volunteer² *v* **1** [I,T] to offer to do something without being told that you must do it: *Ernie volunteered to wash the dishes.* **2** [T] to tell someone something without being asked: *Michael volunteered the information before I had a chance to ask.* **3** [I] to offer to join the army, navy etc: *When the war began, my brother immediately volunteered.*

voluptuous /və'lʌptʃuəs/ *adj* a voluptuous woman has large breasts and an attractively curved body

vomit¹ /'vɒmᵻt $ 'vɑ:-/ *v* [I,T] *formal* if you vomit, food comes up from your stomach and comes out of your mouth

vomit² *n* [U] the food or drink that comes out of your mouth when you vomit

voodoo /'vu:du:/ *n* [U] magical beliefs and practices used as a form of religion, especially in parts of Africa and the Caribbean

voracious /və'reɪʃəs, vɒ- $ vɔ:-, və-/ *adj formal* wanting to do something a lot, especially eating: *a voracious appetite.* —**voracity** /-'ræs‿ti/ *n* [U]

vote¹ /vəʊt $ voʊt/ *v*

1 [I,T] to show by marking a paper, raising your hand etc which person you want to elect or whether you support a particular plan: **+for/ against/in favour of** *He voted for the Labour candidate.* | **+on** *The people now had the chance to vote on the issue.* | **vote to do sth** *Congress voted to increase taxes.*

2 [T] to choose someone or something to win a particular prize by voting for them: *It was voted best film at Cannes.*

vote² *n* [C]

1 an act of voting or the choice that someone makes when they vote: *The bill was passed by 319 votes to 316.* | **+for/against/in favour (of)** *A vote for us is not a wasted vote.*

2 an occasion when people vote to choose or decide something: **+on** *There will be a vote on the matter.* | **take/have a vote (on sth)** *Let's take a vote then.* | **put sth to the/a vote** (=decide something by voting)

3 the vote a) the total number of votes in an election: *The Nationalists won 25% of the vote.* **b)** the right to vote: *In France, women didn't get the vote until 1945.*

→ CASTING VOTE

voter /'vəʊtə $ 'voʊtər/ *n* [C] someone who votes or has the right to vote

vouch /vaʊtʃ/ *v*

vouch for sb/sth *phr v* to say that something is true or good, or that someone can be trusted, which you know from your experience or knowledge of them

voucher /'vaʊtʃə $ -ər/ *n* [C] a kind of ticket that can be used instead of money to pay for things

vow¹ /vaʊ/ *n* [C] a serious promise: *She made a vow to herself that she would never go back.*

vow² *v* [T] to make a serious promise that you will definitely do something or not do something: *I vowed that I would never drink again.* → see box at PROMISE

vowel /'vaʊəl/ *n* [C] one of the sounds shown in English by the letters a, e, i, o, or u, and sometimes y

voyage /'vɔɪ-ɪdʒ/ *n* [C] a long trip, especially in a ship or space vehicle: *The voyage from England to India used to take six months.* | *She made the voyage single-handed.* → see box at JOURNEY

voyeur /vwɑ:'jɜ: $ -'jɜ:r/ *n* [C] someone who gets sexual pleasure from secretly watching other people's sexual activities —**voyeurism** *n* [U] —**voyeuristic** /ˌvwɑ:jə'rɪstɪk‿/ *adj*

vs. also **vs** *BrE* a written abbreviation of **versus**

vulgar /'vʌlgə $ -ər/ *adj* **1** behaving in a way that is not polite, especially by talking in a rude way: *vulgar jokes* **2** *disapproving* not showing good judgment about what is attractive or suitable —**vulgarity** /vʌl'gær‿ti/ *n* [U]

vulnerable /'vʌlnərəbəl/ *adj* easily harmed, hurt, or attacked: *The army was in a vulnerable position.* | *She looked so young and vulnerable.* —**vulnerability** /ˌvʌlnərə'bɪl‿ti/ *n* [U]

vulture /'vʌltʃə $ -ər/ *n* [C] a large wild bird that eats dead animals

vying /'vaɪ-ɪŋ/ *v* the present participle of VIE

W, w

W, w /'dʌbəlju:/ *n* [C,U] plural **W's, w's** the 23rd letter of the English alphabet

W **1** the written abbreviation of **west** or **western** **2** the written abbreviation of **watt**

wacky /'wæki/ *adj informal* silly in an amusing way

wad /wɒd $ wɑːd/ *n* [C] **1** a thick pile of thin sheets of something, especially money: **+of** *a wad of dollar bills* → see picture at PIECE **2** a thick soft mass of material that has been pressed together: **+of** *a wad of cotton*

waddle /'wɒdl $ 'wɑːdl/ *v* [I] to walk with short steps, with your body moving from one side to another, like a duck

wade /weɪd/ *v* [I] to walk through water: *We waded across the stream.* → see box at WALK
　wade through sth *phr v* to read something that is very long and boring → see box at READ

wafer /'weɪfə $ -ər/ *n* [C] a very thin BISCUIT

waffle¹ /'wɒfəl $ 'wɑː-/ *n* **1** [C] a flat cake with a pattern of square holes in it, often eaten for breakfast in the US → see picture on page A5 **2** [U] *informal* talk or writing that uses a lot of words but says nothing important

waffle² also **waffle on** *v* [I] *informal* to talk or write using a lot of words but without saying anything important: **+about** *What's he waffling about now?*

waft /wɑːft, wɒft $ wɑːft, wæft/ *v* [I,T] if smoke or a smell wafts somewhere, or if the wind wafts it, it moves gently through the air: *The smell of bacon wafted up from the kitchen.*

wag /wæg/ *v* [I,T] **wagged, wagging** if a dog wags its tail, or if its tail wags, the tail moves quickly from one side to the other

wage¹ /weɪdʒ/ *n* [singular] also **wages** [plural] the money that someone receives every day or week as payment for working [➡ **salary**]: *I'll get my wages on Friday.* | *the average **weekly wage*** | *He **earns** a good **wage**.* | *a **wage increase*** | *the national **minimum wage*** (=the lowest wage that an employer is allowed to pay by law) → see box at MONEY

wage² *v* [T] to be involved in a war or battle against someone or something: *The police are **waging war** on drug dealers.*

wager /'weɪdʒə $ -ər/ *n* [C] an amount of money that you risk on the result of a game or race

waggle /'wægəl/ *v* [I,T] to move something quickly from side to side, or to move in this way

wagon /'wægən/ *n* [C] **1** a strong vehicle with four wheels, usually pulled by horses [➡ **cart**] **2** *BrE* a vehicle used for carrying goods, which is pulled by a train [= **freight car** *AmE*] **3 be/go on the wagon** *informal* to not drink alcohol any more → STATION WAGON

waif /weɪf/ *n* [C] *literary* a child who is pale and thin and looks as if they do not have a home

wail /weɪl/ *v* [I] **1** to cry or complain loudly because you are sad or in pain: *'But what shall I do?' he wailed.* **2** to make a long, high sound: *Police sirens were wailing.* —**wail** *n* [C]

waist /weɪst/ *n* [C]
1 the narrow part in the middle of your body: *a slim waist*
2 the part of a piece of clothing that goes around your waist: *trousers with an elasticated waist*

waistband /'weɪstbænd/ *n* [C] the part of a skirt, trousers etc that fastens around your waist

waistcoat /'weɪskəʊt, 'weɪskət $ 'weskət/ *n* [C] *BrE* a piece of clothing with buttons down the front and no sleeves that a man wears over a shirt and under a jacket [= **vest** *AmE*]

waistline /'weɪstlaɪn/ *n* [C, usually singular]
1 the measurement around your waist: *his expanding waistline* **2** the part of a piece of clothing that fits around the waist

wait¹ /weɪt/ *v* [I]

1 to stay somewhere or not do something until something else happens or someone arrives: *Hurry up! Everyone's waiting.* | **+for** *Wait for me.* | *We had to wait 45 minutes for a bus.* | **wait to do sth** *Are you waiting to use the phone?* | **+till/until** *I'll wait till you come back.* | *I'm sorry to have **kept** you **waiting** (=made you wait).*

THESAURUS

Wait is never followed directly by a noun. You must say 'wait for': *I'm waiting for a phone call.* Or you can say 'wait to do something': *We're waiting to hear the news.*
Expect can be followed directly by a noun. Use it to say that you believe that something will come, happen etc: *I'm expecting a phone call.* | *The police are expecting trouble.*
Look forward to means to be excited and pleased about something that you know is going to happen: *I'm looking forward to seeing you all.*

2 if you are waiting for something, you expect or hope that it will happen but it has not happened yet: *'Have you heard about the job yet?' 'No, I'm still waiting.'*

3 if something is waiting for you, it is ready for you to use or collect: *I'll **have** dinner **waiting** for you.*

4 wait a minute/second/moment etc used to ask someone not to leave or start doing something immediately: *Wait a moment, just let me think.*

COMMUNICATION

asking someone to wait

hold on/hang on *informal*
just a minute/second
I won't be a minute
wait up *AmE* (=used to tell someone to stop walking or moving away, so that you can talk to them or go with them)
one moment, please *formal*
bear with me (=used to ask someone politely to wait while you do something)

please hold (the line) (=used on the phone by someone who is trying to connect you)

5 can't wait/can hardly wait (to do sth) used to emphasize that someone is very excited about something and is eager for it to happen: *I can't wait to see him again.*
6 sth can/can't wait if something can wait, it is not very urgent. If something can't wait, it is very urgent: *The report can wait till tomorrow.*
7 wait and see used to say that someone should be patient because they will find out about something later
8 (just) you wait *spoken* used to warn or threaten someone
9 wait tables *AmE* to serve food to people at their table in a restaurant

wait around also **wait about** *BrE phr v* to do nothing while you are waiting for something to happen: *The people at the embassy kept us waiting around for hours.*
wait on *sb phr v* to serve food to someone at their table, especially in a restaurant
wait up *phr v* **1** to wait for someone to come back home before you go to bed: **+for** *Please don't wait up for me.* **2** *AmE* to wait for someone: *Hey, wait up. I'm coming.*

wait² *n* [singular] a period of time when you wait for something to happen, someone to arrive etc: **+for** *The average wait for an appointment was eight weeks.* | *We had a three-hour wait before our flight.* ➔ **lie in wait (for sb/sth)** at **LIE¹**

waiter /ˈweɪtə $ -ər/ *n* [C] a man who serves food and drink at the tables in a restaurant ➔ see box at **RESTAURANT**

'waiting list *n* [C] a list of people who have asked for something but who must wait before they can have it

'waiting room *n* [C] a room for people to wait in, for example to see a doctor

waitress /ˈweɪtrɪs/ *n* [C] a woman who serves food and drink at the tables in a restaurant ➔ see box at **RESTAURANT**

waive /weɪv/ *v* [T] to state officially that a right or rule can be ignored: *She waived her right to see a lawyer.*

wake¹ /weɪk/ also **wake up** *v* [I,T] past tense **woke** /wəʊk $ woʊk/ past participle **woken** /ˈwəʊkən $ ˈwoʊ-/
to stop sleeping, or to make someone stop sleeping: *I woke up at 5.00 this morning.* | *Try not to wake the baby.*
wake up to *sth phr v* to start to realize and understand something important: *It's time you woke up to the fact that it's a tough world out there.*

wake² *n* **1 in the wake of sth** happening after something, usually as a result of it: *Famine followed in the wake of the drought.* **2** [C] the track made behind a boat as it moves through the water

waken /ˈweɪkən/ *v* [I,T] *formal* to wake up, or to wake someone up

'wake-up ˌcall *n* [C] something that shocks you into realizing that you must do something to make a situation change: *Getting arrested for fighting was a real wake-up call.*

waking /ˈweɪkɪŋ/ *adj* **waking hours/moments etc** all the time when you are awake: *He spends every waking moment in front of his computer.*

walk¹ /wɔːk $ wɒːk/ *v*
1 [I,T] to move forwards by putting one foot in front of the other: *We must have walked ten miles today.* | **+into/down/up etc** *She walked up to him and kissed him.* | *We missed the bus and had to* **walk home.** | *Is the school* **within walking distance** (=near enough to walk to)? ➔ see picture on page A11

THESAURUS

stride – to walk with long steps in a determined way
stroll – to walk in a relaxed way, especially for pleasure
creep/sneak – to walk quietly when you do not want to be seen or heard
wander – to walk slowly, often when you are not going to any particular place
trudge – to walk in a tired way or when it is difficult to continue walking
wade – to walk through water
limp – to walk with difficulty because one leg is hurt
march – to walk like soldiers, with regular steps
➔ **RUN, TRAVEL**

2 [T] to walk somewhere with someone: *It's late – I'll* **walk** *you home.* | **walk sb to sth** *I'll walk you to the bus stop.*
3 [T] to take a dog out for exercise: *Jude's out walking the dog.*
4 walk all over sb *informal* to treat someone very badly
—**walker** *n* [C] *an area popular with walkers and climbers* —**walking** *n* [U] *We went walking in the hills.*

walk away *phr v* to leave a situation without caring what happens: **+from** *You can't just walk away from 12 years of marriage!*
walk away with *sth phr v informal* to win something easily: *Carrie walked away with the prize.*
walk into *sth phr v* if you walk into a job, you get it very easily
walk off with *sth phr v informal* **1** to steal something: *Someone's walked off with my new jacket!* **2** to win something easily: *He walked off with first prize.*
walk out *phr v* to leave a place suddenly because you are angry
walk out on *sb phr v* to leave your husband or wife: *Mary just walked out on him one day.*

walk² *n* [C]
1 when you walk somewhere: *Let's* **go for a walk.** | **a long/short/ten-minute etc walk** *It's only a short walk to the beach.*
2 a path or road that you walk along, especially one that goes through an interesting or attractive area: *walks through the national park*
3 people from all walks of life people who have very different jobs or positions in society

walkie-talkie /ˌwɔːki ˈtɔːki $ ˌwɒːki ˈtɒːki/ *n* [C] a small radio that you can carry and use to speak to other people who have the same kind of radio

'walking stick n [C] a stick that you use to help support you when you walk

Walkman /'wɔːkmən $ 'wɔːk-/ n [C] plural **Walkmans** *trademark* a small CASSETTE PLAYER with HEADPHONES that you carry with you so that you can listen to music [= **personal stereo**]

walkout /'wɔːk-aʊt $ 'wɔːk-/ n [C] an occasion when people stop working or leave a meeting as a protest

walkover /'wɔːk,əʊvə $ 'wɔːk,oʊvər/ n [C] *informal* a very easy victory

walkway /'wɔːkweɪ $ 'wɔːk-/ n [C] a path built for people to walk along, often above the ground

wall /wɔːl $ wɒl/ n [C]

1 one of the sides of a room or building: *We've decided to paint the walls blue.* | **on a wall** *There were some lovely pictures on the wall.*

2 an upright structure made of stone or brick that divides one area of land from another [➡ **fence**]: *The garden is surrounded by a high wall.*

3 drive sb up the wall *informal* to make someone very angry

—**walled** *adj*: *a walled city*

wallet /'wɒlɪt $ 'wɑː-/ n [C] a small flat case in which you carry paper money, bank cards etc [= **billfold** AmE; ➡ **purse**]

wallop /'wɒləp $ 'wɑː-/ v [T] *informal* to hit someone or something very hard —**wallop** n [singular]

wallow /'wɒləʊ $ 'wɑːloʊ/ v [I] **1** if someone wallows in an unpleasant feeling or situation, they seem to enjoy it and want to be unhappy: *He was **wallowing in self-pity**.* **2** to lie or roll around in mud or water for pleasure

wallpaper /'wɔːl,peɪpə $ 'wɒl,peɪpər/ n [U] **1** paper that you stick onto the walls of a room in order to decorate it **2** the colour, pattern, or picture that you have as the background on the screen of a computer —**wallpaper** v [T]

'Wall Street n [singular] the New York City STOCK EXCHANGE: *Prices fell on Wall Street yesterday.*

,wall-to-'wall *adj* [only before noun] covering the whole floor: *wall-to-wall carpeting*

wally /'wɒli $ 'wɑː-/ n [C] plural **wallies** BrE *informal* someone who behaves in a silly way

walnut /'wɔːlnʌt $ 'wɒl-/ n **1** [C] a nut that you can eat, shaped like a human brain **2** [U] the dark brown wood of the tree on which this nut grows

walrus /'wɔːlrəs $ 'wɒl-, 'wɑːl-/ n [C] a large sea animal with two long TUSKS (=long pointed teeth) coming down from the sides of its mouth

waltz¹ /wɔːls $ wɒlts/ n [C] a fairly slow dance with a regular pattern of three beats

waltz² v [I] **1** to dance a waltz **2** *informal* to walk in a very confident way that annoys other people: **+in/into/up to etc** *Jeff waltzed up to the bar and poured himself a drink.*

wan /wɒn $ wɑːn/ *adj* looking pale, weak, or tired: *a wan smile*

wand /wɒnd $ wɑːnd/ n [C] a thin stick you hold in your hand to do magic tricks

wander /'wɒndə $ 'wɑːndər/ v

1 [I,T] to walk slowly across or around an area, usually without a clear direction or purpose: **+around/in/through etc** *We spent the morning wandering around the old part of the city.* | *He*

*was found **wandering the streets** of New York.*
→ see box at WALK

2 also **wander off** [I] to walk away from where you are supposed to stay: *Don't let the children wander off.*

3 [I] if your mind or your thoughts wander, you stop paying attention to something and start thinking about other things: *She's getting old, and sometimes her mind wanders.*

4 [I] to start to talk or write about something not connected with the main subject: **+from/off** *I wish he'd stop wandering off the subject.*

—**wander** n [singular] *We had a little wander round the town.* —**wanderer** n [C]

wane¹ /weɪn/ v [I] to become gradually weaker or less important: *After a while his enthusiasm for the sport began to wane.*

wane² n **on the wane** becoming weaker or less important: *The president's popularity seems to be on the wane.*

wangle /'wæŋgəl/ v [T] *informal* to succeed in getting something by using clever or slightly dishonest methods: *In the end she wangled an invitation to the wedding.*

wanna /'wɒnə $ 'wɑː-/ *informal* a way of writing or saying 'want to' or 'want a', which many people think is incorrect

wannabe /'wɒnəbi $ 'wɑː-/ n [C] *informal disapproving* someone who tries to look or behave like a famous or popular person: *Tom Cruise wannabes*

want¹ /wɒnt $ wɒnt, wɑːnt/ v [T]

1 to have a desire or need for something: *Do you want a drink?* | *What do you want for your birthday?* | **want to do sth** *I want to go home.* | **want sb/sth to do sth** *Her parents want her to find a rich husband.* | *I don't want the holiday to end.* | **want sth done** *I want that report finished today.*

2 *informal* used to say that something needs to be done: *The car wants a good clean.* | *Those plants want watering.*

3 to ask for someone to come and talk to you: *Sam, mum wants you!* | *You're wanted on the phone.*

4 *informal* used to tell someone what they should do [= **ought to**]: **want to do sth** *You want to be more careful with your money.*

want² n **1 for (the) want of sth** because of a lack of something: *The gallery closed down for want of funding.* **2 wants** [plural] the things you want or need to have

'want ad n [C] AmE a CLASSIFIED AD → see box at ADVERTISEMENT

wanted /'wɒntɪd $ 'wɒn-, 'wɑːn-/ *adj* someone who is wanted is being looked for by the police: **+for** *He is wanted for murder.*

wanting /'wɒntɪŋ $ 'wɒn-, 'wɑːn-/ *adj* **be found wanting** *formal* if something is found wanting, it has been shown to be not good enough: *Traditional solutions had been tried and found wanting.*

wanton /'wɒntən $ 'wɒn-, 'wɑːn-/ *adj formal* deliberately causing damage or harm for no reason: *wanton violence*

war /wɔː $ wɔːr/ n [C,U]

1 when there is fighting between two or more countries or between opposing groups within a country [≠ **peace**]: *the Vietnam War* | **+against/**

W

with *the war with Spain* | **+between** *the war between Iran and Iraq* | *In 1793 England was at war with France.* | *the history of the men who went to war* | *War broke out in 1939.* | **the war years**
2 a situation in which a person or group is fighting for power, influence, or control: *a trade war between Europe and the US*
3 a struggle over a long period of time to control something harmful: **+against/on** *the war against drugs*
➔ **CIVIL WAR, PRISONER OF WAR**

'war crime *n* [C] an illegal and cruel act done during a war —**war criminal** *n* [C]

ward¹ /wɔːd $ wɔːrd/ *n* [C] a large room in a hospital where people who need medical treatment stay

ward² *v*
ward sth ⇔ **off** *phr v* to prevent something from affecting you or attacking you: *a spray to ward off insects*

warden /'wɔːdn $ 'wɔːrdn/ *n* [C] *AmE* the person in charge of a prison [= **governor** *BrE*] ➔ **TRAFFIC WARDEN**

warder /'wɔːdə $ 'wɔːrdər/ *n* [C] *BrE* a prison guard

wardrobe /'wɔːdrəub $ 'wɔːrdroub/ *n* **1** [C] *BrE* a piece of furniture in which you hang clothes [= **closet** *AmE*] ➔ see box at **CLOTHES**
2 [singular] the clothes that someone has: *the latest addition to her wardrobe*

warehouse /'weəhaus $ 'wer-/ *n* [C] a large building for storing goods before they are sold

wares /weəz $ werz/ *n* [plural] *old-fashioned* the things that someone is selling, usually not in a shop

warfare /'wɔːfeə $ 'wɔːrfer/ *n* [U] fighting in a war, especially fighting with a particular type of weapon: **nuclear/chemical/germ etc warfare**

warhead /'wɔːhed $ 'wɔːr-/ *n* [C] the explosive part at the front of a **MISSILE**

warlike /'wɔːlaɪk $ 'wɔːr-/ *adj* people who are warlike like war and are skilful in it: *a warlike nation*

warlord /'wɔːlɔːd $ 'wɔːrlɔːrd/ *n* [C] the leader of an unofficial military group fighting against a government or other groups in a country

warm¹ /wɔːm $ wɔːrm/ *adj*
1 slightly hot, especially in a pleasant way [≠ **cool**; ➔ **warmth**]: *a nice warm bath* | *The weather was lovely and warm.* | *I've put your dinner in the oven to keep it warm.* | **keep/stay warm** *Make sure you keep warm!* ➔ see box at **HOT** ➔ and **WEATHER**
2 clothes or buildings that are warm can keep in heat or keep out cold: *Here, put on your nice warm coat.*
3 friendly: *a warm welcome* | *The Hungarian people are warm and friendly.*
—**warmly** *adv*: *She smiled warmly.*

warm² *v* [T] to make someone or something warm: *I warmed my hands over the fire.*
warm to sb/sth *phr v* to start to like someone or something: *They soon warmed to the idea.* | *I must say I didn't warm to her.*
warm up *phr v* **1** to become warm, or to make something warm: *The house will soon warm up.* | **warm** sth ⇔ **up** *Shall I warm the soup up?*
2 to do gentle exercises to prepare for some

sport: *The athletes were warming up for the race.*
➔ see box at **EXERCISE 3** if a machine warms up, it becomes ready to work properly

,**warm-'blooded** *adj* animals that are warmblooded have a body temperature that remains fairly high whether the temperature around them is hot or cold [≠ **cold-blooded**]

,**warmed-'over** *adj AmE* warmed-over food has been cooked before and then heated again for eating

warm-hearted /,wɔːm 'hɑːtɪd◂ $,wɔːrm 'hɑːr-/ *adj* friendly and kind [≠ **cold-hearted**]: *a warm-hearted old lady*

warmonger /'wɔː,mʌŋgə $ 'wɔːr,mɑːŋgər, -,mʌŋ-/ *n* [C] *disapproving* someone who is eager to start a war —**warmongering** *n* [U]

warmth /wɔːmθ $ wɔːrmθ/ *n* [U] **1** the heat that something produces: **+of** *the warmth of the sun* **2** friendliness: **+of** *the warmth of her smile*

'**warm-up** *n* [C] a set of gentle exercises you do to prepare your body for sport

warn /wɔːn $ wɔːrn/ *v* [T]
1 to tell someone that something bad or dangerous may happen, so that they can avoid it or prevent it: *We tried to warn her, but she wouldn't listen.* | **warn sb (that)** *We warned them that there was a bull in the field.* | **warn sb about/of sth** *Travellers are being warned about the danger of HIV infection.* | **warn sb to do sth** *We warned them to be careful.*

COMMUNICATION

warn someone

be careful: *Be careful on the ice.*
look out/watch out: *Look out! There's a car coming.*
mind: *Mind the step.*
beware of sth *written: Beware of the dog.*

---

2 to advise someone not to do something because it may have had dangerous or unpleasant results: **warn sb against sth** *He warned her against such a risky investment.* | **warn sb not to do sth** *I warned her not to walk home alone.*
3 to tell someone about something before it happens so that they are not worried or surprised by it: **warn sb (that)** *Can you warn your mother that you'll be back late?*

warning /'wɔːnɪŋ $ 'wɔːrn-/ *n* [C,U] something that tells you that something bad or dangerous may happen: *They took no notice of our warnings.* | **+of/about** *They have issued a warning about severe storms this evening.* | **+that** *a warning that the roads will be icy* | *The planes attacked without warning.*

warp /wɔːp $ wɔːrp/ *v* **1** [I,T] if wood or metal warps, or if something warps it, it becomes bent or twisted: *The wood had warped in the heat.*
2 [T] to change someone and make them unpleasant or cruel

warpath /'wɔːpɑːθ $ 'wɔːrpæθ/ *n* **be on the warpath** to be angry and looking for someone to fight or punish

warped /wɔːpt $ wɔːrpt/ *adj* someone who is warped has ideas or thoughts that are unpleasant or cruel: *a warped mind*

warrant¹ /'wɒrənt $ 'wɔː-, 'wɑː-/ *n* [C] a legal document that is signed by a judge, allowing the police to do something: **+for** *The police have a warrant for his arrest.* | *a* **search warrant**

warrant[2] *v* [T] *formal* to be a good enough reason for something to happen or be done [➡ **unwarranted**]: *The story doesn't warrant the attention it's been given in the press.*

warranty /'wɒrənti $ 'wɔː-, 'wɑː-/ *n* [C,U] plural **warranties** a written agreement in which a company selling something promises to repair it if it breaks within a particular period of time [➡ **guarantee**]: *The TV comes with a 3-year warranty.*

warren /'wɒrən $ 'wɔː-, 'wɑː-/ *n* [C] **1** the underground holes that rabbits live in **2** a place with a lot of very narrow streets

warring /'wɔːrɪŋ/ *adj* [only before noun] fighting against each other: *the warring countries*

warrior /'wɒriə $ 'wɔːriər, 'wɑː-/ *n* [C] someone who fought in battles in past times, especially someone who was very brave

warship /'wɔːʃɪp $ 'wɔːr-/ *n* [C] a ship with guns, used in wars → see box at **SHIP**

wart /wɔːt $ wɔːrt/ *n* [C] a small hard raised part on your skin → see box at **MARK**

wartime /'wɔːtaɪm $ 'wɔːr-/ *n* [U] the period of time when a country is fighting a war [≠ **peacetime**]: *Things are different in wartime.*

'war-torn *adj* a war-torn country, city etc is being destroyed by war

wary /'weəri $ 'weri/ *adj* careful because you are worried that someone or something may be dangerous or harmful: **+of** *She was a bit wary of him at first.* —**warily** *adv*

was /wəz; *strong* wɒz $ wəz; *strong* wɑːz/ *v* the past tense of the verb BE in the first and third person singular

wash[1] /wɒʃ $ wɒːʃ, wɑːʃ/ *v*

1 [T] to clean something with water and soap: *He spent the morning washing the car.* | *These jeans need to be washed.* | **wash sth in sth** *I had to wash my hair in cold water.*

2 [I,T] to clean your body with soap and water: *You didn't wash this morning!* | *Go upstairs and wash your hands.* | *I* **got washed** *and went to bed.*

3 [I] if water washes somewhere, it flows there: **+against** *The waves washed softly against the shore.*

4 [T] if something is washed somewhere, the sea or a river carries it there: **wash sth out/into etc** *The body was washed out to sea.*

5 wash your hands of sth/sb to refuse to be responsible for something or someone

wash sth ⇔ **away** *phr v* if water washes something away, it carries it away

wash sth ⇔ **down** *phr v* to drink something with food or medicine: *a big plate of pasta washed down with red wine*

wash off *phr v* **1** if something washes off, you can remove it from the surface of something by washing it: *Don't worry, the mud will wash off.* **2 wash sth** ⇔ **off** to clean dirt or dust from the surface of something by washing it

wash out *phr v* **1** if a substance washes out, you can remove it from a material by washing it **2 wash sth** ⇔ **out** to wash the inside of something: *Wash the bowl out with warm water.*

wash up *phr v* **1** *BrE* to wash the plates, dishes etc after a meal: *Will you help me wash*

up? | **wash sth** ⇔ **up** *It took ages to wash up all the pots.* **2** *AmE* to wash your hands: *Go wash up for supper.* **3 wash sth** ⇔ **up** if waves wash something up, they carry it to the shore: *His body was washed up on the beach.*

wash[2] *n* [singular]

1 a wash when you wash something, or wash yourself using soap and water: *I'm just going to* **have a wash** (=wash myself). | *I'll* **give** *the car* **a wash** *at the weekend.*

2 clothes that are to be washed, are being washed, or have just been washed: **in the wash** *All my jumpers are in the wash.*

washable /'wɒʃəbəl $ 'wɔːʃ-, 'wɑːʃ-/ *adj* **1** washable clothes are not damaged by washing **2** washable paint can be removed from clothing by washing

washbasin /'wɒʃ beɪsən $ 'wɔːʃ-, 'wɑːʃ-/ *n* [C] *especially BrE* a small SINK for washing your hands and face

,washed-'out *adj* **1** no longer having any colour: *washed-out jeans* **2** tired and pale: *You look washed out.*

washer /'wɒʃə $ 'wɒʃər, 'wɑː-/ *n* [C] a small flat ring of metal, plastic, or rubber, used between a NUT and BOLT or in a TAP

washing /'wɒʃɪŋ $ 'wɔː-, 'wɑː-/ *n* [singular,U] *BrE* clothes that need to be washed, are being washed, or have just been washed [= **wash** *AmE*]: *I need to* **do the washing**.

'washing line *n* [C,U] *BrE* a piece of string that you hang wet clothes on outside so that they can dry [= **clothesline**]

'washing ma,chine *n* [C] a machine that washes clothes

'washing ,powder *n* [C,U] *BrE* a powder used for washing clothes

,washing-'up *n* *BrE* **1 do the washing-up** to wash the plates, dishes etc that have been used for a meal **2** [U] plates, knives etc that need to be washed after a meal: *a huge pile of washing-up*

,washing-'up ,liquid *n* [U] *BrE* a liquid used for washing plates, knives etc

washout /'wɒʃaut $ 'wɔːʃ-, 'wɑːʃ-/ *n* [singular] *informal* **1** a failure **2** when rain stops something from happening

washroom /'wɒʃrum, -ruːm $ 'wɔːʃ-, 'wɑːʃ-/ *n* [C] *AmE* a public toilet

wasn't /'wɒzənt $ 'wɑː-/ the short form of 'was not': *He wasn't there.*

wasp /wɒsp $ wɑːsp, wɔːsp/ *n* [C] a black and yellow insect that stings

wastage /'weɪstɪdʒ/ *n* [U] when something is wasted or lost: *The aim is to reduce energy wastage.*

waste[1] /weɪst/ *n*

1 [singular, U] when something such as money, time, or a skill is not used effectively or sensibly: **a waste of time/money/resources etc** *My father thought college would be a complete waste of time.* | **What a waste** *of money!*

2 [U] things that are left after people have used something: **household/domestic waste** *More household waste could be recycled.* | *a* **waste bin** (=container for things that people throw away) | **toxic/hazardous waste** | **nuclear/radioactive**

waste | *Waste disposal* sites are well controlled.
→ see box at **RUBBISH**
3 go to waste to be wasted: *We can't let all this food go to waste.*
4 a waste of space *spoken* someone or something with no good qualities
5 *literary* **wastes** [plural] a large empty area of land: **icy/frozen/snowy etc wastes** *the icy wastes of Antarctica*

waste² *v* [T]
1 to use something such as money, time, or a skill in a way that is not effective or sensible: *They wasted a lot of time trying to fix it themselves.* | **waste sth on sth** *Don't waste your money on that junk!*
2 waste no time (in) doing sth to do something very quickly: *He wasted no time in introducing himself.*
3 be wasted if someone is wasted in a particular situation, their skills are not being fully used: *He's wasted in that job.*
4 be wasted on sb to have no importance for someone or no effect on someone: *He thought education was wasted on women.*
5 waste your breath *spoken* to say something that will have no effect: *You're wasting your breath trying to tell her anything!*
  waste away *phr v* to gradually become thinner and weaker, because you are ill

waste³ *adj* [only before noun] **1** having no use, or no further use: *waste products* | *waste paper* **2** waste ground is empty or not looked after by anyone

wastebasket /ˈweɪstˌbɑːskɪt $ -ˌbæs-/ *n* [C] *especially AmE* a WASTEPAPER BASKET → see box at **BIN** → see picture at **CLASSROOM**

wasted /ˈweɪstɪd/ *adj* **1** having no useful result: *You've had a wasted trip – he's gone.* **2** if someone's body is wasted, it is very thin and weak **3** *informal* very drunk or strongly affected by illegal drugs

wasteful /ˈweɪstfəl/ *adj* using more of something than you should: *the wasteful use of resources*

wasteland /ˈweɪstlænd, -lənd/ *n* [C,U] an area of land which is not looked after, for example with old factories on it: *urban wasteland*

wastepaper basket /ˌweɪstˈpeɪpə ˌbɑːskɪt, ˈweɪstˌpeɪpə- $ ˈweɪstˌpeɪpər ˌbæ-/ *n* [C] *especially BrE* a small container in which you put bits of paper and other things that you do not want [= **wastebasket** *AmE*] → see box at **BIN** → see picture at **CLASSROOM**

watch¹ /wɒtʃ $ wɑːtʃ, wɒːtʃ/ *v*
1 [I,T] to look at and pay attention to something that is happening: *Watch me, I'll show you.* | *Watch carefully and you might learn something.* | **watch sb do sth** *She watched him drive away.* | **watch sb doing sth** *We watched the children playing.* | **watch TV/a film etc** *I was watching the news.* | **+what/how/where etc** *Watch what he does.* → see box at **SEE**
2 [T] to be careful about something: *Watch yourself* (=be careful) *when you cross the road.* | **+(that)** *Watch he doesn't run off on his own.* | **+where/what etc** *Watch what you're doing!*
3 watch it *spoken informal* used to warn someone to be careful: *Hey, watch it – you nearly hit that truck!*

4 watch your step *informal* to be careful because you might make someone angry
5 [T] to take care of someone or something for a short time: *Can you watch my bags for me?*
6 [T] to pay attention to a situation that interests or worries you: *The government will watch the progress of these schemes with interest.*
  watch out *phr v* to be careful and pay attention, because something unpleasant might happen: *Watch out! You might cut yourself.* | **+for** *You can ride your bike here, but watch out for cars.*
  watch over sb/sth *phr v* to take care of someone or something

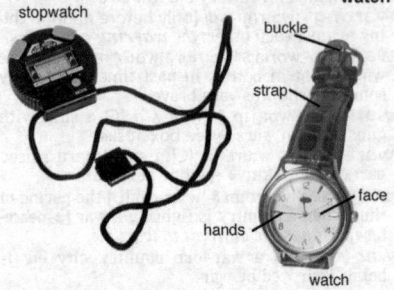

watch

stopwatch

buckle

strap

face

hands

watch

watch² *n*
1 [C] a small clock that you wear on your wrist: *My watch has stopped.* | *He looked at his watch.*
2 keep a (close) watch on/over sth/sb to watch someone or something carefully so that you are ready to deal with anything that happens: *The police are keeping a close watch on the area.*
3 keep watch to look around a place so that you can warn people if there is any danger: *Douglas kept watch while the others slept.*

watchdog /ˈwɒtʃdɒg $ ˈwɑːtʃdɔːg, ˈwɒːtʃ-/ *n* [C] a person or organization that checks that companies behave properly and protects the rights of ordinary people: *a consumer watchdog*

watchful /ˈwɒtʃfəl $ ˈwɑːtʃ-, ˈwɒːtʃ-/ *adj* careful to notice what is happening: *She cooked the meal under the watchful eye of her mother.*

watchword /ˈwɒtʃwɜːd $ ˈwɑːtʃwɜːrd, ˈwɒːtʃ-/ *n* [C] a word or phrase which expresses something that is very important: *Caution is still the watchword.*

water¹ /ˈwɔːtə $ ˈwɒːtər, ˈwɑː-/ *n*
1 [U] the clear liquid that falls as rain and is used for drinking and washing: *Can I have a drink of water?* | *a bowl of hot water* | *The refugees have no clean drinking water.* | *There was no electricity or running water* (=clean water from pipes). | *He prefers mineral water to tap water.*
2 [U] an area of water such as the sea or a lake: **shallow/deep water** *The ship ran aground in shallow water.*
3 waters [plural] a very large area of water, for example an ocean or a large river: *the coastal waters of Alaska* | **international/Arctic/Korean etc waters** *We received permission to*

sail in Japanese waters. | *The flood waters slowly receded.*

4 uncharted/troubled waters a situation that is difficult, dangerous, or unfamiliar

5 in hot/deep water in a lot of trouble

6 be water under the bridge to belong to the past and no longer be important → **keep your head above water** at HEAD¹ → **not hold water** at HOLD¹

water² v

1 [T] to pour water on a plant

2 [I] if your eyes water, liquid comes out of them: *The onions are making my eyes water.*

water sth ⇔ down *phr v* **1** to make a statement or plan less strong or less effective **2** to add water to a drink to make it less strong [➡ dilute]

watercolour *BrE*; **watercolor** *AmE* /ˈwɔːtəˌkʌlə $ ˈwɔːtərˌkʌlər, ˈwɑː-/ *n* [C,U] a kind of paint that you mix with water, or a painting done using this kind of paint

watercress /ˈwɔːtəkres $ ˈwɒtər-, ˈwɑː-/ *n* [U] a small green plant with strong-tasting leaves that grows in water

waterfall /ˈwɔːtəfɔːl $ ˈwɒtərfɒːl, ˈwɑː-/ *n* [C] a place where a river or stream drops down over a cliff or rock

waterfall

waterfront /ˈwɔːtə frʌnt $ ˈwɒtər-, ˈwɑː-/ *n* [C] an area beside a lake, river, or the sea: *Most of the hotels are down on the waterfront.*

waterhole /ˈwɔːtə həʊl $ ˈwɒtərhoʊl, ˈwɑː-/ *n* [C] a small area of water in a dry country

'watering can *n* [C] a container used for pouring water on plants

waterlogged /ˈwɔːtəlɒgd $ ˈwɒtərlɔːgd, ˈwɑː-, -lɑːgd/ *adj* land that is waterlogged is very wet or covered with water: *The pitch was waterlogged.*

watermark /ˈwɔːtəmɑːk $ ˈwɒtərmɑːrk, ˈwɑː-/ *n* [C] a design on a piece of paper, especially on money, that you can see when the paper is held up to the light

watermelon /ˈwɔːtəˌmelən $ ˈwɒtər-, ˈwɑː-/ *n* [C] a large round fruit with thick green skin, red flesh, and black seeds → see picture at FRUIT

'water ,polo *n* [U] a ball game played in water between two teams

waterproof¹ /ˈwɔːtəpruːf $ ˈwɒtər-, ˈwɑː-/ *adj* not allowing water to enter: *waterproof boots* → see picture at CLOTHES —**waterproof** *v* [T] *Plastic sheeting was used to waterproof the shed.*

waterproof² *n* [C usually plural] waterproof clothing

watershed /ˈwɔːtəʃed $ ˈwɒtər-, ˈwɑː-/ *n* [singular] **1** an event or time when very important changes happen: **+in** *The election marked a watershed in American politics.* **2 the watershed** the time in the evening after which programmes may be shown on British television which are not suitable for children

'water-,skiing *n* [U] a sport in which someone wearing SKIS is pulled over water by a boat —**water-ski** *v* [I] —**water skier** *n* [C]

watertight /ˈwɔːtətaɪt $ ˈwɒtər-, ˈwɑː-/ *adj* **1** containing no mistakes or weaknesses, and therefore impossible to criticize: *a watertight explanation* **2** not allowing any water to get in or out: *a watertight container*

waterway /ˈwɔːtəweɪ $ ˈwɒtər-, ˈwɑː-/ *n* [C] a river or CANAL that boats can travel on

watery /ˈwɔːtəri $ ˈwɒː-, ˈwɑː-/ *adj* **1** containing water, especially when this is unpleasant: *watery soup* **2** a watery light is very pale

watt /wɒt $ wɑːt/ *n* [C] a unit for measuring electrical power: *a 100 watt light bulb*

wave¹ /weɪv/ *v*

1 [I,T] to raise your arm and move your hand from side to side as a signal or greeting: **+to/at** *Anne waved at us and we waved back.* | *She waved to me from the other side of the road.* | **wave sb through/away etc** (=show someone where to go by waving) *The policeman waved us through.* | *She waved goodbye to Tony.* | *They stood on the platform and waved us off* (=waved as we were leaving.) → see picture on page A10

2 [I,T] if you wave something, or if it waves, it moves from side to side: **wave sth around/at/ towards etc** *He started shouting and waving his gun around.* | *The crowd were waving flags and cheering.*

wave sth ⇔ aside *phr v* to ignore what someone says

waves

wave² *n* [C]

1 a line of raised water that moves across the surface of the sea: *The children were playing in the waves.* | *She watched the waves breaking on the shore.* | *Huge waves were crashing into the boat.*

2 when something suddenly starts happening a lot: **wave of violence/attacks/bombings etc** *a wave of strikes* | *the latest crime wave to hit the city* | *Wave after wave of aircraft passed overhead.*

3 when someone suddenly feels a particular feeling very strongly: **wave of panic/fear/ enthusiasm etc** *Harriet was overcome by a wave of homesickness.*

4 the movement you make when you wave your hand: *He gave us a quick wave.*

5 the form in which some types of energy move, for example light and sound: **sound/light/radio waves** | *short-wave radio broadcasts*

W

6 make waves to complain or cause problems: *I didn't want to make any waves.*

→ **LONG WAVE, MEDIUM WAVE, NEW WAVE, SHOCK WAVE, TIDAL WAVE**

waveband /'weɪvbænd/ *n* [C] a set of sound waves of a particular length, used to broadcast radio programmes

wavelength /'weɪvleŋθ/ *n* [C] **1** the size of radio wave used by a radio company to broadcast its programmes **2** the distance between two waves of energy such as sound or light **3 be on the same wavelength** to have the same opinions and feelings as someone else

waver /'weɪvə $ -ər/ *v* [I] **1** to be unable to make a decision: *The party wavered between free trade and protectionism.* **2** to become less definite or less strong: *He never wavered in his loyalty.* **3** to shake a little: *His voice wavered.*

wavy /'weɪvi/ *adj* with curves in, not straight: *wavy hair* | *a wavy line* → see picture at **HAIR**

wax¹ /wæks/ *n* [U]

1 a thick substance made of fats or oils, used for making CANDLES and for polishing surfaces **2** the sticky substance in your ears

wax² *v* [T] **1 wax lyrical (about sth)** *humorous* to talk about something in a way that shows you think it is excellent **2 wax and wane** *literary* to increase and decrease: *Friendship can wax and wane like the moon.* **3** to polish a surface using wax **4** to remove hair from your body using wax

waxy /'wæksi/ *adj* having a shiny surface like wax: *waxy leaves*

way¹ /weɪ/

1 [C] a method of doing something: **way of doing sth** *There are different ways of doing this.* | **way to do sth** *What's the best way to get fit?* | *OK, do it your own way.* | **(in) the right/ wrong way** *You're doing this the wrong way.* | **way (a)round sth** (=method of dealing with sth) *There are several ways around this problem.* | **way out (of sth)** *There seemed to be no way out of the crisis.*

2 [C] the manner in which someone does something or in which something happens: **in a ... way** *He looked at me in a strange way.* | *The disease affects different people in different ways.* | *He had cooked the meat just the way I like it.* | **this/that way** *Try doing it this way.* | *I didn't know you felt that way.* | *Things are going to change* **in a big way** (=a lot).

3 [C] the road, path etc that you follow in order to go to a place: **+to** *What's the quickest way to the beach?* | *Could you* **tell me the way** *to the station?* | *He offered to* **show** *us* **the way** *back.* | *I hope someone* **knows the way.** | *They* **lost their way** *coming down off the mountain.* | **way in/out** *We couldn't find the way out.*

4 [C] a particular direction or position: *Which way is north?* | **the right/wrong way** *I think we might have gone the wrong way.* | *Face this way, please.* | *Is this picture* **the right way up?** | *You've got the letters* **the wrong way round.**

5 [singular] a distance or a length of time, especially a long one: *We're still* **a long way** *from the airport.* | **a long way off/away/ahead etc** *A peace settlement seems a long way off.* | *She slept* **most of the way** *home.*

6 by the way *spoken* used when saying something that is not connected with what you were talking about before: *Oh, by the way, I saw Marie yesterday.*

7 no way! *spoken* used to say that you will definitely not do or allow something: *'Dad, can I borrow the car tonight?' 'No way!'*

8 in a way/in some ways used to say that something is true about some parts of something: *Life is much easier now, in some ways.*

9 in the way/in sb's way if something is in the way, it is in front of you and prevents you from going somewhere or seeing something: *There was a big truck in the way.*

10 get in the way of sth to prevent something from happening: *Don't let your social life get in the way of your studies.*

11 make way a) to move so that someone or something can pass **b)** if one thing makes way for another thing, the other thing replaces it: *Several houses were torn down to make way for a new fire station.*

12 make your way to/towards/along etc sth to move towards something, especially when this takes a long time: *They made their way towards the exit.*

13 push/grope/inch etc your way somewhere to move somewhere in the way mentioned: *She elbowed her way to the front.*

14 know/find your way around to know or find out where things are: *It takes a few weeks to find your way around.*

15 on my/your way etc while you are going somewhere: *Could you get some milk on your way back home?*

16 be on its/his etc way to be arriving soon: *The taxi is on its way.*

17 have/get your (own) way to do what you want even if someone else wants something different: *They always let that kid get his own way.*

18 have a way with sb/sth to be especially good at dealing with people or things of a particular type: *He's always had a way with kids.*

19 go out of your way to do sth to make a special effort to do something, especially to help someone or be kind to them: *Ben went out of his way to help us.*

20 out of the way if something is out of the way, it is finished or you have dealt with it: *I want to get my homework out of the way before we leave.*

21 keep/stay out of sb's way to avoid someone: *It's best to stay out of her way when she's in this mood.*

22 in a bad way ill: *He looked in a bad way.*

23 you can't have it both ways *spoken* used to say that someone cannot have the advantages of two opposite things and must choose one

24 split/divide sth two/three etc ways to divide something into two/three etc equal parts

25 sth has come a long way if something has come a long way, it has developed and improved a lot: *Psychiatry has come a long way since the 1920s.*

26 way to go! *AmE spoken* used to say 'well done'

→ **NO WAY, RIGHT OF WAY**

way² *adv informal* **1** by a large amount: *The film was* **way too long.** | **way ahead/behind etc** *She was way ahead of us.* | *We met* **way back** (=a long time ago) *in the 70s.* | *Your guess was* **way**

out (=completely wrong). **2** *informal* extremely: *This is way cool.*

waylay /'weɪleɪ/ v [T] past tense and past participle **waylaid** *literary* to stop or attack someone when they are going somewhere

way of 'life n [C] plural **ways of** life your way of life is the way that you live: *the American way of life*

way-'out adj *informal* very modern or unusual

wayside /'weɪsaɪd/ n **fall/go by the wayside** to stop being successful

wayward /'weɪwəd $ -wərd/ adj behaving badly: *his wayward son*

WC /,dʌbəlju: 'si:/ n BrE *old-fashioned* water closet used on signs to show where there is a public toilet

we /wi; strong wi:/ pron

1 the person who is speaking and one or more other people: *We ordered our meal.* | *He didn't care, but we did.*
2 people in general: *Today we know much more about the disease.*

weak /wi:k/ adj

1 not having much strength or energy [≠ strong]: *She's too weak to feed herself.* | *Her knees felt weak.* | *He managed a weak smile.*
2 unable to support a lot of weight and likely to break: *The bridge was too weak to support the weight of the traffic.*
3 not very powerful or successful: *The president is now in quite a weak position.* | *a weak economy* | *The dollar is still quite weak* (=not worth very much) *compared to other currencies.*
4 *disapproving* easily influenced by other people: *a weak and indecisive man*
5 not good at doing something: *His spelling was weak.* | *one of the weaker students in the class* | **+at** *I'm quite weak at maths.* | *Be honest about your **weak points*** (=things you are not good at).
6 a weak excuse or reason is not easy to believe
7 weak drinks have little taste because they contain a lot of water: *weak tea*
8 a weak sound or light is not very loud or bright [≠ faint]
—**weakly** adv: *She smiled weakly.*

weaken /'wi:kən/ v [I,T] **1** to become less powerful or less strong, or to make someone or something do this: *The earthquake has weakened several buildings.* | *The president's position has weakened.* **2** to make someone less determined, or to become less determined: *Nothing could weaken her resolve.* | *He knew he would weaken.*

weakling /'wi:k-lɪŋ/ n [C] someone who is very weak physically

weakness /'wi:knəs/ n

1 [U] when someone or something is not powerful, determined, or strong: *I dared not show any **sign of weakness**.* | *He caught me in a **moment of weakness**.* | *the weakness of the pound against the dollar*
2 [C] a problem or fault: **+in** *There are several weaknesses in their argument.* | *What are your main **strengths and weaknesses**?*
3 have a weakness for sth to like something very much, especially something that you should not have or do: *He had a weakness for chocolate.*

wealth /welθ/ n

1 [singular,U] a large amount of money or property that a rich person has: *She enjoyed sharing her wealth with her friends.* | *The purpose of industry is to **create wealth**.*
2 a wealth of sth a lot of something good: *The book contains **a wealth of information**.*

wealthy /'welθi/ adj

1 rich: *an extremely wealthy family* | *the wealthy countries of the world* → see box at RICH
2 the wealthy people who have a lot of money or possessions

wean /wi:n/ v [T] to gradually stop feeding a baby on its mother's milk and start giving it ordinary food
wean sb off sth *phr v* to help someone to gradually stop doing or having something: *She wanted to wean him off junk food.*

weapon /'wepən/ n [C]

1 something that is used to attack people or to fight against people: *They were armed with knives and other weapons.* | *Police are still searching for the **murder weapon**.* | **nuclear/chemical/biological etc weapons** *Is he prepared to use nuclear weapons?* | **weapons of mass destruction**
2 something that you can use in order to achieve your aim: *The cameras are another weapon in the fight against car crime.*

weaponry /'wepənri/ n [U] weapons

wear¹ /weə $ wer/ v past tense **wore** /wɔ: $ wɔ:r/ past participle **worn** /wɔ:n $ wɔ:rn/

1 [T] to have something such as clothes, shoes, or jewellery on your body: *She was wearing jeans and a red jumper.* | *What are you wearing to the party?* | *He wears glasses for reading.* | *She never wears make-up.*
2 [T] to have your hair in a particular style: *Fay wore her hair in a bun.*
3 [T] to have a particular expression on your face: *He came out wearing a big grin on his face.*
4 [I,T] to become thinner or weaker after continuous use, or to make something do this: *The carpet was starting to wear at the edges.* | *You've worn a hole in your sock.*
5 wear well to remain in good condition after being used
6 wear thin if an excuse or joke is wearing thin, it has been used a lot and is no longer effective
wear away *phr v* to gradually become thinner or smoother because of being rubbed or touched, or to make this happen: **wear sth ⇔ away** *Look how the rocks have been worn away by the sea.*
wear down *phr v* **1 wear sb ⇔ down** to make someone weaker or less determined: *Lewis gradually wore down his opponent.* **2** to gradually become flatter or smaller because of being rubbed or used, or to make this happen: **wear sth ⇔ down** *You've worn your shoes down at the heel.*
wear off *phr v* if a feeling or effect wears off, it gradually stops: *The drug was starting to wear off.*
wear on *phr v* **as the day/evening etc wore on** used to say that something happened gradually during a particular day, evening etc: *It became hotter as the day wore on.*

W

wear out phr v **1** if something wears out, or if you wear it out, it becomes damaged and useless because it has been used so much: **wear sth ⇔ out** Terry had worn out the soles of his shoes. **2 wear sb ⇔ out** to make someone feel very tired [= exhaust]: The kids are wearing me out. → **WORN OUT**

wear² n [U] **1 children's/women's/casual etc wear** clothing worn by children, by women, on informal occasions etc **2** damage caused when something is used over a long period: The carpets are showing signs of wear. | Check the equipment for wear and tear (=damage). → the worse for wear at **WORSE¹**

wearing /'weərɪŋ $ 'wer-/ adj making you feel tired or annoyed: He can be a bit wearing at times.

wearisome /'wɪərɪsəm $ 'wɪr-/ adj formal making you feel tired or annoyed: a wearisome task

weary¹ /'wɪəri $ 'wɪr-/ adj **1** very tired: She gave a weary sigh. **2** wanting something to stop: +of People were growing weary of the war. —**wearily** adv: We walked wearily home. —**weariness** n [U]

weary² v [I,T] wearied, wearying, wearies formal to make someone tired, or to become tired: The children wearied her.

weasel /'wiːzəl/ n [C] a small wild animal with a long body

weather¹ /'weðə $ -ər/ n
1 [singular, U] the temperature and other conditions such as sun, rain, and wind: What's the weather like today? | The weather was lovely. | We had to cancel the match because of bad weather. | a warning of severe weather over the weekend | We've had a lot of wet weather recently.

THESAURUS

What's the weather like?
It's sunny/fine/lovely/glorious.
It's rainy/wet/cloudy/windy/foggy.
It's cool/chilly.
It's warm.
It's (boiling) hot.
It's (freezing) cold.
It's snowing.
It's raining.
It's pouring (down) BrE/It's pouring (rain) AmE (=raining a lot).
It's drizzling (=raining a little).
→ **RAIN, SNOW, SUN, WIND**

2 under the weather slightly ill: I was feeling a bit under the weather. → see box at **ILL**

weather² v **1** [T] if you weather a difficult period, you manage to continue until things improve: We will have to **weather the storm**. **2** [I,T] if a surface is weathered, or if it weathers, the wind, rain, and sun gradually change its appearance: his weathered skin | The brick had weathered to a lovely pinky-brown.

weather-,beaten adj damaged or changed by the wind and sun: the sailor's weather-beaten face

weather ,forecast n [C] a report on the television or radio that says what the weather will be like: It's going to rain, according to the weather forecast.

weather ,forecaster also **weatherman** /'weðəmæn $ -ðər-/, **weathergirl** /'weðəgɜːl $ -ðərgɜːrl/ n [C] a person on the television or radio whose job is to say what the weather will be like

weather vane n [C] a metal object that moves to show the direction of the wind

weave /wiːv/ v
1 [I,T] past tense **wove** /wəʊv $ woʊv/ past participle , **woven** /'wəʊvən $ 'woʊ-/ to make cloth, a CARPET, a basket etc by crossing threads or thin pieces under and over each other: a beautifully woven carpet
2 [T] past tense **wove** past participle **woven** to join different ideas or subjects together in a clever way: The plot weaves together fact and fiction.
3 [I,T] past tense and past participle **weaved** to move somewhere by turning and changing direction a lot: +in and out/through She watched him weaving in and out of the traffic on his bike. | The snake was **weaving its way** through the grass.
—**weaver** n [C]

web /web/ n **1** [C] a net of thin threads made by a SPIDER to catch insects → see picture at **SPIDER 2 the Web** the system that connects computers around the world together so that people can use and find information on the Internet [= the World Wide Web; ➡ the Internet, the Net]: on the Web a guide to the best education-related sites on the Web **3** [singular] a set of things that are connected with each other in a complicated way: +of a web of lies

webbed /webd/ adj webbed feet have skin between the toes → see picture on page A2

web ,browser n [C] a computer program that finds information on the Internet and shows it on your computer screen

webcam /'webkæm/ n [C] a video camera that broadcasts what it is filming on a website

web page n [C] all the information that you can see in one part of a website

website /'websaɪt/ n [C] a place on the Internet where you can find information about something, especially a particular organization: For more information, visit our website.

wed /wed/ v [I,T] past tense and past participle **wedded** or **wed** literary to marry

Wed. also **Wed** BrE a written abbreviation of **Wednesday**

we'd /wid; strong wiːd/ the short form of 'we had' or 'we would': We'd better go now. | We'd like some more coffee.

wedding /'wedɪŋ/ n [C] a marriage ceremony: Have you been invited to their wedding? | **wedding party/reception** (=a special meal or party after a wedding) | **wedding dress/cake/present** the bride's wedding dress

TOPIC

At a **wedding ceremony/service** the most important people are the **bride** (=woman getting married) and the **bridegroom** (=man getting married). The **best man** helps the bridegroom and the **bridesmaids** help the bride. After the ceremony, there is usually a

reception (=special party). Then the married couple **go on honeymoon** (=special holiday).
→ ENGAGED, MARRIED

'wedding ring n [C] a ring that you wear to show that you are married

wedge¹ /wedʒ/ n [C] a piece of something which is thin and pointed at one end and thick at the other end: **+of** *a wedge of chocolate cake*

wedge² v [T] **1** to force something firmly into a narrow space: *She kept her hands wedged between her knees.* **2 wedge sth open/shut** to put something under a door, window etc to make it stay open or shut

Wednesday /'wenzdi, -deɪ/ n [C,U] written abbreviation **Weds.** or **Wed.** the day between Tuesday and Thursday
→ see examples at MONDAY → see box at DAY

wee¹ /wiː/ adj very small – used especially in Scotland: *a wee child*

wee² v [I] BrE spoken to URINATE (=make liquid waste flow out of your body) – used by or to children —**wee** n [singular]

weed¹ /wiːd/ n [C] a wild plant that grows where you do not want it to grow: *She was pulling up weeds in the garden.*

weed² v [I,T] to remove weeds from a garden or other place
weed sb/sth ⇔ **out** phr v to get rid of people or things that are not very good

weedy /'wiːdi/ adj BrE informal physically weak or having a weak character

week /wiːk/ n [C]
1 a period of seven days, especially one that begins on a Monday and ends on a Sunday: *The movie starts this week.* | **last/next week** (=the week before or after this one) *See you next week.* | *We had drawing lessons once a week.* | *I've been living here for six weeks.*
2 the part of the week between Monday and Friday, when people are working or studying: **during the week** *I don't see the kids much during the week.*
3 (on) Monday week/Tuesday week etc BrE a week after the day that is mentioned: *I'll be back Monday week.*

weekday /'wiːkdeɪ/ n [C] any day of the week except Saturday and Sunday

weekend /ˌwiːk'end◂ 'wiːkend $ 'wiːkend/ n [C] Saturday and Sunday: *What are you doing this weekend* (=the weekend that is coming)? | *We're going to Paris for a long weekend* (=Saturday and Sunday and one or two more days). | **last/next weekend** (=the weekend before or after this one) | **at the weekend** BrE/**on the weekend** AmE: *I like to play golf at the weekend.*

weekly¹ /'wiːkli/ adj happening or done every week: *a weekly newspaper* → see box at REGULAR
—**weekly** adv

weekly² n [C] plural **weeklies** a magazine or newspaper that appears once a week

weep /wiːp/ v [I,T] past tense and past participle **wept** /wept/ literary to cry: *She wept with relief.* → see box at CRY

weigh /weɪ/ v
1 [linking verb] to have a particular weight: *The baby weighs 12 pounds.* | *How much do you weigh?*
2 [T] to measure how heavy someone or something is: *Have you weighed yourself lately?*
3 also **weigh up** [T] to consider something carefully before making a decision: *It is my job to weigh the evidence.* | **weigh sth against sth** *You have to weigh the benefits against the extra costs.*
4 [I] formal to influence someone's opinion and the decision that they make: **+against** *Her age weighs against her.*
weigh sb ⇔ **down** phr v **1** if something weighs you down, it is heavy and difficult to carry **2** if you are weighed down by your problems and responsibilities, you worry a lot about them
weigh on sb/sth phr v to make someone feel worried and upset: *I'm sure there's something weighing on his mind.*
weigh sth ⇔ **out** phr v to measure an amount of something by weighing it: *Could you weigh out half a pound of flour for me?*
weigh sb/sth ⇔ **up** phr v to consider something or someone carefully in order to make a judgment: *She weighed up the options before giving her decision.*

weight¹ /weɪt/ n
1 [C,U] how heavy someone or something is, or the quality of being heavy: *Your weight is about right.* | **put on/lose weight** (=become heavier or lighter) *She's been trying to lose weight for months.* | *I'm watching my weight* (=being careful not to gain weight). | *The roof collapsed under the weight of the snow.*
2 [singular, U] something that makes you feel worried: **+of** *the weight of responsibility* | *The baby's healthy, so that's a weight off our minds* (=it is no longer a cause of worry).
3 weights [plural] heavy pieces of metal, usually fixed to a metal bar, that people lift to make their muscles bigger → see box at EXERCISE
4 [C] a piece of metal weighing a particular amount that is balanced against something to measure how much that thing weighs
5 [C] a heavy object: *Avoid lifting heavy weights.* → **pull your weight** at PULL¹

weight²
weight sth ⇔ **down** phr v to put something heavy on or in something so that it does not move: *The nets are weighted down with lead.*

weighted /'weɪtɪd/ adj **be weighted in favour of sb/against sb** if a system is weighted in favour of or against a group of people, it gives them advantages or disadvantages

weightless /'weɪtləs/ adj something that is weightless seems to have no weight, especially when it is floating in space or water —**weightlessness** n [U]

weigh

scales BrE/
scale AmE

W

weightlifting /ˈweɪtˌlɪftɪŋ/ n [U] the sport of lifting weights attached to the ends of a bar —**weight-lifter** n [C]

ˈweight ˌtraining n [U] a form of exercise in which you lift special pieces of metal

weighty /ˈweɪti/ adj important and serious: a weighty problem

weir /wɪə $ wɪr/ n [C] a wall or fence built across a river to control or stop the flow of water

weird /wɪəd $ wɪrd/ adj informal unusual and strange: I had a really weird dream. → see box at STRANGE
—**weirdly** adv

weirdo /ˈwɪədəʊ $ ˈwɪrdoʊ/ n [C] plural **weirdos** informal someone who seems very strange

welcome¹ /ˈwelkəm/ spoken used to greet someone who has just arrived: +**to** Welcome to Chicago! | **Welcome back** – it's good to see you again.

welcome² adj
1 if you are welcome in a place, the other people want you to be there: I had the feeling I wasn't welcome. | They all did their best to **make** me **feel welcome**.
2 you're welcome! spoken used to reply politely to someone who has just thanked you for something: 'Thanks for the coffee.' 'You're welcome.'
3 if something is welcome, people are pleased that it has happened, because it is useful, pleasant etc: a welcome suggestion | a welcome breeze
4 be welcome to do sth spoken used to invite someone to do something if they would like to: You're welcome to stay for lunch.
5 be welcome to sth spoken used to say that someone can have something if they want it, because you definitely do not want it: If Rob wants that job, he's welcome to it!

welcome³ v [T]
1 to say hello in a friendly way to someone who has just arrived [➡ **greet**]: Jill was welcoming the guests at the door. | They **welcomed** us **warmly**.
2 to be glad when something happens or is done, or to say that you are glad: We would welcome a change in the law.

welcome⁴ n **1** [singular] the way in which you greet someone when they arrive at a place: They gave him a very **warm welcome** when he returned to work. **2 outstay/overstay you welcome** to stay at someone's house longer than they want you to

welcoming /ˈwelkəmɪŋ/ adj pleasant and making you feel welcome: a friendly hotel with a welcoming atmosphere

weld /weld/ v [T] to join metal objects to each other by heating them and pressing them together when they are hot —**welder** n [C]

welfare /ˈwelfeə $ -fer/ n [U] **1** someone's welfare is their health and happiness: We're only concerned with your welfare. **2** help that is provided for people who have personal or social problems: welfare services **3** AmE money paid by the government in the US to people who are very poor or unemployed: **on welfare** Most of the people in this neighborhood are on welfare.

ˌwelfare ˈstate / $ ˈ.. ./ n **the welfare state** a system in which the government provides money, free medical care etc for people who are unemployed, ill, or too old to work

we'll /wɪl; strong wiːl/ the short form of 'we will': We'll have to leave soon.

well¹ /wel/ adv **better** /ˈbetə $ -ər/ **best** /best/
1 in a good, successful, or a satisfactory way: Did you sleep well? | The business is **doing well**. | I hope the party goes well. → see box at GOOD
2 thoroughly or completely: Mix the flour and butter well. | I don't know her very well. | Summer is now **well and truly** (=completely) over.
3 very much or a lot: +**before/after/above/below etc** By the time they finished, it was well after midnight. | The village is well **worth** a visit.
4 as well (as sb/sth) in addition to something or someone else: My sister's going as well. | He's learning French as well as Italian. → see box at ALSO
5 well done spoken used to praise someone when you think they have done something very well: 'I got an 'A' in Spanish.' 'Well done!'
6 may/might/could well used to say that something is likely to happen or is likely to be true: There may well be another earthquake very soon.
7 may/might as well spoken used when you do not particularly want to do something but you decide you should do it: We may as well get started.
8 might/could (just) as well used to say that a course of action that was easier, cheaper etc would have had an equally good result: The taxi was so slow, we might just as well have gone on the bus.
9 can't very well do sth spoken used to say that it does not seem sensible or fair to do something: We can't very well just leave her on her own.

well² adj **better, best**
1 healthy: You're **looking** very well. | I should be better by this weekend. | I hope you **get well** soon. | 'How are you?' 'Very well, thank you.'
2 all is well used to say that a situation is satisfactory: I hope all is well with you.
3 it's just as well (that) spoken used to say that it is lucky or good that things have happened in the way they have done: It's just as well we didn't stay any longer, because it's just started raining.
4 it's/that's all very well spoken used to say that you are not happy or satisfied with something: It's all very well for you to say you're sorry, but I've been waiting here for two hours!
5 it is as well to do sth used to give someone advice: It would be as well to check.

well³ spoken
1 used to pause before saying something, or to emphasize what you are about to say: Well, let's see now, I could meet you on Thursday. | 'James doesn't want to come to the cinema with us.' 'Well then, let's go on our own.'
2 also **oh 'well** used to say that you accept a situation, even though it is not a very good one: Oh well, at least you did your best.
3 also **ˌwell, 'well** used when you are surprised about something: 'She's just got a job with CNN.' 'Well, well.'
4 used when you want to start telling someone more about someone or something that you have just mentioned: You know that guy I was telling you about? Well, he's been arrested!

W

5 well? used to ask someone to reply to you or tell you what has happened: *Well? What did he say?*

well⁴ *n* [C] a deep hole in the ground from which water or oil is taken → OIL WELL

well⁵ *v*

well up *phr v literary* if a liquid wells up, it rises and may start to flow: *I felt tears well up in my eyes.*

,well-'balanced *adj* **1** a well-balanced person is sensible and does not suddenly become angry, upset etc **2** a well-balanced meal or DIET contains all the things you need to stay healthy

,well-be'haved *adj* a well-behaved child behaves in the way he or she should

,well-'being *n* [U] a feeling of being comfortable, healthy, and happy

,well-brought-'up *adj* a well-brought-up child has been taught to be polite and behave well

,well-'built *adj* someone who is well-built is big and strong

,well-con'nected *adj* knowing a lot of powerful important people

,well-'done *adj* meat that is well-done has been cooked thoroughly [➡ **rare, medium**]: *He likes his steak well-done.*

,well-'dressed *adj* wearing good clothes

,well-'earned *adj* deserved, because you have worked hard: *He was enjoying a well-earned rest.*

,well-es'tablished *adj* something that is well-established has existed for a long time and is respected or trusted by people

,well-'fed *adj* a well-fed animal or person gets plenty of good food to eat

,well-'heeled *adj informal* rich

wellies /'weliz/ *n* [plural] *BrE informal* WELLINGTONS

,well-in'formed *adj* someone who is well-informed knows a lot about a subject or different subjects

wellingtons /'welɪŋtənz/ also **'wellington ,boots** *n* [plural] *BrE* long rubber boots that stop your feet getting wet

,well-in'tentioned *adj* well-meaning

,well-'kept *adj* **1** something that is well-kept has been kept neat and tidy: *well-kept gardens* **2** a well-kept secret is one that few people know about

,well-'known *adj* known about by a lot of people: *a well-known artist and writer* → see box at FAMOUS

,well-'meaning *adj* trying to help, but often making the situation worse: *well-meaning advice*

,well-'off *adj* fairly rich: *Her family are quite well-off.* → see box at RICH

,well-'paid *adj* someone who is well-paid receives a lot of money for their work

well-read /,wel 'red◂/ *adj* someone who is well-read has read many books and knows a lot about different subjects

,well-'rounded *adj* someone who is well-rounded has had a wide variety of experiences or is able to do many different things

,well-'spoken *adj* speaking in a correct and socially acceptable way

,well-'stocked *adj* having a large supply and variety of food or drink: *a well-stocked general store*

,well-to-'do *adj* rich and having a high position in society → see box at RICH

'well-,wisher *n* [C] someone who does something to show that they want another person to succeed, become healthy again etc: *She received hundreds of cards from well-wishers.*

welter /'weltə $ -ər/ *n* **a welter of sth** *formal* a large and confusing number of different details or feelings: *a welter of information*

wend /wend/ *v* **wend your way** *literary* to go slowly from one place to another: *People began to wend their way home.*

went /went/ *v* the past tense of GO

wept /wept/ *v* the past tense and past participle of WEEP

we're /wɪə $ wɪr/ the short form of 'we are': *We're going home.*

were /wə; *strong* wɜː $ wər; *strong* wɜːr/ *v* the past tense of BE

weren't /wɜːnt $ wɜːrnt/ the short form of 'were not': *His parents weren't very pleased when they found out.*

werewolf /'weəwʊlf, 'wɪə- $ 'wer-, 'wɪr-/ *n* [C] plural **werewolves** /-wʊlvz/ a person in stories who changes into a WOLF

west¹, **West** /west/ written abbreviation **W** [singular,U]

1 the direction towards the place where the sun goes down: *Which way is west?* | **from/towards the west** *A damp wind blew from the west.* | **to the west (of sth)** *a village to the west of Brussels* → see picture at NORTH¹

2 the west the western part of a country or area: *Rain will spread to the west later today.* | **+of** *the west of the island*

3 the West the western part of the world, especially western Europe and North America

west², **West** written abbreviation **W** *adj* [only before noun]

1 in the west or facing the west: *the west coast of the island* | *West Africa*

2 a west wind comes from the west

west³ written abbreviation **W** *adv* towards the west: *The window faces west.* | **+of** *The meeting took place in Rustenburg, 50 km west of Pretoria.*

westbound /'westbaʊnd/ *adj* travelling or leading towards the west: *westbound traffic*

westerly /'westəli $ -ərli/ *adj* **1** towards or in the west: *We set off in a westerly direction.* **2** a westerly wind comes from the west

western¹, **Western** /'westən $ -ərn/ written abbreviation **W** *adj* **1** in or from the west of a country or area: *the largest city in western Iowa* | *Western Australia* **2 Western** in or from Europe or North America: *Western philosophies*

western², **Western** *n* [C] a film about life in the 19th century in the American West, especially about COWBOYS → see box at FILM

westerner, Westerner /'westənə $ -tərnər/ *n* [C] someone from Europe or North America

westernize also **-ise** *BrE* /'westənaɪz $ -ər-/ *v* [T] if a country becomes westernized, it becomes like countries in North America and Western Europe —**westernization** /,westənaɪ'zeɪʃən $ -tərnə-/ *n* [U]

westernmost /'westənməʊst $ -tərnmoʊst/ *adj* furthest west: *the westernmost part of the island*

W

westwards /-wədz $ -wərdz/ also **westward**
/'westwəd $ -wərd/ adv towards the west: *The
ship turned westwards.* —**westward** adj: *westward flights*

wet¹ /wet/ adj

1 covered in water or another liquid [≠ dry]: *wet
clothes* | *I didn't want to get my hair wet.* |
soaking/dripping wet (=extremely wet) *We
arrived home soaking wet.* | *My jeans are wet
through* (=completely wet).

2 a) rainy: *It's very wet outside.* → see box at
WEATHER **b) the wet** rainy weather: *Come in out
of the wet.*

3 not yet dry: *wet paint*
—**wetness** n [U]

wet² v [T] past tense and past participle **wet** or
wetted, present participle **wetting** **1** to make
something wet: *Wet this cloth and put it on her
forehead.* **2 wet the bed/your pants etc** to
make your bed etc wet because you URINATE by
accident

,**wet 'blanket** / $ '. ,../ n [singular] informal
someone who spoils other people's enjoyment by
not taking part in an activity

'**wet suit** n [C] rubber clothing that people wear
to keep warm when swimming under water

we've /wiv; strong wiːv/ the short form of 'we
have': *We've got to leave soon.*

whack /wæk/ v [T] informal to hit someone or
something hard —**whack** n [C]

whacked /wækt/ adj spoken very tired

whale /weɪl/ n [C] a very large animal that lives
in the sea and looks like a fish

whaling /'weɪlɪŋ/ n [U] the activity of hunting
whales —**whaler** n [C]

wharf /wɔːf $ wɔːrf/ n [C] plural **wharves**
/wɔːvz $ wɔːrvz/ a structure that is built out
into the water so that boats can stop next to it
[= pier]

what /wɒt $ wɑːt, wʌt/ determiner, pron

1 used to ask for information about something:
What are you doing? | *What did Ellen say?* |
What kind of dog is that? → see box at **WHICH**

2 used to talk about something that is not
known or certain: *She asked them what they
wanted for lunch.* | *Tell me what happened.* |
what to do/say/expect etc *I'm not sure what to
do.*

3 the thing which: *I like what you're saying.* |
What you need is a holiday.

4 used at the beginning of a sentence to empha-
size a description: *What an idiot!* | *What a nice
day!*

5 what? spoken **a)** used to ask someone to
repeat something they have just said because
you did not hear it properly: *'Do you want a fried
egg?' 'What?'* **b)** used when you have heard
someone calling to you and you are asking them
what they want: *'Anita?' 'What?' 'Can you come
here for a minute?'* **c)** used when you are surprised or shocked

6 what if...? spoken used to talk about something that might happen, especially something
bad or frightening: *What if he got lost?*

7 what's up (with sb/sth) used to ask what is
wrong with someone or something: *What's up
with Denise?* → see box at **PROBLEM**

8 what with sth spoken used when you are
giving the reasons for something, especially a

bad situation: *I can't afford to run a car, what
with petrol, insurance, and everything.*

9 what's more spoken used to add another
thing to what you have just said, especially
something interesting or surprising

10 ... or what? spoken used to emphasize a
question or to make it a statement: *Are you
afraid of him, or what?* | *Is she brilliant or what*
(=she is brilliant)?

→ **guess what?** at **GUESS¹** → **so what?** at **so¹** →
what about sb/sth? at **ABOUT¹**

whatever¹ /wɒt'evə $ wɑːt'evər, wʌt-/ deter-
miner, pron

1 any or all of the things that are wanted,
needed, or possible: *Just take whatever you
need.* | *He needs whatever help he can get.*

2 used to say that it is not important what
happens, what you do etc because it does not
change the situation: *Whatever I say, she always
disagrees.*

3 ... or whatever spoken used to refer to other
things of the same kind: *You can go swimming,
scuba diving, or whatever.*

4 spoken used in a question when you are surprised or annoyed: *Whatever are you talking
about?*

5 spoken used when you do not know exactly
what something is: *He's doing Communication
Studies, whatever that is.*

whatever² also **whatsoever** /,wɒtsəu'evə
$ -sou'evər, ,wʌt-/ adv used to emphasize a
negative statement: *She had no money whatsoever.*

wheat /wiːt/ n [U] a plant that produces grain
used for making flour, or this grain
→ **WHOLE WHEAT**

wheedle /'wiːdl/ v [I,T] to persuade someone to
do something or give you something: *She managed to wheedle some money out of her parents.*

wheel¹ /wiːl/ n [C]

1 one of the round things under a car, bicycle
etc that turn when it moves: **front/rear wheel** →
see picture at **BICYCLE**

2 a STEERING WHEEL: *He had fallen asleep at the
wheel* (=while driving).

3 a round object joined to a ROD in a machine,
which turns when the machine operates: *a gear
wheel*

wheel² v **1** [T] to move something that has
wheels: *She wheeled her bike into the garage.*

2 [I] to turn around suddenly: **+around** *Anita
wheeled around and started yelling at us.* →
WHEELING AND DEALING

wheelbarrow /'wiːl,bærəu $ -rou/ n [C] an
open container with one wheel and two handles
that you use outdoors to carry things, especially
in the garden

wheelchair /'wiːltʃeə $ -tʃer/ n [C] a chair
with large wheels, used by people who cannot
walk

'**wheel clamp** also **clamp** n [C] a metal object
that is fastened to the wheel of an illegally
parked car so that it cannot be driven away
—**wheel-clamp** v [T]

,**wheeler-'dealer** n [C] someone in business or
politics who uses complicated or slightly dishonest methods to achieve what they want

wheeling and 'dealing n [U] the making of complicated and sometimes dishonest deals, especially in business or politics

wheeze /wiːz/ v [I] to breathe with difficulty, making a noise in your throat and chest → see box at BREATHE —**wheezy** adj

when /wen/ adv, linking word
1 at what time: *When are we leaving?* | *When did you notice he was gone?* | **when to do sth** *I'll tell you when to stop.*
2 at or during the time that something happens: *He was nine when his father died.* | *He always wears glasses except when playing football.* | *The best moment was when Barnes scored the winning goal.*
3 after or as soon as something happens: *I'll phone you when I get home.*
4 even though something is true: *Why do you want a new camera when your old one's perfectly good?*
→ **since when** at SINCE

whenever /wen'evə $ -'evər/ adv, linking word
1 every time: *Whenever we come here, we always see someone we know.*
2 at any time: *Come over whenever you want.* | *Use recycled paper whenever possible.*

where /weə $ wer/ adv, linking word
1 in or to which place: *Where do you live?* | *I think I know where he's gone.* | **where to do sth** *It's hard to know where to get help.*
2 used to talk about a particular place, or to give more information about it: *Stay right where you are.* | *In 1963 we moved to Boston, where my grandparents lived.*
3 in or to any place [= **wherever**]: *You can sit where you like.*
4 used to talk about a part of a process or situation: *It had reached the point where both of us wanted a divorce.*

whereabouts[1] /ˌweərə'bauts $ 'werəbauts/ adv spoken used to ask about a place: *Whereabouts do you live?*

whereabouts[2] /'weərəbauts $ 'wer-/ n [plural, U] the place where someone or something is: *His whereabouts are a mystery.*

whereas /weər'æz $ wer-/ linking word, formal used to say that one person, thing, or situation is different from another: *Nowadays the journey takes six hours, whereas then it took several weeks.*

whereby /weə'baɪ $ wer-/ adv formal by or according to which: *a law whereby all children could receive free education*

wherein /weər'ın $ wer-/ adv formal in which place or part

whereupon /ˌweərə'pɒn $ 'werəpɑːn, -pɔːn/ linking word, formal after which: *One of them called the other a liar, whereupon a fight broke out.*

wherever /weər'evə $ wer'evər/ adv, linking word
1 in any place: *Sit wherever you like.*
2 in every place or situation: *I always have her picture with me wherever I go.* | *We try to use locally produced food wherever possible.*
3 spoken used in a question to show surprise: *Wherever did you find that old thing?*

wherewithal /'weəwɪðɔːl $ 'werwɪðɒːl/ n **the wherewithal to do sth** the money, skills etc you need in order to do something

whet /wet/ v **whetted, whetting** **whet sb's appetite** to make someone want more of something by letting them try it or see what it is like

whether /'weðə $ -ər/ linking word
1 used when talking about a choice you have to make or about something that is not certain: *He asked her whether she was coming.* | *I couldn't decide whether or not I wanted to go.*
2 used to say that something definitely will or will not happen whatever the situation is: *Whether you like it or not, you have to take that test.*

whew /hjuː/ another spelling of PHEW

which /wɪtʃ/ determiner, pron
1 used to ask or talk about one or more members of a group of people or things, when you are uncertain about it or about them: *Which book is yours?* | **+of** *I don't know which of us was more scared.* | *I wondered which dress to buy.*
2 used to say what thing you are talking about, or to give more information about something: *I want a car which doesn't use too much petrol.* | *The house, which was built in the 16th century, is worth several million pounds.* | *One of the boys kept laughing, which annoyed Jane intensely.* | *She may have missed the train,* **in which case** (=if this has happened) *she won't arrive for another hour.* → see box at THAT

GRAMMAR

Which and **what** *are both used when you are asking about one thing out of a number of possible things.*
Use **which** when there is a small number of possibilities *Which house does Tom live in?*
Use **what** when there is a very large number of possibilities *What name have they given the baby? What is the answer to question 12?*
Which can be followed by 'of' but **what** cannot *Which of these dresses do you like best?*

whichever /wɪtʃ'evə $ -'evər/ determiner, pron
1 any of a group of things or people: *You can choose whichever one you like.*
2 used to say that it does not matter which thing or person is chosen because the result will be the same: *Whichever way you look at it, he's guilty.*

whiff /wɪf/ n [C] a slight smell: **+of** *As she walked past, I* **caught** *a whiff of her perfume* (=smelled it).

while[1] /waɪl/ linking word
1 during the time that something is happening: *They arrived while we were having dinner.* | *Thieves broke in while she was asleep.*
2 all the time that something is happening: *Would you look after the children while I go shopping?*
3 although: *While it was a good school, I was not happy there.*
4 used to say that one person, thing, or situation is different from another [= **whereas**]: *Schools in the north tend to be better equipped, while those in the south are relatively poor.*

W

while² *n* **a while** a period of time, especially a short one: **a short/little/long while** *He'll be back in a little while.* → see box at RECENTLY → **(every) once in a while** at ONCE¹ → **be worth sb's while** at WORTH¹

while³ *v* **while away the hours/evening/days etc** to spend time in a pleasant and lazy way: *We whiled away the evenings playing cards.*

whilst /waɪlst/ *linking word especially BrE* while

whim /wɪm/ *n* [C] a sudden desire to do or have something, especially when there is no good reason for it: **on a whim** *I didn't just leave on a whim.*

whimper /'wɪmpə $ -ər/ *v* [I] to make low crying sounds, because you are sad or in pain: *The dog ran off whimpering.* —**whimper** *n* [C]

whimsical /'wɪmzɪkəl/ *adj* unusual or strange and often amusing: *his whimsical sense of humour*

whine /waɪn/ *v* [I] **1** to complain in a sad, annoying voice about something: *Stop whining!* **2** to make a long high sound because you are sad or in pain: *He could hear the dog whining outside.* —**whine** *n* [C]

whinge /wɪndʒ/ *v* [I] present participle **whinging** or **whingeing** *BrE* to complain in an annoying way about something unimportant —**whinge** *n* [C]

whinny /'wɪni/ *v* [I] **whinnied, whinnying, whinnies** if a horse whinnies, it makes a high sound

whip¹ /wɪp/ *n* [C] a long thin piece of leather or rope with a handle, used for making animals move faster or for hitting people as a punishment

whip² *v* **whipped, whipping 1** [T] to hit a person or animal with a whip **2** also **whip up** [T] to mix cream or the clear part of an egg very hard until it becomes stiff [= beat]: *Whip the cream until thick.* **3** [I] to move quickly and violently: **+round/across etc** *A noise made him whip round.* **4** [T] to move or remove something with a quick sudden movement: **+off/out/away** *He whipped his gun out.*

whip sb/sth ⇔ up *phr v* **1** to try to make people feel strongly about something: *an attempt to whip up opposition to the plan* **2** *informal* to quickly make something to eat: *I could whip up a salad.*

'whip-round *n* **have a whip-round** *BrE informal* if a group of people have a whip-round, they all give some money so that they can buy something together

whir /wɜː $ wɜːr/ *v* the usual American spelling of WHIRR

whirl¹ /wɜːl $ wɜːrl/ *v* [I,T] to turn or spin around very quickly, or to make someone or something do this: *The leaves whirled around in the wind.* | *He whirled her around the dance floor.*

whirl² *n* **1** [singular] a lot of activity of a particular kind: *the social whirl* | **+of** *The next two days passed in a whirl of activity.* **2** **give sth a whirl** *informal* to try something that you are not sure you are going to like or be able to do **3** **be in a whirl** to feel very excited or confused about something: *Debbie's head was all in a whirl.* **4** [C usually singular] a spinning movement or an amount of something that is spinning: **+of** *a whirl of dust*

whirlpool /'wɜːlpuːl $ 'wɜːrl-/ *n* [C] a powerful current of water that spins around and can pull things down into it

whirlwind /'wɜːl,wɪnd $ 'wɜːrl-/ *n* [C] **1** an extremely strong wind that moves quickly with a circular movement, causing a lot of damage **2** **whirlwind romance/tour/campaign etc** something that happens or is done very quickly **3** **a whirlwind of activity/work etc** a situation in which there is a lot of activity

whirr also **whir** *AmE* /wɜː $ wɜːr/ *v* [I] **whirred, whirring** if a machine whirrs, it makes a continuous low sound: *Helicopters whirred overhead.* —**whirr** *n* [singular]

whisk¹ /wɪsk/ *v* [T] **1** to mix liquid, eggs etc very quickly so that air is mixed in, using a fork or a whisk: *Whisk the yolks in a bowl.* → see box at RECIPE → see picture on page A4 **2** to take someone or something somewhere quickly: *They whisked her off to hospital.*

whisk² *n* [C] a small kitchen tool made of curved pieces of wire, used for whisking eggs, cream etc

whisker /'wɪskə $ -ər/ *n* [C] **1** one of the long, stiff hairs that grow near the mouth of a cat, mouse etc → see picture on page A2 **2** **whiskers** [plural] the hair that grows on a man's face

whisky, whiskey /'wɪski/ *n* [C,U] plural **whiskies** or **whiskeys** a strong alcoholic drink made from grain, or a glass of this

whisper /'wɪspə $ -ər/ *v*

1 [I,T] to say something very quietly, using your breath rather than your voice: **whisper sth to sb** *He leaned over to whisper something to her.* | *'I've missed you', she whispered in my ear.* → see box at SAY

2 [I] *literary* to make a soft sound like a whisper: *The wind whispered in the trees.*
—**whisper** *n* [C] *He spoke in a whisper.*

whistle¹ /'wɪsəl/ *v*

1 [I,T] to make a high or musical sound by blowing air out through your lips: **+to** *The man whistled to his dog.* | *He whistled a tune as he strolled home.* | *Janet whistled softly* (=because she was shocked or impressed). *'That's pretty expensive!'*

2 [I] to move quickly, making a whistling sound: **+through** *Bullets were whistling through the air.* **3** [I] to make a high sound when air or steam is forced through a small hole: *a whistling kettle*

whistle² *n* [C]

1 a small object that produces a high sound when you blow into it: *The referee **blew his whistle.*** **2** a high sound made by blowing air through a whistle, your lips etc: *a piercing whistle*

white¹ /waɪt/ *adj*

1 having the colour of milk, snow, or salt: *white paint* → see picture at PATTERN **2** belonging to the race of people with pale skin [➡ black]: *Most of the students in this class are white.* **3** looking pale, because of illness, strong emotion etc: *Her face went white.* | *Are you OK? You're as white as a sheet.*

4 *BrE* white coffee has milk or cream in it [➡ **black**]
5 white wine is a clear pale yellow colour [➡ **red**]
—**whiteness** *n* [U]

white² *n*

1 [U] a white colour: *She was dressed completely in white.*
2 also **White** [C] someone who belongs to the race of people with pale skins [➡ **black**]
3 [C,U] the part of an egg which surrounds the YOLK (=yellow part), and becomes white when cooked

whiteboard /'waɪtbɔːd $ -bɔːrd/ *n* [C] a large board with a white smooth surface that teachers write on → see picture at CLASSROOM

,**white-'collar** *adj* [only before noun] white-collar workers do jobs in offices, banks etc [➡ **blue-collar**]

,**white 'elephant** *n* [C] something that is not at all useful, although it may have cost a lot of money

'**White House** *n* the White House used to refer to the president of the US and the people who advise him: *The White House has refused to comment.* | *White House officials*

,**white 'lie** *n* [C] a lie that you tell someone in order to protect them or avoid hurting their feelings

whiten /'waɪtn/ *v* [I,T] to make something white or to become white

whitewash /'waɪtwɒʃ $ -wɔːʃ, -wɑːʃ/ *n* **1** [C usually singular] a report or examination of events that hides the true facts about something so that the person who is responsible will not be punished: *The newspapers are calling the report a whitewash.* **2** [U] a white liquid used for painting walls —**whitewash** *v* [T]

whittle /'wɪtl/ *v* **1** [I,T] to cut a piece of wood into a particular shape by cutting off small pieces **2** also **whittle down** [T] to gradually make something smaller by taking parts away: *I've whittled down the list of guests from 30 to 16.*
whittle away *phr v* to gradually make something smaller or less effective: **whittle sth ⇔ away** *His power has been slowly whittled away.*

whizz¹ *BrE*; **whiz** *AmE* /wɪz/ *v* [I] *informal* to move very quickly: +**past/by/through etc** *Marty whizzed past us on his motorbike.*

whizz² *BrE*; **whiz** *AmE n* [singular] *informal* someone who is very good at doing something

whizzkid /'wɪzkɪd/ *BrE*; '**whiz kid** *AmE n* [C] a young person who is very skilled or successful at something: *financial whizzkids*

who /huː/ *pron*

1 used to ask or talk about which person is involved, or what the name of a person is: *Who do you work for?* | *Who locked the door?* | *I know who sent you that card.*
2 used after a noun to show which person or which people you are talking about, or to add more information about someone: *That's the woman who owns the house.* | *She asked her English teacher, who had studied at Oxford.* → see box at THAT

whoa /wəʊ, həʊ $ woʊ, hoʊ/ *spoken* **1** said when you think something is impressive **2** used to tell someone to do something more slowly

who'd /huːd/ the short form of 'who had' or 'who would': *a young girl who'd been attacked*

whodunit, whodunnit /ˌhuːˈdʌnɪt/ *n* [C] a book, film etc about a murder, in which you do not find out who the killer is until the end

whoever /huːˈevə $ -ˈevər/ *pron*

1 used to talk about a specific person or people, although you do not know who they are: *Whoever did this is in big trouble.*
2 used to say that it does not matter who does something, is in a particular place etc: *Whoever gets there first can find a table.*
3 used in a question to show surprise: *Whoever would do a thing like that to an old woman?*

whole¹ /həʊl $ hoʊl/ *adj*

1 all of something [➡ **entire**]: *She drank a whole bottle of wine.* | *He had not told her the whole truth.*
2 a whole lot a) very much: *I'm feeling a whole lot better.* **b)** a large quantity or number: +**of** *I've got a whole lot of problems.*
3 not divided or broken into parts: *These birds swallow fish whole.*

whole² *n*

1 the whole of sth all of something: *The whole of my body ached.*
2 on the whole generally or usually: *On the whole, life was much quieter after John left.*
3 as a whole used to say that all the parts of something are being considered: *We must look at our educational system as a whole.*

wholefood /'həʊlfuːd $ 'hoʊl-/ *n* [U] food that does not contain harmful chemicals and artificial things, and is as natural as possible

wholehearted /ˌhəʊlˈhɑːtɪd◂ $ ˌhoʊlˈhɑːr-/ *adj* **wholehearted support/approval/co-operation etc** complete support, approval etc: *The plans met with our wholehearted approval.* —**wholeheartedly** *adv*

wholemeal /'həʊlmiːl $ 'hoʊl-/ *adj BrE* whole-meal flour or bread uses all of the grain, including the outside layer [= **whole wheat** *AmE*]

,**whole 'number** *n* [C] a number such as 0, 1, 2 etc, not part of a number

wholesale /'həʊlseɪl $ 'hoʊl-/ *adj* **1** relating to the business of selling goods in large quantities at low prices to other businesses, rather than to the general public [➡ **retail**]: *wholesale prices* **2** affecting a lot of things or people, often in a bad way: *the wholesale destruction of the rainforest* —**wholesale** *adv*

wholesaler /'həʊlˌseɪlə $ 'hoʊlˌseɪlər/ *n* [C] a person or company that buys goods in large quantities and sells them to other businesses

wholesome /'həʊlsəm $ 'hoʊl-/ *adj* **1** good for your health: *a good wholesome breakfast* → see box at FOOD **2** morally good, or having a good moral effect: *good wholesome fun*

'**whole wheat** *adj AmE* whole wheat flour or bread uses all of the grain, including the outside layer [= **wholemeal** *BrE*]

who'll /huːl/ the short form of 'who will': *Who'll be next?*

wholly /'həʊl-li $ 'hoʊl-/ *adv formal* completely: *The rumours are wholly untrue.*

W

whom /huːm/ *pron*

1 many/all/some etc of whom many, all etc of the people just mentioned: *They had four sons, one of whom died young.*

2 *formal* the object form of 'who': *To whom was the letter addressed?*

whoop /wuːp, huːp/ *v* [I] to shout loudly and happily —**whoop** *n* [C]

whooping cough /ˈhuːpɪŋ kɒf $ -kɔːf/ *n* [U] a serious disease that mainly affects children, in which you make a loud noise after you cough

whoops /wʊps/ *spoken* used when you make a small mistake, drop something, or fall

whoosh /wʊʃ $ wuːʃ/ *n* [C] a sound like air or water moving very fast —**whoosh** *v* [I]

whopper /ˈwɒpə $ ˈwɑːpər/ *n* [C] *informal* something that is unusually large

whopping /ˈwɒpɪŋ $ ˈwɑː-/ *adj* [only before noun] *informal* very large: *a whopping fee*

who're /ˈhuːə $ ˈhuːər/ the short form of 'who are': *Who're those two guys?*

who's /huːz/ the short form of 'who is' or 'who has': *Who's sitting next to Reggie?* | *That's Karl, the guy who's come over from Germany.*

whose /huːz/ *determiner, pron*

1 used to ask which person or people a particular thing belongs to: *Whose jacket is this?*

2 used to say which person or thing you mean, or to add more information about a person or thing, by talking about something belonging to them: *families whose relatives have been killed* | *Jurors, whose identities will be kept secret, will be paid $40 a day.*

who've /huːv/ the short form of 'who have': *people who've been in prison*

why /waɪ/ *adv, linking word*

1 used to ask or talk about the reason for something: *Why are these books so cheap?* | *I think I know why I didn't get the job.* | *Tell me the reason why you're leaving.*

2 why don't you/why not ... etc *spoken* used to make a suggestion: *Why don't you try this one?* | *Why not relax and enjoy yourself?*

3 why not? *spoken* used to agree with a suggestion or invitation: *'Do you want to come along?' 'Yeah, why not?'*

wick /wɪk/ *n* [C] the string that burns in a CANDLE or in an oil lamp

wicked /ˈwɪkɪd/ *adj*

1 very bad or evil: *the wicked stepmother in 'Cinderella'*

2 behaving badly in a way that is amusing [➡ **mischievous**]: *a wicked grin*

3 *spoken informal* very good: *That's a wicked bike!*

—**wickedness** *n* [U] —**wickedly** *adv*

wicker /ˈwɪkə $ -ər/ *n* [U] a material made from thin dry branches or stems woven together: *a wicker chair*

wicket /ˈwɪkɪt/ *n* [C] one of the sets of sticks that the BOWLER tries to hit with the ball in CRICKET

wide¹ /waɪd/ *adj*

1 measuring a large distance from one side to the other [≠ **narrow**; = **broad**]: *a wide street* | *a wide grin* | *The earthquake was felt over a wide area.* | *a wide screen TV* (=television that gives a wider picture) → see picture at **NARROW¹**

2 measuring a particular distance from one side to the other: **three feet/five metres etc wide** *The bathtub's three feet wide.* | *How wide is this room?*

3 including a large variety of different people, things etc: *We offer a wide range of vegetarian dishes.*

4 wide difference/gap etc a large and noticeable difference etc: *wide differences of opinion*

5 *literary* wide eyes are fully open, especially when someone is very surprised, excited, or frightened: *Her eyes grew wide in anticipation.*

6 wider wider problems, questions, or parts of a situation are more general and often more important: *The trial also raises a much wider issue.*

7 wide of the mark incorrect: *Their forecasts were hopelessly wide of the mark.*

wide² *adv*

1 if you open something wide, you open it as far as possible: *The windows had been opened wide.* | *Somebody left the door wide open.* | *He stood with his legs wide apart.*

2 be wide awake to be completely awake

3 away from the point that you were aiming at: *His shot went wide.*

wide-eyed *adj, adv* **1** with your eyes wide open, especially because you are surprised or frightened: *a look of wide-eyed amazement* **2** too willing to believe, accept, or admire things because you do not have much experience of life: *wide-eyed innocence*

widely /ˈwaɪdli/ *adv*

1 in a lot of different places or by a lot of people: *products that are widely available* | *a widely read newspaper*

2 to a large degree: *Taxes vary widely from state to state.*

widen /ˈwaɪdn/ *v* [I,T] **1** to become wider, or to make something wider [➡ **narrow**]: *They're widening the road.* **2** to become greater or larger, or to make something do this [➡ **narrow**]: *The gap between rich and poor began to widen.*

wide-ranging *adj* including a lot of different subjects, things, or people: *a wide-ranging discussion*

widespread /ˈwaɪdspred/ *adj* happening in many places, among many people, or in many situations: *the widespread use of illegal drugs*

widow /ˈwɪdəʊ $ -doʊ/ *n* [C] a woman whose husband has died and who has not married again

widowed /ˈwɪdəʊd $ -doʊd/ *adj* **be widowed** if someone is widowed, their husband or wife dies → see box at **MARRIED**

widower /ˈwɪdəʊə $ -doʊər/ *n* [C] a man whose wife has died and who has not married again

width /wɪdθ/ *n* [C,U] the distance from one side of something to the other [➡ **length, breadth**]: **+of** *the width of the window* | *a width of 10 inches* | **two feet/three metres etc in width** *It's about six metres in width.*

wield /wiːld/ *v* [T] **1 wield power/influence/ authority etc** to have a lot of power, influence etc and to use it: *the influence wielded by the church* **2** to use or hold a weapon or tool

wiener /ˈwiːnə $ -ər/ *n* [C] *AmE* a type of SAUSAGE

W

wife /waɪf/ n [C] plural **wives** /waɪvz/ the woman that a man is married to [➞ **husband**]

wig /wɪg/ n [C] artificial hair that you wear on your head

wiggle /ˈwɪɡəl/ v [I,T] to make small movements from side to side or up and down, or to make something move this way: *Jo wiggled her toes.* —**wiggle** n [C]

wigwam /ˈwɪɡwæm $ -wɑːm/ n [C] a round tent used by some Native Americans

wild[1] /waɪld/ adj
1 wild animals and plants live or grow in natural conditions, without being changed or controlled by people [➞ **tame**]: *wild horses* | *wild flowers* | *wild mushrooms* ➔ see box at **NATURAL**
2 a wild area of land is in a completely natural state and does not have farms, towns etc on it: *the wild and beautiful landscape of Nepal*
3 feeling or expressing strong uncontrolled emotions, especially anger, happiness, or excitement: +**with** *He was wild with rage.* | *A wild look* (=crazy look) *came into her eyes.*
4 behaving in an uncontrolled way and not doing what other people tell you to do: *a wild teenager*
5 [only before noun] done or said without thinking carefully or without knowing all the facts: *Take a wild guess.* | *wild accusations*
6 **be wild about sb/sth** spoken to like someone or something very much: *I'm not wild about rap music.*
7 stormy and windy: *a wild night*

wild[2] adv   **1** **go wild** to become very excited or angry: *The audience went wild.*   **2** **run wild** to behave in a very free way, without enough control: *Left on their own, the boys ran wild.*   **3** **grow wild** if plants grow wild somewhere, they have not been planted by people

wild[3] n   **1** **in the wild** in natural conditions, without being changed or controlled by people: *animals in the wild*   **2** **the wilds** areas where there are no towns and not many people live: +**of** *the wilds of Canada*

wilderness /ˈwɪldənɪs $ -dər-/ n [singular,U] a large natural area of land that has never been built on: *the Alaskan wilderness*

wildfire /ˈwaɪldfaɪə $ -faɪr/ n [C,U] a fire that moves quickly and cannot be controlled ➔ **spread like wildfire** at **SPREAD**[1]

,wild ˈgoose ˌchase n [singular] a situation in which you waste a lot of time looking for something that cannot be found

wildlife /ˈwaɪldlaɪf/ n [U] animals and plants living in natural conditions

wildly /ˈwaɪldli/ adv   **1** in a very uncontrolled or excited way: *The audience cheered wildly.*   **2** extremely: *wildly successful*

wiles /waɪlz/ n [plural] clever talk or tricks used to persuade someone to do what you want: *Men could not resist her feminine wiles.*

wilful BrE; **willful** AmE /ˈwɪlfəl/ adj   **1** **wilful damage/neglect etc** deliberate damage etc, when you know that what you are doing is wrong   **2** doing what you want even though people tell you not to: *a wilful child* —**wilfully** adv

will[1] /wɪl/ modal verb, negative short form **won't**

1 used to make future tenses: *I'm sure that will be OK.* | *What time will you arrive?* | *We'll call you later.* | *I hope she won't be angry.* ➔ see box at **SHALL**
2 used to say that someone is willing or ready to do something, or that something is able to do something: *Dr Weir will see you now.* | *Sue won't agree.* | *The car won't start.*
3 used to ask someone to do something or to offer something to someone: *Will you help me carry this?* | *Won't you have a cup of tea?*
4 used to say what always happens or what is generally true: *Some people will always complain.*
5 used to say that you think that something is true: *'Someone's at the door.' 'That'll be Nick.'*
6 used to describe someone's habits, especially when you think that they are annoying: *He will keep on whistling.*

will[2] n
1 [C,U] determination to do something that you have decided to do: **will to do sth** *I had lost the will to live.* | *She had a very strong will.*
2 [C] a legal document that says who you want your money and property to be given to after you die: *Have you made a will?* | **in sb's will** *Grandpa left me $7,000 in his will.*
3 [singular] what someone wants to happen in a particular situation: +**of** *the will of the people* | **against sb's will** (=when someone is forced to do something that they do not want to do) *Lucy was kept there against her will.*
4 **at will** whenever you want and in whatever way you want: *He can't just fire people at will.*
➔ **FREE WILL**, **ILL WILL**

will[3] v [T] to try to make something happen by thinking about it very hard: **will sb/sth to do sth** *The crowd were all willing her to win.*

willful /ˈwɪlfəl/ adj the American spelling of **WILFUL**

willing /ˈwɪlɪŋ/ adj
1 **be willing to do sth** if you are willing to do something, you will agree to do it if someone asks you: *Are you willing to help?* | **quite/ perfectly willing** *I'm perfectly willing to try.*
2 eager and wanting to do something very much: **willing helpers** | *a willing volunteer* —**willingly** adv: *I would willingly have accepted.* —**willingness** n [U]

willow /ˈwɪləʊ $ -loʊ/ n [C] a tree with very long thin branches that grows near water

willowy /ˈwɪləʊi $ -loʊi/ adj tall, thin, and graceful: *her young, willowy figure*

willpower /ˈwɪlˌpaʊə $ -ˌpaʊr/ n [U] the ability to control your mind and body in order to do something: *It took all his willpower to remain calm.*

willy-nilly /ˌwɪli ˈnɪli/ adv   **1** if something happens willy-nilly, it happens whether you want it to or not   **2** without planning

wilt /wɪlt/ v [I] if a plant wilts, it bends over because it is too dry or old

wily /ˈwaɪli/ adj clever at getting what you want, especially by tricking people [= **cunning**]

wimp /wɪmp/ n [C] informal disapproving someone who is afraid to do anything that is slightly dangerous —**wimpish**, **wimpy** adj

win[1] /wɪn/ v past tense and past participle **won** /wʌn/ present participle **winning**

W

1 [I,T] to be the best or most successful in a competition, game, war etc [≠ **lose**]: *Who do you think will win the election?* | *Argentina won the World Cup that year.* | **+at** *I never win at cards.*

come first – to win a competition, game etc
was/came in first/second etc place – used to describe someone's position at the end of a race
be in the lead/be ahead – to be winning at the moment
the winning team/horse etc – the one that wins
If you are the **champion** or you **hold the record for something**, you are the person who has beaten all other people in a series of competitions.

2 [T] to get something as a prize for winning in a competition or game: *He **won** a gold **medal**.* | *I won $200.* → see box at **GAIN**
3 [T] to get something good because of your efforts or abilities [= **gain**]: **win sb's approval/support/trust etc** *Knight quickly won the respect of his colleagues.*
4 sb can't win *spoken* used to say that there is no satisfactory way of dealing with a particular situation
  win sb ⇔ **over** also **win sb** ⇔ **round/around** *BrE phr v* to persuade someone to agree with you, support you, or like you: *their attempt to win over voters*

win² *n* [C] a success or victory, especially in sport [≠ **defeat**]: **+over** *Ireland's 2–1 win over France*

wince /wɪns/ *v* [I] suddenly to change the expression on your face when you see or remember something painful or embarrassing

winch /wɪntʃ/ *n* [C] a machine with a rope or chain used for lifting heavy objects —**winch** *v* [T]

wind¹ /wɪnd/ *n*
1 also **the wind** [C,U] moving air, especially when it moves strongly or quickly: *An icy wind was blowing.* | **strong/high wind** (=powerful wind) | *A sudden **gust of wind** (=a quick powerful wind) blew the door shut.*

breeze – a light wind
gale – very strong wind
hurricane – a violent storm with a very strong fast wind
tornado – an extremely violent storm consisting of air that spins very quickly and causes a lot of damage
→ **RAIN, SNOW, SUN, WEATHER**

2 get wind of sth to hear or find out about something secret or private: *Then the local press got wind of the affair.*
3 [U] *BrE* when you have a lot of air in your stomach [= **gas** *AmE*]: *Baked beans always give me wind.*
4 [U] your ability to breathe properly
5 the wind section the people in an ORCHESTRA who play WIND INSTRUMENTS → see box at **ORCHESTRA**
→ **your second wind** at **SECOND¹**

wind² /waɪnd/ *v past tense and past participle* **wound** /waʊnd/
1 [I,T] to turn or twist something long and thin several times, especially around something else: **wind sth around/round sth** *Wind the bandage around her arm.*
2 also **wind up** [T] to make a machine, toy, clock etc work by turning a small handle several times
3 [I] if a road, river etc winds somewhere, it has many smooth bends and is usually very long: *The road wound up into the hills.*
4 [T] to make a video CASSETTE tape go forwards or backwards
  wind down *phr v* **1 wind sth** ⇔ **down** gradually to reduce the work of a business or organization so that it can be closed down completely **2** to rest and relax after a lot of hard work or excitement: *It's difficult to wind down after work.*
3 wind sth ⇔ **down** *BrE* to make something, especially a car window, move down by turning a handle or pressing a button
  wind up *phr v* **1** to be in an unpleasant situation or place after a lot has happened: *He wound up in prison.* **2 wind sth** ⇔ **up** to end an activity, meeting etc: *Let's wind things up.*
3 wind sb ⇔ **up** *BrE* to say something that will annoy or worry someone, as a joke **4 wind sth** ⇔ **up** *BrE* to make something, especially a car window, move up by turning a handle or pressing a button

wind³ /wɪnd/ *v* [T] if a fall, a blow, or exercise winds you, it causes you to have difficulty breathing —**winded** *adj*

windchill /'wɪndˌtʃɪl/ *n* [U] *technical* the cold effect of the wind

windfall /'wɪndfɔːl $ -fɒːl/ *n* [C] money that you get unexpectedly

winding /'waɪndɪŋ/ *adj* curving or bending many times: *a winding path*

wind instrument /'wɪnd ˌɪnstrᵿmənt/ *n* [C] a musical instrument that you play by blowing into it

windmill /'wɪndˌmɪl/ *n* [C] a building or structure with parts that turn around in the wind, used for producing electrical power or crushing grain

windmill

window /'wɪndəʊ $ -doʊ/ *n* [C]
1 an area of glass in the wall of a building or vehicle that lets in light: *Let's open a window.* | *She looked out of the window.* | *a shop window*
2 one of the areas on a computer screen where different programs operate
→ **BAY WINDOW, FRENCH WINDOWS**

'window box *n* [C] a long narrow container attached to the bottom of a window, used for growing plants

windowpane /'wɪndəʊˌpeɪn $ -doʊ-/ *n* [C] a single whole piece of glass in a window

'window ,shopping n [U] when you look at goods in shop windows without intending to buy them

windowsill /'wɪndəʊ,sɪl $ -doʊ-/ also **'window ledge** n [C] the shelf at the bottom of a window

windpipe /'wɪndpaɪp/ n [C] the tube through which air passes from your mouth to your lungs

windscreen BrE /'wɪndskriːn/, **windshield** AmE /-ʃiːld/ n [C] the large window at the front of a car, bus etc → see picture on page A12

'windscreen ,wiper BrE; **'windshield ,wiper** AmE n [C] a long piece of metal with a rubber edge that moves across a windscreen to remove the rain → see picture on page A12

windsurfing /'wɪnd,sɜːfɪŋ $ -ɜːr-/ n [U] the sport of sailing across water by standing on a special board and holding onto a large sail → see picture on page A9 —**windsurfer** n [C]

windswept /'wɪndswept/ adj a windswept place is often very windy and has few trees or buildings

windy /'wɪndi/ adj if it is windy, there is a lot of wind: a windy day → see box at WEATHER

wine¹ /waɪn/ n [C,U] an alcoholic drink made from GRAPES: a glass of wine | red/white wine | French wines

wine² v **wine and dine sb** to entertain someone with good food, wine etc

winery /'waɪnəri/ n [C] plural **wineries** a place where wine is made and kept

wing /wɪŋ/ n [C]

1 one of the parts of a bird's or insect's body that it moves in order to fly: ducks flapping their wings

2 one of the two flat parts that stick out from the side of a plane and help it stay in the air → see picture at AEROPLANE

3 one of the parts of a large building, especially one that sticks out from the main part: the east wing of the palace | the hospital's maternity wing

4 a group of people within a political party who have particular opinions or aims: the liberal wing of the party

5 **a)** someone who plays on the far left or far right of the field in games such as football **b)** the far left or far right of a sports field

6 BrE the part of a car that is above a wheel [= fender AmE] → see picture on page A12

7 **take sb under your wing** to help or protect someone who is younger or less experienced than you

8 **(waiting) in the wings** ready to do something or be used when the time is right

9 **the wings** [plural] the parts at either side of a stage where the actors cannot be seen

→ LEFT-WING, RIGHT-WING

winged /wɪŋd/ adj having wings: winged insects

wingspan /'wɪŋspæn/ n [C] the distance from the end of one wing to the end of the other

wink /wɪŋk/ v [I] if you wink at someone, you look towards them and quickly close and open one eye, in order to show them that you are joking or being friendly, or as a signal —**wink** n [C] She gave me a little wink.

winner /'wɪnə $ -ər/ n

1 [C] a person or animal that has won a competition, race etc: **+of** the winner of the 100m

2 [C] informal something that is, or is likely to be, very popular and successful: His latest book is another winner.

3 [singular] a GOAL or point that makes someone win a game of tennis, football etc: Moran scored the winner.

winning /'wɪnɪŋ/ adj [only before noun]

1 the winning person or thing is the one that wins a competition or game: the winning goal → see box at WIN **2** making someone attractive or making something successful: a winning smile | As a business, they have found a winning formula. → **a winning streak** at STREAK¹

winnings /'wɪnɪŋz/ n [plural] money that you win in a game or competition

wino /'waɪnəʊ $ -noʊ/ n [C] plural **winos** informal someone who drinks a lot of alcohol and lives on the streets

winter¹ /'wɪntə $ -ər/ n [C,U] the season after autumn and before spring, when the weather is coldest [➔ summer]: **in (the) winter** It often snows in winter. | **this/last/next winter** | long winter evenings | **winter sports** (=sports such as skiing)

winter² v [I] formal to spend the winter somewhere: The birds usually winter in southern France and Spain.

wintry /'wɪntri/ adj typical of winter, especially because it is cold or snowing: wintry weather

,win-'win adj [only before noun] a win-win situation is one that will be successful for everyone involved

wipe /waɪp/ v [T]

1 to remove liquid or dirt from a surface, especially using a cloth or your hand: **wipe sth with/on sth** She wiped her eyes (=removed the tears from her eyes) with the back of her hand. | **wipe sth from/off sth** He wiped the sweat from his face. | Quickly, she wiped away her tears. → see box at REMOVE

2 to remove all the information that is stored on a tape, video, or computer DISK

—**wipe** n [C]

wipe sth ⇔ **down** phr v to clean a surface completely, using a wet cloth

wipe sth ⇔ **out** phr v to destroy something completely: Whole villages were wiped out by the floods.

wipe sth ⇔ **up** phr v to remove liquid from a surface, using a cloth: Could you wipe that mess up?

wiper /'waɪpə $ -ər/ n [C] a WINDSCREEN WIPER

wire¹ /waɪə $ waɪr/ n

1 [C,U] thin metal in the form of a thread, or a piece of this: a wire fence

2 [C] a piece of metal like this, used for carrying electrical currents or signals: electrical wires | telephone wires

→ BARBED WIRE

wire² v [T] **1** also **wire up a)** to connect wires inside a building or piece of equipment so that electricity can pass through: instructions on how to wire a plug **b)** to connect electrical equipment to the electricity supply, using wires: I've

W

wired up the speakers. **2** to send money electronically: *Could you wire me $50?* **3** to fasten two or more things together using wire

wireless /'waɪələs $ 'waɪr-/ *n* [C] *old-fashioned* a radio

wiring /'waɪərɪŋ $ 'waɪr-/ *n* [U] the system of wires that carries electricity in a building, vehicle, or piece of equipment

wiry /'waɪəri $ 'waɪri/ *adj* **1** someone who is wiry is thin but strong **2** wiry hair is stiff and curly

wisdom /'wɪzdəm/ *n*

1 [U] the ability to use your knowledge and experience of life to make good decisions and give good advice
2 the wisdom of sth whether something is sensible: *Some people doubted the wisdom of his decision.*

'wisdom tooth *n* [C] one of the four large teeth at the back of an adult's mouth

wise¹ /waɪz/ *adj*

1 a wise decision or action is sensible: **it is wise to do sth** *It would be wise to phone first.*
2 a wise person is able to use their knowledge and experience of life to make good decisions and give good advice: *He's older and wiser now.*
→ see box at **INTELLIGENT**
3 be none the wiser to still not understand or know something even after it has been explained to you: *He tried to explain, but I was still none the wiser.*
4 work-wise/price-wise/time-wise etc used to refer to a particular feature of a situation: *How are you managing money-wise?*
—**wisely** *adv*

wise² *v*
wise up *phr v informal* to realize the truth about a bad situation

wisecrack /'waɪzkræk/ *n* [C] a quick, funny, and often slightly unkind remark

wish¹ /wɪʃ/ *v*

1 [T] to want something to be true, although you know it is impossible or unlikely: **+(that)** *I wish you hadn't invited him.* | *I wish I didn't have to go to work.* | *We wish we could have done more.* | *She wished Katie would stop crying.*
2 [I,T] *formal* to want to do something: **wish to do sth** *I wish to make a complaint.* | *You may go, if you wish.*
3 [T] to say that you hope someone will be happy, successful, lucky etc: **wish sb sth** *They wished us a happy Christmas.* | *I wish you luck.*
4 [I] if you wish for something, you want it to happen or want to have it, although it seems unlikely or impossible: **+for** *It's no use wishing for the impossible.*

wish² *n* [C]

1 a desire for something: **sb's wish(es)** *We need to respect the wishes of the patient.* | **wish to do sth** *her wish to emigrate* | *I have no wish to see him.* | *He left school against his parents' wishes* (=his parents did not want him to leave school). | *His dearest wish* (=what he most wanted) *was to see his father again.*
2 best/good/warmest etc wishes used, especially in cards and letters, to say that you hope someone will be happy, successful, or healthy: **+for** *Best wishes for your retirement!* | *Please*

give my best wishes to your parents. | **(with) best wishes** (=used at the end of a letter before you sign your name) *With best wishes, Amy.*

wishful 'thinking *n* [U] when you hope that something good will happen, when it is not possible

wishy-washy /'wɪʃi ˌwɒʃi $ -ˌwɒːʃi, -ˌwɑːʃi/ *adj informal disapproving* without any firm or clear ideas: *wishy-washy liberals*

wisp /wɪsp/ *n* [C] **1** a wisp of hair, grass, HAY etc is a thin piece of it that is separate from the rest **2** a wisp of smoke, cloud, steam etc is a small thin line of it that rises upwards —**wispy** *adj*

wistful /'wɪstfəl/ *adj* a little sad because you cannot have something you want: *a wistful smile* —**wistfully** *adv*

wit /wɪt/ *n*

1 [U] the ability to say things that are clever and amusing: *a woman of great wit*
2 wits [plural] your ability to think quickly and make good decisions: **keep/have your wits about you** (=be ready to think quickly to deal with any problems)
3 frighten/scare/terrify sb out of their wits *informal* to frighten someone very much: *I was terrified out of my wits.*
4 be at your wits' end to be very upset and not know what to do because you have tried everything possible to solve a problem

witch /wɪtʃ/ *n* [C] a woman who is believed to have magic powers, especially to do bad things [→ **wizard**]

witchcraft /'wɪtʃkrɑːft $ -kræft/ *n* [U] the use of magic to make strange things happen

'witch ˌdoctor *n* [C] a man who is believed to be able to cure people, using magic

'witch ˌhunt *n* [C] *disapproving* an attempt to find and punish people in a society or organization whose opinions are believed to be wrong or dangerous

with /wɪð, wɪθ/ *prep*

1 used to say that two or more people or things are together in the same place: *She lives with her Mom.* | *Will you come with me?* | *Put this bag with the others.* | *Mix the powder with boiling water.*
2 having or holding something: *a girl with dark hair* | *a house with a garden* | *She came back with an ice cream.*
3 using something: *Chop the onions with a sharp knife.* | *We decorated the church with flowers.*
4 used to say which other person, group, or country is involved in an action or activity: *Discuss the problem with your doctor.* | *She had been arguing with Kevin.* | *the war with France*
5 because of something, or as a result of something: *He was trembling with fear.* | *With Josh away* (=because Josh is away), *I have more time.*
6 used to say what covers or fills something: *His hands were covered with blood.*
7 including: *A double room with breakfast is £45.*
8 used to say what an action or situation is related to: *There's something wrong with the TV.* | *Be careful with that glass.*
9 used to say who or what someone has a particular feeling towards: *Are you angry with me?* | *She's delighted with her new car.*

W

10 used to say how someone does something or how something happens: *Prepare everything with great care.* | *The door closed with a bang.* | *'Hello,' she said with a smile.*
11 used to talk about the position of someone's body: *He stood with his back to the class.*
12 supporting someone or sharing their opinion: *I'm with Harry on this one.*
13 be with me/you *spoken* to understand what someone is saying: *Sorry, I'm not with you.*

withdraw /wɪðˈdrɔː, wɪθ- $ -ˈdrɒː/ *v* past tense **withdrew** /-ˈdruː/ past participle **withdrawn** /-ˈdrɔːn $ -ˈdrɒːn/ **1** [I,T] to stop taking part in a race, competition etc, or to leave an organization: **+from** *Injury forced her to withdraw from the race.* **2** [T] to stop giving support or money to someone or something: *The government has withdrawn its support for the project.* **3** [T] if you withdraw a threat, offer, request etc, you say that you no longer intend to do what you said or no longer want what you asked for **4** [T] *formal* if you withdraw something you have said, you admit that it was untrue **5** [T] to take money out of a bank account: *I need to withdraw $200.* → see box at ACCOUNT **6** [I,T] if an army withdraws, or if it is withdrawn, it moves back away from a place

withdrawal /wɪðˈdrɔːəl, wɪθ- $ -ˈdrɒːəl/ *n* **1** [C,U] when military forces are moved back out of an area: **of** *the withdrawal of NATO forces from Bosnia* **2** [U] the removal or stopping of something such as support, an offer, or a service: **+of** *the withdrawal of government aid* **3** [C,U] the act of taking money from a bank account, or the amount you take out: *I'd like to **make a withdrawal.*** **4** [U] the act of no longer taking part in an activity or being a member of an organization: **+from** *Germany's withdrawal from the talks* **5** [U] when someone stops taking a drug that they were dependent on, and the unpleasant mental and physical effects that this causes: **withdrawal symptoms** (=the unpleasant effects of withdrawal)

withdrawn /wɪðˈdrɔːn, wɪθ- $ -ˈdrɒːn/ *adj* quiet and not wanting to talk to people

wither /ˈwɪðə $ -ər/ also **wither away** *v* [I]
1 if a plant withers, it becomes drier and smaller and starts to die **2** to become weaker and then disappear: *Without commercial sponsorship, sport would wither.*

withering /ˈwɪðərɪŋ/ *adj* **withering look/ remark etc** a look, remark etc that makes someone feel stupid or embarrassed

withhold /wɪðˈhəʊld, wɪθ- $ -ˈhoʊld/ *v* [T] past tense and past participle **withheld** /-ˈheld/ to refuse to give someone something: **withhold sth from sb** *He is accused of **withholding** information from Congress.*

within /wɪðˈɪn $ wɪðˈɪn, wɪθˈɪn/ *adv, prep*
1 before a certain period of time has ended: *Payment must be made within 28 days.* | *Within a year he was dead.*
2 less than a certain distance from a place: *We live within four miles of each other.*
3 inside a group, organization, building, or area: *critics within the party* | *footpaths within the national park*

4 if something stays within a particular limit or set of rules, it does not go beyond that limit: *The company has acted **within the law.***
5 *literary* inside a person's body or mind: *A feeling of happiness grew within her.*

without /wɪðˈaʊt $ wɪðˈaʊt, wɪθˈaʊt/ *adv, prep*
1 not having, doing, or showing something: *a house without a garden* | *The soldiers fired with- out warning.* | **without doing sth** *He left with- out saying goodbye.* | **do/go without (sth)** (=not have something important) *We **had to do** with- **out** water for two days.*
2 not with someone: *If you're late, I'll go without you.*

withstand /wɪðˈstænd, wɪθ- $ -ˈstænd/ *v* [T] past tense and past participle **withstood** /-ˈstʊd/ to not be damaged by heat, pressure, a force etc

witness[1] /ˈwɪtnɪs/ *n* [C]
1 someone who sees an accident, crime etc and can say what happened: **+to** *Police have appealed for witnesses to the accident.*
2 someone who tells a court of law what they know about the case that is being considered: *Will she be **called as a witness** (=asked to speak in court)?* | *Few witnesses are willing to **testify** (=speak in court) against him.* | **prosecution/ defence witness**
3 someone who is present when an official docu- ment is signed, and who signs it to prove this

witness[2] *v* [T] **1** to see something happen, especially an accident or crime: *Several people witnessed the attack.* → see box at SEE **2** to experience an important event or change: *Our generation has witnessed a period of peace.* **3** to be present when someone signs an official docu- ment, and to sign it to prove this

'witness stand also **'witness box** *BrE n* [C] the place where a witness stands when they speak in court

witticism /ˈwɪtɪsɪzəm/ *n* [C] a clever and amusing remark

witty /ˈwɪti/ *adj* funny and clever: **witty speech/remark/story etc** → see box at FUNNY

wives /waɪvz/ *n* the plural of WIFE

wizard /ˈwɪzəd $ -ərd/ *n* [C] **1** a man who is thought to have magic powers **2** someone who is very good at something: *a financial wizard*

wizardry /ˈwɪzədri $ -ər-/ *n* [U] a very impres- sive skill or achievement in a particular subject: *technical wizardry*

wizened /ˈwɪzənd/ *adj* old and with dry and WRINKLEd skin: *wizened apples*

wobble /ˈwɒbəl $ ˈwɑː-/ *v* [I] to move unstead- ily from side to side: *Celia wobbled past on her bike.* → see box at SHAKE —**wobbly** *adj: a wobbly chair* —**wobble** *n* [C]

woe /wəʊ $ woʊ/ *n literary* **1** [U] great sadness **2 woes** [plural] very serious problems

woeful /ˈwəʊfəl $ ˈwoʊ-/ *adj* **1** very bad or disappointing: *The country has a woeful record on human rights.* **2** *literary* sad —**woefully** *adv*

wok /wɒk $ wɑːk/ *n* [C] a large round pan, used in Chinese cooking

woke /wəʊk $ woʊk/ *v* the past tense of WAKE

woken /ˈwəʊkən $ ˈwoʊ-/ *v* the past participle of WAKE

wolf[1] /wʊlf/ *n* [C] plural **wolves** /wʊlvz/ a wild animal similar to a large dog

W

wolf² also **wolf down** v [T] *informal* to eat something very quickly: *She wolfed down her breakfast.* → see box at EAT

woman /'wʊmən/ n [C] plural **women** /'wɪmɪn/
1 an adult female person: *a beautiful woman* | *married women* | **woman priest/doctor etc** *the first woman president* | **women's clothes/magazines/groups etc** (=clothes etc for women)

THESAURUS

Lady is a polite word for a woman.
A **girl** is a young woman.
A **female** teacher, singer etc is a woman who is a teacher.
→ MAN

2 spokeswoman/businesswoman etc a woman who does a particular job or activity
womanhood /'wʊmənhʊd/ n [U] the state of being a woman
womanizer also **-iser** *BrE* /'wʊmənaɪzə $ -ər/ n [C] a man who has sexual relationships with many women
womankind /'wʊmənkaɪnd/ n [U] all women, considered as a group
womanly /'wʊmənli/ adj *approving* behaving, dressing etc in a way that people think is right for a woman
womb /wuːm/ n [C] the part of a woman's body where a baby grows before it is born [= uterus]
women /'wɪmɪn/ n the plural of WOMAN
won /wʌn/ v the past tense and past participle of WIN
wonder¹ /'wʌndə $ -ər/ v [I,T]

1 to think about something you do not know, and want to know it: **+who/where/if etc** *I wonder where she lives these days.* | *I wonder if he'll take the job.* | **+about** *She wondered about the bruise on his cheek.*
2 I was wondering if/whether ... *spoken* used to ask for something politely, or to invite someone to do something: *I was wondering if you could help me – I'm looking for the City Hall.*
wonder² n **1** [U] surprise and admiration [= awe]: **in wonder** *They listened to her tale in wonder.* | *We were filled with wonder.* **2** [C usually plural] something that makes you feel admiration: *the wonders of technology* **3 (it's) no/small/little wonder (that)** *spoken* used to say that something does not surprise you: *No wonder you feel sick after eating all that chocolate.* **4 it's a wonder (that)** *spoken* used to say that something is surprising: *It's a wonder he didn't go mad.* **5 do/work wonders** to be very good at solving a problem
wonder³ adj [only before noun] very good or effective: *a new wonder drug*
wonderful /'wʌndəfəl $ -dər-/ adj very good [= great]: *wonderful news* | *We had a wonderful time.* → see box at NICE
—**wonderfully** adv
wondrous /'wʌndrəs/ adj *literary* wonderful
wonky /'wɒŋki $ 'wɑːŋki/ adj *BrE informal* not straight or level
won't /wəʊnt $ woʊnt/ the short form of 'will not': *Dad won't like it.*
wont /wəʊnt $ wɔːnt/ adj **be wont to do sth** *formal* to have the habit of doing something

woo /wuː/ v [T] **1** to try to persuade someone to support you: *The politicians are busy wooing voters.* **2** *old-fashioned* to try to persuade a woman to love and marry you
wood /wʊd/ n

1 [U] the hard material that trees are made of [→ wooden]: *a boat made of wood* | *a piece of wood* → see picture at PLANT
2 [C] also **the woods** an area of land that is covered in trees [→ forest] → see box at TREE
3 touch wood *BrE* **knock on wood** *AmE spoken* used after you say you have been fortunate, because it is supposed to make your good luck continue
wooded /'wʊdɪd/ adj covered with trees
wooden /'wʊdn/ adj made of wood: *a wooden box* → see picture at MATERIAL¹
woodland /'wʊdlənd, -lænd/ n [C,U] an area of land that is covered with trees
woodpecker /'wʊd,pekə $ -ər/ n [C] a bird with a long beak that makes holes in trees
woodwind /'wʊd,wɪnd/ n [U] wooden or metal musical instruments that you play by blowing into them [→ brass]
woodwork /'wʊdwɜːk $ -wɜːrk/ n [U] **1** *BrE* the skill or activity of making things out of wood [= woodworking *AmE*] **2** the parts of a building that are made of wood **3 crawl/come out of the woodwork** *disapproving* to unexpectedly start to take part in a situation
woodworking /'wʊd,wɜːkɪŋ $ -ɜːr-/ n [U] *AmE* the skill or activity of making things out of wood [= woodwork *BrE*]
woodworm /'wʊdwɜːm $ -wɜːrm/ n [C,U] an insect that makes holes in wood, or the damage this insect causes
woody /'wʊdi/ adj **1** woody plants have thick hard stems **2** a woody area of land is covered with trees
woof /wʊf/ the sound a dog makes when it BARKS
wool /wʊl/ n [U] the soft thick hair of a sheep, used to make cloth or thread: *a ball of wool* | *a pure wool skirt*
→ COTTON WOOL
woollen *BrE*; **woolen** *AmE* /'wʊlən/ adj made of wool —**woollens** n [plural]
woolly *BrE*; **wooly** *AmE* /'wʊli/ adj **1** made of wool or a material similar to wool: *a woolly hat* → see picture at MATERIAL¹ **2** not showing clear thinking: *a woolly argument*
woozy /'wuːzi/ adj *informal* feeling weak and unsteady [= dizzy]
word¹ /wɜːd $ wɜːrd/ n

1 [C] a separate group of sounds or letters that has a particular meaning: **+for** *What's the English word for* (=word that means) *'casa'?* | *a 500-word essay* | *What does this word mean?* | *The weather was inclement – in other words, just plain bad.* | *She found it hard to put her feelings into words* (=say how she felt). | *Say in your own words what happened.* | *a dying man's last words* (=the last thing he said)
2 [singular] something that you say to someone: **a word of warning/advice/thanks etc** *He rode off without a word of thanks.* | **a kind/angry etc word** *His parents never exchanged an angry word.* | **have a word with sb** (=have a short

conversation with someone) *Can I have a* **quick word**? | **put in a good word for sb** (=say something good about someone to an important person) | *He put in a good word for me with the boss* (=said good things about me to help me).

3 not say/understand/believe etc a word not to say, understand etc anything or any part of something: *She didn't understand a word of Italian.* | *Don't breathe a word of what I've told you* (=don't tell anyone).

4 sb's word someone's promise or statement that something is true: *Can you trust her to keep her word?* | *I give you my word that you will not be harmed.* | *I'll have to take his word for it* (=believe what he says because I do not know about it). → see box at PROMISE

5 word for word if you repeat something word for word, you say it using exactly the same words

6 [singular,U] news, information, or a message: *Had any word from Andy?* | *Spread the word* (=tell people) *about the benefits of exercise.* | *Word soon got round about our engagement* (=people soon heard about it). | *I get most of my business by word of mouth* (=by people talking to each other). | **the word is/word has it (that)** (=people are saying that) *The word is they're to marry.*

7 the spoken/written word spoken or written language

8 the last word the last thing said in a discussion, argument etc: *Why must you always have the last word?*

9 not in so many words *spoken* used to say that although someone did not say something directly, you know what they meant: *'So Dad said he'd pay for it?' 'Not in so many words.'*

10 get a word in (edgeways) to manage to say something when other people are saying a lot
→ FOUR-LETTER WORD, LINKING WORD, SWEAR WORD

word[2] *v* [T] to choose the words you use carefully [= phrase]: *a carefully worded statement*

wording /'wɜːdɪŋ $ 'wɜːr-/ *n* [U] the words and phrases used in a piece of writing or speech

wordless /'wɜːdləs $ 'wɜːrd-/ *adj literary* not using words: *She embraced him in wordless grief.*
—**wordlessly** *adv*

'word-play *n* [U] using words in a clever amusing way

'word ,processor *n* [C] computer software or a small computer that you use for writing things
—**word processing** *n* [U]

wordy /'wɜːdi $ 'wɜːrdi/ *adj disapproving* containing too many words

wore /wɔː $ wɔːr/ *v* the past tense of WEAR

work[1] /wɜːk $ wɜːrk/ *v*

1 [I,T] to do a job in order to earn money: **+at/in** *She works in a bank.* | **+for** *Do you enjoy working for the police?* | **+as** *Joe worked as a builder.* | **+with/among** *She wants to work with children.* | *Ted often works late* (=works after most people have finished). | **work days/nights/weekends** (=work during the day, night etc)

THESAURUS

If you work for a company or organization, you are an **employee**.
The person or organization you work for is your **employer**.

Your **employer** pays your **salary** (=monthly pay) or **wages** (=weekly pay).
An organization's **staff** are all the people who work for the organization.
Your **colleagues/co-workers/workmates** are the people you work with.
When you reach the age to stop working permanently, you **retire**.
→ JOB

2 [I,T] to spend time and effort doing something: **+on** *She's working on a new book.* | **work to do sth** *The company is working hard to improve its image.* | *They work the land* (=grow crops) *to feed their families.*

3 a) [I] if a machine works, it does what it is meant to do: *The CD player isn't working.* **b)** [T] to make a machine do what it is meant to do [= operate]: *Do you know how to work the printer?*

4 [I] if a plan, method, medicine etc works, it gives you the results you want: *Most diets don't work.*

5 [I] to gradually move to a new position: *The wheel must have worked loose.* | *He worked his way to the top.*

6 work against sb/work in sb's favour to stop someone succeeding or help them to succeed: *Unfortunately, her low grades worked against her.*

7 [I,T] to use a particular substance in order to make something: **+in/with** *a sculptor who works in steel*

work sth ⇔ **off** *phr v* to do some physical exercise to make yourself feel less worried, angry etc: *Running is a good way of working off stress.*

work out *phr v* **1** to calculate an amount, price, or value: **work sth** ⇔ **out** *Let's work out how much beer we need.* | **+at** *It works out at $50 a night.* → see box at CALCULATE **2 work sth** ⇔ **out** to decide or plan something in order to solve a problem: *He still hasn't worked out where he'll live.* **3** if a situation works out in a particular way, it ends in that way: *Everything worked out OK in the end.* **4** to do exercises that make you stronger

work up sth *phr v* to gradually make yourself have a particular feeling: **work up interest/ energy/enthusiasm etc** *I'm trying to work up the courage to visit the dentist.* | **work up an appetite/thirst** (=make yourself hungry or thirsty)

work up to sth *phr v* to prepare yourself for something difficult

work[2] *n*

1 [U] your job or the activities that you do regularly to earn money: *My dad started work when he was 14.* | **in/out of work** (=with or without a job) *He's been out of work for months.* | **find/look for/seek work** *Jo's hoping to find work in television.* | *I'll be late for work.* | **after work** (=after you have finished working for the day) *Shall we go for a drink after work?* → see box at JOB

2 [U] the place where you do your job: **at work** *When do you have to be at work?*

3 [U] physical or mental activity and effort: *Looking after children can be hard work.* | **+on** *Work on the bridge is continuing.* | **at work** (=working) *Dad was hard at work in the garden.* | **set/get to work** (=start working)

W

4 [U] something you produce for your job, as part of a course etc: *an excellent piece of work* | *The standard of work in colleges is improving.*
5 [C] a painting, book, play, piece of music etc: *a great work of art*
6 do sb's dirty work to do an unpleasant or dishonest action for someone, so that they do not have to do it
7 works [plural] **a)** activities that involve repairing roads, bridges etc **b)** a large building where goods are produced or an industrial process takes place: **gasworks/ironworks etc**
→ **DONKEY WORK**

workable /'wɜːkəbəl $ 'wɜːr-/ *adj* a workable plan, system, idea etc is practical and will work well [≠ **unworkable**]: *a workable solution*

workaholic /ˌwɜːkə'hɒlɪk $ ˌwɜːrkə'hɔː-/ *n* [C] someone who chooses to work so much that they do not have time for anything else

workbench /'wɜːkbentʃ $ 'wɜːrk-/ *n* [C] a strong table used for working with tools

workbook /'wɜːkbʊk $ 'wɜːrk-/ *n* [C] a school book with questions and exercises in it

worked 'up *adj* [not before noun] *informal* upset, nervous, or excited: **+about/over** *Don't get so worked up over little things.*

worker /'wɜːkə $ 'wɜːrkər/ *n* [C]
1 someone who does a particular kind of job for an organization, but who is not a manager: **factory/farm/office etc worker** *training for healthcare workers* | *Even skilled workers are finding it hard to get jobs.* | **manual/blue-collar worker** (=someone who does physical work) | **white-collar worker** (=someone who works in an office)
2 a good/hard/quick etc worker someone who works well etc
→ **DOCK WORKER, SOCIAL WORKER**

workforce /'wɜːkfɔːs $ 'wɜːrkfɔːrs/ *n* [singular] all the people who work in a country or company: *a skilled workforce*

working[1] /'wɜːkɪŋ $ 'wɜːr-/ *adj* [only before noun] **1** relating to the situation or time when you work: **working conditions/environment etc** *poor working conditions* | **working day/week/hours etc** *He spent most of his working life in the same firm.* | *a good working relationship between managers and staff* **2** having a job: *working mothers* **3 be in (good/perfect etc) working order** to be working properly and not broken: *The watch was still in good working order.* **4 working party/group** a group of people formed to examine a particular situation or problem **5 a working knowledge of sth** enough knowledge of a language, subject etc to be able to do something effectively: *a working knowledge of Spanish*

working[2] *n* **1** [singular] also **workings** [plural] the way that something works: *the workings of government* **2** [U] a particular way of working at your job: **part-time/flexible etc working**

working 'class *n* [singular] the group of people in society who usually do physical work and who do not have much money or power
—**working-class** *adj*

workload /'wɜːkləʊd $ 'wɜːrkloʊd/ *n* [C] the amount of work you must do: *a heavy workload* (=a lot of work)

workman /'wɜːkmən $ 'wɜːrk-/ *n* [C] plural **workmen** /-mən/ someone who does physical work, such as building or repairing things

workmanlike /'wɜːkmənlaɪk $ 'wɜːrk-/ *adj* done in a practical and skilful way

workmanship /'wɜːkmənʃɪp $ 'wɜːrk-/ *n* [U] the skill used to make something

workmate /'wɜːkmeɪt $ 'wɜːrk-/ *n* [C] *BrE* someone you work with [= **colleague**] → see box at **WORK**

workout /'wɜːkaʊt $ 'wɜːrk-/ *n* [C] a period of physical exercise done to make your body stronger: *a daily workout in the gym* → see box at **EXERCISE**

'work ˌpermit *n* [C] an official document that you must have to work in a foreign country

workplace /'wɜːkpleɪs $ 'wɜːrk-/ *n* [C usually singular] the room or building where people work: *the problem of bullying in the workplace*

worksheet /'wɜːkʃiːt $ 'wɜːrk-/ *n* [C] a piece of paper with questions and exercises on it

workshop /'wɜːkʃɒp $ 'wɜːrkʃɑːp/ *n* [C] **1** a room or building where people use tools and machines to make or repair things **2** a meeting where people learn about a particular subject by discussing their experiences and doing practical exercises: **drama/writing/music etc workshop**

workstation /'wɜːkˌsteɪʃən $ 'wɜːrk-/ *n* [C] a computer that is part of an office computer system → see box at **OFFICE**

'work-ˌsurface also **'work-top** *n* [C] *BrE* a flat surface for working on (=counter *AmE*): *kitchen worktops* → see picture at **KITCHEN**

world[1] /wɜːld $ wɜːrld/ *n*
1 the world the PLANET we live on, and all the people, countries etc on it [= **earth**]: *Students from all over the world study here.* | *a common disease in some parts of the world* | *the world's tallest building* | **in the world** (=used to emphasize) *You're the best dad in the world!* | *I want the whole world* (=everyone) *to know how happy I am.*
2 [singular] our society, and the way that people live and behave: *I want a better world for my kids.* | *In an ideal world everything would be recycled.*
3 [C usually singular] all the things and people that are connected with a particular subject, activity, place, time, or person: **the world of fashion/politics/sport etc** | **the Arab/Western/English-speaking etc world** *Opinion in the Western world is divided.* | **the industrialized/developing world** | **the ancient/modern etc world** *a history of the ancient world*
4 the animal/plant/insect world animals etc considered as a group
5 [C] another PLANET that is not the Earth
6 the outside world people and events in the rest of the world, where you cannot or do not go: *Prisoners are cut off from the outside world.*
7 a world of difference/worlds apart used to say that two things are very different from each other: *There's a world of difference between being alone and being lonely.*
8 in a world of your own thinking so much that you do not notice other people
9 out of this world *informal* very good: *The graphics are out of this world!*

10 do sb a world of good *informal* to make someone feel much better

11 mean the world to sb/think the world of sb if you mean the world to someone, or they think the world of you, they love or admire you very much

12 the best of both worlds the advantages of two very different things: *With instant access to your money and good interest rates, you* **have the best of both worlds.**

13 be/feel on top of the world to feel happy and healthy

14 move/go up in the world to get a better job, more money etc: *Diamonds! You're going up in the world then?*

15 have the world at your feet to be very successful

world² *adj* [only before noun] involving or affecting all or most of the world: *the world champion* | *World War Two* | *Bains set a new world record in the long jump.*

,**world-'class** *adj* among the best in the world: *a world-class tennis player*

,**world-'famous** *adj* known about by people all over the world

worldly /'wɜːldli $ 'wɜːrld-/ *adj* **1** *literary* **worldly** goods/possessions everything you own **2** knowing a lot about life

'**world ,music** *n* [U] traditional music from the different countries around the world, not the US or Britain

,**world 'power** *n* [C] a country with power and influence over many other countries

worldwide /,wɜːld'waɪd◂ $,wɜːrld-/ *adj, adv* everywhere in the world: *The company employs 2000 people worldwide.* | *a worldwide campaign*

,**World Wide 'Web** *n* **the World Wide Web** the WEB written abbreviation *WWW* [= Internet]

worm¹ /wɜːm $ wɜːrm/ *n* [C]

1 a small long thin creature without bones or legs that lives in soil

2 worms [plural] long thin creatures that can live inside people or animals and make them ill
→ **can of worms** at **CAN²**

worm² *v* **1 worm your way into/through etc sth** to move through a narrow place slowly and with difficulty **2 worm your way into sb's heart/affections/confidence etc** *disapproving* to gradually make someone love and trust you, especially in order to gain an advantage

worm sth out of sb *phr v* to persuade someone to tell you something

worn¹ /wɔːn $ wɔːrn/ *v* the past participle of WEAR

worn² *adj* old and rather damaged: *worn jeans*

,**worn 'out, worn-out** *adj* **1** very tired: *You look worn out.* → see box at **TIRED 2** too old or damaged to use any more: *worn-out shoes*

worried /'wʌrid $ 'wɜːrid/ *adj* if you are worried, you keep thinking about a problem or about something bad that might happen so that you do not feel happy or relaxed: *You look worried.* | +**about** *I'm worried about my exam.* | +**(that)** *I was worried we'd be late.*

anxious: *She was getting anxious about the children.*
concerned: *Many scientists are concerned*

about global warming.
nervous – worried or frightened about something, and unable to relax: *I get really nervous about exams.*
uneasy – worried because you think something bad might happen: *I felt uneasy leaving the kids with him.*
stressed (out) – so worried that you cannot relax: *I'm getting totally stressed out about work.*

worry¹ /'wʌri $ 'wɜːri/ *v* **worried, worrying, worries**

1 [I] to keep thinking about a problem or about something bad that might happen so that you do not feel happy or relaxed: +**about** *Parents always worry about their children.* | +**(that)** *I worry that I won't have enough money.*

2 don't worry *spoken* **a)** used when you are trying to make someone feel less anxious: *Don't worry, Daddy's here.* **b)** used to tell someone that they do not have to do something: +**about** *Don't worry about the washing-up. I'll do it later.*

3 [T] if something worries you, it makes you feel worried: *Changes in the climate are worrying scientists.* | **it worries sb that** *It worries me that my dad lives alone now.*

worry² *n* [C,U] plural **worries** something that makes you feel worried, or the feeling of being worried: *My main worry is finding somewhere to live.* | *money worries* | *She was desperate with worry.*

COLLOCATIONS

slight/minor worry
big/great/major/serious worry
constant worry – one that never goes away

worrying /'wʌri-ɪŋ $ 'wɜː-/ *adj* making you feel worried: *worrying news*

worse¹ /wɜːs $ wɜːrs/ *adj* [the comparative of 'bad']

1 more bad or more unpleasant [➝ **better**]: +**than** *Your singing is even worse than mine!* | *The problem is getting worse.* | *The traffic is* **much worse** *after five o'clock.*

2 [not before noun] more ill: *If you feel worse tomorrow, go to the doctor.*

3 the worse for wear drunk or in a bad condition: *He arrived home at 5 am, looking the worse for wear.*

worse² *n* [U] something worse: *Worse was yet to come.*

worse³ *adv* [the comparative of 'badly']

1 in a more severe or serious way than before: +**than** *It's raining worse than ever.*

2 not as well [➝ **better**]: *He sings even worse than I do!*

worsen /'wɜːsən $ 'wɜːr-/ *v* [I,T] to become worse or make something worse: *His condition is worsening.*

,**worse 'off** *adj* poorer, or in a worse situation: *The tax increase will leave us worse off.*

worship /'wɜːʃɪp $ 'wɜːr-/ *v* **worshipped, worshipping** *BrE*; also **worshiped, worshiping** *AmE*

1 [I,T] to express respect and love for a god

2 [T] to love and admire someone very much: *He absolutely worships her.*

—**worship** *n* [U] —**worshipper** *n* [C]

W

worst¹ /wɜːst $ wɜːrst/ *adj* [the superlative of 'bad'] worse than any other person or thing [➡ **best**]: *the worst movie I've ever seen* | *It all happened at the **worst possible** time.*

worst² *n*

1 the worst someone or something that is worse than every other person or thing [➡ **the best**]: *Of all the exams, that was the worst.* | **worst (that)** *This year's harvest is the worst I can remember.* | *Last month was **by far the worst** for road accidents.* | *When he didn't come home, I **feared the worst**.*

2 at (the) worst if things are as bad as they can be: *At worst, the repairs will cost you $700.*

3 if the worst comes to the worst *especially BrE*; **if worse comes to worst** *especially AmE* if the situation develops in the worst possible way: *If the worst comes to the worst, we'll have to sell the car.*

worst³ *adv* [the superlative of 'badly'] most badly: *the cities that were worst affected by the war* | *She was lost and, **worst of all**, she didn't have any money.*

worth¹ /wɜːθ $ wɜːrθ/ *adj*

1 be worth sth to have a particular value: *Our house is worth $350,000.* | *Each question is worth 4 points.* | *How much is it worth?*

2 a) used to say that something is interesting, useful, or enjoyable: **be worth (doing) sth** *The film is **well worth** seeing.* **b)** used to say that someone should do something because they will gain something from it: **it is worth doing sth** *It's worth checking the bill.* | **be worth the time/effort/work** *It was a great show, and worth the hard work.*

3 it's (not) worth it *informal* used to say that you gain or do not gain something from an action: *Don't argue with her – it's just not worth it.*

4 be worth sb's while *spoken* used to say that someone should spend time or money on something because they will gain something from it

worth² *n* [U]

1 ten pounds' worth/$500 worth etc of sth an amount of something worth ten pounds, $500 etc: *£2000 worth of computer equipment* | *The fire caused thousands of pounds' worth of damage.*

2 ten minutes' worth/a week's worth etc of sth something that takes ten minutes, a week etc to happen, do, or use: *We bought a week's worth of shopping.*

3 how good or useful something or someone is: *The new computer has **proved** its **worth**.*

worthless /ˈwɜːθləs $ ˈwɜːrθ-/ *adj* **1** something that is worthless has no value, importance, or use [≠ **valuable**]: *worthless rubbish* | *The information was worthless to me.* **2** a worthless person has no good qualities or useful skills: *She made him feel completely worthless.*

worthwhile /ˌwɜːθˈwaɪl◂ $ ˌwɜːrθ-/ *adj* if something is worthwhile, it is important or useful, even though you have to spend time, effort, or money doing it: *It's worthwhile comparing prices.*

worthy /ˈwɜːði $ ˈwɜːrði/ *adj* **1** [only before noun] deserving respect from people: *United are worthy winners.* | *a worthy opponent* **2 be worthy of sth** *formal* to deserve something: *A couple of other books are worthy of mention.*

would /wʊd/ *modal verb* negative short form **wouldn't**

1 used when describing what someone said or thought in the past: *He said he would call back later.* | *I never thought she would marry him.*

2 used when talking about a possible situation that you imagine or want to happen: *If I won the lottery, I'd buy a house.* | *I'd be amazed if I got the job.*

3 used when talking about something that might have happened, but it did not happen: *I would have phoned you, but there wasn't time.*

4 used when saying that something happened often in the past: *In summer he would sit out in the garden.*

5 *spoken* used when asking someone politely to do something: *Would you shut the door, please?*

6 *spoken* used when offering something to someone or inviting them politely: *Would you like a cake?*

7 *spoken* used when saying that someone wants something or wants to do something: **would like/love/prefer** *I'd love a coffee.* | *She'd like to meet you.*

8 would not a) used when saying that someone refused to do something: *He wouldn't give us any money.* **b)** used when saying that something did not happen, even though someone was trying to make it happen: *The door wouldn't open, no matter how hard she pulled.*

9 *spoken* used when making a suggestion or giving advice politely: *I'd ask your teacher, if I were you.*

10 I would think/imagine/guess/say *spoken* used when saying what you think is probably true: *I would think she's gone back home.*

11 *spoken* used when you are annoyed about what someone has said or done, because it is typical of them: *You would say that, wouldn't you!*

→ **-'D** → **would rather** at **RATHER**

'would-be *adj* a would-be writer, actor, student etc is someone who wants to be a writer, actor etc

wouldn't /ˈwʊdnt/ the short form of 'would not': *She wouldn't answer.*

would've /ˈwʊdəv/ the short form of 'would have': *You would've enjoyed the film.*

wound¹ /wuːnd/ *n* [C] a deep cut made in your skin by a knife or bullet: *gunshot wounds* | *It took a long time for his **wounds** to **heal**.*

wound² *v* [T] **1** to injure someone with a knife, gun etc: *Six people were wounded in the attack.* → see box at **HURT 2** to make someone feel unhappy or upset —**wounded** *adj*

wound³ /waʊnd/ *v* the past tense and past participle of **WIND**

wound up /ˌwaʊnd ˈʌp/ *adj* [not before noun] very angry, nervous, or excited: *I was too wound up to sleep.*

wove /wəʊv $ woʊv/ *v* the past tense of **WEAVE**

woven /ˈwəʊvən $ ˈwoʊ-/ *v* the past participle of **WEAVE**

wow /waʊ/ *spoken* used when you think something is impressive or surprising: *Wow! Look at that!*

wrangle /ˈræŋɡəl/ *v* [I] to argue with someone angrily for a long time —**wrangle** *n* [C]

wrap /ræp/ v [T] **wrapped, wrapping**

1 also **wrap up** to put paper or cloth over something to cover it completely: **wrap sth in sth** *The present was wrapped in gold paper.* | **wrap sth around sb/sth** *Wrap the blanket around you.*

2 if you wrap your arms, legs, or fingers around something, you use them to hold it: **wrap sth around sb/sth** *She sat with her arms wrapped around her legs.*

→ **GIFT WRAP, PLASTIC WRAP**

wrap up phr v **1** to put on warm clothes: *Make sure you wrap up warm.* **2 wrap sth ⇔ up** *informal* to finish a job, meeting etc: *The project was quickly wrapped up.* **3 be wrapped up in sth** to give so much of your attention to something that you do not have time for anything else

wrapper /'ræpə $ -ər/ n [C] the paper or plastic that covers something you buy → see box at **COVER**

wrapping /'ræpɪŋ/ n [C,U] the cloth, paper, or plastic that is put around something to protect it → see box at **COVER**

'wrapping ,paper n [U] coloured paper used to wrap presents

wrath /rɒθ $ ræθ/ n [U] *formal* extreme anger

wreak /riːk/ v past tense and past participle **wreaked** or **wrought** /rɔːt $ rɒːt/ **wreak havoc (on sth)** to cause a lot of damage or problems

wreath /riːθ/ n [C] a circle of flowers and leaves used as a decoration or to show respect for someone who has died

wreathe /riːð/ v *literary* **be wreathed in sth** to be covered in something: *The mountains were wreathed in mist.*

wreck¹ /rek/ v [T] *informal* to destroy something completely: *The building was wrecked by an explosion.* | *Injury wrecked his career.*

wreck² n [C] **1** a car, plane, or ship that has been very badly damaged **2** *informal* someone who is very tired, unhealthy, or worried: *The attack left her an emotional wreck.* **3** *AmE* a bad car accident or plane accident [= **crash** *BrE*]: *One person survived the wreck.* → see box at **ACCIDENT**

wreckage

wreckage /'rekɪdʒ/ n [singular,U] the broken parts of a vehicle or building that has been destroyed: *She pulled the driver from the wreckage.*

wren /ren/ n [C] a very small brown bird

wrench¹ /rentʃ/ v [T] **1** to twist and pull something from somewhere, using force: *I*

wrenched the box from his grasp. **2** to injure part of your body by twisting it suddenly

wrench² n **1** [C] *especially AmE* a tool that you use for turning NUTS [= **spanner** *BrE*] **2** [singular] if it is a wrench to leave someone or something, it makes you feel very sad: *It was a wrench to leave LA.* **3** [usually singular] a twisting movement that pulls something violently

wrest /rest/ v [T + adv/prep] *formal* to take something from someone with force

wrestle /'resəl/ v **1** [I,T] to fight someone by holding them and trying to push them to the ground **2 wrestle with sth** to try to understand or solve a difficult problem: *He wrestled with the problem for days.*

wrestling /'reslɪŋ/ n [U] a sport in which two people fight and try to push each other to the ground → see box at **FIGHT** —**wrestler** n [C]

wretch /retʃ/ n [C] *old-fashioned* someone that you feel sorry for

wretched /'retʃɪd/ adj **1** someone who is wretched is very unhappy or ill, and you feel sorry for them **2** [only before noun] used when you feel angry with someone or something: *The wretched thing's broken!*

wriggle /'rɪgəl/ v [I,T] to twist quickly from side to side: *She wriggled into the tight dress.* —**wriggle** n [C]

wriggle out of sth phr v to avoid doing something by using clever excuses: *He wriggled out of paying.*

wring /rɪŋ/ v [T] past tense and past participle **wrung** /rʌŋ/ **1** also **wring out** to twist wet cloth tightly to remove water **2 wring sth's neck** to kill an animal by twisting its neck

wrinkle /'rɪŋkəl/ n [C] a small line on your face that you get when you are old —**wrinkled** adj: *his wrinkled face* —**wrinkle** v [I,T]

wrist /rɪst/ n [C] the joint between your hand and your arm → see picture at **HAND¹**

wristwatch /'rɪstwɒtʃ $ -wɑːtʃ, -wɒːtʃ/ n [C] a watch that you wear on your wrist

writ /rɪt/ n [C] a legal document that orders someone to do something

write /raɪt/ v past tense **wrote** /rəʊt $ roʊt/ past participle **written** /'rɪtn/

1 [I,T] to make letters or words on paper, using a pen or pencil: *We teach children to read and write.* | **write sth on/in sth** *Write your name on a piece of paper.* | **written report/agreement/reply etc** (=done on paper, not spoken)

THESAURUS

make a note (of sth) – to write down information that you might need later
jot sth down – to write something very quickly
scribble sth – to write something very quickly and in an untidy way
take/get sth down – to write down what someone is saying
fill sth in/out – to write information about yourself on a form or other official document
sign sth – to write your **signature** (=name) at the end of a letter, document etc
key sth in/enter sth – to write or record information on a computer
→ **READ**

2 [I,T] to produce a letter to send to someone: +**to** *Will you write to me?* | **write sth to sb** *I'm writing a letter to my mum.* | **write sb** *AmE: Ian hasn't written me for a long time.*
3 [I,T] to produce a book, song etc: *He wrote two books.* | *The article is well written.*
4 also **write out** [T] to write information on a cheque, form etc: *I wrote a cheque for £30.*

write back *phr v* to answer someone's letter by sending them a letter: *I sent them a long letter at Christmas, but they never wrote back.*

write sth ⇔ **down** *phr v* to write something on a piece of paper: *He wrote down her phone number.*

write in *phr v* to send a letter to an organization

write off *phr v* **1** to send a letter to an organization asking them to send you something: +**for** *I've written off for an application form.* **2 write sth** ⇔ **off** to decide that someone or something is useless, unimportant, or a failure: *The critics wrote him off.* **3 write sth** ⇔ **off** to officially say that a debt no longer has to be paid, or officially accept that you cannot get back money that you have spent or lost: *The US wrote off debts worth billions of dollars.*

write sth ⇔ **out** *phr v* to write something on paper, especially in a neat and clear way, including all the details: *He wrote out the poem in his best handwriting.*

write sth ⇔ **up** *phr v* to write something using notes you made earlier: *I'm writing up my report.*

'write-off *n* [C] *BrE* a vehicle that is so badly damaged that it can never be used again

writer /'raɪtə $ -ər/ *n* [C] someone who writes books, stories etc, especially as a job [➡ **author**, **playwright**]

'write-up *n* [C] a piece of writing in a newspaper, magazine etc, in which someone gives their opinion about a new book, film etc: *The play got a good write-up.*

writhe /raɪð/ *v* [I] to twist your body, especially because you are in a lot of pain: *He lay writhing in agony.*

writing /'raɪtɪŋ/ *n*
1 [U] words that have been written or printed: *I can't read the writing on the envelope.* | *a T-shirt with Japanese writing on it*
2 [U] books, poems, articles etc by a particular writer or on a particular subject: *some of Greene's most powerful writing*
3 [U] the activity or skill of writing: *She took up writing as a career.*
4 in writing if you get something in writing, it is official proof of an agreement, promise etc
5 writings [plural] the books, stories etc that an important writer has written

written /'rɪtn/ *v* the past participle of WRITE

wrong¹ /rɒŋ $ rɔːŋ/ *adj*

1 not correct – used when someone has made a mistake [≠ **right**]: *Your calculations must be wrong.* | *The letter was delivered to the wrong address.*

THESAURUS

incorrect – used about facts, answers etc that are completely wrong
inaccurate – used about information, numbers

etc that are not exactly right
misleading – used about a statement or piece of information that makes people believe something that is wrong
false – used about facts that are untrue and wrong
be mistaken *formal* – used about a person whose opinion about something is wrong: *No, I've never been there. You must be mistaken.*
→ **RIGHT**

2 be wrong (about sb/sth) not to be right in what you think about someone or something [≠ **right**]: *No, you're wrong. Sue wouldn't do a thing like that.*
3 used to describe a situation where there are problems, or when someone is ill or unhappy: **there is something wrong/something is wrong** *When he didn't come back, I knew that something was wrong.* | +**with** *He's got something wrong with his foot.* | *You look sad. What's wrong?* → see box at **PROBLEM**
4 not morally right or acceptable [≠ **right**]: **it is wrong that** *It's wrong that people should have to sleep on the streets.* | **it is wrong to do sth** *It is wrong to treat children like that.*
5 not suitable [≠ **right**]: *It's the wrong time of year to go skiing.*
6 if something is wrong with a vehicle or machine, it stops working properly: +**with** *There's something wrong with the car.*
7 get on the wrong side of sb to make someone angry with you
8 get (hold of) the wrong end of the stick *BrE informal* to understand a situation in completely the wrong way

wrong² *adv*

1 not in the correct way [≠ **right**]: *You spelt my name wrong.* | *Have I done it wrong?*
2 go wrong if something goes wrong, it starts to have problems or it is unsuccessful: *Something's gone wrong with my watch.* | *His plan went wrong.*
3 get sth wrong to make a mistake in the way you write, judge, or understand something: *He got the answer wrong.* | *We must have got the address wrong.*
4 don't get me wrong *spoken* used when you think that someone may understand your remarks wrongly, or be offended by them: *Don't get me wrong – I like Tim.*

wrong³ *n* **1** [U] behaviour that is not morally correct: *He's too young to know right from wrong.* **2** [C] an action or situation in which someone is treated badly or unfairly: *the wrongs done to these people during the war* **3 be in the wrong** to make a mistake or deserve the blame for something **4 sb can do no wrong** used to say that someone thinks that another person is perfect, especially when you know that they are not

wrong⁴ *v* [T] *formal* to treat someone unfairly

wrongdoing /'rɒŋˌduːɪŋ $ 'rɔːŋˌduːɪŋ/ *n* [C,U] *formal* when someone does something illegal or wrong —**wrongdoer** *n* [C]

wrongful /'rɒŋfəl $ 'rɔːŋ-/ *adj* **wrongful arrest/imprisonment/dismissal etc** a wrongful arrest etc is unfair or illegal because the person affected by it has done nothing wrong —**wrongfully** *adv*

W

wrongly /ˈrɒŋli $ ˈrɔː-/ *adv* **1** not correctly: *His name is wrongly spelt.* **2** in an unfair or immoral way: *He had been wrongly accused of murder.*

wrote /rəʊt $ roʊt/ *v* the past tense of WRITE

wrought /rɔːt $ rɒːt/ *v* the past tense and past participle of WREAK

wrought 'iron *n* [U] long thin pieces of iron formed into shapes: *a wrought iron gate*

wrung /rʌŋ/ *v* the past tense and past participle of WRING

wry /raɪ/ *adj* [only before noun] a wry expression or wry humour shows that you know a situation is bad, but you also think it is slightly amusing: *a wry smile* —**wryly** *adv*

WWW /ˌdʌbəlju: dʌbəlju: ˈdʌbəlju:/ the written abbreviation of **World Wide Web**

XY, xy

X, x /eks/ *n* plural **X's, x's** **1** [C,U] the 24th letter of the English alphabet **2** [C] a mark used on school work to show that an answer is wrong **3** [C] a mark used at the end of a letter to show a kiss **4** [U] a letter used instead of someone's name because you want to keep it secret, or you do not know it: *Ms X*

xenophobia /ˌzenəˈfəʊbiə $ -ˈfoʊ-/ *n* [U] strong fear or dislike of people from other countries —**xenophobic** *adj*

Xerox /ˈzɪərɒks $ ˈzɪrɑːks, ˈziː-/ *n* [C] *trademark* a PHOTOCOPY —**Xerox** *v* [T] → see box at COPY

XL extra large used on clothes to show their size

Xmas /ˈkrɪsməs, ˈeksməs/ *n* [C,U] *written informal* Christmas: *Happy Xmas*

X-ray /ˈeks reɪ/ *n* [C] **1** a beam of RADIATION that can go through solid objects and is used for photographing the inside of the body **2** a photograph of the inside of someone's body, taken using X-rays to see if anything is wrong —**X-ray** *v* [T]

xylophone /ˈzaɪləfəʊn $ -foʊn/ *n* [C] a musical instrument with flat metal bars that you hit with a stick → see picture on page A6

Y, y /waɪ/ *n* [C,U] plural **Y's, y's** the 25th letter of the English alphabet

-y /i/ *suffix* having something or like something: *dusty shelves* (=covered in dust) | *a wintry day* (=typical of winter)

yacht /jɒt $ jɑːt/ *n* [C] **1** a boat with sails used for races or sailing for pleasure → see picture at TRANSPORT **2** a large expensive boat, used for travelling or pleasure

yachting /ˈjɒtɪŋ $ ˈjɑːtɪŋ/ *n* [U] *especially BrE* sailing or racing in a yacht

yachtsman /ˈjɒtsmən $ ˈjɑːts-/ *n* [C] plural **yachtsmen** /-mən/ a man who sails a yacht

yachtswoman /ˈjɒts,wʊmən $ ˈjɑːts-/ *n* [C] plural **yachtswomen** /-,wɪmɪn/ a woman who sails a yacht

yak¹ /jæk/ *n* [C] an animal of central Asia that looks like a cow with long hair

yak² *v* [I] **yakked, yakking** *informal* to talk a lot about unimportant things

yam /jæm/ *n* [C] **1** a tropical plant grown for its root which is eaten as a vegetable **2** *AmE* a SWEET POTATO

yank /jæŋk/ *v* [I,T] *informal* to suddenly pull something quickly and with force: *He yanked the door open.* —**yank** *n* [C] *He gave the rope* **a yank.**

Yank *n* [C] *informal* someone from the US

yap /jæp/ *v* [I] **yapped, yapping** if a small dog yaps, it BARKS in an excited way —**yap** *n* [C]

yard /jɑːd $ jɑːrd/ *n* [C]

1 written abbreviation **yd** a unit for measuring length, equal to three feet or 0.9144 metres: *a hundred yards away* | *9000* **square yards**
2 *AmE* the area around a house, usually covered with grass [= garden *BrE*]: **front/back yard** *The kids were playing in the back yard.*
3 an area of land used for a particular purpose: *a builder's yard* | **prison/school yard** (=an area in a prison or school where people do activities outdoors)

yardstick /ˈjɑːd,stɪk $ ˈjɑːrd-/ *n* [C] something that you compare another thing with, to show how good it is: *Profit is the main yardstick of success for a business.*

yarn /jɑːn $ jɑːrn/ *n* **1** [U] thread that you use to KNIT things **2** [C] *informal* a long story that is not completely true

yawn /jɔːn $ jɒːn/ *v* [I] to open your mouth wide and breathe deeply because you are tired or bored: *He looked at his watch and yawned.* —**yawn** *n* [C]

yawn

yawning /ˈjɔːnɪŋ $ ˈjɒː-/ *adj* **yawning gap/gulf/chasm etc (between sth)** a very big space or difference between things: *the yawning gap between rich and poor*

yd the written abbreviation of **yard**

yeah /jeə/ *adv* *spoken informal* yes

year /jɪə, jɜː $ jɪr/ *n* [C]

1 a period of 365 days or 12 months: *I've been teaching for six years.* | *They got married a year ago.* | **a/per year** (=each year) *How much does he earn a year?* | *Many birds return to the same spot* **year after year** (=every year for many years). | **all (the) year round** (=during the whole year) *It's sunny here all the year round.* | *The house is about 150* **years old.** | **seven-year-old/twenty-year-old etc** (=someone who is seven years old etc)
2 the period from January 1 to December 31: **this/next/last year** *Where are you spending Christmas this year?* | *The movie's set in the year 2052.*

Y

3 school/financial/academic etc year a particular period of 12 months used by schools, businesses etc: *The tax year begins on April 1st.*

4 years *informal* a very long time [= ages]: *It's years since I last saw him.* | **in/for years** *I haven't played tennis for years.*

5 a particular time in someone's life or in history: **sb's early/teenage/retirement etc years** *In his later years he suffered from ill health.* | **sb's years in/at/as sth** *She enjoyed her years as a student.* | **the war/depression/Clinton etc years**

6 *BrE* **a)** a level at school or university which is related to how long you have been at school or university: *You have important exams in year 11.* | **the year above/below (sb)** *My brother's in the year above me.* | *John's in his third year at Oxford.* | *first-year students* **b) first-year/ second-year etc** someone who is in their first, second etc year at school or university: *They must be first-years.* ➔ GAP YEAR, LEAP YEAR, LIGHT YEAR, NEW YEAR

yearbook /'jɪəbʊk, 'jɜ:- $ 'jɪr-/ *n* [C] a book that an organization or school produces every year, with information about its activities

yearly /'jɪəli, 'jɜ:- $ 'jɪrli/ *adj* happening every year or once a year: *The yearly sum of £7000* | **three-yearly/five-yearly etc** (=happening every three etc years) *a five-yearly review* ➔ see box at REGULAR —**yearly** *adv*: *A meeting is held* **twice yearly** (=two times every year).

yearn /jɜ:n $ jɜ:rn/ *v* [I] *formal* to want something very much, especially when it is difficult or impossible to get: +**for** *She yearned for a child.* | **yearn to do sth** *I yearned to go home.* —**yearning** *n* [C,U]

yeast /ji:st/ *n* [U] a substance used to make bread rise and to produce alcohol in beer and wine

yell /jel/ also **yell out** *v* [I,T] to shout something very loudly: +**at** *Someone yelled at her to stop.* ➔ see box at SHOUT —**yell** *n* [C]

yellow /'jeləʊ $ -loʊ/ *adj* having the colour of butter or the sun: **bright/pale yellow** *bright yellow curtains* ➔ see picture at PATTERN —**yellow** *n* [C,U] —**yellow** *v* [I,T] *yellowing newspaper cuttings*

,yellow 'line *n* [C] *BrE* a yellow line at the side of a road which means you can only park there for a short time, or at a particular time: **double yellow lines** (=two lines that mean you cannot park there)

,Yellow 'Pages *n trademark* a book containing the telephone numbers and addresses of businesses in an area

yelp /jelp/ *v* [I] to give a short high cry because of pain or excitement – used especially of dogs —**yelp** *n* [C]

yep /jep/ *adv spoken informal* yes

yes¹ /jes/ *spoken*

1 used as an answer to say that something is true, that you agree, that you want something etc [≠ no]: *'Is that real gold?' 'Yes.'* | *'The movie was great.' 'Yes, it was.'* | *'Would you like some wine?' 'Yes, please.'* | **say yes** (=agree to something or allow something) *Ask Dad. I'm sure he'll say yes.*

2 used to show that you are ready to listen to someone when they call you or want your attention: *'Mum!' 'Yes?'*

3 used to say that a negative statement is not true: *'John doesn't love me any more.' 'Yes he does!'*

4 used when you are very happy or excited: *Yes! I got the job!*

yes² *n* [C] *plural* **yeses** or **yesses** an answer, decision, or vote that agrees with or supports something: *Was that a yes?*

yesterday /'jestədi, -deɪ $ -ər-/ *adv, n* [U] the day before today [➔ tomorrow]: *Did you watch the game yesterday?* | *Yesterday was their anniversary.* | **yesterday morning/afternoon/ evening** *I saw him yesterday afternoon.* | *They arrived* **the day before yesterday** (=two days ago).

yesteryear /'jestəjɪə, -jɜ: $ 'jestərjɪr/ *n* **the ... of yesteryear** *literary* things or people that existed in the past: *the beautiful cars of yesteryear*

yet¹ /jet/ *adv*

1 used in negative sentences and questions to talk about whether something has happened, especially something that you expect to happen: *Have you heard their new song yet?* | *I haven't finished yet.* | *'Is supper ready?' 'No, not yet.'* | **As yet** (=until now) *there is no news.*

2 used in negative sentences to say that it is too early or soon for someone to do something: *You don't have to get up yet.*

3 months/weeks/ages etc yet used to say that a long time will pass before something happens: *My holiday's not for ages yet.* | *It'll be weeks yet before we know the result.*

4 used to emphasize that something could still happen in the future, or that there is still enough time to do something [= still]: **could/may/might yet do sth** *The plan may yet succeed.* | *There's plenty of* **time yet** *to enter the competition.*

5 best/fastest/most etc yet best etc until and including now: *This is their best record yet.*

6 yet another/yet more/yet again used to emphasize that something has increased or has happened again, especially when this is surprising or annoying: *I've spotted yet another mistake!* | *The meeting was cancelled yet again.*

7 have yet to do sth *formal* used to say that something you are expecting has not happened or been done: *He has yet to reply to my letter.*

yet² *linking word* used to add something that is surprising after what you have just said: *It was past midnight, yet she still felt wide awake.* | *a simple yet effective solution*

yew /ju:/ *n* [C] a tree with dark green leaves like needles

Y-fronts /'waɪ frʌnts/ *n* [plural] *trademark BrE* a type of men's underwear

yield¹ /ji:ld/ *v* **1** [T] to produce something, especially a profit or a result: *Our research yielded important results.* **2** [I] to finally agree to do something because people have forced or persuaded you: +**to** *The minister yielded to pressure and resigned.* **3** [I] *AmE* to allow the traffic on another road to go first [= give way *BrE*]: +**to** *Yield to traffic on the left.* **4** [T] to allow someone else to have power or control over something: *The military promised to yield power.*

5 [I] *literary* to stop fighting and admit you have lost [= **surrender**] **6** [I] to bend or move when pressed

yield² *n* [C] the amount of profit, crops etc that something produces: **high/low yields** *investments with high yields*

yikes /jaɪks/ *spoken informal* said when you suddenly notice or realize something: *Yikes! I'm late!*

yippee /jɪˈpiː $ ˈjɪpiː/ *spoken informal* said when you are very happy or excited

yo /jəʊ $ joʊ/ *spoken informal especially AmE* used to say hello to someone or get their attention

yob /jɒb $ jɑːb/ *n* [C] *BrE* a rude and often violent young man: *a gang of yobs*

yodel /ˈjəʊdl $ ˈjoʊdl/ *v* [I] **yodelled, yodelling** *BrE*; **yodeled, yodeling** *AmE* to sing while changing between your natural voice and a very high voice, as traditionally done in the mountains of Switzerland and Austria

yoga /ˈjəʊɡə $ ˈjoʊɡə/ *n* [U] a system of exercises which helps you to relax your body and mind

yoghurt, yogurt /ˈjɒɡət $ ˈjoʊɡərt/ *n* [C,U] a thick liquid food made from milk

yoke /jəʊk $ joʊk/ *n* [singular] something that limits your freedom: **+of** *the yoke of tradition*

yokel /ˈjəʊkəl $ ˈjoʊ-/ *n* [C] *humorous* someone who lives in the countryside and is not very intelligent or educated

yolk /jəʊk $ joʊk, jelk/ *n* [C,U] the yellow part of an egg [➡ **white**]

yonder /ˈjɒndə $ ˈjɑːndər/ *adv, determiner literary* over there

you /jə, jʊ; *strong* juː/ *pron*

1 the person or people that someone is speaking or writing to: *Do you want a cigarette?* | *I can't hear you.* | *Can you all come a bit nearer?* | *You idiot!*

2 people in general: *As you get older, you often forget things.*

you'd /juːd/ **1** the short form of 'you had': *I wish you'd told me.* **2** the short form of 'you would': *I didn't think you'd mind.*

you'll /juːl/ the short form of 'you will': *You'll feel better soon.*

young¹ /jʌŋ/ *adj*

1 not having lived for very long [≠ **old**]: *a game for young children* | *I used to ski when I was young.* | *My brother's younger than me.*

THESAURUS

A **small/little** child is a very young child.
A **teenage** boy or girl is between 13 and 19.
An **adolescent** boy or girl is changing from being a child to an adult.
➔ **OLD**

2 seeming younger than you are [➡ **youthful**]: *I've always looked young for my age.* | *The show is ideal for children and people who are young at heart* (=who have the same attitudes, interests etc as young people).

3 a young country, organization etc has not existed for very long

4 intended for young people: *Is this dress too young for me?*

young² *n* [plural] **1 the young** young people **2** the young animals produced by an animal: *The females care for their young alone.*

youngster /ˈjʌŋstə $ -ər/ *n* [C] a young person

your /jə; *strong* jɔː $ jər; *strong* jɔːr/ *determiner*

1 belonging or relating to you: *Is that your mother?* | *Don't worry, it's not your fault.*

2 belonging or relating to anyone – used when talking about people in general: *On entering the town, the church is on your right.*

you're /jə; *strong* jɔː $ jər; *strong* jʊr, jɔːr/ the short form of 'you are': *You're wrong.*

yours /jɔːz $ jʊrz, jɔːrz/ *pron*

1 the POSSESSIVE form of 'you': *That bag's yours, isn't it?* | *Yours is the nicest car.* | **sth of yours** *Is he a friend of yours': You're wrong.*

2 yours/yours faithfully/yours sincerely/yours truly used at the end of a letter before you sign your name

yourself /jɔːˈself $ jɔːr-/ *pron plural* **yourselves** /-ˈselvz/

1 the REFLEXIVE form of 'you': *Did you hurt yourself?*

2 used to emphasize 'you': *Why don't you do it yourself?* | *You yourself told me.*

3 (all) by yourself alone or without help from anyone else: *You're going to Ecuador by yourself?* | *Did you paint the house all by yourself?*

4 have sth (all) to yourself to be the only person in a place: *You'll have the house to yourself this weekend.*

5 you don't look/seem yourself *spoken* used to tell someone that they seem ill or worried

youth /juːθ/ *n plural* **youths** /juːðz $ juːðz, juːθs/

1 [U] the time when someone is young, or the quality of being young [➡ **old age**]: **in your youth** *In his youth he lived in France.* | *He seemed confident, in spite of his youth.*

2 [C] *disapproving* a boy or young man – used especially in news reports: *Three youths were arrested for stealing.* → see box at MAN

3 [U] young people in general: **+of** *the youth of today* | *a youth training scheme*

youth club *n* [C] a place where young people can meet, play games, dance etc

youthful /ˈjuːθfəl/ *adj* **1** typical of young people: *youthful enthusiasm* **2** seeming younger than you are: *a youthful 50-year-old*

youth hostel *n* [C] a place where people can stay cheaply when they are travelling

you've /juːv/ the short form of 'you have': *You've broken it.*

Yo-Yo /ˈjəʊ jəʊ $ ˈjoʊ joʊ/ *n* [C] plural **yo-yos** *trademark* a round toy that you can make go up and down on a string that you hold

yr. also **yr** *BrE* the written abbreviation of **year**

yuck /jʌk/ *spoken informal* said when you think something looks or tastes very unpleasant

yucky /ˈjʌki/ *adj informal* very unpleasant

Yuletide /ˈjuːltaɪd/ *n* [C,U] *literary* Christmas

yum /jʌm/ *spoken informal* said when you think something tastes good

yummy /ˈjʌmi/ *adj informal* tasting very good

yuppie /ˈjʌpi/ *n* [C] *disapproving* a young person who earns a lot of money and buys expensive things

Y

Z, z

Z, z /zed $ zi:/ n [C,U] plural **Z's, z's** the 26th letter of the English alphabet

zany /ˈzeɪni/ adj funny and unusual: *a zany new TV comedy*

zap /zæp/ v [T] **zapped, zapping** *informal* to attack or destroy something very quickly

zapper /ˈzæpə $ -ər/ n [C] *informal especially AmE* something you use for changing CHANNELS on a television from a distance [= remote control]

zeal /zi:l/ n [U] great eagerness to do something that you believe is important: *political zeal*

zealous /ˈzeləs/ adj having great energy and eagerness —**zealously** adv

zebra /ˈzi:brə, ˈze- $ ˈzi:brə/ n [C] an animal like a horse but with black and white lines on its body

zebra ˈcrossing n [C] *BrE* a place on the road marked with black and white lines, where people can cross safely [= crosswalk *AmE*]

zenith /ˈzenɪθ $ ˈzi:-/ n [singular] the time when something is most successful: *The empire had reached its zenith.*

zero¹ /ˈzɪərəʊ $ ˈzi:roʊ/ number plural **zeros** or **zeroes**

1 the number 0: *Make x greater than or equal to zero.*

THESAURUS

nil: *Our chances of finding her are almost nil.* | *United won the game three-nil.*
nothing: *The score was twenty-two to nothing.*
nought *BrE* – used in calculations and figures: *It's increased by nought point seven five per cent (=0.75%).*
O – used to say the number 0 like the letter O: *The code for Oxford is O one eight six five (=01865).*

---

2 the point between + and − on a scale for measuring something, or the lowest point on a scale that shows how much there is left of something: *The petrol gauge was already at zero.*
3 a temperature of 0°: **above/below zero** *It was five degrees below zero last night.*
4 none at all, or the lowest possible amount: **sb's chances are zero** (=they have no chance of success) *His chances of winning are zero.* | *zero inflation*

zero² v

zero in on sth *phr v* to give your attention to something or move directly towards it: *She zeroed in on the weak point in his argument.*

zest /zest/ n [U] **1** a feeling of eagerness and enjoyment: **+for** *a zest for life* **2** the outer layer of the skin of an orange or LEMON

zigzag¹ /ˈzɪgzæg/ n [C] a line or pattern that looks like a row of w's joined together → see picture at PATTERN

zigzag² v [I] **zigzagged, zigzagging** to move forward by moving first to the left, then to the right etc at sharp angles: **+up/down/through etc** *The path zigzags up the mountain.*

zilch /zɪltʃ/ n [U] *informal* nothing

zillion /ˈzɪljən/ number *informal* an extremely large number or amount

zinc /zɪŋk/ n [U] a metal used to produce or cover other metals

zip¹ /zɪp/ v **zipped, zipping**

1 also **zip up** [T] to fasten something using a zip [≠ unzip]: *John zipped up his jacket.* | **zip sth shut/open** (=close or open something using a zip) *She zipped her case open.* → see box at FASTEN
2 [I] to go somewhere or do something very quickly [= whizz, zoom]: **+along/through/up etc** *An ambulance zipped past us.*

zip² n

1 [C] *BrE* a thing for fastening clothes, bags etc, which consists of two lines of small pieces of metal or plastic that join together [= zipper *AmE*]: **do up/undo a zip** *Can you do up the zip on my dress?*
2 [U] *AmE informal* zero: *We beat them ten to zip.*

ˈzip code n [C] *AmE* a number you write below an address on an envelope, which helps the post office deliver the letter more quickly [= postcode *BrE*]

ˈzip drive n [C] *technical* a small piece of equipment that you connect to your computer and use with computer DISKS that can store large amounts of information

zipper /ˈzɪpə $ -ər/ n [C] *AmE* a zip

zit /zɪt/ n [C] *informal* a small painful raised area on your skin [= spot] → see box at MARK

zodiac /ˈzəʊdiæk $ ˈzoʊ-/ n **sign of the zodiac** in ASTROLOGY, one of the 12 areas of the sky where the sun, the moon etc appear to be at different times of the year. They are named after groups of stars.

zombie /ˈzɒmbi $ ˈzɑ:m-/ n **like a zombie** in a very tired, slow, and confused way

zone /zəʊn $ zoʊn/ n [C] an area that is different from the areas around it, because of particular rules or something that is happening: *a no-parking zone* | *a war zone* → see box at AREA → TIME ZONE

zoo /zu:/ n [C] plural **zoos** a place where a lot of different animals are kept so that people can go to look at them

ˈzoo-ˌkeeper n [C] someone who looks after animals in a zoo

zoology /zu:ˈɒlədʒi, zəʊ-ˈɒ- $ zoʊˈɑ:l-/ n [U] the scientific study of animals and their behaviour —**zoologist** n [C]

zoom /zu:m/ v [I] *informal* to go somewhere or do something very quickly: **+down/along/off etc** *I saw a police car zooming along the highway.*

zoom in *phr v* if a camera zooms in, it makes the person or thing in the picture seem much closer and bigger

ˈzoom ˌlens n [C] a camera LENS that can make the person or thing in the picture look bigger or smaller

zucchini /zʊˈki:ni/ n [C,U] *AmE* a long vegetable with dark green skin [= courgette *BrE*] → see picture at VEGETABLE

IRREGULAR VERBS

Verb	Present participle	Past tense	Past participle
arise	arising	arose	arisen
be	being	was	been
bear	bearing	bore	borne
beat	beating	beat	beaten
become	becoming	became	become
begin	beginning	began	begun
bend	bending	bent	bent
bet	betting	betted *or* bet	betted *or* bet
bind	binding	bound	bound
bite	biting	bit	bitten
bleed	bleeding	bled	bled
blow	blowing	blew	blown
break	breaking	broke	broken
breed	breeding	bred	bred
bring	bringing	brought	brought
build	building	built	built
burn	burning	burned *or* burnt	burned *or* burnt
buy	buying	bought	bought
catch	catching	caught	caught
choose	choosing	chose	chosen
come	coming	came	come
cost	costing	cost	cost
creep	creeping	crept	crept
cut	cutting	cut	cut
deal	dealing	dealt	dealt
die	dying	died	died
dig	digging	dug	dug
dive	diving	dived, dove (*AmE*)	dived
do	doing	did	done
draw	drawing	drew	drawn
dream	dreaming	dreamed *or* dreamt	dreamed *or* dreamt
drink	drinking	drank	drunk
drive	driving	drove	driven
eat	eating	ate	eaten
fall	falling	fell	fallen
feed	feeding	fed	fed
feel	feeling	felt	felt
fight	fighting	fought	fought
find	finding	found	found
fly	flying	flew	flown
forbid	forbidding	forbade	forbidden
forget	forgetting	forgot	forgotten
freeze	freezing	froze	frozen
get	getting	got	got (*BrE*), gotten (*AmE*)
give	giving	gave	given
go	going	went	gone
grow	growing	grew	grown
hang	hanging	hung *or* hanged	hung *or* hanged

Verb	Present participle	Past tense	Past participle
have	having	had	had
hear	hearing	heard	heard
hide	hiding	hid	hidden
hit	hitting	hit	hit
hold	holding	held	held
hurt	hurting	hurt	hurt
keep	keeping	kept	kept
kneel	kneeling	knelt, kneeled (esp *AmE*)	knelt, kneeled (esp *AmE*)
know	knowing	knew	known
lay	laying	laid	laid
lead	leading	led	led
lean	leaning	leaned *or* leant	leaned *or* leant
leap	leaping	leaped *or* leapt	leaped *or* leapt
learn	learning	learned *or* learnt	learned *or* learnt
leave	leaving	left	left
lend	lending	lent	lent
let	letting	let	let
lie[1]	lying	lay	lain
lie[2]	lying	lied	lied
lose	losing	lost	lost
make	making	made	made
mean	meaning	meant	meant
meet	meeting	met	met
mistake	mistaking	mistook	mistaken
outgrow	outgrowing	outgrew	outgrown
overhear	overhearing	overheard	overheard
oversleep	oversleeping	overslept	overslept
overtake	overtaking	overtook	overtaken
panic	panicking	panicked	panicked
pay	paying	paid	paid
put	putting	put	put
quit	quitting	quit	quit
read	reading	read	read
repay	repaying	repaid	repaid
ride	riding	rode	ridden
ring	ringing	rang	rung
rise	rising	rose	risen
run	running	ran	run
saw	sawing	sawed	sawn
say	saying	said	said
see	seeing	saw	seen
seek	seeking	sought	sought
sell	selling	sold	sold
send	sending	sent	sent
set	setting	set	set
sew	sewing	sewed	sewn
shake	shaking	shook	shaken
shine	shining	shone	shone
shoot	shooting	shot	shot
show	showing	showed	shown

Verb	Present participle	Past tense	Past participle
shrink	shrinking	shrank	shrunk
shut	shutting	shut	shut
sing	singing	sang	sung
sink	sinking	sank	sunk
sit	sitting	sat	sat
sleep	sleeping	slept	slept
slide	sliding	slid	slid
sling	slinging	slung	slung
smell	smelling	smelt or smelled	smelt or smelled
sow	sowing	sowed	sown
speak	speaking	spoke	spoken
speed	speeding	speeded or sped	speeded or sped
spell	spelling	spelled or spelt	spelled or spelt
spend	spending	spent	spent
spill	spilling	spilled or spilt	spilled or spilt
spin	spinning	spun	spun
spit	spitting	spat	spat
split	splitting	split	split
spoil	spoiling	spoilt	spoilt
spread	spreading	spread	spread
spring	springing	sprang	sprung
stand	standing	stood	stood
steal	stealing	stole	stolen
sting	stinging	stung	stung
strike	striking	struck	struck
swear	swearing	swore	sworn
sweep	sweeping	swept	swept
swim	swimming	swam	swum
swing	swinging	swung	swung
take	taking	took	taken
teach	teaching	taught	taught
tear	tearing	tore	torn
tell	telling	told	told
think	thinking	thought	thought
throw	throwing	threw	thrown
thrust	thrusting	thrust	thrust
undergo	undergoing	underwent	undergone
understand	understanding	understood	understood
undertake	undertaking	undertook	undertaken
undo	undoing	undid	undone
unwind	unwinding	unwound	unwound
upset	upsetting	upset	upset
wake	waking	waked or woke	woken
wear	wearing	wore	worn
weep	weeping	wept	wept
wet	wetting	wet or wetted	wet or wetted
win	winning	won	won
wind	winding	wound	wound
withdraw	withdrawing	withdrew	withdrawn
write	writing	wrote	written

Single User Licence Agreement: Longman Active Study Dictionary

IMPORTANT: READ CAREFULLY

This is a legally binding agreement between You (the user or purchaser) and Pearson Education Limited. By retaining this licence, any software media or accompanying written materials or carrying out any of the permitted activities You agree to be bound by the terms of the licence agreement below.

If You do not agree to these terms then promptly return the entire publication (this licence and all software, written materials, packaging and any other components received with it) with Your sales receipt to Your supplier for a full refund.

SINGLE USER LICENCE AGREEMENT

YOU ARE PERMITTED TO:

✔ Use (load into temporary memory or permanent storage) a single copy of the software on only one computer at a time. If this computer is linked to a network then the software may only be installed in a manner such that it is not accessible to other machines on the network. If You want to use the software on a network or across a whole site, You need to read the Network version of the User Licence or the Site Licence. You can get these from the email address at the end of this licence

✔ Use the software with a class provided it is only installed on one computer

✔ Transfer the software from one computer to another provided that you only use it on one computer at a time

✔ Print out individual screen extracts from the disk for (a) private study or (b) to include in Your essays or classwork with students

✔ Photocopy individual screen extracts for Your schoolwork or classwork with students

YOU MAY NOT:

✘ Rent, lease or sell the software or any part of the publication

✘ Copy any part of the documentation, except where specifically indicated otherwise

✘ Make copies of the software, even for backup purposes

✘ Reverse engineer, decompile or disassemble the software or create a derivative product from the contents of the databases or any software included in them

✘ Use the software on more than one computer at a time

✘ Install the software on any networked computer or server in a way that could allow access to it from more than one machine on the network

✘ Include any material or software from the disk in any other product or software materials, except as allowed under "You are permitted to"

✘ Use the software in any way not specified above without the prior written consent of Pearson Education Limited

✘ Print out more than one page at a time

✘ Print, download or save any pictures

ONE COPY ONLY

This license is for a single user copy of the software

PEARSON EDUCATION LIMITED RESERVES THE RIGHT TO TERMINATE THIS LICENCE BY WRITTEN NOTICE AND TO TAKE ACTION TO RECOVER ANY DAMAGES SUFFERED BY PEARSON EDUCATION LIMITED IF YOU BREACH ANY PROVISION OF THIS AGREEMENT.

Pearson Education Limited owns the software. You only own the disk on which the software is supplied.

LIMITED WARRANTY

Pearson Education Limited warrants that the disk or CD ROM on which the software is supplied is free from defects in materials and workmanship under normal use for ninety (90) days from the date You receive it. This warranty is limited to You and is not transferable. Pearson Education Limited does not warrant that the functions of the software meet Your requirements or that the media is compatible with any computer system on which it is used or that the operation of the software will be unlimited or error-free.

You assume responsibility for selecting the software to achieve Your intended results and for the installation of, the use of and the results obtained from the software. The entire liability of Pearson Education Limited and your only remedy shall be replacement free of charge of the components that do not meet this warranty.

This limited warranty is void if any damage has resulted from accident, abuse, misapplication, service or modification by someone other than Pearson Education Limited. In no event shall Pearson Education Limited be liable for any damages whatsoever arising out of installation of the software, even if advised of the possibility of such damages. Pearson Education Limited will not be liable for any loss or damage of any nature suffered by any party as a result of reliance upon or reproduction of or any errors in the content of the publication.

Pearson Education Limited does not limit its liability for death or personal injury caused by its negligence.

This licence agreement shall be governed by and interpreted and construed in accordance with English law.

Technical support: only registered users are entitled to free technical help and advice. As a registered user, You may receive technical help by writing to elt-support@pearson.com or your local agent.

New releases and updates: as a registered user You may be able to get new releases and updates, or upgrade to a network version of the software at reduced prices.

Registration: to register as a user, please write to us at the address shown below or email us at elt-support@pearson.com

Longman Dictionaries Division
Pearson Education Limited
Edinburgh Gate
Harlow
Essex
CM20 2JE
England